Benutzerhinweise

Blaue **Stichwörter**.

maßvoll **I.** *adj* moderate

Markierung der **Phrasal Verb** Einträge.

Kennzeichnung gleich geschriebener Wörter mit unterschiedlicher Bedeutung (**Homographen**).

Plastik¹ <-s> ['plas·tɪk] *nt kein pl* plastic
Plastik² <-, -en> ['plas·tɪk] *f* (*Kunstwerk*) ...

Angabe der **Aussprache** in internationaler Lautschrift. Die Trennungspunkte geben die Sprechsilben wider. Diese Trennung entspricht nicht immer der orthographischen Silbentrennung.
Bei Stichwörtern ohne Phonetik wird die Betonung direkt im Stichwort angegeben.

übersehbar [y:bɐ'ze:·ba·ɐ̯] ...
übersehen* [y:bɐ'ze:·ən] ...
übersetzen*¹ [y:bɐ'zɛ·tsn̩] ...

verschneit *adj* ...
verschnörkelt *adj* ...

Unregelmäßige Pluralformen, Verb- und Steigerungsformen werden in spitzen Klammern angegeben.

verschleißen <verschliss, verschlissen> *vi, vt sein* to wear out

Kennzeichnung der **Trennbarkeit von Verben**.

ab|bringen *vt irreg* ...

Die alte Schreibung wird durch das hochgestellte Zeichen ᴬᴸᵀ kenntlich gemacht, die neue durch ᴿᴿ.

Stängelᴿᴿ <-s, -> ['ʃtɛŋl̩] *m* stalk, stem
Stengelᴬᴸᵀ <-s, -> ['ʃtɛŋl̩] *m s.* **Stängel**

Mit **römischen Ziffern** wird ein Eintrag unter grammatischen Gesichtspunkten gegliedert. Die **arabischen Ziffern** bezeichnen die unterschiedlichen Bedeutungen des Stichworts.

langsam ['laŋ·za:m] **I.** *adj* **1.** (*nicht schnell*) slow **2.** (*allmählich*) gradual **II.** *adv* **1.** (*nicht schnell*) slowly ...

Die **Tilde** ersetzt in Wendungen das Stichwort.
Das Zeichen ▶ leitet den Block der **festen Wendungen** ein. Die Unterstreichung dient der besseren Orientierung.

Bach <-[e]s, Bäche> [bax] *m* brook ▶ **den ~ runtergehen** *fam* to go down the drain

Das Symbol ⇄ bei **Phrasal Verb** Einträgen und die Angabe *sep* in Übersetzungen geben an, dass die Reihenfolge von Objekt und Ergänzung auch vertauscht werden kann.

beladen* I. *irreg vt* to load [up *sep*]

Wegweiser zur treffenden Übersetzung:

- **Sachgebietsangaben** (geben den Wissensbereich an)

unfruchtbar ['ʊn·frʊxt·ba·ɐ̯] *adj* MED ...

- **Bedeutungserklärungen, Kontextpartner** oder **Synonyme**

echt [ɛçt] **I.** *adj* **1.** (*nicht künstlich, wirklich*) real; (*Haarfarbe*) natural; (*Silber, Gold*) pure ...

- **Regionale Bedeutungen**

berichten* I. *vt* **1.** (*mitteilen*) to tell **2.** *schweiz* falsch/recht berichtet wrong/right ...

- **Stil-, Alters-** und **rhetorische** Angaben

Bücherwurm *m hum* bookworm

coach [koʊtʃ] **I.** n **1.** SPORT Trainer(in) m(f);
...

bring <brought, brought> [brɪŋ] vt ...
◈ **bring about** vt verursachen

Blue **headwords**.

English **phrasal verbs** come directly after the base verb and are marked with a diamond (◈)

incense¹ ['ɪn·sens] n (in church) Weihrauch m ...
incense² [ɪn·'sens] vt empören

Homographs marked with superscript numbers.

flexibility [flek·sə·'bɪl·ɪ·t̬i] ...
flexible ['flek·sə·bəl] ...
flextime ['fleks·taɪm] ...

Phonetic transcriptions.
Centered dots are used for syllable division. Please note that this does not always correspond with the orthographic division into syllables.

'**time bomb** n ...
'**time-consuming** adj ...

Where no phonetic code is given, the main spoken emphasis of the headword is indicated by a stress mark.

'**daughter-in-law** <pl daughters-> ...
begin <-nn-, began, begun> ...
unruly <-ier, -iest or more ~, most ~> ...

Angle brackets are used to show **irregular plural forms** and, **forms of irregular verbs and adjectives**.

Indication of **separability** of verbs.

Old spellings are marked with a superscript ALT symbol.
New spellings are marked with a superscript RR symbol.

balance ['bæl·ənts] **I.** n **1.** Gleichgewicht nt a. fig **2.** FIN Kontostand m **II.** vt ...

Roman numerals are used for the parts of speech of a word, and **Arabic numerals** for sense divisions.

ballistic [bə·'lɪs·tɪk] adj ... ► **to go** ~ fam ausflippen fam

The **swung dash** substitutes the entry word in phrases.
The ► sign introduces **a block of set expressions, idioms and proverbs.**
Key words are underlined as a guide.

◈ **win back** vt **1.** SPORT **to** ~ **back ⇆ the trophy** den Pokal zurückholen **2.** (customers) zurückgewinnen

The symbol ⇆ in **phrasal verb** entries and the label sep in translations show that the sequence of object and complement can be reversed.

Guides to the correct translation:

horn [hɔrn] n **1.** ZOOL Horn nt **2.** MUS Horn nt

- **Subject labels** (which indicate areas of specialization)

wild [waɪld] **I.** adj **1.** (undomesticated) wild **2.** (uncultivated: landscape) rau, wild; ...

- **Definitions**, **context partners** or **synonyms**

dinner ['dɪn·ər] n **1.** (evening meal) Abendessen nt; dial (warm lunch) Mittagessen nt; **to go out for** ~ essen gehen; ...

- **Regional labels**

jump ['dʒʌmp] **I.** n a. fig Sprung m ...

- **Usage Labels** (which indicate restriction to a particular level or style of usage)

A
B
C
D
E
F
G
H
I
J
K
L
M
N
O
P
Q
R
S
T
U
V
W
X
Y
Z

With the aid of the alphabetical thumb index overleaf (at the edge of the page) you can quickly locate the letter you need to find in the German-English and English-German dictionary. Once you have localized the letter you need on the thumb index, simply flip to the correspondingly marked part of the dictionary.

If you are left-handed, you can use the thumb index at the end of this book.

Mit Hilfe der alphabetischen Daumenleiste am rechten Seitenrand (s. a. Rückseite), kann man die gesuchte Stelle im Alphabet des deutsch-englischen und des englisch-deutschen Wörterbuches schnell finden. Wurde die gewünschte Stelle im Alphabet auf der Leiste ausgewählt, schlägt man das Wörterbuch an der entsprechend markierten Stelle auf und befindet sich dann in der richtigen Buchstabenstrecke.

Falls Sie Linkshänder(in) sind, können Sie die Buchstabenleiste in der hinteren Umschlagklappe benutzen.

BARRON'S

FOREIGN LANGUAGE GUIDES

GERMAN–ENGLISH

Pocket Dictionary

Taschenwörterbuch

DEUTSCH–ENGLISCH

BARRON'S Foreign Language Guides
German-English Pocket Dictionary
Taschenwörterbuch Deutsch-Englisch

First edition for the United States and Canada published in 2008 by Barron's Educational Series, Inc.

© 2008 Ernst Klett Sprachen GmbH, Stuttgart, Germany, and Barron's Educational Series, Inc., Hauppauge, USA.

Editorial management: Anette Dralle
Contributors: Stephen Curtis, Ian Dawson, Monika Finck, Jill Williams

Typesetting: Mariusz Idzikowski, Poznań; Dörr und Schiller GmbH, Stuttgart

All inquiries should be addressed to:
Barron's Educational Series, Inc.
250 Wireless Boulevard
Hauppauge, NY 11788
www.barronseduc.com

ISBN-13: 978-0-7641-4003-7
ISBN-10: 0-7641-4003-5
Library of Congress Control Number 2008920656

Printed in China
9 8 7 6 5 4 3 2 1

Inhalt

Contents

Lautschriftzeichen für Deutsch
German phonetic symbols

Vokale/Vowels

[a]	matt
[ɐ]	bitter
[ɐ̯]	Uhr
[ã]	Arangement
[ã:]	Gourmand
[e]	Etage
[e:]	Beet, Mehl
[ɛ]	Nest, Wäsche
[ɛ:]	wählen
[ɛ̃]	Cousin
[ɛ̃:]	Teint
[ə]	halte
[ɪ]	Bitte
[i]	Vitamin
[i:]	Bier
[i̯]	Studie
[j]	ja
[o]	Oase
[o:]	Boot, drohen
[o̯]	loyal
[ɔ]	Post
[õ]	Fondue
[õ:]	Fonds
[ø]	Ökonomie
[ø:]	Öl
[œ]	Götter
[œ:]	Server
[u]	zunächst
[u:]	Hut
[u̯]	aktuell
[ʊ]	Mutter
[y]	Aerodynamik
[y:]	Typ
[y̆]	Etui
[ʏ]	füllen

Diphthonge/Diphthongs

[ai]	heiß
[au]	Haus
[ɔy]	Mäuse

Konsonanten/Consonants

[b]	Ball
[ç]	ich
[d]	dicht
[dʒ]	Budget, Job
[f]	Fett, viel
[g]	Geld
[h]	Hut
[k]	Kohl, Computer
[kv]	Quadrat
[l]	Last
[l̩]	Nebel
[m]	Meister
[n]	nett
[n̩]	sprechen
[ŋ]	Ring, blinken
[p]	Papst
[pf]	Pfeffer
[r]	Rad
[s]	Rast, besser, heiß
[ʃ]	Schaum, sprechen, Chef
[t]	Test

[ts]	Zaun
[tʃ]	Matsch, Tschüs
[v]	wann
[x]	Schlauch
[ks]	Fix, Axt, Lachs
[z]	Hase, sauer
[ʒ]	Genie

Zeichen/Signs

ʔ	glottal stop
'	primary stress
ˌ	secondary stress
:	length symbol
[·]	syllable division

English phonetic symbols
Lautschriftzeichen für Englisch

Vowels/Vokale

[a]	farm, not
[æ]	cat, man, sad
[e]	best, get, hair, dare
[ə]	Africa, better, actor, potato, anonymous, virus
[ɜ]	bird, berth, curb
[i]	read, meet, belief, hobby
[ɪ]	sit, wish, near
[ɔ]	caught, all, law, sauce, floor
[u]	moose, lose, you
[ʊ]	book, put, sure, tour
[ʌ]	bust, multi
[ã]	genre

Diphthongs/Diphthonge

[aɪ]	ride, my, buy
[aʊ]	house, now
[eɪ]	rate, lame
[ɔɪ]	boy, noise
[oʊ]	rope, piano, road, toe, show, plateau
[ju]	accuse, beauty

Consonants/Konsonanten

[b]	big, blind
[d]	dad, had
[ð]	father, bathe
[dʒ]	edge, juice, object
[f]	fast, wolf
[g]	beg, gold
[h]	hello
[j]	yellow
[ʒ]	pleasure
[k]	cat, king, milk
[l]	little, ill, oil
[m]	man, am
[n]	nice, manner
[ŋ]	long, sing, prank
[p]	paper, happy
[r]	right, dry, current, player, part
[s]	soft, yes, cent, capacity
[ʃ]	shift, station, fish
[t]	take, fat
[t̬]	butter, interstate
[θ]	think, bath
[tʃ]	chip, patch
[v]	vitamin, live
[w]	wish, why, wore
[z]	zebra, jazz, gaze

Signs/Zeichen

'	primary stress
ˌ	secondary stress
[·]	syllable division

A

A, a <-, -> [aː] *nt* **1.** (*Buchstabe*) A, a; **~ wie Anton** A as in Alpha **2.** MUS A, a; **A-Dur/a-Moll** A major/A minor ▶ **das ~ und** [**das**] **O** be all and end all; **von ~ bis Z** from beginning to end

Aal <-[e]s, -e> [aːl] *m* eel

aalen ['aːlən] *vr fam* **sich** *akk* **auf dem Sofa ~** to stretch out on the sofa; **sich** *akk* **in der Sonne ~** to bask in the sun

aalglatt ['aːl·'glat] *adj* slippery

Aas <-es, -e> [aːs] *nt* (*Tierleiche*) carrion

Aasgeier *m* vulture *a. pej*

ab [ap] **I.** *adv* **1.** (*weg, entfernt*) off; **mein Knopf ist ~** I've lost a button; **erst muss die alte Farbe ~** first you have to remove the old paint **2.** **links/rechts ~** off to the left/right **3.** **weit ~ liegen** to be far away ▶ **~ und zu** now and then **II.** *präp* +*dat* from; **Kinder ~ 14 Jahren** children age 14 and older; **~ heute** starting today; **~ Köln** from Cologne

ab|ändern *vt* to amend; (*Programm*) to change

abartig *adj* abnormal

Abbau <-s> *m kein pl* **1.** (*von Bodenschätzen*) mining **2.** (*Verringerung*) **der ~ von Arbeitsplätzen** job cuts *pl*; **der ~ von Vorurteilen** the breaking down of prejudices

ab|bauen I. *vt* **1.** (*Bodenschätze*) to mine **2.** (*Schrank*) to dismantle **3.** (*verringern*) to reduce **II.** *vi* **jd baut ab** sb is wilting; (*geistig*) sb is deteriorating

ab|bekommen* *vt irreg s.* **abkriegen**

ab|bestellen* *vt* (*Zeitung, Reservierung*) to cancel; **den Klempner ~** to tell the plumber he doesn't need to come anymore

ab|bezahlen* *vt* to pay off *sep*

ab|biegen *irreg vi sein* [**nach**] **links/rechts ~** to turn left/right; (*Straße*) to curve

Abbiegespur *f* turning lane

ab|bilden *vt* **auf dem Foto war ... abgebildet** the photo showed ...

ab|blasen *vt irreg fam* to call off *sep*

Abblendlicht *nt* AUTO low beam headlights

ab|blitzen *vi sein fam* **bei jdm ~** to not get anywhere with sb; **jdn ~ lassen** to turn down *sep* sb

ab|brechen *irreg* **I.** *vt haben* **1.** (*lösen*) to break off *sep* **2.** (*beenden*) to stop; **eine Beziehung ~** to break up; **einen Streik ~** to call off *sep* strike; **das Studium ~** to drop out of college; **den Urlaub ~** to cut short *sep* one's vacation **II.** *vi sein* **1.** (*sich lösen*) to break off **2.** (*aufhören*) to stop; (*Beziehung*) to end

ab|bringen *vt irreg* **jdn von etw** *dat* **~** to get sb to give up sth; (*abraten*) to change sb's mind about sth; **jdn davon ~, etw zu tun** to prevent sb from doing sth

Abbruch *m* **1.** (*eines Gebäudes*) demolition **2.** (*einer Beziehung*) break-up

abbruchreif *adj* **1.** (*Gebäude*) dilapidated **2.** *schweiz* (*schrottreif*) ready for the junk yard *pred*

ab|buchen *vt* (*Bank*) to debit; **etw** [**vom Konto**] **~** to deduct sth [from a/one's bank account]

Abc-Schütze, -Schützin [aːbeː'tseː-] *m, f* child attending school for the first time

ab|danken *vi* to resign; (*König*) to abdicate

ab|decken *vt* to cover

ab|dichten *vt* to seal

ab|drehen *vt* to turn off *sep*

Abdruck *m* **1.** <-drücke> (*Spur*) print **2.** <-drucke> (*Veröffentlichung*) printing

ab|drucken *vt* to print

abend ALT *adv s.* **Abend**

Abend <-s, -e> ['aːbnt] *m* evening; **am ~** in the evening; **gestern/morgen ~** yesterday/tomorrow evening; **heute ~** tonight; **~ für ~** night after night; **den ganzen ~ über** the whole evening; **gegen ~** toward evening; **jdm guten ~ wünschen** to wish sb a good evening; **zu ~ essen** to eat dinner

Abendbrot *nt dial s.* **Abendessen**

Abendessen *nt* dinner

abendfüllend *adj* all-night *attr,* lasting all evening *pred*

Abendkasse *f* evening box office

Abendkleid *nt* evening dress

Abendkurs *m* evening class

Abendland *nt kein pl geh* West, Occident

Abendmahl nt [Holy] Communion; **das Letzte ~** the Last Supper

Abendrot <-s> ['a:bnt·ro:t] nt kein pl [red] sunset; **im ~** in the evening glow

abends ['a:bnts] adv in the evening

Abenteuer <-s, -> ['a:bn·tɔye] nt 1. adventure 2. (Liebesabenteuer) fling; **auf [ein] ~ aus sein** to be looking for a one-night stand

abenteuerlich ['a:bn·tɔye·lıç] adj (Geschichte) fantastic; (Vorhaben) risky

Abenteurer, Abenteu(r)erin <-s, -> ['a:bn·tɔye·re, 'a:bn·tɔy·(r)ə·rın] m, f adventurer

aber ['a:be] konj but; **~ dennoch ...** but in spite of this ...; **oder ~** or else

Aber <-s, -> ['a:be] nt but fam; **kein ~!** no buts [about it]!

Aberglaube m superstition

abergläubisch ['a:be·glɔy·bıʃ] adj superstitious

abermals ['a:be·ma:ls] adv once again

abfahrbereit adj, adv ready to depart pred

ab|fahren irreg I. vi sein to depart ▶ **auf jdn/etw ~** fam to be crazy about sb/sth; **jdn ~ lassen** fam to turn down sep sb II. vt 1. sein o haben (Strecke) to [drive along and] check 2. haben (Reifen) to wear down sep

Abfahrt f 1. (Wegfahren) departure 2. (Autobahnabfahrt) exit 3. (beim Skifahren, Rodeln) run; (Abfahrtsstrecke) slope

Abfahrtszeit f departure time

Abfall m garbage

Abfallbeseitigung f garbage [o trash] removal, waste disposal

Abfalleimer m garbage can

abfällig I. adj **~e Bemerkung** derogatory remark II. adv disparagingly; **sich akk ~ über jdn/etw äußern** to make derogatory remarks about sb/sth

Abfallverwertung f recycling

ab|finden irreg I. vt (entschädigen) to compensate II. vr fam **sich** akk **mit etw** dat **~** to put up with sth

Abfindung <-, -en> f compensation; (bei Entlassung) severance pay

ab|flauen vi sein (Wind, Sturm) to abate; (Nachfrage) to decrease; (Lärm) to drop;

(Interesse) to wane

ab|fliegen vi irreg sein to take off

Abflug m departure, takeoff

Abfluss RR m (Rohr) drain pipe

Abfuhr <-, -en> f snub; **jdm eine ~ erteilen** to snub sb

ab|führen I. vt 1. **jdn ~** (Polizei) to lead sb away 2. (Geld) to pay II. vi MED to loosen the bowels

Abführmittel nt laxative

ab|füllen vt 1. (Flüssigkeit) to fill (**in** +akk into); (in Flaschen) to bottle 2. sl (betrunken machen) to get drunk

Abgangszeugnis nt diploma

Abgas nt exhaust

abgasarm adj low-emission

ab|geben irreg I. vt 1. (geben) **jdm etw ~** to give sb sth [o sth to sb]; **jdm die Hälfte [von etw** dat**] ~** to go halves [on sth] with sb; **jdm nichts ~** to not share with sb 2. (Diplomarbeit etc.) to hand in sep sth 3. (hinterlassen) **etw [bei jdm] ~** to leave sth [with sb]; **das Gepäck ~** to check in one's luggage; **den Mantel an der Garderobe ~** to check one's coat 4. (Erklärung, Urteil) to make; **seine Stimme ~** to cast one's vote 5. (darstellen) to be; **die perfekte Hausfrau ~** to be the perfect wife II. vr **sich** akk **mit jdm ~** to associate with sb

abgebrannt adj fam broke

abgebrüht adj fam unscrupulous

abgedroschen adj pej fam hackneyed

ab|gehen irreg vi sein 1. (sich lösen) to come off 2. **von der Schule ~** to drop out of school 3. (abzweigen) to branch off

abgekartet adj fam ▶ **ein ~es Spiel treiben** to play a double game

abgelegen adj remote

abgeneigt adj **nicht ~ sein, etw zu tun** to not be averse to doing sth

Abgeordnete(r) ['ap·gə·ʔɔrd·nə·tə, -tə] f(m) dekl wie adj representative

Abgeordnetenhaus nt ≈ House of Representatives

abgerissen pp von **abreißen**

Abgesandte(r) f(m) dekl wie adj envoy

abgeschieden adj isolated

abgesehen I. adj **es auf jdn ~ haben**

(*schikanieren wollen*) to have it in for sb; **es auf etw** *akk* ~ **haben** to have one's eye on sth; **du hast es nur darauf** ~, **mich zu ärgern** you're just out to annoy me **II.** *adv* ~ **von jdm/etw** except for sb/sth; ~ **davon, dass ...** apart from the fact that ...

abgespannt *adj, adv* tired out

abgestanden *adj* (*Bier, Wasser*) stale

ab|gewöhnen* **I.** *vt* **jdm etw** ~ to get sb to stop doing sth **II.** *vr* **sich** *dat* **etw** ~ to give up sth

abgöttisch *adv* **jdn** ~ **lieben** to idolize sb

Abgrund *m* abyss; **am Rande des** ~**s stehen** to be on the brink of disaster

abgrundtief ['apgrʊnt·'ti:f] *adj* (*Hass*) profound

ab|gucken *vt* **etw** [**von jdm**] ~ to copy sth [from sb]

ab|hacken *vt* to chop down *sep*; (*Finger*) to chop off *sep*

ab|haken *vt* **1.** (*in einer Liste*) to check off *sep* **2.** (*vergessen*) to forget; **die Sache ist abgehakt** the affair is over and done with

ab|halten *vt irreg* **1.** (*hindern*) **jdn von etw** *dat* ~ to keep sb from sth **2.** (*fernhalten: Hitze*) to protect from; (*Insekten*) to repel **3.** (*veranstalten*) to hold; (*Demonstration*) to stage

abhanden|kommen ^{RR} [ap·'handn̩-] *vi irreg* **sein** to get lost

Abhang <-[e]s, Abhänge> *m* slope

ab|hängen *vi irreg* **1.** (*bedingt sein*) to depend (**von** +*dat* on); **das hängt davon ab** that [all] depends **2.** (*angewiesen sein*) to be dependent (**von** +*dat* on) **3.** *sl* (*nichts tun*) to hang out

abhängig *adj* **1.** (*bedingt*) **von etw** ~ **sein** to depend on sth **2.** (*angewiesen*) **von jdm** ~ **sein** to be dependent on sb **3.** (*süchtig*) addicted; [**von etw** *dat*] ~ **sein** to be addicted [to sth]

ab|härten *vt, vi* to harden (**gegen** +*akk* to)

ab|hauen <haute ab, abgehauen> *vi* **sein** *fam* to skip out of town; **hau ab!** get lost!

ab|heben *irreg* **I.** *vi* **1.** (*Flugzeug*) to take off **2.** (*am Telefon*) to answer [the phone] **II.** *vt* (*Geld*) to withdraw

ab|hetzen *vr* **sich** *akk* ~ to stress oneself out

Abhilfe *f kein pl* remedy

ab|holen *vt* to pick up *sep*

Abholzung <-, -en> *f* deforestation

Abi <-s, -s> ['abi] *nt pl selten fam*, **Abitur** <-s, -e> [abi·'tu:ɐ̯] *nt pl selten* Abitur (*written and oral final examination usually taken at the end of the 13th year of school*)

Abiturient(in) <-en, -en> [abi·tu·'rjɛnt] *m(f)* Abitur student (*student who is taking or has passed the Abitur*)

ab|kapseln *vr* **sich** *akk* ~ to cut oneself off

ab|kaufen *vt a. fig* **jdm etw** ~ to buy sth off sb; **das kaufe ich dir nicht ab!** *fig* I don't buy that!

ab|kochen *vt* to boil

ab|kommen *vi irreg* **sein** (*von der Straße*) to veer off; (*vom Weg*) to stray from; **von einer Meinung** ~ to change one's mind; **vom Thema** ~ to digress from the topic

Abkommen <-s, -> *nt* agreement; **ein** ~ **abschließen** to sign a treaty

ab|kratzen **I.** *vt* **haben** to scratch off *sep* **II.** *vi* **sein** *sl* to kick the bucket

ab|kriegen *vt fam* **1.** (*Anteil*) to get one's share; **die Hälfte von etw** *dat* ~ to receive half of sth **2.** (*beschädigt werden*) to get damaged; (*verletzt werden*) to be injured

ab|kühlen **I.** *vi* **sein** to cool [down]; (*Begeisterung*) to wane **II.** *vr* **haben sich** *akk* ~ (*Person*) to cool off; (*Wetter*) to get cooler

ab|kürzen *vt* **1.** (*Wort*) to abbreviate **2.** (*Weg, Gespräch*) to cut short *sep*

Abkürzung *f* **1.** (*eines Wortes*) abbreviation **2.** (*Weg*) shortcut; **eine** ~ **nehmen** to take a shortcut

ab|laden *vt irreg* **1.** (*Müll*) to dump **2.** (*Ladung, Waren*) to unload **3.** *fam* (*absetzen*) **jdn** ~ to drop off *sep* sb **4.** (*abreagieren*) **seinen Ärger bei jdm** ~ to take out one's anger on sb **5.** (*abwälzen*) **etw auf jdn** ~ to shift sth onto sb

ab|lassen *irreg vt* (*Wasser, Öl*) to drain; **Dampf** ~ *a. fig* to let off steam

Ablauf <-es, -läufe> *m* **1.** (*Verlauf*) course; (*von Verbrechen, Unfall*) sequence of events **2.** nach/vor ~ der Frist after/before a deadline

ab|laufen *irreg* **I.** *vi sein* **1.** (*verlaufen*) to proceed **2.** (*abfließen*) to run; **das Badewasser ~ lassen** to drain the bathtub **3.** (*ungültig werden*) to expire **II.** *vt haben* (*Schuhe*) to wear down *sep*

ab|legen I. *vt* **1.** (*an einen Ort*) to put **2. einen Eid ~** to take an oath; **ein Geständnis ~** to make a confession; **eine Prüfung ~** to pass an exam **II.** *vi* NAUT to set sail

ab|lehnen I. *vt* **1.** (*zurückweisen*) to turn down *sep*; (*Person, Antrag*) to reject **2.** (*sich weigern*) **[es] ~, etw zu tun** to refuse to do sth **3.** (*missbilligen*) to disapprove of **II.** *vi* (*nein sagen*) to refuse

Ablehnung <-, -en> *f* **1.** (*Zurückweisung*) rejection **2.** (*Missbilligung*) disapproval; **auf ~ stoßen** to meet with disapproval

ab|lenken I. *vt* to distract; **sich** *akk* **von etw** *dat* **~ lassen** to be distracted by sth; **Gartenarbeit lenkt ihn ab** working in the garden helps him to relax **II.** *vi* to distract; **vom Thema ~** to change the subject

Ablenkung *f* distraction; **zur ~** in order to relax

ab|lesen *irreg vt* (*Messgeräte, Strom*) to read

ab|liefern *vt* (*Paket*) to deliver (**bei** +*dat* to); (*Manuskript*) to hand in *sep*

ab|lösen I. *vt* **1.** (*abmachen*) to remove; (*Pflaster*) to peel off *sep* **2. einen Kollegen ~** to take over for a colleague; **die Wache ~** to change the guard **3.** *fig* (*ersetzen*) to replace **II.** *vr* **sich** *akk* **~ 1.** (*abgehen*) to peel off **2.** (*abwechseln*) to take turns (**bei** +*dat* at); **sich** *akk* **bei der Arbeit ~** to work in shifts

ab|machen *vt* **1.** (*entfernen*) to take off *sep* **2.** (*vereinbaren*) **etw [mit jdm] ~** to arrange sth [with sb]

Abmachung <-, -en> *f* agreement; **sich** *akk* **[nicht] an eine ~ halten** to [not] keep an agreement

ab|melden I. *vt* **1.** jdn von einer Schule ~ to withdraw sb from a school **2. ein Auto ~** to cancel one's car registration; **das Telefon ~** to have one's phone disconnected **II.** *vr* **sich** *akk* **~** (*bei Umzug*) to notify the authorities of a change of address

ab|messen *vt irreg* to measure

ab|nabeln *vr* **sich** *akk* **[von jdm/etw] ~** to become independent [of sb/sth]

Abnahme <-, -n> ['ap·na:·mə] *f* reduction [in]; (*der Kräfte*) weakening

ab|nehmen *irreg* **I.** *vi* **1.** (*an Gewicht*) to lose weight **2.** (*sich verringern*) to decrease; (*Nachfrage*) to drop **3.** (*am Telefon*) to answer [the phone] **II.** *vt* **1.** (*wegnehmen*) **jdm etw ~** to take sth [away *sep*] from sb **2.** (*herunternehmen*) to take down *sep*; **den Hut ~** to take off *sep* one's hat **3. den Telefonhörer ~** to pick up *sep* the phone **4.** (*übernehmen*) **jdm etw ~** to take over *sep* sth for sb; **deine Arbeit kann ich dir nicht ~** I can't do your work for you

Abneigung *f* dislike (**gegen** +*akk* of)

ab|nutzen, ab|nützen *südd, österr* **I.** *vt* to wear out *sep*; **abgenutzt** worn **II.** *vr* **sich** *akk* **~** to wear

abonnieren * [abɔ·'ni:·rən] *vt* to subscribe to

Abordnung *f* delegation

ab|plagen *vr* **sich** *akk* **[mit etw** *dat*] **~** to struggle [with sth]

ab|prallen *vi sein* to rebound (**von** +*dat* off [of]); **an jdm ~** to bounce off sb

ab|putzen *vt* to clean; **putz dir die Schuhe ab!** wipe your shoes!

ab|raten *vi irreg* **jdm von etw** *dat* **~** to advise sb against sth

ab|räumen *vt* **den Tisch ~** to clear the table

ab|reagieren * ['ap·rea·gi:·rən] **I.** *vt* (*Wut, Frust*) to work off *sep* **II.** *vr* **sich** *akk* **~** to calm down

ab|rechnen *vi* (*zur Rechenschaft ziehen*) **mit jdm ~** to call sb to account

Abrechnung *f* **die ~ machen** to add up the bill

ab|regen *vr* *fam* **sich** *akk* **~** to calm down; **reg dich ab!** calm down!, relax!

Abreise *f* kein *pl* departure

ab|reisen *vi sein* to depart

ab|reißen *irreg* **I.** *vt haben* to tear (**von** +*dat* off); (*Gebäude*) to tear down *sep* **II.** *vi sein* **1.** (*sich lösen*) to tear off **2.** (*aufhören*) to break off; **den Kontakt nicht ~ lassen** to not lose contact

ab|riegeln *vt* (*Fenster, Tür*) to bolt; (*Gebiet, Straße*) to cordon off *sep*

ab|rufen *vt irreg* **Daten ~** to retrieve data

ab|runden *vt* **1.** (*Betrag, Zahl*) to round (**auf** +*akk* to) **2.** **ein Essen ~** to round off a meal

ab|rüsten *vi* MIL to disarm

Abrüstung *f kein pl* MIL disarmament

ABS <-> [aːbeːˈɛs] *nt Abk von* **Antiblockiersystem** ABS

ab|sacken *vi sein fam* (*Blutdruck, Boden*) to sink; (*Flugzeug, Leistung*) to drop (**auf** +*akk* to); **sie ist in ihren Leistungen sehr abgesackt** her performance has deteriorated considerably

Absage <-, -n> *f* rejection

ab|sagen **I.** *vt* (*Termin, Verabredung*) to cancel **II.** *vi jdm ~* to decline sb's invitation; **ich muss leider ~** I'm afraid I have to cancel *fam;* **hast du ihr schon abgesagt?** have you already told her you're not going?

ab|sägen *vt* (*Ast*) to saw off *sep;* (*Baum*) to cut down *sep*

Absatz *m* **1.** (*am Schuh*) heel **2.** (*Abschnitt*) paragraph **3.** (*Verkauf*) sales *pl;* **~ finden** to find a market

ab|schaffen *vt* to abolish; **die Todesstrafe ~** to abolish the death penalty

ab|schalten **I.** *vt* (*abstellen*) to turn off *sep* **II.** *vi fam* (*entspannen*) to relax

ab|schätzen *vt* **1.** (*einschätzen*) to assess; **ich kann ihre Reaktion schlecht ~** I can't even guess what her reaction will be **2.** (*ungefähr schätzen*) to estimate

ab|schauen *vt südd, österr, schweiz s.* **abgucken**

Abschaum *m kein pl pej* scum

abscheulich [apˈʃɔʏlɪç] **I.** *adj* revolting; (*Verbrechen*) horrifying **II.** *adv* **~ wehtun** to hurt like hell *fam;* **~ kalt/warm** awfully cold/hot

ab|schieben *irreg vt* (*ausweisen*) to deport

Abschied <-[e]s, -e> [ˈapˈʃiːt] *m* farewell; **der ~ fiel ihr nicht leicht** she found it difficult to say goodbye; **sie gab ihm zum ~ einen Kuss** she gave him a goodbye kiss; **von jdm ~ nehmen** to say goodbye to sb

ab|schlachten *vt* to slaughter

ab|schlagen *irreg vt* **1.** (*abtrennen*) to knock (**von** +*dat* off); (*Ast*) to knock down; **jdm den Kopf ~** to chop off *sep* sb's head **2.** **jdm etw ~** to refuse sb sth; **er kann keinem etwas ~** he can't refuse anybody anything

Abschlag(s)zahlung *f* partial payment

ab|schleppen *vt* **1.** (*Fahrzeug, Schiff*) to tow [away *sep*] **2.** *fam* (*Person*) to pick up *sep;* **jede Woche schleppt er eine andere ab** he comes home with a different girl every week

Abschleppseil *nt* tow rope

Abschleppwagen *m* tow truck

ab|schließen *irreg* **I.** *vt* **1.** (*Tür*) to lock **2.** (*beenden*) to finish; (*Diskussion*) to end **3.** (*vereinbaren: Geschäft*) to close; (*Versicherung*) to take out *sep;* (*Vertrag*) to sign; (*Wette*) to place **II.** *vi* (*zuschließen*) to lock up

abschließend *adj* **~e Bemerkungen** closing remarks

Abschluss [RR] *m* **1.** *kein pl* (*Ende*) conclusion; **zum ~ kommen** to draw to a conclusion; **kurz vor dem ~ stehen** to be nearly over **2.** SCH, UNIV degree; **welchen ~ haben Sie?** what degree do you have? **3.** (*das Vereinbaren*) settlement; (*einer Versicherung*) taking out; (*eines Vertrags*) signing

Abschlussprüfung [RR] *f* SCH final [exam]

Abschlusszeugnis [RR] *nt* SCH diploma

ab|schminken *vr* **1.** (*Make-up entfernen*) **sich** *akk* **~** to take off one's make-up **2.** *fig fam* (*aufgeben*) **sich** *dat* **etw ~** to give up *sep* sth; **das können Sie sich ~!** you can forget about that!

ab|schnallen *vr* **sich** *akk* **~** to unfasten one's seat belt

ab|schneiden *irreg* **I.** *vt* to cut [off *sep*]; **jdm den Weg ~** to intercept sb; **jdm das Wort ~** to cut sb short **II.** *vi fam* **bei etw** *dat* **gut/schlecht ~** to do well/poorly on sth

Abschnitt *m* **1.** (*im Text*) passage **2.** (*Zeitabschnitt*) period; **ein neuer ~ der Geschichte** a new era in history; **ein neuer ~ in seinem Leben** a new chapter of his life **3.** (*Unterteilung*) part; (*einer Autobahn*) section

ab|schrauben *vt* to unscrew

ab|schrecken **I.** *vt* KOCHK to shock **II.** *vi* to deter

abschreckend **I.** *adj* deterrent; **ein ~es Beispiel** a warning **II.** *adv* ~ **wirken** to act as a deterrent

ab|schreiben *irreg vt* **1.** (*Text*) to copy **2.** *fam* (*verloren geben*) to write off *sep*

Abschürfung <-, -en> *f* MED scrape

abschüssig ['ap·ʃy·sɪç] *adj* steep

ab|schütteln *vt* to shake off *sep*

ab|schweifen *vi sein* (*Gedanken*) to deviate; **bitte schweifen Sie nicht ab!** please stick to the point!; **vom Thema ~** to digress [from a topic]

absehbar ['ap·ze:·ba:ɐ̯] *adj* foreseeable; **das Ende ist nicht ~** the end is not in sight; **in ~er Zeit** in the foreseeable future

abseits ['ap·zaits] *präp* +*gen* **ein wenig ~ der Straße** not far from the road

abseits|stehen ^{RR} *vi irreg* to stand on the sidelines

Absender(in) <-s, -> *m(f)* sender

ab|setzen **I.** *vt* **1.** (*Hut, Brille*) to take off *sep* **2.** (*hinstellen*) to put down *sep* **3.** (*aussteigen lassen*) **jdn ~** to drop off *sep* sb **4.** **etw von der Steuer ~** to deduct sth from one's taxes **5.** (*Medikament*) to stop taking **II.** *vr sich akk ~* **1.** (*Dreck, Staub*) to settle **2.** *fam* (*verschwinden*) to clear out; **sich** *akk* **ins Ausland ~** to leave the country

Absicht <-, -en> *f* intention; **~ sein** to be intentional; **das war nicht meine ~!** I didn't mean to do it!; **mit/ohne ~** intentionally/unintentionally; **die ~ haben, etw zu tun** to intend to do sth

absichtlich ['ap·zɪçt·lɪç] *adv* on purpose

absolut [ap·zo·'lu:t] **I.** *adj* absolute; **~e Ruhe** complete calm **II.** *adv fam* absolutely; **~ nicht/nichts** absolutely not/nothing

ab|sondern **I.** *vt* (*ausscheiden*) to secrete **II.** *vr sich akk ~* to keep oneself apart

ab|speichern *vt* COMPUT to store; (*Daten sichern*) to save

abspenstig ['ap·ʃpɛnstɪç] *adj* **jdm etw ~ machen** to take away *sep* sth from sb

ab|sperren **I.** *vt* **1.** (*versperren*) to cordon off *sep* **2.** (*abstellen: Strom, Wasser*) to cut off *sep* **3.** *südd* (*zuschließen*) to lock **II.** *vi südd* (*zuschließen*) to lock up

ab|spielen **I.** *vr* **sich** *akk* **~** to happen; **was hat sich hier abgespielt?** what happened here? **II.** *vt* **1.** (*Musik*) to play **2.** (*Ball*) to pass

Absprache *f* agreement; **eine ~ treffen** to come to an agreement

ab|sprechen *irreg* **I.** *vt* (*vereinbaren*) to agree on **II.** *vr* **sich** *akk* **mit jdm ~** to come to an agreement with sb (**wegen** +*gen* on)

Absprung *m fam* (*Ausstieg*) getting out; **den ~ schaffen** to make a getaway; **den ~ verpassen** to miss the boat

ab|spülen **I.** *vt* to wash off *sep;* **das Geschirr ~** to do the dishes **II.** *vi* to do the dishes

Abstand *m* **1.** (*räumlich*) distance; **ein ~ von 20 Metern** a distance of 65 feet; **in einigem ~** at some distance; **~ halten** to maintain a distance; **fahr nicht so dicht auf, halt ~!** don't tailgate! **2.** (*zeitlich*) interval; **in kurzen/regelmäßigen Abständen** at short/regular intervals **3.** (*emotional*) aloofness

ab|stauben *vt* (*Möbel*) to dust

Abstecher <-s, -> *m* (*Ausflug*) trip

ab|stehen *vi irreg* to stick out; **er hat ~de Ohren** his ears stick out

ab|steigen *vi irreg sein* **1.** (*heruntersteigen*) to dismount; **von einer Leiter ~** to get down off a ladder **2.** *fam* **in einem Hotel ~** to stay in a hotel **3.** *beruflich/gesellschaftlich* **~** to slide down the job/social ladder

ab|stellen *vt* **1.** (*Gerät*) to turn off *sep* **2.** (*Wasser, Strom*) to cut off *sep;* **den Haupthahn ~** to turn off the main shutoff valve **3.** (*absetzen*) to put down *sep* **4.** (*Fahrzeug*) to park

Abstellgleis *nt* siding

ab|stempeln *vt* **1.** (*Brief*) to stamp **2.** *fig*

[als etw *akk*] **abgestempelt** branded [as sth]

ab|sterben *vi irreg sein* (*Blätter, Zellen*) to die; (*Finger, Zehen*) to go numb

Abstieg <-[e]s, -e> *m* descent; **der berufliche/gesellschaftliche ~** descent down the job/social ladder

ab|stimmen I. *vi* to vote; [**über etw** *akk*] **~ lassen** to [have a] vote [on sth] **II.** *vt* (*in Einklang bringen*) **Dinge aufeinander ~** to coordinate things [with each other]; (*Farben, Kleidung*) to match

Abstimmung *f* POL vote (**über** +*akk* on)

abstinent [ap·sti·ˈnɛnt] *adj* abstinent; **~ sein** to be a teetotaler

ab|stoßen *irreg vt* **1.** MED to reject **2.** (*anwidern*) to repel

abstoßend *adj* (*Aussehen*) repulsive; (*Geruch*) disgusting

ab|stottern *vt fam* to pay in installments

abstrakt [ap·ˈstrakt] *adj* abstract

ab|streiten *vt irreg* to deny; **er stritt ab, sie zu kennen** he denied knowing her

ab|stumpfen *vi sein* to blunt (**gegen** +*akk* to)

Absturz *m* fall; (*von Computer, Flugzeug*) crash

ab|stürzen *vi sein* **1.** (*in die Tiefe*) to fall; (*Computer, Flugzeug*) to crash **2.** (*sich betrinken*) to get hammered *sl*

ab|suchen *vt* to search (**nach** +*dat* for)

absurd [ap·ˈzʊrt] *adj* absurd

Abszess RR <-es, -e>, **Abszeß** ALT <-sses, -sse> [aps·ˈtsɛs] *m* MED abscess

Abt, Äbtissin <-[e]s, Äbte> [apt, ɛp·ˈtɪsɪn] *m, f* abbot *masc*, abbess *fem*

ab|tanzen *vi sl* to boogie *fam*

ab|tasten *vt* to search (**nach** +*dat* for); **jdn nach Waffen ~** to frisk sb for weapons

ab|tauen I. *vi sein* (*Eis*) to thaw **II.** *vt haben* (*Kühlschrank*) to defrost

Abtei <-, -en> *f* abbey

Abteil *nt* compartment

ab|teilen *vt* to partition off *sep*

Abteilung *f* department; (*eines Krankenhauses*) ward

Abteilungsleiter(in) *m(f)* department manager

ab|treiben *irreg vt, vi* MED to have an abortion

Abtreibung <-, -en> *f* MED abortion

ab|trennen *vt* **1.** (*ablösen*) to detach **2.** (*abteilen*) to divide off *sep* **3.** (*Körperteil*) to cut off *sep*

ab|treten *irreg vt* **1.** (*übertragen: Rechte*) to transfer; (*Land*) to cede **2.** *fam* (*überlassen*) **jdm etw ~** to give sth to sb; **er hat ihr seinen Platz abgetreten** he gave up his seat to her **3.** **seine Schuhe ~** to wipe off *sep* one's shoes

ab|trocknen *vt* to dry; **das Geschirr ~** to dry the dishes

abturnend [ˈap·tø:ɐ̯·nənt] *adj sl* repulsive

ab|wägen *vt irreg* to weigh; **die Vor- und Nachteile ~** to weigh the advantages and disadvantages

ab|wälzen *vt* **etw [auf jdn] ~** to unload sth [on[to] sb]; (*Kosten*) to pass on *sep*; (*Verantwortung*) to shift

ab|warten I. *vi* to wait **II.** *vt* **etw ~** to wait for sth; **das bleibt abzuwarten** that remains to be seen

abwärts [ˈap·vɛrts] *adv* down, downward[s]; (*bergab*) downhill; **den Fluss ~** downstream

Abwasch[1] <-[e]s> *m kein pl* (*Geschirr*) dirty dishes *pl*; **den ~ machen** to do the dishes

Abwasch[2] <-, -en> *f österr* (*Spülbecken*) sink

ab|waschen *irreg* **I.** *vt* (*Schmutz*) to wash off *sep*; **das Geschirr ~** to do the dishes **II.** *vi* to do the dishes

Abwasser <-wässer> *nt* waste water; (*von Industrieanlagen*) effluent

Abwasserkanal *m* sewer

ab|wechseln [-vɛk·sln] *vr* **sich** *akk* **~** (*bei Tätigkeit*) to take turns

abwechselnd [-vɛk·slnd] *adv* alternately

Abwechslung <-, -en> [-vɛks·lʊŋ] *f* change; **die ~ lieben** to like variety; **zur ~** for a change

abwegig [ˈap·ve:·gɪç] *adj* absurd; (*Idee*) far-fetched; (*Verdacht*) unfounded

ab|wehren *vt* (*Angriff*) to fend off *sep*; (*Ball*) to clear

Abwehrkräfte *pl* the body's defenses

ab|weisen *vt irreg* **1.** (*wegschicken*) to turn away *sep*; **sich** *akk* [**von jdm**] **nicht**

~ lassen to not take no for an answer [from sb] **2.** (*ablehnen*) to turn down *sep*; (*Antrag, Bitte*) to deny

abweisend *adj* cold

ab|wenden *vr reg o irreg* **sich** *akk* ~ to turn away

ab|werben *vt irreg* to entice away *sep*

ab|werten *vt* **1.** (*Währung*) to devalue (**um** +*akk* by) **2.** (*Bedeutung mindern*) to debase

abwesend ['ap·veː·znt] *adj* absent

Abwesenheit <-, -en> *f pl selten* absence

ab|wickeln *vt* (*Auftrag*) to process; (*Geschäft*) to carry out

ab|wimmeln *vt fam* **jdn** ~ to get rid of sb; **etw** ~ to get out of [doing] sth

ab|wischen *vt* to wipe; **sich** *dat* **die Tränen** ~ to dry one's tears; **sich** *dat* **den Schweiß von der Stirn** ~ to wipe the sweat from one's brow

ab|würgen *vt fam* **1.** (*Motor*) to stall **2.** (*unterbrechen*) **jdn** ~ to cut sb short

ab|zahlen *vt* (*in Raten*) to pay in installments

ab|zeichnen **I.** *vt* **1.** (*abmalen*) to copy **2.** (*signieren*) to initial **II.** *vr* (*erkennbar werden*) **sich** *akk* ~ to become apparent

ab|ziehen *irreg* **I.** *vi sein* **1.** (*Truppen*) to withdraw **2.** (*Rauch*) to clear **3.** *fam* (*weggehen*) to go away; **zieh ab!** beat it! *sl* **II.** *vt haben* **1.** (*einbehalten*) to deduct **2.** MATH to subtract **3.** (*Truppen*) to withdraw **4.** (*Bett*) to strip **5.** (*Schlüssel*) to take out *sep* **6.** *schweiz* (*ausziehen*) to take off *sep*

Abzocke <-> *f kein pl pej fam* price gouging

ab|zocken *vt fam* **jdn** ~ to swindle sb

Abzug *m* **1.** ÖKON deduction **2.** (*von Truppen*) withdrawal

abzüglich ['ap·tsyːk·lɪç] *präp* +*gen* minus sth

Abzugshaube *f* exhaust hood

ab|zweigen **I.** *vi sein* to branch off; **nach links/rechts** ~ to turn off to the left/right **II.** *vt fam* **Geld** ~ to put aside *sep* money

Abzweigung <-, -en> *f* turnoff

Ach [ax] *nt* ▶ **mit ~ und** <u>Krach</u> *fam* by

the skin of one's teeth

Achse <-, -n> ['ak·sə] *f* **1.** AUTO axle **2.** (*Linie*) axis ▶ **auf ~ sein** *fam* to be on the move

Achsel <-, -n> ['ak·sl] *f* ANAT armpit; **mit den ~n zucken** to shrug one's shoulders

Achselhöhle *f* armpit

acht¹ [axt] *adj* eight; **das kostet ~ Euro** that costs eight euros; **die Linie ~ fährt zum Bahnhof** the No. 8 [bus/streetcar] goes to the train station; **es steht ~ zu drei** it's eight to three; **~ [Jahre alt] sein/werden** to be/turn eight [years old]; **mit ~ [Jahren]** at the age of eight; **~ Uhr sein** to be eight o'clock; **gegen ~ [Uhr]** [at] about eight [o'clock]; **um ~** at eight [o'clock]; **... [Minuten] nach/vor ~ ...** [minutes] after/to eight [o'clock]; **alle ~ Tage** every eight days; **heute/Freitag in ~ Tagen** a week from today/Friday; **heute/Freitag vor ~ Tagen** a week ago today/Friday

acht² [axt] *adv* **wir waren zu ~** there were eight of us

Acht¹ <-, -en> [axt] *f* eight; **auf dem Eis eine ~ laufen** to skate a figure eight on the ice; **die Kreuzacht** the eight of clubs

Acht RR2 [axt] *f* **~ geben** to be careful; **sie gab genau Acht, was der Professor sagte** she paid careful attention to what the professor said; **auf jdn/etw ~ geben** to look after sb/sth; **etw außer ~ lassen** to not take sth into account; **sich** *akk* [**vor jdm/etw**] **in ~ nehmen** to be wary [of sb/sth]

achte(r, s) ['ax·tə, -tɐ, -təs] *adj* **1.** (*an achter Stelle*) eighth; **an ~r Stelle** [**in**] eighth [place]; **die ~ Klasse** eighth grade **2.** (*Datum*) eighth; **am ~n August** on August eighth

Achte(r) ['ax·tə, -tɐ] *f/m(r) dekl wie adj* **1.** (*Person*) **der/die/das** ~ the eighth; **du bist jetzt der ~, der fragt** you're the eighth person to ask; **als ~ an der Reihe sein** to be the eighth [in line]; **~[r] sein/werden** to be/finish [in] eighth [place]; **als ~r durchs Ziel gehen** to finish eighth, to cross the line in eighth place; **jeder ~** every eighth person, one

in eight [people] **2.** (*bei Datumsangabe*) **der ~** [*o geschrieben* **der 8.**] the eighth *spoken,* the 8th *written;* **heute ist der ~** it's the eighth today; **am ~n** on the eighth **3.** (*Namenszusatz*) **Karl der ~** [*o geschrieben* **Karl VIII.**] Karl the Eighth *spoken* [*o written* Karl VIII]

achtel ['ax·tl̩] *adj* eighth

Achtel <-s, -> ['ax·tl̩] *nt* eighth

achten ['ax·tn̩] **I.** *vt* to respect **II.** *vi* **auf jdn/etw ~** to pay attention to sb/sth; **darauf ~, etw zu tun** to make sure to do sth; **achtet darauf, dass ihr nichts umwerft!** be careful not to knock anything over!

achtens ['ax·tn̩s] *adv* eighthly

Achterbahn *f* roller coaster

achtfach, 8fach ['axt·fax] *adj, adv* eightfold; **die ~e Menge** eight times the amount

achtjährig, 8-jährig [RR] ['axt·jɛː·rɪç] *adj* **1.** (*Alter*) eight-year-old *attr,* eight years old *pred;* **das ~e Jubiläum einer S.** *gen* the eighth anniversary of sth **2.** (*Zeitspanne*) eight-year *attr;* **eine ~e Amtszeit** an eight-year term of office

achtlos I. *adj* careless **II.** *adv* without noticing

achtmal, 8-mal [RR] *adv* eight times

achttägig, 8-tägig [RR] ['axt·tɛː·gɪç] *adj* eight-day *attr,* lasting eight days *pred*

Achtung <-> ['ax·tʊŋ] *f kein pl* respect (**vor** +*dat* for); **~!** attention!

achtzehn ['axt·seːn] *adj* eighteen; **ab ~ frei[gegeben] sein** (*Film*) ≈ NC-17; **~ Uhr** 6 p.m.; MIL 1800 hrs *written; s. a.* **acht**[1]

achtzehnte(r, s) *adj* eighteenth; (*Datum*) 18th; *s. a.* **achte(r, s)** 1, 2

achtzig ['axt·sɪç] *adj* **1.** (*Zahl*) eighty; **die Linie ~ fährt zum Bahnhof** the No. 80 [bus/streetcar] goes to the train station; **~ [Jahre alt] sein** to be eighty [years old]; **mit ~ [Jahren]** at the age of eighty **2.** *fam* (*Stundenkilometer*) eighty [kilometers an hour]; [**mit**] **~ fahren** to do eighty [kilometers an hour] ▶ **jdn auf ~ bringen** *fam* to make sb's blood boil

achtzigste(r, s) ['axt·sɪç·stə, -tə, -təs] *adj* eightieth; *s. a.* **achte(r, s)** 1

Acker <-s, Äcker> ['ake] *m* field

Ackerbau *m kein pl* [arable] farming

Ackerland *nt kein pl* arable [farm]land

Adapter <-s, -> [a'dap·te] *m* adapter

addieren* [a'diː·rən] *vt* to add up *sep*

Adel <-s> ['aːdl̩] *m kein pl* aristocracy

Ader <-, -n> ['aːdɐ] *f* **1.** (*Vene*) vein; (*Schlagader*) artery **2.** (*Begabung*) **eine künstlerische ~ haben** to have an artistic bent

Adjektiv <-s, -e> ['at·jɛk·tiːf] *nt* adjective

Adler <-s, -> ['aːd·le] *m* eagle

adlig ['aːd·lɪç] *adj* aristocratic; **~ sein** to have a title

Adlige(r) ['aːd·lɪ·gə, -gə] *f(m) dekl wie adj* aristocrat

adoptieren* [ad·ɔp·'tiː·rən] *vt* to adopt

Adoption <-, -en> [adɔp·'tsi̯oːn] *f* adoption; **ein Kind zur ~ freigeben** to put a child up for adoption

Adoptiveltern [ad·ɔp·'tiːf·-] *pl* adoptive parents

Adoptivkind *nt* adopted child

Adrenalin <-s> [ad·re·na·'liːn] *nt kein pl* adrenalin

Adressat(in) <-en, -en> [adrɛ·'saːt] *m(f)* addressee

Adressbuch [RR] *nt* address book

Adresse <-, -n> [a'drɛ·sə] *f* address

adressieren* [adrɛ·'siː·rən] *vt* to address (**an** +*akk* to)

Adria <-> ['aːdria] *f* Adriatic [Sea]

Advent <-s, -e> [at·'vɛnt] *m* Advent [season]; **im ~** during [the] Advent [season]; **erster ~** first Sunday of/in Advent

Adverb <-s, -ien> [at·'vɛrp] *nt* adverb

Advokat(in) <-en, -en> [at·vo·'kaːt] *m(f) österr, schweiz* (*Rechtsanwalt*) lawyer

Advokatur <-, -en> [at·vo·ka·'tuːɐ̯] *f schweiz* (*Anwaltskanzlei*) lawyer's office

Affe <-n, -n> ['afə] *m* **1.** (*Tier*) ape, monkey **2.** *fam* (*blöder Kerl*) dope; **ein eingebildeter ~** a conceited jackass

Affekt <-[e]s, -e> [a'fɛkt] *m* affect; **im ~ handeln** to act in the heat of the moment

affektiert [afɛk·'tiːɐ̯t] *adj* affected

Affenhitze ['afn̩·'hɪtsə] *f fam* scorching heat

Afghane, Afghanin <-n, -n> [afˈɡaːnə, -nɪn] *m, f* Afghan; *s. a.* **Deutsche(r)**

Afrika <-s> [ˈaːfriˌka] *nt* Africa

Afrikaner(in) <-s, -> [afriˈkaːnɐ] *m(f)* African

afrikanisch [afriˈkaːnɪʃ] *adj* African

Afroamerikaner(in) [ˈaːfro-] *m(f)* African-American

afroamerikanisch *adj* African-American

After <-s, -> [ˈaf·tɐ] *m* ANAT anus

Agent(in) <-en, -en> [aˈɡɛnt] *m(f)* 1. (*Spion*) spy 2. (*Vertreter*) agent

Agentur <-, -en> [aɡɛnˈtuːɐ] *f* agency

Ägypten <-s> [ɛˈɡʏp·tn̩] *nt* Egypt; *s. a.* **Deutschland**

Ägypter(in) <-s, -> [ɛˈɡʏp·tɐ] *m(f)* Egyptian; *s. a.* **Deutsche(r)**

ägyptisch [ɛˈɡʏp·tɪʃ] *adj* Egyptian; *s. a.* **deutsch**

ähneln [ˈɛːnl̩n] *vt* to resemble, to look like; **du ähnelst meiner Frau** you remind me of my wife

ahnen [ˈaːnən] *vt* to suspect; **das kann/ konnte ich doch nicht ~!** how can/ could I know that?

ähnlich [ˈɛːn·lɪç] **I.** *adj* similar **II.** *adv* similarly; **jdm ~ sehen** to look like sb

Ähnlichkeit <-, -en> *f* resemblance; **mit jdm/etw ~ haben** to resemble sb/sth

Ahnung <-, -en> *f* 1. (*Vermutung*) suspicion; **es ist eher so eine ~** it's more of a hunch *fam* 2. (*Idee*) **hast du eine ~!** *iron fam* that's what you think!; **keine ~ haben** to have no idea; **keine ~!** *fam* [I have] no idea!

ahnungslos *adj* unsuspecting

Ahorn <-s, -e> [ˈaːhɔrn] *m* maple [tree]

Aids <-> [eːts] *nt Akr von* **acquired immune deficiency syndrome** AIDS

Airbag <-s, -s> [ˈɛːɐ·bɛk] *m* airbag

Airbus [ˈɛːɐ·bʊs] *m* airbus

Akademie <-, -n> [aka·deˈmiː] *f* academy

Akademiker(in) <-s, -> [akaˈdeː·mi·kɐ] *m(f)* university graduate

akklimatisieren * [akli·ma·tiˈziː·rən] *vr* **sich** *akk* ~ 1. (*klimatisch*) to become acclimated 2. (*sich einleben*) to get used to sth

Akkordarbeit *f* piecework

Akkordeon <-s, -s> [aˈkɔr·de·ɔn] *nt* accordion

Akku <-s, -s> [ˈaku] *m fam kurz für* **Akkumulator** rechargeable battery

Akkusativ <-s, -e> [ˈaku·za·tiːf] *m* accusative [case]

Akne <-, -n> [ˈaknə] *f* acne

Akrobat(in) <-en, -en> [akro·ˈbaːt] *m(f)* acrobat

akrobatisch *adj* acrobatic

Akt¹ <-[e]s, -e> [akt] *m* 1. (*Gemälde*) nude [painting] 2. (*Handlung*) act; **ein ~ der Rache** an act of revenge 3. THEAT act

Akt² <-[e]s, -e> [akt] *m österr* (*Akte*) file

Akte <-, -n> [ˈaktə] *f* file; **die ~ Borgfeld** the Borgfeld file ▶ **etw zu den ~n legen** to lay sth to rest

Aktenordner *m* file

Aktentasche *f* briefcase

Aktenzeichen *nt* file reference [number]

Aktie <-, -n> [ˈak·tsi̯ə] *f* BÖRSE stock; **die ~n stehen gut/schlecht** the stock is doing well/badly; *fig* things are/aren't looking good

Aktiengesellschaft *f* joint stock company

Aktienkurs *m* stock price

Aktion <-, -en> [akˈtsi̯oːn] *f* action; **in ~ sein** to be [constantly] in action; **in ~ treten** to come into action

Aktionär(in) <-s, -e> [ak·tsi̯o·ˈnɛːɐ] *m(f)* FIN stockholder

aktiv [akˈtiːf] *adj* active

Aktiv <-s, -e> [ˈak·tiːf] *nt pl selten* LING active [voice]

aktivieren * [ak·ti·ˈviː·rən] *vt* to activate

Aktivität <-, -en> [ak·ti·vi·ˈtɛːt] *f* activity

aktualisieren * *vt* to update

aktuell [ak·ˈtu̯ɛl] *adj* current

Akupunktur <-, -en> [aku·pʊŋk·ˈtuːɐ] *f* acupuncture

Akustik <-> [aˈkʊs·tɪk] *f kein pl* acoustics *+ pl vb*

akustisch [aˈkʊs·tɪʃ] *adv* acoustically; **ich habe dich rein ~ nicht verstanden** I just didn't hear what you said

akut [aˈkuːt] *adj* acute

Akzent <-[e]s, -e> [akˈtsɛnt] *m* 1. (*Aussprache*) accent 2. LING (*Zeichen*) accent 3. (*Betonung*) stress 4. (*Schwerpunkt*) emphasis; **den ~ auf etw** *akk*

legen to emphasize sth

akzeptieren* [ak·tsɛp·'tiː·rən] *vt* to accept

Alarm <-[e]s, -e> [a·'larm] *m* alarm; ~ **schlagen** to sound the alarm

Alarmanlage *f* [alarm system]

alarmieren* [alar·'miː·rən] *vt* **die Polizei** ~ to call the police

Albaner(in) <-s, -> [al·'baː·nɐ] *m(f)* Albanian; *s. a.* **Deutsche(r)**

Albanien <-s> [al·'baː·niən] *nt* Albania; *s. a.* **Deutschland**

albanisch [al·'baː·nɪʃ] *adj* Albanian; *s. a.* **deutsch**

albern ['al·bɐn] **I.** *adj* childish **II.** *vi* to fool around

Albtraum ᴿᴿ *m* nightmare

Album <-s, Alben> ['al·bʊm] *nt* album

Alge <-, -n> ['al·gə] *f* alga

Alibi <-s, -s> ['aː·li·bi] *nt* alibi

Alimente [ali·'mɛn·tə] *pl* alimony

Alkohol <-s, -e> ['al·ko·hoːl] *m* alcohol

Alkoholeinfluss ᴿᴿ *m* influence of alcohol

alkoholfrei *adj* nonalcoholic

alkoholhaltig *adj* alcoholic

Alkoholiker(in) <-s, -> [al·ko·'hoː·li·kɐ] *m(f)* alcoholic; ~ **sein** to be an alcoholic

Alkoholismus <-> [al·ko·ho·'lɪs·mʊs] *m kein pl* alcoholism

all [al] *pron indef* all; ~ **ihr Geld** all her money

All <-s> [al] *nt kein pl* space

alle ['alə] *adj pred fam* **1.** (*aufgebraucht*) ~ **sein** to be all gone; **etw** ~ **machen** to finish sth off *sep* **2.** (*erschöpft*) ~ **sein** to be finished

alle(r, s) ['alə, -lə, -ləs] *pron indef* **1.** (*mit Singular*) all; [**ich wünsche dir**] ~**s Gute** [I wish you] all the best **2.** (*mit Plural*) ~**e Anwesenden** all those present **3.** *substantivisch* (*jeder*) ~ everyone; **und damit sind** ~ **gemeint** and that means everyone; **ihr seid** ~ **beide Schlitzohren!** you're both a couple of sly little weasels!; **wir haben** ~ **kein Geld mehr** none of us have any money left; ~ **die[jenigen]**, **die ...** everyone, who ...; ~ **auf einmal** all at once **4.** *substantivisch* (*alle Dinge*) ~**s** everything; **das ist** ~**s** that's everything; **ist das schon** ~**s?** is that

it? **5.** *substantivisch* (*insgesamt*) ~**s** all [that]; **das ist doch** ~**s Unsinn** that's all nonsense **6.** (*bei Zeit- und Maßangaben*) every; ~ **fünf Minuten/Meter** every five minutes/meters ▶ ~**s in** ~**m** all in all; [**wohl**] **nicht mehr** ~ **haben** *fam* to have a screw loose; **vor** ~**m** above all

Allee <-, -n> [a·'leː] *f* avenue

allein [a·'lain] **I.** *adj pred* alone; (*einsam*) lonely; (*ohne Hilfe*) on one's own; **sind Sie** ~ **oder in Begleitung?** are you by yourself or with someone?; **jdn** ~ **lassen** to leave sb alone **II.** *adv* **1.** (*bereits*) just; ~ **der Schaden war schon schlimm genug** the damage alone was bad enough; ~ **der Gedanke daran** the mere thought of it **2.** (*ausschließlich*) exclusively; **das ist** ~ **deine Entscheidung** it's your decision [and yours alone] **3.** (*ohne Hilfe*) by oneself; **er kann sich schon** ~ **anziehen** he can already get himself dressed; ~ **erziehend sein** to be a single parent; **von** ~ by itself/oneself; **ich wäre auch von** ~ **darauf gekommen** I would have thought of it [by] myself

Alleinerziehende(r) *f(m) dekl wie adj* single parent

alleinstehend *adj* single

allemal ['alə·'maːl] *adv* **was er kann, kann ich** ~ whatever he can do, I can do too ▶ **ein für** ~ once and for all

allenfalls ['alən·'fals] *adv* at [the] most

allerbeste(r, s) ['ale·'bɛstə, -tə, -təs] *adj* very best; **ich wünsche dir das A~** I wish you all the best

allerdings ['ale·'dɪŋs] *adv* **1.** (*aber*) although; **ich rufe dich an,** ~ **erst morgen** I'll call you, though not until tomorrow **2.** (*in der Tat*) definitely; ~**!** indeed!, you bet! *fam*; **hast du mit ihm gesprochen?** — ~**!** did you speak to him? — certainly! *fam*

allererste(r, s) ['ale·'ʔeːɐstə, -tə, -təs] *adj* the [very] first; **als A~r** the first; **als A~s** first of all

Allergie <-, -n> [alɛr·'giː] *f* allergy (**gegen** +*akk* to); ~ **auslösend** allergenic

allergisch [a·'lɛr·gɪʃ] **I.** *adj* allergic (**gegen** +*akk* to) **II.** *adv* ~ **auf etw** *akk* **reagie-**

ren MED to have an allergic reaction to sth; *fig* to get steamed up about sth

Allerheiligen <-> ['alɐ'hai·lɪ·ɡn̩] *nt* All Saints' Day

allerlei ['alɐ'lai] *adj* **1.** *substantivisch* a lot; **ich muss noch ~ erledigen** I still have a lot to do **2.** *attr* all sorts of

allerletzte(r, s) ['alɐ·'lɛts·tə, -tɐ, -təs] *adj* [very] last ▸ **das A~ sein** *fam* to be beyond the pale *fam;* **er ist das A~!** he's the worst!

allermeiste(r, s) ['alɐ·'mais·tə, -tɐ, -təs] *adj* most; **am ~n** most of all; **die ~n Leute** the vast majority of the people

allerneueste(r, s) ['alɐ·'nɔy·əs·tə, -tɐ, -təs] *adj* latest; **auf dem ~n Stand** state-of-the-art; **das A~** the latest

Allerseelen <-> ['alɐ·'ze:·lən] *nt* All Souls' Day

allerwenigste(r, s) *adj* **1.** *(zählbar)* fewest; **in den ~n Fällen** in only very few cases **2.** *(unzählbar)* least; **das ~ Geld** the least money; **am ~n** the least

allesamt ['alə·'zamt] *adv* all [of them/ you/us]

allgemein ['al·ɡə·'main] **I.** *adj* general; **von ~em Interesse sein** to be of general interest; **zur ~en Überraschung** to everyone's surprise ▸ **im A~en** *(normalerweise)* generally speaking; *(insgesamt)* on the whole **II.** *adv* generally; **~ bekannt sein** to be common knowledge; **~ gültig** general; **~ verständlich** intelligible to everybody

Allgemeinbildung *f kein pl* general education

Allgemeinheit <-> ['al·ɡə·'main·hait] *f kein pl* general public

allgemeinverständlich *adj s.* **allgemein II**

Allheilmittel *nt* cure-all

Allianz <-, -en> [a'lj̆·ants] *f* alliance

Alliierte(r) [ali·'i:·ɐ·te -te] *f(m) dekl wie adj* ally; **die ~n** the Allies

alljährlich ['al·'jɛ:ɐ·lɪç] *adj attr* annual

allmählich [al·'mɛ:·lɪç] **I.** *adj attr* gradual **II.** *adv* gradually; **~ geht er mir auf die Nerven** he's beginning to get on my nerves; **wir sollten jetzt ~ gehen** it's time we left

Allradantrieb *m* four-wheel drive

Alltag ['al·ta:k] *m kein pl* everyday life

alltäglich ['al·tɛ:k·lɪç] *adj* **1.** *attr (tagtäglich)* daily, everyday **2.** *(gang und gäbe)* usual **3.** *(gewöhnlich)* ordinary

allzu ['al·tsu:] *adv* **~ oft** only too often; **nicht ~ oft** not [all] too often; **~ sehr/ viel** too much

Allzweckhalle *f* multipurpose hall

Allzweckreiniger *m* general-purpose cleaner

Alm <-, -en> [alm] *f* mountain pasture

Alpen ['al·pn̩] *pl* **die ~** the Alps

Alphabet <-[e]s, -e> [al·fa·'be:t] *nt* alphabet

alphabetisch [al·fa·'be:·tɪʃ] *adj* alphabetical

Alptraum ['alp·traum] *m* nightmare

als [als] *konj* **1.** *(zeitlich)* when, as; **ich kam, ~ er ging** I came as he was leaving; **gleich, ~ ...** as soon as ...; **damals, ~ ...** back in the days when ...; **gerade ~ ...** just when ... **2.** *nach Komparativ* than; **Joe ist größer ~ Tom** Joe is taller than Tom **3.** *(wie)* as; **alles andere ~ ...** everything but ...; **anders ~ jd sein** to be different from sb; **niemand anders ~ ...** *a. hum, iron* none other than ... **4.** **...,** **~ habe/könne/sei/würde ...** as if; **..., als habe er es schon geahnt ...,** as if he had already known; **es sieht aus, ~ würde es bald schneien** it looks like snow **5.** *(in der Eigenschaft)* as; **schon ~ Kind hatte er immer Albträume** even as a child, he had nightmares; **sich** *akk* **~ wahr/falsch erweisen** to prove to be true/false

also ['alzo] *adv* so

alt <älter, älteste> [alt] *adj* old; *(von früher)* ancient; **wie ~ ist er? – er ist 8 Jahre ~** how old is he? — he's 8 [years old]; **älter sein/werden** to be/get older; **ältere Mitbürger** senior citizens; **A~ und Jung** young and old alike ▸ **~ aussehen** *fam* to look like a complete fool

Altar <-s, Altäre> [al·'ta:ɐ] *m* altar

altbacken *adj* **1.** *(Backwaren)* stale **2.** *(altmodisch)* old-fashioned

Altbau <-bauten> *m* old building

altbewährt ['alt·bə·'vɛ:ɐt] *adj* tried-and-true

Alter <-s, -> ['altɐ] *nt* **1.** (*Lebensalter*) age; **in jds** *dat* ~ **sein** to be the same age as sb; **er ist in meinem** ~ he's my age; **mittleren ~s** middle-aged **2.** (*Bejahrtheit*) old age; **im** ~ in old age ▸ ~ **schützt vor Torheit nicht** *prov* there's no fool like an old fool *prov*

altern ['altɐn] *vi sein* (*Mensch*) to age

alternativ [altɛrnaˈtiːf] *adv* ~ **leben** to live an alternative lifestyle

Alternative <-, -n> [altɛrnaˈtiːvə] *f* alternative

Altersgruppe *f* age group

Altersheim *nt* retirement home

Altersrente *f* social security

Altersschwäche *f kein pl* infirmity

Altersversorgung *f* pension; (*betrieblich*) retirement plan

Altglascontainer *m* glass recycling container

altklug ['altˈkluːk] *adj* precocious

ältlich ['ɛltlɪç] *adj* oldish

altmodisch **I.** *adj* old-fashioned **II.** *adv* ~ **gekleidet** dressed in old-fashioned clothes; ~ **eingerichtet** furnished in an old-fashioned style

Altöl *nt* used oil

Altpapier *nt* waste paper

Altstadt *f* old town center

Altweibersommer [altˈvaibɐzɔmɐ] *m* Indian summer

Alu ['aːlu] *nt kurz für* **Aluminium**

Alufolie *f* aluminum foil

Aluminium <-s> [aluˈmiːni̯ʊm] *nt kein pl* aluminum

am [am] **1.** = **an dem** *s.* **an 2.** + *superl* **ich fände es ~ besten, wenn ...** I think it would be best if ...; **es wäre mir ~ liebsten, wenn ...** I would prefer it if ...; ~ **schnellsten/schönsten sein** to be [the] fastest/most beautiful

Amateur(in) <-s, -e> [amaˈtøːɐ̯] *m(f)* amateur

Ambulanz <-, -en> [ambuˈlants] *f* **1.** (*im Krankenhaus*) outpatient department **2.** (*Unfallwagen*) ambulance

Ameise <-, -n> ['aːmai̯zə] *f* ant

Ameisenbär *m* anteater

Ameisenhaufen *m* anthill

Amen <-s, -> ['aːmɛn] *nt* Amen

Amerika <-s> [aˈmeːrika] *nt* **1.** (*Kontinent*) America **2.** (*USA*) the USA, the United States, the States *fam*

Amerikaner(in) <-s, -> [ameriˈkaːnɐ] *m(f)* American; *s. a.* **Deutsche(r)**

amerikanisch [ameriˈkaːnɪʃ] *adj* American

Amok ['aːmɔk] *m* ~ **laufen** to run amok

amortisieren * [amɔrtiˈziːrən] *vr sich akk* ~ to pay for itself

Ampel <-, -n> ['ampl̩] *f* traffic light; **die** ~ **ist auf Rot gesprungen** the light turned red; **du hast eine rote** ~ **überfahren** you just ran a red light

Amphibie <-, -n> [amˈfiːbi̯ə] *f* amphibian

amputieren * [ampuˈtiːrən] *vt, vi* to amputate

Amsel <-, -n> ['amzl̩] *f* blackbird

Amt <-[e]s, Ämter> [amt] *nt* **1.** (*Behörde*) office; **aufs** ~ **gehen** *fam* to go to the authorities **2.** (*öffentliche Stellung*) post; **ein** ~ **antreten** to take up one's post; **ein** ~ **innehaben** to hold an office; **im** ~ **sein** to be in office

amtlich *adj* official

Amtsgericht *nt* ≈ district court

Amtsrichter(in) *m(f)* ≈ district court judge

Amtszeit *f* term of office

Amulett <-[e]s, -e> [amuˈlɛt] *nt* amulet

amüsant [amyˈzant] *adj* amusing

amüsieren * [amyˈziːrən] **I.** *vr sich akk* ~ to enjoy oneself; **amüsiert euch gut!** have a good time!; **sich** *akk* **mit jdm** ~ to have a good time with sb; **sich** *akk* **über jdn/etw** ~ to laugh at sb/sth **II.** *vt* **jdn** ~ to amuse sb

an [an] **I.** *präp* **1.** + *dat* (*räumlich*) **etw hängt** ~ **der Wand** sth is hanging on the wall; **am Telefon sein** to be on the phone; **am Tisch sitzen** to sit at the table; **Tür** ~ **Tür wohnen** to be next-door neighbors; ~ **Krücken gehen** to walk on crutches **2.** + *akk* (*räumlich*) **etw** ~ **die Tafel schreiben** to write sth on the board; ~**s Telefon gehen** to answer the telephone; **sich** *akk* ~ **den Tisch setzen** to sit down at the table; **jdn** ~ **die Hand nehmen** to take sb by the hand **3.** + *dat* (*zeitlich*) **am**

Freitag on Friday; **am Morgen** in the morning; **~ jenem Morgen** that morning; **~ Weihnachten** at Christmas; (*25. Dezember*) on Christmas Day **4.** +*dat* (*Eigenschaft*) **das Angenehme ~ etw** *dat* the pleasant thing about sth; **was ist ~ ihm so besonders?** what's so special about him? **5.** +*dat* (*mittels*) **jdn ~ der Stimme erkennen** to recognize sb by his/her voice ▸ **[und für] <u>sich</u> actually II.** *adj pred* (*angeschaltet*) **~ sein** to be on **III.** *adv* (*ungefähr*) **~ die ...** approximately ...

analog [ana·'lo:k] *adj* TECH analog

Analphabet(in) <-en, -en> ['an·ʔal·fa·be:t] *m(f)* illiterate

Analyse <-, -n> [ana·'ly:·zə] *f* analysis

analysieren* [ana·ly·'zi:·rən] *vt* to analyze

Ananas <-, -> ['a·na·nas] *f* pineapple

anatomisch [ana·'to:·mɪʃ] *adj* anatomic

an|bahnen *vr* **sich** *akk* ~ to be in the making; **zwischen ihnen bahnt sich etwas an** there's sth going on there

Anbau¹ *m kein pl* AGR cultivation

Anbau² <-bauten> *m* (*Nebengebäude*) annex

an|bauen *vt* **1.** (*Gemüse*) to grow **2. etw [an etw** *akk*] ~ to build an extension [to sth]

an|beten *vt* to adore; REL to worship

an|biedern ['an·bi:·dən] *vr pej* **sich** *akk* **bei jdm ~** to curry favor with sb

an|bieten *irreg* **I.** *vt* [**jdm**] **etw ~** to offer [sb] sth **II.** *vr* **1.** (*zur Verfügung stellen*) **sich** *akk* ~ to offer one's services; **sich** *akk* ~**, etw zu tun** to offer to do sth **2.** (*naheliegen*) **etw bietet sich an** sth is just the right thing

an|binden *vt irreg* to tie (**an** +*akk* to)

an|blicken *vt* to look at

an|brennen *irreg vi sein* to burn; **etw ~ lassen** to let sth burn; **es riecht hier so angebrannt** something smells burned in here ▸ **nichts ~ <u>lassen</u>** *fam* to not hesitate

Anbruch *m kein pl* **bei ~ des Tages** at the break of day; **bei ~ der Dunkelheit** at dusk

andächtig ['an·dɛç·tɪç] *adv* **1.** REL devoutly **2.** (*ehrfürchtig*) reverently; (*in-*

brünstig) raptly

an|dauern *vi* to continue; (*Gespräche*) to go on

andauernd I. *adj* continuous **II.** *adv* continuously

Andenken <-s, -> *nt* **1.** (*Souvenir*) souvenir **2.** (*Erinnerungsstück*) keepsake **3.** *kein pl* (*Erinnerung*) memory; **zum ~ an jdn** in memory of sb

andere(r, s) ['an·də·rə, -rɐ, -rəs] *pron indef* **1.** (*abweichend*) different, other; **das ist eine ~ Frage** that's another question; **das ~ Geschlecht** the opposite sex; **ein ~s Mal** another time **2.** (*weitere*) other; **haben Sie noch ~ Fragen?** do you have any more questions? **3.** *substantivisch* **es gibt noch ~, die warten!** there are others waiting!; **ein ~r/eine ~** someone else; **alle ~n** all [the] others; **wir ~n** the rest of us; **das T-Shirt ist schmutzig – hast du noch ein ~s** this T-shirt is dirty — do you have another one?; **das ist etwas ganz ~s!** that's something entirely different; **es bleibt uns nichts ~s übrig** there's nothing else we can do; **unter ~m ... ...** among other things

ändern ['ɛn·dɐn] *vt, vr* [**sich** *akk*] ~ to change; **ich kann es nicht ~** I can't do anything about it; **daran kann man nichts ~** there's nothing you can do about it; **es hat sich nichts geändert** nothing's changed; **seine Meinung ~** to change one's mind

anders ['an·dɐs] *adv* differently; **~ als ...** different from [*o* than] ...; **es ging leider nicht ~** I'm afraid I couldn't do anything about it; **~ kann ich es mir nicht erklären** I can't think of another explanation; **~ als sonst** different than usual; **~ denkend** dissenting; **jemand/ niemand ~** somebody/nobody else; **es sich** *dat* **~ überlegen** to change one's mind ▸ **nicht ~ <u>können</u>** *fam* to be unable to help it; **jdm <u>wird</u> ganz ~** sb feels dizzy

anderswo ['an·dɐs·vo:] *adv* somewhere else

anderthalb ['an·dɐt·halp] *adj* one and a half; **~ Stunden** an hour and a half

Änderung <-, -en> *f* change

anderweitig ['an·dɐ·vai·trç] **I.** *adj attr* other **II.** *adv* ~ **beschäftigt sein** to be otherwise busy; **etw** ~ **verwenden** to use sth in a different way

an|deuten *vt* to imply

Andeutung *f* hint; **eine versteckte** ~ **an** insinuation; **eine** ~ **machen** to imply

Andrang *m kein pl* rush

an|eignen *vr* **sich** *dat* **etw** ~ **1.** (*an sich nehmen*) to take sth **2.** (*lernen*) to learn sth

aneinander [an·ʔai'nan·dɐ] *adv* to one another; **etw** ~ **finden** to see sth in each other; ~ **vorbeireden** to be working at cross-purposes

aneinander|geraten * *vi irreg sein* to have a fight

aneinander|reihen *vt* to string together *sep*

an|ekeln *vt* **jdn** ~ to make sb sick; **von etw** *dat* **angeekelt sein** to be disgusted by sth

Anemone <-, -n> [ane·'mo:·nə] *f* BOT anemone

an|erkennen * ['an·ʔɛɐ̯·kɛ·nən] *vt irreg* **1.** (*akzeptieren: Forderung*) to accept; (*Kind*) to acknowledge; (*Meinung*) to respect **2.** (*würdigen*) to appreciate

an|fahren *irreg* **I.** *vi sein* to drive off; (*Zug*) to pull in **II.** *vt haben* **1.** (*mit Fahrzeug*) to hit **2.** (*schelten*) **jdn** ~ to snap at sb **3.** TRANSP to stop at; **einen Hafen** ~ to pull in at a port

Anfall *m* **1.** MED attack; **epileptischer** ~ epileptic seizure **2.** (*Wutanfall*) fit [of rage]; **einen** ~ **kriegen** to throw a fit **3.** (*Anwandlung*) **in einem** ~ **von etw** *dat* in a fit of sth

an|fallen *irreg vt* to attack

anfällig *adj* to be prone (**für** +*akk* to)

Anfang <-[e]s, -fänge> *m* **1.** (*Beginn*) beginning, start; **der Täter war ca.** ~ **40** the perpetrator was in his early 40s; **am** ~ (*zu Beginn*) in the beginning; (*anfänglich*) to begin with; **den** ~ **machen** to start; **einen neuen** ~ **machen** to make a fresh start; ~ **September/der Woche** at the beginning of September/the week; **von** ~ **an** from the [very] start; **von** ~ **bis Ende** from start to finish **2.** (*Ursprung*) origin[s] *usu pl* ▶ **der**

~ **vom Ende** the beginning of the end; **aller** ~ **ist schwer** *prov* the first step is always the hardest

an|fangen *irreg* **I.** *vi* to start **II.** *vt* **1.** (*beginnen*) to start **2.** (*machen*) **anders** ~ to do sth differently **3.** (*zu tun wissen*) **jd kann mit etw** *dat*/ **jdm nichts** ~ sth/sb is [of] no use to sb; **was soll ich damit** ~? what am I supposed to do with that?; **mit jdm ist nichts anzufangen** nothing can be done with sb; **nichts mit sich** *dat* **anzufangen wissen** to not know what to do with oneself

Anfänger(in) <-s, -> *m(f)* beginner; (*im Straßenverkehr*) student driver; ~ **sein** to be a novice

anfänglich *adj attr* initial *attr*

anfangs *adv* at first

Anfangsbuchstabe *m* first letter

Anfangsstadium *nt* initial stage[s] *usu pl*

an|fassen **I.** *vt* to touch **II.** *vi* **mit** ~ to lend a hand

an|fechten *vt irreg* JUR to contest

an|fertigen *vt* to make

an|flehen *vt* to beg (**um** +*akk* for)

Anflug *m* LUFT approach ▶ **ein** ~ **von Eifersucht** a fit of jealousy

an|fordern *vt* to request; (*Katalog*) to order

Anforderung *f* **1.** *kein pl* (*das Anfordern*) request; (*von Katalog*) ordering **2.** *meist pl* (*Anspruch*) demands; ~**en** [**an jdn**] **stellen** to place demands [on sb]; **du stellst zu hohe** ~**en** you're too demanding

Anfrage *f* inquiry; **auf** ~ [up]on request

an|fragen *vi* to ask

an|freunden ['an·frɔyn·dn̩] *vr* **sich** *akk* ~ to become friends; **sich** *akk* **mit jdm** ~ to make friends with sb; **sich** *akk* **mit etw** *dat* ~ to get to like sth

an|führen *vt* **1.** (*Gruppe*) to lead **2.** (*zitieren*) to quote; **ein Beispiel/einen Grund** ~ to give an example/a reason **3.** (*benennen*) to name

Anführer(in) *m(f)* leader

Anführungsstrich *m*, **Anführungszeichen** *nt meist pl* quotation mark[s]

Angabe <-, -n> *f* **1.** *meist pl* (*Information*) details *pl*; **genauere** ~**n** further

details; **~n zur Person** personal details; **~n machen** to give details **2.** *kein pl* (*Prahlerei*) boasting

an|geben *irreg* **I.** *vt* **1.** (*nennen*) to give; **seinen Namen ~** to give one's name; **jdn als Zeugen ~** to cite sb as a witness **2.** (*behaupten*) to claim **3.** (*anzeigen*) to indicate **4.** (*bestimmen*) to set; (*Takt*) to give; **das Tempo ~** to set the pace **II.** *vi* (*prahlen*) to brag (**mit** +*dat* about)

Angeber(in) <-s, -> *m(f)* poser

angeblich ['anˈɡeːplɪç] **I.** *adj attr* alleged **II.** *adv* allegedly; **er hat ~ nichts gewusst** supposedly, he didn't know anything about it

angeboren *adj* innate; MED congenital

Angebot *nt* offer; **im ~** on sale; **~ und Nachfrage** supply and demand

angebracht *adj* **1.** (*sinnvoll*) sensible **2.** (*angemessen*) suitable

angegossen *adj* **wie ~ sitzen** *fam* to fit like a glove

angeheitert ['anˈɡəˈhaiˈtɛt] *adj fam* tipsy

an|gehen *irreg* **I.** *vi sein* **1.** (*Licht, Radio*) to come on **2.** (*bekämpfen*) **gegen jdn/etw ~** to fight sb/sth **II.** *vt haben* (*betreffen*) to concern; **was geht mich das an?** what's that got to do with me?; **das geht dich nichts an!** *fam* that's none of your business!; **was mich angeht, ...** as far as I am concerned, ...

an|gehören * *vi* to belong to

Angehörige(r) *f(m) dekl wie adj* **1.** (*Verwandte(r)*) relative; **die nächsten ~n** the next of kin **2.** (*Mitglied*) member

Angeklagte(r) *f(m) dekl wie adj* accused

Angel <-, -n> ['aŋl] *f* fishing pole

Angelegenheit <-, -en> *f* matter; **sich** *akk* **um seine eigenen ~en kümmern** to mind one's own business

angeln ['aŋln] **I.** *vi* to fish (**nach** +*dat* for) **II.** *vt* to catch; **sich** *dat* **einen Mann ~** *fam* to catch oneself a man

Angelrute *f* fishing rod

angemessen **I.** *adj* appropriate; **~es Verhalten** appropriate behavior **II.** *adv* appropriately; **~ bezahlt** appropriately paid

angenehm *adj* pleasant; (*Nachricht*)

good; (*Wetter*) agreeable ▶ **das A~e mit dem Nützlichen verbinden** to mix business with pleasure

angesehen **I.** *adj* respected; (*Firma*) of good standing **II.** *pp von* **ansehen**

angesichts *präp* +*gen* in the face of

Angestellte(r) *f(m) dekl wie adj* employee

angestrengt *pp von* **anstrengen**

angetan **I.** *adj* **von jdm/etw ~ sein** to be taken with sb/sth; **es jdm ~ haben** to appeal to sb **II.** *pp von* **antun**

angetrunken *adj* tipsy

angewandt **I.** *adj attr* applied **II.** *pp von* **anwenden**

angewiesen **I.** *adj* dependent (**auf** +*akk* [up]on) **II.** *pp von* **anweisen**

an|gewöhnen * *vt* **sich** *dat* **etw ~** to get into the habit of [doing] sth

Angewohnheit *f* habit

Angler(in) <-s, -> ['aŋ·lɐ] *m(f)* angler

angreifbar *adj* contestable

an|greifen *irreg vt, vi* to attack

angrenzend *adj attr* bordering; **die ~en Bauplätze** the adjoining building sites

Angriff *m* attack ▶ **etw in ~ nehmen** to tackle sth

angriffslustig *adj* aggressive

angst [aŋst] *adj* **jdm ist/wird ~ [und bange]** sb is/becomes afraid

Angst <-, Ängste> [aŋst] *f* fear (**vor** +*dat* of); **~ bekommen** to get scared; **~ [vor etw** *dat*] **haben** to be afraid [of sth]; **~ um etw** *akk* **haben** to be worried about sth; **jdm ~ machen** to frighten sb

ängstigen ['ɛŋs·tɪ·ɡn̩] **I.** *vt* to frighten **II.** *vr* **sich** *akk* **~** to be afraid

ängstlich ['ɛŋst·lɪç] *adj* timid

Angstmacherei <-> ['aŋst·ma·xə·rai] *f kein pl* scaremongering

an|haben *vt irreg* **1.** (*Kleidung*) to have on **2.** (*schaden*) **jdm nichts ~ können** to be unable to harm sb

an|halten *irreg* **I.** *vi* **1.** (*stoppen*) to stop **2.** (*fortdauern*) to continue **II.** *vt* (*stoppen*) to bring to a stop

anhaltend *adj* (*Hitze*) continuing; (*Lärm*) incessant; (*Schmerz*) persistent

Anhalter(in) <-s, -> ['an·hal·tɐ] *m(f)* hitchhiker; **per ~ fahren** to hitchhike

Anhang <-[e]s, -hänge> *m* **1.** (*Nach-*

trag) appendix **2.** *kein pl* (*Angehörige*) [close] family, dependants **3.** COMPUT attachment

an|hängen *vt* **1.** *fam* (*anlasten*) **jdm etw ~** to blame sth on sb **2.** COMPUT to attach

Anhänger <-s, -> *m* **1.** AUTO trailer **2.** (*Schmuck*) pendant **3.** (*für Gepäck*) label

Anhänger(in) <-s, -> *m(f)* fan

anhänglich ['an·hɛŋ·lɪç] *adj* devoted; **die Kinder sind sehr anhänglich** the children won't leave their mother's side

an|heben *irreg vt* **1.** (*hochheben*) to lift [up *sep*] **2.** *fig* (*Löhne, Preise*) to increase

Anhieb *m* **auf ~** right away; **das kann ich nicht auf ~ sagen** I can't say off the top of my head

an|himmeln *vt fam* to idolize

an|hören I. *vt* [**sich** *dat*] **etw ~** to listen to sth; **jdm etw ~** to hear sth in sb['s voice]; **dass er Däne ist, hört man ihm nicht an** you can't tell from his accent that he's Danish **II.** *vr* **sich** *akk* **~** to sound

Animateur(in) <-s, -e> [anima·'tø:ɐ̯] *m(f)* host *masc*, hostess *fem*

animieren* [ani·'mi:·rən] *vt* to encourage

Anis <-[es], -e> [a'ni:s] *m* **1.** (*Pflanze*) anise **2.** (*Gewürz*) aniseed

Ankauf *m* buy

Anker <-s, -> ['aŋ·kɐ] *m* anchor; **vor ~ gehen** to drop anchor [somewhere]; **den ~ lichten** to weigh anchor; **vor ~ liegen** to lie at anchor

an|ketten *vt* to chain up (**an** +*akk* to)

Anklage <-, -n> *f* **1.** (*Beschuldigung*) accusation **2.** *kein pl* JUR charge; **gegen jdn ~ [wegen etw** *gen*] **erheben** to charge sb [with sth]; **unter ~ stehen** to be charged

an|klagen *vt* **1.** JUR to charge **2.** (*beschuldigen*) to accuse

Anklang *m* ▶ **finden** to meet with approval

an|klicken *vt* COMPUT to click on

an|klopfen *vi* to knock

an|knüpfen *vt* **etw** *akk* **~** to resume sth

an|kommen *irreg* **I.** *vi sein* to arrive; **seid ihr gut angekommen?** did you

arrive safely?; [**bei jdm**] **~** (*Sache*) to go over well [with sb]; (*Person*) to make an impression [on sb]; **gegen jdn/etw ~** to get the better of sb/sth **II.** *vi impers sein* (*wichtig sein*) **es kommt darauf an, dass ...** what matters is that ... **2.** (*abhängen von*) **auf jdn/etw ~** to be dependent on sb/sth; **das kommt darauf an** it depends

an|kündigen *vt* to announce

Ankündigung *f* announcement

Ankunft <-, -künfte> ['an·kʊnft] *f* arrival

an|kurbeln *vt* ÖKON to boost

an|lächeln *vt* to smile at

Anlass RR <-es, -lässe>, **Anlaß** ALT <-sses, -lässe> ['an·las] *m* **1.** (*Gelegenheit*) occasion; **dem ~ entsprechend** to fit the occasion **2.** (*Grund*) reason; **es besteht kein ~ zu etw** *dat/*, **etw zu tun** there are no grounds for sth/to do sth; [**jdm**] **~ zu etw** *dat* **geben** to give [sb] grounds for sth; **keinen ~ haben, etw zu tun** to have no grounds to do sth; **etw zum ~ nehmen, etw zu tun** to use sth as an opportunity to do sth

an|lassen *irreg vt* **1.** AUTO to start [up *sep*] **2.** *fam* (*Kleidung*) to keep on *sep* **3.** **das Licht ~** to leave on *sep* the light

Anlasser <-s, -> *m* AUTO starter [motor]

anlässlich RR, **anläßlich** ALT ['an·lɛs·lɪç] *präp* +*gen* on the occasion of

Anlauf <-[e]s, -läufe> *m* SPORT **~ nehmen** to take a running start

an|laufen *irreg vi sein* **1.** (*Metall*) to tarnish **2.** **vor Wut rot ~** to turn purple with rage

Anlaufschwierigkeiten *pl meist pl* initial difficulties

Anlaufstelle *f* refuge

an|legen I. *vt* **1.** (*Liste*) to draw up; (*Garten, Park*) to lay out; **Vorräte ~** to stock up **2.** ÖKON (*Geld*) to invest **II.** *vi* (*Schiff*) to berth **III.** *vr* **sich** *akk* **mit jdm ~** to pick a fight with sb

an|lehnen I. *vt* to lean [against]; (*Tür*) to leave ajar **II.** *vr* **sich** *akk* **~ an** to lean against

an|leiern *vt fam* to get going

an|leiten *vt* to instruct

Anleitung *f* instructions *pl*; **unter jds** *dat* **~** under sb's guidance

Anliegen <-s, -> *nt* request

an|locken *vt* to attract; (*Tier*) to lure

an|lügen *vt irreg* to lie to

an|machen *vt* **1.** (*Licht, Gerät*) to turn on *sep;* (*Zigarette*) to light **2.** (*Salat*) to dress **3.** (*aufreizen*) to turn on *sep* **4.** *sl* (*aufreißen wollen*) to pick up *sep* **5.** *sl* (*rüde ansprechen*) **jdn ~** to have a go at sb

an|mailen ['an·mɛɪ·lən] *vt fam* to e-mail

anmaßend ['an·ma:·sn̩t] *adj* arrogant

an|melden **I.** *vt* **1. ein Kind in der Schule ~** to enroll a child at a school; **jdn zu einem Kurs ~** to enroll sb in a course **2. ein Auto ~** to register a car; **ein Fernsehgerät/Radio ~** to get a TV/radio reception license; **das Telefon ~** to get phone service **II.** *vr* **sich** *akk* **~** **1.** (*zu einem Besuch*) to give notice of a visit (**bei** +*dat* to) **2.** (*zu einem Kurs*) to sign up **3.** (*bei einem Umzug*) to register one's change of address with the authorities

Anmeldung <-, -en> *f* **1.** (*Ankündigung*) [advance] notice [of a visit]; **ohne ~** without an appointment **2.** SCH enrollment **3.** (*Registrierung*) registration **4.** (*Anmelderaum*) reception

an|merken *vt* **jdm etw ~** to notice sth in sb; **er ließ sich nichts ~** he didn't let it show

Anmerkung <-, -en> *f* **1.** (*Fußnote*) footnote **2.** (*Kommentar*) comment

anmutig *adj* graceful

an|nähen *vt* **einen Knopf ~** to sew a button on

Annäherungsversuche *pl* advances; **~ machen** to make advances

Annahme <-, -n> *f* **von einer ~ ausgehen** to proceed on the assumption; **in der ~, dass ...** on the assumption that ...

annehmbar *adj* acceptable

an|nehmen *irreg* **I.** *vt* **1.** (*übernehmen*) to accept; (*Auftrag, Job, Patienten, Schüler*) to take on *sep;* (*Kind*) to adopt **2.** (*voraussetzen*) to assume; **angenommen, das stimmt ...** assuming that's right ... **II.** *vr* **1.** (*sich kümmern*) *akk* **jds** *gen* **~** to look after sb **2.** (*erledigen*) **sich** *akk* **einer S.** *gen* **~** to take

care of sth

Annehmlichkeiten <-, -en> *pl* conveniences

Anno, anno ['ano] *adv österr* in the year ▶ **von ~ dazumal** *fam* from long ago

Annonce <-, -n> [a'nõː·sə] *f* advertisement

anonym [ano·'nyːm] *adj* anonymous; **~ bleiben** to remain anonymous

Anorak <-s, -s> ['ano·rak] *m* anorak

an|ordnen *vt* **1.** (*bestimmen*) to order **2.** (*ordnen*) to arrange (**nach** +*dat* according to)

an|packen **I.** *vt* to tackle; **packen wir's an!** let's get started! **II.** *vi* **mit ~** to lend a hand

an|passen **I.** *vt* to adjust **II.** *vr* **sich jdm/etw ~** to fit in with sb/sth; (*gesellschaftlich*) to conform to sth

anpassungsfähig *adj* adaptable

Anpassungsfähigkeit *f* adaptability

an|pflanzen *vt* to grow

an|probieren* *vt* to try on *sep*

an|pumpen *vt fam* **jdn ~** to pump sb for cash *sl;* **jdn um 100 Euro ~** to hit sb up for 100 euros *sl*

an|rechnen *vt* (*gutschreiben*) **die 200 Euro werden auf die Gesamtsumme angerechnet** the 200 euros will be deducted from the total ▶ **dass er ihr geholfen hat, rechne ich ihm hoch an** I think very highly of him for having helped her

an|regen *vt* **1.** (*ermuntern*) **jdn** [**zu etw** *dat*] **~** to encourage sb [to do sth] **2.** (*vorschlagen*) to suggest **3.** (*stimulieren*) to stimulate; **den Appetit ~** to whet the appetite

anregend *adj* stimulating; (*sexuell*) sexually arousing

Anregung *f* **auf jds ~** at sb's suggestion

Anreise *f* trip [here/there]

Anreiz *m* incentive

an|rempeln *vt* to bump into

Anrichte <-, -n> *f* sideboard

an|richten *vt* (*Speisen*) to prepare; (*Schaden, Unheil*) to cause; **was hast du da wieder angerichtet!** what have you done now!; **Unfug ~** to be up to no good

anrüchig ['an·rʏ·çɪç] *adj* indecent

Anruf *m* [phone] call

Anrufbeantworter <-s, -> *m* answering machine

an|rufen *irreg vt, vi* to phone; **angerufen werden** to get a [phone] call

Ansage *f* announcement

an|sagen I. *vt* to announce II. *vr* **sich** *akk* ~ to announce a visit

Ansager(in) <-s, -> ['an·za:·ge] *m(f)* RADIO announcer

ansässig ['an·zɛ·sɪç] *adj* resident; **in einer Stadt** ~ **sein** to reside in a city

an|schaffen I. *vt* to buy; **sich** *dat* **etw** ~ to buy oneself sth II. *vi sl* ~ [gehen] to hook *pej fam*

Anschaffung <-, -en> *f* purchase; **eine** ~ **machen** to make a purchase

an|schalten *vt* to switch on

an|schauen *vt, vr s.* **ansehen**.

anschaulich I. *adj* illustrative; **ein ~es Beispiel** a good example II. *adv* vividly

Anschein *m* appearance; **allem** ~ **nach** to all appearances; **den** ~ **erwecken, als [ob]** ... to give the impression that ...; **den** ~ **haben, als [ob]** ... to seem that ...

anscheinend *adv* apparently

Anschlag *m* attempted assassination; **einen** ~ **auf jdn/etw verüben** to make an attack on sb/sth; **einen** ~ **auf jdn vorhaben** *hum fam* to have a request for sb

an|schließen *irreg* I. *vt* TECH to connect (**an** +*akk* to) II. *vr* 1. (*sich zugesellen*) **sich** *akk* **jdm** ~ to join sb 2. (*beipflichten*) **sich** *akk* **jdm/etw** ~ to fall in with sb/sth; **dem schließe ich mich an** I think I'd go along with that

Anschluss ᴿᴿ *m* 1. TELEK connection; **der** ~ **ist gestört** there's a disturbance in the line 2. **im** ~ **an etw** *akk* after sth 3. *kein pl* (*Kontakt*) contact; ~ **finden** to make friends; ~ **suchen** to try to make friends 4. BAHN, LUFT (*Verbindung*) connection; **den** ~ **verpassen** to miss one's connecting train/flight

an|schmiegen *vr* **sich** *akk* [an jdn/etw] ~ to cuddle up [to sb/sth]; (*Katze, Hund*) to nestle [up to sb/into sth]

anschmiegsam *adj* 1. (*anlehnungsbedürftig*) affectionate 2. (*weich*) soft

an|schnallen *vr* **sich** *akk* ~ to fasten one's seat belt

an|schnauzen *vt fam* to yell at

an|schneiden *vt irreg* (*Brot, Fleisch*) to cut; (*Thema*) to touch on

an|schreiben *irreg* I. *vt* **jdn** ~ to write to sb II. *vi fam* ~ **lassen** to buy on credit

an|schreien *vt irreg* to shout at

Anschrift *f* address

an|schwemmen *vt* to wash up *sep*

an|sehen *irreg vt* 1. (*ins Gesicht sehen*) to look at; **jdn böse** ~ to give sb an angry look 2. (*betrachten: Film*) to watch; (*Theaterstück, Fußballspiel*) to see; **etw genauer** ~ to take a closer look at sth; **hübsch anzusehen sein** to be pretty to look at 3. (*ablesen können*) **jdm sein Alter nicht** ~ sb doesn't look his/her age; **ihre Erleichterung war ihr deutlich anzusehen** her relief was obvious 4. (*hinnehmen*) **etw mit** ~ to stand by and watch sth; **das kann ich nicht länger mit** ~ I can't stand it anymore

Ansehen <-s> *nt kein pl* reputation

ansehnlich *adj* considerable; **eine ~e Leistung** an impressive performance

an|setzen I. *vt* 1. **jdn auf jdn/etw** ~ (*Detektiv*) to put sb on sb/sth 2. **Fett** ~ to put on weight II. *vi* to start; **zum Überholen** ~ to begin to pass

Ansicht <-, -en> *f* opinion; **ich bin ganz Ihrer** ~ I agree with you completely; **in etw** *dat* **geteilter** ~ **sein** to have a different view of sth; **der** ~ **sein, dass** ... to be of the opinion that ...; **meiner** ~ **nach** in my opinion

Ansichtskarte *f* [picture] postcard

Anspannung *f* strain

an|spielen *vi* to allude (**auf** +*akk* to); **worauf willst du** ~? what are you driving at?

Anspielung <-, -en> *f* allusion (**auf** +*akk* to)

an|spornen *vt* to spur on; (*Spieler*) to cheer on

Ansprache *f* speech; **eine** ~ **halten** to make a speech

an|sprechen *irreg* I. *vt* 1. (*anreden*) **jdn** ~ to speak to sb; **jdn [mit Peter/**

mit seinem Namen| ~ to address sb [as Peter/by his name] **2.** (*erwähnen*) **etw** ~ to mention sth **3.** (*gefallen*) **jdn** ~ to appeal to sb **II.** *vi* MED, TECH to respond (**auf** +*akk* to)

ansprechend *adj* appealing

Ansprechpartner(in) *m(f)* contact [person]

an|springen *irreg vi sein* (*Motor*) to start

Anspruch *m* **1.** (*Recht*) claim (**auf** +*akk* to); ~ **auf etw** *akk* **erheben** to make a claim for sth; ~ **auf etw** *akk* **haben** to be entitled to sth **2.** (*Anforderung*) demand; **den Ansprüchen [voll] gerecht werden** to [fully] meet the requirements; **Ansprüche stellen** to be very demanding ▶ **etw in** ~ **nehmen** to claim sth; **jds Hilfe in** ~ **nehmen** to accept help from sb

anspruchslos *adj* undemanding; (*Film, Lektüre*) trivial; **ein ~er Mensch** a modest person

anspruchsvoll *adj* demanding; (*Lesestoff, Film a.*) highbrow; (*Geschmack*) discriminating

Anstalt <-, -en> ['anʃtalt] *f fam* (*für psychisch Kranke*) asylum

Anstand *m kein pl* decency; **keinen** ~ **haben** to have no sense of decency

anständig **I.** *adj* decent **II.** *adv* **1.** (*gesittet*) decently; **sich** *akk* ~ **benehmen** to behave oneself **2.** *fam* (*gut*) properly; ~ **essen/ausschlafen** to get a decent meal/a good night's sleep

an|starren *vt* to stare at

anstatt [an.'ʃtat] **I.** *präp* +*gen* instead of **II.** *konj* ~ **etw zu tun** instead of doing sth

an|stecken **I.** *vt* **1.** (*Gebäude*) to set on fire; (*Zigarette*) to light [up] **2.** (*infizieren*) to infect; **ich möchte dich nicht** ~ I don't want to give you my cold **II.** *vr* **sich** *akk* [**bei jdm**] ~ to catch sth [from sb]; **sich** *akk* **leicht/schnell** ~ to get sick easily

ansteckend *adj* contagious; ~**e Krankheit** contagious disease

an|stehen *vi irreg haben o südd sein* **1.** (*Schlange stehen*) **nach etw** *dat* ~ to line up for sth **2.** (*zu erledigen sein*)

etw steht an sth must be dealt with; **steht bei dir heute etwas an?** are you planning on doing anything today?

an|steigen *vi irreg sein* **1.** (*sich erhöhen*) to go up (**auf** +*akk* to, **um** +*akk* by) **2.** (*steiler werden*) to ascend; **steil** ~ to ascend steeply

anstelle [an.'ʃtɛ.lə] *präp* +*gen* instead of

an|stellen **I.** *vt* **1.** (*einschalten*) to turn on *sep* **2.** (*beschäftigen*) to employ **3.** (*durchführen*) **Nachforschungen [über etw** *akk*] ~ to conduct inquiries [into sth]; **Vermutungen [über etw** *akk*] ~ to make assumptions [about sth] **4.** *fam* (*bewerkstelligen*) to manage; **etw geschickt** ~ to pull sth off **5.** *fam* (*anrichten*) **Blödsinn** ~ to be up to no good; **was hast du da wieder angestellt?** what have you done now? *fam* **II.** *vr* **sich** *akk* ~ **1.** (*Schlange stehen*) to line up; **sich** *akk* **hinten** ~ to get in the back of a line **2.** *fam* (*sich verhalten*) to act; **sich** *akk* **dumm** ~ to play the fool **3.** (*wehleidig sein*) to make a fuss; **stell dich nicht [so] an!** don't make such a fuss!

an|stiften *vt* **jdn [dazu]** ~, **etw zu tun** to incite sb to do sth; **jdn zu einem Verbrechen** ~ to incite sb to commit a crime

Anstoß *m* **1.** (*Ansporn*) impetus (**zu** +*dat* for); **den** ~ **zu etw** *dat* **bekommen** to be encouraged to do sth; **jdm den** ~ **geben**, **etw zu tun** to encourage sb to do sth **2.** (*Ärgernis*) ~ **erregen** to be annoying; **an etw** *dat* ~ **nehmen** to take offense at sth **3.** SPORT start of the game; (*Billard*) break; (/*am.*/ Fußball) kickoff; (*Eishockey*) face-off **4.** *schweiz* (*Angrenzung*) border

an|stoßen *irreg* **I.** *vi* **1.** *sein* **mit dem Kopf an etw** *akk o dat* ~ to bump one's head on sth **2.** *haben* **auf jdn/etw** ~ to drink to sb/sth; **lasst uns** ~! let's drink to it/that! **II.** *vt haben* **1.** (*leicht stoßen*) to bump **2.** (*in Gang setzen*) to set in motion **III.** *vr haben* **sich** *dat* **den Kopf** ~ to bang one's head

anstößig *adj* offensive

an|streichen *vt irreg* **1.** (*mit Farbe*) to paint; **etw neu/frisch** ~ to give sth a

new/fresh coat of paint **2.** (*markieren*)
to mark; **etw rot ~** to mark sth [in] red

Anstreicher(in) <-s, -> *m(f)* [house]
painter

an|strengen I. *vr* **sich** *akk* **~** to try hard;
sich *akk* **mehr ~** to make a greater effort
II. *vt* **jdn ~** to tire sb out

anstrengend *adj* strenuous; (*geistig*) taxing; (*körperlich*) exhausting; **das ist ~
für die Augen** it's a strain on the eyes

Anstrengung <-, -en> *f* effort; **mit letzter ~** with one last effort

Ansturm *m* rush

Antarktis <-> [ant·'?ark·tɪs] *f* Antarctic

antarktisch [ant·'?ark·tɪʃ] *adj* Antarctic
attr

an|tasten *vt* **1.** jds Ehre/Würde **~** to
offend sb's honor/dignity; **jds Rechte
~** to encroach [up]on sb's rights **2.** *Er-
sparnisse/Vorräte* **~** to dip into sav-
ings/supplies

Anteil ['an·tail] *m* share (**an** +*dat* of); **der
~ an Asbest** the proportion of asbestos
▶ **~ an etw** *dat* **nehmen** to show an
interest in sth

anteilig *adj* proportionate

Anteilnahme <-> ['an·tail·na:·mə] *f* kein
pl sympathy

Antenne <-, -n> [an·'tɛ·nə] *f* antenna

antiautoritär [an·ti·?au·to·ri·'tɛ:ɐ̯] *adj*
anti[-]authoritarian

Antibabypille [an·ti·'be:·bi·pɪ·lə] *f* fam
die ~ the [contraceptive] pill

Antibiotikum <-s, -biotika> [an·ti·'bio:-
ti·kʊm] *nt* antibiotic

Antiblockiersystem [an·ti·blɔ·'ki:ɐ̯-] *nt*
antilock [braking] system, ABS

antik [an·'ti:k] *adj* (*Möbel*) antique

Antike <-> [an·'ti:·kə] *f* kein *pl* antiq-
uity; **die Kunst der ~** the art of the
ancient world

Antikörper *m* MED antibody

Antilope <-, -n> [an·ti·'lo:·pə] *f* antelope

Antiquariat <-[e]s, -e> [an·ti·kva·'ria:t]
nt secondhand bookstore

Antiquität <-, -en> [an·ti·kvi·'tɛ:t] *f* antique

Antrag <-[e]s, -träge> ['an·tra:k] *m*
1. (*Beantragung*) application (**auf** +*akk*
for); **einen ~ stellen** to put in an ap-

plication **2.** (*Heiratsantrag*) [marriage]
proposal; **jdm einen ~ machen** to
propose to sb

Antragsformular *nt* application form

an|treffen *vt irreg* jdn **~** to catch sb; **etw
~** to come across sth

an|treiben *irreg vt* **1.** (*vorwärtstreiben*)
to drive [on *sep*] **2.** (*drängen*) jdn **~,
etw zu tun** to urge sb to do sth; (*auf-
dringlicher*) to push sb to do sth **3.** TECH
to drive

Antrieb *m* AUTO, LUFT drive ▶ **aus eigenem ~** on one's own initiative

Antritt *m* kein *pl* **nach ~ seines Am-
tes** after assuming office; **nach ~ der
Erbschaft** after coming into the inheritance

an|tun *vt irreg* jdm etwas/nichts **~** to
do something/not to do anything to sb;
tu mir das nicht an! hum fam spare
me, please! ▶ **sich** *dat* **etwas ~** to
kill oneself

Antwort <-, -en> ['ant·vɔrt] *f* answer
(**auf** +*akk* to); **jdm [eine] ~ geben** to
give sb an answer; **als ~ auf etw** *akk* in
response to sth

antworten ['ant·vɔr·tn̩] *vi* [jdm/auf etw
akk] **~** to answer [sb/sth]; **mit Ja/Nein
~** to answer yes/no; **schriftlich ~** to
answer in writing

an|vertrauen* ['an·fɛɐ̯·trau·ən] **I.** *vt* jdm
etw **~** (*übergeben*) to entrust sb with
sth; (*erzählen*) to confide sth to sb **II.** *vr*
sich *akk* jdm **~** to confide in sb

Anwalt, Anwältin <-[e]s, -wälte> ['an·
valt, 'an·vɛl·tɪn] *m*, *f* lawyer; **sich** *dat*
einen ~ nehmen to hire a lawyer

an|weisen *vt irreg* jdn **~, etw zu tun** to
order sb to do sth

Anweisung <-, -en> *f* order

anwendbar *adj* applicable (**auf** +*akk* to);
in der Praxis ~ practicable

an|wenden *vt reg o irreg* to use (**bei**
+*dat* on)

Anwender(in) <-s, -> *m(f)* COMPUT user

anwenderfreundlich *adj* COMPUT user-
friendly

Anwendung *f* **1.** (*Gebrauch*) use **2.** MED
administration

anwesend *adj* present *pred* (**bei** +*dat* at)

Anwesenheit <-> *f* kein *pl* presence;

(*von Studenten*) attendance; **in jds ~** in sb's presence

an|widern ['an·viː·dən] *vt* to disgust

Anzahl *f kein pl* number

Anzahlung *f* down payment

an|zapfen *vt* to tap

Anzeige <-, -n> *f* **1.** (*Strafanzeige*) charge (**wegen** +*gen* of) **2.** (*Inserat*) ad|vertisement

an|zeigen *vt* **1.** jdn [**wegen einer S.** *gen*] **~** to report sb [for sth] **2.** (*Gerät, Uhr*) to show; (*digital*) to display

an|ziehen *irreg* **I.** *vt* **1.** (*Kleidung*) to put on *sep* **2.** (*festziehen: Schraube*) to tighten; (*Handbremse*) to put on **3.** (*Arm, Bein*) to draw up **4.** (*anlocken*) to attract; **sich** *akk* **von jdm/etw angezogen fühlen** to be attracted to sb/sth **5.** *schweiz* **das Bett frisch ~** to change the bed **II.** *vr* **sich** *akk* **~** to get dressed; **sich** *akk* **warm ~** to dress warm[ly]; **sich** *akk* **schick ~** to dress up

anziehend *adj* attractive

Anziehungskraft *f* **1.** PHYS **~ der Erde** [force of] gravitation **2.** *kein pl fig* **auf jdn eine ~ ausüben** to appeal to sb

Anzug *m* **1.** (*Kleidung*) suit **2.** *schweiz* (*Bezug*) duvet cover

anzüglich ['an·tsyːk·lɪç] *adj* (*Bemerkung*) insinuating; **~ werden** to get personal

an|zünden *vt* (*Feuer, Zigarette*) to light; (*Haus*) to set on fire

apart [a·'part] *adj* striking

Apartment <-s, -s> [a·'part·mənt] *nt* apartment

apathisch [a·'paː·tɪʃ] *adj* apathetic

Apfel <-s, Äpfel> ['ap·fl̩] *m* apple ▶ **in den <u>sauren</u> ~ beißen** *fam* to bite the bullet; **der ~ fällt nicht weit vom <u>Stamm</u>** *prov* like father, like son

Apfelbaum *m* apple tree

Apfelsaft *m* apple juice

Apfelsine <-, -n> [ap·fl̩·'ziː·nə] *f* orange

Apfelwein *m* hard cider

Apostel <-s, -> [a·'pɔs·tl̩] *m* apostle

Apostroph <-s, -e> [apo·'stroːf] *m* apostrophe

Apotheke <-, -n> [apo·'teː·kə] *f* pharmacy

Apotheker(in) <-s, -> [apo·'teː·kɐ] *m(f)* pharmacist

Apparat <-[e]s, -e> [apa·'raːt] *m* **1.** TECH

apparatus *form;* (*kleineres Gerät*) gadget **2.** (*Telefon*) telephone; **am ~ bleiben** to hold on; **am ~!** speaking!

appellieren * [ape·'liː·rən] *vi* **an jds Vernunft ~** to appeal to sb's common sense

Appetit <-[e]s> [ape·'tiːt] *m kein pl* appetite; **guten ~!** enjoy your meal!; **~ auf etw** *akk* **haben** to feel like [having] sth; [**jdm**] **~ machen** to whet sb's appetite; **jdm den ~ verderben** to spoil sb's appetite

appetitlich *adj* appetizing

Appetitlosigkeit <-> *f kein pl* lack of appetite

applaudieren * [aplau·'diː·rən] *vi* to applaud

Applaus <-es, -e> [a·'plaus] *m pl selten* applause

Aprikose <-, -n> [apri·'koː·zə] *f* apricot

April <-s, -e> [a·'prɪl] *m pl selten* April; *s. a.* **Februar** ▶ **~! ~!** April fool!; **jdn in den ~ <u>schicken</u>** to make an April fool of sb

Aprilscherz *m* April fools' joke

apropos [apro·'poː] *adv* by the way; **~ Männer, ...** speaking of men, ...

Aquarell <-s, -e> [akva·'rɛl] *nt* watercolor [painting]

Äquator <-s> [ɛ·'kvaː·toːɐ̯] *m kein pl* equator

Araber(in) <-s, -> ['ara·bɐ] *m(f)* Arab

arabisch [a·'raː·bɪʃ] *adj* **1.** GEOG Arabian; **A~es Meer** Arabian Sea **2.** LING Arabic; **auf ~** in Arabic

Arbeit <-, -en> ['ar·bait] *f* **1.** (*Tätigkeit*) work; **gute/schlechte ~ leisten** to do a good/bad job; **sich** *akk* **an die ~ machen** to get down to work **2.** (*Arbeitsplatz*) job **3.** SCH test; **eine ~ schreiben** to take a test; **eine schriftliche ~** a [term] paper **4.** *kein pl* (*Mühe*) effort; **sich** *dat* **~ machen** to take the trouble ▶ **erst die ~, dann das <u>Vergnügen</u>** *prov* business before pleasure *prov*

arbeiten ['ar·bai·tn̩] *vi* to work; (*Körperorgan*) to function; **an etw** *dat* **~** to be working on sth; **~ gehen** to have a job

Arbeiter(in) <-s, -> *m(f)* (*Industrie*) [blue-collar] worker; (*Landwirtschaft*) laborer

Arbeitgeber(in) <-s, -> *m(f)* employer

Arbeitnehmer(in) <-s, -> *m(f)* employee

Arbeitsamt *nt* unemployment office

Arbeitsbedingungen *pl* working conditions *pl*

Arbeitsbeschaffungsmaßnahme *f* job creation plan

Arbeitserlaubnis *f* work permit

Arbeitsessen *nt* business lunch/dinner

Arbeitsgericht *nt* a court that handles labor disputes

arbeitsintensiv *adj* labor-intensive

Arbeitskleidung *f* work clothes *pl*

Arbeitskraft *f* 1. *kein pl* (*Leistungskraft*) work capacity 2. (*Mitarbeiter*) worker

arbeitslos *adj* unemployed

Arbeitslose(r) *f(m) dekl wie adj* unemployed person; **die ~n** the unemployed

Arbeitslosengeld *nt* unemployment benefit

Arbeitslosenhilfe *f* unemployment aid

Arbeitslosigkeit <-> *f kein pl* unemployment *no indef art, + sing vb*

Arbeitsmarkt *m* job market

Arbeitsniederlegung *f* walkout

Arbeitsplatz *m* 1. (*Arbeitsstätte*) workplace; **am ~** at work 2. (*Stelle*) job; **freier ~** vacancy

Arbeitsspeicher *m* COMPUT main memory

Arbeitstag *m* work day

arbeitsunfähig *adj* unable to work; **jdn ~ schreiben** to put sb on sick leave

Arbeitsunfall *m* work-related accident

Arbeitsvertrag *m* employment contract

Arbeitszeit *f* working hours *pl*; **gleitende ~** flexitime

Arbeitszeugnis *nt* reference

Arbeitszimmer *nt* study

Archäologe, Archäologin <-n, -n> [ar-çɛo·'lo:·gə, arçɛo·'lo:·gɪn] *m, f* archaeologist

Archäologie <-> [arçɛo·lo·'gi:] *f kein pl* archaeology

Architekt(in) <-en, -en> [ar·çi·'tɛkt] *m(f)* architect

Architektur <-, -en> [ar·çi·tɛk·'tu:ɐ̯] *f* architecture

Archiv <-s, -e> [ar·'çi:f] *nt* archives *pl*

Arena <-, Arenen> [a're:·na] *f* 1. (*Manege*) [circus] ring 2. SPORT [sports] arena 3. (*für Stierkampf*) [bull]ring

arg <ärger, ärgste> [ark] *bes südd* I. *adj* bad; (*Enttäuschung*) big II. *adv* badly; **tut es ~ weh?** does it hurt badly?

Argentinien <-s> [ar·gɛn·'ti:·ni·ən] *nt* Argentina; *s. a.* **Deutschland**

Argentinier(in) <-s, -> [ar·gɛn·'ti:·niɐ] *m(f)* Argentinian; *s. a.* **Deutsche(r)**

argentinisch [ar·gɛn·'ti:·nɪʃ] *adj* Argentinian; *s. a.* **deutsch**

Ärger <-s> ['ɛrge] *m kein pl* trouble; **~ bekommen** to get into trouble; **~ haben** to have problems; [jdm] **~ machen** to cause [sb] trouble

ärgerlich *adj* 1. (*verärgert*) annoyed 2. (*unangenehm*) annoying

ärgern ['ɛr·gɐn] I. *vt* 1. (*ungehalten machen*) to annoy 2. (*reizen*) to tease (**wegen** +*gen* about) II. *vr* **sich** *akk* ~ to be annoyed; **ich ärgere mich, dass ich nicht hingegangen bin** I'm upset with myself for not going

arglos *adj* innocent

Argument <-[e]s, -e> [argu·'mɛnt] *nt* argument; **das ist kein ~** (*unsinnig*) that's a poor argument; (*keine Entschuldigung*) that's no excuse

argumentieren * *vi* to argue; **mit etw** *dat* **~** to use sth as an argument

argwöhnisch ['ark·vø:·nɪʃ] *adj* suspicious

Aristokrat(in) <-en, -en> [arɪs·to·'kra:t] *m(f)* aristocrat

aristokratisch *adj* aristocratic

Arktis <-> ['ark·tɪs] *f* Arctic

arktisch ['ark·tɪʃ] *adj* arctic

arm <ärmer, ärmste> [arm] *adj* poor; **~ dran sein** to have a hard time

Arm <-[e]s, -e> [arm] *m* arm; **jdn im ~ halten** to hold sb in one's arms ▶ **jdm** [**mit etw** *dat*] **unter die ~e greifen** to help sb out [with sth]; **jdn auf den ~ nehmen** to pull sb's leg

Armaturenbrett *nt* AUTO dashboard

Armband <-bänder> *nt* 1. (*an Uhr*) [watch] strap 2. (*Schmuck*) bracelet

Armbanduhr *f* [wrist]watch

Armee <-, -n> [ar·'me:] *f* army

Ärmel <-s, -> ['ɛr·ml] *m* sleeve

Ärmelkanal *m* **der ~** the English Channel

Armlehne f armrest

ärmlich ['ɛrm·lɪç] I. adj poor; (Kleidung) shabby; **aus ~en Verhältnissen** from humble backgrounds II. adv poorly; **~ gekleidet sein** to be shabbily dressed

armselig adj 1. (Kleidung) shabby 2. (dürftig) miserable

Armut <-> ['ar·muːt] f kein pl poverty

Aroma <-s, Aromen> [a'roː·ma] nt 1. (Geruch) aroma; (Geschmack) taste 2. (Aromastoff) flavor[ing]

aromatisch [aro·'maː·tɪʃ] adj aromatic; **~ schmecken** to have a distinctive taste

Arrest <-[e]s, -e> [a'rɛst] m JUR detention

arrogant [aro·'gant] adj arrogant

Arroganz <-> [aro·'gants] f kein pl arrogance

Arsch <-[e]s, Ärsche> [arʃ] m derb 1. (Hintern) ass 2. pej (blöder Kerl) asshole ▸ **am ~ der Welt** sl out in the boonies; **jdm in den ~ kriechen** sl to kiss sb's ass sl; **jdn [mal] am ~ lecken können** sl sb can shove it; **im ~ sein** sl to be screwed

Arschkriecher(in) <-s, -> m(f) pej derb ass kisser

Arschloch nt derb asshole

Arsen <-s> [ar·'zeːn] nt kein pl CHEM arsenic

Art <-, -en> [aːgt] f 1. (Sorte) kind 2. (Methode) way; **auf diese ~ und Weise** [in] this way; **das ist doch keine ~!** that's no way to behave! 3. (Wesen) nature 4. BIOL species ▸ **nach ~ des Hauses** à la maison

Artenschutz m protection of species

Arterie <-, -n> [ar·'teː·riə] f artery

artig ['aːg·tɪç] adj well-behaved

Artikel <-s, -> [ar·'tiː·kl] m 1. (in der Zeitung) article 2. (Ware) item 3. LING article

Artischocke <-, -n> [ar·ti·'ʃɔ·kə] f artichoke

Artist(in) <-en, -en> [ar·'tɪst] m(f) performer

Arznei <-, -en> [aːgts·'naɪ] f medicine

Arzneimittel nt drug

Arzt, Ärztin <-es, Ärzte> [aːgtst, 'ɛːgts·tɪn] m, f doctor; **~ für Allgemeinmedizin** family physician, GP

Arzthelfer(in) m(f) doctor's assistant

ärztlich ['ɛːgtst·lɪç] I. adj medical II. adv medically; **sich** akk **~ behandeln lassen** to get medical advice

As ALT <-ses, -se> [as] nt s. **Ass**

Asche <-, -n> ['aʃə] f ash

Aschenbecher m ashtray

Aschermittwoch [aʃɐ·'mɪt·vɔx] m REL Ash Wednesday

Asiat(in) <-en, -en> m(f) Asian

asiatisch [a'zia·tɪʃ] adj Asiatic; (Kultur, Sprache) Asian

Asien <-s> ['aːzi̯ən] nt Asia

asozial ['azo·tsi̯aːl] adj antisocial

Asphalt <-[e]s, -e> [as·'falt] m asphalt

asphaltieren* [as·fal·'tiː·rən] vt to tar

Ass RR <-es, -e> nt ace ▸ **[noch] ein ~ im Ärmel haben** to have an ace up one's sleeve

Assistent(in) <-en, -en> [asɪs·'tɛnt] m(f) assistant

Assistenzarzt, -ärztin m, f [hospital] intern

assistieren* [asɪs·'tiː·rən] vi to assist (**bei** +dat with)

Ast <-[e]s, Äste> [ast] m branch ▸ **auf dem absteigenden ~ sein** fam sb/sth is going downhill

Aster <-, -n> ['as·tɐ] f aster

ästhetisch [ɛs·'teː·tɪʃ] adj aesthetic

Asthma <-s> ['ast·ma] nt kein pl asthma

asthmatisch [ast·'maː·tɪʃ] adj asthmatic

Astrologe, Astrologin <-n, -n> [as·tro·'loː·gə, -gɪn] m, f astrologer

Astrologie <-> [as·tro·lo·'giː] f kein pl astrology

astrologisch [as·tro·'loː·gɪʃ] adj astrological

Astronom(in) <-en, -en> [as·tro·'noːm] m(f) astronomer

Astronomie <-> [as·tro·no·'miː] f kein pl astronomy

Asyl <-s, -e> [a'zyːl] nt asylum; **um ~ bitten** to apply for [political] asylum; **jdm ~ gewähren** to grant sb [political] asylum

Asylbewerber(in) m(f) asylum seeker

Atelier <-s, -s> [atə·'li̯eː] nt KUNST studio

Atem <-s> ['aːtəm] m kein pl breath; **den ~ anhalten** to hold one's breath; **~ ho-**

len to take a breath; **wieder zu ~ kommen** to catch one's breath; **außer ~** out of breath ▶ **den längeren ~ haben** to have the upper hand; **jdn in ~ halten** to keep sb on their toes; **jdm den ~ verschlagen** to take sb's breath away

atemberaubend adj breathtaking

Atemgerät nt respirator; (von Taucher) breathing apparatus

atemlos adv breathlessly

Atemnot f kein pl shortness of breath

Atemweg m respiratory tracts pl

Atemzug m breath

Atheist(in) <-en, -en> [ate·'ɪst] m(f) atheist

Äthiopien <-s> [ɛ'tjoː·pi̯·ən] nt Ethiopia; s. a. **Deutschland**

Äthiopier(in) <-s, -> [ɛ'tjoː·pi̯·ɐ] m(f) Ethiopian; s. a. **Deutsche(r)**

äthiopisch [ɛ'tjoː·pɪʃ] adj Ethiopian; s. a. **deutsch**

Athlet(in) <-en, -en> [at·'leːt] m(f) athlete

athletisch [at·'leː·tɪʃ] adj athletic

Atlantik <-s> [at·'lan·tɪk] m Atlantic

Atlas <-, Atlanten> ['at·las] m atlas

atmen ['aːt·mən] vt, vi to breathe

Atmosphäre <-, -n> [at·mo·'sfɛː·rə] f atmosphere

Atmung <-> f kein pl breathing

Atom <-s, -e> [a'toːm] nt atom

Atombombe f nuclear bomb

Atomenergie f nuclear energy

Atomindustrie f nuclear industry

Atomkraft f kein pl nuclear power

Atomkraftwerk nt nuclear power plant

Attentat <-[e]s, -e> ['atn·taːt] nt attempt on sb's life; **ein ~ auf jdn verüben** to make an attempt on sb's life

Attentäter(in) ['atn·tɛː·tɐ] m(f) assassin

Attest <-[e]s, -e> [a'tɛst] nt certificate; **jdm ein ~ ausstellen** to certify sth

Attrappe <-, -n> [a'trapə] f dummy

ätzend adj 1. (Substanz) corrosive 2. (Geruch) pungent 3. sl (sehr übel) lousy

Aubergine <-, -n> [obɐr·'ʒiː·nə] f eggplant

auch [aux] adv 1. (ebenfalls) too, also, as well; **ich ~** me too; **~ nicht** not ... either, ... [n]either; **ich ~ nicht** me [n]either; **ich**

gehe nicht mit! – ich ~ nicht! I'm not going [along]! — neither am I!; **wenn du nicht hingehst, gehe ich ~ nicht** if you don't go, I won't either 2. (sogar) even; **~ wenn** even if 3. (einräumend) **wie dem ~ sei** whatever

Audienz <-, -en> [au·'diː·ɛnts] f audience

auf [auf] I. präp 1. +dat on; **~ dem Stuhl** on the chair 2. +akk on, onto; **sie fiel ~ den Rücken** she fell on[to] her back 3. +akk (zu) to; **~ die Post/das Fest** to the post office/party 4. +akk (bei Zeitangaben) on; **etw ~ morgen verlegen** to postpone sth until tomorrow II. adv fam 1. (geöffnet) **~ sein** to be open 2. (nicht mehr im Bett) **~ sein** to be up ▶ **~ und ab** up and down; **~ und davon** up and away

auf|**atmen** vi [erleichtert] **~** to heave a sigh of relief

auf|**bauen** vt 1. (zusammenbauen) to assemble 2. (errichten: Zelt) to put up sep; (Haus, Stadt) to build; **ein Haus neu ~** to rebuild a house 3. (aufmuntern) **jdn [wieder] ~** to cheer up sep sb 4. (schaffen: Partei, Existenz) to build

auf|**bekommen*** vt irreg fam 1. (öffnen) to get open sep 2. (Hausaufgaben) to get as homework

auf|**bereiten*** vt (Trinkwasser) to purify

auf|**bessern** vi to improve; (Gehalt) to increase

auf|**bewahren*** vt 1. (aufheben) to keep 2. (lagern) to store

Aufbewahrung <-> f kein pl [safe] keeping

auf|**blasen** irreg vt (Luftballon) to blow up sep

auf|**bleiben** vi irreg sein 1. (nicht zu Bett gehen) to stay up 2. (geöffnet bleiben) to stay open

auf|**blühen** vi sein 1. (Blume) to bloom 2. (aufleben) to blossom out

auf|**brauchen** vt to use up sep

auf|**brausen** vi sein to flare up

auf|**brechen** irreg I. vt haben to break open sep; **ein Auto** to break into a car II. vi sein 1. (aufplatzen) to break up; (Wunde) to open 2. (sich auf den Weg machen) to start off; **ich glaube, wir**

müssen ~ I think we have to go

auf|bringen *vt irreg* (*Geld*) to raise; (*Geduld, Kraft, Mut*) to summon [up *sep*]

Aufbruch *m kein pl* departure

auf|decken *vt* (*Skandal, Verbrechen*) to reveal

auf|donnern *vr fam* **sich** *akk* ~ to doll oneself up

auf|drängen I. *vt* jdm etw ~ to force sth on sb **II.** *vr* **sich** *akk* jdm ~ to impose oneself on sb

auf|drehen I. *vt* **1.** (*öffnen*) to turn on *sep*; (*Flasche, Ventil*) to open; (*Schraubverschluss*) to unscrew **2.** *fam* (*lauter stellen*) to turn up *sep* **II.** *vi fam* **aufgedreht sein** to be full of go

aufdringlich *adj* (*Benehmen*) obtrusive; (*Geruch*) pungent; (*Person*) insistent

auf|drücken *vt* **1.** (*Tür*) to push open *sep* **2.** *fam* (*aufzwingen*) **jdm etw** ~ to impose sth on sb

aufeinander [auf·ʔai·ˈnan·dɐ] *adv* **1.** (*räumlich*) on top of each other **2.** (*zeitlich*) after each other; **dicht ~ folgen** to come hard and fast *a. hum*; **~ folgend** successive **3.** (*gegeneinander*) **~ losgehen** to hit away at each other **4.** (*wechselseitig*) **~ angewiesen sein** to be dependent [up]on each other; **~ zugehen** to approach each other

aufeinander|folgen *vi sein s.* **aufeinander 2**

aufeinanderfolgend *adj s.* **aufeinander 2**

aufeinander|stoßen *vi irreg sein* to clash

Aufenthalt <-[e]s, -e> [ˈauf·ʔɛnt·halt] *m* stay; BAHN stop[over]; **wie lange haben wir in Köln ~?** how long are we stopping in Cologne?

Aufenthaltsort *m* whereabouts + *sing/ pl vb*

Aufenthaltsraum *m* day room; (*in Firma*) employee lounge

Auferstehung <-, -en> *f* REL resurrection; **Christi ~** the Resurrection [of Christ]

auf|essen *irreg vt, vi* to eat up *sep*

Auffahrunfall *m* collision; (*mehrere Fahrzeuge*) pile-up

auffallend I. *adj* striking **II.** *adv* ~

schön strikingly beautiful

auffällig *adj* conspicuous; **an jdm ~ sein** to be noticeable about sb; **etwas A~es** something conspicuous

Auffanglager *nt* reception camp

auf|fassen *vt* to interpret; **etw falsch ~** to misinterpret sth

Auffassung *f* opinion; **ich bin der ~, dass ...** I think [that] ...; **nach jds ~** in sb's opinion

auf|finden *vt irreg* to find

auf|fliegen *vi irreg sein* **1.** (*Tür*) to fly open **2.** *fam* (*bekannt werden*) to leak out; (*Betrug, Machenschaften*) to be exposed; **jdn/etw ~ lassen** to blow the whistle on sb/sth

auf|fordern *vt* jdn ~, etw zu tun to ask sb to do sth; **jdn zum Tanz ~** to ask sb to dance

auf|frischen I. *vt haben* (*Beziehung*) to renew; (*Erinnerung*) to refresh; (*Kenntnisse*) to polish up *sep*; (*Make-up*) to touch up; **sein Englisch ~** to brush up on one's English **II.** *vi sein o haben* (*Wind*) to freshen

Auffrischungskurs *m* refresher course

auf|führen I. *vt* **1.** (*Theaterstück*) to perform **2.** (*auflisten*) to list; (*Beispiele, Zeugen*) to cite **II.** *vr* **sich** *akk* ~ to behave; **sich** *akk* ~, **als ob ...** to act as if ...

Aufführung *f* THEAT performance

auf|füllen *vt* to fill up *sep*

Aufgabe <-, -n> *f* **1.** (*Pflicht*) job, task **2.** *meist pl* (*Übung*) exercise; (*Hausaufgabe*) homework; **eine schwierige ~ lösen** to solve a difficult problem

auf|gabeln *vt fam* to pick up *sep*

Aufgabenbereich *nt* area of responsibility

auf|geben *irreg* **I.** *vt* **1.** (*Brief, Päckchen*) to mail **2.** (*Gepäck*) to register; LUFT to check in **3.** (*Anzeige*) to place **4. eine Gewohnheit ~** to break [with] a habit; **das Rauchen ~** to quit smoking **5.** (*verloren geben*) **jdn ~** to give up on sb **II.** *vi* to give up; MIL to surrender

aufgeblasen I. *adj pej* self-important **II.** *pp von* **aufblasen**

aufgebracht I. *adj* outraged (**über** +*akk* with) **II.** *pp von* **aufbringen**

aufgedunsen adj bloated; (Gesicht) puffy

auf|gehen vi irreg sein 1. (sich öffnen) to open; (Vorhang) to rise; (Knoten, Reißverschluss etc.) to come undone 2. (Sonne, Mond) to rise 3. (Teig) to rise 4. (Erfüllung finden) **in etw** dat **~** to be wrapped up in sth

aufgelegt I. adj gut/schlecht **~ sein** to be in a good/bad mood; **dazu ~ sein, etw zu tun** to feel like doing sth II. pp von **auflegen**

aufgeregt I. adj excited II. pp von **aufregen**

aufgeschmissen adj fam **~ sein** to be in a jam

aufgeweckt I. adj bright II. pp von **aufwecken**

auf|greifen vt irreg **einen Punkt ~** to take up a point; **ein Gespräch ~** to continue a conversation

aufgrund, auf Grund [auf·'grʊnt] präp +gen because of

auf|haben irreg fam I. vt (Hut, Mütze) to wear II. vi (Geschäft, Museum) to be open

auf|halten irreg I. vt 1. **jdn ~** to hold up sb sep; **den Verkehr ~** to tie up traffic 2. **die Hand ~** to hold out sep one's hand; **jdm die Tür ~** to hold open sep the door for sb II. vr 1. (verweilen) **sich** akk **~** to stay somewhere 2. (sich befassen) **sich** akk **mit jdm/etw ~** to spend time [dealing] with sb/sth

auf|hängen I. vt (Bild, Mantel) to hang up sep; (Mensch) to hang II. vr **sich** akk **~** to hang oneself

auf|heben irreg vt 1. (vom Boden) to pick up sep 2. (behalten) to keep 3. (Gesetz) to abolish; (Urteil) to reverse; (Verbot) to lift

auf|heitern I. vt to cheer up sep II. vr impers **sich** akk **~** (Himmel) to brighten up

auf|hetzen vt pej to incite

auf|holen I. vt to make up sep II. vi to catch up; (Läufer, Rennfahrer) to make up ground

auf|horchen vi to prick up one's ears

auf|hören vi to stop

auf|klappen vt (Buch) to open [up sep];

(Messer) to unclasp; (Verdeck) to fold back sep

auf|klären I. vt to inform (über +akk about); (sexuell) to explain the facts of life; (Irrtum, Missverständnis) to resolve; (Verbrechen) to clear up sep II. vr **sich** akk **~** 1. (Geheimnis, Irrtum) to resolve itself 2. (sonniger werden) to brighten [up]

Aufkleber m sticker

auf|kommen vi irreg sein 1. (finanziell) **für etw** akk **~** to pay for sth; **für jdn ~** to pay for sb's upkeep 2. (Nebel, Regen) to set in; (Wind) to pick up

auf|laden irreg vt 1. **etw auf den Wagen ~** to load on[to] a vehicle 2. **jdm etw ~** to burden sb with sth 3. (Batterie) to charge

Auflage <-, -n> f 1. (eines Buchs) edition 2. (Auflagenhöhe: eines Buchs) number of copies; (einer Zeitung) circulation 3. (Bedingung) condition; **die ~ haben, etw zu tun** to be obliged to do sth

auf|lassen vt irreg fam 1. (Fenster, Tür) to leave open sep 2. (Hut) to leave on sep

auf|lauern vi **jdm ~** to lie in wait for sb

Auflauf m KOCHK casserole

auf|laufen vi irreg sein fam **jdn ~ lassen** to show sb up

auf|leben vi sein to liven up

auf|legen vt 1. **ein Buch neu ~** to reprint a book 2. **eine CD ~** to put on sep a CD 3. **den Hörer ~** to hang up

auf|lehnen vr **sich** akk **~** to revolt

auf|leuchten vi sein o haben to light up

auf|lockern vt **die Erde ~** to break up sep the earth 1. SPORT **die Muskeln ~** to loosen up one's muscles 2. **das Gespräch ~** to liven up the conversation

auf|lösen I. vt 1. (in Flüssigkeit) to dissolve 2. (aufklären) to clear up sep 3. (Konto, Geschäft) to close; (Haushalt) to break up sep; (Parlament) to dissolve; (Partei, Verein) to disband II. vr **sich** akk **~** 1. (in Flüssigkeit) to dissolve 2. (sich klären) to resolve itself 3. (Bewölkung) to break up; (Nebel a.) to lift

Auflösung f 1. (eines Geschäfts, Kontos) closing; (eines Haushalts) breaking

up; (*des Parlaments*) dissolution; (*einer Partei, eines Vereins*) disbanding **2.** (*eines Rätsels*) solution **3.** (*Bildqualität*) resolution

auf|machen I. *vt* (*Tür*) to open; (*Knopf*) to undo **II.** *vi* **1.** (*Tür öffnen*) to open the door **2.** (*Geschäft*) to open up **III.** *vr* **sich** *akk* ~ to set out (**nach** +*akk* for)

aufmerksam *adj* attentive; **das ist sehr ~ [von Ihnen]**! that's most kind [of you]; **jdn auf etw** *akk* ~ **machen** to draw sb's attention to sth; **auf etw** *akk* ~ **werden** to take notice of sth

auf|muntern *vt* to cheer up *sep*

aufmüpfig *adj fam* rebellious

Aufnahme <-, -n> *f* **1.** (*von Musik, Videos*) recording **2.** (*von Tätigkeit*) start **3.** (*in Verein*) admission

Aufnahmeprüfung *f* entrance examination

auf|nehmen *vt irreg* **1.** (*Foto*) to take; (*Film, Video*) to record **2. jdn [bei sich** *dat*] ~ to take in *sep* sb **3.** (*verstehen*) **etw** ~ to grasp sth; **wie hat sie es aufgenommen?** how did she take it? **4.** (*auflisten*) to include **5.** (*Tätigkeit*) to take up *sep;* **Kontakt mit jdm** ~ to contact sb

auf|opfern *vr* **sich** *akk* ~ to sacrifice oneself

auf|passen *vi* to pay attention; **pass auf!** (*sei aufmerksam*) [be] careful!; (*Vorsicht*) watch out!; **genau** ~ to pay close attention; **auf die Kinder** ~ to watch the children

auf|peppen [ˈaʊf·pɛpn̩] *vt sl* to jazz up *sep*

Aufprall <-[e]s, -e> *m* impact

auf|prallen *vi sein* **auf etw** *akk* ~ to hit sth; (*Mensch, Fahrzeug a.*) to run into sth

Aufpreis *m* surcharge; **gegen** ~ for an additional charge

auf|pumpen *vt* to pump up *sep*

Aufputschmittel *nt* stimulant

auf|raffen *vr* **sich** *akk* **zu etw** *dat* ~ to bring oneself to do sth

auf|räumen I. *vt* (*Zimmer*) to clean [up *sep*]; (*Schrank*) to clear out; (*Schreibtisch*) to clear [off *sep*]; (*Spielsachen*) to put away *sep* **II.** *vi* to clean up; **mit etw**

dat ~ to do away with sth

aufrecht [ˈaʊf·rɛçt] *adj, adv* upright

aufrecht|erhalten * [ˈaʊf·rɛçt·ʔɛɡ·hal·tn̩] *vt irreg* to maintain; (*Freundschaft*) to keep up *sep;* **seine Behauptung** ~ to stick to one's claim

auf|regen I. *vt* to excite; (*nervös machen*) to make nervous **II.** *vr* **sich** *akk* ~ to get worked up (**über** +*akk* about); **reg dich nicht so auf!** don't get [yourself] so worked up!

Aufregung *f* excitement; **nur keine ~!** don't get flustered; **in heller** ~ in utter confusion; **jdn in** ~ **versetzen** to make sb lose their composure *fam*

auf|reißen *irreg vt haben* **1.** (*öffnen*) (*Augen, Mund*) to open wide *sep;* (*Fenster, Tür*) to fling open *sep;* (*Geschenk, Tüte*) to tear open *sep* **2. eine Frau/einen Mann** ~ *sl* to pick up *sep* a woman/man

aufrichtig *adj* honest; (*Gefühl*) sincere; (*Liebe*) true

Aufrichtigkeit <-> *f kein pl* sincerity

auf|rufen *irreg* **I.** *vt* **1.** (*Schüler, Zeuge*) to call [out *sep*] **2.** COMPUT (*Datei*) to call up *sep;* (*Daten*) to retrieve **II.** *vi* **zu etw** *dat* ~ to call for sth

Aufruhr <-[e]s, -e> [ˈaʊf·ru:ɐ̯] *m* **1.** *kein pl* (*Unruhe*) turmoil; (*in der Stadt/im Volk*) unrest **2.** (*Aufstand*) revolt

aufrührerisch *adj* rebellious

auf|runden *vt* to round up *sep* (**auf** +*akk* to)

auf|sagen *vt* to recite

auf|sammeln *vt* to pick up *sep*

aufsässig [ˈaʊf·zɛ·sɪç] *adj* rebellious

Aufsatz *m* LING essay

auf|schichten *vt* to stack

auf|schieben *vt irreg* (*Termin*) to postpone ▶ **aufgeschoben ist nicht aufgehoben** *prov* there'll be another opportunity

auf|schlagen *irreg* **I.** *vi* **1.** *sein* **mit dem Kopf [auf etw** *akk* o *dat*] ~ to hit one's head [on sth] **2.** *haben* (*sich verteuern*) to go up (**um** +*akk* by) **II.** *vt haben* **1.** (*Buch*) to open; **Seite 35** ~ to turn to page 35 **2.** (*Nuss*) to break open *sep* **3.** (*Zelt*) to put up *sep* **4.** (*verteuern*) to raise (**um** +*akk* by)

auf|schließen *irreg* I. *vt* (*Tür*) to unlock II. *vi* |*jdm*| ~ to unlock the door [for sb]

aufschlussreich ^{RR} *adj* informative; (*enthüllend*) revealing

auf|schnappen *vt fam* to pick up *sep*

Aufschnitt *m kein pl* 1. (*Wurst*) cold cuts *npl* 2. (*Käse*) assorted sliced cheese[s *pl*]

auf|schrauben *vt* to unscrew; (*Flasche*) to take the cap off

auf|schrecken I. *vt* <schreckte auf, aufgeschreckt> **haben** to startle II. *vi* <schreckte auf, aufgeschreckt> **sein** to start [up]

auf|schreiben *vt irreg* to write down *sep;* **sich** *dat* **etw** ~ to make a note of sth

Aufschub *m* delay; **jdm** ~ **gewähren** to grant sb an extension

auf|schwatzen *vt dial fam* **jdm etw** ~ to palm off *sep* sth on sb; **sich** *dat* **etw** ~ **lassen** to get talked into buying sth

Aufschwung *m* 1. (*Auftrieb*) impetus; **jdm neuen** ~ **geben** to give sb a boost 2. (*Aufwärtstrend*) upswing

Aufsehen <-s> *nt kein pl* sensation; **ohne** [**großes**] ~ without any [real] fuss; **etw erregt** [**großes**] ~ sth causes a [great] sensation; ~ **erregend** sensational

auf|setzen I. *vt* 1. (*Hut, Brille*) to put on *sep* 2. (*Essen, Wasser*) to put on *sep* 3. (*zur Schau tragen*) to put on *sep* II. *vr* **sich** *akk* ~ to sit up

Aufsichtsrat *m* supervisory board

auf|spielen *vr fam* **sich** *akk* ~ to show off

auf|spüren *vt* to track down *sep*

auf|stacheln *vt* **jdn** [**zu etw** *dat*] ~ to incite sb [to do sth]; **jdn gegen jdn** ~ to turn sb against sb

Aufstand *m* rebellion

auf|stehen *vi irreg* 1. **sein** (*Person*) to stand up; (*aus dem Bett*) to get up 2. **haben** (*Fenster, Tür*) to be open

auf|stellen *vt* I. *vt* 1. (*aufbauen*) to put up *sep;* (*Maschine*) to install; (*Denkmal*) to erect; (*Falle*) to set 2. (*Rekord*) to set 3. (*Kandidat*) to nominate 4. (*Wache*) to post 5. *schweiz* (*aufmuntern*) to perk up *sep* II. *vr* **sich** *akk* ~ to stand; **sich** *akk* **hintereinander** ~ to line up; **sich** *akk* **im Kreis** ~ to form a circle

Aufstieg <-[e]s, -e> ['auf·ʃtiːk] *m* climb (**auf** +*akk* up); **sozialer** ~ social advancement; **den** ~ **ins Management schaffen** to work one's way up into management

auf|stocken *vt* to increase (**um** +*akk* by); **ein Team** ~ to add players to a team

auf|tanken *vt, vi* to fill up *sep;* (*Flugzeug*) to refuel

auf|tauchen *vi* **sein** 1. (*Taucher*) to come up 2. (*verlorener Gegenstand*) to be found 3. (*plötzlich da sein*) to suddenly appear

auf|tauen I. *vi* **sein** 1. (*Eis*) to thaw 2. *fig* to open up II. *vt* **haben** to thaw [out *sep*]

auf|teilen *vt* 1. (*aufgliedern*) to divide [up *sep*] (**in** +*akk* into) 2. (*verteilen*) to share *sep* (**unter** +*dat* among)

Auftrag <-[e]s, Aufträge> ['auf·traːk] *m* order; **jdm den** ~ **geben, etw zu tun** to instruct sb to do sth; „~ **erledigt!**" "mission accomplished!"

auf|tragen *irreg vt* 1. (*Creme, Farbe*) to apply (**auf** +*akk* to) 2. **jdm etw** ~ to instruct sb to do sth

Auftraggeber(in) <-s, -> *m(f)* client

auf|treiben *vt irreg fam* to get [a] hold of

auf|treten *irreg* I. *vi* **sein** 1. (*Problem, Schwierigkeiten*) to occur 2. THEAT to appear [on the stage] 3. **selbstbewusst** ~ to exhibit self-confidence II. *vt* **haben** (*Tür*) to kick open *sep*

Auftreten <-s> *nt kein pl* behavior

Auftritt *m* MUS, THEAT appearance

auf|tun *irreg vr* **sich** *akk* ~ (*Möglichkeit*) to open [up]

auf|wachen *vi* **sein** to wake [up]

auf|wachsen [-ks-] *vi irreg* **sein** to grow up

Aufwand <-[e]s> ['auf·vant] *m kein pl* expenditure; **der** ~ **war umsonst** it was a waste of energy/money/time; [**großen**] ~ **treiben** to be [very] extravagant

Aufwandsentschädigung *f* expense allowance

auf|wärmen I. *vt* (*Essen*) to heat up *sep* II. *vr* **sich** *akk* ~ to warm oneself [up]

aufwärts ['auf·vɛrts] *adv* up, upward[s]; (*bergauf*) uphill; **den Fluss** ~ upstream

auf|wecken vt to wake [up sep]

auf|weisen vt irreg to show; **zahlreiche Fehler ~** to be full of mistakes

auf|wenden vt irreg o reg to use; (Zeit, Mühe) to expend; (Geld) to spend; **viel Energie ~, etw zu tun** to put a lot of energy into doing sth

auf|werfen irreg vt (Frage) to raise

auf|werten vt **1.** (Währung) to revalue **2.** fig to increase the value of

Aufwertung <-, -en> f **1.** (einer Währung) revaluation **2.** fig enhancement

auf|wischen vt, vi to wipe [up sep]

auf|wühlen vt jdn [innerlich] ~ to stir up sep sb

auf|zählen vt to list

Aufzeichnung f **1.** (Aufnahme) recording; (auf Band a.) taping; (auf Videoband a.) videotaping **2.** meist pl (Notizen) notes

auf|ziehen irreg **I.** vt haben **1.** (Schublade) to open; (Reißverschluss) to unzip; (Vorhänge) to draw back sep **2.** (Kind) to raise **3.** fam (verspotten) to tease (**mit** +dat about) **II.** vi sein (Wolken) to gather

Aufzucht f raising

Aufzug m elevator; [mit dem] ~ **fahren** to take the elevator

Augapfel ['auk·ʔapfl] m eyeball

Auge <-s, -n> ['au·gə] nt eye; **gute/ schlechte ~n haben** to have good/poor eyesight sing ▶ **mit einem blauen ~ davonkommen** fam to get off lightly; **ins ~ gehen** fam to backfire; **jdn nicht aus den ~n lassen** to not let sb out of one's sight; **ins ~ springen** to catch sb's eye; **etw aus den ~n verlieren** to lose track of sth; **sich** akk **aus den ~n verlieren** to lose touch with; **die ~n vor etw** dat **verschließen** to close one's eyes to sth; **unter vier ~n** in private; **ein ~ auf jdn/etw werfen** to have one's eye on sb/sth; **ein ~/beide ~n zudrücken** fam to turn a blind eye to sth; **kein ~ zutun** fam to not sleep a wink; **~n zu und durch** fam take a deep breath and do it

Augenarzt, -ärztin m, f optometrist

Augenblick ['au·gn·blɪk] m moment; **im ersten ~** for a moment; **im letzten ~** at the [very] last moment; ~ **mal!** just a minute!

augenblicklich ['au·gn·blɪk·lɪç] adv **1.** (sofort) immediately; (herausfordernd) at once **2.** (zurzeit) at present

Augenbraue f eyebrow; **die ~n hochziehen** to raise one's eyebrows

Augenlid nt eyelid

Augentropfen pl eye drops npl

Augenzeuge, -zeugin m, f eyewitness (**bei** +dat to)

August <-[e]s, -e> [au·ˈgʊst] m August; s. a. **Februar**

Auktion <-, -en> f auction

Aula <-, Aulen> ['au·la] f [assembly] hall

aus [aus] **I.** präp +dat **1.** (von innen nach außen) out of; ~ **dem Fenster/ der Tür** out of the window/door; **das Öl tropfte ~ dem Fass** the oil was dripping from the barrel **2.** (Herkunft) from; ~ **Stuttgart kommen** to be from Stuttgart; ~ **dem 17. Jahrhundert stammen** to be [from the] 17th century; **Zigaretten ~ dem Automaten** cigarettes from a vending machine **3.** (Ursache) ~ **Angst/Dummheit/Verzweiflung** out of fear/stupidity/desperation; ~ **einer Laune heraus** on a whim; ~ **Unachtsamkeit** due to carelessness **4.** (Material) ~ **Glas/Holz** [made] of glass/wood **II.** adv fam **1.** (gelöscht) out **2.** (ausgeschaltet) off **3.** (zu Ende) ~ **sein** to have finished; (Krieg) to have ended; (Schule) to be out; **mit etw** dat **ist es ~** sth is over; **es ist ~** [zwischen jdm] fam it's over [between sb] ▶ **auf jdn/etw ~ sein** to be after sb/sth; ~ **und vorbei sein** to be over and done with

aus|atmen vt, vi to exhale

aus|bauen vt **1.** (Gebäude) to extend (**zu** +dat into); (innen) to remodel **2.** (herausmontieren) to remove (**aus** +dat from)

aus|bessern vt to repair

aus|beuten vt to exploit

Ausbeutung <-, -en> f exploitation

aus|bezahlen* vt (Betrag) to pay out sep; (Person) to pay off sep

aus|bilden vt to train; (akademisch) to educate; **jdn zum Arzt ~** to train sb to be a doctor

A

Ausbilder(in) <-s, -> m(f), **Aus-**
bildner(in) <-s, -> m(f) österr, schweiz
trainer; MIL instructor

Ausbildung <-, -en> f training; (akademisch) education; **in der ~ sein** to
be in training

Ausbildungsplatz m internship

aus|blenden vt fam (Problem) to forget

aus|brechen irreg vi sein 1. (aus dem
Gefängnis) to escape 2. (Vulkan) to
erupt 3. (Feuer, Seuche, Panik) to break
out 4. **in Gelächter/Tränen ~** to burst
into laughter/tears

aus|breiten I. vt 1. (Decke, Landkarte)
to spread [out sep] 2. (Arme, Flügel)
to spread [out sep] II. vr sich akk ~ to
spread (**auf** +akk to)

Ausbruch m 1. (aus dem Gefängnis)
escape (**aus** +dat from) 2. (Beginn) outbreak 3. (eines Vulkans) eruption

aus|bürsten vt to brush [out sep]

Ausdauer f kein pl endurance

aus|dehnen I. vr sich akk ~ 1. (größer
werden) to expand 2. (sich ausbreiten)
to spread (**auf** +akk to) II. vt 1. (Zeitraum) to extend 2. (erweitern, vergrößern: Aktivitäten, Streik) to expand
(**auf** +akk to)

aus|denken vr irreg **sich** dat **etw ~** to
think up sep sth; **sich** akk **eine Über-**
raschung ~ to plan a surprise

Ausdruck¹ <-drücke> m expression; **etw**
zum ~ bringen to express sth; **als ~**
der Dankbarkeit as an expression of
one's gratitude

Ausdruck² <-drucke> m [computer]
printout; **einen ~ [von etw** dat] **ma-**
chen to run off sep a copy [of sth]

aus|drucken vt to print [out sep]

aus|drücken I. vt 1. (zeigen) to show;
Gefühle ~ to express feelings 2. (formulieren) to put into words; **anders**
ausgedrückt in other words; **einfach**
ausgedrückt put simply 3. (Zigarette)
to snuff out sep II. vr sich akk ~ to express oneself; **sich** akk **falsch ~** to use
the wrong word

ausdrücklich ['aus·drʏk·lɪç] adj attr explicit

ausdruckslos adj inexpressive; (Blick)
vacant; (Gesicht) expressionless

ausdrucksvoll adj expressive

Ausdrucksweise f way one expresses
oneself

auseinander [aus·ʔai·ˈnan·dɐ] adv apart

auseinander|biegen vt to bend apart
sep

auseinander|fallen vi irreg sein to fall
apart

auseinander|falten vt to unfold

auseinander|gehen vi irreg sein
1. (Menschen) to part 2. (Beziehung) to
break up; (Ehe a.) to fall apart 3. (Mei-
nungen) to differ 4. fam (dick werden)
to [start to] fill out a. hum

auseinander|setzen I. vt **jdm etw ~** to
explain sth to sb II. vt sich akk **mit etw**
dat ~ to tackle sth

Auseinandersetzung <-, -en> [aus·ʔai·
ˈnan·de·zɛtsʊŋ] f argument

Ausfahrt f exit; (mit Tor) gateway

aus|fallen vi irreg sein (Veranstaltung)
to be canceled; **etw ~ lassen** to cancel sth

ausfällig adj abusive; **~ werden** to become abusive

aus|findig adj **jdn/etw ~ machen** to
locate sb/sth

aus|flippen ['aus·flɪpn̩] vi sein fam
1. (aus Wut) to freak out 2. (aus Freude) to jump for joy

Ausflucht <-, Ausflüchte> f excuse;
Ausflüchte machen to make excuses

Ausflug m outing; SCH field trip

aus|fragen vt to question

aus|fressen vt irreg fam **etwas/nichts**
ausgefressen haben to have done
something/nothing wrong

Ausfuhr <-> f kein pl export[ation]

Ausfuhrbestimmungen pl export regulations pl

aus|führen vt 1. (Auftrag) to carry out
sep; (Befehl) to execute 2. **jdn zum**
Essen ~ to take sb out sep for dinner
3. (exportieren) to export (**in** +akk to)

ausführlich ['aus·fy:ɐ̯·lɪç] I. adj detailed
II. adv in detail; **sehr ~** in great detail

aus|füllen vt 1. (Formular) to fill in sep
2. **jdn [ganz] ~** to satisfy sb [completely]
3. **seine Zeit mit etw** dat ~ to fill one's
time with sth

Ausgabe f 1. MEDIA, LIT edition 2. pl

(*Kosten*) expenses

Ausgang *m* exit

aus|geben *irreg* I. *vt* 1. (*Geld*) to spend (**für** +*akk* on) 2. (*austeilen*) to distribute (**an** +*akk* to) 3. *fam* (*spendieren*) **jdm etw** ~ to treat sb to sth; **eine Runde** ~ to buy a round; [**jdm**] **einen** ~ *fam* to buy sb a drink II. *vr* **sich** *akk* **als jd/ etw** ~ to pass oneself off as sb/sth

ausgebucht *adj* booked up

ausgedehnt I. *adj* extensive II. *pp von* **ausdehnen**

ausgefallen I. *adj* unusual II. *pp von* **ausfallen**

ausgeglichen I. *adj* (*Mensch*) easy-going II. *pp von* **ausgleichen**

aus|gehen *vi irreg sein* 1. (*zum Essen etc.*) to go out 2. (*Feuer, Licht*) to go out 3. (*Haare*) to fall out 4. **von etw** *dat* ~ to take sth as a basis; **davon** ~, **dass ...** to assume that ...; **davon kann man nicht** ~ you can't go by that 5. (*enden*) to end; **gut/schlecht** ~ to turn out well/badly; (*Buch, Film*) to have a happy/sad ending

ausgelassen I. *adj* wild II. *adv* **es wurde** ~ **gefeiert** there was a lively party going on III. *pp von* **auslassen**

ausgemacht I. *adj attr* ~**er Unsinn** utter nonsense II. *pp von* **ausmachen**

ausgenommen I. *konj* except; **wir kommen,** ~ **es regnet** we'll come, but only if it doesn't rain II. *pp von* **ausnehmen**

ausgepowert [-pauɐt] *adj fam* beat

ausgeprägt *adj* distinctive; (*Interesse*) pronounced

ausgerechnet [ˈausˌɡəˌrɛçˌnət] I. *adv* ~ **er** he of all people; ~ **jetzt** now of all times; ~ **gestern/heute** yesterday/today of all days II. *pp von* **ausrechnen**

ausgeschlossen I. *adj pred* **es ist nicht** ~, **dass ...** it is still possible that ...; [**völlig**] ~! [that's] [completely] out of the question. II. *pp von* **ausschließen**

ausgeschnitten *adj* **tief** ~ (*Kleid, Bluse*) low-cut

ausgesprochen I. *adv* really II. *pp von* **aussprechen**

ausgestorben I. *adj* 1. (*Tier-, Pflanzenart*) extinct 2. (*Straßen*) deserted II. *pp*

von aussterben

ausgesucht *pp von* **aussuchen**

ausgewogen *adj* balanced

ausgezeichnet [ˈausˌɡəˌtsaiçˌnət] I. *adj* excellent II. *adv* extremely well III. *pp von* **auszeichnen**

ausgiebig [ˈausˌɡiːˌbɪç] I. *adj* extensive; (*Mahlzeit*) substantial II. *adv* extensively; ~ **schlafen** to have a good [long] sleep

aus|gleichen *irreg* I. *vt* (*Konto*) to balance; (*Mangel*) to compensate for; (*Unterschied*) to even out II. *vr* **sich** *akk* ~ to balance out

aus|graben *vt irreg* 1. (*aus der Erde*) to dig up sep; (*Altertümer*) to excavate 2. (*hervorholen*) to dig out sep; **alte Geschichten** ~ to bring up sep old stories

Ausgrabungen *pl* excavations *pl*

Ausguss ᴿᴿ *m* (*Spüle*) sink

aus|halten *irreg vt* 1. (*ertragen*) to bear; **hältst du es noch eine Stunde aus?** can you hold out [for] another hour?; **es ist nicht** [**länger**] **auszuhalten** it's [getting to be] unbearable; **es lässt sich hier** ~ it's not a bad place; **den Druck** ~ to [with]stand the pressure; **die Kälte** ~ to endure the cold; **eine hohe Temperatur** ~ to withstand a high temperature; **viel** ~ to take a lot 2. (*finanziell*) to support

aus|händigen [ˈausˌhɛnˌdɪˌɡn̩] *vt* to hand over sep

Aushang *m* notice

aus|harren *vi* to wait [patiently]

aus|helfen *vi irreg* to help out sep

Aushilfe *f* temporary worker; [**bei jdm**] **als** ~ **arbeiten** to temp [for sb] *fam*

aus|horchen *vt fam* to sound out sep

aus|kennen *vr irreg* 1. **sich** *akk* **irgendwo** ~ to know one's way around somewhere 2. **sich** *akk* [**in etw** *dat*] ~ to know a lot [about sth]

Ausklang *m kein pl* **zum** ~ **des Abends** to conclude the evening

aus|klopfen *vt* (*Teppich*) to beat

aus|kommen *vi irreg sein* 1. **mit etw** *dat* ~ to get by on sth; **ohne jdn/etw** ~ to manage without sb/sth 2. **mit jdm** [**gut**] ~ to get along [well] with sb 3. *österr* (*entkommen*) to escape

Auskommen <-s> *nt kein pl* **sein ~ haben** to get by

aus|kosten *vt* **das Leben ~** to enjoy life to the fullest; **den Moment/seine Rache ~** to savor the moment/one's revenge

Auskunft <-, Auskünfte> ['aus·kʊnft] *f* **1.** (*Information*) information; **nähere ~** more information **2.** (*Schalter*) information counter **3.** TELEK **die ~** the operator

aus|lachen *vt* to laugh at

aus|laden *irreg vt* **1.** (*entladen*) to unload; (*Einladung widerrufen*) **jdn ~** to tell sb not to come

Ausland ['aus·lant] *nt kein pl* **[das] ~** foreign countries *pl;* **aus dem ~** from abroad; **im/ins ~** abroad

Ausländer(in) <-s, -> ['aus·lɛn·dɐ] *m(f)* foreigner; JUR alien

Ausländerbeauftragte(r) *f(m) dekl wie adj* Commissioner for Foreigners' Affairs

ausländerfeindlich *adj* racist

ausländisch ['aus·lɛn·dɪʃ] *adj attr* foreign

Auslandseinsatz *m* MIL foreign [military] deployment

Auslandsgespräch *nt* TELEK international call

Auslandskorrespondent(in) *m(f)* foreign correspondent

aus|lassen *irreg* **I.** *vt* **1.** (*weglassen*) to omit; (*überspringen*) to skip **2.** *fam* (*ausgeschaltet*) to keep turned off **3. etw an jdm ~** (*Wut*) to vent sth on sb **II.** *vr* **sich** *akk* **über jdn/etw ~** to go on about sb/sth *pej* **III.** *vi österr* to let go

aus|laufen *irreg vi sein* **1.** (*Schiff*) to [set] sail (**nach** +*dat* for) **2.** (*Vertrag*) to expire **3.** (*undicht sein*) to leak

aus|leeren *vt* (*Gefäß*) to empty [out *sep*]; (*Inhalt*) to pour away *sep*

aus|legen *vt* to interpret; **etw falsch ~** to misinterpret sth

aus|leihen *irreg vt* **jdm etw** *akk* **~** to lend sb sth; [**sich** *dat*] **etw** *akk* **von jdm ~** to borrow sth from sb

Auslese <-> *f kein pl* selection; **die natürliche ~** natural selection

aus|liefern *vt* **1.** (*Waren*) to deliver

2. *fig* **jdm/etw ausgeliefert sein** to be at the mercy of sb/sth

Auslieferung *f* **1.** (*von Waren*) delivery **2.** JUR extradition

aus|löschen *vt* to extinguish

aus|losen *vi* to draw lots

Auslöser <-s, -> *m* **1.** FOTO [shutter] release **2.** (*Anlass*) trigger

Auslosung <-, -en> *f* draw

aus|machen *vt* **1.** (*Feuer*) to extinguish **2.** (*Gerät, Licht*) to turn off *sep* **3.** (*vereinbaren*) to agree [up]on **4.** (*bewirken*) **kaum etwas ~** to hardly make any difference; **nichts ~** to not make any difference; **viel ~** to make a big difference **5.** (*stören*) **es macht jdm nichts/viel aus, etw zu tun** it doesn't mind/really does mind doing sth; **macht es Ihnen etwas aus, wenn ...?** do you mind if ...?

aus|malen *vr* **sich** *dat* **etw ~** to imagine sth

Ausmaß *nt* **1.** (*Größe*) size; **das ~ von etw** *dat* **haben** to cover the area of sth **2.** *fig* (*Tragweite*) extent

aus|messen *vt irreg* to measure [out]

aus|misten *vt* **1.** (*Stall*) to muck out *sep* **2.** *fam* (*Zimmer*) to clean up *sep;* (*alte Sachen*) to throw out *sep*

Ausnahme <-, -n> ['aus·na:mə] *f* exception ▶ **~n bestätigen die Regel** *prov* the exception proves the rule *prov*

Ausnahmezustand *m* POL state of emergency; **den ~ verhängen** to declare a state of emergency (**über** +*akk* in)

ausnahmslos *adv* without exception

ausnahmsweise *adv* for a change

aus|nehmen *irreg vt* **1.** (*Tiere*) to gut; (*Geflügel*) to draw **2.** (*ausschließen*) to exempt; **ich nicht ausgenommen** myself not excepted **3.** *fam* (*Geld abnehmen*) **jdn ~** to fleece sb *fam;* (*beim Glücksspiel*) to clean out *sep* sb *fam*

ausnehmend *adv* exceptionally; **das gefällt mir ~ gut** I really like it a lot

aus|nutzen *vt* **1. jdn ~** to exploit sb **2. etw ~** to make the most of sth; **jds Leichtgläubigkeit ~** to take advantage of sb's gullibility

aus|packen **I.** *vt* to unpack; (*Geschenk*) to unwrap **II.** *vi fam* (*gestehen*) to talk

aus|plaudern vt to let out sep

aus|plündern vt (Menschen) to plunder; (Laden) to loot

aus|posaunen * vt fam to broadcast

aus|pressen vt eine Orange/Zitrone ~ to squeeze an orange/a lemon; **den Saft** ~ to squeeze out sep the juice

aus|probieren * I. vt to try [out sep] II. vi ~, **ob/wie** ... to see whether/how ...

Auspuff <-[e]s, -e> m exhaust system

Auspuffrohr nt exhaust pipe

aus|quetschen vt jdn ~ to pump sb [for information]; (Polizei) to grill sb

aus|radieren * vt (mit Radiergummi) to erase

aus|rangieren * [-raŋ·ʒiː-rən] vt to throw out sep

aus|rauben vt to rob

aus|räumen vt 1. (Möbel) to move out sep; (Zimmer) to clear out sep 2. (Missverständnis, Zweifel) to dispel

aus|rechnen vt to calculate

Ausrede f excuse

aus|reichen vi to be sufficient

aus|reisen vi sein to leave the country

Ausreisevisum [-viː-] nt exit visa

aus|reißen irreg I. vt haben to pull out sep; (Haare) to tear out sep II. vi sein fam to run away

Ausreißer(in) <-s, -> m(f) fam runaway

aus|renken vt to dislocate

aus|richten vt 1. (übermitteln) jdm etw ~ to tell sb sth; **kann ich etwas ~?** can I give him/her a message?; **richten Sie ihr einen Gruß [von mir] aus** give her my regards 2. (erreichen) **bei jdm etwas/nichts** ~ to achieve something/nothing with sb 3. österr (schlechtmachen) to badmouth 4. schweiz (zahlen) jdm etw ~ to pay sb sth

aus|rotten vt (Ungeziefer) to destroy; (Unkraut) to wipe out sep; (Volk) to exterminate

aus|rufen vt irreg to call out sep; (Streik) to call; (Krieg) to declare; **jdn** ~ to put out a call for sb

Ausrufungszeichen nt, **Ausrufezeichen** nt österr, schweiz exclamation point

aus|ruhen vi, vr [sich akk] ~ to rest; **aus-geruht [sein]** [to be] well rested

Ausrüstung <-, -en> f equipment

aus|rutschen vi sein to slip; **sie ist ausgerutscht** she slipped; **mir ist die Hand ausgerutscht** I lost my temper and slapped him/her

Ausrutscher <-s, -> m fam slip-up

Aussage f statement; (Zeugenaussage) evidence; **eine ~ machen** to make a statement

aus|sagen vt etw [über jdn/etw] ~ to say sth [about sb/sth]

aus|schalten vt (Gerät, Licht) to turn off sep

Ausschau f ~ halten to keep an eye out (nach +dat for)

aus|scheiden irreg I. vi sein 1. (aus Amt, Beruf) to retire; (aus Verein) to leave 2. SPORT to drop out 3. (nicht in Betracht kommen) to be ruled out II. vt haben (absondern) to excrete

aus|schlafen irreg vi, vr [sich akk] ~ to sleep in

Ausschlag m MED rash ▶ **bei etw** dat **den ~ geben** to be the decisive factor [for/in sth]

aus|schlagen irreg vt 1. (Angebot) to turn down sep; (höflicher) to decline; **jdm etw** ~ to refuse sb sth; **eine Erbschaft** ~ to disclaim an estate 2. jdm **einen Zahn** ~ to knock out sep one of sb's teeth

ausschlaggebend adj decisive; **von ~er Bedeutung sein** to be of primary importance

aus|schließen irreg I. vt 1. (entfernen) to exclude; (als Strafe a.) to bar; (Mitglied) to expel; (vorübergehend) to suspend 2. (für unmöglich halten) to rule out sep II. vr sich akk ~ to lock oneself out

ausschließlich ['aus-ʃliːs-lɪç] I. adv exclusively; **darüber habe ~ ich zu bestimmen** I'm the one to decide on this matter II. präp excluding; (geschrieben a.) excl.

Ausschluss RR m exclusion; (von Mitglied) expulsion; (vorübergehend) suspension; **unter ~ der Öffentlichkeit stattfinden** to be closed to the public

aus|schneiden vt irreg to cut out sep

Ausschnitt m 1. (an Kleidung) neckline; **ein tiefer ~** a low neckline 2. (Teil) part

aus|schöpfen vt (Möglichkeiten, Reserven) to exhaust

Ausschreitungen pl riots pl

Ausschuss RR m committee

aus|schütten vt (Gefäß) to empty; (Inhalt) to pour out

ausschweifend adj (Leben) hedonistic; (Fantasie) wild

aus|sehen vi irreg to look; **~ wie ...** to look like ...; **es sieht gut/schlecht aus** things are looking good/not looking too good; **nach Schnee/Regen ~** to look like it's going to snow/rain; **wie sieht's aus?** how're things?

Aussehen <-s> nt kein pl appearance; **dem ~ nach** judging by appearances

außen ['ausn] adv on the outside; **links/rechts ~** on the outside left/right; **von ~** from the outside ▶ **jdn/etw ~ vor lassen** to leave sb/sth out; **~ vor sein** to be left out

Außenbezirk m outer district

Außenhandel m foreign trade

Außenminister(in) m(f) Secretary of State

Außenministerium nt State Department

Außenpolitik ['ausn·po·li·ti:k] f foreign policy

außenpolitisch ['ausn·po·li:·tɪʃ] adj foreign policy attr; **~er Sprecher** foreign policy spokesman

Außenseiter(in) ['ausn·zai·te] <-s, -> m(f) outsider

Außenspiegel m AUTO [out]side mirror

außer ['ause] I. präp +dat 1. (abgesehen von) apart from 2. (zusätzlich zu) in addition to 3. **~ Betrieb/Sicht/Gefahr sein** to be out of order/sight/danger ▶ **[über jdn/etw] ~ sich** dat **sein** to be beside oneself [about sb/sth] II. konj **~ wenn** except when

außerdem ['ause·de:m] adv besides

äußere(r, s) ['ɔy·sə·rə, -rə, -rəs] adj outer; **~ Einflüsse/Verletzung** external influences/injury

Äußere(s) ['ɔy·sə·rə, -rəs] nt dekl wie adj outward appearance

außerehelich adj extramarital; (Kind)

illegitimate

außergewöhnlich ['au·sə·gə·'vø:n·lɪç] I. adj unusual; (Leistung) extraordinary; (Mensch) remarkable II. adv extremely

außerhalb ['au·sə·halp] I. adv outside; **von ~** from out of town II. präp +gen outside

äußerlich ['ɔy·se·lɪç] adj external

äußern ['ɔy·sen] I. vr sich akk **über jdn/etw ~** to make comments about sb/sth II. vt to say; (Kritik) to voice; (Wunsch) to express

außerordentlich ['au·se·'?ɔr·dn̩t·lɪç] adj extraordinary

außerplanmäßig ['au·sə·pla:n·mɛ:·sɪç] adj unscheduled; (Ausgaben, Kosten) nonbudgetary

äußerst ['ɔy·sest] adv extremely

außerstande [au·se·'ʃtan·də] adj **~, etw zu tun** unable to do sth

äußerste(r, s) adj 1. (entfernteste) outermost; **am ~n Ende der Welt** at the farthest point of the globe; **der ~ Norden/Süden** the extreme north/south 2. (höchste) utmost; **von ~r Wichtigkeit** of supreme importance; **der ~ Preis** the ultimate price

äußerstenfalls ['ɔy·sestn̩·'fals] adv at the most

Äußerung <-, -en> f comment

aus|setzen I. vt 1. (Kind, Haustier) to abandon 2. **eine Belohnung ~** to offer a reward 3. (preisgeben) **jdn/etw etw** dat **~** to expose sb/sth to sth 4. (bemängeln) **an etw** dat **etwas auszusetzen haben** to find fault with sth; **was hast du an ihr auszusetzen?** what don't you like about her?; **daran ist nichts auszusetzen** there's nothing wrong with that II. vi (versagen) to stop; (Motor) to fail

Aussicht f 1. (Blick) view; **ein Zimmer mit ~ aufs Meer** a room overlooking the sea 2. (Chance) prospect; **die ~ auf etw** akk the chance of sth; **etw in ~ haben** to have good prospects of sth; **jdm etw in ~ stellen** to promise sb sth

aussichtslos adj hopeless

Aussichtsturm m lookout tower

aus|söhnen ['aus·zø:·nən] vr sich akk **~**

to make [it] up; **sich** *akk* **mit jdm/etw ~** to reconcile with sb/to become reconciled with sth

aus|spannen I. *vi* to relax II. *vt* **jdm die Freundin/den Freund ~** *fam* to steal sb's girlfriend/boyfriend

aus|sperren I. *vt* **jdn ~** to lock sb out II. *vr* **sich** *akk* **~** to lock oneself out

aus|spielen *vt* **jdn gegen jdn ~** to play sb off against sb

aus|spionieren* *vt* to spy out

Aussprache *f* **1.** LING pronunciation **2.** (*Unterredung*) talk

aus|sprechen *irreg* I. *vt* **1.** LING to pronounce **2.** (*äußern*) to express; (*Warnung*) to issue; **ein Lob ~** to give a word of praise II. *vr* **sich** *akk* **~ 1.** (*sein Herz ausschütten*) to talk things over **2. sich** *akk* **für/gegen jdn/etw ~** to voice one's support for/opposition against sb/sth III. *vi* to finish [speaking]

Ausstand *m* **1.** (*Streik*) **im ~ sein** to be on strike; **in den ~ treten** to go on strike **2.** *österr, schweiz, südd* (*Ausscheiden aus Stelle o Schule*) going away; **seinen ~ geben** to hold a going-away party

aus|statten ['aus·ʃtatn̩] *vt* to equip; (*Wohnung*) to furnish

aus|stehen *irreg* I. *vt* **jdn/etw nicht ~ können** to not be able to stand sb/sth II. *vi* to be due; **die Antwort steht seit 5 Wochen aus** the reply has been due for 5 weeks

aus|steigen *vi irreg sein* (*aus Bus, Flugzeug, Zug*) to get off; (*aus dem Auto*) to get out of; **du kannst mich dort ~ lassen** you can drop me off over there

aus|stellen *vt* **1.** (*auf Messe, in Museum*) to exhibit **2.** [**jdm**] **eine Rechnung ~** to issue [sb] an invoice; **sie ließ sich die Bescheinigung ~** she had the certificate made out in her name

Ausstellung *f* KUNST exhibition

aus|sterben *vi irreg sein* (*Pflanze, Tier*) to become extinct

Aussteuer <-, -n> *f* dowry

Ausstieg <-[e]s, -e> *m* **1.** (*Öffnung*) exit **2.** *fig* **der ~ aus etw** *dat* abandoning sth; **der ~ aus der Kernenergie** abandoning [of] nuclear energy

aus|stoßen *vt irreg* **1.** (*Gase*) to emit **2.** (*Seufzer*) to utter; (*Schrei*) to give [out]; (*Laute*) to make **3. jdn aus etw ~** to expel sb from sth

Ausstrahlung *f* **1.** (*Charisma*) **eine besondere ~ haben** to have a special charisma **2.** RADIO, TV broadcast[ing]

aus|strecken I. *vt* (*Hände, Beine*) to stretch out II. *vr* **sich** *akk* [**auf dem Sofa**] **~** to stretch oneself out [on the sofa]

aus|suchen *vt* to choose; [**sich** *dat*] **etw ~** to choose sth; [**sich** *dat*] **jdn ~** to pick sb

Austausch *m* exchange

austauschbar *adj* interchangeable; (*defekte Teile, Mensch*) replaceable

aus|tauschen I. *vt* **1.** (*ersetzen*) to replace (**gegen** +*akk* with) **2.** (*miteinander wechseln*) to exchange II. *vr* **sich** *akk* **über jdn/etw ~** to exchange stories about sb/sth

aus|teilen *vt* to distribute

Auster <-, -n> ['aus·tɐ] *f* oyster

Austernpilz *m* oyster mushroom

aus|toben *vr* **sich** *akk* **~** to romp around

aus|tragen *vt irreg* **1.** (*Post, Zeitung*) to deliver **2.** (*Baby*) to carry to [full] term **3. einen Streit mit jdm ~** to have it out with sb **4.** SPORT (*Wettkampf*) to hold

aus|treiben *vt irreg* **1. jdm etw ~** to knock sth out of sb **2.** (*Teufel*) to exorcise

aus|treten *irreg* I. *vi sein* (*Öl*) to leak; (*Gas*) to escape II. *vt haben* **1.** (*Feuer, Zigarette*) to stamp out **2.** (*Schuhe*) to wear out

aus|tricksen *vt fam* to trick

aus|üben *vt* **1.** (*Beruf*) to practice; (*Amt*) to hold; (*Aufgabe, Funktion*) to perform **2.** (*Macht, Recht*) to exercise; (*Druck, Einfluss*) to exert; (*Wirkung*) to have

aus|ufern ['aus·ʔuːfɐn] *vi sein* to escalate (**zu** +*dat* into)

Ausverkauf *m* clearance sale

ausverkauft *adj* sold out

Auswahl *f* **1.** (*Warenangebot*) selection (**an** +*dat* of) **2.** *kein pl* (*das Aussuchen*) **eine ~ treffen** to make one's choice (**unter** +*dat* from) **3.** SPORT all-

star team

aus|wählen *vt, vi* to choose (**unter** +*dat* from)

Auswanderer, -wanderin *m, f* emigrant

aus|wandern *vi sein* to emigrate

auswärtig ['aus·vɛr·tɪç] *adj attr* POL **Auswärtiges ~** State Department

aus|wechseln [-ks-] *vt* to replace (**gegen** +*akk* with); (*Spieler*) to substitute (**gegen** +*akk* for)

Ausweg *m* way out; **der letzte ~** the last resort

ausweglos *adj* hopeless

aus|weichen *vi irreg sein* 1. (*vermeiden*) **|etw** *dat*] **~** to get out of the way [of sth] 2. (*als Alternative*) **auf etw** *akk* **~** to fall back on sth

Ausweis <-es, -e> ['aus·vais] *m* ID, identity card

aus|weisen *irreg* I. *vt* (*abschieben*) to deport II. *vr sich akk* **~** to identify oneself; **können Sie sich ~?** do you have any [means of] identification?

Ausweispapiere *pl* identification [*o* ID] papers *pl*

Ausweisung *f* ADMIN deportation

aus|weiten I. *vt* to expand II. *vr sich akk* **~** to extend; **sich** *akk* **zu etw** *dat* **~** to escalate [into sth]

auswendig *adv* by heart; **etw ~ können** to know sth by heart

aus|wirken *vr sich akk* **~** to have an effect

Auswirkung *f* effect

aus|wischen *vt* to wipe [clean] ▶ **jdm eins ~** *fam* to put one over on sb

aus|zahlen I. *vt* 1. (*Lohn, Betrag*) to pay out 2. (*Kompagnon, Miterben*) to buy out *sep* II. *vr sich akk* **|für jdn] ~** to pay [off] [for sb]

aus|zählen *vt* to count

aus|zeichnen I. *vt* 1. (*Ware*) to price 2. (*ehren*) to honor; **jdn mit einem Preis ~** to give sb an award 3. (*hervorheben*) **jdn ~** to distinguish sb [from all others] II. *vr sich akk* **~** to stand out

Auszeichnung *f* (*Medaille*) medal; (*Orden*) decoration; (*Preis*) award

aus|ziehen *irreg* I. *vt haben* 1. (*Kleidung*) to take off *sep* 2. (*Zahn*) to pull

out *sep* II. *vr haben* **sich** *akk* **ausziehen** to get undressed III. *vi sein* **|aus einem Haus|** **~** to move out [of a house]

Auszubildende(r) *f(m) dekl wie adj* trainee

Auszug *m* 1. (*aus Wohnung*) move 2. (*Ausschnitt*) excerpt 3. (*Kontoauszug*) statement 4. PHARM extract

authentisch [au·'tɛn·tɪʃ] *adj* authentic

Auto <-s, -s> ['au·to] *nt* car; **~ fahren** to drive; **mit dem ~ fahren** to take the car

Autoatlas *m* road atlas

Autobahn *f* highway, freeway; (*in Deutschland a.*) autobahn

Autobahndreieck *nt* highway junction

Autobahnkreuz *nt* highway intersection

Autobahnraststätte *f* service area

Autobiografie RR, **Autobiographie** [au·to·bio·gra·'fi:] *f* autobiography

Autobus ['au·to·bus] *m*, **Autocar** ['au·to·ka:ɐ] *m schweiz* bus

Autofahrer(in) *m(f)* [car] driver

autogen [au·to·'ge:n] *adj* **~es Training** relaxation through self-hypnosis

Autogramm <-s, -e> [au·to·'gram] *nt* autograph

Autokennzeichen *nt* license plate; (*Länderkennzeichen*) international license plate code

Automat <-en, -en> [au·to·'ma:t] *m* (*Geldautomat*) ATM; (*Musikautomat*) jukebox; (*Spielautomat*) slot machine; (*Verkaufsautomat*) vending machine

Automatik <-, -en> [au·to·'ma:·tɪk] *f* AUTO automatic transmission

automatisch [au·to·'ma:·tɪʃ] *adj* automatic

automatisieren* [au·to·ma·ti·'zi:·rən] *vt* to automate

autonom [au·to·'no:m] *adj* POL autonomous

Autonomie <-, -n> [au·to·no·'mi:] *f* POL autonomy

Autopsie <-, -n> [au·tɔ·'psi:] *f* MED autopsy

Autor, Autorin <-s, Autoren> ['au·to:ɐ, au·'to:·rɪn] *m, f* author

Autoradio *nt* car radio

Au̱toreifen m car tire

Au̱torennen nt motor race

autorisieren* [au·to·ri·ˈziː·rən] vt to authorize; **ich habe ihn dazu autorisiert** I gave him authorization for it

autoritär [au·to·ri·ˈtɛːɐ̯] adj authoritarian

Autorität <-, -en> [au·to·ri·ˈtɛːt] f authority

Au̱tovermietung <-, -en> f car rental company

Axt <-, Äxte> [akst] f ax

Azoren [aˈtsoː·rən] pl **die ~** the Azores npl

Azubi [a·ˈtsuː·bi] m <-s, -s> f <-, -s> kurz für **Auszubildende(r)**

B

B, b <-, -> [beː] nt **1.** (Buchstabe) B, b; **~ wie Berta** B as in Bravo **2.** MUS (Note) B flat

Baby <-s, -s> [ˈbeː·bi] nt baby

Babyklappe [ˈbeː·bi·] f hatch or container in which unwanted babies can be left anonymously

Babypause [ˈbeː·bi·] f parental leave

Babysitter(in) <-s, -> [ˈbeː·bi·zɪ·tɐ] m(f) babysitter

Bach <-[e]s, Bäche> [bax] m brook ▶ **den ~ runtergehen** fam to go down the drain

Ba̱ckblech nt baking sheet

Backbord <-[e]s> [ˈbak·bɔrt] nt kein pl NAUT port [side]

Backe <-, -n> [ˈba·kə] f cheek

backen <backt, backte, gebacken> [ˈba·kn̩] vt, vi (im Ofen) to bake; (in Fett) to fry

Ba̱ckenknochen m cheekbone

Ba̱ckenzahn m molar

Bäcker(in) <-s, -> [ˈbɛ·kɐ] m(f) baker; **beim ~** at the baker's [shop]

Bäckerei <-, -en> [bɛ·kə·ˈrai] f bakery

Backfisch [ˈbak·fɪʃ] m batter-fried fish

Ba̱ckform f baking pan

Ba̱ckofen [ˈbak·ʔoː·fn̩] m oven

Ba̱ckpulver nt baking powder

Bad <-[e]s, Bäder> [baːt] nt **1.** bath; **jdm/sich** dat **ein ~ einlassen** to run sb/oneself a bath **2.** (Badezimmer) bathroom **3.** (Schwimmbad) swimming pool **4.** (Heilbad) spa; (Seebad) seaside resort

Ba̱dezug m swimsuit

Ba̱dehose f swim[ming] trunks npl

Ba̱dekappe f swim[ming] cap

Ba̱demantel m bathrobe

Ba̱demeister(in) m(f) lifeguard

baden [ˈbaː·dn̩] I. vi **1.** (in Wanne) to take a bath **2.** (schwimmen) to swim; **~ gehen** to go for a swim II. vt to bathe III. vr sich akk ~ to take a bath

Ba̱deort m ocean resort; (Kurort) spa resort

Ba̱detuch nt bath towel

Ba̱dewanne f bathtub

Ba̱dezimmer nt bathroom

baff [baf] adj fam ~ **sein** to be flabbergasted

Bagatelle <-, -n> [ba·ga·ˈtɛ·lə] f trifle

Bagger <-s, -> [ˈbagɐ] m BAU excavator

Bahamas [ba·ˈhaː·mas] pl **die ~** the Bahamas pl

Bahn <-, -en> [baːn] f **1.** (Eisenbahn) train; (Straßenbahn) streetcar; **mit der ~ fahren** to take the train/streetcar **2.** SPORT track; (beim Schwimmen) lane ▶ **freie ~ haben** to have the go-ahead; **auf die schiefe ~ kommen** to get off the straight and narrow; **jdn aus der ~ werfen** to get sb off course

ba̱hnen vt sich dat **einen Weg durch etw** akk ~ to fight one's way through sth

Ba̱hnfahrt f train trip

Ba̱hnhof m train station ▶ **nur [noch] ~ verstehen** fam to not have the foggiest [idea]

Ba̱hnpolizei f railroad police

Ba̱hnsteig <-[e]s, -e> m [train] platform

Ba̱hnübergang m grade crossing

Ba̱hnverbindung f [train] connection

Bahre <-, -n> [ˈbaː·rə] f stretcher

Bakterie <-, -n> [bak·ˈteː·rjə] f meist pl bacterium

Balance <-, -n> [ba·ˈlãː·sə] f balance

balancieren* [ba·lã·ˈsiː·rən] vt, vi to balance

bald [balt] adv soon; **bis ~!** see you later!; **nicht so ~** not as soon; **wird's ~?** move it!

Baldrian <-s, -e> m BOT valerian

Balearen [ba·le·'a:·rən] pl **die ~** the Balearic Islands pl

Balkan <-s> ['bal·ka:n] m 1. (Halbinsel, Länder) **der ~** the Balkans pl; **auf dem ~** on the Balkans 2. (Gebirge) Balkan Mountains pl

Balken <-s, -> ['bal·kn̩] m (a. sport) beam ▶ **lügen, dass sich die ~ biegen** fam to lie through one's teeth

Balkon <-s, -s> [bal·'kɔŋ] m 1. ARCHIT balcony 2. THEAT dress circle

Ball[1] <-[e]s, Bälle> [bal] m ball ▶ **am ~ bleiben/sein** to stay be on the ball

Ball[2] <-[e]s, Bälle> [bal] m (Fest) ball

Ballast <-[e]s, -e> ['ba·last] m pl selten 1. NAUT, LUFT ballast 2. fig burden

Ballaststoffe pl fiber

ballen ['ba·lən] I. vt (Faust) to clench II. vr **sich** akk **~** to crowd [together]; (Wolken) to gather

Ballett <-[e]s, -e> [ba·'lɛt] nt ballet

Ballon <-s, -s> [ba·'lɔŋ] m balloon

Ballungsgebiet nt metropolitan area

Balsam <-s, -e> ['bal·za:m] m a. fig balm

Baltikum <-s> ['bal·ti·kʊm] nt **das ~** the Baltic States

baltisch ['bal·tɪʃ] adj Baltic; s. a. **deutsch**

Bambus <-ses, -se> ['bam·bʊs] m bamboo

Bambussprossen pl bamboo shoots pl

banal [ba·'na:l] adj banal; (Angelegenheit) trivial

Banane <-, -n> [ba·'na:·nə] f banana

band [bant] imp von **binden**

Band[1] <-[e]s, Bänder> [bant] nt 1. (aus Stoff) ribbon 2. (Tonband) [recording] tape; **etw auf ~ aufnehmen** to tape-[record] sth 3. meist pl ANAT ligament ▶ **am laufenden ~** nonstop

Band[2] <-[e]s, Bände> [bant] m (Buch) volume ▶ **Bände sprechen** to speak volumes

Band[3] <-, -s> [bɛnt] f MUS band

Bandage <-, -n> [ban·'da:·ʒə] f bandage

bandagieren* [ban·da·'ʒi:·rən] vt to bandage

Bandbreite f 1. (Spektrum) range 2. INET, RADIO bandwidth

Bande <-, -n> ['ban·də] f gang

Bänderriss RR ['bɛn·de·] m torn ligament

bändigen ['bɛn·dɪ·gn̩] vt to tame

Bandit(in) <-en, -en> [ban·'di:t] m(f) bandit

Bandmaß nt tape measure

Bandscheibe f ANAT [intervertebral] disc; **es an den ~n haben** to have a slipped disc

Bandwurm m tapeworm

Bank[1] <-, Bänke> [baŋk] f bench ▶ [**alle**] **durch die ~** every single one [of them]; **etw auf die lange ~ schieben** to put sth off

Bank[2] <-, -en> [baŋk] f FIN bank; **ein Konto bei einer ~ haben** to have a bank account

Bankangestellte(r) f(m) bank employee

Bankett <-[e]s, -e> [baŋ·'kɛt] nt banquet

Bankier <-s, -s> [baŋ·'kje:] m banker

Bankkonto nt bank account

bankrott [baŋk·'rɔt] adj bankrupt; **jdn ~ machen** to bankrupt sb

Bankrott <-[e]s, -e> [baŋk·'rɔt] m bankruptcy

bankrott|gehen RR vi irreg sein to go bankrupt

Bankverbindung f bank account

Banner <-s, -> ['ba·ne] nt banner

bar [ba:ɐ̯] adj FIN cash; [**in**] **~ bezahlen** to pay [in] cash

Bar <-, -s> [ba:ɐ̯] f bar

Bär <-en, -en> [bɛ:ɐ̯] m bear; **wie ein ~ schlafen** to sleep like a log ▶ **jdm einen ~en aufbinden** to put sb on

Baracke <-, -n> [ba·'ra·kə] f shack

Bardame f barmaid

barfuß ['ba:ɐ̯·fu:s] adj pred barefoot[ed]

Bargeld nt cash

bargeldlos I. adj cashless II. adv without using cash

Barkauf m cash purchase

barmherzig [barm·'hɛr·tsɪç] adj compassionate; **~ sein** to show compassion

Barmherzigkeit <-> f kein pl mercy

Barmixer(in) <-s, -> *m(f)* bartender

Barock <-[s]> [ba·ˈrɔk] *nt o m kein pl* baroque

Barometer <-s, -> [baro·ˈmeː·tɐ] *nt* barometer

Barren <-s, -> [ˈba·rən] *m* **1.** SPORT parallel bars *pl* **2.** (*Goldbarren*) bar

Barriere <-, -n> [ba·ˈrjeː·rə] *f a. fig* barrier

Barrikade <-, -n> [ba·ri·ˈkaː·də] *f* barricade

barsch [barʃ] *adj* curt

Barsch <-[e]s, -e> [barʃ] *m* perch

Bart <-[e]s, Bärte> [baːɐ̯t] *m* **1.** beard; **sich** *dat* **einen ~ wachsen lassen** to grow a beard **2.** ZOOL whiskers

Barzahlung *f* cash payment

Basar <-s, -e> [ba·ˈzaːɐ̯] *m* bazaar

Base <-, -n> [ˈbaː·zə] *f* **1.** *veraltet* (*Cousine*) cousin **2.** *schweiz s.* **Tante** aunt

basieren* [ba·ˈziː·rən] *vi* to be based

Basilikum <-s> [ba·ˈziː·li·kʊm] *nt kein pl* basil

Basis <-, Basen> [ˈbaː·zɪs] *f* **1.** (*Grundlage*) basis **2.** POL **die ~** the grass roots **3.** MIL base

Baskenland *nt* **das ~** the Basque region

Baskenmütze *f* beret

Bass RR <-es, Bässe>, **Baß** ALT <-sses, Bässe> [bas] *m* bass

basteln [ˈbas·tl̩n] **I.** *vi* **1.** (*als Hobby*) to do arts and crafts **2.** **an etw** *dat* **~** to work on sth **II.** *vt* to make

Batterie <-, -n> [ba·tə·ˈriː] *f* ELEK, MIL battery

batteriebetrieben *adj* battery-powered

Bau <-[e]s, -ten> [bau] *m* **1.** *kein pl* **im ~ sein** to be under construction **2.** (*Gebäude*) building **3.** **auf dem ~ arbeiten** to work on a building site

Bauarbeiten *pl* construction [work] *sing;* **wegen ~ gesperrt** closed for repairs

Bauarbeiter(in) *m(f)* construction worker

Bauch <-[e]s, Bäuche> [baux] *m* belly; **sich** *dat* **den ~ vollschlagen** *fam* to stuff oneself ▶ **aus dem ~** from the heart; **aus dem hohlen ~** [**heraus**] off the top of one's head

Bauchfellentzündung *f* peritonitis

Bauchgefühl *nt kein pl* gut feeling

bauchig [ˈbaux·ɪç] *adj* bulbous

Bauchnabel *m* navel

Bauchschmerzen *pl* stomachache

Bauchspeicheldrüse *f* ANAT pancreas

Bauchtanz *m* belly dance

bauen [ˈbau·ən] **I.** *vt* to build **II.** *vi* **1.** (*Haus*) to build a house **2.** (*vertrauen*) **auf jdn/etw ~** to rely on sb/sth

Bauer, Bäuerin <-n, -n> [ˈbau·ɐ, ˈbɔyə·rɪn] *m, f* **1.** (*Landwirt*) farmer **2.** *pej* (*ungehobelter Mensch*) yokel **3.** (*Schachfigur*) pawn

Bauernhaus *nt* farmhouse

Bauernhof *m* farm

baufällig *adj* dilapidated

Baufirma *f* construction company

Baugelände *nt* construction site

Baugerüst *nt* scaffolding

Baugrube *f* [building] excavation

Bauholz *nt* lumber

Bauingenieur(in) *m(f)* civil engineer

Baujahr *nt* **1.** (*von Gebäude*) year of construction **2.** (*Produktionsjahr*) year of manufacture

Baukasten *m* construction set

Baum <-[e]s, Bäume> [baum] *m* tree ▶ **jd könnte Bäume ausreißen** sb is full of energy

Baumarkt *m* building supplies store

baumeln [ˈbau·ml̩n] *vi* to dangle (**an** +*dat* from)

Baumgrenze *f* tree line

Baumschule *f* tree nursery

Baumstamm *m* tree trunk

Baumsterben *nt* dying[-off] of trees

Baumwolle *f* cotton

Bauplan *m* building plans *pl*

Bauplatz *m* [construction] site

Bauschutt *m* construction waste

bausparen *vi nur infin* to have an account with a mortgage lender

Bausparkasse *f* mortgage lender

Bausparvertrag *m* savings account for home construction

Baustelle *f* construction site

Bauunternehmer(in) *m(f)* builder

Bauwerk *nt* building; (*Brücke etc.*) construction

Bayer(in) <-n, -n> [ˈbai·ɐ] *m(f)* Bavarian; *s. a.* **Deutsche(r)**

bayerisch [ˈbaiə·rɪʃ] *adj* Bavarian; *s. a.* **deutsch**

Bayern <-s> ['bai·ɐn] nt Bavaria; s. a. **Deutschland**

beabsichtigen * [bə·'ʔap·zɪç·tɪ·gn̩] vt to intend; **das hatte ich nicht beabsichtigt!** I didn't mean to do that!

beachten * [bə·'ʔax·tn̩] vt **1.** (befolgen) to observe; (Anweisung, Rat) to follow; **die Vorfahrt ~** to yield [the right of way] **2.** (Aufmerksamkeit schenken) **jdn/etw ~** to pay attention to sb/sth; **bitte ~ Sie, dass ...** please note that ...

beachtlich adj considerable; (Erfolg, Leistung) notable; (Verbesserung) marked

Beachtung f **1.** (Befolgung) observance; **~ der Vorschriften** compliance with the regulations **2.** (Aufmerksamkeit) **~ finden** to receive attention; **keine ~ finden** to be ignored; **jdm/etw ~ schenken** to pay attention to sb/sth

Beamte(r) [bə·'ʔam·tɐ, bə·'ʔam·tə] m dekl wie adj, **Beamtin** <-, -nen> [bə·'ʔam·tɪn] f civil servant

beängstigend adj alarming

beanspruchen * [bə·'ʔan·ʃprʊ·xn̩] vt **1.** (fordern) to claim **2.** (brauchen) to require; (Platz, Zeit) to take up **3.** (Anforderungen stellen) **jdn ~** to make demands on sb; **ich will Sie nicht länger ~** I don't want to take up any more of your time; **etw ~** to demand sth; **jds Zeit ~** to make demands on sb's time; **jds Geduld ~** to try sb's patience

beanstanden [bə·'ʔan·ʃtan·dn̩] vt to complain about; **das ist beanstandet worden** there have been complaints about that

beantragen * vt to apply for; POL to propose

beantworten * vt to answer; **etw mit etw ~** to respond to sth with sth

bearbeiten * vt **1.** (behandeln) to work on; **Holz ~** to work wood **2.** (auf jdn einwirken) **jdn ~** to work on sb; **wir haben ihn so lange bearbeitet, bis er zugesagt hat** we pressed him until he agreed

beatmen * vt to give artificial respiration to

beaufsichtigen * [bə·'ʔauf·zɪç·tɪ·gn̩] vt to supervise; (Kinder) to look after; (bei Prüfung) to proctor

beauftragen * vt (Architekt, Künstler) to commission; (Firma) to hire; **jdn mit etw** dat **~** to give sb the job of doing sth; **jdn ~, etw zu tun** to ask sb to do sth

Beauftragte(r) f(m) dekl wie adj representative

bebauen * vt **1.** (Grundstück) to build on; **dicht bebaut sein** to be heavily built-up **2.** (Acker, Feld) to cultivate

beben ['be:·bn̩] vi to tremble; **vor Zorn ~** to shake with anger

Becher <-s, -> ['bɛ·çɐ] m glass; (aus Plastik) cup; (für Tee/Kaffee) mug

Becken <-s, -> ['bɛ·kn̩] nt **1.** (Bassin) basin; (Spülbecken) sink; (von Toilette) bowl; (Schwimmbecken) pool **2.** ANAT pelvis **3.** MUS cymbals pl

bedacht [bə·'daxt] **I.** pp von **bedenken** **II.** adj **1.** (überlegt) cautious **2. auf etw** akk **~ sein** to be concerned about sth

bedächtig [bə·'dɛç·tɪç] **I.** adj **1.** (ohne Hast) deliberate **2.** (besonnen) thoughtful **II.** adv **1.** (ohne Hast) deliberately; **~ sprechen** to speak in measured tones **2.** (besonnen) carefully

bedanken * vr **sich** akk **~** to express one's thanks; **sich** akk **bei jdm ~** to thank sb; **ich bedanke mich!** thank you!

Bedarf <-[e]s> [bə·'darf] m kein pl need (**an** +dat for); **der tägliche ~ an Vitaminen** the daily requirement of vitamins; **Dinge des täglichen ~s** everyday necessities; **bei ~** if required; **[je] nach ~** as required

bedauerlich adj regrettable; **sehr ~!** how unfortunate!; **~ sein, dass ...** to be unfortunate that ...

bedauerlicherweise adv unfortunately

bedauern * vt **1. etw ~** to regret sth **2. jdn ~** to feel sorry for sb

Bedauern <-s> nt kein pl regret

bedauernswert adj (Mensch) pitiful; **ein ~er Zwischenfall** an unfortunate incident

bedeckt adj pred (bewölkt) overcast
▶ **sich** akk **~ halten** to keep a low profile

bedenken * irreg vt to consider; **[jdm] etw zu ~ geben** to ask [sb] to consider sth; **[jdm] zu ~ geben, dass ...** to ask [sb] to keep in mind that ...

Bedenken <-s, -> nt meist pl doubt; ~ **haben** to have doubts; **moralische** ~ moral scruples; **jdm kommen** ~ sb has second thoughts; **ohne** ~ without hesitation

bedenkenlos adv without hesitation

bedenklich adj 1. (fragwürdig) questionable 2. (Besorgnis erregend) disturbing; (Gesundheitszustand) serious; **jdn** ~ **stimmen** to give sb cause for concern

bedeuten＊ vt to mean; **das hat nichts zu** ~ that doesn't mean a thing; **[jdm] etw** ~ to mean something [to sb]

bedeutend adj 1. (wichtig) important; (Politiker) leading; **eine ~e Rolle spielen** to play a significant role 2. (beachtlich) considerable

bedeutsam adj 1. (wichtig) important 2. (vielsagend) meaningful

Bedeutung <-, -en> f 1. (Sinn) meaning; **in wörtlicher/übertragener** ~ in the literal/figurative sense 2. (Wichtigkeit) importance; **für jdn/etw von** ~ **sein** to be of importance [to sb/sth]; **nichts von** ~ nothing important

bedeutungslos adj insignificant

bedienen＊ I. vt 1. (Kunde, Gast) to serve 2. (Maschine) to operate ▶ **bedient sein** fam to have had enough II. vi to serve; **wird hier nicht bedient?** isn't anyone working here? III. vr sich akk [mit etw akk] ~ to help oneself [to sth]; ~ **Sie sich!** help yourself!

Bedienung <-, -en> f 1. (Kellner) waiter masc, waitress fem 2. kein pl (Handhabung) operation 3. kein pl (Service) service; ~ **inbegriffen** service included

Bedienungsanleitung f [operating] instructions pl

bedingt adv ~ **gültig** of limited validity

Bedingung <-, -en> f 1. (Voraussetzung) condition; **unter der** ~, **dass ...** on the condition that ... 2. pl (Umstände) conditions

bedingungslos adj unconditional; (Gehorsam, Treue) unquestioning

bedrohen＊ vt to threaten

bedrohlich adj threatening

bedrücken＊ vt to depress; **was bedrückt dich?** what's troubling you?

bedrückt adj depressed; ~**es Schweigen** oppressive silence

Beduine, Beduinin <-n, -n> [bedu·ˈiː·nə, bedu·ˈiː·nɪn] m, f Bed[o]uin

Bedürfnis <-ses, -se> [bə·ˈdʏrf·nɪs] nt need; **die ~se des täglichen Lebens** everyday needs; **das** ~ **haben, etw zu tun** to feel the need to do sth

beeilen＊ vr sich akk ~ to hurry [up]; **sich akk** ~, **etw zu tun** to hurry to do sth

beeindrucken＊ [bə·ˈʔain·drʊ·kn̩] vt to impress; **sich** akk **[von etw** dat**] nicht** ~ **lassen** to not be impressed [by sth]

beeinflussen＊ [bə·ˈʔain·flʊ·sn̩] vt to influence

beeinträchtigen＊ [bə·ˈʔain·trɛç·tɪ·gn̩] vt to impair

beenden＊ vt to end

beerdigen＊ [bə·ˈʔeːɐ̯·dɪ·gn̩] vt to bury

Beerdigung <-, -en> f funeral

Beere <-, -n> [ˈbeː·rə] f berry

Beet <-[e]s, -e> [beːt] nt (Blumen) flower bed; (Gemüse) vegetable patch

befahren＊ adj (Straße) used; **kaum/ stark** ~ **sein** to be little/heavily used; **eine viel ~e Kreuzung** a busy intersection

befangen [bə·ˈfa·ŋən] adj JUR biased; **jdn als** ~ **ablehnen** to disqualify sb on grounds of bias

befassen＊ vr sich akk **mit etw** dat ~ to concern oneself with sth; **sich** akk **mit einem Problem** ~ to tackle a problem; **sich** akk **mit jdm** ~ to spend time with sb

Befehl <-[e]s, -e> [bə·ˈfeːl] m order; **jdm den** ~ **geben, etw zu tun** to order sb to do sth

befehlen <befiehlt, befahl, befohlen> [bə·ˈfeː·lən] vt to order; **von dir lasse ich mir nichts** ~! I won't take orders from you!

befestigen＊ vt to fasten (**an** +dat to)

befinden＊ irreg I. vr sich akk **irgendwo** ~ to be somewhere; **unter den Geiseln** ~ **sich zwei Deutsche** the hostages include two Germans II. vi **über etw** akk ~ to decide [on] sth

befolgen＊ vt (Rat) to follow; (Befehl, Vorschrift) to obey

befördern＊ vt 1. (transportieren) to

transport **2.** (*beruflich*) to promote

Beförderung *f* **1.** (*Transport*) transportation **2.** (*beruflich*) promotion

befragen * *vt* to question

befreien * I. *vt* **1.** (*Gefangene*) to free **2.** (*Volk, Land*) to liberate **3.** (*freistellen*) to excuse; (*vom Wehrdienst*) to exempt **4.** (*von Schmerzen, Sorgen*) to free **II.** *vr* **sich** *akk* **von etw** *dat* ~ to rid oneself of sth

Befreiung <-, -en> *f pl selten* **1.** (*von Gefangenen*) release **2.** (*eines Volkes, Landes*) liberation **3.** (*Freistellung*) exemption

befreunden * [bə-'frɔyn-dn̩] *vr* **sich** *akk* **mit jdm** ~ to make friends with sb; **mit jdm befreundet sein** to be friends with sb

befriedigen * [bə-'fri:-dɪ-gn̩] I. *vt* to satisfy; (*Ansprüche, Wünsche*) to fulfill; **leicht/schwer zu** ~ **sein** to be easily/not easily satisfied **II.** *vr* **sich** *akk* [**selbst**] ~ to masturbate

befriedigend *adj* satisfactory; ~ **sein** to be satisfying

befristen * *vt* to limit (**auf** +*akk* to)

befugt [bə-'fu:kt] *adj* authorized

Befund <-[e]s, -e> *m* MED result[s *pl*]; **ohne** ~ negative

befürchten * *vt* to fear; ~, **dass ...** to be afraid that ...

befürworten * [bə-'fy:ɐ̯-vɔr-tn̩] *vt* to be in favor of

Befürworter(in) <-s, -> *m(f)* supporter

begabt [bə-'ga:pt] *adj* gifted, talented; **für etw** *akk* ~ **sein** to have a gift for sth; **künstlerisch sehr** ~ **sein** to be very artistic

Begabung <-, -en> *f* gift, talent

begeben * *vr irreg* **sich** *akk* **in ärztliche Behandlung** ~ to undergo medical treatment; **sich** *akk* **in Gefahr** ~ to expose oneself to danger

begegnen * [bə-'ge:g-nən] I. *vi sein* **jdm** ~ to meet sb **II.** *vr sein* **sich** *dat* ~ to meet

Begegnung <-, -en> *f* encounter

begehren * [bə-'ge:-gn̩] *vt* to desire

begehrenswert *adj* desirable

begehrt *adj* (*Frau, Mann*) desirable; (*Preis*) [much-]coveted; **ein** ~**er Jung-**

geselle an eligible bachelor

begeistern * I. *vt* to fill with enthusiasm **II.** *vr* **sich** *akk* **für jdn/etw** ~ to be enthusiastic about sb/sth

begeistert *adj* enthusiastic (**von** +*dat* about)

Begeisterung <-> *f kein pl* enthusiasm

Begierde <-, -n> [bə-'gi:ɐ̯-də] *f* desire (**nach** +*dat* for)

begierig *adj* **1.** (*gespannt*) eager (**auf** +*akk* for) **2.** (*verlangend*) longing

Beginn <-[e]s> [bə-'gɪn] *m kein pl* beginning, start; **zu** ~ at the beginning

beginnen <begann, begonnen> [bə-'gɪ-nən] *vt, vi* to begin

beglaubigen * [bə-'glau-bɪ-gn̩] *vt* to authenticate; **eine beglaubigte Kopie** a certified copy

begleichen * *vt irreg* (*Schulden*) to pay; (*Rechnung*) to settle

begleiten * *vt a. fig* to accompany; **jdn zur Tür** ~ to show sb to the door

Begleiter(in) <-s, -> *m(f)* companion

Begleitung <-, -en> *f* **1.** company; **kommst du allein oder in** ~? are you coming by yourself or with someone?; **in** [**jds** *gen*] ~ accompanied by sb; **ohne** ~ unaccompanied **2.** (*Begleiter[in]*) companion **3.** MUS accompaniment; **ohne** ~ **spielen** to play unaccompanied

beglückwünschen * *vt* to congratulate (**zu** +*dat* on)

begnadigen * [bə-'gna:-dɪ-gn̩] *vt* to pardon

begnügen * [bə-'gny:-gn̩] *vr* **sich** *akk* **mit etw** *dat* ~ to be satisfied with sth

begraben * *vt irreg* **1.** (*beerdigen*) to bury **2.** (*aufgabe: Hoffnung, Plan*) to abandon; **einen Streit** ~ to bury the hatchet

Begräbnis <-ses, -se> [bə-'grɛp-nɪs] *nt* burial

begreifen * *irreg* I. *vt* to comprehend; ~, **dass ...** to realize that ...; **kaum zu** ~ **sein** to be incomprehensible **II.** *vi* **langsam/schnell** ~ to be slow/quick on the uptake

begreiflich *adj* understandable; **jdm etw** ~ **machen** to make sth clear to sb

begrenzen * *vt* to limit; **die Geschwindigkeit auf ... km/h** ~ to impose a speed limit of ... kmph

Begriff <-[e]s, -e> *m* **1.** (*Ausdruck*) term; **ein ~ aus der Philosophie** a philosophical term **2.** (*Vorstellung*) idea; **jdm ein/kein ~ sein** to mean sth/ nothing to sb; **für jds ~ sein** in sb's opinion ▶ **im ~ sein, etw zu tun** to be about to do sth; **schnell/schwer von ~ sein** *fam* to be quick/slow on the uptake

begriffsstutzig *adj* slow on the uptake

begründen * *vt* to give reasons for; (*Ablehnung, Forderung*) to justify; (*Behauptung, Verdacht*) to substantiate

begründet *adj* well-founded; **in etw** *dat* **~ liegen** to be the result of sth

Begründung <-, -en> *f* reason

begrüßen * *vt* to greet; **es ist zu ~, dass ...** it is a good thing that ...

Begrüßung <-, -en> *f* greeting; **offizielle ~** official welcome

begünstigen * [bəˈɡʏn·stɪ·ɡn̩] *vt* (*Export, Wachstum*) to encourage; **von etw** *dat* **begünstigt werden** to be helped by sth

behagen * [bəˈhaː·ɡn̩] *vi* **etw behagt jdm** sb likes sth

behaglich [bəˈhaːk·lɪç] *adj* **1.** (*gemütlich*) cozy; **es sich** *dat* **~ machen** to make oneself comfortable **2.** **ein ~es Schnurren** a contented purring

behalten * *vt irreg* **1.** (*nicht wegwerfen*) to keep **2.** (*nicht verraten*) **etw für sich** *akk* **~** to keep sth to oneself **3.** **die Nerven ~** to keep one's composure **4.** (*sich merken*) to remember; **etw im Kopf ~** to keep sth in one's head

Behälter <-s, -> *m* container

behandeln * *vt* to treat; **jdn gut/schlecht ~** to treat sb well/badly

Behandlung <-, -en> *f* treatment

beharren * *vi* to insist; **auf seiner Meinung ~** to stick to one's opinion

beharrlich *adv* persistently; **~ schweigen** to persist in remaining silent

behaupten * [bəˈhaup·tn̩] **I.** *vt* to claim; **von jdm ~, dass ...** to say of sb that ...; **es wird behauptet, dass ...** it is said that ...; **seinen Vorsprung gegen jdn ~** *sport* to maintain one's lead over sb **II.** *vr* **sich** *akk* **~** to assert oneself; **sich** *akk* **gegen die Konkurrenz ~ können** to hold one's own against

the competition

Behauptung <-, -en> *f* assertion; **eine ~ aufstellen** to make an assertion

beheben * *vt irreg* (*Fehler, Mangel*) to rectify; (*Missstände*) to remedy; (*Schaden, Störung*) to repair

Behelf <-[e]s, -e> [bəˈhɛlf] *m* [temporary] replacement

beherbergen * *vt* to accommodate

beherrschen * **I.** *vt* **1.** (*Land*) to rule **2.** (*im Griff haben*) to control; **ein Fahrzeug ~** to have control over a vehicle **3.** **ein Instrument ~** to play an instrument well; **eine Sprache ~** to have good command of a language; **alle Tricks ~** to know all the tricks **II.** *vr* **sich** *akk* **~** to control oneself

behilflich [bəˈhɪlf·lɪç] *adj* **jdm ~ sein** to help sb

behindern * *vt* to hinder

behindert *adj* **geistig/körperlich ~** mentally/physically disabled

Behinderte(r) *f(m) dekl wie adj* disabled person; **die B~n** the disabled

Behinderung <-, -en> *f* **1.** TRANSP **es muss mit ~en gerechnet werden** delays should be expected **2.** MED **geistige/körperliche ~** mental/physical disability

Behörde <-, -n> [bəˈhøːɐ̯·də] *f* department; **die ~n** the authorities

bei [bai] *präp* +*dat* **1.** (*in der Nähe*) near; **eine Stadt ~ Köln** a town near Cologne **2.** **~ jdm** [**zu Hause**] at sb's place; **~ uns zu Hause** at our place; **ich war ~ meinen Eltern** [**house**] I was at my parents' [house]; **er ist ~ der Bahn** he works for the railroad; **~ wem nimmst du Klavierstunden?** who's your piano teacher?; **~m Bäcker/Friseur** at the bakery/hairdresser's **3.** **etw ~ sich** *dat* **haben** to have sth on one; **ich habe gerade kein Geld ~ mir** I don't have any money on me at the moment **4.** (*zeitlich*) **~ Tag/ Nacht** by day/night; **~m Lesen kann ich nicht Radio hören** I cannot read and listen to the radio at the same time; **störe mich bitte nicht ~ der Arbeit!** please stop disturbing me while I'm working!; **~ dem Zugunglück starben viele Menschen** many people died in

the train crash **5.** (*Begleitumstände*) **wir können das ja ~ einer Flasche Wein besprechen** let's talk about it over a bottle of wine; **~ deinen Fähigkeiten** with your talents; **~ 45° unter null** at 45° below zero [Celsius]; **~ dieser Hitze/Kälte** in such heat/cold; **~ Nebel/Regen** when it is foggy/raining; **~ Wind und Wetter** come rain or shine **6.** (*ungefähr*) around; **der Preis liegt ~ 1.000 Euro** the price is around 1,000 euros

bei|behalten * *vt irreg* to maintain; (*Tradition, Brauch*) to uphold; (*Meinung*) to stick to

bei|bringen *vt irreg* **jdm etw ~** to teach sb sth ▶ **jdm etw schonend ~** to break sth gently to sb

Beichte <-, -n> [ˈbaiçtə] *f* confession; **die ~ ablegen** to make one's confession; **jdm die ~ abnehmen** to hear sb's confession

beichten [ˈbaiçtn̩] **I.** *vt* [**jdm**] **etw ~** to confess sth [to sb] **II.** *vi* **~ gehen** to go to confession

beide [ˈbaidə] *pron* both; **meine ~n Töchter** my two daughters; **alle ~** both of them; **~ Mal[e]** both times; **keiner von ~n** neither of them; **ihr ~** the two of you; **ihr habt ~ Recht** both of you are right; **wir ~** the two of us; **die ~n** both [of them]; **die ersten/letzten ~n** the first/last two; **einer von ~n** one of the two; **~s** both; **~s ist möglich** both are possible

beiderlei [ˈbaiˈde·lai] *adj attr* both

beieinander [baiˈʔaiˈnanˈde] *adv* together ▶ **gut/schlecht ~ sein** *fam* (*körperlich*) to be in good/bad shape; (*geistig*) to be with it/not all there

Beifahrer(in) *m(f)* front-seat passenger

Beifahrersitz *m* [front] passenger seat

Beifall <-[e]s> *m kein pl* applause; [**jds** *akk*] **~ finden** to meet with [sb's] approval; **~ klatschen** to applaud

bei|fügen *vt* **1.** (*mitsenden*) to enclose **2.** (*hinzufügen*) to add

beige [beːʃ, ˈbeː·ʒə] *adj* beige

bei|geben *vt irreg* ▶ **klein ~** to give in

Beihilfe *f* financial aid

Beil <-[e]s, -e> [bail] *nt* [short-handled] ax

Beilage *f* **1.** (*Speise*) side dish **2.** (*Beiheft*) supplement

beiläufig *adv* **etw ~ erwähnen** to mention sth in passing

bei|legen *vt* **1. einem Brief einen Rückumschlag ~** to enclose a return envelope in a letter **2. einen Streit ~** to settle a dispute

Beileid *nt* condolence[s *pl*]; [**mein**] **herzliches ~** [you have] my heartfelt sympathy; **jdm** [**zu etw** *dat*] **sein ~ aussprechen** to offer sb one's condolences [on sth]

beiliegend *adj* enclosed; **~ finden Sie ...** please find enclosed ...

Bein <-[e]s, -e> [bain] *nt* leg; **jdm auf die ~e helfen** to help sb back on his/her feet; **jdm ein ~ stellen** to trip sb; **die ~e übereinanderschlagen** to cross one's legs; **unsicher auf den ~en sein** to be unsteady on one's feet ▶ **sich** *dat* **die ~e in den Bauch stehen** to be standing around for ages; **wieder auf die ~e kommen** (*gesundheitlich*) to be up on one's feet again; (*finanziell*) to regain one's financial standing; **mit dem linken ~ zuerst aufgestanden sein** to have gotten up on the wrong side of the bed; **auf den ~en sein** (*auf sein*) to be up and about; **etw auf die ~e stellen** to get sth going

beinahe [ˈbaiˈnaːə] *adv* almost

Beinbruch *m* leg fracture ▶ **das ist kein ~!** *fam* it's not as bad as all that!

beinhalten * [bəˈʔɪnˈhalˈtn̩] *vt* to contain

Beipackzettel *m* instruction sheet

beirren * *vt* **sich** *akk* [**nicht**] **~ lassen** to [not] let oneself be put off

Beisammensein *nt* get-together

beiseite [baiˈzaiˈtə] *adv* to one side

beiseite|gehen RR *vi irreg sein* to step aside

beiseite|legen RR *vi irreg* **etw ~** (*weglegen*) to put sth to one side; (*Geld*) to put aside *sep* sth

bei|setzen *vt geh* to inter; (*Urne*) to install

Beisetzung <-, -en> *f geh* interment; (*einer Urne*) installing [in its resting place]

Beispiel <-[e]s, -e> ['bai·ʃpiːl] nt example; **anschauliches ~** illustration; **praktisches ~** demonstration; **zum ~** for example; **wie zum ~** such as ▶ **mit gutem ~ vorangehen** to set a good example

beispielsweise adv for example

beißen <biss, gebissen> ['bai·sn] I. vt to bite ▶ **etw/nichts zu ~ haben** fam to have something/nothing to eat II. vi 1. (mit den Zähnen) **auf/in etw** akk **~** to bite into sth 2. (brennen) to sting; (Säure) to burn; **in den Augen ~** to make one's eyes sting ▶ **an etw** dat **zu ~ haben** to have sth to chew on III. vr 1. **sich** akk o dat **auf die Zunge ~** to bite one's tongue 2. **sich** akk **[mit etw** dat**] ~** (Farben) to clash [with sth]

beißend adj **~er Geruch** pungent smell; **~e Kälte** bitter cold; **~e Kritik** sharp criticism; **~er Witz** caustic humor

bei|stehen vi irreg **jdm ~** to stand by sb

Beitrag <-[e]s, -träge> ['bai·traːk] m 1. (für Verein) fee; (für Versicherung) premium 2. (Artikel) article 3. (Mitwirkung) contribution; **einen ~ zu etw** dat **leisten** to make a contribution to sth 4. schweiz (Subvention) subsidy

beitragspflichtig adj liable to pay contributions

Beitragssatz m membership rate

bei|treten vi irreg **sein** to join [as a member]; **der EU ~** to join the EU

Beitritt m entry (**zu** +dat into); **der ~ zur EU** the accession to the EU

Beiwagen m sidecar

beizeiten [bai·ˈtsai·tn̩] adv in good time

beizen ['bai·tsn̩] vt 1. **etw [braun/schwarz] ~** to stain sth [brown/black] 2. KOCHK to marinate

bejahen* [bə·ˈjaː·ən] vt 1. (Frage) to say yes to 2. (gutheißen) to approve [of]

bekämpfen* I. vt to fight; **Schädlinge ~** to control pests II. vr **sich** akk **[gegenseitig] ~** to fight one another

bekannt [bə·ˈkant] adj 1. (allgemein gekannt) well-known; **etw ist allgemein ~** sth is common knowledge; **etw ~ geben** to announce sth; (Presse) to publish sth; **etw ~ machen** to make sth known to the public 2. (berühmt) **jdn ~ machen** to make sb famous; **~ werden** to become famous; **für etw** akk **~ sein** to be well-known for sth 3. (nicht fremd) familiar; **ist dir dieser Name ~?** are you familiar with this name?; **mit jdm ~ sein** to be acquainted with sb

Bekannte(r) f(m) dekl wie adj acquaintance; **ein guter ~r** a friend

bekannt|geben s. **bekannt 1**

bekanntlich adv as is [generally] known

bekannt|machen vt s. **bekannt 1, 2**

Bekanntschaft <-, -en> f 1. pl selten (das Bekanntsein) acquaintance; **eine nette ~ machen** to meet a nice person; **mit etw** dat **~ machen** iron to get to know sth 2. (Bekannte[r]) acquaintance; (Bekanntenkreis) acquaintances pl

bekehren* vt to convert

bekennen* irreg I. vt to confess II. vr 1. (eintreten für) **sich** akk **zu jdm/etw ~** to declare one's support for sb/sth; **sich** akk **zu einem Glauben ~** to profess a faith 2. (zugeben) **sich** akk **zu einem Irrtum/einer Tat ~** to admit [to] a mistake/doing sth

bekifft [bə·ˈkɪft] adj fam stoned

beklagen* I. vt to lament; **bei dem Unglück waren 23 Tote zu ~** the accident claimed 23 lives II. vr **sich** akk **[bei jdm] ~** to complain [to sb]

beklagenswert adj lamentable; (Irrtum, Versehen) unfortunate

bekleckern* fam I. vt to stain II. vr **sich** akk **mit Soße ~** to spill sauce all over oneself

Bekleidung f clothing

beklommen [bə·ˈklɔ·mən] adj anxious

bekloppt [bə·ˈklɔpt] adj fam s. **bescheuert**

bekömmlich [bə·ˈkœm·lɪç] adj [easily] digestible

bekümmert adj worried

beladen* irreg vt to load [up sep]

Belag <-[e]s, Beläge> [bə·ˈlaːk] m 1. (Schicht) coating 2. (für Pizza, Brot) topping; (für Sandwich) filling 3. (auf Zähnen) film; (auf Zunge) fur

belagern* vt to besiege

belangen* vt JUR to prosecute (**wegen** +gen for)

belanglos adj irrelevant

belassen* vt irreg **1. es bei etw** dat ~ to leave it at sth; ~ **wir es dabei!** let's leave it at that **2. etw an seinem Platz** ~ to leave sth in its place

belasten* vt **1.** (mit Gewicht) to load **2.** (seelisch) to burden; **jdn mit Problemen** ~ to burden sb with problems; **jdn** [**schwer**] ~ to weigh [heavily] on one's mind; ~**d** crippling **3.** (körperlich) to strain; **jdn/etw zu sehr** ~ to overstrain sb/sth; **etw belastet das Herz** sth puts a strain on the heart **4.** JUR to incriminate; ~**des Material** incriminating evidence **5. die Umwelt** ~ to pollute the environment **6.** FIN **ein Konto** [**mit 100 Euro**] ~ to debit [100 euros from] an account; **etw mit einer Hypothek** ~ to mortgage sth

belästigen* [bə-ˈlɛs-tɪ-gn̩] vt to pester; **jdn sexuell** ~ to harass sb sexually

Belästigung <-, -en> f annoyance; **sexuelle** ~ sexual harassment

Belastung <-, -en> f **1.** (Gewicht) load **2.** (seelisch) burden **3.** (körperlich) strain (**für** +akk on) **4.** ÖKOL pollution

belaufen* vr irreg **sich** akk **auf etw** akk ~ to amount to sth

beleben* **I.** vt (Konjunktur) to stimulate; (Party, Unterhaltung) to liven up **II.** vr **sich** akk ~ to liven up; (Konjunktur) to be stimulated

belebend adj refreshing

Beleg <-[e]s, -e> m **1.** ÖKON receipt **2.** (Beweis) proof

belegen* vt **1. ein Brot mit etw** dat ~ to put sth on a slice of bread; **belegte Brote** [open-faced] sandwiches **2. eine Behauptung** ~ to substantiate a claim; **ein Zitat** ~ to give a reference for a quotation **3. einen Kurs** ~ to enroll for a class **4.** (besetzen) to occupy; **belegt sein** to be occupied; **ist der Stuhl hier schon belegt?** is this chair free? **5.** SPORT **den vierten Platz** ~ to take fourth place

Belegschaft <-, -en> f staff; (Arbeiter) workforce

belegt adj (Stimme) hoarse

belehren* vt **sich** akk **von jdm** ~ **lassen** to listen to sb

beleibt [bə-ˈlaipt] adj corpulent

beleidigen* [bə-ˈlai-dɪ-gn̩] vt to insult

Beleidigung <-, -en> f insult

belesen [bə-ˈleː-zn̩] adj well-read

beleuchten* vt **1.** (durch Licht) to light [up sep] **2.** fig (betrachten) to throw light on

Beleuchtung <-, -en> f **1.** pl selten lighting; **die** ~ **der Straßen** street lighting **2.** AUTO lights pl

Belgien <-s> [ˈbɛl-ɡjən] nt Belgium; s. a. **Deutschland**

Belgier(in) <-s, -> [ˈbɛl-ɡiɐ] m(f) Belgian; s. a. **Deutsche(r)**

belgisch [ˈbɛl-ɡɪʃ] adj Belgian; s. a. **deutsch**

Belichtung f FOTO exposure

Belieben nt [**ganz**] **nach** ~ just as you/they etc. like

beliebig [bə-ˈliː-bɪç] **I.** adj any; **eine** ~**e Zahl** any number at all; **jeder B**~**e** anyone at all **II.** adv ~ **lange/viele** as long/many as you like; **etw** ~ **verändern** to change sth at will

beliebt [bə-ˈliːpt] adj popular (**bei** +dat with); **sich** akk **[bei jdm]** ~ **machen** to make oneself popular [with sb]

Beliebtheit <-> f kein pl popularity

beliefern* vt to supply

bellen [ˈbɛ-lən] vi to bark

belohnen* vt to reward

Belohnung <-, -en> f reward; **eine** ~ **aussetzen** to offer a reward

Belüftung f ventilation no indef art

belügen* irreg **I.** vt **jdn** ~ to lie to sb **II.** vr **sich** akk **selbst** ~ to deceive oneself

bemängeln* [bə-ˈmɛ-ŋl̩n] vt to find fault with

bemerkbar adj noticeable; **sich** akk **[bei jdm]** ~ **machen** to attract [sb's] attention; **ich werde mich schon** ~ **machen, wenn ich Sie benötige** I'll let you know when I need you

bemerken* vt **1.** (wahrnehmen) to notice **2.** (äußern) to say

bemerkenswert adj remarkable

Bemerkung <-, -en> f remark; **eine** ~ **über etw** akk **machen** to remark on sth; **eine** ~ **fallen lassen** to drop a remark

bemitleiden* [bə-ˈmɪt-lai-dn̩] **I.** vt to

pity **II.** *vr* **sich** *akk* [**selbst**] ~ to feel sorry for oneself

bemitleidenswert *adj* pitiful

bemühen* *vr* **sich** *akk* ~ to try hard; **sich** *akk* **vergebens** ~ to try in vain; **sich** *akk* **um eine Stelle** ~ to try hard to get a job

Bemühung <-, -en> *f* effort; **danke für Ihre ~en** thank you for your trouble

bemuttern* [bə-'mʊ-tən] *vt* to mother

benachbart [bə-'nax-baːɐt] *adj* neighboring *attr*; **das ~e Haus** the house next door

benachrichtigen* [bə-'naːx-rɪç-tɪgn] *vt* to inform; (*amtlich*) to notify

Benachrichtigung <-, -en> *f* notification

benachteiligen* [bə-'naːx-tai-lɪ-gn] *vt* to put at a disadvantage; (*wegen Rasse, Geschlecht, Glaube*) to discriminate against

Benachteiligung <-, -en> *f* **die ~ einer Person** discrimination against sb

benehmen* *vr irreg* **sich** *akk* ~ to behave [oneself]; **benimm dich!** behave yourself!; **sich** *akk* **gut/schlecht** ~ to behave well/badly

Benehmen <-s> *nt kein pl* manners *pl*

beneiden* *vt* **jdn** [**um etw**] ~ to envy sb [sth]

beneidenswert *adj* enviable

benennen* *vt irreg* to name (**nach** +*dat* after); **Gegenstände** ~ to denote objects

Bengel <-s, -[s]> ['bɛ·ŋl] *m* rascal

benommen [bə-'nɔ-mən] *adj* dazed; **jdn** ~ **machen** to throw sb

benötigen* *vt* to need

benutzen* *vt*, **benützen*** *vt dial, österr* **1.** (*gebrauchen*) to use; **den Aufzug** ~ to take the elevator **2.** (*ausnutzen*) **jdn** ~ to take advantage of sb; **sich** *akk* **benutzt fühlen** to feel [that one has been] used

Benutzer(in) <-s, -> *m(f)*, **Benützer(in)** <-s, -> *m(f) dial, österr* COMPUT user

Benutzerhandbuch *nt* user manual

Benutzername *m* COMPUT user name

Benutzeroberfläche *f* COMPUT user interface

Benutzung *f*, **Benützung** *f dial, österr*

use; **jdm etw zur ~ überlassen** to put sth at sb's disposal

Benzin <-s, -e> [bɛn·'tsiːn] *nt* gas[oline]

Benzintank *m* gas tank

Benzinverbrauch *m* gas consumption

beobachten* [bə-'ʔoːb·ax·tn] *vt* **1.** (*betrachten*) to observe; **jdn** [**bei etw** *dat*] ~ to watch sb [doing sth]; **gut beobachtet!** good observation! **2.** (*überwachen*) **beobachtet werden** to be kept under surveillance; **jdn** ~ **lassen** to put sb under surveillance **3.** (*bemerken*) **etw an jdm** ~ to notice sth in sb

Beobachter(in) <-s, -> *m(f)* observer

Beobachtung <-, -en> *f* **1.** (*das Betrachten*) observation **2.** (*Überwachung*) surveillance **3.** *meist pl* (*Feststellung*) observations *pl*

bequem [bə-'kveːm] *adj* **1.** (*angenehm*) comfortable; **es sich** *dat* ~ **machen** to make oneself comfortable; **ein ~es Leben haben** to have an easy life **2.** *pej* (*träge*) idle

Bequemlichkeit <-, -en> *f* **1.** (*Behaglichkeit*) comfort **2.** (*Trägheit*) idleness; **aus** [**reiner**] ~ out of [sheer] laziness

beraten* *irreg* **I.** *vt* to advise; **jdn finanziell** ~ to give sb financial advice; **sich** *akk* [**von jdm**] ~ **lassen** to ask sb's advice **II.** *vi* **über etw** *akk* ~ to discuss sth **III.** *vr* **sich** *akk* [**über etw** *akk*] ~ to discuss sth; POL to debate sth

Berater(in) <-s, -> *m(f)* advisor

Beratung <-, -en> *f* **1.** *kein pl* (*das Beraten*) advice **2.** (*Besprechung*) discussion; POL debate **3.** (*beratendes Gespräch*) consultation

berauschend *adj* intoxicating

berechenbar [bə-'rɛ·çn·baːɐ] *adj* **1.** MATH calculable **2.** (*voraussehbar*) predictable

berechnen* *vt* **1.** MATH to calculate **2.** (*in Rechnung stellen*) to charge

berechnend *adj pej* scheming

Berechnung *f* **1.** MATH calculation; **nach meiner** ~ according to my calculations **2.** *pej* (*Eigennutz*) scheming; **aus** ~ in cold deliberation

berechtigt [bə-'rɛç-tɪçt] *adj* (*Anspruch, Frage, Hoffnung*) legitimate; **ein ~er Vorwurf** a just accusation; [**dazu**] ~,

etw zu tun to be entitled to do sth
Bereich <-[e]s, -e> *m* area
bereichern * [bə·'rai·çɐn] *vr* **sich** *akk* |**an etw** *dat*| ~ to grow rich [on sth]
bereisen * *vt* **etw** ~ to travel around sth; **die Welt** ~ to travel the world
bereit [bə·'rait] *adj meist pred* **1.** (*fertig*) ready; (*vorbereitet*) prepared **2.** (*willens*) **zu etw** *dat* ~ **sein** to be prepared to do sth; **sich** *akk* ~ **erklären, etw zu tun** to agree to do sth
bereiten * *vt* to cause; (*Freude, Überraschung*) to give; **jdm Kopfschmerzen** ~ to give sb a headache
bereits [bə·'raits] *adv* already; ~ **damals** even then
Bereitschaft <-, -en> [bə·'rait·ʃaft] *f kein pl* **1.** willingness; **seine** ~ **zu etw** *dat* **erklären** to express one's willingness to do sth **2.** *kein pl* (*Bereitschaftsdienst*) emergency service; ~ **haben** (*Apotheke*) to provide emergency services; (*Arzt, Feuerwehr*) to be on call; (*im Krankenhaus*) to be on duty; (*Polizei, Soldaten*) to be on standby
Bereitschaftsdienst *m* emergency service
bereit|stellen *vt* **etw** |**für jdn/etw**| ~ to provide |sb/sth with| sth
bereitwillig **I.** *adj* (*Auskunft*) given willingly; (*Helfer*) willing; (*Verkäufer*) obliging; ~**e Hilfe** eager hands **II.** *adv* readily
bereuen * *vt* to regret; **das wirst du noch** ~! you'll be sorry |for that|!
Berg <-[e]s, -e> [bɛrk] *m* **1.** GEOG mountain; (*kleiner*) hill; **am** ~ **liegen** to lie at the foot of the hill **2.** (*große Menge*) ~**e von etw** *dat* piles of sth; ~**e von Papier** mountains of paper ▶ **über alle** ~**e sein** to be miles away; **mit etw** *dat* **hinterm** ~ **halten** to keep quiet about sth; **über den** ~ **sein** to be out of the woods; **die Patientin ist noch nicht über den** ~ the |female| patient is still in critical condition
bergab [bɛrk·'ʔap] *adv* a. *fig* downhill; **mit seinem Geschäft geht es** ~ his business is going downhill
Bergarbeiter(in) *m(f)* miner
bergauf [bɛrk·'ʔauf] *adv* uphill; **es geht**

wieder ~ *fig* things are looking up
Bergbahn *f* mountain railroad
Bergbau *m kein pl* mining
bergen <birgt, barg, geborgen> ['bɛr·gn̩] *vt* to rescue (**aus** +*dat* from); (*Giftstoffe, Tote*) to recover; (*Schiff*) to salvage
Bergführer(in) *m(f)* mountain guide
Berggipfel *m* mountain top
Bergkette *f* mountain range
Bergrutsch *m* landslide
Bergsteigen <-s> *nt kein pl* mountain climbing
Bergsteiger(in) <-s, -> *m(f)* mountain climber
Bergung <-, -en> *f* rescuing; (*eines Schiffs*) salvaging; (*von Toten*) recovering
Bergwacht <-, -en> *f* mountain rescue service
Bergwand *f* mountain face
Bergwerk *nt* mine
Bericht <-[e]s, -e> [bə·'rɪçt] *m* report
berichten * **I.** *vt* **1.** (*mitteilen*) to tell **2.** *schweiz* **falsch/recht berichtet** wrong/right; **bin ich falsch/recht berichtet, wenn ich annehme ...?** am I wrong/right in assuming ...? **II.** *vi* **1.** **über etw** *akk* ~ to report on sth; **wie unser Korrespondent berichtet** according to our correspondent; **wie soeben berichtet wird, ...** we are just receiving reports that ... **2.** (*Bericht erstatten*) **jdm** ~ to tell sb **3.** *schweiz* (*erzählen*) to talk
Berichterstattung <-, -en> *f* reporting (**über** +*akk* on)
berichtigen * [bə·'rɪç·tɪ·gn̩] *vt* to correct
Berlin <-s> [bɛr·'li:n] *nt* Berlin
Berliner[1] <-s, -> [bɛr·'li:·nɐ] *m* (*Gebäck*) ≈ jelly donut
Berliner[2] [bɛr·'li:·nɐ] *adj attr* Berlin
Bernstein ['bɛrn·ʃtain] *m kein pl* amber
berüchtigt [bə·'rʏç·tɪçt] *adj* notorious (**für** +*akk* for)
berücksichtigen * [bə·'rʏk·zɪç·tɪ·gn̩] *vt* to take into consideration; ~, **dass ...** to bear in mind that ...
Beruf <-[e]s, -e> [bə·'ru:f] *m* occupation; (*Stellung*) job; **sie ist Ärztin von** ~ she's a doctor; **was sind Sie von** ~? what do you do |for a living|?; **ein aka-**

demischer ~ an academic profession; **ein handwerklicher ~** a trade

berufen[1] *adj* **zu etw** *dat* **~ sein** to have a vocation for sth; **sich** *akk* **~ fühlen, etw zu tun** to feel a calling to do sth

berufen[2] *irreg* I. *vt* **jdn zu etw** *dat* **~** to appoint sb to sth II. *vr* **sich** *akk* **auf jdn/etw ~** to refer to sb/sth III. *vi* JUR *österr* (*Berufung einlegen*) to [file an] appeal

beruflich I. *adj* professional; **~e Aussichten** career prospects; **~e Laufbahn** career II. *adv* as far as work is concerned; **was macht sie ~?** what does she do for a living?; **sich** *akk* **~ weiterbilden** to attend professional seminars/workshops; **~ unterwegs sein** to be away on business; **~ verhindert sein** to be detained by work

Berufsakademie *f* university which combines three years of college-level academics with on-the-job training

Berufsausbildung *f* [professional] training; (*zum Handwerker*) apprenticeship

Berufsberater(in) *m(f)* career advisor

Berufsberatung *f* 1. (*Beratungsstelle*) career advisory service 2. (*das Beraten*) career advice

berufserfahren *adj* [professionally] experienced

Berufskrankheit *f* occupational disease

Berufsleben *nt* professional life

Berufspendler(in) *m(f)* commuter

Berufsschule *f* vocational school

berufstätig *adj* working; **~ sein** to be employed; **sie ist nicht mehr ~** she's no longer working

Berufsverkehr *m* rush-hour traffic

Berufung <-, -en> *f* 1. JUR appeal; **in die ~ gehen** to file an appeal 2. (*in ein Amt*) appointment 3. (*innerer Auftrag*) vocation (**zu** +*dat* for) 4. (*das Sichbeziehen*) **unter ~ auf jdn/etw** with reference to sb/sth

beruhen[*] *vi* **auf etw** *dat* **~** to be based on sth ▸ **etw auf sich** *akk* **lassen** to drop sth

beruhigen[*] I. *vt* to calm down *sep*; (*Nerven*) to soothe; (*Schmerzen*) to ease; **dieses Getränk wird deinen Magen ~** this drink will settle

your stomach; **jds Gewissen ~** to ease sb's conscience; **den Verkehr ~** to introduce traffic-calming measures II. *vr* **sich** *akk* **~** to calm down; (*politische Lage*) to stabilize; (*Meer*) to grow calm; (*Unwetter*) to die down

Beruhigungsmittel *nt* sedative

berühmt [bə·ˈryːmt] *adj* famous

Berühmtheit <-, -en> *f* 1. *kein pl* (*Ruf*) fame; **~ erlangen** to rise to fame 2. (*Mensch*) celebrity

berühren[*] *vt* 1. (*anfassen*) to touch 2. (*seelisch*) **etw berührt jdn** sth moves sb; **das berührt mich überhaupt nicht!** I couldn't care less!

besänftigen[*] [bə·ˈzɛnf·tɪ·gn̩] I. *vt* to soothe II. *vr* **sich** *akk* **~** to calm down; (*Sturm, Unwetter*) to die down

Besatzung <-, -en> [bə·ˈza·tsʊŋ] *f* 1. (*Mannschaft*) crew 2. MIL occupation

besaufen[*] *vr irreg fam* **sich** *akk* **~** to get sloshed

beschädigen[*] *vt* to damage

Beschädigung <-, -en> *f* damage

beschaffen[1] I. *vt* **[jdm] etw ~** to get sth [for sb] II. *vr* **sich** *dat* **etw ~** to get sth; **du musst dir Arbeit ~** you've got to find yourself a job

beschaffen[2] *adj* **so ~ sein, dass ...** to be made in such a way that ...

beschäftigen[*] [bə·ˈʃɛf·tɪ·gn̩] I. *vt* 1. (*Firma etc.*) to employ 2. **jdn** [**mit etw** *dat*] **~** to keep sb busy [with sth] 3. (*gedanklich*) **jdn ~** to be on sb's mind; **einer Frage/einem Problem beschäftigt sein** to be preoccupied with a question/problem II. *vr* **sich** *akk* [**mit etw** *dat*] **~** to occupy oneself [with sth]; **hast du genug, womit du dich ~ kannst?** do you have enough to do?; **sich** *akk* **mit jdm ~** to pay attention to sb; **du musst dich mehr mit den Kindern ~** you should spend more time with the children

beschäftigt [bə·ˈʃɛf·tɪçt] *adj* 1. (*angestellt*) employed; **wo bist du ~?** where do you work? 2. (*befasst*) busy

Beschäftigte(r) *f(m) dekl wie adj* employee

Beschäftigung <-, -en> *f* 1. (*Anstel-

B

lung) employment, job **2.** (*Tätigkeit*) occupation **3.** (*mit Literatur, Musik*) study (**mit** +*dat* of)

beschämt *adj* **über etw** *akk* ~ **sein** to be ashamed of sth

beschatten * *vt* to shadow

beschaulich *adj* peaceful; **ein ~es Leben führen** to lead a contemplative life

Bescheid <-[e]s, -e> [bə·ˈʃait] *m* information; ADMIN answer; ~ **erhalten** to be informed; **jdm** ~ **geben** to inform sb; **jdm** ~ **sagen, dass ...** to let sb know that ...; **ich habe noch keinen** ~ I still haven't heard anything; [**über etw** *akk*] ~ **wissen** to know [about sth] ▶ **jdm ordentlich** ~ **sagen** to give sb a piece of one's mind

bescheiden [bə·ˈʃai·dn̩] *adj* modest; **ein ~es Leben führen** to lead a humble life

bescheinigen * [bə·ˈʃai·nɪ·gn̩] *vt* **jdm etw** ~ to certify sth for sb *form;* [**jdm**] ~, **dass ...** to confirm [to sb] in writing that ...; **sich** *dat* **etw** ~ **lassen** to have sth certified

Bescheinigung <-, -en> *f* certification

bescheißen * *irreg derb* **I.** *vt* **jdn** ~ to rip off *sep sl sl* **II.** *vi* [**bei etw** *dat*] ~ to cheat [at sth]

beschenken * *vt* **jdn** ~ to give sb a present; **reich beschenkt werden** to be showered with presents; **sich** *akk* [**gegenseitig**] ~ to give each other presents

Bescherung <-, -en> *f* giving of Christmas presents ▶ [**das ist ja**] **eine schöne** ~! *iron* what a fine mess!

bescheuert *fam* **I.** *adj* **1.** (*blöd*) screwy; **dieser** ~**e Kerl** that stupid idiot; **der ist etwas** ~ he's got a screw loose *fam* **2.** (*unangenehm*) stupid; **so was B~es!** how stupid! **II.** *adv* stupidly; **du siehst total** ~ **aus** you look totally ridiculous; **sich** *akk* ~ **anstellen** to act like an idiot

beschimpfen * *vt* to insult; **sich** *akk* [**gegenseitig**] ~ to insult each other

beschissen *vulg* **I.** *adj* lousy **II.** *adv* in a lousy fashion; **es geht ihr wirklich** ~ she's miserable; ~ **aussehen/**

behandelt werden to look /be treated like shit *vulg*

beschlagen * *irreg vi sein* (*Spiegel, Scheibe*) to fog up

beschlagnahmen * [bə·ˈʃlaːk·naː·mən] *vt* to confiscate

beschleunigen * [bə·ˈʃlɔy·nɪ·gn̩] **I.** *vt* to accelerate; (*Tempo*) to increase; (*Schritte*) to quicken; (*Vorgang*) to speed up **II.** *vi* (*Fahrzeug*) to accelerate

Beschleunigung <-, -en> *f* acceleration

beschließen * *irreg* **I.** *vt* **1.** (*entscheiden*) to decide; **ein Gesetz** ~ to pass a motion **2.** (*beenden*) to conclude **II.** *vi* **über etw** *akk* ~ to decide on sth

Beschluss RR <-es, Beschlüsse> *m* decision

beschmutzen * **I.** *vt* **1.** to dirty up **2.** *fig* to tarnish **II.** *vr* **sich** *akk* ~ to get oneself dirty

Beschneidung <-, -en> *f* MED, REL circumcision

beschönigen * [bə·ˈʃøː·nɪ·gn̩] *vt* to gloss over

beschränken * **I.** *vt* to limit (**auf** +*akk* to); **jdn in seinen Rechten** ~ to limit sb's rights **II.** *vr* **sich** *akk* [**auf etw** *akk*] ~ to restrict oneself [to sth]; **sich** *akk* **auf das Wesentliche** ~ to keep to the essential points

beschränkt *adj* restricted; (*Sicht*) low; (*Intelligenz*) limited; (*Sichtweise*) narrow-minded; **finanziell/räumlich/ zeitlich** ~ **sein** to have a limited amount of cash/space/time; **Gesellschaft mit** ~**er Haftung** corporation

Beschränkung <-, -en> *f* restriction

beschreiben * *vt irreg* (*darstellen*) to describe

Beschreibung <-, -en> *f* description; (*Gebrauchsanweisung*) instructions *pl*

beschriften * [bə·ˈʃrɪf·tn̩] *vt* **einen Umschlag** ~ to address an envelope

beschuldigen * [bə·ˈʃul·dɪ·gn̩] *vt* **jdn** [**einer S.** *gen*] ~ to accuse sb [of sth]

Beschuldigung <-, -en> *f* accusation

beschützen * *vt* to protect (**vor** +*dat* from)

Beschützer(in) <-s, -> *m(f)* protector

Beschwerde <-, -n> [bə·ˈʃveːɐ̯·də] *f*

complaint; **Grund zur ~ haben** to have grounds for complaint; **~n mit etw** *dat* **haben** MED to have problems with sth; **mein Magen macht mir ~n** my stomach is giving me trouble

beschweren * [bə·ˈʃveː·rən] **I.** *vr* **sich** *akk* **~** to complain **II.** *vt* to weight [down]

beschwerlich *adj* difficult; **das Laufen ist für ihn sehr ~** walking is hard for him

beschwichtigen * [bə·ˈʃvɪç·tɪ·gn̩] *vt* to soothe

beschwingt I. *adj* lively; (*Mensch a.*) vivacious **II.** *adv* **sich** *akk* **~ fühlen** to feel elated

beschwipst [bə·ˈʃvɪpst] *adj fam* tipsy

beschwören * *vt irreg* **etw ~** to swear [to] sth; **~ kann ich das nicht** I wouldn't like to swear to it

beseitigen * [bə·ˈzai·tɪ·gn̩] *vt* **1.** (*entfernen*) to dispose of; (*Missverständnis, Zweifel*) to clear up; (*Hindernis*) to clear away; (*Fehler*) to eliminate; (*Ungerechtigkeiten*) to abolish **2.** *euph* (*umbringen*) to eliminate

Besen <-s, -> [ˈbeː·zn̩] *m* **1.** (*Kehrbesen*) broom; (*kleiner*) brush; (*einer Hexe*) broomstick **2.** *pej fam* (*kratzbürstige Frau*) old bag **3.** *südd fam* Swabian vineyard's wine bar, indicated by a broom hanging outside the door
▶ **ich** <u>fresse</u> **einen ~, wenn ...** *fam* I'll eat my hat if ...

besessen [bə·ˈzɛ·sn̩] *adj* obsessed (**von** +*dat* with); **wie ~** like crazy

besetzen * *vt* (*Land, Stühle, Plätze*) to occupy; **die Leitung ist besetzt** the line is busy; **ein Haus ~** to squat in a house; **einen Posten ~** to fill a post

Besetztzeichen *nt* busy signal

besichtigen * [bə·ˈzɪç·tɪ·gn̩] *vt* to visit; (*Betrieb*) to take a tour of; (*Haus, Wohnung*) to view

Besichtigung <-, -en> *f* visiting; (*von Haus, Wohnung etc.*) viewing; **eine ~ der Sehenswürdigkeiten** a sightseeing tour; **die ~ einer Stadt** a tour of a town

Besinnung <-> *f kein pl* consciousness; **die ~ verlieren** to faint; **[wieder] zur ~ kommen** to come around

besinnungslos *adj* **1.** unconscious; **~ werden** to pass out **2.** *fig* (*Wut*) blind; **~ vor Angst** blind with fear

Besitz <-es> [bə·ˈzɪts] *m kein pl* **1.** (*Eigentum*) property; (*Vermögen*) possessions *pl* **2.** (*das Besitzen*) possession; **in den ~ einer S.** *gen* **gelangen** to come into possession of sth; **in privatem/staatlichem ~** privately-/state-owned

besitzen * *vt irreg* **1.** (*Eigentum*) to own **2.** (*haben*) to have [got]; **die Frechheit ~, etw zu tun** to have the nerve to do sth; **jds Vertrauen ~** to have sb's confidence

Besitzer(in) <-s, -> *m(f)* owner; (*eines Geschäfts etc.*) proprietor; **den ~ wechseln** to change hands

besitzergreifend *adj* possessive

besoffen [bə·ˈzɔfn̩] *adj fam* sloshed; **total ~** hammered *sl*

besondere(r, s) [bə·ˈzɔn·də·rə, -əre, -ərəs] *adj* exceptional; **ein ~s Interesse an etw** *dat* **haben** to be especially interested in sth; **von ~r Bedeutung** of great significance; **~n Wert auf etw** *akk* **legen** to attach great importance to sth

besonders [bə·ˈzɔn·des] *adv* **1.** (*außergewöhnlich*) particularly; **[nicht] ~ klug/fröhlich** [not] especially bright/happy; **~ viel** a great deal **2.** (*vor allem*) in particular, above all **3.** *fam* **nicht ~ sein** to be nothing out of the ordinary; **jd fühlt sich** *akk* **nicht ~** sb does not feel too good

besonnen [bə·ˈzɔ·nən] *adj* sensible; **~ bleiben** to stay calm

besorgen * *vt* **1.** (*kaufen*) to buy **2.** (*beschaffen*) to get; **sich** *dat* **einen Job ~** to find oneself a job ▶ **es jdm ~** *fam* (*verprügeln*) to beat up *sep* sb; *derb* (*sexuell befriedigen*) to do sb

besorgt [bə·ˈzɔrkt] *adj* worried (**wegen** +*gen* about); **um jdn/etw ~ sein** to be concerned about sb/sth; **ein ~es Gesicht machen** to look troubled

besprechen * *irreg vt* **1.** (*erörtern*) to discuss; **wie besprochen** as agreed **2.** (*Buch, Film*) to review **3.** (*Kassette*) to make a recording on

Besprechung <-, -en> *f* **1.** (*Konferenz*) meeting **2.** (*Unterredung*) discussion

besser ['bɛ·sɐ] **I.** *adj komp von* **gut** better; (*Qualität*) superior; **etwas/nichts B~es** something/nothing better ▶ **jdn eines B~en belehren** to enlighten sb; **ich lasse mich gerne eines B~en belehren** I'm willing to admit [it when] I'm wrong **II.** *adv* **1.** **es geht jdm ~** sb feels better **2.** *fam* (*lieber*) better; **dem solltest du ~ aus dem Wege gehen!** it would be better if you avoided him! ▶ **es ~ haben** to be better off

bessern ['bɛ·sɐn] *vr sich akk* ~ to improve; (*Person*) to better oneself

Besserung <-> *f kein pl* improvement; **gute ~!** get well soon!; **auf dem Weg der ~ sein** to be on one's way to recovery

Besserwisser(in) <-s, -> *m(f)* *pej* know-it-all

Bestand <-[e]s, Bestände> *m* **1.** *kein pl* (*Fortdauer*) survival; **~ haben** to be long-lasting **2.** (*Vorrat*) supply (**an** +*dat* of)

beständig *adj* **1.** (*gleich bleibend*) consistent; (*Wetter*) steady **2.** (*widerstandsfähig*) resistant (**gegen** +*akk* to)

Bestandteil *m* part; sci component; **notwendiger ~** essential part; **etw in seine ~e zerlegen** to dismantle

bestärken * *vt* **jdn** [**in etw** *dat*] ~ to encourage sb['s sth]; **jdn in einem Verdacht** ~ to reinforce sb's suspicion

bestätigen * [bə·'ʃtɛ:·tɪ·gn̩] **I.** *vt* to confirm; **die Richtigkeit einer S.** *gen* ~ to verify sth **II.** *vr* **sich** *akk* ~ to prove to be true

Bestätigung <-, -en> *f* confirmation; (*Schriftstück*) certification

bestatten * [bə·'ʃta·tn̩] *vt geh* to bury

Bestattung <-, -en> *f geh* funeral

Bestattungsinstitut *nt geh* funeral home

beste(r, s) ['bɛs·tə, 'bɛs·te, 'bɛs·təs] *adj superl von* **gut** *attr* best; **„mit den ~n Wünschen"** "best wishes"; **in ~r Laune** in the best of spirits; **am ~n ...** it would be best if ...; **es wäre am ~n, wenn Sie jetzt gingen** you had better leave now

bestechen * *irreg* **I.** *vt* (*Beamte*) to bribe **II.** *vi* to be impressive; **durch etw** *akk* ~

to impress with sth

bestechlich [bə·'ʃtɛç·lɪç] *adj* corrupt

Bestechung <-, -en> *f* bribery

Besteck <-[e]s, -e> [bə·'ʃtɛk] *nt* KOCHK cutlery *n sing*

bestehen * *irreg* **I.** *vt* (*Prüfung*) to pass; **etw nicht ~** to fail sth; **die Prüfer ließen ihn nicht ~** the inspectors failed him **II.** *vi* **1.** (*existieren*) to be; + *Zeitangabe* to exist; **es ~ gute Aussichten, dass ...** the prospects are good that ...; **es besteht die Gefahr, dass ...** there is a danger of ...; **das Problem/der Unterschied besteht darin, dass ...** the problem/difference is that ...; **es besteht kein Zweifel** there is no doubt; **~ bleiben** to last; (*Versprechen*) to remain; **etw ~ lassen** to retain sth **2.** (*sich zusammensetzen*) to consist (**aus** +*dat* of); (*Material*) to be made (**aus** +*dat* [out] of) **3.** (*beharren*) **auf etw** *dat* ~ to insist on sth; **auf einer Meinung ~** to stick to an opinion; **darauf ~, dass ...** to insist that ...; **wenn Sie darauf ~!** if you insist!

besteigen * *vt irreg* (*Berg*) to climb [[up] onto]; (*Bus*) to get on; (*Flugzeug*) to board; (*Pferd*) to mount; (*Podest*) to get up onto; (*Schiff*) to go on board; (*Taxi*) to get into; (*Thron*) to ascend

bestellen * *vt* **1.** (*Ware*) to order (**bei** +*dat* from) **2.** (*Tisch*) to reserve **3.** (*Handwerker*) to ask to come; (*Taxi*) to call **4.** (*ausrichten*) to tell; **können Sie ihr etwas ~?** may I leave a message for her?; [**jdm**] **Grüße** ~ to send [sb] one's regards ▶ **wie bestellt und nicht abgeholt** *hum fam* standing around looking like a lost sheep; **mit etw** *dat* **ist es schlecht bestellt** things look bad for sth

Bestellnummer *f* order number

Bestellung <-, -en> *f* order

bestenfalls ['bɛs·tn̩·fals] *adv* at best

bestens ['bɛs·tn̩s] *adv* very well

bestialisch [bɛs·'tia:·lɪʃ] **I.** *adj* atrocious; (*Gestank*) revolting; (*Schmerz*) excruciating; **~ stinken** to stink to high heaven **II.** *adv fam* dreadfully

Bestie <-, -n> ['bɛs·tiə] *f* **1.** (*Tier*) beast **2.** (*Mensch*) brute

bestimmen* I. vt 1. (festsetzen) etw ~ to decide on sth; (Ort, Preis, Zeit) to fix 2. (vorsehen) für jdn/etw bestimmt sein to be for sb/sth; füreinander bestimmt meant for each other II. vi über jdn/etw ~ to control sb/sth

bestimmt [bə·ˈʃtɪmt] I. adj 1. (speziell) particular; ganz ~e Vorstellungen very particular ideas 2. (festgelegt: Tag, Termin) set 3. LING ein ~er Artikel a definite article 4. (entschieden: Auftreten) firm II. adv 1. (sicher) definitely; ganz ~ kommt er noch he'll be here [sooner or later]; Sie sind ~ derjenige, der ... you must be the person who ...; das ist ~ für dich (Anruf, Besuch) it must be for you; etw ganz ~ wissen to be positive about sth; ~ nicht certainly not 2. (entschieden) determinedly

Bestimmung <-, -en> f 1. (Vorschrift) regulation 2. (Schicksal) destiny

bestmöglich [ˈbɛst·ˈmøː·k·lɪç] adj best possible

bestrafen* vt to punish; etw wird mit Gefängnis bestraft sth is punishable by imprisonment

Bestrafung <-, -en> f punishment; zur ~ as a punishment

Bestrahlung <-, -en> f MED radiotherapy

bestrebt adj ~ sein, etw zu tun to be eager to do sth

bestreiken* vt to go on strike against; dieser Betrieb wird bestreikt there is a strike in progress at this company

bestreiten* vt irreg 1. (leugnen) to deny; (Behauptung) to reject; es lässt sich nicht ~, dass ... it cannot be denied that ... 2. (finanzieren: Kosten) to cover; seinen Unterhalt ~ to earn a living

bestürmen* vt to bombard

bestürzt I. adj upset; zutiefst ~ deeply dismayed II. adv in a dismayed manner

Besuch <-[e]s, -e> [bə·ˈzuːx] m 1. (das Besuchen) visit (bei/in +dat to); jdm einen ~ abstatten to pay sb a visit; (kurz) to drop in on sb; [bei jdm] auf ~ sein to be visiting [sb]; ich bin hier nur zu ~ I'm just visiting 2. (Besucher) visitor[s]; (eingeladen) guest[s]

besuchen* vt 1. (Menschen, Museum etc.) to visit; (Konzert) to attend; besuch mich bald mal wieder! come again soon! 2. (teilnehmen) einen Kurs ~ to take a class; die Schule ~ to go to school

Besucher(in) <-s, -> m(f) visitor, guest; (Kino) moviegoer; (Theater) theatergoer; (Sportveranstaltung) spectator; ein regelmäßiger ~ a frequenter

Besuchszeit f visiting hours pl

betätigen* I. vt (Schalter) to press; (Hebel) to operate II. vr sich akk ~ to busy oneself; sich akk politisch ~ to be politically active; sich akk sportlich ~ to exercise

betäuben* [bə·ˈtɔy·bn̩] vt 1. (narkotisieren) to anesthetize; die Entführer betäubten ihr Opfer the kidnappers drugged their victim 2. fig (Schmerz) to kill; seinen Kummer mit Alkohol ~ to drown one's sorrows in alcohol

Betäubungsmittel nt anesthetic

beteiligen* [bə·ˈtai·lɪ·gn̩] I. vt to give a share (an +dat of/in) II. vr sich akk [an etw dat] ~ to participate [in sth]; (an einem Unternehmen) to have a share in

beteiligt [bə·ˈtai·lɪçt] adj an etw dat ~ sein 1. (mit dabei) to be involved in sth 2. FIN, ÖKON to hold a stake in sth

beten [ˈbeː·tn̩] I. vi to pray II. vt to recite

beteuern* [bə·ˈtɔy·ɐn] vt jdm ~, dass ... to protest to sb that ...; seine Unschuld ~ to protest one's innocence

Beton <-s, selten -s> [be·ˈtɔŋ, be·ˈtõː] m concrete

betonen* vt 1. (hervorheben) to stress; (die Figur) to accentuate 2. LING (Wort) to stress

betonieren [be·to·ˈniː·rən] vt to concrete

betont I. adj emphatic; ~e Höflichkeit studied politeness II. adv markedly

Betonung <-, -en> f LING stress

Betracht [bə·ˈtraxt] m in ~ kommen to be considered; etw außer ~ lassen to disregard sth; jdn/etw in ~ ziehen to consider sb/sth

betrachten* vt 1. (anschauen) to look

at; **bei näherem B~** [up]on closer examination **2.** (*halten für*) to regard (**als** +*akk* as)

beträchtlich [bə'trɛçt·lɪç] *adj* considerable; (*Schaden*) extensive

Betrag <-[e]s, Beträge> [bə'traːk] *m* amount

betragen* *irreg* **I.** *vi* to be; **die Rechnung beträgt 10 Euro** the bill comes to 10 euros **II.** *vr* **sich** *akk* ~ to behave

Betragen <-s> *nt kein pl* behavior; SCH

betreffen* *vt irreg* **1.** (*angehen*) **jdn** ~ to concern sb; **etw** ~ to affect sth; **was das betrifft, ...** as far as that is concerned **2.** (*bestürzen*) **jdn ...** ~ to affect sb ...

betreffend *adj attr* **1.** (*erwähnt*) in question *pred*; **die ~e Person** the person in question **2.** (*in Bezug auf*) concerning

betreten* [1] *vt irreg* (*Haus, Zimmer*) to enter

betreten [2] *adj* embarrassed

betreuen* [bə'trɔy·ən] *vt* (*Kind*) to look after

Betrieb <-[e]s, -e> [bə'triːp] *m* **1.** (*Firma*) company **2.** *kein pl* (*Betriebsamkeit*) activity; **heute war nur wenig/herrschte großer ~** it was very quiet/busy today **3.** (*Tätigkeit*) operation; **etw in ~ nehmen** to put sth into operation; **außer ~** out of order; **in ~** in operation

Betriebsanleitung *f* [operating] instructions *pl*

Betriebsarzt, -ärztin *m, f* company doctor

Betriebsausflug *m* staff outing

Betriebsferien *pl* vacation close-down

Betriebsklima *nt* work atmosphere

Betriebskosten *pl* operating costs; (*einer Maschine*) running costs

Betriebsleitung *f* management

Betriebsrat *m* employee representative committee

Betriebssystem *nt* COMPUT operating system

Betriebsunfall *m* ≈ occupational accident (*accident at or on the way to or from work*)

Betriebswirtschaft *f* business management

betrinken* *vr irreg* **sich** *akk* [**mit etw**

dat] ~ to get drunk [on sth]

betroffen I. *pp von* **betreffen II.** *adj* shocked; **~es Schweigen** stunned silence **III.** *adv* **jdn ~ anschauen** to look at sb with dismay; **~ schweigen** to be too upset to say anything

betrübt *adj* sad

Betrug <-[e]s, *schweiz* Betrüge> [bə'truːk] *m* fraud

betrügen* *irreg* **I.** *vt* **1.** (*vorsätzlich täuschen*) to cheat (**um** +*akk* out of); **ich fühle mich betrogen!** I feel betrayed! **2.** (*durch Seitensprung*) **jdn [mit jdm]** ~ to be unfaithful to sb [with sb] **II.** *vr* **sich** *akk* **selbst** ~ to deceive oneself

Betrüger(in) <-s, -> [bə'tryː·gɐ] *m(f)* con man

betrunken [bə'trʊŋ·kn̩] *adj* drunken *attr*, drunk *pred*

Bett <-[e]s, -en> [bɛt] *nt* bed; **jdn ins ~ bringen** to put sb to bed; **ins ~ gehen** to go to bed; **jdn aus dem ~ holen** to get sb out of bed; **das ~ hüten müssen** to be confined to [one's] bed

Bettbezug *m* duvet cover

Bettdecke *f* blanket; (*Steppdecke*) duvet

betteln ['bɛ·tl̩n] *vi* to beg (**um** +*akk* for)

bettlägerig *adj* bedridden

Bettlaken *nt s.* **Betttuch**

Bettler(in) <-s, -> ['bɛt·lɐ] *m(f)* beggar

Betttuch RR, **Bettuch** ALT ['bɛt·tuːx] *nt* sheet

Bettwäsche *f* bed linens *pl*

Bettzeug *nt* bedding

betüddeln [bə·'tyː·dl̩n] *vt fam* to coddle

beugen ['bɔy·gn̩] **I.** *vt* **1.** (*neigen*) to bend; (*Kopf*) to bow **2.** LING (*konjugieren*) to conjugate; (*deklinieren*) to decline **II.** *vr* **1.** (*sich neigen*) **sich** *akk* **nach vorn/hinten** ~ to bend forward/backward; **sich** *akk* **aus dem Fenster** ~ to lean out [of] the window **2.** (*sich unterwerfen*) **sich** *akk* [**jdm/etw**] ~ to submit [to sb/sth]; **ich werde mich der Mehrheit** ~ I will bow to the majority

Beule <-, -n> ['bɔy·lə] *f* **1.** (*Delle*) dent **2.** (*Schwellung*) bump

beunruhigen* [bə·'ʔʊn·ruː·ɪ·gn̩] *vt* to worry

beurkunden* [bə·'ʔuːɐ̯·kʊn·dn̩] *vt* to certify

beurlauben* [bə-'ʔuːɐ̯-lau-bn̩] vt 1. (*Urlaub geben*) to give time off; **können Sie mich für eine Woche ~?** can you give me a week off? 2. (*suspendieren*) to suspend; **Sie sind bis auf weiteres beurlaubt** you are suspended until further notice

beurteilen* vt 1. (*einschätzen*) to judge 2. (*abschätzen*) to assess

Beurteilung <-, -en> f assessment

Beute <-> ['bɔy-tə] f kein pl 1. (*Jagdbeute*) prey 2. (*erbeutete Dinge*) loot; [**fette**] **~ machen** to make a [big] haul

Beutel <-s, -> ['bɔy-tl̩] m 1. (*Tasche*) bag 2. ZOOL pouch

Bevölkerung <-, -en> f population

bevölkerungsreich adj populous

bevollmächtigen* vt to authorize

bevor [bə-'foːɐ̯] konj before; **nicht ~** not until

bevormunden* [bə-'foːɐ̯-mʊn-dn̩] vt to treat like a child

bevorstehen vi irreg 1. (*zu erwarten haben*) jdm ~ to await sb; **der schwierigste Teil steht dir erst noch bevor!** the most difficult part is yet to come! 2. (*bald kommen*) etw steht bevor sth is approaching

bevorzugen* [bə-'foːɐ̯-tsuː-gn̩] vt to prefer; **keines unserer Kinder wird bevorzugt** none of our children receive preferential treatment; **hier wird niemand bevorzugt!** there's no favoritism around here!

bewachen* vt to guard

bewahren* vt 1. (*schützen*) to save; **vor etw** dat **bewahrt bleiben** to be spared sth 2. (*behalten*) [sich dat] etw ~ to keep sth

bewähren* vr sich akk ~ 1. (*Gerät, Methode, Medikament*) to prove itself 2. (*Mensch*) to prove oneself; **sich** akk **als Freund ~** to prove to be a friend

bewahrheiten* [bə-'vaːɐ̯-hai-tn̩] vr sich akk ~ to come true

bewährt adj proven

Bewährung <-, -en> f JUR probation; **eine Strafe zur ~ aussetzen** to suspend a sentence

Bewährungshelfer(in) m(f) JUR probation officer

bewältigen* [bə-'vɛl-tɪ-gn̩] vt 1. (*meistern*) to cope with, to handle; (*Schwierigkeiten*) to overcome 2. (*überwinden*) to get over; (*Vergangenheit*) to come to terms with

bewandert [bə-'van-dɐt] adj well-versed

bewässern* vt (*Feld*) to irrigate; (*Garten*) to water

bewegen*¹ [bə-'veː-gn̩] I. vt 1. (*Gegenstand, Körperteil*) to move 2. (*innerlich aufwühlen*) **etw bewegt jdn** sth moves sb 3. (*bewirken*) to achieve; **etwas/nichts/viel/wenig ~** to achieve something/nothing/a lot/little II. vr sich akk ~ 1. (*sich regen*) to move 2. (*sich körperlich betätigen*) to [get some] exercise 3. (*schwanken*) to range; **der Preis bewegt sich um die 3.000 Euro** the price is around 3,000 euros

bewegen*² <bewog, bewogen> [bə-'veː-gn̩] vt (*veranlassen*) **jdn dazu ~, etw zu tun** to move sb to do sth

Beweggrund m motive

beweglich [bə-'veːk-lɪç] adj movable; (*Glieder*) supple

bewegt adj 1. (*innerlich gerührt*) moved; **mit ~er Stimme** in an emotional voice 2. (*Leben, Vergangenheit*) eventful

Bewegung <-, -en> f (a. kunst, pol) movement; **jdn in ~ halten** to keep sb moving; **jd/ein Tier braucht ~** sb/an animal needs exercise

bewegungslos adj motionless

Beweis <-es, -e> [bə-'vais] m proof (**für** +akk of)

beweisen* irreg vt to prove

Beweismaterial nt JUR [body of] evidence

Bewerber(in) <-s, -> m(f) applicant

Bewerbung <-, -en> f application

Bewerbungsgespräch nt [job] interview

Bewerbungsschreiben nt application [letter]

bewerkstelligen* [bə-'vɛrk-ʃtɛ-lɪ-gn̩] vt to manage

bewerten* vt to assess; **jdn/etw nach etw** dat **~** to judge sb/sth according to sth; **etw zu hoch/niedrig ~** to overvalue/undervalue sth

Bewertung f assessment

bewilligen * [bə·ˈvɪ·lɪ·gn̩] *vt* to approve; FIN to grant; (*Stipendium*) to award

bewirken * *vt* **1.** (*verursachen*) to cause **2.** (*erreichen*) **etwas ~** to achieve something

bewirten * *vt* to entertain

bewohnbar *adj* habitable

bewohnen * *vt* **1.** (*Gegend, Insel*) to inhabit **2.** (*Haus*) to live in

Bewohner(in) <-s, -> *m(f)* **1.** (*Einwohner*) inhabitant **2.** (*eines Hauses, Zimmers*) occupant

bewölken * *vr* **sich** *akk* ~ to cloud over

bewölkt *adj* cloudy; **leicht ~** partly cloudy

Bewunderer, Bewunderin <-s, -> [bə·ˈvʊn·də·rɐ, bə·ˈvʊn·də·rɪn] *m, f* admirer

bewundern * *vt* to admire (**wegen** +*gen* for)

bewundernswert *adj* admirable

Bewunderung <-, -en> *f pl selten* admiration

bewusst ᴿᴿ, **bewußt** ᴬᴸᵀ [bə·ˈvʊst] I. *adj* **1.** (*vorsätzlich*) **~es Nichtbefolgen von Anordnungen** willful disobedience of orders **2.** (*überlegt*) considered; **eine ~e Entscheidung** a deliberate decision; **~e Lebensführung** socially and environmentally aware lifestyle **3. jdm etw ~ machen** to make sb realize sth; **sich** *dat* **etw ~ machen** to realize sth; **sich** *dat* **etw** *gen* **~ sein** to be aware of sth; **jdm ~ sein** to be clear to sb II. *adv* **1.** (*vorsätzlich*) deliberately **2.** (*überlegt*) **~ leben** to practice social and environmental awareness

bewusstlos ᴿᴿ, **bewußtlos** ᴬᴸᵀ [bə·ˈvʊst·loːs] *adj* unconscious; **~ werden** to faint

Bewusstsein ᴿᴿ, **Bewußtsein** ᴬᴸᵀ <-s> *nt kein pl* consciousness; **bei [vollem] ~ sein** to be [fully] conscious; **etw aus dem ~ verdrängen** to banish sth from one's mind; **jdm etw ins ~ rufen** to remind sb of sth

bezahlen * I. *vt* to pay; (*Rechnung*) to settle; (*Getränke, Speisen*) to pay for II. *vi* to pay; **~, bitte!** [the] check, please!

Bezahlung *f* (*Lohn*) pay; **gegen ~ für** a fee

bezaubern * *vt, vi* to enchant

bezeichnen * I. *vt* **jdn/etw als jdn/ etw ~** to call sb/sth sb/sth II. *vr* **sich** *akk* **als etw** *akk* **~** to call oneself sth

bezeichnend *adj* typical (**für** +*akk* of)

Bezeichnung *f* term

beziehen * *irreg* I. *vt* **1.** (*überziehen*) to cover; **das Bett neu ~** to change the sheets **2.** (*Haus, Wohnung*) to move into **3.** (*Gehalt*) to receive **4.** (*Standpunkt*) to adopt; **zu etw** *dat* **Stellung ~** to take a stand on sth **5.** (*kaufen*) to obtain **6.** (*in Beziehung setzen*) to apply (**auf** +*akk* to); **warum bezieht er immer alles gleich auf sich?** why does he always take everything personally? **7.** *schweiz* (*einziehen*) to collect II. *vr* **1. sich** *akk* ~ (*Himmel*) to cloud over **2.** (*betreffen, sich berufen*) **sich** *akk* **auf jdn/etw ~** to refer to sb/sth

Beziehung <-, -en> [bə·ˈtsiː·ʊŋ] *f* **1.** (*Verhältnis*) relationship (**zu** +*dat* with); (*sexuell*) [romantic] relationship; **menschliche ~en** human relations **2.** (*Verbindung*) connection; **etw zu etw** *dat* **in ~ setzen** to connect sth to [*o* with] sth **3.** *meist pl* (*fördernde Bekanntschaften*) **~en haben** to have connections; **seine ~en spielen lassen** to pull [some] strings **4.** (*Hinsicht*) **in jeder ~** in every respect; **in mancher ~** in many respects

beziehungsweise *konj* or rather

Bezirk <-[e]s, -e> [bə·ˈtsɪrk] *m* district

bezug ᴬᴸᵀ [bə·ˈtsuːk] *s.* **Bezug 2**

Bezug <-[e]s, Bezüge> [bə·ˈtsuːk] *m* **1.** (*für Kissen*) pillowcase; (*für Bett*) duvet cover **2.** (*Relation*) **in ~ auf etw** *akk* with regard to sth; **~ auf etw** *akk* **nehmen** to refer to sth; **etw zu etw** *dat* **in ~ setzen** to connect sth to [*o* with] sth

bezüglich [bə·ˈtsyː·k·lɪç] *präp* +*gen* regarding

Bezugsperson *f* [personal] role model

bezwecken * [bə·ˈtsvɛ·kn̩] *vt* to aim to achieve; **was willst du damit ~?** what do you hope to achieve by doing that?

bezweifeln * *vt* to doubt

BH <-[s], -[s]> [beː·ˈhaː] *m Abk von* **Büstenhalter** bra

Bibel <-, -n> ['bi:bl] f Bible

Biber <-s, -> ['bi:·bɐ] m beaver

Bibliografie RR, **Bibliographie** <-, -n> [bib·lio·gra·'fi] f bibliography

Bibliothek <-, -en> [bib·lio·'te:k] f library

Bibliothekar(in) <-s, -e> [bib·lio·te·'ka:ɐ̯] m(f) librarian

bieder ['bi:·dɐ] adj pej (spießig) narrow-minded; (Geschmack) conservative

biegen <bog, gebogen> ['bi:·gn] vt, vr |sich akk| to bend

biegsam ['bi:k·za:m] adj (Material) flexible

Biegung <-, -en> f 1. (Kurve) bend; **eine ~ machen** to turn 2. LING österr (Flexion) inflection

Biene <-, -n> ['bi:·nə] f bee

Bienenhonig m [bee] honey

Bienenkönigin f queen bee

Bienenwabe f honeycomb

Bier <-[e]s, -e> [bi:ɐ̯] nt beer; **~ vom Fass** draft beer ▶ **das ist dein** ~ fam that's your business; **das ist nicht mein** ~ fam that has nothing to do with me

Bierdose f beer can

Biest <-[e]s, -er> [bi:st] nt beast

bieten <bot, geboten> ['bi:·tn] I. vt 1. (anbieten) to offer 2. (geben) to give; (Gewähr, Sicherheit, Schutz) to provide 3. (zumuten) **sich** dat **etw nicht ~ lassen** to not stand for sth II. vr **sich** akk |jdm| ~ (Möglichkeit, Gelegenheit) to present itself [to sb]

Bikini <-s, -s> [bi·'ki:·ni] m bikini

Bilanz <-, -en> [bi·'lants] f ÖKON balance sheet ▶ ~ **ziehen** to take stock

Bild <-[e]s, -er> [bɪlt] nt picture ▶ **ein** ~ **für die Götter** fam a sight for sore eyes; **sich** dat **von jdm/etw ein ~ machen** to form an opinion about sb/sth; **im ~e sein** to be in the picture

bilden ['bɪl·dn] I. vt 1. (formen) to form 2. (Ausschuss) to set up sep 3. (darstellen) to make up; (Gefahr, Problem) to constitute 4. (mit Bildung versehen) to educate II. vr 1. (entstehen) **sich** akk ~ to develop; CHEM to form; BOT to grow 2. (sich Bildung verschaffen) **sich** akk ~ to educate oneself 3. (sich formen) **sich** dat **eine Meinung ~** to form an

opinion III. vi **etw bildet** sth broadens the mind

Bilderbuch nt picture book

Bilderrahmen m picture frame

Bildhauer(in) <-s, -> ['bɪlt·hau̯ɐ] m(f) sculptor

bildhübsch ['bɪlt·'hʏpʃ] adj as pretty as a picture

bildlich adv figuratively; **~ gesprochen** metaphorically speaking; **sich** dat **etw ~ vorstellen** to picture sth

Bildschirm m TV, COMPUT screen

Bildschirmschoner m screen saver

bildschön ['bɪlt·'ʃøːn] adj s. **bildhübsch**

Bildtelefon nt videophone

Bildung <-> f kein pl education; **keine ~ haben** to be uneducated

Bildungslücke f gap in one's education

Billard <-s, -e> ['bɪl·jart] nt billiards + sing vb, pool

Billardkugel ['bɪl·jart-] f billiard ball

Billardstock m billiard cue

Billett <-[e]s, -s> [bɪl·'jɛ(t)] nt 1. schweiz (Fahrkarte) ticket 2. schweiz (Eintrittskarte) admission ticket 3. österr (Glückwunschkarte) greeting card

Billiarde <-, -n> [bɪ·'liar·də] f thousand trillion

billig ['bɪ·lɪç] I. adj cheap II. adv cheaply; **~ abzugeben** going cheap ▶ **da-vonkommen** fam to get off lightly

billigen ['bɪ·lɪgn] vt to approve of

Billiglinie f low-cost airline

Billion <-, -en> [bɪ·'liǫ:n] f trillion

binär [bi·'nɛːɐ̯] adj binary

Binde <-, -n> ['bɪn·də] f 1. MED bandage; (Schlinge) sling 2. (Monatsbinde) sanitary napkin

Bindegewebe nt ANAT connective tissue

Bindehaut f ANAT conjunctiva

Bindehautentzündung f conjunctivitis

binden <band, gebunden> ['bɪn·dn] I. vt 1. (befestigen) to tie [up sep (an +akk to) 2. (zusammenbinden) Schnürsenkel) to tie; (Krawatte) to knot (Blumenstrauß, Buch, Kranz) to bind ▶ **mir sind die Hände gebunden** my hands are tied II. vr 1. (sich verpflich ten) **sich** akk **an jdn/etw ~** to commit oneself to sb/sth 2. (feste Partnerschaf

eingehen) **ich will mich momentan nicht ~** I don't want to tie myself down right now

bindend *adj* binding

Bindestrich *m* hyphen

Bindfaden *m* string

Bindung <-, -en> *f* **1.** (*Verbundenheit*) bond (**an** +*dat* to) **2.** (*Verpflichtung*) commitment; **eine vertragliche ~ eingehen** to enter into a binding contract **3.** (*am Ski*) binding

Binnengewässer *nt* inland water *no indef art*

Binnenhafen *m* inland port

Binnenmarkt *m* domestic market; **der [Europäische] ~** the Single [European] Market

Bioabfall *m* ÖKOL organic waste [matter]

Biografie ^{RR} <-, -n> [bio·gra·ˈfiː] *f* **1.** (*Buch*) biography **2.** (*Lebenslauf*) life [history]

biografisch ^{RR} [bio·ˈgra·fɪʃ] *adj* biographical

Biographie <-, -n> [bio·gra·ˈfiː] *f* s. **Biografie**

biographisch [bio·ˈgra·fɪʃ] *adj* s. **biografisch**

Bioladen *m* health food store

Biolandbau *m* kein pl organic farming

Biologe, Biologin <-n, -n> [bio·ˈloː·gə, -gɪn] *m, f* biologist

Biologie <-> [bio·lo·ˈgiː] *f* kein pl biology

biologisch **I.** *adj* biological; (*natürlich*) natural **II.** *adv* biologically; **~ abbaubar** biodegradable

Biotonne *f* garbage container for organic waste

Biowaffe *f* biological weapon

Birke <-, -n> [ˈbɪr·kə] *f* birch [tree]

Birma <-s> [ˈbɪr·ma] *nt* Burma; *s. a.* **Deutschland**

Birnbaum *m* pear [tree]

Birne <-, -n> [ˈbɪr·nə] *f* **1.** (*Frucht*) pear **2.** ELEK (*light*) bulb **3.** *fam* (*Kopf*) noggin *fam*

bis [bɪs] **I.** *präp* +*akk* **1.** *zeitlich* until; (*nicht später als*) by; **~ jetzt** up to now; **~ bald/morgen!** see you soon/tomorrow! **2.** *räumlich* as far as; **~ dort/dorthin/dahin** [up] to there; **~ hierher**

up to this point **3.** (*erreichend*) up to; **ich zähle ~ drei** I'll count [up] to three; **die Tagestemperaturen steigen ~** [**zu**] **30°C** daytime temperatures will reach 30°C; **Kinder ~ sechs Jahre** children up to the age of six **4.** (*mit Ausnahme von*) **~ auf** [*o schweiz* ~ **an**] except [for] **II.** *konj* **1.** (*ungefähre Angabe*) to; **400 ~ 500 Gramm Schinken** 400 to 500 grams of ham **2.** *zeitlich* **~ es dunkel wird, möchte ich zu Hause sein** I want to be home by the time it gets dark; **ich warte noch, ~ es dunkel wird** I'll wait until it gets dark

Bischof, Bischöfin <-s, Bischöfe> [ˈbɪ·ʃɔf, ˈbɪ·ʃœ·fɪn] *m, f* bishop

bisexuell [bi·zɛ·ˈksu̯·ɛl] *adj* bisexual

bisher [bɪs·ˈheːɐ̯] *adv* until now

Biskaya <-> [bɪs·ˈkaːja] *f* **die ~** [the Bay of] Biscay

Biskuit <-[e]s, -s> [bɪs·ˈkviːt] *nt o m* sponge cake

bislang [bɪs·ˈlaŋ] *adv* s. **bisher**

Bison <-s, -e> [ˈbiː·zɔn] *m* bison

biss ^{RR}, **biß** ^{ALT} [bɪs] *imp von* **beißen**

Biss ^{RR} <-es, -e>, **Biß** ^{ALT} <-sses, -sse> [bɪs] *m* bite ▶ **~ haben** to have drive

bisschen ^{RR}, **bißchen** ^{ALT} [ˈbɪs·çən] *pron indef* **1.** + *Substantiv* **ein ~ ...** a little ...; **kein ~ ...** not one [little] bit of ...; **das ~ ...** the little bit of ... **2.** + *adj/adv/vb* **ein ~ ...** a bit ...; **das war ein ~ dumm von ihr!** that was a little stupid of her!; **kein ~ ...** not the slightest bit ...

Bissen <-s, -> [ˈbɪ·sn̩] *m* morsel; **kann ich einen ~ von deinem Brötchen haben?** can I have a bite of your roll?; **er brachte keinen ~ herunter** he couldn't eat a thing

bissig [ˈbɪ·sɪç] *adj* **1.** **ein ~er Hund** a dog that bites **2.** (*sarkastisch*) sarcastic; (*Kritik*) scathing

Bissen <-s, -> → same

Bistum <-s, Bistümer> [ˈbɪs·tuːm] *nt* bishopric

Bit <-[s], -[s]> [bɪt] *nt* COMPUT bit

bitte [ˈbɪ·tə] *interj* **1.** (*auffordernd*) please; **~ nicht!** please don't!; **ja, ~?** (*am Telefon*) hello?; **tun Sie** [**doch**] **~ ...** won't you please ... **2.** (*Dank erwidernd*) **~ schön!** here you are!; **danke für die Auskunft! – ~[, gern**

geschehen] thanks for the information — you're [very] welcome!; **danke, dass du mir geholfen hast! – ~[, gern geschehen]**! thanks for helping me — not at all!; **danke schön! – – schön, war mir ein Vergnügen!** thank you! — don't mention it, my pleasure!; **Entschuldigung! – –!** Excuse me! — go right ahead!

Bitte <-, -n> ['bɪ·tə] f request (**um** +akk for)

bitten <bat, gebeten> ['bɪ·tn̩] vt, vi to ask (**um** +akk for); **könnte ich dich um einen Gefallen ~?** could I ask you a favor? ▸ **wenn ich ~ darf!** if you wouldn't mind!

bitter ['bɪ·tɐ] **I.** adj bitter; (Schokolade) dark; (Reue) deep **II.** adv (sehr) bitterly

bitterböse ['bɪ·tɐ·'bøː·zə] adj furious

bizarr [bi·'tsar] adj bizarre

blähen ['blɛː·ən] **I.** vr sich akk ~ to billow; MED to dilate **II.** vi MED to cause flatulence

Blähung <-, -en> f meist pl ~en haben to have flatulence

Blamage <-, -n> [bla·'maː·ʒə] f disgrace

blamieren * [bla·'miː·rən] **I.** vt to disgrace **II.** vr sich akk ~ to make a fool of oneself

blank [blaŋk] **I.** adj **1.** (glänzend, sauber) shining **2.** (Unsinn) utter **3.** fam (pleite) ~ **sein** to be broke **II.** adv ~ **gewetzt** shiny; ~ **poliert** brightly polished

Blase <-, -n> ['blaː·zə] f **1.** ANAT bladder **2.** MED blister; **sich** dat ~**n laufen** to get blisters on one's feet

blasen <bläst, blies, geblasen> ['blaː·zn̩] vt, vi to blow

Blasenentzündung f bladder infection

Blasinstrument nt wind instrument

Blaskapelle f brass band

blass RR, **blaß** ALT [blas] adj **1.** (bleich, hell) pale; ~ **um die Nase sein** to be green about the gills hum **2.** (schwach) vague; (Erinnerung) dim

Blatt <-[e]s, Blätter> [blat] nt **1.** BOT leaf **2.** (Papierseite) sheet **3.** (Zeitung) paper ▸ **kein ~ vor den Mund nehmen** to

not mince one's words; **das ~ hat sich gewendet** things have changed

blättern ['blɛ·tɐn] vi **in einem Buch ~** to flip through a book

Blätterteig m puff pastry

Blattgold nt gold leaf

Blattlaus f aphid

blau [blau] adj **1.** (Farbe) blue **2. ein ~er Fleck** a bruise; **ein ~es Auge** a black eye **3.** meist pred fam (betrunken) plastered sl

blauäugig adj **1.** (blaue Augen habend) blue-eyed **2.** (naiv) naïve

Blauhelm m blue beret

bläulich adj bluish

Blaulicht nt flashing blue light

blaumachen vi fam to call in sick; SCH to play hooky

Blausäure f hydrocyanic acid

Blazer <-s, -> ['ble:·zɐ] m blazer

Blech <-[e]s, -e> [blɛç] nt **1.** kein p (Material) sheet metal **2.** (Backblech) [baking] tray

Blechdose f tin

blechen ['blɛç·n̩] vt, vi fam to fork out

Blechschaden m AUTO damage to the bodywork

Blei <-[e]s> [blai] nt kein pl lead

Bleibe <-, -n> ['blai·bə] f place to stay

bleiben <blieb, geblieben> ['blai·bn̩] v sein **1.** (verweilen) to stay; **wo bleibs du so lange?** what's taking you so long [to get here]?; **wo sie nur so lang bleibt?** where the heck is she? **2.** (weiterhin sein) to remain; **unbeachtet ~** to go unnoticed; **wach ~** to stay awake **das bleibt unter uns** that's [just] between you and me **3.** (übrig bleiben eine Möglichkeit bleibt uns noch w** still have one possibility left; **es blie mir keine andere Wahl** I was left with no other choice

bleibend adj lasting

bleich [blaiç] adj pale

bleifrei adj lead-free

Bleistift m pencil

blenden ['blɛn·dn̩] vi to be dazzling

blendend I. adj brilliant; **~er Laun sein** to be in a fantastic mood **II.** ad wonderfully; **sich** akk ~ **amüsieren** have a great time

Blick <-[e]s, -e> [blɪk] *m* **1.** (*das Blicken*) look; **er warf einen ~ aus dem Fenster** he glanced out the window; **auf einen ~** at a glance; **auf den ersten ~** at first sight; **auf den zweiten ~** upon closer inspection; **jds ~ ausweichen** to avoid sb's gaze; **einen ~ auf jdn/etw werfen** to glance at sb/sth **2.** (*Augenausdruck*) look in one's eye **3.** (*Aussicht*) view; **ein Zimmer mit ~ auf den Strand** a room overlooking the beach

blicken ['blɪkn̩] *vi* **1.** (*schauen*) to look (**auf** +*akk* at) **2. sich** *akk* **~ lassen** to put in an appearance; **sie hat sich hier nicht wieder ~ lassen** she hasn't shown up here again

Blickkontakt *m* visual contact; **~ haben** to have eye contact

blind [blɪnt] *adj* blind; **~ werden** to go blind; **~ vor Hass/Eifersucht sein** to be blinded by hatred/jealousy

Blinddarm *m* appendix

Blinddarmentzündung *f* appendicitis

Blinde(r) *f(m)* dekl wie adj blind person

Blindenhund *m* guide dog

Blindenschrift *f* Braille *no art*

blinken ['blɪŋkn̩] *vi* **1.** (*funkeln*) to gleam **2.** (*Fahrzeug*) to flash; (*zum Abbiegen*) to put one's turn signal on; **mit der Lichthupe ~** to flash one's [head]lights

Blinker <-s, -> ['blɪŋkɐ] *m* AUTO turn signal

Blitz <-es, -e> [blɪts] *m* lightning; FOTO flash; **vom ~ getroffen werden** to be struck by lightning ▶ **wie vom ~ getroffen** thunderstruck; **wie ein ~ einschlagen** to come as a bombshell; **wie der ~** *fam* like lightning

Blitzableiter <-s, -> *m* lightning rod

blitzblank *adj* squeaky clean

blitzen ['blɪtsn̩] **I.** *vi impers* **es blitzt** there is [a flash of] lightning **II.** *vt* TRANSP **geblitzt werden** to be photographed by a traffic camera

Blitzlicht *nt* FOTO flash[light]

Blitzschlag *m* lightning strike

Block <-[e]s, Blöcke> [blɔk] *m* block; **ein ~ Briefpapier** a stationery pad

Blockflöte *f* recorder

blockieren* [blɔˈkiːrən] **I.** *vt* to block; (*Stromzufuhr*) to interrupt; (*Verkehr*) to

stop **II.** *vi* (*Bremse, Räder*) to lock

blöd [bløːt] **I.** *adj fam* silly; (*stärker*) stupid; (*Situation*) awkward; **ein ~es Gefühl** a funny feeling; **zu ~!** how annoying! **II.** *adv fam* idiotically; **frag doch nicht so ~!** don't ask such stupid questions!; **sich** *akk* **~ anstellen** to act stupid

blödeln ['bløːdl̩n] *vi fam* to tell silly jokes

Blödsinn *m kein pl* nonsense; **machen Sie keinen ~!** don't mess around!

blödsinnig ['bløːtzɪnɪç] *adj* idiotic

blöken ['bløːkn̩] *vi* to bleat

blond [blɔnt] *adj* blond[e]

Blondine <-, -n> [blɔnˈdiːnə] *f* blonde

bloß [bloːs] **I.** *adj* with **~em Auge** with the naked eye; **mit ~em Oberkörper** stripped to the waist **II.** *adv* (*nur*) only **III.** *part* (*verstärkend*) **lass mich ~ in Ruhe!** just leave me alone!; **was er ~ hat?** what's his problem?

bluffen ['blʊfn̩] *vi* to bluff

blühen ['blyːən] *vi* **1.** (*Pflanze*) to bloom **2.** *fig* (*florieren*) to flourish **3.** *fam* (*bevorstehen*) **jdm ~** to be in store for sb; **dann blüht dir aber was!** then you'll be in for it!

blühend *adj* ▶ **eine ~e Fantasie haben** to have a fertile imagination

Blume <-, -n> ['bluːmə] *f* (*Blume*) potted plant ▶ **jdm etw durch die ~ sagen** to say sth in a roundabout way to sb

Blumenbeet *nt* flower bed

Blumenkohl *m kein pl* cauliflower

Blumenstrauß <-sträuße> *m* bouquet of flowers

Blumentopf *m* flowerpot

Blumenvase *f* flower vase

blumig *adj* flowery

Bluse <-, -n> ['bluːzə] *f* blouse

Blut <-[e]s> [bluːt] *nt kein pl* blood; **jdm ~ abnehmen** to take a blood sample from sb ▶ **~ geleckt haben** to have developed a liking for sth; **jdm im ~ liegen** to be in sb's blood; **[nur] ruhig ~!** [just] calm down!; **~ und Wasser schwitzen** to sweat blood [and tears]

Blutbad nt bloodbath

Blutbank <-banken> f blood bank

Blutdruck m kein pl blood pressure

Blüte <-, -n> ['bly:·tə] f 1. (von Blume) bloom; (von Baum) blossom; **in voller ~ stehen** a. fig to be in full bloom; (Baum, Strauch) to be in full blossom; 2. fam (falsche Banknote) fake [bill]

Blutegel m leech

bluten ['blu:·tn̩] vi to bleed

Blütenblatt nt petal

Blütenstaub m pollen

Bluter(in) <-s, -> ['blu:·tɐ] m(f) MED hemophiliac

Bluterguss RR <-es, -ergüsse>, **Bluterguß** ALT <-sses, -ergüsse> m bruise

Blütezeit f 1. BOT blossoming 2. fig heyday

Blutgefäß nt blood vessel

Blutgerinnsel nt blood clot

Blutgruppe f blood group

Bluthund m bloodhound

blutig ['blu:·tɪç] adj 1. bloody; (blutbefleckt) bloodstained 2. KOCHK rare; **sehr ~** very rare

blutjung ['blu:t·'jʊŋ] adj very young

Blutorange f blood orange

Blutplasma nt blood plasma

Blutprobe f 1. (Untersuchung) blood test 2. (Entnahme) blood sample

blutrot adj blood-red

blutrünstig ['blu:t·rʏns·tɪç] adj bloodthirsty

Blutsauger m a. fig bloodsucker

Blutspender(in) m(f) blood donor

blutsverwandt adj related by blood pred

Blutsverwandte(r) f(m) blood relation

Blutung <-, -en> f 1. (das Bluten) bleeding; **innere ~en** internal bleeding 2. [monatliche] ~ menstruation

blutunterlaufen adj (Augen) bloodshot

Blutvergießen <-s> nt kein pl bloodshed

Blutvergiftung f blood poisoning no indef art

Blutverlust m blood loss

Blutwäsche f MED hemodialysis

Blutwurst f blood sausage

Bö <-, -en> [bø:] f gust [of wind]

Bock <-[e]s, Böcke> [bɔk] m 1. ZOOL buck; (Schafsbock) ram; (Ziegenbock) billy goat 2. pej **ein alter ~** an old goat; **ein sturer ~** a stubborn bastard ▶ **~ [auf etw akk] haben** sl to feel like [doing sth]

bockig ['bɔ·kɪç] adj fam stubborn

Bockwurst f bockwurst (type of sausage)

Boden <-s, Böden> ['bo:·dn̩] m 1. (Erdreich) soil; **magerer ~** barren soil 2. (Erdboden) ground; (Fußboden) floor 3. kein pl (Territorium) territory; **auf amerikanischem ~** on American soil 4. (Dachboden) attic 5. (Grund) bottom; (eines Gefäßes a.) base ▶ **am ~ zerstört sein** fam to be devastated; **etw [mit jdm] zu ~ reden** schweiz to chew over sth sep [with sb]

Bodenbelag m floor covering

Bodenfrost m light frost

bodenlos adj outrageous; **das ist eine ~e Frechheit!** that's absolutely outrageous!

Bodennebel m ground fog

Bodenpersonal nt LUFT ground crew

Bodenschätze pl mineral resources pl

Bodensee ['bo:·dn̩·ze:] m **der ~** Lake Constance

Body <-s, -s> ['bɔdi] m bodysuit

Bodybuilding <-s> [-bɪl·dɪŋ] nt kein pl bodybuilding

Bogen <-s, -> ['bo:·gn̩] m 1. (Kurve) curve; **einen ~ machen** to curve [around] 2. (Blatt Papier) sheet [of paper] 3. (Schusswaffe) bow; **Pfeil und ~** bow and arrow[s pl] 4. ARCHIT arch ▶ **in hohem ~ hinausfliegen** fam to be thrown out; **den ~ heraushaben** fam to have got the hang of it; **einen [großen] ~ um jdn/etw machen** fam to steer clear of sb/sth

bogenförmig adj arched

böhmisch ['bø:·mɪʃ] adj Bohemian

Bohne <-, -n> ['bo:·nə] f bean; **dicke/ grüne/rote/weiße ~n** broad/green/ kidney/navy beans

Bohnenkaffee m kein pl real coffee

Bohnenstange f a. hum beanpole a. hum

bohnern ['bo:·nɐn] vt to polish

Bohnerwachs [-vaks] nt floor polish

bohren ['boː·rən] I. vt 1. (Loch) to bore; (mit Bohrmaschine) to drill 2. (hineinstoßen) to sink; **sie bohrte ihm das Messer in den Bauch** she plunged the knife into his stomach II. vi 1. (mit dem Bohrer) to drill 2. **in der Nase ~** to pick one's nose 3. fam (drängen) **so lange ~, bis ...** to keep on asking until ...

Bohrer <-s, -> m drill

Bohrinsel f drilling rig

Bohrturm m derrick

böig ['bøː·ɪç] adj (Wetter) windy

Boiler <-s, -> ['bɔy·lɐ] m hot-water tank

Boje <-, -n> ['boː·jə] f buoy

Bolivianer(in) <-s, -> [boli·'vjaː·nɐ] m(f) Bolivian; s. a. **Deutsche(r)**

Bolivien <-s> [bo·'liː·vi·ən] nt Bolivia; s. a. **Deutschland**

bombardieren * [bɔm·bar·'diː·rən] vt 1. MIL to bomb 2. fig fam to bombard

Bombe <-, -n> ['bɔm·bə] f bomb; **wie eine ~ einschlagen** to come as a bombshell

Bombenerfolg m fam smash hit

Bombengeschäft nt fam booming business

Bombenstimmung f kein pl fam **in ~ sein** to be in a great mood; **auf der Party herrschte eine ~** that was one happening party sl

bombig ['bɔm·bɪç] adj fam fantastic

Bon <-s, -s> [bɔŋ, bõː] m 1. (Kassenzettel) receipt 2. (Gutschein) coupon

Bonbon <-s, -s> [bɔŋ·'bɔŋ] m o österr nt piece of candy

Bonus <-, -> ['boː·nʊs] m FIN bonus

boomen ['buː·mən] vi ÖKON to [be on the] boom

Boot <-[e]s, -e> [boːt] nt boat; (Segelboot) yacht; **~ fahren** to go boating

Bootsfahrt f boat trip

Bootshaus nt boathouse

Bootsverleih m boat rental

Bord¹ [bɔrt] m **an ~** aboard; **an ~ gehen** to board; **über ~ gehen** to go overboard; **Mann über ~!** man overboard!; **von ~ gehen** (Lotse) to leave the plane/ship; (Passagier a.) to disembark

Bord² <-[e]s, -e> [bɔrt] nt shelf

Bordell <-s, -e> [bɔr·'dɛl] nt brothel

Bordkarte f boarding pass

Bordpersonal nt kein pl crew

Bordstein m curb

borgen ['bɔr·gn] vt 1. (sich leihen) to borrow 2. (verleihen) to lend

Borke <-, -n> ['bɔr·kə] f BOT bark

Borkenkäfer m bark beetle

borniert [bɔr·'niːɐt] adj pej bigoted

Börse <-, -n> ['bœr·zə] f FIN stock market; (Gebäude) stock exchange; **an die ~ gehen** to go public; **an der ~ [gehandelt]** [traded] on the exchange

Börsenmakler(in) m(f) stockbroker

Borste <-, -n> ['bɔrs·tə] f bristle

bösartig adj 1. (tückisch) malicious; (Tier) vicious 2. MED malignant

Böschung <-, -en> ['bœ·ʃʊŋ] f embankment

böse ['bøː·zə] I. adj 1. (schlecht) bad; **~ Absicht** malice; **das war keine ~ Absicht!** no harm intended!; **nichts B~s ahnen** to not suspect anything is wrong; **ein ~s Ende nehmen** to end in disaster; **~ Folgen haben** to have dire consequences; **eine ~ Überraschung erleben** to have an unpleasant surprise; **ein ~r Zufall** a terrible coincidence 2. (verärgert) angry; **ein ~s Gesicht machen** to scowl 3. fam (unartig) naughty II. adv 1. (schlecht) badly; **~ ausgehen** to end in disaster; **~ [für jdn] aussehen** to look bad [for sb] 2. (böswillig) **das habe ich nicht ~ gemeint** I meant no harm; **~ lächeln** to give an evil smile 3. fam (sehr) **sich akk ~ irren** to make a serious mistake

Bösewicht <-[e]s, -er> ['bøː·zə·vɪçt] m 1. hum fam little rascal 2. veraltend (Schurke) villain

boshaft ['boːs·haft] I. adj malicious II. adv **~ grinsen** to give an evil grin

Bosheit <-, -en> f malice; (Bemerkung) nasty remark

Boss RR <-es, -e>, **Boß** ALT <-sses, -sse> [bɔs] m boss

böswillig adj malevolent; JUR willful

botanisch [bo·'taː·nɪʃ] adj botanical

Bote, Botin <-n, -n> ['boː·tə, 'boː·tɪn] m, f courier; (mit Nachricht) messenger

Botschaft <-, -en> ['boːt·ʃaft] f 1. (Nach-

richt) message; **hast du schon die freu-dige ~ gehört?** have you heard the good news yet? **2.** POL embassy

Botschafter(in) <-s, -> *m(f)* POL ambassador

Bottich <-[e]s, -e> ['bɔ·tɪç] *m* tub; (*für Wäsche*) washtub

Bouillon <-, -s> [bu̯l·'jɔŋ] *f* (*beef*) bouillon

Boulevardpresse *f fam* yellow press

Boutique <-, -n> [bu·'ti:k] *f* boutique

Bowle <-, -n> ['boː·lə] *f* KOCHK punch

Bowling <-s, -s> ['boː·lɪŋ] *nt* (*tenpin*) bowling

Box <-, -en> [bɔks] *f* **1.** (*Behälter*) box **2.** *fam* (*Lautsprecher*) loudspeaker

boxen ['bɔ·ksn̩] **I.** *vi* to box; **gegen jdn ~** to fight sb **II.** *vt* to punch

Boxen <-s> ['bɔ·ksn̩] *nt kein pl* boxing *no art*

Boxer(in) <-s, -> ['bɔ·ksɐ] *m(f)* boxer

Boxhandschuh *m* boxing glove

Boxkampf *m* boxing match

boykottieren* [bɔɪ·kɔ·'tiː·rən] *vt* to boycott

brach [braːx] *imp von* **brechen**

Branche <-, -n> ['brã·ʃə] *f* ÖKON line of business

Branchenverzeichnis *nt* ≈ Yellow Pages

Brand <-[e]s, Brände> [brant] *m* fire; **in ~ geraten** to catch fire; **etw in ~ stecken** to set sth on fire

brandeilig *adj fam* extremely urgent

Brandherd *m* source of the fire

brandmarken *vt* to brand

brandneu ['brant·'nɔɪ] *adj fam* brand-new

Brandschaden *m* fire damage

Brandschutz *m kein pl* fire protection

Brandstifter(in) <-s, -> *m(f)* arsonist

Brandstiftung *f* arson

Brandung <-, -en> *f* surf

Brandwunde *f* burn

Branntwein [brant·vain] *m* spirits *pl*

Brasilianer(in) <-s, -> [bra·zi·'lja:·nɐ] *m(f)* Brazilian; *s. a.* **Deutsche(r)**

brasilianisch [bra·zi·'lja:·nɪʃ] *adj* Brazilian; *s. a.* **deutsch**

Brasilien <-s> [bra·'ziː·li̯·ən] *nt* Brazil; *s. a.* **Deutschland**

braten <brät, briet, gebraten> ['braː·tn̩] *vt, vi* (*in der Pfanne*) to fry; (*am Spieß*)

to roast

Braten <-s, -> ['braː·tn̩] *m* roast [meat], kalter ~ cold meat ▶ **ein fetter ~** far a good catch; **den ~ riechen** *fam* t smell a rat *fam*

Brathähnchen *nt*, **Brathendl** <-s, -[n]: *nt österr, südd* grilled chicken

Bratkartoffeln *pl* fried potatoes *pl*

Bratpfanne *f* frying pan

Bratsche <-, -n> ['braː·tʃə] *f* MUS viola

Bratwurst *f* bratwurst, (*fried*) sausage (*vor dem Braten*) [frying] sausage

Brauch <-[e]s, Bräuche> [braux] *m* cus tom; [**bei jdm so**] **~ sein** to be custom ary [with sb]

brauchbar *adj* useful; **nicht ~ sein** t be of no use

brauchen ['brau·xn̩] **I.** *vt* **1.** (*benötigen* to need; **wozu brauchst du das?** wha do you need that for?; **ich brauche bi zum Bahnhof eine Stunde** it takes m an hour to get to the train station **2.** *di fam* (*gebrauchen*) to use; **kannst d die Sachen ~?** can you find a use fc these things? **II.** *modal vb* (*müssen*) t need; **etw nicht** [**zu**] **tun ~** to not nee to do sth; **du hättest doch nur etwa** [**zu**] **sagen ~** you should have just sai something **III.** *vt impers schweiz, süd* **es braucht etw** sth is needed

brauen ['brau·ən] *vt* (*Bier*) to brew

Brauerei <-, -en> [brau·ə·'rai] *f* brew ery

braun [braun] *adj* **1.** brown; (*Haut*) [sur tanned **2.** POL *pej hist* **die B~en** *pl* th Brown Shirts *pl*

bräunen ['brɔɪ·nən] **I.** *vt* (*Haut*) to ta **II.** *vr* **sich** *akk* **~** (*sich sonnen*) to get tan; (*braun werden*) to turn brown

Braunkohle *f* lignite

Brausetablette *f* effervescent tablet

Braut <-, Bräute> [braut] *f* bride

Bräutigam <-s, -e> ['brɔɪ·tɪ·gam] /* [bride]groom

Brautjungfer *f* bridesmaid

Brautkleid *nt* wedding dress

brav [braːf] *adj* (*Kind*) good; **sei schön ~** be a good boy/girl!

brechen <bricht, brach, gebrochen> ['brɛ·çn̩] **I.** *vt haben* to break; **sei Schweigen ~** to break one's silenc

II. *vi* **1.** *sein* (*auseinander*) to break [apart] **2.** *haben* **mit jdm ~** to break with sb **3.** (*sich erbrechen*) to throw up

Brechreiz *m kein pl* nausea

Brei <-[e]s, -e> [brai] *m* **1.** KOCHK porridge ▶ **um den** [**heißen**] **~ herumreden** to beat around the bush *fam*

breit [brait] **I.** *adj* wide; (*Schultern*) broad; **etw ~er machen** to widen sth **II.** *adv* **~ gebaut** strongly built; **sich** *akk* **~ hinsetzen** to plump down

Breite <-, -n> ['brai·tə] *f* width; **von 4 cm ~** 4 cm in width; **die ~ des Angebots** the wide range of offers

Breitengrad *m* [degree of] latitude

breitmachen *vr fam* **sich** *akk* **~** to spread oneself [out]

breitschlagen *vt irreg fam* to talk sb into sth

Bremse¹ <-, -n> ['brɛm·zə] *f* (*Bremsvorrichtung*) brake

Bremse² <-, -n> ['brɛm·zə] *f* (*Stechfliege*) horsefly

bremsen ['brɛm·zn̩] **I.** *vi* (*Fahrzeug*) to brake **II.** *vt* **1.** (*Fahrzeug*) to brake **2.** (*aufhalten*) to slow down *sep;* **sie ist nicht zu ~** there's no holding her back

Bremsflüssigkeit *f* brake fluid

Bremsklotz *m* brake pad

Bremslicht *nt* brake light

Bremsspur *f* skid mark

Bremsweg *m* braking distance

brennbar *adj* combustible

brennen <brannte, gebrannt> ['brɛ·nən] **I.** *vi* **1.** (*Feuer*) to burn; (*Gegenstand*) to be on fire; **es brennt!** fire! fire!; **in der Fabrik brennt es** there's a fire in the factory; **lichterloh ~** to be ablaze **2.** (*Licht*) to be burning; **das Licht ~ lassen** to leave the light on **3. auf der Haut ~** to burn the skin ▶ **darauf ~, etw zu tun** to be dying to do sth **II.** *vt* **1.** (*Schnaps*) to distill **2.** (*CD*) to burn

brennend I. *adj* burning; (*Frage*) urgent; (*Wunsch*) fervent **II.** *adv* ▶ **etw interessiert jdn ~** sb is dying to know sth

Brenner <-s, -> ['brɛ·nɐ] *m* TECH burner

Brennerei <-, -en> [brɛ·nə·'rai] *f* distillery

Brennessel ^(ALT) ['brɛn·nɛ·sl̩] *f s.* **Brennnessel**

Brennholz *nt* firewood

Brennnessel ^(RR) ['brɛn·nɛ·sl̩] *f* stinging nettle

Brennspiritus *m* methylated spirit

Brennstoff *m* fuel

brenzlig ['brɛnts·lɪç] *adj fam* dicey; **die Situation wird mir zu ~** things are getting too hot for me

Bretagne <-> [bre·'tan·jə] *f* **die ~** Brittany

Brett <-[e]s, -er> [brɛt] *nt* board; (*Planke*) plank; (*Regalbrett*) shelf; **schwarzes ~** bulletin board ▶ **ein ~ vorm Kopf haben** *fam* to be slow on the uptake

Bretterzaun *m* wooden fence

Brettspiel *nt* board game

Brezel <-, -n> ['bre:·tsl̩] *f* pretzel

Brief <-[e]s, -e> [bri:f] *m* letter

Briefbeschwerer <-s, -> *m* paperweight

Briefbogen *m* [sheet of] writing paper

Brieffreund(in) *m(f)* pen pal

Briefkasten *m* mailbox

Briefmarke *f* [postage] stamp

Brieföffner *m* letter opener

Briefpapier *nt* stationery

Brieftasche *f* wallet

Briefträger(in) *m(f)* mailman *masc,* mailwoman *fem*

Briefumschlag *m* envelope

Briefwahl *f* absentee ballot

Brikett <-s, -s> [bri·'kɛt] *nt* briquette

brillant [brɪl·'jant] *adj* brilliant

Brillant <-en, -en> [brɪl·'jant] *m* brilliant

Brille <-, -n> ['brɪ·lə] *f* **1.** (*Sehhilfe*) [eye] glasses *npl;* **eine ~** a pair of glasses; **eine ~ tragen** to wear glasses **2.** (*Toilettenbrille*) [toilet] seat

Brillenetui *nt* eyeglass case

Brillengestell *nt* [eyeglass] frames

Brillenglas *nt* lens

bringen <brachte, gebracht> ['brɪ·ŋən] *vt* **1.** (*hinbringen*) **jdm etw ~** to bring [sb] sth **2.** (*wegbringen*) **jdn/etw irgendwohin ~** to take sb/sth somewhere; **jdn nach Hause ~** to take sb home; **den Müll nach draußen ~** to take out the garbage; **die Kinder ins Bett ~** to put the children to bed **3.** (*versetzen*) **jdn in Bedrängnis ~** to get sb in[to] trouble; **jdn ins Gefängnis**

~ to put sb in prison; **jdn ins Grab** ~ to be the death of sb; **jdn in Schwierigkeiten** ~ to put sb into a difficult position **4.** (*rauben*) **jdn um etw** *akk* ~ to rob sb of sth; **jdn um den Verstand** ~ to drive sb crazy **5.** (*einbringen*) **das bringt nicht viel** that won't bring in much money [for us] **6.** (*bewegen*) **jdn dazu** ~, **etw zu tun** to get sb to do sth **7.** + *substantiviertem Verb* (*bewerkstelligen*) **jdn zum Laufen/Singen/Sprechen** ~ to make sb run/sing/talk; **jdn zum Schweigen** ~ to silence sb **8.** *fam* (*tun*) **das kannst du doch nicht** ~! you can't [go and] do that! **9.** *fam* (*gut sein*) **sie bringt's** she's got what it takes; **das bringt er nicht** he's not up to it; **das bringt nichts** it's pointless; **das bringt's nicht** that's useless ▶ **etw hinter sich** *akk* ~ to get sth over [and done] with; **etw bringt etw mit sich** sth involves sth; **es nicht über sich** *akk* ~, **etw zu tun** to not be able to bring oneself to do sth

brisant [bri·'zant] *adj* explosive

Brise <-, -n> ['bri:·zə] *f* breeze

Brite, Britin <-n, -n> ['brɪ·tə, 'brɪ·tɪn] *m, f* Briton, Brit *fam*; *s. a.* **Deutsche(r)**

britisch ['brɪ·tɪʃ] *adj* British, Brit *attr fam*; *s. a.* **deutsch**

bröckeln ['brœ·kln] *vi* to crumble

Brocken <-s, -> ['brɔ·kn] *m* **1.** (*Stück*) chunk **2.** *pl* LING **ein paar** ~ **Russisch** a smattering of Russian ▶ **ein harter** ~ **sein** *fam* to be a tough one

Brokkoli <-s, -s> ['brɔ·ko·li] *m* broccoli

Brombeere ['brɔm·be:·rə] *f* blackberry; (*Strauch*) blackberry bush

Bronchie <-, -n> ['brɔn·çjə] *f meist pl* bronchial tube

Bronchitis <-, Bronchitiden> [brɔn·'çi:·tɪs] *f* bronchitis *no art*

Bronze <-, -n> ['brõ:·sə] *f* bronze

Bronzemedaille [-me·dal·jə] *f* bronze medal

Brosche <-, -n> ['brɔ·ʃə] *f* brooch

Broschüre <-, -n> [brɔ·'ʃy:·rə] *f* brochure

Brot <-[e]s, -e> [bro:t] *nt* bread; (*Laib*) loaf [of bread]; **ein** ~ **mit Käse** a slice of bread with cheese; **belegtes** ~ [open-faced] sandwich

Brötchen <-s, -> ['brø:t·çən] *nt* [bread] roll ▶ **sich** *dat* **seine** ~ **verdiene** *fam* to earn one's living

Broteinheit *f* MED carbohydrate unit

Brotkasten *m* bread box

Brotrinde *f* [bread] crust

Browser <-s, -> ['brau·zɐ] *m* INET browser

Bruch <-[e]s, Brüche> [brʊx] *m* **1.** (*eines Vertrags*) infringement; (*von Vertrauen*) breach **2.** (*in Beziehung, Freundschaft*) rift; **in die Brüche gehen** to go to pieces **3.** (*Knochenbruch*) fracture **ein komplizierter** ~ a compound fracture **4.** MED **sich** *dat* **einen** ~ **heben** to give oneself a hernia

bruchfest *adj* unbreakable

brüchig ['brʏ·çɪç] *adj* (*Leder, Stimme*) cracked

Bruchteil *m* **im** ~ **einer Sekunde** in a split second

Brücke <-, -n> ['brʏ·kə] *f* **1.** ARCHIT bridge **2.** (*Teppich*) rug

Brückenpfeiler *m* [bridge] pier

Bruder <-s, Brüder> ['bru:·dɐ] *m* brother; **die Brüder Schmitz/Grimm** the Schmitz brothers/the Brothers Grimm

brüderlich *adv* ~ **teilen** to share and share alike

Bruderschaft <-, -en> *f* REL fraternity

Brühe <-, -n> ['bry:·ə] *f* KOCHK broth

Brühwürfel *m* bouillon cube

brüllen ['brʏ·lən] *vt* **jdm etw ins Ohr** ~ to shout sth in sb's ear

brummen ['brʊ·mən] **I.** *vi* (*Bass*) to rumble; (*Motor*) to drone **II.** *vt* to mumble

Brummschädel *m fam* headache; (*durch Alkohol a.*) hangover

brünett [brʏ·'nɛt] *adj* brunet[te]

Brunnen <-s, -> ['brʊ·nən] *m* **1.** (*Wasserbrunnen*) well **2.** (*Springbrunnen*) fountain

brünstig ['brʏns·tɪç] *adj* (*männliches Tier*) rutting; (*weibliches Tier*) in heat *pred*

brüsk [brʏsk] *adj* brusque

brüskieren * [brʏs·'ki:·rən] *vt* to snub

Brüssel <-s> ['brʏ·sl] *nt* Brussels

Brust <-, Brüste> [brʊst] *f* breast; (*Brustkasten*) chest; **einem Kind die** ~ **geben** to breastfeed a baby; **es auf der** ~ **ha**

ben to have chest trouble ► **schwach auf der ~ sein** hum fam (*schwächlich*) to have weak lungs; (*finanziell*) to be a bit short on cash

Brustbein nt ANAT breastbone

Brustbeutel m [neck] travel pouch

Brustfellentzündung f MED pleurisy

Brustkorb m ANAT chest

Brustkrebs m breast cancer

Brustschwimmen nt breaststroke

Brustwarze f nipple

brutal [bru·'ta:l] adj brutal

Brutalität <-, -en> [bru·ta·li·'tɛ:t] f kein pl brutality

Brutkasten m MED incubator

brutto ['brʊ·to] adv gross; **3.800 Euro ~ verdienen** to have a gross income of 3,800 euros

Bruttoeinkommen nt gross income

Bub <-en, -en> [bu:p] m südd, österr, schweiz boy

Buch <-[e]s, Bücher> [bu:x] nt book

Buchdrucker(in) m(f) (letterpress) printer

Buche <-, -n> ['bu:·xə] f beech

Buchecker <-, -n> f BOT beechnut

Bücherei <-, -en> [by:·çə·'rai] f (lending) library

Bücherregal nt bookshelf

Bücherschrank m bookcase

Bücherwurm m hum bookworm

Buchführung f bookkeeping

Buchhalter(in) m(f) bookkeeper

Buchhandel m book trade; **im ~ erhältlich** available in bookstores

Buchhändler(in) m(f) bookseller

Buchhandlung f bookstore

Büchsenöffner m can opener

Buchstabe <-n[s], -n> ['bu:x·ʃta·bə] m letter

buchstabieren * [bu:x·ʃta·'bi:·rən] vt to spell

Bucht <-, -en> [bʊxt] f bay

Buchung <-, -en> f 1. (*Reservierung*) booking, reservation 2. FIN book entry

Buchweizen m buckwheat

bücken ['bʏ·kn̩] vr **sich** akk [**nach etw** dat] **~** to bend down [to pick sth up]

buddeln ['bʊ·dl̩n] fam I. vi to dig [up] II. vt to dig [out sep]

Buddhismus <-> [bʊ·'dɪs·mʊs] m kein pl Buddhism

Buddhist(in) <-en, -en> [bʊ·'dɪst] m(f) Buddhist

Bude <-, -n> ['bu:·də] f fam (*Wohnung*) pad; **sturmfreie ~ haben** fam to have the place [all] to oneself

Budget <-s, -s> [bʏ·'dʒe:] nt budget

Büfett <-[e]s, -s> [bʏ·'fɛt] nt, **Buffet** <-s, -s> [bʏ·'fe:] nt bes österr, schweiz 1. (*Essen*) buffet 2. (*Anrichte*) sideboard 3. schweiz (*Bahnhofsgaststätte*) train station restaurant

Büffel <-s, -> ['bʏ·fl̩] m buffalo

Bügelbrett nt ironing board

Bügeleisen <-s, -> nt iron

Bügelfalte f crease

bügelfrei adj wrinkle-free

bügeln ['by:·gl̩n] vt, vi to iron

Bühne <-, -n> ['by:·nə] f stage; **auf der ~ stehen** to be on [the] stage; **hinter der ~** behind the scenes ► **etw über die ~ bringen** fam to get sth over with; **über die ~ gehen** fam to take place

Bühnenbild nt scenery

Bühnenbildner(in) <-s, -> m(f) scene painter

Bühnenstück nt [stage] play

Buhruf m [cry of] boo

Bulgare, Bulgarin <-n, -n> [bʊl·'ga:·rə, -rɪn] m, f Bulgarian; s. a. **Deutsche(r)**

Bulgarien <-s> [bʊl·'ga:·ri·ən] nt Bulgaria; s. a. **Deutschland**

bulgarisch [bʊl·'ga:·rɪʃ] adj Bulgarian; s. a. **deutsch**

Bullauge ['bʊl·] nt porthole

Bulldogge f bulldog

Bulldozer <-s, -> ['bʊl·do:·zə] m bulldozer

Bulle <-n, -n> ['bʊ·lə] m 1. ZOOL bull 2. sl (*Polizist*) cop fam

Bullenhitze f kein pl fam stifling heat

Bumerang <-s, -s> ['bu:·mə·raŋ] m boomerang

Bummel <-s, -> ['bʊ·ml̩] m stroll

bummeln ['bʊ·ml̩n] vi 1. sein (*spazieren gehen*) to stroll; **~ gehen** to go for a stroll 2. haben fam (*trödeln*) to dilly-dally

Bummelzug m fam local [passenger] train

bumsen ['bʊm·zn̩] vt, vi derb to screw

Bund[1] <-[e]s, Bünde> [bʊnt] *m* **1.** (*Vereinigung*) association **2.** *fam* (*Bundeswehr*) **der ~** the [German] army; **beim ~ sein** to be serving in the military

Bund[2] <-[e]s, -e> [bʊnt] *nt* bunch; **ein ~ Petersilie** a bunch of parsley

Bündel <-s, -> ['bʏn·dl] *nt* bundle

Bundesbank *f kein pl* **die [Deutsche] ~** [German] Federal [Reserve] Bank

Bundesbürger(in) *m(f)* German citizen

Bundesgebiet *nt brd, österr* federal territory

Bundesgerichtshof *m brd* [German] Federal Supreme Court

Bundeshauptstadt *f* federal capital

Bundesinnenminister(in) *m(f)* [German] Secretary of the Interior

Bundeskanzler(in) *m(f) brd* German Chancellor; *österr* Austrian Chancellor; *schweiz* Head of the Federal Chancellery

Bundesland *nt* federal state; **die alten/ neuen Bundesländer** the federal states of the former West/East Germany

Bundesliga *f kein pl* the highest level sports league, often divided into two subleagues, the 1st and 2nd Bundesliga

Bundespost *f kein pl* [German] Federal Post Office

Bundespräsident(in) *m(f) brd, österr* President of the Federal Republic of Germany/Austria; *schweiz* President of the Confederation

Bundesrat *m* **1.** *brd, österr* Bundesrat, Senate **2.** *schweiz* [Swiss] Federal Council *(executive body)*

Bundesregierung *f* federal government

Bundesrepublik *f* federal republic; **die ~ Deutschland** the Federal Republic of Germany

Bundesstaat *m* **1.** (*Staatenbund*) confederation **2.** (*Gliedstaat*) federal state; **im ~ Kalifornien** in the state of California

Bundesstraße *f brd, österr* highway

Bundestag *m kein pl brd* Bundestag, ≈ House of Representatives

Bundestagswahl *f* Bundestag election

Bundesverfassungsgericht *nt kein pl brd* [German] Federal Constitutional Court *(supreme legal body that settle issues relating to the basic constitution)*

Bundesversammlung *f* POL **1.** *br* Federal Assembly, ≈ U.S. Congres **2.** *schweiz* Parliament

Bundeswehr *f* [Federal] Armed Forces

Bündnis <-ses, -se> ['bʏnt·nɪs] *nt* alliance

Bunker <-s, -> ['bʊŋ·kɐ] *m* MIL bunker

bunt [bʊnt] *adj* colorful

Buntstift *m* colored pencil

Buntwäsche *f* colored laundry

Burg <-, -en> [bʊrk] *f* castle

bürgen *vi* **1. für jdn ~** to vouch fo sb **2.** *fig* **für etw** *akk* **~** to be a guar antee of sth

Bürger(in) <-s, -> ['bʏr·gɐ] *m(f)* citizen

Bürgerinitiative *f* citizens' group

Bürgerkrieg *m* civil war

bürgerlich ['bʏr·gɐ·lɪç] *adj* **1.** *attr (de Staatsbürger betreffend)* civil; **~e Pflich** civic duty **2.** (*dem Bürgerstand angehö rend*) bourgeois *pej*

Bürgermeister(in) ['bʏr·gɐ·mais·te] *m(f* mayor

Bürgerrechtsbewegung *f* civil right movement

Bürgersteig <-[e]s, -e> *m* sidewalk

Bürgerversammlung *f* public meeting

Burgund <-[s]> [bʊr·ˈgʊnt] *nt* Bur gundy

Büro <-s, -s> [by·ˈroː] *nt* office

Büroangestellte(r) *f(m)* office worker

Büroarbeit *f* office work

Büroklammer *f* paper clip

Bürokratie <-, -n> [by·ro·kra·ˈtiː] *f* bu reaucracy

Bürste <-, -n> ['bʏrs·tə] *f* brush

bürsten ['bʏrs·tn] *vt* to brush

Bus <-ses, -se> [bʊs] *m* bus; (*Reise bus*) tour bus

Busbahnhof *m* bus station

Busch <-[e]s, Büsche> [bʊʃ] *m* shru **▶ mit etw** *dat* **hinter dem ~ halte** *fam* to keep sth to oneself; **da ist etv im ~** *fam* sth is up; **bei jdm auf den ~ klopfen** *fam* to sound sb out

Büschel <-s, -> ['bʏ·ʃl] *nt* tuft

Busen <-s, -> ['buː·zn̩] m bust
Busfahrer(in) m(f) bus driver
Bushaltestelle f bus stop
Buslinie f bus route
Bussard <-s, -e> ['bʊ·sart] m buzzard
büßen ['byː·sn̩] I. vt to pay for; **das wirst du mir ~!** I'll make you pay for that! II. vi **dafür wird er mir ~!** I'll make him suffer for that!
Bußgeld nt fine *(for traffic or tax offenses)*
Büste <-, -n> ['bʏs·tə] f bust
Büstenhalter m bra[ssiere]
Butangas nt butane gas
Butter <-> ['bʊ·te] f *kein pl* butter
▶ **weich wie ~** as soft as can be
Butterblume f buttercup
Butterbrot nt slice of buttered bread
Butterbrotpapier nt wax paper
Buttermilch f buttermilk
Butterschmalz nt clarified butter
butterweich ['bʊ·te·vaiç] adj really soft
Byte <-s, -s> [bait] nt byte

C

C, c <-, -> [tseː] nt **1.** C, c; **~ wie Cäsar** C as in Charlie **2.** MUS C, c; **das hohe ~** high C
C *Abk von* **Celsius** C
ca. *Abk von* **circa** approx., ca
Café <-s, -s> [ka·'feː] nt café
Cafeteria <-, -s> [ka·fe·ta·'riː·a] f cafeteria
Camping <-s> ['kɛm·pɪŋ] nt *kein pl* camping
Campingplatz m campsite
CD <-, -s> [tseː·'deː] f *Abk von* **Compactdisc** CD
CD-ROM <-, -s> [tseː·deː·'rɔm] f CD-ROM
CD-Spieler m CD player
Cellist(in) <-en, -en> [tʃɛ·'lɪst] m(f) cellist
Cello <-s, -s> ['tʃɛ·lo] nt cello
Celsius ['tsɛl·zi·ʊs] *kein art* Celsius
Cembalo <-s, -s> ['tʃɛm·ba·lo] nt harpsichord
Cent <-(s), -(s)> ['sɛnt] m cent
Champagner <-s, -> [ʃam·'pan·je] m champagne
Champignon <-s, -s> ['ʃam·pɪn·jɔŋ] m mushroom
Chance <-, -n> ['ʃãː·sə] f chance; **die ~n** *pl* **stehen gut** there's a good chance; **die ~n** *pl* **stehen schlecht** there's little chance
Chancengleichheit f *kein pl* equal opportunity
Chaos <-> ['kaː·ɔs] nt *kein pl* chaos
Chaot(in) <-en, -en> [ka·'oːt] m(f) chaotic person
chaotisch [ka·'oːtɪʃ] adj chaotic
Charakter <-s, -e> [ka·'rak·te, *pl* -'teː·rə] m *(einer Person)* character; *(einer Sache)* nature *no indef art*
Charaktereigenschaft f characteristic
charakterfest adj with strength of character *pred*
charakterisieren * [ka·rak·te·ri·'ziː·rən] vt to characterize
charakteristisch [ka·rak·te·'rɪs·tɪʃ] adj characteristic **(für** +akk of)
Charakterzug m characteristic
charmant [ʃar·'mant] I. adj charming II. adv charmingly
Charme <-s> ['ʃarm] m *kein pl* charm
Chauffeur(in) <-s, -e> [ʃɔ·'føː·ɐ] m(f) chauffeur
Chauvinist(in) <-en, -en> [ʃo·vi·'nɪst] m(f) chauvinist
chauvinistisch [ʃo·vi·'nɪs·tɪʃ] I. adj chauvinistic II. adv chauvinistically
checken ['tʃɛ·kn̩] vt **1.** *(überprüfen)* to check **2.** sl *(begreifen)* to get
Chef(in) <-s, -s> ['ʃɛf] m(f) head; *(einer Firma)* manager
Chefarzt, -ärztin m, f head doctor
Chefkoch, -köchin m, f head cook
Chefredakteur(in) m(f) editor in chief
Chemie <-> [çe·'miː] f *kein pl* chemistry
Chemiefaser f man-made fiber
Chemiker(in) <-s, -> ['çeː·mi·ke] m(f) chemist
chemisch ['çeː·mɪʃ] adj chemical
Chemotherapie f chemotherapy
Chiffre <-, -n> ['ʃɪf·rə] f **1.** *(Kennziffer)* box number **2.** *(Zeichen)* cipher
Chile <-s> ['tʃiː·le] nt Chile; *s. a.* **Deutschland**
Chilene, Chilenin <-n, -n> [tʃi·'leː·nə]

m, f Chilean; *s. a.* **Deutsche(r)**

China <-s> [ˈçiːna] *nt* China; *s. a.* **Deutschland**

Chinese, Chinesin <-n, -n> [çiˈneːzə, çiˈneːzɪn] *m, f* Chinese [person]; *s. a.* **Deutsche(r)**

chinesisch [çiˈneːzɪʃ] *adj* Chinese ► **für jdn sein** *fam* to be all Greek to sb; *s. a.* **deutsch**

Chip <-s, -s> [tʃɪp] *m* 1. COMPUT [micro] chip 2. *meist pl* KOCHK chip *usu pl*

Chirurg(in) <-en, -en> [çiˈrʊrk] *m(f)* surgeon

Chirurgie <-, -n> [çiˈrʊrˈgiː] *f kein pl* surgery

chirurgisch [çiˈrʊrˈgɪʃ] *adj* surgical

Chlor <-s> [kloːɐ̯] *nt kein pl* chlorine

Chloroform <-s> [kloˈroˈfɔrm] *nt kein pl* chloroform

Chlorophyll <-s> [kloˈroˈfʏl] *nt kein pl* chlorophyll

Cholera <-> [ˈkoːlera] *f kein pl* cholera

cholerisch [koˈleːrɪʃ] *adj* choleric

Cholesterin <-s> [kolˈɛsˈteˈriːn] *nt kein pl* cholesterol

Cholesterinspiegel *m* cholesterol level

Chor <-[e]s, Chöre> [koːɐ̯] *m* chorus; REL choir

Choral <-s, Choräle> [koˈraːl] *m* choral[e]

Choreograf RR(**in**) <-en, -en> [koˈreoˈgraːf] *m(f)* choreographer

Choreografie RR <-, -n> [koˈreoˈgraˈfiː] *f* choreography

Christ(in) <-en, -en> [ˈkrɪst] *m(f)* Christian

Christbaum *m dial* Christmas tree

Christentum <-s> *nt kein pl* Christianity

Christkind *nt* 1. (*Jesus*) Christ child 2. (*weihnachtliche Gestalt*) Santa Claus; **ans ~ glauben** to believe in Santa Claus

christlich *adj* Christian

Christmette *f* Christmas mass

Christus <Christi, *dat* -, *akk* -> [ˈkrɪstʊs] *m* Christ; **nach/vor ~** A.D./B.C.; **Christi Himmelfahrt** Ascension

Chrom <-s> [ˈkroːm] *nt kein pl* chrome

Chromosom <-s, -en> [kroˈmoˈzoːm] *nt* chromosome

Chronik <-, -en> [ˈkroːnɪk] *f* chronicle

chronisch [ˈkroːnɪʃ] *adj* chronic; **etw ist bei jdm ~** sb has [a] chronic [case of] sth

chronologisch [kroˈnoˈloːgɪʃ] *adj* chronological

circa [ˈtsɪrˈka] *adv s.* **zirka**

Clip <-s, -s> [ˈklɪp] *m* 1. (*Klemme*) clip 2. (*Ohrschmuck*) clip-on [earring] 3. (*Videoclip*) video

Clique <-, -n> [ˈklɪkə] *f* circle of friends

Clown(in) <-s, -s> [klaun] *m(f)* clown ► **sich** *akk* **zum ~ machen** to make a fool of oneself

Code <-s, -s> *m s.* **Kode**

Computer <-s, -> [kɔmˈpjuːtə] *m* computer; [**etw**] **auf ~ umstellen** to computerize [sth]

computergesteuert I. *adj* computer-controlled II. *adv* under computer control

Computerspiel *nt* computer game

Container <-s, -> [kɔnˈteːnə] *m* container

Cookie <-s, -s> [ˈkʊˌkɪ] *nt* INET cookie

Cord <-s> [ˈkɔrt] *m kein pl* corduroy

Couch <-, -s> [kautʃ] *f o schweiz m* couch

Couchgarnitur *f* couch set

Couchtisch *m* coffee table

couragiert [kuˈraˈʒiːɐ̯t] *adj* bold

Cousin, Cousine <-s, -s> [kuˈzɛ̃ː, kuˈziːnə] *m, f* cousin

Crack[1] <-s, -s> [ˈkrɛk] *m* (*ausgezeichneter Spieler*) ace

Crack[2] <-s> [ˈkrɛk] *nt kein pl* (*Rauschgift*) crack

Creme <-, -s> [ˈkreːm, ˈkrɛːm] *f* 1. (*Salbe*) cream 2. (*Sahnespeise*) mousse

cremefarben *adj* cream-colored

cremig *adj* creamy

Curry <-s, -s> [ˈkœri] *m o nt* curry

D

D, d <-, -> [deː] *nt* 1. (*Buchstabe*) D, d; **~ wie Dora** D as in Delta 2. MUS D, d

da [ˈdaː] I. *adv* 1. (*dort*) there; (*hier*) here; **~ sein** to be there/here; **~ bist du ja!** there you are!; **~ drüben/vor-**

ne over there; ~ **hinten** back there; ~ **draußen/drinnen** out/in there; **der/die/das ...** this ... [over] here [*o* that ... [over] there] **2.** (*dann*) then; **von ~ an herrschte endlich Ruhe** after that it was finally quiet **3.** (*in diesem Fall*) in this case; ~ **bin ich ganz deiner Meinung** I completely agree with you **II.** *konj* (*weil*) since, as

dabei [da·'bai] *adv* **1.** (*örtlich*) with [it/ them]; **die Rechnung war nicht ~** the bill was not enclosed; **direkt/nahe ~** right next to/near it **2.** (*zeitlich*) at the same time; (*währenddessen*) while doing it **3.** (*anwesend, beteiligt*) there; ~ **sein** to be there; **bist du ~?** are you with us? **4.** (*damit verbunden*) through it/them; **was hast du dir denn ~ gedacht?** what [on earth] were you thinking?; **ich habe mir nichts ~ gedacht** I didn't mean anything by it; **da ist** [**doch**] **nichts ~** there's nothing to it; **das Dumme/Schöne ~ ist, ...** the stupid/good thing about it is ...

da|bleiben *vi irreg sein* to stay there

Dach <-[e]s, Dächer> ['dax] *nt* (*Gebäudeteil, a. vom Auto*) roof ► [**von jdm**] **eins aufs ~ kriegen** *fam* to be given a talking-to [by sb]; **jdm aufs ~ steigen** *fam* to jump down sb's throat

Dachboden *m* attic

Dachdecker(in) <-s, -> *m(f)* roofer

Dachfenster *nt* skylight

Dachgepäckträger *m* roof rack

Dachrinne *f* gutter

Dachs <-es, -e> ['daks] *m* badger

Dachstuhl *m* roof truss

Dachziegel *m* [roofing] tile

Dackel <-s, -> ['da·kl̩] *m* dachshund

dadurch [da·'dʊrç] *adv* **1.** *örtlich* through [it/them] **2.** ~, **dass ...** because ... **3.** (*auf diese Weise*) this is how

dafür [da·'fyːɐ̯] *adv* **1.** (*für das*) for it/ this/that; **warum ist er böse? er hat doch keinen Grund ~** why's he angry? he has no reason to be; **es ist ein Beweis ~, dass ...** it's proof that ...; ~ **bin ich ja da** that's what I'm here for **2.** (*als Gegenleistung*) in return **3.** (*andererseits*) **in Mathematik ist er schlecht, ~ kann er gut Fußball spielen** he's

bad at math, but he makes up for it with soccer; **er ist zwar nicht kräftig, ~ aber intelligent** he may not be strong, but [at least] he's smart **4.** (*im Hinblick darauf*) ~, **dass ...** seeing [that] ... **5.** ~ **sein** (*zustimmen*) to be for it/that

dagegen [da·'geː·gn̩] **I.** *adv* **1.** (*räumlich*) against it **2.** (*als Einwand, Ablehnung*) against it/that; ~ **müsst ihr was tun** you have to do something about it; **etwas/nichts ~ haben** to mind/ not mind sth; **ich habe nichts ~** [**einzuwenden**] that's fine by me **3.** (*als Gegenmaßnahme*) **das hilft gut ~** this will help; ~ **lässt sich nichts machen** you can't do anything about it **4.** (*verglichen damit*) compared with it/that/ them **5.** ~ **sein** (*nicht zustimmen*) to be against it **II.** *konj* (*jedoch*) whereas

daheim [da·'haim] *adv südd, österr, schweiz* at home

daher ['daː·heːɐ̯] *adv* **1.** (*von da*) from there **2.** (*aus dieser Quelle*) ~ **hat er das** that's where he got it [from]; ~ **weißt du es also** so that's how you know [that] **3.** (*aus diesem Grund*) [and] that's why; **das kommt ~, dass ...** that is because ...

dahin [da·'hɪn] *adv* **1.** (*an diesen Ort*) there; **kommst du mit ~?** are you coming along?; **ist es noch weit bis ~?** is there still a ways to go? *fam* **2.** (*zeitlich*) **bis ~** until then **3.** (*in dem Sinne*) **er äußerte sich ~ gehend, dass ...** he said something to the effect that ...

dahin|schmelzen *vi irreg sein hum* to melt, to get [all] gooey *fam*

dahinten [da·'hɪn·tn̩] *adv* back there

dahinter [da·'hɪn·tɐ] *adv* behind it/that/ them etc.

Dahlie <-, -n> ['daː·li̯ə] *f* dahlia

damalig ['daː·maː·lɪç] *adj attr* at that time *pred*

Dame <-, -n> ['daː·mə] *f* **1.** lady; **meine ~n und Herren!** ladies and gentlemen! **2.** (*Damespiel*) checkers + *sing vb* **3.** (*bei Schach, Karten*) queen

Damebrett ['daː·mə·brɛt] *nt* checkerboard

Damenbinde *f* sanitary napkin

Damenfahrrad *nt* women's bicycle

Damespiel *nt* [game of] checkers + *sing vb*

damit [daˈmɪt] **I.** *adv* with it/that; **was soll ich ~?** what am I supposed to do with this/that?; **weißt du, was sie ~ meint?** do you know what she means by that?; **ist Ihre Frage ~ beantwortet?** has that answered your question?; **ich habe nichts ~ zu tun** I have nothing to do with this; **hör auf ~!** knock it off!; **sind Sie ~ einverstanden?** do you agree [to/with it/that]? **II.** *konj* so that

dämlich [ˈdɛːmlɪç] *fam* **I.** *adj* stupid **II.** *adv* **sich** *akk* **~ anstellen** to be awkward

Damm <-[e]s, Dämme> [ˈdam] *m* (*Staudamm*) dam; (*Deich*) dike ▶ **wieder auf dem ~ sein** to be on one's feet again

dämmern [ˈdɛmɐn] **I.** *vi* **1.** (*Tag, Morgen*) to dawn; (*Abend*) to approach **2.** *fig* **jdm ~** to [gradually] dawn on sb **II.** *vi impers* **es dämmert** (*morgens*) dawn is breaking; (*abends*) night is falling

Dämmerung <-, -en> *f* twilight; (*abends*) dusk; (*morgens*) dawn

Dämon <-s, Dämonen> [ˈdɛːmɔn] *m* demon

Dampf <-[e]s, Dämpfe> [ˈdampf] *m* steam; *s. a.* **ablassen**

Dampfbügeleisen *nt* steam iron

dampfen [ˈdampfn̩] *vi* to steam

dämpfen [ˈdɛmpfn̩] *vt* **1.** (*Gemüse*) to steam **2.** (*Stimme*) to lower **3.** (*Stoß, Begeisterung*) to dampen

Dampfer <-s, -> [ˈdampfɐ] *m* steamship ▶ **auf dem** falschen **~ sein** to be barking up the wrong tree

Dampfmaschine *f* steam engine

Dampfwalze *f* steamroller

danach [daˈnaːx] *adv* **1.** *zeitlich* after it/that; (*nachher a.*) afterwards; **ein paar Minuten ~** a few minutes later **2.** *örtlich* behind [her/him/it/them etc.] **3.** (*laut dem*) according to that **4.** (*nach dieser Sache*) **~ greifen** to [make a] grab for it; **sich** *akk* **~ sehnen** to long for it/that; **jdm ist ~/nicht ~** sb feels/doesn't feel like it

Däne, Dänin <-n, -n> [ˈdɛːnə, ˈdɛːnɪn] *m, f* Dane; *s. a.* **Deutsche(r)**

daneben [daˈneːbn̩] *adv* **1.** (*räumlich*) next to her/him/it/that etc.; **links/ rechts ~** (*bei Gegenständen*) to the left/right of it/them; (*bei Menschen*) to her/his left/right **2.** (*verglichen damit*) compared with her/him/it/that etc. **3.** (*außerdem*) in addition [to that] ▶ **~ sein** (*unangemessen*) to be inappropriate

daneben|**gehen** *vi irreg sein* **1.** (*Ziel verfehlen*) to miss; (*Pfeil, Schuss a.*) to miss its/their mark **2.** (*scheitern*) to go wrong

Dänemark <-s> [ˈdɛːnəmark] *nt* Denmark; *s. a.* **Deutschland**

dänisch [ˈdɛːnɪʃ] *adj* Danish; *s. a.* **deutsch**

dank [ˈdaŋk] *präp* +*gen a. iron* thanks to

Dank <-[e]s> [ˈdaŋk] *m kein pl* gratitude; **vielen ~!** thank you very much!, thanks a lot! *fam;* **das ist der** [ganze] **~ dafür!** that is/was all the thanks one gets/got!

dankbar [ˈdaŋkbaːɐ̯] *adj* grateful; **jdm ~ sein** to be grateful to sb

Dankbarkeit <-> *f kein pl* gratitude

danke *interj* thank you, thanks *fam*

danken [ˈdaŋkn̩] **I.** *vi* **jdm ~** to thank sb, to express one's thanks to sb; **nichts zu ~** you're welcome **II.** *vt* **jdm etw ~** to repay sb for sth; **wie kann ich Ihnen das jemals ~?** how can I ever thank you?

dann [ˈdan] *adv* **1.** (*danach*) then; **noch eine Woche, ~ ist Weihnachten** one more week until Christmas **2.** (*zu dem Zeitpunkt*) **immer ~, wenn ...** whenever ... **3.** (*unter diesen Umständen*) then; **wenn ..., ~ ...** if ..., [then] ...; **selbst ~** even then **4.** (*außerdem*) **und ~ auch noch ...** on top of that ... ▶ **~ und** wann now and then

daran [daˈran] *adv* **1.** (*räumlich*) **halt deine Hand ~!** put your hand [up] against it; **etw ~ befestigen** to fasten sth to it; **~ riechen** to smell it; **~ vorbei** past it **2.** (*zeitlich*) **im Anschluss ~** following that/this **3.** (*an dieser Sache*) **es ändert sich nichts ~** it won't change; **denk ~!** don't forget!; **das Gute ~ ist, dass ...** the good thing about it is that ...; **kein Interesse ~** no interest in it/that;

~ **arbeiten** to work on it/that; **sich** *akk* ~ **beteiligen** to take part in it/that; **sich** *akk* ~ **erinnern** to remember it/that

daran|gehen *vi irreg sein* to get started

daran|machen *vr* **sich** *akk* ~ to get started

daran|setzen [da-'ran·zɛt·sn̩] *vt* **alles** ~, **etw zu tun** to make every effort to do sth

darauf [da-'rauf] *adv* **1.** (*räumlich*) on it/that/them etc. **2.** (*zeitlich*) after that; **bald** ~ shortly afterwards; **am Abend** ~ the next evening; **im Jahr** ~ [in] the following year **3.** (*auf das*) **wir müssen** ~ **Rücksicht nehmen** we must take that into consideration; ~ **antworten** to reply to it/that; **etw** ~ **sagen** to say sth to it/this/that; **ein Recht** ~ a right to it/that; **sich** *akk* ~ **verlassen** to rely on it/that; **sich** *akk* ~ **vorbereiten** to prepare for it/that

daraufhin [da-rauf·'hɪn] *adv* **1.** (*nachher*) after that **2.** (*infolgedessen*) as a result [of this/that]

daraus [da-'raus] *adv* **1.** (*aus Gefäß, Raum*) out of it/that/them; **etw** ~ **entfernen** to remove sth from it **2.** (*aus diesem Material*) out of it/that/them **3.** (*aus dieser Tatsache*) ~ **folgt, dass ...** the result of which is that ...

Darbietung <-, -en> ['da:ɐ̯·bi:·tʊŋ] *f* performance

darin [da-'rɪn] *adv* **1.** (*in dem/der*) in there; (*in vorher Erwähntem*) in it/them; **was steht** ~ [**geschrieben**]? what does it say? **2.** (*in dem Punkt*) in that respect; ~ **übereinstimmen, dass** *akk* to agree that ...

dar|legen ['da:ɐ̯·le:·gn̩] *vt* to explain

Darm <-[e]s, Därme> ['darm] *m* intestine

Darmgrippe *f* stomach flu

dar|stellen ['da:ɐ̯·ʃtɛ·lən] *vt* **1.** (*wiedergeben*) to portray **2.** (*beschreiben*) to describe; **etw knapp** ~ to give a brief description of sth **3.** (*bedeuten*) to represent

Darstellung <-, -en> *f* **1.** (*bildlich*) portrayal **2.** THEAT performance **3.** (*das Schildern*) representation

darüber [da-'ry:·bɐ] *adv* **1.** (*räumlich*)

over it/that/them; (*direkt auf etwas*) on top [of it/that]; (*oberhalb von etwas*) above [it/that/them]; (*über etwas hinweg*) over [it/that/them] **2.** (*hinsichtlich einer Sache*) about it/that/them; ~ **spricht er nicht gern** he doesn't like to talk about it/that **3.** (*dabei und deswegen*) in the process **4.** (*über dieser Grenze*) above [that]; **Kinder im Alter von 12 Jahren und** ~ children 12 [years] and older/over; **10 Stunden oder** ~ 10 hours and/or longer ► ~ **hinaus** what is more; ~ **hinweg sein** to have gotten over it/that

darum [da-'rom] *adv* **1.** (*deshalb*) that's why **2.** (*um das*) ~ **bitten** to ask for it/that; **es geht nicht** ~, **wer zuerst kommt** it's not a question of who comes first; ~ **geht es ja gerade!** that's just it!, that's exactly what I'm/we're talking about! **3.** (*räumlich*) ~ [**herum**] around it

darunter [da-'rʊn·tɐ] *adv* **1.** (*räumlich*) under it/that/them; (*unterhalb von etw*) below [it/that]; ~ **hervorgucken** to look out [from underneath] **2.** (*unter dieser Sache*) **was verstehst du** ~? what do you understand it/that to mean?; ~ **kann ich mir nichts vorstellen** it doesn't mean anything to me **3.** (*dazwischen*) among[st] them **4.** (*unter dieser Grenze*) lower; **Kinder im Alter von 12 Jahren und** ~ children 12 [years] and younger/under

das[1] <*gen:* des, *dat:* dem, *akk:* das, *pl:* die> ['das] *art def, sing nt* the; ~ **Kind/Tier/Schiff** the child/animal/ship; *s. a.* **der**[1], **die**[1]

das[2] <*gen:* dessen, *dat:* dem, *akk:* das, *pl:* die> ['das] *pron dem, sing nt* that; ~ **Kind/Haus** [**da**] that child/house [there]; **was ist denn** ~? what on earth is that/this?; *s. a.* **der**[2], **die**[3]

das[3] <*gen:* dessen, *dat:* dem, *akk:* das, *pl:* die> ['das] *pron rel, sing nt* that; (*Person a.*) who, whom *form*; (*Gegenstand, Tier a.*) which; **ich sah ein Auto,** ~ **um die Ecke fuhr** I saw a car driving around the corner; **ein Mädchen,** ~ **gut singen kann** a girl who can sing well; *s. a.* **der**[3], **die**[5]

da|sein ᴬᴸᵀ ['daː·zain] *vi irreg sein s.* da I 1

Dasein <-s> ['daː·zain] *nt kein pl* 1. (*Existenz*) existence 2. (*Anwesenheit*) presence

dasjenige <*gen:* desjenigen, *dat:* demjenigen, *akk:* dasjenige, *pl:* diejenigen> ['das·je·nɪ·gə] *pron dem* 1. *substantivisch* ~, was ... that which ... 2. *adjektivisch* ~ Kind, das ... the child that ...; *s. a.* diejenige, derjenige

dass ᴿᴿ, daß ᴬᴸᵀ ['das] *konj* that; ich habe gehört, ~ du Vater geworden bist I heard [that] you became a father; die Tatsache, ~ ... the fact that ...

dasselbe <*gen:* desselben, *dat:* demselben, *akk:* dasselbe, *pl:* dieselben> *pron dem* ~ Kleid the same dress; *s. a.* derselbe, dieselbe

Datei <-, -en> [da·'tai] *f* [data] file

Daten ['daː·tn̩] *pl* 1. (*Angaben*) data 2. *pl von* Datum

Datenabruf *m* data retrieval

Datenaufbereitung *f* data processing

Datenbank <-banken> *f* database

Datenhandschuh *m* data glove

Datenschutz *m* data [privacy] protection

Datensicherung *f* [data] backup

Datenträger *m* data medium

Datenverarbeitung *f* data processing

datieren * [da·'tiː·rən] *vt, vi* to date

Dativ <-s, -e> ['daː·tiːf] *m* dative [case]

Dattel <-, -n> ['da·tl̩] *f* date

Datum <-s, Daten> ['daː·tʊm] *nt* date; welches ~ haben wir heute? what's today's date?

Dauer <-> ['dau·ɐ] *f kein pl* duration; (*eines Aufenthalts*) length ▶ von kurzer ~ sein to be short-lived; auf die ~ in the long run; diesen Lärm kann auf die ~ keiner ertragen nobody can stand this noise for any length of time

dauerhaft I. *adj* (*Beziehung, Schaden*) permanent; (*Frieden, Wirkung*) durable, lasting II. *adv* permanently

dauern ['dau·ɐn] *vi* 1. (*anhalten*) to last; der Film dauert 3 Stunden the film is 3 hours long 2. *impers* (*Zeit erfordern*) to take; es wird nicht lange ~

it won't take long; vier Stunden? das dauert mir zu lange four hours? that's too long for me

dauernd ['dau·ɐnt] I. *adj* constant II. *adv* constantly; etw ~ tun to keep [on] doing sth

Dauerwelle *f* perm

Dauerzustand *m* permanent state of affairs

Daumen <-s, -> ['dau·mən] *m* thumb; am ~ lutschen to suck one's thumb ▶ jdm die ~ drücken to keep one's fingers crossed [for sb]

Daune <-, -n> ['dau·nə] *f* down

Daunendecke *f* duvet

davon [da·'fɔn] *adv* 1. (*räumlich*) links/rechts ~ to the left/right of it/that/them; etw ~ lösen to loosen sth from it/that 2. (*von dieser Sache*) was hältst du ~? what do you think of it/that/them?; ~ weiß ich nichts I don't know anything about that; das Gegenteil ~ the opposite of it/that; die Hälfte ~ half of it/that/them; ~ essen/trinken to eat/drink some of it/that; etwas/nichts ~ haben to have some/not have any of it

davon|fliegen *vi irreg sein* to fly away; (*Vögel a.*) to fly off

davon|kommen *vi irreg sein* mit dem Leben ~ to escape with one's life; mit einem Schock ~ to come away with no more than a shock

davon|laufen *vi irreg sein* jdm ~ 1. (*weglaufen*) to run away from sb 2. (*jdn abhängen*) to run ahead of sb 3. (*überraschend verlassen*) to run out on sb

davon|machen *vr* sich *akk* ~ to slip away

davon|tragen *vt irreg* 1. (*wegtragen*) to take away *sep* 2. *geh* (*Preis*) to carry off *sep*; (*Ruhm*) to achieve; (*Sieg*) to score 3. (*erleiden: Knochenbruch, Verletzung*) to suffer

davor ['daː·foːɐ] *adv* 1. (*räumlich*) in front [of it/that/them]; ~ musst du links abbiegen you have to turn left before [you get to] it 2. (*zeitlich*) before [it/that/them/etc.] 3. *mit Verben* er hat Angst ~ he's afraid of it/that; er hatte mich ~ gewarnt he warned me

about it/that

dazu [daˈtsuː, ˈdaːtsuː] *adv* **1.** (*zu dem gehörend*) with it **2.** (*außerdem*) at the same time **3.** (*zu diesem Ergebnis*) **wie konnte es nur ~ kommen?** how could that happen?; **~ reicht das Geld nicht** we/I don't have enough money for that **4.** **im Gegensatz ~** in contrast to that; **im Vergleich ~** compared to that **5.** (*zu dieser Sache*) **ich würde dir ~ raten** I would advise you to do that; **ich bin noch nicht ~ gekommen** I haven't gotten around to it/that yet; **es gehört viel Mut ~** that takes a lot of courage **6.** (*dafür*) **ich bin ~ nicht bereit** I'm not prepared to do that; **~ ist es da** that's what it's there for **7.** (*darüber*) **er hat sich noch nicht ~ geäußert** he hasn't commented on it/that yet; **was meinst du ~?** what do you think about it/that?

dazu|gehören * *vi* **1.** (*zu der Sache gehören*) to belong [to it/etc.] **2.** (*nicht wegzudenken sein*) be a part of it

dazu|tun *vt irreg* to add

Dazutun *nt* **ohne jds ~** without sb's intervention

dazwischen [daˈtsvɪʃn] *adv* **1.** (*zwischen zwei Dingen*) [in] between; (*darunter*) among[st] them **2.** (*zeitlich*) in between

dazwischen|kommen *vi irreg sein* **wenn nichts dazwischenkommt!** if everything goes according to plan!; **leider ist [mir] etwas dazwischengekommen** I'm afraid something has come up

dealen [ˈdiːlən] *vi sl* **[mit Drogen** *dat*] **~** to deal [drugs]

Dealer(in) <-s, -> [ˈdiːlɐ] *m(f) sl* drug dealer

Debatte <-, -n> [deˈbatə] *f* debate; (*schwächer*) discussion; **zur ~ stehen** to be under discussion; **das steht hier nicht zur ~** that's beside the point

debattieren * [debaˈtiːrən] *vt* to debate; (*schwächer*) to discuss

Deck <-[e]s, -s> [dɛk] *nt* deck

Decke <-, -n> [ˈdɛkə] *f* **1.** (*Zimmerdecke*) ceiling **2.** (*Tischdecke*) tablecloth **3.** (*Wolldecke*) blanket; (*Bettdecke*) cov-

ers *pl* ▶ **jdm fällt die ~ auf den Kopf** sb feels really cooped up; **an die ~ gehen** to go through the roof

Deckel <-s, -> [ˈdɛkl̩] *m* **1.** (*Verschluss*) lid; (*von Glas, Schachtel a.*) top **2.** (*Buchdeckel*) cover ▶ **jdm eins auf den ~ geben** to slap sb upside the head

decken [ˈdɛkn̩] **I.** *vt* **1.** (*Tisch*) to set **2.** (*Dach*) to shingle **3.** (*etw verheimlichen*) **jdn ~** to cover up for sb; **etw ~** to cover up *sep* sth **4.** (*Kosten*) to meet; (*Kosten*) to cover **II.** *vi* **diese Farbe deckt besser** this paint covers better **III.** *vr* **sich** *akk* **~** (*Aussagen*) to correspond

Deckenbeleuchtung *f* ceiling lights *pl*

Deckname *m* code name

Deckung <-, -en> *f* **1.** (*Schutz*) cover **2.** ÖKON **~ der Kosten** to cover the costs; **die ~ der Nachfrage** to meet the demand

defekt [deˈfɛkt] *adj* faulty

Defekt <-[e]s, -e> [deˈfɛkt] *m* defect

Defensive [defɛnˈziːvə] *f* **in die ~ gehen** to go on the defensive

definieren * [defiˈniːrən] *vt* to define

Definition <-, -en> [definiˈtsjoːn] *f* definition

definitiv [definiˈtiːf] **I.** *adj* (*genau*) definite; (*endgültig a.*) definitive **II.** *adv* (*genau*) definitely; (*endgültig a.*) definitely

Defizit <-s, -e> [ˈdeːfiˌtsɪt] *nt* deficit

deftig [ˈdɛftɪç] *adj* (*Mahlzeit*) hearty; (*Witz*) crude

dehnbar *adj* **1.** (*Material*) elastic **2.** (*Begriff*) flexible

dehnen [ˈdeːnən] *vt, vr* [**sich** *akk*] **~** to stretch

Deich <-[e]s, -e> [daɪç] *m* dike

dein [daɪn] *pron poss, adjektivisch* your; **herzliche Grüße, ~e Anita/~ Paul** best wishes, love Anita/Paul

deine(r, s) [ˈdaɪnə] *pron poss, substantivisch* yours; **diese Tasche ist ~** this bag is yours

deinerseits [ˈdaɪnɐˌzaɪts] *adv* (*von dir aus*) on your part; (*auf deiner Seite*) for your part

deinetwegen [ˈdaɪnətˌveːgn̩] *adv*

1. (*wegen dir*) because of you **2.** (*dir zuliebe*) for your sake

Dekan(in) <-s, -e> [de·'ka:n] *m(f)* UNIV dean; REL deacon

deklinieren * [de·kli·'ni:·rən] *vt* to decline

Dekor <-s, -s> [de·'ko:ɐ̯] *m o nt* pattern

Dekorateur(in) <-s, -e> [de·ko·ra·'tø:ɐ̯] *m(f)* (*Schaufensterdekorateur*) window dresser

Dekoration <-, -en> [de·ko·ra·'tsjo:n] *f* decoration

dekorativ [de·ko·ra·'ti:f] *adj* decorative

dekorieren * [de·ko·'ri:·rən] *vt* to decorate

Delegierte(r) *f(m)* dekl wie adj delegate

Delfin RR <-s, -e> [dɛl·'fi:n] *m s.* **Delphin**

delikat [de·li·'ka:t] *adj* **1.** (*wohlschmeckend*) delicious **2.** (*heikel*) sensitive

Delikatesse <-, -n> [de·li·ka·'tɛ·sə] *f* delicacy

Delikt <-[e]s, -e> [de·'lɪkt] *nt* JUR **1.** (*Verstoß*) offense **2.** (*Straftat*) crime

Delirium <-s, -rien> [de·'li:·ri̯·ʊm] *nt* delirium

Delle <-, -n> ['dɛ·lə] *f* dent

Delphin <-s, -e> [dɛl·'fi:n] *m* dolphin

dem ['de:m] I. *art def dat sing von* **der**[1], **das**[1]; **er gab ~ Kind das Geld** he gave the money to the child; **ich werde es ~ Klaus sagen** *fam* I'll tell Klaus II. *pron dem dat sing von* **der**[2], **das**[2]; **das Fahrrad gehört ~ Mann/Kind** [da] the bike belongs to that man/child [[over] there] III. *pron rel dat sing von* **der**[3]; **der Freund, mit ~ ich mich gut verstehe** the [male] friend that I get along so well with; **der Hund, ~ er zu fressen gibt** the dog that he is feeding

dementsprechend ['de:m·ʔɛnt·'ʃprɛ·çn̩t] I. *adj* appropriate II. *adv* accordingly; **sich akk ~ äußern** to utter words to that effect; **~ bezahlt werden** to be paid commensurately *form*

demnach ['de:m·na:x] *adv* therefore

demnächst [de:m·'nɛ:çst] *adv* soon

Demokrat(in) <-en, -en> [de·mo·'kra:t] *m(f)* democrat

Demokratie <-, -n> [de·mo·kra·'ti:] *f* democracy

demokratisch [de·mo·'kra:·tɪʃ] I. *adj* democratic II. *adv* democratically

demolieren * [de·mo·'li:·rən] *vt* (*Auto*) to wreck; (*Gebäude*) to demolish

Demonstrant(in) <-en, -en> [de·mɔn·'strant] *m(f)* demonstrator

Demonstration <-, -en> [de·mɔn·stra·'tsjo:n] *f* demonstration (**für** +*akk* in support of, **gegen** +*akk* against)

demonstrativ [de·mɔn·stra·'ti:f] I. *adj* demonstrative II. *adv* demonstratively

Demonstrativpronomen *nt* demonstrative pronoun

demonstrieren * [de·mɔn·'stri:·rən] *vt, vi* to demonstrate (**für** +*akk* in support of, **gegen** +*akk* against)

Demut <-> ['de:·mu:t] *f kein pl* humility (**gegenüber** +*dat* before)

demütig ['de:·my:·tɪç] I. *adj* humble II. *adv* humbly

demütigen ['de:·my:·tɪ·gn̩] *vt* to humiliate

Demütigung <-, -en> *f* humiliation

den ['de:n] I. *art def* **1.** *akk sing von* **der**[1]; **er kennt ~ Mann** he knows the man; **grüße bitte ~ Klaus von mir** *fam* please give Klaus my regards **2.** *dat pl von* **die**[2]; **sie hilft ~ Armen** she helps the poor II. *pron dem akk sing von* **der**[2]; **~ Mann da** [drüben] that man [over] there III. *pron rel akk sing von* **der**[3]; **der Mann, ~ ich gesehen habe** the man [that] I saw; **der Hund, ~ er füttert** the dog [that] he is feeding

denkbar I. *adj* imaginable II. *adv* **~ das ~ beste/schlechteste Wetter** the best/worst possible weather

Denkblockade *f* PSYCH mental block

denken <dachte, gedacht> ['dɛŋ·kn̩] *vt, vi* **1.** (*überlegen*) to think (**an** +*akk* of); **langsam/schnell ~** to think slowly/quickly **2.** (*meinen*) to think; **ich denke nicht** I don't think so; **wer hätte das [von ihr] gedacht!** who'd have expected that/it [from her]? **3.** (*urteilen*) to think (**über** +*akk* about); **wie ~ Sie darüber?** what's your view [on it/that]? **ich denke genauso darüber** that's exactly what I think **4.** (*sich erinnern*) **solange ich ~ kann** [for] as long as I can remember; **die wird noch an mich ~**

she won't forget me in a hurry! **5. für jdn/etw gedacht sein** to be meant for sb/sth **6.** (*beabsichtigen*) **ich habe mir nichts Böses dabei gedacht**[, **als ...**] I meant no harm [when ...] ▶ **jdm zu ~ geben** to give sb food for thought; **das gab mir zu ~** that made me think

Denkmal <-s, Denkmäler> ['dɛŋkˌma:l] *nt* memorial

Denkmalschutz *m* **unter ~ stehen** to be designated as a historical landmark

denkwürdig *adj* memorable

denn ['dɛn] *konj* **1.** (*weil*) because; **~ sonst** otherwise **2. es sei ~,** [**dass**] **...** unless ... **3. schöner ~ je** more beautiful than ever

dennoch ['dɛ.nɔx] *adv* still

denunzieren * [de.nʊn.'tsi:.rən] *vt* to denounce

Deo <-s, -s> ['de:o] *nt fam* deodorant

Deoroller *m* roll-on [deodorant]

Deponie <-, -n> [de.po.'ni:] *f* disposal site

deponieren * [de.po.'ni:.rən] *vt* to deposit

deportieren * [de.pɔr.'ti:.rən] *vt* to deport

Depot <-s, -s> [de.'po:] *nt* **1.** (*Lager*) depot **2.** (*für Straßenbahnen, Omnibusse*) [streetcar/bus] depot **3.** *schweiz* (*Flaschenpfand*) deposit

Depp <-en, -e[n]> ['dɛp] *m österr, schweiz, südd fam* idiot

Depression <-, -en> [de.prɛ.'sɪoːn] *f* PSYCH, ÖKON depression

depressiv [de.prɛ.'siːf] I. *adj* depressive; (*deprimiert*) depressed II. *adv* **~ veranlagt** prone to depression

deprimieren * [de.pri.'miː.rən] *vt* to be depressing

der[1] <*gen:* des, *dat:* dem, *akk:* den, *pl:* die> ['deːɐ̯] *art def, sing m* the; **~ Nachbar/Hengst/Käse** the neighbor/stallion/cheese; **~ Papa hat's mir erzählt** *fam* dad told me; **~ Andreas lässt dich grüßen** *fam* Andreas says hi; *s. a.* **das**[1], **die**[1]

der[2] <*gen:* dessen, *dat:* dem, *akk:* den, *pl:* die> ['deːɐ̯] *pron dem, sing m* that; **~ Mann/Hengst/Stuhl** [da] that man/stallion/chair [[over] there]; **~ mit den**

roten Haaren the guy/man/one with the red hair; **wo ist dein Bruder? – ~ kommt gleich** where's your brother? — he'll be here soon; *s. a.* **das**[2], **die**[3]

der[3] <*gen:* dessen, *dat:* dem, *akk:* dem, *pl:* die> ['deːɐ̯] *pron rel, sing m* that; (*Person a.*) who; (*Gegenstand, Tier a.*) which; **der Mann, ~ es eilig hatte** the man who was in a hurry; **ein Film, ~ gut ankommt** a highly-acclaimed film; **ein Zahn, ~ wackelt** a tooth that is loose; *s. a.* **das**[3], **die**[5]

der[4] ['deːɐ̯] I. *art def* **1.** *gen sing von* **die**[1]; **die Augen ~ Katze** the eyes of the cat, the cat's eyes **2.** *dat sing von* **die**[1]; **er half ~ Frau** he helped the woman; **an ~ Decke hängen** to hang from the ceiling; **ich werde es ~ Anne sagen** I'll tell Anne **3.** *gen pl von* **die**[2]; **die Wünsche ~ Männer/Frauen/Kinder** the men's/women's/children's wishes; **das Ende ~ Ferien** the end of vacation **II.** *pron dem dat sing von* **die**[3]; **das Fahrrad gehört ~ Frau** [da] the bike belongs to that woman [over there] **III.** *pron rel dat sing von* **die**[5]; **die Freundin, mit ~ ich mich gut verstehe** my [girl]friend that I get along so well with; **die Katze, ~ er zu fressen gibt** the cat [that] he is feeding; **die Hitze, unter ~ sie leiden** the heat [that] they're suffering from

derart ['deːɐ̯.ʔaɐ̯t] *adv s.* **dermaßen**

derartig ['deːɐ̯.ʔaɐ̯.tɪç] *adj, adv* such

derb ['dɛrp] I. *adj* **1.** (*grob*) coarse; (*Manieren*) rough; (*Ausdrucksweise, Witz*) crude **2.** (*fest: Material, Schuhe*) strong II. *adv* **jdn ~ anfassen** to handle sb roughly; **sich** *akk* **~ ausdrücken** to be crude

dergleichen [deːɐ̯.'glaɪ.çn̩] *pron dem* that sort of thing; **nichts ~** nothing like it; **ich will nichts ~ hören!** I'm not interested in hearing any of that!

derjenige <*gen:* desjenigen, *dat:* demjenigen, *akk:* denjenigen, *pl:* diejenigen> ['deːɐ̯.jeː.nɪ.gə] *pron dem* **1.** *substantivisch* **~, der ...** *auf eine Person bezogen* the person who ..., whoever ...; *auf eine Sache bezogen* the one that ... **2.** *adjektivisch* that; **~**

Mann, der ... the man who ...; *s. a.* **dasjenige, diejenige**

dermaßen ['dɛːɐ̯maːsn̩] *adv* such; **jdn ~ unter Druck setzen, dass ...** to put sb under so much pressure that ...

derselbe <*gen:* desselben, *dat:* demselben, *akk:* denselben, *pl:* dieselben> [deːɐ̯'zɛlbə] *pron dem* ~ **Pulli** the same sweater; *s. a.* **dasselbe, dieselbe**

derzeitig ['deːɐ̯tsai̯tɪç] *adj attr* present

des ['dɛs] *art def gen sing von* **der[1], das[1]; das Aussehen ~ Kindes/Mannes** the child's/man's appearance; **ein Zeichen ~ Unbehagens** a sign of uneasiness

desertieren* [dezɛr'tiːrən] *vi sein* to desert

deshalb ['dɛs'halp] *adv* because of it; **~ frage ich ja** that's why I'm asking; **also ~!** [so] that's why!

Design <-s, -s> [di'zain] *nt* design

Designermode *f* designer fashion

Desinfektion <-, -en> [dɛsʔɪnfɛk'tsi̯oːn] *f* disinfection

Desinfektionsmittel *nt* disinfectant; (*für Wunden a.*) antiseptic

desinfizieren* [dɛsʔɪnfiˈtsiːrən] *vt* to disinfect

despotisch [dɛs'poːtɪʃ] I. *adj* despotic II. *adv* despotically

dessen ['dɛsn̩] I. *pron dem gen sing von* **der[2], das[2]; ein Freund und ~ Schwester** a [male] friend and his sister; **ein Buch und ~ Inhalt** a book and its contents II. *pron rel gen von* **der[3], das[3]** whose; (*von Sachen a.*) of which; **ein Junge, ~ Name ich nicht weiß** a boy whose name I do not know; **ein Buch, ~ Seiten verkleckst sind** a book that has stained pages

Dessert <-s, -s> [dɛˈseːɐ̯, dɛˈsɛːɐ̯] *nt* dessert

destillieren* [dɛstɪˈliːrən] *vt* to distill

desto ['dɛsto] *konj* **je einfacher ~ besser** the simpler the better; **~ eher** the earlier; **~ schlimmer** so much the worse

destruktiv [dɛstrʊkˈtiːf] *adj* destructive

Detail <-s, -s> [deˈtai̯, deˈtaːj] *nt* detail

detailliert [detaˈjiːɐ̯t] I. *adj* detailed II. *adv* in detail

Detektiv(in) <-s, -e> [detɛkˈtiːf] *m(f)* (*Privatdetektiv*) private investigator

deuten ['dɔy̯tn̩] I. *vt* to interpret II. *vi* to point (**auf** +*akk* at)

deutlich ['dɔy̯tlɪç] I. *adj* clear; (*Umrisse*) distinct; **das war ~!** that was very clear! II. *adv* clearly; **sich** *akk* **~ ausdrücken** to make oneself clear

Deutlichkeit <-> *f kein pl* clarity; [jdm] **etw in aller ~ sagen** to make sth perfectly clear [to sb]

deutsch ['dɔy̯tʃ] *adj* German; **typisch ~ sein** to be typically German; **~er Abstammung sein** to be of German origin; **die ~e Schweiz** German-speaking Switzerland; **die ~e Sprache** the German language; **die ~e Staatsbürgerschaft besitzen** to be a German citizen; **das ~e Volk** the German people; **die ~e Wiedervereinigung** the reunification of Germany

Deutsch ['dɔy̯tʃ] *nt dekl wie adj* 1. LING German; **können Sie ~?** do you speak/understand German?; **er spricht akzentfrei ~** he speaks German without an accent; **sie spricht fließend ~** she speaks fluent German; **~ lernen** to learn German; **~ sprechen** to speak German; **~ verstehen** to understand German; **kein ~ verstehen** to not understand [any] German; **auf ~ in German; etw auf ~ sagen** to say sth in German; **~ unterrichten** to teach German ▶ **auf gut ~** [gesagt] *fam* in plain English

Deutsche(r) *f(m) dekl wie adj* German; **er hat eine ~ geheiratet** he married a German [woman]; **die ~n** the Germans; **~ sein** to be German

Deutschland <-s> ['dɔy̯tʃlant] *nt* Germany; **aus ~ kommen** to come from Germany; **in ~ leben** to live in Germany

deutschsprachig ['dɔy̯tʃʃpraːxɪç] *adj* 1. (*Person*) German-speaking *attr* 2. (*Literatur etc.*) German[-language] *attr*

Devise <-, -n> [deˈviːzə] *f* motto

Dezember <-s, -> [deˈtsɛmbɐ] *m* December; *s. a.* **Februar**

dezent [deˈtsɛnt] I. *adj* discreet; (*Farbe*) subdued II. *adv* discreetly

dezentralisieren* [detsɛntraliˈziːrən] *vt* to decentralize

dezimieren* [detsiˈmiːrən] *vt geh* to decimate

Dia <-s, -s> ['di:a] *nt* slide

Diabetes <-> [dia·'be:·tɛs] *m kein pl* diabetes

Diabetiker(in) <-s, -> [dia·'be:·ti·kɐ] *m(f)* diabetic

Diagnose <-, -n> [dia·'gno:·zə] *f* diagnosis

diagnostizieren * [dia·gnɔs·ti·'tsi:·rən] *vt* to diagnose

diagonal [dia·go·'na:l] *adj* diagonal

Diagonale <-, -n> [dia·go·'na:·lə] *f* diagonal [line]

Diagramm <-s, -e> [dia·'gram] *nt* diagram

Diakon(in) <-s, -e[n]> [dia·'ko:n] *m(f)* deacon

Dialekt <-[e]s, -e> [dia·'lɛkt] *m* dialect

Dialog <-[e]s, -e> [dia·'lo:k] *m* dialogue

Diamant <-en, -en> [dia·'mant] *m* diamond

Diät <-, -en> [di·'ɛ:t] *f* diet; **~ halten** to keep to a diet; **auf ~ sein** to be on a diet; **jdn auf ~ setzen** to put sb on a diet

dich ['dɪç] **I.** *pron pers akk von* **du** you **II.** *pron refl* yourself; **du solltest ~ da raushalten** you should keep out of that/this; **wie fühlst du ~?** how do you feel?

dicht ['dɪçt] **I.** *adj* **1.** dense; (*Haar*) thick; (*Verkehr*) heavy **2.** (*wasserdicht*) **die Fenster sind wieder ~** [now] the windows are sealed again ▶ **nicht ganz ~ sein** *pej fam* to be out of one's mind *pej fam* **II.** *adv* **1.** (*nah*) closely; **~ vor jdm** just in front of sb; **~ beieinander** close together; **~ gedrängt** squeezed together **2.** (*stark*) **~ bevölkert** densely populated

Dichter(in) <-s, -> ['dɪç·tɐ] *m(f)* poet

dichthalten ['dɪçt·hal·tn] *vi irreg sl* to keep one's mouth shut

Dichtung <-, -en> ['dɪç·tʊŋ] *f* **1.** *kein pl* LING poetry **2.** TECH seal[ing]

dick ['dɪk] **I.** *adj* **1.** (*von großem Umfang: Buch, Kleidung, Stamm*) thick; (*Bauch*) fat; (*Backen*) chubby; **etwa fünf Meter ~** about fifteen feet thick **2.** (*geschwollen*) swollen; (*Beule*) big **3.** (*dickflüssig*) thick **4.** *fam* (*Freunde*) close **II.** *adv* **1.** (*warm*) **sich** *akk* **~ an-**

ziehen to dress warmly **2.** *fig* **mit jdm ~ befreundet sein** to be good friends with sb ▶ **~ auftragen** to lay it on thick *sl*; **jdn/etw ~[e] haben** *fam* to be sick of sb/sth

Dickdarm *m* large intestine

dickflüssig *adj* thick, viscous

Dickicht <-[e]s, -e> ['dɪk·kɪçt] *nt* thicket

dickköpfig *adj* stubborn, obstinate

die¹ <*gen:* der, *dat:* der, *akk:* die, *pl:* die> ['di:] *art def, sing fem* the; **~ Tochter/Stute/Theorie** the daughter/mare/theory; **~ Mama hat's mir erzählt** *fam* mom told me; **ich bin ~ Susi** *fam* I'm Susi; *s. a.* **das¹, der¹**

die² <*gen:* der, *dat:* den, *akk:* die> ['di:] *art def, pl* **~ Männer/Mütter/Pferde** the men/mothers/horses; *s. a.* **das¹, der¹, die¹**

die³ <*gen:* deren, *dat:* der, *akk:* die, *pl:* die> ['di:] *pron dem, sing fem* that; **~ Frau/Stute/Tasche [da]** that woman/mare/bag [[over] there]; **~ mit den roten Haaren** the girl/woman/one with the red hair; **wo ist deine Schwester? – ~ kommt gleich** where's your sister? — she'll be here soon; *s. a.* **das², der²**

die⁴ <*gen:* deren/derer, *dat:* denen, *akk:* die> ['di:] *pron dem, pl* **~ Männer/Frauen/Stühle [da]** the men/women/chairs [over there]; **~ mit den roten Haaren** the girls/women/ones with the red hair; **~ waren es!** it was them!; **welche Bücher? – da? oder ~ hier?** which books? those [over there]? or these [over here]?; *s. a.* **das², der², die³**

die⁵ <*gen:* deren, *dat:* der, *akk:* die> ['di:] *pron rel, sing fem* that; (*Person a.*) who; (*Gegenstand, Tier a.*) which; **die Frau, ~ da drüben läuft** the woman walking along over there; **die Katze, ~ nicht fressen mag** the cat that doesn't want to eat; **eine Geschichte, ~ Millionen gelesen haben** a story [that has been] read by millions; *s. a.* **das³, der³**

die⁶ <*gen:* deren, *dat:* denen, *akk:* die> ['di:] *pron rel, pl* that; (*Person a.*) who; (*Gegenstand, Tier a.*) which; **ich sah zwei Autos, ~ um die Ecke fuhren** I saw two cars driving around the corner; **die Abgeordneten, ~ dagegenstimm-**

ten the members of Congress who voted against it; *s. a.* **das³, der³, die⁵**

Dieb(in) <-[e]s, -e> ['di:p] *m(f)* thief

Diebstahl <-[e]s, -stähle> ['di:p·ʃta:l] *m* theft

Diebstahlsicherung *f* antitheft device

diejenige <*gen:* derjenigen, *dat:* derjenigen, *akk:* diejenige, *pl:* diejenigen> ['di:·je·nɪ·gə] *pron dem* **1.** *substantivisch* ~, **die ...** *auf eine Person bezogen* the person who ...; *auf eine Sache bezogen* the one that ...; ~**n, die ...** *auf Personen bezogen* the people who ...; *auf Gegenstände bezogen* the ones that ... **2.** *adjektivisch* that; ~ **Frau, die ...** the woman who ...; *s. a.* **dasjenige, derjenige**

Diele <-, -n> ['di:·lə] *f* **1.** (*Vorraum*) hall **2.** (*Bodenbrett*) floorboard

dienen ['di:·nən] *vi* **1.** (*nützlich sein*) *etw dat* ~ to be [important] for sth; **einem guten Zweck** ~ to be for a good cause **2.** (*behilflich sein*) **womit kann ich Ihnen** ~? how can I help you?; **jdm ist mit etw** *dat* **nicht/kaum gedient** sth is of no/little use to sb **3.** (*verwendet werden*) **[jdm] als etw** ~ to serve [sb] as sth

Diener¹ <-s, -> ['di:·nɐ] *m* (*Verbeugung*) bow

Diener(in)² <-s, -> ['di:·nɐ] *m(f)* servant

Dienst <-[e]s, -e> ['di:nst] *m* **1.** *kein pl* (*berufliche Tätigkeit*) work; ~ **haben** to be on duty; **im** ~ at work; **während/nach dem** ~ during/outside working hours **2.** *kein pl* (*Amt*) **diplomatischer/öffentlicher** ~ diplomatic/civil service **3.** *kein pl* (*Bereitschaftsdienst*) ~ **haben** to be on call; **der** ~ **habende Arzt** the doctor on duty **4.** (*Service*) service; ~ **am Kunden** customer service ▶ **jdm einen guten/schlechten** ~ **erweisen** to do sb a service/disservice

Dienstag ['di:ns·ta:k] *m* Tuesday; **wir haben heute** ~ today's Tuesday; **treffen wir uns** ~? would you like to get together on Tuesday?; **am** ~ on Tuesday; **[am]** ~ **früh** early Tuesday [morning]; **an** ~**en** on Tuesdays; **an einem** ~ one Tuesday; **am** ~**, den 4. März** on Tuesday, March 4th; **diesen** ~ this Tuesday; **jeden** ~ every Tuesday; **[am] nächsten** ~ next Tuesday; **ab nächstem** ~ from next Tuesday on; ~ **in acht Tagen** a week from Tuesday; ~ **vor acht Tagen** a week ago Tuesday; **letzten** ~ last Tuesday; **seit letztem** ~ since last Tuesday; **den ganzen** ~ **über** all day Tuesday; **eines** ~**s** one Tuesday; **in der Nacht [von Montag] auf** ~ [on] Monday night, in the early hours of Tuesday morning

dienstags ['di:ns·ta:ks] *adv* [on] Tuesdays; ~ **abends/nachmittags/vormittags** [on] Tuesday evenings/afternoons/mornings

Dienstleistung *f meist pl* services *npl*

dienstlich **I.** *adj* official **II.** *adv* ~ **unterwegs sein** to be away on business

Dienstreise *f* business trip

Dienststelle *f* office

Dienststunden *pl* office hours *npl*

Dienstzeit *f* **1.** ADMIN tenure **2.** (*Arbeitszeit*) working hours *pl*

diesbezüglich ['di:s·bə·tsy:k·lɪç] **I.** *adj* relating to this **II.** *adv* with respect to this

diese(r, s) ['di:·zə] *pron dem* **1.** *adjektivisch* this *sing*, these *pl* **2.** *substantivisch* this one *sing*, these *pl*; ~ **und jenes** this and that

Diesel¹ <-s> ['di:·zl] *nt kein pl* diesel

Diesel² <-s, -> ['di:·zl] *m fam* **1.** (*Wagen mit Dieselmotor*) diesel **2.** *s.* **Dieselmotor**

dieselbe <*gen:* derselben, *dat:* derselben, *akk:* dieselbe, *pl:* dieselben> *pron dem* ~ **Frau** the same woman; ~**n Männer** the same men; *s. a.* **dasselbe, derselbe**

Dieselmotor *m* diesel engine

diesig ['di:·zɪç] *adj* misty

diesjährig ['di:s·jɛ:rɪç] *adj attr* this year's

diesmal ['di:s·ma:l] *adv* this time

diesseits ['di:s·zaits] *präp +gen* this side of

Dietrich <-s, -e> ['di:t·rɪç] *m* picklock

differenzieren * [dɪfə·rɛn·'tsi:·rən] *vi* to discriminate

digital [di·gi·'ta:l] *adj* digital

Diktator, Diktatorin <-s, -toren> [dɪk·'ta:·to:ɐ̯, dɪk·ta·'to:·rɪn] *m, f* dictator

Diktatur <-, -en> [dɪk·ta·'tu:ɐ̯] *f* dictatorship

diktieren * [dɪkˈtiː·rən] *vt* to dictate

Diktiergerät *nt* Dictaphone®

Dill <-s, -e> [ˈdɪl] *m* dill

Dimension <-, -en> [di·mɛn·ˈzjoːn] *f* dimension

Ding <-[e]s, -e> [ˈdɪŋ] *nt* 1. (*Gegenstand*) thing 2. *fam* (*Mädchen*) **ein junges ~** a young thing 3. (*Angelegenheit*) matters *pl*; **so wie die ~e liegen** as things stand [at the moment] ▶ **das ist [ja] ein ~!** *fam* wow!, get a load of that!; *sl*; **krumme ~er drehen** *fam* to pull a fast one *sl*; **das ist nicht so ganz mein ~** that's not really my thing; **über den ~en stehen** to be above it all

Dingsbums <-> [ˈdɪŋs·bʊms] *nt kein pl fam* (*Sache*) thingamajig

Dinosaurier <-s, -> [di·no·ˈzau·ri̯·ɐ] *m* dinosaur

Diphtherie <-, -n> [dɪf·te·ˈriː] *f* diphtheria

Diplom <-s, -e> [di·ˈploːm] *nt* (*Hochschulabschluss*) degree; (*Zeugnis, Urkunde*) diploma

Diplomat(in) <-en, -en> [di·plo·ˈmaːt] *m(f)* diplomat

diplomatisch [di·plo·ˈmaː·tɪʃ] I. *adj* diplomatic II. *adv* diplomatically

Diplomingenieur(in) [-ɪn·ʒe·njøːɐ] *m(f)* sb with a Master of Science in engineering

dir [ˈdiːɐ̯] *pron* 1. *pers dat von* **du** you; **ich hoffe, es geht ~ wieder besser** I hope you're feeling better; **Freunde von ~** friends of yours 2. *refl dat von* **sich** yourself, you; **was wünschst du ~ zum Geburtstag?** what would you like for your birthday?; **du solltest ~ die Haare waschen** you should wash your hair

direkt [di·ˈrɛkt] I. *adj* direct; (*Übertragung*) live II. *adv* 1. *fam* (*geradezu*) almost; **das war ja ~ lustig** that was actually funny for a change 2. (*unverblümt*) directly; **etw ~ zugeben** to admit sth outright 3. (*mit Ortsangabe*) direct[ly]; **~ am Bahnhof** right by the train station 4. (*unverzüglich*) immediately

Direktor, Direktorin <-s, -toren> [di·ˈrɛk·toːɐ̯, di·rɛk·ˈtoː·rɪn] *m, f* (*eines Unternehmens*) manager; (*einer öffentlichen* *Einrichtung*) director; (*einer Schule*) principal

Direktübertragung *f* live broadcast

Dirigent(in) <-en, -en> [di·ri·ˈgɛnt] *m(f)* conductor

dirigieren * [di·ri·ˈgiː·rən] *vt, vi* MUS to conduct

Diskette <-, -n> [dɪsˈkɛ·tə] *f* disk

Diskettenlaufwerk *nt* disk drive

Diskothek <-, -en> [dɪs·ko·ˈteːk] *f* discotheque

diskret [dɪsˈkreːt] I. *adj* 1. (*vertraulich*) confidential 2. (*unauffällig*) discreet II. *adv* **etw ~ behandeln** to treat sth confidentially; **sich** *akk* **~ verhalten** to behave discreetly

diskriminieren * [dɪs·kri·mi·ˈniː·rən] *vt* **jdn ~** to discriminate against sb

Diskriminierung <-, -en> *f* discrimination

Diskussion <-, -en> [dɪs·kʊ·ˈsjoːn] *f* discussion

diskutieren * [dɪs·ku·ˈtiː·rən] *vt, vi* to discuss

disqualifizieren * [dɪs·kva·li·fi·ˈtsiː·rən] *vt* to disqualify (**wegen** +*gen* for)

Dissident(in) <-en, -en> [dɪ·si·ˈdɛnt] *m(f)* dissident

Distanz <-, -en> [dɪs·ˈtants] *f* distance

distanzieren * [dɪs·tan·ˈtsiː·rən] *vr* **sich** *akk* **~** to distance oneself (**von** +*dat* from)

Distel <-, -n> [ˈdɪs·tl̩] *f* thistle

Disziplin <-, -en> [dɪs·tsi·ˈpliːn] *f* discipline

diszipliniert [dɪs·tsi·pli·ˈniːɐ̯t] I. *adj* disciplined II. *adv* in a disciplined way

divers [di·ˈvɛrs] *adj attr* diverse

Dividende <-, -n> [di·vi·ˈdɛn·də] *f* dividend

dividieren * [di·vi·ˈdiː·rən] *vt* to divide (**durch** +*akk* by)

DNS <-> [deː·ʔɛn·ˈɛs] *f Abk von* **Desoxyribonukleinsäure** DNA

doch [dɔx] I. *konj* (*aber*) but II. *adv* 1. (*dennoch*) even so; **zum Glück ist aber ~ nichts passiert** fortunately, nothing happened 2. (*einräumend*) **du hattest ~ Recht** you were right after all 3. (*Widerspruch ausdrückend*) **du gehst jetzt ins Bett – nein! – ~!** you

need to go to bed now — no! — oh yes you do! **4.** (*ja*) yes; **hat es dir nicht gefallen? –** ~[, ~]! didn't you enjoy it? — yes, I did!

Docht <-[e]s, -e> ['dɔxt] *m* wick

Dock <-s, -s> ['dɔk] *nt* dock

Dogge <-, -n> ['dɔgə] *f* mastiff

Doktor, Doktorin <-s, -toren> ['dɔk·toːɐ̯, dɔk·'toː·rɪn] *m, f* doctor; **er ist ~ der Physik** he's got a PhD in physics

Doku <-, -s> ['do·ku] *f kurz für* **Dokumentarfilm, -bericht** documentary

Dokument <-[e]s, -e> [do·ku·'mɛnt] *nt* document

Dokumentarfilm *m* documentary [film]

dokumentieren * [do·ku·mɛn·'tiː·rən] *vt* to document

Dolch <-[e]s, -e> ['dɔlç] *m* dagger

Dollar <-[s], -s> ['dɔ·lar] *m* dollar

dolmetschen ['dɔl·mɛt·ʃn̩] *vt, vi* to interpret

Dolmetscher(in) <-s, -> ['dɔl·mɛt·ʃe] *m(f)* interpreter

Dom <-[e]s, -e> ['doːm] *m* (*Kirche*) cathedral

Domäne <-, -n> [do·'mɛː·nə] *f* domain

dominieren * [do·mi·'niː·rən] *vt, vi* to dominate

Dominikanische Republik *f* Dominican Republic

Domino <-s, -s> ['doː·mi·no] *nt* dominoes + *sing vb*

Dompteur(in) <-s, -e> [dɔmp·'tøːɐ̯] *m(f)*, **Dompteuse** <-, -n> [dɔmp·'tøː·zə] *f* animal trainer

Domstadt *f kein pl* Cathedral City *(nickname for the city of Cologne)*

Donau <-> ['doː·nau] *f* **die ~** the Danube

Donner <-s, -> ['dɔ·ne] *m pl selten* thunder

donnern ['dɔ·nen] **I.** *vi impers* **haben hörst du, wie es donnert?** can you hear the thunder?; **es hat geblitzt und gedonnert** there was thunder and lightning **II.** *vi sein* (*krachen*) to crash (**gegen/in** +*akk* into) **III.** *vt haben* (*irgendwohin werfen*) to fling

Donnerstag ['dɔ·nes·taːk] *m* Thursday; *s. a.* **Dienstag**

Donnerwetter ['dɔ·ne·vɛ·te] *nt fam* (*Schelte*) a tongue-lashing; **zum ~!**

[god]damn it!

doof <*doofer*, *doofste*> ['doːf] *adj fam* stupid

Doppel <-s, -> ['dɔpl̩] *nt* **1.** (*Duplikat*) duplicate **2.** sport doubles; **gemischtes ~** mixed doubles

Doppelbett *nt* double bed

Doppeldecker <-s, -> *m* **1.** (*Flugzeug*) biplane **2.** (*Bus*) double-decker [bus]

doppeldeutig ['dɔpl̩·dɔy·tɪç] *adj* ambiguous

Doppelgänger(in) <-s, -> [-gɛŋe] *m(f)* look-alike

Doppelhaus *nt* duplex

Doppelleben *nt* double life

Doppelpunkt *m* colon

doppelt ['dɔplt] **I.** *adj* **1.** (*zweifach*) double; (*Staatsangehörigkeit*) dual; **die ~e Menge** double the amount **2.** (*verdoppelt*) doubled; **mit ~em Einsatz arbeiten** to redouble one's efforts **II.** *adv* **1.** (*zweimal*) twice; **~ so groß/klein** twice as big/small; **~ so viel/viele** twice as much/many **2.** (*umso mehr*) doubly; **~ vorsichtig sein** to be doubly careful ▶ **~ sehen** to see double

Doppelzentner *m* ≈ 2.2 [short] hundredweights *(220 pounds)*

Doppelzimmer *nt* double [room]

Dorf <-[e]s, Dörfer> ['dɔrf] *nt* village

Dorn <-[e]s, -en> ['dɔrn] *m* thorn ▶ **jdm ein ~ im Auge sein** to be a thorn in sb's side

Dornröschen <-> [-'røː·s·çən] *nt kein pl* Sleeping Beauty

Dörrobst *nt* dried fruit

dort ['dɔrt] *adv* there; **~ drüben** over there

dorther ['dɔrt·'heːɐ̯] *adv* from [over] there

dorthin ['dɔrt·'hɪn] *adv* [over] there

dortig ['dɔr·tɪç] *adj attr* local

Dose <-, -n> ['doː·zə] *f* can

dösen ['døː·zn̩] *vi* to doze

Dosenbier *nt* canned beer

Dosenmilch *f* condensed milk

Dosenöffner *m* can opener

Dosenpfand *nt kein pl* deposit

dosieren * [do·'ziː·rən] *vt* to measure out *sep*

Dosis <-, Dosen> ['doː·zɪs] *f* dose

Dotter <-s, -> ['dɔ·te] *m o nt* yolk

Double <-s, -s> ['duː·bl] *nt* double

downloaden ['daʊn·loʊ·dn̩] *vt* INET to download

Dozent(in) <-en, -en> [do·'tsɛnt] *m(f)* lecturer

Drache <-n, -n> ['dra·xə] *m* dragon

Drachen <-s, -> ['dra·xn̩] *m* **1.** (*Spielzeug*) kite; **einen ~ steigen lassen** to fly a kite **2.** (*Fluggerät*) hang glider **3.** *fam* (*zänkisches Weib*) witch

Draht <-[e]s, Drähte> ['draːt] *m* wire ▶ **zu jdm einen guten ~ haben** to be on good terms with sb

Drahtbürste *f* wire brush

Drahtgitter *nt* wire grating

drahtig *adj* wiry

Drahtseil *nt* wire cable

drall ['dral] *adj* well-rounded; (*Mädchen*) shapely

Drama <-s, -men> ['draː·ma] *nt* drama

dramatisch [dra·'maː·tɪʃ] *adj* dramatic

dramatisieren * [dra·ma·ti·'ziː·rən] *vt* **1.** LIT to dramatize **2.** *fig* (*übertreiben*) to express in a dramatic way, to be dramatic about

dran ['dran] *adv fam* **1.** (*fertig*) [zu] **früh/spät ~ sein** to be [too] early/late **2.** (*an der Reihe*) **jetzt bist du ~!** now it's your turn!; **wer ist als Nächster ~?** who's next? **3.** (*zutreffen*) **an dem Gerücht ist etwas/nichts ~** there is something/nothing to the rumor ▶ **besser ~ sein als ...** to be better off than ...; **schlecht ~ sein** (*gesundheitlich*) to be in bad shape; (*schlechte Möglichkeiten haben*) to be having a hard time [of it]

drang ['draŋ] *imp von* **dringen**

Drang <-[e]s, Dränge> ['draŋ] *m* longing; **ein starker ~** a strong desire

drängeln ['drɛŋ·əln] **I.** *vi* to push **II.** *vt* **jdn ~** to pester sb

drängen ['drɛŋ·ən] **I.** *vi* **1.** *irgendwohin* **~** to force one's way somewhere **2.** (*fordern*) **auf etw** *akk* **~** to insist [up]on sth; **warum drängst du so zur Eile?** why are you in such a hurry? **3.** (*pressieren*) **die Zeit drängt** time is running out; **es drängt nicht** there's no hurry **II.** *vt* **1.** (*schiebend drücken*) to push **2.** (*antreiben*) **jdn ~, etw zu tun** to pressure sb into doing sth; **jdn** [**zu etw** *dat*] **~** to

force sb [to do sth] **III.** *vr* **sich** *akk* **~** to crowd; **sich** *akk* **nach vorne ~** to push forward; **sich** *akk* **durch die Menge ~** to force one's way through the crowd

drangsalieren * [draŋ·za·liː·rən] *vt* to plague

drastisch ['dras·tɪʃ] *adj* drastic

drauf ['draʊf] *adv fam* **1.** (*darauf*) on it/them **2.** **gut/schlecht ~ sein** *fam* to be in a good/bad mood ▶ **~ und dran sein, etw zu tun** to be on the verge of doing sth

Draufgänger(in) <-s, -> ['draʊf·gɛŋɐ] *m(f)* go-getter *fam*

drauf|gehen ['draʊf·geː·ən] *vi irreg sein fam* **1.** (*sterben*) to kick the bucket **2.** (*verbraucht werden*) to be spent **3.** (*kaputtgehen*) to break

drauf|haben *vt irreg fam* (*Kenntnisse haben*) **nichts/viel ~** to know nothing/a lot; **Mathe hat er drauf** he's brilliant at math

drauf|zahlen *vi fam* **500 Euro ~** to pay an extra 500 euros; **~ müssen** to lose money

draußen ['draʊ·sn̩] *adv* outside; **nach ~** outside

Dreck <-[e]s> ['drɛk] *m kein pl* **1.** (*Schmutz, Erde*) dirt **2.** (*Schlamm*) mud **3.** (*Müll*) trash ▶ **jdn wie den letzten ~ behandeln** to treat sb like dirt

dreckig ['drɛ·kɪç] **I.** *adj* dirty **II.** *adv* ▶ **jdm geht es ~** sb feels terrible; (*finanziell*) sb is not doing [too] well

Dreckspatz *m* filthy kid

Dreh <-s, -s> ['dreː] *m* ▶ **den ~ raushaben** to get the hang of it

drehbar *adj*, *adv* revolving

Drehbuch *nt* screenplay

Drehbuchautor(in) *m(f)* screenplay writer

drehen ['dreː·ən] **I.** *vt* **1.** (*herumdrehen*) to turn **2.** (*Zigarette*) to roll **3.** FILM to shoot **4. das Radio lauter/leiser ~** to turn the radio up/down ▶ **wie man es auch dreht und wendet** no matter how you look at it **II.** *vi* **1.** FILM to shoot **2. an etw** *dat* **~** to turn sth **3.** (*Wind*) to change **III.** *vr* **1.** (*rotieren*) **sich** *akk* **~** to turn **2.** (*wenden: zur Seite,*

auf den Bauch) to turn **3.** (betreffen) **sich** akk **um** jdn/etw ~ to be about sb/sth; **das Gespräch dreht sich um Sport** the conversation revolves around sports ▶ **jdm dreht sich alles** sb's head is spinning

Drehorgel f barrel organ

Drehtür f revolving door

Drehzahl f [number of] revolutions pl; (eines Motors) revolutions pl per minute

drei ['drai] adj three

Drei <-, -en> ['drai] f **1.** (Zahl) three **2.** (Zeugnisnote) C

Dreieck <-s, -e> ['drai-ʔɛk] nt triangle

dreieckig, 3-eckig RR ['drai-ʔɛ-kɪç] adj triangular

dreifach, 3fach ['drai-fax] **I.** adj threefold; **die ~e Arbeit** triple the work **II.** adv threefold, three times over

dreihundert ['drai-'hʊn-dɛt] adj three hundred

dreijährig, 3-jährig RR adj **1.** (Alter) three-year-old attr; three years old pred; s. a. **achtjährig 1 2.** (Zeitspanne) three-year attr; s. a. **achtjährig 2**

Dreirad nt tricycle

dreißig ['drai-sɪç] adj thirty; s. a. **achtzig 1, 2**

dreißigjährig, 30-jährig RR ['drai-sɪç-jɛː-rɪç] adj attr **1.** (Alter) thirty-year-old attr; thirty years old pred **2.** (Zeitspanne) thirty-year attr

dreißigste(r, s) adj **1.** (an dreißigster Stelle) thirtieth; s. a. **achte(r, s) 1 2.** (Datum) thirtieth, 30th; s. a. **achte(r, s) 2**

dreist ['draist] adj brazen

dreistellig, 3-stellig RR adj three-figure attr

dreiteilig, 3-teilig RR adj three-part; (Besteck) three-piece

dreizehn ['drai-tseːn] adj thirteen; **~ Uhr** 1 p.m.; s. a. **acht¹** ▶ **jetzt schlägt's aber ~** enough is enough

dreizehnte(r, s) adj **1.** (an dreizehnter Stelle) thirteenth; s. a. **achte(r, s) 1 2.** (Datum) thirteenth, 13th; s. a. **achte(r, s) 2**

dreschen <drischt, drosch, gedroschen> ['drɛ-ʃn] vt **1.** AGR to thresh

2. fam (prügeln) to beat

dressieren* [drɛ-'siː-rən] vt to train [an animal]

Dressman <-s, -men> ['drɛs-mən] m male model

Dressur <-, -en> [drɛ-'suːɐ̯] f training [of animals]

drin ['drɪn] adv fam **1.** (darin) in it **2.** (drinnen) inside ▶ **bei jdm ist alles** ~ anything is possible with sb; **für jdn ist noch alles** ~ anything is still possible for sb

dringen <drang, gedrungen> ['drɪŋ-ən] vi **1.** sein (stoßen) **durch/in etw** akk ~ to penetrate sth **2.** sein (vordringen) **an die Öffentlichkeit** ~ to leak to the public **3.** haben (fordern) **auf etw** akk ~ to insist [up]on sth

dringend ['drɪŋ-ənt] **I.** adj urgent, pressing; **eine ~e Bitte** an urgent request **II.** adv urgently; **ich muss dich ~ sehen** I really need to see you

drinnen ['drɪ-nən] adv inside

dritt ['drɪt] adv **wir waren zu ~** there were three of us

dritte(r, s) ['drɪ-tə] adj **1.** (an dritter Stelle) third; s. a. **achte(r, s) 1 2.** (Datum) third, 3rd; s. a. **achte(r, s) 2**

drittel ['drɪ-tl̩] adj third

drittens ['drɪ-tn̩s] adv thirdly, in the third place

Droge <-, -n> ['droː-gə] f drug

drogenabhängig adj addicted to drugs pred

Drogerie <-, -n> [dro-gə-'riː] f drugstore

Drogist(in) <-en, -en> [dro-'gɪst] m(f) pharmacist

Drohbrief m threatening letter

drohen ['droː-ən] vi to threaten

drohend I. adj **1.** (einschüchternd) threatening **2.** (bevorstehend) impending **II.** adv threateningly

dröhnen ['drøː-nən] vi **1.** (dumpf klingen: Donner) to rumble; (Lautsprecher, Musik, Stimme) to boom **2. jdm dröhnt der Kopf** sb's head is ringing; **jdm ~ die Ohren** sb's ears are ringing

Drohung <-, -en> ['droː-ʊŋ] f threat

drollig ['drɔ-lɪç] adj **1.** (belustigend) amusing **2.** (niedlich) cute

Dromedar <-s, -e> [dro·me·'da:ɐ̯] *nt* dromedary

Drossel <-, -n> ['drɔ·sl̩] *f* thrush

drosseln ['drɔ·sl̩n] *vt (Heizung)* to turn down *sep*; *(Produktion)* to cut; *(Tempo)* to reduce

drüben ['dry:·bn̩] *adv* over there

drüber ['dry:·bɐ] *adv fam* s. **darüber**

Druck¹ <-[e]s, Drücke> ['drʊk] *m* pressure; **unter ~ stehen** to be under pressure; **jdn unter ~ setzen** to put pressure on sb

Druck² <-[e]s, -e> ['drʊk] *m* TYPO printing

Druckbuchstabe *m* **in ~n** in print

Drückeberger <-s, -> *m pej* shirker

drucken ['drʊ·kn̩] *vt, vi* to print

drücken ['drʏ·kn̩] **I.** *vi* **1.** *(pressen)* to push; **auf einen Knopf ~** to push a button **2.** *(Kleidung)* to pinch; **die Schuhe ~** the shoes are pinching my feet **II.** *vt* **1.** *(pressen)* to press; **einen Knopf ~** to press a button; **etw aus etw** *dat* **~** to squeeze sth from sth **2.** *(Kleidung)* **jdn ~** to be too tight for sb **3.** *(umarmen)* **jdn ~** to hug sb **4.** *(herabsetzen)* **den Preis ~** to force down the price **III.** *vr* **sich** *akk* **[vor etw** *dat*/**um etw** *akk*] **~** to dodge [sth]

drückend *adj (Hitze, Stimmung)* oppressive; *(Sorgen)* serious

Drucker <-s, -> *m* COMPUT printer

Drucker(in) <-s, -> *m(f)* printer

Drücker *m* ▶ **auf den** <u>letzten</u> **~** at the last minute

Druckerei <-, -en> [drʊ·kə·'rai] *f* printer's, print shop

Druckfehler *m* typographical error

Druckknopf *m* snap

Druckluft *f kein pl* compressed air

Druckmittel *nt* **jdn/etw als ~ benutzen** to use sb/sth as a means of exerting pressure

druckreif *adj* ready for publication *pred*

Drucksache *f* printed matter

Druckschrift *f* **in ~ schreiben** to write in print

drum ['drʊm] *adv fam* s. **darum** ▶ **das D~ und** <u>Dran</u> the whole works, the whole shebang *fam*

drunter ['drʊn·tɐ] *adv fam* s. **darun-**

ter ▶ **alles geht ~ und** <u>drüber</u> it's all chaos

Drüse <-, -n> ['dry:·zə] *f* gland

Dschungel <-s, -> ['dʒʊŋ·əl] *m* jungle

du <*gen:* deiner, *dat:* dir, *akk:* dich> ['du:] *pron pers* you; **bist ~ das, Peter?** is that you, Peter?

Du <-[s], -[s]> ['du:] *nt* you, "du" *(familiar form of address);* **jdm das ~ anbieten** to suggest that sb use the familiar form of address

Dübel <-s, -> ['dy:·bl̩] *m* drywall anchor

dubios [du·'bi̯o:s] *adj* dubious

ducken ['dʊ·kn̩] *vr* **sich** *akk* **~** to duck one's head

Duckmäuser(in) <-s, -> ['dʊk·mɔy·zɐ] *m(f) pej* yes man

Dudelsack ['du:·dl̩·zak] *m* bagpipes *pl*

Duell <-s, -e> [du·'ɛl] *nt* duel

Duft <-[e]s, Düfte> ['dʊft] *m* [pleasant] smell; *(einer Blume, eines Parfüms)* scent; *(von Essen, Kaffee)* aroma

duften ['dʊf·tn̩] *vi* to smell **(nach** +*dat* of)

duftend *adj attr* fragrant

dulden ['dʊl·dn̩] *vt* to tolerate

dumm <dümmer, dümmste> ['dʊm] **I.** *adj* **1.** *(geistig beschränkt)* stupid **2.** *(unklug)* foolish; **kein ~er Vorschlag!** not a bad idea! **3.** *(albern)* silly; **etw wird jdm zu ~** sb has had enough of sth **4.** *(ärgerlich: Geschichte, Sache)* unpleasant; **so etwas D~es!** how stupid! **II.** *adv* stupidly; **frag nicht so ~** don't ask such stupid questions ▶ **~** <u>dastehen</u> to look stupid; **jdn für ~** <u>ver-</u><u>kaufen</u> to take sb for a ride

dummerweise *adv* **1.** *(leider)* unfortunately **2.** *(unklugerweise)* stupidly

Dummheit <-, -en> *f* **1.** *kein pl (geringe Intelligenz)* stupidity **2.** *(unkluge Handlung)* foolish action

Dummkopf *m pej* idiot

dumpf ['dʊmpf] *adj* **1.** *(hohl klingend)* dull; *(Geräusch, Ton)* muffled **2.** *(unbestimmt)* vague; *(Gefühl)* sneaking; *(Schmerz)* dull **3.** *(feucht-muffig)* musty; *(Atmosphäre, Luft)* oppressive

Düne <-, -n> ['dy:·nə] *f* dune

Düngemittel *nt* fertilizer

düngen ['dʏŋən] *vt* to fertilize

Dünger <-s, -> *m* fertilizer

dunkel ['dʊŋ·kl̩] **I.** *adj* **1.** (*nicht hell*) dark; (*Ton*) deep **2.** (*unklar: Erinnerung*) vague; **ein dunkles Kapitel** a dark chapter **3.** *pej* (*zwielichtig: Gestalt*) shady ▸ **im D~n tappen** to be groping around in the dark **II.** *adv* **sich** *akk* ~ **an etw** *akk* **erinnern** to remember sth vaguely

dunkelhäutig *adj* dark-skinned

Dunkelheit <-> *f kein pl* darkness

Dunkelziffer *f* number of unreported cases

dünn [dʏn] **I.** *adj* thin; (*Kleidung*) light; (*Strümpfe*) fine **II.** *adv* thinly; ~ **besiedelt** sparsely populated; ~ **gesät** thinly scattered

Dünndarm *m* small intestine

Dunst <-[e]s, Dünste> ['dʊnst] *m* **1.** (*leichter Nebel*) haze; (*durch Abgase*) smog *npl* **2.** (*Dampf*) steam

dünsten ['dʏns·tn̩] *vt* KOCHK to steam

dunstig ['dʊns·tɪç] *adj* METEO hazy

durch ['dʊrç] **I.** *präp* **1.** (*räumlich*) through; ~ **den Fluss waten** to wade across the river; **mitten** ~ **etw** *akk* through the middle of sth **2.** (*vermittels*) by [means of]; ~ **[einen] Zufall** by chance **3.** (*zeitlich*) throughout; **die ganze Nacht** ~ all night long **4.** MATH divided by **II.** *adj pred* **1.** (*durchgetrennt*) through **2.** (*vorbei*) **es ist schon 12 Uhr** ~ it's already past 12 [o'clock]; **der Zug ist vor zwei Minuten** ~ the train left two minutes ago **3.** (*gar, reif: Steak*) well-done; (*Käse*) ripe **4.** (*fertig*) **mit jdm/etw** ~ **sein** to be through with sb/sth

durch|arbeiten ['dʊrç·ʔar·bai·tn̩] **I.** *vt* to go through **II.** *vi* to keep working [until the end]

durch|atmen ['dʊrç·ʔaːt·mən] *vi* to breathe deeply

durchaus ['dʊrç·ʔaus] *adv* ~ **kein schlechtes Angebot** not a bad offer [at all]; **ich bin** ~ **deiner Meinung, aber ...** I completely agree with you, but ...; ~ **möglich sein** to be quite possible; ~ **nicht schlecht sein** to be by no means bad

durch|blicken ['dʊrç·blɪ·kn̩] *vi* **1.** (**durch etw** *akk*) ~ to look through [sth] **2.** (**den**

Überblick haben) to know what's going on **3.** **etw** ~ **lassen** to hint at sth

durch|braten ['dʊrç·braː·tn̩] *irreg vt* **etw** ~ to cook sth until it is well-done

durch|brechen[1] ['dʊrç·brɛ·çn̩] *irreg* **I.** *vt* **haben** to break in two **II.** *vi sein* (*zerbrechen*) to break in two

durchbrechen[*2] [dʊrç·'brɛ·çn̩] *vt irreg* (*Absperrung, Blockade*) to break through

durch|brennen ['dʊrç·brɛ·nən] *irreg vi sein* **1.** ELEK to burn out; (*Sicherung*) to blow **2.** (*weglaufen*) [**jdm**] ~ to run away [from sb]

durch|bringen ['dʊrç·brɪŋən] *vt irreg* **1.** (*finanziell*) to support **2.** (*einen Kranken*) to pull through

Durchbruch ['dʊrç·brʊx] *m* **1.** breakthrough **2.** (*Öffnung*) opening

durch|drehen ['dʊrç·dreː·ən] *vi fam* to crack up

durch|dringen[1] ['dʊrç·drɪŋən] *irreg vi sein* **zu jdm** ~ to make one's way up to sb

durchdringen[*2] [dʊrç·'drɪŋən] *irreg vt* to penetrate

durcheinander [dʊrç·ʔai·'nan·de] *adj, pred* (*in Unordnung*) in a mess; (*verwirrt*) confused

Durcheinander <-s> [dʊrç·ʔai·'nan·de] *nt kein pl* **1.** (*Unordnung*) mess **2.** (*Wirrwarr*) confusion

durcheinander|bringen *vt irreg* **etw** ~ (*in Unordnung bringen*) to mess up *sep* sth; (*verwechseln*) to mix up *sep* sth; **jdn** ~ to confuse sb

durcheinander|reden *vi* to all talk at once

Durchfahrt ['dʊrç·faːɐ̯t] *f* (*das Durchfahren*) ~ **verboten** do not enter; **auf der** ~ **sein** to be passing through

Durchfall ['dʊrç·fal] *m* diarrhea

durch|fallen ['dʊrç·fa·lən] *vi irreg sein* **1.** (*räumlich*) [**durch etw** *akk*] ~ to fall through [sth] **2.** *fig* (*nicht bestehen*) **bei einer Prüfung** ~ to fail an exam

durch|fragen ['dʊrç·fraː·gn̩] *vr* **sich** *akk* ~ to find one's way by asking

durchführbar *adj* feasible

Durchgang ['dʊrç·gaŋ] *m* (*Passage*) path[way]

Durchgangsverkehr m through traffic

durch|geben ['dʊrç·ɡe:·bn̩] vt irreg (Lottozahlen) to read; **eine Meldung ~** to make an announcement

durch|gehen ['dʊrç·ɡe:·ən] irreg vi sein 1. (hindurchgehen) to go through 2. fam (weglaufen) to run off 3. (angenommen werden) to go through; (Antrag, Gesetz) to pass 4. (Pferd) to bolt 5. (gehalten werden) **für etw** akk ~ to pass for sth ▶ **jdm etw ~ lassen** to let sb get away with sth

durchgehend ['dʊrç·ɡe:·ənt] I. adj 1. (nicht unterbrochen) continuous 2. BAHN direct II. adv **„wir haben von 9 - 18 Uhr ~ geöffnet"** "we're open from 9 a.m. - 6 p.m." (not closed for lunch)

durch|greifen ['dʊrç·ɡrai·fn̩] vi irreg (wirksam vorgehen) to take drastic action; **hart ~** to crack down hard

durchgreifend I. adj (Änderung, Maßnahme) drastic II. adv drastically

durch|halten ['dʊrç·hal·tn̩] irreg I. vt 1. (Belastung) to withstand 2. (beibehalten) to keep up sep II. vi to hold out

Durchhänger <-s, -> m **einen [totalen] ~ haben** fam to be on a [real] downer

durch|kämmen[1] ['dʊrç·kɛ·mən] vt (Haar) to comb through sep

durch|kämmen[2] [dʊrç·ˈkɛ·mən] vt to comb (**nach** +dat for)

durch|kommen ['dʊrç·kɔ·mən] vi irreg sein 1. (durchfahren) [**durch etw** akk] ~ to come through [sth] 2. (Sonne) to come through 3. (Charakterzug) to become noticeable 4. (Erfolg haben) **mit etw** dat ~ to get away with sth 5. (durch eine Öffnung) to get through sep 6. (überleben) to pull through

durch|kreuzen * [dʊrç·ˈkrɔy·tsn̩] vt (vereiteln: Plan) to foil

durchlässig ['dʊrç·lɛ·sɪç] adj porous (**für** +akk to)

durch|lesen ['dʊrç·le:·zn̩] vt irreg to read through sep

durch|machen ['dʊrç·ma·xn̩] I. vt (Phase) to go through; (Krankheit) to suffer II. vi fam 1. (feiern) **die ganze Nacht ~** to stay up all night 2. (durcharbeiten)

to keep working [until the end]

Durchmesser <-s, -> ['dʊrç·me·sɐ] m diameter

durch|mogeln vr fam **sich** akk ~ to fake one's way through

durch|nehmen ['dʊrç·ne:·mən] vt irreg SCH to do

durchqueren * [dʊrç·ˈkve:·rən] vt to cross

Durchsage <-, -n> ['dʊrç·za:·ɡə] f announcement

durch|sagen ['dʊrç·za:·ɡn̩] vt to announce

durchschauen *[1] [dʊrç·ˈʃau·ən] vt (jds Absichten erkennen) **jdn ~** to see through sb

durch|schauen[2] ['dʊrç·ʃau·ən] vt s. **durchsehen**

durch|schlagen ['dʊrç·ʃla:·ɡn̩] irreg I. vt **haben** (in two) to split II. vr haben **sich** akk ~ 1. (seine Existenz behaupten) to struggle along 2. (ans Ziel gelangen) to make one's way through

durchschlagend ['dʊrç·ʃla:·ɡnt] adj 1. (überwältigend) sweeping; (Erfolg) huge; **eine ~e Wirkung haben** to be extremely effective 2. (überzeugend) convincing; (Beweis) conclusive

durch|schneiden ['dʊrç·ʃnai·dn̩] vt irreg to cut through

Durchschnitt ['dʊrç·ʃnɪt] m average; **im ~** on average; **über/unter dem ~ liegen** to be above/below average

durchschnittlich ['dʊrç·ʃnɪt·lɪç] I. adj 1. (Mittelwert betreffend) average attr 2. (mittelmäßig) ordinary II. adv 1. (im Schnitt) on average 2. (mäßig) moderately; **~ intelligent** of average intelligence

Durchschnittsgeschwindigkeit f average speed

durch|sehen ['dʊrç·ze:·ən] irreg I. vt **etw ~** to go over sth II. vi **durch etw** akk ~ to look through sth

durch|setzen ['dʊrç·ze·tsn̩] I. vt (Maßnahmen) to impose; (Reformen) to carry out; (Ziel) to achieve; **etw bei jdm ~** to get sb to agree to sth; **seinen Willen [gegen jdn] ~** to get one's own way [with sb] II. vr 1. (sich Geltung verschaffen) **sich** akk ~ to assert oneself;

sich akk **mit etw** dat ~ to be successful with sth **2.** (Gültigkeit erreichen)
sich akk ~ to gain acceptance; (Trend)
to catch on

Durchsicht ['dʊrç·zɪçt] f inspection; **zur**
~ for inspection

durchsichtig ['dʊrç·zɪç·tɪç] adj transparent a. fig; (Bluse, Kleid) see-through

durch|stehen ['dʊrç·ʃteː·ən] vt irreg
to get through; (Qualen) to endure;
(Schwierigkeiten) to cope

durch|streichen ['dʊrç·ʃtraɪ·çn̩] vt irreg
(Fehler, Wort) to cross out sep

durchsuchen * [dʊrç·ˈzuː·xn̩] vt to search
(**nach** +dat for)

Durchsuchung <-, -en> [dʊrç·ˈzuː·xʊŋ]
f search

durchtrieben [dʊrç·ˈtriː·bn̩] adj crafty

durchwachsen [dʊrç·ˈvak·sn̩] adj
1. (Speck) marbled **2.** pred (mittelmäßig) so-so

durchweg ['dʊrç·vɛk] adv without exception

durch|wühlen [1] ['dʊrç·vyː·lən] vr **sich**
akk [**durch etw** akk] ~ to plow through
[sth]

durchwühlen * [2] [dʊrç·ˈvyː·lən] vt (durchstöbern) to comb (**nach** +dat for)

durch|ziehen ['dʊrç·tsiː·ən] irreg **I.** vt
haben 1. (durch eine Öffnung) to
pull through **2.** fam (vollenden) to see
through **II.** vi sein to come through
III. vr haben **sich** akk **durch etw** akk ~
to occur throughout sth

dürfen ['dʏr·fn̩] **I.** modal vb <darf, durfte, dürfen> **1.** (Erlaubnis haben) **etw**
[**nicht**] **tun** ~ to [not] be allowed to do
sth **2.** verneint **wir** ~ **den Zug nicht
verpassen** we can't miss the train; **du
darfst ihm das nicht übel nehmen**
you shouldn't hold that against him
3. im Konjunktiv (sollen) **das/es dürfte
... that/it should ...; es dürfte wohl das
Beste sein, wenn ...** it would probably
be best if ... **II.** vi <darf, durfte, gedurft>
darf ich nach draußen? may I go outside?; **sie hat nicht gedurft** she wasn't
allowed to **III.** vt <darf, durfte, gedurft>
etw ~ to be allowed to do sth; **darfst du
das?** are you allowed to [do that]?

dürftig ['dʏrf·tɪç] **I.** adj **1.** (karg) paltry; (Unterkunft) poor **2.** (schwach)
poor; (Ausrede) feeble; (Kenntnisse)
little **3.** (spärlich: Informationen) spars
II. adv scantily

dürr ['dʏr] adj **1.** (trocken) dry; (Laub)
withered **2.** (mager) [painfully] thin

Dürre <-, -n> ['dʏ·rə] f drought

Durst <-[e]s> ['dʊrst] m kein pl thirst;
haben to be thirsty

durstig ['dʊrs·tɪç] adj thirsty

durstlöschend adj thirst-quenching

Durststrecke f lean period

Dusche <-, -n> ['duː·ʃə] f shower; **unte
die** ~ **gehen** to take a shower

duschen ['duː·ʃn̩] **I.** vi to take a showe
II. vr **sich** akk ~ to take a shower **III.**
jdn ~ to give sb a shower

Duschgel nt body wash

Duschkabine f shower stall

Düse <-, -n> ['dyː·zə] f **1.** TECH nozzl
2. LUFT jet

düsen ['dyː·zn̩] vi sein fam (fahren) **
race; (schnell gehen) to dash

Düsenantrieb m jet propulsion

Düsenflugzeug nt jet plane

dusselig ['dʊ·sə·lɪç] **I.** adj daft **II.** ad
1. (dämlich) **sich** akk ~ **anstellen**
act stupidly **2.** (enorm viel) **sich** akk
arbeiten to work oneself silly

düster ['dyːs·tɐ] adj (Himmel, Wette
gloomy; **eine** ~**e Ahnung** a dark fore
boding; ~**e Gedanken** black thought
eine ~**e Miene** a gloomy face

Dutzend <-s, -e> ['dʊ·tsn̩t] nt dozen

dutzendweise ['dʊ·tsn̩t·vai·zə] adv b
the dozen

dynamisch [dy·ˈnaː·mɪʃ] **I.** adj dynami
II. adv dynamically

Dynamit <-s> [dy·na·ˈmiːt] nt kein
dynamite

Dynastie <-, -n> [dyn·as·ˈtiː] f dynasty

E

E, e <-, -> [eː] nt **1.** (Buchstabe) E, e;
wie Emil E as in Echo **2.** MUS E, e

Ebbe <-, -n> ['ɛbə] f low tide; (Wa.
serstand) low water; ~ **und Flut** th
tides pl

eben¹ ['e:bn̩] **I.** adj **1.** (flach) flat **2.** (glatt) level **II.** adv evenly

eben² ['e:bn̩] **I.** adv **1.** zeitlich just **2.** (nun einmal) just; **das ist ~ so** that's [just] the way it is **3.** (gerade noch) just [about] **4.** (kurz) **mal ~** for a minute **II.** part **1.** (genau das) precisely **2.** (Abschwächung von Verneinung) **das ist nicht ~ billig** that's/it's not exactly cheap

Ebenbild nt image

ebenbürtig ['e:bn̩·byr·tɪç] adj equal (**an** +dat in); **einander [nicht] ~ sein** to be [un]evenly matched

Ebene <-, -n> ['e:bə·nə] f **1.** (Tiefebene) plain; (Hochebene) plateau **2.** MATH, PHYS plane **3.** fig **auf wissenschaftlicher ~** at the scientific level

ebenfalls ['e:bn̩·fals] adv as well; **danke, ~!** thanks, [and the] same to you

ebenso ['e:bn̩·zo:] adv **1.** (genauso) just as; **er schwimmt ~ gern wie ich** he likes to swim just as much as I do; **~ gut/oft/lang(e)** just as well/often/long; **~ sehr/viel** just as much; **~ wenig** just as little **2.** (auch) as well

Eber <-s, -> ['e:bɐ] m boar

ebnen ['e:b·nən] vt to level [off] ▶ **jdm/ etw den Weg ~** to pave the way for sb/sth

EC¹ <-s, -s> [e:'tse:] m Abk von **Eurocity** Eurocity train

EC² <-s, -s> [e:'tse:] m FIN Abk von **Electronic Cash** electronic cash (a debit card system)

Echo <-s, -s> ['ɛço] nt **1.** (Effekt) echo **2.** (Reaktion) response (**auf** +akk to)

Echse <-, -n> ['ɛk·sə] f lizard

echt ['ɛçt] **I.** adj **1.** (nicht künstlich, wirklich) real; (Haarfarbe) natural; (Silber, Gold) pure **2.** (aufrichtig: Freundschaft, Schmerz) sincere **II.** adv **1.** (typisch) typically **2.** fam (wirklich) really

EC-Karte [e:'tse:-] f debit card

Eckball m SPORT corner [kick]

Ecke <-, -n> ['ɛkə] f **1.** (spitze Kante) corner; (Tischkante) edge **2.** (Straßen-, Zimmerecke) corner **3.** fam (Gegend) area **4.** SPORT corner [kick]

eckig ['ɛk·ɪç] adj **1.** (nicht rund) square; (Gesicht) angular **2.** (ungelenk: Bewegungen) jerky

Eckzahn m canine [tooth]

Ecuador <-s> [ekɥa·'do:ɐ̯] nt Ecuador; s. a. **Deutschland**

Ecuadorianer(in) <-s, -> [ekɥa·do·'rja:·nɐ] m(f) Ecuadorian; s. a. **Deutsche(r)**

edel ['e:dl̩] **I.** adj **1.** (großherzig) generous **2.** (hochwertig) fine **3.** (aristokratisch) noble **II.** adv nobly

Edelgas nt inert gas

Edelmetall nt precious metal

edelmütig ['e:dl̩·my:·tɪç] adj magnanimous

Edelstahl m stainless steel

Edelstein m precious stone

Edelweiß <-[es], -e> ['e:dl̩·vais] nt BOT edelweiss

editieren* [edi·'ti:·rən] vt COMPUT to edit

EDV <-> [e:·de:·'fau] f COMPUT Abk von **elektronische Datenverarbeitung** EDP

Efeu <-s> ['e:fɔy] m kein pl ivy

Effekt <-[e]s, -e> [ɛ'fɛkt] m effect

effektiv [ɛfɛk·'ti:f] **I.** adj **1.** (wirksam) effective; attr (tatsächlich) actual attr **II.** adv **1.** (wirksam) effectively **2.** (tatsächlich) actually

EG <-> [e:'ge:] f kein pl hist Abk von **Europäische Gemeinschaft** EC, European Community

egal [e'ga:l] adj **jdm ~ sein** to be all the same to sb; **das ist mir ~** I don't care; (unhöflicher) I couldn't care less; **~, was/wie/wo/warum ...** no matter what/how/where/why ...

Egoist(in) <-en, -en> [ego·'ɪst] m(f) ego[t]ist

egoistisch [ego·'ɪs·tɪʃ] adj ego[t]istical

ehe ['e:ə] konj before; **~ das Wetter nicht besser wird ...** until the weather changes for the better ...

Ehe <-, -n> ['e:ə] f marriage

Ehebruch m adultery

Ehefrau f s. **Ehemann** wife

Ehegatte m geh **1.** s. **Ehemann 2.** pl (Ehepartner) **die ~n** [married] partners pl

Eheleute pl married couple + sing/pl vb

ehelich ['e:ə·lɪç] adj marital; (Kind) legitimate

ehemalig ['e:ɐ·ma:·lɪç] *adj attr* former

Ehemann <-männer> *m* husband

Ehepaar *nt* [married] couple + *sing/pl vb*

eher ['e:ɐ] *adv* 1. (*früher*) sooner 2. (*wahrscheinlicher*) more likely 3. (*mehr*) more 4. (*lieber*) rather

Ehering *m* wedding ring

Eheschließung *f geh* wedding

ehrbar ['e:ɐ·ba:ɐ] *adj* respectable

Ehre <-, -n> ['e:rə] *f* honor; **jdm eine ~ sein** to be an honor for sb; **jdm wird die ~ zuteil, etw zu tun** sb is given the honor of doing sth ▶ **habe die ~!** *österr, südd* (*ich grüße Sie!*) [I'm] pleased to meet you

ehren ['e:r·ən] *vt* to honor

ehrenamtlich ['e:r·ən·?amt·lɪç] I. *adj* ~**e Tätigkeiten** volunteer work II. *adv* on a voluntary basis

Ehrenbürger(in) *m(f)* honorary citizen

Ehrengast *m* guest of honor

Ehrenkodex *m* code of honor

Ehrenplatz *m* place of honor

Ehrensache *f* matter of honor

ehrenvoll *adj* honorable

ehrenwert *adj s.* ehrbar

Ehrenwort <-worte> *nt* word of honor

Ehrfurcht *f kein pl* respect; (*fromme Scheu*) reverence; **vor jdm/etw ~ haben** to have [great] respect for sb/sth

ehrfürchtig ['e:ɐ·fʏrç·tɪç] I. *adj* reverent II. *adv* reverentially

Ehrgefühl *nt kein pl* sense of honor

Ehrgeiz ['e:ɐ·gaits] *m kein pl* ambition

ehrgeizig ['e:ɐ·gai·tsɪç] *adj* ambitious

ehrlich ['e:ɐ·lɪç] I. *adj* honest; ~**e Zuneigung** genuine affection II. *adv* (*legal*) ~ **verdientes Geld** honestly earned money ▶ ~ **gesagt** ... to be [quite] honest ...

Ehrlichkeit *f kein pl* honesty

Ehrwürden <*bei Voranstellung* -[s] *o bei Nachstellung* -> ['e:ɐ·vʏr·dn̩] *m kein pl, kein art* REL Reverend

ehrwürdig ['e:ɐ·vʏr·dɪç] *adj* venerable

Ei <-[e]s, -er> ['ai] *nt* egg; (*Eizelle*) ovum; **ein hart/weich gekochtes ~** a hard-boiled/soft-boiled egg

Eiche <-, -n> ['ai·çə] *f* (*a. Holz*) oak

Eichel <-, -n> ['ai·çl̩] *f* 1. BOT acorn 2. ANAT glans

eichen ['ai·çn̩] *vt* (*Instrument, Messgerät*) to calibrate

Eichhörnchen ['aiç·hœrn·çən] *nt* squirrel

Eid <-[e]s, -e> ['ait] *m* oath; **einen ~ ablegen** to swear an oath

Eidechse ['ai·dɛk·sə] *f* lizard

Eidgenossenschaft *f* **Schweizerische ~** the Swiss Confederation

Eierbecher *m* egg cup

Eierkuchen *m* pancake

Eierschale *f* eggshell

Eierstock *m* ANAT ovary

Eifer <-s> ['ai·fɐ] *m kein pl* enthusiasm ▶ **im ~ des Gefechts** *fam* in the heat of the moment

Eifersucht ['ai·fɐ·zʊxt] *f kein pl* jealousy

eifersüchtig ['ai·fɐ·zʏç·tɪç] *adj* jealous

eifrig ['ai·frɪç] I. *adj* eager; (*Leser, Sammler*) avid II. *adv* eagerly; ~ **lernen** to study hard

Eigelb <-s, -e *o bei Zahlenangaben* -> *nt* egg yolk

eigen ['ai·gn̩] *adj* 1. (*jdm gehörig*) own; **seine ~e Meinung/Wohnung haben** to have one's own opinion/apartment 2. (*separat*) **mit ~em Eingang** with a separate entrance 3. (*typisch*) **mit dem ihr ~en Optimismus** ... with her characteristic optimism ... 4. (*eigenartig*) peculiar

Eigenart ['ai·gn̩·?a:ɐt] *f* characteristic

eigenartig ['ai·gn̩·?a:ɐ·tɪç] *adj* strange

Eigenbedarf *m* **zum ~** for one's [own] personal use

eigenhändig ['aign̩·hɛn·dɪç] I. *adj* personal; (*Brief*) handwritten; (*Testament*) holographic II. *adv* personally

Eigenheim *nt* home of one's own

eigenmächtig ['aign̩·mɛç·tɪç] *adj* highhanded

Eigenname *m* LING proper noun

Eigennutz <-es> *m kein pl* self-interest

eigennützig ['aign̩·nʏ·tsɪç] *adj* selfish

Eigenschaft <-, -en> ['ai·gn̩·ʃaft] *f* 1. (*Charakteristik*) quality; **gute/ schlechte ~en** good/bad qualities 2. (*Funktion*) capacity

Eigenschaftswort <-wörter> *nt* LING adjective

eigensinnig ['ai·gn̩·zɪ·nɪç] *adj* stubborn

eigentlich ['ai·gn̩t·lɪç] I. *adj* 1. (*wirk-*

lich) real; (*Wesen*) true 2. (*ursprünglich*) original II. *adv* actually; **da hast du ~ Recht** you may be right there III. *part* (*überhaupt*) **was ist ~ mit dir los?** what [on earth] is wrong with you?; **wie alt bist du ~?** how old are you anyway?

Eigentor *nt* own goal

Eigentum <-s, *selten* -e> ['ai·gn·tu:m] *nt* property

Eigentümer(in) <-s, -> ['ai·gn·ty:·mɐ] *m(f)* owner

eigentümlich ['ai·gn·ty:m·lɪç] I. *adj* 1. (*merkwürdig*) strange 2. (*typisch*) **jdm/etw ~** characteristic of sb/sth II. *adv* strangely

Eigentumswohnung *f* condominium

eigenwillig ['ai·gn·vɪ·lɪç] *adj* 1. (*eigensinnig*) stubborn 2. (*unkonventionell*) unconventional

eignen ['aig·nən] *vr* **sich** *akk* **für etw** *akk* **~** to be suited to sth

Eilbrief *m* express letter

Eile <-> ['ai·lə] *f kein pl* haste; **etw hat ~** sth is urgent; **in ~ sein** to be in a hurry

eilen ['ai·lən] I. *vi* **etw eilt** sth is urgent II. *vi impers* **es eilt** it's urgent

eilig ['ai·lɪç] I. *adj* 1. (*schnell*) hurried 2. (*dringend*) urgent; **es ~ haben** to be in a hurry II. *adv* quickly

Eilzug *m* BAHN *a type of express train*

Eimer <-s, -> ['ai·mɐ] *m* bucket

ein¹ ['ain] *adv* (*eingeschaltet*) on; **E~/ Aus** *on/off*

ein² ['ain], **eine** ['ai·nə], **ein** ['ain] I. *adj* one; **mir fehlt noch ~ Cent** I need one more cent ► ~ **für alle Mal** once and for all II. *art indef* 1. (*einzeln*) a/an; **was für ~ Lärm!** what a noise! 2. (*jeder*) a/an

einander [ai·'nan·dɐ] *pron* each other

ein|arbeiten I. *vr* **sich** *akk* **[in etw** *akk*] **~** to get used to [sth] II. *vt* 1. (*praktisch vertraut machen*) **jdn [in etw** *akk*] **~** to train sb [for sth] 2. *österr* (*nachholen: Zeitverlust*) to make up [for] sth

Einarbeitungszeit *f* training period

ein|äschern ['ain·ʔɛʃɐn] *vt* (*Leiche*) to cremate

ein|atmen *vt, vi* to breathe in *sep*

Einbahnstraße *f* one-way street

ein|balsamieren * *vt* (*Leiche*) to embalm

Einband <-bände> ['ain·bant] *m* [book] cover

einbändig ['ain·bɛn·dɪç] *adj* (*Buch*) one-volume *attr*

Einbau <-bauten> *m kein pl* installation

ein|bauen *vt* 1. (*installieren*) **etw [in etw** *akk*] **~** to build sth in[to] sth; (*Batterie, Motor*) to install sth in[to] sth 2. *fam* (*einfügen*) to incorporate sth [into sth]

Einbauküche *f* fitted kitchen

Einbauschrank *m* built-in cupboard; (*im Schlafzimmer*) built-in closet

ein|berufen * *vt irreg* 1. (*Versammlung*) to convene 2. MIL to draft

Einberufung *f* 1. (*einer Versammlung*) convention 2. MIL draft card

ein|betten *vt* to embed

ein|beziehen * *vt irreg* to include

ein|biegen *vi irreg sein* to turn (**in** +*akk* into)

ein|bilden *vr* 1. (*glauben*) **sich** *dat* **etw ~** to imagine sth; **sich** *dat* **~, dass ...** to think that ...; **was bildest du dir eigentlich ein?** *fam* what has gotten into your head? 2. (*stolz sein*) **sich** *dat* **etw auf etw** *akk* **~** to be proud of sth

Einbildung *f kein pl* 1. (*Fantasie*) imagination 2. (*Arroganz*) conceitedness

Einbildungskraft *f kein pl* [powers of] imagination

ein|blenden *vt* to insert; (*Geräusche, Musik*) to dub in

Einblick *m* insight; **~ in etw** *akk* **haben** to have insight into sth

ein|brechen *irreg vi* 1. *sein o haben* (*Einbruch verüben*) to break in 2. *sein* (*Dämmerung, Nacht*) to fall 3. *sein* (*einstürzen*) to cave in

Einbrecher(in) <-s, -> *m(f)* burglar

ein|bringen *irreg* I. *vt* 1. (*Ernte*) to bring in 2. (*finanziell*) to bring; **Zinsen ~** to earn interest 3. **seine Erfahrung ~** to bring one's experience to sth II. *vr* **sich** *akk* **~** to contribute

Einbruch <-[e]s, -brüche> ['ain·brʊx] *m* 1. JUR break-in 2. (*einer Mauer etc.*) collapse 3. (*plötzlicher Beginn*) onset; **bei**

~ der Dunkelheit at nightfall

ein|bürgern ['ain·byr·gən] I. *vt* ADMIN **jdn ~** to naturalize sb II. *vr* **sich** *akk* **~** (*Gewohnheiten etc.*) to become the habit (**bei** +*dat* with)

ein|checken [-ˌt∫ɛkn] I. *vi* to check in II. *vt* to check in *sep*

ein|cremen ['ain·kreː·mən] *vt* **sich** *dat* **etw ~** to put cream on sth

ein|decken *vr* **sich** *akk* **[mit etw** *dat*] **~** to stock up [on sth]

eindeutig ['ain·dɔy·tɪç] I. *adj* 1. (*unmissverständlich*) unambiguous 2. (*unzweifelhaft*) clear II. *adv* 1. (*unmissverständlich*) unambiguously 2. (*klar*) clearly

ein|dicken ['ain·dɪkn̩] I. *vt haben* KOCHK to thicken II. *vi sein* to thicken

ein|dringen *vi irreg sein* **in etw** *akk* **~** to force one's way into sth; MIL to penetrate [into] sth

Eindringling <-s, -e> ['ain·drɪŋ·lɪŋ] *m* intruder

Eindruck <-[e]s, -drücke> ['ain·drʊk] *m* (*Vorstellung*) impression; **den ~ erwecken/haben, dass ...** to give/have the impression that ...

eindrucksvoll *adj* impressive

eine(r, s) ['ai·nə] *pron indef* 1. (*jemand*) someone, somebody; **~s von den Kindern** one of the children 2. *fam* (*man*) one; **und das soll noch ~r glauben?** and I'm expected to swallow that? 3. (*ein Punkt*) **~s** one thing

eineiig ['ain·?ai·ɪç] *adj* BIOL identical

eineinhalb ['ain·?ain·'halp] *adj* one and a half

ein|engen ['ain·ɛŋ·ən] *vt* to restrict

einer ['ai·nɐ] *pron s.* **eine(r, s)**

einerlei ['ai·nə·'lai] *adj pred* (*egal*) **das ist mir ganz ~** it's all the same to me

einerseits ['ai·nɐ·zaits] *adv* **~ ... andererseits ...** on the one hand ..., on the other hand ...

einfach ['ain·fax] I. *adj* 1. (*leicht*) easy 2. (*gewöhnlich*) simple 3. **eine ~e Fahrkarte** a one-way ticket II. *adv* (*leicht*) easily; **~ zu verstehen** easy to understand III. *part* simply; just; **das geht ~ nicht!** we/you just can't do that!

ein|fädeln ['ain·fɛː·d|n̩] I. *vt* 1. (*Faden*) to thread 2. *fam* (*anbahnen*) to engineer *fig* II. *vr* AUTO **sich** *akk* **~** to merge

ein|fahren *irreg* I. *vi sein* **in etw** *akk* **~** to pull in to sth; **auf einem Gleis ~** to arrive on a platform II. *vt haben* 1. (*Antenne, Objektiv*) to retract 2. (*Gewinne*) to make 3. (*Heu, Korn*) to harvest

Einfahrt <-, -en> *f* 1. *kein pl* (*das Einfahren*) entry; (*eines Zuges*) arrival 2. (*Zufahrt*) entrance; (*Auffahrt*) driveway

Einfall ['ain·fal] *m* 1. (*Idee*) idea 2. MIL invasion (**in** +*akk* of)

ein|fallen *vi irreg sein* 1. (*in den Sinn kommen*) **etw fällt jdm ein** sth occurs to sb 2. (*in Erinnerung kommen*) **etw fällt jdm ein** sb remembers sth 3. (*einstürzen*) to collapse 4. MIL **in ein Land ~** to invade a country 5. (*Wangen*) to become hollow

einfallslos *adj* unimaginative

einfältig ['ain·fɛl·tɪç] *adj* naive

Einfaltspinsel *m pej fam* simpleton

Einfamilienhaus *nt* single-family house

ein|fangen *irreg* I. *vt* **jdn/ein Tier [wieder] ~** to [re]capture sb/an animal II. *vr fam* **sich** *dat* **etw ~** to catch sth

einfarbig *adj* in one color

ein|fassen *vt* (*Edelstein, Diamant*) to set

ein|finden *vr irreg* **sich** *akk* **[irgendwo] ~** to arrive [somewhere]

ein|flößen *vt* 1. (*langsam eingeben*) **jdm etw ~** to give sb sth 2. (*erwecken*) **jdm Angst/Vertrauen ~** to instill fear/confidence in sb

Einflugschneise *f* approach [path]

Einfluss [RR], **Einfluß** [ALT] <-flusses, -flüsse> ['ain·flʊs] *m* influence; **auf jdn/etw ~ haben** to have an influence on sb/sth

einflussreich [RR] *adj* influential

einförmig ['ain·fœr·mɪç] I. *adj* monotonous; (*Landschaft*) uniform II. *adv* monotonously

ein|frieren *irreg vt* 1. (*konservieren*) to [deep-]freeze 2. (*suspendieren*) to suspend; (*Projekt*) to shelve 3. ÖKON to freeze

ein|fügen I. *vt* **etw [in etw** *akk*] **~** to fit sth in[to sth] II. *vr* **sich** *akk* **[in etw**

akk] ~ **1.** *(sich anpassen)* to adapt [oneself] [to sth] **2.** *(hineinpassen)* to fit in [with sth]

Einfühlungsvermögen *nt* empathy

Einfuhr <-, -en> ['aɪn·fuːɐ̯] *f* importation

Einfuhrbestimmungen *pl* import regulations *pl*

ein|führen *vt* **1.** *(importieren)* to import **2.** *(bekannt machen)* to introduce; *(Artikel, Firma)* to establish **3.** *(vertraut machen)* **jdn** ~ to introduce sb (*in +akk* to) **4.** *(hineinschieben)* to insert (*in +akk* into)

Einführung *f* introduction

Einführungspreis *m* introductory price

Einfuhrzoll *m* import duty

Eingabe <-, -en> *f* **1.** *(Petition)* petition (*bei +dat* to) **2.** *kein pl (von Daten, Informationen)* entry

Eingabetaste *f* COMPUT enter key

Eingang <-[e]s, -gänge> ['aɪn·gaŋ] *m* **1.** *(Zugang)* entrance; „**kein ~!**" "no entry" **2.** *kein pl (Erhalt)* receipt

ein|geben *irreg vt* **1.** COMPUT **Daten** ~ to input data (*in +akk* into) **2.** **jdm etw** ~ *(Medizin)* to administer sth to sb

eingebildet *adj* **1.** *pej (hochmütig)* conceited **2.** *(imaginär)* imaginary

Eingeborene(r) *f(m)* native

Eingebung <-, -en> *f* *(Inspiration)* inspiration

eingefallen *adj* hollow; *(Gesicht)* gaunt

ein|gehen *irreg* **I.** *vi sein* **1.** *(sich beschäftigen mit)* **auf etw** *akk* ~ to deal with sth; **auf jdn** ~ to pay attention to sb **2.** *(zustimmen)* **auf etw** *akk* ~ to agree to sth; *(sich einlassen)* to accept sth **3.** **in die Geschichte** ~ to go down in history **4.** *(/ab/sterben)* to die (*an +dat* of); *(Laden)* to go bust *fam* **II.** *vt sein* **ein Risiko** ~ to take a risk; **ich gehe jede Wette ein, dass ...** I'll bet you anything that ...

eingehend ['aɪn·geː·ənt] **I.** *adj* detailed; *(Prüfung)* extensive **II.** *adv* in detail

Eingemachte(s) *nt dekl wie adj* KOCHK preserved fruit

eingeschnappt *adj fam* miffed

eingeschrieben *adj* registered

Eingeständnis ['aɪn·gə·ʃtɛnt·nɪs] *nt* admission

ein|gestehen * *irreg* **I.** *vt* to admit **II.** *vr* **sich** *dat* ~, **dass ...** to admit to oneself that ...

eingestellt *adj* **1.** *(gesinnt)* **fortschrittlich/ökologisch** ~ progressively/environmentally minded; **jd ist gegen jdn** ~ sb is set against sb **2.** *(vorbereitet)* **auf etw** *akk* ~ **sein** to be prepared for sth

eingetragen *adj* *(Mitglied, Verein, Warenzeichen)* registered

Eingeweide <-s, -> ['aɪn·gə·vai·də] *nt meist pl* entrails *npl*

ein|gewöhnen * *vr* **sich** *akk* ~ to acclimatize

ein|gießen *vt irreg* s. **einschenken**

eingleisig ['aɪn·glai·zɪç] *adj* single-track

ein|gliedern **I.** *vt* **1.** *(integrieren)* **jdn** ~ to integrate sb (*in +akk* into) **2.** ADMIN, POL *(einbeziehen)* **etw** ~ to incorporate sth (*in +akk* into) **II.** *vr* **sich** *akk* ~ to integrate oneself (*in +akk* into)

ein|greifen *vi irreg* to intervene

Eingriff *m* **1.** *(Einschreiten)* intervention **2.** MED operation

Einhalt ['aɪn·halt] *m kein pl* **jdm/etw** ~ **gebieten** to put a stop to sb/sth

ein|halten *irreg vt* **eine Diät** ~ to stick to a diet; **einen Vertrag** ~ to honor [the terms of] a contract; **die Spielregeln/Vorschriften** ~ to obey the rules

ein|handeln *vr fam* **sich** *dat* **eine Krankheit** ~ to catch a disease

einheimisch ['aɪn·hai·mɪʃ] *adj* **1.** *(ortsansässig)* local **2.** BOT, ZOOL indigenous

Einheit <-, -en> ['aɪn·hait] *f* unity; **Tag der deutschen** ~ Day of German Unity

einheitlich ['aɪn·hait·lɪç] **I.** *adj* **1.** *(gleich)* uniform **2.** *(in sich geschlossen)* integrated; *(Front)* united **II.** *adv* ~ **gekleidet** dressed the same

ein|heizen *vi (gründlich heizen)* to turn the heat on

ein|holen *vt* **1.** *(einziehen)* to pull in *sep; (Fahne, Segel)* to lower **2.** *(Genehmigung)* to ask for **3.** *(erreichen, nachholen)* **jdn/etw** ~ to catch up with sb/sth

einig ['ai·nɪç] *adj pred (einer Meinung)* **sich** *dat* [**über etw** *akk*] ~ **sein** to agree [on sth]

einige(r, s) ['ai·nɪ·gə] *pron indef* **1.** *sing, adjektivisch (etwas)* some; **nach ~r Zeit** after some time **2.** *sing, substantivisch (viel)* **~s** quite a lot **3.** *pl, adjektivisch (mehrere)* several; **vor ~n Tagen** a few days ago **4.** *pl, substantivisch (mehrere)* some; **~ von euch** some of you; **~ wenige** a few

einigen ['ai·nɪgn̩] *vr* **sich** *akk* **~** to agree (**auf** *+akk* on)

einigermaßen ['ai·nɪ·gɐ·'maː·sn̩] *adv* **1.** (*ziemlich*) fairly **2.** (*leidlich*) all right

Einigkeit <-> ['ai·nɪç·kait] *f kein pl* **1.** (*Eintracht*) unity **2.** (*Übereinstimmung*) agreement

Einigung <-, -en> *f* **1.** POL unification **2.** (*Übereinstimmung*) agreement (**über** *+akk* on)

einimpfen *vt* **jdm etw ~** to drum sth into sb

einjährig, 1-jährig RR ['ain·jɛː·rɪç] *adj* **1.** (*Alter*) one-year-old *attr,* one year old *pred; s. a.* **achtjährig 1 2.** BOT annual **3.** (*Zeitspanne*) one-year *attr,* [of] one year *pred; s. a.* **achtjährig 2**

einkalkulieren* *vt* **etw** [**mit**] **~** to take sth into account

einkassieren* *vt* **1.** (*kassieren*) to collect **2.** *fam* (*wegnehmen*) to confiscate

Einkauf *m* **1.** (*das Einkaufen*) shopping; **beim ~ von Lebensmitteln ...** when buying food ... **2.** (*gekaufte Ware*) purchase

einkaufen **I.** *vt* to buy **II.** *vi* **~ gehen** to go shopping **III.** *vr* (*einen Anteil erwerben*) **sich** *akk* **in etw** *akk* **~** to buy [one's way] into sth

Einkaufsbummel *m* shopping trip

Einkaufspassage [-pa·sa:··ʒə] *f* galleria

Einkaufswagen *m* shopping cart

Einkaufszentrum *nt* shopping mall

einkehren *vi sein veraltend* to stop off (**in** *+dat* at)

einklammern *vt* LING to put in parentheses

Einklang *m* harmony

einklemmen *vt* **1.** (*quetschen*) to trap **2.** (*festdrücken*) to clamp

einkochen KOCHK **I.** *vt haben* to preserve **II.** *vi sein* to thicken

Einkommen <-s, -> *nt* income

einladen *irreg vt* **1.** (*zu Hochzeit, Party*) to invite (**zu** *+dat* to) **2.** (*Gegenstände*) to load (**in** *+akk* in[to])

Einladung *f* invitation

Einlage <-, -n> *f* **1.** FIN (*Bankguthaben*) deposit **2.** (*für Schuhe*) insole

einlagern *vt* to store

Einlass RR, **Einlaß** ALT <-lasses, -lässe> ['ain·las] *m* admission

einlassen *irreg* **I.** *vt* **1.** (*hereinlassen*) **jdn ~** to let sb in **2.** (*einlaufen lassen*) **jdm ein Bad ~** to run sb a bath **II.** *v* **1.** (*auf etwas eingehen*) **sich** *akk* **au etw** *akk* **~** to get involved in sth; (*au Abenteuer*) to embark on sth; (*auf Kompromiss*) to accept sth **2.** *bes pej* (*Kontakt aufnehmen*) **sich** *akk* **mit jdm ~** to get involved with sb

einlaufen *irreg* **I.** *vi sein* **1.** (*Kleidung*) to shrink **2.** (*Badewasser*) to run **3.** SPORT **als Erster ~** to come in first **II.** *vt haben* **Schuhe ~** to wear shoes in

einleben *vr* **sich** *akk* **~** to settle in

einlegen *vt* **1.** AUTO **den zweiten Gang ~** to shift into second [gear] **2.** KOCHK **etw** [**in etw** *dat o akk*] **~** to pickle sth [in sth] **3.** **eine Pause ~** to take a break

einleiten *vt* **1.** (*in die Wege leiten*) to introduce; **Schritte** [**gegen jdn**] **~** to take steps [against sb] **2.** MED to induce **3.** ÖKON **Abwässer in einen Fluss ~** to discharge effluent into a river

einleitend **I.** *adj* introductory **II.** *adv* as an introduction

Einleitung *f* (*a. Vorwort*) introduction; (*eines Verfahrens*) institution; (*einer Untersuchung*) opening

einlenken *vi* (*nachgeben*) to give in

einleuchten *vi* to make sense

einleuchtend **I.** *adj* evident; (*Argument*) convincing; (*Erklärung*) plausible **II.** *adv* clearly

einliefern *vt* **jdn ins Krankenhaus ~** to admit sb to the hospital; **jdn ins Gefängnis ~** to send sb to prison

einloggen ['ain·lɔ·gn̩] *vr* **sich** *akk* **~** to log in

einlösen *vt* **1.** (*Scheck*) to cash **2.** (*Pfand*) to redeem (**bei** *+dat* at) **3.** (*Versprechen*) to honor

ein|machen vt to preserve; (in Essig) to pickle sth

Einmachglas nt [preserving] jar

einmal¹, 1-mal RR ['ain·ma:l] adv once; ~ **am Tag/in der Woche** once a day/ week; **es war** ~ once upon a time; **irgendwann** ~ sometime ▶ **auf** ~ (plötzlich) all of a sudden; (an einem Stück) all at once; ~ **ist keinmal** prov just once doesn't matter

einmal² ['ain·ma:l] part 1. (eben) **so liegen die Dinge nun** ~ that's [just] the way things are 2. (einschränkend) **nicht** ~ not even

Einmaleins <-> [ain·ma:l·'?ains] nt kein pl **das** ~ multiplication tables pl

einmalig ['ain·ma:·lɪç] adj 1. (nicht nochmals: Chance, Gelegenheit) unique; (Zahlung) one-off 2. fam (ausgezeichnet) outstanding

Einmischung f interference

einmotorig adj single-engine

einmütig ['ain·my:·tɪç] adj unanimous

Einnahme <-, -n> ['ain·na:·mə] f 1. FIN earnings npl; (bei einem Geschäft) receipts npl 2. kein pl (von Arzneimitteln, Mahlzeiten) taking

ein|nehmen vt irreg 1. (Geld) to take; (Steuern) to collect 2. (zu sich nehmen) to take; (Mahlzeit) to have 3. (Platz) to take 4. (Raum) to take up 5. (Standpunkt) to hold 6. (erobern) to take 7. **jdn für sich** akk ~ to win favor with sb

einnehmend ['ain·ne:·mənt] adj engaging

ein|nicken vi sein fam to doze off

ein|nisten vr sich akk ~ 1. (sich niederlassen) to ensconce oneself (**bei** +dat with) 2. (Ungeziefer) to nest

Einöde ['ain·?ø:də] f wasteland

ein|ordnen I. vt 1. (einsortieren) **etw** ~ to organize sth 2. (klassifizieren) **jdn/etw** ~ to classify sb/sth II. vr TRANSP **sich** akk **links/rechts** ~ to merge [to the] left/right

ein|packen vt 1. (verpacken) to wrap; (zum Verschicken) to pack 2. fam (einmummeln) **jdn** ~ to wrap sb up

ein|parken vt, vi to park; (am Straßenrand) to parallel park

ein|planen vt to plan; **etw [mit]** ~ to take sth into consideration

ein|prägen I. vr 1. **sich** dat **etw** ~ to make a mental note of sth 2. **sich** akk **jdm** ~ (Bilder, Eindrücke, Worte) to be imprinted on sb's memory II. vt **jdm etw** ~ to drum sth into sb's head

einprägsam ['ain·prɛ:k·za:m] adj easy to remember pred; (Melodie) catchy

ein|rahmen vt to frame

ein|räumen vt 1. (hineintun) to place 2. (gewähren) **jdm etw** ~ (Frist, Kredit) to give sb sth

ein|rechnen vt to include

ein|reden I. vt **jdm etw** ~ to talk sb into thinking sth II. vi (bedrängen) **auf jdn** ~ to pester sb fam III. vr **sich** dat **etw** ~ to talk oneself into thinking sth

ein|reichen vt to submit

ein|reihen I. vt **jdn/etw unter etw** akk ~ to classify sb/sth under sth II. vr **sich** akk **in etw** akk ~ to join sth

Einreise f entry [into a country]

Einreisegenehmigung f entry permit

ein|reisen vi sein to enter

ein|renken ['ain·rɛŋ·kn̩] I. vt 1. MED **[jdm] etw** ~ to pop sth back in [place] [for sb] 2. fam (bereinigen) **etw [wieder]** ~ to straighten sth out sep II. vr **fam** (ins Lot kommen) **sich** akk **wieder** ~ to sort itself out

ein|richten I. vt 1. (möblieren) to furnish; (Praxis) to equip 2. (gründen) to set up sep 3. (Konto) to open 4. (arrangieren) **es** ~, **dass ...** arrange it so that ... 5. (vorbereitet sein) **auf etw** akk **eingerichtet sein** to be prepared for sth II. vr 1. (mit Möbeln) **ich richte mich völlig neu ein** I'm completely refurnishing my home 2. (sich einstellen) **sich** akk **auf etw** akk ~ to be prepared for sth

Einrichtung <-, -en> f 1. (Möbel) furnishings npl; (Ausstattung) decorations npl 2. (das Möblieren) furnishing; (das Ausstatten) decorating 3. (das Installieren) installation 4. FIN (eines Kontos) opening 5. (Institution) organization

eins ['ains] I. adj one; s. a. **acht¹** ▶ ~ **A** fam first-class II. adj pred ~ **mit jdm/ sich/etw sein** to be [at] one with sb/ oneself/sth

einsam ['ain·za:m] *adj* 1. (*verlassen*) lonesome; (*Leben*) solitary 2. (*abgelegen*) isolated 3. (*menschenleer*) deserted ▶ **das war ~e Spitze!** it was absolutely fantastic!

ein|sammeln *vt* to collect

Einsatz <-es, Einsätze> *m* 1. (*beim Spiel*) bet 2. (*Verwendung*) use; (*von Truppen*) deployment 3. **im ~ sein** to be on duty 4. (*eingesetzte Leistung*) effort; **unter ~ ihres Lebens** by putting her own life at risk

einsatzbereit *adj* ready for use *pred*; (*Menschen*) ready for action; MIL ready for combat *pred*

ein|schalten I. *vt* 1. (*Gerät, Licht*) to switch on *sep* 2. (*hinzuziehen*) **jdn ~** to call in *sep* sb II. *vr sich akk* [**in etw** *akk*] **~** 1. RADIO, TV to tune in[to sth] 2. (*sich einmischen*) to intervene [in sth]

Einschaltquote *f* [audience] ratings *npl*

ein|schärfen *vt* **jdm etw ~** to impress on sb the importance of sth II. *vr sich dat* **etw ~** to remember sth

ein|schätzen *vt* to assess; **Sie haben ihn richtig eingeschätzt** your opinion of him was right

ein|schenken *vt* **jdm etw ~** to pour sb sth

ein|schiffen *vr sich akk* **~** to embark

ein|schlafen *vi irreg sein* to fall asleep

ein|schläfern ['ain·ʃlɛ:·fən] *vt a.* euph to put to sleep

einschläfernd ['ain·ʃlɛ:·fənt] *adj* MED **ein ~es Mittel** a sleep-inducing drug

ein|schlagen *irreg* I. *vt haben* 1. (*mit Gewalt*) **eine Tür ~** to break down *sep* a door; **jdm die Zähne ~** to knock sb's teeth out 2. (*wählen: Laufbahn, Weg*) to choose II. *vi* 1. *sein o haben* [**in etw** *akk*] **~** (*Blitz*) to strike [sth] 2. *sein* (*Granaten*) to fall 3. *haben* (*einprügeln*) **auf jdn ~** to hit sb 4. *haben* (*Anklang finden*) to catch on

ein|schließen *vt irreg* 1. (*in einen Raum*) **jdn ~** to lock up *sep* sb 2. (*wegschließen*) **etw ~** to lock away *sep* sth 3. (*einbeziehen*) **jdn ~** to include sb 4. (*einkesseln*) **jdn/etw ~** to surround sb/sth

einschließlich ['ain·ʃli:s·lɪç] I. *präp ~*

einer S. *gen* including sth II. *adv* inclusive

ein|schmeicheln *vr* **sich** *akk* [**bei jdm**] **~** to ingratiate oneself [with sb]

ein|schnappen *vi sein* 1. (*Tür*) to click shut 2. *fam* (*beleidigt sein*) to get in a huff

einschneidend ['ain·ʃnai·dnt] *adj* **eine ~e Veränderung** a drastic change

Einschnitt *m* 1. MED incision 2. (*geschichtlich*) turning point

ein|schränken ['ain·ʃrɛŋ·kŋ] I. *vt* 1. (*reduzieren*) to cut [back on] 2. (*beschränken*) to curb II. *vr sich akk* **~** to cut back (**in** +*dat* on)

Einschränkung <-, -en> *f* **ohne ~en** (*in vollem Umfang*) without restrictions (*ohne Vorbehalt*) without reservations

ein|schreiben *irreg vr* SCH, UNI **sich** *akk* **~** to register

Einschreiben *nt* registered letter

ein|schreiten *vi irreg sein* to take action

ein|schüchtern ['ain·ʃʏç·tɐn] *vt* **jdn ~** to intimidate sb

ein|schweißen *vt* (*Bücher, Nahrungsmittel*) to seal

ein|sehen *vt irreg* **~, dass ...** to see that ...

einseitig ['ain·zai·tɪç] I. *adj* 1. MED (*Lähmung*) one-sided 2. (*unausgewogen. Ernährung*) unbalanced 3. (*voreingenommen: Sicht*) bias[s]ed II. *adv* 1. MED (*gelähmt*) on one side 2. (*unausgewogen*) **sich** *akk* **~ ernähren** to have an unbalanced diet 3. (*parteiisch*) from a one-sided point of view

ein|senden *vt irreg* to send (**an** +*akk* to)

Einsendeschluss ᴿᴿ *m* deadline [for entries]

einsetzbar *adj* applicable

ein|setzen I. *vt* 1. (*einfügen*) to insert 2. (*Kommission*) to set up 3. (*zum Einsatz bringen*) to use; SPORT to put in *sep* II. *vi* (*beginnen*) to start III. *vr sich akk* **~** to make an effort; **sich** *akk* **für jdn/ etw ~** to support sb/sth

Einsicht *f* 1. (*Vernunft*) sense; (*Erkenntnis*) insight; **jdn zur ~ bringen** to make sb see reason 2. (*in Akten, Unterlagen*) **~ in etw** *akk* **nehmen** to inspect sth

einsichtig ['ain·zɪç·tɪç] *adj* 1. (*verständ-*

lich: Argument) understandable **2.** (*vernünftig: Person*) reasonable

einsilbig [ˈain·zɪl·bɪç] *adj* (*a. ling*) monosyllabic

ein|spannen *vt* **1.** (*in einen Schraubstock*) to clamp **2.** (*Tiere*) to harness **3. jdn [für etw** *akk*] ~ to call sb in [for sth]; **sehr eingespannt sein** to be very busy

ein|sperren *vt* to lock up *sep*

ein|spielen I. *vr* **1. sich** *akk* ~ (*Methode, Regelung*) to get going; **sich** *akk* **aufeinander** ~ to get used to each other **2.** SPORT **sich** *akk* ~ to warm up **II.** *vt* FILM to bring in *sep*

ein|springen *vi irreg sein fam* **1.** (*vertreten*) [**für jdn**] ~ to cover [for sb] **2.** (*aushelfen*) [**mit etw** *dat*] ~ to help out [with sth]

Einspruch *m* (*a. jur*) objection

einspurig [ˈain·ʃpuː·rɪç] **I.** *adj* **1.** TRANSP one-lane **2.** *pej* **~es Denken** one-track mind **II.** *adv* TRANSP **die Straße ist nur ~ befahrbar** only one lane of the road is open [to traffic]

einst [ˈainst] *adv* **1.** (*früher*) once **2.** (*in der Zukunft*) one day

Einstand *m* **1.** (*Arbeitsanfang*) start of a new job **2.** TENNIS deuce

ein|stecken *vt* **1.** (*Geld, Schlüssel*) to put in one's pocket **2.** (*Brief*) to mail **3.** *fam* (*hinnehmen*) **etw** ~ to put up with sth **4.** ELEK to plug in *sep*

ein|stehen *vi irreg sein* **1.** (*sich verbürgen*) **für jdn/etw** ~ to vouch for sb/sth **2.** (*aufkommen*) **für etw** *akk* ~ to take responsibility for sth

ein|steigen *vi irreg sein* [**in etw** *akk*] ~ **1.** (*besteigen: Auto*) to get in [sth]; (*Bus, Flugzeug*) to get on [sth] **2.** *fam* (*hineinklettern*) to climb in[to sth] **3.** ÖKON to buy into sth **4.** (*sich engagieren*) to get involved [in sth]

ein|stellen I. *vt* **1.** (*anstellen*) to employ **2.** (*beenden*) to stop; (*Suche*) to call off; (*Projekt*) to shelve **3.** MIL to stop; **das Feuer** ~ to cease fire **4.** JUR to abandon **5.** FOTO, TECH to adjust **6.** TV, RADIO to tune **7.** SPORT **den Rekord** ~ to tie the record **II.** *vr* **1.** (*auftreten*) **sich** *akk* ~ (*Bedenken*) to begin; MED (*Fieber, Sym-*

ptome) to develop **2.** (*sich anpassen*) **sich** *akk* **auf jdn/etw** ~ to adapt to sb/sth **3.** (*sich vorbereiten*) **sich** *akk* **auf etw** *akk* ~ to prepare oneself for sth

Einstellung *f* **1.** (*Gesinnung*) attitude **2.** (*Anstellung*) employment **3.** (*Beendigung*) stopping **4.** FOTO adjustment **5.** FILM take **6.** TV, RADIO tuning

Einsturz *m* collapse; (*einer Decke a.*) cave-in; (*einer Mauer*) falling-down

ein|stürzen *vi sein* **1.** (*zusammenbrechen*) to collapse; (*Decke a.*) to cave in **2.** *fig* **auf jdn** ~ to overwhelm sb

einstweilig [ˈainst·ˈvai·lɪç] *adj attr* JUR **~e Verfügung** temporary restraining order

eintägig, 1-tägigRR *adj* one-day *attr*, lasting one day *pred*

Eintagsfliege *f* ZOOL mayfly ▶ **eine ~ sein** to be here today gone tomorrow

ein|tauchen I. *vt haben* to dip sth **II.** *vi sein* [**in etw** *akk*] ~ to dive in[to sth]

ein|teilen *vt* **1.** (*unterteilen*) **etw in etw** *akk* ~ to divide sth up into sth **2.** [**sich** *dat*] **etw** ~ (*Geld, Vorräte, Zeit*) to be careful with sth **3.** (*zu Tätigkeit*) **jdn zu etw** *dat* ~ to assign sb to sth

Einteilung *f* **1.** (*von Vorräten, Zeit*) management **2.** (*Verpflichtung*) **jds ~ zu etw** *dat* sb's assignment to sth

eintönig [ˈain·tø·nɪç] **I.** *adj* monotonous **II.** *adv* monotonously; **~ klingen** to sound monotonous

Eintopf *m* stew

einträchtig [ˈain·trɛç·tɪç] *adj* harmonious

Eintrag <-[e]s, Einträge> [ˈain·traːk] *m* **1.** (*Vermerk*) note **2.** (*im Nachschlagewerk*) entry **3.** ADMIN record

ein|tragen *vt irreg* **1.** (*einschreiben*) **jdn** ~ to record sb's name **2.** (*amtlich registrieren*) to register **3.** (*einzeichnen*) **etw** ~ to note sth [down]

ein|treffen *vi irreg sein* **1.** (*ankommen*) to arrive **2.** (*in Erfüllung gehen*) to come true; (*Ereignis, Katastrophe*) to happen

ein|treiben *vt irreg* **etw [von jdm]** ~ to collect sth [from sb]

ein|treten *irreg* **I.** *vi* **1.** *sein* (*betreten*) to enter **2.** *sein* (*beitreten: in Partei, Verein*) to join **3.** *sein* (*sich ereignen*) to occur; **sollte der Fall ~, dass ...** if

it should happen when ... **4.** *sein* (*sich einsetzen*) **für jdn/etw ~** to stand up for sb/sth **5.** *haben* (*wiederholt treten*) **auf jdn/ein Tier ~** to kick sb/an animal [repeatedly] **II.** *vt haben* **eine Tür ~** to kick in *sep* a door

Eintritt *m* **1.** (*Beitritt*) **jds ~ in etw** *akk* sb's joining sth **2.** (*Eintrittsgeld*) admission **3.** (*das Betreten*) **~ verboten** do not enter

Eintrittskarte *f* [admission] ticket

ein|üben *vt* to practice; (*Rolle, Stück*) to rehearse

ein|verleiben * ['ain·fɛɐ̯·lai·bn̩] *vr* **sich** *dat* **etw ~** ÖKON to incorporate sth **2.** *hum fam* (*verzehren*) to put sth away

Einvernehmen <-s> *nt kein pl* agreement

einverstanden ['ain·fɛɐ̯·ʃtan·dn̩] *adj pred* **~ sein** to agree

Einverständnis ['ain·fɛɐ̯·ʃtɛnt·nɪs] *nt* **sein ~ geben** to give one's consent; **in beiderseitigem ~** by mutual agreement

Einwand <-[e]s, Einwände> ['ain·vant] *m* objection (**gegen** +*akk* to)

Einwanderer, -wand[r]erin *m, f* immigrant

ein|wandern *vi sein* to immigrate

einwandfrei ['ain·vant·frai] *adj* **1.** (*tadellos*) flawless; (*Obst*) perfect; (*Qualität*) excellent; (*Benehmen*) impeccable **2.** (*unzweifelhaft*) irrefutable

Einwegflasche *f* nonreturnable bottle

ein|weichen *vt* to soak sth

ein|weihen *vt* **1.** (*offiziell eröffnen*) **etw ~** to open sth [officially] **2.** (*informieren*) **jdn ~** to initiate sb (**in** +*akk* into)

ein|weisen *vt irreg* **1.** (*unterweisen*) **jdn ~** to brief sb (**in** +*akk* about) **2.** MED to refer

ein|wenden *vt irreg* **etw** [**gegen etw** *akk*] **~** to object [to sth]

ein|werfen *irreg vt* **1.** (*Brief*) to mail **2.** (*Fenster*) to break **3.** SPORT to throw in *sep* **4.** (*Bemerkung*) to throw in *sep*

ein|wickeln *vt* **1.** (*in etwas wickeln*) to wrap [up *sep*] **2.** *fam* (*überlisten*) **jdn ~** to take sb in

ein|willigen ['ain·vɪ·lɪ·gn̩] *vi* to consent (**in** +*akk* to)

ein|wirken *vi* **auf jdn/etw ~** to have an effect on sb/sth

Einwohner(in) <-s, -> ['ain·voː·nɐ] *m/f* inhabitant

Einwohnermeldeamt *nt* ≈ Town Clerk['s Office]

Einwurf *m* **1.** (*von Münzen*) insertion (*von Brief*) mailing **2.** (*beim Fußball*) throw-in **3.** (*Zwischenbemerkung*) interjection

Einzahl ['ain·tsaːl] *f* LING singular

ein|zahlen *vt* to pay [in]

Einzahlung *f* FIN deposit

Einzelfahrschein *m* one-way ticket

Einzelgänger(in) <-s, -> *m(f)* (*Mensch Tier*) loner

Einzelhaft *f* solitary confinement

Einzelhandel *m* retail trade

Einzelhändler(in) *m(f)* retailer

Einzelheit <-, -en> *f* detail

Einzelkind *nt* only child

einzeln ['ain·tsl̩n] **I.** *adj* **1.** (*für sich allein*) individual **2.** (*Detail*) **im E~en** in detail **3.** (*individuell*) individual **jede(r, s)** E~e each [and every] individual **4.** (*alleinstehend*) single **5.** *pl* (*einige wenige*) a few; **~e Schauer** METEO scattered showers **II.** *adv* separately

Einzelteil *nt* separate part

Einzelzimmer *nt* single room

ein|ziehen *irreg* **I.** *vt haben* **1.** (*Beiträge, Gelder*) to collect **2.** (*beschlagnahmen*) to take away *sep* **3.** MIL **jdn** [**zum Militär**] **~** to draft sb [into the army] **4.** (*zurückziehen*) to draw in *sep*; (*Antenne, Periskop*) to retract; **den Kopf ~** to duck one's head **5.** BAU **eine Wand ~** to put in *sep* a wall **II.** *vi sein* **1.** (*in eine Wohnung*) **bei jdm ~** to move in with sb **2.** SPORT, MIL (*einmarschieren*) **in etw** *akk* **~** to march into sth **3.** (*Flüssigkeit*) to soak

einzig ['ain·tsɪç] **I.** *adj* **1.** *attr* only **2.** (*alleinige*) **der/die** E~e the only one; **das** E~e the only thing **II.** *adv* only

einzigartig ['ain·tsɪç·ʔaːɐ̯·tɪç] **I.** *ad* unique **II.** *adv* astoundingly

Eis <-es> ['ais] *nt kein pl* ice; (*Eiscreme*) ice cream

Eisbahn *f* SPORT skating rink

Eisbär *m* polar bear

Eisbecher *m* **1.** (*Behälter*) [ice-cream

carton **2.** (*Eiscreme*) sundae

Eisberg *m* GEOG iceberg

Eisbrecher *m* NAUT icebreaker

Eiscreme [-kre:m] *f* ice cream

Eisdiele *f* ice cream parlor

Eisen <-s, -> ['aizn] *nt kein pl* iron

Eisenbahn ['ai·zn·ba:n] *f* train

Eisenbahner(in) <-s, -> *m(f) fam* railroad employee

Eisenbahnwagen *m* (*Personenwagen*) passenger car; (*Güterwaggon*) freight car

eisern ['ai·zɐn] **I.** *adj* iron **II.** *adv* resolutely

eisgekühlt *adj* ice-cold

Eisglätte *f* black ice

Eishockey *nt* ice hockey

eisig ['ai·zɪç] **I.** *adj* **1.** (*bitterkalt*) icy **2.** (*abweisend*) icy; (*Schweigen*) frosty **3.** (*jäh*) chilling; **ein ~er Schreck durchfuhr sie** a cold shiver ran through her [body] **II.** *adv* coolly

eiskalt ['ais·kalt] **I.** *adj* **1.** ice-cold **2.** *fig* cold-blooded **II.** *adv fig* coolly

Eiskunstlauf *m* figure skating

eis|laufen *vi irreg sein* to ice-skate

Eisprung *m* ovulation

Eiswürfel *m* ice cube

Eiszapfen *m* icicle

Eiszeit *f* Ice Age

eitel ['ai·tl] *adj* vain

Eitelkeit <-, -en> ['ai·tl̩·kait] *f* vanity

Eiter <-s> ['ai·tɐ] *m kein pl* pus

eitern ['ai·tɐn] *vi* to fester

Eiweiß ['ai·vais] *nt* **1.** CHEM protein **2.** KOCHK egg white

Eizelle *f* ovum

Ekel[1] <-s> ['e:kl̩] *m kein pl* disgust; **~ erregend** revolting

Ekel[2] <-s, -> ['e:kl̩] *nt fam* disgusting person

ekelhaft *adj* disgusting

ekeln ['e:kl̩n] **I.** *vt* **jdn ~** to disgust sb **II.** *vt impers* **es ekelt mich vor diesem Geruch** this smell is disgusting **III.** *vr* **sich** *akk* **vor etw** *dat* **~** to find sth disgusting

eklig <-er, -ste> ['e:k·lɪç] *adj s.* **ekelhaft**

Ekstase <-, -n> [ɛk·'sta:·zə] *f* ecstasy

Ekzem <-s, -e> [ɛk·'tse:m] *nt* eczema

elastisch [e'las·tɪʃ] *adj* **1.** (*Binde, Stoff*)

stretchy **2.** (*Gelenk, Muskel, Mensch*) supple; (*Gang*) springy

Elch <-[e]s, -e> ['ɛlç] *m* elk

Elefant <-en, -en> [ele·'fant] *m* elephant

elegant [ele·'gant] *adj* elegant

Elektriker(in) <-s, -> [e'lɛk·tri·kɐ] *m(f)* electrician

elektrisch [e'lɛk·trɪʃ] *adj* electric; **~e Geräte** electrical appliances

elektrisieren* [elɛk·tri·'zi:·rən] *vt* to electrify

Elektrizität <-> [elɛk·tri·tsi·'tɛːt] *f kein pl* electricity

Elektrizitätswerk *nt* [electric] power plant

Elektroherd [e'lɛk·tro·heːɐt] *m* electric stove

Elektromotor [e'lɛk·tro·,mo:·to:ɐ] *m* electric motor

Elektron <-s, -tronen> [elɛk·'tro:n] *nt* electron

Elektronenmikroskop *nt* electron microscope

Elektronik <-, -en> [elɛk·'tro:·nɪk] *f kein pl* electronics + *sing vb*

elektronisch [elɛk·'tro:·nɪʃ] **I.** *adj* electronic **II.** *adv* electronically

Elektrorasierer *m* electric razor

Elektrotechnik [elɛk·tro·'tɛç·nɪk] *f* electrical engineering

Element <-[e]s, -e> [ele·'mɛnt] *nt* element

elend ['e:lɛnt] *adj* **1.** (*beklagenswert*) miserable **2.** (*krank*) wretched **3.** (*erbärmlich*) dreadful **4.** (*gemein*) miserable

Elend <-[e]s> ['e:lɛnt] *nt kein pl* misery

Elendsviertel *nt* slum

elf ['ɛlf] *adj* eleven; *s. a.* **acht**[1]

Elf <-, -en> ['ɛlf] *f* **1.** (*Zahl*) eleven **2.** FBALL team, eleven

Elfe <-, -n> ['ɛl·fə] *f* elf

Elfenbein ['ɛl·fn̩·bain] *nt* ivory

Elfenbeinküste *f* Ivory Coast

Elfmeter [ɛlf·'me:·tɐ] *m* penalty kick; **einen ~ schießen** to take a penalty kick

elfte(r, s) ['ɛlf·tə] *adj* **1.** (*Zahl*) eleventh; *s. a.* **achte(r, s) 1 2.** (*Datum*) eleventh, 11th; *s. a.* **achte(r, s) 2**

elitär [eli·'tɛːɐ] *adj* elitist

E

Elite <-, -n> [e'liː·tə] f elite

Elixier <-s, -e> [eliˈksiːɐ̯] nt elixir

Ellipse <-, -n> [ɛˈlɪp·sə] f MATH ellipse; LING ellipsis

El Salvador <-s> [ɛl zalˈva·ˈdoːɐ̯] nt El Salvador; *s. a.* **Deutschland**

Elsass RR, **Elsaß** ALT <-> [ˈɛl·zas] nt das ~ Alsace

Elsässer(in) <-s, -> [ˈɛlzɛ·sɐ] m(f) inhabitant of Alsace

elsässisch [ˈɛl·zɛ·sɪʃ] adj 1. GEOG Alsatian 2. LING Alsatian

Elster <-, -n> [ˈɛl·stɐ] f magpie

Eltern [ˈɛl·tɐn] pl parents pl

E-Mail <-, -s> [ˈiː·meːl] f e-mail

Emanzipation <-, -en> [eman·tsi·pa·ˈtsi̯oːn] f emancipation

emanzipieren * [eman·tsi·ˈpiː·rən] vr sich akk ~ to emancipate oneself

Embargo <-s, -s> [ɛm·ˈbar·go] nt embargo

Embryo <-s, -s> [ˈɛm·bryo] m o österr nt embryo

Emigrant(in) <-en, -en> [emi·ˈgrant] m(f) emigrant

emigrieren * [emi·ˈgriː·rən] vi sein to emigrate

Emission <-, -en> [emɪ·ˈsi̯oːn] f emission

Emotion <-, -en> [emo·ˈtsi̯oːn] f emotion

emotional [emo·tsi̯o·ˈnaːl] adj emotional

empfahl [ɛm·ˈpfaːl] imp von **empfehlen**

empfand [ɛm·ˈpfant] imp von **empfinden**

Empfang <-[e]s, Empfänge> [ɛm·ˈpfaŋ] m 1. *kein pl* (*das Entgegennehmen*) receipt 2. (*Begrüßung*) reception 3. *kein pl* TV, RADIO reception 4. (*Hotelrezeption*) reception [desk]

empfangen <empfing, empfangen> [ɛm·ˈpfaŋən] vt 1. RADIO, TV to receive 2. (*begrüßen*) jdn mit etw dat ~ to receive sb with sth

Empfänger(in) <-s, -> [ɛm·ˈpfɛŋɐ] m(f) 1. (*Adressat*) addressee 2. FIN payee

Empfänger <-s, -> [ɛm·ˈpfɛŋɐ] m RADIO, TV receiver

empfänglich [ɛm·ˈpfɛŋ·lɪç] adj für etw akk ~ sein 1. (*zugänglich*) to be receptive to sth 2. (*beeinflussbar, anfällig*) to

be susceptible to sth

Empfängnis <-, -se> [ɛm·ˈpfɛŋ·nɪs] f *pl selten* conception

Empfängnisverhütung f contraception

Empfangsbestätigung f [confirmation of] receipt

Empfangsdame f receptionist

empfehlen <empfahl, empfohlen> [ɛm·ˈpfeː·lən] I. vt [jdm] etw ~ to recommend sth [to sb] II. vr impers es empfiehlt sich, etw zu tun it is advisable to do sth

empfehlenswert adj 1. (*wert, empfohlen zu werden*) recommendable 2. (*ratsam*) es ist ~, etw zu tun it is advisable to do sth

Empfehlung <-, -en> f recommendation; **auf ~ von** jdm on the recommendation of sb; **mit den besten ~en** with best regards

empfinden <empfand, empfunden> [ɛm·ˈpfɪn·dn̩] vt to feel

empfindlich [ɛm·ˈpfɪnt·lɪç] I. adj sensitive (**gegen** +akk to); (*Gesundheit*) delicate; ~ **gegen Kälte** sensitive to cold II. adv **auf etw** akk ~ **reagieren** to be very sensitive to sth

empfindsam [ɛm·ˈpfɪnt·zaːm] adj, *ao* sensitive; (*einfühlsam*) empathetic

empfing [ɛm·ˈpfɪŋ] imp von **empfangen**

empfunden [ɛm·ˈpfʊn·dn̩] pp von **empfinden**

emporarbeiten vr sich akk ~ to work one's way up

Empore <-, -n> [ɛm·ˈpoː·rə] f gallery

empören * [ɛm·ˈpø·rən] I. vt jdn ~ to fill sb with indignation II. vr sich akk ~ to be outraged

empörend adj outrageous

empört I. adj scandalized (**über** +akk by) II. adv indignantly

emsig [ˈɛm·zɪç] I. adj busy II. adv industriously; **überall wird** ~ **gebaut** they are busy building everywhere

Ende <-s, -n> [ˈɛn·də] nt 1. (*Schluss*) end; ~ **August/des Monats/~ 2007** the end of August/the month/2007; ~ **20 sein** to be in one's late 20s; **damit muss es jetzt ein** ~ **haben** this must stop now; **etw** dat **ein** ~ **machen** to

put an end to sth; **das nimmt gar kein ~** there's no end to it; **am ~** *fam* finally; **etw zu ~ bringen** to complete sth; **zu ~ sein** to be finished **2.** FILM, LIT ending **3.** (*räumliches Ende*) end ▸ ► **~ gut, alles gut** *prov* all's well that ends well

Endeffekt ['ɛnt-ʔɛfɛkt] *m* **im ~** in the end

enden ['ɛn-dn̩] *vi* **1.** *haben* to end **2.** *haben* LING **auf etw** *akk* **~** to end with sth **3.** *sein fam* (*irgendwo landen*) to end up

Endergebnis *nt* final result

endgültig I. *adj* final; (*Antwort*) definitive **II.** *adv* finally

Endhaltestelle *f* terminal stop

Endlager *nt* ÖKOL permanent disposal site

endlich ['ɛnt-lɪç] **I.** *adv* **1.** (*nunmehr*) at last; **lass mich ~ in Ruhe!** just leave me alone already! **2.** (*schließlich*) finally; **na ~!** *fam* at last! **II.** *adj* ASTRON, MATH finite

endlos I. *adj* endless **II.** *adv* interminably

Endspurt *m* final spurt

Endstation *f* terminus, end of the line, final stop

Endung <-, -en> *f* ending

Endverbraucher(in) *m(f)* end-user

Energie <-, -n> [enɛr-ˈgiː] *f* energy

Energiebedarf *m* energy requirement[s]

Energiegewinnung *f kein pl* energy generation

Energieverbrauch *m* energy consumption

Energieversorgung *f* energy supply

energisch [e'nɛr-gɪʃ] **I.** *adj* **1.** (*Tatkraft ausdrückend*) energetic **2.** (*entschlossen*) firm **II.** *adv* vigorously

eng ['ɛŋ] **I.** *adj* **1.** (*schmal*) narrow **2.** (*knapp sitzend*) tight **3.** (*beengt*) cramped **4.** (*wenig Zwischenraum habend*) close together *pred* **5.** (*intim*) close **6.** (*eingeschränkt*) limited; **im ~eren Sinn** in the stricter sense **II.** *adv* **1.** (*knapp*) **ein ~ anliegendes Kleid** a close-fitting dress **2.** (*dicht*) densely; **~ nebeneinanderstehen** to stand close to each other **3.** (*intim*) closely; **~ befreundet sein** to be close friends **4.** (*akribisch*) **etw zu ~ sehen** to take too narrow a view of sth

Engagement <-s, -s> [āga-ʒə-ˈmãː] *nt* **1.** (*Eintreten*) commitment (**für** +*akk* to) **2.** THEAT engagement

engagieren* [āga-ˈʒiːr-ən] **I.** *vt* **jdn ~** to engage sb **II.** *vr* **sich** *akk* **[für jdn/etw] ~** to be committed [to sb/sth]

engagiert [āga-ˈʒiːrt] *adj* **politisch/sozial ~** politically/socially engaged

Enge <-, -n> ['ɛŋə] *f* **1.** (*schmale Beschaffenheit*) narrowness **2.** *kein pl* (*Beschränktheit*) confinement

Engel <-s, -> ['ɛŋl̩] *m* angel

England <-s> ['ɛŋ-lant] *nt* **1.** (*Teil Großbritanniens*) England **2.** (*falsch für Großbritannien*) Great Britain; *s. a.* **Deutschland**

Engländer(in) <-s, -> ['ɛŋ-lɛn-dɐ] *m(f)* Englishman *masc*, Englishwoman *fem*; **die ~** the English

englisch ['ɛŋ-lɪʃ] *adj* English; *s. a.* **deutsch**

Englisch ['ɛŋ-lɪʃ] *nt dekl wie adj* English; *s. a.* **Deutsch**

Engpass RR *m* **1.** GEOG [narrow] pass **2.** (*Fahrbahnverengung*) bottleneck **3.** (*Verknappung*) bottleneck

engstirnig ['ɛŋ-ʃtɪr-nɪç] *adj* narrow-minded

Enkel(in) <-s, -> ['ɛŋ-kl̩] *m(f)* grandchild

enorm [e'nɔrm] **I.** *adj* enormous; (*Summe*) vast **II.** *adv fam* tremendously; **~ viel/viele** an enormous amount/number

Ensemble <-s, -s> [ā-ˈsãː-bl̩] *nt* ensemble

entbehren* [ɛnt-ˈbeː-rən] *vt* **jdn/etw ~ können** to be able to do without sb/sth

Entbindung *f* delivery

entblößen* [ɛnt-ˈbløː-sn̩] *vt* **sich** *akk* **~** to take one's clothes off

entdecken* *vt* **1.** (*zum ersten Mal finden*) to discover **2.** (*ausfindig machen*) to find; (*Fehler*) to spot

Entdecker(in) <-s, -> [ɛnt-ˈdɛ-kɐ] *m(f)* discoverer

Entdeckung *f* discovery

Entdeckungsreise *f* voyage of discovery

Ente <-, -n> ['ɛn-tə] *f* **1.** ORN duck **2.** *fam*

(*Zeitungsente*) canard ► **lahme** ~ *fam* slowpoke

ent|**eignen*** *vt* jdn ~ to dispossess sb

ent|**erben*** *vt* jdn ~ to disinherit sb

ent|**fachen*** [ɛnt·'fa·çn̩] *vt* 1. (*Feuer*) to kindle; (*Brand*) to start 2. (*entfesseln*) to provoke; (*Leidenschaft*) to arouse

ent|**falten*** I. *vt* (*Fähigkeiten, Kräfte*) to develop II. *vr* 1. (*sich öffnen*) sich *akk* [zu etw *dat*] ~ (*Blüte, Fallschirm*) to open [into sth] 2. (*sich voll entwickeln*) sich *akk* ~ to fully develop

Entfaltung <-, -en> *f* (*Entwicklung*) development

ent|**fernen*** [ɛnt·'fɛr·nən] I. *vt* 1. (*beseitigen*) to remove (aus/von +*dat* from) 2. MED jdm den Blinddarm ~ to take out *sep* sb's appendix 3. (*weit abbringen*) jdn von etw *dat* ~ to take sb away from sth II. *vr* 1. (*weggehen*) sich *akk* ~ to go away (von/aus +*dat* from); sich *akk* vom Weg ~ to go off the path 2. (*nicht bei etwas bleiben*) sich *akk* von etw *dat* ~ to depart from sth

ent|**fernt** I. *adj* 1. (*Verwandte*) distant 2. (*gering: Ähnlichkeit*) slight; (*Ahnung*) vague 3. (*weit weg*) remote 4. weit davon ~ sein, etw zu tun to not have the slightest intention of doing sth II. *adv* vaguely

Entfernung <-, -en> *f* 1. (*Distanz*) distance 2. ADMIN (*Ausschluss*) removal

ent|**fremden*** [ɛnt·'frɛm·dn̩] I. *vt* to estrange; etw seinem Zweck ~ to use sth for a different purpose; (*falscher Zweck*) to use sth for the wrong purpose II. *vr* sich *akk* jdm ~ to become estranged from sb

ent|**führen*** *vt* (*Person*) to abduct; (*Fahrzeug, Flugzeug*) to hijack

Entführer(in) *m(f)* kidnapper; (*eines Fahrzeugs/Flugzeugs*) hijacker

Entführung *f* kidnapping; (*eines Fahrzeugs/Flugzeugs*) hijacking

ent|**gegen** [ɛnt·'ge:·gn̩] I. *adv* toward II. *präp* against

ent|**gegen**|**gehen** *vi irreg sein* jdm ~ to go to meet sb

ent|**gegengesetzt** [ɛnt·'ge:·gn̩·gə·zɛtst] I. *adj* 1. (*gegenüberliegend*) opposite 2. (*einander widersprechend*) oppos-

ing; (*Auffassungen*) conflicting II. *adv* ~ denken/handeln to think/do the exact opposite

ent|**gegen**|**halten** *vt irreg* 1. jdm die Hand ~ to hold out one's hand to sb 2. *fig* (*gegenüberstellen*) ~, dass .... to counter that ...

ent|**gegen**|**kommen** [ɛnt·'ge:·gn̩·kɔ·mən] *vi irreg sein* 1. (*in jds Richtung kommen*) jdm ~ to come [over] to meet sb 2. (*Zugeständnisse machen*) jdm/etw ~ to accommodate sb/sth 3. (*entsprechen*) jds Plänen ~ to fit in sb's plans

Entgegenkommen <-s, -> [ɛnt·'ge:·gn̩·kɔ·mən] *nt kein pl* cooperation

ent|**gegenkommend** *adj* obliging

ent|**gegen**|**treten** *vi irreg sein* 1. (*in den Weg treten*) jdm ~ to walk up to sb 2. (*sich zur Wehr setzen*) etw *dat* ~ to counter sth

ent|**gegnen*** [ɛnt·'ge:g·nən] *vt* to reply

ent|**gehen*** *vi irreg sein* 1. (*entkommen*) jdm/etw ~ to escape sb/sth 2. (*nicht bemerkt werden*) etw entgeht jdm sth escapes sb['s notice] 3. (*versäumen*) sich *dat* etw ~ lassen to miss sth

Entgelt <-[e]s, -e> [ɛnt·'gɛlt] *nt* 1. (*Bezahlung*) payment; (*Entschädigung*) compensation 2. (*Gebühr*) gegen ~ for a fee

ent|**gleisen*** [ɛnt·'glaizn̩] *vi sein* 1. (*Zug*) to derail 2. *fig* (*ausfallend werden*) to make a gaffe

ent|**gleiten*** *vi irreg sein* 1. (*aus den Händen*) etw entgleitet jdm sth loses his/her grip on sth 2. (*verloren gehen*) jdm ~ to slip away from sb

ent|**halten*** *irreg* I. *vt* 1. (*in sich haben*) to contain 2. (*einschließen*) Frühstück im Preis ~ breakfast included II. *vr* sich *akk* ~ POL to abstain

ent|**haltsam** [ɛnt·'halt·za:m] *adj* abstinent

ent|**heben*** *vt irreg geh* jdn eines Amtes ~ to relieve sb of a position

Enthüllung <-, -en> *f* 1. (*Aufdeckung*) disclosure; (*von Lüge, Skandal*) exposure 2. (*das Enthüllen: von Denkmal, Gesicht*) unveiling

ent|**husiastisch** *adj* enthusiastic

entkoffeiniert [ɛntˈkɔ·fei·ˈniːɐ̯t] adj decaffeinated

entkommen * vi irreg sein to escape

Entkommen <-s> nt kein pl escape

entkräften * [ɛntˈkrɛf·tn̩] vt 1. (kraftlos machen) jdn ~ (durch Anstrengung) to weaken sb; (durch Krankheit) to debilitate sb form 2. (widerlegen) etw ~ to refute sth

entladen * irreg I. vt 1. (Ladung) to unload 2. ELEK to drain II. vr sich akk ~ 1. (zum Ausbruch kommen: Gewitter, Sturm) to break 2. ELEK (Akku, Batterie) to run down 3. fig (plötzlich ausbrechen: Begeisterung, Zorn etc.) to be vented

entlang [ɛntˈlaŋ] I. präp (längs) along; **den Fluss** ~ along the river II. adv **an etw** dat ~ along sth

entlarven * [ɛntˈlar·fn̩] vt (Dieb, Spion) to expose

entlassen * vt irreg 1. (kündigen) jdn ~ to dismiss sb 2. MED, MIL to discharge sb 3. (entbinden) jdn aus etw dat ~ to release sb from sth

entlasten * vt 1. JUR jdn (von etw dat) ~ to clear sb [of sth] 2. (von Belastung befreien) jdn ~ to relieve sb

Entlastung <-, -en> f 1. JUR exoneration 2. (das Entlasten) relief

entlaufen [*1] vi irreg sein to run away

entlaufen [²] adj (entflohen) escaped; (weggelaufen) on the run pred

entledigen * [ɛntˈleː·dɪ·gn̩] vr sich akk einer S. gen ~ 1. (ablegen) to put down sep sth; (Kleidungsstück) to remove sth 2. (loswerden) to get rid of sth

entlegen [ɛntˈleː·gn̩] adj remote

entmachten * [ɛntˈmax·tn̩] vt to disempower

entmutigen * [ɛntˈmuː·tɪ·gn̩] vt to discourage

entnehmen * vt irreg 1. (herausnehmen) [etw dat] etw ~ to take sth [from sth] 2. MED jdm etw ~ to take sth from sb 3. fig (aus etwas schließen) aus etw dat ~, dass ... to gather from sth that ...

entpuppen * [ɛntˈpʊ·pn̩] vr fig (sich enthüllen) sich akk [als ...] ~ to turn out to be ...

entreißen * vt irreg 1. (wegreißen) jdm

etw ~ to snatch sth [away] from sb 2. (retten) jdn etw dat ~ to rescue sb from sth

entrümpeln * vt to clear out sep

entrüsten * I. vt (empören) jdn ~ to make sb indignant; (stärker) to outrage sb II. vr (sich empören) sich akk über jdn/etw ~ to be indignant about sb/sth; (stärker) to be outraged by sb/sth

entrüstet I. adj indignant (über +akk about/at) II. adv indignantly

Entschädigung f compensation

entschärfen * vt a. fig to defuse

entscheiden * irreg I. vt to decide; (gerichtlich) to rule II. vi to decide (über +akk on); für/gegen jdn/etw ~ to decide in favor/against sb/sth; (gerichtlich) to rule in favor/against sb/sth III. vr sich [dazu] ~, etw zu tun to decide [to do sth]

entscheidend [ɛntˈʃai·dn̩t] adj decisive; **für jdn/etw ~ sein** to be crucial for sb/sth

Entscheidung f 1. (Beschluss) decision; **eine ~ treffen** to make a decision 2. JUR ruling

entschieden [ɛntˈʃiː·dn̩] I. pp von **entscheiden** II. adj 1. (entschlossen) resolute 2. (eindeutig) definite III. adv 1. (entschlossen) etw ~ ablehnen to categorically reject sth 2. (eindeutig) **diesmal bist du ~ zu weit gegangen** this time you've definitely gone too far

entschließen * vr irreg sich akk [zu etw dat] ~ to decide [on sth]

entschlossen [ɛntˈʃlɔ·sn̩] I. pp von **entschließen** II. adj determined III. adv resolutely

Entschluss [RR], **Entschluß** [ALT] <-schlusses, -schlüsse> [ɛntˈʃlʊs] m decision

entschuldbar [ɛntˈʃʊlt·baːɐ̯] adj excusable

entschuldigen * [ɛntˈʃʊl·dɪ·gn̩] I. vi (als Höflichkeitsformel) ~ Sie excuse me II. vr sich akk ~ 1. (um Verzeihung bitten) to apologize 2. (eine Abwesenheit begründen) to ask to be excused III. vt 1. (als verzeihlich begründen) etw mit etw dat ~ to use sth as an excuse for sth 2. (eine Abwesenheit begründen) jdn bei jdm ~ to ask sb to excuse sb 3. (als

verständlich erscheinen lassen **etw ~** to excuse sth

Entschuldigung <-, -en> *f* **1.** (*Bitte um Verzeihung*) apology **2.** (*Begründung, Rechtfertigung*) **als ~ für etw** *akk* as an excuse for sth **3.** (*als Höflichkeitsformel*) **~!** sorry! **4.** SCH note

ent|setzen* **I.** *vt* (*in Grauen versetzen*) **jdn ~** to horrify sb **II.** *vr* (*die Fassung verlieren*) **sich** *akk* **~** to be horrified (**über** +*akk* at/about)

Entsetzen <-s> *nt kein pl* horror; **mit ~** horrified; **voller ~** filled with horror

entsetzlich [ɛnt·'zɛts·lɪç] **I.** *adj* **1.** (*schrecklich*) horrible **2.** *fam* (*sehr stark*) terrible **II.** *adv* terribly

entsetzt I. *adj* horrified **II.** *adv* (*großes Entsetzen zeigend*) **sie schrie ~ auf** she let out a horrified scream

ent|spannen* **I.** *vr* **sich** *akk* **~** to relax; (*pol a.*) to ease **II.** *vt* **1.** (*lockern*) **etw ~** to relax sth **2.** ÖKON, POL **die Situation ~** to ease the situation

Entspannung *f* **1.** (*innerliche Ruhe*) relaxation **2.** POL easing of tension

ent|sprechen* *vi irreg* **etw** *dat* **~ 1.** (*übereinstimmen mit*) to correspond to sth **2.** (*genügen*) **den Anforderungen ~** to fulfill the requirements

entsprechend [ɛnt·'ʃprɛ·çnt] **I.** *adj* (*angemessen*) appropriate **II.** *präp* in accordance with

ent|stehen* *vi irreg sein* [**aus etw** *dat*/ **durch etw** *akk*] **~ 1.** (*zu existieren beginnen*) to come into being [from sth] **2.** (*verursacht werden*) to arise [from sth] **3.** CHEM (*sich bilden*) to be produced [from/through sth]

Entstehung <-, -en> *f* creation; (*des Lebens*) origin; (*eines Gebäudes*) construction

ent|stellen* *vt* **1.** (*verunstalten*) to disfigure; **jds Gesicht ~** to disfigure sb's face; **der Schmerz entstellte ihre Züge** her features were contorted with pain **2.** (*verzerren*) **etw entstellt wiedergeben** to distort sth

ent|täuschen* **I.** *vt* **1.** (*Erwartungen nicht erfüllen*) **jdn ~** to disappoint sb **2.** (*nicht entsprechen*) **jds Hoffnungen ~** to dash sb's hopes **II.** *vi* (*enttäuschend*

sein) to be disappointing

enttäuscht I. *adj* disappointed (**über** +*akk* about, **von** +*dat* by) **II.** *adv* disappointedly

Enttäuschung *f* disappointment

entwaffnend I. *adj* disarming **II.** *adv* disarmingly

Entwarnung *f* all clear

ent|wässern* *vt* **1.** AGR, BAU to drain **2.** MED to dehydrate

entweder [ɛnt·'ve:·də] *konj* **~ ... oder ...** either...or

ent|werfen* *vt irreg* **1.** (*designen*) to design **2.** (*im Entwurf erstellen*) to draft

ent|wickeln* **I.** *vt* to develop **II.** *vr* **sich** *akk* [**zu etw** *dat*] **~** to develop [into sth]; **na, wie entwickelt sich euer Projekt?** well, how is your project coming along?

Entwicklung <-, -en> *f* **1.** (*das Entwickeln, Foto*) development **2.** (*das Vorankommen*) progression **3.** ÖKON, POL trend

Entwicklungshelfer(in) *m(f)* development aid worker

Entwicklungshilfe *f* development aid

Entwicklungsland *nt* developing country

Entwurf *m* **1.** (*Skizze*) sketch **2.** (*Design*) design **3.** (*Konzept*) draft

ent|ziehen* *irreg* **I.** *vt* **jdm etw ~** to withdraw sth from sb **II.** *vr* **1. sich** *akk* **jdm/etw ~** to evade sb/sth **2. sich** *akk* **etw** *dat* **~: das entzieht sich meiner Kenntnis** that's beyond my knowledge

Entziehungskur *f* treatment for an addiction

ent|ziffern* [ɛnt·'tsɪ·fɐn] *vt* to decipher

ent|zücken* *vt* **jdn ~** to delight sb

Entzücken <-s> *nt kein pl* delight; [**über etw** *akk*] **in ~ geraten** to be ecstatic [about sth]

entzückend [ɛnt·'tsʏ·knt] *adj* delightful

Entzug <-[e]s> *m kein pl* **1.** ADMIN revocation **2.** MED withdrawal; **auf ~ sein** *sl* to go [through] cold turkey **3.**

Entzugserscheinungen *pl* withdrawal symptoms

ent|zünden* *vr* **sich** *akk* **~ 1.** MED to become infected **2.** (*in Brand geraten*) to catch fire

entzündet adj MED infected

Entzündung f MED (eines Gelenks) inflammation

entzwei [ɛnt-'tsvai] adj pred in two [pieces]; (zersprungen) broken

entzwei|**gehen** vi irreg sein to break [in two]

Enzian <-s, -e> ['ɛn·tsi̯·a:n] m 1. BOT gentian 2. (Schnaps) spirit distilled from the roots of gentian

Enzyklopädie <-, -n> [ɛn·tsy·klo·pɛ·'di:] f encyclopedia

Enzym <-s, -e> [ɛn·'tsy:m] nt enzyme

Epidemie <-, -n> [epi·de·'mi:] f epidemic

Epilepsie <-, -n> [epi·lɛ·'psi:] f epilepsy

Epileptiker(in) <-s, -> [epi'lɛp·ti·kɐ] m(f) epileptic

Epoche <-, -n> [e'pɔ·xə] f epoch

Epos <-, Epen> ['e:pɔs] nt epic

er <gen seiner, dat ihm, akk ihn> ['eːɐ̯] pron pers he; **sie ist ein Jahr jünger als** ~ she is a year younger than him

Erachten <-s> [ɛg·'ʔax·tn̩] nt kein pl **meines ~s** in my opinion

Erbanlagen pl hereditary factors

er|**barmen** * [ɛg·'bar·mən] vr **sich** akk **jds/einer S.** ~ to take pity on sb/sth

Erbarmen <-s> [ɛg·'bar·mən] nt kein pl pity; ~ **mit jdm** [**haben**] [to have] pity for sb; **ohne** ~ merciless[ly]

erbärmlich [ɛg·'bɛrm·lɪç] I. adj pej 1. fam (gemein) miserable 2. (jämmerlich: Aussehen, Zustand) wretched II. adv pej 1. (gemein) **sich** akk ~ **verhalten** to behave abominably 2. fam (furchtbar) ~ **kalt** terribly cold

erbarmungslos [ɛg·'bar·mʊŋs·lo:s] adj merciless

er|**bauen** * I. vt 1. (errichten) to build 2. fam (begeistert sein) [**von etw** dat] **erbaut sein** to be enthusiastic [about sth] II. vr (sich innerlich erfreuen) **sich** akk **an etw** dat ~ to be uplifted by sth

Erbauer(in) <-s, -> m(f) architect

Erbe¹ <-s> ['ɛr·bə] nt kein pl 1. (Erbschaft) inheritance 2. fig (Hinterlassenschaft) legacy

Erbe², Erbin <-n, -n> ['ɛr·bə] m, f heir masc, heiress fem

erben ['ɛr·bn̩] I. vt to inherit II. vi (Erbe

sein) to receive an inheritance

er|**beuten** * [ɛg·'bɔy·tn̩] vt (Diebesgut) to carry off sep; (Kriegsbeute) to capture

Erbfaktor m hereditary factor

Erbfolge f [line of] succession

Erbgut nt kein pl genetic makeup

Erbin <-, -nen> ['ɛr·bɪn] f s. **Erbe** heiress

erbittert adj bitter

Erbkrankheit f hereditary disease

er|**blassen** * [ɛg·'bla·sn̩] vi sein to turn pale (**vor** +dat with)

erblich ['ɛrp·lɪç] I. adj hereditary II. adv by inheritance

er|**blinden** * [ɛg·'blɪn·dn̩] vi sein [**durch etw** akk] ~ to go blind [as a result of sth]

er|**brechen** * irreg I. vt (Mageninhalt, Essen) to bring up sep II. vr **sich** akk ~ to throw up fam

er|**bringen** * vt irreg 1. FIN (Erlös) to raise 2. JUR **den Beweis** ~ to produce evidence

Erbschaft <-, -en> ['ɛrp·ʃaft] f inheritance

Erbse <-, -n> ['ɛrp·sə] f pea

Erdachse ['e:gd·aksə] f earth's axis

Erdanziehung f kein pl earth's gravitational pull

Erdapfel m südd, österr (Kartoffel) potato

Erdatmosphäre f Earth's atmosphere

Erdbeben nt earthquake

Erdbeere ['e:gd·be:·rə] f strawberry

Erdboden m ground

Erde <-, -n> ['e:g·də] f 1. kein pl (Welt) earth; **auf der ganzen** ~ in the whole world 2. (Erdreich) earth 3. (Boden) ground; **zu ebener** ~ at street level

erdenklich adj attr conceivable

Erdgas nt natural gas

Erdgeschoss^RR nt first floor

Erdkugel f globe

Erdkunde f geography

Erdnuss^RR f peanut

Erdoberfläche f Earth's surface

Erdöl nt oil

er|**dreisten** * [ɛg·'drai·stn̩] vr **sich** akk ~ to take liberties; **sich** akk ~, **etw zu tun** to have the audacity to do sth

er|**drosseln** * vt to strangle

er|**drücken** * vt 1. (Eigenständigkeit

E

nehmen) jdn [mit etw dat] ~ to stifle sb [with sth] **2.** (*sehr stark belasten*) **jdn** ~ to overwhelm sb

Erdrutsch m a. fig landslide

Erdstoß m seismic shock

Erdteil m continent

er|dulden* vt (*Kränkungen, Leid*) to endure

Erdumdrehung f Earth's rotation

Erdumlaufbahn f [Earth] orbit

er|eifern* vr **sich** akk [**über etw** akk] ~ to get worked up [about sth]

er|eignen* [ɛg·ˈʔaig·nən] vr **sich** akk ~ to occur

Ereignis <-ses, -se> [ɛg·ˈʔaig·nɪs] nt event

ereignisreich adj eventful

er|fahren¹ [ɛg·ˈfaː·rən] irreg **I.** vt **1.** (*zu hören bekommen*) to hear **2.** (*erleben*) to experience **II.** vi (*Kenntnis erhalten*) **von etw** dat/**über etw** akk ~ to learn of sth

erfahren² [ɛg·ˈfaː·rən] adj (*versiert*) experienced

Erfahrung <-, -en> f **1.** (*prägendes Erlebnis*) experience; **nach meiner** ~ in my experience **2.** kein pl (*Übung*) experience; **jahrelange** ~ years of experience **3.** (*Kenntnis*) **etw in** ~ **bringen** to find out sep sth

erfahrungsgemäß adv in sb's experience; ~ **ist ...** experience shows ...

er|fassen* vt **1.** (*mitreißen: Auto, Strömung*) to catch **2.** (*befallen*) **jdn** ~ (*Furcht, Traurigkeit*) to seize sb **3.** (*begreifen*) to understand **4.** ADMIN (*registrieren*) to record **5.** (*eingeben: Daten, Text*) to enter

er|finden* [ɛg·ˈfɪn·dn̩] vt irreg to invent

Erfinder(in) [ɛg·ˈfɪn·de] m(f) inventor

erfinderisch [ɛg·ˈfɪn·də·rɪʃ] adj inventive

Erfindung <-, -en> f invention

Erfolg <-[e]s, -e> [ɛg·ˈfɔlk] m success; ~ **versprechend** promising; **viel** ~! good luck!; **mit dem** ~, **dass ...** with the result that ...

er|folgen* vi sein to occur

erfolglos [ɛg·ˈfɔlk·loːs] adj **1.** (*ohne Erfolg*) unsuccessful **2.** (*vergeblich*) futile

erfolgreich adj successful

Erfolgsdruck m kein pl performance pressure

Erfolgserlebnis nt sense of achievement

erforderlich [ɛg·ˈfɔr·də·lɪç] adj necessary

er|fordern* vt to require

er|forschen* vt **1.** (*durchstreifen und erkunden*) to explore **2.** (*prüfen*) to investigate; (*Gewissen*) to examine

er|freuen* **I.** vt to please **II.** vr **1.** (*Freude haben*) **sich** akk **an etw** dat ~ to take pleasure in sth **2.** (*genießen*) **sich** akk **einer S.** gen ~ to enjoy sth

erfreulich [ɛg·ˈfrɔy·lɪç] **I.** adj (*Anblick*) pleasant; (*Nachricht*) welcome **II.** adv happily

erfreulicherweise adv happily

er|frieren* vi irreg sein **1.** (*durch Frost eingehen*) to be killed by frost **2.** (*Gliedmaßen*) to get frostbitten **3.** (*an Kälte sterben*) to freeze to death

er|frischen* [ɛg·ˈfrɪ·ʃən] **I.** vt **jdn** ~ to refresh sb **II.** vi to be refreshing **III.** vr **sich** akk ~ to refresh oneself

erfrischend adj refreshing

Erfrischung <-, -en> f refreshment

Erfrischungsgetränk nt refreshment

er|füllen* **I.** vt **1.** (*Pflicht, Versprechen, Wunsch*) to fulfill **2.** (*durchdringen*) to fill; **von Angst/Ekel erfüllt sein** to be filled with fear/disgust **II.** vr (*sich bewahrheiten*) **sich** akk ~ to come true

er|gänzen* [ɛg·ˈgɛn·tsn̩] vt **1.** (*auffüllen: Vorräte*) to replenish **2.** (*erweitern: Sammlung*) to complete **3.** **sie** ~ **sich** they complement each other

Ergänzung <-, -en> f **1.** (*das Auffüllen: von Vorräten*) replenishment **2.** (*Erweiterung: einer Sammlung*) completion; **zur** ~ **einer S.** gen for the completion of sth **3.** (*Zusatz*) addition

er|gattern* vt fam to get [a] hold of

er|geben*¹ irreg **I.** vt **1.** MATH **etw** ~ to amount to sth **2.** (*als Resultat haben*) ~, **dass ...** to reveal that ... **II.** vr **1.** (*kapitulieren*) **sich** akk [**jdm**] ~ to surrender [to sb] **2.** (*sich fügen*) **sich** akk **in sein Schicksal** ~ to resign oneself to one's fate **3.** (*sich hingeben*) **sich** akk **dem Glücksspiel** ~ to take to gambling

4. (daraus folgen) sich akk aus etw dat ~ to result from sth

ergeben² adj 1. (demütig) humble 2. (treu) devoted

Ergebnis <-ses, -se> [ɛɐ̯ˈgeːpnɪs] nt result; SPORT score

ergebnislos adj without result

er|gehen* irreg I. vi sein 1. JUR (Beschluss, Urteil) to be enacted 2. (geduldig hinnehmen) etw über sich akk ~ lassen to endure sth II. vi impers sein (widerfahren) und wie ist es dir im Urlaub so ergangen? how did you fare on your holidays?; es ergeht jdm schlecht it's not going well for sb

ergiebig [ɛɐ̯ˈgiːbɪç] adj 1. (sparsam im Verbrauch) economical 2. (nützlich) productive

er|greifen* irreg 1. (fassen) to seize 2. (Maßnahmen) to take 3. JUR (Täter) to apprehend 4. (gefühlsmäßig bewegen) jdn ~ to seize sb; (Angst) to grip sb

ergreifend adj moving

ergriffen [ɛɐ̯ˈgrɪfn̩] adj moved

Erhalt <-[e]s> m kein pl 1. (das Bekommen) receipt; den ~ einer S. gen bestätigen to confirm receipt of sth 2. (das Aufrechterhalten) maintenance

er|halten* irreg I. vt 1. (bekommen) to receive; (Befehl) to be given; einen Eindruck [von jdm/etw] ~ to get an impression of sb/sth 2. (bewahren) to maintain 3. BAU to preserve II. vr 1. (sich halten) sich akk gesund ~ to keep [oneself] healthy 2. (bewahrt bleiben) sich akk ~ to remain preserved

erhältlich [ɛɐ̯ˈhɛltlɪç] adj obtainable

er|härten* I. vt etw ~ (Vermutung, Verdacht) to support sth II. vr sich akk ~ to be reinforced

er|heben* irreg I. vt 1. (hochheben) to raise 2. ADMIN, POL (Gebühr, Steuern) to levy 3. (Daten, Informationen) to gather 4. (zum Ausdruck bringen: Protest) to voice; (Einspruch) to raise II. vr sich akk ~ 1. (aufstehen) to stand up (von +dat from) 2. (sich auflehnen) to revolt 3. (aufragen) to rise up (über +dat above) 4. (entstehen, aufkommen)

to start; (Wind) to pick up; (Sturm) to blow up

erheblich [ɛɐ̯ˈheːplɪç] I. adj 1. (beträchtlich) considerable; (Nachteil, Vorteil a.) great; (Störung, Verspätung a.) major; (Verletzung) serious 2. (relevant) relevant II. adv considerably

er|heitern [ɛɐ̯ˈhaɪtɐn] vt to amuse

er|hellen [ɛɐ̯ˈhɛlən] I. vt 1. (hell machen) to light up sep 2. (klären) to throw light on II. vr sich akk ~ to clear

er|hitzen* [ɛɐ̯ˈhɪtsn̩] I. vt to heat II. vr (sich erregen) sich akk ~ to get excited (an +dat about)

er|hoffen* vt [sich dat] etw ~ to hope for sth

er|höhen* [ɛɐ̯ˈhøː·ən] I. vt 1. (anheben: Löhne, Preise) to raise (um +akk by) 2. (verstärken: Produktion) to increase (auf +akk to, um +akk by) II. vr sich akk ~ to increase (auf +akk to, um +akk by)

er|holen* vr sich akk ~ 1. (von einer Krankheit) to recover (von +dat from) 2. (von der Arbeit) to take a break (von +dat from) 3. BÖRSE to rally

erholsam [ɛɐ̯ˈhoːlˌzaːm] adj relaxing

Erholung <-> f kein pl relaxation

er|innern* [ɛɐ̯ˈʔɪn·ɐn] I. vt jdn an jdn/ etw ~ to remind sb of sb/sth; jdn daran ~, etw zu tun to remind sb to do sth II. vr (sich entsinnen) sich akk an jdn/ etw ~ to remember sb/sth III. vi 1. (in Erinnerung bringen) an jdn/etw ~ to be reminiscent of sb/sth form 2. (ins Gedächtnis rufen) daran ~, dass ... to point out that ...

Erinnerung <-, -en> f memory (an +akk of)

er|kälten* [ɛɐ̯ˈkɛl·tn̩] vr sich akk ~ to catch a cold

Erkältung <-, -en> f cold; eine ~ bekommen to catch a cold

er|kämpfen* vt etw ~ to fight to get sth

erkennbar adj 1. (auf Foto) recognizable 2. an etw dat ~ sein, dass ... to be perceptible from sth that ...

er|kennen* irreg I. vt 1. (identifizieren) to recognize (an +dat by) 2. (einsehen) einen Irrtum ~ to realize one's mistake II. vi ~, dass ... to realize that ...

erkenntlich [ɛɛ̯-'kɛnt-lıç] *adj* grateful; **sich** *akk* ~ **zeigen** to show one's appreciation

Erkenntnis <-, -se> [ɛɛ̯-'kɛnt-nıs] *f* (*Einsicht*) insight; **zu der** ~ **kommen, dass** ... to realize that ...

Erker <-s, -> ['ɛɛ̯-ke] *m* oriel

er|klären* I. *vt* 1. (*erläutern*) [jdm] **etw** ~ to explain sth [to sb]; **wie** ~ **Sie sich, dass** ... how do you explain that ... 2. (*bekannt geben*) to announce 3. (*offiziell bezeichnen*) **jdn für etw** ~ *akk* to pronounce sb sth II. *vr* **sich** *akk* **bereit** ~, **etwas zu tun** to volunteer to do sth

erklärt *adj attr* declared

Erklärung *f* 1. (*Erläuterung*) explanation 2. (*Mitteilung*) statement

Erkrankung <-, -en> *f* illness

er|kunden* [ɛɛ̯-'kʊn-dn̩] *vt* 1. (*auskundschaften*) to scout out *sep* 2. (*in Erfahrung bringen*) to discover

er|kundigen* [ɛɛ̯-'kʊn-dɪ-gn̩] *vr* **sich** *akk* [**nach jdm/etw**] ~ to ask [about sb/sth]

er|langen* [ɛɛ̯-'laŋən] *vt* to obtain

er|lassen* *vt irreg* 1. JUR (*verfügen*) to issue 2. (*von etw befreien*) **jdm etw** ~ to remit sb's sth

er|lauben* [ɛɛ̯-'lau̯-bn̩] I. *vt* 1. (*gestatten*) **jdm etw** ~ to allow sb to do sth 2. (*zulassen*) **ich komme, soweit es meine Zeit erlaubt** if time permits, I'll come ▶ ~ **Sie mal!** what do you think you're doing? II. *vr* 1. (*sich gönnen*) **sich** *dat* **etw** ~ to allow oneself sth 2. (*sich herausnehmen*) **sich** *dat* ~, **etw zu tun** to take the liberty of doing sth

Erlaubnis <-, *selten* -se> *f* permission; (*schriftlich*) permit

er|läutern* *vt* [jdm] **etw** ~ to explain sth [to sb]

Erläuterung <-, -en> *f* explanation

Erle <-, -n> ['ɛɛ̯-lə] *f* alder

er|leben* *vt* 1. (*im Leben mitmachen*) **etw** ~ to live to see sth 2. (*erfahren*) to experience 3. (*durchmachen*) **etw** ~ to go through sth 4. (*mit ansehen*) **es** ~, **dass/wie** ... to see that/how ...; **so wütend habe ich ihn noch nie erlebt** I've never seen him so furious

Erlebnis <-ses, -se> [ɛɛ̯-'le:p-nıs] *nt* experience

er|ledigen* *vt* 1. (*ausführen*) **etw** ~ to take care of sth 2. *fam* (*erschöpfen*) **jdn** ~ to wear out *sep* sb 3. *sl* (*umbringen*) **jdn** ~ to bump off *sep* sb II. *vr* **etw erledigt sich** [**von selbst**] sth sorts itself out [on its own]

er|legen* *vt* 1. (*töten*) **ein Tier** ~ to shoot an animal 2. *österr* (*bezahlen*) to pay

er|leichtern* [ɛɛ̯-'lai̯ç-ten] *vt* 1. (*einfacher machen*) **etw** ~ to make sth easier 2. (*innerlich beruhigen*) **jdn** ~ to be a relief to sb 3. *fam* (*beklauen*) **jdn um etw** *akk* ~ to relieve sb of sth

er|leiden* *vt irreg* to suffer

er|lesen *adj* exquisite

er|liegen* *vi irreg sein* **etw** *dat* ~ ▶ **zum E~ kommen** to come to a standstill

Erlös <-es, -e> [ɛɛ̯-'lø:s] *m* proceeds *npl*

er|mächtigen* [ɛɛ̯-'mɛç-tɪ-gn̩] *vt* to authorize

er|mahnen* *vt* 1. (*warnend mahnen*) **jdn** ~ to warn sb 2. (*anhalten*) **jdn zu etw** *dat* ~ to admonish sb to do sth

Ermäßigung <-, -en> *f* reduction

Ermessen <-s> *nt kein pl* **nach jds** ~ in sb's discretion

er|mitteln* I. *vt* 1. (*herausfinden*) to find out *sep*; **den Täter** ~ to establish the culprit's identity 2. (*errechnen*) to determine; (*Gewinner*) to decide [on] II. *vi* (*eine Untersuchung durchführen*) [**gegen jdn**] ~ to investigate [sb]

Ermittlung <-, -en> *f* 1. *kein pl* (*das Ausfindigmachen*) determining 2. (*Untersuchung*) investigation

er|möglichen* [ɛɛ̯-'møk-lı-çn̩] *vt* **jdm etw** ~ to enable sb to do sth

er|morden* *vt* to murder

er|müden* [ɛɛ̯-'my:-dn̩] I. *vt haben* **jdn** ~ to tire [out *sep*] sb II. *vi sein* 1. (*müde werden*) to become tired 2. TECH to wear

ermüdend *adj* tiring

Ermüdung <-, *selten* -en> *f* 1. (*das Ermüden*) tiredness 2. TECH wear

er|mutigen* [ɛɛ̯-'mu:-tɪ-gn̩] *vt* **jdn** [**zu etw** *dat*] ~ to encourage sb [to do sth]

er|nähren* I. vt (mit Nahrung versorgen) to feed II. vr sich akk von etw dat ~ 1. (essen) to live on sth 2. (sich finanzieren) to support oneself by doing sth

Ernährung <-> f kein pl 1. (das Ernähren) feeding 2. (Nahrung) diet 3. (finanziell) support

Ernährungsberater, -beraterin m, f nutritionist

er|nennen* vt irreg to appoint (zu +dat as)

Ernennung f appointment (zu +dat as)

erneuerbar adj renewable

er|neuern* [ɛɐ̯ˈnɔy·ɐn] vt 1. (auswechseln: Fenster, Reifen) to replace; (Öl) to change 2. (wiederbeleben: Freundschaft) to renew

er|niedrigen* [ɛɐ̯ˈniː·drɪ·gn̩] vt jdn/sich ~ to demean sb/oneself

ernst [ɛrnst] adj 1. (gravierend) serious 2. (aufrichtig) genuine; es ~ meinen [mit jdm/etw] to be serious [about sb/sth]; jdn/etw ~ nehmen to take sb/sth seriously 3. (Anlass) solemn

Ernstfall m emergency

ernsthaft I. adj 1. (gravierend) serious 2. (aufrichtig) sincere II. adv seriously

ernten [ˈɛrn·tn̩] vt 1. (Gemüse, Obst) to harvest 2. (erzielen: Anerkennung) to gain; (Applaus) to win; (Lob, Spott) to earn

er|nüchtern* [ɛɐ̯ˈnʏç·tɐn] vt jdn ~ 1. (wieder nüchtern machen) to sober up sep sb 2. (in die Realität zurückholen) to bring sb back to reality

Ernüchterung <-, -en> f disillusionment

er|obern* [ɛɐ̯ˈʔoː·bɐn] vt 1. (mit Waffengewalt: Gebiet, Land, Stadt) to conquer 2. (Markt) to capture 3. (für sich einnehmen: Mensch) to win sb's heart

Eroberung <-, -en> f 1. (das Erobern) conquest 2. fam (eroberte Person) conquest hum

Eröffnung f 1. (eines Geschäfts, Museums etc.) opening 2. (Mitteilung) revelation

er|örtern* [ɛɐ̯ˈʔœr·tɐn] vt to discuss [in detail]

Erörterung <-, -en> f discussion

Erotik <-> [eˈroː·tɪk] f kein pl eroticism

erotisch [eˈroː·tɪʃ] adj erotic

Erpel <-s, -> [ˈɛr·pl̩] m drake

erpicht [ɛɐ̯ˈpɪçt] adj auf etw akk ~ sein to be after sth

er|pressen* vt jdn ~ to blackmail sb

Erpresser(in) <-s, -> m(f) blackmailer

Erpressung <-, -en> f blackmail

er|proben* vt to test

erprobt adj ein ~es Mittel a reliable remedy

er|raten* vt irreg to guess

er|rechnen* vt to calculate

er|regen* vt 1. (aufregen) jdn ~ to excite sb; (sexuell a.) to arouse sb 2. (hervorrufen) etw ~ (Aufmerksamkeit) to attract; (Aufsehen) to cause

Erreger <-s, -> m pathogen

erreichbar adj [für jdn] ~ sein to be able to be reached [by sb]

er|reichen* vt to reach

er|richten* vt 1. (aufstellen) to erect form 2. (gründen) to found sth

er|röten* vi sein to blush

Errungenschaft <-, -en> [ɛɐ̯ˈrʊŋən·ʃaft] f achievement

Ersatz <-es> [ɛɐ̯ˈzats] m kein pl 1. (ersetzender Mensch) substitute; (ersetzender Gegenstand) replacement 2. (Entschädigung) compensation

Ersatzbank f SPORT bench

Ersatzdienst m nonmilitary service for conscientious objectors

Ersatzmann <-männer o -leute> m substitute

Ersatzreifen m spare tire

Ersatzteil nt spare part

er|schaffen* vt irreg to create

er|scheinen* vi irreg sein 1. (auftreten) to appear 2. (sichtbar werden) to be able to be seen 3. (veröffentlicht werden: Buch, CD etc.) to come out 4. (scheinen) to seem; das erscheint mir recht weit hergeholt that seems pretty far-fetched to me

Erscheinen <-s> nt kein pl 1. (das Auftreten) appearance 2. (die Veröffentlichung) publication

Erscheinung <-, -en> f 1. (Phänomen) phenomenon 2. (Persönlichkeit) eine bestimmte ~ a certain figure 3. (Visi-

E

on) vision ▶ **in ~ treten** to appear

er|**schießen** * *irreg vt* **jdn ~** to shoot sb dead

er|**schlagen** **1 vt* **jdn ~** *irreg* **1.** (*totschlagen*) to beat sb to death **2.** (*durch Darauffallen töten: Gegenstand*) to fall down and kill sb; (*Blitz*) to strike sb dead **3.** *fig* (*überwältigen*) to overwhelm sb

er|**schlagen**² *adj fam* **wie ~ sein** to be pooped *sl*

er|**schließen** * *irreg* **I.** *vt* (*Land*) to develop **II.** *vr* **sich** *dat* **jdm ~** to reveal oneself to sb

er|**schöpfen** * *vt* **1.** (*ermüden*) **jdn ~** to exhaust **2.** (*aufbrauchen*) **etw ~** to exhaust sth

er|**schöpfend** **I.** *adj* **1.** (*zur Erschöpfung führend*) exhausting **2.** (*ausführlich*) exhaustive **II.** *adv* exhaustively

Er**schöpfung** <-, *selten* -en> *f* exhaustion

er|**schrak** *imp von* **erschrecken** II

er|**schrecken** **I.** *vt* <erschreckte, erschreckt> **haben jdn ~ 1.** (*in Schrecken versetzen*) to give sb a scare **2.** (*bestürzen*) to shock sb **II.** *vi* <erschrickt, erschreckte o erschrak, erschreckt o erschrocken> **sein** to be scared (**vor** *+dat* by) **III.** *vr* <erschrickt, erschreckte, erschreckt o erschrocken> **haben** *fam* **sich** *akk* [**über etw** *akk*] **~** to be shocked [by sth]

er**schrocken** **I.** *pp von* **erschrecken** II, III **II.** *adj* alarmed *pred* **III.** *adv* with a start

er|**schüttern** * [ɛɡ·ˈʃy·tɐn] *vt* **1.** (*zum Beben bringen: Boden, Gebäude*) to shake **2.** (*in Frage stellen: Ansehen*) to damage; (*Glaubwürdigkeit*) to undermine; (*Vertrauen*) to shake **3.** (*tief bewegen*) **jdn ~** to shake sb

er|**schweren** * [ɛɡ·ˈʃveː·rən] *vt* to make more difficult

er**schwinglich** [ɛɡ·ˈʃvɪŋ·lɪç] *adj* affordable

er|**sehen** * *vt irreg* to see (**aus** *+dat* from)

er|**setzen** * *vt* **1.** (*austauschen*) **etw** [**durch etw** *akk*] **~** to replace sth [with sth] **2.** (*vertreten*) **jdn/etw ~** to replace sb/sth **3.** (*erstatten*) **jdm etw ~** to re-

imburse sb for sth

er**sichtlich** *adj* apparent; **aus etw** *dat* **~ sein, dass ...** to be apparent from sth that ...

er|**sparen** * *vt* **1.** (*von Ärger verschonen*) **jdm etw ~** to spare sb sth **2.** (*durch Sparen erwerben*) [**sich** *dat*] **etw ~** to save up [to buy] sth

Er**sparnis** <-, -se> [ɛɡ·ˈʃpaːɡ·nɪs] *f* savings *npl*

erst ['eːɡst] **I.** *adv* **1.** (*zuerst*) [at] first **2.** (*nicht früher als*) only; **wecken Sie mich bitte ~ um 8 Uhr!** please don't wake me up until 8 o'clock! **II.** *part* (*verstärkend*) **an deiner Stelle würde ich ~ gar nicht anfangen zu ...** if I were in your shoes I wouldn't even start to ... ▶ **~ recht** all the more

er|**statten** * [ɛɡ·ˈʃtaː·tn̩] *vt* **1.** (*ersetzen*) [**jdm**] **etw ~** to reimburse [sb] for sth **2.** *Anzeige ~* to report a crime

Er**stattung** <-, -en> *f* (*von Auslagen, Unkosten*) reimbursement

Er**staufführung** *f* première

Er**staunen** *nt* amazement; **jdn in ~ versetzen** to amaze sb

er**staunlich** [ɛɡ·ˈʃtaun·lɪç] *adj* amazing

er**staunlicherweise** *adv* amazingly

er**staunt** **I.** *adj* amazed **II.** *adv* in amazement

erste(r, s) ['eːɡs·tə] *adj* **1.** (*an erster Stelle*) first; **das E~, was ...** the first thing that ...; *s. a.* **achte(r, s) 1 2.** (*Datum*) first, 1st; *s. a.* **achte(r, s) 2 3.** (*führend*) leading ▶ **fürs E~** to begin with

Erste-Hilfe-Kasten [eːɡs·tə·ˈhɪl·fə·kas·tn̩] *m* first-aid kit

er|**sticken** * **I.** *vt* **haben 1.** (*durch Ersticken töten*) to suffocate **2.** (*Brand*) to extinguish **II.** *vi* **sein 1.** (*durch Ersticken sterben*) **an etw** *dat* **~** to choke to death on sth **2.** (*erlöschen: Feuer*) to go out **3.** (*übermäßig viel haben*) **in etw** *dat* **~** to drown in sth

erst**klassig** ['eːɡst·klasɪç] *adj* first-class

erst**malig** ['eːɡst·maː·lɪç] **I.** *adj* first **II.** *adv s.* **erstmals**

erst**mals** ['eːɡst·maːls] *adv* for the first time

er|**strecken** * **I.** *vr* **1.** (*sich ausdehnen*)

sich *akk* [**über etw** *akk*] ~ to extend [over sth] **2.** (*betreffen*) **sich** *akk* **auf etw** *akk* ~ to include sth **II.** *vt schweiz* (*verlängern*) to extend

er|**tappen** * *vt*, *vr* **jdn/sich** [**bei etw** *dat*] ~ to catch sb/oneself [doing sth]

Ertrag <-[e]s, Erträge> [ɛɐ̯'traːk] *m* **1.** (*Ernte*) yield; ~ **bringen** to bring yields **2.** *meist pl* (*Einnahmen*) revenue

er|**tragen** * *vt irreg* to bear

er|**träglich** [ɛɐ̯'trɛːk·lɪç] *adj* bearable

er|**trinken** * *vi irreg sein* to drown

er|**übrigen** * [ɛɐ̯'ʔyːbrɪ·gn̩] **I.** *vr* **sich** *akk* ~ to be superfluous **II.** *vt* (*aufbringen*) **etw** ~ **können** (*Geld, Zeit*) to spare sth

er|**wachen** * *vi sein* to wake up

er|**wachsen** * [ɛɐ̯'vak·sn̩] *adj* adult

Erwachsene(r) *f(m)* adult

Erwachsenenbildung [ɛɐ̯'vak·se·nən·] *f* adult education

er|**wägen** * *vt irreg* to consider

er|**wähnen** * *vt* to mention

er|**wärmen** * **I.** *vt* to warm [up] **II.** *vr* **1.** (*warm werden*) **sich** *akk* ~ to warm up **2.** (*sich begeistern*) **sich** *akk* **für jdn/etw** ~ to work up enthusiasm for sb/sth

er|**warten** * **I.** *vt* to expect **II.** *vr* (*sich versprechen*) **sich** *dat* **von jdm/etw** ~ to expect sth from sb/sth

Erwartung <-, -en> *f* **1.** *kein pl* (*Ungeduld*) anticipation **2.** *pl* (*Hoffnung*) expectations *pl;* **den ~en entsprechen** to fulfill expectations

erwartungsvoll **I.** *adj* expectant, full of expectation *pred* **II.** *adv* expectantly

er|**wecken** * *vt* to arouse; **den Eindruck ~, ...** to give the impression ...

er|**weisen** * *irreg* **I.** *vt* **1.** (*nachweisen*) to prove **2.** (*zeigen*) **etw wird ~, dass/ob ...** sth will show that/whether ... **3.** **jdm einen Dienst/Gefallen ~** to do somebody a service/favor **II.** *vr* **1.** (*sich herausstellen*) **sich** *akk* **als etw** ~ to prove to be sth **2.** (*sich zeigen*) **sie sollte sich dankbar** [**ihm gegenüber**] ~ she should be grateful [to him]

er|**weitern** * **I.** *vt* **1.** (*Straße, Kleidung*) to widen (**um** +*akk* by) **2.** (*vergrößern*)

to expand (**um** +*akk* by) **3.** (*umfangreicher machen*) to increase (**um** +*akk* by) **II.** *vr* **1.** (*sich verbreitern*) **sich** *akk* ~ to widen (**um** +*akk* by) **2.** MED, ANAT **sich** *akk* ~ to dilate

Erwerb <-[e]s> [ɛɐ̯'vɛrp] *m kein pl* purchase

er|**werben** * *vt irreg* **1.** (*kaufen*) to purchase **2.** (*gewinnen: Vertrauen*) to win

erwerbsfähig *adj* fit for gainful employment *pred*

erwerbslos *adj* unemployed

erwerbsunfähig *adj* unfit for gainful employment

er|**widern** * [ɛɐ̯'viː·dɐn] *vt* **1.** (*antworten*) to reply **2.** (*zurückgeben: Gefühle, Liebe*) to return

erwiesenermaßen [ɛɐ̯·viː·zə·nɐ·'maː·sn̩] *adv* as has been proved

er|**wischen** * [ɛɐ̯'vɪ·ʃn̩] *vt fam* **1.** (*ertappen*) **jdn** [**bei etw** *dat*] ~ to catch sb [doing sth] **2.** (*ergreifen, erreichen*) **jdn/etw** ~ to catch sb/sth

Erz <-es, -e> ['eːɐ̯ts] *nt* ore

er|**zählen** * **I.** *vt* **1.** (*anschaulich berichten*) to explain **2.** (*sagen*) to tell **II.** *vi* to tell a story/stories

Erzähler(in) <-s, -> [ɛɐ̯'tsɛː·lɐ] *m(f)* storyteller; (*Schriftsteller(in)*) author; (*Romanperson*) narrator

Erzählung *f* **1.** (*Geschichte*) story **2.** *kein pl* (*das Erzählen*) telling

Erzbischof, -bischöfin ['ɛrts·bɪ·ʃɔf, -bɪ·ʃœ·fɪn] *m, f* archbishop

Erzengel ['ɛrts·ʔɛŋl̩] *m* archangel

er|**zeugen** * *vt* **1.** ÖKON (*produzieren*) to produce **2.** ELEK, SCI to generate **3.** (*hervorrufen*) to create

Erzeuger(in) <-s, -> *m(f)* **1.** (*Produzent*) producer **2.** *hum fam* (*Vater*) father

Erzeugnis <-ses, -se> [ɛɐ̯'tsɔyk·nɪs] *nt* product

Erzfeind(in) *m(f)* archenemy

erziehbar *adj* educable; **schwer ~ sein** to have behavioral problems

er|**ziehen** * *vt irreg* **1.** (*aufziehen*) **gut/ schlecht erzogen sein** to be well/ badly brought-up **2.** (*anleiten*) **jdn zu etw** *dat* ~ to teach sb to be sth

Erziehung *f kein pl* **1.** (*das Erziehen*) education **2.** (*anerzogene Manieren*)

manners *npl*

Erziehungsurlaub *m* maternity/paternity leave *(for up to 3 years)*

er|zielen* *vt* **1.** (*erreichen*) to achieve; (*Einigung*) to reach **2.** SPORT to score

er|zwingen* *vt irreg* **etw |von jdm| ~** to force sth |out of sb|; **ein Geständnis |von jdm| ~** to make sb confess

es <*gen* seiner, *dat* ihm, *akk* es> ['ɛs] *pron pers, unbestimmt* **1.** *auf Dinge bezogen* (*das, diese*) it; **wer ist da? – ich bin ~** who's there? — it's me **2.** *auf vorangehenden Satzinhalt bezogen* it; **kommt er auch? – ich hoffe ~** is he coming too? – I hope so **3.** *rein formales Subjekt* it; **hier stinkt ~** something smells bad in here; **~ gefällt mir** I like it **4.** *rein formales Objekt* **er hat ~ gut** he's got it made **5.** *Subjekt bei unpersönl. Ausdrücken* **~ klopft** there's a knock at the door; **~ regnet** it's raining **6.** *Einleitewort mit folgendem Subjekt* **~ waren Tausende** there were thousands

Esche <-, -n> ['ɛʃə] *f* ash

Esel(in) <-s, -> ['eːzl] *m(f)* **1.** (*Tier*) donkey **2.** *nur m fam* (*Dummkopf*) idiot

Eselsbrücke *f fam* mnemonic [device]

Eselsohr *nt* dog-ear

eskalieren* [ɛs·ka·'liː·rən] *vt, vi* to escalate (**zu** +*dat* into)

Eskimo, -frau <-s, -s> ['ɛs·ki·mo] *m, f* Eskimo

Espe <-, -n> ['ɛs·pə] *f* aspen

Espenlaub *nt* ▶ **zittern wie ~** to be shaking like a leaf

essbar^{RR}, **eßbar**^{ALT} *adj* edible

essen <isst, aß, gegessen> ['ɛsn̩] **I.** *vt* to eat; **~ Sie gern Äpfel?** do you like apples?; **etw zum Nachtisch ~** to have sth for dessert **II.** *vi* to eat; **griechisch/ italienisch ~** to eat Greek/Italian food

Essen <-s, -> ['ɛsn̩] *nt* **1.** (*Mahlzeit*) meal **2.** (*Nahrung*) food

Essen(s)marke *f* meal voucher

Essig <-s, -e> ['ɛsɪç] *m* vinegar

Essiggurke *f* pickle

Essigsäure *f* acetic acid

Esskastanie^{RR} *f* sweet chestnut

Esslöffel^{RR} *m* **1.** (*Essbesteck*) soup spoon **2.** (*Maßeinheit beim Kochen*) tablespoon

Esszimmer^{RR} *nt* dining room

Este, Estin <-n, -n> ['eːstə, 'eːs·tɪn] *m, f* Estonian; *s. a.* **Deutsche(r)**

Estland <-s> ['eːst·lant] *nt* Estonia; *s. a.* **Deutschland**

estnisch ['eːst·nɪʃ] *adj* Estonian; *s. a.* **deutsch**

Estragon <-s> ['ɛs·tra·ɡɔn] *m kein pl* tarragon

etabliert *adj geh* established

Etage <-, -n> [e'taː·ʒə] *f* floor; **auf der 5. ~** on the 6th floor

Etagenwohnung [e'taː·ɡən-] *f* apartment *(occupying a whole floor)*

Etappe <-, -n> [e'tapə] *f* **1.** (*Abschnitt*) stage **2.** (*Teilstrecke*) leg **3.** MIL communications zone

Etat <-s, -s> [e'taː] *m* budget

etepetete ['eː·tə·pe·'teː·tə] *adj pred fam* finicky

Ethik <-> ['eːtɪk] *f kein pl* **1.** (*Wissenschaft*) ethics + *sing vb* **2.** (*moralische Haltung*) ethics *npl*

ethisch ['eːtɪʃ] *adj* ethical

Etikett <-[e]s, -e> [eti·'kɛt] *nt* **1.** (*Preisschild*) price tag **2.** (*Aufnäher*) label

etliche(r, s) ['ɛt·lɪ·çə] *pron indef* **1.** *adjektivisch, sing o pl* quite a lot of **2.** *substantivisch, pl* quite a few **3.** *substantivisch, sing* **~s** quite a lot

Etui <-s, -s> [ɛ'tviː, e'tʏiː] *nt* case; (*verziert a.*) etui

etwa ['ɛt·va] **I.** *adv* **1.** (*ungefähr, annähernd*) about; **in ~** more or less **2.** (*zum Beispiel*) **wie ~ mein Bruder** like my brother for instance **II.** *part* **1.** (*womöglich*) **soll das – heißen, dass ...?** is that supposed to mean [that] ...?; **willst du – schon gehen?** you don't want to go already, do you? **2.** (*Verstärkung der Verneinung*) **ist das ~ nicht wahr?** do you mean to say it's not true?

etwaig [ɛt·'va·ɪç] *adj attr* any

etwas ['ɛt·vas] *pron indef* **1.** *substantivisch* (*eine unbestimmte Sache*) something; (*bei Fragen*) anything **2.** *adjektivisch* (*nicht näher bestimmt*) something; (*bei Fragen*) anything; **~ anderes** something else; **[noch] ~ Kaffee** some [more] coffee **3.** *adverbial* (*ein wenig*) a little

Etwas <-> ['ɛt·vas] *nt kein pl* ▶ **das ge-wisse** ~ that certain something

EU [eː'uː] *f Abk von* **Europäische Union** EU, European Union

euch [ɔyç] **I.** *pron pers akk o dat von* **ihr** you[-all], you guys *sl;* **ein Freund/eine Freundin von** ~ a friend of yours **II.** *pron refl* beeilt ~! hurry up!; **macht** ~ **fertig!** get [*fam* yourselves] ready!

euere(r, s) ['ɔyə·rə] *pron poss, substantivisch s.* **eure(r, s)**

Eukalyptus <-, -lypten> [ɔy·ka·'lyp·tʊs] *m* **1.** (*Baum*) eucalyptus [tree] **2.** (*Öl*) eucalyptus [oil]

EU-Kommission *f* EU Commission

EU-Land *nt* EU country

Eule <-, -n> ['ɔy·lə] *f* owl

EU-Mitgliedsland *nt* EU member state

Eunuch <-en, -en> [ɔy·'nuːx] *m* eunuch

Euphorie <-, -n> [ɔy·fo·'riː] *f* euphoria

euphorisch [ɔy·'foː·rɪʃ] *adj* euphoric

eure(r, s) ['ɔy·rə] *pron poss geh* (**der/die/das**) **E~** yours; **tut ihr das E~** you do your part

euretwegen ['ɔy·rət·'veː·gn̩] *adv* (*wegen euch*) because of you; (*euch zuliebe*) for your sake[s]

euretwillen ['ɔy·rət·vɪ·lən] *adv* for your sake[s]

Euro [ɔy·ro] *m* (*Währungseinheit*) euro

Eurocity ['ɔy·ro·sɪti] *m* Eurocity train (*connecting major European cities*)

Europa <-s> [ɔy·'roː·pa] *nt* Europe

Europäer(in) <-s, -> [ɔy·ro·'pɛː·ɐ] *m(f)* European

europäisch [ɔy·ro·'pɛː·ɪʃ] *adj* European; **E~e Einheitswährung** single European currency, euro; **E~e Gemeinschaft** [*o* **EG**] European Community, EC; **E~er Gerichtshof** European Court of Justice; **E~es Parlament** European Parliament; **E~er Rat** European Council

Europameister(in) *m(f)* (*als Einzelner*) European champion; (*als Team, Land*) European champions *pl*

Europaparlament *nt* the European Parliament

Europapokal *m* European cup tournament

Europarat *m kein pl* Council of Europe

Eurozone <-> *f kein pl* Eurozone

Euter <-s, -> ['ɔy·tɐ] *nt o m* udder

evakuieren* [eva·ku·'iː·rən] *vt* to evacuate

evangelisch [evaŋ·'geː·lɪʃ] *adj* Protestant

Evangelium <-s, -lien> [evaŋ·'geː·li·ʊm] *nt* Gospel; *fig* gospel

eventuell [evɛn·'tu·ɛl] **I.** *adj attr* possible; **bei ~en Rückfragen wenden Sie sich bitte an ...** if you have any questions, please contact ... **II.** *adv* possibly

Evolution <-, -en> [evo·lu·'tsjoːn] *f* evolution

EWG <-> [eː·veː·'geː] *f kein pl hist Abk von* **Europäische Wirtschaftsgemeinschaft** EEC, [European] Economic Community

EWI <-[s]> *nt kein pl Abk von* **Europäisches Währungsinstitut** HIST EMI, European Monetary Institute

ewig ['eː·vɪç] **I.** *adj* **1.** (*immer während*) eternal **2.** *pej fam* (*ständig*) **~es Gejammer** never-ending moaning and groaning **II.** *adv* **1.** (*dauernd*) eternally; (*seit jeher*) always **2.** *fam* (*ständig*) always **3.** *fam* (*lange Zeitspanne*) for ages

Ewigkeit <-, -en> ['eː·vɪç·kait] *f* eternity; **eine** [**halbe**] ~ **dauern** *hum fam* to last forever

EWS <-> [eː·veː·'ɛs] *nt kein pl hist Abk von* **Europäisches Währungssystem** EMS, European Monetary System

EWWU <-> [eː·veː·veː·'uː] *f Abk von* **Europäische Wirtschafts- und Währungsunion** EEMU, European Economic and Monetary Union

exakt [ɛ'ksakt] **I.** *adj* exact **II.** *adv* exactly; ~ **arbeiten** to be accurate in one's work

Examen <-s, -> [ɛ'ksaː·mən] *nt* **mündliches/schriftliches** ~ oral/written exam; **das** ~ **bestehen** to pass one's final [exam]; **durch das** ~ **fallen** to fail one's final [exam]

Exemplar <-s, -e> [ɛks·ɛm·'plaːg] *nt* specimen; (*Ausgabe: von Buch, Heft*) copy; (*einer Zeitung*) issue

Exil <-s, -e> [ɛ'ksiːl] *nt* exile

Existenz <-, -en> [ɛksɪs·'tɛnts] *f* **1.** *kein pl* (*das Vorhandensein*) existence

2. (*Lebensgrundlage, Auskommen*) livelihood **3.** (*Dasein, Leben*) life

Existenzgründer(in) *m(f)* founder of a new business

Existenzgrundlage *f* basis of one's livelihood

Existenzminimum *nt* subsistence level

Existenzrecht *nt kein pl* right to existence

existieren* [εksɪs·ˈtiː·rən] *vi* **1.** (*vorhanden sein*) to exist **2.** (*sein Auskommen haben*) [**von etw** *dat*] ~ to live [on sth]

exklusiv [εks·klu·ˈziːf] *adj* exclusive

Exkrement <-[e]s, -e> [εks·kre·ˈmɛnt] *nt meist pl geh* excrement

Exkursion <-, -en> [εks·kʊr·ˈzjoːn] *f* UNIV study trip; SCH field trip

exotisch [ε·ˈksoː·tɪʃ] *adj* **1.** (*aus fernem Land*) exotic **2.** *fam* (*ausgefallen*) unusual

Expedition <-, -en> [εks·pe·di·ˈtsjoːn] *f* expedition

Experiment <-[e]s, -e> [εks·pe·ri·ˈmɛnt] *nt* experiment

experimentieren* [εks·pe·ri·mɛn·ˈtiː·rən] *vi* to experiment

Experte, Expertin <-n, -n> [εks·ˈpɛr·tə] *m, f* expert

explodieren* [εks·plo·ˈdiː·rən] *vi sein a. fig* to explode *a. fig*

Explosion <-, -en> [εks·plo·ˈzjoːn] *f a. fig* explosion *a. fig;* **etw zur ~ bringen** to detonate sth

Explosionsgefahr *f* danger of explosion

explosiv [εks·plo·ˈziːf] *adj* explosive

Export <-[e]s, -e> [εks·ˈpɔrt] *m kein pl* export

Exportartikel *m* exported article; *pl* exports

Exporteur(in) <-s, -e> [εkspɔr·ˈtøːɐ̯] *m(f)* exporter

exportieren* [εks·pɔr·ˈtiː·rən] *vt* to export

Express RR, **Expreß** ALT <Expresses> [εks·ˈprɛs] *m kein pl* **1.** (*Eilzug*) express [train] **2.** (*schnell*) **etw per ~ senden** to send sth express

Expressionismus <-> [εks·prɛ·sjo·ˈnɪs·mʊs] *m kein pl* expressionism

extern [εks·ˈtɛrn] *adj* external

extra [ˈεks·tra] *adv* **1.** (*besonders*) extra **2.** (*zusätzlich*) extra **3.** (*eigens*) just **4.** *fam* (*absichtlich*) on purpose **5.** (*gesondert*) separately; KOCHK on the side

Extrablatt *nt* special supplement

Extrakt <-[e]s, -e> [εks·ˈtrakt] *m o nt* extract

extravagant [εks·tra·va·ˈgant] *adj* extravagant

extravertiert [εks·tra·vɛr·ˈtiːɐ̯t] *adj* extroverted

extrem [εks·ˈtreːm] **I.** *adj* extreme **II.** *adv* (*sehr*) extremely; ~ **links/rechts** POL ultra-left/right

Extremist(in) <-en, -en> [εks·tre·ˈmɪst] *m(f)* extremist

Extremitäten [εks·tre·mi·ˈtɛː·tn̩] *pl* extremities *npl*

exzellent [εks·tsε·ˈlɛnt] *geh* **I.** *adj* excellent **II.** *adv* excellently; **sich** *akk* ~ **fühlen** to feel great; ~ **schmecken** to taste delicious

exzentrisch [εks·ˈtsɛn·trɪʃ] *adj* eccentric

Exzess RR, **Exzeß** ALT <Exzesses, Exzesse> [εks·ˈtsɛs] *m meist pl* excess; **etw bis zum ~ treiben** to take sth to extremes

exzessiv [εks·tsε·ˈsiːf] *adj* excessive

EZB <-> [eː·tsɛt·ˈbeː] *f kein pl* FIN *Abk von* **Europäische Zentralbank** ECB, European Central Bank

F

F, f <-, -> [εf] *nt* F, f; ~ **wie Friedrich** F as in Foxtrot

Fabrik <-, -en> [fa·ˈbriːk] *f* factory

Fabrikarbeiter(in) *m(f)* factory worker

Fabrikgelände *nt* factory site

fabrikneu *adj* brand-new

Fach <-[e]s, Fächer> [fax] *nt* **1.** (*im Schrank*) shelf **2.** (*Sachgebiet*) subject; **vom ~ sein** to be a specialist

Facharbeiter(in) *m(f)* skilled worker

Facharzt, -ärztin *m, f* specialist

Fachausdruck *m* technical term; **juristischer ~** legal term

Fächer <-s, -> [ˈfɛ·çɐ] *m* fan

Fachgebiet *nt* field of expertise

Fachhändler(in) *m(f)* retail dealer

Fachhochschule *f* ≈ University of Applied Sciences

Fachkenntnisse *pl* specialized knowledge *sing*

fachlich *adv* **sich** *akk* ~ **qualifizieren** to gain expertise in one's field

Fachliteratur *f* technical literature

Fachmann, -frau <-leute> *m, f* expert

Fachsprache *f* [technical] jargon

Fachwerkhaus *nt* half-timbered house

Fachwissen *nt* specialized knowledge

Fachwort *nt* technical term

Fachwörterbuch *nt* technical dictionary; **ein medizinisches** ~ a dictionary of medical terms

Fachzeitschrift *f* technical journal

Fackel <-, -n> ['fa·kl̩] *f* torch

Faden <-s, Fäden> ['faː·dn̩] *m* thread; **die Fäden ziehen** MED to remove sb's stitches ▶ **der rote** ~ the central theme; **den** ~ **verlieren** to lose one's train of thought

fähig ['fɛː·ɪç] *adj* able, competent; **zu etw** *dat* [nicht] ~ **sein** to be [in]capable of sth

Fähigkeit <-, -en> *f* ability

fahnden ['faːn·dn̩] *vi* to search (**nach** +*dat* for)

Fahndung <-, -en> *f* search; **eine** ~ **nach jdm einleiten** to put out an APB for sb

Fahne <-, -n> ['faː·nə] *f* flag; (*Alkoholgeruch*) smell of alcohol *no indef art*

Fahrausweis *m* **1.** (*Fahrkarte*) ticket **2.** *schweiz* (*Führerschein*) driver's license

Fahrbahn *f* road; **von der** ~ **abkommen** to leave the road

Fähre <-, -n> ['fɛː·rə] *f* ferry

fahren <fährt, fuhr, gefahren> ['faː·rən] **I.** *vi sein* to go; (*als Fahrer*) to drive; (*losfahren*) to leave; **die Bahn fährt alle 20 Minuten** the train runs every 20 minutes; **mit dem Auto/Bus/Zug** ~ to take the car/bus/train; **in Urlaub** ~ to go on vacation; **gegen etw** *akk* ~ to drive into sth; **was ist denn in dich ge~?** *fig* what's gotten into you?; **gut/ schlecht** ~ *fig* to do/not do well **II.** *vt* **1.** *haben* (*lenken*) to drive **2.** *sein* Fahr-

rad/Motorrad ~ to ride a bicycle/motorcycle; **Schlittschuh** ~ to ice-skate; **90 [km/h]** ~ to be doing 90 kmph **3.** *haben* (*befördern*) to take; **ich fahr dich nach Hause** I'll take you home **III.** *vr haben* **der Wagen fährt sich gut** the car handles well

Fahrer(in) <-s, -> ['faː·rɐ] *m(f)* driver; (*auf Motorrad*) biker *fam*

Fahrerflucht *f* hit-and-run

Fahrgast *m* passenger

Fahrgemeinschaft *f* carpool; **eine** ~ **bilden** to carpool

Fahrkarte *f* ticket (**nach** +*dat* to)

Fahrkartenautomat *m* ticket machine

Fahrkartenschalter *m* ticket office

fahrlässig ['faːɐ̯·lɛ·sɪç] **I.** *adj* negligent; **grob** ~ reckless **II.** *adv* negligently; ~ **handeln** to act with negligence

Fahrlässigkeit <-, -en> *f* negligence; **grobe** ~ recklessness

Fahrlehrer(in) *m(f)* driving instructor

Fahrplan *m* schedule

Fahrpreis *m* fare

Fahrprüfung *f* driving test

Fahrrad ['faːɐ̯·raːt] *nt* bicycle, bike *fam;* ~ **fahren** to ride a bicycle

Fahrradweg *m* bicycle path

Fahrschein *m* ticket

Fahrschule *f* driving school

Fahrschüler(in) *m(f)* student driver

Fahrspur *f* [traffic] lane

Fahrstuhl *m* elevator

Fahrt <-, -en> [faːɐ̯t] *f* trip; **gute** ~! [have a] safe trip!; **eine einfache** ~ a one-way [ticket]; **eine** ~ **ins Blaue** a Sunday drive ▶ **in** ~ **kommen/sein** *fam* (*in Wut*) to get/be all riled up *fam;* (*in Schwung*) to get going

Fährte <-, -n> ['fɛːɐ̯·tə] *f* trail; **auf der falschen/richtigen** ~ **sein** *fig* to be on the wrong/right track

fahrtüchtig *adj* (*Fahrzeug*) roadworthy; (*Mensch*) fit to drive *pred*

Fahrzeug <-s, -e> *nt* vehicle

Fahrzeughalter(in) *m(f)* vehicle owner

Faktor <-s, -toren> ['fak·toːɐ̯] *m* factor

Fakultät <-, -en> [fa·kʊl·'tɛt] *f* department

Falke <-n, -n> ['fal·kə] *m* falcon

Fall <-[e]s, Fälle> [fal] *m* **1.** *kein pl*

(*Sturz*) fall; *fig* (*Untergang*) downfall **2.** (*Umstand*) case, circumstance; **auf alle Fälle** in any case; **auf keinen ~** under no circumstances; **für alle Fälle** just in case; **im besten/schlimmsten ~[e]** at best/worst; **in diesem ~** in this case; **klarer ~!** you bet!; **von ~ zu ~** from case to case **3.** JUR, MED case ▶ **[nicht] jds ~ sein** *fam* to [not] be sb's cup of tea

Falle <-, -n> ['fa·lə] *f* trap; **in der ~ sitzen** to be trapped; **~n stellen** to set traps

fallen <fällt, fiel, gefallen> ['fa·lən] *vi sein* **1.** (*nach unten*) to fall; (*Person, Preise*) to fall; (*Gegenstand, Klappe, Temperatur, Vorhang*) to drop; (*Fieber, Wasserstand*) to go down; **über etw** *akk* **~** to trip over sth **2.** *fig* **eine Bemerkung ~ lassen** to drop a remark; **jdn/etw ~ lassen** to abandon sb/sth **3.** *fam* (*nicht bestehen*) **durch etw** *akk* **~** to fail sth **4.** (*im Krieg*) to be killed **5.** (*stattfinden*) **der 1. Mai fällt auf einen Montag** May 1st falls on a Monday

fällen ['fɛ·lən] *vt* **einen Baum ~** to fell a tree; **eine Entscheidung ~** to come to a decision; **ein Urteil ~** JUR to pass judgment

fällig ['fɛ·lɪç] *adj* due *usu pred*

falls [fals] *konj* if

Fallschirm *m* parachute

Fallschirmspringer(in) *m(f)* parachutist

falsch [falʃ] **I.** *adj* **1.** (*verkehrt*) wrong; **~e Anschuldigung** false accusation; **einen ~en Namen angeben** to give a false name; **~e Scham** false shame; **~e Vorstellung** wrong idea **2.** (*hinterhältig*) two-faced **II.** *adv* wrongly; **etw ~ aussprechen** to mispronounce sth; **jdn ~ informieren** to misinform sb; **~ singen** to sing out of tune

fälschen ['fɛl·ʃn] *vt* to forge; **Geld ~** to counterfeit money; **gefälschter Scheck** forged check

Falschgeld *nt kein pl* counterfeit money

falsch|liegen *vi irreg* [**mit etw** *dat*] **~** to be wrong [in sth]

falsch|spielen *vi* to cheat

Fälschung <-, -en> *f* forgery

fälschungssicher *adj* counterfeit-proof

Faltblatt *nt* leaflet

Falte <-, -n> ['fal·tə] *f* **1.** (*in Kleidung*) crease; **~n bekommen** to get wrinkled **2.** (*in Stoff*) fold; **~n werfen** to fall in folds **3.** (*in Haut*) wrinkle; **die Stirn in ~n legen** to furrow one's brow

falten ['fal·tn] *vt* to fold

Falter <-s, -> ['fal·tɐ] *m* (*Tagfalter*) butterfly; (*Nachtfalter*) moth

faltig ['fal·tɪç] *adj* wrinkled

familiär [fa·mi·'liɛ] *adj* family *attr*; **aus ~en Gründen** for family reasons; **in ~er Atmosphäre** in an informal atmosphere

Familie <-, -n> [fa·'mi:·liə] *f* family; **„~ Lang"** "The Lang Family"; **das liegt in der ~** it runs in the family; **eine vierköpfige ~** a family of four; **~ haben** to have a family

Familienname *m* last name, surname

Familienstand *m* marital status

Fan <-s, -s> [fɛn] *m* fan

Fanatiker(in) <-s, -> [fa·'na:·ti·kɐ] *m(f)* fanatic; **politischer ~** extremist

fanatisch [fa·'na:·tɪʃ] *adj* fanatical

fand ['fant] *imp von* **finden**

Fang <-[e]s, Fänge> [faŋ] *m* catch; **einen guten ~ machen** *a. fig* to make a good catch

fangen <fängt, fing, gefangen> ['faŋən] **I.** *vt, vi* to catch; **F~ spielen** to play catch **II.** *vr* **sich** *akk* **~** to steady oneself

Fangfrage *f* trick question

Fantasie <-, -n> [fan·ta·'zi:] *f kein pl* imagination

fantasieren * [fan·ta·'zi:·rən] *vi* to fantasize (**von** *+dat* about)

fantasievoll *adj* [highly] imaginative

fantastisch *adj* fantastic; **das klingt ~** that sounds incredible

Farbe <-, -n> ['far·bə] *f* color; (*Anstreichmittel*) paint; (*Färbemittel*) dye; **sanfte ~n** soft hues ▶ **~ bekennen** to come clean

färben ['fɛr·bn] **I.** *vt* to dye **II.** *vr* **sich** *akk* **~** to change color; **die Blätter ~ sich gelb** the leaves are turning yellow

farbenblind *adj* color blind

Farbfilm *m* color film

farbig ['far·bɪç] *adj* **1.** (*bunt*) colored

2. (anschaulich) colorful **3.** attr (Hautfarbe) of color; **die ~e Bevölkerung** people of color

Farbige(r) f(m) dekl wie adj person of color; (Schwarzamerikaner) African-American

Farbkopierer m color copier

farblos ['farp·lo:s] adj colorless; (langweilig) dull

Farbskala f color scale

Farbstift m colored pencil

Farbstoff m (in Nahrungsmitteln) artificial coloring

Farbton m shade

Farn <-[e]s, -e> [farn] m, **Farnkraut** nt fern

Fasan <-s, -e[n]> [fa·'za:n] m pheasant

Fasching <-s, -e> ['fa·ʃɪŋ] m südd, österr carnival

Faschismus <-> [fa·'ʃɪs·mʊs] m kein pl fascism

Faschist(in) <-en, -en> [fa·'ʃɪst] m(f) fascist

Faser <-, -n> ['fa:·zɐ] f fiber

faserig ['fa:·zə·rɪç] adj fibrous

Fass RR <-es, Fässer>, **Faß** ALT <-sses, Fässer> [fas] nt barrel; **Bier vom ~** draft beer ▶ **das ~ zum Überlaufen bringen** to be the final straw

fassen ['fasn] I. vt 1. (ergreifen) to grasp; **jdn am Arm ~** to grab sb's arm; **jdn bei der Hand ~** to take sb by the hand; **den Täter ~** to apprehend the culprit 2. fig einen Entschluss/Vorsatz ~ to make a decision/resolution; **keinen klaren Gedanken ~ können** to not be able to think clearly 3. (begreifen) to comprehend; **er konnte sein Glück kaum ~** he could hardly believe his luck 4. (enthalten) to contain II. vi to grip; **fass!** (Hund) sic [him/her]! III. vr **sich** akk **~** to pull oneself together

Fassung <-, -en> f 1. (Rahmen) mounting 2. (Brillengestell) frame 3. (für Lampen) socket 4. (Bearbeitung) version, draft 5. kein pl (Selbstbeherrschung) composure; **die ~ bewahren** to maintain one's composure; **jdn aus der ~ bringen** to rattle sb; **die ~ verlieren** to lose one's self-control

fassungslos I. adj stunned II. adv in

bewildermt; **~ zusehen, wie ...** to watch in disbelief as ...

Fassungsvermögen nt capacity

fast [fast] adv almost; **~ nie** hardly ever

fasten ['fas·tn] vi to fast

Fastenzeit f REL Lent

Fast Food RR, **Fastfood** RR, **Fast food** ALT <-> ['fa:st·fu:t] nt kein pl fast food

Fastnacht ['fast·naxt] f kein pl dial carnival

faszinieren* [fas·tsi·'ni:·rən] vt, vi to fascinate

faszinierend adj fascinating

fatal [fa·'ta:l] adj fatal; **~e Folgen** fatal repercussions; **~e Lage** awkward position

fauchen ['fau·xn] vi 1. (Tier) to hiss 2. (wütend zischen) to spit

faul [faul] adj 1. lazy 2. (verfault) rotten ▶ **an etw** dat **ist etw ~** something is fishy about sth

faulen ['fau·lən] vi sein o haben to rot

faulenzen ['fau·lɛn·tsn] vi to laze around

Faulenzer(in) <-s, -> ['fau·lɛn·tsɐ] m(f) pej slacker pej

Faulheit <-> f kein pl laziness

faulig ['fau·lɪç] adj rotten; (Geruch) foul

Fäulnis <-> ['fɔy·lnɪs] f kein pl decay, rot

Faulpelz m pej fam lazybones pej

Fauna <-, Faunen> ['fau·na] f fauna

Faultier nt ZOOL sloth

Faust <-, Fäuste> [faust] f fist ▶ **auf eigene ~** on one's own initiative

Fausthandschuh m mitten

Faustregel f rule of thumb

Fax <-, -e> [faks] nt fax

faxen ['faksn] vt, vi to fax

Faxen ['faksn] pl ▶ **lass die ~!** stop clowning around!

Fazit <-s, -s> ['fa:·tsɪt] nt result

FCKW <-s, -s> [ɛf·tse:·ka:·'ve:] m Abk von **Fluorchlorkohlenwasserstoff** CFC

Februar <-[s], selten -e> ['fe:·bru·a:ɐ̯] m February; **Anfang/Ende ~** at the beginning/end of February; **Mitte ~** in the middle of February, mid-February; **im ~** in February; **diesen/jeden ~** this/every February; **bis in den ~** [hinein] well into February; **den ganzen ~ über**

throughout February; **am 14. ~** on February 14th; **am Freitag, dem** [o **den**] **14. Februar** on Friday, February [the] 14th; **Hamburg, den 14. ~ 2005** Hamburg, February 14, 2005; **auf den 14. ~ fallen/legen** to fall on/to schedule for February 14th

fechten <ficht, focht, gefochten> [ˈfɛç·tn̩] *vi* to fence

Fechten <-s> [ˈfɛç·tn̩] *nt kein pl* fencing

Feder <-, -n> [ˈfeː·dɐ] *f* **1.** (*von Vögeln*) feather; (*Schreibfeder*) quill **2.** (*aus Metall*) spring **3.** (*Bett*) **raus aus den ~n!** *fam* rise and shine!; **noch in den ~n liegen** *fam* to still be in bed

Federball *m kein pl* badminton

Federbett *nt* duvet

Federgewicht *nt kein pl* SPORT featherweight

federn [ˈfeː·dɐn] *vi* to be springy

Federung <-, -en> *f* springing; (*von Auto*) suspension

Fee <-, -n> [feː] *f* fairy

Fegefeuer [ˈfeː·gə·] *nt* purgatory

fegen [ˈfeː·gn̩] *vt, vi* **1.** (*kehren*) to sweep **2.** *schweiz* (*feucht wischen*) to wipe

Fehlbetrag *m* ÖKON deficit

fehlen [ˈfeː·lən] **I.** *vi* **1.** (*nicht da sein*) **etw fehlt** sth is missing; **jdm fehlt etw** sb is missing sth; **unentschuldigt ~** to be absent without an excuse **2.** (*vermissen*) **jd fehlt jdm** sb misses sb **3.** (*an etw leiden*) **fehlt Ihnen etwas?** is there something wrong [with you]? **II.** *vi impers* **es fehlt etw** sth is missing; **jdm fehlt es an etw** *dat* sb is lacking sth; **jdm fehlt es an nichts** sb wants for nothing

Fehler <-s, -> [ˈfeː·lɐ] *m* mistake; (*Mangel*) defect; **einen ~ machen** to make a mistake; **jds ~ sein** to be sb's fault

Fehlermeldung *f* COMPUT error message

Fehlgeburt *f* miscarriage

Fehlgriff *m* mistake

Fehlkonstruktion *f* **eine totale ~ sein** to be poorly designed

fehlschlagen *vi irreg* to fail

Fehlstart *m* SPORT false start

Feier <-, -n> [ˈfaɪe] *f* celebration; **zur ~ des Tages** in honor of the occasion

Feierabend [ˈfaɪ·ɐ·ʔaː·bn̩t] *m* end of work;

~! that's it for today!; **schönen ~!** have a nice evening!; **hoffentlich ist bald ~** I hope it's time to go home soon!; **~ machen** to finish work for the day

feierlich [ˈfaɪ·ɐ·lɪç] **I.** *adj* (*Akt*) ceremonial; **ein ~er Anlass** a formal occasion **II.** *adv* **etw ~ begehen** to celebrate sth

Feierlichkeiten *pl* celebrations

feiern [ˈfaɪ·ɐn] *vt, vi* to celebrate; **eine Party ~** to have a party

Feiertag [ˈfaɪ·ɐ·taːk] *m* holiday

Feige <-, -n> [ˈfaɪ·gə] *f* fig

Feigheit <-> *f kein pl* cowardice

Feigling <-s, -e> [ˈfaɪk·lɪŋ] *m pej* coward

Feile <-, -n> [ˈfaɪ·lə] *f* file

feilen [ˈfaɪ·lən] *vt, vi* **an etw** *dat* **~** to file sth; *fig* to polish sth

feilschen [ˈfaɪl·ʃn̩] *vi pej* to haggle (**um** +*akk* over)

fein [faɪn] **I.** *adj* **1.** (*nicht grob*) fine; (*zart*) delicate **2.** (*vornehm*) distinguished; **jd ist sich** *dat* **für etw** *akk* **zu ~** sth is beneath sb; **sich** *akk* **~ machen** to get dressed up **3.** (*sehr gut*) exquisite; **vom F~sten** of the highest quality **4.** *fam* (*anständig*) decent; *iron* fine **5.** *fam* (*erfreulich*) **~, dass ...** it's great that ... ▸ **~ raus sein** to be in a nice position **II.** *adv* **~ gemahlen** finely ground; **~ säuberlich** accurate

Feind(in) <-[e]s, -e> [faɪnt] *m(f)* enemy; **sich** *dat* **jdn zum ~ machen** to make an enemy of sb; **ein ~ einer S.** *gen* an opponent of sth

feindlich *adj* hostile; MIL enemy *attr*

Feindschaft <-, -en> *f kein pl* animosity

feindselig [ˈfaɪnt·zeː·lɪç] *adj* hostile

Feindseligkeit <-> *f kein pl* hostility

feinfühlig [ˈfaɪn·fyː·lɪç] *adj* sensitive

Feingefühl *nt kein pl* sensitivity

feinkörnig *adj* fine-grained; (*Foto*) fine grain

Feinkostgeschäft *nt* gourmet shop

Feinmechanik *f* precision engineering

Feinschmecker(in) <-s, -> *m(f)* gourmet

Feld <-[e]s, -er> [fɛlt] *nt* field; (*auf Spielbrett*) square; (*Bereich*) area; **ein weites ~ sein** to be a broad subject ▸ **das ~ räumen** to clear the way; **jdm das**

~ **überlassen** to leave the field open to sb

Feldsalat m mâche

Feldwebel(in) <-s, -> ['fɛlt·veː·bl̩] m(f) sergeant major

Feldweg m field path

Feldzug m campaign

Felge <-, -n> ['fɛl·gə] f rim

Fell <-[e]s, -e> [fɛl] nt fur ▶ **ein dickes ~ haben** to be thick-skinned

Felsblock <-blöcke> m boulder

Felsen <-s, -> ['fɛl·zn̩] m cliff

felsenfest ['fɛl·zn̩ˈfɛst] adv ~ **von etw** dat **überzeugt sein** to be firmly convinced of sth

felsig ['fɛl·zɪç] adj rocky

Felswand f rock face

feminin [fe·mi·ˈniːn] adj feminine

Feminismus <-> [fe·mi·ˈnɪs·mʊs] m kein pl feminism

Feminist(in) <-en, -en> [fe·mi·ˈnɪst] m(f) feminist

feministisch adj feminist

Fenchel <-s> ['fɛn·çl̩] m kein pl BOT fennel

Fenster <-s, -> ['fɛn·stɐ] nt window

Fensterbank <-bänke> f windowsill

Fensterladen m shutter

Fensterplatz m window seat

Fensterputzer(in) <-s, -> m(f) window cleaner

Fensterrahmen m window frame

Fensterscheibe f window pane

Ferien ['feː·ri̯ən] pl vacation; **in die ~ fahren** to go on vacation; **die großen ~** summer vacation; **~ haben** to be on vacation

Ferienhaus nt vacation home

Ferienkurs m summer school

Ferienlager nt vacation camp

Ferienwohnung f vacation apartment

Ferienzeit f vacation

Ferkel <-s, -> ['fɛr·kl̩] nt 1. ZOOL piglet 2. pej fam (unsauberer Mensch) pig; (obszöner Mensch) filthy pig

fern [fɛrn] I. adj distant II. präp +dat far [away] from

Fernbedienung f remote control

fernbleiben vi irreg sein geh to stay away

Ferner ['fɛr·nɐ] I. adj komp von **fern**; **in**

der ~en Zukunft in the distant future II. konj furthermore

Fernfahrer(in) m(f) long-distance truck driver

Ferngespräch nt long-distance call

ferngesteuert adj remote-controlled

Fernglas nt [pair of] binoculars

fernhalten vr irreg **sich** akk **von jdm/ etw** ~ to keep away from sb/sth

Fernkurs m correspondence course

Fernlicht nt AUTO high beams

Fernost ['fɛrn·ˈʔɔst] kein art **aus/in/nach ~** from/in/to the Far East

Fernrohr nt telescope

Fernsehansager(in) m(f) television announcer

Fernsehantenne f television antenna

Fernsehen <-s> ['fɛrn·zeː·ən] nt kein pl television; **im ~ kommen** to be on television

fernsehen ['fɛrn·zeː·ən] vi irreg to watch television

Fernseher <-s, -> m television [set]

Fernsehsender m television station

Fernsehsendung f television program

Fernsehübertragung f television broadcast

Fernsehzeitschrift f TV guide

Fernsicht f view; **bei guter ~** with good visibility

Fernsteuerung f remote control

Fernstudium nt correspondence course

Fernverkehr m long-distance traffic

Fernweh <-[e]s> nt kein pl geh wanderlust

Ferse <-, -n> ['fɛr·zə] f heel ▶ **jdm [dicht] auf den ~n sein** to be [hot] on sb's tail

fertig ['fɛr·tɪç] I. adj 1. (abgeschlossen) finished; **etw ~ haben** to have finished sth; **mit etw** dat **~ sein** to be finished with sth; **mit etw** dat **~ werden** to finish sth 2. (bereit) ready 3. fam (erschöpft) exhausted 4. (im Griff haben) **mit jdm/etw ~ werden** to cope with sb/sth II. adv 1. (zu Ende) **etw ~ bekommen** to complete sth; **etw ~ machen** [o stellen] to finish sth 2. (bereit) **sich** akk **~ machen** to get ready [for sth] ▶ **auf die Plätze, ~, los!** on your marks, get set, go!

Fertiggericht nt instant meal

Fertighaus nt prefabricated house

fertig|machen I. vt, vr s. **fertig** II 1, II 2 II. vt fam 1. (zermürben) **etw macht jdn fertig** sth wears out sep/sl 2. **jdn ~** (schikanieren) to wear sb down sep; sl (zusammenschlagen) to beat sb up sep

fertig|stellen vt s. **fertig** II 1

fesch [fɛʃ] adj südd, österr fam (flott) chic

Fessel <-, -n> ['fɛsl] f 1. meist pl (Kette) shackles npl 2. ANAT (von Mensch) ankle; (von Huftier) pastern

fesseln ['fɛ·sl̩n] vt **jdn ~** to tie sb up; (faszinieren) to captivate sb

fesselnd adj captivating

fest [fɛst] I. adj firm; (erstarrt) solidified; **~e Freundschaft** lasting friendship; **~er Händedruck** firm handshake; **~e Schuhe** sturdy shoes; **~er Termin** fixed date; **~e Zusage** firm promise II. adv 1. (kräftig) firmly; **jdn ~ an sich** akk **drücken** to give someone a big hug 2. (nicht locker) tightly; **~ anziehen** to screw in tightly; **jdm etw ~ versprechen** to make sb a firm promise 3. (dauernd) permanently; **~ angestellt sein** to have a permanent job

Fest <-[e]s, -e> [fɛst] nt celebration; **ein ~ geben** to throw a party; **frohes ~!** Merry Christmas/Happy Easter, etc. ▶ **man soll die ~e feiern, wie sie fallen** prov one should make hay while the sun shines prov

festangestellt adj s. **fest** II 3

Festessen nt banquet

fest|fahren vr irreg **sich** akk **~** to get stuck

fest|halten irreg I. vt to grab (**an** +dat by); (gefangen halten) to detain II. vi **an etw** dat **~** to adhere to sth III. vr **sich** akk **~** to hold on (**an** +dat to)

Festiger <-s, -> m setting lotion

Festland ['fɛst·lant] nt kein pl mainland

fest|legen I. vt to determine; **~, dass ...** to stipulate that ...; **jdn** [**auf etw** akk] **~** to oblige sb [to do sth] II. vr **sich** akk **~** to commit [oneself] (**auf** +akk to)

festlich adv festively; **~ gekleidet sein** to be dressed up

Festlichkeit <-, -en> f festivity

fest|liegen vi irreg to be determined; **die Termine liegen jetzt fest** the schedule have now been set

fest|nageln vt 1. (mit Nägeln) to nail (**a** +akk to) 2. fam (festlegen) **jdn ~** to na sb down (**auf** +akk to)

Festnahme <-, -n> ['fɛst·naː·mə] f an rest

fest|nehmen vt irreg to take into cus tody; **Sie sind festgenommen** you'r under arrest

Festplatte f COMPUT hard disk

Festplattenlaufwerk nt COMPUT har disk drive

fest|schnallen vr **sich** akk **~** to faste one's seat belt

fest|schrauben vt to screw tight sep

fest|sitzen vi irreg to be stuck

fest|stehen vi irreg to be certain; **e steht fest, dass ...** it is certain that .. **steht das Datum schon fest?** has th date been set yet?

fest|stellen vt (bemerken) to detect; **z meinem Erstaunen muss ich ~, das ...** I am astounded to see that ...

Feststellung f remark; (Beobachtung observation; **zu der ~ kommen, das ...** to come to the conclusion that ...; **di ~ machen, dass ...** to see that ...

Festung <-, -en> ['fɛs·tʊŋ] f fortress

fett [fɛt] adj fat; (fetthaltig) fatty; **~ ge druckt** in bold [type] pred

Fett <-[e]s, -e> [fɛt] nt fat; (zum Schmie ren) grease; **~ ansetzen** (Mensch to gain weight; (Tier) to put on fa **pflanzliches/tierisches ~** vegetable animal fat

fettarm adj low-fat

Fettfleck, Fettflecken m grease mark

fettgedruckt adj attr s. **fett**

fettig ['fɛ·tɪç] adj greasy

Fettnäpfchen nt ▶ **ins ~ treten** to p one's foot in one's mouth

Fetzen <-s, -> ['fɛtsn̩] m 1. (Stück) scra **etw in ~ reißen** to tear sth to piec 2. (einer Unterhaltung) fragments 3. sl (billiges Kleid) rag ▶ **... dass d ~ fliegen** fam ... like crazy

feucht [fɔʏçt] adj damp; **~e Hände/Stin** clammy hands/forehead; **~es Klima** h mid climate; **~e Luft** humid air

Feuchtigkeit <-> ['fɔyç·tɪç·kaɪt] f kein pl dampness; (von Luft) humidity; (Wassergehalt) moisture

Feuchtigkeitscreme [-kreːm] f moisturizing cream

Feuer <-s, -> ['fɔy·ɐ] nt **1.** (Flamme, Brand) fire; **am ~** by the fire; **~ fangen** to catch [on] fire; **~ machen** to make a fire; **das olympische ~** the Olympic flame **2.** (für Zigarette) **jdm ~ geben** to give sb a light; **~ haben** to have a light **3.** (Kochstelle) **etw vom ~ nehmen** to take sth off the heat **4.** MIL (Beschuss) fire; **~ frei!** open fire!; **das ~ eröffnen/einstellen** to open/cease fire ▶ **~ und Flamme [für etw] sein** fam to be enthusiastic [about sth]; **mit dem ~ spielen** to play with fire

Feueralarm m fire alarm

Feuerbestattung f cremation

feuerfest adj fireproof; **~es Geschirr** ovenproof dishes

Feuerleiter f fire escape

Feuerlöscher m fire extinguisher

Feuermelder <-s, -> m fire alarm

feuern I. vi to fire II. vt fam to fire fam; **gefeuert werden** to get the ax

feuersicher ['fɔy·ɐ·zɪ·çɐ] adj fireproof

Feuerwehr <-, -en> f fire department

Feuerwehrauto nt fire engine

Feuerwehrmann, -frau <-leute> m, f firefighter, fireman masc, firewoman fem

Feuerwerk nt fireworks npl

Feuerwerkskörper m firework

Feuerzeug nt lighter

Feuilleton <-s, -s> [fœ·jə·'tõː] nt culture section

fichte ['fɪç·tə] f spruce

ficken ['fɪ·kn̩] vt, vi vulg to fuck vulg

Fidschiinseln pl Fiji Islands pl

Fieber <-s, -> ['fiː·bɐ] nt fever; **~ haben** to have a temperature

fieberhaft adj feverish

Fieberthermometer nt [clinical] thermometer

fiebrig ['fiː·brɪç] adj feverish

fiel ['fiːl] imp von **fallen**

fies [fiːs] adj fam mean

Figur <-, -en> [fi·'guːɐ] f figure; FILM, LIT character

Filet <-s, -s> [fi·'leː] nt fillet

Filetsteak [fi·'leː·steːk] nt fillet steak

Filiale <-, -n> [fi·'ljaː·lə] f branch

Filialleiter(in) m(f) branch manager

Film <-[e]s, -e> [fɪlm] m film; (Spielfilm a.) movie; **beim ~ arbeiten** to work in the movie industry

filmen ['fɪl·mən] vt, vi to film

Filmkamera f movie camera

Filmregisseur(in) m(f) movie director

Filmvorschau f [movie] preview

Filter <-s, -> ['fɪl·tɐ] m o nt o m filter

Filterkaffee m filter coffee

filtern ['fɪl·tɐn] vt to filter

Filterpapier nt filter paper

Filterzigarette f filter cigarette

Filz <-es, -e> [fɪlts] m felt

Filzstift m felt-tip pen

Finale <-s, -s> [fi·'naː·lə] nt final

Finanzamt nt **das ~** the Department of the Treasury

Finanzen [fi·'nan·tsn̩] pl finances npl; **jds ~ übersteigen** to be beyond sb's means

finanziell [fi·nan·'tsjɛl] adj financial

finanzieren * [fi·nan·'tsiː·rən] vt to finance; **etw [nicht] ~ können** to [not] be able to afford sth

Finanzierung <-, -en> f financing

Finanzminister(in) m(f) Secretary of the Treasury

Finanzministerium nt Department of the Treasury, Treasury [Department]

finden <fand, gefunden> ['fɪn·dn̩] I. vt **1.** to find; **Unterstützung ~** to receive support; **einen Vorwand [für etw akk] ~** to find an excuse [for sth]; **Zustimmung [bei jdm] ~** to meet with approval [from sb] **2.** (meinen) to think; **ich finde, die Ferien sind zu kurz** I think the vacation is too short; **jdn blöd/nett ~** to think [that] sb is stupid/nice; **es kalt/warm ~** to find it cold/warm ▶ **etwas an jdm/etw ~** to see sth in sb/sth; **nichts an jdm/etw ~** to not think much of sb/sth II. vi **1.** (den Weg finden) **zu jdm/etw ~** to find one's way to sb/sth; **zu sich dat selbst ~** to find oneself **2.** (meinen) to think; **~ Sie?** [do] you think so?

Finderlohn m reward [for the finder]

fing ['fɪŋ] *imp von* **fangen**

Finger <-s, -> ['fɪŋɐ] *m* finger; ~ **weg!** hands off!; **der kleine ~** the little finger ▶ **etw in die ~ bekommen** *fam* to get one's hands on sth; **keinen ~ krumm machen** *fam* to not lift a finger; **die ~ von jdm/etw lassen** *fam* to keep away from sb/sth; **sich** *dat* **etw aus den ~ saugen** *fam* to conjure up *sep* sth; **sich** *dat* **nicht die ~ schmutzig machen** *fam* to not get one's hands dirty; **überall seine ~ im Spiel haben** *fam* to have a finger in every pie

Fingerabdruck *m* fingerprint

Fingerhut *m* thimble

Fingernagel *m* fingernail; **an den Fingernägeln kauen** to bite one's nails

Fink <-en, -en> [fɪŋk] *m* finch

Finne, Finnin <-n, -n> ['fɪnə, 'fɪnɪn] *m, f* Finn, Finnish man/woman/boy/girl; ~ **sein** to be Finnish

finnisch ['fɪnɪʃ] *adj* Finnish

Finnland <-s> ['fɪnlant] *nt* Finland

finster ['fɪnstɐ] *adj* dark; *fig* grim

Firma <-, Firmen> ['fɪrma] *f* company

Firmenwagen *m* company car

Firmung <-, -en> *f* confirmation

First <-[e]s, -e> [fɪrst] *m* roof ridge

Fisch <-[e]s, -e> [fɪʃ] *m* **1.** (*Tier*) fish **2.** *kein pl* ASTROL Pisces ▶ **weder ~ noch Fleisch sein** to be neither fish nor fowl; **ein großer/kleiner ~** a big fish/small fry

fischen ['fɪʃn] *vi* to fish; **das F~** fishing

Fischer(in) <-s, -> ['fɪʃɐ] *m(f)* fisher, fisherman *masc*, fisherwoman *fem*

Fischfang *m kein pl* fishing

Fischhändler(in) *m(f)* fishmonger

Fischotter *m* otter

Fischstäbchen *nt* fish stick

Fischzucht *f* fish farming

Fisole <-, -n> [fi'zoːlə] *f österr* green bean

fit [fɪt] *adj pred* fit; **sich** *akk* ~ **halten** to keep fit

Fitness [RR], **Fitneß** [ALT] <-> ['fɪtnɛs] *f kein pl* fitness

Fitnesscenter [RR] [-sɛn-tɐ] *nt* gym

Fitnessgerät [RR] ['fɪt-nɛs-] *nt* fitness equipment

fix [fɪks] *adj* quick ▶ ~ **und fertig sein**

(*erschöpft*) to be exhausted; (*am Ende*) to be at the end of one's rope; **jdn ~ und fertig machen** *fam* to wear out sb *sep*

fixieren * [fɪk·'siː·rən] *vt* to stare at

FKK-Strand *m* nude beach

flach [flax] **I.** *adj* flat; (*nicht hoch*) low (*nicht steil*) gentle **II.** *adv* ~ **abfallen** to slope down gently; ~ **atmen** to take shallow breaths

Flachbildschirm *m* flat screen

Flachdach *nt* flat roof

Fläche <-, -n> ['flɛ·çə] *f* expanse; (*m Maßangaben*) area

Flachland *nt* lowland

flackern ['flakɐn] *vi* to flicker

Fladenbrot *nt* KOCHK ≈ [thick] pita bread

Flagge <-, -n> ['fla·gə] *f* flag

Flame, Flamin *o* **Flämin** <-n, -n> ['fla·mə, flaː·mɪn, flɛː·mɪn] *m, f* Flemish man/woman/boy/girl

Flamingo <-s, -s> [fla·'mɪŋ·go] *m* flamingo

flämisch ['flɛ·mɪʃ] *adj* Flemish

Flamme <-, -n> ['fla·mə] *f* flame; **in ~ aufgehen** to go up in flames; **etw au großer/kleiner ~ kochen** to cook sth on high/low heat

Flandern <-s> ['flan·dɐn] *nt* Flanders + *sing vb*

Flanke <-, -n> ['flaŋ·kə] *f* **1.** ANAT flank **2.** (*im Fußball*) cross

Flasche <-, -n> ['fla·ʃə] *f* **1.** bottle; **ei nem Kind die ~ geben** to bottle-fee a child **2.** *fig* loser

Flaschenbier *nt* bottled beer

Flaschenöffner *m* bottle opener

flattern ['fla·tɐn] *vi* to flutter

flau [flau] *adj* **ein ~es Gefühl im Mage** a queasy feeling

Flaum <-[e]s> [flaum] *m kein pl* down

flauschig *adj* fleecy

Flaute <-, -n> ['flau·tə] *f* (*Windstille* calm; ÖKON lull

Flechte <-, -n> ['flɛç·tə] *f* BOT, MED l chen

flechten <flocht, geflochten> ['flɛç·tən *vt* (*Haare*) to braid; (*Korb, Kranz*) t weave

Fleck <-[e]s, -e> [flɛk] *m* **1.** (*Schmutz. fleck*) stain; ~**en machen** to stai **2.** (*dunkle Stelle*) mark; **ein blauer**

a bruise **3.** (*Stelle*) spot; **sich** *akk* **nicht vom ~ rühren** to not move [an inch]

fleckig ['flɛ·kɪç] *adj* stained; **~e Haut** blotchy skin

Fledermaus ['fleː·dɐ·maus] *f* bat

Flegel <-s, -> ['fleː·gl̩] *m pej* lout

flehen ['fleː·ən] *vi geh* to beg (**um** +*akk* for)

Fleisch <-[e]s> ['flaiʃ] *nt kein pl* **1.** (*Nahrungsmittel*) meat; **~ fressend** carnivorous **2.** (*Gewebe*) flesh ▶ **jdm in ~ und Blut übergehen** to become sb's second nature; **sich** *dat* o *akk* **ins eigene ~ schneiden** to cut off one's nose to spite one's face

Fleischbrühe *f* bouillon

Fleischer(in) <-s, -> ['flai·ʃɐ] *m(f)* butcher

Fleischklößchen *nt* [small] meatball

Fleischwolf *m* meat grinder

Fleischwurst *f* ≈ pork sausage (*similar to bologna*)

fleißig ['flai·sɪç] *adj* industrious

flexibel [flɛˈksiː·bl̩] *adj* flexible; (*elastisch*) pliable

Flexibilität <-> [flɛk·si·bi·li·ˈtɛːt] *f* flexibility

flicken ['flɪ·kn̩] *vt* to mend; **einen Fahrradschlauch ~** to patch [up *sep*] a bicycle tube

Flicken <-s, -> ['flɪ·kn̩] *m* patch

Flickzeug *nt kein pl* **1.** (*für Fahrräder*) [flat] repair kit **2.** (*Nähzeug*) sewing kit

flieder *m* lilac

Fliege <-, -n> ['fliː·gə] *f* **1.** (*Insekt*) fly **2.** MODE bow tie

fliegen <flog, geflogen> ['fliː·gn̩] *vi sein* to fly

Fliegengewicht *nt kein pl* flyweight

Fliegenklatsche *f* fly swatter

Fliegenpilz *m* fly agaric

Flieger <-s, -> *m fam* plane

fliehen <floh, geflohen> ['fliː·ən] *vi sein* to flee; **aus dem Gefängnis ~** to escape from prison

Fliese <-, -n> [fliː·zə] *f* tile

Fliesenleger(in) <-s, -> *m(f)* tiler

Fließband <-bänder> *nt* assembly line; **am ~ arbeiten** to work on the production line

fließen <floss, geflossen> ['fliː·sn̩] *vi sein* to flow

fließend *adv* **~ Französisch sprechen** to speak French fluently; **~ warmes und kaltes Wasser** running hot and cold water

flimmern ['flɪ·mɐn] *vi* to flicker

flink [flɪŋk] *adj* quick

Flinte <-, -n> ['flɪn·tə] *f* shotgun ▶ **die ~ ins Korn werfen** *fam* to throw in the towel

flippern ['flɪ·pɐn] *vi* to play pinball

flippig *adj fam* hip

flirten ['flø·ɐ·tn̩] *vi* to flirt

Flitterwochen *pl* honeymoon *n sing*

flitzen ['flɪ·tsn̩] *vi sein* to dash

flocht ['flɔxt] *imp von* **flechten**

Flocke <-, -n> ['flɔ·kə] *f* flake

flog ['floːk] *imp von* **fliegen**

Floh <-[e]s, Flöhe> [floː] *m* flea

Flohmarkt *m* flea market

Floskel <-, -n> ['flɔs·kl̩] *f* set phrase

Floß <-es, Flöße> [floːs] *nt* raft

floss ^RR, **floß** ^ALT ['flɔs] *imp von* **fließen**

Flosse <-, -n> ['flɔ·sə] *f* **1.** (*Fischflosse*) fin **2.** (*Schwimmflosse*) flipper

Flöte <-, -n> ['fløː·tə] *f* **1.** MUS pipe; (*Querflöte*) flute; (*Blockflöte*) recorder **2.** (*Kelchglas*) flute [glass]

Flötist(in) <-en, -en> [fløˈtɪst] *m(f)* flutist

flott [flɔt] **I.** *adj* **1.** (*zügig*) quick; **aber ein bisschen ~!** *fam* make it snappy!; **ein ~es Tempo** [a] high speed **2.** (*schick*) smart **II.** *adv* **1.** (*zügig*) fast **2.** (*schick*) smartly

Flotte <-, -n> ['flɔ·tə] *f* fleet

flottmachen *vt* **etw** [wieder] **~** to get sth back in working order; **ein Auto ~** to get a car back on the road

Fluch <-[e]s, Flüche> [fluːx] *m* curse

fluchen ['fluː·xn̩] *vi* to curse (**auf/über** +*akk* at)

Flucht <-, -en> [flʊxt] *f* escape; **auf der ~ sein** to be on the run; **die ~ ergreifen** *geh* to take flight

fluchtartig *adv* hastily

flüchten ['flʏç·tn̩] **I.** *vi sein* to flee; (*entkommen*) to escape **II.** *vr haben* **sich** *akk* **irgendwohin ~** to seek refuge somewhere; **sich** *akk* **in etw** *akk* **~** *fig* to take refuge in sth; **sich** *akk* **in Ausreden ~** to resort to excuses

flüchtig ['flʏç·tɪç] **I.** *adj* **1.** (*geflüchtet*)

fugitive *attr;* ~ **sein** to be a fugitive **2.** (*kurz*) brief **3.** (*oberflächlich*) cursory; **eine ~e Bekanntschaft** a passing acquaintance **II.** *adv* **1.** (*kurz*) briefly **2.** (*oberflächlich*) cursorily; **jdn ~ kennen** to have met sb briefly

Flüchtigkeitsfehler *m* careless mistake

Flüchtling <-s, -> ['flʏçt·lɪŋ] *m* refugee

Flug <-[e]s, Flüge> [fluːk] *m* flight ▶ **wie im** ~[e] in a flash

Flugbegleiter(in) *m(f)* flight attendant, steward *masc*, stewardess *fem*

Flugblatt *nt* flyer

Flügel <-s, -> ['flyː·gl̩] *m* wing; MUS grand piano

Flügeltür *f* double door

Fluggast *m* passenger

Fluggeschwindigkeit *f* (*von Flugzeug*) flying speed; (*von Rakete, Geschoss*) velocity; (*von Vögeln*) speed of flight

Fluggesellschaft *f* airline

Flughafen *m* airport

Flughöhe *f* altitude

Fluglotse, -lotsin *m, f* air traffic controller

Flugplatz *m* airfield

Flugverkehr *m* air traffic

Flugzeit *f* flight time

Flugzeug <-[e]s, -e> *nt* [air]plane; **mit dem** ~ by [air]plane

Flugzeugbesatzung *f* flight crew

Flugzeughalle *f* hangar

Flugzeugträger *m* aircraft carrier

flunkern ['flʊŋ·kɐn] *vi fam* to fib

Fluor <-s> ['fluː·oːɐ̯] *nt kein pl* fluorine

Flur <-[e]s, -e> [fluːɐ̯] *m* hall[way]

Fluss RR <-es, Flüsse>, **Fluß** ALT <-sses, Flüsse> [flʊs] *m* river; **am** ~ next to the river

flussab RR [flʊs·'ʔap], **flussabwärts** RR [flʊs·'ʔap·vɛrts] *adv* downriver

flussaufwärts RR [flʊs·'ʔaʊf·vɛrts] *adv* upriver

Flussbett RR *nt* riverbed

flüssig ['flyː·sɪç] **I.** *adj* liquid **II.** *adv* ~ **lesen** to read effortlessly; ~ **sprechen** to speak fluently

Flüssigkeit <-, -en> *f* liquid

Flusskrebs RR *m* crayfish

Flusspferd RR *nt* hippopotamus

Flussufer RR *nt* river bank

flüstern ['flʏs·tɐn] *vt, vi* to whisper

Flut <-, -en> [fluːt] *f* **1.** GEOL high tide; **bei** ~ at high tide; **die** ~ **geht zurück** the tide is going out; **es ist** ~ the tide's in; **die** ~ **kommt** the tide is coming in **2.** (*große Menge*) **eine** ~ **von etw** *dat* a flood of sth

fluten ['fluː·tn̩] *vt, vi* to flood

Fluthilfe *f* flood relief

Flutlicht *nt kein pl* floodlight

Flutwelle *f* tidal wave

focht [fɔxt] *imp von* **fechten**

Fohlen <-s, -> ['foː·lən] *nt* foal

Föhn RR <-[e]s, -e> [føːn] *m* **1.** (*Wind*) foehn [wind] **2.** (*Haartrockner*) hair dryer

föhnen RR *vt* to blow-dry

Folge <-, -n> ['fɔl·gə] *f* **1.** (*Auswirkung*) consequence; **etw zur** ~ **haben** to result in sth; **als** ~ **von etw** *dat* as a consequence of sth **2.** (*Abfolge*) series; (*von Bildern, Tönen a.*) sequence; **in rascher** ~ in quick succession **3.** (*einer TV-Serie*) episode

folgen ['fɔl·gn̩] *vi sein* **jdm** ~ to follow sb; **auf etw** *akk* ~ to come after sth; **aus etw** *dat* ~ to follow from sth; **es folgt, dass ...** it follows that ...; **wie folgt** as follows; **jdm/etw** ~ **können** to be able to follow sb/sth; **einem Vorschlag** ~ to act on a suggestion

folgend ['fɔl·gn̩t] *adj* following; **F~es** the following; **im F~en** in the following

folgendermaßen ['fɔl·gn̩·de·'maː·sn̩] *adv* as follows

folgenschwer *adj* serious; **eine ~e Entscheidung** a momentous decision

folgerichtig *adj* logical

folgern ['fɔl·gɐn] *vt* to conclude (**aus** +*dat* from)

folglich ['fɔlk·lɪç] *adv* therefore

folgsam ['fɔlk·zaːm] *adj* obedient

Folie <-, -n> ['foː·liə] *f* **1.** (*Plastikfolie*) [plastic] film; KOCHK plastic wrap; (*Metallfolie*) foil **2.** (*Projektorfolie*) slide

Folter <-, -n> ['fɔl·te] *f* torture ▶ **jdn auf die** ~ **spannen** to keep sb on tenterhooks

foltern ['fɔl·tɐn] *vt* to torture

Folterung <-, -en> *f* torture

Fonds <-, -> [fõː] *m* FIN fund

önenALT ['føː·nən] *vt s.* **föhnen**

Fontäne <-, -n> [fɔn·'tɛː·nə] *f* fountain

Förderband <-bänder> *nt* conveyor belt

förderlich *adj* useful

fordern ['fɔr·dən] *vt* 1. (*verlangen*) to demand 2. (*erfordern*) to require 3. (*Leistung abverlangen*) **jdn ~** to make demands on sb

fördern ['fœr·dən] *vt* 1. (*unterstützen*) to support; **jdn ~** (*Sponsor*) to sponsor; **die Verdauung ~** to aid digestion 2. (*steigern*) to promote; **den Umsatz ~** to boost sales 3. (*abbauen*) to mine for; (*Erdöl*) to drill for

Forderung <-, -en> *f* demand; ÖKON debt claim; **jds ~en erfüllen** to meet sb's demands; **~en [an jdn] stellen** to make demands [on sb]

Forelle <-, -n> [fo·'rɛ·lə] *f* trout

Form <-, -en> [fɔrm] *f* 1. (*äußere Gestalt*) shape; **~ annehmen** to take shape; **in ~ bleiben** to stay in shape; **nicht in ~ sein** to be out of shape; **seine ~ verlieren** to lose shape 2. (*Art und Weise*) form; **in ~ von etw** *dat* in the form of sth; **in mündlicher/schriftlicher ~** verbally/in writing; **die ~ wahren** to remain polite 3. (*Gussform*) mold

formal [fɔr·'maːl] *adj* formal

Formalität <-, -en> [fɔr·ma·li·'tɛt] *f* formality

Format <-[e]s, -e> [fɔr·'maːt] *nt* format ▶ **[kein] ~ haben** to have [no] class

formatieren * [fɔr·ma·'tiː·rən] *vt* to format

Formatierung *f* formatting

formbar *adj* malleable

Formel <-, -n> ['fɔr·ml] *f* 1. CHEM, MATH formula 2. (*in Brief, Eid*) wording

formell [fɔr·'mɛl] *adj* official

förmlich ['fœrm·lɪç] I. *adj* (*Bitte, Entschuldigung*) formal II. *adv* 1. (*unpersönlich*) formally 2. (*geradezu*) really

Förmlichkeit <-, -en> *f kein pl* formality

formlos *adj* **~er Antrag** informal application

Formular <-s, -e> [fɔr·mu·'laːɐ̯] *nt* form

formulieren * [fɔr·mu·'liː·rən] *vt* to formulate; **... wenn ich es mal so ~ darf** ... if

I might put it that way

forsch [fɔrʃ] *adj* bold

forschen ['fɔr·ʃn] *vi* to research; **nach jdm/etw ~** to search for sb/sth

Forscher(in) <-s, -> *m(f)* researcher; (*Forschungsreisender*) explorer

Forschung <-, -en> *f* research; **~ und Lehre** research and teaching

Forst <-[e]s, -e[n]> [fɔrst] *m* [commercial] forest

Forstamt *nt* Forest Service

Förster(in) <-s, -> ['fœr·stɐ] *m(f)* forester

Forstwirtschaft *f kein pl* forestry

fort [fɔrt] *adv* 1. (*weg*) away; **nur ~ von hier!** let's get out of here 2. (*weiter*) **und so ~** and so on; **in einem ~** constantly

fort|bewegen * *vt, vr* **[sich** *akk*] **~** to move

Fortbewegung *f kein pl* movement

Fortbewegungsmittel *nt* means of locomotion

fort|bilden *vr* **sich** *akk* **~** to further one's training

Fortbildung *f kein pl* supplementary training

fort|bringen ['fɔrt·brɪŋən] *vt irreg* to take away *sep*

fort|dauern *vi* to continue

fort|fahren *vi sein* 1. (*wegfahren*) to drive [away/off] 2. (*weitermachen*) to continue

fort|führen *vt* 1. (*wegführen*) to lead away 2. (*fortsetzen*) to continue

fort|gehen *vi sein* to go away

fortgeschritten *adj* advanced; **im ~en Alter** at an advanced age

fortgesetzt *adj* constant

fort|jagen *vt* to chase away

fort|laufen *vi irreg sein* to run away; **uns ist unsere Katze fortgelaufen** our cat has disappeared

fortlaufend *adj* consecutive

fort|pflanzen *vr* **sich** *akk* **~** to reproduce

Fortpflanzung *f kein pl* reproduction

fort|schaffen *vt* to get rid of

fort|schicken *vt* to send away

Fortschritt ['fɔrt·ʃrɪt] *m* progress; **[gute] ~e machen** to make progress

fortschrittlich adj progressive

fortsetzen vt, vi to continue

Fortsetzung <-, -en> ['fɔrt·zɛ·tsʊŋ] f (eines Buches, Films) sequel; (einer TV-Serie, eines Hörspiels) episode; „~ folgt" "to be continued"

fortwährend ['fɔrt·vɛː·rənt] adj attr constant

Fossil <-s, -ien> [fɔ·'siːl] nt fossil

Foto <-s, -s> ['foː·to] nt photo, picture; **ein ~ [von jdm/etw] machen** to take a photo [of sb/sth]

Fotoapparat m camera

Fotograf(in) <-en, -en> [fo·to·'graːf] m(f) photographer

Fotografie <-, -n> [fo·to·gra·'fiː] f photography

fotografieren * [fo·to·gra·'fiː·rən] I. vt **jdn/etw ~** to take a picture II. vi to take pictures

Fotokopie [fo·to·ko·'piː] f photocopy

fotokopieren * [fo·to·ko·'piː·rən] vt to photocopy

Fötus <-[ses], Föten> ['føː·tʊs] m fetus

foulen ['fau·lən] vt, vi to foul

Fracht <-, -en> [fraxt] f freight

Frachter <-s, -> ['frax·te] m freighter

Frachtgut nt cargo

Frachtschiff nt cargo boat; (groß) cargo ship

Frack <-[e]s, Fräcke> [frak] m tails npl; **im ~** in tails; **einen ~ tragen** to wear tails

Frage <-, -n> ['fraː·gə] f question; **~en aufwerfen** to raise questions; **eine ~ zu etw** dat **haben** to have a question about sth; **keine ~** no problem; **in ~ kommen** to be worthy of consideration; **nicht in ~ kommen** to be out of the question; **ohne ~** without [a] doubt; **jdm eine ~ stellen** to ask sb a question; **eine strittige ~** a controversial issue; **ungelöste ~en** unresolved issues

Fragebogen m questionnaire

fragen ['fraː·gŋ] I. vi to ask; **man wird ja wohl noch ~ dürfen** I was only asking; **nach jdm ~** to ask for sb; **nach der Uhrzeit/dem Weg ~** to ask for the time/for directions; **nach jds Gesundheit ~** to inquire about sb's health; **ohne zu ~** without asking questions

II. vr **sich** akk **~, ob/wann/wie ..** to wonder whether/when/how ...; **es fragt sich, ob ...** it is doubtful whethe ... III. vt **|jdn| etw ~** to ask [sb] sth

Fragesatz m LING interrogative clause

Fragezeichen nt question mark

fraglich ['fraːk·lɪç] adj 1. (fragwürdig) suspect; **eine ~e Angelegenheit** a sus picious matter 2. (unsicher) doubtful; **es ist ~, ob ...** it's doubtful whether .. 3. attr (betreffend) in question pred; **zu ~en Zeit** at the time in question

fragwürdig ['fraːk·vvr·dɪç] adj dubious

Fraktion <-, -en> [frak·'tsjoːn] f faction

Fraktionsvorsitzende(r) f(m) dekl wie adj chairman of a political party

frankieren * [fraŋ·'kiː·rən] vt to put post age on

Frankreich <-s> ['fraŋk·raiç] nt France s. a. **Deutschland**

Franse <-, -n> ['fran·zə] f fringe

Franzose <-n, -n> [fran·'tsoː·zə] m ad justable wrench

Franzose, Französin <-n, -n> [fran 'tsoː·zə, fran·'tsøː·zɪn] m, f French man masc, Frenchwoman fem; **~ sein** to be French; **die ~n** the French; s. a. **Deutsche(r)**

französisch [fran·'tsøː·zɪʃ] adj French; **~es Bett** double bed; s. a. **deutsch**

Französisch [fran·'tsøː·zɪʃ] nt dek wie adj French; **auf ~** in French; s. a **Deutsch**

Fraß <-es, selten -e> [fraːs] m pej far (schlechtes Essen) slop

fraß [fraːs] imp von **fressen**

Fratze <-, -n> ['fra·tsə] f grotesque face (Grimasse) grimace

Frau <-, -en> [frau] f woman; (Ehefrau wife; (Anrede) Mrs., Ms.; ~ **Dokto** Doctor; **gnädige ~** geh my dear lady

Frauenarzt, -ärztin m, f gynecologist

Frauenbewegung f kein pl women' rights movement

Frauenhaus nt women's shelter

Fräulein <-s, -> ['frɔy·lain] nt hur veraltend young [unmarried] woman (Anrede) Miss

frech [frɛç] adj 1. (dreist) brazen; **~ sein** to be rude; (Kind) to backtalk 2. (kess daring; **~e Frisur** sassy hairstyle

Frechdachs *m fam* little rascal

Frechheit <-, -en> *f* **1.** *kein pl* (*Dreistigkeit*) impudence; **die ~ haben, etw zu tun** to have the nerve to do sth **2.** (*Äußerung*) rude remark; (*Handlung*) insolent behavior

frei [frai] **I.** *adj* **1.** (*nicht gefangen, unabhängig*) free; **~e Meinungsäußerung** freedom of speech; **~er Mitarbeiter/~e Mitarbeiterin** freelance[r]; **aus ~en Stücken** of one's own free will **2.** (*freie Zeit*) **er hat heute ~** he's off today; **~ haben/nehmen** to have/take time off; **eine Woche ~ haben** to have a week off **3.** (*verfügbar*) available; **sich** *akk* [**für jdn/etw**] **~ machen** to make oneself available [for sb/sth] **4.** (*nicht besetzt*) free; (*Stuhl, Zimmer*) vacant; **ist dieser Platz ~?** is this seat taken?; **~e Stelle** vacancy; **eine Zeile ~ lassen** to leave a line **5.** (*kostenlos*) free; „**Eintritt ~**" "admission free"; „**Lieferung ~ Haus**" "free [home] delivery" **6.** (*ohne etw*) **~ von etw** *dat* **sein** to be free of sth; **~e Rede** impromptu speech **7.** (*unbekleidet*) bare; **sich** *akk* **~ machen** to get undressed **8.** (*ungefähr*) **~ nach ...** roughly quoting... **II.** *adv* **er läuft immer noch ~ herum!** he is still on the loose!; **~ atmen** to breathe easy; **sich** *akk* **~ bewegen können** to be able to move [around] freely; **~ erfunden** to be completely made up; **~ laufend** (*Tiere*) free-range; **~ lebend** living in the wild; **~ sprechen** to speak off the cuff

Freibad *nt* outdoor swimming pool

freiberuflich *adj* freelance

Freibetrag *m* allowance

Freie(r) *f(m) dekl wie adj* freeman

freigeben *vt irreg* (*Urlaub geben*) to give time off

freihalten *vt irreg* (*Ausfahrt*) to keep clear; **einen Platz für jdn ~** to save a seat for sb

Freihandelszone *f* free trade zone

freihändig ['frai·hɛn·dɪç] *adv* **~ zeichnen** to draw freehand; **~ Rad fahren** to ride a bike with no hands

Freiheit <-, -en> ['frai·hait] *f* **1.** *kein pl* (*das Nichtgefangensein*) freedom; **in ~ sein** to have escaped **2.** (*[Vor]recht*) liberty; **sich** *dat* **die ~ nehmen, etw zu tun** to take the liberty of doing sth; **dichterische ~** poetic license

Freiheitsstrafe *f* prison sentence

Freikarte *f* free ticket

Freikörperkultur *f kein pl* nudism

freilassen *vt irreg* to free

freilegen *vt* to uncover

Freilichtbühne *f* open-air theater

freimachen **I.** *vt* (*frankieren*) to stamp **II.** *vi fam* (*nicht arbeiten*) to take time off

Freimaurer ['frai·mau·rɐ] *m* Freemason

freimütig ['frai·my:·tɪç] *adj* frank

freischaffend *adj attr* freelance

freisprechen *vt irreg* JUR to acquit

Freispruch *m* acquittal; **auf ~ plädieren** to plead for an acquittal

Freistaat *m* free state

freistehen *vi irreg* **jdm steht es frei, etw zu tun** sb is free to do sth

Freistoß *m* free kick

Freitag <- [e]s, -e> ['frai·ta:k] *m* Friday; *s. a.* **Dienstag**

freiwillig ['frai·vɪ·lɪç] *adv* voluntarily; **sich** *akk* **~ versichern** to take out a voluntary insurance policy

Freiwillige(r) ['frai·vɪ·lɪ·gə, 'frai·vɪ·lɪ·gə] *f(m) dekl wie adj* volunteer

Freizeichen *nt* dial tone

Freizeit *f* free time

Freizeitkleidung *f* leisurewear

Freizeitpark *m* amusement park

freizügig *adj* **~es Kleid** revealing dress

fremd [frɛmt] *adj* **ich bin hier ~** I'm not from around here; **~es Eigentum** somebody else's property; **~e Länder/Sitten** foreign countries/customs

Fremde(r) ['frɛm·dɐ, -ɐɐ] *f(m) dekl wie adj* stranger; (*Ausländer*) foreigner

Fremdenführer(in) *m(f)* [tour] guide

Fremdenlegion *f kein pl* [French] Foreign Legion

Fremdenverkehr *m* tourism

Fremdkörper *m* MED foreign body

Fremdsprache *f* foreign language

fremdsprachlich *adj* foreign-language *attr*

Fremdwort *nt* borrowed word

Frequenz [fre·'kvɛnts] *f* frequency

Fresko <-s, Fresken> ['frɛs·ko] *nt* fresco

Fressalien [frɛ·'sa:·li·ən] *pl fam* grub

Fresse <-, -n> ['frɛsə] f derb (Mund) trap; (Gesicht) mug ▸ **die ~ halten** to shut up, to shut one's face; **jdm die ~ polieren** to smash sb's face in

fressen <fraß, gefressen> ['frɛ·sn̩] I. vi 1. (von Tieren) to eat 2. pej derb (von Menschen) to gobble 3. fig (langsam zerstören) to eat away (**an** +dat at) II. vt 1. (Tiere) to eat; (sich ernähren) to feed on; **etw leer ~** to lick sth clean 2. fig (verbrauchen) **Energie ~** to gobble up sep energy ▸ **jdn zum F~ gernhaben** fam sb is good enough to eat

Frettchen <-s, -> ['frɛt·çən] nt ferret

Freude <-, -n> ['frɔy·də] f joy, delight; **was für eine ~, dich wiederzusehen!** what a pleasure to see you again!; **~ an etw** dat **haben** to get pleasure from sth; **jdm eine ~ machen** to make sb happy; **etw macht jdm ~** sb enjoys sth; **zu unserer großen ~** to our great delight

Freudengeschrei nt cries of joy

freudestrahlend adv joyfully

freudig ['frɔy·dɪç] I. adj joyful; **~es Ereignis** happy event; **~e Nachricht/Überraschung** joyful news/surprise II. adv with joy; **~ überrascht** pleasantly surprised

freudlos ['frɔyt·loːs] adj cheerless

freuen ['frɔy·ən] I. vr sich akk ~ to be happy (**über** +akk about); **sich** akk **auf etw** akk ~ to look forward to sth; **sich** akk **für jdn ~** to be happy for sb; **sich** akk **mit jdm ~** to share sb's happiness II. vt impers **es freut mich, dass ...** I'm pleased that ...

Freund(in) <-[e]s, -e> ['frɔynt, 'frɔyn·dɪn] m(f) friend; (Anhänger) lover; (intimer Bekannter) boyfriend; (intime Bekannte) girlfriend; **jdn zum ~ haben** to be going [out] with sb

freundlich ['frɔynt·lɪç] I. adj friendly; (Person a.) kind; (Farben) cheerful; **das ist sehr ~ von Ihnen** that's very kind of you; **bitte recht ~!** smile please!; **eine ~e Einstellung** a friendly attitude II. adv in a friendly way, kindly

Freundlichkeit <-, -en> f kein pl friendliness, kindness

Freundschaft <-, -en> f kein pl friendship; **~ schließen** to make friends

freundschaftlich I. adj **~e Gefühle** feelings of friendship II. adv **jdm ~ auf die Schulter klopfen** to give sb a friendly slap on the back; **jdm ~ gesinnt sein** to be well-disposed toward sb

Frieden <-s, -> ['friː·dn̩] m peace; **ich traue dem ~ nicht** there's something fishy going on; **im ~** in peacetime; **der häusliche ~** domestic harmony; **jdn in ~ lassen** to leave sb in peace; **~ schließen** to make peace; **~ stiften** to bring about peace

Friedensbewegung f peace movement

Friedenseinsatz m MIL peacekeeping troops pl

Friedensrichter(in) m(f) justice of the peace

Friedensverhandlungen pl peace negotiations

Friedensvertrag m peace treaty

friedfertig adj peaceable

Friedhof m graveyard; (in Städten) cemetery

friedlich ['friːt·lɪç] adj peaceful; (Tier) placid

frieren <fror, gefroren> ['friː·rən] I. vi 1. haben (sich kalt fühlen) **jd friert** sb is freezing 2. sein (gefrieren) to freeze II. vi impers haben **es friert** it's freezing

Frikadelle <-, -n> [fri·ka·'dɛ·lə] f hamburger

frisch [frɪʃ] I. adj fresh; (Farbe) wet; (Wind a.) cool; **sich** akk ~ **machen** to freshen up; **~ und munter sein** fam to be [as] fresh as a daisy II. adv freshly; **die Betten ~ beziehen** to change the sheets; **~ gebacken** freshly baked; **~ gestrichen** newly painted

Frischhaltefolie f plastic wrap

Frischkäse m cream cheese

Friseur <-s, -e> [fri·'zøːɐ̯] m hairdresser's; (Herrensalon) barbershop; **zum ~ gehen** to go to the hairdresser's/barbershop

Friseur(in) <-s, -e> [fri·'zøːɐ̯] m(f), **Friseuse** <-, -n> [fri·'zøː·zə] f hairdresser; (Herrenfriseur) barber

frisieren * [fri·'ziː·rən] vt **jdn ~** to do sb's hair

Frisiersalon m hair stylist['s]; (für Da-

men) hairdresser's; (für Herren) barbershop

Frisör <-s, -e> [fri·'zø:ɐ̯] m, **Frisöse** <-, -n> [fri·'zø:·zə] f s. **Friseur(in)**

Frist <-, -en> [frɪst] f period; (Aufschub) respite; (bei Zahlung) extension; **festgesetzte ~** fixed time; **gesetzliche ~** statutory period; **innerhalb einer ~ von zwei Wochen** within two week deadline

fristlos adv without notice; **jdn ~ entlassen** to fire sb on the spot

Frisur <-, -en> [fri·'zu:ɐ̯] f hairstyle

frittieren * RR, **fritieren** * ALT [frɪ·'ti:·rən] vt to [deep-]fry

froh [fro:] adj happy; **~ sein** to be pleased (**über** +akk with/about); **~e Feiertage!** have a nice holiday!; **~e Ostern/Weihnachten!** Happy Easter/Merry Christmas!; **eine ~e Botschaft** good news; **die F~e Botschaft** REL the Gospel; **~ gelaunt** cheerful

fröhlich ['frø:·lɪç] adj cheerful

Fröhlichkeit <-> f kein pl cheerfulness

fromm <frömmer, frömmste> [frɔm] adj devout

Front <-, -en> [frɔnt] f face, front; **in vorderster ~ stehen** to be on the front lines ▸ **klare ~en schaffen** to clarify one's position

frontal [frɔn·'ta:l] I. adj attr frontal; **~er Zusammenstoß** head-on collision II. adv frontally; **~ zusammenstoßen** to collide head-on

Frontscheibe f AUTO windshield

fror ['fro:ɐ̯] imp von **frieren**

Frosch <-[e]s, Frösche> [frɔʃ] m frog ▸ **einen ~ im Hals haben** fam to have a frog in one's throat

Froschschenkel m frog's leg

Frost <-[e]s, Fröste> [frɔst] m frost; **~ abbekommen** to get frostbitten

frösteln [frœs·tln] vi to shiver

frostig ['frɔs·tɪç] adj frosty

Frostschutzmittel nt antifreeze

Frottee <-s, -s> [frɔ·'te:] nt o m terrycloth

frotzeln ['frɔ·tsln] vi fam to tease

Frucht <-, Früchte> [frʊxt] f fruit; **kandierte Früchte** candied fruit; **Früchte tragen** to bear fruit

fruchtbar ['frʊxt·ba:ɐ̯] adj fertile

Fruchtbarkeit <-> f kein pl fertility

fruchten ['frʊx·tn̩] vi **nichts/wenig ~** to be of no/little use

Fruchtfleisch nt [fruit] pulp

fruchtlos adj fig fruitless

Fruchtsaft m fruit juice

Fruchtwasser nt MED amniotic fluid

Fruchtzucker m fructose

früh [fry:] I. adj early; **~ am Morgen** early in the morning; **der ~e Goethe** the young Goethe; **ein ~er Picasso** an early Picasso II. adv early; **Montag ~** Monday morning; **~ genug** early enough; **von ~ bis spät** from morning until night

Frühaufsteher(in) <-s, -> m(f) early riser

Frühe <-> ['fry:·ə] f kein pl **in aller ~** at the crack of dawn; **in der ~** early in the morning

früher ['fry:·ɐ̯] I. adj 1. (vergangen) earlier; **in ~en Zeiten** in the past 2. (ehemalig) former; (Adresse) previous; **~e Freundin** ex[-girlfriend] II. adv 1. (eher) earlier; **~ geht's nicht** it can't be done any earlier; **~ oder später** sooner or later 2. (ehemals) **ich habe ihn ~ [mal] gekannt** I used to know him; **~ war das alles anders** things were different in the [good] old days; **von ~** from the past

Früherkennung f early diagnosis

frühestens adv at the earliest

Frühgeburt f premature birth; (Baby) premature baby

Frühjahr ['fry:·ja:ɐ̯] nt spring

Frühjahrsmüdigkeit f springtime lethargy

Frühling <-s, -e> ['fry:·lɪŋ] m spring[time]; **es wird ~** spring is coming

Frühlingsrolle f spring roll

frühmorgens [fry:·'mɔr·gn̩s] adv early in the morning

Frühpensionierung f early retirement

frühreif adj precocious

Frühschicht f morning shift; **~ haben** to be on the morning shift

Frühstück <-s, -e> ['fry:·ʃtʏk] nt breakfast; **zum ~** for breakfast; **zweites ~** midmorning snack

frühstücken ['fry:·ʃtʏ·kn̩] vt, vi **[etw] ~** to

have [sth for] breakfast

frühzeitig ['fryːtsaɪ̯tɪç] *adj, adv* early; **möglichst ~** as soon as possible

Frust <-[e]s> [frʊst] *m kein pl fam* frustration; **einen ~ haben** to be frustrated

Frustration <-, -en> [frʊstraˈtsi̯oːn] *f* frustration

frustrieren * [frʊsˈtriːrən] *vt fam* **jdn frustriert etw** sth is frustrating sb

Fuchs, Füchsin <-es, Füchse> [fʊks, ˈfʏksɪn] *m, f* fox; (*weiblich*) vixen

Fuchsbau *m* [fox's] den

Fuchsschwanz *m* 1. ZOOL [fox's] tail 2. (*Säge*) [straight back] hand saw

fuchsteufelswild [fʊks-ˈtɔ̯y-fls-ˈvɪlt] *adj fam* mad as hell

Fuchtel <-, -n> [ˈfʊx-tl̩] *f fam* **unter jds ~ stehen** to be [well] under sb's control

Fuge <-, -n> [ˈfuː-ɡə] *f* joint; **aus den ~n geraten** *fig* to be turned upside down

fügen [ˈfyː-ɡn̩] *vr* **sich** *akk* **~** to toe the line; **sich** *akk* **in etw** *akk* **~** to submit to sth; **sich** *akk* **jdm ~** to bow to sb; **sich** *akk* **den Anordnungen ~** to obey instructions

Fügung <-, -en> *f* stroke of fate; **eine ~ des Schicksals** an act of fate; **eine glückliche ~** a stroke of luck; **eine göttliche ~** divine providence

fühlbar *adj* noticeable

fühlen [ˈfyː-lən] I. *vt, vi* to feel II. *vr* **wie ~ Sie sich?** how do you feel?; **sich** *akk* **besser ~** to feel better

fuhr [fuːɐ̯] *imp von* **fahren**

Fuhre <-, -n> [ˈfuː-rə] *f* [cart]load

führen [ˈfyː-rən] I. *vt* 1. (*leiten*) **ein Geschäft ~** to run a business; **eine Armee ~** to command an army; **jdn ~** to lead sb 2. **etw mit sich** *dat* **~** to carry sth 3. (*geleiten*) **was führt Sie zu mir?** what brings you to me?; **jdn auf Abwege ~** to lead sb astray; **jdn durch ein Museum ~** to show sb around a museum 4. ÖKON to stock II. *vi* 1. SPORT **mit drei Punkten ~** to lead by three points 2. (*verlaufen: Weg*) to lead; (*Kabel*) to run 3. (*als Ergebnis haben*) **zu etw** *dat* **~** to lead to sth

führend *adj* leading *attr*

Führer <-s, -> [ˈfyː-rə] *m* (*Buch*) guide[book]

Führer(in) <-s, -> [ˈfyː-rə] *m(f)* leader; (*Fremdenführer*) [tour] guide; **der ~** HIST (*Hitler*) the Führer

Führerschein *m* driver's license; **den ~ machen** (*Unterricht nehmen*) to learn to drive; (*Prüfung machen*) to take one's driving test

Führerscheinentzug *m* driver's license revocation

Fuhrpark *m* fleet [of vehicles]

Führung <-, -en> *f* 1. (*Besichtigung*) guided tour 2. *kein pl* MIL command 3. *kein pl* (*Vorsprung*) **in ~ liegen/gehen** to be in/take the lead 4. *kein pl* (*Betragen*) **bei guter ~** for good conduct

Führungskraft *f* executive [officer]

Führungszeugnis *nt* **polizeiliches ~** [criminal] background check

Fuhrunternehmen [fuːɐ̯-] *nt* trucking company

Fülle <-> [ˈfʏ-lə] *f kein pl* ▶ **in Hülle und ~** in abundance

füllen [ˈfʏ-lən] I. *vt* to fill; (*Gans, Ente, etc.*) to stuff; **etw in etw** *akk* **~** to put sth into sth; **etw in Flaschen ~** to bottle sth II. *vr* **sich** *akk* **~** to fill [up]

Füller <-s, -> [ˈfʏ-lə] *m* fountain pen; (*mit Patrone*) cartridge pen

Füllung <-, -en> *f* stuffing

fummeln [ˈfʊ-mln̩] *vi fam* 1. (*hantieren*) to fumble [around] 2. (*sexuell*) to pet

fundamental [fʊn-da-mɛn-ˈtaːl] *adj* fundamental

Fundbüro *nt* lost-and-found [office]

Fundsachen *pl* lost and found items

fünf [fʏnf] *adj* five; *s. a.* **acht¹**

Fünf <-, -en> [fʏnf] *f* 1. (*Zahl*) five; *s. a.* **Acht¹** 2. (*Note*) "unsatisfactory", ≈ "F"

fünffach, 5fach [ˈfʏnf-fax] *adj* fivefold; **die ~e Menge** five times the amount

fünfhundert [ˈfʏnf-ˈhʊn-dət] *adj* five hundred

fünfmal, 5-mal ᴿᴿ *adv* five times; *s. a.* **achtmal**

fünftausend [ˈfʏnf-ˈtau̯-znt] *adj* five thousand

fünfte(r, s) [ˈfʏnf-tə, ˈfʏnf-tɐ, ˈfʏnf-təs]

adj (*Zahl*) fifth; (*Datum*) 5th; *s. a.*
achte(r, s) 1, 2

fünftel ['fʏnf·tl̩] *adj* fifth

fünftens ['fʏnf·tns] *adv* in [the] fifth place

fünfzehn ['fʏnf·tse:n] *adj* fifteen; ~ **Uhr** 3
p.m.; *s. a.* **acht**[1]

fünfzehnte(r, s) *adj* (*Zahl*) fifteenth; (*Datum*) 15th; *s. a.* **achte(r, s) 1, 2**

fünfzig ['fʏnf·tsɪç] *adj* fifty; *s. a.* **acht-zig 1, 2**

fünfzigste(r, s) *adj* fiftieth; *s. a.* **achte(r, s) 1, 2**

Funk <-s> [fʊŋk] *m kein pl* radio

Funke <-ns, -n> ['fʊŋ·kə], **Funken** <-s, -> ['fʊŋ·kn̩] *m* spark; ~**n sprühen** to emit sparks; **ein** ~ [**von**] **Anstand** *fig* a shred of decency; **ein** ~ **Hoffnung** *fig* a gleam of hope; **der zündende** ~ *fig* the vital spark

funkeln ['fʊŋ·kl̩n] *vi* to sparkle; (*Edelsteine, Gold*) to glitter

funken ['fʊŋ·kn̩] **I.** *vt* to radio; **SOS** ~ to send out *sep* an SOS **II.** *vi impers fam* (*sich verlieben*) **zwischen den beiden hat's gefunkt** those two have really clicked

Funkgerät *nt* radiotelephone unit; (*Sprechfunkgerät*) walkie-talkie

Funkstille *f* ▶ **bei jdm herrscht** ~ sb is [completely] incommunicado

Funktion <-, -en> [fʊŋk·'tsjo:n] *f* function; **in ihrer** ~ **als etw** in her capacity as sth

Funktionär(in) <-s, -e> [fʊŋk·tsjo·'nɛːɐ̯] *m(f)* official; **ein hoher** ~ a high-ranking official

funktionell [fʊŋk·tsjo·'nɛl] *adj* MED **eine** ~**e Störung** a dysfunction

funktionieren* [fʊŋk·tsjo·'niː·rən] *vi* to work; (*Maschine a.*) to operate; (*Organisation*) to run smoothly

Funkverbindung *f* radio contact

Funkverkehr *m* radio communication *no art*

für [fyːɐ̯] *präp* +*akk* for; ~ **jdn/etw** for sb/sth; **er hat es** ~ **45 Dollar bekommen** he got it for 45 dollars; **sind Sie** ~ **diesen Kandidaten?** do you support this candidate?; ~ **ihr Alter ist sie noch rüstig** she's in great shape for someone her age; ~ **diese Jahreszeit**

ist es ziemlich kalt it's pretty cold for this time of year; **was Sie da sagen, hat manches** ~ **sich** there's something to what you're saying; **ich halte sie** ~ **intelligent** I think she is intelligent; ~ **ganz** *schweiz* (*für immer*) for good, forever; ~ **sich** *akk* **bleiben** to remain by oneself; **was** ~ **ein ...** what ...; **was** ~ **ein Blödsinn!** what nonsense!; **was** ~ **ein Pilz ist das?** what kind of mushroom is that?

Für <-> [fyːɐ̯] *nt* **das** ~ **und Wider** the pros and cons

Furche <-, -n> ['fʊr·çə] *f* furrow

Furcht <-> ['fʊrçt] *f kein pl* fear; ~ [**vor jdm/etw**] **haben** to fear sb/sth; ~ **erregend** terrifying

furchtbar *adj* terrible

fürchten ['fʏrç·tn̩] **I.** *vt* to fear; **zum F~** frightful; ~, **dass ...** to be afraid that ... **II.** *vr* **sich** *akk* ~ to be afraid (**vor** +*dat* of); **sich** *akk* **im Dunkeln** ~ to be afraid of the dark

fürchterlich *adj s.* **furchtbar**

furchterregend *adj s.* **Furcht**

furchtlos *adj* fearless

füreinander [fyːɐ̯·ʔai·'nan·dɐ] *adv* for each other; ~ **einspringen** to help each other out

Furie <-, -n> ['fuː·rjə] *f* fury

Furnier <-s, -e> [fʊr·'niːɐ̯] *nt* veneer

furnieren* [fʊr·'niː·rən] *vt* to veneer

Fürsorge ['fyːɐ̯·zɔr·gə] *f kein pl* **1.** (*Betreuung*) care **2.** *fam* (*Sozialhilfe*) **von der** ~ **leben** to live on welfare

fürsorglich ['fyːɐ̯·zɔrk·lɪç] *adj* considerate

Fürst(in) <-en, -en> [fʏrst] *m(f)* prince *masc*, princess *fem*

Fürstentum *nt* principality; **das** ~ **Monaco** the principality of Monaco

fürstlich ['fʏrst·lɪç] *adv* ~ **speisen** to eat like a king

Furz <-[e]s, Fürze> [fʊrts] *m derb* fart

furzen ['fʊr·tsn̩] *vi derb* to fart

Fusion <-, -en> [fu·'zjoːn] *f* ÖKON merger

Fuß <-es, Füße> [fuːs] *m* foot; **bei** ~**!** heel!; **gut/schlecht zu** ~ **sein** to be steady/not so steady on one's feet; **etw ist zu** ~ **zu erreichen** sth is within walking distance; **zu** ~ **gehen** to walk

▶ **auf eigenen** Füßen stehen to stand on one's own two feet; **auf großem ~[e] leben** to live the high life; **kalte** Füße **bekommen** to get cold feet; **jdm zu** Füßen **liegen** to lie at sb's feet; **keinen ~ vor die Tür setzen** to not set foot outside; **sich** *dat* **die** Füße **vertreten** to stretch one's legs; **auf wackligen** Füßen stehen to rest on shaky ground

Fußball ['fu:s·bal] *m* soccer; (*Ball*) soccer ball

Fußballer(in) <-s, -> ['fu:s·ba·le] *m(f) fam* soccer player

Fußballmannschaft *f* soccer team

Fußballplatz *m* soccer field

Fußballspiel *nt* soccer game

Fußballspieler(in) *m(f)* soccer player

Fußballstadion *nt* soccer stadium

Fußbank <-bänke> *f* footrest

Fußboden *m* floor

fusselig ['fʊ·sə·lɪç] *adj* fluffy, lint-covered *attr*, full of lint *pred*

Fußgänger(in) <-s, -> *m(f)* pedestrian

Fußgängerüberweg *m*, **Fußgängerstreifen** *m schweiz* pedestrian crossing

Fußgängerzone *f* pedestrian zone

Fußgelenk *nt* ankle

Fußnagel *m* toenail

Fußnote *f* LIT footnote

Fußpilz *m kein pl* athlete's foot

Fußstapfen <-s, -> *m* ▶ **in jds ~ treten** to follow in sb's footsteps

Fußtritt *m* kick

Fußweg *m* footpath; **es sind nur 15 Minuten ~** it's only a 15 minute walk

Futter¹ <-s, -> ['fʊ·te] *nt* (*Tiernahrung*) [animal] feed

Futter² <-s-> ['fʊ·te] *nt kein pl* (*Innenstoff*) lining

Futteral <-s, -e> [fʊ·tə·'ra:l] *nt* case

füttern¹ ['fʏ·ten] *vt* (*mit Nahrung*) to feed

füttern² ['fʏ·ten] *vt* (*mit Stofffutter*) to line

futtern ['fʊ·ten] **I.** *vi hum fam* to stuff oneself **II.** *vt hum fam* **etw ~** to scarf sth down *sep sl*

Fütterung <-, -en> *f* feeding

Futur <-s, -e> [fu·'tu:ɐ̯] *nt* LING future [tense]

futuristisch [fu·tu·'rɪs·tɪʃ] *adj* futurist[ic]

G

G, g <-, -> [ge:] *nt* **1.** (*Buchstabe*) G, g; **~ wie Gustav** G as in Golf **2.** MUS G, g

g *Abk von* **Gramm** g

gab [ga:p] *imp von* **geben**

Gabe <-, -n> ['ga:·bə] *f* **1.** *geh* (*Geschenk*) gift; **eine milde ~** alms *p* **2.** (*Begabung*) gift **3.** *schweiz* (*Preis, Gewinn*) prize

Gabel <-, -n> ['ga:·bl̩] *f* **1.** (*Essensgabel*) fork **2.** (*Heu-, Mistgabel*) pitchfork **3.** (*Radgabel*) fork **4.** TELEK cradle

gabeln ['ga:·bl̩n] *vr* **sich** *akk* **~** (*Straße, Ast*) to fork

Gabelstapler <-s, -> [-ʃta:p·le] *m* forklift

Gabelung <-, -en> ['ga:·bə·lʊŋ] *f* fork

gackern ['ga·ken] *vi* **1.** (*Huhn*) to cluck **2.** *fig fam* to cackle

Gage <-, -n> ['ga:·ʒə] *f* THEAT fee

gähnen ['gɛ:·nən] *vi* to yawn

galant [ga·'lant] *adj veraltend* chivalrous

Galeere <-, -n> [ga·'le:·rə] *f* galley

Galerie <-, -n> [ga·lə·'ri:] *f* **1.** ARCHIT gallery **2.** (*Gemäldegalerie*) art gallery; (*Kunsthandlung*) art dealership **3.** *österr, schweiz* (*Tunnel mit fensterartigen Öffnungen*) gallery

Galgen <-s, -> ['gal·gn̩] *m* gallows + *sing vb*

Galgenfrist *f fam* stay of execution

Galle <-, -n> ['ga·lə] *f* **1.** (*Gallenblase*) gall bladder **2.** (*Gallenflüssigkeit*) bile

Galopp <-s, -s> [ga·'lɔp] *m* gallop

galoppieren * [ga·lɔ·'pi:·rən] *vi sein o haben* to gallop

galt [galt] *imp von* **gelten**

Gämse ^RR^ <-, -n> ['gɛm·zə] *f* chamois

Gang¹ <-[e]s, Gänge> ['gaŋ] *m* **1.** *kein pl* (*Gangart*) gait **2.** (*Weg*) walk; (*Besorgung*) errand **3.** (*Ablauf*) course; **alles geht wieder seinen gewohnten ~** everything is back to normal **4.** (*in einer Speisenfolge*) course **5.** AUTO gear; (*Fahrrad a.*) speed **6.** (*eingefriedeter Weg*) passageway; (*Korridor*) corridor; (*im Theater, Flugzeug, Laden*) aisle ▶ **etw in ~ bringen** to get sth going; *a. fig* **in ~ kommen** (*Mensch*) to get go-

ing; (*Geschäft*) to get off the ground

Gang² <-, -s> [gɛŋ] *f* (*Bande*) gang

Gangart *f* walk; (*bei Pferden*) pace

gängig ['gɛŋɪç] *adj* **1.** (*üblich: Praxis*) common **2.** (*gut verkäuflich: Buch, Modell*) popular

Gangschaltung *f* gearshift

Ganove <-n, -n> [ga·'no:·və] *m pej fam* crook

Gans <-, Gänse> ['gans] *f* goose

Gänseblümchen *nt* daisy

Gänsefüßchen *pl fam* quotation marks *pl*

Gänsehaut *f kein pl* goose bumps *pl*

Gänsemarsch *m kein pl* **im ~** in single file

ganz ['gants] **I.** *adj* **1.** (*vollständig*) all; **den ~en Tag** all [*o* the whole] day; **die ~e Wahrheit** the whole truth **2.** (*unbestimmtes Zahlwort*) **eine ~e Menge** quite a lot **3.** *fam* (*unbeschädigt*) intact; **etw wieder ~ machen** to fix sth **4.** *fam* (*nicht mehr als*) **~e 10 Minuten** no more than 10 minutes **II.** *adv* **1.** (*sehr, wirklich*) really; **das war ~ lieb von dir** that was really kind of you; **~ besonders** particularly **2.** (*ziemlich*) quite **3.** (*vollkommen*) completely; **~ und gar** completely; **~ und gar nicht** not at all; **~ hinten/vorne** all the way in [the] back/up front

Ganze(s) *nt* **1.** (*alles zusammen*) whole; **im ~n** on the whole **2.** (*die ganze Angelegenheit*) the whole business

ganzheitlich *adj* **~e Behandlung/Medizin** holistic treatment/medicine

gänzlich ['gɛnts·lɪç] *adv* completely

Ganztagsschule *f* all-day school

gar¹ ['ga:ɐ̯] *adj* KOCHK done

gar² ['ga:ɐ̯] *adv* **1.** (*überhaupt*) at all, whatsoever; **~ keine[r]** no one at all; **hattest du denn ~ keine Angst?** weren't you even the least bit scared?; **~ nichts** nothing at all [*o* whatsoever] **2.** *österr, schweiz, südd* (*sehr*) really

Garage <-, -n> [ga·'ra:·ʒə] *f* garage

Garantie <-, -n> [ga·ran·'ti:] *f* guarantee

garantieren* [ga·ran·'ti:·rən] *vt, vi* to guarantee

Garde <-, -n> ['gar·də] *f* guard

Garderobe <-, -n> [gar·də·'ro:·bə] *f*

1. (*Kleiderablage*) coat rack; (*Aufbewahrungsraum*) cloakroom **2.** *kein pl* (*Kleidung*) wardrobe **3.** THEAT (*Ankleideraum*) dressing room

Gardine <-, -n> [gar·'di:·nə] *f* curtain

gären ['gɛ:·rən] *vi sein o haben* **1.** (*sich in Gärung befinden*) to ferment **2.** *fig* to seethe

Garn <-[e]s, -e> ['garn] *nt* thread

Garnele <-, -n> [gar·'ne:·lə] *f* prawn

garnieren* [gar·'ni:·rən] *vt* KOCHK to garnish

Garnitur <-, -en> [gar·ni·'tu:ɐ̯] *f* set

Garten <-s, Gärten> ['gar·tn̩] *m* garden

Gartenarbeit *f* gardening

Gartenbau *m kein pl* horticulture

Gartenlokal *nt* open-air restaurant

Gärtner(in) <-s, -> ['gɛrt·nɐ] *m(f)* gardener

Gärtnerei <-, -en> [gɛrt·nə·'rai] *f* nursery

Gas <-es, -e> ['ga:s] *nt* gas; **~ geben** to accelerate; *fig* to speed up on it

Gasflasche *f* gas canister

gasförmig *adj* gaseous

Gasheizung *f* gas heating [system]

Gasherd *m* gas stove

Gaskocher *m* camping stove

Gasleitung *f* gas pipe

Gasmaske *f* gas mask

Gaspedal *nt* gas [pedal]

Gasse <-, -n> ['ga·sə] *f* **1.** (*schmale Straße*) alley[way] **2.** *österr* (*Straße*) street

Gast <-es, Gäste> ['gast] *m* guest; **~ in einem Land sein** to be visiting country

Gastarbeiter(in) *m(f)* guest worker

Gästebuch *nt* guest book

Gästezimmer *nt* guestroom

gastfreundlich *adj* hospitable

Gastfreundschaft *f* hospitality

Gastgeber(in) <-s, -> *m(f)* host *masc*, hostess *fem*

Gasthaus, Gasthof *m* inn

Gastritis <-, Gastritiden> [gas·'tri:·tɪs] *f* gastritis

Gastronomie <-,-n> [gas·tro·no·'mi:] *f* **1.** (*Gaststättengewerbe*) catering trade **2.** (*Kochkunst*) gastronomy

gastronomisch *adj* gastronomic

Gastspiel *nt* THEAT guest performance

Gaststätte *f* restaurant

Gastwirt(in) *m(f)* restaurant manager; (*einer Kneipe*) barkeeper

Gastwirtschaft *f s.* **Gaststätte**

Gaszähler *m* gas meter

Gatte, Gattin <-n, -n> ['ga·tə, 'ga·tɪn] *m, f geh* spouse

Gatter <-s, -> ['ga·tɐ] *nt* fence

Gattung <-, -en> ['ga·tʊŋ] *f* 1. BIOL genus 2. KUNST, LIT genre

GAU <-s, -s> ['gau] *m Akr von* **größter anzunehmender Unfall** MCA

Gaudi <-> ['gau·di] *f o nt kein pl österr, südd fam* (*Spaß*) fun

Gaul <-[e]s, Gäule> ['gaul] *m* nag

Gaumen <-s, -> ['gau·mən] *m* palate

Gauner(in) <-s, -> ['gau·nɐ] *m(f)* 1. (*Betrüger*) crook 2. (*Schelm*) rogue

Gaunerei <-, -en> [gau·nə·'rai] *f* cheating

Gazelle <-, -n> [ga·'tsɛ·lə] *f* gazelle

Gebäck <-[e]s, -e> [gə·'bɛk] *nt* 1. *pl selten* (*Plätzchen*) cookies *pl* 2. (*Teilchen*) pastries *pl*

gebacken *pp von* **backen**

geballt I. *adj* 1. (*konzentriert*) concentrated 2. (*zur Faust gemacht*) ~e Fäuste clenched fists II. *adv* in clusters

gebar [gə·'ba:ɐ̯] *imp von* **gebären**

gebärden * [gə·'bɛːɐ̯·dn̩] *vr haben* sich *akk* ~ to behave

gebären <gebiert, gebar, geboren> [gə·'bɛː·rən] I. *vt* 1. (*zur Welt bringen*) **geboren werden** to be born 2. (*eine natürliche Begabung haben*) **zu etw** *dat* **geboren sein** to be born to sth II. *vi* (*ein Kind zur Welt bringen*) to give birth

Gebärmutter *f* womb

Gebäude <-s, -> [gə·'bɔy·də] *nt* building

Gebein <-[e]s, -e> [gə·'bain] *nt* ~e *pl* bones *pl*; (*eines Heiligen*) relics *pl*

geben <gibt, gab, gegeben> ['ge:·bn̩] I. *vt* 1. (*reichen*) **jdm etw** *akk* ~ to give sb sth [*o* sth to sb]; (*beim Kartenspiel*) to deal sb sth; **jdm etw zu tun** ~ to give sb sth to do 2. (*schenken*) **jdm seine Telefonnummer** ~ to give sb one's telephone number 4. (*verkaufen*) ~ **Sie mir bitte fünf Brötchen** I'd like

five rolls please 5. (*spenden*) **Schutz/ Schatten** ~ to give protection/shade 6. TELEK **jdm jdn** ~ to put sb through to sb; ~ **Sie mir bitte Frau Kuhn** can I please speak to Mrs. Kuhn? 7. (*Pressekonferenz*) to hold 8. (*zukommen lassen*) **jdm einen Namen** ~ to name sb 9. (*veranstalten*) **ein Fest** ~ to give a party 10. KOCHK to add 11. (*ergeben*) **7 mal 7 gibt 49** 7 times 7 equals 49; **keinen Sinn** ~ to make no sense 12. (*äußern*) **etw von sich** *dat* ~ to utter sth II. *vi* 1. KARTEN to deal 2. SPORT (*Aufschlag haben*) to serve; **du gibst!** it's your serve III. *vr impers* 1. (*gereicht werden*) **was gibt es zum Frühstück?** what's for breakfast?; **freitags gibt es bei uns immer Fisch** we always have fish on Fridays 2. (*eintreten*) **heute gibt es noch Regen** it's going to rain [later] today 3. (*existieren, passieren*) **das gibt's doch nicht!** *fam* I can't believe it!; **was gibt's?** *fam* what's up? IV. *vr* 1. (*nachlassen*) **etw gibt sich** sth is letting up; (*sich erledigen*) sth sorts itself out 2. (*sich benehmen, aufführen*) **sie gab sich sehr überrascht** she acted very surprised

Gebet <-[e]s, -e> [gə·'be:t] *nt* prayer

gebeten [gə·'be:·tn̩] *pp von* **bitten**

Gebiet <-[e]s, -e> [gə·'bi:t] *nt* 1. (*Fläche*) area; (*Region a.*) region; (*Staatsgebiet*) territory 2. (*Fach*) field

gebieten * [gə·'bi:·tn̩] *irreg vt geh* **etw** *dat* **Einhalt** ~ to put an end to sth; **es ist Vorsicht geboten** care must be taken

Gebilde <-s, -> [gə·'bɪl·də] *nt* 1. (*Ding*) thing 2. (*Form*) shape; (*Struktur*) structure

gebildet *adj* educated

Gebirge <-s, -> [gə·'bɪr·gə] *nt* mountain range

gebirgig [gə·'bɪr·gɪç] *adj* mountainous

Gebiss RR <-es, -e>, **Gebiß** ALT <-sses, -sse> [gə·'bɪs] *nt* 1. (*Zähne*) [set of] teeth 2. (*Zahnprothese*) dentures *npl*

gebissen [gə·'bɪ·sn̩] *pp von* **beißen**

geblasen *pp von* **blasen**

geblieben [gə·'bli:·bn̩] *pp von* **bleiben**

geboren [gə·'bo:·rən] I. *pp von* **gebären** II. *adj* **der ~e Koch sein** to be a

born cook

geborgen [gə·'bɔr·gn̩] **I.** pp von **bergen II.** adj safe

Gebot <-[e]s, -e> [gə·'bo:t] nt **1.** (Gesetz) law; (Verordnung) decree **2.** REL **die zehn ~e** the Ten Commandments **3.** ÖKON bid

geboten [gə·'bo:·tn̩] pp von **bieten, gebieten**

gebracht [gə·'braxt] pp von **bringen**

gebraten pp von **braten**

Gebrauch <-[e]s, Gebräuche> [gə·'braux] m **1.** kein pl (Verwendung) use; (Anwendung) application **2.** meist pl **Sitten und Gebräuche** manners and customs

ge|brauchen* vt (verwenden) to use

gebräuchlich [gə·'brɔyç·lɪç] adj **1.** (allgemein üblich) customary; (in Gebrauch) in use **2.** (herkömmlich) conventional

Gebrauchsanweisung f operating instructions pl, directions pl

gebraucht adj secondhand

Gebrauchtwagen m used car

gebrechlich [gə·'brɛç·lɪç] adj frail

gebrochen [gə·'brɔ·xn̩] **I.** pp von **brechen II.** adj (völlig entmutigt) broken **III.** adv imperfectly; **sie sprach nur ~ Deutsch** she only spoke broken German

Gebrüder [gə·'bry:·də] pl veraltet brothers

Gebühr <-, -en> [gə·'by:ɐ̯] f charge; (Beitrag, Honorar) fee

gebührend [gə·'by:·rənt] **I.** adj (angemessen) appropriate **II.** adv appropriately

gebührenfrei adj, adv free [of charge]

gebührenpflichtig adj, adv subject to a charge

gebunden [gə·'bʊn·dn̩] **I.** pp von **binden II.** adj **~es Buch** hardcover; **vertraglich ~ sein** to be bound by contract

Geburt <-, -en> [gə·'bu:ɐ̯t] f birth

gebürtig [gə·'byr·tɪç] adj by birth; **er ist ~er Brasilianer** he is a native Brazilian

Geburtsdatum nt date of birth

Geburtsjahr nt year of birth

Geburtsort m place of birth

Geburtstag m birthday; (Geburtsdatum) date of birth; **„herzlichen Glück-**

wunsch zum ~" "Happy Birthday [to you]"

Geburtsurkunde f birth certificate

Gebüsch <-[e]s, -e> [gə·'bʏʃ] nt bushes pl; (Unterholz) undergrowth

gedacht [gə·'daxt] pp von **denken, gedenken**

Gedächtnis <-ses, -se> [gə·'dɛçt·nɪs] nt memory

Gedanke <-ns, -n> [gə·'daŋ·kə] m **1.** (das Gedachte, Überlegung) thought; **jdn auf andere ~n bringen** to take sb's mind off [of] sth; **sich** dat **über etw** akk **~n machen** to be worried about sth **2.** (Einfall) idea

gedankenlos adj thoughtless

Gedankenstrich m dash

Gedeck <-[e]s, -e> [gə·'dɛk] nt place setting

ge|denken* vi irreg geh **1.** (ehrend zurückdenken) **jds/einer S. ~** to remember sb/sth **2.** (beabsichtigen) **~, etw zu tun** to intend to do sth

Gedenken <-s> [gə·'dɛŋ·kn̩] nt kein pl memory

Gedenkfeier f commemoration

Gedenkminute f moment of silence

Gedenktag m day of remembrance

Gedicht <-[e]s, -e> [gə·'dɪçt] nt poem

gediegen [gə·'di:gn̩] adj **1.** (solide gearbeitet) high quality **2.** (gründlich) **~e Kenntnisse haben** to have sound knowledge

Gedränge <-s> [gə·'drɛŋə] nt kein pl **1.** (drängende Menschenmenge) crowd **2.** (das Drängen) jostling

gedroschen [gə·'drɔ·ʃn̩] pp von **dreschen**

gedrungen [gə·'drʊŋən] **I.** pp von **dringen II.** adj (Körperbau) stocky

Geduld <-> [gə·'dʊlt] f kein pl patience

ge|dulden* vr **sich** akk **~** to be patient

geduldig [gə·'dʊl·dɪç] adj patient

gedurft [gə·'dʊrft] pp von **dürfen**

geehrt adj honored; **sehr ~e Damen, sehr ~e Herren!** ladies and gentlemen!; (Anrede in Briefen) **sehr ~e Damen und Herren!** Dear Sir or Madam

geeignet [gə·'ʔaig·nət] adj suitable

Gefahr <-, -en> [gə·'fa:ɐ̯] f danger; **jdn in ~ bringen** to endanger sb; **auf eige-**

ne ~ at one's own risk

ge|fährden * [gə·ˈfɛːɐ̯·dn̩] vt sich/jdn/etw ~ to endanger oneself/sb/sth; den Erfolg einer S. gen ~ to jeopardize the success of sth

gefahren pp von fahren

gefährlich [gə·ˈfɛːɐ̯·lɪç] adj dangerous; (risikoreich) risky

gefahrlos [gə·ˈfaːɐ̯·loːs] adj safe

ge|fallen <gefiel, gefallen> I. vi etw gefällt jdm sth pleases sb, sb likes sth II. vr fam sich dat etw ~ lassen to put up with sth

Gefallen <-s, -> m favor; jdn um einen ~ bitten to ask sb for a favor; jdm einen ~ tun to do sb a favor

Gefallene(r) f(m) soldier killed in action

gefällig [gə·ˈfɛ·lɪç] adj 1. (hilfsbereit) helpful 2. (ansprechend) pleasant 3. a. iron form (gewünscht) Kaffee ~? would you care for [some] coffee? form

Gefälligkeit <-, -en> f 1. (Gefallen) favor 2. kein pl (Hilfsbereitschaft) helpfulness

gefangen [gə·ˈfaŋən] I. pp von fangen II. adj 1. (in Gefangenschaft) jdn ~ halten to hold sb captive; jdn ~ nehmen MIL to take sb prisoner; (verhaften) to arrest sb 2. (beeindruckt) jdn ~ halten to captivate sb

Gefangene(r) f(m) captive; (im Gefängnis) prisoner; (im Krieg) prisoner of war

gefangen|halten ALT vt irreg s. gefangen II 2

Gefangennahme <-, -n> f 1. MIL capture 2. (Verhaftung) arrest

Gefangenschaft <-, selten -en> f captivity

Gefängnis <-ses, -se> [gə·ˈfɛŋ·nɪs] nt 1. (Haftanstalt) prison, jail; ins ~ kommen to be sent to prison 2. kein pl (Haftstrafe) imprisonment

Gefängnisstrafe f prison sentence

Gefäß <-es, -e> [gə·ˈfɛːs] nt 1. (Behälter) container 2. MED (Ader) vessel

gefasst RR, gefaßt ALT I. adj 1. (beherrscht) composed 2. (eingestellt) auf etw akk ~ sein to be prepared for sth II. adv calmly

Gefecht <-[e]s, -e> [gə·ˈfɛçt] nt a. fig battle

Gefieder <-s, -> [gə·ˈfiː·dɐ] nt plumage

geflochten [gə·ˈflɔx·tn̩] pp von flechten

geflogen [gə·ˈfloː·gn̩] pp von fliegen

geflohen [gə·ˈfloː·ən] pp von fliehen

geflossen [gə·ˈflɔ·sn̩] pp von fließen

Geflügel <-s> [gə·ˈflyː·gl̩] nt kein pl poultry

geflügelt [gə·ˈflyː·gl̩t] adj winged

gefochten [gə·ˈfɔx·tn̩] pp von fechten

Gefolge <-s, -> [gə·ˈfɔl·gə] nt retinue

gefräßig [gə·ˈfrɛː·sɪç] adj 1. (fressgierig) voracious 2. pej (unersättlich) greedy

gefressen [gə·ˈfrɛ·sn̩] pp von fressen

ge|frieren * vi irreg sein to freeze

Gefrierfach nt freezer [compartment]

Gefrierpunkt m freezing point

gefroren [gə·ˈfroː·rən] pp von frieren, gefrieren

gefügig [gə·ˈfyː·gɪç] adj compliant

Gefühl <-[e]s, -e> [gə·ˈfyːl] nt feeling; ein ~ für etw akk [haben] [to have] a feeling for sth

gefühllos I. adj 1. (Bein, Fuß) numb 2. (herzlos) insensitive II. adv insensitively

Gefühlsausbruch m emotional outburst

gefühlsbetont adj emotional

gefühlsmäßig adv instinctively

gefühlvoll I. adj sensitive II. adv with feeling

gefunden [gə·ˈfʊn·dn̩] pp von finden

gegangen [gə·ˈgaŋən] pp von gehen

gegebenenfalls [gə·ˈgeː·bə·nən·fals] adv if necessary

gegen [ˈgeː·gn̩] I. präp +akk 1. (wider) against; (jur, sport a.) versus; ~ jdn/etw sein to be against sb/sth; etwas ~ eine Erkältung sth for a cold 2. (für) ~ Kaution/Quittung with a deposit/receipt 3. (verglichen mit) compared with 4. (ungefähr) ~ Abend/Morgen toward evening/morning II. adv er kommt ~ drei Uhr an he's arriving around three o'clock

Gegenangriff m counterattack

Gegenargument nt counterargument

Gegend <-, -en> [ˈgeː·gn̩t] f 1. (Gebiet) region; durch die ~ fahren/laufen to drive/walk around 2. (Wohngegend) neighborhood 3. (Nähe) area

Gegendarstellung f MEDIA reply

gegeneinander [ge:·gn·ʔai·'nan·de] adv against each other

gegeneinander|prallen vi sein to collide

Gegengift nt antidote

Gegenleistung f **eine/keine ~ erwarten** to expect something/nothing in return

Gegensatz m 1. (Gegenteil) opposite; **im ~ zu jdm/etw** unlike sb/sth 2. pl differences; **unüberbrückbare Gegensätze** irreconcilable differences

gegensätzlich ['ge:·gn·zɛts·lɪç] I. adj conflicting; (Menschen, Temperamente) different II. adv differently

Gegenseite f other side

gegenseitig ['ge:·gn·zai·tɪç] adj mutual

Gegenseitigkeit <-> f kein pl **auf ~ beruhen** to be mutual

Gegenspieler(in) m(f) opponent

Gegenstand <-[e]s, Gegenstände> m 1. (Ding) object 2. (Thema) subject

Gegenteil ['ge:·gn·tail] nt opposite

gegenteilig ['ge:·gn·tai·lɪç] I. adj opposite II. adv to the contrary

gegenüber [ge:·gn·'?y:·be] I. präp +dat **jdm/etw ~** 1. (örtlich) opposite sb/sth 2. (in Bezug auf) toward sb/sth 3. (im Vergleich zu) in comparison with sb/sth II. adv opposite

gegenüberliegend adj attr opposite

gegenüber|stehen irreg I. vi 1. (örtlich) **jdm ~** to stand opposite sb 2. (eingestellt sein) **jdm/etw [...] ~** to have a [...] attitude toward sb/sth II. vr sich dat **~** to face each other

gegenüber|stellen vt 1. (konfrontieren) **jdm jdn ~** to confront sb with sb 2. (vergleichen) **etw dat etw ~** to compare sth with sth

Gegenüberstellung f JUR police lineup

Gegenverkehr m oncoming traffic

Gegenwart <-> ['ge:·gn·vart] f kein pl 1. (jetziger Augenblick) present 2. (heutiges Zeitalter) present [day]; **die Literatur/Musik der ~** contemporary literature/music 3. LING present [tense] 4. (Anwesenheit) presence

gegenwärtig ['ge:·gn·vɛr·tɪç] I. adj attr (derzeitig) present II. adv currently

Gegenwind m headwind

gegessen [gə·'gɛ·sn] pp von **essen**

geglichen [gə·'glɪ·çn] pp von **gleichen**

geglitten [gə·'glɪ·tn] pp von **gleiten**

Gegner(in) <-s, -> ['ge:g·ne] m(f) 1. (Feind) enemy 2. (Gegenspieler, Sport) opponent

gegnerisch adj attr opposing

gegolten [gə·'gɔl·tn] pp von **gelten**

gegoren [gə·'go:·ran] pp von **gären**

gegossen [gə·'gɔ·sn] pp von **gießen**

graben [gə·'gra:·bn] pp von **graben**

gegriffen [gə·'grɪ·fn] pp von **greifen**

Gehalt¹ <-[e]s, Gehälter> [gə·'halt] nt o österr m salary

Gehalt² <-[e]s, -e> [gə·'halt] m (Anteil) content (**an** +dat of)

Gehaltserhöhung f pay raise

gehaltvoll adj (nahrhaft) nutritious

gehangen [gə·'haŋən] pp von **hängen**

gehässig [gə·'hɛ·sɪç] adj spiteful

gehauen pp von **hauen**

Gehäuse <-s, -> [gə·'hɔy·zə] nt casing; (einer Kamera a.) body

gehbehindert adj **leicht/stark ~ sein** to have a slight/severe mobility handicap

Gehege <-s, -> [gə·'he:·gə] nt enclosure

geheim [gə·'haim] I. adj secret II. adv secretly; **etw [vor jdm] ~ halten** to keep sth secret [from sb]

Geheimagent(in) m(f) secret agent

Geheimdienst m secret service

geheim|halten ALT vt irreg s. **geheim** II

Geheimnis <-ses, -se> [gə·'haim·nɪs] nt secret

geheimnisvoll adj mysterious

Geheimnummer f 1. TELEK unlisted number 2. (Geheimzahl) PIN

Geheimtipp RR m inside tip

Geheimzahl f FIN PIN

geheißen pp von **heißen**

gehen <ging, gegangen> ['ge:·ən] I. vi sein 1. (sich fortbewegen) to go; (zu Fuß) to walk 2. (besuchen) **zu jdm ~** to go [and] visit sb; **in die Kirche/ Schule/ins Theater ~** to go to church/ school/the theater 3. (weggehen) to go; (abfahren a.) to leave; **ich muss jetzt ~** I have to go; **wann geht der Zug nach Hamburg?** when does the train

G

to Hamburg leave? **4.** (*führen*) to go; **die Brücke geht über den Fluss** the bridge crosses the river; **wohin geht dieser Weg?** where does this path lead [to]? **5.** (*funktionieren*) to work; **meine Uhr geht nicht mehr** my watch [has] stopped **6.** (*gelingen*) **versuch's einfach, es geht ganz leicht** just try it — it's really easy; **kannst du mir bitte erklären, wie das Spiel geht?** can you please explain how the game goes? **7.** ÖKON **das Geschäft geht vor Weihnachten immer gut** business is always good before Christmas **8.** (*hineinpassen*) **es ~ über 450 Besucher in das neue Theater** the new theater holds over 450 people; **wie viele Leute ~ in deinen Wagen?** how many people [can] fit in your car? **9.** (*dauern*) **der Film geht drei Stunden** the movie lasts three hours **10.** (*reichen*) **der Rock geht ihr bis zum Knie** the skirt goes down to her knee; **in die Tausende ~** to run into the thousands **11.** KOCHK (*Teig*) to rise **12.** (*möglich sein*) **haben Sie am nächsten Mittwoch Zeit? – nein, das geht [bei mir] nicht** are you free next Wednesday? — no, that's no good [for me]; **ich muss mal telefonieren – geht das?** I have to make a phone call — would that be alright? **13.** (*beeinträchtigen*) **zu viel Alkohol geht auf die Leber** too much alcohol is bad for your liver; **das geht [mir] ganz schön an die Nerven** that really wears on my nerves **14.** (*gerichtet sein*) **an jdn ~** to be addressed to sb **15.** *fam* (*liiert sein*) **mit jdm ~** to be going out with sb **16.** (*überschreiten*) **zu weit ~** to go too far **17.** *fam* (*akzeptabel sein*) **er geht gerade noch, aber seine Frau ist furchtbar** he's not that bad, but his wife is awful; **wie ist das Hotel? – es geht [so]** how's the hotel? — it's ok **➤ es geht nichts über jdn/etw** *akk* there's nothing like sb/sth **II.** *vi impers sein* **1.** + *adv* (*sich befinden*) **wie geht es Ihnen? – danke, mir geht es gut!** how are you? — fine, thank you!; **nachher ging es ihr wieder besser** afterwards she felt better again **2.** + *adv* (*verlaufen*)

wie war denn die Prüfung? – ach, es ging ganz gut how was the exam? — oh, it went quite well **3.** (*sich handeln um*) **worum geht es in diesem Film?** what is this movie about? **4.** (*wichtig sein*) **worum geht es dir eigentlich?** what are you trying to say?; **es geht mir ums Prinzip** it's a matter of principle **5.** (*ergehen*) **mir ist es ähnlich/genauso gegangen** it was the same/just the same with me; **lass es dir gut ~!** take care of yourself! **6.** (*sich machen lassen*) **ich werde arbeiten, solange es geht** I will continue working as long as possible; **geht es, oder soll ich dir tragen helfen?** can you manage, or should I help you carry it/them? **7.** (*nach jds Kopf gehen*) **wenn es nach mir ginge** if it were up to me **III.** *vr haben* **1.** *impers* **in diesen Schuhen geht es sich bequem** these shoes are very comfortable for walking **2.** (*sich nicht beherrschen*) **sich** *akk* **~ lassen** to lose one's self-control; (*nachlässig sein*) to let oneself go

gehen|lassen * *vr irreg s.* **gehen III 2**
geheuer [gə-'hɔy-ɐ] *adj* **[jdm] nicht [ganz] ~ sein** to seem [a bit] suspicious [to sb]
Gehilfe, Gehilfin <-n, -n> [gə-'hɪl-fə, gə-'hɪl-fɪn] *m, f* assistant
Gehirn <-[e]s, -e> [gə-'hɪrn] *nt* brain
Gehirnerschütterung *f* concussion
Gehirnschlag *m* stroke
geholfen [gə-'hɔl-fn̩] *pp von* **helfen**
Gehör <-[e]s, *selten* -e> [gə-'hø:ɐ̯] *nt* hearing; **sich** *dat* **~ verschaffen** to make oneself heard
gehorchen * *vi* **jdm/etw ~** to obey sb/sth
ge|hören * **I.** *vi* **1.** (*jds Eigentum sein*) **jdm ~** to belong to sb; **ihm ~ mehrere Häuser** he owns several houses **2.** (*jdm zugewandt sein*) **jdm/etw ~** to belong to sb/sth; **ihre ganze Liebe gehört ihrem Sohn** she gives all her love to her son **3.** (*den richtigen Platz haben*) **die Kinder ~ ins Bett** the children belong in bed **4.** (*angebracht sein*) **nicht zum Thema ~** to be beside the point **5.** (*Mitglied sein*) **zu jdm/etw ~** to belong to

sb/sth; **zur Familie ~** to be one of the family **6.** (*Teil sein von*) **zu etw** *dat* **~** to be [a] part of sth **7.** (*Voraussetzung, nötig sein*) to require; **es gehört viel Mut dazu, ...** it takes a lot of courage to ... **II.** *vr* **sich** *akk* **~** to be fitting; **wie es sich gehört** as it should be; **sich** *akk* [**einfach**] **nicht ~** to be [simply] not good manners

gehörig [gə·ˈhøː·rɪç] **I.** *adj* **1.** *attr fam* (*beträchtlich*) good *attr* **2.** *geh* (*gehörend*) belonging (**zu** +*dat* to) **II.** *adv fam* **jdn ~ ausschimpfen** to really tell sb off

Gehörlose(r) *f/m* deaf person

gehorsam [gə·ˈhoːɐ̯·za:m] *adj* obedient

Gehorsam <-s> [gə·ˈhoːɐ̯·za:m] *m kein pl* obedience

Gehweg *m* **1.** *s.* **Bürgersteig 2.** (*Fußweg*) walk

Geier <-s, -> [ˈgai·ɐ] *m* vulture

Geige <-, -n> [ˈgai·gə] *f* violin, fiddle *fam*

geil [gail] **I.** *adj* **1.** (*lüstern*) lecherous; **~ auf jdn sein** to have the hots for sb **2.** *sl* (*toll*) cool **II.** *adv* **1.** (*lüstern*) lecherously **2.** *sl* (*toll*) cool

Geisel <-, -n> [ˈgai·zl̩] *f* hostage

Geiselnehmer(in) <-s, -> *m(f)* kidnapper, abductor

Geist <-[e]s, -er> [gaist] *m* **1.** *kein pl* (*Vernunft*) mind **2.** *kein pl* (*Esprit*) wit **3.** *kein pl* (*Wesen, Sinn, Gesinnung*) spirit **4.** (*körperloses Wesen*) ghost; **böse/gute ~er** evil/good spirits; **der Heilige ~** the Holy Ghost ▶ **den ~ aufgeben** *fam* to give up the ghost; **von allen guten ~ern verlassen sein** *fam* to have taken leave of one's senses

geistesabwesend *adj* absent-minded

geistesgegenwärtig I. *adj* quick-witted **II.** *adv* with great presence of mind

geistesgestört *adj* mentally disturbed

Geisteskrankheit *f* mental illness

Geisteswissenschaften *pl* humanities

geistig [ˈgais·tɪç] *adj* **~es Eigentum** JUR intellectual property

Geistliche(r) *f/m* clergyman *masc*, clergywoman *fem*

geistlos *adj* **1.** (*dumm*) witless **2.** (*einfallslos*) inane

geistreich *adj* **1.** (*Mensch*) witty **2.** *iron*

(*dumm*) bright *iron*

geizen [ˈgai·tsn̩] *vi* **mit etw** *dat* **~ 1.** (*knauserig sein*) to be stingy with sth **2.** (*zurückhaltend sein*) to be sparing with sth

Geizhals *m* cheapskate

geizig [ˈgai·tsɪç] *adj* stingy

Gejammer <-s> [gə·ˈja·mɐ] *nt kein pl pej fam* whining

gekannt [gə·ˈkant] *pp von* **kennen**

geklungen [gə·ˈklʊŋən] *pp von* **klingen**

gekniffen [gə·ˈknɪ·fn̩] *pp von* **kneifen**

gekommen *pp von* **kommen**

Gekritzel <-s> [gə·ˈkrɪtsl̩] *nt kein pl pej* scrawl

gekrochen [gə·ˈkrɔ·xn̩] *pp von* **kriechen**

Gel <-s, -e> [geːl] *nt* gel

Gelächter <-s, *selten* -> [gə·ˈlɛç·tɐ] *nt* laughter

geladen I. *pp von* **laden II.** *adj fam pred* (*wütend*) furious

gelähmt *adj* paralyzed

Gelände <-s, -> [gə·ˈlɛn·də] *nt* **1.** (*Land*) terrain **2.** (*bestimmtes Stück Land*) site

Geländer <-s, -> [gə·ˈlɛn·dɐ] *nt* handrail; (*Treppengeländer*) banister

Geländewagen *m* all-terrain vehicle, ATV

gelang [gə·ˈlaŋ] *imp von* **gelingen**

gelangen* *vi sein* **1.** (*hinkommen*) **ans Ziel ~** to reach one's destination **2.** (*erwerben*) **zu etw** *dat* **~** to achieve sth; (*Ruhm, Reichtum*) to gain

gelassen [gə·ˈla·sn̩] **I.** *pp von* **lassen II.** *adj* calm

Gelassenheit <-> *f kein pl* calmness

gelaufen *pp von* **laufen**

geläufig [gə·ˈlɔy·fɪç] *adj* familiar

gelaunt [gə·ˈlaunt] *adj pred* **gut/schlecht ~ sein** to be in a good/bad mood

gelb [gɛlp] *adj* yellow

Gelb <-s, -> [gɛlp] *nt* yellow

Geld <-[e]s, -er> [gɛlt] *nt kein pl* (*Zahlungsmittel*) money ▶ **jdm das ~ aus der Tasche ziehen** to squeeze money out of sb

Geldanlage *f* [financial] investment

Geldautomat *m* automated teller machine, ATM

Geldbeutel m südd, **Geldbörse** f österr (sonst geh: Portmonee) wallet

Geldschein m bill

Geldstrafe f fine

Geldwechsel m foreign exchange

Gelee <-s, -s> [ʒeˈleː, ʒəˈleː] m o nt jelly

gelegen [ɡəˈleːɡn̩] I. pp von **liegen** II. adj (passend) convenient; **jdm ~ kommen** to come at the right time for sb

Gelegenheit <-, -en> [ɡəˈleːɡn̩haɪt] f 1. (günstiger Moment) opportunity 2. (Anlass) occasion

Gelegenheitsarbeiter(in) m(f) casual laborer

gelegentlich [ɡəˈleːɡn̩tlɪç] I. adj attr occasional II. adv 1. (manchmal) occasionally 2. (bei Gelegenheit) **wenn Sie ~ in der Nachbarschaft sind ...** if you happen to be in the neighborhood ...

gelehrt adj learned

Geleitschutz m escort; **jdm/etw ~ geben** to escort sb/sth

Gelenk <-[e]s, -e> [ɡəˈlɛŋk] nt ANAT, TECH joint

Gelenkentzündung f arthritis

gelenkig [ɡəˈlɛŋkɪç] adj supple

gelesen pp von **lesen**

Geliebte(r) f(m) lover

geliehen [ɡəˈliːən] pp von **leihen**

gelingen [ɡəˈlɪŋən] vi sein **jdm gelingt es, etw zu tun** sb manages to do sth; **jdm gelingt es nicht, etw zu tun** sb fails to do sth

gelitten [ɡəˈlɪtn̩] pp von **leiden**

gelogen [ɡəˈloːɡn̩] pp von **lügen**

gelten <gilt, galt, gegolten> [ˈɡɛltn̩] I. vi 1. (gültig sein) **[für jdn]** ~ (Regelung) to be valid [for sb]; (Bestimmungen) to apply [to sb]; (Gesetz) to be in force 2. (bestimmt sein für) **jdm/etw** ~ to be meant for sb/sth; (Buhrufe) to be aimed at sb/sth; (Frage) to be directed at sb 3. (gehalten werden) **als etw** ~ to be regarded as sth ▶ **etw ~ lassen** to accept sth II. vi impers **es gilt, etw zu tun** it is necessary to do sth; **das gilt nicht!** that's not allowed!

geltend adj attr 1. (gültig) current 2. (vorherrschend: Meinung) prevailing

3. **Ansprüche/Forderungen** ~ **machen** to make claims/demands

Geltung <-> f kein pl (Gültigkeit) validity ▶ **etw zur** ~ **bringen** to show off sep sth to its advantage

Gelübde <-s, -> [ɡəˈlʏpdə] nt geh vow

gelungen [ɡəˈlʊŋən] I. pp von **gelingen** II. adj attr successful

Gemälde <-s, -> [ɡəˈmɛːldə] nt painting

gemäß [ɡəˈmɛːs] I. präp +dat in accordance with; ~ **§ 198** according to § 198 II. adj **jdm/etw** ~ appropriate for sb/sth

gemäßigt adj 1. METEO temperate 2. (moderat) moderate

gemein [ɡəˈmaɪn] I. adj 1. (niederträchtig) mean; (böse) nasty 2. attr, kein komp/superl BOT, ZOOL common 3. pred (gemeinsam) **etw mit jdm/etw ~ haben** to have sth in common with sb/sth II. adv fam horribly

Gemeinde <-, -n> [ɡəˈmaɪndə] f 1. ADMIN (politische Einheit) municipality 2. REL (Pfarrgemeinde) parish; (Gläubige a.) parishioners pl

Gemeindehaus nt REL parish house

Gemeinderat[1] m (Organ der Gemeinde) town council

Gemeinderat, -rätin[2] m, f (Gemeinderatsmitglied) councilman masc, councilwoman fem

Gemeindeverwaltung f town council

gemeingefährlich adj constituting a public danger pred

Gemeinheit <-, -en> f 1. kein pl (Niedertracht) meanness 2. (niederträchtige Bemerkung, Handlung) **so eine ~!** that was a mean thing to say/do!

gemeinnützig [ɡəˈmaɪnnʏtsɪç] adj charitable

gemeinsam [ɡəˈmaɪnzaːm] I. adj 1. (mehreren gehörend) common; (Konto) joint; (Freund) mutual; **etw ~ haben** to have sth in common 2. (von mehreren unternommen) joint attr II. adv jointly

Gemeinschaft <-, -en> f 1. POL community 2. kein pl (gegenseitige Verbundenheit) sense of community

Gemeinschaftspraxis f joint practice

Gemenge <-s, -> [gə·ˈmɛŋə] nt 1. (Mischung) mixture (aus +dat of) 2. (Gewühl) crowd 3. (Durcheinander) jumble

Gemetzel <-s, -> [gə·ˈmɛ·tsl̩] nt bloodbath

gemieden [gə·ˈmiː·dn̩] pp von **meiden**

Gemisch <-[e]s, -e> [gə·ˈmɪʃ] nt mixture (aus +dat of)

gemischt adj mixed

gemocht [gə·ˈmɔxt] pp von **mögen**

gemolken [gə·ˈmɔl·kn̩] pp von **melken**

Gemse ᴬᴸᵀ <-, -n> f s. **Gämse**

Gemüse <-s, selten -> [gə·ˈmyː·zə] nt vegetables pl; **ein ~** a vegetable

Gemüsehändler(in) m(f) produce market

gemusst ᴿᴿ, **gemußt** ᴬᴸᵀ [gə·ˈmʊst] pp von **müssen**

gemustert adj patterned

gemütlich I. adj 1. (bequem) cozy; **es sich/jdm ~ machen** to make oneself/sb comfortable 2. (gesellig) pleasant; (ungezwungen) informal II. adv 1. (gemächlich) leisurely 2. (behaglich) comfortably

Gemütlichkeit <-> f kein pl 1. (Behaglichkeit) coziness 2. (Ungezwungenheit) informality

Gemütsmensch m fam good-natured person

Gemütsruhe f **in aller ~** fam at one's own pace

Gemütszustand m mood

Gen <-s, -e> [ˈgeːn] nt gene

genannt [gə·ˈnant] pp von **nennen**

genau [gə·ˈnau] I. adj 1. (exakt) exact; **man weiß noch nichts G~es** nobody knows any details yet 2. (gewissenhaft) meticulous II. adv exactly; **~ in der Mitte** right in the middle; **~ genommen** strictly speaking

genaugenommen adv s. **genau** II

Genauigkeit <-> [gə·ˈnau·ɪç·kait] f kein pl exactness; (von Daten) accuracy

genauso [gə·ˈnau·zoː] adv just the same; **~ gut/viel/wenig** just as well/much/little

Gendefekt m ʙɪᴏʟ, ᴍᴇᴅ genetic defect

genlnehmigen* [gə·ˈneː·mɪ·gn̩] I. vt **jdm etw ~** to grant [sb] permission

to do sth II. vr **sich** dat **etw ~** to indulge in sth

Genehmigung <-, -en> f 1. (das Genehmigen) approval 2. (Berechtigungsschein) permit

geneigt adj **~ sein, etw zu tun** to be inclined to do sth

General(in) <-[e]s, -e> [ge·nə·ˈraːl] m(f) general

Generaldirektor(in) m(f) general manager

Generalprobe f 1. ᴛʜᴇᴀᴛ dress rehearsal 2. ᴍᴜs final rehearsal

Generalstreik m general strike

Generaluntersuchung f complete checkup

Generation <-, -en> [ge·nə·ra·ˈtsi̯oːn] f generation

Generator <-s, -toren> [ge·nə·ˈraː·toːɐ̯] m generator

generell [ge·nə·ˈrɛl] I. adj general II. adv generally

genervt [gə·ˈnɛrft] adj annoyed; (stärker) at the end of one's rope

Genesung <-, selten -en> [gə·ˈneː·zʊŋ] f geh convalescence

Genetik <-> [ge·ˈneː·tɪk] f kein pl genetics + sing vb

genetisch [ge·ˈneː·tɪʃ] adj genetic

Genforschung f genetic research

genial [ge·ˈni̯aːl] adj 1. (überragend) brilliant; (erfinderisch) ingenious 2. (Idee) inspired

Genick <-[e]s, -e> [gə·ˈnɪk] nt neck ▶ **jdm das ~ brechen** to finish [off sep] sb

Genie <-s, -s> [ʒe·ˈniː] nt genius

genieren* [ʒe·ˈniː·rən] vr **sich** akk **~** to be embarrassed

genlließen <genoss, genossen> [gə·ˈniː·sn̩] vt 1. (auskosten) to enjoy 2. (essen) to eat

Genießer(in) <-s, -> m(f) gourmet

Genitiv <-s, -e> [ˈgeː·ni·tiːf] m genitive [case]

genommen [gə·ˈnɔ·mən] pp von **nehmen**

genormt adj standardized

genoss ᴿᴿ, **genoß** ᴬᴸᵀ [gə·ˈnɔs] imp von **genießen**

Genosse, Genossin <-n, -n> [gə·ˈnɔ·sə,

gə·'nɔ·sɪn] *m, f* comrade

genossen [gə·'nɔ·sn̩] *pp von* **genießen**

Genossenschaft <-, -en> [gə·'nɔ·sn̩· ʃaft] *f* cooperative

Gentechnik *f* genetic engineering

genug [gə·'nu:k] *adv* enough

Genüge [gə·'ny:·gə] *f kein pl* **zur ~** [quite] enough; *(oft genug)* often enough

ge|nügen * [gə·'ny:·gn̩] *vi* **1.** *(ausreichen)* [jdm] **~** to be enough [for sb] **2.** *(gerecht werden)* **etw** *dat* **~** to fulfill sth

genügsam [gə·'ny:k·za:m] *adj (bescheiden)* modest

Genugtuung <-, selten -en> [gə·'nu:k· tu:·ʊŋ] *f* satisfaction

Genus <-, Genera> ['gɛ·nʊs] *nt* gender

Genuss^{RR} <-es, Genüsse>, **Genuß**^{ALT} <-sses, Genüsse> [gə·'nʊs] *m* **1.** *(Köstlichkeit)* [culinary] delight **2.** *kein pl (das Zusichnehmen)* consumption **3.** *(das Genießen)* enjoyment; **in den ~ einer S.** *gen* **kommen** to [come to] enjoy sth; *(aus etw Nutzen ziehen a.)* to benefit from sth

genüsslich^{RR}, **genüßlich**^{ALT} I. *adj* pleasurable II. *adv* with [great] pleasure

Genussmittel^{RR} *nt* luxury foods, alcohol and tobacco

Geograf^{RR}(in) <-en, -en> *m(f)* s. **Geograph**

Geografie^{RR} <-> *f kein pl* s. **Geographie**

geografisch^{RR} *adj* s. **geographisch**

Geograph(in) <-en, -en> [geo·'gra:f] *m(f)* geographer

Geographie <-> [geo·gra·'fi:] *f kein pl* geography

geographisch [geo·'gra:·fɪʃ] *adj* geographic[al]

geologisch [geo·'lo:·gɪʃ] *adj* geological

Geometrie <-> [geo·me·'tri:] *f kein pl* geometry

geometrisch [geo·'me:·trɪʃ] *adj* geometric

Gepäck <-[e]s> [gə·'pɛk] *nt kein pl* luggage, baggage

Gepäckabfertigung *f* luggage [*o* baggage] check-in

Gepäckausgabe *f* luggage [*o* baggage] claim

Gepäckstück *nt* piece of luggage [*o* baggage]

Gepäckträger *m (am Fahrrad)* rear rack

Gepäckträger(in) *m(f)* porter

Gepäckwagen *m* luggage cart

gepfeffert *adj fam* s. **gesalzen**

gepfiffen [gə·'pfɪ·fn̩] *pp von* **pfeifen**

gepflegt *adj* **1.** *(nicht vernachlässigt)* well looked after; *(Aussehen)* well-groomed; *(Garten)* well-tended; *(Park)* well-kept **2.** *fam (kultiviert)* civilized; *(Ausdrucksweise)* sophisticated

gepriesen [gə·'pri:·zn̩] *pp von* **preisen**

gequollen [gə·'kvɔ·lən] *pp von* **quellen**

gerade [gə·'ra:·də] I. *adj* **1.** *(nicht krumm)* straight; *(aufrecht)* upright; **~ sitzen/stehen** to sit/stand up straight **2.** MATH even II. *adv fam* **1.** *(im Augenblick, soeben)* just; **haben Sie ~ einen Moment Zeit?** do you have a minute?; **da du ~ da bist, ...** while you're here, ...; **ich wollte mich ~ ins Bad begeben, da ...** I was just about to take a bath when ...; **da wir ~ von Geld sprechen, ...** speaking of money, ... **2.** *(knapp)* just; **sie hat die Prüfung ~ so bestanden** she [just] barely passed the exam **3.** *(genau)* just; **~ heute habe ich an dich gedacht** I was just thinking of you today III. *part (ausgerechnet)* **warum ~ er/ich?** why him/me of all people?; **warum ~ jetzt?** why now of all times?; **~ deswegen** that's exactly why ▶ **das hat ~ noch gefehlt!** *iron* that's all I need!; **~, weil ...** especially because ...

Gerade <-n, -n> [gə·'ra:·də] *f* MATH straight line

geradeaus [gə·ra:·də·'ʔaʊs] *adv* straight ahead

gerade|biegen *vt irreg fam (in Ordnung bringen)* to straighten out *sep*

geradeheraus [gə·ra:·də·hɛ·'raʊs] I. *adj pred* straightforward II. *adv* frankly

gerade|stehen^{ALT1} *vi irreg (aufrecht stehen)* s. **gerade** I 1

gerade|stehen² *vi irreg (einstehen)* **für jdn/etw ~** to answer for sb/sth

geradezu [gə·ra:·də·tsu:] *adv* really

geradlinig *adj, adv* straight

Geranie <-, -n> [ge·'ra:·njə] *f* geranium

gerann [gə·'ran] *imp von* **gerinnen**

gerannt [gə·'rant] *pp von* **rennen**

Gerät <-[e]s, -e> [gə·'rɛ:t] *nt* 1. (*Vorrichtung*) device, gadget 2. ELEK, TECH appliance; (*Fernseher, Radio*) set 3. (*Werkzeug*) tool 4. SPORT (*Turngerät*) apparatus 5. *kein pl* (*Ausrüstung*) equipment; (*eines Handwerkers*) tools *pl*

ge|raten[1] <gerät, geriet, geraten> *vi sein* 1. (*unbeabsichtigt kommen*) **in etw** *akk* **~** to get into sth; **in Schwierigkeiten/eine Schlägerei ~** to get into difficulties/a fight; **in Armut ~** to end up in poverty; **in Brand ~** to catch fire; **in eine Falle ~** to fall into a trap; **in Gefangenschaft ~** to be taken prisoner; **ins Schleudern ~** to go into a skid; **in einen Stau ~** to get stuck in a traffic jam; **ins Schwärmen/Träumen ~** to fall into a rapture/dream; **in einen Sturm ~** to get caught in a storm; **in Vergessenheit ~** to fall into oblivion 2. (*erfüllt werden von*) **in Panik ~** to start to panic; **in Verlegenheit/Wut ~** to get embarrassed/angry 3. **zu groß/klein ~** to turn out too big/short 4. (*gelingen*) to turn out; **das Soufflé ist mir nicht ~** my soufflé turned didn't turn out well 5. *fam* (*kennen lernen*) **an jdn ~** to come across sb 6. (*arten*) **nach jdm ~** to take after sb

geraten[2] *pp von* **raten**

Geratewohl [gə·ra:·tə·'vo:l] *nt* ▶ **aufs ~** *fam* (*auf gut Glück*) on the off chance; (*willkürlich*) randomly

geräumig [gə·'rɔy·mɪç] *adj* spacious

Geräusch <-[e]s, -e> [gə·'rɔyʃ] *nt* sound; (*unerwartet, unangenehm a.*) noise

geräuschempfindlich *adj* sensitive to noise *pred*

geräuschlos *adj* silent

geräuschvoll *adj* loud

gerben ['gɛr·bn̩] *vt* to tan

gerecht [gə·'rɛçt] I. *adj* just; **etw** *dat* **~ werden** to fulfill sth; **Erwartungen ~ werden** to meet expectations II. *adv* justly

Gerechtigkeit <-> [gə·'rɛç·tɪç·kait] *f kein pl* justice

Gerede <-s> [gə·'re:·də] *nt kein pl* gossip; (*Geschwätz*) talk; **kümmere dich**

nicht um das ~ der Leute don't worry about what [other] people are saying

gereizt I. *adj* (*verärgert*) irritated; (*nervös*) edgy II. *adv* irritably

Gericht[1] <-[e]s, -e> [gə·'rɪçt] *nt* (*Speise*) dish

Gericht[2] <-[e]s, -e> [gə·'rɪçt] *nt* 1. JUR court [of justice]; (*Gebäude*) law courts *pl* 2. (*die Richter*) court ▶ **mit jdm ins ~ gehen** to sharply criticize sb

gerichtlich I. *adj attr* judicial II. *adv* legally; **~ gegen jdn vorgehen** to take sb to court

Gerichtshof *m* court of law

Gerichtssaal *m* courtroom

Gerichtsverfahren *nt* legal proceedings *pl;* **ein ~ gegen jdn einleiten** to take legal action against sb

Gerichtsverhandlung *f* trial; (*zivil*) hearing

Gerichtsvollzieher(in) <-s, -> *m(f)* U.S Marshal

geriet [gə·'ri:t] *imp von* **geraten**[1]

gering [gə·'rɪŋ] *adj* 1. (*niedrig*) low; (*Anzahl, Menge*) small; **das stört mich nicht im G~sten** it doesn't bother me in the slightest; **von ~em Wert** of little value 2. (*unerheblich*) slight; (*Bedeutung*) minor; (*Chance*) slim

geringfügig [gə·'rɪŋ·fy:·gɪç] I. *adj* insignificant; (*Betrag, Einkommen*) small; (*Unterschied*) slight; (*Vergehen, Verletzung*) minor II. *adv* slightly

geringschätzig [gə·'rɪŋ·ʃɛ·tsɪç] *adj s.* **abfällig**

ge|rinnen <gerann, geronnen> *vi sein* to coagulate; (*Blut a.*) to clot; (*Milch a.*) to curdle

Gerippe <-s, -> [gə·'rɪ·pə] *nt* skeleton

gerissen [gə·'rɪ·sn̩] I. *pp von* **reißen** II. *adj fam* crafty; (*Plan*) cunning

geritten [gə·'rɪ·tn̩] *pp von* **reiten**

Germane, Germanin <-n, -n> [gɛr·'ma:·nə, gɛr·'ma:·nɪn] *m, f* Teuton

germanisch [gɛr·'ma:·nɪʃ] *adj* 1. HIST Teutonic 2. LING Germanic

Germanistik <-> [gɛr·ma·'nɪs·tɪk] *f kein pl* German [studies *npl*]

gern(e) <lieber, am liebsten> ['gɛr·n(ə)] *adv* 1. (*freudig*) with pleasure; **ich mag ihn sehr ~** I like him a lot; **etw ~ tun**

to like doing/to do sth; **seine Arbeit ~ machen** to enjoy one's work; **ich hätte ~ gewusst, ...** I would like to know ... **2.** (*ohne weiteres*) **das kannst du ~ haben** you're welcome to [have] it; **das glaube ich ~!** I [really] believe it! ▶ **~ geschehen!** don't mention it!

gerochen [gə·'rɔ·xn̩] *pp von* **riechen**

Geröll <-[e]s, -e> [gə·'rœl] *nt* scree *spec*, talus; (*größer*) boulders *pl*

Gerste <-, -n> ['gɛrs·tə] *f* barley

Geruch <-[e]s, Gerüche> [gə·'rʊx] *m* smell; (*einer Blume, eines Parfüms*) scent; (*Gestank*) stench

geruchlos *adj* odorless

Geruch(s)sinn *m kein pl* sense of smell

Gerücht <-[e]s, -e> [gə·'rʏçt] *nt* rumor; **ein ~ in die Welt setzen** to start a rumor

gerufen *pp von* **rufen**

Gerümpel <-s> [gə·'rʏm·pl̩] *nt kein pl* junk

Gerundium <-s, -ien> [ge·'rʊn·di·ʊm] *nt* gerund *spec*

gerungen [gə·'rʊŋən] *pp von* **ringen**

Gerüst <-[e]s, -e> [gə·'rʏst] *nt* **1.** BAU scaffold[ing] **2.** (*Grundplan*) framework

gesalzen [gə·'zal·tsn̩] *adj fam* (*Preis, Strafe*) steep

gesamt [gə·'zamt] *adj attr* whole, entire; (*Kosten*) total

Gesamtbetrag *m* total [amount]

Gesamteindruck *m* overall impression

Gesamtkosten *pl* total cost[s *pl*]

Gesamtschule *f* ≈ integrated school

gesandt [gə·'zant] *pp von* **senden²**

Gesandte(r) [gə·'zan·tə] *f(m)* envoy

Gesang <-[e]s, Gesänge> [gə·'zaŋ] *m* **1.** *kein pl* (*das Singen*) singing **2.** (*Lied*) song; **ein Gregorianischer ~** a Gregorian chant

Gesangbuch *nt* hymn book

Gesangverein *m* glee club

Gesäß <-es, -e> [gə·'zɛːs] *nt* rear end *fam*

geschaffen *pp von* **schaffen²**

Geschäft <-[e]s, -e> [gə·'ʃɛft] *nt* **1.** (*Laden*) store, shop **2.** (*Gewerbe, Handel*) business; **mit jdm ins ~ kommen** (*einmalig*) to make a deal with sb; (*dauer-*

haft) to do business with sb; **wie gehen die ~e?** how's business? **3.** (*Geschäftsabschluss*) deal; **ein gutes ~ machen** to get a good deal ▶ **kleines/großes ~** *fam* number one/number two

geschäftig [gə·'ʃɛf·tɪç] *adj* busy

geschäftlich [gə·'ʃɛft·lɪç] **I.** *adj* business *attr* **II.** *adv* on business; **~ verreist** away on business

Geschäftsbrief *m* business letter

Geschäftsfrau *f s.* **Geschäftsmann** businesswoman *fem*

Geschäftsführer(in) *m(f)* **1.** ADMIN manager **2.** (*in einem Verein*) secretary

Geschäftsmann *m* businessman

Geschäftsreise *f* business trip

Geschäftsschluss ^RR *m* (*Ladenschluss*) closing time

Geschäftsstelle *f* (*Büro*) office; (*einer Bank, Firma*) branch

geschäftstüchtig *adj* business-minded

Geschäftszeit *f* business hours *pl*

geschah [gə·'ʃaː] *imp von* **geschehen**

ge|schehen <geschah, geschehen> [gə·'ʃeː·ən] *vi sein* **1.** (*stattfinden*) to happen; **es muss etwas ~** something has to be done **2.** (*widerfahren*) **jdm geschieht etw** sth happens to sb; **das geschieht dir recht!** [it] serves you right!; **nicht wissen, wie einem geschieht** to not know whether one is coming or going **3.** (*hin und weg sein*) **als sie ihn sah, war es um sie ~** she was lost the moment she set eyes on him

Geschehen <-s, -> [gə·'ʃeː·ən] *nt* events *pl*

gescheit [gə·'ʃait] *adj* clever

Geschenk <-[e]s, -e> [gə·'ʃɛŋk] *nt* present

Geschenkpapier *nt* wrapping paper

Geschichte <-, -n> [gə·'ʃɪçtə] *f* **1.** *kein pl* (*Historie*) history; **Alte/Neue ~** ancient/modern history **2.** (*Erzählung*) story **3.** *fam* (*Angelegenheit, Sache*) business; **die ganze ~** everything; **das sind ja schöne ~n!** *iron* that's a fine state of affairs!

geschichtlich [gə·'ʃɪçt·lɪç] *adj* historical

Geschichtsbuch *nt* history book

Geschick¹ <-[e]s> [gə·'ʃɪk] *nt kein pl*

(Fertigkeit) skill

Geschick² <-[e]s, -e> [gə·ˈʃɪk] *nt (Schicksal)* fate

Geschicklichkeit <-> *f kein pl* skill

geschickt I. *adj* skillful; *(Verhalten)* diplomatic II. *adv* skillfully

geschieden [gə·ˈʃiː·dn̩] I. *pp von* **scheiden** II. *adj* divorced

geschienen [gə·ˈʃiː·nən] *pp von* **scheinen**

Geschirr <-[e]s, -e> [gə·ˈʃɪr] *nt* 1. *kein pl (Haushaltsgefäße)* dishes *pl* 2. *(Service)* [tea/dinner] service 3. *(Riemenzeug)* harness

Geschirrspülmaschine *f* dishwasher

Geschirrspülmittel *nt* dish soap

Geschirrtuch *nt* dishcloth

geschissen [gə·ˈʃɪ·sn̩] *pp von* **scheißen**

geschlafen *pp von* **schlafen**

geschlagen *pp von* **schlagen**

Geschlecht <-[e]s, -er> [gə·ˈʃlɛçt] *nt* 1. *kein pl* BIOL gender; **das andere ~** the opposite sex; **männlichen/weiblichen ~s** male/female 2. *(Sippe)* family 3. LING gender

Geschlechtskrankheit *f* sexually transmitted disease

Geschlechtsteil *nt* genitals *npl*

Geschlechtsverkehr *m* sexual intercourse

geschlichen [gə·ˈʃlɪ·çn̩] *pp von* **schleichen**

geschliffen [gə·ˈʃlɪ·fn̩] I. *pp von* **schleifen²** II. *adj* polished

geschlossen [gə·ˈʃlɔ·sn̩] I. *pp von* **schließen** II. *adj* 1. *(gemeinsam)* united; *(Ablehnung)* unanimous 2. *(nicht geöffnet)* closed III. *adv (einheitlich)* unanimously

geschlungen [gə·ˈʃlʊŋən] *pp von* **schlingen**

Geschmack <-[e]s, Geschmäcke> [gə·ˈʃmak] *m* 1. *kein pl (Aroma)* taste 2. *kein pl (Geschmackssinn)* sense of taste 3. *(ästhetisches Empfinden)* taste; **einen guten/keinen guten ~ haben** to have good/bad taste; **auf den ~ kommen** to acquire a taste for sth ▶ **über ~ lässt sich [nicht] streiten** *prov* there's no accounting for taste

geschmacklos *adj* 1. KOCHK bland 2. *(taktlos)* tasteless

Geschmacklosigkeit <-, -en> *f* 1. *(Taktlosigkeit)* tastelessness; *(taktlose Bemerkung)* tasteless remark 2. KOCHK tastelessness

geschmackvoll *adj* tasteful

geschmeidig [gə·ˈʃmai·dɪç] I. *adj* 1. *(weich)* sleek; *(Haar, Fell)* silky; *(Haut)* soft; *(Leder)* supple; *(Masse, Teig)* smooth 2. *(biegsam)* supple II. *adv (biegsam)* supplely

geschmissen [gə·ˈʃmɪ·sn̩] *pp von* **schmeißen**

geschmolzen [gə·ˈʃmɔl·tsn̩] *pp von* **schmelzen**

geschnitten [gə·ˈʃnɪ·tn̩] *pp von* **schneiden**

geschoben [gə·ˈʃo·bn̩] *pp von* **schieben**

gescholten [gə·ˈʃɔl·tn̩] *pp von* **schelten**

geschoren [gə·ˈʃoː·rən] *pp von* **scheren¹**

Geschoss RR <-es, -e>, **Geschoß** ALT <-sses, -sse> [gə·ˈʃɔs] *nt* 1. MIL projectile 2. *(Wurfgeschoss)* missile 3. *(Stockwerk)* floor, story

geschossen [gə·ˈʃɔ·sn̩] *pp von* **schießen**

geschraubt *adj pej* affected

Geschrei <-s> [gə·ˈʃrai] *nt kein pl* 1. *(Schreien)* shouting; *(schrill)* shrieking 2. *fam (Lamentieren)* fuss

geschrieben [gə·ˈʃriː·bn̩] *pp von* **schreiben**

geschrie(e)n [gə·ˈʃriː(·ə)n] *pp von* **schreien**

geschritten [gə·ˈʃrɪ·tn̩] *pp von* **schreiten**

geschunden [gə·ˈʃʊn·dn̩] *pp von* **schinden**

Geschwätz <-es> [gə·ˈʃvɛts] *nt kein pl pej fam* 1. *(dummes Gerede)* hot air *pej fam* 2. *(Klatsch)* gossip

geschwätzig [gə·ˈʃvɛ·tsɪç] *adj pej* talkative

geschweige [gə·ˈʃvai·gə] *konj* ~ [**denn**] never mind, let alone

geschwiegen [gə·ˈʃviː·gn̩] *pp von* **schweigen**

geschwind [gə·ˈʃvɪnt] *adv dial* quickly

Geschwindigkeit <-, -en> [gə·ˈʃvɪn·dɪç·kait] *f* speed

Geschwindigkeitsbegrenzung f speed limit

Geschwister [gə·ˈʃvɪs·tɐ] pl siblings pl

geschwollen [gə·ˈʃvɔ·lən] I. pp von **schwellen** II. adj pej pompous III. adv in a pompous way

geschwommen [gə·ˈʃvɔ·mən] pp von **schwimmen**

Geschworene(r) f(m) juror; **die ~n** the jury

Geschwulst <-, Geschwülste> [gə·ˈʃvʊlst] f tumor

geschwunden [gə·ˈʃvʊn·dn̩] pp von **schwinden**

Geschwür <-s, -e> [gə·ˈʃvyːɐ̯] nt ulcer

gesehen pp von **sehen**

ge|sellen* [gə·ˈzɛ·lən] vr 1. (sich anschließen) **sich** akk **zu jdm ~** to join sb 2. (hinzukommen) **sich** akk **zu etw** dat **~** to add to sth

gesellig [gə·ˈzɛ·lɪç] I. adj sociable; (Abend) convivial; **ein ~es Beisammensein** a friendly get-together II. adv **~ zusammensitzen** to sit together and chat

Geselligkeit <-, -en> f gregariousness

Gesellschaft <-, -en> [gə·ˈzɛl·ʃaft] f 1. POL, SOZIOL society 2. ÖKON corporation 3. (Fest) party 4. (Kreis von Menschen) group of people; **in schlechte ~ geraten** to get in with the wrong crowd; **jdm ~ leisten** to join sb 5. (Umgang) company

Gesellschafter(in) <-s, -> m(f) (Teilhaber) shareholder

gesellschaftlich adj social

gesellschaftsfähig adj socially acceptable

gesessen [gə·ˈzɛ·sn̩] pp von **sitzen**

Gesetz <-es, -e> [gə·ˈzɛts] nt law

Gesetzbuch nt statute book; **Bürgerliches ~** Civil Code

Gesetzentwurf m draft legislation

Gesetzgeber <-s, -> m legislator

Gesetzgebung <-, -en> f legislation

gesetzlich [gə·ˈzɛts·lɪç] adj legal

Gesetzmäßigkeit <-, -en> f 1. (Gesetzlichkeit) legality 2. (Rechtmäßigkeit) legitimacy 3. (Regelmäßigkeit) regularity

gesetzt I. adj dignified II. konj **~, ...** (an-

genommen, ...) assuming that ...; (vorausgesetzt, dass ...) providing that ...

gesichert I. pp von **sichern** II. adj secure[d]; (Erkenntnisse) solid; **~es Einkommen** fixed income; **~e Existenz** secure livelihood

Gesicht <-[e]s, -er> [gə·ˈzɪçt] nt face; **jdm etw** akk **vom ~ ablesen** to see sth from sb's expression; **ein böses/trauriges ~ machen** to look angry/sad ▸ **jdm wie aus dem ~ geschnitten sein** to be the spitting image of sb; **sein wahres ~ zeigen** to show one's true colors

Gesichtsfarbe f complexion

Gesichtspunkt m point of view

Gesindel <-s> [gə·ˈzɪn·dl̩] nt kein pl pej riffraff

gesinnt [gə·ˈzɪnt] adj meist pred minded; **jdm gut/übel ~ sein** to be well-disposed/ill-disposed toward sb

Gesinnungswandel m change in attitude

gesittet [gə·ˈzɪ·tət] I. adj well-brought up II. adv **sich** akk **~ benehmen** to be well-behaved

gesoffen [gə·ˈzɔ·fn̩] pp von **saufen**

gesogen [gə·ˈzoː·gn̩] pp von **saugen**

gespalten [gə·ˈʃpal·tn̩] pp von **spalten**

gespannt adj 1. (sehr erwartungsvoll) expectant; **~ sein, ob/was ...** to be anxious to see whether/what ... 2. (konfliktträchtig) tense

Gespenst <-[e]s, -er> [gə·ˈʃpɛnst] nt ghost

gespenstisch [gə·ˈʃpɛns·tɪʃ] adj eerie

gesponnen [gə·ˈʃpɔ·nən] pp von **spinnen**

Gespött <-[e]s> [gə·ˈʃpœt] nt kein pl mockery; **sich/jdn zum ~ [der Leute] machen** to make a laughing stock of oneself/sb

Gespräch <-[e]s, -e> [gə·ˈʃprɛːç] nt 1. (Unterredung) conversation; **mit jdm ins ~ kommen** to get into a conversation with sb 2. (Anruf) [tele]phone call

gesprächig [gə·ˈʃprɛː·çɪç] adj talkative

gesprochen [gə·ˈʃprɔ·xn̩] pp von **sprechen**

gesprossen [gə·ˈʃprɔ·sn̩] pp von **sprießen**

gesprungen [gə·ˈʃprʊŋən] pp von **sprin-**

gen

Gespür <-s> [gəˈʃpyːɐ̯] nt kein pl instinct; **ein gutes ~ für Farben** a good feel for colors

Gestalt <-, -en> [gəˈʃtalt] f 1. (Mensch) figure; **eine verdächtige ~** a suspicious character 2. (Wuchs) build 3. (Person, Persönlichkeit) character; **in ~ jds** in the form of sb ▶ **~ annehmen** to take shape

gestalten * [gəˈʃtal·tn̩] I. vt to design; (Garten) to lay out; (Schaufenster) to dress; **etw anders/neu ~** to redesign sth II. vr **sich** akk **irgendwie ~** to turn out to be somehow

Gestaltung <-, -en> f 1. (das Einrichten) design; (eines Gartens) laying out; (eines Schaufensters) window dressing 2. (das Organisieren) organization 3. ARCHIT building

gestand imp von **gestehen**

geständig [gəˈʃtɛn·dɪç] adj **~ sein** to have confessed

Geständnis <-ses, -se> [gəˈʃtɛnt·nɪs] nt admission; (eines Verbrechens) confession

Gestank <-[e]s> [gəˈʃtaŋk] m kein pl stench

ge|**statten** * [gəˈʃta·tn̩] I. vt s. **erlauben** I 1,2 II. vi **wenn Sie ~, das war mein Platz!** if you don't mind, that was my seat! III. vr s. **erlauben** II

Geste <-, -n> [ˈɡeːs·tə] f gesture

ge|**stehen** <gestand, gestanden> vt, vi to confess

Gestein <-[e]s, -e> [gəˈʃtain] nt rock

Gestell <-[e]s, -e> [gəˈʃtɛl] nt 1. (Brett-terregal) shelves pl 2. (Brillengestell) frame

gestern [ɡɛs·tɐn] adv (der Tag vor heute) yesterday; **~ vor einer Woche** a week ago yesterday ▶ **nicht von ~ sein** fam to not be born yesterday

gestiegen [gəˈʃtiː·ɡn̩] pp von **steigen**

gestochen [gəˈʃtɔ·xn̩] I. pp von **stechen** II. adv **~ scharf** crystal clear

gestohlen [gəˈʃtoː·lən] pp von **stehlen**

gestorben [gəˈʃtɔr·bn̩] pp von **sterben**

gestoßen [gəˈʃtoː·sn̩] pp von **stoßen**

Gestotter <-s> [gəˈʃtɔ·tɐ] nt kein pl stammering

gestreift adj striped

gestrichen [gəˈʃtrɪ·çn̩] I. pp von **streichen** II. adj level III. adv **~ voll** full to the brim

gestrig [ˈɡɛst·rɪç] adj attr yesterday's attr, [of] yesterday pred

gestritten [gəˈʃtrɪ·tn̩] pp von **streiten**

Gestrüpp <-[e]s, -e> [gəˈʃtrʏp] nt undergrowth

gestunken [gəˈʃtʊŋ·kn̩] pp von **stinken**

gesucht adj (gefragt) in demand pred, much sought-after

gesund <gesünder, gesündeste> [gəˈzʊnt] adj healthy; **Rauchen ist nicht ~** smoking is bad for you; **geistig und körperlich ~** of sound mind and body; **~ und munter** in good shape

Gesundheit <-> f kein pl health; **~!** gesundheit!, bless you!

gesundheitlich I. adj health; **aus ~en Gründen** for health reasons II. adv (hinsichtlich der Gesundheit) with regard to health; **wie geht es Ihnen ~?** how are you doing, healthwise?

Gesundheitsamt nt local public health department

gesungen [gəˈzʊŋən] pp von **singen**

gesunken [gəˈzʊŋ·kn̩] pp von **sinken**

getan [gəˈtaːn] pp von **tun**

getragen [gəˈtraː·ɡn̩] pp von **tragen**

Getränk <-[e]s, -e> [gəˈtrɛŋk] nt drink

Getränkeautomat m drink dispenser

ge|**trauen** * vr (wagen) **sich** akk **~, etw zu tun** to dare to do sth

Getreide <-s, -> [gəˈtrai·də] nt cereal; (geerntet) grain

getrennt adj separate

getreten pp von **treten**

Getriebe <-s, -> [gəˈtriː·bə] nt TECH transmission

getrieben [gəˈtriː·bn̩] pp von **treiben**

getroffen [gəˈtrɔ·fn̩] pp von **treffen**

getrogen [gəˈtroː·ɡn̩] pp von **trügen**

getrost [gəˈtroːst] adv (ohne weiteres) safely

getrunken [gəˈtrʊŋ·kn̩] pp von **trinken**

Getto <-s, -s> [ˈɡɛ·to] nt ghetto

Getue <-s> [gəˈtuː·ə] nt kein pl pej fuss

geübt adj experienced; (Auge, Griff, Ohr) trained

G

gewachsen I. pp von **wachsen**[1] **II.** adj (ebenbürtig) equal; **sie ist der Aufgabe ~** she is certainly up to the task; **einem Gegner ~ sein** to be a match for an opponent

Gewächshaus nt greenhouse

gewagt adj **1.** (kühn) audacious; (gefährlich) risky **2.** (freizügig) risqué

Gewähr <-> [gə·ˈveːɐ̯] f kein pl guarantee; **ohne ~** subject to change

ge|währen* [gə·ˈveː·rən] vt **1.** (einräumen) [jdm] etw ~ to grant [sb] sth; **jdm einen Rabatt ~** to give sb a discount; **jdn ~ lassen** to give sb free rein **2.** (zuteilwerden lassen: Trost) to afford

gewährleisten* [gə·ˈveːɐ̯·lais·tn̩] vt to guarantee

Gewalt <-, -en> [gə·ˈvalt] f **1.** (Machtbefugnis, Macht) power; **in jds ~ sein** to be in sb's hands; **höhere ~** JUR act of God; **ein Gebiet/Land in seine ~ bringen** to bring a region/country under one's control; **~ über jdn haben** to exercise [complete] control over sb; **sich** akk **in der ~ haben** to have oneself under control **2.** kein pl (gewaltsames Vorgehen) force; (Gewalttätigkeit) violence; **nackte ~** brute force; **sich** dat **~ antun** to force oneself **3.** kein pl (Heftigkeit) force

Gewaltherrschaft f kein pl tyranny

gewaltig [gə·ˈval·tɪç] **I.** adj **1.** (heftig) enormous; (Orkan) violent **2.** (riesig, wuchtig) huge; (Bauwerke) monumental; (Last) heavy **3.** fam (sehr groß) tremendous **II.** adv fam (sehr) considerably; **sich** akk **~ irren** to be very much mistaken

gewaltlos I. adj nonviolent **II.** adv without violence

Gewaltlosigkeit <-> f kein pl nonviolence

gewaltsam [gə·ˈvalt·zaːm] **I.** adj violent **II.** adv by force

gewalttätig adj violent

Gewalttätigkeit f violence

gewandt [gə·ˈvant] **I.** pp von **wenden II.** adj skillful; (Auftreten) confident; (Bewegung) deft; (Redner) good

gewann [gə·ˈvan] imp von **gewinnen**

gewaschen pp von **waschen**

Gewässer <-s, -> [gə·ˈvɛ·sɐ] nt body of water

Gewebe <-s, -> [gə·ˈveː·bə] nt **1.** (Stoff) fabric **2.** ANAT, BIOL tissue

Gewehr <-[e]s, -e> [gə·ˈveːɐ̯] nt rifle; (Schrotflinte) shotgun

Geweih <-[e]s, -e> [gə·ˈvai] nt antlers pl

Gewerbe <-s, -> [gə·ˈvɛr·bə] nt **1.** (Betrieb) [commercial] business **2.** (Handwerk, Handel) trade

Gewerbesteuer f business tax

gewerblich [gə·ˈvɛrp·lɪç] **I.** adj (handwerklich) trade; (kaufmännisch) commercial; (industriell) industrial **II.** adv **Räume ~ nutzen** to use rooms for commercial purposes

Gewerkschaft <-, -en> [gə·ˈvɛrk·ʃaft] f [trade] union

Gewerkschaft(l)er(in) <-s, -> [gə·ˈvɛrk·ʃaft(l)ɐ] m(f) trade unionist

Gewerkschaftsmitglied nt [trade] union member

gewichen [gə·ˈvɪ·çn̩] pp von **weichen**

Gewicht <-[e]s, -e> [gə·ˈvɪçt] nt **1.** kein pl (Schwere eines Körpers) weight + sing vb; **ein geringes/großes ~ haben** to be very light/heavy **2.** kein pl fig (Wichtigkeit) weight; **ins ~ fallen** to count; **auf etw** akk **[großes] ~ legen** to attach importance to sth **3.** (Metallstück zum Beschweren) weight

gewichtig [gə·ˈvɪç·tɪç] adj significant

Gewichtszunahme f weight gain

gewieft [gə·ˈviːft] fam **I.** adj crafty **II.** adv with cunning

gewiesen [gə·ˈviː·zn̩] pp von **weisen**

Gewimmel <-s> [gə·ˈvɪ·ml̩] nt kein pl (von Insekten) swarm; (von Menschen) throng

Gewinde <-s, -> [gə·ˈvɪn·də] nt TECH thread

Gewinn <-[e]s, -e> [gə·ˈvɪn] m **1.** ÖKON profit; **~ bringen** to make a profit **2.** (Preis) prize; (beim Lotto, Wetten) winnings npl **3.** kein pl ([innere] Bereicherung) gain

Gewinnbeteiligung f profit sharing

ge|winnen <gewann, gewonnen> [gə·ˈvɪ·nən] **I.** vt **1.** (als Gewinn erhalten) to win **2.** (überzeugen) **jdn ~** to win sb over; **jdn als Freund ~** to win sb as

a friend; **jdn als Kunden ~** to gain sb as a customer **3.** (*erzeugen*) to obtain; (*Kohle, Metall*) to extract (**aus** +*dat* from) **4.** (*Einfluss, Selbstsicherheit*) to gain **II.** *vi* **1.** (*Gewinner sein*) to win (**bei/in** +*dat* at) **2.** (*profitieren*) to profit (**bei** +*dat* from)

gewinnend *adj* charming

Gewinner(in) <-s, -> *m(f)* winner; (*mil a.*) victor

Gewinnung <-> *f kein pl* extraction

gewiss RR, **gewiß** ALT [gə'vɪs] **I.** *adj* **1.** *attr* (*nicht näher bezeichnet*) certain; **eine ~e Frau Schmidt** a (certain) Ms. Schmidt **2.** (*sicher*) **sich** *dat* **etw** *gen* **~ sein** to be certain of sth **II.** *adv* *geh* certainly; **aber ~!** sure!

Gewissen <-s> [gə'vɪ·sn̩] *nt kein pl* conscience; **jdn/etw auf dem ~ haben** to have sb/sth on one's conscience; **jdm ins ~ reden** to appeal to sb's conscience

gewissenhaft *adj* conscientious

gewissenlos I. *adj* unscrupulous **II.** *adv* without scruple[s pl]

Gewissensbisse *pl* **~ haben** to have a bad conscience

Gewissenskonflikt *m* moral conflict

gewissermaßen *adv* so to speak

Gewissheit RR, **Gewißheit** ALT <-, -en> *f selten pl* certainty; **~ haben** to be certain; **sich** *dat* ~ [**über etw** *akk*] **verschaffen** to find out for certain [about sth]

Gewitter <-s, -> [gə'vɪ·tɐ] *nt* thunderstorm

ge|wittern * *vi impers* **es gewittert** it's thundering

gewittrig [gə'vɪt·rɪç] *adj* thundery; **~e Schwüle** oppressive heat

gewoben [gə'vo:·bn̩] *pp von* **weben**

gewogen [gə'vo:·gn̩] **I.** *pp von* **wiegen** **II.** *adj* **jdm/etw ~ sein** to be well-disposed toward[s] sb/sth

ge|wöhnen * **I.** *vt* **jdn an etw** *akk* **~** to accustom sb to sth **II.** *vr* **sich** *akk* **an jdn/etw ~** to get used to sb/sth; **sich** *akk* **daran ~, etw zu tun** to get used to doing sth

Gewohnheit <-, -en> *f* habit

Gewohnheitsmensch *m* creature of habit

Gewohnheitsrecht *nt* (*als Rechtssystem*) common law *no art*

gewöhnlich [gə'vø:n·lɪç] **I.** *adj* **1.** *attr* (*üblich*) usual **2.** (*normal*) normal **3.** *pej* (*ordinär*) common **II.** *adv* (*üblicherweise*) usually; **für ~** normally; **wie ~** as usual

gewohnt [gə'vo:nt] *adj* usual; (*Umgebung*) familiar; **etw ~ sein** to be used to sth; **es ~ sein, etw zu tun** to be used to doing sth

Gewölbe <-s, -> [gə'vœl·bə] *nt* vault

gewölbt *adj* (*Dach, Decke*) vaulted; (*Stirn*) domed; (*Rücken*) rounded

gewonnen [gə'vɔ·nən] *pp von* **gewinnen**

geworben [gə'vɔr·bn̩] *pp von* **werben**

geworden [gə'vɔr·dn̩] *pp von* **werden**

geworfen [gə'vɔr·fn̩] *pp von* **werfen**

Gewühl <-[e]s> [gə'vy:l] *nt kein pl* **1.** (*Gedränge*) throng **2.** *pej* (*andauerndes Kramen*) rummaging around

gewunken [gə'vʊŋ·kn̩] *dial pp von* **winken**

Gewürz <-es, -e> [gə'vʏrts] *nt* spice

Gewürzgurke *f* gherkin

gewusst RR, **gewußt** ALT [gə'vʊst] *pp von* **wissen**

gezackt *adj* jagged; (*Hahnenkamm*) toothed; (*Blatt*) serrated

Gezeiten [gə'tsai·tn̩] *pl* tide[s pl]

Gezeter <-s> [gə'tse:·tɐ] *nt kein pl pej fam* racket

gezielt I. *adj* well-directed; (*Fragen*) specific **II.** *adv* specifically; **~ fragen** to ask questions with sth mind

geziert *adj* *pej* affected

gezogen [gə'tso:·gn̩] *pp von* **ziehen**

Gezwitscher <-s> [gə'tsvɪ·tʃɐ] *nt kein pl* chirping

gezwungen [gə'tsvʊŋən] **I.** *pp von* **zwingen** **II.** *adj* (*gekünstelt*) forced; (*Benehmen*) stiff **III.** *adv* (*gekünstelt*) stiffly; **~ lachen** to give a forced laugh

gezwungenermaßen *adv* of necessity

Ghetto <-s, -s> *nt* s. **Getto**

Gicht <-> ['gɪçt] *f kein pl* gout

Giebel <-s, -> ['gi:·bl̩] *m* gable [end]

Gier <-> ['gi:ɐ̯] *f kein pl* greed (**nach** +*dat* for); (*nach etw Ungewöhnlichem*) craving (**nach** +*dat* for)

gierig ['giː·rɪç] **I.** adj greedy **II.** adv greedily; **etw ~ trinken** to gulp down sep sth

gießen <goss, gegossen> ['giː·sn̩] **I.** vt **1.** (bewässern) to water **2.** (schütten) to pour (**auf** +akk on, **über** +akk over) **3.** TECH to cast **II.** vi impers (stark regnen) **es gießt in Strömen** it's pouring

Gießkanne f watering can

Gift <-[e]s, -e> ['gɪft] nt poison; (Schlangengift) venom ▶ **~ und Galle spucken** fam to vent one's spleen; **darauf kannst du ~ nehmen** fam you can bet your life on that

Giftgas nt poison gas

giftig ['gɪf·tɪç] **I.** adj **1.** (Gift enthaltend) poisonous **2.** (boshaft) venomous **3.** (grell) garish **II.** adv pej **~ antworten** to give a nasty reply

Giftmüll m toxic waste

Giftschlange f poisonous snake

Giftstoff m toxic substance

Gigant(in) <-en, -en> [gi·ˈgant] m(f) giant; fig a. colossus

gigantisch [gi·ˈgan·tɪʃ] adj gigantic

ging ['gɪŋ] imp von **gehen**

Ginster <-s, -> ['gɪns·tɐ] m broom

Gipfel <-s, -> ['gɪp·fl̩] m **1.** (Bergspitze) peak; (höchster Punkt) summit; dial (Wipfel) treetop **2.** fig (Zenit) peak; (Höhepunkt) height **3.** POL summit

Gipfeltreffen nt summit [meeting]

Gips <-es, -e> ['gɪps] m **1.** (Baumaterial) plaster; (in Mineralform) gypsum; (zum Modellieren) plaster of Paris **2.** (Kurzform für Gipsverband) [plaster] cast; **den Fuß in ~ haben** to have one's foot in a cast

Gipsbein nt fam leg in a cast

gipsen ['gɪp·sn̩] vt **1.** (Wand) to plaster **2.** MED (Bruch) to put in a cast

Gipsverband m plaster cast

Giraffe <-, -n> [gi·ˈra·fə] f giraffe

Girlande <-, -n> [gɪr·ˈlan·də] f garland (**aus** +dat of)

Girokonto ['ʒiː·ro·] nt ≈ checking account

Gischt <-[e]s, -e (m) o -, -en (f)> ['gɪʃt] m o f pl selten [sea] spray

Gitarre <-, -n> [gi·ˈta·rə] f guitar

Gitarrist(in) <-en, -en> [gi·ta·ˈrɪst] m(f) guitarist

Gitter <-s, -> ['gɪtɐ] nt (Absperrung) fencing; (vor Türen, Fenstern: engmaschig) screen; (grobmaschig) grate; (parallel laufende Stäbe) bars pl; (für Gewächse) trellis ▶ **jdn hinter ~ bringen** fam to put sb behind bars

Gitterfenster nt barred window

glamourös [gla·mu·ˈrøːs] adj glamorous

Glanz <-es> ['glants] m kein pl **1.** (das Glänzen) shine; (von Augen) sparkle; (von Lack) gloss; (von Perlen, Seide) sheen **2.** (herrliche Pracht) splendor

glänzen ['glɛn·tsn̩] vi **1.** (widerscheinen) to shine; (polierte Oberfläche) to gleam; (Augen) to sparkle; (Haut, Stoff) to be shiny; (Wasseroberfläche) to glisten; (Sterne) to twinkle **2.** fig (sich hervortun) to shine

glänzend ['glɛn·tsn̩t] **I.** adj **1.** (widerscheinend) shining; (Oberfläche) gleaming; (Augen) sparkling; (Haar) shiny; (Papier) glossy **2.** (hervorragend) brilliant **II.** adv (sehr) splendidly; **sich** akk **~ amüsieren** to have a great time

Glanzleistung f brilliant achievement

glanzvoll adj brilliant

Glas <-es, Gläser> ['glaːs] nt **1.** (Werkstoff) glass no indef art, + sing vb; **„Vorsicht ~!"** "glass — handle with care" **2.** (Trinkgefäß) glass

Glascontainer [-kɔn·teː·nɐ] m recycling container for glass

Glaserei [gla·zə·ˈrai] f glazier's workshop

Glasfaserkabel nt fiber optic cable

glasig ['glaː·zɪç] adj KOCHK (Zwiebeln) transparent

glasklar **I.** adj **1.** (durchsichtig) transparent **2.** fig (klar und deutlich) crystal clear **II.** adv (klar und deutlich) in no uncertain terms

Glasscheibe f **1.** (dünne Glasplatte) sheet of glass **2.** (Fensterscheibe) pane of glass

Glasscherbe f glass shard

Glasur [gla·ˈzuːɐ] f **1.** (Keramikglasur) glaze **2.** KOCHK icing

glatt <-er o fam glätter, -este o fam glätteste> ['glat] **I.** adj **1.** (Fläche, Haut) smooth; (Gesicht) unlined; (Haar)

straight; **~ rasiert** clean-shaven; **etw ~ streichen** to smooth out *sep* sth **2.** (*Straße*) slippery **3.** (*problemlos*) smooth **4.** *attr fam* (*eindeutig*) outright; (*Lüge*) downright **II.** *adv fam* (*rundweg*) plainly; (*ohne Umschweife*) straight up; (*leugnen*) flatly

Glatteis *nt* [thin sheet of] ice; „**Vorsicht ~!**" "danger — black ice" ▶ **sich** *akk* **auf ~** **begeben** to skate on thin ice

glätten ['glɛ·tn̩] **I.** *vt* (*glatt streichen*) to smooth out *sep* sth **II.** *vr* **sich** *akk* **~ 1.** (*Meer, Wellen*) to subside **2.** *fig* (*Wut, Erregung*) to die down

glattweg ['glat·vɛk] *adv fam* just like that; **etw ~ ablehnen** to turn sth down flat out; **etw ~ abstreiten** to flatly deny sth

Glatze <-, -n> ['glatsə] *f* bald head; **eine ~ bekommen/haben** to go/be bald

Glatzkopf *m fam* **1.** (*Kopf*) bald head **2.** (*Mann*) baldy

Glaube <-ns> ['glau·bə] *m kein pl* **1.** (*Überzeugung*) belief (**an** +*akk* in); (*gefühlsmäßige Gewissheit*) faith (**an** +*akk* in); **in gutem ~n** in good faith; **den festen ~n haben, dass ...** to firmly believe that ...; **jdm/etw** [**keinen**] **~n schenken** to [not] believe sb/sth; **den ~n an jdn/etw verlieren** to lose faith in sb/sth **3.** REL (*religious*) faith

glauben ['glau·bn̩] **I.** *vt* **1.** (*für wahr halten*) to believe; **kaum zu ~** incredible **2.** (*wähnen*) **sich** *akk* **unbeobachtet ~** to think [that] nobody is watching **II.** *vi* (*vertrauen*) **jdm ~** to believe sb; **jdm aufs Wort ~** to take sb's word for it; **an jdn/etw ~** to believe in sth **2.** (*für wirklich halten*) **an etw** *akk* **~** to believe in sth ▶ **dran ~** **müssen** *sl* (*sterben müssen*) to kick the bucket; (*weggeworfen werden müssen*) to get tossed out; (*etw tun müssen*) to be stuck with it

Glaubensbekenntnis *nt* (*Religionszugehörigkeit*) profession [of faith]

gläubig ['glɔy·bɪç] *adj* (*religiös*) religious

Gläubige(r) ['glɔy·bɪ·gə] *f/m* believer

Gläubiger(in) <-s, -> ['glɔy·bɪ·gɐ] *m(f)* ÖKON creditor

glaubwürdig *adj* credible

Glaubwürdigkeit <-> *f kein pl* credibility

gleich ['glaiç] **I.** *adj* **1.** (*übereinstimmend*) same; **2 mal 2** [**ist**] **~ 4** 2 times 2 is 4; **~ alt** the same age; **~ groß** equal in size; **~ schwer** equally heavy; **~ gesinnt** like-minded **2.** (*unverändert*) **es ist immer das** [**ewig**] **G~e** it's always the same [old thing]; **~ bleibend gut** consistently good **3.** (*gleichgültig*) **jdm ~ sein** to be all the same to sb; **ganz ~ wer/was** [...] no matter who/what [...] **II.** *adv* **1.** (*sofort, bald*) right away; **bis ~!** see you soon!; (*sofort*) see you in a minute!; **ich komme ~!** I'll be right there!; **~ darauf** soon afterward; (*sofort*) right away; **~ morgen** [first thing] tomorrow; **~ nach dem Frühstück** right after breakfast **2.** (*unmittelbar daneben/danach*) immediately; **~ als ...** as soon as ...; **~ daneben** right beside it **3.** (*zugleich*) at once **III.** *part* **1.** *in Aussagesätzen emph* just as well **2.** *in Fragesätzen* (*noch*) again; **wie war doch ~ Ihr Name?** what was your name again?

gleichalt(e)rig ['glaiç·ʔalt(ə)·rɪç] *adj* [of] the same age *pred*

gleichberechtigt *adj* **~ sein** to have equal rights

Gleichberechtigung *f kein pl* equal rights + *sing/pl vb*

gleichbleibend *adj, adv s.* **gleich I 2**

gleichen <glich, geglichen> ['glai·çn̩] *vt* **jdm/etw ~** to be [just] like sb/sth; **sich** *dat* **~** to be alike

gleichfalls *adv* likewise; **danke ~!** thanks, [and the] same to you! *a. iron*

gleichförmig *adj* uniform

gleichgesinnt *adj s.* **gleich I 1**

Gleichgewicht *nt kein pl* balance; **im ~ sein** to be balanced; **aus dem ~ kommen** to lose one's balance

gleichgültig **I.** *adj* **1.** (*uninteressiert*) indifferent (**gegenüber** +*dat* to[ward]) **2.** (*teilnahmslos*) apathetic (**gegenüber** +*dat* toward) **3.** (*unwichtig*) immaterial; **etw ist jdm vollkommen ~** sb couldn't care less about sth **II.** *adv* **1.** (*uninteressiert*) with indifference **2.** (*teilnahmslos*) with apathy

Gleichgültigkeit [ˈglaiç·gyl·tɪç·kait] *f kein pl* indifference

Gleichheitszeichen *nt* equal|s| sign

gleichmäßig I. *adj* even; (*Bewegungen*) regular; (*Puls, Tempo*) steady II. *adv* 1. (*in gleicher Stärke/Menge*) equally; ~ **atmen** to breathe regularly; ~ **schlagen** (*Herz, Puls*) to beat steadily 2. (*ohne Veränderungen*) consistently

Gleichnis <-ses, -se> [ˈglaiç·nɪs] *nt* allegory; (*aus der Bibel*) parable

gleich|setzen *vt* to equate (**mit** +*dat* with)

Gleichstand *m kein pl* tie

Gleichstrom *m* ELEK direct current

Gleichung <-, -en> [ˈglai·çʊŋ] *f* equation

gleichwertig *adj* equal; ~ **sein** to be equally matched

gleichzeitig I. *adj* simultaneous II. *adv* 1. (*zur gleichen Zeit*) simultaneously 2. (*ebenso, zugleich*) at the same time

Gleis <-es, -e> [ˈglais] *nt* track; (*einzelne Schiene*) rail; (*Bahnsteig*) platform; ~ **2** track 2

gleiten <glitt, geglitten> [ˈglai·tn̩] *vi* 1. *sein* (*schweben*) to glide; (*Wolke*) to sail 2. *sein* (*streichen, huschen*) **über etw** *akk* ~ (*Augen*) to wander over sth; (*Blick*) to pass over sth; (*Finger*) to explore sth; (*Hand*) to slide over sth 3. *sein* (*rutschen*) to slide; **ins Wasser** ~ to slip into the water

Gleitmittel *nt* lubricant

Gleitzeit *f fam* flextime

Gletscher <-s, -> [ˈglɛ·tʃɐ] *m* glacier

Gletscherspalte *f* crevasse

glich [ˈglɪç] *imp von* **gleichen**

Glied <-[e]s, -er> [ˈgliːt] *nt* 1. (*Körperteil*) limb 2. (*Penis*) |male| member *form* 3. (*Kettenglied*) link *a. fig* 4. (*Teil*) part

gliedern [ˈgliː·dɐn] I. *vt* (*Aufsatz, Buch*) to |sub|divide (**in** +*akk* into) II. *vr* **sich** *akk* **in etw** *akk* ~ to be |sub|divided into sth

Gliederschmerz *pl* rheumatic pains

Gliedmaßen *pl* limbs

Glimmstängel RR, **Glimmstengel** ALT *m hum fam* smoke

glimpflich [ˈglɪmpf·lɪç] I. *adj* 1. (*ohne schlimmere Folgen*) without serious consequences *pred* 2. (*mild: Strafe*) mild II. *adv* 1. (*ohne schlimmere Folgen*) ~ **abgehen** to pass |by| without serious consequences; ~ **davonkommen** to get off lightly 2. (*mild*) **mit jdm** ~ **umgehen** to treat sb leniently

glitschig [ˈglɪt·ʃɪç] *adj fam* slippery

glitt [ˈglɪt] *imp von* **gleiten**

glitz(e)rig [ˈglɪ·ts(ə)·rɪç] *adj* sparkly

glitzern [ˈglɪ·tsɐn] *vi* to glitter; (*Stern*) to twinkle

global [glo·ˈbaːl] I. *adj* 1. (*weltweit*) global 2. (*umfassend*) general II. *adv* 1. (*weltweit*) globally 2. (*ungefähr*) generally

Globalisierung <-> *f* globalization

Globus <-, Globen> [ˈgloː·bʊs] *m* globe

Glocke <-, -n> [ˈglɔ·kə] *f* 1. (*Läutewerk*) bell 2. (*glockenförmiger Deckel*) |glass| cover ▶ **etw an die große** ~ **hängen** *fam* to shout sth from the rooftops

Glockenblume *f* bellflower

Glockenspiel *nt* 1. (*in Kirch- oder Stadttürmen*) carillon 2. (*Musikinstrument*) glockenspiel

Glockenturm *m* belfry

Glossar <-s, -e> [glɔ·ˈsaːɐ̯] *nt* glossary

glotzen [ˈglɔ·tsn̩] *vi pej fam* to gape (**auf** +*akk* at)

Glück <-[e]s> [ˈglʏk] *nt kein pl* 1. (*günstige Fügung*) luck, fortune; **ein** ~, **dass** ... it is/was lucky that ...; **viel** ~ |**bei etw** *dat*|! good luck |with sth|!; ~/**kein** ~ **haben** to be lucky/unlucky; **zum** ~ luckily 2. (*Freude*) happiness ▶ **etw auf gut** ~ **tun** to do sth on the off chance; ~ **im Unglück haben** it could have been much worse |for sb|; **mehr** ~ **als Verstand haben** to have more luck than brains

glücken [ˈglʏ·kn̩] *vi sein* (*gelingen*) to be successful; **jdm glückt etw** sb succeeds in sth

gluckern [ˈglʊ·kɐn] *vi* to gurgle

glücklich [ˈglʏk·lɪç] I. *adj* 1. (*vom Glück begünstigt*) lucky 2. (*vorteilhaft, erfreulich*) happy; (*Umstand*) fortunate 3. (*froh*) happy (**mit** +*dat* with, **über** +*akk* about) II. *adv* 1. (*vorteilhaft, erfreulich*) happily 2. (*froh und zufrieden*)

~ [mit jdm] verheiratet sein to be happily married [to sb]

glücklicherweise adv luckily

Glücksbringer <-s, -> m lucky charm

Glücksfall m stroke of luck

Glückspilz m fam lucky devil

Glückssache f etw ist [reine] ~ sth's a matter of [sheer] luck

Glücksspiel nt game of chance

Glückstreffer m stroke of luck; (beim Schießen) lucky shot

Glückwunsch m congratulations npl (zu +dat on)

Glückwunschkarte f greeting card

Glühbirne f light bulb

glühen ['glyː·ən] vi to glow; **vor Scham** ~ to burn with shame

glühend I. adj 1. (rot vor Hitze) glowing; (Metall) [red-]hot 2. (brennend, sehr heiß) burning; (Hitze) blazing **II.** adv ~ heiß burning hot

Glühwein m [hot] mulled wine

Glühwürmchen <-s, -> nt glowworm; (fliegend) firefly

Glut <-, -en> ['gluːt] f embers npl

glutrot adj fiery red

GmbH <-, -s> [geː·ʔɛm·beː·haː] f Abk von **Gesellschaft mit beschränkter Haftung** ≈ Inc.

Gnade <-, -n> ['gnaː·də] f mercy; ~ **vor Recht ergehen lassen** to temper justice with mercy

Gnadenfrist f [temporary] reprieve

gnadenlos adj merciless

gnädig ['gnɛː·dɪç] **I.** adj 1. (herablassend) gracious a. iron 2. (Nachsicht zeigend) merciful 3. veraltet (verehrt) ~**e Frau** madam; ~**es Fräulein** madam; (jünger) miss; ~**er Herr** veraltet sir **II.** adv 1. (herablassend) graciously 2. (milde) leniently

Gnom <-en, -en> ['gnoːm] m pej gnome

Gold <-[e]s> ['gɔlt] nt kein pl gold ▶ **es ist nicht alles ~, was glänzt** prov all that glitters is not gold

Goldbarren m gold ingot

golden ['gɔl·dn̩] **I.** adj attr gold[en liter] **II.** adv like gold

Goldfisch m goldfish

goldgelb adj golden yellow; KOCHK golden brown

Goldgrube f fig goldmine

Goldhamster m [golden] hamster

goldig ['gɔl·dɪç] adj 1. fam (allerliebst) cute 2. pred dial fam (rührend nett) sweet a. iron 3. dial iron fam **du bist aber ~!** very funny!

Goldmedaille [-me·dal·jə] f gold [medal]

goldrichtig adj fam 1. (völlig richtig) absolutely right 2. pred (in Ordnung) all right

Goldschmied(in) m(f) goldsmith

Goldstück nt 1. veraltet piece of gold 2. (Kosewort) treasure pet

Golf¹ <-[e]s, -e> ['gɔlf] m GEOL gulf

Golf² <-s> ['gɔlf] nt kein pl SPORT golf

Golfplatz m golf course + sing/pl vb

Golfspieler(in) m(f) golfer

Golfstaat m **die ~en** the Gulf States

Golfstrom m GEOL **der ~** the Gulf Stream

Gondel <-, -n> ['gɔn·dl̩] f 1. (Boot in Venedig) gondola 2. (Seilbahngondel) cable car 3. (Ballongondel) basket

gönnen ['gœ·nən] **I.** vt 1. (gern zugestehen) **jdm etw** ~ to not begrudge sb sth; **ich gönne ihm diesen Erfolg von ganzem Herzen!** I'm absolutely delighted that he succeeded! 2. iron **es jdm** ~, **dass** ... to be pleased [to see] that sb ... iron **II.** vr sich dat etw ~ to allow oneself sth; **sich** akk **ein Glas Wein** ~ to treat oneself to a glass of wine

gor ['goːɐ̯] imp von **gären**

Göre <-, -n> ['gøː·rə] f fam brat

Gorilla <-s, -s> [go·ˈrɪ·la] m gorilla

goss RR, **goß** ALT ['gɔs] imp von **gießen**

Gotik <-> ['goː·tɪk] f kein pl Gothic period

gotisch ['goː·tɪʃ] adj Gothic

Gott, Göttin <-es, Götter> ['gɔt] m, f 1. (ein Gott) god masc, goddess fem 2. kein pl (das höchste Wesen) God; ~ **sei Dank!** a. fig fam thank God! ▶ **ach ~** (resignierend) oh God!; (tröstend) oh dear; **ach du lieber ~** good heavens!; ~ **bewahre!** God forbid!; **wie ~ in Frankreich leben** to live in the lap of luxury; **grüß ~!** bes südd, österr hello!; **um ~es willen!** emph (o je!) [oh] my God!; (bitte) for God's sake!; ~ **weiß was/wann** ... fam God [only] knows what/when ...; **über ~ und die Welt reden** to talk

about everything under the sun

Gottesdienst *m* [church] service

Gotteslästerung *f* blasphemy

Göttin <-, -nen> ['gœtɪn] *f s.* **Gott** goddess

göttlich ['gœtlɪç] *adj* divine

gottlos *adj* godless

gottverlassen *adj emph fam* godforsaken *pej*

Grab <-[e]s, Gräber> ['graːp] *nt* grave ▶ **sich** *dat* **sein eigenes ~ schaufeln** to dig one's own grave; **schweigen können wie ein ~** to be [as] silent as the grave; **jd würde sich** *akk* **im ~[e] umdrehen, wenn ...** *fam* sb would turn in their grave if ...

graben <gräbt, gegraben> ['graːbn̩] **I.** *vi* to dig (**nach** +*dat* for) **II.** *vt* (*Loch*) to dig

Graben <-s, Gräben> ['graːbn̩] *m* **1.** (*Vertiefung in der Erde*) ditch **2.** MIL trench **3.** (*Festungsgraben*) moat

Grabmal *nt* **1.** (*Grabstätte*) mausoleum **2.** (*Gedenkstätte*) memorial

Grabstein *m* gravestone

Grad <-[e]s, -e> ['graːt] *m* **1.** SCI, MATH degree; **2 ~ unter/über null** 2 degrees below/above [zero] **2.** (*Maß, Stufe*) level; **in hohem ~[e]** to a great extent ▶ **um [ein]hundertachtzig ~** *fam* complete[ly]

Graf <-en, -en> ['graːf] *m, f* count *masc*, countess *fem*

Grafik ['graːfɪk] *f* **1.** *kein pl* (*grafische Technik*) graphic arts *pl* **2.** (*grafische Darstellung*) graphic **3.** (*Schaubild*) diagram

Grafiker(in) <-s, -> ['graːfɪke] *m(f)* graphic artist

Grafikkarte *f* COMPUT graphics card

Gräfin <-, -nen> ['grɛːfɪn] *f s.* **Graf** countess *fem*

Grafit RR <-s, -e> [gra·'fiːt] *m s.* **Graphit**

Grafschaft <-, -en> *f* HIST count's land

Gramm <-s, -e *o bei Zahlenangaben* -> ['gram] *nt* gram

Grammatik <-, -en> [gra·'ma·tɪk] *f* grammar

grammatisch [gra·'ma·tɪʃ] *adj* grammatical

Granat <-[e]s, -e *o österr* -en> [gra·'naːt] *m* garnet

Granate <-, -n> [gra·'naː·tə] *f* shell

grandios [gran·'di̯oːs] *adj* magnificent

Granit <-s, -e> [gra·'niːt] *m* granite

Grapefruit <-, -s> ['greːp·fruːt] *f* grapefruit

Graphik <-, -en> *f s.* **Grafik**

Graphit <-s, -e> [gra·'fiːt] *m* graphite

Gras <-es, Gräser> ['graːs] *nt* BOT grass ▶ **ins ~ beißen** *sl* to bite the dust; **das ~ wachsen hören** to have a sixth sense; **über etw** *akk* **wächst ~** *fam* [the] dust settles on sth

grasen ['graː·zn̩] *vi* to graze

Grashalm *m* blade of grass

Grashüpfer <-s, -> *m fam* grasshopper

grässlich RR, **gräßlich** ALT ['grɛs·lɪç] **I.** *adj* horrible; **was für ein ~es Wetter!** what lousy weather! **II.** *adv fam* terribly

Grat <-[e]s, -e> ['graːt] *m* **1.** (*oberste Kante*) ridge **2.** ARCHIT hip

Gräte <-, -n> ['grɛː·tə] *f* [fish]bone

gratis ['graː·tɪs] *adv* free [of charge]

Gratisprobe *f* free sample

gratulieren * [gra·tu·'liː·rən] *vi* [jdm] ~ to congratulate [sb] (**zu** +*dat* on); [**ich**] **gratuliere!** [my] congratulations!; **jdm zum Geburtstag ~** to wish sb a happy birthday

grau ['grau] *adj* **1.** (*Farbe*) gray; **~ meliert** (*leicht ergraut*) graying; MODE flecked with gray *pred* **2.** (*trostlos*) drab; **der ~e Alltag** the dullness of everyday life

Graubrot *nt dial* (*Mischbrot*) bread made from rye and wheat flour

Gräueltat RR *f* atrocity

grauen ['grau·ən] *vi impers* **es graut jdm vor jdm/etw** sb is terrified of sb/sth

Grauen <-s> ['grau·ən] *nt kein pl* horror, ~ **erregend** terrible

grauenerregend *adj s.* **Grauen**

grauenhaft *adj* **1.** (*furchtbar*) terrible **2.** *fam* (*schlimm*) dreadful

grauhaarig *adj* gray-haired

gräulich ['grɔy·lɪç] *adj* grayish

Graupelschauer *m* sleet shower

grausam ['grau·za·m] *adj* **1.** (*brutal*) cruel **2.** (*furchtbar*) terrible

Grausamkeit <-, -en> *f* **1.** *kein pl* (*Brutalität*) cruelty **2.** (*grausame Tat*)

act of cruelty

Gravierung <-, -en> f engraving

Gravitation <-> [gra·vi·ta·'tsjo:n] f kein pl gravitation[al pull]

greifbar adj 1. pred (verfügbar) etw ~ **haben** to have sth handy 2. (konkret) tangible

greifen <griff, gegriffen> ['grai·fn̩] I. vt [sich dat] etw ~ to take hold of sth II. vi 1. (fassen) to reach (in +akk into, nach +dat for); zu Drogen/zur Zigarette ~ to turn to drugs/reach for a cigarette 2. TECH etw greift (Reifen, Zahnrad) sth grips 3. (wirksam werden: Methoden) to take effect ▶ um sich akk ~ (sich ausbreiten) to spread

Greis(in) <-es, -e> ['grais] m(f) very old man/woman

grell ['grɛl] I. adj 1. (hell: Licht, Sonne) glaring 2. (schrill: Stimme, Schrei) piercing 3. (auffallend: Muster) loud II. adv 1. (sehr hell) dazzlingly 2. (schrill) ~ **klingen** to sound shrill

Gremium <-s, -ien> ['gre:·mi̯·ʊm] nt committee

Grenze <-, -n> ['grɛn·tsə] f 1. (Landesgrenze) border; **an der** ~ on the border; **über die** ~ **fahren** to cross the border 2. (Trennlinie) boundary 3. (äußerstes Maß) limit; **alles hat seine ~n** there is a limit to everything; **seine** ~n **kennen** to know one's limitations; **sich** akk **in** ~n **halten** to be limited

grenzen ['grɛn·tsn̩] vi to border (an +akk on)

grenzenlos I. adj 1. (unbegrenzt) endless 2. (maßlos) extreme; (Vertrauen) blind II. adv extremely

Grenzfall m borderline case

Grenzgebiet nt POL border area

Grenzlinie f SPORT line [marking the boundary of a playing surface]

Grenzübergang m border crossing point

Grenzwert m limiting value

Grieche, Griechin <-n, -n> ['gri:·çə] m, f Greek; s. a. **Deutsche(r)**

Griechenland <-s> ['gri:·çn̩·lant] nt Greece; s. a. **Deutschland**

griechisch ['gri:·çɪʃ] adj Greek; s. a. **deutsch**

Grieß <-es, -e> ['gri:s] m semolina

Grießbrei m semolina

griff ['grɪf] imp von **greifen**

Griff <-[e]s, -e> ['grɪf] m 1. (Zugriff) grip 2. (Handgriff) movement; **mit einem** ~ in a flash 3. SPORT hold 4. (Öffnungsmechanismus: einer Tür, eines Revolvers) handle; (eines Messers) hilt ▶ **etw in den** ~ **bekommen** fam to get the hang of sth; **jdn/etw im** ~ **haben** to have sb/ sth under control

griffbereit adj etw ~ **haben** to have sth handy

Grill <-s, -s> ['grɪl] m 1. (Gerät) grill 2. (Grillrost) barbecue; **vom** ~ grilled

Grille <-, -n> ['grɪ·lə] f cricket

grillen ['grɪ·lən] I. vi to have a barbecue II. vt to grill

Grimasse <-, -n> [gri·'ma·sə] f grimace; ~n **schneiden** to make faces

grimmig ['grɪ·mɪç] adj grim

grinsen ['grɪn·zn̩] vi to grin; **frech** ~ to smirk; **höhnisch** ~ to sneer

Grinsen <-s> ['grɪn·zn̩] nt kein pl grin; **freches** ~ smirk; **höhnisches** ~ sneer

Grippe <-, -n> ['grɪ·pə] f influenza, flu fam

grob <gröber, gröbste> ['gro:p] I. adj 1. (nicht fein) coarse 2. (ungefähr) rough 3. (unhöflich) rude 4. (unsanft, unsensibel) rough ▶ **aus dem Gröbsten heraus sein** the worst is over II. adv 1. (nicht fein) coarsely; ~ **gemahlen** coarsely ground 2. (in etwa) roughly; ~ **geschätzt** at a rough estimate 3. (unhöflich) rudely 4. (unsanft, unsensibel) roughly 5. (schlimm) **sich** akk ~ **täuschen** to be badly mistaken

Groll <-[e]s> ['grɔl] m kein pl resentment; [einen] ~ **gegen jdn hegen** to harbor a grudge against sb

grollen ['grɔ·lən] vi [jdm] ~ to be resentful [of sb]

Grönland ['grø:n·lant] nt Greenland; s. a. **Deutschland**

groß <größer, größte> ['gro:s] I. adj 1. (flächenmäßig) large, big 2. (lang) long 3. (hoch: Gebäude) high 4. (hoch gewachsen) tall; **du bist** ~ **geworden** you've grown; **er ist 1,78 m** ~ he is 1.78 m [o 5 feet 10 inches] [tall] 5. (das Maß oder Ausmaß betreffend) **in** ~en

Größen in large sizes; **mit ~er Geschwindigkeit** at high speed; **die ~e Masse** the majority of [the] people **6.** *fig* (*bedeutend, beträchtlich*) great; (*Durchbruch, Reinfall*) major; (*Misserfolg*) abject; (*Nachfrage*) big; (*Schrecken*) nasty; (*Schwierigkeiten*) serious; (*Unternehmen*) leading; **~e Angst haben** to be terribly afraid **7.** *fig* (*in Eigennamen*) **Friedrich der G~e** Frederick the Great ▶ **im G~en und Ganzen [gesehen]** on the whole **II.** *adv* **1.** *fam* (*besonders*) **was soll man da schon ~ sagen?** there's really not much to say; **ich habe mich nie ~ für Politik interessiert** I've never been particularly interested in politics **2.** MODE **etw größer machen** to let out *sep* sth **3.** (*von weitem Ausmaß*) **~ angelegt** large-scale

großartig ['gro:s·ʔa:ɐ̯·tɪç] **I.** *adj* **1.** (*prächtig*) magnificent **2.** (*hervorragend*) brilliant **3.** (*wundervoll*) wonderful **II.** *adv* magnificently

Großaufnahme *f* close-up

Großbetrieb *m* large business; AGR large farm

Großbritannien <-s> [gro:s·bri·'tanjən] *nt* Great Britain; *s. a.* **Deutschland**

Großbuchstabe *m* capital [letter]

Größe <-, -n> ['grø:·sə] *f* **1.** (*räumliche Ausdehnung, Mode*) size **2.** (*Höhe, Länge*) height **3.** MATH, PHYS quantity **4.** *kein pl* (*Erheblichkeit*) magnitude; (*eines Problems*) seriousness; (*eines Erfolgs*) extent **5.** *kein pl* (*Bedeutsamkeit*) significance

Großeinkauf *m* bulk purchase

Großeltern *pl* grandparents *pl*

großenteils *adv* largely

Größenwahn(sinn) *m* megalomania

Großfahndung *f* large-scale search

Großfamilie *f* extended family

Großhandel *m* wholesale trade; **etw im ~ kaufen** to buy sth wholesale

Großhändler(in) *m(f)* wholesaler

großherzig *adj* magnanimous

Großhirn *nt* cerebrum

Großkind *nt schweiz* (*Enkelkind*) grandchild

großkotzig *adj pej sl* swanky

Großmaul *nt pej fam* big mouth

Großmutter *f* grandmother, grandma *fam*, granny *fam*

Großraum *m* **im ~ Berlin** in Greater Berlin

Großraumbüro *nt* open-plan office

großspurig *adj pej* boastful

Großstadt ['gro:s·ʃtat] *f* [big] city

großstädtisch ['gro:s·ʃtɛ:·tɪʃ] *adj* big-city *attr*

Großteil *m* **1.** (*ein großer Teil*) **ein ~** a large part **2.** (*der überwiegende Teil*) **der ~** the majority; **zum ~** for the most part

größtenteils *adv* for the most part

Großvater *m* grandfather, grandpa *fam*

groß|ziehen ['gro:s·tsi:ən] *vt irreg* (*Kind*) to raise; (*Tier*) to rear

großzügig *adj* **1.** (*generös*) generous **2.** (*nachsichtig*) lenient **3.** (*in großem Stil*) grand

Großzügigkeit <-> *f kein pl* **1.** (*Generosität*) generosity **2.** (*Toleranz*) leniency **3.** (*Weiträumigkeit*) spaciousness

grotesk [gro·'tɛsk] *adj* grotesque

Grotte <-, -n> ['grɔ·tə] *f* grotto

grub [gru:p] *imp von* **graben**

Grube <-, -n> ['gru:·bə] *f* **1.** (*größeres Erdloch*) [large] hole **2.** (*Bergwerk*) pit ▶ **wer andern eine ~ gräbt, fällt selbst hinein** *prov* you can easily fall into your own trap

grübeln ['gry:·bl̩n] *vi* to brood (**über** *+akk* over)

Gruft <-, Grüfte> ['grʊft] *f* (*Grabgewölbe*) vault; (*Kirche*) crypt

grün ['gry:n] *adj* (*Farbe, Politik*) green ▶ **sich** *akk* **~ und blau ärgern** to be furious; **jdn ~ und blau schlagen** *fam* to beat sb black and blue

Grün <-s, -> ['gry:n] *nt* **1.** (*Farbe*) green ▶ **das ist dasselbe in ~** *fam* it's one and the same [thing]

Grünanlage *f* green space

Grund <-[e]s, Gründe> ['grʊnt] *m* **1.** (*Ursache, Veranlassung*) reason (**zu** *+dat* for); **keinen/nicht den geringsten ~** no/not the slightest reason; **jdm ~ [zu etw** *dat*] **geben** to give sb reason [to do sth] **2.** (*Motiv*) grounds *pl*; **~ zu der Annahme haben, dass ...** to have reason to believe that ...; **aus finanziel-**

len/gesundheitlichen Gründen** for financial/health reasons; **aus gutem ~** with good reason; **aus unerfindlichen Gründen** for some obscure reason; **aus diesem/welchem ~[e]** for this/what reason **3.** *kein pl* (*Erdboden*) ground **4.** *dial* (*Land, Acker*) land; **~ und Boden** land **5.** (*eines Gewässers*) bottom ▸ **auf ~ einer S.** *gen* on the basis of sth; **jdn in ~ und Boden reden** to shoot sb's arguments to pieces; **im ~e jds Herzens** in one's heart of hearts; **im ~e [genommen]** basically; **von ~ auf** completely; (*von Anfang an*) from scratch

Grundausbildung *f* basic training
Grundbesitz *m* real estate
Grundbesitzer(in) *m(f)* landowner
Grundbuch *nt* real property register
gründen ['grʏn·dn̩] **I.** *vt* to found; (*Firma*) to set up; (*Partei*) to form **II.** *vr* **sich** *akk* **auf etw** *akk* **~** to be based on sth
Gründer(in) *m(f)* <-s, -> founder
Grundfläche *f* area
Grundgebühr *f* basic charge
Grundgesetz *nt* basic [*o* fundamental] law
grundieren * ['grʊn·ˈdiː·rən] *vt* to prime
Grundlage *f* basis
grundlegend *adj* fundamental
gründlich ['grʏnt·lɪç] **I.** *adj* thorough **II.** *adv* **1.** *fam* (*total*) completely **2.** (*gewissenhaft*) thoroughly
Gründlichkeit <-> *f kein pl* thoroughness
grundlos **I.** *adj* (*unbegründet*) unfounded **II.** *adv* groundlessly
Grundnahrungsmittel *nt* basic food[stuff]
Gründonnerstag [grʏn·ˈdɔnɐs·taːk] *m* Maundy Thursday
Grundrecht *nt* basic right
Grundriss RR *m* **1.** BAU floor plan **2.** (*Abriss*) outline
Grundsatz ['grʊnt·zats] *m* principle
grundsätzlich ['grʊnt·zɛts·lɪç] **I.** *adj* **1.** (*grundlegend*) fundamental; (*Bedenken, Zweifel*) serious **2.** (*prinzipiell*) in principle *pred* **II.** *adv* **1.** (*völlig*) completely **2.** (*prinzipiell*) in principle **3.** (*kategorisch*) absolutely

Grundschule *f* elementary school
Grundstein *m* foundation stone; **den ~ zu etw** *dat* **legen** to lay the foundation for sth
Grundstück *nt* [piece of] property
Grundstücksmakler(in) *m(f)* real estate agent
Gründung <-, -en> *f* **1.** (*das Gründen*) foundation; (*eines Betriebs*) establishment **2.** BAU foundation
grundverschieden ['grʊnt·fɛɐ̯·ˈʃiː·dn̩] *adj* completely different
Grundwasser *nt* ground water
Grundwasserspiegel *m* groundwater level
Grundwortschatz *m* basic vocabulary
Grüne(r) ['grʏː·nə] *f(m)* POL [member of the] Green [Party]; **die ~n** the Green Party
Grüner Punkt *indicates that cartons and other packages can be recycled according to a special recycling system*
Grünfläche *f* green space
Grünkohl *m* [curly] kale
grünlich ['gryː·n·lɪç] *adj* greenish
Grünschnabel *m fam* greenhorn
Grünspan ['grʏː·n·ʃpaːn] *m kein pl* verdigris
Grünstreifen *m* median [strip]; (*am Straßenrand*) grassy shoulder
grunzen ['grʊn·tsn̩] *vt, vi* to grunt
Grünzeug *nt fam* **1.** (*Kräuter*) herbs *pl* **2.** (*Salat*) green salad **3.** (*Gemüse*) greens *pl*
Gruppe <-, -n> ['grʊ·pə] *f* group
Gruppenarbeit *f kein pl* teamwork
gruppenweise *adv* in groups
gruppieren * [grʊ·ˈpiː·rən] **I.** *vt* to group **II.** *vr* **sich** *akk* **~** to be grouped
Gruppierung <-, -en> *f* **1.** (*Gruppe*) group **2.** (*Aufstellung*) grouping
Gruselgeschichte *f* horror story
Gruß <-es, Grüße> ['gruːs] *m* **1.** (*Begrüßung*) greeting; MIL salute; **einen [schönen] ~ an Ihre Frau** [please] give my regards to your wife, say hi to your wife for me *fam* **2.** (*am Briefschluss*) regards; **mit freundlichen Grüßen** sincerely; **herzliche Grüße** best wishes
grüßen ['grʏː·sn̩] **I.** *vt* **1.** (*begrüßen*) to greet; **grüß dich!** *dial* hello [there]!

G

2. (*Grüße übermitteln*) **jdn von jdm ~** to send sb sb's regards; **jdn ~ lassen** to say hello to sb **II.** *vi* to say hello to sb **III.** *vr* **sich** *akk* ~ to say hello to one another

gucken ['gʊ·kn̩] *vi* **1.** (*sehen*) to look; (*heimlich*) to peek; **was guckst du so dumm!** wipe that silly look off your face! **2.** (*ragen*) **aus etw** *dat* ~ to stick out of sth

Guckloch *nt* peephole

Guerillakrieg [ɡeˈrɪ·lja-] *m* guerrilla war[fare]

Gulasch <-[e]s, -e> ['ɡu·laʃ] *nt o m* goulash

gültig ['ɡʏl·tɪç] *adj* **1.** (*Geltung besitzend*) valid; **der Sommerfahrplan tritt ab dem 1. April ~** the summer schedule takes effect April 1st **2.** (*allgemein anerkannt*) universal

Gummi <-s, -s> ['ɡʊmi] *nt o m* **1.** (*Material*) rubber **2.** *fam* (*Radiergummi*) eraser **3.** *fam* (*Gummiband*) rubber band **4.** (*Gummizug*) elastic **5.** *fam* (*Kondom*) rubber *sl*

Gummiband *nt* rubber band

Gummibaum *m* **1.** (*Kautschukbaum*) rubber tree **2.** (*Zimmerpflanze*) rubber plant

Gummihandschuh *m* rubber glove

Gummizelle *f* padded cell

Gunst <-> ['ɡʊnst] *f kein pl* **1.** (*Wohlwollen*) goodwill; **in jds ~ stehen** to be in sb's favor **2.** (*Vergünstigung*) **zu jds ~en** in sb's favor

günstig ['ɡʏns·tɪç] *adj* **1.** (*zeitlich gut gelegen*) convenient **2.** (*begünstigend*) favorable **3.** (*preisgünstig*) reasonable

Gurgel <-, -n> ['ɡʊr·ɡl̩] *f* throat

gurgeln ['ɡʊr·ɡln̩] *vi* **1.** (*den Rachen spülen*) to gargle **2.** (*von ablaufender Flüssigkeit*) to gurgle

Gurke <-, -n> ['ɡʊr·kə] *f* cucumber; (*Essiggurke*) pickle

gurren ['ɡʊ·rən] *vi* (*Tauben*) to coo; *fam* (*Mensch*) to purr

Gurt <-[e]s, -e> ['ɡʊrt] *m* **1.** (*Riemen*) strap **2.** (*Sicherheitsgurt*) seat belt **3.** (*breiter Gürtel*) belt

Gürtel <-s, -> ['ɡʏr·tl̩] *m* belt

Gürtelschnalle *f* belt buckle

Gürtpflicht *f* seatbelt law

Guss ^RR <-es, Güsse>, **Guß** ^ALT <-sses, Güsse> ['ɡʊs] *m* **1.** *fam* (*Regenguss*) downpour **2.** (*Zuckerguss*) icing

Gusseisen ^RR *nt* cast iron

Gussform ^RR *f* mold

gut <besser, beste> ['ɡuːt] **I.** *adj* **1.** (*nicht schlecht*) good (**in** +*dat* at, **gegen** +*akk* for); **jdm geht es ~/nicht ~** sb is fine/not well **2.** *attr* (*lieb*) good; (*Freund, Freundin*) close **3.** (*in Wünschen*) good; **~en Appetit!** enjoy your meal!; **~e Besserung!** get well soon!; **~e Fahrt!** have a nice trip!; **ein ~es neues Jahr!** Happy New Year! ▶ **~!** (*in Ordnung!*) OK!; **also ~!** well, all right then!; **~ beieinander sein** to be a bit chubby; **~ drauf sein** *fam* to be in a good mood; **das kann nicht ~ gehen!** this won't be good!; **lass mal ~ sein!** *fam* let's drop the subject!; **schon ~!** *fam* all right!; **~ so!** that's great! [*o* perfect!]; **und das ist auch ~ so** and it's/that's a good thing, too; **sei so ~ und ...** would you be kind enough to ...; **wer weiß, wozu es ~ ist** perhaps it's for the best; **etw wird wieder ~ werden** sth will be all right; **wozu ist das ~?** *fam* what's the use of that?; **[wie] ~, dass ...** it's a good thing that ... **II.** *adv* **1.** (*nicht schlecht*) well; **du sprichst aber ~ Englisch!** your English is really good!; **~ aussehend** *attr* good-looking; **~ bezahlt** *attr* well-paid; **~ gehend** *attr* flourishing; **~ gelaunt** in a good mood; **~ gemeint** *attr* well-meant; **~ verdienend** *attr* high-income *attr* **2.** (*geschickt*) well **3.** (*reichlich*) **es dauert noch ~ eine Stunde, bis Sie an der Reihe sind** it'll be a good hour before it's your turn **4.** (*einfach, recht*) **ich kann ihn jetzt nicht ~ im Stich lassen** I can't just leave him like that [now] **5.** (*leicht, mühelos*) **hast du die Prüfung ~ hinter dich gebracht?** did you make it through the exam all right?; **~ leserlich** very legible **6.** (*angenehm*) **hm, wonach riecht das denn so ~ in der Küche?** hmm, what's that great smell coming from the kitchen?; **schmeckt es dir auch ~?** do you like it, too? ▶ **~ und gern** easily; **so ~ es geht** as best one can; [**das hast du**] **~**

gemacht! good job!; **es ~ haben** to be lucky; **das kann ~ sein** that's quite possible; **mach's ~!** *fam* bye!; **pass ~ auf!** be [very] careful!; **sich** *akk* **~ mit jdm stellen** to get in good with sb

Gut <-[e]s, Güter> ['gu:t] *nt* 1. (*Landgut*) estate 2. (*Ware*) commodity

Gutachten <-s, -> ['gu:t·ʔax·tn̩] *nt* [expert's] report

Gutachter(in) <-s, -> *m(f)* expert

gutartig *adj* 1. MED benign 2. (*nicht widerspenstig*) good-natured

gutbürgerlich ['gu:t·bʏr·gə·lɪç] *adj* middle-class; КОСНК home-style; **~e Küche** home-style cooking

Gute(s) *nt* 1. (*Positives*) [*etwas*] **~s** [something] good; **man hört viel ~s über ihn** you hear a lot of good things about him; **alles ~!** all the best!; **das ~ daran** the good thing about it; [*auch*] **sein ~s haben** to have its good points [too]; **ein ~s hat die Sache** there is one good thing about it; **jdm schwant nichts ~s** sb has a bad feeling about sth; **~s tun** to do good; **was kann ich dir denn ~s tun?** how can I spoil you?; **nichts ~s versprechen** to not sound very promising; **sich** *akk* **zum ~n wenden** to take a turn for the better 2. (*friedlich*) **im ~n** amicably; **lass dir's im ~n gesagt sein, dass ich das nicht dulde** take a bit of friendly advice — I won't put up with it/that!; **sich** *akk* **im ~n trennen** to part on friendly terms 3. (*gute Charakterzüge*) **das ~ im Menschen** the good in man ▶ **alles hat sein ~s** *prov* every cloud has a silver lining *prov*; **Gut und Böse** good and evil; **im ~n wie im Bösen** (*mit Güte wie mit Strenge*) every way possible; (*in guten und schlechten Zeiten*) through good [times] and bad; **des ~n zu viel sein** to be too much [of a good thing]; **das ist wirklich des ~n zu viel!** that's really overdoing it/things!

Güte <-> ['gy:tə] *f kein pl* 1. (*milde Einstellung*) kindness; **die ~ haben, zu ...** to be so kind as to ... 2. (*Qualität*) [good] quality ▶ **erster ~** *fam* of the first order; **ach du liebe ~!** *fam* oh my goodness! *fam*; **in ~** amicably

Güterbahnhof *m* freight depot

Gütergemeinschaft *f* JUR community property; **in ~ leben** to have community property

Gütertrennung *f* JUR separation of property; **in ~ leben** to have separate property

Güterzug *m* freight train

Gütezeichen *nt* mark of quality

gutgläubig *adj* gullible

gut|haben *vt irreg* **etw bei jdm ~** to be owed sth by sb

Guthaben <-s, -> *nt* credit balance

gut|heißen *vt irreg* to approve of

gütig ['gy:tɪç] *adj* kind; **würden Sie so ~ sein, zu ...** *geh* would you be so kind as to ...; [**danke,**] **zu ~!** *iron* [thank you,] you're too kind!

gutmütig ['gu:t·my:·tɪç] *adj* good-natured

Gutsbesitzer(in) *m(f)* landowner

Gutschein *m* coupon

gut|schreiben *vt irreg* **jdm etw** *akk* **~** to credit sb with sth

Gutschrift *f* ÖKON voucher

Gutshof *m* estate, manor

gutwillig *adj* (*entgegenkommend*) obliging

Gymnasiast(in) <-en, -en> [gʏm·na·'zjast] *m(f)* ≈ high-school student

Gymnasium <-s, -ien> [gʏm·'na:·zjʊm] *nt* ≈ high school

Gymnastik <-> [gʏm·'nas·tɪk] *f kein pl* gymnastics + *sing vb*

Gynäkologe, Gynäkologin <-n, -n> [gʏ·nɛ·ko·'lo:·gə] *m, f* gynecologist

H

H, h <-, -> [ha:] *nt* 1. (*Buchstabe*) H, h; **~ wie Heinrich** H as in Hotel 2. MUS B, b

h *Abk von* **hora[e]** hr. 1. *gesprochen:* Uhr (*Stunde der Uhrzeit*) **22 ~** 2200 hrs.; **Abfahrt des Zuges: 9 h 17** train departure: 9:17 a.m. 2. *gesprochen:* Stunde (*Stunde*) h

ha [ha:] *Abk von* **Hektar** ha

Haar <-[e]s, -e> [ha:ɐ̯] *nt* 1. (*einzel-*

nes Haar) hair **2.** *sing o pl* (*gesamtes Kopfhaar*) hair; **graue ~e bekommen** to go gray; **sich** *dat* **die ~e schneiden lassen** to have one's hair cut ▶ **jdm stehen die ~e zu Berge** sb's hair is standing on end; **sich** *dat* **in die ~e geraten** to argue; **etw ist an den ~en herbeigezogen** sth is far-fetched; **um ein ~** within a hair's breadth

Haarausfall *m* hair loss

Haarbürste *f* hairbrush

haaren ['haːrən] *vi* to molt

Haarfarbe *f* color of one's hair

haarig ['haːrɪç] *adj* **1.** (*behaart*) hairy **2.** *fig* (*heikel*) hairy; (*Angelegenheit*) tricky

Haarnadel *f* hairpin

haarscharf *adv* (*ganz knapp*) by a hair's breadth

Haarschnitt *m* haircut

Haarspalterei <-, -en> [haːɐ̯ʃpalteˈraɪ] *f pej* splitting hairs

Haarspange *f* barrette

haarsträubend ['haːɐ̯ʃtrɔybn̩t] *adj* hair-raising

Haartrockner *m* hair dryer

Hab [haːp] *nt* **~ und Gut** belongings *npl*

haben <hätte, gehabt> ['haːbn̩] **I.** *vt* **1.** (*besitzen, aufweisen*) to have **2.** (*erhalten*) to have; **ich hätte gern ein Bier** I'd like a beer, please **3.** *in Maßangaben* **ein Meter hat 100 Zentimeter** there are 100 centimeters in a meter **4.** (*von etw erfüllt sein*) **Angst/Durst/Hunger/Sorgen ~** to be afraid/thirsty/hungry/worried; **gute/schlechte Laune ~** to be in a good/bad mood **5.** (*herrschen*) **wir ~ heute den 13.** it's the 13th today **6.** + *adj* **es bei jdm gut ~** to have got it made with sb **7.** (*tun müssen*) **etw zu tun ~** to have sth to do; **ich habe noch zu arbeiten** I still have work to do **8.** *dial* (*geben*) **es hat ... ** there is/are ... **9.** + *prep* **etw an sich** *dat* **~** to be sth about one; **jetzt weiß ich, was ich an ihr habe** now I know how lucky I am to have her; **das hast du jetzt davon!** now look where it's gotten you!; **nichts davon ~** to not gain a thing from it; **jdn vor sich** *dat* **haben** to deal with sb; **wissen Sie**

überhaupt, wen Sie vor sich haben? do you have any idea who you are dealing with? ▶ **noch/nicht mehr zu ~ sein** *fam* to still/no longer be available; **da haben wir's!** *fam* there you are!; **was hat es damit auf sich?** what's all this about?; **wie gehabt** as usual **II.** *aux vb* **etw getan ~** to have done sth; **also, ich hätte das nicht gemacht** well, I wouldn't have done that

Haben <-s> ['haːbn̩] *nt kein pl* credit; **mit etw** *dat* **im ~ sein** to be in the black by sth

Habenichts <-[es], -e> ['haːbənɪçts] *m fam* have-not *usu pl*

habgierig ['haːpɡiːrɪç] *adj pej* greedy

Habicht <-s, -e> ['haːbɪçt] *m* hawk

Habseligkeiten ['haːpzeːlɪçkaɪtn̩] *pl* [meager] belongings *npl*

Hackbraten *m* meat loaf

Hacke <-, -n> ['hakə] *f* **1.** (*Gartengerät*) hoe **2.** *österr* (*Axt*) ax **3.** *dial* (*Ferse*) heel

hacken[1] ['hakn.] **I.** *vt* **1.** (*Gemüse, Nüsse*) to chop [*up sep*] **2.** (*Boden*) to hoe **3.** (*in Stücke zerteilen*) to hack (**in** +*akk* into) **II.** *vi* **1.** (*mit dem Schnabel*) to peck **2.** (*mit der Hacke*) to hoe

hacken[2] ['hɛkn̩] *vi* COMPUT *sl* **das H~** hacking

Hacker(in) <-s, -> ['hɛkə] *m(f) sl* (*Computerpirat*) hacker

Hackfleisch *nt* ground meat

hadern ['haːdɐn] *vi* to argue (**mit** +*dat* with); **mit seinem Schicksal ~** to rail against one's fate

Hafen <-s, Häfen> ['haːfn̩] *m* harbor, port

Hafenarbeiter(in) *m(f)* docker

Hafenstadt *f* port [city]

Hafer <-s, -> ['haːfə] *m* oats *pl*

Haferflocken *pl* oatmeal

Haft <-> [haft] *f kein pl* **1.** (*Haftstrafe*) imprisonment **2.** (*Haftzeit*) prison sentence; **in ~ sein** to be in custody

haftbar ['haftbaːɐ̯] *adj* **für etw** *akk* **~ sein** to be liable for sth; **jdn für etw** *akk* **~ machen** to hold sb responsible for sth

Haftbefehl *m* [arrest] warrant

haften[1] ['haftn̩] *vi* **1.** ÖKON to be liable

(**für** +*akk* for, **mit** +*dat* with) **2.** (*die Haftung übernehmen*) to be responsible (**für** +*akk* for)

haften² ['haf·tn̩] *vi* (*festkleben*) to adhere (**an/auf** +*dat* to)

Häftling <-s, -e> ['hɛft·lɪŋ] *m* prisoner

Haftnotiz *f* sticky note, Post-it®

Haftpflicht *f* **1.** (*Schadenersatzpflicht*) liability **2.** *fam s.* **Haftpflichtversicherung**

Haftpflichtversicherung *f* personal liability insurance; AUTO third-party insurance

Haftung¹ <-, -en> ['haf·tʊŋ] *f* JUR liability

Haftung² <-> ['haf·tʊŋ] *f kein pl* AUTO road handling

Hagebutte <-, -n> ['ha:·gə·bu·tə] *f* rose hip

Hagel <-s> ['ha:·gl̩] *m kein pl* METEO hail

Hagelkorn <-körner> *nt* hailstone

hageln ['ha:·gl̩n] **I.** *vi impers* to hail **II.** *vt impers fam* **es hagelt etw** there is a hail of sth

hager ['ha:·gɐ] *adj* gaunt

Hahn¹ <-[e]s, Hähne> [ha:n] *m* rooster

Hahn² <-[e]s, Hähne> [ha:n] *m* **1.** (*Wasserhahn*) faucet **2.** (*an Schusswaffen*) hammer

Hai <-[e]s, -e> [hai] *m*, **Haifisch** ['hai·fɪʃ] *m* shark

Hain <-[e]s, -e> [hain] *m geh, poet* grove

Haiti <-s> [ha·'i:ti] *nt* Haiti; *s. a.* **Deutschland**

häkeln ['hɛ·kl̩n] *vt, vi* to crochet

Häkelnadel *f* crochet hook

Haken <-s, -> ['ha:·kn̩] *m* **1.** (*gebogene Halterung*) hook **2.** (*beim Boxen*) hook **3.** (*hakenförmiges Zeichen*) check [mark] **4.** *fam* (*hindernde Schwierigkeit*) **einen ~ haben** *fam* to have a catch

Hakennase *f* hooked nose

halb [halp] **I.** *adj* **1.** (*die Hälfte von*) half **2.** (*halbe Stunde der Uhrzeit*) **es ist genau ~ sieben** it is exactly six[-]thirty **3.** *kein art* (*ein Großteil*) ▶ **Deutschland verfolgt die Fußballweltmeisterschaft** half of Germany is following the World Cup ▶ **nichts H~es und nichts Ganzes** neither this nor that **II.** *adv*

1. *vor vb* (*zur Hälfte*) half; **etw nur ~ machen** to only half do sth; **~ so ... sein** to be half as ...; **~ ..., ~ ...** half ..., half ... **2.** *vor adj, adv* (*halbwegs*) **~ nackt/voll** half-naked/half-full ▶ [**mit jdm**] **~e~~e machen** to go halves with sb; **das ist ~ so schlimm** it's not as bad as all that

Halbbruder *m* half brother

halber ['hal·bɐ] *präp +gen nachgestellt* **der ... ~** for the sake of ...

halbfertig *adj attr* half-finished

Halbgott, -göttin *m, f* demigod *masc*, demigoddess *fem*

halbieren * [hal·'bi:·rən] *vt* **1.** (*teilen*) to divide in half **2.** (*um die Hälfte vermindern*) to halve

Halbinsel ['halp·ʔɪn·zl̩] *f* peninsula

Halbjahr *nt* half year

halbjährig ['halp·jɛː·rɪç] *adj attr* **1.** (*ein halbes Jahr dauernd*) six-month *attr* **2.** (*ein halbes Jahr alt*) six-month-old *attr*

halbjährlich ['halp·jɛː·ɐ·lɪç] **I.** *adj* half-yearly **II.** *adv* every six months, twice a year

Halbkreis *m* semicircle

Halbkugel *f* hemisphere

Halbmond *m* **1.** ASTRON half moon **2.** (*Figur*) crescent

Halbpension *f* breakfast and dinner

Halbschuh *m* low shoe

Halbschwester *f* half sister

halbtags *adv* on a part-time basis; **~ arbeiten** to work half-time

halbwegs ['halp·ve:ks] *adv* **1.** (*einigermaßen*) partly **2.** (*nahezu*) almost **3.** *veraltend* (*auf halbem Wege*) halfway

Halbwert(s)zeit *f* PHYS half-life

Halbwüchsige(r) *f(m) dekl wie adj* adolescent

Halbzeit *f* halftime

Halde <-, -n> ['hal·də] *f* **1.** (*Müllhalde*) landfill **2.** BERGB slag heap **3.** (*unverkaufte Ware*) stockpile

half [half] *imp von* **helfen**

Hälfte <-, -n> ['hɛlf·tə] *f* half; **um die ~** by half

Halle <-, -n> ['halə] *f* **1.** (*großer Raum*) hall **2.** (*Werkshalle*) workshop

3. (*Sporthalle*) gymnasium; **in der ~** indoors

hallen ['ha·lən] *vi* to echo

Hallenbad *nt* indoor swimming pool

Halligalli <-s> ['ha·li·ga·li] *nt kein pl meist pej fam* hubbub

hallo [ha·'loː] *interj* hello

Hallo <-s, -s> [ha·'loː] *nt* hello

Halm <-[e]s, -e> [halm] *m* **1.** (*Stängel*) stalk **2.** (*Trinkhalm*) straw

Hals <-es, Hälse> [hals] *m* **1.** ANAT neck; **den ~ recken** to crane one's neck **2.** (*Kehle*) throat **3.** (*Flaschenhals*) neck ▶ **~ über Kopf** in a hurry; **aus vollem ~[e]** at the top of one's voice

Halsabschneider(in) *m(f) pej fam* shark

Halsband *nt* **1.** (*für Haustiere*) collar **2.** (*Samtband*) choker

halsbrecherisch ['hals·brɛ·çə·rɪʃ] *adj* breakneck *attr*

Halsentzündung *f* sore throat

Halskette *f* necklace

Halsschlagader *f* carotid [artery]

Halsschmerzen *pl* sore throat

Halstuch *nt* neckerchief

halt¹ [halt] *interj* halt!

halt² [halt] *adv dial s.* **eben I 2**

Halt <-[e]s, -e> [halt] *m* **1.** (*Stütze*) hold; **~ geben** to support; **den ~ verlieren** to lose one's grip **2.** (*inneres Gleichgewicht*) stability **3.** (*Stopp*) stop; **~ machen** to stop

haltbar ['halt·baːɐ̯] *adj* **1.** (*nicht leicht verderblich*) nonperishable; **~ sein** to keep; **~ machen** to preserve **2.** (*widerstandsfähig*) durable

Haltbarkeit <> *f kein pl* **1.** (*Lagerfähigkeit*) shelf life **2.** (*Widerstandsfähigkeit*) durability

Haltbarkeitsdatum *nt* sell-by date

halten <hielt, gehalten> ['hal·tn̩] **I.** *vt* **1.** (*festhalten, stützen*) to hold **2.** (*aufhalten*) to stop **3.** (*zurückhalten*) to keep **4.** (*in Position bringen*) to put; **er hielt die Hand in die Höhe** he put his hand up **5.** (*besitzen*) to keep **6.** (*weiter innehaben*) to hold on to **7.** (*in einem Zustand erhalten*) to keep **8.** (*abhalten: Rede, Vortrag*) to give **9.** (*erfüllen*) **der Film hält nicht, was der Titel verspricht** the film doesn't live up to its title ▶ **das kannst du ~, wie du willst** that's completely up to you; **viel/nichts davon ~,** **etw zu tun** to consider/not consider it important to do sth; **jdn/etw für jdn/etw ~** to take sb/sth for sb/sth; **etw von jdm/etw ~** to think sth of sb/sth **II.** *vi* **1.** (*festhalten*) to hold **2.** (*haltbar sein*) to keep **3.** (*anhalten*) to stop ▶ **an sich** *akk* **~** to control oneself; **zu jdm ~** to stand by sb **III.** *vr* **1.** (*sich festhalten*) **sich** *akk* **an etw** *dat* **~** to hold on to sth **2.** METEO (*konstant bleiben*) **sich** *akk* **~** to last **3.** (*eine Richtung beibehalten*) **sich** *akk* **irgendwohin/nach ... ~** to keep to somewhere/heading toward ... **4.** (*sich richten nach*) **sich** *akk* **an etw** *akk* **~** to stick to sth **5.** (*eine bestimmte Haltung haben*) **sich** *akk* **irgendwie ~** to carry oneself in a certain manner ▶ **sich** *akk* **gut gehalten haben** *fam* to have worn well

Haltestelle *f* stop

Halteverbot *nt kein pl* no stopping [any time]; **eingeschränktes ~** ≈ loading/unloading zone

haltlos *adj* **1.** (*labil*) weak; (*Mensch*) unsteady **2.** (*unbegründet*) unfounded

Haltung¹ <-, -en> ['hal·tʊŋ] *f* **1.** (*Körperhaltung*) posture; (*typische Stellung*) stance **2.** (*Einstellung*) attitude **3.** *kein pl* (*Verhalten*) manner ▶ **~ bewahren** to keep one's composure

Haltung² <-> ['hal·tʊŋ] *f kein pl* (*von Tieren*) keeping

Halunke <-n, -n> [ha·'lʊŋ·kə] *m* **1.** *pej* (*Gauner*) scoundrel **2.** *hum* (*Schlingel*) rascal

hämisch ['hɛː·mɪʃ] *adj* malicious

Hammel <-s, -> ['ha·ml̩] *m* **1.** (*Tier*) wether **2.** *kein pl* (*Fleisch*) mutton

Hammelfleisch *nt* mutton

Hammer <-s, Hämmer> ['ha·mɐ] *m* **1.** (*Werkzeug*) hammer **2.** SPORT (*Wurfgerät*) hammer **3.** *fam* (*schwerer Fehler*) major mistake **4.** *fam* (*Unverschämtheit*) outrageous thing

hämmern ['hɛ·mɐn] *vt, vi* **1.** (*mit dem Hammer arbeiten*) to hammer **2.** (*wie Hammerschläge ertönen*) to make a hammering noise **3.** *fam* (*auf dem Kla-*

vier spielen) to hammer away on the piano **4.** (*rasch pulsieren*) to pound

Hämorrhoide <-, -n> [hɛ·mɔ·ˈriː·də] *f meist pl* hemorrhoids *pl*

Hampelmann <-männer> [ˈham·pl·man] *m* **1.** (*Spielzeug*) jumping jack **2.** *pej fam* (*labiler Mensch*) puppet

Hamster <-s, -> [ˈham·stɐ] *m* hamster

hamstern [ˈham·stɐn] *vt, vi* to hoard

Hand <-, Hände> [hant] *f* **1.** ANAT hand; **Hände hoch!** hands up!; **jdm etw in die ~ drücken** to slip sth into sb's hand; **jdm die ~ geben** to shake sb's hand; **etw in die ~ nehmen** to pick up *sep* sth; **Hände weg!** [get your] hands off! **2.** *kein pl* SPORT (*Handspiel*) handball **3.** (*Besitz*) hands; **der Besitz gelangte in fremde Hände** the property passed into foreign hands ▶ **an ~ einer S.** *gen* with the aid of sth; [**bar**] **auf die ~** *fam* cash in hand; **mit der bloßen ~** with one's bare hand[s]; **aus erster/ zweiter ~** firsthand/secondhand; **in festen Händen sein** *fam* to be spoken for; **~ und Fuß haben** to be well thought-out; **etw gegen jdn in der ~ haben** to have sth on sb; **~ in ~** hand in hand; [**klar**] **auf der ~ liegen** *fam* to be [perfectly] obvious; **jds rechte ~** to be sb's right-hand man; **die Hände in den Schoß legen** to sit back and do nothing; [**bei etw** *dat*] **die Hände im Spiel haben** to have a hand in sth; **eine starke ~** a firm hand; **alle Hände voll zu tun haben** to have one's hands full; **von ~** by hand; **zu Händen von jdm** attn: sb, for sb's attention; **zur ~ sein** to be on hand

Handarbeit *f* **1.** (*Gegenstand*) handicraft; **~ sein** to be handmade **2.** (*Nähen, Stricken etc.*) needlework; (*Gegenstand*) needlework

Handball *m o fam nt* SPORT handball

Handbewegung *f* gesture

Handbremse *f* hand brake

Handbuch *nt* manual

Händchen <-s, -> [ˈhɛnt·çən] *nt dim von* **Hand** small hand ▶ **für etw** *akk* **ein ~ haben** *fam* to have a knack for sth; **~ halten** *fam* to hold hands

Händedruck *m kein pl* handshake

Handel <-s> [ˈhan·dl] *m kein pl* **1.** (*Wirtschaftszweig der Händler*) commerce **2.** (*Warenverkehr*) trade; **im ~ sein** to be on the market **3.** *fam* (*Abmachung, Geschäft*) deal **4.** (*das Handeln*) dealing (**mit** +*dat* in)

handeln [ˈhan·dln] **I.** *vi* **1.** (*kaufen und verkaufen*) to trade (**mit** +*dat* in); **mit Drogen ~** to deal drugs **2.** (*feilschen*) to haggle (**um** +*akk* about/over) **3.** (*agieren*) to act **4.** (*befassen*) **von etw** *dat* **~** to be about [o deal with] sth **II.** *vr impers* **sich akk um jdn/etw ~** to concern [o be about] sb/sth **III.** *vt* (*angeboten und verkauft werden*) [**für etw** *akk*] **gehandelt werden** to be traded [at/for sth]

Handelsbank *f* merchant bank

Handelsbeziehungen *pl* trade relations

Handelskammer *f* chamber of commerce

Handelsregister *nt* register of business names

Handelsschule *f* business school

Handelsvertreter(in) *m(f)* commercial agent

Handelsware *f* commodity

Handfeger <-s, -> *m* hand brush

Handfeuerwaffe *f* handgun

Handfläche *f* palm of one's hand

handgearbeitet *adj* handmade

Handgelenk *nt* wrist ▶ **etw aus dem ~ schütteln** *fam* to do sth effortlessly

Handgemenge *nt* scuffle

Handgepäck *nt* carry-on luggage

handgeschrieben *adj* handwritten

handgreiflich [ˈhant·graif·lɪç] *adj* violent (**gegen** +*akk* toward)

Handgriff *m* **1.** (*Aktion*) movement; **mit einem ~** with a flick of the wrist **2.** (*Griff*) handle

handhaben [ˈhant·ha·bn] *vt* **1.** (*bedienen*) to handle; (*Maschine a.*) to operate **2.** (*anwenden*) to apply **3.** (*verfahren*) to manage

Handkoffer *m* small suitcase

Handkuss [RR] *m* kiss on the hand

Handlanger(in) <-s, -> [ˈhant·laŋe] *m(f)* **1.** (*Helfer*) laborer **2.** *pej* (*Erfüllungsgehilfe*) stooge

H

Händler(in) <-s, -> ['hɛnd·lɐ] m(f) dealer;
fliegender ~ hawker

handlich ['hant·lɪç] adj 1. (bequem zu
handhaben) easy to handle 2. (leicht
lenkbar) maneuverable

Handlung <-, -en> ['hand·lʊŋ] f 1. (Tat)
act 2. (im Buch, Film etc.) plot

Handlungsweise f conduct

Handrücken m back of the hand

Handschelle f meist pl handcuffs pl

Handschrift ['hant·ʃrɪft] f 1. (Schrift)
handwriting 2. (Text) manuscript

handschriftlich I. adj handwritten
II. adv (von Hand) by hand

Handschuh m glove

Handschuhfach nt glove compartment

Handtasche f purse

Handtuch <-tücher> nt towel

Handumdrehen ['hant·ʔʊm·dreː·ən] nt
▶ **im ~** in a jiffy

Handvoll <-, -> f handful

Handwerk nt trade ▶ **jdm das ~ legen**
to put an end to sb's game; **sein ~ verstehen** to know one's job

Handwerker(in) <-s, -> m(f) tradesman

Handy <-s, -s> ['hɛn·di] nt TELEK cell[ular]
[tele]phone

Handzettel m leaflet

Hanf <-[e]s> [hanf] m kein pl hemp

Hang <-[e]s, Hänge> [haŋ] m 1. (Abhang) slope 2. kein pl (Neigung) tendency; **sie hat einen ~ zu Übertreibungen** she tends to exaggerate; **den
~ haben, etw zu tun** to be inclined
to do sth

Hängebrücke f suspension bridge

Hängematte f hammock

hängen ['hɛŋ·ən] I. vi <hing, gehan-
gen> 1. (angebracht sein: Gegenstand,
Verbrecher) to hang (**an** +dat on, **über**
+dat over, **von** +dat from) 2. (sich
neigen) to lean 3. (befestigt sein) **an
etw** dat **~** (Anhänger, Wohnwagen)
to be attached to sth 4. fam (angeschlossen sein) **an etw** dat **~** (Patient) to be
connected to sth 5. fam (emotional)
an jdm/etw ~ to be attached to sb/
sth 6. (festhängen) [**mit etw** dat] **an
etw** dat **~ bleiben** to get [sth] caught
on sth 7. fam (sich aufhalten) **er hängt**

den ganzen Tag vorm Fernseher he
spends all day in front of the television
8. fam (zu erledigen sein) **etw bleibt
an jdm ~** sth is up to sb 9. fam (in der
Erinnerung bleiben) [**bei jdm**] **~ bleiben** to stick in sb's mind) 10. (nach
unten) **etw ~ lassen** to dangle sth II. vt
<hängte o dial hing, gehängt o dial ge-
hangen> 1. (anbringen) to hang (**an/
auf** +akk on) 2. (henken) to hang
3. (anschließen) to attach (**an** +akk on)
4. (im Stich lassen) **jdn ~ lassen** to let
sb down III. vr <hängte o dial hing,
gehängt o dial gehangen> 1. (sich festhalten) **sich** akk **an jdn/etw ~** to hang
on to sb/sth 2. (sich gehen lassen) **sich**
akk **~ lassen** to let oneself go

Hanse <-> ['hanzə] f kein pl HIST Han-
seatic League

hänseln ['hɛn·z|n] vt to tease (**wegen**
+gen about)

Hantel <-, -n> ['han·t|] f SPORT dumbbell

hantieren* [han·'tiː·rən] vi 1. (sich beschäftigen) to be busy (**mit** +dat with)
2. (herumwerkeln) to work (**an** +dat
on)

hapern ['haː·pɐn] vi impers fam 1. (fehlen) **an etw** dat **~** to be lacking sth
2. (schlecht bestellt sein) **es hapert
[bei jdm] mit etw** dat sb has a problem with sth

Happen <-s, -> ['hapn] m fam (kleine
Mahlzeit) snack

happig ['ha·pɪç] adj fam (hoch: Preis)
steep

Harfe <-, -n> ['har·fə] f harp

harmlos I. adj 1. (ungefährlich) harmless 2. (arglos) innocent II. adv 1. (ungefährlich) harmlessly 2. (arglos) innocently

Harmonie <-, -n> [har·mo·'niː] f harmony

harmonieren* [har·mo·'niː·rən] vi 1. (zu-
sammenklingen) to harmonize 2. (zwei-
nander passen) to go with 3. (gut zusammenpassen) to get along well [with
each other]

Harmonika <-, -s> [har·'moː·ni·ka] f accordion

harmonisch [har·'moː·nɪʃ] adj harmonious

Harn <-[e]s, -e> [harn] *m* urine

Harnblase *f* bladder

Harpune <-, -n> [har·ˈpuː·nə] *f* harpoon

hart <härter, härteste> [hart] **I.** *adj*
1. (*nicht weich*) hard; (*straff*) firm
2. (*heftig: Aufprall, Ruck, Winter*) severe
3. (*Akzent*) harsh **4.** (*Schnaps*) strong;
(*Drogen*) hard; (*Pornografie*) hard-core
5. (*brutal: Film, Konflikt*) violent **6.** (*abgehärtet: Kerl*) tough **7.** (*streng, unerbittlich: Gesetze, Regime, Worte*) harsh;
(*Mensch*) hard; (*Strafe*) severe; ~ **mit
jdm sein** to be hard on sb **8.** (*schwer
zu ertragen*) cruel; (*Zeiten*) hard; (*Realität, Wahrheit*) harsh; **der Tod ihres
Mannes war für sie ein ~er Schlag**
the death of her husband was a cruel
blow for her **9.** (*mühevoll*) tough; (*Arbeit*) hard ▶ **in etw dat ~ bleiben** to
remain firm [about sth]; ~ **im Nehmen
sein** to be resilient **II.** *adv* **1.** (*nicht
weich*) hard; ~ **gefroren** frozen hard
pred; ~ **gekocht** hard-boiled **2.** (*rau*)
harshly; **die Sprache klingt ziemlich ~**
the language sounds quite harsh **3.** (*mühevoll*) hard; ~ **arbeiten** to work hard
▶ **jdn ~ treffen** to hit sb hard

Härte <-, -n> [ˈhɛr·tə] *f* **1.** (*Härtegrad*) hardness **2.** *kein pl* (*Wucht*)
force **3.** *kein pl* (*Robustheit*) robustness
4. *kein pl* (*Stabilität*) stability **5.** *kein
pl* (*Strenge*) severity; (*Unerbittlichkeit*)
relentlessness **6.** (*schwere Erträglichkeit*) cruelty

Härtefall *m* hardship case

Härtetest *m* endurance test

hartherzig *adj* hard-hearted

hartnäckig **I.** *adj* **1.** (*beharrlich*) persistent **2.** (*langwierig*) stubborn **II.** *adv*
(*beharrlich*) persistently

Harz <-es, -e> [haːɐ̯ts] *nt* resin

harzig [ˈhaːɐ̯·tsɪç] *adj* resinous

Haschisch <-[s]> [ˈha·ʃɪʃ] *nt o m kein
pl* hashish

Hase <-n, -n> [ˈhaː·zə] *m* **1.** (*wild lebendes Nagetier*) hare **2.** (*Kaninchen*)
rabbit

Haselnuss ^RR <-, Haselnüsse> [ˈhaː·zl̩·nʊs] *f* **1.** (*Nuss*)
hazelnut **2.** (*Hasel*) hazel

Hass ^RR <-es>, **Haß** ^ALT <-sses> [has] *m
kein pl* hatred; **aus ~** out of hatred; **ei-**
nen ~ **auf jdn haben** to hate sb

hassen [ˈha·sn̩] *vt* to hate; **es ~, etw zu
tun** to hate doing sth

hasserfüllt ^RR *adj, adv* full of hate

hässlich ^RR, **häßlich** ^ALT [ˈhɛs·lɪç] **I.** *adj*
1. (*unschön*) ugly **2.** (*gemein*) nasty
3. (*unerfreulich*) unpleasant **II.** *adv*
(*gemein*) nastily

Hässlichkeit ^RR, **Häßlichkeit** ^ALT <-, -en>
f ugliness

hasten [ˈhas·tn̩] *vi sein geh* to hurry

hastig [ˈhas·tɪç] **I.** *adj* hurried; **nicht so
~!** not so fast! **II.** *adv* hastily

hätscheln [ˈhɛ:·tʃl̩n] *vt* **1.** (*liebkosen*) to
cuddle **2.** (*gut behandeln*) to pamper
3. (*gerne pflegen*) to cherish

hatte [ˈha·tə] *imp von* **haben**

Haube <-, -n> [ˈhau·bə] *f* **1.** (*weibliche
Kopfbedeckung*) bonnet **2.** (*Trockenhaube*) hair dryer **3.** (*Motorhaube*)
hood **4.** *österr, südd* (*Mütze*) cap

Hauch <-[e]s, -e> [haux] *m* **1.** (*Atemhauch*) breath **2.** (*Luftzug*) breath of air
3. (*leichter Duft*) whiff **4.** (*Flair*) aura

hauchdünn [ˈhaux·ˈdʏn] *adj* **1.** (*äußerst
dünn*) wafer-thin; (*Stoff*) airy **2.** (*äußerst knapp: Mehrheit*) narrow

hauchen [ˈhau·xn̩] *vt* (*flüstern*) to whisper

Haue <-, -n> [ˈhauə] *f* **1.** *südd, schweiz,
österr* (*Hacke*) hoe **2.** *kein pl fam* (*Prügel*) thrashing

hauen <haute, gehauen *o dial* gehaut>
[ˈhauən,] **I.** *vt* **1.** *fam* (*schlagen*) to hit
2. *fam* (*verprügeln*) to hit; **sie ~ sich**
they're beating each other up **3.** (*meißeln*) to carve **II.** *vr fam* (*sich setzen,
legen*) **sich** *akk* **auf/in etw** *akk* ~ to
throw oneself onto/into sth

Haufen <-s, -> [ˈhau·fn̩] *m* **1.** (*Anhäufung*) heap, pile **2.** *fam* (*große Menge*)
ton; **du erzählst da einen ~ Quatsch!**
what a bunch of nonsense! **3.** (*Schar*)
crowd **4.** (*Gruppe, Gemeinschaft*)
bunch ▶ **auf einem ~** *fam* in one
place; **jdn über den ~ fahren/rennen**
fam to run over *sep* sb; **etw über den ~
werfen** *fam* to mess up *sep* sth

haufenweise *adv* **1.** (*in Haufen*) in piles
2. *fam* in great quantities; **etw ~ haben**
to have tons of sth

häufig ['hɔy·fɪç] I. *adj* frequent II. *adv* frequently

Häufigkeit <-, -en> *f* frequency

Haupt <-[e]s, Häupter> [haupt] *nt geh* head; **gesenkten/erhobenen ~es** with one's head bowed/raised

Hauptbahnhof *m* main [train] station

hauptberuflich I. *adj* full-time II. *adv* on a full-time basis

Hauptdarsteller(in) *m(f)* leading actor

Haupteingang *m* main entrance

Hauptfach *nt* SCH major

Hauptgericht *nt* main course

Hauptgeschäftszeit *f* peak shopping hours *pl*, main business hours *pl*

Hauptgewinn *m* first prize

Häuptling <-s, -e> ['hɔypt·lɪŋ] *m* chief

Hauptperson *f* LIT main character

Hauptquartier *nt* headquarters *npl*

Hauptrolle *f* leading role ▶ |**bei etw** *dat*| **die ~ spielen** to play a leading part [in sth]

Hauptsache ['haupt·za·xə] *f* main thing; **~, du bist glücklich!** the main thing is that you're happy!

hauptsächlich ['haupt·zɛç·lɪç] I. *adj* main II. *adv* mainly

Hauptsaison [-zɛ·zɔŋ] *f* peak season

Hauptsatz *m* LING main clause

Hauptschlagader *f* aorta

Hauptschule *f* ≈ junior high school *(a school for grades 5 to 10 in Germany or grades 5 to 8 in Austria)*

Hauptstadt *f* capital [city]

Hauptverkehrsstraße *f* main road

Hauptverkehrszeit *f* rush hour

Hauptwort *nt* noun

Haus <-es, Häuser> [haus] *nt* 1. *(Gebäude)* house; **jdn nach ~e bringen** to take sb home; **außer ~** to be out; **sich** *akk* **wie zu ~e fühlen** to feel at home; **frei ~ liefern** to deliver free of charge; **nach ~e** |*o österr, schweiz a.* **nachhause**| home; **zu ~e essen** |*o österr, schweiz a.* **zuhause**| at home; **bei jdm zu ~e** |*o österr, schweiz a.* **zuhause**| at sb's house 2. *(Familie)* household; **er ist ein alter Freund des ~es** he's an old friend of the family; **aus gutem ~e** from a good family 3. *(Unternehmen)* company; **im ~e sein** to be in; **das** **erste ~ am Platze** the best company in the area 4. POL *(Kammer)* House ▶ **~ halten** to be economical; **von ~e aus** originally

Hausangestellte(r) *f(m)* domestic servant

Hausarbeit *f* 1. *(Arbeit im Haushalt)* housework 2. SCH *(Schulaufgaben)* homework; *(wissenschaftliche Arbeit)* assignment

Hausarrest *m* 1. *(elterliche Strafe)* ~ **haben** to be grounded 2. JUR house arrest

Hausarzt, -ärztin *m, f* family physician

Hausaufgaben *pl* SCH homework *sing*

Hausbesitzer(in) *m(f)* homeowner; *(Vermieter)* landlord

Hausbewohner(in) *m(f)* tenant

Häuschen <-s, -> ['hɔys·çən] *nt* 1. *dim von* **Haus** small house 2. *schweiz (Kästchen auf kariertem Papier)* square

Hauseingang *m* entrance [to a house]

hausen ['hau·zn] *vi* 1. *pej fam (erbärmlich wohnen)* to live [in poor conditions] 2. *(wüten)* to wreak havoc

Hausflur *m* entrance hall

Hausfrau *f* 1. *(nicht berufstätige Frau)* housewife 2. *österr, südd (Zimmerwirtin)* landlady

Hausfriedensbruch *m* trespassing

Hausgebrauch *m* **für den ~** for domestic use; *(für durchschnittliche Ansprüche)* for average requirements

Haushalt <-[e]s, -e> *m* 1. *(Hausgemeinschaft)* household 2. *(Haushaltsführung)* housekeeping; **|jdm| den ~ führen** to keep house [for sb] 3. MED, BIOL balance 4. ÖKON budget

haushalten *vi irreg* to be economical *(mit +dat* with)

Haushaltsgeld *nt* money for household expenses

Hausherr(in) <-en, -en> *m(f)* head of the household; *(Gastgeber)* host

haushoch ['haus·hox] I. *adj* 1. *euph (sehr hoch)* huge; *(Flammen, Wellen)* gigantic 2. SPORT *(eindeutig)* clear; *(Niederlage)* crushing; *(Sieg)* overwhelming; *(Favorit)* obvious II. *adv (eindeutig)* clearly

hausieren* [hau·ˈziː·rən] *vi* to hawk; **H~**

verboten! no soliciting!

Hausierer(in) <-s, -> *m(f)* solicitor

Hauslehrer(in) *m(f)* private tutor

häuslich ['hɔys·lɪç] I. *adj* 1. (*die Hausgemeinschaft betreffend*) domestic 2. (*das Zuhause liebend*) home-loving II. *adv* **sich** *akk* ~ **einrichten** to make oneself at home; **sich** *akk* ~ **niederlassen** to settle down

Hausmädchen *nt* maid

Hausmann ['haus·man] *m* house husband

Hausmannskost *f kein pl* KOCHK home cooking

Hausmeister(in) *m(f)* janitor

Hausmittel *nt* household remedy

Hausordnung *f* house rules *pl*

Hausrat *m kein pl* household contents *pl*

Hausratversicherung *f* home owner's insurance

Hausschlüssel *m* house key

Hausschuh *m* slipper

Haustier *nt* pet

Haustür *f* front door

Haut <-, Häute> [haut] *f* skin; **nass bis auf die** ~ soaked to the skin [*o* bone] ▶ **aus der** ~ **fahren** *fam* to hit the roof; **auf der faulen** ~ **liegen** *fam* to take it easy; **mit** ~ **und Haar[en]** *fam* completely; **mit heiler** ~ **davonkommen** *fam* to escape unscathed; **jd möchte nicht in jds** ~ **stecken** sb would not like to be in sb's shoes; **sich** *akk* **nicht wohl in seiner** ~ **fühlen** *fam* to not feel too good

Hautabschürfung *f* graze

Hautausschlag *m* [skin] rash

Hautcreme *f* skin cream

häuten ['hɔy·tn̩] I. *vt* to skin II. *vr* **sich** *akk* ~ (*Schlange*) to shed one's skin

hauteng *adj, adv* skin-tight

Hebamme <-, -n> ['he:p·ʔamə] *f* midwife

Hebebühne *f* hydraulic lift

Hebel <-s, -> ['he:·bl̩] *m* lever ▶ **am längeren** ~ **sitzen** *fam* to hold the upper hand

heben <hob, gehoben> ['he:·bn̩] I. *vt* 1. (*nach oben bewegen*) to raise 2. (*verbessern: Stimmung, Niveau*) to improve 3. *südd* (*halten*) to hold II. *vr* **sich** *akk* ~ (*Vorhang*) to rise III. *vi* 1. (*Lasten*

hochhieven) to lift loads; **er musste den ganzen Tag schwer** ~ he had to do a lot of heavy lifting all day 2. *südd* (*haltbar sein: Lebensmittel*) to keep

Hebräer(in) <-s, -> [he·'brɛː·ɐ] *m(f)* Hebrew

hebräisch [he·'brɛː·ɪʃ] *adj* Hebrew

Hecht <-[e]s, -e> [hɛçt] *m* pike ▶ **ein toller** ~ *fam* an incredible guy

Heck <-[e]s, -e> [hɛk] *nt* 1. AUTO rear, back 2. NAUT stern 3. LUFT tail

Hecke <-, -n> ['hɛ·kə] *f* hedge

Heckenschütze, -schützin *m, f* sniper

Heckklappe *f* AUTO tailgate

Heckscheibe *f* AUTO rear window

Heer <-[e]s, -e> ['heːɐ] *nt* 1. (*Armee*) armed forces *npl* 2. *fig* (*große Anzahl*) **ein** ~ **von ...** an army of ...

Hefe <-, -n> ['he:·fə] *f* yeast

Hefeteig *m* yeast dough

Heft <-[e]s, -e> [hɛft] *nt* 1. (*Schreibheft*) notebook 2. (*Zeitschrift*) magazine; (*Ausgabe*) issue

heften ['hɛf·tn̩] *vt* 1. (*befestigen*) to stick (**an** +*akk* to) 2. (*mit Heftklammer*) to staple (**an** +*akk* to) 3. (*nähen: Naht, Saum*) to baste

Hefter <-s, -> *m* 1. (*Mappe*) [loose-leaf] folder 2. (*Heftmaschine*) stapler

heftig ['hɛf·tɪç] I. *adj* 1. (*stark: Aufprall, Schlag*) violent; (*Kämpfe*) fierce; (*Kopfschmerzen*) splitting; (*Regen, Schneefall*) heavy 2. (*intensiv: Leidenschaft, Sehnsucht*) intense 3. (*scharf: Kritik*) fierce; (*Reaktion*) vehement II. *adv* **etw** ~ **dementieren** to vehemently deny sth

Heftklammer *f* staple

Heftpflaster *nt* Band-Aid®

Heftzwecke *f* thumbtack

Heide <-, -n> ['hai·də] *f* 1. (*Heideland*) heath, moor 2. *s.* **Heidekraut**

Heide, Heidin <-n, -n> ['hai·də, 'hai·dɪn] *m, f* REL heathen, pagan

Heidekraut *nt* BOT heather

Heidelbeere ['hai·dl̩·beː·rə] *f* blueberry

Heidenangst *f* mortal fear; **eine** ~ **vor etw** *dat* **haben** to be scared stiff of sth

Heidenspaß *m fam* great fun

heikel ['hai·kl̩] *adj* delicate; (*Frage, Situation a.*) tricky

heil [hail] *adj, adv* **1.** (*unverletzt*) uninjured **2.** (*unbeschädigt*) intact

heilbar *adj* curable

Heilbutt <-s, -e> ['hail·bʊt] *m* halibut

heilen ['hai·lən] **I.** *vi sein* (*gesund werden*) to heal [up] **II.** *vt* **1.** (*gesund machen*) to cure (**von** +*dat* of) **2.** (*kurieren*) **von jdm/etw geheilt sein** to have gotten over sb/sth

heilfroh ['hail·'fro:] *adj pred fam* really glad

heilig ['hai·lıç] *adj* **1.** (*geweiht*) holy; **die ~e Kommunion** Holy Communion **2.** (*bei Namen von Heiligen*) Saint; **die H~e Jungfrau** the Blessed Virgin

Heiligabend [hai·lıç·'ʔa:bn̩t] *m* Christmas Eve

Heilige(r) ['hai·lı·gə, -gə] *f(m) dekl wie adj* saint

heiligsprechen *vt irreg* to canonize

Heilkraft *f* healing power

Heilkraut *nt meist pl* medicinal herb

Heilkunde *f kein pl* medicine

heillos ['hail·lo:s] **I.** *adj* terrible **II.** *adv* hopelessly

Heilpflanze *f* medicinal plant

Heilpraktiker(in) *m(f)* nonmedical practitioner

Heilquelle *f* medicinal spring

heilsam ['hail·za:m] *adj* salutary

Heilung <-, -en> ['hai·lʊŋ] *f* **1.** (*Genesungsprozess*) recovery **2.** (*Krankenbehandlung*) curing **3.** (*Abheilen einer Wunde*) healing

heim [haim] *adv dial* home

Heim <-[e]s, -e> [haim] *nt* **1.** (*Zuhause*) home **2.** (*Seniorenheim, Jugendanstalt*) home **3.** (*Stätte eines Clubs*) club[house] **4.** (*Erholungsheim*) convalescent home

Heimat <-, -en> ['hai·ma:t] *f* hometown; (*Heimatland*) homeland; ʙoт, ᴢooʟ natural habitat

heimatlich *adj* native; (*Brauchtum, Lieder*) local

heimatlos *adj* homeless; ᴘoʟ stateless

Heimatstadt *f* hometown

Heimfahrt *f* trip [*o* ride] home

heimisch ['hai·mıʃ] *adj* **1.** (*einheimisch*) native; **sich** *akk* ~ **fühlen** to feel at home **2.** (*bewandert*) **in etw** *dat* ~ **sein**

to be at home with sth

Heimkehr <-> *f kein pl* return home

heimkehren ['haim·ke:·rən] *vi sein* to return home (**aus/von** +*dat* from)

heimlich ['haim·lıç] *adj* **1.** (*geheim*) secret **2.** (*verstohlen*) furtive

Heimlichtuerei <-, -en> [haim·lıç·tu:ə·'rai] *f pej* secretiveness

Heimreise *f* trip home

heimtückisch ['haim·tʏ·kıʃ] *adj* **1.** (*tückisch*) malicious **2.** (*gefährlich*) insidious

Heimweg *m* way home; **sich** *akk* **auf den** ~ **machen** to head home

Heimweh <-[e]s> *nt kein pl* homesickness; *kein pl, kein art* ~ **haben** to be homesick (**nach** +*dat* for)

heimzahlen *vt* **jdm etw** ~ to pay sb back for sth

Heirat <-, -en> ['hai·ra:t] *f* marriage

heiraten ['hai·ra:·tn̩] **I.** *vt* to marry **II.** *vi* to get married; **sie hat reich geheiratet** she married into money

Heiratsantrag *m* [marriage] proposal; **jdm einen** ~ **machen** to propose to sb

heiser ['hai·ze] **I.** *adj* (*Stimme*) hoarse; (*rauchig*) husky **II.** *adv* hoarsely

Heiserkeit <-, selten -en> *f* hoarseness

heiß [hais] **I.** *adj* **1.** (*sehr warm*) hot; **jdm ist/wird es** ~ sb is/is getting hot; **etw** ~ **machen** to heat up *sep* sth **2.** (*Debatte*) heated; (*Kampf*) fierce **3.** (*Liebe*) burning; (*Wunsch*) fervent **4.** *fam* (*aufreizend*) hot; (*Kleid*) sexy **5.** *fam* (*gestohlen*) hot **6.** (*brisant*) ein ~es Thema an explosive issue **7.** (*aufregend: Musik, Party*) hot **8.** *attr fam* (*aussichtsreich*) hot; **die Polizei ist auf einer** ~**en Fährte** the police are on a hot trail **9.** *sl* (*großartig*) fantastic; **echt** ~ really cool **10.** *fam* (*brünstig*) in heat **II.** *adv* **1.** (*sehr warm*) hot; ~ **laufen** (*Maschinenteil*) to overheat **2.** (*innig*) ardently; ~ **ersehnt** greatly longed for; ~ **geliebt** dearly beloved **3.** (*erbittert*) fiercely; ~ **umstritten** hotly disputed

heißblütig ['hais·bly:·tıç] *adj* **1.** (*impulsiv*) hot-tempered **2.** (*leidenschaftlich*) passionate

heißen <hieß, geheißen> ['hai·sn̩] **I.** *vi* **1.** (*den Namen haben*) to be called;

wie ~ Sie? what's your name? **2.** (*bedeuten*) to mean; **„ja" heißt auf Japanisch „hai"** "hai" is Japanese for "yes"; **was heißt eigentlich „Liebe" auf Russisch?** how do you say "love" in Russian?; **was soll das [denn] ~?** what's that supposed to mean?; **das heißt, ...** that is to say ...; (*vorausgesetzt*) that is, ...; (*sich verbessernd*) or should I say, ... **3.** (*lauten*) **das Sprichwort heißt anders** that's not how the proverb goes **II.** *vi impers* **1.** (*zu lesen sein*) **Auge um Auge, wie es im Alten Testament heißt** an eye for an eye, as it says in the Old Testament **2.** (*als Gerücht kursieren*) **es heißt, dass ...** there is a rumor [going around] that ...

Heißhunger *m* craving; **mit ~** ravenously

Heißluft *f kein pl* hot air

heiter ['haitɐ] *adj* **1.** (*fröhlich*) cheerful **2.** (*fröhlich stimmend*) amusing **3.** METEO (*Wetter*) bright

Heizanlage *f* heater

Heizdecke *f* electric blanket

heizen ['haitsn] **I.** *vi* **1.** (*die Heizung betreiben*) **mit Gas/Öl ~** to heat with natural gas/oil **2.** (*Wärme abgeben*) to give off heat **II.** *vt* **1.** (*beheizen*) to heat **2.** (*anheizen*) to stoke

Heizkessel *m* boiler

Heizkissen *nt* heating pad

Heizkörper *m* radiator

Heizlüfter *m* fan heater

Heizöl *nt* fuel oil

Heizung <-, -en> *f* **1.** (*Zentralheizung*) heating **2.** (*Heizkörper*) radiator

Heizungskeller *m* boiler room

Hektar <-s, -e *o bei Maßangaben* -> [hɛkˈtaːɐ] *m o nt* hectare

Hektik <-> ['hɛktɪk] *f kein pl* hectic pace; **nur keine ~!** take it easy!

hektisch ['hɛktɪʃ] **I.** *adj* hectic **II.** *adv* frantically

Held(in) <-en, -nen> [hɛlt] *m(f)* hero *masc*, heroine *fem*

heldenhaft *adj* heroic

Heldentat *f* heroic deed

helfen <half, geholfen> ['hɛlfn] *vi* **1.** (*unterstützen*) to help (**bei** +*dat* with); **warte mal, ich helfe dir** wait,

I'll help you **2.** (*dienen, nützen*) **jdm ist mit etw** *dat* **geholfen/nicht geholfen** sth is of help/no help to sb; **Knoblauch soll gegen Arteriosklerose ~** garlic is supposed to help prevent arteriosclerosis ► **ich kann mir nicht ~, [aber] ...** I'm sorry, but ...; **man muss sich** *dat* **nur zu ~ wissen** you just have to be resourceful

Helfer(in) <-s, -> ['hɛlfɐ] *m(f)* **1.** (*unterstützende Person*) helper; (*Komplize*) accomplice **2.** *fam* (*nützliches Gerät*) aid

hell [hɛl] **I.** *adj* **1.** (*nicht dunkel*) light; **es wird ~** it's getting light [out] **2.** (*kräftig leuchtend*) bright **3.** (*gering gefärbt*) light-colored; (*Haar, Haut*) fair **4.** (*Stimme, Ton*) clear **5.** *fam* (*aufgeweckt*) bright; **du bist ein ~es Köpfchen** you've got brains **6.** *attr* (*rein, pur: Freude*) sheer, pure **II.** *adv* **1.** (*licht*) brightly **2.** (*hoch*) high and clear

hellhörig ['hɛlhøːrɪç] *adj* badly soundproofed ► **~ werden** to prick up one's ears

Helligkeit <-, -en> *f* **1.** *kein pl* (*Lichtfülle*) lightness; (*helles Licht*) [bright] light **2.** (*Lichtstärke*) brightness **3.** ASTRON (*Leuchtkraft*) luminosity

Hellseher(in) ['hɛlzeːɐ] *m(f)* clairvoyant

hellwach ['hɛlˈvax] *adj* wide-awake

Helm <-[e]s, -e> ['hɛlm] *m* helmet

Hemd <-[e]s, -en> [hɛmt] *nt* shirt; (*Unterhemd*) undershirt

hemmen [hɛˈmən] *vt* **1.** (*ein Hemmnis sein*) to hinder **2.** (*bremsen*) to stop **3.** PSYCH to inhibit

Hemmschwelle *f* PSYCH inhibition level

Hemmung <-, -en> *f* **1.** *kein pl* (*das Hemmen*) obstruction **2.** (*Bedenken, Skrupel*) **~en haben** to feel inhibited; **nur keine ~en!** don't hold back! **3.** *pl* PSYCH inhibitions *pl*

hemmungslos I. *adj* **1.** (*zügellos*) unrestrained **2.** (*skrupellos*) unscrupulous **II.** *adv* **1.** (*zügellos*) without restraint **2.** (*skrupellos*) unscrupulously

Hengst <-[e]s, -e> [hɛŋst] *m* (*männliches Pferd*) stallion; (*männlicher Esel, männliches Kamel*) male

Henkel <-s, -> ['hɛŋkl] *m* handle

Henne <-, -n> ['hɛ·nə] f hen

Hepatitis <-, Hepatitiden> [he·pa·'tiː·tɪs] f MED hepatitis

her [heːɐ̯] adv 1. (raus) here, to me; ~ damit! fam give it here! 2. (herum) um jdn ~ all around sb 3. (von einem Punkt aus) von etw dat ~ räumlich from sth; von weit ~ from a long way away; von ... ~ zeitlich from ...; ich kenne ihn von meiner Studienzeit ~ I know him from my college days; lang ~ sein, dass ... to have been a long time since ... 4. (verfolgen) hinter etw dat ~ sein to be after sth

herab|lassen irreg I. vt geh (herunterlassen) to let down sep II. vr sich [zu etw dat] ~ to lower oneself [to [do] sth]; sich akk [dazu] ~, etw zu tun to condescend to doing sth

herablassend adj condescending

herab|sehen vi irreg to look down (auf +akk [up]on)

herab|setzen vt 1. (reduzieren: Geschwindigkeit, Preise) to reduce 2. (schlechtmachen) to belittle

heran [hɛ·'ran] adv near, close up (an +akk to)

heran|kommen vi irreg sein 1. (herbeikommen) to approach; (bis an etwas kommen) to get to 2. (herangelangen können) to reach 3. (sich beschaffen können) to get [a] hold of 4. (in persönlichen Kontakt kommen) an jdn ~ to get a hold of sb 5. (gleichwertig sein) to be up to the standard of

heran|machen vr fam sich akk an jdn ~ to approach sb

heran|wachsen [-'vak·sn̩] vi irreg sein geh to grow up (zu +dat into)

heran|wagen vr sich akk an etw akk ~ 1. (heranzukommen wagen) to dare to go near sth 2. (sich zu beschäftigen wagen) to dare to attempt sth

heran|ziehen irreg vt 1. (näher holen) to pull (an +akk to/toward) 2. (einsetzen) jdn [zu etw dat] ~ to use sb [for [o as] sth]

herauf [hɛ·'rauf] I. adv von da unten bis oben ~ from down there all the way up here II. präp +akk up; sie ging die Treppe ~ she went up the stairs

herauf|beschwören* vt irreg 1. (wachrufen) to evoke 2. (herbeiführen) to cause

herauf|kommen vi irreg sein to come up (zu +dat to)

herauf|ziehen irreg I. vt haben to pull up sep II. vi sein (Gewitter) to approach

heraus [hɛ·'raus] adv 1. (nach draußen) out; aus etw dat ~ out of sth 2. (entfernt sein) ~ sein to have been taken out [o removed] 3. MEDIA (veröffentlicht sein) ~ sein to be out 4. (hinter sich haben) aus etw dat ~ sein to leave behind sep sth; aus dem Alter bin ich ~ that's all behind me 5. (gesagt worden sein) ~ sein to have been said

heraus|bekommen* vt irreg 1. (entfernen) to get out (aus +dat of) 2. (herausfinden) to find out sep 3. (ausgezahlt bekommen) to get back

heraus|bringen vt irreg 1. (nach draußen bringen) to bring sth out[side] 2. (auf den Markt bringen) to launch 3. (der Öffentlichkeit vorstellen) to publish 4. (sagen) to utter

heraus|finden irreg I. vt 1. (dahinterkommen) to find out 2. (herauslesen) to find (aus +dat from amongst) II. vi (den Weg finden) to find one's way out (aus +dat of)

Herausforderer, -forderin <-s, -> m, f challenger

heraus|fordern I. vt 1. (auffordern) to challenge (zu +dat to) 2. (provozieren) to provoke 3. (herausfbeschwören) to invite; (Gefahr) to court; das Schicksal ~ to tempt fate II. vi etw fordert zu etw dat heraus sth invites sth

herausfordernd adj provocative

Herausforderung f challenge

heraus|geben irreg I. vt 1. (veröffentlichen) to publish 2. (Geld) to return II. vi to give change; falsch ~ to give [back] the wrong change

Herausgeber(in) <-s, -> m(f) MEDIA (Verleger) publisher; (editierender Lektor) editor

heraus|gehen vi irreg sein 1. (herauskommen) to go out (aus/von +dat of) 2. (entfernt werden können) to

come out (**aus** +dat of) **3.** (lebhaft werden) **aus sich** dat ~ to come out of one's shell

heraus|greifen vt irreg to pick out sep (**aus** +dat from)

heraus|halten irreg I. vt **1.** (nach draußen halten) to hold out (**aus** +dat of) **2.** (nicht verwickeln) to keep out (**aus** +dat of) II. vr **sich** akk [**aus etw** dat] ~ to keep out [of sth]

heraus|kommen [hɛraus·kɔ·mən] vi irreg sein **1.** (nach draußen kommen) to come out (**aus** +dat of) **2.** (etw verlassen können) **aus etw** dat ~ to get out of sth **3.** (aufhören können) **aus etw** dat **kaum/nicht** ~ to hardly/not be able to stop doing sth **4.** (überwinden können) **aus Schwierigkeiten** ~ to get over one's difficulties **5.** (auf den Markt kommen) to be launched; (erscheinen) to come out **6.** (bekannt gegeben werden) to be published; (Gesetz, Verordnung) to be enacted **7.** (bekannt werden) **es kam heraus, dass ...** it came out that ... **8.** (zur Sprache bringen) **mit etw** dat ~ to come out with sth **9.** (als Resultat haben) **bei etw** dat ~ to come of sth; **und was soll dabei ~?** and what good will that do?; **auf dasselbe** ~ to amount to the same thing ▶ **groß** ▶ fam to be a great success

heraus|nehmen irreg I. vt **1.** (entnehmen) to take out (**aus** +dat of); (Zahn) to pull **2.** (aus einer Umgebung entfernen) **jdn aus etw** dat ~ to take sb away from sth II. vr **1.** pej (frech für sich reklamieren) **sich** dat **etw** ~ to take liberties; **sich** dat **zu viel** ~ to go too far **2.** (sich erlauben) **sich** dat ~, **etw zu tun** ~ to have the nerve to do sth

heraus|ragen vi s. **hervorragen**

heraus|reißen vt irreg **1.** (aus etw reißen) to tear out (**aus** +dat of); (Baum, Wurzel) to pull out **2.** (ablenken) **jdn aus seiner Arbeit** ~ to interrupt sb in their work **3.** fam (wettmachen) to save

heraus|rutschen vi sein **1.** (aus etw rutschen) to slip out [of sth] **2.** fam (ungewollt entschlüpfen) **etw rutscht jdm heraus** sb lets sth slip out

heraus|stellen I. vt **1.** (nach draußen stellen) to put outside **2.** (hervorheben) to emphasize II. vr **1.** (ans Licht kommen) **sich** akk ~ to come to light **2.** (sich erweisen) **sich** akk **als ...** ~ to be shown to be ...; **es stellte sich heraus, dass ...** it turned out that ...

herb [hɛrp] I. adj **1.** (bitter-würzig) sharp, astringent; (Duft, Parfüm) tangy; (Wein) dry **2.** (schmerzlich) bitter; (Erkenntnis) sobering **3.** (etwas streng) severe; (Schönheit) austere **4.** (scharf: Kritik) harsh II. adv ~ **duften** to smell tangy; ~ **schmecken** to taste sharp

herbei|eilen vi sein to rush over

herbei|führen [hɛɐ̯·ˈbai·fyː·rən] vt (bewirken) to bring about sep

Herberge <-, -n> [ˈhɛr·bɛr·ɡə] f hostel

Herbst <-[e]s, -e> [hɛrpst] m pl selten fall

herbstlich [ˈhɛrpst·lɪç] adj fall attr, autumnal

Herd <-[e]s, -e> [heːɐ̯t] m **1.** (Küchenherd) stove **2.** (Krankheitsherd) focus **3.** GEOL (Zentrum) epicenter

Herde <-, -n> [ˈheːɐ̯·də] f herd; (Schafherde) flock

herein [hɛ·ˈrain] adv in [here]; ~! come in!

herein|brechen [hɛ·ˈrain·brɛ·çn̩] vi irreg sein [**über jdn/etw**] ~ (Katastrophe, Unglück) to befall [sb/sth]

herein|fallen vi irreg sein **1.** (nach innen fallen) to fall (**in** +akk in[to]) **2.** fam (betrogen werden) to be taken in (**auf** +akk by)

herein|kommen vi irreg sein to come in; **wie bist du hier hereingekommen?** how did you get in here?

herein|lassen vt irreg to let in

herein|legen vt **1.** fam (betrügen) to cheat (**mit** +dat with) **2.** (nach drinnen legen) to put in

herein|platzen vi sein fam [**bei jdm**] ~ to burst in [on sb]; **bei etw** dat ~ to burst into sth

Herfahrt f trip [over] here; **auf der** ~ on the way here

her|fallen vi irreg sein **1.** (überfallen) **über jdn** ~ to attack sb; (kritisieren) to tear sb to pieces; (mit Fragen) to besiege

sb (**mit** +*dat* with) **2.** (*sich stürzen*) **über jdn/etw** ~ to fall upon sth

Hergang <-[e]s> *m kein pl* course of events

her|geben *irreg* **I.** *vt* **1.** (*weggeben*) to give away *sep* **2.** (*aushändigen*) to hand over *sep* [to] **3.** *fam* (*erbringen*) to say; **der Artikel gibt eine Fülle an Information her** the article contains a lot of information **4.** (*leihen*) **seinen guten Namen für etw** *akk* ~ to lend one's name to sth **II.** *vr* **sich** *akk* **für etw** *akk* ~ to have something to do with sth

her|gehen *irreg* **I.** *vi sein* **1.** (*entlanggehen*) **neben/vor jdm** ~ to walk beside/ in front of sb **2.** (*sich erdreisten*) ~ **und ...** to just go [ahead] and ... **3.** *südd, österr* (*herkommen*) to come [[over] here] **II.** *vi impers sein fam* (*zugehen*) **bei der Diskussion ging es heiß her** it was a heated discussion

Hering <-s, -e> ['heː·rɪŋ] *m* **1.** (*Fisch*) herring **2.** (*Zeltpflock*) [tent] peg

her|kommen *vi irreg sein* **1.** (*herbeikommen*) to come [over] here **2.** (*herstammen*) to come from

Herkunft <-, *selten* Herkünfte> ['heːɐ̯·kʊnft] *f* **1.** (*Abstammung*) origins *pl*, descent **2.** (*Ursprung*) origin

Herkunftsland *nt* country of origin

her|machen *vr fam* **1.** (*beschäftigen*) **sich** *akk* **über etw** *akk* ~ to dive into sth **2.** (*Besitz ergreifen*) **sich** *akk* **über etw** *akk* ~ to pounce on sth **3.** (*herfallen*) **sich** *akk* **über jdn** ~ to attack sb **II.** *vt fam* **das macht doch nicht viel her!** that's not very impressive!

Hermelin <-s, -e> [hɛr·mə·'liːn] *nt* ZOOL (*braun*) stoat; (*weiß*) ermine

hermetisch [hɛr·'meː·tɪʃ] *adj* hermetic

Heroin <-s> [he·ro·'iːn] *nt kein pl* heroin

Herpes <-> ['hɛr·pɛs] *m kein pl* herpes

Herr(in) <-n, -en> [hɛr] *m(f)* **1.** *nur m* (*männliche Anrede*) Mr.; **die ~en Schmidt und Schrader** Mr. Schmidt and Mr. Schrader; **sehr geehrter ~ ...** Dear Mr. ...; **sehr geehrte ~en!** Dear Sirs! **2.** *nur m* geh (*Mann*) gentleman **3.** (*Herrscher*) ruler (**über** +*akk* of); **~ der Lage sein** to be master of

the situation; **sein eigener ~ sein** to be one's own boss **4.** REL (*Gott*) Lord
▶ **aus aller ~en Länder** from all over the world

Herrenbekleidung *f* menswear

Herren(fahr)rad *nt* men's bicycle

Herrenhaus *nt* manor house

herrenlos *adj* abandoned; (*Hund, Katze*) stray

Herrentoilette *f* men's restroom

Herrgott ['hɛr·gɔt] *m südd, österr fam* **der ~** the Lord

Herrin <-, -nen> *f s.* **Herr** mistress

herrisch ['hɛ·rɪʃ] **I.** *adj* overbearing; (*Ton*) commanding **II.** *adv* imperiously

herrlich I. *adj* **1.** (*prächtig*) marvelous; (*Aussicht*) magnificent; (*Sonnenschein*) glorious; (*Urlaub*) delightful; **das Wetter ist ~ heute!** the weather is great today! **2.** (*köstlich*) delicious **II.** *adv* (*prächtig*) **sich ~ amüsieren** to have a wonderful time

Herrschaft <-, -en> ['hɛr·ʃaft] *f* **1.** *kein pl* (*Macht, Kontrolle*) reign **2.** *pl* (*Damen und Herren*) ~en ladies and gentlemen; **darf ich den ~en sonst noch etwas bringen?** would any of you ladies or gentlemen care for anything else?

herrschaftlich *adj* grand

herrschen ['hɛrʃn] **1.** *vi* to rule (**über** +*akk* over); (*Meinung*) to prevail; (*Ruhe, Stille*) to reign; (*Hunger, Krankheit, Not*) to be rampant **II.** *vi impers* **es herrscht ... there is ...**

herrschend *adj* ruling; (*Meinung*) prevailing; (*Mode*) current

Herrscher(in) <-s, -> *m(f)* ruler (**über** +*akk* of)

Herrscherhaus *nt* [ruling] dynasty

herrschsüchtig *adj* domineering

her|rühren *vi* **von etw** *dat* ~ to come from sth

her|stellen *vt* **1.** (*erzeugen*) to produce **2.** (*gesundheitlich*) **jdn wieder** ~ to restore sb back to health **3.** (*irgendwohin stellen*) to put [over] here

Hersteller(in) <-s, -> *m(f)* producer

Herstellung *f kein pl* production

herüber [hɛ·'ryː·bə] *adv* over here

herum [hɛ·'rʊm] *adv* **1.** (*um etw im Kreis*) **um etw** *akk* ~ around sth **2.** (*überall in*

jds Nähe) **um jdn** ~ [all] around sb **3.** *(gegen)* **um ...** ~ around ...

herum|ärgern *vr fam* **sich** *akk* **mit jdm/ etw** ~ to keep getting worked up about sb/sth

herum|drehen I. *vt* **1.** *(um die Achse drehen)* to turn **2.** *(wenden)* to turn over **II.** *vr* **sich** *akk* ~ to turn around

herum|führen I. *vt* **jdn** ~ to show sb around **II.** *vi* **um etw** *akk* ~ to go around sth

herum|gehen *vi irreg sein* **1.** *(einen Kreis gehen)* to walk around *(in a circular pattern)* **2.** *(ziellos umhergehen)* to wander around **3.** *(herumgereicht werden)* to be passed around **4.** *(weitererzählt werden)* to go around **5.** *(vorübergehen)* to pass

herum|kommandieren * I. *vt fam* to boss around **II.** *vi fam* to give orders

herum|kommen *vi irreg sein fam* **1.** *(herumfahren können)* to get around **2.** *(vermeiden können)* to get out of **3.** *(reisen)* to get around; **viel** ~ to do a lot of traveling

herum|laufen *vi irreg sein* **1.** *(um etwas laufen)* to run around **2.** *fam (umherlaufen)* to go around; **[noch] frei** ~ to be [still] at large

herum|liegen *vi irreg fam* to lie around; **etw** ~ **lassen** to leave sth lying around

herum|lungern *vi fam* to hang around; JUR to loiter

herum|schlagen *irreg vr fam* **sich** *akk* **mit jdm/etw** ~ to struggle with sb/sth

herum|schnüffeln *vi pej fam (spionieren)* to snoop around *(in +dat* in)

herum|stehen *vi irreg sein* **1.** *fam (irgendwo in der Gegend stehen)* to stand around **2.** *(gruppiert sein)* **um jdn/etw** ~ to stand around sb/sth

herum|treiben *vr irreg* **sich** *akk* **irgendwo** ~ to hang around somewhere

herum|ziehen *irreg vi sein* **mit jdm** ~ to move around with sb

herunter [hɛˈrʊn·tɐ] **I.** *adv* down; **sie liefen den Berg** ~ they ran down the hill **II.** *präp nachgestellt* **etw** ~ down sth

herunter|fallen *vi irreg sein* to fall off; **mir ist der Hammer heruntergefallen** I dropped the hammer

herunter|gehen *vi irreg sein* **1.** *(nach unten gehen)* to go down **2.** *fig (sinken: Preise)* to drop **3.** *(Flughöhe verringern)* to descend **4.** *(reduzieren)* to reduce; **mit der Geschwindigkeit** ~ to slow down

heruntergekommen *adj pej* **1.** *(abgewohnt)* rundown, dilapidated **2.** *(verwahrlost)* down-and-out

herunter|handeln *vt fam* to talk down *sep*

herunter|kippen *vt fam (Schnaps, Bier)* to chug [down *sep*]

herunter|klappen *vt* to put down *sep; (Kragen)* to turn down; *(Deckel)* to close

herunter|kommen *vi irreg sein* to come down

herunter|laden *vt* COMPUT to download

herunter|machen *vt fam* **1.** *(schlechtmachen)* to tear to pieces **2.** *(zurechtweisen)* to tell off

herunter|wirtschaften *vt pej fam* to ruin

hervor|heben *vt irreg* to emphasize, to stress

hervor|holen *vt* to take out *sep* **(aus** *+dat* from)

hervor|ragen [hɛɡ·ˈfoːɐ̯·raː·gn̩] *vi* **1.** *(vorstehen)* to jut out **(aus** *+dat* from) **2.** *fig (sich auszeichnen)* to stand out

hervorragend *adj* excellent, outstanding

hervor|rufen *vt irreg* to evoke; *(Bestürzung, Entsetzen)* to cause

hervor|treten *vi irreg sein* **1.** *(heraustreten)* to step out **(hinter** *+dat* from behind) **2.** *(Wangenknochen, Kinn)* to protrude **3.** *(erkennbar werden)* to become evident

hervor|tun *vr irreg fam* **sich** *akk* ~ to distinguish oneself **(mit** *+dat* with)

Herz <-ens, -en> [hɛrts] *nt* **1.** ANAT heart **2.** *(Gemüt, Gefühl)* heart; **mit ganzem ~en** wholeheartedly; **von ganzem ~en** sincerely; **im Grunde seines ~ens** in his heart of hearts; **leichten ~ens** lightheartedly; **schweren ~ens** with a heavy heart; **jds** ~ **erweichen** to soften up *sep* sb **3.** *(Zentrum)* heart **4.** *(Schatz, Liebling)* dear, love **5.** KARTEN hearts *pl*
▶ **jdm das** ~ **brechen** to break sb's

heart; **etw nicht übers ~ bringen** to not have the heart to do sth; **etw auf dem ~en haben** to have sth on one's mind; **jds ~ hängt an etw** *dat* sb is attached to sth; **jds ~ höherschlagen lassen** to make sb's heart beat faster; **jdm etw ans ~ legen** to entrust sb with sth; **jdm liegt etw am ~en** sb is concerned about sth; **jdn in sein ~ schließen** to take sb into one's heart; **ein ~ und eine Seele sein** to be the best of friends; **seinem ~en einen Stoß geben** to pluck up the courage; **jd wächst jdm ans ~** sb is growing fond of sb

Herzanfall *m* heart attack
herzensgut ['hɛr·tsns·'guːt] *adj* good-hearted
herzergreifend *adj* heart-rending
Herzfehler *m* heart defect
herzhaft **I.** *adj* **1.** (*würzig-kräftig*) savory; (*Essen, Eintopf*) hearty **2.** (*kräftig*) substantial **II.** *adv* **1.** (*würzig-kräftig*) **~ schmecken** to be tasty **2.** (*kräftig*) heartily; **~ gähnen** to yawn loudly
herzig ['hɛr·tsɪç] *adj* cute
Herzinfarkt *m* heart attack
Herzklopfen *nt kein pl* pounding of the heart, palpitations *pl*
herzkrank *adj* **~ sein** to have a heart condition
herzlich **I.** *adj* **1.** (*warmherzig*) warm, friendly, cordial; (*Lachen*) hearty **2.** (*in Grußformeln*) kind **II.** *adv* **1.** (*aufrichtig*) warmly; **sich** *akk* **bei jdm ~ bedanken** to thank sb very much; **jdn ~ gratulieren** to congratulate sb warmly **2.** (*recht*) really; **~ wenig** precious little
Herzlichkeit <-> *f kein pl* warmth
herzlos *adj* heartless
Herzog(in) <-s, Herzöge> ['hɛr·tso:k] *m(f)* duke *masc*, duchess *fem*
Herzogtum <-s, -tümer> *nt* duchy, dukedom
Herzschlag *m* MED **1.** (*Kontraktion des Herzmuskels*) heartbeat **2.** (*Herzstill-*

stand) heart failure
Herzschrittmacher *m* MED pacemaker
Herzstillstand *m* MED cardiac arrest
herzzerreißend *adj* heart-rending
heterosexuell [he·te·ro·zɛ·'ksu·ɛl] *adj* heterosexual
hetzen ['hɛtsn] **I.** *vi* **1.** *haben* (*sich abhetzen*) to rush around **2.** *sein* (*eilen*) to rush **3.** *haben pej* (*Hass schüren*) to stir up hatred (**gegen** +*akk* against) **II.** *vt haben* **1.** (*jagen*) to hunt **2.** (*losgehen lassen*) **jdn/einen Hund auf jdn ~** to set sb/a dog on sb **3.** *fam* (*antreiben*) to rush **4.** (*vertreiben*) to chase (**von** +*dat* off)
Hetzkampagne *f pej* smear campaign
Heu <-[e]s> [hɔy] *nt kein pl* hay ▶ **Geld wie ~ haben** to have heaps of money
Heuchelei <-, -en> [hɔy·çə·'lai] *f pe,* **1.** (*Heucheln*) hypocrisy **2.** (*heuchlerische Äußerung*) hypocritical remark
heucheln ['hɔy·çln] **I.** *vi* to be hypocritical **II.** *vt* to feign
Heuchler(in) <-s, -> ['hɔy·çle] *m(f) pe,* hypocrite
heuchlerisch *adj pej* hypocritical
heuer ['hɔy·ɐ] *adv* südd, österr, schweiz (*in diesem Jahr*) this year
heulen ['hɔy·lən] *vi* **1.** *fam* (*weinen*) to cry; **es ist zum H~** *fam* it's enough to make you cry **2.** (*Sturm, Wolf*) to howl (*Motor*) to wail; (*Flugzeug, Motorrad* to roar
Heuschnupfen *m* hay fever
Heuschrecke <-, -n> *f* grasshopper (*Wanderheuschrecke*) locust
heute ['hɔy·tə] *adv* **1.** (*an diesem Tag*) today; **~ Abend** this evening; **~ Nach** tonight; **~ früh** [early] this morning; **ab ~** as of today; **~ in/vor acht Tagen** a week from today/ago today **2.** (*der Gegenwart*) today; **von ~ auf morgen** al of a sudden, overnight **3.** (*heutzutage* nowadays
heutig ['hɔy·tɪç] *adj attr* **1.** (*heute stattfindend*) today's **2.** (*von heute: Nachrichten, Zeitung*) today's; **der ~e An lass** this occasion **3.** (*gegenwärtig*) **die ~e Zeit** nowadays; **der ~e Stand de Technik** today's technology
heutzutage ['hɔyt·tsu·ta:·gə] *adv* nowa

days, these days

Hexe <-, -n> ['hɛ·ksə] f 1. (böses Fabelwesen) witch 2. pej fam (zeternde Frau) shrew; **eine alte ~** an old hag

hexen ['hɛ·ksn̩] vi to cast spells, to do magic; **ich kann doch nicht ~** fig I can't work miracles

Hexenschuss RR m kein pl fam lumbago

Hexerei <-, -en> [hɛ·ksə·ˈrai] f sorcery

hieb ['hi:p] imp von **hauen**

Hieb <-[e]s, -e> [hi:p] m 1. (Schlag) blow 2. pl (Prügel) beating sing, thrashing sing

hieb- und stichfest adj irrefutable; (Alibi) iron

hielt ['hi:lt] imp von **halten**

hier [hi:ɐ̯] adv 1. here; **er müsste doch schon längst wieder ~ sein!** he should have been back a long time ago!; **~ ist/spricht Dr. Günther** [this is] Dr. Günther [speaking]; **~ draußen/drinnen** out/in here; **~ entlang** this way; **~ oben/unten** up/down here; **~ vorn/hinten** here at the front/at the back; **von ~ aus** from here; **von ~ sein** to be from here 2. (in diesem Moment) at this point ▶ **~ und da** (stellenweise) here and there; (gelegentlich) now and then

Hierarchie <-, -n> [hie·rar·ˈçi:] f hierarchy

hierauf ['hi:r·ˈauf] adv 1. (obendrauf) here, on this 2. (daraufhin) as a result of this/that

hieraus ['hi:r·ˈaus] adv 1. (aus diesem Gegenstand) from [o out of] here 2. (aus diesem Material) out of this 3. (aus dem Genannten) from this

hierbei ['hi:ɐ̯·ˈbai] adv 1. (währenddessen) while doing this 2. (dabei) here; **~ sind gewisse Punkte zu beachten** you need to pay attention to certain things here

hierdurch ['hi:ɐ̯·ˈdʊrç] adv 1. (hier hindurch) through here 2. (dadurch) in this way

hierfür ['hi:ɐ̯·ˈfy:ɐ̯] adv for this

hierher ['hi:ɐ̯·ˈhe:ɐ̯] adv here; **bis ~** up to here; **bis ~ und nicht weiter** this far and no farther

hierin ['hi:r·ˈɪn] adv 1. (in diesem Raum) in here 2. (was angeht) in this

hiermit ['hi:g·ˈmɪt] adv with this; **~ erkläre ich, dass ...** I hereby declare that ...; **~ wird bescheinigt, dass ...** this is to certify that ...; **~ ist die Angelegenheit erledigt** that is the end of the matter

hierüber ['hi:r·ˈyːbɐ] adv 1. (über diese Stelle) over here 2. (über diese Angelegenheit) about this

hiervon ['hi:g·ˈfɔn] adv 1. (von diesem Gegenstand) of this/these 2. (über dieses Thema) about this

hierzu ['hi:ɐ̯·ˈtsu:] adv 1. (dazu) with it 2. (zu dieser Kategorie) **~ gehört ...** this includes ... 3. (zu diesem Punkt) to this; **sich** akk **~ äußern** to say something about this

hierzulande, hier zu Lande ['hi:ɐ̯·tsu·ˈlan·də] adv [here] in these parts, around here fam

hieß ['hi:s] imp von **heißen**

Hi-Fi-Anlage ['hai·fi·] f stereo system, hi-fi

Hilfe <-, -n> ['hɪl·fə] f 1. kein pl (Beistand, Unterstützung) help, assistance; **jdn um ~ bitten** to ask sb for help; **jdm zu ~ kommen** to come to sb's assistance; **um ~ rufen** to call for help; **[zu] ~!** help!; **ohne fremde ~** without outside help; **erste ~** first aid 2. (Zuschuss) **finanzielle ~** financial aid; (für Notleidende) relief; **wirtschaftliche ~** economic aid 3. (Hilfsmittel) aid 4. (Haushaltshilfe) help

Hilferuf m cry for help

hilflos ['hɪlf·lo:s] I. adj 1. (auf Hilfe angewiesen) helpless 2. (ratlos) at a loss pred II. adv 1. (schutzlos) helplessly; **jdm/etw ~ ausgeliefert sein** to be at the mercy of sb/sth 2. (ratlos) at a loss

hilfreich adj helpful; (nützlich a.) useful

Hilfsaktion f aid program

hilfsbedürftig adj 1. (auf Hilfe angewiesen) in need of help pred 2. FIN (bedürftig) needy

hilfsbereit adj helpful

Hilfsmittel nt 1. MED [health] aid [product] 2. pl (Geldmittel) [financial] aid

Himbeere ['hɪm·beːˌrə] f raspberry

Himmel <-s, poet -> ['hɪ·ml̩] m 1. (Fir-

mament) sky; **unter freiem ~** outdoors **2.** (*Himmelreich*) heaven; **in den ~ kommen** to go to heaven **3.** (*Baldachin*) canopy **4.** AUTO [interior] roof ▶ **aus heiterem ~** out of the blue; **um ~s willen** *fam* for heaven's sake

himmelblau ['hɪ·ml·blau] *adj* sky-blue

Himmelfahrt *f* ascension into heaven; **Christi ~** Ascension Day

Himmelskörper *m* celestial body

Himmelsrichtung *f* direction; **die vier ~en** the four points of the compass

himmelweit I. *adj fam* enormous; (*Unterschied*) considerable II. *adv* **sich** *akk* ~ **unterscheiden** to be completely different

himmlisch ['hɪm·lɪʃ] I. *adj attr* divine II. *adv* divinely, wonderfully

hin [hɪn] *adv* **1.** räumlich (*dahin*) there; ~ **und her laufen** to run back and forth; **der Balkon liegt zur Straße ~** the balcony faces the street; ~ **und zurück** there and back **2.** zeitlich (*sich hinziehend*) **über die Jahre** ~ over the years **3.** *fig* **auf jds Bitte/Vorschlag** ~ at sb's request/suggestion; **auf jds Rat** ~ on sb's advice; **auf die Gefahr ~, dass ich mich wiederhole** at the risk of repeating myself ▶ **nach langem H~ und Her** after careful consideration; ~ **und wieder** from time to time

hinarbeiten *vi* **auf etw** *akk* ~ to work [one's way] toward sth

hinauf [hɪ·ˈnauf] *adv* up; **den Fluss ~** upstream; **bis ~ zu etw** *dat* up to sth

hinauffahren *irreg vi sein* to go up

hinaufgehen *vi irreg sein* **1.** (*nach oben gehen*) to go up (**auf** +*akk* to) **2.** (*steigen: Preise*) to go up **3.** (*hochgehen*) **mit dem Preis** ~ to raise the price

hinaufsteigen *vi irreg sein* to climb up (**auf** +*akk* onto)

hinaus [hɪ·ˈnaus] I. *interj* (*nach draußen*) get out [of here]! II. *adv* **1.** (*von hier nach draußen*) out; **hier/dort ~ bitte!** this/that way out, please!; **aus etw** *dat* ~ out of sth; **nach hinten/vorne ~ liegen** to be [situated] at the back/front [of a house] **2.** *fig* **über etw** *akk* ~ **sein** to be past sth; **über etw** *akk* ~ **reichen** to include sth **3.** (*zeitlich*) **auf Jahre**

~ for years to come; **über etw** *akk* ~ more than sth

hinausgehen [hɪ·ˈnaus·ge·ən] *irreg* I. *vi sein* **1.** (*nach draußen gehen*) to go out (**aus** +*dat* of); **auf die Straße** ~ to go out to the street **2.** (*gerichtet sein*) **auf etw** *akk* ~ to look out onto sth; **nach Osten** ~ to face east **3.** (*überschreiten*) [**weit**] **über etw** *akk* ~ to go [far] beyond sth II. *vi impers sein* **es geht dort hinaus!** that's the way out!

hinauslaufen *vi irreg sein* **1.** (*nach draußen laufen*) to run out **2.** (*gleichbedeutend mit etw sein*) **auf etw** *akk* ~ to be the same as sth; **auf was soll das ~?** what's that supposed to mean?; **auf dasselbe** ~ to come to the same thing

hinauslehnen *vr* **sich** *akk* ~ to lean out

hinausschieben *vt irreg* **1.** (*nach draußen schieben*) to push out **2.** (*auf später verschieben*) to put off

hinauswerfen *vt irreg* **1.** (*nach draußen werfen*) to throw out (**aus** +*dat* of) **2.** *fam* (*entlassen*) to fire

hinauswollen *vi* **1.** (*nach draußen wollen*) **auf den Hof/in den Garten** ~ to want to go out into the courtyard/garden **2.** (*etw anstreben*) **auf etw** *akk* ~ to get at sth; **worauf wollen Sie hinaus?** what are you getting at?

hinauszögern I. *vt* to put off *sep*, to delay II. *vr* **sich** *akk* ~ to be delayed

hinbiegen *vt irreg fam* **1.** (*bereinigen*) to sort out *sep*; (*Problem a.*) to iron out **2.** *pej* (*drehen*) **es so ~, dass ...** to manage it so that ...

Hinblick *m* **im ~ auf etw** *akk* (*angesichts*) in view of sth; (*in Bezug auf*) with regard to sth

hinderlich ['hɪn·dɐ·lɪç] *adj* **1.** (*behindernd*) ~ **sein** to be a hindrance **2.** (*ein Hindernis darstellend*) **jdm/für etw** *akk* ~ **sein** to be an obstacle for sb/sth

hindern ['hɪn·dɐn] *vt* **1.** (*abhalten*) **jdn daran ~, etw zu tun** to prevent sb from doing sth **2.** (*hemmen*) **jdn bei etw** *akk* ~ to hamper sb in [doing] sth

Hindernis ['hɪn·dɐ·nɪs] *nt* <-ses, -se> obstacle; **jdm ~se in den Weg legen** to put obstacles in sb's way; (*bei Leichtathletik*) hurdle

hin|deuten *vi* **auf etw** *akk* ~ to suggest sth

Hindu <-[s], -[s]> ['hɪn·du] *m* Hindu

hindurch [hɪn·'dʊrç] *adv* **1.** *räumlich* through **2.** *zeitlich* through, throughout; **die ganze Zeit** ~ all the time

hinein [hɪ·'naɪn] *adv* in; ~ **mit dir!** *fam* in with you!, get in there!

hinein|gehen *vi irreg sein* **1.** (*betreten*) to go in[to], to enter **2.** *fam s.* **hineinpassen**

hinein|passen *vi* **in etw** *akk* ~ to fit in[to] sth

hinein|reden *vi* **jdm in seine Angelegenheiten** ~ to meddle in sb's affairs

hinein|stecken *vt* **1.** (*in etw stecken*) to put in[to]; (*Nadel*) to stick in[to] **2.** (*investieren*) to put in[to]

hinein|versetzen* *vr* **sich** *akk* **in jdn** ~ to put oneself in sb's place; **sich** *akk* **in etw** *akk* ~ to acquaint oneself with sth

hin|fahren *irreg* **I.** *vi sein* **irgendwo** ~ to go somewhere **II.** *vt haben* **jdn** ~ to take sb; **jdn zum Flughafen** ~ to drive sb to the airport

Hinfahrt *f* drive, trip; **auf der** ~ on the way there

hin|fallen *vi irreg sein* to fall [down]

hinfällig *adj* **1.** (*gebrechlich*) frail **2.** (*ungültig*) invalid

Hinflug *m* flight

hin|führen **I.** *vt* (*irgendwohin geleiten*) **jdn** [*irgendwo*] ~ to take sb [somewhere] **II.** *vi* (*in Richtung auf etw verlaufen*) to lead [to]

hing ['hɪŋ] *imp von* **hängen**

Hingabe *f kein pl* (*rückhaltlose Widmung*) dedication; (*zu einem Mensch*) devotion; **sie spielt die Flöte mit** ~ she plays the flute with passion

hin|geben *irreg vr* **sich** *akk* **etw** *dat* ~ to abandon oneself to sth

hingebungsvoll **I.** *adj* dedicated; (*Blick, Pflege*) devoted **II.** *adv* with dedication

hingegen [hɪn·'ge:·gn̩] *konj* but, however

hin|gehen *vi irreg sein* **1.** (*dorthin gehen*) to go **2.** *geh* (*vergehen*) to pass

hin|halten *vt irreg* **1.** (*entgegenhalten*) **jdm etw** ~ to hold sth out to sb **2.** (*aufhalten*) to keep waiting

hin|hauen *irreg* **I.** *vi fam* **1.** (*klappen*) to work **2.** (*ausreichen*) to be enough **3.** (*zuschlagen*) to take a swing **II.** *vr sl* **sich** *akk* ~ **1.** (*schlafen*) to turn in **2.** (*sich hinflegeln*) to plunk [oneself] down **III.** *vt fam* (*schlampig erledigen*) to rush through; (*Schriftstück*) to dash off

hinken ['hɪŋ·kn̩] *vi* **1.** *haben* (*das Bein nachziehen*) to limp **2.** *haben* (*nicht ganz zutreffen*) **der Vergleich hinkt** that's not a good comparison

hin|knien *vi, vr* *vi: sein* to kneel down

hin|legen **I.** *vt* **1.** (*niederlegen*) to put down **2.** (*flach lagern*) to lay down **3.** (*ins Bett bringen*) to put to bed **4.** *fam* (*bezahlen: Geldbetrag*) to fork out **II.** *vr* **sich** *akk* ~ **1.** (*schlafen gehen*) to go sleep **2.** *fam* (*hinfallen*) to fall [over]

hin|nehmen *vt irreg* to accept; **eine Niederlage/einen Verlust** ~ [**müssen**] to [have to] suffer a defeat/a loss

hinreichend *adj* sufficient; (*Gehalt, Einkommen*) adequate

Hinreise *f* trip [somewhere]; (*mit dem Auto*) drive

hin|reißen *vt irreg* **1.** (*begeistern*) to enchant **2.** (*spontan verleiten*) **sich** *akk* **zu etw** *dat* ~ **lassen** to allow oneself to be provoked into doing sth

hinreißend *adj* enchanting, captivating; (*Schönheit*) striking

hin|richten *vt* to execute

Hinrichtung *f* execution

hin|schmeißen *vt irreg fam s.* **hinwerfen**

hin|setzen **I.** *vr* **sich** *akk* ~ to sit down **II.** *vt* to put down

Hinsicht *f kein pl* **in gewisser** ~ in certain respects

hinsichtlich *präp +gen* with regard to

hin|stellen **I.** *vt* **1.** (*an einen Platz*) to put **2.** *fam* (*bauen*) to put up **3.** (*Fahrzeug*) to park **4.** (*charakterisieren*) **jdn als ...** ~ to make sb out to be ... **II.** *vr* **sich** *akk* ~ to stand up straight; **sich** *akk* **vor jdn** ~ to plant oneself in front of sb

hinten ['hɪn·tn̩] *adv* at the back; ~ **im Buch** at the back of the book; **sich** *akk* ~ **anstellen** to get in line [at the back]; **das**

wird weiter ~ erklärt that's explained further toward the end

hinter ['hɪn·tɐ] **I.** *präp* +dat **1.** (*dahinter*) behind; **~ dem Baum** behind the tree **2.** (*jenseits von etw*) **~ der Grenze** on the other side of the border **3.** *fig* (*herausfinden*) **~ etw kommen** to find out about sth **4.** (*unterstützen*) **sich akk ~ jdn stellen** to back sb up **II.** *präp* +akk **1.** (*örtlich*) behind **2.** *zeitlich* after; **etw ~ sich** *akk* **bringen** to get sth over with **III.** *part fam* s. **dahinter**

Hinterachse [-ak·sə] *f* rear axle

Hinterbein *nt* hind leg

hintere(r, s) ['hɪn·tə·rə, -rə, -rəs] *adj* **der/die/das ~ ...** the rear ...

hintereinander [hɪn·tɐ·ʔain·'an·dɐ] *adv* **1.** *räumlich* one behind the other **2.** *zeitlich* one after the other; **mehrere Tage ~** several days in a row

Hintergedanke *m* ulterior motive

hintergehen * [hɪn·tɐ·'geː·ən] *vt irreg* (*betrügen*) to deceive; (*sexuell*) to two-time; (*um Profit zu machen*) to double-cross

Hintergrund *m* background; **die Hintergründe einer S.** *gen* the [true] facts about sth

Hinterhalt *m pej* ambush

hinterhältig ['hɪn·tɐ·hɛl·tɪç] **I.** *adj pej* underhanded **II.** *adv pej* in an underhanded manner

hinterher [hɪn·tɐ·'heːɐ] *adv* **1.** *räumlich* behind; **jdm ~ sein** to be after sb **2.** *zeitlich* after that, afterwards

hinterher|laufen [hɪn·tɐ·'heːɐ·lau·fn̩] *vi irreg sein* to run after

Hinterhof *m* courtyard; (*Garten*) backyard

Hinterland *nt kein pl* hinterland

hinterlassen * [hɪn·tɐ·'la·sn̩] *vt irreg* to leave; **bei jdm einen Eindruck ~** to leave an impression on sb

hinterlegen * [hɪn·tɐ·'leː·gn̩] *vt* **etw [bei jdm] ~** to leave sth [with sb]; (*Sicherheitsleistung, Betrag*) to supply [sb with] sth

hinterlistig *adj* shifty

Hintermann <-männer> *m* **1.** (*räumlich*) the person behind **2.** *meist pl* (*Drahtzieher*) ringleader, brains [behind the operation]

hintern ['hɪn·tɐn] = **hinter den** *s.* **hinter**

Hintern <-s, -> ['hɪn·tɐn] *m fam* (*Gesäß*) butt

Hinterrad *nt* rear wheel

Hinterradantrieb *m* rear-wheel drive

hinterrücks ['hɪn·tɐ·rʏks] *adv* **1.** (*von hinten*) from behind **2.** (*im Verborgenen*) behind sb's back

hinterste(r, s) ['hɪn·tes·tə, -stə, -stəs] *adj superl von* **hintere(r, s)** last; (*entlegenste*) farthest

Hintertür *f*, **Hintertürl** <-s, -[n]> *nt* österr **1.** (*hintere Eingangstür*) back entrance; (*zu einem privaten Haus*) back door **2.** *fam* (*Ausweg*) back door, loophole

hinterziehen * [hɪn·tɐ·'tsiː·ən] *vt irreg* **Steuern ~** to evade tax[es]

hinüber [hɪ·'nyː·bɐ] *adv* **1.** (*nach drüben*) across, over **2.** *fam* (*verdorben*) bad **3.** *fam* (*kaputt, erschöpft*) **etw/jd ist ~** sth has had it

hinunter [hɪ·'nʊn·tɐ] *adv* down

hinunter|gehen [hɪ·'nʊn·tɐ·geː·ən] *vi irreg sein* **1.** (*nach unten gehen*) to go down **2.** (*die Flughöhe verringern*) to descend (**auf** +akk to)

hinunter|schlucken *vt* **1.** (*schlucken*) to swallow [down *sep*] **2.** *fam* (*sich verkneifen*) to suppress; **eine Antwort ~** to stifle a reply

hinunter|spülen *vt* **1.** (*wegspülen*) to flush down *sep* **2.** (*mit einem Getränk*) to wash down *sep*

hinunter|werfen *vt irreg* to throw down

hinweg [hɪn·'vɛk] *adv* **über jdn/etw ~ sein** to have gotten over sb/sth

Hinweg ['hɪn·veːk] *m* way there

hinweg|gehen [hɪn·'vɛk·geː·ən] *vi irreg sein* **über etw** *akk* **~** to disregard sth

hinweg|kommen *vi irreg sein* **über etw** *akk* **~** to get over sth

hinweg|sehen *vi irreg* **über jdn/etw ~ 1.** (*darüber sehen*) to see over sb['s head]/sth **2.** (*nicht wichtig nehmen*) to overlook sb/sth

hinweg|setzen *vr* **sich** *akk* **über etw** *akk* **~** to disregard sth

Hinweis <-es, -e> ['hɪn·vais] m 1. (Rat) advice, tip 2. (Anhaltspunkt) clue

hin|weisen irreg I. vt jdn darauf ~, dass ... to point out [to sb] that ... II. vi auf jdn/etw ~ to point to sb/sth

hin|werfen irreg vt 1. (zuwerfen) jdm etw ~ to throw sth to sb 2. (auf den Boden werfen) to throw down sep 3. fam (aufgeben) to give up sep 4. (Bemerkung) to drop 5. (flüchtig zu Papier bringen) to dash off

hin|ziehen irreg I. vt haben 1. (zu sich ziehen) jdn/etw zu sich dat ~ to pull sb/sth toward oneself 2. (anziehen) es zieht jdn zu jdm/etw hin dat sb is attracted to sb/sth 3. (hinauszögern) to delay II. vi sein (an einen Ort) to move III. vr sich akk ~ 1. (zeitlich) to drag on 2. (räumlich) to extend along

hinzu [hɪn·ˈtsu:] adv in addition, besides

hinzu|kommen [hɪn·ˈtsu:·kɔ·mən] vi irreg sein 1. (eintreffen) to arrive; **die anderen Gäste kommen dann später hinzu** the other guests will come along later 2. (sich noch ereignen) **es kommt [noch] hinzu, dass ...** there is also the fact that ... 3. (zu einem Kauf) **kommt sonst noch etwas hinzu?** can I get you anything else?

hinzu|ziehen vt irreg to consult

Hirn <-[e]s, -e> [hɪrn] nt 1. (Gehirn) brain 2. (Hirnmasse) brains pl

Hirngespinst nt fantasy

Hirnhautentzündung f MED meningitis

hirnrissig adj pej fam harebrained

Hirntod m MED brain death

hirnverbrannt adj fam s. **hirnrissig**

Hirsch <-es, -e> [hɪrʃ] m 1. (Rothirsch) deer 2. (Hirschfleisch) venison

Hirschgeweih nt antlers pl

Hirschkuh f hind

Hirse <-, -n> ['hɪr·zə] f millet

Hirt(in) <-en, -en> ['hɪrt] m(f) herdsman masc; (Schafhirt) shepherd masc, shepherdess fem

historisch [hɪs·ˈto:·rɪʃ] adj s. **geschichtlich**

Hitze <-, fachspr -n> ['hɪ·tsə] f heat; **bei mittlerer ~ backen** to bake at medium heat

hitzebeständig adj heat-resistant

Hitzewelle f heat wave

hitzig ['hɪ·tsɪç] I. adj 1. (leicht aufbrausend: Mensch) hotheaded, quick-tempered; (Reaktion) heated; (Temperament) fiery 2. (leidenschaftlich) passionate; (Debatte) heated II. adv passionately

Hitzkopf m fam hothead

Hitzschlag m heatstroke; (von der Sonne a.) sunstroke

HIV <-[s]> [ha:·ʔi:·ˈfau] nt Abk von **human immunodeficiency virus** HIV

HIV-infiziert [ha:·ʔi:·ˈfau-] adj HIV-positive

HIV-positiv [ha:·ʔi:·ˈfau-ˈpo:·zi·ti:f] adj HIV-positive

H-Milch ['ha:] f UHT milk

hob ['ho:p] imp von **heben**

Hobby <-s, -s> ['hɔ·bi] nt hobby

Hobel <-s, -> ['ho:·bl] m 1. (Werkzeug) plane 2. (Küchengerät) slicer

hobeln ['ho:·bln] vt, vi 1. (mit dem Hobel glätten) to plane 2. (mit dem Hobel schneiden) to slice

hoch [ho:x] I. adj <attr hohe(r, s), höher, attr höchste(r, s)> 1. (räumlich: Berg) high; (Gebäude a.) tall; (Baum) tall 2. (beträchtlich, groß) large; (Kosten) high; (Druck, Geschwindigkeit, Lebensstandard) high; (Verlust) severe; (Sachschaden) extensive 3. (bedeutend) great, high; (Position) senior ► **etw ist jdm zu hoch** sth is above sb's head II. adv <höher, am höchsten> 1. (nach oben) **etw ~ halten** to hold up sep sth 2. (in einiger Höhe) **~ gelegen** highlying attr; **~ oben** high up 3. (sehr) highly; **~ konzentriert arbeiten** to be completely focused on one's work; **jdm etw ~ anrechnen** to give sb a lot of credit for sth; **jdn/etw ~ schätzen** to appreciate sb/sth very much 4. (eine hohe Summe umfassend) highly; **~ gewinnen** to win big fam; **~ verschuldet** deep in debt pred 5. MATH (Bezeichnung der Potenz) **2 ~ 4** 2 to the power of 4 ► **etw ~ und heilig versprechen** to promise sth faithfully; **wenn es ~ kommt** fam at the most

Hoch <-s, -s> [ho:x] nt METEO high

Hochachtung f deep respect

hochachtungsvoll *adv geh* your obedient servant *dated form*

hochaktuell *adj* **1.** (*äußerst aktuell*) [most] up-to-date **2.** MODE highly fashionable, all the rage *pred*

hocharbeiten *vr* **sich** *akk* ~ to work one's way up

Hochbahn *f* elevated railroad

Hochbau *m kein pl* structural engineering

hochbetagt *adj geh* aged

Hochbetrieb *m* intense activity; ~ **haben** to be very busy

Hochburg *f* stronghold

hochdeutsch ['hoːxˈdɔytʃ] *adj* Standard German

Hochdruck *m kein pl* high pressure

Hochebene *f* plateau

hocherfreut *adj* overjoyed

Hochgebirge *nt* high mountains *pl*

Hochgefühl *nt* elation

hochgehen *vi irreg sein* **1.** (*hinaufgehen*) to go up **2.** *fam* (*detonieren*) to go off *sep* **3.** *fam* (*wütend werden*) to blow one's top **4.** *fam* (*Preise*) to go up **5.** *fam* (*enttarnt werden*) to get caught

Hochgenuss RR *m* real delight

Hochgeschwindigkeitszug *m* high-speed train

Hochglanz *m* FOTO high gloss

Hochglanzmagazin *nt* glossy magazine

hochgradig *adj* extreme

hochhalten *vt irreg* **1.** (*in die Höhe halten*) to hold up *sep* **2.** *fig* (*ehren*) to uphold

Hochhaus *nt* high-rise building

hochheben *vt irreg* **1.** (*Last*) to lift up *sep* **2.** (*Arm, Hand, Kind*) to put up *sep*

hochkant ['hoːxˈkant] *adv* **etw** ~ **stellen** to stand sth on end

Hochkonjunktur *f* (*economic*) boom

Hochland ['hoːxˈlant] *nt* highland *usu pl*

Hochleistung *f* first-rate performance

hochmodern **I.** *adj* ultramodern **II.** *adv* in the latest fashion[s]

hochmütig ['hoːxˈmyːtɪç] *adj pej* arrogant

hochnäsig ['hoːxˈnɛːzɪç] *adj pej fam* conceited

Hochofen *m* blast furnace

Hochrechnung *f* projection

Hochsaison *f* **1.** (*Zeit stärksten Betriebes*) busy season **2.** (*Hauptsaison*) high season

Hochschule ['hoːxˈʃuːlə] *f* **1.** (*Universität*) university **2.** (*Fachhochschule*) college

Hochschullehrer(in) *m(f)* college/university professor

hochschwanger *adj* in an advanced stage of pregnancy *pred*

Hochseefischerei *f* deep-sea fishing

Hochsommer *m* midsummer, height of summer

Hochspannung *f* **1.** ELEK high voltage **2.** *kein pl* (*Belastung*) enormous tension

Hochsprung *m* high jump

höchst [høːçst] *adv* most, extremely

Hochstapler(in) <-s, -> ['hoːxˈʃtaːplɐ] *m(f) pej* con man

höchste(r, s) *attr* **I.** *adj superl von* hoch **1.** (*räumlich: Baum*) tallest; (*Berg*) highest **2.** (*bedeutendste*) highest; (*Profit*) largest; **aufs H~** extremely, most; **von ~r Bedeutung sein** to be of the utmost importance **II.** *adv* **1.** (*räumlich*) the highest **2.** (*in größtem Ausmaß*) the most, most of all **3.** (*die größte Summe umfassend*) the most

höchstens ['høːçstns] *adv* **1.** (*bestenfalls*) at [the] most, at best **2.** (*nicht mehr als*) not more than

Höchstgeschwindigkeit *f* **1.** (*mögliche Geschwindigkeit*) maximum speed **2.** (*zulässige Geschwindigkeit*) speed limit

Höchstmaß *nt* maximum amount

höchstpersönlich *adv* in person, personally

höchstwahrscheinlich ['høːçstˈvaːɐˌʃainlɪç] *adv* most likely

Hochtour *f* **1.** SPORT (*Hochgebirgstour*) high-altitude mountain climbing trip **2.** *pl* TECH (*größte Leistungsfähigkeit*) **auf ~en laufen** to operate at full speed; *fig* to be in full swing

hochtrabend *adj pej* pompous

Hochverrat *m* high treason

Hochwasser *nt* **1.** (*Flut*) high tide **2.** (*überhoher Wasserstand*) high [level]

of] water **3.** (*Überschwemmung*) flood

hochwertig ['hoːxˌveːɐ̯ɡˌtɪç] *adj* **1.** (*von hoher Qualität*) [of *pred*] high quality **2.** (*von hohem Nährwert*) highly nutritious

Hochzeit¹ <-, -en> ['hɔxˌtsait] *f* (*Heirat*) wedding

Hochzeit² <-, -en> ['hoːxˌtsait] *f geh* (*Blütezeit*) golden age

Hochzeitsfeier *f* wedding reception

Hochzeitsreise *f* honeymoon

Hochzeitstag *m* **1.** (*Tag der Hochzeit*) wedding day **2.** (*Jahrestag*) wedding anniversary

hoch|ziehen *irreg vt* **1.** (*nach oben*) to pull up *sep* **2.** *fam* (*rasch bauen*) to build [rapidly]

Hocke <-, -n> ['hɔkə] *f* **1.** (*Körperhaltung*) crouching position; **in die ~ gehen** to squat [down] **2.** (*Turnübung*) squat vault

hocken ['hɔkn̩] *vi* **1.** *haben* (*kauern*) to crouch, to squat **2.** *haben fam* (*sitzen*) to sit **3.** *sein* SPORT to squat-vault (**über** +*akk* over)

Hocker <-s, -> *m* stool

Höcker <-s, -> ['hœkɐ] *m* (*eines Kamels*) hump

Hoden <-s, -> ['hoːdn̩] *m* testicle

Hodensack *m* ANAT, MED scrotum

Hof <-[e]s, Höfe> [hoːf] *m* **1.** (*Innenhof*) courtyard; (*Schulhof*) schoolyard, playground **2.** (*Bauernhof*) farm **3.** HIST (*Fürstensitz, Hofstaat*) court

hoffen ['hɔfn̩] **I.** *vi* to hope (**auf** +*akk* for) **II.** *vt* **das will ich ~** I hope so

hoffentlich ['hɔfn̩tlɪç] *adv* hopefully; **~ nicht** I hope not

Hoffnung <-, -en> ['hɔfnʊŋ] *f* hope (**auf** +*akk* for/of); **jds letzte ~ sein** to be sb's last hope; **sich** *dat* **~en machen** to have hope

hoffnungslos I. *adj* hopeless **II.** *adv* **1.** (*ohne Hoffnung*) without hope **2.** (*völlig*) hopelessly; **sich** *akk* **~ in jdn verlieben** to fall head over heels in love with sb

Hoffnungsschimmer *m* glimmer of hope

höflich ['høːflɪç] *adj* polite

hohe(r, s) ['hoːə, 'hoːˌe, 'hoːˌəs] *adj s.* **hoch**

Höhe <-, -n> ['høːə] *f* **1.** (*Ausdehnung nach oben*) height; **aus der ~** from above; **auf halber ~** halfway up; **in einer ~ von** at a height of **2.** (*Gipfel*) summit, top **3.** (*Ausmaß*) amount, level; **ein Betrag in ~ von ...** an amount totaling ...; **die ~ des Schadens** the extent of the damage; **in die ~ gehen** (*Preise*) to rise ▶ **das ist doch die ~!** *fam* enough is enough [already]!

Hoheit <-, -en> ['hoːhait] *f* **1.** (*Mitglied einer fürstlichen Familie*) member of the royal family; **Ihre Königliche ~** Your Royal Highness **2.** *kein pl* (*oberste Staatsgewalt*) sovereignty

Hoheitsgebiet *nt* sovereign territory

Hoheitsgewässer *pl* territorial waters *npl*

Höhenmesser *m* LUFT altimeter

Höhenunterschied *m* difference in altitude

Höhepunkt *m* **1.** (*bedeutendster Teil*) high point; (*einer Veranstaltung*) highlight **2.** (*Gipfel*) height, peak; **die Krise hatte ihren ~ erreicht** the crisis had reached its climax **3.** (*Orgasmus*) climax

höher ['høːɐ] **I.** *adj komp von* **hoch** **1.** (*räumlich*) higher, taller **2.** (*bedeutender, größer: Druck, Forderungen, Verlust*) greater; (*Gewinn, Preis, Temperatur*) higher; (*Strafe*) more severe **II.** *adv komp von* **hoch** **1.** (*weiter nach oben*) higher, taller **2.** (*mit gesteigertem Wert*) higher; **sich** *akk* **~ versichern** to increase one's insurance

hohl [hoːl] *adj, adv* **1.** (*leer*) hollow; **mit der ~en Hand** with cupped hands; **~e Wangen** sunken cheeks **2.** *fig, pej* (*nichts sagend*) empty

Höhle <-, -n> ['høːlə] *f* **1.** (*Felshöhle*) cave **2.** (*Tierbehausung*) cave, den **3.** (*Höhlung*) hollow

Hohlraum *m* cavity, hollow space

Hohlspiegel *m* concave mirror

Hohn <-[e]s> [hoːn] *m kein pl* scorn, mockery

höhnisch ['høːnɪʃ] *adj* sneering

holen ['hoːlən] **I.** *vt* **1.** (*hervorholen*) to get (**aus** +*dat* out of, **von** +*dat* from) **2.** (*herholen*) **Sie können den Patienten jetzt ~** you can send for the patient

now; **jdn ~ lassen** to go get sb; **Hilfe ~** to get help **II.** *vr fam* **sich** *dat* **etw ~ 1.** (*sich nehmen*) to get oneself sth (**aus** +*dat* out of, **von** +*dat* from) **2.** (*sich zuziehen*) to catch sth (**an** +*dat* from, **bei** +*dat* in); **bei dem kalten Wetter holst du dir eine Erkältung** you'll catch a cold in this chilly weather **3.** (*sich einhandeln: Abfuhr, Rüge*) to get

Holland <-s> ['hɔ·lant] *nt* **1.** *fam* (*Niederlande*) the Netherlands *npl*, Holland; *s. a.* **Deutschland 2.** (*Provinz der Niederlande*) Holland

Holländer <-s> ['hɔ·lɛn·dɐ] *m kein pl* (*Käse*) Dutch cheese

Holländer(in) <-s, -> ['hɔ·lɛn·dɐ] *m(f) fam* Dutchman *masc*, Dutchwoman *fem*; **die ~** the Dutch + *pl vb*

holländisch ['hɔ·lɛn·dɪʃ] *adj fam* Dutch; *s. a.* **deutsch**

Hölle <-, -n> ['hœ·lə] *f pl selten* ► **jdm die ~ heißmachen** *fam* to give sb hell; **die ~ ist los** *fam* all hell has broken loose

Höllenlärm ['hœ·lən·ˈlɛrm] *m* racket

höllisch ['hœ·lɪʃ] *adj* **1.** *attr* infernal **2.** *fam* (*fürchterlich*) terrible *pred*; **ein ~er Lärm** an awful noise

holp(e)rig ['hɔl·p(ə)·rɪç] *adj* **1.** (*Straße*) bumpy, uneven **2.** (*Sprache, Stil*) clumsy

Holunder <-s, -> [ho·ˈlʊn·dɐ] *m* elder

Holz <-es, Hölzer> [hɔlts] *nt* **1.** *kein pl* (*Material*) wood; **~ fällen** to cut down *sep* trees; **tropische Hölzer** tropical wood; **aus ~** wood[en]; **massives ~** solid wood **2.** *pl* (*Bauhölzer*) timber **3.** SPORT (*beim Golf*) wood

hölzern ['hœl·tsɐn] *adj* wooden

Holzfäller(in) <-s, -> *m(f)* lumberjack

Holzhammer *m* mallet

Holzhammermethode *f fam* sledgehammer approach

Holzklotz *m* wooden block

Holzkohle *f* charcoal

Holzschuh *m* clog, wooden shoe

Holzwurm *m* woodworm

Homo-Ehe *f fam* gay marriage

homogenisieren * [ho·mo·ge·ni·ˈziː·rən] *vt* to homogenize

homöopathisch [ho·møo·ˈpaː·tɪʃ] *adj*

homeopathic

homosexuell [ho·mo·zɛ·ˈksu̯·ɛl] *adj* homosexual

Homosexuelle(r) *f(m) dekl wie adj* homosexual

Honig <-s, -e> ['hoː·nɪç] *m* honey; **türkischer ~** halva[h] ► **jdm ~ ums Maul schmieren** *fam* to butter up *sep* sb

Honigbiene *f* honeybee

Honigmelone *f* honeydew melon

Honorar <-s, -e> [ho·no·ˈraːɐ̯] *nt* fee, (*eines Autors*) royalties *npl*; **gegen ~** for a fee

honorieren * [ho·no·ˈriː·rən] *vt* **1.** (*würdigen*) to appreciate **2.** (*bezahlen*) to pay

Hopfen <-s, -> ['hɔp·fn̩] *m* hops *pl* ► **bei jdm ist ~ und Malz verloren** *fam* sb is a hopeless case

hoppla ['hɔp·la] *interj* **1.** (*o je!*) [wh]oops! **2.** (*Moment!*) hang on!; **~, wer kommt denn da?** hello, who's that [coming over this way]?

hopsen ['hɔp·sn̩] *vi sein fam* to skip; (*auf einem Bein*) to hop

hörbar *adj* audible

Hörbuch *nt* audio book

horchen ['hɔr·çn̩] *vi* to listen in (**an** +*dat* on); (*heimlich a.*) to eavesdrop

Horde <-, -n> ['hɔr·də] *f* (*wilde Schar*) horde

hören ['høː·rən] **I.** *vt* **1.** (*mit dem Gehör vernehmen*) to hear; **..., wie ich höre** I hear ...; **wie man hört, ...** word has it ...; **nie gehört!** never heard of him/her/it!; **das will ich nicht gehört haben** I'll ignore that comment; **sich akk gern reden ~** to like the sound of one's own voice **2.** (*anhören*) to listen ► **etwas [von jdm] zu ~ bekommen** to get chewed out [by sb]; **ich kann das nicht mehr ~!** enough [of that] already!; **etw/nichts von sich** *dat* **~ lassen** to keep/ not keep in touch **II.** *vi* **1.** (*zuhören*) to listen; **hör mal!/~ Sie mal!** listen! **2.** (*vernehmen*) **~, was/wie ...** to hear what/how ...; **gut/schlecht ~** to have good/poor hearing **3.** (*erfahren*) **~, dass ...** to hear [that] ...; **von jdm/etw ~** to hear of [*o* about] sb/sth **4.** (*gehorchen*) to listen (**auf** +*akk* to); **auf dich**

hört er! he listens to you! ▶ **lass von dir/lassen Sie von sich ~!** keep in touch!; **na hör/~ Sie mal!** euph [now] look here!; **man höre und staune!** would you believe it!

Hörensagen ['hø·rən·za:·gn] nt **vom ~** from hearsay

Hörer <-s, -> m (Telefonhörer) receiver; **den ~ auflegen** to hang up [on sb]

Hörer(in) <-s, -> m(f) listener

Hörfunk m radio

Hörgerät nt hearing aid

hörig ['hø:·rɪç] adj (sexuell abhängig) sexually dependent

Horizont <-[e]s, -e> [ho·ri·'tsɔnt] m horizon; **am ~** on the horizon; **über jds ~ gehen** to be beyond sb

horizontal [ho·ri·tsɔn·'ta:l] adj horizontal

Horizontale [ho·ri·tsɔn·'ta:·lə] f dekl wie adj horizontal [line]

Hormon <-s, -e> [hɔr·'mo:n] nt hormone

Hörmuschel f TELEK earpiece

Horn <-[e]s, Hörner> [hɔrn] nt horn; **das ~ von Afrika** the Horn of Africa

Hörnchen <-s, -> ['hœrn·çən] nt **1.** dim von **Horn** small horn **2.** (Gebäck) crescent roll; (aus Plunderteig) croissant

Hornhaut f **1.** (des Auges) cornea **2.** (der Haut) callus

Hornisse <-, -n> [hɔr·'nɪ·sə] f hornet

Hornochs(e) m fam stupid idiot

Horoskop <-s, -e> [ho·ro·'sko:p] nt horoscope

Hörsaal m lecture hall

Hörspiel nt **1.** kein pl (Gattung) radio drama **2.** (Stück) radio play

Horst <-[e]s, -e> [hɔrst] m **1.** (Nest) nest, aerie **2.** MIL (Fliegerhorst) military airbase

Hörsturz m sudden hearing loss

horten ['hɔr·tn] vt to hoard

Hörweite f hearing range, earshot; **in/außer ~** within/out of earshot

Hose <-, -n> ['ho:·zə] f pants npl, trousers npl; **kurze ~[n]** shorts npl ▶ **in die ~ gehen** to be a failure; **jdm ist das Herz in die ~ gerutscht** fam sb's heart was in their mouth; **[sich** dat**] in die ~[n] machen** to wet oneself; **tote ~** sl boring as hell; **jd hat die ~n [gestrichen] voll** sl sb is scared shitless

Hosenanzug m pantsuit

Hosenschlitz m fly; **dein ~ ist offen!** your fly is down!

Hosentasche f pants pocket

Hosenträger pl suspenders npl

Hospital <-s, -e> [hɔs·pi·'ta:l] nt dial hospital

Hostie <-, -n> ['hɔs·tjə] f REL host

Hotel <-s, -s> [ho·'tɛl] nt hotel

Hotelfachschule f school of hotel management

Hotelier <-s, -s> [ho·tə·'lje:] m hotelier

Hotellerie <-> [ho·tɛ·lə·'ri:] f kein pl hospitality

HTML <-, -> [ha:·te:·?ɛm·'?ɛl] nt o f kein pl COMPUT Abk von **hypertext markup language** HTML

Hubraum m cubic capacity

hübsch [hʏpʃ] adj **1.** (Aussehen) pretty; **na, ihr zwei H~en?** fam well, my two lovelies?; **sich** akk **~ machen** to get all dressed up **2.** fam (beträchtlich) real, pretty; **ein ~es Sümmchen** a pretty penny **3.** fam (sehr angenehm) nice and ...; **das wirst du ~ bleiben lassen** you'll do no such thing

Hubschrauber <-s, -> m helicopter

huckepack ['hʊ·kə·pak] adv piggyback; **jdn ~ nehmen** to give sb a piggyback ride

Huf <-[e]s, -e> [hu:f] m hoof

Hufeisen nt horseshoe

Hüfte <-, -n> ['hʏf·tə] f **1.** (Körperpartie) hip **2.** kein pl KOCH (Fleischstück) inside round; (vom Rind) top sirloin

Hüftgelenk nt hip joint

Hügel <-s, -> ['hy:·gl] m hill; (Erdhaufen) mound

hüg(e)lig ['hy:·g(ə)·lɪç] adj hilly; **eine ~e Landschaft** rolling countryside

Huhn <-[e]s, Hühner> [hu:n] nt **1.** (Haushuhn) hen, chicken; **frei laufende Hühner** free-range chickens **2.** (Hühnerfleisch) chicken **3.** (Person) **dummes ~!** pej fam stupid idiot!; **ein verrücktes ~** a nutcase ▶ **da lachen ja die Hühner** fam you must be joking

Hühnchen <-s, -> ['hy:n·çən] nt dim von **Huhn** spring chicken ▶ **mit jdm ein ~ zu rupfen haben** fam to have a bone to pick with sb

Hühnerauge nt corn

Hühnerei nt chicken egg

Hühnerstall m hencoop

Hühnerstange f chicken roost

Hülle <-, -n> ['hʏl·lə] f cover ► **in ~ und Fülle** geh in abundance

hüllenlos adj naked, in one's birthday suit hum

Hülse <-, -n> ['hʏl·zə] f **1.** BOT (Schote) pod **2.** (röhrenförmige Hülle) capsule

Hülsenfrucht ['hʏl·zn̩-] f meist pl legume

human [hu·'maːn] adj **1.** (menschenwürdig) humane; (Strafe) lenient **2.** (Chef, Lehrer) considerate (**gegenüber** +dat toward) **3.** (Menschen betreffend) human

humanitär [hu·ma·ni·'tɛːɐ̯] adj humanitarian

Hummel <-, -n> ['hʊ·ml̩] f bumblebee ► **~n im Hintern haben** fam to have ants in one's pants

Hummer <-s, -> ['hʊ·mɐ] m lobster

Humor <-s, -e> [hu·'moːɐ̯] m pl selten **1.** (Laune) good humor, cheerfulness **2.** (Witz, Wesensart) [sense of] humor; **etw mit ~ nehmen** to take sth good-humoredly; [**einen Sinn für**] **~ haben** to have a sense of humor

humorlos adj humorless

humorvoll adj humorous

humpeln ['hʊm·pl̩n] vi sein o haben to limp

Humus ['huː·mʊs] m kein pl humus

Hund <-[e]s, -e> [hʊnt] m **1.** (Tier) dog; (Jagdhund) hound; „**Vorsicht**,] **bissiger ~!**" "beware of dog!" **2.** (Mensch) swine; **ein armer ~ sein** fam to be a poor soul; [**du**] **gemeiner ~** [you] dirty dog ► **da liegt der ~ begraben** fam that's the crux of the matter; **~e, die bellen, beißen nicht** prov sb's bark is worse than their bite; **bekannt sein wie ein bunter ~** fam to be known far and wide; **das ist ja ein dicker ~** sl that is absolutely outrageous

hundeelend ['hʊn·də·'ʔeːlɛnt] adj fam jd **fühlt sich** akk **~** sb feels awful

Hundehütte f doghouse

Hundeleine f dog leash

hundemüde ['hʊn·də·'myː·də] adj pred

fam dog-tired

hundert ['hʊn·dɐt] adj **1.** (Zahl) [a [o one]] hundred **2.** fam (sehr viele) a hundred, hundreds **3.** pl, auch großgeschrieben (viele hundert) hundreds pl; s. a. **Hundert¹ 2**

Hundert¹ <-s, -e> ['hʊn·dɐt] nt **1.** (Einheit von 100) hundred; **mehrere ~** several hundred **2.** pl, auch kleingeschrieben (viele hundert) hundreds pl; **einige/viele ~e ...** a few/ several hundred ...; **~e von ...** hundreds of ...; **in die ~e gehen** fam (Kosten, Schaden) to run into the hundreds; **~e und aber ~e** hundreds upon hundreds

Hundert² <-, -en> ['hʊn·dɐt] f [one [o a]] hundred

hundertprozentig ['hʊn·dɐt·pro·tsɛn·tɪç] **I.** adj **1.** (100 % umfassend) one hundred percent; (Alkohol) pure **2.** fam (typisch) through and through; **er ist ein ~er Bayer** he's a Bavarian through and through **II.** adv fam absolutely, completely; **das weiß ich ~** I know that for certain; **sich** dat **~ sicher sein** to be absolutely sure

Hundertstel <-s, -> ['hʊn·dɐts·tl̩] nt o schweiz m hundredth

Hündin ['hʏn·dɪn] f bitch

Hüne <-n, -n> ['hyː·nə] m giant

hünenhaft adj gigantic

Hunger <-s> ['hʊŋɐ] m kein pl **1.** (Hungergefühl) hunger; **~ bekommen/haben** to get/be hungry; **~ auf etw** akk **haben** to feel like [eating] sth; **~ leiden** to starve; **~ wie ein Bär haben** to be [as] hungry as a bear **2.** (Hungersnot) famine **3.** (großes Verlangen) jds **~ nach etw** dat sb's thirst for sth ► **~ ist der beste Koch** prov hunger is the best sauce prov

Hungerhilfe f kein pl famine relief

Hungerlohn m pej pittance; **für einen ~ arbeiten** to work for peanuts

hungern vi **1.** (Hunger leiden) to starve; fam (fasten) to fast **2.** fig (verlangen) to hunger (**nach** +dat for)

Hungersnot f famine

Hungerstreik m hunger strike; **in den ~ treten** to go on a hunger strike

hungrig ['hʊŋ·rɪç] adj hungry; **etw**

macht ~ sth works up an appetite

Hupe <-, -n> ['hu:·pə] *f* horn; **auf die ~ drücken** to honk the horn

hupen ['hu:·pn̩] *vi* to honk [the horn]

hüpfen ['hyp·fn̩] *vi sein* to hop; (*Lamm, Zicklein*) to frolic; (*Ball*) to bounce; **vor Freude ~** to jump for joy

Hürde <-, -n> ['hyr·də] *f* SPORT hurdle; **110 Meter ~n laufen** to run the 110-meter hurdles ▸ **eine ~ nehmen** to overcome an obstacle

Hürdenlauf *m* hurdling, hurdles *npl*

Hure <-, -n> ['hu:·rə] *f* whore

huschen ['hʊ·ʃn̩] *vi sein* to dart, to flit; (*Maus*) to scurry; (*Licht*) to flash; **ein Lächeln huschte über ihr Gesicht** a smile flitted across her face

husten ['hu:s·tn̩] **I.** *vi* to cough **II.** *vt* (*auswerfen*) **Blut/Schleim ~** to cough up blood/mucus

Husten <-s> ['hu:s·tn̩] *m kein pl* cough

Hustenbonbon *m o nt* cough drop

Hustenreiz *m* tickly throat

Hustensaft *m* cough syrup

Hut¹ <-[e]s, Hüte> [hu:t] *m* **1.** (*Kopfbedeckung*) hat; **den ~ abnehmen/aufsetzen** to take off/put on one's hat **2.** BOT (*von Pilzen*) cap ▸ **~ ab [vor jdm]!** *fam* hats off to sb!; **etw unter einen ~ bringen** to reconcile sth; (*Termine*) to fit in *sep* sth; **mit etw dat nichts am ~ haben** *fam* to not really have anything in common with sth; **vor jdm/etw den ~ ziehen** to take one's hat off to sb/sth

Hut² <-> [hu:t] *f* **auf der ~ [vor etw dat] sein** to be on one's guard [against sth]

hüten ['hy:·tn̩] **I.** *vt* (*Schafe*) to tend **II.** *vr* (*sich in Acht nehmen*) **sich** *akk* **vor etw** *dat* **~** to be on one's guard against sth; **sich** *akk* **~, etw zu tun** to take care not to do sth

Hütte <-, -n> ['hy·tə] *f* **1.** (*kleines Haus*) hut; (*ärmlich*) shack **2.** (*Berghütte*) [mountain] hut; (*Holzhütte*) cabin

Hüttenkäse *m* cottage cheese

Hyäne <-, -n> ['hyɛ·nə] *f* hyena

Hyazinthe <-, -n> [hy̆a·ˈtsɪn·tə] *f* hyacinth

Hydrant <-en, -en> [hy·ˈdrant] *m* hydrant

hydraulisch [hy·ˈdrau·lɪʃ] *adj* hydraulic

Hydrokultur *f* hydroponics + *sing vb spec*

Hygiene <-> [hy·ˈgie̯·nə] *f kein pl* hygiene

hygienisch [hy·ˈgie̯·nɪʃ] *adj* hygienic

Hymne <-, -n> ['hʏm·nə] *f* hymn

Hyperaktivität [hype·ak·ti·vi·ˈtɛt] *f* hyperactivity

Hypnose <-, -n> [hʏp·ˈno:·zə] *f* hypnosis; **jdn in ~ versetzen** to hypnotize sb

hypnotisieren* *vt* to hypnotize

Hypothek <-, -en> [hy·po·ˈte:k] *f* mortgage

Hypothese <-, -n> [hy·po·ˈte:·zə] *f* hypothesis; **eine ~ aufstellen/widerlegen** to advance/refute a hypothesis

hypothetisch [hy·po·ˈte:·tɪʃ] *adj* hypothetical

Hysterie <-, -n> [hʏs·te·ˈri:] *f* hysteria

hysterisch [hʏs·ˈte:·rɪʃ] *adj* hysterical

I

I, i <-, -> [i:] *nt* I, i; **~ wie Ida** I as in India

i [i:] *interj fam* (*Ausdruck von Ablehnung, Ekel*) ugh; **~, wie ekelig** yuck, how disgusting ▸ **~ wo!** *dial* no way! *fam*

IC <-s, -s> [i:·ˈtse:] *m Abk von* **Intercity**

ICE <-s, -s> [i:·tse:·ˈʔe:] *m Abk von* **Intercity Express** *a high-speed train*

ich <*gen* meiner, *dat* mir, *akk* mich> ['ɪç] *pron pers* I, me; **~ bin/war es** it's/it was me; **~ nicht!** not me!; **~ selbst** I myself

Ich <-[s], -s> ['ɪç] *nt* **1.** (*das Selbst*) self **2.** PSYCH (*Ego*) ego; **jds anderes ~** sb's alter ego; **jds besseres ~** sb's better self

ideal [ide·ˈa:l] *adj* ideal

Ideal <-s, -e> [ide·ˈa:l] *nt* ideal

Idee <-, -n> [i'de:] *f* **1.** (*Einfall, Vorstellung*) idea; **eine fixe ~** an obsession; **keine ~ haben** to have no idea; **jdn auf eine ~ bringen** to give sb an idea; **jdn auf andere ~n bringen** to take sb's mind off of sth/it; **auf eine ~ kommen**

to get an idea **2.** *fam (ein wenig)* **keine ~ besser sein** to be not one bit better; **eine ~ ...** a little bit ...

identifizieren * [iden·ti·fi·ˈtsiː·rən] **I.** *vt* to identify **II.** *vr* **sich** *akk* **mit jdm/etw ~** to identify with sb/sth

identisch [iˈdɛn·tɪʃ] *adj* identical (**mit** +*dat* to)

Ideologie <-, -n> [ideo·lo·ˈgiː] *f* ideology

idiomatisch [idjo·ˈmaː·tɪʃ] *adj* idiomatic

Idiot(in) <-en, -en> [iˈdi̯·oːt] *m(f) pej fam* idiot

idiotisch [iˈdi̯o·tɪʃ] *adj fam* idiotic

Idol <-s, -e> [iˈdoːl] *nt* idol

idyllisch [iˈdʏ·lɪʃ] *adj* idyllic

Igel <-s, -> [ˈiː·gl̩] *m* hedgehog

igitt(igitt) [iˈgɪt·(igɪt)] *interj* ugh, yuck

Ignoranz <-> [ɪg·no·ˈrants] *f kein pl pej geh* ignorance

ignorieren * [ɪg·no·ˈriː·rən] *vt* to ignore

ihm [iːm] *pron pers dat von* **er, es 1.** *(dem Genannten)* him; **es geht ~ nicht gut** he's not feeling very well; *nach Präpositionen* him; **ich war gestern bei ~** I was at his place yesterday; **das ist ein Freund von ~** that's a friend of his **2.** *bei Tieren und Dingen (dem genannten Tier oder Ding)* it; *(bei Haustieren)* him

ihn [iːn] *pron pers akk von* **er 1.** *(den Genannten)* him **2.** *bei Tieren und Dingen (das genannte Tier oder Ding)* it; *(bei Haustieren)* him

ihnen [ˈiː·nən] *pron pers dat pl von* **sie** them; *nach Präpositionen* them; **ich war die ganze Zeit bei ~** I was at their place the whole time

Ihnen [ˈiː·nən] *pron pers dat sing o pl von* **Sie** you; *nach Präpositionen* you

ihr[1] *<gen* euer, *dat* euch, *akk* euch*>* [ˈiːɐ̯] *pron pers* **2.** *pers pl nomin von* **sie** you [all]

ihr[2] [ˈiːɐ̯] *pron pers dat sing von* **sie** *(der Genannten)* her

ihr[3] [ˈiːɐ̯] *pron poss, adjektivisch* **1.** *sing* her **2.** *pl* their

ihre(r, s) *pron poss, substantivisch* **1.** *sing (dieser weiblichen Person)* her; **das ist nicht seine Aufgabe, sondern ~** he's not responsible for doing that, she

is; **der/die/das ~** hers **2.** *pl* theirs

Ihre(r, s)[1] *pron poss, substantivisch, auf „Sie" bezüglich* **1.** *sing* your; **der/die/das ~** yours **2.** *pl* your; **der/die/das ~** yours **3.** *sing und pl (Angehörige)* **die ~n** your loved ones **4.** *sing und pl (Eigentum)* **das ~** yours; **Sie haben alle das ~ getan** you have all done your part

Ihre(r, s)[2] *pron poss, substantivisch, auf „sie" sing bezüglich* **1.** *(Angehörige)* **der/[die] ~[n]** her loved one[s] **2.** *(Eigentum)* **das ~** hers

Ihre(r, s)[3] *pron poss, substantivisch, auf „sie" pl bezüglich* **1.** *(Angehörige)* **der/[die] ~[n]** their loved ones **2.** *(Eigentum)* **das ~** their things

ihrer *pron pers gen von* **sie 1.** *sing geh* her **2.** *pl* them

Ihrer *pron pers geh gen von* **Sie 1.** *sing [of] you* **2.** *pl* them

ihresgleichen [ˈiː·rəs·ˈglai·çn̩] *pron* **1.** *sing* people *npl* like her; *pej (Leute wie sie)* her [own] kind **2.** *pl* people like them; *pej (Leute wie sie)* their [own] kind

Ihresgleichen [ˈiː·rəs·ˈglai·çn̩] *pron* **1.** *sing* people like you **2.** *pl pej (Leute wie Sie)* your [own] kind; **ich kenne [Sie und] ~** I know your kind!

illegal [ˈɪl·le·gaːl] *adj* illegal

Illusion <-, -en> [ɪlu·ˈzi̯oːn] *f* illusion; **sich** *akk* **der ~ hingeben, [dass]** to be under the illusion [that]; **sich** *dat* **keine ~en machen** to not have any illusions

illusorisch [ɪlu·ˈzoː·rɪʃ] *adj* **1.** *(trügerisch)* illusory **2.** *(zwecklos)* futile

Illustration <-, -en> [ɪlus·tra·ˈtsi̯oːn] *f* illustration

illustrieren * [ɪlus·ˈtriː·rən] *vt* to illustrate

Illustrierte <-n, -n> *f* magazine

Iltis <-ses, -se> [ˈɪl·tɪs] *m* polecat

im [ˈɪm] = **in dem 1.** *(örtlich)* in the; **~ Bett/Haus** in bed/the house; **~ Januar** in January **2.** *(zeitlich)* while; **~ Bau sein** to be under construction; **~ Begriff sein, etw zu tun** to be about to do sth; **etw ist ~ Kommen** sth is coming

Image <-[s], -s> [ˈɪm·ɪtʃ] *nt* image

Imbiss [RR] <-es, -e> [ˈɪm·bɪs], **Imbiß** [ALT]

<-sses, -sse> *m* **1.** (*kleine Mahlzeit*) snack **2.** *fam* s. **Imbissstube**

Imbissstube RR *f* snack bar

imitieren * [imi·'tiː·rən] *vt* to imitate sth; (*im Kabarett*) to impersonate

Imker(in) <-s, -> ['ɪm·kɐ] *m(f)* beekeeper

immatrikulieren * [ɪma·tri·ku·'liː·rən] *vr* **sich** *akk* ~ to matriculate

immer ['ɪmɐ] **I.** *adv* **1.** (*ständig, jedes Mal*) always, all the time; **für** ~ forever; ~ **und ewig** for ever and ever; ~ **wenn** every time; **wie** ~ as usual; ~ **mit der Ruhe** take it easy; **etw** ~ **wieder tun** to keep on doing sth **2.** (*zunehmend*) increasingly; ~ **häufiger** more and more frequently; ~ **mehr** more and more **3.** *fam* (*jeweils*) each; ~ **am vierten Tag** every fourth day **II.** *part* [*nur*] ~ **her damit!** *fam* hand it/them over!; ~ **mal** *fam* now and again; ~ **noch** still; ~ **noch nicht** still not; **wann/was/wer/ wie/wo** [**auch**] ~ whenever/whatever/ whoever/however/wherever

immerhin ['ɪmɐ·'hɪn] *adv* **1.** (*wenigstens*) at least **2.** (*schließlich*) after all **3.** (*allerdings, trotz allem*) all the same

Immigrant(in) <-en, -en> [ɪmi·'grant] *m(f)* immigrant

Immobilie <-, -n> [ɪmo·'biː·li̯ə] *f meist pl* real estate; ~**n** property

Immobilienmakler(in) *m(f)* real estate agent

immun [ɪ'muːn] *adj a. fig* immune (**gegen** +*akk* to)

Immunsystem *nt* immune system

Imperativ <-s, -e> ['ɪm·pe·ra·tiːf] *m* LING imperative [form] *spec*

Imperfekt <-s, -e> ['ɪm·pɛr·fɛkt] *nt* imperfect [tense] *spec*

Imperialismus <-, *selten* -lismen> [ɪm·pe·ri̯a·'lɪs·mʊs] *m* imperialism

impfen ['ɪm·pfn̩] *vt* to vaccinate (**gegen** +*akk* against)

Impfpass RR *m* vaccination card

Impfstoff *m* vaccine

Impfung <-, -en> *f* vaccination

implantieren [ɪm·plan·'tiː·rən] *vt* [**jdm**] **etw** ~ to implant sth [into sb]

imponieren * [ɪm·po·'niː·rən] *vi* to impress

imponierend *adj* impressive

Import <-[e]s, -e> [ɪm·'pɔrt] *m* import

importieren * [ɪm·pɔr·'tiː·rən] *vt* to import

imprägnieren * [ɪm·prɛg·'niː·rən] *vt* (*wasserabweisend machen*) to waterproof

Impressionismus <-> [ɪm·prɛ·si̯o·'nɪs·mʊs] *m* Impressionism

impressionistisch *adj* Impressionist

improvisieren * [ɪm·pro·vi·'ziː·rən] *vt, vi* to improvise

impulsiv [ɪm·pʊl·'ziːf] *adj* impulsive

imstande, im Stande [ɪm·'ʃtan·də] *adj pred* **zu etw** *dat* ~ **sein** to be capable of doing sth; ~ **sein, etw zu tun** to be able to do sth; **zu allem** ~ **sein** to be capable of anything; **zu nichts mehr** ~ **sein** to be exhausted

in¹ ['ɪn] *präp* **1.** +*dat* (*darin befindlich*) in; **bist du schon mal** ~ **New York gewesen?** have you ever been to New York?; **ich arbeite seit einem Jahr** ~ **dieser Firma** I've been working for this company for a year **2.** +*akk* (*hin zu einem Ziel*) into; ~ **die Kirche/ Schule gehen** to go to church/school **3.** +*dat* (*innerhalb von*) in; ~ **diesem Augenblick** at the moment; ~ **diesem Jahr/Monat/Sommer** this year/ month/summer; ~ **einem Jahr bin ich 18** in a year I'll be 18 **4.** +*akk* (*bis zu einer Zeit*) until **5.** +*dat* (*Verweis auf ein Objekt*) in; **er ist Fachmann** ~ **seinem Beruf** he is an expert in his field; **sich** *akk* ~ **jdm täuschen** to be wrong about sb **6.** +*dat* (*auf eine Art und Weise*) in; ~ **Wirklichkeit** in reality

in² ['ɪn] *adj fam* in *fam*; ~ **sein** to be in

inbegriffen ['ɪn·bə·grɪ·fn̩] *adj pred* inclusive; **in etw** *dat* ~ **sein** to be included in sth

indem [ɪn·'deːm] *konj* (*dadurch, dass*) by

Inder(in) <-s, -> ['ɪn·dɐ] *m(f)* Indian; *s. a.* **Deutsche(r)**

indessen [ɪn·'dɛ·sn̩] **I.** *adv* **1.** (*inzwischen*) in the meantime **2.** (*dagegen*) however **II.** *konj geh* while

Indianer(in) <-s, -> [ɪn·'di̯aː·nɐ] *m(f)* Indian *esp pej*, Native American

Indien <-s> ['ɪn·di̯ən] *nt* India; *s. a.* **Deutschland**

Indikativ <-s, -e> ['ɪn·di·ka·tiːf] *m* indicative [mood] *spec*

indirekt ['ɪn·di·rɛkt] *adj* indirect

indisch ['ɪn·dɪʃ] *adj* Indian; *s. a.* **deutsch**

individuell [ɪn·di·vi·ˈdu̯·ɛl] *adj* individual

Individuum <-s, -duen> [ɪn·di·ˈviː·du·ʊm] *nt* individual

Indiz <-es, -ien> [ɪn·ˈdiːts] *nt* 1. JUR piece of circumstantial evidence 2. (*Anzeichen*) **ein ~ für etw** *akk* **sein** to be a sign of sth

Indonesien <-s> [ɪn·do·ˈneː·zi̯·ən] *nt* Indonesia; *s. a.* **Deutschland**

indonesisch [ɪn·do·ˈneː·zɪʃ] *adj* Indonesian; *s. a.* **deutsch**

Industrie <-, -n> [ɪn·dʊs·ˈtriː] *f* industry *no art*

Industriegebiet *nt* industrial area

Industrie- und Handelskammer *f* Chamber of Commerce

Industriezweig *m* branch of industry

ineinander [ɪn·ʔai̯·ˈnan·dɐ] *adv* in each other; **~ verliebt sein** to be in love with each other; **~ übergehen** to merge

ineinander|greifen *vi irreg* to mesh

Infektion <-, -en> [ɪn·fɛk·ˈtsi̯oːn] *f* 1. (*Ansteckung*) infection 2. *fam* (*Entzündung*) inflammation

Infinitiv <-s, -e> ['ɪn·fi·ni·tiːf] *m* infinitive *spec*

infizieren* [ɪn·fi·ˈtsiː·rən] I. *vt* to infect II. *vr* **sich** *akk* **[an etw** *dat***/bei jdm] ~** to be infected [by sth/sb]

Inflation <-, -en> [ɪn·fla·ˈtsi̯oːn] *f* 1. ÖKON inflation 2. (*übermäßig häufiges Auftreten*) proliferation

infolge [ɪn·ˈfɔl·gə] I. *präp* +*gen* owing to II. *adv* **~ von etw** *dat* as a result of sth

infolgedessen [ɪn·fɔl·gə·ˈdɛ·sn̩] *adv* consequently

Informatik <-> [ɪn·fɔr·ˈmaː·tɪk] *f kein pl* computer science

Informatiker(in) <-s, -> [ɪn·fɔr·ˈmaː·ti·kɐ] *m(f)* computer specialist

Information <-, -en> [ɪn·fɔr·ma·ˈtsi̯oːn] *f* 1. (*Mitteilung, Hinweis*) (a piece of) information 2. (*das Informieren*) informing; **zu Ihrer ~** for your information 3. (*Informationsstand*) information desk

informativ [ɪn·fɔr·ma·ˈtiːf] I. *adj* infor-mative II. *adv* in an informative manner *pred*

informieren* [ɪn·fɔr·ˈmiː·rən] I. *vt* to inform (**über** +*akk* about); **jd ist gut informiert** sb is well-informed II. *vr* **sich** *akk* **[über etw** *akk***] ~** to find out [about sth]

Ingenieur(in) <-s, -e> [ɪn·ʒe·ˈni̯øːɐ̯] *m(f)* engineer

Ingwer <-s> ['ɪŋ·vɐ] *m kein pl* ginger

Inhaber(in) <-s, -> ['ɪn·haː·bɐ] *m(f)* 1. (*Besitzer*) owner 2. (*Halter*) holder; (*von Scheck*) bearer

Inhalt <-[e]s, -e> ['ɪn·halt] *m* 1. (*enthaltene Gegenstände*) contents *pl* 2. (*Sinngehalt*) content 3. (*wesentliche Bedeutung*) meaning 4. MATH (*Flächeninhalt*) area; (*Volumen*) volume

Inhaltsangabe *f* summary; (*von Buch, Film, Theaterstück*) synopsis

Inhaltsverzeichnis *nt* table of contents *npl*

Initiative <-, -en> [in·itsi̯a·ˈtiː·və] *f* 1. (*erster Anstoß*) initiative; **aus eigener ~** on one's own initiative; **[in etw** *dat***] die ~ ergreifen** to take the initiative [in sth] 2. *kein pl* (*Unternehmungsgeist*) drive 3. (*Bürgerinitiative*) pressure group 4. *schweiz* (*Volksbegehren*) demand for a referendum

Injektion <-, -en> [ɪn·jɛk·ˈtsi̯oːn] *f* injection

inklusive [ɪn·klu·ˈziː·və] I. *präp* +*gen* including II. *adv* **vom 25. bis zum 28. ~** from 25th to 28th inclusive

Inkrafttreten <-s> *nt kein pl* coming into effect

Inlandflug *m* domestic flight

innen ['ɪnən] *adv* 1. (*im Inneren*) on the inside; **~ und außen** [on the] inside and outside; **nach ~** inside; **die Tür geht nach ~ auf** the door opens inwards; **von ~** from the inside 2. (*auf der Innenseite*) on the inside 3. *bes öster* (*drinnen*) inside

Innendienst *m* office work

Innenminister(in) *m(f)* Secretary of the Interior, Interior Secretary

Innenministerium *nt* Department of the Interior

Innenpolitik *f* domestic policy

Innenraum m interior

Innenspiegel m AUTO rearview mirror

Innenstadt f downtown

innere(r, s) ['ɪnə·rə] adj 1. (Tasche) inside 2. (a. med, anat) inner, internal

Innere(s) ['ɪnə·rə] nt 1. (innerer Teil) inside 2. PSYCH **tief in seinem ~n war ihm klar, dass ...** deep down, he knew that ...

Innereien [ɪnə·'rai·ən] pl KOCHK innards npl

innerhalb ['ɪnə·halp] I. präp +gen 1. (räumlich) inside 2. (zeitlich) within II. adv ~ **von etw** dat within sth

innerlich ['ɪnə·lɪç] I. adj 1. MED internal 2. PSYCH inner II. adv 1. (im Inneren des Körpers) internally 2. PSYCH inwardly; ~ **war er sehr aufgewühlt** he was in inner turmoil

innerste(s) ['ɪnɐs·tə(s)] nt core being; **tief in ihrem ~n wusste sie ...** deep down, she knew ...

innig ['ɪnɪç] I. adj 1. (tief empfunden) deep; (Dank) heartfelt 2. (Beziehung) intimate II. adv deeply

Innovation <-, -en> [ɪno·va·'tsjo:n] f innovation

innovativ [ɪno·va·'ti:f] adj innovative

Innung <-, -en> ['ɪn·ʊŋ] f guild

inoffiziell adj unofficial

in puncto [ɪn 'pʊŋk·to] adv fam concerning

ins ['ɪns] = **in das** s. **in**

Insasse, Insassin <-n, -n> ['ɪn·za·sə] m, f (eines Gefängnisses, Lagers) inmate

insbesondere [ɪns·bə·'zɔn·də·rə] adv especially

Insekt <-[e]s, -en> [ɪn·'zɛkt] nt insect

Insektenstich m insect sting

Insel <-, -n> ['ɪn·zl] f island

Inserat <-[e]s, -e> [ɪn·ze·'ra:t] nt advertisement

inserieren * [ɪn·ze·'ri:·rən] vt, vi to advertise

insgeheim [ɪns·gə·'haim] adv secretly

insgesamt [ɪns·gə·'zamt] adv 1. (alles zusammen) altogether 2. (im Großen und Ganzen) on the whole

insofern [ɪn·zo·'fɛrn, ɪn·'zo:·fɛrn] I. adv in this respect; ~ **...**, **als** in that II. konj

österr (vorausgesetzt, dass) if; ~ **als** insofar as

insoweit [ɪn·'zo·vait] adv, konj s. **insofern**

Inspektion <-, -en> [ɪn·spɛk·'tsjo:n] f 1. (technische Wartung) service 2. (Überprüfung) inspection

Inspektor, Inspektorin <-s, -en> [ɪn·'spɛk·to:g] m, f 1. ADMIN executive officer; (Kriminalpolizei) inspector 2. (Prüfer) supervisor

Installateur(in) <-s, -e> [ɪn·sta·la·'tø:g] m(f) 1. (Elektroinstallateur) electrician 2. (Klempner) plumber

installieren * [ɪn·sta·'li:·rən] vt 1. TECH (einbauen) **[jdm]** etw ~ to install sth [for sb] 2. COMPUT (einprogrammieren) **[jdm]** etw **[auf etw** akk] ~ to install sth [for sb] [on sth]

instand, in Stand [ɪn·'ʃtant] adj in working order; **etw ~ halten** to keep sth in good condition; **etw ~ setzen** to repair sth

inständig ['ɪn·ʃtɛn·dɪç] I. adj (Bitte etc.) urgent II. adv urgently; ~ **um etw** akk **bitten** to beg for sth

Instanz <-, -en> [ɪn·'stants] f 1. ADMIN authority 2. (Stufe eines Gerichtsverfahrens) **in erster/zweiter/oberster ~** trial court/appellate court/supreme court

Instinkt <-[e]s, -e> [ɪn·'stɪŋkt] m instinct

instinktiv [ɪn·stɪŋk·'ti:f] adj instinctive

Institut <-[e]s, -e> [ɪn·sti·'tu:t] nt institute

Institution <-, -en> [ɪn·sti·tu·'tsjo:n] f institution

Instrument <-[e]s, -e> [ɪn·stru·'mɛnt] nt 1. MUS instrument; (Gerät für wissenschaftliche Zwecke) instrument 2. a. fig geh (Werkzeug) tool

Insulin <-s> [ɪn·zu·'li:n] nt kein pl insulin

inszenieren * [ɪns·tse·'ni:·rən] vt 1. (dramaturgisch gestalten) to stage 2. pej to stage-manage

Inszenierung <-, -en> f 1. FILM, MUS, THEAT production 2. pej (Bewerkstelligung) engineering

intakt [ɪn·'takt] adj 1. (unversehrt) in-

tact **2.** (*voll funktionsfähig*) in working order

Integration <-, -en> [ɪn·te·gra·ˈtsjoːn] *f* integration

integrieren * [ɪn·te·ˈgriː·rən] **I.** *vt* (*eingliedern*) to integrate (**in** +*akk* into) **II.** *vr* (*sich einfügen*) **sich** *akk* [**in etw** *akk*] ~ to become integrated [into sth]

Intellekt <-[e]s> [ɪn·te·ˈlɛkt] *m kein pl* intellect

intellektuell [ɪn·te·lɛk·ˈtu̯·ɛl] *adj* intellectual

Intellektuelle(r) *f(m)* intellectual

intelligent [ɪn·tɛ·li·ˈɡɛnt] *adj* intelligent, smart

Intelligenz <-, -en> [ɪn·tɛ·li·ˈɡɛnts] *f kein pl* intelligence

Intensität <-, *selten* -en> [ɪn·tɛn·zi·ˈtɛːt] *f* intensity

intensiv [ɪn·tɛn·ˈziːf] **I.** *adj* **1.** (*gründlich*) intensive **2.** (*eindringlich, durchdringend: Duft, Schmerz*) intense **II.** *adv* **1.** (*gründlich*) intensively; ~ **bemüht sein, etw zu tun** to make intense efforts to do sth **2.** (*eindringlich, durchdringend*) strongly

intensivieren * [ɪn·tɛn·zi·ˈviː·rən] *vt* to intensify

Intensivkurs *m* intensive course

Intensivstation *f* intensive care unit

interaktiv [ɪn·tɐ·ʔak·ˈtiːf] *adj* interactive

Intercity <-s, -s> [ɪn·tɐ·ˈsɪ·ti] *m* intercity [train]

interessant [ɪn·tə·rɛ·ˈsant] **I.** *adj* **1.** (*Interesse erweckend*) interesting; **sich** *akk* [**bei jdm**] ~ **machen** to attract [sb's] attention **2.** (*Angebot, Gehalt*) attractive **II.** *adv* interestingly; **der Vorschlag hört sich ~ an** the proposal sounds interesting

Interesse <-s, -n> [ɪn·tə·ˈrɛ·sə] *nt* **1.** *kein pl* (*Aufmerksamkeit*) interest; ~ [**an jdm/etw**] **haben** to be interested [in sb/sth]; **hätten Sie ~ daran, für uns tätig zu werden?** would you be interested in working for us? **2.** *pl* (*Neigungen*) interests *pl*; **aus** ~ out of interest **3.** *pl* (*Belange*) interests *pl* **4.** (*Nutzen*) interest; [**für jdn**] **von** ~ **sein** to be of interest [to sb]; **in jds** ~ **liegen** to be in sb's interest

Interessengemeinschaft *f* community of interests

Interessent(in) <-en, -en> [ɪn·tə·rɛ·ˈsɛnt] *m(f)* **1.** (*an einer Teilnahme Interessierter*) interested party **2.** (*an einem Kauf Interessierter*) potential buyer

interessieren * [ɪn·tə·rɛ·ˈsiː·rən] **I.** *vt* to interest **II.** *vr* **sich** *akk* **für jdn/etw** ~ to be interested in sb/sth

Internat <-[e]s, -e> [ɪn·tɐ·ˈnaːt] *nt* boarding school

international [ɪn·tɐ·na·tsjo·ˈnaːl] *adj* international

Internet <-s> [ˈɪntɐ·nɛt] *nt kein pl* Internet; **im ~ surfen** to surf the Internet

Internist(in) <-en, -en> [ɪn·tɐ·ˈnɪst] *m(f)* internist

interpretieren * [ɪn·tɐ·pre·ˈtiː·rən] *vt* to interpret

Interpunktion <-> [ɪn·tɐ·pʊŋk·ˈtsjoːn] *f kein pl* punctuation

Interview <-s, -s> [ˈɪn·tɐ·vjuː] *nt* interview

interviewen * [ɪn·tɐ·ˈvjuː·ən] *vt* **1.** (*durch ein Interview befragen*) **jdn** [**zu etw** *dat*] ~ to interview sb [about sth]; **sich** *akk* [**von jdm**] ~ **lassen** to give [sb] an interview **2.** *hum fam* (*befragen*) **jdn** ~ [**ob/wann/wo etc.**] to consult sb about [whether/when/where, etc.]

intim [ɪn·ˈtiːm] *adj* **1.** (*innig, persönlich*) intimate; (*Bekannter, Freund*) close **2.** (*sexuell liiert*) **mit jdm** ~ **sein/werden** to be/become intimate with sb

Intimität <-, -en> [ɪn·ti·mi·ˈtɛːt] *f* intimacy

Intimsphäre *f* private life

intolerant [ˈɪn·to·le·rant] *adj* intolerant

intransitiv [ˈɪn·tran·zi·tiːf] *adj* intransitive

Intrige <-, -n> [ɪn·ˈtriː·ɡə] *f* conspiracy

introvertiert [ɪn·tro·vɛr·ˈtiːɐt] *adj* introverted

invalide [ɪn·va·ˈliː·də] *adj* invalid

Invalide, Invalidin <-n, -n> [ɪn·va·ˈliː·də] *m, f* invalid

Invasion <-, -en> [ɪn·va·ˈzjoːn] *f* invasion

Inventar <-s, -e> [ɪn·vɛn·ˈtaːɐ] *nt* inventory

Inventur <-, -en> [ɪn·vɛn·ˈtuːɐ] *f* inven

tory; ~ **machen** to take inventory

nvestieren* [ɪn·vɛs·ˈtiː·rən] *vt* to invest

nvestition <-, -en> [ɪn·vɛs·tɪ·ˈtsjoːn] *f* investment

nwiefern [ɪn·viˈfɛrn] *adv* in what way

nzucht [ˈɪn·tsʊxt] *f* inbreeding

nzwischen [ɪn·ˈtsvɪ·ʃn] *adv* in the meantime

rak <-s> [iˈraːk] *m* [**der**] ~ Iraq; *s. a.* **Deutschland**

raker(in) <-s, -> [iˈraː·ke] *m(f)* Iraqi; *s. a.* **Deutsche(r)**

ran <-s> [iˈraːn] *m* **der** ~ Iran; *s. a.* **Deutschland**

raner(in) <-s, -> [iˈraː·ne] *m(f)* Iranian; *s. a.* **Deutsche(r)**

re, Irin <-n, -n> [ˈiːrə] *m, f* Irishman *masc*, Irishwoman *fem*; **die** ~**n** the Irish; [**ein**] ~ **sein** to be Irish; *s. a.* **Deutsche(r)**

rgend [ˈɪr·gn̩t] *adv* at all; **wenn** ~ **möglich** if at all possible; "**wer war am Apparat?**" – "**ach, wieder** ~ **so ein Spinner!**" "who was that on the phone?" — "oh, some lunatic again"

rgendein [ˈɪr·gn̩t·ˈʔain], **irgendeine(r, s)** [ˈɪr·gn̩t·ˈʔainə], **irgendeins** [ˈɪr·gn̩t·ˈʔains] *pron indef* 1. *adjektivisch* some; **haben Sie noch irgendeinen Wunsch?** would you like anything else?; **ich will nicht irgendein Buch, sondern diesen Roman** I don't just want any old book, I want this novel 2. *substantivisch* any [old] one; **ich werde doch nicht irgendeinen einstellen** I'm not going to hire just anybody

rgendetwas RR [ˈɪr·gn̩t·ˈʔɛt·vas] *pron indef* something; (*bei Fragen*) anything; ~ **anderes** something else; **nicht** [**einfach**] ~ not just anything

rgendjemand RR [ˈɪr·gn̩t·ˈʔjeː·mant] *pron indef* someone, somebody; (*fragend, verneinend*) anyone, anybody; ~ **anderer** sb else; **nicht** [**einfach**] ~ not just anybody

rgendwann [ˈɪr·gn̩t·ˈvan] *adv* some time or other

rgendwas [ˈɪr·gn̩t·ˈvas] *pron indef fam s.* **irgendetwas**

rgendwie [ˈɪr·gn̩t·ˈviː] *adv* somehow [or other]; **Sie kommen mir** ~ **bekannt**

vor you seem familiar somehow

irgendwo [ˈɪr·gn̩t·ˈvoː] *adv* somewhere [or other]

irisch [ˈiː·rɪʃ] *adj* Irish; *s. a.* **deutsch**

Irland [ˈɪr·lant] *nt* Ireland, Eire; *s. a.* **Deutschland**

Ironie <-, *selten* -n> [iro·ˈniː] *f* irony

ironisch [iˈroː·nɪʃ] **I.** *adj* ironic **II.** *adv* ironically; ~ **lächeln** to give an ironic smile

irrational [ˈɪra·tsjo·naːl] *adj* irrational

Irre <-> [ˈɪrə] *f* **jdn in die** ~ **führen** to mislead sb

irre|**führen** *vt* to mislead; **sich** *akk* **von jdm/etw** ~ **lassen** to be misled by sb/sth

irreführend *adj* misleading

irren [ˈɪrən] **I.** *vi* to be wrong ▶ **I~ ist menschlich** *prov* to err is human **II.** *vr* **sich** *akk* ~ to be wrong (**in** +*dat* about); **da irrst du dich** you're wrong there; **wenn ich mich nicht irre, ...** if I am not mistaken ...

Irrenhaus *nt veraltet pej* insane asylum; **wie im** ~ *fam* like [in] a loony bin

irritieren* [ɪri·ˈtiː·rən] *vt* 1. (*verwirren*) to confuse 2. (*stören*) to annoy

Irrsinn [ˈɪr·zɪn] *m kein pl* 1. *veraltet* (*psychische Krankheit*) insanity 2. *fam* (*Unsinn*) [sheer] madness

irrsinnig [ˈɪr·zɪ·nɪç] **I.** *adj* 1. *veraltet* (*psychisch krank*) insane 2. *fam* (*völlig wirr, absurd*) crazy 3. *fam* (*stark, intensiv*) tremendous; (*Hitze, Kälte, Verkehr*) incredible; (*Kopfschmerzen*) terrible **II.** *adv fam* (*äußerst*) terribly

Irrtum <-[e]s, Irrtümer> [ˈɪr·tuːm] *m* 1. (*irrige Annahme*) error; [**schwer**] **im** ~ **sein** to be [badly] mistaken 2. (*fehlerhafte Handlung*) mistake

irrtümlich [ˈɪr·tyːm·lɪç] *adj attr* mistaken

Ischias <-> [ˈɪʃias] *m o nt kein pl* sciatica

Islam <-s> [ɪsˈlaːm, ˈɪs·lam] *m kein pl* Islam; **der** ~ Islam

islamisch [ɪsˈlaː·mɪʃ] *adj* Islamic

Island [ˈiːs·lant] *nt* Iceland; *s. a.* **Deutschland**

Isländer(in) <-s, -> [ˈiːs·lɛn·de] *m(f)* Icelander; ~ **sein** to be an Icelander; *s. a.* **Deutsche(r)**

isländisch ['iːs·lɛn·dɪʃ] *adj* Icelandic; *s. a.* **deutsch**

Isolation <-, -en> [iz·ola·'tsi̯oːn] *f* **1.** TECH insulation **2.** (*das Isolieren: von Patienten, Häftlingen, etc.*) isolation **3.** (*Abgeschlossenheit*) isolation (**von** *+dat* from)

isolieren* [izo·'liː·rən] **I.** *vt* **1.** TECH to insulate (**gegen** *+akk* against) **2.** JUR, MED to isolate (**von** *+dat* from) **II.** *vr* (*sich absondern*) **sich** *akk* [**von jdm/etw**] **~** to isolate oneself [from sb/sth]

Israel <-s> ['ɪs·ra·eːl] *nt* Israel; *s. a.* **Deutschland**

Israeli [ɪs·ra·'eːli] *m* <-[s], -[s]> *f* <-, -[s]> Israeli; *s. a.* **Deutsche(r)**

israelisch [ɪs·ra·'eːlɪʃ] *adj* Israeli; *s. a.* **deutsch**

Italien <-s> [i'taː·li̯·ən] *nt* Italy; *s. a.* **Deutschland**

Italiener(in) <-s, -> [ita·'li̯eː·nɐ] *m(f)* Italian; **~ sein** to be [an] Italian; *s. a.* **Deutsche(r)**

italienisch [ita·'li̯eː·nɪʃ] *adj* Italian; *s. a.* **deutsch**

IWF <-> [iː·veː·'ʔɛf] *m kein pl Abk von* **Internationaler Währungsfonds** IMF

J

J, j <-, -> [jɔt] *nt* J, j; **~ wie Julius** J as in Juliet

ja ['jaː] *part* **1.** (*bestätigend: so ist es*) yes; **~, bitte?** yes, [how] may I help you?; **das sag ich ~!** *fam* that's exactly what I'm talking about!; **aber ~!** [yes,] of course! **2.** (*fragend: so? tatsächlich?*) really?; **ach ~?** [oh] really? **3.** (*warnend: bloß*) make sure; **sei ~ vorsichtig mit dem Messer!** be sure to be careful with the knife! **4.** (*abschwächend, einschränkend: schließlich*) after all; **ich kann es ~ mal versuchen** I can certainly give it a try **5.** (*revidierend, steigernd: und zwar*) in fact **6.** (*anerkennend, triumphierend: doch*) **siehst du, ich habe es ~ immer gesagt!** see — what did I tell you?; **es musste ~ mal so kommen!** it was bound to happen!; **wo steckt nur der verfluchte Schlüssel? ach, da ist er ~!** where's the damn key? oh, there it is! **7.** (*bekräftigend: allerdings*) **das ist ~ kaum zu glauben!** that is really hard to believe!; **ich verstehe das ~, aber trotzdem finde ich's nicht gut** I do understand what you're saying, but I still don't think it's okay; **das ist ~ die Höhe!** that is [absolutely] outrageous!; **es ist ~ immer dasselbe** some things will never change **8.** (*na*) well **9.** (*als Satzabschluss: nicht wahr?*) isn't it?; **es bleibt doch bei unserer Abmachung, ~?** we're sticking to what we agreed to, right? **10.** (*ratlos: nur*) **ich weiß ~ nicht, wie ich es ihm beibringen soll** I have no idea how [I'm going] to teach him that **11.** (*beschwichtigend*) **ich komm ~ schon!** okay! okay! I'm coming! ▶ **~ und amen zu etw sagen** *fam* to give sth one's blessing; **wenn ~** if so

Ja <-s, -[s]> ['jaː] *nt* yes

Jacke <-, -n> ['ja·kə] *f* **1.** (*Stoffjacke*) jacket **2.** (*Strickjacke*) cardigan

Jackett <-s, -s> [ʒa·'kɛt] *nt* jacket

Jagd <-, -en> ['jaːkt] *f* **1.** (*das Jagen*) hunting; **auf der ~ sein** to be [out] hunting **2.** (*Verfolgung*) hunt (**auf** *+akk* for) **3.** (*wildes Streben*) pursuit (**nach** *+dat* of)

Jagdhund *m* hound

Jagdrevier *nt* preserve

Jagdschein *m* hunting license

jagen ['jaː·gn̩] **I.** *vt* **1.** (*auf der Jagd verfolgen*) to hunt **2.** (*hetzen*) to pursue **3.** *fam* (*antreiben, vertreiben*) **jdn aus etw** *dat* **~** to drive sb out of sth ▶ **jdn mit etw** *dat* **~ können** *fam* to not be able to stand sth **II.** *vi* to hunt

Jäger(in) <-s, -> ['jɛː·gɐ] *m(f)* hunter

Jaguar <-s, -e> ['jaː·gu̯·aːɐ̯] *m* jaguar

jäh ['jɛː] *adj* **1.** (*abrupt, unvorhergesehen*) abrupt; (*Bewegung*) sudden **2.** (*steil*) steep

Jahr <-[e]s, -e> ['jaːɐ̯] *nt* **1.** (*Zeitraum von 12 Monaten*) year; **die 20er-/30er-~e** the twenties/thirties + *sing/pl vb;* **anderthalb ~e** a year and a half; **ein dreiviertel ~** nine months; **das ganze ~ über** throughout the whole year, all year long; **das neue ~** the New Year;

~ **für** ~ year after year; **zweimal im** ~ twice a year; **letztes/nächstes** ~ last/next year; **in diesem/im nächsten** ~ this/next year; **vor einem** ~ a year ago; **alle ~e wieder** every year; **Buch des ~es** book of the year 2. (*Lebensjahre*) **er ist 10 ~e alt** he's 10 years old ▶ **in den besten ~en** [sein] [to be] in one's prime; **in die ~e kommen** *euph fam* to be getting on in years

ahrelang ['jaːrəlaŋ] I. *adj attr* lasting for years; **die Früchte ~er Forschungen** the fruits of years of research II. *adv* for years

Jahrestag *m* anniversary

Jahreswechsel *m* turn of the year; **zum ~** at the turn of the year

Jahreszahl *f* year

Jahreszeit *f* season

Jahrgang *m* 1. (*Personen eines Geburtsjahrs*) people born in the same year; (*Gesamtheit der Schüler eines Schuljahres*) class of [a year] 2. (*Erntejahr von Wein*) vintage

Jahrhundert <-s, -e> [jaːɐ̯ˈhʊndɐt] *nt* century

Jahrhundertwende *f* turn of the century

jährlich ['jɛːɐ̯lɪç] *adj* annual

Jahrmarkt *m* fair

Jahrtausend <-s, -e> [jaːɐ̯ˈtau̯zn̩t] *nt* millennium

Jahrzehnt <-[e]s, -e> [jaːɐ̯ˈtseːnt] *nt* decade

jähzornig *adj* irascible

Jalousie <-, -n> [ʒaluˈziː] *f* venetian blind

jämmerlich ['jɛmɐlɪç] *adj attr* 1. (*beklagenswert*) wretched 2. (*kummervoll*) sorrowful 3. *fam* (*Ausrede*) pathetic 4. *pej fam* (*verächtlich*) miserable

jammern ['jamɐn] *vi* 1. *a. pej* (*lamentieren*) to whine (**über** +*akk* about, **wegen** +*dat* about); **lass das J~** stop [your] moaning 2. (*wimmernd verlangen*) to beg (**nach** +*dat* for)

Jänner <-s, -> ['jɛnɐ] *m österr* January

Januar <-[s], *selten* -e> ['januaːɐ̯] *m* January; *s. a.* **Februar**

Japan <-s> ['jaːpan] *nt* Japan; *s. a.* **Deutschland**

Japaner(in) <-s, -> [jaˈpaːnɐ] *m(f)* Japanese; **die** ~ the Japanese; *s. a.* **Deutsche(r)**

japanisch [jaˈpaːnɪʃ] *adj* Japanese; *s. a.* **deutsch**

Jasmin <-s, -e> [jasˈmiːn] *m* jasmine

jäten ['jɛːtn̩] I. *vt* 1. (*aushacken*) to hoe 2. (*von Unkraut befreien*) to weed II. *vi* to weed

jauchzen ['jau̯xtsn̩] *vi geh* to shout with joy

jaulen ['jau̯lən] *vi* to howl

Jawort *nt* **jdm das ~ geben** to agree to marry sb; (*bei Trauung*) to say "I do"

Jazz <-> ['dʒɛs, 'jats] *m kein pl* jazz

je ['jeː] I. *adv* 1. (*jemals*) ever 2. (*jeweils*) each II. *präp* +*akk* (*pro*) per III. *konj* ~ **öfter du übst, desto besser kannst du dann spielen** the more you practice, the better you will be able to play; ~ **nachdem!** it [all] depends!; ~ **nachdem, ob/wann/wie ...** depending on whether/when/how ...

Jeans <-, -> ['dʒiːnz] *f meist pl* jeans *npl*

jede(r, s) ['jeːdə] *pron indef* 1. *attr* (*alle einzelnen*) each, every; **~s Mal** every time; ~ **Woche** each week 2. *attr* (*jegliche*) **ohne ~ Anstrengung** without any effort 3. *attr* (*beliebige*) **zu ~r Zeit** at any time 4. *substantivisch* everyone; (*stärker*) each and every one; **das weiß doch ein ~r!** everybody knows that!; *dial* (*jeweils der/die einzelne*) each [one]; ~**e(r, s) zweite/dritte ...** one in two/three ...

jedenfalls ['jeːdn̩fals] *adv* 1. (*immerhin*) in any case 2. (*auf jeden Fall*) anyhow, anyway

jederzeit ['jeːdɐtsai̯t] *adv* 1. (*zu jeder beliebigen Zeit*) at any time 2. (*jeden Augenblick*) at any moment

jedesmal ^ALT *adv s.* **Mal**[1]

jedoch [jeˈdɔx] *konj, adv* however

jemals ['jeːmaːls] *adv* ever

jemand ['jeːmant] *pron indef* somebody; (*bei Fragen, Negation etc.*) anyone

jene(r, s) ['jeːnə] *pron dem geh* that *sing*, those *pl*

jenseits ['jeːnzai̯ts] I. *präp* +*gen* (*auf der anderen Seite*) on the other side

II. adv (über ... hinaus) ~ **von etw** dat beyond sth

Jenseits <-> ['jɛn·zaits] nt kein pl hereafter

Jesuit <-en, -en> [je·zu·'iːt] m Jesuit

Jesus <gen o dat Jesu, akk Jesum> ['jeː·zʊs] m Jesus; ~ **Christus** Jesus Christ

jetzig ['jɛt·sɪç] adj attr current

jetzt ['jɛtst] adv **1.** (zurzeit) now; **bis ~** so far; ~ **gleich** right now; ~ **oder nie!** [it's] now or never!; ~ **schon?** already? **2.** (verstärkend: nun) now; **habe ich ~ den Brief eingeworfen oder nicht?** did I just mail the letter or not?; **wer ist das ~ schon wieder?** now who is it? **3.** (heute) now[a]days

jeweils ['jeː·vails] adv **1.** (jedes Mal) each time; **die Miete ist ~ monatlich im Voraus fällig** the rent is due each month in advance **2.** (immer zusammengenommen) each; ~ **drei Pfadfinder mussten sich einen Teller Eintopf teilen** there was only one plate of stew for every three scouts **3.** (zur entsprechenden Zeit) at the time

jobben ['dʒɔ·bn̩] vi fam to work odd jobs

Jockey <-s, -s> ['dʒɔ·ke, 'dʒɔ·kiː] m jockey

jodeln ['joː·dl̩n] vi to yodel

Joga <-[s]> ['joː·ga] m o nt kein pl yoga

joggen ['dʒɔ·gn̩] vi **1.** haben (eine Strecke laufen) to jog **2.** sein **irgendwohin ~** to jog somewhere

Jogger(in) <-s, -> ['dʒɔ·ge] m(f) jogger

Jogginganzug ['dʒɔ·gɪŋ-] m tracksuit

Joghurt, Jogurtᴿᴿ <-[s], -[s]> ['joː·gʊrt] m o nt yog[h]urt

Johannisbeere [jo·'ha·nɪs-] f currant; **rote/schwarze ~** red/black currant

johlen ['joː·lən] vi to yell

Jo-Jo <-s, -s> [joː'joː] nt yo-yo

jonglieren* [ʒɔŋ·'liː·rən] vi to juggle

Jordanien <-s> [jɔr·'daː·ni·ən] nt Jordan; s. a. **Deutschland**

Jordanier(in) <-s, -> [jɔr·'daː·ni·ɐ] m(f) Jordanian; s. a. **Deutsche(r)**

jordanisch [jɔr·'daː·nɪʃ] adj Jordanian; s. a. **deutsch**

Journal <-s, -e> [ʒʊr·'naːl] nt journal

Journalist(in) <-en, -en> [ʒʊr·na·'lɪst] m(f) journalist

jubeln ['juː·bl̩n] vi [über etw akk] ~ to celebrate [sth]

Jubiläum <-s, Jubiläen> [ju·bi·'lɛː·ʊm] nt anniversary

jucken ['jʊ·kn̩] **I.** vi (Juckreiz erzeugen) to itch **II.** vi impers to itch **III.** vi impers **1.** (zum Kratzen reizen) **mich juckt's am Rücken** my back's itching **2.** fam (reizen) **jdn juckt es, etw zu tun** sb's itching to do sth **IV.** vt **1.** (kratzen) **das Unterhemd juckt mich** my undershirt is itchy **2.** meist verneint fam (kümmern) **das juckt mich doch nicht** I couldn't care less **V.** vr fam (sich kratzen) **sich** akk [an etw dat] ~ to scratch [one's sth]

Juckreiz m itch[ing]

Jude, Jüdin <-n, -n> ['juː·də] m, f Jew masc, Jewess fem; ~ **sein** to be Jewish

Judentum <-s> nt kein pl Jewry, Jews pl

Jüdin <-, -nen> ['jyː·dɪn] f s. **Jude**

jüdisch ['jyː·dɪʃ] adj Jewish

Judo <-s> ['juː·do] nt kein pl judo

Jugend <-> ['juː·gn̩t] f kein pl **1.** (Jugendzeit) youth; **frühe/früheste ~** early/earliest youth; **in jds ~** in sb's youth; **in meiner ~ ...** when I was young, ... **2.** (Jungsein) youthfulness **3.** (junge Menschen) **die heutige ~** young people today

Jugendherberge f youth hostel

jugendlich ['juː·gn̩t·lɪç] adj **1.** (jung) young **2.** (jung wirkend) youthful

Jugendliche(r) f(m) young person

Jugoslawien <-s> [ju·go·'sla·vi·ən] nt hist Yugoslavia; s. a. **Deutschland**

jugoslawisch [ju·go·'sla·vɪʃ] adj hist Yugoslav[ian]; s. a. **deutsch**

Juli <-[s], -s> ['juː·li] m July; s. a. **Februar**

jung <jünger, jüngste> ['jʊŋ] **I.** adj young; **jünger [als jd] sein** to be younger [than sb]; **der/die Jüngere/der/die Jüngste** the younger/the youngest; **das hält ~!** it keeps you young! **II.** adv (in jungen Jahren) young; ~ **heiraten** to marry

Junge <-n, -n> ['jʊŋə] m boy ▶ **alter ~** fam old buddy, dude sl; **mein** ~ fam my boy, son; **~, ~!** fam boy, oh boy!

Junge(s) ['jʊŋə(s)] *nt* ORN, ZOOL young

jünger ['jʏŋɐ] *adj komp von* jung younger

Jünger(in) <-s, -> ['jʏŋɐ] *m(f)* disciple

Jungfrau ['jʊŋ·frau] *f* 1. (*Frau*) virgin; **die ~ Maria** the Virgin Mary; **die ~ von Orléans** Joan of Arc 2. ASTROL Virgo

jungfräulich ['jʊŋ·frɔy·lɪç] *adj a. fig* virgin

Junggeselle, -gesellin ['jʊŋ·gə·zɛ·lə] *m, f* bachelor

Jüngling <-s, -e> ['jʏŋ·lɪŋ] *m geh* young man

jüngste(r, s) *adj* 1. *superl von* jung youngest; [auch] **nicht mehr der/die Jüngste sein** *hum* to be no spring chicken anymore [either] 2. (*nicht lange zurückliegend*) [most] recent 3. (*neueste*) latest

Juni <-[s], -s> ['ju:·ni] *m* June; *s. a.* Februar

junior, Juniorin <-s, -en> ['ju:·njo:ɐ̯] *m, f* 1. (*Juniorchef*) boss' [*o* owner's] son *masc*/daughter *fem* 2. *fam* (*Sohn*) junior 3. *pl* (*junge Sportler zwischen 18 und 23*) [*members of the*] junior team

Jura¹ ['ju:·ra] *kein art* SCH law

Jura² <-s> ['ju:·ra] *m* GEOL Jurassic [period/system]

Jura³ <-s> ['ju:·ra] *m kein pl* GEOG 1. (*Gebirge in der Ostschweiz*) Jura Mountains *pl* 2. (*Schweizer Kanton*) Jura

Jurist(in) <-en, -en> [ju·'rɪst] *m(f)* jurist

Jury <-, -s> [ʒy·'ri:] *f* jury

Justiz <-> [jʊs·'ti:ts] *f kein pl* JUR 1. (*Gerichtsbarkeit*) justice 2. (*Justizbehörden*) legal authorities *pl*

Justizbeamte(r) *m*, **Justizbeamtin** *f* judicial officer

Justizminister, -ministerin *m, f* Attorney General

Justizministerium *nt* Department of Justice

Juwel¹ <-s, -en> [ju·'ve:l] *m o nt* 1. (*Schmuckstein*) gem[stone], jewel 2. *pl* (*Schmuck*) jewelry

Juwel² <-s, -en> [ju·'ve:l] *nt gem*; **das ~ der Sammlung** the jewel of the collection; **ein ~ von einer Köchin sein** to be a great cook

Jux <-es, *selten* -e> ['jʊks] *m fam* (*Scherz*)

joke; **aus ~** as a joke; **aus [lauter] ~ und Tollerei** *fam* out of sheer fun

K

K, k <-, -> [ka:] *nt* K, k; **~ wie Kaufmann** K as in Kilo

Kabarett <-s, -e> [ka·ba·'rɛt] *nt* cabaret

Kabel <-s, -> ['ka:·bl̩] *nt* 1. ELEK wire; (*größer*) cable 2. TELEK, TV cable

Kabelfernsehen *nt* cable TV

Kabeljau <-s, -e> ['ka:·bl̩·jau] *m* cod

Kabine <-, -n> [ka·'bi:·nə] *f* 1. (*Umkleidekabine*) changing room 2. NAUT cabin

Kabinett <-s, -e> [ka·bi·'nɛt] *nt* POL cabinet

Kachel <-, -n> ['ka·xl̩] *f* tile

Kachelofen ['ka·xl̩·ʔo:fn̩] *m* tiled masonry heater

Kadaver <-s, -> [ka·'da:·vɐ] *m* carcass

Kader <-s, -> ['ka:·dɐ] *m* 1. MIL cadre 2. SPORT squad

Käfer <-s, -> ['kɛ·fɐ] *m* 1. ZOOL beetle 2. *fam* (*Volkswagen*) [VW] bug [*o* beetle]

Kaff <-s, -s> ['kaf] *nt pej fam* hole

Kaffee <-s, -s> ['ka·fe] *m* coffee

Kaffeehaus *nt österr* coffee house

Kaffeekanne *f* coffeepot

Kaffeemaschine *f* coffeemaker

Kaffeepause *f* coffee break

Käfig <-s, -e> ['kɛ·fɪç] *m* cage

kahl [ka:l] I. *adj* 1. (*ohne Kopfhaar*) bald 2. (*Baum, Wand*) bare; (*Landschaft*) barren II. *adv* **etw ~ fressen** to strip sth bare; **jdn ~ scheren** to shave sb's head; **~ geschoren** shaved

Kahlkopf *m* bald head

kahlköpfig *adj* bald-headed

Kahn <-[e]s, Kähne> [ka:n] *m* (*flaches Boot*) small boat; (*Schleppkahn*) barge

Kai <-s, -e> [kai] *m* quay

Kaiser(in) <-s, -> ['kai·ze] *m(f)* emperor *masc*, empress *fem*

kaiserlich ['kai·ze·lɪç] *adj* imperial

Kaiserschmarr(e)n *m* KOCH *österr, südd* a warm dessert of sliced crepes and raisins, topped with powdered sugar, often served with apple sauce or plum jam

Kaiserschnitt m Caesarean [section]

Kajüte <-, -n> [ka·ˈjyː·tə] f cabin

Kakao <-s, -s> [ka·ˈkau] m cocoa; (heiß) hot chocolate; (Pulver) cocoa [powder]

Kakerlake <-, -n> [ˈkaː·kɐ·la·kə] f cockroach

Kaktus <-, Kakteen> [ˈkak·tʊs] m cactus

Kalb <-[e]s, Kälber> [kalp] nt calf

kalben [ˈkal·bn̩] vi to calve

Kalbfleisch nt veal

Kalbsschnitzel nt veal cutlet

Kalender <-s, -> [ka·ˈlɛn·dɐ] m calendar

Kalenderjahr nt calendar year

Kalifornien <-s> [ka·li·ˈfɔr·ni̯·ən] nt California

Kalium <-s> [ˈkaː·li̯·ʊm] nt kein pl potassium

Kalk <-[e]s, -e> [kalk] m 1. (Kalziumkarbonat) lime 2. BAU whitewash 3. (Kalzium) calcium

kalkhaltig adj chalky; (Wasser) hard

Kalkulation <-, -en> [kal·ku·la·ˈtsi̯oːn] f calculation

kalkulierbar adj calculable

kalkulieren * [kal·ku·ˈliː·rən] vt, vi to calculate (mit +dat with)

Kalorie <-, -n> [ka·lo·ˈriː] f calorie

kalorienarm I. adj low-calorie II. adv ~ essen to eat diet food

kalt <kälter, kälteste> [kalt] I. adj cold; mir ist ~ I'm cold II. adv 1. (mit kaltem Wasser) ~ duschen to take a cold shower 2. (ohne Aufwärmen) etw ~ essen to eat sth cold 3. (an einen kühlen Ort) etw ~ stellen to chill sth ▶ jdn überläuft es ~ cold shivers run down sb's back

kaltblütig [ˈkalt·blyː·tɪç] I. adj cold-blooded II. adv in cold blood

Kälte <-> [ˈkɛl·tə] f kein pl cold; vor ~ with cold

kälteempfindlich adj sensitive to cold pred

Kälteschutzmittel nt antifreeze

kaltlassen vi irreg etw lässt jdn kalt sth leaves sb cold

Kaltluft f cold air

kaltschnäuzig fam I. adj callous II. adv callously

Kalzium <-s> [ˈkal·tsi̯·ʊm] nt kein pl calcium

Kamel <-[e]s, -e> [ka·ˈmeːl] nt camel

Kamera <-, -s> [ˈka·me·ra] f camera

Kamerad(in) <-en, -en> [ka·mə·ˈraːt] m(f) comrade

kameradschaftlich I. adj friendly II. adv on a friendly basis

Kamerun <-s> [ˈka·mə·ruːn] nt Cameroon; s. a. Deutschland

Kamille <-, -n> [ka·ˈmɪ·lə] f camomile

Kamin <-s, -e> [ka·ˈmiːn] m o dia nt 1. (offene Feuerstelle) fireplace 2. (Schornstein) chimney

Kaminfeger(in) <-s, -> m(f) dia (Schornsteinfeger) chimney sweep

Kamm <-[e]s, Kämme> [kam] m 1. (Frisierkamm) comb 2. (eines Vogels) comb 3. (Bergrücken) ridge

kämmen [ˈkɛ·mən] vt to comb

Kammer <-, -n> [ˈkamɐ] f 1. (kleine Raum) small room 2. POL, JUR chamber 3. (Berufsvertretung) professional association

Kampagne <-, -n> [kam·ˈpan·i̯ə] f campaign

Kampf <-[e]s, Kämpfe> [kampf] m 1. a fig (Auseinandersetzung) fight (gegen +akk against) 2. (innerlich) struggle 3. (das Ringen) struggle (um +akk for) 4. MIL battle 5. SPORT fight (um +akk for) ▶ jdm/etw den ~ ansagen to declare war on sb/sth

kämpfen [ˈkɛmp·fn̩] I. vi 1. to fight 2. (ringen) mit sich dat/etw dat ~ to struggle with oneself/sth II. vr sich akk durch etw akk ~ to struggle through sth

kämpferisch I. adj 1. SPORT attacking 2. (Kampfgeist aufweisend) aggressive 3. MIL fighting II. adv aggressively

Kampfhund m fighting dog

Kampfsport m kein pl martial arts pl

kampieren * [kam·ˈpiː·rən] vi to camp [out]

Kanada <-s> [ˈka·na·da] nt Canada; s. a. Deutschland

Kanadier(in) <-s, -> [ka·ˈnaː·di̯ɐ] m(f) Canadian; s. a. Deutsche(r)

kanadisch [ka·ˈnaː·dɪʃ] adj Canadian s. a. deutsch

Kanal <-s, Kanäle> [ka·ˈnaːl] m 1. NAUT TRANSP canal 2. (Abwasserkanal) sewer

3. *kein pl (Ärmelkanal)* **der** ~ the [English] Channel **4.** RADIO, TV channel

Kanalinseln *pl* **die** ~ the Channel Islands *pl*

Kanalisation <-, -en> [ka·na·li·za·'tsi̯oːn] *f* sewage system

Kanaltunnel *m* **der** ~ the Channel Tunnel

Kandidat(in) <-en, -en> [kan·di·'daːt] *m(f)* candidate

kandidieren * [kan·di·'diː·rən] *vi* POL [**für etw** *akk*] ~ to run [for sth]

kandiert *adj* candied

Kandiszucker ['kan·dɪs-] *m kein pl* rock candy

Känguru RR, **Känguruh** ALT <-s, -s> ['kɛŋ·gu·ru] *nt* kangaroo

Kaninchen <-s, -> [ka·'niːn·çən] *nt* rabbit

Kanister <-s, -> [ka·'nɪs·tɐ] *m* canister

Kanne <-, -n> ['kanə] *f* (*Wasserkanne*) pitcher; (*Kaffee-, Teekanne*) pot; (*Gießkanne*) watering can

Kannibale <-n, -n> [ka·ni·'baː·lə] *m* cannibal

Kanone <-, -n> [ka·'noː·nə] *f* **1.** (*Geschütz*) cannon **2.** *sl* (*Pistole*) pistol ▶ **unter aller** ~ **sein** *fam* to be lousy

Kante <-, -n> ['kan·tə] *f* (*Rand*) edge ▶ **etw auf die hohe** ~ **legen** *fam* to put sth away [for a rainy day]

kantig ['kan·tɪç] *adj* angular

Kantine <-, -n> [kan·'tiː·nə] *f* cafeteria

Kanton <-s, -e> [kan·'tɔːn] *m* canton

Kanu <-s, -s> ['kaː·nu] *nt* canoe

Kanzlei <-, -en> [kants·'lai̯] *f* office

Kanzler(in) <-s, -> ['kants·lɐ] *m(f)* chancellor

Kanzleramt *nt* POL **1.** (*Büro*) chancellor's office **2.** *kein pl* (*Amt*) chancellorship

Kap <-s, -s> [kap] *nt* cape; ~ **der Guten Hoffnung** Cape of Good Hope

Kapazität <-, -en> [ka·pa·tsi·'tɛt] *f* capacity

Kapelle¹ <-, -n> [ka·'pɛ·lə] *f* REL chapel

Kapelle² <-, -n> [ka·'pɛ·lə] *f* MUS orchestra

Kaper <-, -n> ['kaː·pɐ] *f* caper

kapieren * [ka·'piː·rən] *vt fam* to get; ~**, dass/wie ...** to understand that/how ...

Kapital <-s, -e> [ka·pi·'taːl] *nt* FIN, ÖKON capital ▶ ~ **aus etw** *dat* **schlagen** to cash in on sth

Kapitalismus <-> [ka·pi·ta·'lɪs·mʊs] *m kein pl* capitalism

Kapitalist(in) <-en, -en> [ka·pi·ta·'lɪst] *m(f)* capitalist

kapitalistisch *adj* capitalist[ic]

Kapitalverbrechen *nt* capital offense

Kapitän(in) <-s, -e> [ka·pi·'tɛːn] *m(f)* captain

Kapitel <-s, -> [ka·'pɪ·tl̩] *nt* chapter

Kapitulation <-, -en> [ka·pi·tu·la·'tsi̯oːn] *f* capitulation

kapitulieren * [ka·pi·tu·'liː·rən] *vi* to capitulate; **vor etw** *dat* ~ to give up in the face of sth

Kaplan <-s, Kapläne> [ka·'plaːn] *m* chaplain

Kappe <-, -n> ['ka·pə] *f* **1.** (*Mütze*) cap, hat **2.** (*Verschluss*) top

kappen ['ka·pn̩] *vt* **1.** (*durchtrennen*) to cut **2.** *fam* (*beschneiden: Zuschüsse*) to cut back [on]

Kapsel <-, -n> ['kap·sl̩] *f* PHARM, RAUM capsule

kaputt [ka·'pʊt] *adj fam* **1.** (*zerbrochen*) broken **2.** (*beschädigt*) damaged **3.** (*erschöpft*) shattered **4.** (*ruiniert*) ruined

kaputt|gehen *vi irreg sein fam* **1.** (*zerstört werden*) to break; (*Gerät*) to break down **2.** (*beschädigt werden*) to become damaged **3.** (*ruiniert werden*) [**an etw** *dat*] ~ to be ruined [because of sth]; (*Ehe, Partnerschaft*) to break up [because of sth]

kaputt|lachen *vr fam* **sich** *akk* ~ to die laughing

kaputt|machen *fam* **I.** *vt* **1.** (*zerstören*) to break **2.** (*ruinieren*) to ruin **3.** (*erschöpfen*) **jdn** ~ to wear sb out **II.** *vr* **sich** *akk* ~ to wear oneself out

Kapuze <-, -n> [ka·'puː·tsə] *f* hood

Karaffe <-, -n> [ka·'ra·fə] *f* carafe

Karambolage <-, -n> [ka·ram·bo·'laː·ʒə] *f* pile-up

Karamel ALT, **Karamell** RR <-s> [ka·ra·'mɛl] *m kein pl* caramel

Karate <-[s]> [ka·'raː·tə] *nt kein pl* karate

Kardamom <-s> [kar·da·'moːm] *m o nt*

K

kein pl cardamom

Kardinal <-s, Kardinäle> [kar·di·'na:l] *m* REL, ORN cardinal

Kardinalzahl *f* cardinal number

Karfiol <-s> [kar·'fjo:l] *m kein pl südd, österr* (*Blumenkohl*) cauliflower

Karfreitag [ka:ɐ̯·'frai·ta:k] *m* Good Friday

karg [kark] I. *adj* 1. (*unfruchtbar*) barren 2. (*dürftig*) sparse; (*Einkommen, Mahl*) meager II. *adv* sparsely; **die Portionen sind ~ bemessen** they're stingy with the portions

kärglich ['kɛrk·lɪç] *adj* 1. (*ärmlich*) shabby 2. (*sehr dürftig*) meager; **ein ~er Lohn** a pittance

Karibik <-> [ka·'ri:·bɪk] *f* **die ~** the Caribbean

kariert [ka·'ri:rt] *adj* 1. (*Stoff*) plaid 2. (*Papier*) squared

Karies <-> ['ka·ri·ɛ:s] *f kein pl* tooth decay

Karikatur <-, -en> [ka·ri·ka·'tu:ɐ̯] *f a. pej* caricature

karikieren * [ka·ri·'ki:·rən] *vt* to caricature

Karneval <-s, -e> ['kar·nə·val] *m* carnival

Kärnten <-s> ['kɛrn·tn̩] *nt* Carinthia

Karo <-s, -s> ['ka:·ro] *nt* 1. (*Raute*) rhombus 2. *kein pl* KARTEN diamonds *pl*

Karosse <-, -n> [ka·'rɔ·sə] *f* (*Prunkkutsche*) state carriage

Karosserie <-, -n> [ka·rɔ·sə·'ri:] *f* bodywork

Karotte <-, -n> [ka·'rɔ·tə] *f* carrot

Karpfen <-s, -> ['kar·pfn̩] *m* carp

Karren <-s, -> ['ka·rən] *m* 1. *fam* (*Auto*) old clunker 2. (*Schubkarre*) wheelbarrow 3. (*offener Pferdewagen*) cart ▶ **den ~ [für jdn] aus dem Dreck ziehen** to get [sb] out of a mess

Karriere <-, -n> [ka·'rjɛ:·rə] *f* career

Karrierefrau *f* career woman

Karte <-, -n> ['kar·tə] *f* 1. (*Ansichtskarte*) [post]card 2. (*Eintritts-, Fahrkarte*) ticket 3. (*Visitenkarte*) [business] card 4. FBALL **die gelbe/rote ~** the yellow/red card 5. (*Auto-, Landkarte*) map 6. (*Speisekarte*) menu 7. (*Spielkarte*) card

Kartei <-, -en> [kar·'tai] *f* card index

Karteikarte *f* index card

Kartenspiel *nt* 1. (*Spiel*) game of cards 2. (*Satz Karten*) pack of cards

Kartentelefon *nt a public telephone that accepts phone cards*

Kartenvorverkauf *m* advance ticket sales

Kartoffel <-, -n> [kar·'tɔ·fl̩] *f* potato

Kartoffelbrei *m* mashed potatoes *pl*

Kartoffelchips *pl* [potato] chips *pl*

Kartoffelpuffer <-s, -> *m* potato pancake, latke

Kartoffelsalat *m* potato salad

Karton <-s, -s> [kar·'tɔŋ] *m* 1. (*Schachtel*) cardboard box 2. (*Pappe*) cardboard

Karussell <-s, -s> [ka·rʊ·'sɛl] *nt* merrygo-round

Karzinom <-s, -e> [kar·tsi·'no:m] *nt* carcinoma

kaschieren * [ka·'ʃi:·rən] *vt* to conceal

Kaschmir[1] <-s> ['kaʃ·mi:ɐ̯] *nt* GEOG Kashmir

Kaschmir[2] <-s, -e> ['kaʃ·mi:ɐ̯] *m* (*Wolle*) cashmere

Käse <-s, -> ['kɛ:·zə] *m* 1. (*Lebensmittel*) cheese; **weißer ~** *dial* quark (*low-fat curd cheese*) 2. *pej fam* (*Quatsch*) nonsense

Käsekuchen *m* cheesecake

käsig ['kɛ·sɪç] *adj fam* (*Aussehen*) pasty

Kasse <-, -n> ['ka·sə] *f* 1. (*Zahlstelle*) [cash] register; (*im Supermarkt*) checkout counter 2. (*Kartenverkauf*) ticket office 3. (*Registrierkasse*) cash register ▶ **gut/schlecht bei ~ sein** *fam* to be well-off/not well-off; **jdn zur ~ bitten** to ask sb to pay

Kassenautomat *m* pay station

Kassenbon *m* [sales] receipt

Kassenpatient(in) *m(f)* ≈ HMO patient

Kassenzettel *m s.* Kassenbon

Kassette <-, -n> [ka·'sɛ·tə] *f* 1. (*Videokassette*) videotape; (*Musikkassette*) [cassette] tape 2. (*Kästchen*) case 3. (*Schutzkarton*) box

Kassettenrekorder *m* cassette recorder

kassieren * [ka·'si:·rən] I. *vt* (*Miete*) to collect; (*Abfindung, Zinsen*) to pick up II. *vi* to settle the bill; **darf ich schon [bei Ihnen] ~?** would you mind paying

the check now?

Kassierer(in) <-s, -> [ka·'si:·rɐ] *m(f)* cashier

Kastanie <-, -n> [kas·'ta:·njə] *f* (*Rosskastanie*) [horse] chestnut; (*Esskastanie*) chestnut

Kasten <-s, Kästen> ['kas·tn̩] *m* 1. (*kantiger Behälter*) box 2. (*offene Kiste*) crate 3. *österr, schweiz* (*Schrank*) cupboard

kastrieren * [kas·'tri:·rən] *vt* to castrate

Kasus <-, -> ['ka:·zʊs] *m* LING case

Katalog <-[e]s, -e> [ka·ta·'lo:k] *m* catalog

Katalysator <-s, -toren> [ka·ta·ly·'za:·to:ɐ̯] *m* 1. AUTO catalytic converter; **geregelter ~** regulated catalytic converter 2. CHEM catalyst

Katarr RR, **Katarrh** <-s, -e> [ka·'tar] *m* catarrh

katastrophal [ka·tas·tro·'fa:l] I. *adj* catastrophic II. *adv* catastrophically

Katastrophe <-, -n> [ka·ta·'stro:·fə] *f* catastrophe

Katastrophenhilfe *f kein pl* disaster aid

Kategorie <-, -n> [ka·te·go·'ri:] *f* category

kategorisch [ka·te·'go:·rɪʃ] I. *adj* categorical II. *adv* categorically

Kater[1] <-s, -> ['ka:·tɐ] *m* tomcat

Kater[2] <-s, -> ['ka:·tɐ] *m fam* hangover

Kathedrale <-, -n> [ka·te·'dra:·lə] *f* cathedral

Katholik(in) <-en, -en> [ka·to·'li:k] *m(f)* [Roman] Catholic

katholisch [ka·'to:·lɪʃ] *adj* Roman Catholic

katzbuckeln ['kats·bʊ·kl̩n] *vi pej fam* to grovel

Katze <-, -n> ['ka·tsə] *f* cat ▶ **die ~ aus dem Sack lassen** *fam* to let the cat out of the bag; **die ~ im Sack kaufen** *fam* to buy a pig in a poke

Katzenjammer *m fam* the blues + *sing vb*

Katzensprung *m fam* [nur] **einen ~ entfernt sein** to be [only] a stone's throw away

Katzenwäsche *f hum fam* ≈ quick shower

Kauderwelsch <-[s]> ['kau·dɐ·vɛlʃ] *nt kein pl pej* (*Sprachgemisch*) gibberish

kauen ['kau·ən] *vt, vi* to chew (**an** +*dat* on)

kauern ['kau·ɐn] I. *vi* to be huddled [up] II. *vr* **sich** *akk* **hinter etw** *akk* ~ to crouch behind sth; **sich** *akk* **in eine Ecke** ~ to cower in a corner

Kauf <-[e]s, Käufe> [kauf] *m* buying; **etw zum ~ anbieten** to offer sth for sale ▶ **etw in ~ nehmen** to accept sth

kaufen ['kau·fn̩] *vt* 1. (*einkaufen*) to buy 2. *fam* (*bestechen*) **jdn ~** to buy sb [off *sep*]

Käufer(in) <-s, -> ['kɔy·fɐ] *m(f)* buyer

Kauffrau *f* businesswoman

Kaufhaus *nt* department store

Kaufkraft *f* 1. (*Geldwert*) purchasing power 2. (*Finanzkraft*) spending power

käuflich *adj* 1. (*zu kaufen*) for sale *pred* 2. (*bestechlich*) bribable

Kaufmann <-leute> ['kauf·man] *m* businessman

kaufmännisch *adj* commercial

Kaufpreis *m* purchase price

Kaufvertrag *m* bill of sale

Kaugummi *m* chewing gum

kaum [kaum] *adv* hardly

Kaution <-, -en> [kau·'tsjo:n] *f* 1. JUR bail 2. (*Mietkaution*) deposit

Kauz <-es, Käuze> [kauts] *m* 1. (*Eulenvogel*) [tawny] owl 2. (*Sonderling*) oddball *fam*

Kavalier <-s, -e> [ka·va·'li:ɐ̯] *m* gentleman

Kavaliersdelikt *nt* petty offense

Kaviar <-s, -e> ['ka:·vi·ar] *m* caviar[e]

keck [kɛk] I. *adj* cheeky II. *adv* cheekily

Kegel <-s, -> ['ke:·gl̩] *m* 1. (*Spielfigur*) pin 2. MATH, GEOG cone

Kegelbahn *f* (*Anlage*) bowling alley

kegeln ['ke:·gl̩n] *vi* to go bowling

Kehle <-, -n> ['ke:·lə] *f* throat

Kehlkopf *m* larynx

kehren[1] ['ke:·rən] *vt* ▶ **jdm/etw den Rücken ~** to turn one's back on sb/sth

kehren[2] ['ke:·rən] *vt, vi dial* (*fegen*) to sweep

Kehrschaufel *f* dustpan

Kehrseite *f* (*Schattenseite*) downside

kehrlmachen *vi* to turn [around and go] back

Kehrwoche *f südd* a week in which it is a resident's turn to clean the common

areas in and around an apartment building

keifen ['kai·fn̩] *vi pej* to nag

Keil <-[e]s, -e> [kail] *m* TECH wedge

Keilerei <-, -en> [kai·lə·'rai] *f fam* scuffle

Keilriemen *m* AUTO fan belt

Keim <-[e]s, -e> [kaim] *m* **1.** BOT shoot **2.** (*befruchtete Eizelle*) embryo **3.** (*Erreger*) germ ▶ **etw im ~ ersticken** to nip sth in the bud

keimen ['kai·mən] *vi* **1.** BOT to germinate **2.** *fig* to stir

keimfrei *adj* sterile; **etw ~ machen** to sterilize sth

Keimling <-s, -e> *m* BOT shoot

kein [kain] **I.** *pron indef, attr* **1.** (*verneint Substantiv*) no, not any; **ich habe ~ Geld/~e Freunde** I don't have any money/friends, I have no money/friends; **ich habe jetzt wirklich ~e Zeit** I really don't have any time now; **er sagte ~ Wort** he didn't say a word **2.** (*verneint Adjektiv*) not; **das ist ~ dummer Gedanke** that's not a bad idea; **das ist ~ großer Unterschied** that's not much of a difference **3.** (*vor Zahlwörtern*) less than, not; **er wartete ~e 3 Minuten** he waited less than 3 minutes; **die Reparatur dauert ~e 5 Minuten** it won't even take 5 minutes to repair it **II.** *pron indef, substantivisch* **1.** (*von Menschen*) nobody, no one; **~e(r) von uns** none of us; **ich habe ~en gesehen** I didn't see anyone; **~e(r) von beiden** neither [of them] **2.** (*von Gegenständen*) none, any; **ist Saft da? – nein, ich habe ~en gekauft** is there any juice? — no, I didn't buy any; **~s von beiden** neither [of them]; **~s von beiden gefällt mir** I don't like either of them **3.** (*nachgestellt*) **Lust habe ich schon, aber Zeit habe ich ~e** I'd like to, it's just that I don't have time; **ich gehe zu der Verabredung, aber Lust hab ich ~e** I'm going to keep the appointment, but I don't feel like going

keinerlei ['kai·nɐ·lai] *adj attr* no ... at all

keinesfalls ['kai·nəs·fals] *adv* under no circumstances

keineswegs ['kai·nəs·'veːks] *adv* by no means

Keks <-es, -e> [keːks] *m* cookie ▶ **jdm auf den ~ gehen** *fam* to get on someone's nerves

Keller <-s, -> ['kɛ·lɐ] *m* cellar

Kellergeschoss RR *nt* basement

Kellner(in) <-s, -> ['kɛl·nɐ] *m(f)* waiter *masc*, waitress *fem*

Kelte, Keltin <-n, -n> ['kɛl·tə, 'kɛl·tɪn] *m, f* Celt

keltern ['kɛl·tɐn] *vt* to press

Keltin <-, -nen> *f s.* **Kelte**

Kenia <-s> ['keː·nja] *nt* Kenya; *s. a.* **Deutschland**

kennen <kannte, gekannt> ['kɛ·nən] *vt* **1.** (*jdm bekannt sein*) **jdn/etw ~** to know sb/sth; **du kennst dich doch!** you know what you're like; **kennst du mich noch?** do you remember me?; **so kenne ich dich gar nicht** I've never seen you like this; **jdn ~ lernen** to get to know sb; **sich** *akk* **~ lernen** (*erstmals begegnen*) to meet **2.** (*jdm vertraut sein*) **etw ~** to be familiar with sth; **kennst du das Buch/diesen Film?** have you read this book/seen this movie?; **das ~ wir** [schon] *iron* we've heard all that before ▶ **jdn noch ~ lernen** *fam* to still have sb to deal with

Kenner(in) <-s, -> ['kɛ·nɐ] *m(f)* expert

Kenntnis <-, -se> ['kɛnt·nɪs] *f* **1.** *kein pl* (*Vertrautheit*) knowledge; **etw zur ~ nehmen** to make [a] note of sth; **zur ~ nehmen, dass ...** to note that ...; **jdn von etw** *dat* **in ~ setzen** *geh* to inform sb of sth **2.** *pl* (*Wissen*) knowledge

Kennwort <-wörter> *nt* **1.** (*Codewort*) code word **2.** (*Losungswort*) password

Kennzeichen *nt* **1.** (*Autokennzeichen*) license plate **2.** (*Merkmal*) mark

kennzeichnen ['kɛn·tsai·ç·nən] *vt* **1.** (*markieren*) to mark **2.** (*charakterisieren*) to characterize

kentern ['kɛn·tɐn] *vi sein* to capsize

Keramik <-, -en> [ke·'raː·mɪk] *f* **1.** *kein pl* (*Töpferwaren*) pottery *no indef art* **2.** (*einzelner Gegenstand*) piece of pottery

Kerbe <-, -n> ['kɛr·bə] *f* notch ▶ **in die gleiche ~ hauen** *fam* to take the same line

Kerl <-s, -e> [kɛrl] *m fam* guy

Kern <-[e]s, -e> [kɛrn] *m* **1.** (*von Kernobst*) pip; (*von Steinobst*) pit **2.** (*Atom-, Zellkern*) nucleus **3.** (*wichtigster Teil*) core ▶ **in ihr steckt ein guter ~** she's good at heart; **einen wahren ~ haben** to contain a core of truth

kerngesund *adj* fit as a fiddle *pred*

kernig ['kɛr·nɪç] *adj* **1.** (*voller Obstkerne*) pithy **2.** (*urwüchsig*) earthy

Kernkraft *f* nuclear power

Kernkraftwerk *nt* nuclear power plant

Kernseife *f* tallow soap

Kernstück *nt* crucial part

Kerosin <-s, -e> [ke·ro·'zi:n] *nt* kerosene

Kerze <-, -n> ['kɛr·tsə] *f* **1.** (*Wachskerze*) candle **2.** AUTO spark plug

kerzengerade **I.** *adj* erect **II.** *adv* [as] straight as an arrow

Kerzenlicht *nt* kein pl candlelight

Kerzenständer *m* candlestick

kess [RR], **keß** [ALT] [kɛs] **I.** *adj* **1.** (*frech und pfiffig*) cheeky **2.** (*flott*) jaunty **II.** *adv* cheekily

Kessel <-s, -> ['kɛ·səl] *m* **1.** (*Wasserkessel*) kettle **2.** (*großer Kochtopf*) pot

Ketchup, Ketschup [RR] <-[s], -s> ['kɛt·ʃap] *m o nt* ketchup

Kette <-, -n> ['kɛ·tə] *f* **1.** chain; (*zum Schmuck*) necklace **2.** (*Serie*) line; **eine ~ von Ereignissen** a chain of events; **eine ~ von Unglücksfällen** a series of accidents

Kettenraucher(in) *m(f)* chain smoker

Kettenreaktion *f* chain reaction

Ketzer(in) <-s, -> ['kɛ·tsɐ] *m(f)* heretic

ketzerisch *adj* heretical

keuchen ['kɔy·çn] *vi* to pant

Keuchhusten *m* whooping cough *no art*

Keule <-, -n> ['kɔy·lə] *f* **1.** (*Waffe*) club **2.** KOCHK leg

keusch [kɔyʃ] **I.** *adj* chaste **II.** *adv* **~ leben** to lead a chaste life

Kichererbse ['kɪçɐ·ʔɛrp·sə] *f* chickpea

kichern ['kɪ·çɐn] *vi* to giggle

kidnappen ['kɪt·nɛ·pn] *vt* to kidnap

Kiefer[1] <-, -n> ['ki:·fɐ] *f* BOT pine

Kiefer[2] <-s, -> ['ki:·fɐ] *m* ANAT jaw [bone]

Kieferorthopäde, -orthopädin <-n, -n> *m, f* orthodontist

Kieme <-, -n> ['ki:·mə] *f* gill

Kies <-es, -e> [ki:s] *m* gravel

Kieselstein *m* pebble

Kilo <-s, -[s]> ['ki:·lo] *nt* kilo

Kilobyte ['ki:·lo·bait] *nt* kilobyte

Kilogramm *nt* kilogram

Kilometer [ki·lo·'me:·tɐ] *m* kilometer

Kilometerzähler *m* mileage counter

Kind <-[e]s, -er> [kɪnt] *nt* child; **ein ~ [von jdm] bekommen** to be expecting a baby [from sb]; **von ~ auf** from an early age; **ein großes ~ sein** to be a big baby ▶ **mit ~ und Kegel** *hum fam* with the whole family; **wir werden das ~ schon schaukeln** *fam* we'll manage to sort it out; **kein ~ von Traurigkeit sein** *hum* to be sb who enjoys life

Kinderarzt, -ärztin *m, f* pediatrician

Kindergarten *m* kindergarten

Kindergärtner(in) *m(f)* kindergarten teacher

Kindergeld *nt a monthly government subsidy paid to parents or guardians for each child under 18*

Kinderhort *m* day-nursery

Kinderkrankheit *f* **1.** (*Krankheit*) childhood disease **2.** meist pl (*Anfangsproblem*) teething troubles *pl*

Kinderlähmung *f* polio

kinderleicht ['kɪn·dɐ·'laiçt] *fam* **I.** *adj* very easy; **~ sein** to be child's play **II.** *adv* very easily

kinderlieb ['kɪn·dɐ·li:p] *adj* fond of children *pred*

kinderlos *adj* childless

Kindermädchen *nt* nanny

kinderreich *adj* with many children *pred*; **eine ~e Familie** a large family

Kindersitz *m* (*im Auto*) child safety seat; (*am Fahrrad*) child carrier [seat]

Kinderspiel *nt* children's game ▶ **[für jdn] ein ~ sein** to be child's play [for sb]

Kinderspielplatz *m* playground

Kinderteller *m* child's portion

Kinderwagen *m* baby carriage

Kindheit <-> *f* kein pl childhood; **von ~ an** from childhood

kindisch ['kɪn·dɪʃ] **I.** *adj* childish **II.** *adv* childishly

kindlich ['kɪnt·lɪç] *adj* childlike

Kinn <-[e]s, -e> [kɪn] *nt* chin

Kinnhaken *m* hook to the chin

Kino <-s, -s> ['ki:·no] *nt* [movie] theater; **im ~ kommen** to be playing at the movies

Kiosk <-[e]s, -e> ['ki:·ɔsk] *m* kiosk

Kipfe(r)l <-s, -[n]> *nt* österr (*Hörnchen*) croissant

Kippe <-, -n> ['kɪ·pə] *f fam* 1. (*Deponie*) dump 2. (*Zigarettenstummel*) cigarette butt; (*Zigarette*) cigarette ▶ **es steht auf der ~, ob ...** it's touch and go whether ...

kippen ['kɪ·pn̩] I. *vt haben* 1. (*schütten*) to tip 2. (*schräg stellen*) to tilt 3. *fam* (*scheitern lassen: Gesetzesvorlage*) to vote down *sep;* (*Urteil*) to overturn ▶ **gerne einen/ein paar ~** *fam* to like a drink [or two] II. *vi sein* 1. (*umfallen*) to topple over 2. (*fallen*) **von etw** *dat* **~** to fall off [of] sth 3. (*scheitern: System*) to collapse

Kirche <-, -n> ['kɪr·çə] *f* 1. (*Gebäude, Gottesdienst*) church 2. (*Glaubensgemeinschaft, Institution*) Church

Kirchenchor *m* church choir

Kirchenfest *nt* religious festival

Kirchengemeinde *f* 1. (*Bezirk*) parish 2. (*Angehörige*) church members *pl*

Kirchenlied *nt* hymn

Kirchensteuer *f* taxes taken out of one's paycheck which are allotted to the state church one belongs to

kirchlich ['kɪrç·lɪç] I. *adj* church *attr,* ecclesiastical; **ein ~er Feiertag** a religious holiday II. *adv* ~ **bestattet werden** to have a church funeral; **sich** *akk* ~ **trauen lassen** to get married in church

Kirchturm *m* [church] steeple

Kirschbaum ['kɪrʃ·baʊm] *m* cherry tree

Kirsche <-, -n> ['kɪr·ʃə] *f* cherry

Kissen <-s, -> ['kɪ·sn̩] *nt* (*Kopfkissen*) pillow; (*Zierkissen*) cushion

Kissenbezug *m* (*für Kopfkissen*) pillowcase; (*für Zierkissen*) cushion cover

Kiste <-, -n> ['kɪs·tə] *f* 1. (*Behälter*) box, crate 2. *fam* (*Auto*) [old] clunker 3. *fam* (*Fernseher*) tube 4. *fam* (*Bett*) sack; **ab in die ~!** hit the sack!

Kitsch <-es> [kɪtʃ] *m kein pl* kitsch

kitschig ['kɪt·ʃɪç] *adj* kitschy

Kittchen <-s, -> ['kɪt·çən] *nt fam* slammer *sl*

Kittel <-s, -> ['kɪ·tl̩] *m* smock; (*eines Arztes/Laboranten*) lab coat

kitten ['kɪ·tn̩] *vt* 1. (*verspachteln*) to putty 2. *fig* (*in Ordnung bringen*) to patch up *sep*

kitzelig ['kɪt·tsə·lɪç] *adj* ticklish

kitzeln ['kɪ·tsl̩n] I. *vt* **jdn irgendwo ~** to tickle sb somewhere II. *vi* to tickle III. *vt impers* (*jucken*) **es kitzelt mich** it tickles 2. *fig* (*reizen*) **es kitzelt mich sehr, da mitzumachen** I'm really itching to join in

Kiwi <-, -s> ['ki:·vi] *f* kiwi [fruit]

klaffen ['kla·fn̩] *vi* to yawn; (*Schnitt, Wunde*) to gape

kläffen ['klɛ·fn̩] *vi pej fam* to yap

Klage <-, -n> ['kla:·gə] *f* 1. *geh* (*Wehklage*) lament[ation] 2. (*Beschwerde*) complaint (**über** *+akk* about) 3. JUR [legal] action; **eine ~ abweisen** to dismiss a suit; **eine ~ auf Schadenersatz** a claim for compensation

klagen ['kla:·gn̩] I. *vi* 1. (*jammern*) to moan (**über** *+akk* about) 2. (*sich beklagen*) to complain (**über** *+akk* about); **ich kann nicht ~** I can't complain; **ohne zu ~** without complaining 3. JUR to take legal action (**gegen** *+akk* against); **auf Schadenersatz ~** to sue for damages II. *vt* 1. **jdm sein Leid ~** to tell sb one's troubles 2. österr (*verklagen*) **jdn ~** to take legal action against sb

Kläger(in) <-s, -> *m(f)* JUR plaintiff

klamm [klam] *adj* 1. (*Finger*) numb 2. (*Kleidung, Wäsche*) dank 3. *sl* (*knapp bei Kasse*) ~ **sein** to be [a little] strapped for cash *fam*

Klammer <-, -n> ['kla·mɐ] *f* 1. (*Wäscheklammer*) clothespin; (*Heftklammer*) staple; (*Haarklammer*) [hair] clip; MED clip 2. (*Zahnklammer*) braces *pl* 3. (*grafisches Zeichen: rund*) parentheses; (*eckig*) square bracket; (*spitz*) angle bracket; **in ~n** (*rund*) in parentheses; (*eckig o spitz*) in brackets

Klammeraffe *m* 1. ZOOL spider monkey 2. INET "at" symbol

klammheimlich ['klam·'haɪm·lɪç] *fam* I. *adj* clandestine II. *adv* clandestinely; **sich** *akk* ~ **fortstehlen** to slip away [unseen]

klang [klaŋ] *imp von* **klingen**

Klang <-[e]s, Klänge> [klaŋ] *m* sound

klangvoll *adj* sonorous; *(Melodie)* tuneful; *(Stimme)* melodious

Klappe <-, -n> ['kla·pə] *f* **1.** *(Deckel)* flap **2.** *sl (Mund)* trap; **halt die ~!** shut up!; **eine große ~ haben** to have a big mouth

klappen ['kla·pn̩] **I.** *vt* to fold **II.** *vi fam (funktionieren)* to work out; **alles hat geklappt** everything went as planned

Klapperkiste *f fam (Auto)* rattletrap

klappern ['kla·pɐn] *vi* to rattle

Klapperschlange *f* rattlesnake

Klappfahrrad *nt* folding bicycle

Klappmesser *nt* switchblade

klapprig ['klap·rɪç] *adj* rickety

Klappstuhl *m* folding chair

Klaps <-es, -e> [klaps] *m fam* smack

Klapsmühle *f sl* funny farm *pej*

klar [klaːɐ̯] **I.** *adj* clear; *(Antwort)* straight; *(Frage)* direct; *(Ergebnis)* clear-cut; **alles ~?** *fam* is everything okay?; **na ~!** *fam* of course!; **jdm ~ sein** to be clear to sb; **sich** *dat* **über etw** *akk* **~ werden** to get sth clear in one's mind **II.** *adv* clearly; **etw ~ erkennen** to see sth clearly; **~ und deutlich** clearly and unambiguously; **~ denkend** clear-thinking; **jdm etw ~ zu verstehen geben** to make sth clear to sb; **~ im Vorteil sein** to be at a clear advantage

Kläranlage *f* sewage plant

klären ['klɛ·rən] **I.** *vt* **1.** *(aufklären)* to clear up *sep*; *(Frage)* to settle; *(Problem)* to resolve **2.** *(Abwässer)* to treat **II.** *vr (sich aufklären)* **sich** *akk* **~** to be cleared up

klargehen *vi irreg sein fam* to go okay

klarkommen *vi irreg sein fam* **1.** *(bewältigen)* **mit etw** *dat* **~** to manage [sth] **2.** *(zurechtkommen)* **mit jdm ~** to cope with sb

klarmachen *vt* **jdm etw ~** to make sth clear to sb; **sich** *dat* **etw ~** to realize sth

Klartext *m* ▸ **mit jdm ~ reden** *fam* to be frank with sb

klasse ['kla·sə] *fam* **I.** *adj* fantastic, great **II.** *adv* fantastically, very well

Klasse <-, -n> ['kla·sə] *f* **1.** *(Schulklasse)* class, grade; **eine ~ wiederholen/überspringen** to repeat/skip a grade **2.** *(einer Gesellschaft)* class **3.** *(Güteklasse)* class; **wir fahren immer erster ~** we always travel first class

Klassenkamerad(in) *m(f)* classmate

Klassenlehrer(in) *m(f)* teacher

Klassenzimmer *nt* classroom

klassifizieren * [kla·si·fi·ˈtsiː·rən] *vt* to classify *(als* as)

Klassik <-> ['kla·sɪk] *f kein pl (Musik)* classical music

klassisch ['kla·sɪʃ] *adj* KUNST, LIT, MUS classical

Klatsch <-[e]s> [klatʃ] *m kein pl pej fam* ~ [und Tratsch] gossip

klatschen ['klat·ʃn̩] **I.** *vi* **1.** *(mit den Händen)* to clap; **in die Hände ~** to clap one's hands **2.** *(applaudieren)* to applaud **3.** *fam (tratschen)* to gossip *(über +akk* about) **II.** *vt* **1.** *(applaudieren)* **jdm Beifall ~** to applaud sb **2.** *fam (werfen)* **etw irgendwohin ~** to chuck sth somewhere

klatschnass ^RR *adj fam* soaking wet; **~ sein/werden** to be/get soaked

Klatschspalte *f pej fam* gossip column

Klaue <-, -n> ['klaʊə] *f* claw

klauen ['klaʊ·ən] *fam* **I.** *vt* **[jdm] etw ~** to steal sth [from sb] **II.** *vi* to steal [things]

Klausel <-, -n> ['klaʊ·zl̩] *f (eines Vertrags)* clause

Klavier <-s, -e> [kla·ˈviːɐ̯] *nt* piano

Klavierspieler(in) *m(f)* pianist

kleben ['kleː·bn̩] **I.** *vi* **1.** *(klebrig sein)* to be sticky **2.** *(haften)* to stick **(an** *+dat* to); **[an jdm/etw] ~ bleiben** to stick [to sth/sth] **3.** *fig (festhalten)* to cling **(an** *+dat* to) **II.** *vt* **1.** *(reparieren)* to glue **2.** *(befestigen)* to stick **(an** *+akk* to) ▸ **jdm eine ~** *fam* to clock sb

klebrig ['kleː·brɪç] *adj* sticky

Klebstoff *m* adhesive

Klebstreifen *m* [adhesive] tape

kleckern ['klɛ·kɐn] *fam* **I.** *vt* **etw irgendwohin ~** to spill sth somewhere **II.** *vi (beim Essen)* to make a mess; **mit etw** *dat* **~** to spill sth ▸ **nicht ~, sondern klotzen!** think big!

Klecks <-es, -e> ['klɛks] *m* **1.** *(Fleck)* stain **2.** *(kleine Menge)* blob

K

klecksen ['klɛk·sn̩] vi **1.** haben (*Kleckse verursachen*) [mit etw dat] ~ to make a mess [with sth] **2.** sein (*tropfen*) etw kleckst irgendwohin sth is spilling on[to] sth

Klee <-s> [kle:] m kein pl clover

Kleeblatt nt cloverleaf; **vierblättriges ~** four-leaf clover

Kleid <-[e]s, -er> [klait] nt **1.** (*Damenkleid*) dress **2.** pl (*Bekleidungsstücke*) clothes npl

kleiden ['klai·dn̩] vt, vr (**sich** akk) ~ to dress

Kleiderbügel m coat hanger

Kleiderbürste f clothes brush

Kleiderhaken m coat hook

Kleiderschrank m clothes closet

Kleidung <-, -en> f pl selten clothing

Kleidungsstück nt garment

klein [klain] **I.** adj small, little **II.** adv **~ gedruckt** attr in small print pred; **etw ~ hacken** to chop up sep sth ▶ **~ beigeben** to give in [quietly]; **von ~ auf** from childhood

Kleinasien [klain·'ʔa:zi̯·ən] nt Asia Minor

Kleingeld nt [small] change

Kleinholz nt kein pl chopped wood ▶ **aus jdm/etw ~ machen** fam to make mincemeat [out] of sb/sth

Kleinigkeit <-, -en> ['klai·nɪç·kait] f **1.** (*Bagatelle*) small matter; **muss ich mich um jede ~ kümmern?** do I have to do every little thing myself?; **wegen jeder ~** for the slightest reason, at every opportunity **2.** (*ein wenig*) **eine ~ zu hoch/tief** a little too high/low **3.** (*Sache*) little something; **ich habe dir eine ~ mitgebracht** I brought you a little something; **eine ~ essen** to have a bite to eat ▶ **[jdn] eine ~ kosten** iron to cost [sb] a pretty penny

kleinkariert I. adj **1.** (*mit kleinen Karos*) finely checkered **2.** fam (*engstirnig*) narrow-minded **II.** adv in a narrow-minded way

Kleinkind nt toddler

Kleinkram m fam **1.** (*Zeug*) odds and ends **2.** (*Trivialitäten*) trivialities pl

klein|kriegen vt fam **1.** (*kaputtmachen*) to smash **2.** (*gefügig machen*) **jdn ~** to bring sb into line

kleinlaut I. adj sheepish; (*gefügig*) subdued **II.** adv sheepishly

kleinlich ['klain·lɪç] adj pej **1.** (*knauserig*) mean **2.** (*engstirnig*) petty

Kleinstadt f small town

kleinstädtisch adj small-town attr

Kleinwagen m subcompact car

Klemme <-, -n> ['klɛ·mə] f fam (*schwierige Lage*) jam

klemmen ['klɛ·mən] **I.** vt to stick **II.** vr **sich** dat **den Finger in der Tür ~** to get one's finger caught in the door ▶ **sich** akk **hinter etw ~** to get on sth; **ich werde mich mal hinter die Sache ~** I'll get on it **III.** vi **1.** (*blockieren*) to jam **2.** (*angeheftet sein*) to be stuck

Klempner(in) <-s, -> ['klɛmp·nɐ] m(f) plumber

Klerus <-> ['kle:·rʊs] m kein pl clergy

Klette <-, -n> ['klɛ·tə] f **1.** (*Pflanze*) burdock **2.** pej fam (*anhänglicher Mensch*) nuisance; **an jdm wie eine ~ hängen** fam to stick to sb like glue

klettern ['klɛ·tɐn] vi sein to climb; **auf einen Baum ~** to climb a tree

Klettverschluss^RR m Velcro® fastener

Klima <-s, Klimata> ['kli:·ma] nt climate

Klimaanlage f air-conditioning

klimatisiert adj air-conditioned

Klimaveränderung f climate change

klimpern ['klɪm·pɐn] vi (*Münzen*) to jingle; (*Schlüssel*) to jangle; **auf einer Gitarre ~** to pluck away on a guitar fam

Klinge <-, -n> ['klɪŋə] f blade

Klingel <-, -n> ['klɪŋl̩] f bell

klingeln ['klɪŋl̩n] vi to ring; **an der Tür ~** to ring the doorbell ▶ **hat es jetzt endlich geklingelt?** do you get it, finally?

klingen <klang, geklungen> ['klɪŋən] vi **1.** (*erklingen: Glas*) to clink; (*Glocke*) to ring **2.** (*sich anhören*) to sound; **das klingt gut/interessant** that sounds good/interesting

Klinik <-, -en> ['kli:·nɪk] f clinic

Klinke <-, -n> ['klɪn·kə] f [door] handle

Klippe <-, -n> ['klɪ·pə] f cliff; (*im Meer*) [coastal] rock

klirren ['klɪ·rən] vi **1.** (*Gläser*) to tinkle;

(*Fensterscheiben*) to rattle **2.** (*Lautsprecher, Mikrophon*) to crackle

Klo <-s, -s> [kloː] *nt fam* john

Kloake <-, -n> [kloˈaːkə] *f a. fig* cesspool

klobig [ˈkloː·bɪç] *adj* bulky; (*Hände*) massive

klonen [ˈkloː·nən] *vt* to clone

klönen [ˈkløː·nən] *vi fam* to chat

klopfen [ˈklɔp·fn̩] **I.** *vi* to knock (**auf** +*akk* on, **gegen** +*akk* against); **jdm auf etw** *akk* ~ (*mit der flachen Hand*) to pat sb on sth; (*mit dem Finger*) to tap sb on sth **II.** *vt* (*Teppich, Fleisch*) to beat

kloppen [ˈklɔ·pn̩] *vr dial fam* **sich** *akk* [**mit jdm**] ~ to fight [with sb]

Klops <-es, -e> [klɔps] *m* (*Fleischkloß*) meatball

Klosett <-s, -e> [kloˈzɛt] *nt veraltend* privy *old*

Kloß <-es, Klöße> [kloːs] *m* dumpling ▶ **einen** ~ **im** **Hals haben** *fam* to have a lump in one's throat

Kloster <-s, Klöster> [ˈkloːs·tɐ] *nt* (*Mönchskloster*) monastery; (*Nonnenkloster*) convent

Klotz <-es, Klötze> [klɔts] *m* block [of wood]; (*hässliches Gebäude*) monstrosity ▶ **jdm] ein ~ am** **Bein sein** *fam* to be a heavy burden for sb

Klub <-s, -s> [klʊp] *m* club

Kluft[1] <-, Klüfte> [klʊft] *f* GEOG [deep] fissure

Kluft[2] <-, -en> [klʊft] *f dial hum* uniform

klug <klüger, klügste> [kluːk] **I.** *adj* **1.** (*vernünftig*) smart, clever; (*vernünftig*) wise; (*Entscheidung*) prudent; (*Rat*) sound; **es wäre klüger, ...** it would be more sensible ...; **da soll einer draus ~ werden** I can't make heads or tails of it; **genauso ~ wie zuvor sein** to be none the wiser **II.** *adv a. iron* cleverly

klumpen [ˈklʊm·pn̩] *vi* to get lumpy; (*Salz*) to cake

Klumpen <-s, -> [ˈklʊm·pn̩] *m* lump; ~ **bilden** to get lumpy

Klüngel <-s, -> [ˈklʏŋl̩] *m pej fam* clique

knabbern [ˈknaˈbɐn] **I.** *vi* **1.** (*essen*) to nibble (**an** +*dat* on) **2.** (*emotional verarbeiten*) to chew (**an** +*dat* on) **II.** *vt*

to nibble; **etwas zum K~** something to nibble on

Knabe <-n, -n> [ˈknaː·bə] *m veraltend geh* boy; **na, alter ~!** *fam* hey, dude! *sl*

Knäckebrot *nt* crispbread

knacken [kna·kn̩] **I.** *vt* to crack **II.** *vi* to crack; (*Diele*) to creak; (*Zweige*) to snap

Knacker <-s, -> *m dial fam* guy; **ein alter ~** an old geezer

Knacki <-s, -s> [ˈkna·ki] *m sl* ex-con

Knackpunkt *m fam* crucial point

Knacks <-es, -e> [knaks] *m* **1.** (*Laut*) crack **2.** (*Schaden*) problem; **einen ~ haben** (*Ehe*) to be in trouble; (*Freundschaft*) to be suffering; (*Mensch*) to have a screw loose

Knall <-[e]s, -e> [knal] *m* bang; (*vom Korken*) pop; (*einer Tür*) bang ▶ ~ **auf** **Fall** *fam* all of a sudden; **einen ~ haben** *fam* to be off one's rocker

knallen [ˈknalən] **I.** *vi* **1.** *haben* (*ertönen*) to bang; (*Auspuff*) to backfire; (*Feuerwerkskörper*) to [go] bang; (*Korken*) to [go] pop; (*Schuss*) to ring out **2.** *sein fam* (*stoßen*) to bang (**auf** +*akk* on, **gegen** +*akk* against) **II.** *vi impers haben* **es knallt** there's a bang; **..., sonst knallt's!** *fam* (*oder es gibt eine Ohrfeige!*) ... or I'll slap you!; (*oder ich schieße!*) ... or I'll shoot! **III.** *vt* (*werfen*) to slam ▶ **jdm** **eine** ~ *fam* to whack sb

knallhart [ˈknalˈhart] *fam* **I.** *adj* **1.** (*rücksichtslos*) really tough, [as] tough as nails *pred* **2.** (*Schuss*) fierce; (*Schlag*) crushing **II.** *adv* brutally; ~ **verhandeln** to drive a hard bargain

knallrot [ˈknalˈroːt] *adj* bright red

knapp [knap] **I.** *adj* **1.** (*gering*) meager; (*Geld*) tight; [**mit etw** *dat*] ~ **sein** to be short [on sth] **2.** (*eng*) tight[-fitting] **3.** (*noch genügend*) just enough; (*Mehrheit, Sieg*) narrow; (*Ergebnis*) close **4.** (*nicht ganz*) almost; **in einer ~en Stunde** in just under an hour **5.** (*Antwort, Worte*) succinct **II.** *adv* **1.** (*mäßig*) sparingly; **seine Zeit ist ~ bemessen** he only has a limited amount of time **2.** (*nicht ganz*) almost; ~ **eine Stunde** just under an hour **3.** (*haarscharf*) narrowly

K

Knarre <-, -n> ['kna·rə] *f sl* gun

knarren ['kna·rən] *vi* to creak

Knast <-[e]s, Knäste> [knast] *m sl* prison; **im ~** in the slammer; **im ~ sitzen** to do time

knattern ['kna·tɐn] *vi* to clatter; *(Motorrad)* to roar

Knäuel <-s, -> ['knɔ·yəl] *m o nt* ball

Knauf <-[e]s, Knäufe> [knauf] *m* knob

knauserig ['knau·zə·rɪç] *adj pej fam* stingy

knausern ['knau·zɐn] *vi pej fam* to be stingy **(mit** +*dat* with)

knautschen ['knau·tʃn] *vi* to crease

Knebel <-s, -> ['kne:·bl̩] *m* gag

knebeln ['kne:·bl̩n] *vt a. fig* to gag

kneifen <kniff, gekniffen> ['knai·fn̩] **I.** *vt* to pinch; **jdn in etw** *akk* **~** to pinch sb's sth **II.** *vi* **1.** *(zwicken)* to pinch **2.** *fam (zurückscheuen)* **[vor etw** *dat]* **~** to chicken out [of sth]; **vor jdm ~** to shy away from sb

Kneipe <-, -n> ['knai·pə] *f fam* bar

Knete <-> ['kne:·tə] *f kein pl* **1.** *sl (Geld)* bread **2.** *fam* Play-Doh®

kneten ['kne:·tn̩] *vt* **1.** *(durchwalken)* to knead **2.** *(formen)* to model

knicken ['knɪ·kn̩] *vt* to fold; **„nicht ~!"** "[please] do not bend!"

knickerig ['knɪ·kə·rɪç] *adj fam (knauserig)* penny-pinching, stingy

Knie <-s, -> [kni:] *nt* knee ▶ **etw übers ~ brechen** *fam* to rush into sth; **weiche ~ bekommen** *fam* to go weak at the knees

Kniebeuge *f* kneebend

Kniegelenk *nt* knee joint

Kniekehle *f* back of the knee

knien [kni:n] **I.** *vi* to kneel **II.** *vr* **sich** *akk* **~** **1.** *(auf die Knie gehen)* to kneel [down] **(auf** +*akk* on) **2.** *fam (sich intensiv beschäftigen)* **sich** *akk* **in etw** *akk* **~** to get down to sth

Kniescheibe *f* kneecap

Kniestrumpf *m* knee sock

kniff [knɪf] *imp von* **kneifen**

Kniff <-[e]s, -e> [knɪf] *m* **1.** *(Kunstgriff)* trick **2.** *(Falte)* fold; *(unabsichtlich a.)* crease

knifflig ['knɪf·lɪç] *adj fam* tricky

Knilch <-s, -e> [knɪlç] *m pej sl (Scheiß-kerl)* bastard *vulg;* *(Niete)* loser *fam*

knipsen ['knɪp·sn̩] **I.** *vt* **1.** *fam (fotografieren)* **jdn/etw ~** to take a picture of sb/sth **2.** *(lochen)* to punch **II.** *vi fam* to take pictures; *(wild drauflos)* to snap away

knirschen ['knɪr·ʃn̩] *vi* to crunch; *(Getriebe)* to grind

knistern ['knɪs·tɐn] *vi (Feuer)* to crackle; *(Papier)* to rustle; **mit etw** *dat* **~** to rustle sth

knittern ['knɪ·tɐn] *vt, vi* to crease

knobeln ['kno:·bl̩n] *vi (würfeln)* to play dice

Knoblauch <-[e]s> *m kein pl* garlic

Knoblauchzehe *f* clove of garlic

Knöchel <-s, -> ['knœ·çl̩] *m* **1.** *(Fußknöchel)* ankle **2.** *(Fingerknöchel)* knuckle

Knochen <-s, -> ['knɔ·xn̩] *m* bone ▶ **bis auf die ~ abgemagert sein** to be all skin and bone[s]

Knochenarbeit *f fam* backbreaking work

Knochenbruch *m* fracture

Knochengerüst *nt* skeleton

Knochenmark *nt* bone marrow

knochig ['knɔ·xɪç] *adj* bony

Knödel <-s, -> ['knø:·dl̩] *m südd, österr* dumpling

Knolle <-, -n> ['knɔ·lə] *f* **1.** BOT nodule; *(der Kartoffel)* tuber **2.** *fam (dicke Nase)* bulbous nose

Knopf <-[e]s, Knöpfe> [knɔpf] *m* button

Knopfloch *nt* buttonhole

Knorpel <-s, -> ['knɔr·pl̩] *m* ANAT cartilage; KOCHK gristle

knorpelig ['knɔr·pə·lɪç] *adj* ANAT cartilaginous *spec;* KOCHK gristly

Knospe <-, -n> ['knɔs·pə] *f* bud

knoten ['kno:·tn̩] *vt* to knot

Knoten <-s, -> ['kno:·tn̩] *m* **1.** *(Verschlingung)* knot **2.** MED lump **3.** *(Haarknoten)* bun

Knotenpunkt *m* AUTO, BAHN junction

knotig ['kno:·tɪç] *adj* **1.** *(Finger)* knotty; *(Haar)* full of knots *pred* **2.** MED nodular

Knüller <-s, -> ['kny·lɐ] *m fam (Nachricht)* scoop

knüpfen ['knʏp·fn̩] I. vt 1. (verknoten) to tie; (Netz) to mesh; (Teppich) to knot 2. (gedanklich) **eine Bedingung an etw** akk ~ to attach a condition to sth; **Hoffnungen an etw** akk ~ to pin hopes on sth II. vr **sich** akk **an etw** akk ~ to be linked with sth

Knüppel <-s, -> ['knʏ·pl̩] m cudgel, club; (Polizeiknüppel) nightstick

knurren ['knʊ·rən] vt, vi to growl; (wütend) to snarl

knusprig ['knʊs·prɪç] adj (Brot, Braten) crisp[y]; (Brot a.) crusty; (Gebäck, Nüsse) crunchy

knutschen ['knu:·tʃn̩] fam I. vt to kiss II. vi to smooch (**mit** +dat with)

Knutschfleck m fam love bite

Koalition <-, -en> [ko·ʔali·'tsi̯oːn] f coalition

Koch, Köchin <-s, Köche> [kɔx, 'kœ·çɪn] m, f cook

Kochbuch nt cookbook

kochen ['kɔ·xn̩] I. vi 1. (Speisen zubereiten) to cook 2. (brodeln) to boil; **etw zum K~ bringen** to bring sth to a boil; **~d heiß** boiling hot 3. (in Aufruhr sein) to seethe; **vor Wut ~** to seethe with rage II. vt 1. (zubereiten) to cook; **Kaffee/Suppe ~** to make coffee/soup 2. (Wäsche) to wash hot

Köchin <-, -nen> ['kœ·çɪn] f s. **Koch**

Kochlöffel m wooden spoon

Kochnische f kitchenette

Kochplatte f 1. (Herdplatte) hotplate 2. (transportabler Kocher) small [electric] stove

Kochrezept nt recipe

Kochtopf m [cooking] pot; (mit Stiel) saucepan

Kochwäsche f laundry that can be washed in boiling-hot water

Kode <-s, -s> ['koːt] m code

Köder <-s, -> ['køː·dɐ] m bait

ködern ['køː·den] vt to lure; **sich** akk **von jdm/etw ~ lassen** to be tempted by sb/sth

Koffein <-s> [kɔ·fe·'iːn] nt kein pl caffeine

koffeinfrei adj decaffeinated

Koffer <-s, -> ['kɔ·fɐ] m suitcase

Kofferraum m trunk

Kognak <-s, -s> ['kɔn·jak] m brandy

Kohl <-[e]s, -e> [koːl] m cabbage

Kohle <-, -n> ['koː·lə] f 1. (Brennstoff) coal 2. sl (Geld) dough no indef art ▶ **wie auf** ⟨glühenden⟩ **~n sitzen** to be on tenterhooks

Kohlendioxid nt kein pl carbon dioxide

Kohlenhydrat <-[e]s, -e> nt carbohydrate

Kohlensäure f carbonic acid; **mit/ohne ~** carbonated/noncarbonated

kohlrabenschwarz ['koːl·l·raː·bn̩·'ʃvarts] adj jet-black

Kohlrabi <-[s], -[s]> [koːl·'raː·bi] m kohlrabi

Koje <-, -n> ['koː·jə] f NAUT bunk

Kojote <-n, -n> [ko·'joː·tə] m coyote

Kokain <-s> [ko·ka·'iːn] nt kein pl cocaine

kokett [ko·'kɛt] I. adj flirtatious II. adv flirtatiously

kokettieren * [ko·kɛ·'tiː·rən] vi (flirten) to flirt

Kokosnuss ᴿᴿ f coconut

Koks¹ <-es, -e> [koːks] m (Brennstoff) coke

Koks² <-es> [koːks] m o nt kein pl sl (Kokain) coke fam

Kolben <-s, -> ['kɔl·bn̩] m 1. AUTO piston 2. (Gewehrkolben) butt 3. CHEM retort 4. (Maiskolben) cob

Kolik <-, -en> ['koː·lɪk] f colic

Kollaps <-es, -e> ['kɔ·laps] m collapse

Kollege, Kollegin <-n, -n> [kɔ·'leː·gə] m, f colleague

kollegial [kɔ·le·'gi̯aːl] I. adj considerate and friendly (towards one's colleagues) II. adv in a considerate and friendly way

kollidieren * [kɔ·li·'diː·rən] vi 1. sein (zusammenstoßen) to collide 2. sein o haben (unvereinbar sein) to clash

Kollision <-, -en> [kɔ·li·'zi̯oːn] f collision

Köln <-s> [kœln] nt Cologne

Kölnisch Wasser ['kœl·nɪʃ·va·sɐ] nt [eau de] cologne

Kolonie <-, -n> [ko·lo·'niː] f colony

kolonisieren * [ko·lo·ni·'ziː·rən] vt to colonize

Kolonne <-, -n> [ko·'lɔ·nə] f AUTO line [of

K

traffic]; (*von Polizei*) convoy

Koloss RR <-es, -e>, **Koloß** ALT <-sses, -sse> [ko·'lɔs] *m* 1. *fam* (*riesiger Mensch*) colossus 2. (*gewaltiges Gebilde*) colossal thing

kolossal [ko·lɔ·'saːl] I. *adj* colossal; **eine ~e Dummheit begehen** to do sth incredibly stupid II. *adv* tremendously; **sich** *akk* **~ verschätzen** to make a huge miscalculation

Kolumbien <-s> [ko·'lʊm·bi̯·ən] *nt* Colombia; *s. a.* **Deutschland**

Kolumne <-, -n> [ko·'lʊm·nə] *f* column

Kolumnist(in) <-en, -en> [ko·lʊm·'nɪst] *m(f)* columnist

Koma <-s, -s> ['koː·ma] *nt* coma

Kombi <-s, -s> ['kɔm·bi] *m fam* station wagon

Kombination <-, -en> [kɔm·bi·na·'tsi̯oːn] *f* 1. (*Verbindung*) combination 2. MODE outfit

kombinieren * [kɔm·bi·'niː·rən] I. *vt* to combine II. *vi* to deduce; **gut ~ können** to be good at deducing; **falsch/ richtig ~** to come to the wrong/right conclusion

Komet <-en, -en> [ko·'meːt] *m* comet

Komfort <-s> [kɔm·'foːɐ̯] *m kein pl* comfort

komfortabel [kɔm·fɔr·'taː·bl] *adj* 1. (*großzügig ausgestattet*) luxurious 2. (*bequem*) comfortable

Komiker(in) <-s, -> ['koː·mɪ·kɐ] *m(f)* comedian

komisch ['koː·mɪʃ] I. *adj* 1. (*zum Lachen reizend*) funny 2. (*sonderbar*) strange; **etw kommt jdm ~ vor** (*eigenartig*) sth seems funny/strange to sb; (*suspekt*) sth seems fishy to sb; **sich** *akk* **~ fühlen** to feel funny II. *adv* (*eigenartig*) strangely

Komitee <-s, -s> [ko·mi·'teː] *nt* committee

Komma <-s, -s> ['kɔ·ma] *nt* 1. (*Satzzeichen*) comma 2. MATH [decimal] point

Kommando <-s, -s> [kɔ·'man·do] *nt* command; **auf ~** on command; **das ~ haben** to be in command

kommen <kam, gekommen> ['kɔ·mən] I. *vi sein* 1. (*eintreffen, hinkommen*) to come; **ich komme schon!** I'm coming!;

der Zug kommt aus Paris the train is coming from Paris; **da kommt Anne/ der Bus** there's Anne/the bus; **ist Post für mich gekommen?** was there any mail for me?; **wann soll das Baby ~?** when's the baby due?; **das Schlimmste kommt noch** the worst is yet to come; **als Erster/Letzter ~** to be the first/ last to arrive; **mit dem Auto/Fahrrad ~** to come by car/bike; **zu Fuß ~** to come on foot 2. (*besuchen*) **zu jdm ~** to visit sb, to come and see sb 3. (*gelangen*) **irgendwohin ~** to get somewhere; **wie komme ich von hier zum Bahnhof?** how do I get to the train station from here?; **zu Fuß kommt man am schnellsten dahin** the quickest way [to get] there is to walk; **ans Ziel ~** to reach the finish line; **zu der Erkenntnis ~, dass ...** to realize that ...; **zu Geld ~** to come into money; **zu Kräften ~** to gain strength; **zu sich** *dat* **~** to regain consciousness 4. (*gehen, fahren*) to come; **kommst du mit uns ins Kino?** are you coming to the movies with us?; **durch einen Ort/Tunnel ~** to pass through a place/tunnel 5. (*stammen*) **irgendwoher ~** to come from somewhere; **woher kommst du?** where are you from?; **ich komme aus Germersheim** I'm from Germersheim 6. (*an der Reihe sein*) **jd kommt an die Reihe** it's sb's turn; **ich komme zuerst an die Reihe** I'm first; **wer kommt [jetzt]?** whose turn is it [now]? 7. (*Aufenthalt beginnen*) **ins Gefängnis/Krankenhaus ~** to go to prison/to be admitted to a hospital; **in die Schule/Lehre ~** to start school/ an apprenticeship 8. **den Arzt/ein Taxi ~ lassen** to send for the doctor/a taxi 9. (*herannahen*) to approach; (*eintreten, geschehen*) to come about; **das kam doch anders als erwartet** it/that turned out differently than expected; **es kam eins zum anderen** one thing led to another; **und so kam es, dass ...** and that's how it came about that ...; **wie kommt es, dass ...?** how come ...?; **es musste ja so ~** it/that was bound to happen; **es hätte viel schlimmer ~ können** it could have been much worse;

was auch immer ~ mag whatever happens; **so weit ~, dass ...** to get to the point where ... **10.** (*erfassen*) **über jdn ~** (*Gefühl*) to come over sb; **jdm ~ die Tränen** sb is starting to cry; **jdm ~ Zweifel, ob ...** sb doubts whether ... **11.** (*geraten*) **wir kamen plötzlich ins Schleudern** we suddenly started to skid; **in Gefahr/Not ~** to get into danger/difficulty; **in Verlegenheit ~** to get embarrassed **12.** (*Grund haben*) **das kommt davon, dass ...** that's because ...; **das kommt davon, wenn ...** that's what happens when ... **13.** (*sich erinnern*) **auf etw** akk **~** to remember sth **14.** (*Idee haben*) **auf etw** akk **~: wie kommst du darauf?** what makes you think that? **15. hinter etw** akk **~** (*Pläne*) to find out sep sth; **hinter ein Geheimnis ~** to uncover a secret **16.** RADIO, TV (*gesendet werden*) to be on TV **17.** (*Zeit finden*) **zu etw** dat **~** to get around to doing sth **18.** (*ansprechen*) **auf etw** akk **zu sprechen ~** to get around to [talking about] sth **19.** sl (*Orgasmus haben*) to come II. vt sein fam **die Reparatur kam mich sehr teuer** the repairs cost a lot [of money]

kommend adj coming, next; **in den ~en Jahren** in the years to come

Kommentar <-s, -e> [kɔ·mɛnˈtaːg] m **1.** (*Stellungnahme*) statement; **kein ~!** no comment! **2.** (*Meinung*) opinion; **einen ~** [**zu etw** dat] **abgeben** to comment [on] sth **3.** (*kommentierendes Werk*) commentary

kommentieren * [kɔ·mɛnˈtiː·rən] vt to comment on

Kommissar(in) <-s, -e> [kɔ·mɪˈsaːg] m(f) (*bei der Polizei*) inspector

Kommission <-, -en> [kɔ·mɪˈsjoːn] f **1.** (*Gremium, Ausschuss*) committee **2.** (*EU-Kommission*) Commission **3.** (*Auftrag*) commission; **etw in ~ geben** to commission sb to sell sth

Kommode <-, -n> [kɔˈmoː·də] f bureau, dresser

kommunal [kɔ·muˈnaːl] adj municipal

Kommunalpolitik f local politics pl

Kommunalwahl f local [government] elections pl

Kommune <-, -n> [kɔˈmuː·nə] f **1.** (*Gemeinde*) local authority **2.** (*Wohngemeinschaft*) commune

Kommunikation <-, -en> [kɔ·mu·ni·kaˈtsjoːn] f communication

Kommunion <-, -en> [kɔ·muˈnjoːn] f REL Holy Communion; (*Erstkommunion*) First Communion

Kommunismus <-> [kɔ·muˈnɪs·mʊs] m kein pl communism

Kommunist(in) <-en, -en> [kɔ·muˈnɪst] m(f) communist

kommunistisch [kɔ·muˈnɪs·tɪʃ] adj communist

Komödie <-, -n> [ko·ˈmø·djə] f **1.** (*Bühnenstück*) comedy **2.** pej (*Verstellung*) play-acting

kompakt [kɔmˈpakt] adj compact

Komparativ <-s, -e> [ˈkɔm·pa·ra·tiːf] m comparative

Kompass RR <-es, -e>, **Kompaß** ALT <-sses, -sse> [ˈkɔm·pas] m compass

kompatibel [kɔm·paˈtiː·bl̩] adj compatible

kompensieren * [kɔm·pɛnˈziː·rən] vt to compensate

kompetent [kɔm·peˈtɛnt] I. adj **1.** (*sachverständig*) competent **2.** (*zuständig*) responsible II. adv competently

komplett [kɔmˈplɛt] I. adj complete II. adv completely

komplex [kɔmˈplɛks] I. adj complex II. adv complexly, in a complicated manner pred

Komplex <-es, -e> [kɔmˈplɛks] m complex

Komplikation <-, -en> [kɔm·pli·kaˈtsjoːn] f complication

Kompliment <-[e]s, -e> [kɔm·pliˈmɛnt] nt compliment; **jdm ein ~ machen** to pay sb a compliment

Komplize, Komplizin <-n, -n> [kɔmˈpliː·tsə] m, f accomplice

kompliziert I. adj complicated II. adv in a complicated manner pred

Komplizin <-, -nen> f s. **Komplize**

Komplott <-[e]s, -e> [kɔmˈplɔt] nt plot

komponieren * [kɔm·po·niˈrən] vt, vi to compose

Komponist(in) <-en, -en> [kɔm·poˈnɪst] m(f) composer

Kompost <-[e]s, -e> [kɔm·'pɔst] *m* compost

kompostieren * [kɔm·pɔs·'tiː·rən] *vt* to compost

Kompott <-[e]s, -e> [kɔm·'pɔt] *nt* compote

komprimieren * [kɔm·pri·'miː·rən] *vt* to compress

Kompromiss RR <-es, -e>, **Kompromiß** ALT <-sses, -sse> [kɔm·pro·'mɪs] *m* compromise; **fauler ~** false compromise

kompromisslos RR *adj* uncompromising

kondensieren * [kɔn·dɛn·'ziː·rən] *vt, vi sein o haben* to condense

Kondensmilch *f* condensed milk

Konditor(in) <-s, -toren> [kɔn·'diː·toːɐ̯, kɔn·di·'toː·rɪn] *m(f)* pastry chef, confectioner

Konditorei <-, -en> [kɔn·di·to·'raɪ̯] *f* pastry shop

Kondom <-s, -e> [kɔn·'doːm] *m o nt* condom

Kondor <-s, -e> ['kɔn·doːɐ̯] *m* condor

Konfekt <-[e]s, -e> [kɔn·'fɛkt] *nt* confections *pl*

Konfektionsgröße *f* size

Konferenz <-, -en> [kɔn·fe·'rɛnts] *f* conference

Konfession <-, -en> [kɔn·fɛ·'sjoːn] *f* denomination

konfessionslos *adj* not belonging to any denomination

Konfirmation <-, -en> [kɔn·fɪr·ma·'tsjoːn] *f* confirmation

konfiszieren * [kɔn·fɪs·'tsiː·rən] *vt* to confiscate

Konfitüre <-, -n> [kɔn·fi·'tyː·rə] *f* jam, preserves *pl*

Konflikt <-s, -e> [kɔn·'flɪkt] *m* conflict

Konfrontation <-, -en> [kɔn·frɔn·ta·'tsjoːn] *f* confrontation

konfrontieren * [kɔn·frɔn·'tiː·rən] *vt* to confront

konfus [kɔn·'fuːs] I. *adj* confused II. *adv* confusedly

Kongress RR <-es, -e>, **Kongreß** ALT <-sses, -sse> [kɔn·'grɛs] *m* 1. (*Fachtagung*) congress 2. (*Parlament der USA*) **der ~** Congress

König <-s, -e> ['køː·nɪç] *m* king

Königin <-, -nen> ['køː·nɪ·gɪn] *f s.* **König** queen

königlich ['køː·nɪk·lɪç] *adj* 1. (*dem König gehörend*) royal 2. (*großzügig*) handsome

Königreich ['køː·nɪk·raɪ̯ç] *nt* kingdom

Konjugation <-, -en> [kɔn·ju·ga·'tsjoːn] *f* conjugation

konjugieren * [kɔn·ju·'giː·rən] *vt* to conjugate

Konjunktur <-, -en> [kɔn·jʊnk·'tuːɐ̯] *f* state of the economy; **steigende/rückläufige ~** [economic] boom/slump

konkret [kɔn·'kreːt] I. *adj* concrete II. *adv* specifically; **das kann ich Ihnen noch nicht ~ sagen** I can't tell you for sure yet

konkretisieren * [kɔn·kre·ti·'ziː·rən] *vt* to clearly define

Konkurrent(in) <-en, -en> [kɔn·kʊ·'rɛnt] *m(f)* competitor

Konkurrenz <-, -en> [kɔn·kʊ·'rɛnts] *f* 1. (*Konkurrent*) competitor; **keine ~ [für jdn] sein** to be no competition [for sb] 2. *kein pl* (*Wettbewerb*) competition; **mit jdm in ~ stehen** to be in competition with sb; **außer ~** unofficially

konkurrieren * [kɔn·kʊ·'riː·rən] *vi* to compete

Konkurs <-es, -e> [kɔn·'kʊrs] *m* bankruptcy; **~ machen** *fam* to go bankrupt; **~ anmelden** to declare oneself bankrupt

können ['kœ·nən] I. *vt* <kann, konnte, gekonnt> 1. (*beherrschen*) **etw ~** to know sth; **eine Sprache ~** to speak a language 2. (*verantwortlich sein*) **etwas/nichts für etw** *akk* **~** to be able/to not be able to do anything about sth ▶ **du kannst mich mal** *euph sl* kiss my ass! *vulg*, fuck off! *vulg* II. *vi* <kann, konnte, gekonnt> to be able; **nicht mehr ~** (*erschöpft sein*) to not be able to go on; (*überfordert sein*) to have had enough; (*satt sein*) to be full; **noch ~** (*weitermachen können*) to be able to continue; (*weiteressen können*) to be able to eat more; **wie konntest du nur!** how could you?! III. *modal vb* <kann, konnte, können> 1. (*fähig sein*) **etw tun ~** to be able to do sth 2. (*dürfen*) **kann ich das Foto sehen?** can

I see the picture? **3.** (*möglicherweise sein*) **solche Dinge ~ eben manchmal passieren** these things [can] happen sometimes; **[ja,] kann sein** [yes,] that's possible; **könnte es nicht sein, dass ...?** could it be that ...?

Können <-s> [ˈkœ·nən] *nt kein pl* ability

konsequent [kɔn·ze·ˈkvɛnt] **I.** *adj* consistent; **~ sein** to be consistent (**bei/in** +*dat* in) **II.** *adv* consistently

Konsequenz <-, -en> [kɔn·ze·ˈkvɛnts] *f* **1.** (*Folge*) consequence; **~en** [**für jdn**] **haben** to have consequences [for sb]; **die ~en tragen** to take the consequences **2.** *kein pl* (*Unbeirrbarkeit*) consistency

konservativ [kɔn·zɛr·va·ˈtiːf] **I.** *adj* conservative **II.** *adv* **~ eingestellt sein** to have a conservative attitude

Konserve <-, -n> [kɔn·ˈzɛr·və] *f* preserved food

Konservendose *f* can

konservieren * [kɔn·zɛr·ˈviː·rən] *vt* to preserve

Konservierungsmittel *nt* preservative

Konsonant <-en, -en> [kɔn·zo·ˈnant] *m* consonant

konstant [kɔn·ˈstant] **I.** *adj* constant **II.** *adv* constantly

Konstante <-[n], -n> [kɔn·ˈstan·tə] *f* constant

Konstitution <-, -en> [kɔn·sti·tu·ˈtsjoːn] *f* constitution

konstitutionell [kɔn·sti·tu·tsjo·ˈnɛl] *adj* constitutional; **~e Monarchie** constitutional monarchy

konstruieren * [kɔn·stru·ˈiː·rən] *vt* **1.** (*aufbauen*) to construct **2.** (*entwerfen*) to design

Konstruktion <-, -en> [kɔn·strʊk·ˈtsjoːn] *f* **1.** (*Bauweise*) construction **2.** (*Entwurf*) design

konstruktiv [kɔn·strʊk·ˈtiːf] **I.** *adj* constructive **II.** *adv* constructively

Konsul(in) <-s, -n> [ˈkɔn·zʊl] *m(f)* consul

Konsulat <-[e]s, -e> [kɔn·zʊ·ˈlaːt] *nt* consulate

konsultieren * [kɔn·zʊl·ˈtiː·rən] *vt* to consult (**wegen** +*gen* about)

Konsum <-s> [kɔn·ˈzuːm] *m kein pl* consumption

Konsument(in) <-en, -en> [kɔn·zu·ˈmɛnt] *m(f)* consumer

Konsumgesellschaft *f* consumer society

Konsumgüter *pl* consumer goods

konsumieren * [kɔn·zu·ˈmiː·rən] *vt* to consume

Kontakt <-[e]s, -e> [kɔn·ˈtakt] *m* (*a. elek*) contact; **mit jdm ~ aufnehmen** to get in touch with sb; [**mit jdm**] **in ~ bleiben** to keep in touch [with sb]; **keinen ~ mehr** [**zu jdm**] **haben** to have lost touch [with sb]; **mit jdm in ~ kommen** to come into contact with sb

kontaktfreudig *adj* sociable

Kontaktlinse *f* contact lens

kontern [ˈkɔn·tɛn] *vt, vi* to counter

Kontext <-[e]s, -e> [ˈkɔn·tɛkst] *m* context

Kontinent <-[e]s, -e> [ˈkɔn·ti·nɛnt] *m* continent

Kontingent <-[e]s, -e> [kɔn·tɪŋ·ˈgɛnt] *nt* **1.** MIL contingent **2.** (*Teil einer Menge*) quota

kontinuierlich [kɔn·ti·nu·ˈiːɐ̯·lɪç] **I.** *adj* continuous **II.** *adv* continuously

Kontinuität <-> [kɔn·ti·nui·ˈtɛt] *f kein pl geh* continuity

Konto <-s, Konten> [ˈkɔn·to] *nt* account ▶ **auf jds ~ gehen** (*verantworten*) to be sb's fault; (*bezahlen*) to be on sb

Kontoauszug *m* bank statement

Kontoinhaber(in) *m(f)* account holder

Kontonummer *f* account number

Kontostand *m* account balance

Kontrahent(in) <-en, -en> [kɔn·tra·ˈhɛnt] *m(f) geh* adversary

konträr [kɔn·ˈtrɛːɐ̯] *adj geh* contrary

Kontrast <-[e]s, -e> [kɔn·ˈtrast] *m* contrast

Kontrastprogramm *nt* alternative program

kontrastreich *adj* rich in contrast

Kontrolle <-, -n> [kɔn·ˈtrɔ·lə] *f* **1.** (*Überprüfung*) check **2.** (*Überwachung*) monitoring **3.** (*Herrschaft*) control (**über** +*akk* of); **etw unter ~ bringen** to bring sth under control; **jdn/etw unter ~ haben** to have sb/sth under control; **die ~ über sich** *akk/***etw** *akk* **verlieren** to

lose control of sth/oneself

kontrollierbar adj 1. (beherrschbar) controllable 2. (überprüfbar) verifiable

kontrollieren * [kɔn·tro·ˈliː·rən] vt 1. (überprüfen) to check (auf +akk for) 2. (überwachen) to monitor 3. (beherrschen) to control

Kontrolllampe RR f indicator light

Kontrollturm m control tower

Kontroverse <-, -n> [kɔn·tro·ˈvɛr·zə] f conflict

Kontur <-, -en> [kɔn·ˈtuːɐ̯] f meist pl contour

Konvention <-, -en> [kɔn·vɛn·ˈtsi̯oːn] f convention

Konventionalstrafe f fixed penalty

konventionell [kɔn·vɛn·tsi̯o·ˈnɛl] I. adj conventional II. adv conventionally

Konversation <-, -en> [kɔn·vɛr·za·ˈtsi̯oːn] f conversation

konvertieren * [kɔn·vɛr·ˈtiː·rən] vi sein o haben to convert (zu +dat to)

Konvoi <-s, -s> [ˈkɔn·vɔy] m convoy

Konzentrat <-[e]s, -e> [kɔn·tsɛn·ˈtraːt] nt concentrate

Konzentration <-, -en> [kɔn·tsɛn·tra·ˈtsi̯oːn] f concentration (auf +akk on)

Konzentrationsfähigkeit f kein pl ability to concentrate

Konzentrationslager nt concentration camp

konzentrieren * [kɔn·tsɛn·ˈtriː·rən] vt, vr (sich akk) ~ to concentrate (auf +akk on)

Konzept <-[e]s, -e> [kɔn·ˈtsɛpt] nt 1. (Entwurf) draft 2. (Plan) plan, concept; jdn aus dem ~ bringen to throw sb for a loop fam; aus dem ~ geraten to lose one's train of thought; jdm nicht ins ~ passen to not fit in with sb's plans

Konzern <-s, -e> [kɔn·ˈtsɛrn] m group

Konzert <-[e]s, -e> [kɔn·ˈtsɛrt] nt concert

Konzertflügel m concert grand

konzipieren * [kɔn·tsi·ˈpiː·rən] vt to plan

Kooperation <-, -en> [ko·ʔope·ra·ˈtsi̯oːn] f cooperation

Koordination <-, -en> [ko·ʔɔr·di·na·ˈtsi̯oːn] f coordination

koordinieren * [ko·ʔɔr·di·ˈniː·rən] vt to coordinate

Kopf <-[e]s, Köpfe> [kɔpf] m 1. (Haupt) head; von ~ bis Fuß from head to toe; einen roten ~ bekommen to go red [in the face] 2. (oberer Teil) head; (Briefkopf) letterhead; ~ oder Zahl? (bei Münzen) heads or tails? 3. (Gedanken) head; sich dat etw durch den ~ gehen lassen to mull sth over; nichts als Sport im ~ haben to think of nothing but sports; sich dat [über etw akk] den ~ zerbrechen fam to rack one's brain [over sth]; nicht ganz richtig im ~ sein fam to be not quite right in the head 4. (Wille) mind; seinen eigenen ~ haben fam to have a mind of one's own; seinen ~ durchsetzen to get one's way 5. (Person) head; der ~ einer S. gen the person behind sth; pro ~ per person ▶ nicht auf den ~ gefallen sein fam to not have been born yesterday; etw auf den ~ hauen fam to spend all of sth; ~ hoch! [keep your] chin up!; [bei etw dat] ~ und Kragen riskieren fam to risk life and limb [doing sth]; etw auf den ~ stellen (gründlich durchsuchen) to turn sth upside down; (ins Gegenteil verkehren) to turn sth on its head; jdn vor den ~ stoßen to offend sb; mit dem ~ durch die Wand [rennen] wollen fam to be determined to get one's way

Kopfball m header

Kopfbedeckung f headgear

Köpfchen [ˈkœpf·çən] nt ▶ ~ haben fam to have brains

köpfen [ˈkœp·fn̩] vt fam (enthaupten) to behead

Kopfende nt head

Kopfhaut f scalp

Kopfhörer m headphones pl

Kopfkissen nt pillow

kopflos I. adj (verwirrt) confused II. adv in a bewildered manner

Kopfrechnen nt mental arithmetic

Kopfsalat m lettuce

Kopfschmerz m meist pl headache

Kopfstand m headstand

Kopfsteinpflaster nt cobblestones pl

Kopfstütze f headrest

Kopftuch nt headscarf

kopfüber [kɔpf·ˈʔyː·bɐ] adv head first

Kopfweh nt dial s. **Kopfschmerz**

Kopie <-, -n> [koˈpiː] f copy

kopieren * [koˈpiː·rən] vt to copy

Kopierer <-s, -> m [photo]copier

Koppel <-, -n> [ˈkɔ·pl̩] f pasture

Koralle <-, -n> [koˈra·lə] f coral

Koran <-s> [koˈraːn] m kein pl Koran

Korb <-[e]s, Körbe> [kɔrp] m 1. (a. sport) basket 2. kein pl (Weidengeflecht) wicker 3. fam (Abfuhr) rejection; **[von jdm] einen ~ bekommen** (bei einer Verabredung) to be rejected [by sb]; (bei einer Verabredung) to get stood up [by sb]; **jdm einen ~ geben** to turn sb down; (bei einer Verabredung) to stand sb up

Korbball m netball (a game that resembles basketball without the backboards)

Kord <-[e]s, -e> [kɔrt] m s. **Cord**

Korea <-s> [koˈreːa] nt Korea; s. a. **Deutschland**

Koreaner(in) <-s, -> [ko·reˈaː·nɐ] m(f) Korean; s. a. **Deutsche(r)**

Koriander <-s, -> [koˈri̯an·dɐ] m coriander

Korinthe <-, -n> [koˈrɪn·tə] f currant

Kork <-[e]s, -e> [kɔrk] m cork

Korken <-s, -> [ˈkɔr·kn̩] m cork

Korkenzieher <-s, -> m corkscrew

Korn¹ <-[e]s, Körner> [kɔrn] nt 1. (Samenkorn) grain 2. (Getreide) corn, grain

Korn² <-[e]s, -> [kɔrn] m (Kornbranntwein) schnapps

Körper <-s, -> [ˈkœr·pɐ] m body; **am ganzen ~** all over

Körperbau m kein pl physique

Körperbehinderte(r) f/m(f) physically disabled person

Körpergewicht nt weight

Körpergröße f size

körperlich I. adj physical II. adv physically; **~ arbeiten** to do physical labor

Körperpflege f personal hygiene

Körpersprache f body language

Körperteil m part of the body, body part

Körperverletzung f bodily harm; **fahrlässige ~** bodily injury caused by negligence; **schwere ~** aggravated assault

korpulent [kɔr·puˈlɛnt] adj geh corpulent

korrekt [kɔˈrɛkt] I. adj correct II. adv correctly

Korrektur <-, -en> [kɔ·rɛkˈtuːɐ̯] f correction; (von Schularbeiten) grading; **[etw] ~ lesen** to proofread [sth]

Korrespondent(in) <-en, -en> [kɔ·rɛs·pɔnˈdɛnt] m(f) correspondent

Korrespondenz <-, -en> [kɔ·rɛs·pɔnˈdɛnts] f correspondence

korrespondieren * vi 1. (in Briefwechsel stehen) to correspond (**mit** +dat with) 2. geh (entsprechen) **mit etw** dat ~ to correspond to sth

Korridor <-s, -e> [ˈkɔ·ri·doːɐ̯] m corridor

korrigieren * [kɔ·riˈgiː·rən] vt to correct; (Klassenarbeit, Aufsatz) to grade; (Manuskript) to proofread

korrupt [kɔˈrʊpt] adj corrupt

Korruption <-, -en> [kɔ·rʊpˈtsi̯oːn] f corruption

Korse, Korsin <-n, -n> [ˈkɔr·zə] m, f Corsican; s. a. **Deutsche(r)**

Korsin <-, -nen> f s. **Korse**

koscher [ˈkoː·ʃɐ] I. adj kosher ▸ **nicht [ganz] ~ sein** to not be [entirely] on the level II. adv according to kosher requirements

Kosename m pet name

Kosewort nt term of endearment

Kosmetik <-> [kɔsˈmeː·tɪk] f kein pl cosmetics pl

Kosmetiker(in) <-s, -> [kɔsˈmeː·ti·kɐ] m(f) beautician

kosmetisch [kɔsˈmeː·tɪʃ] I. adj cosmetic II. adv cosmetically

kosmisch [ˈkɔs·mɪʃ] adj cosmic

Kosmopolit(in) <-en, -en> [kɔs·mo·poˈliːt] m(f) geh cosmopolitan

Kosmos <-> [ˈkɔs·mɔs] m kein pl cosmos

Kost <-> [kɔst] f kein pl food; **[freie] ~ und Logis** [free] room and board

kostbar [ˈkɔst·baːɐ̯] adj valuable, precious; **jdm ~ sein** to mean a lot to sb

Kostbarkeit <-, -en> f 1. (Gegenstand) precious object 2. kein pl (Erlesenheit) preciousness

kosten¹ [ˈkɔs·tn̩] vt 1. (als Preis haben) to cost 2. (erfordern) to take [up]

kosten² [ˈkɔs·tn̩] vt, vi (probieren) to taste

K

Kosten ['kɔs·tn̩] pl costs pl, expenses pl; auf ~ von jdm/etw dat at the expense of sb/sth ▶ auf seine ~ **kommen** to get one's money's worth

kostendeckend I. adj cost-effective II. adv cost-effectively

kostenlos adj, adv free [of charge]

Kostenvoranschlag m quotation; **sich** dat einen ~ **machen lassen** to get an estimate

köstlich ['kœst·lɪç] I. adj 1. (herrlich) delicious 2. fam (amüsant) priceless II. adv (herrlich) deliciously; **sich** akk ~ **amüsieren** to have a wonderful time

Kostprobe f (Vorgeschmack) sample

kostspielig adj expensive

Kostüm <-s, -e> [kɔs·'tyːm] nt 1. MODE suit 2. HIST, THEAT costume

Kot <-[e]s> [koːt] m kein pl excrement

Kotelett <-s, -s> [kɔt·'lɛt] nt chop

Köter <-s, -> ['køː·tɐ] m pej mutt

Kotflügel m wing

Kotzbrocken m pej sl slimeball

Kotze <-> ['kɔ·tsə] f kein pl fam puke sl

kotzen ['kɔ·tsn̩] vi fam to puke; **das ist zum K~** that makes me want to puke sl

Krabbe <-, -n> ['kra·bə] f 1. ZOOL (Taschenkrebs) crab 2. KOCHK (Garnele) prawn

krabbeln ['kra·bl̩n] vi sein to crawl

Krach <-[e]s, Kräche> [krax] m 1. kein pl (Lärm) noise 2. fam (Streit) quarrel; **sie haben** ~ they're not on speaking terms; **mit jdm** ~ **kriegen** to get into trouble with sb

krachen ['kra·xn̩] vi 1. haben (laut hallen) to crash; (Ast) to creak; (Schuss) to ring out 2. sein fam (prallen) to crash

krächzen ['krɛç·tsn̩] vt, vi 1. ORN to caw 2. fam (heiser sprechen) to croak

Kraft <-, Kräfte> [kraft] f 1. ([körperliche] Stärke) strength; **mit frischer** ~ with renewed energy; **mit letzter** ~ with one's last ounce of strength; **mit vereinten Kräften** with combined efforts; **aus eigener** ~ by oneself; **die treibende** ~ the driving force; **wieder zu Kräften kommen** to regain one's strength; **über jds Kräfte gehen** to be more than sb can cope with 2. (Geltung) power; **in** ~ **sein** to be in effect;

in ~ **treten** to take effect; **außer** ~ **sein** to be no longer in effect; **etw außer** ~ **setzen** to cancel sth 3. PHYS (Energie) power 4. meist pl (Einfluss ausübende Gruppe) force

Kraftakt m act of strength

Kraftfahrer(in) m(f) driver

Kraftfahrzeug nt motor vehicle

Kraftfahrzeugbrief m title

Kraftfahrzeugsteuer f motor vehicle tax

Kraftfahrzeugversicherung f auto insurance

kräftig ['krɛf·tɪç] I. adj 1. (stark) strong (Händedruck) firm; (Haarwuchs) healthy; (Stimme) powerful; (Farbe) rich 2. KOCHK hearty II. adv 1. (angestrengt) vigorously 2. METEO (stark) heavily

kraftlos I. adj weak II. adv feebly

Kraftprobe f test of strength

Kraftrad nt motorcycle

Kraftstoff m fuel

kraftvoll I. adj strong; (Stimme) powerful II. adv forcefully; ~ **zubeißen** to take a hearty bite

Kraftwagen m motor vehicle

Kraftwerk nt power plant

Kragen <-s, -> ['kra·gən] m collar ▶ jdm **geht** es an den ~ derb sb is in for it; **etw kostet jdn den** ~ derb sth is sb's downfall; **jdm platzt der** ~ fam sb is blowing his/her top

Kragenweite f collar size ▶ **genau** **nicht jds** ~ **sein** fam to be just/not sb's cup of tea

Krähe <-, -n> ['krɛː·ə] f crow

Krake <-n, -n> ['kra·kə] m octopus

krakeelen * [kra·'keː·lən] vi pej fam to make a racket

Kralle <-, -n> ['kra·lə] f ORN, ZOOL claw ▶ jdn **in seine** ~n **bekommen** to get one's claws into sb

krallen ['kra·lən] I. vr sich akk an jdn/ etw ~ to cling onto sb/sth II. vt etw in etw akk ~ to dig sth into sth

Kram <-[e]s> [kraːm] m kein pl fam 1. (Krempel) junk 2. (Angelegenheit) affairs pl; **den ganzen** ~ **hinschmeißen** to pack it all in; **jdm in den** ~ **passen** to suit sb fine; **jdm nicht in den** ~ **passen** to be a real nuisance to sb

Krampf <-[e]s, Krämpfe> [krampf] *m* cramp

krampfhaft I. *adj* **1.** (*angestrengt*) desperate **2.** MED convulsive **II.** *adv* desperately

Kran <-[e]s, Kräne> [kra:n] *m* TECH crane

rank <kränker, kränkste> [kraŋk] *adj* sick, ill ▶ **du bist wohl ~!** are you out of your mind?; **jdn** [mit etw *dat*] ~ **machen** to get on sb's nerves [with sth]

Kranke(r) *f(m) dekl wie adj* sick person

ränkeln ['krɛŋ·kln] *vi* to be in poor health

ränken ['krɛŋ·kn̩] *vt* **jdn** ~ to hurt sb's feelings; **gekränkt sein** to feel hurt; **es kränkt jdn, dass ...** it hurts sb['s feelings], that ...; **~d** hurtful

Krankengeld *nt* sick pay

Krankengymnastik *f* physical therapy

Krankenhaus *nt* hospital, clinic; **ins ~ kommen/müssen** to go/have to go to the hospital; **im ~ liegen** to be in a hospital

Krankenkasse *f* health insurance company

Krankenpflege *f* nursing

Krankenpfleger(in) *m(f)* male nurse

Krankenschwester *f* nurse

Krankenversicherung *f* health insurance

Krankenwagen *m* ambulance

rank|feiern *vi fam* to call in sick

rankhaft I. *adj* morbid **II.** *adv* morbidly

rankheit <-, -en> *f* disease

Krankheitserreger *m* pathogen

ränklich ['krɛŋk·lɪç] *adj* sickly

rank|melden RR *vr* **sich** *akk* ~ to call in sick

rankmeldung *f* notification of illness

rank|schreiben RR *vt* **jdn** ~ to excuse sb from [going to] work because he/she is sick

ränkung <-, -en> *f* insult

ranz <-es, Kränze> [krants] *m* **1.** (*Ring aus Pflanzen*) wreath **2.** dial (*Hefekranz*) Danish ring

rass RR, **kraß** ALT [kras] **I.** *adj* (*Beispiel*) glaring; (*Bemerkung*) crass; (*Unter-*

schied) extreme **II.** *adv sl* crassly

Krätze <-> ['krɛ·tsə] *f kein pl* scabies

kratzen ['kra·tsn̩] **I.** *vt* **1.** (*mit den Nägeln ritzen*) to scratch; **etw von etw** *dat* ~ to scratch sth off [of] sth **2.** *fam* (*kümmern*) **das kratzt mich nicht** I couldn't care less about that **II.** *vi* to scratch

Kratzer <-s, -> ['kra·tsɐ] *m* scratch

kraulen[1] ['krau·lən] *vi sein o haben* (*schwimmen*) to do [o swim] the crawl

kraulen[2] ['krau·lən] *vt* (*streicheln*) to fondle; **einen Hund zwischen den Ohren** ~ to scratch a dog between its ears

kraus [kraus] *adj* (*Haare*) frizzy; (*Stirn*) wrinkled

Kraut <-[e]s, Kräuter> [kraut] *nt* **1.** BOT herb **2.** *kein pl dial* (*Kohl*) cabbage; (*Sauerkraut*) sauerkraut ▶ **wie ~ und Rüben durcheinanderliegen** *fam* to lie around all over the place

Kräutertee *m* herbal tea

Krawall <-s, -e> [kra·'val] *m* **1.** (*Tumult*) riot **2.** *kein pl fam* (*Aufruhr, Lärm*) racket

Krawatte <-, -n> [kra·'va·tə] *f* tie

kreativ [krea·'ti:f] **I.** *adj* creative **II.** *adv* creatively

Kreativität <-> [krea·ti·vi·'tɛt] *f kein pl* creativity

Krebs <-es, -e> [kre:ps] *m* **1.** ZOOL crayfish **2.** *kein pl* KOCHK (*Krebsfleisch*) crab **3.** MED cancer **4.** *kein pl* ASTROL Cancer

Krebserreger *m* carcinogen

Krebsfrüherkennung *f kein pl* early cancer diagnosis

Krebsgeschwür *nt* cancerous ulcer

Krebsvorsorgeuntersuchung *f* cancer checkup

Kredit <-[e]s, -e> [kre·'di:t] *m* credit; (*Darlehen*) loan

Kreditkarte *f* credit card

Kreide <-, -n> ['krai·də] *f* chalk

kreidebleich *adj* as white as a sheet

Kreidezeichnung *f* chalk drawing

kreieren * [kre·'i:·rən] *vt* to create

Kreis <-es, -e> [krais] *m* **1.** (*a. math*) circle; **die Hochzeit fand im engsten ~ statt** only close friends and family were invited to the wedding **2.** ADMIN district

kreischen ['krai·ʃn̩] *vi* **1.** ORN to squawk

2. (*hysterisch schreien*) to shriek
3. (*Bremsen, Reifen*) to screech

Kreisel <-s, -> ['krai·zl̩] *m* 1. (*Spielzeug*) top 2. TRANSP *fam* traffic circle

kreisen ['krai·zn̩] *vi sein o haben* 1. ASTRON, RAUM **um etw** *akk* ~ to orbit sth 2. LUFT, ORN to circle (**über** +*dat* above) 3. (*in einem Kreislauf sein*) to circulate (**in** +*dat* through) 4. *fig* **um jdn/etw** ~ to revolve around sb/sth

kreisförmig I. *adj* circular II. *adv* in a circle

Kreislauf *m* 1. MED circulation 2. (*Zirkulation*) cycle

Kreislaufstörungen *pl* circulatory disorder

Kreisstadt *f* county seat

Kreisverkehr *m* traffic circle

Krematorium <-s, -rien> [kre·ma·'to:·rɪ·ʊm] *nt* crematorium

Krempe <-, -n> ['krɛm·pə] *f* brim

Krempel <-s> ['krɛm·pl̩] *m kein pl pej fam* 1. (*ungeordnete Sachen*) stuff 2. (*Ramsch*) junk ▶ **den ganzen** ~ **hinwerfen** to throw in the towel

krepieren * [kre·'pi:·rən] *vi sein sl* (*zugrunde gehen*) to croak

Kresse <-, -n> ['krɛ·sə] *f* cress

kreuz [krɔyts] ▶ ~ **und quer** all over the place

Kreuz <-es, -e> [krɔyts] *nt* 1. (*Zeichen X*) cross; **über** ~ crosswise 2. REL cross; (*Kruzifix*) crucifix; **ans** ~ **schlagen** to crucify sb 3. *fam* (*Teil des Rückens*) **es im** ~ **haben** *fam* to have back trouble 4. (*Autobahnkreuz*) intersection 5. *kein pl* KARTEN clubs *pl* ▶ **jdn aufs** ~ **legen** *fam* to fool sb; **drei** ~**e machen** *fam* to be so relieved; **das Rote** ~ the Red Cross

Kreuzer <-s, -> ['krɔy·tsɐ] *m* NAUT cruiser

Kreuzfahrt *f* cruise

Kreuzfeuer *nt* crossfire ▶ **ins** ~ [**der Kritik**] **geraten** to come under fire

kreuzigen ['krɔy·tsɪ·gn̩] *vt* to crucify

Kreuzigung <-, -en> *f* crucifixion

Kreuzotter *f* adder

Kreuzspinne *f* cross [*o* garden] spider

Kreuzung <-, -en> *f* 1. (*Straßenkreuzung*) crossroad *usu pl* 2. *kein pl* BIOL (*das Kreuzen*) crossbreeding 3. ZOOL,

BIOL (*Bastard*) mongrel

Kreuzworträtsel *nt* crossword [puzzle]

Kreuzzug *m* crusade

kribbeln ['krɪ·bl̩n] *vi* (*prickeln*) **das kribb belt so schön auf der Haut** it's so nic and tingly on the skin

Kricket <-s, -s> ['krɪ·kət] *nt* SPORT cricke

kriechen <kroch, gekrochen> ['kri:·çɐ *vi* 1. *sein* (*auf dem Bauch*) to craw 2. *sein* (*Zeit*) to creep by; (*Verkehr*) t creep 3. *sein o haben pej* (*unterwürfi sein*) to grovel (**vor** +*dat* before)

Krieg <-[e]s, -e> [kri:k] *m* war

kriegen ['kri:·gn̩] *vt fam* 1. (*bekommer* to get; **den Schrank in den Aufzug** to get the cupboard into the elevator **ich kriege noch 20 Euro von dir** yo still owe me 20 euros; **hast du die Ar beit auch bezahlt gekriegt?** did yo get paid for the work?; **ein Kind** ~ t have a baby; **eine Krankheit** ~ to ge a disease 2. (*erwischen*) to catch; **den Zug** ~ to catch the train 3. (*es schaffen* **jdn dazu** ~, **etw zu tun** to get sb to d sth; **ich kriege das schon geregelt** I' take care of it ▶ **es mit jdm zu tun** to be in trouble with sb

Krieger(in) <-s, -> ['kri:·gɐ] *m(f)* warric

kriegerisch I. *adj* 1. (*kämpferisch*) warlike 2. (*militärisch*) military II. *ac* belligerently

Kriegsausbruch *m* outbreak of war

Kriegsbeil *nt* tomahawk ▶ **das** ~ **be graben** to bury the hatchet

Kriegsberichterstatter(in) *m(f)* wa correspondent

Kriegsbeschädigte(r) *f(m) dekl w. adj* sb wounded in action, disable vet[eran]

Kriegsdienstverweigerer <-s, -> conscientious objector

Kriegsgefangene(r) *f(m)* prisoner of wa

Kriegsgefangenschaft *f* captivity; **in geraten** to become a prisoner of war

Kriegsgericht *nt* court martial

Kriegsschiff *nt* warship

Kriegsverbrecher(in) *m(f)* war crimina

Krimi <-s, -s> ['krɪ·mi] *m fam* 1. (*Buc* detective novel 2. (*Film*) [crime] thrille

Kriminalbeamte(r) *m*, **-beamtin** *f* de tective

Kriminalität <-> [kri·mi·na·li·'tɛt] *f kein pl* criminality

Kriminalpolizei *f* criminal investigation department

Kriminalroman *m* detective novel

kriminell [kri·mi·'nɛl] *adj* criminal

Kriminelle(r) [kri·mi·'nɛ·lə, -lɐ] *f(m) dekl wie adj* criminal

Krimskrams <-es> ['krɪms·krams] *m kein pl fam* junk

Kringel <-s, -> ['krɪŋl] *m* **1.** KOCHK ring-shaped cookie **2.** (*Schnörkel*) squiggle

Kripo <-, -s> ['kri·po] *f fam kurz für* **Kriminalpolizei**

Krippe <-, -n> ['krɪ·pə] *f* **1.** manger **2.** *s.* **Kinderhort**

Krise <-, -n> ['kri:·zə] *f* crisis

kriseln ['kri:·z|n] *vi impers fam* **es kriselt** a crisis is looming

krisenfest *adj* crisis-proof

Krisenherd *m* trouble spot

Kristall <-s, -e> [krɪs·'tal] *m* crystal

Kriterium <-s, -rien> [kri·'te:·ri·ʊm] *nt* criterion

Kritik <-, -en> [kri·'ti:k] *f* **1.** *kein pl* (*Beurteilung*) criticism; **an jdm/etw ~ üben** to criticize sb/sth **2.** MEDIA (*Rezension*) review; **gute/schlechte ~en bekommen** to receive good/bad reviews ▶ **unter aller ~ sein** *pej* to be beneath contempt

Kritiker(in) <-s, -> ['kri:·ti·kɐ] *m(f)* critic

kritiklos **I.** *adj* uncritical **II.** *adv* uncritically

kritisch ['kri:·tɪʃ] **I.** *adj* critical **II.** *adv* critically

kritisieren * [kri·ti·'zi:·rən] *vt* to criticize

Kritzelei <-, -en> [krɪ·tsə·'lai] *f pej fam* (*Gekritzel*) scribble

kritzeln ['krɪ·tsln] *vt, vi* to scribble

Krokette <-, -n> [kro·'kɛ·tə] *f* croquette

Krokodil <-s, -e> [kro·ko·'di:l] *nt* crocodile

Krokodilstränen *pl fam* crocodile tears *pl*

Krone <-, -n> ['kro:·nə] *f* **1.** (*Kopfschmuck, Zahnkrone*) crown **2.** (*Baumkrone*) top **3.** (*Währungseinheit: in Skandinavien*) krone; (*in der Tschechei*) crown ▶ **einen in der ~ haben** *fam* to have had one too many; **die ~ sein** *fam* to beat everything

krönen ['krø:·nən] *vt* to crown

Kronprinz, -prinzessin *m, f* crown prince *masc*, crown princess *fem*

Krönung <-, -en> *f* **1.** (*Höhepunkt*) high point **2.** (*das Krönen*) coronation

Kropf <-[e]s, Kröpfe> [krɔpf] *m* ORN crop

Kröte <-, -n> ['krø:·tə] *f* **1.** ZOOL toad **2.** *pl sl* (*Geld*) pennies *pl* **3.** *pej* (*Kind*) brat

Krücke <-, -n> ['krʏ·kə] *f* crutch; **an ~ gehen** to walk on crutches

Krug <-[e]s, Krüge> [kru:k] *m* (*Gefäß*) jug; (*Trinkgefäß*) tankard

Krümel <-s, -> ['kry:·ml] *m* crumb

krümelig ['kry:·mə·lɪç] *adj* crumbly

krumm [krʊm] **I.** *adj* **1.** (*verbogen*) crooked; **~ und schief** askew **2.** (*gebogen: Nase*) hooked; (*Rücken*) hunched; (*Beine*) bowed **3.** *pej fam* (*unehrlich*) crooked; **ein ~es Ding drehen** to pull a fast one *sl*; **es auf die ~e Tour versuchen** to try to pull some monkey business with sth *sl* **II.** *adv* **~ gehen** to walk with a stoop ▶ **sich** *akk* **~ und schief lachen** *fam* to bust a gut laughing

krümmen ['krʏ·mən] **I.** *vt* to bend **II.** *vr* **sich** *akk* **~** (*Fluss*) to wind; (*Straße*) to bend; **sich** *akk* **vor Schmerzen/ Lachen ~** to double up in pain/with laughter

krumm|nehmen *vt irreg fam* [jdm] **etw ~** to take offense at sth [sb said or did]

Kruste <-, -n> ['krʊs·tə] *f* crust; (*eines Bratens*) cracklings *pl*; (*einer Wunde*) scab

Kruzifix <-es, -e> ['kru:·tsi·fɪks] *nt* crucifix

Krypta <-, Krypten> ['krʏp·ta] *f* crypt

Kuba <-s> ['ku:·ba] *nt* Cuba; *s. a.* **Deutschland**

Kubaner(in) <-s, -> [ku·'ba:·nɐ] *m(f)* Cuban; *s. a.* **Deutsche(r)**

Kübel <-s, -> ['ky:·bl] *m* **1.** (*großer Eimer*) bucket **2.** (*Pflanzkübel*) container

Kubikmeter [ku·'bi:k-] *m o nt* cubic meter

Küche <-, -n> ['kʏ·çə] *f* kitchen

Kuchen <-s, -> ['ku:·xn] *m* cake

Küchenchef(in) *m(f)* chef

Kuchenform *f* cake pan

Küchenherd m stove

Küchenschabe f cockroach

Kuckuck <-s, -e> ['kʊ·kʊk] m ORN cuckoo ▶ [das] weiß der ~! fam God only knows!; zum ~ [noch mal]! fam [god] damn it!

Kuddelmuddel <-s> m o nt kein pl fam 1. muddle; (Unordnung) mess 2. (Verwirrung) confusion

Kugel <-, -n> ['ku:·gl] f 1. MATH sphere 2. SPORT ball; (Kegelkugel) bowling ball 3. (Geschoss) bullet ▶ eine ruhige ~ schieben fam to have it pretty easy

kugelförmig adj spherical

kugeln ['ku:·gln] vi sein to roll ▶ zum K~ sein fam to be hilarious

kugelrund [ku:·gl·'rʊnt] adj 1. (kugelförmig) round as a ball pred 2. fam (dick) tubby

Kugelschreiber m ballpoint pen

kugelsicher adj bulletproof

Kuh <-, Kühe> [ku:] f 1. ZOOL cow 2. pej fam (Frau) bitch; blöde ~ stupid chick

Kuhhandel m pej fam horse trade

kühl [ky:l] I. adj 1. (recht kalt) cool 2. (reserviert) cool II. adv 1. (recht kalt) etw ~ lagern to store sth in a cool place 2. (reserviert) coolly

Kühlbox f cooler

kühlen ['ky:·lən] I. vt to chill II. vi to cool

Kühler <-s, -> ['ky:·lɐ] m AUTO radiator

Kühlerhaube f hood

Kühlraum m cold [o refrigerated] storage room

Kühlschrank m refrigerator, fridge fam

Kühltruhe f freezer [chest]

Kühlwasser nt kein pl coolant

kühn [ky:n] adj 1. (wagemutig) brave 2. (gewagt: Behauptung etc.) bold

Kuhstall m cowshed

Küken <-s, -> ['ky:·kn] nt chick

kulant [ku·'lant] adj obliging

Kuli <-s, -s> ['ku:·li] m fam pen

kulinarisch [ku·li·'na:·rɪʃ] adj culinary

Kulisse <-, -n> [ku·'lɪ·sə] f THEAT scenery ▶ hinter die ~n blicken to look behind the scenes

kullern ['kʊ·lɐn] vi sein fam to roll

Kult <-[e]s, -e> [kʊlt] m cult

Kultfigur f cult figure

kultivieren * [kʊl·ti·'vi:·rən] vt to cultivate

kultiviert [kʊl·ti·'vi:·ɐt] I. adj (gepflegt: Mensch) cultured; (Benehmen) refined II. adv (gepflegt) in a refined manner

Kultstätte f place of ritual worship

Kultur <-, -en> [kʊl·'tu:ɐ] f culture

Kulturbanause m pej fam philistine

Kulturbeutel m toiletries bag

kulturell [kʊl·tu·'rɛl] I. adj cultural II. adv culturally

Kümmel <-s, -> ['ky·ml] m caraway

Kummer <-s> ['kʊ·mɐ] m kein pl grief

kümmerlich ['ky·mɐ·lɪç] I. adj 1. pej (armselig) miserable; (Mahlzeit) measly 2. (miserabel) pitiful II. adv (notdürftig) in a miserable way

kümmern ['ky·mɐn] I. vt etw/jd kümmert jdn sth/sb concerns sb; was kümmert mich das? what concern is that of mine? II. vr sich akk um jdn ~ to look after sb; sich akk um etw ~ to take care of sth; sich akk darum ~, dass ... to see to it that ...; kümmere dich um deine eigenen Angelegenheiten mind your own business

Kumpan(in) <-s, -e> [kʊm·'pa:n] m(f) pej fam pal

Kumpel <-s, -> m 1. (Bergmann) miner 2. fam (Kamerad) buddy

Kunde, Kundin <-n,-n> ['kʊn·də, 'kʊn·dɪn] m, f customer

Kundendienst m customer service

Kundenkarte f customer card

Kundennummer f customer account number

Kundgebung <-, -en> f rally

kündigen ['kyn·dɪ·gn] I. vi 1. (Arbeitsverhältnis beenden) jdm ~ to give sb notice, to lay off sep sb; jdm fristlos ~ to lay off sep sb without notice 2. (Mietverhältnis beenden) dem Mieter/Vermieter ~ to give a tenant/landlord notice II. vt (Arbeitsverhältnis beenden) jdn ~ to give sb notice, to lay off sep sb; jdn fristlos ~ to lay off sep sb without notice

Kündigung <-, -en> f 1. (durch den Arbeitnehmer) handing in one's notice; (durch den Arbeitgeber) dismissal, layoff; fristlose ~ dismissal without notice

2. (*eines Abonnements, Kredits*) cancellation; (*eines Vertrags*) termination
Kündigungsfrist *f* period of notice
Kundin <-, -nen> *f s.* **Kunde**
Kundschaft <-, -en> ['kʊnt.ʃaft] *f* customers *pl;* (*bei Dienstleistungen*) clientele
künftig ['kʏnf.tɪç] **I.** *adj* future **II.** *adv* in the future
Kunst <-, Künste> [kʊnst] *f* art ▶ **keine ~ <u>sein</u>** *fam* to be easy
Kunstausstellung *f* art exhibit[ion]
Kunstfaser *f* synthetic fiber
kunstfertig **I.** *adj* skillful **II.** *adv* skillfully
Kunstgegenstand *m* objet d'art, piece of art
Kunstgriff *m* trick
Kunstleder *nt* imitation leather
Künstler(in) <-s, -> ['kʏnst.lɐ] *m(f)* [visual] artist
künstlerisch ['kʏnst.lə.rɪʃ] **I.** *adj* artistic **II.** *adv* artistically
Künstlername *m* pseudonym; (*eines Schauspielers*) stage name
künstlich ['kʏnst.lɪç] **I.** *adj* artificial **II.** *adv* artificially
Kunstsammlung *f* art collection
Kunstseide *f* imitation silk
Kunststoff *m* synthetic material
Kunststück *nt* **1.** (*artistische Leistung*) trick **2.** (*schwierige Leistung*) feat; **das ist doch kein ~!** *fam* there's nothing to it!
Kunstwerk *nt* work of art
kunterbunt ['kʊn.tɐ.bʊnt] *adj* **1.** (*vielfältig*) varied **2.** (*sehr bunt*) colorful **3.** (*wahllos gemischt*) motley; **ein ~es Durcheinander** a jumble **II.** *adv* (*ungeordnet*) **~ durcheinander** completely jumbled up
Kupfer <-s, -> ['kʊ.pfɐ] *nt* copper
Kuppe <-, -n> ['kʊ.pə] *f* **1.** (*Bergkuppe*) [rounded] hilltop **2.** (*Fingerkuppe*) tip
Kuppel <-, -n> ['kʊ.pl̩] *f* dome
kuppeln ['kʊ.pl̩n] **I.** *vi* AUTO to work the clutch **II.** *vt* to couple (**an** +*akk* to)
Kupplung <-, -en> ['kʊp.lʊŋ] *f* **1.** AUTO clutch **2.** (*Anhängevorrichtung*) coupling
Kur <-, -en> [kuːɐ̯] *f* treatment [at a health resort]
Kurbel <-, -n> ['kʊr.bl̩] *f* crank
Kurbelwelle *f* crankshaft
Kürbis <-ses, -se> ['kʏr.bɪs] *m* pumpkin
Kurhaus *nt* main facility at a spa
Kurier <-s, -e> [ku.'riːɐ̯] *m* courier
Kurierdienst *m* courier [service]
kurieren* [ku.'riː.rən] *vt* to cure (**von** +*dat*)
kurios [ku.'riː.oːs] *geh* **I.** *adj* curious **II.** *adv* curiously
Kuriosität <-, -en> [ku.ri̯o.zi.'tɛt] *f* *geh* **1.** *kein pl* (*kuriose Art*) oddity **2.** (*kurioser Gegenstand*) curiosity
Kurort *m* spa, health resort
Kurs <-es, -e> [kʊrs] *m* **1.** (*Richtung*) course **2.** (*Lehrgang*) course **3.** (*Wechselkurs*) exchange rate
kursieren* [kʊr.'ziː.rən] *vi* (*Falschgeld*) to be in circulation; (*Gerücht*) to circulate
kursiv [kʊr.'ziːf] **I.** *adj* italic **II.** *adv* in italics
Kursivschrift *f* italics
Kurve <-, -n> ['kʊr.və] *f* **1.** MATH, TRANSP curve; **aus der ~ fliegen** *fam* to wipe out on a curve **2.** *pl* (*Körperrundung*) curves *pl* ▶ **die ~ <u>kratzen</u>** *fam* to scram *sl*, to beat it *sl*
kurvig ['kʊr.vɪç] *adj* curvy
kurz <kürzer, kürzeste> [kʊrts] **I.** *adj* **1.** (*räumlich*) short **2.** (*zeitlich*) brief, short **3.** (*knapp*) brief ▶ **den Kürzeren <u>ziehen</u>** *fam* to draw the short straw **II.** *adv* **1.** (*räumlich*) short; [jdm] **etw kürzer machen** MODE to shorten sth [for sb] **2.** (*zeitlich*) for a short time; **etw ~ braten** to flash-fry sth; **~ gesagt** in a word; **jdn ~ sprechen** to have a quick word with sb; **~ bevor** just before; **~ nachdem** shortly after; **vor ~em** just a little while ago; **bis vor ~em** up until recently ▶ **~ <u>entschlossen</u>** without a moment's hesitation; **~ und <u>gut</u>** in a word; [bei etw *dat*] **zu ~ <u>kommen</u>** to lose out [on sth]; **über ~ oder <u>lang</u>** sooner or later; **~ und <u>schmerzlos</u>** *fam* quick[ly] and painless[ly]
Kurzarbeit *f* *kein pl* reduced working hours

kurz|arbeiten *vi* to work reduced hours

kurzärm(e)lig *adj* short-sleeved

kürzen ['kʏr·tsn̩] *vt* 1. (*Länge/Umfang verringern*) to shorten (**um** +*akk* by) 2. (*verringern*) to cut, to reduce

kurzerhand ['kʊr·tse·'hant] *adv* there and then

Kurzfassung *f* abridged version

Kurzfilm *m* short film

Kurzform *f* shortened form

kurzfristig ['kʊrts·frɪs·tɪç] I. *adj* 1. (*innerhalb kurzer Zeit*) on short notice 2. (*für kurze Zeit*) short-term II. *adv* 1. (*innerhalb kurzer Zeit*) within a short [period of] time 2. (*für kurze Zeit*) briefly

Kurzgeschichte *f* short story

kurzlebig ['kʊrts·le:·bɪç] *adj* short-lived

kürzlich ['kʏrts·lɪç] *adv* not long ago

Kurznachrichten *pl* news in brief + *sing vb*

Kurzschluss RR *m* ELEK short circuit

Kurzschlussreaktion RR *f* knee-jerk reaction

kurzsichtig I. *adj a. fig* shortsighted II. *adv* (*beschränkt*) in a shortsighted manner

Kurzstreckenflug *m* short-haul flight

Kürzung <-, -en> *f* 1. (*Text*) abridgement 2. FIN cut

Kurzwaren *pl* dry goods *npl*

kurzweilig ['kʊrts·vai·lɪç] *adj* entertaining

Kurzwelle *f* short wave

Kurzzeitgedächtnis *m* short-term memory

kuscheln ['ku·ʃl̩n] I. *vr* sich *akk* an jdn ~ to cuddle up to sb; sich *akk* in etw *akk* ~ to snuggle up in sth II. *vi* to cuddle (**mit** +*dat* with)

Kuschelrock <-s, -> *m kein pl* MUS soft rock

kuschen ['ku·ʃn̩] *vi* (**vor jdm**) ~ to obey [sb]

Kusine <-, -n> [ku·'zi:·nə] *f s.* **Cousin** cousin

Kuss RR <-es, Küsse>, **Kuß** ALT <-sses, Küsse> [kʊs] *m* kiss

küssen ['kʏ·sn̩] *vt, vi* to kiss

Küste <-, -n> ['kʏs·tə] *f* coast

Küstengewässer *pl* coastal waters *pl*

Küstenschifffahrt RR *f kein pl* coastal shipping

Kutsche <-, -n> ['kʊt·ʃə] *f* carriage

Kutte <-, -n> ['kʊ·tə] *f* habit

Kuttel <-, -n> ['kʊ·tl̩] *f meist pl* tripe *sing*

Kutter <-s, -> ['kʊ·te] *m* cutter

Kuvert <-s, -s> [ku·'ve:ɐ] *nt* envelope

Kuwait <-s> ['ku:·vait] *nt* Kuwait; *s. a.* **Deutschland**

Kuwaiter(in) *m(f)* Kuwaiti; *s. a.* **Deutsche(r)**

KZ <-s, -s> [ka:·'tsɛt] *nt Abk von* **Konzentrationslager**

L

L, l <-, -> [ɛl] *nt* L, l; ~ **wie Ludwig** L as in Lima

l [ɛl] *Abk von* **Liter** l

labil [la·'bi:l] *adj* 1. MED (*Gesundheit, Kreislauf etc.*) poor 2. *geh* (*instabil*) unstable

Labor <-s, -s> [la·'bo:ɐ] *nt* laboratory, lab *fam*

Laborant(in) <-en, -en> [la·bo·'rant] *m(f)* laboratory technician

Labyrinth <-[e]s, -e> [la·by·'rɪnt] *nt* maze

Lache <-, -n> ['la·xə] *f* (*zusammengelaufene Flüssigkeit*) puddle

lächeln ['lɛ·çl̩n] *vi* to smile

Lächeln <-s> ['lɛ·çl̩n] *nt kein pl* smile

lachen ['la·xn̩] *vi* to laugh (**über** +*akk* at) ▶ **gut ~ haben** to be all right for sb to laugh

Lachen <-s> ['la·xn̩] *nt kein pl* 1. (*Gelächter*) laughter 2. (*Lache*) laugh

lächerlich ['lɛ·çe·lɪç] I. *adj* 1. (*albern*) ridiculous; **sich/jdn ~ machen** to make a fool of oneself/sb 2. (*geringfügig*) trivial II. *adv* (*sehr*) ridiculously

lachhaft *adj* laughable

Lachs <-es, -e> [laks] *m* salmon

Lack <-[e]s, -e> [lak] *m* 1. (*Lackierung*) paint [job] 2. (*Lackfarbe*) glossy paint; (*transparent*) varnish

lackieren* [la·'ki:·rən] *vt* (*a. Fingernägel*) to paint; (*Holz*) to varnish

Lackleder <-s> *nt* patent leather

den¹ \<lädt, lud, gel<u>a</u>den\> [ˈlaːdn̩] **I.** vt **1.** (packen) to load (**auf** +akk on[to], **in** +akk in[to]), to unload (**aus** +dat from/ out of) **2.** COMPUT to load **3.** (sich aufbürden) **etw auf sich** akk **~** to saddle oneself with sth **4.** (mit Munition versehen) to load (**mit** +dat with) **5.** ELEK to charge **II.** vi ▶ **gel<u>a</u>den <u>sein</u>** fam to be hopping mad

den² \<lädt, lud, gel<u>a</u>den\> [ˈlaːdn̩] vt JUR to summon

aden¹ \<-s, Läden\> [ˈlaːdn̩] m (Geschäft) store, shop

aden² \<-s, Läden\> [ˈlaːdn̩] m shutter

adendieb(in) m(f) shoplifter

adenhüter m pej slow seller

adenpreis m retail price

adenschluss RR m kein pl closing time

aderampe f loading ramp

aderaum m LUFT, NAUT cargo space

idieren* [lɛˈdiːrən] vt to damage

adung¹ \<-, -en\> f **1.** (Fracht) load; (von Flugzeug, Schiff) cargo **2.** fam (größere Menge) load **3.** (Munition, Sprengstoff) charge

adung² \<-, -en\> f JUR summons + sing vb

age \<-, -n\> [ˈlaːgə] f **1.** (geographisch) location **2.** (Liegeposition) position **3.** (Situation) situation; **zu etw** dat **in der ~ sein** to be in a position to do sth; **sich** akk **in jds ~ versetzen** to put oneself in sb's position **4.** (Schicht) layer

ager \<-s, -> [ˈlaːgə] nt **1.** (Warenlager) warehouse; **etw auf ~ haben** to have sth in stock **2.** (vorübergehende Unterkunft) camp **3.** (ideologische Gruppierung) camp **4.** TECH bearing

agerfeuer nt campfire

agern [ˈlaːgən] **I.** vt (aufbewahren) to store **II.** vi **1.** (aufbewahrt werden) **dunkel/kühl ~** to be stored in the dark/a cold place **2.** (liegen) to lie (**auf** +dat on) **3.** (sich niederlassen) to camp

agerraum m **1.** (Raum) storeroom **2.** (Fläche) storage space

agerung \<-, -en\> f storage, warehousing

hm [laːm] adj **1.** (gelähmt: Arm, Bein) lame **2.** fam (steif) stiff **3.** fam (ohne Schwung arbeitend) sluggish **4.** fam (schwach) lame; (Erklärung) feeble

lähmen [ˈlɛːmən] vt to paralyze

lahm|legen vt (Verkehr) to bring to a standstill

Lähmung \<-, -en\> f paralysis

Laib \<-[e]s, -e\> [laip] m bes südd loaf; (Käse) block

Laich \<-[e]s, -e\> [laiç] m spawn

laichen [ˈlai̯çn̩] vi to spawn

Laie, Laiin \<-n, -n\> [ˈlaiə, ˈlai·ɪn] m, f layman, layperson

Lake \<-, -n\> [ˈlaː·kə] f brine

Laken \<-s, -> [ˈlaː·kn̩] nt sheet

Lakritze \<-, -n\> [la·ˈkrɪt·sə] f licorice

lallen [ˈla·lən] vt, vi to slur

Lama \<-s, -s\> [ˈlaː·ma] nt ZOOL llama

Lamelle \<-, -n\> [la·ˈmɛ·lə] f **1.** (dünne Platte) slat **2.** (Segment) rib **3.** BOT lamella

Lametta \<-s\> [la·ˈmɛ·ta] nt kein pl tinsel

Lamm \<-[e]s, Lämmer\> [lam] nt (a. Fleisch) lamb

Lämmfell nt lambskin

Lampe \<-, -n\> [ˈlam·pə] f lamp

Lampenfieber nt stage fright

Lampenschirm m lampshade

Land \<-[e]s, Länder\> [lant] nt **1.** (Staat) country; **andere Länder, andere Sitten** every country has its own customs **2.** (Bundesland) [federal] state **3.** NAUT land; **~ in Sicht!** land ahoy!; **an ~ gehen** to go ashore; **jdn/etw an ~ ziehen** to pull sb/sth ashore **4.** kein pl (Gelände) land **5.** kein pl (ländliche Gegend) country; **auf dem ~[e]** in the country

Landarbeiter(in) m(f) farm hand

Landebahn f runway

landeinwärts adv inland

landen [ˈlan·dn̩] **I.** vi sein **1.** (niedergehen: Flugzeug, Raumschiff, Vogel) to land (**auf** +dat on) **2.** fam (hingelangen o enden) to end up **3.** fam (Eindruck machen) **mit deinen Schmeicheleien kannst du bei mir nicht ~** your flattery won't get you very far with me **II.** vt haben vt LUFT, RAUM, MIL to land

Ländereien [lɛn·də·ˈrai·ən] pl estates pl

Landesgrenze f **1.** (Staatsgrenze) border **2.** (Grenze eines Bundeslandes) state border [o line]

L

Landesinnere(s) *nt* interior

Landesregierung *f* state government

Landesverrat *m* treason

Landfriedensbruch *m* disturbing the peace

Landgericht *nt* district court

Landhaus *nt* country manor

Landkarte *f* map

Landkreis *m* administrative district

landläufig *adj* generally accepted; (*Ansicht*) popular

Landleben *nt* country life

ländlich ['lɛnt·lɪç] *adj* rural; (*Idylle*) pastoral

Landschaft <-, -en> ['lant·ʃaft] *f* landscape

landschaftlich *adv* ~ **schön** scenic

Landsmann, -männin <-leute> *m, f* compatriot

Landstraße *f* country road

Landstreicher(in) <-s, -> *m(f)* tramp

Landtag *m* state parliament

Landung <-, -en> *f* (*a. mil*) landing

Landungsbrücke *f* pier

Landvermessung *f* [land] surveying

Landwirt(in) *m(f)* farmer

Landwirtschaft *f* **1.** *kein pl* (*Tätigkeit*) agriculture **2.** (*landwirtschaftlicher Betrieb*) farm

landwirtschaftlich **I.** *adj* agricultural; (*Betrieb*) farm **II.** *adv* agriculturally

lang <länger, längste> [laŋ] **I.** *adj* **1.** (*räumlich ausgedehnt*) long **2.** (*zeitlich ausgedehnt*) long; **noch/schon ~** for a long time **3.** *fam* (*groß gewachsen*) tall **II.** *adv* **1.** (*eine lange Dauer*) long; **die Verhandlungen ziehen sich schon ~e hin** the negotiations have been dragging on for a long time; **wo bist du denn so ~e geblieben?** where have you been all this time? **2.** (*für die Dauer von etwas*) **sie hielt einen Moment ~ inne** she paused for a moment **3.** (*der Länge nach*) **~ gestreckt** long; **~ gezogen** prolonged

langatmig *adj pej* long-winded

lange ['laŋə] *adv s.* **lang II 1**

Länge <-, -n> ['lɛŋə] *f* **1.** (*räumlich*) length; **der ~ nach** lengthwise; **Pfähle von drei Metern ~** ten-foot-long poles **2.** (*zeitlich*) length, duration; **in voller** ~ in its entirety; **sich** *akk* **in die ~ zi**hen to drag on **3.** *fam* (*Größe*) heiɡ **4.** SPORT length **5.** (*Abstand vom N*ɡ *meridian*) longitude

langen ['laŋən] **I.** *vi fam* **1.** (*ausreiche* [jdm] ~ to be enough [for sb] **2.** (*fasse* *reichen*) to reach; **lange bloß nicht m** der Hand an die Herdplatte ma sure you don't touch the hot plate wɡ your hand **3.** *impers fam* **jetzt lang**ɡ **aber!** I've just about had enough! **II.** *fam* (*reichen*) **jdm etw ~** to hand sth ▶ **jdm eine ~** *fam* to smack sb the mouth

Längengrad *m* degree of longitude

längerfristig **I.** *adj* fairly long-teɡ **II.** *adv* on a fairly long-term basis

Langeweile <-> ['laŋə·vai·lə] *f* kein boredom

langfristig **I.** *adj* long-term **II.** *adv* oɡ long-term basis

langjährig *adj* of many years' standiɡ (*Freundschaft*) long-standing

Langlauf *m kein pl* cross-country skiɡ

langlebig *adj* **1.** (*lange lebend*) loɡ lived **2.** (*lange Zeit zu gebrauche*ɡ long-lasting **3.** (*hartnäckig*) persisterɡ

länglich ['lɛŋ·lɪç] *adj* longish

längs [lɛŋs] **I.** *präp +gen* ~ **einer** ɡ *gen* along sth **II.** *adv* (*der Länge na*ɡ lengthwise; ~ **gestreift** with vertiɡ stripes

langsam ['laŋ·zaːm] **I.** *adj* **1.** (*ni*ɡ *schnell*) slow **2.** (*allmählich*) gradɡ **II.** *adv* **1.** (*nicht schnell*) slowly **2.** *f*ɡ (*allmählich*) gradually

Langsamkeit <-> *f kein pl* slowness

Langschläfer(in) *m(f)* late riser

längst [lɛŋst] *adv* **1.** (*lange*) long sinɡ for a long time **2.** (*bei weitem*) ~ niɡ by no means

längste(r, s) *adj, adv superl von* langɡ

längstens ['lɛŋ·stn̩s] *adv* **1.** (*höchste*ɡ at the most **2.** (*spätestens*) at the ɡ est

Langstreckenflug *m* long-haul flight

Languste <-, -n> [laŋ·ɡʊs·tə] *f* crayfɡ

langweilen ['laŋ·vai·lən] **I.** *vt* to bɡ **II.** *vi pej* to be boring **III.** *vr* **sich** ɡ ~ to be bored

langweilig ['laŋ·vai·lɪç] **I.** *adj* borɡ

II. *adv* boringly

.angwelle *f* long wave

angwierig ['laŋ·viː·rɪç] *adj* long-drawn-out

.angzeitarbeitslose(r) *f(m) dekl wie adj* long-term unemployed person

.angzeitarbeitslosigkeit *f* long-term unemployment

.angzeitgedächtnis *nt* long-term memory

Lanze <-, -n> ['lan·tsə] *f* lance

Lappalie <-, -n> [la·ˈpaː·li̯ə] *f* trifle

Lappen <-s, -> ['lapn̩] *m* rag ▶ **jdm durch die ~ gehen** *fam* to slip through sb's fingers

läppisch ['lɛpɪʃ] I. *adj* 1. *fam* (*lächerlich: Betrag*) ridiculous 2. *pej* (*albern*) silly II. *adv pej* in a silly manner

Laptop <-s, -s> ['lɛp·tɔp] *m* laptop

Lärche <-, -n> ['lɛr·çə] *f* BOT larch

Lärm <-[e]s> [lɛrm] *m kein pl* noise

Lärmbelästigung *f* noise pollution

lärmempfindlich *adj* sensitive to noise

lärmen ['lɛr·mən] *vi* to be noisy

Lärmpegel *m* noise level

Lärmschutz *m* noise protection

Larve <-, -n> ['lar·fə] *f* larva, grub

lasch [laʃ] I. *adj fam* 1. (*schlaff*) feeble; (*Händedruck*) limp 2. (*nachsichtig*) lax II. *adv pej* (*schlaff*) limply

Lasche <-, -n> ['la·ʃə] *f* flap; (*Kleidung*) loop

Laser <-s, -> ['leː·zɐ] *m* laser

Laserdrucker *m* laser printer

lassen <lässt, ließ, gelassen> ['la·sn̩] I. *vt* 1. (*unterlassen*) to stop; **wenn du keine Lust dazu hast, dann lass es doch** if you don't feel like it, [then] don't do it; **er kann es nicht ~** he can't help [*o* stop] it 2. (*zurücklassen*) **jdn/etw irgendwo ~** to leave sb/sth somewhere 3. (*überlassen, behalten lassen*) **jdm etw ~** to let sb have sth; **ich lasse dir das Auto** you can have the car 4. (*gehen lassen*) to let; **lass den Hund nicht nach draußen** don't let the dog out 5. (*in einem Zustand lassen*) **jdn ohne Aufsicht ~** to leave sb unsupervised 6. (*loslassen*) **jdn/etw ~** to let sb/sth go 7. (*in Ruhe lassen*) **jdn ~** to leave sb alone 8. (*gewähren lassen*)

ich möchte so gerne mit, lässt du mich? I really want to go along — will you let me? 9. (*hineinlassen*) **frische Luft ins Zimmer ~** to let some fresh air into the room 10. (*hinauslassen*) **sie haben mir die Luft aus den Reifen gelassen!** they let the air out of my tires! 11. (*zugestehen*) **eines muss man ihm ~, er versteht sein Handwerk** you have to give him one thing: he knows his job ▶ **einen ~** *fam* to let one rip II. *aux vb* <lässt, ließ, lassen> *modal* 1. (*veranlassen*) **jdn etw tun ~** to have sb do sth; **jdn kommen ~** to send for sb; **~ Sie Herrn Braun hereinkommen** send Mr. Braun in; **der Chef hat es nicht gerne, wenn man ihn warten lässt** the boss doesn't like to be kept waiting; **etw machen ~** to have sth done; **ich lasse mir die Haare schneiden** I'm going to get a haircut 2. (*zulassen*) **jdn etw tun ~** to let sb do sth; **lass sie gehen!** let her go!; **er lässt sich nicht so leicht betrügen** it won't be that easy to trick him; **das lasse ich nicht mit mir machen** I won't stand for it!; **viel mit sich machen ~** to put up with a lot 3. (*belassen*) **das Wasser sollte man eine Minute kochen ~** the water should be allowed to boil for one minute 4. (*Möglichkeit ausdrückend*) **das lässt sich machen!** that can be done! 5. *mit imper* **lass uns jetzt lieber gehen** let's go now III. *vi* <lässt, ließ, gelassen> (*ablassen*) **sie kann einfach nicht von ihm ~** she simply can't part from him; **vom Alkohol ~** to give up alcohol; **lass nur!** that's all right!

lässig ['lɛsɪç] I. *adj* (*ungezwungen*) casual II. *adv* 1. (*ungezwungen*) casually 2. *fam* (*mit Leichtigkeit*) no problem

Last <-, -en> [last] *f* 1. (*zu tragender Gegenstand*) load 2. (*schweres Gewicht*) weight 3. (*Bürde*) burden 4. *pl* (*finanzielle Belastung*) burden; **zu jds ~en gehen** to be charged to sb ▶ **jdm zur ~ fallen** to become a burden on sb

lasten ['las·tn̩] *vi* 1. (*als Last liegen auf*) to rest (**auf** +*dat* on) 2. (*eine Bürde sein*) **auf jdm ~** (*Verantwortung*) to rest with sb 3. (*stark belasten*) **auf etw** *dat*

~ to weigh heavily on sth

Laster¹ <-s, -> ['las·tɐ] m fam (Lastwagen) truck

Laster² <-s, -> ['las·tɐ] nt (schlechte Gewohnheit) vice

lästern ['lɛs·tɐn] vi to make disparaging remarks (**über** +akk about)

lästig ['lɛs·tɪç] adj **1.** (unangenehm: Husten, Kopfschmerzen etc.) irritating **2.** (störend, nervend) annoying; (Person a.) tiresome

Lastwagen m truck

Lastzug m tractor-trailer

Lasur <-, -en> [la·'zu:ɐ̯] f [clear] varnish

Latein <-s> [la·'tain] nt Latin ▶ **mit seinem ~ am Ende sein** to be at one's wits' end

Lateinamerika nt Latin America

Lateinamerikaner(in) <-s, -> m(f) Latin American; s. a. **Deutsche(r)**

lateinamerikanisch adj Latin American; s. a. **deutsch**

lateinisch adj Latin

Laterne <-, -n> [la·'tɛr·nə] f lantern; (Straßenlaterne) street lamp

Laternenpfahl m lamppost

Latex <-, Latizes> ['la:·tɛks] m latex

latschen ['la:t·ʃn] vi sein fam **1.** (schlurfen) to trudge **2.** (lässig gehen) to wander

Latschen <-s, -> ['la:t·ʃn] m fam **1.** (Hausschuh) slipper **2.** pej (ausgetretener Schuh) worn-out shoe ▶ **aus den ~ kippen** fam to keel over; (sehr überrascht sein) to be bowled over

Latschenkiefer f mountain pine

Latte <-, -n> ['latə] f **1.** (kantiges Brett) slat **2.** SPORT bar **3.** (Torlatte) crossbar ▶ **eine ganze ~ von etw** dat fam a slew of sth

Lattenzaun m picket fence

Latz <-es, Lätze o österr -e> [lats] m bib

Latzhose f overalls npl

lau [lau] adj **1.** (mild) mild **2.** (lauwarm) lukewarm; (mäßig) moderate **3.** (halbherzig) half-hearted

Laub <-[e]s> [laup] nt kein pl foliage

Laubbaum m deciduous tree

Laube <-, -n> ['lau·bə] f arbor

Laubfrosch m tree frog

Laubsäge f jigsaw

Laubwald m deciduous forest

Lauch <-[e]s, -e> [laux] m leek

Lauer <-> ['lauɐ] f **auf der ~ liegen** to lie in wait

lauern ['lau·ɐn] vi **1.** (in einem Versteck warten) to lie in wait (**auf** +akk for) **2.** fam **die anderen lauerten nur darauf, dass sie einen Fehler machte** the others were just waiting for her to make a mistake

Lauf <-[e]s, Läufe> [lauf] m **1.** kein pl (das Laufen) run **2.** SPORT (Durchgang) round; (Rennen) heat **3.** kein pl (eines Flusses) course; (eines Sterns) path **4.** (Verlauf, Entwicklung) course; **das ist der ~ der Dinge** that's the way things go; **seinen ~ nehmen** to take its course **5.** (Gewehrlauf) barrel ▶ **etw** dat **freien ~ lassen** to give sth free rein

Laufbahn f career

laufen <läuft, lief, gelaufen> ['lau·fn] **I.** vi sein **1.** (rennen, Sport) to run **2.** fam (gehen) to go **3.** (zu Fuß gehen) to walk **4.** (fließen) to run; **jdm eiskalt über den Rücken ~** fig a chill runs down sb's spine **5.** (funktionieren) to work; (Getriebe, Maschine, Motor) to run; (eingeschaltet sein) to be on **6.** FILM, THEAT (gezeigt werden) **was läuft** [im Kino]? what's playing [at the movies]? **7.** (gültig sein: Vertrag) to run **8.** (seinen Gang gehen) to go; **wie läuft es?** how's it going? **9.** (geführt werden) **auf jds Namen ~** to be issued in sb's name ▶ **die Sache ist gelaufen** it's too late now **II.** vt haben o sein **1.** SPORT to run; **einen Rekord ~** to set a record **2.** (zurücklegen) to run **3.** (fahren) **Rollschuh/Schlittschuh/Ski ~** to roller-skate/ice-skate/ski **III.** vr impers haben **mit diesen Schuhen wird es sich besser ~** it will be easier to walk in these shoes

laufend I. adj attr **1.** geh (derzeitig) current **2.** (ständig) constant ▶ **jdn** [über etw akk] **auf dem L~en halten** to keep sb up-to-date [on sth] **II.** adv fam constantly

Läufer¹ <-s, -> ['lɔy·fɐ] m **1.** (Schachfigur) bishop **2.** (Teppich) runner

Läufer(in)² <-s, -; -nen> ['lɔy·fɐ] m(f) runner

läufig [ˈlɔy·frɪç] adj in heat

Laufkundschaft f kein pl window-shoppers

Laufmasche f run

Laufschritt m im ~ at a quick pace; MIL double time

Laufstall m playpen

Laufsteg m catwalk

Laufwerk nt (einer Maschine) drive mechanism; (einer Uhr) clockwork; (eines Computers) disk drive

Lauge <-, -n> [ˈlau·gə] f **1.** (Seifenlauge) soapy water, suds **2.** (wässrige Lösung einer Base) lye; (von Salz) salt solution

Laune <-, -n> [ˈlau·nə] f **1.** (Stimmung) mood; **schlechte ~ haben** to be in a bad mood; **seine ~ an jdm auslassen** to take it out on sb fig fam **2.** (abwegige Idee) whim

Laus <-, Läuse> [laus] f **1.** (Blut saugendes Insekt) louse **2.** (Blattlaus) aphid

lauschen [ˈlau·ʃn] vi (heimlich zuhören) to eavesdrop

lauschig [ˈlau·ʃɪç] adj veraltend (gemütlich) snug

lausen [ˈlau·zn] vt to delouse

lausig [ˈlau·zɪç] pej **I.** adj **1.** fam (entsetzlich: Arbeit, Zeiten etc.) awful, lousy **2.** fam (geringfügig) measly **II.** adv **1.** (entsetzlich) terribly **2.** (geringfügig) ~ **bezahlt** paid badly

laut¹ [laut] **I.** adj **1.** (weithin hörbar) loud; **etw ~er stellen** to turn up sep sth; **musst du immer gleich ~ werden?** do you always have to get so upset right away? **2.** (voller Lärm) noisy **II.** adv (weithin hörbar) loudly; **kannst du ~er sprechen?** can you speak up?; **~ denken** to think out loud

laut² [laut] präp +gen o dat ~ **Zeitungsberichten** ... according to newspaper reports ...

Laut <-[e]s, -e> [laut] m noise; **keinen ~ von sich geben** to not make a sound

lauten [ˈlau·tn] vi **1.** (zum Inhalt haben) to read; **wie lautet die Frage?** what is the question?; **wie lautet der letzte Absatz?** how does the final paragraph go?; **die Anklage lautete auf Erpressung** the charge is blackmail **2.** (ausgestellt sein) **die Papiere ~ auf seinen**

Namen the papers are in his name

läuten [ˈlɔy·tn] **I.** vi (Klingel, Telefon) to ring; (Glocke a.) to chime; (feierlich) to toll **II.** vi impers **es hat geläutet** there was a ring at the door

lauter [ˈlau·tɐ] adj just; **das sind ~ Lügen** that's nothing but lies; **vor ~ Arbeit** because of all the work I have

lauthals [ˈlaut·hals] adv at the top of one's lungs pred

lautlos [ˈlaut·loːs] **I.** adj noiseless, silent **II.** adv noiselessly, silently

Lautschrift f phonetic alphabet

Lautsprecherbox f speaker

lautstark **I.** adj loud; (Protest) strong **II.** adv loudly, strongly

Lautstärke f volume

lauwarm [ˈlau·varm] adj lukewarm

Lava <-, Laven> [ˈlaː·va] f lava

Lavendel <-s, -> [la·ˈvɛn·dl] m lavender

Lawine <-, -n> [la·ˈviː·nə] f a. fig avalanche

lax [laks] adj lax

Lazarett <-[e]s, -e> [la·tsa·ˈrɛt] nt military hospital

leben [ˈleː·bn] vi to live; **Gott sei Dank, er lebt** [noch] thank God, he's [still] alive; **vegetarisch ~** to be [a] vegetarian; **getrennt ~** to live apart; **vom Schreiben ~** to make a living as a writer ▶ **leb[e] wohl!** farewell!

Leben <-s, -> [ˈleː·bn] nt life; **am ~ sein** to be alive; [bei etw dat] **ums ~ kommen** to die [doing sth]; **sich** dat **das ~ nehmen** euph to take one's life; **das tägliche ~** everyday life; **so ist das ~** [eben] that's life ▶ **nie im ~** fam never; **etw ins ~ rufen** to establish sth; [bei etw dat] **sein ~ aufs Spiel setzen** to risk one's life [doing sth]; **es geht um ~ und Tod** it's a matter of life and death

lebend I. adj living **II.** adv alive

lebendig [le·ˈbɛn·dɪç] adj **1.** (lebend) living; ~ **sein** to be alive **2.** (anschaulich, lebhaft) vivid; (Kind) lively

Lebendigkeit <-> f kein pl vividness

Lebensabend m geh twilight years pl

Lebensabschnitt m chapter in one's life

Lebensbedingungen pl living conditions

Lebensdauer f 1. (*Dauer des Lebens*) life span 2. (*Dauer der Funktionsfähigkeit*) [working] life

Lebenserfahrung f life experience

Lebenserwartung f life expectancy

Lebensfreude f kein pl love of life

lebensfroh adj full of life pred

Lebensgefahr f mortal danger; **jd ist in/außer ~** sb's life is in/no longer in danger

lebensgefährlich I. adj extremely dangerous; (*Krankheiten*) life-threatening II. adv 1. (*mit Lebensgefahr verbunden*) **~ verletzt** seriously injured 2. fam (*sehr gefährlich*) dangerously

Lebensgefährte, -gefährtin m, f partner

Lebenshaltungskosten pl cost of living

Lebenslage f situation [in life]

lebenslänglich ['le:bn̩s·lɛn·lɪç] I. adj JUR life attr; for life pred; „**~**" **bekommen** fam to get life [in prison] II. adv all one's life

Lebenslauf m résumé

Lebensmittel nt meist pl food

Lebensmittelgeschäft nt grocery store

Lebensmittelvergiftung f food poisoning

Lebensqualität f kein pl quality of life

Lebensraum m (*Biotop*) habitat

Lebensretter(in) m(f) lifesaver

Lebensstandard m kein pl standard of living

Lebensunterhalt m kein pl living; **das deckt noch nicht einmal meinen ~** that doesn't even cover my basic needs

Lebensversicherung f life insurance

Lebensweise f lifestyle

Lebensweisheit f 1. (*weise Lebenserfahrung*) worldly wisdom 2. (*Wahlspruch*) maxim

lebenswert adj worth living pred

lebenswichtig adj vital, essential

Lebenszeichen nt a. fig sign of life

Lebenszeit f lifetime; **auf ~** for life

Leber <-, -n> ['le:·bɐ] f liver

Leberfleck m liver spot; (*Muttermal*) mole

Leberpastete f liver pâté

Lebertran m cod-liver oil

Leberwurst f liver sausage

Lebewesen nt living thing; **menschli〈ches ~** human being

Lebewohl <-[e]s, -s o geh -e> [le:·ba 'vo:l] nt geh farewell

lebhaft ['le:p·haft] I. adj 1. (*temperamentvoll*) lively 2. (*angeregt*) lively (*Beifall*) thunderous 3. (*belebt*) lively (*Verkehr*) brisk 4. (*anschaulich: Da stellung*) vivid II. adv 1. (*anschaulich*) vividly 2. (*sehr stark*) intensely

Lebkuchen ['le:p·ku:·xn̩] m gingerbread

leblos ['le:p·lo:s] adj lifeless

Lebzeiten pl **zu jds ~** (*Zeit*) in sb's day (*Leben*) in sb's lifetime

lechzen ['lɛ·çtsn̩] vi geh to long (**nach** +dat for)

Leck <-[e]s, -s> [lɛk] nt leak

lecken ['lɛ·kn̩] vi (*schlecken*) to lick

lecker ['lɛ·kɐ] I. adj delicious II. ad deliciously

Leckerbissen m delicacy

Leder <-s, -> ['le:·de] nt leather; **zäh wi ~** fam tough as nails

Lederjacke f leather jacket

Lederwaren pl leather goods

ledig ['le:·dɪç] adj single

lediglich ['le:·dɪk·lɪç] adv geh merely

leer [le:g] I. adj empty; (*Blatt Papier* blank; (*Blick*) vacant; (*Versprechunger Worte*) empty II. adv **wie ~ gefegt sei** to be deserted ► **[bei etw** dat**] ~ ausgehen** to go away empty-handed

Leere <-> ['le:·rə] f kein pl emptiness

leeren ['le:·rən] vt, vr [**sich** akk**] ~ t** empty; **sie leerte ihre Tasse nur hal** she only drank half of her cup

Leergut nt kein pl empties pl fam

Leerlauf m 1. (*Gangeinstellung*) neutr [gear] 2. (*unproduktive Phase*) unpro ductiveness

Leertaste f space bar

Leerung <-, -en> f emptying; (*von Pos* collection

legal [le·'ga:l] I. adj legal II. adv legally

legalisieren * [le·ga·li·'zi·rən] vt to le galize

Legalität <-> [le·ga·li·'tɛ:t] f kein legality

Legastheniker(in) <-s, -> [le·gas·'te:·n ke] m(f) dyslexic

gen ['le:·gn̩] I. *vt* 1. *jdn/etw irgend-wohin* ~ to put sb/sth somewhere; **seinen Arm um jdn** ~ to put one's arm around sb; ~ **Sie ihn auf den Rücken** lay him on his back 2. **die Stirn in Falten** ~ to frown 3. *(Teppich, Kabel, Eier)* to lay II. *vr* **sich** *akk* ~ 1. *(hinlegen)* to lie down; **sich** *akk* **ins Bett/in die Sonne/auf den Rücken** ~ to go to bed/lie down in the sun/lie on one's back 2. *(nachlassen: Aufregung, Empörung, Sturm, Begeisterung)* to subside; *(Nebel)* to lift

gendär [le·gɛn·'dɛ:ɐ̯] *adj* legendary

egende <-, -n> [le·'gɛn·də] *f* 1. *(fromme Sage)* legend 2. *(Lügenmärchen)* myth

ger [le·'ʒe:ɐ̯] I. *adj* 1. *(bequem)* loose-fitting 2. *(ungezwungen)* casual II. *adv* casually

egierung <-, -en> *f* alloy

egion <-, -en> [le·'gio:n] *f* legion

egionär <-s, -e> [le·gio·'nɛ:ɐ̯] *m* legionary

egislative <-n, -n> [le·gɪs·la·'ti:·və] *f* legislative power

egislaturperiode [le·gɪs·la·'tu:ɐ̯-] *f* legislative period

ehm <-[e]s, -e> [le:m] *m* clay

hmig ['le:·mɪç] *adj (aus Lehm bestehend)* clay; *(voller Lehm)* clayey; *(Weg)* muddy

ehne <-, -n> ['le:·nə] *f (Armlehne)* armrest; *(Rückenlehne)* back

hnen ['le:·nən] I. *vt (anlehnen)* to lean *(an/gegen* +*akk* against) II. *vi (schräg angelehnt sein)* to lean *(an* +*dat* against) III. *vr (sich beugen)* **sich** *akk* **an jdn/etw** ~ to lean on sb/sth; **sich** *akk* **über etw** *akk* ~ to lean over sth

ehnstuhl *m* armchair

ehramt ['le:ɐ̯-] *nt geh* **das** ~ the position of teacher; *(Studiengang)* teacher training [program]

ehrbeauftragte(r) *f(m)* visiting [*o* adjunct] lecturer

ehrberuf *m* teaching profession

ehre <-, -n> ['le:·rə] *f* 1. *(/handwerkliche/ Ausbildung)* apprenticeship 2. *(Erfahrung, aus der man lernt)* lesson; **jdm eine** ~ **erteilen** to teach sb a les-

son 3. *(ideologisches System)* doctrine 4. *(Theorie)* theory

lehren ['le:·rən] *vt (unterrichten)* to teach; **die Erfahrung hat uns gelehrt, dass ...** experience has taught us that ...

Lehrer(in) <-s, -> ['le:·rɐ] *m(f)* teacher

Lehrfach *nt* subject

Lehrgang <-gänge> *m* course; **auf einem** ~ **sein** to be at a seminar

Lehrkörper *m* teaching staff + *sing/pl vb*

Lehrling <-s, -e> ['le:ɐ̯·lɪŋ] *m veraltend s.* **Auszubildende(r)**

Lehrmittel *nt fachspr* teaching aid

Lehrplan *m* syllabus

lehrreich *adj* instructive

Lehrsatz *m* theorem

Lehrstelle *f* apprenticeship

Lehrstuhl *m* chair, professorship

Leib <-[e]s, -er> [laip] *m (Körper)* body; **etw** *akk* **am eigenen** ~ **erfahren** to experience sth firsthand; **bei lebendigem** ~ alive ▶ **mit** ~ **und Seele** wholeheartedly

Leibgericht *nt* favorite meal

leiblich ['laip·lɪç] *adj* 1. *(körperlich)* physical 2. *(blutsverwandt)* natural; ~**e Verwandte** blood relations

Leibwächter(in) *m(f)* bodyguard

Leiche <-, -n> ['lai·çə] *f* corpse, body ▶ **über** ~**n gehen** *pej fam* to stop at nothing

leichenblass^{RR} *adj* deathly pale

Leichenhalle *f* mortuary

Leichenschauhaus *nt* morgue

Leichenverbrennung *f* cremation

Leichnam <-s, -e> ['laiç·na:m] *m geh* corpse, body

leicht [laiçt] I. *adj* 1. *(geringes Gewicht habend)* light 2. *(dünn)* light 3. *(einfach)* easy; **nichts** ~**er als das!** no problem!; ~**e Lektüre** light reading 4. METEO *(schwach: Regen)* light; *(Donner)* distant 5. *(sacht)* light; *(Akzent)* slight; *(Schlag)* gentle 6. *(Eingriff, Verbrennung)* minor 7. *(nicht belastend: Mahlzeit)* light; *(Zigarette)* mild 8. *(unbeschwert)* **jdm ist** ~ sb is relieved 9. *(nicht massiv)* lightweight II. *adv* 1. ~ **bekleidet** dressed in light clothing 2. *(einfach)* easily; **etw geht [ganz]** ~

L

sth is [quite] easy; **es jdm ~ machen** to make it easy for sb 3. METEO (*schwach*) lightly 4. (*nur wenig, etwas*) lightly; **~ verärgert sein** to be slightly annoyed 5. (*schnell*) easily; **das sagst du so ~!** that's easy for you to say!; **~ zerbrechlich** fragile 6. (*problemlos*) easily

Leichtathlet(in) *m(f)* track and field athlete

Leichtathletik *f* track and field + *sing vb, no art*

leichtfertig I. *adj* thoughtless II. *adv* thoughtlessly

Leichtgewicht *nt* 1. *kein pl* (*Gewichtsklasse*) lightweight category 2. *fig* (*Sportler*) lightweight *a. fig*

leichtgläubig *adj* gullible

Leichtigkeit <-> *f* 1. *kein pl* (*Einfachheit*) simplicity; **mit ~** effortlessly 2. (*Leichtheit*) lightness

Leichtmetall *nt* light metal

leicht|nehmen *vt irreg* **etw ~** to take sth lightly

Leichtsinn ['laiçt·zɪn] *m kein pl* carelessness

leichtsinnig ['laiçt·zɪnɪç] I. *adj* careless II. *adv* carelessly

leid [lait] *adj pred* (*überdrüssig*) **ich bin es ~, das immer tun zu müssen** I'm sick of having to do this all the time

Leid <-[e]s> [lait] *nt kein pl* sorrow; **jdm ~ sein ~ klagen** to tell sb one's troubles

leiden <litt, gelitten> ['lai·dn] I. *vi* to suffer; (*Möbelstück, Stoff*) to get damaged; **an etw** *dat* **~** to suffer from sth; **unter jdm ~** to suffer because of sb; **unter etw** *dat* **~** to suffer from sth II. *vt* ▶ **jdn/etw ~ können** to like sb/sth; **ich kann das nicht ~** I can't stand that

Leiden <-s, -> ['lai·dn] *nt* 1. (*chronische Krankheit*) ailment 2. *pl* (*leidvolle Erlebnisse*) suffering

Leidenschaft <-, -en> ['lai·dn̩·ʃaft] *f* passion

leidenschaftlich I. *adj* passionate II. *adv* passionately; **etw ~ gern tun** to love doing sth; **ich esse ~ gern Himbeereis** I [absolutely] love raspberry ice cream

leidenschaftslos I. *adj* dispassionate II. *adv* dispassionately

leider ['lai·de] *adv* unfortunately; i◼ **habe das ~ vergessen** I'm sorry, I f◼ got about that; **das ist ~ so** that's ju the way it is

leidig ['lai·dɪç] *adj attr pej* tedious; i◼ **mer das ~e Geld!** it always com◼ down to money!

Leidtragende(r) *f(m)* **der/die ~** t◼ one to suffer

leid|tun RR *vi irreg* **es tut mir leid** I sorry; **es tut mir [so] leid, dass ...** I [so] sorry that ...; **er tut mir leid** I fe◼ sorry for him

leidvoll *adj geh* sorrowful *liter*

Leidwesen *nt kein pl* **zu jds ~** mu◼ to sb's regret

Leier <-, -n> ['laie] *f* MUS lyre

Leierkasten *m fam s.* **Drehorgel**

Leihbücherei *f* lending library

leihen <lieh, geliehen> ['lai·ən] 1. (*ausleihen*) to lend 2. (*borgen*) si◼ *dat* **etw** *akk* **[von jdm] ~** to borro◼ sth [from sb]

Leihgabe *f* loan

Leihhaus *nt* pawn shop

Leihmutter *f* surrogate mother

leihweise *adv* on loan

Leim <-[e]s, -e> [laim] *m* glue

leimen ['lai·mən] *vt* 1. (*kleben*) to gl◼ together 2. *fam* (*hereinlegen*) **jdn ~** take sb for a ride

Leine <-, -n> ['lai·nə] *f* 1. (*dünnes Se◼* rope 2. (*Wäscheleine*) [clothes]lin◼ 3. (*Hundeleine*) leash

Leinen <-s, -> ['lai·nən] *nt* linen

Leinsamen *m* linseed

Leintuch <-tücher> *nt dial* (*Lake◼* sheet

Leinwand *f* 1. (*Projektionswand*) scree◼ 2. *kein pl* (*Gewebe aus Flachsfaser◼* canvas

leise ['lai·zə] I. *adj* 1. (*nicht laut*) quie◼ **etw ~ stellen** to turn down *sep* s◼ 2. (*gering*) slight; (*Ahnung, Verdach◼* vague; **es fiel ~r Regen** it was drizzli◼ II. *adv* 1. (*nicht laut*) quietly 2. (*kau◼ merklich*) slightly

Leiste <-, -n> ['lais·tə] *f* 1. (*schmale La◼ te*) strip 2. ANAT groin

leisten ['lais·tn̩] I. *vt* 1. (*erbringen*) **ga◼ ze Arbeit ~** to do a good job; **viel ~** ◼

get a lot done **2.** TECH, PHYS to generate **3.** *Funktionsverb* **Hilfe ~** to help; **eine Anzahlung ~** to make a down payment; **gute Dienste ~** to serve sb well **II.** *vr* **1.** (*sich gönnen*) **sich** *dat* **etw ~** to treat oneself to sth **2.** (*sich herausnehmen*) **da hast du dir ja was geleistet!** you've really outdone yourself!; **er hat sich eine Dummheit geleistet** he behaved stupidly; (*tragen können*) **tolles Kleid – sie kann es sich ~, bei der Figur!** great dress — she can certainly get away with it with a figure like that! **3.** (*finanziell in der Lage sein*) **sich** *dat* **etw ~ können** to be able to afford sth; **es sich** *dat* **~ können, etw zu tun** to be able to afford to do sth

Leistenbruch *m* hernia

Leistung <-, -en> *f* **1.** *kein pl* (*das Leisten*) performance **2.** (*geleistetes Ergebnis*) accomplishment; **eine hervorragende/sportliche ~** an outstanding piece of work/athletic achievement; **schulische ~en** performance at school; **ihre ~en lassen zu wünschen übrig** her work leaves a lot to be desired **3.** TECH, PHYS power; (*einer Fabrik*) output **4.** FIN (*Entrichtung*) payment

Leistungsdruck *m kein pl* pressure to perform

leistungsfähig *adj* **1.** (*zu hoher Arbeitsleistung fähig*) efficient **2.** (*zu hoher Produktionsleistung fähig*) productive **3.** (*zur Abgabe großer Energie fähig*) powerful **4.** FIN competitive

Leistungsgesellschaft *f* meritocracy

Leitartikel *m* editorial [article]

Leitbild *nt* [role] model

leiten ['laɪ̯tn̩] **I.** *vt* **1.** (*verantwortlich sein: Firma*) to run; **eine Abteilung/ Schule ~** to be head of a department/ school **2.** (*den Vorsitz führen*) to lead; (*Sitzung, Debatte*) to chair **3.** TECH (*transportieren*) to conduct; (*Erdöl*) to pipe **4.** TRANSP (*Zug*) to divert **5.** (*führen*) to lead, to guide; **sich** *akk* **durch etw** *akk* **~ lassen** to [let oneself] be guided by sth; **sich** *akk* **von etw** *dat* **~ lassen** to [let oneself] be governed by sth **II.** *vi* PHYS to conduct; **gut/schlecht ~** to be a good/bad conductor

leitend **I.** *adj* **1.** (*führend*) leading **2.** (*in hoher Position*) managerial; **~er Angestellter** executive; **~er Redakteur** editor in chief **3.** PHYS conductive **II.** *adv* **~ tätig sein** to hold a managerial position

Leiter¹ <-, -n> ['laɪ̯tɐ] *f* (*Sprossenleiter*) ladder; (*Stehleiter*) stepladder

Leiter² <-s, -> ['laɪ̯tɐ] *m* PHYS conductor

Leiter(in) <-s, -> ['laɪ̯tɐ] *m(f)* head; (*einer Firma, eines Geschäfts*) manager; (*einer Schule*) principal; **~ einer Diskussion** person chairing a discussion

Leitfaden *m* MEDIA compendium

Leitgedanke *m* central idea

Leitmotiv *nt* central theme; (*in der Musik, Literatur*) leitmotiv

Leitplanke *f* guardrail

Leitung <-, -en> *f* **1.** *kein pl* (*Führung*) management **2.** (*leitendes Gremium*) management **3.** (*Rohr*) pipe **4.** (*Kabel*) cable **5.** TELEK line; **die ~ ist gestört** it's a bad connection ▶ **eine lange ~ haben** *hum fam* to be slow on the uptake

Leitungsrohr *nt* pipe

Leitungswasser *nt* tap water

Leitzins *m* prime rate

Lektion <-, -en> [lɛkˈtsi̯oːn] *f* SCH (*Kapitel*) chapter; (*Stunde*) lesson ▶ **jdm eine ~ erteilen** to teach sb a lesson

Lektor(in) <-s, -toren> ['lɛktoːɐ̯, lɛkˈtoːrɪn] *m(f)* **1.** (*in einem Verlag*) editor **2.** (*an der Universität*) lecturer who teaches in his/her native language at a university in a foreign country

Lektüre <-, -n> [lɛkˈtyːrə] *f* **1.** *kein pl* (*das Lesen*) reading **2.** (*Lesestoff*) reading material

Lende <-, -n> ['lɛndə] *f* ANAT, KOCHK loin

Lendenschurz *m* loincloth

Lendenstück *nt* KOCHK tenderloin

lenken ['lɛŋkn̩] **I.** *vt* to direct; (*Fahrzeug, Unterhaltung*) to steer; (*politisch*) to control; **jds Aufmerksamkeit auf etw** *akk* **~** to draw sb's attention to sth **II.** *vi* to drive

Lenker <-s, -> *m* handlebar *usu pl*

Lenkrad *nt* steering wheel

Leopard <-en, -en> [leoˈpart] *m* leopard

Lepra <-> ['leːpra] *f kein pl* leprosy

L

Lerche <-, -n> ['lɛr·çə] f ORN lark

lernbehindert adj with learning difficulties pred; ~ **sein** to have learning difficulties

lernen ['lɛr·nən] I. vt 1. (sich als Kenntnis aneignen) to learn 2. fam (eine Ausbildung machen) **etw** ~ to train to be sth ▶ **gelernt ist [eben] gelernt** once learned, never forgotten; **etw will gelernt sein** sth takes [a lot of] practice II. vi 1. (für die Schule) to study, to [do school]work 2. (beim Lernen unterstützen) **mit jdm** ~ to tutor sb 3. (eine Ausbildung machen) to apprentice (**bei** +dat with); **er hat bei verschiedenen Firmen gelernt** he has apprenticed with several companies; **sie lernt noch** she is still an apprentice

lesbar ['le:s·ba:ɐ̯] adj (Handschrift) legible

Lesbe <-, -n> ['lɛs·bə] f lesbian

lesbisch ['lɛs·bɪʃ] adj lesbian

Lesebuch nt reader

Leselampe f reading lamp

lesen <liest, las, gelesen> ['le:·zn̩] I. vt to read II. vi 1. (als Lektüre) to read 2. (Hochschulwesen) to lecture (**über** +akk on/about) III. vr **etw liest sich leicht** sth is easy to read

lesenswert adj worth reading pred

Leser(in) <-s, -> ['le:·ze] m(f) reader

Leseratte f hum fam bookworm

Leserbrief m letter to the editor

leserlich adj legible; **gut** ~ **sein** to be easy to read

Lesesaal m reading room

Lesestoff m reading material

Lesezeichen nt bookmark

Lesung <-, -en> f reading

Lette, Lettin <-n, -n> ['lɛ·tə] m, f Latvian; s. a. **Deutsche(r)**

lettisch ['lɛ·tɪʃ] adj Latvian; s. a. **deutsch**

Lettland ['lɛt·lant] nt Latvia; s. a. **Deutschland**

letzte(r, s) adj 1. (am Ende einer Reihenfolge) last; (Angebot, Versuch) final; (Zug) last; **sie saß in der** ~ **Reihe** she sat in the back row; **sie ging als** ~ **Läuferin durchs Ziel** she was the last runner to cross the finish line; **das** ~ **Brot** the last of the bread; **L**~**(r) werden** to

finish last; **der L**~ **des Monats** the last [day] of the month; **das ist das L**~**, was ...** this is the last thing that ...; **in** ~**r Minute** at the last minute; **es ist das** ~ **Mal, dass ...** this is the last time that ...; **zum** ~**n Mal** the last time 2. (vorig) **beim** ~**n Mal** last time; **im** ~**n Jahr** last year 3. (neueste: Nachricht, Mode) latest 4. fam (schlechteste) **das ist doch der** ~ **Kerl!** what a total loser!

letztendlich ['lɛtst·ʔɛnt·lɪç] adv s. **letztlich**

letztens ['lɛts·tn̩s] adv recently; **erst** ~ just the other day

letztlich ['lɛtst·lɪç] adv in the end

Leuchtboje f light buoy

Leuchte <-, -n> ['lɔʏç·tə] f (Stehlampe) floor lamp ▶ **nicht gerade eine** ~ **sein** fam to not be all that bright

leuchten ['lɔʏç·tn̩] vi 1. (Licht ausstrahlen) to shine; (Abendsonne) to glow; **leuchte mit der Lampe mal hier in die Ecke** shine the light over here in the corner [please] 2. (Licht reflektieren) to glow; **die Kinder hatten vor Freude** ~**de Augen** the children's eyes were sparkling with joy

leuchtend adj 1. (strahlend) bright; (Farben) glowing, bright 2. **ein** ~**es Beispiel** a shining example

Leuchter <-s, -> m candlestick; (mehrarmig) candelabra

Leuchtfeuer nt beacon; (auf der Landebahn) runway lights

Leuchtrakete f [rocket] flare

Leuchtreklame f neon sign

Leuchtschrift f neon lettering pl

Leuchtturm m lighthouse

leugnen ['lɔʏg·nən] I. vt to deny; **es ist nicht zu** ~, **dass ...** there is no denying the fact that ... II. vi to deny it

Leukämie <-, -n> [lɔʏ·kɛ·'mi:] f leukemia

Leute ['lɔʏ·tə] pl 1. (Menschen) people npl; **alle/keine/kaum** ~ everybody/nobody/hardly anybody; **unter** ~ **gehen** to get out and about 2. fam (Kameraden, Verwandte) folks npl 3. MIL, NAUT (Mitarbeiter) men pl ▶ **etw unter die** ~ **bringen** fam to make sth known

Leviten [le·'vi:·tən] pl ▶ **jdm die**

~ **lesen** fam to read sb the riot act

Lexikon <-s, Lexika> ['lɛk·si·kɔn] nt encyclopedia

Libanese, Libanesin <-n, -n> [li·ba·'ne:·zə] m, f Lebanese; s. a. **Deutsche(r)**

libanesisch [li·ba·'ne:·zɪʃ] adj Lebanese; s. a. **deutsch**

Libanon <-[s]> ['li:·ba·nɔn] m **der** ~ Lebanon; s. a. **Deutschland**

Libelle <-, -n> [li·'bɛ·lə] f dragonfly

liberal [li·be·'ra:l] adj liberal

liberalisieren * [li·be·ra·li·'zi:·rən] vt to liberalize

Liberia <-s> [li·'be:·rja] nt Liberia; s. a. **Deutschland**

Libero <-s, -s> ['li:·be·ro] m FBALL sweeper

Libyen <-s> ['li:·bў·ən] nt Libya; s. a. **Deutschland**

Libyer(in) <-s, -> ['li:·bў·ɐ] m(f) Libyan; s. a. **Deutsche(r)**

libysch ['li:·bўʃ] adj Libyan; s. a. **deutsch**

Licht <-[e]s, -er> [lɪçt] nt **1.** kein pl (Helligkeit) light **2.** ELEK light; **das ~ brennt** the light is on; **das ~ ausschalten** to turn out the light[s]; **etw gegen das ~ halten** to hold sth up to the light ▶ **etw erscheint in einem anderen** ~ sth appears in a different light; **etw ans ~ bringen** to bring sth to light; **jdn hinters ~ führen** to hoodwink sb; **mir geht ein ~ auf** fam now I see, it has suddenly dawned on me; **kein großes** ~ **sein** fam to be no great genius; **grünes** ~ **[für etw** akk**] geben** to give [sth] the go-ahead; **das** ~ **der Welt erblicken** geh to [first] see the light of day

Lichtbild nt veraltend geh (Passbild) passport photograph

Lichtblick m ray of hope

lichtdurchlässig adj translucent

lichtempfindlich adj sensitive to light pred; FOTO photosensitive

lichten ['lɪç·tn̩] **I.** vt HORT to thin out sep **II.** vr **sich** akk ~ **1.** (dünner werden) to [grow] thin **2.** (spärlicher werden) to go down **3.** (klarer werden) to be cleared up

lichterloh ['lɪç·te·'lo:] adv ~ **brennen** to be ablaze

Lichtgeschwindigkeit f kein pl **mit ~** at the speed of light

Lichthupe f **die** ~ **betätigen** to flash one's high beams

Lichtjahr nt light year

Lichtmaschine f generator

Lichtquelle f light source

Lichtschacht m light well

Lichtschalter m light switch

Lichtschutzfaktor m [sun] protection factor

Lichtstrahl m light beam

lichtundurchlässig adj opaque

Lichtung <-, -en> f clearing

Lichtverhältnisse pl lighting conditions pl

Lid <-[e]s, -er> [li:t] nt [eye]lid

Lidschatten m eye shadow

Lidstrich m eyeliner

lieb [li:p] adj **1.** (liebenswürdig) kind, nice; **seien Sie/sei so ~ und ...** would you be so kind as to ... **2.** (artig) good; **sei ein ~es Mädchen!** be a good girl! **3.** (niedlich) cute **4.** (geschätzt) dear; **L~er Karl, L~e Amelie,** (als Anrede in Briefen) Dear Karl and Amelie,; **[mein] L~es** [my] love; **[ach] du ~e Güte** fam good heavens!; **jdn ~ haben** to love sb; **man muss ihn einfach ~ haben** it's impossible not to like him **5.** (angenehm) welcome; **das wäre mir weniger ~** I'd rather you didn't [do it]

liebäugeln ['li:p·ʔɔy·gln̩] vi **mit etw** dat ~ to have one's eye on sth; **damit ~, etw** akk **zu tun** to toy with the idea of doing sth

Liebe <-, -n> ['li:·bə] f **1.** kein pl (Gefühl starker Zuneigung) love; **aus ~ zu jdm** out of love for sb; **aus ~ zu etw** dat for the love of sth; **aus ~ heiraten** to marry for love **2.** (Mensch) love; **die ~ meines Lebens** the love of my life ▶ ~ **auf den ersten Blick** love at first sight; ~ **macht blind** prov love is blind

lieben ['li:·bn̩] **I.** vt **1.** (Liebe entgegenbringen) to love; **jdn** akk ~ to love each other **2.** (gerne mögen) to love **3.** euph (Geschlechtsverkehr miteinander haben) **jdn** ~ to make love to sb; **sich** akk ~ to make love **II.** vi to be in love

liebenswert adj lovable

li̱ebenswürdig *adj* kind

Li̱ebenswürdigkeit <-, -en> *f* kindness; **würden Sie die ~ haben, ...?** *geh* would you be so kind as to ...?

li̱eber ['li:·bɐ] **I.** *adj komp von* **lieb; mir wäre es ~, wenn ...** I would prefer it if ...; **was ist Ihnen ~, das Theater oder das Kino?** would you prefer to go to the theater or the movies? **II.** *adv* **1.** *komp von* **gern(e)** rather; **etw ~ mögen** to prefer sth; **ich würde ~ in der Karibik als an der Ostsee Urlaub machen** I would rather take a vacation in the Caribbean than on the Baltic **2.** *(besser)* better; **darüber schweige ich ~** I think it's better to remain silent; **wir sollten ~ gehen** we [really] should get going; **das hätten Sie ~ nicht gesagt** you shouldn't have said that; **das möchte ich dir ~ nicht sagen** I'd rather not tell you that

Li̱ebesbrief *m* love letter

Li̱ebeserklärung *f* declaration of love; **jdm eine ~ machen** to declare one's love to sb

Li̱ebeskummer *m* lovesickness; **~ haben** to be lovesick

Li̱ebeslied *nt* love song

Li̱ebespaar *nt* lovers *pl*

li̱ebevoll **I.** *adj* loving; *(Kuss)* affectionate **II.** *adv* **1.** *(zärtlich)* affectionately **2.** *(mit besonderer Sorgfalt)* lovingly

Li̱ebhaber(in) <-s, -> ['li:p·ha:·bɐ] *m(f)* **1.** *(Partner)* lover **2.** *(Freund (der Künste))* enthusiast

Li̱ebhaberei <-, -en> [li:p·ha:·bə·'raɪ] *f* hobby

li̱ebkosen* [li:p·'ko:·zn̩] *vt geh* to caress

li̱eblich ['li:p·lɪç] **I.** *adj* **1.** *(angenehm süß)* sweet; *(Wein)* medium sweet **2.** *(erhebend)* lovely; *(Töne)* melodious **II.** *adv* **~ duften/schmecken** to smell/taste sweet

Li̱ebling <-s, -e> ['li:p·lɪŋ] *m* **1.** *(Geliebte(r))* darling **2.** *(Favorit)* favorite

li̱eblos ['li:p·lo:s] **I.** *adj* **1.** *(herzlos)* unloving **2.** *(Nachlässigkeit zeigend)* unfeeling **II.** *adv* *(nachlässig)* carelessly

Li̱eblosigkeit <-, -en> *f* **1.** *kein pl* *(Herzlosigkeit)* lack of feeling **2.** *(herzlose Handlung)* unkind act

li̱ebste(r, s) ['li:ps·tə, -tɐ, -təs] *adj superl von* **lieb** dearest; **das mag ich am ~n** I like that the best; **ich mag Vollmilchschokolade am ~n** milk chocolate is my favorite; **am ~n möchte ich schlafen** I'd really just like to sleep; **am ~n hätte ich ja abgelehnt** I would have rather said no

Li̱ebste(r) ['li:ps·tə, -tɐ] *f(m)* sweetheart

Lied <-[e]s, -er> [li:t] *nt* song ▶ **es ist immer das alte ~** *fam* it's always the same old story; **ein ~ von etw** *dat* **singen können** to be able to tell sb a thing or two about sth

Li̱ederbuch *nt* songbook

Li̱edermacher(in) *m(f)* singer-songwriter

Li̱eferant(in) <-en, -en> [li·fə·'rant] *m(f)* **1.** *(Firma)* supplier **2.** *(Auslieferer)* deliveryman *masc,* deliverywoman *fem*

li̱eferbar *adj* **1.** *(erhältlich)* available, in stock **2.** *(zustellbar)* **Ihre Bestellung ist leider erst später ~** unfortunately, we won't be able to ship your order until a later date

Li̱eferbedingungen *pl* terms of delivery

li̱efern ['li:·fɐn] **I.** *vt* **1.** *(ausliefern)* **[jdm] etw** *akk* **~** to deliver sth [to sb] **2.** *(Beweis)* to provide **3.** *(erzeugen)* to yield **4.** SPORT **ein spannendes Spiel ~** to put on an exciting game **II.** *vi* to deliver

Li̱eferschein *m* packing slip

Li̱eferung <-, -en> *f* **1.** *(das Liefern)* delivery; **bei ~** on delivery **2.** *(gelieferte Ware)* consignment

Li̱eferwagen *m* delivery van; *(offen)* pickup truck

Li̱ege <-, -n> ['li:·gə] *f* **1.** *(Bett ohne Fuß-/Kopfteil)* day bed **2.** *s.* **Liegestuhl**

li̱egen <lag, gelegen> ['li:·gn̩] *vi* haben *o südd sein* **1.** *(sich in horizontaler Lage befinden)* to lie; **ich liege noch im Bett** I'm still [lying] in bed; **deine Brille müsste eigentlich auf dem Schreibtisch ~** your glasses must be on the desk; **in diesem Liegestuhl liegt man am bequemsten** this is the most comfortable lounge chair [to lie in]; **~ bleiben** *(nicht aufstehen)* to stay in bed; *(nicht mehr aufstehen)* to remain

lying down; **etw ~ lassen** to leave sth [where it is] **2.** (*sich abgesetzt haben*) **hier liegt oft bis Mitte April noch Schnee** there will often be snow on the ground until mid-April here; **über allen Möbeln lag eine dicke Staubschicht** a thick layer of dust covered all the furniture **3.** (*lagern*) **Hände weg, das Buch bleibt [da] ~!** hands off — that book's not going anywhere!; **~ bleiben** (*nicht verkauft werden*) to remain unsold **4.** (*vergessen werden*) **irgendwo ~ bleiben** to be left behind somewhere **5.** (*geografisch gelegen sein*) to lie; **Cannes liegt in Frankreich** Cannes is in France **6.** (*eine bestimmte Lage haben*) to be situated; **ihr Haus liegt an einem See** they have a house on a lake; **diese Wohnung liegt zur Straße** this apartment faces [out onto] the street **7.** (*begraben sein*) **irgendwo ~** to be buried somewhere **8.** NAUT to be moored **9.** AUTO **~ bleiben** to break down **10.** SPORT to be; **wie ~ unsere Schwimmer im Wettbewerb?** how are our swimmers doing in the competition? **11.** (*angesiedelt sein*) **der Preis dürfte bei 4.500 Euro ~** the price is probably around 4,500 euros **12.** (*verursacht sein*) **das liegt nur an dir** it's all your fault; **woran mag es nur ~, dass ...** why is it that ... **13.** (*wichtig sein*) **du weißt doch, wie sehr mir daran liegt** you know how important it is to me; **mir ist viel daran gelegen** this means a lot to me **14.** *meist verneint* (*zusagen*) **Sport liegt mir nicht** I don't like sports; **körperliche Arbeit liegt ihr nicht** she's not really cut out for physical work **15.** (*lasten*) **auf jdm ~** (*Schuld*) to weigh down on sb **16.** (*abhängig sein*) **das liegt ganz bei Ihnen** it's entirely up to you **17.** (*nicht ausgeführt werden*) **~ bleiben** (*Arbeit*) to be left undone ▶ **an mir <u>soll</u> es nicht ~!** don't let me stop you!

Liegesitz *m* recliner

Liegestuhl *m* chaise longue; (*Stuhl*) deck chair

Liegewagen *m* couchette car

Lift <-[e]s, -e> [lɪft] *m* elevator

Liga <-, Ligen> ['liː·ga] *f* league

Likör <-s, -e> [li·ˈkøːɐ̯] *m* liqueur

lila ['liː·la] *adj* purple

Lilie <-, -n> ['liː·liə] *f* lily

Liliputaner(in) <-s, -> [li·li·pu·ˈtaː·nɐ] *m(f)* dwarf

Limonade <-, -n> [li·mo·ˈnaː·də] *f* lemon-lime soda

Limousine <-, -n> [li·mu·ˈziː·nə] *f* sedan; (*größerer Luxuswagen*) limousine

Linde <-, -n> ['lɪn·də] *f* BOT linden [tree]

lindern ['lɪn·dɐn] *vt* to alleviate; (*Husten, Sonnenbrand*) to soothe

Linderung <-> *f kein pl* relief

Lineal <-s, -e> [li·ne·ˈaːl] *nt* ruler

Linie <-, -n> ['liː·niə] *f a.* TRANSP line; **nehmen Sie am besten die ~ 19** it's best if you take the [number] 19 ▶ **die schlanke ~** *fam* one's figure

Linienbus *m* regular [service] bus

Linienflug *m* scheduled flight

Linienrichter *m* (*beim Fußball*) linesman; (*beim Tennis*) line judge

liniert *adj* lined

link [lɪŋk] *adj fam* shady

Link <-s, -s> [lɪŋk] *nt* COMPUT link

Linke <-n, -n> ['lɪŋ·kə] *f* **1.** (*linke Hand*) left hand **2.** (*im Boxen*) left **3.** POL **die ~** the left

linke(r, s) *adj attr* **1.** left; (*Fahrbahn, Spur*) left-hand **2.** POL left-wing

linken ['lɪŋ·kn̩] *vt sl* to take for a ride *fam*

linkisch ['lɪŋ·kɪʃ] *adj* clumsy

links [lɪŋks] **I.** *adv* **1.** (*auf der linken Seite*) on the left; **~ neben/von ...** to the left of ...; **~ oben/unten** in the top [*o* upper]/bottom [*o* lower] left-hand corner; **nach ~** [to the] left; **von ~** from the left **2.** TRANSP **~ abbiegen** to turn [to the] left; **sich** *akk* **~ einordnen** to go into the left lane; **sich** *akk* **~ halten** to keep [to the] left **3.** MODE **~ stricken** to purl **4.** **etw auf ~ waschen** to wash sth inside out **5.** POL left-wing; **~ stehen** to be left-wing **6.** MIL **~ um!** left face! ▶ **jdn ~ liegen lassen** *fam* to ignore sb; **mit ~** *fam* easily **II.** *präp* +*gen* **~ einer S.** to the left of sth

Linksaußen <-, -> [lɪŋks·ˈʔau·sn̩] *m* **1.** SPORT left winger **2.** POL *fam* extreme left-winger

Linkshänder(in) <-s, -> ['lɪŋks·hɛn·de] m(f) left-hander

Linkskurve f left-hand curve

linksradikal adj radical left-wing attr

Linoleum <-s> [li·'no:·le·ʊm] nt kein pl linoleum

Linse <-, -n> ['lɪn·zə] f 1. meist pl BOT, KOCHK lentil 2. ANAT, PHYS lens

Lippe <-, -n> ['lɪpə] f ANAT lip ▶ **etw nicht über die ~n bringen** to not be able to bring oneself to say sth

Lippenstift m lipstick

Liquidität <-> [li·kvi·di·'tɛ:t] f kein pl ÖKON [financial] solvency

lispeln ['lɪs·p|n] vi to lisp

List <-, -en> [lɪst] f trick ▶ **mit ~ und Tücke** fam with cunning and trickery

Liste <-, -n> ['lɪs·tə] f list ▶ **auf der schwarzen ~ stehen** to be blacklisted

listig ['lɪs·tɪç] adj cunning

Litauen <-s> ['li:·tau·ən] nt Lithuania; s. a. **Deutschland**

Litauer(in) <-s, -> ['li:·tau·e] m(f) Lithuanian; s. a. **Deutsche(r)**

litauisch ['li:·tau·ɪʃ, 'lɪ·tau·ɪʃ] adj Lithuanian; s. a. **deutsch**

Liter <-s, -> ['li:·te] m o nt liter

literarisch [lɪ·tə·'ra:·rɪʃ] adj literary

Literatur <-, -en> [lɪ·tə·ra·'tu:ɐ̯] f literature

Literaturangabe f bibliographical reference

Literaturpreis m literary prize

Literaturwissenschaft f literary studies pl

Litfaßsäule ['lɪt·fas·zɔy·lə] f advertising column

live [laif] adj pred live

Livesendung RR f live broadcast

Lizenz <-, -en> [li·'tsɛnts] f license

Lizenziat RR <-[e]s, -e> [li·tsɛn·tsi̯a:t] m schweiz (akademischer Grad) licentiate

Lob <-[e]s, selten -e> [lo:p] nt praise

Lobby <-, -s> ['lɔbi] f lobby

loben ['lo:·bn̩] vt, vi to praise

lobenswert adj commendable

löblich ['lø:p·lɪç] adj s. lobenswert

Loch <-[e]s, Löcher> [lɔx] nt 1. (offene Stelle) hole; **ein ~ im Reifen** a puncture; **schwarzes ~** ASTRON black hole

2. fam (elende Wohnung) hole ▶ **jdn ein ~ in den Bauch fragen** fam to floo_ sb with questions; **auf dem letzten -** **pfeifen** fam (finanziell am Ende sein) to be broke; (völlig erschöpft sein) to b_ on one's last legs; **saufen wie ein ~** fa_ to drink like a fish

Locher <-s, -> ['lɔ·xe] m hole punch[er]

Locke <-, -n> ['lɔ·kə] f curl; **~n habe** to have curly hair

locken¹ ['lɔ·kn̩] vt, vr (sich akk) ~ to cur_

locken² ['lɔ·kn̩] vt 1. (anlocken) to lure_ **mich lockt es jedes Jahr in die Ka** **ribik** every year I feel the lure of th_ Caribbean 2. (verlocken) to tempt; **Ih** **Vorschlag könnte mich schon ~** I'm [very] tempted by your offer

Lockenstab m curling iron

Lockenwickler <-s, -> m roller

locker ['lɔ·ke] I. adj 1. (nicht stramm_ loose 2. (nicht fest) loose, loosely-packe_ attr, loosely packed pred 3. KOCHK ligh_ 4. (nicht gespannt) slack; (Muskeln_ relaxed; **ein ~es Mundwerk habe_** fig fam to have a big mouth 5. (lege_ unverkrampft) relaxed, laid-back att_ fam, laid back pred fam 6. (oberfläch lich) casual II. adv 1. (nicht stramm_ loosely; **~ sitzen** (Kleidungsstück) t_ be loose 2. sl (ohne Schwierigkeiten_ **das mache ich ganz ~** I can do it n_ problem fam

lockerlassen vi irreg fam **lass nicht -** don't give up

lockermachen vt fam to shell out

lockern ['lɔ·ken] I. vt 1. (locker machen_ to loosen 2. (entspannen: Muskeln) t_ loosen up sep 3. (weniger streng ge stalten: Regeln) to relax II. vr sich ak_ ~ 1. (locker werden: Backstein, Schrau_ be, Zahn) to work loose; (Bremsen) t_ come loose; (Bewölkung, Nebel) to lif_ 2. SPORT (die Muskulatur entspannen_ to loosen up 3. (sich entkrampfen) di_ **Verkrampfung lockerte sich zuse_** **hends** the tension eased visibly

lockig ['lɔ·kɪç] adj (Haar) curly

Lockvogel m a. pej decoy

lodern ['lo:·den] vi (Feuer) to blaze

Löffel <-s, -> ['lœ·fl̩] m 1. (als Besteck_ spoon 2. (Maßeinheit) a spoonful [o_

▶ **den ~ abgeben** *sl* to kick the bucket; **sich** *dat* **etw hinter die ~ schreiben** to get sth into one's head

oge <-, -n> ['lo:·ʒə] *f* 1. FILM, THEAT box 2. (*Pförtnerloge*) lodge 3. (*Geheimgesellschaft von Freimaurern*) lodge

ogik <-> ['lo:·gɪk] *f kein pl* logic

gisch ['lo:·gɪʃ] *adj* 1. (*in sich stimmig*) logical 2. *fam* (*selbstverständlich*) [**na,**] ~! of course!

ogo <-s, -s> ['lo:·go] *nt* logo

ogopäde, Logopädin <-n, -n> [lo·go·ˈpɛː·də] *m, f* speech therapist

ohn <-[e]s, Löhne> [lo:n] *m* 1. (*Arbeitsentgelt*) wage[s *pl*], pay 2. *kein pl* (*Belohnung*) reward

ohnen ['lo:·nən] I. *vr* 1. (*sich bezahlt machen*) **sich** *akk* [**für jdn**] ~ to be worthwhile [for sb]; **unsere Mühe hat sich gelohnt** our efforts were worth it 2. (*es wert sein*) **sich** *akk* ~**, etw zu tun** to be worth doing sth II. *vt* 1. (*rechtfertigen*) **das lohnt den Aufwand kaum** it is hardly worth the effort 2. (*belohnen*) **sie hat mir meine Hilfe mit Undank gelohnt** she repaid my help with ingratitude

ohnend *adj* 1. (*einträglich*) lucrative 2. (*nutzbringend*) worthwhile

ohnerhöhung *f* pay raise

ohnfortzahlung *f* continued payment of wages

ohnsteuer *f* income tax

ohnsteuerjahresausgleich *m* ≈ tax return

ohnsteuerkarte *f* ≈ W-2 [form]

okal [lo·ˈkaːl] *adj* local

okal <-s, -e> [lo·ˈkaːl] *nt* bar, pub; (*Restaurant*) restaurant

okalisieren * [lo·ka·li·ˈziː·rən] *vt* 1. (*örtlich bestimmen*) to locate 2. (*eingrenzen*) to localize (**auf** +*akk* in)

okomotive <-, -n> [lo·ko·mo·ˈtiː·və] *f* locomotive

okomotivführer(in) *m(f)* engineer

orbeer <-s, -en> [ˈlɔr·beːɐ] *m* 1. (*Baum*) laurel [tree] 2. (*Gewürz*) bay leaf ▶ **sich** *akk* **auf seinen ~en ausruhen** *fam* to rest on one's laurels

---

los [lo:s] I. *adj pred* 1. (*von etwas getrennt*) ~ **sein** to have come off 2. *fam* (*losgeworden*) **jdn/etw ~ sein** to be rid of sb/sth; **er ist sein ganzes Geld ~** he's lost all his money ▶ **mit jdm ist etwas ~** *fam* sth's up with sb; **dort ist nichts ~** *fam* nothing is going on there; **da ist immer viel ~** *fam* that's where the action always is; **mit jdm ist nichts ~** *fam* (*jd ist langweilig*) sb is really boring; **was ist ~?** *fam* what's up?; **was ist denn hier/da ~?** *fam* what's going on here/there? II. *adv* 1. (*fortgegangen*) **Ihre Frau ist schon vor fünf Minuten ~** your wife left five minutes ago 2. (*gelöst*) **etw ist ~** sth is loose; **noch ein paar Umdrehungen, dann ist die Schraube ~!** just a couple more turns and the screw is out! ▶ **~! (mach!)** come on!

Los <-es, -e> [lo:s] *nt* 1. (*Lotterielos*) [lottery] ticket; (*Kirmeslos*) [raffle] ticket 2. (*für Zufallsentscheidung*) lot 3. *kein pl geh* (*Schicksal*) fate ▶ **jd hat mit jdm/etw das große ~ gezogen** sb has hit the jackpot with sb/sth

los|binden *vt irreg* to untie (**von** +*dat* from)

los|brechen *irreg* I. *vt haben* to break off II. *vi sein* 1. (*abbrechen*) to break off 2. (*plötzlich beginnen*) to break out

löschen [ˈlœ·ʃn] I. *vt* 1. (*auslöschen: Feuer, Flammen*) to extinguish; (*Licht*) to turn off 2. (*tilgen*) to delete 3. (*Musikkassette, Videokassette*) to erase II. *vi* to extinguish a fire

Löschfahrzeug *nt* fire engine

Löschpapier *nt* blotting paper

lose [ˈlo:·zə] *adj* loose

Lösegeld [ˈlø:·zə-] *nt* ransom

losen [ˈlo:·zn] *vi* to draw lots (**um** +*akk* for)

lösen [ˈlø:·zn] I. *vt* 1. (*ablösen*) to remove (**von** +*dat* from) 2. (*aufbinden*) to untie; (*Fesseln, Knoten*) to undo 3. (*Bremse*) to release 4. (*Schraube, Verband*) to loosen 5. (*klären*) to solve; (*Konflikt, Schwierigkeit*) to resolve 6. (*aufheben, annullieren*) to break off; (*Verbindung*) to sever; (*Vertrag*) to cancel 7. (*zergehen lassen*) to dissolve

II. *vr* sich *akk* ~ **1.** (*sich ablösen*) to come off (**von** +*dat* of) **2.** (*sich freimachen, trennen*) to free oneself (**von** +*dat* of) **3.** (*sich aufklären*) to be solved **4.** (*sich auflösen*) to dissolve (**in** +*akk* in) **5.** (*sich lockern*) to loosen; **langsam löste sich die Spannung** *fig* the tension [slowly] faded away

los|fahren *vi irreg sein* to drive off, to leave

los|gehen *irreg* **I.** *vi sein* **1.** (*weggehen*) to leave [on foot] **2.** (*auf ein Ziel zu*) **auf etw** *akk* ~ to set off for/toward sth; **wir gingen früh los** we set off early **3.** *fam* (*beginnen*) to start; **das Konzert geht erst in einer Stunde los** the concert doesn't start for another hour **4.** (*angreifen*) [**mit etw** *dat*] **auf jdn** ~ to lay into sb [with sth] **5.** (*Schusswaffen*) to go off **II.** *vi impers sein fam* (*beginnen*) to start; **jetzt geht's los** *fam* here we go

los|kommen *vi irreg sein fam* **1.** (*wegkommen*) to get away **2.** (*sich befreien*) **von jdm** ~ to free oneself of sb; **von einer Sucht** ~ to overcome an addiction

los|lassen *vt irreg* **1.** (*nicht mehr festhalten*) to let go **2.** (*beschäftigt halten*) **der Gedanke lässt mich nicht mehr los** I can't get the thought out of my mind

löslich ['lø:s·lɪç] *adj* soluble

Lösung <-, -en> ['lø:·zʊŋ] *f* **1.** CHEM solution **2.** (*Aufhebung*) cancellation; (*einer Beziehung/Verlobung*) breaking off **3.** (*das Sichlösen*) breaking away (**von** +*dat* from)

Lösungsmittel *nt* solvent

los|werden *vt irreg sein* **1.** (*sich entledigen*) to get rid of **2.** (*aussprechen*) to tell **3.** *fam* (*ausgeben*) to shell out **4.** *fam* (*verkaufen*) to sell [off], to move

Lot <-[e]s, -e> [lo:t] *nt* ▸ **im** ~ **sein** *fig* to be all right

löten ['lø:·tn̩] *vt* to solder (**an** +*akk* to)

Lothringen <-s> ['lo:·trɪŋən] *nt* Lorraine

Lotion <-, -en> [lo·'tsjo:n] *f* lotion

Lötkolben ['lø:t-] *m* soldering iron

Lotse, Lotsin <-n, -n> ['lo:·tsə] *m, f* pilot

lotsen ['lo:·tsn̩] *vt* **1.** (*als Lotse dirigie-*

ren) to pilot **2.** *fam* (*führen*) jdn i **gendwohin** ~ to take sb somewhere

Lotterielos *nt* lottery ticket

Lotto <-s, -s> ['lɔto] *nt* (*Zahlenlotto*) lo tery; ~ **spielen** to play the lottery

Löwe ['lø:·və] *m* **1.** (*Raubtierart*) lio **2.** ASTROL Leo

Löwenzahn *m kein pl* dandelion

loyal [loa·'ja:l] *adj* loyal

Loyalität <-, *selten* -en> [loa·ja·li·'tɛ:t] loyalty (**gegenüber** +*dat* to)

Luchs <-es, -e> [lʊks] *m* lynx

Lücke <-, -n> ['lʏ·kə] *f* **1.** (*Zwischer raum*) gap **2.** (*Unvollständigkeit*) gap (*Gesetzeslücke*) loophole

lückenhaft *adj* **1.** (*leere Stellen au weisend*) full of gaps **2.** (*unvollstän dig*) fragmentary; (*Wissen, Sammlung* incomplete; (*Bericht, Erinnerung* sketchy

lückenlos *adj* (*vollständig*) complete (*Alibi*) solid; (*Kenntnisse*) thorough

Luft <-, *liter* Lüfte> [lʊft] *f* **1.** *kein p* (*Atemluft*) air; **die ~ anhalten** to hol one's breath; **an die [frische] ~ gehe** to get some fresh air; [**tief**] ~ **holen** t take a deep breath; **nach ~ schnap pen** to gasp for breath **2.** *pl geh* (*Raur über dem Erdboden*) air; **in die ~ ge hen** *a. fig fam* to explode; **etw ist au der ~ gegriffen** *fig* sth is completel made up **3.** (*Platz, Spielraum* space ▸ **sich in ~ auflösen** to vanisl into thin air; **da ist dicke ~** *fam* the mood is tense; **die ~ ist rein** *fam* the coast is clear

Luftabwehr *f* air defense

Luftangriff *m* air raid

Luftballon *m* balloon

Luftblase *f* bubble

luftdicht *adj* airtight

Luftdruck *m kein pl* air pressure

lüften ['lʏf·tn̩] **I.** *vt* **1.** (*mit Frischluft ver sorgen*) to air **2.** (*preisgeben*) to reveal (*Geheimnis*) to disclose **II.** *vi* (*Luft her einlassen*) to let some air in

Luftfahrt *f kein pl geh* aviation

Luftfeuchtigkeit *f* humidity

Luftfracht *f* **1.** (*Frachtgut*) air freigh **2.** (*Frachtgebühr*) air freight charge

Luftgewehr *nt* air gun

luftig ['lʊf·tɪç] adj 1. (gut belüftet) well ventilated 2. (dünn und luftdurchlässig) airy; (Kleid) light

Luftkissenboot nt air-cushion vehicle

Luftkurort m health resort area with particularly good air

luftleer adj pred vacuous

Luftlinie f as the crow flies

Luftmatratze f inflatable mattress

Luftpost f airmail (**per** +dat by)

Luftpumpe f pump; (für Fahrrad) bicycle pump

Luftraum m airspace

Luftröhre f windpipe

Luftschlange f [paper] streamer

Luftschutzbunker m air raid bunker

Lüftung <-, -en> f 1. (das Lüften) ventilation 2. (Ventilationsanlage) ventilation system

Luftverschmutzung f air pollution

Luftwaffe f air force + sing vb

Luftzufuhr f kein pl air supply

Luftzug m breeze; (durch das Fenster) draft

Lüge <-, -n> ['ly:·gə] f lie ▶ ~n haben kurze <u>Beine</u> prov the truth will come out

lügen <log, gelogen> ['ly:·gn̩] vi to lie; **das ist gelogen!** that's a lie! ▶ ~ **wie** <u>gedruckt</u> fam to lie one's head off

Lügner(in) <-s, -> ['ly:g·nɐ] m(f) pej liar

Luke <-, -n> ['lu:·kə] f 1. BES NAUT (verschließbarer Einstieg) hatch 2. (Dachluke) skylight; (Kellerluke) trapdoor

lukrativ [lu·kra·'ti:f] adj geh lucrative

Lumpen <-s, -> ['lʊm·pn̩] m 1. pl neg (zerschlissene Kleidung, Stofffetzen) rags pl 2. dial (Putzlappen) rag

Lunge <-, -n> ['lʊŋə] f lung

Lungenentzündung f pneumonia

Lupe <-, -n> ['lu:·pə] f magnifying glass ▶ **jdn/etw unter die ~** <u>nehmen</u> fam to examine sb/sth with a fine-tooth[ed] comb

Lust <-> [lʊst] f kein pl desire; **~/keine ~ zu etw** dat **haben** to feel like/not feel like doing sth

lüstern ['lʏs·tɐn] adj lustful

lustig ['lʊs·tɪç] adj cheerful; (Abend) fun; **sich** akk **über jdn/etw ~ machen** to

make fun of sb/sth

lustlos adj listless

Lustschloss ᴿᴿ nt summer residence

Lustspiel nt comedy

lutschen ['lʊ·tʃn̩] vt, vi to suck

Lutscher <-s, -> ['lʊ·tʃɐ] m lollipop

Luxemburg <-s> ['lʊ·ksm̩·bʊrk] nt Luxembourg; s. a. **Deutschland**

Luxemburger(in) <-s, -> ['lʊ·ksm̩·bʊr·gɐ] m(f) Luxembourger; s. a. **Deutsche(r)**

luxemburgisch ['lʊ·ksm̩·bʊr·gɪʃ] adj Luxembourgian; s. a. **deutsch**

luxuriös [lʊ·ksu·'rjø:s] adj luxurious

Luxus <-> ['lʊ·ksʊs] m kein pl luxury

Luxusartikel m luxury item

Luxushotel nt luxury hotel

Lymphknoten m lymph node

lynchen ['lʏn·çn̩] vt a. hum to lynch

Lyrik <-> ['ly:·rɪk] f kein pl lyric [poetry]

M

M, m <-, -> [ɛm] nt M, m; **~ wie Martha** M as in Mike

m m kurz für **Meter** m

Machart f style

machen ['ma·xn̩] I. vt 1. (tun, unternehmen) to do; **eine Reise/einen Spaziergang ~** to go on a trip/for a walk 2. (erzeugen, verursachen) to make; (Fotos) to take; **jdm Angst ~** to frighten sb; **sich** dat **Sorgen ~** to worry; **jdm Hoffnung/Mut ~** to give sb hope/courage 3. (zubereiten: Tee, Kaffee) to make 4. (absolvieren) to do; **einen Kurs ~** to take a course; **eine Ausbildung ~** to train to be sth 5. (kosten) **das macht zehn Euro** that's ten euros [please]; **was macht das zusammen?** what does that come to? 6. (ausmachen) [das] **macht** [doch] **nichts!** never mind!; **macht das was?** does it matter? ▶ **mach's** <u>gut</u> fam take care [o it easy] II. vi 1. (werden lassen) **Liebe macht blind** love is blind 2. (aussehen lassen) **Querstreifen ~ dick** horizontal stripes make you look fat III. vr 1. (viel leisten) **die neue Sekretärin macht sich gut**

the new secretary is doing a good job **2.** (*passen*) **das Bild macht sich gut an der Wand** the picture looks good on the wall **3.** (*sich begeben*) **sich** *akk* **an die Arbeit ~** to get down to work **4.** (*gewinnen*) **sich** *dat* **Feinde ~** to make enemies **5.** **+** *adj* (*werden*) **sich** *akk* **verständlich ~** to make oneself understood **6.** (*gelegen sein*) **sich** *dat* **etwas/viel/ wenig aus jdm/etw ~** to care/care a lot/not care much for sb/sth

Macher(in) <-s, -> *m(f) fam* doer

Macho <-s, -s> ['ma·tʃo] *m fam* macho

Macht <-, Mächte> ['maxt] *f* power; **an die ~ kommen** to come [in]to power

Machthaber(in) <-s, -> [-ha:·bɐ] *m(f)* ruler

mächtig I. *adj* **1.** (*einflussreich*) powerful **2.** (*gewaltig*) mighty **II.** *adv fam* (*sehr*) extremely

Machtkampf *m* power struggle

machtlos *adj* powerless

Machtprobe *f* test of strength

Macke <-, -n> ['ma·kə] *f fam* **1.** (*Schadstelle*) defect **2.** *fam* (*Tick, Eigenart*) quirk

Mädchen <-s, -> ['mɛːt·çən] *nt* girl ▶ **für alles** *fam* jack-of-all-trades

mädchenhaft *adj* girlish

Mädchenname *m* **1.** (*Vorname*) girl's name **2.** (*Geburtsname einer Ehefrau*) maiden name

Made <-, -n> ['ma:·də] *f* maggot ▶ **wie die ~[n] im Speck leben** *fam* to live the life of Riley

madig ['ma:·dɪç] *adj* worm-eaten

madigmachen^RR *vt* to belittle; **jdm etw ~** *fam* to spoil sth for sb

Magazin <-s, -e> [ma·ga·'tsi:n] *nt* magazine

Magen <-s, Mägen> ['ma:·gn̩] *m* stomach; **auf nüchternen ~** on an empty stomach ▶ **jdm dreht sich der ~ um** sb's stomach is turning; **etw schlägt jdm auf den ~** *fam* sth gets to sb

Magenbitter <-s, -> *m* bitters *npl*

Magengeschwür *nt* stomach ulcer

Magensäure *f* stomach acid

Magenschmerzen *pl* stomachache

Magenverstimmung *f* upset stomach

mager ['ma:·gɐ] *adj* **1.** (*dünn*) thin

2. (*fettarm*) low-fat; (*Fleisch*) lean **3.** (*dürftig*) feeble; (*Ernte*) poor

Magermilch *f* skim milk

Magersucht *f kein pl* anorexia

Magie <-> [ma·'gi:] *f kein pl* magic

Magier(in) <-s, -> ['ma:·gi·ɐ] *m(f)* magician

magisch ['ma:·gɪʃ] *adj* magic

Magister Artium *m* the most commonly awarded degree in the humanities and social sciences at German universities

Magnesium <-s> [ma·'gne:·zi·ʊm] *nt kein pl* magnesium

Magnet <-[e]s, -e[n]> [ma·'gne:t] *m* magnet

Magnetfeld *nt* magnetic field

magnetisch [ma·'gne:·tɪʃ] *adj* magnetic

Mahagoni <-s> [ma·ha·'go:·ni] *nt kein pl* mahogany

Mähdrescher <-s, -> *m* combine harvester

mähen ['mɛː·ən] *vt* (*Gras*) to mow; (*Feld*) to harvest

Mahl <-[e]s, -e> ['ma:l] *nt pl selten geh* meal

mahlen <mahlte, gemahlen> ['ma:·lən] *vt* to grind

Mahlzeit ['ma:l·tsait] *f* meal; **~!** *dial fam* ≈ [good] afternoon! (*greeting used during the lunch break in parts of Germany and Austria*)

Mähne <-, -n> ['mɛː·nə] *f* mane

mahnen ['ma:·nən] *vt* **1.** (*nachdrücklich erinnern*) to warn **2.** (*an eine Rechnung erinnern*) to remind

Mahnung <-, -en> *f* **1.** (*mahnende Äußerung*) warning **2.** (*Mahnbrief*) reminder

Mai <-[e]s, -e> ['mai] *m* May; *s. a.* **Februar**

Maiglöckchen *nt* lily of the valley

Mailand <-s> ['mai·lant] *nt* Milan

Mailbox <-, -en> ['me:l·bɔks] *f* INET mailbox

Mais <-es, -e> ['mais] *m* **1.** (*Anbaupflanze*) corn **2.** (*Maisfrucht*) sweet corn

Maiskolben *m* corncob

majestätisch [ma·jɛs·'tɛː·tɪʃ] *adj* majestic

Majonäse <-, -n> [ma·jo·'nɛː·zə] *f* mayonnaise

Majoran <-s, -e> ['ma:·jo·ran] *m* marjoran

makaber [ma'ka:·bɐ] *adj* macabre

Makel <-s, -> ['ma:·kl̩] *m* flaw

makellos *adj* 1. (*untadelig: Ruf*) untarnished 2. (*fehlerlos*) perfect

mäkeln ['mɛ:·kl̩n] *vi* to whine [about sth]

Make-up <-s, -s> [me:k·'ʔap] *nt* make-up

Makkaroni [ma·ka·'ro:·ni] *pl* macaroni

Makler(in) <-s, -> ['ma:·klɐ] *m(f)* broker; (*Immobilienmakler*) realtor

Makrele <-, -n> [ma·'kre:·lə] *f* mackerel

mal¹ ['ma:l] *adv* 1. MATH times; **drei ~ drei ergibt neun** three times three is nine 2. (*eben so*) **gerade ~** *fam* only

mal² [ma:l] *adv fam kurz für* **einmal**

Mal¹ <-[e]s, -e *o nach Zahlwörtern:* -> [ma:l] *nt* (*Zeitpunkt*) time; **einige/etliche ~e** sometimes/very often; **ein/kein einziges ~** once/not once; **jedes ~** every time; **zum ersten/letzten ~** for the first/last time; **bis zum nächsten ~!** see you [around]!; **das x-te ~** *fam* the millionth time; **das eine oder andere ~** [every] now and again ► **ein für alle ~** once and for all; **mit einem ~[e]** all of a sudden

Mal² <-[e]s, -e> ['ma:l] *nt* mark; (*Muttermal*) birthmark

Malaria <-> [ma·'la:·rja] *f kein pl* malaria

Malaysia <-s> [ma·'lai·zja] *nt* Malaysia; *s. a.* **Deutschland**

malen ['ma:·lən] *vt, vi* 1. (*ein Bild herstellen*) to paint 2. *dial* (*anstreichen*) to paint

Maler(in) <-s, -> ['ma:·lɐ] *m(f)* painter

Malerei <-, -en> [ma·lə·'rai] *f* 1. *kein pl* (*Malkunst*) painting 2. *meist pl* (*Gemälde*) picture, painting

malerisch *adj* picturesque

Malheur <-s, -s> [ma·'løːɐ] *nt* mishap

Malta <-s> ['mal·ta] *nt* Malta; *s. a.* **Deutschland**

Malteser(in) <-s, -> [mal·'te:·zɐ] *m(f)* Maltese; *s. a.* **Deutsche(r)**

maltesisch [mal·'te:·zɪʃ] *adj* Maltese; *s. a.* **deutsch**

Malz <-es> ['malts] *nt kein pl* malt

Mama <-, -s> ['ma·ma] *f*, **Mami** <-, -s>

['ma·mi] *f fam* mommy

man <*dat* einem, *akk* einen> ['man] *pron indef* 1. (*irgendjemand*) one *form*, you; **das hat ~ mir gesagt** that's what I was told 2. (*die Leute*) people; **so etwas tut ~ nicht** that's not the way things work [around here] 3. (*ich*) **~ versteht sein eigenes Wort nicht** I can't hear myself think

Management <-s, -s> ['mɛn·ɪtʃ·mənt] *nt* management + *sing/pl* vb

Manager(in) <-s, -> ['mɛ·nɪ·dʒɐ] *m(f)* manager

manche(r, s) *pron indef* 1. + *pl* (*einige*) some 2. + *sing* **~r Mann/~ Frau** many a man/woman

mancherlei ['man·çe·'lai] *pron indef, adjektivisch* various

manchmal ['mançˌma:l] *adv* 1. (*gelegentlich*) sometimes 2. *schweiz* (*oft*) often

Mandarine <-, -n> [man·da·'ri:·nə] *f* mandarin

Mandel <-, -n> ['man·dl̩] *f* 1. (*Frucht*) almond 2. *meist pl* ANAT tonsils *pl*

Mandelentzündung *f* tonsillitis

Manege <-, -n> [ma·'ne:·ʒə] *f* ring

Mangel¹ <-s, Mängel> ['ma·ŋl̩] *m* 1. (*Fehler*) flaw 2. *kein pl* (*Knappheit*) lack (**an** + *dat* of); **ein ~ an Vitamin C** vitamin C deficiency

Mangel² ['ma·ŋl̩] *f* ► **jdn in die ~ nehmen** *fam* to grill sb

Mangelerscheinung *f* deficiency symptom

mangelhaft *adj* 1. (*unzureichend*) inadequate 2. (*Mängel aufweisend*) faulty 3. (*Schulnote*) ≈ E

mangeln ['ma·ŋl̩n] *vi* **es mangelt an etw** *dat* there is a shortage of sth

Mango <-, -gonen> ['maŋ·go] *f* mango

Manie <-, -n> [ma·'ni:] *f geh* obsession

Manifest <-[e]s, -e> [ma·ni·'fɛst] *nt* manifesto

Maniküre <-> [ma·ni·'ky:·rə] *f kein pl* manicure

Manipulation <-, -en> [ma·ni·pu·la·'tsjo:n] *f* manipulation

manipulieren * [ma·ni·pu·'li:·rən] *vt* to manipulate

Mann <-[e]s, Männer> ['man] *m*

1. (*männlicher Mensch*) man; **Männer** men; (*im Gegensatz zu den Frauen a.*) males **2.** (*Ehemann*) husband ▶ der ~ **auf der Straße** the man in the street, John Doe; **jd ist ein gemachter** ~ sb has got it made

Mannequin <-s, -s> [ˈmanəkɛ̃] *nt* model

männlich [ˈmɛnlɪç] *adj* **1.** male; (*Aussehen, Duft, Züge*) masculine **2.** LING masculine

Mannschaft <-, -en> *f* **1.** SPORT team **2.** (*Schiffs- o Flugzeugbesatzung*) crew **3.** (*Gruppe von Mitarbeitern*) staff + *sing/pl vb*

Manöver <-s, -> [maˈnøːvɐ] *nt* **1.** MIL maneuver **2.** *pej* (*Winkelzug*) trick

Mantel <-s, Mäntel> [ˈmantl̩] *m* coat

manuell [maˈnuɛl] **I.** *adj* manual **II.** *adv* manually

Mappe <-, -n> [ˈmapə] *f* **1.** (*Schnellhefter*) folder **2.** (*Aktenmappe*) briefcase

Maracuja <-, -s> [maraˈkuːja] *f* passion fruit

Marathon <-s, -s> [ˈmaːratɔn] *m a. fig* marathon

Märchen <-s, -> [ˈmɛːɐ̯çən] *nt* fairy tale

Marder <-s, -> [ˈmardɐ] *m* marten

Margarine <-, -n> [marɡaˈriːnə] *f* margarine

Marienkäfer *m* ladybug

Marille <-, -n> [maˈrɪlə] *f österr* apricot

Marine <-, -n> [maˈriːnə] *f* NAUT, MIL navy; **bei der** ~ in the navy

Marionette <-, -n> [marioˈnɛtə] *f* puppet *a. fig*

Mark[1] <-, - *o hum* Märker> [mark] *f hist* mark; **Deutsche** ~ German mark

Mark[2] <-[e]s> [mark] *nt kein pl* marrow ▶ **etw geht jdm durch** ~ **und Bein** sth sets sb's teeth on edge

markant [marˈkant] *adj* **1.** (*ausgeprägt*) bold **2.** (*auffallend*) striking

Marke <-, -n> [ˈmarkə] *f* **1.** *fam* (*Briefmarke*) stamp; **eine** ~ **zu 55 Cent** a 55-cent stamp **2.** (*Warensorte*) brand; **das ist** ~ **Eigenbau** *hum* I made it myself

Markenartikel *m* brand-name product

Markenzeichen *nt* trademark *a. fig*

markieren* [marˈkiːrən] *vt* **1.** (*kennzeichnen*) to mark **2.** *fam* (*vortäuschen*) to play

Markierung <-, -en> *f* marking

Markise <-, -n> [marˈkiːzə] *f* awning

Markt <-[e]s, Märkte> [ˈmarkt] *m* **1.** (*Wochenmarkt*) market **2.** (*Marktplatz*) marketplace **3.** ÖKON, FIN market; **etw auf den** ~ **bringen** to put sth on the market

Marktführer *m* market leader

Marktlücke *f* niche in the market

Marktplatz *m* marketplace

Marmelade <-, -n> [marməˈlaːdə] *f* jam; (*aus Zitrusfrüchten*) marmalade

Marmor <-s, -e> [ˈmarmoːɐ̯] *m* marble

Marokkaner(in) <-s, -> [marɔˈkaːnɐ] *m(f)* Moroccan; *s. a.* **Deutsche(r)**

marokkanisch [marɔˈkaːnɪʃ] *adj* Moroccan; *s. a.* **deutsch**

Marokko <-s> [maˈrɔko] *nt* Morocco; *s. a.* **Deutschland**

Marone <-, -n> [maˈroːnə] *f* [edible] chestnut

Mars <-> [mars] *m* **der** ~ Mars

Marsch <-[e]s, Märsche> [marʃ] *m* (*a. mus*) march

marschieren* [marˈʃiːrən] *vi sein* **1.** MIL to march **2.** (*zu Fuß gehen*) to walk quickly

Märtyrer(in) <-s, -> [ˈmɛrtyːrɐ, ˈmɛrtyːrərɪn] *m(f) a. fig* martyr

Marxismus <-> [marˈksɪsmʊs] *m kein pl* Marxism

Marxist(in) <-en, -en> [marˈksɪst] *m(f)* Marxist

März <-[es], -e> [mɛrts] *m* March; *s. a.* **Februar**

Marzipan <-s, -e> [martsiˈpaːn] *nt o m* marzipan

Masche <-, -n> [ˈmaʃə] *f* **1.** (*Strickmasche*) stitch **2.** *fam* (*Trick*) trick

Maschendraht *m* wire mesh

Maschine <-, -n> [maˈʃiːnə] *f* **1.** (*Automat*) machine **2.** (*Motorrad*) bike **3.** (*Schreibmaschine*) typewriter; ~ **schreiben** to type

maschinell [maʃiˈnɛl] **I.** *adj* machine *attr* **II.** *adv* by machine

Maschinenbau *m kein pl* **1.** (*das Bau*) machine construction **2.** (*Fachgebiet*)

mechanical engineering

Masern ['ma:·zen] *pl* measles

Maske <-, -n> ['mas·kə] *f a. fig* mask

maskieren* [mas·'ki:·rən] **I.** *vt* to disguise **II.** *vr* **sich** *akk* ~ **1.** (*sich verkleiden*) to dress up **2.** (*sich vermummen*) to put on a mask

Masochist(in) <-en, -en> [ma·zɔ·'xɪst] *m(f)* masochist

masochistisch *adj* masochistic

maß ['ma:s] *imp von* **messen**

Maß¹ <-es, -e> ['ma:s] *nt* **1.** (*Maßeinheit*) measure **2.** *pl* (*gemessene Größe*) measurements; (*Raum*) dimensions; **bei jdm ~ nehmen** to measure sb **3.** (*Ausmaß*) extent ▶ **in ~en** in moderation; **das ~ ist voll** enough is enough

Maß² <-, -> ['ma:s] *f südd* liter [*mug*] of beer

Massage <-, -n> [ma·'sa:·ʒə] *f* massage

Massaker <-s, -> [ma·'sa:·kɐ] *nt* massacre

massakrieren* [ma·sa·'kri:·rən] *vt* to massacre

Masse <-, -n> ['ma·sə] *f* **1.** (*breiige Material*) mass **2.** (*Menschenmasse*) crowd **3.** (*große Anzahl*) mass; **eine [ganze] ~** a lot [of] **4.** PHYS mass

Massenandrang *m* crush [of people]

Massenarbeitslosigkeit *f* mass unemployment *no art*

massenhaft I. *adj* on a huge scale **II.** *adv fam* in droves

Massenmedien *pl* mass media + *sing/ pl vb*

Massentierhaltung *f* factory farming

Massentourismus *m kein pl* mass tourism

Masseur(in) <-s, -e> [ma·'søːɐ̯] *m(f)* masseur *masc*, masseuse *fem*

Masseuse <-, -n> [ma·'søː·zə] *f* **1.** *veraltend s.* **Masseur 2.** *euph* (*Prostituierte*) masseuse

maßgeblich ['ma:s·geːp·lɪç] **I.** *adj* **1.** (*ausschlaggebend*) decisive **2.** (*bedeutend*) significant **II.** *adv* decisively; **an etw** *dat* ~ **beteiligt sein** to play a leading role in sth

massieren* [ma·'siː·rən] *vt* to massage

massig ['ma·sɪç] *adj* massive

mäßig ['mɛː·sɪç] **I.** *adj* **1.** (*maßvoll, ge-*

ring) moderate **2.** (*mittelmäßig*) mediocre, indifferent **II.** *adv* **1.** (*in Maßen*) with moderation **2.** (*nicht besonders*) indifferently

mäßigen ['mɛː·sɪ·gn̩] **I.** *vt* to curb **II.** *vr* **sich** *akk* ~ to restrain oneself

massiv [ma·'siːf] *adj* **1.** (*solide*) solid *attr* **2.** (*wuchtig*) solid, massive **3.** (*drastisch, heftig*) serious; (*Kritik*) heavy

Massiv <-s, -e> [ma·'siːf] *nt* massif

maßlos I. *adj* extreme; ~ **sein** to be immoderate **II.** *adv* **1.** (*äußerst*) extremely **2.** (*unerhört*) hugely

Maßlosigkeit <-> *f kein pl* lack of moderation

Maßnahme <-, -n> ['ma:s·na:·mə] *f* measure

Maßstab ['ma:s·ʃta:p] *m* **1.** (*Größenverhältnis*) scale; **im ~ 1:250.000** on a scale of 1:250,000 **2.** (*Kriterium*) criterion

maßstab(s)gerecht *adj* true to scale

maßvoll I. *adj* moderate **II.** *adv* moderately

Mast¹ <-[e]s, -en> ['mast] *m* **1.** NAUT mast **2.** (*Stange*) pole

Mast² <-, -> ['mast] *f pl selten* (*das Mästen*) fattening

mästen ['mɛs·tn̩] *vt* to fatten

masturbieren* [mas·tʊr·'biː·rən] *vi* to masturbate

Material <-s, -ien> [ma·te·'rɪ̯a:l] *nt* material

Materialismus <-> [ma·te·rɪ̯a·'lɪs·mʊs] *m kein pl* materialism

Materialist(in) <-en, -en> [ma·te·rɪ̯a·'lɪst] *m(f)* materialist

materialistisch [ma·te·rɪ̯a·'lɪs·tɪʃ] *adj* materialist[ic]

Materie <-, -n> [ma·'te:·rɪ̯ə] *f* **1.** *kein pl* PHYS, CHEM matter **2.** (*Thema*) subject

materiell [ma·te·'rɪ̯ɛl] *adj* **1.** (*stofflich*) material **2.** (*finanziell*) financial

Mathematik <-> [ma·te·ma·'tik] *f kein pl* mathematics + *sing vb*, math *fam*

mathematisch [ma·te·ma·'tɪʃ] *adj* mathematical

Matratze <-, -n> [ma·'tra·tsə] *f* mattress

Matrose <-n, -n> [ma·'tro:·zə] *m* sailor

Matsch <-[e]s> ['matʃ] *m kein pl* **1.** (*schlammige Erde*) mud; (*Schnee-*

matsch) slush **2.** (*breiige Masse*) mush

matschig ['mat·ʃɪç] *adj fam* **1.** (*Erde*) muddy; (*Schnee*) slushy **2.** (*breiig*) mushy

matt ['mat] **I.** *adj* **1.** (*erschöpft, schwach*) weak; (*Händedruck*) limp; (*Lächeln, Stimme*) faint; (*Licht*) dim **2.** (*glanzlos*) matt[te]; (*Augen*) dull; (*Farben*) pale **II.** *adv* **1.** (*schwach*) dimly **2.** (*ohne Nachdruck*) feebly

Matte¹ <-, -n> ['ma·tə] *f* (*Fußmatte etc.*) mat

Matte² <-, -n> ['ma·tə] *f schweiz, österr* (*Bergwiese*) alpine meadow

Mauer <-, -n> ['mau·ɐ] *f a. fig* wall

mauern ['mau·ɐn] *vt* to build

Maul <-[e]s, Mäuler> ['maul] *nt* **1.** (*bei Tieren*) mouth; (*Raubtier*) jaws *pl* **2.** *derb* (*Mund*) trap ▸ **halt's ~!** *vulg* shut up!; **jdm das ~ stopfen** *vulg* to shut sb up

Maulesel ['maul·ʔe·zl̩] *m* mule

Maulkorb *m* muzzle

Maultaschen *pl* KOCHK *südd* large pasta squares filled with meat, cheese, spinach, etc.

Maultier ['maul·tiːɐ̯] *nt s.* **Maulesel**

Maulwurf <-[e]s, -würfe> ['maul·vʊrf] *m a. fig* mole

Maurer(in) <-s, -> ['mau·rɐ] *m(f)* bricklayer

Maus <-, Mäuse> ['maus] *f* **1.** (*a. comput*) mouse **2.** *pl sl* (*Geld*) dough *sing*

Mausefalle *f* mousetrap

Maut <-, -en> ['maut] *f* toll [charge]

maximal [ma·ksi·'maːl] **I.** *adj* maximum *attr;* (*höchste a.*) highest *attr* **II.** *adv* at maximum; **das ~ zulässige Gesamtgewicht** the maximum weight; **~ 25.000 Euro** 25,000 euros at most

Maximum <-s, Maxima> ['ma·ksi·mʊm] *nt* maximum (**an** +*dat* of)

Mayonnaise <-, -n> [ma·jɔ·'nɛː·zə] *f s.* **Majonäse**

Mazedonien <-s> [ma·tse·'doː·ni·ən] *nt* Macedonia; *s. a.* **Deutschland**

Mechanik <-, -en> [me·'çaː·nɪk] *f* mechanics + *sing vb*

Mechaniker(in) <-s, -> [me·'çaː·nɪ·kɐ] *m(f)* mechanic

mechanisch [me·'çaː·nɪʃ] *adj a. fig* mechanical

Mechanismus <-, -nismen> [me·ça·'nɪs·mʊs] *m* mechanism

meckern ['mɛ·kɐn] *vi* **1.** (*der Ziege*) to bleat **2.** *fig fam* to complain, to bellyache *fam* (**über** +*akk* about)

Medaille <-, -n> [me·'dal·jə] *f* medal

Medien ['meː·di·ən] *pl* **die ~** the media + *sing/pl vb*

Medikament <-[e]s, -e> [me·di·ka·'mɛnt] *nt* medicine

Medikamentenmissbrauch ᴿᴿ *m* drug abuse

medikamentös [me·di·ka·mɛn·'tøːs] *adj* medicinal

Meditation <-, -en> [me·di·ta·'tsjoːn] *f* meditation (**über** +*akk* about/on)

mediterran [me·di·tɛ·'raːn] *adj* Mediterranean

meditieren * [me·di·'tiː·rən] *vi* to meditate

Medizin <-, -en> [me·di·'tsiːn] *f* **1.** *kein pl* (*Heilkunde*) medicine **2.** *fam* (*Medikament*) medicine

Mediziner(in) <-s, -> [me·di·'tsiː·nɐ] *m(f)* doctor

medizinisch [me·di·'tsiː·nɪʃ] **I.** *adj* **1.** (*ärztlich*) medical **2.** (*heilend*) medicinal **II.** *adv* medically; **jdn ~ behandeln** to give sb medical treatment

Medizinmann <-männer> [-man] *m* (*indianisch*) medicine man; (*afrikanisch*) witch doctor

Meer <-[e]s, -e> ['meːɐ̯] *nt* sea; (*Weltmeer*) ocean; **am ~** by the water; **ans ~ fahren** to go to the ocean; **das Schwarze/Tote ~** the Black/Dead Sea

Meerenge *f* strait

Meeresalge *f* seaweed + *sing vb*

Meeresfrüchte *pl* seafood + *sing vb*

Meeresspiegel *m* sea level

Meerrettich *m* horseradish

Meerschweinchen *nt* guinea pig

Meerwasser *nt* sea water

Megabyte ['meː·ga·bait] *nt* COMPUT megabyte

Mehl <-[e]s, -e> ['meːl] *nt* flour

mehlig ['meː·lɪç] *adj* (*Kartoffeln*) floury

mehr ['meːɐ̯] **I.** *pron indef komp vo* **viel** more; **immer ~** more and more

~ **oder weniger** more or less **II.** *adv* more; **nicht** ~ no longer; **es war keiner** ~ **da** there was nobody left; **ich kann nicht** ~ I can't take it any longer; **nie** ~ never again; **niemand** ~ nobody else

mehrdeutig *adj* ambiguous

mehrdimensional *adj* multidimensional

mehrere ['me:·rə·rə] *pron indef* **1.** *adjektivisch* (*einige*) several *attr;* (*verschiedene*) various **2.** *substantivisch* (*einige*) several; ~ **davon** several [of them]

Mehrfamilienhaus [-liən-] *nt* multi-family house

mehrfarbig *adj* multicolored

Mehrheit <-, -en> *f* majority

mehrjährig *adj attr* several years of *attr,* of several years *pred*

Mehrkosten *pl* additional costs *pl*

mehrmals ['me:g·ma:ls] *adv* repeatedly

mehrsprachig *adj* multilingual

mehrstündig *adj* lasting several hours *pred*

mehrtägig *adj* lasting several days *pred*

Mehrwegflasche *f* deposit [*o* returnable] bottle

Mehrwegverpackung *f* reusable packaging

Mehrwertsteuer *f* ≈ sales tax

mehrwöchig *adj* lasting several weeks *pred*

Mehrzahl *f kein pl* **1.** (*Mehrheit*) majority **2.** LING plural [form]

meiden <mied, gemieden> ['mai·dn] *vt* to avoid

Meile <-, -n> ['mai·lə] *f* mile

Meilenstein *m a. fig* milestone

meilenweit ['mai·lən·vait] *adv* for miles

mein ['main] *pron poss, adjektivisch* my

meine(r, s) ['mai·nə] *pron poss, substantivisch* mine

Meineid ['main·?ait] *m* JUR perjury; **einen** ~ **leisten** to commit perjury

meinen ['mai·nən] *vt, vi* **1.** (*denken, annehmen*) to think; **und was** ~ **Sie dazu?** and what do you think about that?; ~ **Sie?** [do] you think so? **2.** (*sagen wollen*) **was** ~ **Sie** [damit]**?** what do you mean [by that]? **3.** (*ansprechen*) **damit bist du gemeint** that means you **4.** (*beabsichtigen*) to mean, to intend;

ich meine es ernst I'm serious [about it]; **es gut** ~ to mean well; **es gut mit jdm** ~ to do one's best for sb; **so war das nicht gemeint** I didn't mean it like that

meinetwegen ['mai·nət·'ve:·gn] *adv* **1.** (*wegen mir*) because of me **2.** (*mir zuliebe*) for my sake **3.** (*von mir aus*) as far as I'm concerned; **darf ich?** — ~**!** may I? — sure! [*o* go right ahead!]

Meinung <-, -en> ['mai·nʊŋ] *f* opinion; (*Anschauung a.*) view; **jdm die** ~ **sagen** to give sb a piece of one's mind

Meinungsforschung *f kein pl* opinion polling

Meinungsumfrage *f* opinion poll

Meinungsverschiedenheit *f* **1.** (*unterschiedliche Ansichten*) difference of opinion **2.** (*Auseinandersetzung*) argument

Meise <-, -n> ['mai·zə] *f* ORN tit ▶ **eine** ~ **haben** *fam* to have a screw loose

meist ['maist] *adv s.* **meistens**

meiste(r, s) *pron indef superl von* **viel** **1.** *adjektivisch* most; **das** ~ **Geld** the most money; (*als Anteil*) most of the money; **die** ~ **Zeit** the most time; (*meistens*) most of the time **2.** *substantivisch* **die** ~**n** most people; **die** ~**n von uns** most of us; **das** ~ most of it; (*als Anteil*) the most; **das** ~ **von dem, was ...** most of what ...; **am** ~**n** [the] most

meistens ['mais·tns] *adv* mostly, more often than not; (*zum größten Teil*) for the most part

Meister(in) <-s, -> ['mais·te] *m(f)* **1.** (*Handwerksmeister*) master [craftsman]; **seinen** ~ **machen** to take one's master craftsman's exam **2.** SPORT champion ▶ **es ist noch kein** ~ **vom** <u>**Himmel**</u> **gefallen** *prov* practice makes perfect

meisterhaft I. *adj* masterly; (*geschickt*) masterful **II.** *adv* in a masterly manner; (*geschickt*) masterfully

meistern ['mais·ten] *vt* to master

Meisterschaft <-, -en> *f* **1.** (*Wettkampf*) championship; (*Veranstaltung*) championships *pl* **2.** *kein pl* (*Können*) mastery

Melancholie <-, -n> [me·laŋ·ko·'li:] *f* melancholy

M

melancholisch [me·laŋ·ˈkoː·lɪʃ] *adj* melancholy

Meldeamt *nt fam* ≈ city/town clerk|'s office|

melden [ˈmɛl·dn̩] I. *vt* 1. (*anzeigen*) to report 2. RADIO, TV to report; **für morgen ist Schneefall gemeldet** snow is in the forecast for tomorrow ▸ **nichts zu ~ haben** *fam* to have no say II. *vr* 1. (*sich zur Verfügung stellen*) **sich** *akk* **zu etw** *dat* **freiwillig ~** to volunteer for sth 2. **sich** *akk* |**am Telefon**| **~** to answer the telephone; **es meldet sich keiner** there's no answer 3. (*in Kontakt bleiben*) **sich** *akk* |**bei jdm**| **~** to get in touch |with sb|

Meldepflicht *f kein pl* obligation to report sth; **polizeiliche ~** *legal obligation in Germany to register one's residence with the local authorities*

meldepflichtig *adj* **~e Krankheit** disease doctors are required to report

Meldung <-, -en> *f* 1. (*Nachricht*) piece of news 2. (*offizielle Mitteilung*) report

meliert [me·ˈliːɐ̯t] *adj* 1. (*Haar*) graying 2. (*Gewebe*) flecked, mottled

Melisse <-, -n> [me·ˈlɪ·sə] *f* |lemon| balm

melken <melkte, gemolken *o* gemelkt> [ˈmɛl·kn̩] *vt* 1. (*Kuh*) to milk 2. *fam* (*Person*) to fleece

Melodie <-, -n> [me·lo·ˈdiː] *f* melody, tune

melodisch [me·ˈloː·dɪʃ] I. *adj* melodic II. *adv* melodically

Melone <-, -n> [me·ˈloː·nə] *f* 1. (*Frucht*) melon 2. *fam* (*Hut*) bowler |hat|, derby

Memoiren [me·mo·ˈaː·rən] *pl* memoirs

Menge <-, -n> [ˈmɛ·ŋə] *f* 1. (*bestimmte Anzahl*) amount, quantity 2. (*große Anzahl*) **eine ~ Geld** a lot of money; **eine ~ zu sehen** a lot to see; **jede ~ Arbeit** a ton of work 3. (*Menschenmenge*) crowd ▸ **in rauen ~n** *fam* in vast quantities

Mensa <-, Mensen> [ˈmɛn·za] *f* university cafeteria

Mensch <-en, -en> [ˈmɛnʃ] *m* 1. (*menschliches Lebewesen*) man; **die ~en** man *sing*, *no art*, human beings *pl*;

auch nur ein ~ sein to be only human 2. (*Person, Persönlichkeit*) person; **~en** people; **kein ~** no one ▸ **wie der erste ~** *fam* very clumsily

Menschenaffe *m* |anthropoid| ape

Menschenfresser(in) <-s, -> *m(f)* cannibal

Menschenhandel *m kein pl* human trafficking

Menschenkenner(in) <-s, -> *m(f)* judge of character

Menschenkenntnis *f kein pl* ability to judge character

Menschenleben *nt* 1. (*Todesopfer*) life 2. (*Lebenszeit*) lifetime

menschenleer *adj* 1. (*unbesiedelt*) uninhabited 2. (*unbelebt*) deserted

Menschenrecht *nt meist pl* human right *usu pl*

Menschenrechtsverletzung *f* human rights violation

Menschenseele [ˈmɛn·ʃn̩·ˈzeː·lə] *f* human soul; **keine ~** not a |living| soul

menschenunwürdig I. *adj* inhumane; (*Behausung*) unfit for human habitation II. *adv* in an inhumane way, inhumanely

Menschenverstand *m* **gesunder ~** common sense

Menschenwürde *f kein pl* human dignity

Menschheit <-> *f kein pl* **die ~** mankind, humanity

menschlich [ˈmɛnʃ·lɪç] *adj* 1. (*des Menschen*) human 2. (*human*) humane; (*Vorgesetzter*) sympathetic

Menschlichkeit <-> *f kein pl* humanity

Menstruation <-, -en> [mɛns·trua·ˈtsjoːn] *f* menstruation

Mentalität <-, -en> [mɛn·ta·li·ˈtɛːt] *f* mentality

Menü <-s, -s> [me·ˈnyː] *nt* (*a. comput*) menu

merken [ˈmɛr·kn̩] I. *vt, vi* 1. (*spüren*) to feel; **es war kaum zu ~** it was barely noticeable 2. (*wahrnehmen*) to notice; **ich habe nichts davon gemerkt** I didn't notice a thing 3. (*behalten*) **leicht zu ~ sein** to be easy to remember II. *vr* (*im Gedächtnis behalten*) **sich** *dat* **etw ~** to remember sth

erkmal <-s, -e> ['mɛrk·ma:l] *nt* feature

erkwürdig I. *adj* strange **II.** *adv* strangely

eßbarRR, **meßbar**ALT *adj* measurable

esse¹ <-, -n> ['mɛ·sə] *f* (*Gottesdienst*) mass

esse² <-, -n> ['mɛ·sə] *f* (*Ausstellung*) trade show, convention

essehalle *f* exhibit hall

essen <misst, maß, gemessen> ['mɛ·n] **I.** *vt* **1.** (*Ausmaß oder Größe ermitteln*) to measure; (*Blutdruck, Temperatur*) to take **2.** (*beurteilen nach*) to judge (**an** +*dat* by) **II.** *vr geh* **sich** *akk* **mit jdm ~ können** to be able to compete with sb

esser <-s, -> ['mɛ·sə] *nt* knife ▶ **bis aufs ~** *fam* to the bitter end; **jdn ans ~ liefern** *fam* to betray sb

esserspitze *f* tip of a knife; **eine ~ Muskat** a pinch of nutmeg

essias <-> [mɛ·ˈsi:as] *m* REL Messiah

essing <-s> ['mɛ·sɪŋ] *nt kein pl* brass

essinstrumentRR *nt* measuring instrument

etall <-s, -e> [me·ˈtal] *nt* metal

etallarbeiter(in) *m(f)* metalworker

etallisch [me·ˈta·lɪʃ] **I.** *adj* **1.** (*aus Metall*) metal **2.** (*metallartig*) metallic **II.** *adv* like metal

etapher <-, -n> [me·ˈta·fɐ] *f* metaphor

etastase <-, -n> [me·ta·ˈsta·zə] *f* MED metastasis

eteorologe, Meteorologin <-n, -n> [me·teo·ro·ˈlo:·gə, me·teo·ro·ˈlo:·gɪn] *m, f* meteorologist

eter <-s, -> ['me:·tɐ] *m o nt* meter

ethode <-, -n> [me·ˈto:·də] *f* method

etropole <-, -n> [me·tro·ˈpo:·lə] *f* metropolis

etzger(in) <-s, -> ['mɛts·gɐ] *m(f)* butcher

etzgerei <-, -en> [mɛts·gə·ˈrai] *f* butcher shop

eute <-, -n> ['mɔy·tə] *f* **1.** *pej* (*Gruppe*) mob **2.** (*Jägersprache*) pack (of hounds)

euterei <-, -en> [mɔy·tə·ˈrai] *f* mutiny

euterer <-s, -> *m* mutineer

eutern ['mɔy·tɐn] *vi* **1.** (*sich auflehnen*) to mutiny **2.** *fam* (*meckern*) to grumble, complain

Mexikaner(in) <-s, -> [mɛ·ksi·ˈka:·nɐ] *m(f)* Mexican; *s. a.* **Deutsche(r)**

mexikanisch [mɛ·ksi·ˈka:·nɪʃ] *adj* Mexican; *s. a.* **deutsch**

Mexiko <-s> ['mɛ·ksi·ko] *nt* Mexico; *s. a.* **Deutschland**

miauen* [mi·ˈau·ən] *vi* to meow

mich ['mɪç] **I.** *pron pers akk von* **ich** me **II.** *pron refl* myself; **ich fühle ~ nicht so gut** I don't feel very well

Mief <-s> ['mi:f] *m kein pl fam* stench

Miene <-, -n> ['mi:·nə] *f* expression ▶ **ohne eine ~ zu verziehen** without turning a hair

mies ['mi:s] *adj fam* lousy, rotten

miesmachen *vt fam s.* **madigmachen**

Miesmuschel ['mi:s·mʊ·ʃl] *f* (blue) mussel

Mietauto *nt* rental car

Miete <-, -n> ['mi:·tə] *f* rent; **zur ~ wohnen** to rent

mieten ['mi:·tn] *vt* (*Boot, Wagen*) to rent; (*Haus, Wohnung, Büro a.*) to lease

Mieter(in) <-s, -> *m(f)* tenant

Mietshaus *nt* apartment building

Mietvertrag *m* rental agreement

Mietwagen *m* rental car

Mietwohnung *f* rented apartment

Migräne <-, -n> [mi·ˈgrɛ:·nə] *f* migraine

Mikrochip [-tʃɪp] *m* microchip

Mikrofon <-s, -e> [mi·kro·ˈfo:n] *nt* microphone

Mikroskop <-s, -e> [mi·kro·ˈsko:p] *nt* microscope

Mikrowelle ['mi:·kro·vɛ·lə] *f* microwave

Milbe <-, -n> ['mɪl·bə] *f* mite

Milch <-> ['mɪlç] *f kein pl* milk

Milchflasche *f* milk bottle; (*für Babys*) baby's bottle

Milchkaffee *m* (caffe) latte

Milchprodukt *nt* milk product

Milchpulver *nt* powdered milk

Milchreis *m* **1.** (*Gericht*) rice pudding **2.** (*Reis*) arborio rice

Milchstraße *f* **die ~** the Milky Way

Milchzahn *m* milk tooth

mild ['mɪlt] *adj, adv* mild

mildern ['mɪl·dɐn] *vt* to alleviate; **~de Umstände** mitigating circumstances

M

Milieu <-s, -s> [mi·'ljøː] nt environment

Militär <-s> [mi·li·'tɛːɐ̯] nt kein pl armed forces pl, military

Militärdiktatur f military dictatorship

militärisch [mi·li·'tɛː·rɪʃ] adj military

Miliz <-, -en> [mi·'liːts] f 1. (Bürgerwehr) militia 2. (in sozialistischen Staaten: Polizei) police

Milliardär(in) <-s, -e> [mɪ·ljar·'dɛːɐ̯] m(f) billionaire

Milliarde <-, -n> [mɪ·'ljar·də] f billion

Millimeter <-s, -> [ˈmɪ·li·meː·tɐ] m o nt millimeter

Million <-, -en> [mɪ·'ljoːn] f million

Millionär(in) <-s, -e> [mɪ·ljo·'nɛːɐ̯] m(f) millionaire masc, millionairess fem

Millionenstadt f city with a million inhabitants or more

Milz <-, -en> [mɪlts] f spleen

Mimik <-> [ˈmiː·mɪk] f kein pl [gestures and] facial expression[s]

Minderheit <-, -en> f minority

minderjährig [ˈmɪn·dɐ·jɛː·rɪç] adj underage

Minderjährige(r) f(m) dekl wie adj minor

mindern [ˈmɪn·dɐn] vt to reduce (um +akk by)

minderwertig adj inferior

Minderwertigkeit <-> f kein pl inferiority

Minderwertigkeitsgefühl nt feeling of inferiority

Minderwertigkeitskomplex m inferiority complex

Minderzahl f kein pl minority

Mindestalter nt minimum age

mindeste(r, s) adj attr slightest; **das wäre das M~ gewesen** that's the least he/she/you etc. could have done

mindestens [ˈmɪn·dəs·tn̩s] adv at least

Mine <-, -n> [ˈmiː·nə] f 1. (eines Bleistifts) lead; (eines Filz-, Kugelschreibers) refill 2. (Sprengkörper) mine 3. (Bergwerk) mine

Mineral <-s, -e> [mi·ne·'raːl] nt mineral

Mineralöl nt mineral oil

Mineralölsteuer f tax on oil

Mineralwasser nt mineral water

minimal [mi·ni·'maːl] adj minimal

Minimum <-s, Minima> [ˈmiː·ni·mʊm] nt

minimum (**an** +dat of)

Minirock m miniskirt

Minister(in) <-s, -> [mi·'nɪs·tɐ] m(f) Secretary

Ministerium <-s, -rien> [mi·nɪs·'teː·ʊm] nt POL department

Ministerpräsident(in) m(f) (eines L des) prime minister; (eines Bun landes) minister-president (leader German state)

minus [ˈmiː·nʊs] präp, konj, adv mi ~ 15°C minus 15°C

Minus <-, -> [ˈmiː·nʊs] nt 1. (Mir zeichen) minus 2. ÖKON (Fehlbet deficit; ~ **machen** to lose money; **etw** dat **im ~ sein** to be in the [with sth]

Minuszeichen nt minus sign

Minute <-, -n> [mi·'nuː·tə] f minute letzter ~ at the last minute; **auf di** on the dot

Minutenzeiger m minute hand

Minze <-, -n> [ˈmɪn·tsə] f mint

mir [miːɐ̯] pron 1. pers dat von me; **eine alte Bekannte von ~** old acquaintance of mine; **komm zu ~** come back to my place 2. dat von sich one's; **ich wasche ~ Haare morgen** I'll wash my hair morrow ► **~ nichts, dir nichts** just like that

Mirabelle <-, -n> [mi·ra·'bɛlə] f M belle [plum]

Mischbrot nt bread made from rye wheat flour

Mischehe f mixed marriage

mischen [ˈmɪ·ʃn̩] I. vt to mix; KA to shuffle II. vr sich akk ~ 1. (vermengen) to mix (mit +dat v 2. (sich mengen) to mingle (unter - with) 3. (sich einmischen) to inter (in +akk in)

Mischling <-s, -e> [ˈmɪʃ·lɪŋ] 1. (Mensch) person of mixed paren 2. ZOOL half-breed; (Hund) mongrel

Mischung <-, -en> f mixture; (Ka, Tee, Tabak) blend

miserabel [mi·zə·'raː·bl̩] I. adj miser II. adv ~ **schlafen** to sleep really ba

Misere <-, -n> [mi·'zeː·rə] f geh mis

missachten * RR, **mißachten** * ALT [

'?ax·tn̩] vt **1.** (*ignorieren*) to disregard **2.** (*gering schätzen*) **jdn ~** to be disdainful of sb; **etw ~** to disdain sth

ißachtung RR, **Mißachtung** ALT ['mɪs·'?ax·tʊŋ] f **1.** (*Ignorierung*) disregard **2.** (*Geringschätzung*) disdain

ißbilligen * RR, **mißbilligen** * ALT ['mɪs·'bɪ·lɪ·gn̩] vt to disapprove of

ißbilligung RR, **Mißbilligung** ALT <-, -en> [mɪs·'bɪ·lɪ·gʊŋ] f pl selten disapproval

ißbrauch RR, **Mißbrauch** ALT ['mɪs·braux] m abuse

ißbrauchen * RR, **mißbrauchen** * ALT [mɪs·'brau·çn̩] vt to abuse

issen ['mɪ·sn̩] vt **jdn/etw nicht ~ wollen** geh not to want to do without sb/sth; **mein Telefon möchte ich nicht ~** I wouldn't want to have to do without my [tele]phone

ißerfolg RR, **Mißerfolg** ALT ['mɪs·] m failure

ißfallen * RR, **mißfallen** * ALT [mɪs·'fa·lən] vi irreg **jdm missfällt etw [an jdm]** sb dislikes sth [about sb]

ißgeburt RR, **Mißgeburt** ALT ['mɪs·gə·buːɐ̯t] f pej monster

ißgeschick RR, **Mißgeschick** ALT <-[e]s, -e> ['mɪs·gə·ʃɪk] nt mishap

ißglücken * RR, **mißglücken** * ALT [mɪs·'glʏ·kn̩] vi sein to fail

ißgönnen * RR, **mißgönnen** * ALT [mɪs·'gœ·nən] vt **jdm seinen Erfolg ~** to resent sb's success

ißgunst RR, **Mißgunst** ALT ['mɪs·gʊnst] f envy

ißgünstig RR, **mißgünstig** ALT **I.** adj envious **II.** adv enviously

isshandeln * RR, **mißhandeln** * ALT [mɪs·'han·dl̩n] vt to mistreat

isshandlung RR, **Mißhandlung** ALT [mɪs·'hand·lʊŋ] f mistreatment

ission <-, -en> [mɪ·'sjoːn] f mission

issionar(in) <-s, -e> [mɪ·sjo·'naːɐ̯] m(f) missionary

isslingen RR, **mißlingen** ALT <misslang, misslungen> [mɪs·'lɪŋən] vi sein to fail

isslingen RR, **Mißlingen** ALT <-s> [mɪs·'lɪŋən] nt kein pl failure

issmut RR, **Mißmut** ALT ['mɪs·muːt] m moroseness

issmutig RR, **mißmutig** ALT adj mo-

rose, sullen

missraten * RR, **mißraten** * ALT [mɪs·'raː·tn̩] vi irreg **sein** to go wrong; **ein ~es Kind** a child who has turned out badly

Missstand RR, **Mißstand** ALT m sorry state of affairs; **soziale Missstände** social evils

misstrauen * RR, **mißtrauen** * ALT [mɪs·'trau·ən] vi to mistrust

misstrauisch RR, **mißtrauisch** ALT ['mɪs·trau·ɪʃ] **I.** adj mistrustful; (*argwöhnisch*) suspicious **II.** adv mistrustfully; (*argwöhnisch*) suspiciously

missverständlich RR, **mißverständlich** ALT **I.** adj unclear; **~ sein** to be easily misunderstood **II.** adv unclearly

Missverständnis RR, **Mißverständnis** ALT <-ses, -se> ['mɪs·fɛɐ̯·ʃtɛnt·nɪs] nt misunderstanding

missverstehen * RR, **mißverstehen** * ALT ['mɪs·fɛɐ̯·ʃteː·ən] vt irreg to misunderstand

Mist <-es> ['mɪst] m kein pl **1.** (*Stalldünger*) dung; (*~ Vieh*) **2.** fam shit! vulg **2.** fam (*Quatsch*) nonsense **3.** fam (*Schund*) junk ▶ **~ bauen** fam to screw up; **so ein ~!** fam damn [it]!

Mistel <-, -n> ['mɪs·tl̩] f mistletoe

Misthaufen m dunghill

Miststück nt fam bastard masc vulg, bitch vulg

mit ['mɪt] **I.** präp +dat **1.** with; **~ jdm [zusammen]** [together] with sb **2.** (*per*) by; **~ der Bahn/dem Fahrrad/der Post** by train/bicycle/mail **3.** **~ 18 [Jahren]** at [the age of] 18 **II.** adv too, as well; **~ dabei sein** to be there [too]

Mitarbeit f kein pl **1.** (*Arbeitsbeteiligung*) collaboration **2.** SCH participation

mitarbeiten ['mɪt·?ar·bai·tn̩] vi **1.** (*als Mitarbeiter*) to collaborate (**bei** +dat on) **2.** SCH to participate (**in** +dat in)

Mitarbeiter(in) m(f) employee; **freier ~** freelancer

mitbekommen * vt irreg **1.** (*mitgegeben bekommen*) **etw [von jdm] ~** to be given sth [by sb] **2.** (*wahrnehmen*) **etw ~** to be aware of sth **3.** (*verstehen*) **hast du etwas davon ~?** did you catch any of that? **4.** fam (*vererbt bekommen*)

M

etw von jdm ~ to get sth from sb

mit|benutzen * *vt*, **mit|benützen** * *vt südd* to share

mit|bestimmen* I. *vi* to have a say (**bei** +*dat* in) II. *vt* to have an influence on

Mitbestimmung *f kein pl* participation

Mitbewohner(in) *m(f)* housemate; (*in einem Zimmer*) roommate

mit|bringen ['mɪt·ʔbrɪŋən] *vt irreg* 1. to bring; **hast du denn niemanden mitgebracht?** didn't you bring anyone along? 2. (*Vorraussetzungen*) to meet

Mitbürger(in) *m(f)* fellow citizen

mit|denken *vi irreg* **bei etw** ~ to follow sth

miteinander [mɪt·ʔai·'nan·de] *adv* 1. (*jeder mit dem anderen*) with each other; ~ **reden** to talk to each other 2. (*zusammen*) together; **alle** ~ all together

mit|erleben * *vt* (*Ereignisse*) to live through; (*eine Zeit*) to witness; (*im Fernsehen*) to follow

Mitesser <-s, -> *m* blackhead

mit|fahren *vi irreg sein* 1. (*begleiten*) **bei jdm** [**im Auto**] ~ to go [*o* ride along] with sb [in his/her car] 2. (*Mitfahrgelegenheit haben*) **darf ich** [**bei Ihnen**] ~? can you give me a lift [*o* ride]?

Mitfahrer(in) *m(f)* fellow passenger

mit|fühlen *vi* **mit jdm** ~ to sympathize with sb; **ich kann** ~, **wie dir zu Mute sein muss** I can imagine how you must feel

mitfühlend *adj* sympathetic

mit|geben *vt irreg* **jdm etw** ~ to give sb sth to take with him/her

Mitgefühl *nt kein pl* sympathy

mit|gehen *vi irreg sein* 1. (*begleiten*) **mit jdm** ~ to come [*o* go] [along] with sb 2. (*stehlen*) **etw** ~ **lassen** to walk off with sth

mitgenommen I. *adj fam* worn-out II. *pp von* **mitnehmen**

Mitglied ['mɪt·gliːt] *nt* member

mit|halten *vi irreg fam* to keep up (**bei** +*dat* with)

mit|helfen *vi irreg* to help (**bei** +*dat* with)

Mithilfe ['mɪt·hɪl·fə] *f kein pl* assistance

mit|hören *vt*, *vi* to listen in; **ein Gespräch** ~ to listen in on a conversation;

(*zufällig*) to overhear a conversation

mit|kommen *vi irreg sein* 1. (*begle ten*) to come along 2. (*Schritt halte können*) to keep up 3. *fam* (*versteher* **da komme ich nicht mit** that's [*o* it' beyond me

mit|kriegen *vt fam s.* **mitbekommen**

Mitleid ['mɪt·lait] *nt kein pl* sympath (**mit** +*dat* for), pity; **ein** ~ **erregende Anblick** a sorry sight

Mitleidenschaft *f* **jdn in** ~ **ziehen** t affect sb

mitleidig ['mɪt·lai·dɪç] I. *adj* 1. (*mitfüt lend*) sympathetic 2. (*verächtlich*) pity ing II. *adv* 1. (*voller Mitgefühl*) sympa thetically 2. (*verächtlich*) pityingly

mit|machen I. *vi* 1. (*teilnehmen*) t take part (**bei** +*dat* in) 2. *fam* (*gt funktionieren*) **wenn das Wetter mi macht** if the weather cooperates; **solan ge meine Beine** ~ as long as my leg hold out II. *vt fam* 1. (*hinnehmen*) t go along with 2. (*erleiden*) **viel** ~ to g through a lot

Mitmensch *m* fellow man

mit|nehmen *vt irreg* 1. (*mit sich nel men*) to take [along] 2. (*transportie ren*) to take [along]; **könnten Sie mich** ~? (*im Auto*) could you give me a lift [*o* ride] 3. (*erschöpfen*) to take it ou of sb

mit|reden *vi* 1. (*mitbestimmen*) to hav a say (**bei** +*dat* in) 2. (*beim Gespräch* **da kann ich nicht** ~ I wouldn't knov anything about that

Mitreisende(r) *f(m)* fellow passenger

mit|reißen *vt irreg* 1. (*mit sich re ßen*) to sweep away 2. (*begeistern* to get going

mit|schicken *vt* (*im Brief*) to enclose to include

mit|schreiben *irreg* I. *vt* to write [*o* take down II. *vi* to take notes

mit|schuldig *adj* **an etw** ~ **sein** to b partly to blame for sth

Mitschüler(in) *m(f)* classmate

mit|singen *irreg vi* to sing along

mit|spielen *vi* 1. SPORT to play 2. FILM THEAT to act (**bei/in** +*dat* in) 3. (*bei Kin derspielen*) to play 4. *fam* (*mitmacher* to go [along] with it; **das Wetter spielte**

nicht mit the weather didn't cooperate **5.** (*wichtig sein*) to play a [big] part (**bei** +*dat* in) **6.** jdm übel ~ to play a nasty trick on sb

Mitspracherecht *nt kein pl* right to have a say; **ein ~ bei etw** *dat* **haben** to have a say in sth

Mittag <-[e]s, -e> ['mɪ·taːk] *m* **1.** (*zwölf Uhr*) noon, midday; (*Essenszeit*) lunchtime; **gegen ~** around noon; [etw] **zu ~ essen** to have [sth for] lunch **2.** *fam* (*Mittagspause*) **~ machen** to take one's lunch break

Mittagessen *nt* lunch

mittags ['mɪ·taːks] *adv* in the middle of the day, at lunchtime

Mittagspause *f* lunch break

Mittagsschlaf *m* [afternoon] nap; **einen ~ machen** to take a nap

Mittagszeit *f kein pl* lunchtime; **in der ~** at lunchtime

Mittäter(in) *m(f)* accomplice

Mitte <-, -n> ['mɪ·tə] *f* **1.** (*räumlich*) middle; **in der ~ zwischen ...** halfway between ... **2.** (*Mittelpunkt*) center **3.** (*zur Hälfte*) **~ Januar** mid-January; **~ des Jahres** in the middle of the year; **sie ist ~ dreißig** she's in her mid-thirties ► **die goldene ~** a happy medium

mit|teilen ['mɪt·tai·lən] **I.** *vt* to tell **II.** *vr* **sich** *akk* [jdm] ~ to communicate [with sb]

Mitteilung *f* notification

Mittel <-s, -> ['mɪ·tl] *nt* **1.** (*Hilfsmittel*) means *sing*; **es gibt ein ~, das herauszufinden** there is a way to find that out **2.** (*Heilmittel*) remedy (**gegen** +*akk* for) **3.** *pl* (*Geldmittel*) funds **4.** (*Mittelwert*) average; **im ~** on average ► **ein ~ zum Zweck** a means to an end

Mittelalter ['mɪ·tl·ʔal·tɐ] *nt kein pl* **das ~** the Middle Ages *npl*

mittelalterlich ['mɪ·tl·ʔal·tɐ·lɪç] *adj* medieval

Mittelamerika ['mɪ·tl·ʔa'me:·ri·ka] *nt* Central America

Mitteleuropa ['mɪ·tl·ʔɔy·'ro:·pa] *nt* Central Europe

mitteleuropäisch ['mɪ·tl·ʔɔy·ro·'pɛː·ɪʃ] *adj* Central European

Mittelfinger *m* middle finger

mittellos *adj* destitute

mittelmäßig **I.** *adj* average; *pej* mediocre **II.** *adv* **er spielte nur ~** his performance was just mediocre

Mittelmäßigkeit <-> *f kein pl* mediocrity

Mittelmeer ['mɪ·tl·me:ɐ] *nt* **das ~** the Mediterranean [Sea]

Mittelpunkt *m* center

mittels ['mɪ·tls] *präp* +*gen geh* by means of

Mittelstand *m* **1.** SOZIOL middle class **2.** (*Unternehmen*) medium-sized business

mittelständisch *adj* medium-sized

Mittelweg *m* middle course ► **der goldene ~** a happy medium

mitten ['mɪ·tn] *adv* **~ auf/in** *dat* in the middle of; **~ unter Menschen** in the midst of people

Mitternacht ['mɪ·tɐ·naxt] *f kein pl* midnight *no art*

mittlere(r, s) ['mɪ·tlə·rə] *adj attr* **1.** (*in der Mitte zwischen zweien*) middle; **mein ~r Bruder** my second oldest/youngest [*o* middle] brother **2.** (*durchschnittlich*) average *attr o pred* **3.** (*mittelgroß*) medium-sized

mittlerweile ['mɪ·tlɐ·'vai·lə] *adv* (*unterdessen*) in the meantime; (*seit dem*) since then; (*bis zu diesem Zeitpunkt*) by now

Mittwoch <-s, -e> ['mɪt·vɔx] *m* Wednesday; *s. a.* **Dienstag**

mittwochs ['mɪt·vɔxs] *adv* [on] Wednesdays; *s. a.* **dienstags**

mitverantwortlich *adj* jointly responsible *pred*

mit|wirken *vi* (*beteiligt sein*) to collaborate (**bei/an** +*dat* on)

mit|wollen ['mɪt·vɔ·lən] *vi* to want to go [*o* come], too

mit|zählen **I.** *vi* to count **II.** *vt* to include

mixen ['mɪ·ksn] *vt* to mix

Mixer <-s, -> ['mɪ·ksɐ] *m* blender

Mobbing <-s> ['mɔ·bɪŋ] *nt kein pl* bullying in the workplace

Möbel <-s, -> ['møː·bl] *nt* **1.** *sing* piece of furniture **2.** *pl* furniture

mobil [mo·'biːl] *adj* **1.** (*beweglich*) mo-

bile **2.** *fam* (*munter*) lively

Mobilfunk *m* mobile communications *pl*

Mobilität <-> [mo·bi·li·ˈtɛːt] *f kein pl* mobility

Mobiltelefon *nt* cell phone

möblieren* [mø·ˈbliː·rən] *vt* to furnish

Mode <-, -n> [ˈmoː·də] *f* fashion, style; **aus der/in ~ kommen** to go out of/ come into fashion

Modell <-s, -e> [mo·ˈdɛl] *nt* model

Modem <-s, -s> [ˈmoː·dɛm] *nt o m* TELEK modem

Modenschau *f* fashion show

Moderator, Moderatorin <-s, -toren> [mo·de·ˈraː·toɐ̯, mo·de·ra·ˈtoː·rɪn] *m, f* RADIO, TV host, presenter

modern[1] [ˈmoː·dɐn] *vi* sein *o* haben to decay, to get moldy

modern[2] [mo·ˈdɛrn] *adj* **1.** (*zeitgemäß*) modern; **~ste Technik** state-of-the-art technology **2.** (*modisch*) fashionable

modernisieren* [mo·dɐr·ni·ˈziː·rən] *vt* to modernize

Modeschmuck *m* costume jewelry

Modeschöpfer(in) *m(f)* fashion designer

modisch [ˈmoː·dɪʃ] **I.** *adj* fashionable **II.** *adv* fashionably

Modus <-, Modi> [ˈmoː·dʊs] *m* COMPUT mode

Mofa <-s, -s> [ˈmoː·fa] *nt* moped

mogeln [ˈmoː·gln] *vi fam* to cheat (**bei** +*dat* at/on)

mögen [ˈmøː·gn] **I.** *modal vb* <mag, mochte, mögen> **1.** (*wollen*) etw tun ~ to want to do sth; **ich möchte gerne kommen** I'd like to come **2.** (*Vermutung*) **sie mag Recht haben** she may be right; **das mag schon stimmen** that might [well] be true; **was mag das wohl bedeuten?** what's that supposed to mean? **II.** *vt* <mag, mochte, gemocht> **1.** (*gernhaben*) to like; (*lieben*) to love **2.** (*Gefallen finden*) ~ **Sie Fisch?** do you like fish?; **ich mag lieber Bier** I prefer beer; **am liebsten mag ich Eintopf** stew is my favorite [meal] **3.** (*haben wollen*) to want; **möchtest du ein Bier?** would you like a beer?; **ich möchte ein Stück Kuchen** I'd like a piece of cake

möglich [ˈmøː·k·lɪç] *adj* possible; **alle ~en ...** all kinds [*o* sorts] of ...; **es für ~ halten, dass ...** to consider it possible that ...; **sein M~stes tun** to do everything in one's power; **schon ~** *fam* maybe

möglicherweise *adv* possibly

Möglichkeit <-, -en> *f* **1.** (*Gelegenheit*) opportunity **2.** (*Möglichsein*) possibility; **nach ~** if possible

möglichst *adv* ~ **bald** as soon as possible

Mohn <-[e]s, -e> [moːn] *m* poppy; (*Mohnsamen*) poppy seed

Möhre <-, -n> [ˈmøː·rə] *f* carrot

Mokka <-s, -s> [ˈmɔ·ka] *m* mocha

Molke <-> [ˈmɔl·kə] *f kein pl* whey

Molkerei <-, -en> [mɔl·kə·ˈrai̯] *f* dairy

mollig [ˈmɔ·lɪç] *adj fam* **1.** (*rundlich*) plump **2.** (*behaglich*) cozy **3.** (*angenehm warm*) snug

Moment <-[e]s, -e> [mo·ˈmɛnt] *m* moment; **im ~** at the moment; **im ersten ~** at first; **im falschen/letzten ~** at the wrong/last moment; **einen [kleinen] ~!** just a minute!

momentan [mo·mɛn·ˈtaːn] **I.** *adj* **1.** (*derzeitig*) present *attr*, current *attr* **2.** (*vorübergehend*) momentary **II.** *adv* **1.** (*derzeit*) at present **2.** (*vorübergehend*) momentarily

Monarch(in) <-en, -en> [mo·ˈnarç, mo·ˈnar·çɪn] *m(f)* monarch

Monarchie <-, -n> [mo·nar·ˈçiː] *f* monarchy

Monat <-[e]s, -e> [ˈmoː·nat] *m* month; **im vierten ~ sein** to be four month pregnant

monatlich [ˈmoː·nat·lɪç] *adj, adv* monthly

Monatsbinde *f* sanitary napkin

Monatsblutung *f s.* **Menstruation**

Mönch <-[e]s, -e> [ˈmœnç] *m* monk

Mond <-[e]s, -e> [ˈmoːnt] *m* moon; **der ~ nimmt ab/zu** the moon is waning, waxing ▶ **hinter dem ~ leben** to be out of touch [with the world]

Mondfinsternis *f* eclipse of the moon

Mondschein *m* moonlight

Mongole, Mongolin <-n, -n> [mɔŋ·ˈgoː·lə] *m, f* Mongol, Mongolian; *s. a.* **Deutsche(r)**

Mongolei <-> [mɔŋ·goˈlaɪ] f die ~ Mongolia; s. a. **Deutschland**

mongolisch [mɔŋˈgoːlɪʃ] adj Mongolian; s. a. **deutsch**

Monitor <-s, -toren> [ˈmoːniˌtoːɐ] m monitor

Monolog <-[e]s, -e> [mono·ˈloːk] m monolog[ue]

Monopol <-s, -e> [mono·ˈpoːl] nt monopoly (**auf** +akk on)

monoton [mono·ˈtoːn] I. adj monotonous II. adv monotonously

Monotonie <-, -n> [mono·to·ˈniː] f monotony

Monster <-s, -> [ˈmɔnstɐ] nt monster

Monsun <-s, -e> [mɔnˈzuːn] m monsoon

Montag <-s, -e> [ˈmoːnˌtaːk] m Monday; s. a. **Dienstag**

Montage <-, -n> [mɔnˈtaːʒə] f 1. (Zusammenbau) assembly 2. fam **auf ~ sein** to be away on a job

Monteur(in) <-s, -e> [mɔnˈtøːɐ] m(f) mechanic, fitter

montieren* [mɔnˈtiːrən] vt 1. (zusammenbauen) to assemble 2. (installieren) to install (**an/auf** +akk to)

Monument <-[e]s, -e> [mo·nu·ˈmɛnt] nt monument

Moor <-[e]s, -e> [ˈmoːɐ] nt swamp

Moos <-es, -e> [ˈmoːs] nt 1. (Pflanze) moss 2. kein pl fam (Geld) dough

Moped <-s, -s> [ˈmoːpɛt] nt moped

Mops <-es, Möpse> [ˈmɔps] m 1. (Hund) pug [dog] 2. fam (dicke Person) pudge 3. pl fam (Brüste) boobs pl sl, tits pl vulg

Moral <-> [mo·ˈraːl] f kein pl 1. (ethische Grundsätze) morals pl 2. (einer Geschichte) moral

moralisch [mo·ˈraːlɪʃ] I. adj moral II. adv morally

Moralpredigt f homily

Mord <-[e]s, -e> [ˈmɔrt] m murder
▶ **dann gibt es ~ und Totschlag** there'll be hell to pay

Mordanschlag m attempt on sb's life; (pol a.) assassination attempt

Morddrohung f death threat

morden [ˈmɔr·dn̩] vi to murder, to kill

Mörder(in) <-s, -> [ˈmœr·dɐ] m(f) murderer, killer

Mordfall m murder case

Mordkommission f homicide [division]

Mordsglück nt fam incredibly good luck; **ein ~ haben** to be incredibly lucky

Mordskrach m fam 1. kein pl (Lärm) terrible racket, a real commotion 2. (Streit) big argument

morgen [ˈmɔr·gn̩] adv tomorrow; ~ **Früh/Mittag** tomorrow morning/at lunchtime; **bis ~!** see you tomorrow!

Morgen <-s, -> [ˈmɔr·gn̩] m morning; **am ~** in the morning; **eines ~s** one morning; **den ganzen ~ [über]** all morning [long]; **guten ~!** good morning!; **zu ~ essen** schweiz (frühstücken) to have breakfast

morgendlich [ˈmɔr·gn̩t·lɪç] adj 1. (morgens üblich) morning attr 2. (morgens stattfindend) in the morning pred

Morgenessen nt schweiz (Frühstück) breakfast

Morgengrauen <-s, -> nt daybreak

Morgenmuffel <-s, -> m fam **ein [großer] ~ sein** to always be [very] grumpy in the morning

morgens [ˈmɔr·gn̩s] adv in the morning

morgig [ˈmɔr·gɪç] adj attr tomorrow's; **der ~e Termin** tomorrow's appointment

Morphium <-s> [ˈmɔr·fi̯·ʊm] nt kein pl morphine

morsch [ˈmɔrʃ] adj rotten

Mosaik <-s, -e[n]> [mo·za·ˈiːk] nt mosaic

Moschee <-, -n> [mo·ˈʃeː] f mosque

Mosel <-> [ˈmoː·zl̩] f die ~ the Moselle

Moskito <-s, -s> [mɔs·ˈkiː·to] m mosquito

Moslem, Moslemin <-s, -s> [ˈmɔs·lɛm, mɔs·ˈleː·mɪn] m, f Muslim

moslemisch [mɔs·ˈleː·mɪʃ] adj attr Muslim

Most <-[e]s> [ˈmɔst] m kein pl 1. (Fruchtsaft) fruit juice 2. südd, schweiz, österr (Obstwein) hard cider

Motiv <-s, -e> [mo·ˈtiːf] nt motive

Motivation <-, -en> [mo·ti·va·ˈtsi̯oːn] f motivation

motivieren* [mo·ti·ˈviː·rən] vt to motivate

Motor <-s, Motoren> ['mo:·to:ɐ̯] m (*Verbrennungsmotor*) engine; (*Elektromotor*) motor

Motorboot nt motor boat

Motorhaube f hood

Motorrad [mo·'to:rat] nt motorcycle, motorbike *fam*

Motorradfahrer(in) m(f) motorcyclist

Motorroller m [motor] scooter

Motorschaden m engine damage

Motte <-, -n> ['mɔ·tə] f moth

Motto <-s, -s> ['mɔ·to] nt motto

motzen ['mɔ·tsn̩] vi fam to complain (**über** +*akk* about)

Möwe <-, -n> ['møː·və] f [sea]gull

Mücke <-, -n> ['mʏ·kə] f mosquito ▶ **aus einer ~ einen Elefanten machen** to make a mountain out of a molehill

Mückenstich m mosquito bite

Mucks ['mʊks] m fam **keinen ~ sagen** to not say a word; **ohne einen ~** without a murmur

mucksmäuschenstill ['mʊks·mɔys·çən·'ʃtɪl] adj fam completely quiet; **~ sein** to not make a sound

müde ['myː·də] adj 1. (*schlafbedürftig*) tired 2. (*überdrüssig*) **einer S.** gen **~ sein/werden** to be/grow tired of sth; **nicht ~ werden, etw zu tun** to never tire of doing sth

Müdigkeit <-> ['myː·dɪç·kait] f kein pl tiredness

Muffel <-s, -> ['mʊ·fl̩] m fam grouch

muffig ['mʊ·fɪç] I. adj 1. (*dumpf*) musty 2. (*schlecht gelaunt*) grumpy II. adv 1. (*dumpf*) musty 2. (*lustlos*) listlessly

Mühe <-, -n> ['myː·ə] f trouble; **der ~ wert sein** to be worth the trouble; **sich** dat [große] **~ geben[, etw zu tun]** to take [great] pains [to do sth]; **sich** dat **keine ~ geben[, etw zu tun]** to make no effort [to do sth]; **~ haben, etw zu tun** to have trouble doing sth; **[jdn] ~ kosten** to be hard work [for sb]; **machen Sie sich keine ~!** [please] don't go to any trouble! ▶ **mit ~ und Not** [just] barely

mühelos I. adj effortless II. adv effortlessly

Mühle <-, -n> ['myː·lə] f mill

mühsam ['myː·zaːm] I. adj arduous II. adv laboriously

Mulde <-, -n> ['mʊl·də] f (*Bodenvertiefung*) hollow

Müll <-[e]s> ['mʏl] m kein pl garbage

Müllabfuhr <-, -en> f garbage [o trash] collection

Müllbeseitigung f kein pl garbage [o trash] collection

Mullbinde f MED gauze bandage

Mülldeponie f garbage [o trash] dump

Mülleimer m s. **Mülltonne**

Mülltonne f garbage [o trash] can

mulmig ['mʊl·mɪç] adj fam (*unbehaglich*) uneasy; **jdm ist ~ zumute** sb has butterflies in their stomach

multikulturell adj multicultural

multiplizieren* [mʊl·ti·pli·'tsiː·rən] vt to multiply (**mit** +*dat* by)

Mumie <-, -n> ['muː·mi̯ə] f mummy

Mumm <-s> ['mʊm] m kein pl guts npl

Mumps <-> ['mʊmps] m kein pl MED [the] mumps + sing/pl vb

Mund <-[e]s, Münder> ['mʊnt] m mouth ▶ **halt den ~!** shut up!; **den ~ [zu] voll nehmen** to talk [too] big

münden ['mʏn·dn̩] vi sein o haben (*Fluss*) to flow (**in** +*akk* into); (*Weg*) to lead (**in** +*akk* into)

Mundgeruch m bad breath no indef art, halitosis no indef art

Mundharmonika f harmonica

mündig ['mʏn·dɪç] adj **~ sein/werden** to be/come of age

mündlich ['mʏnt·lɪç] I. adj oral II. adv orally

Mundpropaganda f word of mouth

Mündung <-, -en> ['mʏn·dʊŋ] f 1. (*eines Flusses*) mouth 2. (*einer Schusswaffe*) muzzle

Mundwasser nt mouthwash

Mundwerk nt **ein loses ~ haben** to be foul-mouthed

Mund-zu-Mund-Beatmung f mouth-to-mouth resuscitation

Munition <-, -en> [mu·ni·'tsi̯oːn] f am munition

Münster <-s, -> ['mʏns·tə] nt cathedral

munter ['mʊn·tə] adj 1. (*aufgeweckt*) bright 2. (*heiter*) lively 3. (*wach*) awake

Münzautomat m vending machine

Münze <-, -n> ['mʏn·tsə] f coin ▶ etw für bare ~ nehmen to take sth at face value

murmeln ['mʊr·m|n] I. vi to murmur II. vt to mutter

Murmeltier ['mʊr·m|·tiːɐ̯] nt marmot, woodchuck ▶ wie ein ~ schlafen to sleep like a log

mürrisch ['mʏ·rɪʃ] I. adj grumpy II. adv grumpily

Muschel <-, -n> ['mʊ·ʃl] f 1. (a. kochk) mussel 2. (Muschelschale) [sea] shell

Museum <-s, Museen> [mu·ˈzeː·ʊm] nt museum

Musik <-, -en> [mu·ˈziːk] f music

musikalisch [mu·zi·ˈkaː·lɪʃ] I. adj musical II. adv musically

Musikant(in) <-en, -en> [mu·zi·ˈkant] m(f) musician

Musiker(in) <-s, -> ['muː·zi·kɐ] m(f) musician

Musikinstrument nt [musical] instrument

Musikkapelle f band

musizieren* [mu·zi·ˈtsiː·rən] vi to play a musical instrument

Muskel <-s, -n> ['mʊs·kl] m muscle

Muskelkater m kein pl sore muscles pl

Muskelprotz <-es, -e> m fam muscleman

Muskelzerrung f pulled muscle

Muskulatur <-, -en> [mʊs·ku·la·ˈtuːɐ̯] f musculature

muskulös [mʊs·ku·ˈløːs] I. adj muscular II. adv ~ gebaut sein to have a muscular build

Müsli <-[s], -s> ['myːs·li] nt muesli

nuss^RR, **muß**^ALT ['mʊs] 3. pers sing pres von **müssen**

Muße <-> ['muː·sə] f kein pl leisure

müssen ['mʏ·sn] I. modal vb <muss, musste, müssen> 1. (gezwungen sein) etw tun ~ to have to do sth 2. (notwendig sein) etw [nicht] tun ~ to [not] need to do sth; warum muss es heute regnen? why does it have to rain today?; muss das [denn] sein? is that really necessary? 3. (eigentlich sollen) ought to; jd müsste etw tun sb should do sth; ich hätte es ahnen ~! I should have known! 4. (Vermutung)

es müsste jetzt acht Uhr sein it must be eight o'clock [now]; es müsste bald ein Gewitter geben there's supposed to be a thunderstorm soon; das muss wohl stimmen that must be true II. vi <muss, musste, gemusst> 1. (gehen müssen) to have to go; ich muss zur Post I have to go to the post office 2. (gebracht werden müssen) irgendwohin ~ to have to get somewhere; dieser Brief muss heute noch zur Post this letter has to be mailed today 3. euph fam [mal] ~ to have to go [to the bathroom]

müßig ['myː·sɪç] adj geh (zwecklos) futile, pointless

Muster <-s, -> ['mʊs·tɐ] nt 1. (Warenmuster) sample 2. MODE pattern

Musterknabe m iron paragon of virtue

mustern ['mʊs·tɐn] vt (eingehend betrachten) to scrutinize

Mut <-[e]s> ['muːt] m kein pl courage

mutig ['muː·tɪç] I. adj brave II. adv bravely

mutlos adj discouraged

Mutlosigkeit <-> f kein pl discouragement

Mutter^1 <-, Mütter> ['mʊ·tɐ] f mother; ~ werden to be having a baby

Mutter^2 <-, -n> ['mʊ·tɐ] f TECH nut

Mutterleib m womb

mütterlich ['mʏ·tɐ·lɪç] adj 1. (von der Mutter) maternal 2. (umsorgend) motherly; ein ~er Typ sein to be the maternal type

Mutterliebe f motherly love

Muttermal nt birthmark; (kleiner) mole

Muttermilch f breast milk

Muttersöhnchen <-s, -> nt pej fam mama's boy fam

Muttersprache f native language

Muttersprachler(in) <-s, -> [-ʃpraː·xlɐ] m(f) native speaker

Muttertag m Mother's Day

Mutti <-, -s> ['mʊ·ti] f fam mommy

Mütze <-, -n> ['mʏ·tsə] f cap, hat

MwSt. f Abk von **Mehrwertsteuer** VAT, ≈ sales tax

mysteriös [mʏs·tə·ˈrjøːs] adj mysterious

Mythos <-, Mythen> ['myː·tɔs] m myth

M

N

N, n <-, -> [ɛn] *nt* N, n; ~ **wie Nordpol** N as in November

Nabel <-s, -> ['na:-bl̩] *m* navel

Nabelschnur *f a. fig* umbilical cord

nach [na:x] *präp +dat* **1.** (*räumlich: bis hin zu*) to; **der Weg führt ~ ...** this is the way to ... **2.** (*räumlich: hinter*) behind; **du stehst ~ mir auf der Liste** you're after me on the list **3.** (*zeitlich: im Anschluss an*) after **4.** (*gemäß*) according to; **~ allem, was ich gehört habe** from what I've heard **5.** (*in Anlehnung an*) after ▶ **~ und ~** little by little; **~ wie vor** still

nach|ahmen *vt* **1.** (*imitieren*) to imitate **2.** (*kopieren*) to copy

Nachahmung <-, -en> *f* **1.** *kein pl* (*Imitation*) imitation **2.** (*Kopie*) copy

Nachbar(in) <-n, -n> ['nax-ba:ɐ̯] *m(f)* neighbor; (*nebenan sitzend*) sb sitting next to one

Nachbarhaus *nt* house next door

Nachbarschaft <-, -en> *f* **1.** (*nähere Umgebung*) neighborhood **2.** (*die Nachbarn*) neighbors

Nachbildung *f* reproduction; (*exakt*) copy

nachdem [na:x-'de:m] *konj* **1.** *zeitlich* after **2.** (*da*) since

nach|denken *vi irreg* to contemplate (**über** +*akk* about); **laut ~** to think out loud

nachdenklich ['na:x-dɛŋk-lɪç] *adj* pensive; **jdn ~ machen** to make sb think

Nachdruck¹ *m kein pl* emphasis; **~ auf etw** *akk* **legen** to stress sth; **etw mit ~ sagen** to say sth emphatically

Nachdruck² <-[e]s, -e> *m* VERLAG **1.** (*nachgedrucktes Werk*) reprint **2.** *kein pl* (*das Nachdrucken*) reprinting

nachdrücklich ['na:x-drʏk-lɪç] **I.** *adj* insistent; (*Warnung*) firm **II.** *adv* firmly

nach|eifern *vi geh* to emulate

nacheinander [na:x-ʔai-'nan-dɐ] *adv* one after another

nach|empfinden* *vt irreg* **etw ~ können** to empathize with sth

nach|erzählen* *vt* to retell

nach|fahren *vi irreg sein* **1.** (*hinterherfahren*) to follow **2.** (*später fahren*) to come [along] later

Nachfolger(in) <-s, -> *m(f)* successor

Nachforschung *f* inquiry; (*polizeilich*) investigation

Nachfrage *f* ÖKON demand (**nach** +*dat* for)

nach|fragen *vi* to inquire

nach|fühlen *vt s.* **nachempfinden**

nach|füllen *vt* (*Behältnis*) to refill; **Zucker ~** to fill back up with sugar

Nachfüllpack <-s, -s> *m* refill [pack]

nach|geben *irreg vi* **1.** (*einlenken*) to give in **2.** (*nicht standhalten: Boden, Knie*) to give way

nach|gehen *vi irreg sein* **1.** (*hinterhergehen*) to follow **2.** (*Uhr*) to be slow **3.** *fig* (*verfolgen*) **einem Problem ~** to look into a problem **4.** *form* (*ausüben*) to practice; (*Interessen*) to pursue

nachgiebig ['na:x-gi:-bɪç] *adj* accommodating; **jdm gegenüber** **zu ~ sein** to be too soft [on sb]

nach|gucken *vt, vi s.* **nachsehen** 1, 2, II

nachhaltig ['na:x-hal-tɪç] **I.** *adj* lasting **II.** *adv* **jdn ~ beeindrucken** to leave lasting impression on sb

nach|helfen *vi irreg* **1.** (*zusätzlich beeinflussen*) to help along *sep* **2.** (*auf die Sprünge helfen*) **jdm ~** to give sb helping hand

nachher ['na:x-e:ɐ̯] *adv* **1.** (*danach*) afterwards **2.** (*irgendwann später*) later; **bis ~!** see you later! **3.** *fam* (*womöglich*) possibly

Nachhilfe *f* private tutoring

Nachhilfestunde *f* private lesson

nach|holen *vt* **1.** (*aufholen*) to make up for **2.** (*zu sich holen*) **seine Familie ~** to have one's family join one

nach|jagen *vi sein* **1.** (*zu erreichen trachten*) to pursue **2.** (*eilends hinterherlaufen*) to chase after

nach|kaufen *vt* to buy later

Nachkomme <-n, -n> ['na:x-kɔ-mə] *m* descendant

nach|kommen *vi irreg sein* **1.** (*folgen*) to come [along] later; **jdn ~ lassen**

have sb join one later; **sein Gepäck ~ lassen** to have one's luggage sent on **2.** (*Schritt halten*) to keep up **3.** (*erfüllen*) to fulfill; (*Anordnung, Pflicht*) to carry out *sep;* (*Forderung*) to meet **4.** *schweiz* (*verstehen*) to follow

Nachkriegszeit *f* postwar period

Nachlass RR <-es, -e> *m* **1.** (*hinterlassene Werke*) unpublished works *npl* **2.** (*hinterlassener Besitz*) estate **3.** (*Rabatt*) discount (**auf** +*akk* on)

nach|lassen *irreg* **I.** *vi* to diminish; (*Druck, Schmerz*) to ease off; (*Gehör, Sehkraft*) to deteriorate; (*Nachfrage*) to fall; (*Sturm*) to die down **II.** *vt* [jdm] **10 % vom Preis ~** to give [sb] a 10% discount

nachlässig ['naːxˌlɛ·sɪç] **I.** *adj* careless; (*Arbeit a.*) slipshod *pej* **II.** *adv* carelessly

Nachlässigkeit <-, -en> *f* **1.** *kein pl* (*Art*) carelessness **2.** (*Handlung*) negligence

nach|laufen *vi irreg sein a. fig* to run after

nach|lösen *vi* **eine** [**Fahr**]**karte ~** to buy a ticket (*after boarding a train, bus etc.*)

nach|machen *vt* **1.** (*imitieren*) to imitate **2.** (*nachahmen*) **jdm etw ~** to copy sth from sb **3.** *fam* (*nachträglich anfertigen*) to make up *sep*

nach|messen *irreg vt* to measure again

Nachmieter(in) *m(f)* new tenant *no indef art*

Nachmittag ['naːxˌmɪ·taːk] *m* afternoon; **am** [**frühen**] **~** in the [early] afternoon; **im Laufe des ~s** during [the course of] the afternoon

nachmittags *adv* in the afternoon

Nachnahme <-, -n> ['naːxˌnaː·mə] *f* cash [*o* collect] on delivery; **etw per ~ schicken** to send sth COD

Nachname *m* surname, last name

nach|prüfen *vt, vi* to verify

Nachrede *f* **üble ~** slander, defamation [of character] *form*

nach|reichen *vt* to hand [*o* turn] in later

Nachricht <-, -en> ['naːxˌrɪçt] *f* **1.** MEDIA news *no indef art,* + *sing vb;* **eine ~** a news item; **die ~en** the news + *sing vb*

2. (*Mitteilung*) message; **eine gute ~** [a piece of] good news; **jdm ~ geben** to let sb know

Nachrichtenagentur *f* news agency

Nachrichtendienst *m* **1.** (*Geheimdienst*) intelligence service **2.** *s.* **Nachrichtenagentur**

Nachrichtensprecher(in) *m(f)* newscaster

nach|rüsten I. *vt* to update; (*Computer*) to upgrade **II.** *vi* MIL to deploy new arms

nach|sagen *vt* **1.** (*von jdm behaupten*) **jdm Schlechtes ~** to say bad things about sb; **es wird ihr nachgesagt, dass ...** she is accused of ..., supposedly she ... **2.** (*nachsprechen*) [jdm] **etw ~** to repeat sth [after sb]

Nachsaison [-zɛˌzõː, -zɛˈzɔ̃] *f* off-season

nach|schauen *vt, vi s.* **nachsehen** I 1, 2, II

nach|schicken *vt* **1.** (*nachsenden*) to forward **2.** (*hinterher schicken*) **jdn ~** to send sb after sb

nach|schlagen *irreg* **I.** *vt* to look up *sep* (**in** +*dat* in) **II.** *vi* **1.** **haben in einem Wörterbuch ~** to consult a dictionary **2.** *sein geh* (*ähneln*) **jdm ~** to take after sb

nach|sehen *irreg* **I.** *vt* **1.** (*nachschlagen*) to look up *sep* (**in** +*dat* in) **2.** (*überprüfen: Auto, Schularbeiten*) to check **3.** (*verzeihen*) **jdm etw ~** to forgive sb for sth **II.** *vi* **1.** (*mit Blicken folgen*) **jdm/etw ~** to follow sb/sth with one's eyes **2.** (*hingehen und prüfen*) to have a look **3.** (*nachschlagen*) to look it up

Nachsehen *nt* ▶ [**bei etw** *dat*] **das ~ haben** to come off worse [in sth]; (*leer ausgehen*) to be left empty-handed [in sth]; (*keine Chance haben*) to not get anywhere [with sth]

nach|senden *vt irreg* to forward

nachsichtig I. *adj* lenient; (*verzeihend*) merciful **II.** *adv* leniently

Nachspeise *f* dessert

Nachspiel *nt* (*unangenehme Folgen*) consequences *pl*

nach|sprechen *irreg vt* [jdm] **etw ~** to

repeat sth [after sb]

nächste(r, s) ['nɛːçs·tə] *adj superl von* **nahe** 1. *räumlich* (*zuerst folgend*) next; **im ~n Haus** next door; (*nächstgelegen*) nearest 2. (*Angehörige*) close 3. *temporal* (*darauf folgend*) next; **bis zum ~n Mal!** until next time!; **am ~n Tag** the next day; **in den ~n Tagen** in the next few days; **als N~s** next

nach|stellen I. *vt* 1. LING [etw *dat*] **nachgestellt werden** to be put after [sth] 2. TECH (*neu einstellen*) to adjust; (*wieder einstellen*) to readjust; (*korrigieren*) to correct; (*Uhr*) to turn back *sep* 3. (*nachspielen*) to reconstruct II. *vi* **jdm ~** 1. *geh* (*verfolgen*) to follow sb 2. (*umwerben*) to pester sb

Nächstenliebe *f* compassion

nächstliegend *adj attr* most plausible

Nacht <-, Nächte> [naxt] *f* night; **~ sein/werden** to be/get dark; **bis weit in die ~** far into the night; **bei ~** at night; **in der ~** at night; **über ~** overnight; **über ~ bleiben** to stay the night; **diese/letzte ~** tonight/last night ▶ **bei ~ und Nebel** *fam* in the dead of night; **die ~ zum Tage machen** to stay up all night; **zu ~ essen** *südd, österr* to have dinner

Nachteil <-[e]s, -e> ['naːx·tail] *m* disadvantage; **sich** *akk* **zu seinem ~ verändern** to change for the worse

nachteilig ['naːx·tai·lɪç] I. *adj* disadvantageous (**für** +*akk* for) II. *adv* unfavorably

nächtelang ['nɛç·tə·laŋ] *adv* for nights on end

Nachtessen *nt südd, österr, schweiz* (*Abendessen*) dinner, supper

Nachthemd *nt* nightgown

Nachtigall <-, -en> ['nax·tɪgal] *f* nightingale

Nachtisch *m s.* **Nachtspeise**

Nachtleben *nt* nightlife

Nachtlokal *nt* nightclub

Nachtrag <-[e]s, -träge> ['naːx·tra:k] *m* 1. (*im Brief*) postscript 2. *pl* (*Ergänzungen*) supplement

nach|tragen *vt irreg* 1. (*hinterhertragen*) to carry after 2. (*nachträglich ergänzen*) to add 3. (*nicht verzeihen können*) **jdm**

etw ~ to hold sth against sb; **jdm ~ dass ...** to hold it against sb that ...

nachtragend ['naːx·tra:·gnt] *adj* unforgiving

nachträglich ['naːx·trɛːk·lɪç] I. *adj* later, (*verspätet*) belated II. *adv* later, belatedly

nach|trauern *vi* **jdm/etw ~** to shed a tear for sb/sth

nachts ['naxts] *adv* at night; **montags ~** [on] Monday nights

Nachtschicht *f* night shift

Nachtschwester *f* night nurse

Nachttisch *m* bedside table

Nachtwache *f* night duty

Nachtwächter(in) *m(f)* night watchman

Nachuntersuchung *f* follow-up examination

nachvollziehbar *adj* comprehensible; **es ist für mich nicht ganz ~, wie ...** I don't quite understand how ...

nach|vollziehen * *vt irreg* to understand

nach|weinen *vi* **jdm/etw ~** to shed a tear for sb/sth

Nachweis <-es, -e> ['naːx·vais] *m* proof

nachweisbar I. *adj* provable; (*Giftstoffe*) detectable; (*Fehler*) demonstrable II. *adv* provably

nach|weisen *vt irreg* 1. (*beweisen*) to establish proof of; **man kann mir nichts ~** nothing can be proved against me 2. (*finden*) to detect (**in** +*dat* in)

nach|werfen *vt irreg* 1. (*hinterherwerfen*) **jdm etw ~** to throw sth at sb 2. *fam* (*überlassen*) **jdm etw ~** to [practically] give sth away to sb

Nachwirkung *f* aftereffect; *fig* consequence

Nachwuchs *m kein pl* 1. *fam* (*Kinder*) offspring 2. (*junge Fachkräfte*) young professionals *pl*

nach|zahlen *vt* 1. (*nachträglich*) to pay at a later date 2. (*zusätzlich*) to pay extra

Nachzahlung *f* 1. (*nachträglich*) back payment 2. (*zusätzlich*) additional payment

nach|ziehen *irreg vt* 1. (*Schraube*) to tighten [up *sep*] 2. (*Bein*) to drag 3. (*Linie*) to go over; **sich** *dat* **die Au-**

genbrauen ~ to pencil in *sep* one's eyebrows

Nachzügler(in) <-s, -> ['naːxˌtsyːkˌlɐ] *m(f)* late arrival

Nacken <-s, -> ['nakn̩] *m* neck ► **jdm im** ~ **sitzen** to breathe down sb's neck

nackt ['nakt] I. *adj* 1. (*unbekleidet*) naked, nude; (*Haut, Arme*) bare 2. (*kahl: Wand*) bare 3. (*unverblümt*) naked; (*Tatsachen*) bare; (*Wahrheit*) plain II. *adv* naked, in the nude

Nadel <-, -n> ['naːdl̩] *f* 1. (*Nähnadel, Tannennadel*) needle 2. (*Zeiger*) needle ► **an der** ~ **hängen** *sl* to be hooked on heroin

Nadelbaum *m* conifer

Nagel <-s, Nägel> ['naːɡl̩] *m* (*Metallstift, Fingernagel*) nail ► **jdm brennt es unter den Nägeln, etw zu tun** *fam* sb is dying to do sth; **etw an den** ~ **hängen** *fam* to give up *sep* sth; **sich** *dat* **etw unter den** ~ **reißen** *sl* to steal [*o* make off with] sth

Nagelfeile *f* nail file

Nagellack *m* nail polish

Nagellackentferner *m* nail polish remover

nageln ['naːɡln̩] *vt* to nail (**an** +*akk* to)

nagelneu ['naːɡlˈnɔy] *adj fam* brand-new

nagen ['naːɡn̩] I. *vt, vi* to gnaw (**an** +*dat* at/on) II. *vi* (*quälen*) **an jdm** ~ to nag [at] sb

nagend ['naːɡn̩t] *adj* nagging; (*Hunger*) gnawing

Nagetier *nt* rodent

nah ['naː] *adj, adv s.* **nahe** ► **von** ~ **und fern** from near and far

nahe <näher, nächste> ['naːə] I. *adj* 1. *räumlich* nearby, close [by] *pred;* **von** ~**m** from close up 2. *zeitlich* near, approaching 3. (*eng*) close; **jdm** ~ **sein** to be close to sb II. *adv* 1. *räumlich* nearby, close [by]; ~ **an/bei** **etw** *dat* close to sth 2. *zeitlich* close 3. (*fast*) **sie war** ~ **am Aufgeben** she almost gave up 4. (*eng*) closely; ~ **mit jdm verwandt sein** to be a close relative of sb ► **jdm zu** ~ **treten** to offend sb III. *präp* +*dat* near to

Nähe <-> ['nɛːə] *f kein pl* (*geringe Entfernung*) proximity; **aus der** ~ from close up; **in der** ~ near

nahebei ['naːəˈbai] *adv* nearby

nahekommen *vr irreg sein* **sich** *dat* ~ to become close

nahelegen *vt* **jdm** ~, **etw zu tun** to advise sb to do sth

naheliegend *adj* ~ **sein** to seem to suggest itself; **aus** ~**en Gründen** for obvious reasons

nahen ['naːən] *vi sein geh* to approach

nähen ['nɛːən] *vt* to sew; MED to stitch

näher ['nɛːe] I. *adj komp von* **nahe** 1. (*in geringerer Entfernung*) nearer, closer 2. (*kürzer bevorstehend*) closer, sooner *pred;* (*Zukunft*) near 3. (*detaillierter*) further *attr;* **die** ~**en Umstände** the precise circumstances 4. (*enger*) closer; (*Verwandte*) immediate II. *adv komp von* **nahe** 1. (*in geringeren Abstand*) closer, nearer; **kommen Sie** ~! come closer! 2. (*eingehender*) in more detail; **etw** ~ **ansehen** to have a closer look at sth; **sich** *akk* ~ **mit etw** *dat* **befassen** to go into sth in greater detail 3. (*enger*) closer; **jdn/etw** ~ **kennen** to know sb/sth well; **jdn/etw** ~ **kennen lernen** to get to know sb/sth better

nähern ['nɛːen] *vr* 1. (*näher herankommen*) **sich** *akk* [**jdm/etw**] ~ to get closer [to sb/sth] 2. (*einen Zeitpunkt erreichen*) **sich** *akk* **etw** *dat* ~ to get close to sth; **unser Urlaub nähert sich seinem Ende** our vacation is drawing to a close

nahestehen *vr irreg* **sich** *dat* ~ to be close

nahezu ['naːəˈtsuː] *adv* almost, virtually

Nähgarn *nt* cotton

Nähmaschine *f* sewing machine

Nähnadel *f* [sewing] needle

nahrhaft *adj* nutritious

Nährstoff *m* nutrient

Nahrung <-> ['naːrʊŋ] *f kein pl* food; **flüssige/feste** ~ liquids/solids *pl*

Nahrungsmittel *nt* food

Nährwert *m* nutritional value

Naht <-, Nähte> ['naːt] *f* 1. (*bei Kleidung*) seam 2. MED suture *spec* 3. TECH weld

Nahverkehr *m* local traffic; **der öffentli-**

che ~ local public transportation

Nahverkehrszug m local train

naiv [na·'i:f] adj naive

Naivität <-> [na·ivi·'tɛ:t] f kein pl naivety

Name <-ns, -n> ['na:·mə] m name; **in jds ~n** on behalf of sb; **jdn nur dem ~n nach kennen** to only know sb by name

namenlos adj nameless; (Helfer, Spender) anonymous

namens ['na:·məns] adv by the name of

Namenstag m Saint's day

nämlich ['nɛ:m·lɪç] adv namely

Napf <-[e]s, Näpfe> ['napf] m bowl

Narbe <-, -n> ['nar·bə] f scar

Narkose <-, -n> [nar·'ko:·zə] f anesthesia

Narr, Närrin <-en, -en> ['nar, 'nɛ·rɪn] m, f fool; **jdn zum ~en halten** to make a fool of sb; **sich** akk **zum ~en machen** to make a fool of oneself

närrisch ['nɛ·rɪʃ] adj (verrückt) crazy; (unvernünftig) foolish; [ganz] ~ **auf jdn/ etw sein** fam to be crazy about sb/sth

Narzisse <-, -n> [nar·'tsɪ·sə] f narcissus

naschen ['na·ʃn] I. vi to snack, to nosh fam; **etwas zum N~** something sweet [to snack on] II. vt (essen) **etw ~** to snack on sth

Naschkatze f fam person with a sweet tooth

Nase <-, -n> ['na:·zə] f nose; **sich** dat **die ~ putzen** to blow one's nose ▶ **jdm etw auf die ~ binden** fam to tell sb sth; **sich** dat **an seine eigene ~ fassen** fam to blame oneself; **auf die ~ fliegen** fam to fall flat on one's face; **sich** dat **eine goldene ~ verdienen** to earn a fortune; **die ~ vorn haben** to be one step ahead; **jdn an der ~ herumführen** to lead sb on; **jdm auf der ~ herumtanzen** fam to walk all over sb; **pro ~** hum fam per person; **die ~ von jdm/etw voll haben** fam to be fed up with sb/sth; **jdm etw aus der ~ ziehen** fam to get sth out of sb

Nasenbluten <-s-> nt kein pl nosebleed

Nasenspitze f tip of the nose ▶ **jdm etw an der ~ ansehen** to be able to tell sth from sb's face

Naseweis <-es, -e> ['na:·zə·vais] m

(Besserwisser) know-it-all fam, wis**** guy fam

Nashorn nt rhino[ceros]

nass RR, **naß** ALT <nasser o nässer, nas**** seste o nässeste> ['nas] adj wet; ~ **ge**** **schwitzt** soaked with sweat pred

Nässe <-> ['nɛ·sə] f kein pl wetness; **vo** **~ triefen** to be soaking wet

nasskalt RR adj cold and damp

Nation <-, -en> [na·'tsjo:n] f nation; **die Vereinten ~en** the United Nations

national [na·tsjo·'na:l] I. adj 1. nationa 2. (patriotisch) nationalist II. adv nationalistic

Nationalhymne f national hymn

Nationalist(in) <-en, -en> [na·tsjo·na 'lɪst] m(f) nationalist

nationalistisch adj, adv nationalist[ic]

Nationalität <-, -en> [na·tsjo·na·li·'tɛ:t] f nationality

Nationalmannschaft f national team

Nationalrat m kein pl 1. österr National Assembly 2. schweiz National Council

Nationalsozialismus [na·tsjo·'na:l·zo tsja·lɪs·mʊs] m National Socialism

Natter <-, -n> ['na·tɐ] f adder

Natur <-, -en> [na·'tu:ɐ] f 1. kein pl BIOL nature 2. kein pl (Landschaft) countryside; **in freier ~** in the wild 3. (Wesensart) nature; **von ~ aus** by nature

Naturereignis nt natural phenomenon

Naturfreund(in) m(f) nature lover

naturgetreu adj, adv true to life

Naturkatastrophe f natural disaster

Naturkostladen m health food store

natürlich [na·'ty:ɐ·lɪç] I. adj natural II. adv naturally, of course

Natürlichkeit <-> f kein pl naturalness

Naturprodukt nt natural product

Naturschutz m [nature] conservation; **unter ~ stehen** to be protected

Naturschutzgebiet nt nature reserve

Naturvolk nt primitive people

Naturwissenschaften pl natural sciences pl

Naturwissenschaftler(in) m(f) natural scientist

naturwissenschaftlich adj natural-scientific

Nazi <-s, -s> ['na:·tsi] m Nazi

Nebel <-s, -> ['ne:·bl] m 1. fog; **bei ~ in**

foggy conditions **2.** ASTRON nebula

Nebelscheinwerfer *m* fog light

neben ['ne:·bn̩] *präp* **1.** +*akk, dat* beside, next to **2.** +*dat (außer)* apart from **3.** +*dat (verglichen mit)* compared to

nebenan [ne:·bn̩·'ʔan] *adv* next door

nebenbei [ne:·bn̩·'bai] *adv* **1.** (*neben der Arbeit*) on the side **2.** (*beiläufig*) incidentally; ~ [**bemerkt**] by the way

Nebenbeschäftigung *f* side job, sideline

Nebenbuhler(in) <-s, -> *m(f)* rival

nebeneinander [ne:·bn̩·ʔai·'nan·dɐ] *adv* **1.** (*Seite an Seite*) side by side **2.** (*gleichzeitig*) simultaneously, at the same time

Nebenfluss RR *m* tributary

Nebengebäude *nt* (*benachbartes Gebäude*) neighboring building

nebenher [ne:·bn̩·'he:ɐ] *adv* in addition

Nebenkosten *pl* additional costs *pl*

Nebenmann <-es, -männer> *m* neighbor; **mein ~** the person next to me

Nebenrolle *f* FILM, THEAT supporting role

Nebensache *f* trivial matter; **~ sein** to be irrelevant

nebensächlich *adj* irrelevant

Nebensaison *f* off-season

Nebenverdienst *m* additional income

Nebenwirkung *f* side effect

Nebenzimmer *nt* next room [over]

neblig ['ne:·blɪç] *adj* foggy

necken ['nɛ·kn̩] *vt* to tease

Neffe <-n, -n> ['nɛ·fə] *m* nephew

negativ ['ne:·ga·ti:f] **I.** *adj* negative **II.** *adv* negatively

Negativ <-s, -e> ['ne:·ga·ti:f] *nt* negative

nehmen <nimmt, nahm, genommen> ['ne:·mən] *vt* **1.** to take; **nimm dir noch Kuchen** help yourself to more cake; **jdn ~, wie er ist** to take sb as he is; **den Bus/die Bahn/ein Taxi ~** to take the bus/the train/a taxi; **jdm etw ~** to take sth [away] from sb; **jdm die Sicht ~** to block sb's view ▶ **es sich** *dat* **nicht ~ lassen, etw zu tun** to insist on doing sth

Neid <-[e]s> ['nait] *m kein pl* jealousy, envy (**auf** +*akk* of)

neidisch ['nai·dɪʃ] *adj* jealous, envious

(**auf** +*akk* of)

neigen ['nai·gn̩] **I.** *vr* **sich** *akk* **~ 1.** (*sich beugen*) **sich** *akk* **zu jdm ~** to lean over to sb; **sich** *akk* **nach vorne ~** to lean forward **2.** (*schräg abfallen*) to slope **3.** (*sich biegen: Äste*) to bow down **II.** *vt* (*beugen*) to bend **III.** *vi* **1.** (*anfällig sein für*) **zu etw** *dat* **~** (*Krankheiten*) to be prone to sth **2.** (*tendieren*) **zu etw** *dat* **~** to tend to [do] sth

Neigung <-, -en> *f* **1.** (*Vorliebe*) inclination **2.** (*Tendenz*) tendency **3.** (*Gefälle*) slope

nein ['nain] *adv* no

Nein <-s> ['nain] *nt kein pl* no

Neinstimme *f* no, "no" vote

Nektar <-s, -e> ['nɛk·tar] *m* nectar

Nektarine <-, -n> [nɛk·ta·'ri:·nə] *f* nectarine

Nelke <-, -n> ['nɛl·kə] *f* **1.** BOT carnation **2.** KOCHK clove

nennen <nannte, genannt> ['nɛ·nən] *vt* **1.** (*anreden, benennen*) to call; **wie nennt man das?** what do you call that? **2.** (*sagen: Namen*) to name; (*Grund*) to give; **können Sie mir einen guten Anwalt ~?** can you give me the name of a good lawyer?

Neofaschismus <-> ['ne:·o·fa·ʃɪs·mʊs] *m kein pl* neofascism

Neon <-s> ['ne:·ɔn] *nt kein pl* neon

Neonazi <-s, -s> ['ne:·o·na:·tsi] *m kurz für* **Neonazist** neo-Nazi

Neonlicht *nt* neon light

Nerv <-s, -en> ['nɛrf] *m* nerve ▶ **die -en behalten/verlieren** to keep calm/lose one's cool; **jdm auf die ~en gehen** *fam* to get on sb's nerves; **du hast vielleicht ~en!** *fam* you've got some nerve!

nerven ['nɛr·fn̩] *vt fam* **jdn** [**mit etw** *dat*] **~** to bug sb [with sth]

nervenaufreibend *adj* nerve-racking

Nervenbündel *nt fam* bundle of nerves

Nervensäge *f fam* pain in the neck

Nervensystem *nt* nervous system

Nervenzusammenbruch *m* nervous breakdown

nervös [nɛr·'vø:s] *adj* nervous

Nervosität <-> [nɛr·vo·zi·'tɛːt] *f kein pl* nervousness

N

Nerz <-es, -e> ['nɛrts] *m* mink

Nessel <-, -n> ['nɛ·sl] *f* BOT nettle ▶ **sich** *akk* **in die ~n setzen** *fam* to put one's foot in one's mouth

Nest <-[e]s, -er> [nɛst] *nt* **1.** ORN nest **2.** *fam* (*Kaff*) hole ▶ **sich** *akk* **ins gemachte ~ setzen** *fam* to have got it made

Netiquette <-, -n> [nɛ·ti·'kɛ·tə] *f* netiquette

nett ['nɛt] *adj* nice; **sei so ~ und ...** would you mind ...

netto ['nɛ·to] *adv* net

Nettoeinkommen *nt* net income

Nettogewicht *nt* net weight

Netz <-es, -e> [nɛts] *nt* **1.** (*a. sport*) net **2.** (*Einkaufsnetz*) string bag **3.** (*Gepäcknetz*) baggage net **4.** (*Spinnennetz*) web **5.** ELEK, TELEK network; (*Strom*) power grid **6.** *kein pl* COMPUT network; **das ~** the Net **7.** TRANSP system, network

Netzhaut *f* retina

Netzstecker *m* power plug

Netzwerk *nt* network

neu ['nɔy] **I.** *adj* **1.** (*nicht alt*) new; **die ~este Mode** the latest fashion; **ein ~eres System** a more up-to-date system; **was gibt's N~es?** *fam* what's new?; **was gibt's N~es?** what's new?; **der/die N~e** the newcomer; **das N~e** [an *etw dat*] the new thing [about sth]; **das N~este** the latest [thing] **2.** (*abermalig*) new; **einen ~en Anfang machen** to make a fresh start ▶ **auf ein N~es!** here's to a fresh start!; **seit ~[e]stem** [since] recently; **von ~em** all over again **II.** *adv* **1.** (*von vorn*) ~ **bearbeitet** MEDIA revised; ~ **anfangen** to start all over again; ~ **gestalten** to redesign **2.** (*zusätzlich*) anew; **33 Mitarbeiter ~ einstellen** to hire 33 new employees **3.** (*erneut*) again **4.** (*seit kurzem da*) newly; ~ **eröffnet** newly opened; (*erneut eröffnet*) reopened ▶ **wie ~ geboren** like a new man/woman

Neuankömmling <-s, -e> *m* newcomer

neuartig ['nɔy·ʔaːɐ̯·tɪç] *adj* new, new type of

Neuauflage *f* **1.** (*unveränderter Nachdruck*) reprint **2.** (*veränderte Neuausgabe*) new edition

Neubau <-bauten> ['nɔy·bau] *m* **1.** *kei pl* (*neue Errichtung*) [new] buildin **2.** (*neu erbautes Gebäude*) new build ing

Neubaugebiet *nt* development area (*schon bebaut*) new development

Neubauwohnung *f* newly built apart ment

neuerdings ['nɔy·ɐ·dɪŋs] *adv* recently

Neuerscheinung *f* new publication

Neuerung <-, -en> ['nɔy·ə·rʊŋ] *f* re form

Neufundland <-s> [nɔy·'fʊnt·lant] *r* Newfoundland

Neugeborene(s) *nt* newborn

Neugier(de) <-> ['nɔy·giːɐ̯(·də)] *f* *kei* *pl* curiosity

neugierig **I.** *adj* curious; ~ **sein, ob ..** to be curious [to know] whether ...; **se nicht so ~!** don't be so nosy! **II.** *adv* curiously, full of curiosity

Neuigkeit <-, -en> ['nɔy·ɪç·kait] *f* news

Neujahr *nt* *kein pl* New Year; **prost ~!** here's to the New Year!

neulich ['nɔy·lɪç] *adv* the other day

Neuling <-s, -e> ['nɔy·lɪŋ] *m* beginner

neumodisch *adj pej* newfangled

Neumond *m* *kein pl* new moon

neun ['nɔyn] *adj* nine; *s. a.* **acht**[1]

neunte(r, s) ['nɔyn·tə(ɐ̯, s)] *adj* **1.** (*an neunter Stelle*) ninth; *s. a.* **achte(r, s) 1 2.** (*Datum*) ninth, 9th; *s. a.* **achte(r, s) 2**

neuntel ['nɔyn·tl̩] *nt* ninth

neunzehn ['nɔyn·tseːn] *adj* nineteen; *s. a.* **acht**[1]

neunzehnte(r, s) *adj* **1.** (*an neunzehnter Stelle*) nineteenth; *s. a.* **achte(r, s) 1 2.** (*Datum*) nineteenth, 19th; *s. a.* **achte(r, s) 2**

neunzig ['nɔyn·tsɪç] *adj* ninety; *s. a.* **achtzig 1, 2**

neunzigste(r, s) ['nɔyn·tsɪç·stə] *adj* ninetieth; *s. a.* **achte(r, s) 1**

Neurologe, Neurologin <-n, -n> [nɔy·ro·'loː·gə] *m, f* neurologist

Neurose <-, -n> [nɔy·'roː·zə] *f* neurosis

Neurotiker(in) <-s, -> [nɔy·'roː·ti·kɐ] *m(f)* neurotic

neurotisch [nɔy·'roː·tɪʃ] *adj* neurotic

Neuschnee *m* fresh snow

Neuseeland <-s> [nɔy·'zeː·lant] *nt* New

Zealand; *s. a.* **Deutschland**

Neuseeländer(in) <-s, -> [nɔy·'ze:·lɛn·dɐ] *m(f)* New Zealander; *s. a.* **Deutsche(r)**

neuseeländisch [nɔy·'ze:·lɛn·dɪʃ] *adj* New Zealand *attr,* from New Zealand *pred*

neutral [nɔy·'tra:l] *adj, adv* neutral

Neutralität <-> [nɔy·tra·li·'tɛ:t] *f kein pl* neutrality

neuwertig *adj* as new

nicht [nɪçt] *adv* not; **ich weiß ~** I don't know; **ich bin es ~ gewesen** it wasn't me; **~ öffentlich** *attr* not open to the public *pred;* **~ [ein]mal** not even; **~ mehr** not any more, no longer; **~ mehr als ...** no more than ...; **bitte ~!** please don't!

Nichtbeachtung *f* noncompliance

Nichte <-, -n> ['nɪç·tə] *f* niece

Nichterscheinen <-s> *nt kein pl* failure to appear

nichtig ['nɪç·tɪç] *adj* **1.** (*ungültig*) invalid **2.** *geh* (*belanglos*) trivial

Nichtigkeit <-, -en> *f* **1.** *kein pl* (*Ungültigkeit*) invalidity **2.** *meist pl geh* triviality

Nichtraucher(in) *m(f)* nonsmoker

nichts ['nɪçts] *pron indef* **1.** (*nicht etwas*) not anything, nothing; **es ist ~** it's nothing; **~ als ...** (*nur*) nothing but ...; **~ mehr** nothing more [*o* else]; **~ wie raus!** let's get out of here!; **~ ahnend** unsuspecting; **~ sagend** meaningless; **damit will ich ~ zu tun haben** I don't want anything to do with it **2.** *vor substantiviertem adj* nothing; **~ anderes [als ...]** nothing other [than ...]; **hoffentlich ist es ~ Ernstes** I hope it's nothing serious ▶ **~ da!** *fam* no chance!; **für ~** for nothing; **für ~ und wieder ~** *fam* [all] for nothing

Nichts <-, -e> ['nɪçts] *nt* **1.** *kein pl* (*leerer Raum*) void **2.** (*unbedeutender Mensch*) nonentity ▶ **aus dem ~ auftauchen** to show up from out of nowhere; **vor dem ~ stehen** to be left with nothing

Nichtschwimmer(in) *m(f)* non-swimmer

nichtsdestoweniger [nɪçts·dɛs·to·'ve:·nɪ·gɐ] *adv* nevertheless

Nichtsnutz <-es, -e> ['nɪçts·nʊts] *m pej* good-for-nothing

Nickel <-s> ['nɪ·kl̩] *nt kein pl* nickel

nicken ['nɪ·kn̩] *vi* to nod

Nickerchen <-s, -> ['nɪ·kɐ·çən] *nt fam* nap; **ein ~ machen** to take a nap

nie ['niː] *adv* never; **~ mehr** never again; **das hätte ich ~ im Leben gedacht** I never would have thought that ▶ **~ und nimmer** never ever

Niedergang <-[e]s> *m kein pl* decline

niedergeschlagen [-gə·ʃlaː·gn̩] *adj* downcast

Niederlage *f* defeat

Niederlande ['niː·dɐ·lan·də] *pl* **die ~** the Netherlands; *s. a.* **Deutschland**

Niederländer(in) <-s, -> ['niː·dɐ·lɛn·də] *m(f)* Dutchman *masc,* Dutchwoman *fem; s. a.* **Deutsche(r)**

niederländisch ['niː·dɐ·lɛn·dɪʃ] *adj* Dutch; *s. a.* **deutsch**

nieder|lassen *vr irreg* **sich** *akk* **~ 1.** (*ansiedeln*) to settle down **2.** (*beruflich etablieren*) to establish oneself; **niedergelassener Arzt** licensed doctor with his/her own practice **3.** *geh* (*hinsetzen*) to sit down (**auf** +*akk* on); (*Vogel*) to settle (**auf** +*akk* on)

Niederlassung <-, -en> *f* (*Zweigstelle*) branch

nieder|legen *vt* **1.** (*hinlegen*) to put down *sep* **2.** (*aufgeben*) to give up; (*Amt, Mandat*) to resign; (*Arbeit*) to stop

Niederschlag *m* (*Regen*) rainfall; (*Schnee*) snowfall; (*Hagel*) hail

nieder|schlagen *irreg* **I.** *vt* **1.** (*zu Boden schlagen*) to floor **2.** (*unterdrücken*) to crush; (*Streik*) to break up; (*Unruhen*) to suppress **II.** *vr* **sich** *akk* **~ 1.** (*kondensieren*) to condense (**an** +*dat* on) **2.** (*zum Ausdruck kommen*) to find expression (**in** +*dat* in)

niederschmetternd ['niː·dɐ·ʃmɛ·tɐnt] *adj* deeply distressing; (*Nachricht*) devastating

Niedertracht <-> *f kein pl* **1.** (*Gesinnung*) malice **2.** (*Tat*) despicable act

niederträchtig *adj* contemptible; (*Einstellung, Lüge, Person a.*) despicable

niedlich ['niːt·lɪç] **I.** *adj* cute, sweet

N

II. *adv* sweetly

niedrig ['niː·drɪç] I. *adj* 1. (*nicht hoch*) low 2. (*gering*) low; (*Betrag*) small II. *adv* low

niemals ['niː·maːls] *adv* never

niemand ['niː·mant] *pron indef* nobody, no one; (*bei Fragen und Verneinung*) anyone, anybody

Niemandsland ['niː·mants·lant] *nt kein pl* no man's land

Niere <-, -n> ['niː·rə] *f* kidney ▶ **jdm an die ~ gehen** *fam* to get to sb

Nierenstein *m* kidney stone

Nierenversagen *nt kein pl* kidney failure

nieseln ['niː·z̩ln] *vi impers* **es nieselt** it's drizzling

Nieselregen ['niː·z̩l-] *m* drizzle

niesen ['niː·zn̩] *vi* to sneeze

Niete[1] <-, -n> ['niː·tə] *f* 1. (*Nichttreffer*) blank 2. *fam* (*Versager*) loser

Niete[2] <-, -n> ['niː·tə] *f* TECH rivet

niet- und nagelfest ['niːt·ʔʊnt·'naː·ɡl̩·fɛst] *adj* ▶ **alles, was nicht ~ ist** *fam* everything that's not nailed down

Nikolaus <-, -e> ['niː·ko·laus] *m* 1. (*verkleidete Gestalt*) St. Nicholas (*figure who brings children presents on December 6*) 2. *kein pl* (*6. Dezember*) St. Nicholas' Day

Nikotin <-s> [ni·ko·'tiːn] *nt kein pl* nicotine

nikotinfrei *adj* nicotine-free

Nilpferd *nt* hippo[potamus]

nippen ['nɪ·pn̩] *vi* to sip (**an** +*dat* on)

Nippes ['nɪ·pəs, 'nɪps, 'nɪp] *pl* knickknacks *pl*

nirgends ['nɪr·ɡn̩ts], **nirgendwo** ['nɪr·ɡn̩t·'voː] *adv* nowhere; **ich konnte ihn ~ finden** I couldn't find him anywhere

Nische <-, -n> ['niː·ʃə] *f* niche

nisten ['nɪs·tn̩] *vi* to nest

Nitrat <-[e]s, -e> [ni·'traːt] *nt* nitrate

Niveau <-s, -s> [ni·'voː] *nt* 1. (*Anspruch*) caliber; **~ haben** to have class; **kein ~ haben** to be lowbrow; **das ist unter meinem ~** this is beneath me *fig* 2. (*Höhe einer Fläche*) level

niveaulos [ni·'voː-] *adj* primitive

niveauvoll *adj* intellectually stimulating

Nixe <-, -n> ['nɪk·sə] *f* mermaid

nobel ['noː·b̩l] I. *adj* 1. (*edel*) noble 2. (*luxuriös*) luxurious 3. (*großzügig*) generous II. *adv* 1. (*edel*) honorably 2. (*großzügig*) generously

Nobelpreis [no·'bɛl·prais] *m* Nobel Prize

noch ['nɔx] I. *adv* 1. (*bis jetzt*) still; **ein ~ ungelöstes Problem** an as yet unsolved problem; **~ immer** [**nicht**] still [not]; **~ nicht** not yet; **~ nichts** nothing yet; **~ nie** never 2. (*irgendwann*) some time; **er kommt schon ~** he will eventually come 3. (*nicht später als*) by the end of; **~ gestern habe ich davon nichts gewusst** even yesterday I didn't know a thing about it; **~ heute** today 4. (*bevor etw anderes geschieht*) **bleib ~ ein wenig** stay a little longer 5. (*womöglich*) **wir kommen ~ zu spät** we're going to end up being late 6. (*zusätzlich*) in addition; **möchtest du ~ etwas essen?** would you like something else to eat?; **möchten Sie ~ eine Tasse Kaffee?** would you like another cup of coffee?; **~ eine(r, s)** another 7. *vor komp* (*mehr als*) even [more] II. *konj* **weder ... ~ ...** neither ... nor ...

nochmals ['nɔx·maːls] *adv* again

Nomade, Nomadin <-n, -n> [no·'maː·də] *m, f* nomad

Nominativ <-[e]s, -e> ['noː·mi·na·tiːf] *m* nominative

nominieren* [no·mi·'niː·rən] *vt* to nominate

Nonne <-, -n> ['nɔ·nə] *f* nun

Nordamerika ['nɔrt·ʔa·me:·ri·ka] *nt* North America

Norden <-s> ['nɔr·dn̩] *m kein pl, kein indef art* 1. (*Himmelsrichtung*) north; **aus/im/nach ~** from/in/to the north; **in Richtung ~** to[ward] the north 2. (*nördliche Gegend*) north; **er wohnt im ~ der Stadt** he lives in the northern part of town

Nordeuropa ['nɔrt·ʔɔy·'roː·pa] *nt* Northern Europe

Nordhalbkugel *f* Northern Hemisphere

Nordirland ['nɔrt·'ʔɪr·lant] *nt* Northern Ireland

nördlich ['nœrt·lɪç] I. *adj* 1. (*Himmelsrichtung*) northern 2. (*im Norden liegend*) northern; **weiter ~ liegen** to

lie farther [to the] north **3.** (*von/nach Norden*) northerly; **in ~e Richtung** northward **II.** *adv* **~ von ...** north of ... **III.** *präp* +*gen* **~ der Stadt** [to the] north of the town

Nordosten [nɔrt·'ʔɔs·tn̩] *m kein indef art* northeast; *s. a.* **Norden**

nordöstlich [nɔrt·'ʔœst·lɪç] **I.** *adj* **1.** (*Himmelsrichtung*) northeastern **2.** (*im Nordosten liegend*) northeastern **3.** (*von/nach Nordosten*) northeastward **II.** *adv* **~ von ...** northeast of ... **III.** *präp* +*gen* northeast of; *s. a.* **nördlich**

Nordpol ['nɔrt·po:l] *m kein pl* **der ~** the North Pole

Nordsee ['nɔrt·ze:] *f* **die ~** the North Sea; **an der ~** on the North Sea coast

Nordwesten [nɔrt·'vɛs·tn̩] *m kein indef art* northwest; *s. a.* **Norden**

nordwestlich [nɔrt·'vɛst·lɪç] **I.** *adj* **1.** (*Himmelsrichtung*) northwestern **2.** (*im Nordwesten liegend*) northwestern **3.** (*von/nach Nordwesten*) northwestward **II.** *adv* **~ von ...** northwest of ... **III.** *präp* +*gen* northwest of; *s. a.* **nördlich**

Nordwind *m* north wind

Nörgelei <-, -en> *f* **1.** (*Äußerung*) moaning [and groaning] **2.** *kein pl* (*das Nörgeln*) nagging

nörgeln ['nœr·gl̩n] *vi* to moan (**über** +*akk* about)

Norm <-, -en> ['nɔrm] *f* **1.** (*festgelegte Größe*) standard **2.** (*verbindliche Regel*) norm **3.** (*Durchschnitt*) **die ~** the norm

normal [nɔr·'ma:l] **I.** *adj* **1.** (*üblich*) normal **2.** *meist verneint fam* (*zurechnungsfähig*) right in the head; **du bist wohl nicht ~!** you are out of your mind! **II.** *adv* normally

Normalbenzin *nt* regular [unleaded] [gas]

Normalverbraucher(in) *m(f)* average consumer; **Otto ~** *fam* the man in the street

normen ['nɔr·mən] *vt* to standardize

Norwegen <-s> ['nɔr·ve:·gn̩] *nt* Norway; *s. a.* **Deutschland**

Norweger(in) <-s, -> ['nɔr·ve:·gɐ] *m(f)* Norwegian; *s. a.* **Deutsche(r)**

norwegisch ['nɔr·ve:·gɪʃ] *adj* Norwegian;

s. a. **deutsch**

Nostalgie <-> [nɔs·tal·'gi:] *f kein pl geh* nostalgia

nostalgisch [nɔs·'tal·gɪʃ] *adj geh* nostalgic

Not <-, Nöte> ['no:t] *f* **1.** *kein pl* (*Armut*) poverty **2.** (*Bedrängnis*) distress; **in ~ geraten** to be in dire straits; **jdm seine ~ klagen** to pour out one's troubles to sb ▶ **~ macht erfinderisch** *prov* necessity is the mother of invention; **mit knapper ~** just; **zur ~** if need[s] be

Notar(in) <-s, -e> [no·'ta:ɐ̯] *m(f)* notary [public]

Notariat <-[e]s, -e> [no·ta·'rja:t] *nt* (*Kanzlei*) notary's office

Notarzt, -ärztin *m, f* **1.** (*bei Unfällen*) emergency doctor **2.** (*Arzt im Notdienst*) on-call physician

Notaufnahme *f* **1.** (*eines Kranken*) emergency admission **2.** (*Krankenhausstation*) emergency room

Notausgang *m* emergency exit

Notbremse *f* emergency brake

Notdienst *m* **~ haben** to be on duty

Note <-, -n> ['no:·tə] *f* **1.** MUS note; **~n lesen** to read music **2.** SCH, UNIV grade **3.** (*Banknote*) [bank]note

Notebook <-s, -s> ['noʊt·bʊk] *nt* COMPUT notebook

Notfall *m* emergency

notfalls ['no:t·fals] *adv* if need be

notgedrungen *adv* willy-nilly

notieren * [no·'ti:·rən] *vt* to write down

nötig ['nø:·tɪç] *adj* necessary; **alles N~e** everything necessary; **das N~ste** the essentials; **etw** [**bitter**] **~ haben** to be in [urgent] need of sth; **das haben wir nicht ~!** we don't have to put up with that!

Nötigung <-, -en> *f* (*Zwang*) coercion

Notiz <-, -en> [no·'ti:ts] *f* **1.** (*Vermerk*) note **2.** (*Zeitungsmeldung*) short report ▶ [**keine**] **~** [**von jdm/etw**] **nehmen** to take [no] notice [of sb/sth]

Notizblock <-blöcke> *m* notepad

Notlage *f* desperate situation

Notlandung *f* emergency landing

Notlösung *f* stopgap [solution]

notorisch [no·'to:·rɪʃ] **I.** *adj geh* notorious **II.** *adv geh* notoriously

Notruf m 1. (*Anruf*) emergency call 2. (*Notrufnummer*) emergency number

Notstand m 1. (*Notlage*) desperate situation 2. JUR [state of] emergency

Notstandsgebiet nt disaster area

Notunterkunft f emergency accommodations pl

Notwehr <-> f kein pl self-defense

notwendig ['noːt·vɛn·dɪç] I. adj necessary II. adv necessarily

Notwendigkeit <-, -en> [noːt·'vɛn·dɪç·kait] f necessity

Nougat <-s, -s> ['nuː·gat] m o nt s. **Nugat**

November <-s, -> [noˈvɛm·bɐ] m November; s. a. **Februar**

Nu [nuː] m **im** ~ in a flash

nüchtern ['nʏç·tɐn] adj 1. (*mit leerem Magen*) with an empty stomach 2. (*nicht betrunken*) sober 3. (*realitätsbewusst*) down-to-earth 4. (*Tatsachen*) plain; (*Einrichtung*) austere

Nudel <-, -n> ['nuː·dl] f meist pl pasta + sing vb, no indef art; (*Suppennudel*) noodle usu pl

Nugat <-s, -s> m o nt nougat

nuklear [nuˈkleˈaːɐ] I. adj attr nuclear II. adv with nuclear weapons

null [nʊl] adj zero ▸ **gleich ~ sein** to be [practically] zero, to be extremely unrealistic; **in ~ Komma nichts** fam in a flash; **~ und nichtig sein** to be null and void

Null <-, -en> [nʊl] f 1. (*Zahl*) zero 2. fam (*Versager*) nothing

Nulldiät f starvation diet

Nullpunkt m kein pl freezing point ▸ **auf den ~ sinken** to reach rock bottom

numerieren * ALT [nuˈməˈriː·rən] vt s. **nummerieren**

Numerus <-, Numeri> ['nuː·me·rʊs] m number; **~ clausus** enrollment limits

Nummer <-, -n> ['nʊ·mɐ] f 1. (*Zahl, Telefonnummer*) number 2. MEDIA (*Ausgabe*) issue 3. (*Größe*) size 4. sl (*Koitus*) fuck vulg; **eine ~ [mit jdm] schieben** sl to get it on [with sb] sl ▸ **auf ~ Sicher gehen** fam to play it safe

nummerieren * RR vt to number

Nummernschild nt license plate

nun [nuːn] adv 1. (*jetzt*) now 2. (*eben*) **es ist ~ [ein]mal so** that's [just] the way it is

nur ['nuːɐ] adv 1. (*lediglich*) only; **sie fährt gut, ~ zu schnell** she drives well, but too fast 2. (*bloß*) just; **wie konnte ich das ~ vergessen!** how on earth could I forget that! 3. (*ruhig*) just; **~ zu!** go [right] ahead!

nuscheln ['nʊ·ʃln] vt, vi fam to mumble

Nuss RR, **Nuß** ALT <-, Nüsse> ['nʊs] f nut ▸ **dumme ~** moron, idiot

Nussbaum RR m nut tree

Nutte <-, -n> ['nʊ·tə] f sl whore

nutz ['nʊts] adj pred südd, österr s. **nütze**

nütze ['nʏ·tsə] adj pred **zu etw** dat ~ **sein** to be useful for sth; **zu nichts ~ sein** to be good for nothing

nutzen ['nʊ·tsn], **nützen** ['nʏ·tsn] I. vi (*von Nutzen sein*) to be of use; **[jdm] nichts ~** to not do [sb] any good II. vt 1. (*in Gebrauch nehmen*) to use 2. (*ausnutzen*) to exploit; **eine Gelegenheit ~** to take advantage of an opportunity

Nutzen <-s> ['nʊ·tsn] m kein pl benefit; **welchen ~ versprichst du dir davon?** what do you hope to gain from it?; **[jdm] ~ bringen** to be advantageous [to sb]; **[jdm] von ~ sein** to be of use [to sb]

nützlich ['nʏts·lɪç] adj 1. (*nutzbringend*) useful 2. (*hilfreich*) helpful

nutzlos I. adj useless II. adv in vain pred

Nutzlosigkeit <-> f kein pl uselessness

Nutzpflanze f [economically] useful plant

Nutzung <-, -en> f use

O

O, o <-, -> [oː] nt O, o; ~ **wie Otto** O as in Oscar

Oase <-, -n> [oˈaː·zə] f oasis

ob ['ɔp] konj whether; **~ er morgen kommt?** I wonder if he's coming tomorrow?

Obdach <-[e]s> ['ɔp·dax] nt kein pl geh shelter

Qbdachlos *adj* homeless

Qbdachlose(r) *f(m)* homeless person

Qbdachlosenheim *nt* homeless shelter

Q-Beine *pl* bow legs *pl*

oben ['o:bn̩] *adv* **1.** (*in der Höhe*) top; **ich möchte die Flasche ~ links** I'd like the bottle [that's] on the top left; **~ auf etw** *dat o akk* on top of sth; **dort/ hier ~** up there/here; **ganz ~** at the very top; **hoch ~** high; **bis ~** [**hin**] up to the top; **nach ~** up; **nach ~ zu** further up; **von ~** (*vom oberen Teil*) from above **2.** (*im oberen Stockwerk*) upstairs; **nach ~** upstairs; **von ~** from upstairs **3.** *fam* (*auf höherer Ebene*) **der Befehl kommt von ~** the order comes from the top **4.** (*vorher*) above; **der/die/das ~ erwähnte** the above-mentioned ▶ **dieser Job steht mir bis** [**hier**] **~** *fam* I'm fed up with this job *sl*; **~ ohne** *fam* topless; **von ~ bis unten** from top to bottom; **ich weiß nicht mehr, wo ~ und unten ist** *fam* I don't know whether I'm coming or going *sl*

obendrein ['o:bn̩·'drain] *adv* on top

Qber <-s, -> ['o:bɐ] *m* waiter

Qberarm *m* upper arm

Qberarzt, -ärztin *m, f* assistant medical director

Qberbefehlshaber(in) *m(f)* commander in chief

Qberbegriff *m* generic term

Qberbürgermeister(in) ['o:bɐ·byr·gə·maistɐ] *m(f)* mayor

obere(r, s) ['o:bə·rə, -rə, -rəs] *adj attr* **1.** (*oben befindlich*) top **2.** (*rangmäßig höher*) higher **3.** (*vorhergehend*) previous **4.** (*höher gelegen*) upper

Qberfläche ['o:bɐ·flɛ·çə] *f* surface

oberflächlich ['o:bɐ·flɛç·lɪç] **I.** *adj* superficial **II.** *adv* superficially; (*flüchtig*) in a slapdash manner *pred*

Qberflächlichkeit <-> *f kein pl* superficiality

Qbergeschoss ᴿᴿ *nt* top floor

oberhalb ['o:bɐ·halp] **I.** *präp* +*gen* above **II.** *adv* above

Qberhaupt *nt* head

oberirdisch **I.** *adj* aboveground; (*Leitung*) overhead **II.** *adv* aboveground

Qberkörper *m* torso

Qberlippe *f* upper lip

Qberschenkel *m* thigh

Qberschicht *f* (*der Gesellschaft*) upper class

Qberseite *f* top

oberste(r, s) ['o:bɐ·stə, -stə, -stəs] *adj* **1.** (*räumlich*) top **2.** (*rangmäßig*) highest

Qberstufe *f* ≈ sixth grade

obgleich [ɔp·'glaiç] *konj* although

Objekt <-[e]s, -e> [ɔp·'jɛkt] *nt* **1.** (*Gegenstand, a. Grammatik*) object **2.** (*Immobilie*) [piece of] property **3.** (*Kunstgegenstand*) objet d'art, work of art

objektiv [ɔpjɛk·'ti:f] **I.** *adj* objective **II.** *adv* objectively

Objektiv <-s, -e> [ɔpjɛk·'ti:f] *nt* lens

Objektivität <-> [ɔpjɛk·tivi·'tɛːt] *f kein pl* objectivity

obligatorisch [obliga·'to:·rɪʃ] *adj geh* mandatory

Obst <-[e]s> ['o:pst] *nt kein pl* fruit

Qbstbaum *m* fruit tree

Qbstkuchen *m* fruit tart

Qbstsalat *m* fruit salad

obszön [ɔps·'tsøːn] *adj* obscene

Obszönität <-, -en> [ɔps·tsø·ni·'tɛːt] *f* obscenity

obwohl [ɔp·'vo:l] *konj* although

Qchse <-n, -n> ['ɔksə] *m* ox

Qchsenschwanzsuppe *f* oxtail soup

öde ['øːdə] *adj* **1.** (*verlassen*) desolate **2.** (*fade: Landschaft*) dull **3.** (*langweilig*) tedious, dull

oder ['o:dɐ] *konj* **1.** (*eines oder anderes*) or; **~ aber** or else; **~ auch** or [even]; **~ auch nicht** or [maybe] not **2.** (*stimmt's?*) **der Film hat dir auch gut gefallen, ~?** you liked the movie too, didn't you?; **er schuldet dir noch Geld, ~?** he still owes you money, doesn't he?

Ofen <-s, Öfen> ['o:fn̩] *m* **1.** (*Heizofen*) heater; (*Kohle-, Kachel-, Ölofen*) stove **2.** (*Backofen*) oven **3.** *dial* (*Herd*) stove ▶ **jetzt ist der ~ aus** *fam* that does it

Qfenheizung *f* stove heating

offen ['ɔfn̩] **I.** *adj* **1.** (*Punkt*) moot; (*Problem, Rechnung*) unsettled; (*Frage*) unanswered; **bei ~em Fenster** with the window open; **~er Wein** wine by the

glass/carafe; ~ **haben** (*Laden, Geschäft*) to be open **II.** *adv* openly; ~ **gestanden** to be [perfectly] honest

offenbar [ɔfn̩·'baːɐ] **I.** *adj* obvious **II.** *adv* obviously

Offenheit <-> *f kein pl* openness; **in aller** ~ quite frankly

offenherzig *adj* **1.** (*freimütig*) open **2.** *hum fam* (*tief ausgeschnitten*) revealing

offensichtlich ['ɔfn̩·zɪçt·lɪç] **I.** *adj* obvious; (*Irrtum, Lüge*) blatant **II.** *adv* obviously

öffentlich ['œfn̩·tlɪç] *adj* public **II.** *adv* publicly

Öffentlichkeit <-> *f kein pl* **die** ~ the [general] public + *sing/pl vb*; **in aller** ~ in public; **etw an die** ~ **bringen** to make sth public

offiziell [ɔfi·'tsi̯ɛl] **I.** *adj* **1.** (*amtlich*) official **2.** (*förmlich: Empfang, Feier*) formal **II.** *adv* officially

Offizier(in) <-s, -e> [ɔfi·'tsiːɐ] *m(f)* officer

Offlinebetrieb ᴿᴿ, **Off-line-Betrieb** ᴬᴸᵀ ['ɔf·lain-] *m kein pl* offline operation

öffnen ['œf·nən] **I.** *vt* to open **II.** *vi* [*jdm*] ~ to open the door [for sb] **III.** *vr* **1.** (*aufgehen*) **sich** *akk* ~ (*Tür*) to open; (*Blüte, Fallschirm*) to open up **2.** (*sich zuwenden*) **sich** *akk* [*jdm/etw*] ~ to open up [to sb/sth]

Öffnung <-, -en> *f* **1.** (*offene Stelle*) opening **2.** *kein pl* (*das Öffnen*) opening

Öffnungszeiten *pl* hours of business *pl*

oft <öfter, am öftesten> ['ɔft] *adv* often

öfter(s) ['œf·tə(s)] *adv* [every] once in a while; **ist dir das schon** ~ **passiert?** has that happened to you often?

oftmals *adv s.* **oft**

ohne ['oːnə] **I.** *präp* +*akk* **1.** (*nicht versehen mit*) without; ~ **Geld** without any money; ~ **Schutz** unprotected **2.** (*nicht eingerechnet*) excluding; ~ **mich!** count me out! **II.** *konj* ~ **etw zu tun** without doing sth; ~, **dass etw geschieht** without sth happening; ~, **dass jd etw tut** without sb doing sth

Ohnmacht <-, -en> ['oːn·maxt] *f* **1.** (*Bewusstseinszustand*) faint; **in** ~ **fallen**

to faint **2.** *geh* (*Machtlosigkeit*) powerlessness

ohnmächtig ['oːn·mɛç·tɪç] **I.** *adj* **1.** (*bewusstlos*) unconscious; ~ **werden** to faint **2.** *geh* (*machtlos*) powerless **3.** *attr* (*Wut*) helpless **II.** *adv* helplessly

Ohr <-[e]s, -en> ['oːɐ] *nt* ear ▶ **es faustdick hinter den ~en haben** to be a sly one; **ganz** ~ **sein** *hum fam* to be all ears; **jdm eins hinter die ~en geben** *fam* to whack sb on the back of the head; **viel um die ~en haben** *fam* to have a lot on one's plate; **jdn übers** ~ **hauen** *fam* to pull a fast one on sb; **jdm** [**mit etw** *dat*] **in den ~en liegen** to nag sb [about sth]; **die ~en spitzen** *fam* to prick up one's ears; **bis über beide ~en verliebt sein** to be head over heels in love

ohrenbetäubend I. *adj* deafening **II.** *adv* deafeningly

Ohrfeige <-, -en> *f* slap in the face

ohrfeigen *vt* **jdn** ~ to give sb a slap in the face

Ohrläppchen <-s, -> *nt* earlobe

Ohrring *m* earring

Ökologie <-> [øko·lo·'giː] *f kein pl* ecology

ökologisch [øko·'loː·gɪʃ] **I.** *adj* ecological **II.** *adv* ecologically

ökonomisch [øko·'noː·mɪʃ] **I.** *adj* **1.** (*die Wirtschaft betreffend*) economic **2.** (*sparsam*) economical **II.** *adv* economically

Ökosteuer *f* environmental tax (*tax on products or processes which damage the environment*)

Ökosystem *nt* ecosystem

Oktober <-s, -> [ɔk·'toː·bɐ] *m* October *s. a.* **Februar**

Öl <-[e]s, -e> ['øːl] *nt* (*fette Flüssigkeit, a. Erdöl*) oil; (*Heizöl*) fuel oil; (*Schmieröl*) lubricating oil ▶ ~ **ins Feuer gießen** to add fuel to the fire

Oldtimer <-s, -> ['ɔlt·taimɐ] *m* (*Auto*) vintage car; (*Flugzeug*) vintage airplane

ölen ['øːlən] *vt* to oil

Ölfarbe *f* oil-based paint; KUNST oil [paint]

Ölgemälde *nt* oil painting

Ölheizung *f* oil heater

ölig ['øː·lɪç] *adj* oily; (*fettig*) greasy

Olive <-, -n> [oˈliː·və] f olive

Olivenöl nt olive oil

olivgrün adj olive-green, olive attr

Ölleitung f oil pipe; (Pipeline) oil pipeline

Ölpest f oil pollution

Ölquelle f oil well

Ölsardine f sardine [in oil] ▶ **wie die ~n** fam like sardines

Ölstand m kein pl oil level

Ölstandsmesser m oil pressure gauge

Öltanker m oil tanker

Ölwechsel m oil change

Olympiade <-, -n> [olʏmˈpi̯aː·də] f Olympic Games pl

olympisch [oˈlʏm·pɪʃ] adj Olympic attr

Oma <-, -s> [ˈoːma] f fam granny fam, grandma fam

Omelett <-[e]s, -e> nt, **Omelette** <-, -n> [ɔm(ə)·ˈlɛt] f omelet

Omnibus [ˈɔmni·bʊs] m bus

Omnibushaltestelle f bus stop

Onkel <-s, -> [ˈɔŋ·kl̩] m uncle

Onlinebanking <-[s]> [ˈɔn·lain·bɛŋ·kɪŋ] nt kein pl online banking

Onlinebetrieb [ˈɔn·lain-] m kein pl online operation

Onlinedienst [ˈɔn·lain-] m online service

Opa <-s, -s> [ˈoːpa] m fam grandpa

Oper <-, -n> [ˈoː·pɐ] f opera

Operation <-, -en> [opəˈra·ˈtsi̯oːn] f operation

Operationssaal m operating room

operieren * [opəˈriː·rən] vt jdn/etw ~ to operate on sb/sth; **jdn am Bein** ~ to operate on sb's leg; **sich** dat **etw** ~ **lassen** to have sth operated on; **sich** akk ~ **lassen** to have an operation

Opernsänger(in) m(f) opera singer

Opfer <-s, -> [ˈɔ·pfɐ] nt 1. (verzichtende Hingabe) sacrifice; ~ **bringen** to make sacrifices 2. (geschädigte Person) victim; (von Unfall, Krieg) casualty; **jdm/etw zum ~ fallen** to fall victim to sb/sth

opfern [ˈɔ·pfɐn] vt to sacrifice

Opiat <-[e]s, -e> [oˈpi̯aːt] nt opiate

Opium <-s> [ˈoː·pi̯ʊm] nt kein pl opium

Opportunismus <-> [ɔpɔr·tu·ˈnɪs·mʊs] m kein pl geh opportunism

Opportunist(in) <-en, -en> [ɔp·ɔr·tu·ˈnɪst] m(f) opportunist

opportunistisch adj opportunistic

Opposition <-, -en> [ɔpo·zi·ˈtsi̯oːn] f POL **die** ~ the opposition

Oppositionsführer(in) m(f) opposition leader

Optiker(in) <-s, -> [ˈɔp·ti·kɐ] m(f) optometrist

optimal [ɔp·ti·ˈmaːl] I. adj optimal II. adv in the best possible way

optimieren * [ɔp·ti·ˈmiː·rən] vt to optimize

Optimismus <-> [ɔp·ti·ˈmɪs·mʊs] m kein pl optimism

Optimist(in) <-en, -en> [ɔp·ti·ˈmɪst] m(f) optimist

optimistisch I. adj optimistic II. adv optimistically

optisch [ˈɔp·tɪʃ] adj (Eindruck, Täuschung) optical

orange [oˈrãː·ʒə] adj orange

Orange <-, -n> [oˈrãː·ʒə] f orange

Orangensaft m orange juice

Orangenschale f orange peel

Orang-Utan <-s, -s> [ˈoːraŋ·ˈʔuːtan] m orangutan

Orchester <-s, -> [ɔrˈkɛs·tɐ] nt orchestra

Orchidee <-, -n> [ɔr·çi·ˈdeː(ə)] f orchid

Orden <-s, -> [ˈɔr·dn̩] m 1. (Ehrenzeichen) decoration, medal; **jdm einen ~ [für etw** akk] **verleihen** to decorate sb [for sth] 2. (Gemeinschaft) [holy] order

ordentlich [ˈɔr·dn̩·tlɪç] I. adj 1. (aufgeräumt) neat 2. (ordnungsliebend: Person) orderly, neat 3. (anständig: Benehmen) respectable; (Leute) proper 4. fam (tüchtig) proper; (Portion) decent II. adv 1. (säuberlich) neatly 2. (anständig) **sich** akk ~ **benehmen** to [really] behave oneself 3. fam (tüchtig) properly; ~ **essen** to eat well

Ordinalzahl [ɔr·di·ˈnaːl-] f ordinal [number]

ordinär [ɔr·di·ˈnɛːɐ̯] I. adj 1. (vulgär) vulgar 2. (alltäglich) ordinary II. adv crudely

ordnen [ˈɔrd·nən] vt to arrange; **neu** ~ to rearrange

Ordner <-s, -> m file; (Hefter) binder

Ordnung <-> [ˈɔrd·nʊŋ] f kein pl order; **die öffentliche** ~ public order; ~ **schaf-**

O

fen to straighten things up ▶ **etw in ~ bringen** (*aufräumen*) to clean sth up; (*klären*) to sort sth out; (*reparieren*) to fix sth; **es [ganz] in ~ finden, dass ...** to find it [perfectly] all right that ...; **geht in ~!** *fam* that's OK; **etw ist mit jdm/etw nicht in ~** there's something wrong with sb/sth; **wieder in ~ kommen** to turn out all right; **in ~ sein** *fam* to be OK; **nicht in ~ sein** (*nicht funktionieren*) to not be working right; (*sich nicht gehören, nicht richtig sein*) to not be OK

Ordnungsamt *nt* municipal authority responsible for registration, licensing, and regulating public events

ordnungsgemäß I. *adj* according to the rules *pred* II. *adv* in accordance with the regulations

Ordnungsstrafe *f* fine

ordnungswidrig I. *adj* improper II. *adv* improperly

Ordnungswidrigkeit *f* infringement [of the rules/law]

Organ <-s, -e> [ɔr·ˈgaːn] *nt* **1.** ANAT organ **2.** *fam* (*Stimme*) voice **3.** *form* (*offizielle Zeitschrift/Einrichtung*) organ

Organhandel *m* organ trafficking

Organisation <-, -en> [ɔr·ga·ni·za·ˈtsi̯oːn] *f* organization

Organisationstalent *nt* **1.** *kein pl* (*Eigenschaft*) organizational ability **2.** (*Mensch*) skilled organizer

organisatorisch [ɔr·ga·ni·za·ˈtoː·rɪʃ] I. *adj* organizational II. *adv* organizationally

organisch [ɔr·ˈgaː·nɪʃ] I. *adj* organic II. *adv* organically

organisieren* [ɔr·ga·ni·ˈziː·rən] I. *vt, vi* to organize; **er kann ausgezeichnet ~** he's an excellent organizer II. *vt* *fam* (*beschaffen*) to get hold of; **wer organisiert einen CD-Spieler für die Party?** who is going to arrange for a CD player for the party? III. *vr* **sich** *akk* **~** to get organized

Organismus <-, -nismen> [ɔr·ga·ˈnɪs·mʊs] *m* organism

Organspende *f* organ donation

Organspender(in) *m(f)* organ donor

Organtransplantation *f*, **Organverpflanzung** *f* organ transplant

Orgasmus <-, Orgasmen> [ɔr·ˈgas·mʊs] *m* orgasm

Orgel <-, -n> [ˈɔr·gl̩] *f* organ

Orgie <-, -n> [ˈɔr·gi̯ə] *f* orgy

Orient <-s> [ˈoːri·ɛnt, oˈri̯ɛnt] *m kein p[l]* **der ~** the Orient; **der Vordere ~** the Middle East

Orientale, Orientalin <-n, -n> [o·ri̯ɛn·ˈta·lə] *m, f* Oriental

orientalisch [o·ri̯ɛn·ˈta·lɪʃ] *adj* oriental

orientieren* [o·ri̯ɛn·ˈtiː·rən] I. *vr* **sich** *akk* **~ 1.** (*sich zurechtfinden*) to use as a point of reference; **sich** *akk* **an den Sternen ~** to get one's bearings by looking at the stars **2.** (*sich ausrichten*) **sich** *akk* **an etw** *dat* **~** (*Bericht*) to be based on; (*Person*) to adapt oneself to; **ich bin eher links orientiert** I tend more to the left II. *vt* to inform (**über** +*akk* about)

Orientierung <-, -en> [o·ri̯ɛn·ˈtiː·rʊŋ] *f* orientation; **die ~ verlieren** to lose one's sense of direction

Orientierungssinn *m kein pl* sense of direction

original [o·ri·gi·ˈnaːl] I. *adj* **1.** (*echt*) genuine **2.** (*ursprünglich*) original II. *adv* in the original [condition]

Original <-s, -e> [o·ri·gi·ˈnaːl] *nt* **1.** (*Urversion*) original **2.** (*Mensch*) character

originell [o·ri·gi·ˈnɛl] *adj* original

Orkan <-[e]s, -e> [ɔr·ˈkaːn] *m* hurricane

orkanartig *adj* hurricane-force *attr*

Ornament <-[e]s, -e> [ɔr·na·ˈmɛnt] *nt* ornament

Ort¹ <-[e]s, -e> [ˈɔrt] *m* place ▶ **an ~ und Stelle** on the spot

Ort² [ˈɔrt] *nt fam* ▶ **vor ~** on site

Orthografie RR, **Orthographie** <-, -n> [ɔr·to·gra·ˈfiː] *f* orthography, spelling

orthografisch RR, **orthographisch** [ɔr·to·ˈgra·frɪʃ] I. *adj* orthographic[al] *spec* II. *adv* orthographically *spec*

Orthopäde, Orthopädin <-n, -n> [ɔr·to·ˈpɛː·də] *m, f* orthopedist

orthopädisch [ɔr·to·ˈpɛː·dɪʃ] *adj* orthopedic

örtlich [ˈœrt·lɪç] I. *adj* **1.** (*lokal*) local **2.** METEO localized II. *adv* locally; **jdn ~ betäuben** to give sb a local anesthetic

Ortsangabe f (*Standortangabe*) [name of] location; (*in Anschrift*) [name of the] city/town

Ortsausgang m village/town exit

Ortschaft <-, -en> f village/[small] town; **eine geschlossene ~** a built-up area

Ortseingang m village/town entrance

ortsfremd adj ~ **sein** to be a stranger

Ortsgespräch nt local call

Ortsname m place name

Ortsschild nt sign for a town

Ortstarif m local [call] rate

Ortsteil m part of a town

Ortszeit f local time

Öse <-, -n> ['ø:·zə] f eye[let]

Ossi <-, -s> ['ɔsi] m o f fam East German

Ostasien nt East[ern] Asia

ostdeutsch ['ɔst·dɔytʃ] adj East German

Ostdeutschland ['ɔst·dɔytʃ·lant] nt East Germany

Osten <-s> ['ɔs·tn̩] m kein pl, no indef art 1. (*Himmelsrichtung*) east; **der Ferne/Nahe ~** the Far/Middle East; *s. a.* **Norden 1** 2. (*östliche Gegend*) east; *s. a.* **Norden 2**

Osterei nt Easter egg

Osterglocke f BOT daffodil

Osterhase m Easter bunny

Ostermontag ['o:s·te·'mo:n·ta:k] m Easter Monday

Ostern <-, -> ['o:s·ten] nt Easter; **frohe ~!** Happy Easter!

Österreich <-s> ['ø:s·tə·raiç] nt Austria; *s. a.* **Deutschland**

Österreicher(in) <-s, -> ['ø:s·tə·rai·çɐ] m(f) Austrian; *s. a.* **Deutsche(r)**

österreichisch ['ø:s·tə·rai·çɪʃ] adj Austrian; *s. a.* **deutsch**

Ostersonntag ['o:s·te·'zɔn·ta:k] m Easter Sunday

Osteuropa ['ɔst·ʔɔy·'ro:·pa] nt Eastern Europe

Ostfriese, -friesin <-n, -n> ['ɔst·'fri:·zə] m, f East Frisian

ostfriesisch ['ɔst·'fri:·zɪʃ] adj East Frisian

Ostfriesland ['ɔst·'fri:s·lant] nt East Friesland

östlich ['œst·lɪç] **I.** adj 1. (*Himmelsrichtung*) eastern; *s. a.* **nördlich I 1** 2. (*im Osten liegend*) eastern; *s. a.*

nördlich I 2 3. (*von/nach Osten*) eastward; (*Richtung, Wind*) easterly; *s. a.* **nördlich I 3 II.** adv ~ **von ...** east of ... **III.** präp +gen [to the] east of

Ostsee ['ɔst·ze:] f **die ~** the Baltic [Sea]

Oststaaten pl (*in den USA*) Eastern states pl

Ost-West-Beziehungen ['ɔst·'vɛst-] pl East-West relations pl

Otter¹ <-, -n> ['ɔtɐ] f (*Schlangenart*) adder

Otter² <-s, -> ['ɔtɐ] m (*Fischotter*) otter

oval [o·'va:l] adj oval

Oxidation <-, -en> [ɔ·ksi··da·'tsjo:n] f oxidation

oxidieren * [ɔ·ksi·'di:·rən] vt, vi sein o haben to oxidize

Ozean <-s, -e> ['o:·tsea:n] m ocean

Ozon <-s> [o·'tso:n] nt o m kein pl ozone

Ozonloch nt ozone hole

Ozonschicht f kein pl ozone layer

P

P, p <-, -> [pe:] nt P, p; **~ wie Paula** P as in Papa

paar [pa:ɐ] adj **ein ~ ...** a few ...; **ein ~ Mal** a couple of times; **alle ~ Tage** every few days

Paar <-, -e> [pa:ɐ] nt 1. (*Menschen*) couple 2. (*Dinge*) pair; **ein ~ Würstchen** a couple [of] sausages

paaren [pa:·rən] vr sich akk ~ 1. (*kopulieren*) to mate 2. (*sich verbinden*) to be coupled

paarweise adv in pairs

Pacht <-, -en> [paxt] f lease

pachten ['pax·tn̩] vt to lease

Pächter(in) <-s, -> ['pɛç·tɐ] m(f) tenant

Pack¹ <-[e]s, -e> [pak] m (*Stapel*) stack; (*zusammengeschnürt*) pack

Pack² <-s> [pak] nt kein pl pej (*Pöbel*) riffraff + pl vb

Päckchen <-s, -> ['pɛk·çən] nt 1. (*Postsendung*) small package 2. (*Packung*) pack, packet 3. (*kleiner Packen*) small bundle

packen ['pa·kn̩] vt 1. (*ergreifen*) to grab

[hold of] (**bei, an** +dat by) **2.** (*vollpacken, verstauen*) to pack (**in** +akk in[to]); **ein Paket ~** to box up *sep* a package **3.** (*überkommen*) to seize; **von Ekel gepackt** utterly disgusted **4.** sl (*bewältigen*) to manage; (*Prüfung*) to pass

Packen <-s, -> ['pakn] m stack; (*unordentlich a.*) pile; (*zusammengeschnürt*) bundle

packend adj absorbing; (*Buch, Film*) thrilling

Packung <-, -en> f pack[age]; **eine ~ Pralinen** a box of chocolates

Pädagoge, Pädagogin <-n, -nen> [pɛ·da·'go:·gə] m, f **1.** (*Lehrer*) teacher **2.** (*Erziehungswissenschaftler*) education[al] theorist

Pädagogik <-> [pɛ·da·'go:·gɪk] f kein pl pedagogy *spec*

pädagogisch [pɛ·da·'go:·gɪʃ] **I.** adj educational attr; **~e Fähigkeiten** teaching ability **II.** adv educationally

Paddel <-s, -> ['pa·dl̩] nt paddle

Paddelboot nt canoe

paddeln ['pa·dl̩n] vi sein o haben to paddle

Page <-n, -n> ['pa:·ʒə] m page

Paket <-[e]s, -e> [pa·'ke:t] nt **1.** (*Postsendung*) package, parcel **2.** (*umhüllter Packen*) package **3.** (*Packung*) pack, packet **4.** (*Gesamtheit*) package **5.** (*Stapel*) stack

Pakistan <-s> ['pa:·kɪ·sta:n] nt Pakistan; *s. a.* **Deutschland**

Pakt <-[e]s, -e> [pakt] m pact

Palast <-[e]s, Paläste> [pa·'last] m palace

Palästina <-s> [pa·lɛs·'ti:·na] nt Palestine; *s. a.* **Deutschland**

Palästinenser(in) <-s, -> [pa·lɛs·ti·'nɛn·zɐ] m(f) Palestinian; *s. a.* **Deutsche(r)**

palästinensisch [pa·lɛs·ti·'nɛn·zɪʃ] adj Palestinian; *s. a.* **deutsch**

Palme <-, -n> ['pal·mə] f palm [tree] ▶ **jdn auf die ~ bringen** *fam* to drive sb up the wall

Palmsonntag [palm·'zɔn·ta:k] m Palm Sunday

Pampelmuse <-, -n> [pam·pl̩·'mu:·zə] f grapefruit

Panama <-s> ['pa·na·ma] nt Panama; *s. a.* **Deutschland**

Panamaer(in) <-s, -> ['pa·na·ma·ɐ] m(f) Panamanian; *s. a.* **Deutsche(r)**

panieren * [pa·'ni:·rən] vt to bread

Paniermehl nt breadcrumbs pl

Panik <-, -en> ['pa:·nɪk] f panic; **in ~ geraten** to panic

panisch ['pa:·nɪʃ] **I.** adj attr panic-stricken **II.** adv in panic

Panne <-, -n> ['pa·nə] f **1.** AUTO, TECH breakdown **2.** (*Missgeschick*) mishap

Pannendienst <-es, -e> m tow[ing] service

Panorama <-s, Panoramen> [pa·no·'ra:·ma] nt panorama

panschen ['pan·ʃn̩] vt to water down *sep* (*an alcoholic drink*)

Panter RR, **Panther** <-s, -> ['pan·tɐ] m panther

Pantoffel <-s, -n> [pan·'tɔ·fl̩] m [backless] slipper

Pantoffelheld m fam henpecked husband

Panzer <-s, -> ['pan·tsɐ] m **1.** MIL tank **2.** (*Schutzhülle*) shell; (*eines Krokodils*) bony plate; (*eines Nashorns, Sauriers*) armor

panzern ['pan·tsɐn] vt to armor-plate

Papa <-s, -s> ['pa·pa] m fam dad, daddy *esp childspeak*

Papagei <-s, -en> [pa·pa·'gai] m parrot

Papi <-s, -s> ['pa·pi] m fam s. **Papa**

Papier <-s, -e> [pa·'pi:ɐ̯] nt **1.** kein pl (*Material*) paper **2.** (*Schriftstück*) paper, document **3.** (*Ausweise*) ~e [identification] papers pl

Papierkorb m waste paper basket

Papierstau m paper jam

Papiertaschentuch nt tissue

Pappbecher m paper cup

Pappe <-, -n> ['pa·pə] f cardboard

Pappel <-, -n> ['pa·pl̩] f poplar

pappig ['pa·pɪç] adj fam **1.** (*klebrig*) sticky **2.** (*breiig*) mushy

Pappkarton m **1.** *Pappschachtel*) cardboard box **2.** (*Pappe*) cardboard

Pappteller m paper plate

Paprika <-s, -[s]> ['pa·pri·ka] m **1.** (*Strauch, Schote*) pepper **2.** kein pl (*Gewürz*) paprika

Papst <-[e]s, Päpste> [pa:pst] m **der ~** the Pope

päpstlich ['pɛːpst·lɪç] *adj* papal *a. pej*

Parabolantenne [pa·ra·'boːl-] *f* satellite dish

Para**debeispiel** *nt* perfect example

Paradeiser <-s, -> [pa·ra·'dai·zɐ] *m* *österr* (*Tomate*) tomato

Paradies <-es, -e> [pa·ra·'diːs] *nt* paradise *no def art* ▶ **das ~ auf Erden** heaven on earth

paradox [pa·ra·'dɔks] *geh* **I.** *adj* paradoxical **II.** *adv* paradoxically

Paragraf^{RR}, **Paragraph** <-en, -en> [pa·ra·'ɡraf] *m* paragraph

parallel [pa·ra·'leːl] *adj, adv* parallel

Parallele <-, -n> [pa·ra·'leː·lə] *f a. fig* parallel; **eine ~** [**zu etw** *dat*] **ziehen** to draw a parallel [to *o* with] sth

paramilitärisch ['paː·ra·mi·li·tɛ·rɪʃ] *adj* paramilitary

Parasit <-en, -en> [pa·ra·'ziːt] *m* parasite

Parfüm <-s, -e> [par·'fyːm] *nt* perfume

Parfümerie <-, -n> [par·fy·mə·'riː] *f* perfumery

parfümieren * [par·fy·'miː·rən] *vr* **sich** *akk* **~** to put on *sep* perfume

Pariser[1] [pa·'riː·zɐ] *adj attr* **1.** (*in Paris befindlich*) in Paris **2.** (*aus Paris stammend*) Parisian

Pariser[2] <-s, -> [pa·'riː·zɐ] *m sl* (*Kondom*) condom

Park <-s, -s> [park] *m* park

parken ['par·kn̩] *vt, vi* to park

Parkett <-s, -e> [par·'kɛt] *nt* **1.** (*Holzfußboden*) parquet [flooring] **2.** (*Tanzfläche*) dance floor

Parkgebühr *f* parking fee

Parkhaus *nt* parking garage

Parklücke *f* parking space

Parkplatz *m* **1.** (*Parkbereich*) parking lot **2.** (*Parklücke*) parking space

Parkscheibe *f* parking disk *(for parking spaces with time limits to show what time the car was parked)*

Parksünder(in) *m(f)* parking offender

Parkuhr *f* parking meter

Parkverbot *nt* **1.** (*Verbot zu parken*) parking ban **2.** (*Parkverbotszone*) no-parking zone

Parkwächter(in) *m(f)* parking lot attendant

Parlament <-[e]s, -e> [par·la·'mɛnt] *nt* parliament

Parmesan(käse) <-s> [par·me·'zaːn-] *m kein pl* Parmesan [cheese]

Partei <-, -en> [par·'tai] *f* **1.** POL, JUR party **2.** (*Mietpartei*) tenant ▶ **für/ gegen jdn ~ ergreifen** to side with/ against sb

Parteigenosse, -genossin <-n, -n> *m, f* party member

parteiisch [par·'tai·ɪʃ] **I.** *adj* biased **II.** *adv* in a biased way

parteilos *adj* independent

Parteimitglied *nt* party member

Parteipolitik *f* party politics + *sing vb*

Parteiprogramm *nt* party platform

Parteitag *m* **1.** (*Parteikonferenz*) party conference **2.** (*Beschlussorgan*) party executive

Parteivorsitzende(r) *f(m)* party chairperson, party chairman *masc* [*o fem* -woman]

parterre [par·'tɛr] *adv* on the ground floor

Partie <-, -n> [par·'tiː] *f* **1.** (*Körperbereich*) area **2.** SPORT game; **eine ~ Schach** a game of chess ▶ **eine gute ~ machen** to marry well; **mit von der ~ sein** to be in on it

Partizip <-s, -ien> [par·ti·'tsiːp] *nt* participle

Partner(in) <-s, -> ['part·nɐ] *m(f)* partner

Partnerschaft <-, -en> *f* partnership; **in einer ~ leben** to live with somebody

Partnerstadt *f* sister city

Party <-, -s> ['paː·ɐ·ti] *f* party

Partyservice ['paː·ɐ·ti·zøːɐ·vɪs] *m* catering service

Pass^{RR}, **Paß**^{ALT} <Passes, Pässe> [pas] *m* **1.** (*Dokument*) passport **2.** GEOG pass

Passage <-, -n> [pa·'saː·ʒə] *f* **1.** LIT, NAUT passage **2.** (*Ladenstraße*) [shopping] galleria

Passagier(in) <-s, -e> [pa·sa·'ʒiːɐ] *m(f)* passenger ▶ **ein blinder ~** a stowaway

Passagierliste *f* passenger list

Passant(in) <-en, -en> [pa·'sant] *m(f)* passer-by

P

Passbild ᴿᴿ nt passport photo[graph]

passen ['pa·sn̩] vi 1. (von der Größe/Form her) to fit 2. (harmonieren) zu jdm ~ to suit sb; zu etw dat ~ to go well with sth; **sie passt einfach nicht in unser Team** she simply doesn't fit in with our team 3. (gelegen sein) jdm ~ to suit sb; **der Termin passt mir zeitlich gar nicht** that day/time isn't convenient for me at all; **würde Ihnen der Dienstag besser ~?** would Tuesday be better for you?; **passt es Ihnen, wenn wir ...** is it okay with you if we ... 4. (gefallen) jdm passt etw nicht [an jdm] sb does not like sth [about sb] 5. fam [bei etw dat] ~ müssen (überfragt sein) to have to pass [on sth]

passend adj 1. (Größe, Form) fitting 2. (Farbe, Stil) matching 3. (genehm) convenient 4. (richtig) suitable; (angemessen) appropriate; (Bemerkung) fitting; **die ~en Worte finden** to find the right words 5. fam **es ~ haben** (Geldbetrag) to have exact change

Passfoto ᴿᴿ nt s. **Passbild**

passieren* [pa·'siː·rən] I. vi sein to happen; **ist was passiert?** has something happened?; **wie konnte das nur ~?** how could that happen?; **... passiert war!** fam ... or else!; **so etwas passiert eben** shit happens fam vulg II. vt haben 1. (vorbeigehen, -fahren) to pass 2. (überqueren) to cross

passioniert [pa·sio̯·'niːɐ̯t] adj geh passionate

Passionsfrucht f passion fruit

passiv ['pa·siːf] I. adj passive II. adv passively

Passiv <-s, -e> ['pa·siːf] nt passive

Passivrauchen nt passive smoking

Passkontrolle ᴿᴿ f 1. (das Kontrollieren) passport check 2. (Kontrollstelle) passport checkpoint

Passstraße ᴿᴿ f pass

Passwort ᴿᴿ <-es, -wörter> nt password

Paste <-, -n> ['pas·tə] f paste

Pastellfarbe f pastel color

Pastete <-, -n> [pas·'teː·tə] f pâté

Pastor, Pastorin <-s, -toren> ['pas·toːɐ̯, pas·'toː·rɪn] m, f dial s. **Pfarrer**

Pate, Patin <-n, -n> ['paː·tə, 'paː·tɪn] m, godfather masc, godmother fem

Patenkind nt godchild

Patenonkel m godfather

Patent <-[e]s, -e> [pa·'tɛnt] nt 1. (amtlicher Schutz) patent 2. schweiz (staatliche Erlaubnis) permit

Patentamt nt Patent Office

Patentante f godmother

patentieren* [pa·tɛn·'tiː·rən] vt [jdm etw ~ to patent sth [for sb]

Patient(in) <-en, -en> [pa·'tsi̯ɛnt] m(f) patient; **stationärer ~** inpatient

patriarchalisch [pa·tri·ar·'çaː·lɪʃ] adj patriarchal

Patriot(in) <-en, -en> [pa·tri·'oːt] m(f) patriot

patriotisch [pa·tri·'oː·tɪʃ] I. adj patriotic II. adv patriotically

Patriotismus <-> [pa·trio̯·'tɪs·mʊs] m kein pl patriotism

Patrone <-, -n> [pa·'troː·nə] f cartridge

Patsche ['pat·ʃə] f ▶ **jdm aus der ~ helfen** fam to get sb out of a jam; **in der ~ sitzen** fam to be in a jam

patschnass ᴿᴿ ['patʃ·'nas] adj fam soaking wet

Patzer <-s, -> m 1. fam (Fehler) slip-up 2. österr (Klecks) blob

patzig ['pa·tsɪç] adj fam snotty

Pauke <-, -n> ['pau̯·kə] f MUS kettledrum ▶ **auf die ~ hauen** fam (angeben) to toot one's [own] horn; (ausgelassen feiern) to paint the town red

pauken ['pau̯·kn̩] vt, vi fam to cram; **Mathe/Vokabeln ~** to cram for a math/vocabulary test

Pauker(in) <-s, -> ['pau̯·kɐ] m(f) fam teacher

pauschal [pau̯·'ʃaːl] I. adj 1. (undifferenziert) sweeping 2. FIN flat-rate attr all-inclusive II. adv 1. (allgemein) etw ~ beurteilen to make a wholesale judgment on sth 2. FIN at a flat rate

Pauschalbetrag m lump sum

Pauschale <-, -n> [pau̯·'ʃaː·lə] f flat rate

Pauschalpreis m all-inclusive price

Pause <-, -n> ['pau̯·zə] f 1. (Unterbrechung) break; SCH, POL recess; [eine] ~ machen to take a break 2. (Sprechpause) pause

pausenlos *adj, adv s.* **ständig**

Pazifik <-s> [pa·ˈtsiː·fɪk] *m* **der ~** the Pacific

Pazifist(in) <-en, -en> [pa·tsi·ˈfɪst] *m(f)* pacifist

pazifistisch *adj* pacifist

PC <-s, -s> [peː·ˈtseː] *m Abk von* **Personal Computer** PC

Pech <-[e]s> [pɛç] *nt kein pl* bad luck; **[bei etw** *dat***] ~ haben** to be unlucky [in/with sth]; **~ gehabt!** *fam* tough luck [*o fam vulg* shit]!

Pechvogel *m fam* walking disaster *hum*

Pedal <-s, -e> [pe·ˈdaːl] *nt* pedal

Pedant(in) <-en, -en> [pe·ˈdant] *m(f)* pedant

pedantisch [pe·ˈdan·tɪʃ] I. *adj* pedantic II. *adv* pedantically

Pegelstand [ˈpeː·ɡl̩-] *m* water level

peinlich [ˈpain·lɪç] *adj* **1.** (*unangenehm*) embarrassing; (*Frage, Lage, Situation*) awkward; **es war ihr sehr ~** she was really embarrassed [about it] **2.** (*äußerst*) painstaking; (*Genauigkeit*) meticulous; (*Sauberkeit*) scrupulous

Peitsche <-, -n> [ˈpai·tʃə] *f* whip

peitschen [ˈpai·tʃn̩] I. *vt haben* to whip II. *vi sein* (*Regen*) to lash (**gegen** +*akk* against)

Pelikan <-s, -e> [ˈpeː·li·kaːn] *m* pelican

Pelle <-, -n> [ˈpɛ·lə] *f fam* (*Haut*) skin ▶ **jdm auf die ~ rücken** *fam* (*sich dicht herandrängen*) to crowd sb; (*jdn bedrängen*) to badger sb

pellen [ˈpɛ·lən] *vt fam* to peel

Pellkartoffeln *pl* potatoes boiled in their skin

Pelz <-es, -e> [pɛlts] *m* fur

Pelzmantel *m* fur coat

Pendel <-s, -> [ˈpɛn·dl̩] *nt* pendulum

pendeln [ˈpɛn·dl̩n] *vi* **1.** *haben* (*schwingen*) **[hin und her] ~** to swing [to and fro] **2.** *sein* TRANSP to commute

Pendelverkehr *m* **1.** (*Nahverkehrsdienst*) shuttle service **2.** (*Berufsverkehr*) commuter traffic

Pendler(in) <-s, -> [ˈpɛnd·le] *m(f)* commuter

penetrant [pe·ne·ˈtrant] I. *adj* **1.** (*durchdringend*) penetrating; (*Geruch*) pungent **2.** (*aufdringlich*) overbearing

II. *adv* penetratingly

penibel [pe·ˈniː·bl̩] *adj geh* (*Ordnung*) meticulous; (*Mensch*) fastidious (**in** +*dat* about)

Penis <-, -se> [ˈpeː·nɪs] *m* penis

Penizillin <-s, -e> [pe·ni·tsɪ·ˈliːn] *nt* penicillin

pennen [ˈpɛ·nən] *vi fam* to sleep

Penner(in) <-s, -> [ˈpɛ·ne] *m(f) pej fam* (*Stadtstreicher*) bum

Pension <-, -en> [pã·ˈzjoːn, pɛn·ˈzjoːn] *f* **1.** TOURIST guesthouse **2.** (*Ruhegehalt*) pension; **in ~ gehen/sein** to retire/ be retired

pensionieren* [pã·zjo·ˈniː·rən] *vt* **pensioniert werden** to be retired off; **sich** *akk* **~ lassen** to retire

Pensum <-s, Pensa> [ˈpɛn·zʊm] *nt geh* work quota

Peperoni [pe·pe·ˈroː·ni] *pl* **1.** (*scharfe Paprikas*) chili peppers *pl* **2.** *schweiz* (*Gemüsepaprikas*) bell peppers *pl*

peppig [ˈpɛ·pɪç] *adj fam* peppy

per [pɛr] *präp* **1.** (*durch*) by; **~ Post** by mail **2. mit jdm ~ du/Sie sein** to address sb with "du"/"Sie"

perfekt [pɛr·ˈfɛkt] I. *adj* perfect II. *adv* perfectly

Perfekt <-s, -e> [ˈpɛr·fɛkt] *nt* perfect [tense]

Perfektion <-> [pɛr·fɛk·ˈtsjoːn] *f kein pl* perfection

Pergamentpapier *nt* wax paper

Periode <-, -n> [pe·ˈrjoː·də] *f* (*a. biol*) period

Perle <-, -n> [ˈpɛr·lə] *f* **1.** (*Schmuckperle*) pearl **2.** (*Kügelchen, Tropfen*) bead

Perlenkette *f* pearl necklace

permanent [pɛr·ma·ˈnɛnt] *geh* I. *adj* permanent II. *adv* permanently

perplex [pɛr·ˈplɛks] *adj* dumbfounded

Perserteppich *m* Persian rug

Person <-, -en> [pɛr·ˈzoːn] *f* (*a. ling*) person

Personal <-s> [pɛr·zo·ˈnaːl] *nt kein pl* staff

Personalausweis *m* identity card, ID

Personalien [pɛr·zo·ˈnaː·li̯ən] *pl* particulars *npl*

Personalpronomen *nt* personal pronoun

Pers<u>o</u>nenkraftwagen m automobile

Pers<u>o</u>nenverkehr m passenger transportation

persönlich [pɛrˈzøːnˌlɪç] **I.** *adj* personal; ~ **werden** to get personal **II.** *adv* personally; ~ **erscheinen** to appear in person

Persönlichkeit <-, -en> f **1.** *kein pl* (*Eigenart*) personality **2.** (*markanter Mensch*) character **3.** (*Prominenter*) celebrity

Perspektive <-, -n> [pɛrsˈpɛkˈtiːvə] f **1.** (*Blickwinkel*) perspective **2.** *geh* (*Zukunftsaussicht*) prospect *usu pl*

perspektivlos *adj* without prospects

Perücke <-, -n> [peˈrʏkə] f wig

pervers [pɛrˈvɛrs] *adj* **1.** (*widernatürlich*) perverted **2.** *fam* (*abartig*) perverse

Perversion <-, -en> [pɛrvɛrˈzjoːn] f perversion

Pessimismus <-> [pɛsiˈmɪsˌmʊs] m *kein pl* pessimism

Pessimist(in) <-en, -en> [pɛsiˈmɪst] *m(f)* pessimist

pessimistisch [pɛsiˈmɪstɪʃ] **I.** *adj* pessimistic **II.** *adv* pessimistically

Pest <-> [pɛst] f *kein pl* **die ~** the plague ▶ **jdn wie die ~ hassen** *fam* to hate sb's guts; **wie die ~ stinken** *fam* to stink to high heaven

Petersilie <-, -n> [peˈtɐˈziːˌliˌə] f parsley

Petroleum <-s> [peˈtroːˌleˌʊm] *nt kein pl* kerosene

petto [ˈpɛto] *adv* ▶ **etw in ~ haben** *fam* to have sth up one's sleeve

petzen [ˈpɛtsn̩] **I.** *vt pej fam* [**jdm**] **etw ~** to tell [sb] about sth **II.** *vi pej fam* to tell

Pfad <-[e]s, -e> [pfaːt] m path

Pfadfinder(in) <-s, -> *m(f)* Boy Scout; (*Mädchen*) Girl Scout

Pfahl <-[e]s, Pfähle> [pfaːl] m post, stake

Pfand <-[e]s, Pfänder> [pfant] *nt* deposit

pfänden [ˈpfɛndn̩] *vt* **1.** (*beschlagnahmen*) to impound **2.** (*Pfandsiegel anbringen*) **jdn ~** to seize some of sb's possessions

Pfandflasche f deposit bottle

Pfanne <-, -n> [ˈpfanə] f **1.** (*Bratpfanne*) [*frying*] pan **2.** *schweiz* (*Topf*) pot ▶ **jdn in die ~ hauen** *sl* to play a mean trick on sb

Pfannkuchen m pancake; (*dünner*) crepe

Pfarramt *nt* vicarage

Pfarrei <-, -en> [pfaˈrai] f **1.** (*Gemeinde*) parish **2.** *s.* **Pfarramt**

Pfarrer(in) <-s, -> [ˈpfarɐ] *m(f)* (*katholisch*) priest; (*evangelisch*) minister

Pfau <-[e]s, -en> [pfau] m peacock

Pfeffer <-s, -> [ˈpfɛfɐ] m pepper ▶ **hingehen, wo der ~ wächst** *fam* to go to hell

Pfefferminze f *kein pl* peppermint

Pfefferminztee m peppermint tea

Pfeffermühle f pepper mill

pfeffern [ˈpfɛfɐn] *vt* KOCHK to season with pepper

Pfeife <-, -n> [ˈpfaifə] f **1.** (*Musikinstrument, Orgelpfeife*) pipe **2.** (*Trillerpfeife*) whistle **3.** (*Tabakpfeife*) pipe **4.** *fam* (*Nichtskönner*) twit ▶ **nach jds ~ tanzen** to dance to sb's tune

pfeifen <pfiff, gepfiffen> [ˈpfaifn̩] **I.** *vt, vi* to whistle **II.** *vi* **auf etw** *akk* ~ *fam* to not give a damn about sth

Pfeifton m whistle

Pfeil <-s, -e> [pfail] m (*a. Richtungspfeil*) arrow

Pfeiler <-s, -> [ˈpfaiˌlɐ] m pillar

Pfennig <-s, -e o meist nach Zahlenangaben -> [ˈpfɛnɪç] m *hist* pfennig; **keinen ~** [**Geld**] **haben** to be penniless ▶ **jeden ~ umdrehen** *fam* to think twice about every penny one spends; **keinen ~ wert sein** *fam* to be worthless

Pferd <-[e]s, -e> [pfeːɐt] *nt* **1.** (*Tier*) horse **2.** (*Schachfigur*) knight ▶ **die ~e scheu machen** *fam* to put people off; **ich glaub' mich tritt ein ~!** *fam* well I'll be damned!

Pferderennen *nt* horse race

Pferdeschwanz m **1.** (*vom Pferd*) horse's tail **2.** (*Frisur*) ponytail

Pferdestall m stable

pfiff [pfɪf] *imp von* **pfeifen**

Pfiff <-s, -e> [pfɪf] m *fam* (*Reiz*) pizzazz

Pfifferling <-[e]s, -e> [ˈpfɪfɐˌlɪŋ] m chan-

terelle ▶ **keinen ~ <u>wert</u> sein** to be worthless

pfiffig [ˈpfɪ.fɪç] **I.** adj smart **II.** adv smartly

Pfingsten <-, -> [ˈpfɪŋs.tn̩] nt meist ohne art Whitsuntide

Pfingstsonntag m Pentecost, Whitsunday

Pfirsich <-s, -e> [ˈpfɪr.zɪç] m peach

Pflanze <-, -n> [ˈpflan.tsə] f plant

pflanzen [ˈpflan.tsn̩] vt to plant

Pflanzenschutzmittel nt pesticide

pflanzlich adj attr **1.** (vegetarisch) vegetarian **2.** (aus Pflanzen gewonnen) plant-based

Pflaster <-s, -> [ˈpflas.tɐ] nt **1.** MED band-aid **2.** BAU pavement ▶ **ein gefährliches ~** fam a dangerous place

Pflasterstein m paving stone

Pflaume <-, -n> [ˈpflau.mə] f **1.** (Frucht) plum **2.** fam s. **Pfeife**

Pflege <-> [ˈpfleː.gə] f kein pl **1.** (eines Kranken) [nursing] care **2.** (des Körpers) grooming **3.** (von Pflanzen, des Gartens) care

pflegebedürftig adj in need of care pred

Pflegeeltern pl foster parents pl

Pflegefall m sb who needs long-term care

Pflegeheim nt nursing home

Pflegekind nt foster child

pflegeleicht adj **1.** (Waschprogramm) permanent press; (Textilien) easy-care attr **2.** (Mensch, Tier) easy-going attr, easy going pred

pflegen [ˈpfleː.gn̩] **I.** vt **1.** (Kranke) to care for, to look after **2.** (Körper) to treat **3.** (Pflanzen, Garten) to tend **4.** (gewöhnlich tun) **etw zu tun ~** to usually do sth **II.** vr sich akk ~ to take care of one's appearance

Pfleger(in) <-s, -> m(f) [male] nurse masc, nurse fem

Pflegesatz m [daily] hospital charges pl

Pflicht <-, -en> [pflɪçt] f duty

pflichtbewusst RR adj conscientious

Pflichtgefühl nt kein pl sense of duty

Pflichtverteidiger(in) m(f) court-appointed defense lawyer

pflücken [ˈpflʏ.kn̩] vt to pick

Pflug <-es, Pflüge> [pfluːk] m plow

pflügen vt, vi to plow

Pforte <-, -n> [ˈpfɔr.tə] f gate

Pförtner(in) <-s, -> [ˈpfœrt.nɐ] m(f) doorman

Pfosten <-s, -> [ˈpfɔs.tn̩] m (a. sport) post

Pfote <-, -n> [ˈpfoː.tə] f **1.** (von Tieren) paw **2.** fam (Hand) paw

Pfund <-[e]s, -e o nach Zahlenangaben -> [pfʊnt] nt **1.** (500 Gramm) ≈ pound **2.** (Währungseinheit) pound; **in ~** in pounds

pfuschen [ˈpfuː.ʃn̩] vi **1.** (schlampen) to be sloppy **2.** dial (mogeln) to cheat (**bei** +dat at/in/on)

Pfuscherei <-, -en> [pfuː.ʃɛˈrai] f bungling

Pfütze <-, -n> [ˈpfʏ.tsə] f puddle

Phänomen <-s, -e> [fɛ.noˈmeːn] nt phenomenon

phänomenal [fɛ.no.meˈnaːl] adj phenomenal

Phantasie <-, -n> [fan.taˈziː] f s. **Fantasie**

phantasieren * [fan.taˈziː.rən] s. **fantasieren**

phantasievoll adj s. **fantasievoll**

phantastisch [fanˈtas.tɪʃ] adj, adv s. **fantastisch**

Phantom <-s, -e> [fanˈtoːm] nt phantom

Phantombild nt composite sketch

Pharmazie <-> [far.maˈtsiː] f kein pl pharmacy

Philippinen [fi.lɪˈpiː.nən] pl **die ~** the Philippines pl

Philippiner(in) <-s, -> [fi.lɪˈpiː.nɐ] m(f) Filipino; s. a. **Deutsche(r)**

philippinisch [fi.lɪˈpiː.nɪʃ] adj Filipino; s. a. **deutsch**

Philologe, Philologin <-n, -n> [fi.loˈloː.gə] m, f philologist

Philosoph(in) <-en, -en> [fi.loˈzoːf] m(f) philosopher

Philosophie <-, -n> [fi.lo.zoˈfiː] f philosophy

philosophieren * [fi.lo.zoˈfiː.rən] vi geh to philosophize (**über** +akk about)

philosophisch [fi.loˈzoː.fɪʃ] adj philosophical

Phobie <-, -n> [foˈbiː] f phobia

P

Phosphat <-[e]s, -e> [fɔsˈfaːt] *nt* phosphate

Phosphor <-s> [ˈfɔsfoːɐ̯] *m kein pl* phosphorus

Phrase <-, -n> [ˈfraːzə] *f pej* empty phrase

Physik <-> [fyˈziːk] *f kein pl* physics + *sing vb, no art*

physikalisch [fyziˈkaːlɪʃ] *adj* physical

Physiker(in) <-s, -> [ˈfyːzike] *m(f)* physicist

Physiotherapeut(in) <-en, -en> [fyzjoteraˈpɔyt] *m(f)* physical therapist

Physiotherapie [fyzjoteraˈpiː] *f kein pl* physical therapy

physisch [ˈfyːzɪʃ] *adj* physical

Pianist(in) <-en, -en> [pjaˈnɪst] *m(f)* pianist

Piano <-s, -s> [ˈpjaːno] *nt* piano

Pickel <-s, -> [ˈpɪkl̩] *m* **1.** (*Hautunreinheit*) pimple, zit *fam* **2.** (*Spitzhacke*) pickax; (*Eispickel*) ice pick

pickelig [ˈpɪkəlɪç] *adj* pimply

picken [ˈpɪkn̩] *vi* ORN to peck (**nach** +*dat* at)

Picknick <-s, -s> [ˈpɪknɪk] *nt* picnic

piepen [ˈpiːpn̩] *vi* to peep; (*Maus*) to squeak; (*Gerät*) to beep

Pier <-s, -s> [piːɐ̯] *m* pier

pietätlos *adj geh* irreverent

pikant [piˈkant] **I.** *adj* **1.** KOCHK spicy **2.** (*frivol*) racy **II.** *adv* piquantly

pikiert [piˈkiːɐ̯t] *geh* **I.** *adj* peeved **II.** *adv* peevishly

piksen [ˈpiːksn̩] **I.** *vt fam* to prick (**mit** +*dat* with) **II.** *vi fam* to prickle

Pilger(in) <-s, -> [ˈpɪlge] *m(f)* pilgrim

pilgern [ˈpɪlgen] *vi sein* **1.** (*wallfahren*) to make a pilgrimage (**nach** to) **2.** *fam* (*gehen, marschieren*) to wend one's way

Pille <-, -n> [ˈpɪlə] *f* pill; **die ~** (*Antibabypille*) the pill; **die ~ danach** the morning-after pill

Pilot(in) <-en, -en> [piˈloːt] *m(f)* pilot

Pils <-, -> [pɪls] *nt* pilsner

Pilz <-es, -e> [pɪlts] *m* **1.** BOT fungus; (*Speisepilz*) mushroom **2.** MED fungal skin infection ▶ **wie ~e aus dem Boden schießen** to shoot up

Pilzerkrankung *f* fungal disease

Pinguin <-s, -e> [ˈpɪŋguiːn] *m* penguin

pinkeln [ˈpɪŋkl̩n] *vi fam* to pee

Pinnwand *f* bulletin board

Pinsel <-s, -> [ˈpɪnzl̩] *m* brush

Pinte <-, -n> [ˈpɪntə] *f fam* bar, pub

Pinzette <-, -n> [pɪnˈtseːtə] *f* tweezers *npl*

Pionier(in) <-s, -e> [pjoˈniːɐ̯] *m(f) geh* (*Wegbereiter*) pioneer

Pirat(in) <-en, -en> [piˈraːt] *m(f)* pirate

pissen [ˈpɪsn̩] *vi* **1.** *derb* (*urinieren*) to piss **2.** *impers sl* (*stark regnen*) **es pisst** it's pouring

Pistazie <-, -n> [pɪsˈtaːtsjə] *f* pistachio

Piste <-, -n> [ˈpɪstə] *f* **1.** (*Skipiste*) ski slope [*o* run] **2.** (*Rollbahn*) runway

Pistole <-, -n> [pɪsˈtoːlə] *f* pistol ▶ **jdm die ~ auf die Brust setzen** *fam* to hold a gun to sb's head

Plackerei <-, -en> [plakəˈrai] *f fam* grind

plädieren * [plɛˈdiːrən] *vi* **1.** JUR **auf etw** *akk* **~** to plead sth; **auf schuldig ~** to plead guilty **2.** *fig geh* **für etw** *akk* **~** to plead for sth

Plädoyer <-s, -s> [plɛdoaˈjeː] *nt* JUR summation

Plage <-, -n> [ˈplaːgə] *f* nuisance

plagen [ˈplaːgn̩] **I.** *vt* **1.** (*mit Fragen, Bitten*) to pester **2.** (*quälen*) to bother; **Zweifel plagten ihn** he was plagued with doubt **II.** *vr* **sich** *akk* **[mit etw** *dat*] **~** **1.** (*sich abrackern*) to slave away [over sth] **2.** (*sich herumplagen*) to be bothered [by sth]

Plakat <-[e]s, -e> [plaˈkaːt] *nt* poster

Plakette <-, -n> [plaˈkɛtə] *f* (*Anstecker*) badge; (*Aufkleber, TÜV-Plakette*) sticker

Plan <-[e]s, Pläne> [plaːn] *m* **1.** (*Vorhaben*) plan; **nach ~ laufen** to go according to plan; **jds Pläne durchkreuzen** to thwart sb's plans **2.** GEOG, TRANSP map **3.** (*zeichnerische Darstellung*) plan

Plane <-, -n> [ˈplaːnə] *f* tarp *fam*

planen [ˈplaːnən] *vt* to plan

Planet <-en, -en> [plaˈneːt] *m* planet

Planetarium <-s, -tarien> [planeˈtaːrjʊm] *nt* planetarium

Planierraupe *f* bulldozer

Planke <-, -n> [ˈplaŋkə] *f* plank

lanlos *adj* 1. (*ziellos*) aimless 2. (*ohne System*) unsystematic

olanmäßig I. *adj* 1. TRANSP scheduled 2. (*systematisch*) systematic **II.** *adv* 1. TRANSP as scheduled, according to schedule 2. (*systematisch*) systematically

Planschbecken *nt* kiddie pool

planschen ['plan·ʃn] *vi* to splash around

Plantage <-, -n> [plan·'taː·ʒə] *f* plantation

Planung <-, -en> *f* planning

Plappermaul *nt bes pej fam* blabbermouth

plappern ['pla·pen] *fam* **I.** *vi* to chatter **II.** *vt* **Unsinn ~** to babble nonsense

Plastik[1] <-s> ['plas·tɪk] *nt kein pl* plastic

Plastik[2] <-, -en> ['plas·tɪk] *f* (*Kunstwerk*) sculpture

Plastikbecher *m* plastic cup

Plastikfolie *f* plastic wrap

Plastiktüte *f* plastic bag

Platin <-s> ['plaː·tiːn] *nt kein pl* platinum

platonisch [pla·'toː·nɪʃ] *adj geh* platonic

plätschern ['plɛ·tʃen] *vi* (*Brunnen*) to splash; (*Bach*) to babble; (*Regen*) to patter

platt [plat] **I.** *adj* 1. (*flach*) flat 2. (*geistlos*) dull 3. *fam* (*verblüfft*) **~ sein** to be flabbergasted **II.** *adv* flat; **~ drücken** to flatten

Platt <-[s]> [plat] *nt kein pl*, **Plattdeutsch** ['plat·dɔytʃ] *nt* Low German

Platte <-, -n> ['pla·tə] *f* 1. (*Steinplatte*) slab 2. (*Metallplatte*) sheet 3. (*Schallplatte*) record 4. (*Servierteller, Gericht*) platter 5. (*Kochplatte*) burner

Plattenspieler *m* record player

Plattform *f* (*a. comput*) platform

Platz <-es, Plätze> [plats] *m* 1. (*Ort, Stelle*) place 2. (*öffentlicher Platz*) square 3. (*Sitzplatz*) seat; **~ nehmen** *geh* to take a seat 4. (*freier Raum*) room 5. (*Sportplatz*) playing field 6. (*Rang*) place; **er liegt jetzt auf ~ drei** he's now in third place ▶ **fehl am ~[e] sein** to be out of place

Platzangst *f* 1. *fam* claustrophobia 2. (*Agoraphobie*) agoraphobia

Plätzchen <-s, -> ['plɛts·çən] *nt* 1. *dim* von **Platz** spot 2. (*Keks*) cookie

platzen ['pla·tsn] *vi sein* 1. (*zerplatzen*) to burst; **vor Ärger/Neugier ~** *fig* to be bursting with anger/curiosity 2. (*aufplatzen*) to split 3. (*fam (scheitern)*) to fall through; **das Fest ist geplatzt** the party is off

platzieren * RR [pla·'tsiː·rən] *vt* to place

Platzkarte *f* seat reservation

Platzregen *m* cloudburst

Platzwunde *f* laceration

plaudern ['plau·den] *vi* 1. (*sich gemütlich unterhalten*) to [have a] chat 2. *fam* (*ausplaudern*) to gossip

plausibel [plau·'ziː·bl] *adj* plausible

Playboy <-s, -s> ['pleː·bɔy] *m* playboy

Plazenta <-, -s> [pla·'tsɛn·ta] *f* placenta

plazieren * ALT [pla·'tsiː·rən] *vt s.* **platzieren**

pleite ['plai·tə] *adj fam* broke

Pleite <-, -n> ['plai·tə] *f fam* 1. (*Bankrott*) bankruptcy; **~ machen** to go bust 2. (*Reinfall*) flop

pleite|gehen RR *vi irreg sein* to go bankrupt

Plombe <-, -n> ['plɔm·bə] *f* 1. MED (*im Zahn*) filling 2. (*Bleisiegel*) lead seal

plombieren * [plɔm·'biː·rən] *vt* 1. MED (*Zahn*) to fill 2. (*amtlich versiegeln*) to seal

plötzlich ['plœts·lɪç] **I.** *adj* sudden **II.** *adv* suddenly, all of a sudden; **das kommt alles etwas/so ~** it's all happening rather/so suddenly

plump [plʊmp] **I.** *adj* 1. (*massig*) plump 2. (*schwerfällig*) ungainly 3. (*dummdreist*) obvious; (*Lüge*) blatant **II.** *adv* 1. (*schwerfällig*) clumsily 2. (*dummdreist*) crassly

Plunder <-s> ['plʊn·de] *m kein pl* junk

plündern ['plʏn·den] **I.** *vt* 1. (*ausrauben*) to plunder 2. *fam* (*leeren*) to raid **II.** *vi* to plunder

Plural <-s, -e> ['pluː·raːl] *m* plural

plus [plʊs] *konj, präp, adv* plus; **6 ~ 4 ist 10** 6 plus 4 is 10; **wir haben fünf Grad ~** it's five degrees above zero

Plus <-, -> [plʊs] *nt* 1. (*Pluszeichen*) plus 2. ÖKON surplus; **~ machen** to make a profit; **[mit etw** *dat*] **im ~ sein** to be in the black [with sth]

P

Plüsch <-[e]s, -e> [plyʃ] m plush

Plüschtier nt stuffed animal

Plusquamperfekt <-s, -e> ['plʊs·kvam·pɛr·fɛkt] nt past perfect, pluperfect

Po <-s, -s> [po:] m fam butt

pochen ['pɔ·xn̩] vi 1. (anklopfen) to knock (**gegen/auf** +akk against/on) 2. (Herz, Blut) to pound 3. (bestehen) to insist (**auf** +akk on)

Pocken pl smallpox no art

Podest <-[e]s, -e> [po·'dɛst] nt o m podium, rostrum

Poesie <-> [poe·'zi:] f kein pl poetry

Poet(in) <-en, -en> [po·'e:t] m(f) poet

poetisch [po·'e:·tɪʃ] adj poetic[al]

Pointe <-, -n> ['pɔɛ̃·tə] f (einer Erzählung) point; (eines Witzes) punch line

Pokal <-s, -e> [po·'ka:l] m 1. (Trinkbecher) goblet 2. sport trophy, cup

Poker <-s> ['po:·ke] nt kein pl poker

pokern ['po:·ken] vi 1. karten to play poker; **um etw ~** to gamble for sth 2. (viel riskieren) to stake a lot

Pol <-s, -e> [po:l] m elek, geog, phys pole ▶ **der ruhende ~** the calming influence

Polarkreis m polar circle; **nördlicher/südlicher ~** Arctic/Antarctic circle

Polarstern m Polaris

Pole, Polin <-n, -n> ['po:·lə] m, f Pole; s. a. **Deutsche(r)**

polemisch [po·'le:·mɪʃ] adj geh polemical

Polen <-s> ['po:·lən] nt Poland; s. a. **Deutschland**

polieren* [po·'li:·rən] vt to polish

Politesse <-, -n> [po·li·'tɛsə] f meter maid

Politik <-, -en> [po·li·'ti:k] f 1. kein pl politics + sing vb, no art 2. (Strategie) policy

Politiker(in) <-s, -> [po·'li:·ti·ke] m(f) politician

politisch [po·'li:·tɪʃ] I. adj 1. pol political 2. (klug) politic II. adv 1. pol politically 2. (klug) judiciously

Politologe, Politologin <-n, -n> [po·li·to·'lo:·gə] m, f political scientist

Polizei <-, -en> [po·li·'tsai] f pl selten 1. (Institution) **die ~** the police + sing/pl vb; **bei der ~ sein** to be a police officer 2. kein pl (Dienstgebäude) police

Polizeibeamte(r) m, **-beamtin** f police officer

polizeilich I. adj attr police attr II. ad by the police; **~ gemeldet sein** to be registered with the police

Polizeipräsident(in) m(f) chief of police

Polizeipräsidium nt police headquarters + sing/pl vb

Polizeirevier nt 1. (Dienststelle) police station 2. (Bezirk) [police] precinct

Polizeischutz m police protection

Polizeistreife f police patrol

Polizist(in) <-en, -en> [po·li·'tsɪst] m(f) police officer, policeman masc, policewoman fem

Pollen <-s, -> ['pɔ·lən] m pollen

Pollenflug m kein pl pollen dispersal

polnisch ['pɔl·nɪʃ] adj Polish; s. a. **deutsch**

Polster <-s, -> ['pɔls·te] nt o österr m 1. (von Möbeln) upholstery 2. (an Kleidung) pad 3. (Rücklage) cushion **ein finanzielles ~** financial reserves p 4. österr (Kissen) cushion

Polterabend ['pɔl·te-] m party at the house of the bride's parents on the eve of a wedding, at which dishes are smashed to bring good luck

poltern ['pɔl·ten] vi 1. haben (rumpeln) to bang 2. sein (krachend fallen) **de Schrank polterte die Treppe hinunter** the cupboard went crashing down the stairs 3. sein (lärmend gehen) to stomp

Polyester <-s, -> [po·ly·'ʔɛs·te] m polyester

Polygamie <-> [po·ly·ga·'mi:] f kein pl polygamy

Pomade <-, -n> [po·'ma:·də] f pomade

Pommes ['pɔ·məs] pl fam, **Pommes frites** [pɔm·'frɪt] pl [French] fries pl

pompös [pɔm·'pøːs] I. adj grandiose II. adv grandiosely

Pony¹ <-s, -s> ['pɔ·ni] nt (Pferd) pony

Pony² <-s, -s> ['pɔ·ni] m bangs npl

Popo <-s, -s> [po·'po:] m fam butt

populär [po·pu·'lɛːɐ̯] adj popular

Popularität <-> [po·pu·la·ri·'tɛːt] f kein pl popularity

Pore <-, -n> ['po:·rə] f pore

Porno <-s, -s> ['pɔr·no] m fam porn

Pornografie[RR], **Pornographie** <-> [pɔr·no·gra·'fi:] f kein pl pornography

porös [po·'rø:s] adj porous

Portal <-s, -e> [pɔr·'ta:l] nt portal

Portemonnaie <-s, -s> [pɔrt·mɔ·'ne:] nt s. **Portmonee**

Portier <-s, -s> [pɔr·'tje:] m doorman

Portion <-, -en> [pɔr·'tsjo:n] f 1. (beim Essen) portion 2. fam (Anteil) amount
▶ eine <u>halbe</u> ~ fam a half-pint

Portmonee[RR] <-s, -s> [pɔrt·mɔ·'ne:] nt wallet, change purse

Porto <-s, -s> ['pɔr·to] nt postage

Porträt <-s, -s> [pɔr·'trɛ:] nt portrait

Portugal <-s> ['pɔr·tu·gal] nt Portugal; s. a. **Deutschland**

Portugiese, Portugiesin <-n, -n> [pɔr·tu·'gi:·zə] m, f Portuguese; s. a. **Deutsche(r)**

portugiesisch [pɔr·tu·'gi:·zɪʃ] adj Portuguese; s. a. **deutsch**

Portugiesisch [pɔr·tu·'gi:·zɪʃ] nt dekl wie adj Portuguese; s. a. **Deutsch 1**

Portwein ['pɔrt·vain] m port [wine]

Porzellan <-s, -e> [pɔr·tsɛ·'la:n] nt 1. (Material) porcelain 2. kein pl (Geschirr) china

Posaune <-, -n> [po·'zau·nə] f trombone

Pose <-, -n> ['po:·zə] f pose

Position <-, -en> [po·zi·'tsjo:n] f position

positiv ['po:·zi·ti:f] I. adj positive; ~ [für jdn] sein to be good news [for sb] II. adv positively; etw ~ beeinflussen to have a positive influence on sth; sich akk ~ verändern to change for the better

Post <-> [pɔst] f kein pl 1. (Institution) Post Office; etw mit der/per ~ schicken to send sth in the mail, to mail sth 2. (Dienststelle) post office; auf die/zur ~ gehen to go to the post office 3. (Briefsendungen) mail; elektronische ~ electronic mail

Postamt nt post office

Postbeamte(r) m, **-beamtin** f post office clerk

Postbote, -botin m, f mail carrier, post-

man masc, mailman masc

Posten <-s, -> ['pɔs·tn̩] m 1. (zugewiesene Position) post 2. (Anstellung) position 3. ÖKON (Position) item

Postfach nt 1. (Schließfach) post office [o PO] box 2. (offenes Fach) pigeonhole

Postgiroamt [-ʒi·ro-] nt bank operated by the post office

Postgirokonto [-ʒi·ro-] nt postal checking account

Postkarte f postcard

Postleitzahl f Zip Code

Postscheck m postal check

Poststempel m (Abdruck) postmark

Potenz <-, -en> [po·'tɛnts] f (sexuell) potency

Pott <-[e]s, Pötte> [pɔt] m fam (Topf) pot

Pracht <-> [praxt] f kein pl splendor
▶ eine <u>wahre</u> ~ sein fam to be [really] great

prächtig ['prɛç·tɪç] adj 1. (prunkvoll) magnificent 2. (großartig) splendid

Prädikat <-[e]s, -e> [prɛ·di·'ka:t] nt 1. LING predicate 2. (Auszeichnung) rating

Präfix <-es, -e> [prɛ·'fɪks, 'prɛ:·fɪks] nt prefix

Prag <-s> [pra:k] nt Prague

prägen ['prɛ:·gn̩] vt 1. (Münzen) to mint 2. (Wort) to coin 3. fig (formen) jdn ~ to leave its/their mark on sb

pragmatisch [prag·'ma:·tɪʃ] I. adj pragmatic II. adv pragmatically

prähistorisch [prɛ·hɪs·'to:·rɪʃ] adj prehistoric

prahlen ['pra:·lən] vi to boast, to brag pej fam (mit +dat about)

Prahler(in) <-s, -> m(f) bragger

prahlerisch adj boastful

Praktik <-, -en> ['prak·tɪk] f meist pl practice

Praktikant(in) <-en, -en> [prak·ti·'kant] m(f) intern

praktisch ['prak·tɪʃ] I. adj practical; (Beispiel) concrete II. adv 1. (so gut wie) practically 2. (in der Praxis) in practice

praktizieren* [prak·ti·'tsi:·rən] vt, vi to practice; ~der Arzt practicing doctor

Praline <-, -n> [pra·'li:·nə] *f* praline, [piece of] chocolate

prall [pral] *adj* **1.** (*sehr voll: Brüste*) well-rounded; (*Schenkel, Waden*) sturdy; (*Euter*) swollen **2.** (*Sonne*) blazing **3. eine ~ gefüllte Brieftasche** a bulging wallet

prallen ['pra·lən] *vi sein* to crash (**gegen** +*akk* into); (*Ball*) to bounce

Prämie <-, -n> ['prɛː·mi̯ə] *f* **1.** (*zusätzliche Vergütung*) bonus **2.** (*Versicherungsbeitrag*) [insurance] premium **3.** (*staatliche Prämie*) [government] premium

Pranke <-, -n> ['praŋ·kə] *f* paw; *hum a.* mitt *sl*

Präposition <-, -en> [prɛ·po·zi·'tsi̯oːn] *f* preposition

Prärie <-, -n> [prɛ·'riː] *f* prairie

Präsens <-, Präsentia> ['prɛː·zɛns] *nt* present tense

Präsentation <-, -en> [prɛ·zɛn·ta·'tsi̯oːn] *f* presentation

präsentieren * [prɛ·zɛn·'tiː·rən] *vt* **jdm etw** *akk* **~** to present sb with sth

Präservativ <-s, -e> [prɛ·zɛr·va·'tiːf] *nt* condom

Präsident(in) <-en, -en> [prɛ·zi·'dɛnt] *m(f)* president

Präsidium <-s, Präsidien> [prɛ·'ziː·di̯·um] *nt* **1.** (*Vorstand, Vorsitz*) chairmanship **2.** (*Führungsgruppe*) committee **3.** (*Polizeipräsidium*) [police] headquarters + *sing/pl vb*

Praxis <-, Praxen> ['prak·sɪs] *f* **1.** (*Arztpraxis*) doctor's office; (*Anwaltspraxis*) law practice **2.** *kein pl* (*Erfahrung*) [practical] experience **3.** *kein pl* (*Anwendung*) practice *no art;* **etw in die ~ umsetzen** to put sth into practice

präzise [prɛ·'tsiː·zə] *adj geh* precise; (*Beschreibung*) exact

predigen ['preː·di·gn̩] *vt, vi* to preach; **jdm etw** *akk* **~** *fam* to lecture sb on/about sth

Prediger(in) <-s, -> *m(f)* preacher

Predigt <-, -en> ['preː·dɪçt] *f a. fam* sermon

Preis <-es, -e> [prais] *m* **1.** (*Kaufpreis*) price (**für** +*akk* of); **zum halben ~ a** [*o* for] half-price **2.** (*Gewinn*) prize; **der erste ~** [the] first prize ► **um jeder ~** at all costs

Preisanstieg *m* price increase

Preisausschreiben *nt* competition, contest

Preiselbeere ['prai·zl̩·beː·rə] *f* [mountain *spec*] cranberry

Preisempfehlung *f* recommended price

preisen <pries, gepriesen> ['prai·zn̩] *v* *geh* to praise

Preisermäßigung *f* price reduction

Preisfrage *f* **1.** (*Quizfrage*) contest question **2.** (*vom Preis abhängende Entscheidung*) question of price

preisgeben ['prais·geː·bn̩] *vt irreg geh* **1.** (*Geheimnis*) to divulge; **jdm etw** *akk* **~** to betray sth to sb **2. jdn der Lächerlichkeit ~** to expose sb to ridicule

preisgekrönt *adj* award-winning *attr*

preisgünstig *adj* inexpensive; (*Angebot*) very reasonable; **etw ~ bekommen** to get a good deal on sth

Preis-Leistungs-Verhältnis *nt kein p* cost-effectiveness, cost-benefit ratio

Preisnachlass [RR] *m* discount

Preisrätsel *nt* puzzle competition

Preisschild *nt* price tag

Preissenkung *f* reduction in prices

Preissteigerung *f* price increase

preiswert *adj s.* **preisgünstig**

Prellung <-, -en> *f* contusion *spec* (**ar** +*dat* on)

Premiere <-, -n> [prə·'mi̯eː·rə] *f* première

Premierminister(in) *m(f)* prime minister

Presse <-, -n> ['prɛ·sə] *f* **1.** (*Gerät*) press (*Fruchtpresse*) juice extractor **2.** *kein pl* **die ~** (*Zeitungen und Zeitschriften*) the press

Presseagentur *f* press agency

Pressefreiheit *f kein pl* freedom of the press

Pressekonferenz *f* press conference

Pressemeldung *f* press report

pressen ['prɛ·sn̩] *vt* to press; (*Saft*) to squeeze (**aus** +*dat* out of)

Pressesprecher(in) *m(f)* spokesman

Prestige <-s> [prɛs·'tiː·ʒə] *nt kein pl geh* prestige

preußisch ['prɔy·sɪʃ] *adj* Prussian

prickeln ['prɪ·kl̩n] *vi* 1. (*kribbeln*) to tingle; **ein P~ in den Beinen** pins and needles in one's legs 2. (*erregen, reizen*) to thrill

prickelnd *adj* (*Gefühl*) tingling; (*Humor*) piquant; (*Champagner*) sparkling

Priester(in) <-s, -> ['priːs·te] *m(f)* priest *masc*, priestess *fem*

prima ['priː·ma] *adj fam* great; **es läuft alles ~** everything is going really well

primitiv [pri·mi·'tiːf] *adj* primitive; **ein ~er Kerl** a big ape

Prinz <-en, -en> [prɪnts] *m* prince

Prinzessin <-, -nen> ['prɪn·tsɛ·sɪn] *f* princess

Prinzip <-s, -ien> [prɪn·'tsiːp] *nt* principle; **aus/im ~** on/in principle

prinzipiell [prɪn·tsi·'pi̯ɛl] I. *adj* fundamental II. *adv* (*aus Prinzip*) on principle; (*im Prinzip*) in principle

Priorität <-, -en> [pri̯o·ri·'tɛːt] *f geh* priority (**vor** +*dat* over)

Prise <-, -n> ['priː·zə] *f* pinch

privat [pri·'vaːt] I. *adj* private II. *adv* privately; **sich** *akk* **~ versichern** to take out private insurance

Privatdetektiv(in) *m(f)* private investigator

Privatgrundstück *nt* private property *npl*

Privatleben *nt kein pl* private life

Privatpatient(in) *m(f)* private patient

Privatschule *f* private school

Privatsekretär(in) *m(f)* private secretary

Privatsphäre *f kein pl* privacy

Privileg <-[e]s, -ien> [pri·vi·'leːk] *nt geh* privilege

pro [proː] *präp* per; **~ Kopf** a head; **~ Person** per person; **~ Stück** each

Pro <-> [proː] *nt kein pl* [**das**] **~ und** [**das**] **Kontra** *geh* the pros and cons *pl*

Probe <-, -n> ['proː·bə] *f* 1. (*Warenprobe, Testmenge*) sample 2. (*Theater*) rehearsal 3. (*Prüfung*) test ▶ **auf ~** on probation; **jds Geduld auf eine harte ~ stellen** to try sb's patience; **jdn auf die ~ stellen** to put sb to the test;

zur ~ on a trial basis

Probealarm *m* fire drill

Probefahrt *f* test drive

proben ['proː·bn̩] *vt, vi* to rehearse

Probezeit *f* probationary period

probieren* [pro·'biː·rən] *vt, vi* to try; **von etw** *dat* **~** to try some of sth; **~, ob ...** to try and see whether ...

Problem <-s, -e> [pro·'bleːm] *nt* problem

problematisch [pro·ble·'maː·tɪʃ] *adj* problematic[al]; (*Kind*) difficult

problemlos I. *adj* problem-free, unproblematic *attr* II. *adv* without any problems

Produkt <-[e]s, -e> [pro·'dʊkt] *nt* product

Produktion <-, -en> [pro·dʊk·'tsi̯oːn] *f* production

produktiv [pro·dʊk·'tiːf] *adj geh* productive

Produzent(in) <-en, -en> [pro·du·'tsɛnt] *m(f)* producer

produzieren* [pro·du·'tsiː·rən] *vt* to produce

professionell [pro·fɛ·si̯o·'nɛl] *adj* professional

Professor, Professorin <-s, -soren> [pro·'fɛ·soːɐ̯, pro·fɛ·'soː·rɪn] *m, f* 1. (*Universitätsprofessor*) professor 2. *österr* (*Gymnasiallehrer*) ≈ high-school teacher

Profi <-s, -s> ['proː·fi] *m fam* pro

Profil <-s, -e> [pro·'fiːl] *nt* 1. (*eines Reifens, einer Schuhsohle*) tread 2. (*Seitenansicht*) profile

Profit <-[e]s, -e> [pro·'fiːt, pro·'fɪt] *m* profit

profitabel [pro·fi·'taː·bl̩] *adj* profitable; (*stärker*) lucrative

profitieren* [pro·fi·'tiː·rən] *vi* to profit (**von, bei** +*dat* from/with)

pro forma [proː·'fɔr·ma] *adv* pro forma, as a formality

Prognose <-, -n> [pro·'gnoː·zə] *f* prognosis; (*Wetter*) forecast

Programm <-s, -e> [pro·'gram] *nt* 1. (*geplanter Ablauf*) program; (*Tagesordnung*) agenda; (*Zeitplan*) schedule; **ein volles ~ haben** to have a full day/week etc. ahead [of oneself]; **was**

P

steht für heute auf dem ~? what's the agenda/program/schedule for today? **2.** RADIO, TV (*Sender*) channel **3.** (*Programmheft*) program **4.** COMPUT [computer] program

Programmfehler m COMPUT program error, bug

programmieren * [pro·gra·'mi:·rən] vt COMPUT to program

Programmierer(in) <-s, -> m(f) programmer

progressiv [pro·grɛ·'si:f] adj geh progressive

Projekt <-[e]s, -e> [pro·'jɛkt] nt project

Projektleiter(in) <-s, -> m(f) project manager

Projektor <-s, -toren> [pro·'jɛk·to:ɐ̯] m projector

projizieren * [pro·ji·'tsi:·rən] vt a. fig to project (**auf** +akk on[to])

Pro-Kopf-Einkommen [pro·'kɔpf-] nt per capita income

Prolet <-en, -en> [pro·'le:t] m pej redneck pej sl

Proll <-s, -s> ['prɔl] m pej sl s. **Prolet**

Prolog <-[e]s, -e> [pro·'lo:k] m prolog[ue]

Promenade <-, -n> [pro·mə·'na:·də] f promenade

Promille <-[s], -> [pro·'mɪ·lə] nt **1.** (*Tausendstel*) per mill[l] **2.** pl fam (*Alkoholpegel*) [blood] alcohol level; **0,5 ~** blood alcohol level of 0.05 [percent]

Promillegrenze f legal [alcohol] limit

prominent [pro·mi·'nɛnt] adj prominent

Prominenz <-> [pro·mi·'nɛnts] f kein pl (*die Prominenten*) prominent figures pl

prompt [prɔmpt] **I.** adj prompt **II.** adv **1.** (*sofort*) promptly **2.** meist iron **er ist ~ auf den Trick hereingefallen** naturally, he fell for the trick

Pronomen <-s, -> [pro·'no:·mən] nt pronoun

Propaganda <-> [pro·pa·'gan·da] f kein pl **1.** POL a. pej propaganda **2.** (*Werbung*) publicity

Propangas nt kein pl propane [gas]

Propeller <-s, -> [pro·'pɛ·le] m propeller

Prophet(in) <-en, -en> [pro·'fe:t] m(f) prophet masc, prophetess fem

prophezeien * [pro·fe·'tsai·ən] vt to prophesy, to predict

Prophezeiung <-, -en> f prophecy

prophylaktisch [pro·fy·'lak·tɪʃ] adj prophylactic

Proportion <-, -en> [pro·pɔr·'tsjo:n] f geh proportion

proportional [pro·pɔr·tsjo·'na:l] adj geh proportional (**zu** +dat to)

Prosa <-> ['pro:·za] f kein pl prose

Prospekt <-[e]s, -e> [pros·'pɛkt] m (*Werbebroschüre*) brochure; (*Werbezettel*) flier

prost [pro:st] interj cheers

Prostata <-, Prostatae> ['prɔs·ta·ta] f ANAT prostate gland

Prostituierte(r) [pros·ti·tu·'i:ɐ̯·tə, -tɐ] f(m) prostitute

Prostitution <-> [pros·ti·tu·'tsjo:n] f kein pl prostitution

Protein <-s, -e> [pro·te·'i:n] nt protein

Protest <-[e]s, -e> [pro·'tɛst] m protest

Protestant(in) <-en, -en> [pro·tɛs·'tant] m(f) Protestant

protestieren * [pro·tɛs·'ti:·rən] vi to protest

Prothese <-, -n> [pro·'te:·zə] f prosthesis spec

Protokoll <-s, -e> [pro·to·'kɔl] nt **1.** (*Niederschrift*) record[s pl]; (*einer Sitzung*) minutes npl; **etw zu ~ geben** (*bei der Polizei*) to make a statement **2.** dial (*Strafmandat*) ticket **3.** kein pl (*Zeremoniell*) **gegen das ~ verstoßen** to break with protocol

protzen ['prɔ·tsn̩] vi fam [**mit etw** dat] **~** to flaunt [sth]

protzig ['prɔ·tsɪç] adj fam showy; (*Auto*) fancy

Proviant <-s, -e> [pro·'vi̯ant] m pl selten provisions; MIL supplies

Provinz <-, -en> [pro·'vɪnts] f **1.** (*Verwaltungsgebiet*) province **2.** kein pl (*rückständige Gegend*) provinces pl a. pej; **in der ~ leben** to live [out] in the sticks fam

provinziell [pro·vɪn·'tsi̯ɛl] adj provincial a. pej

Provision <-, -en> [pro·vi·'zi̯o:n] f commission

provisorisch [pro·vi·'zo:·rɪʃ] **I.** adj provisional; (*Unterkunft*) temporary **II.** adv temporarily

Provokation <-, -en> [pro·vo·ka·'tsjo:n] f provocation

provozieren * [pro·vo·'tsi:·rən] vt to provoke; (Streit) to cause; **jdn zu etw** dat ~ to provoke sb into [doing] sth

Prozent <-[e]s, -e> [pro·'tsɛnt] nt **1.** (Hundertstel) percent **2.** (Alkoholgehalt) alcohol content **3.** pl (Rabatt) discount

Prozentsatz m percentage

ProzessRR <-es, -e>, **Prozeß**ALT <-sses, -sse> [pro·'tsɛs] m **1.** (Gerichtsverfahren) [court] case; (Strafverfahren) trial; **einen ~ [gegen jdn] führen** to take legal action [against sb] **2.** geh (Vorgang) process ▶ **mit jdm/etw kurzen ~ machen** fam to make short work of sb/sth

prozessieren * [pro·tsɛ·'si:·rən] vi [gegen jdn] ~ to take [sb] to court

Prozession <-, -en> [pro·tsɛ·'sjo:n] f procession

ProzesskostenRR pl court costs

Prozessor <-s, -soren> [pro·'tsɛ·so:ɐ̯, -'so:·rən] m COMPUT processor

prüde ['pry:·də] adj pej prudish

prüfen ['pry:·fn̩] vt **1.** (überprüfen, untersuchen) to check (auf +akk for); (Material) to test **2.** (Kenntnisse abfragen) to examine

Prüfung <-, -en> f **1.** (Examen) exam[ination]; (für den Führerschein) test; **mündliche ~ [in etw** dat] oral exam[ination] [in sth] **2.** (Überprüfung) checking; (von Material) test **3.** geh (Heimsuchung) trial

Prüfungsangst f pre-exam jitters

Prügel ['pry:·gl̩] pl thrashing; **jdm eine Tracht ~ verabreichen** to give sb a [good] beating

Prügelei <-, -en> [pry:·gə·'lai] f fam [fist] fight

Prügelknabe m fam whipping boy

prügeln ['pry:·gl̩n] I. vt, vi to hit II. vr **sich** akk ~ to fight

Prügelstrafe f **die** ~ corporal punishment

Prunk <-s> [prʊŋk] m kein pl magnificence

prusten ['pru:s·tn̩] vi fam to snort; (beim Trinken) to splutter

Pseudonym <-s, -e> [psɔy·do·'ny:m] nt pseudonym

Psyche <-, -n> ['psy:·çə] f psyche

Psychiater(in) <-s, -> [psy'çia:·te] m(f) psychiatrist

Psychiatrie <-, -n> [psyçia·'tri:] f **1.** kein pl (Fachgebiet) psychiatry no art **2.** fam (Abteilung) psychiatric ward

psychiatrisch [psy'çia:·trɪʃ] adj psychiatric

psychisch ['psy:·çɪʃ] adj psychological, mental

Psychoanalytiker(in) [psy·ço·ʔana·'ly:·ti·ke] m(f) psychoanalyst

Psychologe, Psychologin <-n -n> [psy·ço·'lo:·gə] m, f psychologist

psychologisch [psy·ço·'lo:·gɪʃ] adj psychological

Psychopath(in) <-en, -en> [psy·ço·'pa:t] m(f) psychopath

Psychose <-, -n> [psy·'ço:·zə] f psychosis

psychosomatisch [psy·ço·zo·'ma:·tɪʃ] adj psychosomatic

Psychotherapeut(in) [psy·ço·te·ra·'pɔyt] m(f) psychotherapist

Pubertät <-> [pu·bɛr·'tɛ:t] f kein pl puberty no art

Publikum <-s> ['pu:·bli·kʊm] nt kein pl audience; (im Theater a.) house; (beim Sport) crowd

publizieren * [pu·bli·'tsi:·rən] vt to publish

Pudding <-s, -s> ['pʊ·dɪŋ] m KOCHK pudding

Pudel <-s, -> ['pu:·dl̩] m poodle

pudelwohl ['pu:·dl̩·'vo:l] adj fam **sich** akk ~ **fühlen** to feel like a million bucks

Puder <-s, -> ['pu:·de] m o fam nt powder

pudern ['pu:·den] vt to powder

Puderzucker m powdered [o confectioner's] sugar

Puff¹ <-[e]s, Püffe> [pʊf] m fam (Stoß) thump; (in die Seite) prod

Puff² <-[e]s, -s> [pʊf] m fam brothel, whorehouse

Puffer <-s, -> ['pʊ·fe] m **1.** BAHN bumper **2.** (Kartoffelpuffer) potato pancake, ≈ latke

Pullover <-s, -s> [pʊ·'lo:·ve] m sweater

P

Puls <-es, -e> [pʊls] *m* pulse

Pult <-[e]s, -e> [pʊlt] *nt* **1.** (*Rednerpult*) lectern **2.** (*Schaltpult*) control panel

Pulver <-s, -> ['pʊl·vɐ] *nt* powder

Pulverkaffee *m* instant coffee

Pulverschnee *m* powder[y] snow

Puma <-s, -s> ['puː·ma] *m* puma, mountain lion, cougar

pummelig ['pʊ·mə·lɪç] *adj fam* chubby

Pump ['pʊmp] *m* ► **auf ~** *fam* on credit

Pumpe <-, -n> ['pʊm·pə] *f* **1.** (*Gerät*) pump **2.** *fam* (*Herz*) heart

pumpen ['pʊm·pn̩] *vt* **1.** (*mittels einer Pumpe*) to pump **2.** *fam* (*leihen*) **jdm etw** *akk* **~** to lend sb sth; **sich** *dat* **etw** *akk* [**bei/von jdm**] **~** to borrow sth [from sb]

Punker(in) <-s, -> ['paŋ·kɐ] *m(f)* punk [rocker]

Punkt <-[e]s, -e> [pʊŋkt] *m* **1.** (*runder Fleck*) spot; (*in der Mathematik*) point **2.** (*Stelle*) spot; (*genauer*) point; **bis zu einem gewissen ~** up to a certain point **3.** (*Satzzeichen*) period; (*auf i, Auslassungszeichen*) dot **4.** (*Bewertungseinheit*) point **5.** (*Detailpunkt*) point; (*auf der Tagesordnung*) point **6. um ~ acht** [**Uhr**] at exactly eight [o'clock] ► **ein dunkler ~** [**in jds Vergangenheit**] a dark chapter [in sb's past]; **ohne ~ und Komma reden** *fam* to rattle on and on; **nun mach aber mal einen ~!** *fam* come off it!; **der springende ~** the crucial point

pünktlich ['pʏŋkt·lɪç] **I.** *adj* punctual **II.** *adv* punctually

Pünktlichkeit <-> *f kein pl* punctuality

Punktzahl *f* SPORT score

Punsch <-es, -e> [pʊnʃ] *m* [hot] punch

Pupille <-, -n> [pu·'pɪ·lə] *f* pupil

Puppe <-, -n> ['pʊ·pə] *f* (*Spielzeug*) doll ► **bis in die ~n** *fam* until the wee hours of the morning; **bis in die ~n schlafen** *fam* to sleep until all hours

Puppentheater *nt* puppet theater

pur [puːɐ̯] *adj* **1.** (*rein, unverdünnt*) pure; **etw ~ trinken** to drink sth straight **2.** *fam* (*blank, bloß*) sheer, pure; (*Wahnsinn*) absolute

Püree <-s, -s> [py·'reː] *nt* **1.** (*passiertes Gemüse/Obst*) purée **2.** (*Kartoffelbrei*) mashed potatoes *pl*

Purzelbaum ['pʊr·ts|-] *m fam* somersault

purzeln ['pʊr·ts|n̩] *vi sein* (*a. Preise*) to tumble

Puste <-> ['puː·stə] *f kein pl fam* breath; **aus der ~ kommen** to get out of breath

Pustel <-, -n> ['pʊs·tl̩] *f* pimple

pusten ['puː·s·tn̩] *vt, vi fam* to blow

Puter <-s, -> ['puː·tɐ] *m* tom, gobbler

puterrot ['puː·tɐ·'roːt] *adj* scarlet

Putsch <-[e]s, -e> [pʊtʃ] *m* coup [d'état]

Putschist(in) <-en, -en> [pʊt·'ʃɪst] *m(f)* rebel

Putz <-es> [pʊts] *m kein pl* (*Wandverkleidung*) plaster; (*bei Außenmauern*) [soft lime] stucco ► **auf den ~ hauen** *fam* (*angeben*) to show off; (*übermütig sein*) to go wild [*o* to town]

putzen ['pʊ·tsn̩] **I.** *vt* to clean; (*Gemüse*) to prepare; (*Spinat*) to wash; **putz dir den Dreck von den Schuhen!** wipe the mud off your shoes!; **sich** *dat* **die Nase ~** to blow one's nose; **sich** *dat* **die Zähne ~** to brush one's teeth **II.** *vi* ► **~ gehen** to work as a housekeeper

Putzfrau *f* maid, cleaning lady

putzig ['pʊ·tsɪç] *adj fam* (*niedlich*) sweet; (*Tier*) cute

Putzlappen *m* rag

Putzmittel *nt* detergent

Puzzle <-s, -s> ['pʊ·z|, 'pa·z|] *nt* jigsaw [puzzle]

Pyjama <-s, -s> [py·'dʒa·ma] *m* pajamas *npl*

Pyramide <-, -n> [py·ra·'miː·də] *f* pyramid

Pyrenäen [py·re·'nɛː·ən] *pl* **die ~** the Pyrenees *npl*

Pythonschlange *f* python

Q

Q, q <-, -> [kuː] *nt* Q, q; **~ wie Quelle** Q as in Quebec

q [kuː] *schweiz, österr Abk von* **Zentner** 100 kg

Quadrat <-[e]s, -e> [kva·'dra:t] *nt* square

quadratisch *adj* square

Quadratmeter *m* square meter

quaken ['kva:·kn̩] *vi* (*Frosch*) to croak; (*Ente*) to quack

Qual <-, -en> ['kva:l] *f* 1. (*Quälerei*) struggle 2. *meist pl* (*Pein*) agony ▶ **die ~ der Wahl haben** *hum* to be spoiled for choice

quälen ['kvɛː·lən] I. *vt* 1. (*misshandeln: Mensch, Tier*) to be cruel to 2. (*peinigen: Gedanken, Gefühle*) to torment *fig*; (*Schmerzen*) to trouble II. *vr* 1. (*leiden*) **sich** *akk* **~** to suffer 2. (*sich herumquälen*) **sich** *akk* **mit etw** *dat* **~** (*mit Gedanken, Gefühlen*) to torment oneself with sth; (*mit Hausaufgaben, Arbeit*) to struggle [hard] with sth 3. (*sich mühsam bewegen*) **sich** *akk* **~** to struggle

Quälerei <-, -en> [kvɛː·lə·'rai] *f* (*körperlich, seelisch*) torture

Qualifikation <-, -en> [kva·li·fi·ka·'tsi̯o:n] *f* 1. (*beruflich*) qualifications *pl* 2. SPORT qualifier

qualifizieren * [kva·li·fi·'tsi:·rən] I. *vr* **sich** *akk* **[für etw** *akk*] **~** to qualify [for sth] II. *vt* **jdn für etw** *akk* **~** to qualify sb for sth

Qualität <-, -en> [kva·li·'tɛ:t] *f* 1. (*Güte, Beschaffenheit*) quality 2. *pl* (*gute Eigenschaften*) qualities *pl*

qualitativ ['kva·li·ta·ti:f] I. *adj* qualitative II. *adv* qualitatively

Qualle <-, -n> ['kva·lə] *f* jellyfish

Qualm <-[e]s> ['kvalm] *m kein pl* [thick] smoke

qualmen ['kval·mən] I. *vi a. fam* (*rauchen*) to smoke II. *vt fam* to puff away at

qualvoll I. *adj* agonizing II. *adv* **~ sterben** to die in agony

Quäntchen RR <-s, -> *nt* **ein ~ Glück** a little bit of luck; **ein ~ Hoffnung** a glimmer of hope

Quantität <-, -en> [kvan·ti·'tɛ:t] *f* quantity

quantitativ ['kvan·ti·ta·ti:f] *adj* quantitative

Quarantäne <-, -n> [ka·ran·'tɛ:·nə] *f* quarantine; **unter ~ stehen/stellen** to

be in/place under quarantine

Quark <-s> ['kvark] *m kein pl* 1. KOCHK quark, ≈ fromage frais 2. *fam* (*Quatsch*) nonsense

Quartal <-s, -e> [kvar·'ta:l] *nt* quarter

Quartier <-s, -e> [kvar·'ti:ɐ̯] *nt* accommodation

Quarz <-es, -e> ['kva:ɐ̯ts] *m* quartz

quasi ['kva:·zi] *adv* almost, more or less *fam*

quasseln ['kva·sl̩n] *vi fam* to babble

Quasselstrippe <-, -n> *f fam* 1. *hum* (*Telefon*) **an der ~ hängen** to be on the phone 2. *pej* (*Person*) windbag

Quatsch <-es> ['kvatʃ] *m kein pl fam* nonsense; **~ machen** to mess [*o fam* screw] around

quatschen ['kva·tʃn̩] *fam* I. *vt* **dummes Zeug ~** to talk nonsense II. *vi fam* 1. (*viel und dumm reden*) to babble 2. (*sich unterhalten*) to chat 3. (*etw ausplaudern*) to blab

Quatschkopf *m pej fam* babbling idiot

Quecksilber ['kvɛk·zɪl·bɐ] *nt* mercury

Quelle <-, -n> ['kvɛ·lə] *f* source

quellen <quillt, quoll, gequollen> ['kvɛ·lən] *vi sein* 1. (*herausfließen*) [**aus etw** *dat*] **~** to pour out [of sth] 2. (*aufquellen*) to swell [up]

Quellwasser *nt* spring water

quengeln ['kvɛ·ŋl̩n] *vi fam* 1. (*weinerlich sein*) to whine 2. (*nörgeln*) to moan

Quentchen ALT <-s, -> ['kvɛnt·çən] *nt s.* **Quäntchen**

quer ['kve:ɐ̯] *adv* 1. (*der Breite nach*) diagonally; **~ gestreift** horizontally striped 2. **~ durch/über etw** *akk* straight through/across sth

Quere ['kve:·rə] *f* ▶ **jdm in die ~ kommen** to get in sb's way

querfeldein [kve:ɐ̯·fɛlt·'ʔain] *adv* through the countryside

Querflöte *f* flute

Querkopf *m fam* person with a different agenda from everyone else's

Querschnitt *m* cross section

Querstraße *f* crossroad

Querulant(in) <-en, -en> [kve·ru·'lant] *m(f)* querulous person

quetschen ['kvɛt·ʃn̩] I. *vt* **jdn gegen die Mauer ~** to crush sb against the wall;

Q

Kleider in einen Koffer ~ to stuff clothes into a suitcase II. *vr* 1. (*verletzen*) sich *dat* den Fuß ~ to crush one's foot 2. (*sich zwängen*) sich *akk* in die U-Bahn ~ to squeeze into the subway train

Quetschung <-, -en> *f* MED bruise

quietschen ['kvi:tʃn] *vi* (*Tür, Bett*) to squeak; mit ~den Bremsen/Reifen with screeching brakes/tires; unter lautem Q~ kam das Fahrzeug zum Stehen the vehicle came to a halt with a loud screech

quietschfidel ['kvi:tʃ·fi·'de:l], quietschvergnügt ['kvi:tʃ·fɛɐ·'gny:kt] *adj fam* chipper *pred*

quitt [kvɪt] *adj* [mit jdm] ~ sein (*abgerechnet haben*) to be even [with sb] *fam*; (*sich getrennt haben*) to be finished [with sb]

Quitte <-, -n> ['kvɪ·tə] *f* quince

quittieren* [kvɪ·'ti:·rən] *vt* ÖKON etw ~ to acknowledge [the] receipt of sth; jdm etw ~ to give sb a receipt for sth; sich *dat* etw ~ lassen to obtain a receipt for sth

Quittung <-, -en> ['kvɪ·tʊŋ] *f* 1. ÖKON receipt; jdm eine ~ [für etw *akk*] ausstellen to give sb a receipt [for sth] 2. (*Folgen*) das ist die ~ für deine Faulheit that's what you get for being so lazy

Quiz <-, -> [kvɪs] *nt* quiz

Quote <-, -n> ['kvo:·tə] *f* 1. (*Anteil*) proportion 2. (*Rate*) rate, quota; TV ratings *npl*

R

R, r <-, -> [ɛr] *nt* R, r; ~ wie Richard R as in Romeo; das ~ rollen to roll one's r's

Rabatt <-[e]s, -e> [ra·'bat] *m* discount (auf +*akk* on)

Rabe <-n, -n> ['ra:·bə] *m* raven

rabenschwarz ['ra:·bn̩·'ʃvarts] *adj* jet-black

rabiat [ra·'bi̯a:t] I. *adj* 1. (*gewalttätig*) aggressive 2. (*rigoros*) ruthless II. *adv* ruthlessly

Rache <-> ['ra·xə] *f kein pl* revenge

Racheakt *m* act of revenge

Rachen <-s, -> ['ra·xn̩] *m* 1. (*von Mensch*) throat 2. (*von Tier*) jaws *pl*

rächen ['rɛ·çn̩] I. *vt* etw ~ to take revenge for sth; jdn ~ to avenge sb II. *vr* sich *akk* ~ to take [one's] revenge (an +*dat* on, für +*akk* for)

Rachitis <-> [ra·'xi:·tɪs] *f kein pl* rickets

rachsüchtig *adj* vindictive

Rad <-[e]s, Räder> [ra:t] *nt* 1. (*Fahrrad*) bicycle, bike *fam*; ~ fahren to ride a bicycle, to bike *fam* 2. (*eines Fahrzeugs*) wheel ▶ ein ~ ab haben *sl* to have a screw loose *hum fam*

Radar <-s> [ra·'da:ɐ] *m o nt kein pl* radar

Radarkontrolle *f* radar speed enforcement

Radau <-s> [ra·'dau] *m kein pl fam* racket

radeln ['ra:·dl̩n] *vi sein fam* to bike

Radfahrer(in) *m(f)* bicyclist

Radieschen <-s, -> [ra·'di:s·çən] *nt* radish

radikal [ra·di·'ka:l] I. *adj* 1. POL radical 2. (*völlig: Beseitigung, Bruch*) complete 3. (*tief greifend: Veränderung*) drastic II. *adv* 1. POL radically 2. (*völlig: brechen, entfernen*) completely 3. (*tief greifend*) drastically

Radio <-s, -s> ['ra:·di̯o] *nt o schweiz, südd m* radio; im ~ on the radio

radioaktiv [ra·di̯o·ʔak·'ti:f] I. *adj* radioactive II. *adv* ~ verseucht contaminated by radioactivity

Radioaktivität <-> [ra·di̯o·ʔak·ti·vi·'tɛ:t] *f kein pl* radioactivity

Radiowecker *m* alarm clock radio

Radius <-, Radien> ['ra:·di̯·ʊs] *m* radius

Radkappe *f* AUTO hub cap

Radrennen *nt* bike race

Radsport *m* cycling

Radtour [-tu:ɐ] *f* bike ride

raffen ['ra·fn̩] *vt* 1. (*eilig greifen*) to grab 2. (*in Falten legen*) to gather

raffgierig *adj* greedy

Raffinerie <-, -n> [ra·fi·nə·'ri:] *f* refinery

Raffinesse <-, -n> [ra·fi·'nɛ·sə] *f* 1. *kein pl* (*Durchtriebenheit*) cunning 2. (*Feinheit*) refinement

raffiniert I. *adj* 1. (*Öl, Zucker*) re-

fined **2.** (*gerissen: Person, Plan*) cunning **3.** (*ausgefallen: Kleidung*) stylish **II.** *adv* **1.** (*durchtrieben*) cunningly **2.** (*ausgefallen*) stylishly

ragen ['ra:gn̩] *vi* **1.** (*in die Höhe*) to rise up (**aus** +*dat* out of); (*Gebirge*) to tower up **2.** (*aus etwas heraus*) to stick out

Ragout <-s, -s> [ra·'gu:] *nt* ragout

Rahm <-[e]s> [ra:m] *m kein pl bes südd, schweiz* (*Sahne*) cream

rahmen ['ra:mən] *vt* to frame; (*Dia*) to mount

Rahmen <-s, -> ['ra:mən] *m* **1.** (*Einfassung*) frame **2.** (*Gestell: eines Fahrrads*) frame; (*eines Autos*) chassis **3.** (*begrenzter Umfang/Bereich*) framework; **sich** *akk* **im ~ halten** to stay within reasonable limits; [**mit etw** *dat*] **aus dem ~ fallen** to stand out [because of sth]

Rahmsoße *f* cream[y] sauce

Rakete <-, -n> [ra·'ke:·tə] *f* rocket; MIL missile

Rallye <-, -s> ['ra·li, 'rɛ·li] *f* rally

rammen ['ra·mən] *vt* to ram (**in** +*akk* into)

Rampe <-, -n> ['ram·pə] *f* ramp; (*Laderampe*) loading ramp

Rampenlicht *nt* THEAT spotlight, footlight ▶ **im ~** [**der Öffentlichkeit**] **stehen** to be in the limelight

ramponieren * [ram·po·'ni:·rən] *vt fam* to ruin

Ramsch <-[e]s> [ramʃ] *m kein pl fam* junk

Rand <-es, Ränder> [rant] *m* **1.** (*obere Begrenzung: eines Glases, einer Tasse*) brim; (*einer Wanne*) rim **2.** (*äußere Begrenzung*) edge; (*eines Huts*) brim **3.** (*eines Blatts Papier*) margin **4.** (*Schatten, Spur*) mark; **Ränder um die Augen haben** to have rings [o bags] around one's eyes ▶ **am ~e** in passing; **außer ~ und Band geraten** *fam* to be beside oneself; **mit jdm/etw zu ~e** **kommen** to get along with sb/cope with sth

rang [raŋ] *imp von* **ringen**

Rang <-[e]s, Ränge> [raŋ] *m* **1.** (*gesellschaftliche Position*) [social] standing **2.** *kein pl* (*Stellenwert*) status **3.** MIL rank ▶ **alles, was ~ und Namen hat**

everybody who is anybody

Rangelei <-, -en> [raŋə·'lai] *f fam* scuffle

rangeln ['ra·ŋln̩] *vi fam* to scuffle

rangieren * [rã·'ʒi:·rən] *vi* to rank, to be ranked

Rangliste *f* rankings, ranking list

Rangordnung *f* hierarchy

ranken ['raŋ·kn̩] *vr* **sich** *akk* **um etw** *akk* **~** (*Pflanze*) to wind itself around sth; **sich** *akk* **um jdn/etw ~** (*Legende, Sage*) to have grown up around sb/developed around sth

Ranzen <-s, -> ['ran·tsn̩] *m* **1.** SCH ≈ backpack **2.** *fam* (*Bauch*) gut

ranzig ['ran·tsɪç] *adj* rancid

rappelvoll *adj fam* jam-packed

Raps <-es, -e> [raps] *m* rape[seed]

rar [ra:ɐ̯] *adj* rare; **~ sein/werden** to be/become hard to find

Rarität <-, -en> [ra·ri·'tɛ:t] *f* rarity

rasant [ra·'zant] **I.** *adj* fast, rapid; (*Tempo*) breakneck **II.** *adv* rapidly

rasch [raʃ] **I.** *adj* quick **II.** *adv* quickly

rascheln ['ra·ʃl̩n] *vi* to rustle

rasen ['ra:·zn̩] *vi* **1.** *sein* (*schnell fahren*) to speed; **gegen/in etw** *akk* **~** to crash into sth **2.** *sein* (*Zeit*) to fly [by] **3.** *haben* **sie raste** [**vor Wut**] she was beside herself [with rage]

Rasen <-s, -> ['ra:·zn̩] *m* lawn

rasend *adj* **1.** (*schnell*) breakneck **2.** (*wütend*) furious; **~ vor Wut sein** to be infuriated **3.** (*furchtbar*) terrible; (*Durst*) burning; (*Schmerz*) excruciating; (*Wut*) blind **4.** (*Beifall*) thunderous **II.** *adv fam* very; **ich würde das ~ gern tun** I'd love to do it

Rasenmäher <-s, -> *m* lawnmower

Raser(in) <-s, -> ['ra·zɐ] *m(f) fam* speeder

Rasierapparat *m* **1.** (*Elektrorasierer*) [electric] shaver **2.** (*Nassrasierer*) [safety] razor

rasieren * [ra·'zi:·rən] *vt, vr* [**sich** *akk*] **~** to shave; **sich** *akk* **trocken/nass ~** to dry-shave/wet-shave; **sich** *dat* **die Beine ~** to shave one's legs

Rasierklinge *f* razor blade

Rasierschaum *m* shaving cream

Rasierwasser *nt* aftershave

Raspel <-, -n> ['ras·pl̩] *f* KOCHK grater

raspeln ['ras·pl̩n] *vt* KOCHK to grate

Rasse <-, -n> ['ra·sə] *f* (*bei Menschen*) race; (*bei Tieren*) breed

rasseln ['ra·sl̩n] *vi* 1. **haben** to rattle; **mit etw** *dat* ~ to rattle sth 2. **sein** *fam* **durch eine Prüfung** ~ to fail [*o* flunk] an exam

Rassendiskriminierung *f* racial discrimination

rassig ['ra·sɪç] *adj* spirited

Rassismus <-> [ra·'sɪs·mʊs] *m kein pl* racism

Rassist(in) <-en, -en> [ra·'sɪst] *m(f)* racist

rassistisch *adj* racist

Rast <-, -en> [rast] *f* break

rasten ['ras·tn̩] *vi* to take a break

rastlos *adj* 1. (*unermüdlich*) tireless 2. (*unruhig*) restless

Rastplatz *m* rest area [*o* stop]

Rat¹ <-[e]s> [ra:t] *m kein pl* advice; **jdm den ~ geben, etw zu tun** to advise sb to do sth; **sich** *dat* **keinen ~ [mehr] wissen** to be at one's wit's end; **jdn/ etw zu ~e ziehen** to consult sb/sth

Rat² <-[e]s, Räte> [ra:t] *m* POL council

Rate <-, -n> ['ra:·tə] *f* installment

raten <rät, riet, geraten> ['ra:·tn̩] I. *vi* 1. (*Ratschläge geben*) [jdm] **zu etw** ~ to advise [sb to do] sth 2. (*schätzen*) to guess II. *vt* 1. (*als Ratschlag geben*) **jdm etw** ~ to advise sb to do sth 2. (*erraten*) to guess

Ratenkauf *m* installment plan

Ratenzahlung *f* 1. *kein pl* (*Zahlung in Raten*) payment in installments 2. (*einzelne Zahlung*) installment payment

Rathaus *nt* city [*o* town] hall

Ration <-, -en> [ra·'tsi̯oːn] *f* ration

rational [ra·tsi̯o·'naːl] I. *adj* rational II. *adv* rationally

rationell [ra·tsi̯o·'nɛl] I. *adj* efficient II. *adv* efficiently

rationieren [ra·tsi̯o·'niː·rən] *vt* to ration

ratlos I. *adj* helpless; **ich bin völlig ~** I'm completely at a loss II. *adv* helplessly

ratsam ['ra:t·za:m] *adj* advisable

Ratschlag <-s, Ratschläge> ['ra:t·ʃla:k] *m* advice; **~ fahren** to drive at breakneck speed

Rätsel <-s, -> ['rɛː·tsl̩] *nt* 1. (*Geheimnis*) mystery; **es ist [jdm] ein ~, warum/ wie ...** it is a mystery [to sb] why/how ... 2. (*Denkaufgabe*) riddle

rätselhaft *adj* mysterious

Ratte <-, -n> ['ra·tə] *f a. fig* rat

rattern ['ra·tɐn] *vi* 1. **haben** (*klappern*) to rattle 2. **sein** (*sich fortbewegen*) to rattle along

rau ^{RR} [rau] *adj* 1. (*spröde: Hände, Haut*) rough; (*Lippen*) chapped 2. (*heiser: Stimme*) hoarse; (*verführerisch*) husky 3. (*unwirtlich: Klima, Wetter*) harsh; (*Gegend*) inhospitable 4. (*ungehobelt: Benehmen, Sitten*) uncouth

Raub <-[e]s, -e> [raup] *m pl selten* 1. (*das Rauben*) robbery 2. (*das Geraubte*) loot

rauben ['rau·bn̩] I. *vt* (*stehlen*) to rob; **das hat mir viel Zeit geraubt** this has cost me a lot of time II. *vi* to rob

Räuber(in) <-s, -> ['rɔy·bɐ] *m(f)* robber

Raubkatze *f* big [predatory] cat

Raubkopie *f* pirate[d] copy

Raubmord *m* murder robbery

Raubtier *nt* predator

Raubüberfall *m* robbery; (*auf Geldtransport etc. a.*) holdup

Raubvogel *m* bird of prey

Rauch <-[e]s> [raux] *m kein pl* smoke ▶ **sich in ~ auflösen** to go up in smoke

rauchen ['rau·xn̩] *vt, vi* to smoke

Raucher(in) <-s, -> *m(f)* smoker

Raucherabteil *nt* BAHN smoking compartment [*o* car]

Räucherlachs *m* smoked salmon

räuchern ['rɔy·çɐn] *vt, vi* to smoke

rauchig ['rau·xɪç] *adj* smoky

Rauchverbot *nt* smoking ban

Rauchwolke *f* cloud of smoke

raufen ['rau·fn̩] *vi, vr* [**sich** *akk*] ~ to fight (**um** +*akk* over)

rauh ^{ALT} [rau] *adj s.* **rau**

Raum <-[e]s, Räume> [raum] *m* 1. (*Zimmer*) room 2. *kein pl* (*Platz*) room *no art*, space *no art* 3. GEOG (*Gebiet*) region, area; **im ~ Hamburg** in the Hamburg area ▶ **im ~ stehen** to be unresolved; **etw in den ~ stellen** to raise sth

räumen ['rɔy·mən] *vt* **1.** (*entfernen*) to remove (**aus/von** +*dat* from) **2.** (*einsortieren*) to put away *sep* (**in** +*akk* in/into) **3.** (*Wohnung*) to vacate; (*Straße*) to clear **4.** (*evakuieren*) to evacuate

Raumfähre *f* space shuttle

Raumfahrt *f* space travel *no art;* (*einzelner Raumflug*) space flight

Räumfahrzeug *nt* bulldozer; (*für Schnee*) snowplow

räumlich ['rɔym·lɪç] **I.** *adj* **1.** (*den Raum betreffend*) spatial **2.** (*dreidimensional*) three-dimensional **II.** *adv* **1.** (*platzmäßig*) spatially **2.** (*dreidimensional*) three-dimensionally

Raumpfleger(in) *m(f)* cleaner

Raumschiff *nt* spaceship

Raumstation *f* space station

Räumungsverkauf *m* clearance sale

Raupe <-, -n> ['rau·pə] *f* **1.** ZOOL caterpillar **2.** (*Planierraupe*) bulldozer

Rausch <-[e]s, Räusche> [rauʃ] *m* **1.** (*Trunkenheit*) intoxication; **einen ~ haben** to be drunk; **seinen ~ ausschlafen** to sleep it off **2.** (*Ekstase*) ecstasy

rauschen ['rau·ʃn] *vi* **1.** haben (*anhaltendes Geräusch erzeugen: Wasser, Verkehr*) to roar; (*sanft*) to murmur; (*Baum, Blätter*) to rustle; (*Lautsprecher*) to hiss; (*Rock, Vorhang*) to swish **2.** sein (*sich geräuschvoll bewegen: Wasser*) to rush; (*Vogelschwarm*) to swoosh **3.** sein (*zügig gehen*) to sweep (**aus** +*dat* out of, **in** +*akk* into)

Rauschgift *nt* drug

Rauschgifthändler(in) *m(f)* drug dealer; (*international*) drug trafficker

rauschgiftsüchtig *adj* addicted to drugs *pred*

Rauschgiftsüchtige(r) *f(m)* drug addict

raus|fliegen *vi irreg sein fam* **1.** (*hinausgeworfen werden*) **aus der Schule ~** to be kicked out of school; **aus einem Betrieb ~** to be given the boot **2.** (*weggeworfen werden*) to get thrown out

räuspern ['rɔys·pɛn] *vr* **sich** *akk* **~** to clear one's throat

raus|schmeißen *vt irreg fam* to throw out

Rausschmeißer <-s, -> *m fam* bouncer

Razzia <-, Razzien> ['ra·tsja] *f* raid

Reagenzglas *nt* test tube

reagieren * [rea·'gi:·rən] *vi* (*a. chem*) to react (**auf** +*akk* to, **mit** +*dat* with)

Reaktion <-, -en> [reak·'tsjo:n] *f* reaction (**auf** +*dat* to)

Reaktor <-s, -toren> [re·'ak·to:ɐ] *m* reactor

real [re·'a:l] *adj* real

realisierbar *adj* realizable; **schwer ~e Pläne** plans that are hard to accomplish

realisieren * [rea·li·'zi:·rən] *vt* to realize

realistisch [rea·'lɪs·tɪʃ] **I.** *adj* realistic **II.** *adv* realistically

Realität <-, -en> [rea·li·'tɛ:t] *f* **1.** (*Wirklichkeit*) reality **2.** *pl* (*Gegebenheiten*) facts **3.** *pl österr* (*Immobilien*) real estate

realitätsfern *adj* unrealistic; (*Person*) out of touch with reality

realitätsnah *adj* realistic; (*Person*) in touch with reality

Realschule *f* ≈ junior high school (*a school for grades 5–10 that prepares students either for the Gymnasium or for an apprenticeship in a trade or industry*)

Rebe <-, -n> ['re:·bə] *f* (*grape*)vine

Rebell(in) <-en, -en> [re·'bɛl] *m(f)* rebel

rebellieren * [re·bɛ·'li:·rən] *vi* to rebel (**gegen** +*akk* against)

Rebellion <-, -en> [re·bɛ·'ljo:n] *f* rebellion; (*von Studenten*) revolt

rebellisch [re·'bɛ·lɪʃ] *adj* rebellious

Rechenaufgabe *f* math problem

Rechenfehler *m* calculation mistake

Rechenschaft <-> *f kein pl* account; **jdm** [**über etw** *akk*] **~ schulden** to be accountable to sb [for sth]; **jdn** [**für etw** *akk*] **zur ~ ziehen** to call sb to account [for sth]

Recherche <-, -n> [re·'ʃɛr·ʃə] *meist pl f* research

recherchieren * [re·ʃɛr·'ʃi:·rən] *vt, vi* to investigate, to research

rechnen ['rɛç·nən] **I.** *vt* **1.** (*mathematisch lösen*) to calculate **2.** (*veranschlagen*) to estimate; **wir müssen mindestens zehn Stunden ~** we have to count on at least ten hours **3.** (*berücksichti-*

R

gen) to take into account **4.** (*einstufen, gehören*) to count (**zu** +*dat* among); **ich rechne sie zu meinen besten Freundinnen** I consider her one of my best [girl]friends **II.** *vi* **1.** (*Rechenaufgaben lösen*) to do math; **ich konnte noch nie gut ~** I was never [any] good at math **2.** (*sich verlassen*) **auf jdn/etw ~** to count on sb/sth **3.** (*einkalkulieren*) **mit etw** *dat* ~ to count on sth; **wann ~ Sie mit einer Antwort?** when do you expect an answer?; **mit allem/dem Schlimmsten ~** to be prepared for anything/the worst **4.** *fam* (*Haus halten*) to economize; **wir müssen mit jedem Cent ~** we have to watch every penny **III.** *vr* (*Gewinn einbringen*) **etw rechnet sich** [**nicht**] *akk* sth is [not] profitable

Rechnung <-, -en> *f* **1.** (*schriftliche Abrechnung*) bill; (*im Restaurant a.*) check; **das geht auf meine ~** I'll pay [for it], [you can] put that on my tab; [**jdm**] **etw in ~ stellen** to charge [sb] for sth **2.** (*Berechnung*) calculation; **die ~ stimmt nicht** the numbers don't add up ▶ **er hatte die ~ ohne den Wirt gemacht** there was one thing he failed to take into consideration

recht [rɛçt] **I.** *adj* **1.** (*passend*) right **2.** (*richtig*) right; **ganz ~!** that's right [all right]! **3.** (*angenehm*) **jdm ist etw ~** sth is all right with sb; **dieser Kompromiss ist mir durchaus nicht ~** I'm not at all happy with this compromise **4.** *schweiz, südd* (*anständig*) decent; (*angemessen*) appropriate ▶ **jdm ~ geschehen** to serve sb right; **nach dem R~en sehen** to make sure that everything's okay **II.** *adv* **1.** (*richtig*) correctly; **höre ich ~?** am I hearing things?; **versteh mich bitte ~** please don't misunderstand me **2.** (*genau*) really; **nicht ~ wissen** to not really know **3.** (*ziemlich*) rather; (*gehörig*) properly **4.** *fam* (*gelegen*) **jdm gerade ~ kommen** to come just in time for sb; *iron* to be all sb needs [right now]; **man kann es nicht allen ~ machen** you can't please everyone ▶ **jetzt erst ~** now more than ever

Recht <-[e]s, -e> [rɛçt] *nt* **1.** *kein pl*

(*Rechtsordnung*) law **2.** (*Anspruch*) right; **jds gutes ~ sein** to be sb's [lega] right; **jdm ~ geben** to agree with sb; **~ haben** to be [in the] right; **ein ~ au jdn/etw haben** to have a right to sb. sth **3.** (*Befugnis*) right; **mit welchem ~?** by what right?; **mit ~** rightly; **un das mit ~!** and rightly so!

Rechte <-n, -n> [ˈrɛçtə] *f* **1.** (*recht Hand*) right [hand] **2.** POL right

Rechteck <-[e]s, -e> *nt* rectangle

rechteckig *adj* rectangular

rechtfertigen I. *vt* to justify (**gegen über** +*dat* to) **II.** *vr* **sich** *akk* ~ to jus tify oneself

Rechtfertigung *f* justification

rechthaberisch *adj pej* dogmatic

rechtlich I. *adj* legal **II.** *adv* legally

rechtlos *adj* without rights *pred*

rechtmäßig *adj* **1.** (*legitim*) lawfu **2.** (*legal*) legal

rechts [rɛçts] **I.** *adv* **1.** (*auf der rechte Seite*) on the right; **dein Schlüssel bund liegt ~ neben dir** your keys ar just to your right; **~ oben/unten** o the top/bottom right; **nach/von ~** to from the right **2.** TRANSP (*nach rechts* [to the] right; **halte dich ganz ~** keep [to the] right; **~ abbiegen/ranfahrer** to turn off/pull over to the right **3.** PO right; **~ eingestellt sein** to lean to the right ▶ **nicht mehr wissen, wo ~ und links ist** *fam* to not know whethe one is coming or going **II.** *präp* +*gen* t [*o on*] the right of

Rechtsabteilung *f* legal department

Rechtsanwalt, -anwältin *m, f* lawyer attorney; (*vor Gericht*) lawyer

Rechtschreibfehler *m* spelling mistake

Rechtschreibreform *f* German spell ing reform which went into effect on August 1, 2006

Rechtschreibung *f* spelling

Rechtsextremismus *m kein pl* right wing extremism

Rechtsextremist(in) *m(f)* right-wing extremist

rechtskräftig I. *adj* legally valid; (*Ur teil*) final **II.** *adv* with the force of law; **jdn ~ verurteilen** to pass final sen tence on sb

Rechtskurve f right-hand curve

Rechtslage f legal position

Rechtsprechung <-, -en> f pl selten dispensation of justice

rechtsradikal I. adj ultra-right-wing II. adv with ultra right-wing tendencies

Rechtsschutzversicherung f insurance that covers legal expenses

Rechtsstaat m state founded on the rule of law

rechtsstaatlich adj under the rule of law pred

Rechtsstreit m lawsuit

rechtswidrig adj unlawful

rechtzeitig I. adj punctual II. adv on time; **Sie hätten mich ~ informieren müssen** you should have given me enough [advance] notice

recken ['rɛ·kn̩] vt, vr [sich] akk ~ to stretch

Recycling <-s> [ri·'sai·klɪŋ] nt kein pl recycling

Redakteur(in) <-s, -e> [re·dak·'tø:ɐ] m(f) editor

Redaktion <-, -en> [re·dak·'tsjo:n] f 1. (Büro) editorial department 2. (Redaktionsmitglieder) editorial staff 3. kein pl (das Redigieren) editing

Rede <-, -n> ['re:·də] f 1. (Ansprache) speech 2. (das Reden, Gespräch) talk; **wovon ist die ~?** what's it [all] about?; **es war gerade von dir die ~** we/they were just talking about you; **die ~ kam auf jdn/etw** the conversation turned to sb/sth ▶ **jdm ~ und Antwort stehen** to justify oneself to sb; **davon kann keine ~ sein** that's out of the question; **jdn zur ~ stellen** to take sb to task; **nicht der ~ wert sein** to be not worth mentioning

redegewandt adj eloquent

reden ['re:·dn̩] I. vi 1. (sprechen) to talk (mit +dat to/with, über +akk about) 2. (eine Rede halten) to speak (über +akk about/on) 3. (diskutieren) **darüber lässt sich ~** that's not out of the question; **mit sich dat [über etw akk] ~ lassen** to be willing to discuss [sth] ▶ **du hast gut ~** that's easy for you to say II. vt 1. (sagen) to say 2. (klatschen) **etw [über jdn/etw] ~** to say

sth [about sb/sth]; **es wird über uns geredet** they're talking about us

Redewendung f idiom

redlich ['re:t·lɪç] I. adj honest II. adv honestly

Redner(in) <-s, -> [re:d·nɐ] m(f) speaker

redselig ['re:t·ze:·lɪç] adj talkative

reduzieren * [re·du·'tsi:·rən] vt to reduce

Reederei <-, -en> [re:·də·'rai] f shipping company

reell [re·'ɛl] adj 1. (tatsächlich) real 2. (anständig) straight; (Angebot, Preis) fair; (Geschäft) sound

Referat <-[e]s, -e> [re·fe·'ra:t] nt (seminar) paper; SCH project; **ein ~ [über jdn/etw] halten** to give a presentation [on sb/sth]

Referenz <-, -en> [re·fe·'rɛnts] f meist pl (Beurteilung) **gute ~en aufzuweisen haben** to have good references

reflektieren * [re·flɛk·'ti:·rən] I. vt to reflect II. vi 1. (zurückstrahlen) to reflect 2. (nachdenken) to reflect (über +akk on/upon)

Reflex <-es, -e> [re·'flɛks] m 1. (Nervenreflex) reflex 2. (Lichtreflex) reflection

Reflexion <-, -en> [re·flɛ·'ksjo:n] f reflection

Reform <-, -en> [re·'fɔrm] f reform

reformbedürftig adj in need of reform pred

Reformhaus nt health food store

reformieren * [re·fɔr·'mi:·rən] vt to reform

Reformkost f health food

Refrain <-s, -s> [re·'frɛ:, rə-] m refrain

Regal <-s, -e> [re·'ga:l] nt shelf, shelving, rack

Regatta <-, Regatten> [re·'ga·ta] f regatta

rege ['re:·gə] I. adj (lebhaft) lively; (Anteilnahme, Beteiligung) active II. adv actively

Regel <-, -n> ['re:·gl̩] f 1. (Grundsatz) rule; **sich dat etw zur ~ machen** to make a habit of sth; **in der ~** as a rule 2. (Menstruation) period ▶ **nach allen ~n der Kunst** with all the tricks of the trade

R

regelmäßig I. *adj* regular **II.** *adv* **1.** (*immer wieder*) regularly **2.** (*ständig*) always; **sie kommt ~ zu spät** she is always late

Regelmäßigkeit <-> *f* *kein pl* regularity

regeln ['re:ɡln] **I.** *vt* **1.** (*in Ordnung bringen*) to settle; (*Problem*) to resolve **2.** (*regulieren*) to regulate **II.** *vr* **sich** *akk* [**von selbst**] ~ to sort itself out

regelrecht ['re:ɡl·rɛçt] **I.** *adj* real; (*Frechheit*) downright **II.** *adv* really; ~ **betrunken sein** to be hammered *sl*

Regelung <-, -en> ['re:ɡə·lʊŋ] *f* **1.** (*festgelegte Vereinbarung*) arrangement; (*Bestimmung*) ruling **2.** *kein pl* (*das Regulieren*) regulation

regelwidrig I. *adj* against the rules *pred* **II.** *adv* against the rules

regen ['re:ɡn] *vr* **sich** *akk* ~ **1.** (*sich bewegen*) to move **2.** *geh* (*Zweifel, Gewissen, Hoffnung*) to stir

Regen <-s, -> ['re:ɡn] *m* rain; **saurer ~** acid rain; **bei strömendem ~** in [the] pouring rain ► **vom ~ in die Traufe kommen** *prov* to jump out of the frying pan into the fire; **jdn im ~ stehen lassen** *fam* to leave sb in the lurch

Regenbogen *m* rainbow

Regenmantel *m* raincoat

Regenschauer *m* rain shower

Regenschirm *m* umbrella

Regent(in) <-en, -en> [re·'ɡɛnt] *m(f)* ruler; (*Vertreter des Herrschers*) regent

Regenwald *m* rainforest

Regenwurm *m* earthworm

Regie <-, -n> [re·'ʒi:] *f* FILM, THEAT direction; RADIO production; [**bei etw** *dat*] **die ~ haben** to direct [sth] ► **in eigener ~** on one's own

regieren * [re·'ɡi:·rən] *vt, vi* to rule (**über** +*akk* over); (*Monarch a.*) to reign

Regierung <-, -en> [re·'ɡi:·rʊŋ] *f* POL **1.** (*Kabinett*) government **2.** (*Herrschaftsgewalt*) rule; **die ~ antreten** to take power [*o* office]; **an der ~ sein** to be in power

Regierungschef(in) *m(f)* head of a government

Regierungserklärung *f* government statement

Regierungspartei *f* ruling party

Regierungssprecher(in) *m(f)* government spokesperson

Regime <-s, -s> [re·'ʒi:m] *nt pej* regime

Region <-, -en> [re·'ɡio:n] *f* region

regional [re·ɡio·'na:l] **I.** *adj* regional **II.** *adv* regionally

Regisseur(in) <-s, -e> [re·ʒɪ·'sø:ɐ] *m(f)* FILM, THEAT director; RADIO producer

registrieren * [re·ɡɪs·'tri:·rən] *vt* to register

Regler <-s, -> ['re:ɡ·lɐ] *m* ELEK regulator; AUTO governor

reglos ['re:k·lo:s] *adj* s. **regungslos**

regnen ['re:ɡ·nən] *vi impers* to rain; **es regnet** it's raining

regnerisch *adj* rainy

regulär [re·ɡu·'lɛ:ɐ] *adj* **1.** (*vorgeschrieben*) regular **2.** (*normal*) normal

regulieren * [re·ɡu·'li:·rən] **I.** *vt* (*einstellen*) to regulate **II.** *vr* **sich** *akk* [**von selbst**] ~ to regulate itself

Regung <-, -en> *f* **1.** (*Bewegung*) movement **2.** (*Empfindung*) feeling; **menschliche ~** human emotion

regungslos *adj* motionless; (*Miene*) impassive

Reh <-[e]s, -e> [re:] *nt* roe deer

Rehabilitationszentrum *nt* rehabilitation center]

rehabilitieren * [re·ha·bi·li·'ti:·rən] *vt* to rehabilitate

Reibe <-, -n> ['rai·bə] *f* grater

Reibekuchen *m* KOCHK *dial* (*Kartoffelpuffer*) potato pancake, ~ latke

reiben <rieb, gerieben> ['rai·bn] **I.** *vt* **1.** (*zerkleinern*) to grate **2.** (*reibend verteilen*) **etw auf/in etw** *akk* ~ to rub sth onto/into sth **3.** (*reibend entfernen*) **etw aus/von etw** *dat* ~ to rub sth out of/off sth **II.** *vr* **sich** *dat* **die Augen/Hände** ~ to rub one's eyes/hands

Reibereien [rai·bə·'rai·ən] *pl fam* friction

Reibung <-, -en> *f* *kein pl* PHYS friction

reibungslos I. *adj* smooth **II.** *adv* smoothly

reich [raiç] **I.** *adj* **1.** (*sehr wohlhabend*) rich, wealthy **2.** (*in Fülle habend*) rich (**an** +*dat* in); ~ **an Erfahrung sein** to have a wealth of experience **3.** (*ergiebig*) rich; (*Ernte*) abundant; (*Ölquel-*

le) productive; (*Mahlzeit*) lavish; (*Erbschaft*) substantial **4.** (*vielfältig*) wide; (*Möglichkeiten, Leben*) rich; (*Auswahl, Wahl*) large; (*Bestände*) copious **II.** *adv* **1.** (*reichlich*) richly; **jdn ~ beschenken** to shower sb with presents **2.** (*mit viel Gelderwerb verbunden*) ~ **heiraten/erben** to marry into/inherit money **3.** (*reichhaltig*) richly

Reich <-[e]s, -e> [raiç] *nt* **1.** (*Imperium*) empire; **das ~ Gottes** the Kingdom of God; **das Dritte ~** HIST the Third Reich; **das Römische ~** HIST the Roman Empire **2.** *fig* (*Bereich*) realm

reichen ['rai·çn̩] **I.** *vi* **1.** (*ausreichen*) to be enough; **die Vorräte ~ noch Monate** there are enough supplies to last for months **2.** (*überdrüssig sein*) **etw reicht jdm** sth is enough for sb; **mir reicht's!** I've had enough [of this]!; **jetzt reicht's [mir] [aber]!** enough is enough! **3.** (*sich erstrecken*) **bis zu etw** *dat* ~ to reach to sth **II.** *vt geh* **1.** (*geben*) **jdm etw** ~ to give [o *pass*] sb sth **2.** (*zur Begrüßung*) **jdm die Hand** ~ to hold out one's hand to sb; **sich** *dat* **die Hand** ~ to shake hands

reichhaltig ['raiç·hal·tɪç] *adj* **1.** (*vielfältig*) wide; (*Programm*) varied **2.** (*Bibliothek, Sammlung*) well-stocked **3.** (*üppig*) rich

reichlich ['raiç·lɪç] **I.** *adj* large; (*Belohnung*) ample; (*Trinkgeld*) generous; ~ **Geld/Zeit haben** to have plenty of money/time **II.** *adv* (*ziemlich*) rather

Reichstag *m* seat of the federal government in Germany

Reichtum <-[e]s, Reichtümer> ['raiç·tu:m] *m* **1.** *kein pl* (*große Wohlhabenheit*) wealth; **zu ~ kommen** to get rich **2.** *pl* (*materieller Besitz*) riches *npl* **3.** *kein pl* (*Reichhaltigkeit*) wealth (**an** +*dat* of)

Reichweite *f* range

reif [raif] *adj* **1.** AGR, HORT ripe **2.** (*ausgereift: a. Persönlichkeit*) mature; **im ~en Alter von ...** at the ripe old age of ... **3.** *fam* ~ **für etw** *akk* **sein** to be ready for sth

Reif <-[e]s> [raif] *m kein pl* METEO hoarfrost

Reife <-> ['rai·fə] *f kein pl* (*charakterlich*) maturity

reifen ['rai·fn̩] *vi sein* **1.** AGR, HORT to ripen **2.** (*sich entwickeln*) to mature (**zu** +*dat* into)

Reifen <-s, -> ['rai·fn̩] *m* tire

Reifendruck *m* tire pressure

Reifenpanne *f* flat [tire]

reiflich ['raif·lɪç] **I.** *adj* thorough; **nach ~er Überlegung** after [very] careful consideration **II.** *adv* thoroughly, carefully

Reihe <-, -n> ['raiə] *f* **1.** (*fortlaufende Folge*) row; **außer der ~** out of [the usual] order; **der ~ nach** in order **2.** (*das Drankommen*) **jd ist an der ~** it's sb's turn; **ich war jetzt an der ~!** I was next!; **jeder kommt an die ~** everyone will get a turn **3.** (*Menge*) **eine [ganze] ~ von** a [whole] lot of; **eine ganze ~ von Beschwerden** a slew of complaints **4.** (*Linie von Menschen*) line; **sich** *akk* **in ~n aufstellen** to form lines ▶ **etw auf die ~ kriegen** (*kapieren*) to get sth into one's head; (*in Ordnung bringen*) to get sth together; **aus der ~ tanzen** to step out of line

Reihenfolge *f* order

Reihenhaus *nt* townhouse

reihenweise *adv* **1.** (*in großer Zahl*) by the dozen **2.** (*nach Reihen*) in rows

reihum [rai·ˈʔʊm] *adv in* turn; **etw ~ gehen lassen** to pass sth around

Reim <-[e]s, -e> [raim] *m* **1.** (*Endreim*) rhyme **2.** *pl* (*Verse*) verse[s]

reimen ['rai·mən] **I.** *vt, vr* **sich** *akk* ~ to rhyme (**auf** +*akk* with, **mit** +*dat* with) **II.** *vt* **etw ~** to rhyme sth **III.** *vi* to make up rhymes

rein¹ [rain] *adv fam s.* **herein, hinein**

rein² [rain] **I.** *adj* **1.** (*unvermischt*) pure; (*Wahrheit*) plain **2.** *fam* (*absolut: Zufall, Glück*) pure; (*Blödsinn*) sheer; (*Unsinn*) utter; **das Kinderzimmer ist der ~ste Schweinestall!** the children's room is an absolute pigsty! **3.** (*sauber*) clean; (*Kleidung*) fresh **4.** (*makellos*) clear ▶ **etw [für jdn] ins R~e bringen** to clear up sth *sep* [for sb]; **mit sich** *dat* [**selbst**]/**etw ins R~e kommen** to come to terms with oneself/sth; **etw ins R~e schreiben** to make a fair copy of

sth **II.** adv **1.** (ausschließlich) purely; **eine ~ persönliche Meinung** a purely personal opinion **2.** fam (absolut) absolutely; **~ zufällig** purely by chance

Reinfall ['rain·fal] m fam disaster

rein|fallen vi irreg sein fam **1.** (eine schwere Enttäuschung erleben) to be taken in (**mit** +dat by) **2.** (hineinfallen) to fall in

Reinheitsgebot nt **Deutsches ~** German beer purity regulation

Reingewinn m net profit

reinigen ['rai·nɪ·gn] vt to clean

Reinigung <-, -en> f **1.** kein pl (das Reinigen) cleaning **2.** (Reinigungsbetrieb) cleaner's; **die chemische ~** the dry cleaner's

reinlich adj clean

reinrassig adj thoroughbred

Reis <-es, -e> [rais] m AGR, BOT rice

Reise <-, -n> ['rai·zə] f trip, journey; **gute ~!** have a nice trip!; **eine ~ machen** to take a trip

Reiseandenken nt souvenir

Reisebüro nt travel agency

Reiseführer m travel [o tour] guide

Reisegepäck nt luggage

Reisegruppe f tour group

Reiseleiter(in) m(f) guide

reisen ['rai·zn] vi sein to travel (**nach** to)

Reisende(r) f(m) dekl wie adj traveler

Reisepass RR m passport

Reisescheck m traveler's check

Reisetasche f travel bag

Reiseveranstalter(in) m(f) tour operator

Reiseversicherung f travel insurance

Reiseziel nt destination

reißen <riss, gerissen> ['rai·sn] **I.** vi **1.** sein (zerreißen: Seil, Faden) to break; (Papier, Stoff) to tear **2.** haben (zerren) to pull **II.** vt haben **1.** **etw in Stücke ~** to tear sth to pieces **2.** (abreißen) **etw von etw** dat **~** (Ast, Bauteil) to break sth off [o] sth; (Papier, Stoff) to tear sth off [o] sth **3.** (wegreißen) **jdm etw aus der Hand ~** to snatch [o grab] sth from sb's hands **4.** (sich bemächtigen) **etw an sich** akk **~** to seize sth **III.** vr **haben** fam **sich** akk **um jdn/etw ~** to scramble to get/see sb/sth; **um diese**

Arbeit reiße ich mich nicht I'm not in any hurry to do this work

Reißverschluss RR m zipper

Reißzwecke <-, -n> f thumbtack

reiten <ritt, geritten> ['rai·tn] **I.** vi sein to ride [a horse/pony]; **im Galopp/Trab ~** to gallop/trot **II.** vt haben to ride

Reiter(in) <-s, -> ['rai·te] m(f) [horseback] rider

Reiz <-es, -e> [raits] m **1.** (Verlockung) appeal, attraction; **für jdn den ~ verlieren** to lose its appeal [for sb] **2.** (Stimulus) stimulus

reizbar adj irritable

reizen ['rai·tsn] vt **1.** (verlocken) **jdn ~** to appeal to sb; **es reizt jdn, etw zu tun** sb is tempted to do sth **2.** MED to irritate **3.** (provozieren) to provoke (**zu** +dat into)

reizend I. adj delightful, charming; **das ist ja ~!** iron that's charming! iron **II.** adv charmingly

reizlos adj dull

Reizthema nt emotional topic

Reizüberflutung f overstimulation

Reizung <-, -en> f irritation

reizvoll adj attractive

Reklamation <-, -en> [re·kla·ma·ˈtsjo:n] f complaint

Reklame <-, -n> [re·ˈkla:·mə] f **1.** (Werbeprospekt) flyer **2.** (Werbung) commercials pl

reklamieren* [re·kla·ˈmi:·rən] vt (bemängeln) to complain about

rekonstruieren* [re·kɔn·stru·ˈi:·rən] vt to reconstruct

Rekord <-s, -e> [re·ˈkɔrt] m record

Rekordzeit f record time

Relation <-, -en> [re·la·ˈtsjo:n] f proportion; **in ~ zu etw** dat **stehen** to be proportional to sth; **in keiner ~ zu etw** dat **stehen** to bear no relation to sth

relativ [re·la·ˈti:f] **I.** adj relative **II.** adv relatively

Religion <-, -en> [re·li·ˈgjo:n] f religion

Religionsfreiheit f freedom of religion

religiös [re·li·ˈgjø:s] **I.** adj religious **II.** adv in a religious manner

Rendezvous <-, -> [rã·de·ˈvu:] nt rendezvous a. hum

Rennbahn f racetrack

rennen <rannte, gerannt> ['rɛ·nən] *vi sein* **1.** (*laufen*) to run **2.** (*stoßen*) **gegen etw** akk ~ to bump into sth

Rennen <-s, -> ['rɛ·nən] *nt* race

Renner <-s, -> ['rɛ·nɐ] *m fam* big seller

Rennfahrer(in) *m(f)* **1.** (*Autorennen*) racecar driver **2.** (*Radrennen*) bicycle racer

Rennsport *m* **1.** (*Motorrennen*) motor racing **2.** (*Radrennsport*) bicycle racing **3.** (*Pferderennsport*) horse racing

Rennwagen *m* racecar

renovieren * [re·no·'vi:·rən] *vt* to renovate

Renovierung <-, -en> *f* renovation

rentabel [rɛn·'ta:·bl̩] **I.** *adj* profitable **II.** *adv* profitably

Rente <-, -n> ['rɛn·tə] *f* **1.** (*Ruhestand*) **in ~ gehen/sein** *fam* to retire/be retired **2.** (*Altersruhegeld*) pension; (*staatlich*) social security

Rentenalter *nt* retirement age

Rentenversicherung *f* Social Security

Rentier ['rɛn·ti:ɐ] *nt* reindeer

rentieren * [rɛn·'ti:·rən] *vr* **sich** akk ~ to be worthwhile

Rentner(in) <-s, -> *m(f)* retiree

Reparatur <-, -en> [re·pa·ra·'tu:ɐ] *f* repair

reparieren * [re·pa·'ri:·rən] *vt* to repair

Repertoire <-s, -s> [re·pɛr·'toa:ɐ] *nt* repertoire

Reportage <-, -n> [re·pɔr·'ta:·ʒə] *f* documentary

Reporter(in) <-s, -> [re·'pɔr·tɐ] *m(f)* reporter

Repräsentant(in) <-en, -en> [re·prɛ·zɛn·'tant] *m(f)* representative

repräsentativ [re·prɛ·zɛn·ta·'ti:f] **I.** *adj* **1.** (*aussagekräftig: Ergebnis, Querschnitt*) representative **2.** (*vorzeigbar: Aufmachung, Auftreten*) prestigious **II.** *adv* imposingly

repräsentieren * [re·prɛ·zɛn·'ti:·rən] **I.** *vt* to represent **II.** *vi* to perform official and social functions

Reptil <-s, -ien> [rɛp·'ti:l] *nt* reptile

Republik <-, -en> [re·pu·'bli:k] *f* republic

Republikaner(in) <-s, -> [re·pu·bli·'ka:·nɐ] *m(f)* **1.** (*in den USA*) Republican

2. (*in Deutschland*) member of the German Republican Party (*an ultra right-wing party*)

Reservat <-[e]s, -e> [re·zɛr·'va:t] *nt* reservation

Reserve <-, -n> [re·'zɛr·və] *f a. fig* reserve; **jdn aus der ~ locken** to bring sb out of his/her shell

Reservekanister *m* gas can

Reserverad *nt* spare tire

Reservespieler(in) *m(f)* substitute

reservieren * [re·zɛr·'vi:·rən] *vt* to reserve

Residenz <-, -en> [re·zi·'dɛnts] *f* residence

resolut [re·zo·'lu:t] **I.** *adj* resolute **II.** *adv* resolutely

Respekt <-s> [re·'spɛkt, rɛ-] *m kein pl* respect (**vor** +*dat* for); **jdm** [**bei jdm**] **~ verschaffen** to earn [sb's] respect

respektieren * [re·spɛk·'ti:·rən, rɛ-] *vt* to respect

respektlos **I.** *adj* disrespectful **II.** *adv* disrespectfully

respektvoll **I.** *adj* respectful **II.** *adv* respectfully

Rest <-[e]s, -e *o schweiz a.* -en> [rɛst] *m* rest; (*von Essen*) leftovers *npl*; **der ~ ist für Sie!** (*beim Bezahlen*) keep the change! ▶ **jdm den ~ geben** *fam* to be the final straw for sb

Restaurant <-s, -s> [rɛ·sto·'rã:] *nt* restaurant

restaurieren * [rɛ·stau·'ri:·rən, rɛ-] *vt* to restore

restlich *adj* remaining

Resultat <-[e]s, -e> [re·zʊl·'ta:t] *nt* result

resultieren * [re·zʊl·'ti:·rən] *vi geh* to result (**aus** +*dat* from, **in** +*dat* in)

Retourbillett ['rə·tu:ɐ·bɪl·jɛt] *nt schweiz* (*Rückfahrkarte*) round-trip ticket

Retourgeld *nt schweiz* (*Wechselgeld*) change

retten ['rɛ·tn̩] **I.** *vt* to save (**vor** +*dat* from) ▶ **bist du noch zu ~?** *fam* are you out of your mind? **II.** *vr* **sich** akk ~ to save oneself (**vor** +*dat* from) ▶ **rette sich, wer kann!** run for your lives!; **sich** akk **vor etw** *dat* **nicht mehr ~ können** to not have a chance against sth

R

Retter(in) <-s, -> *m(f)* rescuer

Rettich <-s, -e> ['rɛ·tɪç] *m* radish

Rettung <-, -en> *f* rescue; **für jdn gibt es keine ~ mehr** there is no saving sb ▶ **jds letzte ~ sein** to be sb's last hope

Rettungsboot *nt* lifeboat

Rettungsring *m* **1.** NAUT life preserver **2.** *hum fam* (*Fettpolster*) spare tire

Rettungswagen *m* ambulance

Reue <-> ['rɔʏə] *f kein pl* remorse

reumütig ['rɔʏ·myː·tɪç] **I.** *adj* remorseful; (*Sünder*) repentant **II.** *adv* remorsefully

Revanche <-, -n> [re·ˈvãː·ʃə, re·ˈvaŋ·ʃə] *f* **1.** (*Revanchespiel*) rematch **2.** (*Rache*) revenge

revanchieren * [re·vã·ˈʃiː·rən] *vr* (*sich erkenntlich zeigen*) **sich** *akk* **bei jdm für eine Einladung ~** to return sb's invitation

Revier <-s, -e> [re·ˈviːɐ̯] *nt* **1.** (*Polizeidienststelle*) police station **2.** (*Jagdrevier*) preserve **3.** (*Zuständigkeitsbereich*) area of responsibility

Revision <-, -en> [re·vi·ˈzjoːn] *f* **1.** FIN, ÖKON audit **2.** JUR appeal **3.** TYPO final proofreading

Revolte <-, -n> [re·ˈvɔl·tə] *f* revolt

Revolution <-, -en> [re·vo·lu·ˈtsjoːn] *f* revolution

revolutionär [re·vo·lu·tsjo·ˈnɛːɐ̯] *adj* revolutionary

Revolutionär(in) <-s, -e> [re·vo·lu·tsjo·ˈnɛːɐ̯] *m(f)* POL revolutionary

Revolver <-s, -> [re·ˈvɔl·ve] *m* revolver

Revue <-, -n> [re·ˈvyː, rə·ˈvyː] *f* THEAT revue

Rezension <-, -en> [re·tsɛn·ˈzjoːn] *f* review

Rezept <-[e]s, -e> [re·ˈtsɛpt] *nt* **1.** KOCHK recipe **2.** MED prescription

Rezeption <-, -en> [re·tsɛp·ˈtsjoːn] *f* reception

rezeptpflichtig *adj* requiring a prescription; **~ sein** to be available only with a prescription

Rhabarber <-s, -> [ra·ˈbar·be] *m* rhubarb

Rhein <-s> [rain] *m* Rhine

rhetorisch [re·ˈtoː·rɪʃ] **I.** *adj* rhetorical

II. *adv* rhetorically

Rheuma <-s> ['rɔʏ·ma] *nt kein pl fam* rheumatism

rheumatisch [rɔʏ·ˈmaː·tɪʃ] *adj* rheumatic

Rheumatismus <-> [rɔʏ·ma·ˈtɪs·mus] *m kein pl* rheumatism

Rhinozeros <-[ses], -se> [ri·ˈnoː·tse·rɔs] *nt* rhinoceros

rhythmisch ['rʏt·mɪʃ] *adj* rhythmic[al]

Rhythmus <-, Rhythmen> ['rʏt·mus] *m* rhythm

richten ['rɪç·tn̩] **I.** *vr* **1.** (*bestimmt sein*) **sich** *akk* **an jdn ~** to be directed at sb **2.** (*sich orientieren*) **sich** *akk* **nach jdm/etw ~** to comply with sb/sth; **wir richten uns ganz nach Ihnen** [we'll do] whatever is best for you **II.** *vt* **1.** (*lenken*) **etw** *akk* (*auf +akk* toward/at); **eine Schusswaffe auf jdn ~** to point a gun at sb **2.** (*adressieren*) to address (**an** +*akk* to) **3.** *dial* (*reparieren*) to fix **III.** *vi geh* to pass judgment (**über** +*akk* on)

Richter(in) <-s, -> ['rɪç·te] *m(f)* judge

Richtgeschwindigkeit *f* recommended speed limit

richtig ['rɪç·tɪç] **I.** *adj* **1.** (*korrekt*) right; (*Lösung*) correct **2.** (*angebracht*) right; **es war ~, dass du gegangen bist** you were right to leave **3.** (*am richtigen Ort*) **irgendwo/bei jdm ~ sein** to be in the right place/at the right address **4.** (*echt*) real; **ein ~er Winter mit viel Schnee** a real winter with lots of snow **5.** *fam* (*regelrecht*) **du bist ein ~er Idiot!** you're a real idiot! **6.** (*passend*) right (**für** +*dat* for) **7.** *fam* (*in Ordnung*) all right **II.** *adv* **1.** (*korrekt*) correctly; **Sie haben irgendwie nicht ~ gerechnet** you've miscalculated somehow; **ich höre doch wohl nicht ~?** you must be joking [*o* kidding]!; **eine ~ gehende Uhr** an accurate watch; **sehr ~!** that's correct! **2.** *fam* (*regelrecht*) really; **das schmeckt ~ gut** this tastes really good

richtig|liegen *vi irreg fam* [**mit etw** *dat*] **~** to be right [about sth]; **bei jdm ~** to have come to the right person

richtig|stellen *vt* **etw ~** to correct sth

Richtlinie *f meist pl* guideline *usu pl*

Richtung <-, -en> ['rɪç·tʊŋ] *f* direction

richtungweisend *adj* pointing the way [ahead]

Richtwert *m* guideline

riechen <roch, gerochen> ['riːçn̩] **I.** *vi* **1.** (*duften*) to smell (**nach** +*dat* of); (*stinken a.*) to stink *pej* **2.** (*schnuppern*) **an jdm/etw** ~ to smell sb/sth **II.** *vt* to smell; **riechst du nichts?** don't you smell anything? ▶ **jdn nicht** ~ **können** to not be able to stand sb; **das konnte ich nicht** ~! how was I supposed to know that!

Riegel <-s, -> ['riːgl̩] *m* **1.** (*Verschluss*) bolt; **vergiss nicht, den** ~ **vorzulegen** don't forget to bolt the door **2.** (*Schokoriegel*) bar ▶ **etw** *dat* **einen** ~ **vorschieben** to put a stop to sth

Riemen <-s, -> ['riːmən] *m* (*schmaler Streifen*) strap ▶ **sich** *akk* **am** ~ **reißen** to pull oneself together

Riese, Riesin <-n, -n> ['riːzə, 'riːzɪn] *m, f* giant

rieseln ['riːzl̩n] *vi sein* **1.** (*rinnen*) to trickle (**auf** +*akk* onto) **2.** (*bröckeln*) **von etw** *dat* ~ to flake off [of] sth

riesengroß ['riːzn̩'groːs] *adj fam* colossal, enormous; **eine ~e Dummheit** something really stupid; **eine ~e Enttäuschung/Überraschung** a huge disappointment/surprise

Riesenrad *nt* Ferris wheel

riesig ['riːzɪç] **I.** *adj* **1.** (*ungeheuer groß*) gigantic **2.** (*gewaltig*) enormous; (*Anstrengung, Enttäuschung*) huge **3.** *pred fam* (*gelungen*) great; **die Party war einfach** ~ the party was really great **II.** *adv fam* enormously; **das war** ~ **nett von Ihnen** that was terribly nice of you

Riff <-[e]s, -e> [rɪf] *nt* reef

Rille <-, -n> ['rɪlə] *f* groove

Rind <-[e]s, -er> [rɪnt] *nt* **1.** (*Kuh*) cow **2.** *kein pl* (*Rindfleisch*) beef

Rinde <-, -n> ['rɪndə] *f* **1.** (*eines Baums*) bark **2.** (*von Brot*) crust; (*von Käse*) rind

Rinderbraten *m* roast beef

Rinderfilet *nt* fillet of beef

Rinderwahnsinn *m kein pl* mad cow disease *fam*

Rindfleisch *nt* beef

Rindvieh <-viecher> *nt* **1.** *kein pl* (*Rinder*) cattle *no art*, + *pl vb* (*Dummkopf*) **2.** *sl* (*Dummkopf*) ass

Ring <-[e]s, -e> [rɪŋ] *m* **1.** (*Fingerring, Öse*) ring **2.** (*Ringstraße*) beltway **3.** (*Boxring*) ring

ringen <rang, gerungen> ['rɪŋən] *vi* **1.** (*im Ringkampf kämpfen*) to wrestle **2.** (*kämpfen*) **mit sich** *dat* ~ to wrestle with oneself **3.** (*schnappen*) **nach Atem** ~ to gasp for breath **4.** (*sich bemühen*) **um etw** *akk* ~ to struggle for sth

Ringen <-s> ['rɪŋən] *nt kein pl* wrestling

Ringer(in) <-s, -> *m(f)* wrestler

Ringfinger *m* ring finger

Ringkampf *m* wrestling match

ringsum ['rɪŋs-'ʔʊm] *adv* [all] around

Rinne <-, -n> ['rɪnə] *f* **1.** (*Furche*) furrow **2.** (*Dachrinne, Regenrinne*) gutter

rinnen <rann, geronnen> ['rɪnən] *vi sein* **1.** (*fließen*) to run **2.** (*sickern: Tränen*) to trickle

Rinnstein *m* **1.** (*Gosse*) gutter **2.** (*Bordstein*) curb

Rippchen <-s, -> ['rɪpçən] *nt* smoked pork ribs *pl*, spare rib *usu pl*

Rippe <-, -n> ['rɪpə] *f* ANAT, KOCHK rib

Rippenfellentzündung *f* pleurisy

Risiko <-s, -s *o österr* Risken> ['riːziko] *nt* risk

Risikogruppe *f* [high-]risk group

riskant [rɪs-'kant] *adj* risky

riskieren* [rɪs-'kiː-rən] *vt* to risk; **ich riskiere es!** I'll chance it!; **[es]** ~, **etw zu tun** to risk doing sth; **seinen Job** ~ to put one's job at risk; **sein Leben** ~ to risk one's life

riss^{RR}, **riß**^{ALT} [rɪs] *imp von* **reißen**

Riss^{RR} <-es, -e>, **Riß**^{ALT} <Risses, Risse> [rɪs] *m* (*in Kleidung, Muskel, Wand*) tear

rissig ['rɪsɪç] *adj* (*Leder, Wand*) cracked; (*Hände, Lippen*) chapped

ritt [rɪt] *imp von* **reiten**

Ritt <-[e]s, -e> [rɪt] *m* ride

Ritter <-s, -> ['rɪtɐ] *m* knight

Ritual <-s, -e> [ri-'tu-aːl] *nt* ritual

Ritze <-, -n> ['rɪtsə] *f* crack

ritzen ['rɪtsn̩] **I.** *vt* to carve **II.** *vr* **sich** *akk* ~ to cut oneself

Rivale, Rivalin <-n, -n> [riˈvaːlə, riˈvaːlɪn] m, f rival

rivalisieren * [ri·va·li·ˈziː·rən] vi geh **mit jdm ~** to compete with sb

Rivalität <-, -en> [ri·va·li·ˈtɛːt] f geh rivalry

Robbe <-, -n> [ˈrɔbə] f seal

Robe <-, -n> [ˈroː·bə] f 1. (langes Abendkleid) evening gown 2. (Talar) robe[s pl]

Roboter <-s, -> [ˈroː·bɔ·tɐ] m robot

robust [roˈbʊst] adj robust

röcheln [ˈrœ·çln] vi to breath rattles; (Sterbender) to give the death rattle liter

Rock <-[e]s, Röcke> [rɔk] m 1. (Damenrock) skirt 2. dial (Jackett) jacket 3. schweiz (Kleid) dress

Rodelbahn f toboggan run

rodeln [ˈroː·dln] vi sein o haben to sled, to toboggan

Rogen <-s, -> [ˈroː·gn] m roe

Roggen <-s> [ˈrɔ·gn] m kein pl rye

Roggenbrot nt rye bread

roh [roː] I. adj 1. (nicht zubereitet) raw 2. (unbearbeitet) crude; (Holzklotz) rough 3. (grob) rough; **mit ~er Gewalt** by brute force, with brute strength II. adv (grob) roughly

Rohbau <-bauten> m shell

Rohkost f raw vegetables npl

Rohling <-s, -e> [ˈroː·lɪŋ] m (brutaler Kerl) brute

Rohöl nt crude oil

Rohr <-[e]s, -e> [roːɐ̯] nt 1. (Röhre) pipe; (kleinerer Durchmesser, flexibel) tube 2. südd, österr (Backofen) oven

Rohrbruch m burst pipe

Röhre <-, -n> [ˈrøː·rə] f 1. (Hohlkörper) tube 2. (Leuchtstoffröhre) neon tube 3. (Backofen) oven

Rohrleitung f pipe

Rohrzucker m cane sugar

Rohstoff m raw material

Rollladen ALT <-s, Rolläden> m s. **Rollladen**

Rollbahn f LUFT runway

Rolle <-, -n> [ˈrɔ·lə] f 1. (Gerolltes) roll; **eine ~ Draht/Toilettenpapier** a roll of wire/toilet paper 2. (Garnrolle) reel 3. (Laufrad) roller; (Möbelrolle) caster 4. (Turnübung) roll 5. FILM, THEAT role,

part; **eine ~ spielen** to play a pa[rt] 6. (Beteiligung, Part) role, part; **da** spielt doch keine ~! that doesn't mat[ter!] 7. SOZIOL rolle ▸ **aus der ~ falle[n]** to behave badly

rollen [ˈrɔ·lən] I. vi sein to roll ▸ **etw[ins R~ bringen** to set sth in motio[n] II. vt 1. (zusammenrollen) to roll [u, sep] 2. (rollend fortbewegen) to ro[III. vr sich akk ~ to curl up

Rollenspiel nt role play

Roller <-s, -> [ˈrɔ·lɐ] m 1. (Kinderfah[r] zeug) scooter 2. (Motorroller) [moto[r] scooter 3. österr (Rollo) [roller] blind[[o shade]

Rolli <-s, -s> [ˈrɔ·lli] m MODE fam turtle[neck

Rollkragen m turtleneck

Rollladen RR <-s, Rollläden> m storm[shutters npl

Rollschuh m roller skate; **~ laufen** t[roller-skate

Rollstuhl m wheelchair

Rollstuhlfahrer(in) m(f) wheelchair use[r]

rollstuhlgerecht adj wheelchair-acces[sible

Rolltreppe f escalator

Rom <-s> [roːm] nt kein pl Rome

Roman <-s, -e> [roˈmaːn] m novel

romanisch [roˈmaː·nɪʃ] adj 1. LING, GEO[Romance 2. HIST Romanesque spe[3. schweiz (rätoromanisch) Rhaeto[Romanic

Romanistik <-> [ro·ma·ˈnɪs·tɪk] f kein p[Romance studies

Romanschriftsteller(in) m(f) novelist

Romantik <-> [roˈman·tɪk] f kein p[1. (Epoche) **die ~** the Romantic perio[2. (gefühlsbetonte Stimmung) romanti[cism; [einen] **Sinn für ~ haben** to b[e] a romantic

romantisch [roˈman·tɪʃ] I. adj 1. (zu[r] Romantik gehörend) Romantic 2. (ge[fühlvoll) romantic 3. (malerisch) pictur[esque II. adv picturesquely

Römer(in) <-s, -> m(f) Roman

römisch [ˈrøː·mɪʃ] adj Roman

röntgen [ˈrœnt·gn] vt to X-ray; **sich ak[~ lassen** to be X-rayed

Röntgenstrahlen pl X-rays pl

rosa [ˈroː·za] adj pink

Rose <-, -n> ['roːzə] f **1.** (*Strauch*) rose bush **2.** (*Blüte*) rose

Rosenkohl m [Brussels] sprouts

Rosenmontag m the Monday before Shrove Tuesday, the climax of the German carnival celebration

rosig ['roːzɪç] adj rosy

Rosine <-, -n> [roˈziːnə] f raisin

Rosmarin <-s> ['roːsmaˈriːn] m kein pl rosemary

Rosskastanie ᴿᴿ [-kaˈstaːnjə] f [horse] chestnut

Rost¹ <-[e]s> [rɔst] m kein pl (*auf Eisen, Stahl*) rust

Rost² <-[e]s, -e> [rɔst] m **1.** (*Gitter*) grating **2.** (*Grillrost*) grill **3.** (*Bettrost*) base

rosten ['rɔstn] vi sein o haben to rust

rösten ['rœstn] vt to roast; (*Brot*) to toast

rostfrei adj stainless

Rösti ['røːsti] pl schweiz ≈ hash browns pl

rostig ['rɔstɪç] adj rusty

rot <-er o röter, -este o röteste> [roːt] adj red; ~ **werden** to turn red; (*aus Scham a.*) to blush

rotblond adj (*Frau*) strawberry blond[e]; (*Mann*) sandy-haired

rotbraun adj reddish brown

Röteln ['røːtln] pl rubella spec

röten ['røːtn] vr **sich** akk ~ to turn red; (*Wangen a.*) to blush

rothaarig adj red-haired; ~ **sein** to have red hair

rotieren* [roˈtiːrən] vi **1.** (*sich drehen*) to rotate **2.** fam (*hektisch agieren*) to run around like crazy

Rotkohl m, **Rotkraut** nt österr, südd red cabbage

rötlich ['røːtlɪç] adj reddish

Rotlichtviertel nt red-light district

Rotstift m red pencil/pen

Rotwein m red wine

Roulade <-, -n> [ruˈlaːdə] f KOCHK roulade spec

Route <-, -n> ['ruːtə] f route

Routine <-> [ruˈtiːnə] f kein pl routine

routiniert [rutiˈniːɐt] adj experienced

Rowdy <-s, -s> ['rauˌdi] m hooligan

rubbeln ['rʊbln] vt, vi to rub hard

Rübe <-, -n> ['ryːbə] f KOCHK, BOT turnip; **Gelbe ~** südd, schweiz carrot; **Rote ~** beet

Rubrik <-, -en> [ruˈbriːk] f **1.** (*Kategorie*) category **2.** (*Spalte*) column

Ruck <-[e]s, -e> [rʊk] m Jolt ▶ **sich** dat **einen ~ geben** to pull oneself together

ruckartig I. adj jerky, jolting attr II. adv with a jerk

rücken ['rʏkn] I. vi sein to move; **zur Seite ~** to move aside; (*auf einer Bank a.*) to scoot over fam II. vt haben to move

Rücken <-s, -> ['rʏkn] m **1.** ANAT back; **jdm den ~ zudrehen** to turn one's back on sb; **auf dem ~** on one's back; **hinter jds ~** a. fig behind sb's back **2.** KOCHK saddle **3.** (*Buchrücken*) spine ▶ **jdm läuft es [eis]kalt über den ~** cold shivers run down sb's spine; **jdm in den ~ fallen** to stab sb in the back; **jdm den ~ stärken** to give sb moral support

Rückenmark nt spinal cord

Rückenschmerzen pl back pain, backache

Rückenschwimmen nt backstroke

Rückenwind m tail wind

Rückerstattung f refund; (*von Verlusten*) reimbursement form

Rückfahrkarte f return ticket

Rückfahrt f return trip

Rückfall m **1.** MED relapse form **2.** JUR second offense

rückfällig adj **1.** JUR (*Täter*) recidivist attr **2.** (*Alkoholiker, Raucher, Patient*) relapsed; ~ **werden** to suffer a relapse

Rückflug m return flight

Rückfrage f question (**zu** +dat regarding)

Rückgabe f return

Rückgang m drop, fall

rückgängig adj **etw ~ machen** to cancel sth

Rückgrat <-[e]s, -e> nt **1.** (*Wirbelsäule*) spine **2.** kein pl fig (*Stehvermögen*) backbone

Rückhalt m support

Rückkehr <-> f kein pl return

Rücklage f (*Ersparnisse*) savings npl

rückläufig ['rʏkˌlɔɪfɪç] adj declining, falling

Rücklicht nt tail light; (eines Fahrrads a.) rear light

Rückreise f return trip

Rucksack ['rʊk·zak] m backpack

Rückschlag m 1. (Verschlechterung) setback; **einen ~ erleiden** to suffer a setback 2. (von Schusswaffe) recoil

Rückschritt m step backwards

Rückseite f 1. (von Blatt, Buch, Münze) reverse [side] 2. (von Gebäude, Gerät) back, rear

Rücksicht <-, -en> ['rʏk·zɪçt] f consideration; **~ [auf jdn] nehmen** to show consideration [for sb]; **~ auf etw** akk **nehmen** to take sth into consideration

rücksichtslos I. adj inconsiderate (**gegenüber** +dat toward) II. adv inconsiderately

Rücksichtslosigkeit <-> f kein pl thoughtlessness

rücksichtsvoll I. adj considerate (**zu** +dat toward) II. adv considerately

Rücksitz m rear seat

Rückspiegel m rearview mirror

Rückspiel nt rematch

Rückstand m 1. (Verzug) arrears npl; **mit der Miete in ~ sein** to be behind on the rent 2. pl (fällige Zahlungen) outstanding payments pl 3. (von Chemikalien) residue form

rückständig ['rʏk·ʃtɛn·dɪç] adj 1. (überfällig) overdue 2. (zurückgeblieben) backward

Rückstrahler <-s, -> m reflector

Rücktritt m 1. (Amtsniederlegung) resignation 2. (von einem Vertrag) withdrawal (**von** +dat from)

Rückwand f 1. (rückwärtige Mauer) back wall 2. (rückwärtige Platte) back [panel]

rückwärts ['rʏk·vɛrts] adv 1. (rücklings) backwards; **~ einparken** to back into a parking space 2. (nach hinten) backward; **Salto ~** backward somersault

Rückwärtsgang m reverse [gear]

Rückweg m way back; **sich** akk **auf den ~ machen** to head back

rückwirkend I. adj retroactive II. adv retroactively

Rückzahlung f repayment

Rückzieher <-s, -> m **einen ~ machen** fam (eine Zusage zurückziehen) to back out [of a commitment]; (nachgeben) to back down

Rückzug m MIL retreat; **den ~ antreten** to retreat

Rüde <-n, -n> ['ry:·də] m [male] dog

Rudel <-s, -> ['ru:·dl] nt herd; (von Wölfen) pack; (von Menschen) swarm

Ruder <-s, -> ['ru:·dɐ] nt 1. (langes Paddel) oar 2. (Steuerruder) helm; (eines kleineren Bootes a.) rudder

Ruderboot nt rowboat

Ruderer, Ruderin <-s, -> m, f rower

rudern ['ru:·dɐn] vi sein o haben to row

Ruf <-[e]s, -e> [ru:f] m 1. (Ausruf) shout; (an jdn gerichtet) call 2. kein pl (Ansehen) reputation

rufen <rief, gerufen> ['ru:·fn] I. vi 1. (schreien) to cry out 2. a. fig (nach jdm/etw verlangen) [nach jdm] ~ to call [for sb]; **die Pflicht ruft** duty calls II. vt 1. (ausrufen) to shout 2. (herbestellen) to call; **jdn zu sich** dat ~ to summon sb; **jdn ~ lassen** to send for sb

Rufmord m slander, character assassination

Rufname m name that sb is called

Rufnummer f [tele]phone number

Ruhe <-> ['ru:·ə] f kein pl 1. (Stille) quiet, silence; **~!** [be] quiet!, shhh! 2. (Frieden) peace; **jdn [mit etw** dat] **in ~ lassen** to leave sb alone [about sth] 3. (Erholung) rest; **sich** dat **keine ~ gönnen** to not allow oneself any rest; **jdm keine ~ lassen** to not give sb a moment's rest 4. (Gelassenheit) calm[ness]; **[die] ~ bewahren** to keep calm; **jdn aus der ~ bringen** to throw sb [for a loop]; **sich** akk **[von jdm/etw] nicht aus der ~ bringen lassen** to not let oneself get rattled [by sb/sth]; **in [aller] ~** [really] calmly; **immer mit der ~!** fam take it easy!, easy does it! ▶ **keine ~ geben, bis ...** to not rest until ...; **sich** akk **zur ~ setzen** to retire; **die ~ weghaben** fam to be unflappable

Ruhelosigkeit <-> f kein pl restlessness

ruhen ['ru:·ən] vi 1. (ausruhen) to rest 2. (eingestellt sein) to be suspended

Ruhestand m kein pl retirement; **in den**

~ gehen to retire; **im ~** retired
Ruheständler(in) <-s, -> ['ruː·əʃtɛnt·lɐ] m(f) retiree
Ruhestörung f disturbance of the peace
Ruhetag m (arbeitsfreier Tag) day off; (Feiertag) day of rest
ruhig ['ruː·ɪç] I. adj 1. (still) quiet; **sei ~!** fam [be] quiet!, shhh! 2. (geruhsam: Abend) quiet 3. (unbewegt: Meer) calm; (Blick, Hand) steady 4. (gelassen: Person, Stimme) calm; (Gewissen) clear II. adv (gelassen) calmly III. part fam geh **~, ich komme schon alleine zurecht** it's okay if you leave; I can manage on my own; **du kannst ~ hierbleiben** you're welcome to stay here
Ruhm <-es> [ruːm] m kein pl fame
rühmen ['ryː·mən] I. vt to praise II. vr **sich** akk **einer S.** gen **~** to brag about sth
rühmlich adj praiseworthy
Rührei ['ryːɐ·ʔai] nt scrambled eggs pl
rühren ['ryː·rən] I. vt 1. (umrühren) to stir 2. (innerlich: Herz) to touch; **jdn ~** to move sb II. vr (sich bewegen) **sich** akk **~** to move
rührend I. adj touching, moving II. adv touchingly
rührselig adj tear-jerking fam; **ein ~er Film/ein ~es Buch** a tearjerker fam
Rührung <-> f kein pl emotion
Ruin <-s> [ru·'iːn] m kein pl ruin
Ruine <-, -n> [ru·'iː·nə] f ruin[s pl]
ruinieren* [rui·'niː·rən] vt to ruin
rülpsen ['rʏlp·sn̩] vi to burp
Rum <-s, -s> [rʊm] m rum
Rumäne, Rumänin <-n, -n> [ru·'mɛː·nə, ru·'mɛː·nɪn] m, f Romanian; s. a. **Deutsche(r)**
Rumänien <-s> [ru·'mɛː·ni·ən] nt Romania; s. a. **Deutschland**
rum|kriegen vt sl 1. (zu etw bewegen) **jdn** [**zu etw** dat] **~** to talk sb into [doing] sth 2. (verbringen) **den Tag irgendwie ~** to get through the day somehow
Rummel <-s> ['rʊ·ml̩] m kein pl 1. fam (Aufhebens) [hustle and] bustle 2. (Betriebsamkeit) commotion 3. dial s. **Rummelplatz**
Rummelplatz m fairground
Rumpf <-[e]s, Rümpfe> [rʊmpf] m

1. (Torso) torso 2. (eines Flugzeugs) fuselage; (eines Schiffes) hull
Rumpsteak ['rʊmp·ʃteːk] nt rump steak
rund [rʊnt] I. adj 1. (kreisförmig) round 2. (rundlich) plump; (Hüften) well-rounded; (Wangen) chubby 3. fam **eine ~e Summe** a round sum; **~e fünf Jahre** a good five years 4. (Geschmack) full II. adv 1. **~ um ...** around ... 2. (etwa) around; **~ 100 Euro** approximately 100 euros
Runde <-, -n> ['rʊn·də] f 1. (Gesellschaft) company 2. (Rundgang) rounds pl; (eines Polizisten) beat; (eines Briefträgers) route 3. sport lap; (im Boxen) round 4. (Bestellung) round [of drinks]; **eine ~ spendieren** to buy a [o the next] round ▶ [**mit etw** dat] **über die ~n kommen** to make ends meet [with sth]
Rundfahrt f (sightseeing) tour
Rundflug m sightseeing flight
Rundfunk m 1. geh radio; **im ~** on the radio 2. (Sendeanstalt) broadcasting
Rundgang m walk; (zur Besichtigung) tour
rundlich ['rʊnt·lɪç] adj plump; (Hüften) well-rounded; (Wangen) chubby
Rundreise f tour (**durch** +akk of)
Rundung <-, -en> f 1. (Wölbung) curve 2. pl fam curves
Runzel <-, -n> ['rʊn·tsl̩] f wrinkle
runzelig ['rʊn·tsə·lɪç] adj wrinkled
runzeln ['rʊn·tsl̩n] vt to crease; (Stirn) to wrinkle
Rüpel <-s, -> ['ryː·pl̩] m lout
rupfen ['rʊp·fn̩] vt 1. (Huhn) to pluck 2. (zupfen) to pull up sep (**aus** +dat out of)
ruppig ['rʊ·pɪç] I. adj gruff; (Antwort) abrupt II. adv gruffly
Rüsche <-, -n> ['ryː·ʃə] f frill
Ruß <-es> [ruːs] m kein pl soot; (beim Dieselmotor) particulate
Russe, Russin <-n, -n> ['rʊ·sə] m, f Russian; s. a. **Deutsche(r)**
Rüssel <-s, -> ['rʏ·sl̩] m snout; (eines Elefanten a.) trunk
rußig ['ruː·sɪç] adj blackened [with soot pred]; (verschmutzt a.) sooty
russisch ['rʊ·sɪʃ] adj Russian; s. a. **deutsch**

R

Russland^{RR}, **Rußland**^{ALT} <-s> ['rʊs·lant] nt Russia; s. a. Deutschland

rüsten ['rʏs·tn̩] vi to arm

rüstig ['rʏs·tɪç] adj sprightly

rustikal [rʊs·ti·'ka:l] I. adj rustic II. adv in a rustic style

Rüstung <-, -en> ['rʏs·tʊŋ] f 1. kein pl (das Rüsten) [re]armament 2. (Ritterrüstung) armor

Rüstungsindustrie f weapons industry

Rute <-, -n> ['ru:·tə] f 1. (Gerte) switch 2. (Angelrute) fishing rod

Rutsch <-es, -e> [rʊtʃ] m landslide ▶ **in einem ~** fam in one go; **guten ~!** fam Happy New Year!

rutschen ['rʊt·ʃn̩] vi sein 1. (ausrutschen) to slip; (Auto) to skid 2. fam (rücken) to move; **auf dem Stuhl hin und her ~** to fidget in one's chair; **rutsch mal!** scoot over! 3. (gleiten) to slide; (Kleidung) to slip [down]

rutschfest adj nonslip

rutschig ['rʊt·ʃɪç] adj slippery

rütteln ['rʏ·tln̩] I. vt to shake II. vi an etw dat ~ to shake sth; **daran ist nicht zu ~** (kein Zweifel) there's no doubt about it

S

S, s <-, -> [ɛs] nt S, s; **~ wie Siegfried** S as in Sierra

s. Abk von **siehe**

Saal <-[e]s, Säle> [za:l] m hall

Saat <-, -en> [za:t] f 1. kein pl (das Säen) sowing 2. (Saatgut) seed[s pl]

Sabbat <-s, -e> ['za·bat] m the Sabbath

Säbel <-s, -> ['zɛː·bl̩] m saber

Sabotage <-, -n> [za·bo·'ta:·ʒə] f sabotage

Sachbearbeiter(in) m(f) (in einer Behörde) official in charge

Sachbeschädigung f vandalism

Sachbuch nt nonfiction book

Sache <-, -n> ['za·xə] f 1. (Ding) thing 2. (Angelegenheit) matter; **eine gute ~** a good cause; **das ist meine ~** that's my business 3. (Aufgabe) **mit jdm gemeinsame ~ machen** to collude with

sb; **sie macht keine halben ~n** she finishes what she starts; **er macht seine ~ gut** he's doing well 4. (Sachlage) **sich** dat **seiner ~ sicher sein** to be confident about what one's doing; **zur ~ kommen** to get to the point; **bei der ~ sein** to concentrate, to pay attention; **nichts zur ~ tun** to be irrelevant

Sachgebiet nt field

sachkundig adj [well-]informed

sachlich ['zax·lɪç] I. adj 1. (objektiv) objective 2. (inhaltlich: Fehler) factual 3. (schmucklos: Stil) functional II. adv 1. (objektiv) objectively 2. (inhaltlich) factually

Sachschaden m property damage

Sachsen <-s> ['zak·sn̩] nt Saxony

sächsisch ['zɛk·sɪʃ] adj Saxon, of Saxony pred

sachte ['zax·tə] adv gently

Sachverständige(r) f(m) dekl wie adj expert

Sachwert m real value

Sack <-[e]s, Säcke> [zak] m 1. (großer Beutel) sack, bag 2. südd, österr, schweiz (Hosentasche) [pants] pocket ▶ **jdm auf den ~ gehen** derb to get on sb's nerves

Sackgasse f a. fig dead end a. fig

Sadismus <-> [za·'dɪs·mʊs] m kein pl sadism

Sadist(in) <-en, -en> [za·'dɪst] m(f) sadist

sadistisch I. adj sadistic II. adv sadistically

säen ['zɛː·ən] vt, vi to sow

Safari <-, -s> [za·'fa:·ri] f safari

Safran <-s, -e> ['zaf·ra:n] m saffron

Saft <-[e]s, Säfte> [zaft] m 1. (Fruchtsaft) [fruit] juice 2. (Pflanzensaft) sap 3. fam (Strom) juice

saftig ['zaf·tɪç] adj 1. (Früchte) juicy 2. fig (Rechnung) steep

Sage <-, -n> ['za·gə] f legend

Säge <-, -n> ['zɛː·gə] f 1. (Werkzeug) saw 2. österr (Sägewerk) sawmill

sagen ['za·gn̩] I. vt 1. (äußern) to say; **warum haben Sie das nicht gleich gesagt?** why didn't you say so before? **was ich noch ~ wollte, ...** [oh, and one more thing ...] 2. (mitteilen) to tell

wem ~ Sie das! you don't need to tell me [that]!; **das ist nicht gesagt** that is by no means certain; **nichts zu ~ haben** to have nothing to say **3.** (*meinen*) **was ~ Sie dazu?** what do you think?; **das kann man wohl ~!** you can say that again! **4.** (*bedeuten*) **jdm etwas ~** to mean something to sb; **das hat nichts zu ~** it doesn't mean a thing **II.** *vi* **sag/~ Sie, ...** tell me, ...; **unter uns gesagt** between you and me; **sag bloß!** you don't say!

sägen ['zɛ:·gn̩] *vt, vi* to saw

Sahara <-> [za·'ha:·ra] *f kein pl* **die ~** the Sahara

Sahne <-> ['za:·nə] *f kein pl* cream; (*Schlagsahne*) whipping cream

Sahnetorte *f* layer cake (*filled with whipped cream*)

Saison <-, -s *o südd, österr* -en> [zɛ·'zõ:] *f* season; **außerhalb der ~** in the off-season

Saisonarbeiter(in) *m(f)* seasonal worker

Saite <-, -n> ['zai·tə] *f* MUS string ▶ **andere ~n aufziehen** to get tough

Saiteninstrument *nt* string[ed] instrument

Sakko <-s, -s> ['zako] *m o nt* sports coat

Sakrament <-[e]s, -e> [za·kra·'mɛnt] *nt* sacrament

Salamander <-s, -> [za·la·'man·dɐ] *m* salamander

Salami <-, -s> [za·'la:·mi] *f* salami

Salat <-[e]s, -e> [za·'la:t] *m* **1.** (*Pflanze*) lettuce **2.** (*Gericht*) salad

Salatgurke *f* cucumber

Salatsoße *f* salad dressing

Salbe <-, -n> ['zal·bə] *f* ointment

Salbei <-s> ['zal·bai] *m kein pl* sage

Saldo <-s, -s> ['zal·do] *m* FIN balance

Salmonellenvergiftung *f* salmonella poisoning

salopp [za·'lɔp] **I.** *adj* **1.** (*leger*) casual **2.** (*ungezwungen: Ausdrucksweise*) slangy **II.** *adv* **1.** (*leger*) casually **2.** (*ungezwungen*) **sich** *akk* **~ ausdrücken** to use slang[y] expressions

Salto <-s, -s> ['zal·to] *m* somersault; **einen ~ machen** to somersault

Salz <-es, -e> [zalts] *nt* salt

salzen <salzte, gesalzen> ['zal·tsn̩] **I.** *vt* to salt **II.** *vi* to add salt

salzig ['zal·tsɪç] *adj* salty

Salzkartoffeln *pl* boiled potatoes

Salzsäure *f kein pl* hydrochloric acid

Salzstreuer <-s, -> *m* salt shaker

Salzwasser *nt kein pl* salt water

Samen <-s, -> ['za:·mən] *m* **1.** (*Pflanzensamen*) seed **2.** *kein pl* (*Sperma*) sperm

sammeln ['za·mln̩] **I.** *vt* **1.** (*aufsammeln, zusammentragen*) to gather; (*Belege*) to keep **2.** (*Briefmarken, Münzen, Unterschriften*) to collect **II.** *vr* **sich** *akk* **~** (*sich konzentrieren*) to collect oneself **III.** *vi* **für einen guten Zweck ~** to collect for a good cause

Sammler(in) <-s, -> *m(f)* collector

Sammlung <-, -en> *f* collection

Samstag <-[e]s, -e> ['zams·ta:k] *m* Saturday; *s. a.* **Dienstag**

samstags *adv* [on] Saturdays

Samt <-[e]s, -e> [zamt] *m* velvet

sämtlich ['zɛmt·lɪç] *adj* all

Sanatorium <-, -rien> [za·na·'to:·ri̯ʊm] *nt* sanatorium

Sand <-[e]s, -e> [zant] *m* sand ▶ **das gibt es wie ~ am Meer** there are tons of them; **im ~e verlaufen** to peter out

Sandale <-, -n> [zan·'da:·lə] *f* sandal

Sandbank <-bänke> *f* sandbank

sandig ['zan·dɪç] *adj* sandy, full of sand *pred*

Sandkasten *m* sandbox

Sandstein *m* sandstone

Sandstrand *m* sandy beach

sanft [zanft] **I.** *adj* **1.** (*Berührung, Stimme*) gentle **2.** (*Farben, Musik*) soft **II.** *adv* gently

sanftmütig *adj* gentle

Sänger(in) <-s, -> ['zɛŋɐ] *m(f)* singer

sanieren* [za·'ni:·rən] *vt* **1.** (*Gebäude*) to refurbish **2.** (*Unternehmen*) to rehabilitate

Sanierung <-, -en> *f* **1.** (*eines Gebäudes*) renovation **2.** (*eines Unternehmens*) rehabilitation

sanitär [zani·'tɛːɐ̯] *adj attr* sanitary; **~e Anlagen** sanitation

Sanitäter(in) <-s, -> [zani·'tɛː·tɐ] *m(f)* paramedic

S

Sanktion <-, -en> [zaŋkˈtsɪoːn] f sanction

sanktionieren* [zaŋktsɪoˈniːrən] vt to sanction

Saphir <-s, -e> [zaˈfiːɐ] m sapphire

Sardelle <-, -n> [zarˈdɛlə] f anchovy

Sardine <-, -n> [zarˈdiːnə] f sardine

Sarg <-[e]s, Särge> [zark] m coffin, casket

Satan <-s, -e> [ˈzaːtan] m kein pl Satan

satanisch [zaˈtaːnɪʃ] I. adj attr satanic, diabolical II. adv diabolically

Satellit <-en, -en> [zateˈliːt] m satellite

Satin <-s, -s> [zaˈtɛ̃ː] m satin

Satire <-, -n> [zaˈtiːrə] f kein pl satire (**auf** +akk about/on)

satt [zat] adj 1. (gesättigt) full pred fam; **ich bin ~** I'm full; **Nudeln machen ~** pasta is filling; **sich** akk [**an etw** dat] **~ essen** to eat one's fill [of sth] 2. (kräftig: Farben) rich, deep 3. fam (überdrüssig) **etw ~ sein** to be fed up with sth

Sattel <-s, Sättel> [ˈza·tl̩] m saddle

satt|haben RR vi irreg **etw ~** to be fed up with sth

sättigen [ˈzɛ·tɪ·gn̩] vi to be filling

sättigend adj filling

Saturn <-s> [zaˈtʊrn] m kein pl Saturn

Satz[1] <-es, Sätze> [zats] m 1. LING sentence 2. (Set) set; **ein ~ Weingläser** a set of wine glasses 3. SPORT set

Satz[2] <-es, Sätze> [zats] m leap, jump; **einen ~ machen** to leap

Satz[3] <-es> [zats] m kein pl dregs npl; (Kaffeesatz) grounds npl

Satzung <-, -en> [ˈza·tsʊŋ] f constitution, statutes npl

Satzzeichen nt LING punctuation mark

Sau <-, Säue> [zau] f 1. (weibliches Schwein) sow 2. sl (schmutziger Mensch) filthy pig ▶ **jdn zur ~ machen** to chew sb out; **die ~ rauslassen** to let it all hang out; **das ist unter aller ~** it's enough to make you puke

sauber [ˈzau·bɐ] I. adj 1. (rein) clean 2. (stubenrein) **~ sein** (Tier) to be housebroken; (Kind) to be potty trained 3. (sorgfältig) neat 4. (anständig) honest II. adv (sorgfältig) neatly

Sauberkeit <-> f kein pl cleanliness

säuberlich [ˈzɔy·bɐ·lɪç] I. adj neat

II. adv neatly

säubern [ˈzɔy·bɐn] vt 1. (reinigen) to clean 2. euph (befreien) to purge (**von** +dat of)

Sauce <-, -n> [ˈzoː·sə] f s. **Soße**

sauer [ˈzau·ɐ] adj 1. (nicht süß) sour; (sauer eingelegt) pickled 2. (Säure enthaltend) acid[ic] 3. (übel gelaunt) mad (**auf** +akk at), pissed off pred (**auf** +akk at/with)

Sauerampfer <-, -n> m sorrel

Sauerbraten m sauerbraten (beef roast marinated in vinegar and herbs)

Sauerei <-, -en> [zauəˈrai] f fam 1. (schmutziger Zustand) mess 2. (unmögliches Benehmen) [downright] disgrace

Sauerkirsche f sour cherry

Sauerkraut nt dial sauerkraut

Sauerstoff [ˈzauɐ·ʃtɔf] m kein pl oxygen

Sauerstoffmangel m kein pl lack of oxygen

Sauerteig m sourdough

saufen <säuft, soff, gesoffen> [ˈzau·fn̩] I. vt fam to drink; (schneller) to knock back sep II. vi to drink

Säufer(in) <-s, -> [ˈzɔy·fɐ] m(f) fam drunk[ard], boozer

Sauferei <-, -en> [zau·fəˈrai] f fam 1. (Besäufnis) drinking party 2. (übermäßiges Trinken) boozing fam

saugen <sog o saugte, gesogen o gesaugt> [ˈzau·gn̩] vt, vi to suck (**an** +dat on)

säugen [ˈzɔy·gn̩] vt sein Junges ~ to suckle its young

Säugetier nt mammal

Säugling <-s, -e> [ˈzɔyk·lɪŋ] m baby

Säule <-, -n> [ˈzɔy·lə] f 1. ARCHIT column 2. a. fig (Stütze) pillar

Saum <-[e]s, Säume> [zaum] m hem

Sauna <-, -s> [ˈzau·na] f sauna

Säure <-, -n> [ˈzɔy·rə] f 1. CHEM acid 2. (saure Beschaffenheit) acidity, sourness

Saurier <-s, -> [ˈzau·riɐ] m dinosaur

sausen [ˈzau·zn̩] vi sein (sich schnell bewegen) to dash [off]; (schnell fahren) to roar ▶ **etw ~ lassen** to forget sth; **lass deine Verabredung doch ~** forget about your date

S<u>au</u>stall m fam pigsty

S<u>au</u>wetter nt fam lousy weather no indef art

Savanne <-, -n> [za·ˈvanə] f savanna[h]

Saxof<u>o</u>nᴿᴿ, **Saxophon** <-[e]s, -e> [zak·soˈfoːn] nt saxophone

SB [ɛsˈbeː] Abk von **Selbstbedienung** self-service

S-Bahn [ˈɛs-] f rapid transit train

Schabe <-, -n> [ˈʃaː·bə] f (cock)roach

schaben [ˈʃaː·bn̩] vt to scrape

sch<u>ä</u>big [ˈʃɛː·bɪç] adj 1. (unansehnlich) shabby 2. (gemein) mean 3. (dürftig) paltry

Schabl<u>o</u>ne <-, -n> [ʃaˈbloː·nə] f stencil

Schach <-s> [ʃax] nt kein pl 1. (Spiel) chess; **eine Partie ~** a game of chess 2. (Stellung) check; **~ und matt!** checkmate!

Schachbrett nt chessboard

Schachfigur f chess piece

schachmatt [ʃaxˈmat] adj checkmate

Schacht <-[e]s, Schächte> [ʃaxt] m 1. ʙᴇʀɢʙ shaft 2. (eines Brunnens) well

Schachtel <-, -n> [ˈʃaxtl̩] f box; **eine ~ Zigaretten** a pack of cigarettes

Schachzug m move

schade [ˈʃaː·də] adj pred 1. (bedauerlich) **wie ~!** that's too bad, what a shame; **ich finde es ~, dass ...** it's too bad that ...; **es ist ~ um ihn** it's a shame about him 2. (zu gut) **für etw** akk **zu ~ sein** to be too good for sth

Sch<u>ä</u>del <-s, -> [ˈʃɛː·dl̩] m skull ▸ **jdm br<u>u</u>mmt der ~** fam sb's head is throbbing; **einen d<u>i</u>cken ~ haben** fam to have a hangover

schaden [ˈʃaː·dn̩] vi **jdm ~** to [do] harm [to] sb; **etw** dat **~** to damage sth

Schaden <-s, Schäden> [ˈʃaː·dn̩] m damage (**durch** +akk caused by)

Schadenfreude f schadenfreude

schadenfroh I. adj malicious, gloating; **~ sein** to delight in others' misfortunes II. adv **~ grinsen** to grin maliciously

sch<u>ä</u>digen [ˈʃɛː·dɪɡn̩] vt to harm (**durch** +akk with)

sch<u>ä</u>dlich [ˈʃɛːt·lɪç] adj harmful

Sch<u>ä</u>dling <-s, -e> [ˈʃɛːt·lɪŋ] m pest

Schädlingsbekämpfungsmittel nt pesticide

Sch<u>a</u>dstoff m harmful substance; (in der Umwelt) pollutant

sch<u>a</u>dstoffarm adj (Motor) low-emission

Sch<u>a</u>dstoffbelastung f pollution

Schaf <-[e]s, -e> [ʃaːf] nt sheep

Sch<u>a</u>fbock m ram

Sch<u>ä</u>fer(in) <-s, -> [ˈʃɛː·fɐ] m(f) shepherd masc, shepherdess fem

Sch<u>ä</u>ferhund m German shepherd

Sch<u>a</u>ffell nt sheepskin

schaffen¹ <schaffte, geschafft> [ˈʃafn̩] vt 1. (bewältigen) to manage; (Examen) to pass; **es ist geschafft** it's done; **es ~, etw zu tun** to manage to do sth; **Ordnung ~** to tidy things up 2. (gelangen) **wir müssen es bis zur Grenze ~** we have to get to the border

schaffen² <schuf, geschaffen> [ˈʃafn̩] vt (herstellen) to create; **dafür bist du wie ge~** that's right up your alley fam

schaffen³ <schaffte, geschafft> [ˈʃafn̩] vi 1. südd, österr, schweiz (arbeiten) to work 2. bes südd, österr, schweiz (tun) **nichts mit jdm/etw zu ~ haben** to have nothing to do with sb/sth ▸ **jdm zu ~ machen** to give sb a hard time, to cause sb trouble

Schaffner(in) <-s, -> [ˈʃaf·nɐ] m(f) conductor

Sch<u>a</u>fherde f flock of sheep

Schaf<u>o</u>tt <-[e]s, -e> [ʃaˈfɔt] nt scaffold

Schakal <-s, -e> [ʃaˈkaːl] m jackal

Schal <-s, -s> [ʃaːl] m scarf

Schale¹ <-, -n> [ˈʃaː·lə] f 1. (Nussschale) shell 2. (Fruchtschale) skin; (abgeschält) peel ▸ **eine r<u>au</u>e ~ haben** to be a rough diamond

Schale² <-, -n> [ˈʃaː·lə] f bowl

sch<u>ä</u>len [ˈʃɛː·lən] vt, vr **sich** akk **~** to peel

Schall <-s, -e> [ʃal] m sound

Sch<u>a</u>lldämpfer <-s, -> m (einer Schusswaffe) silencer; (eines Auspuffs) muffler

sch<u>a</u>lldicht adj soundproof

schallen [ˈʃalən] vi to resound

Sch<u>a</u>llgeschwindigkeit f kein pl ᴘʜʏs speed of sound

S

Schallplatte f record

Schallwelle f sound wave

schalten ['ʃaltn̩] I. vi 1. AUTO to change gears, to shift 2. fam (begreifen) to get it 3. (sich einstellen) **auf ~ Rot** to switch to red II. vt (einstellen) to switch, to turn (**auf** +akk to)

Schalter <-s, -> ['ʃaltɐ] m 1. ELEK switch 2. ADMIN, BAHN counter

Schaltjahr nt leap year

Schaltknüppel m gearshift

Schaltung <-, -en> f 1. AUTO gearshift 2. ELEK circuit

Scham <-> [ʃaːm] f kein pl 1. (Beschämung) shame 2. (Verlegenheit) embarrassment

Schambein nt pubic bone

schämen ['ʃɛːmən] vr **sich** akk **~** to be ashamed (**wegen** +dat of); **sich** akk **vor jdm ~** to be embarrassed in front of sb; **schäm dich!** shame on you!

Schamhaar nt pubic hair

schamhaft adj shy, bashful

Schamlippen pl labia pl

schamlos adj shameless, rude

Schande <-> ['ʃandə] f kein pl disgrace, shame

schänden ['ʃɛndn̩] vt (Denkmal, Grab) to desecrate

Schanze <-, -n> ['ʃantsə] f ski jump

Schar <-, -en> [ʃaːɐ] f (von Vögeln) flock; (von Menschen) crowd

scharen ['ʃaːran] I. vt **Dinge/Menschen um sich** akk **~** to gather things/people around oneself II. vr **sich** akk **um jdn/etw ~** to gather around sb/sth

scharenweise adv in hordes

scharf <schärfer, schärfste> [ʃarf] I. adj 1. (gut geschliffen) sharp 2. (spitz zulaufend) sharp; **eine ~e Kurve** a hairpin turn 3. KOCHK spicy; (hochprozentig) strong 4. (ätzend: Reinigungsmittel) aggressive 5. (schonungslos, heftig) harsh, severe, tough; (Kontrolle) rigorous; (Konkurrenz) fierce 6. (Bombe) live 7. (konzentriert, präzise) careful; (Beobachtung) astute 8. (Foto, Umrisse) sharp; (Augen) keen 9. fam (aufreizend) spicy; **auf jdn ~ sein** to have the hots for sb; **auf etw** akk **~ sein** to be really

interested in sth 10. fam (toll) fantastic, great II. adv 1. (intensiv gewürzt) **etw ~ würzen** to season sth highly; **ich esse gerne ~** I like [eating] spicy food 2. (heftig) sharply; (kritisieren) harshly; (verurteilen) strongly 3. (präzise) **~ beobachten** to observe carefully 4. (abrupt) abruptly; **~ bremsen** to slam on the brakes; **~ links/rechts abbiegen** to take a sharp left/right

Schärfe <-, -n> ['ʃɛrfə] f 1. (von Messer, Degen) sharpness 2. (Heftigkeit) severity; (von Kritik) sharpness; (von Worten) harshness; (der Augen) keenness 3. (von Foto, Bild) sharpness; (einer Brille) strength

schärfen ['ʃɛrfn̩] vt to sharpen

scharfmachen vt fam (sexuell reizen) **jdn ~** to turn sb on

Scharfschütze, -schützin m, f marksman masc, markswoman fem

Scharfsinn m kein pl astuteness

scharfsinnig I. adj astute, perceptive II. adv astutely, perceptively

Scharlach <-s> ['ʃarlax] m kein pl MED scarlet fever

Scharlatan <-s, -e> ['ʃarlaːtan] m (Betrüger) fraud

Scharnier <-s, -e> [ʃarˈniːɐ] nt hinge

Schaschlik <-s, -s> ['ʃaʃlɪk] nt shish kebab

Schatten <-s, -> ['ʃatn̩] m 1. (schattige Stelle) shade; **30°C im ~** 30°C in the shade 2. (schemenhafte Gestalt, Umriss) shadow; **einen ~ [auf etw** akk**] werfen** to cast a shadow [over sth] ▶ **in jds ~ stehen** to be overshadowed by sb; **jdn/etw in den ~ stellen** to outshine sb/sth

Schattenseite f dark side

schattig ['ʃatɪç] adj shady

Schatz <-es, Schätze> [ʃats] m 1. (kostbare Dinge) treasure 2. fam (Liebling) sweetheart

schätzen ['ʃɛtsn̩] I. vt 1. (einschätzen) to guess; **meistens werde ich jünger geschätzt** people usually think I'm younger than I am; **grob geschätzt** roughly 2. (wertmäßig einschätzen) to assess (**auf** +akk at) 3. (würdigen) to value (**als** +akk as); **jdn ~** to hold sb

in high esteem; **etw ~** to appreciate sth **II.** *vi* to guess

Schätzung <-, -en> *f* **1.** *kein pl* (*wertmäßiges Einschätzen*) valuation **2.** (*Anschlag*) estimate

schätzungsweise *adv* approximately

Schau <-, -en> [ʃau] *f* show; **etw zur ~ stellen** to display sth

Schaubild *nt* diagram

Schauder <-s, -> [ˈʃaudɐ] *m* shudder

schauderhaft *adj s.* **schauerlich**

schaudern [ˈʃaudɐn] **I.** *vt impers* **es schaudert mich bei dem Gedanken** the thought alone makes me shudder **II.** *vi* (*erschauern*) to shudder; (*vor Kälte*) to shiver

schauen [ˈʃauən] *vi südd, österr, schweiz* **1.** (*blicken*) to look (**auf** +*akk* at) **2.** (*darauf achten*) **auf etw** *akk* **~** to pay attention to sth **3.** (*sich kümmern*) **nach jdm/etw ~** to look after sb/sth **4.** (*suchen*) [**nach etw** *dat*] **~** to look [for sth] ▶ **da schaust du aber!** *fam* how about that!

Schauer <-s, -> [ˈʃauɐ] *m* **1.** (*Regenschauer*) shower **2. s. Schauder**

schauerlich *adj* (*grässlich*) ghastly, horrific; (*furchtbar*) awful

Schaufel <-, -n> [ˈʃaufl̩] *f* shovel; (*für Mehl o. Ä.*) scoop; (*für Kehricht*) dustpan

schaufeln [ˈʃaufl̩n] *vt, vi* to shovel, to dig

Schaufenster *nt* store window

Schaufensterpuppe *f* mannequin

Schaukel <-, -n> [ˈʃaukl̩] *f* swing

schaukeln [ˈʃaukl̩n] **I.** *vi* to swing; (*auf und ab wippen*) to rock **II.** *vt* to swing; (*Baby*) to rock

Schaukelpferd *nt* rocking horse

Schaukelstuhl *m* rocking chair

Schaum <-s, Schäume> [ʃaum] *m* foam; (*auf einer Flüssigkeit*) froth; (*Seifenschaum*) lather

Schaumbad *nt* bubble bath

schäumen [ˈʃɔymən] *vi* to foam; (*Flüssigkeit*) to froth; (*Seife*) to lather

Schaumgummi *m* foam rubber

schaumig [ˈʃaumɪç] *adj* frothy

Schaumwein *m* sparkling wine

Schauplatz *m* scene

schaurig [ˈʃaurɪç] *adj* **1.** (*unheimlich*)

eerie **2.** (*gruselig*) macabre, scary

Schauspiel [ˈʃauʃpiːl] *nt* **1.** THEAT play, drama *no indef art* **2.** (*Anblick*) spectacle

Schauspieler(in) [ˈʃauʃpiːlɐ] *m(f)* actor *masc*, actress *fem*

Schauspielhaus *nt* theater, playhouse

Schauspielschule *f* drama school

Scheck <-s, -s> [ʃɛk] *m* check (**über** +*akk* for)

Scheckkarte *f* debit card

Scheibe <-, -n> [ˈʃaibə] *f* **1.** (*dünnes Glasstück*) [piece of] glass; (*Fensterscheibe*) window [pane] **2.** KOCHK slice **3.** (*kreisförmiger Gegenstand*) disk

Scheibenwischer <-s, -> *m* windshield wiper

Scheich <-s, -e> [ʃaiç] *m* sheikh

Scheide <-, -n> [ˈʃaidə] *f* **1.** (*Schwert-/Dolchscheide*) scabbard **2.** (*Vagina*) vagina

scheiden <schied, geschieden> [ˈʃaidn̩] **I.** *vt haben* to divorce; **die Ehe wurde 2002 geschieden** the marriage was dissolved in 2002; **sich** *akk* **~ lassen** to get divorced (**von** +*dat* from) **II.** *vi sein* **aus einem Amt ~** to retire from a position

Scheidung <-, -en> *f* divorce; **die ~ einreichen** to start divorce proceedings

Schein <-[e]s, -e> [ʃain] *m* **1.** *kein pl* (*Lichtschein*) light **2.** *kein pl* (*Anschein*) appearance; **den ~ wahren** to keep up appearances **3.** (*Banknote*) bill, banknote **4.** *fam* (*Bescheinigung*) certificate **5.** UNIV certificate (*after successfully completing a seminar*)

scheinbar *adj* apparent, seeming

scheinen <schien, geschienen> [ˈʃainən] *vi* **1.** (*leuchten*) to shine **2.** (*den Anschein haben*) to appear, to seem

Scheinfirma *f* bogus company

scheinheilig [ˈʃainˌhaiˌlɪç] **I.** *adj* hypocritical; **~ tun** to play the innocent **II.** *adv* hypocritically

Scheinwerfer *m* **1.** (*Strahler*) spotlight **2.** AUTO headlight

Scheinwerferlicht *nt* spotlight ▶ **im ~ stehen** to be in the public eye

Scheiß <-> [ʃais] *m kein pl vulg* (*Quatsch*) crap; **he, was soll der ~!** hey, what [the

S

hell] are you doing?; **lass doch den ~** quit screwing around!; **mach keinen ~!** don't fuck around! *vulg;* **so ein ~!** shit! *vulg*

Scheiße <-> ['ʃai·sə] *f kein pl* **1.** *vulg (Darminhalt)* shit **2.** *vulg (Mist)* ~! shit! *vulg* ▸ **in der ~ sitzen** *vulg* to be in deep shit *vulg*

scheißen <schiss, geschissen> ['ʃai·sn̩] *vi* **1.** *derb* to shit **2.** *vulg (verzichten können)* to shit **(auf** +*akk* about)

Scheitel <-s, -> ['ʃai·tl̩] *m* part

schellfisch *m* haddock

schelmisch *adj* mischievous

schelten <schilt, schalt, gescholten> ['ʃɛl·tn̩] *vt* to scold

Schema <-s, -ta> ['ʃe:·ma] *nt* **1.** *(Muster)* pattern **2.** *(Diagramm)* diagram

schematisch [ʃe·'ma:·tɪʃ] **I.** *adj* schematic **II.** *adv* schematically; **etw ~ darstellen** to show sth with a chart

Schemel <-s, -> ['ʃe:·ml̩] *m* stool

Schenkel <-s, -> ['ʃɛŋ·kl̩] *m* thigh

schenken ['ʃɛŋ·kn̩] **I.** *vt* to give; **jdm etw ~** to give sb sth [as a present]; **jdm Aufmerksamkeit ~** to pay attention to sb; **jdm Vertrauen ~** to trust sb **II.** *vi* to give presents **III.** *vr (sich sparen)* **sich** *dat* **etw ~** to spare oneself sth

Scherbe <-, -n> ['ʃɛr·bə] *f* [sharp] piece; *(von Glas)* piece of glass

Schere <-, -n> ['ʃe:·rə] *f (Werkzeug)* scissors *npl*

scheren¹ <schor, geschoren> ['ʃe:·rən] *vt (Fell)* to shear; *(Bart)* to crop; *(Hecke)* to prune

scheren² ['ʃe:·rən] *vr fam (sich kümmern)* **sich** *akk* **um etw** *akk* **~** to care about sth

Scherz <-es, -e> ['ʃɛrts] *m* joke

scherzen ['ʃɛr·tsn̩] *vi geh* to crack a joke/jokes; **mit ihm ist nicht zu ~** you shouldn't joke around with him

scherzhaft **I.** *adj* jocular **II.** *adv* jokingly

scheu [ʃɔy] *adj* shy

Scheu <-> [ʃɔy] *f kein pl* shyness

scheuchen ['ʃɔy·çn̩] *vt (treiben)* to shoo; *(Tiere)* to drive

scheuen ['ʃɔy·ən] **I.** *vt* **Auseinandersetzungen ~** to avoid conflict **II.** *vi (Pferd)* to shy **(vor** +*dat* at)

scheuern ['ʃɔy·ɐn] **I.** *vt* to scour ▸ **jdm eine ~** *fam* to hit somebody **II.** *vi* to rub, to chafe

Scheune <-, -n> ['ʃɔy·nə] *f* barn

scheußlich ['ʃɔys·lɪç] **I.** *adj* **1.** *(ekelhaft)* disgusting, revolting **2.** *fam (schlimm)* awful **II.** *adv* **1.** *(widerlich)* in a disgusting manner **2.** *fam (schlimm)* terribly

Schicht <-, -en> ['ʃɪçt] *f* **1.** *(Lage)* layer; *(Farbe)* coat **2.** *(Gesellschaftsschicht)* class **3.** *(Arbeitsschicht)* shift; **~ arbeiten** to do shift work

Schichtarbeiter(in) *m(f)* shift worker

schichten ['ʃɪç·tn̩] *vt* to stack [up *sep*], to layer **(auf** +*akk* on/on top of)

Schichtwechsel [-vɛksl̩] *m* shift change

schick [ʃɪk] **I.** *adj* chic **II.** *adv* fashionably

schicken ['ʃɪkn̩] **I.** *vt* to send; **etw mit der Post ~** to send sth by mail **II.** *vi* **nach jdm ~** to send for sb **III.** *vr* **etw schickt sich** *akk* **nicht [für jdn]** sth is not suitable [for sb]

Schicksal <-s, -e> ['ʃɪk·za:l] *nt* fate

Schicksalsschlag *m* stroke of fate

Schiebedach *nt* sunroof

schieben <schob, geschoben> ['ʃi:·bn̩] *vt* **1.** *(vorwärtsbewegen)* to push **2.** *(stecken)* to put, to stick; **die Pizza in den Ofen ~** to stick the pizza in the oven **3.** *(zuweisen)* **etw auf jdn/etw ~** to blame sb/sth for sth; **die Schuld auf jdn ~** to lay the blame on sb **4.** *(abweisen)* **etw von sich** *dat* **~** to reject sth

Schiebetür *f* sliding door

Schiebung <-> *f kein pl* **1.** *(Begünstigung)* string-pulling **2.** SPORT fix

Schiedsgericht *nt* arbitration court

Schiedsrichter(in) *m(f)* SPORT referee; *(bei Tennis, Baseball)* umpire

schief [ʃi:f] **I.** *adj* crooked, not straight *pred* **II.** *adv* askew; **das Bild hängt ~** that picture isn't hanging straight ▸ **jdn ~ ansehen** to look at sb suspiciously

schiefgehen *vi irreg sein fam* to go wrong

schiefliegen *vi irreg fam* to miss the mark

schielen ['ʃiː·lən] *vi* **1.** MED to squint, to be cross-eyed **2.** (*haben wollen*) **nach etw** *dat* ~ to steal a glance at sth

Schienbein ['ʃiːn·bain] *nt* shin, tibia

Schiene <-, -n> ['ʃiː·nə] *f* **1.** (*Führungsschiene*) rail *usu pl* **2.** MED splint

Schießbude *f* shooting gallery

schießen <schoss, geschossen> ['ʃiː·sn] *vt, vi* **1.** haben (*feuern*) to shoot (**auf** +*akk* at) **2.** haben FBALL to shoot; **ein Tor** ~ to score (a goal) **3.** *sein* (*schnell bewegen*) **das Auto kam um die Ecke geschossen** the car came flying around the corner; **jdm durch den Kopf** ~ to flash through sb's mind

Schießerei <-, -en> [ʃiː·sə·'rai] *f* shooting

Schießpulver *nt* gunpowder

Schiff <-[e]s, -e> [ʃɪf] *nt* ship

SchiffahrtALT *f s.* **Schifffahrt**

Schiffbau *m kein pl* shipbuilding

Schiffbruch *m* shipwreck; ~ **erleiden** to be shipwrecked

SchifffahrtRR [ʃɪf·faːɐt] *f* shipping

Schikane <-, -n> [ʃi·'kaː·nə] *f* harassment *no indef art*

schikanieren * [ʃi·ka·'niː·rən] *vt* to harass

Schild[1] <-[e]s, -er> [ʃɪlt] *nt* (*Hinweisschild*) sign

Schild[2] <-[e]s, -e> [ʃɪlt] *m* shield ▶ **etw im ~e führen** to be up to sth

Schilddrüse *f* thyroid [gland]

schildern ['ʃɪl·dɐn] *vt* to describe

Schilderung <-, -en> *f* description; (*von Ereignissen a.*) account

Schildkröte ['ʃɪlt·krøː·tə] *f* tortoise; (*Seeschildkröte*) turtle

Schilf <-[e]s, -e> [ʃɪlf] *nt* reeds *pl*

schillernd *adj* shimmering; (*Persönlichkeit*) flamboyant

Schimmel[1] <-s> [ʃɪml] *m kein pl* mold

Schimmel[2] <-s, -> [ʃɪml] *m* (*Tier*) white horse

schimmelig ['ʃɪmə·lɪç] *adj* moldy; (*Leder, Buch*) mildewed

schimmeln ['ʃɪmln] *vi sein o haben* to get moldy

Schimmer <-s> ['ʃɪmɐ] *m kein pl* shimmer; **ein ~ von Hoffnung** a glimmer of hope ▶ **keinen blassen ~ [von etw**

dat] haben *fam* to not have the faintest idea [about sth]

schimmern ['ʃɪmɐn] *vi* to shimmer

Schimpanse <-n, -n> [ʃɪm·'pan·zə] *m* chimpanzee

schimpfen ['ʃɪm·pfn] *vi* **1.** (*sich ärgerlich äußern*) to grumble (**über/auf** +*akk* about) **2.** (*fluchen*) to swear **3.** (*zurechtweisen*) **mit jdm** ~ to scold sb, to tell sb off

Schimpfwort *nt* swear word

schinden <schindete, geschunden> ['ʃɪn·dn] *vr* **sich** *akk* ~ to slave [away]

Schinken <-s, -> ['ʃɪŋ·kn] *m* ham

Schirm <-[e]s, -e> [ʃɪrm] *m* (*Regenschirm*) umbrella; (*Sonnenschirm*) sunshade; (*tragbar*) parasol

schissRR, **schiß**ALT [ʃɪs] *imp von* **scheißen**

SchissRR <-es>, **Schiß**ALT <-sses> [ʃɪs] *m kein pl* ~ **[vor jdm/etw] haben** *sl* to be scared shitless [of sb/sth]

schizophren [ʃi·tso·'freːn] *adj* schizophrenic

Schizophrenie <-, *selten* -n> [ʃi·tso·fre·'niː] *f* schizophrenia

Schlacht <-, -en> [ʃlaxt] *f* battle

schlachten ['ʃlax·tn] *vt, vi* to slaughter

Schlächter(in) <-s, -> *m(f) dial s.* **Fleischer**

Schlachtfeld *nt* battlefield

Schlachtfest *nt* KOCHK slaughter festival (*celebration and feast following the slaughtering of a farm animal*)

Schlachthof *m* slaughterhouse

Schlaf <-[e]s> [ʃlaːf] *m kein pl* sleep; **einen festen/leichten** ~ **haben** to be a deep [*o* sound]/light sleeper; **jdm den** ~ **rauben** to keep sb awake ▶ **nicht im ~ an etw** *akk* **denken** to not dream of [doing] sth; **etw im ~ können** *fam* to be able to do sth in one's sleep

Schlafanzug *m* pajamas *npl*

Schläfe <-, -n> ['ʃlɛː·fə] *f* temple

schlafen <schlief, geschlafen> ['ʃlaː·fn] *vi* to sleep; **er schläft noch** he is still asleep; ~ **gehen** to go to bed

schlaff [ʃlaf] **I.** *adj* **1.** (*locker fallend*) slack **2.** (*nicht straff*) sagging; (*Händedruck*) limp **II.** *adv* **1.** (*locker fallend*) slackly **2.** (*kraftlos*) feebly

S

Schlafgelegenheit f place to sleep

Schlaflosigkeit <-> f kein pl insomnia

Schlafmittel nt sleeping pill

schläfrig ['ʃlɛːfrɪç] adj sleepy, drowsy

Schlafsaal m dormitory

Schlafsack m sleeping bag

Schlaftablette f sleeping pill

Schlafwagen m sleeper

Schlafwandler(in) <-s, -> m(f) sleep-walker

Schlafzimmer nt bedroom

Schlag <-[e]s, Schläge> [ʃlaːk] m 1. (Hieb) blow, wallop fam; (mit der Faust) punch; (mit der Hand) slap; SPORT stroke, hit; (Baseball) hit; **Schläge bekommen** to get beaten up 2. (rhythmisches Geräusch) **die Schläge des Herzens** the heartbeats 3. (Schicksalsschlag) blow 4. österr (Schlagsahne) whipped cream 5. (Stromstoß) shock; **einen ~ kriegen** to get an electric shock 6. (Schlaganfall) stroke; **einen ~ bekommen** to suffer a stroke 7. MODE **eine Hose mit ~** flared pants ▶ **auf ~** in rapid succession; **jdn trifft der ~** fam sb is flabbergasted [o shocked]; **etw auf einen ~ tun** to get things done all at once

Schlagader f artery

Schlaganfall m stroke

schlagen <schlug, geschlagen> ['ʃlaːgn̩] I. vt haben 1. (hauen) to hit; (mit der Faust) to punch; (mit der Hand) to slap; **einen Nagel in die Wand ~** to hammer a nail into the wall 2. (prügeln) to beat; **jdn bewusstlos ~** to beat sb senseless 3. (besiegen) to defeat; SPORT to beat (**in** +dat at) 4. (Sahne) to whip; **Eier in die Pfanne ~** to crack eggs into the [frying] pan 5. (legen) **ein Bein über das andere ~** to cross one's legs; **die Decke zur Seite ~** to throw the blanket aside II. vi 1. haben (hauen) to hit; [mit etw dat] um sich akk ~ to lash out [with sth] 2. sein (auftreffen) to strike (**gegen** +akk against) 3. haben (pochen) to beat 4. haben (läuten: Uhr) to strike 5. sein fam (jdm ähneln) **nach jdm ~** to take after sb III. vr haben sich akk ~ to fight (**umm** +akk over)

Schlager <-s, -> ['ʃlaː·gɐ] m MUS 1. (Lied) pop song 2. (Erfolg) [big] hit, great success

Schläger <-s, -> ['ʃlɛː·gɐ] m SPORT (beim Tennis) racket; (beim Tischtennis) paddle; (beim Golf) golf club

Schlägerei <-, -en> ['ʃlɛː·gə·ˈraɪ] f fight

schlagfertig I. adj quick-witted II. adv quick-wittedly

Schlaginstrument nt percussion instrument

Schlagloch nt pothole

Schlagsahne f (flüssig) whipping cream; (geschlagen) whipped cream

Schlagzeile f headline

Schlagzeug <-[e]s, -e> nt drums pl; (im Orchester) percussion

Schlagzeuger(in) <-s, -> m(f) drummer; (im Orchester) percussionist

Schlamassel <-s, -> [ʃla·ˈma·sl̩] m o nt mess

Schlamm <-[e]s, -e> [ʃlam] m mud; (breiige Rückstände) sludge

schlammig ['ʃlamɪç] adj muddy

Schlammlawine f GEOG mudslide

Schlampe <-, -n> ['ʃlam·pə] f slut

schlampig ['ʃlam·pɪç] I. adj 1. (nachlässig) (liederlich) slovenly 2. (ungepflegt) unkempt II. adv 1. (nachlässig) sloppily 2. (ungepflegt) in an unkempt way

Schlange <-, -n> ['ʃlaŋə] f 1. ZOOL snake 2. (lange Reihe) line; ~ **stehen** to stand in line

schlängeln ['ʃlɛŋ·l̩n] vr sich akk ~ (sich winden) to crawl; (Fluss, Straße) to meander

schlank ['ʃlaŋk] adj thin, slim; (Handgelenk) slender; **du bist ~ geworden** you have lost weight

Schlankheitskur f diet

schlapp [ʃlap] adj 1. pred (erschöpft) worn out 2. (ohne Antrieb) feeble, listless

schlau [ʃlaʊ] adj 1. (gescheit) clever; **ich werde nicht ~ aus der Bedienungsanleitung** I can't make heads or tails of the operating instructions 2. (gerissen) crafty, wily; (Plan) ingenious

Schlauch <-[e]s, Schläuche> [ʃlaʊx] m 1. (biegsame Leitung) tube; (für Wasser) hose 2. (Reifenschlauch) [inner] tube

schlauchboot nt rubber boat

chlauchen ['ʃlau·xn̩] vt, vi to wear sb out; **das schlaucht ganz schön!** that really takes it out of you!

chlaufe <-, -n> ['ʃlau·fə] f loop; (aus Leder) strap

schlecht [ʃlɛçt] I. adj 1. (nicht gut) bad; (Augen) weak; (Gehalt, Leistung, Qualität) poor; (Zeiten) hard 2. (moralisch verkommen) bad, wicked, evil; **ein ~es Gewissen haben** to have a bad conscience 3. (übel) **mir ist ~** I feel sick 4. (verdorben) bad; **das Fleisch ist ~ geworden** the meat has spoiled ▶ **es sieht ~ aus** things don't look good II. adv 1. (nicht gut) badly, poorly; **so ~ habe ich selten gegessen** I've rarely had such bad food; **die Geschäfte gehen ~** business is bad; **~ gelaunt sein** in a bad mood pred; (dauernd) bad-tempered 2. MED **jdm geht es ~** sb doesn't feel good; **~ hören** to be hard of hearing; **~ sehen** to have poor eyesight

schlecht|machen vt **jdn ~** to badmouth sb

chleichen <schlich, geschlichen> ['ʃlai·çn̩] I. vi sein 1. (leise gehen) to creep, to sneak 2. (langsam gehen/fahren) to crawl along II. vr haben **sich** akk **in das Zimmer ~** to sneak into the room; **sich** akk **aus dem Haus ~** to steal away softly

chleier <-s, -> ['ʃlai·ɐ] m veil

chleierhaft adj **~ sein** to be a mystery

chleife <-, -n> ['ʃlai·fə] f 1. MODE bow 2. (Straße) loop

chleifen¹ ['ʃlai·fn̩] I. vt haben (ziehen) to drag II. vi 1. haben (reiben) to rub (**an** +dat against) 2. sein o haben (gleiten) to slide; (Schleppe) to trail

chleifen² <schliff, geschliffen> ['ʃlai·fn̩] vt 1. (schärfen) to sharpen 2. (in Form polieren) to polish; (mit Sandpapier) to sand; (Edelsteine) to cut

chleifmaschine f sander

chleim <-[e]s, -e> [ʃlaim] m 1. MED mucus; (in Bronchien) phlegm 2. (klebrige Masse) slime

chleimhaut f mucous membrane

chleimig ['ʃlai·mɪç] I. adj 1. MED mucous 2. (glitschig) slimy 3. pej (unterwürfig) slimy, obsequious II. adv pej in a slimy way, obsequiously

schlemmen ['ʃlɛ·mən] vi to have a feast

schlendern ['ʃlɛn·dɐn] vi sein to stroll along

schlenkern ['ʃlɛŋ·kɐn] vi to dangle

Schleppe <-, -n> ['ʃlɛ·pə] f MODE train

schleppen ['ʃlɛ·pn̩] I. vt 1. (tragen) to carry, to lug fam 2. (zerren) to drag 3. (abschleppen) to tow II. vr **sich** akk **~** to drag oneself; (Verhandlungen) to drag on

schleppend I. adj 1. (zögerlich) slow 2. (schwerfällig) shuffling II. adv 1. (zögerlich) slowly; **~ in Gang kommen** to be slow in getting started 2. (schwerfällig) **~ gehen** to shuffle along

Schleppkahn m barge

Schlepplift m ski tow

schleudern ['ʃlɔy·dɐn] I. vt haben 1. (werfen) to hurl 2. (Wäsche) to spin II. vi sein to skid; **ins S~ geraten** to go into a skid; fig to be losing control of a situation

schleunigst adv right away, at once

Schleuse <-, -n> ['ʃlɔy·zə] f lock; (Tor) sluice [gate]

schlicht [ʃlɪçt] I. adj 1. (einfach) simple, plain 2. (wenig gebildet) simple, unsophisticated 3. attr (bloß) plain II. part (ganz einfach) simply

schließen <schloss, geschlossen> ['ʃliː·sn̩] I. vi 1. (zugehen, zumachen) to close 2. (schlussfolgern) to conclude; **etw lässt auf etw** akk **~** sth indicates sth II. vt 1. (zumachen) to close; (Lücke) to fill 2. (eingehen: Frieden, einen Pakt) to make; **Freundschaft ~** to become friends; **einen Kompromiss ~** to reach a compromise 3. (schlussfolgern) to conclude (**aus** +dat from) 4. (umfassen) **jdn in die Arme ~** to take sb in one's arms

Schließfach nt (Gepäckschließfach) locker; (Bankschließfach) safe-deposit box; (Postfach) post office box

schließlich ['ʃliːs·lɪç] adv 1. (endlich) at last, finally 2. (immerhin) after all

schlimm [ʃlɪm] I. adj 1. (übel) bad, terrible; **etwas S~es/S~eres** sth terrible/worse; **das ist nicht so ~** that's

not so bad **2.** (*ernst*) serious **3.** (*moralisch schlecht*) bad; (*Verbrechen*) serious ▶ **das ist halb so ~** it's not as bad as all that; **ist nicht ~!** no problem!, don't worry [about it]! **II.** *adv* **1.** (*gravierend*) seriously **2.** (*äußerst schlecht*) dreadfully; **es hätte ~er kommen können** it could have been worse; **~ dran sein** *fam* to be hard up; **umso ~er** so much the worse

schlimmstenfalls [ˈʃlɪm·stn̩·ˈfals] *adv* if worst comes to worst

Schlinge <-, -n> [ˈʃlɪŋə] *f* (*Schlaufe*) loop; (*um jdn aufzuhängen*) noose

schlingen[1] <schlang, geschlungen> [ˈʃlɪŋən] **I.** *vt* to wind (**um** +*akk* around); **die Arme um jdn ~** to wrap one's arms around sb **II.** *vr* **sich** *akk* **um etw** *akk* **~** to wind itself around sth

schlingen[2] <schlang, geschlungen> [ˈʃlɪŋən] *vi fam* to gobble one's food

Schlingpflanze *f* creeper

Schlips <-es, -e> [ʃlɪps] *m* tie

Schlitten <-s, -> [ˈʃlɪ·tn̩] *m* **1.** (*Rodel*) sledge, sled; (*Rodelschlitten*) toboggan; (*mit Pferden*) sleigh **2.** *sl* (*Auto*) wheels *pl*

Schlittschuh [ˈʃlɪt·ʃuː] *m* [ice] skate; **~ laufen** to [ice-]skate

Schlittschuhbahn *f* ice rink

Schlittschuhläufer(in) <-s, -> *m(f)* [ice] skater

Schlitz <-es, -e> [ʃlɪts] *m* **1.** (*Einsteckschlitz*) slot **2.** (*schmale Öffnung*) slit

Schlitzohr *nt* rogue

schloss RR, **schloß** ALT [ʃlɔs] *imp von* **schließen**

Schloss RR <-es, Schlösser>, **Schloß** ALT <-sses, Schlösser> [ʃlɔs] *nt* **1.** (*Palast*) castle, palace **2.** (*Türschloss*) lock; **ins ~ fallen** to snap shut **3.** (*Verschluss*) catch ▶ **jdn hinter ~ und Riegel bringen** to put sb behind bars

Schlosser(in) <-s, -> [ˈʃlɔsɐ] *m(f)* locksmith

Schlosserei <-, -en> [ʃlɔ·səˈrai] *f* locksmith's store

Schlucht <-, -en> [ʃlʊxt] *f* gorge

schluchzen [ˈʃlʊxtsn̩] *vi* to sob

Schluck <-[e]s, -e> [ʃlʊk] *m* mouthful; (*größer*) gulp; (*kleiner*) sip

Schluckauf <-s> [ˈʃlʊk·ʔauf] *m kein pl*

hiccup

schlucken [ˈʃlʊkn̩] *vt, vi a. fig* to swallow (*Auto*) to guzzle

Schluckimpfung *f* oral vaccination

schlummern [ˈʃlʊ·mɐn] *vi* to slumber

Schlund <-[e]s, Schlünde> [ʃlʊnt] *[...]* throat

schlüpfen [ˈʃlʏp·fn̩] *vi sein* **1.** ORN, ZOO[...] to hatch (**aus** +*dat* out [of]) **2.** (*rasc[...] kleiden*) to slip (**aus** +*dat* out of, **i[...]** +*akk* into)

Schlüpfer <-s, -> [ˈʃlʏp·fɐ] *m* panties *np[...]*

schlürfen [ˈʃlʏr·fn̩] *vt, vi* to slurp

Schluss RR <-es, Schlüsse>, **Schluß** AL[...] <-sses, Schlüsse> [ʃlʊs] *m* **1.** *kei[...]* *pl* (*räumlich, zeitlich*) end; **~ für heute** that's enough for today!; **~ damit!** sto[...] it!; **~ [jetzt]!** [that's] enough [already]!; **zum ~ kommen** to finish; **[mit etw[...]** *dat*] **~ machen** *fam* to stop [sth]; **[mi[...]** **jdm] ~ machen** to break up [with sb[...] **zum ~** at the end; (*schließlich*) in th[...] end **2.** (*Folgerung*) conclusion

Schlüssel <-s, -> [ˈʃlʏ·sl̩] *m* key

Schlüsselbein *nt* clavicle

Schlüsselloch *nt* keyhole

Schlussfolgerung RR, **Schlußfolge[...] rung** ALT <-, -en> *f* conclusion

Schlussverkauf RR *m* sale

schmächtig [ˈʃmɛç·tɪç] *adj* slight

schmackhaft *adj* tasty ▶ **jdm etw ~[...] machen** to make sth tempting for sb

schmal <-er *o* schmäler, -ste *o* schmäls[...] te> [ʃmaːl] *adj* narrow; (*Mensch*) slim

Schmalz <-es, -e> [ʃmalts] *nt* KOCHK drip[...] pings *npl*; (*vom Schwein*) lard

schmalzig [ˈʃmal·tsɪç] *adj pej fam[...]* schmaltzy, corny

Schmarotzer <-s, -> *m* parasite

Schmarren [ˈʃma·rən] *m südd, öster[...]* **1.** KOCHK *a warm dessert of sliced crepe[...]* *and raisins, topped with powdered sug[...]* *ar, often served with apple sauce o[...]* *plum jam* **2.** *fam* (*Quatsch*) nonsense

schmatzen [ˈʃma·tsn̩] *vi* to eat/drin[...] noisily

schmecken [ˈʃmɛ·kn̩] **I.** *vi* **1.** (*Ge[...]* *schmack haben*) to taste (**nach** +*dat* o[...] **2.** (*munden*) **hat es geschmeckt?** di[...] you enjoy it?; **das schmeckt aber gu[...]** this tastes wonderful; **lass es dir ~!** er[...]

joy your meal! **3.** *südd, österr, schweiz* (*riechen*) smell **II.** *vt* to taste

Schmeichelei <-, -en> [ʃmai·çə·ˈlai] *f* flattery

schmeichelhaft *adj* flattering

schmeicheln [ˈʃmai·çl̩n] *vi* to flatter; **es schmeichelte ihm, dass ...** he was flattered that ...

schmeißen <schmiss, geschmissen> [ˈʃmai·sn̩] **I.** *vt, vi fam* **1.** (*werfen*) to throw; (*mit Kraft*) to hurl, to fling **2.** *sl* (*spendieren: Party*) to throw **3.** *sl* (*managen*) to run **4.** *fam* (*abbrechen*) to quit **II.** *vr* (*sich fallen lassen*) **sich** *akk* ~ to throw oneself (**auf** +*akk* onto, **vor** +*akk* in front of)

Schmeißfliege *f* blowfly

schmelzen <schmolz, geschmolzen> [ˈʃmɛl·tsn̩] **I.** *vi sein* to melt **II.** *vt haben* to melt; (*Metall*) to smelt

Schmelzkäse *m* KOCHK **1.** (*in Scheiben*) processed cheese **2.** (*streichfähig*) cheese spread

Schmelzpunkt *m* melting point

Schmerz <-es, -en> [ʃmɛrts] *m* pain; ~**en haben** to be in pain

schmerzempfindlich *adj* sensitive to pain *pred*

schmerzen [ˈʃmɛr·tsn̩] *vi* to hurt; ~**d** painful, aching

Schmerzensgeld *nt* compensation

schmerzhaft *adj* painful

schmerzlich I. *adj* painful, distressing **II.** *adv* painfully

schmerzlos *adj* painless ▶ **kurz und** ~ short and sweet

Schmerzmittel *nt* painkiller; MED analgesic

schmerzstillend *adj* painkilling; ~ **sein** to be a painkiller

Schmerztablette *f* painkiller

Schmetterling <-s, -e> [ˈʃmɛ·tɐ·lɪŋ] *m* butterfly

schmettern [ˈʃmɛ·tɐn] *vt* **1.** (*schleudern*) to fling **2.** SPORT to smash **3.** MUS to blare out; (*Lied*) to bawl out

Schmied(in) <-[e]s, -e> [ʃmiːt] *m(f)* smith

schmiedeeisern *adj* wrought-iron

schmieden [ˈʃmiː·dn̩] *vt* **1.** (*glühend hämmern*) to forge **2.** (*aushecken: Plan*) to make

schmiegen [ˈʃmiː·gn̩] *vr* to snuggle (**an** +*akk* up to); **sich** *akk* [**an jdn**] ~ to cuddle up close [to sb]

schmieren [ˈʃmiː·rən] **I.** *vt* **1.** (*streichen*) to spread; (*Creme etc.*) to rub, to smear **2.** (*fetten*) to lubricate, to grease **3.** *fam* (*bestechen*) **jdn** ~ to grease sb's palm ▶ **jdm eine** ~ *fam* to whack sb; **wie geschmiert** *fam* like clockwork **II.** *vt pej* (*unsauber schreiben*) to scribble; (*Kuli*) to smudge

Schmiergeld *nt fam* bribe, kickback

schmierig [ˈʃmiː·rɪç] *adj* **1.** (*nass und klebrig*) greasy **2.** *pej* (*schleimig*) slimy

Schmieröl *nt* lubricating oil

Schmierseife *f* soft soap

Schmierzettel *m* piece of scratch paper

Schminke <-, -n> [ˈʃmɪŋ·kə] *f* makeup

schminken [ˈʃmɪŋ·kn̩] **I.** *vt* to put makeup on **II.** *vr* **sich** *akk* ~ to put on makeup

Schmirgelpapier [ˈʃmɪrgl̩-] *nt* sandpaper

schmollen [ˈʃmɔ·lən] *vi* to sulk

Schmorbraten [ˈʃmoːɐ̯-] *m* pot roast

schmoren [ˈʃmoː·rən] *vt, vi* **1.** KOCHK to braise **2.** *fam* (*schwitzen*) to swelter ▶ **jdn lassen** *fam* to let sb stew

Schmuck <-[e]s> [ʃmʊk] *m kein pl* **1.** (*Schmuckstücke*) jewelry **2.** (*Verzierung*) decoration, ornamentation

schmücken [ˈʃmʏ·kn̩] **I.** *vt* (*dekorieren*) to decorate, to embellish **II.** *vr* **sich** *akk* ~ to wear jewelry

schmuddelig [ˈʃmʊdə·lɪç] *adj* grubby

Schmuggel <-s> [ˈʃmʊgl̩] *m kein pl* smuggling

schmuggeln [ˈʃmʊgl̩n] *vt* to smuggle

Schmuggelware *f* smuggled goods *pl*, contraband

Schmuggler(in) <-s, -> [ˈʃmʊg·lɐ] *m(f)* smuggler

schmunzeln [ˈʃmʊn·tsl̩n] *vi* to grin quietly to oneself (**über** +*akk* about)

Schmunzeln <-s> [ˈʃmʊn·tsl̩n] *nt kein pl* grin

schmusen [ˈʃmuː·zn̩] *vi fam* to cuddle, to neck

Schmutz <-es> [ʃmʊts] *m kein pl* dirt ▶ **jdn/etw in den** ~ **ziehen** to ruin sb's name/sth's reputation

S

schmutzig ['ʃmʊ·tsɪç] *adj* **1.** (*dreckig*) dirty; **sich** *akk* [**bei etw** *dat*] **~ machen** to get dirty [doing sth] **2.** (*obszön*) smutty, lewd; (*Witz*) dirty **3.** *pej* (*unlauter*) dubious, crooked; (*Geld*) dirty; (*Geschäfte*) shady

Schnabel <-s, Schnäbel> ['ʃnaː·bl̩] *m* **1.** (*Vogelschnabel*) beak **2.** (*lange Tülle*) spout **3.** *fam* (*Mund*) trap; **halt den ~!** shut up!

Schnake <-, -n> ['ʃnaː·kə] *f* **1.** (*Weberknecht*) daddy longlegs *fam* **2.** *dial* (*Stechmücke*) mosquito

Schnalle <-, -n> ['ʃnalə] *f* buckle

Schnäppchen <-s, -> ['ʃnɛp·çən] *nt* bargain

Schnäppchenmarkt *m* ÖKON *fam* bargain basement

schnappen ['ʃna·pn̩] **I.** *vi* to grab (**nach** +*dat* for), to snatch (**nach** +*dat* at); (*mit den Zähnen*) to snap (**nach** +*dat* at) **II.** *vt fam* **1.** (*ergreifen*) [**sich** *dat*] **etw ~** to grab sth; **etwas frische Luft ~** to get a breath of fresh air **2.** (*festnehmen*) to catch

Schnappschuss ᴿᴿ *m* snapshot

Schnaps <-es, Schnäpse> [ʃnaps] *m* schnapps

schnarchen ['ʃnar·çn̩] *vi* to snore

schnattern ['ʃna·ten] *vi* **1.** ORN to cackle **2.** *fam* (*schwatzen*) to chatter

schnauben <schnaubte, geschnaubt> ['ʃnau·bn̩] *vi* to snort

schnaufen ['ʃnau·fn̩] *vi* **1.** (*angestrengt atmen*) to puff, to pant **2.** *bes südd* (*atmen*) to breathe

Schnauzbart *m* walrus mustache

Schnauze <-, -n> ['ʃnau·tsə] *f* **1.** ZOOL snout **2.** *sl* (*Mund*) trap; **eine große ~ haben** to have a big mouth; **die ~ halten** to shut up ▶ [**mit etw** *dat*] **auf die ~ fallen** *sl* to fall flat on one's face [with sth]; **die ~** [**von etw** *dat*] **voll haben** *sl* to be fed up [with sth]

schnäuzen ᴿᴿ ['ʃnɔy·tsn̩] *vr* **sich** *akk* **~** to blow one's nose

Schnecke <-, -n> ['ʃnɛ·kə] *f* **1.** ZOOL snail; (*Nacktschnecke*) slug **2.** (*Gebäck*) ≈ cinnamon roll with raisins ▶ **jdn zur ~ machen** to chew sb out

Schneckenhaus *nt* snail shell

Schneckentempo *nt* **im ~** at a snail's pace

Schnee <-s> [ʃneː] *m kein pl* snow ▶ **~ von gestern** [ancient] history

Schneeball *m* snowball

Schneebesen *m* whisk

Schneefall *m* snowfall

Schneeflocke *f* snowflake

Schneeglöckchen <-s, -> *nt* snowdrop

Schneegrenze *f* snow line

Schneekette *f meist pl* snow chain[s *pl*]

Schneemann *m* snowman

Schneematsch *m* slush

Schneepflug *m* snowplow

Schneeregen *m* sleet

Schneeschaufel *f* snow shovel

Schneesturm *m* snowstorm

Schneewittchen <-s> [ʃneː·ˈvɪt·çən] *nt* Snow White

schneiden <schnitt, geschnitten> ['ʃnai·dn̩] **I.** *vt* **1.** (*zerteilen*) to cut **2.** (*kürzen*) to cut, to trim; (*Baum*) to prune **3.** (*knapp einscheren: Auto*) to cut **4.** FILM to edit **5.** (*meiden*) to snub **II.** *vr* **sich** *akk* **in den Finger ~** to cut one's finger

schneidend *adj* **1.** (*durchdringend*) biting **2.** (*scharf*) sharp

Schneider(in) <-s, -> ['ʃnai·de] *m(f)* tailor ▶ **aus dem ~ sein** to be in the clear

Schneidezahn *m* incisor

schneien ['ʃnai·ən] *vi impers* to snow

Schneise <-, -n> ['ʃnai·zə] *f* aisle

schnell [ʃnɛl] **I.** *adj* **1.** (*mit hoher Geschwindigkeit*) fast **1.** (*zügig*) prompt, rapid **3.** *attr* (*baldig*) swift, speedy **II.** *adv* **1.** (*mit hoher Geschwindigkeit*) fast **2.** (*zügig*) quickly; **es geht ganz ~** it won't take long; **~ machen** to hurry up

Schnellhefter *m* loose-leaf binder

Schnelligkeit <-, *selten* -en> *f* speed

Schnellimbiss ᴿᴿ *m* fast-food stand

Schnellkochtopf *m* pressure cooker

Schnellkurs *m* crash course

schnellstens *adv* as soon as possible

Schnellstraße *f* expressway

Schnellzug *m* fast train

schneuzen ᴬᴸᵀ ['ʃnɔy·tsn̩] *vr* s. **schnäuzen**

schniefen ['ʃniː·fn̩] *vi* to sniffle

schnippisch [ˈʃnɪ·pɪʃ] *adj* snippy, snotty

Schnipsel <-s, -> [ˈʃnɪp·sl̩] *m o nt* shred

schnitt [ʃnɪt] *imp von* **schneiden**

Schnitt <-[e]s, -e> [ʃnɪt] *m* cut ▶ **im ~** on average

Schnitte <-, -n> [ˈʃnɪ·tə] *f* 1. KOCHK slice 2. *dial* (*belegtes Brot*) [open-faced] sandwich

Schnittlauch [ˈʃnɪt·laux] *m kein pl* chives *npl*

Schnittpunkt *m* point of intersection

Schnittstelle *f* COMPUT interface

Schnittwunde *f* cut

Schnitzel¹ <-s, -> [ˈʃnɪ·tsl̩] *nt* KOCHK veal cutlet; **Wiener ~** Wiener schnitzel

Schnitzel² <-s, -> [ˈʃnɪ·tsl̩] *m o nt* shred

schnitzen [ˈʃnɪ·tsn̩] *vt, vi* to carve

Schnorchel <-s, -> [ˈʃnɔr·çl̩] *m* snorkel

schnorren [ˈʃnɔ·rən] *vt, vi* to sponge [*o* mooch]

Schnorrer(in) <-s, -> *m(f)* moocher, scrounger

schnüffeln [ˈʃnʏ·fl̩n] *vi* 1. (*schnuppern*) to sniff 2. *fam* (*spionieren*) to nose around

Schnuller <-s, -> [ˈʃnʊ·lɐ] *m* pacifier, Binky® *fam*

Schnulze <-, -n> [ˈʃnʊl·tsə] *f* corny love song

schnupfen [ˈʃnʊpfn̩] I. *vi* to sniff II. *vt* (*Tabak, Kokain*) to snort

Schnupfen <-s, -> [ˈʃnʊp·fn̩] *m* cold; **[ei-nen] ~ haben** to have a cold

schnuppern [ˈʃnʊ·pɐn] *vt, vi* to sniff (**an** *+dat* at)

Schnur <-, Schnüre> [ʃnuːɐ̯] *f* cord

schnüren [ˈʃnyː·rən] *vt* to tie up *sep* (**zu** *+dat* into); (*Schuhe*) to tie

schnurlos *adj* cordless

Schnurrbart [ˈʃnʊr·baːɐ̯t] *m* mustache

schnurren [ˈʃnʊ·rən] *vi* 1. (*Katze*) to purr 2. (*surren*) to whir

Schnürsenkel *m* shoelace

Schnürstiefel *m* lace-up boot

Schock <-[e]s, -s> [ʃɔk] *m* shock; **unter ~ stehen** to be in [a state of] shock

schockieren * [ʃɔ·kiː·rən] *vt* to shock; **schockiert sein** to be shocked (**über** *+akk* about)

Schöffe, Schöffin <-n, -n> [ˈʃœfə, ˈʃœ·fɪn] *m, f* juror

Schokolade <-, -n> [ʃo·ko·ˈlaː·də] *f* (*Kakaomasse*) chocolate; (*Kakaogetränk*) hot chocolate

Scholle <-, -n> [ˈʃɔ·lə] *f* 1. ZOOL plaice 2. (*flacher Erdklumpen*) clod [of earth] 3. (*Eisbrocken*) [ice] floe

schon [ʃoːn] I. *adv* 1. (*bereits*) already, yet; **sind wir ~ da?** are we there yet?; **du willst ~ gehen?** you want to leave already?; **~ damals** even at that time; **~ lange** for a long time; **~ mal** ever; **~ oft** several times [already] 2. (*allein*) **aus dem Grund** for that reason alone; **~ die Tatsache, dass ...** the fact alone that ... 3. (*irgendwann*) in the end, one day; **es wird ~ noch klappen** it will [all] work out in the end 4. (*denn*) **was macht das ~?** what does it matter? 5. (*irgendwie*) all right; **danke, es geht ~** thanks, I can manage 6. (*ja*) **ich sehe ~, ...** I can see, ...; **~ immer** always; **~ längst** for ages, ages ago; **~ wieder** [once] again; **und wenn ~!** so what? II. *part* 1. (*auffordernd*) **geh ~!** go on!; **gib ~ her!** come on, give it here!; **mach ~!** hurry up!; **[nun] sag ~!** come on, tell me! 2. (*nur*) **wenn ich das ~ höre!** I'm sick of hearing that!

schön [ʃøːn] I. *adj* 1. (*hübsch*) beautiful; (*ansprechend*) nice 2. (*angenehm*) good, great, nice; (*Tag*) beautiful; **ich wünsche euch ~e Ferien** have a nice vacation; **[das ist ja alles] ~ und gut, aber ...** that's all very well, but ...; **na ~** all right then 3. *iron* (*unschön*) great; **das sind ja ~e Aussichten!** the future sure looks bright!; **das wird ja immer ~er!** things are getting worse and worse!; **das S~ste kommt erst noch** the best is yet to come 4. (*beträchtlich*) great, good II. *adv* 1. (*ansprechend*) well; **~ singen** to sing well 2. *fam* (*genau*) thoroughly 3. *fam* (*besonders*) **groß** nice and big 4. *iron* (*ziemlich*) really; **das hat ganz ~ wehgetan!** that really hurt!

schonen [ˈʃoː·nən] I. *vt* 1. (*pfleglich behandeln*) to take care of 2. (*nicht überbeanspruchen*) to go easy on; **das schont die Gelenke** it's easy on the joints 3. (*verschonen*) to spare II. *vr*

S

sich *akk* ~ to take it easy

schonend I. *adj* 1. (*nicht strapazierend*) gentle; (*pfleglich*) careful 2. (*rücksichtsvoll*) considerate II. *adv* 1. (*pfleglich*) carefully, with care 2. (*rücksichtsvoll*) **jdm etw ~ beibringen** to break sth to sb gently

Schönheit <-, -en> *f* beauty

Schönheitsfehler *m* 1. (*kosmetisch*) blemish 2. (*kleiner Makel*) flaw

Schonung <-> *f kein pl* 1. (*das pflegliche Behandeln*) care 2. (*Schutz*) protection 3. (*Rücksichtnahme*) consideration

schonungslos I. *adj* blunt, merciless; (*Kritik*) savage; (*Offenheit*) unabashed II. *adv* bluntly, mercilessly

schöpfen[1] ['ʃœpfn] *vt* 1. (*mit einem Behältnis entnehmen*) to scoop; (*Suppe*) to ladle 2. (*Kraft*) to summon [up]

schöpfen[2] ['ʃœpfn] *vt* (*erschaffen*) to create; (*Ausdruck, Wort*) to coin

Schöpfer(in) <-s, -> *m(f)* creator; **der ~** (*Gott*) the Creator

schöpferisch ['ʃœpfərɪʃ] I. *adj* creative II. *adv* creatively

Schöpfung <-, -en> *f* creation; **die ~** REL the Creation

Schöpfungsgeschichte *f kein pl* **die ~** the story of the Creation

Schorf <-[e]s, -e> [ʃɔrf] *m* scab

Schornstein ['ʃɔrn·ʃtain] *m* chimney

Schornsteinfeger(in) <-s, -> *m(f)* chimney sweep

schoss[RR], **schoß**[ALT] [ʃɔs] *imp von* **schießen**

Schoß <-es, Schöße> [ʃɔs] *m* 1. ANAT lap 2. (*Mutterleib*) womb ▶ **etw fällt jdm in den ~** sth falls into sb's lap

Schoßhund *m* lapdog

Schote <-, -n> ['ʃo·tə] *f* pod

Schotte, Schottin <-n, -n> ['ʃɔ·tə, 'ʃɔ·tɪn] *m, f* Scot, Scotsman *masc*, Scotswoman *fem*; *s. a.* **Deutsche(r)**

Schottenrock *m* 1. (*Rock mit Schottenmuster*) plaid skirt 2. (*Kilt*) kilt

schottisch ['ʃɔ·tɪʃ] *adj* Scottish; *s. a.* **deutsch**

Schottland ['ʃɔt·lant] *nt* Scotland; *s. a.* **Deutschland**

schraffieren * [ʃra·'fiː·rən] *vt* to hatch

schräg [ʃrɛːk] I. *adj* sloping; (*Linien*) diagonal II. *adv* *s.* **schief** II

Schrägstrich *m* slash

Schramme <-, -n> ['ʃra·mə] *f* 1. (*Schürfwunde*) scrape 2. (*Kratzer*) scratch

Schrank <-[e]s, Schränke> [ʃraŋk] *m* (*Geschirrschrank*) cupboard; (*Kleiderschrank*) closet

Schranke <-, -n> ['ʃraŋ·kə] *f* 1. BAHN barrier, gate 2. (*Grenze*) limit; **jdn in seine ~n weisen** to put sb in his/her place

schrankenlos *adj* unlimited, boundless

Schraube <-, -n> ['ʃrau·bə] *f* 1. TECH screw 2. NAUT propeller 3. SPORT twist ▶ **bei jdm ist eine ~ locker** *fam* has a screw loose

schrauben ['ʃrau·bn] *vt* to screw (**an** +*akk* into, **auf** +*akk* onto)

Schraubenschlüssel *m* wrench

Schraubenzieher <-s, -> *m* screwdriver

Schraubverschluss[RR] *m* screw top

Schrebergarten ['ʃreː·bɐ] *m* small garden plot on a piece of land managed by a gardening club

Schreck <-s> [ʃrɛk] *m kein pl* fright; **einen ~ bekommen** to get a fright; **jdm einen ~ einjagen** to give sb a scare

Schrecken <-s, -> ['ʃrɛ·kn] *m* 1. *kein pl s.* **Schreck** 2. *pl* (*Gräuel*) horrors *pl*

Schreckgespenst *nt* bogey

schreckhaft *adj* jumpy

schrecklich ['ʃrɛk·lɪç] I. *adj* terrible, awful II. *adv* terribly, awfully

Schrei <-[e]s, -e> [ʃrai] *m* scream, cry ▶ **der letzte ~** *fam* the latest craze

Schreibblock <s, -blöcke> *m* writing pad

schreiben <schrieb, geschrieben> ['ʃrai·bn] I. *vt* to write; **etw falsch/richtig ~** to spell sth wrong/right II. *vi* to write; **jdm ~** to write to sb III. *vr* **wie schreibt sich das Wort?** how do you spell that word?

Schreiben <-s, -> ['ʃrai·bn] *nt* letter

Schreibkraft *f* typist

Schreibmaschine *f* typewriter

Schreibtisch *m* desk

Schreibung <-, -en> *f* spelling

schreien <schrie, geschrie[e]n> ['ʃrai·ən] I. *vi* 1. (*brüllen*) to yell 2. ORN, ZOOL to

Schreihals *m fam* screamer

Schrein <-[e]s, -e> [ʃraɪn] *m geh* shrine

Schreiner(in) <-s, -> [ʃraɪ·nɐ] *m(f)* carpenter

Schreinerei <-, -en> [ʃraɪ·nə·ˈraɪ] *f (Tischlerei)* carpenter's workshop

schreiten <schritt, geschritten> [ˈʃraɪ·tn̩] *vi sein* 1. *(gehen)* to stride 2. *(etw in Angriff nehmen)* to proceed (**zu** +*dat* with)

Schrift <-, -en> [ʃrɪft] *f* 1. *(Handschrift)* [hand]writing 2. *(Schriftsystem)* script 3. TYPO *(Druckschrift)* type; COMPUT font 4. *(Abhandlung)* paper; **die Heilige ~** the [Holy] Scriptures *pl*

schriftlich [ˈʃrɪft·lɪç] I. *adj* written II. *adv* in writing

Schriftsprache *f* standard language

Schriftsteller(in) <-s, -> [ˈʃrɪft·ʃtɛ·lɐ] *m(f)* author, writer

schritt [ʃrɪt] *imp von* **schreiten**

Schritt <-[e]s, -e> [ʃrɪt] *m* 1. *(Tritt)* step; **[mit jdm/etw] ~ halten** to keep up [with sb/sth]; **~ für ~** step by step 2. *kein pl (Gang)* walk, gait 3. *(Maßnahme)* measure, step; **~e [gegen jdn/etw] unternehmen** to take steps [against sb/sth] 4. MODE crotch

Schrittempoᴬᴸᵀ *nt s.* **Schritttempo**

Schrittgeschwindigkeit *f* walking speed

Schrittmacher <-s, -> *m* pacemaker

Schritttempoᴿᴿ *nt* walking speed

schrittweise I. *adj* gradual II. *adv* gradually

schroff [ʃrɔf] I. *adj* 1. *(barsch)* curt, brusque 2. *(steil)* steep II. *adv* 1. *(barsch)* curtly, brusquely 2. *(steil)* steeply

Schrot <-[e]s, -e> [ʃroːt] *m o nt* 1. *kein pl* AGR coarsely ground whole wheat 2. *(aus Blei)* shot

Schrotflinte *f* shotgun

Schrott <-[e]s, -e> [ʃrɔt] *m kein pl* 1. *(Metallmüll)* scrap metal 2. *fam (wertloses Zeug)* junk; **ein Auto zu ~ fahren** *fam*

to total a car

Schrotthändler(in) *m(f)* scrap dealer

Schrottplatz *m* junkyard

schrubben [ˈʃrʊbn̩] *vt, vi* to scrub

Schrubber <-s, -> [ˈʃrʊ·bɐ] *m* scrubbing brush

schrumpfen [ˈʃrʊmp·fn̩] *vi sein* to shrink; *(Frucht)* to shrivel; *(Muskeln)* to atrophy

Schubkarre *f* wheelbarrow

Schublade <-, -n> [ˈʃuːp·laː·də] *f* drawer

Schubs <-es, -e> [ʃʊps] *m fam* shove

schubsen [ˈʃʊp·sn̩] *vt fam* to shove

schüchtern [ˈʃʏç·tɐn] *adj* shy; *(Versuch)* half-hearted

Schüchternheit <-> *f kein pl* shyness

Schuft <-[e]s, -e> [ʃʊft] *m* villain

schuften [ˈʃʊf·tn̩] *vi fam* to slave away

Schufterei <-, -en> [ʃʊf·tə·ˈraɪ] *f fam* drudgery

Schuh <-[e]s, -e> [ʃuː] *m* shoe ▶ **jdm etw in die ~e schieben** *fam* to put the blame for sth on sb

Schuhgeschäft *nt* shoe store

Schuhgröße *f* shoe size

Schuhmacher(in) <-s, -> [ˈʃuː·ma·xɐ] *m(f)* shoemaker, cobbler

Schuhsohle *f* sole [of a/one's shoe]

Schularbeiten *pl* 1. *s.* **Hausaufgaben** 2. *österr (Klassenarbeit)* [written] test

Schulbildung *f kein pl* school education

Schulbuch *nt* schoolbook, textbook

Schulbus *m* school bus

schuld [ʃʊlt] *adj* **~ sein** to be to blame (**an** +*dat* for)

Schuld <-> [ʃʊlt] *f kein pl* 1. *(Verschulden)* fault, blame; **jdm [die] ~ geben** to blame sb; **es ist jds ~, dass ...** it is sb's fault that ...; **die ~ auf sich nehmen** to take the blame 2. *(verschuldete Missetat)* guilt; REL sin; **er ist sich keiner ~ bewusst** he's not aware of having done anything wrong 3. *meist pl* FIN debt; **~en machen** to go into debt

schuldbewusstᴿᴿ I. *adj* guilty II. *adv* guiltily

schulden [ˈʃʊl·dn̩] *vt* to owe

schuldenfrei *adj* free of debt

Schuldgefühl *nt* guilty feelings *pl*

schuldig [ˈʃʊl·dɪç] *adj* 1. JUR guilty; **sich**

akk ~ **bekennen** to plead guilty; **jdn ~ sprechen** to find sb guilty **2. jdm etw ~ sein** (Geld, einen Gefallen etc.) to owe sb sth

Schuldige(r) f(m) dekl wie adj guilty party

schuldlos I. adj blameless **II.** adv blamelessly

Schuldner(in) <-s, -> ['ʃʊld·nɐ] m(f) debtor

Schule <-, -n> ['ʃuː·lə] f school; **in die ~ gehen** to go to school; **in die ~ kommen** to start school; **in der ~** at school

schulen ['ʃuː·lən] vt to train

Schüler(in) <-s, -> ['ʃyː·lɐ] m(f) student; (sch a.) schoolchild

Schüleraustausch m high school exchange program

Schülerausweis m student ID [card]

Schulfach nt [school] subject

Schulferien pl summer vacation

schulfrei adj ~ **haben** to not have school

Schulgeld nt tuition

Schulheft nt notebook

Schulhof m school playground

Schuljahr nt SCH **1.** (Zeitraum) school year **2.** (Klasse) grade

Schulklasse f [school] class

Schulleiter(in) m(f) principal

Schulmedizin f classical medicine

Schulpflicht f kein pl mandatory school attendance

schulpflichtig adj of school age; ~ **sein** to be required to attend school

Schulschwänzer(in) ['ʃuːl·ʃvɛn·tsɐ] m(f) SCH fam truant

Schulsprecher(in) m(f) student body president

Schulter <-, -n> ['ʃʊl·tɐ] f shoulder; **mit den ~n zucken** to shrug one's shoulders ▶ **jdm die kalte ~ zeigen** to give sb the cold shoulder; **jd nimmt etw auf die leichte ~** sb takes sth very lightly, sb doesn't take sth very seriously

Schulterblatt nt shoulder blade

schulterlang adj shoulder-length

Schulung <-, -en> f training

Schulunterricht m kein pl [in-]class instruction

Schulverweis m SCH referral; (befristet) suspension

Schulweg m way to/from school

Schulzeit f kein pl school days pl

Schulzeugnis nt report card

schummeln ['ʃʊ·mln] vi fam to cheat

schummrig ['ʃʊm·rɪç] adj dim

Schund <-[e]s> [ʃʊnt] m kein pl pej trash

Schuppe <-, -n> ['ʃʊpə] f **1.** ZOOL scale **2.** pl MED dandruff

schuppen ['ʃʊ·pn] **I.** vt KOCHK to remove the scales **II.** vr sich akk ~ (Haut) to flake

Schuppen <-s, -> ['ʃʊ·pn] m **1.** (Verschlag) shed **2.** fam (Lokal) joint

Schuppenflechte f MED psoriasis

schuppig ['ʃʊ·pɪç] adj (Haut) flaky; ~ **Haare haben** to have dandruff

Schürfwunde f scrape

Schurke <-n, -n> ['ʃʊr·kə] m veraltend scoundrel

Schurwolle f wool; „**reine ~**" "pure new wool"

Schürze <-, -n> ['ʃʏr·tsə] f apron

Schuss RR <-es, Schüsse>, **Schuß** AL <-sses, Schüsse> [ʃʊs] m **1.** (mit einer Waffe) shot **2.** FBALL shot **3.** sl (Drogeninjektion) shot; **sich** dat **einen ~ setzen** to shoot up **4.** (Spritzer) splash; **ein ~ Rum** a splash of rum; **mit ~ with** a shot (of alcohol) ▶ **in ~** in top shape; **weit vom ~ sein** fam to be miles away

Schüssel <-, -n> ['ʃʏ·sl] f bowl, dish

schusssicher RR adj bulletproof

Schussverletzung RR f bullet wound

Schusswaffe RR f firearm

Schusswechsel RR m exchange of fire

Schuster(in) <-s, -> ['ʃuːs·tɐ] m(f) s Schuhmacher

Schutt <-[e]s> [ʃʊt] m kein pl rubble no indef art ▶ **in ~ und Asche liegen** to be in ruins

Schüttelfrost m chills and fever

schütteln ['ʃʏ·tln] vt to shake

schütten ['ʃʏ·tn] **I.** vt to pour **II.** vi e~ **schüttet** impers fam it's pouring

Schutz <-es, -e> [ʃʊts] m kein pl (Sicherheit) protection (**vor** +dat from) ▶ ~ **suchen** to seek refuge; **im ~[e] der Dunkelheit** under cover of darkness; **zu Ihrem ~** for your own protection; **jdn [vor etw** dat] **in ~ nehmen** to protect sb [from sth]

Schutzanzug *m* protective clothing

Schutzbrille *f* protective goggles *npl*

Schütze, Schützin <-n, -n> [ˈʃʏtsə, ˈʃʏtsɪn] *m, f* **1.** SPORT marksman *masc*, markswoman *fem*; (*beim Fußball, Eishockey*) scorer **2.** (*Jagdwesen*) hunter **3.** MIL private, rifleman **4.** *kein pl* ASTROL Sagittarius

schützen [ˈʃʏtsn̩] **I.** *vt* to protect (**vor** +*dat* against/from) **II.** *vi* to give protection (**vor** +*dat* from)

schützend *adj* protective

Schutzengel *m* REL guardian angel

Schutzgebühr *f* nominal fee

Schutzhelm *m* protective helmet, hard hat

Schutzimpfung *f* vaccination

Schützling <-s, -e> [ˈʃʏts·lɪŋ] *m* protégé

schutzlos I. *adj* defenseless **II.** *adv* ~ **jdm ausgeliefert sein** to be at sb's mercy

Schutzmaske *f* protective mask

Schutzmaßnahme *f* precaution, precautionary measure

Schutzpatron(in) <-s, -e> *m(f)* REL patron saint

Schutzumschlag *m* dust jacket [*o* cover]

Schutzvorrichtung *f* safety device

Schutzweste *f* bulletproof vest

schwach <schwächer, schwächste> [ʃvax] **I.** *adj* **1.** (*nicht stark*) weak **2.** (*wenig leistend*) weak; (*Schüler*) poor; (*Batterie*) low **3.** (*gering*) weak; (*Anzeichen*) slight; (*Beteiligung*) poor; (*Interesse, Trost*) little **4.** (*leicht: Atmung*) faint; (*Bewegung*) slight; (*Druck, Wind, Strömung*) light; **schwächer werden** to become fainter ▶ [**bei jdm/etw**] ~ **werden** *fam* to be unable to refuse [sb/sth] **II.** *adv* **1.** (*leicht*) faintly **2.** (*dürftig*) poorly

Schwäche <-, -n> [ˈʃvɛ·çə] *f* **1.** *kein pl* (*geringe Stärke*) weakness **2.** *kein pl* (*Unwohlsein*) [feeling of] faintness **3.** (*Vorliebe*) weakness

schwächen [ˈʃvɛ·çn̩] **I.** *vt* to weaken; **geschwächt** weakened **II.** *vi* to have a weakening effect

Schwachkopf *m fam* idiot, bonehead

schwächlich [ˈʃvɛç·lɪç] *adj* weakly, feeble

Schwächling <-s, -e> [ˈʃvɛç·lɪŋ] *m* weakling

Schwachsinn *m kein pl fam* (*Quatsch*) nonsense

schwachsinnig *adj fam* (*blödsinnig*) idiotic, ridiculous

Schwachstelle *f* weak spot

Schwager, Schwägerin <-s, Schwäger> [ˈʃva·ɡɐ, ˈʃvɛː·ɡər·ɪn] *m, f* brother-in-law *masc*, sister-in-law *fem*

Schwalbe <-, -n> [ˈʃval·bə] *f* ORN swallow

Schwall <-[e]s, -e> [ʃval] *m* torrent

schwamm [ʃvam] *imp von* **schwimmen**

Schwamm <-[e]s, Schwämme> [ʃvam] *m* **1.** (*zur Reinigung*) sponge **2.** *südd, öster, schweiz* (*essbarer Pilz*) mushroom ▶ ~ **drüber!** let's forget it!

schwammig [ˈʃvamɪç] **I.** *adj* **1.** (*weich und porös*) spongy **2.** (*aufgedunsen*) puffy, bloated **3.** (*vage*) vague, woolly **II.** *adv* vaguely

Schwan <-[e]s, Schwäne> [ʃvaːn] *m* swan

schwanger [ˈʃvaŋɐ] *adj* pregnant (**von** +*dat* by)

Schwangere *f dekl wie adj* pregnant woman

Schwangerschaft <-, -en> *f* pregnancy

Schwangerschaftsabbruch *m* abortion

schwanken [ˈʃvaŋ·kn̩] *vi* **1.** *haben* (*schwingen*) to sway **2.** *sein* (*wanken*) to stagger **3.** *haben* (*nicht stabil sein*) to fluctuate **4.** *haben* (*unentschlossen sein*) to be undecided; **zwischen zwei Dingen** ~ to be torn between two things

Schwankung <-, -en> *f* fluctuation

Schwanz <-es, Schwänze> [ʃvants] *m* **1.** ZOOL tail **2.** ORN train, tail **3.** *sl* (*Penis*) dick, cock ▶ **den** ~ **einziehen** *fam* to back down

schwänzen [ˈʃvɛn·tsn̩] *vt, vi* SCH *fam* to play hooky

Schwarm¹ <-[e]s, Schwärme> [ʃvarm] *m* swarm; (*von Fischen*) school

Schwarm² <-[e]s> [ʃvarm] *m fam* (*verehrter Mensch*) heartthrob

schwärmen¹ [ˈʃvɛr·mən] *vi sein* to swarm

S

schwärmen² ['ʃvɛr·mən] vi 1. haben (begeistert reden) to gush fam (von +dat about) 2. (sich begeistern) für jdn ~ to be crazy about sb; für etw akk ~ to have a passion for sth

Schwärmerei <-, -en> [ʃvɛr·mə·'rai] f 1. (Wunschtraum) [pipe] dream 2. (Passion) passion

Schwarte <-, -n> ['ʃvar·tə] f KOCHK rind

schwarz <schwärzer, schwärzeste> [ʃvarts] I. adj 1. (Farbe) black 2. attr fam (illegal) illicit; (Geld) untaxed ▶ ~ auf **weiß** in black and white II. adv 1. (mit schwarzer Farbe) black 2. fam (auf illegale Weise) illicitly

Schwarz <-[es]> [ʃvarts] nt kein pl black

Schwarzarbeit f kein pl work that pays cash

schwarz|arbeiten vi to work under the table [o for cash]

Schwarzarbeiter(in) m(f) worker who gets paid under the table [o in cash]

Schwarzbrot nt dial 1. (Roggenbrot) sourdough rye bread 2. (festes Vollkornbrot) ≈ pumpernickel

Schwarze(r) f(m) dekl wie adj (Mensch) black

schwarz|fahren vi irreg sein to ride [public transportation] without paying the fare

Schwarzhandel m kein pl black market (mit +dat for)

Schwarzmarkt m black market

schwarz|sehen vi irreg [für jdn/etw] ~ to be pessimistic [about sb/sth]

schwatzen ['ʃvatsn] vi, **schwätzen** ['ʃvɛtsn] vi südd, österr 1. (sich unterhalten) to chat 2. (etw ausplaudern) to blab fam 3. (im Unterricht reden) to talk during class

Schwebe <-> ['ʃve·bə] f kein pl in der ~ sein to be in the balance; etw in der ~ lassen to leave sth undecided

Schwebebahn f 1. (an Schienen) suspension railway 2. s. **Seilbahn**

schweben ['ʃve·bn] vi haben to float; (Vogel) to hover; in Lebensgefahr ~ to be in danger of one's life; (Patient) to be in critical condition

Schwede, Schwedin <-n, -n> ['ʃve·də, 'ʃve·dɪn] m, f Swede; s. a. Deutsche(r)

Schweden <-s> ['ʃve·dn] nt Sweden s. a. Deutschland

schwedisch ['ʃve·dɪʃ] adj Swedish; s. deutsch

Schwefel <-s> ['ʃve·fl] m kein pl sulfur

Schwefeldioxid nt sulfur dioxide

schwefelhaltig adj sulfurous

schweifen ['ʃvai·fn] vi sein to roam, t wander; seine Blicke ~ lassen to le one's gaze wander

Schweigegeld nt hush money

Schweigeminute f minute of silence

schweigen <schwieg, geschwiegen ['ʃvai·gn] vi to remain silent ▶ **ganz z** ~ von [etw] dat let alone [sth]

Schweigen <-s> ['ʃvai·gn] nt kein pl si lence; jdn zum ~ bringen to silence s

Schweigepflicht f obligation to [main tain] confidentiality; der ~ unterliege to be bound to maintain confidentiality

schweigsam ['ʃvaik·za:m] adj taciturn

Schwein <-s, -e> [ʃvain] nt 1. ZOOL pi 2. kein pl (Schweinefleisch) pork 3. pe fam (gemeiner Kerl) bastard 4. fam (ur sauberer Mensch) pig 5. fam (obszöne Mensch) lewd person, pervert 6. far (bedauernswerter Mensch) [ein] arme ~ [an] unlucky bastard ▶ [großes] **haben** fam to be [really] lucky; **kein** fam nobody

Schweinebraten m roast pork

Schweinefleisch nt pork

Schweinerei <-, -en> [ʃvai·nə·'rai] f far 1. (Unordnung) mess 2. (Gemeinhei dirty trick; ~! bullshit! vulg sl 3. (Skar dal) scandal

Schweinestall m [pig]sty, [pig]pen

Schweiß <-es> [ʃvais] m kein pl sweat jdm bricht der ~ aus sb breaks ou in a sweat

schweißen ['ʃvai·sn] vt, vi to weld

Schweißfuß m meist pl sweaty foot

schweißgebadet adj bathed in sweat pred

Schweiz <-> [ʃvaits] f Switzerland; die französische/italienische ~ French speaking/Italian-speaking Switzerland s. a. Deutschland

Schweizer adj attr Swiss

Schweizer(in) <-s, -> ['ʃvai·tse] m(f) Swiss; s. a. Deutsche(r)

Schweizerdeutsch <-[s]> [ˈʃvai·tsə·dɔytʃ] *nt dekl wie adj* LING Swiss German; *s. a.* **Deutsch**

schwelgen [ˈʃvɛl·ɡn̩] *vi* to indulge oneself (**in** +*dat* in); **in Erinnerungen ~** to wallow in memories

Schwelle <-, -n> [ˈʃve·lə] *f* 1. (*Türschwelle*) threshold 2. (*Bahnschwelle*) [railroad] tie

schwellen <schwoll, geschwollen> [ˈʃve·lən] *vi sein* MED to swell [up]

Schwellung <-, -en> *f* swelling

Schwemme <-, -n> [ˈʃvɛ·mə] *f* (*Überangebot*) glut

schwemmen [ˈʃve·mən] *vt* **etw an Land ~** to wash sth ashore

schwenken [ˈʃvɛŋ·kn̩] **I.** *vt* 1. (*Fahne, Stab*) to wave 2. KOCHK to toss **II.** *vi* TV, FILM (*Kamera*) to pan

schwer <schwerer, schwerste> [ˈʃveːɐ̯] **I.** *adj* 1. (*nicht leicht*) heavy; **30 kg ~ sein** to weigh 30 kilos 2. (*beträchtlich*) serious; (*Verlust*) bitter; **~e Mängel aufweisen** to be badly defective; **~e Verwüstung[en] anrichten** to cause utter devastation 3. (*hart*) hard; (*Schicksal*) cruel; (*Strafe*) harsh 4. (*körperlich belastend*) serious, grave; (*Operation*) difficult 5. (*schwierig*) hard, difficult; (*Lektüre*) heavy 6. *attr* (*heftig: Sturm, Gewitter, Kämpfe*) heavy **II.** *adv* 1. (*hart*) hard; **~ arbeiten** to work hard; **jdm ~ zu schaffen machen** to give sb a hard time 2. (*mit schweren Lasten*) heavily; **~ bepackt sein** to be heavily laden 3. *fam* (*sehr*) deeply; **~ betrunken** plastered *sl* 4. (*mit Mühe*) with [great] difficulty; **ein ~ erziehbares Kind** a problem child; **~ verdaulich** indigestible 5. (*ernstlich*) seriously; **sich** *akk* **~ erkälten** to catch a bad cold; **~ verunglückt sein** to have had a bad accident; **~ wiegend** serious 6. (*schwierig*) difficult, not easy; **~ verständlich** (*kaum nachvollziehbar*) barely comprehensible; (*kaum zu verstehen*) hard to understand *pred*; **jdm das Leben ~ machen** to make life difficult for sb

Schwerarbeit *f kein pl* heavy labor

Schwerbehinderte(r) *f(m) dekl wie adj* severely disabled person

schwerelos *adj* weightless

schwer|fallen *vi irreg sein* **etw fällt jdm schwer** sth is difficult for sb [to do]

schwerfällig <-er, -ste> **I.** *adj* (*plump*) clumsy **II.** *adv* (*plump*) clumsily

Schwergewicht *nt* 1. (*Gewichtsklasse*) heavyweight 2. (*Schwerpunkt*) emphasis

schwerhörig *adj* hard of hearing *pred*

Schwerkraft *f kein pl* gravity

Schwermetall *nt* heavy metal

Schwermut <-> *f kein pl* melancholy

schwermütig <-er, -ste> [ˈʃveːɐ̯·myː·tɪç] *adj* melancholy

schwer|nehmen *vt irreg* **etw ~** to take sth to heart

Schwerpunkt *m* 1. (*Hauptgewicht*) main emphasis; **~e setzen** to set priorities 2. PHYS center of gravity

Schwert <-[e]s, -er> [ʃveːɐ̯t] *nt* sword

Schwertfisch *m* swordfish

Schwertlilie *f* iris

Schwerverbrecher(in) *m(f)* dangerous criminal, felon

Schwerverletzte(r) *f(m) dekl wie adj* critically injured person

Schwester <-, -n> [ˈʃves·te] *f* 1. (*weibliches Geschwisterteil*) sister 2. (*Krankenschwester*) nurse 3. (*Nonne*) nun

Schwiegereltern [ˈʃviː·ɡe·] *pl* parents-in-law *pl*, in-laws *pl fam*

Schwiegermutter *f* mother-in-law

Schwiegersohn *m* son-in-law

Schwiegertochter *f* daughter-in-law

Schwiegervater *m* father-in-law

Schwiele <-, -n> [ˈʃviː·lə] *f* callus

schwierig [ˈʃviː·rɪç] **I.** *adj* 1. (*nicht einfach*) difficult, hard 2. (*verwickelt*) complicated; (*Situation*) tricky **II.** *adv* with difficulty

Schwierigkeit <-, -en> *f* 1. *kein pl* (*Problematik*) difficulty; (*einer Lage, eines Problems*) complexity; (*einer Situation*) trickiness 2. *pl* (*Probleme*) problems *pl*; **jdn in ~en bringen** to get sb into trouble; **in ~en geraten** to get into trouble

Schwimmbad *nt* swimming pool

Schwimmbecken *nt* [swimming] pool

schwimmen <schwamm, geschwommen> [ˈʃvɪ·mən] *vt, vi sein o haben* to

S

swim; **~ gehen** to go swimming

Schwimmer(in) <-s, -> ['ʃvɪ·mɐ] *m(f)* swimmer

Schwimmflosse *f* flipper

Schwimmweste *f* life jacket

Schwindel <-s> ['ʃvɪn·dl̩] *m kein pl* **1.** (*Betrug*) swindle, fraud **2.** MED dizziness, vertigo; **~ erregend** *fig* astronomical

Schwindelanfall *m* MED dizzy spell

schwindelfrei *adj* **~ sein** to not suffer from vertigo

schwindelig ['ʃvɪn·də·lɪç] *adj pred* dizzy, giddy

schwindeln ['ʃvɪn·dl̩n] **I.** *vi* to lie **II.** *vi impers* **mir schwindelt** [es] I feel dizzy

schwinden <schwand, geschwunden> ['ʃvɪn·dn̩] *vi sein geh* (*Interesse*) to be waning; (*Wirkung*) to be wearing off; (*Zuversicht*) to be failing

Schwindler(in) <-s, -> ['ʃvɪnd·lɐ] *m(f)* **1.** (*Betrüger*) swindler **2.** (*Lügner*) liar

schwingen <schwang, geschwungen> ['ʃvɪŋən] **I.** *vt haben* to swing; (*Axt*) to brandish; (*Fahne*) to wave **II.** *vi sein o haben* (*pendeln*) to swing **III.** *vr haben* **sich** *akk* **auf/in etw** *akk* **~** to jump onto/into sth; **sich** *akk* **aufs Fahrrad ~** to hop on one's bike

Schwingung <-, -en> *f* oscillation

Schwips <-es, -e> [ʃvɪps] *m fam* **einen ~ haben** to be tipsy

schwirren ['ʃvɪ·rən] *vi sein* (*Mücken*) to buzz; (*Vogel*) to whir

schwitzen ['ʃvɪtsn̩] *vi* to sweat; **nass geschwitzt** drenched with sweat

schwören <schwor, geschworen> ['ʃvøː·rən] **I.** *vi* to swear (**auf** +*akk* by) **II.** *vt* to promise

schwul [ʃvuːl] *adj fam* gay

schwül [ʃvyːl] *adj* humid, muggy

Schwule(r) *m dekl wie adj fam* gay

Schwüle <-> ['ʃvyː·lə] *f kein pl* humidity, mugginess

schwülstig ['ʃvʏls·tɪç] **I.** *adj pej* overly ornate, florid; (*Stil*) bombastic **II.** *adv pej* bombastically

Schwung <-[e]s, Schwünge> [ʃvʊŋ] *m* swing ▸ **in ~ kommen** to get going;

[richtig] **in ~ sein** to be in full swing

schwungvoll I. *adj* **1.** (*weit ausholend*) sweeping **2.** (*mitreißend*) lively; (*Rede*) passionate **II.** *adv* lively

Schwur <-[e]s, Schwüre> [ʃvuːɐ̯] *m* **1.** (*Versprechen*) vow **2.** (*Eid*) oath

Schwurgericht *nt* jury court

sechs [zɛks] *adj* six; *s. a.* **acht**[1]

Sechs <-, -en> [zɛks] *f* **1.** (*Zahl*) six **2.** SCH (*schlechteste Zensur*) ≈ **F 3.** *schweiz* (*beste Zensur*) ≈ A

Sechseck *nt* hexagon

sechshundert ['zɛks·'hʊn·dɐt] *adj* six hundred

sechstausend ['zɛks·'tau·znt] *adj* six thousand

sechste(r, s) ['zɛks·tə, -tə, -təs] *adj* **1.** (*an sechster Stelle*) sixth; *s. a.* **achte(r, s) 1 2.** (*Datum*) sixth, 6th; *s. a.* **achte(r, s) 2**

Sechstel ['zɛks·tl̩] *adj* sixth

Sechstel <-s, -> ['zɛks·tl̩] *nt* sixth

sechstens ['zɛks·tn̩s] *adv* sixthly, in sixth place

sechzehn ['zɛç·tse·n] *adj* sixteen; *s. a.* **acht**[1]

sechzehnte(r, s) *adj* **1.** (*an sechzehnter Stelle*) sixteenth; *s. a.* **achte(r, s) 1 2.** (*Datum*) sixteenth, 16th; *s. a.* **achte(r, s) 2**

sechzig ['zɛç·tsɪç] *adj* sixty; *s. a.* **achtzig 1, 2**

sechzigste(r, s) *adj* sixtieth; *s. a.* **achte(r, s) 1**

Secondhandladen *m* secondhand store

See[1] <-s, -n> [zeː] *m* lake

See[2] <-, -n> [zeː] *f* **1.** (*Meer*) sea; **an der ~** by the sea; **auf ~** at sea; **auf hoher ~** on the high seas; **in ~ stechen** to put to sea **2.** (*Seegang*) heavy sea

Seefahrer *m* seafarer

Seefahrt *f kein pl* sea travel, seafaring *no art*

Seefisch *m* saltwater fish

Seehund *m* seal

Seekarte *f* nautical chart

seekrank *adj* seasick

Seelachs *m* coalfish

Seele <-, -n> ['zeː·lə] *f* soul; **mit Leib und ~** wholeheartedly; **das tut mir in der ~ weh** it breaks my heart ▸ **ein**

Herz und eine ~ sein to be inseparable

seelenruhig ['ze:·lən·'ru:ɪç] adv calmly

Seeleute pl von Seemann

seelisch ['ze:·lɪʃ] I. adj psychological,
emotional; ~es Gleichgewicht mental
balance II. adv ~ bedingt sein to have
psychological causes

Seelöwe, -löwin <-n, -n> m, f sea lion

Seelsorge f kein pl spiritual guidance

Seelsorger(in) <-s, -> ['ze:l·ˌzɔr·gə] m(f)
pastor

Seemacht f naval power

Seemann <-leute> ['ze:·man] m sailor,
seaman

Seemeile f nautical mile

Seenot f kein pl distress [at sea]

Seepferd(chen) nt sea horse

Seeräuber(in) m(f) pirate

Seereise f voyage; (Kreuzfahrt) cruise

Seerose f water lily

Seestern m starfish

Seetang m seaweed

seetüchtig adj seaworthy

Seeufer nt lakefront, lakeshore

Seeweg m sea route; auf dem ~ by sea

Seezunge f sole

Segel <-s, -> ['ze:·gl] nt sail

Segelboot nt sailboat

Segelflugzeug nt glider

segeln ['ze:·gln] vi sein to sail

Segeln <-s> ['ze:·gln] nt kein pl sailing

Segelschiff nt sailing ship

Segen <-s, -> ['ze:·gn] m kein pl blessing; ein wahrer ~ sein to be a real
godsend

Segler(in) <-s, -> ['ze:·glɐ] m(f) yachtsman masc, yachtswoman fem

Segment <-[e]s, -e> [zɛg·'mɛnt] nt segment

segnen ['ze:g·nən] vt to bless

sehen <sah, gesehen> ['ze:·ən] I. vt
1. (erblicken, bemerken) to see; ich
kann kein Blut ~ I can't stand the
sight of blood; das muss man ge~ haben! you have to see it to believe it!;
das sehe ich gar nicht gern! I don't
like that at all!; das wollen wir [doch]
erst mal ~! [well,] we'll see about that!;
gut/schlecht zu ~ sein to be easily/
poorly visible; etw kommen ~ to see

sth coming; sich akk ~ lassen können
to be something to be proud of; so ge~
from that point of view 2. (ansehen,
zusehen) to watch 3. (treffen) jdn ~ to
meet sb 4. (einschätzen) ich sehe das
so: ... the way I see it, ... II. vi 1. (Sehvermögen haben) to see; gut/schlecht
~ to have good/bad eyesight 2. (ansehen) to look; lass mal ~ let me see
3. (blicken) to look; aus dem Fenster
~ to look out [of] the window 4. (bemerken) ~ Sie!/siehste! fam [you] see?
5. (sich kümmern um) nach jdm/etw
~ to check on sb/sth; ich werde ~, was
ich für Sie tun kann I'll see what I can
do for you 6. (abwarten) to wait and see
III. vr sich akk gezwungen ~, etw zu
tun to feel compelled to do sth

sehenswert adj worth seeing

Sehenswürdigkeit <-, -en> f sight

Sehfehler m visual defect

Sehkraft f kein pl [eye]sight

Sehne <-, -n> ['ze:·nə] f ANAT tendon,
sinew

sehnen ['ze:·nən] vr sich akk nach jdm/
etw ~ to long for sb/sth

Sehnerv m optic nerve

sehnig ['ze:·nɪç] adj sinewy

Sehnsucht <-, -süchte> ['ze:n·zʊxt] f
longing (nach +dat for)

sehnsüchtig ['ze:n·zʏç·tɪç] adj attr longing, yearning; (Blick) wistful; (Verlangen,
Wunsch) ardent

sehr <[noch] mehr, am meisten> ['ze:ɐ̯]
adv 1. vor vb (in hohem Maße) very
much, a lot; danke ~! thanks a lot;
bitte ~, bedienen Sie sich! go ahead
and help yourself!; das will ich doch ~
hoffen I very much hope so 2. vor adj,
adv (besonders) very; jdm ~ dankbar
sein to be very grateful to sb

Sehschärfe f visual acuity

Sehstörung f visual defect

Sehtest m eye test

seicht [zaɪçt] adj shallow

Seide <-, -n> ['zai·də] f silk

seiden ['zai·dn̩] adj attr silk

Seidenraupe f silkworm

seidig ['zai·dɪç] adj silky

Seife <-, -n> ['zai·fə] f soap

Seifenoper f TV soap opera

S

Seil <-[e]s, -e> [zaɪl] *nt* rope; (*Draht-seil*) cable

Seilbahn *f* (*Standseilbahn*) funicular; (*Drahtseilbahn*) gondola

seil|springen *vi irreg, nur infin und pp sein* to skip rope

Seiltänzer(in) *m(f)* tightrope acrobat

sein¹ <bin, bist, ist, sind, seid, war, gewesen> [zaɪn] **I.** *vi sein* **1.** (*existieren, sich befinden*) to be, to exist; **ich bin wieder da** I'm back [again]; **ist da jemand?** is anybody there? **2.** (*Eigenschaft haben*) to be; **böse/klug ~** to be angry/clever; **er war so freundlich und hat das überprüft** he was kind enough to check it out; **sei so lieb und ...** I would be grateful if ... **3.** (*gehören*) **das Buch ist meins** the book is mine **4.** MATH to be, to equal **5.** (*sich ereignen*) to be, to take place; **was ist mit dir?** what is the matter with you?; **was ist [denn schon wieder]?** what is it [now]?; **war was?** *fam* did anything happen?; **das wär's dann** that's it; **das darf doch nicht wahr ~!** that can't be true!; **muss das ~?** do you [really] have to?; **was ~ muss, muss ~** what will be will be; **etw ~ lassen** *fam* to stop [doing sth] **6.** (*hergestellt sein*) **aus etw** *dat* **~** to be [made of] sth **7.** (*sich fühlen*) **mir ist heiß/kalt** I'm hot/cold; **mir ist übel** I feel sick **II.** *vi impers* **1.** (*bei Zeitangaben*) **es ist jetzt 9 Uhr** it is now 9 o'clock; **es ist Januar/Nacht** it is January/night[time] **2.** (*der Fall sein*) **mir ist es zu kalt** I'm too cold; **es sei denn, dass ...** unless ...; **wie wäre es mit ...?** how about ...?; **es war einmal ...** once upon a time ...; **wie dem auch sei** be that as it may, in any case **III.** *aux vb* **1.** *zur Bildung des Perfekts* **jd ist gefahren/gegangen** sb drove/went **2.** *zur Bildung des Zustandspassivs* **jd ist gebissen/verurteilt worden** sb has been bitten/convicted

sein² [zaɪn] *pron poss, adjektivisch* **1.** (*einem Mann gehörend*) his; (*zu einem Gegenstand gehörend*) its; (*einem Mädchen gehörend*) her; (*zu einer Stadt, einem Land gehörend*) its **2.** *auf „man" bezüglich* one's; *auf „jeder"*

bezüglich his, their *fam*; **jeder bekam ~ eigenes Zimmer** everyone got his/her own room

Sein <-s> [zaɪn] *nt kein pl* existence

seine(r, s) ['zaɪ·nə, -nə, -nəs] *pron poss substantivisch geh* **das S~** his [own]; **jedem das S~** to each his own; **die S~n** his family

seinerseits ['saɪ·nə·ˈzaɪts] *adv* (*von ihm aus*) on his part, as far as he is concerned

seinetwegen ['zaɪ·nət·ˈveː·gn̩] *adv* because of him

seinetwillen ['zaɪ·nət·ˈvɪ·lən] *adv* **um ~** for his sake

seit [zaɪt] **I.** *präp +dat* **1.** (*Anfangspunkt*) since; **~ wann?** since when?; **~ Juni** since June; **~ neuestem** recently **2.** (*Zeitspanne*) for; **~ drei Wochen** for three weeks; **~ einiger Zeit** for a while **II.** *konj* (*seitdem*) since

seitdem [zaɪt·ˈdeːm] **I.** *adv* since then **II.** *konj* since

Seite <-, -n> ['zaɪ·tə] *f* **1.** (*Fläche eines Körpers*) side; **die vordere/hintere/untere/obere ~** the front/back/bottom/top **2.** (*rechts oder links der Mitte*) **zur ~ gehen** to step aside; **jdn zur ~ nehmen** to take sb aside **3.** (*Papierblatt*) page; **gelbe ~n** Yellow Pages **4.** (*Beistand*) **jdm zur ~ stehen** to stand by sb **5.** (*Aspekt*) **alles hat [seine] zwei ~n** there are two sides to everything; **auf der einen ~...**, **auf der anderen [~] ...** on the one hand, ..., on the other [hand], ...; **sich** *akk* **von seiner besten ~ zeigen** to be on one's best behavior; **jds starke ~ sein** *fam* to be sb's forte **6.** (*Partei, Gruppe*) side; **auf jds ~ stehen** to be on sb's side; **die ~n wechseln** to change sides ▶ **etw auf die ~ legen** to put sth aside

Seitenangabe *f* page reference

Seitenausgang *m* side exit

Seiteneingang *m* side entrance

seitens ['zaɪ·tn̩s] *präp +gen* on the part of

Seitensprung *m fam* affair

Seitenstechen *nt kein pl* stitch [in one's side]

Seitenstreifen *m* hard shoulder

Seitenwind *m* crosswind

Seitenzahl *f* 1. (*Anzahl der Seiten*) number of pages 2. (*Ziffer*) page number

seither [zait·'he:ɐ] *adv* since then

seitlich ['zait·lɪç] I. *adj* side *attr* II. *adv* sideways III. *präp +gen* ~ **der Straße** at the side of the road

seitwärts ['zait·vɛrts] *adv* sideways

Sekretär(in) <-s, -e> [zek·re·'tɛ:ɐ] *m(f)* secretary

Sekretariat <-[e]s, -e> [zek·re·ta·'rjat] *nt* administrative office

Sekt <-[e]s, -e> [zɛkt] *m* sparkling wine

Sekte <-, -n> ['zɛk·tə] *f* sect

sekundär [ze·kʊn·'dɛ:ɐ] *adj* secondary

Sekunde <-, -n> [ze·'kʊn·də] *f* second; **auf die ~ genau** to the second

Sekundenzeiger *m* second hand

selbst [zɛlpst] I. *pron dem* 1. (*persönlich*) myself/yourself/himself etc. 2. (*ohne Hilfe, alleine*) by oneself; **etw ~ machen** to do sth by oneself; **von ~** automatically; **das versteht sich von ~** it goes without saying ▶ **er ist die Ruhe ~** he is calmness itself II. *adv* 1. (*eigen*) self; **~ ernannt** self-appointed; **~ gemacht** homemade; **~ gestrickt** hand-knit 2. (*sogar*) even; **~ wenn** even if

Selbstachtung *f* self-respect

selbständig ['zɛlp·ʃtɛn·dɪç] *adj s.* **selbstständig**

Selbständigkeit <-> *f kein pl s.* **Selbstständigkeit**

Selbstauslöser *m* self-timer

Selbstbedienungsladen *m* ≈ supermarket

Selbstbefriedigung *f* masturbation

Selbstbeherrschung *f* self-control

Selbstbestimmungsrecht *nt kein pl* right to self-determination

selbstbewusst RR *adj* self-confident

Selbstbewusstsein RR *nt* self-confidence

Selbsterhaltungstrieb *m* survival instinct

selbstgefällig *adj* self-satisfied

Selbstgespräch *nt* monologue; **Selbstgespräche führen** to talk to oneself

Selbsthilfegruppe *f* self-help group

selbstklebend *adj* self-adhesive

Selbstkostenpreis *m* cost; **zum ~** at cost

Selbstkritik *f kein pl* self-criticism; **~ üben** to criticize oneself

selbstlos *adj* selfless, unselfish

Selbstmitleid *nt* self-pity

Selbstmord *m* suicide; **~ begehen** to commit suicide

Selbstmörder(in) *m(f)* suicidal person

Selbstmordversuch *m* suicide attempt

Selbstschutz *m* self-protection

selbstsicher *adj* self-confident

selbstständig RR ['zɛlpst·ʃtɛn·dɪç] *adj* 1. (*eigenständig*) independent 2. (*beruflich unabhängig*) self-employed; **sich akk ~ machen** to start up *sep* one's own business

Selbstständigkeit <-> *f kein pl* 1. (*Eigenständigkeit*) independence 2. (*selbstständige Stellung*) self-employment

Selbsttäuschung *f* self-delusion

Selbstüberschätzung *f* overestimation of one's abilities

Selbstüberwindung *f* self-discipline

selbstverständlich I. *adj* natural; **das ist doch ~** don't mention it; **etw für ~ halten** to take sth for granted II. *adv* naturally, of course; **[aber] ~!** [but] of course!

Selbstverständlichkeit <-, -en> *f* naturalness; **eine ~ sein** to be the least that could be done

Selbstverteidigung *f* self-defense

Selbstvertrauen *nt* self-confidence

Selbstverwaltung *f* self-government

Selbstverwirklichung *f* self-realization

Selbstzweck *m kein pl* end in itself

Selen <-s> [ze'le:n] *nt* selenium

selig ['ze:·lɪç] *adj* (*überglücklich*) overjoyed ▶ **wer's glaubt, wird ~** *iron fam* that's a likely story

Sellerie <-s, -[s]> ['zɛ·ləri] *m* 1. (*Knollensellerie*) celeriac 2. (*Stangensellerie*) celery

selten ['zɛl·tn̩] I. *adj* rare II. *adv* rarely

Seltenheit <-, -en> *f* 1. *kein pl* (*seltenes Vorkommen*) rare occurrence 2. (*seltene Sache*) rarity

seltsam ['zɛlt·za:m] *adj* strange, weird, peculiar

S

Semester <-s, -> [zeˈmɛsˌtɐ] nt semester, term

Semikolon <-s, -s> [zeˈmiˈkoːˌlɔn] nt semicolon

Seminar <-s, -e o österr -ien> [zeˈmiˈnaːɐ̯] nt **1.** (*Lehrveranstaltung*) seminar **2.** (*Universitätsinstitut*) department

Semit(in) <-en, -en> [zeˈmiːt] m(f) Semite

semitisch [zeˈmiːtɪʃ] adj Semitic

Semmel <-, -n> [ˈzɛml] f dial roll ▶ **weggehen wie warme ~n** fam to go like hot cakes

Senat <-[e]s, -e> [zeˈnaːt] m senate

Senator, Senatorin <-s, -toren> [zeˈnaːtoːɐ̯, zeˈnaˈtoːˌrɪn] m, f senator

Sendegebiet nt broadcast area

senden[1] [ˈzɛnˌdn̩] **I.** vt to broadcast; (*Botschaft*) to transmit **II.** vi to be on the air

senden[2] <sandte o sendete, gesandt o gesendet> [ˈzɛnˌdn̩] vt to send; (*Truppen*) to dispatch

Sender <-s, -> [ˈzɛnˌdɐ] m **1.** (*Sendeanstalt*) TV channel; RADIO station **2.** (*Sendegerät*) transmitter

Sendeschluss RR m end of a broadcast

Sendezeit f airtime; **zur besten ~** at prime time

Sendung[1] <-, -en> f TV, RADIO program; **auf ~ gehen/sein** to go/be on the air

Sendung[2] <-, -en> f (*Paketsendung*) package; (*Warensendung*) shipment

Senf <-[e]s, -e> [zɛnf] m mustard ▶ **seinen ~ dazugeben** dat fam to have one's say

senil [zeˈniːl] adj senile

Senior <-s, Senioren> [ˈzeːˌnjoːɐ̯] m meist pl (*älterer Mensch*) senior citizen

Seniorenheim nt nursing [o retirement] home

senken [ˈzɛŋkn̩] **I.** vt **1.** (*niedriger machen*) to lower; (*Fieber*) to reduce **2.** (*abwärtsbewegen*) **den Kopf ~** to bow one's head **II.** vr **sich** akk **~** to sink, to drop

senkrecht [ˈzɛŋkrɛçt] adj vertical

Senkung <-, -en> f **1.** kein pl (*der Preise*) reduction; (*der Löhne*) cut; (*der Steuern*) decrease **2.** (*das Senken*) drop,

subsidence; (*der Stimme*) lowering

Sensation <-, -en> [zɛnzaˈtsi̯oːn] f sensation

sensationell [zɛnzaˈtsi̯oˈnɛl] adj sensational

sensibel [zɛnˈziːbl̩] adj sensitive

Sensibilität <-, -en> [zɛnˈziˈbiˈliˈtɛːt] f sensitivity

Sensor <-s, -soren> [ˈzɛnˌzoːɐ̯] m sensor

sentimental [zɛntiˈmɛnˈtaːl] adj sentimental

Sentimentalität <-, -en> [zɛntiˈmɛnˈtaˈliˈtɛːt] f sentimentality

separat [zeˈpaˈraːt] adj separate

Separatist(in) <-en, -en> [zeˈpaˈraˈtɪst] m(f) separatist

September <-[s], -> [zɛpˈtɛmˌbɐ] m September; *s. a.* **Februar**

Serbien <-s> [ˈzɛrˌbi̯ən] nt Serbia; *s. a.* **Deutschland**

Serenade <-, -n> [zeˈreˈnaːˌdə] f serenade

Serie [ˈzeːˌri̯ə] f (*a. media, tv*) series + *sing vb*

serienmäßig adj **1.** (*in Serienfertigung*) mass-produced **2.** (*bereits eingebaut sein*) standard

Seriennummer f serial number

seriös [zeˈri̯øːs] **I.** adj (*Mensch*) respectable; (*Angebot*) serious; (*Unternehmen*) reputable **II.** adv respectably

Serpentine <-, -n> [zɛrˈpɛnˈtiːˌnə] f winding road

Service[1] <-, -s> [ˈzœrˌvɪs] m kein pl (*Bedienung*) service

Service[2] <-[s], -> [zɛrˈviːs] nt (*Set*) dinner/coffee service

servieren * [zɛrˈviːˌrən] vt to serve

Serviette <-, -n> [zɛrˈvi̯ɛˌtə] f napkin

Servolenkung f power[-assisted] steering

servus [ˈzɛrˌvʊs] interj österr, südd (*hallo*) hi; (*tschüs*) [good]bye

Sessel <-s, -> [ˈzɛˌsl̩] m armchair

Sessellift m chair lift

setzen [ˈzɛˌtsn̩] **I.** vt haben **1.** (*platzieren*) to put, to place **2.** (*festlegen*) to set; **eine Frist/ein Ziel ~** to set a deadline/a goal **3.** (*bringen*) **etw in Betrieb ~** to set sth in motion; **jdn auf**

Diät ~ to put sb on a diet **4.** (*pflanzen*) to plant **5.** (*wetten*) **Geld auf jdn/etw ~** to bet money on sb/sth **6.** TYPO to set **II.** *vr* haben **sich** *akk* **~ 1.** (*sich niederlassen*) to sit [down]; **bitte ~ Sie sich doch!** please sit down!; **sich** *akk* **zu jdm ~** to sit next to sb; **wollen Sie sich nicht zu uns ~?** won't you join us?; **sich** *akk* **ins Auto ~** to get in the car **2.** (*sich senken: Kaffeesatz*) to settle **III.** *vi* **1.** haben (*wetten*) **auf jdn/etw ~** to bet on sb/sth **2.** sein *o* haben **über etw** *akk* **~** (*springen*) to jump over sth; (*überschiffen*) to cross sth

Seuche <-, -n> ['zɔy·çə] *f* epidemic

Seuchenbekämpfung *f* epidemic control

seufzen ['zɔyf·tsn̩] *vi* to sigh

Seufzer <-s, -> *m* sigh

Sex <-[es]> [zɛks] *m* kein pl sex

siamesisch [zja·'me:·zɪʃ] *adj* Siamese

Sibirien <-s> [zi·'biː·ri̯ən] *nt* Siberia

sich [zɪç] *pron refl* **1.** *akk* oneself; **er/sie/es ... ~** he/she/it ... himself/herself/itself; **Sie ... ~** you ... yourself/yourselves; **sie ... ~** they ... themselves; **man fragt ~, was das soll** one wonders what it's all about; **~ freuen/wundern** to be pleased/surprised; **~ schämen** to be ashamed of oneself **2.** *dat* one's; **~ etw einbilden** to imagine sth; **~ etw kaufen** to buy sth for oneself; **die Katze leckte ~ die Pfote** the cat licked its paw **3.** *pl* (*einander*) each other, one another; **~ lieben** to love each other **4.** *unpersönlich* **das Auto fährt ~ prima** the car drives really well **5.** + *prep* **er denkt immer nur an ~** he only ever thinks of himself; **wieder zu ~ kommen** to regain consciousness; **etw von ~ aus tun** to do sth of one's own accord

Sichel <-, -n> ['zɪ·çl̩] *f* **1.** (*Werkzeug*) sickle **2.** (*Gebilde, von Mond*) crescent

sicher ['zɪ·çɐ] **I.** *adj* **1.** (*gewiss*) certain, sure; (*Zusage*) definite; **sind Sie ~?** are you sure?; **es ist nicht ~, dass er kommt** it is not certain that he will come; **sich** *dat* **etw** *gen* **~ sein** to be sure of sth **2.** (*ungefährdet*) safe (**vor**

+*dat* from); (*Anlage, Arbeitsplatz*) secure; **~ ist ~** you can't be too careful **3.** (*zuverlässig*) reliable; (*Methode*) foolproof **4.** (*geübt*) competent **5.** (*selbstsicher*) self-assured **II.** *adv* **1.** (*gewiss*) surely; [*aber*] **~!** *fam* sure!; **ich weiß das ganz ~** I know that for sure **3.** (*ungefährdet*) **sich** *akk* **~ fühlen** to feel safe

Sicherheit <-, -en> *f* **1.** kein pl (*gesicherter Zustand*) safety; **etw in ~ bringen** to get sth to a safe place; **in ~ sein** to be safe **2.** kein pl (*Gewissheit*) certainty; **mit ~** for certain **3.** kein pl (*Gewandtheit*) competence **4.** (*Kaution*) surety

Sicherheitsabstand *m* safe distance

Sicherheitsgurt *m* seat [*o* safety] belt

sicherheitshalber *adv* to be on the safe side

Sicherheitsnadel *f* safety pin

Sicherheitsrat *m* kein pl POL Security Council

sicherlich *adv* surely

sichern ['zɪ·çɐn] *vt* **1.** (*schützen*) to safeguard (**gegen** +*akk* against) **2.** (*Schusswaffe*) to put a safety on **3.** (*absichern*) to protect; (*Bergsteiger, Tatort, Tür*) to secure; **gesichert sein** to be protected **4.** COMPUT to save

sicher|stellen *vt* **1.** (*in Gewahrsam nehmen*) to confiscate **2.** (*gewährleisten*) to guarantee; **~, dass ...** to ensure that ...

Sicherung <-, -en> *f* **1.** (*das Sichern*) securing, safeguarding **2.** ELEK fuse **3.** (*Schutzvorrichtung*) safety [catch] **4.** COMPUT backup

Sicherungskopie *f* COMPUT backup copy

Sicht <-, selten -en> [zɪçt] *f* **1.** (*Aussicht*) view; **du nimmst mir die ~** you're blocking my view; **die ~ beträgt heute nur 20 Meter** visibility is down to 20 meters today; **in ~ sein** to be in sight; **Land in ~!** land ahoy!; **etw ist in ~** *fig* sth is on the horizon; **auf kurze/lange ~** *fig* in the short/long term **2.** (*Meinung*) [point of] view; **aus jds ~** from sb's point of view

sichtbar *adj* visible

sichten ['zɪ·çtn̩] *vt* **1.** (*ausmachen*) to

sight **2.** (*durchsehen*) **die Akten ~** to look through the files

sichtlich *adv* ~ **beeindruckt sein** to be visibly impressed

Sichtverhältnisse *pl* visibility

Sichtweite *f* visibility; **außer/in ~ sein** to be out of/in sight

sickern ['zɪ·kɐn] *vi sein* to seep (**aus** +*dat* from, **durch** +*akk* through)

sie [ziː] *pron pers*, 3. *pers* **1.** <*gen* ihrer, *dat* ihr, *akk* sie> *sing* she; ~ **ist es!** it's her!; (*weibliche Sache bezeichnend*) it; (*Tier bezeichnend*) it; (*bei weiblichen Haustieren*) she **2.** <*gen* ihrer, *dat* ihnen, *akk* sie> *pl* they

Sie[1] <*gen* ihrer, *dat* Ihnen, *akk* Sie> [ziː] *pron pers*, 2. *pers sing o pl* (*förmliche Anrede*) you

Sie[2] <-s> [ziː] *nt* **jdn mit ~ anreden** to address sb using the "Sie" form

Sieb <-[e]s, -e> [ziːp] *nt* (*Küchensieb*) sieve; (*größer*) colander; (*Kaffeesieb, Teesieb*) strainer

sieben[1] ['ziː·bn̩] *adj* seven; *s. a.* **acht**[1]

sieben[2] ['ziː·bn̩] *vt* to sieve

siebenhundert ['ziː·bn̩·ˈhʊn·dɐt] *adj* seven hundred

siebte(r, s) ['ziːp·tə, -tɐ, -təs] *adj* **1.** (*an siebter Stelle*) seventh; *s. a.* **achte(r, s) 1 2.** (*Datum*) seventh, 7th; *s. a.* **achte(r, s) 2**

Siebtel <-s, -> ['ziːp·tl̩] *nt* seventh

siebzehn ['ziːp·tseːn] *adj* seventeen; *s. a.* **acht**[1]

siebzehnte(r, s) *adj* **1.** (*an siebzehnter Stelle*) seventeenth; *s. a.* **achte(r, s) 1 2.** (*Datum*) seventeenth, 17th; *s. a.* **achte(r, s) 2**

siebzig ['ziːp·tsɪç] *adj* seventy; *s. a.* **achtzig 1, 2**

siebzigste(r, s) *adj* seventieth; *s. a.* **achte(r, s) 1**

siedeln ['ziː·dln̩] *vi* to settle

sieden <siedete, gesiedet> ['ziː·dn̩] *vi* to boil

Siedepunkt *m* boiling point

Siedler(in) <-s, -> ['ziːd·lɐ] *m(f)* settler

Siedlung <-, -en> ['ziːd·lʊŋ] *f* **1.** (*Wohnhausgruppe*) housing development **2.** (*Ansiedlung*) settlement

Sieg <-[e]s, -e> [ziːk] *m* victory (**über** +*akk* over)

Siegel <-s, -> ['ziː·gl̩] *nt* seal; (*privates a.*) signet

siegen ['ziː·gn̩] *vt, vi* to win

Sieger(in) <-s, -> *m(f)* **1.** MIL victor **2.** SPORT winner

Siegerehrung *f* SPORT victory ceremony

Siegerurkunde *f* SPORT winner's certificate

siegessicher *adj* certain of victory *pred*

siegreich **I.** *adj* **1.** MIL victorious **2.** SPORT winning *attr*, successful **II.** *adv* in triumph

sieh(e) ['ziː(·ə)] *imp sing von* **sehen**

Signal <-s, -e> [zɪ·ˈgnaːl] *nt* signal

signalisieren * [zɪ·gna·li·ˈziː·rən] *vt* to signal

Signatur <-, -en> [zɪ·gna·ˈtuːɐ̯] *f* signature

signieren * [zɪ·ˈgniː·rən] *vt* to sign; (*bei einer Autogrammstunde*) to autograph; **signiert** signed, autographed

Silbe <-, -n> ['zɪl·bə] *f* syllable

Silbentrennung *f* hyphenation

Silber <-s> ['zɪl·bɐ] *nt kein pl* silver

Silberhochzeit *f* silver wedding anniversary

Silbermedaille *f* silver medal

silbern ['zɪl·bɐn] *adj* **1.** (*aus Silber bestehend*) silver **2.** (*Farbe*) silver[y]

Silhouette <-, -n> [zi·ˈlʏɛtə] *f* silhouette

Silizium <-s> [zi·ˈliː·tsi̯·ʊm] *nt kein pl* silicon

Silvester <-s, -> [zɪl·ˈvɛs·tɐ] *m o nt* New Year's Eve

simpel ['zɪm·pl̩] **I.** *adj* simple **II.** *adv* simply

Sims <-es, -e> [zɪms] *m o nt* (*Fenstersims*) windowsill; (*Kaminsims*) mantelpiece

simsen ['zɪm·zən] *vt, vi* TELEK *fam* to text, to send a text message

Simulant(in) <-en, -en> [zi·mu·ˈlant] *m(f)* malingerer

simulieren * [zi·mu·ˈliː·rən] **I.** *vi* to malinger **II.** *vt* SCI to [computer-]simulate

simultan [zi·mʊl·ˈtaːn] **I.** *adj* simultaneous **II.** *adv* simultaneously; ~ **dolmetschen** to simultaneously interpret

Sinfonie <-, -n> [zɪn·fo·ˈniː] *f* symphony

singen <sang, gesungen> ['zɪŋ·ən] *vt, vi* to sing

Singular <-s, -e> ['zɪŋ·gu·laɐ̯] *m* LING singular

Singvogel *m* songbird

sinken <sank, gesunken> ['zɪŋ·kn̩] *vi sein* 1. (*versinken*) to sink; (*Schiff*) to go down 2. (*abnehmen*) to go down; (*Fieber, Preis*) to fall; (*Hoffnung*) to sink ▶ **den** <u>Mut</u> ~ **lassen** to lose courage

Sinn <-[e]s, -e> [zɪn] *m* 1. *meist sg* (*Organ der Wahrnehmung*) sense; **bist du noch bei ~en?** have you taken leave of your senses?; **von ~en sein** to be out of one's mind 2. *kein pl* (*Bedeutung*) meaning; **im wahrsten ~e des Wortes** in the truest sense of the word; **im übertragenen ~e** in the figurative sense; **in diesem ~e** in that respect 3. (*Zweck*) point; **der ~ des Lebens** the meaning of life; **es hat keinen ~[, etw zu tun]** there's no point [in doing sth] 4. *kein pl* (*Verständnis*) ▶ **für etw** *akk* **haben** to appreciate sth 5. (*Intention, Gedanke*) inclination; **in jds** *dat* ~ **handeln** to act according to sb's wishes; **was hast du mit ihm im ~?** what do you have in mind with him?

sinnbildlich I. *adj* symbolic II. *adv* symbolically

Sinnesorgan *nt* sense organ

Sinnestäuschung *f* hallucination

sinngemäß *adv* **etw ~ wiedergeben** to give the gist of sth

sinnlich I. *adj* 1. (*sexuell*) carnal *form* 2. (*sexuell verlangend*) sensual; (*stärker*) voluptuous 3. (*gern genießend*) sensuous, sensual 4. (*die Sinne ansprechend*) sensory, sensorial II. *adv* (*mit den Sinnen*) sensuously

Sinnlichkeit <-> *f kein pl* sensuality

sinnlos *adj* 1. (*unsinnig*) senseless; (*Bemühungen*) futile; (*Geschwätz*) meaningless; **das ist doch ~!** that's pointless! 2. *pej* (*maßlos*) frenzied; (*Hass, Wut*) blind

Sinnlosigkeit <-, -en> *f* futility

sinnvoll I. *adj* 1. (*zweckmäßig*) practical, appropriate 2. (*Erfüllung bietend*) meaningful 3. (*eine Bedeutung habend*) meaningful, coherent II. *adv* sensibly

Sintflut ['zɪnt·fluːt] *f* **die ~** the Flood ▶ <u>nach</u> **mir die ~** *fam* I don't care what happens after I leave

Sippe <-, -n> ['zɪ·pə] *f* 1. SOZIOL [extended] family 2. *hum fam* (*Verwandtschaft*) family, clan *fam*

Sirene <-, -n> [zi·'reː·nə] *f* siren

Sirup <-s, -e> ['ziː·rʊp] *m* syrup

Sitte <-, -n> ['zɪtə] *f* custom ▶ **andere** <u>Länder, andere</u> **~n** other countries, other customs

Sittlichkeitsverbrechen *nt* sex crime

Situation <-, -en> [zi·tu̯a·'tsi̯oːn] *f* situation; (*persönlich a.*) position

Sitz <-es, -e> [zɪts] *m* 1. (*Sitzgelegenheit*) seat 2. (*Amtssitz*) seat; (*von Verwaltung*) headquarters + *sing/pl vb*; (*von Unternehmen*) head office

sitzen <saß, gesessen> ['zɪtsn̩] *vi haben o südd, österr, schweiz sein* 1. (*sich gesetzt haben*) to sit; **im S~** while seated, sitting down; **bitte bleiben Sie ~!** please don't get up! 2. (*beschäftigt sein*) **an einem Aufsatz ~** to be laboring over an essay 3. *fam* (*inhaftiert sein*) to do time 4. MODE (*Hosen, Rock*) to fit 5. SCH ▶ **bleiben** *fam* to repeat a grade 6. (*nicht absetzen können*) **auf etw** *dat* ~ **bleiben** to be left with sth ▶ **sie hat** <u>einen</u> ~ *fam* she's had one too many; **jdn** ~ **lassen** *fam* (*im Stich lassen*) to leave sb in the lurch; (*versetzen*) to stand sb up; (*nicht heiraten*) to jilt sb; **das lasse ich nicht** <u>auf</u> **mir ~!** I won't stand for this/that!

Sitzgelegenheit *f* seats *pl*, seating [accommodation]

Sitzplatz *m* seat

Sitzung <-, -en> *f* meeting; (*im Parlament*) [parliamentary] session

Sitzungssaal *m* conference hall

Sizilien <-s, -e> [zi·'tsiː·li̯ən] *nt* Sicily; *s. a.* **Deutschland**

Skala <-, Skalen> ['ska·la] *f* 1. (*Maßeinteilung*) scale 2. (*Palette*) range

Skandal <-s, -e> [skan·'daːl] *m* scandal

skandalös [skan·da·'løːs] 1. *adj* scandalous, outrageous II. *adv* outrageously, shockingly

Skandinavien <-s> [skan·di·'naː·vi̯ən] *nt* Scandinavia

S

skandinavisch [skan·di·ˈnaː·vɪʃ] *adj*
Scandinavian

Skateboard <-s, -s> [ˈskɛːt·boːɐ̯t] *nt*
skateboard; ~ **fahren** to skateboard

Skelett <-[e]s, -e> [ske·ˈlɛt] *nt* skeleton

Skepsis <-> [ˈskɛp·sɪs] *f kein pl* skepticism

skeptisch [ˈskɛp·tɪʃ] **I.** *adj* skeptical
II. *adv* skeptically

Ski <-s, -> [ʃiː, ˈʃiːə] *m* ski; ~ **laufen**
to ski

Skianzug *m* ski suit

Skifahrer(in) *m(f)* skier

Skilift *m* ski lift

Skinhead <-s, -s> [ˈskɪn·hɛt] *m* skinhead

Skipiste *f* ski run

Skispringen *nt kein pl* ski jumping

Skizze <-, -n> [ˈskɪ·tsə] *f* sketch

skizzieren * [skɪ·ˈtsiː·rən] *vt* **1.** (*umreißen: Plan*) to outline **2.** KUNST (*als Skizze darstellen*) to sketch

Sklave, Sklavin <-n, -n> [ˈsklaː·və, ˈsklaː·vɪn] *m, f* slave

Sklavenhandel *m kein pl* slave trade

Sklaverei <-, -en> [sklaː·və·ˈrai] *f* slavery *no art*

Skorpion <-s, -e> [skɔr·ˈpjoːn] *m* **1.** ZOOL
scorpion **2.** ASTROL Scorpio

Skrupel <-s, -> [ˈskruː·pl̩] *m meist pl*
scruple, qualms *pl*

skrupellos *pej* **I.** *adj* unscrupulous
II. *adv* without scruple

Skrupellosigkeit <-> *f kein pl* unscrupulousness

Skulptur <-, -en> [skʊlp·ˈtuːɐ̯] *f* sculpture

Slalom <-s, -s> [ˈslaː·lɔm] *m* slalom

Slawe, Slawin <-n, -n> [ˈslaː·və, ˈslaː·vɪn] *m, f* Slav; *s. a.* **Deutsche(r)**

slawisch [ˈslaː·vɪʃ] *adj* Slav[on]ic; *s. a.*
deutsch

Slip <-s, -s> [slɪp] *m* panties *pl*

Slipeinlage *f* panty liner

Slowakei <-> [slo·va·ˈkai] *f* die ~ Slovakia; *s. a.* **Deutschland**

Slowenien <-s> [slo·ˈveː·njən] *nt* Slovenia; *s. a.* **Deutschland**

Slum <-s, -s> [slam] *m* slum

Smaragd <-[e]s, -e> [sma·ˈrakt] *m* emerald

Smog <-[s], -s> [smɔk] *m* smog

Smogalarm *m* smog alert

Smoking <-s, -s> [ˈsmoː·kɪŋ] *m* tuxedo,
dinner jacket

SMS <-, -> [ɛs·ʔɛm·ˈɛs] *f* MEDIA, TELEK
Abk von **Short Message Service** text
[message], IM

so [zoː] **I.** *adv* **1.** + *adj/adv* (*derart*) so,
es ist ~, wie du sagst it is [just] as you
say; das ist ~ weit richtig, aber ...
generally speaking that is right, but ...; ~
viel [wie] as much [as]; ~ **weit sein** *fam*
to be ready; ~ **wenig wie möglich** as
little as possible **2.** + *vb* (*derart*) **sie hat**
sich ~ darauf gefreut she was really
looking forward to it; **ich habe mich**
~ **über ihn geärgert!** I was so angry
with him **3.** (*auf diese Weise*) like this/
that, this/that way, thus *form;* ~ **musst**
du es machen this is how you have to
do it; ~ **ist das nun mal** *fam* that's the
way things are; ~ **ist es** that's [just] the
way it is; ~, **als ob** ... as if ...; ~ **oder**
~ either way, in the end; **und** ~ **weiter**
[und + **fort**] et cetera[, et cetera]; ~ **ge-**
nannt so-called **4.** (*solch*) ~ **ein Buch**
haben wir nicht we don't have a book
like that; ~ **etwas** such a thing; ~ **etwas**
sagt man nicht you shouldn't say such
things **5.** *fam* (*etwa*) **wir treffen uns**
~ **gegen 7 Uhr** we'll meet at around 7
o'clock **6.** *fam* **und/oder** ~ or so; **ich**
gehe um 5 oder ~ I'm going around
5 or so **7.** *fam* (*umsonst*) for nothing;
das können Sie ~ **haben** you can have
it [for free] **II.** *konj* **1.** (*konsekutiv*) ~
dass so that **2.** (*obwohl*) ~ **leid es mir**
auch tut as sorry as I am **III.** *inter*
1. (*also*) so, right; ~, **jetzt gehen wir**
einkaufen so, now let's go shopping
2. (*ätsch*) so there! **3.** (*ach*) ~, ~! *fam*
is that a fact! *iron*

sobald [zo·ˈbalt] *konj* as soon as

Socke <-, -n> [ˈzɔ·kə] *f* sock ► **sich**
akk **auf die -n machen** *fam* to get a
move on

Sockel <-s, -> [ˈzɔ·kl̩] *m* **1.** (*von Statue*) plinth, pedestal **2.** (*von Gebäude*)
plinth, base course

Sodbrennen [zoːt·] *nt* heartburn

soeben [zo·ˈʔeːbn̩] *adv geh* just

Sofa <-s, -s> ['zo:·fa] *nt* sofa

sofern [zo·'fɛrn] *konj* if, provided that

sofort [zo·'fɔrt] *adv* immediately

sofortig [zo·'fɔr·tɪç] *adj* immediate; **mit ~er Wirkung** with immediate effect

Softie <-s, -s> ['zɔf·ti] *m fam* softie

Software <-, -s> ['zɔft·vɛːɐ̯] *f* software

sogar [zo·'gaːɐ̯] *adv* even

Sohle <-, -n> ['zoː·lə] *f* sole

Sohn <-[e]s, Söhne> [zoːn] *m* son

Sojabohne *f* soybean

solange [zo·'laŋə] *konj* as long as

Solarenergie *f* solar energy

Solarium <-s, -rien> [zo·'laː·ri̯·ʊm] *nt* solarium

solch [zɔlç] *adj* such

solche(r, s) *adj* **1.** *attr* such; **~ Frauen** women like that; **ich soll mir ~ Sorgen** I was really worried; **sie hatte ~ Angst ...** she was so afraid ... **2.** *substantivisch* (*solche Menschen*) people like that; **es gibt ~ und ~ Kunden** there are customers and then there are customers; **als ~(r, s)** as such, in itself; **der Mensch als ~r** man as such

Sold <-[e]s> [zɔlt] *m kein pl* MIL pay

Soldat <-en, -en> [zɔl·'daːt] *m(f)* soldier

Söldner(in) <-s, -> ['zœld·nɐ] *m(f)* mercenary

solidarisieren * [zo·li·da·ri·'ziː·rən] *vr* **sich** *akk* **~** to show [one's] solidarity

Solidarität <-> [zo·li·da·ri·'tɛːt] *f kein pl* solidarity

Solidaritätszuschlag *m* POL solidarity tax (*a tax to help finance the cost of the German reunification*)

solide [zo·'liː·də] **I.** *adj* **1.** (*haltbar, fest*) solid; (*Kleidung*) durable **2.** (*fundiert: Kenntnisse*) sound, thorough **3.** (*untadelig: Leben*) respectable **4.** (*seriös: Unternehmen*) well-established *attr,* sound **II.** *adv* (*haltbar, fest*) solidly

Solist(in) <-en, -en> [zo·'lɪst] *m(f)* MUS soloist

Soll <-[s], -[s]> [zɔl] *nt* **1.** (*Sollseite*) debit side; **~ und Haben** debit and credit **2.** (*Produktionsnorm*) target; **sein ~ erfüllen** to reach one's target

sollen ['zɔ·lən] **I.** *aux vb* <sollte, sollen> **1.** (*etw zu tun haben*) **du sollst herkommen, habe ich gesagt!** I said [you should] come here!; **man hat mir gesagt, ich soll Sie fragen** I was told to ask you; **was ~ wir machen?** what should we do? **2.** (*falls*) **sollte das passieren, ...** should that happen ... **3.** (*eigentlich müssen*) **du sollst dich schämen!** you should be ashamed [of yourself]; **das solltest du unbedingt sehen** you have to see this; **so soll es sein** that's how it ought to be **4.** (*angeblich sein, tun*) to be supposed to; **sie soll sehr reich sein** she is said to be very rich; **was soll das heißen?** what's that supposed to mean? **5.** (*dürfen*) **du hättest das nicht tun** ~ you should not have done that **6.** *in der Vergangenheit* **es sollte ganz anders kommen** things were supposed to turn out quite differently **II.** *vi* <sollte, gesollt> **1.** (*eine Anweisung befolgen*) **soll er reinkommen? – ja, er soll** should he come in? — yes, he should **2.** (*müssen*) **du sollst sofort nach Hause** you should go home right away **3.** (*bedeuten*) **was soll der Blödsinn?** *fam* what's all this nonsense about?; **was soll das?** *fam* what's that supposed to mean?; **was soll's?** *fam* who cares?

Solo <-s, Soli> ['zoː·lo] *nt* MUS solo

somit [zo·'mɪt] *adv* therefore, hence form

Sommer <-s, -> ['zɔ·mɐ] *m* summer

sommerlich I. *adj* summer *attr;* **~es Wetter** summer weather **II.** *adv* like in summer; **sich** *akk* **~ kleiden** to wear summer clothing

Sommersprosse *f meist pl* freckle

Sonate <-, -n> [zo·'naː·tə] *f* sonata

Sonde <-, -n> ['zɔn·də] *f* **1.** MED (*Schlauchsonde*) tube; (*Operationssonde*) probe **2.** (*Raumsonde*) probe

Sonderangebot *nt* special offer; **etw im ~ haben** to have sth on sale

sonderbar ['zɔn·dɐ·baːɐ̯] **I.** *adj* peculiar, strange, odd **II.** *adv* strangely

Sonderfall *m* special case

Sonderling <-s, -e> ['zɔn·dɐ·lɪŋ] *m* oddball

Sondermüll *m* hazardous waste

sondern ['zɔn·dɐn] *konj* but; **nicht sie**

S

war es, ~ er it wasn't her, it was him

Sonderpreis m special [reduced] [o sale] price

Sonderregelung f special provision

Sonderschule f school for special education

Sonderstellung f special position

Sonderzug m special [o chartered] train

Sonett <-[e]s, -e> [zɔ·ˈnɛt] nt sonnet

Sonnabend [ˈzɔn·ˌʔa:bn̩t] m dial (Samstag) Saturday

sonnabends adv dial (samstags) [on] Saturdays

Sonne <-, -n> [ˈzɔnə] f kein pl sun; **die ~ geht auf/unter** the sun rises/sets

sonnen [ˈzɔ·nən] vr 1. (sonnenbaden) **sich** akk ~ to sunbathe 2. (genießen) **sich** akk **in etw** dat ~ to bask in sth

Sonnenaufgang m sunrise, sunup

Sonnenbad nt sunbathing; **ein ~ nehmen** to sunbathe

Sonnenblume f sunflower

Sonnenbrand m sunburn no art

Sonnenbrille f sunglasses npl, shades npl sl

Sonnenenergie f solar energy

Sonnenfinsternis f solar eclipse

Sonnenlicht nt kein pl sunlight

Sonnenmilch f suntan lotion

Sonnenschein m sunshine

Sonnenschirm m sunshade; (tragbar) parasol

Sonnenstich m sunstroke no art

Sonnenstrahl m sunbeam

Sonnensystem nt solar system

Sonnenuntergang m sunset, sundown

sonnig [ˈzɔ·nɪç] adj sunny

Sonntag [ˈzɔn·ta:k] m Sunday; s. a. **Dienstag**

sonntäglich adj [regular] Sunday attr

sonntags adv [on] Sundays

sonst [zɔnst] adv 1. (andernfalls) or [else], otherwise 2. (gewöhnlich) usually; **du hast doch ~ keine Bedenken** you don't usually have any doubts; **kälter als ~** colder than usual 3. (außerdem) **~ noch Fragen?** any more questions?; **gibt es ~ noch etwas?** is there anything else?; **~ keine(r, s)** nothing/nobody else; **~ nichts** nothing else; **~ was** whatever

sonstig [ˈzɔns·tɪç] adj attr (weitere[s]) other; „**Sonstiges**" "miscellaneous"

Sopran <-s, -e> [zo·ˈpraːn] m kein p. soprano

Sorge <-, -n> [ˈzɔr·gə] f worry; **keine ~!** fam don't [you] worry; **sich** akk **um etw** akk ~ **machen** to worry about sth; **~n haben** to have problems

sorgen [ˈzɔr·gn̩] I. vi 1. (sich kümmern) **für jdn** ~ to provide for [o look after] sb 2. (besorgen) **ich sorge dafür, dass ...** I'll see to it then ...; **dafür ist gesorgt** that's taken care of 3. (bewirken) **für Aufsehen** ~ to cause a sensation II. vr **sich** akk **um jdn/etw** ~ to be worried about sb/sth

Sorgerecht nt kein pl custody

Sorgfalt <-> [ˈzɔrk·falt] f kein pl care

sorgfältig [ˈzɔrk·fɛl·tɪç] I. adj careful II. adv carefully

sorglos [ˈzɔrk·loːs] I. adj 1. (achtlos) careless 2. (sorgenfrei) carefree II. adv 1. (achtlos) carelessly 2. (sorgenfrei) free of care

Sorte <-, -n> [ˈzɔr·tə] f 1. (Art) kind, variety 2. (Marke) brand

sortieren* [zɔr·ˈtiː·rən] vt to sort

Sortiment <-[e]s, -e> [zɔr·ti·ˈmɛnt] nt range [of products]

Soße <-, -n> [ˈzoː·sə] f sauce; (Bratensoße) gravy

Souterrain <-s, -s> [ˈzuː·tɛ·rɛ̃] nt basement

Souvenir <-s, -s> [zu·və·ˈniːɐ] nt souvenir

souverän [zu·və·ˈrɛːn] I. adj 1. (unabhängig) sovereign attr 2. (überlegen) superior II. adv with superior ease

Souveränität <-> [zu·və·rɛ·ni·ˈtɛːt] f kein pl sovereignty; (Überlegenheit) supremacy

soviel [zo·ˈfiːl] konj as far as; **~ ich weiß ...** as far as I know ...; **~ ich auch trinke ...** no matter how much I drink ...

soweit [zo·ˈvait] konj as far as

sowie [zo·ˈviː] konj 1. (sobald) as soon as, the moment [that] 2. (und auch) as well as

sowieso [zo·vi·ˈzoː] adv anyway, anyhow

sowohl [zoˈvoːl] *konj* ~ ... als auch ... both ... and ..., ... as well as ...

sozial [zoˈtsi̯aːl] I. *adj* 1. (*gesellschaftlich*) social 2. (*für Hilfsbedürftige gedacht*) welfare *attr* 3. (*gesellschaftlich verantwortlich*) public-spirited II. *adv* ~ **schwache Familien** low-income families; ~ **denken** to be socially minded

Sozialabgaben *pl* social security contributions

Sozialamt *nt* Department of Social Services

Sozialarbeiter(in) *m(f)* social worker

Sozialdemokrat(in) *m(f)* social democrat

sozialdemokratisch *adj* social democratic

Sozialhilfe *f kein pl* welfare

Sozialismus <-> [zoˈtsi̯aˈlɪsmʊs] *m kein pl* socialism

Sozialist(in) <-en, -en> [zoˈtsi̯aˈlɪst] *m(f)* socialist

sozialistisch [zoˈtsi̯aˈlɪstɪʃ] *adj* 1. (*Sozialismus betreffend*) socialist 2. *österr* (*sozialdemokratisch*) social democratic

Sozialleistungen *pl* social security benefits

Sozialstaat *m* welfare state

Sozialwohnung *f* [housing] project

Soziologe, Soziologin <-n, -n> [zoˈtsi̯oˈloːɡə, -ˈloːɡɪn] *m, f* sociologist

Soziologie <-> [zoˈtsi̯oˈloˈgiː] *f kein pl* sociology

sozusagen [zoːtsuˈzaːɡn̩] *adv* as it were, so to speak

Spachtel <-s, -> [ˈʃpaˈxtl̩] *m* putty knife

Spagetti RR, **Spaghetti** [ʃpaˈɡɛti] *pl* spaghetti + *sing vb*

spähen [ˈʃpɛːən] *vi* 1. (*suchend blicken*) to peek (**durch** +*akk* through) 2. (*Ausschau halten*) to look out (**nach** +*dat* for)

Spalt <-[e]s, -e> [ʃpalt] *m* gap; (*Riss*) crack; (*Felsspalt*) crevice; **die Tür einen** ~ **öffnen/offen lassen** to open the door slightly/leave the door ajar

Spalte <-, -n> [ˈʃpalˈtə] *f* 1. (*Öffnung*) fissure; (*Felsspalte a.*) crevice 2. TYPO, MEDIA column

spalten [ˈʃpalˈtn̩] I. *vt* <*pp* gespalten *o* gespaltet> 1. (*zerteilen*) to split;

(*Holz a.*) to chop 2. (*trennen*) to divide II. *vr* <*pp* gespalten> **sich** *akk* ~ 1. (*der Länge nach reißen*) to split 2. (*sich teilen*) to divide

Span <-[e]s, Späne> [ʃpaːn] *m* (*Holzspan*) [wood] chip; (*Bohrspan*) swarf, turnings *pl*

Spanferkel [ˈʃpaːnˌfɛrkl̩] *nt* suckling pig

Spange <-, -n> [ˈʃpaŋə] *f* 1. (*Haarspange*) barrette 2. (*Zahnspange*) braces *pl*, retainer

Spanien <-s> [ˈʃpaːni̯ən] *nt* Spain; *s. a.* **Deutschland**

Spanier(in) <-s, -> [ˈʃpaːni̯ɐ] *m(f)* Spaniard; **die** ~ the Spanish; *s. a.* **Deutsche(r)**

spanisch [ˈʃpaːnɪʃ] *adj* Spanish; *s. a.* **deutsch**

spann [ʃpan] *imp von* **spinnen**

Spannbetttuch RR *nt* fitted sheet

Spanne <-, -n> [ˈʃpanə] *f* 1. (*Gewinnspanne*) [profit] margin 2. (*Zeitspanne*) span

spannen [ˈʃpanən] I. *vt* 1. (*straffen*) to tighten 2. (*aufspannen: Wäscheleine*) to put up *sep*; (*Seil*) to stretch (**zwischen** +*akk* between) 3. (*anspannen: Tier*) to harness (**vor** +*akk* to) II. *vr refl* **sich** *akk* ~ (*Seil*) to become taut III. *vi* (*zu eng sitzen: Hose*) to be [too] tight

spannend *adj* exciting; (*stärker*) thrilling

Spannung <-, -en> *f* 1. *kein pl* (*gespannte Erwartung*) suspense; **etw mit** ~ **erwarten** to anxiously await sth 2. *meist pl* (*Anspannung*) tension 3. ELEK voltage; **unter** ~ **stehen** to be live

Sparbuch *nt* bankbook

Sparbüchse *f* piggy bank

sparen [ˈʃpaːrən] I. *vt* 1. (*einsparen*) to save 2. (*ersparen*) **sich/jdm etw** ~ to spare oneself/sb sth; **den Weg hätten wir uns** ~ **können** we could have saved ourselves that trip; **deine Ratschläge kannst du dir** ~ [you can] keep your advice to yourself II. *vi* 1. FIN (*Geld zurücklegen*) to save; **für etw** *akk* ~ to save [up] for sth 2. (*sparsam sein*) to economize (**an** +*dat* on)

Sparer(in) <-s, -> *m(f)* saver

Spargel <-s, -> ['ʃpar·gl̩] *m* asparagus

Sparkasse *f* bank *(supported publicly by a commune or district)*

spärlich ['ʃpɛːɐ̯·lɪç] **I.** *adj (Haarwuchs, Vegetation)* sparse; *(Ausbeute, Reste)* meager **II.** *adv* sparsely; ~ **bekleidet** scantily dressed; ~ **besucht** poorly attended

Sparmaßnahme *f* cost-cutting measure

Sparpreis *m* budget [*o* economy] price

sparsam ['ʃpaːɐ̯·zaːm] **I.** *adj* thrifty; *(ökonomisch im Verbrauch)* economical **II.** *adv* thriftily; *(ökonomisch beim Verbrauch)* sparingly

Sparsamkeit <-> *f* *kein pl* thriftiness

Sparschwein *nt* piggy bank

Sparte <-, -n> ['ʃpar·tə] *f* **1.** *(Branche)* line of business **2.** *(Spezialbereich)* area, branch **3.** *(Rubrik)* section, column

Spaß <-es, Späße> [ʃpaːs] *m* **1.** *kein pl (Vergnügen)* fun; **es macht mir ~, das zu tun** I enjoy doing that; **viel ~!** have fun! **2.** *(Scherz)* joke; **da hört der ~ auf** that's going a bit too far; ~ **muss sein** *fam* there's no harm in a joke; **keinen ~ verstehen** to not have a sense of humor; ~ **beiseite** joking apart; **[nur] ~ machen** to be [just] kidding ▶ **ein teurer ~ sein** to be an expensive business

spaßen ['ʃpaː·sn̩] *vi* to joke; **mit etw** *dat* **ist nicht zu ~** sth is no joking matter

spaßig ['ʃpaː·sɪç] *adj* funny

Spaßverderber(in) <-s, -> *m(f)* spoilsport

Spaßvogel *m* joker

spät [ʃpɛːt] **I.** *adj* late; **am ~en Abend** late in the evening **II.** *adv* late; **du kommst zu ~** you're too late; **wie ~ ist es?** what time is it?; **wie ~ kommst du heute nach Hause?** what time are you coming home today?; ~ **dran sein** to be [running] late

Spaten <-s, -> ['ʃpaː·tn̩] *m* spade

später ['ʃpɛː·tɐ] **I.** *adj* later **II.** *adv* later [*on*]; **bis ~!** see you later!; **nicht ~ als** not later than; ~ **[ein]mal** some other time

spätestens ['ʃpɛː·təs·tn̩s] *adv* at the [very] latest

Spätschicht *f* late shift

Spätvorstellung *f* late show[ing]

Spatz <-en, -en> [ʃpats] *m* ORN sparrow

spazieren * [ʃpa·ˈtsiː·rən] *vi sein* to walk; ~ **fahren/gehen** to go for a drive/walk

Spazierfahrt *f* drive; **eine ~ machen** to go for a drive

Spaziergang <-gänge> *m* walk, stroll; **einen ~ machen** to go for a walk

Spaziergänger(in) <-s, -> *m(f)* stroller

Specht <-[e]s, -e> [ʃpɛçt] *m* woodpecker

Speck <-[e]s, -e> [ʃpɛk] *m* bacon

Spediteur(in) <-s, -e> [ʃpe·di·ˈtøːɐ̯] *m(f)* freight forwarder, shipper

Spedition <-, -en> [ʃpe·di·ˈtsi̯oːn] *f* *(Transportunternehmen)* trucking company; *(Umzugsunternehmen)* moving company

Speerwerfen *nt* *kein pl* SPORT the javelin

Speiche <-, -n> ['ʃpai̯·çə] *f* spoke

Speichel <-s> ['ʃpai̯·çl̩] *m* *kein pl* saliva

Speicher <-s, -> ['ʃpai̯·çɐ] *m* **1.** *(Dachboden)* attic, loft; **auf dem ~** in the attic **2.** *(Lagerhaus)* storehouse **3.** COMPUT memory

speichern ['ʃpai̯·çɐn] *vt, vi* COMPUT to save; *(Nummern im Handy)* to store

Speicherplatz *m* COMPUT memory space; *(auf Festplatte)* disk space

Speicherung <-, -en> *f* COMPUT storage

Speise <-, -n> ['ʃpai̯·zə] *f* *meist pl* meal

Speisekarte *f* menu

speisen ['ʃpai̯·zn̩] *vi* to dine, to eat

Speiseöl *nt* cooking oil

Speiseröhre *f* esophagus, gullet

Speisewagen *m* dining car

spektakulär [ʃpɛk·ta·ku·ˈlɛːɐ̯] *adj* spectacular

Spekulant(in) <-en, -en> [ʃpe·ku·ˈlant] *m(f)* speculator

spekulieren * [ʃpe·ku·ˈliː·rən] *vi* to speculate *(mit +dat* in, *auf +akk* on)

spendabel [ʃpɛn·ˈdaː·bl̩] *adj* generous

Spende <-, -n> ['ʃpɛn·də] *f* donation

spenden ['ʃpɛn·dn̩] *vt, vi* to donate; *(Blut)* to give

Spender <-s, -> ['ʃpɛn·dɐ] *m* *(Dosierer)* dispenser

Spender(in) <-s, -> ['ʃpɛn·dɐ] *m(f)* **1.** *(jd, der spendet)* don[at]or **2.** MED donor

spendieren * [ʃpɛn·ˈdiː·rən] *vt fam* [*jdm*]

etw ~ to buy [sb] sth; **das Essen spendiere ich** [the] dinner's on me

Sperling <-s, -e> ['ʃpɛr·lɪŋ] *m* sparrow

Sperma <-s, Spermen> ['ʃpɛr·ma, 'ʃpɛr·mə] *nt* sperm

Sperre <-, -n> ['ʃpɛ·rə] *f* 1. (*Sperrvorrichtung*) barrier 2. (*Spielverbot*) ban

sperren ['ʃpɛ·rən] I. *vt* 1. *südd, österr* (*schließen*) to close off (**für** +*akk* to) 2. (*blockieren*) to block; (*Konto*) to freeze; (*Scheck*) to stop payment on 3. (*einschließen*) to lock [up] 4. (*ein Spielverbot verhängen*) to ban II. *vr* **sich** *akk* ~ to back away (**gegen** +*akk* from)

Sperrmüll *m* bulky trash

Sperrstunde *f* closing time

Spesen ['ʃpe:·zn̩] *pl* expenses *npl*

Spezialgebiet *nt* special field

spezialisieren * [ʃpe·tsi̯a·li·'zi:·rən] *vr* **sich** *akk* ~ to specialize (**auf** +*akk* in)

Spezialisierung <-, -en> *f* specialization

Spezialist(in) <-en, -en> [ʃpe·tsi̯a·'lɪst] *m(f)* specialist

Spezialität <-, -en> [ʃpe·tsi̯a·li·'tɛːt] *f* specialty

speziell [ʃpe·'tsi̯ɛl] I. *adj* special II. *adv* [e]specially

spezifisch [ʃpe·'tsi:·fɪʃ] I. *adj* specific II. *adv* typically

Sphäre <-, -n> ['sfɛː·rə] *f* sphere

spicken ['ʃpɪ·kn̩] *vt* 1. KOCHK (*durchsetzen*) to lard 2. *fam* (*abschreiben*) to copy

Spiegel <-s, -> ['ʃpi:·gl̩] *m* mirror

Spiegelbild *nt* mirror image

Spiegelei *nt* egg sunny side up

spiegeln ['ʃpi:·gl̩n] I. *vi* to reflect II. *vr* **sich** *akk* **in etw** *dat* ~ to be reflected in sth

Spiegelreflexkamera *f* reflex camera

Spiel <-[e]s, -e> [ʃpi:l] *nt* game; (*im Tennis, Volleyball*) match ▶ **ein abgekartetes** ~ *fam* a fix; **jdn/etw aus dem** ~ **lassen** to keep sb/sth out of it; **leichtes** ~ **haben** to have an easy job of it; [**bei etw**] **im** ~ **sein** to be involved [in sth]; **etw aufs** ~ **setzen** to put sth on the line; **auf dem** ~ **stehen** to be at stake; **jdm das** ~ **verderben** *fam* to

ruin sb's plans

Spielautomat *m* gambling machine

Spielbank *f* casino

spielen ['ʃpi:·lən] I. *vt* to play ▶ **was wird hier gespielt?** what's going on here? II. *vi* 1. to play; (*beim Glücksspiel*) to gamble 2. (*als Szenario haben*) **in Italien/im Mittelalter** ~ to be set in Italy/in the Middle Ages

spielend *adv* easily

Spieler(in) <-s, -> ['ʃpi:·le] *m(f)* 1. (*Mitspieler*) player 2. (*Glücksspieler*) gambler

spielerisch I. *adj* playful II. *adv* playfully

Spielfeld ['ʃpi:l·fɛlt] *nt* [playing] field

Spielfilm *m* feature film

Spielkamerad(in) *m(f)* playmate

Spielkarte *f* playing card

Spielkasino *nt* casino

Spielplatz *m* playground

Spielraum *m* leeway

Spielregel *f meist pl* rules *pl*

Spielsachen *pl* toys *pl*

Spielverderber(in) <-s, -> *m(f)* spoilsport

Spielzeit *f* 1. THEAT season 2. SPORT playing time

Spielzeug *nt* toy

Spieß <-es, -e> [ʃpi:s] *m* 1. (*Bratspieß*) spit; (*kleiner*) skewer 2. (*Stoßwaffe*) spike ▶ **wie am** ~ **brüllen** to scream at the top of one's lungs; **den** ~ **umdrehen** to turn the tables

Spießbürger(in) *m(f)* s. **Spießer**

spießen ['ʃpi:·sn̩] *vt* **etw auf etw** *akk* ~ to skewer sth on sth

Spießer(in) <-s, -> ['ʃpi:·se] *m(f) fam* narrow-minded person

spießig ['ʃpi:·sɪç] *adj fam* narrow-minded

Spießigkeit <-> *f kein pl pej fam* narrow-mindedness

Spinat <-[e]s> [ʃpi'na:t] *m kein pl* spinach

Spinne <-, -n> ['ʃpɪ·nə] *f* spider

spinnen <spann, gesponnen> ['ʃpɪ·nən] I. *vt* 1. (*Wolle*) to spin 2. (*Geschichte*) to invent II. *vi fam* (*nicht bei Trost sein*) to be crazy [*o sl* nuts]; **sag mal, spinnt der?** is he out of his mind?

Spinner(in) <-s, -> ['ʃpɪ·ne] *m(f) fam* nutcase

S

Spinnerei <-, -en> [ʃpɪ·nə·ˈraɪ] f 1. (Betrieb) spinning mill 2. kein pl fam (Blödsinn) nonsense

Spion(in) <-s, -e> [ʃpi·ˈoːn] m(f) spy

Spionage <-> [ʃpi̯o·ˈnaː·ʒə] f kein pl espionage

spionieren* [ʃpi̯o·ˈniː·rən] vi to spy

Spirale <-, -n> [ʃpi·ˈraː·lə] f 1. (gewundene Linie) spiral 2. MED IUD

Spirituosen [ʃpi·ri·ˈtu̯oː·zn̩, sp-] pl spirits pl

Spital <-s, Spitäler> [ʃpi·ˈtaːl] nt österr, schweiz hospital

spitz [ʃpɪts] I. adj 1. (mit einer Spitze) pointed; (Bleistift, Messer) sharp 2. (spitz zulaufend) tapered; (Nase, Kinn) pointy 3. (Bemerkung) sharp II. adv 1. (V-förmig) tapered 2. (spitzzüngig) sharply

Spitze <-, -n> [ˈʃpɪtsə] f 1. (spitzes Ende) point 2. (vorderster Teil) front 3. (erster Platz, höchste Stelle eines Bergs) top 4. (Höchstwert) peak 5. pl (führende Leute: der Gesellschaft) the top; (eines Unternehmens) the heads 6. MODE lace ► ~ **sein** fam to be great; etw auf die ~ **treiben** to take sth to extremes

Spitzel <-s, -> [ˈʃpɪtsl̩] m informer

spitzen [ˈʃpɪtsn̩] vt to sharpen

Spitzenleistung f outstanding [o firstrate] performance

spitzfindig adj hairsplitting

Spitzname m nickname

Splitter <-s, -> [ˈʃplɪ·tɐ] m splinter

Sponsion f academic ceremony in Austria at which Master's degrees are awarded

Sponsor, Sponsorin <-s, -soren> [ˈʃpɔn·zɐ, ʃpɔn·ˈzoː·rɪn] m, f sponsor

spontan [ʃpɔn·ˈtaːn, sp-] adj spontaneous

sporadisch [ʃpo·ˈraː·dɪʃ, sp-] adj sporadic

Sport <-[e]s, selten -e> [ʃpɔrt] m 1. SPORT sport[s pl]; ~ **treiben** to play sports 2. SCH PE, gym

Sportart f discipline, kind of sport

Sportlehrer(in) m(f) PE [o gym] teacher

Sportler(in) <-s, -> [ˈʃpɔrt·lɐ] m(f) athlete

sportlich [ˈʃpɔrt·lɪç] I. adj 1. (den Sport betreffend) sporting 2. (trainiert: Figur) athletic; (Mensch) sporty 3. MODE casual II. adv 1. SPORT (in einer Sportart) in sports 2. (flott) casually

Sportplatz m [playing [o sports] field

Sportveranstaltung f sports event

Sportverein m sports club

Sportwagen m AUTO sports car

Spott <-[e]s> [ʃpɔt] m kein pl mockery

spotten [ˈʃpɔ·tn̩] vi to mock; [über jdn/etw] ~ to make fun [of sb/sth]

spöttisch [ˈʃpœ·tɪʃ] adj mocking

sprachbegabt adj linguistically talented; ~ **sein** to be good at languages

Sprache <-, -n> [ˈʃpraː·xə] f 1. (Kommunikationssystem) language 2. kein pl (Sprechweise) way of speaking 3. kein pl (das Sprechen) speech; etw zur ~ **bringen** to bring up sep sth; zur ~ **kommen** to come up ► mit der ~ **herausrücken** fam to come out with it; jdm die ~ **verschlagen** to leave sb speechless; **heraus mit der ~!** fam out with it!

Sprachfehler m speech impediment

Sprachkenntnisse pl language skills pl

Sprachkurs m language class [o course]

sprachlos adj speechless

Sprachwissenschaft f linguistics + sing vb

Spray <-s, -s> [ʃpreː, spre:] m o nt spray

sprechen <spricht, sprach, gesprochen> [ˈʃprɛ·çn̩] I. vi 1. (reden) to speak, to talk; **sprich nicht so laut** don't talk so loud; **sprich nicht in diesem Ton mit mir!** don't speak to me like that!; **wovon ~ Sie eigentlich?** what are you talking about?; **sein Benehmen spricht für sich [selbst]** his behavior speaks for itself; **mit sich selbst ~** to talk to oneself; „**hallo, wer spricht denn da?**" "hello, who's speaking?" 2. (empfehlen) **für jdn/etw ~** to speak well for sb/sth; **gegen jdn/etw ~** to not be in sb's/sth's favor II. vt 1. (können) to speak; ~ **Sie Chinesisch?** can you speak Chinese? 2. (sich unterreden) **jdn ~** to speak to sb ► **nicht gut auf jdn zu ~ sein** to be on bad terms with sb; **wir ~ uns noch!** you haven't heard the last of this!; **für jdn**

niemanden zu ~ sein to be available for sb/to not be available for anyone

Sprecher(in) <-s, -> *m(f)* 1. (*Wortführer*) spokesperson 2. (*Beauftragter*) speaker 3. RADIO, TV announcer; (*Nachrichtensprecher*) newscaster, anchorperson

Sprechstunde *f* office hours *pl*

Sprechstundenhilfe *f* receptionist

Sprechzimmer *nt* consultation room

spreizen ['ʃprai̯·tsn̩] *vt* to spread

sprengen¹ ['ʃprɛŋən] I. *vt* 1. (*zur Explosion bringen*) to blow up *sep* 2. (*bersten lassen*) to burst 3. (*gewaltsam auflösen*) to break up *sep* II. *vi* to blast

sprengen² ['ʃprɛŋən] *vt* (*Rasen*) to water

Sprengkörper *m* explosive device

Sprengkraft *f kein pl* explosive force

Sprengstoff *m* explosive

Sprengstoffanschlag *m* bomb attack

Sprichwort <-wörter> ['ʃprɪç·vɔrt] *nt* proverb

sprießen <spross *o* sprießte, gesprossen> ['ʃpriː·sn̩] *vi sein* BOT to sprout; (*Haare*) to grow

Springbrunnen *m* fountain

springen¹ <sprang, gesprungen> ['ʃprɪŋən] *vi sein* to shatter; (*einen Sprung bekommen*) to crack

springen² <sprang, gesprungen> ['ʃprɪŋən] *vi sein* to jump; (*im Sprünge*) to leap; **er sprang hin und her** he jumped around ▶ **etw ~ lassen** *fam* to fork out sth

Springflut *f* spring tide

Spritze <-, -n> ['ʃprɪ·tsə] *f* 1. (*Injektionsspritze*) syringe, needle 2. (*Injektion*) injection, shot

spritzen ['ʃprɪtsn̩] I. *vi* 1. *haben* (*in Tropfen*) to spray; (*Fett*) to spit; (*Farbe*) to splash 2. *sein* (*im Strahl*) to spurt II. *vt haben* 1. (*im Strahl verteilen*) to squirt 2. (*bewässern*) to sprinkle 3. (*injizieren*) to inject 4. (*mit Bekämpfungsmittel besprühen*) to spray (**gegen** +*akk* against)

Spritzer <-s, -> *m* splash

spritzig ['ʃprɪ·tsɪç] *adj* 1. (*prickelnd*) tangy 2. (*flott*) sparkling

spröde ['ʃprøː·də] *adj* 1. (*unelastisch*) brittle 2. (*rau*) rough; (*Haar*) brittle;

(*Lippen*) chapped 3. (*abweisend*) aloof

sproß ^RR, **sproß** ^ALT ['ʃprɔs] *imp von* **sprießen**

Sproß ^RR <-es, -e>, **Sproß** ^ALT <-sses, -sse> ['ʃprɔs] *m* BOT shoot

Sprosse <-, -n> ['ʃprɔ·sə] *f* rung, step

Spruch <-[e]s, Sprüche> ['ʃprʊx] *m* 1. (*Ausspruch*) saying; (*Parole*) slogan 2. (*Richterspruch*) verdict ▶ **Sprüche klopfen** *fam* to talk big

Sprudel <-s, -> ['ʃpruː·dl̩] *m* 1. (*Mineralwasser*) sparkling mineral water 2. *dial* (*Erfrischungsgetränk*) soft drink

sprudeln ['ʃpruː·dl̩n] *vi* 1. *haben* (*aufschäumen*) to bubble, to foam 2. *sein* (*heraussprudeln*) to bubble out

Sprühdose *f* aerosol [*o* spray] can

sprühen ['ʃpryː·ən] I. *vt* to spray II. *vi* **vor Begeisterung ~** to bubble with excitement

Sprung <-[e]s, Sprünge> ['ʃprʊŋ] *m* 1. (*Riss*) crack 2. (*Satz*) leap, jump ▶ [**mit etw** *dat*] **keine großen Sprünge machen können** *fam* to not be able to live it up [with sth]; **jdm auf die Sprünge helfen** to give sb a helping hand; **auf dem ~ sein** to be in a hurry; **auf einen ~ [bei jdm] vorbeikommen** *fam* to pop in [to see sb]

Sprungbrett *nt* 1. (*ins Wasser*) diving board 2. (*Turngerät*) springboard

Sprungschanze *f* ski jump

Spucke <-> ['ʃpʊ·kə] *f kein pl fam* spit ▶ **jdm bleibt die ~ weg** sb is flabbergasted

spucken ['ʃpʊ·kn̩] I. *vi* to spit II. *vt* to spit out *sep*

spuken ['ʃpuː·kn̩] *vi impers* to haunt; **hier spukt es** this place is haunted

Spüle <-, -n> ['ʃpyː·lə] *f* [kitchen] sink

spülen ['ʃpyː·lən] I. *vi* 1. (*Geschirr*) to do the dishes 2. (*Toilette*) to flush II. *vt* 1. (*abspülen*) **das Geschirr ~** to do the dishes 2. *s.* **schwemmen**

Spülmaschine *f* dishwasher

Spülmittel *nt* dish soap

Spülung <-, -en> *f* 1. (*Wasserspülung*) flush 2. (*Haarspülung*) conditioner

Spur <-, -en> ['ʃpuːɐ̯] *f* 1. (*Anzeichen*) trace; **~en hinterlassen** to leave traces; (*Schicksal a.*) to leave its mark;

S

(*Verbrecher a.*) to leave clues; **jdm auf der ~ sein** to be on sb's trail; **auf der falschen/richtigen ~ sein** to be on the wrong/right track; **eine heiße ~** a firm lead; **jdm auf die ~ kommen** to be onto sb **2.** (*Fußspuren*) track|s pl, trail **3.** (*kleine Menge*) trace; (*von Knoblauch, etc.*) touch **4.** (*Fahrstreifen*) lane

spüren ['ʃpyː·rən] **I.** vt to feel; **etw zu ~ bekommen** to feel the brunt of sth **II.** vi ~, **dass ...** to sense that ...; **jdn ~ lassen, dass ...** to leave sb with no doubt that ...

Spürhund m tracker dog

spurlos I. adj without a trace pred **II.** adv without [leaving] a trace; **die Scheidung ging nicht ~ an ihm vorüber** the divorce left its mark on him

Spurt <-s, -s> [ʃpʊrt] m spurt

spurten ['ʃpʊr·tn̩] vi sein to spurt

Squash <-> [skvɔʃ] nt squash

Staat <-[e]s, -en> [ʃtaːt] m **1.** (*Land*) country **2.** (*staatliche Institutionen*) state **3.** pl (*USA*) **die ~en** the States

Staatenbund <-bünde> m confederation [of states]

staatlich I. adj **1.** (*staatseigen*) state-owned; (*staatlich geführt*) state-run; **~e Einrichtungen** government facilities **2.** (*den Staat betreffend*) state attr, national **3.** (*aus dem Staatshaushalt stammend*) government attr, state attr **II.** adv ~ **anerkannt** state-approved; SCH, UNIV state-accredited; ~ **gefördert** government-sponsored

Staatsakt m state ceremony

Staatsangehörige(r) f/m dekl wie adj citizen

Staatsangehörigkeit f nationality

Staatsanwalt, -anwältin m, f district attorney

Staatsbeamte(r), -beamtin m, f civil servant

Staatsbesuch m state visit

Staatsbürger(in) m(f) citizen

Staatsdienst m civil service

Staatseigentum nt state [o government] property

Staatsexamen nt state exam[ination]; (*zur Übernahme in den Staatsdienst*)

civil service exam[ination]

Staatsform f form of government

Staatsgebiet nt national territory

Staatshaushalt m national budget

Staatskosten pl public expenses pl

Staatsminister(in) <-s, -> m(f) secretary of state

Staatsoberhaupt nt head of state

Staatspräsident(in) m(f) president [of a republic]

Staatsstreich m coup [d'état]

Stab <-[e]s, Stäbe> [ʃtaːp] m **1.** (*runde Holzlatte*) rod; (*Gitterstab*) bar **2.** (*Stabhochsprungstab*) pole; (*Staffelstab*) baton **3.** (*beigeordnete Gruppe*) staff; (*von Experten*) panel

Stabhochsprung m pole vault

stabil [ʃtaˈbiːl, st-] adj **1.** (*strapazierfähig*) sturdy **2.** (*beständig: Preise, Währung, Zustand*) stable **3.** (*nicht labil*) steady; (*Gesundheit*) sound

stabilisieren [ʃta·bi·liˈziː·rən] vt, vr |**sich akk**| ~ to stabilize

Stabilität <-> [ʃta·bi·liˈtɛːt, st-] f kein pl stability, solidity

Stachel <-s, -n> ['ʃta·xl̩] m **1.** (*von Rose*) thorn; (*von Kakteen*) spine **2.** (*Giftstachel*) sting

Stachelbeere f gooseberry

Stacheldraht m barbed wire

stachelig ['ʃta·xə·lɪç] adj prickly; (*Rosen*) thorny; (*Kakteen*) spiny

Stachelschwein nt porcupine

Stadion <-s, Stadien> ['ʃta·di·ɔn] nt stadium, bowl

Stadium <-s, Stadien> ['ʃta·di·ʊm] nt stage; **im letzten ~** MED at a terminal stage

Stadt <-, Städte> [ʃtat] f **1.** (*Ort*) town; (*Großstadt*) city **2.** (*Stadtverwaltung*) city/town council

Stadtbibliothek f city/town library

Städtepartnerschaft f sister city arrangement

Städter(in) <-s, -> ['ʃtɛː·tɐ] m(f) city/town dweller

Stadtgebiet nt municipal area

städtisch ['ʃtɛː·tɪʃ] adj **1.** (*kommunal*) municipal, city/town attr **2.** (*urban*) urban

Stadtmauer f city/town wall

Stadtmitte f downtown

Stadtplan m [street] map [of a city/town]

Stadtrand m edge of town, outskirts npl of the city

Stadtrat m city/town council

Stadtrundfahrt f sightseeing tour of a city/town

Stadtteil m district, part of town

Stadtverwaltung f city/town council

Stadtviertel nt district

Stadtwerke pl public utilities pl

Stadtzentrum nt city/town center

Staffel <-, -n> [ˈʃta·fl̩] f 1. SPORT relay team 2. MIL (Luftwaffeneinheit) squadron 3. TV season

Staffelei <-, -en> [ʃta·fə·ˈlai] f easel

Staffellauf m SPORT relay [race]

Stagnation <-, -en> [ʃta·gna·ˈtsi̯oːn, st-] f stagnation

stagnieren * [ʃta·ˈgniː·rən, st-] vi to stagnate

stahl [ʃtaːl] imp von **stehlen**

Stahl <-[e]s, -e> [ʃtaːl] m steel

Stahlbeton m reinforced concrete

Stahlhelm m steel helmet

Stahlindustrie f kein pl steel industry

Stall <-[e]s, Ställe> [ʃtal] m (Hühnerstall) coop; (Kaninchenstall) hutch; (Kuhstall) cowshed, [cow] barn; (Pferdestall) stable; (Schweinestall) [pig]sty, [pig]pen

Stamm <-[e]s, Stämme> [ʃtam] m 1. (Baumstamm) [tree] trunk 2. LING stem 3. (Volksstamm) tribe

Stammbaum m family tree

stammeln [ˈʃta·ml̩n] vt, vi to stammer

stammen [ˈʃta·mən] vi to be (aus +dat from)

Stammgast m regular [guest]

Stammkunde, -kundin m, f regular [customer]

Stammlokal nt usual [o favorite] café/restaurant/bar

Stammplatz m usual [o favorite] seat

Stammtisch m 1. (Tisch für Stammgäste) table reserved for the regulars 2. (regelmäßiges Zusammentreffen) [group of] regulars

stampfen [ˈʃtamp·fn̩] I. vi 1. haben (aufstampfen) mit dem Fuß auf den Boden ~ to stomp one's foot 2. sein s.

stapfen II. vt haben KOCHK (Gemüse, Kartoffeln) to mash

stand [ʃtant] imp von **stehen**

Stand <-[e]s, Stände> [ʃtant] m 1. (Verkaufsstand) stand 2. (Anzeige) reading; **laut ~ des Barometers** according to the barometer [reading] 3. kein pl (Zustand) state; **der ~ der Dinge** the [present] state of affairs; **sich** akk **auf dem neuesten ~ befinden** to be up-to-date 4. (Spielstand) score

Standard <-s, -s> [ˈʃtan·dart, 'st-] m standard

standardisieren * [ʃtan·dar·di·ˈziː·rən, st-] vt to standardize

Ständer <-s, -> [ˈʃtɛn·dɐ] m 1. (Gestell) stand 2. sl (erigierter Penis) hard-on

Standesamt nt justice of the peace['s office]

standesamtlich adv **sich** akk ~ **trauen lassen** to be married by the Justice of the Peace

Standesbeamte(r), -beamtin m, f Justice of the Peace

standhaft I. adj steadfast II. adv steadfastly

stand|halten [ˈʃtant·hal·tn̩] vi irreg **etw** dat ~ to hold out against sth

ständig [ˈʃtɛn·dɪç] I. adj constant II. adv constantly

Standlicht nt kein pl parking lights pl

Standort <-[e]s, -e> m location

Standpunkt m [point of] view, standpoint; **den ~ vertreten, dass ...** to take the view that ...

Standspur f TRANSP shoulder

Standuhr f grandfather clock

Stange <-, -n> [ˈʃtaŋə] f 1. (Stab) pole; (kürzer) rod 2. (Metallstange) bar 3. **eine ~ Zigaretten** a carton of cigarettes ▸ **bei der ~ bleiben** fam to keep it up; **eine [schöne] ~ Geld kosten** fam to cost a pretty penny; **von der ~** fam off the rack

StängelRR <-s, -> [ˈʃtɛŋl̩] m stalk, stem

stänkern [ˈʃtɛŋ·kɐn] vi to stir things up

stanzen [ˈʃtan·tsn̩] vt **Löcher in etw** akk ~ to punch holes in sth

Stapel <-s, -> [ˈʃtaː·pl̩] m stack

Stapellauf m NAUT launch[ing]

stapeln [ˈʃtaː·pl̩n] I. vt to stack [up sep]

S

II. *vr* sich *akk* ~ to pile up

stapfen ['ʃtap·fn̩] *vi sein* to tramp (**durch** +*akk* through)

Star[1] <-[e]s, -e> [ʃtaːɐ̯] *m* 1. (*Vogel*) starling 2. MED [**grauer**] ~ cataract; **grüner** ~ glaucoma

Star[2] <-s, -s> [ʃtaːɐ̯, st-] *m* (*berühmte Person*) star

stark <stärker, stärkste> [ʃtark] I. *adj* 1. (*kräftig*) strong 2. (*mächtig*) powerful, strong 3. (*dick*) thick 4. (*Hitze, Kälte*) severe; (*Regen*) heavy; (*Strömung*) strong; (*Sturm*) violent 5. (*Erkältung*) bad; (*Fieber*) high 6. (*Schlag*) hard; (*Druck*) high 7. (*Gefühle, Schmerzen*) intense; (*Bedenken*) considerable; (*Liebe*) deep 8. (*leistungsfähig*) powerful 9. (*Medikamente, Schnaps*) strong II. *adv* 1. (*heftig*) a lot; ~ **regnen** to rain heavily 2. (*erheblich*) ~ **beschädigt** badly damaged; ~ **bluten** to bleed profusely; ~ **erkältet sein** to have a bad cold; ~ **gewürzt** very spicy 3. (*in höherem Maße*) greatly, a lot; ~ **vertreten** strongly represented

Stärke <-, -n> ['ʃtɛr·kə] *f* 1. (*Kraft*) strength 2. (*Macht, von Motor*) power 3. (*Dicke*) thickness 4. (*zahlenmäßiger Ausmaß*) size; (*einer Armee*) strength 5. (*Fähigkeit*) jds ~ **sein** to be sb's strong point 6. CHEM starch

stärken ['ʃtɛr·kn̩] I. *vt* to strengthen II. *vi* ~**d** fortifying III. *vr* sich *akk* ~ to fortify oneself

stark|machen RR *vr fam* sich *akk* **für jdn/etw** ~ to stand up for sb/sth

Starkstrom *m* high voltage

Stärkung <-, -en> *f kein pl* strengthening

starr [ʃtar] *adj* 1. (*steif*) rigid 2. (*erstarrt*) stiff; ~ **vor Angst** paralyzed with fear; ~ **vor Kälte** numb with cold; ~**er Blick** [fixed] stare 3. (*rigide*) inflexible; (*Haltung*) unbending

starren ['ʃtar·rən] *vi* to stare

starrsinnig *adj* stubborn

Start <-s, -s> [ʃtart, start] *m* 1. LUFT takeoff; RAUM liftoff, launch 2. SPORT start 3. (*Beginn*) start; (*eines Projekts*) launch[ing]

Startbahn *f* LUFT runway

startbereit *adj* 1. LUFT ready for takeoff *pred* 2. SPORT ready to go *pred*

starten ['ʃtar·tn̩, 'st-] I. *vi sein* 1. LUFT to take off; RAUM to lift off 2. SPORT to start 3. (*beginnen*) to start; (*Projekt*) to be launched II. *vt haben* 1. (*Auto*) to start 2. (*Computer*) to initialize, to boot [up *sep*]; (*Programm*) to run 3. (*beginnen lassen*) to launch, to start

Starterlaubnis *f* takeoff clearance

Startkapital *nt* seed money

Startschuss RR *m* starting signal

Statik <-> ['ʃta·tɪk, 'st-] *f* PHYS statics + *sing vb*

Station <-, -en> [ʃta·'tsjoːn] *f* 1. (*Haltestelle*) stop 2. (*Aufenthalt*) stopover; ~ **machen** to make a stop 3. (*Klinikabteilung*) ward 4. METEO, SCI, RADIO station

stationär [ʃta·tsjo·'nɛːɐ̯] I. *adj* MED inpatient *attr;* **ein** ~**er Aufenthalt** a stay in a hospital II. *adv* MED in the hospital

stationieren* [ʃta·tsjo·'niː·rən] *vt* **Truppen** ~ to station troops

Stationsschwester *f* senior nurse

Statist(in) <-en, -en> [ʃta·'tɪst] *m(f)* extra

Statistik <-, -en> [ʃta·'tɪs·tɪk] *f* statistics + *sing vb*

statistisch [ʃta·'tɪs·tɪʃ] I. *adj* statistical II. *adv* statistically

Stativ <-s, -e> [ʃta·'tiːf] *nt* tripod

statt [ʃtat] I. *präp* +*gen* instead of II. *konj* (*anstatt*) instead of

Stätte <-, -n> ['ʃtɛ·tə] *f* place

statt|finden ['ʃtat·fɪn·dn̩] *vi irreg* to take place; (*Veranstaltung a.*) to be held

stattlich ['ʃtat·lɪç] *adj* 1. (*imposant*) imposing 2. (*beträchtlich*) considerable

Statue <-, -n> ['ʃta·tuə] *f* statue

Status <-, -> ['ʃta·tʊs, 'st-] *m* status, position

Statussymbol *nt* status symbol

Stau <-[e]s, -e> [ʃtau] *m* 1. (*Verkehrsstau*) traffic jam 2. (*von Wasser etc.*) build-up

Staub <-[e]s, -e> [ʃtaup] *m kein pl* dust; ~ **saugen** to vacuum; ~ **wischen** to dust ▶ sich *akk* **aus dem** ~[e] **machen** *fam* to bolt

staubig ['ʃtau·bɪç] *adj* dusty

staubsaugen <*pp* staubgesaugt>, **Staub saugen** <*pp* Staub gesaugt>

vt, vi to vacuum

Staubsauger *m* vacuum [cleaner]

Staubtuch *nt* dust cloth

Staudamm *m* dam

Staude <-, -n> ['ʃtau·də] *f* HORT perennial [plant]

stauen ['ʃtau·ən] **I.** *vt* to dam [up *sep*] **II.** *vr* sich *akk* ~ **1.** (*sich anstauen*) to collect; (*von Wasser a.*) to rise **2.** (*Schlange bilden: Autos*) to pile up

staunen ['ʃtau·nən] *vi* to be astonished (*über* +*akk* at)

Stausee *m* reservoir

stechen <sticht, stach, gestochen> ['ʃtɛ·çn̩] **I.** *vi* **1.** (*piksen*) to prick **2.** (*von Insekten*) to sting; (*Mücken*) to bite **3.** (*mit spitzem Gegenstand eindringen*) to stab **4.** KARTEN to take the trick **II.** *vt* to stab; (*Insekt*) to sting; (*Mücken*) to bite **III.** *vr* sich *akk* ~ to prick oneself

stechend *adj* **1.** (*scharf*) sharp **2.** (*durchdringend: Schmerzen*) stabbing **3.** (*beißend: Geruch*) acrid

Stechmücke *f* mosquito

Stechuhr *f* time clock

Steckbrief *m* "wanted" poster

Steckdose *f* [wall] socket, electrical outlet

stecken ['ʃtɛ·kn̩] **I.** *vi* <steckte *o geh* stak, gesteckt> **1.** (*festsitzen*) in etw *dat* ~ to be stuck in sth; ~ bleiben to get stuck **2.** (*eingesteckt sein*) hinter/in/zwischen etw *dat* ~ to be behind/in/among sth; den Schlüssel ~ lassen to leave the key in the lock **3.** (*verborgen sein*) wo hast du denn gesteckt? *fam* where have you been [hiding]?; wo steckt er denn bloß wieder? *fam* where did he disappear to again? **4.** (*verwickelt sein*) in einer Krise ~ to be in the middle of a crisis; in Schwierigkeiten ~ to be in trouble **5.** (*stocken*) ~ bleiben (*in einer Rede*) to falter; (*im Verkehr*) to get stuck **II.** *vt* <steckte, gesteckt> **1.** (*schieben*) etw hinter/in/unter etw *akk* ~ to put sth behind/in[to]/under sth **2.** *fam* (*befördern*) jdn ins Gefängnis ~ to stick sb in prison **3.** *fam* (*investieren*) Geld in eine Firma ~ to put money into a company; viel Zeit in etw *akk* ~ to devote

a lot of time to sth

Stecker <-s, -> *m* ELEK plug

Stecknadel *f* pin

Steckrübe *f* rutabaga

Steg <-[e]s, -e> [ʃteːk] *m* **1.** (*schmale Holzbrücke*) footbridge **2.** (*Bootssteg*) dock, pier

stehen <stand, gestanden> ['ʃteː·ən] **I.** *vi* wir haben *o südd, österr, schweiz sein* **1.** (*in aufrechter Stellung sein*) to stand **2.** (*hingestellt sein*) to be; wo steht das Auto? where did you park the car?; etw ~ lassen to leave sth; (*nicht verrücken*) to leave sth where it is; (*vergessen*) to leave sth behind; jdn einfach ~ lassen to walk out on sb; das Essen ~ lassen to leave the food untouched; alles ~ und liegen lassen to drop everything **3.** (*gedruckt sein*) wo steht das? where does it say that?; das steht auf Seite sechs that's on page six; was steht in seinem Brief? what does his letter say? **4.** (*nicht mehr in Betrieb sein*) to have stopped; (*von Maschine a.*) to be at a standstill; zum S~ kommen to come to a stop **5.** (*anhalten*) ~ bleiben to stop **6.** (*von etw betroffen sein*) unter Drogen ~ to be under the influence of drugs; unter Schock ~ to be in a state of shock **7.** (*passen zu*) jdm [gut] ~ to suit sb [well]; das steht dir nicht it doesn't suit you **8.** (*einen bestimmten Spielstand haben*) wie steht das Spiel? what's the score? **9.** *fam* (*fest sein: Abmachung, Termin*) to be finally settled **10.** (*unterstützen*) hinter jdm/etw ~ to support sb/sth; zu jdm/etw ~ to stand by sb/sth **11.** (*eingestellt sein*) wie ~ Sie dazu? what is your opinion on this? **12.** (*anzeigen*) auf etw *dat* ~ to indicate sth; die Ampel steht auf Rot the traffic light is red **13.** *fam* (*gut finden*) auf jdn ~ to be crazy about sb; stehst du auf Techno? do you into techno? ► jdm steht etw bis hier *fam* sb is sick and tired of sth **II.** *vi impers* (*gesundheitlich*) es steht gut/schlecht um jdn sb is in good/bad shape

Stehlampe *f* floor lamp

stehlen <stahl, gestohlen> ['ʃteː·lən] **I.** *vt, vi* to steal; das S~ stealing ► jdm

die **Zeit** ~ to take up sb's time; **das kann mir gestohlen <u>bleiben</u>!** *fam* to hell with it! II. *vr* to sneak; **sich** *akk* **von etw** *dat* ~ to sneak away from sth

steif [ʃtaif] I. *adj* 1. (*starr*) stiff; (*Begrüßung*) formal 2. (*erigiert*) erect ▶ **etw ~ und <u>fest</u> behaupten** to stubbornly maintain sth II. *adv* stiffly

Steigbügel [ˈʃtaik-] *m* stirrup

steigen <stieg, gestiegen> [ˈʃtai·gn̩] I. *vi sein* 1. (*klettern*) **auf etw** *akk* ~ (*auf einen Berg*) to climb [up] sth; (*aufs Fahrrad, Pferd*) to get on[to] sth 2. (*einsteigen*) **in etw** *akk* ~ to get in[to] sth; **in einen Zug** ~ to get on a train 3. (*aussteigen*) **aus etw** *dat* ~ to get out of sth; **aus einem Bus** ~ to get off a bus 4. (*absteigen*) **von etw** *dat* ~ to get off [of] sth 5. (*sich aufwärts bewegen*) to rise [up]; **der Sekt ist mir zu Kopf gestiegen** the sparkling wine has gone to my head 6. (*Achtung*) to rise; (*Flut*) to swell; (*Preis, Wert*) to increase; (*Temperatur*) to climb 7. (*sich intensivieren*) to increase; (*Spannung, Ungeduld, a.*) to mount II. *vt sein* **Treppen** ~ to climb [up] stairs

steigend *adj* 1. (*sich erhöhend: Preise, Löhne*) rising 2. (*sich intensivierend: Spannung, Ungeduld*) mounting

steigern [ˈʃtai·gn̩] I. *vt* 1. (*erhöhen*) to increase (**auf** +*akk* to, **um** +*akk* by) 2. (*verbessern*) to improve II. *vr sich akk* ~ to increase 1. (*sich intensivieren: Spannung a.*) to mount 2. (*seine Leistung verbessern*) to improve

Steigerung <-, -en> *f* 1. (*Erhöhung*) increase, rise 2. (*Verbesserung*) improvement

Steigung <-, -en> *f* 1. (*ansteigende Strecke*) ascent 2. (*Anstieg*) slope; **eine ~ von 10 %** a 10% gradient

steil [ʃtail] I. *adj* 1. (*stark abfallend/ansteigend*) steep 2. (*sehr rasch*) rapid II. *adv* steeply

Steilhang *m* steep slope

Steilküste *f* bluff

Stein <-[e]s, -e> [ʃtain] *m* 1. (*Gesteinsstück*) stone, rock 2. (*Obstkern*) stone ▶ **bei jdm einen ~ im <u>Brett</u> haben** *fam* to be in good with sb; **mir fällt ein**

~ **vom <u>Herzen</u>!** that's [taken] a load of [off] my mind!; **den ~ ins <u>Rollen</u> bringen** *fam* to start the ball rolling; **jdm ~-e in den <u>Weg</u> legen** to put obstacles in sb's way

Steinbock *m* 1. ZOOL ibex 2. ASTROL Capricorn

Steinbruch *m* quarry

steinig [ˈʃtai·nɪç] *adj* stony

steinigen [ˈʃtai·nɪ·gn̩] *vt* to stone

Steinpilz *m* porcino

steinreich [ˈʃtain-ˈraiç] *adj* filthy rich

Steinschlag *m* falling rocks *pl*

Steinzeit *f kein pl* **die** ~ the Stone Age

Steißbein *nt* ANAT coccyx

Stelle <-, -n> [ˈʃtɛ·lə] *f* 1. (*Platz*) place; (*genauer*) spot; **an dieser** ~ in this place, here; *fig* at this point; **an andere** ~ elsewhere; **an erster/zweiter** ~ in the first/second place; **~ von etw** *dat* instead of sth 2. (*umrissener Bereich*) spot; (*in einem Buch*) passage; **fettige/rostige** ~ grease/rust spot 3. MATH digit; **eine Zahl mit sieben ~n** a seven-digit number 4. (*Posten*) place; **an jds** ~ **treten** to take sb's place; **an deiner** ~ **würde ich ...** if I were you, I would ... 5. (*Arbeitsplatz*) job; **eine freie** ~ a vacancy ▶ **zur** ~ **sein** to be on hand; **auf der** ~ **treten** to not make any progress; **auf der** ~ at once; **er war auf der** ~ **to** he died instantly

stellen [ˈʃtɛ·lən] I. *vt* 1. (*hin-, abstellen*) to put; **das Auto in die Garage** ~ to put the car in the garage; **den Wein kalt** ~ to chill the wine 2. (*aufrecht hinstellen*) to stand [up *sep*] 3. (*einstellen*) **die Heizung höher/kleiner** ~ to turn up/down *sep* the heat; **den Fernseher lauter/leiser** ~ to turn the television up/down; **den Wecker auf 7 Uhr** ~ to set the alarm for 7 o'clock 4. (*vorgeben: Aufgabe*) to set; (*Bedingungen*) to stipulate; **[jdm] eine Frage** ~ to ask [sb] a question 5. (*richten*) **einen Antrag** ~ to put forward a motion; **Forderungen** ~ to make demands ▶ **auf sich** *akk* **selbst gestellt sein** to have to fend for oneself II. *vr* 1. (*sich hinstellen*) **sich** *akk* ~ to take up position 2. (*entgegentreten*) **sich** *akk* **jdm/etw** ~ to face sb.

sth **3.** (*sich melden*) **sich** *akk* **der Po-**
lizei ~ to turn oneself in to the police
4. (*etw vorgeben*) **sich** *akk* **ahnungs-**
los ~ to play innocent; **sich** *akk* **tot ~** to
pretend to be dead

Stellenangebot *nt* job offer; „**~e**" "job
market", "help wanted"

Stellenbeschreibung *f* job description

Stellengesuch *nt* "employment wanted"
advertisement

Stellenvermittlung *f* **1.** (*das Vermitteln*)
job placement **2.** (*Einrichtung*) employment agency

Stellplatz *m* parking space

Stellung <-, -en> *f* **1.** (*Arbeitsplatz*)
job **2.** (*Rang, Körperhaltung, Position*)
position **3.** (*Standpunkt*) **~ zu etw** *dat*
beziehen to take a stand on sth; **~ zu**
etw *dat* **nehmen** to express an opinion
about/on sth

Stellungnahme <-, -n> *f* statement

stellvertretend **I.** *adj attr* (*vorüberge-*
hend) acting *attr*; (*an zweiter Stelle*
stehend) deputy *attr* **II.** *adv* **- für jdn**
on sb's behalf

Stellvertreter(in) *m(f)* deputy, substitute

Stemmeisen *nt* chisel

stemmen ['ʃtɛ·mən] **I.** *vt* (*hochdrücken*)
to lift **II.** *vr* **sich** *akk* **gegen etw** *akk* **~**
to brace oneself against sth

Stempel <-s, -> ['ʃtɛm·pl̩] *m* stamp

stempeln ['ʃtɛm·pl̩n] *vt, vi* to stamp

Stengel ALT <-s, -> ['ʃtɛŋl̩] *m* s. **Stängel**

Stenografie <-, -n> [ʃte·no·gra·'fiː] *f*
shorthand, stenography

Stenographie <-, -n> [ʃte·no·gra·'fiː] *f*
s. **Stenografie**

Stenotypist(in) <-en, -en> [ʃte·no·ty·
'pɪst] *m(f)* stenographer

Steppdecke *f* comforter

Steppe <-, -n> ['ʃtɛ·pə] *f* steppe

Sterbehilfe *f* *kein pl* euthanasia

sterben <starb, gestorben> ['ʃtɛr·bn̩] *vi*
sein to die (**an** +*dat* of); **ich sterbe vor**
Durst *fig* I'm dying of thirst ▶ **für jdn**
ist jd/etw gestorben sb is finished with
sb/sth; **er ist für mich gestorben** I'm
finished with him

Sterberate *f* death rate

Sterbeurkunde *f* death certificate

sterblich ['ʃtɛrp·lɪç] *adj geh* mortal

Sterblichkeit <-> *f kein pl* mortality

Stereo <-> ['ʃteː·reo, 'st-] *nt kein pl* stereo

Stereoanlage *f* stereo [system]

stereotyp [ʃte·reo·'tyːp, st-] **I.** *adj* stereotype *attr*; stereotypical **II.** *adv* ste-
reotypically

Stereotyp <-s, -e> [ʃte·reo·'tyːp, st-]
stereotype

steril [ʃte·'riːl, st-] *adj* sterile

Sterilisation <-, -en> [ʃte·ri·li·za·'tsi̯oːn,
st-] *f* sterilization

sterilisieren * [ʃte·ri·li·'ziː·rən] *vt* to sterilize; **sich** *akk* **~ lassen** to get sterilized

Stern <-[e]s, -e> [ʃtɛrn] *m star* ▶ **in den**
~en stehen to be written in the stars

Sternbild *nt* constellation

Sternschnuppe <-, -n> *f* shooting star

Sternwarte *f* observatory

Stethoskop <-s, -e> [ʃte·to·'skoːp] *nt*
stethoscope

stetig ['ʃte·tɪç] **I.** *adj* steady **II.** *adv*
steadily

stets [ʃteːts] *adv* at all times

Steuer¹ <-s, -> ['ʃtɔy·ɐ] *nt* **1.** AUTO [steer-
ing] wheel **2.** NAUT helm

Steuer² <-, -n> ['ʃtɔy·ɐ] *f* ÖKON tax; **etw**
von der ~ absetzen to deduct sth from
one's taxes

steuerbegünstigt *adj* tax-deductible

Steuerbelastung *meist sing f* tax burden

Steuerberater(in) *m(f)* tax consultant

Steuerbescheid *m* tax assessment

Steuerbord ['ʃtɔy·ɐ·bɔrt] *nt kein pl* star-
board

Steuererhöhung *f* tax increase

Steuererklärung *f* tax return

Steuerermäßigung *f* FIN tax reduction

steuerfrei **I.** *adj* tax-exempt *attr*, exempt from tax *pred* **II.** *adv* without
paying tax

Steuergelder *pl* taxes *pl*, tax revenue[s
pl]

Steuerhinterziehung *f* tax evasion

Steuerklasse *f* tax category

Steuermann <-männer> ['ʃtɔy·ɐ·man] *m*
NAUT helmsman

steuern ['ʃtɔy·ɐn] **I.** *vt* **1.** (*lenken*) to
steer **2.** LUFT to fly **3.** (*regulieren*) to

S

control **II.** *vi* AUTO to drive

steuerpflichtig *adj* **1.** (*zu versteuern*) taxable **2.** (*zur Steuerzahlung verpflichtet*) obligated to pay tax *pred*

Steuerrad *nt* wheel, helm

Steuerruder *nt* rudder

Steuersatz *m* tax rate

Steuersenkung *f* tax cut

Steuerzahler(in) *m(f)* taxpayer

Steward <-s, -s> ['stjuː·ɐt, 'ʃt(j)uː·ɐt] *m* steward

Stewardess RR <-, -en>, **Stewardeß** ALT <-, -ssen> [stjuːɐ·'dɛs] *f* stewardess

Stich <-[e]s, -e> [ʃtɪç] *m* **1.** (*Messerstich*) stab; (*Stichwunde*) stab wound **2.** (*Insektenstich*) sting; (*Mückenstich*) bite **3.** (*stechender Schmerz*) stabbing pain **4.** (*Nadelstich*) stitch **5.** KUNST engraving ▶ **jdn im ~ lassen** to leave sb in the lurch

sticheln ['ʃtɪ·çln] *vi* to make nasty remarks

stichhaltig I. *adj* (*Alibi*) solid; (*Argumentation*) sound; (*Beweis*) conclusive; [**nicht**] **~ sein** to [not] hold water **II.** *adv* (*schlüssig*) conclusively

Stichprobe *f* spot check

Stichtag *m* deadline

Stichwort ['ʃtɪç·vɔrt] *nt* **1.** LING (*Haupteintrag*) headword **2.** THEAT cue **3.** *meist pl* (*Wort als Gedächtnisstütze*) **sich** *dat* **~e machen** to take notes

Stichwunde *f* knife wound

sticken ['ʃtɪ·kn̩] *vt, vi* to embroider

stickig ['ʃtɪ·kɪç] *adj* stuffy; (*Luft*) stale

Stickstoff ['ʃtɪk·ʃtɔf] *m kein pl* nitrogen

Stiefbruder ['ʃtiːf-] *m* stepbrother

Stiefel <-s, -> ['ʃtiː·fl̩] *m* boot

Stiefeltern *pl* stepparents *pl*

Stiefkind *nt* stepchild

Stiefmutter *f* stepmother

Stiefmütterchen *nt* BOT pansy

Stiefschwester *f* stepsister

Stiefsohn *m* stepson

Stieftochter *f* stepdaughter

Stiefvater *m* stepfather

Stiel <-[e]s, -e> [ʃtiːl] *m* **1.** (*Handgriff*) handle; (*Besenstiel*) broomstick **2.** (*Blumenstiel*) stem, stalk

Stier <-[e]s, -e> [ʃtiːɐ] *m* **1.** (*Bulle*) bull **2.** ASTROL Taurus

stieren ['ʃtiː·rən] *vi* to stare

Stierkampf *m* bullfight

Stift <-[e]s, -e> [ʃtɪft] *m* **1.** (*Stahlstift*) [steel] pin [*o* tack] **2.** (*zum Schreiben*) pen, pencil

stiften ['ʃtɪf·tn̩] *vt* **1.** (*spenden*) to donate **2.** (*verursachen*) to cause; **Unruhe ~** to create unrest

Stiftung <-, -en> *f* **1.** (*Organisation*) foundation **2.** (*Schenkung*) donation

Stigmatisierung [ʃtɪg·ma·ti·'ziː·rʊŋ] *geh* stigmatization

Stil <-[e]s, -e> [ʃtiːl, st-] *m* (*Ausdrucksform*) style ▶ **im großen ~** on grand scale

still [ʃtɪl] *adj* **1.** (*ruhig*) quiet, peaceful; **sei ~!** be quiet!; **in einer ~en Stunde** in a quiet moment **2.** (*geräuschlos*) silent; (*Vorwurf*) silent **3.** (*unbewegt*) still; **etw ~ halten** to keep sth still ▶ **im S~en hoffen** to secretly hope

Stille <-> ['ʃtɪ·lə] *f kein pl* **1.** (*Ruhe*) quiet; (*ohne Geräusch*) silence; **in aller ~** quietly **2.** (*Abgeschiedenheit*) peace

Stilleben ALT *nt s.* **Stillleben**

stillegen ALT <stillgelegt> *vt s.* **stilllegen**

stillen ['ʃtɪ·lən] *vt* **1.** (*säugen*) to breastfeed **2.** (*befriedigen*) to satisfy; **den Durst ~** to quench sb's thirst **3.** (*aufhören lassen*) to stop; (*Blutverlust*) to stanch

stillhalten *vi irreg* to keep still, to not move

Stillleben RR ['ʃtɪl·leː·bn̩] *nt* still life

stilllegen RR <stillgelegt> *vt* to close [down *sep*]

stillsitzen *vi irreg sein o haben* to sit still

Stillstand *m kein pl* standstill; **zum ~ kommen** (*zum Erliegen*) to come to a standstill; (*aufhören*) to stop

stillstehen *vi irreg sein o haben* **1.** (*außer Betrieb sein*) to stand idle; (*Verhandlungen, Verkehr*) to be at a standstill **2.** *a. fig* (*sich nicht bewegen*) to stand still

Stilmöbel *nt meist pl* period furniture

Stimmband *nt meist pl* vocal cord

stimmberechtigt *adj* entitled to vote *pred*

timmbruch *m* er war mit 12 im ~ his voice broke when he was 12

timme <-, -n> [ˈʃtɪ·mə] *f* 1. (*Art des Sprechens*) voice 2. POL vote; **sich** *akk* **der** ~ **enthalten** to abstain 3. (*Meinungsäußerung*) voice

timmen[1] [ˈʃtɪ·mən] *vi* 1. (*zutreffen*) to be right; **es stimmt, dass ...** it is true that ...; **stimmt!** right! 2. (*korrekt sein*) to be correct; **da stimmt was nicht** there's something wrong here; **stimmt so** keep the change

timmen[2] [ˈʃtɪ·mən] *vt* MUS to tune

timmengleichheit *f* tie

timmenmehrheit *f* majority of votes

timmenthaltung *f* abstention

timmgabel *f* tuning fork

timmrecht *nt* right to vote

timmung <-, -en> *f* 1. (*Gemütslage*) mood; **in der ~ sein** to be in the mood **(zu** for); **in ~ kommen** to get in the [right] mood 2. (*Atmosphäre*) atmosphere

timmzettel *m* ballot

timulieren * [ʃti·mu·ˈliː·rən] *vt* to stimulate

tinken <stank, gestunken> [ˈʃtɪŋ·kn̩] *vi* 1. (*unangenehm riechen*) to stink (**nach** +*dat* of) 2. (*verdächtig sein*) **die Sache stinkt** the whole business stinks 3. *fam* (*zuwider sein*) **jdm stinkt etw** sb is sick and tired of sth

tinktier *nt* skunk

tipendium <-s, -dien> [ʃti·ˈpɛn·di̯·ʊm] *nt* scholarship

tirn <-, -en> [ʃtɪrn] *f* forehead; **die ~ runzeln** to frown ▸ **jdm die ~ bieten** to stand up to sb

tirnband <-bänder> *nt* headband

tirnhöhle *f* sinus

töbern [ˈʃtøː·ben] *vi* to rummage (**in** +*dat* in)

tock[1] <-[e]s, Stöcke> [ʃtɔk] *m* 1. (*Holzstange*) stick 2. (*Topfpflanze*) plant

tock[2] <-[e]s, -> [ʃtɔk] *m* floor, story; **der** 1. ~ the second floor

tockbesoffen [ˈʃtɔk·bə·ˈzɔ·fn̩] *adj fam* plastered *fam*

tockdunkel [ˈʃtɔk·ˈdʊŋ·kl̩] *adj* pitch-dark

töckelschuh *m* high-heeled shoe

stocken [ˈʃtɔ·kn̩] *vi* 1. (*innehalten*) to falter 2. (*zeitweilig stillstehen*) to come to a halt

stockend *adj* 1. (*Unterhaltung*) flagging 2. (*Verkehr*) stop-and-go

Stockwerk *nt s.* Stock[2]

Stoff <-[e]s, -e> [ʃtɔf] *m* 1. (*Textil*) material, fabric 2. (*Material*) material 3. CHEM substance 4. (*thematisches Material*) material 5. (*Lehrstoff*) subject material 6. *kein pl sl* (*Rauschgift*) dope

Stofftier *nt* stuffed animal

Stoffwechsel [-vɛksl̩] *m* metabolism

stöhnen [ˈʃtøː·nən] *vi* to moan; (*vor Schmerz*) to groan

Stollen <-s, -> [ˈʃtɔ·lən] *m* 1. BERGB tunnel 2. KOCHK stollen (*a sweet Christmas bread-like cake made with dried fruit, often filled with marzipan*)

stolpern [ˈʃtɔl·pen] *vi sein* to trip, to stumble

stolz [ʃtɔlts] I. *adj* proud II. *adv* proudly

Stolz <-es> [ʃtɔlts] *m kein pl* pride; **jds ganzer ~ sein** to be sb's pride and joy

Stop[ALT] <-s, -s> [ʃtɔp] *m s.* Stopp

stopfen [ˈʃtɔp·fn̩] I. *vt* 1. (*hineinzwängen*) to stuff; (*Loch*) to fill 2. (*mit Nadel und Faden*) to darn II. *vi* (*die Verdauung hemmen*) to cause constipation

Stopp[RR] <-s, -s> [ʃtɔp] *m* stop

Stoppelbart *m* stubbly beard

stoppen [ˈʃtɔ·pn̩] *vt, vi* 1. (*anhalten*) to stop 2. (*Zeit nehmen*) to time

Stoppschild <-schilder> *nt* stop sign

Stoppuhr *f* stopwatch

Stöpsel <-s, -> [ˈʃtœp·sl̩] *m* stopper; (*für Badewanne*) plug

Storch <-[e]s, Störche> [ʃtɔrç] *m* stork

stören [ˈʃtøː·rən] I. *vt* 1. (*unterbrechen*) to disturb; **jdn bei der Arbeit ~** to disturb sb while he/she is working; **entschuldigen Sie, wenn ich Sie störe** I'm sorry to bother you 2. (*beeinträchtigen*) **jds Pläne ~** to interfere with sb's plans 3. (*unangenehm berühren*) **stört es Sie, wenn ich ...?** do you mind if I ...?; **das stört mich nicht** that doesn't bother me; **das stört mich!** that's getting on my nerves [*o* annoying [me]]! II. *vi* 1. (*bei etw unterbrechen*) to dis-

S

turb; **ich will nicht ~, aber ...** I'm sorry to bother you, but ... **2.** (*lästig sein*) to be irritating **III.** *vr* **er stört sich aber auch an allem** he lets absolutely everything bother him

stornieren * [ʃtɔr·'niː·rən] *vt* to cancel

Stornierung <-, -en> *f* **1.** HANDEL (*eines Auftrags*) cancellation **2.** FIN (*einer Buchung*) reversal, cancellation of an entry

störrisch ['ʃtœ·rɪʃ] **I.** *adj* obstinate, stubborn **II.** *adv* obstinately, stubbornly

Störung <-, -en> *f* **1.** (*Unterbrechung*) interruption, disruption, disturbance **2.** (*Störsignale*) interference **3.** (*technischer Defekt*) fault; (*Fehlfunktion*) malfunction

Stoß <-es, Stöße> [ʃtoːs] *m* **1.** (*Schubs*) push; (*mit dem Ellbogen*) dig; (*mit der Faust*) punch; (*mit dem Fuß*) kick **2.** (*Erschütterung*) bump **3.** (*Stapel*) pile, stack ► **sich** *dat* **einen ~ geben** to pull oneself together

Stoßdämpfer *m* shock absorber

stoßen <stößt, stieß, gestoßen> ['ʃtoː·sn̩] **I.** *vt* (*schubsen*) to push, to shove (**aus** +*dat* out of, **von** +*dat* off) **II.** *vr* **sich** *akk* [**an etw** *dat*] ~ to hurt oneself [on sth]; **sich** *dat* **den Kopf** ~ to bang one's head **III.** *vi* **1.** *sein* (*aufschlagen*) **an/gegen etw** *akk* ~ to bump against/into sth; **mit dem Kopf an etw** *akk* ~ to bang one's head on sth **2.** *sein* (*grenzen*) **an etw** *akk* ~ to border on sth **3.** *sein* (*treffen*) **zu jdm** ~ to join sb **4.** *sein* (*finden*) **auf etw** *akk* ~ to find sth; **auf Erdöl** ~ to strike oil **5.** *sein* (*konfrontiert werden*) **auf Ablehnung/Zustimmung** ~ to meet with disapproval/approval **6.** *schweiz* (*schieben*) to push, to shove

Stoßstange *f* bumper

Stoßzeit *f* **1.** (*Hauptverkehrszeit*) rush hour **2.** (*Hauptgeschäftszeit*) peak business hour[s *pl*], busy time of day

stottern ['ʃtɔ·tɐn] *vi* **1.** (*stockend sprechen*) to stutter **2.** (*Motor*) to splutter

Strafanstalt *f* penal institution

Strafanzeige *f* [criminal] charge

Strafarbeit *f* extra work *(assigned as punishment)*

Strafbank *f* SPORT penalty box

strafbar *adj* punishable [by law]; **sic** *akk* ~ **machen** to make oneself liab to prosecution

Strafe <-, -n> ['ʃtraː·fə] *f* **1.** (*Bestrafun* punishment; JUR penalty; **zur** ~ as a pu ishment **2.** (*Geldstrafe*) fine; (*Haftstr fe*) sentence; **seine** ~ **absitzen** to serv [out] one's sentence

strafen ['ʃtraː·fn̩] *vt* to punish; **jdn m Verachtung** ~ to treat sb with co tempt

Straferlass RR *m* remission of a sentenc

straff [ʃtraf] **I.** *adj* **1.** (*fest gespann* taut, tight **2.** (*nicht schlaff*) firm **II.** *a* tightly

straffällig *adj* JUR punishable, crimin *attr*; ~ **werden** to become a criminal

straffen ['ʃtra·fn̩] *vt* **1.** (*straff anziehe* to tighten **2.** (*kürzen: Artikel, Text*) shorten; (*präziser machen*) to tighte up *sep*

straffrei *adj* unpunished; ~ **bleiben** go unpunished

Straffreiheit *f kein pl* immunity fro criminal prosecution

Strafgefangene(r) *f(m) dekl wie a* prisoner

Strafgesetzbuch *nt* penal code

sträflich ['ʃtrɛː·f·lɪç] *adj* criminal *attr*

Sträfling <-s, -e> ['ʃtrɛː·f·lɪŋ] *m* prisone

Strafmaß *nt* sentence

strafmildernd *adj* mitigating

Strafprozess RR *m* trial

Strafpunkt *m* SPORT penalty point

Strafraum *m* FBALL penalty area [*o* box

Strafrecht *nt* criminal law

Strafstoß *m* SPORT penalty [kick]

Straftat *f* [criminal] offense

Strafverteidiger(in) *m(f)* defense a torney

Strafvollzug *m* penal system

Strafzettel *m* ticket

Strahl <-[e]s, -en> [ʃtraːl] *m* **1.** (*Lich strahl*) ray [of light]; (*Sonnenstrah* sunbeam; (*konzentriertes Licht*) bea **2.** (*Wasserstrahl*) jet

strahlen ['ʃtraː·lən] *vi* **1.** (*leuchten*) shine **2.** (*Radioaktivität abgeben*) be radioactive **3.** (*ein freudiges G sicht machen*) to beam (**vor** +*dat* wit

4. (*glänzen*) to shine

trahlenbelastung f radiation, radioactive contamination

trahlentherapie f radiotherapy

trahlenverseucht adj contaminated with radioactivity *pred*

trahlung <-, -en> f PHYS radiation; **radioaktive ~** radioactivity

trähne <-, -n> ['ʃtrɛːnə] f strand

tramm [ʃtram] **I.** adj **1.** (*straff*) tight; **etw ~ ziehen** to tighten sth **2.** (*kräftig*) strong, brawny, strapping *hum fam* **3.** (*drall*) taut; (*Beine*) sturdy **4.** (*Marsch*) brisk **II.** adv **1.** (*eng anliegend*) tightly **2.** fam (*intensiv*) intensively; **~ marschieren** to march briskly

trammstehen vi irreg to stand at attention

trampeln ['ʃtram·pl̩n] vi **1.** (*heftig treten*) to kick around **2.** fam (*sich abmühen*) to struggle

trand <-[e]s, Strände> [ʃtrant] m beach

tranden ['ʃtran·dn̩] vi sein (*auf Grund laufen*) to run aground ▶ **irgendwo gestrandet sein** to be stranded somewhere

trandkorb m beach chair

trangulieren * [ʃtraŋ·ɡu·ˈliː·rən] vt to strangle

trapaze <-, -n> [ʃtra·ˈpaː·tsə] f stress, strain

trapazieren * [ʃtra·pa·ˈtsiː·rən] **I.** vt **1.** (*stark beanspruchen*) to wear; (*abnutzen*) to wear out *sep* **2.** (*überanspruchen*) **jds Geduld ~** to tax sb's patience; **jds Nerven ~** to get on sb's nerves **II.** vr **sich** akk [**bei etw** dat] **~** to overdo it [when doing sth], to wear oneself out

trapazierfähig adj durable

trapaziös [ʃtra·pa·ˈtsjøːs] adj strenuous

traps <-es, -e> [ʃtraps] m meist pl garter

traße <-, -n> [ʃtraː·sə] f (*Verkehrsweg*) road; (*bewohnte Straße*) street; (*enge Straße auf dem Land*) lane ▶ **auf die ~ gehen** to demonstrate; **jdn auf die ~ setzen** to throw sb out; **auf der ~ sitzen** to be [out] on the streets; **auf of-**

fener ~ in broad daylight

Straßenbahn f streetcar

Straßenbahnhaltestelle f streetcar stop

Straßenbahnlinie f streetcar line

Straßenbau m kein pl road construction *no art*

Straßenbelag m road surface

Straßengraben m [roadside] ditch

Straßenkarte f road map

Straßenschild nt street sign

Straßensperre f roadblock

Straßenverkehr m [road] traffic

Strategie <-, -en> [ʃtra·te·ˈɡiː] f strategy

strategisch [ʃtra·ˈteː·ɡɪʃ] **I.** adj strategic **II.** adv strategically

sträuben ['ʃtrɔy·bn̩] vr **1.** (*sich widersetzen*) **sich** akk [**gegen etw** akk] **~** to resist [sth] **2.** (*sich aufrichten: Fell, Haar*) to stand on end

Strauch <-[e]s, Sträucher> [ʃtraux] m shrub, bush

Strauß¹ <-es, Sträuße> [ʃtraus] m bunch [of flowers], bouquet

Strauß² <-es, -e> [ʃtraus] m ZOOL ostrich

streben ['ʃtreː·bn̩] vi (*sich bemühen*) to strive (**nach** +dat for)

Streber(in) <-s, -> ['ʃtreː·bɐ] m(f) pej fam dweeb sl

strebsam ['ʃtreːp·zaːm] adj industrious

Strecke <-, -n> ['ʃtrɛ·kə] f **1.** (*Wegstrecke*) distance; **auf halber ~** halfway; **über weite ~n** for long stretches **2.** BAHN stretch; **auf freier ~** between stations ▶ **auf der ~ bleiben** dat fam to fall by the wayside; **jdn zur ~ bringen** to hunt sb down

strecken ['ʃtrɛ·kn̩] **I.** vt to stretch; (*Drogen etc.*) to dilute **II.** vr **sich** akk **~** to stretch

streckenweise adv in parts

Streich <-[e]s, -e> [ʃtraiç] m prank; **jdm einen ~ spielen** to play a trick on sb

streicheln ['ʃtrai·çl̩n] vt to caress; (*Katze, Hund*) to pet

streichen <strich, gestrichen> ['ʃtrai·çn̩] **I.** vt haben **1.** (*anmalen*) to paint **2.** (*schmieren*) to spread **3.** (*ausstreichen*) to delete **4.** (*zurückziehen: Auftrag, Projekt*) to cancel; (*Zuschüsse*) to withdraw **II.** vi **1.** haben (*darüber-*

S

fahren) **über etw** *akk* ~ to stroke sth
2. *sein* (*streifen*) to prowl

Streichholz *nt* match

Streichinstrument *nt* string[ed] instrument

Streichwurst *f* spreadable sausage

streifen ['ʃtrai·fn̩] *vt* **1.** (*flüchtig berühren*) to touch; **ein Thema nur** ~ to just touch on a subject **2.** (*überziehen*) **etw auf/über etw** *akk* ~ to slip sth on/over sth **3.** (*abstreifen*) **etw von etw** *dat* ~ to slip sth off [of] sth

Streifen <-s, -> ['ʃtrai·fn̩] *m* **1.** (*schmaler Abschnitt*) stripe **2.** (*schmales Stück*) strip

Streifenwagen *m* patrol car

Streik <-[e]s, -s> [ʃtraik] *m* strike; **in den** ~ **treten** to go on strike

Streikbrecher(in) *m(f)* strikebreaker, scab *pej fam*

streiken ['ʃtrai·kn̩] *vi* **1.** (*nicht arbeiten*) to be on strike, to strike **2.** *hum fam* (*nicht funktionieren*) to call it quits **3.** *fam* (*sich weigern*) to go on strike

Streikposten *m* picket; ~ **aufstellen** to set up a picket line

Streikrecht *nt kein pl* right to strike

Streit <-[e]s, -e> [ʃtrait] *m* argument, dispute, fight; [**mit jdm**] ~ [**wegen etw** *dat*] **bekommen** to get into an argument [with sb] [about sth]; ~ **haben/suchen** to have/be looking for an argument; **im** ~ during an argument

streiten <stritt, gestritten> ['ʃtrai·tn̩] *vi, vr* to argue, to fight (**über** +*akk* about); **sich** *akk* **um etw** *akk* ~ to argue [*o* fight] over sth

Streiterei <-, -en> [ʃtrai·tə·'rai] *f fam* arguing

Streitfall *m* dispute, conflict; **im** ~ in case of dispute

streitig ['ʃtrai·tɪç] *adj* disputed; JUR contentious

Streitkräfte *pl* [armed] forces *pl*

streitlustig *adj* argumentative

streitsüchtig *adj* quarrelsome, contentious

streng [ʃtrɛŋ] **I.** *adj* strict; (*Winter*) severe; (*Geruch*) pungent **II.** *adv* strictly; **was riecht hier so** ~? what's that strong smell?

Strenge <-> ['ʃtrɛŋə] *f kein pl* **1.** (*Unnachsichtigkeit*) strictness **2.** (*Härte*) severity **3.** (*von Geschmack*) sharpness (*von Geruch*) pungency

Stress RR <-es, -e>, **Streß** ALT <-sses, -sse> [ʃtrɛs, st-] *m* stress; ~ **haben** t experience stress; **im** ~ **sein** to be un der stress; **ich bin voll im** ~ I am com pletely stressed out

stressen ['ʃtrɛ·sn̩] *vt* to put under stress

stressig ['ʃtrɛ·sɪç] *adj* stressful

streuen ['ʃtrɔy·ən] **I.** *vt* **1.** (*hinstreuen*, to scatter, to spread **2.** (*verbreiten*) t spread **II.** *vi* (*Streumittel anwenden*) t put down sand; (*Salz*) to salt [the roads

streunen *vi sein o haben* to roam aroun ~**de Hunde** stray dogs

Streuselkuchen *m* streusel [cake]

strich [ʃtrɪç] *imp von* **streichen**

Strich <-[e]s, -e> [ʃtrɪç] *m* **1.** (*gezoge ne Linie*) line **2.** *fam* (*Prostitution*) **au den** ~ **gehen** to become a streetwalke ▶ **nach** ~ **und** Faden *fam* good an proper; **jd/etw macht jdm einen** ~ **durch die** Rechnung *fam* sb/sth messes u sb's plans; **jdm gegen den** ~ **gehen** *fa* to go against the grain; **einen** ~ **unte etw** *akk* **ziehen** to put an end to sth **unterm** ~ *fam* at the end of the day

stricheln ['ʃtrɪ·çln̩] *vt* to sketch in *sep*; **ge strichelte Linie** dotted line; (*auf Stra ße*) broken line

Stricher <-s, -> *m sl* young male pros titute

Strichpunkt *m* semicolon

Strick <-[e]s, -e> [ʃtrɪk] *m* rope ▶ **wen alle** ~**e** reißen *fam* if all else fails

stricken ['ʃtrɪ·kn̩] *vt, vi* to knit

Strickgarn *nt* knitting yarn

Strickjacke *f* cardigan

Strickwaren *pl* knitwear

striegeln ['ʃtri·gln̩] *vt* to groom

strikt [ʃtrɪkt, st-] **I.** *adj* strict; (*Weigerun* point-blank **II.** *adv* strictly

Striplokal ['strɪp·lo·ka:l] *nt fam* strip joint

strittig ['ʃtrɪ·tɪç] *adj* contentious; (*Fal* controversial; (*Grenze*) disputed; ~ **sei** to be in dispute; **der** ~**e Punkt** th point at issue

Stroh <-[e]s> [ʃtro:] *nt kein pl* straw

strohblond *adj* (*Mensch*) with sandy blonde hair; (*Haare*) sandy [blonde]

Strohhalm *m* straw

Strohhut *m* straw hat

Strohmann *m* front man

Strom <-[e]s, Ströme> [ʃtroːm] *m* **1.** ELEK electricity; **elektrischer ~** electric current; **unter ~ stehen** (*elektrisch geladen sein*) to be live; (*überaus aktiv sein*) to be a live wire *fig* **2.** (*großer Fluss*) [large] river **3.** (*Schwarm: von Besuchern etc.*) stream ▶ **in Strömen gießen** to pour [down] [rain]; **mit dem/ gegen den ~ schwimmen** to swim with/against the current

stromabwärts [ʃtroːmˈʔapˌvɛrts] *adv* downstream

stromaufwärts [ʃtroːmˈʔaufˌvɛrts] *adv* upstream

Stromausfall *m* power outage

strömen [ˈʃtrøːmən] *vi sein* to stream (**aus** +*dat* out of)

Stromerzeugung *f* electricity generation

Stromkabel *nt* power line

Stromkreis *m* [electric[al]] circuit

Stromnetz *nt* power grid

Stromstärke *f* current [strength]

Stromstoß *m* electric shock

Strömung <-, -en> *f* **1.** (*fließendes Wasser*) current **2.** (*Tendenz*) trend

Stromverbrauch *m* power consumption

Stromversorgung *f* power supply

Stromzähler *m* electric meter

Strophe <-, -n> [ˈʃtroː-fə] *f* verse

Strudel <-s, -> [ˈʃtruː-dl̩] *m* **1.** (*Wasserwirbel*) whirlpool; (*kleiner*) eddy **2.** (*Gebäck*) strudel

Struktur [ʃtrʊkˈtuːɐ̯] *f* **1.** (*Aufbau*) structure **2.** (*von Stoff etc.*) texture

strukturell [ʃtrʊk-tuˈrɛl] *adj* structural

strukturschwach *adj* economically underdeveloped

Strumpf <-[e]s, Strümpfe> [ʃtrʊmpf] *m* **1.** (*Kniestrumpf*) knee-high; (*Socke*) sock **2.** (*Damenstrumpf*) stocking

Strumpfhalter <-s, -> *m* garter

Strumpfhose *f* pantyhose, stockings; (*fester*) tights *npl*

struppig [ˈʃtrʊ-pɪç] *adj* (*Haare*) tousled; (*Fell*) shaggy

Stube <-, -n> [ˈʃtuː-bə] *f dial* (*Wohnzimmer*) living room

Stubenarrest *m* **~ haben** *fam* to be confined to one's room

stubenrein *adj* housebroken

Stuck <-[e]s> [ʃtʊk] *m kein pl* stucco, cornices *pl*

Stück <-[e]s, -e *o nach Zahlenangaben* -> [ʃtʏk] *nt* **1.** (*einzelnes Teil*) piece; **ein ~ Kuchen** a piece of cake; **etw in ~e reißen** to tear sth to pieces; **~ für ~** bit by bit; **am ~** in one piece; **geschnitten oder am ~?** sliced or unsliced?; **5 Euro das ~** 5 euros each **2.** (*besonderer Gegenstand*) piece, item **3.** (*Abschnitt*) part; **ich begleite dich noch ein ~** I'll go part of the way with you; **ein ~ Land** a plot of land **4.** THEAT play **5.** MUS piece ▶ **jds bestes ~** *hum fam* sb's pride and joy; **aus freien ~en** of one's own free will; **große ~e auf jdn halten** *fam* to think highly of sb

Stückpreis *m* unit price

Student(in) <-en, -en> [ʃtuˈdɛnt] *m(f)* student

Studentenausweis *m* [college] student ID [card]

Studie <-, -n> [ˈʃtuː-diə] *f* study

Studienfach *nt* subject

Studiengebühren *pl* tuition

Studienrat, -rätin *m, f* ≈ school board member

Studienreise *f* study trip

studieren* [ʃtuˈdiː-rən] *vt, vi* to study; **sie studiert noch** she is still a student; **ich will ~** I want to go to college

Studio <-s, -s> [ˈʃtuː-diɔ] *nt* studio

Studium <-, Studien> [ˈʃtuː-diˌʊm] *nt* **1.** (*an Universität*) studies *pl*; **ein ~ aufnehmen** to begin one's studies **2.** (*eingehende Beschäftigung*) study

Stufe <-, -n> [ˈʃtuː-fə] *f* **1.** (*Treppenabschnitt*) step **2.** (*Niveau*) level **3.** (*Abschnitt*) stage, phase

stufenlos I. *adj* continuously variable **II.** *adv* smoothly

Stufenschnitt *m* (*Frisur*) layered cut

Stuhl <-[e]s, Stühle> [ʃtuːl] *m* chair

Stuhlbein *nt* chair leg

Stuhllehne *f* chair back

stumm [ʃtʊm] **I.** *adj* **1.** (*nicht sprechen*

S

könnend) dumb **2.** (*schweigend*) silent; **~ werden** to go silent **3.** LING silent **II.** *adv* silently

Stummel <-s, -> [ˈʃtʊ·ml̩] *m* (*Glied*) stump; (*von Bleistift, Kerze*) stub

Stummfilm *m* silent movie

Stümper(in) <-s, -> [ˈʃtʏm·pɐ] *m(f) pej* incompetent

stumpf [ʃtʊmpf] *adj* **1.** (*nicht scharf*) blunt **2.** (*glanzlos*) dull **3.** (*abgestumpft*) apathetic

stumpfsinnig *adj* **1.** (*geistig träge*) apathetic **2.** (*stupide*) mindless, tedious

Stunde <-, -n> [ˈʃtʊn·də] *f* **1.** (*60 Minuten*) hour; **nur noch eine knappe ~** just under an hour to go; **zu später ~** at a late hour; **in einer stillen ~** in a quiet moment, fifteen minutes; **eine halbe ~** half an hour; **anderthalb ~n** an hour and a half; **volle ~** on the hour; **der Zug fährt jede volle ~** the train departs every hour on the hour; **alle** [**halbe**] **~** every [half [an]] hour **2.** *kein pl* (*festgesetzter Zeitpunkt*) time, hour *form*; **zur gewohnten ~** at the usual time **3.** (*Unterrichtsstunde*) lesson, period **4.** *meist pl* (*Zeitraum von kurzer Dauer*) times *pl*; **sich** *akk* **nur an die angenehmen ~n erinnern** to only remember the good times ▶ **jds große ~** sb's big moment; **jds letzte ~ hat geschlagen** sb's hour has come; **die ~ der Wahrheit** the moment of truth

stunden [ˈʃtʊn·dn̩] *vt* **jdm etw ~** to give sb time to pay [for] sth

Stundenkilometer *pl* kilometers *pl* per hour

stundenlang I. *adj* lasting several hours *pred* **II.** *adv* for hours

Stundenlohn *m* hourly wage

Stundenplan *m* timetable, schedule

stundenweise I. *adv* for an hour or two [at a time] **II.** *adj* for a few hours *pred*

stündlich [ˈʃtʏnt·lɪç] **I.** *adj* hourly **II.** *adv* hourly, every hour

Stupsnase *f* snub nose

stur [ʃtuːɐ̯] **I.** *adj* stubborn, obstinate **II.** *adv* obstinately; **sich** *akk* **~ stellen** *fam* to dig one's heels in

Sturheit <-> *f kein pl* stubbornness,

obstinacy

Sturm <-[e]s, Stürme> [ʃtʊrm] *m* **1.** (*starker Wind*) storm **2.** FBALL forward line **3.** (*heftiger Andrang*) rush (**auf** +*akk* for) ▶ **gegen etw** *akk* **~ laufen** to be up in arms against sth; **~ läuten** to keep ringing the doorbell

stürmen [ˈʃtʏr·mən] **I.** *vi impers haben* **es stürmt** it's really windy out **II.** *vi* **1.** *haben* SPORT to attack **2.** *sein* (*rennen*) to storm **III.** *vt haben* to storm

Stürmer(in) <-s, -> [ˈʃtʏr·mɐ] *m(f)* forward; FBALL striker

Sturmflut *f* storm tide

stürmisch [ˈʃtʏr·mɪʃ] **I.** *adj* **1.** METEO blustery; (*mit Regen*) stormy; (*See*) rough **2.** (*vehement*) tumultuous; (*Mensch*) impetuous; (*Beziehung*) passionate; **nicht so ~!** take it easy! **II.** *adv* tumultuously

Sturmwarnung *f* storm warning

Sturz <-es, Stürze> [ʃtʊrts] *m* **1.** (*Fall*) fall **2.** (*drastisches Absinken*) **ein ~ der Temperaturen um 15° C** a drop in temperature of 15° C **3.** (*eines Diktators, einer Regierung*) overthrow

stürzen [ˈʃtʏr·tsn̩] **I.** *vi sein* **1.** (*fallen*) to fall (**von** +*dat* off) **2.** (*rennen*) to rush; **ins Zimmer ~** to burst into the room **II.** *vt haben* **1.** (*werfen*) **sich/jdn aus dem Fenster ~** to throw oneself/sb out of the window **2.** POL (*absetzen*) to bring down; (*Minister*) to force to resign; (*Diktator*) to overthrow; (*Regierung*) to topple **3.** KOCHK (*aus der Form kippen*) to turn upside down **III.** *vr* **1.** (*sich werfen*) **sich** *akk* **auf jdn ~** to pounce on sb; **die Gäste stürzten sich aufs kalte Büfett** the guests stormed the cold buffet **2.** (*sich mit etw belasten*) **sich** *akk* **in etw** *akk* **~** to plunge into sth; **sich** *akk* **in große Unkosten ~** to go to great expense

Sturzflug *m* LUFT nosedive; ORN steep dive

Sturzhelm *m* crash helmet

Stute <-, -n> [ˈʃtuː·tə] *f* mare

Stütze <-, -n> [ˈʃtʏ·tsə] *f* **1.** (*Stützpfeiler*) support [pillar] **2.** (*Halt*) support, prop **3.** (*Unterstützung*) support **4.** *fam* (*finanzielle Hilfe vom Staat*) welfare

stutzen¹ ['ʃtuː·tsn̩] *vi* to hesitate, to stop short

stutzen² ['ʃtuː·tsn̩] *vt* **1.** HORT to prune **2.** ZOOL to clip; **gestutzte Flügel** clipped wings **3.** (*kürzen*) to trim

stützen ['ʃtʏ·tsn̩] **I.** *vt* **1.** (*Halt geben*) to support **2.** (*aufstützen*) **etw auf etw** *akk* ~ to rest sth on sth **3.** (*gründen*) **etw auf etw** *akk* ~ to base sth on sth **4.** (*untermauern*) to back up *sep*; (*Theorie*) to support **II.** *vr* **1.** (*sich aufstützen*) **sich** *akk* **auf jdn/etw** ~ to lean on sb/sth **2.** (*basieren*) **sich** *akk* **auf etw** *akk* ~ to be based on sth

stutzig ['ʃtuː·tsɪç] *adj* **jdn ~ machen** to make sb suspicious; **~ werden** to begin to wonder

Stützpunkt *m* MIL base

Subjekt <-[e]s, -e> [zʊpˈjɛkt] *nt* subject

subjektiv ['zʊp·jɛk·tiːf] **I.** *adj* subjective **II.** *adv* subjectively

Substantiv <-s, -e> ['zʊp·stan·tiːf] *nt* noun

Substanz <-, -en> [zʊpˈstants] *f* substance

subtrahieren* [zʊp·traˈhiː·rən] *vt, vi* to subtract (**von** +*dat* from)

Subtraktion <-, -en> [zʊp·trakˈtsi̯oːn] *f* subtraction

Subunternehmer(in) <-s, -> ['zʊp·ʔʊn·te·neː·me] *m(f)* subcontractor

Subvention <-, -en> [zʊp·vɛnˈtsi̯oːn] *f* subsidy

subventionieren* [zʊp·vɛn·tsi̯oˈniː·rən] *vt* to subsidize

Suche <-, -n> ['zuː·xə] *f* search (**nach** +*dat* for); **sich** *akk* **auf die ~** [**nach jdm/etw**] **machen** to go in search [of sb/sth]; **auf der ~** [**nach jdm/etw**] **sein** to be looking [for sb/sth]

suchen ['zuː·xn̩] **I.** *vt* **1.** (*zu finden versuchen*) to look for; (*intensiver*) to search for; **du hast hier nichts zu ~!** you've got no business being here! **2.** (*erstreben: Arbeit, Asyl, Schutz*) to seek **II.** *vi* to search, to look (**nach** +*dat* for)

Suchfunktion *f* COMPUT search function

Suchlauf *m* search process

Suchmaschine *f* search engine

Sucht <-, Süchte> [zʊxt] *f* **1.** (*Abhängigkeit*) addiction; **~ erzeugend** addictive

2. (*Verlangen*) obsession; **jds ~ nach etw** *dat* sb's craving for sth

Suchtgefahr *f* danger of addiction

süchtig ['zʏç·tɪç] *adj* **1.** (*abhängig*) addicted *pred*; **~ machen** to be addictive **2.** (*begierig*) **~ sein** to be hooked (**nach** +*dat* on)

Süchtige(r) *f(m) dekl wie adj* addict

Suchtkranke(r) <-n, -n> *f (m) dekl wie adj* addict

Südafrika ['zyː·tˈʔaːf·ri·ka] *nt* South Africa; *s. a.* **Deutschland**

südafrikanisch ['zyː·tˈʔafri·ˈkaː·nɪʃ] *adj* South African; *s. a.* **deutsch**

Südamerika ['zyː·tˈʔaˈmeː·ri·ka] *nt* South America; *s. a.* **Deutschland**

südamerikanisch *adj* South American; *s. a.* **deutsch**

süddeutsch ['zyː·tˈdɔytʃ] *adj* Southern German; *s. a.* **deutsch**

Süddeutschland ['zyː·tˈdɔytʃ·lant] *nt* Southern Germany; *s. a.* **Deutschland**

Süden <-s> ['zyː·dn̩] *m kein pl, kein indef art* **1.** (*Himmelsrichtung*) south; *s. a.* **Norden 1 2.** (*südliche Gegend*) south; *s. a.* **Norden 2**

Südfrucht *f* tropical fruit

Südhalbkugel *f* Southern Hemisphere

südlich ['zyː·t·lɪç] **I.** *adj* **1.** (*Himmelsrichtung*) southern; *s. a.* **nördlich I 1 2.** (*im Süden liegend*) southern; *s. a.* **nördlich I 2 3.** (*von/nach Süden*) southward, southerly; *s. a.* **nördlich I 3 II.** *adv* ~ **von ...** south of ... **III.** *präp* +*gen* ~ **der Stadt** [to the] south of the city/town

Südosten [zyː·tˈʔɔs·tn̩] *m kein pl, kein indef art* southeast

südöstlich [zyː·tˈʔœst·lɪç] **I.** *adj* **1.** (*im Südosten gelegen*) southeastern **2.** (*von/nach Südosten*) southeastward, southeasterly **II.** *adv* southeast **III.** *präp* +*gen* [to the] southeast of sth

Südpol ['zyː·tpoːl] *m* **der ~** the South Pole

Südsee ['zyː·tˈzeː] *f kein pl* **die ~** the South Seas *pl*, the South Pacific

Südstaaten ['zyː·tˈʃtaː·tn̩] *pl* (*in den USA*) **die ~** the South

Südwesten [zyː·tˈvɛs·tn̩] *m kein pl, kein indef art* southwest

südwestlich [zyː·tˈvɛst·lɪç] **I.** *adj* **1.** (*im*

Südwesten liegend) southwestern **2.** (*von/nach Südwesten*) southwestward **II.** *adv* [to the] southwest **III.** *präp* +*gen* [to the] southwest of sth

suggerieren * [zʊˈɡeˈriːrən] *vt* to suggest

sühnen [ˈzyːnən] *vt* etw ~ to atone for sth

Sultan, Sultanin <-s, -e> [ˈzʊlˈtaːn, ˈzʊlˈtaˈnɪn] *m, f* sultan *masc*, sultana *fem*

Summe <-, -n> [ˈzʊˈmə] *f* **1.** (*Additionsergebnis*) sum, total **2.** (*Betrag*) sum, amount

summen [ˈzʊmən] *vt, vi* to hum; (*Biene*) to buzz

summieren * [zʊˈmiːrən] **I.** *vt* to add up *sep* **II.** *vr* sich *akk* auf etw *akk* ~ to amount [*o* add up] to sth

Sumpf <-[e]s, Sümpfe> [zʊmpf] *m* marsh, swamp; (*Moor*) bog

Sumpffieber *nt* malaria

Sumpfgebiet *nt* marsh[land], swamp[land]

sumpfig [ˈzʊmˈpfɪç] *adj* marshy, swampy

Sünde <-, -n> [ˈzʏnˈdə] *f* sin

Sündenbock *m* scapegoat

Sünder(in) <-s, -> *m(f)* sinner

sündig [ˈzʏnˈdɪç] *adj* **1.** REL sinful **2.** (*lasterhaft*) dissolute

super [ˈzuːˈpɐ] **I.** *adj* super **II.** *adv* super well

Super <-s> [ˈzuːˈpɐ] *nt kein pl* AUTO super, premium

Superlativ <-[e]s, -e> [ˈzuːˈpɐˈlaˈtiːf] *m* superlative

Supermacht *f* superpower

Supermarkt [ˈzuːˈpɐˈmarkt] *m* supermarket

superreich [ˈzuːˈpɐ-] *adj pej* superrich

Suppe <-, -n> [ˈzʊˈpə] *f* soup; **klare ~** consommé, broth ▶ **die ~ auslöffeln müssen** *fam* to have to face the music

Suppenhuhn *nt* boiling chicken

Suppenschüssel *f* soup tureen

Suppenteller *m* soup plate [*o* bowl]

Surfbrett [ˈzœɐf-] *nt* **1.** (*zum Windsurfen*) windsurfer **2.** (*zum Wellensurfen*) surfboard

Surfen <-s> [ˈzœːɐˈfn̩] *nt kein pl* surfing

surfen [ˈzœrˈfn̩] *vi* to surf; **im Internet ~** to surf the Internet

Surfer(in) <-s, -> *m(f)* surfer

surren [ˈzʊˈrən] *vi* (*Insekt*) to buzz; (*Motor*) to hum

suspekt *adj geh* suspicious; **jdm ~ sein** to look suspicious to sb

suspendieren * [zʊsˈpɛnˈdiːrən] *vt* to suspend (**von** +*dat* from)

süß [zyːs] **I.** *adj* sweet **II.** *adv* sweetly

süßen [ˈzyːsn̩] *vt* to sweeten

Süßigkeit <-, -en> [ˈzyːsɪçˈkait] *f meist pl* sweets *pl*, candy

süßlich *adj* sickly sweet

süßsauer [ˈzyːsˈzauˈɐ] *adj* sweet-and-sour

Süßspeise *f* dessert

Süßstoff *m* sweetener

Süßwasser *nt* fresh water

Symbol <-s, -e> [zʏmˈboːl] *nt* symbol

symbolisch [zʏmˈboːˈlɪʃ] **I.** *adj* symbolic **II.** *adv* symbolically

symbolisieren * [zʏmˈboˈliˈziːrən] *vt* to symbolize

symmetrisch [zʏˈmeːˈtrɪʃ] **I.** *adj* symmetrical **II.** *adv* symmetrically

Sympathie <-, -en> [zʏmˈpaˈtiː] *f* sympathy

Sympathisant(in) <-en, -en> [zʏmˈpatiˈzant] *m(f)* sympathizer

sympathisch [zʏmˈpaːˈtɪʃ] *adj* nice, likeable; **sie war mir gleich ~** I liked her right away

Symphonie <-, -en> [zʏmˈfoˈniː] *f* symphony

Symptom <-s, -e> [zʏmpˈtoːm] *nt* symptom (**für** +*akk* of)

Synagoge <-, -n> [zyˈnaˈɡoːˈɡə] *f* synagogue

synchronisieren * [zʏnˈkroˈniˈziːrən] *vt* **1.** FILM, TV to dub **2.** (*zeitlich abstimmen*) to synchronize

synonym [zyˈnoˈnyːm] *adj* synonym

Synonym <-s, -e> [zyˈnoˈnyːm] *nt* synonym

Syntax <-, -en> [ˈzʏnˈtaks] *f* syntax

Synthese <-, -n> [zʏnˈteːˈzə] *f* synthesis

synthetisch [zʏnˈteːˈtɪʃ] **I.** *adj* synthetic **II.** *adv* synthetically

Syphilis <-> [ˈzyːˈfiˈlɪs] *f kein pl* syphilis

System <-s, -e> [zʏsˈteːm] *nt* system; **mit ~** systematically

systematisch [zʏs·te·ma·tɪʃ] **I.** *adj* systematic **II.** *adv* systematically

Systemfehler *m* system error

Szene <-, -n> ['stse:·nə] *f* **1.** THEAT, FILM scene **2.** (*Krach*) scene; **eine ~ machen** to make a scene **3.** *kein pl* (*Milieu*) scene

Szeneladen *m fam* (*Kneipe*) trendy bar; (*Disco oder Club*) trendy club

Szenenwechsel *m* change of scene

T

T, t <-, -> [te:] *nt* T, t; **~ wie Theodor** T as in Tango

t *Abk von* **Tonne**

Tabak <-s, -e> ['ta:·bak, 'ta·bak] *m* tobacco

Tabaksteuer *f* tobacco tax

Tabakwaren *pl* tobacco products *pl*

Tabelle <-, -n> [ta·'bɛ·lə] *f* table; SPORT [league] standings

Tabellenführer(in) *m(f)* SPORT league leader

Tablett <-[e]s, -s> [ta·'blɛt] *nt* tray

Tablette <-, -n> [ta·'blɛ·tə] *f* pill

tabu [ta·'bu:] *adj* taboo

Tachometer *m o nt* speedometer

Tadel <-s, -> ['ta:·dl̩] *m* reprimand

tadellos **I.** *adj* (*einwandfrei*) perfect **II.** *adv* perfectly

tadeln *vt* to reprimand, to reproach

Tafel <-, -n> ['ta:·fl̩] *f* **1.** (*Platte*) board, plaque; SCH [black]board **2.** **eine ~ Schokolade** a bar of chocolate **3.** *geh* (*festlicher Esstisch*) table

Tafelwasser *nt* table water

Tafelwein *m* table wine

Tag <-[e]s, -e> [ta:k] *m* **1.** (*Abschnitt von 24 Stunden*) day; **ein freier ~** a day off; **den ganzen ~** [lang] all day; **guten ~!** hello!, good afternoon/morning!; **~ für ~** every day, day after day; **von einem ~ auf den anderen** overnight; **eines** [schönen] **~es** one [fine] day **2.** (*Datum*) day; **~ der offenen Tür** open house; **der ~ X** D-Day; **bis zum heutigen ~** up to the present day **3.** (*Tageslicht*) light; **am ~** dur-ing the day **4.** *pl fam* (*Menstruation*) period ▶ **es ist noch nicht aller ~e Abend** it's not over yet; **man soll den ~ nicht vor dem Abend loben** *prov* don't count your chickens before they're hatched; **etw kommt an den ~** sth comes to light; **in den ~ hinein leben** to live from day to day; **über/unter ~e** above/below ground

Tagebau *m kein pl* strip mining

Tagebuch *nt* diary

tagelang **I.** *adj* lasting for days; **nach ~em Warten** after days of waiting **II.** *adv* for days

Tagelöhner(in) <-s, -> ['ta:·gə·løː·ne] *m(f) veraltend* day laborer

tagen *vi* to meet; **der Kongress tagt** Congress is in session

Tagesablauf *m* daily routine

Tagesanbruch *m* daybreak

Tagesgeschäft *nt* BÖRSE day order

Tageskarte *f* **1.** (*Speisekarte*) menu of the day **2.** (*Eintrittskarte*) [one-] day pass

Tageslicht *nt kein pl* daylight (**bei** by/in)

Tagesmutter *f* nanny

Tagesordnung *f* agenda; **etw auf die ~ setzen** to put sth on the agenda; **auf der ~ stehen** to be on the agenda ▶ [wie-der] **zur ~ übergehen** to carry on [with business] as usual

Tageszeit *f* time [of day]

Tageszeitung *f* daily [[news]paper]

täglich ['tɛːk·lɪç] *adj, adv* daily

tagsüber ['ta:ks·ʔy:be] *adv* during the day

Tagung <-, -en> *f* **1.** (*Fachtagung*) con-ference **2.** (*Sitzung*) meeting

Taifun <-s, -e> [tai·'fu:n] *m* typhoon

Taille <-, -n> ['tal·jə] *f* waist

Takt <-[e]s, -e> ['takt] *m* **1.** MUS bar **2.** *kein pl* (*Rhythmus*) rhythm; **den ~ angeben** to beat time; **im ~** in time to sth **3.** *kein pl* (*Taktgefühl*) tact

Taktgefühl *nt* **1.** (*Feingefühl*) sense of tact **2.** MUS sense of rhythm

taktieren* [tak·'ti:·rən] *vi* to use tactics

Taktik <-, -en> ['tak·tɪk] *f* tactics *pl*

taktisch ['tak·tɪʃ] **I.** *adj* tactic[al] **II.** *adv* tactically

taktlos adj tactless

Taktlosigkeit <-, -en> f tactlessness; **so eine ~!** what a tactless thing to do!

Taktstock m baton

taktvoll adj tactful

Tal <-[e]s, Täler> [taːl] nt valley

Talar <-s, -e> [taˈlaːɐ̯] m JUR robe; REL cassock; SCH gown

Talent <-[e]s, -e> [taˈlɛnt] nt talent

talentiert [talɛnˈtiːɐ̯t] I. adj talented II. adv in a talented way

Talisman <-s, -e> [ˈtaːlɪsman] m lucky charm

Talkshow ᴿᴿ <-, -s> [ˈtɔːkʃoː] f talk show

Tampon <-s, -s> [ˈtampɔn] m tampon

Tang <-[e]s, -e> [taŋ] m seaweed

Tangente <-, -n> [taŋˈɡɛntə] f MATH tangent

Tango <-s, -s> [ˈtaŋɡo] m tango

Tank <-s, -s> [taŋk] m tank

tanken [ˈtaŋkn̩] I. vi (Auto) to get gas; (Flugzeug) to refuel II. vt 1. (als Tankfüllung) **Benzin ~** to fill up a car with gas 2. fam (in sich aufnehmen) **frische Luft/Sonne ~** to get some fresh air/sun ▶ [ganz schön] **getankt** haben fam to have drunk a fair share

Tanker <-s, -> [ˈtaŋkɐ] m tanker

Tankstelle f gas station

Tankwart(in) m(f) gas station attendant

Tanne <-, -n> [ˈtanə] f fir

Tannenbaum m 1. (Weihnachtsbaum) Christmas tree 2. s. **Tanne**

Tannenzapfen m pinecone

Tante <-, -n> [ˈtantə] f aunt

Tanz <-es, Tänze> [ˈtants] m dance

tanzen [ˈtantsn̩] vt, vi to dance

Tänzer(in) <-s, -> [ˈtɛntsɐ] m(f) dancer

Tanzfläche f dance floor

Tanzmusik f dance music

Tanzschule f dance school

Tapete <-, -n> [taˈpeːtə] f wallpaper

tapezieren * [tapeˈtsiːrən] vt to wallpaper

tapfer [ˈtapfɐ] adj brave

Tapferkeit <-> f kein pl courage

tappen [ˈtapn̩] vi sein **schlaftrunken tappte er zum Telefon** he shuffled drowsily to the phone

Tarantel <-, -n> [taˈrantl̩] f tarantula

Tarif <-[e]s, -e> [taˈriːf] m 1. (Gehaltsvereinbarung) pay scale 2. (Gebühr) charge

Tarifgruppe f wage group

tariflich I. adj negotiated II. adv by negotiation

Tariflohn m standard wage

Tarifverhandlungen pl collective bargaining negotiations pl

Tarifvertrag m collective bargaining agreement

tarnen [ˈtarnən] vt 1. MIL to camouflage (**gegen** +akk against) 2. (Identität wechseln) **sich** akk **~** to disguise oneself

Tarnung <-, -en> f 1. kein pl (das Tarnen) camouflage 2. (tarnende Identität) cover

Tasche <-, -n> [ˈtaʃə] f bag; (in Kleidung) pocket ▶ **jdm auf der ~ liegen** fam to live off [of] sb['s money]; **jdn in die ~ stecken** fam to be head and shoulders above sb

Taschenbuch nt paperback

Taschendieb(in) m(f) pickpocket

Taschengeld nt allowance, spending money

Taschenlampe f [pocket] flashlight

Taschenmesser nt pocketknife

Taschenrechner m pocket calculator

Taschentuch nt handkerchief

Taschenuhr f pocket watch

Tasse <-, -n> [ˈtasə] f cup; **eine ~ Tee** a cup of tea ▶ **nicht alle ~n im Schrank haben** fam to have a screw loose

Tastatur <-, -en> [tastaˈtuːɐ̯] f keyboard

Taste <-, -n> [ˈtastə] f key; (am Telefon) button

tasten [ˈtastn̩] vt, vi to feel (**nach** +dat for)

Tastsinn m kein pl sense of touch

tat [taːt] imp von **tun**

Tat <-, -en> [taːt] f 1. (Handlung) act; **eine gute ~** a good deed; **etw in die ~ umsetzen** to put sth into effect 2. (Straftat) crime; **jdn auf frischer ~ ertappen** to catch sb red-handed fig ▶ **in der ~** indeed

Tatbestand m 1. (Sachlage) facts [of the matter] 2. JUR elements of an offense

tatenlos adj idle; **~ zusehen** to stand back and do nothing

Täter(in) <-s, -> ['tɛː·tɐ] m(f) perpetrator

tätig ['tɛː·tɪç] adj 1. (beschäftigt) employed; **[irgendwo] ~ sein** to work [somewhere] 2. (aktiv) active; **[in etw dat] ~ werden** geh to act [on sth]

Tätigkeit <-, -en> f occupation

Tatkraft f kein pl drive

tatkräftig adj active

Tatort m scene of the crime

tätowieren* [tɛ·to·ˈviː·rən] vt to tattoo

Tätowierung <-, -en> f 1. tattoo 2. kein pl (das Tätowieren) tattooing

Tatsache ['taːt·za·xə] f fact; **~ ist [aber], dass ...** the fact of the matter is [however] that ... ▶ **den ~n ins Auge sehen** to face the facts

tatsächlich [taːt·ˈzɛç·lɪç] I. adj attr actual attr, real II. adv 1. (in Wirklichkeit) actually 2. (in der Tat) really

tätscheln ['tɛːt·ʃln] vt to pat

Tatze <-, -n> ['ta·tsə] f a. pej paw

Tau¹ <-[e]s> ['tau] m kein pl (Wasser) dew

Tau² <-[e]s, -e> ['tau] nt (Seil) rope

taub ['taup] adj 1. (gehörlos) deaf 2. (gefühllos) numb 3. (Nuss) empty

Taube <-, -n> ['tau·bə] f pigeon

Taubheit <-> f kein pl 1. (Gehörlosigkeit) deafness 2. (Gefühllosigkeit) numbness

taubstumm adj deaf and dumb

Taubstumme(r) f(m) deaf-mute

tauchen [tau·xn] I. vi haben o sein to dive (**nach** +dat for) II. vt haben 1. (eintauchen) to dip 2. (untertauchen) to duck

Tauchen <-s> ['tau·xn] nt kein pl diving

Taucher(in) <-s, -> ['tau·xɐ] m(f) (a. orn) diver

Taucheranzug m diving suit

Tauchsieder <-s, -> m immersion heater

tauen ['tau·ən] vi 1. haben es taut it's thawing [o starting to thaw] 2. sein (schmelzen) to melt

Taufbecken nt baptismal font

Taufe <-, -n> ['tau·fə] f REL baptism

taufen ['tau·fn] vt 1. (die Taufe vollziehen) to baptize 2. (in der Taufe benennen) to christen 3. fam (benennen) to christen

Taufpate, -patin m, f godfather masc, godmother fem

taugen ['tau·gn] vi 1. (wert sein) **etwas/viel/nichts ~** to be useful/very useful/useless 2. (geeignet sein) to be suitable (**als/zu/für** for)

tauglich ['tauk·lɪç] adj 1. (geeignet) suitable 2. MIL fit [for military service]

taumeln ['tau·mln] vi sein to stagger

Tausch <-[e]s> ['tauʃ] m kein pl swap, trade; **im ~ gegen [etw akk]** in exchange for [sth]

tauschen ['tau·ʃn] I. vt 1. (einwechseln) to swap [o trade] (**mit** +dat with, **gegen** +akk for) 2. (austauschen) to exchange II. vi to swap [o trade] ▶ **mit niemandem ~ wollen** to not wish to trade places with anyone

täuschen ['tɔy·ʃn] I. vt (irreführen) to deceive; **wenn mich nicht alles täuscht ...** if I'm not completely mistaken ...; **sich akk [von jdm/etw] nicht ~ lassen** to not be fooled [by sb/sth] II. vr (sich irren) **sich akk ~** to be mistaken [o wrong] (**in** +dat about) III. vi to be deceptive

täuschend I. adj (trügerisch) deceptive; (Ähnlichkeit) striking II. adv (trügerisch) deceptively; **sie sieht ihrer Mutter ~ ähnlich** she bears a striking resemblance to her mother

Täuschung <-, -en> ['tɔy·ʃʊŋ] f 1. (Betrug) deception 2. (Irrtum) error; **optische ~** optical illusion

tausend ['tau·znt] adj 1. (Zahl) a [o one] thousand 2. fam (sehr viele) thousands of ...

Tausend¹ <-s, -e o -> ['tau·znt] nt 1. (Einheit von 1000) a [o one] thousand 2. pl, auch kleingeschrieben (viele tausend) thousands pl (**von** +dat of); s. a. Hundert¹ 2

Tausend² <-, -en> ['tauznt] f thousand

Tausendfüßler <-s, -> ['tau·znt·fy:s·lɐ] m centipede

Tausendstel ['tau·znt·stl] nt o schweiz m thousandth

Tauwetter nt thaw

T

Taxi <-s, -s> ['tak·si] *nt* taxi, cab

Taxifahrer(in) *m(f)* taxi [*o* cab] river

Taxistand *m* taxi [*o* cab] stand

Team <-s, -s> [ti:m] *nt* team

Teamarbeit ['ti:m-] *f* teamwork

Technik <-, -en> ['teç·nɪk] *f* 1. *kein pl* (*Technologie*) technology 2. *kein pl* (*technische Ausstattung*) technical equipment 3. (*Methode*) technique 4. österr (*technische Hochschule*) college of technology

Techniker(in) <-s, -> ['teç·nɪ·kɐ] *m(f)* technician

technisch ['teç·nɪʃ] I. *adj* technical II. *adv* technically

Technologie <-, -n> [tɛç·no·lo·'gi:] *f* technology

Tee <-s, -s> [te:] *m* tea; (*Kräutertee*) herbal tea; **eine Tasse ~** a cup of tea; **grüner/schwarzer ~** green/black tea ▶ **abwarten und ~ trinken** *fam* to wait and see

Teebeutel *m* tea bag

Teefilter *m* tea strainer

Teekanne *f* teapot

Teelöffel *m* 1. (*Löffel*) teaspoon 2. (*Menge*) teaspoon[ful]

Teer <-[e]s, -e> [te:ɐ] *m* tar

Teeservice *nt* tea set

Teich <-[e]s, -e> [taiç] *m* pond

Teig <-[e]s, -e> [taik] *m* (*Hefe-, Rühr-, Nudelteig*) dough; (*Mürbe-, Blätterteig*) pastry; (*flüssig*) batter

Teigwaren *pl* pasta + *sing vb*

Teil¹ <-[e]s, -e> [tail] *m* 1. (*Bruchteil*) part; **zum ~** partly; (*gelegentlich*) on occasion; **zum größten ~** for the most part 2. (*Anteil*) share; **zu gleichen ~en** equally 3. (*Bereich: einer Strecke*) stretch; (*eines Gebäudes, einer Zeitung, eines Buches*) section ▶ **sich** *dat* **seinen ~ denken** to draw one's own conclusions

Teil² <-[e]s, -e> [tail] *nt* component

teilbar *adj* MATH divisible (**durch** +*akk* by)

Teilchen <-s, -> *nt* 1. (*Partikel*) particle 2. KOCHK *dial* pastries *pl*

teilen ['tai·lən] I. *vt* 1. (*aufteilen*) to share 2. MATH (*dividieren*) to divide (**durch** +*akk* by) II. *vr* 1. (*sich aufteilen, trennen*) **sich** *akk* **~** *akk* to split up 2. (*gemeinsam benutzen, essen etc.*) **sich** *dat* **etw** [**mit jdm**] **~** to share sth [with sb] III. *vi* (*abgeben*) to share

Teilhaber(in) <-s, -> *m(f)* partner

Teilnahme <-, -en> ['tail·na:·mə] *f* participation (**an** +*dat* in)

teilnahmslos *adj* apathetic

teilnehmen *vi irreg* 1. (*anwesend sein*) [**an etw** *dat*] **~** to attend [sth] 2. (*sich beteiligen*) to take part (**an** +*dat* in)

Teilnehmer(in) <-s, -> *m(f)* 1. (*Anwesender*) person present 2. (*Beteiligter*) participant (**an** +*dat* in) 3. (*Telefoninhaber*) subscriber

teils [tails] *adv* partly; **~, ~** yes and no

Teilung <-, -en> *f* division

teilweise I. *adv* partly II. *adj attr* partial

Teilzeitarbeit *f* part-time work

Teint <-s, -s> ['tɛ̃:] *m* complexion

Telebanking ['te:·lə·bɛŋ·kɪŋ] *nt* home banking

Telefon <-s, -e> ['te:·le·fo:n] *nt* [tele] phone

Telefonat <-[e]s, -e> [te·le·fo·'na:t] *nt* telephone call, phone *fam*

Telefonauskunft *f* directory assistance

Telefonbuch *nt* [tele]phone book

Telefongespräch *nt* [tele]phone call

telefonieren * [te·le·fo·'ni:·rən] *vi* to be on the phone; **mit jdm ~** to talk on the phone with sb

telefonisch I. *adj* [tele]phone II. *adv* by [tele]phone

Telefonkarte *f* calling card

Telefonleitung *f* [tele]phone line

Telefonnummer *f* [tele]phone number

Telefonrechnung *f* [tele]phone bill

Telefonzelle *f* phone booth

telegrafieren * [te·le·gra·'fi:·rən] *vt, vi* to telegraph

Telegramm <-s, -e> [te·le·'gram] *nt* telegram

Telekommunikation *f* telecommunication

Teleobjektiv *nt* telephoto lens

Telepathie <-> [te·le·pa·'ti:] *f kein pl* telepathy

Teleskop <-s, -e> [te·le·'sko:p] *nt* telescope

Teller <-s, -> ['tɛ·lɐ] *m* 1. (*Geschirrteil*) plate; **flacher/tiefer ~** dinner/soup plate 2. (*Menge*) plate[ful]

Tempel <-s, -> ['tɛm·pl̩] *m* temple

Temperament <-[e]s, -e> [tɛm·pə·ra·'mɛnt] *nt* 1. (*Wesensart*) temperament 2. *kein pl* (*Lebhaftigkeit*) vivacity; **~ haben** to be very lively

temperamentvoll I. *adj* lively, vivacious II. *adv* vivaciously

Temperatur <-, -en> [tɛm·pə·ra·'tuːɐ̯] *f* temperature; **seine ~ messen** to take one's temperature; [**erhöhte**] **~ haben** to have a temperature

Tempo <-s, -s> ['tɛm·po] *nt* speed; **mit hohem ~** at high speed

Tempolimit *nt* speed limit

Tendenz <-, -en> [tɛn·'dɛnts] *f* 1. (*Trend*) trend 2. (*Neigung*) tendency (**zu** +*dat*)

tendieren * [tɛn·'diː·rən] *vi* to tend (**zu** +*dat* toward); **dazu ~, etw zu tun** to tend to do sth

Tennis <-> ['tɛ·nɪs] *nt kein pl* tennis

Tennisplatz *m* 1. (*Spielfeld*) tennis court 2. (*Anlage*) outdoor tennis complex

Tennisschläger *m* tennis racket

Tennisspiel *nt* 1. (*Sportart*) tennis 2. (*Einzelspiel*) game of tennis

Tenor <-s, Tenöre> [te·'noːɐ̯] *m* MUS tenor

Teppich <-s, -e> ['tɛ·pɪç] *m* carpet; (*klein*) rug

Teppichboden *m* wall-to-wall carpeting

Termin <-s, -e> [tɛr·'miːn] *m* 1. (*verabredeter Zeitpunkt*) appointment; **einen ~ vereinbaren/verpassen** to set up/miss an appointment; **sich** *dat* **einen ~** [**für etw** *akk*] **geben lassen** to make an appointment [for sth] 2. (*Stichtag*) deadline

Terminal <-s, -s> ['tøːɐ̯·mi·nl̩] *nt* COMPUT, LUFT, TRANSP terminal

Terminkalender *m* [appointment] calendar

Termite <-, -n> [tɛr·'miː·tə] *f* termite

Terpentin <-s, -e> [tɛr·pɛn·'tiːn] *nt o österr m* turpentine; (*Terpentinöl a.*) oil of turpentine

Terrain <-s, -s> [tɛ·'rɛ̃ː] *nt* 1. (*Gelände*) terrain 2. a. *fig* (*[Bau]grundstück*) site

Terrasse <-, -n> [tɛ·'ra·sə] *f* terrace

Territorium <-s, -rien> [tɛ·ri·'toː·rɪ·ʊm] *nt* territory

Terror <-s> ['tɛ·roːɐ̯] *m kein pl* 1. (*terroristische Aktivitäten*) terrorism 2. (*Furcht und Schrecken*) terror 3. *fam* (*Stunk*) huge fuss

Terroranschlag *m* terror[ist] attack

terrorisieren * [tɛ·ro·ri·'ziː·rən] *vt* 1. *fam* (*schikanieren*) to intimidate 2. (*in Angst und Schrecken versetzen*) to terrorize

Terrorismus <-> [tɛ·ro·'rɪs·mʊs] *m kein pl* terrorism

Terrorist(in) <-en, -en> [tɛ·ro·'rɪst] *m(f)* terrorist

terroristisch *adj* terrorist *attr*

Terzett <-[e]s, -e> [tɛr·'tsɛt] *nt* MUS trio

Test <-[e]s, -s> [tɛst] *m* test

Testament <-[e]s, -e> [tɛs·ta·'mɛnt] *nt* 1. JUR will 2. REL **Altes/Neues ~** Old/New Testament

testamentarisch [tɛs·ta·mɛn·'taː·rɪʃ] I. *adj* testamentary II. *adv* in the will

Testamentseröffnung *f* reading of the will

testen ['tɛs·tn̩] *vt* to test (**auf** +*akk* for)

teuer ['tɔy·ɐ] I. *adj* 1. (*viel kostend*) expensive 2. (*geschätzt*) dear II. *adv* (*zu einem hohen Preis*) expensively; **das hast du aber zu ~ eingekauft** you paid too much for that ▶ **etw** *akk* **bezahlen müssen** to pay a high price for sth; **jdn ~ zu stehen kommen** to cost sb dearly

Teuerungsrate *f* rate of price increase

Teufel <-s, -> ['tɔy·fl̩] *m* 1. *kein pl* (*Satan*) **der ~** the Devil 2. (*teuflischer Mensch*) devil ▶ **geh zum ~!** *fam* go to hell!; **soll jdn** [**doch**] **der ~ holen** *fam* to hell with sb; **in ~s Küche kommen** *fam* to get into a hell of a mess; **irgendwo ist der ~ los** *fam* all hell is breaking loose somewhere; **den ~ an die Wand malen** to imagine the worst; **weiß der ~** *fam* who the hell knows

Teufelskreis *m* vicious circle

teuflisch ['tɔy·flɪʃ] I. *adj* diabolical II. *adv* 1. (*diabolisch*) diabolically 2. *fam* (*höllisch*) like hell

Text <-[e]s, -e> [tɛkst] *m* text; (*eines*

T

Lieds) lyrics; *(einer Rede)* script

Texter(in) <-s, -> *m(f)* songwriter; *(in der Werbung)* copywriter

Textilien [tɛksˈtiːli̯ən] *pl* textiles *pl*

Textilindustrie *f* textile industry

Textstelle *f* passage

Textverarbeitungsprogramm *nt* word processing program

Theater <-s, -> [teˈaːtə] *nt* **1.** *(Gebäude)* theater **2.** *kein pl (Schauspielkunst)* theater; **~ spielen** to act **3.** *kein pl fam (Umstände)* fuss; [**ein**] **~ machen** to make a fuss

Theateraufführung *f* theater performance

Theaterbesucher(in) *m(f)* theatergoer

Theaterstück *nt* play

Theke <-, -n> [ˈteːkə] *f* counter; *(in einem Lokal)* bar

Thema <-s, Themen> [ˈteːma] *nt* **1.** *(Gesprächsthema)* topic; **jdn vom ~ abbringen** to get [*o* throw] sb off the subject; **beim ~ bleiben** to stick to the subject; **ein ~ ist [für jdn] erledigt** a matter is closed [as far as sb is concerned] **2.** *(schriftliches Thema)* subject **3.** MUS theme ▶ **ein/kein ~ sein** to be/not be an issue

Thematik <-> [teˈmaːtɪk] *f kein pl* topic

Theologe, Theologin <-n, -n> [teoˈloːɡə] *m, f* theologian

Theologie <-, -n> [teolo-ˈɡiː] *f* theology

theoretisch [teoˈreːtɪʃ] **I.** *adj* theoretical **II.** *adv* theoretically

Theorie <-, -n> [teoˈriː] *f* theory

Therapeut(in) <-en, -en> [tera-ˈpɔyt] *m(f)* therapist

Therapie <-, -n> [teraˈpiː] *f* therapy

therapieren [teraˈpiːrən] *vt* to treat

Thermalquelle [tɛrˈmaːl-] *f* thermal spring

Thermometer <-s, -> [tɛrmoˈmeːtə] *nt* thermometer

Thermometerstand *m* temperature

Thermostat <-[e]s, -e[n]> [tɛrmoˈstaːt] *m* thermostat

These <-, -n> [ˈteːzə] *f geh* thesis

Thrombose <-, -n> [trɔmˈboːzə] *f* thrombosis

Thron <-[e]s, -e> [ˈtroːn] *m* throne

Thronfolge *f* line of succession

Thronfolger(in) <-s, -> *m(f)* heir t the throne

Thunfisch [ˈtuːnfɪʃ] *m* tuna [fish]

Thüringen <-s> [ˈtyːrɪŋən] *nt* Thürin gia

Thüringer(in) <-s, -> [ˈtyːrɪŋe] *m(* Thuringian

thüringisch [ˈtyːrɪŋɪʃ] *adj* Thuringian

Thymian <-s, -e> [ˈtyːmi̯aːn] *m* thyme

ticken [ˈtɪkn̩] *vi* to tick ▶ **nicht richti ~ sl** to be off one's rocker *sl*

tief [ˈtiːf] **I.** *adj* **1.** deep; **ein Meter ~** meter deep **2.** *(niedrig: Temperaturer Tisch)* low; *(Ausschnitt)* low **3.** *(Stim me)* deep **4.** *(intensiv: Bedauern, Schla Schmerz)* deep **5. im ~sten Winter** i the middle of winter **II.** *adv* **1.** *(in di Tiefe)* deep; **er stürzte 300 Meter ~** he fell 300 meters [down] **2.** *(niedrig low;* **~ liegend** low-lying; **~ stehend** *fi* low-level **3.** *(weit eindringend)* deep ~ greifend far-reaching **4.** *(dumpf tö nend)* low; **zu ~ singen** to sing fla **5.** *(intensiv)* deeply; **etw ~ bedauern** to deeply regret sth; **~ schlafen** t sleep soundly

Tief <-[e]s, -s> [ˈtiːf] *nt* **1.** METEO low **2.** *(depressive Phase)* low [point]

Tiefe <-, -n> [ˈtiːfə] *f* depth

Tiefebene *f* lowland plain

Tiefenschärfe *f kein pl* depth of field

Tiefgang *m* NAUT draft ▶ **~ haben** t be profound

tiefgreifend *adj s.* **tief** II 3

Tiefkühlkost *f* frozen food

Tiefkühltruhe *f* freezer chest

Tiefland [ˈtiːflant] *nt* lowlands *pl*

Tiefpunkt *m* low point

tiefsinnig *adj* profound

Tier <-[e]s, -e> [ˈtiːɐ̯] *nt* animal

Tierart *f* animal species + *sing vb*

Tierarzt, -ärztin *m, f* veterinarian, vet *fam*

tierisch [ˈtiːrɪʃ] **I.** *adj* **1.** *(Fett, Produkt* animal *attr* **2.** *fam (gewaltig)* **einer ~en Durst/Hunger haben** to be dyin of thirst/hunger *fig* **II.** *adv fam (hef tig)* like hell; **~ schuften/schwitzen** to work/sweat like hell; **~ wehtun** t hurt like crazy

Tierkreiszeichen nt zodiac sign

tierlieb adj animal-loving attr; ~ **sein** to be an animal lover

Tierquälerei [ti:ɐ̯·kvɛː·lə·ˈraɪ] f cruelty to animals

Tierschutz m protection of animals

Tierschützer(in) m(f) animal welfare activist

Tierversuch m animal testing

Tiger <-s, -> [ˈtiː·ɡe] m tiger

tilgen [ˈtɪlɡn̩] vt FIN (Schulden) to pay off

Tilgung <-, -en> f FIN (von Schulden) repayment

Tinte <-, -n> [ˈtɪn·tə] f ink ▶ **in der ~ sitzen** fam to be in a scrape

Tintenfisch m squid

Tintenstrahldrucker m ink-jet printer

TippRR, **Tip**ALT <-s, -s> [tɪp] m tip; **guter ~** good bet

tippen¹ [ˈtɪpn̩] I. vi 1. (Lotto spielen) to play the lottery 2. fam (raten) to guess; **darauf ~, dass ...** to bet that ... II. vt **eine Zahl ~** to play a number

tippen² [ˈtɪpn̩] I. vi 1. fam (Schreibmaschine schreiben) to type 2. (kurz anstoßen) to tap (**an/auf** +akk on, **gegen** +akk against) II. vt fam to type

Tippfehler m typo

Tirol <-s> [ti·ˈroːl] nt Tyrol

Tiroler(in) <-s, -> [ti·ˈroː·le] m(f) Tyrolean

Tisch <-[e]s, -e> [tɪʃ] m table ▶ **unter den ~ fallen** fam to fall by the wayside; **reinen ~ machen** to sort things out; **vom ~ sein** to be [all] cleared up; **sich** akk [**mit jdm**] **an einen ~ setzen** to come to the table [with sb]; **jdn über den ~ ziehen** fam to pull a fast one on sb

Tischdecke f tablecloth

Tischler(in) <-s -> [ˈtɪʃ·le] m(f) carpenter

Tischlerei <-, -en> [tɪʃ·lə·ˈraɪ] f carpenter's workshop

Tischtennis nt table tennis, ping-pong

Tischtennisplatte f table-tennis [o ping-pong] table

Tischtennisschläger m table-tennis [o ping-pong] paddle

Titel <-s, -> [ˈtiː·tl̩] m 1. (Überschrift) heading 2. (Namenszusatz) [academ-

ic] title 3. (Adelstitel) title 4. MEDIA, SPORT title

Titelbild nt cover [picture]

Titelblatt nt (einer Zeitung) front page; (einer Zeitschrift) cover

Titelverteidiger(in) m(f) title holder

Toast <-[e]s, -e> [toːst] m 1. kein pl (Toastbrot) toast 2. (Scheibe Toastbrot) **ein ~** a slice of toast

Toaster <-s, -> [ˈtoːs·te] m toaster

toben [ˈtoː·bn̩] vi 1. haben (wüten) to be raging (**vor** +dat with) 2. haben (ausgelassen spielen) to romp [around] 3. sein fam (sich ausgelassen fortbewegen) **irgendwohin ~** to romp somewhere

Tobsuchtsanfall m fam fit of rage

Tochter <-, Töchter> [ˈtɔx·te] f 1. (weibliches Kind) daughter 2. s. **Tochtergesellschaft**

Tochtergesellschaft f subsidiary [company]

Tod <-[e]s, -e> [toːt] m death ▶ **jdn/etw auf den ~ nicht ausstehen können** fam to be unable to stand sb/sth; **sich** dat **den ~ holen** fam to catch one's death [of cold]; **sich** akk **zu ~e langweilen** fam to be bored to death

todernst [ˈtoːt·ˈʔɛrnst] I. adj deadly serious II. adv in a deadly serious manner

Todesangst f 1. fam (große Angst) mortal fear; **Todesängste ausstehen** fam to be scared to death 2. (Angst vor dem Sterben) fear of death

Todesanzeige f obituary

Todesfall m death

Todesopfer nt casualty

Todesstrafe f death penalty; **auf etw** akk **steht die ~** sth is punishable by death

Todestag m anniversary of sb's death

Todesursache f cause of death

Todesurteil nt death sentence

todkrank [ˈtoːt·ˈkraŋk] adj terminally ill

tödlich [ˈtøːt·lɪç] I. adj deadly II. adv 1. ~ **verunglücken** to be killed in an accident 2. fam (entsetzlich) **sich** akk ~ **langweilen** to be bored to death

Todsünde f deadly sin

Toilette <-, -n> [tɔa·ˈlɛ·tə] f restroom, bathroom fam; **ich muss mal auf die ~** I need to go to the restroom; **öffentliche ~** public restroom

Toilettenpapier nt toilet paper

tolerant [to·le·'rant] adj tolerant (**gegenüber** +dat toward)

Toleranz <-, -en> [to·le·'rants] f kein pl tolerance (**gegenüber** +dat toward)

tolerieren * [to·le·'ri:·rən] vt to tolerate

toll ['tɔl] I. adj fam (sehr gut) great II. adv fam (sehr gut) very well

Tollpatsch RR <-es, -e> ['tɔl·patʃ] m fam clumsy fool

Tollwut f rabies

Tollpatsch ALT <-es, -e> m s. **Tollpatsch**

Tölpel <-s, -> ['tœl·pl] m fam fool

Tomate <-, -n> [to·'ma:·tə] f tomato
▶ ~n auf den Augen haben fam to be blind; du treulose ~! fam you're a fine friend! iron

Tomatenketchup RR, **Tomatenketchup** nt [tomato] ketchup [o catsup]

Tomatenmark nt tomato paste

Tombola <-, -s> ['tɔm·bo·la] f raffle

Tomographie RR, **Tomografie** RR <-, -n> [to·mo·gra·'fi:] f tomography

Ton¹ <-[e]s, -e> ['to:n] m (Material) clay

Ton² <-[e]s, Töne> ['to:n] m 1. (Laut) sound 2. (Tonfall) tone; **ich verbitte mir diesen ~!** I will not be spoken to like that!; **einen anderen ~ anschlagen** to change one's tune 3. (Farbton) tone ▶ den ~ angeben to set the tone; **große Töne spucken** fam to brag about sth fam; **keinen ~ herausbringen** to not be able to utter a word; **der ~ macht die Musik** prov it's not what you say, but the way you say it

Tonart f MUS key

Tonband nt tape; **etw** akk **auf ~ aufnehmen** to tape sth

tönen ['tø:·nən] vt to tint; (Haare) to color

Tonfall m tone of voice

Tonfilm m sound film

Tonhöhe f pitch

Tonleiter f scale

tonlos adj (Stimme) flat

Tonne <-, -n> ['tɔ·nə] f 1. (Behälter) barrel 2. (Mülltonne) garbage can; **grüne ~** recycling container for paper 3. (Gewichtseinheit) ton 4. fam (fetter Mensch) fatso sl

Tonstörung f sound interference

Tontechniker(in) m(f) sound technician

Tonträger m sound carrier

Tönung <-, -en> f 1. (das Tönen) tinting 2. (Produkt für Haare) hair color 3. (Farbton) shade

Topf <-[e]s, Töpfe> ['tɔpf] m 1. (Kochtopf) pot, sauce pan 2. (Nachttopf) bedpan 3. (für Kleinkinder) potty fam ▶ alles in einen ~ werfen to lump everything together

Töpferei <-, -en> [tœp·fə·'rai] f pottery

Töpferscheibe f potter's wheel

Töpferwaren pl pottery

Topflappen m pot holder

Topfpflanze f potted plant

Tor <-[e]s, -e> ['to:ɐ̯] nt 1. (breite Tür) gate; (Garage) door 2. (Torbau) gateway 3. SPORT goal; **ein ~ schießen** to score a goal; **im ~ stehen** to be the goalkeeper [o goalie]

Torbogen m archway

Torf <-[e]s, -e> ['tɔrf] m peat

töricht ['tœ·rɪçt] I. adj geh foolish II. adv geh foolishly

torkeln ['tɔr·kl̩n] vi sein 1. (taumeln) to reel 2. (irgendwohin taumeln) to stagger

Torlinie f goal line

Tornado <-s, -s> [tɔr·'na:·do] m tornado, twister

Torpedo <-s, -s> [tɔr·'pe:·do] m torpedo

Torschlusspanik RR f fam **~ haben** to be afraid of missing the boat

Torschütze, -schützin m, f scorer

Torte <-, -n> ['tɔr·tə] f torte, cake; (Obstkuchen) tart

Torwart(in) m(f) goalkeeper, goalie

tot ['to:t] adj dead; **sich** akk **~ stellen** to play dead; **~ umfallen** to drop dead

total [to·'ta:l] adj total

totalitär [to·ta·li·'tɛːɐ̯] I. adj totalitarian II. adv in a totalitarian manner

Totalschaden m write-off

Tote(r) ['to:·tə] f(m) dead person; (Todesopfer) fatality

töten ['tø:·tn̩] vt to kill

Totenschein m death certificate

totfahren vt irreg fam to run over [and kill]

Totgeburt f stillbirth

tot|schießen vt irreg fam to shoot dead

Totschlag m kein pl manslaughter

tot|schlagen vt irreg fam to beat to death

Tötung <-, selten -en> f killing; **fahrlässige ~** [involuntary] manslaughter

Toupet <-s, -s> [tuˈpeː] nt toupee

toupieren* [tuˈpiː·rən] vt **sich/jdm die Haare ~** to tease one's/sb's hair

Tour <-, -en> [tuːɐ] f **1.** (Geschäftsfahrt) trip **2.** (Ausflugsfahrt) tour; **eine ~ machen** to go on a tour ▶ **jdm auf die dumme ~ kommen** to try to cheat sb; **in einer ~** fam nonstop; **auf ~en kommen** fam to get into high gear

Tourismus <-> [tuˈrɪs·mʊs] m kein pl tourism

Tourist(in) <-en, -en> [tuˈrɪst] m(f) tourist

Tournee <-, -n> [tʊrˈneː] f tour; **auf ~ gehen** to go on tour

toxisch [ˈtɔk·sɪʃ] adj toxic

Trab <-[e]s> [traːp] m kein pl trot ▶ **jdn auf ~ bringen** fam to make sb get a move on

traben [ˈtraː·bn̩] vi **1.** haben o sein (im Trab laufen o reiten) to trot **2.** sein (sich irgendwohin bewegen) to trot

Tracht <-, -en> [traxt] f **1.** (Volkstracht) traditional attire **2.** (Berufskleidung) uniform ▶ **eine ~ Prügel** fam a walloping

trächtig [ˈtrɛç·tɪç] adj (Tier) pregnant

Tradition <-, -en> [tra·di·ˈtsi̯oːn] f tradition

traditionell [tra·di·tsi̯oˈnɛl] adj meist attr traditional

tragbar adj **1.** (portabel) portable **2.** (akzeptabel) acceptable

träge [ˈtrɛː·gə] **I.** adj **1.** (schwerfällig) lethargic **2.** PHYS, CHEM inert **II.** adv lethargically

tragen <trägt, trug, getragen> [ˈtraː·gn̩] **I.** vt **1.** (schleppen) to carry **2.** (mit sich führen) **etw bei sich dat ~** to carry sth on one; **tragen Sie Waffen bei sich?** do you have any weapons on you? **3.** MODE to wear; **einen Bart ~** to have a beard; **das Haar kurz/lang ~** to have short/long hair **4.** (stützen) to support **5.** AGR, HORT to produce **6.** (für etwas aufkommen) to bear **II.** vi **1.** AGR, HORT to produce **2.** (trächtig sein) to be pregnant **3.** (das Begehen aushalten) to withstand weight **4.** MODE to wear; **sie trägt lieber kurz** she prefers to wear short clothing ▶ **zum T~ kommen** to come into effect **III.** vr **1.** geh **sich** akk **mit dem Gedanken ~, etw zu tun** dat to contemplate the idea of doing sth **2.** FIN **sich** akk **~** to pay for itself

Träger <-s, -> m **1.** meist pl MODE strap **2.** BAU girder

Tragetasche f [tote] bag

Tragfläche f wing

Trägheit <-, selten -en> f **1.** kein pl (Schwerfälligkeit) sluggishness; (Faulheit) laziness **2.** PHYS inertia

Tragik <-> [ˈtraː·gɪk] f kein pl tragedy

tragisch [ˈtraː·gɪʃ] **I.** adj tragic; **es ist nicht [so] ~** fam it's not the end of the world **II.** adv tragically; **nimm's nicht so ~!** fam don't take it to heart!

Tragödie <-, -n> [traˈgøː·di̯ə] f tragedy

Tragweite f scale; (einer Entscheidung, Handlung) consequence

Trainer(in) <-s, -> [ˈtrɛː·nɐ] m(f) coach

Trainer <-s, -> [ˈtrɛː·nɐ] m schweiz tracksuit

trainieren* [trɛˈniː·rən] **I.** vt **1.** (üben) to practice **2.** (auf Wettkämpfe vorbereiten) **jdn ~** to coach sb **II.** vi **1.** (üben) to practice **2.** (sich auf Wettkämpfe vorbereiten) to train

Training <-s, -s> [ˈtrɛː·nɪŋ] nt practice

Trainingsanzug [ˈtrɛː·nɪŋs-] m tracksuit

Trakt <-[e]s, -e> [ˈtrakt] m ARCHIT wing

Traktor <-s, -toren> [ˈtrak·toːɐ] m tractor

Tram <-, -s o o. -s> [ˈtram] f o nt schweiz streetcar

trampen [ˈtrɛmpn̩] vi sein to hitchhike

Trampolin <-s, -e> [ˈtram·po·liːn] nt trampoline

Träne <-, -n> [ˈtrɛː·nə] f tear; **in ~n aufgelöst** in tears; **den ~ nahe sein** to be close to tears; **jdm kommen die ~n** sb is starting to cry

tränken [ˈtrɛŋ·kn̩] vt **1.** (durchnässen) to soak **2.** (Tier) to water

Transfer <-s, -s> [transˈfeːɐ] m transfer

T

Transformator <-s, -en> [trans·fɔr·'maː·toːɐ̯] m transformer

Transistor <-s, -en> [tran·'zɪs·toːɐ̯] m transistor

transitiv ['tran·zi·tiːf] adj LING transitive

Transitverkehr [tran·'zɪt-] m transit traffic

transparent [trans·pa·'rɛnt] adj transparent

Transparent <-[e]s, -e> [trans·pa·'rɛnt] nt banner

Transport <-[e]s, -e> [trans·'pɔrt] m transport

Transporter <-s, -> [trans·'pɔr·te] m (Lieferwagen) van

transportfähig adj transportable

transportieren * [trans·pɔr·'tiː·rən] vt 1. (befördern) to transport; (Person) to move 2. FOTO to wind

Transportmittel nt means of transportation

Transportunternehmen nt trucking company

transsexuell [trans·zɛ·'ksu̯·ɛl] adj transsexual

Transvestit <-en, -en> [trans·vɛs·'tiːt] m transvestite

Trapez <-es, -e> [tra·'peːts] nt 1. MATH trapezoid 2. (Artistenschaukel) trapeze

tratschen ['traː·tʃn̩] vi fam to gossip (**über** +akk about)

Traube <-, -n> ['trau̯·bə] f (Weintraube) grape usu pl

Traubensaft m grape juice

Traubenzucker m glucose

trauen[1] ['trau̯·ən] vt to join in marriage; **sich ~ lassen** to marry

trauen[2] ['trau̯·ən] I. vi (vertrauen) to trust II. vr **sich** akk ~, **etw** akk **zu tun** to dare to do sth

Trauer <-> ['trau̯·ɐ] f kein pl grief

Trauerfall m bereavement

Trauerkleidung f mourning attire [o dress]

trauern ['trau̯·ɐn] vi to mourn (**um** +akk for)

Traum <-[e]s, Träume> ['traum] m dream; **es war immer mein ~, mal so eine Luxuslimousine zu fahren** I've always dreamed of driving a luxury

car like this ▶ **aus der ~!** so much for that!; **etw fällt jdm im ~ nicht ein** sb wouldn't dream of it

Trauma <-s, Traumen> ['trau̯·ma] nt trauma

traumatisch [trau̯·'maː·tɪʃ] adj traumatic

träumen ['trɔy̯·mən] vt, vi to dream (**von** +dat about); **schlecht ~** to have bad dreams

Träumer(in) <-s, -> ['trɔy̯·mɐ] m(f) [day]dreamer

traurig ['trau̯·rɪç] I. adj sad; [**es ist**] **~, dass ...** it's unfortunate that ..., unfortunately ... II. adv sadly ▶ **mit etw** dat **sieht es ~ aus** sth doesn't look too good

Traurigkeit <-> f kein pl sadness

Trauring m wedding ring [o band]

Trauung <-, -en> ['trau̯·ʊŋ] f marriage [o wedding] ceremony

Trauzeuge, -zeugin m, f best man, witness to a marriage

Treff <-s, -s> [trɛf] m fam 1. (Treffen) get-together 2. (Treffpunkt) meeting point

treffen <trifft, traf, getroffen> ['trɛ·fn̩] I. vt **haben** 1. (zusammenkommen) to meet 2. (antreffen) to find; **ich habe ihn zufällig in der Stadt getroffen** I bumped into him in town 3. (mit einem Wurf, Schlag etc.) to hit 4. (Abmachung, Entscheidung) to make; (Maßnahmen, Vorkehrungen) to take 5. (wählen) **den richtigen Ton ~** to strike the right chord; **auf dem Foto bis du wirklich gut getroffen** that's a really good picture of you; **du hättest es auch schlechter ~ können** it could have been worse 6. (kränken) to hurt II. vi 1. sein (antreffen) **auf jdn ~** to meet sb 2. haben (ins Ziel) to hit 3. haben (verletzen) to hurt III. vr haben **sich** akk [**mit jdm**] **~** to meet [sb]; **das trifft sich [gut]** that works out [great]

Treffen <-s, -> [trɛ·fn̩] nt meeting

treffend adj appropriate

Treffer <-s, -> m 1. (aufs Ziel) hit 2. (Tor) goal 3. (Gewinnlos) winner

Treffpunkt m meeting point

treiben <trieb, getrieben> ['trai̯·bn̩] I. vt

haben 1. (*drängen*) to drive; **jdn in den Wahnsinn ~** to drive sb mad **2.** (*fortbewegen*) **jdn/etw** [*irgendwohin*] **~** (*durch Wasser*) to wash sb/sth [somewhere]; (*durch Wind*) to blow sb/sth [somewhere] **3.** (*Nagel*) to drive (**in** +*akk* into) **4.** bot to sprout **5.** *fam* (*anstellen*) **etw ~** to be up to sth; **dass ihr mir bloß keinen Blödsinn treibt!** don't you [guys] try to pull any nonsense now!; **es zu bunt/wild ~** to go too far **6.** (*betreiben: Gewerbe*) to carry out; (*Handel*) to trade **7.** *sl* (*Sex haben*) **es** [**mit jdm**] **~** to do it [with sb] **II.** *vi* **1.** *sein* (*sich fortbewegen*) to drift; **sich** *akk* [**von etw** *dat*] **~ lassen** to let oneself be carried along [by sth] **2.** *haben* bot to sprout **3.** *haben* kochk to rise **4.** *haben* (*diuretisch wirken*) to have a diuretic effect ▶ **sich** *akk* **~ lassen** to drift

Treiben <-s> ['trai·bn̩] *nt kein pl* **1.** *pej* (*üble Aktivität*) dirty tricks **2.** (*geschäftige Aktivität*) hustle and bustle

Treibhaus *nt* greenhouse

Treibhauseffekt *m kein pl* **der ~** the greenhouse effect

Treibstoff *m* fuel

Trend <-s, -s> ['trɛnt] *m* trend; **voll im ~ liegen** to be very popular at the moment

trennen ['trɛ·nən] **I.** *vt* **1.** (*abtrennen*) **etw von etw** *dat* **~** to cut sth off sth **2.** (*auseinanderbringen, teilen*) to separate (**von** +*dat* from) **3.** ling (*Wort*) to divide **II.** *vr* **sich** *akk* **~ 1.** (*getrennt weitergehen*) to part company **2.** (*die Beziehung lösen*) to split up (**von** +*dat* with) **3.** (*wegwerfen*) to part (**von** +*dat* with) **III.** *vi* to differentiate (**zwischen** +*dat* between)

Trennung <-, -en> *f* **1.** (*Scheidung*) separation; **in ~ leben** to be separated **2.** (*Unterscheidung*) distinction **3.** ling division

Trennungsstrich *m* hyphen

Trennwand *f* partition [wall]

Treppe <-, -n> ['trɛ·pə] *f* stairs *pl*

Treppengeländer *nt* handrail

Treppenhaus *nt* stairwell

Treppenstufe *f* step

Tresen <-s, -> ['treː·zn̩] *m* **1.** (*Theke*) bar

2. (*Ladentisch*) counter

Tresor <-s, -e> [tre·'zoːɐ̯] *m* **1.** (*Safe*) safe **2.** (*Tresorraum*) strong room

treten <tritt, trat, getreten> ['treː·tn̩] **I.** *vt haben* to kick **II.** *vi* **1.** *haben* (*mit dem Fuß*) to kick **2.** *sein* (*einen Schritt machen*) to step; **~ Sie bitte zur Seite** please step aside; **pass auf, wohin du trittst** watch where you step [*o* your step] **3.** *sein o haben* (*den Fuß setzen*) to tread (**auf** +*akk* on) **4.** *sein o haben* (*betätigen*) to step (**auf** +*akk* on); **auf die Bremse ~** to put on the brakes

treu ['trɔy] **I.** *adj* **1.** (*loyal*) loyal; **sich** *dat* **selbst ~ bleiben** to remain true to oneself **2.** (*verlässlich*) loyal **3.** (*keinen Seitensprung machend*) faithful **II.** *adv* **1.** (*loyal*) loyally **2.** (*treuherzig*) trustingly

Treue <-> ['trɔyə] *f kein pl* **1.** (*Loyalität, Verlässlichkeit*) loyalty **2.** (*monogames Verhalten*) fidelity

treulos *adj* unfaithful

Tribüne <-, -n> [tri·'byː·nə] *f* stand

Trichter <-s, -> ['trɪç·tɐ] *m* **1.** (*Einfülltrichter*) funnel **2.** (*Explosionskrater*) crater

Trick <-s, -s> ['trɪk] *m* trick

Trickbetrüger(in) *m(f)* con artist [*o* man]

Trickfilm *m* cartoon [*o* animated] movie

trieb ['triːp] *imp von* **treiben**

Trieb¹ <-[e]s, -e> ['triːp] *m* bot shoot

Trieb² <-[e]s, -e> ['triːp] *m* psych [sex] drive

Triebwerk *nt* engine

triefen <triefte *o geh* troff, getrieft> ['triː·fn̩] *vi* to run; (*Auge*) to water; **aus etw** *dat* **~** to pour from [*o* out of] sth; **vor Nässe ~** to be dripping wet

triftig ['trɪf·tɪç] **I.** *adj* good; (*Argument, Grund*) convincing **II.** *adv* convincingly

Trikot¹ <-s> [tri·'koː, 'trɪ·ko] *m o nt kein pl* (*dehnbares Gewebe*) tricot

Trikot² <-s, -s> [tri·'koː, 'trɪ·ko] *nt* mode, sport jersey

Trillerpfeife ['trɪ·lɐ·] *f* whistle

trinkbar *adj* drinkable

trinken <trank, getrunken> ['trɪŋ·kn̩] **I.** *vt* to drink; **möchten Sie lieber Kaffee oder Tee ~?** would you prefer cof-

fee or tea [to drink]?; **etwas zu ~** something to drink; **jdm mit jdm] einen ~ gehen** *fam* to go for a drink [with sb] **II.** *vi* **auf jdn/etw ~** to drink to sb/sth

Trinker(in) <-s, -> *m(f)* drunk[ard]

Trinkgeld *nt* tip; **~ geben** to give a tip

Trinkspruch *m* toast

Trinkwasser *nt* drinking water

Trinkwasseraufbereitung *f* drinking water purification

tritt [trɪt] *3. pers sing pres von* **treten**

Tritt <-[e]s, -e> [trɪt] *m* **1.** (*Fußtritt*) kick **2.** (*Schritt*) step

Triumph <-[e]s, -e> [tri-'ʊmf] *m* triumph

Triumphbogen *m* triumphal arch

triumphieren * [tri-ʊm-'fiː-rən] *vi* **1.** (*frohlocken*) to rejoice **2.** (*erfolgreich sein*) to triumph (**über** +*akk* over)

triumphierend I. *adj* triumphant **II.** *adv* triumphantly

trocken ['trɔ-kn̩] **I.** *adj* dry; (*Buch*) dull; **im T~en** out of the rain; **~er Wein** dry wine ▶ **auf dem T~en sitzen** *fam* to be broke **II.** *adv* **etw ~ aufbewahren** to keep sth in a dry place; **sich** *akk* **~ rasieren** to use an electric razor, to dry shave

Trockenheit <-, *selten* -en> *f* **1.** (*Dürreperiode*) drought **2.** (*trockene Beschaffenheit: a. eines Gebietes*) dryness

trocken|legen *vt* **1.** (*windeln*) **ein Baby ~** to change a baby['s diaper] **2.** (*entwässern*) to drain

Trockenzeit *f* dry season

trocknen ['trɔk-nən] **I.** *vi sein* to dry **II.** *vt haben* to dry

trödeln ['trøː-dl̩n] *vi* **1.** *haben* (*langsam sein*) to dilly-dally **2.** *sein* (*langsam schlendern*) to [take a] stroll

Trödler(in) <-s, -> ['trøːd-lɐ] *m(f)* **1.** (*Altwarenhändler*) second-hand dealer **2.** *fam* (*trödelnder Mensch*) dilly-dallier

Trommel <-, -n> ['trɔ-ml̩] *f* drum

Trommelfell *nt* eardrum

trommeln ['trɔ-ml̩n] *vi* to drum

Trompete <-, -n> [trɔm-'peː-tə] *f* trumpet

Trompeter(in) <-s, -> *m(f)* trumpeter

Tropen ['troː-pn̩] *pl* **die ~** the tropics *pl*

Tropenkrankheit *f* tropical disease

Tropf <-[e]s, -e> ['trɔpf] *m* MED drip

tropfen ['trɔp-fn̩] *vi* **1.** *haben* to drip; (*Nase*) to run **2.** *sein* **aus etw** *dat* [*irgendwohin*] **~** to drip from sth [somewhere]

Tropfen <-s, -> ['trɔp-fn̩] *m* **1.** (*kleine Menge Flüssigkeit*) drop **2.** *pl* PHARM, MED **drops** *pl* ▶ **ein ~ auf den heißen Stein** *fam* just a drop in the ocean

Tropfsteinhöhle *f* cave with stalactites and stalagmites

Trophäe <-, -n> [tro-'fɛː-ə] *f* trophy

tropisch ['troː-prɪʃ] *adj* tropical

Trost <-[e]s> ['troːst] *m kein pl* **1.** (*Linderung*) consolation; **das ist ein schöner ~** *iron* some comfort that is; **ein schwacher ~ sein** to be of little consolation **2.** (*Zuspruch*) words of comfort; **jdm ~ spenden** to comfort sb ▶ **nicht [ganz] bei ~ sein** *fam* to have taken leave of one's senses

trösten ['trøːs-tn̩] **I.** *vt* to comfort; **etw tröstet jdn** sth is of consolation to sb **II.** *vr* **sich** *akk* [**mit jdm**] **~** to find consolation [with sb]; **sich** *akk* [**mit etw** *dat*] **~** to console oneself [with sth]

tröstlich *adj* comforting

trostlos *adj* **1.** (*deprimierend*) miserable **2.** (*öde und hässlich*) desolate; (*Landschaft*) bleak

Trostpreis *m* consolation prize

Trott <-[e]s> ['trɔt] *m kein pl* routine

Trottel <-s, -> ['trɔ-tl̩] *m fam* bonehead *sl*

trotten ['trɔ-tn̩] *vi sein* to trudge [along]

trotz ['trɔts] *präp* +*gen* despite

Trotz <-es> ['trɔts] *m kein pl* defiance; **aus ~** [**gegen jdn/etw**] out of spite [for sb/sth]; **jdm/etw zum ~** in defiance of sb/sth

Trotzalter *nt* difficult age, the terrible twos

trotzdem ['trɔts-deːm] *adv* nevertheless; (*aber*) still

trotzen ['trɔ-tsn̩] *vi* **jdm/etw ~** to defy sb/sth

trotzig ['trɔ-tsɪç] *adj* defiant

trübe ['tryː-bə] *adj* **1.** (*unklar*) murky; (*Saft, Urin*) cloudy; (*Glas, Spiegel*) dull **2.** (*matt*) dim **3.** (*Himmel*) dull **4.** (*deprimierend*) bleak; (*Stimmung*) gloomy

▶ **mit etw** *dat* **sieht es ~ aus** the prospects [for sth] are [looking] bleak

Trubel <-s> ['truː·bl̩] *m kein pl* hustle and bustle

trüben ['tryː·bn̩] **I.** *vt* **etw ~ 1.** (*unklar machen*) to make sth murky [o cloudy] **2.** (*beeinträchtigen*) to cast a cloud over sth; (*Beziehungen, ein Verhältnis*) to strain **II.** *vr* **sich** *akk* **~** to become murky

trübselig *adj* **1.** (*betrübt*) miserable; (*Miene*) gloomy **2.** (*trostlos*) bleak

Trübung <-, -en> *f* **1.** (*von Wasser etc.*) clouding **2.** (*von Beziehungen*) straining

Trüffel <-, -n> ['trʏfl̩] *f* (*Pilz, Praline*) truffle

trügen <trog, getrogen> ['tryː·gn̩] **I.** *vt* **wenn mich nicht alles trügt** unless I'm very much mistaken **II.** *vi* to be deceptive

Truhe <-, -n> ['truː·ə] *f* chest

Trümmer ['trʏ·mɐ] *pl* rubble; (*eines Flugzeugs*) wreckage; **in ~n liegen** to lie in ruins *pl*

Trumpf <-[e]s, Trümpfe> ['trʊmpf] *m* **1.** KARTEN trump [card]; **~ sein** to be trumps **2.** *fig* (*entscheidender Vorteil*) trump card; **noch einen ~ in der Hand haben** to have another ace up one's sleeve

Trunkenheit <-> *f kein pl* drunkenness; **~ am Steuer** drunk driving

Truppe <-, -n> ['trʊ·pə] *f* **1.** MIL troop; **Rückzug der ~n** troop withdrawal **2.** THEAT company

Truthahn ['truːt·haːn] *m* turkey

Tschad <-s> ['tʃat] *nt* Chad; *s. a.* **Deutschland**

Tscheche, Tschechin <-n, -n> ['tʃɛ·çə] *m, f* Czech; *s. a.* **Deutsche(r)**

tschechisch ['tʃɛ·çɪʃ] *adj* Czech; *s. a.* **deutsch**

Tschechische Republik *f* Czech Republic; *s. a.* **Deutschland**

T-Shirt <-s, -s> ['tiː·ʃøːɐ̯t] *nt* T-shirt

Tube <-, -n> ['tuː·bə] *f* tube ▶ **auf die ~ drücken** *fam* to step on it

Tuberkulose <-, -n> [tu·bɛr·ku·'loː·zə] *f* tuberculosis

Tuch <-[e]s, Tücher> ['tuːx] *nt* **1.** (*Kopftuch*) [head]scarf; (*Halstuch*) scarf **2.** (*dünne Decke*) cloth

tüchtig ['tʏç·tɪç] **I.** *adj* **1.** (*fähig*) capable; (*fleißig*) hard-working **2.** *fam* (*groß*) big **II.** *adv fam* **~ essen** to eat heartily; **~ regnen/schneien** to rain/snow hard

Tücke <-, -n> ['tʏkə] *f* **1.** *kein pl* (*Heimtücke*) malice **2.** (*Unwägbarkeiten*) **~n** *pl* vagaries *pl*; **~ sein** to be temperamental ▶ **das ist die ~ des Objekts** these things have a will of their own!

tückisch ['tʏ·kɪʃ] *adj* **1.** (*hinterhältig*) malicious **2.** (*Krankheit*) pernicious **3.** (*gefährlich*) treacherous

tüfteln ['tyf·tl̩n] *vi fam* to fiddle around (**an** +*dat* with)

Tugend <-, -en> ['tuː·gn̩t] *f* virtue

Tulpe <-, -n> ['tʊl·pə] *f* tulip

tummeln ['tʊ·ml̩n] *vr* **sich** *akk* **~** to romp [around]

Tumor <-s, -en> ['tuː·moːɐ̯] *m* tumor

Tumult <-[e]s, -e> [tu·'mʊlt] *m* **1.** *kein pl* (*lärmendes Durcheinander*) commotion **2.** *meist pl* (*Aufruhr*) disturbance

tun <tat, getan> ['tuːn] **I.** *vt* **1.** + *unbestimmtem Objekt* (*machen*) to do; **was sollen wir bloß ~?** what the heck should we do?; **was tut er nur den ganzen Tag?** what does he do all day?; **so etwas tut man nicht!** you just don't do [things like] that!; **noch viel ~ müssen** to still have a lot to do; **etw aus Liebe ~** to do sth out of love; **~ und lassen können, was man will** to do as one pleases; **~, was man nicht lassen kann** to do sth if one has to **2.** (*unternehmen*) **etwas/nichts/einiges für jdn ~** to do something/nothing/a lot for sb; **was tut man nicht alles für seine Kinder!** the things we do for our children!; **was kann ich für Sie ~?** ÖKON (*o may*) I help you?; **etw gegen etw** *akk* **~** (*gegen Belästigungen, Pickel, Unrecht etc.*) to do sth about sth; **ich will sehen, was ich da ~ lässt** I'll see what I can do [about it] [*o* do what I can] **3.** *fam* (*legen o stecken*) **etw irgendwohin ~** to put sth somewhere **4.** *fam* (*funktionieren*)

tut es dein altes Tonbandgerät eigentlich noch? [by the way,] is your old tape recorder still working? **5.** *fam* (*ausmachen*) **das tut nichts** it doesn't matter, no problem **6.** *fam* (*genug sein*) **für heute tut's das** that'll do for today **7.** *sl* (*Sex haben*) **es [mit jdm]** ~ to do it [with sb] **II.** *vr impers* **etwas/nichts/einiges tut sich** something/nothing/a lot is happening **III.** *vi* **1.** (*sich benehmen*) to act; **er ist doch gar nicht wütend, er tut nur so[, als ob]** he's not angry at all; he's just pretending [to be] **2.** (*Dinge erledigen*) **zu** ~ **haben** to be busy ▶ **es mit jdm zu** ~ **bekommen** *fam* to get into trouble with sb; **es mit jdm zu** ~ **haben** to be dealing with sb; **etwas/nichts mit jdm/etw zu** ~ **haben** to have something/nothing to do with sb/sth **IV.** *aux vb modal* **1.** + *vorgestelltem Infinitiv* *fam* **singen tut sie ja gut** she sure is a good singer **2.** + *nachgestelltem Infinitiv* *dial* **ich tu nur schnell den Braten anbraten** I'll just quickly sear the roast **3.** *konjunktivisch,* + *vorgestelltem Infinitiv* *dial* **er täte zu gerne wissen, warum ...** he would love to know why ...

Tunesien <-s> [tu·'neː·ziən] *nt* Tunisia; *s. a.* **Deutschland**

Tunesier(in) <-s, -> [tu·'neː·zie] *m(f)* Tunisian; *s. a.* **Deutsche(r)**

tunesisch [tu·'neː·zɪʃ] *adj* Tunisian; *s. a.* **deutsch**

Tunfisch [RR] *m s.* **Thunfisch**

Tunnel <-s, -> ['tʊnl] *m* tunnel; (*für Fußgänger*) pedestrian underpass

Tür <-, -en> ['tyːɐ] *f* door; **an die** ~ **gehen** to get the door ▶ **zwischen** ~ **und Angel** *fam* in passing; **jdm** [fast] **die** ~ **einrennen** *fam* to pester sb constantly; **mit der** ~ **ins Haus fallen** *fam* to blurt it [right] out; [bei jdm] [mit etw dat] **offene** ~**en einrennen** to be preaching to the choir [with sth]; **jdn vor die** ~ **setzen** *fam* to kick sb out; **vor der** ~ **sein** (*ganz in der Nähe*) to be just around the corner

turbulent [tʊr·bu·'lɛnt] **I.** *adj* turbulent **II.** *adv* turbulently; ~ **verlaufen** to be turbulent

Türgriff *m* door handle, doorknob

Türke(in) <-n, -n> ['tyr·kə] *m(f)* Turk ; *s. a.* **Deutsche(r)**

Türkei <-> [tyr·'kai] *f* **die** ~ Turkey; *s. a.* **Deutschland**

türkis [tyr·'kiːs] *adj* turquoise

türkisch ['tyr·kɪʃ] *adj* Turkish; *s. a.* **deutsch**

Turm <-[e]s, Türme> ['tʊrm] *m* **1.** ARCHIT tower; (*spitzer Kirchturm*) spire, steeple **2.** SPORT (*Sprungturm*) diving platform **3.** (*Schachfigur*) castle

türmen[1] ['tyr·mən] *vt, vr* (**sich** *akk*) ~ *da* to pile up *sep*

türmen[2] ['tyr·mən] *vi sein fam* **aus dem Knast** ~ to break out of jail

Turmspringen *nt kein pl* high diving

turnen ['tʊr·nən] *vi haben* **1.** SPORT to do gymnastics **2.** *sein fam* (*sich flink bewegen*) to dash

Turnen <-s> ['tʊr·nən] *nt kein pl* **1.** SPORT gymnastics + *sing vb* **2.** SCH physical education, PE

Turner(in) <-s, -> ['tʊr·ne] *m(f)* gymnast

Turnhalle *f* gymnasium, gym *fam*

Turnier <-s, -e> [tʊr·'niːɐ] *nt* HIST, SPORT (*längerer Wettbewerb*) tournament; (*der Springreiter*) show jumping competition

Turnschuh *m* tennis shoe

Turnübung *f* gymnastics exercise

Türöffner *m* automatic door opener

Türschild *nt* nameplate

Tusche <-, -n> ['tʊ·ʃə] *f* Indian ink

tuscheln ['tʊ·ʃln] *vi* [**über jdn/etw**] ~ to gossip secretly [about sb/sth]

Tüte <-, -n> ['tyː·tə] *f* bag; **eine** ~ **Popcorn** a bag of popcorn; **Suppe aus der** ~ **instant soup** ▶ [**das**] **kommt nicht in die** ~! *fam* no way!

TÜV <-s, -s> [tʏf] *m Akr von* **Technischer Überwachungsverein** Technical Inspection Association (*performs vehicle inspections*); **jds/der** ~ **läuft ab** sb's/the annual car inspection needs to be renewed; **durch den** ~ **kommen** to get [a vehicle] through its inspection

TV <-[s], -s> [teː·'faʊ, a. tiː·'viː] *nt Abk von* **Television** TV

Typ <-s, -en> ['tyːp] *m* **1.** (*Ausführung*)

model **2.** (*Art Mensch*) type [of person] *fam*; **was ist er für ein ~, dein neuer Chef?** what type of person is your new boss?; **der ~ ... sein, der ...** to be the type of ... who ...; **dein ~ ist nicht gefragt** *fam* we don't want your type [around] here **3.** *sl* (*Kerl, Freund*) guy **4.** *fam* (*merkwürdiger Mensch*) character; **was ist denn das für ein ~?** what a weirdo!

typisch ['ty:·pɪʃ] **I.** *adj* typical (**für** +*akk* for); [**das ist**] **~!** *fam* [that's] [just] typical! **II.** *adv* **~ jd** [that's] typical of sb; **~ Frau/ Mann!** typical woman/man!; **~ amerikanisch/deutsch** typically American/ German

Tyrann(in) <-en, -en> [ty·'ran] *m(f)* tyrant

tyrannisch [ty·'ra·nɪʃ] **I.** *adj* tyrannical **II.** *adv* tyrannically

tyrannisieren * [ty·ra·ni·'zi:·rən] *vt* to tyrannize; **sich** *akk* [**von jdm/etw**] **~ lassen** to [allow oneself to] be tyrannized [by sb/sth]

U

U, u <-, -> [u:] *nt* U, u; **~ wie Ulrich** U as in Uniform

u. *konj Abk von* **und**

U-Bahn [u:-] *f* subway

übel ['y:bl̩] **I.** *adj* **1.** (*schlimm*) bad, nasty; (*Affäre*) ugly **2.** (*unangenehm*) nasty **3.** (*verkommen*) rotten; (*Stadtviertel*) bad **4.** (*schlecht*) **jdm ist/wird ~** sb feels nauseous **II.** *adv* **1.** (*unangenehm*) **was riecht hier so ~?** what's that awful smell [[in] here]? **2.** (*schlecht*) badly; **nicht ~** not that bad [at all]; **jdn ~ behandeln** to treat sb badly

Übel <-s, -> ['y:bl̩] *nt* evil ▶ **das kleinere ~** the lesser evil; **ein notwendiges ~** a necessary evil

Übelkeit <-, -en> *f* nausea

Übeltäter(in) *m(f)* wrongdoer

üben ['y:bn̩] **I.** *vt, vi* to practice **II.** *vr* **sich** *akk* **in etw** *dat* **~** to practice sth

über ['y:bɐ] **I.** *präp* **1.** +*dat* (*oberhalb von*) above **2.** +*akk* (*quer hinüber*) over **3.** +*akk* (*höher als*) above, over **4.** +*akk* (*etw erfassend*) over; **ein Überblick ~ etw** an overview of sth **5.** +*akk* (*quer darüber*) over; **er strich ihr ~ das Haar/die Wange** he stroked her hair/ cheek **6.** +*akk* (*jdn/etw betreffend*) about **7.** +*dat* (*zahlenmäßig größer als*) above **8.** (*durch jdn/etw*) through **9.** (*via*) via **10.** (*während*) over; **habt ihr ~ die Feiertage/das Wochenende schon was vor?** do you have anything planned for the holiday/weekend? ▶ **~ alles** more than anything **II.** *adv* **1.** (*älter als*) over **2.** (*mehr als*) more than ▶ **~ und ~** completely **III.** *adj fam* (*übrig*) **~ sein** to be left [over]; (*Essen*) to be left [over]

überall [y:bɐ·'ʔal] *adv* **1.** (*an allen Orten*) everywhere; (*an jeder Stelle*) all over [the place]; **~ wo** wherever **2.** (*wer weiß wo*) anywhere **3.** (*in allen Dingen*) everything; **er kennt sich ~ aus** he knows something about everything **4.** (*bei jedermann*) everyone; **er ist ~ beliebt** everyone likes him

überanstrengen * [y:bɐ·'ʔan·ʃtrɛŋ·ən] **I.** *vt* **etw ~** to put too great a strain on sth **II.** *vr* **sich** *akk* **~** to overexert oneself

überarbeiten * [y:bɐ·'ʔar·bai·tn̩] **I.** *vt* to revise **II.** *vr* **sich** *akk* **~** to overwork oneself

überaus ['y:bɐ·ʔaus] *adv* extremely

überbacken * [y:bɐ·'ba·kn̩] *vt irreg* **etw mit Käse ~** to top sth with cheese and bake it

überbelasten * *vt* to overload

überbelichten * *vt* to overexpose

überbewerten * *vt* **du überbewertest diese Äußerung** you're placing too much importance on this comment

überbieten * [y:bɐ·'bi:·tn̩] *vt irreg* **1.** SPORT to better (**um** +*akk* by); (*Rekord*) to break **2.** (*durch höheres Gebot*) to outbid (**um** +*akk* by)

Überbleibsel <-s, -> ['y:bɐ·blaip·sl̩] *nt fam* **1.** (*Relikt*) relic **2.** (*Rest*) remnant

Überblick ['y:bɐ·blɪk] *m* view (**über** +*akk* of); **den ~ [über etw** *akk*] **verlieren** to lose track [of sth]

U

überblicken * [y:bɐ·ˈblɪ·kn̩] vt 1. (Sicht haben) to look out over 2. (erfassen: Lage, Situation etc.) to have an overview of

überbringen * [y:bɐ·ˈbrɪ·ŋən] vt irreg to deliver

überbrücken * [y:bɐ·ˈbrʏ·kn̩] vt to bridge

überdenken * [y:bɐ·ˈdɛŋ·kn̩] vt irreg to think over sep

Überdosis f overdose (**an** +dat of)

Überdruck m excess pressure

Überdruss RR <-es-, **Überdruß** ALT <-sses> [ˈy:bɐ·drʊs] m kein pl aversion; **bis zum ~** ad nauseam

überdrüssig [ˈy:bɐ·drʏ·sɪç] adj jds/einer S. gen ~ **sein/werden** to be/grow tired of sb/sth

überdurchschnittlich I. adj above-average attr, above average pred II. adv above average

übereinander [y:bɐ·ˈʔai·ˈnan·dɐ] adv 1. (eins über dem anderen/das andere) on top of each other 2. (über sich) about each other

übereinander|schlagen vt irreg **die Beine ~** to cross one's legs

überein|kommen [y:bɐ·ˈʔain·kɔ·mən] vi irreg sein to agree

überein|stimmen [y:bɐ·ˈʔain·ʃtɪ·mən] vi 1. (der gleichen Meinung sein) to agree (**in** +dat on) 2. (sich gleichen) [**mit etw dat**] ~ to match [sth]

Übereinstimmung f agreement (**in** +dat on)

überempfindlich adj oversensitive; MED hypersensitive (**gegen** +akk to)

überfahren * [y:bɐ·ˈfa:·rən] vt irreg 1. (niederfahren) to run over sep 2. (nicht beachten) **eine rote Ampel ~** to run a red light 3. fam (übertölpeln) **jdn ~** to railroad sb

Überfall m attack; (Raubüberfall) robbery

überfallen * [y:bɐ·ˈfal·ən] vt irreg 1. (angreifen) to mug; (Bank) to rob; (Land) to attack; MIL to raid 2. (überraschend besuchen) **jdn ~** to descend [up]on sb 3. (bestürmen) to bombard (**mit** +dat with)

überfliegen * [y:bɐ·ˈfli:·gn̩] vt irreg 1. LUFT to fly over 2. (flüchtig ansehen) to take a quick look at; (Text a.) to skim through

Überfluss RR m kein pl abundance; **im ~ vorhanden sein** to be in plentiful supply; **etw im ~ haben** to have plenty of sth ▶ **zu allem ~** to top it all off

überflüssig adj superfluous; (Anschaffungen, Bemerkung) unnecessary

überfluten * [y:bɐ·ˈflu:·tn̩] vt a. fig to flood

überfordern * [y:bɐ·ˈfɔr·dɐn] vt to be too much for; **überfordert sein** to be out of one's league

überführen * [y:bɐ·ˈfy:·rən] vt 1. (transportieren) to transfer; (Leiche) to transport 2. JUR to convict; **jdn des Mordes ~** to convict sb of murder

überfüllt adj overcrowded

Übergabe f 1. (das Übergeben) handing over 2. MIL surrender

Übergangszeit f transition; (zwischen Jahreszeiten) off-season

übergeben * [y:bɐ·ˈge:·bn̩] irreg I. vt 1. (überreichen) [**jdm**] **etw ~** to hand over sep sth [to sb] 2. (ausliefern) **jdn jdm ~** to hand over sep sb to sb 3. MIL (überlassen) to surrender II. vr **sich akk ~** to vomit

über|gehen[1] [ˈy:bɐ·ge:·ən] vi irreg sein 1. (wechseln) **zu etw** dat ~ to move on to sth 2. **in anderen Besitz ~** to become sb else's property 3. **in Fäulnis/Gärung/Verwesung ~** to begin to rot/ferment/decay 4. (verschwimmen) **ineinander ~** to merge into one another

übergehen * [2] [y:bɐ·ˈge:·ən] vt irreg 1. (nicht berücksichtigen) to pass over sep 2. (nicht beachten) to ignore 3. (auslassen) to skip [over sep]

übergeordnet adj 1. (vorrangig) superior 2. (vorgesetzt) higher

Übergewicht nt kein pl 1. (zu hohes Körpergewicht) excess weight; **~ haben** to be overweight 2. (vorrangige Bedeutung) predominance

übergewichtig adj overweight

überglücklich I. adj extremely happy, overjoyed pred II. adv **~ lächeln** to smile blissfully

über|greifen vi irreg to spread (**auf** +akk to)

Übergröße f extra large size

überhängen [ʸːbɐ·hɛ·ŋən] vt **sich/jdm etw ~** dat to put sth around one's/sb's shoulders

überhäufen * [ʸːbɐ·hɔy·fn̩] vt **jdn mit etw ~** dat a. fig to heap sth [up]on sb

überhaupt [ʸːbɐ·haupt] I. adv **~ kein(e, r)** nobody/nothing/none at all; **~ kein Geld haben** to have no money at all; **~ nicht/nichts** not/nothing at all; **~ [noch] nie** never [at all] II. part (eigentlich) **was soll das ~?** what's that supposed to mean?; **wissen Sie ~, wer ich bin?** don't you even know who I am?

überheblich [ʸːbɐ·he·p·lɪç] I. adj arrogant II. adv arrogantly

Überheblichkeit <-> f kein pl arrogance

überhöht adj excessive; **mit ~er Geschwindigkeit fahren** to speed

überholen * [ʸːbɐ·ho·ln̩] vt 1. (vorbeifahren) to pass 2. (übertreffen) to surpass 3. (Motor, Gerät) to overhaul

Überholspur f fast lane

überholt adj outdated

Überholverbot nt restriction on passing; (Strecke) no passing zone

überhören * [ʸːbɐ·hø·rən] vt 1. (nicht hören) to not hear 2. (nicht hören wollen) to ignore

überkochen [ʸːbɐ·kɔ·xn̩] vi sein to boil over

überladen * [ʸːbɐ·la·dn̩] vt irreg to overload

überlassen * [ʸːbɐ·la·sn̩] vt irreg 1. (zur Verfügung stellen) **jdm etw ~** to let sb have sth 2. (entscheiden lassen) **jdm etw ~** to leave sth to sb 3. (preisgeben) **sich** dat **selbst ~ sein** to be left to one's own devices

Überlastung <-, -en> f 1. (eines Menschen) excess strain 2. TRANSP (des Verkehrs) congestion

überlaufen *¹ [ʸːbɐ·lau·fn̩] vt irreg **es überlief mich kalt** a cold shiver ran down my spine

überlaufen² [ʸːbɐ·lau·fn̩] vi irreg sein 1. (über den Rand) to overflow; (Tasse a.) to run over a. poet 2. (überkochen) to boil over 3. MIL to desert

überlaufen³ [ʸːbɐ·lau·fn̩] adj overrun

überleben * [ʸːbɐ·le·bn̩] I. vt 1. (lebend überstehen) to survive 2. (lebend überdauern) **etw ~** to live through sth 3. (über jds Tod hinaus leben) **jdn ~** to outlive sb II. vi to survive

Überlebende(r) f(m) dekl wie adj survivor

überlegen *¹ [ʸːbɐ·le·gn̩] I. vt, vi to think [about it]; **überleg [doch] mal!** just [stop and] think about it!; **das wäre zu ~** it is worth considering; **nach kurzem/langem Ü~** after short/long deliberation; **ohne zu ~** without thinking II. vr **sich** dat **etw ~** to consider sth; **ich will es mir noch einmal ~** I'll think it over again; **wenn man es sich recht überlegt** on second thought; **sich** dat **etw reiflich ~** to give serious thought to sth; **es sich** dat [anders] **~** to change one's mind

überlegen² [ʸːbɐ·le·gn̩] I. adj superior; (Sieg) convincing; **jdm ~ sein** to be superior to sb (**auf/in** +dat in) II. adv 1. (mit großem Vorsprung) convincingly 2. (herablassend) superciliously pej

überlegt [ʸːbɐ·le·kt] I. adj [well-]considered II. adv with consideration

Überlegung <-, -en> f consideration

überleiten vi to lead (**zu** +dat to)

überliefern * [ʸːbɐ·li·fen] vt to hand down sep

Überlieferung f tradition; **mündliche ~** oral tradition

überlisten * [ʸːbɐ·lɪs·tn̩] vt to outwit

übermächtig adj 1. (überlegen) superior 2. (überwältigend) overpowering; (Verlangen) overwhelming

Übermaß nt kein pl excess

übermäßig I. adj excessive; (Freude, Trauer) intense; (Schmerz) violent II. adv excessively; **sich** akk **~ anstrengen** to try too hard

übermorgen [ʸːbɐ·mɔr·gn̩] adv the day after tomorrow

übermüdet [ʸːbɐ·my·dət] adj overtired; (erschöpft a.) overfatigued form

Übermut m high spirits npl; **aus ~** just for the hell of it fam

übermütig [ʸːbɐ·my·tɪç] I. adj high-spirited; (zu dreist) cocky fam II. adv boisterously

übernächste(r, s) ['y:bɐ·nɛːçs·tə, -tɐ, -təs] *adj attr* ~s **Jahr/**~ **Woche** the year/week after next, in two years/ weeks; **die** ~ **Tür** two doors down

übernachten* [y:bɐ·'nax·tn̩] *vi* [**bei jdm**] ~ to spend the night [at sb's place]

Übernachtung <-, -en> *f* 1. *kein pl* (*das Übernachten*) spending the night [o a]; (*bei Kindern*) sleepover 2. (*verbrachte Nacht*) overnight stay; **mit zwei** ~**en in Bangkok** with two nights in Bangkok; ~ **mit Frühstück** bed and breakfast

Übernahme <-, -n> ['y:bɐ·naː·mə] *f* 1. (*Inbesitznahme*) taking possession 2. (*das Übernehmen*) assumption; (*von Verantwortung a.*) acceptance 3. ÖKON takeover

übernatürlich *adj* supernatural

übernehmen* [y:bɐ·'neː·mən] *irreg* I. *vt* 1. (*in Besitz nehmen*) to take; (*kaufen*) to buy; (*Geschäft*) to take over *sep* 2. (*auf sich nehmen, annehmen*) to accept; (*Auftrag, Verantwortung a.*) to take on *sep*; (*Kosten*) to pay; (*Verpflichtungen*) to assume 3. (*weiterbeschäftigen*) to take over *sep*; **jdn ins Angestelltenverhältnis** ~ to employ sb on a permanent basis II. *vr sich akk* ~ to take on too much

überprüfen* [y:bɐ·'pryː·fn̩] *vt* 1. (*durchchecken*) to vet; (*Papiere, Rechnung*) to check (**auf** +*akk* for) 2. (*die Funktion nachprüfen*) to examine 3. (*erneut bedenken*) to examine

überqueren* [y:bɐ·'kveː·rən] *vt* 1. (*sich über etw hinweg bewegen*) to cross [over] 2. (*über etw hinwegführen*) to lead over

überragen*¹ [y:bɐ·'raː·gn̩] *vt* 1. (*größer sein*) to tower above (**um** +*akk* by); (*Mensch*) to be taller than 2. (*übertreffen*) to outclass

über|ragen² ['y:bɐ·raː·gn̩] *vi* (*überstehen*) to project

überraschen* [y:bɐ·'ra·ʃn̩] *vt* to surprise (**mit** +*dat* with); **lassen wir uns** ~! *fam* let's wait and see [what happens]; **jdn dabei** ~, **wie er etw tut** to catch sb doing sth; **vom Regen überrascht werden** to get caught in the rain

überraschend I. *adj* unexpected II. *adv* unexpectedly

Überraschung <-, -en> *f* surprise

überreden* [y:bɐ·'reː·dn̩] *vt* to persuade; **jdn zu etw** *dat* ~ to talk sb into [doing] sth

überreichen* [y:bɐ·'rai·çn̩] *vt* **jdm etw** ~ to hand over *sep* sth to sb; (*feierlich*) to present sth to sb

Überrest *m meist pl* remains *npl*; **jds sterbliche** ~**e** *sb's* [mortal] remains

überschätzen* [y:bɐ·'ʃɛ·tsn̩] I. *vt* to overestimate II. *vr sich akk* ~ to think too highly of oneself

überschlagen* [y:bɐ·'ʃlaː·gn̩] *irreg* I. *vt* 1. (*Buchseite*) to skip [over] 2. (*ungefähr berechnen*) to [roughly] estimate II. *vr sich akk* ~ 1. (*Fahrzeug*) to overturn; (*Mensch*) to fall head over heels 2. (*Ereignisse*) to follow in quick succession 3. (*Stimme*) to crack

überschneiden* [y:bɐ·'ʃnai·dn̩] *vr irreg* **sich** *akk* ~ 1. (*zeitlich*) to overlap (**um** +*akk* by) 2. (*Linien*) to intersect

überschreiten* [y:bɐ·'ʃrai·tn̩] *vt irreg* 1. *geh* (*zu Fuß*) to cross [over] 2. (*über etw hinausgehen*) to exceed (**um** +*akk* by)

Überschrift *f* title; (*Zeitung*) headline

Überschuss^RR *m* 1. (*Reingewinn*) profi 2. (*überschüssige Menge*) surplus (**an** +*dat* of)

überschüssig ['y:bɐ·fy·sɪç] *adj* surplus *attr*

überschwänglich^RR I. *adj* effusive II. *adv* effusively

überschwemmen* [y:bɐ·'ʃvɛ·mən] *v* to flood

Überschwemmung <-, -en> *f* flood[ing]

überschwenglich^ALT ['y:bɐ·fvɛŋ·lɪç] *adj adv s.* **überschwänglich**

Übersee ['y:bɐ·zeː] *kein art* **aus** ~ from overseas; **in/nach** ~ overseas

übersehbar [y:bɐ·'zeː·baːɐ̯] *adj* 1. (*abschätzbar: Auswirkungen*) containable; (*Dauer, Kosten, Schäden*) assessable; (*Konsequenzen*) clear; **etw ist/ist noch nicht** ~ sth is in sight/sth is still now known 2. (*mit Blicken zu erfassen*) visible

übersehen* [y:bɐ·'zeː·ən] *vt irreg* 1. (*nicht bemerken*) to overlook 2. (*ab*

schätzen) to assess **3.** (*mit Blicken erfassen*) to have a view of

übersetzen*[1] [y:bɐ'zɛ·tsn̩] *vt, vi* to translate; [etw] ~ **aus dem Deutschen ins Englische** ~ to translate [sth] from German into English

über|setzen[2] [y:bɐ·ze·tsn̩] **I.** *vt haben* **jdn** ~ to ferry across *sep* sb **II.** *vi sein* to cross [over]

Übersetzer(in) <-s, -> *m(f)* translator

Übersetzung <-, -en> *f* **1.** LING translation **2.** TECH transmission ratio

Übersicht <-, -en> *f* **1.** *kein pl* (*Überblick*) overall view **2.** (*knappe Darstellung*) outline

übersichtlich I. *adj* **1.** (*rasch erfassbar*) clear **2.** (*gut zu überschauen*) open *attr* **II.** *adv* clearly

übersinnlich *adj* paranormal

überspitzt I. *adj* exaggerated **II.** *adv* in an exaggerated fashion

überspringen*[1] [y:bɐ·'ʃprɪ·ŋən] *vt irreg* **1.** (*über etw hinüber*) to jump; (*Mauer*) to vault **2.** (*auslassen*) to skip [over] **3.** SCH (*Klasse*) to skip

über|springen[2] [y:bɐ·ʃprɪ·ŋən] *vi irreg sein* to spread (**auf** +*akk* to)

überstehen* [y:bɐ·ʃte:·ən] *vt irreg* to get through; (*Krankheit, Operation*) to get over; **die nächsten Tage** ~ to make it through the next few days

übersteigen* [y:bɐ·'ʃtai·gn̩] *vt irreg* **1.** (*über etw klettern*) to climb over; (*Mauer*) to scale **2.** (*über etw hinausgehen*) to exceed

überstimmen* [y:bɐ·'ʃtɪ·mən] *vt* **1.** (*mit Stimmenmehrheit besiegen*) to outvote **2.** (*mit Stimmenmehrheit ablehnen*) to defeat

Überstunde *f* hour of overtime; ~**n** overtime

überstürzen* [y:bɐ·'ʃtʏr·tsn̩] **I.** *vt* **etw** ~ to rush into sth **II.** *vr* **sich** *akk* ~ to follow in quick succession

übertragbar [y:bɐ·'tra:k·ba:ɐ̯] *adj* **1.** (*Krankheit*) communicable *form* (**auf** +*akk* to); (*durch Berührung*) contagious **2.** (*anderweitig anwendbar*) to be applicable (**auf** +*akk* to) **3.** (*Ticket*) transferable

übertragen*[1] [y:bɐ·'tra:·gn̩] *irreg* **I.** *vt*

1. (*senden*) to broadcast **2.** (*Krankheit*) to communicate (**auf** +*akk* to) **3.** (*übergeben: Besitz*) to transfer (**auf** +*akk* to); **jdm die Verantwortung** ~ to entrust sb with the responsibility **4.** *geh* (*übersetzen*) to translate **II.** *vr* **1.** MED **sich** *akk* [**auf jdn**] ~ to be communicated [to sb] **2.** (*beeinflussen*) **sich** *akk* **auf jdn** ~ to spread to sb

übertragen[2] [y:bɐ·'tra:·gn̩] **I.** *adj* figurative **II.** *adv* figuratively

übertreffen* [y:bɐ·'trɛ·fn̩] *vt irreg* **1.** (*besser/größer sein*) to surpass (**an/in** +*dat* in) **2.** (*über etw hinausgehen*) to exceed (**um** +*akk* by)

übertreiben* [y:bɐ·'trai·bn̩] *irreg* **I.** *vi* to exaggerate **II.** *vt* to overdo; **ohne zu** ~ I'm not joking

Übertreibung <-, -en> *f* exaggeration

über|treten[1] [y:bɐ·'tre:·tn̩] *vi irreg sein* **1.** (*konvertieren*) to convert (**zu** +*dat* to) **2.** SPORT to overstep

übertreten*[2] [y:bɐ·'tre:·tn̩] *vt irreg* (*Gesetz, Vorschrift*) to break

Übertretung <-, -en> [y:bɐ·'tre:·tʊŋ] *f* violation

übertrieben I. *adj* exaggerated; (*Vorsicht*) excessive **II.** *adv* excessively

überwachen* [y:bɐ·'va:·xn̩] *vt* **1.** (*heimlich beobachten: Verdächtigen*) to keep under surveillance; (*Telefon*) to bug **2.** (*kontrollieren*) to supervise; (*durch eine Kamera*) to monitor

Überwachung <-, -en> *f* **1.** (*heimliches Beobachten: eines Verdächtigen*) surveillance; (*eines Telefons*) bugging **2.** (*Kontrolle*) supervision; (*durch eine Kamera*) monitoring

überwältigen* [y:bɐ·'vɛl·tɪ·gn̩] *vt* **1.** (*bezwingen*) to overpower **2.** (*übermannen*) **etw überwältigt jdn** sth overwhelms sb

überwältigend *adj* overwhelming; (*Schönheit*) stunning; (*Sieg*) crushing

überweisen* [y:bɐ·'vai·sn̩] *vt irreg* **1.** (*Geld*) to transfer **2.** (*Patienten*) to refer (**an** +*akk* to)

Überweisung <-, -en> *f* **1.** (*von Geld*) transfer **2.** (*eines Patienten*) referral (**an** +*akk* to); (*Überweisungsformular*) referral form

überwiegend ['y:bɐ·vi:·gn̩t] **I.** *adj* predominant; (*Mehrheit*) vast **II.** *adv* mainly

überwinden * [y:bɐ·'vɪn·dn̩] *irreg* **I.** *vt* to overcome **II.** *vr* **sich** *akk* ~ to overcome one's feelings/inclinations etc.; **sich** *akk* **zu etw** *dat* ~ to force oneself to do sth

Überwindung <-> *f kein pl* **1.** (*das Überwinden*) overcoming **2.** (*Selbstüberwindung*) conscious effort; **jdn** ~ **kosten[, etw zu tun]** to take sb a lot of will power [to do sth]

überwintern * [y:bɐ·'vɪn·ten] *vi* to [spend the] winter; (*Pflanzen*) to overwinter

überzeugen * [y:bɐ·'tsɔy·gn̩] **I.** *vt* to convince (**von** +*dat* of); (*umstimmen a.*) to persuade **II.** *vi* **1.** (*überzeugend sein*) to be convincing **2.** (*sich bewähren*) **bei etw** *dat* ~ to prove oneself in sth **III.** *vr* **sich** *akk* [**selbst**] ~ to convince oneself; ~ **Sie sich selbst!** [go and] see for yourself!

überzeugend I. *adj* convincing; (*umstimmend a.*) persuasive **II.** *adv* convincingly

Überzeugung <-, -en> [y:bɐ·'tsɔy·gʊŋ] *f* convictions *npl*; **zu der** ~ **gelangen, dass ...** to become convinced that ...

überziehen * ¹ [y:bɐ·'tsi:·ən] *vt irreg* **1.** (*bedecken*) to cover; (*Kuchen mit Glasur*) to coat **2.** (*Konto*) to overdraw (**um** +*akk* by) **3.** (*zu weit treiben*) **etw** ~ to carry sth too far; **überzogen** exaggerated

überziehen ² [y:bɐ·tsi:·ən] *vt irreg* (*anziehen*) [**sich** *dat*] **etw** ~ to put on *sep* sth

Überzug *m* coat[ing]; (*dünner*) film; (*Zuckerguss*) frosting

üblich ['y:p·lɪç] *adj* usual; **es ist bei uns hier** [**so**] ~ that's the custom around here

U-Boot ['u:·bo:t] *nt* submarine

übrig ['y:·brɪç] *adj* remaining, rest of *attr*; (*andere a.*) other *attr*; **die Ü~en** the remaining ones; **das Ü~e** the rest; ~ **sein** to be left [over]; **es wird ihm nichts anderes** ~ **bleiben** he won't have any [other] choice; **[jdm] etw** ~ **lassen** to leave sth [for sb]

übrigens ['y:·brɪ·gn̩s] *adv* by the way

übrig|haben RR *vt irreg* **für jdn/etw nichts/viel** ~ to be not at all/very interested in sb/sth

Übung <-, -en> ['y:bʊŋ] *f* **1.** *kein pl* (*das Üben*) practice; **das ist alles nur** ~ i[all] comes with practice; **zur** ~ for practice **2.** (*Übungsstück*) exercise **3.** SPORT exercise **4.** (*Probe für den Ernstfall*) drill **5.** (*Lehrveranstaltung*) lab (**zu** +*dat* on) ▶ ~ **macht den Meister** *prov* practice makes perfect

Ufer <-s, -> ['u:fɐ] *nt* (*Flussufer*) bank; (*Seeufer*) shore; **ans** ~ **schwimmen** to swim ashore

Ufo, UFO <-[s], -s> ['u:fo] *nt Abk von* **Unbekanntes Flugobjekt** UFO

Uganda <-> [u'gan·da] *nt* Uganda; *s. a.* **Deutschland**

Ugander(in) <-s, -> [u'gan·dɐ] *m(f)* Ugandan; *s. a.* **Deutsche(r)**

ugandisch [u'gan·dɪʃ] *adj* Ugandan; *s. a.* **deutsch**

Uhr <-s, -en> [u:ɐ] *f* **1.** (*Gerät*) clock; (*Armbanduhr*) watch; **die** ~ [**auf Sommer-/Winterzeit**] **umstellen** to set the clock/one's watch [an hour forward/backward at daylight saving time]; **diese** ~ **geht nach/vor** this watch is slow/fast; **rund um die** ~ round-the-clock, 24 hours a day **2.** (*Zeitangabe*) o'clock; **wie viel** ~ **ist es?** what time is it?; **um wie viel** ~? [at] what time?; **um 10** ~ at ten [o'clock]; **10** ~ **morgens/abends** ten [o'clock] in the morning/in the evening; **15** ~ 3 o'clock [in the afternoon], 3 p.m.; **7** ~ 30 half past 7 seven thirty; **8** ~ **23** 23 minutes after 8 eight twenty-three

Uhrzeigersinn *m im* ~ clockwise; **gegen den** ~ counterclockwise

Uhrzeit *f* time [of day]

Uhu <-s, -s> ['u:hu] *m* eagle owl

Ukraine <-> [ukra·'i:nə] *f* **die** ~ [the] Ukraine; *s. a.* **Deutschland**

Ukrainer(in) <-s, -> [ukra·'i:nɐ] *m(f)* Ukrainian; *s. a.* **Deutsche(r)**

ukrainisch [ukra·'i:nɪʃ] *adj* Ukrainian *s. a.* **deutsch**

ulkig ['ʊl·kɪç] *adj* **1.** (*lustig*) funny **2.** (*seltsam*) odd

Ultimatum <-s, -s> [ʊl·ti·'ma:·tʊm] *n*

ultimatum; **jdm ein ~ stellen** to give sb an ultimatum

Ultraschall ['ʊl·tra·ʃal] *m* ultrasound

Ultraschalluntersuchung *f* ultrasound

ultraviolett [ʊl·tra·vjo·'lɛt] *adj* ultraviolet

um [ʊm] **I.** *präp* +*akk* **1.** (*etw umgebend*) ~ **etw** [**herum**] around sth; **ganz um etw** [**herum**] all around sth **2.** (*gegen*) ~ **Ostern/den 15./die Mitte des Monats** [**herum**] around Easter/the 15th/the middle of the month **3.** (*über*) ~ **etw streiten** to argue about sth **4.** *Unterschiede im Vergleich ausdrückend* ~ **einiges besser** quite a bit better; ~ **einen Kopf größer/kleiner** taller/shorter by a head; ~ **10 cm länger/kürzer** 4 inches longer/shorter **5.** (*wegen*) ~ **jds/einer S.** *gen* **willen** for sb's sake/for the sake of sth; ~ **meinetwillen** for my sake **6.** (*für*) **Minute** ~ **Minute** minute by minute **7.** (*nach allen Richtungen*) ~ **sich** *akk* **schlagen/treten** to hit/kick out in all directions **8.** (*vorüber*) ~ **sein** to be over; (*Zeit*) to be up; (*Frist*) to expire **II.** *konj* ~ **etw zu tun** [in order] to do sth **III.** *adv* ~ **die 80 Meter** about 250 feet

um|ändern *vt* to alter

umarmen* [ʊm·'ʔar·mən] *vt* to embrace; (*fester*) to hug

Umarmung <-, -en> *f* embrace, hug

um|bauen ['ʊm·bau·ən] **I.** *vt* to rebuild **II.** *vi* to renovate

um|benennen* *vt irreg* to rename

um|biegen *irreg* **I.** *vt haben* to bend **II.** *vi sein* (*kehrtmachen*) to turn back

um|binden ['ʊm·bɪn·dn̩] *vt irreg* **jdm ein Tuch** ~ to put a scarf around sb's neck; (*mit Knoten a.*) to tie a scarf around sb's neck; **sich** *dat* **etw** ~ to put [*o* tie] on *sep* sth

um|blättern *vi* to turn over

um|blicken *vr* **1.** (*nach hinten*) **sich** *akk* ~ to look back; **sich** *akk* **nach jdm/etw** ~ to turn around to look at sb/sth **2.** (*zur Seite*) **sich** *akk* **nach links/rechts/allen Seiten** ~ to look to the left/right/in all directions; (*vor Straßenüberquerung a.*) to look left/right/both ways

um|bringen *irreg* **I.** *vt* to kill; (*vorsätz-*

lich a.) to murder (**durch** +*akk* with); **jdn mit einem Messer** ~ to stab sb to death **II.** *vr* **1. sich** *akk* ~ to kill oneself **2. sich** *akk* **vor Freundlichkeit/Höflichkeit** [*fast*] ~ to go out of one's way to be friendly/polite

Umbruch ['ʊm·brʊx] *m* radical change

um|buchen *vt* **1.** (*Reise*) to change one's booking/reservation (**auf** +*akk* to); **den Flug auf einen anderen Tag** ~ to change one's flight reservation to another day **2.** (*Geld*) to transfer (**auf** +*akk* to)

um|definieren* *vt* to redefine

um|denken *vi irreg* to change one's ideas/views (**in** +*dat* of)

um|drehen I. *vt haben* **1.** (*auf die andere Seite*) to turn over *sep* **2.** (*herumdrehen*) to turn **II.** *vr haben* **sich** *akk* ~ to turn around **III.** *vi sein o haben* to turn around; (*Mensch a.*) to turn back

Umdrehungszahl *f* number of revolutions [per minute/second]

umeinander [ʊm·ʔai·'nan·dɐ] *adv* about each other

um|fahren ['ʊm·fa:·rən] *vt irreg fam* to run over *sep;* **umgefahren werden** to be hit by a vehicle

um|fallen *vi irreg sein* **1.** (*umkippen*) to topple over; (*Baum a.*) to fall [down] **2.** (*zu Boden fallen*) to fall over; (*schwerfällig*) to slump to the floor/ground; **tot** ~ to drop dead **3.** *fam* (*die Aussage widerrufen*) to retract one's statement

Umfang <-[e]s, Umfänge> *m* **1.** (*Perimeter*) circumference; (*vom Bauch*) girth **2.** (*Ausdehnung*) area **3.** (*Ausmaß*) **in großem** ~ on a large scale; **in vollem** ~ completely

umfangreich *adj* extensive; (*Buch*) thick

umfassen* [ʊm·'fa·sn̩] *vt* **1.** (*umschließen*) to clasp; (*umarmen*) to embrace **2.** (*aus etw bestehen*) to comprise

umfassend *adj* **1.** (*weitgehend*) extensive **2.** (*alles enthaltend*) full **II.** *adv* ~ **über etw** *akk* **berichten** to report all the details of sth; **jdn** ~ **informieren** to keep sb informed about everything

Umfeld *nt* sphere

Umfrage *f* survey; POL [opinion] poll; **eine** ~ **machen** to conduct a survey (**zu** +*dat*

U

on/about, **über** +akk on/about)

Umgang m 1. (gesellschaftlicher Verkehr) dealings pl; **kein ~ für jdn sein** to not be fit company for sb 2. (Beschäftigung) **jds ~ mit etw** dat sb's dealing[s] with sth

umgänglich ['ʊm·gɛŋ·lɪç] adj friendly; (entgegenkommend) obliging

Umgangsformen pl [social] manners pl

Umgangssprache f LING colloquial speech; **die deutsche ~** colloquial German

Umgangston m way of speaking

umgeben * [ʊm·'ge:·bn̩] irreg I. vt to surround II. vr **sich** akk **mit jdm/etw ~** to surround oneself with sb/sth

Umgebung <-, -en> [ʊm·'ge:·bʊŋ] f 1. (umgebende Landschaft) environment, surroundings pl; (einer Stadt a.) environs npl; (Nachbarschaft) vicinity 2. (jdn umgebender Kreis) people around one

umgehen[1] ['ʊm·ge:·ən] vi irreg sein 1. (behandeln) to treat; **mit jdm nicht ~ können** to not know how to deal with sb; **mit etw** dat **gleichgültig/vorsichtig ~** to handle sth indifferently/carefully 2. (Gerücht) to circulate

umgehen *[2] [ʊm·'ge:·ən] vt irreg (vermeiden) to avoid

Umgehungsstraße [ʊm·'ge:·ʊŋs-] f bypass

umgekehrt I. adj reverse attr; (Richtung) opposite; **in ~er Reihenfolge** in reverse order; **[es ist] gerade ~!** [it's] just the opposite! II. adv the other way around

umgraben vt irreg to dig over sep

Umhang m cape

umhängen ['ʊm·hɛ·ŋən] vt **sich** dat **etw ~** to put on sep sth; **jdm etw ~** to wrap sth around sb

Umhängetasche f shoulder bag

umher [ʊm·'he:ɐ] adv around; **überall ~** everywhere

umhören vr **sich** akk **~** to ask around

umkehren I. vi sein to turn back II. vt haben to reverse

umkippen 1. vi sein 1. (seitlich umfallen) to tip over; (Stuhl, Fahrrad) to fall over 2. fam (bewusstlos umfallen) to pass out 3. fam (die Meinung ändern)

to come around 4. ÖKOL to become polluted 5. (ins Gegenteil umschlagen: Laune) to change; **in etw** akk **~** to turn into sth II. vt haben to tip over sep

umklammern * [ʊm·'kla·mɐn] vt **jdn ~** to cling [on] to sb; **etw ~** to hold sth tight

Umkleideraum m changing room

umkommen vi irreg sein 1. (sterben) to be killed (**bei/in** +dat in) 2. fam (verderben) to go bad 3. fam (es nicht mehr aushalten) **vor Hunger/Durst ~** to be dying of hunger/thirst; **vor Langeweile ~** to be bored to death

Umkreis m vicinity; **im ~ von 100 Metern** within a radius of 100 Meters

umkreisen * [ʊm·'krai·zn̩] vt ASTRON, RAUM to orbit

umkrempeln vt (grundlegend umgestalten) **jdn/etw ~** to shake up sep sb/sth

Umlauf ['ʊm·lauf] m 1. ASTRON rotation 2. **etw in ~ bringen** to circulate sth; (Gerücht, Lüge) to spread sth; (Geld) to put into circulation

Umlaufbahn f orbit

Umlaut m umlaut

umlegen ['ʊm·le:·gn̩] vt 1. (Schalter) to turn 2. (um Körperteil legen) **sich/jdm etw ~** dat to put sth around oneself/sb 3. sl (umbringen) **jdn ~** to bump off sep sb 4. (auf einen anderen Zeitpunkt verlegen) to reschedule (**auf** +akk for)

umleiten vt to divert

Umleitung f detour

umpflügen ['ʊm·pfly:·gn̩] vt to plow up sep

umräumen I. vi to rearrange II. vt (Möbel, Zimmer) to rearrange

Umrechnungskurs m exchange rate

umrennen vt **jdn/etw ~** to [run into and] knock sb/sth over

Umriss[RR] m meist pl contour, outline; **in ~en** in outline

umrühren vt, vi to stir

Umsatz m turnover

Umsatzsteuer f sales tax

umschalten vi 1. RADIO, TV to switch over; **auf einen anderen Sender ~** to change the channel 2. (Ampel) to change; **auf Rot/Grün ~** to turn red/green 3. fam (sich einstellen) to shift gears fig (**auf** +akk to)

um|schauen vr s. **umsehen**

Umschlag m 1. (Briefumschlag) envelope 2. (Schutzumschlag) jacket 3. MED compress 4. kein pl ÖKON transfer

um|schlagen [ʊmˈʃlaːgn̩] irreg I. vt haben 1. (Kragen) to turn down sep; (Ärmel) to turn up sep 2. (umladen) to transfer II. vi sein METEO to change

umschließen * [ʊmˈʃliːsn̩] vt irreg 1. (umgeben, umzingeln) to enclose 2. (umarmen) **jdn/etw mit den Armen** ~ to take sb/sth into one's arms

umschlingen * [ʊmˈʃlɪŋ·ən] vt irreg 1. (eng umfassen) to embrace; **jdn mit den Armen** ~ to wrap one's arms around sb 2. BOT to climb

um|schulen vt 1. (für andere Tätigkeit ausbilden) to retrain (**zu** +dat as) 2. (auf andere Schule schicken) to transfer to another school

Umschwung m 1. (plötzliche Veränderung) drastic change 2. schweiz (umgebendes Gelände) surrounding property

um|sehen vr irreg 1. (in Augenschein nehmen) **sich akk irgendwo/bei jdm** ~ to have a look around somewhere/in sb's home 2. (nach hinten blicken) **sich akk** ~ to look back 3. (suchen) **sich akk nach jdm/etw** ~ to look around for sb/sth

um|setzen ['ʊm·zɛ·tsn̩] vt 1. (an anderen Platz) to move 2. (umwandeln) to convert (**in** +akk to); **etw in die Praxis** ~ to put sth [in]to practice 3. (verkaufen) to turn over

umsonst [ʊmˈzɔnst] adv 1. (gratis) for free, free of charge 2. (vergebens) in vain; ~ **sein** to be pointless; **nicht** ~ not without reason

Umstand m 1. (wichtige Tatsache) fact; **mildernde Umstände** JUR mitigating circumstances; **den Umständen entsprechend** [gut] [as good] as can be expected under the circumstances; **unter diesen Umständen** under these circumstances; **unter Umständen** possibly 2. pl (Schwierigkeiten) trouble; **bitte keine Umstände!** please don't go to any trouble! ▸ **in anderen Umständen sein** to be expecting

umständlich ['ʊm·ʃtɛnt·lɪç] I. adj 1. (mit großem Aufwand verbunden) laborious; (Anweisung, Beschreibung) elaborate; (Aufgabe, Reise) complicated; (Erklärung, Anleitung) long-winded 2. (unpraktisch veranlagt) ~ **sein** to be awkward II. adv 1. (weitschweifig) long-windedly 2. (mühselig und aufwändig) laboriously

um|steigen vi irreg sein 1. TRANSP to change 2. (überwechseln) to switch [over] (**auf** +akk to)

um|stellen¹ ['ʊm·ʃtɛ·lən] I. vt 1. (Möbel) to move 2. **die Uhr** ~ to turn the clock back/forward 3. **die Ernährung** ~ to change one's diet II. vi **auf etw** akk ~ to change over to sth III. vr (sich anpassen) **sich akk** ~ to adapt (**auf** +akk to)

umstellen *² [ʊmˈʃtɛ·lən] vt (umringen) **jdn/etw** ~ to surround sb/sth

Umstellung f change (**auf** +akk to)

um|stimmen vt **jdn** ~ to change sb's mind; **sich** akk **[von jdm]** ~ **lassen** to let oneself be persuaded [by sb]

umstritten [ʊmˈʃtrɪ·tn̩] adj controversial

Umsturz m coup [d'état]

um|stürzen I. vi sein to fall II. vt haben to knock over sep; (politisches Regime etc.) to overthrow

Umtausch m exchange

um|tauschen vt to exchange (**in/gegen** +akk for); (Währung) to change (**in** +akk into)

um|wandeln ['ʊm·van·dln̩] vt to convert (**in** +akk into); **wie umgewandelt sein** to be a changed person

Umweg m detour

Umwelt ['ʊm·vɛlt] f kein pl environment

Umweltbelastung f environmental damage

Umweltbewusstsein RR nt kein pl environmental consciousness

umweltfeindlich adj harmful to the environment

umweltfreundlich adj environmentally friendly

Umweltgefährdung f environmental threat

Umweltpolitik f environmental policy

Umweltschäden pl environmental damage

U

Umweltschutz m environmental protection

Umweltschützer(in) m(f) environmentalist

Umweltverschmutzung f pollution

umweltverträglich adj environmentally friendly

Umweltzerstörung f destruction of the environment

umwerben* [ʊmˈvɛrbn̩] vt irreg to woo

um|werfen vt irreg **1.** (zum Umfallen bringen) to knock over sep **2.** fam (fassungslos machen) to bowl over sep **3.** (zunichtemachen: Ordnung, Plan) to upset

um|ziehen [ˈʊmtsiːən] irreg **I.** vi sein to move [house] **II.** vr sich akk ~ to get changed

Umzug m **1.** (Wohnungswechsel) move **2.** (Parade) parade

unabhängig [ˈʊnʔapˌhɛˌŋɪç] adj **1.** (von niemandem abhängig) independent (von +dat of/from) **2.** (ungeachtet) ~ von etw dat regardless of sth; ~ davon, ob/wann ... regardless of whether/ when ...; ~ voneinander separately

Unabhängigkeit f kein pl a. POL independence (von +dat of/from)

unabsichtlich [ˈʊnʔapˌzɪçtˌlɪç] **I.** adj unintentional; (Beschädigung) accidental **II.** adv accidentally

Unachtsamkeit f carelessness

unangebracht [ˈʊnʔanˌɡəˌbraxt] adj inappropriate

unangemessen [ˈʊnʔanˌɡəˌmɛˌsn̩] **I.** adj **1.** (Preise) unreasonable **2.** (Verhalten) inappropriate **II.** adv unreasonably

unangenehm [ˈʊnʔanˌɡəˌneːm] **I.** adj **1.** (nicht angenehm) unpleasant **2.** (peinlich) jdm ist etw ~ sb feels bad about sth **3.** (unsympathisch) unpleasant; **sie kann ganz schön ~ werden** she can get quite nasty **II.** adv unpleasantly

Unannehmlichkeit [ˈʊnʔanˌneːmˌlɪçˌkait] f meist pl trouble

unanständig [ˈʊnʔanˌʃtɛnˌdɪç] **I.** adj **1.** (obszön) dirty **2.** (rüpelhaft) rude **II.** adv rudely

unappetitlich [ˈʊnʔapeˌtiːtˌlɪç] adj **1.** (nicht appetitlich) unappetizing **2.** (ekelhaft) disgusting

unartig [ˈʊnʔaːɐ̯ˌtɪç] adj naughty

unauffällig [ˈʊnʔaufˌfɛˌlɪç] **I.** adj discrete **II.** adv discretely

unaufgefordert [ˈʊnʔaufˌɡəˌfɔrˌdɛt] adv without having been asked; ~ **eingesandte Manuskripte** unsolicited manuscripts

unaufhörlich [ʊnʔaufˈhøːɐ̯ˌlɪç] **I.** adj constant **II.** adv **1.** (fortwährend) constantly **2.** (ununterbrochen) incessantly

unaufmerksam [ˈʊnʔaufˌmɛrkˌzaːm] adj **1.** (nicht aufmerksam) inattentive **2.** (nicht zuvorkommend) thoughtless

Unaufmerksamkeit f kein pl **1.** (unaufmerksames Verhalten) inattentiveness **2.** (unzuvorkommende Art) thoughtlessness

unausgeglichen [ˈʊnʔausˌɡəˌɡlɪˌçn̩] adj unbalanced; (Mensch) moody; (Wesensart) uneven

unausstehlich [ʊnʔausˈʃteːˌlɪç] adj intolerable; (Mensch, Art a.) insufferable

unausweichlich [ʊnʔausˈvaiçˌlɪç] **I.** adj inevitable **II.** adv inevitably

unbarmherzig [ˈʊnˌbarmˌhɛrˌtsɪç] **I.** adj merciless **II.** adv mercilessly

unbeabsichtigt I. adj **1.** (versehentlich) accidental **2.** (nicht beabsichtigt) unintentional **II.** adv accidentally

unbedenklich [ˈʊnˌbəˌdɛŋkˌlɪç] **I.** adj harmless; (Situation, Vorhaben) acceptable **II.** adv quite safely

unbedeutend [ˈʊnˌbəˌdɔyˌtn̩t] **I.** adj **1.** (nicht bedeutend) insignificant **2.** (geringfügig) minimal; (Änderung) minor **II.** adv insignificantly

unbedingt [ˈʊnˌbəˌdɪŋt] **I.** adj attr absolute **II.** adv (auf jeden Fall) really; **erinnere mich ~ daran, sie anzurufen** [whatever you do,] don't forget to remind me to call her; **nicht** ~ not necessarily; ~! absolutely!

unbefangen [ˈʊnˌbəˌfaŋˌən] **I.** adj **1.** (unvoreingenommen) objective; (Ansicht) unbiased **2.** (nicht gehemmt) uninhibited **II.** adv **1.** (unvoreingenommen) objectively **2.** (nicht gehemmt) uninhibitedly

unbefriedigend [ˈʊn·bə·friː·dɪ·gn̩t] I. *adj* unsatisfactory II. *adv* in an unsatisfactory way

unbefristet [ˈʊn·bə·frɪs·tət] I. *adj* lasting for an indefinite period; (*Aufenthaltserlaubnis, Visum*) permanent; ~ **sein** to be [valid] for an indefinite period II. *adv* indefinitely

unbefugt [ˈʊn·bə·fuːkt] I. *adj* unauthorized II. *adv* without authorization

unbegrenzt [ˈʊn·bə·grɛntst] I. *adj* unlimited; (*Vertrauen*) boundless II. *adv* indefinitely

unbegründet [ˈʊn·bə·grʏn·dət] *adj* 1. (*grundlos*) unfounded; (*Kritik, Maßnahme*) unwarranted 2. JUR unfounded

unbehaglich [ˈʊn·bə·haːk·lɪç] *adj* uneasy II. *adv* uneasily

unbeholfen [ˈʊn·bə·hɔl·fn̩] I. *adj* (*schwerfällig*) clumsy; (*wenig gewandt*) awkward II. *adv* clumsily

unbekannt [ˈʊn·bə·kant] *adj* unknown; **jdm ~ sein** to be unknown to sb; (*Gesicht, Name, Wort*) to be unfamiliar to sb; **"~ verzogen"** "moved — address unknown"

Unbekannte(r) *f(m)* stranger

unbekümmert [ˈʊn·bə·kʏ·mɐt] I. *adj* carefree II. *adv* in a carefree manner

unbelastet [ˈʊn·balas·tət] I. *adj* 1. (*frei*) free (**von** +*dat* of) 2. FIN unencumbered II. *adv* freely

unbeliebt [ˈʊn·bəliːpt] *adj* unpopular

unbenutzt [ˈʊn·bə·nʊtst] *adj* unused; (*Bett*) not slept in *pred;* (*Kleidung*) unworn

unbeobachtet [ˈʊn·bə·ʔoːbax·tət] *adj* unnoticed; (*Gebäude, Platz*) unwatched

unbequem [ˈʊn·bə·kveːm] I. *adj* 1. (*Stuhl, Sofa*) uncomfortable 2. (*Frage*) awkward II. *adv* 1. (*nicht bequem*) uncomfortably 2. (*lästig*) awkwardly

unberechenbar [ˈʊn·bə·ˈrɛ·çn̩·baːɐ̯] *adj* 1. (*nicht einschätzbar: Gegner, Mensch*) unpredictable 2. (*nicht vorhersehbar*) unforeseeable

unberührt [ˈʊn·bə·ry·ɐ̯t] *adj* 1. (*im Naturzustand erhalten*) unspoiled 2. (*nicht benutzt*) untouched

unbeschädigt *adj, adv* undamaged

unbeschränkt [ˈʊn·bə·ʃrɛŋkt] *adj* unrestricted; (*Macht*) limitless; (*Möglichkeiten*) unlimited

unbeschreiblich [ˈʊn·bɛ·ʃraip·lɪç] I. *adj* 1. (*maßlos*) tremendous 2. (*nicht zu beschreiben*) indescribable II. *adv* **sich** *akk* ~ **ärgern/freuen** to be terribly angry/enormously happy

unbeschwert [ˈʊn·bə·ʃveːɐ̯t] *adj* carefree

unbesiegbar [ʊn·bə·ˈziːk·baːɐ̯] *adj* 1. MIL *a. fig* invincible 2. SPORT unbeatable

unbesorgt [ˈʊn·bə·zɔrkt] *adj* unconcerned; **sei/seinen Sie ~!** don't worry! II. *adv* without worrying; **die Pilze kannst du ~ essen** you needn't worry about eating the mushrooms

unbeständig [ˈʊn·bə·ʃtɛn·dɪç] *adj* 1. METEO unsettled 2. (*wankelmütig*) fickle

unbestechlich [ˈʊn·bɛ·ʃtɛç·lɪç] *adj* 1. (*nicht bestechlich*) incorruptible 2. (*nicht zu täuschen*) unerring

unbestimmt [ˈʊn·bə·ʃtɪmt] *adj* 1. (*unklar*) vague 2. (*nicht festlegbar*) indefinite; (*Alter*) uncertain; (*Anzahl, Menge*) indeterminate; (*Grund, Zeitspanne*) unspecified

unbestritten [ˈʊn·bɛ·ʃtrɪ·tn̩] I. *adj* 1. (*nicht bestritten*) undisputed; (*Argument*) irrefutable 2. JUR uncontested II. *adv* 1. (*wie nicht bestritten wird*) unquestionably 2. (*unstreitig*) unarguably

unbeteiligt [ˈʊn·bə·tai·lɪçt] *adj* 1. (*an etw nicht beteiligt*) uninvolved 2. (*desinteressiert*) indifferent; (*in einem Gespräch*) uninterested

unbeweglich [ˈʊn·bɛ·veːk·lɪç] *adj* 1. (*starr*) fixed; (*Konstruktion, Teil*) immovable 2. (*unveränderlich*) inflexible; (*Gesichtsausdruck*) rigid; *fig* unmoved

unbewohnt *adj* 1. (*nicht besiedelt*) uninhabited 2. (*nicht bewohnt*) unoccupied

unbewusst[RR] [ˈʊn·bə·vʊst] I. *adj* unconscious II. *adv* unconsciously

unbezahlbar [ʊn·bə·ˈtsaːl·ba·ɐ̯] *adj* 1. (*nicht aufzubringen*) unaffordable 2. (*äußerst nützlich*) invaluable 3. (*immens wertvoll*) priceless

unblutig [ˈʊn·bluː·tɪç] I. *adj* bloodless II. *adv* without bloodshed

U

unbrauchbar ['ʊn·braux·ba·ɐ̯] *adj* useless

und [ʊnt] *konj* and; ~ **dann?** then what?; (*nun*) well?; **na ~?** so what?

undankbar ['ʊn·daŋk·ba·ɐ̯] *adj* **1.** (*nicht dankbar*) ungrateful **2.** (*nicht lohnend*) thankless

undenkbar [ʊn·'dɛŋk·ba·ɐ̯] *adj* unthinkable

undeutlich ['ʊn·dɔyt·lɪç] **I.** *adj* indistinct; (*Schrift*) illegible **II.** *adv* ~ **sprechen** to mumble

undicht ['ʊn·dɪçt] *adj* (*luftdurchlässig*) not airtight; (*wasserdurchlässig*) not watertight

Unding ['ʊn·dɪŋ] *nt kein pl* **ein ~ sein[, etw zu tun]** to be absurd [to do sth]

undurchsichtig ['ʊn·dʊrç·zɪç·tɪç] *adj* **1.** (*nicht transparent*) nontransparent; (*Glas*) opaque **2.** *fig* (*Geschäfte*) shadowy; (*Motive*) obscure

uneben ['ʊn·'e:bn̩] *adj* uneven; (*Straße*) bumpy

unecht ['ʊn·ʔɛçt] *adj* **1.** (*imitiert*) fake *usu pej*; (*Haar*) artificial; (*Zähne*) false **2.** (*unaufrichtig*) false

unehelich ['ʊn·ʔe:ə·lɪç] *adj* (*Kind*) illegitimate

uneigennützig ['ʊn·ʔai·gn̩·ny·tsɪç] *adj* selfless

uneingeschränkt ['ʊn·ʔain·gə·ʃrɛŋkt] **I.** *adj* absolute; (*Handel*) free; (*Lob*) unreserved **II.** *adv* absolutely, unreservedly

unempfindlich ['ʊn·ʔɛmp·fɪnt·lɪç] *adj* insensitive (**gegen** +*akk* to); (*durch Erfahrung*) hardened, seasoned; (*Pflanze*) hardy; (*Material*) practical

unendlich [ʊn·'ʔɛnt·lɪç] *adj* **1.** (*nicht überschaubar*) infinite **2.** (*unbegrenzt*) endless

Unendlichkeit <-> *f kein pl* infinity

unentbehrlich ['ʊn·ʔɛnt·be:ɐ̯·lɪç] *adj* **1.** (*unbedingt erforderlich*) essential **2.** (*unverzichtbar*) indispensable

unentgeltlich ['ʊn·ʔɛnt·gɛlt·lɪç] **I.** *adj* free of charge; **die ~e Benutzung von etw** *dat* the free use of sth **II.** *adv* for free

unentschieden ['ʊn·ʔɛnt·ʃi:·dn̩] **I.** *adj* **1.** SPORT tied **2.** (*noch nicht entschie-*

den) undecided **II.** *adv* SPORT ~ **ausgehen** to end in a tie; ~ **spielen** to tie

Unentschieden <-s, -> ['ʊn·ʔɛnt·ʃi:·dn̩] *nt* SPORT tie

Unentschlossenheit *f* indecision

unerbittlich [ʊn·ʔɛɐ̯·'bɪt·lɪç] *adj* **1.** (*nicht umzustimmen*) unrelenting **2.** (*gnadenlos*) merciless

unerfahren ['ʊn·ʔɛɐ̯·fa:·rən] *adj* inexperienced

unerfreulich ['ʊn·ʔɛɐ̯·frɔy·lɪç] **I.** *adj* unpleasant; (*Neuigkeiten, Nachrichten*) bad; (*Zwischenfall*) unfortunate **II.** *adv* unpleasantly

unergründbar [ʊn·ʔɛɐ̯·'grʏnt·ba·ɐ̯], **unergründlich** [ʊn·ʔɛɐ̯·'grʏnt·lɪç] *adj* puzzling; (*Blick, Lächeln*) enigmatic

unerhört ['ʊn·ʔɛɐ̯·'høːɐ̯t] *adj attr* **1.** *pej* (*skandalös*) outrageous **2.** (*außerordentlich*) incredible

unerklärbar [ʊn·ʔɛɐ̯·'klɛːɐ̯·ba·ɐ̯], **unerklärlich** [ʊn·ʔɛɐ̯·'klɛːɐ̯·lɪç] *adj* inexplicable; **jdm ist ~, warum/wie ...** sb cannot understand why/how ...

unerlaubt ['ʊn·ʔɛɐ̯·laupt] **I.** *adj* unauthorized; JUR illegal **II.** *adv* without permission

unermüdlich [ʊn·ʔɛɐ̯·'my:t·lɪç] **I.** *adj* tireless **II.** *adv* tirelessly

unerreichbar [ʊn·ʔɛɐ̯·'raiç·ba·ɐ̯] *adj* unattainable; (*telefonisch*) unavailable

unersättlich [ʊn·ʔɛɐ̯·'zɛt·lɪç] *adj* insatiable; (*Wissensdurst*) unquenchable

unerschütterlich [ʊn·ʔɛɐ̯·'ʃʏ·tə·lɪç] **I.** *adj* unshakable **II.** *adv* unshakably

unerschwinglich [ʊn·ʔɛɐ̯·'ʃvɪŋ·lɪç] *adj* exorbitant; **für jdn ~ sein** to be beyond sb's means

unersetzlich [ʊn·ʔɛɐ̯·'zɛts·lɪç] *adj* indispensable; (*Wertgegenstand*) irreplaceable; (*Schaden*) irreparable

unerträglich [ʊn·ʔɛɐ̯·'trɛːk·lɪç] **I.** *adj* **1.** (*nicht auszuhalten: Lärm, Schmerzen*) unbearable **2.** *pej* (*Mensch*) impossible **II.** *adv* (*nicht auszuhalten*) unbearably

unerwartet ['ʊn·ʔɛɐ̯·var·tət] **I.** *adj* unexpected **II.** *adv* unexpectedly

unerwünscht ['ʊn·ʔɛɐ̯·vʏnʃt] *adj* **1.** (*nicht willkommen*) unwelcome **2.** (*lästig*) undesirable

ınfähig ['ʊn·fɛː·ɪç] *adj* **1.** (*inkompetent*) incompetent **2.** (*nicht imstande*) incapable (**zu** +*dat* of)

ınfair ['ʊn·fɛːɐ̯] **I.** *adj* unfair (**gegenüber** +*dat* to[ward]) **II.** *adv* unfairly

ınfall ['ʊn·fal] *m* accident

ınfallflucht *f* leaving the scene of an accident, hit-and-run

ınfallversicherung *f* accident insurance

ınfassbar^RR, **unfaßbar**^ALT [ʊn·'fas·baːɐ̯], **unfasslich**^RR, **unfaßlich**^ALT [ʊn·'fas·lɪç] *adj* **1.** (*unbegreiflich*) incomprehensible; (*Phänomen*) incredible **2.** (*unerhört*) outrageous

ınfehlbar [ʊn·'feːl·baːɐ̯] **I.** *adj* infallible; (*Geschmack*) impeccable; (*Gespür, Instinkt*) unerring **II.** *adv* without fail

ınförmig ['ʊn·fœr·mɪç] **I.** *adj* shapeless; (*groß*) cumbersome; (*Gesicht*) misshapen; (*Bein*) unshapely **II.** *adv* shapelessly

ınfreiwillig ['ʊn·frai·vɪ·lɪç] **I.** *adj* **1.** (*gezwungen*) compulsory **2.** (*unbeabsichtigt*) unintentional **II.** *adv* **etw ~ tun** to be forced to do sth

ınfreundlich ['ʊn·frɔynt·lɪç] **I.** *adj* **1.** (*nicht liebenswürdig*) unfriendly **2.** (*unangenehm*) unpleasant; (*Klima*) inhospitable; (*Jahreszeit, Tag*) dreary; (*Raum*) cheerless **II.** *adv* **jdn ~ behandeln** to be unfriendly to sb

ınfruchtbar ['ʊn·frʊxt·baːɐ̯] *adj* MED infertile; (*agr a.*) barren

ınfruchtbarkeit *f kein pl* **1.** MED infertility **2.** AGR barrenness

ınfug <-s> ['ʊn·fuːk] *m kein pl* nonsense; **~ machen** to be up to no good

ıngar(in) <-n, -n> ['ʊŋ·gar] *m(f)* Hungarian; *s. a.* **Deutsche(r)**

ıngarisch ['ʊŋ·ga·rɪʃ] *adj* Hungarian; *s. a.* **deutsch**

ıngarn <-s> ['ʊŋ·garn] *nt* Hungary; *s. a.* **Deutschland**

ıngebeten ['ʊn·gə·beː·tn̩] **I.** *adj* unwelcome **II.** *adv* **1.** (*ohne eingeladen zu sein*) without being invited **2.** (*ohne aufgefordert zu sein*) without an invitation

ıngebildet ['ʊn·gə·bɪl·dət] *adj* uneducated

ungeboren ['ʊn·gəbo·ːrən] *adj* unborn

ungebräuchlich ['ʊn·gə·brɔyç·lɪç] *adj* uncommon, not in use *pred*

ungebunden ['ʊn·gə·bʊn·dn̩] *adj* unattached

Ungeduld ['ʊn·gə·dʊlt] *f* impatience

ungeduldig ['ʊn·gə·dʊl·dɪç] **I.** *adj* impatient **II.** *adv* impatiently

ungeeignet ['ʊn·gə·ʔaig·nət] *adj* unsuitable (**für** +*akk* for/to)

ungefähr ['ʊn·gə·fɛːɐ̯] **I.** *adv* **1.** (*zirka*) approximately, about *fam;* **um ~ ...** (*Zeit*) at around ... **2.** (*etwa*) ~ **da/ hier** around there/here; **~ so** something like this/that **3.** (*in etwa*) more or less **II.** *adj attr* approximate

ungefährlich ['ʊn·gəfɛːɐ̯·lɪç] *adj* harmless; **~ sein, etw zu tun** to be safe to do sth

ungeheuer ['ʊn·gə·hɔy·ɐ] **I.** *adj* **1.** (*ein gewaltiges Ausmaß besitzend*) enormous **2.** (*größte Intensität, Bedeutung besitzend*) tremendous **II.** *adv* **1.** (*äußerst*) terribly **2.** (*ganz besonders*) enormously

Ungeheuer <-s, -> ['ʊn·gə·hɔy·ɐ] *nt* monster

ungehindert ['ʊn·gə·hɪn·dɐt] **I.** *adj* unhindered **II.** *adv* without hindrance

ungehorsam ['ʊn·gə·hoːɐ̯·za:m] *adj* disobedient (**gegenüber** +*dat* toward)

Ungehorsam ['ʊn·gə·hoːɐ̯·za:m] *m* disobedience

ungeklärt ['ʊn·gəklɛːɐ̯t] *adj, adv* **1.** (*nicht aufgeklärt*) unsolved **2.** (*Abwässer*) untreated

ungelegen ['ʊn·gə·leː·gn̩] *adj* inconvenient; **jdm] ~ kommen** to be inconvenient [for sb]; (*zeitlich*) to be an inconvenient time [for sb]

ungelernt ['ʊn·gə·lɛrnt] *adj attr* unskilled

ungemütlich ['ʊn·gə·my:t·lɪç] *adj* **1.** (*nicht gemütlich*) uninviting **2.** (*unerfreulich*) uncomfortable ▶ **~ werden** *fam* to become nasty

ungenau ['ʊn·gə·nau] **I.** *adj* **1.** (*nicht exakt*) vague **2.** (*nicht korrekt*) inaccurate **II.** *adv* **1.** (*nicht exakt*) vaguely **2.** (*nicht korrekt*) incorrectly

Ungenauigkeit <-, -en> *f* inaccuracy

U

ungenießbar ['ʊn·gə·niːsˈbaːɐ̯] *adj*
1. (*nicht zum Genuss geeignet*) inedible; (*Getränke*) undrinkable **2.** (*schlecht schmeckend*) unpalatable **3.** *fam* (*unausstehlich*) unbearable

ungenügend ['ʊn·gə·nyː·gn̩t] I. *adj*
1. (*nicht ausreichend*) insufficient; (*Information*) inadequate **2.** SCH unsatisfactory, ≈ F II. *adv* insufficiently, inadequately

ungenutzt ['ʊn·gə·nʊtst] *adj* unused; (*materielle/personelle Ressourcen*) unexploited; (*Gelegenheit*) missed

ungepflegt ['ʊn·gə·pfleːkt] *adj* (*Haus, Garten*) neglected; (*Person*) unkempt

ungerade ['ʊn·gə·raː·də] *adj* odd

ungerecht ['ʊn·gə·rɛçt] I. *adj* unjust; ~ **sein** to be unfair (**gegen** +*akk* to) II. *adv* unjustly, unfairly

Ungerechtigkeit <-, -en> *f* injustice

ungern ['ʊn·gɛrn] *adv* reluctantly

ungeschickt ['ʊn·gə·ʃɪkt] *adj* **1.** (*unbeholfen*) clumsy; (*unbedacht*) careless **2.** *dial, südd* (*unhandlich*) unwieldy; (*ungelegen*) awkward

ungeschoren ['ʊn·gə·ʃoː·rən] I. *adj* unshorn II. *adv* unscathed; ~ **davonkommen** to get away with it

ungesetzlich ['ʊn·gə·zɛts·lɪç] *adj* unlawful

ungestört ['ʊn·gə·ʃtøːɐ̯t] I. *adj* undisturbed; ~ **sein wollen** to want to be left alone II. *adv* without being disturbed

ungestraft ['ʊn·gə·ʃtraːft] *adv* with impunity; ~ **davonkommen** to get away scot-free

ungestüm ['ʊn·gə·ʃtyːm] I. *adj* (*Art, Temperament*) impetuous; (*Begrüßung*) enthusiastic II. *adv* enthusiastically

ungesund ['ʊn·gə·zʊnt] I. *adj* unhealthy II. *adv* unhealthily

ungeübt ['ʊn·gə·ʔyːpt] *adj* unpracticed; (*Lehrlinge*) inexperienced; **in etw** *dat* ~ **sein** to lack experience in sth

ungewiss^RR ['ʊn·gə·vɪs] *adj* uncertain

Ungewissheit^RR <-, -en> *f* uncertainty

ungewöhnlich ['ʊn·gə·vøːn·lɪç] I. *adj* **1.** (*vom Üblichen abweichend*) unusual **2.** (*außergewöhnlich*) remarkable II. *adv* **1.** (*äußerst*) exceptionally **2.** (*in nicht üblicher Weise*) unusually

ungewohnt ['ʊn·gə·voːnt] *adj* unusual

ungewollt ['ʊn·gə·vɔlt] I. *adj* unintentional; (*Schwangerschaft*) unwanted II. *adv* unintentionally; **ich musste ~ grinsen** I couldn't help grinning

Ungeziefer <-s> ['ʊn·gə·tsiː·fɐ] *nt kein pl* pests *pl*

ungezogen ['ʊn·gə·tsoː·gn̩] I. *adj* (*Kind*) naughty II. *adv* impertinently; **sich** *akk* ~ **benehmen** to behave badly

ungezwungen ['ʊn·gə·tsvʊŋən] *adj* informal

ungläubig ['ʊn·glɔy·bɪç] *adj* **1.** (*etw nicht glauben wollend*) disbelieving; **ein ~es Kopfschütteln** an incredulous shake of the head **2.** REL unbelieving

unglaublich ['ʊn·glaup·lɪç] I. *adj* **1.** (*nicht glaubhaft*) unbelievable **2.** (*unerhört*) outrageous II. *adv fam* (*überaus*) incredibly

unglaubwürdig ['ʊn·glaup·vʏr·dɪç] I. *adj* implausible; (*Zeuge*) unreliable II. *adv* implausibly

ungleich ['ʊn·glaiç] I. *adj* unequal; (*Belastung*) uneven; (*Paar*) odd; (*Gegenstände*) dissimilar II. *adv* **1.** (*unterschiedlich*) unequally **2.** *vor komp* (*weitaus*) far III. *präp* +*dat geh* unlike

ungleichmäßig ['ʊn·glaiç·mɛː·sɪç] I. *adj* **1.** (*unregelmäßig*) irregular **2.** (*nicht zu gleichen Teilen*) uneven II. *adv* **1.** (*unregelmäßig*) irregularly **2.** (*ungleich*) unevenly

Unglück <-glücke> ['ʊn·glʏk] *nt* **1.** *kein pl* (*Pech*) bad luck; **zu allem ~** to make matters worse **2.** (*katastrophales Ereignis*) disaster **3.** *kein pl* (*Elend*) unhappiness ▶ **ein ~ kommt selten allein** *prov* when it rains it pours

unglücklich ['ʊn·glʏk·lɪç] I. *adj* **1.** (*betrübt*) unhappy **2.** (*ungünstig, ungeschickt*) unfortunate II. *adv* unfortunately; ~ **verliebt sein** to be lovelorn

unglücklicherweise *adv* unfortunately

Unglücksfall *m* **1.** (*Unfall*) accident **2.** (*unglückliche Begebenheit*) mishap

ungültig ['ʊn·gʏl·tɪç] *adj* **1.** (*nicht mehr gültig*) invalid; (*Tor, Treffer*) disallowed **2.** (*nichtig*) [null and] void

ungünstig ['ʊn·gʏns·tɪç] *adj* (*Zeit/punkt*) inconvenient; (*Wetter*) inclement

ungut ['ʊn·guːt] *adj* bad; (*Verhältnis*) strained ▶ **nichts für ~!** no offense!

unhandlich ['ʊn·hant·lɪç] *adj* unwieldy

Unheil ['ʊn·haɪl] *nt* disaster; **großes ~ anrichten** to wreak havoc

unheilbar ['ʊn·haɪl·baːɐ̯] I. *adj* incurable II. *adv* incurably

unheimlich ['ʊn·haɪm·lɪç] I. *adj* 1. (*Grauen erregend*) eerie 2. *fam* (*unglaublich, sehr*) incredible 3. *fam* (*sehr groß, sehr viel*) terrific *fig* II. *adv fam* incredibly

unhöflich ['ʊn·høːf·lɪç] *adj* impolite II. *adv* impolitely

unhygienisch ['ʊn·hy·gje:·nɪʃ] *adj* unhygienic

Uniform <-, -en> [uni·'fɔrm, 'ʊni·fɔrm] *f* uniform

Universität <-, -en> [uni·vɛr·zi·'tɛ:t] *f* university

Universum <-s, Universen> [uni·'vɛr·zʊm] *nt* universe

unkenntlich ['ʊn·kɛnt·lɪç] *adj* unrecognizable; (*Eintragung*) indecipherable

Unkenntnis ['ʊn·kɛnt·nɪs] *f kein pl* ignorance

unklar ['ʊn·klaːɐ̯] I. *adj* 1. (*unverständlich*) unclear 2. (*ungeklärt*) unclear; [**sich** *dat*] **im U~en sein** to be uncertain (**über** +*akk* about); **jdn im U~en lassen** to leave sb in the dark (**über** +*akk* about) 3. (*verschwommen*) indistinct; (*Wetter*) hazy; (*Umrisse*) blurred; (*Erinnerungen*) vague II. *adv* (*unverständlich*) unclearly

Unklarheit <-, -en> *f* 1. *kein pl* (*Ungewissheit*) uncertainty 2. (*Undeutlichkeit*) lack of clarity

unklug ['ʊn·kluːk] *adj* unwise

unkompliziert ['ʊn·kɔmp·li·tsiːɐ̯t] *adj* straightforward; (*Fall*) simple; (*Mensch*) uncomplicated

unkonzentriert ['ʊn·kɔn·tsɛn·triːɐ̯t] *adj* distracted

Unkosten ['ʊn·kɔs·tn̩] *pl* costs *npl*

Unkraut ['ʊn·kraut] *nt* weed

unkündbar ['ʊn·kʏnt·baːɐ̯] *adj* (*Stellung*) tenured; (*Vertrag*) not subject to termination

unleserlich ['ʊn·leː·zɐ·lɪç] I. *adj* (*Schrift*) illegible II. *adv* illegibly

unlogisch I. *adj* illogical II. *adv* illogically

unlöslich [ʊn·'løːs·lɪç] I. *adj* 1. (*nicht zu lösen: Problem*) unsolvable; (*Widerspruch*) irreconcilable 2. CHEM insoluble II. *adv* (*untrennbar*) indissolubly

Unlust ['ʊn·lʊst] *f kein pl* reluctance

unmäßig ['ʊn·mɛː·sɪç] I. *adj* excessive II. *adv* excessively

unmenschlich ['ʊn·mɛnʃ·lɪç] I. *adj* 1. (*Bedingungen, Verhältnisse*) appalling, inhuman[e]; (*Diktator, Grausamkeit*) brutal 2. (*Hitze, Leid*) tremendous II. *adv* 1. (*grausam*) in an inhuman[e] manner 2. (*entsetzlich*) appallingly

unmerklich ['ʊn·mɛrk·lɪç] I. *adj* imperceptible II. *adv* imperceptibly

unmissverständlich ^{RR} ['ʊn·mɪs·fɛɐ̯·ʃtɛnt·lɪç] I. *adj* unequivocal; (*Antwort*) blunt II. *adv* unequivocally

unmittelbar ['ʊn·mɪ·tl̩·baːɐ̯] I. *adj* direct; **in ~er Nähe von etw** in the immediate vicinity of sth II. *adv* 1. (*sofort*) immediately 2. (*ohne Umweg*) directly

unmöglich ['ʊn·møːk·lɪç] I. *adj* 1. (*nicht machbar*) impossible; (*Vorhaben*) infeasible 2. *pej fam* (*nicht tragbar, lächerlich*) impossible II. *adv fam* not possibly

unmoralisch ['ʊn·mo·raː·lɪʃ] *adj* immoral

unmündig ['ʊn·mʏn·dɪç] *adj* 1. (*noch nicht volljährig*) underage 2. (*geistig unselbstständig*) dependent

unmusikalisch ['ʊn·mu·zi·kaː·lɪʃ] *adj* unmusical

unnachahmlich ['ʊn·naːx·ʔaːm·lɪç] *adj* inimitable

unnachgiebig ['ʊn·naːx·giː·bɪç] I. *adj* adamant II. *adv* adamantly

unnahbar [ʊn·'naː·baːɐ̯] *adj* unapproachable

unnatürlich ['ʊn·na·tyːɐ̯·lɪç] *adj* 1. (*nicht natürlich*) unnatural; (*abnorm*) abnormal 2. (*gekünstelt*) artificial

unnötig ['ʊn·nøː·tɪç] *adj* unnecessary

unordentlich ['ʊn·ʔɔr·dn̩t·lɪç] I. *adj* messy; (*Schrift*) sloppy II. *adv* messily; (*schreiben*) sloppily; **~ arbeiten** to work carelessly

Unordnung ['ʊn·ʔɔrd·nʊŋ] *f kein pl* mess

U

unparteiisch ['ʊn·par·tai·ɪʃ] I. *adj* impartial II. *adv* impartially

unpassend ['ʊn·pa·sn̩t] *adj* 1. (*unangebracht*) inappropriate 2. (*ungelegen*) inconvenient; (*Augenblick*) inopportune

unpersönlich ['ʊn·pɛr·zøːn·lɪç] *adj* 1. (*distanziert: Mensch*) distant; (*Gespräch, Art*) impersonal 2. LING impersonal

unpraktisch ['ʊn·prak·tɪʃ] *adj* 1. (*nicht handwerklich veranlagt*) unpractical 2. (*nicht praxisgerecht*) impractical

unpünktlich ['ʊn·pʏŋkt·lɪç] I. *adj* 1. (*generell nicht pünktlich*) unpunctual 2. (*verspätet*) late II. *adv* late

Unrecht ['ʊn·rɛçt] *nt kein pl* 1. (*unrechte Handlung*) wrong; **jdm ein ~ antun** to do sb an injustice 2. (*dem Recht entgegengesetztes Prinzip*) **im ~ sein** to be [in the] wrong; **zu ~** wrongly

unrechtmäßig ['ʊn·rɛçt·mɛː·sɪç] I. *adj* illegal II. *adv* illegally

unregelmäßig ['ʊn·reː·ɡl̩·mɛː·sɪç] I. *adj* irregular II. *adv* irregularly

unreif ['ʊn·raif] *adj* 1. AGR, HORT unripe, green 2. (*Person*) immature

Unruhe ['ʊn·ruː·ə] *f* 1. (*Ruhelosigkeit*) restlessness 2. (*ständige Bewegung*) agitation 3. (*erregte Stimmung*) agitation; **~ stiften** to cause trouble 4. (*Aufstand*) **~n** *pl* riots *pl*

unruhig ['ʊn·ruː·ɪç] I. *adj* 1. (*ständig gestört*) restless; (*Zeit*) troubled; (*ungleichmäßig*) uneven; (*Herzschlag*) irregular 2. (*laut*) noisy 3. (*ruhelos*) agitated; (*Leben*) eventful; (*Geist*) restless; (*Schlaf*) fitful II. *adv* 1. (*ruhelos*) anxiously 2. (*unter ständigen Störungen*) restlessly

uns [ʊns] I. *pron pers* 1. *dat von* **wir** [to/for] us; **bei ~** at our house 2. *akk von* **wir** us II. *pron refl* 1. *akk o dat von* **wir** ourselves 2. (*einander*) each other

unsachgemäß ['ʊn·zax·gə·mɛːs] I. *adj* improper II. *adv* improperly

unsanft ['ʊn·zanft] I. *adj* rough; (*Erwachen*) rude II. *adv* roughly

unsauber ['ʊn·zau·bɐ] *adj* 1. (*schmutzig*) dirty 2. (*unordentlich, nachlässig*) careless; (*unpräzise*) unclear II. *adv*

carelessly

unschädlich ['ʊn·ʃɛːt·lɪç] *adj* harmless

unscharf ['ʊn·ʃarf] I. *adj* 1. (*ohne klare Konturen*) blurred 2. (*nicht scharf*) out of focus 3. (*nicht präzise*) imprecise II. *adv* 1. (*nicht präzise*) out of focus 2. (*nicht exakt*) imprecisely

unscheinbar ['ʊn·ʃain·baːɐ] *adj* inconspicuous

unschlagbar [ʊn·ˈʃlaːk·baːɐ] *adj* unbeatable (**in** *+dat* at)

unschlüssig ['ʊn·ʃlʏ·sɪç] *adj* indecisive

Unschuld ['ʊn·ʃʊlt] *f* 1. (*Schuldlosigkeit*) innocence 2. (*Reinheit*) purity; (*Naivität*) innocence 3. *veraltend* (*Jungfräulichkeit*) virginity

unschuldig ['ʊn·ʃʊl·dɪç] I. *adj* innocent II. *adv* 1. JUR despite sb's/one's innocence 2. (*arglos*) innocently

unselbständig ['ʊn·zɛlp·ʃtɛn·dɪç], **unselbstständig** RR ['ʊn·zɛlp·ʃtʃtɛn·dɪç] *adj* dependent (**on** others)

unser ['ʊn·ze] I. *pron poss, adjektivisch* our II. *pron pers gen von* **wir** *geh* of us

unsere(r, s) ['ʊn·zə·rə, -zəre, -zə·rəs] *pron poss, substantivisch geh* ours

unseresgleichen ['ʊn·zes·ˈglai·çn̩] *pron* people *npl* like us

unsicher ['ʊn·zɪ·çɐ] I. *adj* 1. (*gefährlich*) unsafe; (*Gegend*) dangerous 2. (*gefährdet*) insecure, at risk *pred* 3. (*nicht selbstsicher*) unsure; (*Blick*) uncertain 4. (*unerfahren, ungeübt*) **sich** *akk* **~ fühlen** to feel unsure of oneself 5. (*schwankend*) unsteady; (*Hand*) shaky 6. (*ungewiss*) uncertain 7. (*nicht verlässlich*) unreliable *fam* II. *adv* 1. (*schwankend*) unsteadily 2. (*nicht selbstsicher*) **~ fahren** to drive with little confidence

Unsicherheit *f* 1. *kein pl* (*mangelnde Selbstsicherheit*) insecurity 2. *kein pl* (*mangelnde Verlässlichkeit*) unreliability 3. *kein pl* (*Ungewissheit*) uncertainty 4. (*Gefährlichkeit*) dangers *pl* 5. *meist pl* (*Unwägbarkeit*) uncertainty

Unsinn ['ʊn·zɪn] *m kein pl* nonsense; **~ machen** to mess around

unsinnig ['ʊn·zɪ·nɪç] I. *adj* ridiculous II. *adv fam* (*unerhört*) terribly

unsittlich ['ʊn·zɪt·lɪç] I. *adj* indecent

II. *adv* indecently

unsozial ['ʊn·zo·tsi̯aːl] I. *adj* antisocial II. *adv* antisocially

unsportlich ['ʊn·ʃpɔrt·lɪç] I. *adj* 1. (*Person*) unathletic 2. (*nicht fair*) unsportsmanlike II. *adv* (*nicht fair*) **sich** *akk* ~ **verhalten** to behave in an unsportsmanlike way

unsterblich ['ʊn·ʃtɛrp·lɪç] I. *adj* 1. (*ewig lebend*) immortal 2. (*unvergänglich: Liebe*) undying II. *adv fam* (*über alle Maßen*) incredibly

Unsterblichkeit <-> *f kein pl* immortality

unsympathisch ['ʊn·zʏm·paː·tɪʃ] *adj* unpleasant

untätig ['ʊn·tɛː·tɪç] I. *adj* idle II. *adv* idly

untauglich ['ʊn·tauk·lɪç] *adj* unsuitable; MIL unfit

unteilbar [ʊn·'tail·baːɐ] *adj* indivisible

unten ['ʊn·tn̩] *adv* 1. (*an einer tieferen Stelle*) down; **dort** ~ down there; **weiter** ~ farther down; **ich habe die Bücher** ~ **ins Regal gelegt** I put the books down below on the shelf; ~ **links/ rechts** on the bottom left/right 2. (*Unterseite*) bottom 3. (*in einem tieferen Stockwerk*) downstairs; **der Aufzug fährt nach** ~ the elevator is going down 4. (*in sozial niedriger Position*) bottom 5. (*hinten im Text*) **siehe** ~ see below 6. (*am hinteren Ende*) at the bottom

unter ['ʊn·tɐ] I. *präp* 1. +*dat* (*unterhalb von etw*) under, underneath; ~ **freiem Himmel** outdoors 2. +*akk* (*unterhalb von etw*) under; **sich** *akk* ~ **einen Baum stellen** to stand under a tree 3. +*dat* (*weniger, niedriger*) less; ~ **dem Durchschnitt liegen** to be below average 4. +*dat* (*zwischen*) among[st]; (*von*) among; ~ **uns gesagt** between you and me; ~ **anderem** among other things 5. +*dat* (*begleitet von, hervorgerufen durch*) under; ~ **Zwang** under duress; ~ **Lebensgefahr** at risk to one's life; ~ **der Bedingung, dass ...** on the condition that ...; ~ **Umständen** possibly 6. +*dat* (*in einem Zustand*) under; ~ **Druck stehen** to be under pressure; ~ **einer Krankheit leiden** to suffer

from an illness 7. +*dat südd* (*während*) during; ~ **der Woche** during the week II. *adv* 1. (*jünger als*) under 2. (*weniger als*) less than

Unterarm ['ʊn·te·ʔarm] *m* forearm

Unterbewusstsein ᴿᴿ ['ʊn·te·bə·vʊst·zain] *nt* **das/jds** ~ the/sb's subconscious; **im** ~ subconsciously

unterbrechen * [ʊn·te·'brɛ·çn̩] *vt irreg* 1. (*vorübergehend beenden*) to interrupt 2. (*räumlich auflockern*) to break up *sep*

unterbringen *vt irreg* 1. (*Unterkunft verschaffen*) **jdn** ~ to put sb up; **die Kinder sind gut untergebracht** the children are being well looked after 2. (*abstellen*) **etw** ~ to put sth somewhere 3. *fam* (*eine Anstellung verschaffen*) **jdn** ~ to get sb a job

unterdrücken * [ʊn·te·'drʏ·kn̩] *vt* 1. (*niederhalten*) **jdn** ~ to oppress sb 2. (*zurückhalten*) **etw** ~ to suppress sth

Unterdrückung <-, -en> *f* 1. *kein pl* (*das Unterdrücken: der Bürger, Einwohner, des Volks*) oppression; (*von Aufstand, Unruhen*) suppression; (*das Unterdrücktsein*) oppression

untere(r, s) ['ʊn·tə·rə, -tə·rə, -tə·rəs] *adj attr* lower

untereinander [ʊn·te·ʔai·'nan·dɐ] *adv* 1. (*räumlich*) one below the other 2. (*gegenseitig*) among yourselves/ themselves etc.; **sich** *akk* ~ **helfen** to help each other

unterernährt *adj* undernourished

Unterführung [ʊn·te·'fyː·rʊŋ] *f* underpass

Untergang *m* 1. (*eines Schiffs*) sinking 2. (*der Sonne*) setting 3. (*Zerstörung*) destruction; (*einer Zivilisation*) decline

Untergebene(r) *f(m) dekl wie adj* subordinate

untergehen *vi irreg sein* 1. (*versinken*) to sink 2. (*Sonne*) to set 3. (*zugrunde gehen*) to be destroyed

untergeordnet *adj* 1. (*zweitrangig*) secondary 2. (*subaltern*) subordinate

Untergeschoss ᴿᴿ *nt* basement

Untergrund ['ʊn·te·grʊnt] *m* 1. GEOL subsoil 2. *kein pl* (*politische Illegalität*) underground; **im** ~ underground

U

3. KUNST (*unterste Farbschicht*) under-coat

unterhalb ['ʊn·tɐ·halp] **I.** *präp +gen* (*darunter befindlich*) below **II.** *adv* (*tiefer gelegen*) below; (*eines Flusses*) downstream; **~ von etw** *dat* below sth

Unterhalt <-[e]s> ['ʊn·tɐ·halt] *m kein pl* **1.** (*Lebensunterhalt*) keep; (*Unterhaltsgeld*) alimony **2.** (*Instandhaltung*) upkeep

unterhalten * [ʊn·tɐ·'hal·tn̩] *irreg* **I.** *vt* **1.** (*für jds Lebensunterhalt sorgen*) to support **2.** (*instand halten, pflegen*) to maintain **3.** (*betreiben*) to run **4.** (*die Zeit vertreiben*) to entertain **II.** *vr* **1.** (*sich vergnügen*) **sich** *akk* **~** to keep oneself amused **2.** (*sprechen*) **sich** *akk* [**mit jdm**] **~** to talk [to sb] (**über** *+akk* about); **wir müssen uns mal ~!** we need to have a talk

unterhaltsam [ʊn·tɐ·'halt·za:m] *adj* entertaining

Unterhaltspflicht *f kein pl* obligation to pay maintenance

Unterhaltung <-, -en> *f* **1.** *kein pl* (*Instandhaltung*) maintenance **2.** *kein pl* (*Betrieb*) running **3.** (*Gespräch*) conversation **4.** *kein pl* (*Zeitvertreib*) entertainment; **gute ~!** enjoy [yourselves]!

Unterhaus ['ʊn·tɐ·haus] *nt* lower house, ≈ House of Representatives

Unterhemd ['ʊn·tɐ·hɛmt] *nt* undershirt

Unterhose ['ʊn·tɐ·ho:·zə] *f* underwear

unterirdisch ['ʊn·tɐ·ʔɪr·dɪʃ] **I.** *adj* underground; (*Fluss*) subterranean **II.** *adv* underground

Unterkunft <-, Unterkünfte> ['ʊn·tɐ·kʊnft] *f* accommodation; **~ mit Frühstück** bed and breakfast; **~ und Verpflegung** room and board

Unterlage ['ʊn·tɐ·la:·gə] *f* **1.** (*zum Unterlegen*) mat **2.** *pl* (*Dokumente*) **~n** documents

unterlassen * [ʊn·tɐ·'la·sn̩] *vt irreg* **1.** (*nicht ausführen*) **etw ~** to fail to do sth **2.** (*mit etw aufhören*) **etw ~** to refrain from doing sth

unter|legen¹ ['ʊn·tɐ·le:·gn̩] *vt* (*darunter platzieren*) to put under[neath]

unterlegen *² [ʊn·tɐ·'le:·gn̩] *vt* **einen Film mit Musik ~** to put music to

a film

unterlegen³ [ʊn·tɐ·'le:·gn̩] *adj* **1.** (*schwächer als andere*) inferior; **zahlenmäßig ~ sein** to be outnumbered **2.** SPORT **jdm ~ sein** to be defeated by sb

Unterleib *m* [lower] abdomen

unterliegen * ['ʊn·tɐ·li:·gn̩] *vi irreg* **1.** *sein* (*besiegt werden*) [**jdm**] **~** to lose [to sb] **2.** *haben* (*unterworfen sein*) **einer Täuschung ~** to be the victim of deception; **der Schweigepflicht ~** to be bound to maintain confidentiality

Unterlippe *f* lower lip

Untermiete ['ʊn·tɐ·mi:·tə] *f* subtenancy; **jdn in ~ nehmen** to sublet a room/apartment to sb; **zur ~ wohnen** to rent [a room/apartment] from an existing tenant

Untermieter(in) *m(f)* subtenant

unternehmen * [ʊn·tɐ·'ne:·mən] *vt irreg* **1.** (*in die Wege leiten*) **etwas/nichts ~** to take action/no action (**gegen** *+akk* against) **2.** (*machen*) **wollen wir nicht etwas zusammen ~?** why don't we do something together?; **einen Ausflug ~** to take a trip; **einen Versuch ~** to make an attempt

Unternehmen <-s, -> [ʊn·tɐ·'ne:·mən] *nt* **1.** ÖKON company **2.** (*Vorhaben*) venture

Unternehmensberater(in) *m(f)* management consultant

Unternehmer(in) <-s, -> [ʊn·tɐ·'ne:·mɐ] *m(f)* entrepreneur

unternehmungslustig *adj* enterprising

Unteroffizier ['ʊn·tɐ·ʔɔfi·tsi:ɐ̯] *m* non-commissioned officer

unter|ordnen **I.** *vt* **1.** (*hintanstellen*) **etw etw** *dat* **~** to put sth before sth **2.** (*jdm/einer Institution unterstellen*) **jdm/etw untergeordnet sein** to be subordinate to sb/sth **II.** *vr* **sich** *akk* [**jdm**] **~** to take on a subordinate role [to sb]

Unterricht <-[e]s, -e> ['ʊn·tɐ·rɪçt] *m pl selten* lesson, class; **der ~ beginnt um zehn vor acht** classes begin at ten to eight; **heute fällt der ~ in Mathe aus** there's no math class today; **im ~ sein** to be in class; **theoretischer/praktischer ~** theoretical/practical classes

unterrichten * [ʊn·te·ˈrɪç·tn̩] I. vt 1. (lehren) to teach 2. (informieren) to inform (**über** +akk about) II. vi to teach

Unterrichtsstunde f lesson, class

Unterrock [ˈʊn·te·rɔk] m petticoat

untersagen * [ʊn·te·ˈzaː·gn̩] vt form s. **verbieten**

Untersatz [ˈʊn·te·zats] m mat

unterschätzen * [ʊn·te·ˈʃɛ·tsn̩] vt to underestimate

unterscheiden * [ʊn·te·ˈʃai·dn̩] irreg I. vt 1. (differenzieren) to distinguish (**zwischen** +dat between) 2. (auseinanderhalten) to tell the difference between; **ich kann die beiden nie** ~ I can never tell the difference between the two; **etw von etw** dat ~ to tell sth from sth II. vi [**zwischen Dingen**] ~ to differentiate [between things] III. vr **sich** akk **von jdm/etw** ~ to differ from sb/sth

Unterschenkel m lower leg; (vom Hähnchen) drumstick

Unterschied <-[e]s, -e> [ˈʊn·te·ʃiːt] m difference; **im** ~ **zu dir bin ich vorsichtiger** unlike you, I'm more careful; **ohne** ~ indiscriminately; **einen/keinen** ~ [**zwischen Dingen**] **machen** to draw a/no distinction [between things]

unterschiedlich [ˈʊn·te·ʃiːt·lɪç] I. adj different; **~er Auffassung sein** to have different views II. adv differently

unterschlagen * [ʊn·te·ˈʃlaː·gn̩] vt irreg 1. (unrechtmäßig für sich behalten) to misappropriate; (Geld) to embezzle; (Brief, Beweise) to withhold 2. (vorenthalten) **jdm etw** ~ to withhold sth from sb

unterschreiben * [ʊn·te·ˈʃrai·bn̩] vt, vi irreg to sign

Unterschrift [ˈʊn·te·ʃrɪft] f 1. (eigene Signatur) signature 2. (Bildunterschrift) caption

Unterseite f underside

untersetzt [ʊn·te·ˈzɛtst] adj stocky

unterste(r, s) [ˈʊn·tes·ta, -tes·te, -tes·tas] adj superl von **untere(r, s)** ▸ **das U~ zuoberst kehren** fam to turn everything upside down

unterstehen *¹ [ʊn·te·ˈʃteː·ən] irreg I. vi **jdm/etw** ~ to be subordinate to sb/sth

II. vr **sich** akk ~ **etw zu tun** to have the audacity to do sth; **untersteh dich!** don't you dare!

unter|stehen² [ˈʊn·te·ˌʃteː·ən] vi irreg haben südd, österr, schweiz (Schutz suchen) to take shelter

unterstellen *¹ [ʊn·te·ˈʃtɛ·lən] vt 1. (unterordnen) **jdm jdn/etw** ~ to put sb in charge of sb/sth 2. (unterschieben) **jdm etw** ~ to imply that sb has said/done sth

unter|stellen² [ˈʊn·te·ˌʃtɛ·lən] I. vt 1. (abstellen) **etw irgendwo** ~ to store sth somewhere; **ein Auto bei jdm** ~ to leave one's car at sb's house 2. (darunterstellen) **einen Eimer** ~ to put a bucket underneath II. vr **sich** akk ~ to take shelter

Unterstellung f (falsche Behauptung) insinuation

unterstreichen * [ʊn·te·ˈʃtrai·çn̩] vt irreg 1. (markieren) to underline 2. (betonen) to emphasize

unterstützen * [ʊn·te·ˈʃty·tsn̩] vt 1. (helfen) to support (**bei/in** +dat in) 2. (sich dafür einsetzen) to back

Unterstützung f 1. kein pl (Hilfe) support 2. (finanzielle Hilfe) financial aid; (Arbeitslosenunterstützung) unemployment benefit

untersuchen * [ʊn·te·ˈzuː·xn̩] vt 1. (den Gesundheitszustand überprüfen) to examine (**auf** +akk for) 2. (überprüfen) to investigate; (Fahrzeug) to check 3. (genau betrachten) to scrutinize 4. (durchsuchen) to search (**auf** +akk for) 5. (aufzuklären suchen) to investigate

Untersuchung <-, -en> f 1. (Überprüfung des Gesundheitszustandes) [medical] examination 2. (Durchsuchung) search 3. (Überprüfung) investigation 4. (analysierende Arbeit) investigation

Untersuchungshaft f custody; **in** ~ **sein** to be in detention pending trial

Untersuchungsrichter(in) m(f) magistrate judge

Untertasse f saucer

unter|tauchen * [ˈʊn·te·tau·xn̩] I. vt haben **jdn** ~ to dunk sb's head under the water II. vi sein 1. (tauchen) to dive [under]; (U-Boot) to submerge

2. (*sich verstecken*) to go underground; **irgendwo ~** to disappear somewhere; **bei jdm ~** to hide out at sb's place

Untertitel ['ʊn·tɐ·tiː·tl̩] *m* subtitle

untervermieten* *vt, vi* to sublet

unterversorgt *adj* undersupplied

Unterversorgung *f kein pl* shortage

Unterwäsche <-> ['ʊn·tɐ·vɛ·ʃə] *f kein pl* underwear

unterwegs [ʊn·tɐ·'veːks] *adv* on the way; **er hat mich von ~ angerufen** he called me while he was on the road; **für ~** for the trip

Unterwelt ['ʊn·tɐ·vɛlt] *f kein pl* underworld

unterwerfen* [ʊn·tɐ·'vɛr·fn̩] *irreg* I. *vt* to subjugate II. *vr* **sich** *akk* **jdm/etw ~** to submit to sb/sth

unterzeichnen* [ʊn·tɐ·'tsaɪç·nən] *vt* to sign

unterziehen*¹ [ʊn·tɐ·'tsiː·ən] *irreg vr* **sich** *akk* **etw** *dat* **~** to undergo sth

unter|ziehen² ['ʊn·tɐ·tsiː·ən] *vt irreg* (*Kleidung*) to put on *sep* underneath

untragbar [ʊn·'traːk·baːɐ̯] *adj* **1.** (*unerträglich*) unbearable **2.** (*nicht tolerabel*) intolerable

untrennbar [ʊn·'trɛn·baːɐ̯] *adj* inseparable

untreu ['ʊn·trɔy] *adj* unfaithful; **jdm ~ sein** to be unfaithful to sb; **sich** *dat* **~ werden** to be untrue to oneself; **etw** *dat* **~ werden** to be disloyal to sth

Untreue *f* **1.** (*untreues Verhalten*) unfaithfulness **2.** JUR embezzlement

untröstlich [ʊn·'trøːst·lɪç] *adj* inconsolable

untypisch *adj* untypical

unübersichtlich ['ʊn·ʔyː·bɐ·zɪçt·lɪç] *adj* **1.** (*nicht übersichtlich*) confusing **2.** (*schwer zu überblicken*) unclear

unübertroffen [ʊn·ʔyː·bɐ·'trɔ·fn̩] *adj* unsurpassed; (*Rekord*) unbroken

unumstritten [ʊn·ʔʊm·'ʃtrɪ·tn̩] I. *adj* undisputed II. *adv* undisputedly

ununterbrochen ['ʊn·ʔʊn·tɐ·brɔ·xn̩] I. *adj* **1.** (*unaufhörlich andauernd*) incessant **2.** (*nicht unterbrochen*) uninterrupted II. *adv* incessantly

unveränderlich [ʊn·fɛɐ̯·'ʔɛn·dɐ·lɪç] *adj* unchanging

unverändert ['ʊn·fɛɐ̯·ʔɛn·dɐt] *adj* **1.** (*keine Änderungen aufweisend*) unrevised **2.** (*gleich bleibend*) unchanged; (*Einsatz, Fleiß*) unchanging

unverantwortlich [ʊn·fɛɐ̯·'ʔant·vɔrt·lɪç] I. *adj* irresponsible II. *adv* irresponsibly

unverbesserlich [ʊn·fɛɐ̯·'bɛ·sə·lɪç] *adj* incorrigible; (*Optimist*) incurable

unverbindlich ['ʊn·fɛɐ̯·bɪnt·lɪç] I. *adj* **1.** (*nicht verpflichtend*) not binding *pred* **2.** (*distanziert*) detached II. *adv* without obligation

unvereinbar [ʊn·fɛɐ̯·'ʔaɪn·baːɐ̯] *adj* incompatible; (*Gegensätze*) irreconcilable

unvergänglich ['ʊn·fɛɐ̯·gɛŋ·lɪç] *adj* **1.** (*Eindruck*) lasting **2.** (*nicht vergänglich*) immortal

unvergesslichᴿᴿ [ʊn·fɛɐ̯·'gɛs·lɪç] *adj* unforgettable

unvergleichlich [ʊn·fɛɐ̯·'glaɪç·lɪç] I. *adj* incomparable II. *adv* incomparably

unverhältnismäßig ['ʊn·fɛɐ̯·hɛlt·nɪs·mɛː·sɪç] *adv* excessively

unverhofft ['ʊn·fɛɐ̯·hɔft] I. *adj* unexpected II. *adv* unexpectedly

unverkäuflich ['ʊn·fɛɐ̯·kɔyf·lɪç] *adj* not for sale *pred*

unverkennbar [ʊn·fɛɐ̯·'kɛn·baːɐ̯] *adj* unmistakable; **~ sein, dass ...** to be clear that ...

unverletzt ['ʊn·fɛɐ̯·lɛtst] *adj* unhurt

unvermeidlich [ʊn·fɛɐ̯·'maɪt·lɪç] *adj* unavoidable

unvermindert ['ʊn·fɛɐ̯·mɪn·dɐt] I. *adj* undiminished II. *adv* unabated

Unvermögen ['ʊn·fɛɐ̯·møː·gn̩] *nt kein pl* powerlessness; **jds ~, etw zu tun** sb's inability to do sth

unvermutet ['ʊn·fɛɐ̯·muː·tət] I. *adj* unexpected II. *adv* unexpectedly

unvernünftig ['ʊn·fɛɐ̯·nʏnf·tɪç] *adj* unreasonable

unverschämt ['ʊn·fɛɐ̯·ʃɛːmt] I. *adj* (*Lüge, Preise*) outrageous II. *adv* outrageously

Unverschämtheit <-, -en> *f* **1.** *kein pl* (*Dreistigkeit*) insolence **2.** (*Bemerkung*) impertinent remark; **[das ist eine] ~!** that's outrageous! **3.** (*Handlung*) impertinence

unverschuldet [ˈʊn·fɛɐ̯·ʃʊl·dət] *adj, adv* through no fault of one's own

unversöhnlich [ˈʊn·fɛɐ̯·zøː·n·lɪç] *adj* irreconcilable

unverständlich [ˈʊn·fɛɐ̯·ʃtɛnt·lɪç] *adj* 1. (*akustisch nicht zu verstehen*) unintelligible 2. (*unbegreiflich*) incomprehensible

unverträglich [ˈʊn·fɛɐ̯·trɛ·k·lɪç] *adj* indigestible

unverwechselbar [ʊn·fɛɐ̯·ˈvɛk·sl̩·baːɐ̯] *adj* unmistakable

unverwundbar [ʊn·fɛɐ̯·ˈvʊnt·baːɐ̯] *adj* invulnerable

unverwüstlich [ʊn·fɛɐ̯·ˈvyːst·lɪç] *adj* tough; (*Gesundheit*) robust

unverzeihlich [ʊn·fɛɐ̯·ˈtsai·lɪç] *adj* inexcusable

unvollständig [ˈʊn·fɔl·ʃtɛn·dɪç] I. *adj* incomplete II. *adv* incompletely

unvorbereitet [ˈʊn·foːɐ̯·bə·rai·tət] I. *adj* unprepared II. *adv* 1. (*ohne sich vorbereitet zu haben*) without [any] preparation 2. (*unerwartet*) unexpectedly

unvoreingenommen [ˈʊn·foːɐ̯·ʔain·gə·nɔ·mən] I. *adj* unbiased II. *adv* impartially

unvorhergesehen [ˈʊn·foːɐ̯·he·ɐ̯·gə·zeː·ən] I. *adj* unforeseen; (*Besuch*) unexpected II. *adv* unexpectedly

unvorsichtig [ˈʊn·foːɐ̯·zɪç·tɪç] I. *adj* 1. (*unbedacht*) rash 2. (*nicht vorsichtig*) careless II. *adv* 1. (*unbedacht*) rashly 2. (*nicht vorsichtig*) carelessly

unvorstellbar [ʊn·foːɐ̯·ˈʃtɛl·baːɐ̯] I. *adj* inconceivable II. *adv* inconceivably

unwahr [ˈʊn·vaːɐ̯] *adj* untrue, false

unwahrscheinlich [ˈʊn·vaːɐ̯·ʃain·lɪç] I. *adj* 1. (*kaum denkbar*) unlikely; (*Zufall*) remarkable 2. *fam* (*unerhört*) incredible II. *adv fam* incredibly

unweigerlich [ˈʊn·vai·gɐ·lɪç] I. *adj attr* inevitable II. *adv* inevitably

unweit [ˈʊn·vait] *adv* ~ **von etw** *dat* not far from sth

Unwetter <-s, -> [ˈʊn·vɛ·tɐ] *nt* thunderstorm

unwichtig [ˈʊn·vɪç·tɪç] *adj* unimportant

unwiderstehlich [ʊn·vi·dɐ·ˈʃteː·lɪç] *adj* irresistible

unwillig [ˈʊn·vɪ·lɪç] I. *adj* 1. (*verärgert*) angry 2. (*widerwillig*) reluctant II. *adv* reluctantly

unwillkürlich [ˈʊn·vɪl·ky·ɐ̯·lɪç] I. *adj* involuntary II. *adv* involuntarily

unwirklich [ˈʊn·vɪrk·lɪç] *adj* unreal

unwirksam [ˈʊn·vɪrk·zaːm] *adj* ineffective

Unwissenheit <-> [ˈʊn·vɪ·sn̩·hait] *f kein pl* ignorance

unwohl [ˈʊn·voːl] *adj* **jdm ist ~** 1. (*gesundheitlich nicht gut*) sb feels sick 2. (*unbehaglich*) sb feels uneasy

Unwohlsein <-s> [ˈʊn·voːl·zain] *nt kein pl* |slight| nausea

unwürdig [ˈʊn·vʏr·dɪç] *adj* 1. (*nicht würdig*) unworthy 2. (*schändlich*) disgraceful

unzählig [ʊn·ˈtsɛː·lɪç] *adj* countless

unzerbrechlich [ˈʊn·tsɛɐ̯·brɛç·lɪç] *adj* unbreakable

unzufrieden [ˈʊn·tsu·friː·dn̩] *adj* dissatisfied

Unzufriedenheit *f* dissatisfaction

unzugänglich [ˈʊn·tsuː·gɛŋ·lɪç] *adj* 1. (*schwer erreichbar*) inaccessible 2. (*nicht aufgeschlossen*) unapproachable

unzulänglich [ˈʊn·tsuː·lɛŋ·lɪç] I. *adj* inadequate; (*Erfahrungen, Kenntnisse*) insufficient II. *adv* inadequately

unzulässig [ˈʊn·tsuː·lɛ·sɪç] *adj* inadmissible

unzumutbar [ˈʊn·tsuː·muːt·baːɐ̯] *adj* unreasonable

unzurechnungsfähig [ˈʊn·tsuː·rɛç·nʊŋs·fɛː·ɪç] *adj* of unsound mind *pred;* **jdn für ~ erklären** to certify [*o* declare] sb mentally incompetent

unzusammenhängend [ˈʊn·tsu·za·mən·hɛŋ·ənt] *adj* incoherent

unzuverlässig [ˈʊn·tsuː·fɛɐ̯·lɛ·sɪç] *adj* unreliable

üppig [ˈʏpɪç] *adj* 1. (*Figur*) voluptuous 2. (*Mahlzeit*) sumptuous

uralt [ˈuːɐ̯·ʔalt] *adj* 1. (*sehr alt*) very old 2. (*schon lange existent*) ancient 3. *fam* (*schon lange bekannt*) ancient; (*Problem*) old, perennial

Uran <-s> [uˈraːn] *nt kein pl* uranium

Uraufführung *f* (*eines Theaterstücks*) first performance; (*eines Films*) first release

U

Ureinwohner(in) *m(f)* indigenous person

Urenkel(in) ['uːɐ̯·ʔɛŋ·kl̩] *m(f)* great-grandchild, great-grandson *masc*, great-granddaughter *fem*

Urgeschichte ['uːɐ̯·ɡə·ʃɪç·tə] *f kein pl* prehistory

Urgroßeltern ['uːɐ̯·ɡroːs·ʔɛl·tɐn] *pl* great-grandparents *pl*

Urgroßmutter ['uːɐ̯·ɡroːs·mʊ·tɐ] *f* great-grandmother

Urgroßvater *m* great-grandfather

Urheberrecht *nt* **1.** (*Recht des Autors*) copyright (**an** +*dat* on) **2.** (*urheberrechtliche Bestimmungen*) copyright law

urheberrechtlich **I.** *adj* copyright *attr* **II.** *adv* ~ **geschützt** copyright[ed]

Urin <-s, -e> [uˈriːn] *m* urine

urinieren * [ur·iˈniː·rən] *vi geh* to urinate

Urkunde <-, -n> ['uːɐ̯·kʊn·də] *f* (*Auszeichnung*) certificate; (*rechtskräftig*) document

Urkundenfälschung *f* document forgery

Urlaub <-[e]s, -e> ['uːɐ̯·laup] *m* vacation; ~ **machen** to go on vacation; **in** ~ **sein** to be on vacation

Urlauber(in) <-s, -> *m(f)* vacationer

Urlaubsgeld *nt* vacation pay

Urne <-, -n> ['ʊr·nə] *f* **1.** (*Graburne*) urn **2.** (*Wahlurne*) ballot box

Ursache *f* cause (**für** +*akk* of) ▶ **keine** ~**!** you're welcome!

Ursprung ['uːɐ̯·ʃprʊŋ] *m* origin

ursprünglich ['uːɐ̯·ʃpryŋ·lɪç] **I.** *adj* **1.** *attr* (*anfänglich*) original **2.** (*im Urzustand befindlich*) unspoiled **3.** (*urtümlich*) ancient **II.** *adv* originally

Urteil <-s, -e> ['ʊr·tail] *nt* **1.** JUR judgment, verdict **2.** (*Meinung*) opinion (**über** +*akk* on)

urteilen ['ʊr·tai·lən] *vi* to pass judgment (**über** +*akk* on)

Urteilsbegründung *f* basis for a judgment

Urwald ['uːɐ̯·valt] *m* primeval [*o* virgin] forest

urwüchsig *adj* **1.** (*im Urzustand erhalten*) unspoiled **2.** (*unverbildet*) earthy **3.** (*ursprünglich*) original

Urzeit *f* **die** ~ primeval times *pl* ▶ **seit** ~**en** for eons; **vor** ~**en** eons ago

Urzustand *m kein pl* original state

Utopie <-, -n> [uto·ˈpiː] *f* Utopia

utopisch [uˈtoː·pɪʃ] *adj* utopian

UV-Strahlen *pl* UV rays *pl*

V

V, v <-, -> [fau] *nt* V, v; ~ **wie Viktor** V as in Victor

V *Abk von* **Volt** V

Vagabund(in) <-en, -en> [va·ɡa·ˈbʊnt] *m(f)* vagabond

vage ['vaː·ɡə] **I.** *adj* vague **II.** *adv* vaguely

Vagina <-, Vaginen> ['vaː·ɡi·na] *f* vagina

Vakuum <-s, Vakuen> ['vaː·ku·ʊm] *nt* vacuum

vakuumverpackt *adj* vacuum-packed

Vampir <-s, -e> [vamˈpiːɐ̯] *m* vampire

Vandale, Vandalin <-n, -n> [van·ˈdaː·lə, van·ˈdaː·lɪn] *m, f* vandal

Vandalismus <-> [van·da·ˈlɪs·mʊs] *m kein pl* vandalism

Vanille <-, -en> [va·ˈnɪlə] *f* vanilla

variabel [va·ˈrĭaː·bl̩] *adj* variable

Variante <-, -n> [va·ˈrĭan·tə] *f* **1.** (*Abwandlung*) variation **2.** (*veränderte Ausführung*) variant

variieren * [va·ri·ˈiːrən] *vi* to vary

Vase <-, -n> ['vaː·zə] *f* vase

Vater <-s, Väter> ['faː·tɐ] *m* father

Vaterland *nt* fatherland

väterlich ['fɛ·tɐ·lɪç] **I.** *adj* **1.** (*dem Vater gehörend*) **das** ~**e Geschäft** his/her father's business **2.** (*zum Vater gehörend*) paternal **3.** (*fürsorglich*) fatherly **II.** *adv* like a father

väterlicherseits *adv* on sb's father's side

Vaterschaftsklage *f* paternity suit

Vaterunser <-s, -> [faː·tɐ·ˈʔʊn·zɐ] *nt* REL **das** ~ the Lord's Prayer

Vati <-s, -s> ['faː·ti] *m fam* daddy

Vatikan <-s> [va·ti·ˈkaːn] *m* Vatican

V-Ausschnitt ['faʊ-] *m* V-neck; **ein Pullover mit** ~ a V-neck sweater

Vegetarier(in) <-s, -> [veˑgeˑ'taːrɪˌɐ] *m(f)* vegetarian

vegetarisch [veˑgeˑ'taːrɪʃ] **I.** *adj* vegetarian **II.** *adv* **sich** *akk* ~ **ernähren** to be a vegetarian

Vegetation <-, -en> [veˑgeˑtaˑ'tsjoːn] *f* vegetation

Veilchen <-s, -> ['failçən] *nt* violet

Velo <-s, -s> ['veːˑlo] *nt schweiz* (*Fahrrad*) bicycle, bike *fam*

Velours <-, -> [vəˑ'luːɐ] *nt*, **Veloursleder** *nt* suede

Vene <-, -n> ['veːnə] *f* vein

Ventil <-s, -e> [vɛn'tiːl] *nt* valve

Ventilator <-s, -toren> [vɛntiˑ'laːˑtoːɐ] *m* fan

verabreden * **I.** *vr* **sich** *akk* [**mit jdm**] ~ to set up a date [*o* make plans] [with sb]; [**mit jdm**] **verabredet sein** to have plans [*o* a date] [with sb] **II.** *vt* **etw** [**mit jdm**] ~ to arrange [*o* set up] sth [with sb]; **verabredet** agreed

Verabredung <-, -en> *f* **1.** (*Treffen*) meeting; (*Rendezvous*) date **2.** (*Vereinbarung*) arrangement

verabscheuen * *vt* to detest, to loathe

verabschieden * **I.** *vr* **sich** *akk* ~ to say goodbye (**von** +*dat* to) **II.** *vt* (*Gesetz*) to pass

verachten * *vt* **1.** (*verächtlich finden*) to despise **2.** (*nicht achten*) to scorn; **nicht zu** ~ **sein** [sth is] not to be sneezed at *fam*

verächtlich [fɛɐ'ʔɛçtˌlɪç] **I.** *adj* **1.** (*Verachtung zeigend*) contemptuous, scornful **2.** (*verabscheuungswürdig*) despicable **II.** *adv* contemptuously, scornfully

Verachtung *f* contempt, scorn

verallgemeinern * **I.** *vt* **etw** ~ to generalize about sth **II.** *vi* to generalize

veralten * [fɛɐ'ʔalˌtn̩] *vi sein* to become obsolete; (*Ansichten, Methoden*) to become outdated; **veraltet** obsolete; (*Reiseführer, Stadtplan*) old

Veranda <-, Veranden> [veˑ'ranˑda] *f* veranda

veränderlich *adj* variable

verändern * *vt, vr* to change

Veränderung *f* change; (*leicht*) alteration, modification

veranlagt [fɛɐ'ʔanˌlaːkt] *adj* **ein künst-**lerisch ~**er Mensch** a person with an artistic disposition; **er ist praktisch** ~ he is practically minded

Veranlagung <-, -en> *f* disposition (**zu** +*dat* to)

veranlassen * *vt* **1.** (*in die Wege leiten*) to arrange; ~, **dass etw geschieht** to see to it that sth happens **2.** (*dazu bringen*) **jdn zu etw** *dat* ~ to cause sb to do sth

Veranlassung <-, -en> *f* cause; **auf jds** ~ at sb's instigation

veranschaulichen * [fɛɐ'ʔanˌʃauˑlɪˌçn̩] *vt* to illustrate

veranstalten * [fɛɐ'ʔanˌʃtalˌtn̩] *vt* to organize

Veranstalter(in) <-s, -> *m(f)* organizer

Veranstaltung <-, -en> *f* **1.** *kein pl* (*das Durchführen*) organizing **2.** (*Ereignis*) event

Veranstaltungsort *m* venue

verantworten * **I.** *vt* **etw** ~ to take responsibility for sth **II.** *vr* **sich** *akk* [**vor jdm**] ~ to answer [to sb] (**für** +*akk* for)

verantwortlich *adj* responsible

Verantwortung <-, -en> *f* responsibility; **die** ~ [**für etw** *akk*] **tragen/übernehmen** to be responsible/take responsibility [for sth]; **auf eigene** ~ on one's own responsibility, at one's own risk

verantwortungsbewusst ᴿᴿ **I.** *adj* responsible **II.** *adv* responsibly

verantwortungslos I. *adj* irresponsible **II.** *adv* irresponsibly

verarbeiten * *vt* **1.** (*verwenden*) to use; (*Lebensmittel, Rohstoffe*) to process; **etw zu etw** *dat* ~ to make sth into sth **2.** ᴘꜱʏᴄʜ to assimilate, to come to terms with

verärgern * *vt* to annoy

Verarmung <-, -en> *f* impoverishment

verarschen * [fɛɐ'ʔarˌʃn̩] *vt derb* **jdn** ~ to mess around with sb

verarzten * [fɛɐ'ʔaːɐtsˌtn̩] *vt fam* to treat

verausgaben * [fɛɐ'ʔausˌgaˑbn̩] *vr* **sich** *akk* ~ (*körperlich*) to overexert; (*finanziell*) to overspend

Verb <-s, -en> [vɛrp] *nt* verb

verbal [vɛr'baːl] **I.** *adj* verbal **II.** *adv* verbally

Verband <-[e]s, Verbände> [fɛɐ'bant] *m*

V

1. (*Bund*) association **2.** MED bandage, dressing

Verband(s)kasten *m* first-aid kit

Verbannung <-, -en> *f* exile, banishment

verbergen * *vt irreg* to hide, to conceal (**vor** +*dat* from)

verbessern * **I.** *vt* **1.** (*besser machen*) to improve **2.** (*korrigieren*) to correct **II.** *vr* **sich** *akk* ~ to improve

Verbesserung <-, -en> *f* **1.** (*qualitative Anhebung*) improvement **2.** (*Korrektur*) correction

verbeugen *vr* **sich** *akk* ~ to bow

Verbeugung *f* bow

verbiegen * *vt, vr irreg* [**sich** *akk*] ~ to bend; **verbogen** bent

verbieten <verbot, verboten> *vt* to forbid, to ban; (*offiziell*) to outlaw; **jdm ~, etw zu tun** to forbid sb to do sth; **ich habe es dir doch verboten** I told you you weren't allowed to do that

verbinden *[^*1] *vt irreg* (*Wunde*) to dress; **jdn ~** to dress sb's wound[s]

verbinden *[^*2] *vt irreg* **1.** (*zusammenfügen*) to join (**mit** +*dat* to) **2.** TELEK **jdn** [**mit jdm**] ~ to connect sb [to sb]; **falsch verbunden!** wrong number! **3.** TRANSP to connect, to link **4.** (*verknüpfen*) to combine; **das Nützliche mit dem Angenehmen ~** to combine business with pleasure **5.** (*assoziieren*) **etw mit etw** *dat* ~ to associate sth [with sth]

verbindlich [fɛɐ̯·ˈbɪnt·lɪç] **I.** *adj* **1.** (*bindend*) binding **2.** (*entgegenkommend*) friendly **II.** *adv* **1.** (*bindend*) ~ **zusagen** to make a binding commitment **2.** (*entgegenkommend*) in a friendly manner

Verbindung *f* **1.** (*direkte Beziehung*) contact; **in ~ bleiben** to keep in touch; **~en zu jdm/etw haben** to have connections *pl* with sb/sth; **sich** *akk* **mit jdm in ~ setzen** to contact sb **2.** TELEK, TRANSP connection (**nach** +*dat* to) **3.** (*Zusammenhang*) **jdn mit etw** *dat* **in ~ bringen** to connect sb with sth; **in ~ mit** in connection with **4.** CHEM compound **5.** UNIV fraternity

verbissen I. *adj* **1.** (*hartnäckig*) dogged **2.** (*verkrampft*) grim **II.** *adv* doggedly

verbitten * *vr irreg* **sich** *dat* **etw ~** to

not tolerate sth

verbittert I. *adj* embittered, bitter **II.** *adv* bitterly

Verbitterung <-, *selten* -en> *f* bitterness

verblassen * *vi sein* **1.** (*blasser werden*) to pale **2.** (*schwächer werden*) to fade

verbleit *adj* leaded

verblöden * [fɛɐ̯·ˈbløː·dn̩] *vi sein fam* to turn into a zombie

verblüffen * [fɛɐ̯·ˈblʏ·fn̩] *vt* to astonish

verblühen * *vi sein* to wilt

verbluten * *vi sein* to bleed to death

verbohrt *adj* obstinate

verborgen *adj* hidden

Verbot <-[e]s, -e> [fɛɐ̯·ˈboːt] *nt* ban

verboten [fɛɐ̯·ˈboː·tn̩] *adj* prohibited, forbidden; **Parken ~!** you're not allowed to park here!

Verbotsschild *nt* sign prohibiting sth

Verbrauch *m kein pl* consumption (**an** +*dat* of)

verbrauchen * *vt* **1.** to consume **2.** (*Vorräte*) to use up *sep*

Verbraucher(in) <-s, -> *m(f)* consumer

verbraucherfreundlich *adj* consumer-friendly

verbraucht *adj* (*aufgebraucht*) exhausted; (*Mensch a.*) burned-out *fam*

verbrechen <verbrach, verbrochen> *vt fam* to be up to

Verbrechen <-s, -> *nt* crime

Verbrecher(in) <-s, -> *m(f)* criminal

verbrecherisch *adj* criminal

verbreiten * *vt, vr* to spread

verbreitern * [fɛɐ̯·ˈbraɪ·tɐn] *vt* to widen

verbreitet *adj* popular; [**weit**] ~ **sein** to be [very] widespread

Verbreitung <-, -en> *f* **1.** *kein pl* (*das Verbreiten*) dissemination **2.** MEDIA distribution **3.** MED spread

verbrennen * *irreg* **I.** *vt haben* to burn **II.** *vr haben* **sich** *dat* **die Zunge ~** to burn one's tongue; **sich** *dat* **die Finger** [**an etw** *dat*] ~ to burn one's fingers [on sth] **III.** *vi sein* to burn; **verbrannt** burned

Verbrennung <-, -en> *f* **1.** *kein pl* (*das Verbrennen*) burning **2.** MED burn

verbrühen * *vt* to scald

verbuchen * *vt* to mark up *sep* (**als** +*akk* as)

verbummeln * vt fam 1. (vertrödeln) to waste 2. (verlieren) to misplace

verbünden * [fɛɐ̯ˈbʏn·dn̩] vr sich akk ~ to form an alliance

Verbundenheit <-> f kein pl closeness

Verbündete(r) f(m) dekl wie adj ally

verbürgen * I. vr sich akk für jdn/etw ~ to vouch for sb/sth II. vt to guarantee

verbüßen * vt JUR to serve

verchromt adj chrome-plated

Verdacht <-[e]s> [fɛɐ̯ˈdaxt] m kein pl suspicion; ~ erregen to arouse suspicion; jdn im ~ haben to suspect sb

verdächtig [fɛɐ̯ˈdɛç·tɪç] I. adj suspicious; jdm ~ vorkommen to seem suspicious to sb; sich akk ~ machen to arouse suspicion II. adv suspiciously

Verdächtige(r) f(m) dekl wie adj suspect

verdächtigen * [fɛɐ̯ˈdɛç·tɪ·gn̩] vt to suspect

verdammen * [fɛɐ̯ˈda·mən] vt to condemn

verdammt adj fam 1. (Ärger ausdrückend) damned; ~! damn! 2. (sehr groß) wir hatten ~es Glück! we were damn lucky!

verdampfen * vi sein to evaporate

verdanken * vt 1. (durch etw erhalten) diesen Erfolg verdanke ich dir thanks to you, this has been a success 2. schweiz (Dank aussprechen) [jdm] etw ~ to express one's thanks [to sb]

verdauen * [fɛɐ̯ˈdau·ən] vt 1. (Nahrung) to digest 2. (Niederlage etc.) to get over

verdaulich adj digestible; gut/schwer ~ easy/hard to digest

Verdauung <-> f kein pl digestion

Verdeck <-[e]s, -e> nt convertible top

verdecken * vt 1. (die Sicht nehmen) to cover [up sep] 2. (maskieren) to conceal

verderben <verdarb, verdorben> [fɛɐ̯ˈdɛr·bn̩] I. vt haben 1. (moralisch) to corrupt 2. (zunichtemachen: Spaß) to spoil 3. (verscherzen) es sich dat mit niemandem ~ wollen to try to please everyone II. vi sein to spoil; (Lebensmittel) to go bad

verderblich [fɛɐ̯ˈdɛrp·lɪç] adj (Lebensmittel) perishable

verdeutlichen * [fɛɐ̯ˈdɔyt·lɪ·çn̩] vt to explain

verdichten * I. vt PHYS to compress II. vr sich akk ~ (Eindruck, Gefühl) to intensify; (Verdacht) to grow

verdienen * I. vt 1. (als Verdienst bekommen) to earn 2. (Gewinn machen) to make (an +dat off of) 3. (zustehen) to deserve II. vi 1. (einen Verdienst bekommen) to earn [money] 2. (Gewinn machen) to make a profit (an +dat off of)

Verdienst[1] <-[e]s, -e> [fɛɐ̯ˈdiːnst] m FIN income, earnings npl

Verdienst[2] <-[e]s, -e> [fɛɐ̯ˈdiːnst] nt merit; es ist sein ~, dass ... it's thanks to him [o to his credit] that ...

Verdienstausfall m loss of earnings pl

verdoppeln * I. vt 1. (erhöhen) to double 2. (verstärken) to redouble II. vr sich akk ~ to double

verdorben [fɛɐ̯ˈdɔr·bn̩] I. pp von verderben II. adj 1. (ungenießbar) bad 2. (moralisch korrumpiert) corrupt 3. MED einen ~en Magen haben to have an upset stomach

verdorren * [fɛɐ̯ˈdɔ·rən] vi sein to wither

verdrängen * vt 1. (vertreiben) to drive out 2. (unterdrücken: Erinnerung, Gefühl) to suppress

verdrehen * vt 1. (wenden) to twist; (Augen) to roll 2. (Tatsachen) to distort ► jdm den Kopf ~ to turn sb's head

verdreifachen * [fɛɐ̯ˈdrai·fa·xn̩] I. vt to triple II. vr sich akk ~ to triple

verdrießlich [fɛɐ̯ˈdriːs·lɪç] adj (Gesicht) sullen; (Stimmung) morose

verdrossen [fɛɐ̯ˈdrɔ·sn̩] adj sullen, morose

verdrücken * I. vt fam (verzehren) to polish off sep II. vr fam (verschwinden) sich akk ~ to slip away

Verdruss[RR] <-es, -e>, **Verdruß**[ALT] <-sses, -sse> [fɛɐ̯ˈdrʊs] m meist sing annoyance; jdm ~ bereiten to annoy sb

verdunkeln * I. vt 1. (abdunkeln) to black out 2. (verdüstern) to darken II. vr (dunkler werden) sich akk ~ to darken

      V

verdünnen * [fɛɐ̯ˈdʏ·nən] *vt* to dilute

verdunsten * *vi sein* to evaporate

verdursten * *vi sein* to die of thirst

verdutzt [fɛɐ̯ˈdʊtst] I. *adj fam* 1. (*verwirrt*) baffled, confused 2. (*überrascht*) taken aback *pred* II. *adv* in a baffled manner

verehren * *vt* 1. (*bewundernd*) to admire 2. REL to worship

Verehrer(in) <-s, -> *m(f)* admirer

Verehrung *f kein pl* 1. (*Bewunderung*) admiration 2. REL worship

vereidigen * [fɛɐ̯ˈʔai·dɪ·gn̩] *vt* to swear in *sep*

vereidigt [fɛɐ̯ˈʔai·dɪçt] *adj* sworn; **gerichtlich** ~ certified before the court

Verein <-[e]s, -e> [fɛɐ̯ˈʔain] *m* club, association; **eingetragener** ~ registered association; **gemeinnütziger** ~ charitable organization

vereinbar *adj* compatible (**mit** +*dat* with)

vereinbaren * [fɛɐ̯ˈʔain·ba:·rən] *vt* 1. (*absprechen*) **etw** [**mit jdm**] ~ to agree to [o arrange] sth [with sb] 2. (*in Einklang bringen*) to reconcile; **sich** *akk* ~ **lassen** to be compatible

Vereinbarung <-, -en> *f* 1. *kein pl* (*das Vereinbaren*) arranging 2. (*Abmachung*) agreement; **laut** ~ as agreed; **nach** ~ by arrangement

vereinen * *vt* to unite

vereinfachen * [fɛɐ̯ˈʔain·fa·xn̩] *vt* to simplify

vereinheitlichen * [fɛɐ̯ˈʔain·hait·lɪ·çn̩] *vt* to standardize

vereinigen * *vr* **sich** *akk* ~ to merge

vereinsamen * [fɛɐ̯ˈʔain·za:·mən] *vi sein* to become lonely

vereinsamt *adj* lonely

Vereinsamung <-> *f kein pl* loneliness

vereinzelt [fɛɐ̯ˈʔain·tsl̩t] *adj* occasional

vereisen * I. *vi sein* to ice up; **eine vereiste Fahrbahn** an icy road II. *vt haben* (*lokal anästhesieren*) to freeze

vereiteln * [fɛɐ̯ˈʔaitl̩n] *vt* to thwart

vereitern * *vi sein* to go septic

vererben * I. *vt* [**jdm**] **etw** ~ 1. (*hinterlassen*) to leave [sb] sth 2. (*durch Vererbung weitergeben*) to pass on *sep* sth [to sb] 3. (*schenken*) to hand down *sep* sth [to sb] II. *vr* **sich** *akk* ~ to be hereditary

vererblich *adj* hereditary

verewigen * [fɛɐ̯ˈʔe:vɪ·gn̩] I. *vr* **sich** *akk* ~ to leave one's mark [for posterity] II. *vt* (*unsterblich machen*) to immortalize

verfahren *¹ [fɛɐ̯ˈʔfa:·rən] *vi irreg sein* 1. (*vorgehen*) to proceed 2. (*umgehen*) **mit jdm** ~ to deal with sb

verfahren *² [fɛɐ̯ˈʔfa:·rən] *irreg* I. *vt* (*Benzin*) to use up *sep* II. *vr* **sich** *akk* ~ to get lost [while driving]

verfahren³ [fɛɐ̯ˈʔfa:·rən] *adj* muddled; **völlig** ~ **sein** to be a total mess

Verfahren <-s, -> [fɛɐ̯ˈʔfa:·rən] *nt* 1. (*Methode*) process 2. (*Gerichtsverfahren*) [legal [o criminal]] proceedings *npl*

Verfall [fɛɐ̯ˈfal] *m kein pl* 1. (*Verwahrlosung*) dilapidation 2. (*moralisch*) decline

verfallen *¹ *vi irreg sein* 1. (*zerfallen*) to decay 2. (*immer schwächer werden*) to deteriorate 3. (*ungültig werden: Ticket, Gutschein*) to expire; (*Anspruch*) to lapse 4. (*erliegen*) **jdm** ~ to be captivated by sb; **etw** *dat* ~ to become addicted to sth

verfallen² *adj* 1. (*völlig baufällig*) dilapidated 2. (*abgelaufen*) expired

Verfallsdatum *nt* ÖKON 1. (*der Haltbarkeit*) use-by date 2. (*der Gültigkeit*) expiration date

verfälschen * *vt* 1. (*falsch darstellen*) to distort 2. (*in der Qualität mindern*) to adulterate (**durch** +*akk* with)

verfärben * I. *vr* **sich** *akk* ~ to change color; (*Wäsche*) to discolor II. *vt* to discolor

verfassen * *vt* to write; (*Gesetz, Urkunde*) to draw up

Verfasser(in) <-s, -> [fɛɐ̯ˈfa·sɐ] *m(f)* author

Verfassung *f* 1. *kein pl* (*Zustand*) condition; (*körperlich*) state [of health]; (*seelisch*) state [of mind] 2. POL constitution

Verfassungsschutz *m* domestic intelligence agency

verfassungswidrig *adj* unconstitutional

verfaulen * *vi sein* to rot

Verfechter(in) *m(f)* advocate, champion

verfehlen * *vt* 1. (*nicht treffen, verpassen*) to miss; **nicht zu ~ sein** to be impossible to miss 2. (*nicht erreichen*) to not achieve; **das Thema ~** to be off the subject; **seinen Beruf ~** to miss one's calling

verfeinden * [fɛɐ̯·ˈfain·dn̩] *vr* **sich** *akk* ~ to fall out; **verfeindet sein** to be enemies; **verfeindete Staaten** enemy states

verfeinern * [fɛɐ̯·ˈfai·nɐn] *vt* 1. (*verbessern*) KOCHK to improve (**mit** +*dat* with) 2. (*raffinierter gestalten: Methode, Stil*) to refine

Verfilmung <-, -en> *f* 1. *kein pl* (*das Verfilmen*) filming 2. (*Film*) film

verfinstern * [fɛɐ̯·ˈfɪns·tɐn] *vr* **sich** *akk* ~ to darken

verfliegen * *vi irreg sein* 1. (*Zorn*) to pass; (*Kummer*) to vanish 2. (*Geruch*) to evaporate

verfluchen * *vt* to curse

verflüssigen * [fɛɐ̯·ˈfly·sɪ·ɡn̩] *vt, vr* to liquefy

verfolgen * *vt* 1. (*nachgehen*) to follow 2. (*aus politischen etc. Gründen*) to persecute 3. (*zu erreichen suchen*) to pursue; **eine Absicht ~** to have sth in mind 4. (*belasten*) **vom Pech verfolgt sein** to be dogged by bad luck

Verfolger(in) <-s, -> *m(f)* pursuer

Verfolgte(r) [fɛɐ̯·ˈfɔlk·tə, -tə] *f(m) dekl wie adj* victim of persecution

Verfolgung <-, -en> *f* 1. (*das Verfolgen*) pursuit 2. (*aus politischen Gründen*) persecution 3. JUR prosecution

Verfolgungsjagd *f* pursuit, chase

Verfolgungswahn *m* persecution complex

verformen * I. *vt* to distort II. *vr* **sich** *akk* ~ to become distorted [*o* misshapen]

verfressen * *adj pej fam* [overly] greedy

verfrüht *adj* premature

verfügbar *adj* available

verfügen * I. *vi* **über etw** *akk* ~ to have sth at one's disposal II. *vt* (*anordnen*) to order

Verfügung <-, -en> *f* 1. (*Anordnung*) order; **einstweilige ~** JUR temporary injunction 2. (*Disposition*) **etw zur ~ haben** to have sth at one's disposal;

jdm zur ~ stehen to be available to sb; **[jdm] etw zur ~ stellen** to make sth available [to sb]

verführen * *vt* 1. (*verleiten*) to entice; (*sexuell*) to seduce 2. *hum* (*verlocken*) to tempt

verführerisch [fɛɐ̯·ˈfy·rə·rɪʃ] *adj* 1. (*verlockend*) tempting 2. (*aufreizend*) seductive

Verführung *f* 1. (*Verleitung*) seduction; **~ Minderjähriger** JUR seduction of minors 2. (*Verlockung*) temptation

Vergabe [fɛɐ̯·ˈɡaː·bə] *f* (*von Arbeit, Studienplätzen*) allocation; (*eines Auftrags, Preises*) award

vergammeln <-er, -este> *adj fam* scruffy

vergangen *adj* past, former

Vergangenheit <-, *selten* -en> [fɛɐ̯·ˈɡaŋən·hait] *f* 1. *kein pl* (*Vergangenes*) past 2. LING past [tense]

vergänglich [fɛɐ̯·ˈɡɛŋ·lɪç] *adj* transient

Vergaser <-s, -> *m* AUTO carburetor

vergeben * *irreg* I. *vi* to forgive II. *vt* 1. (*verzeihen*) to forgive 2. (*zuteilen*) to allocate sth (**an** +*akk* to); (*Preis, Auftrag*) to award

vergeblich [fɛɐ̯·ˈɡeːp·lɪç] I. *adj* (*erfolglos bleibend*) futile II. *adv* (*umsonst*) in vain

Vergebung <-, -en> *f* forgiveness

vergehen * [fɛɐ̯·ˈɡeː·ən] *irreg* I. *vi* 1. (*Zeit*) to pass II. *vr haben* **sich** *akk* **an jdm ~** to sexually assault sb

Vergehen <-s, -> [fɛɐ̯·ˈɡeː·ən] *nt* offense

vergelten *vt irreg* **[jdm] etw ~** to repay sb for sth

Vergeltung <-, -en> *f* revenge

Vergeltungsschlag *m* retaliatory strike

vergessen * *vt irreg* (*vergisst, vergaß, vergessen*) [fɛɐ̯·ˈɡɛ·sn̩] I. *vt* 1. (*nicht mehr daran denken*) to forget; **nicht zu ~ ...** keep [*o* bear] in mind that ... 2. (*liegen lassen*) to leave behind II. *vr* (*die Beherrschung verlieren*) **sich** *akk* ~ to lose oneself

vergesslich RR, **vergeßlich** ALT [fɛɐ̯·ˈɡɛs·lɪç] *adj* forgetful

vergeuden * [fɛɐ̯·ˈɡɔy·dn̩] *vt* to waste

vergewaltigen * [fɛɐ̯·ɡə·ˈval·tɪ·ɡn̩] *vt* to rape

Vergewaltigung <-, -en> *f* rape

V

vergewissern * [fɛɐ̯·gə·ˈvɪ·sɐn] *vr* **sich akk ~, dass ...** to make sure that ...

vergießen * *vt irreg* (*Tränen, Blut*) to shed

vergiften * *vt* to poison

Vergiftung <-, -en> *f kein pl* poisoning

vergilbt *adj* yellowed

Vergissmeinnicht ᴿᴿ, **Vergißmeinnicht** ᴬᴸᵀ <-[e]s, -[e]> [fɛɐ̯·ˈgɪs·main·nɪçt] *nt* forget-me-not

Vergleich <-[e]s, -e> [fɛɐ̯·ˈglaiç] *m* comparison; **im ~** |**zu jdm/etw**| in comparison |with sb/sth|, compared to |sb/sth| ▶ **der ~ hinkt** that's a poor comparison

vergleichbar *adj* comparable (**mit** +*dat* to/with)

vergleichen * *vt irreg* to compare (**mit** +*dat* to/with)

vergleichsweise *adv* comparatively; **das ist ~ wenig/viel** that is a little/a lot in comparison

vergnügen * [fɛɐ̯·ˈgnyː·gn̩] *vr* **sich akk ~** to amuse [*o* enjoy] oneself

Vergnügen <-s, -> [fɛɐ̯·ˈgnyː·gn̩] *nt* (*Freude*) enjoyment; (*Genuss*) pleasure ▶ **viel ~!** have a good time!

vergnügt [fɛɐ̯·ˈgnyːkt] **I.** *adj* happy, cheerful **II.** *adv* happily, cheerfully

Vergnügungspark *m* amusement park

vergöttern * [fɛɐ̯·ˈgœ·tɐn] *vt* to idolize

vergraben * *irreg* **I.** *vt* to bury **II.** *vr* **sich akk in Arbeit ~** to bury oneself in work

vergreifen * *vr irreg* **1.** (*stehlen*) **sich akk an etw** *dat* **~** to steal sth **2.** (*Gewalt antun*) **sich akk an jdm ~** to assault sb **3.** (*sich unpassend ausdrücken*) **sich akk im Ton ~** to adopt the wrong tone

vergriffen *adj* (*Buch*) out of print *pred;* (*Ware*) unavailable

vergrößern [fɛɐ̯·ˈgrøː·sɐn] **I.** *vt* **1.** (*Fläche, Umfang*) to extend, to enlarge (**um** +*akk* by, **auf** +*akk* to) **2.** (*Distanz*) to increase **3.** (*Firma*) to expand **4.** (*größer erscheinen lassen*) to magnify **5.** ꜰᴏᴛᴏ to enlarge, to blow up *sep* **II.** *vr* **sich akk ~** (*anschwellen*) to become enlarged

Vergrößerung <-, -en> *f* **1.** (*das Vergrößern*) enlargement, increase; (*einer Firma*) expansion; (*technisch*) magnification **2.** (*vergrößertes Foto*) enlargement, blowup **3.** (*Anschwellung*) enlargement

Vergrößerungsglas *m* magnifying glass

Vergünstigung <-, -en> *f* **1.** (*finanzieller Vorteil*) perk **2.** (*Ermäßigung*) reduction, concession

Vergütung <-, -en> *f* **1.** (*das Ersetzen*) refund, reimbursement **2.** (*Geldsumme*) payment, remuneration; (*Honorar*) fee

verhaften * *vt* to arrest; **Sie sind verhaftet!** you're under arrest!

Verhaftung <-, -en> *f* arrest

verhalten * [fɛɐ̯·ˈhal·tn̩] *vr irreg* **sich akk ~** to behave

Verhalten <-s> [fɛɐ̯·ˈhal·tn̩] *nt kein pl* behavior

Verhaltensforschung *f kein pl* behavioral research

verhaltensgestört *adj* disturbed

Verhaltensweise *f* behavior

Verhältnis <-ses, -se> [fɛɐ̯·ˈhɛlt·nɪs] *nt* **1.** (*Relation*) ratio; **im ~** in a ratio (**von** +*dat* of, **zu** +*dat* to); **in keinem ~ zu etw** *dat* **stehen** to bear no relation to sth **2.** (*persönliche Beziehung*) relationship (**zu** +*dat* with); (*Affäre*) affair **3.** *pl* (*Bedingungen*) conditions *pl;* **klare ~se schaffen** to get things straightened out **4.** *pl* (*Lebensumstände*) circumstances *pl;* **über seine ~se** *pl* **leben** to live beyond one's means *pl*

verhältnismäßig *adv* relatively

verhandeln * **I.** *vi* to negotiate **II.** *vt* **1.** (*aushandeln*) to negotiate **2.** ᴊᴜʀ to hear

Verhandlung *f* **1.** *meist pl* (*das Verhandeln*) negotiations *npl* **2.** ᴊᴜʀ trial, hearing

Verhängnis <-, -se> [fɛɐ̯·ˈhɛŋ·nɪs] *nt* disaster; **jdm zum ~ werden** to be sb's undoing

verhängnisvoll *adj* disastrous, fatal

verharmlosen * [fɛɐ̯·ˈharm·loː·zn̩] *vt* to play down *sep*

verharren * *vi sein o haben geh* to pause

verhaspeln * *vr* **sich akk ~** to get [all] mixed up

verhasst ᴿᴿ, **verhaßt** ᴬᴸᵀ [fɛɐ̯·ˈhast] *adj* hated

verhätscheln *vt* to spoil, to pamper

verhauen * <verhaute, verhauen> *vt fam* **1.** (*verprügeln*) to beat up *sep* **2.** SCH *fam* **ich habe den Aufsatz** [**gründlich**] **~!** I've made a [complete] mess of the essay!

verheddern * [fɛɐ̯ˈhɛ·dən] *vr* **sich** *akk* **~ 1.** (*sich verfangen*) to get tangled up **2.** (*sich versprechen*) to get [all] mixed up

verheerend I. *adj* devastating **II.** *adv* **sich** *akk* **~ auswirken** to have a devastating effect

verheilen * *vi sein* to heal [up]

verheimlichen * [fɛɐ̯ˈhaim·lɪ·çn̩] *vt* [jdm] **etw ~** (*sth conceal sth* [*o keep sth secret*] [from sb]) **ich habe nichts zu ~** I have nothing to hide

verheißungsvoll I. *adj* promising; **wenig ~** not very promising **II.** *adv* full of promise

verhelfen * *vi irreg* **jdm zu etw** *dat* **~** to help sb [to] achieve sth

verherrlichen * [fɛɐ̯ˈhɛr·lɪ·çn̩] *vt* to glorify

verhexen * *vt* to bewitch

verhindern * *vt* to prevent

verhöhnen * *vt* to mock

Verhör <-[e]s, -e> [fɛɐ̯ˈhøːɐ̯] *nt* questioning, interrogation

verhüllen * *vt* to cover

verhungern * *vi sein* to starve [to death]

verhüten * **I.** *vt* to prevent **II.** *vi* (*Verhütungsmittel anwenden*) to use contraception

Verhütung <-, -en> *f* **1.** (*das Verhindern*) prevention **2.** (*Empfängnisverhütung*) contraception

Verhütungsmittel *nt* contraceptive

verirren * *vr* **sich** *akk* **~** to get lost

verjagen * *vt* to chase away *sep*

verkabeln * *vt* to connect to the cable network

verkalken * *vi sein* **1.** (*Kalk einlagern*) to clog up; **verkalkt** clogged up **2.** (*Arterien*) to harden

Verkalkung <-, -en> *f* **1.** (*das Verkalken*) clogging **2.** (*von Arterien*) hardening

verkatert [fɛɐ̯ˈkaː·tɛt] *adj fam* hung-over *pred*

Verkauf <-s, Verkäufe> [fɛɐ̯ˈkauf] *m*

1. (*das Verkaufen*) sale, selling; **zum ~ stehen** to be [up] for sale **2.** *kein pl* (*Verkaufsabteilung*) sales *no art,* + *sing/pl vb*

verkaufen * **I.** *vt* to sell (**an** +*akk* to); **zu ~ sein** to be for sale **II.** *vr* **sich** *akk* **~** to sell; **das Buch verkauft sich gut** the book is selling well

Verkäufer(in) [fɛɐ̯ˈkɔy·fɐ] *m(f)* **1.** (*in Geschäft*) sales assistant **2.** (*verkaufender Eigentümer*) seller; JUR vendor

verkäuflich *adj* for sale *pred*

Verkaufspreis *m* retail price

Verkehr <-[e]s> [fɛɐ̯ˈkeːɐ̯] *m kein pl* **1.** (*Straßenverkehr*) traffic **2.** (*Umgang*) contact, dealings *pl* **3.** (*Handel*) **etw aus dem ~ ziehen** to withdraw sth from circulation **4.** (*Geschlechtsverkehr*) intercourse

verkehren * **I.** *vi* **1.** *sein o haben* (*fahren*) to run; **der Zug verkehrt nur zweimal am Tag** the train only runs twice a day **2.** *haben* (*häufiger Gast sein*) to visit regularly **3.** *haben* (*Umgang pflegen*) **[mit jdm] ~** to associate [with sb] **II.** *vr haben* (*sich umkehren*) **sich** *akk* **in etw** *akk* **~** to turn into sth

Verkehrsampel *f* traffic lights *pl*

verkehrsberuhigt *adj* traffic-calmed

Verkehrschaos *nt* traffic mess

Verkehrsfunk *m* traffic report

Verkehrskontrolle *f* police checkpoint

Verkehrsmittel *nt* means + *sing/pl vb* of transportation; **öffentliches/privates ~** public/private transportation

Verkehrsnetz *nt* transportation system

Verkehrsregel *f* traffic regulation

Verkehrsschild *nt* traffic sign

Verkehrssünder(in) *m(f) fam* traffic offender

Verkehrstote(r) *f(m) dekl wie adj* traffic fatality

Verkehrsverein *m* tourist [information] office

verkehrswidrig *adj* in violation of traffic regulations *pl*

Verkehrszeichen *nt s.* **Verkehrsschild**

verkehrt I. *adj* wrong; **die ~e Richtung** the wrong direction; **der V~e** the wrong person **II.** *adv* wrong; **~ herum** the

wrong way around

verklagen* vt jdn ~ to take sb to court; **jdn auf Schadenersatz ~** to sue sb for damages

verkleiden* I. vt 1. (*kostümieren*) to dress up *sep* 2. (*überdecken*) to cover; (*innen*) to line II. vr sich akk ~ to dress up

Verkleidung f 1. (*zur Tarnung*) disguise; (*Kostüm*) costume 2. (*Auskleidung*) lining

verkleinern* [fɛɐ̯ˈklai̯·nɐn] I. vt 1. (*verringern*) to reduce 2. FOTO to reduce; COMPUT to scale down II. vr sich akk ~ 1. (*sich verringern*) to be reduced in size 2. (*schrumpfen*) to shrink

Verkleinerungsform f LING diminutive [form]

verklemmt adj uptight [about sex *pred*]

Verknappung f shortage

verkneifen vr irreg fam **sich** dat etw ~ 1. (*nicht offen zeigen*) to repress sth; **ich konnte mir ein Grinsen nicht ~** I couldn't help grinning 2. (*sich versagen*) to do without sth

verknittern* vt to crumple

verknoten* vt etw miteinander ~ to knot together *sep* sth

verknüpfen* vt 1. (*verknoten*) to tie [together *sep*] 2. (*verbinden*) to combine 3. (*in Zusammenhang bringen*) to link (**mit** +dat to)

verkommen*[1] vi irreg sein (*Gebäude*) to decay; (*Mensch*) to go to the dogs; (*Moral*) to degenerate

verkommen[2] adj 1. (*verfallen: Anwesen, Gebäude*) dilapidated 2. (*verwahrlost: Mensch*) down-at-heel attr, down at heel pred 3. (*moralisch*) degenerate

verkorkst <-er, -este> adj screwed-up; (*Magen*) upset

verkörpern* [fɛɐ̯ˈkœr·pɐn] vt 1. FILM, THEAT to play [the part of] 2. (*personifizieren*) to personify

verkrachen vr fam **sich** akk ~ to fall out

verkraften* [fɛɐ̯ˈkraf·tn̩] vt etw ~ to cope with sth

verkrampft I. adj tense II. adv tensely

verkriechen* vr irreg **sich** akk ~ to crawl away

verkrüppelt <-er, -este> adj 1. (*Pflan-*

zen) stunted 2. (*Mensch, Körperteil*) crippled

verkümmern* vi sein 1. (*eingehen*) to [shrivel up and] die 2. (*verloren gehen*) to wither away 3. (*die Lebenslust verlieren*) to waste away

verkürzen* I. vt 1. (*kürzer machen*) to shorten (**auf** +akk to, **um** +akk by) 2. (*zeitlich vermindern*) to reduce (**auf** +akk to, **um** +akk by); (*Urlaub*) to cut short *sep* II. vr sich akk ~ to become shorter

Verkürzung f 1. (*das Verkürzen*) shortening, cutting short 2. (*zeitliche Verminderung*) reduction

verladen* vt irreg to load

Verlag <-[e]s, -e> [fɛɐ̯ˈlaːk] m publisher, publishing house

verlagern* vt to move; **den Schwerpunkt ~** to shift the emphasis

verlangen* I. vt 1. (*fordern*) to demand (**von** +dat of); (*Preis*) to ask 2. (*erfordern*) to require 3. (*erwarten*) to expect; **das ist nicht zu viel verlangt** that is not too much to expect II. vi **nach etw** dat ~ 1. (*fordern*) to demand sth 2. (*um etw bitten*) to ask for sth

Verlangen <-s, -> nt 1. (*dringender Wunsch*) desire (**nach** +dat for) 2. (*Forderung*) demand; **auf ~** [up]on demand; **auf ihr ~ [hin]** at her request

verlängern* [fɛɐ̯ˈlɛŋɐn] I. vt 1. (*länger machen*) to lengthen, to extend (**um** +akk by) 2. (*länger dauern lassen*) to extend; (*Leben*) to prolong; (*Vertrag*) to renew II. vr sich akk ~ to increase (**um** +akk by), to become longer (**um** +akk by); (*Leben, Leid*) to be prolonged

Verlängerung <-, -en> f 1. kein pl (*räumlich*) lengthening; (*durch ein Zusatzteil*) extension 2. kein pl (*zeitliche*) extension 3. SPORT overtime

Verlängerungskabel nt, **Verlängerungsschnur** f extension cord

verlangsamen* [fɛɐ̯ˈlaŋ·zaː·mən] I. vt to slow down *sep* II. vr sich akk ~ to slow [down]

verlassen*[1] irreg I. vt 1. (*im Stich lassen*) to abandon; **der Mut verließ ihn** he lost [his] courage 2. (*fortgehen*) to leave II. vr sich akk auf jdn/etw ~

to rely on sb/sth; **worauf du dich ~ kannst!** you bet!, I guarantee it!

verlassen² adj deserted; (verwahrlost) desolate

verlässlich RR, **verläßlich** ALT [fɛɐ̯ˈlɛs-lɪç] adj reliable

Verlauf [fɛɐ̯ˈlaʊf] m course; **einen guten ~ nehmen** to go well; **im ~ der nächsten Monate** over the course of the next few months

verlaufen * irreg **I.** vi sein **1.** (ablaufen) **das Gespräch verlief nicht wie erhofft** the discussion didn't go as hoped **2.** (sich erstrecken) to run **II.** vr (sich verirren) **sich** akk ~ to get lost

Verlaufsform f LING continuous form

verlebt adj ruined, haggard

verlegen *¹ [fɛɐ̯ˈleː-gn̩] vt **1.** (Schlüssel etc.) to misplace **2.** (Termin) to postpone **(auf** +akk until) **3.** (Gleise, Kabel, Teppich) to lay **4.** (Buch) to publish **5.** (Abteilung, Patient) to transfer

verlegen² [fɛɐ̯ˈleː-gn̩] **I.** adj embarrassed; **er ist nie um eine Entschuldigung ~** he's never lost for an excuse **II.** adv in embarrassment

Verlegenheit <-, -en> f kein pl embarrassment

Verleger(in) <-s, -> m(f) publisher

Verleih <-[e]s, -e> [fɛɐ̯ˈlaɪ] m **1.** (Unternehmen) rental company **2.** kein pl (das Verleihen) renting out

verleihen * vt irreg **1.** (verborgen) to lend **(an** +akk to); **(gegen Geld)** to rent out sep **2.** (jdn mit etw auszeichnen) **jdm einen Preis ~** to award sb a prize **3.** (geben: Kraft) to give

verleiten * vt **jdn** [zu etw dat] **~ 1.** (dazu bringen) to persuade sb [to do sth] **2.** (verführen) to entice sb [to do sth]

verlernen * vt to forget; **das Tanzen ~** to forget how to dance

verletzbar adj s. **verletzlich**

verletzen * [fɛɐ̯ˈlɛtsn̩] vt **1.** (verwunden) to injure [o hurt] **2.** (kränken) to offend; (Gefühle) to hurt **3.** (übertreten) to violate

verletzend adj hurtful

verletzlich adj vulnerable

Verletzte(r) f(m) dekl wie adj injured person; (Opfer) casualty; **die ~n** the

injured + pl vb

Verletzung <-, -en> f **1.** MED injury **2.** kein pl (Übertretung) violation

verleugnen * vt to deny

verleumden * [fɛɐ̯ˈlɔym-dn̩] vt to slander; (schriftlich) to libel

Verleumdung <-, -en> f slander, libel

verlieben * vr **sich** akk [**in jdn**] **~** to fall in love [with sb]; (für jdn schwärmen) to have a crush on sb

verliebt adj infatuated; **~ sein** to be in love **(in** +akk with)

verlieren <verlor, verloren> [fɛɐ̯ˈliː-rən] **I.** vt to lose ▶ **du hast hier nichts verloren** fam you have no business being here **II.** vr **sich** akk ~ to disappear

Verlierer(in) <-s, -> m(f) loser

Verlies <-es, -e> [fɛɐ̯ˈliːs] nt dungeon

verloben * vr **sich** akk ~ to get engaged **(mit** +dat to)

Verlobte(r) f(m) dekl wie adj fiancé masc, fiancée fem

Verlobung <-, -en> f engagement

verlockend adj tempting

verlogen [fɛɐ̯ˈloː-gn̩] adj **1.** (lügnerisch) lying attr; **~ sein** (Behauptung) to be a lie; (Mensch) to be a liar **2.** (heuchlerisch) insincere, phony

verloren [fɛɐ̯ˈloː-rən] **I.** pp von **verlieren II.** adj **~ gehen** to get lost

verlosen * vt to raffle

Verlosung f raffle, drawing

Verlust <-[e]s, -e> [fɛɐ̯ˈlʊst] m loss; **~e machen** to be losing money

vermachen * vt to bequeath

Vermächtnis <-ses, -se> [fɛɐ̯ˈmɛçt·nɪs] nt legacy

vermählen * [fɛɐ̯ˈmɛː-lən] vr geh **sich** akk [**mit jdm**] **~** to marry [sb] attr

vermarkten * vt to market

vermasseln * [fɛɐ̯ˈma·sl̩n] vt to mess up sep

vermehren * vr **sich** akk ~ **1.** (sich fortpflanzen) to reproduce; (stärker) to multiply **2.** (zunehmen) to increase **(um** +akk by)

Vermehrung <-, -en> f **1.** (Fortpflanzung) reproduction; (stärker) multiplying **2.** (das Anwachsen) increase

vermeiden * vt irreg to avoid; **sich** akk **nicht ~ lassen** to be inevitable

Vermerk <-[e]s, -e> [fɛɐ̯ˈmɛrk] *m* note

vermessen **1 [fɛɐ̯ˈmɛ·sn̩] *vt irreg* to measure; (*Grundstück, Gebäude*) to survey

vermessen² [fɛɐ̯ˈmɛ·sn̩] *adj* presumptuous

vermieten * *vt* to rent out *sep* (**an** +*akk* to); „ **zu ~** " "for rent"

Vermieter(in) *m(f)* landlord *masc*, landlady *fem*

vermindern * **I.** *vt* to reduce **II.** *vr* **sich** *akk* ~ to decrease, to diminish

vermischen * **I.** *vt* to mix; (*um eine bestimmte Qualität zu erreichen*) to blend **II.** *vr* **sich** *akk* [**miteinander**] ~ to mix

vermissen * *vt* **1.** (*das Fehlen bemerken*) **etw** ~ to have lost sth **2.** (*jds Abwesenheit bedauern*) **jdn** ~ to miss sb **3.** (*jds Abwesenheit feststellen*) **wir** ~ **unsere Tochter** our daughter is missing

Vermisste(r) ᴿᴿ, **Vermißte(r)** ᴬᴸᵀ *f(m) dekl wie adj* missing person

vermitteln * **I.** *vt* **1.** (*beschaffen*) **jdm eine Stellung** ~ to find sb a job; **jdn an eine Firma** ~ to place sb with a company **2.** (*weitergeben*) to pass on *sep*; **jdm ein schönes Gefühl** ~ to give sb a good feeling **3.** (*arrangieren*) to arrange **II.** *vi* to mediate

Vermittlung <-, -en> *f* **1.** (*Vermitteln: einer Stelle, Wohnung*) finding **2.** (*Schlichtung*) mediation **3.** (*Telefonzentrale*) operator **4.** (*das Weitergeben*) imparting

Vermögen <-s, -> [fɛɐ̯ˈmøː·gn̩] *nt* FIN assets *pl*; (*Geld*) capital; (*Eigentum*) property; (*Reichtum*) fortune, wealth

vermögend [fɛɐ̯ˈmøː·gn̩t] *adj* wealthy

Vermögenssteuer *f* property tax

vermummt *adj* masked

vermuten * *vt* to suspect

vermutlich **I.** *adj attr* probable, likely **II.** *adv* probably

Vermutung <-, -en> *f* assumption

vernachlässigen * [fɛɐ̯ˈnax·lɛ·sɪ·gn̩] *vt* **1.** (*sich nicht genügend kümmern*) to neglect **2.** (*unberücksichtigt lassen*) to ignore

vernarben * *vi sein* to form a scar; **vernarbt** scarred

vernehmen * *vt irreg* JUR to question

Vernehmung <-, -en> *f* JUR questioning

verneigen * *vr* **sich** *akk* ~ to bow

verneinen * [fɛɐ̯ˈnai·nən] *vt* **1.** (*negieren*) to say no; **eine Frage** ~ to answer a question in the negative **2.** (*leugnen*) to deny

Verneinung <-, -en> *f* LING negative

vernetzen *vt* **1.** COMPUT to network, to link up *sep* **2.** *fig* (*verknüpfen*) [**mit**] **etw** *dat*] **vernetzt sein** to be linked [up] [to sth]

vernetzt *adj* COMPUT networked

vernichten * [fɛɐ̯ˈnɪç·tn̩] *vt* **1.** (*zerstören*) to destroy **2.** (*ausrotten*) to exterminate

vernichtend **I.** *adj* devastating; (*Niederlage*) crushing **II.** *adv* **jdn** ~ **schlagen** to inflict a crushing defeat on sb

Vernichtung <-, -en> *f* **1.** (*Zerstörung*) destruction **2.** (*Ausrottung*) extermination

Vernunft <-> [fɛɐ̯ˈnʊnft] *f kein pl* reason, common sense; **jdn zur ~ bringen** to bring sb to his/her senses

vernünftig [fɛɐ̯ˈnʏnf·tɪç] **I.** *adj* **1.** (*klug*) reasonable, sensible **2.** *fam* (*ordentlich*) proper; (*anständig, gut*) decent; **~e Preise** decent prices **II.** *adv fam* properly, decently

veröffentlichen * [fɛɐ̯ˈʔœfn̩t·lɪ·çn̩] *vt* to publish

Veröffentlichung <-, -en> *f* publication

verordnen * *vt* MED to prescribe

verpachten * *vt* to lease (**an** +*akk* to)

verpacken * *vt* to pack [up *sep*]; (*als Geschenk*) to wrap [up *sep*]

Verpackung <-, -en> *f* **1.** *kein pl* (*das Verpacken*) packing **2.** (*Hülle*) packaging

verpassen * *vt* **1.** (*versäumen*) to miss **2.** *fam* (*aufzwingen*) **jdm etw** ~ to give sb sth; **jdm einen Denkzettel** ~ to give sb a warning

verpesten * [fɛɐ̯ˈpɛs·tn̩] *vt* to pollute

verpetzen * *vt fam* **jdn** ~ to tell on sb

verpfänden * *vt* to pawn; (*Grundstück, Haus*) to mortgage

verpflanzen * *vt* **1.** (*umpflanzen*) to replant **2.** MED **jdm ein Organ** ~ to give sb an organ transplant

verpflegen * vt to cater for

Verpflegung <-, selten -en> f **1.** kein pl (das Verpflegen) catering; **mit voller ~** with full board **2.** (Nahrung) food

verpflichten * [fɛɐ̯ˈpflɪçtn̩] I. vt **1.** (eine Pflicht auferlegen) jdn [zu etw dat] ~ to oblige sb to do sth **2.** (einstellen) jdn [für etw akk] ~ to hire sb [to do sth] II. vr sich akk zu etw dat ~ to commit oneself to doing sth

Verpflichtung <-, -en> f **1.** meist pl (Pflichten) duty; **seinen ~en nachkommen** to fulfill one's obligations; **finanzielle ~en** financial commitments **2.** kein pl (das Engagieren) engagement

verpfuschen * vt etw ~ to make a mess of sth

verplappern * vr sich akk ~ to blab

verpönt [fɛɐ̯ˈpøːnt] adj deprecated

verprassen * vt to squander

verprügeln * vt to beat up sep; (als Strafe) to give sb a beating

Verputz m plaster

verputzen * vt **1.** (mit Putz versehen) to plaster **2.** fam (aufessen) to polish off sep

verqualmt <-er, -este> adj smoke-filled attr, full of smoke pred

verquollen adj swollen

Verrat <-[e]s> [fɛɐ̯ˈraːt] m **1.** kein pl betrayal (an +dat of) **2.** JUR treason

verraten (verriet, verraten) I. vt **1.** (ausplaudern) to give away sep **2.** (Verrat üben, preisgeben) to betray **3.** (erkennen lassen) to show II. vr sich akk ~ to give oneself away

Verräter(in) <-s, -> [fɛɐ̯ˈrɛːtɐ] m(f) traitor

verrechnen * I. vr sich akk ~ to miscalculate II. vt etw mit etw dat ~ to set off sep sth against sth

Verrechnungsscheck m a check [endorsed] for deposit only

verregnet <-er, -este> adj spoiled by rain; (Tag) rainy

verreisen * vi sein to go away; **geschäftlich verreist sein** to be away on business

verrenken * vt to twist; **sich dat ein Gelenk ~** to dislocate a joint

Verrenkung <-, -en> f distortion; (Gelenk) dislocation

verrichten * vt to perform

verriegeln * vt to bolt

verringern * [fɛɐ̯ˈrɪŋɐn] I. vt to reduce (um +akk by) II. vr sich akk ~ to decrease

Verringerung <-> f kein pl reduction

verrosten * vi sein to rust

verrotten * [fɛɐ̯ˈrɔtn̩] vi sein **1.** (faulen) to rot **2.** (verwahrlosen) to decay

verrücken * vt to move

verrückt [fɛɐ̯ˈrʏkt] adj **1.** (wahnsinnig) nuts, crazy; **bist du ~?** are you out of your mind?; **jdn ~ machen** to drive sb crazy **3.** (in starkem Maße) **wie** ~ like crazy **3.** (ausgefallen) crazy, wild **4.** (versessen) ~ **nach jdm/etw sein** to be crazy about sb/sth

Verrückte(r) f(m) dekl wie adj lunatic

verrufen adj disreputable

verrühren * vt to stir

verrutschen * vi sein to slip

Vers <-es, -e> [fɛrs] m verse, lines pl

versagen * I. vi to fail, to choke sl II. vt **jdm etw ~** to refuse sb sth

Versagen <-s> nt kein pl failure; **menschliches ~** human error

Versager(in) <-s, -> m(f) failure

versalzen * vt irreg to put too much salt in/on

versammeln * I. vr sich akk ~ to gather, to assemble II. vt (zusammenkommen lassen) to call together; (Truppen) to rally

Versammlung f **1.** (Zusammenkunft) meeting **2.** (versammelte Menschen) assembly

Versand <-[e]s> [fɛɐ̯ˈzant] m kein pl **1.** (das Versenden) dispatch **2.** (Versandabteilung) dispatch, distribution

Versandhandel m mail order no art

Versandhaus nt mail-order company

versäumen * vt to miss

verschaffen * vt sich/jdm etw ~ to get [a hold of] sth for oneself/sb; **jdm eine Stellung ~** to get sb a job; **sich dat Gewissheit ~** to make certain

verschämt [fɛɐ̯ˈʃɛːmt] adj shy, bashful

verschanzen * vr sich akk ~ **1.** MIL to take up a fortified position **2.** (verste-

cken) to take refuge

verschärfen* I. *vr* **sich** *akk* ~ to get worse; (*Krise*) to intensify II. *vt* 1. (*rigoroser machen*) to make more rigorous; (*Strafe*) to make more severe 2. (*zuspitzen: Situation*) to aggravate

verschenken* *vt* 1. (*schenken*) to give away *sep* (**an** +*akk* to) 2. (*ungenutzt lassen*) to waste

verscherzen *vr* **sich** *dat* **etw** ~ to lose sth; **es sich** *dat* **mit jdm** ~ to have a falling out with sb

verscheuchen* *vt* to chase away *sep*

verschicken* *vt* to send

verschieben* *irreg* I. *vt* 1. (*Gegenstand*) to move (**um** +*akk* by) 2. (*Termin*) to postpone (**auf** +*akk* until, **um** +*akk* by) II. *vr* **sich** *akk* ~ 1. (*später stattfinden*) to be postponed 2. (*verrutschen*) to slip

Verschiebung *f* postponement

verschieden [fɛɐ̯·ˈʃiː·dn̩] I. *adj* 1. (*unterschiedlich*) different; (*mehrere*) various 2. *attr* (*einige*) several *attr,* a few *attr;* **V~es** various things *pl* II. *adv* differently

verschiedenartig *adj* different kinds of *attr,* diverse

Verschiedenheit <-, -en> *f* (*Unterschiedlichkeit*) difference; (*Unähnlichkeit*) dissimilarity

verschimmeln* *vi sein* to get moldy

verschlafen*¹ *irreg* I. *vi* to oversleep II. *vt* 1. *fam* to miss 2. (*schlafend verbringen*) to sleep through

verschlafen² *adj* sleepy

verschlagen*¹ *vt irreg* 1. (*nehmen*) **jdm die Sprache** ~ to leave sb speechless 2. (*geraten*) **es hatte mich nach Argentinien** ~ I ended up in Argentina

verschlagen² I. *adj* devious, sly *pej;* **ein ~er Blick** a furtive glance II. *adv* slyly; (*verdächtig*) shiftily

verschlampen* *vt* **etw** ~ to manage to lose sth

verschlechtern* [fɛɐ̯·ˈʃlɛç·tɐn] I. *vt* to make worse II. *vr* **sich** *akk* ~ to get worse, to worsen

Verschlechterung <-, -en> *f* worsening

verschleiern* [fɛɐ̯·ˈʃlai·ɐn] *vt* 1. (*mit einem Schleier bedecken*) to cover with a veil 2. (*verdecken*) to cover up *sep*

verschleiert *adj* (*Gesicht*) veiled

Verschleiß <-es, -e> [fɛɐ̯·ˈʃlais] *m* wear [and tear]

verschleißen <verschliss, verschlissen> *vt, vi sein* to wear out

verschleppen* *vt* 1. (*deportieren*) to take away *sep* 2. (*hinauszögern*) to prolong 3. MED to delay treatment

verschleudern* *vt* to sell off *sep* cheaply

verschließen* *irreg* I. *vt* 1. (*zumachen*) to close 2. (*zuschließen*) to lock 3. (*wegschließen*) to lock away *sep* 4. (*versagt bleiben*) **jdm verschlossen bleiben** to be closed off to sb II. *vr* **sich** *akk* **etw** *dat* ~ to ignore sth

verschlimmern* I. *vt* to make worse II. *vr* **sich** *akk* ~ to get worse; (*Zustand, Lage a.*) to deteriorate

Verschlimmerung <-, -en> *f* deterioration

verschlingen* *vt irreg* (*Essen, Buch*) to devour

verschlissen I. *pp von* **verschleißen** II. *adj* worn-out

verschlossen [fɛɐ̯·ˈʃlɔ·sn̩] *adj* 1. (*zugemacht*) closed 2. (*abgeschlossen*) locked 3. (*zurückhaltend*) reserved; (*schweigsam*) taciturn

verschlucken* I. *vt* 1. (*hinunterschlucken*) to swallow 2. (*undeutlich aussprechen*) to slur; (*nicht aussprechen*) to bite back II. *vr* **sich** *akk* ~ to choke (**an** +*dat* on)

verschlungen I. *pp von* **verschlingen** II. *adj* entwined

Verschluss ᴿᴿ, **Verschluß** ᴬᴸᵀ *m* 1. (*von Tasche, Brosche*) clasp; **etw unter ~ halten** to keep sth under lock and key 2. (*Deckel*) lid; (*Flasche*) top

verschlüsseln* [fɛɐ̯·ˈʃlʏ·sl̩n] *vt* to [en]code

verschmähen* *vt* to reject; (*stärker*) to scorn

verschmelzen* *irreg* I. *vi sein* to melt together II. *vt* (*löten*) to solder; (*verschweißen*) to weld

verschmieren* I. *vt* 1. (*verstreichen*)

to apply; (*Creme etc.*) to spread **2.** (*verwischen*) to smear **3.** (*beschmieren*) to make dirty **II.** *vi* to smear, to get smeared

verschmutzen * **I.** *vt* to make dirty; ÖKOL to pollute **II.** *vi sein* to get dirty; ÖKOL to get polluted

verschneit *adj* snow-covered *attr*, covered in snow *pred*

verschnörkelt *adj* adorned with flourishes

verschnupft [fɛɐ̯ˈʃnʊpft] *adj fam* ~ **sein 1.** (*erkältet*) to have a cold **2.** (*indigniert*) to be in a huff

verschnüren * *vt* to tie up *sep* [with a string]

verschollen [fɛɐ̯ˈʃɔ·lən] *adj* missing

verschonen * *vt* to spare; **verschone mich mit den Einzelheiten!** spare me the details!; **von etw** *dat* **verschont bleiben** to escape sth

verschönern * [fɛɐ̯ˈʃøː·nen] *vt* to brighten up *sep*

verschränken *vt* **die Arme/Beine ~** to fold one's arms/cross one's legs

verschreiben * *irreg* **I.** *vt* **jdm etw ~** to prescribe sb sth (**gegen** +*akk* for) **II.** *vr* **1.** (*falsch schreiben*) **sich** *akk* **~** to make a slip of the pen **2.** (*sich widmen*) **sich** *akk* **etw** *dat* **~** to devote oneself to sth

verschreibungspflichtig *adj* available by prescription only *pred*

verschrotten * *vt* to scrap

verschüchtert *adj* intimidated

verschulden * **I.** *vt* **etw ~** to be to blame for sth **II.** *vi sein* **verschuldet sein** to be in debt **III.** *vr* **sich** *akk* **~** to get into debt

Verschulden <-s> *nt kein pl* fault

Verschuldung <-, -en> *f* (*Schulden*) debts *pl*

verschütten * [fɛɐ̯ˈʃʏ·tən] *vt* **1.** (*danebenschütten*) to spill **2.** (*unter etw begraben*) to bury

verschwägert [fɛɐ̯ˈʃvɛː·ɡet] *adj* related by marriage *pred*

verschweigen * *vt irreg* to keep secret (**vor** +*dat* from); (*Informationen*) to withhold; **jdm ~, dass ...** to keep from sb the fact that ...

verschwenden * *vt* to waste

Verschwender(in) <-s, -> *m(f)* wasteful person; (*Geld a.*) spendthrift

verschwenderisch **I.** *adj* **1.** (*sinnlos ausgebend*) wasteful **2.** (*sehr üppig*) extravagant, sumptuous **II.** *adv* wastefully

Verschwendung <-, -en> *f* waste

verschwiegen [fɛɐ̯ˈʃviː·ɡn̩] *adj* discreet

verschwimmen * *vi irreg sein* to become blurred

verschwinden * *vi irreg sein* **1.** (*nicht mehr da sein*) to disappear; **verschwunden** [sein] [to be] missing; **etw in etw** *dat* **~ lassen** to slip sth into sth **2.** (*sich auflösen*) to vanish **3.** *fam* (*sich davonmachen*) to disappear; **verschwinde!** beat it!, scram!

Verschwinden <-s> *nt kein pl* disappearance

verschwommen *adj* **1.** (*undeutlich*) blurred **2.** (*unklar*) hazy, vague

verschwören * *vr irreg* **sich** *akk* **~** to conspire [*o* plot] (**gegen** +*akk* against)

Verschwörung <-, -en> *f* conspiracy, plot

Versehen <-s, -> [fɛɐ̯ˈzeː·ən] *nt* mistake; **aus ~** inadvertently; (*aufgrund einer Verwechslung*) by mistake

versehentlich [fɛɐ̯ˈzeː·ənt·lɪç] *adv* inadvertently; (*aufgrund einer Verwechslung a.*) by mistake

versenden * *vt irreg o reg* to send

versenken * *vt* to sink

versessen [fɛɐ̯ˈzɛ·sn̩] *adj* **auf etw** *akk* **~ sein** to be crazy about sth

versetzen * **I.** *vt* **1.** (*an eine andere Stelle*) to move; (*aus Berufsgründen*) to transfer **2.** SCH **einen Schüler ~** to move up *sep* [*o* promote] a student **3.** (*bringen*) **jdn in Begeisterung ~** to fill sb with enthusiasm; **jdn in Panik/ Wut ~** to send sb into a panic/a rage **4.** (*verpfänden*) to pawn **5.** (*warten lassen*) **jdn ~** to stand sb up **6.** (*mischen*) **etw mit etw** *dat* **~** to mix sth with sth **II.** *vr* (*sich hineindenken*) **sich** *akk* **in jdn ~** to put oneself in sb's place

Versetzung <-, -en> *f* **1.** (*beruflich*) transfer **2.** SCH moving up, promotion

verseuchen * [fɛɐ̯ˈzɔy·çn̩] *vt* to contaminate; (*Umwelt*) to pollute

versichern*¹ *vt* to insure

versichern*² *vt* jdm ~, |dass| ... to assure sb |that| ...

Versicherte(r) *f(m) dekl wie adj* insured

Versicherung¹ *f* 1. (*Vertrag*) insurance policy 2. (*Gesellschaft*) insurance company

Versicherung² *f* (*Beteuerung*) assurance

Versicherungsschutz *m kein pl* insurance coverage

Versicherungsvertreter(in) *m(f)* insurance agent

versickern* *vi sein* to seep away

versiegeln* *vt* to seal |up *sep*|

versinken *vi irreg sein* to sink

versöhnen* [fɛɐˈzøː·nən] I. *vr* sich *akk* mit jdm ~ to make up with sb II. *vt* 1. (*aussöhnen*) to reconcile 2. (*besänftigen*) to mollify

Versöhnung <-, -en> *f* reconciliation

versorgen* *vt* 1. (*betreuen*) jdn ~ to take care of [*o* look after] sb 2. (*versehen*) to supply; sich *akk* mit etw *dat* ~ to provide oneself with sth; sich *akk* selbst ~ to look after oneself

Versorgung <-> *f kein pl* 1. (*das Versorgen*) care 2. (*das Ausstatten*) supply

verspäten* [fɛɐˈʃpɛː·tn̩] *vr* sich *akk* ~ to be |running| late

verspätet I. *adj* 1. (*zu spät eintreffend*) delayed 2. (*zu spät erfolgend*) late II. *adv* late; (*nachträglich*) belatedly

Verspätung <-, -en> *f* delay; ~ haben to be late; mit einer Stunde ~ ankommen to arrive an hour late

versperren* *vt* to block

verspielen* *vt* 1. (*beim Glücksspiel*) to gamble away *sep* 2. (*Chance*) to squander

verspotten* *vt* to mock

versprechen* *irreg* I. *vt* to promise II. *vr* 1. (*sich erhoffen*) sich *dat* etw von jdm/etw ~ to hope for sth from sb/sth; ich verspreche mir nicht viel davon I don't expect much 2. (*falsch sprechen*) sich *akk* ~ to misspeak

Versprechen <-s, -> *nt* promise

verspritzen* *vt* to spray

verstaatlichen* [fɛɐˈʃtaːt·lɪ·çn̩] *vt* to nationalize

verstand [fɛɐˈʃtant] *imp von* **verstehen**

Verstand <-[e]s> [fɛɐˈʃtant] *m kein p* reason; du bist wohl nicht bei ~ you're out of your mind!; bei klarem ~ sein to be lucid; jdn um den ~ bringen to drive sb out of his/her mind

verständig [fɛɐˈʃtɛn·dɪç] *adj* (*einsichtig* cooperative

verständigen* [fɛɐˈʃtɛn·dɪ·gn̩] I. *vt* t notify (von +*dat* of) II. *vr* sich *akk* ~ 1. (*sich verständlich machen*) to communicate 2. (*sich einigen*) to reach ar agreement

Verständigung <-, selten -en> *f* 1. (*Benachrichtigung*) notification 2. (*Kommunikation*) communication 3. (*Einigung*) agreement, understanding

verständlich [fɛɐˈʃtɛnt·lɪç] I. *adj* 1. (*begreiflich*) understandable; sich *akk* ~ machen to make oneself understood 2. (*gut zu hören*) clear, intelligible 3. (*leicht zu verstehen*) clear, comprehensible II. *adv* 1. (*vernehmbar*) clearly 2. (*verstehbar*) comprehensibly

Verständnis <-ses, selten -se> [fɛɐ ˈʃtɛnt·nɪs] *nt* understanding; für etw *akk* ~ haben to have sympathy for sth

verständnislos I. *adj* uncomprehending; ein ~er Blick a blank look II. *adv* uncomprehendingly, blankly

verständnisvoll *adj* understanding, sympathetic

verstärken* *vt* 1. (*stärker machen*) to strengthen; (*durch stärkeres Material a.*) to reinforce 2. (*intensivieren: Gefühle*) to intensify 3. (*erhöhen*) to increase

Verstärker <-s, -> *m* TECH amplifier, amp *fam*

Verstärkung *f* 1. (*das Verstärken*) strengthening 2. (*Vergrößerung*) reinforcement 3. (*Erhöhung*) increase

verstauchen* *vt* sich *dat* das Handgelenk ~ to sprain one's wrist

verstauen* *vt* to pack |away *sep*|

Versteck <-[e]s, -e> [fɛɐˈʃtɛk] *nt* hiding place

verstecken* *vt* to hide (vor +*da* from)

versteckt *adj* 1. (*verborgen*) hidden, (*vorsätzlich a.*) concealed 2. (*abgele*

gen) secluded **3.** (*unausgesprochen*) veiled

erstehen <verstand verstanden> I. *vt*
1. (*hören*) to hear; ~ **Sie mich gut?** can you hear me okay? **2.** (*begreifen*) to understand **3.** (*können*) to understand; **es** ~, **etw zu tun** to know how to do sth; **er versteht nichts von Musik** he doesn't know a thing about music **4.** (*auslegen*) **was verstehst du unter teuer?** what's "expensive" to you?; **wie darf ich das** ~? how am I supposed to interpret that?; **dieser Brief ist als Drohung zu** ~ this letter has to be taken as a threat II. *vr* **1.** (*auskommen*) **sich** *akk* **mit jdm** ~ to get along with sb **2.** (*beherrschen*) **sich** *akk* **auf etw** *akk* ~ to know all about sth **3.** (*zu verstehen sein*) **etw versteht sich von selbst** sth goes without saying III. *vi* **verstehst du?** [do you] understand?, you know?

ersteifen * *vr* **sich** *akk* ~ **1.** (*auf etw beharren*) to insist (**auf** +*akk* on) **2.** MED to stiffen [up]

ersteigern * *vt* to auction [off]

Ersteigerung *f* auction

Ersteinerung <-, -en> *f* fossil

erstellbar *adj* adjustable

erstellen * I. *vt* **1.** (*anders einstellen*) to adjust **2.** (*woandershin stellen*) to move **3.** (*unzugänglich machen*) to block **4.** (*verändern*) to disguise II. *vr* **sich** *akk* ~ to put on an act

ersteuern * *vt* **etw** ~ to pay tax on sth

erstimmt *adj* **1.** MUS out of tune **2.** (*verärgert*) ~ **sein** to be disgruntled **3.** (*Magen*) upset

erstockt *adj* obstinate

erstohlen [fɛɐ̯ˈʃtoːlən] I. *adj* furtive II. *adv* furtively

erstopfen * I. *vt* to block up *sep* II. *vi sein* to get blocked [up]

erstopft *adj* blocked, congested

Erstopfung <-, -en> *f* MED constipation; ~ **haben** to be constipated

erstorben [fɛɐ̯ˈʃtɔrbn̩] *adj* deceased, late *attr*

Erstorbene(r) *f(m) dekl wie adj* deceased

erstört [fɛɐ̯ˈʃtøːɐ̯t] I. *adj* distraught II. *adv* in distress

Verstoß [fɛɐ̯ˈʃtoːs] *m* violation (**gegen** +*akk* of); JUR offense

verstoßen * *irreg* I. *vi* **gegen etw** *akk* ~ to violate sth II. *vt* **jdn** ~ to expel sb

verstreichen * *irreg* I. *vt* (*Farbe*) to apply; (*Butter*) to spread II. *vi sein* (*Zeit*) to pass [by]; (*Zeitspanne a.*) to elapse

Verstümmelung <-, -en> *f* mutilation

Versuch <-[e]s, -e> [fɛɐ̯ˈzuːx] *m* **1.** (*Bemühen*) attempt, try **2.** (*Experiment*) experiment

versuchen * *vt* **1.** (*probieren*) to try; ~, **etw zu tun** to try doing/to do sth; **es mit jdm/etw** ~ to give sb/sth a try **2.** (*in Versuchung sein*) **versucht sein, etw zu tun** to be tempted to do sth

Versuchskaninchen *nt* guinea pig

Versuchstier *nt* laboratory animal

Versuchung <-, -en> *f* temptation; **jdn in** ~ **führen** to tempt sb; **in** ~ **geraten** to be tempted

versunken [fɛɐ̯ˈzʊŋkn̩] *adj* **1.** (*untergegangen*) sunken **2. in Gedanken** ~ **sein** to be lost in thought

versüßen * *vt* to sweeten

vertagen * *vt* to adjourn (**auf** +*akk* until); (*Entscheidung*) to postpone

vertauschen * *vt* to switch; (*unabsichtlich*) to mix up *sep*

verteidigen * [fɛɐ̯ˈtai̯dɪ·gn̩] *vt, vi* to defend

Verteidiger(in) <-s, -> *m(f)* **1.** JUR defense counsel **2.** SPORT defender

Verteidigung <-, -en> *f* defense

Verteidigungsministerium *nt* Defense Department

verteilen * I. *vt* **1.** (*austeilen*) to distribute (**an** +*akk* to) **2.** (*platzieren*) to place **3.** (*ausstreuen, verstreichen*) to spread (**auf** +*dat* on) II. *vr* (*sich verbreiten*) **sich** *akk* ~ to spread out

Verteilung *f* distribution

verteuern * [fɛɐ̯ˈtɔy̯ɐn] I. *vt* to increase the price (**um** +*akk* by) II. *vr* **sich** *akk* ~ to become more expensive

vertiefen * I. *vt* to deepen II. *vr* **sich** *akk* **in etw** *akk* ~ to become absorbed in sth; **in Gedanken vertieft sein** to be deep in thought

Vertiefung <-, -en> *f* **1.** (*vertiefte Stelle*) depression **2.** *kein pl* (*von Beziehung,*

Freundschaft) deepening

vertikal [vɛr·ti·ˈkaːl] I. *adj* vertical II. *adv* vertically

vertippen * *vr fam* **sich** *akk* ~ to make a typo *fam*

Vertrag <-[e]s, Verträge> [fɛɐ̯·ˈtraːk] *m* contract; (*international*) treaty; **jdn unter ~ nehmen** to contract sb

vertragen * *irreg* I. *vt* 1. (*aushalten*) to bear, to stand 2. (*wegstecken können*) to tolerate 3. *fam* (*zu sich nehmen können*) **ich vertrage keinen Alkohol** alcohol doesn't agree with me 4. *fam* (*benötigen*) **das Haus könnte einen neuen Anstrich ~** the house could use a new coat of paint 5. *schweiz* (*austragen*) to deliver II. *vr* 1. (*auskommen*) **sich** *akk* **mit jdm ~** to get along with sb 2. (*zusammenpassen*) **sich** *akk* **mit etw** *dat* ~ to go with sth

vertraglich [fɛɐ̯·ˈtraːk·lɪç] I. *adj* contractual II. *adv* contractually, by contract; **~ festgelegt sein** to be laid down in a contract

verträglich [fɛɐ̯·ˈtrɛːk·lɪç] *adj* 1. (*umgänglich*) good-natured 2. (*bekömmlich*) **gut/schwer ~** easily digestible/hard to digest; (*Medikament*) well[-]/not well[-]tolerated

Vertragsabschluss RR *m* acceptance of the terms and conditions of a contract

Vertragsbruch *m* breach of contract

vertrauen * *vi* **jdm ~** to trust sb; **auf jdn ~** to trust in sb; **auf Gott ~** to put one's trust in God; **darauf ~, dass ...** to be confident that ...

Vertrauen <-s> *nt kein pl* trust, confidence (**zu** +*dat* in); **~ erweckend sein** to inspire confidence; **im ~ [gesagt]** [told] in [strict] confidence

Vertrauensbruch *m* breach of confidence

vertrauensvoll I. *adj* trusting, based on trust II. *adv* trustingly

vertrauenswürdig *adj* trustworthy

vertraulich I. *adj* 1. (*geheim*) [streng] ~ [strictly] confidential 2. (*freundschaftlich*) familiar, chummy *fam* II. *adv* confidentially

verträumt *adj* 1. (*idyllisch*) sleepy 2. (*realitätsfern*) dreamy

vertraut *adj* 1. (*wohlbekannt*) familiar; **sich** *akk* **mit etw** *dat* ~ **machen** to familiarize oneself with sth; **sich** *akk* **mit dem Gedanken ~ machen, dass ...** to get used to the idea that ... 2. (*eng verbunden*) close, intimate

Vertraute(r) *f(m) dekl wie adj* confidant masc, confidante fem

vertreiben * *vt irreg* (*verjagen*) to drive away [*o* out] *sep*

vertretbar *adj* 1. (*zu vertreten*) tenable 2. (*akzeptabel*) justifiable

vertreten *[1] *vt irreg* 1. (*vorübergehend ersetzen*) **jdn ~** to cover for sb; **durch jdn ~ werden** to be replaced by sb 2. (*repräsentieren*) to represent 3. (*verfechten: Ansicht*) to take; (*Meinung*) to hold

vertreten *[2] *vr irreg* (*verstauchen*) **sich** *dat* **den Fuß ~** to twist one's ankle ▶ **sich** *dat* **die Beine ~** to stretch one's legs

Vertreter(in) <-s, -> *m(f)* 1. (*Stellvertreter*) deputy, stand-in 2. (*Handelsvertreter*) sales representative 3. (*Repräsentant*) representative

Vertretung <-, -en> *f* 1. (*Stellvertreter*) deputy, ÖKON agency

Vertrieb <-[e]s, -e> *m* 1. *kein pl* (*das Vertreiben*) sale[s *pl*] 2. (*Vertriebsabteilung*) sales department

Vertriebene(r) *f(m) dekl wie adj* deportee, displaced person

vertrocknen * *vi sein* (*Vegetation*) to dry out

vertrösten * *vt* to put off *sep* (**auf** +*akk* until)

vertuschen * *vt* to hush up *sep*

verübeln * [fɛɐ̯·ˈʔyː·bl̩n] *vt* **jdm etw** ~ to hold sth against sb

verunglücken * [fɛɐ̯·ˈʔʊn·ɡlʏ·kn̩] *vi sein* to have an accident; **tödlich ~** to be killed in an accident

verunsichern * [fɛɐ̯·ˈʔʊn·zɪ·çən] *vt* to unsettle

verunsichert <-er, -este> *adj* insecure

verunstalten * [fɛɐ̯·ˈʔʊn·ʃtal·tn̩] *vt* to disfigure

veruntreuen * [fɛɐ̯·ˈʔʊn·trɔy·ən] *vt* to embezzle

verursachen * [fɛɐ̯·ˈʔuː·ɐ̯·za·xn̩] *vt* to cause

Verursacher(in) <-s, -> m(f) (Person) person responsible

verurteilen * vt 1. (für schuldig befinden) to convict; **jdn zu etw** dat ~ to sentence sb to sth 2. (verdammen) to condemn; **zum Scheitern verurteilt sein** to be bound to fail

Verurteilung <-, -en> f conviction

verwählen * vr TELEK **sich** akk ~ to dial the wrong number

verwahrlost <-er, -este> adj neglected

verwaist adj orphaned; fig (verlassen) deserted, abandoned

verwalten * vt 1. FIN, ADMIN to administer; (Besitz) to manage 2. COMPUT to manage

Verwalter(in) <-s, -> m(f) administrator; (Gut) manager; (Nachlass) trustee

Verwaltung <-, -en> f administration

Verwaltungsbezirk m administrative district

verwandeln * I. vt 1. (umwandeln) **jdn in etw** akk ~ to turn sb into sth; **er ist wie verwandelt** he is a changed person 2. TECH to convert 3. (anders erscheinen lassen) to transform II. vr **sich** akk **in etw** akk ~ to turn into sth

Verwandlung f 1. (Umformung) transformation 2. TECH conversion

verwandt¹ [fɛɐ̯ˈvant] adj related (mit +dat to); (Methoden) similar

verwandt² [fɛɐ̯ˈvant] pp von **verwenden**

Verwandte(r) f(m) dekl wie adj relative, relation

Verwandtschaft <-, -en> f 1. (die Verwandten) relatives pl 2. (gemeinsamer Ursprung) affinity

Verwarnung f warning, caution

Verwechslung <-, -en> [-ˈvɛks·lʊŋ] f mix-up, confusion

verwegen [fɛɐ̯ˈveː·gn̩] adj daring, bold

verweigern * vt, vi to refuse

Verweigerung f refusal

verweint adj (Augen) red from crying; (Gesicht) tear-stained

Verweis <-es, -e> [fɛɐ̯ˈvais] m 1. (Tadel) reprimand 2. (Hinweis) reference (auf +akk to); (Querverweis) cross-reference

verweisen * vt, vi irreg to refer (an/auf +akk to)

verwelken * vi sein to wilt

verwendbar adj usable

verwenden <verwendete o verwandte, verwendet o verwandt> vt to use (für +akk for)

Verwendung <-, -en> f use

Verwendungszweck m purpose

verwerten * vt 1. (ausnutzen, heranziehen) to use 2. (nutzbringend anwenden) to exploit

Verwertung <-, -en> f use

verwesen * [fɛɐ̯ˈveː·zn̩] vi sein to rot, to decompose

Verwesung <-> f kein pl decomposition

verwickeln I. vt **jdn in etw** akk ~ to involve sb in sth; **jdn in ein Gespräch** ~ to engage sb in conversation II. vr **sich** akk ~ to get tangled up

verwickelt adj complicated, intricate

verwildert adj 1. (Garten) overgrown 2. (Tier) feral

verwirren * vt to confuse

verwirrt <-er, -este> adj confused

Verwirrung <-, -en> f 1. (Verstörtheit) confusion 2. (Chaos) chaos

verwitwet [fɛɐ̯ˈvɪt·vət] adj widowed

verwöhnt adj (anspruchsvoll) discriminating

verworren [fɛɐ̯ˈvɔ·rən] adj confused

verwunderlich adj odd, strange; **das ist nicht** ~ that's not surprising

Verwunderung <-> f kein pl amazement

verwundet adj fig a. wounded, hurt

Verwundete(r) f(m) dekl wie adj casualty, wounded person

Verwundung <-, -en> f wound

verwünschen * vt 1. (verfluchen) to curse 2. (verzaubern) to cast a spell on

verwurzelt adj rooted

verwüsten * vt to devastate; (Wohnung) to wreck; (Land) to ravage

Verwüstung <-, -en> f meist pl devastation

verzählen vr **sich** akk ~ to miscount

verzaubern * vt 1. (verhexen) **jdn** ~ to cast a spell on sb; **jdn in einen Vogel** ~ to turn sb into a bird 2. (betören) to enchant

Verzehr <-[e]s> [fɛɐ̯ˈtseː·ɐ̯] m kein pl

V

consumption

verzehren* *vt* **1.** (*essen*) to consume **2.** (*verbrauchen*) to use up **II.** *vr* **sich** *akk* **nach jdm ~** to pine for sb

Verzeichnis <-ses, -se> *nt* list; (*Tabelle*) table; (*Computer*) directory

verzeihen <verzieh, verziehen> **I.** *vt* to forgive **II.** *vi* to excuse; (*Unrecht, Sünde*) to forgive; **~ Sie!** excuse me!, I beg your pardon!

Verzeihung <-> *f kein pl* forgiveness; **|jdn| um ~ bitten** to apologize |to sb|; **~!** sorry!

verzerren* **I.** *vt* **1.** (*verziehen, entstellen*) to distort **2.** (*Muskel*) to pull; (*Sehne*) to strain **II.** *vr* (*sich verziehen*) **sich** *akk* **~** to become contorted

verzichten* [fɛɐ̯ˈtsɪçtn̩] *vi* to go without; **auf Alkohol/Zigaretten ~** to abstain from drinking/smoking

verziehen*[1] *vr irreg* **sich** *akk* **~** to disappear; (*Gewitter*) to pass; **verzieh dich!** beat it!, scram!

verziehen*[2] *irreg* **I.** *vt* **das Gesicht ~** to grimace **II.** *vr* **sich** *akk* **~** (*Holz*) to warp

verziehen[3] *pp von* **verziehen**

verzieren* *vt* to decorate

Verzierung <-, -en> *f* decoration; (*an Gebäuden*) ornamentation

verzinsen* *vt* **etw |mit 3 Prozent| ~** to pay |3 Percent| interest on sth

verzogen [fɛɐ̯ˈtsoːɡn̩] *adj* badly brought up; (*Kinder*) spoiled

verzögern* **I.** *vt* **1.** (*später erfolgen lassen*) to delay (**um** +*akk* by/for) **2.** (*verlangsamen*) to slow down **II.** *vr* (*später erfolgen*) **sich** *akk* **~** to be delayed (**um** +*akk* by/for)

Verzögerung <-, -en> *f* delay, holdup *fam;* (*Verlangsamung*) slowing down

verzollen* *vt* **etw ~** to pay customs on sth; **haben Sie etwas zu ~?** do you have anything to declare?

Verzug <-[e]s> *m kein pl* delay; **|mit etw *dat*| in ~ geraten** to fall behind |with sth|

verzweifeln* *vi sein* to despair (**an** +*dat* of)

verzweifelt I. *adj* **1.** (*völlig verzagt*) despairing; **ein ~es Gesicht machen** to

look desperate **2.** (*hoffnungslos*) desperate **II.** *adv* (*völlig verzagt*) despairingly, desperately

Verzweiflung <-> *f kein pl* (*Gemütszustand*) despair; (*Ratlosigkeit*) desperation; **jdn zur ~ bringen** to drive sb to despair

verzwickt [fɛɐ̯ˈtsvɪkt] *adj* tricky

Veteran <-en, -en> [ve·te·ˈraːn] *m* veteran

Veto <-s, -s> [ˈveːto] *nt* veto

Vetorecht *nt* right of veto

Vetter <-s, -n> [ˈfɛ·te] *m* cousin

Vetternwirtschaft *f kein pl* nepotism

Viadukt <-[e]s, -e> [via·ˈdʊkt] *m o nt* viaduct

Vibration <-, -en> [vi·bra·ˈtsi̯oːn] *f* vibration

Videoaufzeichnung *f* video recording

Videokamera *f* video camera

Vieh <-[e]s> [fiː] *nt kein pl* **1.** AGR livestock; (*Rinder*) cattle **2.** *fam* (*Tier*) animal, beast

Viehzucht *f* cattle [*o* livestock] breeding

viel [fiːl] **I.** *adj* <mehr, meiste> **1.** *sing, adjektivisch* a lot of; **er braucht ~ Geld** he needs lots of money; **~ Erfolg!** good luck!; **~ Spaß!** have a good time! **2.** *sing, + art, poss* **das ~e Essen ist mir nicht bekommen** all that food hasn't done me any good **3.** *substantivisch* a lot, much; **ich habe zu ~ zu tun** I have too much to do; **obwohl er ~ weiß, ...** although he knows a lot, ... **4.** *pl, adjektivisch* **~e** a lot of, many; **und ~e andere** and many others **5.** + *pl, substantivisch* (*eine große Anzahl*) **~e** a lot; (*von Menschen a.*) many [people] **II.** *adv* <mehr, am meisten> **1.** (*häufig*) a lot; **~ diskutiert** much-discussed; **eine ~ befahrene Straße** a [very] busy street **2.** (*wesentlich*) a lot; **~ zu groß** much too big

vieldeutig *adj* ambiguous

Vielfalt <-> [ˈfiːl·falt] *f* diversity, [great] variety (**an** +*dat* of)

vielfältig [ˈfiːl·fɛl·tɪç] *adj* diverse, varied

vielleicht [fiˈlaɪ̯çt] **I.** *adv* **1.** (*eventuell*) perhaps, maybe **2.** (*ungefähr*) about **II.** *part* **1.** (*bitte /mahnend/*) please; **würdest du mich ~ einmal ausreden**

lassen? would you please let me finish what I'm saying for once? **2.** (*etwa*) by any chance; **erwarten Sie ~, dass ich Ihnen das Geld gebe?** I don't suppose you expect me to give you the money, do you? **3.** (*wirklich*) really; **du erzählst ~ einen Quatsch** what are you talking about?

vielmehr ['fiːl·meːɐ̯] *adv* rather

vielseitig ['fiːl·zai·tɪç] **I.** *adj* (*Mensch, Maschine*) versatile; (*Angebot, Arbeit*) varied **II.** *adv* **1.** (*in vieler Hinsicht*) widely **2.** (*in verschiedener Weise*) **etw ist ~ anwendbar** sth can be used in a variety of ways

Vielzahl *f kein pl* **eine ~ von etw** *dat* a large amount of sth

vier [fiːɐ̯] *adj* four; *s. a.* **acht**[1] ▶ **ein Gespräch unter ~ Augen führen** to have a private conversation

Vier <-, -en> [fiːɐ̯] *f* **1.** (*Zahl*) four **2.** (*Zeugnisnote*) **er hat in Deutsch eine ~ ≈** he got a D in German ▶ **auf allen ~en** on all fours

Viereck ['fiːɐ̯·ʔɛk] *nt* square; MATH quadrilateral

viereckig ['fiːɐ̯·ʔɛkɪç] *adj* rectangular

vierfach, 4fach I. *adj* fourfold; **die ~e Menge** four times the amount **II.** *adv* fourfold, four times over

vierhundert ['fiːɐ̯·'hʊn·dɐt] *adj* four hundred

viermal, 4-mal [RR] ['fiːɐ̯·maːl] *adv* four times; *s. a.* **achtmal**

Vierradantrieb *m* four-wheel drive

vierspurig *adj* four-lane *attr*

vierstellig *adj* **eine ~e Zahl** a four-digit number

vierte(r, s) ['fiːɐ̯·tə -te -təs] *adj* **1.** (*an vierter Stelle*) fourth; *s. a.* **achte(r, s) 1 2.** (*Datum*) fourth, 4th; *s. a.* **achte(r, s) 2**

viertel ['fɪr·tl] *adj* quarter, fourth; **drei ~** three-quarters, three-fourths

Viertel[1] <-s, -> ['fɪr·tl] *nt* district, quarter

Viertel[2] <-s, -> ['fɪr·tl] *nt o schweiz m* **1.** (*der vierte Teil*) quarter **2.** (*15 Minuten*) **vor/nach drei** [a] quarter to [*o of*]/after three

Vierteljahr [fɪr·tl·'jaːɐ̯] *nt* three months, quarter *spec*

vierteljährlich ['fɪr·tl·jɛːɐ̯·lɪç] *adj, adv* quarterly

Viertelstunde [fɪr·tl·'ʃtʊn·də] *f* quarter of an hour, fifteen minutes

vierzehn ['fɪr·tseːn] *adj* fourteen; **~ Tage** two weeks; *s. a.* **acht**[1]

vierzehntägig ['fɪr·tseːn-] *adj* two-week *attr*

vierzehnte(r, s) *adj* **1.** (*an vierzehnter Stelle*) fourteenth; *s. a.* **achte(r, s) 1 2.** (*Datum*) fourteenth, 14th; *s. a.* **achte(r, s) 2**

vierzig ['fɪr·tsɪç] *adj* forty; *s. a.* **achtzig 1, 2**

vierzigste(r, s) *adj* fortieth; *s. a.* **achte(r, s) 1**

Vietnam <-s> [vjɛt·'nam] *nt* Vietnam; *s. a.* **Deutschland**

Vikar(in) <-s, -e> [vi·'kaːɐ̯] *m(f)* vicar

Villa <-, Villen> ['vɪla] *f* villa

violett [vjo·'lɛt] *adj* violet, purple

Violine <-, -n> [vjo·'liː·nə] *f* violin

virtuell [vɪr·'tu·ɛl] *adj* virtual

Virus <-, Viren> ['viː·rʊs] *nt o m* virus

Vision <-, -en> [vi·'zjoːn] *f* vision

Visite <-, -n> [vi·'ziː·tə] *f* (*Arztbesuch*) round

Visitenkarte [vi·'ziː·tən-] *f* business card

Viskose <-> [vɪs·'koː·zə] *f kein pl* viscose

Visum <-s, Visa> ['viː·zʊm] *nt* visa

vital [vi·'taːl] *adj* **1.** (*Lebenskraft besitzend*) lively, vigorous **2.** (*lebenswichtig*) vital

Vitalität <-> [vi·ta·li·'tɛt] *f kein pl* vitality, vigor

Vitamin <-s, -e> [vi·ta·'miːn] *nt* vitamin

Vitaminmangel *m* vitamin deficiency

Vitrine <-, -n> [vi·'triː·nə] *f* (*Schaukasten*) display case; (*Glasvitrine*) glass cabinet

Vizepräsident(in) *m(f)* vice president

Vogel <-s, Vögel> ['foː·gl] *m* **1.** (*Tier*) bird **2.** *fam* (*auffallender Mensch*) **ein lustiger ~** a real joker; **ein seltsamer ~** a strange bird ▶ **einen ~ haben** to have a screw loose

Vogelfutter *nt* bird food

Vogelscheuche <-, -n> *f* scarecrow

Vokabel <-, -n> [vo·'kaː·bl] *f* word; **~n** *pl* **lernen** to memorize vocabulary words

Vokabular <-s, -e> [vo·ka·bu·'laːɐ̯] *nt*

V

vocabulary

Vokal <-s, -e> [vo·'ka:l] *m* vowel

Volk <-[e]s, Völker> [fɔlk] *nt* **1.** (*Nation*) nation, people **2.** *kein pl* (*Menschen*) people *npl;* **sich** *akk* **unters ~ mischen** to mingle with the people

Völkergemeinschaft *f* international community

Völkerkunde <-> *f kein pl* ethnology

Völkermord *m* genocide

Völkerrecht *nt kein pl* international law

Volksabstimmung *f* referendum

Volksfest *nt* folk festival

Volksheld(in) *m(f)* national hero

Volkshochschule *f* adult education center

Volkslied *nt* folk song

Volksstamm *m* tribe

Volkstanz *m* folk dance

volkstümlich ['fɔlks·ty:m·lɪç] *adj* traditional

Volkswirtschaft *f* national economy

Volkszählung *f* [national] census

voll [fɔl] **I.** *adj* **1.** (*gefüllt*) full; **eine Hand ~ Reis** a handful of rice; **~ sein** *fam* (*satt*) to be full **2.** (*vollständig*) full, whole; **etw in ~en Zügen genießen** to enjoy sth to the fullest; **jede ~e Stunde** every hour on the hour; **bei ~em Bewusstsein** fully conscious **3.** (*kräftig: Stimme*) rich; (*Haar*) thick **4.** *fam* (*betrunken*) **~ sein** to be hammered ▶ **sie nimmt ihn nicht für ~** she doesn't take him seriously; **aus dem V~en schöpfen** to draw on plentiful resources **II.** *adv* **1.** (*vollkommen*) completely **2.** (*uneingeschränkt*) fully; **~ und ganz** totally **3.** (*mit aller Wucht*) right, smack; **der Wagen war ~ gegen den Pfeiler geprallt** the car ran smack into the pillar

vollautomatisch I. *adj* fully automatic **II.** *adv* fully automatically

Vollbart *m* full beard

Vollblut *nt* thoroughbred

vollbringen * *vt irreg* to accomplish; (*Wunder*) to perform

Volleyball ['vɔli-] *m* volleyball

Vollgas *nt kein pl* full speed; **~ geben** to put one's foot down

völlig ['fœ·lɪç] **I.** *adj* complete **II.** *adv* completely; **Sie haben ~ recht** you'r absolutely right

volljährig ['fɔl·jɛ:·rɪç] *adj* of age; **~ werden** to come of age

Vollkaskoversicherung *f* comprehensive car insurance [coverage]

vollklimatisiert *adj* fully air-conditione

vollkommen [fɔl·'kɔ·mən] **I.** *adj* **1.** (*perfekt*) perfect **2.** (*völlig*) complete **II.** *adv* completely

Vollkornbrot *nt* whole-grain bread

Vollmacht <-, -en> ['fɔl·maxt] *f* authori zation; (*Schriftstück*) power of attorney; **jdm [die] ~ für etw** *akk* **geben** to au thorize sb to do sth; **eine ~ haben** t have power of attorney

Vollmilch *f* whole milk

Vollmond *m kein pl* full moon; **bei ~** when there's a full moon

Vollpension *f kein pl* [mit] ~ full board

vollschlank *adj* plump

vollständig ['fɔl·ʃtɛn·dɪç] **I.** *adj* complete **II.** *adv* completely

Vollstreckung <-, -en> *f* execution

Volltreffer *m* **1.** (*direkter Treffer*) bull' eye *fig fam* **2.** *fam* (*voller Erfolg*) com plete success

Vollversammlung *f* general meeting

vollwertig *adj* **1.** ~e **Kost** whole food **2.** (*Ersatz*) fully adequate

Vollwertkost *f kein pl* whole foods *pl*

vollzählig ['fɔl·tsɛ:·lɪç] **I.** *adj* (*komplett* complete, whole; **~ sein** to be all presen **II.** *adv* at full strength

vollziehen * [fɔl·'tsi:·ən] *irreg* **I.** *vt* t carry out *sep;* (*Urteil*) to execute; (*Ehe* consummate **II.** *vr* **sich** *akk* ~ to tak place

Vollzugsanstalt *f* penal institution

Volontär(in) <-s, -e> [vo·lɔn·'tɛ:ɐ̯] *m(* intern, trainee

Volt <-[e]s, -> [vɔlt] *nt* volt

Volumen <-s, -> [vo·'lu:·mən] *nt* volume

von [fɔn] *präp* +*dat* **1.** *räumlich* (*ab, her kommend*) from; **~ woher...?** where .. from?, from where...?; **~ rechts** from the right; **~ diesem Fenster kann man alles sehen** you can see every thing from this window; **~ unserem eigenen Garten** from our own garden

(aus ... herab/heraus) off; **er fiel ~ der Leiter** he fell off [o from] the ladder 2. *räumlich (etw entfernend)* from, off; **die Wäsche ~ der Leine nehmen** to take the laundry off the line; **Schweiß ~ der Stirn wischen** to wipe sweat from one's brow 3. *zeitlich (stammend)* from; **die Zeitung ~ gestern** yesterday's [news]paper; **ich kenne sie ~ früher** I know her from a long time ago; **~ jetzt an** from now on 4. *(Urheber, Ursache)* ~ **jdm gelobt werden** to be praised by sb; ~ **wem ist dieses Geschenk?** who is this present from?; ~ **wem weißt du das?** who told you that?; ~ **wem ist dieser Roman?** who wrote this novel?; **das war nicht nett ~ dir!** that wasn't nice of you! 5. *statt gen (Zugehörigkeit)* of; **die Musik ~ Beethoven** Beethoven's music 6. *(Gruppenangabe)* of; **einer ~ vielen** one of many; **keiner ~ uns** none of us; **ein Student ~ mir** a student of mine, one of my students 7. *(bei Maßangaben)* of; **ein Abstand ~ zwei Metern** a distance of six feet; **eine Pause ~ zehn Minuten** a ten-minute break ▶ **~ wegen!** no way!

oneinander [fɔn·ʔai·ˈnan·dɐ] *adv* from each other; **die beiden Städte sind 25 Kilometer ~ entfernt** the two cities are 25 kilometers apart

or [fɔɐ̯] **I.** *präp* 1. *(räumlich)* in front of; **8 km ~ der Stadt** 8 km outside of town 2. *(zeitlich)* before; **es ist zehn ~ zwölf** it is ten to twelve; **ich war ~ dir dran** I was before you; **vor kurzem/hundert Jahren** a short time/a hundred years ago 3. *(bedingt durch)* with; **starr ~ Schreck** scared stiff; **~ Kälte zittern** to shiver [with cold]; **~ und zurück** forwards and backwards **II.** *adv* forward; **~ und zurück** forwards and backwards

orabend [ˈfoːɐ̯·ʔaːbn̩t] *m* **am ~** *[einer S. gen]* on the evening before [sth], on the eve [of sth]

orahnung *f* premonition

oran|gehen *vi irreg sein* 1. *(an der Spitze gehen)* **jdm ~** to go ahead of sb 2. *a. impers (Fortschritte machen)* to make progress; **die Arbeiten gehen zügig voran** the work is progressing rapidly 3. *(einer Sache vorausgehen)*

to precede

voran|kommen *vi irreg sein* 1. *(vorwärtskommen)* to make headway 2. *(Fortschritte machen)* to make progress; **wie kommt ihr voran mit der Arbeit?** how's your work coming along[, guys]?

Voranmeldung [ˈfoːɐ̯·ʔan·mɛl·dʊŋ] *f* appointment, booking

Vorarbeiter(in) *m(f)* foreman *masc,* forewoman *fem*

voraus [fo·ˈraus] *adv* in front, ahead; **jdm ~ sein** to be ahead of sb; **im V~** in advance

voraus|gehen [fo·ˈraus·geː·ən] *vi irreg sein* to go on ahead; **einem Unwetter geht meistens ein Sturm voraus** bad weather is usually preceded by a storm

vorausgesetzt *adj* ~, [**dass**] ... provided [that] ...

Voraussage <-, -en> *f* prediction

voraus|sagen *vt* to predict

voraus|setzen *vt* 1. *(als selbstverständlich erachten)* to assume 2. *(erfordern)* to require

Voraussetzung <-, -en> *f* 1. *(Vorbedingung)* condition; ~**en** *(für eine Arbeit)* qualifications *npl*; **unter der ~, dass ...** on the condition that ...; **unter bestimmten ~en** under certain conditions 2. *(Annahme)* assumption, premise

voraussichtlich [fo·ˈraus·zɪçt·lɪç] **I.** *adj (erwartet)* expected **II.** *adv (wahrscheinlich)* probably

Vorauszahlung *f* advance payment

Vorbehalt <-[e]s, -e> [ˈfoɐ̯·bə·halt] *m* reservation (**gegen** +*akk* about); **ohne ~** without reservation; **unter ~** with reservations *pl*

vorbehaltlos I. *adj* unreserved **II.** *adv* unreservedly, without reservation

vorbei [foːɐ̯·ˈbai] *adv* 1. *(vorüber)* **an etw** *dat* ~ past sth; **wir sind schon an München ~** we already passed Munich; **schon wieder ~, ich treffe nie** missed again — I never hit the target 2. *(vergangen)* ~ **sein** to be over; **es ist drei Uhr ~** it's [already] past three o'clock; **aus und ~** over and done with

vorbei|fahren *vi irreg sein* 1. *(vorüberfahren)* to drive past; **im V~** while

driving past **2.** (*kurz aufsuchen*) **bei etw** *dat* ~ (*Apotheke, Supermarkt*) to stop off at sth

vorbei|gehen [foː'ɡ·bai·geː·ən] *vi irreg sein* **1.** (*vorübergehen*) to go past; (*überholen*) to pass; (*danebengehen: Schuss*) to miss; **sie ging dicht an uns vorbei** she walked right past us **2.** (*aufsuchen*) to go to; **gehe doch bitte bei der Apotheke vorbei** please stop off at the drugstore **3.** (*vergehen*) **die Ferien gingen schnell** ~ vacation went by fast

vorbei|kommen *vi irreg sein* **1.** (*passieren*) to pass **2.** (*besuchen*) to drop in (**bei** +*dat* at) **3.** (*vorbeigehen können*) to get past

vorbei|lassen *vt irreg* to let past; **lassen Sie uns bitte vorbei!** please let us through!

vorbei|reden *vi* **am Thema** ~ to miss the point; **aneinander** ~ to be talking at cross-purposes *pl*

vorbelastet *adj* at a disadvantage; **erblich** ~ **sein** to have a genetic predisposition

vor|bereiten* **I.** *vt* to prepare **II.** *vr sich akk* ~ to prepare oneself

Vorbereitung <-, -en> *f* preparation

Vorbesitzer(in) <-s, -> *m(f)* previous owner

vor|bestellen* *vt* to order in advance; **ich möchte zwei Karten** ~ I'd like to reserve two tickets

Vorbestellung *f* advance booking

vorbestraft *adj* previously convicted (**wegen** +*dat* for/of); **nicht** ~ **sein** to not have a criminal record

vor|beugen I. *vt* (*nach vorne beugen*) to bend forward **II.** *vi* (*Prophylaxe betreiben*) to take preventive measures; **etw** *akk* ~ (*Gefahr, Krankheit*) to prevent sth **III.** *vr sich akk* ~ to lean forward

Vorbeugung <-, -en> *f* prevention; **zur** ~ [**gegen etw** *akk*] as a preventive measure [against sth]

Vorbild <-[e]s, -er> ['foːɡ·bɪlt] *nt* example; [**jdm**] **als** ~ **dienen** to serve as an example [for sb]

vorbildlich I. *adj* exemplary **II.** *adv* in an exemplary manner

vor|bringen *vt irreg* (*Argument*) to put forward; (*Bedenken*) to express; (*Einwand*) to raise

vorchristlich *adj attr* **in** ~**er Zeit** in pre-Christian times

Vorderachse *f* front axle

Vorderasien <-s> *nt* Near East

vordere(r, s) ['fɔr·də·rə, -rə, -rəs] *adj* front

Vordergrund *m* foreground

Vordermann *m* **mein** ~ the person in front of me

Vorderrad *nt* front wheel

Vorderradantrieb *m* front-wheel drive

Vorderseite *f* front [side]

vorderste(r, s) ['fɔr·dɐ·sta, -stə, -stəs] *adj superl von* **vordere(r, s)** foremost; **die** ~**n Plätze** the seats at the very front

vor|drängeln, vor|drängen *vr sich akk* ~ to push one's way to the front

vor|dringen *vi irreg sein* to reach, to get as far as

vorehelich *adj attr* premarital

voreilig ['foːɡ·ʔai·lɪç] **I.** *adj* rash, over-hasty **II.** *adv* rashly, hastily

voreingenommen ['foːɡ·ʔain·gə·nɔ·mən] *adj* prejudiced (**gegenüber** +*da* against)

Vorentscheidung *f* preliminary decision

vorerst ['foːɡ·ʔeːɐst] *adv* for the time being

Vorfahr(in) <-en, -en> ['foːɡ·faːɐ] *m(f)* ancestor

Vorfahrt ['foːɡ·faːɐt] *f kein pl* right of way; **jdm die** ~ **nehmen** to not yield to sb

Vorfahrtsstraße *f* main road

Vorfall *m* incident, occurrence

vor|fallen *vi irreg sein* to happen, to occur

vor|finden *vt irreg* to find

Vorfreude *f* [excited] anticipation (**auf** +*akk* of)

vor|führen *vt* **1.** (*Gerät*) to demonstrate **2.** (*darbieten*) to perform

Vorführung *f* FILM screening

Vorgang <-gänge> *m* **1.** (*Geschehnis*) event **2.** (*Prozess*) process

Vorgänger(in) <-s, -> *m(f)* predecessor

Vorgarten *m* front yard

vor|geben vt irreg **1.** (vorschützen) to use as an excuse; **~, dass ...** to pretend that ... **2.** (festlegen) to set in advance

Vorgebirge nt foothills pl

vor|gehen vi irreg sein **1.** (vorausgehen) to go on ahead **2.** (zu schnell gehen) to be fast; **meine Uhr geht fünf Minuten vor** my watch is five minutes fast **3.** (Priorität haben) to have priority, to come first **4.** (Schritte ergreifen) to take action **5.** (sich abspielen) to be going on; **was ging in ihr vor?** what was going on inside her? **6.** (verfahren) to proceed (**bei** +dat in/with)

Vorgeschmack m kein pl foretaste

Vorgesetzte(r) f(m) dekl wie adj superior

vorgestern ['foːɐ̯ɡɛstɐn] adv the day before yesterday; **~ Morgen/Nacht** the morning/night before last

vor|haben ['foːɐ̯haːbn̩] vt irreg to have planned; **hast du etwa vor, noch weiterzuarbeiten?** do you intend to keep on working?

Vorhaben <-s, -> ['foːɐ̯haːbn̩] nt plan, project

vor|halten irreg I. vt jdm etw ~ **1.** (vorwerfen) to reproach sb for sth **2.** (davorhalten: Spiegel) to hold sth in front of sb II. vi to last

vorhanden ['foːɐ̯handn̩] adj **1.** (verfügbar) available **2.** (existierend) existing

Vorhang <-s, Vorhänge> ['foːɐ̯haŋ] m curtain

Vorhängeschloss RR nt padlock

Vorhaut f ANAT foreskin

vorher [foːɐ̯ˈheːɐ̯] adv beforehand; **kurz ~** just before; **ich muss ~ noch essen** I have to eat first

vorher|bestimmen* vt to predetermine; **vorherbestimmt sein** to be predestined

vorherig [foːɐ̯ˈheːrɪç] adj attr prior; (Abmachung, Vereinbarung) previous

Vorhersage [foːɐ̯ˈheːɐ̯zaːɡə] f **1.** METEO forecast **2.** (Voraussage) prediction

vorher|sagen vt to predict

vorhersehbar adj foreseeable

vorher|sehen vt irreg to foresee

vorhin [foːɐ̯ˈhɪn] adv a moment ago, just [now]

vorig ['foːrɪç] adj attr last, previous

Vorjahr nt last year

Vorkehrung <-, -en> f precaution; **~en treffen** to take precautions

vor|kochen vt KOCHK to precook

vor|kommen vi irreg sein **1.** (passieren) to happen; **es kommt vor, dass ...** it can happen that ...; **das kann [schon mal]** ~ these things [can] happen **2.** (vorhanden sein) to be found, to occur **3.** (erscheinen) to seem; **jdm bekannt ~** to sound familiar to sb; **du kommst dir wohl sehr schlau vor?** you think you're real clever, don't you? **4.** (nach vorn kommen) to come [up] to the front **5.** (zum Vorschein kommen) [hinter etw dat] ~ to come out [from behind sth]

Vorkommen <-s, -> nt **1.** kein pl (Auftreten) incidence **2.** meist pl GEOL deposit

Vorkriegszeit f prewar period

Vorladung f JUR **1.** (das Vorladen) summoning **2.** (Schreiben) summons

Vorlage f **1.** kein pl (das Vorlegen) presentation **2.** (Muster) pattern **3.** schweiz (Vorleger) mat

vor|lassen vt irreg **1.** (den Vortritt lassen) to let go first **2.** (nach vorn durchlassen) to let past

Vorläufer(in) m(f) precursor

vorläufig ['foːɐ̯lɔy̯fɪç] I. adj temporary; (Ergebnis) provisional; (Regelung) interim II. adv for the time being

vorlaut ['foːɐ̯laut] adj cheeky, impertinent

vor|lesen irreg I. vt [jdm] etw ~ to read out sep sth [to sb] II. vi to read aloud (**aus** +dat from)

Vorlesung f lecture (**über** +akk on)

vorletzte(r, s) ['foːɐ̯lɛtstə, -stɐ, -stəs] adj before last pred

Vorliebe [foːɐ̯ˈliːbə] f preference; **eine ~ für jdn/etw haben** to be particularly fond of sb/sth

vor|liegen vi irreg **1.** (eingereicht sein) **jdm ~** to have been received by sb; **uns liegen keine Beweise vor** we have no proof **2.** (bestehen) to be

vor|lügen vt irreg **jdm etw ~** to lie to sb

V

vor|machen vt 1. (täuschen) sich/jdm etw ~ to fool oneself/sb; machen wir uns doch nichts vor let's not kid ourselves 2. (demonstrieren) jdm etw ~ to show sb [how to do] sth

vor|merken vt ich habe mir den Termin vorgemerkt I've made a note of the appointment

Vormittag ['foːɐ̯·mɪ·taːk] m morning; am [frühen/späten] ~ [early/late] in the morning

vormittags ['foːɐ̯·mɪ·taːks] adv in the morning

Vormund <-[e]s, -e> ['foːɐ̯·mʊnt] m guardian

Vormundschaft <-, -en> ['foːɐ̯·mʊnt·ʃaft] f guardianship

vorn [fɔrn] adv at the front; ~ im Bus at the front of the bus; nach ~ to the front; von ~ (von der Vorderseite her) from the front; (von Anfang an) from the beginning; jetzt kann ich wieder von ~ anfangen now I have to start from scratch all over again; von ~ bis hinten fam from beginning to end

Vorname m first name

vornehm ['foːɐ̯·neːm] adj 1. (elegant) elegant; (Mensch, Benehmen) distinguished 2. (luxuriös: Gegend, Restaurant) exclusive ▶ ~ tun pej to put on airs

vor|nehmen irreg I. vt (ausführen) to carry out sep; Änderungen ~ to make changes II. vr (planen) sich dat etw ~ to plan sth

vornherein ['fɔrn·hɛ·rain] adv von ~ from the start

Vorort ['foːɐ̯·ʔɔrt] m suburb

Vorplatz m forecourt

vorprogrammiert adj pre-programmed; (vorbestimmt) predetermined

Vorrang m kein pl 1. (Priorität) priority (vor +dat over) 2. österr (Vorfahrt) right of way

vorrangig I. adj priority attr, of prime importance pred; ~ sein to have priority II. adv as a matter of priority

Vorrat <-[e]s, Vorräte> ['foːɐ̯·raːt] m stock, supply (an +dat of); Vorräte anlegen to stock up on sth; so lange der ~ reicht while supplies last

vorrätig ['foːɐ̯·rɛ·tɪç] adj in stock prec etw ~ haben to have sth in stock

Vorrecht nt privilege

Vorrichtung <-, -en> f device, gadget

vor|rücken I. vi sein 1. MIL to advance (gegen +akk on) 2. (nach vorn rücken) to move forward II. vt haben to move forward

Vorruhestand m early retirement

Vorrunde f SPORT preliminary round

Vorsaison f low season

Vorsatz <-[e]s, Vorsätze> ['foːɐ̯·zats] r resolution; den ~ fassen, etw zu tur to resolve to do sth

vorsätzlich ['foːɐ̯·zɛts·lɪç] I. adj deliberate, intentional II. adv deliberately intentionally

vor|schieben vt irreg 1. (vorschützen) to use as an excuse 2. (für sich agieren lassen) jdn ~ to use sb as a front man/woman 3. (nach vorn schieben) to push forward 4. (vor etw schieben: Riegel) to push across

vor|schießen vt irreg (Geld) to advance

Vorschlag m suggestion; [jdm] einen ~ machen to make a suggestion [to sb]; auf jds ~ [hin] on sb's recommendation

vor|schlagen vt irreg 1. (als Vorschlag unterbreiten) to suggest 2. (empfehlen) to recommend

vor|schreiben vt irreg jdm etw ~ to stipulate sth to sb; schreib mir nicht vor, was ich machen soll! don't tell me what to do!

Vorschrift f ADMIN regulation, rule; (Anweisung) instructions pl; (polizeilich) orders pl; ~ sein to be the rule[s]; jdm ~en machen to tell sb what to do

vorschriftsmäßig adj, adv according to [the] regulations

Vorschulalter nt kein pl preschool age im ~ sein to be of preschool age

Vorschule f preschool

Vorschuss RR <-es, Vorschüsse>, **Vorschuß** ALT <-sses, Vorschüsse> ['foːɐ̯·ʃʊs] m advance

vor|schweben vi to have in mind

vor|sehen irreg I. vr sich akk ~ to watch out (vor +dat for); sieh dich vor! watch it! II. vt (planen) es ist vorgesehen

dass ... it is planned that ...; **das Geld war für den Urlaub vorgesehen** the money was intended for the vacation; **Sie hatte ich für eine andere Aufgabe vorgesehen** I had you in mind for a different job

Vorsehung <-> ['foːɐ̯·zeː·ʊŋ] f kein pl providence

Vorsicht <-> ['foːɐ̯·zɪçt] f kein pl caution; **~!** watch out!

vorsichtig I. adj **1.** (umsichtig) careful **2.** (zurückhaltend) cautious **II.** adv **1.** (umsichtig) carefully **2.** (zurückhaltend) cautiously

vorsichtshalber adv as a precaution, just to be on the safe side

Vorsichtsmaßnahme f precaution; **~n treffen** to take precautions

Vorsilbe f prefix

vor|singen vt irreg to sing first

Vorsitzende(r) f(m) dekl wie adj chairman/-woman/-person

Vorsorge f provisions pl; **~ für etw** akk **treffen** to make provisions for sth

vor|sorgen vi to provide

Vorsorgeuntersuchung f medical checkup

Vorspeise f starter, appetizer

Vorspiel nt **1.** MUS prelude; (zur Probe) audition **2.** (vor dem Liebesakt) foreplay

vor|spielen I. vt **1.** MUS to play **2.** (vorheucheln) to put on **II.** vi MUS to play

Vorsprung m lead

Vorstadt f suburb

Vorstand m **1.** (Geschäftsführung) [management] board; (einer Partei, eines Vereins) [executive] committee **2.** (Vorstandsmitglied) director, board member; (einer Partei) executive; (eines Vereins) [member of the] executive [committee]

Vorsteher(in) <-s, -> ['foːɐ̯·ʃteː·ɐ] m(f) head

vor|stellen I. vt **1.** (gedanklich sehen) **sich** dat **etw ~** to imagine sth; **das muss man sich mal ~!** just imagine [it]! **2.** (als angemessen betrachten) **sich** dat **etw ~** to have sth in mind **3.** (bekannt machen) **jdm jdn ~** to introduce sb to sb **4.** (präsentieren) **jdm etw ~** to pres-

ent sth to sb **5.** (vorrücken: Uhr) to set forward **II.** vr **sich** akk **~ 1.** (bekannt machen) to introduce oneself **2.** (bei Arbeitgeber) to have an interview

Vorstellung f **1.** (gedankliches Bild) idea; **falsche ~en haben** to have false hopes **2.** THEAT performance; FILM screening

Vorstellungsgespräch nt interview

Vorstellungskraft f kein pl, **Vorstellungsvermögen** nt kein pl [powers npl of] imagination

Vorstrafe f previous conviction

Vortag m **am ~** the day before; **vom ~** from yesterday

vor|täuschen vt (Unfall) to fake; (Interesse) to feign

Vorteil <-s, -e> ['foːɐ̯·tail] m advantage; **er ist nur auf seinen ~ bedacht** he only ever thinks of his own interests; **im ~ sein** to have an advantage (**gegenüber** +dat over); **von ~ sein** to be advantageous (**für** +akk for/to)

vorteilhaft adj favorable (**für** +akk for); (Geschäft) lucrative, profitable

Vortrag <-[e]s, Vorträge> ['foːɐ̯·traːk] m lecture; **einen ~ halten** to give a lecture (**über** +akk about/on)

vor|tragen vt irreg **1.** (berichten) to present; (Wunsch) to express **2.** (rezitieren) to recite; (Lied) to sing

vortrefflich [foːɐ̯·trɛf·lɪç] **I.** adj excellent; (Gedanke, Idee a.) splendid **II.** adv excellently

vor|treten vi irreg sein **1.** (nach vorn treten) to step forward **2.** (vorstehen) to jut out

Vortritt¹ m precedence, priority; **jdm den ~ lassen** to let sb go first

Vortritt² m kein pl schweiz (Vorfahrt) right of way

vorüber [foˈryː·bɐ] adv **~ sein 1.** räumlich to have gone past **2.** zeitlich to be over; (Schmerz) to be gone

vorüber|gehen [foˈryː·bɐ·geː·ən] vi irreg sein to pass; (Schmerz) to go

vorübergehend I. adj temporary **II.** adv for a short time; **~ geschlossen** temporarily closed

Vorurteil ['foːɐ̯·ʔʊr·tail] nt prejudice; **~e haben** to be prejudiced (**gegenüber** +dat against)

V

Vorverkaufsstelle *f* advance ticket office

vor|verlegen* *vt* to move up (**auf** +*akk* to)

Vorwahl *f* **1.** (*vorherige Auswahl*) preselection [process] **2.** POL primary [election] **3.** TELEK area code

Vorwand <-[e]s, Vorwände> ['fo:ɐ̯·vant] *m* pretext, excuse; **unter einem ~** on a pretext

vorwärts ['fo:ɐ̯·vɛrts] *adv* forward; **~!** onward!, move it!

vorwärts|bringen *vt irreg* **jdn ~** to help sb make progress

Vorwärtsgang <-gänge> *m* forward gear

vorwärts|kommen *vi irreg sein* to make progress

vorweg|nehmen [fo:ɐ̯·ˈvɛk·neː·mən] *vt irreg* to anticipate

vorweihnachtlich *adj* pre-Christmas

vor|werfen *vt irreg* **jdm etw ~** to reproach sb for [doing] sth

vorwiegend *adv* predominantly, mainly

vorwitzig *adj* cocky

Vorwort <-worte> *nt* foreword, preface

Vorwurf <-[e]s, Vorwürfe> *m* reproach; **jdm Vorwürfe machen** to reproach sb (**wegen** +*gen* for)

vorwurfsvoll **I.** *adj* reproachful **II.** *adv* reproachfully

Vorzeichen *nt* **1.** (*Omen*) omen **2.** (*Anzeichen*) sign

vor|zeigen *vt* to show

vorzeitig ['fo:ɐ̯·tsai·tɪç] *adj* early; (*Tod*) untimely

vor|ziehen *vt irreg* **1.** (*bevorzugen*) to prefer **2.** (*zuerst erfolgen lassen: Termin*) to move up **3.** (*nach vorn ziehen*) to pull forward

Vorzimmer *nt* **1.** (*Sekretariat*) secretary's office **2.** *österr* (*Diele*) hall

Vorzug <-[e]s, Vorzüge> ['fo:ɐ̯·tsu:k] *m* **1.** (*gute Eigenschaft*) asset **2.** (*Vorteil*) advantage **3.** (*Bevorzugung*) **etw** *dat* **den ~ geben** to prefer sth

vorzüglich [fo:ɐ̯·ˈtsy:g·lɪç] **I.** *adj* excellent **II.** *adv* excellently

Vorzugspreis *m* discount fare

Votum <-s, Voten> ['vo:·tʊm] *nt* **1.** (*Entscheidung*) decision **2.** POL vote

vulgär [vʊl·ˈgɛːɐ̯] **I.** *adj* vulgar **II.** *adv*

sich *akk* **~ ausdrücken** to use vulgar language

Vulkan <-[e]s, -e> [vʊl·ˈka:n] *m* volcano

Vulkanausbruch [vʊ-] *m* volcanic eruption

vulkanisch [vʊl·ˈka:·nɪʃ] *adj* volcanic

W

W, w <-, -> [veː] *nt* W, w; **~ wie Wilhelm** W as in Whiskey

Waage <-, -n> ['va:·gə] *f* **1.** TECH scale **2.** *kein pl* ASTROL Libra

waagerecht ['va:·gə·rɛçt] **I.** *adj* horizontal **II.** *adv* horizontally

wach [vax] *adj* awake; **~ werden** to wake up

Wache <-, -n> ['va·xə] *f* **1.** *kein pl* (*Wachdienst*) guard duty; **~ stehen** to be on guard duty **2.** (*Wachposten*) guard **3.** (*Polizeiwache*) police station

wachen ['va·xn] *vi* **1.** (*Wache halten*) to keep watch **2.** **über etw** *akk* **~** to ensure that sth is done

wach|rufen *vt irreg* (*Erinnerungen*) to evoke

Wachs <-es, -e> [vaks] *nt* wax

wachsam ['vax·za:m] **I.** *adj* vigilant, watchful **II.** *adv* vigilantly, watchfully

wachsen¹ <wächst, wuchs, gewachsen> ['vak·sn] *vi sein* to grow (**um** +*akk* by)

wachsen² ['vak·sn] *vt* (*mit Wachs einreiben*) to wax

Wächter(in) <-s, -> ['vɛç·tɐ] *m(f)* **1.** (*einer Anstalt*) guard; (*Wachmann*) [night] watchman **2.** (*[moralischer] Hüter*) guardian

Wackelkontakt *m* loose connection

wackeln ['va·kln] *vi* (*Konstruktion*) to shake

Wade <-, -n> ['va:·də] *f* calf

Waffe <-, -n> ['va·fə] *f* weapon

Waffel <-, -n> ['va·fl] *f* waffle

Waffenhandel *m* arms trade

Waffenruhe *f* ceasefire

Waffenschein *m* gun license

Waffenstillstand *m* armistice

wagemutig *adj* daring

wagen ['vaːɡn̩] I. vt 1. (riskieren) to risk 2. (sich trauen) es ~, etw zu tun to dare [to] do sth ▶ wer nicht wagt, der nicht gewinnt prov nothing ventured, nothing gained II. vr sich akk irgendwohin ~ to venture out to somewhere

Wagen <-s, - o südd, österr Wägen> ['vaːɡn̩] m (Auto, Zug) car

Wagenheber <-s, -> m jack

Waggon <-s, -s> [va'ɡɔ̃] m RAIL car

waghalsig ['vaːkˌhalzɪç] adj daring

Wagnis <-ses, -se> ['vaːkˌnɪs] nt 1. (riskantes Vorhaben) risky venture 2. (Risiko) risk

Wagon <-s, -s> [va'ɡɔ̃] m s. **Waggon**

Wahl <-, -en> [vaːl] f 1. POL election 2. (Auswahl) choice; jdm keine ~ lassen to leave sb no choice

wahlberechtigt adj entitled to vote pred

Wahlbeteiligung f [voter] turnout

wählen ['vɛːlən] vt, vi 1. (auswählen) to choose 2. POL to vote; jdn ~ to vote for sb; jdn zu etw dat ~ to elect sb as sth 3. TELEK to dial

Wähler(in) <-s, -> m(f) voter

Wahlergebnis nt election result

wählerisch ['vɛːləˌrɪʃ] adj particular, choosy fam; (Kunde) discerning

Wahlkampf m election campaign

wahllos ['vaːlˌloːs] I. adj indiscriminate II. adv indiscriminately

Wahlniederlage f electoral defeat

Wahlplakat nt election poster

Wahlrecht nt kein pl [right to] vote

Wahlsieg m election victory

Wahlspruch m motto, slogan

wahlweise adv as desired

Wahn <-[e]s> [vaːn] m kein pl 1. (irrige Vorstellung) delusion 2. (Manie) mania

Wahnsinn m kein pl 1. (Geisteskrankheit) insanity 2. fam (Unsinn) madness; ~! amazing!

wahnsinnig I. adj 1. (geisteskrank) insane; jdn ~ machen fam to drive sb crazy 2. fam (unsinnig) crazy 3. attr fam (gewaltig) terrible, dreadful II. adv 1. fam (sehr) terribly, dreadfully; ~ viel a whole lot

Wahnsinnige(r) f(m) dekl wie adj lunatic

wahr [vaːɐ̯] adj 1. (zutreffend) true 2. attr (wirklich) real; ~ werden to become a reality ▶ das darf doch nicht ~ sein! (verärgert) I don't believe this [is happening]!; (entsetzt) this can't be true!; da ist etwas W~es dran there is some truth in it; (als Antwort) you're right about that; etw ist [auch] nicht das W~e sth is not the real McCoy fam

während ['vɛːrənt] I. präp +gen during II. konj 1. (zur selben Zeit) while 2. (wohingegen) whereas

wahrhaben vt etw nicht ~ wollen to not want to admit sth

Wahrheit <-, -en> ['vaːɐ̯haɪt] f truth

wahrnehmbar adj perceptible; (Geräusch) audible

wahrnehmen ['vaːɐ̯neːmən] vt irreg 1. (merken) to perceive; (Geräusch, Geschmack) to detect 2. (Gelegenheit) to take advantage of; (Interessen) to look after; (Termin) to keep

Wahrnehmung <-, -en> f (Geräusch) detection; (Geruch) perception

wahrsagen ['vaːɐ̯zaːɡn̩] vi to tell fortunes

Wahrsager(in) <-s, -> ['vaːɐ̯zaːɡɐ] m(f) fortune teller

wahrscheinlich [vaːɐ̯'ʃaɪnlɪç] I. adj probable, likely II. adv probably

Wahrscheinlichkeit <-, -en> f probability; aller ~ nach in all probability

Währung <-, -en> ['vɛːrʊŋ] f currency

Währungsreform f currency reform

Wahrzeichen ['vaːɐ̯tsaɪçn̩] nt landmark

Waise <-, -n> ['vaɪzə] f orphan

Waisenhaus nt orphanage

Wal <-[e]s, -e> [vaːl] m whale

Wald <-[e]s, Wälder> [valt] m forest, woods pl

Waldbrand m forest fire

Waldsterben nt [forest] dieback

Waldweg m forest path

Wales <-> [weɪls] nt Wales; s. a. **Deutschland**

Waliser(in) <-s, -> [va'liːzɐ] m(f) Welshman masc, Welshwoman fem; s. a. **Deutsche(r)**

walisisch [va'liːzɪʃ] adj Welsh; s. a. **deutsch**

W

Wall <-[e]s, Wälle> [val] *m* embankment; (*Burg*) rampart

Wallfahrer(in) *m(f)* pilgrim

Wallfahrt ['val·faːɐ̯t] *f* pilgrimage

Walnuss ^RR ['val·nʊs] *f* walnut

Walpurgisnacht *f* eve of May 1st, according to German folklore: the night of the Witches' Sabbat on the Blocksberg

Walross ^RR <-es, -e>, **Walroß** ^ALT <-rosses, -rosse> ['val·rɔs] *nt* walrus

Walze <-, -n> ['val·tsə] *f* roller

wälzen ['vɛl·tsn̩] I. *vt* 1. (*rollen*) to roll 2. (*Probleme*) to turn over in one's mind 3. (*Bücher*) to pore over II. *vr* sich *akk* ~ to roll (**in** +*dat* in); **sie wälzte sich im Bett hin und her** she tossed and turned in bed

Walzer <-s, -> ['val·tsɐ] *m* waltz

Wampe <-, -n> ['vam·pə] *f* *fam* [beer] belly

wand *imp von* **winden**

Wand <-, Wände> [vant] *f* wall

Wandel <-s> ['van·dl̩] *m* *kein pl* change

wandeln ['van·dl̩n] *vt, vr* [sich *akk*] ~ to change

Wanderausstellung *f* traveling exhibit

Wanderer, Wanderin <-s, -> ['van·də·rɐ] *m, f* hiker

Wanderkarte *f* trail map

wandern ['van·den] *vi sein* 1. (*eine Wanderung machen*) to hike 2. zool to migrate

Wanderung <-, -en> ['van·də·rʊŋ] *f* hike

Wandschrank *m* built-in wall closet

Wange <-, -n> ['va·ŋə] *f* cheek

wankelmütig ['van·kl̩·myː·tɪç] *adj* inconsistent

wanken ['van·kn̩] *vi* 1. *haben* (*schwanken*) to sway 2. *sein* (*wankend gehen*) to stagger

wann [van] *adv* when; **seit** ~ since when; ~ [**auch**] **immer** whenever

Wanne <-, -n> ['va·nə] *f* tub

Wanst <-[e]s, Wänste> [vanst] *m* belly

Wanze <-, -n> ['van·tsə] *f* bug

wappnen ['vap·nən] *vr* sich *akk* [**gegen etw** *akk*] ~ to prepare oneself [for sth]

Ware <-, -n> ['vaː·rə] *f* article, product

Warenangebot *nt* range of products

Warenhaus *nt* department store

warm <wärmer, wärmste> [varm] *adj* warm; **etw** ~ **halten** to keep sth warm; **etw** ~ **machen** to heat sth up; **den Motor** ~ **laufen lassen** to let the engine warm up; **mir ist zu** ~ I'm hot ▸ **etw wärmstens empfehlen** to highly recommend sth; **mit jdm** ~ **werden** to warm to sb

Wärme <-> ['vɛr·mə] *f* *kein pl* warmth

wärmen ['vɛr·mən] I. *vt* to warm up II. *vi* to be warm III. *vr* sich *akk* **gegenseitig** ~ to keep each other warm

Wärmeregler *m* thermostat

Wärmflasche *f* hot-water bottle

warmherzig *adj* warm-hearted

Warmstart *m* COMPUT soft reset

Warnblinkanlage *f* AUTO hazard lights *pl*, hazards *pl* *fam*

Warndreieck *nt* hazard warning triangle

warnen ['var·nən] *vt* to warn (**vor** +*dat* about)

Warnlicht *nt* AUTO hazard lights *pl*

Warnschild *nt* warning sign

Warnschuss ^RR *m* warning shot

Warnstreik *m* warning strike

Warnung <-, -en> *f* warning (**vor** +*dat* about)

Warschau <-s> ['var·ʃau] *nt* Warsaw

Wartehalle *f* waiting room

Warteliste *f* waiting list

warten ['var·tn̩] I. *vi* to wait (**auf** +*akk* for); **auf sich** *akk* ~ **lassen** to be a long time [in] coming; **warte mal!** hold on!; **na warte!** just you wait! II. *vt* (*Gerät*) to service

Wärter(in) <-s, -> ['vɛr·tɐ] *m(f)* 1. (*Gefängniswärter*) prison guard 2. (*Tierpfleger*) keeper

Warteraum *m* waiting room

Warteschlange *f* line

Wartezeit *f* wait

Wartezimmer *nt* waiting room

Wartung <-, -en> *f* service, maintenance

warum [va·rʊm] *adv* why

Warze <-, -n> ['var·tsə] *f* wart

was [vas] I. *pron interrog* what; ~ **bedeutet das?** what does that mean?; ~ **kostet das?** how much does that cost?; ~ **ist?** what's up?; ~ **für ein ...**

what kind of ...; ~ für ein Glück! what luck! **II.** *pron rel* what; **alles, ~ du willst** everything you want; **alles, ~ ich weiß** all [that] I know **III.** *pron indef fam* (*etwas*) something; (*in Fragesätzen*) anything; **ist ~?** is anything wrong?; **gibt es ~ Neues?** have you heard anything [new]?

Waschanlage *f* car wash

waschbar *adj* washable

Waschbär *m* raccoon

Waschbecken *nt* sink

Wäsche <-> *f kein pl* **1.** (*das Waschen, Schmutzwäsche*) laundry, wash **2.** (*Unterwäsche*) underwear **3.** (*Haushaltswäsche*) linens *pl*

waschecht *adj* **1.** (*typisch*) genuine, real **2.** (*nicht verbleichend*) colorfast

Wäscheklammer *f* clothespin

Wäschekorb *m* laundry basket

Wäscheleine *f* [clothes]line

waschen <wäscht, wusch, gewaschen> ['va·ʃn] *vt* to wash

Wäscherei <-, -en> [vɛ·ʃə·ˈrai] *f* laundry

Wäscheschrank *m* linen cupboard

Wäscheständer *m* clotheshorse, drying rack

Wäschetrockner <-s, -> *m* drier

Waschküche *f* laundry room

Waschlappen *m* **1.** (*Lappen*) washcloth **2.** *fam* (*Feigling*) wimp

Waschmaschine *f* washing machine

Waschmittel *nt* detergent

Waschpulver *nt* laundry powder

Waschraum *m* laundry room

Waschsalon *m* laundromat

Waschstraße *f* car wash

Wasser <-s, -> ['va·sɐ] *nt* water; **~ abweisend** water-repellent ▶ **ins ~ fallen** to fall through; **das ~ bis zum Hals stehen haben** to be up to one's ears in debt; **sich** *akk* **über ~ halten** to keep oneself above water; **jdm läuft das ~ im Mund zusammen** *fam* sb's mouth is watering

Wasseranschluss RR *m* water main connection

Wasseraufbereitungsanlage *f* water treatment plant

Wasserball *m* **1.** *kein pl* (*Sport*) water polo **2.** (*Ball*) beach ball

Wasserbett *nt* waterbed

Wasserdampf *m* steam

wasserdicht *adj* watertight, waterproof

Wasserfall *m* waterfall

Wasserglas *nt* glass, tumbler

Wasserhahn *m* [water] faucet

Wasserkraftwerk *nt* hydroelectric power station

Wasserleitung *f* water pipe

Wassermann ['va·sə·man] *m* ASTROL Aquarius

Wassermelone *f* watermelon

wässern ['vɛ·sɐn] *vt* to water

Wasserpistole *f* water pistol

Wasserrohr *nt* water pipe

wasserscheu *adj* scared of water

Wasserschutzgebiet *nt* water protection area

Wasserski *m* **1.** *kein pl* (*Sportart*) waterskiing **2.** (*Sportgerät*) waterski

Wassersport *m* water sports *pl*

Wasserstand *m* water level

Wasserstrahl *m* jet of water

Wasserverbrauch *m* water consumption

Wasserversorgung *f* water supply

Wasserwaage *f* level

Wasserwerk *nt* waterworks + *sing/pl vb*

wässrig RR, **wäßrig** ALT ['vɛ·rɪç] *adj* **1.** (*Augen, Suppe*) watery **2.** CHEM (*Lösung*) aqueous

waten ['va:·tn] *vi sein* to wade

watscheln ['va:·tʃln] *vi sein* to waddle

Watt¹ <-s, -> [vat] *nt* PHYS watt

Watt² <-[e]s, -en> [vat] *nt* mud flats *pl*

Watte <-, -n> ['va·tə] *f* cotton wool

Wattestäbchen *nt* cotton swab, Q-tip®

wattieren* [va·ˈti:·rən] *vt* to pad

weben <webte *o geh* wob, gewebt *o geh* gewoben> ['ve:·bn] *vt, vi* to weave

Webseite *f* INET Web page

Website <-, -s> ['wɛbˌsait] *f* INET Web site

Wechsel <-s, -> ['vɛk·sl] *m* change

Wechselgeld *nt kein pl* change

wechselhaft ['vɛk·sl-] *adj* changeable

Wechseljahre *pl* menopause

Wechselkurs *m* exchange rate

wechseln ['vɛk·sln] *vt, vi* to change

wechselseitig *adj* mutual

Wechselstrom *m* alternating current

Wechselstube f exchange booth

Wechselwirkung f interaction

wecken ['vɛ·kn̩] vt 1. (aufwecken) to wake [up] 2. (hervorrufen) to bring back sep; (Assoziationen) to create; (Interesse, Verdacht) to arouse

Wecker <-s, -> ['vɛ·kɐ] m alarm clock

wedeln ['ve:·dl̩n] vi mit etw dat ~ to wave sth; (mit dem Schwanz) to wag sth

weder ['ve:·dɐ] konj ~ ... noch ... neither ... nor ...; ~ du noch er neither you nor him; ~ noch neither

weg [vɛk] adv 1. (fort) ~ sein to have left, to be gone; ~ mit dir! go away!; nichts wie ~ hier! let's get out of here!; ~ da! [get] out of the way! 2. fam (hinweggekommen) über etw akk ~ sein to have gotten over sth

Weg <-[e]s, -e> [ve:k] m 1. (Pfad) path 2. (unbefestigte Straße) track 3. (Strecke) way; auf dem ~ sein to be on one's way; auf jds ~ liegen to be on sb's way; sich akk auf den ~ machen to take off 4. (Methode) way ▶ auf dem ~e der <u>Besserung</u> sein to be on the road to recovery; jdm auf <u>halbem</u> ~e entgegenkommen to meet sb halfway; jdm/etw aus dem ~ <u>gehen</u> to avoid sb/sth; jdm über den ~ <u>laufen</u> to run into sb; etw in die ~e <u>leiten</u> to arrange sth; etw aus dem ~ <u>räumen</u> to remove sth; sich akk jdm in den ~ <u>stellen</u> to block sb's path; jdm nicht über den ~ <u>trauen</u> to not trust sb for a second

weg|bleiben vi irreg sein to stay away; bleib nicht so lange weg! don't stay out too long

weg|bringen vt irreg to take away

wegen ['ve:·gn̩] präp +gen 1. (aufgrund von) because of, due to; ~ ihm fam because of him 2. (bezüglich) regarding

weg|fahren irreg I. vi sein 1. (abfahren) to drive off, to leave 2. (verreisen) to leave on a trip II. vt haben (wegbringen) to drive [o take] away

weg|fallen vi irreg sein to cease to apply

weg|fliegen vi irreg sein 1. (Vogel) to fly away 2. (Hut, Blätter) to be blown away, to fly off

weg|führen vt, vi to lead away

weg|geben vt irreg to give away sep

weg|gehen vi irreg sein 1. (fortgehen) to walk away 2. (ausgehen) to go out 3. fam (sich entfernen lassen) to go away; der Fleck geht nicht weg the stain won't come out

weg|jagen vt to drive away sep

weg|kommen vi irreg sein fam 1. (weggehen können) to get away 2. (abhandenkommen) to disappear 3. fam (abschneiden) [bei etw dat] gut/schlecht ~ to do/not do well [on sth] ▶ mach, dass du wegkommst! get out of here!

weg|lassen vt irreg 1. (auslassen) to leave out sep 2. (weggehen lassen) to let go

weg|laufen vi irreg sein to run away (vor +dat from)

weg|legen vt 1. (beiseitelegen) to put down sep 2. (aufbewahren) to put aside sep

weg|müssen vi irreg to have to go

weg|nehmen vt irreg to take (von +dat off); jdm etw ~ to take away sth sep from sb; etw [von etw dat] ~ to take sth sep [off sth]

weg|räumen vt to clear away sep

weg|schaffen vt to remove

weg|schicken vt 1. (Person) to send away 2. (Brief) to send off sep

weg|schmeißen vt irreg fam s. wegwerfen

weg|schütten vt to pour away sep

weg|sehen vi irreg to look away

weg|stecken vt 1. (einstecken) to put away sep 2. (verkraften) to get over

weg|stellen vt to move out of the way

weg|stoßen vt irreg to push away sep; (mit dem Fuß) to kick away sep

weg|tragen vt irreg to carry away sep

weg|tun vt irreg 1. (wegwerfen) to throw away sep 2. (weglegen) to put down sep

Wegweiser <-s, -> m signpost

weg|werfen vt irreg to throw away sep

weg|wischen vt to wipe away sep

weg|ziehen irreg I. vi sein to move away II. vt haben to pull away sep

wehen ['ve:·ən] vi 1. (Wind) to blow 2. (Haare) to blow around; (Fahne) to flutter

wehleidig *adj* oversensitive

wehmütig ['veː·myː·tɪç] *adj* melancholy; (*Erinnerung*) nostalgic

Wehr [veːɐ̯] *f* **sich** *akk* **zur ~ setzen** to defend oneself

Wehrdienst *m kein pl* military service

Wehrdienstverweigerer *m* conscientious objector

wehren ['veː·rən] *vr* **1.** (*sich widersetzen*) **sich** *akk* **gegen etw** *akk* ~ to fight against sth **2.** (*sich sträuben*) **sich** *akk* **dagegen ~, etw zu tun** to resist doing sth

wehrlos **I.** *adj* defenseless (**gegen** +*akk* against) **II.** *adv* in a defenseless state; **etw** *dat* **~ gegenüberstehen** to be defenseless against sth

Wehrpflicht *f kein pl* mandatory military service

wehrpflichtig *adj* obliged to enlist for military service

Weib <-[e]s, -er> [vaɪp] *nt* woman

Weibchen <-s, -> ['vaɪp·çən] *nt* female

Weiberheld *m pej* lady-killer *sl*

weiblich ['vaɪp·lɪç] *adj* **1.** (*fraulich*) feminine **2.** ANAT female **3.** LING feminine

Weiblichkeit <-> *f kein pl* femininity

weich [vaɪç] **I.** *adj* soft ▸ ~ **werden** to weaken **II.** *adv* softly

weichen <wich, gewichen> ['vaɪ·çn̩] *vi sein* (*weggehen*) to go; **er wich nicht von der Stelle** he didn't budge from the spot; **jdm nicht von der Seite ~** to not leave sb's side

weichherzig *adj* soft-hearted

Weichkäse *m* soft cheese

Weichling <-s, -e> ['vaɪç·lɪŋ] *m pej* weakling

Weide <-, -n> ['vaɪ·də] *f* **1.** BOT willow **2.** AGR meadow

weiden ['vaɪ·dn̩] **I.** *vi* (*grasen*) to graze **II.** *vr* **sich** *akk* **an etw** *dat* ~ to feast one's eyes on sth; (*schadenfroh*) to revel in sth

weigern ['vaɪ·ɡɐn] *vr* **sich** *akk* ~ to refuse

Weigerung <-, -en> *f* refusal

Weihnachten <-, -> ['vaɪ·nax·tn̩] *nt* Christmas, Xmas *fam;* **fröhliche ~!** Merry Christmas!

weihnachtlich **I.** *adj* Christmassy, festive **II.** *adv* festively

Weihnachtsabend *m* Christmas Eve

Weihnachtsbaum *m* Christmas tree

Weihnachtsfest *nt* Christmas

Weihnachtsgeld *nt* Christmas bonus

Weihnachtsgeschenk *nt* Christmas present

Weihnachtslied *nt* [Christmas] carol

Weihnachtsmann *m* Santa Claus, Father Christmas

Weihnachtsmarkt *m* Christmas market

weil [vaɪl] *konj* because, since

Weile <-> ['vaɪ·lə] *f kein pl* while; **eine ganze ~** quite a while

Wein <-[e]s, -e> [vaɪn] *m* **1.** (*Getränk*) wine **2.** *kein pl* (*Weinrebe*) [grape]vines *pl* ▸ **jdm reinen ~ einschenken** to tell sb the truth

Weinbeere *f* **1.** (*Traube*) grape **2.** *südd, österr, schweiz* (*Rosine*) raisin

Weinberg *m* vineyard

Weinbrand *m* brandy

weinen ['vaɪ·nən] *vi* to cry (**um** +*akk* for)

weinerlich **I.** *adj* tearful **II.** *adv* tearfully

Weinflasche *f* wine bottle

Weinglas *nt* wine glass

Weingut *nt* winery

Weinkeller *m* wine cellar

Weinlese *f* grape harvest

Weinprobe *f* wine tasting

Weinrebe *f* grape[vine]

weinrot *adj* burgundy[-colored]

Weinstube *f* wine bar

Weintraube *f* grape

weise ['vaɪ·zə] **I.** *adj* wise **II.** *adv* wisely

Weise <-, -n> ['vaɪ·zə] *f* way; **auf diese/eine bestimmte ~** in this/a certain way; **in gewisser ~** in certain respects

weisen <wies, gewiesen> ['vaɪ·zn̩] **I.** *vt* **1.** **jdm den Weg ~** to show sb the way **2.** **etw von sich** *dat* ~ to reject sth **II.** *vi* **irgendwohin ~** to point somewhere

Weisheit <-, -en> ['vaɪs·haɪt] *f* **1.** *kein pl* (*Klugheit*) wisdom **2.** *meist pl* (*weiser Rat*) words *pl* of wisdom ▸ **mit seiner ~ am Ende sein** to be at one's wits' end

Weisheitszahn *m* wisdom tooth

weis|machen *vt* **jdm etw ~** to lead sb to believe sth

weiß¹ [vaɪs] *adj* white

W

weiß² [vais] *3. pers sing pres von* **wissen**

Weissagung <-, -en> *f* prophecy

Weißbrot *nt* white bread

Weiße(r) *f(m) dekl wie adj* white, white man/woman; **die ~n** white people

Weißglut *f* ▶ **jdn zur ~ bringen** to make sb livid with rage

Weißkohl *m,* **Weißkraut** *nt südd, österr* white cabbage

Weißwein *m* white wine

weit [vait] **I.** *adj* long; *(Kleidung)* baggy; **bis dahin ist es noch ~** we still have a way to go before we get there **II.** *adv* **1.** *(räumlich)* far; **~ weg** far away; **es noch ~ haben** to have a long way to go; **8 km ~er** 8 km ahead; **etw ~ öffnen** to open sth wide **2.** *(erheblich)* s. **weitaus 1 3. ~ reichend** extensive; **~ verbreitet** widespread **4.** *(zeitlich)* **~ zurückliegen** to be a long time ago ▶ **bei/von ~em** by/from far; **bei ~em nicht** not nearly; **~ und breit** for miles around; **~ hergeholt** far-fetched; **mit etw** *dat* **ist es nicht ~ her** sth is nothing much to write home about

weitab ['vait-'ʔap] *adv* far away; **~ von etw** *dat* far from sth

weitaus ['vait-'ʔaus] *adv* **1.** *vor komp (erheblich)* far, much; **~ schlechter sein** to be far [o much] worse **2.** *vor superl (bei weitem)* [by] far

weiten ['vai-tn] **I.** *vt* MODE to widen **II.** *vr* **sich** *akk* **~** to widen; *(Pupille)* to dilate

weiter ['vai-tɐ] *adv* **1.** *(sonst)* **wenn es ~ nichts ist, ...** well, if that's all ... **2.** *(weiterhin)* **~ bestehen** to continue to exist

weiter|bilden *vr* **sich** *akk* **in etw** *dat* **~** to [further] develop one's knowledge of sth

Weiterbildung *f kein pl* continuing education

weiter|bringen *vt irreg* to help along

weiter|empfehlen * *vt irreg* to recommend

weiter|führen *vt (fortsetzen)* to continue

weiter|geben *vt irreg* to pass on *sep* (**an** +*akk* **to**)

weiter|gehen *vi irreg sein* **1.** *(seinen Weg fortsetzen)* to keep going **2.** *(sei-*

nen Fortgang nehmen) to go on; **so kann es nicht ~** things can't go on like this

weiter|helfen *vi irreg* to keep helping; *(auf die Sprünge helfen)* to help along

weiterhin ['vai-tɐ-'hɪn] *adv* **1.** *(immer noch)* still **2.** *(außerdem)* furthermore, in addition

weiter|kommen *vi irreg sein* to get farther along

weiter|machen *vi* to continue

weiter|sagen *vt* to pass on *sep;* **nicht ~!** don't tell anyone!

weitgehend I. *adj (umfassend)* extensive **II.** *adv* extensively, to a large extent

weitläufig ['vait-lɔy-fɪç] **I.** *adj* **1.** *(ausgedehnt)* extensive **2.** *(entfernt)* distant **II.** *adv* extensively, distantly

weitreichend *adj* extensive

weitsichtig ['vait-zɪç-tɪç] *adj (a. med)* farsighted

Weizen <-s, -> ['vai-tsn] *m* wheat

welche(r, s) I. *pron interrog* which **II.** *pron rel (der, die, das: Mensch)* who; *(Sache)* which **III.** *pron indef* **1.** *(etwas)* some; **wenn du Geld brauchst, kann ich dir ~s leihen** if you need money, I can lend you some **2.** *pl (einige)* some; **~, die ...** some [people], who

welk [vɛlk] *adj* **1.** *(verwelkt)* wilted **2.** *(schlaff)* worn-out

welken ['vɛl-kn] *vi sein* to wilt

Wellblech *nt* corrugated iron

Welle <-, -n> ['vɛ-lə] *f* wave

wellen ['vɛ-lən] *vr* **sich** *akk* **~** to be/become wavy; *(Papier)* to crinkle

Wellenbrecher <-s, -> *m* breakwater

Wellenlänge *f* PHYS wavelength

Wellenreiten *nt* surfing

Wellensittich *m* parakeet

wellig ['vɛ-lɪç] *adj* **1.** *(gewellt)* wavy **2.** *(wellenförmig)* uneven

Welpe <-n, -n> ['vɛl-pə] *m* puppy, whelp

Welt <-, -en> [vɛlt] *f* world; **auf der ~** in the world ▶ **alle ~** *fam* the whole world; **in aller ~** all over the world; **die Dritte ~** the Third World; **auf die ~ kommen** to be born; **in einer anderen ~ leben** to live on another planet; **um nichts in der ~** not for the world

Weltall *nt* universe

Weltanschauung f worldview, philosophy of life

Weltausstellung f world's fair

weltberühmt adj world-famous

Weltbevölkerung f kein pl world population

Weltenbummler(in) <-s, -> m(f) globetrotter

weltfremd adj unworldly

Weltkarte f world map

Weltkrieg m world war; **der Erste/Zweite ~** World War I/II

weltlich ['vɛlt·lɪç] adj 1. (irdisch) worldly 2. (profan) mundane

Weltmacht f world power

Weltmeer nt ocean

Weltmeister(in) m(f) world champion (**in** +dat in)

Weltmeisterschaft f world championship

Weltraum m kein pl [outer] space

Weltraumfähre f space shuttle

Weltreise f **eine ~ machen** to go on a trip around the world

Weltrekord m world record

Weltsicherheitsrat m [United Nations] Security Council

Weltstadt f international city

Weltuntergang m end of the world

weltweit I. adj global, worldwide II. adv globally

Weltwirtschaft f world economy

Weltwirtschaftsgipfel m world economic summit

Weltwunder nt **die sieben ~** the Seven Wonders of the World

wem [ve:m] I. pron indef dat von **wer** fam to/for somebody II. pron interrog who ... to, to whom form; **~ gehört dieser Schlüssel?** who does this key belong to?; **mit/von ~** with/from whom III. pron rel **~ ...,** [**der**] **...** the person to whom ..., the person who ... to

wen [ve:n] I. pron indef akk von **wer** fam somebody II. pron interrog who, whom; **an/für ~** to/for whom form, who ... to/for III. pron rel **~ ...,** [**der**] **...** the person who[m] ...; **an/für ~** to/for whom form, who ... to/for

Wende <-, -n> ['vɛn·də] f change, turn

Wendekreis m AUTO turning circle

Wendeltreppe f spiral staircase

wenden ['vɛn·dn̩] I. vr <wendete o geh wandte, gewendet o geh gewandt> 1. (sich drehen) **sich** akk **nach links/rechts ~** to turn left/right 2. (kontaktieren) **sich** akk [**in etw** dat] **an jdn ~** to turn to sb [regarding sth] 3. (zielen) **sich** akk **an jdn ~** to be directed at sb 4. (entgegentreten) **sich** akk **gegen jdn ~** to turn against sb; **sich** akk **gegen etw** akk **~** to oppose sth 5. (sich verkehren) **sich** akk **zum Besseren/Schlechteren ~** to take a turn for the better/worse II. vt <wendete, gewendet> (umdrehen) to turn over sep III. vi <wendete, gewendet> AUTO to turn

Wendepunkt m turning point

wendig ['vɛn·dɪç] adj maneuverable

Wendung <-, -en> f 1. (Veränderung) turn 2. (Redewendung) expression

wenig ['ve:·nɪç] I. pron indef 1. sing (nicht viel) little; **~ Zeit/Geld haben** to have little time/money; **zu ~ Freizeit** not enough free time; **zu ~ sein** to be not [very] much 2. pl (nicht viele) **~e** a few; **~e Stunden später** a few hours later; **das wissen nur ~e** only a few [people] know about it II. adv little; **~ interessant** of little interest; **zu ~ schlafen** to not get enough sleep

weniger ['ve:·nɪ·ɡɐ] I. adj komp von **wenig**; **~ als ...** less ... than II. pron indef 1. (unzählbar: Zeit, Geld) less 2. (zählbar: Menschen, Bücher) fewer III. adv less; **~ bekannt sein** to be less known

wenigste(r, s) I. pron **die ~n** very few; **das ~, was ...** the least that ... II. adv least; pl fewest; **am ~n** least of all

wenigstens ['ve:·nɪçs·tn̩s] adv at least

wenn [vɛn] konj 1. (falls) if; **~ das so ist** if that's true [o the way it is] 2. (sobald) as soon as

wenngleich [vɛn·'glaɪç] konj although

wer <gen **wessen,** dat **wem,** akk **wen**> [ve:ɐ̯] I. pron interrog who; **~ von beiden?** which of the two? II. pron rel **~ ... das sagt,** [**der**] **lügt** whoever says that is lying III. pron indef fam s. **jemand**
▶ **~ sein** to be somebody fam

Werbeagentur f advertising agency

Werbefernsehen nt commercials pl

Werbefilm m promotional film

Werbegeschenk nt promotional gift

Werbekampagne f advertising campaign

werben <wirbt, warb, geworben> ['vɛr-bn̩] I. vt jdn [für etw akk] ~ to recruit sb [for sth] II. vi 1. (Reklame machen) für etw akk ~ to advertise [o promote] sth 2. (zu erhalten suchen) um eine Frau ~ to woo a woman; um neue Wähler ~ to try to attract new voters

Werbeslogan m advertising slogan

Werbespot m commercial

Werbung <-> f kein pl 1. (Reklame) advertisement; ~ für etw akk machen to advertise sth 2. (Werbespot) commercial; (Werbeprospekt) promotional brochure 3. (Branche) advertising

Werdegang m career

werden ['veːɐ̯-dn̩] I. vi <wird, wurde, geworden> sein 1. (seinen Zustand ändern) to become, to get; es wird dunkel it is getting dark; es wird besser ~ it is going to get better; es wird Sommer summer is coming [o almost here]; sie ist gerade 98 geworden she [has] just turned 98; alt/älter ~ to get old/older; kalt ~ to get cold; jdm wird heiß/übel sb feels hot/sick; Wirklichkeit ~ to become reality 2. (eine Ausbildung machen) to become; sie will Ärztin werden she wants to become a doctor; was möchtest du einmal ~? what do you want to be [when you grow up]? 3. (sich entwickeln) zu etw dat ~ to turn into sth; es wird schon [wieder] ~ it'll turn out okay in the end II. aux vb 1. zur Bildung des Futurs etw tun ~ to be going to do sth; es wird etw geschehen sth is going to happen; jd wird etw getan haben sb will have done sth 2. zur Bildung des Konjunktivs jd würde etw tun sb would do sth 3. mutmaßend es wird gegen 20 Uhr sein it's probably [o I'm guessing it's] about 8 o'clock III. aux vb <wird, wurde, worden> sein zur Bildung des Passivs du wirst gerufen you are being called; gebissen ~ to be bitten; sie wurde entlassen she was

laid off [o fired]; das wird bei uns häufig gemacht we do that a lot here

werfen <wirft, warf, geworfen> ['vɛr-fn̩] vt, vi 1. (schleudern) to throw (nach +dat at) 2. (Junge gebären) to throw spec, to give birth

Werft <-, -en> [vɛrft] f shipyard

Werk <-[e]s, -e> [vɛrk] nt 1. (Buch, Kunstwerk) work 2. (Gesamtwerk) works pl 3. (Fabrik) factory ▶ ein gutes ~ tun to do a good deed

Werk(s)angehörige(r) f(m) dekl wie adj factory employee

Werksgelände nt factory premises npl

Werkstatt f 1. (Arbeitsraum) workshop 2. AUTO garage

Werktag m workday

werktags adv on workdays

werktätig ['vɛrk-tɛː-tɪç] adj die ~e Bevölkerung the working population

Werkzeug <-[e]s, -e> nt tool usu sg

Werkzeugkasten m toolbox

wert [veːɐ̯t] adj 1. (einen Wert besitzen) [jdm] etw ~ sein to be worth sth [to sb] 2. (verdienen) einer S. gen ~ sein to be worthy of sth

Wert <-[e]s, -e> [veːɐ̯t] m 1. (Preis) value; im ~ steigen to increase in value; an ~ verlieren to decrease in value; im ~e von etw dat worth sth 2. pl (Daten) results pl 3. (Wichtigkeit) ~ auf etw akk legen to think sth is important 4. (Wertvorstellung) value ▶ das hat keinen ~ fam it's useless

werten vt to rate

wertfrei adj impartial

wertlos adj worthless

Wertschätzung f esteem

wertvoll adj valuable

Wertvorstellung f meist pl moral concept usu pl

Wesen <-s, -> ['veː-zn̩] nt 1. (Geschöpf) being; (tierisch) creature 2. kein pl (Grundzüge) nature

Wesenszug m characteristic

wesentlich ['veː-zn̩t-lɪç] I. adj 1. (erheblich) considerable 2. (wichtig) essential; das W~e the essential part; im W~en essentially II. adv considerably

weshalb [vɛs-'halp] adv why

Wespe <-, -n> ['vɛs-pə] f yellow jacket

wessen ['vɛ·sn̩] *pron interrog gen von* **wer** whose

Wessi <-, -s> ['vɛ·si] *m o f fam* West German

Weste <-, -n> ['vɛs·tə] *f* vest

Westen <-s> ['vɛs·tn̩] *m kein pl, kein indef art* **1.** (*Himmelsrichtung*) west; *s. a.* **Norden 1 2.** (*südliche Gegend*) west; **der Wilde ~** the Wild West; *s. a.* **Norden 2**

Westentasche *f* vest pocket

Western <-[s], -> ['vɛs·tɐn] *m* western

Westfalen <-s> [vɛst·'faː·lən] *nt* Westphalia

Westküste *f* West Coast

westlich ['vɛst·lɪç] **I.** *adj* **1.** (*Himmelsrichtung*) western; *s. a.* **nördlich I 1 2.** (*im Westen liegend*) western; *s. a.* **nördlich I 2 3.** (*von/nach Westen*) westward, westerly; *s. a.* **nördlich I 3 II.** *adv* **~ von** to the west of **III.** *präp* +*gen* [to the] west of

weswegen [vɛs·'veː·gn̩] *adv* why

Wettbewerb <-[e]s, -e> ['vɛt·bə·vɛrp] *m* competition

Wettbewerber(in) *m(f)* competitor

Wette <-, -n> ['vɛ·tə] *f* bet; **die ~ gilt!** you're on!; **jede ~ eingehen, dass ...** to bet anything that ...; **um die ~ laufen** to race [each other]

wetteifern *vi* **miteinander ~** to contend with each other

wetten ['vɛ·tn̩] *vt, vi* to bet (**auf** +*akk* on); [**mit jdm**] **um etw** *akk* **~** to bet [sb] sth; [**wollen wir**] **~?** [do you] want to bet?

Wetter <-s> ['vɛ·tɐ] *nt kein pl* weather; **bei jedem ~** rain or shine

Wetterbericht *m* weather report

Wetterdienst *m* weather service

wetterfühlig *adj* sensitive to weather changes *pred*

Wetterhahn *m* rooster weathervane

Wetterkarte *f* weather map

Wetterlage *f* weather situation

wettern ['vɛ·tɐn] *vi* [**gegen jdn/etw**] **~** to curse [sb/sth]

Wetterumschwung *m* sudden change in the weather

Wettervorhersage *f* weather forecast

Wettkampf *m* competition

Wettlauf *m* race

wettlmachen ['vɛt·ma·xn̩] *vt* **1.** (*aufholen*) to make up **2.** (*gutmachen*) to make up for

Wettrennen *nt* race

Wettrüsten <-s> *nt kein pl* arms race

Wettstreit ['vɛt·ʃtrait] *m* competition

wetzen ['vɛ·tsn̩] **I.** *vt haben* **1.** (*schleifen*) to whet **2.** (*reiben*) to rub (**an** +*dat* on) **II.** *vi sein fam* (*rennen*) to scoot [off]

WG <-, -s> [veː·'geː:] *f Abk von* **Wohngemeinschaft**

wichsen ['vɪk·sn̩] **I.** *vi vulg* to jack [*o* jerk] off *vulg sl* **II.** *vt* (*Schuhe*) to polish

wichtig ['vɪç·tɪç] *adj* important

Wichtigtuer(in) <-s, -> [-tuːɐ] *m(f)* stuffed shirt

wickeln ['vɪ·kln̩] *vt* **1.** (*binden*) to wrap (**um** +*akk* around, **in** +*akk* in) **2.** (*Baby*) to change

Widder <-s, -> ['vɪ·dɐ] *m* **1.** ZOOL ram **2.** *kein pl* ASTROL Aries

widerfahren * [viː·dɐ·'faː·rən] *vi irreg sein* to happen, to befall

Widerhall <-[e]s, -e> ['viː·dɐ·hal] *m* echo

widerlegen * [viː·dɐ·'leː·gn̩] *vt* to refute

widerlich ['viː·dɐ·lɪç] **I.** *adj* **1.** (*ekelhaft*) disgusting **2.** (*unsympathisch*) repulsive **II.** *adv* (*überaus: süß, kalt*) awfully

Widerrede ['viː·dɐ·reː·də] *f* **keine ~!** don't argue [with me]!

widerrufen * [viː·dɐ·'ruː·fn̩] *vt irreg* **1.** (*für ungültig erklären*) to revoke **2.** (*zurücknehmen*) to retract

Widersacher(in) <-s, -> ['viː·dɐ·za·xɐ] *m(f)* antagonist

widersetzen * [viː·dɐ·'zɛ·tsn̩] *vr* **sich** *akk* **jdm ~** to resist sb; **sich** *akk* **etw** *dat* **~** to refuse to comply with sth

widerspenstig ['viː·dɐ·ʃpɛns·tɪç] *adj* unruly; (*Mensch, Pferd*) stubborn; (*Haar*) unmanageable

widerlspiegeln ['viː·dɐ·ʃpiː·gl̩n] **I.** *vt* to mirror, to reflect **II.** *vr* **sich** *akk* **~** to be reflected

widersprechen * [viː·dɐ·'ʃprɛ·çn̩] *irreg* **I.** *vi* to contradict **II.** *vr* **sich** *dat* **~** (*Aussage, Angaben*) to be contradictory

Widerspruch ['viː·dɐ·ʃprʊx] *m* **1.** *kein pl* (*das Widersprechen*) contradiction; **auf ~ stoßen** to meet with opposition

W

2. (*Unvereinbarkeit*) inconsistency; **in ~ zu etw** *dat* **stehen** to conflict with sth

widersprüchlich ['viː·dɐ·ʃprʏç·lɪç] *adj* inconsistent; **~ sein** to be contradictory

widerspruchslos *adv* without protest

Widerstand <-[e]s, -stände> ['viː·dɐ·ʃtant] *m* **1.** *kein pl* (*Gegenwehr*) opposition, resistance **2.** ELEK (*Schaltelement*) resistor

widerstandsfähig *adj* resistant (**gegen** +*akk* to)

Widerstandskraft *f* robustness, resistance (**gegen** +*akk* to)

widerstandslos *adv* without resistance

widerstehen * [viː·dɐ·ˈʃteː·ən] *vi irreg* **1.** (*standhalten*) to withstand **2.** (*nicht nachgeben: Person, Versuchung*) to resist

widerstreben * [viː·dɐ·ˈʃtreː·bn̩] *vi* **jdm widerstrebt es, etw zu tun** sb is reluctant to do sth

Widerstreben <-s> [viː·dɐ·ˈʃtreː·bn̩] *nt kein pl* reluctance

widerwärtig ['viː·dɐ·vɛr·tɪç] **I.** *adj* disgusting; (*Kerl*) nasty **II.** *adv* disgustingly

Widerwille ['viː·dɐ·vɪlə] *m* distaste (**gegen** +*akk* for)

widerwillig I. *adj* reluctant **II.** *adv* reluctantly

widmen ['vɪt·mən] **I.** *vt* to dedicate to **II.** *vr* **1.** (*sich kümmern*) **sich** *akk* **jdm ~** to attend to sb **2.** (*sich beschäftigen*) **sich** *akk* **etw** *dat* **~** to devote oneself to sth

Widmung <-, -en> ['vɪt·mʊŋ] *f* dedication

widrig ['viː·drɪç] *adj* adverse; (*Umstände, Verhältnisse*) unfavorable

wie [viː] **I.** *adv* how; **~ geht es dir?** how are you?; **~ heißt er?** what's his name?; **~ war das Wetter?** what was the weather like?; **~ viel/viele** how much/many; **~ sehr** how much; **wär's mit ...?** how about ...? **II.** *konj* **1.** (*vergleichend*) **so alt/groß ~ ...** as big/old as ...; **er ist genau ~ du** he's just like you **2.** (*beispielsweise*) like

wieder ['viː·dɐ] *adv* again, once more; **~ mal** again; **Verhandlungen ~ aufnehmen** to resume negotiations; **Kontakt ~**

aufnehmen to reestablish contact; **etw ~ einführen** to reintroduce sth

Wiederaufbau [viː·dɐ·ˈʔauf·bau] *m kein. pl* reconstruction

wiederbekommen * *vt irreg* to get back

wiederbeleben * *vt* to revive

wiederbringen ['viː·dɐ·brɪ·ŋən] *vt irreg* to bring back *sep*

wiedererkennen * *vt irreg* to recognize; **nicht wiederzuerkennen sein** to be unrecognizable

Wiedereröffnung *f* reopening

wiederfinden *irreg* **I.** *vt* **1.** (*auffinden*) to find again **2.** (*Fassung*) to regain **II.** *vr* **sich** *akk* **~** to turn up again

Wiedergabe <-, -n> ['viː·dɐ·ga:·bə] *f* **1.** (*Schilderung*) account, report **2.** PHOTO, TYPO reproduction

wiedergeben ['viː·dɐ·ge:·bn̩] *vt irreg* **1.** (*zurückgeben*) to give back **2.** (*zitieren*) to quote

wiedergewinnen * ['viː·dɐ·gə·vɪ·nən] *vt irreg* **1.** (*zurückgewinnen*) to reclaim **2.** (*wiedererlangen*) to regain

Wiedergutmachung <-, -en> *f* compensation

wiederherstellen [viː·dɐ·ˈheːɐ̯·ʃtɛ·lən] *vt* **1.** (*restaurieren*) to restore **2.** (*Ordnung, Kontakt, Gesundheit*) to reestablish

wiederholen *1 [viː·dɐ·ˈho:·lən] **I.** *vt* **1.** (*erneut sagen/machen*) to repeat **2.** (*Lernstoff*) to revise **II.** *vr* **sich** *akk* **~** (*Ereignis*) to happen again; (*Person*) to repeat oneself

wiederholen² ['viː·dɐ·ho:·lən] *vt s.* **zurückholen**

wiederholt I. *adj* repeated **II.** *adv* repeatedly

Wiederholung <-, -en> [viː·dɐ·ˈho:·lʊŋ] *f* **1.** (*erneutes Tun*) repetition **2.** (*im Radio/TV*) repeat **3.** (*von Lernstoff*) review

wiederkehren ['viː·dɐ·ke·rən] *vi sein* **1.** (*Mensch*) to return **2.** (*Problem*) to reoccur

wiederkommen ['viː·dɐ·kɔ·mən] *vi irreg sein* **1.** (*zurückkommen*) to come back **2.** (*erneut kommen*) to come again; (*Gelegenheit*) to reoccur

wiedersehen ['viː·dɐ·ze:·ən] *irreg* **I.** *vt*

jdn ~ to see sb again II. *vr* sich *akk* ~ to meet again

Wiedersehen <-s, -> ['viː·dɐ·zeː·ən] *nt* [another] meeting; (*nach längerer Zeit*) reunion; [auf] ~ sagen to say goodbye

wiederum ['viː·dɐ·ʊm] *adv* 1. (*abermals*) again 2. (*andererseits*) on the other hand, though 3. (*für jds Teil*) in turn

wieder|vereinigen* *vt* POL to reunify

Wiedervereinigung ['viː·dɐ·fɛg·ʔaɪ·nɪ·gʊŋ] *f* POL reunification

Wiederverwertung *f* recycling

Wiederwahl ['viː·dɐ·vaːl] *f* POL reelection

Wiege <-, -n> ['viː·gə] *f* cradle

wiegen <wog, gewogen> ['viː·gŋ] *vt, vi* to weigh

Wiegenlied *nt* lullaby

wiehern ['viː·ɐn] *vi* to neigh

Wien <-s> [viːn] *nt* Vienna

Wiener ['viː·nɐ] *adj attr* Viennese

Wiese <-, -n> [viː·zə] *f* meadow

Wiesel <-s, -> ['viː·zl] *nt* weasel

wieso [vi·ˈzoː] *adv* why

wild [vɪlt] I. *adj* 1. BOT, ZOOL wild 2. (*Kampf*) frenzied 3. (*illegal*) illegal 4. (*sehr gereizt*) furious; ~ werden to go wild ▶ halb so ~ sein *fam* to not be important; ~ auf jdn/etw sein *fam* to be crazy about sb/sth; wie ~ *fam* wildly II. *adv* 1. (*ungeordnet*) strewn around 2. (*hemmungslos*) wildly, furiously 3. (*in freier Natur*) wild *pred*

Wild <-[e]s> [vɪlt] *nt kein pl* 1. KOCHK game 2. ZOOL wild animals

Wilderer, Wilderin <-s, -> ['vɪl·də·re] *m, f* poacher

wildern ['vɪl·dɐn] *vi* to poach

wildfremd ['vɪlt·ˈfrɛmt] *adj* completely strange

Wildhüter(in) <-s, -> *m(f)* gamekeeper

Wildnis <-, -se> ['vɪlt·nɪs] *f* wilderness

Wildschwein *nt* wild boar

Wildwestfilm [vɪlt·ˈvɛst-] *m* western

Wille <-ns> ['vɪ·lə] *m kein pl* will; seinen eigenen ~n haben to have a mind of one's own; seinen ~n durchsetzen to get one's way ▶ jds letzter ~ sb's last will and testament

willenlos *adj* spineless

Willenskraft *f kein pl* willpower

willensstark *adj* strong-willed

willig ['vɪ·lɪç] *adj* willing

willkommen [vɪl·ˈkɔ·mən] *adj* welcome; [jdm] ~ sein to be welcomed [by sb]; jdn ~ heißen to welcome sb

Willkommen <-s, -> [vɪl·ˈkɔ·mən] *nt* welcome; ein herzliches ~ a warm welcome

Willkür <-> ['vɪl·kyːɐ] *f kein pl* arbitrariness

willkürlich ['vɪl·kyːɐ·lɪç] I. *adj* arbitrary II. *adv* arbitrarily

wimmeln ['vɪ·mln] *vi impers* es wimmelt von etw *dat* it is teeming with sth; (*Menschen*) it is swarming with

wimmern ['vɪ·mɐn] *vi* to whimper

Wimper <-, -n> ['vɪm·pɐ] *f* [eye]lash ▶ ohne mit der ~ zu zucken without batting an eyelid

Wimperntusche *f* mascara

Wind <-[e]s, -e> [vɪnt] *m* wind ▶ viel ~ um etw machen to make a fuss about sth; bei ~ und Wetter rain or shine

Winde <-, -n> ['vɪn·də] *f* TECH winch

Windel <-, -n> ['vɪn·dl] *f* diaper

windelweich *adv* jdn ~ schlagen to beat sb black and blue

winden <wand, gewunden> ['vɪn·dn] I. *vr* sich *akk* ~ 1. (*nach Ausflüchten suchen*) to attempt to wriggle out 2. (*sich krümmen*) to writhe (vor +*dat* in) 3. BOT to wind [itself] (um +*akk* around) II. *vt* etw um etw *akk* ~ to wind sth around sth

Windenergie *f* wind energy

windgeschützt I. *adj* sheltered [from the wind] II. *adv* in a sheltered place

windig ['vɪn·dɪç] *adj* windy

Windjacke *f* windbreaker

Windmühle *f* windmill

Windpocken *pl* chickenpox *sing*

Windrad *nt* wind turbine

windschief *adj* crooked

Windschutzscheibe *f* windshield

Windstärke *f* wind force

windstill *adj* windless; ~ sein to be calm

Windstoß *m* gust of wind

Wink <-[e]s, -e> [vɪŋk] *m* 1. (*Hinweis*) hint; einen ~ bekommen to receive a tip 2. (*Handbewegung*) signal ▶ ein ~

W

mit dem <u>Zaunpfahl</u> a broad hint

Winkel <-s, -> ['vɪŋ·kl] *m* **1.** MATH angle; **rechter** ~ right angle **2.** (*Ecke*) corner
▶ <u>toter</u> ~ blind spot

winken <gewinkt *o dial* gewunken> ['vɪŋ·kn] I. *vi* to wave; **mit etw** *dat* ~ to wave sth; **einem Taxi** ~ to hail a taxi II. *vt* **jdn zu sich** *dat* ~ to beckon sb over [to one's side]

winseln ['vɪn·zln] *vi* to whimper; **um etw** *akk* ~ to plead for sth

Winter <-s, -> ['vɪn·tɐ] *m* winter

Wintergarten *m* winter garden

Winterkleidung *f* winter clothes *pl*

winterlich ['vɪn·tə·lɪç] I. *adj* wintry; **~e Temperaturen** winter temperatures II. *adv* ~ **gekleidet** dressed for winter

Wintermantel *m* winter coat

Winterreifen *m* winter tire

Winterschlaf *m* hibernation; ~ **halten** to hibernate

Wintersport *m* winter sport

Winzer(in) <-s, -> ['vɪn·tse] *m(f)* wine grower

winzig ['vɪn·tsɪç] *adj* tiny; ~ **klein** minute

Winzling <-s, -e> ['vɪnts·lɪŋ] *m* tiny thing

Wippe <-, -n> ['vɪ·pə] *f* seesaw

wippen ['vɪ·pn] *vi* to bob up and down (**auf** +*dat* on); (*auf einer Wippe*) to seesaw

wir <*gen* unser, *dat* uns, *akk* uns> [viːɐ̯] *pron pers* we; ~ **nicht** not us

Wirbel <-s, -> ['vɪr·bl] *m* **1.** (*Rückenwirbel*) vertebra **2.** (*Haarwirbel*) cowlick **3.** *fam* (*Trubel*) turmoil

Wirbelsäule *f* spinal column

Wirbelsturm *m* whirlwind

wirken ['vɪr·kn] *vi* **1.** (*Wirkung haben*) to have an effect; (*beabsichtigten Effekt haben*) to work; **dieses Medikament wirkt sofort** this medicine takes effect immediately; **etw auf sich** *akk* ~ **lassen** to take sth in **2.** (*erscheinen*) to seem, to appear

wirklich ['vɪrk·lɪç] I. *adj* real II. *adv* really

Wirklichkeit <-, -en> *f* reality; ~ **werden** to come true

wirksam ['vɪrk·za:m] I. *adj* effective II. *adv* effectively

Wirkstoff *m* active ingredient

Wirkung <-, -en> ['vɪr·kʊŋ] *f* effect

wirkungslos *adj* ineffective

wirkungsvoll *adj* effective

wirr [vɪr] *adj* **1.** (*unordentlich*) tangled **2.** (*verworren*) weird **3.** (*durcheinander*) confused

Wirren ['vɪ·rən] *pl* confusion *sing*

Wirrwarr <-s> ['vɪr·var] *m* *kein pl* **1.** (*Durcheinander*) confusion **2.** (*Unordnung*) tangle

Wirt(in) <-[e]s, -e> [vɪrt] *m(f)* innkeeper, ≈ restaurant/tavern manager/owner

Wirtschaft <-, -en> ['vɪrt·ʃaft] *f* **1.** ÖKON economy **2.** (*Gastwirtschaft*) tavern, pub

wirtschaftlich ['vɪrt·ʃaft·lɪç] I. *adj* **1.** ÖKON economic **2.** (*sparsam*) economical II. *adv* economically

Wirtschaftsabkommen *nt* economic agreement [*o* treaty]

Wirtschaftsflüchtling *m* economic refugee

Wirtschaftshilfe *f* economic aid

Wirtschaftskriminalität *f* white-collar crime

Wirtschaftslage *f* economic situation

Wirtschaftsminister(in) *m(f)* Secretary of Commerce, Commerce Secretary

Wirtschaftsministerium *nt* Department of Commerce, Commerce Department

Wirtschaftspolitik *f* economic policy

Wirtschaftswachstum *nt* economic growth

Wirtschaftswissenschaft *f* *meist pl* economics *sing*

Wirtschaftszweig *m* branch of industry

Wirtshaus *nt* tavern, restaurant, inn

wischen ['vɪ·ʃn] *vt* **1.** (*abwischen*) to wipe **2.** *schweiz* (*fegen*) to sweep

Wischlappen *m* cloth

wispern ['vɪs·pen] *vt, vi* to whisper

wissbegierig RR, **wißbegierig** ALT *adj* eager to learn

wissen <weiß, wusste, gewusst> ['vɪ·sn] *vt, vi* **1.** (*Kenntnis haben*) to know; **man kann nie ~!** you never know!; **woher soll ich das ~?** how should I know that?; **wenn ich nur wüsste, ...** if only I knew ...; **soviel ich weiß** as far as I know; **jdn etw ~ lassen** to let sb

know sth **2.** (*sich erinnern*) **weißt du noch?** do you remember? **3.** (*können*) **etw zu schätzen ~** to appreciate sth; **sich** *dat* **zu helfen ~** to be resourceful ▶ **von jdm/etw nichts [mehr] ~ wollen** *fam* to not want to have anything [more] to do with sb/sth

Wissen <-s> ['vɪsn̩] *nt kein pl* knowledge

Wissenschaft <-, -en> ['vɪsn̩ʃaft] *f* science

Wissenschaftler(in) <-s, -> *m(f)* scientist

wissenschaftlich ['vɪsn̩ʃaftlɪç] **I.** *adj* scientific; (*akademisch*) academic **II.** *adv* scientifically; (*akademisch*) academically

Wissensdrang *m*, **Wissensdurst** *m* thirst for knowledge

Wissensgebiet *nt* field of knowledge

wissenswert *adj* worth knowing

wissentlich ['vɪsn̩tlɪç] **I.** *adj* deliberate **II.** *adv* deliberately, knowingly

wittern ['vɪtɐn] *vt* (*ahnen*) to suspect

Witterung <-, -en> *f* METEO weather

Witterungsverhältnisse *pl* weather conditions *pl*

Witwe <-, -n> ['vɪtvə] *f s.* **Witwer** widow *fem;* **~ werden** to be widowed

Witwer <s, -> ['vɪtvɐ] *m* widower *masc;* **~ werden** to be widowed

Witz <-es, -e> [vɪts] *m* **1.** (*Scherz*) joke; **einen ~ machen** to tell a joke **2.** *kein pl* (*Esprit*) wit

Witzbold <-[e]s, -e> *m* joker

witzeln ['vɪtsl̩n] *vi* to joke (**über** +*akk* about)

witzig ['vɪtsɪç] *adj* funny

WM <-, -s> *f Abk von* **Weltmeisterschaft** world championship; (*im Fußball*) World Cup

wo [vo:] **I.** *adv* **1.** (*räumlich*) where; **pass auf, ~ du hintrittst!** watch your step! [*o* where you're going!] **2.** (*zeitlich*) when; **zu dem Zeitpunkt, ~ ...** when ... **II.** *konj* (*zumal*) when, as; **~ er doch wusste, dass ich keine Zeit hatte** when he knew that I had no time

woanders [vo-'ʔan·dɐs] *adv* somewhere else, elsewhere

wobei [vo-'bai] *adv* **1.** *interrog* how; **~**

ist das passiert? how did that happen? **2.** *rel* in which; **~ mir gerade einfällt ...** which reminds me ...

Woche <-, -n> ['vɔ·xə] *f* week

Wochenblatt *nt* weekly

Wochenende ['vɔ·xn̩·ʔɛn·də] *nt* weekend; **schönes ~!** have a nice weekend!; **am ~** on the weekend

Wochenkarte *f* TRANSP weekly pass

wochenlang ['vɔ·xn̩·laŋ] *adj, adv* for weeks

Wochentag *m* weekday; **was ist heute für ein ~?** what day of the week is it today?

wöchentlich ['vœ·çn̩t·lɪç] *adj, adv* weekly

wodurch [vo·'dʊrç] *adv* **1.** *interrog* how **2.** *rel* which

wofür [vo·'fy:ɐ] *adv* **1.** *interrog* for what, what ... for; **~ hast du denn so viel Geld bezahlt?** what did you pay so much money for? **2.** *rel* for which

Woge <-, -n> ['vo:·gə] *f* wave ▶ **wenn sich die ~n geglättet haben** when things have calmed down

wogegen [vo·'ge:·gn̩] *adv* **1.** *interrog* against what; **~ hilft dieses Mittel?** what is this medicine for? **2.** *rel* against what/which

woher [vo·'he:ɐ] *adv* **1.** *interrog* where ... from; **~ hast du dieses Buch?** where did you get this book [from]? **2.** *rel* from which, where ... [from]

wohin [vo·'hɪn] *adv* **1.** *interrog* where [to]; **~ damit?** where should I put it? **2.** *rel* where

wohl [vo:l] *adv* **1.** (*gut, gesund*) well; **sich** *akk* **~ fühlen** to feel well; **sich** *akk* **irgendwo ~ fühlen** to feel at home somewhere **2.** (*gut*) **~ geformt** well-formed; (*Körperteil*) shapely; **~ überlegt** well thought out **3.** (*wahrscheinlich*) probably; **~ kaum** hardly **4.** **jdm ist ~ bei etw** *dat* sb is comfortable with sth; **jdm ist nicht ~ bei etw** *dat* sb is uneasy about sth **5.** (*zirka*) about **6.** ▶ **~ oder übel** whether you like it or not

Wohl <-[e]s> [vo:l] *nt kein pl* welfare, well-being; **auf jds ~ trinken** to drink to sb's health; **zum ~!** cheers!

wohlauf [vo:l·'ʔauf] *adj pred* **~ sein** to

be well

Wohlbefinden <-s> *nt kein pl* well-being

Wohlbehagen <-s> *nt kein pl* feeling of well-being

wohlbehalten *adv* safe and sound

Wohlfahrtsstaat *m* welfare state

Wohlgefallen ['vo:l·gə·fa·lən] *nt* ▸ **sich** *akk* **in ~ auflösen** *fam* to vanish into thin air

wohlgesinnt <wohlgesinnter, wohlgesinnteste> *adj* ▸ **jdm ~ sein** to be well-disposed toward sb

wohlhabend <wohlhabender, wohlhabendste> *adj* well-to-do

wohlriechend <wohlriechender, wohlriechendste> *adj* fragrant

wohlschmeckend <wohlschmeckender, wohlschmeckendste> *adj* palatable

Wohlstand *m kein pl* affluence, prosperity

Wohlstandsgesellschaft *f* affluent society

Wohltat *f* 1. *kein pl* (*Erleichterung*) relief 2. (*Unterstützung*) good deed

Wohltäter(in) *m(f)* benefactor *masc*, benefactress *fem*

wohltätig *adj* charitable

Wohltätigkeitsveranstaltung *f* charity event

wohltuend <wohltuender, wohltuendste> *adj* agreeable

Wohlwollen <-s> ['vo:l·vɔ·lən] *nt kein pl* goodwill

wohlwollend <wohlwollender, wohlwollendste> I. *adj* benevolent II. *adv* benevolently

Wohnanlage *f* housing development

Wohnblock *m* apartment building

wohnen ['vo:·nən] *vi* to live; (*im Hotel*) to stay

Wohnfläche *f* living space

Wohngebiet *nt* residential area

Wohngeld *nt* housing subsidy

Wohngemeinschaft *f* communal residence, shared house [*o* apartment]; **in einer ~ leben** to share a house/apartment with sb

Wohnhaus *nt* residential building

Wohnheim *nt* (*Studentenwohnheim*) res-

idence hall, dormitory; (*Arbeiterwohnheim*) rooming house [for workers]

Wohnküche *f* eat-in kitchen

wohnlich ['vo:n·lɪç] *adj* cozy

Wohnmobil <-s, -e> *nt* camper

Wohnort *m* place of residence

Wohnsitz *m* ADMIN domicile; **erster ~** permanent residence; **ohne festen ~** without a fixed residence

Wohnung <-, -en> *f* apartment

Wohnungsmarkt *m* housing market

Wohnungsnot *f kein pl* serious housing shortage

Wohnungssuche *f* apartment hunting; **auf ~ sein** to be apartment hunting

Wohnviertel *nt* residential area

Wohnwagen *m* (*zum Campen*) RV

Wohnzimmer *nt* living room

wölben ['vœl·bn] *vr* 1. (*sich biegen*) **sich** *akk* ~ to bend 2. (*überspannen*) **sich** *akk* **über etw** *akk* ~ to arch over sth

Wolf <-[e]s, Wölfe> [vɔlf] *m* wolf

Wolke <-, -n> ['vɔl·kə] *f* cloud ▸ **aus allen** ~**n fallen** *fam* to be flabbergasted

Wolkenbruch *m* cloudburst

Wolkendecke *f* cloud cover

Wolkenkratzer *m* skyscraper

wolkenlos *adj* cloudless

wolkig ['vɔl·kɪç] *adj* cloudy

Wolldecke *f* [wool] blanket

Wolle <-, -n> ['vɔ·lə] *f* wool

wollen ['vɔ·lən] I. *aux vb* <will, wollte, wollen> *modal* 1. (*zu tun beabsichtigen*) **etw tun ~** to want to do sth; **etw gerade tun ~** to be [just] about to do sth; **etw haben ~** to want [to have] sth; **~ wir uns nicht setzen?** why don't we sit down? 2. (*behaupten*) **etw getan haben ~** to claim to have done sth; **und so jemand will Arzt sein!** and he calls himself a doctor! 3. *passivisch* **diese Aktion will gut vorbereitet sein** this operation has to be carefully planned II. *vi* <will, wollte, gewollt> 1. (*den Willen haben*) to want; **ob du willst oder nicht** whether you like it or not; **wenn du willst** if you['d] like; [**ganz**] **wie du willst** whatever is good for you, as you wish 2. (*gehen wollen*) **irgendwohin ~** to want to go somewhere; **zu wem ~ Sie?** who[m] do you wish to see? III. *vt*

<will, wollte, gewollt> 1. (*haben wollen*) etw [von jdm] ~ to want sth [from sb]; **willst du lieber Tee oder Kaffee?** would you prefer tea or coffee?; **ich will, dass du jetzt sofort gehst!** I want you to go right now [*o* leave immediately] 2. (*bezwecken*) etw mit etw *dat* ~ to want sth with [*o* for] sth; **ohne es zu ~** without wanting to

Wolljacke *f* wool cardigan

wollüstig ['vɔ-lʏs-tɪç] *adj* lascivious

womit [vo-'mɪt] *adv* 1. *interrog* with what, what ... with; ~ **reinigt man Seidenhemden?** what do you use to clean silk shirts [with]?; ~ **habe ich das verdient?** what did I do to deserve this? 2. *rel* with which

womöglich [vo-'mø:k-lɪç] *adv* possibly

wonach [vo-'na:x] *adv* 1. *interrog* what ... for, what ... of; ~ **suchst du?** what are you looking for?; ~ **riecht das hier?** what's that smell [in here]? 2. *rel* which [*o* what] ... for, of which

Wonne <-, -n> ['vɔ-nə] *f* joy, delight

woran [vo-'ran] *adv* 1. *interrog* (*an welchem/welchen Gegenstand*) what ... on, on what; ~ **soll ich das befestigen?** what should I fasten this to? 2. *interrog* (*an welchem/welchen Umstand*) what ... of, of what; ~ **haben Sie ihn erkannt?** how did you recognize him?; ~ **denkst du?** what are you thinking of?; ~ **ist sie gestorben?** what did she die of? 3. *rel* (*an welchem/welchen Gegenstand*) on which; **das Seil, ~ der Kübel befestigt war,** riss the rope [that] the pail was fastened to broke 4. *rel* (*an welchem/welchen Umstand*) by which; **das ist das einzige, ~ ich mich noch erinnere** that's the only thing I can remember

worauf [vo-'rauf] *adv* 1. *interrog* on what ..., what ... on; ~ **wartest du noch?** what are you waiting for?; ~ **stützen sich deine Behauptungen?** what do you base your claims on? 2. *rel* on which; **das Bett, ~ wir liegen ...** the bed [that] we're lying on ...

woraus [vo-'raus] *adv* 1. *interrog* what ... out of, out of what; **und ~ schließen Sie das?** and what do you base your

conclusion[s] on? 2. *rel* from which, what ... out of, out of which

worin [vo-'rɪn] *adv* 1. *interrog* in what, what ... in; ~ **besteht der Unterschied?** where is the difference? 2. *rel* in which; **es gibt etwas, ~ sich Original und Fälschung unterscheiden** there is something that the original and the forgery do not have in common

Wort <-[e]s, Wörter> [vɔrt] *nt* 1. word; **mit anderen ~en** in other words; **etw in ~e fassen** to put sth into words; **jdm fehlen die ~e** sb is speechless; **ein ernstes ~ mit jdm reden** to have a serious talk with sb 2. *kein pl* (*Ehrenwort*) **jdm sein ~ geben** to give sb one's word; **sein ~ brechen/halten** to break/keep one's word; **das glaube ich dir aufs ~** I can believe it, trust me, I believe you 3. *kein pl* (*Rede[erlaubnis]*) **jdm ins ~ fallen** to interrupt sb; **zu ~ kommen** to get a chance to speak ▶ **das ist ein ~!** [it's [*o* that's] a] deal!; **jdm das ~ im <u>Munde</u> herumdrehen** to twist sb's words

wortbrüchig *adj* treacherous

Wörterbuch *nt* dictionary

wortkarg *adj* taciturn

Wortklauberei <-, -en> [vɔrt-klau-bə-'rai] *f pej* hairsplitting

wörtlich ['vœrt-lɪç] I. *adj* 1. (*Wiedergabe*) word-for-word, verbatim 2. (*Übersetzung*) literal II. *adv* 1. (*wiedergeben*) word for word 2. (*übersetzen*) literally

wortlos I. *adj* silent II. *adv* silently, without saying a word

Wortschatz *m* vocabulary

Wortspiel *nt* play on words

Wortwechsel *m* verbal exchange

wortwörtlich ['vɔrt-'vœrt-lɪç] I. *adj* word-for-word II. *adv* word for word

worüber [vo-'ry:-bə] *adv* what ... about, about what; ~ **habt ihr euch unterhalten?** what was it you talked about? [*o fam* did you guys talk about?]

worum [vo-'rʊm] *adv* what ... about; ~ **handelt es sich?** what is it about?

worunter [vo-'rʊn-tə] *adv* what ... from; ~ **leidet Ihre Frau?** what is your wife suffering from?

W

wovon [voˈfɔn] *adv* what ... about; **~ bist du denn so müde?** what has made you so tired?; **~ soll ich leben?** what am I supposed to live on?

wovor [voˈfoːɐ̯] *adv* what ... of; **~ fürchtest du dich denn?** what are you afraid of?

wozu [voˈtsuː] *adv* why, how come, what ... for; **~ soll das gut sein?** what's the purpose of that?

Wrack <-[e]s, -s> [vrak] *nt* 1. (*Schiffswrack*) wreck; (*Flugzeug-, Autowrack*) wreckage 2. *pej* (*Mensch*) wreck

Wucher <-s> [ˈvuː·xe] *m kein pl* extortion; (*Zinsen*) usury; **das ist ~!** that's highway robbery!

wuchern [ˈvuː·xen] *vi sein o haben* 1. (*Pflanze*) to grow rampant 2. (*Geschwür*) to proliferate

Wucherpreis *m pej* extortionate price

wuchs [vuːks] *imp von* **wachsen**[1]

Wucht <-> [vʊxt] *f kein pl* force; (*eines Schlags*) brunt; **mit voller ~** with full force ▶ **eine ~ sein** *fam* to be smashing

wuchtig [ˈvʊx·tɪç] *adj* 1. (*mit großer Wucht*) forceful; (*Schlag*) powerful 2. (*massig*) massive

wühlen [ˈvyː·lən] I. *vi* **in etw** *dat* [**nach etw** *dat*] **~** (*kramen*) to rummage through sth [for sth] II. *vr* **sich durch etw** *akk* **~** to burrow one's way through sth

Wühltisch *m* discount table

Wulst <[e]s, Wülste> [vʊlst] *f* <-, Wülste> bulge

wulstig [ˈvʊls·tɪç] *adj* bulging; (*Lippen*) thick

wund [vʊnt] I. *adj* sore II. *adv* **sich** *akk* **~ liegen** to get bedsores; **sich** *dat* **die Füße ~ laufen** to walk until one's feet are sore

Wunde <-, -n> [ˈvʊn·də] *f* wound

Wunder <-s, -> [ˈvʊn·de] *nt* miracle; **wie durch ein ~** miraculously ▶ **sein blaues ~ erleben** *fam* to be in for a nasty surprise; **es ist kein ~, dass ...** *fam* it is no wonder that ...; **~ wirken** *fam* to work wonders

wunderbar [ˈvʊn·de·baːɐ̯] I. *adj* 1. (*herrlich*) wonderful, marvelous 2. (*wie ein Wunder*) miraculous II. *adv fam* wonderfully

Wunderkind *nt* child prodigy

wunderlich [ˈvʊn·de·lɪç] *adj* odd, strange

wundern [ˈvʊn·den] I. *vt* **~** to surprise sb; **das wundert mich [nicht]** I'm [not] surprised at that II. *vr* **sich** *akk* **~** to be surprised (**über** +*akk* at/about); **du wirst dich ~!** you'll be surprised!

wunderschön [ˈvʊn·de·ʃøːn] *adj* wonderful

wundervoll *adj, adv s.* **wunderbar**

Wundsalbe *f* ointment

Wundstarrkrampf *m kein pl* tetanus

Wunsch <-[e]s, Wünsche> [vʊnʃ] *m* 1. (*Verlangen*) wish; (*stärker*) desire; (*Bitte*) request; **jdm jeden ~ erfüllen** to grant sb's every wish; **auf jds ~ [hin]** at/on sb's request 2. *meist pl* (*Glückwunsch*) wish; **mit besten Wünschen** best wishes

Wunschdenken <-s> *nt kein pl* wishful thinking

wünschen [ˈvʏn·ʃn̩] *vt* 1. (*als Geschenk erbitten*) **sich** *dat* **etw [von jdm] ~** to ask for sth [from sb]; **was wünschst du dir?** what would you like? [*o* can I get [for] you?]; **nun darfst du dir etwas ~** now you can say what you'd like for a present 2. (*erhoffen*) to wish; **ich wünschte, der Regen würde aufhören** I wish the rain would stop; **jdm etw ~** to wish sb sth; **jdm zum Geburtstag alles Gute ~** to wish sb a happy birthday; **ich will dir ja nichts Böses ~** I don't mean to wish you any harm; **~, dass** to hope that 3. (*haben wollen*) **sich** *dat* **etw ~** to want sth; **man hätte sich kein besseres Wetter ~ können** one couldn't have wished for better weather ▶ **nichts/viel zu ~ übrig lassen** to leave nothing/much to be desired

wünschenswert *adj* desirable

Wunschkind *nt* planned child

Wunschtraum *m* dream

Wunschzettel *m* wish list

Würde <-> [ˈvʏr·də] *f kein pl* dignity

würdig [ˈvʏr·dɪç] I. *adj* 1. (*ehrbar*) dignified 2. (*wert*) worthy; **einer S.** *gen* **[nicht] ~ sein** to [not] be worthy of sth

II. *adv* **1.** (*mit Würde*) with dignity **2.** (*gebührend*) worthy

würdigen ['vʏr·dɪ·gn] *vt* **1.** (*anerkennend erwähnen*) to acknowledge **2.** (*schätzen*) **etw zu ~ wissen** to appreciate sth

Wurf <-[e]s, Würfe> [vʊrf] *m* **1.** (*das Werfen*) throw **2.** (*Tierjunge*) litter

Würfel <-s, -> ['vʏr·fl] *m* **1.** (*Spielwürfel*) dice *pl*, die **2.** (*Kubus*) cube; **etw in ~ schneiden** to dice sth ▶ **die ~ sind gefallen** the die is cast

Würfelbecher *m* shaker

Würfelspiel *nt* dice game

Würfelzucker *m kein pl* sugar cube[s]

würgen ['vʏr·gn] **I.** *vt* to strangle **II.** *vi* **an etw** *dat* **~** to choke on sth

Wurm <-[e]s, Würmer> [vʊrm] *m* worm ▶ **da ist der ~ drin** *fam* there's something fishy about it

wurmen ['vʊr·mən] *vt fam* to bug; **das wurmt mich sehr** that really bugs me

wurmstichig ['vʊrm·ʃtɪ·çɪç] *adj* (*Apfel*) maggoty; (*Holz*) full of woodworms

Wurst <-, Würste> [vʊrst] *f* sausage; (*Brotauflage*) cold cuts *pl* ▶ **jetzt geht es um die ~** *fam* the moment of truth has come

Würstchen <-s, -> ['vʏrst·çən] *nt dim von* **Wurst** little sausage; **Frankfurter/ Wiener ~** hot dog, frankfurter

Würstchenbude *f*, **Würstchenstand** *m* hot dog stand

Wurzel <-, -n> ['vʊr·tsl] *f* a. *fig* root; **~n schlagen** a. *fig* to put down roots

wurzeln ['vʊr·tsln] *vi* to be rooted (**in** +*dat* in)

würzen ['vʏr·tsn] *vt* to season

würzig ['vʏr·tsɪç] **I.** *adj* tasty **II.** *adv* tastily

wüst [vy:st] **I.** *adj* **1.** (*öde*) waste, desolate **2.** *fig* (*wild, derb*) vile, rude **3.** (*unordentlich*) hopeless, terrible **II.** *adv* vilely, terribly; **jdn ~ beschimpfen** to curse at sb

Wüste <-, -n> [vy:s·tə] *f* desert, wasteland *fig;* **die ~ Gobi** the Gobi Desert

Wüstling <-s, -e> ['vy:st·lɪŋ] *m pej* lecher

Wut <-> [vu:t] *f kein pl* fury, rage; **eine ~ [auf jdn] haben** to be furious [with sb]; **vor ~ kochen** to seethe with rage

Wutausbruch *m* tantrum

wüten ['vy:·tn] *vi* to rage; (*Sturm*) to cause havoc

wütend I. *adj* furious (**auf** +*akk* with) **II.** *adv* furiously, in a rage

WWW <-[s]> [ve:·ve:·ˈve:] *nt* INET *Abk von* **World Wide Web** WWW

X

X, x <-, -> [ɪks] *nt* **1.** (*Buchstabe*) X, x; **~ wie Xanthippe** X as in X-ray **2.** (*eine unbestimmte Zahl*) x amount of; **~ Bücher** x number of books

X-Beine ['ɪks·baɪ·nə] *pl* knock-knees *pl*

x-beliebig [ɪks·bə·ˈli:·bɪç] **I.** *adj fam* any old; **jeder ~e Ort** any old place **II.** *adv fam* as often as one likes

x-mal ['ɪks·ma:l] *adv fam* umpteen times

Xylofon ᴿᴿ, **Xylophon** <-s, -e> [ksy·lo·ˈfo:n] *nt* xylophone

Y

Y, y <-, -> ['ʏpsi·lɔn] *nt* Y, y; **~ wie Ypsilon** Y as in Yankee

Yacht <-, -en> [jaxt] *f* yacht

Yoga <-[s]> ['jo:·ga] *m o nt* yoga

Ypsilon <-[s], -s> ['ʏpsi·lɔn] *nt s.* **Y**

Yuppie <-s, -s> ['jʊ·pi] *m* yuppie

Z

Z, z <-, -> [tsɛt] *nt* Z, z; **~ wie Zacharias** Z as in Zulu

zackig ['tsa·kɪç] *adj* **1.** (*gezackt*) jagged; (*Stern*) pointed **2.** (*schnell: Bewegungen*) brisk; (*Musik*) upbeat

zaghaft ['tsa:k·haft] *adj* timid

zäh [tsɛ:] **I.** *adj* **1.** (*eine feste Konsistenz aufweisend*) tough **2.** (*zähflüssig*) glutinous **3.** (*hartnäckig*) tenacious; (*Gespräch*) long-drawn-out; (*Verhandlungen*) tough **II.** *adv* tenaciously

zähflüssig *adj* thick; *fig* (*Verkehr*) slow-moving

X
Y
Z

Zahl <-, -en> [tsaːl] f number; **arabische/römische ~en** Arabic/Roman numerals

zahlen ['tsaː·lən] vt, vi to pay; **~ bitte!** the check please!

zählen ['tsɛː·lən] I. vt 1. (addieren) to count 2. (dazurechnen) **sich/jdn zu etw** dat **~** to regard oneself/sb as belonging to sth II. vi to count ▸ **auf jdn/etw ~** to count on sb/sth; **zu etw** dat **~** to belong to sth

zahlenmäßig I. adj numerical II. adv (an Anzahl) in number

Zahlenschloss^RR nt combination lock

Zähler <-s, -> m 1. TECH meter 2. MATH numerator

zahllos adj countless

zahlreich I. adj 1. (sehr viele) numerous 2. (eine große Anzahl) large II. adv (in großer Anzahl) **~ erscheinen** to appear in large numbers

Zahlung <-, -en> f payment

Zählung <-, -en> f count

Zahlungsmittel nt means of payment + sing vb

Zahlungsverkehr m payment transactions pl

Zahlwort <-wörter> nt numeral

zahm [tsaːm] adj tame

zähmen ['tsɛː·mən] vt to tame

Zahn <-[e]s, Zähne> [tsaːn] m 1. (Teil des Gebisses) tooth; **Zähne bekommen** to be teething; **sich** dat **die Zähne putzen** to brush one's teeth; **sich** dat **einen ~ ziehen lassen** to have a tooth pulled 2. fam (Tempo) **einen ~ draufhaben** to drive at breakneck speed; **einen ~ zulegen** to step on it ▸ **sich** dat **an jdm/etw die Zähne ausbeißen** fam to have a tough time with sb/sth; **jdm auf den ~ fühlen** fam to grill sb

Zahnarzt, -ärztin m, f dentist

Zahnbehandlung f dental treatment

Zahnbelag m kein pl plaque

Zahnbürste f toothbrush

zahnen ['tsaː·nən] vi (Baby) to teethe

Zahnfäule f kein pl tooth decay

Zahnfleisch nt gum[s pl]

Zahnfüllung f filling

Zahnlücke f gap between the teeth

Zahnpasta f toothpaste

Zahnpflege f kein pl dental hygiene

Zahnprothese f dentures pl

Zahnrad nt AUTO gearwheel; TECH cogwheel

Zahnradbahn f cog railway [o railroad]

Zahnschmelz m [tooth] enamel

Zahnschmerzen pl toothache

Zahnseide f dental floss

Zahnspange f braces pl

Zahnstein m kein pl tartar

Zahnstocher <-s, -> m toothpick

Zange <-, -n> ['tsaŋə] f pliers npl, a pair of pliers; (von Hummer, Krebs) pincers npl; MED forceps npl; (für Zucker) tongs npl ▸ **jdn in die ~ nehmen** fam to give sb the third degree

Zank <-[e]s> [tsaŋk] m kein pl fight

zanken ['tsaŋ·kn̩] I. vi to fight II. vr **sich** akk **~** to have a fight (um +akk over)

zänkisch ['tsɛŋ·kɪʃ] adj quarrelsome

Zäpfchen <-s, -> ['tsɛpf·çən] nt MED suppository

zapfen ['tsap·fn̩] vt (Bier) to draw

Zapfen <-s, -> ['tsap·fn̩] m 1. BOT, ANAT cone 2. (Eiszapfen) icicle

Zapfhahn m tap

Zapfsäule f gas pump

zappelig ['tsa·pə·lɪç] adj 1. (sich unruhig bewegend) fidgety 2. (voller Unruhe) restless

zappeln ['tsa·pl̩n] vi to fidget ▸ **jdn ~ lassen** fam to keep sb in suspense

Zar(in) <-en, -en> [tsaːɐ̯] m(f) czar masc, czarina fem

zart [tsaːɐ̯t] adj 1. (mürbe) tender; (Gebäck) delicate 2. (weich) delicate; (Haut) soft 3. (leicht) mild; (Berührung, Andeutung) gentle; (Farbe, Duft) delicate

zärtlich ['tsɛːɐ̯t·lɪç] I. adj tender, affectionate II. adv tenderly, affectionately

Zärtlichkeit <-, -en> f 1. kein pl (zärtliches Wesen) tenderness 2. pl (Liebkosung) caresses pl; (zärtliche Worte) tender words pl

Zauber <-s, -> ['tsau·bɐ] m 1. (magische Handlung) magic; (magische Wirkung) spell 2. kein pl (Faszination, Reiz) charm

Zauberei <-, -en> [tsau·bə·'rai] *f kein pl* magic

Zauberer, Zauberin <-s, -> ['tsau·bə·re, 'tsau·bə·rɪn] *m, f* **1.** (*Magier*) sorcerer *masc*, sorceress *fem*, wizard **2.** (*Zauberkünstler*) magician

zauberhaft *adj* enchanting; (*Kleid*) gorgeous; (*Abend, Urlaub*) splendid

Zauberkünstler(in) *m(f)* magician

Zauberkunststück *nt* magic trick

zaubern ['tsau·bɐn] **I.** *vt* to conjure (**aus** +*dat* from); **einen Hasen aus einem Hut ~** to pull a rabbit out of a hat **II.** *vi* **1.** (*Magie anwenden*) to do magic **2.** (*Zauberkunststücke vorführen*) to do magic tricks

Zauberspruch *m* magic spell

Zauberstab *m* magic wand

Zaum <-[e]s, Zäume> [tsaum] *m* bridle; **sich/jdn/etw in ~ halten** *fig* to keep oneself/sb/sth in check

zäumen ['tsɔy·mən] *vt* (*Tier*) to bridle

Zaun <-[e]s, Zäune> [tsaun] *m* fence

Zaunkönig *m* wren

Zebra <-s, -s> ['tse:·bra] *nt* zebra

Zebrastreifen *m* pedestrian crossing, crosswalk

Zecke <-, -n> ['tsɛ·kə] *f,* **Zeck** <-[e]s, -en> [tsɛk] *m* österr fam tick

Zeckenbiss RR *m* tick bite

Zeh <-s, -en> [tse:] *m,* **Zehe** <-, -n> ['tse:·ə] *f* ANAT toe

Zehennagel *m* toenail

Zehenspitze *f* tip of the toe; **auf den ~n** on one's tiptoes

zehn [tse:n] *adj* ten; *s. a.* **acht**[1]

Zehn <-, -en> [tse:n] *f* ten; *s. a.* **Acht**[1]

Zehnerkarte *f* TRANSP ten-trip ticket; TOURIST ticket good for ten admissions

Zehnkampf ['tse:n·kampf] *m* decathlon

zehnmal, 10-mal RR ['tse:n·ma:l] *adv* ten times; *s. a.* **achtmal**

zehntausend ['tse:n·'tau·znt] *adj* **1.** (*Zahl*) ten thousand **2.** (*sehr viele*) **Z~e von ...** tens of thousands of ...

zehnte(r, s) ['tse:n·tl] *adj* tenth

Zehntel <-s, -> ['tse:n·tl] *nt* **ein ~** a tenth

zehren ['tse:·rən] *vi* **an jdm/etw ~** to wear sb/sth out; **an jds Gesundheit ~** to ruin sb's health

Zeichen <-s, -> ['tsai·çn] *nt* **1.** (*Symbol*) symbol; (*Schriftzeichen*) character; (*Satzzeichen*) punctuation mark **2.** (*Markierung*) sign **3.** (*Hinweis*) sign **4.** (*Symptom*) symptom **5.** (*Signal*) signal **6.** ASTROL sign

Zeichenblock <-blöcke> *m* sketch pad

Zeichenbrett *nt* drawing board

Zeichenerklärung *f* key; (*Landkarte*) legend

Zeichensetzung <-> *f kein pl* punctuation

Zeichensprache *f* sign language

Zeichentrickfilm *m* cartoon

zeichnen ['tsaiç·nən] **I.** *vt* KUNST, ARCHIT to draw **II.** *vi* KUNST **an etw** *dat* ~ to draw sth

Zeichnung <-, -en> *f* **1.** KUNST drawing **2.** BOT, ZOOL markings *pl* **3.** FIN subscription

Zeigefinger *m* index finger

zeigen ['tsai·gn] **I.** *vt* **1.** (*deutlich machen*) to show **2.** (*vorführen*) to show; **zeig mal, was du kannst!** *fam* let's see what you can do!; **es jdm ~** *fam* to show sb it **II.** *vi* **1.** (*deuten*) to point (**auf** +*akk* at); **nach rechts/hinten ~** to point to the right/back **2.** (*erkennen lassen*) ~, **dass ...** to show that ... **III.** *vr* **sich** *akk* **~ 1.** (*sich sehen lassen*) to show oneself; **komm, zeig dich mal!** come on, let me see what you look like!; **sich** *akk* **von seiner besten Seite ~** to show oneself at one's best **2.** (*erkennbar werden*) to appear

Zeiger <-s, -> ['tsai·gɐ] *m* (*Uhrzeiger*) hand

Zeile <-, -n> ['tsai·lə] *f* line; **jdm ein paar ~n schrieben** to drop sb a line

zeit [tsait] *präp* +*gen* ~ **meines Lebens** all my life

Zeit <-, -en> [tsait] *f* **1.** *kein pl* (*verstrichener zeitlicher Ablauf*) time; **mit der ~** in time; ~ **raubend** time-consuming; ~ **sparend** time-saving **2.** (*Zeitraum*) time; **eine ~ lang** for a while; **die ganze ~** (*über*) the whole time; **in letzter ~** lately; **in nächster ~** in the near future; **auf unbestimmte ~** for an indefinite period; ~ **gewinnen** to gain time; **zwei Tage ~ haben**[, **etw zu tun**] to have two days [to do sth]; **haben Sie einen**

Z

Augenblick ~? do you have a moment to spare?; **das hat noch ~** that can wait; **sich** *dat* **[mit etw** *dat* **] ~ lassen** to take one's time [with sth]; **jdm die ~ stehlen** to waste sb's time **3.** (*Zeitpunkt*) time; **es ist höchste Zeit, dass wir die Tickets kaufen** it's about time we bought the tickets; **seit dieser ~** since then; **von ~ zu ~** from time to time; **zur ~** at the moment; **zu jeder ~** [at] any time **4.** (*Epoche, Lebensabschnitt*) time, age **5.** LING tense **6.** SPORT time; **eine gute ~ laufen** to run a good time

Zeitalter *nt* age; **in unserem ~** nowadays

Zeitarbeit *f kein pl* temporary work

Zeitbombe *f* time bomb

Zeitdruck *m kein pl* time pressure

Zeiteinteilung *f* time management

zeitgemäß *adj, adv* up-to-date, modern

Zeitgenosse, -genossin ['tsait·gə·nɔ·sə, -gənɔ·sɪn] *m, f* contemporary

zeitgenössisch ['tsait·gə·nœ·sɪʃ] *adj* contemporary

Zeitgeschichte *f kein pl* contemporary history

zeitig ['tsai·tɪç] *adj, adv* early

Zeitkarte *f* TRANSP monthly/weekly/weekend pass

zeitlebens [tsait·'le:·bns] *adv* all one's life

zeitlich I. *adj* chronological II. *adv* etw ~ **abstimmen** to synchronize sth; ~ **begrenzt** for a limited time

zeitlos *adj* timeless; (*Kleidung*) classic

Zeitlupe *f kein pl* slow motion *no art*

Zeitlupentempo *nt* **im ~** in slow motion

Zeitplan *m* schedule

Zeitpunkt *m* time; **zum jetzigen ~** at this moment in time

Zeitraffer <-s> *m kein pl* time-lapse photography

Zeitraum *m* period of time

Zeitrechnung *f* calendar; **vor unserer ~** before Christ, BC; **unserer ~** anno Domini, AD

Zeitschrift ['tsait·ʃrɪft] *f* magazine; (*wissenschaftlich*) journal

Zeitspanne *f* period of time

Zeitung <-, -en> ['tsai·tʊŋ] *f* newspaper

Zeitungsanzeige *f* newspaper advertisement

Zeitungsartikel *m* newspaper article

Zeitungspapier *nt* newspaper

Zeitverschiebung *f* time difference

Zeitverschwendung *f kein pl* waste of time

Zeitvertreib <-[e]s, -e> *m* pastime; **zum ~** to pass the time

zeitweise *adv* **1.** (*gelegentlich*) occasionally **2.** (*vorübergehend*) temporarily

zelebrieren * [tse·le·'bri:·rən] *vt* to celebrate

Zelle <-, -n> ['tsɛ·lə] *f* cell

Zellgewebe *nt* cell tissue

Zellkern *m* nucleus [of a cell]

Zellstoff ['tsɛl·ʃtɔf] *m s.* **Zellulose**

Zellteilung *f* cell division

Zellulitis <-, Zelluliden> [tsɛ·lu·'li:·tɪs] *meist sing* MED cellulitis

Zellulose <-, -n> [tse·lu·'lo:·zə] *f* cellulose

Zelt <-[e]s, -e> [tsɛlt] *nt* tent; (*Festzelt*) exhibit tent; (*Zirkuszelt*) big top

zelten ['tsɛl·tn] *vi* to camp

Zeltlager *nt* camp

Zement <-[e]s, -e> [tse·'mɛnt] *m* cement

zementieren * [tse·mɛn·'ti:·rən] *vt a. fig* to cement

Zenit <-[e]s> [tse·'ni:t] *m kein pl* zenith

zensieren * [tsɛn·'zi:·rən] *vt* **1.** SCH to grade **2.** (*der Zensur unterwerfen*) to censor

Zensur <-, -en> [tsɛn·'zu:ɡ] *f* **1.** SCH grade **2.** *kein pl* (*prüfende Kontrolle*) censorship

Zentimeter [tsɛn·ti·'me:·tə] *m o nt* centimeter

Zentner <-s, -> ['tsɛnt·nɐ] *m* 50 kg *(110 lbs)*; *österr, schweiz* 100 kg *(220 lbs)*

zentral [tsɛn·'tra:l] I. *adj* central II. *adv* centrally

Zentrale <-, -n> [tsɛn·'tra:·lə] *f* **1.** (*Hauptgeschäftsstelle: Bank, Firma*) head office; (*Militär, Polizei, Taxiunternehmen*) headquarters + *sing/pl vb*; (*Busse*) depot **2.** TELEK operator; (*Firma*) switchboard

Zentralheizung *f* central heating

zentralisieren * [tsɛn·tra·li·'zi:·rən] *vt* to centralize

Zentralverriegelung <-, -en> f power locks npl

Zentrifugalkraft f centrifugal force

Zentrifuge <-, -n> [tsɛn·tri·ˈfuː·gə] f centrifuge

Zentrum <-s, Zentren> [ˈtsɛn·trʊm] nt center

zerbeißen * [tsɛɐ̯·ˈbai·sn̩] vt irreg 1. (kaputtbeißen) to chew; (Bonbon) to crunch 2. (überall stechen) to bite

zerbrechen * irreg I. vt haben (in Stücke zerbrechen) **etw** ~ to break [in]to pieces; (Glas, Teller) to smash; (Kette) to break II. vi sein 1. (entzweibrechen) to break [in]to pieces 2. (in die Brüche gehen) to be destroyed; (Partnerschaft) to break up 3. (seelisch zugrunde gehen) **an etw** dat ~ to be destroyed by sth

zerbrechlich adj 1. (leicht zerbrechend) fragile 2. (zart) frail

zerbröckeln * I. vt haben to crumble II. vi sein to crumble

zerdrücken * vt 1. (zu einer Masse pressen) to crush; (Kartoffeln) to mash 2. (Zigarette) to put out sep 3. (Stoff) to crease

Zeremonie <-, -n> [tse·re·mo·ˈniː] f ceremony

zerfallen * vi irreg sein 1. (sich zersetzen: Fassade, Gebäude) to disintegrate; (Körper, Materie) to decompose; (Gesundheit) to decline 2. (auseinanderbrechen: Reich, Sitte) to decline

zerkleinern * [tsɛɐ̯·ˈklai·nɐn] vt to cut up sep

zerknirscht [tsɛɐ̯·ˈknɪrʃt] adj remorseful

zerknittern * vt to crease

zerknüllen * vt to crumple up sep

zerkratzen * vt to scratch

zerlassen * vt irreg (Butter) to melt

zerlegen * vt 1. KOCHK to cut [up sep]; (Braten) to carve 2. (auseinandernehmen) to take apart sep; (Maschine) to dismantle; (Getriebe, Motor) to strip down sep

zerlumpt adj ragged; ~ **sein** to be in tatters

zermürben * [tsɛɐ̯·ˈmʏr·bn̩] vt to wear down sep

zerquetschen * vt to squash

zerreiben * vt irreg to crush

zerreißen * irreg I. vt haben 1. (in Stücke) to tear to pieces 2. (durchreißen) to tear; (Brief, Scheck) to tear up sep II. vi sein to tear; (Seil, Faden) to break

zerren [ˈtsɛ·rən] I. vt to drag II. vi to tug (**an** +dat at/on); **an den Nerven** ~ to be nerve-racking III. vr MED **sich** dat **einen Muskel** ~ to pull a muscle

Zerrung <-, -en> f MED (Muskelzerrung) pulled muscle; (Sehnenzerrung) pulled tendon

zerrütten * [tsɛɐ̯·ˈrʏ·tn̩] vt to destroy; (Ehe) to ruin

zerschellen * vi sein to be smashed to pieces

zerschlagen *1 irreg I. vt 1. (Glas, Teller etc.) to smash to pieces 2. (zerstören) to break up sep; (Angriff) to crush; (Plan) to shatter II. vr **sich** akk ~ (Plan) to fall through

zerschlagen2 adj pred shattered

zerschneiden * vt irreg 1. (in Stücke) to cut up sep 2. (durchschneiden) to cut in two

zersetzen * vr (sich auflösen) **sich** akk ~ to decompose

zerstäuben * vt to spray

Zerstäuber <-s, -> m atomizer

zerstochen adj (von Stechmücken) covered in bites, bitten all over

zerstören * vt to destroy; (Plan, Gesundheit) to ruin

zerstörerisch I. adj destructive II. adv destructively

Zerstörung <-, -en> f 1. kein pl destruction 2. (Verwüstung) devastation

zerstreuen * I. vt (Ängste, Sorgen) to dispel II. vr (entspannen) **sich** akk ~ to amuse oneself

zerstreut adj 1. (gedankenlos) absentminded 2. (weit verteilt) scattered

Zerstreuung <-, -en> f (Unterhaltung) diversion

zerteilen * vt to cut up sep (**in** +akk into)

zertrümmern * [tsɛɐ̯·ˈtrʏ·mɐn] vt to smash

zetern [ˈtseː·tɐn] vi pej to nag

Zettel <-s, -> [ˈtsɛ·tl̩] m piece of paper

Zeug <-[e]s> [tsɔyk] nt kein pl fam 1. (Sachen) stuff; **altes** ~ junk 2. (Quatsch) crap fam ▸ **was das** ~ **hält** fam for all

Z

one is worth; **sich** *akk* **ins ~ legen** *fam* to put one's shoulder to the wheel

Zeuge, Zeugin <-n, -n> ['tsɔy·gə, 'tsɔy·gɪn] *m, f* witness

zeugen[1] ['tsɔy·gn̩] *vt* (*Kind*) to father

zeugen[2] ['tsɔy·gn̩] *vi* **von etw** *dat* **~** to show sth

Zeugenaussage *f* testimony

Zeugenstand *m* witness stand

Zeugnis <-ses, -se> ['tsɔyk·nɪs] *nt* **1.** SCH report card **2.** (*Empfehlung*) certificate of recommendation; (*Arbeitszeugnis*) reference

zeugungsfähig *adj* fertile

zeugungsunfähig *adj* sterile

z. H(d). *Abk von* **zu Händen** attn.

zicken ['tsɪ·kən] *vi fam* to kick up a fuss

Zickzack ['tsɪk·tsak] *m* zigzag

Ziege <-, -n> ['tsi:·gə] *f* goat

Ziegel <-s, -> ['tsi:·gl̩] *m* **1.** (*Ziegelstein*) brick **2.** (*Dachziegel*) tile

Ziegelstein *m* brick

Ziegenbock *m* billy goat

Ziegenkäse *m* goat cheese

Ziegenpeter <-s, -> ['tsi:·gn̩·pe:·tə] *m fam* (*Mumps*) mumps + *sing/pl vb*

ziehen <zog, gezogen> ['tsi:·ən] **I.** *vt haben* **1.** (*hinter sich her schleppen, zerren*) to pull; (*fester*) to drag **2.** (*Handbremse*) to put on *sep* **3.** (*herausziehen: Fäden, Zahn*) to take out *sep*; (*Revolver, Spielkarte*) to draw **4.** (*züchten: Pflanzen*) to grow; (*Tiere*) to breed **5.** (*Kreis, Linie*) to draw **6.** (*anziehen*) **etw auf sich** *akk* **~** to attract sth **7.** (*zur Folge haben*) **etw nach sich** *dat* **~** to have consequences **II.** *vi* **1.** *haben* (*zerren*) to pull (**an** +*dat* on) **2.** *sein* (*umziehen*) to move; **zu jdm ~** to move in with sb; **nach München ~** to move to Munich **3.** *sein* (*irgendwohin gehen: Menschenmenge*) to march; (*Rauch, Wolke*) to drift; (*Gewitter*) to move; **durch die Stadt ~** to wander through [the] town/the city; **in den Krieg ~** to go to war **4.** *haben* (*saugen*) **an einer Zigarette ~** to drag on a cigarette **5.** *haben* (*Tee*) to brew **III.** *vi impers haben* **es zieht** there is a draft **IV.** *vt impers haben* **es zog ihn in die weite Welt** he felt a strong urge to see the world; **was zieht**

dich hierhin? what brings you here? **V.** *vr haben* **sich** *akk* **~** (*Gespräch, Verhandlungen*) to drag on

Ziehharmonika *f* concertina

Ziel <-[e]s, -e> [tsi:l] *nt* **1.** (*angestrebtes Ergebnis*) goal, aim; **am ~ sein** to be at one's destination **2.** SPORT, MIL target; **durchs ~ gehen** to cross the finish line **3.** (*Reiseziel*) destination ▶ **über das ~ hinausschießen** *fam* to overshoot the mark

zielen ['tsi:·lən] *vi* to aim (**auf** +*akk* at)

Zielfernrohr *nt* scope

Zielgerade *f* home stretch

Zielgruppe *f* target group

ziellos I. *adj* aimless **II.** *adv* aimlessly

Zielort *m* destination

Zielscheibe *f* target

Zielsetzung <-, -en> *f* aim

zielsicher *adj* unerring

zielstrebig ['tsi:l·ʃtre:·bɪç] **I.** *adj* singleminded **II.** *adv* single-mindedly

ziemlich ['tsi:m·lɪç] **I.** *adj attr* (*beträchtlich*) considerable **II.** *adv* **1.** (*weitgehend*) quite **2.** (*beinahe*) almost; **so ~ more or less; so ~ alles** just about everything; **so ~ dasselbe** pretty much the same

Zierde <-, -n> ['tsi:ɐ̯·də] *f* decoration

zieren ['tsi:·rən] **I.** *vr* **sich** *akk* **~** to make a fuss; (*Mädchen*) to act coyly; **ohne sich** *akk* **zu ~** without having to be pressed **II.** *vt* to adorn

zierlich ['tsi:ɐ̯·lɪç] *adj* dainty

Zierpflanze *f* ornamental plant

Ziffer <-, -n> ['tsɪ·fɐ] *f* **1.** (*Zahlzeichen*) digit **2.** *s.* **Zahl**

zig [tsɪç] *adj fam* umpteen; **~mal** umpteen times

Zigarette <-, -n> [tsi·ga·'rɛ·tə] *f* cigarette

Zigarillo <-s, -s> [tsi·ga·'rɪ·lo] *m o n* cigarillo

Zigarre <-, -n> [tsi·'ga·rə] *f* cigar

Zigeuner(in) <-s, -> [tsi·'gɔy·nɐ] *m(f)* Gypsy

Zimmer <-s, -> ['tsɪ·mɐ] *nt* room; **~ frei haben** to have vacancies

Zimmerantenne *f* indoor antenna

Zimmerdecke *f* ceiling

Zimmermädchen *nt* [chamber]maid

Zimmermann <-leute> *m* carpenter

zimmern ['tsɪ·mɐn] *vt* to make from wood

Zimmerpflanze *f* house plant

Zimmervermittlung *f* accommodations service

zimperlich ['tsɪm·pɐ·lɪç] *adj* squeamish

Zimt <-[e]s, -e> [tsɪmt] *m* cinnamon

Zink <-[e]s> [tsɪŋk] *nt kein pl* zinc

Zinn <-[e]s> [tsɪn] *nt kein pl* tin

zinnoberrot *adj* vermilion

Zinsertrag *m* interest yield

Zinseszins *m* compound interest

zinslos *adj* interest-free

Zipfelmütze *f* pointed cap

zirka ['tsɪr·ka] *adv* about

Zirkel <-s, -> ['tsɪr·kl̩] *m* **1.** (*Gerät*) compass **2.** (*Gruppe*) group

Zirkus <-, -se> ['tsɪr·kʊs] *m* circus; **mach nicht so einen ~!** *fig fam* don't make such a fuss!

Zirkuszelt *nt* big top

zischen ['tsɪ·ʃn̩] *vi haben* to hiss; (*Fett*) to sizzle

Zischen <-s> ['tsɪ·ʃn̩] *nt kein pl* hiss

Zitat <-[e]s, -e> [tsi·'taːt] *nt* quotation

zitieren* [tsi·'tiː·rən] *vt* to quote

Zitrone <-, -n> [tsi·'troː·nə] *f* lemon

Zitronenschale *f* lemon peel

Zitrusfrucht ['tsiː·trʊs-] *f* citrus fruit

zittern ['tsɪ·tɐn] *vi* to tremble; **vor Angst ~** to tremble with fear

zittrig ['tsɪt·rɪç] *adj* shaky

Zivil <-s> [tsi·'viːl] *nt kein pl* **in ~** in civilian clothes

Zivilbevölkerung *f* civilian population

Zivildienst *m kein pl* community service as an alternative to military service

Zivilisation <-, -en> [tsi·vi·li·za·'tsi̯oːn] *f* civilization

zivilisiert **I.** *adj* civilized **II.** *adv* civilly

Zivilist(in) <-en, -en> [tsi·vi·'lɪst] *m(f)* civilian

Zivilrecht *nt* civil law

zocken ['tsɔ·kn̩] *vi sl* to gamble

Zoff <-s> [tsɔf] *m kein pl fam* trouble

zögern ['tsø·ɡɐn] *vi* to hesitate; **ohne zu ~** without hesitation

Zölibat <-[e]s, -e> [tsø·li·'baːt] *nt o m* celibacy

Zoll¹ <-[e]s, -> [tsɔl] *m* (*Maß*) inch

Zoll² <-[e]s, Zölle> [tsɔl] *m* **1.** ÖKON cus-

toms *npl*, duty; **für etw** *akk* **~ bezahlen** to pay customs on sth **2.** *kein pl* (*Zollverwaltung*) customs *npl*

Zollbeamte(r), -beamtin *m, f* customs officer

Zollfahndung *f* customs investigation department

zollfrei *adj, adv* duty-free

zollpflichtig *adj* dutiable

Zollstock *m* ruler

Zone <-, -n> ['tsoː·nə] *f* zone

Zoo <-s, -s> [tsoː] *m* zoo

Zoologie <-> [tsoo·lo·'ɡiː] *f kein pl* zoology

zoomen ['zuː·mən, 'tsoː·mən] *vt* **jdn/etw ~** to zoom in on sb/sth

Zopf <-[e]s, Zöpfe> [tsɔpf] *m* braid

Zorn <-[e]s> [tsɔrn] *m kein pl* anger

zornig ['tsɔr·nɪç] *adj* angry (**auf** +*akk* with/at)

zottelig ['tsɔ·tə·lɪç] *adj fam* shaggy

zu [tsuː] **I.** *präp* +*dat* **1.** (*wohin*) to; **ich muss ~m Arzt** I have to go see a doctor; **~ Fuß/Pferd** on foot/horseback **2.** (*örtlich: Richtung*) **~m Meer/~r Stadtmitte hin** toward the sea/downtown; **das Zimmer liegt ~r Straße hin** the room faces the street **3.** (*neben*) **~ jdm/etw** next to sb/sth; **setz dich ~ uns** [come and] sit with us **4.** *zeitlich* at; **~ Ostern/Weihnachten** at Easter/Christmas; **~m Wochenende fahren wir weg** we're going away on the weekend **5.** (*anlässlich*) **etw ~m Geburtstag bekommen** to get sth for one's birthday; **jdn ~m Essen einladen** to invite sb for a meal; **~ dieser Frage möchte ich Folgendes sagen** I would like to say the following regarding this question **6.** (*für etw bestimmt*) **das Zeichen ~m Aufbruch** the signal to leave; **~m Frühstück trinkt sie immer Tee** she always has tea with breakfast **7.** (*um etw herbeizuführen*) **~r Entschuldigung** in apology; **~ was soll das gut sein?** what is that [supposed to be good] for? **8.** + *substantiviertem Infinitiv* **nichts ~m Essen** nothing to eat; **etwas ~m Spielen** something to play with; **das ist ja ~m Lachen** that's ridiculous **9.** (*Veränderung*) **~ etw werden** to turn into sth;

Z

~m Vorsitzenden **gewählt werden** to be elected [to the post of] chairman **10.** (*Beziehung*) **Liebe ~ jdm** love for sb; **aus Freundschaft ~ jdm** because of one's friendship with sb; **meine Beziehung ~ ihr** my relationship with her **11.** (*Verhältnis*) **im Verhältnis 1 ~ 4** in a 1:4 [*o* 1 to 4] ratio; **unsere Chancen stehen 50 ~ 50** we have a fifty-fifty chance; SPORT **sie gewannen mit 5 ~ 1** they won 5-1, 5 to 1 **12.** *bei Mengenangaben* **~ drei Prozent** at three percent; **sechs** [**Stück**] **~ fünfzig Cent** six for fifty cents; **~m halben Preis** at [*o* for] half price; **~m ersten Mal** for the first time **13.** (*örtlich: Lage*) in; **~ Hause** at home; **~ seiner Rechten/Linken** on his right/left[-hand] side **14.** (*in Wendungen*) **~m Beispiel** for example; **~r Belohnung/Strafe** as a reward/punishment; **~m Glück** luckily; **jdm ~ Hilfe kommen** to come to sb's aid; **~ Hilfe!** help!; **~r Probe** on a trial basis; *schweiz* **~r Hauptsache** mainly **II.** *adv* **1.** (*allzu*) too; **~ sehr** too much; **ich wäre ~ gern mitgefahren** I would have loved to have gone along **2.** (*geschlossen*) shut, closed; **Tür ~!** shut the door!; **mach die Augen ~** close your eyes **3.** *fam* (*betrunken sein*) **~ sein** to be drunk **4.** (*in Wendungen*) **nur ~!** go [right] ahead; **mach ~** hurry up **III.** *konj* **1.** + *infin* to; **etw ~ essen** sth to eat; **sie hat ~ gehorchen** she has to obey; **ohne es ~ wissen** without knowing it **2.** + *part* **~ bezahlende Rechnungen** outstanding bills; **nicht ~ unterschätzende Probleme** problems [that are] not to be underestimated

zuallerletzt [tsu·'?alɐ·'?ɛʁst] *adv* first of all

zuallerletzt [tsu·'?alɐ·lɛtst] *adv* last of all

Zubehör <-[e]s, *selten* -e> ['tsu:·bə·hø:ɐ̯] *nt o* m accessories *pl*

zu|beißen *vi irreg* to bite

zu|bereiten * *vt* to prepare

Zubereitung <-, -en> *f* preparation

zu|billigen *vt* **jdm etw ~** to grant sb sth

zu|binden *vt irreg* (*Schuhe*) to tie

Zucchini <-, -> [tsʊ·'ki:·ni] *f meist pl* zucchini

Zucht <-, -en> [tsʊxt] *f kein pl* (*Pflanzenzucht*) cultivation; (*Tierzucht*) breeding

züchten ['tsʏç·tn̩] *vt* (*Pflanzen*) to grow; (*Tiere*) to breed

Züchter(in) <-s, -> *m(f)* (*Tierzüchter*) breeder; (*Pflanzenzüchter*) grower

Zuchthaus *nt* HIST prison

Zuchthengst *m* stud horse

züchtigen ['tsʏç·tɪ·gn̩] *vt* to beat

zucken ['tsʊ·kn̩] *vi* **1.** *haben* (*ruckartig bewegen: Augenlid*) to flutter; (*Mundwinkel*) to twitch; **mit den Achseln ~** to shrug one's shoulders **2.** *haben* (*Blitz*) to flash

zücken ['tsʏ·kn̩] *vt* (*Messer*) to draw

Zucker[1] <-s, -> ['tsʊ·kɐ] *m* sugar

Zucker[2] <-s> ['tsʊ·kɐ] *m kein pl* MED diabetes

Zuckerguss RR *m* icing

Zuckerhut ['tsʊ·kɐ·hu:t] *m* GEOL sugar loaf

zuckerkrank *adj* diabetic

Zuckerkranke(r) *f(m)* diabetic

Zuckerrohr *nt* sugar cane

Zuckerrübe *f* sugar beet

zuckersüß ['tsʊ·kɐ·'zy:s] *adj* as sweet as sugar *pred*

Zuckung <-, -en> *f meist pl* twitch

zu|decken *vt* to cover [up *sep*]

zu|drehen *vt* **1.** (*verschließen*) to screw on *sep* **2.** (*abstellen*) to turn off *sep* **3.** (*festdrehen*) to tighten **4.** (*abwenden*) **jdm den Rücken ~** to turn one's back on sb

zudringlich ['tsu:·drɪŋ·lɪç] *adj* pushy

zu|drücken *vt* to press shut *sep*

zueinander [tsu·?ai·'nan·dɐ] *adv* to each other; **~ passen** (*Menschen*) to suit each other; (*Farben, Kleider*) to go well together

zuerst [tsu·'?e·ʁst] *adv* **1.** (*als Erster*) the first; (*als Erstes*) first **2.** (*anfangs*) at first **3.** (*zum ersten Mal*) for the first time

Zufahrt ['tsu:·fa:ɐ̯t] *f* entrance

Zufall *m* coincidence; (*Schicksal*) chance; **etw dem ~ überlassen** to leave sth to chance

zu|fallen *vi irreg sein* **1.** (*Tür*) to close **2.** (*zuteilwerden*) **jdm ~** to go to sb

zufällig **I.** *adj* chance *attr* **II.** *adv* by

Zufallstreffer m fluke fam

Zuflucht <-, -en> ['tsuː·flʊxt] f refuge
▶ jds **letzte** ~ **sein** to be sb's last resort

Zufluss RR, **Zufluß** ALT m 1. kein pl (das Zufließen) inflow 2. (Nebenfluss) tributary

zu|flüstern vt jdm etw ~ to whisper sth to sb

zufolge [tsu·ˈfɔl·gə] präp +dat according to

zufrieden [tsu·ˈfriː·dn̩] I. adj (befriedigt) satisfied (**mit** +dat with); (glücklich) contented (**mit** +dat with) II. adv with satisfaction; (glücklich) contentedly; ~ **stellend** satisfactory

zufrieden|geben vr irreg **sich** akk [**mit etw** dat] ~ to be satisfied [with sth]

Zufriedenheit <-> f kein pl satisfaction; (Glücklichsein) contentedness

zufrieden|lassen vt irreg jdn ~ to leave sb alone

zu|frieren vi irreg sein to freeze [over]

zu|fügen vt to cause; jdm **Schaden** ~ to harm sb; jdm **Unrecht** ~ to do sb an injustice

Zufuhr <-, -en> ['tsuː·fuːɐ̯] f supply

Zug¹ <-[e]s, Züge> [tsuːk] m train ▶ **der** ~ **ist abgefahren** fam you missed the boat

Zug² <-[e]s, Züge> [tsuːk] m 1. (inhalierte Menge) puff (**an** +dat on/at) 2. kein pl (Luftzug) draft 3. (Spielzug) move; **am** ~ **sein** to be sb's move 4. (Kolonne) procession 5. (Gesichtszug) feature 6. (Charakterzug) characteristic 7. (Schritt) ~ **um** ~ step by step; **in einem** ~ in one stroke 8. (Umriss) **in groben Zügen** in broad terms

Zugabe ['tsuː·ɡaː·bə] f MUS encore

Zugabteil nt train compartment

Zugang <-[e]s, Zugänge> ['tsuː·ɡaŋ] m 1. (Eingang) entrance 2. kein pl (Zutritt, Zugriff) access (**zu** +dat to)

zugänglich ['tsuː·ɡɛŋ·lɪç] adj 1. (erreichbar) accessible 2. (Mensch) approachable; **für etw** akk ~ **sein** to be receptive to sth

Zugbrücke f drawbridge

zu|geben vt irreg to admit

zugegen [tsu·ˈɡeː·ɡn̩] adj **bei etw** dat ~ **sein** to be present at sth

zu|gehen irreg I. vi sein 1. (Tür) to shut 2. (zubewegen) **auf jdn/etw** ~ to approach sb/sth 3. (sich versöhnen) **aufeinander** ~ to become reconciled II. vi impers sein **auf ihren Partys geht es immer sehr lustig zu** her parties are always great fun

zugehörig ['tsuː·ɡə·høː·rɪç] adj attr accompanying attr

Zugehörigkeit <-> f kein pl (Verbundenheit) affiliation (**zu** +dat to); **ein Gefühl der** ~ a sense of belonging

zugeknöpft adj 1. (Hemd) buttoned-up 2. (Mensch) reserved

Zügel <-s, -> ['tsyː·ɡl̩] m reins npl

zügellos adj unrestrained

zügeln ['tsyː·ɡl̩n] I. vt 1. (im Zaum halten) to rein in sep 2. (beherrschen) to curb 3. (zurückhalten) **sich/jdn** ~ to restrain oneself/sb II. vi sein schweiz (umziehen) [**irgendwohin**] ~ to move [somewhere]

Zugeständnis ['tsuː·ɡə·ʃtɛnt·nɪs] nt concession

zu|gestehen* vt irreg to concede

zugetan ['tsuː·ɡə·taːn] adj jdm/etw ~ **sein** to be taken with sb/sth

Zugführer(in) m(f) BAHN conductor

zugig ['tsuː·ɡɪç] adj drafty

zugleich [tsu·ˈɡlaɪç] adv 1. (ebenso) both 2. (gleichzeitig) at the same time

Zugluft f kein pl draft

Zugmaschine f AUTO tractor

Zugpferd nt 1. (Tier) draft horse 2. (besondere Attraktion) crowd pleaser

zu|greifen vi irreg 1. (sich bedienen) to help oneself 2. COMPUT **auf etw** akk ~ to access sth

Zugrestaurant nt dining car

Zugriffsberechtigung f COMPUT access authorization

zugrunde, zu Grunde RR [tsu·ˈɡrʊn·də] adv [**an etw** dat] ~ **gehen** to be destroyed [by sth]; **etw** dat ~ **liegen** to form the basis of sth

Zugschaffner(in) m(f) train conductor

zugunsten, zu Gunsten RR [tsu·'gʊns·tn̩] *präp +gen* in favor of

zugute|halten RR [tsu·'gu:·tə-] *vt irreg* **jdm etw ~** to make allowances for sb's sth

zugute|kommen RR *vi irreg sein* **jdm/etw ~** to be for the benefit of sb/sth

Zugverbindung *f* train connection

Zugvogel *m* migratory bird

zu|haben *vi irreg fam* to be closed

zu|halten *vt irreg* to hold closed; **sich/ jdm den Mund ~** to hold one's hand over one's/sb's mouth; **sich** *dat* **die Nase ~** to hold one's nose

Zuhälter(in) <-s, -> ['tsu:·hɛl·tɐ] *m(f)* pimp

Zuhause <-s> [tsu·'hau·zə] *nt kein pl* home

zu|hören *vi* **jdm ~** to listen to sb

Zuhörer(in) *m(f)* listener; **die ~** (*Publikum*) the audience + *sing/pl vb;* (*Radiozuhörer a.*) the listeners

zu|jubeln *vi* to cheer

zu|knöpfen *vt* to button up *sep*

zu|kommen *vi irreg sein* **1.** (*sich nähern*) **auf jdn/etw ~** to come toward sb/sth **2.** (*bevorstehen*) **auf jdn ~** to be in store for sb; **alles auf sich ~ lassen** to take things as they come **3.** (*geben*) **jdm etw ~ lassen** to send sb sth

Zukunft <-> ['tsu:·kʊnft] *f kein pl* **1.** (*das Bevorstehende*) future; **in ferner/naher ~** in the distant/near future **2.** LING future [tense]

zukünftig ['tsu:·kʏnf·tɪç] **I.** *adj* future *attr* **II.** *adv* in future

Zukunftsaussichten *pl* future prospects *pl*

Zukunftsmusik *f* ▶ **~ sein** *fam* to be a long way off

zu|lächeln *vi* **jdm ~** to smile at sb

zu|langen *vi fam* **1.** (*zugreifen*) to help oneself **2.** (*zuschlagen*) to land a punch **3.** (*hohe Preise fordern*) to ask a fortune

zu|lassen *vt irreg* **1.** (*dulden*) to allow **2.** *fam* (*Tür*) to keep shut *sep* **3.** (*die Genehmigung erteilen*) **jdn ~** to admit sb (**zu** *+dat* to) **4.** (*anmelden*) to register

zulässig ['tsu:·lɛ·sɪç] *adj* permissible

Zulassung <-, -en> *f* **1.** *kein pl* (*Genehmigung*) authorization; (*Lizenz*) license; **die ~ entziehen** to revoke sb's license **2.** (*Anmeldung*) registration **3.** (*Fahrzeugschein*) [motor vehicle] registration

Zulassungsbeschränkung *f* admission restriction

Zulassungsprüfung *f* ADMIN, SCH entrance exam

zu|legen I. *vt fam* (*zunehmen*) to put on *sep* ▶ **einen Zahn ~** *fam* to step on it **II.** *vi* **1.** *fam* (*zunehmen*) to put on weight **2.** *fam* (*das Tempo steigern*) to get a move on; (*Läufer*) to increase the pace **III.** *vr fam* **sich** *dat* **jdn/etw ~** to get oneself sb/sth

zuleide, zu Leide RR [tsu·'lai·də] *adv* **jdm etwas/nichts ~ tun** *veraltend* to harm/ not harm sb

zuletzt [tsu·'lɛtst] *adv* **1.** (*als Letzte[r]*) **~ eingetroffen** to be the last to arrive; **~ durchs Ziel gehen** to finish last **2.** (*zum Schluss*) **bis ~** until the end; **ganz ~** right at the end **3.** (*letztmalig*) last; **nicht ~** not least [of all]

zuliebe [tsu·'li:·bə] *adv* **jdm/etw ~** for sb['s sake]

zum [tsʊm] = **zu dem** *s.* **zu**

zu|machen *vt, vi* **1.** (*verschließen*) to close; **eine Flasche/ein Glas ~** to put the top on a bottle/lid on a jar **2.** (*zukleben: Brief*) to seal **3.** (*zuknöpfen*) to button [up *sep*] **4.** (*den Betrieb einstellen*) to close [down *sep*]

zumal [tsu·'ma:l] **I.** *konj* particularly as **II.** *adv* particularly

zumindest [tsu·'mɪn·dəst] *adv* at least

zumute, zu Mute RR [tsu·'mu:·tə] *adv* **mir ist nicht zum Scherzen ~** I'm not in a joking mood

zu|muten ['tsu:·mu:·tn̩] *vt* **jdm etw ~** to expect sth of sb; **jdm zu viel ~** to expect too much of sb; **sich** *dat* **etw ~** to undertake sth; **sich** *dat* **zu viel ~** to overtax oneself

Zumutung *f* unreasonable demand; **das ist eine ~!** it's just too much!

zunächst [tsu·'nɛçst] *adv* **1.** (*anfangs*) initially **2.** (*vorerst*) for the moment

Zunahme <-, -n> ['tsu:·na:·mə] *f* increase

Zuname ['tsuː·naː·mə] *m geh* surname

zünden ['tsʏndn̩] *vt, vi* **1.** TECH. to fire *spec* **2.** (*zu brennen anfangen*) to catch fire; (*Streichholz*) to light

zündend *adj* (*Rede*) stirring; (*Idee*) great

Zünder <-s, -> ['tsʏn·de] *m* detonator

Zündholz <-es, -hölzer> *nt dial* match

Zündholzschachtel *f dial* matchbox

Zündkabel *nt* ignition cable

Zündkerze *f* spark plug

Zündschlüssel *m* ignition key

Zündschnur *f* fuse

Zündung <-, -en> *f* **1.** AUTO ignition **2.** TECH firing

zu|nehmen *vi irreg* **1.** (*Gewicht*) to gain weight **2.** (*sich verstärken*) to increase

zu|neigen **I.** *vi* etw ~ to be inclined toward sth **II.** *vr sich akk* **dem Ende** ~ to draw to a close

Zuneigung *f* affection

Zunft <-, Zünfte> [tsʊnft] *f* HIST guild

zünftig ['tsʏnf·tɪç] *adj veraltend fam* proper

Zunge <-, -n> ['tsʊŋə] *f* tongue; **auf der ~ zergehen** to melt in one's mouth ► **etw liegt jdm auf der ~** sth is on the tip of sb's tongue

Zungenbrecher <-s, -> *m fam* tongue twister

Zungenkuss RR *m* French kiss

Zungenspitze *f* tip of the tongue

zunichte|machen RR [tsu·'nɪç·tə-] *vt* to wreck; (*Hoffnungen*) to ruin

zunutze, zu Nutze RR [tsu·'nʊ·tsə] *adv* **sich** *dat* **etw ~ machen** to make use of sth

zu|ordnen ['tsuː·ʔɔrd·nən] *vt* etw etw *dat* ~ to assign sth to sth

zu|packen *vi* **1.** (*zufassen*) to grip; (*schneller*) to make a grab **2.** (*mithelfen*) [**mit**] ~ to lend a [helping] hand

zupfen ['tsʊp·fn̩] *vt* **1.** (*ziehen*) jdn an etw *dat* ~ to pluck at sb's sth; (*stärker*) to tug at sb's sth **2.** (*herausziehen*) etw **aus/von etw** ~ to pull sth out of/ off [of] sth; **sich** *dat* **die Augenbrauen ~** to pluck one's eyebrows

zur [tsuːɐ̯, tsʊr] = **zu der** *s.* **zu**

zurechnungsfähig *adj* JUR responsible for one's [own] actions *pred*

zurecht|finden [tsu·'rɛçt·fɪn·dn̩] *vr irreg*

sich *akk* **irgendwo ~** to get used to a place; **sich** *akk* **in einer Großstadt ~** to find one's way around a city

zurecht|kommen *vi irreg sein* **1.** (*auskommen*) to get along (**mit** +*dat* with) **2.** (*klarkommen*) to cope (**mit** +*dat* with)

zurecht|legen *vr* **sich** *dat* **etw ~** (*sich etw griffbereit hinlegen*) to get sth ready; (*sich im Voraus überlegen*) to work out *sep* sth

zurecht|machen **I.** *vt* **1.** (*vorbereiten*) to get ready **2.** (*zubereiten*) to prepare **II.** *vr* **sich** *akk* ~ to put on *sep* one's makeup

zurecht|weisen *vt irreg* to reprimand (**wegen** +*gen* for)

zu|reden ['tsuː·reː·dn̩] *vi* jdm [**gut**] ~ to encourage sb

zu|richten ['tsuː·rɪç·tn̩] *vt* jdn **übel ~** to beat up *sep* sb badly; **etw übel ~** to make a mess of sth

Zurschaustellung *f meist pej* flaunting

zurück [tsu·'rʏk] *adv* **1.** (*wieder da*) back (**von** +*dat* from) **2.** (*Rückfahrt, -flug*) return; **hin und ~ oder einfach?** round-trip or one-way? ► **~! back up!**

zurück|bekommen * *vt irreg* to get back *sep*

zurück|bezahlen * *vt* to repay, to pay back *sep*

zurück|bleiben *vi irreg sein* **1.** (*nicht mitkommen*) to stay behind **2.** (*zurückgelassen werden*) to be left [behind] **3.** (*nicht mithalten können*) to fall behind

zurück|blicken [tsu·'rʏk·blɪ·kn̩] *vi* to look back (**auf** +*akk* on/at)

zurück|bringen *vt irreg* to bring back *sep*

zurück|denken *vi irreg* to think back (**an** +*akk* to)

zurück|drängen *vt* to force back *sep*

zurück|erstatten * *vt* [jdm] **etw ~** to refund [sb's] sth

zurück|fahren *irreg* **I.** *vi sein* (*zum Ausgangspunkt fahren*) to drive back **II.** *vt* **1.** (*rückwärtsfahren*) to reverse **2.** (*mit dem Auto*) to drive back *sep* **3.** (*reduzieren*) to cut back *sep*

zurück|fallen *vi irreg sein* **1.** SPORT to fall

behind **2.** (*in früheren Zustand*) to lapse back (**in** +*akk* in) **3.** (*angelastet werden*) **auf jdn** ~ to reflect on sb

zurück|finden *vi irreg* to find one's way back

zurück|fordern *vt* to demand back (**von** +*dat* from)

zurück|führen *vt* **1.** (*Ursache bestimmen*) **etw auf etw** *akk* ~ to attribute sth to sth **2.** (*zum Ausgangsort zurückbringen*) **jdn irgendwohin** ~ to take sb back somewhere

zurück|geben *vt irreg* to return; **ein Kompliment** ~ to return a compliment

zurückgeblieben *adj* slow

zurück|gehen *vi irreg sein* **1.** (*zurückkehren*) to return, to go back **2.** (*abnehmen*) to go down **3.** MED (*sich zurückbilden*) to go down; (*Geschwulst*) to be in recession

zurückgezogen *adj, adv* secluded

zurück|greifen *vi irreg* **auf etw** *akk* ~ to fall back [up]on sth

zurück|halten *irreg* **I.** *vr* **sich** *akk* ~ **1.** (*sich beherrschen*) to restrain oneself **2.** (*reserviert sein*) to be reserved **II.** *vt* **1.** (*aufhalten*) to hold up *sep* **2.** (*abhalten*) **jdn** [**von etw** *dat*] ~ to keep sb from doing sth

zurückhaltend I. *adj* **1.** (*reserviert*) reserved **2.** (*vorsichtig*) cautious **II.** *adv* cautiously

Zurückhaltung *f kein pl* reserve

zurück|holen *vt* (*zurückbringen*) to bring back *sep*; (*in seinen Besitz*) to get back *sep*

zurück|kehren *vi sein* to return (**zu** +*dat* to); **nach Hause** ~ to return home

zurück|kommen *vi irreg sein* **1.** (*erneut zum Ausgangsort kommen*) to return; **nach Hause/aus dem Ausland** ~ to return home/from abroad **2.** (*erneut aufgreifen*) **auf etw** *akk* ~ to come back to sth; **auf jdn** ~ to get back to sb

zurück|lassen *vt irreg* to leave behind *sep*

zurück|legen *vt* **1.** (*wieder hinlegen*) to put back *sep* **2.** (*reservieren*) **jdm etw** ~ to set sth aside for sb **3.** (*hinter sich bringen*) **5 km** ~ to go 5 km; (*zu Fuß a.*)

to walk 5 km; (*mit dem Auto a.*) to drive 5 km **4.** (*sparen*) to put away *sep*

zurück|liegen *vi irreg* **etw liegt vier Jahre zurück** it's been four years since sth

zurück|nehmen *vt irreg* **1.** (*als Retour annehmen*) to take back *sep* **2.** (*widerrufen*) to take back *sep* **3.** (*rückgängig machen*) to withdraw; **ich nehme alles zurück** I take it all back

zurück|reisen *vi sein* to travel back

zurück|rufen *irreg* **I.** *vt* **1.** (*zurück telefonieren*) to call back *sep* **2.** (*zurückbeordern*) to recall **II.** *vi* to call back

zurück|schalten *vi* AUTO to downshift (**in** +*akk* into)

zurück|schauen *vi* to look back (**auf** +*akk* on/at)

zurück|schicken *vt* to send back *sep*

zurück|schlagen *irreg* **I.** *vt* **1.** SPORT to hit back **2.** (*umschlagen*) to turn back *sep* **II.** *vi* **auf jdn/etw** ~ to have an effect on sb/sth

zurück|schrecken *vi irreg sein* **1.** (*Bedenken vor etw haben*) to shrink (**vor** +*dat* from); **vor nichts** ~ (*völlig skrupellos sein*) to stop at nothing; (*keine Angst haben*) to not flinch at anything **2.** (*erschrecken*) to start back

zurück|sehnen *vr* **sich** *akk* **nach Hause** ~ to long to return home

zurück|stecken I. *vt* to put back *sep* **II.** *vi* to back down

zurück|stehen *vi irreg* **1.** (*weiter entfernt stehen*) to stand back **2.** (*hintangesetzt werden*) [**hinter jdm**] ~ to be behind [sb]

zurück|stellen *vt* **1.** (*wieder hinstellen*) to put back *sep* **2.** (*nach hinten stellen*) to move back *sep* **3.** (*Heizung*) to turn down *sep* **4.** (*aufschieben*) to put back *sep*; (*verschieben*) to postpone; **die Uhr** ~ to turn back *sep* the clock **5.** (*Wünsche*) to put aside *sep* **6.** *österr* (*zurückgeben*) to return

zurück|stufen *vt* to downgrade

zurück|treten *vi irreg sein* **1.** (*nach hinten treten*) to step back (**von** +*dat* from) **2.** (*von einem Amt*) to resign

zurück|versetzen* *vr* **sich** *akk* ~ to be transported back

zurück|weichen *vi irreg sein* to draw back (**vor** +*dat* from)

zurück|weisen *vt irreg* **jdn ~** to turn away *sep* sb; **etw ~** to reject sth

zurück|werfen *vt irreg* **1.** (*jdm etw wieder zuwerfen*) to throw back *sep* **2.** (*Position verschlechtern*) **das wirft uns um Jahre zurück** that will set us back years

zurück|zahlen *vt* [jdm] **etw ~** to repay [sb] sth

zurück|ziehen *irreg* **I.** *vt* **1.** (*nach hinten ziehen*) to pull back *sep;* (*Vorhang*) to draw back *sep* **2.** (*widerrufen*) to withdraw **II.** *vr* **sich** *akk* **~** to withdraw (**aus** +*dat* from) **III.** *vi sein* **nach Hamburg ~** to move back to Hamburg

zu|rufen *vt irreg* **jdm etw ~** to shout sth to sb

zurzeit [tsur·'tsait] *adv* at present

Zusage ['tsu·za·gə] *f* acceptance

zu|sagen I. *vt* to promise **II.** *vi* **jdm ~ 1.** (*die Teilnahme versichern*) to accept sb **2.** (*gefallen*) to appeal to sb

zusammen [tsu·'za·mən] *adv* **1.** (*gemeinsam*) together (**mit** +*dat* with); **mit jdm ~ sein** to be with sb **2.** (*ein Paar sein*) **~ sein** to be going out **3.** (*insgesamt*) altogether

Zusammenarbeit *f kein pl* cooperation

zusammen|arbeiten *vi* **mit jdm ~** to cooperate [*o* work [together]] with sb

zusammen|bauen *vt* to assemble

zusammen|beißen *vt* **die Zähne ~** to clench one's teeth

zusammen|bleiben *vi irreg sein* to stay together; **mit jdm ~** to stay with sb

zusammen|brechen *vi irreg sein* to collapse

zusammen|bringen *vt irreg* **1.** (*in Kontakt bringen*) **jdn** [mit jdm] **~** to introduce sb [to sb] **2.** (*anhäufen*) to amass

Zusammenbruch *m* collapse

zusammen|drücken *vt* **1.** (*zerdrücken*) to crush **2.** (*aneinanderdrücken*) to press together

zusammen|fahren *vi irreg sein* to start; (*vor Schmerzen*) to flinch

zusammen|fallen *vi irreg sein* **1.** (*einstürzen*) [in sich] **~** to collapse; (*Gebäude a.*) to cave in **2.** (*gleichzeitig stattfinden: Ereignisse*) to coincide

zusammen|falten *vt* to fold [up *sep*]

zusammen|fassen I. *vt* **1.** (*resümieren*) to summarize **2.** (*vereinigen*) **jdn/ etw in etw** *dat* **~** to unite sb/sth into sth; **die Bewerber in Gruppen ~** to divide the applicants into groups **II.** *vi* to summarize; **..., wenn ich kurz ~ darf** to sum up, ...

Zusammenfassung *f* summary

zusammen|fügen I. *vt* to assemble; **die Teile eines Puzzles ~** to piece together a jigsaw puzzle **II.** *vr* **die Teile fügen sich nahtlos zusammen** the parts fit together seamlessly

zusammen|führen *vt* to bring together *sep;* (*eine Familie*) to reunite

zusammen|gehören * *vi* **1.** (*zueinander gehören*) to belong together **2.** (*ein Ganzes bilden*) to go together; (*Socken*) to form a pair

Zusammengehörigkeit <-> *f kein pl* unity

Zusammengehörigkeitsgefühl *nt kein pl* sense of togetherness

zusammengesetzt *adj* compound *attr*

zusammengestöpselt [tsu·'za·mən·gə·ʃtœp·slt] *adj pej fam* [hastily] thrown together

zusammengewürfelt *adj* mismatched

Zusammenhalt *m kein pl* solidarity

zusammen|halten *irreg* **I.** *vi* to stick together **II.** *vt* **1.** (*beisammenhalten*) **seine Gedanken ~** to keep one's thoughts together; **sein Geld ~ müssen** to have to be careful with one's money **2.** (*verbinden*) to hold together

Zusammenhang <-[e]s, -hänge> *m* connection; (*Verbindung*) link (**zwischen** +*dat* between); **jdn/etw mit etw** *dat* **in ~ bringen** to connect sb/sth with [*o* to] sth; **etw aus dem ~ reißen** to take sth out of context; **im ~ mit etw** *dat* in connection with [*o* to] sth; **im ~ mit etw** *dat* **stehen** to be connected with [*o* to] sth

zusammen|hängen *vi irreg* **1.** (*in Zusammenhang stehen*) **mit etw** *dat* **~** to be connected with [*o* to] sth **2.** (*verbunden sein*) to be joined [together]

zusammenhängend I. *adj* **1.** (*kohä-*

Z

rent) coherent **2.** (*betreffend*) **mit etw** *dat* ~ connected with [*o* to] sth **II.** *adv* coherently

zusammenhang(s)los I. *adj* incoherent **II.** *adv* incoherently

zusammen|klappen I. *vt haben* to fold up *sep* **II.** *vi sein a. fig fam* to collapse

zusammen|kommen *vi irreg sein* **1.** (*sich treffen*) to come together; **mit jdm** ~ to meet sb; **zu einer Besprechung** ~ to get together for a discussion **2.** (*sich akkumulieren*) to combine; **heute kommt wieder alles zusammen!** it's another of those days! **3.** (*Schulden*) to mount [up]; (*Spenden*) to be collected

zusammen|krachen *vi sein fam* **1.** (*einstürzen: Brücke*) to crash down; (*Bett, Stuhl*) to collapse with a crash; (*Börse, Wirtschaft*) to crash **2.** (*zusammenstoßen*) to smash together; (*Auto a.*) to crash [into each other]

zusammen|laufen *vi irreg sein* to meet (**in** +*dat* at), to converge (**in** +*dat* at); (*Flüsse*) to flow together; (*Menschen*) to gather

zusammen|leben *vi* to live together

Zusammenleben *nt kein pl* living together *no art*

zusammen|legen I. *vt* **1.** (*zusammenfalten*) to fold [up *sep*] **2.** (*vereinigen*) to combine (**mit** +*dat* with), to join **II.** *vi* (*Geld sammeln*) to pitch in

zusammen|nehmen *irreg* **I.** *vt* to summon [up *sep*]; **den Verstand** ~ to get one's thoughts together; **alles zusammengenommen** all in all **II.** *vr* **sich** *akk* ~ to control oneself

zusammen|passen *vi* (*Menschen*) to suit each other; **gut/schlecht** ~ to be well-matched/a poor match; (*Farben*) to go together; (*Kleidungsstücke*) to match

Zusammenprall *m* collision

zusammen|prallen *vi sein* to collide

zusammen|pressen *vt* to press together *sep*; **die Faust** ~ to clench one's fist; **zusammengepresste Lippen** pinched lips

zusammen|rechnen *vt* to add up *sep*; **alles zusammengerechnet** all in all

zusammen|reimen *vr* **sich** *dat* **etw** ~ to put two and two together from [doing] sth

zusammen|reißen *vr irreg fam* **sich** *akk* ~ to pull oneself together, to get a grip *fam*

zusammen|rücken I. *vi sein* (*enger aneinanderrücken*) to move up closer; (*enger zusammenhalten*) to join in a common cause **II.** *vt haben* to move closer together

zusammen|schlagen *vt irreg haben* **1.** (*verprügeln*) to beat up *sep* **2.** (*zertrümmern*) to smash [up *sep*]

zusammen|schließen *irreg* **I.** *vt* to lock together *sep* **II.** *vr* **sich** *akk* ~ **1.** (*sich vereinigen*) to join together **2.** (*sich verbinden*) to join forces

Zusammenschluss [RR], **Zusammenschluß** [ALT] *m* union; (*Firmen*) merger

zusammen|schreiben *vt irreg* to write as one word

zusammen|schustern *vt pej fam* to throw together *sep*

Zusammensein <-s> *nt kein pl* meeting; (*zwanglos*) get-together

zusammen|setzen I. *vt* **1.** (*aus Teilen herstellen*) to assemble **2.** (*nebeneinandersetzen*) **Schüler/Tischgäste** ~ to seat students/guests beside each other **II.** *vr* **1.** (*sich zueinandersetzen*) **sich** *akk* ~ to sit together; (*um etw zu besprechen*) to get together **2.** (*bestehen*) **sich** *akk* **aus etw** *dat* ~ to be composed of sth

Zusammensetzung <-, -en> *f* **1.** (*Struktur*) composition; (*Mannschaft*) lineup **2.** (*Kombination der Bestandteile*) ingredients *pl*; (*Rezeptur, Präparat*) composition; (*Teile*) assembly

Zusammenspiel *nt kein pl* **1.** sport teamwork **2.** mus ensemble playing **3.** *fig* interplay

zusammen|stellen *vt* **1.** (*auf einen Fleck stellen*) to place side by side **2.** (*aufstellen*) to compile; (*Delegation*) to assemble

Zusammenstoß *m* **1.** (*Zusammenprall*) collision **2.** (*Auseinandersetzung*) clash

zusammen|stoßen *vi irreg sein* **1.** (*kol-*

lidieren) to collide; **mit jdm ~** to bump into sb **2.** (*aneinandergrenzen*) to adjoin

usammen|stürzen *vi sein* to collapse

usammen|tragen *vt irreg* to collect

usammen|treffen *vi irreg sein* **1.** (*sich treffen*) to meet; **mit jdm ~** to meet sb; (*unverhofft*) to encounter sb **2.** (*Umstände*) to coincide

usammentreffen *nt* **1.** (*Treffen*) meeting **2.** (*von Umständen*) coincidence

usammen|tun *irreg* **I.** *vt fam* to put together **II.** *vr fam* **sich** *akk* **~** to get together

usammen|wirken *vi* **1.** (*gemeinsam tätig sein*) to work together **2.** (*vereint wirken*) to combine

usammen|zählen *vt* to add up *sep;* **alles zusammengezählt** all in all

usammen|ziehen *irreg* **I.** *vi sein* to move in together **II.** *vr* **sich** *akk* **~ 1.** (*sich verengen*) to contract; (*Schlinge*) to tighten **2.** (*Sturm, Unheil*) to be brewing; (*Wolken*) to gather **III.** *vt* **die Augenbrauen ~** to frown

Zusatz ['tsu:·zats] *m* **1.** (*zugefügter Teil*) appendix **2.** (*Nahrungszusatz*) additive; **ohne ~ von Farbstoffen** no artificial colors added

Zusatzgerät *nt* attachment; COMPUT peripheral [device]

usätzlich ['tsu:·zɛts·lɪç] **I.** *adj* further *attr;* (*Kosten*) additional **II.** *adv* in addition; **jdn ~ belasten** to put extra pressure on sb

zu|schauen *vi s.* **zusehen**

Zuschauer(in) <-s, -> *m(f)* **1.** SPORT spectator; TV viewer **2.** FILM, THEAT **die ~** the audience

Zuschauerraum *m* auditorium

Zuschauertribüne *f* stands *pl*

zu|schicken *vt* to send; **sich** *dat* **etw ~ lassen** to send for sth

Zuschlag <-[e]s, Zuschläge> *m* **1.** (*Preisaufschlag*) surcharge **2.** (*zusätzliches Entgelt*) bonus

zu|schlagen *irreg* **I.** *vt haben* **1.** (*schließen*) to slam [shut] *sep;* (*Buch*) to close **2.** (*zuspielen*) **jdm den Ball ~** to kick [*o* hit] the ball to sb **II.** *vi* **1.** *haben* (*einen Hieb versetzen*) to strike **2.** *sein*

(*Tür*) to slam shut

zu|schließen *vt irreg* to lock

zu|schneiden *vt irreg* **1.** MODE (*Stoff*) to cut out *sep* **2.** *fig* **auf jdn [genau] zugeschnitten sein** to be cut out for sb

zu|schnüren *vt* **1.** (*durch Schnüren verschließen*) to tie **2.** *fig* **die Angst schnürte ihr die Kehle zu** she was choked with fear

zu|schreiben *vt irreg* **1.** (*beimessen*) **jdm etw ~** to attribute sth to sb **2.** (*zur Last legen*) **jdm/etw die Schuld an etw** *dat* **~** to blame sb/sth for sth

Zuschrift *f geh* reply

zuschulden, zu Schulden RR [tsu·ʃʊl·dn̩] *adv* **sich** *dat* **etwas/nichts ~ kommen lassen** to do something/nothing wrong

Zuschuss RR <-es, Zuschüsse>, **Zuschuß** ALT <-sses, Zuschüsse> ['tsu:·ʃʊs] *m* subsidy

zu|sehen *vi irreg* **1.** (*mit Blicken verfolgen*) to watch **2.** (*etw geschehen lassen*) **etw ~** to sit back and watch sth; **tatenlos musste er ~, wie ...** he could only stand and watch while ... **3.** (*dafür sorgen*) **~, dass ...** to see [to it] that ...

zusehends ['tsu:·ze:·ənts] *adv* noticeably

zu|senden *vt irreg s.* **zuschicken**

zu|setzen **I.** *vt* (*etw* *dat*) **etw ~** to add sth [to sth] **II.** *vi* (*bedrängen*) **jdm ~** to badger sb

zu|sichern *vt* **jdm etw ~** to assure sb of sth; **jdm seine Hilfe ~** to promise to help sb

zu|spielen *vt* **1.** SPORT **jdm den Ball ~** to pass the ball to sb **2.** (*zukommen lassen*) **etw der Presse ~** to leak sth [to the press]

zu|spitzen **I.** *vr* **sich** *akk* **~** to come to a head **II.** *vt* to sharpen

Zuspruch *m kein pl* **1.** (*Popularität, Anklang*) **etw erfreut sich großen ~s** sth is very popular **2.** (*Worte*) **ermutigender ~** words of encouragement

Zustand <-[e]s, Zustände> ['tsu:·ʃtant] *m* **1.** (*Verfassung*) state, condition; **im wachen ~** while awake **2.** *pl* (*Verhältnisse*) conditions; **das ist doch kein ~!**

what a disgrace!

zustande, zu Stande ^{RR} [tsu·'ʃtan·də] *adv* etw ~ **bringen** to manage [to do] sth; **die Arbeit ~ bringen** to get the work done; **eine Einigung ~ bringen** to reach an agreement; **~ kommen** to materialize; (*stattfinden*) to take place

zuständig ['tsu·ʃtɛn·dɪç] *adj* responsible; **der ~e Beamte** the official in charge; **dafür ist er ~** that's his responsibility

zu|stecken *vt* **jdm etw ~** to slip sb sth

zu|stehen *vi irreg* **1.** (*gehören*) **etw steht jdm zu** sb is entitled to sth **2.** (*zukommen*) **es steht dir nicht zu, so über ihn zu reden** it's not for you to speak of him like that

zu|stellen *vt* **1.** *form* (*überbringen*) **[jdm] etw ~** to deliver sth [to sb] **2.** *fam* (*blockieren*) to block

Zustellung <-, -en> *f* delivery

zu|stimmen *vi* **jdm/etw** *dat* **~** to agree [with sb/to sth]

Zustimmung *f* agreement; (*Einwilligung*) consent

zu|stoßen *irreg* **I.** *vi sein* **jdm ~** to happen to sb **II.** *vt* **die Tür mit dem Fuß ~** to kick the door shut

zutage, zu Tage ^{RR} [tsu·'ta:·gə] *adj* etw **~ bringen** to bring sth to light; **~ treten** to come to light

zu|teilen *vt* to allocate; **jdm eine Aufgabe/Rolle ~** to assign a task/role to sb

zuteil|werden ^{RR} [tsu·'tail-] *vi* **jdm wird etw zuteil** sb is given sth; **jdm etw ~ lassen** to grant sb sth

zutiefst [tsu·'ti:·fst] *adv* deeply

zu|trauen *vt* **jdm viel Mut ~** to believe sb has great courage; **sich** *dat* **nichts ~** to have no self-confidence; **sich** *dat* **zu viel ~** to take on too much; **das hätte ich dir nie zugetraut!** I never would have expected that from you!

Zutrauen <-s> *nt kein pl* confidence (**zu** +*dat* in)

zutraulich ['tsu·trau·lɪç] *adj* trusting; (*Hund*) friendly

zu|treffen *vi irreg* **1.** (*richtig sein*) to be correct; (*wahr sein*) to be true **2.** (*anwendbar sein*) **auf jdn [nicht] ~** to [not] apply to sb; **genau auf jdn ~** (*Beschreibung*) to fit sb['s description] perfectly

zutreffend I. *adj* **1.** (*richtig*) correc **Z~es bitte ankreuzen** [please] chec where applicable **2.** (*anwendbar*) **ein auf jdn ~e Beschreibung** a fitting de scription sb **II.** *adv* correctly

Zutritt *m kein pl* admission (**zu** +*dat* to (*Zugang*) access; **[keinen] ~ zu etw** *da* **haben** to [not] be admitted to sth; **~ ver boten!** [*o* kein ~!] no admittance

Zutun *nt* **ohne jds ~** (*ohne jds Hilfe* without sb's help; (*ohne jds Schula* through no fault of sb's own

zuverlässig ['tsu:·fɛg·lɛ·sɪç] *adj* reliable

Zuverlässigkeit <-> *f* kein pl reliabilit

Zuversicht <-> ['tsu:·fɛg·zɪçt] *f* kein p confidence

zuversichtlich *adj* confident

zuvor [tsu·'fo:ɐ̯] *adv* before; (*zunächst* beforehand; **im Jahr ~** the year before **noch nie ~** never before

zuvor|kommen *vi irreg sein* **1.** (*schnel ler handeln*) **jdm ~** to beat sb to i **2.** (*verhindern*) **etw** *dat* **~** to forestall

zuvorkommend I. *adj* (*gefällig*) accom modating; (*höflich*) courteous **II.** *ad* (*gefällig*) obligingly; (*höflich*) courte ously

Zuvorkommenheit <-> *f* kein pl cour tesy

Zuwachs <-es, Zuwächse> ['tsu:·vaks *m* increase

zu|wachsen *vi irreg sein* **1.** (*überwu chert werden*) to become overgrowr **2.** (*Wunde*) to heal [over *o* up]]

Zuwachsrate *f* growth rate

zuwege, zu Wege ^{RR} [tsu·'ve:·gə] *ad* **gut ~ sein** to be in good health; **etw ~ bringen** to achieve sth

zu|weisen *vt irreg* **jdm etw ~** (*Aufgabe* to assign sth to sb

zu|wenden *irreg* **I.** *vt* **jdm das Gesicht/ den Rücken ~** to turn one's face to ward/back on sb; **etw** *dat* **seine Auf merksamkeit ~** to turn one's attention to sth **II.** *vr* **sich** *akk* **jdm/etw ~** to de vote oneself to sb/sth; **wollen wir uns dem nächsten Thema ~?** shall we g on to the next topic?

Zuwendung *f* **1.** *kein pl* (*intensive Hin wendung*) love and care **2.** (*Geld*) [fi nancial] contribution

:uwider¹ [tsu·ˈviː·dɐ] *adv* jdm ist jd/ etw ~ sb finds sb/sth unpleasant; (*stärker*) sb loathes sb/sth

:uwider² [tsu·ˈviː·dɐ] *präp* etw *dat* ~ contrary to sth; **allen Verboten** ~ in defiance of all bans

:u|ziehen *irreg* **I.** *vt haben* **1.** (*Schnur*) to tighten **2.** (*Gardinen*) to draw; (*Tür*) to pull **3.** (*Experten, Gutachter*) to consult **II.** *vr haben* **1.** (*erleiden*) **sich** *dat* **eine Krankheit** ~ to catch a disease; **sich** *dat* **eine Verletzung** ~ to sustain an injury *form* **2.** (*einhandeln*) **sich** *dat* **jds Zorn** ~ to incur sb's wrath *form* **3.** (*sich eng zusammenziehen*) **sich** *akk* ~ to tighten **III.** *vi sein* to move into the area

:uzüglich [ˈtsuː·tsy·ɡ·lɪç] *präp* ~ **einer S.** *gen* plus sth

:wang [tsvaŋ] *imp von* **zwingen**

Zwang <-[e]s, Zwänge> [tsvaŋ] *m* **1.** (*Gewalt*) force; (*Druck*) pressure; **gesellschaftliche Zwänge** social constraints **2.** (*Notwendigkeit*) compulsion; **aus** ~ out of necessity

zwängen [ˈtsvɛŋ·ən] *vt* **Sachen in einen Koffer** ~ to cram things into a suitcase; **sich** *akk* **durch die Menge** ~ to force one's way through the crowd

zwanglos I. *adj* (*ungezwungen*) casual; (*ohne Förmlichkeit*) informal **II.** *adv* (*ungezwungen*) casually; (*ohne Förmlichkeit*) informally

Zwangsarbeit *f* kein pl hard labor

Zwangsjacke *f* straitjacket

Zwangslage *f* predicament

zwangsläufig I. *adj* inevitable **II.** *adv* inevitably; **dazu musste es ja ~ kommen** it had to happen

Zwangsräumung *f* eviction

Zwangsversteigerung *f* foreclosure sale

zwangsweise I. *adj* compulsory **II.** *adv* compulsorily

zwanzig [ˈtsvan·tsɪç] *adj* twenty; *s. a.* **achtzig 1, 2**

zwanzigjährig, 20-jährig ᴿᴿ [ˈtsvan·tsɪç· jɛː·rɪç] *adj* twenty-year-old *attr*; twenty years old *pred*

zwanzigste(r, s) [ˈtsvan·tsɪç·stə, -stə, -stəs] *adj* **1.** (*an zwanzigster Stelle*) twentieth; *s. a.* **achte(r, s) 1 2**. **2.** (*Datum*)

twentieth, 20th; *s. a.* **achte(r, s) 2**

zwar [tsvaːɐ̯] *adv* (*einschränkend*) **sie ist ~ 47, sieht aber wie 30 aus** she may be 47, but she looks like 30; **das mag ~ stimmen, aber ...** that may be true, but ...; **und ~** namely

Zweck <-[e]s, -e> [tsvɛk] *m* **1.** (*Verwendungszweck*) purpose; **ein guter ~** a good cause **2.** (*Absicht*) aim; **seinen ~ verfehlen** to fail to achieve its/one's object; **zu welchem ~?** for what purpose? **3.** (*Sinn*) point; **das hat doch alles keinen ~!** there's no point in any of that ▸ **der ~ heiligt die Mittel** *prov* the end justifies the means

zweckentfremden * *vt* to use for an unintended purpose

zwecklos *adj* futile

zweckmäßig *adj* **1.** (*geeignet*) suitable **2.** (*sinnvoll*) appropriate

zwecks [tsvɛks] *präp* ~ **einer S.** *gen* for the purpose of sth

zwei [tsvai] *adj* two; *s. a.* **acht¹**

Zweibettzimmer *nt* double room

zweideutig [ˈtsvai·dɔy·tɪç] **I.** *adj* ambiguous; (*anrüchig*) suggestive **II.** *adv* ambiguously; (*anrüchig*) suggestively

zweidimensional I. *adj* two-dimensional **II.** *adv* in two dimensions

Zweidrittelmehrheit *f* two-thirds majority

zweifach, 2fach [ˈtsvai·fax] **I.** *adj* **die ~e Menge** twice as much; **in ~er Ausfertigung** in duplicate **II.** *adv* **etw ~ ausfertigen** to issue sth in duplicate

Zweifamilienhaus [tsvai·fa·ˈmiː·ljən· haus] *nt* two-family house

Zweifel <-s, -> [ˈtsvai·fl̩] *m* doubt; **da habe ich meine ~!** I'm not sure about that!; **jdm kommen ~** sb begins to doubt; **es steht außer ~, dass ...** it is beyond [all] doubt that ...

zweifelhaft *adj* **1.** (*anzuzweifeln*) doubtful **2.** *pej* dubious

zweifellos [ˈtsvai·fl̩·loːs] *adv* undoubtedly

zweifeln [ˈtsvai·fl̩n] *vi* **an jdm/etw ~** to doubt sb/sth; **[daran] ~, ob ...** to doubt whether ...

Zweifelsfall *m* **im ~** if [*o* when] in doubt

Z

Zweig <-[e]s, -e> [tsvaik] m 1. (*Ast*) branch; (*kleiner*) twig 2. (*Sparte*) branch ▸ **auf keinen grünen ~ kommen** *fam* to get nowhere

zweigleisig [ˈtsvai·glai·zɪç] I. *adj* two-track *attr* II. *adv* 1. on two tracks 2. *fig* **~ fahren** to pursue a dual-track policy

Zweigstelle f branch office

zweihundert [ˈtsvai·ˈhʊn·dɐt] *adj* two hundred

zweijährig, 2-jährigRR *adj* 1. (*Alter*) two-year-old *attr*; two years old *pred*; *s. a.* **achtjährig** 1 2. (*Zeitspanne*) two-year *attr*; two years *pred*; *s. a.* **achtjährig** 2

Zweikampf m duel

Zweiklassengesellschaft f SOZIOL, POL divided society

zweimal, 2-malRR [ˈtsvai·maːl] *adv* twice, two times; **sich** *dat* **etw ~ überlegen** to think over *sep* sth carefully; *s. a.* **achtmal**

Zweirad nt (*Fahrrad*) bicycle; (*Motorrad*) motorcycle

zweireihig [ˈtsvai·rai·ɪç] *adj* (*Anzug*) double-breasted

zweischneidig [ˈtsvai·ʃnai·dɪç] *adj* two-edged ▸ **ein ~es Schwert** a double-edged sword

zweisprachig [ˈtsvai·ʃpraː·xɪç] I. *adj* bilingual II. *adv* **~ erzogen sein** to be brought up speaking two languages

zweit [tsvait] *adv* **wir sind zu ~** there are two of us

zweitens [ˈtsvai·tn̩s] *adv* secondly; (*bei Aufzählung a.*) second

zweitklassig *adj pej* second-rate

Zweitstimme f second vote

Zweitürer m two-door [car]

Zweitwohnung f second home

Zwerchfell [ˈtsvɛr·çfɛl] nt diaphragm

Zwerg(in) <-[e]s, -e> [tsvɛrk] m(f) dwarf

Zwergwuchs m dwarfism

Zwetschge <-, -n> [ˈtsvɛtʃ·gə] f damson plum

Zwetschgenwasser nt plum brandy

zwicken [ˈtsvɪ·kn̩] vt, vi to pinch

Zwickmühle f ▸ **in der ~ sein** *fam* to be in a dilemma

Zwieback <-[e]s, -e> [ˈtsviː·bak] m zwieback

Zwiebel <-, -n> [ˈtsviː·bl̩] f 1. (*Gemüse*■ onion 2. (*Blumenzwiebel*) bulb

Zwiebelturm m cupola

Zwielicht [ˈtsviː·lɪçt] nt kein pl twilight

zwielichtig *adj pej* dubious

Zwiespalt [ˈtsviː·ʃpalt] m kein pl con■ flict

zwiespältig [ˈtsviː·ʃpɛl·tɪç] *adj* conflict■ ing; (*Charakter*) ambivalent; (*Gefüh*■ *le*) mixed

Zwietracht <-> [ˈtsviː·traxt] f kein p■ discord

Zwilling <-s, -e> [ˈtsvɪ·lɪŋ] m 1. *meist* ■ twin 2. pl ASTROL Gemini

Zwillingsbruder m twin brother

Zwillingsschwester f twin sister

zwingen <zwang, gezwungen> [ˈtsv■ ŋən] I. vt to force; **gezwungen sein**■ **etw zu tun** to be forced into doing [*o t*■ do] sth II. vr **sich** akk **zu etw dat ~** t■ force oneself to do sth

zwingend I. *adj* urgent; (*Gründe*) com■ pelling II. *adv* **sich** akk **~ ergeben** t■ follow conclusively

Zwinger <-s, -> [ˈtsvɪ·ŋɐ] m cage

zwinkern [ˈtsvɪŋ·kɐn] vi to blink; (*mit e*■ *nem Auge*) to wink

Zwirn <-s, -e> [tsvɪrn] m thread

zwischen [ˈtsvɪ·ʃn̩] *präp* 1. +dat (*räum*■ *lich: zwischen 2 Personen, Dingen*) between; (*zwischen mehreren: unter*■ among[st] 2. +dat (*zeitlich*) between■ 3. +dat (*Beziehung*) **~ dir und mir** be■ tween you and me

Zwischenaufenthalt m stopover

Zwischenbemerkung f interruption

Zwischenbilanz f FIN interim balance

zwischendurch [tsvɪ·ʃn̩·ˈdʊrç] *ad*■ 1. *zeitlich* in between times 2. *örtlic*■ in between [them]

Zwischenfall m 1. (*unerwartetes Ereig*■ *nis*) incident 2. pl (*Ausschreitungen*■ serious incidents

Zwischengröße f in-between size

Zwischenhändler(in) m(f) middleman

Zwischenlandung f stopover

zwischenmenschlich *adj* interpersonal■

Zwischenprüfung f ≈ qualifying ex-■ ams npl

Zwischenraum m 1. (*Lücke*) gap■ 2. (*zeitlicher Intervall*) interval

Zwischenruf *m* interruption; **~e** heckling

Zwischenstation *f* stop; **in einer Stadt ~ machen** to stop [off] in a town

Zwischenstück *nt* connecting [*o* middle] piece

Zwischenzeit *f* **in der ~** [in the] meantime

Zwischenzeitlich *adv* meanwhile

Zwischenzeugnis *nt* (*vorläufiges Schulzeugnis*) midterm report card

Zwist <-es, -e> [tsvɪst] *m* discord

Zwitschern ['tsvɪt·ʃən] *vt, vi* to twitter, to chirp

Zwitter <-s, -> ['tsvɪ·tɐ] *m* hermaphrodite

Zwo [tsvoː] *adj fam* two

Zwölf [tsvœlf] *adj* twelve; *s. a.* **acht**[1]

Zwölffingerdarm [tsvœlf·'fɪŋɐ·darm] *m* duodenum

Zyankali <-s> [tsy̆·aːn·'kaː·li] *nt kein pl* potassium cyanide

Zyklon <-s, -e> [tsy·'kloːn] *m* cyclone

Zyklus <-, Zyklen> ['tsyː·klʊs] *m* cycle; (*von Vorträgen*) series

Zylinder <-s, -> [tsi·'lɪn·dɐ] *m* **1.** MATH, TECH cylinder **2.** (*Hut*) top hat

Zylinderkopf *m* cylinder head

Zyniker(in) <-s, -> ['tsyː·ni·kɐ] *m(f)* cynic

Zynisch ['tsyː·nɪʃ] **I.** *adj* cynical **II.** *adv* cynically

Zypern ['tsyː·pɐn] *nt* Cyprus; *s. a.* **Deutschland**

Zypresse <-, -n> [tsy·'prɛ·sə] *f* cypress

Zyste <-, -n> ['tsʏs·tə] *f* cyst

Z

A <pl -'s>, **a** <pl -'s> [eɪ] n **1.** (letter) A nt, a nt; ~ **as in Alpha** A wie Anton **2.** MUS A nt, a nt

[eɪ, ə], before vowel **an** [æn, ən] art indef **1.** (undefined) ein(e) **2.** after neg **not** ~ kein(e); **there was not** ~ **person to be seen** es war niemand zu sehen **3.** (one) ein(e); **can I have** ~ **knife and fork, please?** kann ich bitte Messer und Gabel haben?; **one and** ~ **half** eineinhalb **4.** before profession, nationality **she's** ~ **teacher** sie ist Lehrerin **5.** (per) **three times** ~ **day** dreimal täglich

aback [ə-'bæk] adv **to be taken** ~ erstaunt sein

abacus <pl -es> ['æb-ə-kəs] n MATH Abakus m

abandon [ə-'bæn-dən] vt **1.** (leave) verlassen; (baby) aussetzen; **to** ~ **sb to his/her fate** jdn seinem Schicksal überlassen **2.** zurücklassen; (car) stehen lassen **3.** aufgeben; (attempt) abbrechen

abandoned [ə-'bæn-dənd] adj **1.** (discarded) verlassen; (baby) ausgesetzt **2.** (building) leer stehend

abashed [ə-'bæʃt] adj verlegen

abattoir ['æb-ə-twar] n Schlachthof m

abbreviate [ə-'bri-vi-eɪt] vt abkürzen

abbreviation [ə,bri-vi-'eɪ-ʃən] n Abkürzung f

ABC [eɪ-bi-'si] n (alphabet) ABC nt; **as easy as** ~ kinderleicht

abdicate ['æb-dɪ-keɪt] vi (monarch) abdanken

abdomen ['æb-də-mən] n MED Unterleib m

abduction [æb-'dʌk-ʃən] n Entführung f

aberration [,æb-ə-'reɪ-ʃən] n (deviation) Abweichung f

abeyance [ə-'beɪ-əns] n **in** ~ [vorübergehend] außer Kraft [gesetzt]

abhorrent [æb-'hɔr-ənt] adj abscheulich

abide [ə-'baɪd] vt <abode or abided, abode or abided> usu neg (not like) ausstehen

◆ **abide by** vt (rules) befolgen; **to** ~ **by the law** sich an das Gesetz halten

ability [ə-'bɪl-ɪ-ti] n (capability) Fähig-

keit f; **to the best of my** ~ so gut ich kann

ablaze [ə-'bleɪz] adj **1.** (burning) **to be** ~ in Flammen stehen **2.** fig (impassioned) **to be** ~ **with anger** vor Zorn glühen

able ['eɪ-bəl] adj <more or better ~, most or best ~> (can do) **to** [not] **be** ~ **to do sth** etw [nicht] tun können

able-bodied [,eɪ-bəl-'bad-ɪd] adj gesund

ABM [eɪ-bi-'em] n abbr of **antiballistic missile** Antiraketenrakete f

abnormal [æb-'nɔr-məl] adj anormal; (weather a.) ungewöhnlich

abnormality [,æb-nɔr-'mæl-ɪ-ti] n **1.** MED Anomalie f **2.** (unusualness) Abnormität f

aboard [ə-'bɔrd] adv, prep (on plane, ship) an Bord; (on train) im Zug

abode [ə-'boud] n **1.** hum (home) Wohnung f **2. of no fixed** ~ ohne festen Wohnsitz

abolish [ə-'bal-ɪʃ] vt abschaffen; (law) aufheben

abolition [æb-ə-'lɪʃ-ən] n Abschaffung f; (of a law) Aufhebung f

abominable [ə-'bam-ə-nə-bəl] adj furchtbar

abomination [ə,bam-ə-'neɪ-ʃən] n (loathing) Abscheu m

abort [ə-'bɔrt] vt (baby, fetus) abtreiben; (pregnancy) abbrechen

abortion [ə-'bɔr-ʃən] n Abtreibung f

abortive [ə-'bɔr-tɪv] adj (attempt) gescheitert; (plan) misslungen

about [ə-'baʊt] I. prep **1.** (on the subject of) über +akk; **anxiety** ~ **the future** Angst f vor der Zukunft; **to ask sb** ~ **sth/sb** jdn nach etw/jdm fragen **2.** (affecting) gegen +akk; **to do something** ~ **sth** etw gegen etw machen **3.** after vb (expressing movement) **to wander** ~ **the house** im Haus herumlaufen ▶ **how** ~ **sb/sth?** wie wäre es mit jdm/etw?; **what** ~ **it?** was ist damit? II. adv **1.** (approximately) ungefähr; ~ **eight** [o'clock] [so] gegen acht [Uhr] **2.** (almost) fast **3.** (intending) **we're just** ~ **to have supper** wir wollen gerade zu Abend essen ▶ **that's** ~ **all** [or **it**] das wär's

about-face n **1.** esp MIL Kehrtwendung f

2. *fig* **they've done a complete ~** sie haben ihre Meinung um 180° geändert

above [ə·'bʌv] **I.** *prep* **1.** (*over*) über +*dat* **2.** (*greater than*) über +*akk;* **to be barely ~ freezing** kaum über dem Gefrierpunkt sein **3.** (*more importantly than*) **they value freedom ~ all else** für sie ist die Freiheit wichtiger als alles andere; **~ all** vor allem **II.** *adv* **1.** (*on higher level*) oberhalb, darüber; **they live in the apartment ~** sie wohnen in der Wohnung darüber **2.** (*overhead*) **from ~** von oben **3.** (*earlier in text*) oben **III.** *adj* obige(r, s); **the ~ address** die oben genannte Adresse

above'board *adj fam* einwandfrei

above'mentioned *adj* oben genannte(r, s)

abracadabra [ˌæb·rə·kə·'dæb·rə] *interj fam* Simsalabim!

abrasion [ə·'breɪ·ʒən] *n* (*injury*) Abschürfung *f*

abrasive [ə·'breɪ·sɪv] **I.** *adj* abreibend; **~ cleaner** Scheuermittel *nt* **II.** *n* MECH Schleifmittel *nt*

abreast [ə·'brest] *adv* **1.** (*side by side*) nebeneinander **2.** (*up to date*) **to keep ~ of sth** sich über etw *akk* auf dem Laufenden halten

abridge [ə·'brɪdʒ] *vt* kürzen

abroad [ə·'brɒd] *adv* (*in foreign country*) im Ausland; **to go ~** ins Ausland fahren

abrupt [ə·'brʌpt] *adj* **1.** (*sudden*) abrupt; (*departure*) plötzlich **2.** (*brusque*) schroff

ABS [ˌeɪ·bi·'es] *n abbr of* **antilock braking system** ABS *nt*

abscess <*pl* -es> ['æb·ses] *n* Abszess *m*

absence ['æb·səns] *n* **1.** (*nonappearance*) Abwesenheit *f*; (*from school, work*) Fehlen *nt* **2.** (*lack*) Fehlen *nt;* **in the ~ of sth** in Ermangelung einer S. *gen*

absent **I.** *adj* ['æb·sənt] **1.** (*not there*) abwesend; **to be ~ from work/school** auf der Arbeit/in der Schule fehlen **2.** (*lacking*) **to be ~** fehlen **II.** *vt* [əb·'sent] **to ~ oneself** sich zurückziehen

absentee [ˌæb·sən·'ti] *n* Abwesende(r) *f(m)*, Fehlende(r) *f(m)*

absenteeism [ˌæb·sən·'ti·ɪz·əm] *n* häufiges Fernbleiben

absent-'minded *adj* (*momentarily*) geis tesabwesend; (*habitually*) zerstreut

absent-mindedness *n* (*momentary* Geistesabwesenheit *f*; (*habitual*) Zer streutheit *f*

absolute ['æb·sə·lut] *adj* **1.** absolu **2.** (*angel*) wahr; (*disaster*) einzig; (*ru er*) unumschränkt

absolutely [ˌæb·sə·'lut·li] *adv* absolut; ~ **not!** nein, überhaupt nicht!; ~ **deli cious** einfach köstlich; ~ **nothing** über haupt nichts

absorb [əb·'sɔrb] *vt* **1.** (*soak up*) aufneh men **2.** (*blow*) abfangen; (*light*) absor bieren; (*noise*) dämpfen **3. to be ~e in sth** in etw *akk* vertieft sein

absorbent [əb·'sɔr·bənt] *adj* absorptions fähig; (*cotton, paper*) saugfähig

absorbing [əb·'sɔr·bɪŋ] *adj* fesselnd (*problem*) kniffelig

absorption [əb·'sɔrp·ʃən] *n* Aufnahme *f*

abstain [əb·'steɪn] *vi* **to ~ [from sth]** sich [einer S. *gen*] enthalten

abstinence ['æb·stə·nəns] *n* Abstinenz ,

abstract **I.** *adj* ['æb·strækt] abstrakt; ~ **noun** Abstraktum *nt* **II.** *n* **1.** (*summa ry*) Zusammenfassung *f* **2.** (*generalized form*) **the ~** das Abstrakte

abstraction [əb·'stræk·ʃən] *n* Abstraktion ,

absurd [əb·'sɜrd] *adj* absurd; **to look ~** lächerlich aussehen

abundance [ə·'bʌn·dəns] *n* Fülle *f*; **in ~** in Hülle und Fülle

abundant [ə·'bʌn·dənt] *adj* reichlich; (*harvest*) reich

abuse **I.** *n* [ə·'bjus] **1.** (*affront*) [**verbal**] ~ Beschimpfung[en] *f[pl]*; **a term of ~** ein Schimpfwort *nt* **2.** (*mistreatment, misuse*) Missbrauch *m;* **child ~** Kindes missbrauch *m* **II.** *vt* [ə·'bjuz] **1.** (*verbal ly*) beschimpfen **2.** (*maltreat, exploit*) missbrauchen

abusive [ə·'bju·sɪv] *adj* **1.** (*insulting*) beleidigend **2.** (*mistreating*) misshan delnd

abysmal [ə·'bɪz·məl] *adj* entsetzlich

abyss [ə·'bɪs] *n a. fig* Abgrund *m*

AC [ˌeɪ·'si] *n* **1.** *abbr of* **air conditioning 2.** *abbr of* **alternating current** WS

academic [ˌæk·ə·'dem·ɪk] *adj* akademisch; ~ **year** Studienjahr *nt*

academy [ə·ˈkæd·ə·mi] n Akademie f

accelerate [ək·ˈsel·ə·reɪt] vt, vi beschleunigen

acceleration [ək·ˌsel·ə·ˈreɪ·ʃən] n Beschleunigung f

accelerator [ək·ˈsel·ə·reɪ·tər] n (in car) Gas[pedal] nt

accent [ˈæk·sent] n 1. LING Akzent m 2. (stress) Betonung f; to put the ~ on sth etw in den Mittelpunkt stellen

accentuate [ək·ˈsen·tʃu·eɪt] vt betonen

accept [ək·ˈsept] vt 1. (take) annehmen; (award) entgegennehmen; (bribe) sich bestechen lassen 2. (acknowledge) anerkennen; (blame) auf sich akk nehmen; (decision) akzeptieren

acceptable [ək·ˈsep·tə·bəl] adj (satisfactory) akzeptabel (to für +akk)

acceptance [ək·ˈsep·təns] n 1. (accepting) Annahme f; (of idea) Zustimmung f 2. (recognition) Anerkennung f

accepted [ək·ˈsep·tɪd] adj anerkannt

access [ˈæk·ses] I. n Zugang m; (to information) Zugriff m II. vt COMPUT (data) zugreifen auf +akk

accessibility [æk·ˌses·ə·ˈbɪl·ɪ·ti] n Zugänglichkeit f

accessible [ək·ˈses·ə·bəl] adj 1. (approachable) [leicht] erreichbar 2. to be ~ to sb jdm zugänglich sein

accessory [ək·ˈses·ə·ri] n 1. FASHION Accessoire nt 2. (equipment) Zubehör nt 3. (criminal) Helfershelfer(in) m(f)

accident [ˈæk·sɪ·dənt] n 1. (with injury) Unfall m; car ~ Verkehrsunfall m 2. (chance) Zufall m; by ~ zufällig

accidental [ˌæk·sɪ·ˈden·təl] adj 1. (unintentional) unbeabsichtigt 2. (chance) zufällig

acclimate [ˈə·klaɪ·mɪt] vt, vi sich akklimatisieren (to an +akk); (to new conditions) sich gewöhnen

acclimation [æk·lə·ˈmeɪ·ʃən], **acclimatization** [ə·ˌklaɪ·mə·tɪ·ˈzeɪ·ʃən] n Akklimatisation f

acclimatize [ə·ˈklaɪ·mə·taɪz] vt, vi see acclimate

accommodate [ə·ˈkam·ə·deɪt] vt (have room for) unterbringen

accommodation [ə·ˌkam·ə·ˈdeɪ·ʃən] n (lodging) ~s pl Unterkunft f

accompaniment [ə·ˈkʌm·pə·ni·mənt] n Begleitung f; to be the perfect ~ to ... ideal passen zu ...

accompanist [ə·ˈkʌm·pə·nɪst] n MUS Begleiter(in) m(f)

accompany <-ie-> [ə·ˈkʌm·pə·ni] vt begleiten

accomplice [ə·ˈkam·plɪs] n Komplize m, Komplizin f

accomplish [ə·ˈkam·plɪʃ] vt schaffen; (goal) erreichen

accomplished [ə·ˈkam·plɪʃt] adj fähig; (actor) versiert

accomplishment [ə·ˈkam·plɪʃ·mənt] n 1. Vollendung f 2. usu pl (skill) Fähigkeit f

accord [ə·ˈkɔrd] n (treaty) Vereinbarung f ▶ of one's/its own ~ (voluntarily) von sich dat aus; (without external cause) von alleine

accordance [ə·ˈkɔr·dəns] prep in ~ with gemäß +dat

accordingly [ə·ˈkɔr·dɪŋ·li] adv (appropriately) [dem]entsprechend

according to [ə·ˈkɔr·dɪŋ·tə] prep nach +dat

accordion [ə·ˈkɔr·di·ən] n Akkordeon nt

account [ə·ˈkaʊnt] n 1. (description) Bericht m; by [or from] all ~s nach allem, was man so hört 2. (at bank) Konto nt 3. (bill) Rechnung f 4. (records) ~s pl [Geschäfts]bücher pl 5. (reason) on ~ of aufgrund +gen; on my ~ meinetwegen 6. (importance) to be of no ~ keinerlei Bedeutung haben ▶ to settle ~s with sb mit jdm abrechnen

◆ **account for** vt (explain) erklären

accountability [ə·ˌkaʊn·tə·ˈbɪl·ɪ·ti] n Verantwortlichkeit f

accountable [ə·ˈkaʊn·tə·bəl] adj verantwortlich

accountant [ə·ˈkaʊn·tənt] n [Bilanz]buchhalter(in) m(f)

accredit [ə·ˈkred·ɪt] vt 1. (approve) to have been ~ed (degree, school) anerkannt worden sein 2. (authorize) to be ~ed to sb/sth (ambassador) bei jdm/ etw akkreditiert sein

acct. n abbr of account Kto.

accumulate [ə·ˈkjum·jə·leɪt] vt, vi [sich] ansammeln

accuracy ['æk·jər·ə·si] *n* Genauigkeit *f*

accurate ['æk·jər·ɪt] *adj* genau

accusation [,æk·ju·'zeɪ·ʃən] *n* 1. (*charge*) Anschuldigung *f*; LAW Anklage *f* 2. (*accusing*) Vorwurf *m*

accusative [ə·'kju·zə·tɪv] *n* ~ **(case**) Akkusativ *m*

accuse [ə·'kjuz] *vt* 1. (*charge*) **to ~ sb [of sth]** jdn [wegen einer S. *gen*] anklagen 2. (*claim*) **to ~ sb of sth** jdn einer S. *gen* beschuldigen

accused <*pl* -> [ə·'kjuzd] *n* **the ~** die/der Angeklagte

accustomed [ə·'kʌs·təmd] *adj* **to be ~ to sth** etw gewohnt sein

AC/DC [,eɪ·si·'di·si] I. *n abbr of* **alternating current/direct current** WS/GS II. *adj sl* (*bisexual*) bi *fam*

ace [eɪs] I. *n* Ass *nt* II. *adj fam* klasse III. *vt fam* **to ~ a test** einen Test mit Leichtigkeit bestehen

acetic 'acid *n* Essigsäure *f*

ache [eɪk] I. *n* (*pain*) Schmerz[en] *m[pl]* II. *vi* (*feel pain*) schmerzen

achieve [ə·'tʃiv] *vt* erreichen; (*fame*) erlangen; (*success*) erzielen

achievement [ə·'tʃiv·mənt] *n* Leistung *f*

acid ['æs·ɪd] I. *n* 1. CHEM Säure *f* 2. *sl* (*LSD*) Acid *nt sl* II. *adj* sauer

acid 'rain *n* saurer Regen

acid test *n fig* Feuerprobe *f*

acknowledge [ək·'nɑl·ɪdʒ] *vt* 1. (*admit*) zugeben 2. (*respect*) anerkennen 3. (*greeting*) erwidern; (*receipt*) bestätigen

acne ['æk·ni] *n* Akne *f*

acorn ['eɪ·kɔrn] *n* Eichel *f*

acoustic [ə·'ku·stɪk] *adj* akustisch

acoustic gui'tar *n* Akustikgitarre *f*

acoustics [ə·'ku·stɪks] *n* Akustik *f*

acquaint [ə·'kweɪnt] *vt* vertraut machen

acquaintance [ə·'kweɪn·təns] *n* Bekannte(r) *f(m)*

acquiesce [,æk·wi·'es] *vi* **to ~ [to sth]** in etw *akk* einwilligen

acquire [ə·'kwaɪr] *vt* erwerben; (*reputation*) bekommen

acquisition [,æk·wɪ·'zɪʃ·ən] *n* 1. (*purchase*) Anschaffung *f* 2. (*acquiring*) Erwerb *m*; (*of company*) Übernahme *f*

acquit <-tt-> [ə·'kwɪt] *vt* freisprechen

acquittal [ə·'kwɪt·əl] *n* Freispruch *m*

acre ['eɪ·kər] *n* (*unit*) ≈ Morgen *m*

acrid ['æk·rɪd] *adj* (*smell*) stechend; (*smoke*) beißend

acrobat ['æk·rə·bæt] *n* Akrobat(in) *m(f)*

acrobatic [,æk·rə·'bæt·ɪk] *adj* akrobatisch

acronym ['æk·rə·nɪm] *n* Akronym *nt*

across [ə·'krɔs] I. *prep* 1. (*on other side of*) über +*dat*; ~ **town** am anderen Ende der Stadt 2. (*from one side to other*) über +*akk* ► **~ the board** allgemein II. *adv* 1. (*to other side*) hinüber; (*from other side*) herüber 2. (*on other side*) drüben; ~ **from sb/sth** jdm/etw gegenüber 3. (*wide*) breit ► **to get one's point ~** sich verständlich machen

act [ækt] I. *n* 1. (*deed*) Tat *f*; ~ **of kindness** Akt *m* der Güte 2. (*of a play*) Akt *m* 3. (*pretence*) Schau *f* ► **to get in on the ~** mitmischen; **to get one's ~ together** sich am Riemen reißen II. *vi* 1. (*take action*) handeln; **to ~ [up]on sb's advice** jds Rat befolgen 2. (*represent*) **to ~ for sb** jdn vertreten 3. (*behave*) sich benehmen 4. (*play*) spielen

act out *vt* (*realize*) ausleben

act up *vi fam* 1. (*person*) Theater machen 2. (*thing*) Ärger machen

acting ['æk·tɪŋ] *adj* stellvertretend

action ['æk·ʃən] *n* 1. (*activeness*) Handeln *nt*; (*proceeding*) Vorgehen *nt*; **course of ~** Vorgehensweise *f*; **to put into ~** in die Tat umsetzen 2. (*act*) Handlung *f*, Tat *f* 3. (*combat*) Einsatz *m*; **to go into ~** ins Gefecht ziehen; **to be killed in ~** fallen ► **to want a piece of the ~** eine Scheibe vom Kuchen abhaben wollen

action-packed *adj* spannungsgeladen

activate ['æk·tə·veɪt] *vt* aktivieren; (*alarm*) auslösen

active ['æk·tɪv] *adj* aktiv; (*children*) lebhaft

activist ['æk·tə·vɪst] *n* Aktivist(in) *m(f)*

activity [æk·'tɪv·ɪ·ti] *n* Aktivität *f*

actor ['æk·tər] *n* Schauspieler *m*

actress <*pl* -es> ['æk·trɪs] *n* Schauspielerin *f*

actual ['æk·tʃʊ·əl] *adj* (*real*) eigentlich; (*facts*) konkret; **in ~ fact** tatsächlich

actually ['æk·tʃʊ·ə·li] *adv* 1. (*in fact*) eigentlich 2. (*really*) wirklich; **did you ~ say that?** hast du das tatsächlich gesagt?

actuate ['æk·tʃʊ·eɪt] *vt* in Gang setzen

acupuncture ['æk·jʊ·pʌŋk·tʃər] *n* Akupunktur *f*

acute [ə·'kjut] *adj* 1. (*serious*) akut; (*anxiety*) ernsthaft 2. (*hearing*) fein; (*sense of smell*) ausgeprägt 3. (*angle*) spitz

acutely [ə·'kjut·li] *adv* äußerst

ad [æd] *n fam short for* **advertisement** Anzeige *f*

AD [,eɪ·'di] *adj abbr of* **anno Domini** n. Chr.

Adam's 'apple *n* Adamsapfel *m*

adapt [ə·'dæpt] **I.** *vt* 1. (*modify*) anpassen (**to** an +*akk*) 2. (*rewrite*) bearbeiten **II.** *vi* **to ~** (**to sth**) sich (einer S. *dat*) anpassen

adaptable [ə·'dæp·tə·bəl] *adj* anpassungsfähig

adaptation [,æd·æp·'teɪ·ʃən] *n* 1. (*adapting*) Anpassung *f* 2. (*modification*) Umbau *m*

adapter, adaptor [ə·'dæp·tər] *n* ELEC Adapter *m*

add [æd] *vt* 1. hinzufügen 2. MATH **to ~ [together]** addieren; **to ~ sth to sth** etw zu etw *dat* [dazu]zählen

◆**add up I.** *vi* 1. *fam* (*make sense*) **it doesn't ~ up** es macht keinen Sinn 2. (*total*) **to ~ up to sth** (*bill*) sich auf etw *akk* belaufen **II.** *vt* addieren

adder ['æd·ər] *n* Otter *f*

addict ['æd·ɪkt] *n* Süchtige(r) *f(m)*; **drug ~** Drogenabhängige(r) *f(m)*

addicted [ə·'dɪk·tɪd] *adj* süchtig (**to** nach +*dat*)

addiction [ə·'dɪk·ʃən] *n* Sucht *f*

addictive [ə·'dɪk·tɪv] *adj* süchtig

addition [ə·'dɪʃ·ən] *n* 1. MATH Addition *f* 2. (*extra*) Ergänzung *f* 3. **in ~** außerdem

additional [ə·'dɪʃ·ən·əl] *adj* zusätzlich; **~ charge** Aufpreis *m*, Zuschlag *m*

additionally [ə·'dɪʃ·ən·əl·i] *adv* außerdem

additive ['æd·ɪ·tɪv] *n* Zusatz *m*

address ['æd·res] **I.** *n* <*pl* -es> Adresse *f* **II.** *vt* 1. (*write address*) adressieren (**to** an +*akk*) 2. (*speak to*) anreden

addressee [æd·re·'si] *n* Empfänger(in) *m(f)*

adept [ə·'dept] *adj* geschickt (**at** in +*dat*)

adequacy ['æd·ɪ·kwə·si] *n* Angemessenheit *f*

adequate ['æd·ɪ·kwət] *adj* ausreichend

adhere [æd·'hɪr] *vi* kleben (**to** an +*akk*)

adhesive [æd·'hi·sɪv] **I.** *adj* haftend **II.** *n* Klebstoff *m*

adjacent [ə·'dʒeɪ·sənt] *adj* angrenzend

adjectival [,ædʒ·ɪk·'taɪ·vəl] *adj* adjektivisch

adjective ['ædʒ·ɪk·tɪv] *n* Adjektiv *nt*

adjoining [ə·'dʒɔɪ·nɪŋ] *adj* angrenzend

adjourn [ə·'dʒɜrn] **I.** *vt* (*interrupt*) unterbrechen; (*suspend*) verschieben **II.** *vi* (*stop temporarily*) eine Pause einlegen

adjust [ə·'dʒʌst] **I.** *vt* (*set*) [richtig] einstellen **II.** *vi* (*adapt*) **to ~ to sth** sich an etw *akk* anpassen

adjustable [ə·'dʒʌst·ə·bəl] *adj* verstellbar

adjustment [ə·'dʒʌst·mənt] *n* 1. (*mental*) Anpassung *f* 2. (*mechanical*) Einstellung *f*

ad-lib <-bb-> [,æd·'lɪb] *vt, vi* improvisieren

admin ['əd·mɪn] *n fam short for* **administration**

administration [əd·,mɪn·ɪ·'streɪ·ʃən] *n* 1. Verwaltung *f* 2. (*government*) Regierung *f*

administrative [əd·'mɪn·ɪ·streɪ·tɪv] *adj* administrativ, Verwaltungs-

administrator [əd·'mɪn·ɪ·streɪ·tər] *n* Verwaltungsbeamte(r) *m* /-beamtin *f*

admirable ['æd·mər·ə·bəl] *adj* bewundernswert

admiral ['æd·mər·əl] *n* Admiral(in) *m(f)*

admiration [,æd·mə·'reɪ·ʃən] *n* Bewunderung *f*

admire [əd·'maɪr] *vt* bewundern

admirer [əd·'maɪr·ər] *n* Anhänger(in) *m(f)*

admissible [æd·'mɪs·ə·bəl] *adj* zulässig

admission [æd·'mɪʃ·ən] *n* 1. Zutritt *m*; (*into a hospital*) Einlieferung *f* 2. (*entrance fee*) Eintritt[spreis] *m*

admit <-tt-> [æd·'mɪt] *vt* 1. (*acknowledge*) zugeben 2. (*allow entrance*) hereinlassen/hineinlassen; **to ~ sb to**

the hospital jdn ins Krankenhaus einliefern

admittance [æd·'mɪt·əns] n Zutritt m; **"no ~"** „Betreten verboten"

admittedly [æd·'mɪt·ɪd·li] adv zugegebenermaßen

adolescence [ˌæd·əl·'es·əns] n Jugend[zeit] f

adolescent [ˌæd·əl·'es·ənt] I. adj heranwachsend, jugendlich II. n Jugendliche(r) f/m)

adopt [ə·'dɑpt] vt 1. (raise) adoptieren 2. (put into practice) annehmen; (strategy) verfolgen

adoption [ə·'dɑp·ʃən] n 1. Adoption f 2. (taking on) Annahme f; (of a technology) Übernahme f

adorable [ə·'dɔr·ə·bəl] adj entzückend

adore [ə·'dɔr] vt 1. (love) über alles lieben 2. (like very much) **to ~ sth** etw wunderbar finden

adoring [ə·'dɔr·ɪŋ] adj (devoted) hingebungsvoll

adorn [ə·'dɔrn] vt schmücken

adrenalin(e) [ə·'dren·ə·lɪn] n Adrenalin nt

adrift [ə·'drɪft] adv **to cut ~** losmachen

adroit [ə·'drɔɪt] adj geschickt

adult [ə·'dʌlt] I. n Erwachsene(r) f/m) II. adj (grown-up) erwachsen; (animal) ausgewachsen; (behavior) reif

adult edu'cation n Erwachsenenbildung f

adultery [ə·'dʌl·tə·ri] n Ehebruch m

advance [əd·'væns] I. vi 1. (make progress) Fortschritte machen 2. (move forward) sich vorwärtsbewegen; MIL vorrücken II. vt 1. (career) vorantreiben 2. (money) vorschießen III. n 1. (progress) Fortschritt m 2. (ahead of time) **in ~** im Voraus IV. adj vorherig

advanced [əd·'vænst] adj 1. (in skills) fortgeschritten 2. (in development) fortschrittlich

advancement [əd·'væns·mənt] n 1. (furtherance) Förderung f 2. (in career) Aufstieg m

advance 'notice n Vorankündigung f

advantage [əd·'væn·tɪdʒ] n Vorteil m; **to take ~ of sb** pej jdn ausnutzen

advent ['æd·vent] n REL **A~** Advent m

adventure [æd·'ven·tʃər] n Abenteuer nt

adventurous [əd·'ven·tʃər·əs] adj (daring) abenteuerlustig

adverb ['æd·vɜrb] n Adverb nt

adverbial [æd·'vɜr·bi·əl] adj adverbial

adverse [æd·'vɜrs] adj ungünstig; (criticism, effect) negativ

advertise ['æd·vər·taɪz] I. vt Werbung machen für +akk; (in a newspaper) inserieren II. vi 1. (publicize) werben 2. (in a newspaper) inserieren

advertisement [ˌæd·vər·'taɪz·mənt] n Werbung f; (in a newspaper) Anzeige f; **TV ~** Werbespot m; fig Reklame f

advertising ['æd·vər·ˌtaɪ·zɪŋ] n Werbung f

'advertising agency n Werbeagentur f

'advertising campaign n Werbekampagne f

advice [æd·'vaɪs] n (recommendation) Rat m; **some ~** ein Rat[schlag] m; **to take sb's ~** jds Rat[schlag] m befolgen

advisable [æd·'vaɪ·zə·bəl] adj ratsam

advise [æd·'vaɪz] I. vt beraten; **to ~ sb to do sth** jdm [dazu] raten, etw zu tun II. vi raten

adviser, advisor [əd·'vaɪ·zər] n Berater(in) m(f)

advisory [æd·'vaɪ·zə·ri] adj beratend

aerate ['er·eɪt] vt durchlüften; (soil) auflockern

aerial ['er·i·əl] I. adj Luft- II. n Antenne f

aerobatics [ˌer·ə·'bæt·ɪks] n + sing vb Kunstflug m

aerobics [ə·'roʊ·bɪks] n (exercise) Aerobic nt

aerodynamic [ˌer·oʊ·daɪ·'næm·ɪk] adj aerodynamisch

aerodynamics [ˌer·oʊ·daɪ·'næm·ɪks] n Aerodynamik f

aeronautics [ˌer·ə·'nɔ·t̬ɪks] n + sing vb Luftfahrt[technik] f

aerosol ['er·ə·sɔl] n Spraydose f

aesthetic [es·'θet̬·ɪk] adj ästhetisch

afar [ə·'far] adv **from ~** aus der Ferne

affair [ə·'fer] n 1. (matter, event) Angelegenheit f 2. (situation, relationship) Affäre f

affect [ə·'fekt] vt **to ~ sb/sth** sich auf jdn/etw auswirken; (concern) jdn/etw

betreffen

affected [ə·ˈfek·tɪd] *adj* 1. (*insincere*) affektiert 2. (*influenced*) betroffen

affection [ə·ˈfek·ʃən] *n* Zuneigung *f*

affectionate [ə·ˈfek·ʃə·nɪt] *adj* liebevoll

affiliate [ə·ˈfɪl·i·eɪt] *n* Konzernunternehmen *nt*

affiliation [ə·ˌfɪl·i·ˈeɪ·ʃən] *n* Angliederung *f*

affirmative [ə·ˈfɜr·mə·tɪv] I. *adj* zustimmend; (*answer*) positiv II. *n* Bejahung *f*; **to answer in the ~** mit Ja antworten III. *interj* ~! jawohl!

affix [ə·ˈfɪks] *vt* (*attach*) befestigen (**to** an +*dat*); (*stick on*) ankleben (**to** an +*akk*)

afflict [ə·ˈflɪkt] *vt* plagen

affluence [ˈæf·lʊ·əns] *n* Wohlstand *m*

affluent [ˈæf·lʊ·ənt] *adj* reich

afford [ə·ˈfɔrd] *vt* (*have money, time for*) sich *dat* leisten; **you can't ~ to miss this opportunity** diese Gelegenheit darfst du dir nicht entgehen lassen

affordable [ə·ˈfɔr·də·bəl] *adj* erschwinglich

Afghan [ˈæf·gæn] I. *n* 1. (*person*) Afghane *m*, Afghanin *f* 2. (*dog*) Afghane *m* II. *adj* afghanisch

Afghanistan [æf·ˈgæn·ɪ·stæn] *n* Afghanistan *nt*

afloat [ə·ˈfloʊt] *adj a. fig* über Wasser; **to be ~** schwimmen

afraid [ə·ˈfreɪd] *adj* 1. (*frightened*) verängstigt; **to be ~** [of sb/sth] Angst haben [vor jdm/etw]; **to be ~ that ...** befürchten, dass ... 2. (*expressing regret*) **I'm ~ so** leider ja

Africa [ˈæf·rɪ·kə] *n* Afrika *nt*

African [ˈæf·rɪ·kən] I. *n* Afrikaner(in) *m(f)* II. *adj* afrikanisch

African American [ˌæf·rɪ·kən·ə·ˈmer·ɪ·kən], **Afro-American** [ˌæf·roʊ·ə·ˈmer·ɪ·kən] *n* Afroamerikaner(in) *m(f)*

after [ˈæf·tər] I. *prep* 1. (*later than*) nach +*dat*; **~ lunch** nach dem Mittagessen; **[a] quarter ~ six** [um] Viertel nach Sechs 2. (*following*) nach +*dat* 3. **~ all** schließlich; (*in spite of*) trotz +*gen*; **he couldn't come ~ all** er konnte doch nicht kommen II. *adv* danach; **shortly ~** kurz darauf

aftereffect *n* Nachwirkung *f*

aftermath [-mæθ] *n* Folgen *pl*

afternoon [ˌæf·tər·ˈnun] *n* Nachmittag *m*; **good ~!** guten Tag!; **late ~** am späten Nachmittag; **in the ~** am Nachmittag, nachmittags

aftershave *n* Aftershave *nt*

aftershock *n usu pl* GEOL Nachbeben *nt*

aftertaste *n* Nachgeschmack *m*

afterthought *n* **as an ~** im Nachhinein

afterward, **afterwards** [ˈæf·tər·wərdz] *adv* (*later*) später; **shortly ~** kurz danach

again [ə·ˈgen] *adv* 1. (*as a repetition*) wieder; (*one more time*) noch einmal; **~ and ~** immer wieder 2. (*anew*) noch einmal

against [ə·ˈgenst] I. *prep* gegen +*akk*; **~ one's better judgment** wider besseres Wissen II. *adv* gegen; **only 14 voted ~** es gab nur 14 Gegenstimmen

age [eɪdʒ] I. *n* 1. (*length of existence*) Alter *nt*; **he's about your ~** er ist ungefähr so alt wie du; **to be 45 years of ~** 45 [Jahre alt] sein; **sb looks their ~** man sieht jdm sein Alter an 2. (*era*) Zeitalter *nt* 3. (*long time*) **an ~** eine Ewigkeit; **the meeting took ~s** die Besprechung dauerte ewig [lang] II. *vi* altern III. *vt* (*make look older*) älter machen

age bracket *n* Altersgruppe *f*

aged¹ [eɪdʒd] *adj* **children ~ 8 to 12** Kinder [im Alter] von 8 bis 12 Jahren

aged² [ˈeɪ·dʒɪd] *adj* (*old*) alt

age group *n* Altersgruppe *f*

age limit *n* Altersgrenze *f*

agency [ˈeɪ·dʒən·si] *n* 1. (*private business*) Agentur *f* 2. (*of government*) Behörde *f*

agenda [ə·ˈdʒen·də] *n* Tagesordnung *f*

agent [ˈeɪ·dʒənt] *n* Agent(in) *m(f)*

aggravate [ˈæg·rə·veɪt] *vt* 1. (*worsen*) verschlechtern 2. *fam* (*annoy*) auf die Nerven gehen

aggravating [ˈæg·rə·veɪ·t̬ɪŋ] *adj fam* (*annoying*) ärgerlich

aggregate [ˈæg·rɪ·gɪt] *adj* Gesamt-

aggression [ə·ˈgreʃ·ən] *n* Aggression *f*; **act of ~** Angriffshandlung *f*

aggressive [ə·ˈgres·ɪv] *adj* aggressiv; (*salesman*) aufdringlich

agile [ˈædʒ·əl] *adj* geschickt; (*fingers*)

flink; (*mind*) rege

agility [ə·'dʒɪl·ɪ·t̬i] *n* Flinkheit *f*

aging ['eɪ·dʒɪŋ] *adj* (*person*) alternd; (*machinery*) veraltend

agitate ['ædʒ·ɪ·teɪt] *vt* 1. (*make nervous*) aufregen 2. (*shake*) schütteln

agitation [ˌædʒ·ɪ·'teɪ·ʃən] *n* Aufregung *f*

agitator ['ædʒ·ɪ·teɪ·t̬ər] *n* Agitator(in) *m(f)*

agnostic [æg·'nɑs·tɪk] *n* Agnostiker(in) *m(f)*

ago [ə·'goʊ] *adv* **a year ~** vor einem Jahr; **[not] long ~** vor [nicht] langer Zeit

agonize ['æg·ə·naɪz] *vi* **to ~ about** [*or* **over**] **sth** sich über etw *akk* den Kopf zermartern

agonizing ['æg·ə·naɪ·zɪŋ] *adj* (*pain*) unerträglich

agony ['æg·ə·ni] *n* Todesqualen *pl;* **to be in ~** große Schmerzen leiden

agree [ə·'gri] I. *vi* 1. (*have same opinion*) zustimmen; **to ~ with sb** mit etw *dat* einverstanden sein; **to ~ with sb** mit jdm einer Meinung sein 2. (*consent to*) zustimmen; **~d!** einverstanden! II. *vt* **to ~ that ...** sich darauf einigen, dass ...

agreeable [ə·'gri·ə·bəl] *adj* 1. (*pleasant*) angenehm; (*weather*) freundlich 2. (*acceptable*) **to be ~ to sb** für jdn akzeptabel sein

agreement [ə·'gri·mənt] *n* 1. (*same opinion*) Übereinstimmung *f;* **to be in ~ with sb** mit jdm übereinstimmen 2. (*contract*) Vertrag *m*

agricultural [ˌæg·rɪ·'kʌl·tʃər·əl] *adj* landwirtschaftlich

agriculture ['æg·rɪ·kʌl·tʃər] *n* Landwirtschaft *f*

aground [ə·'graʊnd] *adv* **to run ~** auf Grund laufen

ah [ɑ] *interj* (*in realization*) ach so; (*in happiness*) ah; (*in sympathy*) oh

ahead [ə·'hed] *adv* 1. (*in front*) vorn; **full speed ~** volle Kraft voraus; **to go ~** (*project*) vorangehen 2. (*in the future*) **to look ~** nach vorne sehen

AI [ˌer·'aɪ] *n* 1. COMPUT *abbr of* **artificial intelligence** künstliche Intelligenz 2. SCI *abbr of* **artificial insemination** künstliche Befruchtung

aid [eɪd] I. *n* 1. (*assistance*) Hilfe *f* 2. (*helpful tool*) [Hilfs]mittel *nt;* **hearing ~** Hörgerät *nt* II. *vt* helfen +*dat*

aide [eɪd] *n* 1. (*advisor*) Berater(in) *m(f)* 2. (*assistant*) Hilfskraft *f (im Unterricht)*

AIDS [eɪdz] *n abbr of* **acquired immune deficiency syndrome** Aids *nt*

aim [eɪm] I. *vi* 1. (*point*) zielen (**at** *au* +*akk*) 2. (*try to achieve*) **to ~ at** [*or* **for**] **sth** etw zum Ziel haben; **to ~ to please** gefallen wollen ▶ **to ~ high** hoch hi naus wollen II. *vt* **to ~ sth at sb/sth** mit etw *dat* auf jdn/etw zielen III. *n* (*goal*) Ziel *nt*

aimless ['eɪm·lɪs] *adj* ziellos

ain't [eɪnt] *sl* 1. = **am not, is not, are not** *see* **be** 2. = **has not, have not** *see* **have**

air [er] I. *n* 1. Luft *f;* **by ~** mit dem Flugzeug 2. TV, RADIO Äther *m;* **on/off the ~** auf Sendung/nicht mehr auf Sendung sein II. *vt* 1. (*ventilate*) lüften; (*clothes*) auslüften [lassen] 2. (*express: thoughts*) äußern III. *vi* 1. TV, RADIO gesendet werden 2. (*ventilate*) auslüften

'air bag *n* Airbag *m*

'airbase *n* Luftwaffenstützpunkt *m*

'airborne *adj* (*disease*) durch die Luft übertragen; **~ troops** Luftlandetruppen *pl*

'air brake *n* Druckluftbremse *f*

'air bubble *n* Luftblase *f*

'air-conditioned *adj* klimatisiert

'air conditioner *n* Klimaanlage *f*

'air conditioning *n* Klimaanlage *f*

'air-cooled *adj* luftgekühlt

'aircraft <*pl* -> *n* Luftfahrzeug *nt*

'aircraft carrier *n* Flugzeugträger *m*

'aircrew *n* Crew *f*, Flugpersonal *nt*

'airfield *n* Flugplatz *m*

'air force *n* Luftwaffe *f*

'air freight *n* Luftfracht *f*

airless ['er·lɪs] *adj* stickig

'airline *n* Fluggesellschaft *f*

'airliner *n* Verkehrsflugzeug *nt*

'airmail *n* Luftpost *f* II. *vt* per Luftpost schicken

'airman *n* MIL Flieger *m*

airplane ['er·pleɪn] *n* Flugzeug *nt*

'airport *n* Flughafen *m*

'air raid *n* Luftangriff *m*

'airspace *n* Luftraum *m*

'airstrip *n* Start- und Landebahn *f*

airtight *adj* luftdicht; *fig* hieb- und stichfest

air traffic *n* Flugverkehr *m*

air traffic con'trol *n* Flugleitung *f*

air traffic con'troller *n* Fluglotse *m*, Flug-
lotsin *f*

airway *n see* **airline**

airy ['eːr·i] *adj* luftig

aisle [aɪl] *n* Gang *m;* (*of church*) Sei-
tenschiff *nt*

AK *abbr of* **Alaska**

aka [ˌeɪ·keɪ·'eɪ] *abbr of* **also known
as** alias

AL, Ala. *abbr of* **Alabama**

Alabama [ˌæl·ə·'bæm·ə] *n* Alabama *nt*

alarm [ə·'lɑrm] **I.** *n* **1.** (*worry*) Angst *f;* **to
give sb cause for** ~ jdm einen Grund
zur Sorge geben **2.** (*signal*) Alarm *m*
3. (*device*) Alarmanlage *f* **II.** *vt* **1.** erschrecken **2.** (*warn of danger*) alarmieren

'alarm clock *n* Wecker *m*

alarming [ə·'lɑr·mɪŋ] *adj* (*worrying*) beunruhigend; (*frightening*) erschreckend

Alas. *abbr of* **Alaska**

Alaska [ə·'læs·kə] *n* Alaska *nt*

Albania [æl·'beɪ·ni·ə] *n* Albanien *nt*

albatross <*pl* -es> ['æl·bə·trɔs] *n* Al-
batros *m*

albino [æl·'baɪ·noʊ] *n* Albino *m*

album ['æl·bəm] *n* Album *nt*

alcohol ['æl·kə·hɔl] *n* Alkohol *m*

alcohol-free [ˌæl·kə·hɔl·'fri] *adj* alkoholfrei

alcoholic [ˌæl·kə·'hɔ·lɪk] **I.** *n* Alkoholi-
ker(in) *m(f)* **II.** *adj* (*person*) alkohol-
süchtig; (*drink*) alkoholisch

alcoholism ['æl·kə·hɔ·lɪz·əm] *n* Alkoholismus *m*

alcove ['æl·koʊv] *n* Nische *f*

ale [eɪl] *n* Ale *nt*

alert [ə·'lɜrt] **I.** *adj* **1.** (*mentally*) aufgeweckt **2.** (*watchful*) wachsam; (*at-
tentive*) aufmerksam **II.** *n* Alarmbe-
reitschaft *f;* **to be on the** ~ [**for sth**]
[vor etw] auf der Hut sein **III.** *vt* **to** ~
sb to [*or of*] **sth** (*warn*) jdn vor etw
dat warnen

algae <*pl* -e> ['æl·gə] *n usu pl* Alge *f*

Algeria [æl·'dʒɪr·i·ə] *n* Algerien *nt*

alias ['eɪ·li·əs] **I.** *n* Deckname *m* **II.** *adv*

alias

alibi ['æl·ə·baɪ] *n* Alibi *nt*

alien ['eɪ·li·ən] **I.** *adj* fremd **II.** *n* **1.** (*foreigner*) Ausländer(in) *m(f)* **2.** (*from
space*) Außerirdische(r) *f(m)*

alienate ['eɪ·li·ə·neɪt] *vt* befremden

alight [ə·'laɪt] *vi* **1.** (*from train*) aussteig-
en (**from** aus +*dat*) **2.** (*bird*) landen
(**on** auf +*dat*)

align [ə·'laɪn] *vt* **to** ~ **sth** [**with sth**] etw
[auf etw *akk*] ausrichten

alignment [ə·'laɪn·mənt] *n* Ausrichten *nt*

alike [ə·'laɪk] **I.** *adj* **1.** (*identical*) gleich
2. (*similar*) ähnlich **II.** *adv* gleich; **to
look** ~ sich *dat* ähnlich sehen

alimony ['æl·ɪ·moʊ·ni] *n* Unterhalt *m*

alive [ə·'laɪv] *adj* lebendig, lebend; **to
keep sb** ~ jdn am Leben erhalten; **to
make sth come** ~ (*story*) etw lebendig
werden lassen

alkali <*pl* -s> ['æl·kə·laɪ] *n* Alkali *nt*

alkaline ['æl·kə·laɪn] *adj* alkalisch

all [ɔl] **I.** *adj* **1.** + *pl n* (*every one of*) alle;
~ **her children** alle ihre Kinder; **on** ~
fours auf allen Vieren; ~ **the people**
alle [Leute]; **why her, of** ~ **people?** warum ausgerechnet sie? **2.** + *sing n* (*the
whole* (*amount*) *of*) der/die/das ganze;
~ **her life** ihr ganzes Leben; ~ **week** die
ganze Woche **3.** (*the greatest possible*)
all; **in** ~ **honesty** ganz ehrlich **II.** *pron*
1. (*every one*) alle; **the best of** ~ der
Beste von allen **2.** (*everything*) alles; ~
it takes is a little luck man braucht nur
etwas Glück; **for** ~ **I know, ...** soviel ich
weiß ...; **first of** ~ zuerst; (*most importantly*) vor allem; **most of** ~ am meisten **3.** (*for emphasis*) **at** ~ überhaupt;
nothing at ~ überhaupt nichts **III.** *adv*
1. (*entirely*) ganz; **she's been** ~ **over
the world** sie war schon überall in der
Welt; ~ **along** die ganze Zeit; **to be** ~
over aus und vorbei sein **2.** ~ **the** ...
umso ...; ~ **the better!** umso besser!; ~
but fast **3.** (*for emphasis*) **that's** ~ **very
well, but ...** das ist ja schön und gut,
aber ...; ~ **too** ... nur zu ...; **not** ~ **there**
fam nicht ganz richtig [im Kopf]

Allah ['æl·ə] *n* Allah

all-'around *adj* Allround-

all 'clear *n* Entwarnung *f;* **to give the** ~

Entwarnung geben

allegation [ˌæl·ɪ·'geɪ·ʃən] n Behauptung f; **to make an ~ against sb** jdn beschuldigen

allege [ə·'ledʒ] vt behaupten

alleged [ə·'ledʒd] adj angeblich

allegiance [ə·'li·dʒəns] n Loyalität f; **to pledge ~ to sb** jdm Treue schwören

allergen ['æl·ər·dʒən] n Allergen nt

allergic [ə·'lɜr·dʒɪk] adj allergisch (**to** gegen +akk)

allergy ['æl·ər·dʒi] n Allergie f

alleviate [ə·'li·vi·eɪt] vt (fears) abbauen; (pain) lindern

alley ['æl·i] n (between buildings) Gasse f

alliance [ə·'laɪ·əns] n Allianz f; **to form an ~** ein Bündnis schließen

allied ['æl·aɪd] adj (united) verbündet; MIL alliiert

alligator ['æl·ɪ·geɪ·tər] n Alligator m

allocate ['æl·ə·keɪt] vt zuteilen; (funds) bereitstellen

allocation [ˌæl·ə·'keɪ·ʃən] n usu sing (assignment) Zuteilung f; (of funds) Bereitstellung f

all-'out adj umfassend; **~ attack** Großangriff m

allow [ə·'laʊ] vt (permit) erlauben

◆**allow for** vt berücksichtigen; (error, delay) einkalkulieren

allowable [ə·'laʊ·ə·bəl] adj zulässig

allowance [ə·'laʊ·əns] n **1.** (permitted amount) Zuteilung f **2.** (pocket money) Taschengeld nt **3.** (additional pay) Zulage f

alloy ['æl·ɔɪ] n Legierung f; **~ wheels** Alu-Felgen pl

all-'purpose adj Allzweck-

all 'right I. adj **1.** (OK) in Ordnung; **that's ~** (apologetically) das macht nichts; (you're welcome) keine Ursache; **to be ~ with sb** jdm recht sein **2.** (healthy) gesund; (safe) gut II. interj (in agreement) o. k., in Ordnung III. adv **1.** (doubtless) auf jeden Fall **2.** (quite well) ganz gut

all-'round adj see **all-around**

alluring [ə·'lʊr·ɪŋ] adj anziehend

allusion [ə·'lu·ʒən] n Anspielung f

'all-weather adj Allwetter-

ally I. n ['æl·aɪ] Verbündete(r) f/m II. v <-ie-> [ə·'laɪ] **to ~ oneself with** sich verbünden mit +dat

almond ['ɑ·mənd] n Mandel f

almost ['ɔl·moʊst] adv fast, beinahe; **we're ~ there** wir sind gleich da

aloe vera [ˌal·oʊ·'ver·ə] n Aloe vera f

alone [ə·'loʊn] adj, adv allein; **to leave sb ~** jdn in Ruhe lassen ▶ **to go it ~** sich selbständig machen; (act independently) etw im Alleingang machen

along [ə·'lɑŋ] I. prep entlang before n + dat; **the trees ~ the river** die Bäume entlang dem Fluss after n + akk; **~ the way** unterwegs II. adv **you go ahead — I'll be ~ in a minute** geh du vor – ich komme gleich nach; **~ with** [zusammen] mit +dat; **to bring ~** mitbringen

alongside [ə·'lɑŋ·saɪd] I. prep neben +dat II. adv daneben; **the truck pulled up ~** der Laster fuhr heran

aloof [ə·'luf] adj zurückhaltend

aloud [ə·'laʊd] adv laut

alphabet ['æl·fə·bet] n Alphabet nt

alphabetical [ˌæl·fə·'bet·ɪ·kəl] adj alphabetisch

alpine ['æl·paɪn] n BOT [Hoch]gebirgspflanze f

already [ɔl·'red·i] adv schon

alright [ɔl·'raɪt] adj, adv, interj see **all right**

also ['ɔl·soʊ] adv **1.** (too) auch **2.** (furthermore) außerdem

altar ['ɔl·tər] n Altar m

alter ['ɔl·tər] I. vt ändern; **that doesn't ~ the fact that ...** das ändert nichts an der Tatsache, dass ... II. vi sich ändern

alteration [ˌɔl·tər·'eɪ·ʃən] n Änderung f

alternate I. vi ['ɔl·tər·neɪt] abwechseln II. vt **he ~d working in the office with working at home** abwechselnd arbeitete er mal im Büro und mal zu Hause III. adj ['ɔl·tɜr·nət] attr (by turns) abwechselnd

alternating ['ɔl·tər·neɪ·t̬ɪŋ] adj alternierend

alternative [ɔl·'tɜr·nə·t̬ɪv] I. n Alternative f II. adj alternativ

alternatively [ɔl·'tɜr·nə·t̬ɪv·li] adv stattdessen

although [ɔl·'ðoʊ] conj obwohl

A

altitude ['æl·tə·tud] *n* Höhe *f*

alto ['æl·toʊ] *n* **1.** (*singer*) Altist(in) *m(f)* **2.** (*vocal range*) Altstimme *f*

altogether [ˌɔl·tə·'geð·ər] *adv* **1.** (*completely*) völlig **2.** (*in total*) insgesamt

aluminum [ə·'lu·mə·nəm] *n* Aluminium *nt*

aluminum 'foil *n* Alufolie *f*

always ['ɔl·weɪz] *adv* immer

am [əm, *stressed:* æm] *vi first pers. sing of* **be**

a.m. [ˌeɪ·'em] *abbr of* **ante meridiem; at 6 ~** um sechs Uhr morgens

amalgamate [ə·'mæl·gə·meɪt] **I.** *vt* (*companies*) fusionieren **II.** *vi* sich zusammenschließen

amalgamation [ə·ˌmæl·gə·'meɪ·ʃən] *n* Vereinigung *f*

amass [ə·'mæs] *vt* anhäufen

amateur ['æm·ə·tʃər] **I.** *n* Amateur(in) *m(f)* **II.** *adj* Hobby-; SPORT Amateur-

amateurish [ˌæm·ə·'tʃɜr·ɪʃ] *adj pej* dilettantisch

amaze [ə·'meɪz] *vt* erstaunen

amazement [ə·'meɪz·mənt] *n* Verwunderung *f*

amazing [ə·'meɪ·zɪŋ] *adj* **1.** (*very surprising*) erstaunlich **2.** *fam* (*excellent*) toll

Amazon ['æm·ə·zan] *n* the ~ [River] der Amazonas

ambassador [æm·'bæs·ə·dər] *n* Botschafter(in) *m(f)*

amber ['æm·bər] *n* Bernstein *m*

ambidextrous [ˌæm·bɪ·'dek·strəs] *adj* beidhändig

ambiguity [ˌæm·bɪ·'gju·ɪ·ti] *n* Zweideutigkeit *f*

ambiguous [æm·'bɪg·ju·əs] *adj* zweideutig

ambition [æm·'bɪʃ·ən] *n* **1.** (*wish to succeed*) Ehrgeiz *m* **2.** (*aim*) Ambition[en] *f[pl]*

ambitious [æm·'bɪʃ·əs] *adj* ehrgeizig; (*target*) hochgesteckt

amble ['æm·bəl] *vi* schlendern

ambulance ['æm·bju·ləns] *n* Krankenwagen *m;* ~ **service** Rettungsdienst *m*

ambush ['æm·bʊʃ] **I.** *vt* to be ~ed aus dem Hinterhalt überfallen werden **II.** *n* Überfall *m* aus dem Hinterhalt

ameba <*pl* -s> [ə·'mi·bə] *n see* **amoeba**

amen [eɪ·'men] *interj* Amen

amend [ə·'mend] *vt* [ab]ändern

amendment [ə·'mend·mənt] *n* Änderung *f;* **the Fifth A~** der Fünfte Zusatzartikel [zur Verfassung]

amenities [ə·'men·ə·tiz] *n* Freizeiteinrichtungen *pl*

America [ə·'mer·ɪ·kə] *n* Amerika *nt*

American [ə·'mer·ɪ·kən] **I.** *adj* amerikanisch **II.** *n* Amerikaner(in) *m(f)*

American Indian *n* Indianer(in) *m(f)*

Americanize [ə·'mer·ɪ·kə·naɪz] *vt* amerikanisieren

American Revolutionary War *n* amerikanischer Unabhängigkeitskrieg

amethyst ['æm·ɪ·θɪst] *n* Amethyst *m*

amiable ['eɪ·mi·ə·bəl] *adj* freundlich

amicable ['æm·ɪ·kə·bəl] *adj* freundlich; (*settlement*) gütlich

amid [ə·'mɪd], **amidst** [ə·'mɪdst] *prep* inmitten +*gen*

ammonia [ə·'moʊn·jə] *n* **1.** (*gas*) Ammoniak *nt* **2.** (*liquid*) Salmiakgeist *m*

ammunition [ˌæm·jə·'nɪʃ·ən] *n* Munition *f*

amnesia [æm·'ni·ʒə] *n* Amnesie *f*

amnesty ['æm·nɪ·sti] *n* Amnestie *f*

amoeba <*pl* -s> [ə·'mi·bə] *n* Amöbe *f*

among [ə·'mʌŋ], **amongst** [ə·'mʌŋst] *prep* **1.** (*between*) unter +*dat;* ~ **other things** unter anderem **2.** (*in midst of*) inmitten +*gen*

amoral [ˌeɪ·'mɔr·əl] *adj* amoralisch

amorous ['æm·ər·əs] *adj* amourös; (*look*) verliebt

amortization [æm·ˌər·tɪ·'zeɪ·ʃən] *n* Amortisation *f*

amortize [ə·'mɔr·taɪz] *vt* amortisieren

amount [ə·'maʊnt] *n* (*quantity*) Menge *f;* (*of money*) Betrag *m*

amp [æmp] **1.** *short for* **ampere** Ampere *nt* **2.** *short for* **amplifier** Verstärker *m*

ampere ['æm·pɪr] *n* Ampere *nt*

amphibian [æm·'fɪb·i·ən] *n* (*animal*) Amphibie *f*

amphibious [æm·'fɪb·i·əs] *adj* amphibisch

ample <-r, -st> ['æm·pəl] *adj* reichlich

amplifier ['æm·plə·faɪ·ər] n Verstärker m

amplify <-ie-> ['æm·plə·faɪ] vt verstärken

amputate ['æm·pju·teɪt] vt, vi amputieren

amuse [ə·'mjuz] vt 1. (make laugh) amüsieren 2. (entertain) unterhalten

amusement [ə·'mjuz·mənt] n Belustigung f

a'musement park n Freizeitpark m

amusing [ə·'mju·zɪŋ] adj amüsant

an [ən, stressed: æn] art indef ein(e) (unbestimmter Artikel vor Vokalen oder stimmlosem h); see also **a**

anabolic steroid [æn·ə·'bɒl·ɪk·'ster·ɔɪd] n anaboles Steroid

anachronism [ə·'næk·rə·nɪz·əm] n Anachronismus m

anagram ['æn·ə·græm] n Anagramm nt

analgesic [æn·əl·'dʒi·zɪk] n Analgetikum nt

analogy [ə·'næl·ə·dʒi] n (similarity) Analogie f

analysis <pl -ses> [ə·'næl·ə·sɪs] n 1. Analyse f 2. PSYCH [Psycho]analyse f

analyst ['æn·ə·lɪst] n FIN Analyst(in) m(f); (psychoanalyst) Psychoanalytiker(in) m(f)

analytical [æn·ə·'lɪt·ɪ·kəl] adj analytisch

analyze ['æn·ə·laɪz] vt analysieren

anarchist ['æn·ər·kɪst] n Anarchist(in) m(f)

anarchy ['æn·ər·ki] n Anarchie f

anatomical [æn·ə·'tɒm·ɪ·kəl] adj anatomisch

anatomy [ə·'næt·ə·mi] n Anatomie f

ancestor ['æn·ses·tər] n Vorfahr[e] m, Vorfahrin f

ancestry ['æn·ses·tri] n Abstammung f

anchor ['æŋ·kər] I. n 1. Anker m 2. TV Moderator(in) m(f) II. vt 1. verankern 2. (radio/TV program) moderieren

anchorage ['æŋ·kər·ɪdʒ] n Ankerplatz m

'anchorman n TV Moderator m

'anchorwoman n TV Moderatorin f

anchovy ['æn·tʃoʊ·vi] n An[s]chovis f, Sardelle f

ancient ['eɪn·ʃənt] adj alt; fam uralt

and [ænd, ənd] conj und; **more ~ more** immer mehr; **~ so on** und so weiter

Andes ['æn·diz] npl **the ~** die Anden pl

android ['æn·drɔɪd] n Androide m

anemia [ə·'ni·mi·ə] n Anämie f

anemic [ə·'ni·mɪk] adj anämisch; fig saftund kraftlos

anesthesia [æn·ɪs·'θi·ʒə] n Anästhesie f

anesthesiologist [æn·ɪs·θi·zi·'ɒl·ə·dʒɪst] n Narkosearzt, -ärztin m, f

anesthetic [æn·ɪs·'θet·ɪk] n Betäubungsmittel nt

anesthetize [ə·'nes·θɪ·taɪz] vt betäuben

angel ['eɪn·dʒl] n Engel m

angelic [æn·'dʒel·ɪk] adj engelhaft

anger ['æŋ·gər] n Ärger m; (fury) Wut f

angle ['æŋ·gəl] n 1. Winkel m 2. (perspective) Blickwinkel m

angler ['æŋ·glər] n Angler(in) m(f)

angling ['æŋ·glɪŋ] n Angeln nt

angora [æŋ·'gɔ·rə] n Angorawolle f

angry ['æŋ·gri] adj (annoyed) verärgert; (enraged) wütend

angst [æŋkst] n [neurotische] Angst

anguish ['æŋ·gwɪʃ] n Qual f

angular ['æŋ·gju·lər] adj kantig

animal ['æn·ɪ·məl] n Tier nt

animal 'rights npl das Recht der Tiere auf Leben und artgerechte Haltung

animate ['æn·ɪ·meɪt] vt beleben

animated ['æn·ɪ·meɪ·tɪd] adj 1. lebhaft 2. **~ cartoon** [Zeichen]trickfilm m

animator ['æn·ɪ·meɪ·tər] n Trickfilmzeichner(in) m(f)

anise ['æn·ɪs] n Anis m

ankle ['æŋ·kəl] n [Fuß]knöchel m

'ankle bone n Sprungbein nt

'ankle-deep adj knöcheltief

'ankle sock n Söckchen nt

annex I. vt [ə·'neks] annektieren II. n <pl -es> ['æn·eks] 1. (building) Anbau m 2. (to a letter) Anlage f; (to an e-mail) Anhang m

annihilate [ə·'naɪ·ə·leɪt] vt vernichten

annihilation [ə·naɪ·ə·'leɪ·ʃən] n Vernichtung f

anniversary [æn·ə·'vɜr·sə·ri] n Jahrestag m

announce [ə·'naʊns] vt bekannt geben

announcement [ə·'naʊns·mənt] n Bekanntmachung f; (at airport) Durchsage f

announcer [ə·'naʊn·sər] n [Fernseh]sprecher(in) m(f)

annoy [ə·'nɔɪ] vt ärgern

annoyance [ə·'nɔɪ·əns] n (anger) Är-

A

ger m; (weaker) Verärgerung f

annoying [ə·'nɔɪ·ɪŋ] adj ärgerlich

annual ['æn·ju·əl] adj jährlich; **~ income** Jahreseinkommen nt

annually ['æn·ju·ə·li] adv [all]jährlich

annul <-ll-> [ə·'nʌl] vt annullieren; (contract) auflösen

anomaly [ə·'nam·ə·li] n Anomalie f

anonymous [ə·'nan·ə·məs] adj anonym

anorak ['æn·ə·ræk] n Anorak m

anorexia [ˌæn·ə·'rek·si·ə], **anorexia nervosa** [ˌæn·ə·'rek·si·ə nɜr·'vou·sə] n Magersucht f

anorexic [ˌæn·ə·'rek·sɪk] adj magersüchtig

another [ə·'nʌð·ər] I. adj 1. (one more) noch eine(r, s) 2. (similar to one) ein zweiter/zweites/eine zweite; **the Gulf War could have been ~ Vietnam** der Golfkrieg hätte ein zweites Vietnam sein können 3. (not the same) ein anderer/anderes/eine andere; **that's ~ story** das ist eine andere Geschichte II. pron 1. (different one) ein anderer/eine andere/ein anderes; **one way or ~** irgendwie 2. (additional one) noch eine(r, s) 3. (each other) **one ~** einander

answer [æn·sər] I. n 1. (reply) Antwort f; (reaction a.) Reaktion f 2. MATH Ergebnis nt II. vt beantworten, antworten auf +akk; **to ~ the telephone** ans Telefon gehen; **to ~ sb** jdm antworten III. vi antworten

◆**answer for** vt Verantwortung tragen für +akk

◆**answer to** vt **to ~ to sb** jdm Rede und Antwort stehen

'answering machine n Anrufbeantworter m

ant [ænt] n Ameise f

antagonism [æn·'tæg·ə·nɪz·əm] n Feindseligkeit f

antagonize [æn·'tæg·ə·naɪz] vt sich dat zum Feind machen

Antarctica [ænt·'ark·tɪ·kə] n die Antarktis

antelope <pl -s> ['æn·tɪ·loup] n Antilope f

antenna [æn·'ten·ə] n 1. <pl -nae> (of an insect) Fühler m 2. <pl -s> (aerial) Antenne f

anthem ['æn·θəm] n Hymne f

anthill ['ænt·hɪl] n Ameisenhaufen m

anthracite ['æn·θrə·saɪt] n Anthrazit m

anthropologist [ˌæn·θrə·'pal·ə·dʒɪst] n Anthropologe m, Anthropologin f

anthropology [ˌæn·θrə·'pal·ə·dʒi] n Anthropologie f

anti ['æn·ti] prep gegen +akk

anti'aircraft adj Flugabwehr- f

antibiotic [ˌæn·tɪ·baɪ·'at·ɪk] n Antibiotikum nt

'antibody n Antikörper m

anticipate ['æn·'tɪs·ə·peɪt] vt (expect) erwarten; (foresee) vorhersehen

anti'climax n Enttäuschung f

anti'cyclone n Hochdruckgebiet nt

antide'pressant n Antidepressivum nt

antidote ['æn·tɪ·dout] n Gegenmittel nt

'antifreeze n Frostschutzmittel nt

anti'histamine n Antihistamin nt

antilock 'braking system n Antiblockiersystem nt

anti'oxidant n Antioxidationsmittel nt

antiperspirant [ˌæn·tɪ·'pɜr·spər·ənt] n Antitranspirant nt

antiquarian [ˌæn·tɪ·'kwer·i·ən] n Antiquitätensammler(in) m(f)

antiquated ['æn·tɪ·kweɪ·tɪd] adj antiquiert

antique [æn·'tik] I. n iron a. Antiquität f II. adj antik

anti'rust adj Rostschutz-

anti-'Semitic adj antisemitisch

anti'septic I. n Antiseptikum nt II. adj antiseptisch; fig steril

anti'social adj 1. (harmful) unsozial 2. (not sociable) ungesellig

anti'static adj antistatisch

antler ['ænt·lər] n Geweihstange f

antonym ['æn·tə·nɪm] n Antonym nt

antsy ['ænt·si] adj fam (child) zappelig fam

anus ['eɪ·nəs] n Anus m

anvil ['æn·vɪl] n Amboss m

anxiety [æŋ·'zaɪ·ɪ·ti] n 1. (feeling of concern) Sorge f 2. (concern) Angst f

anxious ['æŋk·ʃəs] adj 1. (concerned) besorgt 2. (eager) bestrebt

any ['en·i] I. adj 1. in questions, conditional [irgend]ein(e); with uncountables etwas; **do you have ~**

brothers or sisters? haben Sie Geschwister? **2.** (*with neg*) **I don't have ~ money** ich habe kein Geld **3.** (*every*) jede(r, s); **in ~ case** (*whatever happens*) auf jeden Fall; (*anyway*) außerdem **4.** (*whichever you like*) jede(r, s) [beliebige]; (*all*) alle; (*not important which*) irgendein(e); (*with pl n*) irgendwelche **II.** *pron* **1.** (*some of many*) welche; (*one of many*) eine(r, s); **do you have ~** [at all]? haben Sie [überhaupt] welche? **2.** (*some of a quantity*) welche(r, s); **hardly ~** kaum etwas **3.** (*with negative*) **don't you have ~ at all?** haben Sie denn überhaupt keine? **4.** (*not important which*) irgendeine(r, s); **~ will do** egal welche **III.** *adv* **1.** (*emphasizing*) noch; (*a little*) etwas; (*at all*) überhaupt; **are you feeling ~ better?** fühlst du dich [denn] etwas besser?; **~ more** noch mehr **2.** (*expressing termination*) **not ~ longer/more** nicht mehr

anybody ['en·ɪ·bad·i] *pron* **1.** (*each person*) jede(r, s) **2.** (*someone*) jemand; **does ~ else want coffee?** möchte noch jemand Kaffee?

anyhow ['en·ɪ·hau] *adv* (*in any case*) sowieso

anyone ['en·ɪ·wʌn] *pron see* **anybody**

anyplace ['en·ɪ·pleɪs] *adv fam* irgendwo

anything ['en·ɪ·θɪn] *pron* **1.** (*each thing*) alles **2.** (*something*) **is there ~ I can do to help?** kann ich irgendwie helfen?; **hardly ~** kaum etwas **3.** (*nothing*) **not ~** nichts; **not ~ like ...** nicht annähernd ... ▶ [**as**] **...** **as** ~ ausgesprochen ...

anytime ['en·i·taɪm] *adv* jederzeit

anyway ['en·ɪ·weɪ] *adv*, **anyways** ['en·ɪ·weɪz] *adv fam* **1.** (*in any case*) sowieso **2.** (*well*) jedenfalls; **~!** na ja!

anywhere ['en·ɪ·wer] *adv* **1.** (*in any place*) überall; **~ else** irgendwo anders **2.** (*some place*) irgendwo; **I'm not getting ~** ich komme einfach nicht weiter; **to go ~** irgendwohin gehen

apart [ə·'part] *adv* **1.** (*not together*) auseinander **2.** **~ from** abgesehen von +*dat*

apartment [ə·'part·mənt] *n* Wohnung *f*

a'partment building, a'partment house *n* Wohnhaus *nt*; (*with smaller apartments*) Ap[p]art[e]menthaus *nt*

apathy ['æp·ə·θi] *n* Apathie *f*

ape [eɪp] *n* [Menschen]affe *m*

aperitif [ə‚per·ə·'tif] *n* Aperitif *m*

aperture ['æp·ər·tʃʊr] *n* [kleine] Öffnung; PHOT Blende *f*

apex <*pl* -es> ['eɪ·peks] *n* Spitze *f*

aphid ['eɪ·fɪd] *n* Blattlaus *f*

aphrodisiac [‚æf·rə·'dɪ·zi·æk] *n* Aphrodisiakum *nt*

apiece [ə·'pis] *adv* das Stück; (*per person*) jeder

apocalypse [ə·'pak·ə·lɪps] *n* Apokalypse *f*

apologetic [ə‚pal·ə·'dʒet·ɪk] *adj* entschuldigend

apologize [ə·'pal·ə·dʒaɪz] *vi* sich entschuldigen (**to** bei +*dat*)

apology [ə·'pal·ə·dʒi] *n* Entschuldigung *f*

apostrophe [ə·'pas·trə·fi] *n* Apostroph *m*

Appalachian Mountains *npl* **the ~** die Appalachen *pl*

appall [ə·'pɔl] *vt* entsetzen

appalling [ə·'pɔ·lɪn] *adj* entsetzlich

apparatus [‚æp·ə·'ræt·əs] *n* [**piece of**] **~ Gerät** *nt*

apparent [ə·'pær·ənt] *adj* **1.** (*obvious*) offensichtlich **2.** (*seeming*) scheinbar

apparently [ə·'pær·ənt·li] *adv* **1.** (*obviously*) offensichtlich **2.** (*seemingly*) anscheinend

appeal [ə·'pil] **I.** *vi* **1.** (*attract*) **to ~ to sb/sth** jdn/etw reizen; (*aim to please*) jdn/etw ansprechen **2.** (*protest formally*) Einspruch einlegen **3.** (*plead*) bitten **II.** *n* **1.** (*attraction*) Reiz *m* **2.** (*formal protest*) Einspruch *m*; **Court of A~** Berufungsgericht *nt*

appealing [ə·'pi·lɪn] *adj* **1.** (*attractive*) attraktiv; (*idea*) verlockend **2.** (*beseeching*) flehend

appealingly [ə·'pi·lɪn·li] *adv* (*attractively*) reizvoll

appear [ə·'pɪr] *vi* **1.** (*become visible*) erscheinen; (*be seen a.*) sich *dat* zeigen; (*arrive a.*) auftauchen **2.** (*film*) anlaufen; (*newspaper*) erscheinen **3.** (*seem*) scheinen

appearance [ə·'pɪr·əns] *n* **1.** (*instance of appearing*) Erscheinen *nt*; (*on TV, the-*

ater) Auftritt _m;_ **to make an** ~ auftreten **2.** (_looks_) Aussehen _nt_

appendicitis [əˌpen·dɪ·ˈsaɪ·tɪs] _n_ Blinddarmentzündung _f_

appendix [ə·ˈpen·dɪks] _n_ **1.** <_pl_ -es> (_body part_) Blinddarm _m_ **2.** <_pl_ -dices> (_in book_) Anhang _m_

appetite [ˈæp·ə·taɪt] _n_ Appetit _m_

appetizer [ˈæp·ə·taɪ·zər] _n_ Vorspeise _f_

applaud [ə·ˈplɔd] **I.** _vi_ applaudieren **II.** _vt_ **1.** (_clap_) **to ~ sb** jdm applaudieren **2.** (_decision_) begrüßen

applause [ə·ˈplɔz] _n_ [**a round of**] ~ Applaus _m_

apple [ˈæp·əl] _n_ Apfel _m_

'apple juice _n_ Apfelsaft _m_

apple 'pie _n_ FOOD gedeckter Apfelkuchen

'applesauce _n_ Apfelmus _nt_

'apple tree _n_ Apfelbaum _m_

appliance [ə·ˈplaɪ·əns] _n_ Gerät _nt_

applicable [ˈæp·lɪ·kə·bəl] _adj_ anwendbar (**to** auf +_akk_); (_on application form_) **not** ~ nicht zutreffend

applicant [ˈæp·lɪ·kənt] _n_ Bewerber(in) _m(f)_

application [ˌæp·lɪ·ˈkeɪ·ʃən] _n_ **1.** (_for a job_) Bewerbung _f;_ (_for a permit_) Antrag _m_ **2.** (_implementation_) Anwendung _f_ **3.** COMPUT Anwendung _f_

appli'cation form _n_ (_for job_) Bewerbungsformular _nt;_ (_for permit_) Antragsformular _nt_

applied [ə·ˈplaɪd] _adj_ angewandt

apply <-ie-> [ə·ˈplaɪ] **I.** _vi_ **1.** **to ~** [**to sb**] [**for sth**] (_for a job_) sich [bei jdm] [um etw _akk_] bewerben; (_for permission, passport_) etw [bei jdm] beantragen **2.** (_pertain_) gelten; **to ~ to** betreffen **II.** _vt_ **1.** (_put on_) anwenden (**to** auf +_akk_); (_makeup_) auftragen **2.** (_use_) gebrauchen; (_force_) anwenden

appoint [ə·ˈpɔɪnt] _vt_ **to ~ sb** [**as**] **sth** jdn zu etw _dat_ ernennen

appointed [ə·ˈpɔɪn·tɪd] _adj_ **1.** (_selected_) ernannt **2.** (_designated_) vereinbart

appointment [ə·ˈpɔɪnt·mənt] _n_ **1.** (_being selected_) Ernennung _f_ **2.** (_official meeting_) Verabredung _f;_ **by ~ only** nur nach Absprache

appraisal [ə·ˈpreɪ·zəl] _n_ Bewertung _f_

appreciate [ə·ˈpri·ʃi·eɪt] _vt_ **1.** (_value_)

schätzen; (_be grateful for_) zu schätzen wissen **2.** (_understand_) Verständnis haben für +_akk_

appreciation [əˌpri·ʃi·ˈeɪ·ʃən] _n_ **1.** (_gratitude_) Anerkennung _f_ **2.** (_understanding_) Verständnis _nt_

appreciative [ə·ˈpri·ʃə·tɪv] _adj_ **1.** (_grateful_) dankbar (**of** für +_akk_) **2.** (_showing appreciation_) anerkennend

apprehensive [ˌæp·rɪ·ˈhen·sɪv] _adj_ besorgt; (_scared_) ängstlich

apprentice [ə·ˈpren·tɪs] _n_ Auszubildende(r) _f(m)_

apprenticeship [ə·ˈpren·tɪs·ʃɪp] _n_ **1.** (_training_) Ausbildung _f_ **2.** (_period of training_) Lehrzeit _f_

approach [ə·ˈprouʧ] **I.** _vt_ **1.** (_come closer_) **to ~ sb/sth** sich jdm/etw nähern; (_come toward[s]_) auf jdn/etw zukommen **2.** (_ask_) **to ~ sb** jdn ansprechen (**about** wegen +_gen_) **3.** (_problem, issue_) angehen **II.** _vi_ sich nähern **III.** _n_ **1.** (_coming_) Nähern _nt_ **2.** (_preparation to land_) [Lande]anflug _m_ **3.** (_method_) Ansatz _m_

approachable [ə·ˈprou·ʧə·bəl] _adj_ (_person_) umgänglich

appropriate _adj_ [ə·ˈprou·pri·ət] angemessen

approval [ə·ˈpru·vəl] _n_ (_consent_) Zustimmung _f_ ▶ **on** ~ ECON zur Ansicht; (_to try_) zur Probe

approve [ə·ˈpruv] **I.** _vi_ **1.** (_agree with_) **to ~ of sth** etw _dat_ zustimmen **2.** (_like_) **to ~ of sth** etw gutheißen **II.** _vt_ (_permit_) genehmigen; (_consent to_) billigen

approved [ə·ˈpruvd] _adj_ **1.** (_agreed_) bewährt **2.** (_sanctioned_) [offiziell] anerkannt

approving [ə·ˈpru·vɪŋ] _adj_ zustimmend

approvingly [ə·ˈpru·vɪŋ·li] _adv_ anerkennend

approx. _adv abbr of_ **approximately** ca.

approximately [ə·ˈprak·sɪ·mət·li] _adv_ ungefähr

approximation [əˌprak·sɪ·ˈmeɪ·ʃən] _n_ Annäherung _f_

APR [ˌeɪ·piˈar] _n_ FIN _abbr of_ **annual percentage rate** Jahreszinssatz _m_

Apr. _n abbr of_ **April** Apr.

apricot [ˈeɪ·prɪ·kat] _n_ Aprikose _f_

April ['eɪ·prəl] n April m; see also **February**

April 'Fools' Day n der erste April

apron ['eɪ·prən] n Schürze f

apt [æpt] adj passend; (remark) treffend

'aptitude test n Eignungstest m

aquarium <pl -s> [ə·'kwer·i·əm] n Aquarium nt

Aquarius [ə·'kwer·i·əs] n ASTROL Wassermann m

aquatic [ə·'kwæt·ɪk] adj Wasser-

AR abbr of **Arkansas**

Arab ['ær·əb] I. n Araber(in) m(f) II. adj arabisch

Arabic ['ær·ə·bɪk] I. n Arabisch nt II. adj arabisch

arbitrary ['ar·bɪ·trer·i] adj willkürlich

arbitrate ['ar·bɪ·treɪt] vi vermitteln

arbitrator ['ar·bɪ·treɪ·tər] n Schlichter(in) m(f)

arbor ['ar·bər] n Laube f

arc [ark] n Bogen m

arcade [ær·'keɪd] n 1. (for playing games) Spielhalle f 2. ARCHIT Arkade f

arch [artʃ] I. n Bogen m II. vt (back) krümmen

archaic [ar·'keɪ·ɪk] adj veraltet

arch'enemy n Erzfeind(in) m(f)

archeologist [ˌar·ki·'al·ə·dʒɪst] n Archäologe m, Archäologin f

archeology [ˌar·ki·'al·ə·dʒi] n Archäologie f

archery ['ar·tʃə·ri] n Bogenschießen nt

archipelago <pl -s> [ˌar·kə·'pel·ə·goʊ] n Archipel m

architect ['ar·kɪ·tekt] n Architekt(in) m(f)

architecture ['ar·kɪ·tek·tʃər] n Architektur f

archive ['ar·kaɪv] n Archiv nt

'archway n Torbogen m

'arc lamp, 'arc light n Bogenlampe f

Arctic ['ark·tɪk] I. n the ~ die Arktis II. adj arktisch; (expedition) Arktis-

ardent ['ar·dənt] adj leidenschaftlich

arduous ['ar·dʒu·əs] adj anstrengend

are [ər, stressed: ar] vt, vi see **be**

area ['er·i·ə] n 1. Gebiet nt 2. (surface measure) Fläche f

'area code n Vorwahl f

arena [ə·'ri·nə] n Arena f

Argentina [ˌar·dʒən·'ti·nə] n Argentinien nt

arguably ['ar·gju·ə·bli] adv wohl

argue ['ar·gju] vi 1. (disagree) [sich] streiten; **don't ~ [with me]!** kein Widerrede! 2. (reason) argumentieren

argument ['ar·gjə·mənt] n 1. (heated discussion) Auseinandersetzung f 2. (case) Argument nt

argumentative [ˌar·gjə·'men·tə·tɪv] adj streitsüchtig

aria ['a·ri·ə] n Arie f

arid ['ær·ɪd] adj dürr

Aries ['er·iz] n ASTROL Widder m

arise <arose, arisen> [ə·'raɪz] vi (come about) sich ergeben

arisen [ə·'rɪz·ən] pp of **arise**

aristocrat [ə·'rɪs·tə·kræt] n Aristokrat(in) m(f)

aristocratic [e·ˌrɪs·tə·'kræt·ɪk] adj aristokratisch

arithmetic [ə·'rɪθ·mɪ·tɪk] Arithmetik f

Ariz. abbr of **Arizona**

Arizona [ˌær·ɪ·'zoʊ·nə] n Arizona nt

ark [ark] n Arche f

Ark. abbr of **Arkansas**

Arkansas ['ar·kən·sɔ] n Arkansas nt

Arlington National Cemetery n Nationalfriedhof Arlington, der Gräber von mehr als 60.000 amerikanischen Soldaten sowie die bekannter amerikanischer Persönlichkeiten beherbergt

arm¹ [arm] n 1. ANAT, GEOG Arm m 2. (armrest) Armlehne f ► **to keep sb at ~'s length** jdn auf Distanz halten

arm² [arm] I. vt 1. (supply with weapons) bewaffnen 2. (bomb) scharf machen II. n ~s pl Waffen pl

'armband n Armbinde f

'armchair n Sessel m

armed [armd] adj bewaffnet

armed 'forces npl Streitkräfte pl

armful ['arm·fʊl] n Armvoll m

armhole ['arm·hoʊl] n Armloch m

armor-'plated adj gepanzert

'armpit n Achselhöhle f

'armrest n Armlehne f

'arms control n Abrüstung f

'arms race n Wettrüsten nt

army ['ar·mi] n Armee f; **to join the ~** zum Militär gehen

aroma [ə·'roʊ·mə] n Duft m

aroma'therapy n Aromatherapie f

aromatic [ˌær·ə·ˈmæt·ɪk] *adj* aromatisch

arose [ə·ˈroʊz] *pt of* **arise**

around [ə·ˈraʊnd] **I.** *adv* **1.** (*on all sides*) rundum; **from miles ~** von weither; **he's the biggest crook ~** er ist der größte Gauner, den es gibt **2.** (*with circular motion*) umher **3.** (*here and there*) herum; **to show sb ~** jdn herumführen ▶ **see you ~** bis demnächst mal **II.** *prep* **1.** um +*akk*; **from all ~ the world** aus aller Welt **2.** ungefähr

arouse [ə·ˈraʊz] *vt* **1.** (*suspicion*) erregen **2.** (*sexually excite*) erregen

arrange [ə·ˈreɪndʒ] **I.** *vt* **1.** (*organize*) arrangieren; (*matters*) regeln **2.** (*put in order*) ordnen **II.** *vi* festlegen; **to ~ to do sth** etw vereinbaren

arrangement [ə·ˈreɪndʒ·mənt] *n* **1.** **~s** *pl* (*preparations*) Vorbereitungen *pl* **2.** (*agreement*) Abmachung *f*; **by** [**prior**] **~** nach [vorheriger] Absprache

arrears [ə·ˈrɪrz] *npl* Rückstände *pl*; **in ~** in Verzug

arrest [ə·ˈrest] **I.** *vt* verhaften **II.** *n* Verhaftung *f*

arrival [ə·ˈraɪ·vəl] *n* (*at a destination*) Ankunft *f*; (*of a baby*) Geburt *f*

arrive [ə·ˈraɪv] *vi* (*bus*) ankommen; (*baby, mail*) kommen

arrogant [ˈær·ə·gənt] *adj* arrogant

arrow [ˈær·oʊ] *n* Pfeil *m*

arson [ˈɑr·sən] *n* Brandstiftung *f*

art [ɑrt] *n* Kunst *f*; **the ~s** *pl* die Kunst

artery [ˈɑr·tə·ri] *n* Arterie *f*

arthritis [ɑr·ˈθraɪ·tɪs] *n* Gelenkentzündung *f*

artichoke [ˈɑr·tɪ·tʃoʊk] *n* Artischocke *f*

article [ˈɑr·tɪ·kəl] *n* Artikel *m*; **~ of clothing** Kleidungsstück *nt*

articulate [ɑr·ˈtɪk·jə·lət] *adj* **1.** (*person*) redegewandt **2.** (*speech*) verständlich

artificial [ˌɑr·tə·ˈfɪʃ·əl] *adj* **1.** (*not natural*) künstlich; **~ leg** Beinprothese *f* **2.** *pej* (*not genuine*) aufgesetzt; (*smile*) unecht

artillery [ɑr·ˈtɪl·ə·ri] *n* Artillerie *f*

artist [ˈɑr·tɪst] *n* Künstler(in) *m(f)*

artiste [ɑr·ˈtist] *n* THEATER, TV Artist(in) *m(f)*

artistic [ɑr·ˈtɪs·tɪk] *adj* künstlerisch; (*arrangement*) kunstvoll

ˈartwork *n* Illustrationen *pl*

arty [ˈɑr·ti], **artsy** [ˈɑrt·si] *adj* gewollt bohemienhaft

as [æz, əz] **I.** *conj* **1.** (*while*) während **2.** (*in the way that, like*) wie; **~ it were** sozusagen; **~ if** [*or* **though**] als ob **3.** (*because*) weil ▶ **~ for ...** was ... betrifft; **~ of** ab **II.** *prep* als; **~ a child** als Kind; **~ a matter of principle** aus Prinzip **III.** *adv* **1.** (*in comparisons*) wie; [**just**] **~ ... ~ ...** [genau] so ... wie ... **2.** (*indicating an extreme*) **~ little ~** nur

asbestos [æs·ˈbes·təs] *n* Asbest *m*

ascend [ə·ˈsend] **I.** *vt* hinaufsteigen **II.** *vi* aufsteigen; (*elevator*) hinauffahren

ascent [ə·ˈsent] *n* Aufstieg *m*

asexual [ˌeɪ·ˈsek·ʃu·əl] *adj* asexuell; (*reproduction*) ungeschlechtlich

ash[1] [æʃ] *n* (*from burning*) Asche *f*; **~es** *pl* Asche *f* *kein pl*

ash[2] [æʃ] *n* (*tree*) Esche *f*

ashamed [ə·ˈʃeɪmd] *adj* **to be ~** [**of sb/ sth**] sich [für jdn/etw] schämen

ashore [ə·ˈʃɔr] *adv* **to swim ~** ans Ufer schwimmen

ˈashtray *n* Aschenbecher *m*

Ash ˈWednesday *n* Aschermittwoch *m*

Asia [ˈeɪ·ʒə] *n* Asien *nt*

Asian [ˈeɪ·ʒən] **I.** *n* Asiat *m*, Asiatin *f* **II.** *adj* asiatisch

aside [ə·ˈsaɪd] *adv* zur Seite; **to leave sth ~** etw [weg]lassen

aside from *prep* abgesehen von +*dat*

ask [æsk] **I.** *vt* **1.** (*request information*) fragen; **to ~ a question** [**about sth**] [zu etw *dat*] eine Frage stellen **2.** (*request*) bitten [um +*dat*]; **she ~ed me for help** sie bat mich, ihr zu helfen **3.** (*invite*) einladen **II.** *vi* (*request information*) fragen; **to ~ about sb/sth** nach jdm/ etw fragen

askew [ə·ˈskju] *adj*, *adv* schief

asking [ˈæs·kɪŋ] *n* **it's yours for the ~** du kannst es gerne haben

asleep [ə·ˈslip] *adj* **to be ~** schlafen; **to fall ~** einschlafen

asparagus [ə·ˈspær·ə·gəs] *n* Spargel *m*

aspect [ˈæs·pekt] *n* Aspekt *m*

aspen [ˈæs·pən] *n* Espe *f*

asphalt [ˈæs·fɔlt] *n* Asphalt *m*

asphyxiation [əsˌfɪkˈsɪˈeɪˈʃən] n Erstickung f

aspiration [ˌæsˈpəˈreɪˈʃən] n Ambition f

aspire [əˈspaɪr] vi anstreben

aspirin [ˈæsˈpəˈrɪn] n Aspirin nt

aspiring [əˈspaɪrˈɪŋ] adj aufstrebend

ass¹ <pl -es> [æs] n Esel m

ass² <pl -es> [æs] n vulg (rear end) Arsch m ▸ **my ~!** fam (emphatically not) wahrlich nicht

assassin [əˈsæsˈɪn] n Mörder(in) m(f); (esp political) Attentäter(in) m(f)

assassination [əˌsæsˈəˈneɪˈʃən] n Attentat nt

assault [əˈsɔlt] I. n Angriff m II. vt angreifen

assemble [əˈsemˈbəl] I. vi sich versammeln II. vt zusammenbauen

assembly [əˈsemˈbli] n 1. (gathering) Versammlung f; **the A~** das Unterhaus 2. TECH Montage f; **~ line** Fließband nt

assert [əˈsɜrt] vt 1. (state firmly) beteuern 2. (independence) behaupten

assertion [əˈsɜrˈʃən] n 1. (claim) Behauptung f 2. (of authority) Geltendmachung f

assertive [əˈsɜrˈtɪv] adj **to be ~** Durchsetzungsvermögen zeigen

assertiveness [əˈsɜrˈtɪvˈnɪs] n Durchsetzungsvermögen nt

assess [əˈses] vt einschätzen; (damage) schätzen (**at** auf +akk)

assessment [əˈsesˈmənt] n 1. (of damage) Schätzung f 2. (evaluation) Beurteilung f

asset [ˈæsˈet] n 1. Pluspunkt m 2. FIN **~s** pl Vermögenswerte pl

assign [əˈsaɪn] vt zuweisen; (task) zuteilen

assignment [əˈsaɪnˈmənt] n Aufgabe f

assimilate [əˈsɪmˈəˈleɪt] vt integrieren; (information) aufnehmen

assimilation [əˌsɪmˈəˈleɪˈʃən] n Eingliederung f

assist [əˈsɪst] vt, vi helfen (**with** bei +dat)

assistance [əˈsɪsˈtəns] n Hilfe f

assistant [əˈsɪsˈtənt] n Assistent(in) m(f); (in store) Verkäufer(in) m(f)

associate I. n [əˈsoʊˈʃiˈət] Kollege m, Kollegin f; **business ~** Geschäftspartner(in) m(f) II. vt [əˈsoʊˈʃiˈeɪt] in Verbindung bringen

association [əˌsoʊˈsiˈeɪˈʃən] n 1. (organization) Vereinigung f 2. (mental connection) Assoziation f

assorted [əˈsɔrˈtɪd] adj gemischt; (colors) verschieden

assortment [əˈsɔrtˈmənt] n Sortiment nt

assume [əˈsum] vt 1. (regard as true) annehmen 2. (adopt) annehmen; (role) übernehmen

assumed [əˈsumd] adj **under an ~ name** unter einem Decknamen

assumption [əˈsʌmpˈʃən] n (supposition) Annahme f; (presupposition) Voraussetzung f

assurance [əˈʃurˈəns] n 1. (promise) Zusicherung f 2. (self-confidence) Selbstsicherheit f

assure [əˈʃur] vt 1. (confirm certainty) zusichern 2. (promise) **to ~ sb of sth** jdm etw zusichern

assured [əˈʃurd] adj selbstsicher

asterisk [ˈæsˈtəˈrɪsk] n Sternchen nt

asteroid [ˈæsˈtəˈrɔɪd] n Asteroid m

asthma [ˈæzˈmə] n Asthma nt

asthmatic [æzˈmætˈɪk] adj asthmatisch

astonish [əˈstanˈɪʃ] vt erstaunen

astonishing [əˈstanˈɪʃˈɪŋ] adj erstaunlich

astound [əˈstaʊnd] vt verblüffen

astounding [əˈstaʊnˈdɪŋ] adj erstaunlich; (fact) verblüffend

astray [əˈstreɪ] adv verloren

astride [əˈstraɪd] prep rittlings auf +dat

astrologer [əˈstralˈəˈdʒər] n Astrologe m, Astrologin f

astrology [əˈstralˈəˈdʒi] n Astrologie f

astronaut [ˈæsˈtrəˈnɔt] n Astronaut(in) m(f)

astronomer [əˈstranˈəˈmər] n Astronom(in) m(f)

astronomical [ˌæsˈtrəˈnamˈɪˈkəl] adj a. fig astronomisch

astronomy [əˈstranˈəˈmi] n Astronomie f

asylum [əˈsaɪˈləm] n (protection) Asyl nt; **~ seeker** Asylbewerber(in) m(f)

asymmetric(al) [ˌeɪˈsɪˈmetˈrɪk(əl)] adj asymmetrisch

at [ət, æt] prep 1. (in location of) an +dat; **~ the bakery** beim Bäcker; **~**

home zu Hause; **~ work** bei der Arbeit
2. (*during time of*) **~ night** in der Nacht,
nachts; **~ 10:00** [**a.m.**] um 10:00 Uhr;
~ the same time (*simultaneously*) zur
gleichen Zeit; (*on the other hand*) auf
der anderen Seite **3.** (*to amount of*) **~
80 miles per hour** mit 80 Meilen pro
Stunde; **~ regular intervals** in regel-
mäßigen Abständen **4.** (*in state of*) **~
a disadvantage** im Nachteil; **~
fault** im Unrecht **5.** (*in ability to*) bei +*dat*;
good ~ math gut in Mathematik ▶ **~
all** überhaupt; **not ~ all** (*definitely not*)
keineswegs

ate [eɪt] *pt of* **eat**

atheism [ˈeɪ·θi·ɪz·əm] *n* Atheismus *m*

atheist [ˈeɪ·θi·ɪst] *n* Atheist(in) *m(f)*

athlete [ˈæθ·lit] *n* Athlet(in) *m(f)*

athletic [æθ·ˈleṯ·ɪk] *adj* athletisch, sportlich

athletics [æθ·ˈleṯ·ɪks] *n* SCH, UNIV [Schul]
sport *m kein pl*

Atlantic [ət·ˈlæn·tɪk] *n* **the ~** [**Ocean**]
der Atlantik

atlas <*pl* -es> [ˈæt·ləs] *n* Atlas *m*

ATM [ˌeɪ·ti·ˈem] *n abbr of* **automated
teller machine** Geldautomat *m*

atmosphere [ˈæt·mə·sfɪr] *n* Atmosphäre *f a. fig*

atom [ˈæt·əm] *n* Atom *nt*

atom bomb *n* Atombombe *f*

atomic [ə·ˈtam·ɪk] *adj* Atom-

atrocious [ə·ˈtroʊ·ʃəs] *adj* grässlich;
(*weather*) scheußlich

atrocity [ə·ˈtras·ɪ·ṯi] *n* Gräueltat *f*

attach [ə·ˈtætʃ] *vt* **1.** (*fix*) befestigen (**to
an** +*dat*) **2.** (*connect*) verbinden (**to mit**
+*dat*) **3.** (*send as enclosure*) **to ~ sth**
[**to sth**] etw [etw *dat*] beilegen

atta'ché case *n* Aktenkoffer *m*

attachment [ə·ˈtætʃ·mənt] *n* **1.** (*fond-
ness*) Sympathie *f* **2.** (*for appliances*)
Zusatzgerät *nt* **3.** COMPUT Anhang *m*

attack [ə·ˈtæk] **I.** *n* Angriff *m* **II.** *vt, vi*
angreifen

attacker [ə·ˈtæ·kər] *n* Angreifer(in) *m(f)*

attainable [ə·ˈteɪn·ə·bəl] *adj* erreichbar

attempt [ə·ˈtempt] **I.** *n* Versuch *m* **II.** *vt*
versuchen

attend [ə·ˈtend] **I.** *vt* (*be present at*) besuchen **II.** *vi* (*be present*) teilnehmen

attendance [ə·ˈten·dəns] *n* **1.** (*being
present*) Anwesenheit *f* **2.** (*number of
people present*) Besucherzahl *f*

attendant [ə·ˈten·dənt] *n* Aufseher(in) *m(f)*

attention [ə·ˈten·ʃən] *n* **1.** (*notice*) Aufmerksamkeit *m*; **~!** Achtung!; **to pay
~ to sth** auf etw *akk* achten **2.** MED
Behandlung *f*

at'tention span *n* Konzentrationsver-
mögen *f*

attentive [ə·ˈten·tɪv] *adj* aufmerksam

attic [ˈæṯ·ɪk] *n* Dachboden *m*

attitude [ˈæṯ·ɪ·tud] *n* Einstellung *f*

attorney [ə·ˈtɜr·ni] *n* Anwalt *m*, Anwältin *f*

attorney 'general <*pl* attornies gener-
al> *n* Justizminister [und Generalstaats-
anwalt], Justizministerin [und General-
staatsanwältin] *m, f*

attract [ə·ˈtrækt] *vt* anziehen; (*attention*)
erregen

attraction [ə·ˈtræk·ʃən] *n* **1.** Anziehung *f*
2. (*appeal*) Reiz *m*

attractive [ə·ˈtræk·tɪv] *adj* attraktiv

attribute [ˈæt·rɪ·bjut] *n* Eigenschaft *f*

auburn [ˈɔ·bərn] *adj* rotbraun

auction [ˈɔk·ʃən] **I.** *n* Auktion *f*, Versteige-
rung *f* **II.** *vt* **to ~** [**off**] versteigern

auctioneer [ˌɔk·ʃə·ˈnɪr] *n* Auktiona-
tor(in) *m(f)*

audible [ˈɔ·də·bəl] *adj* hörbar

audience [ˈɔ·di·əns] *n* (*at performance*)
Publikum *nt*; (*theater a.*) Besucher *pl*;
TV Zuschauer *pl*

audio [ˈɔ·di·oʊ] *adj* Audio-

audit [ˈɔ·dɪt] **I.** *n* Rechnungsprüfung *f*
II. *vt* [amtlich] prüfen

audition [ɔ·ˈdɪʃ·ən] **I.** *n* (*for actor*) Vorsprechen *nt*; (*for singer*) Vorsingen *nt*
II. *vi* vorsprechen, vorsingen **III.** *vt* vor-
sprechen/vorsingen lassen

auditor [ˈɔ·də·ṯər] *n* Rechnungsprü-
fer(in) *m(f)*

auditorium <*pl* -s> [ˌɔ·də·ˈtɔr·i·əm] *n*
THEAT Zuschauerraum *m*; (*for concerts*)
Konzerthalle *f*

Aug. *n abbr of* **August** Aug.

August [ˈɔ·gəst] *n* August *m*; *see also*
February

aunt [ænt] *n* Tante *f*

aural [ˈɔr·əl] *adj* akustisch

austere [ɔ·ˈstɪr] *adj* karg; (*room*) schmucklos

austerity [ɔ·ˈster·ɪ·t̬i] *n* 1. (*absence of comfort*) Rauheit *f* 2. (*sparseness*) Kargheit *f*

Australia [ɔ·ˈstreɪl·jə] *n* Australien *nt*

Austria [ˈɔ·stri·ə] *n* Österreich *nt*

Austrian [ˈɔ·stri·ən] I. *n* (*person*) Österreicher(in) *m(f)* II. *adj* österreichisch

authentic [ɔ·ˈθen·tɪk] *adj* authentisch

authenticate [ɔ·ˈθen·tɪ·keɪt] *vt* [die Echtheit] bestätigen

authenticity [ˌɔ·θən·ˈtɪs·ɪ·t̬i] *n* Echtheit *f*

author [ˈɔ·θər] *n* Schriftsteller(in) *m(f)*

authoritative [ə·ˈθɔr·ə·teɪ·tɪv] *adj* maßgebend

authority [ə·ˈθɔr·ɪ·t̬i] *n* 1. (*right of control*) Autorität *f*; **in ~** verantwortlich 2. (*permission*) Befugnis *f*; (*to act on sb's behalf*) Vollmacht *f* 3. (*organization*) Behörde *f*

authorization [ˌɔ·θər·ɪ·ˈzeɪ·ʃən] *n* Genehmigung *f*

authorize [ˈɔ·θə·raɪz] *vt* genehmigen

auto [ˈɔ·t̬oʊ] I. *n* Auto *nt* II. *adj* 1. (*concerning cars*) Auto- 2. (*automatic*) automatisch

autobiography [ˌɔ·t̬ə·baɪ·ˈag·rə·fi] *n* Autobiografie *f*

autograph [ˈɔ·t̬ə·græf] I. *n* Autogramm *nt* II. *vt* signieren

automate [ˈɔ·t̬ə·meɪt] *vt* automatisieren

automated ˈteller machine *n* Geldautomat *m*

automatic [ˌɔ·t̬ə·ˈmæt̬·ɪk] I. *adj* automatisch II. *n* 1. (*nonmanual machine*) Automat *m* 2. (*rifle*) Selbstladegewehr *nt*

automatic ˈpilot *n* Autopilot *m*

automatic ˈteller machine *n see* **automated teller machine**

automation [ˌɔ·t̬ə·ˈmeɪ·ʃən] *n* Automatisierung *f*

automobile [ˈɔ·t̬ə·moʊ·bil] *n* Auto *nt*

autopsy [ˈɔ·tap·si] *n* Autopsie *f*

autumn [ˈɔ·t̬əm] *n* Herbst *m*

auxiliary [ɔɡ·ˈzɪl·jə·ri] I. *n* 1. Hilfskraft *f* 2. LING Hilfsverb *nt* II. *adj* Hilfs-; (*additional*) Zusatz-

available [ə·ˈveɪ·lə·bəl] *adj* 1. verfügbar; **to make ~** zur Verfügung stellen 2. ECON erhältlich; (*in stock*) lieferbar

avalanche [ˈæv·ə·læntʃ] *n* Lawine *f*

avant-garde [ˌa·vant·ˈgard] *adj* avantgardistisch

Ave. *n abbr of* **avenue**

avenue [ˈæv·ə·nu] *n* 1. (*street*) Avenue *f* 2. *fig* (*possibility*) Weg *m*

average [ˈæv·ər·ɪdʒ] I. *n* Durchschnitt *m* **on ~** im Durchschnitt II. *adj* durchschnittlich; **~ income** Durchschnittseinkommen *nt* III. *vt* im Durchschnitt betragen

aversion [ə·ˈvɜr·ʒən] *n* Abneigung *f*

avert [ə·ˈvɜrt] *vt* verhindern

avg. *n adj abbr of* **average**

aviation [ˌeɪ·vi·ˈeɪ·ʃən] *n* Luftfahrt *f*; **~ industry** Flugzeugindustrie *f*

avid [ˈæv·ɪd] *adj* eifrig, begeistert

avocado <*pl* -s> [ˌæv·ə·ˈka·doʊ] *n* Avocado *f*

avoid [ə·ˈvɔɪd] *vt* 1. (*stay away from*) meiden 2. (*prevent sth from happening*) vermeiden

avoidable [ə·ˈvɔɪd·ə·bəl] *adj* vermeidbar

avoidance [ə·ˈvɔɪd·əns] *n* Vermeidung *f*; (*of taxes*) Umgehung *f*

await [ə·ˈweɪt] *vt* erwarten; **long ~ed** lang ersehnt

awake [ə·ˈweɪk] *adj* wach

awakening [ə·ˈweɪ·kə·nɪŋ] *n* **rude ~** böses Erwachen

award [ə·ˈwɔrd] *n* Auszeichnung *f*

aware [ə·ˈwer] *adj* 1. (*knowing*) **to be ~ of sth** sich *dat* einer S. *gen* bewusst sein 2. (*physically sensing*) **to be ~ of sb/sth** jdn/etw [be]merken 3. (*well informed*) informiert

awareness [ə·ˈwer·nɪs] *n* Bewusstsein *nt*

awash [ə·ˈwaʃ] *adj* **to be ~** unter Wasser stehen

away [ə·ˈweɪ] I. *adv* 1. (*distant*) weg; **to be ~ on business** geschäftlich unterwegs sein; **two days ~** in zwei Tagen 2. SPORT auswärts II. *adj* SPORT **~ game** Auswärtsspiel *nt*

awe [ɔ] *n* Ehrfurcht *f*

ˈawe-inspiring *adj* Ehrfurcht gebietend

awesome [ˈɔ·səm] *adj* 1. (*impressive*) beeindruckend 2. *sl* (*very good*) spitze

awful [ˈɔ·fəl] *adj* 1. (*extremely bad*) furchtbar; **to look ~** schrecklich aussehen 2. (*great*) außerordentlich; **an ~ lo**

eine riesige Menge

wfully ['ɔ-fə-li] *adv* furchtbar; ~ **good** besonders gut

wkward ['ɔk-wərd] *adj* **1.** (*difficult*) schwierig **2.** (*embarrassing*) peinlich **3.** (*inconvenient*) ungünstig

wning ['ɔ-nɪŋ] *n* (*on building*) Markise *f*; (*on camper*) Vorzelt *nt*

x, axe [æks] *n* Axt *f*

xis <*pl* axes> ['æk-sɪs] *n* Achse *f*

xle ['æk-səl] *n* Achse *f*

ye [aɪ] *interj* NAUT ~, ~, **sir!** zu Befehl, Herr Kapitän!

AZ *abbr of* **Arizona**

zalea [ə-'zeɪl-jə] *n* Azalee *f*

zure ['æʒ-ər] *adj* azur[blau]

B

B <*pl* -'s>, **b** <*pl* -'s> [bi] *n* **1.** (*letter*) B *nt*, b *nt*; ~ **as in Bravo** B wie Berta **2.** MUS H *nt*, h *nt* **3.** (*school mark*) ≈ Zwei *f*

BA [bi'eɪ] *n abbr of* **Bachelor of Arts** B.A.

babble ['bæb-əl] **I.** *n* Geplapper *nt* **II.** *vt, vi* plappern; (*stammer*) stammeln; (*baby*) babbeln

babe [beɪb] *n fam* **1.** (*address*) Schatz *m* **2.** (*person*) Süße(r) *f(m)*

baboon [bæ-'bun] *n* Pavian *m*

baby ['beɪ-bi] **I.** *n* **1.** (*child*) Baby *nt*; **to have a** ~ ein Baby bekommen **2.** *fam* (*address*) Baby *nt* **II.** *adj* klein

baby carriage *n* Kinderwagen *m*

baby-sit *vi* babysitten *fam* **II.** *vt* **to** ~ **sb** auf jdn aufpassen

babysitter *n* Babysitter(in) *m(f)*

bachelor ['bætʃ-ə-lər] *n* **1.** Junggeselle *m* **2.** UNIV **B~ of Arts/Science** Bakkalaureus *m* der philosophischen/naturwissenschaftlichen Fakultät (*unterster akademischer Grad in englischsprachigen Ländern*)

back [bæk] **I.** *n* (*of body*) Rücken *m*; (*of building, page*) Rückseite *f*; (*of car*) Heck *nt*; (*of chair*) Lehne *f* **II.** *adj* Hinter-; ~ **pocket** Gesäßtasche *f*; (*of body*) Rücken- **III.** *adv* (*to previous*

place) [wieder] zurück; **there and** ~ hin und zurück; ~ **and forth** hin und her; (*in past*) **that was** ~ **in 1950** das war [schon] 1950 **IV.** *vt* (*support*) unterstützen

◆**back away** *vi* zurückweichen

◆**back down** *vi* nachgeben

◆**back off** *vi* ~ **off!** lass mich in Ruhe!

◆**back out** *vi* einen Rückzieher machen

◆**back up I.** *vi* (*traffic*) sich stauen **II.** *vt* **1.** (*support*) unterstützen **2.** COMPUT sichern **3.** (*reverse*) zurücksetzen

'**backbone** *n* Rückgrat *nt a.* fig

back 'door *n* Hintertür *f*

'**backfire** *vi* **1.** AUTO fehlzünden **2.** (*go wrong*) fehlschlagen

background ['bæk-graʊnd] *n* Hintergrund *m*

backing ['bæk-ɪŋ] *n* Unterstützung *f*

'**backlash** *n* Gegenreaktion *f*

'**backlog** *n usu sing* Rückstand *m*

'**backpack I.** *n* Rucksack *m* **II.** *vi* mit dem Rucksack reisen

'**backpacker** *n* Rucksackreisende(r) *f(m)*

'**back seat** *n* Rücksitz *m*

'**backside** *n fam* Hintern *m*

'**backstroke** *n* Rückenschwimmen *nt*

'**back talk** *n fam* Widerrede *f*

'**backtrack** *vi* **1.** (*go back*) [wieder] zurückgehen **2.** (*change opinion*) einlenken

'**backup** ['bæk-ʌp] *n* **1.** (*support*) Unterstützung *f* **2.** COMPUT Sicherung *f*, Backup *nt*

backward ['bæk-wərd] *adj* **1.** (*facing rear*) rückwärtsgewandt; (*reversed*) Rück[wärts]- *m* **2.** (*slow to learn*) zurückgeblieben **3.** (*underdeveloped*) rückständig

backward(s) ['bæk-wərd(z)] *adv* **1.** (*toward the back*) nach hinten **2.** (*in reverse*) rückwärts **3.** (*into past*) zurück

back'yard *n* Hinterhof *m*

bacon ['beɪ-kən] *n* (*Schinken*)speck *m*

bacteria [bæk-'tɪr-i-ə] *npl* Bakterien *pl*

bad <worse, worst> [bæd] **I.** *adj* schlecht; (*dream*) böse; (*smell*) übel **II.** *adv fam* sehr

badge [bædʒ] *n* Abzeichen *nt*

badger ['bædʒ-ər] **I.** *n* Dachs *m* **II.** *vt* bedrängen

badly <worse, worst> ['bæd·li] *adv*
1. *(poorly)* schlecht 2. *(very much)* sehr
badminton ['bæd·mɪn·tən] *n* Federball *m*
baffle ['bæf·əl] *vt* verwirren
baffling ['bæf·əl·ɪŋ] *adj* verwirrend, rätselhaft
bag [bæg] *n* Tasche *f*; *(of plastic etc)*
Tüte *f*; *(handbag)* Handtasche *f*
bagel ['beɪ·gəl] *n* Bagel *m*
baggage ['bæg·ɪdʒ] *n* Gepäck *nt*
'baggage allowance *n* Freigepäck *nt*
'baggage check *n* Gepäckkontrolle *f*
'baggage claim *n* Gepäckausgabe *f*
baggy ['bæg·i] *adj* [weit] geschnitten
'bagpipes *npl* Dudelsack *m*
Bahamas [bə·'ha·məz] *npl* the ~ die
Bahamas
bail [beɪl] I. *n* Kaution *f* II. *vt* to ~ **sb**
gegen Kaution freilassen
◆ **bail out** I. *vt* to ~ **out ⇆ sb** für jdn [die]
Kaution stellen II. *vi* AVIAT [mit dem Fall-
schirm] abspringen
bailiff ['beɪ·lɪf] *n* Justizwachtmeis-
ter(in) *m(f)*
bait [beɪt] *n* Köder *m a. fig*
bake [beɪk] *vt, vi* backen
baker ['beɪ·kər] *n* Bäcker(in) *m(f)*
bakery ['beɪ·kə·ri] *n* Bäckerei *f*
'baking powder *n* Backpulver *nt*
'baking soda *n* Natron *nt*
balance ['bæl·ənts] I. *n* 1. Gleichgewicht *nt a. fig* 2. FIN Kontostand *m* II. *vt*
balancieren; *(achieve equilibrium)* ein
Gleichgewicht herstellen
balcony ['bæl·kə·ni] *n* Balkon *m*
bald [bɔld] *adj* glatzköpfig; to go ~ eine
Glatze bekommen
bale [beɪl] *n* Ballen *m*
balk [bɔk] *vi* zurückschrecken
ball [bɔl] *n* 1. Ball *m* 2. *(dance)* Ball *m*
▶ to **have** a ~ Spaß haben
ballad ['bæl·əd] *n* Ballade *f*
ballast ['bæl·əst] *n* Ballast *m*
ball 'bearing *n* Kugellager *nt*
ballerina [ˌbæl·ə·'ri·nə] *n* Ballerina *f*
ballet [bæ·'leɪ] *n* Ballett *nt*
bal'let dancer *n* Balletttänzer(in) *m(f)*
'ball game *n* Baseballspiel *nt*
ballistic [bə·'lɪs·tɪk] *adj* ballistisch ▶ to
go ~ *fam* ausflippen *fam*
balloon [bə·'lun] *n* Ballon *m*

ballot ['bæl·ət] *n* 1. Stimmzettel *m*
2. *(vote)* geheime Abstimmung; *(election)* Geheimwahl *f*
'ballot box *n* Wahlurne *f*
'ballpark *n* Baseballstadion *nt*
'ballplayer *n* Baseballspieler(in) *m(f)*
ballpoint, ballpoint 'pen *n* Kugelschreiber *m*
'ballroom *n* Ballsaal *m*
ballroom 'dancing *n* Gesellschaftstanz *m*
balls ['bɔlz] *n pl vulg, sl (testicles)* Eier
pl derb
Baltic ['bɔl·tɪk] *n* the ~ die Ostsee
bamboo [bæm·'bu] *n* Bambus *m*
bamboozle [bæm·'bu·zəl] *vt fam*
1. *(confuse)* verwirren 2. *(trick)* über[s]
Ohr hauen
ban [bæn] I. *n* Verbot *nt* II. *vt* <-nn-≥
(act, event) verbieten; *(person)* ausschließen
banal [bə·'nal] *adj* banal
banana [bə·'næn·ə] *n* Banane *f*
band¹ [bænd] *n* 1. *(of metal, cloth)*
Band *nt* 2. *(of color)* Streifen *m*
band² [bænd] *n* MUS Band *f*; *(traditional)*
Kapelle *f*; *(of criminals)* Bande
bandage ['bæn·dɪdʒ] I. *n* Verband *m*;
(of cloth) Binde *f* II. *vt* bandagieren;
(wound) verbinden
'Band-Aid® *n* Pflaster *nt*
B & B [ˌbi·ən(d)·'bi] *n abbr of* **bed and
breakfast**
bandit ['bæn·dɪt] *n* Bandit(in) *m(f)*
'bandwagon *n* ▶ to **jump** on the ~ auf
den fahrenden Zug aufspringen
bang [bæŋ] I. *n* 1. *(sound)* Knall *m*
2. *(blow)* Schlag *m* 3. ~s *pl (fringe)*
[kurzer] Pony II. *vi* Krach machen;
(door) knallen III. *vt (door)* zuschlagen
bangle ['bæŋ·gəl] *n* Armreif[en] *m*
banister ['bæn·ə·stər] *n usu pl* [Treppen]
geländer *nt*
banjo <pl -s> ['bæn·ʒoʊ] *n* Banjo *nt*
bank¹ [bæŋk] *n* Ufer *nt*; *(raised area)*
Abhang *m*
bank² [bæŋk] I. *n* FIN Bank *f* II. *vi* to ~
with sb bei jdm ein Konto haben
◆ **bank on** *vt* to ~ **on sth** *(rely on)* auf
etw *dat* zählen; *(expect)* mit etw *dat*
rechnen

bank account n Bankkonto nt
bank balance n Kontostand m
banker ['bæŋ·kər] n Banker(in) m(f)
banking ['bæŋ·kɪŋ] n Bankwesen nt
bank robber n Bankräuber(in) m(f)
bankrupt ['bæŋk·rʌpt] I. adj bankrott; to go ~ in Konkurs gehen II. n Konkursschuldner(in) m(f)
bankruptcy ['bæŋk·rəp·si] n Konkurs m
bank statement n Kontoauszug m
banner ['bæn·ər] n Banner nt
banquet ['bæŋ·kwət] n Bankett nt
baptism ['bæp·tɪz·əm] n Taufe f
Baptist ['bæp·tɪst] n Baptist(in) m(f)
baptize ['bæp·taɪz] vt taufen
bar [bar] I. n 1. (rod) Stange f; (of cage) Gitterstab m; to be behind ~s hinter Schloss und Riegel sein 2. (of chocolate) Riegel m; (of soap) Stück nt 3. (for drinking) Lokal nt, Bar f; (counter) Theke f 4. LAW to be admitted to the ~ als Anwalt/Anwältin [vor Gericht] zugelassen werden II. vt <-rr-> 1. (fasten) verriegeln 2. (obstruct) blockieren 3. (prohibit: something) verbieten; (somebody) ausschließen III. prep außer
barbarian [bar·'ber·i·ən] n Barbar(in) m(f)
barbaric [bar·'ber·ɪk] adj barbarisch
barbecue ['bar·bɪ·kju] I. n Grill m; (event) Grillparty f II. vt grillen
barbed 'wire n Stacheldraht m
barber ['bar·bər] n [Herren]friseur m
'bar code n Strichcode m
bare [ber] adj 1. nackt, bloß 2. the ~ essentials das Allernotwendigste
'bareback I. adj auf ungesatteltem Pferd nach n II. adv ohne Sattel
'barefaced adj unverschämt
'barefoot, 'barefooted I. adj barfüßig II. adv barfuß
barely ['ber·li] adv 1. (hardly) kaum 2. (scantily) karg
bargain ['bar·gɪn] I. n 1. Handel m 2. (good buy) guter Kauf II. vi [ver]handeln; (haggle) feilschen
  bargain for vt rechnen mit +dat
barge [bardʒ] I. n Lastkahn m II. vi to ~ into sb jdn anrempeln
baritone ['ber·ə·toʊn] n Bariton m
bark¹ [bark] n (of tree) [Baum]rinde f
bark² [bark] I. vi (dog) bellen II. n

Bellen nt
barley ['bar·li] n Gerste f
'barmaid n Bardame f
'barman n Barmann m
barn [barn] n Scheune f
barometer [bə·'ram·ə·tər] n Barometer nt
baroque [bə·'roʊk] adj barock
barracks ['bær·əks] npl + sing/pl vb Kaserne f
barrel ['bær·əl] n 1. Fass nt 2. (of gun) Lauf m
barren ['bær·ən] adj unfruchtbar; (landscape) karg
barrette [bə·'ret] n Haarspange f
barricade ['bær·ə·keɪd] I. n Barrikade f II. vt verbarrikadieren
barrier ['bær·i·ər] n Barriere f; (manmade) Absperrung f; RAIL Schranke f
barring ['bar·ɪŋ] prep ausgenommen
barrio [ba·rioʊ] n Barrio m (spanischsprachiges Viertel in amerikanischen Städten)
barrow ['bær·oʊ] n Schubkarren m
bartender ['bar·ten·dər] n Barkeeper m
barter ['bar·tər] I. n Tausch[handel] m II. vi Tauschhandel [be]treiben
base [beɪs] I. n 1. (bottom) Fuß m 2. (HQ) Hauptsitz m; MIL Basis f 3. SPORT Base f II. vt 1. to be ~d (company) seinen Sitz haben; (soldier) stationiert sein 2. (taken from) to be ~d on sth auf etw dat basieren
'baseball n Baseball m o nt
bash [bæʃ] fam I. n <pl -es> 1. (blow) [heftiger] Schlag 2. (party) Party f II. vi to ~ into zusammenstoßen mit +dat III. vt verhauen
bashful ['bæʃ·fəl] adj schüchtern
basic ['beɪ·sɪk] I. adj 1. (fundamental) grundlegend 2. (very simple) [sehr] einfach II. n the ~s pl die Grundlagen
basically ['beɪ·sɪ·kə·li] adv im Grunde
basil ['beɪ·zəl] n Basilikum nt
basin ['beɪ·sɪn] n Schüssel f; (washbasin) Waschbecken nt
basis <pl **bases**> ['beɪ·sɪs] n Basis f, Grundlage f
bask [bæsk] vi sich akk aalen a. fig
basket ['bæs·kɪt] n Korb m
'basketball n Basketball m
bass¹ [beɪs] n MUS Bass m

bass² [bæs] n (fish) Barsch m

bassoon [bə'suːn] n Fagott nt

bastard ['bæs·tərd] n Bastard m

bat¹ [bæt] n ZOOL Fledermaus f

bat² [bæt] I. n SPORT Schläger m II. vt, vi <-tt-> SPORT schlagen

batch <pl -es> [bætʃ] n Stapel m

bated ['beɪ·tɪd] adj with ~ breath mit angehaltenem Atem

bath [bæθ] n Bad nt; to take [or have] a ~ ein Bad nehmen, baden; (tub) [Bade]wanne f

bathe [beɪð] I. vi ein Bad nehmen; (swim) schwimmen II. vt baden

bather ['beɪ·ðər] n Badende(r) f(m)

bathing ['beɪ·ðɪŋ] n Baden nt

'bathing suit n Badeanzug m; (trunks) Badehose f

'bathrobe n Bademantel m

'bathroom n Bad[ezimmer] nt; to go to the ~ auf die Toilette gehen

'bathtub n Badewanne f

baton [bə'tɑn] n 1. (conductor's) Taktstock m 2. SPORT Staffelholz nt 3. (majorette) [Kommando]stab m

battalion [bə'tæl·jən] n Bataillon nt

batter¹ ['bæt·ər] n FOOD [Back]teig m

batter² ['bæt·ər] n SPORT Schlagmann m

batter³ ['bæt·ər] I. vt to ~ sb jdn verprügeln; to ~ sth auf etw akk einschlagen II. vi schlagen; (with fists) hämmern

battered ['bæt·ərd] adj 1. (beaten) misshandelt 2. (damaged) böse zugerichtet; (car) verbeult 3. FOOD paniert

battery ['bæt·ə·ri] n Batterie f

'battery charger n [Batterie]ladegerät nt

battle ['bæt·əl] I. n Kampf m, Schlacht f II. vi kämpfen a. fig

'battlefield, 'battleground n Schlachtfeld nt

'battleship n Schlachtschiff nt

bawl [bɔl] I. vi (weep) heulen, plärren; (bellow) brüllen II. vt schreien

bay [beɪ] n Bucht f

'bay leaf n Lorbeerblatt nt

bayonet [ˌbeɪ·ə·'net] n Bajonett nt

bazaar [bə·'zɑr] n Basar m

BC [ˌbi·'si] adv abbr of before Christ v. Chr.

be <was, been> [bi] vi + n/adj 1. (de-

scribes) sein; **she's a doctor** sie ist Ärztin; **what do you want to ~ when you grow up?** was willst du einmal werden, wenn du erwachsen bist? 2. (location) sein; (town, country) liegen; **there is/ are ...** es gibt ... 3. (in imperatives) ~ **quiet!** sei still!; **please ~ seated!** setzen Sie sich bitte! 4. (expressing continuation) **it's raining** es regnet; **you're always complaining** du beklagst dich dauernd 5. (expressing passive) **to ~ asked** gefragt werden; **what is to ~ done?** was kann getan werden?

beach [bitʃ] n <pl -es> Strand m

'beach ball n Wasserball m

'beachwear n Strandkleidung f

bead [bid] n Perle f

beak [bik] n Schnabel m

beaker ['bi·kər] n Becherglas nt

beam [bim] I. n 1. (light) [Licht]strahl m 2. (rafter) Balken m II. vi strahlen

bean [bin] n Bohne f; **baked ~s** Baked Beans pl

'bean sprouts npl Sojabohnensprossen pl

bear¹ [ber] n (animal) Bär(in) m(f)

bear² <bore, born(e)> [ber] I. vt 1. (carry) tragen 2. (endure) ertragen; (suspense) aushalten 3. (harbor) **to ~ sb a grudge** einen Groll gegen jdn hegen 4. (keep) **I'll ~ that in mind** ich werde das berücksichtigen II. vi **to ~ right** sich rechts halten

beard [bɪrd] n Bart m

bearded ['bɪr·dɪd] adj bärtig

bearing ['ber·ɪŋ] n Peilung f; **to lose one's ~s** die Orientierung verlieren

beast [bist] n Tier nt; ~ **of burden** Lasttier nt; (person) Biest nt, Bestie f

beastly ['bist·li] adj scheußlich, ekelhaft

beat [bit] I. n 1. (throb) Schlag m 2. (act) Schlagen nt; (of heart) Klopfen nt 3. MUS Takt m 4. usu sing (route) Runde f II. adj fam fix und fertig III. vt <beat, beaten or beat> 1. (hit) schlagen; **to ~ sth** gegen/auf etw akk schlagen; **to ~ sb to death** jdn totschlagen 2. FOOD schlagen; (defeat) schlagen; **it ~s me how/why ...** fam es ist mir ein Rätsel, wie/warum ... ▶ ~ **it!** fam hau ab! IV. vi <beat, beaten or beat> 1. (throb) schlagen; (heart a.) klopfen

2. (*strike*) **to ~ against/on sth** gegen etw *akk* schlagen

beat down I. *vi* (*rain*) [her]niederprasseln; (*sun*) [her]niederbrennen **II.** *vt* herunterhandeln

beat off *vt* abwehren; MIL zurückschlagen

beat up I. *vt* zusammenschlagen **II.** *vi* **to ~ up on** verprügeln

eater ['biːtər] *n* Rührbesen *m*

eautician [bjuːˈtɪʃ·ən] *n* Kosmetiker(in) *m(f)*

eautiful ['bjuː·tə·fəl] *adj* **1.** (*attractive*) schön **2.** (*uplifting*) herrlich, großartig

eauty ['bjuː·ti] *n* Schönheit *f*

beauty contest, 'beauty pageant *n* Schönheitswettbewerb *m*

beauty parlor *n* Schönheitssalon *m*

eaver ['biː·vər] *n* Biber *m*

ecame [bɪˈkeɪm] *pt of* **become**

ecause [bɪˈkɔz] **I.** *conj* weil; (*since*) da; (*for*) denn **II.** *prep* **~ of** wegen +*gen*

eckon ['bek·ən] *vi* winken *a. fig*

ecome <became, become> [bɪˈkʌm] *vt, vi* werden; **what became of ...?** was ist aus ... geworden?

ecoming [bɪˈkʌm·ɪŋ] *adj* (*clothes*) vorteilhaft

ed [bed] *n* **1.** Bett *nt;* **to go to ~** ins Bett gehen **2.** (*for flowers*) Beet *nt*

ed and 'breakfast *n* Zimmer *nt* mit Frühstück

edclothes *npl* Bettzeug *nt kein pl*

edding ['bed·ɪŋ] *n* **1.** Bettzeug *nt* **2.** AGR [Ein]streu *f*

ed linen *n* Bettwäsche *f*

edridden *adj* bettlägerig

edroom *n* Schlafzimmer *nt*

edside 'table *n* Nachttisch *m*

edspread *n* Tagesdecke *f*

edtime *n* Schlafenszeit *f*

ee [biː] *n* Biene *f*

eech [biːtʃ] *n* Buche *f*

eef [biːf] *n* Rindfleisch *nt*

eefsteak *n* Beefsteak *nt*

eefy ['biː·fi] *adj fam* muskulös

eehive *n* Bienenstock *m;* (*rounded*) Bienenkorb *m*

eeline *n* **to make a ~ for sb/sth** schnurstracks auf jdn/etw zugehen

een [bɪn] *pp of* **be**

beep [biːp] **I.** *vt* **1.** (*toot*) **to ~ one's horn** hupen **2.** (*on pager*) anpiepen **II.** *vi* piepen; (*in car*) hupen **III.** *n* Piep[s] ton *m;* (*of car*) Hupen *nt*

beeper ['biː·pər] *n* Piepser *m*

beer [bɪr] *n* Bier *nt*

'beer garden *n* Biergarten *m*

beet [biːt] *n* (*plant*) [Runkel]rübe *f;* (*edible root*) Rote Bete

beetle ['biː·əl] *n* Käfer *m*

before [bɪˈfɔr] **I.** *prep* **1.** (*earlier*) vor +*dat;* **~ long** in Kürze **2.** (*in front of*) vor +*dat; with verbs of motion* vor +*akk* **II.** *conj* **1.** (*at previous time*) bevor **2.** (*rather than*) bevor, ehe **3.** (*until*) bis; **not ~** erst, wenn **III.** *adv* zuvor, vorher; **I have never seen that ~** das habe ich noch nie gesehen **IV.** *adj after n* zuvor

beforehand [bɪˈfɔrˌhænd] *adv* vorher

befriend [bɪˈfrend] *vt* sich anfreunden mit +*dat*

beg <-gg-> [beg] **I.** *vt* bitten; **to ~ sb's forgiveness** um Verzeihung bitten; **I ~ your pardon** entschuldigen Sie bitte **II.** *vi* **1.** (*seek charity*) betteln **2.** (*request*) **to ~ for mercy** um Gnade flehen **3.** (*dog*) Männchen machen

began [bɪˈgæn] *pt of* **begin**

beggar ['beg·ər] *n* Bettler(in) *m(f)*

begin <-nn-, began, begun> [bɪˈgɪn] *vt, vi* anfangen, beginnen; **she was ~ning to get angry** sie wurde allmählich wütend; **to ~ with** zunächst einmal

beginner [bɪˈgɪn·ər] *n* Anfänger(in) *m(f)*

beginning [bɪˈgɪn·ɪŋ] *n* Anfang *m;* (*in time*) Beginn *m;* **at** [*or* **in**] **the ~** am Anfang

begrudge [bɪˈgrʌdʒ] *vt* **to ~ sb sth** jdm etw missgönnen

begun [bɪˈgʌn] *pp of* **begin**

behalf [bɪˈhæf] *n* **on ~ of sb** [*or* **on sb's ~**] (*speaking for*) im Namen einer Person; (*as authorized by*) im Auftrag von jdm

behave [bɪˈheɪv] **I.** *vi* **1.** (*people*) sich benehmen; **~!** benimm dich! **2.** (*object, substance*) sich verhalten **II.** *vt* **to ~ oneself** sich [anständig] benehmen

behavior [bɪˈheɪ·jər] *n* Benehmen *nt,* Verhalten *nt*

behind [bɪˈhaɪnd] **I.** *prep* **1.** hinter

+*dat*; with verbs of motion hinter +*akk*
2. *fig* I'm ~ you all the way ich stehe voll hinter dir **II.** *adv* hinten **III.** *adj* **1.** (*in arrears*) im Rückstand **2.** (*slow*) to be [way] ~ [weit] zurück sein **IV.** *n fam* Hintern *m*

beige [beɪʒ] *adj* beige[farben]

being ['biːɪŋ] **I.** *n* **1.** (*creature*) Wesen *nt* **2.** (*existence*) Dasein *nt* **II.** *adj* for the time ~ vorerst

belated [bɪˈleɪˌtɪd] *adj* verspätet

belch [beltʃ] **I.** *n* <*pl* -es> Rülpser *m* **II.** *vi* rülpsen

belfry ['bel·fri] *n* Glockenturm *m*

Belgian ['bel·dʒən] **I.** *n* Belgier(in) *m(f)* **II.** *adj* belgisch

Belgium ['bel·dʒəm] *n* Belgien *nt*

belief [bɪˈliːf] *n* **1.** (*faith*) Glaube *m kein pl* **2.** (*view*) Überzeugung *f*

believable [bɪˈliː·və·bəl] *adj* glaubwürdig

believe [bɪˈliːv] **I.** *vt* **1.** glauben; would you ~ it? kannst du dir das vorstellen? **2.** (*pretend*) to make ~ [that] ... so tun, als ob ... **II.** *vi* **1.** (*be certain of*) glauben (in an +*akk*) **2.** (*have confidence*) to ~ in sb/sth auf jdn/etw vertrauen **3.** (*support sincerely*) to ~ in sth viel von etw *dat* halten **4.** (*think*) glauben; I ~ so ich glaube schon

believer [bɪˈliː·vər] *n* Gläubige(r) *f(m)*

bell [bel] *n* Glocke *f*; (*smaller*) Glöckchen *nt*; (*on door*) [Tür]klingel *f*

bellboy *n* [Hotel]page *m*

belligerent [bɪˈlɪdʒ·ər·ənt] *adj* kampflustig

bellow ['bel·oʊ] **I.** *vt, vi* brüllen **II.** *n* Gebrüll *nt*

bellows ['bel·oʊz] *npl* Blasebalg *m*

belly ['bel·i] *n* Bauch *m*

bellyache *n fam* Bauchschmerzen *pl*, Bauchweh *nt kein pl*

belly button *n fam* [Bauch]nabel *m*

belly dancer *n* Bauchtänzerin *f*

belong [bɪˈlɑŋ] *vi* **1.** (*be owned*) to ~ to sb jdm gehören; where do these spoons ~? wohin gehören diese Löffel? **2.** (*fit in*) [dazu]gehören

belongings [bɪˈlɑŋ·ɪŋz] *npl* Hab und Gut *nt kein pl*

beloved [bɪˈlʌv·ɪd] **I.** *n* Geliebte(r) *f(m)*

II. *adj* geliebt

below [bɪˈloʊ] **I.** *adv* **1.** (*lower*) unter darunter **2.** (*on page*) unten **II.** *pre* unter +*dat*; with verbs of motion un ter +*akk*

belt [belt] **I.** *n* Gürtel *m*; (*conveyor* Band *nt*; (*area*) Gebiet *nt* **II.** *vt fam* hauen; (*ball*) knallen

bemused [bɪˈmjuːzd] *adj* verwirrt

bench <*pl* -es> [bentʃ] *n* Bank *f*; LAW th ~ die [Richter]bank

benchmark *n* Maßstab *m*

benchwarmer *n* SPORT Ersatzspie ler(in) *m(f)* (*der/die kaum eingesetz wird*)

bend [bend] **I.** *n* (*in road*) Kurve *f*; (*i river*) Biegung *f* **II.** *vi* <bent, bent **1.** (*turn: road*) biegen; to ~ forwar sich vorbeugen **2.** (*be flexible*) sic biegen; (*tree*) sich neigen **III.** *vt* biegen (*deform*) verbiegen; to ~ the rules *fi* sich nicht ganz an die Regeln halten

bend down *vi* sich niederbeugen

beneath [bɪˈniːθ] **I.** *prep* unter +*da* with verbs of motion unter +*akk* **II.** *ac* unten, darunter

benefactor ['ben·ə·fæk·tər] *n* Wohltä ter(in) *m(f)*

beneficiary [ˌben·ə·ˈfɪʃ·i·ər·i] *n* Nutznie ßer(in) *m(f)*

benefit ['ben·ə·fɪt] **I.** *n* **1.** (*advantage* Vorteil *m*; (*profit*) Nutzen *m* **2.** (*we fare*) Beihilfe *f* **II.** *vi* <-t-> to ~ from sth von etw *dat* profitieren **III.** *vt* <-t-> to ~ sb/sth jdm/etw nützen

bent [bent] **I.** *pt, pp of* **bend II.** *n* Nei gung *f* **III.** *adj* umgebogen; (*wire*) ver bogen; (*person*) gekrümmt

bequest [bɪˈkwest] *n* Vermächtnis *nt*

bereaved [bɪˈriːvd] **I.** *adj* trauernd **II.** the ~ *pl* die Hinterbliebenen

bereavement [bɪˈriːv·mənt] *n* Trauer fall *m*

beret [bəˈreɪ] *n* Baskenmütze *f*; MIL Ba rett *nt*

Bermuda shorts [bərˌmjuː·də·ˈʃɔrts] *np* Bermudas *pl*

berry ['ber·i] *n* Beere *f*

berserk [bərˈsɜrk] *adj* außer sich *dat* t go ~ [fuchsteufels]wild werden

berth [bɜrθ] *n* (*for ship*) Liegeplatz *m*

B

(*bed*) [Schlaf]koje *f*; RAIL Schlafwagenbett *nt*

beside [bɪˈsaɪd] *prep* 1. (*next to*) neben +*dat*; *with verbs of motion* neben +*akk* 2. (*irrelevant to*) ~ **the point** nicht der Punkt

besides [bɪˈsaɪdz] I. *adv* außerdem II. *prep* 1. (*in addition to*) außer +*dat* 2. (*except for*) abgesehen von +*dat*

besiege [bɪˈsiːdʒ] *vt* belagern

best [best] I. *adj superl of* **good** 1. (*finest*) **the ~ ...** der/die/das beste ...; ~ **wishes** herzliche Grüße 2. (*most favorable*) **what's the ~ way to ...** wie komme ich am besten zum/zur ...; **to be ~** am besten sein II. *adv superl of* **well** ~ **of all** am allerbesten III. *n* 1. (*finest person, thing*) **the ~** der/die/das Beste 2. (*most favorable*) **all the ~!** *fam* alles Gute!; **at ~** bestenfalls

best 'man *n* Trauzeuge *m* (*des Bräutigams*)

best'seller *n* Bestseller *m*

bet [bet] I. *n* Wette *f*; **to make a ~ with sb** mit jdm wetten II. *vt, vi* <-tt-, bet *or* -ted, bet *or* -ted> wetten; **I ~ you 25 dollars that ...** ich wette mit dir um 25 Dollar, dass ...

betray [bɪˈtreɪ] *vt* 1. (*be disloyal to*) verraten; (*deceive*) betrügen 2. (*reveal: feelings*) zeigen

betrayal [bɪˈtreɪ·əl] *n* Verrat *m*

better [ˈbet·ər] I. *adj comp of* **good** besser; **she is much ~ at tennis than I am** sie spielt viel besser Tennis als ich; **to get ~** sich erholen II. *adv comp of* **well** 1. (*more skillfully*) besser 2. (*to a greater degree*) mehr; **there's nothing I like ~ than ...** ich tue nichts lieber als ... III. *n* **to change for the ~** sich zum Guten wenden; **all** [*or* **so much**] **the ~** umso besser

betting [ˈbet·ɪŋ] *n* Wetten *nt*

between [bɪˈtwin] I. *prep* zwischen +*dat*; *with verbs of motion* zwischen +*akk*; ~ **you and me** unter uns gesagt II. *adv* [in] ~ dazwischen

beverage [ˈbev·ər·ɪdʒ] *n* Getränk *nt*

beware [bɪˈwer] *vt, vi* sich in Acht nehmen (*of* vor +*dat*); **"~ of the dog"** „[Vorsicht,] bissiger Hund!"

bewilder [bɪˈwɪl·dər] *vt* verwirren

bewilderment [bɪˈwɪl·dər·mənt] *n* Verwirrung *f*

bewitch [bɪˈwɪtʃ] *vt* 1. (*by magic*) verzaubern 2. (*delight*) bezaubern

beyond [bɪˈjɑnd] I. *prep* 1. (*on other side*) über +*akk*, jenseits +*gen* 2. (*after*) nach +*dat* 3. (*further than*) über +*akk* 4. (*surpassing*) ~ **help** nicht mehr zu helfen II. *adv* (*in space*) jenseits; (*in time*) darüber hinaus

biannual [ˌbaɪˈæn·ju·əl] *adj* halbjährlich

bias [ˈbaɪ·əs] I. *n usu sing* 1. (*prejudice*) Vorurteil *nt* 2. (*predisposition*) Neigung *f* II. *vt* <-s-> **to ~ sb against sth** jdn gegen etw *akk* einnehmen

biased [ˈbaɪ·əst] *adj* voreingenommen

bib [bɪb] *n* Lätzchen *nt*

Bible [ˈbaɪ·bəl] *n* Bibel *f*

'Bible belt *n* Bibelgürtel *m* (*sehr christliche Gebiete der USA*)

biblical [ˈbɪb·lɪ·kəl] *adj* biblisch

bibliography [ˌbɪb·liˈɑg·rə·fi] *n* Bibliografie *f*

bicarbonate [ˌbaɪˈkar·bə·nɪt], **bicarbonate of 'soda** *n* Natriumbikarbonat *nt*; (*in cooking*) Natron *nt*

bicentennial [ˌbaɪ·senˈten·i·əl], **bicentenary** [ˌbaɪ·senˈten·ə·ri] *n* zweihundertjähriges Jubiläum

biceps <pl -> [ˈbaɪ·seps] *n* Bizeps *m*

bicker [ˈbɪk·ər] *vi* sich zanken

bicycle [ˈbaɪ·sɪk·əl] *n* Fahrrad *nt*

bid¹ <-dd-, bid *or* bade, bid *or* bidden> [bɪd] *vt* **to ~ sb farewell** jdm Lebewohl sagen

bid² [bɪd] I. *n* 1. (*offer*) Angebot *nt*; (*at auction*) Gebot *nt* 2. (*attempt*) Versuch *m* II. *vt, vi* <-dd-, bid, bid> bieten

biennial [baɪˈen·i·əl] *adj* zweijährlich

big <-gg-> [bɪɡ] *adj* 1. groß; (*tip*) großzügig 2. (*significant*) bedeutend

bigamist [ˈbɪɡ·ə·mɪst] *n* Bigamist(in) *m(f)*

bigamy [ˈbɪɡ·ə·mi] *n* Bigamie *f*

Big 'Apple *n fam* **the ~** New York *nt*

big 'cheese *n fam* hohes Tier *fam*

Big 'Easy *n fam* **the ~** New Orleans *nt*

bigot [ˈbɪɡ·ət] *n* Eiferer, Eiferin *m, f*

bigoted [ˈbɪɡ·ə·tɪd] *adj* fanatisch

bigotry [ˈbɪɡ·ə·tri] *n* Fanatismus *m*

'**big shot** n fam hohes Tier

'**big time** n fam **to hit the ~** den großen Durchbruch schaffen

bike [baɪk] n fam (bicycle) [Fahr]rad nt; (motorcycle) Motorrad nt

biker ['baɪ·kər] n fam (bicycle rider) Fahrradfahrer; (motorcycle rider) Motorradfahrer(in) m(f); (in gang) Rocker(in) m(f)

bikini [bɪ·ˈki·ni] n Bikini m

bile [baɪl] n Galle f

bilious ['bɪl·jəs] adj MED ~ **attack** Gallenkolik f

bill[1] [bɪl] n 1. (invoice) Rechnung f; **could we have the ~, please?** könnten wir bitte zahlen? 2. (money) Geldschein m; **[one-]dollar ~** Dollarschein m 3. (placard) Plakat nt

bill[2] [bɪl] n (of bird) Schnabel m

'**billboard** n Reklamefläche f

'**billfold** n Brieftasche f

billiards ['bɪl·jərdz] n + sing vb Billard nt

billion ['bɪl·jən] n Milliarde f

'**billy goat** n Ziegenbock m

bimbo <pl -es> ['bɪm·boʊ] n pej fam Puppe f pej

bin [bɪn] n (for garbage) Mülleimer m; (for storage) Behälter m

binary ['baɪ·nə·ri] adj binär

bind [baɪnd] I. n fam 1. **to be a ~** lästig sein 2. **to be in a ~** in der Klemme stecken II. vt <bound, bound> **to ~ sb** jdn fesseln; **to ~ sth** etw festbinden

binder ['baɪn·dər] n Einband m

binding ['baɪn·dɪŋ] I. n 1. (covering) Einband m 2. (on ski) Bindung f II. adj verbindlich

binge [bɪndʒ] n fam Gelage nt

bingo ['bɪŋ·goʊ] I. n Bingo nt II. interj bingo

binoculars [bɪ·ˈnak·jə·lərz] npl **[pair of] ~** Fernglas nt

bio'chemistry n Biochemie f

biode'gradable adj biologisch abbaubar

'**biofuel** n Biotreibstoff m

'**biogas** n Biogas nt

biographer [baɪ·ˈag·rə·fər] n Biograf(in) m(f)

biographical [ˌbaɪ·oʊ·ˈgræf·ɪ·kəl] adj biografisch

biography [baɪ·ˈag·rə·fi] n Biografie f

biological [ˌbaɪ·ə·ˈladʒ·ɪ·kəl] adj biologisch

biologist [baɪ·ˈal·ə·dʒɪst] n Biologe, -in m, f

biology [baɪ·ˈal·ə·dʒi] n Biologie f

biopsy ['baɪ·ap·si] n Biopsie f

biped ['baɪ·ped] n Zweifüß[l]er(in) m(f)

birch <pl -es> [bɜrtʃ] n Birke f

bird [bɜrd] n Vogel m

'**birdcage** n Vogelkäfig m

birdie ['bɜr·di] n 1. esp childspeak Piepmatz m 2. SPORT Federball m

'**birdseed** n Vogelfutter m

'**bird's-eye 'view** n Vogelperspektive f

'**bird watching** n das Beobachten von Vögeln

birth [bɜrθ] n 1. (event) Geburt f; **date of ~** Geburtsdatum nt; **to give ~ to a child** ein Kind zur Welt bringen 2. (family) Abstammung f; **American by ~** gebürtiger Amerikaner/gebürtige Amerikanerin

'**birth certificate** n Geburtsurkunde f

'**birth control** n Geburtenkontrolle f

birthday ['bɜrθ·deɪ] n Geburtstag m; **happy ~ [to you]!** alles Gute zum Geburtstag!

'**birthday cake** n Geburtstagstorte f

'**birthday card** n Geburtstagskarte f

'**birthday party** n Geburtstagsparty f

'**birthday present** n Geburtstagsgeschenk nt

'**birthmark** n Muttermal nt

'**birthplace** n Geburtsort m

biscuit ['bɪs·kɪt] n Brötchen nt

bisect ['baɪ·sekt] vt zweiteilen

bisexual [ˌbaɪ·ˈsek·ʃʊ·əl] I. n Bisexuelle(r) f(m) II. adj bisexuell

bishop ['bɪʃ·əp] n 1. REL Bischof m 2. CHESS Läufer m

bison <pl -s> ['baɪ·sən] n Bison m; (European) Wisent m

bit[1] [bɪt] n 1. (piece) Stück nt 2. (part) Teil m; (of a story) Stelle f 3. (a little) **a ~** ein bisschen 4. (quite a lot) **[quite] a ~ of money** ziemlich viel Geld

bit[2] [bɪt] vt, vi pt of **bite**

bitch [bɪtʃ] n <pl -es> 1. pej fam Miststück nt 2. (dog) Hündin f

bite [baɪt] I. n Biss m; (of insect) Stich m;

to have a ~ to eat *fam* eine Kleinigkeit essen II. *vt* <bit, bitten> beißen; (*insect*) stechen; **to ~ one's nails** an seinen Nägeln kauen III. *vi* <bit, bitten> (*dog, snake*) beißen; (*insect*) stechen

bitten ['bɪt·ən] *vt, vi pp of* **bite**

bitter ['bɪt·ər] *adj* <-er, -est> 1. (*taste*) bitter 2. *fig* bitter 3. (*resentful*) verbittert

bitterly ['bɪt·ər·li] *adv* bitter; **~ cold** bitterkalt; **~ disappointed** schwer enttäuscht

bitterness ['bɪt·ər·nɪs] *n* Verbitterung *f*; FOOD Bitterkeit *f*

bizarre [bɪ·'zar] *adj* bizarr; (*behavior*) seltsam

blab <-bb-> [blæb] *vi fam* ausplaudern

black [blæk] I. *adj* schwarz *a. fig*; **~ and blue** grün und blau II. *n* 1. (*person*) Schwarze(r) *f/m* 2. (*color*) Schwarz *nt*

blackberry ['blæk·ˌber·i] *n* Brombeere *f*

blackbird *n* Amsel *f*

blackboard *n* Tafel *f*

black 'box *n* AEROSP Flugschreiber *m*

black 'eye *n* blaues Auge

blackhead *n* Mitesser *m*

black 'hole *n* schwarzes Loch *a. fig*

blackjack ['blæk·dʒæk] *n* CARDS Siebzehnundvier *nt*

blacklist I. *n* schwarze Liste II. *vt* auf die schwarze Liste setzen

blackmail I. *n* Erpressung *f* II. *vt* erpressen

blackmailer *n* Erpresser(in) *m(f)*

black 'market *n* Schwarzmarkt *m*

blackout ['blæk·aʊt] *n* 1. (*unconsciousness*) Ohnmachtsanfall *m* 2. ELEC [Strom]ausfall *m*

Black 'Sea *n* **the ~** das Schwarze Meer

bladder ['blæd·ər] *n* [Harn]blase *f*

blade [bleɪd] *n* Klinge *f*; **~ of grass** Grashalm *m*

blame [bleɪm] I. *vt* **to ~ sb/sth for sth** [*or* **sth on sb/sth**] jdm/etw die Schuld an etw *dat* geben II. *n* Schuld *f*; **to take the ~** die Schuld auf sich nehmen

blameless ['bleɪm·lɪs] *adj* schuldlos; (*life*) untadelig

bland [blænd] *adj* fade; *fig* vage

blank [blæŋk] I. *adj* 1. (*empty*) leer; **my mind went ~** ich hatte ein totales Blackout 2. (*without emotion*) ausdruckslos; (*without comprehension*) verständnislos II. *n* Leerstelle *f*, Lücke *f*

blanket ['blæŋ·kɪt] I. *n* Decke *f* II. *vt* bedecken

blare [bler] I. *n* Geplärr[e] *nt* II. *vi* (*radio*) plärren; (*music*) dröhnen

blast [blæst] I. *n* 1. (*explosion*) Explosion *f* 2. **~ of air** Luftstoß *m*; **at full ~** (*radio*) in voller Lautstärke II. *vt* sprengen

blasted ['blæs·tɪd] *adj attr fam* verdammt

blastoff ['blæst·af] *n* [Raketen]start *m*

blatant ['bleɪ·tənt] *adj* offensichtlich; (*lie*) unverfroren

blaze [bleɪz] I. *n* 1. (*fire*) Brand *m* 2. (*light*) Glanz *m* II. *vi* (*fire*) [hell] lodern; (*eyes*) glänzen; (*sun*) brennen

blazer ['bleɪ·zər] *n* Blazer *m*

blazing ['bleɪ·zɪŋ] *adj* (*fire*) lodernd; (*argument*) heftig; (*sun*) grell

bleach [blitʃ] I. *vt* bleichen II. *n* <*pl* -es> Bleichmittel *nt*; (*for hair*) Blondierungsmittel *nt*

bleachers ['bli·tʃərz] *npl* unüberdachte [Zuschauer]tribüne

bleak [blik] *adj* öde; *fig* trostlos

bleary ['blɪr·i] *adj* (*sleepy*) verschlafen; (*eyes*) müde

bleat [blit] *vi* (*sheep*) blöken; (*person*) jammern

bled [bled] *pt, pp of* **bleed**

bleed [blid] *vi* <bled, bled> bluten

bleep [blip] I. *n* Piepton *m* II. *vi* piepsen

blemish <*pl* -es> ['blem·ɪʃ] *n* Makel *m*

blend [blend] I. *n* Mischung *f* II. *vt* [miteinander] vermischen III. *vi* (*not be noticed*) **to ~ into sth** mit etw *dat* verschmelzen

blender ['blen·dər] *n* Mixer *m*

bless <-ed *or* blest, -ed *or* blest> [bles] *vt* segnen ▶ **[him/her]!** der/die Gute!; **~ you!** (*after a sneeze*) Gesundheit!; (*as thanks*) das ist lieb von dir!

blessing ['bles·ɪŋ] *n* Segen *m*

blew [blu] *pt of* **blow**

blind [blaɪnd] I. *n* 1. Jalousie *f* 2. (*people*) **the ~** *pl* die Blinden II. *vt* blind machen; (*temporarily*) blenden III. *adj* blind *a. fig*

blind 'alley n Sackgasse f a. fig

blinders ['blaɪn·dərz] n pl Scheuklappen pl a. fig

blindfold ['blaɪnd·foʊld] I. n Augenbinde f II. vt **to ~ sb** jdm die Augen verbinden

blinding ['blaɪnd·ɪŋ] adj blendend, grell

blindness ['blaɪnd·nɪs] n Blindheit f

blink [blɪŋk] I. vi blinzeln; (intentionally) zwinkern; (of light) blinken II. n Blinzeln nt; (intentionally) Zwinkern nt

blinker ['blɪŋ·kər] n AUTO Blinker m

bliss [blɪs] n [Glück]seligkeit f

blissful ['blɪs·fəl] adj glückselig; (smile) selig

blister ['blɪs·tər] I. n Blase f II. vi (paint) Blasen werfen; (skin) Blasen bekommen

blitz [blɪts] I. n [plötzlicher] Luftangriff m II. vt bombardieren

blizzard ['blɪz·ərd] n Schneesturm m

bloated ['bloʊ·t̬ɪd] adj aufgedunsen; (overindulged) vollgestopft

blob [blab] n 1. (spot) Klecks m 2. (mass) Klümpchen nt

block [blak] I. n 1. Block m; (of wood) Holzklotz m 2. (neighborhood) [Häuser]block m II. vt blockieren; (artery, pipeline) verstopfen; (exit, passage) versperren

♦ **block up** vt blockieren; (clog) verstopfen

blockade [bla·'keɪd] I. n Blockade f II. vt abriegeln

blockage ['blak·ɪdʒ] n Verstopfung f

block 'capitals, block 'letters npl Blockbuchstaben; **in ~** in Blockschrift

blond(e) [bland] I. adj blond II. n Blonde(r) f(m); (woman a.) Blondine f

blood [blʌd] n Blut nt

'**blood bank** n Blutbank f

'**bloodbath** n Blutbad nt

'**bloodcurdling** adj markerschütternd

'**blood donor** n Blutspender(in) m(f)

'**blood group** n Blutgruppe f

'**blood poisoning** n Blutvergiftung f

'**blood pressure** n Blutdruck m

'**bloodshed** n Blutvergießen nt

'**bloodshot** adj blutunterlaufen

'**bloodsucker** n Blutsauger m a. fig

'**blood test** n Bluttest m

'**bloodthirsty** adj blutrünstig

'**blood type** n Blutgruppe f

'**blood vessel** n Blutgefäß nt

bloody ['blʌd·i] adj blutig

bloom [blum] I. n Blüte f II. vi blühen

blossom ['blas·əm] I. n [Baum]blüte f II. vi blühen a. fig

blot [blat] n Klecks m

blotch <pl -es> [blatʃ] n Fleck m

blotchy ['blatʃ·i] adj fleckig

blouse [blaʊs] n Bluse f

blow¹ [bloʊ] I. vi <blew, blown> (wind) wehen; (exhale) blasen; (fuse) durchbrennen; (tire) platzen II. vt <blew, blown> 1. blasen; (wind) wehen; **to ~ one's nose** sich dat die Nase putzen 2. fam **you've ~n it!** du hast es vermasselt!

♦ **blow away** I. vt (wind) wegwehen; fam (kill) wegpusten; fig fam (impress) umhauen fig fam II. vi wegfliegen, verwehen

♦ **blow down** I. vi umgeweht werden II. vt umwehen

♦ **blow out** I. vt 1. (extinguish) ausblasen 2. **to ~ out ⇄ one's brains** sich dat eine Kugel durch den Kopf jagen II. vi 1. (candle) verlöschen 2. (tire) platzen

♦ **blow up** I. vi explodieren; fig (get angry) an die Decke gehen II. vt (inflate) aufblasen; fig (exaggerate) hochspielen; (enlarge) vergrößern; (destroy) [in die Luft] sprengen

blow² [bloʊ] n 1. (hit) Schlag m 2. (setback) [Schicksals]schlag m

'**blow-dry** I. vt <-ie-> fönen II. n Fönen nt

blown [bloʊn] vt, vi pp of **blow**

blowout ['bloʊ·aʊt] n 1. (of tire) Platzen nt [eines Reifens] 2. fam (meal) Schlemmerei f

'**blowup** n PHOT Vergrößerung f; fam (argument) Krach m

blue [blu] I. adj <-r, -st> 1. blau 2. (depressed) traurig II. n Blau nt

'**bluebell** n [blaue Wiesen]glockenblume f

'**blueberry** n Heidelbeere f

'**blueprint** n Blaupause f; fig Plan m

blues [bluz] npl 1. fam **to have the ~** melancholisch drauf sein fam 2. (music) Blues m

bluff [blʌf] **I.** vi bluffen **II.** vt täuschen **III.** n Bluff m

blunder ['blʌn·dər] **I.** n schwer[wiegend]er Fehler **II.** vi **1.** (make mistake) einen groben Fehler machen **2. to ~ into sth** in etw akk hineinplatzen

blunt [blʌnt] adj **1.** (not sharp) stumpf **2.** (outspoken) direkt

bluntly ['blʌnt·li] adv direkt

blur [blɜr] **I.** vi <-rr-> verschwimmen **II.** vt <-rr-> verschwimmen lassen

blurred [blɜrd], **blurry** ['blɜr·i] adj verschwommen; (picture) unscharf

blush [blʌʃ] **I.** vi erröten **II.** n (Scham-)röte

blusher ['blʌʃ·ər] n Rouge nt

bluster ['blʌs·tər] **I.** vi poltern **II.** n Theater nt fig

boa ['boʊ·ə] n Boa f

board [bɔrd] **I.** n **1.** Brett nt; (blackboard) Tafel f; (bulletin board) Schwarzes Brett; (sign) [Aushänge]schild nt **2.** ADMIN Behörde f; ~ **of directors** Vorstand m **3. on** ~ an Bord a. fig **II.** vt **1. to** ~ **up** mit Brettern vernageln; (plane, ship) besteigen; (bus, train) einsteigen in +akk **III.** vi **1.** SCH im Internat wohnen **2.** AVIAT **Flight 345 is now ready for ~ing** Flug 345 ist nun fertig zum Einsteigen

boarder ['bɔr·dər] n **1.** SCH Internatsschüler(in) m(f) **2.** (lodger) Pensionsgast m

board game n Brettspiel nt

'boarding card n Bordkarte f

'boarding house n Pension f

'boarding pass n Bordkarte f

'boarding school n Internat nt

'boardwalk n Uferpromenade f (aus Holz)

boast [boʊst] **I.** vi angeben **II.** n großspurige Behauptung

boat [boʊt] n Boot nt; (bigger) Schiff nt

'boat trip n Bootsfahrt f

bob¹ [bɑb] n abbr of **bobsleigh** Bob m

bob² <-bb-> [bɑb] vi to ~ [up and down] sich auf und ab bewegen

'bobsled n Bob[sleigh] m

bode [boʊd] vt, vi to ~ **well/ill** etwas Gutes/Schlechtes bedeuten

bodice ['bɑd·ɪs] n Oberteil nt

bodily ['bɑd·əl·i] **I.** adj körperlich **II.** adv gewaltsam

body ['bɑd·i] n **1.** Körper m **2.** (group)

Gruppe f **3.** (central part) Hauptteil m **4.** (corpse) Leiche f; (of animal) Kadaver m **5.** (substance: of hair) Fülle f

'body bag n Leichensack m

'bodyguard n Bodyguard m; (group) Leibwache f

'body language n Körpersprache f

'body lotion n Körperlotion f

'body search n Leibesvisitation f

'bodywork n AUTO Karosserie f

bog [bɑg] n Sumpf m

'bogeyman n Schreckgespenst nt

boggle ['bɑg·əl] vi sprachlos [or fassungslos] sein

bogus ['boʊ·gəs] adj unecht; (documents, name) falsch

boil [bɔɪl] **I.** n **1. to come to a ~** anfangen zu kochen **2.** MED Furunkel m o nt **II.** vi **1.** kochen **2.** CHEM den Siedepunkt erreichen **III.** vt kochen; (bring to boil) zum Kochen bringen

boiler ['bɔɪ·lər] n Boiler m

'boiler room n Kesselraum m

boiling ['bɔɪ·lɪŋ] adj kochend; (weather) sehr heiß; **I'm ~** ich komme um vor Hitze

'boiling point n Siedepunkt m a. fig

boisterous ['bɔɪ·stər·əs] adj **1.** (rough) wild; (noisy) laut **2.** (exuberant) übermütig

bold [boʊld] adj **1.** (brave) mutig **2.** (colors) kräftig; (pattern) auffällig **3.** ~ **type** Fettdruck m

bologna [bə·'loʊ·ni] n ≈ Fleischwurst f

bolster ['boʊl·stər] **I.** n Nackenrolle f **II.** vt **1.** (prop up) stützen **2.** (increase) erhöhen

bolt [boʊlt] **I.** vi (move quickly) rasen; (run away) ausreißen; (horse) durchgehen **II.** vt **1.** (gulp down) hinunterschlingen **2.** (lock) verriegeln **III.** n **1.** (of lightning) Blitz[schlag] m **2.** (lock) Riegel m **3.** (screw) Schraubenbolzen m

bomb [bɑm] **I.** n Bombe f **II.** vt bombardieren

bombard [bɑm·'bɑrd] vt bombardieren a. fig

bomber ['bɑm·ər] n (plane) Bombenflugzeug nt; (person) Bombenleger(in) m(f)

bombing ['bam·ɪŋ] *n* MIL Bombardierung *f*; (*terrorist attack*) Bombenanschlag *m*

'**bombproof** *adj* bombensicher

'**bombshell** *n* Bombe *f a. fig*; **to drop a ~** *fig* die Bombe platzen lassen

bona fide [ˌboʊ·nə·'faɪd] *adj* echt; (*offer*) seriös

bonanza [bə·'næn·zə] *n* Goldgrube *f*

bond [band] I. *n* 1. Bindung *f* 2. FIN Schuldschein *m* II. *vi* haften

bondage ['ban·dɪdʒ] *n* 1. (*slavery*) Sklaverei *f* 2. (*sexual act*) Fesseln *nt*

bone [boʊn] *n* Knochen *m*; (*of fish*) Gräte *f*

'**bone marrow** *n* Knochenmark *nt*

bonfire ['ban·faɪr] *n* Freudenfeuer *nt*

bonnet ['ban·ɪt] *n* Mütze *f*; (*dated*) Haube *f*

bonus ['boʊ·nəs] *n* Prämie *f*, Bonus *m*

bony ['boʊ·ni] *adj* 1. knochig 2. (*full of bones: fish*) voller Gräten; (*meat*) knochig

boo [bu] I. *interj* 1. (*to surprise*) huh 2. (*to show disapproval*) buh II. *vi* buhen III. *vt* ausbuhen IV. *n* Buhruf *m*

boob [bub] *n usu pl sl* **big ~s** große Titten *derb*

'**booby prize** *n* Trostpreis *m*

'**booby trap** *n* getarnte Bombe

book [bʊk] I. *n* 1. Buch *nt* 2. *pl* FIN **the ~s** die [Geschäfts]bücher *pl* II. *vt* buchen; **to ~ sth for sb** etw für jdn reservieren; **to be fully ~ed** (*hotel*) ausgebucht sein III. *vi* buchen, reservieren

'**bookcase** *n* Bücherschrank *m*

bookie ['bʊk·i] *n fam* Buchmacher(in) *m(f)*

booking ['bʊk·ɪŋ] *n* Reservierung *f*

'**bookkeeper** *n* Buchhalter(in) *m(f)*

'**bookkeeping** *n* Buchhaltung *f*

booklet ['bʊk·lɪt] *n* Broschüre *f*

'**bookmark** *n* (*in book, Internet*) Lesezeichen *nt*

'**book review** *n* Buchbesprechung *f*

'**bookseller** *n* Buchhändler(in) *m(f)*

'**bookshelf** *n* Bücherregal *nt*

'**bookstore** *n* Buchgeschäft *nt*

boom[1] [bum] ECON I. *vi* florieren II. *n* Aufschwung *m*

boom[2] [bum] I. *n* Dröhnen *nt kein pl* II. *vi* dröhnen

boomerang ['bu·mə·ræŋ] *n* Bumerang *m*

boost [bust] I. *n* Auftrieb *m* II. *vt* ansteigen lassen; (*morale*) heben

'**booster seat** *n* AUTO Kindersitz *m*

boot [but] *n* 1. Stiefel *m* 2. *fam* **to get the ~** *fig fam* hinausfliegen; **to give sb the ~** *fig fam* jdn hinauswerfen

◆**boot out** *vt fam* rausschmeißen

booth [buθ] *n* 1. (*cubicle*) Kabine *f*, (*in restaurant*) Sitzecke *f* 2. (*at fair*) Stand *m*

'**bootleg** *adj* 1. (*sold illegally*) geschmuggelt 2. (*illegally made*) illegal hergestellt

booty ['bu·ti] *n* Beutegut *nt*

booze [buz] *fam* I. *n* Alk *m* II. *vi* saufen

border ['bɔr·dər] *n* Grenze *f*; (*edge*) Begrenzung *f*; (*of picture*) Umrahmung *f*; FASHION Borte *f*; (*in garden*) Rabatte *f*

◆**border on** *vi* grenzen an +*akk*

borderline ['bɔr·dər·laɪn] I. *n* Grenze *f* II. *adj* Grenz-

bore[1] [bɔr] I. *n* (*thing*) langweilige Sache; (*person*) Langweiler(in) *m(f)* II. *vt* langweilen

bore[2] [bɔr] *pt of* **bear**

bore[3] [bɔr] *vt, vi* bohren

bored [bɔrd] *adj* gelangweilt

boredom ['bɔr·dəm] *n* Langeweile *f*

boring ['bɔr·ɪŋ] *adj* langweilig

born [bɔrn] *adj* geboren

'**born-again** *adj* überzeugt

borne [bɔrn] *vi pt of* **bear**

borough ['bɜr·oʊ] *n* Verwaltungsbezirk *m*

borrow ['bar·oʊ] *vt* leihen; (*from library*) ausleihen

borrower ['bar·oʊ·ər] *n* (*from bank*) Kreditnehmer(in) *m(f)*; (*from library*) Entleiher(in) *m(f)*

Bosnia ['baz·ni·ə] *n* Bosnien *nt*

bosom ['bʊz·əm] *n usu sing* Busen *m*

bosom buddy *n* Busenfreund(in) *m(f)*

boss [bas] I. *n* Chef(in) *m(f)* II. *vt* **to ~ [around** ⇆**] sb** jdn herumkommandieren

bossy ['ba·si] *adj fam* herrschsüchtig

botanical [bə·'tæn·ɪ·kəl] *adj* botanisch

botanist ['bat·ən·ɪst] *n* Botaniker(in) *m(f)*

botany ['bat·ən·i] *n* Botanik *f*

botch [batʃ] *vt fam* verpfuschen

both [bouθ] **I.** *adj, pron* beide **II.** *adv* ~ **men and women** sowohl Männer als auch Frauen

bother ['baθ·ər] **I.** *n* **1.** (*effort*) Mühe *f*; (*work*) Aufwand *m*; **not worth the** ~ kaum der Mühe wert **2.** (*nuisance*) **to be a** ~ lästig sein **II.** *vi* **no, don't** ~ nein, nicht nötig **III.** *vt* **1.** (*worry*) beunruhigen; **what's ~ing you?** was hast du?; **it doesn't** ~ **me** das macht mir nichts aus **2.** (*disturb*) stören; **I'm sorry to ~ you, but ...** entschuldigen Sie bitte [die Störung], aber ... **3.** (*annoy*) belästigen

bottle ['bat·əl] *n* Flasche *f*

'bottle-feed *vt* mit der Flasche füttern

'bottleneck *n* Engpass *m a. fig*

'bottle opener *n* Flaschenöffner *m*

bottom ['bat·əm] *n* **1.** Boden *m*; **pajama** ~**s** Pyjamahose *f*; **from top to** ~ von oben bis unten **2.** (*end*) **at the** ~ **of the street** am Ende der Straße **3.** ANAT Hinterteil *m* ▸ **to get to the** ~ **of sth** einer Sache *dat* auf den Grund gehen **II.** *adj* untere(r, s)

bottom 'line *n usu sing* **1.** FIN Bilanz *f* **2.** *fig* (*main point*) Wahrheit *f*

bought [bɔt] *vt pt of* **buy**

boulder ['boul·dər] *n* Felsbrocken *m*

boulevard ['bʊl·ə·vard] *n* Boulevard *m*

bounce [baʊns] **I.** *n* (*of ball*) Aufprall; (*spring*) Sprungkraft *f*; (*hair*) Elastizität *m* **II.** *vi* **1.** (*ball*) aufspringen; (*bob*) hüpfen **2.** *fam* (*check*) platzen **III.** *vt* **1.** aufspringen lassen; (*baby*) schaukeln **2.** *fam* (*check*) platzen

bouncer ['baʊn·sər] *n* Rausschmeißer(in) *m(f)*

bound[1] [baʊnd] **I.** *vi* springen; (*kangaroo*) hüpfen **II.** *n* Sprung *m*

bound[2] [baʊnd] *adj* **to be ~ for X** unterwegs nach X sein

bound[3] [baʊnd] **I.** *pt, pp of* **bind** **II.** *adj* **it was ~ to happen** das musste so kommen

boundary ['baʊn·də·ri] *n* Grenze *f*

bounds [baʊndz] *npl* Grenzen *pl*; **to be out of ~s** (*ball*) im Aus sein; (*area*) Sperrgebiet sein

bounty ['baʊn·ti] *n* **1.** Kopfgeld *nt* **2.** *liter* (*generosity*) Freigebigkeit *f*

bouquet [bou·'keɪ] *n* Bukett *nt*

bourbon ['bɜr·bən] *n* Bourbon *m*

bourgeois [bʊr·'ʒwa] *adj* [spieß]bürgerlich

bout [baʊt] *n* **1.** Anfall *m* **2.** (*in boxing*) Boxkampf *m*; (*in wrestling*) Ringkampf *m*

boutique [bu·'tik] *n* Boutique *f*

bow[1] [bou] *n* **1.** (*weapon*) Bogen *m* **2.** MUS Bogen *m* **3.** (*knot*) Schleife *f*

bow[2] [baʊ] **I.** *vi* sich verbeugen **II.** *vt* **to** ~ **one's head** den Kopf senken **III.** *n* **1.** (*gesture*) Verbeugung *f* **2.** NAUT Bug *m*

bowel ['baʊ·əl] *n usu pl* MED ~**s** Darm *m*

'bowel movement *n* Stuhl[gang] *m*

bowl[1] [boul] *n* Schüssel *f*; (*shallower*) Schale *f*; (*for doing dishes*) Spülschüssel *f*

bowl[2] [boul] SPORT **I.** *vi* bowlen; (*lawn bowling*) Bowls spielen **II.** *vt* (*bowling*) werfen; (*lawn bowling*) rollen **III.** *n* Kugel *f*

bowler ['bou·lər] *n* **1.** Bowlingspieler(in) *m(f)*; (*lawn bowling*) Bowlsspieler(in) *m(f)* **2.** (*hat*) Melone *f*

bowling ['bou·lɪŋ] *n* Bowling *nt*

'bowling alley *n* Bowlingbahn *f*

bow 'tie *n* Fliege *f*

box[1] [baks] *vi* boxen

box[2] [baks] *n* **1.** (*container*) Kiste *f*; (*carton*) Karton *m*; (*of candy, matches*) Schachtel *f* **2.** (*space*) Kästchen *nt*

boxer ['bak·sər] *n* **1.** (*dog*) Boxer *m* **2.** (*person*) Boxer(in) *m(f)*

boxers ['bak·sərz], **'boxer shorts** *npl* Boxershorts *pl*

boxing ['bak·sɪŋ] *n* Boxen *nt*

'boxing gloves *npl* Boxhandschuhe *pl*

'boxing match *n* Boxkampf *m*

'boxing ring *n* Boxring *m*

'box office *n* Kasse *f* (*im Theater oder Kino*)

boy [bɔɪ] **I.** *n* **1.** Junge *m* **2.** *fam* (*friends*) **the ~s** *pl* die Kumpels *pl* **II.** *interj* [oh] ~! Junge, Junge!

boycott ['bɔɪ·kat] **I.** *vt* boykottieren **II.** *n* Boykott *m*

'boyfriend *n* Freund *m*

boyhood ['bɔɪ·hʊd] *n* Kindheit *f*

boyish ['bɔɪ·ɪʃ] *adj* jungenhaft

'Boy Scout *n* Pfadfinder *m*

bra [brɑ] *n* BH *m*

brace [breɪs] **I.** *n* Stützapparat *m;* (*for teeth*) ~s *pl* Zahnspange *f* **II.** *vt* 1. (*prepare for*) **to ~ oneself for sth** sich auf etw *akk* vorbereiten 2. (*support*) [ab]-stützen; (*horizontally*) verstreben

bracelet ['breɪs·lɪt] *n* Armband *nt*

bracken ['bræk·ən] *n* Adlerfarn *m*

bracket ['bræk·ɪt] **I.** *n* 1. *usu pl* in [round/square/angle] ~s in [runden/eckigen/spitzen] Klammern *f* 2. (*class*) Klasse *f*, Gruppe *f* 3. (*support*) [Winkel]-stütze *f* **II.** *vt* in Klammern setzen

brag <-gg-> [bræg] *vt, vi* **to ~** [**about sth**] [mit etw] prahlen

braid [breɪd] **I.** *n* 1. (*on cloth*) Borte *f;* (*on uniform*) Litze *f;* (*with metal threads*) Tresse[n] *f[pl]* 2. (*in hair*) Zopf *m* **II.** *vt, vi* flechten

Braille [breɪl] *n* Blindenschrift *f*

brain [breɪn] *n* 1. (*organ*) Gehirn *nt;* ~s *pl* [Ge]hirn *nt* 2. (*intelligence*) Verstand *m;* ~s *pl* Intelligenz *f kein pl*

'brain dead *adj* [ge]hirntot

'brainstorm *n fam* (*idea*) Geistesblitz *m*

'brainstorming *n* Brainstorming *nt*

'brainwash *vt* einer Gehirnwäsche unterziehen

'brainwashing *n* Gehirnwäsche *f*

'brainwave *n* Geistesblitz *m*

brainy ['breɪ·ni] *adj fam* gescheit

braise [breɪz] *vt* FOOD schmoren

brake [breɪk] **I.** *n* Bremse *f* **II.** *vi* bremsen

'brake fluid *n* Bremsflüssigkeit *f*

bran [bræn] *n* Kleie *f*

branch [bræntʃ] *n* 1. Zweig *m;* (*of trunk*) Ast *m* 2. (*office*) Zweigstelle *f*, Filiale *f*

brand [brænd] **I.** *n* 1. (*product*) Marke *f* 2. *fig* (*type*) Art *f* 3. (*mark*) Brandzeichen *nt* **II.** *vt* brandmarken

brandish ['bræn·dɪʃ] *vt* [drohend] schwingen

'brand name *n* Markenname *m*

brand 'new *adj* [funkel]nagelneu

brandy ['bræn·di] *n* Weinbrand *m*

brash [bræʃ] *adj* 1. (*cocky*) dreist 2. (*gaudy*) grell

brass [bræs] *n* 1. (*metal*) Messing *nt*

2. + *sing/pl vb* MUS **the ~** die Blechinstrumente *pl*

brass 'band *n* Blaskapelle *f*

brat [bræt] *n hum o pej* Balg *m o nt*

brave [breɪv] *adj* 1. mutig 2. (*stoical*) tapfer

bravery ['breɪ·və·ri] *n* Tapferkeit *f,* Mut *m*

brawl [brɔl] **I.** *n* [lautstarke] Schlägerei **II.** *vi* sich [lautstark] schlagen

brawn [brɔn] *n* Muskelkraft *f*

brawny ['brɔ·ni] *adj fam* muskulös

bray [breɪ] **I.** *vi* (*donkey*) schreien; (*person*) kreischen **II.** *n* [Esels]schrei *m*

brazen ['breɪ·zən] *adj* unverschämt

Brazil [brə·'zɪl] *n* Brasilien *nt*

Brazilian [brə·'zɪl·jən] **I.** *n* Brasilianer(in) *m(f)* **II.** *adj* brasilianisch

Bra'zil nut *n* Paranuss *f*

breach [britʃ] **I.** *n* 1. (*infringement*) Verletzung *f;* **~ of contract** Vertragsbruch *m* 2. (*estrangement*) Bruch *m* **II.** *vt* 1. (*break*) verletzen; (*contract*) brechen 2. (*defense*) durchbrechen

bread [bred] *n* Brot *nt*

bread and 'butter *n* Butterbrot *nt*

'breadcrumb *n* Brotkrume *f;* ~s *pl* (*for coating food*) Paniermehl *nt kein pl*

breadth [bredθ] *n* Breite *f;* *fig* Ausdehnung *f*

'breadwinner *n* Ernährer(in) *m(f)*

break [breɪk] **I.** *n* 1. (*fracture*) Bruch *m* 2. (*gap*) Lücke *f* 3. (*interruption*) Unterbrechung *f;* (*shorter*) Pause *f;* **to take a ~** eine Pause machen 4. (*opportunity*) Chance *f* **II.** *vt* <broke, broken> 1. (*shatter*) zerbrechen; (*damage*) kaputtmachen; (*window*) einschlagen; **to ~ one's arm** sich *dat* den Arm brechen 2. (*momentarily interrupt*) unterbrechen 3. (*put an end to*) brechen; (*habit*) aufgeben 4. (*violate: agreement*) verletzen; (*law*) übertreten; (*promise*) brechen 5. (*code*) entschlüsseln **III.** *vi* <broke, broken> 1. (*stop working*) kaputtgehen, zusammenbrechen, auseinanderbrechen; (*shatter*) zerbrechen 2. (*voice*) **the boy's voice is ~ing** der Junge ist [gerade] im Stimmbruch 3. METEO (*dawn, day*) anbrechen; (*storm*) losbrechen 4. (*news*) bekannt werden 5. (*billiards*) anstoßen; (*boxing*)

sich trennen

break down I. *vi* 1. (*stop working*) stehen bleiben; (*engine*) versagen 2. (*dissolve*) sich auflösen; (*marriage*) scheitern 3. (*emotionally*) zusammenbrechen II. *vt* 1. (*force open*) aufbrechen; (*with foot*) eintreten 2. (*separate into parts*) aufgliedern; CHEM aufspalten

break in I. *vi* 1. einbrechen 2. (*interrupt*) unterbrechen II. *vt* 1. (*shoes*) einlaufen 2. (*tame*) zähmen; (*train*) abrichten; (*horse*) zureiten

break into *vt* 1. einbrechen in +*akk*; (*car*) aufbrechen 2. **to ~ into a run** [plötzlich] zu rennen anfangen

break off I. *vt* abbrechen; (*terminate*) beenden; (*engagement*) lösen II. *vi* abbrechen

break out *vi* 1. (*escape*) ausbrechen 2. (*begin*) ausbrechen; (*storm*) losbrechen

break up I. *vt* 1. (*end*) beenden; (*marriage*) zerstören; (*split up*) aufspalten; (*family*) auseinanderreißen II. *vi* 1. (*end relationship*) sich trennen 2. (*come to an end*) enden; (*marriage*) scheitern 3. (*fall apart*) auseinandergehen; (*aircraft, ship*) zerschellen

breakage ['breɪ·kɪdʒ] *n* Bruch *m*

breakdown *n* 1. (*collapse*) Zusammenbruch *m*; (*failure*) Scheitern *nt* 2. AUTO Panne *f* 3. (*list*) Aufschlüsselung *f* 4. PSYCH [Nerven]zusammenbruch *m*

breakfast ['brek·fəst] *n* Frühstück *nt*

'**break-in** *n* Einbruch *m*

'**breakthrough** *n* Durchbruch *m*

'**breakup** *n* Auseinanderbrechen *nt*; (*of marriage*) Scheitern *nt*; (*of group*) Auflösung *f*

'**breakwater** *n* Wellenbrecher *m*

breast [brest] *n* Brust *f*

'**breastbone** *n* Brustbein *nt*

'**breast cancer** *n* Brustkrebs *m*

'**breastfeed** <-fed, -fed> *vt, vi* stillen

'**breaststroke** *n* Brustschwimmen *nt*

breath [breθ] *n* Atem *m*; (*inhalation*) Atemzug *m*; **bad ~** Mundgeruch *m*; **out of ~** außer Atem; **to catch one's ~** [*or* **get one's ~ back**] verschnaufen; **to take a deep ~** tief Luft holen; **to take sb's ~ away** jdm den Atem rauben

Breathalyzer® ['breθ·ə·laɪ·zər] *n* Alcotest® *m*

breathe [brið] I. *vi* atmen II. *vt* (*exhale*) [aus]atmen

breathing ['bri·ðɪŋ] *n* Atmung *f*

'**breathing apparatus** *n* Sauerstoffgerät *nt*

'**breathing room**, '**breathing space** *n* *fig* Bewegungsfreiheit *f*

breathless ['breθ·lɪs] *adj* atemlos

'**breathtaking** *adj* atemberaubend

'**breath test** *n* Alkoholtest *m*

bred [bred] *pt, pp of* **breed**

breed [brid] I. *vt* <bred, bred> züchten II. *vi* <bred, bred> sich fortpflanzen; (*birds*) brüten; (*rabbits*) sich vermehren III. *n* (*of animal*) Rasse *f*; (*of plant*) Sorte *f*

breeder ['bri·dər] *n* Züchter(in) *m(f)*

breeze [briz] *n* 1. Brise *f* 2. *fam* Kinderspiel *nt*

breezy ['bri·zi] *adj* 1. windig 2. unbeschwert

brevity ['brev·ɪ·t̬i] *n* Kürze *f*

brew [bru] I. *n* Gebräu *nt*; *fig* Mischung *f* II. *vi fig* (*trouble*) sich zusammenbrauen III. *vt* brauen

brewer ['bru·ər] *n* [Bier]brauer(in) *m(f)*

brewery ['bru·ə·ri] *n* Brauerei *f*

bribe [braɪb] I. *vt* bestechen II. *n* Bestechung *f*

bribery ['braɪ·bə·ri] *n* Bestechung *f*

bric-a-brac ['brɪk·ə·bræk] *n* Nippes *pl*

brick [brɪk] *n* Backstein *m*

'**bricklayer** *n* Maurer(in) *m(f)*

'**brickwork** *n* Mauerwerk *nt*

bride [braɪd] *n* Braut *f*

bridegroom ['braɪd·ˌgrum] *n* Bräutigam *m*

'**bridesmaid** *n* Brautjungfer *f*

bridge [brɪdʒ] *n* 1. Brücke *f* 2. (*for teeth*) [Zahn]brücke *f*; (*of nose*) Nasenrücken *m*; (*of glasses*) Brillensteg *m* 3. (*on ship*) Kommandobrücke *f* 4. (*card game*) Bridge *nt*

bridle ['braɪ·dəl] *n* Zaumzeug *nt*

brief [brif] I. *adj* kurz II. *n* 1. LAW Unterlagen *pl* zu einer Rechtssache *f*. **~s** *pl* (*for men*) Herrenunterhose *f*; (*for women*) Slip *m*, [Damen]schlüpfer *m* III. *vt* informieren

briefcase ['brif·keis] n Aktentasche f

briefing ['bri·fin] n [Einsatz]besprechung f

briefly ['brif·li] adv kurz

brigade [bri·'geid] n Brigade f

bright [brait] adj 1. (light) hell; (blinding) grell; (star) leuchtend; (sunshine) strahlend 2. (vivid) ~ **blue** strahlend blau; ~ **red** leuchtend rot 3. intelligent; (idea) glänzend a. iron

brighten ['brait·ən] vi to ~ [up] 1. fröhlicher werden 2. METEO sich aufklären

brilliant ['bril·jənt] adj 1. (color, eyes) leuchtend; (smile, sun) strahlend 2. (person) hoch begabt; (plan) brillant; (idea) glänzend

brim [brim] n 1. (of hat) Krempe f 2. (top) Rand m; **full to the ~** randvoll

brine [brain] n [Salz]lake f

bring <brought, brought> [brin] vt 1. (convey) mitbringen 2. (cause to come, happen) bringen; **so what ~s you here to Chicago?** was hat dich hier nach Chicago verschlagen? 3. LAW to ~ **charges against sb** Anklage gegen jdn erheben

♦ **bring about** vt verursachen

♦ **bring around** vt 1. (persuade) überreden 2. (bring back to consciousness) wieder zu Bewusstsein bringen 3. (bring along) mitbringen

♦ **bring back** vt zurückbringen; (memories) wecken; (reintroduce) wieder einführen

♦ **bring off** vt zustande bringen

♦ **bring on** vt herbeiführen; MED verursachen

♦ **bring out** vt 1. (get out) herausbringen 2. COMM (launch) herausbringen

♦ **bring up** vt 1. (carry up) heraufbringen 2. (rear) großziehen 3. (mention) zur Sprache bringen

brink [brink] n Rand m a. fig

brisk [brisk] adj 1. zügig; (walk) stramm 2. (busy) lebhaft 3. (wind) frisch

bristle ['bris·əl] n Borste f; (on face) [Bart]stoppel f meist pl

bristly ['bris·li] adj borstig; (chin) stoppelig

Brit [brit] n fam Brite, -in m, f

Britain ['brit·ən] n Großbritannien nt

British ['brit·iʃ] I. adj britisch II. np **the ~** die Briten pl

British Isles npl **the ~** die Britischen Inseln

Briton ['brit·ən] n Brite, -in m, f

brittle ['brit·əl] adj zerbrechlich; (bones) brüchig

broach [broutʃ] vt (subject) anschneiden

broad [brɔd] adj 1. (wide) breit 2. (general) allgemein; (generalization) grob 3. (wide-ranging) weitreichend; (interests) vielseitig

broadband n INET Breitband nt

broadcast ['brɔd·kæst] I. n Übertragung f; (program) Sendung f II. vt vi <broadcast or broadcasted, broadcast or broadcasted> senden; (game) übertragen

broaden ['brɔd·ən] I. vi breiter werden II. vt 1. (make wider) verbreitern 2. fig vergrößern; (discussion) ausweiten

broadly ['brɔd·li] adv 1. (widely) breit 2. (generally: agree) weitgehend

broad-'minded adj tolerant

Broadway n der Broadway

broccoli ['brak·ə·li] n Brokkoli m

brochure [brou·'ʃur] n Broschüre f

broil [brɔil] vt grillen

broiler ['brɔi·lər] n Bratrost nt

broke [brouk] I. pt of **break** II. adj pred fam pleite

broken ['brou·kən] I. pp of **break** II. adj (arm) gebrochen; (bottle) zerbrochen; (watch) kaputt

'broken-down adj 1. (not working) kaputt 2. (dilapidated) verfallen

broken'hearted adj untröstlich

broker ['brou·kər] n 1. ECON [Börsen]makler(in) m(f) 2. (negotiator) Vermittler(in) m(f)

bronchitis [bran·'kai·tis] n Bronchitis f

bronze [branz] I. n Bronze f II. adj the **B~ Age** die Bronzezeit; ~ **medal** Bronzemedaille f

brooch <pl -es> [broutʃ] n Brosche f

brood [brud] I. n Brut f a. fig II. vi to ~ **on sth** über etw dat brüten

brook [bruk] n Bach m

broom [brum] n 1. (brush) Besen m 2. BOT Ginster m

broomstick ['brʊmˌstɪk] n Besenstiel m
broth [brɒθ] n Brühe f
brothel ['brɒθ·əl] n Bordell nt
brother ['brʌð·ər] n 1. Bruder m; ~s **and sisters** Geschwister pl 2. fam Kumpel m
brotherhood ['brʌð·ər·hʊd] n 1. (group) Bruderschaft f 2. (feeling) Brüderlichkeit f
'brother-in-law <pl brothers-in-law> n Schwager m
brotherly ['brʌð·ər·li] adj brüderlich
brought [brɔt] pt, pp of **bring**
brow [braʊ] n Augenbraue f, Stirn f
browbeat <-beat, -beaten> ['braʊ·bit] vt einschüchtern
brown [braʊn] I. n Braun nt II. adj braun
brown 'bread n locker gebackenes Brot aus dunklerem Mehl, etwa wie Mischbrot
brownie ['braʊ·ni] n FOOD kleiner Schokoladenkuchen mit Nüssen
Brownie ['braʊ·ni] n (Girl Scout) junge Pfadfinderin
'brownie point n hum fam Pluspunkt m
brown 'rice n ungeschälter Reis
browse [braʊz] I. vi to ~ through a magazine eine Zeitschrift durchblättern; to ~ [around a store] sich [in einem Geschäft] umsehen II. vt COMPUT durchsehen
bruise [bruz] I. n blauer Fleck; (on fruit) Druckstelle f II. vt to ~ one's arm sich am Arm stoßen
brunch <pl -es> [brʌntʃ] n Brunch m
brunette [bru·'net] I. n Brünette f II. adj brünett
brunt [brʌnt] n to bear the ~ of sth etw am stärksten zu spüren bekommen
brush [brʌʃ] I. n <pl -es> 1. (for hair, cleaning) Bürste f; (broom) Besen m; (for painting) Pinsel m 2. (act) Bürsten nt 3. (encounter) Zusammenstoß m II. vt 1. abbürsten; to ~ one's hair sich dat die Haare bürsten 2. (touch lightly) leicht berühren III. vi to ~ against sb/ sth jdn/etw streifen
brush aside vt 1. (push aside) wegschieben 2. (dismiss: thing) abtun; (person) ignorieren
brush up I. vi to ~ up on sth etw auffrischen II. vt auffrischen
'brush-off n to get the ~ from sb von jdm einen Korb bekommen
brusque [brʌsk] adj schroff
Brussels ['brʌs·əlz] n Brüssel nt
Brussel(s) 'sprout n ~s pl Rosenkohl m kein pl
brutal ['brut·əl] adj brutal a. fig
brutality [bru·'tæl·ɪ·ti] n Brutalität f
brute [brut] I. n brutaler Kerl II. adj ~ **force** rohe Gewalt
BS [ˌbi·'es] n 1. abbr of **Bachelor of Science** Bakkalaureus m der Naturwissenschaften 2. vulg abbr of **bullshit**
bubble ['bʌb·əl] I. n Blase f II. vi kochen a. fig; (water, fountain) sprudeln; (champagne) perlen
'bubble bath n Schaumbad nt
'bubblegum n Bubblegum m o nt
bubbly ['bʌb·li] I. n fam Schampus m fam II. adj (drink) sprudelnd; (person) temperamentvoll
buck¹ [bʌk] n fam Dollar m
buck² [bʌk] I. n <pl -> (deer) Bock m; (rabbit) Rammler m II. vi bocken
buck³ [bʌk] n fam to pass the ~ [to sb] die Verantwortung [auf jdn] abwälzen
buck up I. vi (wieder) Mut fassen; ~ up! Kopf hoch! II. vt aufmuntern
bucket ['bʌk·ɪt] n Eimer m
buckle ['bʌk·əl] I. n Schnalle f II. vt 1. (belt) [zu]schnallen 2. (bend) verbiegen III. vi sich verbiegen
buckle up vi AUTO fam sich anschnallen
buckskin ['bʌk·skɪn] n Wildleder nt
bud [bʌd] I. n Knospe f II. vi <-dd-> knospen
Buddhism ['bu·dɪz·əm] n Buddhismus m
Buddhist ['bu·dɪst] I. n Buddhist(in) m(f) II. adj buddhistisch
budding ['bʌd·ɪŋ] adj fig angehend
buddy ['bʌd·i] n fam Kumpel m
budge [bʌdʒ] I. vi 1. (move) sich [vom Fleck] rühren 2. (change mind) nachgeben II. vt 1. (move) [von der Stelle] bewegen 2. (cause to change mind) umstimmen
budget ['bʌdʒ·ɪt] I. n Budget nt II. vi to ~ for sth etw [im Budget] vorsehen III. adj preiswert

buff[1] [bʌf] I. *adj.* 1. (*color*) gelbbraun 2. *sl* muskulös II. *vt* to ~ [up] sth etw polieren

buff[2] [bʌf] *n fam* Fan *m*

buffalo <*pl* -> ['bʌf·ə·ləʊ] *n* Büffel *m*

buffer ['bʌf·ər] *n* Puffer *m*

buffet [bə·'feɪ] *n* Büfett *nt*

buffoon [bə·'fun] *n* Clown *m*

bug [bʌg] I. *n* 1. Wanze *f*; ~s *pl* (*insects*) Ungeziefer *nt kein pl* 2. MED Bazillus *m* 3. COMPUT Bug *m* 4. (*listening device*) Wanze *f* II. *vt* <-gg-> 1. *fam* (*annoy*) to ~ sb jdm auf die Nerven gehen *dat* 2. (*install bugs*) verwanzen 3. (*eavesdrop on*) abhören

'**bugbear** *n* Ärgernis *nt*

buggy ['bʌg·i] *n* 1. (*horse-drawn*) leichter Einspänner 2. (*for baby*) Buggy *m*

bugle ['bju·gəl] *n* Horn *nt*

bugler ['bju·glər] *n* Hornist(in) *m(f)*

build [bɪld] I. *n* Körperbau *m* II. *vt* <built, built> 1. (*construct*) bauen 2. *fig* aufbauen III. *vi* <built, built> 1. (*construct*) bauen 2. (*increase*) zunehmen; (*tension*) steigen

◆ **build up** I. *vt* aufbauen; (*lead*) ausbauen; (*speed*) erhöhen II. *vi* zunehmen; (*traffic*) sich verdichten

builder ['bɪl·dər] *n* Bauarbeiter(in) *m(f)*; (*contractor*) Bauherr(in) *m(f)*

building ['bɪl·dɪŋ] *n* Gebäude *nt*

'**building contractor** *n* Bauunternehmer(in) *m(f)*

'**building site** *n* Baustelle *f*

'**buildup** *n* 1. (*increase*) Zunahme *f* 2. (*hype*) Werbung *f* 3. (*preparations*) Vorbereitung *f*

built [bɪlt] *pt, pp of* **build**

built-in ['bɪlt·ɪn] *adj* eingebaut, Einbau-

built-up ['bɪlt·ʌp] *adj* (*area*) verbaut

bulb [bʌlb] *n* 1. BOT Zwiebel *f* 2. ELEC [Glüh]birne *f*

Bulgaria [bʌl·'ger·i·ə] *n* Bulgarien *nt*

Bulgarian [bʌl·'ger·i·ən] I. *adj* bulgarisch II. *n* 1. (*person*) Bulgare, -in *m, f* 2. (*language*) Bulgarisch *nt*

bulge [bʌldʒ] I. *n* Wölbung *f*; (*in tire*) Wulst *m* II. *vi* sich runden; (*eyes*) hervortreten

bulimia [bu·'li·mi·ə] *n* Bulimie *f*

bulk [bʌlk] *n* 1. (*mass*) Masse *f* 2. (*size*)

Ausmaß *nt* 3. (*quantity*) **in** ~ in großen Mengen 4. (*largest part*) Großteil *m*

bulky ['bʌl·ki] *adj* 1. (*luggage*) sperrig 2. (*person*) massig

bull [bʊl] *n* (*steer*) Stier *m*; (*elephant, walrus also*) Bulle *m*

'**bulldog** *n* Bulldogge *f*

'**bulldozer** ['bʊl·doʊ·zər] *n* Bulldozer *m*

bullet ['bʊl·ɪt] *n* Kugel *f*

bulletin ['bʊl·ə·tɪn] *n* Bulletin *nt*, [kurzer] Lagebericht

'**bulletin board** *n* Schwarzes Brett

'**bulletproof** *adj* kugelsicher

'**bullfight** *n* Stierkampf *m*

'**bullfighter** *n* Stierkämpfer(in) *m(f)*

'**bullfrog** *n* Ochsenfrosch *m*

bullion ['bʊl·jən] *n* **gold** ~ Goldbarren *pl*

bullock ['bʊl·ək] *n* Ochse ~

'**bullring** *n* Stierkampfarena *f*

'**bull's eye** *n* Zentrum *nt* der Zielscheibe; **to hit the** ~ einen Volltreffer landen *a. fig*

'**bullshit** *vulg, sl* I. *n* Schwachsinn *m* II. *vt* <-tt-> verscheißern *derb* III. *vi* <-tt-> Scheiß erzählen *pej derb*

bully ['bʊl·i] I. *n* Tyrann *m* II. *vt* <-ie-> tyrannisieren

bum [bʌm] *fam* I. *n* Penner(in) *m(f)* II. *vt* <-mm-> to ~ sth off sb etw von jdm schnorren

◆ **bum around** *vi fam* 1. (*hang out*) herumgammeln *fam* 2. (*travel*) herumziehen

bumblebee ['bʌm·bəl·bi] *n* Hummel *f*

bumbling ['bʌm·blɪŋ] *adj* tollpatschig

bump [bʌmp] I. *n* 1. (*on head*) Beule *f*; (*in road*) Unebenheit *f* 2. (*light blow*) leichter Stoß 3. (*thud*) Bums *m* II. *vt* 1. zusammenstoßen mit +*dat*; **to** ~ **oneself** sich [an]stoßen 2. *usu passive* **to get** ~ed **from a flight** von der Passagierliste gestrichen werden

◆ **bump into** *vi* to ~ **into sth** gegen etw *akk* stoßen; **to** ~ **into sb** (*knock*) mit jdm zusammenstoßen; (*meet*) jdm [zufällig] in die Arme laufen

◆ **bump off** *vt fam* umlegen

bumper ['bʌm·pər] *n* Stoßstange *f*; RAIL Prellbock *m*

'**bumper car** *n* [Auto]skooter *m*

'**bumper sticker** *n* Autoaufkleber *m*

bumpy ['bʌm·pi] *adj* holp[e]rig; *(flight, ride)* unruhig

bun [bʌn] *n* **1.** Brötchen *nt (für Hamburger verwendetes, weiches Brötchen)* **2.** [Haar]knoten *m* **3.** *fam (buttock)* ~**s** Hintern *m kein pl fam*

bunch <*pl* -es> [bʌntʃ] *n (of bananas)* Büschel *m; (of carrots)* Bund *m; (of flowers)* Strauß *m; (of people)* Haufen *m;* ~ **of grapes** Weintraube *f;* ~ **of keys** Schlüsselbund *m*

bundle ['bʌn·dəl] I. *n* Bündel *nt* II. *vt* **to ~ sb into a car** jdn in ein Auto verfrachten

'**bungee jumping** ['bʌn·ˌdʒi-] *n* Bungeespringen *nt*

bungle ['bʌŋ·gəl] *vt* verpfuschen

bunk [bʌŋk] *n* **1.** *(in boat)* Koje *f* **2.** *(part of bed)* **bottom/top** ~ unteres/oberes Bett *(eines Etagenbetts)*

'**bunk bed** *n* Etagenbett *nt*

bunker ['bʌŋ·kər] *n* Bunker *m*

bunny ['bʌn·i] *n* Häschen *nt*

buoy [bɔɪ] *n* Boje *f*

buoyant ['bɔɪ·jənt] *adj* schwimmfähig, tragend

burden ['bɜr·dən] I. *n* Last *f; fig* Belastung *f* II. *vt* beladen; *(bother)* belasten

burdensome ['bɜr·dən·səm] *adj* belastend

bureau <*pl* -x> ['bjʊr·oʊ] *n* **1.** Amt *nt*, Behörde *f* **2.** *(office)* [Informations]büro *nt* **3.** *(furniture)* Kommode *f*

bureaucracy [bjʊ·'rak·rə·si] *n* Bürokratie *f*

bureaucrat ['bjʊr·ə·kræt] *n* Bürokrat(in) *m(f)*

bureaucratic [ˌbjʊr·ə·'kræt·ɪk] *adj* bürokratisch

burger ['bɜr·gər] *n short for* **hamburger** [Ham]burger *m*

burglar ['bɜr·glər] *n* Einbrecher(in) *m(f)*

'**burglar alarm** *n* Alarmanlage *f*

burglarize ['bɜr·glə·raɪz] *vt* einbrechen in +*akk*

burglary ['bɜr·glə·ri] *n* Einbruch[diebstahl] *nt*

burgundy ['bɜr·gən·di] *n* Burgunder *m*

burial ['ber·i·əl] *n* Beerdigung *f*

burly ['bɜr·li] *adj* kräftig [gebaut]

burn [bɜrn] I. *n* **1.** *(injury)* Verbren-

nung *f*, Brandwunde *f* **2.** *(damage)* Brandfleck *m* II. *vi* <burned *or* burnt, burned *or* burnt> **1.** brennen **2.** FOOD anbrennen **3.** *(sunburn)* einen Sonnenbrand bekommen III. *vt* <burned *or* burnt, burned *or* burnt> **1.** *(damage with heat)* verbrennen; *(village)* niederbrennen **2.** FOOD anbrennen lassen **3.** *(calories)* verbrennen; *(oil)* verbrauchen

◆**burn down** I. *vt* abbrennen II. *vi (building)* niederbrennen; *(forest)* abbrennen; *(candle, fire)* herunterbrennen

◆**burn out** I. *vi* **1.** *(fire, candle)* herunterbrennen **2.** *(rocket)* ausbrennen II. *vt* **to ~ [oneself] out** sich völlig verausgaben

◆**burn up** I. *vi* **1.** verbrennen **2.** *fig (be feverish)* glühen **3.** *(rocket)* verglühen II. *vt* verbrauchen; *(calories)* verbrennen

burner ['bɜr·nər] *n* Brenner *m; (on stove)* Kochplatte *f*

burning ['bɜr·nɪŋ] *adj* brennend *a. fig*

burnt [bɜrnt] I. *vt, vi pt, pp of* **burn** II. *adj (completely)* verbrannt; *(partly: food)* angebrannt; *(from sun)* verbrannt

burp [bɜrp] I. *n* Rülpser *m; (of baby)* Bäuerchen *nt* II. *vi* rülpsen *fam; (baby)* ein Bäuerchen machen

burrow ['bɜr·oʊ] I. *n* Bau *m* II. *vt* graben III. *vi* einen Bau graben

burst [bɜrst] I. *n* Ausbruch *m* II. *vi* <burst, burst> **1.** *(explode)* platzen *a. fig; (bubble)* zerplatzen; *(dam)* bersten **2. to be ~ing** *(be full: suitcase)* zum Bersten voll sein *vt* <burst, burst> zum Platzen bringen; *(balloon)* platzen lassen

◆**burst in** *vi* herein-/hineinstürzen

◆**burst out** *vi* **1.** herausstürzen **2. to ~ out crying/laughing** in Tränen-/Gelächter ausbrechen

bury <-ie-> ['ber·i] *vt (person)* begraben; *(thing)* vergraben *a. fig*

bus [bʌs] *n* <*pl* -es> [Omni]bus *m*

'**bus driver** *n* Busfahrer(in) *m(f)*

bush <*pl* -es> [bʊʃ] *n* Busch *m*

bushy ['bʊʃ·i] *adj* buschig

busily ['bɪz·ɪ·li] *adv* eifrig

business <*pl* -es> ['bɪz·nɪs] *n* **1.** (*commerce*) Handel *m*; **to do ~ with sb** mit jdm Geschäfte machen; **on ~** geschäftlich **2.** (*profession*) Branche *f* **3.** (*company*) Unternehmen *nt* **4.** (*matter*) Angelegenheit *f*; **that's none of your ~** das geht dich nichts an

'**business card** *n* Visitenkarte *f*

'**business class** *n* Businessclass *f*

'**business hours** *npl* Geschäftszeiten *pl*

'**businesslike** *adj* geschäftsmäßig

'**businessman** *n* Geschäftsmann *m*

'**business trip** *n* Dienstreise *f*, Geschäftsreise *f*

'**businesswoman** *n* Geschäftsfrau *f*

'**bus station** *n* Busbahnhof *m*

'**bus stop** *n* Bushaltestelle *f*

bust¹ [bʌst] *n* **1.** (*statue*) Büste *f* **2.** (*breasts*) Büste *f*; (*measurement*) Oberweite *f*

bust² [bʌst] *fam* **I.** *n* **1.** (*recession*) [wirtschaftlicher] Niedergang *m* **2.** (*raid*) Razzia *f* **II.** *adj* **1.** (*broken*) kaputt **2.** (*bankrupt*) **to go ~** Pleite machen **III.** *vt* <bust *or* busted, bust *or* busted> **1.** (*break*) kaputtmachen **2.** (*arrest*) festnehmen

bustle ['bʌs·əl] *n* Getriebe *nt*

busy ['bɪz·i] *adj* **1.** (*occupied*) [viel] beschäftigt **2.** (*life*) bewegt; (*street*) belebt **3.** TELEC besetzt

'**busybody** *n* Wichtigtuer(in) *m(f)*

'**busy signal** *n* TELEC Besetztzeichen *nt*

but [bʌt] **I.** *conj* **1.** (*although, however*) aber **2.** (*except*) als **3.** (*rather*) sondern; **not only ... ~ also ...** nicht nur[,] ... sondern auch ... **II.** *prep* außer; **nothing ~ trouble** nichts als Ärger

butch [bʊtʃ] *adj* maskulin

butcher ['bʊtʃ·ər] **I.** *n* Metzger(in) *m(f)* **II.** *vt* **1.** (*slaughter*) schlachten **2.** (*murder*) niedermetzeln

butler ['bʌt·lər] *n* Butler *m*

butt [bʌt] **I.** *n* **1.** (*of rifle*) Kolben *m*; (*of cigarette*) Stummel *m* **2.** *fam* Hintern *m* **II.** *vt* **to ~ sb** (*person*) jdm einen Stoß mit dem Kopf versetzen; (*goat*) jdn mit den Hörnern stoßen

butter ['bʌt·ər] **I.** *n* Butter *f* **II.** *vt* mit Butter bestreichen

'**buttercup** *n* Butterblume *f*

butterfly ['bʌt·ər·flaɪ] *n* **1.** Schmetterling *m* **2.** (*in swimming*) Butterfly *m*

'**buttermilk** *n* Buttermilch *f*

buttock ['bʌt·ək] *n* [Hinter]backe *f*; **~s** *pl* Gesäß *nt*

button ['bʌt·ən] **I.** *n* **1.** Knopf *m* **2.** (*badge*) Button *m* **II.** *vt* zuknöpfen

♦ **button up** *vt* zuknöpfen

'**buttonhole** **I.** *n* Knopfloch *nt* **II.** *vt* *fam* zu fassen kriegen

buy [baɪ] **I.** *vt* <bought, bought> **1.** kaufen **2.** *fam* (*believe*) abkaufen

buyer ['baɪ·ər] *n* Käufer(in) *m(f)*; (*as job*) Einkäufer(in) *m(f)*

'**buyout** *n* Übernahme *f*

buzz [bʌz] **I.** *vi* (*bee, buzzer*) summen; (*fly*) brummen; (*ears*) dröhnen **2.** *vt* *fam* anrufen **II.** *n* <*pl* -es> **1.** (*of bee, buzzer*) Summen *nt*; (*of fly*) Brummen *nt* **2.** *fam* (*call*) **to give sb a ~** jdn anrufen

buzzard ['bʌz·ərd] *n* Truthahngeier *m*

buzzer ['bʌz·ər] *n* Summer *m*

by [baɪ] **I.** *prep* **1.** (*beside*) neben +*akk*/*dat* **2.** (*not later than*) bis +*akk*; **~ February 14**[th] [spätestens] bis zum 14.02.; **~ now** inzwischen **3.** (*during*) bei +*dat*; **~ day/night** tagsüber/nachts **4.** (*happening progressively*) **little ~ little** nach und nach; **day ~ day** Tag für Tag **5.** (*agent*) von +*dat* **6.** (*by means of*) durch +*akk*, mit +*dat*; **~ hand** mit der Hand; **~ boat/bus** mit dem Schiff/Bus **7.** (*amount*) um +*akk*; **to go up ~ 20%** um 20 % steigen **II.** *adv* **1.** (*past*) vorbei **2.** *close* **~** ganz in der Nähe ▶ **~ and large** im Großen und Ganzen; **~ oneself** (*alone*) allein; (*unaided*) selbst

bye [baɪ] *interj* *fam* tschüs

bye-bye [ˌbaɪˈbaɪ] *interj* *fam* tschüs

'**bygone** **I.** *adj attr* vergangen **II.** *n* ▶ **to let ~s be ~s** die Vergangenheit ruhen lassen

'**bylaw** *n* Gemeindeverordnung *f*

'**bypass** **I.** *n* **1.** Umgehungsstraße *f* **2.** MED Bypass *m* **II.** *vt* **1.** (*detour*) umfahren **2.** (*not consult*) übergehen

'**byproduct** *n* Nebenprodukt *nt*

'bystander *n* Zuschauer(in) *m(f)*

'byway *n* Nebenstraße *f*, Seitenweg *m*

C

C <*pl* -'s>, **c** <*pl* -'s> [si:] *n* **1.** (*letter*) C *nt*, c *nt*; **~ as in Charlie** C wie Cäsar **2.** MUS C *nt*, c *nt* **3.** (*school grade*) ≈ Drei *f*

C *after n abbr of* **Celsius** C

CA *abbr of* **California**

cab [kæb] *n* **1.** (*taxi*) Taxi *nt* **2.** (*of truck*) Führerhaus *nt*

cabaret [,kæb·ə·'reɪ] *n* Varieté *nt*

cabbage ['kæb·ɪdʒ] *n* Kohl *m kein pl*, Kraut *nt kein pl bes südd*

cabbie, cabby ['kæb·i], **'cabdriver** *n* Taxifahrer(in) *m(f)*

cabin ['kæb·ɪn] *n* **1.** (*wooden house*) [Block]hütte *f*; (*for vacation*) Ferienhütte *f* **2.** (*on ship*) Kabine *f*

cabinet ['kæb·ɪ·nɪt] *n* **1.** Schrank *m* **2.** POL Kabinett *nt*

cable ['keɪ·bəl] *n* **1.** ELEC [Leitungs]kabel *nt*, Leitung *f* **2.** NAUT Tau *nt* **3.** TV Kabelfernsehen *nt*

'cable car *n* Drahtseilbahn *f*; (*on street*) Kabelbahn *f*

cable 'television, cable 'TV *n* Kabelfernsehen *nt*

cache [kæʃ] *n* **1.** (*hiding place*) Versteck *nt* **2.** COMPUT Cache *m*

cackle ['kæk·əl] I. *vi* gackern II. *n* (*chicken noise*) Gackern *nt kein pl*; (*laughter*) Gegacker *nt*

cactus <*pl* -es> ['kæk·təs] *n* Kaktus *m*

caddie, caddy ['kæd·i] *n* Caddie *m*

cadet [kə·'det] *n* MIL Kadett *m*

Caesarean [sɪ·'ze·ri·ən] *n* MED Kaiserschnitt *m*

café, cafe [kæ·'feɪ] *n* Café *nt*

cafeteria [,kæf·ɪ·'tɪr·i·ə] *n* Cafeteria *f*; UNIV Mensa *f*

caffeine ['kæf·in] *n* Koffein *nt*

cage [keɪdʒ] *n* Käfig *m*

cagey ['keɪ·dʒi] *adj fam* vorsichtig

cake [keɪk] *n* **1.** Kuchen *m*; (*layered*) Torte *f* **2.** (*patty*) Küchlein *nt* ▶ **a piece of ~** *fam* ein Klacks

calcium ['kæl·si·əm] *n* Kalzium *nt*

calculate ['kæl·kjə·leɪt] I. *vt* berechnen; (*estimate*) veranschlagen II. *vi* rechnen

calculated ['kæl·kjə·leɪ·t̬ɪd] *adj* beabsichtigt; (*risk*) kalkuliert

calculating ['kæl·kjə·leɪ·t̬ɪŋ] *adj* berechnend

calculation [,kæl·kjə·'leɪ·ʃən] *n* **1.** Berechnung *f*; (*estimate*) Schätzung *f* **2.** (*process*) Rechnen *nt*

calculator ['kæl·kjə·leɪ·t̬ər] *n* Rechner *m*

calendar ['kæl·ən·dər] *n* Kalender *m*

calf <*pl* calves> [kæf] *n* **1.** (*animal*) Kalb *nt* **2.** ANAT Wade *f*

caliber ['kæl·ə·bər] *n* **1.** (*diameter*) Kaliber *nt* **2.** (*quality*) Niveau *nt*

California [,kæl·ə·'fɔr·njə] *n* Kalifornien *nt*

call [kɔl] I. *n* **1.** (*on phone*) [Telefon]anruf *m*, [Telefon]gespräch *nt* **2.** (*visit*) Besuch *m* **3.** (*shout*) Ruf *m*; **to be on ~** Bereitschaftsdienst haben II. *vt* **1.** (*on phone*) anrufen; **to ~ sb back** jdn zurückrufen **2.** (*name*) nennen; **what's that animal ~ed?** wie heißt dieses Tier? **3.** (*summon*) [auf]rufen; **to ~ a doctor** einen Arzt rufen III. *vi* **1.** rufen; (*animal*) schreien; **to ~ for sb** jdn rufen; **to ~ for help** um Hilfe rufen **2.** (*telephone*) anrufen; **who's ~ing, please?** wer ist am Apparat? **3.** (*drop by*) vorbeischauen

◆ **call for** *vi* **1.** (*taxi, food*) bestellen **2. this ~s for a celebration** das muss gefeiert werden

◆ **call in** I. *vt* (*specialist, expert*) hinzuziehen; (*ask to come*) kommen lassen II. *vi* sich telefonisch melden; **to ~ in sick** sich [telefonisch] krankmelden

◆ **call off** *vt* **1.** (*cancel*) absagen; (*stop*) abbrechen **2.** (*order back: dog*) zurückrufen

◆ **call on** *vt* **1.** (*visit*) bei jdm vorbeischauen **2.** (*appeal to*) **to ~ on sb to do sth** jdn dazu auffordern, etw zu tun **3.** (*use*) in Anspruch nehmen

◆ **call out** *vt* **1.** (*shout*) rufen **2.** (*fire department*) alarmieren

◆ **call up** *vt* **1.** (*telephone*) anrufen **2.** COMPUT aufrufen **3.** MIL einberufen

◆ **call upon** *vi see* **call on**

caller ['kɔ·lər] n **1.** (on telephone) Anrufer(in) m(f) **2.** (visitor) Besucher(in) m(f)

callous ['kæl·əs] adj hartherzig

calm [kam] **I.** adj ruhig **II.** n **1.** Ruhe f **2.** METEO Windstille f **III.** vt beruhigen
⬩**calm down I.** vt beruhigen **II.** vi sich akk beruhigen

calorie ['kæl·ə·ri] n Kalorie f

Cambodia [kæm·'bou·di·ə] n Kambodscha nt

came [keɪm] vi pt of **come**

camel ['kæm·əl] n Kamel nt

cameo <pl -os> ['kæm·i·ou] n Kamee f

camera ['kæm·ə·ə] n Kamera f

'cameraman n Kameramann m

'camerawoman n Kamerafrau f

camomile ['kæm·ə·mil] n Kamille f

camouflage ['kæm·ə·ˌflaʒ] **I.** n a. fig Tarnung f **II.** vt a. fig tarnen

camp [kæmp] **I.** n MIL [Feld]lager nt **II.** vi zelten

campaign [kæm·'peɪn] **I.** n **1.** Kampagne f; (for election) Wahlkampf m **2.** MIL Feldzug m **II.** vi kämpfen, sich engagieren

camper ['kæm·pər] n **1.** (person) Camper(in) m(f) **2.** (vehicle) Wohnmobil nt

'campfire n Lagerfeuer nt

'campground n Campingplatz m

camping ['kæm·pɪŋ] n Camping nt; **to go ~** zelten gehen

'campsite n Campingplatz m

campus ['kæm·pəs] n Campus m; **on ~** auf dem Campus

can[1] <could, could> [kæn] aux vb (be able to) können; (be allowed to) dürfen; (less formal) können; **~ you hear me?** kannst du mich hören?, hörst du mich?; **you ~'t park here** hier dürfen Sie nicht parken

can[2] [kən] n **1.** Dose f, Büchse f; (of paint) Farbtopf m **2.** sl (bathroom) Klo nt

Canada ['kæn·ə·də] n Kanada nt

Canadian [kə·'neɪ·di·ən] **I.** n Kanadier(in) m(f) **II.** adj kanadisch

canal [kə·'næl] n Kanal m

canary [kə·'ner·i] n Kanarienvogel m

cancel <-l-> ['kæn·səl] **I.** vt **1.** (call off)
absagen **2.** (remove from schedule) streichen **3.** (check, reservation) stornieren **4.** (discontinue) beenden; (subscription) kündigen; COMPUT abbrechen **II.** vi absagen

cancellation [ˌkæn·sə·'leɪ·ʃən] n **1.** Absage f **2.** (from schedule) Streichung f **3.** (revocation) Widerruf m; FIN Stornierung f **4.** (discontinuation) Kündigung f; (of subscription) Abbestellung f

cancer ['kæn·sər] n **1.** a. fig (disease) Krebs m **2.** (growth) Krebsgeschwulst f

Cancer ['kæn·sər] n ASTROL Krebs m

cancerous ['kæn·sər·əs] adj krebsartig

candelabra <pl -> [ˌkæn·dəl·'a·brə] n Leuchter m

candid ['kæn·dɪd] adj offen

candidate ['kæn·dɪ·dət] n Kandidat(in) m(f)

candle ['kæn·dəl] n Kerze f

'candlelight n Kerzenlicht nt

'candlestick n Kerzenständer m

candor ['kæn·dər] n Offenheit f

candy ['kæn·di] n Süßigkeiten pl; (piece) Bonbon m o nt

'candy bar n Schokoriegel m

'candy store n Süßwarenladen m

cane [keɪn] n **1.** (of plant) Rohr nt; **~ sugar** Rohrzucker m **2.** (stick) [Rohr]stock m

canine ['keɪ·naɪn] adj Hunde-

canister ['kæn·ɪ·stər] n Behälter m; (for oil, gasoline) Kanister m

cannabis ['kæn·ə·bɪs] n Cannabis m

cannibal ['kæn·ɪ·bəl] n Kannibale m, Kannibalin f

cannibalism ['kæn·ɪ·bəl·ɪz·əm] n Kannibalismus m

cannon ['kæn·ən] n Kanone f

'cannonball n Kanonenkugel f

cannot ['kæn·at] aux vb = **can not** see **can**

canoe [kə·'nu] n Kanu n

canoeist [kə·'nu·ɪst] n Kanufahrer(in) m(f)

'can opener n Dosenöffner m

canopy ['kæn·ə·pi] n Baldachin m

can't [kænt] fam = **cannot** see **can**

cantankerous [kæn·'tæŋ·kər·əs] adj streitsüchtig

canteen [kæn·'tin] n Feldflasche f

canter ['kæn·ʧər] **I.** n Handgalopp m

II. *vi* leicht galoppieren

anvas <*pl* -es> ['kæn·vəs] *n* Segeltuch *nt;* (*for painting*) Leinwand *f*

canvass ['kæn·vəs] *vt* 1. (*poll*) befragen 2. POL werben

canyon ['kæn·jən] *n* Schlucht *f*

cap [kæp] I. *n* 1. (*hat*) Mütze *f*, Kappe *f* 2. (*top*) Verschlusskappe *f* II. *vt* <-pp-> bedecken; (*teeth*) überkronen

capability [ˌkeɪ·pə·'bɪl·ɪ·ti] *n* Fähigkeit *f*

capable ['keɪ·pə·bəl] *adj* 1. (*competent*) fähig; (*worker*) tüchtig 2. (*able*) fähig

capacity [kə·'pæs·ɪ·ti] *n* 1. Fassungsvermögen *nt* 2. Kapazität *f* 3. (*position*) Funktion *f;* (*role*) Eigenschaft *f*

cape[1] [keɪp] *n* FASHION Umhang *m*, Cape *nt*

cape[2] [keɪp] *n* GEOG Kap *nt;* **C~ Horn** Kap Hoorn

capital ['kæp·ɪ·təl] *n* 1. (*city*) Hauptstadt *f* 2. (*letter*) Großbuchstabe *m* 3. FIN Kapital *nt*

capitalism ['kæp·ɪ·təl·ɪz·əm] *n* Kapitalismus *m*

capitalist ['kæp·ɪ·təl·ɪst] I. *n* Kapitalist(in) *m(f)* II. *adj* kapitalistisch

capitalize ['kæp·ɪ·tə·laɪz] *vt* 1. LING großschreiben 2. FIN kapitalisieren

capital 'letter *n* Großbuchstabe *m*

capital 'punishment *n* Todesstrafe *f*

Capitol ['kæ·pə·təl] *n* **the ~** das Kapitol

Capitol 'Hill *n* Capitol Hill; **on ~** im amerikanischen Kongress

capitulate [kə·'pɪtʃ·ə·leɪt] *vi* kapitulieren

cappuccino <*pl* -s> [ˌkæp·ə·'tʃi·nou] *n* Cappuccino *m*

Capricorn ['kæp·rɪ·kɔrn] *n* ASTROL Steinbock *m*

capsize ['kæp·saɪz] *vi* NAUT kentern

capsule ['kæp·səl] *n* Kapsel *f*

captain ['kæp·tɪn] *n* Kapitän(in) *m(f);* (*in army*) Hauptmann *m*

caption ['kæp·ʃən] *n* 1. Bildunterschrift *f* 2. TV, FILM Untertitel *m* 3. (*heading*) Überschrift *f*

captivate ['kæp·tə·veɪt] *vt* faszinieren

captive ['kæp·tɪv] *n* Gefangene(r) *f(m)*

captivity [kæp·'tɪv·ɪ·ti] *n* Gefangenschaft *f*

capture ['kæp·tʃər] I. *vt* 1. gefangen nehmen; (*police*) festnehmen 2. COMPUT erfassen II. *n* (*of a person*) Gefangennahme *f;* (*by police*) Festnahme *f*

car [kar] *n* 1. Auto *nt*, Wagen *m* 2. RAIL Waggon *m*, Wagen *m*

carafe [kə·'ræf] *n* Karaffe *f*

caramel ['kar·məl] *n* Karamellbonbon *m;* (*burnt sugar*) Karamell *m*

carat <*pl* -s> ['ker·ət] *n* Karat *nt*

caraway ['kar·ə·weɪ] *n* Kümmel *m*

carbohydrate [ˌkar·bou·'haɪ·dreɪt] *n* Kohle[n]hydrat *nt*

'car bomb *n* Autobombe *f*

carbon ['kar·bən] *n* CHEM Kohlenstoff *m*

carbonated ['kar·bə·neɪ·tɪd] *adj* sprudelnd

'carbon copy *n* Durchschlag *m; fig* Ebenbild *nt*

carbon di'oxide *n* Kohlendioxid *nt*

carbon mon'oxide *n* Kohlenmonoxid *nt*

carbs *n pl fam short for* **carbohydrates** Kohle[n]hydrat *nt*

carbuncle ['kar·bʌŋ·kəl] *n* MED Karbunkel *m*

carburetor ['kar·bə·reɪ·tər] *n* Vergaser *m*

carcinogenic [ˌkar·sɪn·ə·'dʒen·ɪk] *adj* Krebs erregend

card [kard] *n* Karte *f;* (*postcard*) [Post]karte *f;* [**game of**] **~s** *pl* Kartenspiel *nt*

'cardboard *n* Pappe *f*

cardiac ['kar·di·æk] *adj* Herz-

cardigan ['kar·dɪ·gən] *n* Strickjacke *f*

cardinal ['kar·dɪn·əl] I. *n* REL Kardinal *m* II. *adj* **~ number** Kardinalzahl *f*

care [ker] I. *n* 1. (*looking after*) Betreuung *f;* (*of children etc.*) Pflege *f;* (*in a hospital*) Versorgung *f;* **take ~** [**of yourself**]! pass auf dich auf!; **to take ~ of sth** für etw *akk* sorgen; **~ of ...** zu Händen von ... 2. (*carefulness*) Sorgfalt *f;* **to handle sth with ~** etw vorsichtig behandeln 3. (*worry*) Sorge *f;* **to not have a ~ in the world** keinerlei Sorgen haben II. *vi* 1. **who ~s?** (*it's not important*) wen interessiert das schon?; (*so what*) was soll's? 2. (*look after*) **to ~ for sb/sth** sich um jdn/etw kümmern 3. **to ~ for sth** (*drink, dessert*) etw mögen III. *vt* **sb does not ~ what/who/whether ...** jdm ist es egal, was/wer/ob ...

career [kə·'rɪr] *n* 1. (*profession*) Beruf *m*

2. (*working life*) Karriere *f*, Laufbahn *f*

ca'reer woman *n* Karrierefrau *f*

'carefree *adj* sorgenfrei

careful ['ker·fəl] *adj* **1.** (*cautious*) vorsichtig; (*driver*) umsichtig **2.** (*meticulous*) sorgfältig, gründlich; (*consideration*) reiflich

careless ['ker·lɪs] *adj* **1.** (*inattentive*) unvorsichtig; (*driver*) leichtsinnig **2.** (*casual: remark*) unbedacht; (*talk*) gedankenlos **3.** (*not painstaking*) nachlässig

carelessness ['ker·lɪs·nɪs] *n* **1.** (*neglecting*) Nachlässigkeit *f* **2.** (*not careful*) Unvorsichtigkeit *f*

caress [kə·'res] **I.** *n* <*pl* -es> Streicheln *nt*; -es *pl* Zärtlichkeiten *pl* **II.** *vt* streicheln

'caretaker *n* Hausverwalter(in) *m(f)*

cargo <*pl* -s> ['kar·goʊ] *n* Fracht *f*; (*load*) Ladung *f*

Caribbean [ˌker·ə·'bi·ən] **I.** *n* **the ~** die Karibik **II.** *adj* karibisch; **the ~ Islands** die Karibischen Inseln

caricature ['ker·ə·kə·tʃʊr] **I.** *n* Karikatur *f* **II.** *vt* (*draw*) karikieren; (*parody*) parodieren

caring ['ker·ɪŋ] *adj* warmherzig; (*person*) fürsorglich

'car insurance *n* Kfz-Versicherung *f*

'carjacking *n* Autoentführung *f*

carnage ['kar·nɪdʒ] *n* Gemetzel *nt*

carnation [kar·'neɪ·ʃən] *n* Nelke *f*

carnival ['kar·nə·vəl] *n* **1.** Volksfest *nt*; (*traveling amusement park*) Jahrmarkt *m* **2.** (*pre-Lent*) Karneval *m*, Fasching *m bes südd, österr*

carnivore ['kar·nə·vɔr] *n* Fleischfresser *m*

carnivorous [kar·'nɪv·ər·əs] *adj* Fleisch fressend

carol ['ker·əl] *n* [**Christmas**] ~ Weihnachtslied *nt*

carousel [ˌkær·ə·'sel] *n* **1.** Karussell *nt* **2.** AVIAT [Gepäck]ausgabeband *nt*

carp <*pl* -> [karp] *n* Karpfen *m*

carpenter ['kar·pən·tər] *n* Zimmermann *m*

carpet ['kar·pət] **I.** *n* Teppich *m*; (*fitted*) Teppichboden *m* **II.** *vt* [mit einem Teppich] auslegen

'carpet sweeper *n* Teppichkehrer *m*

'carpool *n* Fahrgemeinschaft *f*

'car rental *n* Autovermietung *f*

carriage ['ker·ɪdʒ] *n* Kutsche *f*

carrier ['kær·i·ər] *n* **1.** (*person*) Träger(in) *m(f)*; MED [Über]träger(in) *m(f*; **2.** (*company*) Spedition *f*; (*person*) Spediteur(in) *m(f*

carrot ['ker·ət] *n* Möhre *f*, Karotte *f*

carry <-ie-> ['ker·i] **I.** *vt* **1.** (*bear*) tragen *a. fig* **2.** (*transport*) transportieren **3.** (*transmit*) MED übertragen; (*electricity, oil*) leiten **4.** *usu passive* (*motion*) annehmen **II.** *vi* (*sound*) zu hören sein

◆carry away *vt* **1.** (*take away*) wegtragen **2.** *usu passive* **to get carried away** (*be overcome by*) sich mitreißen lassen; (*be enchanted by*) hingerissen sein

◆carry off *vt* **1.** (*take away*) wegtragen; SPORT vom Spielfeld tragen **2.** (*succeed*) hinbekommen

◆carry on **I.** *vt* **1.** fortführen; (*discussion*) fortsetzen **2.** (*conduct*) führen **II.** *vi* **1.** (*continue*) weitermachen **2.** *fam* (*behave stupidly*) sich danebenbenehmen; (*make a fuss*) ein [furchtbares] Theater machen

◆carry out *vt* **1.** hinaus-/heraustragen **2.** (*perform*) durchführen; (*order, plan*) ausführen; (*threat*) wahr machen

cart [kart] **I.** *n* Wagen *m*, Karren *m*; (*in supermarket*) Einkaufswagen *m* **II.** *vt fam* schleppen

cartilage ['kar·təl·ɪdʒ] *n* MED Knorpel *m*

carton ['kar·tən] *n* Karton *m*; (*small*) Schachtel *f*

cartoon [kar·'tun] *n* **1.** (*drawing*) Cartoon *m o nt* **2.** FILM Zeichentrickfilm *m*

cartoonist [kar·'tun·ɪst] *n* **1.** Karikaturist(in) *m(f)* **2.** FILM Trickzeichner(in) *m(f)*

cartridge ['kar·trɪdʒ] *n* (*for ink, ammunition*) Patrone *f*; (*for film*) Kassette *f*

'cartwheel *n* SPORT Rad *nt*; **to turn a ~** ein Rad schlagen

carve [karv] *vt* **1.** ART schnitzen; (*with a chisel*) meißeln; (*cut a pattern*) [ein]ritzen **2.** FOOD tranchieren

carving ['kar·vɪŋ] *n* (*in wood*) Schnitzerei *f*; (*in stone*) Skulptur *f*

'carving knife *n* Tranchiermesser *nt*

'car wash *n* Autowaschanlage *f*

cascade [kæs·'keɪd] **I.** *n* (*natural*) Wasserfall *m*; (*artificial*) Kaskade *f a. fig*

II. *vi* sich ergießen

case¹ [keɪs] *n* **1.** (*instance*) Fall *m;* **in ~ of** [an] **emergency** im Notfall; **in most ~s** meistens; **in ~ ... falls** ...; **in any ~** (*regardless*) jedenfalls **2.** LAW [Rechts] fall *m;* (*suit*) Verfahren *nt* **3.** LING Fall *m,* Kasus *m*

case² [keɪs] *n* **1.** (*container*) Schatulle *f;* (*for eyeglasses*) Etui *nt;* (*for CD, umbrella*) Hülle *f;* (*of beer*) Kiste *f* **2.** (*suitcase*) Koffer *m*

cash [kæʃ] **I.** *n* Bargeld *nt;* **to pay** [in] **~** bar bezahlen **II.** *vt* **to ~** [in] ⇆ **sth** einlösen; (*chips*) etw eintauschen **III.** *vi* **to ~ in on sth** von etw *dat* profitieren

cashew ['kæʃ·u] *n* Cashewnuss *f*

cashier [kæ·'ʃɪr] *n* Kassierer(in) *m(f)*

cash machine *n* Geldautomat *m,* Bankomat *m schweiz, österr*

cashmere ['kæʒ·mɪr] *n* Kaschmir *m*

cash register *n* [Registrier]kasse *f*

casino <*pl* -os> [kə·'si·nou] *n* [Spiel]-kasino *nt*

casket ['kæs·kɪt] *n* **1.** (*coffin*) Sarg *m* **2.** (*box*) Kästchen *nt*

casserole ['kæs·ə·roʊl] *n* Auflaufform *f;* Schmortopf *m;* **tuna/potato ~** Thunfisch-/Kartoffelauflauf *m*

cassette [kə·'set] *n* Kassette *f*

cas'sette player, cas'sette recorder *n* Kassettenrecorder *m*

cast [kæst] **I.** *n* **1.** THEAT, FILM Besetzung *f* **2.** MED Gips[verband] *m* **II.** *vt* <*cast, cast*> **1.** (*throw*) werfen *a. fig;* (*fishing line*) auswerfen **2.** (*ballots, votes*) abgeben **3.** THEAT, FILM (*part, role*) besetzen; (*person*) eine Rolle geben **4.** (*make in a mold*) gießen

cast off NAUT **I.** *vt* losmachen **II.** *vi* ablegen

castanet [ˌkæs·tə·'net] *n* Kastagnette *f*

caster ['kæs·tər] *n* (*wheel*) Laufrolle *f*

casting vote *n* entscheidende Stimme

cast-'iron *n* Gusseisen *nt*

cast-'iron *adj* **1.** aus Gusseisen **2.** *fig* (*alibi*) wasserdicht

castle ['kæs·əl] *n* **1.** (*fortress*) Burg *f;* (*mansion*) Schloss *nt* **2.** CHESS *fam* Turm *m*

castoff **I.** *n* **~s** *pl* abgelegte Kleidung **II.** *adj* (*secondhand*) gebraucht; (*dis-*carded) abgelegt

castor ['kæs·tər] *n see* **caster**

castrate ['kæs·treɪt] *vt* kastrieren

casual ['kæʒ·u·əl] *adj* **1.** (*informal*) lässig, salopp; (*clothing*) leger **2.** (*not planned*) zufällig; (*acquaintance, glance*) flüchtig

casualty ['kæʒ·u·əl·ti] *n* (*accident victim*) [Unfall]opfer *nt;* (*injured*) Verletzte(r) *f(m);* (*dead*) Todesfall *m*

cat [kæt] *n* Katze *f*

catalog ['kæt·əl·ag] **I.** *n* Katalog *m* **II.** *vt* katalogisieren

catalyst ['kæt·ə·lɪst] *n* Katalysator *m*

catamaran [ˌkæt·ə·mə·'ræn] *n* Katamaran *m*

catapult ['kæt·ə·pʌlt] **I.** *n* Katapult *nt* **II.** *vt* katapultieren

cataract ['kæt·ə·rækt] *n* **1.** MED grauer Star **2.** GEOG Katarakt *m*

catastrophe [kə·'tæs·trə·fi] *n* Katastrophe *f*

catastrophic [ˌkæt·ə·'straf·ɪk] *adj* katastrophal

catch [kætʃ] **I.** *n* <*pl* -es> **1.** (*of ball*) Fang *m* **2.** (*fish*) Fang *m kein pl* **3.** (*fastener*) Verschluss *m;* (*bolt*) Riegel *m;* (*hook*) Haken *m* **4.** (*disadvantage*) Haken *m* **II.** *vt* <*caught, caught*> **1.** (*ball*) fangen; (*light*) einfangen; (*person*) auffangen **2.** (*person*) ergreifen; (*arrest*) festnehmen; (*animal*) fangen; (*escaped animal*) einfangen **3.** (*surprise*) erwischen; **to be caught in a thunderstorm** von einem Gewitter überrascht werden **4.** MED **to ~** [a] **cold** sich erkälten **5.** (*take: bus/train*) nehmen; (*arrive in time for*) kriegen **6.** **to ~ sight** [*or* **a glimpse**] **of sb/sth** etw [kurz] sehen; (*by chance*) etw [zufällig] sehen **III.** *vi* <*caught, caught*> **to ~ on sth** an etw *dat* hängen bleiben

catch on *vi fam* **1.** (*understand*) kapieren **2.** (*become popular*) sich durchsetzen

catch up *vi* **to ~ up with sb** jdn einholen *a. fig;* **to ~ up on sth** etw aufarbeiten; **to ~ up on sleep** Schlaf nachholen

catcher ['kætʃ·ər] *n* Fänger(in) *m(f);* (*in baseball*) Catcher *m*

catching ['kætʃ·ɪŋ] *adj* ansteckend

'catch phrase n Slogan m

catchy ['kæt·ʃi] adj eingängig

categorical [ˌkæt·ə·'gɔr·ɪ·kəl] adj kategorisch

category ['kæt·ə·gɔr·i] n Kategorie f

cater ['keɪ·tər] vi 1. für Speise und Getränke sorgen; (company) Speisen und Getränke liefern 2. sich kümmern (to um +akk)

caterer ['keɪ·tər·ər] n (company) Cateringservice m; (for parties) Partyservice m

caterpillar ['kæt·ər·pɪl·ər] n Raupe f

'catfish n <pl -> Seewolf m

cathedral [kə·'θi·drəl] n Kathedrale f, Dom m

Catholic ['kæθ·ə·lɪk] I. n Katholik(in) m(f) II. adj katholisch

Catholicism [kə·'θal·ə·sɪz·əm] n Katholizismus m

'catkin n BOT Kätzchen nt

catnap fam I. n Nickerchen nt II. vi <-pp-> kurz schlafen

cattle ['kæt·əl] npl Rinder pl

catty ['kæt·i] adj gehässig; (remark) bissig

'catwalk n Laufsteg m

Caucasian [kɔ·'keɪ·ʒən] I. n Weiße(r) f(m) II. adj weiß

caught [kɔt] pt, pp of catch

cauliflower ['kɔ·lɪ·ˌflaʊ·ər] n Blumenkohl m, Karfiol m südd, österr

cause [kɔz] I. n 1. (of effect) Ursache f; (reason) Grund m 2. a good ~ ein guter Zweck II. vt verursachen; (trouble) stiften

'cause [kəz] conj fam abbr of because

causeway ['kɔz·weɪ] n Damm m

caustic ['kɔ·stɪk] adj ätzend a. fig; (humor) beißend

caution ['kɔ·ʃən] I. n (carefulness) Vorsicht f; (warning) Vorwarnung f II. vt form warnen

cautious ['kɔ·ʃəs] adj (careful) vorsichtig; (prudent) umsichtig

cavalry ['kæv·əl·ri] n usu + pl vb the ~ die Kavallerie

cave [keɪv] n Höhle f

◆cave in vi 1. (collapse) einstürzen 2. (give in) kapitulieren

'caveman n Höhlenmensch m

cavern ['kæv·ərn] n Höhle f

caviar(e) ['kæv·i·ar] n Kaviar m

cavity ['kæv·ɪ·ti] n Loch nt; (hollow space) Hohlraum m; (in tooth) Loch nt

cayenne [kar·'en], cayenne 'pepper [kar·'en-] n Cayennepfeffer m

CB [ˌsi·'bi] n RADIO abbr of citizens band CB-Funk m

CD [ˌsi·'di] n abbr of compact disc CD f

C'D player n CD-Spieler m

CD-ROM [ˌsi·di·'ram] n abbr of compact disc read-only memory CD-ROM f

cease [sis] form I. vi aufhören II. vt beenden; (fire) einstellen

'ceasefire n Waffenruhe f

cedar ['si·dər] n Zeder f

ceiling ['si·lɪŋ] n [Zimmer]decke f; fig Obergrenze f

celebrate ['sel·ɪ·breɪt] vt, vi feiern

celebrated ['sel·ɪ·breɪ·tɪd] adj berühmt

celebration [ˌsel·ɪ·'breɪ·ʃən] n Feier f

celebrity [sə·'leb·rɪ·ti] n berühmte Persönlichkeit

celeriac [sə·'ler·i·æk] n [Knollen]sellerie m o f

celery ['sel·ə·ri] n [Stangen]sellerie m o f

celibate ['sel·ɪ·bət] adj zölibatär

cell [sel] n 1. BIOL Zelle f 2. (in prison) Zelle f 3. fam see cell phone

cellar ['sel·ər] n Keller m

cellist ['tʃel·ɪst] n Cellist(in) m(f)

cello <pl -s> ['tʃel·oʊ] n Cello nt

cellophane ['sel·ə·feɪn] n Cellophan® nt

'cell phone n Handy nt

cellulite ['sel·jə·laɪt] n Zellulitis f

celluloid ['sel·jʊ·lɔɪd] n Zelluloid nt

cellulose ['sel·jʊ·loʊs] n Zellulose f

Celsius ['sel·si·əs] n Celsius m

cement [sɪ·'ment] I. n Zement m II. vt 1. (with concrete) betonieren; (with cement) zementieren; (with glue) kitten 2. a. fig (bind) festigen

ce'ment mixer n Betonmischmaschine f

cemetery ['sem·ə·ter·i] n Friedhof m

censor ['sen·sər] I. n Zensor(in) m(f) II. vt zensieren

censorship ['sen·sər·ʃɪp] n Zensur f

censure ['sen·ʃər] I. n Tadel m II. vt tadeln

census ['sen·səs] n Zählung f

cent [sent] n Cent m

centenarian [ˌsen·tə·'ner·i·ən] n Hundertjährige(r) f(m)

centennial [sen·'teni·əl] n Hundertjahrfeier f

center ['sen·tər] n 1. Zentrum nt, Mittelpunkt m; POL Mitte f 2. SPORT Center m

centigrade ['sen·tə·greɪd] n Celsius

centimeter ['sen·tə·ˌmi·tər] n Zentimeter m

centipede ['sen·tə·pid] n Tausendfüßler m

central ['sen·trəl] adj 1. (middle) zentral 2. (vital) wesentlich

centrifugal [sen·'trɪf·jə·gəl] adj zentrifugal

century ['sen·tʃə·ri] n Jahrhundert nt

CEO [ˌsi·i·'oʊ] n abbr of chief executive officer Generaldirektor(in) m(f)

ceramics [sə·'ræm·ɪks] n + sing vb Keramik f

cereal ['sɪr·i·əl] n 1. (for breakfast) Frühstückszerealien pl (Cornflakes, Müsli ...) 2. (crop) Getreide nt

ceremonial [ˌser·ə·'moʊ·ni·əl] adj zeremoniell

ceremonious [ˌser·ə·'moʊ·ni·əs] adj förmlich

ceremony ['ser·ə·moʊ·ni] n Zeremonie f, Feier f

certain ['sɜr·tən] adj 1. (sure) sicher; (unavoidable) bestimmt; to make ~ [that ...] darauf achten, dass ...]; for ~ ganz sicher 2. (particular) gewiss

certainly ['sɜr·tən·li] adv 1. (surely) sicher[lich]; (without a doubt) bestimmt, gewiss 2. (gladly) gern[e]; (of course) [aber] selbstverständlich; ~ not auf [gar] keinen Fall

certainty ['sɜr·tən·ti] n Gewissheit f

certificate [sər·'tɪf·ɪ·kət] n (document) Urkunde f; (attestation) Bescheinigung f

certified ['sɜr·tə·faɪd] adj 1. (copy) beglaubigt 2. (trained) ausgebildet, -meister, -in m, f; (by the state) staatlich anerkannt

certify <-ie-> ['sɜr·tə·faɪ] vt bescheinigen, bestätigen; LAW beglaubigen

cervical ['sɜr·vɪ·kəl] adj ANAT 1. (of neck) zervikal 2. (of cervix) Gebärmutterhals-

cervix <pl -es> ['sɜr·vɪks] n Gebärmutterhals m

cesspit ['ses·pɪt], cesspool ['ses·pul] n Jauchegrube f; fig, pej Sumpf m

CFC [ˌsi·ef·'si] n abbr of chlorofluorocarbon FCKW nt

chafe [tʃeɪf] vt [wund]scheuern

chain [tʃeɪn] I. n 1. Kette f 2. fig (of shops) [Laden]kette f II. vt [an]ketten

chain re'action n Kettenreaktion f

'chain saw n Kettensäge f

'chain smoker n Kettenraucher(in) m(f)

'chain store n Kettenladen m

chair [tʃer] I. n 1. Stuhl m 2. UNIV Lehrstuhl m 3. (chairperson) Vorsitzende(r) f(m) II. vt to ~ sth bei etw dat den Vorsitz führen

'chair lift n Sessellift m

'chairman n Vorsitzende(r) m

'chairmanship n Vorsitz m

'chairperson n Vorsitzende(r) f(m)

'chairwoman n Vorsitzende f

chalk [tʃɔk] I. n Kreide f; (rock) Kalkstein m II. vt mit Kreide schreiben/ zeichnen

challenge ['tʃæl·ɪndʒ] I. n Herausforderung f II. vt 1. herausfordern 2. (findings) in Frage stellen

challenger ['tʃæl·ɪn·dʒər] n (for title) Titelanwärter(in) m(f)

challenging ['tʃæl·ɪn·dʒɪŋ] adj [heraus]fordernd

chamber ['tʃeɪm·bər] n 1. (judge's offices) ~s Amtszimmer nt 2. (in firearm) Patronenlager 3. old Kammer f

'chambermaid n Zimmermädchen nt

'chamber music n Kammermusik f

chameleon [kə·'mi·li·ən] n Chamäleon nt a. fig

chamois <pl -> ['ʃæm·i] n 1. ZOOL Gämse f 2. (cloth) Fensterleder nt

champ [tʃæmp] n short for champion Champion m

champagne [ʃæm·'peɪn] n Champagner m

champion ['tʃæm·pi·ən] n 1. Champion m 2. Verfechter(in) m(f)

championship ['tʃæm·pi·ən·ʃɪp] n Meisterschaft f

chance [tʃæns] I. n 1. Zufall m; by ~ zufällig 2. (prospect) Chance f; no ~!

fam niemals! **3.** (*risk*) Risiko *nt;* **to take ~s** [*or* **a ~**] etwas riskieren **II.** *vt fam* riskieren; **to ~ it** es wagen

chancellor ['tʃæn·sə·lər] *n* **1.** Kanzler(in) *m(f)* **2.** UNIV Rektor(in) *m(f)*

chandelier [ʃæn·də·'lɪr] *n* Kronleuchter *m*

change ['tʃeɪndʒ] **I.** *n* **1.** (*alteration*) [Ver]änderung *f* **2.** (*substitution*) Wechsel *m* **3.** (*variety*) Abwechslung *f;* **for a ~** zur Abwechslung **4.** (*coins*) Kleingeld *nt;* (*money returned*) Wechselgeld *nt,* Retourgeld *nt schweiz* **II.** *vi* **1.** sich [ver]ändern; (*traffic light*) umspringen; (*weather*) umschlagen; (*wind*) sich drehen **2.** (*substitute*) **to ~ to sth** zu etw *dat* wechseln **3.** TRANSP umsteigen **4.** (*dress*) sich umziehen **III.** *vt* **1.** (*make different*) [ver]ändern; (*transform*) verwandeln; **to ~ one's mind** seine Meinung ändern **2.** (*exchange*) wechseln; **to ~ places with sb** mit jdm den Platz tauschen; *fig* mit jdm tauschen **3.** (*make fresh: baby*) [frisch] wickeln; (*bed*) neu beziehen; (*socks, underwear*) wechseln; **to get ~d** sich umziehen **4.** (*money*) wechseln; **to ~ $100 into euros** $100 in Euros umtauschen **5.** TRANSP (*buses, trains*) umsteigen

changeable ['tʃeɪn·dʒə·bəl] *adj* unbeständig; (*moods*) wechselnd

changeover *n usu sing* Umstellung *f*

channel ['tʃæn·əl] **I.** *n* **1.** Programm *nt* **2.** [Fluss]bett *nt;* (*artificial*) Kanal *m* **II.** *vt* <-l-> (*direct*) leiten; (*one's energies, money*) stecken

chant [tʃænt] **I.** *n* **1.** REL [Sprech]gesang *m* **2.** SPORT Sprechchor *m* **II.** *vt* **1.** REL singen **2.** SPORT im Sprechchor rufen

chaos ['keɪ·as] *n* Chaos *nt,* Durcheinander *nt*

chaotic [keɪ·'at·ɪk] *adj* chaotisch

chap <-pp-> ['tʃæp] *vt, vi* aufspringen

chapel ['tʃæp·əl] *n* Kapelle *f*

chaplain ['tʃæp·lɪn] *n* Kaplan *m*

Chap Stick® *n* ≈ Labello® *m*

chapter ['tʃæp·tər] *n* Kapitel *nt*

char <-rr-> [tʃar] *vt, vi* verkohlen

character ['ker·ək·tər] *n* **1.** Charakter *m* **2.** LIT [Roman]figur *f* **3.** TYPO Zeichen *nt*

characteristic [ker·ək·tə·'rɪs·tɪk] **I.** *n* charakteristisches Merkmal **II.** *adj* charakteristisch, typisch

characterize ['ker·ək·tə·raɪz] *vt* kennzeichnen

charcoal ['tʃar·koʊl] *n* Holzkohle *f;* (*for drawing*) Kohle *f*

charge [tʃardʒ] **I.** *n* **1.** (*cost*) Gebühr *f;* **free of ~** kostenlos **2.** LAW Anklage *f* ~**s** *pl* Anklagepunkte *pl;* (*in civil cases*) Ansprüche *pl* **3.** (*responsibility*) Verantwortung *f;* **to be in ~** die Verantwortung tragen; **she's in ~ of the department** sie leitet die Abteilung **4.** ELEC Ladung *f* **5.** (*attack*) Angriff *m* **II.** *vi* **1.** (*attack*) [vorwärts]stürmen **2.** (*move quickly*) stürmen **III.** *vt* **1.** (*demand payment*) berechnen; **how much do you ~ for that?** was kostet das bei Ihnen? **2.** LAW **to ~ sb with murder** jdn des Mordes anklagen **3.** (*battery*) aufladen

chariot ['tʃær·i·ət] *n* Streitwagen *m*

charisma [kə·'rɪz·mə] *n* Charisma *nt*

charismatic [kə·rɪz·'mæt·ɪk] *adj* charismatisch

charitable ['tʃer·ɪ·tə·bəl] *adj* **1.** (*generous*) großzügig; (*uncritical*) gütig **2.** (*of charity*) karitativ; ~ **organization** Wohltätigkeitsorganisation *f*

charity ['tʃer·ɪ·ti] *n* **1.** (*generosity*) Barmherzigkeit *f* **2.** Wohltätigkeitsorganisation *f;* **the proceeds go to ~** die Erträge sind für wohltätige Zwecke bestimmt

charm [tʃarm] *n* **1.** (*quality*) Charme *m* **2.** (*jewelry*) Anhänger *m;* **lucky ~** Glücksbringer *m*

charming ['tʃar·mɪŋ] *adj* bezaubernd, reizend

chart [tʃart] *n* **1.** (*visual*) Diagramm *nt* **2.** MUS **the ~s** *pl* die Charts

charter ['tʃar·tər] **I.** *n* **1.** (*constitution*) Charta *f;* (*of society*) Satzung *f* **2.** TRANSP Charter *m* **II.** *vt* chartern

charter flight *n* Charterflug *m*

chase [tʃeɪs] **I.** *n* **1.** Verfolgungsjagd *f* **2.** HUNT Jagd *f* **II.** *vi* **to ~ after sb** hinter jdm herlaufen **III.** *vt* **1.** (*pursue*) verfolgen **2.** **to ~ away** vertreiben, verjagen

chasm ['kæz·əm] *n* Kluft *f a. fig*

chassis <*pl* -> ['ʃæs·i] *n* Fahrgestell *nt*

chaste [tʃeɪst] *adj form* keusch

hastity ['tʃæs·tɪ·ti] n Keuschheit f

hat [tʃæt] I. n fam Schwatz m; **to have a ~ [with sb]** [mit jdm] quatschen II. vi <-tt-> 1. plaudern 2. COMPUT chatten

chat room n Chatroom m

hatter ['tʃæt·ər] I. n Geschwätz nt II. vi 1. (converse) plaudern 2. (teeth) klappern; (machines) knattern

hatty ['tʃæt·i] adj fam (person) gesprächig; pej geschwätzig

hauffeur ['ʃoʊ·fər] n Chauffeur(in) m(f)

heap [tʃip] adj billig a. fig; (reduced) ermäßigt

heapskate n pej fam Geizkragen m

heat [tʃit] I. n 1. (person) Betrüger(in) m(f); (in school) Schummler(in) m(f) 2. (fraud) Täuschung f II. vi betrügen; (in exam) abschreiben; **to ~ on sb** jdn betrügen III. vt täuschen; (financially) betrügen

heck [tʃek] I. n 1. (inspection) Kontrolle f 2. (search) Suchlauf m 3. (restraint) Kontrolle f 4. (mark) Haken m 5. (chess) Schach nt 6. FIN Scheck m; (bill) Rechnung f 7. (pattern) Karo[muster] nt II. vt 1. (inspect) überprüfen 2. (advance) aufhalten 3. CHESS Schach bieten 4. (box) abhaken III. vi 1. (examine) nachsehen 2. (consult) **to ~ with sb** bei jdm nachfragen

check in I. vi (airport) einchecken; (hotel) sich [an der Rezeption] anmelden II. vt (passengers) abfertigen; (hotel guests) anmelden; (luggage) einchecken

check out I. vi sich abmelden II. vt 1. (investigate) untersuchen 2. sl (observe) **~ it out!** schau dir bloß mal das an!

check up vi **to ~ up on sb/sth** jdn/etw überprüfen [or kontrollieren]

heckbook n Scheckheft nt

hecked [tʃekt] adj kariert

heckerboard n Damebrett nt

heckered ['tʃek·ərd] adj 1. (patterned) kariert 2. fig (past, career) bewegt

heck-in ['tʃek·ɪn] n 1. (for flight) Einchecken nt 2. see **check-in counter**

heck-in counter, **check-in desk** n (airport) Abfertigungsschalter m; (hotel) Rezeption f

checking account n Girokonto nt

checklist n Checkliste f

checkmate n CHESS Schachmatt nt

checkout n Kasse f

check room n (for coats) Garderobe f; (for luggage) Gepäckaufbewahrung f

checkup n [Kontroll]untersuchung f

cheek [tʃik] n 1. (of face) Backe f 2. (impertinence) Frechheit f

cheekbone n usu pl Backenknochen m

cheeky ['tʃi·ki] adj frech

cheep [tʃip] I. n (sound) Piepser m; (action) Piepen nt II. vi piep[s]en

cheer [tʃɪr] I. n 1. Beifallsruf m; **three ~s for ...** ein dreifaches Hoch auf +akk ... 2. Aufmunterung f II. vi mit Beifall begrüßen

cheer up I. vi **~ up!** Kopf hoch! II. vt aufmuntern

cheerful ['tʃɪr·fʊl] adj 1. (happy) fröhlich, heiter 2. (bright) heiter; (tune) fröhlich

cheering ['tʃɪr·ɪŋ] I. n Jubel m II. adj jubelnd

cheerleader n Cheerleader m

cheers [tʃɪrz] interj fam prost

cheese [tʃiz] n Käse m

cheeseburger n Cheeseburger m

cheesecake n Käsekuchen m

cheesy ['tʃi·zi] adj 1. käsig 2. pej fam abgedroschen fam

cheetah ['tʃi·tə] n Gepard m

chef [ʃef] n Koch m, Köchin f

chemical ['kem·ɪ·kəl] I. n (substance) Chemikalie f; (additive) chemischer Zusatz II. adj chemisch

chemist ['kem·ɪst] n Chemiker(in) m(f)

chemistry ['kem·ɪ·stri] n Chemie f

chemotherapy [ˌki·moʊ·'θer·ə·pi] n Chemotherapie f

cherish ['tʃer·ɪʃ] vt hegen

cherry ['tʃer·i] n Kirsche f

cherry to'mato n Cocktailtomate f

chervil ['tʃɜr·vɪl] n Kerbel m

chess [tʃes] n Schach[spiel] nt

chessboard n Schachbrett nt

chessman, **chesspiece** n Schachfigur f

chest [tʃest] n 1. Brust f 2. (trunk) Truhe f; (box) Kiste f

chestnut ['tʃes·nʌt] I. n Kastanie f II. adj kastanienbraun

chesty ['tʃes·ti] *adj fam* **1.** (*arrogant*) eingebildet **2.** (*big-bosomed*) vollbusig

chew [tʃu] *vt, vi* kauen

'chewing gum *n* Kaugummi *m o nt*

chic [ʃik] **I.** *n* Schick *m* **II.** *adj* schick

chick [tʃik] *n* **1.** (*chicken*) Küken *nt* **2.** *sl* (*woman*) Puppe *f pej*

chicken ['tʃik·ən] *n* **1.** (*bird*) Huhn *nt* **2.** (*meat*) Hähnchen *nt* **3.** *pej sl* Angsthase *m*

'chickenpox *n* Windpocken *pl*

'chick flick *n sl* Frauenfilm *f (Film mit besonders emotionaler Handlung)*

chickpea ['tʃik·pi] *n* Kichererbse *f*

chicory ['tʃik·ə·ri] *n* Chicorée *m o f*; (*in drink*) Zichorie *f*

chief [tʃif] **I.** *n* **1.** (*boss*) Chef(in) *m(f)* **2.** (*leader*) Führer(in) *m(f)*; (*head of clan*) Oberhaupt *nt*; (*head of tribe*) Häuptling *m* **II.** *adj* Haupt-, oberste(r, s)

chief ex'ecutive *n* Präsident(in) *m(f)*; (*of organization*) ~ [**officer**] Generaldirektor(in) *m(f)*

chief 'justice *n* Oberrichter(in) *m(f)*

chiefly ['tʃif·li] *adv* hauptsächlich

chiffon [ʃi·'fan] *n* Chiffon *m*

child <*pl* -dren> [tʃaɪld] *n* Kind *nt*

'child abuse *n* Kindesmisshandlung *f*

'childbirth *n* Geburt *f*

childhood ['tʃaɪld·hʊd] *n* Kindheit *f*

childish ['tʃaɪl·dɪʃ] *adj pej* kindisch

'childlike *adj* kindlich

'childproof *adj* kindersicher

children ['tʃɪl·drən] *n pl of* **child**

chili <*pl* -es> ['tʃɪl·i] *n* Chili *m*

chili con carne [,tʃɪ·li·kan·'kar·ni] *n* Chili con Carne *nt*

chill [tʃɪl] **I.** *n* Kühle *f*; (*feeling of coldness*) Kältegefühl *nt* **II.** *vi* **1.** abkühlen **2.** *fam* ~ [**out**] chillen *sl* **III.** *vt* [ab]kühlen [lassen]

chilling ['tʃɪl·ɪŋ] *adj* **1.** (*freezing*) eisig **2.** (*frightening*) abschreckend

chilly ['tʃɪl·i] *adj* kühl *a. fig*, frostig

chime [tʃaɪm] **I.** *n* Glockenspiel *nt*; (*of single one*) Glockenschlag *m*; (*of doorbell*) Läuten *nt kein pl* **II.** *vi* klingen; (*church bells*) läuten

chimney ['tʃɪm·ni] *n* Schornstein *m*; (*of factory*) Schlot *m*

'chimney sweep *n* Schornsteinfeger(in) *m(f)*

chimpanzee [tʃɪm·'pæn·zi] *n* Schimpanse *m*

chin [tʃɪn] *n* Kinn *nt*

china ['tʃaɪ·nə] *n* Porzellan *nt*

China ['tʃaɪ·nə] *n* China *nt*

Chinese <*pl* -> [tʃaɪ·'niz] **I.** *n* **1.** (*person*) Chinese, -in *m, f*; **the** ~ *pl* die Chinesen **2.** (*language*) Chinesisch *r* **II.** *adj* chinesisch

chink [tʃɪŋk] *n* Spalt *m*

'chin-up *n* Klimmzug *m*

chip [tʃɪp] **I.** *n* **1.** Splitter *m*; (*of wood*) Span *m* **2. this cup has a ~ in it** dies Tasse ist angeschlagen **3.** *usu pl* FOO| [**potato**] ~s Chips *pl* **4.** COMPUT Chip *r* **II.** *vt* <-pp-> **1.** (*damage*) abschlager (*break off*) abbrechen **2.** SPORT (*ba| puck*) chippen

chip in *vt, vi* etw beisteuern

chipmunk ['tʃɪp·mʌŋk] *n* Backenhörr chen *nt*

chiropractor ['kaɪ·rou·,præk·tər] *n* Chi ropraktiker(in) *m(f)*

chirp [tʃɜrp] **I.** *n* Zwitschern *nt* **II.** *v vi* zwitschern

chisel ['tʃɪz·əl] **I.** *n* Meißel *m* **II.** *vt* <-l-: meißeln

chitchat ['tʃɪt·,tʃæt] *n fam* Geplauder *nt*

chivalrous ['ʃɪv·əl·rəs] *adj* ritterlich

chives [tʃaɪvz] *npl* Schnittlauch *m kein p*

chlorine ['klɔr·in] *n* Chlor *nt*

chlorofluorocarbon [,klɔr·ou·,flʊr·ou 'kar·bən] *n* Fluorchlorkohlenwasse| stoff *m*

chlorophyll ['klɔr·ə·fɪl] *n* Chlorophyll *n*

chock [tʃak] *n* Bremsklotz *m*

chock-'full *adj fam* proppenvoll, vol| gestopft

chocolate ['tʃak·lət] *n* **1.** Schokolade | **dark** ~ Zartbitterschokolade *f* **2.** (*i box*) Praline *f*

chocolate 'chip *n* Schokoladenstück| chen *nt*

choice [tʃɔɪs] **I.** *n* **1.** (*selection*) Wahl | **to make a ~** eine Wahl treffen **2.** (*var ety*) Auswahl *f* **II.** *adj* ausgesucht

choir ['kwaɪr] *n* Chor *m*

choke [tʃouk] **I.** *n* AUTO Choke *m* **II.** | **1.** erwürgen; (*suffocate*) ersticke|

2. (*block*) verstopfen **III.** *vi* **1.** keine Luft bekommen; **to ~ to death** ersticken **2.** *sl* (*fail*) versagen

cholera [ˈkɑl·ər·ə] *n* Cholera *f*

cholesterol [kəˈles·tə·rɑl] *n* Cholesterin *nt*

choose <chose, chosen> [tʃuz] **I.** *vt* [aus]wählen **II.** *vi* (*select*) wählen; (*decide*) sich entscheiden

choosy [ˈtʃu·zi] *adj fam* wählerisch

chop [tʃɑp] **I.** *vt* <-pp-> (*wood*) hacken; **to ~ sth ⇆ [up]** etw klein schneiden **II.** *vi* <-pp-> hacken **III.** *n* **1.** (*meat*) Kotelett *nt* **2.** (*blow*) Schlag *m*

◆**chop down** *vt* fällen

◆**chop off** *vt* abhacken

chopper [ˈtʃɑp·ər] *n* **1.** *sl* (*helicopter*) Hubschrauber *m* **2.** *sl* (*motorcycle*) Chopper *m* **3.** (*ax, cleaver*) Hackbeil *nt*

chopping board *n* Hackbrett *nt*

choppy [ˈtʃɑp·i] *adj* NAUT bewegt

chopstick *n usu pl* [Ess]stäbchen *nt*

choral [ˈkɔr·əl] *adj* Chor-

chord [kɔrd] *n* Akkord *m*

chore [tʃɔr] *n* Hausarbeit *f*

choreographer [ˌkɔr·iˈɑg·rə·fər] *n* Choreograf(in) *m(f)*

choreography [ˌkɔr·iˈɑg·rə·fi] *n* Choreografie *f*

chorus [ˈkɔr·əs] *n* <pl -es> **1.** Refrain *m* **2.** Chor *m*

chose [tʃoʊz] *pt of* **choose**

chosen [ˈtʃoʊ·zən] *pp of* **choose**

chowder [ˈtʃaʊ·dər] *n* sämige Suppe mit Fisch, Muscheln etc.

Christ [kraɪst] *n* Christus *m*

christen [ˈkrɪs·ən] *vt* **1.** (*baptize, name*) taufen **2.** (*use for first time*) einweihen

christening [ˈkrɪs·ə·nɪŋ] *n* Taufe *f*

Christian [ˈkrɪs·tʃən] **I.** *n* Christ(in) *m(f)* **II.** *adj* christlich

Christianity [ˌkrɪs·tʃiˈæn·ɪ·t̬i] *n* Christentum *nt*

Christmas <pl -es> [ˈkrɪs·məs] *n* Weihnachten *nt;* **Merry ~!** Frohe [*or* Fröhliche] Weihnachten!

'Christmas card *n* Weihnachtskarte *f*

'Christmas carol *n* Weihnachtslied *nt*

Christmas 'Day *n* erster Weihnachts-

feiertag

Christmas 'Eve *n* Heiligabend *m*

'Christmas tree *n* Weihnachtsbaum *m*

chrome [kroʊm], **chromium** [ˈkroʊ·mi·əm] *n* Chrom *nt*

chromosome [ˈkroʊ·mə·soʊm] *n* Chromosom *nt*

chronic [ˈkrɑn·ɪk] *adj* chronisch

chronological [ˌkrɑn·əˈlɑdʒ·ɪ·kəl] *adj* chronologisch

chubby [ˈtʃʌb·i] *adj* pummelig; (*face*) pausbäckig

chuck [tʃʌk] *vt fam* **1.** (*throw*) schmeißen **2.** (*throw out*) wegschmeißen

◆**chuck out** *vt fam* wegschmeißen

chuckle [ˈtʃʌk·əl] **I.** *n* Gekicher *nt kein pl* **II.** *vi* in sich hineinlachen

chug [tʃʌg] *vi* <-gg-> tuckern

chum [tʃʌm] *n fam* Freund(in) *m(f)*

chummy [ˈtʃʌm·i] *adj fam* freundlich

chump [tʃʌmp] *n fam* Trottel *m*

chump change *n sl* Kleingeld

chunk [tʃʌŋk] *n* Brocken *m;* (*of bread*) [großes] Stück; *fig fam* großer Batzen

chunky [ˈtʃʌŋ·ki] *adj* (*person*) stämmig; (*peanut butter*) mit ganzen Stücken

church [tʃɜrtʃ] *n* <pl -es> Kirche *f*

'churchgoer *n* Kirchgänger(in) *m(f)*

churn [tʃɜrn] **I.** *n* Butterfass *nt* **II.** *vt* (*milk*) quirlen; (*ground, sea*) aufwühlen **III.** *vi fig* sich heftig drehen

chute¹ [ʃut] *n* Rutsche *f*

chute² [ʃut] *n short for* **parachute** Fallschirm *m*

CIA [ˌsi·aɪˈeɪ] *n abbr of* **Central Intelligence Agency** CIA *m o f*

cider [ˈsaɪ·dər] *n* Apfelwein *m*

cigar [sɪˈgɑr] *n* Zigarre *f*

cigarette [ˌsɪg·əˈret] *n* Zigarette *f*

cigarette butt *n* Kippe *f*

cinch <pl -es> [sɪntʃ] *n usu sing* **a** ~ ein Kinderspiel *nt*

cinder [ˈsɪn·dər] *n* Zinder *m;* **~s** *pl* Asche *f kein pl*

Cinderella [ˌsɪn·dəˈrel·ə] *n* Aschenputtel *nt*

cinema [ˈsɪn·ə·mə] *n* Kino *nt*

cinnamon [ˈsɪn·ə·mən] *n* Zimt *m*

cipher [ˈsaɪ·fər] *n* [Geheim]code *m;* (*symbol*) Chiffre *f*

circle [ˈsɜr·kəl] **I.** *n* Kreis *m* **II.** *vt*

1. (*draw around*) umkringeln **2.** (*walk around*) umkreisen **III.** *vi* kreisen

circuit ['sɜr·kɪt] *n* **1.** ELEC Stromkreis *m*; **short ~** Kurzschluss *m* **2.** (*circular route*) Rundgang *m*

circular ['sɜr·kjə·lər] **I.** *adj* (*kreis*)rund **II.** *n* Rundschreiben *nt*; (*advertisement*) Wurfsendung *f*

circular 'saw *n* Kreissäge *f*

circulate ['sɜr·kjə·leɪt] **I.** *vt* (*news*) in Umlauf bringen; (*petition*) herumgehen lassen **II.** *vi* zirkulieren; (*rumors*) kursieren

circulation [,sɜr·kjʊ·'leɪ·ʃən] *n* **1.** MED [Blut]kreislauf *m*, Durchblutung *f* **2.** (*copies sold*) Auflage *f*

circumcise ['sɜr·kəm·saɪz] *vt* beschneiden

circumcision [,sɜr·kəm·'sɪʒ·ən] *n* Beschneidung *f*

circumference [sər·'kʌm·fər·əns] *n* Umfang *m*

circumstance ['sɜr·kəm·stæns] *n* Umstand *m*; **in** [*or* **under**] **no**/**these ~s** unter keinen/diesen Umständen

circumstantial [,sɜr·kəm·'stæn·ʃəl] *adj* indirekt; **~ evidence** Indizienbeweis *m*

circus ['sɜr·kəs] *n* Zirkus *m*

cistern ['sɪs·tərn] *n* Wasserspeicher *m*

citation [saɪ·'teɪ·ʃən] *n* **1.** Zitat *nt* **2.** JUR Vorladung *f*

cite [saɪt] *vt* **1.** (*mention*) anführen **2.** (*quote*) zitieren **3.** LAW vorladen

citizen ['sɪt·ɪ·zən] *n* [Staats]bürger(in) *m(f)*

citizenship ['sɪt·ɪ·zən·ʃɪp] *n* Staatsbürgerschaft *f*

citrus <*pl* -> ['sɪt·rəs] *n* Zitrusgewächs *nt*; **~ fruit** Zitrusfrucht *f*

city ['sɪt·i] *n* [Groß]stadt *f*

city 'clerk *n* Magistratsbeamte(r), -beamtin *m, f*

city 'council *n* Stadtrat *m*, Stadtverwaltung *f*

city 'hall *n* Rathaus *nt*

City 'Hall *n* Stadtverwaltung *f*

'city slicker *n* *pej fam* Großstädter(in) *m(f)*

civic ['sɪv·ɪk] *adj* städtisch; (*of citizenship*) bürgerlich

civics ['sɪv·ɪks] *n* + *sing vb* SCH Gemeinschaftskunde *f*

civil ['sɪv·əl] *adj* **1.** (*nonmilitary*) zivil; (*ordinary citizens*) bürgerlich **2.** (*courteous*) höflich

civil 'court *n* Zivilgericht *nt*

civil engi'neer *n* Bauingenieur(in) *m(f)*

civilian [sɪ·'vɪl·jən] **I.** *n* Zivilist(in) *m(f)* **II.** *adj* Zivil-

civility [sɪ·'vɪl·ɪ·ti] *n* Höflichkeit *f*

civilization [,sɪv·ə·lɪ·'zeɪ·ʃən] *n* Zivilisation *f*

civilize ['sɪv·ə·laɪz] *vt* zivilisieren

civil 'law *n* Zivilrecht *nt*

civil 'rights *npl* Bürgerrechte *pl*

civil 'servant *n* [Staats]beamte(r) *m*, [Staats]beamte [*or* -in] *f*

civil 'service *n* öffentlicher Dienst

civil 'war *n* Bürgerkrieg *m*

claim [kleɪm] **I.** *n* **1.** (*assertion*) Behauptung *f* **2.** (*demand for money*) Forderung *f* **3.** (*right*) Anspruch *m* **4. insurance ~** Versicherungsanspruch *m* **II.** *vt* **1.** (*declare ownership*) auf etw *akk* Anspruch erheben; (*luggage*) abholen; (*throne*) beanspruchen **2.** (*demand*) beantragen; (*damages, refund*) fordern **3.** (*assert*) behaupten; (*responsibility*) übernehmen; (*victory*) für sich in Anspruch nehmen **4.** (*take violently: lives*) fordern

clairvoyant [,kler·'vɔɪ·ənt] **I.** *n* Hellseher(in) *m(f)* **II.** *adj* **to be ~** hellsehen können

clam [klæm] *n* Venusmuschel *f*

clamber ['klæm·bər] *vi* klettern

clam 'chowder *n* [sämige] Muschelsuppe

clammy ['klæm·i] *adj* feuchtkalt

clamor ['klæm·ər] **I.** *vi* schreien (**for** nach +*dat*) **II.** *n* (*outcry*) Aufschrei *m*; (*demand*) lautstarke Forderung; (*noise*) Lärm *m*

clamp [klæmp] *n* Klammer *f*; (*screwable*) Klemme *f*

clan [klæn] *n* Clan *m*

clandestine [klæn·'des·tɪn] *adj* heimlich

clang [klæŋ] **I.** *vi* scheppern; (*bell*) [laut] läuten **II.** *vt* klappern mit +*dat*, schlagen **III.** *n* *usu sing* Scheppern *nt*; (*bell*) [lautes] Läuten

clank [klæŋk] **I.** *vi* klirren; (*chain*) rasseln **II.** *vt* klirren mit +*dat* **III.** *n* *usu sing* Klirren *nt*

lap [klæp] I. n 1. (*applause*) Klatschen nt 2. ~ **of thunder** Donner|schlag m II. <-pp-> **to ~ one's hands** [**together**] in die Hände klatschen III. vi <-pp-> [Bei-fall] klatschen

larification [ˌkler·ɪ·fɪˈkeɪ·ʃən] n Klar-stellung f

larify <-ie-> [ˈkler·ɪ·faɪ] vt klarstellen

larinet [ˌkler·əˈnet] n Klarinette f

larity [ˈkler·ɪ·ti] n Klarheit f

lash [klæʃ] I. vi 1. (*conflict*) zusam-menstoßen 2. (*compete against*) auf-einandertreffen 3. (*contradict*) im Wi-derspruch stehen 4. (*colors*) sich beißen II. n <pl -es> 1. (*hostile encounter*) Zusammenstoß m 2. (*contest*) Aufein-andertreffen nt

lasp [klæsp] I. n 1. (*fastener*) Ver-schluss m 2. (*firm grip*) Griff m II. vt umklammern

lass [klæs] I. n <pl -es> 1. (*lesson*) [Unterrichts]stunde f; SPORT Kurs[us] m 2. (*students*) [Schul]klasse f 3. (*in so-ciety*) Klasse f, Schicht f 4. (*category*) Klasse f II. vt einstufen

lassic [ˈklæs·ɪk] I. adj klassisch II. n Klassiker m

lassical [ˈklæs·ɪ·kəl] adj klassisch

lassification [ˌklæs·ə·fɪˈkeɪ·ʃən] n Klas-sifikation f

lassified [ˈklæs·ɪ·faɪd] adj geheim; ~ **advertisement** Kleinanzeige f

lassify <-ie-> [ˈklæs·ɪ·faɪ] vt klassifi-zieren

lassmate n Klassenkamerad(in) m(f)

lassroom n Klassenzimmer nt

latter [ˈklæt̬·ər] I. vt klappern mit +dat II. vi klappern III. n Klappern nt

lause [klɔz] n 1. (*in sentence*) Satz-glied nt 2. (*in contract*) Klausel f

laustrophobia [ˌklɔ·strəˈfoʊ·bi·ə] n Klaustrophobie f

laustrophobic [ˌklɔ·strəˈfoʊ·bɪk] adj (*person*) klaustrophobisch

law [klɔ] n Kralle f; (*of bird of prey, big cat*) Klaue[n] f[pl]; (*of sea creature*) Schere[n] f[pl]

lay [kleɪ] n Lehm m; (*for pottery*) Ton m

lean [klin] I. adj 1. sauber; (*sheets*) frisch 2. (*not offensive*) sauber; (*joke*)

anständig II. adv 1. sauber 2. fam (*completely*) total, glatt III. vt (*re-move dirt*) sauber machen, reinigen; (*car*) waschen; (*floor*) wischen; (*shoes, teeth*) putzen IV. vi 1. (*remove dirt*) reinigen 2. (*become free of dirt*) sich reinigen lassen

◆**clean out** vt 1. [gründlich] sauber ma-chen; (*with water*) auswaschen 2. fam (*person*) [wie eine Weihnachtsgans] aus-nehmen

◆**clean up** I. vt 1. (*make clean*) sauber machen; (*room, mess*) aufräumen 2. fig säubern II. vi 1. (*make clean*) aufräu-men; (*freshen oneself*) sich frisch ma-chen 2. sl (*make profit*) absahnen

clean-cut adj anständig

cleaner [ˈkli·nər] n 1. (*substance*) Reini-ger m 2. (*person*) Reinigungskraft f

cleaning [ˈkli·nɪŋ] n **to do the ~** sau-ber machen

cleaning lady, **cleaning woman** n Putzfrau f

cleanliness [ˈklen·lɪ·nɪs] n Sauberkeit f

cleanly [ˈklen·li] adv sauber

cleanse [klenz] vt reinigen

cleanser [ˈklen·zər] n Reiniger m; (*for skin*) Reinigungscreme f

clean-shaven adj glatt rasiert

clear [klɪr] I. adj 1. klar; (*definite*) ein-deutig; (*signs*) deutlich; **to make one-self ~** sich deutlich ausdrücken 2. **to be ~ about sth** sich dat über etw akk im Klaren sein 3. (*glass*) durchsichtig; (*liquid*) klar 4. (*unobstructed: path, view*) frei 5. (*conscience*) rein 6. (*pic-ture*) scharf II. n **to be in the ~** außer Verdacht sein III. vt 1. (*remove clutter from*) [weg]räumen; **to ~ one's throat** sich räuspern 2. (*empty*) ausräumen; (*building*) räumen; (*table, desks*) abräu-men 3. (*acquit*) freisprechen; (*name*) reinwaschen 4. (*give permission*) ge-nehmigen IV. vi (*weather*) sich [auf]-klären; (*fog*) sich auflösen

◆**clear out** I. vt ausräumen; (*attic*) ent-rümpeln II. vi fam verschwinden

◆**clear up** I. vt klären; (*mystery*) aufklä-ren; fig (*put in order: mess*) aufräumen II. vi 1. METEO aufhören zu regnen; (*brighten up*) sich aufklären 2. (*become*

C

cured) verschwinden, sich legen

clearance ['klɪr·əns] n 1. (*action*) Beseitigung f; (*of slums*) Sanierung f 2. (*space*) Spielraum m; (*of a door*) lichte Höhe 3. (*official permission*) Genehmigung f

'**clearance sale** n Räumungsverkauf m

'**clear-cut** *adj* 1. (*sharply outlined*) klar umrissen 2. (*not ambiguous*) klar; (*case*) eindeutig

clearing ['klɪr·ɪŋ] n Lichtung f

clearly ['klɪr·li] *adv* 1. (*distinctly*) klar, deutlich 2. (*obviously*) offensichtlich; (*unambiguously*) eindeutig; (*undoubtedly*) zweifellos

cleavage ['kli·vɪdʒ] n Dekolletee nt

cleaver ['kli·vər] n Hackbeil nt

clef [klef] n [Noten]schlüssel m

cleft [kleft] I. *adj* gespalten; ~ **palate** Gaumenspalte f II. n Spalt m

clematis <pl -> ['klem·ə·tɪs] n Klematis f

clemency ['klem·ən·si] n Milde f

clench [klentʃ] *vt* (*fist*) ballen; (*teeth*) fest zusammenbeißen

clergy ['klɜr·dʒi] n + *sing/pl vb* **the** ~ die Geistlichkeit

'**clergyman** n Geistliche(r) m

'**clergywoman** n Geistliche f

clerk [klɜrk] n Büroangestellte(r) f(m); (*in hotel*) Empfangschef m /Empfangsdame f

clever ['klev·ər] *adj* 1. (*intelligence*) klug, clever a. *pej*; (*trick*) raffiniert 2. (*dexterous*) geschickt

cleverness ['klev·ər·nɪs] n 1. (*intelligence*) Klugheit f 2. (*dexterity*) Geschicklichkeit f

cliché [kli·'ʃeɪ] n Klischee nt

click [klɪk] I. n 1. (*sound*) Klicken nt; (*of lock*) Einschnappen nt 2. COMPUT Klick m II. vi 1. (*make sound*) klicken; (*lock*) einschnappen 2. *fam* (*become friendly*) sich auf Anhieb verstehen 3. *fam* (*become understandable*) [plötzlich] klar werden 4. COMPUT **to ~ on sth** etw anklicken III. vt 1. (*heels*) zusammenklappen; **to ~ one's fingers** [mit den Fingern] schnippen 2. COMPUT anklicken

client ['klaɪ·ənt] n Kunde m, Kundin f; LAW

Klient(in) m(f)

clientele [ˌklaɪ·ən·'tel] n Kundschaft f

cliff [klɪf] n Klippe f

'**cliffhanger** n Thriller m

climate ['klaɪ·mɪt] n Klima nt

'**climate change** n Klimaveränderung f

climax ['klaɪ·mæks] n 1. (*culmination*) Höhepunkt m 2. (*orgasm*) Orgasmus m

climb [klaɪm] I. n Aufstieg m II. vt **to ~ [up] a hill** auf einen Hügel [hinauf]steigen; **to ~ [up] a tree** auf einen Baum [hoch]klettern III. vi 1. (*ascend*) [auf]steigen; (*plant*) hochklettern 2. (*increase rapidly*) [an]steigen

◆**climb down** vi heruntersteigen; (*from summit*) absteigen; (*from tree*) herunterklettern

climber ['klaɪ·mər] n 1. (*mountaineer*) Bergsteiger(in) m(f); (*of rock faces*) Kletterer, Kletterin m, f 2. (*plant*) Kletterpflanze f

clinch [klɪntʃ] I. n <pl -es> Umschlingung f II. vt entscheiden; (*deal*) perfekt machen

cling <clung, clung> [klɪŋ] vi 1. (*hole tightly*) [sich] klammern (**to** an +*akk* 2. (*stick*) kleben

clinic ['klɪn·ɪk] n MED Klinik f, Ärztepraxis f

clinical ['klɪn·ɪ·kəl] *adj* 1. MED klinisch 2. (*emotionless*) distanziert

clink [klɪŋk] I. vt, vi klirren [mit] +*dat* (*esp metal*) klimpern [mit] +*dat* II. n Klirren nt; (*of coins*) Klimpern nt

clip¹ [klɪp] I. n 1. (*trim*) Haarschnitt m 2. FILM Ausschnitt m II. vt <-pp-> 1. (*dog*) trimmen; (*hedge*) stutzen; (*sheep*) scheren; (*nails*) schneiden 2. (*cut out: coupons*) abtrennen, abschneiden

clip² [klɪp] I. n 1. Klipp m; (*for hair*) [Haar]spange f 2. (*for gun*) Ladestreifen m II. vt <-pp-> anheften, anklammern

clipping ['klɪp·ɪŋ] n (*from newspaper*) Zeitungsausschnitt m

clique [klik] n *pej* Clique f

clitoris ['klɪt·ər·əs] n Klitoris f, Kitzler m

cloak [kloʊk] I. n 1. Umhang m 2. *fig* Deckmantel m II. vt verhüllen

'**cloakroom** n Garderobe f

:lock [klak] n Uhr f

◆clock in, clock out vi stechen

:lock 'radio n Radiowecker m

:lockwise ['klak·waɪz] adj, adv im Uhrzeigersinn

clockwork n Uhrwerk nt

clod [klad] n Klumpen m

clog [klag] I. n Holzschuh m; (modern) Clog[s] m/pl/ II. vt, vi <-gg-> to ~ [up] verstopfen

cloister ['klɔɪ·stər] n usu pl Kreuzgang m

clone [kloʊn] I. n Klon m II. vt klonen

close¹ [kloʊs] I. adj 1. (near) nah[e]; to be ~ to sth in der Nähe einer S. gen liegen 2. (intimate) eng; (relatives) nah; to be ~ to sb jdm [sehr] nahestehen 3. (almost equal) knapp 4. (exact) genau; to pay ~ attention to sb jdm gut zuhören II. adv (near) nahe; she came ~ to getting the job fast hätte sie die Stelle bekommen; to hold sb ~ jdn fest an sich drücken; ~ together dicht beieinander

close² [kloʊz] I. vt 1. schließen; (factory a.) stilllegen; (book, mouth) zumachen; (curtains) zuziehen; (road) sperren 2. (end) abschließen; (bank account) auflösen; (meeting) beenden II. vi 1. (shut: door) zugehen; (shop) schließen; (eyes) zufallen 2. (shut down: shop) zumachen 3. (end) zu Ende gehen; (meeting) schließen III. n Ende nt, Schluss m

◆close down I. vi (business) schließen, zumachen; (factory) stillgelegt werden II. vt schließen; (factory) stilllegen

◆close in vi to ~ in on sb/sth sich jdm/etw nähern; (surround) jdn/etw umzingeln

◆close up I. vi 1. (lock up) abschließen 2. (shut: flower, wound) sich schließen 3. (get nearer: people) zusammenrücken; (troops) aufschließen II. vt [ab] schließen

closed [kloʊzd] adj geschlossen, zu; behind ~ doors fig hinter verschlossenen Türen

'close-knit adj (family) eng verbunden

closely ['kloʊs·li] adv 1. (near) dicht 2. (intimately) eng 3. (exactly) genau

4. (carefully) sorgfältig

closeness ['kloʊs·nɪs] n Nähe f; (intimacy) Vertrautheit f

closet ['klaz·ɪt] n Abstellraum m ▶ to come out of the ~ seine Homosexualität bekennen

'close-up n Nahaufnahme f

closing ['kloʊ·zɪŋ] adj abschließend

'closing date n Einsendeschluss m

'closing time n (for shop) Ladenschluss m; (for staff) Feierabend m; (for bars) Sperrstunde f

closure ['kloʊ·ʒər] n (of institution) Schließung f; (of street) Sperrung f; (of factory) Stilllegung f

clot [klat] I. n MED [Blut]gerinnsel nt II. vi <-tt-> gerinnen

cloth [klɔθ] n 1. (material) Tuch nt, Stoff m 2. (for cleaning) Lappen m

clothe [kloʊð] vt <clothed or clad, clothed or clad> [be]kleiden a. fig

clothes [kloʊz] npl Kleider pl; (collectively) Kleidung f kein pl

'clothes hanger n Kleiderbügel m

'clothesline n Wäscheleine f

'clothespin n Wäscheklammer f

clothing ['kloʊ·ðɪŋ] n Kleidung f

cloud [klaʊd] I. n Wolke f; (of insects) Schwarm m II. vt (issue) verschleiern

◆cloud over vi sich bewölken

'cloudburst n Wolkenbruch m

cloudless ['klaʊd·lɪs] adj wolkenlos

cloudy ['klaʊ·di] adj 1. (overcast) bewölkt, bedeckt 2. (liquid) trüb

clout [klaʊt] n fam 1. fam (influence) Schlagkraft f 2. (hit) Schlag m

clove [kloʊv] n 1. Gewürznelke f 2. (of garlic) Knoblauchzehe f

clover ['kloʊ·vər] n Klee m

clown [klaʊn] I. n 1. Clown m 2. (funny person) Kasper m; pej Trottel m II. vi to ~ around herumalbern

club [klʌb] n 1. (group) Klub m, Verein m 2. (nightclub) Diskothek f, Klub m 3. (golf) Schläger m 4. (weapon) Knüppel m 5. CARDS Kreuz nt

clubbing ['klʌb·ɪŋ] n to go ~ clubben gehen

'club foot n MED Klumpfuß m

'clubhouse n Klubhaus nt

club 'soda n Sodawasser nt

cluck [klʌk] *vi* gackern

clue [kluː] *n* 1. Hinweis *m;* (*hint*) Tipp *m;* (*in police work*) Spur *f* 2. (*idea*) I **don't have a ~!** [ich hab'] keine Ahnung!

clueless ['kluː·lɪs] *adj fam* ahnungslos

clump [klʌmp] *n* 1. (*group*) Gruppe *f* 2. (*lump*) Klumpen *m*

clumsiness ['klʌm·zɪ·nɪs] *n* Ungeschicktheit *f*

clumsy ['klʌm·zi] *adj* 1. (*bungling*) ungeschickt, unbeholfen 2. (*ungainly*) klobig

clung [klʌŋ] *pt, pp of* **cling**

cluster ['klʌs·tər] I. *n* Bündel *nt;* (*of people*) Traube *f* II. *vi* **to ~ around sth** sich um etw *akk* scharen

clutch [klʌtʃ] I. *vi* sich klammern (**at** an +*akk*) II. *vt* umklammern III. *n* 1. *usu sing* AUTO Kupplung *f* 2. **to fall into the ~es of sb** jdm in die Klauen fallen

clutter ['klʌt·ər] I. *n* 1. (*mess*) Durcheinander *nt* 2. (*unorganized stuff*) Kram *m* II. *vt* durcheinanderbringen

cm <*pl* -> *n abbr of* **centimeter** cm

c'mon [kə·man] *fam see* **come on**

CO [ˌsiˈoʊ] *n* 1. GEOG *abbr of* **Colorado** 2. MIL *abbr of* **Commanding Officer** Befehlshaber(in) *m(f)*

Co. [koʊ] *n abbr of* **company**

c/o [ˌsiˈoʊ] *abbr of* **care of** c/o, bei

coach [koʊtʃ] I. *n* 1. SPORT Trainer(in) *m(f);* (*teacher*) Nachhilfelehrer(in) *m(f)* 2. (*horse-drawn*) Kutsche *f;* RAIL [Eisenbahn]wagen *m* II. *vt* 1. SPORT trainieren 2. (*help to learn*) Nachhilfe geben

coaching ['koʊtʃ·ɪŋ] *n* 1. SPORT Training *nt* 2. (*teaching*) Nachhilfe *f*

coal [koʊl] *n* Kohle *f*

coalition [ˌkoʊ·əˈlɪʃ·ən] *n* Koalition *f*

'coal mine *n* Kohlenbergwerk *nt*

'coal mining *n* Kohle[n]bergbau *m*

coarse [kɔrs] *adj* 1. (*rough*) grob 2. (*vulgar*) derb

coast [koʊst] I. *n* Küste *f* II. *vi* die Küste entlangfahren; **to ~** [**along**] mühelos vorankommen

coastal ['koʊ·stəl] *adj* Küsten-

coaster ['koʊ·stər] *n* 1. (*for glass*) Untersetzer *m* 2. (*ship*) Küstenmotorschiff *nt* 3. (*roller coaster*) Achterbahn

'coast guard, **'Coast Guard** *n* Küstenwache *f*

'coastline *n* Küste[nlinie] *f*

coat [koʊt] I. *n* 1. (*garment*) Mantel *m* 2. (*of animal*) Fell *nt* 3. (*layer*) Schicht II. *vt* überziehen

'coat hanger *n* Kleiderbügel *m*

coating ['koʊ·tɪŋ] *n* Schicht *f,* Überzug *m;* (*of paint*) Anstrich *m*

coax [koʊks] *vt* **to ~ sb into doing sth** jdn dazu bringen, etw zu tun

cobble together *vt* zusammenschustern

cobbled ['kab·əld] *adj* (*street*) mit Kopfsteinpflaster

cobbler ['kab·lər] *n* [Flick]schuster *m*

'cobblestone *n* Kopfstein *m*

cobra ['koʊ·brə] *n* Kobra *f*

cobweb ['kab·web] *n* Spinnennetz *nt*

cocaine [koʊ·ˈkeɪn] *n* Kokain *nt*

cock [kak] I. *n* 1. (*chicken*) Hahn *m* 2. *vulg, sl* (*penis*) Schwanz *m* II. *vt* (*head*) auf die Seite legen; (*ears*) spitzen

cock-a-doodle-doo [ˌkak·ə·ˌduˈdəlˈdu] *n* Kikeriki *nt*

cockatoo <*pl* -s> ['kak·ə·ˈtu] *n* Kakadu *m*

cockeyed ['kak·aɪd] *adj fam* 1. (*not straight*) schief 2. (*ridiculous*) verrückt

cockle ['kak·əl] *n* Herzmuschel *f*

cockpit ['kak·pɪt] *n* Cockpit *nt*

cockroach ['kak·roʊtʃ] *n* Küchenschabe *f*

cocktail ['kak·teɪl] *n* Cocktail *m*

cocky ['kak·i] *adj fam* großspurig

cocoa ['koʊ·koʊ] *n* Kakao *m*

coconut ['koʊ·kə·nʌt] *n* Kokosnuss *f*

cocoon [kə·ˈkun] I. *n* Kokon *m* II. *vt* fig abschirmen

cod <*pl* -> [kad] *n* Kabeljau *m*

coddle ['kad·əl] *vt* 1. verhätscheln 2. (*cook gently*) langsam köcheln lassen; (*eggs*) pochieren

code [koʊd] I. *n* 1. (*cipher*) Kode *m* 2. LAW Kodex *m* II. *vt* chiffrieren

codeine ['koʊ·din] *n* Kodein *nt*

'code name *n* Deckname *m*

code of 'conduct *n* Verhaltensregeln *pl*

'code word *n* Kennwort *nt*

cod-liver 'oil *n* Lebertran *m*

co-ed [ˌkoʊ·ˈed] *adj* SCH gemischt

oefficient [ˌkoʊ·ɪ·ˈfɪʃ·ənt] n Koeffizient m

oerce [koʊ·ˈɜrs] vt form **to ~ sb into doing sth** jdn dazu zwingen, etw zu tun

oercion [koʊ·ˈɜr·ʒən] n form Zwang m

oexist [ˌkoʊ·ɪɡ·ˈzɪst] vi nebeneinander bestehen

oexistence [ˌkoʊ·ɪɡ·ˈzɪs·təns] n Koexistenz f

offee [ˈkɔ·fi] n Kaffee m

offee bean n Kaffeebohne f

offee break n Kaffeepause f

offee cup n Kaffeetasse f

offee grinder n Kaffeemühle f

offeemaker n Kaffeemaschine f

offeepot n Kaffeekanne f

offee shop n Café nt

offee table n Couchtisch m

offin [ˈkɔ·fɪn] n Sarg m

og [kɑɡ] n 1. (part of wheel) Zahn m 2. (wheel) Zahnrad nt

ognac [ˈkoʊn·jæk] n Cognac m

ohabit [koʊ·ˈhæb·ɪt] vi form zusammenleben; LAW in eheähnlicher Gemeinschaft leben

ohabitation [koʊ·ˌhæb·ɪ·ˈteɪ·ʃən] n Zusammenleben nt; LAW eheähnliche Gemeinschaft

oherence [koʊ·ˈhɪr·əns] n Zusammenhang m

oherent [koʊ·ˈhɪr·ənt] adj zusammenhängend

oherently [koʊ·ˈhɪr·ənt·li] adv zusammenhängend; (speak) verständlich

ohesion [koʊ·ˈhi·ʒən] n Zusammenhalt m

oil [kɔɪl] I. n 1. (spiral) Rolle f 2. ELEC Spule f II. vi sich winden III. vt aufwickeln

oiled [kɔɪld] adj gewunden; **~ spring** Sprungfeder f

oin [kɔɪn] n Münze f

oincide [ˌkoʊ·ɪn·ˈsaɪd] vi 1. (happen at same time) zusammenfallen 2. (correspond) übereinstimmen

oincidence [koʊ·ˈɪn·sɪ·dəns] n 1. (chance event) Zufall m 2. (simultaneity) Zusammenfallen nt

oincidental [koʊ·ˌɪn·sɪ·ˈden·təl] adj zufällig

oincidentally [koʊ·ˌɪn·sɪ·ˈdən·təl·i] adv zufällig[erweise]

coke [koʊk] n sl Koks m

Coke® [koʊk] n short for **Coca Cola®** Cola f

col. [kɑl] n abbr of **column** Sp.

Col. n abbr of **colonel**

colander [ˈkʌl·ən·dər] n Sieb nt

cold [koʊld] I. adj kalt; **as ~ as ice** eiskalt; **to feel ~** frieren; **I'm ~** mir ist kalt II. n 1. (low temperature) Kälte f 2. MED Erkältung f, Schnupfen m; **to have a ~** erkältet sein

cold-blooded [ˌkoʊld·ˈblʌd·ɪd] adj kaltblütig

'**cold cuts** npl Aufschnitt m kein pl

cold-'hearted adj kaltherzig

coldness [ˈkoʊld·nɪs] n Kälte f

'**cold sore** n Bläschenausschlag m

cold 'storage n **to put in ~** kühl lagern; fig auf Eis legen

cold 'turkey n sl kalter Entzug

'**cold war** n kalter Krieg

coleslaw [ˈkoʊl·slɔ] n Krautsalat m

colic [ˈkɑl·ɪk] n Kolik f

collaborate [kə·ˈlæb·ə·reɪt] vi 1. zusammenarbeiten 2. (with enemy) kollaborieren

collaboration [kə·ˌlæb·ə·ˈreɪ·ʃən] n 1. Zusammenarbeit f 2. (with enemy) Kollaboration f

collaborative [kə·ˈlæb·ə·rə·tɪv] adj (effort) gemeinsam

collaborator [kə·ˈlæb·ə·reɪ·tər] n 1. (colleague) Mitarbeiter(in) m(f) 2. pej (traitor) Kollaborateur(in) m(f)

collapse [kə·ˈlæps] I. vi 1. (things, buildings) zusammenbrechen, einstürzen; (people) zusammenbrechen 2. (fail) zusammenbrechen; (enterprise) zugrunde gehen; (talks) scheitern II. n 1. (fall) Einsturz m, Zusammenbruch m 2. (failure) Zusammenbruch m 3. MED Kollaps m

collar [ˈkɑl·ər] I. n Kragen m; (for animals) Halsband nt II. vt fam schnappen

'**collarbone** n Schlüsselbein nt

collateral 'damage n Kollateralschaden m

colleague [ˈkɑl·iɡ] n [Arbeits]kollege, -in m, f

collect [kə-'lekt] I. *adj* TELEC ~ call R-Gespräch *nt* II. *adv* TELEC to call [sb] ~ jdn per R-Gespräch anrufen III. *vi* (*gather*) sich versammeln; (*accumulate*) sich ansammeln IV. *vt* 1. (*gather*) einsammeln; (*money, stamps*) sammeln 2. (*pick up*) abholen

collected [kə-'lek-tɪd] *adj* beherrscht

collection [kə-'lek-ʃən] *n* 1. (*of money, objects*) Sammlung *f*; (*in church*) Kollekte *f*; (*of people*) Ansammlung *f* 2. FASHION Kollektion *f* 3. (*act of collecting*) Abholung *f*; (*from mailbox*) [Briefkasten]leerung *f*

collective [kə-'lek-tɪv] *adj* gemeinsam; (*leadership*) kollektiv

collective 'bargaining *n* Tarifverhandlungen *pl*

collector [kə-'lek-tər] *n* Sammler(in) *m(f)*

college [ˈka-lɪdʒ] *n* 1. (*institution*) Universität *f*, College *nt*, Hochschule *f*; to go to ~ studieren 2. (*division of an institution*) Abteilung *f*, Fakultät *f*

collide [kə-'laɪd] I. *vi* to ~ with [with sb/sth] [mit jdm/etw] zusammenstoßen

collie [ˈka-li] *n* Collie *m*

collision [kə-'lɪʒ-ən] *n* Zusammenstoß *m*

colloquial [kə-'lou-kwi-əl] *adj* umgangssprachlich; ~ language Umgangssprache *f*

Colo. *abbr of* Colorado

colon [ˈkou-lən] *n* 1. ANAT Dickdarm *m* 2. LING Doppelpunkt *m*

colonel [ˈkɜr-nəl] *n* Oberst *m*

colonial [kə-'lou-ni-əl] I. *adj* Kolonial- II. *n* Kolonist(in) *m(f)*

colonize [ˈka-lə-naɪz] *vt* kolonisieren

colony [ˈka-lə-ni] *n* Kolonie *f*

color [ˈkʌl-ər] I. *n* 1. Farbe *f*; ~ photos Farbfotos *pl* 2. (*of complexion*) Gesichtsfarbe *f*; (*of skin*) Hautfarbe *f*; (*of hair*) Haarfarbe *f* II. *vt* 1. (*change color of*) färben 2. (*distort*) beeinflussen III. *vi* (*face*) rot werden; (*leaves*) sich *akk* verfärben

Colorado [ˌka-lə-rad-'ou] *n* Colorado *nt*

coloration [ˌkʌl-ə-'reɪ-ʃən] *n* Färbung *f*

'colorblind *adj* farbenblind

colored [ˈkʌl-ərd] *adj* farbig; ~ pencil Buntstift *m*

'colorfast *adj* farbecht

colorful [ˈkʌl-ər-fəl] *adj* 1. (*paintings*) farbenfroh; (*clothing*) bunt 2. (*vivid*) lebendig; (*description*) anschaulic 3. (*past*) bewegt

coloring [ˈkʌl-ər-ɪŋ] *n* 1. (*complexion*) Gesichtsfarbe *f* 2. (*chemical*) Farb stoff *m*

colorless [ˈkʌl-ər-lɪs] *adj* farblos

colossal [kə-'las-əl] *adj* ungeheuer, riesi

colossus <*pl* -es> [kə-'las-əs] *n* Gigant(in) *m(f)*

colt [koʊlt] *n* [Hengst]fohlen *nt*

Columbus Day *n* wird in den USA a zweiten Montag im Oktober zu Ehre der Entdeckung der Neuen Welt durc Christoph Kolumbus gefeiert

column [ˈka-ləm] *n* 1. (*pillar*) Säule *f* 2. JOURN Kolumne *f*, Spalte *f* 3. (*vertic row*) Kolonne *f*, Reihe *f*

coma [ˈkou-mə] *n* Koma *nt*

comb [koʊm] I. *n* Kamm *m* II. 1. kämmen 2. (*search*) durchkämmer

combat [ˈkam-bæt] I. *n* Kampf *m* II. <-tt- *or* -t-> bekämpfen

combatant [kəm-'bæt-ənt] *n* Kämp fer(in) *m(f)*

combination [ˌkam-bə-'neɪ-ʃən] *n* Kom bination *f*

combine¹ [kəm-'baɪn] I. *vt* verbinde II. *vi* 1. (*mix together*) sich verbinde 2. (*work together*) sich verbünden

combine² [ˈkam-baɪn] *n* Mähdre scher *m*

combined [kəm-'baɪnd] *adj* vereint

come [kʌm] *vi* <came, come> 1. (*mov towards*) kommen 2. (*arrive*) ankom men; Christmas is coming bald is Weihnachten; to ~ for sb/sth jdn/etw abholen 3. (*accompany someone*) mi kommen 4. (*originate from*) stammer where is that awful smell comin from? wo kommt dieser schrecklich Gestank her? 5. (*have priority*) to before sth wichtiger als etw sein; t ~ first [bei jdm] an erster Stelle stehe 6. (*happen*) geschehen; ~ what ma komme, was wolle; you could see coming das war ja zu erwarten; ho ~? wieso? 7. (*be, become*) to ~ unde pressure unter Druck geraten; all m dreams came true all meine Träum

haben sich erfüllt; **nothing came of it** daraus ist nichts geworden ▸ ~ **again?** [wie] bitte?

◆**come about** *vi* passieren

◆**come across** *vi* (*person*) [zufällig] begegnen +*dat*; **to ~ across sth** [zufällig] auf etw *akk* stoßen

◆**come along** *vi* 1. mitgehen, mitkommen; **I'll ~ along later** ich komme später nach 2. (*job, opportunity*) sich bieten 3. **how's your German coming along?** wie geht's mit deinem Deutsch voran?

◆**come apart** *vi* auseinanderfallen

◆**come around** *vi* 1. [wieder] zu sich kommen 2. seine Meinung ändern

◆**come back** *vi* zurückkommen; (*name*) wieder einfallen

◆**come by** *vi* 1. (*visit*) vorbeikommen 2. (*obtain*) kriegen

◆**come down** *vi* 1. fallen; (*pants*) rutschen; (*collapse*) einstürzen; (*move down*) herunterkommen; (*become less*) sinken 2. **to ~ down with the flu** die Grippe bekommen

◆**come forward** *vi* sich melden

◆**come in** *vi* 1. hereinkommen; **~ in!** herein! 2. (*mail*) ankommen; (*results*) eintreffen; (*train*) einfahren; (*tide*) kommen; (*money*) reinkommen; (*news*) hereinkommen 3. + *adj* (*be*) **to ~ in handy** gelegen kommen; **to ~ in useful** sich als nützlich erweisen 4. (*play a part*) **where do I ~ in?** welche Rolle spiele ich dabei?

◆**come off** *vi* (*detach itself*) abgehen

◆**come on** *vi* **~ on!** (*impatient*) komm jetzt [endlich]!; (*encouraging*) komm schon!; (*expressing disbelief*) ach, komm!; (*annoyed*) jetzt hör aber auf!

◆**come out** *vi* 1. herauskommen; (*go out socially*) ausgehen 2. (*book, CD*) herauskommen; (*movie*) anlaufen 3. (*become known*) bekannt werden 4. (*end up*) herauskommen, enden 5. (*flowers, buds*) herauskommen; (*stars*) zu sehen sein 6. (*reveal homosexuality*) sich outen

◆**come over** *vi* vorbeikommen

◆**come through** *vi* 1. (*be noticeable*) durchkommen 2. (*survive*) überleben

◆**come to** *vi* 1. (*regain consciousness*) [wieder] zu sich kommen 2. **the total ~s to 25 dollars** das macht 25 Dollar 3. (*reach*) **to ~ to the point** zum Punkt kommen 4. **when it ~s to traveling ...** wenn's ums Reisen geht, ...

◆**come under** *vi* 1. (*be listed under*) stehen unter 2. **to ~ under fire** unter Beschuss geraten

◆**come up** *vi* 1. hochkommen; (*sun, moon*) aufgehen 2. (*be mentioned*) aufkommen; (*name*) erwähnt werden 3. (*happen unexpectedly*) [unerwartet] passieren 4. (*plants*) herauskommen

comeback ['kʌm·bæk] *n* Comeback *nt*

comedian [kə·'mi·di·ən] *n* Komiker(in) *m(f)*

comedienne [kə·ˌmi·di·'ɛn] *n* Komikerin *f*

comedown ['kʌm·daʊn] *n fam* Abstieg *m*

comedy ['kam·ə·di] *n* Komödie *f*

come-on ['kʌm·ɔn] *n fam* Anmache *f*

comet ['kam·ɪt] *n* Komet *m*

comfort ['kʌm·fərt] **I.** *n* 1. Bequemlichkeit *f* 2. (*consolation*) Trost *m* 3. (*pleasurable things*) **~s** *pl* Komfort *m kein pl* **II.** *vt* trösten

comfortable ['kʌm·fər·tə·bəl] *adj* bequem; (*house, room*) komfortabel; (*temperature*) angenehm; **to feel ~** sich wohl fühlen; **to make oneself ~** es sich *dat* bequem machen

comforter ['kʌm·fər·tər] *n* Oberbett *nt*, Federbett *nt*

comforting ['kʌm·fər·t̬ɪŋ] *adj* (*thoughts*) beruhigend; (*words*) tröstend

comfy ['kʌm·fi] *adj fam* bequem

comic ['kam·ɪk] **I.** *n* Komiker(in) *m(f)* **II.** *adj* komisch

comical ['kam·ɪ·kəl] *adj* komisch

comics ['kam·ɪks] *npl* Comic-Heft *nt sing*

comma ['kam·ə] *n* Komma *nt*

command [kə·'mænd] **I.** *vt* 1. (*order*) befehlen 2. MIL (*company*) leiten; (*ship*) befehligen; **to ~ sth** den Oberbefehl über etw *akk* haben **II.** *n* 1. (*order*) Befehl *m* 2. (*authority*) Kommando *nt* 3. (*knowledge*) Beherrschung *f*

commandant ['kam·ən·dænt] *n* Kommandant(in) *m(f)*

commandeer [ˌkam·ən·ˈdɪr] vt beschlagnahmen

commander [kə·ˈmæn·dər] n 1. MIL Kommandant(in) m(f) 2. NAUT Fregattenkapitän(in) m(f)

commanding [kə·ˈmæn·dɪŋ] adj 1. (authoritative) gebieterisch 2. (position, lead) beherrschend

commandment [kə·ˈmænd·mənt] n REL **the Ten C~s** die Zehn Gebote pl

commemorate [kə·ˈmem·ə·reɪt] vt gedenken +gen

commemoration [kə·ˌmem·ə·ˈreɪ·ʃən] n Gedenken nt

commemorative [kə·ˈmem·ər·ə·tɪv] adj Gedenk-

commence [kə·ˈmens] vi form beginnen, anfangen

commencement [kə·ˈmens·mənt] n form 1. Beginn m, Anfang m 2. SCH, UNIV Abschlussfeier (mit Verleihung der Diplome)

commend [kə·ˈmend] vt 1. (praise) loben 2. (recommend) empfehlen

commendable [kə·ˈmen·də·bəl] adj lobenswert

comment [ˈkam·ent] I. n Kommentar m II. vi einen Kommentar abgeben, sich äußern über +akk

commentary [ˈkam·ən·ter·i] n Kommentar m

commentator [ˈkam·ən·teɪ·tər] n Kommentator(in) m(f), Reporter(in) m(f)

commerce [ˈkam·ərs] n Handel m

commercial [kə·ˈmɜr·ʃəl] I. adj 1. kaufmännisch, Handels- 2. (profit-orientated) kommerziell II. n Werbespot m

commiserate [kə·ˈmɪz·ə·reɪt] vi **to ~ with sb** mit jdm mitfühlen

commiserations [kə·ˌmɪz·ə·ˈreɪ·fənz] npl Beileid nt kein pl

commission [kə·ˈmɪʃ·ən] I. vt (portrait, work) in Auftrag geben II. n 1. (order) Auftrag m 2. (system of payment) Provision f 3. (investigative body) Kommission f 4. **in/out of ~** (machine) in/außer Betrieb

commissioner [kə·ˈmɪʃ·ə·nər] n Beauftragte(r) f(m)

commit <-tt-> [kə·ˈmɪt] I. vt 1. (crime) begehen 2. (money) bereitstellen; **to ~** oneself to doing sth sich verpflichten, etw zu tun II. vi to ~ to sth sich auf etw akk festlegen

commitment [kə·ˈmɪt·mənt] n 1. (obligation) Verpflichtung f 2. (dedication) Engagement nt

committed [kə·ˈmɪt·ɪd] adj 1. verpflichtet 2. (dedicated) engagiert

committee [kə·ˈmɪt·i] n + sing/pl vb Ausschuss m, Komitee nt

commodity [kə·ˈmad·ɪ·ti] n (product) Ware f; (raw material) Rohstoff m

common [ˈkam·ən] adj <-er, -est or more ~, most ~> 1. üblich, gewöhnlich; (disease) weit verbreitet; (name) gängig 2. **it is ~ knowledge/practice ...** es ist allgemein bekannt/üblich ... 3. gemeinsam; **in ~** gemeinsam 4. <-er, -est> pej (behavior) vulgär

commonly [ˈkam·ən·li] adv häufig; (usually) gemeinhin

commonplace I. adj 1. (normal) alltäglich 2. pej (trite) banal II. n Gemeinplatz m

common sense n gesunder Menschenverstand

commotion [kə·ˈmoʊ·ʃən] n (fuss) Theater nt; (noisy confusion) Spektakel m

communal [kə·ˈmju·nəl] adj gemeinsam

communicate [kə·ˈmju·nɪ·keɪt] I. vt mitteilen; (knowledge) vermitteln II. vi 1. (give information) kommunizieren 2. (be in touch) in Verbindung stehen; (socially) sich verstehen

communication [kə·ˌmju·nɪ·ˈkeɪ·ʃən] n 1. Kommunikation f 2. (of ideas) Vermittlung f; (of information) Übermittlung f; (of emotions) Ausdruck m

communicative [kə·ˈmju·nə·keɪ·tɪv] adj gesprächig

Communion [kəm·ˈjun·jən] n [**Holy** ~] (Protestant) das [heilige] Abendmahl; (Catholic) die [heilige] Kommunion

communism [ˈkam·jə·nɪz·əm] n Kommunismus m

communist [ˈkam·jə·nɪst] I. n Kommunist(in) m(f) II. adj kommunistisch

community [kə·ˈmju·nɪ·ti] n Gemeinde f; **the business ~** die Geschäftswelt; **the ~** die Allgemeinheit

commute [kə·ˈmjuːt] *vi* pendeln

commuter [kə·ˈmjuː·tər] *n* Pendler(in) *m(f)*

com'muter train *n* Pendlerzug *m*

compact [ˈkam·pækt] I. *adj* kompakt; (*snow*) fest; (*style*) knapp II. *n* 1. (*cosmetics*) Puderdose *f* 2. AUTO Kompaktwagen *m*

compact 'disc, compact 'disk *n* Compactdisc *f*

companion [kəm·ˈpæn·jən] *n* Begleiter(in) *m(f)*; (*associate*) Gefährte, -in *m, f*

companionship [kəm·ˈpæn·jən·ʃɪp] *n* (*company*) Gesellschaft *f*; (*friendship*) Kameradschaft *f*

company [ˈkʌm·pə·ni] *n* 1. Firma *f*, Unternehmen *nt* 2. (*companionship*) Gesellschaft *f* 3. (*visitors*) Besuch *m kein pl* 4. THEAT Schauspieltruppe *f*; MIL Kompanie *f*

comparable [ˈkam·pər·ə·bəl] *adj* vergleichbar (**to/with** mit +*dat*)

comparative [kəm·ˈper·ə·tɪv] I. *n* Komparativ *m* II. *adj* 1. (*involving comparison*) vergleichend 2. (*relative*) relativ

comparatively [kəm·ˈper·ə·tɪv·li] *adv* 1. (*relatively*) verhältnismäßig 2. (*by comparison*) im Vergleich

compare [kəm·ˈper] I. *vt* vergleichen (**to/with** mit +*dat*) II. *vi* vergleichbar sein

comparison [kəm·ˈper·ɪ·sən] *n* Vergleich *m*

compartment [kəm·ˈpart·mənt] *n* RAIL [Zug]abteil *nt*, Coupé *nt österr*

compass <*pl* -es> [ˈkʌm·pəs] *n* 1. (*showing north*) Kompass *m* 2. (*for drawing circles*) Zirkel *m*

compassion [kəm·ˈpæʃ·ən] *n* Mitgefühl *nt*

compassionate [kəm·ˈpæʃ·ə·nɪt] *adj* mitfühlend

compatibility [kəm·ˌpæt·ə·ˈbɪl·ɪ·ti] *n* Vereinbarkeit *f*

compatible [kəm·ˈpæt·ə·bəl] *adj* 1. **to be ~** zusammenpassen 2. COMPUT, MED kompatibel 3. (*consistent*) vereinbar

compel <-ll-> [kəm·ˈpel] *vt* **to ~ sb to do sth** jdn [dazu] zwingen, etw zu tun

compelling [kəm·ˈpel·ɪŋ] *adj* (*reason*) zwingend; (*performance*) fesselnd

compensate [ˈkam·pən·seɪt] I. *vt* [finanziell] entschädigen II. *vi* kompensieren; **to ~ for sth** etw ausgleichen

compensation [ˌkam·pen·ˈseɪ·ʃən] *n* Entschädigung[sleistung] *f*, Schadenersatz *m*

compete [kəm·ˈpit] *vi* konkurrieren; **to ~ [with sb]** [gegen jdn] kämpfen (**for** um +*akk*)

competence [ˈkam·pɪ·təns], **competency** [ˈkam·pɪ·tən·si] *n* 1. Fähigkeiten *pl*, Kompetenz *f* 2. LAW Zuständigkeit *f*

competent [ˈkam·pɪ·tənt] *adj* 1. fähig; (*qualified*) kompetent 2. LAW zuständig

competition [ˌkam·pə·ˈtɪʃ·ən] *n* 1. (*contest*) Wettbewerb *m*; COMM Konkurrenz *f*, Wettbewerb *m*

competitive [kəm·ˈpet·ɪ·tɪv] *adj* 1. kampfbereit; **~ sports** Leistungssport *m* 2. COMM konkurrenzfähig, wettbewerbsfähig

competitiveness [kəm·ˈpet·ə·tɪv·nɪs] *n* 1. (*ambition*) Konkurrenzdenken *nt* 2. COMM Wettbewerbsfähigkeit *f*

competitor [kəm·ˈpet·ɪ·tər] *n* 1. (*opponent*) [Wettkampf]gegner(in) *m(f)*; (*participant*) [Wettbewerbs]teilnehmer(in) *m(f)* 2. COMM Konkurrent(in) *m(f)*

compile [kəm·ˈpaɪl] *vt* 1. (*list*) erstellen 2. COMPUT kompilieren

complacence [kəm·ˈpleɪ·səns], **complacency** [kəm·ˈpleɪ·sən·si] *n pej* Selbstzufriedenheit *f*

complacent [kəm·ˈpleɪ·sənt] *adj pej* selbstzufrieden

complain [kəm·ˈpleɪn] *vi* klagen, sich beklagen (**about/of** über +*akk*)

complaint [kəm·ˈpleɪnt] *n* 1. Beschwerde *f*, Klage *f* 2. LAW Klageschrift *f*

complement [ˈkam·plɪ·mənt] I. *vt* ergänzen; **to ~ each other** sich [gegenseitig] ergänzen II. *n* Ergänzung *f*

complementary [ˌkam·plə·ˈmen·tə·ri] *adj* [einander] ergänzend

complete [kəm·ˈplit] I. *vt* 1. vervollständigen; (*form*) [vollständig] ausfüllen 2. (*finish*) fertigstellen; (*course*) absolvieren; (*studies*) zu Ende bringen II. *adj* 1. (*with nothing missing*) vollständig,

komplett **2.** (*including*) ~ **with** inklusive **3.** (*total*) absolut; (*breakdown*) total; (*darkness, stranger, surprise*) völlig
completely [kəm·'plit·li] *adv* völlig
completeness [kəm·'plit·nɪs] *n* Vollständigkeit *f*
completion [kəm·'pli·ʃən] *n* Fertigstellung *f*
complex ['kam·pleks] **I.** *adj* komplex; (*complicated*) kompliziert; (*issue, personality*) vielschichtig; (*plot*) verwickelt **II.** *n* <*pl* -es> Komplex *m*
complexion [kəm·'plek·ʃən] *n* Teint *m*
complexity [kəm·'plek·sɪ·ti] *n* Komplexität *f*
complicate ['kam·plɪ·keɪt] *vt* [noch] komplizierter machen
complicated ['kam·plɪ·keɪ·t̬ɪd] *adj* kompliziert
complication [ˌkam·plɪ·'keɪ·ʃən] *n* Komplikation *f*
compliment ['kam·plə·mənt] **I.** *n* Kompliment *nt*; **to pay sb a** ~ jdm ein Kompliment machen **II.** *vt* **to** ~ **sb** jdm ein Kompliment machen
complimentary [ˌkam·plə·'men·tə·ri] *adj* **1.** schmeichelhaft **2.** (*free*) Frei-
comply [kəm·'plaɪ] *vi* sich fügen
component [kəm·'pou·nənt] *n* [Bestand]teil *m*
compose [kəm·'pouz] **I.** *vi* komponieren **II.** *vt* **1.** MUS komponieren **2.** LIT verfassen **3.** (*comprise*) **to be** ~**d of sth** aus etw *dat* bestehen
composer [kəm·'pou·zər] *n* Komponist(in) *m(f)*
composition [ˌkam·pə·'zɪʃ·ən] *n* **1.** (*piece*) Komposition *f* **2.** (*arrangement*) Gestaltung *f*; (*of painting*) Komposition *f*; CHEM Zusammenstellung *f*; CHEM Zusammensetzung *f*
compost ['kam·poust] *n* Kompost *m*
composure [kəm·'pou·ʒər] *n* Fassung *f*
compound ['kam·paund] **I.** *adj* zusammengesetzt **II.** *n* **1.** (*combination*) Mischung *f* **2.** CHEM Verbindung *f*
compound 'interest *n* FIN Zinseszins *m* meist *pl*
comprehend [ˌkam·prɪ·'hend] *vt, vi* begreifen, verstehen
comprehensible [ˌkam·prɪ·'hen·sə·bəl]

adj verständlich
comprehension [ˌkam·prɪ·'hen·ʃən] *n* Verständnis *nt*
comprehensive [ˌkam·prɪ·'hen·sɪv] *adj* umfassend; (*list*) vollständig
compress[1] [kəm·'pres] *vt* **1.** (*squeeze together*) zusammendrücken; (*air, gas*) komprimieren **2.** (*condense*) zusammenfassen
compress[2] <*pl* -es> ['kam·pres] *n* MED Kompresse *f*
compressed [kəm·'prest] *adj* komprimiert; ~ **air** Druckluft *f*
comprise [kəm·'praɪz] *vt form* umfassen
compromise ['kam·prə·maɪz] **I.** *n* Kompromiss *m* **II.** *vi* Kompromisse eingehen
compromising ['kam·prə·maɪ·zɪŋ] *adj* kompromittierend
compulsion [kəm·'pʌl·ʃən] *n* Zwang *m*
compulsive [kəm·'pʌl·sɪv] *adj* **1.** (*obsessive*) zwanghaft; (*liar*) notorisch **2.** (*captivating*) fesselnd
compulsory [kəm·'pʌl·sə·ri] *adj* obligatorisch; ~ **subject** Pflichtfach *nt*
compute [kəm·'pjut] *vt* berechnen
computer [kəm·'pju·tər] *n* Computer *m*
com'puter game *n* Computerspiel *nt*
computerize [kəm·'pju·tə·raɪz] *vt* **1.** (*store on computer*) [im Computer] speichern **2.** (*equip with computers*) computerisieren
computer 'programmer *n* Programmierer(in) *m(f)*
computing [kəm·'pju·t̬ɪŋ] *n* **1.** (*calculating*) Berechnen *nt* **2.** COMPUT EDV *f*
comrade ['kam·ræd] *n* **1.** POL Genosse, -in *m, f* **2.** (*friend*) Kamerad(in) *m(f)*
con[1] [kan] *fam* **I.** *vt* <-nn-> reinlegen **II.** *n* (*trick*) Schwindel *m kein pl*
con[2] [kan] *n sl* (*convict*) Knacki *m sl*
concave ['kan·keɪv] *adj* konkav
conceal [kən·'sil] *vt* verbergen
concealment [kən·'sil·mənt] *n* Verheimlichung *f*; (*of feelings*) Verbergen *nt*
concede [kən·'sid] **I.** *vt* **1.** (*acknowledge*) zugeben; **to** ~ **defeat** sich geschlagen geben **2.** (*grant: privileges, rights*) einräumen **II.** *vi* sich geschlagen geben

conceit [kən-ˈsit] *n* Einbildung *f*

conceited [kən-ˈsi-tɪd] *adj* eingebildet

conceivable [kən-ˈsiv-ə-bəl] *adj* vorstellbar

conceive [kən-ˈsiv] **I.** *vt* sich *dat* vorstellen **II.** *vi* **1.** (*imagine*) **to ~ of sth** sich *dat* etw vorstellen **2.** (*become pregnant*) empfangen

concentrate [ˈkan-sən-treɪt] **I.** *vi* **to ~ [on sth]** sich *akk* [auf etw *akk*] konzentrieren **II.** *vt* konzentrieren

concentrated [ˈkan-sən-treɪ-tɪd] *adj* konzentriert; (*attack*) geballt; (*effort*) gezielt

concentration [ˌkan-sən-ˈtreɪ-ʃən] *n* Konzentration *f*

concen·tration camp *n* Konzentrationslager *nt*

concept [ˈkan-sept] *n* **1.** (*idea*) Vorstellung *f* **2.** (*plan*) Entwurf *m*, Konzept *nt*

conception [kən-ˈsep-ʃən] *n* **1.** (*basic understanding*) Vorstellung *f* **2.** (*idea*) Idee *f*, Konzept *nt* **3.** BIOL Empfängnis *f*

concern [kən-ˈsɜrn] **I.** *n* **1.** (*interest*) Anliegen *nt*, Angelegenheit *f* **2.** (*worry*) Sorge *f*, Besorgnis *f* **3.** COMM Handelsunternehmen *nt* **II.** *vt* **1.** (*be about*) handeln von +*dat* **2.** (*apply to*) angehen; (*affect*) betreffen; **as far as I'm ~ed** was mich betrifft **3.** (*involve*) **to ~ oneself with sth** sich mit etw *dat* befassen **4.** (*worry*) beunruhigen

concerning [kən-ˈsɜr-nɪŋ] *prep* bezüglich +*gen*

concert [ˈkan-sərt] *n* Konzert *nt*

concerted [kən-ˈsɜr-tɪd] *adj* (*effort*) gemeinsam

concerto <*pl* -s> [kən-ˈtʃer-tou] *n* Konzert *nt*

concession [kən-ˈseʃ-ən] *n* **1.** Zugeständnis *nt* **2.** (*admission of defeat*) Eingeständnis *nt* [einer Niederlage] **3.** ECON Konzession *f*

conciliatory [kən-ˈsɪl-i-ə-tɔr-i] *adj* versöhnlich; (*mediating*) beschwichtigend

concise [kən-ˈsaɪs] *adj* präzise; (*answer*) kurz und bündig; (*style a.*) knapp

conclude [kən-ˈklud] **I.** *vi* enden, schließen **II.** *vt* **1.** (*finish*) [ab]schließen **2.** (*infer*) **to ~ [from sth] that ...** [aus etw] schließen, dass ...

concluding [kən-ˈklu-dɪŋ] *adj* abschließend

conclusion [kən-ˈklu-ʒən] *n* **1.** (*end*) Abschluss *m*; (*of a story*) Schluss *m* **2.** (*decision*) **to come to a ~** einen Beschluss fassen **3.** (*inference*) Schluss *m*, Schlussfolgerung *f*

conclusive [kən-ˈklu-sɪv] *adj* **1.** (*convincing*) schlüssig **2.** (*decisive*) eindeutig; (*evidence*) stichhaltig

concoct [kən-ˈkakt] *vt* ausdenken; (*dish*) zusammenstellen; (*drink*) mixen

concoction [kən-ˈkak-ʃən] *n* Erfindung *f*; (*dish*) Kreation *f*; (*drink*) Gebräu *nt*

concrete [ˈkan-krit] **I.** *n* Beton *m* **II.** *adj* **1.** (*surface*) betoniert **2.** (*proof*) eindeutig; (*suggestion*) konkret **III.** *vt* betonieren

ˈconcrete mixer *n* Betonmischmaschine *f*

concur <-rr-> [kən-ˈkɜr] *vi* übereinstimmen

concurrent [kən-ˈkʌr-ənt] *adj* gleichzeitig

concussion [kən-ˈkʌʃ-ən] *n* Gehirnerschütterung *f*

condemn [kən-ˈdem] *vt* **1.** verurteilen; *fig* verdammen **2.** (*declare unsafe*) für unbrauchbar erklären; (*building*) für unbewohnbar erklären

condemnation [ˌkan-dem-ˈneɪ-ʃən] *n* Verurteilung *f*; *fig* Verdammung *f*

condensation [ˌkan-den-ˈseɪ-ʃən] *n* Kondensation *f*; (*droplets*) Kondenswasser *nt*

condense [kən-ˈdens] **I.** *vt* **1.** (*gas*) komprimieren; (*liquid*) eindicken; **~d milk** Kondensmilch *f* **2.** (*shorten*) zusammenfassen **II.** *vi* kondensieren

condescending [ˌkan-dɪ-ˈsen-dɪŋ] *adj* herablassend

condiment [ˈkan-də-mənt] *n* Würzmittel *nt*; (*sauce*) Soße *f*

condition [kən-ˈdɪʃ-ən] **I.** *n* **1.** (*state*) Zustand *m*; (*of person*) Verfassung *f* **2.** (*circumstances*) **~s** *pl* Bedingungen *pl* **3.** (*stipulation*) Bedingung *f* **II.** *vt* **1.** (*train*) konditionieren **2.** (*accustom*) gewöhnen; (*hair*) eine Pflegespülung machen

conditional [kən-ˈdɪʃ-ə-nəl] **I.** *adj* bedingt

II. n LING **the ~** der Konditional

conditionally [kən·ˈdɪʃ·ə·nə·li] adv unter Vorbehalt

conditioner [kən·ˈdɪʃ·ə·nər] n Pflegespülung f

condo [ˈkan·doʊ] n fam short for **condominium** Eigentumswohnung f

condolences [kən·ˈdoʊ·lənsɪz] npl Beileid nt kein pl

condom [ˈkan·dəm] n Kondom nt

condominium [ˌkan·də·ˈmɪn·i·əm] n Eigentumswohnung f; (building) Wohnblock m [mit Eigentumswohnungen]

condone [kən·ˈdoʊn] vt [stillschweigend] dulden

conduct **I.** vt [ˌkən·ˈdʌkt] **1.** (carry out) durchführen; (negotiations) führen; (service) abhalten **2.** (direct) leiten; (orchestra) dirigieren **3.** ELEC leiten **4.** (guide) führen **II.** vi [ˌkən·ˈdʌkt] MUS dirigieren **III.** n [ˈkan·dʌkt] Benehmen nt, Verhalten nt

conductor [kən·ˈdʌk·tər] n **1.** MUS Dirigent(in) m(f) **2.** PHYS Leiter m **3.** RAIL Schaffner(in) m(f)

conduit [ˈkan·du·ɪt] n (pipe) [Rohr]leitung f; (channel) Kanal m

cone [koʊn] n MATH Kegel m; BOT Zapfen m; **ice cream ~** Eistüte f

confectioner [kən·ˈfek·ʃə·nər] n Süßwarenhändler(in) m(f)

confectionery [kən·ˈfek·ʃə·ner·i] n (candy) Süßwaren pl; (chocolate) Konfekt nt

confederacy [kən·ˈfed·ər·ə·si] n Konföderation f; **the C~** HIST die Konföderierten Staaten pl von Amerika

confederate [kən·ˈfed·ər·ət] **I.** n Komplize, -in m, f **II.** adj HIST **C~** Südstaaten-

confederation [kən·ˌfed·ə·ˈreɪ·ʃən] n POL Bund m; ECON Verband m

confer <-rr-> [kən·ˈfɜr] **I.** vt **to ~ sth [up]on sb** jdm etw verleihen **II.** vi sich beraten

conference [ˈkan·fər·əns] n Konferenz f, Tagung f

confess [kən·ˈfes] vt, vi **1.** (admit) zugeben; **to ~ [to] sth** etw gestehen **2.** REL beichten

confession [kən·ˈfeʃ·ən] n Geständnis nt; REL Beichte f

confessional [kən·ˈfeʃ·ə·nəl] n Beichtstuhl m

confessor [kən·ˈfes·ər] n Beichtvater m

confetti [kən·ˈfet·i] n Konfetti nt

confidant [ˈkan·fɪ·dant] n Vertraute(r) m

confidante [ˈkan·fɪ·dant] n Vertraute f

confide [kən·ˈfaɪd] **I.** vt gestehen **II.** vi **to ~ in sb** sich jdm anvertrauen

confidence [ˈkan·fɪ·dəns] n **1.** (trust) Vertrauen nt **2.** no pl (self-assurance) Selbstvertrauen nt

confident [ˈkan·fɪ·dənt] adj **1.** (certain) zuversichtlich; **to be ~ of sth** von etw dat überzeugt sein **2.** (self-assured) selbstbewusst

confidential [ˌkan·fɪ·ˈden·ʃəl] adj vertraulich

confidentially [ˌkan·fɪ·ˈden·ʃə·li] adv vertraulich

configure [kən·ˈfɪg·jər] vt konfigurieren

confine vt [kən·ˈfaɪn] **1.** (restrict) beschränken (**to** auf +akk) **2.** (shut in) einsperren

confinement [kən·ˈfaɪn·mənt] n **1.** Einsperrung f; **solitary ~** Einzelhaft f **2.** MED Geburt f

confirm [kən·ˈfɜrm] **I.** vt **1.** (verify) bestätigen **2.** REL **to be ~ed** (Catholic) gefirmt werden; (Protestant) konfirmiert werden **II.** vi bestätigen

confirmation [ˌkan·fər·ˈmeɪ·ʃən] n **1.** (verification) Bestätigung f **2.** REL (Catholic) Firmung f; (Protestant) Konfirmation f

confiscate [ˈkan·fɪ·skeɪt] vt beschlagnahmen

conflict **I.** n [ˈkan·flɪkt] (clash) Konflikt m; (battle) Kampf m **II.** vi [kən·ˈflɪkt] (dates, events) sich überschneiden; **to ~ with sth** im Widerspruch zu etw dat stehen

conflicting [kən·ˈflɪk·tɪŋ] adj widersprüchlich; (claims) entgegengesetzt

conform [kən·ˈfɔrm] vi sich einfügen; **to ~ to [or with] sth** etw dat entsprechen

conformist [kən·ˈfɔr·mɪst] **I.** n Konformist(in) m(f) **II.** adj konformistisch

confront [kən·ˈfrʌnt] vt **1.** (face) **to ~ sth** sich etw dat stellen; (danger) ins Auge sehen; **to ~ sb** jdn zur Rede stellen gen **2.** (compel to deal with) konfrontieren

confrontation [ˌkan·frən·ˈteɪ·ʃən] n Konfrontation f

confuse [kən·ˈfjuz] vt verwirren, durcheinanderbringen; (misidentify) verwechseln

confused [kən·ˈfjuzd] adj (person) verwirrt, durcheinander; (situation) verworren

confusing [kən·ˈfju·zɪŋ] adj verwirrend

confusion [kən·ˈfju·ʒən] n 1. (perplexity) Verwirrung f 2. (mix-up) Verwechslung f 3. (disorder) Durcheinander nt

congeal [kən·ˈdʒil] vi fest werden

congenial [kən·ˈdʒin·jəl] adj angenehm; (people) sympathisch

congenital [kən·ˈdʒen·ɪ·təl] adj angeboren

congested [kən·ˈdʒes·tɪd] adj 1. überfüllt; (road) verstopft 2. MED verstopft

congestion [kən·ˈdʒes·tʃən] n Überfüllung f; (on roads) Stau m; nasal ~ MED verstopfte Nase

conglomerate [kən·ˈglam·ə·reɪt] n Konglomerat nt

congratulate [kən·ˈgrætʃ·ə·leɪt] vt to ~ sb [on sth] jdm [zu etw] gratulieren

congratulation [kən·ˌgrætʃ·ə·ˈleɪ·ʃən] n Glückwunsch m; ~s! herzlichen Glückwunsch!

congregate [ˈkaŋ·grɪ·geɪt] vi sich [ver]sammeln

congregation [ˌkaŋ·grɪ·ˈgeɪ·ʃən] n REL [Kirchen]gemeinde f

congress [ˈkaŋ·gres] n Kongress m; C~POL der Kongress

congressional [kəŋ·ˈgreʃ·ə·nəl] adj Kongress-

'congressman n [Kongress]abgeordneter m

'congresswoman n [Kongress]abgeordnete f

conifer [ˈkan·ə·fər] n Nadelbaum m

conjecture [kən·ˈdʒek·tʃər] n Vermutung f

conjunction [kən·ˈdʒʌŋk·ʃən] n 1. LING Bindewort nt 2. (combination) in ~ with sth in Verbindung mit etw dat in ~ with sb zusammen mit jdm

conjunctivitis [kən·ˌdʒʌŋk·tə·ˈvaɪ·tɪs] n Bindehautentzündung f

conjure [ˈkan·dʒər] vi zaubern

◆**conjure up** vt (images, pictures) hervorzaubern; (meal) zaubern

conjurer [ˈkan·dʒər·ər] n Zauberkünstler(in) m(f)

'con man n Schwindler m

Conn. abbr of **Connecticut**

connect [kə·ˈnekt] I. vi 1. (plug in) to ~ to sth an etw akk angeschlossen werden 2. (feel affinity) to ~ with sb sich auf Anhieb gut mit jdm verstehen II. vt 1. ELEC verbinden (to/with mit +dat); (plug in) anschließen (to/with an +akk) 2. (associate) in Verbindung bringen dat 3. TELEC verbinden

Connecticut [kə·ˈnet·ɪ·kət] n Connecticut nt

connection [kə·ˈnek·ʃən] n 1. (joining, link) Verbindung f (to/with mit +dat); ELEC Anschluss m (to an +akk) 2. TRANSP Verbindung f; (connecting train, flight) Anschluss m 3. (contacts) ~s pl Beziehungen pl 4. in that/this ~s in diesem Zusammenhang m

conniving [kə·ˈnaɪ·vɪŋ] adj hinterhältig

conquer [ˈkaŋ·kər] vt (person, disease) besiegen; (thing) erobern a. fig

conqueror [ˈkaŋ·kər·ər] n (of sth) Eroberer, Eroberin m, f; (of sb) Sieger(in) m(f)

conquest [ˈkan·kwest] n (of thing) Eroberung f; (of person) Sieg m

conscience [ˈkan·ʃəns] n Gewissen nt

conscientious [ˌkan·ʃi·ˈen·ʃəs] adj gewissenhaft; (dutiful) pflichtbewusst; (work) gründlich

conscious [ˈkan·ʃəs] adj 1. MED bei Bewusstsein 2. (decision) bewusst 3. (aware) bewusst; fashion-~ modebewusst

consciousness [ˈkan·ʃəs·nɪs] n Bewusstsein nt

conscript I. n [ˈkan·skrɪpt] Wehrpflichtige(r) m II. vt [kən·ˈskrɪpt] einziehen, einberufen

conscription [kən·ˈskrɪp·ʃən] n MIL Wehrpflicht f; (act of conscripting) Einberufung f

consecrate [ˈkan·sə·kreɪt] vt weihen

consecration [ˌkan·sə·ˈkreɪ·ʃən] n Weihe f

consecutive [kən·ˈsek·jə·tɪv] adj (days,

months) aufeinanderfolgend; (*numbers*) fortlaufend

consecutively [kən·'sek·jə·t̬ɪv·li] *adv* hintereinander

consensus [kən·'sen·səs] *n* Übereinstimmung *f*

consent [kən·'sent] *form* I. *n* Zustimmung *f* II. *vi* to ~ to sth etw *dat* zustimmen; **to ~ to do sth** einwilligen, etw zu tun

consequence ['kan·sɪ·kwəns] *n* 1. (*result*) Folge *f*, Auswirkung *f* 2. (*significance*) Bedeutung *f*; **of no** ~ unwichtig

consequent ['kan·sɪ·kwənt], **consequential** [ˌkan·sɪ·'kwən·ʃəl] *adj* daraus folgend

consequently ['kan·sɪ·kwənt·li] *adv* folglich

conservation [ˌkan·sər·'veɪ·ʃən] *n* Schutz *m*; (*preservation*) Erhaltung *f*

conservationist [ˌkan·sər·'veɪ·ʃə·nɪst] *n* Naturschützer(in) *m(f)*

conservative [kən·'sɜr·və·tɪv] I. *adj* 1. (*in dress, opinion*) konservativ 2. (*estimate*) vorsichtig II. *n* POL Konservative(r) *f(m)*

conservatory [kən·'sɜr·və·tɔr·i] *n* 1. (*for plants*) Wintergarten *m* 2. MUS Konservatorium *nt*

conserve I. *vt* [kən·'sɜrv] (*save*) sparen; (*strength*) schonen II. *n* ['kan·sɜrv] Eingemachtes *nt kein pl*

consider [kən·'sɪd·ər] *vt* 1. (*think about*) **to ~ sth** sich *dat* etw *akk* überlegen 2. (*look at*) betrachten; (*think of*) denken an +*akk;* (*take into account*) bedenken 3. (*regard as*) **to ~ sb/sth [as** [*or* to be]] sth jdn/etw für etw *akk* halten

considerable [kən·'sɪd·ər·ə·bəl] *adj* erheblich, beträchtlich

considerate [kən·'sɪd·ər·ɪt] *adj* rücksichtsvoll

consideration [kən·ˌsɪd·ə·'reɪ·ʃən] *n* 1. (*thought*) Überlegung *f*; **to take into** ~ berücksichtigen 2. (*factor*) Gesichtspunkt *m* 3. (*regard*) Rücksicht *f*

considered [kən·'sɪd·ərd] *adj* (*opinion*) wohl überlegt

considering [kən·'sɪd·ər·ɪŋ] I. *prep* ~ **how/what ...** wenn man bedenkt, wie/ was ... II. *conj* ~ **that ...** dafür, dass ...

consignment [kən·'saɪn·mənt] *n* Warensendung *f*

consist [kən·'sɪst] *vi* to ~ **of sth** aus etw *dat* bestehen

consistency [kən·'sɪs·tən·si] *n* 1. (*firmness*) Konsistenz *f* 2. (*constancy*) Beständigkeit *f*

consistent [kən·'sɪs·tənt] *adj* 1. (*compatible*) vereinbar, übereinstimmend 2. (*steady*) beständig; (*improvement*) ständig

consolation [ˌkan·sə·'leɪ·ʃən] *n* Trost *m*

console[1] [kən·'soʊl] *vt* trösten

console[2] ['kan·soʊl] *n* Schaltpult *nt;* COMPUT Konsole *f*

consolidate [kən·'sal·ə·deɪt] *vt, vi* 1. (*unite*) [sich] vereinigen 2. (*strengthen*) [sich] festigen

consonant ['kan·sə·nənt] *n* Konsonant *m*

consortium <*pl* -s> [kən·'sɔr·t̬i·əm] *n* Konsortium *nt*

conspicuous [kən·'spɪk·ju·əs] *adj* (*noticeable*) auffallend; (*clearly visible*) unübersehbar

conspiracy [kən·'spɪr·ə·si] *n* Verschwörung *f*

conspirator [kən·'spɪr·ə·t̬ər] *n* Verschwörer(in) *m(f)*

conspire [kən·'spaɪr] *vi a. fig* sich verschwören

constant ['kan·stənt] *adj* 1. (*continuous*) ständig 2. (*unchanging*) gleich bleibend; MATH konstant

constantly ['kan·stənt·li] *adv* ständig

constellation [ˌkan·stə·'leɪ·ʃən] *n* Sternbild *nt*

consternation [ˌkan·stər·'neɪ·ʃən] *n* Bestürzung *f*

constipated ['kan·stə·peɪ·t̬ɪd] *adj* verstopft; **to be** ~ [eine] Verstopfung haben

constipation [ˌkan·stə·'peɪ·ʃən] *n* Verstopfung *f*

constituency [kən·'stɪtʃ·u·ən·si] *n* POL Wahlkreis *m*

constituent [kən·'stɪtʃ·u·ənt] *n* 1. (*voter*) Wähler(in) *m(f)* 2. (*part*) Bestandteil *m*

constitute ['kan·stɪ·tut] *vt* 1. (*make up*) bilden 2. *form* (*be*) sein

constitution [ˌkan·stɪ·'tu·ʃən] *n* 1. (*structure*) Zusammensetzung *f* 2. POL Verfas-

sung f 3. (health) Konstitution f

constitutional [ˌkan-strɪ-ˈtu-ʃə-nəl] I. adj konstitutionell II. n hum [regelmäßiger] Spaziergang m

constraint [kən-ˈstreɪnt] n 1. (compulsion) Zwang m 2. (restriction) Beschränkung f

constrict [kən-ˈstrɪkt] I. vt 1. verengen; (squeeze) einschnüren 2. (hinder) behindern II. vi sich zusammenziehen

constriction [kən-ˈstrɪk-ʃən] n 1. Verengung f; (squeezing) Einschnüren nt 2. (hindrance) Behinderung f

construct [kən-ˈstrʌkt] vt 1. (build) bauen; (dam) errichten 2. (theory) entwickeln

construction [kən-ˈstrʌk-ʃən] n 1. (activity) Bau m; **the ~ industry** die Bauindustrie; **under ~** im Bau 2. (how sth is built) Bauweise f 3. (object) Konstruktion f; (building) Gebäude nt

constructive [kən-ˈstrʌk-tɪv] adj konstruktiv

consul [ˈkan-səl] n Konsul(in) m(f)

consulate [ˈkan-sə-lət] n Konsulat nt

consult [kən-ˈsʌlt] I. vi sich beraten II. vt 1. (ask) um Rat fragen; (doctor, lawyer) konsultieren, zu Rate ziehen 2. (look at: dictionary) nachschlagen in +dat

consultancy [kən-ˈsʌl-tən-si] n (company) Beratungsdienst m

consultant [kən-ˈsʌl-tənt] n Berater(in) m(f)

consultation [ˌkan-səl-ˈteɪ-ʃən] n 1. Beratung f; (with lawyer, accountant) Rücksprache f 2. MED Konsultation f

consume [kən-ˈsum] vt 1. (eat, drink) konsumieren 2. (use up) verbrauchen

consumer [kən-ˈsu-mər] n Verbraucher(in) m(f)

consumerism [kən-ˈsu-mə-rɪz-əm] n Konsumdenken nt

consumption [kən-ˈsʌmp-ʃən] n Verbrauch m, Konsum m

contact [ˈkan-tækt] I. n 1. (communication) Kontakt m, Verbindung f 2. (person) Kontaktperson f; **business ~s** Geschäftskontakte pl 3. (touch) Kontakt m II. vt **to ~ sb** sich mit jdm in Verbindung setzen; (by phone) jdn [telefonisch] erreichen

contact lens n Kontaktlinse f

contagious [kən-ˈteɪ-dʒəs] adj ansteckend

contain [kən-ˈteɪn] vt 1. (hold) enthalten 2. (limit) in Grenzen halten; (hold back) aufhalten; **she could barely ~ herself** sie konnte kaum an sich halten

container [kən-ˈteɪ-nər] n 1. Behälter m 2. TRANSP Container m

contaminate [kən-ˈtæm-ə-neɪt] vt verunreinigen; (with radioactivity etc.) verseuchen

contamination [kən-ˌtæm-ɪ-ˈneɪ-ʃən] n Verunreinigung f; (by radioactivity etc.) Verseuchung f

contemplate [ˈkan-təm-pleɪt] I. vi nachdenken II. vt 1. (consider) in Erwägung ziehen; (reflect upon) über etw akk nachdenken; (suicide) denken an +akk 2. (gaze at) betrachten

contemplation [ˌkan-təm-ˈpleɪ-ʃən] n 1. (thought) Nachdenken nt 2. (gazing) Betrachtung f

contemplative [kən-ˈtem-plə-tɪv] adj 1. (mood) nachdenklich 2. REL besinnlich; (life) beschaulich

contemporary [kən-ˈtem-pə-rer-i] I. n 1. (from same period) Zeitgenosse, -in m, f 2. (of same age) Altersgenosse, -in m, f II. adj zeitgenössisch

contempt [kən-ˈtempt] n 1. (scorn) Verachtung f; (disregard) Geringschätzung f 2. LAW **~ [of court]** Missachtung f [des Gerichts]

contemptuous [kən-ˈtemp-tʃu-əs] adj verächtlich

contend [kən-ˈtend] vi **to ~ with sth** mit etw dat fertigwerden müssen

contender [kən-ˈten-dər] n Bewerber(in) m(f), Anwärter(in) m(f)

content¹ [ˈkan-tent] n 1. Inhalt m 2. Gehalt m; **to have a high/low fat ~** einen hohen/niedrigen Fettgehalt aufweisen

content² [kən-ˈtent] I. adj zufrieden II. vt **to ~ oneself with sth** sich mit etw dat zufriedengeben

contented [kən-ˈten-tɪd] adj zufrieden

contention [kən-ˈten-ʃən] n **in ~ for sth** [noch] im Rennen um etw akk

contentious [kən-ˈten-ʃəs] adj umstritten

contentment [kən·'tent·mənt] n Zufriedenheit f

contents ['kan·tents] npl Inhalt m; [**table of**] ~ Inhaltsverzeichnis nt

contest I. n ['kan·test] 1. (event) Wettbewerb m; SPORT Wettkampf m 2. Wettstreit m II. vt [kən·'test] 1. (compete for) kämpfen um +akk 2. (dispute) bestreiten

contestant [kən·'tes·tənt] n (in competition) Wettbewerbsteilnehmer(in) m(f); SPORT Wettkampfteilnehmer(in) m(f); (on game show) Kandidat(in) m(f)

context ['kan·tekst] n Kontext m, Zusammenhang m

continent ['kan·tə·nənt] n GEOG Kontinent m, Erdteil m

continental [ˌkan·tə·'nən·təl] adj 1. kontinental 2. (of the American colonies) Kontinental-; **C~ Congress** Kontinentalkongress m

contingent [kən·'tɪn·dʒənt] n 1. Gruppe f 2. MIL [Truppen]kontingent nt

continual [kən·'tɪn·ju·əl] adj ständig, andauernd

continually [kən·'tɪn·ju·əl·i] adv ständig, [an]dauernd

continuation [kən·ˌtɪn·ju·'eɪ·ʃən] n Fortsetzung f

continue [kən·'tɪn·ju] I. vi 1. (persist) andauern; (go on) weitergehen; (in an activity) weitermachen; **to ~ doing/to do sth** weiter[hin] etw tun 2. (remain) bleiben 3. (resume) weitergehen; (speaking) fortfahren II. vt 1. (carry on) fortführen; (an action) mit etw dat weitermachen; (education) fortsetzen 2. (resume) fortsetzen

continuity [ˌkan·tə·'nu·ɪ·ṭi] n 1. (consistency) Kontinuität f 2. FILM Drehbuch nt

continuous [kən·'tɪn·ju·əs] adj ununterbrochen; (steady) stetig; (unbroken) durchgehend; (line a.) durchgezogen; (pain) anhaltend

contort [kən·'tɔrt] vi (in pain) sich verzerren

contortion [kən·'tɔr·ʃən] n Verrenkung f

contortionist [kən·'tɔr·ʃə·nɪst] n Schlangenmensch m

contour ['kan·tʊr] n 1. (outline) Kontur f

meist pl 2. GEOG Höhenlinie f

contraband ['kan·trə·bænd] n 1.Schmuggelware f II. adj geschmuggelt

contraception [ˌkan·trə·'sep·ʃən] n [Empfängnis]verhütung f

contraceptive [ˌkan·trə·'sep·tɪv] I. Verhütungsmittel nt II. adj empfängnisverhütend

contract[1] I. n ['kan·trækt] Vertrag m II. vi **to ~ to do sth** sich vertraglich verpflichten, etw zu tun
♦ **contract out** vt vergeben (**to** an +akk

contract[2] [kən·'trækt] I. vt 1. (muscles) zusammenziehen; (shrink) zusammenschrumpfen 2. MED bekommen; (pneumonia) sich dat zuziehen II. vi [kən·'trækt] sich zusammenziehen; (pupils) sich verengen

contraction [kən·'træk·ʃən] n 1. (shrinkage) Zusammenziehen nt 2. (of muscle) Kontraktion f 3. LING Kontraktion f

contractor ['kan·træk·tər] n (person) Auftragnehmer(in) m(f); (company) beauftragte Firma

contractual [kən·'træk·tʃu·əl] adj vertraglich

contradict [ˌkan·trə·'dɪkt] vt widersprechen

contradiction [ˌkan·trə·'dɪk·ʃən] n Widerspruch m

contradictory [ˌkan·trə·'dɪk·tə·ri] adj widersprüchlich

contralto <pl -s> [kən·'træl·toʊ] n 1. (singer) Altist(in) m(f) 2. (voice) Alt m

contrary ['kan·trer·i] I. n Gegenteil nt, **on the ~** ganz im Gegenteil II. adj 1. (interests, views) entgegengesetzt; ~ **to** im Gegensatz zu +dat 2. (argumentative) widerspenstig

contrast I. n ['kan·træst] Gegensatz m, Kontrast m (**to/with** zu +dat) II. vt [kən·'træst] **to ~ sth with sth** etw etw dat gegenüberstellen III. vi [kən·'træst] kontrastieren

contrasting [kən·'træs·tɪŋ] adj gegensätzlich; (colors, flavors) konträr

contribute [kən·'trɪb·jut] vt, vi (money, food, equipment) beisteuern; (ideas) beitragen; (to retirement plan etc.) einen Beitrag leisten

contribution [ˌkan·trɪ·ˈbjuˌ·ʃən] n Beitrag m; (to charity) Spende f

contributor [kən·ˈtrɪb·jə·tər] n 1. (donor) Spender(in) m(f) 2. (writer) Mitarbeiter(in) m(f)

contrive [kən·ˈtraɪv] I. vt 1. (devise) sich dat ausdenken 2. (fabricate) entwerfen, einfädeln II. vi to ~ to do sth es schaffen, etw zu tun

control [kən·ˈtroʊl] I. n 1. Kontrolle f; (of a company) Leitung f; out of ~ außer Kontrolle 2. TECH Schalter m, Regler m II. vt <-ll-> 1. (direct) kontrollieren; (car) steuern; (company) leiten 2. TECH (limit: valve, volume) regulieren; (inflation) eindämmen 3. (emotions) beherrschen; (temper) zügeln

controller [kən·ˈtroʊ·lər] n (director) Leiter(in) m(f); (of radio station) Intendant(in) m(f); (supervisor) Aufseher(in) m(f)

controversial [ˌkan·trə·ˈvɜr·ʃəl] adj umstritten

controversy [ˈkan·trə·vɜr·si] n Kontroverse f

convalesce [ˌkan·və·ˈles] vi genesen

convalescence [ˌkan·və·ˈles·əns] n Genesung f; (time) Genesungszeit f

convalescent [ˌkan·və·ˈles·ənt] I. n Genesende(r) f(m) II. adj 1. (recovering) genesend 2. (for convalescents) Genesungs-

convene [kən·ˈvin] form I. vi sich versammeln; (committee) zusammentreten II. vt zusammenrufen; (committee, meeting) einberufen

convenience [kən·ˈvin·jəns] n 1. (comfort) Annehmlichkeit f 2. (device) Annehmlichkeit f

con'venience store n Laden m an der Ecke

convenient [kən·ˈvin·jənt] adj 1. (useful) zweckmäßig; (comfortable) bequem; (excuse) passend 2. (date, time) passend, günstig 3. (accessible: location) günstig gelegen

convent [ˈkan·vənt] n [Nonnen]kloster nt

convention [kən·ˈven·ʃən] n 1. (custom) Brauch m; (social code) Konvention f 2. (agreement) Abkommen nt; (on human rights) Konvention f 3. (assembly) [Mitglieder]versammlung f; (conference) Konferenz f; ~ **center** Tagungszentrum nt

conventional [kən·ˈven·ʃə·nəl] adj konventionell; ~ **medicine** Schulmedizin f

converge [kən·ˈvɜrdʒ] vi (lines) zusammenlaufen

conversation [ˌkan·vər·ˈseɪ·ʃən] n Gespräch nt, Unterhaltung f

conversational [ˌkan·vər·ˈseɪ·ʃə·nəl] adj Gesprächs-, Unterhaltungs-

converse[1] [kən·ˈvɜrs] vi form sich akk unterhalten

converse[2] [ˈkan·vɜrs] n form **the** ~ das Gegenteil

conversely [kən·ˈvɜrs·li] adv umgekehrt

conversion [kən·ˈvɜr·ʒən] n 1. (change) Umwandlung f; TECH Umrüstung f 2. REL Konversion f, Bekehrung f 3. MATH Umrechnung f 4. (in football) Conversion f; (in hockey, soccer) Verwandlung f

convert I. n [ˈkan·vɜrt] REL Bekehrte(r) f(m); **to become a ~ to Islam** zum Islam übertreten II. vi [kən·ˈvɜrt] 1. REL übertreten 2. (change in function) sich verwandeln lassen III. vt [kən·ˈvɜrt] 1. REL a. fig bekehren 2. (change) to ~ sth [into] etw umwandeln [in] +akk; ARCHIT etw umbauen [zu]; TECH etw umrüsten [zu] 3. (calculate) umrechnen; (exchange) umtauschen 4. (in football: extra point) erfolgreich abschließen; (in hockey, soccer: penalty) verwandeln

convertible [kən·ˈvɜr·ţə·bəl] I. n Kabrio[lett] nt, Kabriole nt österr II. adj 1. (changeable) verwandelbar 2. FIN konvertierbar

convex [ˈkan·veks] adj konvex

convey [kən·ˈveɪ] vt 1. (transport) befördern 2. (transmit) überbringen; (impart) vermitteln; (make clear) deutlich machen

conveyor [kən·ˈveɪ·ər] n ~ **belt** Förderband nt; (in factory) Fließband nt

convict I. n [ˈkan·vɪkt] Strafgefangene(r) f(m) II. vi [kən·ˈvɪkt] auf schuldig erkennen III. vt [kən·ˈvɪkt] verurteilen

conviction [kən·ˈvɪk·ʃən] n 1. (judgment) Verurteilung f (for wegen +dat) 2. (belief) Überzeugung f

convince [kən·'vɪns] *vt* überzeugen

convincing [kən·'vɪn·sɪŋ] *adj* überzeugend

convoluted [ˌkɑn·və·'luːtɪd] *adj form* (*sentence*) verschachtelt; (*plot*) verschlungen

convoy ['kɑn·vɔɪ] *n* Konvoi *m*

convulsion [kən·'vʌl·ʃən] *n usu pl* Krampf *m*

coo [kuː] *vi* gurren

cook [kʊk] **I.** *n* Koch, Köchin *m, f* **II.** *vt, vi* kochen

'cookbook *n* Kochbuch *nt*

cookie ['kʊk·i] *n* **1.** (*cake*) Keks *m*, Plätzchen *nt* **2.** *sl* (*person*) **a tough ~** eine harte Nuss **3.** COMPUT Cookie *nt* ▶ **that's the way the ~ crumbles** *saying* so ist das nun mal im Leben

cooking ['kʊk·ɪŋ] *n* **1.** (*act*) Kochen *nt* **2.** (*style*) Küche *f*

cool [kuːl] **I.** *adj* **1.** (*pleasantly cold*) kühl; (*unpleasantly cold*) kalt; (*clothing, material*) luftig **2.** (*calm*) ruhig, besonnen **3.** (*reception*) kühl **4.** *fam* (*trendy, great*) cool *sl*, geil *sl* **II.** *n* **1.** (*cold*) Kühle *f* **2.** (*calm*) Ruhe *f* **III.** *vi* **1.** (*lose heat*) abkühlen **2.** (*tempers*) nachlassen **IV.** *vt* **1.** (*make cold*) kühlen; (*cool down*) abkühlen **2.** *sl* [**just**] **~ it!** reg dich ab!

cooler ['kuː·lər] *n* Kühlbox *f*; (*for wine bottles*) Kühler *m*

cool'headed *adj* besonnen

coolly ['kuː·li] *adv* kühl, distanziert; (*in a relaxed manner*) cool *sl*

coolness ['kuːl·nɪs] *n* **1.** (*low temperature*) Kühle *f* **2.** (*unfriendliness*) Kühle *f*, Distanziertheit *f*

coop [kuːp] **I.** *n* Hühnerstall *m* **II.** *vt* **to ~ up** einsperren

co-op ['koʊ·ɑp] *n abbr of* **cooperative I**

cooperate [koʊ·'ɑp·ə·reɪt] *vi* **1.** (*help*) kooperieren; (*comply a.*) mitmachen **2.** (*act jointly*) kooperieren, zusammenarbeiten

cooperation [koʊ·ˌɑp·ə·'reɪ·ʃən] *n* **1.** (*assistance*) Kooperation *f*, Mitarbeit *f* **2.** (*joint work*) Zusammenarbeit *f*, Kooperation *f*

cooperative [koʊ·'ɑp·ər·ə·tɪv] **I.** *n* Genossenschaft *f*, Kooperative *f* **II.** *adj* **1.** ECON genossenschaftlich, kooperativ **2.** (*willing*) kooperativ

coordinate [ˌkoʊ·'ɔr·dɪn·eɪt] **I.** *n usu pl* MATH Koordinate *f* **II.** *vi* [gut] zusammenarbeiten **III.** *vt* koordinieren

coordination [ˌkoʊ·ˌɔr·də·'neɪ·ʃən] *n* **1.** (*coordinating*) Koordination *f* **2.** (*dexterity*) Sinn *m* für Koordination

coordinator [koʊ·'ɔr·də·neɪ·tər] *n* Koordinator(in) *m(f)*

cop [kɑp] **I.** *n fam* Bulle *m* **II.** *vt* <-pp-> **to ~ a plea** LAW *sich schuldig bekennen und dafür eine mildere Strafe aushandeln*

cope [koʊp] *vi* **1.** (*mentally*) zurechtkommen; **to ~ with a problem** ein Problem bewältigen **2.** (*physically*) gewachsen sein

copier ['kɑp·i·ər] *n* Kopiergerät *nt*

copilot ['koʊ·ˌpaɪ·lət] *n* Kopilot(in) *m(f)*

copious ['koʊ·pi·əs] *adj* zahlreich

copper ['kɑp·ər] *n* Kupfer *nt*

copy ['kɑp·i] **I.** *n* **1.** (*duplicate*) Kopie *f*; (*of document*) Abschrift *f*; (*of photo*) Abzug *m* **2.** (*issue*) Exemplar *nt* **II.** *vt* <-ie-> **1.** (*duplicate*) kopieren; (*write down: from text*) abschreiben; (*from speech*) niederschreiben **2.** (*person*) nachmachen; (*style*) nachahmen; (*picture*) abmalen **3.** (*plagiarize*) abschreiben

'copycat *n pej fam* Nachmacher(in) *m(f)*

copyright ['kɑp·i·raɪt] *n* Copyright *nt*, Urheberrecht *nt*

'copywriter *n* [Werbe]texter(in) *m(f)*

coral ['kɔr·əl] *n* Koralle *f*

'coral reef *n* Korallenriff *nt*

cord [kɔrd] *n* (*for package*) Schnur *f*; ELEC Kabel *nt*

cordial ['kɔr·dʒəl] **I.** *adj* **1.** freundlich, herzlich; (*relations*) freundschaftlich **2.** *form* (*fervent*) heftig; (*dislike*) tief **II.** *n* Likör *m*

cordless ['kɔrd·lɪs] *adj* schnurlos

cordon ['kɔr·dən] **I.** *n* Kordon *m* **II.** *vt* **to ~ off ⇆ sth** etw absperren

corduroy ['kɔr·də·rɔɪ] *n* **1.** (*material*) Cordsamt *m;* **~ jacket** Cordjacke *f* **2.** (*pants*) **~s** *pl* Cordhose *f*

core [kɔr] **I.** *n* (*of apple*) Kerngehäuse *nt*;

(of rock) Innere[s] nt; (of planet) Mittelpunkt m; (of reactor) [Reaktor]kern m; fig Kern m **II.** adj zentral

coriander ['kɔr·i·æn·dər] n Koriander m

cork [kɔrk] **I.** n **1.** (material) Kork m **2.** (stopper) Korken m **II.** vt zukorken

'**corkscrew** n Korkenzieher m

corn¹ [kɔrn] n FOOD Mais m

corn² [kɔrn] n MED Hühnerauge nt

'**corncob** n Maiskolben m

corner ['kɔr·nər] **I.** n **1.** Ecke f; (of table) Kante f; **out of the ~ of one's eye** aus dem Augenwinkel **2.** (in soccer) Ecke f, Eckball m ▶ **to cut ~s** (financially) Kosten sparen; (in procedure) das Verfahren abkürzen **II.** adj Eck- **III.** vt in die Enge treiben **IV.** vi (vehicle) eine Kurve/Kurven nehmen

'**cornerstone** n a. fig Eckstein m

cornet [kɔr·'net] n MUS Kornett nt

'**corn flakes** npl Cornflakes pl

'**cornstarch** n Maisstärke f

corny ['kɔr·ni] adj fam (sentimental) kitschig; (dopey) blöd

coronary ['kɔr·ə·ner·i] **I.** n Herzinfarkt m **II.** adj koronar, Herzkranz-

coronation [ˌkɔr·ə·'neɪ·ʃən] n Krönung[s-zeremonie] f

coroner ['kɔr·ə·nər] n Coroner m (Beamter, der unter verdächtigen Umständen eingetretene Todesfälle untersucht)

corp. [kɔrp] n **1.** short for **corporation** **2.** short for **corporal**

corporal ['kɔr·pər·əl] n Unteroffizier m

corporate ['kɔr·pər·ət] adj (of corporation) körperschaftlich

corporation [ˌkɔr·pə·'reɪ·ʃən] n COMM [Kapital]gesellschaft f

corps <pl -> [kɔr] n Korps nt

corpse [kɔrps] n Leiche f

corpuscle ['kɔr·pʌs·əl] n Blutkörperchen nt

corral [kə·'ræl] **I.** n [Fang]gehege nt **II.** vt <-ll-> einpferchen

correct [kə·'rekt] **I.** vt korrigieren **II.** adj richtig; (proper a.) korrekt

correction [kə·'rek·ʃən] n **1.** (change) Korrektur f **2.** (improvement) Verbesserung f, Berichtigung f

correctional [kə·'rek·ʃə·nəl] adj ~ **facility** Strafanstalt für junge Straftäter

corrective [kə·'rek·tɪv] **I.** adj **1.** (counteractive) korrigierend; ~ **surgery** Korrekturoperation f **2.** (improving behavior) Besserungs- **II.** n Korrektiv nt

correctly [kə·'rekt·li] adv korrekt, richtig

correctness [kə·'rekt·nɪs] n Korrektheit f, Richtigkeit f

correspond [ˌkɔr·ə·'spand] vi **1.** (be equivalent of) **to ~ to sth** etw dat entsprechen; (be same as) übereinstimmen (**with** mit +dat) **2.** (write) korrespondieren

correspondence [ˌkɔr·ə·'span·dəns] n Korrespondenz f

correspondent [ˌkɔr·ə·'span·dənt] n **1.** (letter writer) Briefschreiber(in) m(f) **2.** (journalist) Berichterstatter(in) m(f), Korrespondent(in) m(f)

corresponding [ˌkɔr·ə·'span·dɪŋ] adj entsprechend

corridor ['kɔr·ɪ·dər] n Gang m, Korridor m

corroborate [kə·'rab·ə·reɪt] vt bestätigen

corroboration [kə·ˌrab·ə·'reɪ·ʃən] n Bestätigung f

corrode [kə·'roʊd] vt, vi korrodieren

corrosion [kə·'roʊ·ʒən] n Korrosion f

corrosive [kə·'roʊ·sɪv] adj korrosiv; (acid) ätzend

corrugated ['kɔr·ə·geɪ·t̬ɪd] adj (iron, cardboard) gewellt

corrupt [kə·'rʌpt] **I.** adj **1.** (dishonest) korrupt, bestechlich **2.** (file) unlesbar; (disk) kaputt **II.** vt **1.** (ethically) korrumpieren; (morally) [moralisch] verderben; (bribe) bestechen **2.** COMPUT (data, file) ruinieren

corruption [kə·'rʌp·ʃən] n **1.** (of moral standards) Korruption f; (of computer file) Zerstörung f **2.** (dishonesty) Unehrenhaftigkeit f; (bribery) Korruption f

corset ['kɔr·sɪt] n Korsett nt; MED Stützkorsett nt

cosmetic [kaz·'met·ɪk] **I.** n Kosmetik f; ~**s** pl Kosmetika pl **II.** adj kosmetisch

cosmic ['kaz·mɪk] adj kosmisch

cosmology [kaz·'mal·ə·dʒi] n Kosmologie f

cosmonaut ['kaz·mə·nɔt] n Kosmonaut(in) m(f)

cosmopolitan [ˌkaz·mə·'pal·ɪ·tən] adj kosmopolitisch

cosmos ['kaz·məs] *n* Kosmos *m*

cost [kɔst] I. *vt* 1. <cost, cost> kosten 2. <-ed, -ed> FIN (*job, project*) [durch] kalkulieren II. *n* 1. Preis *m*, Kosten *pl* (of für +*akk*) 2. *fig* Aufwand *m kein pl*; **at all ~|s|** [*or* **at any ~**] um jeden Preis

costly ['kɔst·li] *adj* kostspielig

costume ['kas·tum] *n* Kostüm *nt*

cosy ['koʊ·zi] *adj*, *vi see* **cozy**

cot [kat] *n* (*camping bed*) Feldbett *nt*; (*foldout bed*) Klappbett *nt*; (*for children*) Kinderbett *nt*

cottage ['kat·ɪdʒ] *n* Cottage *nt*

cottage 'cheese *n* Hüttenkäse *m*

cotton ['kat·ən] I. *n* Baumwolle *f*; (*thread*) Garn *nt* II. *adj* Baumwoll- III. *vi fam* **to ~ |on| to |sth|** [etw] kapieren

cotton 'candy *n* Zuckerwatte *f*

'cotton mill *n* Baumwollspinnerei *f*

couch [kaʊtʃ] I. *n* <*pl* -es> Couch *f* II. *vt* formulieren

'couch potato *n fam jd, der den ganzen Tag nur auf der Couch sitzt und fernsieht*

cougar ['ku·gər] *n* ZOOL Puma *m*

cough [kɔf] I. *n* Husten *m* II. *vt, vi* husten

◆cough up I. *vt* 1. (*blood*) husten 2. *fam* (*pay*) herausrücken II. *vi fam* herausrücken

'cough medicine *n* (*in liquid form*) Hustensaft *m*

could [kʊd] *pt, subjunctive of* **can**

council ['kaʊn·səl] *n* Rat *m*

councilor, councillor ['kaʊn·sə·lər] *n* Ratsmitglied *nt*

counsel ['kaʊn·səl] I. *vt* <-l-> empfehlen, raten II. *n* Anwalt, Anwältin *m, f*; **~ for the defense** Verteidiger(in) *m(f)*

counseling, counselling ['kaʊn·sə·lɪŋ] *n* psychologische Betreuung

counselor, counsellor ['kaʊn·sə·lər] *n* 1. (*advisor*) Berater(in) *m(f)* 2. (*lawyer*) Anwalt *m*, Anwältin *f*

count¹ [kaʊnt] I. *n* 1. (*action*) Zählung *f*; POL Auszählung *f* 2. (*total*) [An]zahl *f*, Ergebnis *nt* 3. LAW Anklagepunkt *m* 4. (*in boxing*) (*in baseball*) Count *m*, Zählung *f* II. *vt* 1. (*number*) zählen; (*change*) nachzählen 2. **to ~ sb as a friend** jdn als Freund betrach-

ten; **to ~ oneself lucky** sich glücklich schätzen III. *vi* zählen; **to ~ against sb** gegen jdn sprechen; **that's what ~s** darauf kommt es an

◆count down *vi* rückwärts bis null zählen; AEROSP den Countdown durchführen

◆count on *vi* zählen auf +*akk*

count² [kaʊnt] *n* Graf *m*

countdown ['kaʊnt·daʊn] *n* Countdown *m*

counter¹ ['kaʊn·tər] I. *vt* ausgleichen; (*arguments*) widersprechen II. *adv* entgegen; **to run ~ to sth** etw *dat* zuwiderlaufen

counter² ['kaʊn·tər] *n* 1. (*in store*) Theke *f*; (*in bank, post office*) Schalter *m*; **over the ~** (*medication*) rezeptfrei; **under the ~** *fig* unterm Ladentisch 2. (*disc*) Spielmarke *f*

counter'act *vt* entgegenwirken +*dat*; (*poison*) neutralisieren

'counterbalance I. *n* Gegengewicht *nt* II. *vt* [ˌkaʊn·tər·'bæl·əns] ausgleichen; *fig* ein Gegengewicht zu etw *dat* darstellen

counter'attack I. *n* Gegenangriff *m* II. *vt* im Gegenzug angreifen III. *vi* zurückschlagen; SPORT kontern

counterbalance *n* [ˈkaʊn·tər·ˌbæl·əns] Gegengewicht *nt* II. *vt* [ˌkaʊn·tər·ˈbæl·əns] ausgleichen; *fig* ein Gegengewicht zu etw *dat* darstellen

counter'clockwise *adv* gegen den Uhrzeigersinn

counter'espionage *n* Spionageabwehr *f*

counterfeit ['kaʊn·tər·fɪt] I. *adj* gefälscht II. *vt* fälschen III. *n* Fälschung *f*

counterin'telligence *n* Spionageabwehr *f*

'countermeasure *n* Gegenmaßnahme *f*

'counterpart *n* Gegenstück *nt*; POL Amtskollege, -in *m, f*

counterpro'ductive *adj* kontraproduktiv

counter'terrorism *n* Terrorismusbekämpfung *f*

countess <*pl* -es> ['kaʊn·tɪs] *n* Gräfin *f*

countless ['kaʊnt·lɪs] *adj* zahllos

country ['kʌn·tri] I. *n* 1. (*nation*) Land *nt* 2. (*rural areas*) **in the ~** auf dem Land 3. (*land*) Land *nt*, Gebiet *nt*; **open ~** freies Land 4. (*music*) Countrymusic *f* II. *adj* (*cottage, road*) Land-; (*customs*) ländlich

'country club *n* Country Club *m*

'countryman *n* [**fellow**] ~ Landsmann *m*

'country music *n* Countrymusic *f*

'**countryside** *n* Land *nt;* (*scenery*) Landschaft *f*

'**countrywide I.** *adj* landesweit **II.** *adv* im ganzen Land

'**countrywoman** *n* [**fellow**] ~ Landsmännin *f*

county ['kaʊn·ti] *n* [Verwaltungs]bezirk *m*

county 'seat *n* Bezirkshauptstadt *f*

coup [ku] *n* **1.** (*achievement*) Coup *m* **2.** POL Staatsstreich *m*

coup de grâce <*pl* coups de grâce> [ˌku·də·'ɡrɑs] *n* Gnadenstoß *m*

coup d'état <*pl* coups d'état> [ˌku·deɪ·'tɑ] *n* Staatsstreich *m*

coupé [kuː·'peɪ] *n* Coupé *nt*

couple ['kʌp·əl] **I.** *n* **1.** (*a few*) **a** ~ **of** ... einige ..., ein paar ... **2.** (*two people*) Paar *nt* **II.** *vt* **1.** (*join*) koppeln (**to** mit +*dat*) **2.** *usu passive* (*put together*) **to be ~d with sth** mit etw *dat* verbunden sein

couplet ['kʌp·lɪt] *n* Verspaar *nt*

coupling ['kʌp·lɪŋ] *n* Kupplung *f*

coupon ['ku·pɑn] *n* Coupon *m*, Gutschein *m*

courage ['kɜr·ɪdʒ] *n* Mut *m*

courageous [kə·'reɪ·dʒəs] *adj* mutig

courier ['kʊr·i·ər] *n* Kurier(in) *m(f)*

course [kɔrs] *n* **1.** (*series*) SCH, UNIV Kurs *m;* MED (*of treatment*) Behandlung *f* **2.** (*of aircraft, ship*) Kurs *m;* **off** ~ nicht auf Kurs; *fig* aus der Bahn geraten; **on** ~ auf Kurs; *fig* auf dem [richtigen] Weg **3.** (*of road*) Verlauf *m;* (*of river, history*) Lauf *m* **4.** (*of action*) Vorgehen *nt* **5. in the** ~ **of sth** im Verlauf einer S. *gen* **6.** (*part of meal*) Gang *m* **7.** (*for golf*) Golfplatz *m* ▶ **of** ~ natürlich; **of** ~ **not** natürlich nicht

court [kɔrt] *n* **1.** LAW Gericht *nt;* **to go to** ~ vor Gericht gehen; **out of** ~ außergerichtlich; **to take sb to** ~ jdn vor Gericht bringen **2.** (*room*) Gerichtssaal *m* **3.** (*playing area*) [Spiel]platz *m* **4.** (*of king, queen*) Hof *m*

courteous ['kɜr·ti·əs] *adj* höflich

courtesy ['kɜr·tə·si] *n* (*politeness, polite gesture*) Höflichkeit *f* ▶ ~ **of sb/sth** (*thanks to*) dank jdm/etw; (*with the permission to*) mit freundlicher Genehmigung von jdm/etw

'**courthouse** *n* Gerichtsgebäude *nt*

courtier ['kɔr·ti·ər] *n* Höfling *m*

court-'martial I. *n* <*pl* -s *or form* courts martial> Kriegsgericht *nt* **II.** *vt* <-l-> vor ein Kriegsgericht stellen

'**courtroom** *n* Gerichtssaal *m*

courtship ['kɔrt·ʃɪp] *n* Werben *nt*

'**courtyard** *n* Hof *m;* (*walled-in*) Innenhof *m*

cousin ['kʌz·ɪn] *n* Cousin, Cousine *m, f*

cove [koʊv] *n* kleine Bucht

covenant ['kʌv·ə·nənt] *n* **1.** (*legal agreement*) vertragliches Abkommen **2.** REL Bündnis *nt*

cover ['kʌv·ər] **I.** *n* **1.** (*covering*) Abdeckung *f;* (*sheath-like*) Hülle *f;* (*protective top*) Deckel *m;* (*for bed*) [Bett]decke *f;* (*for furniture*) [Schon]bezug *m;* **the ~s** *pl* das Bettzeug **2.** (*of a book*) Einband *m;* (*of a magazine*) Titelseite *f* **3.** (*shelter*) Schutz *m;* **to take** ~ (*from rain*) sich unterstellen; (*from danger*) sich verstecken **4.** MIL Deckung *f* **II.** *vt* **1.** (*put over*) bedecken; (*against dust a.*) überziehen **2.** (*protect*) abdecken **3.** (*hide*) verdecken **4.** (*extend over*) sich erstrecken über +*akk; fig* zuständig sein für +*akk* **5.** (*travel*) fahren; **to** ~ **a lot of ground** eine große Strecke zurücklegen; (*make progress*) gut vorankommen; (*be wide-ranging*) sehr umfassend sein **6.** (*deal with*) sich befassen mit +*dat* **7.** (*report on*) berichten über +*akk* **8.** (*insure*) versichern (**against/for** gegen +*akk*) **9.** MIL decken **III.** *vi* (*substitute*) **to** ~ **for sb** jdn vertreten

◆**cover up I.** *vt* **1.** (*hide*) verdecken; (*spot*) abdecken **2.** (*keep secret*) vertuschen **II.** *vi* alles vertuschen; **to** ~ **up for sb** jdn decken

coverage ['kʌv·ər·ɪdʒ] *n* **1.** (*reporting*) Berichterstattung *f* **2.** (*dealing with*) Behandlung *f* **3.** (*insurance*) Versicherungsschutz *m*

'**coveralls** *npl* Overall *m*

'**cover charge** *n* (*in nightclub*) Eintritt *m;* (*in restaurant*) Kosten *pl* für das Gedeck

covered ['kʌv·ərd] *adj* **1.** (*roofed*) überdacht; ~ **wagon** Planwagen *m* **2.** (*insured*) versichert

'cover girl n Covergirl nt

covering ['kʌv·ər·ɪŋ] n Bedeckung f, Überzug m

'cover letter n Begleitschreiben nt

'cover story n Titelgeschichte f

covert ['koʊ·vərt] adj verdeckt, geheim; (glance) verstohlen

'cover-up n Vertuschung f

cow [kaʊ] n Kuh f

coward ['kaʊ·ərd] n Feigling m

cowardice ['kaʊ·ər·dɪs], cowardliness ['kaʊ·ərd·lɪ·nɪs] n Feigheit f

cowardly ['kaʊ·ərd·li] adj feige

'cowboy n Cowboy m

cower ['kaʊ·ər] vi kauern

'cowhide n Rindsleder nt

cowl [kaʊl] n Kapuze f

coworker ['koʊ·wɜr·kər] n Mitarbeiter(in) m(f)

coxswain ['kak·sən] n Steuermann m (beim Rudern)

coy [kɔɪ] adj 1. (pretending to be shy) geziert 2. (secretive) geheimnistuerisch

coyote [kaɪ·'oʊ·ti] n Kojote m

coziness ['koʊ·zɪ·nɪs] n Gemütlichkeit f

cozy, cosy ['koʊ·zi] I. adj 1. gemütlich, behaglich; (atmosphere) heimelig 2. pej bequem; ~ deal Kuhhandel m II. vi <-ie-> to ~ up to sb/sth 1. (snuggle up) sich an jdn/etw anschmiegen 2. fam (ingratiate oneself) mit jdm/etw einen Kuhhandel machen

CPA [ˌsi·pi·'eɪ] n ECON, FIN abbr of certified public accountant Wirtschaftsprüfer(in) m(f)

Cpl, Cpl., CPL. n short for corporal

crab[1] [kræb] n Krebs m

crab[2] [kræb] vi <-bb-> fam nörgeln

crabby ['kræb·i] adj fam mürrisch

crack [kræk] I. n 1. (fissure) Riss m; (narrow space) Ritze f 2. (of a breaking branch) Knacken nt; (of breaking ice, thunder) Krachen nt 3. (sharp blow) Schlag m 4. (illegal drug) Crack nt o m 5. (attempt) Versuch m II. vt 1. (break) to ~ sth einen Sprung in etw akk machen 2. (open) to ~ sth ⇆ [open] etw aufbrechen; (bottle) aufmachen; (egg) aufschlagen; (nuts, safe) knacken 3. (hit) to ~ one's head open sich den

Kopf aufschlagen 4. (make noise) to ~ one's knuckles mit den Fingern knacken; to ~ a whip mit einer Peitsche knallen ▶ to ~ a joke einen Witz reißen III. vi 1. (break) [zer]brechen, zerspringen; (lips, paint) aufspringen, rissig werden 2. (break down) zusammenbrechen; (voice) versagen 3. (make noise: ice, thunder) krachen; (shot, whip) knallen

◆ crack up I. vi fam 1. (laugh) lachen müssen 2. (have nervous breakdown) zusammenbrechen; (go crazy) durchdrehen II. vt 1. it's not all it's ~ed up to be es hält nicht alles, was es verspricht 2. fam (amuse) zum Lachen bringen

'crackdown n scharfes Vorgehen

cracked [krækt] adj rissig; (cup, glass) gesprungen; (lips) aufgesprungen

cracker ['kræk·ər] n 1. Kräcker m 2. Knallbonbon nt

crackle ['kræk·əl] I. vi knistern a. fig; (telephone line) knacken II. n (on telephone line, radio) Knacken nt; (of paper) Knistern nt; (of fire a.) Prasseln nt

crackling ['kræk·lɪŋ] n 1. see crackle 2. (pork skin) ~s pl (Braten)kruste f

'crackpot n fam Spinner(in) m(f)

cradle ['kreɪ·dəl] I. n 1. Wiege f 2. (hanging platform) Hängebühne f II. vt (sanft) halten; (sb's head) betten

craft [kræft] n 1. <pl -> (ship) Schiff nt; (boat) Boot nt 2. (trade) Handwerk nt kein pl; ~s pl Kunsthandwerk nt kein pl

'craftsman n gelernter Handwerker

crafty ['kræf·ti] adj schlau, gerissen

crag [kræg] n Felsmassiv nt

craggy ['kræg·i] adj zerklüftet; (features) markant

cram <-mm-> [kræm] I. vt stopfen II. vi büffeln, pauken

cramp [kræmp] I. n [Muskel]krampf m II. vt einengen

cramped [kræmpt] adj beengt

cranberry ['kræn·ˌber·i] n Kranichbeere f

crane [kreɪn] I. n 1. (device) Kran m 2. (bird) Kranich m II. vt to ~ one's neck den Hals recken

crank [kræŋk] I. n 1. MECH Kurbel f 2. fam (eccentric) Spinner(in) m(f) II. vt to ~ sth [up] (make louder: mu-

sic, *volume*) aufdrehen

crankshaft *n* Kurbelwelle *f*

cranky ['kræŋ·ki] *adj fam* mürrisch

cranny ['kræn·i] *n* Ritze *f*

crap [kræp] **I.** *vi <-pp-> vulg* kacken *vulg* **II.** *n usu sing vulg* Mist *m*

crash [kræʃ] **I.** *n <pl -es>* **1.** Unfall *m;* (*of plane*) Absturz *m* **2.** (*noise*) Krach *m kein pl* **3.** COMM Zusammenbruch *m* **4.** COMPUT Absturz *m* **II.** *vi* **1.** (*driver, car*) verunglücken; (*plane*) abstürzen **2.** (*collide with*) **to ~ into sb/sth** mit etw/jdm zusammenstoßen **3.** (*move noisily*) poltern; (*door*) knallen **4.** COMM (*stock market*) zusammenbrechen **5.** COMPUT abstürzen **6.** *sl* (*sleep*) pennen *sl* **III.** *vt* **1.** (*damage in accident*) zu Bruch fahren; **to ~ a plane** eine Bruchlandung machen; (*deliberately*) einen Unfall/Absturz absichtlich verursachen **2.** *fam* **to ~ a party** uneingeladen zu einer Party kommen

crash course *n* Intensivkurs *m*

crash helmet *n* Sturzhelm *m*

crash landing *n* Bruchlandung *f*

crass [kræs] *adj* krass, grob; (*behavior*) derb

crate [kreɪt] *n* Kiste *f;* (*for bottles*) [Getränke]kasten *m*

crater ['kreɪ·tər] *n* Krater *m;* (*made by bomb*) Trichter *m*

crave [kreɪv] *vt* begehren

craving ['kreɪ·vɪŋ] *n* heftiges Verlangen (**for** nach +*dat*)

crawfish ['krɔ·fɪʃ] *n* Languste *f*

crawl [krɔl] **I.** *vi* **1.** (*on all fours*) krabbeln **2.** (*move slowly*) kriechen **II.** *n* **1.** (*slow pace*) **to move at a ~** im Schneckentempo fahren **2.** (*swimming style*) Kraulen *nt*

crayfish ['kreɪ·fɪʃ] *n* Flusskrebs *m*

crayon ['kreɪ·ɑn] *n* Buntstift *m*

craze [kreɪz] *n* Mode[erscheinung] *f,* Fimmel *m pej,* Begeisterung *f* (**for** für +*akk*)

crazed [kreɪzd] *adj* wahnsinnig

crazy ['kreɪ·zi] *adj* verrückt (**about** nach +*dat*); **to drive sb ~** jdn zum Wahnsinn treiben

creak [krik] *vi* (*furniture*) knarren; (*door*) quietschen

cream [krim] **I.** *n* **1.** FOOD Sahne *f,* Obers *nt österr* **2.** (*cosmetic*) Creme *f* **3.** (*color*) Creme *nt* **4.** *fig* (*the best*) Elite *f* **II.** *adj* cremefarben

cream 'cheese *n* [Doppelrahm]frischkäse *m*

creamy ['kri·mi] *adj* **1.** (*smooth*) cremig, sahnig **2.** (*off-white*) cremefarben

crease [kris] **I.** *n* [Bügel]falte *f* **II.** *vt* zerknittern **III.** *vi* knittern

create [kri·'eɪt] *vt* **1.** (*make*) erschaffen **2.** (*cause*) erzeugen; (*confusion*) stiften; (*impression*) erwecken; (*sensation*) erregen

creation [kri·'eɪ·ʃən] *n* **1.** (*making*) [Er]-schaffung *f;* (*founding*) Gründung *f;* REL Schöpfung *f* **2.** (*product*) Produkt *nt;* FASHION Kreation *f*

creative [kri·'eɪ·tɪv] *adj* kreativ, schöpferisch

creator [kri·'eɪ·tər] *n* Schöpfer(in) *m(f)*

creature ['kri·tʃər] *n* Kreatur *f,* Wesen *nt,* Geschöpf *nt*

credentials [krɪ·'den·ʃəlz] *npl* **1.** (*documents*) Zeugnisse *pl* **2.** (*letter of recommendation*) Empfehlungsschreiben *nt sing*

credibility [ˌkred·ə·'bɪl·ɪ·ti] *n* Glaubwürdigkeit *f*

credible ['kred·ə·bəl] *adj* glaubwürdig

credit ['kred·ɪt] **I.** *n* **1.** (*recognition*) Anerkennung *f;* (*respect*) Achtung *f;* (*honor*) Ehre *f* **2.** COMM Kredit *m* **3.** FIN Haben *nt* **4.** FILM, TV **~s** *pl* Abspann *m* **5.** UNIV Credit [Point] *m,* Leistungspunkt *m* **II.** *vt* **1.** (*believe*) glauben **2.** (*attribute*) zuschreiben **3.** FIN gutschreiben

creditable ['kred·ɪ·tə·bəl] *adj* ehrenwert; (*result*) verdient

'credit card *n* Kreditkarte *f*

creditor ['kred·ɪ·tər] *n* Gläubiger(in) *m(f)*

'credit slip *n* Gutschrift *f*

credulous ['kredʒ·ə·ləs] *adj form* leichtgläubig

creed [krid] *n* Glaubensbekenntnis *nt*

creek [krik] *n* Bach *m;* (*tributary*) Nebenfluss *m*

creep [krip] **I.** *n fam* **1.** (*person*) Mistkerl *m* **2.** (*feeling*) **the ~s** *pl* das Gruseln *kein pl* **II.** *vi <crept, crept>* kriechen

◆**creep up** vi 1. (increase steadily) [an]steigen 2. (sneak up on) sich anschleichen a. fig (**behind/on** an +akk)

creeper ['kri·pər] n BOT Kriechgewächs nt; (up a wall) Kletterpflanze f

creepy ['kri·pi] adj fam grus[e]lig, schaurig

creepy-'crawly [-'krɔ·li] n fam Krabbeltier nt

cremate ['kri·meɪt] vt einäschern

cremation [krɪ·'meɪ·ʃən] n Einäscherung f

crematorium <pl -s> [ˌkri·mə·'tɔr·i·əm], **crematory** ['kri·mə·tɔr·i] n Krematorium nt

crêpe [kreɪp] n 1. FOOD Crêpe f 2. (fabric) Krepp m

crept [krept] pt, pp of **creep**

crescent ['kres·ənt] n 1. (moon) Mondsichel f 2. halbkreisförmige Straße

crest [krest] n 1. (peak) Kamm m 2. (of rooster) Kamm m; (of bird) Schopf m 3. (insignia) Emblem nt

'crestfallen adj niedergeschlagen

Crete [krit] n Kreta nt

cretin ['kri·tən] n pej fam Schwachkopf m

crevasse [krə·'væs] n Gletscherspalte f

crevice ['krev·ɪs] n Spalte f

crew [kru] n 1. AVIAT, NAUT Crew f, Besatzung f 2. fam (gang) Bande f

crib [krɪb] n 1. Kinderbett nt, Gitterbett nt 2. REL Krippe f

'crib death n see **sudden infant death syndrome**

crib sheet n SCH fam Spickzettel m, Schummler m österr

cricket[1] ['krɪk·ɪt] n ZOOL Grille f

cricket[2] ['krɪk·ɪt] n SPORT Kricket nt

crime [kraɪm] n 1. (illegal act) Verbrechen nt 2. (criminality) Kriminalität f

criminal ['krɪm·ə·nəl] I. n Verbrecher(in) m(f) II. adj 1. verbrecherisch; (behavior) kriminell; (offense) strafbar 2. fig schändlich

criminality [ˌkrɪm·ə·'næl·ɪ·ti] n Kriminalität f

crimson ['krɪm·zən] I. n Purpur|rot] nt II. adj purpurrot

cringe [krɪndʒ] vi 1. (cower) sich ducken 2. (shiver) schaudern

crinkle ['krɪŋ·kəl] I. vt [zer]knittern II. vi (dress, paper) knittern; (face, skin [Lach]fältchen bekommen

crinkly ['krɪŋ·kli] adj 1. (paper) zerknittert; (skin) knittrig 3. (wavy and curly) gekräuselt

cripple ['krɪp·əl] I. n Krüppel m II. v (person) zum Krüppel machen; (thing gefechtsunfähig machen; fig lahmlegen

crippling ['krɪp·əl·ɪŋ] adj (debts) erdrückend; (pain) lähmend

crisis <pl -ses> ['kraɪ·sɪs] n Krise f

crisp [krɪsp] I. adj 1. (hard and brittle knusprig; (snow) knirschend 2. (apple lettuce) knackig 3. (paper, tablecloth steif; (banknote) druckfrisch 4. (style; (reply) knapp II. n 1. **burnt te a** ~ verkohlt 2. FOOD Obstdessert nt (m Streuseln überbacken)

'crispbread n Knäckebrot nt

'crisscross I. vt durchqueren II. v sich kreuzen

criterion <pl -ria> [kraɪ·'tɪr·i·ən] n Kriterium nt

critic ['krɪt·ɪk] n Kritiker(in) m(f)

critical ['krɪt·ɪ·kəl] adj 1. (judgmen tal) kritisch 2. (crucial) entscheiden 3. MED (condition) kritisch

criticism ['krɪt·ɪ·sɪz·əm] n Kritik f

criticize ['krɪt·ɪ·saɪz] vt, vi kritisch beur teilen, kritisieren

critter ['krɪt·ər] n fam (creature) Lebewe sen nt, Kreatur f

croak [kroʊk] vi 1. (frog) quaken; (per son) krächzen 2. sl (die) abkratzen sl

Croatia [kroʊ·'eɪ·ʃə] n Kroatien nt

crochet [kroʊ·'ʃeɪ] vt, vi häkeln

crockery ['krɑk·ə·ri] n Geschirr nt

crocodile <pl -> ['krɑk·ə·daɪl] n Kro kodil nt

crocus ['kroʊ·kəs] n Krokus m

croissant [krwɑ·'sɑŋ] n Croissant nt

crony ['kroʊ·ni] adj pej fam Spießgesel le m, Haberer m österr

crook [krʊk] I. n 1. fam (rogue) Gau ner m 2. (staff) Hirtenstab m II. v (arm) beugen; (finger) krümmen

crooked ['krʊk·ɪd] adj 1. fam (dishones unehrlich; (illegal) krumm; (politician cop) korrupt 2. (not straight) krumm (grin, teeth) schief

:rop [krɑp] **I.** n **1.** (plant) Feldfrucht f; (harvest) Ernte f **2.** (hair cut) Kurzhaarschnitt m **3.** (whip) Reitgerte f **II.** vt <-pp-> **1.** (hair) kurz schneiden **2.** PHOT zurechtschneiden

crop up vi fam auftauchen

croquet [kroʊ·ˈkeɪ] n Krocket[spiel] nt

:ross [krɔs] **I.** n **1.** Kreuz nt **2.** (hybrid) Kreuzung f; fig Mittelding nt (**between** zwischen +dat); (person) Mischung f (**between** aus +dat) **3.** (in soccer) Flanke f **II.** vt **1.** (go over) überqueren; (bridge, road also) gehen über; (border) passieren; (threshold) überschreiten; (traverse) durchqueren **2.** (in soccer) flanken **3.** (place crosswise) [über]kreuzen; (arms) verschränken; (legs) übereinanderschlagen **4.** REL **to ~ oneself** sich bekreuz[ig]en **5.** (breed) kreuzen ▶ **to keep one's fingers ~ed** [for sb] [jdm] die Daumen drücken; **to ~ one's mind** jdm einfallen **III.** vi **1.** (intersect) sich kreuzen **2.** (traverse a road) die Straße überqueren; (on foot) über die Straße gehen

cross off vt streichen [von]

cross out vt ausstreichen, [durch]streichen

cross over vi hinübergehen, überqueren; (on boat) übersetzen

crossbar n SPORT Querlatte f; (of bicycle) [Quer]stange f

crossbow n Armbrust f

crossbreed n ZOOL Kreuzung f; (half-breed) Mischling m

crosscheck vt nachprüfen

:ross-ˈcountry I. adj **~ race** Geländerennen nt; **~ skiing** Langlauf m **II.** adv quer durchs Land; (through countryside) querfeldein

:ross-examiˈnation n Kreuzverhör nt

:ross-exˈamine vt ins Kreuzverhör nehmen a. fig

:ross-eyed adj schielend; **to be ~** schielen

crossfire n Kreuzfeuer nt; **to be caught in the ~** ins Kreuzfeuer geraten a. fig

:rossing [ˈkrɔ·sɪŋ] n **1.** (place to cross) Übergang m; (crossroads) [Straßen]kreuzung f **2.** (journey) Überfahrt f

:ross-ˈlegged [ˌkrɔs·ˈleg·əd] adv **to sit ~** im Schneidersitz [da]sitzen

cross-ˈreference n Querverweis m

ˈcrossroads <pl -> n Kreuzung f; fig Wendepunkt m

cross-ˈsection n Querschnitt m

ˈcrosswalk n Fußgängerübergang m

ˈcrossword, **ˈcrossword puzzle** n Kreuzworträtsel nt

crotch [krɑtʃ] n Unterleib m; (of pants) Schritt m

crotchety [ˈkrɑtʃ·ə·ti] adj fam quengelig

crouch [kraʊtʃ] **I.** n usu sing Hocke f **II.** vi sich kauern

crow[1] [kroʊ] n Krähe f ▶ **as the ~ flies** [in der] Luftlinie

crow[2] [kroʊ] vi <crowed, crowed> **1.** (cry: rooster) krähen **2.** (express happiness) jauchzen; (gloatingly) triumphieren

ˈcrowbar n Brecheisen nt

crowd [kraʊd] **I.** n **1.** (throng) [Menschen]menge f; SPORT, MUS Zuschauermenge f **2.** fam (clique) Clique f **II.** vt **1.** (fill: stadium) füllen; (streets) bevölkern **2.** fam (pressure) [be]drängen **III.** vi **to ~ into sth** sich in etw akk hineindrängen

crowd out vt herausdrängen

crowded [ˈkraʊ·dɪd] adj überfüllt; (schedule) übervoll

crown [kraʊn] **I.** n **1.** (of monarch) Krone f **2.** (top of head) Scheitel m; (of tooth, tree, hat) Krone f **II.** vt krönen; (teeth) überkronen

crown ˈjewels npl Kronjuwelen pl

crown ˈprince n Kronprinz m

ˈcrow's feet npl (wrinkles) Krähenfüße pl

crucial [ˈkru·ʃəl] adj (decisive) entscheidend (**to** für +akk); (critical) kritisch; (very important) äußerst wichtig

crucible [ˈkru·sɪ·bəl] n TECH Schmelztiegel m

crucifix [ˈkru·sɪ·fɪks] n Kruzifix nt

crucifixion [ˌkru·sɪ·ˈfɪk·ʃən] n Kreuzigung f

crucify [ˈkru·sɪ·faɪ] vt kreuzigen; fig fam verreißen

crude [krud] **I.** adj **1.** (rudimentary) primitiv **2.** (vulgar) derb **3.** (unprocessed) roh; **~ oil** Rohöl nt **II.** n Rohöl nt

cruel <l> ['kruːəl] *adj* **1.** (*unkind*) grausam; (*remark*) gemein **2.** (*harsh*) hart; (*disappointment*) schrecklich

cruelty ['kruːəltɪ] *n* Grausamkeit *f*; **~ to animals** Tierquälerei *f*; **~ to children** Kindesmisshandlung *f*

cruise [kruːz] **I.** *n* Kreuzfahrt *f* **II.** *vi* **1.** (*take a cruise*) eine Kreuzfahrt machen; (*ship*) kreuzen **2.** (*go at constant speed: airplane*) [mit Reisegeschwindigkeit] fliegen; (*car*) [konstante Geschwindigkeit] fahren **3.** *fam* (*drive around aimlessly*) herumfahren

cruise control *n* Temporegler *m*

cruiser ['kruːzər] *n* **1.** (*warship*) Kreuzer *m* **2.** (*pleasure boat*) Motoryacht *f* **3.** *see* **squad car**

cruise ship *n* Kreuzfahrtschiff *nt*

crumb [krʌm] *n* **1.** Krümel *m*, Brösel *m* österr. *nt;* (*of bread a.*) Krume *f* **2.** *fig* **a ~ of comfort** ein kleiner Trost

crumble ['krʌmbəl] **I.** *vt* zerkrümeln, zerbröckeln **II.** *vi* **1.** (*disintegrate*) zerbröckeln **2.** *fig* (*opposition, relationship*) [allmählich] zerbrechen; (*resistance*) schwinden; (*support*) abbröckeln

crummy ['krʌmɪ] *adj fam* mies; (*house*) schäbig

crumple ['krʌmpəl] **I.** *vt* zerknittern, zerknüllen; (*paper*) zerknüllen, zusammenknüllen **II.** *vi* **1.** (*become wrinkled*) sich verziehen **2.** (*collapse*) zusammenbrechen

crunch [krʌntʃ] **I.** *n* **1.** *usu sing* (*noise*) Knirschen *nt kein pl* **2.** *fam* (*difficult situation*) Krise *f* **II.** *vt* FOOD geräuschvoll verzehren **III.** *vi* (*gravel, snow*) knirschen

crunch time *n* **it's ~** *fam* jetzt kommt es drauf an!

crunchy ['krʌntʃɪ] *adj* (*apple*) knackig; (*cereal, toast*) knusprig; (*snow*) verharscht

crusade [kruːˈseɪd] *n* Kreuzzug *m;* **the C~s** *pl* HIST die Kreuzzüge *pl*

crush [krʌʃ] **I.** *vt* **1.** (*compress*) zusammendrücken; (*causing serious damage*) zerquetschen; MED [sich] etw quetschen **2.** FOOD zerdrücken; (*grapes*) zerstampfen; (*ice*) zerstoßen **3.** (*defeat*) vernichten; (*hopes*) zunichtemachen; (*rebellion*) niederschlagen; (*resistance*) zer-

schlagen **II.** *n* **1.** (*crowd*) Gedränge *n* **2.** (*drink*) Fruchtsaft *m* mit zerstoßenem Eis **3.** (*infatuation*) Schwarm *m;* **to have a ~ on sb** in jdn verknallt sein

crushing ['krʌʃɪŋ] *adj* schrecklich; (*blow*) hart; (*defeat*) vernichtend

crust [krʌst] *n* Kruste *f;* (*pastry shell*) Boden *m*

crustacean [krʌˈsteɪʃən] *n* Krustentier *n*

crusty ['krʌstɪ] *adj* (*bread*) knusprig

crutch [krʌtʃ] *n* **1.** MED Krücke *f* **2.** *fig* Stütze *f*, Halt *m*

crux [krʌks] *n* Kernfrage *f*

cry <-ie-> [kraɪ] **I.** *n* **1.** (*loud utterance*) Schrei *m;* (*shout a.*) Ruf *m;* **~ for help** Hilferuf *m* **2.** ZOOL, ORN Schreien *nt kein pl,* Geschrei *nt kein pl* **II.** *vi* weinen; (*baby*) schreien **III.** *vt* (*exclaim*) rufen

cry out I. *vi* **1.** (*shout*) aufschreien **2.** *fig* (*need*) **to be ~ing out for sth** nach etw *dat* schreien **II.** *vt* rufen; (*scream*) schreien

crypt [krɪpt] *n* Krypta *f*

cryptic ['krɪptɪk] *adj* rätselhaft; (*message a.*) geheimnisvoll

crystal ['krɪstəl] *n* **1.** CHEM Kristall *m* **2.** (*glass*) Kristallglas *nt* **3.** (*on a watch, clock*) [Uhr]glas *nt*

crystal ball *n* Kristallkugel *f*

crystal clear *adj* **1.** (*transparent: water*) kristallklar **2.** (*obvious*) glasklar; **she made it ~ that ...** sie stellte unmissverständlich klar, dass ...

crystallize ['krɪstəlaɪz] **I.** *vi* CHEM kristallisieren; *fig* (*feelings*) fassbar werden **II.** *vt fig* herausbilden

CST [ˌsiːesˈtiː] *n abbr of* **Central Standard Time** Zentral Standardzeit *f*

CT *abbr of* **Connecticut**

cub [kʌb] *n* **1.** ZOOL Junge[s] *nt* **2.** (*Cub Scout*) Wölfling *m*

Cuba ['kjuːbə] *n* Kuba *nt*

cubbyhole ['kʌbɪhoʊl] *n* Kämmerchen *nt*

cube [kjuːb] **I.** *n* **1.** (*shape*) Würfel *m* **2.** MATH Kubikzahl *f* **II.** *vt* **1.** FOOD in Würfel schneiden **2.** MATH hoch drei nehmen; **2 ~d equals 8** 2 hoch 3 ist 8

cubic ['kjuːbɪk] *adj* MATH Kubik-

cubicle ['kjuːbɪkəl] *n* (*for working*) Arbeitsnische *f*

cuckoo [ˈku·ku] I. n ORN Kuckuck m
II. adj fam übergeschnappt

cuckoo clock n Kuckucksuhr f

cucumber [ˈkju·kʌm·bər] n [Salat]gurke f

cuddle [ˈkʌd·əl] I. n [liebevolle] Umarmung II. vt liebkosen III. vi kuscheln

cuddly [ˈkʌd·əl·i] adj knudd[e]lig

cue¹ [kju] n (billiards) Queue nt österr a.
m, Billardstock m

cue² [kju] n THEAT Stichwort m; fig a.
Zeichen nt

cuff¹ [kʌf] n 1. (of sleeve) Manschette f
2. (of pants leg) [Hosen]aufschlag m
3. fam ~s pl Handschellen pl ▶ off the
~ aus dem Stegreif

cuff² [kʌf] vt to ~ sb (strike) jdm einen
Klaps geben

cuff link n Manschettenknopf m

cuisine [kwɪˈzin] n Küche f

cul-de-sac <pl -s or culs-de-sac> [ˈkʌl·
də·sæk] n Sackgasse f a. fig

culinary [ˈkʌl·ə·ner·i] adj kulinarisch

cull [kʌl] I. vt (kill) erlegen (um den Bestand zu reduzieren) II. n Abschlachten nt kein pl; fig Abschuss m kein pl

culminate [ˈkʌl·mɪ·neɪt] vi gipfeln (in
in +dat)

culmination [ˌkʌl·mɪˈneɪ·ʃən] n Höhepunkt m

culpable [ˈkʌl·pə·bəl] adj form schuldig

culprit [ˈkʌl·prɪt] n Schuldige(r) f(m); hum
Missetäter(in) m(f)

cult [kʌlt] n Kult m

cultivate [ˈkʌl·tə·veɪt] vt 1. (crops) anbauen; (land) bestellen 2. fig form entwickeln; (accent, contacts) pflegen

cultivated [ˈkʌl·tə·veɪ·tɪd] adj 1. (field)
bestellt; (land, soil a.) bebaut 2. fig
kultiviert

cultivation [ˌkʌl·tə·ˈveɪ·ʃən] n (of crops,
vegetables) Anbau m; (of land) Bebauung m, Bestellung m

cultivator [ˈkʌl·tə·veɪ·tər] n Grubber m

cultural [ˈkʌl·tʃər·əl] adj kulturell

culture [ˈkʌl·tʃər] n Kultur f

cultured [ˈkʌl·tʃərd] adj kultiviert

cumbersome [ˈkʌm·bər·səm] adj (luggage) unhandlich; (clothing) unbequem

cumin [ˈkju·mɪn] n Kreuzkümmel m

cumulative [ˈkju·mjə·lə·tɪv] adj kumulativ

cunning [ˈkʌn·ɪŋ] I. adj (ingenious: idea)
clever, raffiniert; (person a.) schlau, gerissen II. n Cleverness f, Gerissenheit f

cup [kʌp] n 1. (container) Tasse f; a
~ of coffee/tea eine Tasse Kaffee/
Tee; (made of paper, plastic) Becher m
2. SPORT Pokal m 3. (part of bra) Körbchen nt; (size) Körbchengröße f

cupboard [ˈkʌb·ərd] n Schrank m, Kasten m österr

curator [ˈkjʊ·reɪ·tər] n Konservator(in) m(f)

curb [kɜrb] I. vt zügeln; (expenditures)
senken; (inflation) bremsen II. n 1. (beside road) Randstein m 2. (restraint)
Beschränkung f

curd [kɜrd] n Quark m

curdle [ˈkɜr·dəl] I. vi gerinnen II. vt gerinnen lassen

cure [kjʊr] I. vt 1. (heal) heilen a. fig (of
von +dat); (cancer) besiegen 2. FOOD
haltbar machen; (by smoking) räuchern;
(by salting) pökeln; (by drying) trocknen
II. n (remedy) [Heil]mittel nt (for gegen
+akk); fig (solution) Lösung f

curfew [ˈkɜr·fju] n Ausgangssperre f

curiosity [ˌkjʊr·i·ˈas·ɪ·ti] n 1. (feeling)
Neugier[de] f 2. (object) Kuriosität f

curious [ˈkjʊr·i·əs] adj 1. (inquisitive)
neugierig (about auf +akk) 2. (peculiar)
seltsam, merkwürdig

curl [kɜrl] I. n 1. (of hair) Locke f
2. (spiral) Kringel m II. vi (hair) sich
locken III. vt 1. to ~ one's hair sich
dat Locken drehen 2. (lips, leaves)
kräuseln

curler [ˈkɜr·lər] n Lockenwickler m

curling [ˈkɜr·lɪŋ] n SPORT Curling nt, Eisstockschießen nt

'curling iron n Lockenstab m

curly [ˈkɜr·li] adj (leaves) gewellt, gekräuselt; (hair a.) lockig

currency [ˈkɜr·ən·si] n 1. (money) Währung f; [foreign] ~ Devisen pl 2. (acceptance) [weite] Verbreitung f

current [ˈkɜr·ənt] I. adj gegenwärtig;
(issue) aktuell II. n 1. (of air, water)
Strömung f 2. ELEC Strom m

current affairs, current e'vents npl POL
Zeitgeschehen nt kein pl

currently [ˈkɜr·ənt·li] adv zurzeit

curriculum vitae <*pl* -s *or* curricula vitae> [-'vi·taɪ] *n* Lebenslauf *m*

curry ['kɜr·i] *n* FOOD Curry *nt o m*

curse [kɜrs] I. *vi* fluchen II. *vt* 1. (*swear at*) verfluchen 2. (*put under spell*) verwünschen; **to be ~d with sth** mit etw *dat* geschlagen sein III. *n* Fluch *m*; **to put a ~ on sb** jdn verwünschen

cursor ['kɜr·sər] *n* COMPUT Cursor *m*

cursory ['kɜr·sə·ri] *adj form* (*glance*) flüchtig; (*examination*) oberflächlich

curt [kɜrt] *adj pej* schroff, barsch

curtail [kər·'teɪl] *vt* 1. (*reduce*) kürzen 2. (*shorten*) verkürzen

curtain ['kɜr·tən] *n* 1. Vorhang *m*, Gardine *f* 2. *fig* Schleier *m*, Vorhang *m*

curtsy, curtsey ['kɜrt·si] I. *vi* knicksen (**to** vor +*dat*) II. *n* [Hof]knicks *m*

curvature ['kɜr·və·tʃər] *n* Krümmung *f*; **~ of the spine** Rückgratverkrümmung *f*

curve [kɜrv] I. *n* 1. (*of a figure, vase*) Rundung *f*, Wölbung *f*; (*of a road*) Kurve *f*; (*of a river*) Bogen *m* 2. MATH Kurve *f* II. *vi* (*river, road*) eine Kurve machen; (*line*) eine Kurve beschreiben III. *vt* biegen

cushion ['kʊʃ·ən] I. *n* 1. (*pillow*) Kissen *nt*, Polster *m österr* 2. *fig* (*buffer*) Polster *nt o österr a. m* II. *vt* dämpfen *a. fig*

cushy ['kʊʃ·i] *adj pej fam* bequem; (*job*) ruhig

custard ['kʌs·tərd] *n* (*dessert*) ≈ Vanillepudding *m*

custodial [kʌs·'toʊ·di·əl] *adj* **~ sentence** Freiheitsstrafe *f*

custodian [kʌs·'toʊ·di·ən] *n* 1. (*janitor*) Hausmeister(in) *m(f)* 2. (*keeper*) Aufseher(in) *m(f)*; (*of valuables*) Hüter(in) *m(f)*

custody ['kʌs·tə·di] *n* 1. (*guardianship*) Obhut *f*; LAW Sorgerecht *nt* (**of** für +*akk*) 2. (*detention*) Haft *f*; **to keep sb in ~** jdn in Gewahrsam halten; **to take sb into ~** jdn verhaften

custom ['kʌs·təm] I. *n* 1. (*tradition*) Brauch *m*, Sitte *f* 2. (*habit*) Gewohnheit *f* II. *adj attr* maßgeschneidert

customary ['kʌs·tə·mer·i] *adj* üblich

'custom-built *adj* spezialangefertigt

customer ['kʌs·tə·mər] *n* 1. (*buyer*) Kun-

de, -in *m, f* 2. *fam* (*person*) Typ *m*

customer 'service *n* Kundendienst *m*

customize ['kʌs·tə·maɪz] *vt* nach Kundenwünschen anfertigen

custom-'made *adj* auf den Kunden zu geschnitten; (*shirt*) maßgeschneider▪ (*shoes*) maßgefertigt

customs ['kʌs·təmz] *npl* Zoll *m*

'customs declaration *n* Zollerklärung *f*

'customs duties *npl* Zollabgaben *pl*

'customs officer, 'customs official Zollbeamte(r), -in *m, f*

cut [kʌt] I. *n* 1. (*act*) Schnitt *m* 2. (*c meat*) Stück *nt* 3. (*fit*) [Zu]schnitt *m* (*of shirt, pants*) Schnitt *m* 4. (*wound* Schnittwunde *f* 5. (*decrease*) Sen kung *f*; **~ in production** Produktions einschränkung *f*; **~ in staff** Personal abbau *m* 6. (*less spending*) **~s** *pl* Kür zungen *pl* II. *adj* 1. (*sliced: bread*) [auf geschnitten; **~ flowers** Schnittblume: *pl* 2. (*fitted: glass, gemstones*) geschlif fen III. *interj* FILM **~!** Schnitt! IV. <-tt-, cut, cut> 1. (*slice*) schneiden (*bread*) aufschneiden; (*slice of bread* abschneiden; **to ~ sth in[to] severa pieces** etw in mehrere Teile zerschnei den; **to ~ open** aufschneiden 2. (*sever* durchschneiden 3. (*trim*) [ab]schneider (*hair, fingernails*) schneiden; (*grass*) mä hen; **to have** [*or* get] **one's hair ~** sich *dat* die Haare schneiden lassen 4. (*de crease: costs*) senken; (*prices*) herab setzen; (*overtime*) reduzieren; (*wages* kürzen 5. (*film*) kürzen; (*scene*) heraus schneiden; **to ~ sb short** jdn unterbre chen 6. CARDS abheben V. *vi* <-tt-, cu▪ cut> 1. (*slice: knife*) schneiden 2. (*slic easily: material*) sich schneiden lassen

✦ cut away *vt* wegschneiden

✦ cut back I. *vt* 1. FIN kürzen; (*produc tion*) zurückschrauben 2. HORT zurück schneiden II. *vi* **to ~ back on sth** etw kürzen; (*on spending*) die Ausgabe reduzieren

✦ cut down I. *vt* 1. (*fell: tree*) umhaue 2. (*reduce*) einschränken; (*workforce* abbauen; (*production*) zurückfahre 3. (*abridge*) kürzen II. *vi* **to ~ down on sth** (*smoking, spending*) etw ein schränken

cut in I. *vi* 1. (*interrupt*) unterbrechen 2. AUTO einscheren; **to ~ in in front of sb** jdn schneiden 3. (*jump line*) sich vordränge[l]n; **to ~ in on** [*or* **in front of**] **sb** sich vor jdn drängeln 4. (*activate*) sich einschalten II. *vt* **to ~ sb in** (*share with*) jdn [am Gewinn] beteiligen

cut off *vt* 1. (*remove*) abschneiden; **to ~ sth off** [**of**] **sth** etw von etw *dat* abschneiden 2. (*interrupt*) unterbrechen 3. (*disconnect*) unterbinden; (*electricity*) abstellen; (*gas supply*) abdrehen; (*phone conversation*) unterbrechen 4. (*isolate*) abschneiden; **to ~ oneself off** sich zurückziehen

cut out I. *vt* 1. (*excise*) herausschneiden; (*from paper*) ausschneiden 2. (*delete*) streichen 3. *fam* (*desist*) aufhören mit; **~ it out!** [*or* **that**] hör auf damit! 4. (*disinherit*) **to ~ sb out of one's will** jdn aus seinem Testament streichen ▶ **to have one's work ~ out for one** alle Hände voll zu tun haben; **to be ~ out for sth** für etw *akk* geeignet sein II. *vi* 1. (*stop operating*) sich ausschalten; (*plane's engine*) aussetzen 2. AUTO ausscheren

cut up *vt* (*slice*) zerschneiden; (*food for a child*) klein schneiden

ut-and-'dried *adj* 1. (*fixed*) abgemacht; (*decision*) klar 2. (*routine*) eindeutig

utback ['kʌt·bæk] *n* Kürzung *f*

ute <-r, -st> [kjut] *adj* 1. (*sweet*) süß, niedlich 2. (*clever*) schlau

uticle ['kju·tə·kəl] *n* Nagelhaut *f*

utlery ['kʌt·lə·ri] *n* Besteck *nt*

utlet ['kʌt·lɪt] *n* 1. (*meat*) Kotelett *nt* 2. (*patty*) Frikadelle *f*

utoff ['kʌt·ɔf] *n* 1. (*limit*) Obergrenze *f* 2. (*stop*) Beendigung *f*; **~ date** Endtermin *m*

utoffs *npl* abgeschnittene Jeans *f*

utout ['kʌt·aʊt] *n* 1. (*shape*) Ausschneidefigur *f* 2. (*stereotype*) **cardboard ~** [Reklame]puppe *f* 3. (*switch*) Unterbrecher *m*

ut-price *adj* (*goods*) Billig-; (*clothing*) herabgesetzt

utter ['kʌt·ər] *n* 1. (*tool*) Schneider *m* 2. (*person*) [Zu]schneider(in) *m(f)*; FILM Cutter(in) *m(f)*

'cutthroat *adj* (*competition, pricing*) gnadenlos

cutting ['kʌt·ɪŋ] I. *n* HORT Ableger *m* II. *adj* 1. (*that cuts: tool*) schneidend 2. (*abrasive: comment*) scharf; (*remark*) bissig

cutting 'edge I. *n* 1. (*blade*) Schneide *f* 2. (*latest stage*) **to be at the ~** an vorderster Front stehen II. *adj attr* supermodern, Hightech-

cyanide ['saɪ·ə·naɪd] *n* Zyanid *nt*

cybernetics [ˌsaɪ·bər·ˈnet·ɪks] *n + sing vb* Kybernetik *f*

cyberspace ['saɪ·bər·speɪs] *n* Cyberspace *m*

cycle¹ ['saɪ·kəl] *short for* **bicycle** I. *n* [Fahr]rad *nt* II. *vi* Rad fahren

cycle² ['saɪ·kəl] *n* Zyklus *m*; (*of washing machine*) Arbeitsgang *m*

cyclist ['saɪ·klɪst] *n* Radfahrer(in) *m(f)*

cyclone ['saɪ·kloʊn] *n* METEO Zyklon *m*

cygnet ['sɪg·nɪt] *n* junger Schwan

cylinder ['sɪl·ɪn·dər] *n* 1. AUTO, MATH Zylinder *m* 2. TECH Walze *f*

cylindrical [sɪ·ˈlɪn·drɪ·kəl] *adj* zylindrisch

cymbal ['sɪm·bəl] *n* **~s** Becken *nt*

cynic ['sɪn·ɪk] *n* Zyniker(in) *m(f)*

cynical ['sɪn·ɪ·kəl] *adj* zynisch

cynicism ['sɪn·ɪ·sɪz·əm] *n* Zynismus *m*

cypher *n see* **cipher**

cypress ['saɪ·prəs] *n* Zypresse *f*

Cyprus ['saɪ·prəs] *n* Zypern *nt*

cyst [sɪst] *n* MED Zyste *f*

cystitis [sɪ·ˈstaɪ·tɪs] *n* Blasenentzündung *f*

czar [zar] *n* Zar *m*

czarina [za·ˈri·nə] *n* Zarin *f*

Czech [tʃek] I. *n* 1. (*person*) Tscheche, -in *m, f* 2. (*language*) Tschechisch *nt* II. *adj* tschechisch

Czech Re'public *n* **the ~** die Tschechische Republik

D

D <*pl* -'s>, **d** <*pl* -'s> [di] *n* 1. (*letter*) D *nt*, d *nt*; **~ as in Delta** D wie Dora 2. MUS D *nt*, d *nt* 3. (*school grade*) ≈ Vier *f*

DA [ˌdiːˈeɪ] n LAW abbr of **district attorney**

dab [dæb] vt, vi <-bb-> betupfen

dabble ['dæb·əl] vi dilettieren; **to ~ in** [or with] sth sich nebenbei mit etw dat beschäftigen

dad [dæd] n fam Papa m

daddy ['dæd·i] n fam Vati m, Papi m

daddy 'longlegs <pl -> n fam Weberknecht m

daffodil ['dæf·ə·dɪl] n Osterglocke f

daffy ['dæf·i] adj fam doof pej sl, blöd fam, bescheuert sl

dagger ['dæg·ər] n Dolch m

daily ['deɪ·li] I. adj, adv täglich II. n Tageszeitung f

dainty ['deɪn·ti] adj fein

dairy ['der·i] n 1. (company) Molkerei f; ~ **products** Molkereiprodukte pl 2. (farm) Milchbetrieb m; ~ **farmer** Milchbauer, Milchbäuerin m, f

daisy ['deɪ·zi] n Gänseblümchen nt

dam [dæm] I. n [Stau]damm m II. vt <-mm-> stauen

damage ['dæm·ɪdʒ] I. vt **to ~ sth** 1. (wreck: vehicle) etw [be]schädigen 2. (blemish: reputation) etw dat schaden II. n Schaden m

damn [dæm] fam I. interj (in anger) ~ [it]! verdammt [noch mal]! II. adj 1. (cursed) Scheiß- 2. emph (extreme) verdammt; **to be a ~ sight better** entschieden besser sein III. vt 1. (curse) verfluchen; ~ **you!** hol dich der Teufel! 2. (condemn) verurteilen IV. adv vulg verdammt V. n **to not give a ~ about sb/sth** sich nicht den Teufel um jdn/etw scheren fam

damnation [dæmˈneɪ·ʃən] I. n Verdammnis f II. interj verdammt!

damned [dæmd] I. adj vulg 1. (cursed) Scheiß- 2. emph (extreme) verdammt II. adv vulg verdammt

damning ['dæm·ɪŋ] adj (evidence) erdrückend; (report) belastend

damp [dæmp] I. adj feucht II. n Feuchtigkeit f

dance [dæns] I. vt, vi tanzen a. fig II. n Tanz m

'dance music n Tanzmusik f

dancer ['dæn·sər] n Tänzer(in) m(f)

dancing ['dæn·sɪŋ] n Tanzen nt

dandelion ['dæn·də·laɪ·ən] n Löwenzahn m

dandruff ['dæn·drəf] n [Kopf]schuppen pl

Dane [deɪn] n Däne, -in m, f

danger ['deɪn·dʒər] n Gefahr f

dangerous ['deɪn·dʒər·əs] adj gefährlich

dangle ['dæŋ·gəl] I. vi herabhängen (earrings) baumeln (from an +dat II. vt 1. (swing) **to ~ one's feet** m den Füßen baumeln 2. (tempt with) **to ~ sth in front of sb** jdm etw [verlockend] in Aussicht stellen

Danish ['deɪ·nɪʃ] I. n <pl -es> 1. (language) Dänisch nt 2. (cake) see **Danish pastry** II. adj dänisch

Danish 'pastry n Blätterteiggebäck nt

dank [dæŋk] adj nasskalt

Danube ['dæn·jub] n the ~ die Donau

dappled ['dæp·əld] adj (horse) scheckig (light) gesprenkelt

dare [der] I. vt herausfordern; I ~ **you** trau dich! II. vi sich trauen; **to ~ [to] d sth** es wagen, etw zu tun ▶ **don't you** ~! unterstehs dich!; I ~ **say** (supposing) ich nehme an; (confirming) das glaub ich gern III. n Mutprobe f

'daredevil fam I. n Draufgänger(in) m, II. adj tollkühn; (stunt, tactics) halsbrecherisch

daring ['der·ɪŋ] I. adj (person) kühn wagemutig; (action) waghalsig II. Kühnheit f

dark [dark] I. adj 1. (unlit) dunkel, fin. ter; (gloomy) düster 2. (in color) dunkel 3. fig (period) dunkel; (look) finster II. n the ~ die Dunkelheit; after ~ nach Einbruch der Dunkelheit ▶ **to keep s in the ~** jdn im Dunkeln lassen

'Dark Ages npl HIST the ~ das früh Mittelalter

darken ['dar·kən] I. vi 1. (sky) dunkler werden 2. (face, mood) sich verdüster II. vt verdunkeln; (room) abdunkeln

darkness ['dark·nɪs] n 1. (no light) Dunkelheit f 2. (night) Finsternis f

'darkroom n Dunkelkammer f

darling ['dar·lɪŋ] I. n Liebling r Schatz m, Schätzchen nt II. adj ent zückend

darn[1] [darn] I. vt stopfen II. n gestop

te Stelle

darn² [darn] *interj euph see* **damn**

dart [dart] **I.** *n* **1.** (*weapon*) Pfeil *m* **2.** SPORT Wurfpfeil *m*; **~s** + *sing vb* (*game*) Darts *nt* **II.** *vi* flitzen

'dartboard *n* Dartscheibe *f*

dash [dæʃ] **I.** *n* <*pl* -es> **1.** (*rush*) Hetze *f*; **to make a ~ for the door** zur Tür stürzen **2.** SPORT Kurzstreckenlauf *m* **3.** (*little bit*) **a ~** [**of**] ein kleiner Zusatz **4.** (*punctuation*) Gedankenstrich *m* **II.** *vi* (*hurry*) sausen; **I've got to ~** ich muss fort **III.** *vt* **1.** (*strike forcefully*) schleudern **2.** (*destroy: hopes*) zunichtemachen

'dashboard *n* Armaturenbrett *nt*

dashing ['dæʃ·ɪŋ] *adj* schneidig

data ['deɪ·t̬ə] *npl* + *sing/pl vb* Daten *pl*

'database *n* Datenbank *f*

data 'processing *n* Datenverarbeitung *f*

date¹ [deɪt] **I.** *n* **1.** (*by calendar*) Datum *nt*; **out of ~** überholt; **up to ~** (*technology*) auf dem neuesten Stand; (*style*) zeitgemäß **2.** (*on coins*) Jahreszahl *f* **3.** (*engagement: business*) Termin *m*; (*social*) Verabredung *f*; (*romantic*) Date *nt*; **to make a ~** sich verabreden; **to go out on a ~** ausgehen **4.** (*person*) Date *nt* **II.** *vt* **1.** (*have relationship*) **to ~ sb** mit jdm gehen **2.** (*find age of*) datieren **III.** *vi* **1.** (*have a relationship*) miteinander gehen **2.** (*go back to*) **to ~ from sth** auf etw *akk* zurückgehen; (*tradition*) aus etw *dat* stammen

date² [deɪt] *n* FOOD Dattel *f*

dated ['deɪ·t̬ɪd] *adj* überholt

'date rape *n* Vergewaltigung *f* durch einen dem Opfer bekannte Person

dative ['deɪ·t̬ɪv] *n* LING Dativ *m*

daub [dɔb] **I.** *vt* beschmieren **II.** *n* Spritzer *m*; (*of paint*) Farbklecks *m*

daughter ['dɔ·t̬ər] *n* Tochter *f a. fig*

'daughter-in-law <*pl* daughters-> *n* Schwiegertochter *f*

daunting ['dɔn·t̬ɪŋ] *adj* entmutigend

dawdle ['dɔd·əl] *vi* trödeln

dawn [dɔn] **I.** *n* **1.** (*daybreak*) [Morgen]dämmerung *f*; **at ~** bei Tagesanbruch, im Morgengrauen **2.** *fig* Anfang *m* **II.** *vi* **1.** (*start*) anbrechen *a. fig* **2.** (*become apparent*) bewusst werden, dämmern; **it**

suddenly **~ed on me that ...** auf einmal fiel mir siedend heiß ein, dass ...

day [deɪ] *n* Tag *m*; **any ~** [**now**] jeden Tag; **one ~** eines Tages; **the other ~** neulich; **some ~** irgendwann [einmal]; **the ~ after tomorrow** übermorgen; **the ~ before yesterday** vorgestern; **these ~s** (*recently*) in letzter Zeit; (*nowadays*) heutzutage; (*at the moment*) zurzeit; **one of these ~s** eines Tages; (*soon*) demnächst [einmal]; **in those ~s** damals ▸ **to call it a ~** Schluss machen [für heute]

'daybreak *n* **at ~** bei Tagesanbruch

'daycare *n* (*of preschoolers*) Vorschulkinderbetreuung *f*; (*of the elderly*) Altenbetreuung *f*; **~ center** (*for preschoolers*) Kindertagesstätte *f*, Kinderkrippe *f*; (*for the elderly*) Altentagesstätte *f*

'daydream I. *vi* vor sich *akk* hinträumen **II.** *n* Tagtraum *m*

'daylight *n* Tageslicht *nt*; **in broad ~** am helllichten Tag[e]

'daytime *n* Tag *m*; **in the ~** tagsüber

day-to-'day *adj* (*daily*) [tag]täglich; (*normal*) alltäglich

'day trip *n* Tagesausflug *m*

daze [deɪz] **I.** *n* Betäubung *f*; **in a ~** ganz benommen **II.** *vt* **to be ~d** wie betäubt sein

dazzle ['dæz·əl] *vt* **1.** (*blind*) blenden **2.** (*amaze*) verwundern

'dazzled *adj* geblendet *a.fig*, überwältigt *fig*

DC [ˌdi·'si] *n* **1.** ELEC *abbr of* **direct current** Gleichstrom *m* **2.** *abbr of* **District of Columbia** D.C.

DE *abbr of* **Delaware**

dead [ded] **I.** *adj* **1.** (*not alive*) tot; **~ body** Leiche *f* **2.** (*custom*) ausgestorben; (*fire, match, volcano*) erloschen; (*language*) tot **3.** (*numb: limbs*) taub **4.** (*deserted: city*) wie ausgestorben; (*party*) öde **5.** *fam* (*exhausted*) tot *fam*, kaputt *fam* **6.** (*not functioning: phone*) tot; (*batteries*) leer **II.** *adv* **1.** *fam* (*totally*) absolut; **~ certain** todsicher *fam*; **~ drunk** stockbetrunken; **~ silent** totenstill **2.** (*exactly*) genau; **~ on time** auf die Minute genau **III.** *n* **1.** (*people*) **the ~** *pl* die Toten **2.** (*middle*) **in the ~**

of night mitten in der Nacht

'**deadbeat** n sl **1.** (debtor) Schnorrer(in) m(f) **2.** (lazy person) Faulpelz m; (feckless person) Gammler(in) m(f)

deaden ['dedən] vt **1.** (numb: pain) abtöten a. fig **2.** (diminish: sound) dämpfen

dead 'end n Sackgasse f a. fig

dead-'end adj (job) aussichtslos

dead 'heat n totes Rennen

'**deadline** n letzter Termin, Deadline f

'**deadlock** ['ded·lak] n toter Punkt

deadly ['ded·li] I. adj **1.** (able to kill: weapon) tödlich **2.** (implacable) ~ **enemies** Todfeinde pl **3.** pej fam (very boring) todlangweilig II. adv ~ **serious** todernst

'**deadpan** adj ausdruckslos; (humor) trocken

Dead 'Sea n the ~ das Tote Meer

deaf [def] I. adj (unable to hear) taub; (hard of hearing) schwerhörig II. n the ~ pl die Tauben

deafen ['def·ən] vt taub machen; fig betäuben

deafening ['def·ə·nɪŋ] adj ohrenbetäubend

deaf-'mute n Taubstumme(r) f(m)

deafness ['def·nɪs] n (complete) Taubheit f; (partial) Schwerhörigkeit f

deal [dil] I. n **1. a great** [or good] ~ eine Menge **2.** (in business) Geschäft nt, Deal m sl; **to do a** ~ **with sb** mit jdm ein Geschäft abschließen **3.** (agreement) Abmachung f; **it's a** ~ abgemacht **4.** (treatment) **a raw** [or rough] ~ eine ungerechte Behandlung **5.** CARDS Geben nt ▶ **big** ~! fam was soll's? II. vi <-t, -t> **1.** CARDS geben **2.** sl (sell drugs) dealen III. vt <-t, -t> **1.** (give) **to** ~ |**out**| verteilen; **to** ~ **sb a blow** jdm einen Schlag versetzen a. fig **2.** (sell) **to** ~ **sth** (drugs) mit etw dat dealen

⬩**deal with** vi **1.** (handle) sich befassen mit, sich kümmern um **2.** (treat) handeln von **3.** (do business) Geschäfte machen mit

dealer ['di·lər] n **1.** COMM Händler(in) m(f); (of drugs) Dealer(in) m(f) **2.** CARDS [Karten]geber(in) m(f)

dealership ['di·lər·ʃɪp] n Verkaufsstelle f

dealing ['di·lɪŋ] n **1.** ~ **s** pl (transactions) Geschäfte pl; (contact) Umgang m kein pl **2.** (behavior) Verhalten nt; (in business) Geschäftsgebaren nt

dealt [delt] pt, pp of **deal**

dean [din] n Dekan(in) m(f)

dear [dɪr] I. adj **1.** (much loved) lieb; (lovely: baby, kitten) süß **2.** (in letters) D~ **Mr. Jones** Sehr geehrter Herr Jones; D~ **Jane** Liebe Jane **3.** (costly) teuer II. interj ~ **me!** du liebe Zeit!; **oh** ~! du meine Güte! III. n **1.** (nice person) Schatz m **2.** (term of endearment) **my** ~|**est**| [mein] Liebling m

dearly ['dɪr·li] adv (love) von ganzem Herzen; **to pay** ~ fig teuer bezahlen

dearth [dɜrθ] n form Mangel m (of a +dat)

death [deθ] n Tod m; **to be bored to** ~ sich zu Tode langweilen

'**death certificate** n Sterbeurkunde f

deathly ['deθ·li] adj, adv tödlich

'**death penalty** n Todesstrafe f

'**death 'row** n Todestrakt m

'**death sentence** n Todesurteil nt

'**death trap** n Todesfalle f

debacle [dɪ·'ba·kəl] n Debakel nt

debatable [dɪ·'beɪ·tə·bəl] adj umstritten; **it's** ~ **whether ...** es ist fraglich, ob ...

debate [dɪ·'beɪt] I. n Debatte f II. vt, vi debattieren

debauchery [dɪ·'bɔ·tʃə·ri] n Ausschweifungen pl

debilitating [dɪ·'bɪl·ɪ·tei·tɪŋ] adj schwächend

debit ['deb·ɪt] I. n Debet nt, Soll nt II. vt abbuchen

'**debit card** n Debitkarte f, Geldautomatenkarte f

debris [də·'bri] n Trümmer pl

debt [det] n Schuld f; **to be** |**heavily**| **in** ~ |**to sb**| [große] Schulden [bei jdm] haben

'**debt collector** n Schuldeneintreiber(in) m(f)

debtor ['det·ər] n Schuldner(in) m(f)

debug <-gg-> [ˌdi·'bʌg] vt **to** ~ **sth 1.** COMPUT bei etw dat die Fehler beseitigen **2.** (remove microphones) etw entwanzen

debut [deɪ·'bju] I. n (of performer) De-

büt *nt* II. *vi* debütieren

Dec. *n abbr of* **December** Dez.

decade ['dek·eɪd] *n* Jahrzehnt *nt*

decadence ['dek·ə·dəns] *n* Dekadenz *f*

decadent ['dek·ə·dənt] *adj* dekadent; *hum* üppig

decaf ['di·kæf] *fam* I. *adj abbr of* **decaffeinated** entkoffeiniert, koffeinfrei II. *n* entkoffeinierter Kaffee

decaffeinated [di·kæf·ɪ·neɪ·t̬ɪd] *adj* entkoffeiniert, koffeinfrei

decant [dɪ·ˈkænt] *vt* umfüllen

decanter [dɪ·ˈkæn·tər] *n* Karaffe *f*

decapitate [dɪ·ˈkæp·ɪ·teɪt] *vt* köpfen

decathlon [dɪ·ˈkæθ·lɑn] *n* Zehnkampf *m*

decay [dɪ·ˈkeɪ] I. *n* 1. (*deterioration*) Verfall *m* 2. BIOL Verwesung *f*; BOT Fäulnis *f*; PHYS Zerfall *m* II. *vi* 1. (*deteriorate*) verfallen 2. BIOL verwesen, [ver]faulen; BOT verblühen; PHYS zerfallen

deceased [dɪ·ˈsist] *form* I. *n* <*pl* -> the ~ der/die Verstorbene, die Verstorbenen *pl* II. *adj* verstorben

deceit [dɪ·ˈsit] *n* Betrug *m*

deceitful [dɪ·ˈsit·fəl] *adj* [be]trügerisch

deceive [dɪ·ˈsiv] *vt* betrügen; **to ~ oneself** sich [selbst] täuschen; **to be ~d by sth** von etw *dat* getäuscht werden

December [dɪ·ˈsem·bər] *n* Dezember *m*; *see also* **February**

decency ['di·sən·si] *n* (*respectability*) Anstand *m*; (*goodness*) Anständigkeit *f*

decent ['di·sənt] *adj* 1. (*socially acceptable*) anständig 2. (*good: person*) nett 3. (*appropriate*) angemessen 4. (*good-sized*) anständig 5. (*helping*) ordentlich 5. (*acceptable: job, proposal*) annehmbar 6. *fam* (*dressed*) angezogen

deception [dɪ·ˈsep·ʃən] *n* Täuschung *f*

deceptive [dɪ·ˈsep·tɪv] *adj* täuschend

decibel ['des·ə·bəl] *n* Dezibel *nt*

decide [dɪ·ˈsaɪd] I. *vi* sich entscheiden (**on** für +*akk*); **to ~ to do sth** beschließen [*or* sich entschließen], etw zu tun II. *vt* entscheiden

decided [dɪ·ˈsaɪ·dɪd] *adj* (*definite*) entschieden; (*dislike*) ausgesprochen

deciduous [dɪ·ˈsɪdʒ·u·əs] *adj* ~ **tree** Laubbaum *m*

decimal ['des·ə·məl] *n* Dezimalzahl *f*,

Dezimale *f*; ~ **place** Dezimalstelle *f*; ~ **point** Komma *nt*

decipher [dɪ·ˈsaɪ·fər] *vt* entziffern; (*code*) entschlüsseln

decision [dɪ·ˈsɪʒ·ən] *n* Entscheidung *f*, Entschluss *m*; **to come to** [*or* **reach**] **a** ~ zu einer Entscheidung gelangen; **to make a** ~ eine Entscheidung treffen

decisive [dɪ·ˈsaɪ·sɪv] *adj* 1. (*determining*) bestimmend; (*battle*) entscheidend 2. (*firm: measure*) entschlossen

deck [dek] *n* 1. (*on ship, bus*) Deck *nt*; **on** ~ an Deck 2. (*raised porch*) Veranda *f* 3. CARDS [Karten]spiel *nt*

declaration [de·klə·ˈreɪ·ʃən] *n* Erklärung *f* **Declaration of Independence** *n* Unabhängigkeitserklärung *f (der Vereinigten Staaten)*

declare [dɪ·ˈkler] *vt* 1. (*make known*) verkünden; (*intention*) kundtun; (*support*) zusagen 2. (*state*) erklären; **to** ~ **war on sb** jdm den Krieg erklären 3. (*for customs, tax*) deklarieren; **do you have anything to ~?** haben Sie etwas zu verzollen?

decline [dɪ·ˈklaɪn] I. *n* 1. (*decrease*) Rückgang *m* 2. (*deterioration*) Verschlechterung *f* II. *vi* 1. (*refuse*) ablehnen 2. (*diminish: popularity*) sinken, nachlassen; (*health*) sich verschlechtern; (*strength*) abnehmen III. *vt* 1. (*refuse*) ablehnen 2. LING deklinieren, beugen

decode [di·ˈkoʊd] *vt* entschlüsseln

decompose [di·kəm·ˈpoʊz] *vi* sich zersetzen

decomposition [di·kam·pə·ˈzɪʃ·ən] *n* Zersetzung *f*

decongestant [di·kən·ˈdʒes·tənt] *n* abschwellendes Mittel, Mittel, das die Atemwege frei macht

decontaminate [di·kən·ˈtæm·ɪ·neɪt] *vt* entseuchen

decontamination [di·kən·ˌtæm·ɪ·ˈneɪ·ʃən] *n* Entseuchung *f*

decor ['deɪ·kɔr] *n* Ausstattung *f*; THEAT Dekor *m o nt*

decorate ['dek·ə·reɪt] *vt* 1. (*adorn*) schmücken; (*cake, store window*) dekorieren 2. *usu passive* (*honor*) **to be** ~ [**for sth**] [für etw *akk*] ausgezeichnet werden

decoration [ˌdek·ə·'reɪ·ʃən] *n* **1.** (*for party*) Dekoration *f*; (*for Christmas tree*) Schmuck *m kein pl* **2.** (*medal*) Auszeichnung *f*

decorative ['dek·ə·ə·ˌtɪv] *adj* dekorativ

decorum [dɪ·'kɔr·əm] *n form* Schicklichkeit *f*

decoy ['di·kɔɪ] *n* Lockvogel *m*

decrease I. *vi* [dɪ·'kris] abnehmen, zurückgehen II. *vt* [dɪ·'kris] reduzieren III. *n* ['di·kris] Abnahme *f*; (*numbers*) Rückgang *m*

decree [dɪ·'kri] *n form* Erlass *m*

decrepit [dɪ·'krep·ɪt] *adj* klapprig

dedicate ['ded·ɪ·keɪt] *vt* widmen

dedicated ['ded·ɪ·keɪ·ˌtɪd] *adj* engagiert

dedication [ˌded·ɪ·'keɪ·ʃən] *n* **1.** (*hard work*) Engagement *nt* **2.** (*in book*) Widmung *f*

deduce [dɪ·'dus] *vt* folgern; **to ~ whether ...** feststellen, ob ...

deduct [dɪ·'dʌkt] *vt* abziehen; FIN ausgleichen

deductible [dɪ·'dʌk·tə·bəl] *adj* absetzbar

deduction [dɪ·'dʌk·ʃən] *n* **1.** (*inference*) Schlussfolgerung *f* **2.** (*subtraction*) Abzug *m*

deed [did] *n* **1.** (*action*) Tat *f*; **to do a good ~** eine gute Tat vollbringen **2.** LAW Eigentumsurkunde *f*

deep [dip] *adj, adv* tief; (*disappointment*) schwer; (*regret*) groß; **the snow was 3 feet ~** der Schnee lag 3 Fuß hoch; **to be in ~ trouble** in großen Schwierigkeiten stecken; **~ blue** tiefblau; **~ space** äußerer Weltraum

deepen ['di·pən] I. *vt* **1.** (*make deeper*) tiefer machen **2.** (*intensify*) vertiefen II. *vi* **1.** (*voice, water*) tiefer werden **2.** (*intensify*) sich vertiefen; (*crisis*) sich verschärfen

'**deep freeze** *n* Tiefkühlschrank *m*; (*chest*) Tiefkühltruhe *f*

deep-'fry *vt* frittieren

'**deep fryer** *n* Fritteuse *f*

deeply ['dip·li] *adv* tief, äußerst

deep-'seated *adj* tief sitzend

deer <*pl* -> [dɪr] *n* Hirsch *m*; (*roe deer*) Reh *nt*

deface [dɪ·'feɪs] *vt* verunstalten

defamation [ˌdef·ə·'meɪ·ʃən] *n form* Diffamierung *f*

defamatory [dɪ·'fæm·ə·tɔr·i] *adj form* diffamierend

default [dɪ·'fɔlt] I. *vi* FIN in Verzug geraten (**on** mit +*dat*) II. *n* **1.** (*of contract*) Nichterfüllung *f*; (*failure to pay debt*) Versäumnis *nt* **2. by ~** automatisch **3.** COMPUT Voreinstellung *f* III. *adj* Standard-

defeat [dɪ·'fit] I. *vt* besiegen; (*at games, sports*) schlagen; (*proposal, government, bill*) ablehnen II. *n* Niederlage *f*

defeatism [dɪ·'fi·ˌtɪ·zəm] *n pej* Defätismus *m*, Defaitismus *m schweiz*

defeatist [dɪ·'fi·tɪst] I. *adj* defätistisch, defaitistisch *schweiz* II. *n* Defätist(in) *m(f)*, Defaitist(in) *m(f) schweiz*

defecate ['def·ə·keɪt] *vi form* den Darm entleeren

defect[1] ['di·fekt] *n* Fehler *m*; TECH Defekt *m*

defect[2] [dɪ·'fekt] *vi* POL überlaufen (**to** in +*akk*)

defection [dɪ·'fek·ʃən] *n* Flucht *f*; POL Überlaufen *nt*

defective [dɪ·'fek·tɪv] *adj* fehlerhaft; TECH defekt

defend [dɪ·'fend] *vt, vi* verteidigen; **to ~ oneself** sich wehren

defendant [dɪ·'fen·dənt] *n* LAW Angeklagte(r) *f(m)*

defense[1] [dɪ·'fens] *n* **1.** Verteidigung ; *a. fig*; **~ witness** Zeuge, -in *m, f* der Verteidigung **2.** MED **~s** *pl* Abwehrkräfte *pl*

defense[2] ['di·fens] *n esp* SPORT Abwehr *f*; **to play** [**on**] **~** Abwehrspieler/Abwehrspielerin sein

defenseless [dɪ·'fens·lɪs] *adj* wehrlos

De'fense Secretary *n* Verteidigungsminister(in) *m(f)*

defensible [dɪ·'fen·sə·bəl] *adj* vertretbar

defensive [dɪ·'fen·sɪv] I. *adj* defensiv II. **to be on the ~** in der Defensive sein

defer <-rr-> [dɪ·'fɜr] I. *vi form* **to ~ to sb/sth** sich jdm/etw beugen; (*to sb's judgment*) sich fügen II. *vt* verschieben; FIN, LAW aufschieben

deference ['def·ər·əns] *n form* Respekt *m*

deferential [ˌdef·ə·ˈren·tʃəl] *adj* respektvoll

defiance [dɪ·ˈfaɪ·əns] *n* Aufsässigkeit *f*; **in ~ of sb/sth** jdm/etw zum Trotz

defiant [dɪ·ˈfaɪ·ənt] *adj* aufsässig

deficiency [dɪ·ˈfɪʃ·ən·si] *n* Mangel *m*

deficient [dɪ·ˈfɪʃ·ənt] *adj* unzureichend; **to be ~ in sth** an etw *dat* mangeln

deficit [ˈdef·ɪ·sɪt] *n* Defizit *nt*

define [dɪ·ˈfaɪn] *vt* **1.** (*word, meaning*) definieren **2.** (*specify*) festlegen

definite [ˈdef·ə·nɪt] *adj* sicher; (*answer*) klar; (*improvement, increase*) eindeutig; (*place, time limit*) bestimmt

definite 'article *n* LING bestimmter Artikel

definitely [ˈdef·ɪ·nət·li] *adv* eindeutig; **to decide sth ~** etw endgültig beschließen

definition [ˌdef·ɪ·ˈnɪʃ·ən] *n* **1.** (*meaning*) Definition *f* **2.** (*distinctness*) Schärfe *f*

definitive [dɪ·ˈfɪn·ɪ·t̬ɪv] *adj* **1.** (*conclusive*) endgültig; (*proof*) eindeutig **2.** (*most authoritative*) ultimativ

deflate [dɪ·ˈfleɪt] **I.** *vt* **1.** Luft aus etw *dat* ablassen **2.** ECON (*currency*) deflationieren **II.** *vi* Luft verlieren

deflation [dɪ·ˈfleɪ·ʃən] *n* ECON Deflation *f*

deflect [dɪ·ˈflekt] **I.** *vt* ablenken; (*ball*) abfälschen; (*blow*) abwehren **II.** *vi* **to ~ off sb/sth** (*ball*) von jdm/etw *dat* abprallen

deflection [dɪ·ˈflek·ʃən] *n* Ablenkung *f*; SPORT Abpraller *m*

defogger [ˌdi·ˈfɔ·ɡər] *n* AUTO Gebläse *nt*

deforestation [ˌdi·fɔr·ɪ·ˈster·ʃən] *n* Abholzung *f*, Entwaldung *f*

deform [dɪ·ˈfɔrm] **I.** *vt* deformieren **II.** *vi* sich verformen

deformed [dɪ·ˈfɔrmd] *adj* verformt

deformity [dɪ·ˈfɔr·mɪ·t̬i] *n* Missbildung *f*

defraud [dɪ·ˈfrɔd] *vt* betrügen

defray [dɪ·ˈfreɪ] *vt form* (*costs*) tragen

defrost [ˌdi·ˈfrɔst] *vt, vi* auftauen; (*refrigerator*) abtauen; (*window, windshield*) enteisen

deft [deft] *adj* geschickt

defunct [dɪ·ˈfʌŋkt] *adj form* gestorben; (*institution*) ausgedient

defy <-ie-> [dɪ·ˈfaɪ] *vt* **to ~ sb/sth** sich jdm/etw widersetzen; *fig* (*resist, with-*

stand) sich etw *dat* entziehen

deg. *n abbr of* **degree**

degenerate I. *vi* [dɪ·ˈdʒen·ə·reɪt] degenerieren; **to ~ into sth** etw *dat* entarten **II.** *adj* [dɪ·ˈdʒen·ə·rət] degeneriert **III.** *n* [dɪ·ˈdʒen·ə·rət] *jd, der keine moralischen Werte mehr hat*

degrade [dɪ·ˈɡreɪd] *vt* **1.** (*person*) erniedrigen **2.** CHEM abbauen

degree [dɪ·ˈɡri] *n* **1.** (*amount*) Maß *nt*; (*extent*) Grad *m*; **by ~s** nach und nach; **to some ~** bis zu einem gewissen Grad **2.** MATH, METEO Grad *m* **3.** UNIV Abschluss *m*; (*document*) Abschlusszeugnis *nt*

dehydrate [ˌdi·haɪ·ˈdreɪt] **I.** *vt* **to become ~d** austrocknen **II.** *vi* MED dehydrieren

dehydration [ˌdi·haɪ·ˈdreɪ·ʃən] *n* MED Dehydration *f*

deice [ˌdi·ˈaɪs] *vt* enteisen

deity [ˈdi·ə·t̬i] *n* Gottheit *f*

dejected [dɪ·ˈdʒek·tɪd] *adj* niedergeschlagen

dejection [dɪ·ˈdʒek·ʃən] *n* Niedergeschlagenheit *f*

Del. *abbr of* **Delaware**

Delaware [ˈdel·ə·wer] *n* Delaware *nt*

delay [dɪ·ˈleɪ] **I.** *vt* **1.** (*postpone*) verschieben **2.** (*hold up*) **to be ~ed** [**by 10 minutes**] [zehn Minuten] Verspätung haben; **I was ~ed** ich wurde aufgehalten; **~ tactics** Verzögerungstaktiken *pl* **II.** *vi* verschieben **III.** *n* Verzögerung *f*; TRANSP Verspätung *f*

delectable [dɪ·ˈlek·tə·bəl] *adj* (*food, drink*) köstlich; *esp hum* (*person*) bezaubernd

delegate I. *n* [ˈdel·ɪ·ɡət] Delegierte(r) *f(m)* **II.** *vt* [ˈdel·ɪ·ɡeɪt] **1.** (*appoint*) als Vertreter(in) [aus]wählen; **to ~ sb to do sth** jdn dazu bestimmen, etw zu tun **2.** (*assign*) **to ~ sth to sb** etw auf jdn übertragen **II.** *vi* [ˈdel·ɪ·ɡeɪt] delegieren

delegation [ˌdel·ɪ·ˈɡeɪ·ʃən] *n* Delegation *f*

delete [dɪ·ˈlit] *vt* **1.** (*in writing*) streichen **2.** COMPUT löschen

deletion [dɪ·ˈli·ʃən] *n* Streichung *f*, Löschung *f*; (*of a file*) Löschen *nt*

deli ['del·i] *n fam short for* **delicatessen** Feinkostgeschäft *nt;* (*in supermarket*) Frischtheke, an der Wurst- und Käseaufschnitt, frische Salate etc. verkauft werden

deliberate I. *adj* [dɪˈlɪb·ər·ət] **1.** (*intentional*) absichtlich; (*decision, lie*) bewusst **2.** (*careful: pace*) vorsichtig **II.** *vi* [dɪˈlɪb·ə·reɪt] *form* (*gründlich*) nachdenken (**on** über +*akk*)

deliberately [dɪˈlɪb·ər·ət·li] *adv* absichtlich

deliberation [dɪˌlɪb·ə·ˈreɪ·ʃən] *n* **1.** (*carefulness*) Bedächtigkeit *f* **2.** *form* (*consideration*) Überlegung *f*

delicacy ['del·ɪ·kə·si] *n* **1.** FOOD Delikatesse *f* **2.** (*discretion*) Feingefühl *nt* **3.** (*fineness*) Feinheit *f;* (*of features*) Zartheit *f*

delicate ['del·ɪ·kət] *adj* **1.** (*sensitive*) empfindlich; (*china*) zerbrechlich **2.** (*tricky*) heikel **3.** (*fine*) fein; (*aroma, color*) zart; ~ **cycle** Feinwaschgang *m*

delicatessen [ˌdel·ɪ·kə·ˈtes·ən] *n* Feinkostgeschäft *nt*

delicious [dɪ·ˈlɪʃ·əs] *adj* köstlich, lecker

delight [dɪ·ˈlaɪt] **I.** *n* Freude *f* **II.** *vt* erfreuen

delighted [dɪ·ˈlaɪ·tɪd] *adj* hocherfreut; (*smile*) vergnügt; **to be ~ to do sth** etw mit [großem] Vergnügen tun

delightful [dɪ·ˈlaɪt·fəl] *adj* wunderbar; (*evening, village*) reizend; (*smile, person*) charmant

delinquency [dɪ·ˈlɪŋ·kwən·si] *n* Straffälligkeit *f*

delinquent [dɪ·ˈlɪŋ·kwənt] **I.** *n* Delinquent(in) *m(f)* **II.** *adj* straffällig

delirious [dɪ·ˈlɪr·i·əs] *adj* **1.** im Delirium **2.** (*extremely happy*) außer sich *dat* [vor Freude]

deliver [dɪ·ˈlɪv·ər] **I.** *vt* **1.** (*bring*) liefern; (*by mail*) zustellen; (*newspapers*) austragen; (*message*) überbringen **2.** (*recite: speech*) halten; (*verdict*) verkünden **3.** (*direct: blow*) geben; (*rebuke*) halten **4.** (*give birth*) zur Welt bringen; (*aid in giving birth*) entbinden **II.** *vi* **1.** (*supply*) liefern **2.** (*fulfill*) **to ~ on sth** (*promise*) etw einhalten

delivery [dɪ·ˈlɪv·ə·ri] *n* **1.** (*of goods*) Liefe-

rung *f;* (*of mail*) Zustellung *f* **2.** (*manner of speaking*) Vortragsweise *f* **3.** (*birth*) Entbindung *f*

de'livery room *n* Kreißsaal *m*

de'livery van *n* Lieferwagen *m*

delta ['del·tə] *n* Delta *nt*

delude [dɪ·ˈlud] *vt* täuschen

deluge ['del·judʒ] **I.** *n* **1.** (*downpour*) Regenguss *m;* (*flood*) Flut *f* **2.** *fig* Flut *f* **II.** *vt* **to be ~d** überflutet werden; *fig* überschüttet werden

delusion [dɪ·ˈlu·ʒən] *n* Täuschung *f*

deluxe [dɪ·ˈlʌks] *adj* Luxus-

demand [dɪ·ˈmænd] **I.** *vt* **1.** (*insist on*) verlangen **2.** (*need: skill, patience*) erfordern **II.** *n* **1.** (*request*) Forderung *f* (**for** nach +*dat*) **2.** (*requirement*) Bedarf *m;* COMM Nachfrage *f;* **in ~** gefragt **3.** (*expectations*) **to make ~s on sb/sth** Anforderungen *pl* an jdn/etw stellen

demanding [dɪ·ˈmæn·dɪŋ] *adj* (*child, work*) anstrengend; (*job, person, test*) anspruchsvoll

demeanor [dɪ·ˈmi·nər] *n form* (*behavior*) Verhalten *nt;* (*bearing*) Erscheinungsbild *nt*

demented [dɪ·ˈmen·tɪd] *adj* verrückt

demerit [dɪ·ˈmer·ɪt] *n* **1.** (*fault*) Schwäche *f* **2.** (*black mark*) Minuspunkt *m*

demise [dɪ·ˈmaɪz] *n form* Ableben *nt*

democracy [dɪ·ˈmak·rə·si] *n* Demokratie *f*

democrat ['dem·ə·kræt] *n* Demokrat(in) *m(f)*

democratic [ˌdem·ə·ˈkræt·ɪk] *adj* demokratisch

demolish [dɪ·ˈmal·ɪʃ] *vt* **1.** (*building*) abreißen; (*wall*) einreißen **2.** (*refute*) zunichtemachen; (*argument*) widerlegen

demolition [ˌdem·ə·ˈlɪʃ·ən] *n* Abriss *m*

demon ['di·mən] *n* (*evil spirit*) Dämon *m; fig* (*wicked person*) Fiesling *m*

demonic [dɪ·ˈman·ɪk] *adj* **1.** (*devilish*) dämonisch **2.** (*evil*) bösartig

demonstrable [dɪ·ˈman·strə·bəl] *adj* nachweislich

demonstrate ['dem·ən·streɪt] **I.** *v* **1.** (*show*) zeigen; (*operation*) vorführen; (*authority, knowledge*) demonstrieren; (*loyalty*) beweisen **2.** (*prove*)

nachweisen **II.** *vi* demonstrieren

demonstration [ˌdem·ən·ˈstreɪ·ʃən] *n* **1.** (*act of showing*) Demonstration *f*, Vorführung *f* **2.** (*proof*) Beweis *m* **3.** (*protest*) Demonstration *f*

demonstrator [ˈdem·ən·streɪ·t̬ər] *n* **1.** (*of product*) Vorführer(in) *m(f)* **2.** (*protester*) Demonstrant(in) *m(f)*

demoralize [dɪ·ˈmɔr·ə·laɪz] *vt* demoralisieren

demote [dɪ·ˈmoʊt] *vt* zurückstufen; MIL degradieren

demotion [dɪ·ˈmoʊ·ʃən] *n* MIL Degradierung *f*

demure [dɪ·ˈmjʊr] *adj* **1.** (*shy*) [sehr] schüchtern **2.** (*composed and reserved*) gesetzt

den [den] *n* **1.** (*lair*) Bau *m* **2.** (*study*) Arbeitszimmer *nt*; (*private room*) Bude *f*, Hobbyraum *m* **3.** (*children's playhouse*) Verschlag *m*

denial [dɪ·ˈnaɪ·əl] *n* **1.** (*statement*) Dementi *nt*; (*action*) Leugnen *nt kein pl* **2.** (*refusal*) Ablehnung *f* **3.** PSYCH **to be in ~** sich der Realität verschließen

denim [ˈden·ɪm] *n* **1.** (*material*) Denim® *m* **2.** *fam* **~s** *pl* Jeans *f/pl*

Denmark [ˈden·mark] *n* Dänemark *nt*

denomination [dɪ·ˌnam·ə·ˈneɪ·ʃən] *n* **1.** REL Konfessionsgemeinschaft *f* **2.** (*unit of value*) Währungseinheit *f*

denominator [dɪ·ˈnam·ə·neɪ·t̬ər] *n* MATH Nenner *m*

denote [dɪ·ˈnoʊt] *vt* bedeuten

denounce [dɪ·ˈnaʊns] *vt* **1.** (*criticize*) anprangern **2.** (*accuse*) entlarven; **to ~ sb to sb** jdn bei jdm denunzieren

dense <-r, -st> [dens] *adj* **1.** (*thick*) dicht **2.** *fam* (*stupid*) dumm

densely [ˈdens·li] *adv* dicht

density [ˈden·sə·t̬i] *n* Dichte *f*

dent [dent] **I.** *n* Beule *f*, Delle *f* **II.** *vt* einbeulen

dental [ˈden·təl] *adj* Zahn-

dentist [ˈden·tɪst] *n* Zahnarzt, Zahnärztin *m, f*

dentistry [ˈden·tɪ·stri] *n* Zahnmedizin *f*

dentures [ˈden·tʃərz] *npl* [Zahn]prothese *f*

denunciation [dɪ·ˌnʌn·si·ˈeɪ·ʃən] *n* **1.** (*condemnation*) Anprangerung *f*

2. LAW (*denouncing*) Denunziation *f*

Denver boot *n* Parkkralle *f*

deny <-ie-> [dɪ·ˈnaɪ] *vt* **1.** (*declare untrue*) abstreiten; (*accusation*) zurückweisen **2.** (*refuse to grant*) **to ~ sth to sb** [*or* sb sth] jdm etw verweigern; (*request*) ablehnen

deodorant [di·ˈoʊ·dər·ənt] *n* Deo[dorant] *nt*

dep. [dep] *n* **1.** TRANSP *short for* **departure** Abf.; (*aircraft*) Abfl. **2.** *short for* **department** Abt.

depart [dɪ·ˈpart] *vi* **1.** (*leave*) fortgehen; (*plane*) abfliegen, starten; (*train*) abfahren; (*ship a.*) ablegen **2.** (*differ*) abweichen (**from** *a.* +*dat*)

department [dɪ·ˈpart·mənt] *n* **1.** UNIV Institut *nt*; **the Philosophy D~** die philosophische Fakultät **2.** COMM Abteilung *f* **3.** POL Ministerium *nt* ADMIN Amt *nt*

departmental [ˌdi·part·ˈmen·təl] *adj* **1.** UNIV Instituts- **2.** COMM Abteilungs- **3.** POL Ministerial- **4.** ADMIN Amts-

Department of De'fense *n* Verteidigungsministerium *nt*

Department of Motor 'Vehicles *n* Kfz-Zulassungsstelle *f*

de'partment store *n* Kaufhaus *nt*

departure [dɪ·ˈpar·tʃər] *n* **1.** (*on trip*) Abreise *f*, Abfahrt *f*; (*ship a.*) Ablegen *nt*; (*plane*) Abflug *m* **2.** (*deviation*) Abweichung *f*; (*from policy*) Abkehr *f*

de'parture lounge *n* Abfahrthalle *f*; AVIAT Abflughalle *f*

de'parture time *n* Abfahrtzeit *f*; AVIAT Abflugzeit *f*

depend [dɪ·ˈpend] *vi* **1.** (*be dictated by*) **to ~ [up]on sth** von etw *dat* abhängen; **that ~s** kommt darauf an **2.** (*get help from*) **to ~ [up]on sb/sth** von jdm/etw abhängig sein; (*financially*) finanziell auf jdn/etw angewiesen sein **3.** (*rely on*) **to ~ [up]on sb/sth** sich auf jdn/etw verlassen

dependability [dɪ·ˌpen·də·ˈbɪl·ɪ·t̬i] *n* Zuverlässigkeit *f*, Verlässlichkeit *f*

dependable [dɪ·ˈpen·də·bəl] *adj* zuverlässig, verlässlich

dependence [dɪ·ˈpen·dəns] *n* Abhängigkeit *f*

dependent [dɪ·ˈpen·dənt] **I.** *adj* **1.** (*con-*

ditional) **to be ~ [up]on** sth von etw *dat* abhängen **2.** (*reliant on*) **to be ~ [up]on** sth von etw *dat* abhängig sein; (*help, goodwill*) auf etw *akk* angewiesen sein **II.** *n* [finanziell] abhängige(r) Angehörige(r) *f(m)*

depict [dɪ·ˈpɪkt] *vt form* darstellen

depiction [dɪ·ˈpɪk·ʃən] *n* Darstellung *f*

deplete [dɪ·ˈpliːt] *vt* vermindern

depleted [dɪ·ˈpliː·tɪd] *adj* verbraucht

depletion [dɪ·ˈpliː·ʃən] *n* Abbau *m*; (*of resources, capital*) Erschöpfung *f*

deplorable [dɪ·ˈplɔːr·ə·bəl] *adj* beklagenswert; (*conditions*) erbärmlich

deplore [dɪ·ˈplɔːr] *vt* **1.** (*disapprove*) verurteilen **2.** (*regret*) beklagen

deploy [dɪ·ˈplɔɪ] *vt* einsetzen

deployment [dɪ·ˈplɔɪ·mənt] *n* Einsatz *m*

deport [dɪ·ˈpɔːrt] *vt* ausweisen; (*prisoner*) deportieren

deportation [ˌdiː·pɔːr·ˈteɪ·ʃən] *n* Ausweisung *f*, Abschiebung *f*; (*of prisoner*) Deportation *f*

deportment [dɪ·ˈpɔːrt·mənt] *n form* Benehmen *nt*

depose [dɪ·ˈpoʊz] *vt* absetzen; (*monarch*) entthronen

deposit [dɪ·ˈpaz·ɪt] **I.** *vt* **1.** (*leave: person*) absetzen; (*thing*) ablegen, abstellen; (*luggage*) deponieren **2.** (*in bank*) einzahlen; (*as first installment*) anzahlen **II.** *n* **1.** (*sediment*) Bodensatz *m*; (*layer*) Ablagerung *f* **2.** (*in bank*) Einzahlung *f*; (*first installment*) Anzahlung *f*; (*security*) Kaution *f*; (*on bottle*) Pfand *nt*

deposition [ˌdep·ə·ˈzɪʃ·ən] *n* **1.** *form* (*removal from power*) Absetzung *f* **2.** LAW (*written statement*) Aussage *f*

depot [ˈdiː·poʊ] *n* Depot *nt*

depraved [dɪ·ˈpreɪvd] *adj* verdorben

depravity [dɪ·ˈpræv·ɪ·ti] *n* Verdorbenheit *f*

depreciate [dɪ·ˈpriː·ʃi·eɪt] **I.** *vi* an Wert verlieren **II.** *vt* entwerten

depreciation [dɪˌpriː·ʃi·ˈeɪ·ʃən] *n* Wertminderung *f*; (*of currencies*) Entwertung *f*

depress [dɪ·ˈpres] *vt* **1.** (*deject*) deprimieren **2.** (*reduce: prices*) drücken **3.** (*push: button, lever*) niederdrücken

depressed [dɪ·ˈprest] *adj* **1.** (*dejected*)

deprimiert (**about/at/by/over** wegen +*gen*) **2.** (*reduced: levels*) reduziert, verringert **3.** ECON (*region, sector*) heruntergekommen *fam*

depressing [dɪ·ˈpres·ɪŋ] *adj* deprimierend

depression [dɪ·ˈpreʃ·ən] *n* **1.** (*sadness*) Depression *f* **2.** ECON Wirtschaftskrise *f* **3.** METEO Tiefdruckgebiet *nt*

depressive [dɪ·ˈpres·ɪv] **I.** *n* Depressive(r) *f(m)* **II.** *adj* depressiv

deprivation [ˌdep·rɪ·ˈveɪ·ʃən] *n* Entbehrung *f*

deprive [dɪ·ˈpraɪv] *vt* **to ~** sb [**of**] sth jdm etw entziehen [*or* vorenthalten]

deprived [dɪ·ˈpraɪvd] *adj* sozial benachteiligt

dept. *n abbr of* **department** Abt.

depth [depθ] *n* Tiefe *f a. fig*; **in the ~s of the forest** mitten im Wald; **in the ~s of despair** zutiefst verzweifelt; **in ~** gründlich

deputation [ˌdep·jə·ˈteɪ·ʃən] *n* Abordnung *f*

deputize [ˈdep·jə·taɪz] *vi* **to ~ for** sb für jdn einspringen, jdn vertreten

deputy [ˈdep·jə·ti] **I.** *n* Stellvertreter(in) *m(f)* **II.** *adj* stellvertretend

derail [dɪ·ˈreɪl] *vt* **1.** (*train*) entgleisen lassen; **to be ~ed** entgleisen **2.** (*plan, process*) zum Scheitern bringen

deranged [dɪ·ˈreɪndʒd] *adj* geistesgestört

derby [ˈdɑːr·bi] *n* **1.** SPORT Derby *nt* **2.** (*hat*) Melone *f*

derelict [ˈder·ə·lɪkt] **I.** *adj* verlassen **II.** *n* Obdachlose(r) *f(m)*

dereliction [ˌder·ə·ˈlɪk·ʃən] *n* **1.** (*negligence*) **~ of duty** Pflichtvernachlässigung *f* **2.** (*dilapidation*) Verwahrlosung *f*

derision [dɪ·ˈrɪʒ·ən] *n* Spott *m*

derisive [dɪ·ˈraɪ·sɪv] *adj* spöttisch

derisory [dɪ·ˈraɪ·sə·ri] *adj* **1.** (*derisive*) spöttisch **2.** (*ridiculously small*) lächerlich

derivation [ˌder·ɪ·ˈveɪ·ʃən] *n* **1.** (*origin*) Ursprung *m* **2.** (*process*) Ableitung *f*

derivative [dɪ·ˈrɪv·ə·tɪv] **I.** *adj pej* nachgemacht **II.** *n* Ableitung *f*, Derivat *nt*

derive [dɪ·ˈraɪv] **I.** *vt* gewinnen **II.** *vi*

to ~ from sth sich von etw *dat* ableiten [lassen]

dermatitis [ˌdɜr·mə·'taɪ·t̬əs] n Hautreizung f, Dermatitis f

dermatologist [ˌdɜr·mə·'tal·ə·dʒɪst] n Dermatologe, -in m, f, Hautarzt, Hautärztin m, f

dermatology [ˌdɜr·mə·'tal·ə·dʒi] n Dermatologie f

derogatory [dɪ·'rag·ə·tɔr·i] adj abfällig

derrick ['der·ɪk] n 1. (crane) Lastkran m 2. (over oil well) Bohrturm m

desalination [di·ˌsæl·ɪ·'neɪ·ʃən] n Entsalzung f

descend [dɪ·'send] I. vi 1. (go down: path) herunterführen; (person) heruntergehen 2. (be related) **to be ~ed from sb/sth** von jdm/etw abstammen 3. (fall) herabsinken II. vt hinuntersteigen

descendant [dɪ·'sen·dənt] n Nachkomme m

descent [dɪ·'sent] n 1. (by plane) [Lande]anflug m 2. (way down) Abstieg m kein pl 3. fig (ancestry) Abstammung f

describe [dɪ·'skraɪb] vt beschreiben; (experience) schildern

description [dɪ·'skrɪp·ʃən] n Beschreibung f; **of every ~** jeglicher Art

descriptive [dɪ·'skrɪp·tɪv] adj beschreibend

desecrate ['des·ɪ·kreɪt] vt schänden

desecration [ˌdes·ɪ·'kreɪ·ʃən] n Schändung f

desegregate [ˌdi·'seg·rɪ·geɪt] vt **to ~ schools/universities** die Rassentrennung in der Schule/an der Universität aufheben

desegregation [di·ˌseg·rɪ·'geɪ·ʃən] n Aufhebung f der Rassentrennung

desert[1] ['dez·ərt] n Wüste f a. fig; **~ island** verlassene Insel

desert[2] [dɪ·'zɜrt] I. vi MIL desertieren II. vt verlassen

deserted [dɪ·'zɜr·t̬ɪd] adj verlassen; (of town) ausgestorben

deserter [dɪ·'zɜr·t̬ər] n Deserteur(in) m(f)

desertion [dɪ·'zɜr·ʃən] n Verlassen nt; MIL Desertion f

deserts [dɪ·'zɜrts] npl **to get one's [just] ~** seine Quittung bekommen

deserve [dɪ·'zɜrv] vt verdienen

deservedly [dɪ·'zɜr·vɪd·li] adv verdientermaßen

deserving [dɪ·'zɜr·vɪŋ] adj verdienstvoll

design [dɪ·'zaɪn] I. vt 1. (plan) entwerfen; (cars) konstruieren 2. (intend) **to be ~ed for sb** für jdn konzipiert sein; **these measures are ~ed to reduce pollution** diese Maßnahmen sollen die Luftverschmutzung verringern II. n 1. (plan) Entwurf m 2. (art) Design nt; (of building) Bauart f; (of machine) Konstruktion f; (pattern) Muster nt

designate ['dez·ɪg·neɪt] I. vt **to ~ sb** jdn ernennen (**as** zu +dat) II. adj after n designiert

designated 'driver n Person, die sich bereit erklärt, nüchtern zu bleiben und die Freunde sicher nach Hause zu fahren

designer [dɪ·'zaɪ·nər] I. n 1. Designer(in) m(f) II. adj Designer-

desirable [dɪ·'zaɪr·ə·bəl] adj 1. (worth having) erstrebenswert; (popular) begehrt; (advantageous) erwünscht 2. (sexually attractive) begehrenswert

desire [dɪ·'zaɪr] I. vt 1. (want) wünschen 2. (sexually) begehren II. n 1. (strong wish) Verlangen nt; (stronger) Sehnsucht f; (request) Wunsch m 2. (sexual need) Begierde f

desist [dɪ·'sɪst] vi form innehalten

desk [desk] n 1. (for writing) Schreibtisch m 2. (counter) Schalter m

'desk lamp n Schreibtischlampe f

'desktop n 1. COMPUT Desktop m 2. (desk surface) Tischoberfläche f

desolate ['des·ə·lət] adj 1. (barren) trostlos 2. (unhappy) niedergeschlagen

desolation [ˌdes·ə·'leɪ·ʃən] n 1. (barrenness) Trostlosigkeit f 2. (sadness) Verzweiflung f

despair [dɪ·'sper] I. n Verzweiflung f; **in ~** verzweifelt II. vi verzweifeln (**at/of** an +dat); **to ~ of doing sth** die Hoffnung aufgeben, etw zu tun

despairing [dɪ·'sper·ɪŋ] adj verzweifelt

despatch [dɪ·'spætʃ] n vt see **dispatch**

desperate ['des·pər·ɪt] adj (attempt) verzweifelt; (great) dringend; **to be ~ for sth** etw dringendst brauchen

desperation [ˌdes·pə·'reɪ·ʃən] n Verzweif-

lung f; **in** ~ aus Verzweiflung

despicable [dɪ'spɪk·ə·bəl] adj abscheulich

despise [dɪ'spaɪz] vt verachten

despite [dɪ'spaɪt] prep trotz +gen

despondent [dɪ'span·dənt] adj niedergeschlagen

dessert [dɪ'zɜrt] n Nachtisch m, Dessert nt

destination [ˌdes·tə·'neɪ·ʃən] n Ziel nt; (of trip) Reiseziel nt; (of letter) Bestimmungsort m

destiny ['des·tə·ni] n Schicksal nt

destitute ['des·tɪ·tut] **I.** adj mittellos **II.** n **the ~** pl die Bedürftigen

destitution [ˌdes·tɪ·'tu·ʃən] n Armut f

destroy [dɪ'strɔɪ] vt **1.** (demolish: structure) zerstören **2.** (do away with: possibility) vernichten **3.** (kill: herd) abschlachten; (pet) einschläfern **4.** (ruin: reputation) ruinieren

destroyer [dɪ'strɔɪ·ər] n MIL Zerstörer m

destruction [dɪ'strʌk·ʃən] n Zerstörung f; **mass ~** Massenvernichtung f

destructive [dɪ'strʌk·tɪv] adj zerstörerisch; (influence, person) destruktiv

desultory ['des·əl·tɔr·i] adj form halbherzig

detach [dɪ'tætʃ] vt abnehmen; (without reattaching) abtrennen

detachable [dɪ'tætʃ·ə·bəl] adj abnehmbar

detached [dɪ'tætʃt] adj **1.** (separated) abgelöst **2.** (aloof) distanziert

detachment [dɪ'tætʃ·mənt] n **1.** (aloofness) Distanziertheit f **2.** (of soldiers) Einsatztruppe f

detail [dɪ'teɪl] **I.** n **1.** (item of information) Detail nt, Einzelheit f; **further ~s** nähere Informationen; **to go into ~** ins Detail gehen, auf die Einzelheiten eingehen; **in ~** im Detail **2.** (unimportant item) Kleinigkeit f **3. ~s** pl (vital statistics) Personalien pl **II.** vt **1.** (explain) ausführlich erläutern **2.** (specify) einzeln aufführen

detailed [dɪ'teɪld] adj detailliert; (description, report) ausführlich; (study) eingehend

detain [dɪ'teɪn] vt **1.** LAW in Haft nehmen, inhaftieren **2.** form (delay) aufhalten

detainee [ˌdi·teɪ·'ni] n Häftling m

detect [dɪ'tekt] vt **1.** (discover) entdecken; (disease) feststellen; (smell) bemerken; (sound) wahrnehmen **2.** (catch in act) ertappen

detectable [dɪ'tek·tə·bəl] adj feststellbar (change) wahrnehmbar

detection [dɪ'tek·ʃən] n **1.** Entdeckung f (of disease) Feststellung f **2.** (by detective) Ermittlungsarbeit f

detective [dɪ'tek·tɪv] n **1.** (police officer) Kriminalbeamte(r) m, Kriminalbeamte [or -in] f **2.** (private) [Priva] detektiv(in) m(f)

detention [dɪ'ten·ʃən] n **1.** (state) Haft f **2.** (act) Festnahme f **3.** SCH Nachsitzen nt kein pl; **to get ~** nachsitzen müssen

de'tention center n Untersuchungsgefängnis nt

deter <-rr-> [dɪ'tɜr] vt verhindern; (put off: person) abschrecken, abhalten (**from** von +dat)

detergent [dɪ'tɜr·dʒənt] n Reinigungsmittel nt; (for clothes) Waschmittel nt

deteriorate [dɪ'tɪr·i·ə·reɪt] vi **1.** (become worse) sich verschlechtern **2.** (disintegrate) verfallen; (leather, wood) sich zersetzen; (rubber, leather) brüchig werden

deterioration [dɪ·ˌtɪr·i·ə·'reɪ·ʃən] n **1.** (worsening) Verschlechterung f **2.** ECON, TECH Qualitätsverlust m **3.** (disintegration) Verfall m; (of metal, wood) Zersetzung f

determination [dɪ·ˌtɜr·mɪ·'neɪ·ʃən] n **1.** (resolve) Entschlossenheit f **2.** (determining) Bestimmung f

determine [dɪ'tɜr·mɪn] vt **1.** (decide) entscheiden **2.** (find out) ermitteln feststellen, herausfinden **3.** (influence) bestimmen

determined [dɪ'tɜr·mɪnd] adj entschlossen

deterrent [dɪ'tɜr·ənt] n Abschreckung f Abschreckungsmittel nt

detest [dɪ'test] vt verabscheuen

detonate ['det·ə·neɪt] vt, vi detonieren

detonation [ˌdet·ə·'neɪ·ʃən] n Detonation f

detonator ['det·ə·neɪ·t̬ər] n [Spreng]zünder m

detour ['di·tʊr] n 1. TRANSP Umleitung f 2. (deviation) Umweg m

detox ['di·taks] n short for **detoxification** Entzug m

detract [dɪ·'trækt] vi to ~ from sth etw beeinträchtigen

detriment ['det·rə·mənt] n Nachteil m

detrimental [ˌdet·rɪ·'men·t̬əl] adj schädlich

deuce [dus] n 1. (cards, dice) Zwei f 2. TENNIS Einstand m

devaluation [ˌdi·væl·ju·'eɪ·ʃən] n Abwertung f

devalue [ˌdi·'væl·ju] vt abwerten

devastate ['dev·ə·steɪt] vt vernichten; (region) verwüsten; fam umhauen

devastated ['dev·ə·steɪ·t̬ɪd] adj völlig fertig fam, total down sl

devastating ['dev·ə·steɪ·t̬ɪŋ] adj 1. (destructive) verheerend, vernichtend a. fig 2. fig fam (positively overwhelming) umwerfend; (negatively) niederschmetternd

devastation [ˌdev·ə·'steɪ·ʃən] n 1. (destruction) Verwüstung f 2. (of person) Verzweiflung f

develop [dɪ·'vel·əp] I. vi sich entwickeln (into zu +dat); (abilities) sich entfalten II. vt 1. entwickeln; (habit) annehmen; (plan) ausarbeiten; (skills) weiterentwickeln 2. ARCHIT erschließen [und bebauen] 3. PHOT entwickeln

developed [dɪ·'vel·əpt] adj 1. entwickelt 2. ARCHIT erschlossen

developer [dɪ·'vel·ə·pər] n 1. (person) Bauunternehmer(in) m(f); (company) Baufirma f, Bauunternehmen nt 2. PHOT Entwickler m

development [dɪ·'vel·əp·mənt] n 1. (act, event, process) Entwicklung f 2. ARCHIT Bau m; (area) Baugebiet nt; (buildings) housing ~ Siedlung f

deviant ['di·vi·ənt] SOCIOL I. n to be a [sexual] ~ [im sexuellen Verhalten] von der Norm abweichen II. adj (behavior) abweichend

deviate ['di·vi·eɪt] vi (from norm) abweichen; (from route) sich entfernen

deviation [ˌdi·vi·'eɪ·ʃən] n Abweichung f

device [dɪ·'vaɪs] n 1. (machine) Gerät nt, Vorrichtung f 2. (method) Verfahren nt 3. (bomb) Sprengsatz m

devil ['dev·əl] n 1. REL Teufel m 2. fig Teufel(in) m(f) 3. fam (affectionately) **little ~** kleiner Schlingel fam; **lucky ~** Glückspilz m

devilish ['dev·ə·lɪʃ] adj teuflisch; (situation) verteufelt

devious ['di·vi·əs] adj 1. (dishonest: person) verschlagen; (plan) krumm 2. (roundabout) gewunden

devise [dɪ·'vaɪz] vt erdenken; (plan) aushecken

devoid [dɪ·'vɔɪd] adj to be ~ of sth ohne etw sein

devolve [dɪ·'valv] vi form übergehen ([up]on auf +akk)

devote [dɪ·'voʊt] vt widmen; (one's time) opfern

devoted [dɪ·'voʊ·t̬ɪd] adj (admirer) begeistert; (dog) anhänglich; (follower, friend) treu; (husband, mother) hingebungsvoll

devotee [ˌdev·ə·'ti] n (of an artist) Verehrer(in) m(f); (of a leader) Anhänger(in) m(f); (of a cause) Verfechter(in) m(f); (of music) Liebhaber(in) m(f)

devotion [dɪ·'voʊ·ʃən] n 1. (loyalty) Ergebenheit f 2. (dedication) Hingabe f (to an +akk) 3. (affection: of husband, wife) Liebe f; (of children) Anhänglichkeit f; (of an admirer) Verehrung f

devour [dɪ·'vaʊ·ər] vt verschlingen a. fig

devout [dɪ·'vaʊt] adj REL fromm; fig [sehr] engagiert; (hope, wish) sehnlich

dew [du] n Tau m

'dewdrop n Tautropfen m

dexterity [dek·'ster·ɪ·t̬i] n Geschicklichkeit f

dexterous ['dek·stər·əs] adj gewandt; (fingers) geschickt

dextrous ['dek·strəs] adj see **dexterous**

diabetes [ˌdaɪ·ə·'bi·t̬ɪz] n Zuckerkrankheit f

diabetic [ˌdaɪ·ə·'bet̬·ɪk] I. n Diabetiker(in) m(f) II. adj 1. (having diabetes) zuckerkrank 2. (for diabetics) Diabetiker-

diabolical [ˌdaɪ·ə·'bal·ɪ·kəl] adj 1. (of

Devil) Teufels- **2.** (*evil*) teuflisch

diagnose [ˌdaɪ·əɡ·ˈnoʊs] *vt* **1.** MED diagnostizieren **2.** (*discover*) erkennen; (*fault, problem*) feststellen

diagnosis <*pl* -ses> [ˌdaɪ·əɡ·ˈnoʊ·sɪs] *n* **1.** (*of disease*) Diagnose *f* **2.** (*of problem*) Beurteilung *f*

diagnostic [ˌdaɪ·əɡ·ˈnɑs·tɪk] *adj* diagnostisch

diagonal [daɪ·ˈæɡ·ə·nəl] **I.** *adj* (*line*) diagonal, schräg **II.** *n* Diagonale *f*

diagram [ˈdaɪ·ə·ɡræm] *n* schematische Darstellung, Diagramm *nt*

dial [ˈdaɪ·əl] **I.** *n* (*of clock*) Zifferblatt; (*of instrument, radio*) Skala *f*; (*of telephone*) Wählscheibe *f* **II.** *vt, vi* <-l-> wählen; **to ~ the wrong number** sich verwählen

dialect [ˈdaɪ·ə·lekt] *n* Dialekt *m*

dialogue, dialog [ˈdaɪ·ə·lɑɡ] *n* Dialog *m*

'dial tone *n* Wählton *m*

dialysis [daɪ·ˈæl·ə·sɪs] *n* Dialyse *f*

diameter [daɪ·ˈæm·ə·t̬ər] *n* Durchmesser *m*

diametrically [ˌdaɪ·ə·ˈmet·rɪ·kə·li] *adv* ~ **opposed** völlig entgegengesetzt

diamond [ˈdaɪ·ə·mənd] *n* **1.** (*stone*) Diamant *m* **2.** MATH Raute *f*, Rhombus *m* **3.** CARDS Karo *nt*

diamond anni'versary *n* diamantene Hochzeit

diaper [ˈdaɪ·pər] *n* Windel *f*

diaphragm [ˈdaɪ·ə·fræm] *n* **1.** ANAT Zwerchfell *nt* **2.** (*contraceptive*) Diaphragma *nt*, Pessar *nt*

diarrhea [ˌdaɪ·ə·ˈri·ə] *n* Durchfall *m*

diary [ˈdaɪ·ə·ri] *n* **1.** (*journal*) Tagebuch *nt* **2.** (*schedule*) [Termin]kalender *m*

dice [daɪs] **I.** *n* **1.** *pl of* **die** Würfel *m* **2.** (*game*) Würfelspiel *nt* ▶ **no ~** *sl* kommt [überhaupt] nicht in Frage *fam*; (*of no use*) vergiss es *fam* **II.** *vt* FOOD würfeln

dicey [ˈdaɪ·si] *adj fam* riskant

dick [dɪk] *n* **1.** *vulg* (*penis*) Schwanz *m* **2.** *offensive* (*jerk*) Idiot *m pej*

Dictaphone® [ˈdɪk·tə·foʊn] *n* Diktaphon® *nt*

dictate [ˈdɪk·teɪt] **I.** *vt* **1.** (*command*) befehlen **2.** (*letter, memo*) diktieren **II.** *vi* **1.** (*issue commands*) **to ~ to sb** jdm

Vorschriften machen **2.** (*read aloud*) diktieren

dictation [dɪk·ˈteɪ·ʃən] *n* Diktat *nt*

dictator [ˈdɪk·teɪ·t̬ər] *n* Diktator *m*

dictatorial [ˌdɪk·tə·ˈtɔr·i·əl] *adj* diktatorisch

dictatorship [dɪk·ˈteɪ·t̬ər·ʃɪp] *n* Diktatur *f*

diction [ˈdɪk·ʃən] *n* Ausdrucksweise *f*

dictionary [ˈdɪk·ʃə·ner·i] *n* Wörterbuch *nt*

did [dɪd] *pt of* **do**

diddle [ˈdɪd·əl] *vi fam* **to ~ [around] with sth** an etw *dat* [he]rummachen

didn't [ˈdɪd·ənt] = **did not** *see* **do**

die¹ <-y-> [daɪ] *vi* **1.** sterben, umkommen (**of** vor +*dat*); **to ~ of cancer** an Krebs sterben; **to ~ laughing** sich totlachen, sich kaputtlachen; **to ~ of hunger** verhungern; **to ~ of thirst** verdursten **2.** *fig fam* (*stop functioning*) kaputtgehen; (*engine*) stehen bleiben; (*battery*) leer werden; (*flame, light*) verlöschen ▶ **to be dying to do sth** darauf brennen, etw zu tun; **to be dying for sth** großes Verlangen nach etw *dat* haben

die away *vi* schwinden; (*sound*) verhallen

die down *vi* (*noise*) leiser werden; (*rain, wind*) schwächer werden; (*storm*) sich legen; (*excitement*) abklingen

die off *vi* aussterben; BOT absterben

die out *vi* aussterben

die² [daɪ] *n* <*pl* dice> (*for games*) Würfel *m*

'diehard I. *n pej* Dickschädel *m* **II.** *adj* unermüdlich; (*liberal*) Erz-

diesel [ˈdi·zəl] *n* **1.** (*fuel*) Diesel-[kraftstoff] *m* **2.** (*vehicle*) Dieselfahrzeug *nt*, Diesel *m*

'diesel engine *n* Dieselmotor *m*

'diesel oil *n* Dieselöl *nt*

diet [ˈdaɪ·ət] **I.** *n* **1.** (*food and drink*) Nahrung *f* **2.** MED Diät *f*, Schonkost *f* **3.** (*for losing weight*) Diät *f*, Schlankheitskur *f*; **to go on a ~** eine Diät machen **II.** *vi* Diät halten **III.** *adj* Diät-

dietary [ˈdaɪ·ɪ·ter·i] *adj* **1.** (*of usual food*) Ernährungs-, Ess- **2.** (*of medical diet*) Diät-

dietary 'fiber *n* Ballaststoffe *pl*

dietician, dietitian [ˌdaɪ·ə·ˈtɪʃ·ən] *n* Diätassistent(in) *m(f)*

differ ['dɪf·ər] vi 1. (be unlike) sich unterscheiden 2. (not agree) verschiedener Meinung sein

difference ['dɪf·ər·əns] n 1. Unterschied m; to make all the ~ die Sache völlig ändern 2. FIN Differenz f; MATH (after subtraction) Rest m 3. (disagreement) ~ [of opinion] Meinungsverschiedenheit f

different ['dɪf·ər·ənt] adj 1. anders pred, andere(r, s) attr; to be ~ from [or than] sb/sth sich von jdm/etw unterscheiden 2. (unusual) ungewöhnlich

differential [,dɪf·ə·'ren·tʃəl] I. n 1. MATH Differenzial nt 2. MECH Differenzial[getriebe] nt 3. (difference) Unterschied m; ECON Gefälle nt II. adj 1. (different) unterschiedlich f 2. MATH, MECH Differenzial-

differentiate [,dɪf·ə·'ren·tʃi·eɪt] vt, vi unterscheiden

difficult ['dɪf·ɪ·kəlt] adj schwierig, schwer; (job, trip) beschwerlich

difficulty ['dɪf·ɪ·kəl·ti] n 1. (effort) with ~ mit Mühe 2. (problematic nature) Schwierigkeit f 3. (trouble) Problem nt, Schwierigkeit f; to have ~ doing sth Schwierigkeiten dabei haben, etw zu tun

diffident ['dɪf·ɪ·dənt] adj form 1. (shy) zaghaft 2. (reserved) zurückhaltend

dig [dɪg] I. n 1. ARCHEOL Ausgrabung f 2. (thrust) Stoß m II. vi <-gg-, dug, dug> graben III. vt <-gg-, dug, dug> 1. (with shovel) graben; (ditch) ausheben 2. to ~ sb in the ribs jdn [mit dem Ellenbogen] anstoßen

dig in I. vi 1. MIL sich eingraben 2. fam (start eating) reinhauen fam II. vt (fertilizer) untergraben

dig up vt 1. (turn over) umgraben 2. (remove) ausgraben; ARCHEOL freilegen 3. fig (find out) herausfinden

digest vt [daɪ·'dʒest] 1. verdauen a. fig 2. CHEM auflösen

digestion [daɪ·'dʒes·tʃən] n Verdauung f

digit ['dɪdʒ·ɪt] n 1. MATH Ziffer f 2. (finger) Finger m; (toe) Zehe f

digital ['dɪdʒ·ɪ·təl] adj digital, Digital-

digital 'radio n Digitalradio nt

dignified ['dɪg·nɪ·faɪd] adj würdig, würdevoll

dignitary ['dɪg·nə·ter·i] n Würdenträger(in) m(f)

dignity ['dɪg·nɪ·ti] n Würde f

digress [daɪ·'gres] vi abschweifen

dike¹ [daɪk] n 1. (wall) Deich m 2. (drainage channel) [Abfluss]graben m

dike² n pej sl (lesbian) see **dyke²**

dilapidated [dɪ·'læp·ɪ·deɪ·tɪd] adj (house) verfallen; (car) klapprig

dilate [daɪ·leɪt] I. vi sich weiten II. vt erweitern

dilemma [dɪ·'lem·ə] n Dilemma nt

diligence ['dɪl·ɪ·dʒəns] n 1. (industriousness) Fleiß m; (enthusiasm) Eifer m 2. LAW (carefulness) Sorgfalt f

diligent ['dɪl·ɪ·dʒənt] adj 1. (hardworking) fleißig; (enthusiastic) eifrig 2. (painstaking) sorgfältig

dill [dɪl] n Dill m

dilly-dally <-ie-> ['dɪl·i·dæl·i] vi pej fam schwanken

dilute [daɪ·'lut] vt verdünnen

dim <-mm-> [dɪm] I. adj 1. (not bright) schwach, trüb; (poorly lit) schumm[e]rig 2. (indistinct) undeutlich; (recollection, shape) verschwommen 3. fam (slow to understand) schwer von Begriff II. vt abdunkeln; (headlights) abblenden

dime [daɪm] n Dime m, Zehncentstück nt ▶ a ~ a **dozen** spottbillig

dimension [dɪ·'men·ʃən] n Dimension f

diminish [dɪ·'mɪn·ɪʃ] I. vt vermindern II. vi sich vermindern; (pain) nachlassen; (influence, value) abnehmen

diminutive [dɪ·'mɪn·jə·tɪv] I. adj 1. (tiny) winzig 2. LING diminutiv II. n LING Verkleinerungsform f

dimmer ['dɪm·ər], **dimmer switch** ['dɪm·ər-] n Dimmer m, Helligkeitsregler m; AUTO Abblendschalter m

dimple ['dɪm·pəl] n (in cheeks, chin) Grübchen nt

dimpled ['dɪm·pəld] adj mit Grübchen

din [dɪn] n liter Lärm m

dine [daɪn] vi form speisen

diner ['daɪ·nər] n 1. (person) Speisende(r) f(m); (in restaurant) Gast m 2. (café) Restaurant am Straßenrand mit Theke und Tischen 3. RAIL see **dining car**

dinghy ['dɪŋ·i] n Ding[h]i nt

dingy ['dɪn·dʒi] adj düster, schmuddelig; (color) trüb

dining car ['daɪ·nɪŋ,-] n RAIL Speisewagen m

'dining room n (in house) Esszimmer nt; (in public building) Speisesaal m

dinky ['dɪŋ·ki] adj pej fam klein

dinner ['dɪn·ər] n 1. (evening meal) Abendessen nt; dial (warm lunch) Mittagessen nt; to go out for ~ essen gehen 2. (formal meal) Diner nt, Festessen nt

'dinner party n Abendgesellschaft f [mit Essen]

'dinner table n (in house) Esstisch m; (at formal event) Tafel f

'dinnertime n Essenszeit f

dinosaur ['daɪ·nə·sɔr] n Dinosaurier m a. fig

diocese ['daɪ·ə·sɪs] n Diözese f

dip [dɪp] I. n 1. FOOD Dip m 2. (brief swim) kurzes Bad; to go for a ~ kurz reinspringen 3. (in road) Vertiefung f, Senke f II. vi <-pp-> 1. (go down) [ver]sinken; (lower) sich senken 2. (decline) fallen; (profits) zurückgehen III. vt <-pp-> 1. (immerse) [ein]tauchen; FOOD [ein]tunken 2. (lower) senken; (flag) dippen

◆dip into vi 1. (study casually) to ~ into sth (book) einen kurzen Blick auf etw akk werfen 2. (savings) angreifen

diphtheria [dɪf·'θɪr·i·ə] n MED Diphtherie f

diphthong ['dɪf·θɑŋ] n LING Doppellaut m

diploma [dɪ·'ploʊ·mə] n 1. SCH, UNIV Diplom nt 2. (honorary document) [Ehren]urkunde f

diplomacy [dɪ·'ploʊ·mə·si] n Diplomatie f a. fig

diplomat ['dɪp·lə·mæt] n Diplomat(in) m(f) a. fig

diplomatic [ˌdɪp·lə·'mæt·ɪk] adj diplomatisch a. fig

'dipstick n 1. AUTO [Öl]messstab m 2. sl (idiot) Idiot(in) m(f) pej, Dummkopf m pej

dire ['daɪr] adj 1. (dreadful) entsetzlich, furchtbar; (situation) aussichtslos; in ~ straits in einer ernsten Notlage 2. (omi-

nous: warning, forecast) unheilvoll

direct [dɪ·'rekt] I. adj direkt; the ~ opposite das genaue Gegenteil II. adv direkt III. vt 1. (control) leiten, führen; (traffic) regeln 2. (aim) richten (at, to an +akk; (attention) lenken (at, to auf +akk) 3. (give directions) to ~ sb to sth jdm den Weg zu etw dat zeigen 4. THEAT, FILM Regie führen bei; MUS dirigieren

direct 'current n ELEC Gleichstrom m

direct 'hit n Volltreffer m

direction [dɪ·'rek·ʃən] n 1. (course) Richtung f; in the ~ of the bedroom in Richtung Schlafzimmer; sense of ~ Orientierungssinn m; in opposite ~s in entgegengesetzter Richtung; to give sb ~s jdm den Weg beschreiben 2. (supervision) Leitung f, Führung f 3. (instructions) ~s pl Anweisungen pl

directive [dɪ·'rek·tɪv] n [An]weisung f

directly [dɪ·'rekt·li] adv direkt

direct 'object n direktes Objekt

director [dɪ·'rek·tər] n 1. ADMIN (of company) Direktor(in) m(f) 2. FILM, THEAT Regisseur(in) m(f); (of orchestra) Dirigent(in) m(f); (of choir) Chorleiter(in) m(f)

directory [dɪ·'rek·tə·ri] n (phone book) Telefonbuch nt; (list) Verzeichnis nt

directory as'sistance n [Telefon]auskunft f kein pl

dirt [dɜrt] n 1. (filth) Schmutz m, Dreck m 2. (soil) Erde f

dirt 'cheap adj fam spottbillig

dirt 'road n Schotterstraße f

dirty ['dɜr·ti] I. adj 1. (unclean) dreckig, schmutzig; (needle) benutzt 2. fam (nasty) gemein; (liar) dreckig; (rascal) gerissen 3. fam (lewd) vulgär; (language) vulgär 4. (unfriendly: look) böse II. adv 1. (dishonestly) unfair 2. (obscenely) vulgär III. vt beschmutzen

disability [ˌdɪs·ə·'bɪl·ɪ·ti] n Behinderung f; ~ benefit Erwerbsunfähigkeitsrente f

disable [dɪs·'eɪ·bəl] vt (person) arbeitsunfähig machen; (thing) funktionsunfähig machen

disabled [dɪs·'eɪ·bəld] I. adj 1. (handicapped) behindert 2. (for the handicapped) Behinderten- II. n the ~ pl

die Behinderten

disadvantage [ˌdɪs·əd·ˈvæn·tɪdʒ] I. n Nachteil m; (state) Benachteiligung f; **to put sb at a ~** jdn benachteiligen II. vt benachteiligen

disadvantageous [ˌdɪs·ˌæd·væn·ˈteɪ·dʒəs] adj nachteilig

disaffected [ˌdɪs·ə·ˈfek·tɪd] adj form (dissatisfied) unzufrieden; (estranged) entfremdet

disagree [ˌdɪs·ə·ˈgri] vi 1. (dissent) nicht übereinstimmen; (with plan, decision) nicht einverstanden sein; (with sb else) anderer Meinung sein 2. (argue) eine Auseinandersetzung haben 3. FOOD **something that ~s with me** etwas, das mir nicht bekommt

disagreeable [ˌdɪs·ə·ˈgri·ə·bəl] adj 1. (unpleasant) unangenehm 2. (unfriendly) unsympathisch

disagreement [ˌdɪs·ə·ˈgri·mənt] n 1. (lack of agreement) Uneinigkeit f 2. (argument) Meinungsverschiedenheit f

disallow [ˌdɪs·ə·ˈlaʊ] vt 1. nicht erlauben; SPORT nicht anerkennen; (goal) annullieren 2. LAW abweisen

disappear [ˌdɪs·ə·ˈpɪr] vi verschwinden

disappearance [ˌdɪs·ə·ˈpɪr·əns] n Verschwinden nt

disappoint [ˌdɪs·ə·ˈpɔɪnt] vt enttäuschen

disappointed [ˌdɪs·ə·ˈpɔɪn·tɪd] adj enttäuscht (**at/about** über +akk, **in/with** mit +dat)

disappointing [ˌdɪs·ə·ˈpɔɪn·t̬ɪŋ] adj enttäuschend

disappointment [ˌdɪs·ə·ˈpɔɪnt·mənt] n Enttäuschung f

disapproval [ˌdɪs·ə·ˈpru·vəl] n Missbilligung f

disapprove [ˌdɪs·ə·ˈpruv] vi dagegen sein; **to ~ of sth** etw missbilligen; **to ~ of sb** jdn ablehnen

disarm [dɪs·ˈarm] I. vt (person) entwaffnen a. fig; (bomb) entschärfen II. vi abrüsten

disarmament [dɪs·ˈar·mə·mənt] n Abrüstung f

disarming [dɪs·ˈar·mɪŋ] adj entwaffnend

disarray [ˌdɪs·ə·ˈreɪ] n 1. (disorder) Unordnung f 2. (confusion) Verwirrung f

disaster [dɪ·ˈzæs·tər] n Katastrophe f a. fig

disastrous [dɪ·ˈzæs·trəs] adj katastrophal

disband [dɪs·ˈbænd] I. vi sich auflösen II. vt (meeting, club) auflösen

disbelief [ˌdɪs·bɪ·ˈlif] n Unglaube m

disbelieve [ˌdɪs·bɪ·ˈliv] vt form **to ~ sb** jdm nicht glauben; **to ~ sth** etw bezweifeln

disc [dɪsk] n see **disk**

discard [ˈdɪs·kard] vt 1. (throw away) wegwerfen 2. CARDS abwerfen

'disc brake n Scheibenbremse f

discern [dɪ·ˈsɜrn] vt form wahrnehmen

discernible [dɪ·ˈsɜr·nə·bəl] adj wahrnehmbar, erkennbar

discerning [dɪ·ˈsɜr·nɪŋ] adj urteilsfähig; (palate) fein; (reader) kritisch

discernment [dɪ·ˈsɜrn·mənt] n (good judgment) Urteilskraft f

discharge I. vt [dɪs·ˈtʃardʒ] 1. (release) entlassen (**from** aus +dat); (soldier) verabschieden 2. (emit) absondern; (sewage) ablassen 3. (pay off: debt) begleichen II. vi [dɪs·ˈtʃardʒ] (pour out) sich ergießen; (wound) eitern III. n [ˈdɪs·tʃardʒ] 1. (of person) Entlassung f 2. (of liquid) Ausströmen nt kein pl 3. (liquid emitted) Ausfluss m kein pl; (from wound) Absonderung f

disciple [dɪ·ˈsaɪ·pəl] n Anhänger(in) m(f); (of Jesus) Jünger m

disciplinary [ˈdɪs·ə·plə·ner·i] adj Disziplinar-

discipline [ˈdɪs·ə·plɪn] I. n Disziplin f II. vt (punish) bestrafen

'disc jockey n Diskjockey m

disclaim [dɪs·ˈkleɪm] vt abstreiten; (responsibility) ablehnen

disclaimer [dɪs·ˈkleɪ·mər] n Verzichtserklärung f

disclose [dɪs·ˈkloʊz] vt 1. (reveal) bekannt geben 2. (uncover) enthüllen

disclosure [dɪs·ˈkloʊ·ʒər] n form (of information) Bekanntgabe f; (of secret) Enthüllung f

disco [ˈdɪs·koʊ] n short for **discotheque** Disco f, Disko f

discolor [dɪs·ˈkʌl·ər] I. vi sich verfärben II. vt verfärben

discomfort [dɪsˈkʌm·fərt] *n* 1. (*slight pain*) Beschwerden *pl* 2. (*inconvenience*) Unannehmlichkeit *f*

disconcert [ˌdɪs·kənˈsɜrt] *vt* beunruhigen

disconnect [ˌdɪs·kəˈnekt] *vt* trennen; (*electricity, gas, phone*) abstellen

disconnected [ˌdɪs·kəˈnek·tɪd] *adj* 1. (*turned off*) [ab]getrennt; (*left without supply*) abgestellt 2. (*incoherent: speech*) zusammenhang[s]los

disconsolate [dɪsˈkan·sə·lət] *adj* (*dejected*) niedergeschlagen; (*inconsolable*) untröstlich

discontent [ˌdɪs·kənˈtent] *n* Unzufriedenheit *f*

discontented [ˌdɪs·kənˈten·tɪd] *adj* unzufrieden (**with** mit +*dat*)

discontinue [ˌdɪs·kənˈtɪn·ju] *vt* abbrechen; (*product*) auslaufen lassen; (*service*) einstellen; (*visits*) aufgeben

discord [ˈdɪs·kord] *n* 1. *form* Uneinigkeit *f*, Zwietracht *f* 2. MUS Disharmonie *f*

discordant [dɪsˈkor·dənt] *adj* 1. (*entgegengesetzt*) entgegengesetzt; (*views*) gegensätzlich 2. MUS disharmonisch

discotheque [ˈdɪs·kə·tek] *n* Diskothek *f*

discount I. *n* [ˈdɪs·kaʊnt] Rabatt *m*; ~ **for cash** Skonto *nt o m* II. *vt* [dɪsˈkaʊnt] 1. (*disregard*) unberücksichtigt lassen; (*possibility*) nicht berücksichtigen; (*testimony*) nicht einbeziehen 2. (*reduce: article*) herabsetzen; (*price*) reduzieren

discourage [dɪsˈkɜr·ɪdʒ] *vt* 1. (*dishearten*) entmutigen 2. (*dissuade*) **to ~ sth** von etw *dat* abraten; **to ~ sb from doing sth** jdm davon abraten, etw zu tun

discouragement [dɪsˈkɜr·ɪdʒ·mənt] *n* 1. (*feeling*) Mutlosigkeit *f* 2. (*deterrence*) Abschreckung *f*; (*dissuasion*) Abraten *nt*

discouraging [dɪsˈkɜr·ɪdʒ·ɪŋ] *adj* entmutigend

discourteous [dɪsˈkɜr·ti·əs] *adj form* unhöflich

discover [dɪsˈkʌv·ər] *vt* 1. (*find out*) herausfinden 2. (*find first*) entdecken *a. fig* 3. (*find*) finden

discovery [dɪsˈkʌv·ə·ri] *n* Entdeckung *f* *a. fig*

discredit [dɪsˈkred·ɪt] I. *vt* 1. (*disgrace*) in Verruf bringen, diskreditieren 2. (*cause to appear false*) unglaubwürdig machen II. *n* Misskredit *m*

discreet [dɪsˈskrit] *adj* 1. (*unobtrusive*) diskret; (*color, pattern*) dezent 2. (*tactful*) taktvoll

discrepancy [dɪsˈskrep·ən·si] *n form* Diskrepanz *f*

discretion [dɪsˈskreʃ·ən] *n* 1. (*behavior*) Diskretion *f* 2. (*good judgment*) **to use one's ~** nach eigenem Ermessen handeln

discriminate [dɪsˈskrɪm·ə·neɪt] *vi* 1. (*differentiate*) unterscheiden 2. (*be prejudiced*) diskriminieren; **to ~ in favor of sb** jdn bevorzugen; **to ~ against sb** jdn diskriminieren

discriminating [dɪsˈskrɪm·ə·neɪ·tɪŋ] *adj approv* kritisch; (*palate*) fein

discrimination [dɪsˌskrɪm·ɪˈneɪ·ʃən] *n* 1. (*prejudice*) Diskriminierung *f* 2. (*taste*) [kritisches] Urteilsvermögen

discriminatory [dɪsˈskrɪm·ɪ·nə·tɔr·i] *adj* diskriminierend

discus <*pl* -es> [ˈdɪs·kəs] *n* SPORT Diskus *m*; (*event*) Diskuswerfen *nt*

discuss [dɪsˈskʌs] *vt* 1. (*talk about*) besprechen 2. (*debate*) erörtern, diskutieren

discussion [dɪsˈskʌʃ·ən] *n* Diskussion *f*

disdain [dɪsˈdeɪn] I. *n* Verachtung *f* II. *vt* (*despise*) verachten; (*reject*) verschmähen

disdainful [dɪsˈdeɪn·fəl] *adj form* verächtlich

disease [dɪˈziz] *n* Krankheit *f a. fig*

diseased [dɪˈzizd] *adj* krank; (*plant*) befallen

disembark [ˌdɪs·ɪmˈbark] *vi* von Bord gehen

disentangle [ˌdɪs·ɪnˈtæŋ·gəl] *vt* entwirren; *fig* herauslösen (**from** aus +*dat*); **to ~ oneself** sich befreien

disfavor [ˌdɪsˈfeɪ·vər] *n* Missfallen *nt*

disfigure [dɪsˈfɪg·jər] *vt* entstellen

disfigurement [dɪsˈfɪg·jər·mənt] *n* Entstellung *f*

disgrace [dɪsˈgreɪs] I. *n* Schande *f* II. *vt* Schande bringen über +*akk*

disgraceful [dɪsˈgreɪs·fəl] *adj* schändlich;

(*behavior*) skandalös

disgruntled [dɪsˈɡrʌntəld] *adj* verstimmt

disguise [dɪsˈɡaɪz] **I.** *vt* verbergen; (*voice*) verstellen; **to ~ oneself** sich verkleiden **II.** *n* (*for body*) Verkleidung *f;* (*for face*) Maske *f;* **in ~** verkleidet

disgust [dɪsˈɡʌst] **I.** *n* **1.** (*revulsion*) Ekel *m* **2.** (*indignation*) Empörung *f;* **in ~** entrüstet, empört **II.** *vt* **1.** (*sicken*) anwidern, anekeln **2.** (*appall*) entrüsten, empören

disgusted [dɪsˈɡʌs·tɪd] *adj* **1.** (*sickened*) angeekelt, angewidert **2.** (*indignant*) empört, entrüstet

disgusting [dɪsˈɡʌs·tɪŋ] *adj* **1.** (*repulsive*) widerlich **2.** (*unacceptable*) empörend

dish <*pl* -es> [dɪʃ] *n* **1.** (*for serving*) Schale *f;* (*plate*) Teller *m* **2.** (*after meal*) **the ~es** *pl* das Geschirr *kein pl;* **to do** [*or* **wash**] **the ~es** [ab]spülen **3.** (*meal*) Gericht *nt* **4.** TELEC Schüssel *f*

◆**dish out** *vt* **1.** (*give freely*) großzügig verteilen (**to** an +*akk*) **2.** (*serve: food*) servieren

◆**dish up** *vt fam* auftischen

'**dishcloth** *n* Geschirrtuch *nt*

dishearten [dɪsˈhar·tən] *vt* entmutigen

disheveled [dɪˈʃev·əld] *adj* unordentlich; (*hair*) zerzaust

dishonest [dɪsˈan·ɪst] *adj* unehrlich

dishonesty [dɪsˈan·əs·ti] *n* Unehrlichkeit *f*

dishonor [dɪsˈan·ər] *form* **I.** *n* Schande *f* **II.** *vt* **1.** (*disgrace*) **to ~ sb/sth** dem Ansehen einer Person/Sache schaden **2.** (*not respect: agreement*) verletzen; (*promise*) nicht einlösen

dishonorable [dɪsˈan·ər·ə·bəl] *adj* unehrenhaft

'**dishtowel** *n* Geschirrtuch *nt*

'**dishwasher** *n* **1.** (*machine*) Geschirrspülmaschine *f* **2.** (*person*) Tellerwäscher(in) *m(f)*

'**dishwater** *n* Spülwasser *nt a. fig*

disillusion [ˌdɪs·ɪˈlu·ʒən] **I.** *vt* desillusionieren **II.** *n* Ernüchterung *f*

disillusioned [ˌdɪs·ɪˈlu·ʒənd] *adj* desillusioniert

disinclination [ˌdɪs·ɪn·klɪˈneɪ·ʃən] *n* Abneigung *f*

disinclined [ˌdɪs·ɪnˈklaɪnd] *adj* abgeneigt

disinfect [ˌdɪs·ɪnˈfekt] *vt* desinfizieren

disinfectant [ˌdɪs·ɪnˈfek·tənt] *n* Desinfektionsmittel *nt*

disingenuous [ˌdɪs·ɪnˈdʒen·ju·əs] *adj form* unaufrichtig

disinherit [ˌdɪs·ɪnˈher·ɪt] *vt* enterben

disintegrate [dɪsˈɪn·tə·ɡreɪt] *vi* zerfallen

disintegration [dɪs·ˌɪn·tə·ˈɡreɪ·ʃən] *n* Zerfall *m*

disinterested [dɪsˈɪn·trɪ·stɪd] *adj* (*impartial*) unparteiisch

disjointed [dɪsˈdʒɔɪn·tɪd] *adj* zusammenhanglos

disk, disc [dɪsk] *n* **1.** (*object*) Scheibe *f;* MED Bandscheibe *f* **2.** MUS (*CD*) CD *f;* (*record*) [Schall]platte *f* **3.** COMPUT Diskette *f;* **~ drive** Laufwerk *nt*

'**disk brake** *n see* **disc brake**

'**disk jockey** *n see* **disc jockey**

dislike [dɪsˈlaɪk] **I.** *vt* nicht mögen; **to ~ doing sth** etw nicht gern tun **II.** *n* Abneigung *f* (**of/for** gegen +*akk*)

dislocate [dɪsˈloʊ·keɪt] *vt* **to ~ sth** sich *dat* etw ausrenken

dislodge [dɪsˈladʒ] *vt* (*thing*) lösen; (*person*) verdrängen

disloyal [dɪsˈlɔɪ·əl] *adj* illoyal (**to** gegenüber +*dat*)

dismal [ˈdɪz·məl] *adj* **1.** (*dreary*) düster, trostlos; (*outlook, weather*) trüb **2.** (*inadequate: performance*) kläglich

dismantle [dɪsˈmæn·təl] *vt* zerlegen

dismay [dɪsˈmeɪ] **I.** *n* Bestürzung *f* **II.** *vt* schockieren

dismayed [dɪsˈmeɪd] *adj* bestürzt; (*expression*) betroffen

dismember [dɪsˈmem·bər] *vt* zerstückeln

dismiss [dɪsˈmɪs] *vt* **1.** (*ignore*) abtun; **to ~ a thought** [**from one's mind**] sich *dat* einen Gedanken aus dem Kopf schlagen **2.** (*send away*) wegschicken; (*class*) gehen lassen **3.** (*fire*) entlassen

dismissal [dɪsˈmɪs·əl] *n* **1.** (*disregard*) Abtun *nt* **2.** (*firing*) Entlassung *f*

dismissive [dɪsˈmɪs·ɪv] *adj* geringschätzig

dismount [dɪs·ˈmaʊnt] *vi* absteigen

disobedience [ˌdɪs·ə·ˈbiː·di·əns] *n* Ungehorsam *m*

disobedient [ˌdɪs·ə·ˈbiː·di·ənt] *adj* ungehorsam

disobey [ˌdɪs·ə·ˈbeɪ] *vt* (*person*) nicht gehorchen; (*orders*) nicht befolgen; (*rules*) sich nicht halten an +*akk*

disorder [dɪs·ˈɔr·dər] *n* 1. (*disarray*) Unordnung *f* 2. MED [Funktions]störung *f* 3. (*riot*) Aufruhr *m*

disorderly [dɪs·ˈɔr·dər·li] *adj* 1. (*untidy*) unordentlich *m* 2. (*unruly*) aufrührerisch

disorganized [dɪs·ˈɔr·gə·naɪzd] *adj* schlecht organisiert

disorient [dɪs·ˈɔr·i·ent] *vt usu passive* 1. (*lose bearings*) to be/get [totally] ~ed [völlig] die Orientierung verloren haben/verlieren 2. (*be confused*) to be ~ed orientierungslos sein

disown [dɪs·ˈoʊn] *vt* verleugnen; *hum a.* nicht mehr kennen

disparaging [dɪ·ˈsper·ɪdʒ·ɪŋ] *adj* geringschätzig

disparity [dɪ·ˈsper·ɪ·t̬i] *n* Ungleichheit *f*

dispassionate [dɪs·ˈpæʃ·ə·nɪt] *adj* objektiv

dispatch [dɪ·ˈspætʃ] I. *n* <*pl* -es> (*sending*) Verschicken *nt;* (*of a person*) Entsendung *f* II. *vt* (*thing*) senden; (*person*) entsenden

dispel <-ll-> [dɪ·ˈspel] *vt* (*mist*) auflösen; (*rumors*) zerstreuen

dispensable [dɪ·ˈspen·sə·bəl] *adj* entbehrlich

dispensary [dɪ·ˈspen·sə·ri] *n* [Krankenhaus]apotheke *f*

dispense [dɪ·ˈspens] I. *vt* austeilen; (*medicine*) ausgeben II. *vi* to ~ with sth auf etw *akk* verzichten

dispenser [dɪ·ˈspen·sər] *n* Automat *m*

dispersal [dɪ·ˈspɜr·səl] *n* 1. (*scattering*) Zerstreuung *f;* (*of a crowd*) Auflösung *f* 2. (*wide distribution*) Verstreutheit *f*

disperse [dɪ·ˈspɜrs] I. *vt* 1. (*dispel*) auflösen; (*crowd*) zerstreuen 2. (*distribute*) verteilen II. *vi* (*crowd*) auseinandergehen; (*mist*) sich auflösen

dispirited [dɪ·ˈspɪr·ɪ·t̬ɪd] *adj* entmutigt

displace [dɪs·ˈpleɪs] *vt* 1. (*force out*) vertreiben 2. (*replace*) ersetzen

displaced person *n* Heimatlose(r) *f(m)*

display [dɪ·ˈspleɪ] I. *vt* 1. (*on board*) aushängen; (*in store window*) auslegen 2. (*demonstrate: strength*) zeigen II. *n* 1. (*in museum, store*) Auslage *f;* to be on ~ ausgestellt sein 2. (*demonstration*) Demonstration *f* 3. COMPUT Display *nt*

display case, display cabinet *n* Vitrine *f*

displease [dɪs·ˈpliːz] *vt* to ~ sb jdm missfallen

displeasure [dɪs·ˈpleʒ·ər] *n* Missfallen *nt*

disposable [dɪ·ˈspoʊ·zə·bəl] *adj* 1. (*articles*) Wegwerf- *m* 2. FIN (*income*) verfügbar

disposal [dɪ·ˈspoʊ·zəl] *n* 1. Beseitigung *f;* (*of waste*) Entsorgung *f* 2. (*control*) Verfügung *f;* to be at sb's ~ zu jds Verfügung stehen

dispose of *vt* (*get rid of*) beseitigen; (*sell*) veräußern

disposed [dɪ·ˈspoʊzd] *adj* to be well ~ toward sb/sth jdm/etw wohlgesinnt sein

disposition [ˌdɪs·pə·ˈzɪʃ·ən] *n* 1. (*nature*) Art *f* 2. (*tendency*) Veranlagung *f*

dispossess [ˌdɪs·pə·ˈzes] *vt* enteignen

disproportionate [ˌdɪs·prə·ˈpɔr·ʃə·nɪt] *adj* unangemessen

disprove [dɪs·ˈpruv] *vt* widerlegen

disputable [dɪ·ˈspju·t̬ə·bəl] *adj* strittig

dispute [dɪ·ˈspjut] I. *vt* 1. (*argue*) sich streiten über +*akk* 2. (*oppose*) bestreiten II. *vi* streiten III. *n* (*argument*) Streit *m;* to be beyond ~ außer Frage stehen

disqualification [dɪs·ˌkwal·ə·fɪ·ˈkeɪ·ʃən] *n* Ausschluss *m;* SPORT Disqualifikation *f*

disqualify <-ie-> [dɪs·ˈkwal·ə·faɪ] *vt* ausschließen; SPORT disqualifizieren

disregard [ˌdɪs·rɪ·ˈgard] I. *vt* ignorieren II. *n* Gleichgültigkeit *f;* (*for a rule, the law*) Missachtung *f*

disrepair [ˌdɪs·rɪ·ˈper] *n* Baufälligkeit *f;* to fall into ~ verfallen

disreputable [dɪs·ˈrep·jə·t̬ə·bəl] *adj* verrufen

disrepute [ˌdɪs·rɪ·ˈpjut] *n* Verruf *m kein pl*

disrespect [ˌdɪs·rɪ·ˈspekt] I. *n* Respektlo-

sigkeit f II. vt fam beleidigen

disrespectful [ˌdɪs·rɪ·ˈspekt·fəl] adj respektlos

disrupt [dɪs·ˈrʌpt] vt stören

disruption [dɪs·ˈrʌp·ʃən] n 1. (interruption) Unterbrechung f 2. (disrupting) Störung f

disruptive [dɪs·ˈrʌp·tɪv] adj störend

dissatisfaction [dɪs·ˌsæt·ɪs·ˈfæk·ʃən] n Unzufriedenheit f

dissatisfied [dɪs·ˈsæt·ɪs·faɪd] adj unzufrieden

dissect [dɪ·ˈsekt] vt 1. (cut open) sezieren 2. fig analysieren

dissent [dɪ·ˈsent] I. n 1. (disagreement) Meinungsverschiedenheit f 2. (protest) Widerspruch m II. vi dagegen stimmen; (disagree) anderer Meinung sein

dissenter [dɪ·ˈsen·tər] n Andersdenkende(r) f(m); POL Dissident(in) m(f)

dissertation [ˌdɪs·ər·ˈteɪ·ʃən] n Dissertation f

disservice [ˌdɪs·ˈsɜr·vɪs] n to do sb a ~ jdm einen schlechten Dienst erweisen

dissident [ˈdɪs·ɪ·dənt] I. n Dissident(in) m(f) II. adj regimekritisch

dissimilar [ˌdɪ·ˈsɪm·ɪ·lər] adj unterschiedlich

dissimilarity [ˌdɪ·sɪm·ɪ·ˈler·ɪ·ti] n Unterschied m

dissipate [ˈdɪs·ɪ·peɪt] I. vi allmählich verschwinden; (crowd, mist) sich auflösen II. vt 1. (disperse) auflösen 2. (squander) verschwenden

dissipated [ˈdɪs·ɪ·peɪ·tɪd] adj liter ausschweifend

dissociate [dɪ·ˈsoʊ·ʃi·eɪt] vt getrennt betrachten; to ~ oneself from sb/sth sich von jdm/etw distanzieren

dissolute [ˈdɪs·ə·lut] adj liter (life) ausschweifend; (person) zügellos

dissolve [dɪ·ˈzɑlv] I. vi 1. (in liquid) sich auflösen 2. (subside) to ~ in[to] tears in Tränen ausbrechen II. vt 1. (liquefy) [auf]lösen 2. (annul) auflösen; (marriage) scheiden

dissuade [dɪ·ˈsweɪd] vt abbringen

distance [ˈdɪs·təns] I. n (to a place) Strecke f; (between places) Entfernung f; in the ~ in der Ferne; from [or at] a distance von weitem II. vt to ~ oneself

sich distanzieren

'distance learning n Fernunterricht m

distant [ˈdɪs·tənt] adj 1. (far away) fern; fig (look) abwesend; (relative) entfernt 2. (aloof) unnahbar

distantly [ˈdɪs·tənt·li] adv ~ related entfernt verwandt

distaste [dɪs·ˈteɪst] n Widerwille m

distasteful [dɪs·ˈteɪst·fəl] adj abscheulich

distill [dɪ·ˈstɪl] vt CHEM destillieren; (brandy) brennen

distiller [dɪ·ˈstɪl·ər] n 1. (company) Destillerie f 2. (person) Destillateur m

distillery [dɪ·ˈstɪl·ə·ri] n Brennerei f

distinct [dɪ·ˈstɪŋkt] adj 1. (different) verschieden; as ~ from sth im Unterschied zu etw dat 2. (clear) deutlich

distinction [dɪ·ˈstɪŋk·ʃən] n 1. (difference) Unterschied m 2. (eminence) of |great| ~ von hohem Rang 3. (award) Auszeichnung f; with ~ ausgezeichnet

distinctive [dɪ·ˈstɪŋk·tɪv] adj charakteristisch

distinguish [dɪ·ˈstɪŋ·gwɪʃ] I. vi unterscheiden II. vt 1. (tell apart) unterscheiden 2. (discern) ausmachen [können] 3. (excel) to ~ oneself in sth sich in etw dat auszeichnen

distinguished [dɪ·ˈstɪŋ·gwɪʃt] adj 1. (eminent: career) hervorragend; (person) von hohem Rang 2. (stylish) distinguiert

distort [dɪ·ˈstɔrt] vt 1. (twist) verzerren 2. fig verdrehen

distortion [dɪ·ˈstɔr·ʃən] n 1. (twisting) Verzerrung f 2. fig Verdrehung f

distract [dɪ·ˈstrækt] vt ablenken (from von +dat)

distracted [dɪ·ˈstræk·tɪd] adj verwirrt; (worried) besorgt

distraction [dɪ·ˈstræk·ʃən] n 1. (disturbance) Störung f 2. (diversion) Ablenkung f

distraught [dɪ·ˈstrɔt] adj verzweifelt, außer sich dat

distress [dɪ·ˈstres] I. n 1. (pain) Leid nt; (anguish) Kummer m, Sorge f 2. (trouble) Not f II. vt quälen

distressed [dɪ·ˈstrest] adj 1. (unhappy) bekümmert 2. (shocked) erschüttert (at

distressing über +*dat* **3.** (*old-looking: fabric*) verwaschen; (*jeans, furniture*) Used-Look-

distressing [dɪ·'stres·ɪŋ], **distressful** [dɪ·'stres·fəl] *adj* **1.** (*worrying*) erschreckend **2.** (*painful*) schmerzlich

distribute [dɪ·'strɪb·jut] *vt* verteilen; (*goods*) vertreiben

distribution [ˌdɪs·trɪ·'bju·ʃən] *n* **1.** (*sharing*) Verteilung *f* **2.** (*scattering*) Verbreitung *f* **3.** ECON Vertrieb *m*

distributor [dɪ·'strɪb·jə·tər] *n* **1.** COMM Vertriebsgesellschaft *f* **2.** AUTO Verteiler *m*

district ['dɪs·trɪkt] *n* (*area*) Gebiet *nt*; (*within a town / country*) Bezirk *m*

district at'torney *n* Staatsanwalt, Staatsanwältin *m, f*

district 'court *n* [Bundes]bezirksgericht *nt*

District of Columbia *n* amerikanischer Regierungsbezirk

distrust [dɪs·'trʌst] **I.** *vt* misstrauen +*dat* **II.** *n* Misstrauen *nt* (*of* gegen +*akk*)

distrustful [dɪs·'trʌst·fəl] *adj* misstrauisch

disturb [dɪ·'stɜrb] *vt* **1.** (*interrupt*) stören; "**do not ~**" „bitte nicht stören" **2.** (*worry*) beunruhigen

disturbance [dɪ·'stɜr·bəns] *n* **1.** (*annoyance*) Belästigung *f* **2.** (*riot*) **to cause a ~** Unruhe stiften

disturbed [dɪ·'stɜrbd] *adj* **1.** (*worried*) beunruhigt **2.** PSYCH (*geistig*) verwirrt; **mentally ~** psychisch gestört

disturbing [dɪ·'stɜr·bɪŋ] *adj* beunruhigend

disuse [dɪs·'jus] *n* Nichtgebrauch *m*; **to fall into ~** nicht mehr benutzt werden

ditch [dɪtʃ] **I.** *n* <*pl* -es> Graben *m* **II.** *vt fam* **1.** (*discard*) wegwerfen; (*proposal, job*) aufgeben; (*car*) stehen lassen **2.** (*abandon: person*) versetzen **3.** (*plane*) im Bach landen **III.** *vi* AVIAT auf dem Wasser landen

dither ['dɪð·ər] **I.** *n* **in a ~** ganz aufgeregt **II.** *vi* schwanken

ditto ['dɪt·ou] *adv* (*likewise*) dito; (*me too*) ich auch

divan [dɪ·'van] *n* Diwan *m*

dive [daɪv] **I.** *n* **1.** (*into water*) [Kopf]sprung *m* **2.** (*by plane*) Sturzflug *m* **3.** (*drop in price*) [Preis]sturz *m* **4.** *fam*

(*dingy place*) Spelunke *f* **II.** *vi* <dived *or* dove, dived *or* dove> **1.** (*into water*) einen Kopfsprung ins Wasser machen; (*underwater*) tauchen **2.** (*plane*) einen Sturzflug machen **3.** (*bird*) Taucher *m* (*move quickly*) **to ~ for sth** nach etw *dat* hechten

diver ['daɪ·vər] *n* **1.** (*underwater*) Taucher(in) *m(f)*; SPORT Turmspringer(in) *m(f)* **2.** (*bird*) Taucher *m*

diverge [dɪ·'vɜrdʒ] *vi* auseinandergehen

divergence [dɪ·'vɜr·dʒəns] *n* **1.** (*difference*) Divergenz *f* **2.** (*deviation*) Abweichung *f*

divergent [dɪ·'vɜr·dʒənt] *adj* (*differing*) abweichend; (*opinions*) auseinandergehend

diverse [dɪ·'vɜrs] *adj* **1.** (*varied*) vielfältig **2.** (*not alike*) unterschiedlich

diversification [dɪ·ˌvɜr·sɪ·fɪ·'keɪ·ʃən] *n* Diversifikation *f*

diversify <-ie-> [dɪ·'vɜr·sɪ·faɪ] **I.** *vi* vielfältiger werden **II.** *vt* umfangreicher machen

diversion [dɪ·'vɜr·ʃən] *n* **1.** (*rerouting*) Verlegung *f*; (*of traffic*) Umleitung *f* **2.** (*distraction*) Ablenkung *f*

diversity [dɪ·'vɜr·sɪ·ti] *n* Vielfalt *f*

divert [dɪ·'vɜrt] *vt* **1.** (*reroute*) verlegen; (*traffic*) umleiten **2.** (*reallocate: funds*) anders einsetzen **3.** (*distract*) ablenken

diverting [dɪ·'vɜr·tɪŋ] *adj* unterhaltsam

divest [dɪ·'vest] *vt* **1.** (*deprive*) berauben **2.** (*sell*) verkaufen

divide [dɪ·'vaɪd] **I.** *n* **1.** (*gulf*) Kluft *f* **2.** GEOG (*watershed*) Wasserscheide *f* **II.** *vt* **1.** (*split*) teilen **2.** (*share: profits*) aufteilen; **to ~ sth equally** [*or* **evenly**] etw in gleichen Teilen aufteilen **3.** MATH teilen (**by** durch +*akk*) **4.** (*separate*) trennen **III.** *vi* sich teilen

♦ **divide off** *vt* [ab]teilen

♦ **divide up I.** *vt* aufteilen **II.** *vi* sich teilen

divided [dɪ·'vaɪ·dɪd] *adj* uneinig

divided 'highway *n* Schnellstraße *f*

dividend ['dɪv·ɪ·dend] *n* FIN Dividende *f*; *fig* **to pay ~s** sich bezahlt machen

dividers [dɪ·'vaɪ·dərz] *npl* [**a pair of**] ~ [ein] Zirkel *m*

di'viding line *n* Trennlinie *f*

divine [dɪ·'vaɪn] **I.** *adj* **1.** (*of God*) gött-

lich 2. (*splendid*) himmlisch II. *vt* erraten; (*future*) vorhersehen

diving ['daɪ·vɪŋ] *n* 1. (*into water*) Tauchen *nt*; SPORT Turmspringen *nt* 2. (*underwater*) Tauchen *nt*

'**diving board** *n* Sprungbrett *nt*

'**diving suit** *n* Taucheranzug *m*

di'vining rod *n* Wünschelrute *f*

divisible [dɪ·'vɪz·ə·bəl] *adj* teilbar (**by** durch +*akk*)

division [dɪ·'vɪʒ·ən] *n* 1. (*sharing*) Verteilung *f* 2. (*breakup*) Teilung *f* 3. MATH Division *f* 4. (*section*) Teil *m* 5. (*department*) Abteilung *f* 6. (*league*) Liga *f* 7. (*disagreement*) Meinungsverschiedenheit *f*

divisive [dɪ·'vaɪ·sɪv] *adj* entzweiend

divorce [dɪ·'vɔrs] I. *n* LAW Scheidung *f* II. *vt* **to ~ sb** [*or* **get ~d from sb**] sich von jdm scheiden lassen III. *vi* sich scheiden lassen

divorcé [dɪ·'vɔr·seɪ] *n* Geschiedener *m*

divorced [dɪ·'vɔrst] *adj* geschieden

divorcée [dɪ·'vɔr·seɪ] *n* Geschiedene *f*

divulge [dɪ·'vʌldʒ] *vt* enthüllen; (*information*) weitergeben

dizziness ['dɪz·ɪ·nɪs] *n* Schwindel *m*

dizzy ['dɪz·i] *adj* 1. (*unsteady*) schwindlig; **~ spells** Schwindelanfälle *pl* 2. (*rapid*) atemberaubend 3. *fam* (*scatterbrained*) dumm, einfältig

DJ ['di·dʒeɪ] *n abbr of* **disc jockey** DJ *m*

DMV [ˌdi·em·'vi] *n abbr of* **Department of Motor Vehicles** Kfz-Zulassungsstelle *f*

DNA [ˌdi·en·'eɪ] *n abbr of* **deoxyribonucleic acid** DNS *f*

do [du] I. *aux vb* <does, did, done> 1. (*negating verb*) **Fred ~esn't like olives** Fred mag keine Oliven; **I ~n't want to go yet!** ich will noch nicht gehen! 2. (*forming question*) **~ you like children?** magst du Kinder?; **what did you say?** was hast du gesagt? 3. (*for emphasis*) **can I come? — please ~!** kann ich mitkommen? — aber bitte!; **you ~ look tired** du siehst wirklich müde aus 4. (*replacing verb*) **she runs much faster than he ~es** sie läuft viel schneller als er; **who ate the cake? — I**

did!/didn't! wer hat den Kuchen gegessen? — ich!/ich nicht!; **... so ~ I ...** ich auch II. *vt* <does, did, done> 1. tun, machen; **that was a stupid thing to ~** das war dumm!; **what did you ~ with my coat?** wo hast du meinen Mantel hingetan?; **what ~es your father ~?** was macht dein Vater beruflich?; **where ~ you get your hair done?** zu welchem Friseur gehst du?; **let me ~ the talking** überlass mir das Reden 2. *fam* (*finish*) **are you done?** bist du jetzt fertig? 3. (*travel at*) **to ~ 80 80** fahren 4. (*suffice*) **to ~ sb** jdm genügen 5. *fam* (*cheat*) **to ~ sb out of sth** jdn übers Ohr hauen 6. *vulg, sl* (*have sex with*) **to ~ it with sb** mit jdm schlafen *euph* ▸ **that ~es it!** so, das war's jetzt! III. *vi* <does, did, done> 1. (*behave*) tun; **~ as you're told** tu, was man dir sagt; **to ~ well to do sth** gut daran tun, etw zu tun 2. (*fare*) **sb is ~ing fine** jdm geht es gut; **mother and baby are ~ing well** Mutter und Kind sind wohlauf; **our daughter is ~ing well in school** unsere Tochter ist gut in der Schule 3. (*suffice*) **that'll ~** das ist o. k. so; (*angrily*) jetzt reicht's aber!; **will this room ~?** ist dieses Zimmer o. k. für Sie? ▸ **how ~ you ~?** *form* (*as introduction*) angenehm IV. *n* 1. **the ~s and ~n'ts** was man tun und was man nicht tun sollte 2. *fam* (*party*) Fete *f*

◆**do away with** *vi* 1. (*discard*) abschaffen 2. *fam* (*kill*) um die Ecke bringen

◆**do up** *vt* 1. (*dress*) **to ~ oneself up** sich zurechtmachen 2. (*adorn*) herrichten; (*house*) renovieren 3. (*close*) zumachen

◆**do with** *vi* 1. *fam* (*need*) brauchen; **I could ~ with some sleep** ich könnte jetzt etwas Schlaf gebrauchen 2. (*be related to*) um etw *akk* gehen; **to have nothing to ~ with sth** mit etw *dat* nichts zu tun haben 3. (*concern*) **sth has nothing to ~ with sb** etw geht jdn nichts an

◆**do without** *vi* 1. (*not have*) auskommen ohne 2. (*prefer not to have*) verzichten auf +*akk*

docile ['das·əl] *adj* sanftmütig

dock¹ [dak] I. n 1. (*wharf*) Dock nt; **the ~s** pl die Hafenanlagen pl; **dry ~** Trockendock nt 2. (*pier*) Kai m II. vi 1. NAUT anlegen 2. AEROSP andocken (**with** an +akk)

dock² [dak] n LAW Anklagebank f

dock³ [dak] vt 1. (*reduce*) kürzen; (*deduct*) abziehen 2. (*cut off*) [den Schwanz] kupieren

docker ['dak·ər] n Hafenarbeiter(in) m(f)

'dockyard n Werft f

doctor ['dak·tər] I. n 1. (*medic*) Arzt, Ärztin m, f; **good morning, D~ Smith** guten Morgen, Herr/Frau Doktor Smith 2. (*academic*) Doktor m II. vt 1. (*falsify*) fälschen, frisieren 2. (*poison*) vergiften

doctorate ['dak·tər·ət] n Doktor[titel] m

doctrine ['dak·trɪn] n 1. (*set of beliefs*) Doktrin f 2. (*belief*) Grundsatz m

document ['dak·jə·mənt] I. n Dokument nt II. vt dokumentieren

documentary [ˌdak·jə·'men·tə·ri] I. n Dokumentation f, Dokumentarfilm m II. adj dokumentarisch, Dokumentar-

doddering ['dad·ər·ɪŋ] adj fam tattrig

dodge [dadʒ] I. vt 1. (*avoid: blow*) ausweichen +dat 2. (*evade*) sich entziehen; (*military service*) sich drücken vor; (*question*) ausweichend beantworten II. vi ausweichen III. n fam Trick m

doe [doʊ] n 1. (*deer*) Hirschkuh f, [Reh]geiß f 2. (*hare or rabbit*) Häsin f

does [dʌz] vt, vi, aux vb 3rd pers. sing of **do**

doesn't ['dʌz·ənt] = **does not** see **do** I, II

dog [dɔg] I. n 1. (*canine*) Hund m 2. pej sl (*ugly woman*) Bratze f II. vt <-gg-> 1. (*follow*) ständig verfolgen 2. (*beset*) begleiten

'dog biscuit n Hundekuchen m

'dog collar n 1. (*for dog*) Hundehalsband nt 2. fam (*of a minister*) Halskragen m [eines Geistlichen]

'dog-eared adj mit Eselsohren

dogged ['dɔ·gɪd] adj verbissen, zäh

doggerel ['dɔ·gər·əl] n Knittelvers m

'doghouse n Hundehütte f ▶ **to be** in **the** ~ in Ungnade gefallen sein

dogma ['dɔg·mə] n Dogma nt

dogmatic [dɔg·'mæt·ɪk] adj dogmatisch

dog-'tired adj fam hundemüde

doing ['du·ɪŋ] n 1. (*sb's work*) **to be sb's ~** jds Werk sein; **to take some ~** ganz schön anstrengend sein 2. pl (*activities*) **~s** Tätigkeiten pl

do-it-yourself [ˌdu·ɪt·jər·'self] n Heimwerken nt

doldrums ['doʊl·drəmz] npl fig **to be in the ~** 1. (*in low spirits*) deprimiert sein; (*in stagnant state*) in einer Flaute stecken

dole [doʊl] vt **to ~ out** sparsam austeilen

doll [dal] I. n 1. (*toy*) Puppe f 2. fam (*attractive woman*) Puppe f II. vt **to ~ oneself up** sich herausputzen

dollar ['dal·ər] n Dollar m

dollop ['dal·əp] n Klacks m kein pl

dolly ['dal·i] n 1. TRANSP [Transport]wagen m 2. esp childspeak (*doll*) Püppchen nt

dolphin ['dal·fɪn] n Delphin m

domain [doʊ·'meɪn] n 1. Reich nt, Gebiet nt 2. COMPUT Domäne f; TELEC Domain f

dome [doʊm] n Kuppel f

domestic [də·'mes·tɪk] adj 1. (*household*) häuslich; ~ **appliance** [elektrisches] Haushaltsgerät 2. ECON, POL inländisch, Inland[s]-; ~ **policy** Innenpolitik f; ~ **market** Binnenmarkt m

domesticate [də·'mes·tɪ·keɪt] vt 1. (*tame*) zähmen 2. (*accustom to home life*) häuslich machen

domesticity [ˌdoʊ·me·'stɪs·ɪ·ţi] n Häuslichkeit f, häusliches Leben

domestic 'violence n Gewalt f in der Familie, häusliche Gewalt

domicile ['dam·ə·saɪl] form I. n Wohnsitz m II. vi **to be ~d in ...** in ... ansässig sein

dominance ['dam·ə·nəns] n 1. (*superior position*) Vormacht[stellung] f 2. (*being dominant*) Dominanz f, Vorherrschaft f

dominant ['dam·ə·nənt] adj 1. (*controlling: color, culture*) vorherrschend; (*issue, position*) beherrschend; (*personality*) dominierend 2. BIOL, MUS dominant

dominate ['dam·ə·neɪt] vt 1. beherrschen 2. PSYCH dominieren

domineering [ˌdam·ə·'nɪr·ɪŋ] adj herrschsüchtig, herrisch

domino <pl -es> ['dam·ə·nou] n **1.** (piece) Dominostein m **2.** (game) ~es + sing vb, no art Domino|spiel nt

don [dan] n sl Mafiaboss m

donate ['dou·neɪt] vt, vi spenden (**to** für +akk)

donation [dou·'neɪ·ʃən] n **1.** (contribution) [Geld]spende f; (endowment) Stiftung f; LAW Schenkung f; **charitable ~s** Spenden pl für wohltätige Zwecke **2.** (act of donating) Spenden nt

done [dʌn] pp of **do**

donkey ['dɑŋ·ki] n Esel m a. fig

donor ['dou·nər] n Spender(in) m(f); (of large sums) Stifter(in) m(f); LAW Schenker(in) m(f)

don't [dount] see **do not** see **do** I, II

donut ['dou·nʌt] n see **doughnut**

doodle ['du·dəl] I. vi vor sich akk hinkritzeln II. n Gekritzel nt kein pl

doom [dum] n **1.** (grim destiny) Verhängnis nt kein pl, [schlimmes] Schicksal **2.** (disaster) Unheil nt

doomed [dumd] adj **1.** (destined to end badly) verdammt **2.** (condemned) verurteilt

door [dɔr] n **1.** (entrance) Tür f; **out of ~s** im Freien, draußen **2.** (house) **two ~s away** zwei Häuser weiter; **next ~** nebenan; **~ to** von Tür zu Tür

'doorbell n Türklingel f

'doorframe n Türrahmen m

'doorknob n Türknauf m

'doorman n Portier m

'doormat n **1.** (thing) Fußmatte f, Fußabstreifer m bes südd **2.** fig, pej (person) Waschlappen m

'doorstep n Türstufe f; **right on one's ~** fig direkt vor der Haustür

door-to-'door adj von Haus zu Haus

'doorway n [Tür]eingang m

doozy ['du·zi] n sl (difficult job) **to be a [real] ~** eine Heidenarbeit sein

dope [doup] I. n **1.** fam (illegal drug) Rauschgift nt, Stoff m sl **2.** sl (stupid person) Trottel m II. vt dopen

dopey ['dou·pi] adj **1.** (drowsy) benebelt **2.** pej (stupid) blöd

dorm [dɔrm] n Studentenwohnheim nt

dormant ['dɔr·mənt] adj **1.** (inactive: volcano) untätig **2.** BOT, BIOL **to be ~** ru-

hen; **to lie ~** schlafen; (seeds) ruhen

dormer [dɔr·mər], **dormer window** [dɔr·mər'-] n Mansardenfenster nt

dormitory ['dɔr·mɪ·tɔr·i] n **1.** (student housing) Studentenwohnheim nt **2.** (sleeping quarters) Schlafsaal m

dormouse ['dɔr·maus] n Haselmaus f

dorsal ['dɔr·səl] adj Rücken-

dosage ['dou·sɪdʒ] n (size of dose) Dosis f

dose [dous] I. n (dosage) Dosis f a. fig II. vt [medizinisch] behandeln

dossier ['das·i·eɪ] n Dossier nt

dot [dat] I. n Punkt m; (on material) Tupfen m II. vt <-tt-> **1.** (make a dot) mit einem Punkt versehen **2.** usu passive (scatter) **to be ~ted with sth** mit etw dat übersät sein

doting ['dou·tɪŋ] adj vernarrt

double ['dʌb·əl] I. adj **1.** (twice, two) doppelt; **~ the price** doppelt so teuer; **the number is: six, ~ three, five** die Nummer ist die sechs, zweimal die drei, fünf **2.** (with two parts) Doppel-; (pneumonia) doppelseitig; **~ life** Doppelleben nt II. adv **1.** (twice as much) doppelt so viel; **to charge sb ~** jdm das Doppelte berechnen **2.** (two times) **to see ~** doppelt sehen **3.** (in the middle) **to be bent ~** sich niederbeugen; (with laughter, pain) sich krümmen III. n **1.** (double quantity) das Doppelte [or Zweifache] **2.** (whiskey, gin) Doppelte(r) m **3.** (person) Doppelgänger(in) m(f); FILM Double nt **4.** SPORT **~s** pl Doppel nt; **mixed ~s** gemischtes Doppel **5.** (in baseball) Double m IV. vt **1.** verdoppeln **2.** (fold in two) doppelt nehmen V. vi **1.** (increase twofold) sich verdoppeln **2.** (serve a second purpose) **the kitchen table ~s as my desk** der Küchentisch dient auch als mein Schreibtisch **3.** (in baseball) einen Double schlagen

● **double back** vi kehrtmachen

◆ **double up** vi **1.** (bend over) sich krümmen (**in/with** vor +dat) **2.** (share a room) sich dat ein Zimmer teilen

double-'barreled adj (gun) doppelläufig

double 'bass n Kontrabass m

double 'bed n Doppelbett nt

double-'breasted adj zweireihig

double-'check vt noch einmal überprüfen

double 'chin n Doppelkinn nt

double-'click COMPUT I. vt doppelt anklicken II. vi doppelklicken

double-'cross[1] vt **to ~ sb** mit jdm ein falsches Spiel treiben

double-'cross[2], **double 'cross** n <pl -es> Doppelspiel nt

double-'dealing pej I. n Betrügerei f II. adj betrügerisch

double-'decker n Doppeldecker m

double-'edged adj zweischneidig a. fig

double-'park vt, vi in der zweiten Reihe parken

doubly ['dʌb·li] adv doppelt

doubt [daʊt] I. n 1. (lack of certainty) Zweifel m (**about** an +dat); **no ~** zweifellos; **to cast ~ on sth** etw in Zweifel ziehen 2. (feeling of uncertainty) Ungewissheit f, Bedenken pl; **to have ~s about sth** Zweifel an etw dat haben II. vt **to ~ sb** (mistrust) jdm misstrauen; (not believe) jdm nicht glauben; **to ~ sth** Zweifel an etw dat haben; **to ~ that ...** bezweifeln, dass ...

doubtful ['daʊt·fəl] adj 1. (expressing doubt) zweifelnd 2. (uncertain) unsicher, unschlüssig; **to be ~ about sth** über etw akk im Zweifel sein 3. (questionable) fragwürdig, zweifelhaft

doubtless ['daʊt·lɪs] adv sicherlich

dough [doʊ] n 1. (for baking) Teig m 2. sl (money) Knete f, Kohle f

doughnut ['doʊ·nʌt] n Donut m

dour [dʊr] adj (person) mürrisch; (expression) finster; (struggle) hart[näckig]

douse [daʊs] vt 1. (drench) übergießen 2. (extinguish) ausmachen; (fire) löschen

dove[1] [dʌv] n Taube f a. fig

dove[2] [doʊv] vi pt of **dive**

'dovetail I. vi übereinstimmen II. vt TECH (in wood) verschwalben; (in metal) verzinken III. n (wood) Schwalbenschwanz m; (metal) Zinken m

dowdy ['daʊ·di] adj pej ohne jeden Schick

down[1] [daʊn] I. adv 1. (to lower position) hinunter; (toward the speaker) herunter 2. (downwards) nach unter 3. (in a lower position) unten; ~ **there** dort unten 4. (in the south) im Süden unten fam; (toward the south) in der Süden, runter fam 5. (ill) **to be ~ with sth** an etw dat erkrankt sein 6. SPORT im Rückstand 7. (including) **from the mayor ~** angefangen beim Bürgermeister 8. (written) **to have sth ~ in writing** [or **on paper**] etw schriftlich haben 9. (as initial payment) als Anzahlung; **to pay 100 dollars ~** 100 Dollar anzahler 10. (in crosswords) senkrecht II. prep 1. (downward/downhill) hinunter; (toward the speaker) herunter 2. (along) entlang; **go ~ the street** gehen Sie die Straße entlang III. adj 1. (moving downward) abwärtsführend 2. fam (unhappy) niedergeschlagen, down fam 3. (not functioning) außer Betrieb; (telephone lines) tot IV. vt 1. (knock down, person) zu Fall bringen 2. (shoot down, plane) abschießen V. n (in football) Versuch m VI. interj "~!" (to a dog) „Platz!"; ~ **with the dictator!** nieder mit dem Diktator!

down[2] [daʊn] n (soft feathers) Daunen pl

down-and-'out I. adj heruntergekommen II. n pej Penner(in) m(f)

'downbeat adj (sad) pessimistisch, düster

'downcast adj 1. (sad) niedergeschlagen 2. (looking down) gesenkt

'downfall n 1. (ruin) Untergang m, Fall m fig; (of government) Sturz m 2. (cause of ruin) Ruin m

'downgrade I. vt (person) degradieren; (thing) herunterstufen II. n Gefälle nt

down'hearted adj niedergeschlagen

'downhill adv (downwards) bergab, abwärts; **to go ~** (person) heruntergehen; (vehicle) herunterfahren; (road, path) bergab führen; fig (person) bergab gehen; (situation) sich verschlechtern

'download vt COMPUT herunterladen (**to** auf +akk)

down'market adj weniger anspruchsvoll, für den Massenmarkt

down 'payment n Anzahlung f

down'play vt herunterspielen

'downpour n Regenguss m, Platzregen m

'downright I. *adj* völlig; (*lie*) glatt; (*nonsense*) komplett **II.** *adv* (*completely*) ausgesprochen

'downside *n* Kehrseite *f*

'downsize *vi* ECON Personal abbauen

'downstairs I. *adv* (*to lower floor*) treppab, die Treppe hinunter, nach unten; (*on lower floor*) unten **II.** *adj* **1.** (*one floor down*) im unteren Stockwerk **2.** (*on the ground floor*) im Erdgeschoss **III.** *n* Erdgeschoss *nt*

'downstream *adv* stromabwärts

'downtime *n* MECH Ausfallzeit *f*

down-to-'earth *adj* nüchtern

'downtown I. *n* Innenstadt *f*, Zentrum *nt* **II.** *adj, adv* in der Innenstadt, im Zentrum; (*go*) in die Innenstadt, ins Zentrum

'downtrodden *adj* unterdrückt

'downturn *n* ECON Rückgang *m*

downward ['daʊn·wəd] **I.** *adj* nach unten [gerichtet] **II.** *adv* **1.** (*in/toward a lower position*) abwärts, nach unten, hinunter **2.** (*to a lower amount*) nach unten

downwards ['daʊn·wədz] *adv see* **downward**

dowry ['daʊ·ri] *n* Mitgift *f*

dowse [daʊz] *vt see* **douse**

doze [doʊz] **I.** *n* Nickerchen *nt* **II.** *vi* to ~ [off] dösen

dozen ['dʌz·ən] *n* Dutzend *nt;* **half a ~** ein halbes Dutzend

Dr. *n abbr of* **doctor** Dr.

drab <-bb-> [dræb] *adj* trist; (*colors*) trüb; (*surroundings*) trostlos

draft [dræft] **I.** *n* **1.** (*air current*) [Luft]zug *m kein pl* **2. on ~** vom Fass **3.** MIL Einberufung *f* **4.** (*preliminary version*) [first/rough] [erster/roher] Entwurf *m* **II.** *adj* **1.** ~ **animal** Zugtier *nt* **2.** ~ **beer** Fassbier *nt* **3.** MIL Einberufungs-; ~ **board** Wehrersatzbehörde *f* **4.** (*preliminary*) Entwurfs-; ~ **contract** Vertragsentwurf *m* **III.** *vt* **1.** (*prepare*) entwerfen; (*bill*) verfassen; (*contract*) aufsetzen; (*proposal*) ausarbeiten **2.** MIL **to** ~ **sb into the army** jdn zum Wehrdienst einberufen

'draft dodger *n* (*shirker*) Drückeberger(in) *m(f)*; (*conscientious objector*)

Wehrdienstverweigerer, -in *m, f*

'draftsman *n* [technischer] Zeichner

drafty ['dræf·ti] *adj* zugig

drag [dræg] **I.** *n* **1.** PHYS Widerstand *m;* AVIAT Luftwiderstand *m* **2.** *fig* (*impediment*) Hemmschuh *m* **3.** *fam* (*bore*) langweilige Sache; **what a ~!** so'n Mist! *sl* **4.** *fam* (*puff*) Zug *m* **5.** *fam* (*road*) **the main** ~ die Hauptstraße **6.** *fam* (*clothing of opposite sex*) Fummel *m;* ~ **queen** *Künstler, der in Frauenkleidern auftritt* **II.** *vt* <-gg-> **1.** (*pull along*) ziehen; **to** ~ **one's feet** schlurfen; *fig* sich *dat* Zeit lassen; **to** ~ **oneself along** sich dahinschleppen **2.** (*take despite resistance*) schleifen; **I don't want to** ~ **you away** ich will dich hier nicht wegreißen **3.** (*force*) **to** ~ **sth out of sb** etw aus jdm herausbringen **III.** *vi* <-gg-> **1.** (*trail along*) schleifen **2.** *pej* (*proceed tediously*) sich [da]hinziehen

◆**drag in** *vt* (*person*) hineinziehen; (*thing*) aufs Tapet bringen

◆**drag on** *vi pej* sich [da]hinziehen

◆**drag out** *vt* in die Länge ziehen

dragon ['dræg·ən] *n* **1.** (*mythical creature*) Drache *m* **2.** (*woman*) Drachen *m*

'dragonfly *n* Libelle *f*

drain [dreɪn] **I.** *n* **1.** (*pipe*) Rohr *nt;* (*under sink*) Abflussrohr *nt;* (*in road*) Gully *m;* **to go down the** ~ *fig* vor die Hunde gehen, in den Bach runtergehen *fam* **2.** (*constant outflow*) Belastung *f* (**on** für +*akk*) **II.** *vt* **1.** (*remove liquid*) entwässern; (*liquid*) ablaufen lassen; (*vegetables*) abgießen; (*noodles/rice*) abtropfen lassen; (*abscess*) drainieren **2.** *form* (*empty*) austrinken **3.** (*exhaust*) [völlig] auslaugen **III.** *vi* **1.** (*flow away*) ablaufen **2.** (*empty*) leeren

◆**drain away** *vi* (*liquid*) ablaufen; *fig* [dahin]schwinden

◆**drain off** *vt* (*water*) abgießen

drainage ['dreɪ·nɪdʒ] *n* **1.** (*water removal*) Entwässerung *f* **2.** (*system: for land*) Entwässerungssystem *nt;* (*for houses*) Kanalisation *f*

'drain board *n* Abtropfbrett *nt*

'drainpipe *n* (*for rainwater*) Regenrohr *nt;* (*for sewage*) Abflussrohr *nt*

drake [dreɪk] n Enterich m, Erpel m

drama ['drɑ·mə] n 1. (theater art) Schauspielkunst f 2. (play, event) Drama nt a. fig 3. (dramatic quality) Dramatik f

dramatic [drə·'mæt·ɪk] adj 1. dramatisch 2. pej (theatrical) theatralisch

dramatist ['dræm·ə·tɪst] n Dramatiker(in) m(f)

dramatization [ˌdræm·ə·tɪ·'zeɪ·ʃən] n 1. (of a work) Dramatisierung f; THEAT Bühnenbearbeitung f; FILM Kinobearbeitung f; TV Fernsehbearbeitung f 2. usu pej (exaggeration) Dramatisieren nt

dramatize ['dræm·ə·taɪz] vt 1. (adapt) bearbeiten 2. usu pej (exaggerate) dramatisieren

drank [dræŋk] pt of drink

drape [dreɪp] I. vt 1. (cover loosely) bedecken (in/with mit +dat) 2. (place on) drapieren, legen II. n ~s pl Vorhänge pl

drastic ['dræs·tɪk] adj drastisch; (change, measures) radikal

draw [drɔ] I. n 1. (celebrity) Publikumsmagnet m; (popular film, etc.) Kassenschlager m 2. (in chess, soccer) Unentschieden nt; to end in a ~ unentschieden ausgehen 3. (drawing lots) Verlosung f II. vt <drew, -n> 1. (make a picture) zeichnen; (line) ziehen 2. (depict) darstellen 3. (pull) ziehen; (close: curtains) zuziehen; (open) aufziehen 4. (attract) anlocken; to ~ [sb's] attention [to sb/sth] [jds] Aufmerksamkeit f [auf jdn/etw] lenken; to feel ~n to sb sich zu jdm hingezogen fühlen 5. (formulate: comparison) anstellen; (conclusion, parallel) ziehen 6. (pull out: weapon) ziehen 7. (earn, get from source) beziehen, erhalten 8. (select by chance) ziehen, auslosen; to ~ lots for sth um etw akk losen 9. FIN (money) abheben; (check) ausstellen III. vi <drew, -n> 1. (make pictures) zeichnen 2. (make use of) to ~ on sth auf etw akk zurückgreifen 3. (in chess, soccer) unentschieden spielen

♦**draw out** vt in die Länge ziehen; (vowels) dehnen

♦**draw up** vt aufsetzen; (agenda, list) aufstellen; (guidelines) festlegen; (plan)

entwerfen; (proposal, questionnaire) ausarbeiten; (report) erstellen; (will) errichten

'**drawback** n Nachteil m

drawer [drɔr] n 1. (storage) Schublade f; **chest of ~s** Kommode f 2. hum ~s pl (underwear) Unterwäsche f

drawing ['drɔ·ɪŋ] n 1. (art) Zeichnen nt 2. (picture) Zeichnung f

'**drawing board** n Zeichenbrett nt; to **go back to the ~** fig noch einmal von vorn anfangen

'**drawing room** n form Wohnzimmer nt

drawl [drɔl] I. n schleppende Sprache II. vi schleppend sprechen

drawn [drɔn] I. pp of draw II. adj abgespannt

dread [dred] I. vt to ~ sth sich vor etw dat [sehr] fürchten; to ~ doing sth [große] Angst haben, etw zu tun II. n Furcht f

dreadful ['dred·fəl] adj 1. (awful) schrecklich, furchtbar 2. (of very bad quality) miserabel, erbärmlich

dreadfully ['dred·fə·li] adv 1. (in a terrible manner) schrecklich, entsetzlich 2. (extremely) schrecklich, furchtbar

dream [drim] I. n Traum m a. fig; **in your ~s!** du träumst wohl! II. vt, vi <dreamed or dreamt, dreamed or dreamt> träumen a. fig; **I wouldn't ~ of asking him for money!** es würde mir nicht im Traum einfallen, ihn um Geld zu bitten

♦**dream up** vt sich dat ausdenken

dreamt [dremt] pt, pp of dream

dreamy ['dri·mi] adj 1. (lost in thought) verträumt 2. fam (gorgeous) zum Träumen

dreary ['drɪr·i] adj 1. (depressing) trostlos; (day) trüb 2. (monotonous) eintönig

dredge [dredʒ] I. n [Schwimm]bagger m II. vt (river) ausbaggern

dredger ['dredʒ·ər] n [Schwimm]bagger m

dregs [dregz] npl 1. (of drink) [Boden]satz m kein pl 2. fig Abschaum m kein pl

drench [drentʃ] vt durchnässen

dress [dres] I. n <pl -es> 1. (woman's

garment) Kleid *nt* **2.** (*clothing*) Kleidung *f* **II.** *vi* **1.** (*put on clothing*) to ~ [*or* get ~ed] sich anziehen **2.** (*wear clothing*) sich kleiden; to ~ casually sich leger anziehen **III.** *vt* **1.** (*put on clothing*) to ~ sb/oneself jdn/sich anziehen **2.** FOOD (*salad*) anmachen **3.** (*treat: wound*) verbinden

◆dress up **I.** *vi* **1.** (*wear nice clothes*) sich fein anziehen **2.** (*disguise oneself*) sich verkleiden **II.** *vt* **1.** (*in a costume*) verkleiden **2.** (*improve*) verschönern

dressing ['dres-ɪŋ] *n* **1.** (*for salad*) Dressing *nt* **2.** (*for injury*) Verband *m*

dressing-'down *n fam* Standpauke *f*

'dressing room *n* (*in theater*) [Künstler]-garderobe *f*; SPORT Umkleidekabine *f*

'dressing table *n* Schminktisch *m*, Frisierkommode *f*

'dressmaker *n* [Damen]schneider(in) *m(f)*

'dressmaking *n* Schneidern *nt*

dress re'hearsal *n* THEAT Generalprobe *f*

dressy ['dres-i] *adj fam* **1.** (*stylish*) elegant **2.** (*requiring formal clothes*) vornehm

drew [dru] *pt of* draw

dribble ['drɪb-əl] **I.** *vi* **1.** (*trickle*) tropfen **2.** (*baby*) sabbern **3.** SPORT dribbeln **II.** *vt* SPORT dribbeln mit **III.** *n* **1.** (*saliva*) Sabber *m* **2.** SPORT Dribbling *nt kein pl*

dried [draɪd] **I.** *pt, pp of* dry **II.** *adj* getrocknet

dried up *adj pred,* dried-up *adj attr* ausgetrocknet

drift [drɪft] **I.** *vi* treiben; (*balloon*) schweben; (*mist, fog, clouds*) ziehen; (*snow*) angeweht werden; to ~ along *fig* sich treiben lassen; to ~ away (*people*) davonschlendern **II.** *n* **1.** (*slow movement*) Strömen *nt* **2.** (*snowdrift*) Verwehung *f* **3.** (*general idea*) Kernaussage *f*; to catch sb's ~ verstehen, was jd sagen will

◆drift apart *vi* einander fremd werden

◆drift off *vi* einschlummern

drifter ['drɪf-tər] *n* Gammler(in) *m(f)*

'drift ice *n* Treibeis *nt*

'driftwood *n* Treibholz *nt*

drill [drɪl] **I.** *n* **1.** (*tool*) Bohrer *m* **2.** (*exercise*) Übung *f*; MIL Drill *m* **3.** *fam* (*rou-

tine procedure*) to know the ~ wissen, wie es geht **II.** *vt* **1.** (*holes*) bohren **2.** MIL, SCH drillen **III.** *vi* **1.** (*make holes*) bohren **2.** MIL exerzieren

'drilling platform *n* Bohrinsel *f*

drink [drɪŋk] **I.** *n* **1.** Getränk *nt;* can I get you a ~? kann ich Ihnen etwas zu trinken bringen?; to have a ~ etw trinken **2.** (*alcoholic drink*) Drink *m*, Gläschen *nt* **3.** (*alcohol*) Alkohol *m* **II.** *vt, vi* <drank, drunk> trinken; to ~ and drive unter Alkoholeinfluss fahren; I'll ~ to that darauf trinke ich; *fig* dem kann ich nur zustimmen

◆drink in *vt* [begierig] in sich *akk* aufnehmen

drinker ['drɪŋ-kər] *n* Trinker(in) *m(f)*

drinking ['drɪŋ-kɪŋ] **I.** *n* Trinken *nt* **II.** *adj* Trink-

'drinking water *n* Trinkwasser *nt*

drip [drɪp] **I.** *vi* <-pp-> (*continually*) tropfen; (*in individual drops*) tröpfeln **II.** *vt* <-pp-> [herunter]tropfen lassen **III.** *n* **1.** (*act of dripping*) Tropfen *nt;* (*of rain*) Tröpfeln *nt* **2.** (*drop*) Tropfen *m* **3.** MED Tropf *m* **4.** *fam* (*fool*) Flasche *f pej fam*, Null *f pej fam*

drip-dry **I.** *vt* <-ie-> tropfnass aufhängen **II.** *vi* (*clothes, dishes*) abtropfen **III.** *adj* bügelfrei

dripping ['drɪp-ɪŋ] **I.** *adj* **1.** (*dropping drips*) tropfend **2.** (*extremely wet*) klatschnass **3.** *hum, iron* (*be covered with sth*) to be ~ with sth über und über mit etw *dat* behängt sein **II.** *adv* ~ wet klatschnass

drive [draɪv] **I.** *n* **1.** (*trip*) Fahrt *f*; to go for a ~ eine Spazierfahrt machen; it is a 20-minute ~ to the airport zum Flughafen sind es [mit dem Auto] 20 Minuten **2.** (*driveway*) Einfahrt *f*; (*to larger building*) Auffahrt *f*; (*approach road*) Zufahrt[straße] *f* **3.** (*energy*) Tatkraft *f*; (*vigor*) Schwung *m*, Elan *m*, Drive *m*; (*motivation*) Tatendrang *m*; PSYCH Trieb *m* **4.** (*campaign*) Aktion *f* **5.** COMPUT Laufwerk *nt* **II.** *vt* <drove, -n> **1.** fahren **2.** (*force onwards*) antreiben; to ~ sb to suicide jdn in den Selbstmord treiben; to ~ sb mad/crazy jdn wahnsinnig/verrückt machen

3. (*power: engine*) antreiben; COMPUT treiben **III.** *vi* <drove, -n> **1.** fahren **2.** (*rain, snow*) peitschen; (*clouds*) jagen **3.** *fig* **what are you driving at?** worauf wollen Sie [eigentlich] hinaus?

◆ **drive away I.** *vt* **1.** (*transport*) wegfahren **2.** (*expel*) vertreiben **3.** *fig* (*dispel*) zerstreuen **II.** *vi* wegfahren

◆ **drive back I.** *vt* **1.** (*in vehicle*) zurückfahren **2.** (*force back*) zurückdrängen; (*animals*) zurücktreiben; (*enemy*) zurückschlagen **II.** *vi* zurückfahren

◆ **drive off I.** *vt* **1.** (*expel*) vertreiben **2.** (*repel*) zurückschlagen **II.** *vi* wegfahren

◆ **drive out** *vt* hinausjagen; *fig* austreiben

◆ **drive up I.** *vt* (*prices*) hochtreiben **II.** *vi* vorfahren

'**drive-in I.** *adj* Drive-in- **II.** *n* **1.** (*restaurant*) Drive-in *nt* **2.** (*movie theater*) Autokino *nt*

drivel ['drɪv·əl] *n pej* Gefasel *nt*

driven ['drɪv·ən] **I.** *pp of* **drive II.** *adj* **1.** (*very ambitious*) ehrgeizig **2.** (*powered*) angetrieben

driver ['draɪ·vər] *n* **1.** Fahrer(in) *m(f)*; (*of locomotive*) Führer(in) *m(f)* **2.** (*golf club*) Driver *m*

'**driver's license** *n* Führerschein *m*

'**drive-through I.** *adj attr* Drive-through- **II.** *n* Durchfahrt *f*

'**driveway** *n* (*to small building*) Einfahrt *f*; (*to larger building*) Auffahrt *f*; (*longer*) Zufahrt[sstraße] *f*

driving ['draɪ·vɪŋ] **I.** *n* (*of vehicle*) Fahren *nt* **II.** *adj* **1.** (*on road*) Fahr-; ~ **conditions** Straßenverhältnisse *pl* **2.** (*lashing: rain*) peitschend **3.** (*powerfully motivating*) treibend; (*force, ambition*) stark

'**driving instructor** *n* Fahrlehrer(in) *m(f)*

'**driving lesson** *n* Fahrstunde *f*

'**driving license** *n see* **driver's license**

'**driving school** *n* Fahrschule *f*

'**driving test** *n* Fahrprüfung *f*

drizzle ['drɪz·əl] **I.** *n* METEO Nieselregen *m* **II.** *vi impers* nieseln **III.** *vt* FOOD träufeln

droll [droʊl] *adj* drollig

drone [droʊn] **I.** *n* **1.** (*male bee*) Drohne *f* **2.** (*aircraft*) ferngesteuertes Flug-

zeug; (*missile*) ferngesteuerte Rakete **3.** (*of a machine*) Brummen *nt;* (*of insects*) Summen *nt* **II.** *vi* **1.** (*make sound*) summen; (*engine*) brummen **2.** (*speak monotonously*) leiern

drool [druːl] **I.** *vi* **1.** (*dribble*) sabbern **2.** *fig* **to** ~ **over sb/sth** von jdm/etw hingerissen sein **II.** *n* Sabber *m*

droop [druːp] *vi* **1.** (*hang down*) schlaff herunterhängen; (*flowers*) die Köpfe hängen lassen; (*eyelids*) zufallen **2.** (*lack energy*) schlapp sein

droopy ['druː·pi] *adj* [schlaff] herabhängend *attr*

drop [drɑp] **I.** *n* **1.** (*vertical distance*) Gefälle *nt* **2.** (*decrease*) Rückgang *m* **3.** (*of liquid*) Tropfen *m;* ~**s** *pl* MED Tropfen *pl* **II.** *vt* <-pp-> **1.** (*cause to fall*) fallen lassen; (*anchor*) [aus]werfen; (*bomb, leaflets*) abwerfen **2.** (*lower*) senken **3.** (*dismiss*) entlassen **4.** (*give up*) aufgeben; (*charges*) fallen lassen; (*demands*) abgehen von; **to** ~ **everything** alles stehen und liegen lassen **5.** (*abandon*) **to** ~ **sb** *fig* jdn fallen lassen; (*end a relationship*) mit jdm Schluss machen **6.** *fam* (*tell indirectly*) **to** ~ [**sb**] **a hint** [jdm gegenüber] eine Anspielung machen **III.** *vi* <-pp-> **1.** (*descend*) [herunter]fallen; (*jaw*) herunterklappen **2.** (*become lower: land*) sinken; (*prices, temperatures*) fallen **3.** *fam* (*become exhausted*) umfallen; ~ **dead!** *fam* scher dich zum Teufel!

◆ **drop behind** *vi* zurückfallen

◆ **drop in** *vi fam* vorbeischauen (**on** bei +*dat*)

◆ **drop off I.** *vt fam* (*person*) abliefern; (*thing*) absetzen **II.** *vi* **1.** (*fall off*) abfallen **2.** (*decrease*) zurückgehen; (*support, interest*) nachlassen **3.** (*fall asleep*) einschlafen

◆ **drop out** *vi* **1.** (*give up membership*) ausscheiden; **to** ~ **out of college** das Studium abbrechen **2.** (*of society*) aussteigen

drop-down '**menu** *n* COMPUT Pull-down-Menü *nt*

'**dropout** *n* **1.** (*from university*) [Studien]abbrecher(in) *m(f)*; (*from school*) Schulabgänger(in) *m(f)* **2.** (*from conventional*

lifestyle) Aussteiger(in) *m(f)*

dropper ['drap·ər] *n* Tropfer *m*

droppings ['drap·ɪŋz] *npl (of bird)* Vogeldreck *m; (of horse)* Pferdeäpfel *pl; (of rodents, sheep)* Köttel *pl*

drop shot *n* TENNIS Stopp[ball] *m*

dross [dras] *n* Schrott *m a. fig*

drought [draʊt] *n* Dürre[periode] *f*

drove [droʊv] *pt of* **drive**

drown [draʊn] **I.** *vt* **1.** *(kill)* ertränken; **to be ~ed** ertrinken **2.** *(make inaudible)* übertönen **II.** *vi* ertrinken *a. fig*

♦**drown out** *vt* niederschreien

drowsy ['draʊ·zi] *adj* schläfrig; *(after waking up)* verschlafen

drudge [drʌdʒ] *n (person)* Kuli *m*

drudgery ['drʌdʒ·ə·ri] *n* Schufterei *f*

drug [drʌg] **I.** *n* **1.** *(medicine)* Medikament *m* **2.** *(narcotic)* Droge *f*, Rauschgift *nt* **II.** *vt* <-gg-> **1.** MED Beruhigungsmittel verabreichen **2.** *(secretly)* unter Drogen setzen

'drug abuse *n* Drogenmissbrauch *m*

'drug addict *n* Drogensüchtige(r) *f(m)*

'drug addiction *n* Drogenabhängigkeit *f*

'drug dealer *n* Drogenhändler(in) *m(f)*, Dealer(in) *m(f)*

'drugstore *n* Drogerie *f* [in der man auch Medikamente erhält]

'drug trafficker *n* Drogenhändler(in) *m(f)*

'drug trafficking *n* Drogenhandel *m*

drum [drʌm] **I.** *n* **1.** MUS Trommel *f;* **~s** *pl (drum kit)* Schlagzeug *nt* **2.** *(for storage, machine part)* Trommel *f* **II.** *vi* <-mm-> **1.** MUS trommeln; *(on a drum kit)* Schlagzeug spielen **2.** *(strike repeatedly)* trommeln **(on** auf +*akk***)** **III.** *vt* <-mm-> *fam* **1.** *(make noise)* **to ~ one's fingers** [**on the table**] [mit den Fingern] auf den Tisch trommeln **2.** *(repeat)* **to ~ sth into sb** jdm etw einhämmern

'drumbeat *n* Trommelschlag *m*

drummer ['drʌm·ər] *n* MUS Trommler(in) *m(f); (playing a drum kit)* Schlagzeuger(in) *m(f)*

'drumstick *n* **1.** MUS Trommelstock *m* **2.** FOOD Keule *f*, Schlegel *m südd, österr*

drunk [drʌŋk] **I.** *adj* **1.** *(inebriated)* betrunken; **to get ~** sich betrinken; **~**

driving Trunkenheit *f* am Steuer **2.** *fig (overcome)* trunken **II.** *n pej* Betrunkene(r) *f(m)* **III.** *vt, vi pp of* **drink**

drunkard ['drʌŋ·kərd] *n pej* Trinker(in) *m(f)*

drunken ['drʌŋ·kən] *adj pej* **1.** *(person)* betrunken **2.** *(involving alcohol)* **~ brawl** Streit *m* zwischen Betrunkenen

drunkenness ['drʌŋ·kən·nɪs] *n* Betrunkenheit *f*

dry [draɪ] **I.** *adj* <-ier, -iest *or* -er, -est> **1.** trocken **2.** *(without alcohol)* alkoholfrei **II.** *vt* <-ie-> trocknen; *(fruit, meat)* dörren; *(dry out)* austrocknen; *(dry up)* abtrocknen; **~ your eyes!** wisch dir die Tränen ab!; **to ~ one's hands** sich *dat* die Hände abtrocknen **III.** *vi* <-ie-> **1.** *(lose moisture)* trocknen **2.** *(dry up)* abtrocknen

♦**dry up I.** *vi* **1.** *(become dry)* austrocknen; *(spring, well)* versiegen **2.** *(dry the dishes)* abtrocknen **3.** *fig (run out: funds)* schrumpfen; *(source)* versiegen; *(supply)* ausbleiben; *(conversation)* versiegen **II.** *vt* **1.** *(dishes)* abtrocknen **2.** *(dry out)* austrocknen

'dry-clean *vt* chemisch reinigen

'dry cleaner *n* Reinigung *f*

'dry cleaning *n* [chemische] Reinigung *f*

dryer ['draɪ·ər] *n* **1.** *(for laundry)* [Wäsche]trockner *m* **2.** *(for hair)* Fön *m; (overhead)* Trockenhaube *f*

dry 'land *n* Festland *nt*

'dry rot *n* **1.** *(in wood)* Hausschwamm *m* **2.** *(in plants)* Trockenfäule *f*

DSL [ˌdi·es·'el] *n* INET, COMPUT, TELEC *acr for* **digital subscriber line** DSL *kein art*

dual ['du·əl] *adj (double)* doppelt; *(two different)* zweierlei; **~ role** Doppelrolle *f*

dub <-bb-> [dʌb] *vt* **1.** FILM synchronisieren **2.** *(call)* nennen

dubbing ['dʌb·ɪŋ] *n* FILM Synchronisation *f*

dubious ['du·bi·əs] *adj* **1.** *(questionable)* zweifelhaft, fragwürdig **2.** *(unsure)* unsicher; **to feel ~ about sth** an etw *dat* zweifeln

duchess <*pl* -es> ['dʌtʃ·ɪs] *n* Herzogin *f*

duck[1] [dʌk] *n* Ente *f*

duck[2] [dʌk] **I.** *vi* sich ducken; *(out of*

sight) sich verstecken; **to ~ under water** [unter|tauchen II. *vt* **1. to ~ one's head** den Kopf einziehen **2.** (*avoid*) **to ~ sth** etw *dat* ausweichen a. *fig*

duckling ['dʌk·lɪŋ] *n* Entenküken *nt*, Entchen *nt*

duct [dʌkt] *n* **1.** (*pipe*) [Rohr]leitung *f* **2.** ANAT Kanal *m*

dud [dʌd] *fam* **I.** *n* **1.** (*bomb*) Blindgänger *m* **2.** (*useless thing*) **this pen is a ~** dieser Füller taugt nichts; (*failure*) Reinfall *m* **II.** *adj* (*worthless*) mies; (*checks*) gefälscht

dude [dud] *n fam* **1.** (*smartly dressed urbanite*) feiner Pinkel **2.** (*fellow*) Typ *m*, Kerl *m;* **what's up, ~?** wie geht's, Alter? *sl*

due [du] **I.** *adj* **1.** (*payable*) fällig; **~ date** Fälligkeitstermin *m* **2.** (*appropriate*) gebührend; **with** [**all**] **~ respect** bei allem [gebotenen] Respekt **3.** (*expected*) **in ~ course** zu gegebener Zeit; **~ date** (*for work*) Abgabetermin *m;* (*for entries*) Einsendeschluss *m;* **their baby is ~ in January** sie erwarten ihr Baby im Januar **4.** (*because of*) **~ to sth** wegen [*or auf* Grund] einer S. *gen* **to be ~ to sb/sth** jdm/etw zuzuschreiben sein **II.** *n* **1.** (*fair treatment*) **to give sb his/her ~** jdm Gerechtigkeit widerfahren lassen **2.** (*fees*) **~s** *pl* Gebühren *pl* **III.** *adv* **~ north** genau nach Norden

duel [dul] **I.** *n* Duell *nt* **II.** *vi* <-l-> sich duellieren

duet [du·'et] *n* (*for instruments*) Duo *nt;* (*for voices*) Duett *nt*

dug [dʌg] *pt, pp of* **dig**

'**dugout** *n* **1.** MIL Schützengraben *m* **2.** (*in baseball, soccer*) [überdachte] Spielerbank **3.** (*canoe*) Einbaum *m*

duke [duk] *n* Herzog *m*

dull [dʌl] **I.** *adj* **1.** *pej* (*boring*) langweilig, eintönig **2.** (*not bright: animal's coat*) glanzlos; (*weather*) trüb; (*color*) matt **II.** *vt* (*lessen*) schwächen; (*pain*) betäuben

dullness ['dʌl·nɪs] *n* Langweiligkeit *f*, Eintönigkeit *f*

duly ['du·li] *adv* **1.** (*appropriately*) gebührend **2.** (*at the expected time*) wie erwartet

dumb [dʌm] *adj* **1.** *pej fam* (*stupid*) dumm **2.** (*mute*) stumm

'**dumbfounded** *adj* sprachlos

'**dumbstruck** *adj* sprachlos

dummy ['dʌm·i] **I.** *n* **1.** (*mannequin*) Schaufensterpuppe *f;* (*for crash tests*) Dummy *m;* (*for ventriloquist*) [Bauchredner]puppe *f* **2.** *pej* (*fool*) Dummkopf *m* **II.** *adj* (*duplicate*) nachgemacht; (*false*) falsch

dump [dʌmp] **I.** *n* **1.** (*for garbage*) Müll[ablade]platz *m; fig, pej* (*messy place*) Dreckloch *nt;* (*badly run place*) Sauladen *m* **2.** (*storage place*) Lager *nt* **3.** COMPUT Speicherabzug *m* **II.** *vt* **1.** (*offload*) abladen **2.** (*put down carelessly*) hinknallen **3.** *fam* (*abandon: plan*) fallen lassen; (*sth unwanted*) loswerden **4.** *fam* (*end a relationship*) **to ~ sb** jdm den Laufpass geben, mit jdm Schluss machen **III.** *vi* **1.** (*throw out garbage*) **"No ~ing"** "Müll abladen verboten" **2.** *fam* (*treat unfairly*) **to ~ on sb** jdn fertigmachen

dumpling ['dʌmp·lɪŋ] *n* Knödel *m*, Kloß *m*

'**dump truck** *n* Kipper *m*

dumpy ['dʌm·pi] *adj* pummelig

dunce [dʌns] *n pej* (*poor pupil*) schlechter Schüler, schlechte Schülerin; (*stupid person*) Dummkopf *m*

dune [dun] *n* Düne *f*

dung [dʌŋ] *n* Dung *m*

dungarees [ˌdʌŋ·gəˈriz] *npl* Jeans[hose] *f*

dungeon ['dʌn·dʒən] *n* Verlies *nt*, Kerker *m*

dunk [dʌŋk] **I.** *vt* **1.** (*immerse*) [ein]tunken **2.** SPORT (*basketball*) dunken **II.** *vt* SPORT dunken **III.** *n* SPORT Dunking *m*

duo ['du·oʊ] *n* Duo *nt*

duodenum <*pl* -na> [ˌdu·ə·ˈdi·nəm] *n* Zwölffingerdarm *m*

dupe [dup] **I.** *n* Betrogene(r) *f(m)* **II.** *vt* betrügen

duplex ['du·pleks] *n* <*pl* -es> **1.** (*house*) Doppelhaus *nt* **2.** (*apartment*) Maisonette[wohnung] *f*

duplicate I. *vt* ['du·plɪ·keɪt] **to ~ sth** eine zweite Anfertigung von etw *dat* machen; (*repeat an activity*) etw noch einmal machen **II.** *adj* ['du·plɪ·kət] Zweit-; **~ key** Nachschlüssel *m* **III.** *n* ['du·plɪ·kət] Du-

plikat nt; (of a document) Zweitschrift f; **in** ~ in zweifacher Ausfertigung

duplicity [du·ˈplɪs·ɪ·t̬i] n pej (in speech) Doppelzüngigkeit f; (in behavior) Doppelspiel nt

durability [ˌdʊr·ə·ˈbɪl·ɪ·t̬i] n (of a product) Haltbarkeit f; (of a machine) Lebensdauer f

durable [ˈdʊr·ə·bəl] adj 1. (long-lasting) strapazierfähig, dauerhaft 2. ECON (goods) langlebig

duration [dʊ·ˈreɪ·ʃən] n Dauer f

duress [dʊ·ˈres] n form Zwang m, Nötigung f

during [ˈdʊr·ɪŋ] prep während +gen

dusk [dʌsk] n [Abend]dämmerung f

dusky [ˈdʌs·ki] adj dunkel

dust [dʌst] I. n Staub m; **covered in** ~ (outside) staubbedeckt; (inside) völlig verstaubt II. vt 1. (clean: objects) abstauben; (rooms) Staub wischen in 2. (spread over finely) bestäuben; (using grated material) bestreuen III. vi Staub wischen

ˈ**dust cover** n (for furniture) Schonbezug m; (for devices) Abdeckhaube f; (on a book) Schutzumschlag m; (for clothes) Staubschutz m kein pl

duster [ˈdʌs·tər] n Staubtuch nt

ˈ**dust jacket** n Schutzumschlag m

ˈ**dust mite** n Hausmilbe f

ˈ**dustpan** n Schaufel f

ˈ**dust storm** n Staubsturm m

dusty [ˈdʌs·ti] adj staubig; (objects) verstaubt

Dutch [dʌtʃ] I. adj holländisch, niederländisch II. n 1. (language) Holländisch nt, Niederländisch nt 2. (people) **the** ~ pl die Holländer III. adv **to go** ~ getrennte Kasse machen

ˈ**Dutchman** n Holländer m

ˈ**Dutchwoman** n Holländerin f

dutiful [ˈduː·t̬ɪ·fəl] adj 1. (person) pflichtbewusst; (obedient) gehorsam 2. (act) pflichtschuldig

duty [ˈduː·t̬i] I. n 1. (obligation) Pflicht f 2. (work) Dienst m; **to be off** ~ [dienst]frei haben; **to be on** ~ Dienst haben 3. (revenue) Zoll m; **customs duties** Zollabgaben pl; **to pay** ~ **on sth** etw verzollen II. adj (nurse, officer) diensthabend

duty-ˈfree adj zollfrei

duvet [du·ˈveɪ] n Steppdecke f, Daunendecke f

DVD [ˌdi·vi·ˈdi] n abbr of **digital video disk** DVD f

DVR [ˌdi·vi·ˈar] n abbr of **digital video recorder** digitaler Videorecorder m

dwarf [dwɔrf] I. n <pl -s> Zwerg(in) m(f) II. adj Zwerg- III. vt überragen; fig in den Schatten stellen

dwell <dwelt or dwelled, dwelt or dwelled> [dwel] vi 1. (reside) wohnen 2. (think about) nachdenken (**on** über +akk)

dweller [ˈdwel·ər] n form Bewohner(in) m(f)

dwelling [ˈdwel·ɪŋ] n form Wohnung f

dwelt [dwelt] pt, pp of **dwell**

dwindle [ˈdwɪn·dəl] vi abnehmen; (numbers) zurückgehen; (money, supplies) schrumpfen

dye [daɪ] I. vt färben II. n Färbemittel nt

dyed-in-the-ˈwool adj Erz-

dying [ˈdaɪ·ɪŋ] adj sterbend; fig aussterbend

dyke¹ [daɪk] n (wall) see **dike¹**

dyke² [daɪk] n offensive sl (lesbian) Lesbe f

dynamic [daɪ·ˈnæm·ɪk] adj dynamisch

dynamics [daɪ·ˈnæm·ɪks] n Dynamik f

dynamite [ˈdaɪ·nə·maɪt] I. n Dynamit nt a. fig II. vt mit Dynamit sprengen

dynasty [ˈdaɪ·nə·sti] n Dynastie f

dysentery [ˈdɪs·ən·ter·i] n Ruhr f

dysfunctional [dɪs·ˈfʌŋk·ʃə·nəl] adj SOCIOL gestört

dyslexia [dɪ·ˈsleksiə] n Legasthenie f

dyslexic [dɪs·ˈlek·sɪk] adj legasthenisch

E

E <pl -'s> [i], **e** <pl -'s> [i] n E nt, e nt; ~ **as in Echo** E wie Emil

E n 1. abbr of **east** O 2. (in baseball) abbr of **error** Fehlpass m

each [itʃ] adj, adv, pron jede(r, s); ~ **one** jedes einzelne; **one of** ~ von jedem eins

each ˈother pron after vb einander; **for** ~ füreinander

eager <-er, -est> ['i·gər] *adj* begierig; (*expectant*) erwartungsvoll

eagerness ['i·gər·nəs] *n* Eifer *m*

eagle ['i·gəl] *n* Adler *m*

'eagle-eyed *adj* scharfsichtig

ear [ɪr] *n* **1.** Ohr *nt* **2.** (*grain*) Ähre *f;* **from ~ to ~** von einem Ohr zum anderen ▸ **to be <u>all</u> ~s** ganz Ohr sein

'earache *n* Ohrenschmerzen *pl*

'eardrum *n* Trommelfell *nt*

earl [ɜrl] *n* Graf *m*

'earlobe *n* Ohrläppchen *nt*

early <-ier, -iest> ['ɜr·li] **I.** *adj* früh; (*ahead*) vorzeitig; **from an ~ age** von klein auf **II.** *adv* früh; (*ahead*) vorzeitig; (*prematurely*) zu früh; (*earlier*) [früh]zeitig

'earmuffs *npl* Ohrenschützer *pl*

earn [ɜrn] *vt* verdienen; (*respect*) gewinnen

earnest ['ɜr·nɪst] **I.** *adj* ernst[haft] **II.** *n* Ernst *m;* **in ~** ernst

'earphone *n* Kopfhörer *m*

'earplug *n usu pl* Ohrenstöpsel *nt*

'earring *n* Ohrring *m*

'earshot *n* **[with]in/out of ~** in/außer Hörweite

earth [ɜrθ] *n* (*planet, soil*) Erde *f;* **on ~** in der Welt; **how on ~ ...** wie um alles in der Welt ... ▸ **down to ~** natürlich und umgänglich

Earth Day *n* wird seit 1990 alljährlich am 22. April begangen, um auf die globale Gefährdung unserer Umwelt aufmerksam zu machen

earthly ['ɜrθ·li] *adj fam* **of no ~ use** nicht im Geringsten nützlich

'earthquake *n* Erdbeben *nt*

'earthworm *n* Regenwurm *m*

'earwax *n* Ohrenschmalz *m*

'earwig *n* Ohrwurm *m*

ease [iz] **I.** *n* Leichtigkeit *f;* **to be at ~** sich *akk* wohl fühlen **II.** *vt* (*pain*) lindern; (*strain*) mindern **III.** *vi* nachlassen; (*tension*) sich beruhigen

◆ **ease off** *vi* nachlassen; **to ~ off on sb** jdn in Ruhe lassen

◆ **ease up** *vi* nachlassen; (*relax*) sich *akk* entspannen

easel ['i·zəl] *n* Staffelei *f*

easily ['i·zə·li] *adv* leicht; (*effortlessly*)

mühelos; (*probably*) [sehr] leicht; **to be ~ the ...** + *superl* bei weitem der/die/das ... sein

east [ist] **I.** *n* Osten *m;* **to the ~** nach Osten; **the E~** der Osten **II.** *adj* östlich; **~ wind** Ostwind *m* **III.** *adv* nach Osten

Easter ['i·stər] *n* Ostern *nt*

'Easter egg *n* Osterei *nt*

eastern ['i·stərn] *adj* **1.** östlich; **the ~ seaboard** die Ostküste **2.** E~ orientalisch

easterner ['i·stər·nər] *n* Oststaatler(in) *m(f)*

Easter 'Sunday *n* Ostersonntag *m*

East 'Germany *n* HIST Ostdeutschland *nt*

eastwards ['ist·wərdz] *adj, adv* nach Osten

easy <-ier, -iest> ['i·zi] **I.** *adj* einfach; (*effortless*) mühelos; (*trouble-free*) angenehm **II.** *adv* **[take it]** ~ **[now]**! immer mit der Ruhe!; **to take things** ~ *fam* sich *akk* schonen; (*rest*) sich *dat* keinen Stress machen **III.** *interj fam* locker

'easy-care *adj* pflegeleicht

'easy chair *n* Sessel *m*

easy'going *adj* unkompliziert; (*relaxed*) gelassen

eat <ate, eaten> [it] **I.** *vt* essen; (*animal*) fressen; **to ~ breakfast** frühstücken ▸ **what's ~ing you?** was bedrückt dich? **II.** *vi* essen; (*animal*) fressen

◆ **eat out** *vi* essen gehen

◆ **eat up** *vt, vi* aufessen; (*animal*) auffressen

eaten ['i·tən] *pp* of **eat**

eatery ['i·tə·ri] *n fam* Esslokal *nt*

eau de cologne [ˌou·də·kə·'loun] *n* Kölnischwasser *nt*

eavesdrop <-pp-> ['ivz·drap] *vi* [heimlich] lauschen; **to ~ on sb/sth** jdn/etw belauschen

ebb [eb] *n* Ebbe *f; fig* **to be at a low ~** auf einem Tiefstand sein; (*funds*) knapp bei Kasse sein

ebony ['eb·ə·ni] *n* Ebenholz *nt*

EC [ˌi·'si] *n* HIST *abbr of* **European Community; the ~** die EG

eccentric [ɪk·'sen·trɪk] **I.** *n* Exzentriker(in) *m(f)* **II.** *adj* exzentrisch

ecclesiastic [ɪˌkli·zi·'æs·tɪk] *form* **I.** *n* Geistliche(r) *m* **II.** *adj* kirchlich, geistlich

ECG [ˌiˑsiˑˈdʒi] n abbr of **electrocardiogram** EKG nt

echo [ˈekˑoʊ] I. n <pl -es> Echo nt; fig Anklang m II. vi [wider]hallen; (repeat) wiederholen III. vt wiedergeben; (rot) wiederholen

eclipse [ɪˈklɪps] I. n Finsternis f; fig Niedergang m II. vt verfinstern; fig in den Schatten stellen

ecological [ˌiˑkəˈladʒˑɪˑkəl] adj ökologisch; ~ **disaster** Umweltkatastrophe f

ecologist [iˈkalˑəˑdʒɪst] n Ökologe, -in m, f

ecology [iˈkalˑəˑdʒi] n Ökologie f

e-commerce [ˈiˑkamˑɜrs] n short for **electronic commerce** E-Commerce m

economic [ˌiˑkəˈnamˑɪk] adj wirtschaftlich; (profitable) rentabel

economical [ˌiˑkəˈnamˑɪˑkəl] adj wirtschaftlich; (frugal) sparsam

economics [ˌiˑkəˈnamˑɪks] n + sing vb Wirtschaftswissenschaft[en] f[pl]; (aspect) wirtschaftlicher Aspekt

economist [ɪˈkanˑəˑmɪst] n Wirtschaftswissenschaftler(in) m(f)

economize [ɪˈkanˑəˑmaɪz] vi sparen

economy [ɪˈkanˑəˑmi] n Wirtschaft f; (thriftiness) Sparsamkeit f kein pl

e'conomy class n Touristenklasse f

e'conomy pack, e'conomy size n Sparpackung f

ecosystem [ˈeˑkoʊˌ-] n Ökosystem nt

ecstasy [ˈekˑstəˑsi] n Ekstase f; **E~** Ecstasy f

ecstatic [ekˈstætˑɪk] adj ekstatisch

eddy [ˈedˑi] I. vi <-ie-> wirbeln II. n Wirbel m

edge [edʒ] n Rand m; (sharp) Kante f; (sharpness) Schärfe f

edgewise [ˈedʒˑwaɪz] adv to [not] get a word in ~ [nicht] zu Wort kommen

edgy <-ier, -iest> [ˈedʒˑi] adj fam nervös

edible [ˈedˑɪˑbəl] adj essbar

edifying [ˈedɪˑfaɪˑɪŋ] adj erbaulich

edit [ˈedˑɪt] vt redigieren; (text) bearbeiten

edit out vt [heraus]streichen; (scene) herausschneiden

edition [ɪˈdɪˑʃən] n Ausgabe f

editor [ˈedˑɪˑtər] n Herausgeber(in) m(f); (of newspaper) Redakteur(in) m(f)

editorial [ˌedˑəˈtɔrˑiˑəl] I. n Leitartikel m II. adj ~ **staff** Redaktion f

educate [ˈedʒˑəˑkeɪt] vt unterrichten; (train) ausbilden; (enlighten) aufklären

educated [ˈedʒˑəˑkeɪˌtɪd] adj gebildet; **to be Harvard-~** in Harvard studiert haben

education [ˌedʒˑʊˈkeɪˑʃən] n Bildung f; (system) Erziehungswesen nt

educational [ˌedʒˑʊˈkeɪˑʃəˑnəl] adj Bildungs-; (school) schulisch; (enlightening) lehrreich

eel [il] n Aal m

eerie <-r, -st> [ˈɪrˑi] adj unheimlich

effect [ɪˈfekt] I. n Auswirkung f; (success) Erfolg m; **in** ~ eigentlich; **to come into** ~ in Kraft treten II. vt bewirken

effective [ɪˈfekˑtɪv] adj effektiv; (successful) erfolgreich; (real) tatsächlich; ~ **January 1** mit Wirkung vom 1. Januar

effectively [ɪˈfekˑtɪvˑli] adv effektiv; (successfully) erfolgreich; (basically) eigentlich

effectiveness [ɪˈfekˑtɪvˑnəs] n Effektivität f

efficiency [ɪˈfɪʃˑənˑsi] n Leistungsfähigkeit f

efficient [ɪˈfɪʃˑənt] adj leistungsfähig

effort [ˈefˑərt] n Anstrengung f; **to make an** ~ sich anstrengen

effortless [ˈefˑərtˑlɪs] adj mühelos

EFL [ˌiˑefˈel] n abbr of **English as a Foreign Language** Englisch nt als Fremdsprache

e.g. [ˌiˈdʒi] abbr of **exempli gratia** z. B.

e-generation [ˌiˑdʒenˑəˈreɪˑʃən] n Internetgeneration f

egg [eg] I. n Ei nt ▶ **to put all one's ~s in one basket** alles auf eine Karte setzen II. vt **to** ~ **on** ⇆ **sb** jdn anstacheln

'eggplant n Aubergine f

'egg timer n Eieruhr f

ego [ˈiˑgoʊ] n Ego nt

egocentric [ˌiˑgoʊˈsenˑtrɪk] adj egozentrisch

egoism [ˈiˑgoʊˑɪzˑəm] n Egoismus m

egoist [ˈiˑgoʊˑɪst] n Egoist(in) m(f)

egoistic [ˌiˑgoʊˈɪsˑtɪk] adj egoistisch

'ego trip n Egotrip m

Egypt ['i·dʒɪpt] n Ägypten nt

Egyptian [ɪ·'dʒɪp·fən] I. n Ägypter(in) m(f) II. adj ägyptisch

eh [eɪ] interj ~? (pardon?) hä?; (you know?) nicht [wahr?]

eiderdown ['aɪ·dər·daʊn] n [Eider]daunen pl

eight [eɪt] I. adj acht; **there are ~ of us** wir sind [zu] acht; **~ times** achtmal; **one in ~** jeder Achte; **at ~ [o'clock]** um acht [Uhr]; **half past ~** halb neun; **at ~ twenty/forty-five** um zwanzig nach acht/Viertel vor neun II. n Acht f; **~ of clubs** Kreuzacht f

eighteen [ˌeɪ·'tin] I. adj achtzehn II. n Achtzehn f; see also **eight**

eighteenth [ˌeɪ·'tinθ] I. adj achtzehnte(r, s) II. n **1. the ~** der/die/das Achtzehnte **2. (fraction)** Achtzehntel nt

eighth [eɪtθ] I. adj achte(r, s); **every ~ person** jeder Achte; **the ~ largest ...** der/die/das achtgrößte ... II. n **1. the ~** der/die/das Achte **2. the ~ [of the month]** der 8. [des Monats]; **on February ~** am 8. Februar **3. (fraction)** Achtel nt

eightieth ['eɪ·t̮ɪ·əθ] I. adj achtzigste(r, s) II. n **1. the ~** der/die/das Achtzigste **2. (fraction)** Achtzigstel nt; see also **eighth**

eighty ['eɪ·t̮i] I. adj achtzig; see also **eight** II. n Achtzig f; **in one's eighties** in den Achtzigern; **the eighties** pl die 80er Jahre

Eire ['erə] n Eire nt

either ['i·ðər] I. conj **~ ... or ...** entweder ... oder ... II. adv + neg **I don't/haven't ~** ich auch nicht; **it's good and not very expensive** ~ es ist gut – und nicht einmal sehr teuer III. adj **1. (each) on ~ side** auf beiden Seiten **2. (one)** eine(r, s) [von beiden] IV. pron **~ of you** eine(r) von euch beiden

eject [ɪ·'dʒekt] vt hinauswerfen

elaborate [ɪ·'læb·ər·ət] adj kompliziert; (decorations) kunstvoll [gearbeitet]

elaboration [ɪˌlæb·ə·'reɪ·fən] n (of plan) Ausarbeitung f

elastic [ɪ·'læs·tɪk] I. adj elastisch II. n Gummi m

elastic 'band n see **rubber band**

elbow ['el·boʊ] I. n Ellbogen m II. vt **she ~ed him in the ribs** sie stieß ihm den Ellbogen in die Rippen

'elbow grease n Muskelkraft f

elder[1] ['el·dər] I. n Ältere(r) f(m); **church ~** Kirchenälteste(r) f(m) II. adj ältere(r, s)

elder[2] ['el·dər] n (tree) Holunder m

elderly ['el·dər·li] I. adj ältere(r, s) II. **the ~** pl ältere Menschen

eldest ['el·dɪst] I. adj älteste(r, s) II. **the ~** der/die Älteste

elect [ɪ·'lekt] vt wählen

election [ɪ·'lek·fən] n Wahl f

e'lection campaign n Wahlkampf m

E'lection Day n Wahltag m

electoral 'college n Wahlausschuss m (of US president) Wahlmännergremium nt

electric [ɪ·'lek·trɪk] adj elektrisch; (exciting) elektrisierend

electrical [ɪ·'lek·trɪ·kəl] adj elektrisch

electrician [ɪˌlek·'trɪf·ən] n Elektriker(in) m(f)

electricity [ɪˌlek·'trɪs·ə·t̮i] n [elektrischer] Strom; **heated by ~** elektrisch beheizt

electrify [ɪ·'lek·trɪ·faɪ] vt elektrifizieren fig elektrisieren

electrocute [ɪ·'lek·trə·kjut] vt durch einen Stromschlag töten; (execute) auf dem elektrischen Stuhl hinrichten

electrocution [ɪˌlek·trə·'kju·fən] n Tötung f durch Stromschlag; (execution) Hinrichtung f durch den elektrischen Stuhl

electron [ɪ·'lek·tran] n Elektron nt

electronic [ɪˌlek·'tran·ɪk] adj elektronisch

electronics [ɪˌlek·'tran·ɪks] n + sing vb Elektronik f kein pl

elegance ['el·ɪ·gəns] n Eleganz f

elegant ['el·ɪ·gənt] adj elegant

element ['el·ə·mənt] n Element nt

ele'mentary school n Grundschule f

elephant ['el·ə·fənt] n Elefant m

elevate ['el·ə·veɪt] vt [empor]heben

elevated ['el·ə·veɪ·t̮ɪd] adj erhöht; (important) gehoben

elevation [ˌel·ɪ·'veɪ·fən] n [Boden]erhebung f; (promotion) Beförderung f

elevator ['el·ə·veɪ·t̮ər] n Aufzug m

eleven [ɪˈlev·ən] I. adj elf II. n Elf f; see also **eight**

eleventh [ɪˈlev·ənθ] I. adj elfte(r, s) II. n 1. the ~ der/die/das Elfte 2. (fraction) Elftel nt; see also **eighth**

elf <pl **elves**> [elf] n Elf m, Elfe f

eligibility [ˌel·ɪ·dʒə·ˈbɪl·ə·ti] n Eignung f; (entitlement) Berechtigung f

eligible [ˈel·ɪ·dʒə·bəl] adj 1. to be ~ for sth für etw akk qualifiziert sein; (entitled) zu etw dat berechtigt sein 2. (desirable) begehrt

eliminate [ɪˈlɪm·ɪ·neɪt] vt beseitigen; (exclude) ausschließen; **to be ~d** SPORT ausscheiden

elimination [ɪˌlɪm·ɪ·ˈneɪ·ʃən] n Beseitigung f; **process of ~** Ausleseverfahren nt

elite [ɪˈlit] n Elite f

elitism [ɪˈli·tɪz·əm] n Elitedenken nt

elitist [ɪˈli·tɪst] adj elitär

elk <pl ~> [elk] n Wapitihirsch m

ellipse [ɪˈlɪps] n Ellipse f

elliptic(al) [ɪˈlɪp·tɪ·k(əl)] adj elliptisch

elm [elm] n Ulme f

elope [ɪˈloʊp] vi durchbrennen fam

elopement [ɪˈloʊp·mənt] n Durchbrennen nt fam

eloquent [ˈel·ə·kwənt] adj sprachgewandt

else [els] adv 1. **anybody** ~ jeder andere; **anywhere/nowhere** ~ irgendwo/nirgendwo anders; **everybody** ~ alle anderen; **everything** ~ alles andere; **everywhere** ~ überall sonst; **nobody/nothing** ~ niemand/nichts anders; **someone/something** ~ jemand/etwas anders; **somewhere** ~ woanders; **why** ~ ...? warum sonst ...? 2. (additional) sonst noch; **I don't want anyone** ~ **to come but you** ich will, dass außer dir [sonst] keiner kommt; **there's nothing** ~ **to do** es gibt nichts mehr zu tun; **nobody/nothing** ~ sonst niemand/nichts; **somewhere** ~ noch woanders 3. **or** ~! fam sonst gibt's was!

elsewhere [ˈels·wer] adv woanders

elusive [ɪˈlu·sɪv] adj ausweichend; (hard to find) schwer zu fassen

elves [elvz] n pl of **elf**

emaciated [ɪˈmeɪ·ʃi·eɪ·tɪd] adj [stark] abgemagert

e-mail [ˈi·meɪl] I. n abbr of **electronic mail** E-Mail f II. vt [e-]mailen

emancipated [ɪˈmæn·sə·peɪt̬·ɪd] adj emanzipiert

emancipation [ɪˌmæn·sɪ·ˈpeɪ·ʃən] n Emanzipation f

embalm [em·ˈbam] vt [ein]balsamieren

embankment [em·ˈbæŋk·mənt] n Damm m

embargo [em·ˈbar·goʊ] n <pl -es> Embargo nt

embarrass [em·ˈbær·əs] vt in Verlegenheit bringen

embarrassed [em·ˈbær·əst] adj verlegen

embarrassing [em·ˈbær·əsɪŋ] adj peinlich; (generosity) beschämend

embarrassment [em·ˈbær·əs·mənt] n Peinlichkeit f; (feeling) Verlegenheit f

embassy [ˈem·bə·si] n Botschaft f

embellish [em·ˈbel·ɪʃ] vt schmücken; (truth) beschönigen

embers [ˈem·bərz] npl Glut f

embezzle [ɪm·ˈbez·əl] vt unterschlagen

embezzlement [ɪm·ˈbez·əl·mənt] n Unterschlagung f

emblem [ˈem·bləm] n Emblem nt

embodiment [em·ˈbad·ɪ·mənt] n Verkörperung f; **the ~ of virtue** die Tugend selbst

embody [em·ˈbad·i] vt verkörpern; (show) zum Ausdruck bringen

embrace [em·ˈbreɪs] I. vt umarmen; fig [bereitwillig] übernehmen II. n Umarmung f

embroider [em·ˈbrɔɪ·dər] vt, vi sticken; (cloth) besticken

embroidery [em·ˈbrɔɪ·də·ri] n Stickerei f

embryo [ˈem·bri·oʊ] n Embryo m o österr a. nt

emcee [em·ˈsi] n fam Conférencier m; TV Showmaster m

emerald [ˈem·ər·əld] n Smaragd m

emerge [ɪ·ˈmɜrdʒ] vi herauskommen; (surface) auftauchen; (truth) an den Tag kommen

emergence [ɪ·ˈmɜr·dʒəns] n Auftauchen nt; (of country) Entstehung f; (of ideas) Aufkommen nt

emergency [ɪ·ˈmɜr·dʒən·si] n 1. Not-

fall *m*; **state of ~** Ausnahmezustand *m*
2. (*emergency room*) Notaufnahme *f*

e'mergency room, ER *n* Notaufnahme *f*

'**emery board** *n* Nagelfeile *f*

emigrant ['em·ɪ·grənt] *n* Auswanderer, -in *m*, *f*

emigrate ['em·ɪ·greɪt] *vi* auswandern

emigration [ˌem·ɪ·'greɪ·ʃən] *n* Auswanderung *f*

eminent ['em·ɪ·nənt] *adj* [hoch] angesehen

eminently ['em·ɪ·nənt·li] *adv* überaus

emission [ɪ·'mɪʃ·ən] *n* Emission *f*; (*of gas, liquid*) Ausströmen *nt*; (*of heat, light*) Ausstrahlen *nt*

emit <-tt-> [ɪ·'mɪt] *vt* abgeben; (*fumes, cry*) ausstoßen; (*gas, odor*) verströmen; (*heat, sound*) abgeben; (*rays*) aussenden

emoticon [ɪ·'moʊ·tɪ·kan] *n* INET Emoticon *nt*

emotion [ɪ·'moʊ·ʃən] *n* Gefühl *nt*

emotional [ɪ·'moʊ·ʃə·nəl] *adj* emotional; (*reception*) herzlich; (*speech*) gefühlsbetont

emotionless [ɪ·'moʊ·ʃən·lɪs] *adj* emotionslos; (*face*) ausdruckslos

emperor ['em·pər·ər] *n* Kaiser *m*

emphasis <*pl* -ses> ['em·fə·sɪs] *n* Betonung *f*

emphasize ['em·fə·saɪz] *vt* betonen

empire ['em·paɪr] *n* Imperium *nt*

employ [em·'plɔɪ] *vt* beschäftigen; (*staff*) einstellen

employee ['em·plɔɪ·'i] *n* Angestellte(r) *f(m)*; **~s** *pl* (*staff*) Belegschaft *f*

employer [em·'plɔɪ·ər] *n* Arbeitgeber(in) *m(f)*

employment [em·'plɔɪ·mənt] *n* 1. Beschäftigung *f*; (*taking on*) Anstellung *f*; **in ~** erwerbstätig 2. (*profession*) Beruf *m*

em'ployment agency *n* Stellenvermittlung *f*

empress <*pl* -es> ['em·prɪs] *n* Kaiserin *f*

emptiness ['emp·tɪ·nɪs] *n* Leere *f*

empty ['emp·ti] I. *adj* leer; (*house*) leer stehend; (*stomach*) nüchtern II. *vt* <-ie-> [ent]leeren; (*pour*) schütten III. *vi* <-ie-> sich leeren IV. *n* **empties** *pl* Leergut *nt*

empty out I. *vt* ausleeren; (*pour*) ausschütten II. *vi* sich leeren

empty-'handed *adj* mit leeren Händer; **nach ~**

empty-'headed *adj* hohlköpfig

emu <*pl* -> ['i·mju] *n* Emu *m*

emulsion [ɪ·'mʌl·ʃən] *n* Emulsion *f*

enable [ɪ·'neɪ·bəl] *vt* **to ~ sb to do sth** jdm ermöglichen, etw zu tun

enact [ɪ·'nækt] *vt* (*role*) spielen; (*play*) aufführen; LAW erlassen

enamel [ɪ·'næm·əl] *n* Email *nt*; (*dental*) Zahnschmelz *m*

encapsulate [ɪn·'kæp·sə·leɪt] *vt* ummanteln

encased [en·'keɪs] *adj* ummantelt

enchant [en·'tʃænt] *vt* entzücken

enchanting [en·'tʃæn·tɪŋ] *adj* entzückend

encircle [en·'sɜr·kəl] *vt* umgeben; MIL umzingeln

encl. *adj, n abbr of* **enclosed, enclosure** Anl.

enclose [en·'kloʊz] *vt* umgeben; (*shut in*) einschließen; (*mail*) beilegen

enclosure [en·'kloʊ·ʒər] *n* eingezäuntes Grundstück; (*for animals*) Gehege *nt*; (*in mail*) Anlage *f*

encompass [en·'kʌm·pəs] *vt* umfassen

encore ['an·kɔr] *n* Zugabe *f*

encounter [en·'kaʊn·tər] I. *vt* stoßen auf +*akk*; (*meet*) [unerwartet] treffen II. *n* Begegnung *f*; MIL Zusammenstoß *m*

encourage [en·'kɜr·ɪdʒ] *vt* 1. ermutigen; (*give hope*) unterstützen; **to ~ sb to do sth** jdn [dazu] ermuntern, etw zu tun; (*advise*) jdm [dazu] raten, etw zu tun 2. (*promote*) fördern

encouragement [en·'kɜr·ɪdʒ·mənt] *n* Ermutigung *f*; (*urging*) Ermunterung *f*; (*support*) Unterstützung *f*

encouraging [en·'kɜr·ɪdʒ·ɪŋ] *adj* ermutigend

encyclopedia [en·ˌsaɪ·klə·'pi·di·ə] *n* Lexikon *nt*

encyclopedic [en·ˌsaɪ·klə·'pi·dɪk] *adj* universal

end [end] I. *n* 1. Ende *nt*; (*completion*) Schluss *m*; **until the ~** bis zuletzt; **no ~ of trouble** reichlich Ärger; **~ to ~** der Länge nach; **on ~** hochkant 2. *usu*

pl (*aims*) Ziel *nt*; (*purpose*) Zweck *m*
3. SPORT [Spielfeld]hälfte *f* ▸ **at the ~ of the day** [*or* **in the ~**] (*all considered*) letzten Endes; (*finally*) schließlich; **to go off the deep ~** hochgehen; **to make ~s meet** mit seinem Geld zurechtkommen **II.** *vt* beenden **III.** *vi* enden; **to ~ in a tie** unentschieden ausgehen

end up *vi* enden; **to ~ up in prison** [schließlich] im Gefängnis landen; **to ~ up teaching** schließlich Lehrer/Lehrerin werden

endanger [en·'deɪn·dʒər] *vt* gefährden; **an ~ed species** eine vom Aussterben bedrohte Art

endearing [en·'dɪr·ɪŋ] *adj* lieb[enswert]; (*smile*) gewinnend

endeavor [en·'dev·ər] **I.** *vi* sich bemühen **II.** *n* Bemühung *f*

ending ['en·dɪŋ] *n* Schluss *m*; (*of story, book*) Ausgang *m*; **happy ~** Happyend *nt*

endive ['en·daɪv] *n* Endivie *f*

endless ['end·lɪs] *adj* endlos; (*countless*) unzählig

endorse [en·'dɔrs] *vt* billigen; (*promote*) unterstützen; (*check*) auf der Rückseite unterschreiben

endorsement [en·'dɔrs·mənt] *n* Billigung *f*; (*signature*) Giro *nt* fachspr

endow [en·'daʊ] *vt* (*prize*) stiften; **to be ~ed with sth** mit etw *dat* ausgestattet sein

endowment [en·'daʊ·mənt] *n* Stiftung *f*

endurable [en·'dʊr·ə·bəl] *adj* erträglich

endurance [en·'dʊr·əns] *n* Ausdauer *f*

endure [en·'dʊr] **I.** *vt* ertragen; (*suffer*) erleiden **II.** *vi* fortdauern

enemy ['en·ə·mi] **I.** *n* Feind(in) *m(f)* **II.** *adj* feindlich

energetic [ˌen·ər·'dʒet̬·ɪk] *adj* energiegeladen; (*resolute*) energisch

energy ['en·ər·dʒi] *n* Energie *f*; (*vigor also*) Kraft *f*; **~ crisis** Energiekrise *f*

enforce [en·'fɔrs] *vt* durchsetzen

enforcement [en·'fɔrs·mənt] *n* Erzwingung *f*; (*of regulation*) Durchsetzung *f*; (*of law*) Vollstreckung *f*

engage [en·'geɪdʒ] *vt* (*employ*) anstellen; (*clutch*) einschalten; MIL angreifen

engaged [en·'geɪdʒd] *adj* verlobt; **to get**

~ [**to sb**] sich [mit jdm] verloben

engagement [en·'geɪdʒ·mənt] *n* Verlobung *f*; (*appointment*) Verabredung *f*

en'gagement ring *n* Verlobungsring *m*

engaging [en·'geɪ·dʒɪŋ] *adj* einnehmend; (*smile*) gewinnend

engine ['en·dʒɪn] *n* Motor *m*; (*jet*) Triebwerk *nt*; RAIL Lok[omotive] *f*

engineer [ˌen·dʒɪ·'nɪr] **I.** *n* Ingenieur(in) *m(f)*; (*train driver*) Lok[omotiv]führer(in) *m(f)* **II.** *vt* konstruieren; (*contrive*) arrangieren

engineering [ˌen·dʒɪ·'nɪr·ɪŋ] *n* Technik *f*; (*studies*) Ingenieurwissenschaft *f*

England ['ɪŋ·glənd] *n* England *nt*

English ['ɪŋ·glɪʃ] **I.** *n* Englisch *nt*; **the ~** *pl* die Engländer **II.** *adj* englisch; **~ department** Institut *nt* für Anglistik

'Englishman *n* Engländer *m*

'Englishwoman *n* Engländerin *f*

engrave [en·'greɪv] *vt* [ein]gravieren; (*on stone*) einmeißeln; (*on wood*) einschnitzen

engraving [en·'greɪ·vɪŋ] *n* **1.** (*print*) Stich *m*; (*from wood*) Holzschnitt *m* **2.** (*design*) Gravur *f*

engulf [en·'gʌlf] *vt* verschlingen

enhance [ɪn·'hæns] *vt* verbessern; (*intensify*) hervorheben

enigma [ɪ·'nɪg·mə] *n* Rätsel *nt*

enjoy [en·'dʒɔɪ] *vt* genießen; **did you ~ the movie?** hat dir der Film gefallen?; **to ~ doing sth** etw gern[e] tun; **to ~ oneself** sich amüsieren; **~ yourself!** viel Spaß!

enjoyable [en·'dʒɔɪ·ə·bəl] *adj* angenehm; (*entertaining*) unterhaltsam

enjoyment [en·'dʒɔɪ·mənt] *n* Vergnügen *nt*

enlarge [en·'lardʒ] *vt* vergrößern; (*expand*) erweitern

enlighten [en·'laɪ·tən] *vt* aufklären

enlightened [en·'laɪ·tənd] *adj* aufgeklärt

enlightenment [en·'laɪ·tən·mənt] *n* **the E~** die Aufklärung

enlist [en·'lɪst] **I.** *vi* sich melden **II.** *vt* anwerben; (*support*) gewinnen

en masse [an·'mæs] *adv* alle zusammen

enormity [ɪ·'nɔr·mə·ti] *n* ungeheures Ausmaß

enormous [ɪ·'nɔr·məs] *adj* enorm; (*dif-*

ficulties) ungeheuer

enough [ɪ·ˈnʌf] I. *adj* genug; **that should be ~** das dürfte reichen; **just ~ room** gerade Platz genug II. *adv* **1. are you warm ~?** ist es dir warm genug? **2. he seems nice ~** er scheint so weit recht nett zu sein; **strangely ~** seltsamerweise III. *pron* **there's ~ for everybody** es ist für alle genug da; **that's ~!** jetzt reicht es!

enquire [en·ˈkwaɪr] *vi see* **inquire**

enquiry [en·ˈkwaɪr·i] *n see* **inquiry**

enrage [en·ˈreɪdʒ] *vt* wütend machen

enraged [en·ˈreɪdʒd] *adj* wütend

enrich [en·ˈrɪtʃ] *vt* bereichern

enroll, enrol [en·ˈroʊl] *vi* sich einschreiben; *(for course)* sich anmelden

enrollment, enrolment [en·ˈroʊl·mənt] *n* Einschreibung *f*; *(for course)* Anmeldung *f*

en route [ˌɑn·ˈrut] *adv* unterwegs

ensemble [ɑn·ˈsɑm·bəl] *n* Ensemble *nt*

enslave [en·ˈsleɪv] *vt* zum Sklaven machen

ensure [en·ˈʃʊr] *vt* sicherstellen

entangle [en·ˈtæŋ·gəl] *vt* **to get ~d in sth** sich in etw *dat* verfangen; *fig* sich in etw *akk* verwickeln

enter [ˈen·tər] I. *vt* **1.** hineingehen in +*akk*; *(room)* betreten; *(phase)* eintreten in +*akk*; *(penetrate)* eindringen in +*akk* **2.** *(data)* eingeben; *(in register)* eintragen **3.** *(join)* beitreten +*dat*; **to ~ sb in sth** jdn für etw *akk* anmelden II. *vi* **1.** THEAT auftreten **2.** *(register)* **to ~ in sth** sich für etw *akk* [an]melden

enter into *vi* **to ~ into an alliance** ein Bündnis schließen; **to ~ into negotiations** in Verhandlungen eintreten

'enter key *n* COMPUT Eingabetaste *f*

enterprise [ˈen·tər·praɪz] *n* Unternehmen *nt*; *(initiative)* Unternehmungsgeist *m*

enterprising [ˈen·tər·praɪ·zɪŋ] *adj* unternehmungslustig; *(ingenious)* einfallsreich

entertain [ˌen·tər·ˈteɪn] I. *vt* unterhalten; *(guests)* zu sich einladen; *(give meal)* bewirten II. *vi* Gäste haben

entertainer [ˌen·tər·ˈteɪ·nər] *n* Entertainer(in) *m(f)*

entertaining [ˌen·tər·ˈteɪ·nɪŋ] I. *adj* unterhaltsam II. *n* **to do a lot of ~** häufig Leute bewirten

entertainment [ˌen·tər·ˈteɪn·mənt] *n* Unterhaltung *f*

enthusiasm [en·ˈθu·zi·æz·əm] *n* Begeisterung *f*

enthusiast [ɪn·ˈθu·zi·æst] *n* Enthusiast(in) *m(f)*

enthusiastic [en·ˌθu·zi·ˈæs·tɪk] *adj* begeistert

entire [en·ˈtaɪr] *adj* ganz; *(complete)* vollständig

entirely [en·ˈtaɪr·li] *adv* ganz; *(agree)* völlig

entirety [en·ˈtaɪ·rə·ti] *n* Gesamtheit *f*

entitle [en·ˈtaɪ·təl] *vt* **to be ~d to do sth** dazu berechtigt sein, etw zu tun

entrails [ˈen·treɪlz] *npl* Eingeweide *pl*

entrance [ˈen·trəns] *n* Eingang *m*; *(for car)* Einfahrt *f*; *(entering)* Eintritt *m*; THEAT Auftritt *m*

'entrance exam(ination) *n* Aufnahmeprüfung *f*

entrepreneur [ˌɑn·trə·prə·ˈnɜr] *n* Unternehmer(in) *m(f)*

entrust [en·ˈtrʌst] *vt* **to ~ sth to sb** jdm etw anvertrauen

entry [ˈen·tri] *n* **1.** Eintritt *m*; *(by car)* Einfahrt *f*; *(into country)* Einreise *f*; *(into organization)* Aufnahme *f*; **"no ~"** „Zutritt verboten" **2.** *(entrance)* Eingang *m*; *(road)* Einfahrt *f*

'entry form *n* Antragsformular *nt*; *(for competition)* Teilnahmeformular *nt*

envelop [en·ˈvel·əp] *vt* einhüllen

envelope [ˈen·və·loʊp] *n* Briefumschlag *m*

enviable [ˈen·vi·ə·bəl] *adj* beneidenswert

envious [ˈen·vi·əs] *adj* neidisch

environment [en·ˈvaɪ·ərn·mənt] *n* **1. the ~** die Umwelt **2.** *(surroundings)* Umgebung *f*; *(social)* Milieu *nt*

environmental [en·ˌvaɪ·ərn·ˈmen·təl] *adj* Umwelt-

environmentalist [en·ˌvaɪ·ərn·ˈmen·təl·ɪst] *n* Umweltschützer(in) *m(f)*

environmentally [en·ˌvaɪ·rən·ˈmen·təl] *adv* **~ damaging** umweltschädlich

environment-'friendly *adj* umweltfreundlich

envoy ['an·vɔɪ] n Gesandte(r) f(m)

envy ['en·vi] **I.** n Neid m; **he's the ~ of the school with his new car** die ganze Schule beneidet ihn um sein neues Auto **II.** vt <-ie-> **to ~ sb sth** jdn um etw akk beneiden

enzyme ['en·zaɪm] n Enzym nt

eon ['i·an] n Äon m

epic ['ep·ɪk] **I.** n Epos m **II.** adj episch; fig abenteuerlich; **~ poet** Epiker(in) m(f); **~ proportions** unvorstellbare Ausmaße

epicenter ['ep·ɪ·sen·tər] n Epizentrum nt

epidemic [ˌep·ɪ'dem·ɪk] n Epidemie f

epilepsy ['ep·ɪ·lep·si] n Epilepsie f

epileptic [ˌep·ɪ'lep·tɪk] **I.** n Epileptiker(in) m(f) **II.** adj epileptisch

epilogue, epilog ['ep·ɪ·lag] n Epilog m

Epiphany [ɪ'pɪf·ə·ni] n Dreikönigsfest nt

episode ['ep·ɪ·soud] n Episode f

epitaph ['ep·ɪ·tæf] n Grabinschrift f

epitome [ɪ'pɪt·ə·mi] n Inbegriff m; **the ~ of elegance** die Eleganz selbst

epoch ['ep·ək] n Epoche f

equal ['i·kwəl] **I.** adj 1. (same) gleich; **of ~ size** gleich groß 2. (able) **to be ~ to a task** einer Aufgabe gewachsen sein **II.** n Gleichgestellte(r) f(m); **to have no ~** unübertroffen sein **III.** vt <-l- or -ll-> 1. MATH ergeben 2. (match) herankommen an +akk; (record) erreichen

equality [ɪ'kwal·ə·ti] n Gleichberechtigung f; **racial ~** Rassengleichheit f

equally ['i·kwə·li] adv ebenso; **~ good** gleich gut; **to divide sth ~** etw gleichmäßig aufteilen

equal opportunity n Chancengleichheit f

equal sign n Gleichheitszeichen nt

equation [ɪ'kweɪ·ʒən] n Gleichung f

equator [ɪ'kweɪ·tər] n Äquator m; **on the ~** am Äquator

equilibrium [ˌi·kwɪ'lɪb·ri·əm] n Gleichgewicht nt

equip <-pp-> [ɪ'kwɪp] vt ausstatten; fig rüsten

equipment [ɪ'kwɪp·mənt] n Ausstattung f

equivalence [ɪ'kwɪv·ə·ləns] n Äquivalenz f

equivalent [ɪ'kwɪv·ə·lənt] **I.** adj äquivalent; **to be ~ to sth** etw dat entsprechen

II. n Äquivalent nt

equivocal [ɪ'kwɪv·ə·kəl] adj zweideutig

ER [ˌi·'ar] n abbr of **emergency room** Notaufnahme f

era ['ɪr·ə] n Ära f

erase [ɪ'reɪs] vt entfernen; (memories) auslöschen; (rub out) ausradieren

eraser [ɪ'reɪ·sər] n Radiergummi m

erect [ɪ'rekt] **I.** adj aufrecht; (penis) erigiert **II.** vt errichten; (upright) aufstellen

erection [ɪ'rek·ʃən] n Errichtung f; (penis) Erektion f

ergonomic [ˌɜr·gə·'nam·ɪk] adj ergonomisch

ermine ['ɜr·moʊd] n Hermelin nt

erode [ɪ'roʊd] **I.** vt erodieren; (soil) abtragen; fig untergraben **II.** vi erodiert werden; (soil) abgetragen werden

erosion [ɪ'roʊ·ʒən] n Erosion f; fig (Dahin)schwinden nt

erotic [ɪ'rat·ɪk] adj erotisch

errand ['er·ənd] n Besorgung f

erratic [ɪ'ræt·ɪk] adj sprunghaft

erroneous [ɪ'roʊ·ni·əs] adj falsch

error ['er·ər] n Fehler m; (in baseball) Fehlpass m

error message n COMPUT Fehlermeldung f

error-prone adj fehleranfällig

erupt [ɪ'rʌpt] vi ausbrechen; fig explodieren

eruption [ɪ'rʌp·ʃən] n Ausbruch m

escalate ['es·kə·leɪt] **I.** vi eskalieren **II.** vt ausweiten

escalation [ˌes·kə·'leɪ·ʃən] n Eskalation f; (of fighting) Ausweitung f

escalator ['es·kə·leɪ·tər] n Rolltreppe f

escapade [ˌes·kə·'peɪd] n Eskapade f

escape [ɪ'skeɪp] **I.** vi 1. fliehen; (successfully) entkommen; (from cage, prison) ausbrechen; (zoo animal) entlaufen; (bird) entfliegen 2. (avoid harm) [mit dem Leben] davonkommen; **to ~ unhurt** unverletzt bleiben **II.** vt 1. fliehen; (successfully) entkommen; **to ~ the fire** dem Feuer entkommen 2. (avoid) entgehen +dat; **she was lucky to ~ injury** sie hatte Glück, dass sie nicht verletzt wurde 3. **to ~ sb's attention** jds Aufmerksamkeit entgehen **III.** n Flucht f;

(*from prison*) Ausbruch *m*; (*avoidance*) Entkommen *nt*; **that was a lucky ~!** da haben wir wirklich noch einmal Glück gehabt!; **to have a narrow ~** gerade noch einmal davongekommen sein

e'scape key *n* COMPUT Esc-Taste *f*

escapism [ɪ·'skeɪ·pɪz·əm] *n* Realitätsflucht *f*

escort I. *vt* [ɪs·'kɔrt, es·'kɔrt] eskortieren; MIL Geleitschutz geben +*dat*; **to ~ sb upstairs** jdn hinaufbringen **II.** *n* ['es·kɔrt] Begleitung *f*; (*guard*) Eskorte *f*

esp. *adv abbr of* **especially** bes.

especially [ɪ·'speʃ·ə·li] *adv* besonders

espionage ['es·pi·ə·naʒ] *n* Spionage *f*

espresso [ɪ·'spres·oʊ] *n* Espresso *m*

essay ['es·eɪ] *n* Essay *m o nt*

essence ['es·əns] *n* Wesen *nt*; (*gist*) Wesentliche(s) *nt*; FOOD Essenz *f*

essential [ɪ·'sen·ʃəl] **I.** *adj* unbedingt erforderlich; (*vitamins*) lebenswichtig; (*difference*) grundlegend **II.** *n* **the ~s** *pl* das Wesentliche

essentially [ɪ·'sen·ʃə·li] *adv* im Grunde [genommen]

EST [ˌi·es·'ti] *n abbr of* **Eastern Standard Time** Ostküsten Standardzeit *f*

est. *adj* **1.** *abbr of* **estimated 2.** *abbr of* **established** gegr.

establish [ɪ·'stæb·lɪʃ] *vt* **1.** gründen; (*relations*) aufbauen; (*rule*) aufstellen; **to ~ order** für Ordnung sorgen **2.** (*prove*) feststellen; (*claim*) nachweisen

established [ɪ·'stæb·lɪʃt] *adj* (*standard*) fest; (*proven*) nachgewiesen; (*founded*) gegründet; **it is ~ practice ...** es ist üblich, ...

establishment [ɪ·'stæb·lɪʃ·mənt] *n* **1.** Gründung *f*; (*institution*) Unternehmen *nt*; **educational ~** Bildungseinrichtung *f* **2. the ~** das Establishment

estate [ɪ·'steɪt] *n* Gut *nt*; **country ~** Landgut *nt*

esteem [ɪ·'stim] *n* **to hold sb in high ~** jdn hoch schätzen

esthetic [es·'θet·ɪk] *adj see* **aesthetic**

estimate I. *vt* ['es·tɪ·meɪt] [ein]schätzen **II.** *n* ['es·tɪ·mɪt] Schätzung *f*

estimated ['es·tɪ·meɪ·tɪd] *adj* geschätzt; (*expected*) voraussichtlich

estimation [ˌes·tɪ·'meɪ·ʃən] *n* Einschät-

zung *f*; **in my ~** meiner Ansicht nach

estranged [ɪ·'streɪndʒd] *adj* (*couple*) getrennt

estrogen ['es·trə·dʒən] *n* Östrogen *nt*

estuary ['es·tʃu·er·i] *n* Flussmündung *f*

ETA [ˌi·ti·'eɪ] *n abbr of* **estimated time of arrival** voraussichtliche Ankunft

etc. *adv abbr of* **et cetera** usw., etc.

etch [etʃ] *vt* ätzen; (*in copper*) kupfer stechen

eternal [ɪ·'tɜr·nəl] *adj* ewig; (*complaints*) endlos

eternity [ɪ·'tɜr·nə·ti] *n* Ewigkeit *f*

ethical ['eθ·ɪkəl] *adj* ethisch

ethics ['eθ·ɪks] *n* Ethik *f*

ethnic ['eθ·nɪk] *adj* ethnisch; **~ costume** Landestrachten *pl*

etiquette ['et·ɪ·kɪt] *n* Etikette *f*

eunuch ['ju·nək] *n* Eunuch *m*

euphemism ['ju·fə·mɪz·əm] *n* Euphemismus *m*

euphemistic [ˌju·fə·'mɪs·tɪk] *adj* euphemistisch

euphoria [ju·'fɔr·i·ə] *n* Euphorie *f*

euphoric [ju·'fɔr·ɪk] *adj* euphorisch

euro ['jʊr·oʊ] *n* Euro *m*

Europe ['jʊr·əp] *n* Europa *nt*

European [ˌjʊr·ə·'pi·ən] **I.** *adj* europäisch **II.** *n* Europäer(in) *m(f)*

European 'Union *n* Europäische Union

euthanasia [ˌju·θə·'neɪ·ʒə] *n* Sterbehilfe *f*

evacuate [ɪ·'væk·ju·eɪt] *vt* (*people*) evakuieren; (*area*) räumen

evacuation [ɪ·ˌvæk·ju·'eɪ·ʃən] *n* Evakuierung *f*; (*of building*) Räumung *f*

evade [ɪ·'veɪd] *vt* ausweichen +*dat*; (*police*) entgehen +*dat*; (*taxes*) hinterziehen

evaluate [ɪ·'væl·ju·eɪt] *vt* bewerten; (*results*) auswerten

evaluation [ɪ·ˌvæl·ju·'eɪ·ʃən] *n* Schätzung *f*

evangelical [ˌi·væn·'dʒel·ɪ·kəl] *adj* evangelisch

evangelist [ɪ·'væn·dʒə·lɪst] *n* Wanderprediger(in) *m(f)*

evaporate [ɪ·'væp·ə·reɪt] *vi* verdunsten; *fig* sich in Luft auflösen

evaporation [ɪ·ˌvæp·ə·'reɪ·ʃən] *n* Verdunstung *f*

evasion [ɪ·'veɪ·ʒən] *n* Ausweichen *n*

(*avoidance*) Umgehung *f;* **tax ~** Steuerhinterziehung *f*

vasive [ɪ·ˈveɪ·sɪv] *adj* **to take ~ action** ein Ausweichmanöver machen; **to be ~** ausweichen

ve [iːv] *n* Vorabend *m*

Eve [iːv] *n* Eva *f*

ven [ˈiː·vən] **I.** *adv* **1.** (*also*) selbst; **~ Chris was there** selbst Chris war da **2.** (*indeed*) sogar; **not ~** [noch] nicht einmal; **did he ~ read it?** hat er es überhaupt gelesen? **3.** (*despite*) **~ if ...** selbst wenn ...; **~ so/then** trotzdem **4.** + *comp* **~ colder** noch kälter **II.** *adj* **1.** (*flat*) eben; (*row*) gerade **2.** (*equal*) gleich (*groß*); (*distribution*) gleichmäßig; (*in race*) gleichauf; (*in points*) punktegleich **3.** MATH gerade

even out I. *vt* ausgleichen **II.** *vi* sich ausgleichen

evening [ˈiːv·nɪŋ] *n* Abend *m;* **on Friday ~s** freitagabends

evenly [ˈiː·vən·li] *adv* gleichmäßig; (*calmly*) gelassen

event [ɪ·ˈvent] *n* **1.** Ereignis *nt;* *sporting* **~** Sportveranstaltung *f* **2.** (*case*) **in the ~ that ...** falls ...; **in any ~** auf jeden Fall **3.** SPORT Wettkampf *m*

eventful [ɪ·ˈvent·fəl] *adj* ereignisreich

eventual [ɪ·ˈven·tʃʊ·əl] *adj* schließlich; (*possible*) etwaig

eventuality [ɪ·ˌven·tʃʊ·ˈæl·ə·ti] *n* Eventualität *f*

eventually [ɪ·ˈven·tʃʊ·ə·li] *adv* schließlich; (*some day*) irgendwann

ever [ˈev·ər] *adv* **1.** (*at any time*) je[mals]; **nothing ~ happens here** hier ist nie was los; **have you ~ been there?** bist du schon einmal dort gewesen?; **hardly ~** kaum; **worse than ~** schlimmer als je zuvor **2.** (*always*) **~ since ...** seitdem ... **3.** (*of all time*) **the first performance ~** die allererste Darbietung **4.** (*as intensifier*) **how could anyone ~ ...?** wie kann jemand nur ...?; **when are we ~ going to get this finished?** wann haben wir das endlich fertig?

everglade *n* Sumpfgebiet *nt;* **the E~s** *pl* die Everglades *pl*

evergreen I. *n* immergrüne Pflanze; (*tree*) immergrüner Baum **II.** *adj* im-

mergrün; *fig* immer aktuell

everlasting [ˌev·ər·ˈlæs·tɪŋ] *adj* immerwährend; (*gratitude*) ewig; (*unceasing*) endlos

every [ˈev·ri] *adj* **1.** (*each*) jede(r, s) **2.** (*as emphasis*) ganz und gar; **~ bit as ... as ...** genauso ... wie ...

everybody [ˈev·ri·ˌbad·i], **everyone** [ˈev·ri·wʌn] *pron indef,* + *sing vb* jede(r); **~ but Jane** alle außer Jane

everyday *adj* alltäglich; **~ life** Alltagsleben *nt*

everyone [ˈev·ri·wʌn] *pron see* **everybody**

everything [ˈev·ri·θɪŋ] *pron indef* alles

everywhere [ˈev·ri·wer] *adv* überall

evict [ɪ·ˈvɪkt] *vt* kündigen +*dat*

eviction [ɪ·ˈvɪk·ʃən] *n* Zwangsräumung *f;* **~ order** Räumungsbefehl *m*

evidence [ˈev·ɪ·dəns] *n* **1.** (*proof*) Beweis[e] *m[pl];* **to find no ~ of sth** keinen Anhaltspunkt für etw *akk* haben **2.** LAW Beweisstück *nt*

evil [ˈiː·vəl] **I.** *adj* böse **II.** *n* Übel *nt;* **the lesser of two ~s** das kleinere von zwei Übeln

evolution [ˌev·ə·ˈluː·ʃən] *n* Evolution *f; fig* Entwicklung *f*

evolve [ɪ·ˈvalv] **I.** *vi* sich entwickeln **II.** *vt* entwickeln

ewe [juː] *n* Mutterschaf *nt*

ex <*pl* -es> [eks] *n fam* Ex-Mann, Ex-Frau *m, f;* (*lover*) Ex-Freund(in) *m(f)*

exact [ɪɡ·ˈzækt] *adj* genau; **the ~ opposite** ganz im Gegenteil

exactly [ɪɡ·ˈzækt·li] *adv* **1.** genau; **~!** ganz genau! **2.** **not ~** eigentlich nicht

exaggerate [ɪɡ·ˈzædʒ·ə·reɪt] *vt, vi* übertreiben

exaggerated [ɪɡ·ˈzædʒ·ə·reɪ·ṭɪd] *adj* übertrieben

exaggeration [ɪɡ·ˌzædʒ·ə·ˈreɪ·ʃən] *n* Übertreibung *f*

exam [ɪɡ·ˈzæm] *n* Prüfung *f;* UNIV Examen *nt*

examination [ɪɡ·ˌzæm·ɪ·ˈneɪ·ʃən] *n* **1.** Prüfung *f;* UNIV Examen *nt* **2.** (*investigation*) Untersuchung *f;* (*of evidence*) Überprüfung *f;* **to be under ~** untersucht werden

examine [ɪɡ·ˈzæm·ɪn] *vt* prüfen; (*scruti-*

nize) untersuchen

examiner [ɪɡ·ˈzæm·ɪn·ər] n Prüfer(in) m(f); **medical ~** Gerichtsmediziner(in) m(f)

example [ɪɡ·ˈzæm·pəl] n Beispiel nt; **for ~** zum Beispiel; **to make an ~ of sb** an jdm ein Exempel statuieren

exasperate [ɪɡ·ˈzæs·pə·reɪt] vt zur Verzweiflung bringen

exasperating [ɪɡ·ˈzæs·pə·reɪ·tɪŋ] adj ärgerlich

exasperation [ɪɡ·ˌzæs·pə·ˈreɪ·ʃən] n Verzweiflung f

excavate [ˈek·skə·veɪt] I. vt (*site*) ausgraben; (*hole*) ausheben II. vi Ausgrabungen machen

excavation [ˌek·skə·ˈveɪ·ʃən] n Ausgrabung f; (*of hole*) Ausheben nt

excavator [ˈek·skə·veɪ·tər] n Bagger m

exceed [ɪk·ˈsid] vt übersteigen; (*limit*) überschreiten

exceedingly [ɪk·ˈsi·dɪŋ·li] adv äußerst

excel <-ll-> [ɪk·ˈsel] I. vi **to ~ at sth** sich bei etw dat hervortun II. vt **to ~ one-self** sich akk selbst übertreffen

excellence [ˈek·sə·ləns] n Vorzüglichkeit f; (*of performance*) hervorragende Qualität

Excellency [ˈek·sə·lən·si] n **His/Your ~** Seine/Eure Exzellenz

excellent [ˈek·sə·lənt] adj ausgezeichnet

except [ɪk·ˈsept] I. prep **~ [for]** außer +dat II. conj 1. (*only*) **I want to buy it, ~ I don't have any money** fam ich will es kaufen, ich habe nur kein Geld 2. (*besides*) außer

excepting [ɪk·ˈsep·tɪŋ] prep außer +dat; **not ~** nicht ausgenommen

exception [ɪk·ˈsep·ʃən] n Ausnahme f; **without ~** ausnahmslos

exceptional [ɪk·ˈsep·ʃə·nəl] adj außergewöhnlich

excerpt [ˈek·sɜrpt] n Auszug m

excess [ɪk·ˈses] n <pl -es> Übermaß nt; (*surplus*) Überschuss m

excessive [ɪk·ˈses·ɪv] adj übermäßig; (*claim*) übertrieben

exchange [ɪks·ˈtʃeɪndʒ] I. vt austauschen; (*in store*) umtauschen; (*looks, words*) wechseln II. n 1. Tausch m; **in ~** dafür 2. (*interchange*) Wortwech-

sel m; **~ of blows** Schlagabtausch m

ex'change rate n Wechselkurs m

ex'change student n Austausch schüler(in) m(f); UNIV Austauschstu dent(in) m(f)

excitable [ɪk·ˈsaɪ·tə·bəl] adj erregbar

excite [ɪk·ˈsaɪt] vt begeistern; (*imagina tion*) anregen

excited [ɪk·ˈsaɪ·tɪd] adj aufgeregt (*thrilled*) begeistert; **to be ~ about sth** (*now*) von etw dat begeistert sein; (*in near future*) sich auf etw akk freuen

excitement [ɪk·ˈsaɪt·mənt] n Aufregung f

exciting [ɪk·ˈsaɪ·tɪŋ] adj aufregend; (*story*) spannend

excl. adj, prep abbr of **excluding, ex clusive** exkl.

exclaim [ɪk·ˈskleɪm] I. vi **to ~ in deligh** vor Freude aufschreien II. vt ausrufen

exclamation [ˌek·sklə·ˈmeɪ·ʃən] n Aus ruf m

excla'mation point, excla'mation mar n Ausrufezeichen nt

exclude [ɪk·ˈsklud] vt ausschließen

excluding [ɪk·ˈsklu·dɪŋ] prep ausgenom men +gen

exclusion [ɪk·ˈsklu·ʒən] n Ausschluss m

exclusive [ɪk·ˈsklu·sɪv] I. adj ausschließ lich; (*select*) exklusiv II. n Exklusiv bericht m

excommunicate [ˌeks·kə·ˈmju·nɪ·keɪt] v exkommunizieren

excommunication [ˌeks·kə·ˌmju·nɪ·ˈkeɪ ʃən] n Exkommunikation f

excrement [ˈek·skrə·mənt] n Exkremen te pl

excruciating [ɪk·ˈskru·ʃi·eɪ·tɪŋ] ad schmerzhaft; (*suffering*) entsetzlich

excursion [ɪk·ˈskɜr·ʒən] n Ausflug m

excuse I. vt [ɪk·ˈskjuz] entschuldigen (*ignore*) hinwegsehen über +akk; ~ **me!** entschuldigen Sie bitte!, Entschul digung!; ~ **me?** wie bitte?; **to ~ sb from sth** jdn von etw dat befreien II. n [ɪk· ˈskjus] Entschuldigung f; (*justification*) Ausrede f; **doctor's ~** Krankmeldung f

execute [ˈek·sɪ·kjut] vt ausführen; (*kill*) hinrichten

execution [ˌek·sɪ·ˈkju·ʃən] n Ausführung f; (*killing*) Hinrichtung f

executioner [ˌek·sɪ·ˈkju·ʃə·nər] n Scharf

richter *m*

xecutive [ɪɡ·ˈzek·jʊ·tɪv] **I.** *n* leitender Angestellter/leitende Angestellte; **junior/senior ~** untere/höhere Führungskraft **II.** *adj* ~ **editor** Chefredakteur(in) *m(f);* ~ **producer** leitender Produzent/leitende Produzentin

xemplary [ɪɡ·ˈzem·plə·ri] *adj* vorbildlich

xempt [ɪɡ·ˈzempt] **I.** *vt* befreien; *(draftee)* freistellen **II.** *adj* ~ **from tax** gebührenfrei

xercise [ˈek·sər·saɪz] **I.** *vt* **1.** trainieren; *(dog)* spazieren führen; *(horse)* bewegen **2.** *(use)* üben; *(authority, control)* ausüben; *(right)* geltend machen **II.** *vi* trainieren **III.** *n* **1.** Bewegung *f;* *(training)* Übung *f;* **to do ~s** Gymnastik machen **2.** MIL Übung *f;* SCH, UNIV Aufgabe *f*

xercise bike *n* Heimfahrrad *nt*

xercise book *n* Heft *nt*

xerciser [ˈek·sər·saɪ·zər] *n* Trainingsgerät *nt*

xert [ɪɡ·ˈzɜrt] *vt* ausüben; *(influence)* geltend machen; **to ~ oneself** sich anstrengen

xertion [ɪɡ·ˈzɜr·ʃən] *n* Anstrengung *f*

xhale [eks·ˈheɪl] *vt, vi* ausatmen

xhaust [ɪɡ·ˈzɔst] **I.** *vt* ermüden; *(use up)* erschöpfen; **to ~ oneself** sich strapazieren **II.** *n* **1.** ~ [fumes] Abgase *pl* **2.** *(tailpipe)* Auspuff *m*

xhausted [ɪɡ·ˈzɔs·tɪd] *adj* erschöpft; *(used up)* aufgebraucht

xhausting [ɪɡ·ˈzɔs·tɪŋ] *adj* anstrengend

xhaustion [ɪɡ·ˈzɔs·tʃən] *n* Erschöpfung *f*

xhaustive [ɪɡ·ˈzɔs·tɪv] *adj* erschöpfend; *(inquiry)* eingehend; *(list)* vollständig; *(research)* tief greifend

x'haust pipe *n* Auspuffrohr *nt*

xhibit [ɪɡ·ˈzɪb·ɪt] **I.** *n* **1.** Ausstellungsstück *nt* **2.** LAW *(evidence)* Beweisstück *nt* **II.** *vt, vi* ausstellen

xhibition [ˌek·sɪ·ˈbɪʃ·ən] *n* Ausstellung *f*

xhibitor [ɪɡ·ˈzɪb·ɪ·tər] *n* Aussteller(in) *m(f)*

xhilarating [ɪɡ·ˈzɪl·ə·reɪ·tɪŋ] *adj* aufregend; *(energizing)* belebend

xhilaration [ɪɡ·ˈzɪl·ə·reɪ·ʃən] *n* Hochgefühl *nt*

exhumation [ˌeg·zju·ˈmeɪ·ʃən] *n* Exhumierung *f*

exhume [ɪɡ·ˈzum] *vt* exhumieren

exile [ˈek·saɪl] **I.** *n* **1.** Exil *nt;* **to go into ~** ins Exil gehen **2.** *(person)* Verbannte(r) *f(m);* **tax ~** Steuerflüchtling *m* **II.** *vt* verbannen

exist [ɪɡ·ˈzɪst] *vi* existieren; *(survive)* überleben

existence [ɪɡ·ˈzɪs·təns] *n* Existenz *f;* **means of ~** Lebensgrundlage *f*

existent [ɪɡ·ˈzɪs·tent] *adj* vorhanden

existing [ɪɡ·ˈzɪs·tɪŋ] *adj* bestehend; *(rules)* gegenwärtig

exit [ˈeg·sɪt] **I.** *n* **1.** Ausgang *m;* *(road)* Ausfahrt *f* **2.** *(departure)* Weggehen *nt* kein *pl;* *(from room)* Hinausgehen *nt* kein *pl* **II.** *vt* verlassen **III.** *vi* hinausgehen; *(in car)* eine Ausfahrt nehmen

'exit visa *n* Ausreisevisum *nt*

exodus <*pl* -es> [ˈek·sə·dəs] *n* Auszug *m;* **general ~** allgemeiner Aufbruch

exorbitant [ɪɡ·ˈzɔr·bə·tənt] *adj* überhöht

exorcism [ˈek·sɔr·sɪz·əm] *n* Exorzismus *m*

exorcist [ˈek·sɔr·sɪst] *n* Exorzist(in) *m(f)*

exotic [ɪɡ·ˈzɑt·ɪk] *adj* exotisch

expand [ɪk·ˈspænd] **I.** *vi* zunehmen; *(physically)* sich ausdehnen; *(economy a.)* expandieren; *(horizons)* sich erweitern **II.** *vt* erweitern; *(physically)* ausdehnen

expanse [ɪk·ˈspæns] *n* Weite *f;* ~ **of lawn** ausgedehnte Rasenfläche

expansion [ɪk·ˈspæn·ʃən] *n* Erweiterung *f;* *(physically)* Ausdehnung *f;* *(of territory)* Expansion *f*

expansionism [ɪk·ˈspæn·ʃə·nɪz·əm] *n* Expansionspolitik *f*

expansive [ɪk·ˈspæn·sɪv] *adj* umgänglich; *(effusive)* überschwänglich

expatriate *n* [ek·ˈspeɪ·tri·ət] [ständig] im Ausland Lebende(r) *f(m)*

expect [ɪk·ˈspekt] *vt* **1.** erwarten; **that was to be ~ed** das war zu erwarten; **to ~ to do sth** damit rechnen, etw zu tun **2.** *fam* **I ~ so** ich denke schon

expectancy [ɪk·ˈspek·tən·si] *n* Erwartung *f;* **with an air of ~** erwartungsvoll

expectant [ɪk·ˈspek·tənt] *adj* erwartungsvoll; *(mother)* werdend

expectation [ˌek·spek·'teɪ·ʃən] n Erwartung f

expedition [ˌek·spɪ·'dɪʃ·ən] n Expedition f; MIL Feldzug m

expel <-ll-> [ɪk·'spel] vt ausschließen; SCH verweisen; (breath) ausstoßen

expenditure [ɪk·'spen·dɪ·tʃər] n Ausgabe f; (sum spent) Aufwendungen pl

expense [ɪk·'spens] n 1. [Un]kosten pl; ~s pl (offsettable) Spesen pl; at one's own ~ auf eigene Kosten 2. fig at sb's ~ auf jds Kosten pl ▶ no ~s spared [die] Kosten spielen keine Rolle

ex'pense account n Spesenrechnung f

expensive [ɪk·'spen·sɪv] adj teuer; (overly) kostspielig

experience [ɪk·'spɪr·i·əns] I. n Erfahrung f; (event also) Erlebnis nt; to learn by ~ durch Erfahrung lernen II. vt erleben; (endure) erfahren; (difficulties) stoßen auf +akk; (feel) empfinden

experienced [ɪk·'spɪr·i·ənst] adj erfahren; (eye) geschult; to be ~ at sth Erfahrung in etw dat haben

experiment I. n [ɪk·'sper·ɪ·mənt] Experiment nt II. vi [ɪk·'sper·ɪ·ment] experimentieren

experimental [ɪk·ˌsper·ɪ·'men·təl] adj Versuchs-

expert ['ek·spɜrt] I. n Experte, -in m, f, II. adj 1. fachmännisch; (skilled) erfahren 2. (excellent) ausgezeichnet; (liar) perfekt

expertise [ˌek·spɜr·'tiz] n Fachkenntnis f; (skill) Können nt

expert o'pinion n Expertenmeinung f; LAW Sachverständigengutachten nt

expire [ɪk·'spaɪr] vi ablaufen; (contract) auslaufen; (die) verscheiden

expiry [ɪk·'spaɪ·ri] n Ablauf m

explain [ɪk·'spleɪn] vt erklären; you'd better ~ yourself du solltest mir das erklären

♦**explain away** vt eine [einleuchtende] Erklärung für etw akk haben

explanation [ˌek·splə·'neɪ·ʃən] n Erklärung f; by way of ~ [for sth] als Erklärung [für etw akk]

explanatory [ɪk·'splæn·ə·tɔr·i] adj erklärend

explicit [ɪk·'splɪs·ɪt] adj deutlich; (agree-

ment) ausdrücklich; (detailed) unve hüllt

explode [ɪk·'sploʊd] I. vi explodiere (tire) platzen; to ~ with anger vor W platzen II. vt (bomb) zünden; (contai er) sprengen; (argument) widerlegen

exploit I. n ['ek·splɔɪt] Heldentat f II. [ɪk·'splɔɪt] (worker) ausbeuten; (frien ausnutzen; (utilize) nutzen

exploitation [ˌek·splɔɪ·'teɪ·ʃən] n Ausbe tung f; (of friend) Ausnutzung f; (us Nutzung f

exploration [ˌek·splə·'reɪ·ʃən] n Erfo schung f; (examination) Untersu chung f

exploratory [ɪk·'splɔr·ə·tɔr·i] adj Fo schungs-; (drilling, well) Probe-; ~ talk Sondierungsgespräche pl

explore [ɪk·'splɔr] I. vt erforschen; (e. amine) untersuchen II. vi sich um schauen

explorer [ɪk·'splɔr·ər] n Forscher(in) m

explosion [ɪk·'sploʊ·ʒən] n Explosion

explosive [ɪk·'sploʊ·sɪv] I. adj explo siv; (issue) [hoch] brisant II. n Spreng stoff m kein pl

export I. vt, vi [ɪk·'spɔrt] exportiere II. n ['ek·spɔrt] Export m; (product) Ex portartikel m

exporter [ɪk·'spɔr·tər] n Exporteur n (country) Exportland nt

expose [ɪk·'spoʊz] vt freilegen; (to dar ger, ridicule) aussetzen; (reveal) offer baren; (scandal) aufdecken; (spy) ent larven

exposed [ɪk·'spoʊzd] adj ungeschütz (position) exponiert; (bare) freigelegt

exposure [ɪk·'spoʊ·ʒər] n 1. Ausse zung f; (to weather) Ausgesetztsein 2. (contact) Kontakt m 3. (of plo Aufdeckung f; (of affair) Enthüllung (of person) Entlarvung f 4. (photo Aufnahme f

express [ɪk·'spres] I. vt 1. ausdrücker (say) aussprechen; to ~ oneself sich aus drücken 2. (send) per Express schicke II. adj 1. by ~ delivery per Expres 2. (explicit) ausdrücklich; for the purpose eigens zu dem Zweck III. ac per Express IV. n Express[zug] m

expression [ɪk·'spreʃ·ən] n Ausdruck m

(on face) [Gesichts]ausdruck *m;* **freedom of ~** Freiheit *f* der Meinungsäußerung

xpressionless [ɪkˈspreʃ·ən·lɪs] *adj* ausdruckslos

xpressive [ɪkˈspres·ɪv] *adj* ausdrucksvoll; *(voice)* ausdrucksstark

xpressly [ɪkˈspres·li] *adv* ausdrücklich; *(particularly)* extra

k'pressway *n* Schnellstraße *f*

xpulsion [ɪkˈspʌl·ʃən] *n* Ausschluss *m;* *(from country)* Ausweisung *f;* *(from school)* Verweisung *f*

xquisite [ˈek·skwɪ·zɪt] *adj* exquisit

xtend [ɪkˈstend] **I.** *vt* ausstrecken; *(prolong)* verlängern; *(pull out)* verlängern; *(ladder, table)* ausziehen; *(expand)* erweitern; *(influence)* ausdehnen **II.** *vi* sich erstrecken; *(over time)* sich hinziehen

xtended [ɪkˈsten·dɪd] *adj* verlängert; *(bulletin)* umfassend

xtension [ɪkˈsten·ʃən] *n* **1.** Ausstrecken *nt;* *(of muscles)* Dehnung *f;* *(lengthening)* Verlängerung *f;* *(expansion)* Erweiterung *f;* *(of power)* Ausdehnung *f;* *(prolongation)* Verlängerung *f;* ~ **table** Ausziehtisch *m;* **by ~** im weiteren Sinne **2.** *(annex)* Anbau *m* **3.** *(phone line)* Nebenanschluss *m;* *(number)* [Haus]apparat *m*

x'tension cord *n* Verlängerungskabel *nt*

xtensive [ɪkˈsten·sɪv] *adj* ausgedehnt; *(grounds)* weitläufig; *(far-reaching)* weitreichend; *(damage)* beträchtlich; *(knowledge)* breit; *(repairs)* umfangreich

xtent [ɪkˈstent] *n* Ausdehnung *f;* *(range)* Umfang *m;* *(degree)* Maß *nt kein pl;* **to a certain/great ~** in gewissem/hohem Maße

xterior [ɪkˈstɪr·i·ər] **I.** *n* Außenseite *f;* *(look)* Äußere *nt* **II.** *adj* Außen-

xternal [ɪkˈstɜr·nəl] *adj* äußerlich; *(from outside)* äußere(r, s); *(on surface)* äußerlich; **~ affairs** Außenpolitik *f*

xtinct [ɪkˈstɪŋkt] *adj* ausgestorben; *(language)* erloschen; *(inactive)* erloschen; **to become ~** aussterben; *(volcano)* erlöschen

xtinction [ɪkˈstɪŋk·ʃən] *n* Aussterben *nt;*

(deliberate act) Ausrottung *f;* *(inactivity)* Erlöschen *nt*

extinguish [ɪkˈstɪŋ·gwɪʃ] *vt* [aus]löschen

extinguisher [ɪkˈstɪŋ·gwɪʃ·ər] *n* Feuerlöscher *m*

extort [ɪkˈstɔrt] *vt* erzwingen; *(money)* erpressen

extortion [ɪkˈstɔr·ʃən] *n* Erzwingung *f;* *(of money)* Erpressung *f;* **that's sheer ~!** das ist ja Wucher!

extortionate [ɪkˈstɔr·ʃə·nɪt] *adj* übermäßig; *(using force)* erpresserisch; **~ prices** Wucherpreise *pl*

extra [ˈek·strə] **I.** *adj* zusätzlich; **some ~ money** etwas mehr Geld; **to take ~ care** besonders vorsichtig sein; **~ charge** Aufschlag *m* **II.** *adv* **1.** mehr; **to charge ~** einen Aufpreis verlangen; **postage and handling ~** zuzüglich Porto und Versand **2.** *(especially)* besonders **III.** *n* **1.** *(charge)* Aufschlag *m;* *(perk)* Zusatzleistung *f;* *(option)* Extra *nt* **2.** *(newspaper)* Sonderausgabe *f*

extract I. *vt* [ɪkˈstrækt] [heraus]ziehen; *(bullet)* entfernen; *(tooth)* ziehen; *(confession)* abringen **II.** *n* [ˈek·strækt] **1.** *(excerpt)* Auszug *m* **2.** *(concentrate)* Extrakt *m*

extraction [ɪkˈstræk·ʃən] *n* Herausziehen *nt;* *(of bullet)* Entfernen *nt;* *(of tooth)* [Zahn]ziehen *nt;* *(of confession)* Abringen *nt*

extradite [ˈek·strə·daɪt] *vt* ausliefern

extradition [ˌek·strə·ˈdɪʃ·ən] *n* Auslieferung *f*

extraneous [ɪkˈstreɪ·ni·əs] *adj* **~ substance** Fremdstoff *m*

extraordinary [ɪkˈstrɔr·də·ner·i] *adj* außerordentlich; *(coincidence)* merkwürdig

extraterrestrial [ˈek·strə·tə·ˈres·tri·əl] **I.** *adj* außerirdisch **II.** *n* außerirdisches [Lebe]wesen

extravagance [ɪkˈstræv·ə·gəns] *n* Verschwendungssucht *f;* *(luxury)* Luxus *m kein pl*

extravagant [ɪkˈstræv·ə·gənt] *adj* extravagant; *(wasteful)* verschwenderisch

extravaganza [ɪkˌstræv·ə·ˈgæn·zə] *n* opulente Veranstaltung

extreme [ɪkˈstrim] **I.** *adj* äußerste(r, s);

(*difficulties, weather*) extrem **II.** *n* Extrem *nt;* **to go from one ~ to the other** von einem Extrem ins andere fallen

extremely [ɪkˈstriːm·li] *adv* äußerst

extreme sports *npl* Extremsportarten *pl*

extremism [ɪkˈstriː·mɪz·əm] *n* Extremismus *m*

extremist [ɪkˈstriː·mɪst] **I.** *n* Extremist(in) *m(f)* **II.** *adj* radikal

extrovert [ˈek·strə·vɜrt] *n* extravertierter Mensch

extroverted [ˈek·strə·vɜr·tɪd] *adj* extravertiert

exuberance [ɪgˈzuː·bər·əns] *n* Überschwänglichkeit *f;* (*of feelings*) Überschwang *m*

exuberant [ɪgˈzuː·bər·ənt] *adj* überschwänglich; (*mood*) überschäumend

exultant [ɪgˈzʌl·tənt] *adj* jubelnd; (*laugh*) triumphierend

eye [aɪ] **I.** *n* **1.** Auge *nt;* **black ~** blaues Auge; **as far as the ~ can see** so weit das Auge reicht **2.** (*eyelet*) Öse *f;* (*in needle*) Öhr ▸ **to keep an** [*or* **one's**] **~ on sb/sth** ein [wachsames] Auge auf jdn/etw haben; **to keep one's ~s open** [*or* **peeled**] die Augen offen halten; **with one's ~s shut** mit geschlossenen Augen; **to turn a blind ~** [**to sth**] [bei etw] beide Augen zudrücken **II.** *vt* <-d, -d, -ing *or* eying> beäugen; **to ~ sb up and down** (*carefully*) jdn von oben bis unten mustern; (*with desire*) mit begehrlichen Blicken betrachten

eyeball I. *n* Augapfel *m* **II.** *vt fam* mit einem durchdringenden Blick ansehen; (*measure*) nach Augenmaß einschätzen

eyebrow *n* Augenbraue *f*

eye-catching *adj* auffallend

eye contact *n* **to make ~** [**with sb**] Blickkontakt [mit jdm] aufnehmen

eyedrops *n pl* Augentropfen *pl*

eyeful *n* **to get an ~ of dust** Staub ins Auge bekommen ▸ **to get an ~ of sth** einen Blick auf etw *akk* werfen

eyelash *n* Wimper *f*

eyelid *n* Augenlid *nt*

eyeliner *n* Eyeliner *m*

eye opener *n* **to be an ~ for sb** (*enlightening*) jdm die Augen öffnen; (*startling*) alarmierend für jdn sein

eye shadow *n* Lidschatten *m*

eyesight *n* Sehvermögen *nt*

eyesore *n* Schandfleck *m*

eyetooth *n* Augenzahn *m;* **I'd give m eyeteeth for that** *fig* ich würde all darum geben

eyewash *n* Augenwasser *nt; fam* (*no sense*) Blödsinn *m*

eye'witness *n* Augenzeuge, -in *m, f*

F

F <*pl* -'s>, **f** <*pl* -'s> [ef] *n* (*letter*) F *n* f *nt;* **~ as in Foxtrot** F wie Friedrich

fable [ˈfeɪ·bəl] *n* Fabel *f*

fabric [ˈfæb·rɪk] *n* Stoff *m*

fabulous [ˈfæb·jə·ləs] *adj* fabelhaft

façade [fəˈsad] *n* Fassade *f a. fig*

face [feɪs] **I.** *n* **1.** Gesicht *n a. fig;* **wit a smile on one's** ~ mit einem Lächel im Gesicht; **~ down/up** mit dem Ge sicht nach unten/oben; **to look sb i the ~** jdm in die Augen schauen; **t shut the door in sb's ~** jdm die Tü vor der Nase zuschlagen; **~ to ~** vo Angesicht zu Angesicht; **to come ~ t ~ with sth** direkt mit etw *dat* konfron tiert werden **2.** (*of a building*) Fassade (*of a mountain*) Wand *f* **3.** (*reputation* **to lose/save ~** das Gesicht verlieren wahren ▸ **get out of my face!** *far* lass mich in Ruhe!; **in the ~ of sth** (*de spite*) trotz einer S. *gen* **to show one'** ~ sich blicken lassen **II.** *vt* **1.** (*loo toward: person*) **to ~ sb/sth** sich jdm etw zuwenden; **to ~** [*or* **sit facing**] **s** jdm gegenübersitzen **2.** (*look toward* **to ~ sth** (*object*) zu etw *dat* hinzeige (*be situated across from*) gegenübe etw *dat* liegen **3.** (*confront*) **to ~ sth** sb etw/jdm ins Auge sehen; **it's tim we ~d** [the] **facts** es wird Zeit, dass w den Tatsachen ins Auge sehen ▸ **to ~ the music** für die Folgen geradestehe **III.** *vi* **1.** (*point*) **to ~ backward**[**s**] nach hinten zeigen **2.** (*look onto*) **to ~ south** (*garden*) nach Süden liegen **3.** (*look person*) blicken; **facing forward**[**s**] m dem Gesicht nach vorne

face out vi nach außen zeigen

face up vi to ~ up to sth/sb etw/jdm ins Auge sehen; **to ~ up to one's problems** sich seinen Problemen stellen

face cream n Gesichtscreme f

facelift n [Face]lifting nt

face pack n Gesichtsmaske f

facet ['fæs·ɪt] n Facette f a. fig

facetious [fə-'si·ʃəs] adj usu pej [gewollt] witzig

face 'value n Nennwert m; **to take sth at ~** etw für bare Münze nehmen

facial ['feɪ·ʃəl] n [kosmetische] Gesichtsbehandlung

facilitate [fə-'sɪl·ɪ·teɪt] vt erleichtern

facilitator [fə-'sɪl·ɪ·teɪ·tɚr] n Vermittler(in) m(f)

facility [fə-'sɪl·ə·ti] n 1. (natural ability) Begabung f (**for** für +akk) 2. (building and equipment) Einrichtung f, Anlage f; **sports** ~ Sportanlage f

facsimile [fæk·'sɪm·ə·li] n Faksimile nt

fact [fækt] n 1. (truth) Wirklichkeit f 2. (single truth) Tatsache f

fact-finding adj Untersuchungs-

faction ['fæk·ʃən] n POL [Splitter]gruppe f

factor ['fæk·tɚr] n Faktor m; **by a ~ of four** um das Vierfache

factory ['fæk·tə·ri] n Fabrik f

factory 'farm n [voll] automatisierter landwirtschaftlicher Betrieb

factual ['fæk·tʃu·əl] adj sachlich

faculty ['fæk·əl·ti] n 1. SCH, UNIV Lehrkörper m 2. Fähigkeit f

fad [fæd] n Modeerscheinung f

fade [feɪd] I. vi 1. (lose color) ausbleichen 2. (lose intensity) nachlassen; **the light is fading** es wird dunkel; (sound) verklingen; (color) verbleichen II. vt ausbleichen

fade away vi (hope) schwinden; (memories) verblassen; (beauty) verblühen

fade in vt FILM, TV einblenden

fade out vt ausblenden

fag [fæg] n pej fam (homosexual) Schwule(r) m

fail [feɪl] I. vi 1. (person) versagen; (plan) scheitern; **if all else ~s** zur Not 2. (not do) **to ~ to do sth** versäumen, etw zu tun; **I ~ to see what ...** ich verstehe nicht, was ... 3. SCH, UNIV durch-

fallen 4. (brakes) versagen; (harvest) ausfallen II. vt 1. (not pass) durchfallen; **to ~ sb** (not grant a passing grade) jdn durchfallen lassen ▷ (let down) im Stich lassen III. n ▶ **without ~** auf jeden Fall

failing ['feɪ·lɪŋ] I. adj ~ **eyesight** Sehschwäche f II. n Schwäche f

'fail-safe adj abgesichert

failure ['feɪl·jɚr] n 1. (lack of success) Scheitern nt; (of business) Bankrott m; (of crop) Missernte f; ~ **rate** SCH, UNIV Durchfallquote f 2. Misserfolg m 3. MED, TECH Versagen nt kein pl

faint [feɪnt] I. adj 1. (light, smile) matt; (sound, suspicion) leise; (scent, pattern) zart; (chance) gering; **to not have the ~est idea** nicht die geringste Ahnung haben 2. (line) undeutlich 3. (physically weak) **to feel** ~ sich schwach fühlen; **to be ~ with hunger** vor Hunger fast umfallen II. vi ohnmächtig werden

faint-'hearted adj zaghaft; **to be not for the ~** nichts für schwache Nerven sein

faintly ['feɪnt·li] adv 1. (weakly) leicht 2. (not clearly) schwach; ~ **visible** schwach zu sehen

fair[1] [fer] I. adj 1. (reasonable) fair; (salary) angemessen; (legitimate) berechtigt; **you're not being ~** das ist unfair; **it's ~ to say that ...** man kann [wohl] sagen, dass ... 2. (just, impartial) gerecht, fair; **to get one's ~ share** seinen Anteil bekommen 3. (large) ziemlich; **there's still a ~ bit of work to do** es gibt noch einiges zu tun 4. (skin) hell; (hair) blond II. adv (according to rules) **to play** ~ fair sein

fair[2] [fer] n 1. (carnival) Jahrmarkt m 2. (trade) Messe f

'fairground n Rummel[platz] m bes nordd

fair-'haired <fairer-, fairest- or more ~, most ~> adj blond

fairly ['fer·li] adv 1. (quite) ziemlich 2. (justly) fair

fair-'minded <fairer-, fairest- or more ~, most ~> adj unvoreingenommen

fairness ['fer·nɪs] n 1. Fairness f 2. (of hair) Helligkeit f

fair 'play n Fairplay nt

fairy ['feːrˑi] n Fee f

'fairy tale n Märchen nt a. fig

faith [feɪθ] n 1. (trust) Vertrauen nt; to put one's ~ in sb/sth auf jdn/etw vertrauen 2. REL Glaube m 3. (sincerity) to act in good ~ in gutem Glauben handeln

faithful ['feɪθ·fəl] adj 1. (loyal) treu 2. (accurate) originalgetreu; (account) detailliert

faithfully ['feɪθ·fəl·i] adv 1. (loyally) treu 2. (exactly) genau; (reproduce) originalgetreu

fake [feɪk] I. n 1. (counterfeit object) Fälschung f 2. (impostor) Hochstapler(in) m(f) II. adj Kunst–; (jewel) imitiert; (passport) gefälscht III. vt 1. (make a copy) fälschen 2. (pretend) vortäuschen; (illness) simulieren

falcon ['fæl·kən] n Falke m

fall [fɔl] I. n 1. (drop) Fall m; (harder) Sturz m; she broke her leg in the ~ sie brach sich bei dem Sturz das Bein; the bushes broke his ~ die Büsche haben seinen Sturz abgefangen 2. (decrease) Rückgang m; (in support) Nachlassen nt (in +gen); ~ in value Wertverlust m 3. (of a regime) Sturz m; the ~ of the Roman Empire der Untergang des Römischen Reiches 4. (autumn) Herbst m ▶ to take a [or the] ~ for sb/sth für jdn/etw die Schuld auf sich akk nehmen II. adj Herbst– III. vi <fell, fallen> 1. (tumble) fallen; (harder) stürzen; (person) hinfallen; (tree) umfallen; to ~ to one's death in den Tod stürzen; to ~ flat on one's face auf die Nase fallen; to ~ down dead tot umfallen 2. (hang) fallen; her hair fell to her waist ihr Haar reichte ihr bis zur Taille 3. (decrease) sinken, fallen; church attendance has ~en dramatically die Anzahl der Kirchenbesucher ist drastisch zurückgegangen 4. (become) to ~ asleep einschlafen; to ~ ill krank werden 5. (enter a particular state) to ~ out of favor [with sb] [bei jdm] nicht mehr gefragt sein; to ~ in love [with sb/sth] sich [in jdn/etw] verlieben

◆**fall apart** vi 1. (disintegrate) auseinanderfallen 2. fig (fail) auseinander-

(system) zusammenbrechen; (marriage) auseinandergehen

◆**fall away** vi 1. (detach itself) abfallen 2. (decrease) sinken, zurückgehen

◆**fall back** vi 1. zurückweichen 2. (resort to: thing) zurückgreifen ([up]on auf +akk)

◆**fall behind** vi 1. (slow) zurückfallen 2. (achieve less) zurückbleiben; (at school) hinterherhinken; to ~ behind with sth mit etw dat in Verzug geraten

◆**fall down** vi 1. (tumble) hinunterfallen; (topple: person) hinfallen; (object) umfallen; to ~ down sth etw hinunterfallen; (hole, well) hineinfallen in +akk 2. (collapse) einstürzen; (tent) zusammenfallen

◆**fall for** vt 1. (love) sich verlieben in +akk 2. (be deceived by) hereinfallen auf +akk

◆**fall in** vi 1. (drop) hineinfallen 2. (collapse) einstürzen

◆**fall off** vi 1. to ~ off sth von etw dat fallen 2. (decrease) zurückgehen

◆**fall on** vi 1. (attack) to ~ on sb über jdn herfallen 2. (be assigned to) to ~ on sb jdm zufallen

◆**fall out** vi 1. (drop) herausfallen; (hair) ausfallen 2. (argue) to ~ out [with sb] sich [mit jdm] [zer]streiten

◆**fall over** vi 1. (topple: person) hinfallen; (object) umfallen 2. (trip) to ~ over sth über etw akk fallen

◆**fall through** vi scheitern

fallacy ['fæl·ə·si] n Irrtum m

fallen ['fɔ·lən] adj 1. (apple) abgefallen; (tree) umgestürzt 2. (dictator) gestürzt

'fall guy n sl Prügelknabe m

fallible ['fæl·ə·bəl] adj (person) fehlbar; (thing) fehleranfällig

'fall-off n Rückgang m

'fallout n 1. radioaktive Strahlung; ~ shelter Atombunker m 2. fig Konsequenzen pl

false [fɔls] adj falsch; ~ start Fehlstart m a. fig

falsehood ['fɔls·hʊd] n Unwahrheit f

falseness ['fɔls·nɪs] n Falschheit f

false 'teeth n pl Gebiss nt

falsify <-ie-> ['fɔl·sɪ·faɪ] vt fälschen

falter ['fɔl·tər] vi stocken

fame [feɪm] n Ruhm m

familiar [fə·'mɪl·jər] adj 1. (well-known) vertraut; (faces) bekannt 2. (acquainted) to be ~ with sth etw/jdn kennen 3. (informal) vertraulich; the ~ form (of the second person) LING die Du-Form

familiarity [fə·ˌmɪl·i·'er·ə·t̬i] n 1. (well-known quality) Vertrautheit f 2. (knowledge) Kenntnis f

familiarize [fə·'mɪl·jə·raɪz] vt to ~ oneself/sb with sth sich/jdn mit etw dat vertraut machen; (with work) sich/jdn einarbeiten (with in +akk)

family ['fæm·ə·li] n Familie f

family 'doctor n Hausarzt, Hausärztin m, f

famine ['fæm·ɪn] n Hungersnot f

famished ['fæm·ɪʃt] adj fam ausgehungert

famous ['feɪ·məs] adj berühmt

fan[1] [fæn] n (enthusiast, admirer) Bewunderer, Bewunderin m, f; a football ~ ein Footballfan

fan[2] [fæn] I. n Ventilator m II. vt <-nn-> (flames) anfachen; fig schüren

fanatic [fə·'næt̬·ɪk] n 1. pej (obsessed) Fanatiker(in) m(f) 2. (enthusiast) fitness ~ ein Fitnessfan m

fanatical [fə·'næt̬·ɪ·kəl] adj (obsessed) besessen (about von +dat); (support) bedingungslos

'fan belt n AUTO Keilriemen m

'fan club n Fanclub m

fancy ['fæn·si] I. adj 1. (decorations) aufwändig; (car) schick; fig (talk) geschwollen; **nothing** ~ nichts Ausgefallenes 2. (whimsical) versponnen II. n 1. (liking) Vorliebe f; **to take a** ~ **to sth/sb** Gefallen an etw/jdm finden 2. (whim) Laune f III. vt <-ie-> ~ that! stell dir das (mal) vor!

fanfare ['fæn·fer] n Fanfare f

fang [fæŋ] n Giftzahn m

'fan mail n Fanpost f

fanny ['fæn·i] n fam Hintern m

fantasize ['fæn·tə·saɪz] vi fantasieren

fantastic [fæn·'tæs·tɪk] adj fam (wonderful) fantastisch, toll; **to look** ~ (person) umwerfend aussehen

fantasy ['fæn·tə·si] n Fantasie f; **to have fantasies about** (doing) **sth** von etw dat träumen; LIT Fantasy f

fanzine ['fæn·zin] n Fanmagazin nt

far <farther or further, farthest or furthest> [far] I. adv 1. (in space) weit; **how much farther is it?** wie weit ist es denn noch?; ~ **and wide** weit und breit 2. (in time) weit; **some time** ~ **in the future** irgendwann in ferner Zukunft; ~ **into the night** bis spät in die Nacht hinein; **to plan further ahead** weiter voraus planen 3. (in progress) weit; **to not get very** ~ **with** (doing) **sth** mit etw dat nicht besonders weit kommen 4. (much) weit, viel; ~ **better** viel besser ▶ **as** ~ **as** (in space) bis; **as** ~ **as the eye can see** so weit das Auge reicht; (in degree) **as** ~ **as I know** soweit ich weiß; ~ **and away** mit Abstand; **I'd** ~ **rather ...** ich würde viel lieber ...; ~ **from it!** weit gefehlt; **sb will go** ~ jd wird es zu etwas bringen; **so** ~, **so good** so weit, so gut; **so** ~ (until now) bisher II. adj 1. (further away) **at the** ~ **end** am anderen Ende 2. (distant) fern ▶ **to be a** ~ **cry from sth/sb** mit etw/jdm nicht zu vergleichen sein

faraway ['far·ə·weɪ] adj 1. (distant) fern 2. (dreamy: look) verträumt

fare [fer] n Fahrpreis m

farewell [ˌfer·'wel] I. interj form leb wohl; **to bid** (or say) ~ **to sb/sth** sich von jdm/etw verabschieden II. n Abschied m

far-'fetched adj weit hergeholt

far-'flung adj 1. (widespread) weitläufig 2. (remote) abgelegen

farm [farm] I. n Bauernhof m II. vt bebauen

◆**farm out** vt (work) abgeben (**to** an +akk)

farmer ['far·mər] n Bauer, Bäuerin m, f

farmhand n Landarbeiter(in) m(f)

'farmhouse n Bauernhaus nt

'farmland n Ackerland nt

'farmstead n Farm f

'farmyard n Hof m

far-off adj fern

far-'reaching adj weit reichend

'farsighted adj (decision) weitsichtig; (person) vorausschauend

fart [fɑrt] **I.** n vulg Furz m **II.** vi vulg furzen

farther ['fɑr·ðər] **I.** adv comp of **far** weiter; **how much ~ is it to the airport?** wie weit ist es noch zum Flughafen? **II.** adj comp of **far**; **at the ~ end** am anderen Ende; see also **further**

farthest ['fɑr·ðɪst] **I.** adv superl of **far** am weitesten **II.** adj superl of **far** am weitesten

fascinate ['fæs·ə·neɪt] vt faszinieren

fascinating ['fæs·ə·neɪ·t̬ɪŋ] adj faszinierend

fascination [fæs·ə·'neɪ·ʃən] n Faszination f

fascism ['fæʃ·ɪz·əm] n Faschismus m

fascist ['fæʃ·ɪst] n Faschist(in) m(f)

fashion ['fæʃ·ən] n **1.** (style) Mode f; **to be in ~** in Mode sein **2.** ~ [or **the ~ industry**] die Modebranche

fashionable ['fæʃ·ə·nə·bəl] adj modisch

'fashion designer n Modedesigner(in) m(f)

'fashion show n Modenschau f

fast[1] [fæst] **I.** adj **1.** schnell; **to be a ~ runner** schnell laufen **2.** (clock) **to be ~** vorgehen **II.** adv schnell

fast[2] [fæst] **I.** vi fasten **II.** n Fastenzeit f

fasten ['fæs·ən] **I.** vt **1.** (close) schließen; (coat) zumachen; **to ~ one's seat belt** sich anschnallen **2.** (secure) befestigen (on/to an +dat); (with glue) festkleben **II.** vi (close) sich schließen lassen

◆**fasten down** vt befestigen

◆**fasten up** vt zumachen; (buttons) zuknöpfen

fastener ['fæs·ə·nər] n Verschluss m

fast 'food n Fast Food nt

fast-'forward vt, vi vorspulen

fastidious [fə·'stɪd·i·əs] adj wählerisch; **to be very ~ about doing sth** sehr sorgsam darauf bedacht sein, etw zu tun

fat [fæt] **I.** adj <-tt-> **1.** (fleshy) dick; (animal) fett **2.** (thick) dick **II.** n Fett nt

fatal ['feɪt̬·əl] adj tödlich

fatalist ['feɪt̬·əl·ɪst] n Fatalist(in) m(f)

fatality [fer·'tæl·ə·t̬i] n Todesopfer nt

fatally ['feɪt̬·əl·i] adv **1.** (mortally) tödlich; **~ ill** sterbenskrank **2.** (disastrously) hoffnungslos

'fat cat n pej Bonze m

fate [feɪt] n Schicksal nt

'fat-free adj fettfrei

'fathead n fam Schafskopf m

father ['fɑ·ðər] n Vater m

'father-in-law <pl fathers-> n Schwiegervater m

fatherless ['fɑ·ðər·lɪs] adj vaterlos

fatherly ['fɑ·ðər·li] adj väterlich

fatigue [fə·'tig] n **1.** Ermüdung f; **donor ~** Nachlassen nt der Spendenfreudigkeit **2.** MIL **~s** pl (uniform) Arbeitskleidung f kein pl

fattening ['fæt·ən·ɪŋ] adj **to be ~** dick machen

fatty ['fæt̬·i] adj **1.** (containing fat) fetthaltig **2.** (consisting of fat) Fett-

faucet ['fɔ·sɪt] n Wasserhahn m

fault [fɔlt] n **1.** (responsibility) Schuld f; **it's your own ~** du bist selbst schuld daran; **to find ~ with sb/sth** etw an jdm/etw auszusetzen haben; **through no ~ of his own** ohne sein eigenes Verschulden **2.** TENNIS Fehler m **II.** vt **to ~ sb/sth** [einen] Fehler an jdm/etw finden

faultless ['fɔlt·lɪs] adj fehlerfrei

faulty ['fɔl·ti] adj **1.** (unsound) fehlerhaft **2.** (defective) defekt

favor ['feɪ·vər] **I.** n **1.** (approval) **in ~ of** für; **to be in ~** dafür sein; **all those in ~, ...** alle, die dafür sind, ...; **to fall out of ~** in Ungnade fallen **2.** (advantage) **in ~ of** für; **to reject sb/sth in ~ of sb/ sth** jdm/etw gegenüber jdm/etw den Vorzug geben **3.** (kind act) Gefallen m kein pl; **to do sb a ~** [or a **~ for sb**] jdm einen Gefallen tun **II.** vt **1.** (prefer) vorziehen **2.** (approve) gutheißen; **to ~ doing sth** es gutheißen, etw zu tun

favorable ['fer·vər·ə·bəl] adj **1.** (approving) positiv **2.** (advantageous) günstig (**to** für +akk)

favored ['feɪ·vərd] adj **1.** (preferred) bevorzugt **2.** (privileged) begünstigt

favorite ['feɪ·vər·ɪt] **I.** adj Lieblings-**II.** n **1.** (best-liked: person) Liebling m; (thing) **which one's your ~?** welches magst du am liebsten? **2.** (contestant) Favorit(in) m(f)

favoritism ['feɪ·vər·ɪ·t̬ɪz·əm] n pej Begünstigung f

fawn [fɔn] **I.** n Rehkitz nt **II.** adj rehbraun

fax [fæks] I. n Fax nt II. vt faxen

fax machine n Fax[gerät] nt

FBI [ˌef·bi·'aɪ] n abbr of **Federal Bureau of Investigation** FBI nt

fear [fɪr] I. n 1. (dread) Angst f, Furcht f; **to have a ~ of sth** vor etw dat Angst haben 2. (worry) ~s for sb's safety Sorge f um jds Sicherheit II. vt fürchten; **nothing to** ~ nichts zu befürchten III. vi **to** ~ **for sb/sth** sich dat um jdn/etw Sorgen machen

fearful ['fɪr·fəl] adj 1. (anxious) ängstlich 2. (terrible) schrecklich

fearless ['fɪr·lɪs] adj furchtlos

feasibility [ˌfi·zə·'bɪl·ɪ·t̬i] n Machbarkeit f

feasible ['fi·zə·bəl] adj durchführbar; **technically** ~ technisch machbar

feast [fist] n Festessen nt

feat [fit] n 1. (brave deed) Heldentat f 2. (skillful action) [Meister]leistung f; **no mean** ~ keine schlechte Leistung

feather ['feð·ər] n Feder f

featherweight n Federgewicht nt

feathery ['feð·ə·ri] adj fed[e]rig

feature ['fi·tʃər] I. n 1. (aspect) Merkmal nt, Kennzeichen nt; **special** ~ Besonderheit f 2. (of face) ~s pl Gesichtszüge pl 3. FILM, TV (report) Sonderbeitrag m; (film) Spielfilm m II. vt 1. (show) aufweisen 2. (star) **featuring sb** mit jdm in der Hauptrolle

Feb. n abbr of **February** Febr.

February ['feb·ru·er·i] n Februar m, Feber m österr; **at the beginning of** [or **in early**] ~ Anfang Februar; **in the middle of** ~ Mitte Februar; **in the first half of** ~ in der ersten Februarhälfte; **for the whole of** ~ den ganzen Februar über; **last/next/this** ~ vergangenen [or letzten]/kommenden [or nächsten]/diesen Februar; **in/during** ~ im Februar; **on** ~ **14**[th] am 14. Februar

feces ['fi·siz] npl form Fäkalien pl

Fed [fed] n fam 1. (bank) Zentralbankrat m 2. (police) FBI-Agent(in) m(f)

federal ['fed·ər·əl] adj föderativ; ~ **law** Bundesgesetz nt; ~ **income tax** nationale Einkommensteuer

federalism ['fed·ər·ə·lɪz·əm] n Föderalismus m

federation [ˌfed·ə·'reɪ·ʃən] n Föderation f

fed up adj fam **to be** ~ **up** [**with sb/sth**] die Nase voll haben [von jdm/etw]

fee [fi] n Gebühr f; **membership** ~[s] Mitgliedsbeitrag m

feeble <-r, -st> ['fi·bəl] adj schwach

feed [fid] I. n 1. (fodder) Futter nt 2. TECH (supply) Zufuhr f II. vt <fed, fed> 1. (give food to) **to** ~ **sb** jdm zu essen geben; (animal, baby) füttern; (plant) düngen; **to** ~ **sth to an animal** etw an ein Tier verfüttern 2. (provide food for) ernähren 3. (thread) fädeln; (rope) fädeln III. vi <fed, fed> (eat: animal) weiden; (baby) gefüttert werden

◆**feed off, feed on** vi sich ernähren von

feedback n Feedback nt

feel [fil] I. vt <felt, felt> 1. (sense, touch) fühlen; **to** ~ **one's age** sein Alter spüren; **to** ~ **nothing for sb** für jdn nichts empfinden; ich musste mich die Wand entlangtasten 2. (think) halten; **to** ~ **that ...** der Meinung sein, dass ... II. vi <felt, felt> 1. + adj (have a feeling) sich fühlen; **my mouth** ~s **dry** mein Mund fühlt sich trocken an; **my eyes** ~ **sore** meine Augen brennen; **how do you** ~ **about it?** was sagst du dazu?; **to** ~ **angry** wütend sein; **to** ~ **better** sich besser fühlen; **to** ~ **foolish** sich dat dumm vorkommen; **to** ~ **free to do sth** etw ruhig tun; **sb** ~s **hot** jdm ist heiß; **to** ~ **as if one were doing sth** das Gefühl haben, etw zu tun; **to** ~ **like sth** sich akk wie etw fühlen; **to** ~ **like one's old self** [**again**] [wieder] ganz der/die Alte sein 2. + adj (seem) scheinen 3. (search) tasten (**for** nach +dat) 4. (want) **to** ~ **like sth** zu etw dat Lust haben III. n 1. (texture) **the** ~ **of wool** das Gefühl von Wolle 2. (touch) Berühren nt 3. (talent) Gespür nt; ~ **for language** Sprachgefühl nt

◆**feel up** I. vt fam begrapschen II. vi **to** ~ **up to sth** sich etw dat gewachsen fühlen

feeler ['fi·lər] n usu pl Fühler m

feel-good adj ein Wohlgefühl erzeugend

feeling ['fi·lɪŋ] n 1. Gefühl nt; **to cause bad** ~s böses Blut verursachen; **no hard** ~s! nichts für ungut!; **to have**

a ~ that ... das Gefühl haben, dass ...
2. (opinion) Ansicht f

feet [fit] n pl of **foot**

feign [feɪn] vt vortäuschen

feline ['fiː.laɪn] adj katzenartig

fell¹ [fel] pt of **fall**

fell² [fel] vt (cut down) fällen

fellow ['fel.oʊ] **I.** n **1.** fam (man) Kerl m **2.** (graduate student) Fellow m **II.** adj ~ **citizen** Mitbürger(in) m(f); ~ **sufferer** Leidensgenosse, -in m, f

felt¹ [felt] pt, pp of **feel**

felt² [felt] n Filz m

'felt tip, felt tip 'pen n Filzstift m

female ['fiː.meɪl] **I.** adj weiblich **II.** n **1.** (animal) Weibchen nt **2.** (woman) Frau f

feminine ['fem.ə.nɪn] adj weiblich

feminism ['fem.ə.nɪz.əm] n Feminismus m

feminist ['fem.ə.nɪst] n Feminist(in) m(f)

fence [fens] **I.** n **1.** (barrier) Zaun m **2.** sl (criminal) Hehler(in) m(f) **II.** vi fechten

fencer ['fen.sər] n Fechter(in) m(f)

fencing ['fen.sɪŋ] n SPORT Fechten nt

fend [fend] vi (care) **to ~ for oneself** für sich selbst sorgen

◆**fend off** vt **to ~ off ⇆** sb/sth jdn/etw abwehren; (criticism ⇆) zurückweisen

fender ['fen.dər] n AUTO Kotflügel m

ferment I. vt [fər.'ment] fermentieren **II.** vi [fər.'ment] gären

fermentation [ˌfɜr.mən.'teɪ.ʃən] n Gärung f

fern [fɜrn] n Farn m

ferocious [fə.'roʊ.ʃəs] adj wild; (fighting) heftig

ferociousness [fə.'roʊ.ʃəs.nɪs], **ferocity** [fə.'ras.ə.ti] n Wildheit f; (of attack, storm) Heftigkeit f

Ferris wheel ['fer.ɪs.ˌhwil] n Riesenrad nt

ferry ['fer.i] n Fähre f

fertile ['fɜr.təl] adj fruchtbar; fig (imagination) lebhaft

fertilization [ˌfɜr.təl.ɪ.'zeɪ.ʃən] n Befruchtung f

fertilize ['fɜr.təl.aɪz] vt **1.** AGR düngen **2.** BIOL befruchten

fertilizer ['fɜr.təl.aɪ.zər] n Dünger m

fervent ['fɜr.vənt] adj form (supporter)

glühend

fester ['fes.tər] vi **1.** MED eitern **2.** fig gären

festival ['fes.tɪ.vəl] n Festival nt

festive ['fes.tɪv] adj festlich

festivity [fes.'tɪv.ɪ.ti] n **1.** (celebrations) **festivities** pl Feierlichkeiten pl **2.** (festiveness) Feststimmung f

fetal ['fiː.təl] adj fetal

fetch [fetʃ] vt **1.** (get, collect) abholen **2.** (be sold for) erzielen

fetching ['fetʃ.ɪŋ] adj schick

fetid ['fet.ɪd] adj übel riechend

fetish ['fet.ɪʃ] n Fetisch m

fetus ['fiː.təs] n Fetus m

feud [fjud] n Fehde f

fever ['fiː.vər] n **1.** (temperature) Fieber nt kein pl **2.** (excitement) Aufregung f

feverish ['fiː.vər.ɪʃ] adj fiebrig

few [fju] **I.** adj **1.** (some) **a ~** ein paar, einige; **quite a ~** ziemlich viele **2.** (not many) wenige; **~er people** weniger Menschen; **as ~ as ...** nur ... ▶ **~ and far between** dünn gesät **II.** pron **1.** (some) **a ~ of us** einige von uns **2.** (not many) wenige; **the ~ who came ...** die paar, die kamen, ...; **~ of the houses** wenige der Häuser

fiancé [ˌfi.ɑn.'seɪ] n Verlobte(r) m

fiancée [ˌfi.ɑn.'seɪ] n Verlobte f

fib [fɪb] vi <-bb-> fam schwindeln

fiber ['faɪ.bər] n **1.** Faser f **2.** FOOD Ballaststoffe pl

'fiberglass n glasfaserverstärkter Kunststoff

fiber optic 'cable n Glasfaserkabel nt

fiber 'optics n + sing vb TELEC, COMPUT Glasfasertechnik f

fickle ['fɪk.l] adj pej wankelmütig

fiction ['fɪk.ʃən] n LIT Erzählliteratur f

fictional ['fɪk.ʃə.nəl] adj erfunden

fictitious [fɪk.'tɪʃ.əs] adj **1.** (false) falsch **2.** (imaginary) [frei] erfunden; (character) fiktiv

fiddle ['fɪd.l] **I.** n fam MUS Fidel f ▶ [as] **fit as a ~** kerngesund **II.** vi MUS geigen

fiddler ['fɪd.lər] n fam Geiger(in) m(f)

fidget ['fɪdʒ.ɪt] vi zappeln

field [fild] **I.** n **1.** Feld nt **2.** SPORT [Spiel]feld nt, Platz m **3.** (area of knowledge) Gebiet nt **II.** vi SPORT als Fänger m

spielen, fielden III. *vt* 1. (*ball*) fangen 2. (*questions*) parieren; (*phone calls*) abweisen

fielder ['fil·dər] *n* SPORT Fielder(in) *m(f)*, Fänger(in) *m(f)*

'field glasses *npl* Feldstecher *m*

'field trip *n* Exkursion *f*

'fieldwork *n* Feldforschung *f*

fierce [fɪrs] *adj* 1. (*animal*) wild 2. (*attack, competition*) scharf; (*fighting*) erbittert

fierceness ['fɪrs·nɪs] *n* Wildheit *f*

fiery ['faɪr·i] *adj* (*passionate*) leidenschaftlich

fifteen [fɪf·'tin] I. *adj* fünfzehn II. *n* Fünfzehn *f; see also* **eight**

fifteenth [fɪf·'tinθ] I. *adj* fünfzehnte(r, s) II. *n* 1. (*order*) **the** ~ der/die/das Fünfzehnte 2. (*date*) **the** ~ der Fünfzehnte 3. (*fraction*) Fünfzehntel *nt*

fifth [fɪfθ] I. *adj* fünfte(r, s); **every** ~ **person** jeder Fünfte II. *n* 1. (*order*) **the** ~ der/die/das Fünfte 2. (*date*) **the** ~ der Fünfte 3. (*fraction*) Fünftel *nt; see also* **eighth**

fiftieth ['fɪf·ti·əθ] I. *adj* fünfzigste(r, s) II. *n* 1. (*order*) **the** ~ der/die/das Fünfzigste 2. (*fraction*) Fünfzigstel *nt* III. *adv* fünfzigstens; *see also* **eighth**

fifty ['fɪf·ti] I. *adj* fünfzig II. *n* 1. (*number*) Fünfzig *f* 2. (*paper money*) Fünfziger *m; see also* **eight**

fig [fɪg] *n* FOOD Feige *f*

fig. [fɪg] *n abbr of* **figure** Abb. *f*

fight [faɪt] I. *n* Kampf *m;* **to put up a** ~ sich wehren II. *vi* <fought, fought> 1. kämpfen; (*children*) sich raufen; **to** ~ **with sb** (*against*) gegen jdn kämpfen; (*on same side*) an jds Seite *f* kämpfen 2. (*argue*) sich streiten (**about/over** um +*akk*) III. *vt* <fought, fought> 1. kämpfen (**against** gegen +*akk*); (*battle*) schlagen; (*fire*) bekämpfen; (*disease*) ankämpfen gegen 2. (*in boxing*) boxen gegen +*akk*

◆**fight back** I. *vi* zurückschlagen II. *vt* (*tears*) unterdrücken

◆**fight off** *vt* **to** ~ **off** ⇆ **sb** jdn abwehren

fighter ['faɪ·tər] *n* 1. Kämpfer(in) *m(f)* 2. (*boxer*) Boxer(in) *m(f)*

fighting ['faɪ·tɪŋ] I. *n* Kämpfe *pl* II. *adj* kämpferisch

figure ['fɪg·jər] I. *n* 1. (*shape*) Figur *f* 2. (*person*) Gestalt *f* 3. MATH (*digit*) Ziffer *f;* (*numeral*) Zahl *f;* **he is good with** ~**s** er ist ein guter Rechner II. *vt* 1. (*envisage*) voraussehen; (*estimate*) schätzen III. *vi* 1. (*count on*) **to** ~ **on sth** mit etw *dat* rechnen 2. (*make sense*) **that** [*or* **it**] ~**s** das hätte ich mir denken können

◆**figure out** *vt* 1. (*work out*) herausfinden; MATH ausrechnen 2. (*understand*) begreifen; **to** ~ **out** ⇆ **sth/sb** etw/jdn verstehen

'figure skater *n* Eiskunstläufer(in) *m(f)*

filament ['fɪl·ə·mənt] *n* 1. (*fiber*) Faden *m* 2. ELEC Glühfaden *m*

file¹ [faɪl] I. *n* 1. (*folder*) [Akten]hefter *m* 2. (*database*) Akte *f* 3. COMPUT Datei *f* II. *vt* 1. (*put in folder*) ablegen, abheften; (*in order*) einordnen 2. (*submit*) abgeben; JOURN einsenden

file² [faɪl] *n* (*line*) Reihe *f*

file³ [faɪl] I. *n* Feile *f* II. *vt* feilen

filet [fɪ·'leɪ, 'fɪ·leɪ] *n vt see* **fillet**

filibuster ['fɪl·ɪ·bʌs·tər] *n* Obstruktion *f*

filing ['faɪ·lɪŋ] *n* 1. (*archiving*) Ablage *f* 2. (*registration*) Einreichung *f*

'filing cabinet *n* Aktenschrank *m*

fill [fɪl] I. *n* **to have one's** ~ **of sth** genug von etw *dat* haben II. *vt* 1. (*make full*) füllen; (*gap*) schließen; (*vacancy*) besetzen 2. (*pervade: room*) erfüllen

◆**fill in** I. *vt* 1. (*inform*) **to** ~ **in** ⇆ **sb** [**on sth**] jdn [über etw *akk*] informieren 2. (*complete: form*) ausfüllen II. *vi* **to** ~ **in** [**for sb**] [für jdn] einspringen

◆**fill out** I. *vt* ausfüllen II. *vi* fülliger werden

◆**fill up** I. *vt* 1. (*make full*) vollfüllen 2. (*occupy entire space*) ausfüllen 3. AUTO volltanken II. *vi* 1. (*become full*) sich füllen 2. AUTO [voll]tanken

filler ['fɪl·ər] *n* Spachtelmasse *f*

fillet ['fɪl·ɪt], **filet** [fɪ·'leɪ, 'fɪ·leɪ] I. *n* FOOD Filet *nt* II. *vt* 1. (*remove bones: fish*) entgräten; (*meat*) entbeinen 2. (*cut into pieces*) filetieren

filling ['fɪl·ɪŋ] I. *n* 1. (*for teeth*) Füllung *f* 2. FOOD Füllung *f* II. *adj* sättigend

'filling station *n* Tankstelle *f*

film [fɪlm] **I.** n **1.** FILM, PHOT Film m **2.** (layer) Schicht f; ~ **of oil** Ölfilm m **II.** vt filmen **III.** vi filmen, drehen

filter ['fɪl·tər] **I.** n Filter m **II.** vt **1.** (purify) filtern **2.** fig selektieren

◆**filter through** vi (light) durchscheinen; (liquid) durchsickern

filth [fɪlθ] n **1.** (dirt) Dreck m **2.** pej (obscenity) Schmutz m

filthy ['fɪl·θi] adj **1.** (dirty) schmutzig, dreckig fam **2.** (temper) aufbrausend **3.** pej fam (obscene) schmutzig

filtration [fɪl·'treɪ·ʃən] n Filterung f

fin [fɪn] n Flosse f

final ['faɪ·nəl] **I.** adj **1.** (last) letzte(r, s); **in the ~ analysis** letzten Endes; ~ **score** Endstand m **2.** (decisive) endgültig; **that's ~!** und damit basta! **II.** n **1.** (concluding match) Endspiel nt **2.** ~**s** pl UNIV [Schluss]examen nt

finale [fɪ·'næl·i] n Finale nt

finalist ['faɪ·nə·lɪst] n Finalist(in) m(f)

finalize ['faɪ·nə·laɪz] vt zum Abschluss bringen

finally ['faɪ·nə·li] adv **1.** endlich **2.** (in conclusion) zum Schluss

finance ['faɪ·næns] **I.** n **1.** (money management) Finanzwirtschaft f **2.** (money) ~**s** pl Geldmittel pl **II.** vt finanzieren

'finance company n Finanzierungsgesellschaft f

financial [faɪ·'næn·ʃəl] adj finanziell, Finanz-

finch <pl -es> [fɪntʃ] n Fink m

find [faɪnd] vt <found, found> finden; (money for sth) aufbringen; **she was found unconscious** sie wurde bewusstlos aufgefunden; **to ~ sb/sth** [**to be sth**] jdn/etw [als etw] empfinden; **to ~ sb guilty** jdn für schuldig erklären; **to ~ that ...** feststellen, dass ...; (come to realize) sehen, dass ...; **I wish I could ~ more time for reading** ich wünschte, ich hätte mehr Zeit zum Lesen

◆**find out** vt **1.** (detect) erwischen **2.** (discover) herausfinden

finding ['faɪn·dɪŋ] n **1.** (discovery) Entdeckung f **2.** usu pl (result of investigation) Ergebnis nt

fine¹ [faɪn] **I.** adj **1.** (acceptable) in Ordnung; **seven's ~ by me** sieben [Uhr] passt mir gut **2.** (excellent) glänzend; (wine) erlesen **3.** (slender, cut small) fein; (slice) dünn **4.** METEO schön **II.** adv **1.** (all right) fein, [sehr] gut **2.** (thinly) fein

fine² [faɪn] **I.** n (punishment) Geldstrafe f **II.** vt (person) zu einer Geldstrafe verurteilen

fineness ['faɪn·nɪs] n Feinheit f

fine 'print n **the ~** das Kleingedruckte

finesse [fɪ·'nes] n **1.** (delicacy) Feinheit f **2.** (skill) Geschick nt

fine-tooth 'comb, fine-toothed 'comb n ► **to go through** [or **over**] sth **with a ~** etw sorgfältig unter die Lupe nehmen

fine-'tune vt **to ~ sth** etw fein abstimmen

finger ['fɪŋ·gər] **I.** n Finger m ► **to keep one's ~s crossed** [**for sb**] [jdm] die Daumen drücken; **to put one's ~s on sth** etw genau ausmachen **II.** vt **1.** anfassen **2.** fam (inform on) verpfeifen (**to** bei +dat)

'fingernail n Fingernagel m

'fingerprint I. n Fingerabdruck m **II.** vt **to ~ sb** jdm die Fingerabdrücke abnehmen

'fingertip n Fingerspitze f

finish ['fɪn·ɪʃ] **I.** n **1.** (final stage) Ende nt; (of race) Finish nt; (finishing line) Ziel nt **2.** (final treatment) letzter Schliff **II.** vi enden, aufhören; (conclude) schließen; **to ~ second** als Zweiter fertig sein; SPORT Zweiter werden; **to ~ with sth** etw nicht mehr brauchen **III.** vt **1.** (bring to end) beenden; (book) zu Ende lesen; **to ~ doing sth** mit etw dat fertig sein **2.** (give final treatment) etw dat den letzten Schliff geben **3.** (food) aufessen; (drink) austrinken

◆**finish off I.** vt **1.** (get done) fertigstellen **2.** (make nice) den letzten Schliff geben **3.** sl (murder) erledigen **II.** vi **1.** (end) abschließen; **2.** (get work done) fertig werden

◆**finish up I.** vi fertig werden **II.** vt (food) aufessen; (drink) austrinken

finished ['fɪn·ɪʃt] adj **1.** fertig; **the ~ product** das Endprodukt **2.** (ruined) erledigt; (career) zu Ende

'finish line n SPORT Ziellinie f

Finland ['fɪn·lənd] n Finnland nt

fir [fɜr] n Tanne f

fire ['faɪr] I. n 1. Feuer nt; **to play with ~** mit dem Feuer spielen a. fig 2. (destructive burning) Brand m; **destroyed by ~** völlig abgebrannt; **to be on ~** brennen; **to catch ~** Feuer fangen, in Brand geraten; **to set sth on ~** etw in Brand stecken 3. MIL Feuer nt; **to open ~** das Feuer eröffnen II. vt 1. (shoot) abfeuern; (gun) schießen; fig **to ~ questions at sb** jdn mit Fragen bombardieren 2. (dismiss) feuern 3. (excite) begeistern III. vi 1. (shoot) feuern, schießen (**at** auf +akk) 2. (start up) zünden

'fire off vt abfeuern

'fire up vt (person) begeistern (**about** für +akk); (engine) zünden

'fire alarm n Feuermelder m

'firearm n Schusswaffe f

'firebomb n Brandbombe f

'firecracker n Kracher m

'fire department n Feuerwehr f

'fire drill n Feueralarmübung f

'fire engine n Feuerwehrauto nt

'fire escape n Feuertreppe f

'fire exit n Notausgang m

'fire extinguisher n Feuerlöscher m

'firefighter n Feuerwehrmann, -frau m, f

'firefly n Leuchtkäfer m

'fire house n see **fire station**

'fire hydrant n Hydrant m

'fire insurance n Feuerversicherung f

'fireman n Feuerwehrmann m

'firepower n Feuerkraft f

'fireproof I. adj feuerfest II. vt feuerfest machen

'fire station n Feuerwache f

'firewall n 1. ARCHIT Brandmauer f 2. COMPUT Firewall f

'firewoman n Feuerwehrfrau f

'firewood n Brennholz nt

'firework n ~s pl (display) Feuerwerk nt; fig [Riesen]krach m kein pl

firing ['faɪr·ɪŋ] n 1. (shooting) Abfeuern nt 2. (dismissal) Rauswurf m

'firing line n fig Schusslinie f

'firing squad n Exekutionskommando nt

firm¹ [fɜrm] I. adj fest; COMM stabil; (offer) verbindlich; **to be ~ with sb** jdm gegenüber bestimmt auftreten II. adv fest; **to hold** [or **stand**] **~** standhaft bleiben

firm² [fɜrm] n Firma f

firmness ['fɜrm·nɪs] n 1. (solidity) Festigkeit f 2. (resoluteness) Entschlossenheit f

first [fɜrst] I. adj erste(r, s); **~ thing tomorrow** morgen als Allererstes ▶ **in the ~ place** (at beginning) zunächst [einmal]; (most importantly) in erster Linie; **~ things ~** eins nach dem anderen II. adv 1. (before doing something else) zuerst; **~ of all** zu[aller]erst 2. (before other things, people) als Erste(r, s) ▶ **~ and foremost** vor allem III. n 1. **the ~** der/die/das Erste 2. (start) **at ~** anfangs

first 'aid n erste Hilfe; **~ kit** Verbandskasten m

'firstborn n Erstgeborene(r) f(m)

'first-class adj Erste[r]-Klasse-

first class adv erster Klasse

first-degree 'murder adj schwerer Mord

first 'floor n Erdgeschoss nt

'firsthand¹ adj attr aus erster Hand; **to experience sth ~** etw am eigenen Leib erfahren

first'hand² adv aus erster Hand

first 'lady n **the ~** die First Lady

firstly ['fɜrst·li] adv erstens

'first name n Vorname m

first-'rate adj erstklassig

first 'strike n MIL Erstschlag m

fiscal ['fɪs·kəl] adj fiskalisch

fiscal year n Geschäftsjahr nt

fish [fɪʃ] I. n <pl -es> Fisch m II. vi 1. (catch fish) fischen; (with rod) angeln (**for** auf +akk) 2. (look for) herumsuchen; **to ~ for sth** fig nach etw dat suchen; **to ~ for information** auf der Suche nach Informationen sein

'fish bone n [Fisch]gräte f

'fishbowl n [Gold]fischglas nt

'fisherman n (professional) Fischer m; (for hobby) Angler m

'fishhook n Angelhaken m

fishing ['fɪʃ·ɪŋ] n (catching fish) Fischen nt; (with rod) Angeln nt

'fishing line n Angelleine f

'fishing rod n Angel[rute] f

'fish stick n Fischstäbchen nt

fishy ['fɪʃ·i] adj **1.** (tasting of fish) fischig **2.** pej fam (dubious) verdächtig

fission ['fɪʃ·ən] n PHYS [Kern]spaltung f

fist [fɪst] n Faust f

fit¹ [fɪt] **I.** adj <-tt-> **1.** (suitable) geeignet; **that's all he's ~ for** das ist alles, wozu er taugt **2.** (appropriate) angebracht **3.** (healthy) fit **II.** n FASHION Sitz m **III.** vt <fitted or fit, fitted or fit> **1.** (be the right size) **to ~ sb** jdm passen **2.** (be appropriate) **to ~ sb/sth** sich für jdn/etw eignen **3.** (correspond with) **to ~ sth** etw dat entsprechen; **the key ~s the lock** der Schlüssel passt ins Schloss **4.** (install) montieren **5.** (supply) **to ~ sth with sth** etw mit etw dat versehen **IV.** vi <fitted or fit, fitted> **1.** (be correct size) passen; **~ well** gut sitzen; **to ~ into sth** in etw akk hineinpassen **2.** (agree: facts) übereinstimmen

◆fit in vi **1.** (get along well) sich einfügen **2.** (conform) dazupassen

fit² [fɪt] n Anfall m; **to be in ~s of laughter** sich kaputtlachen

fitness ['fɪt·nɪs] n Fitness f

fitted ['fɪt·ɪd] adj (jacket) tailliert

fitter ['fɪt·ər] n TECH [Maschinen]schlosser(in) m(f)

fitting ['fɪt·ɪŋ] n Anprobe f

five [faɪv] **I.** adj fünf **II.** n **1.** (number, symbol) Fünf f **2.** (five minutes) **to take ~** fam sich dat eine kurze Pause genehmigen; see also **eight**

'fivefold adj, adv fünffach

fiver ['faɪ·vər] n fam Fünfdollarschein m

fix [fɪks] **I.** n **1.** fam (dilemma) Klemme f **2.** sl (drugs) Schuss m, Fix m **3.** NAUT, AVIAT Position f **II.** vt **1.** (repair) reparieren, in Ordnung bringen **2.** (fasten) festmachen (**to** an +akk) **3.** (decide) festlegen **4.** fam (prepare) **to ~ one's hair** sich frisieren; **shall I ~ you something?** soll ich dir was zu essen machen? **5.** (concentrate: eyes, thoughts) richten (**on** auf +akk) **III.** vi sl (drugs) fixen

◆fix on vt **to ~ on** [or upon] **sth** sich auf etw akk festlegen

◆fix up vt **1.** (supply) **to ~ sb ⇆ up** jdn versorgen **2.** (arrange) arrangieren; (time to meet) vereinbaren **3.** fam (re-

pair) in Ordnung bringen

fixation [fɪk·'seɪ·ʃən] n PSYCH Fixierung f

fixed [fɪkst] adj fest; (gaze) starr; (idea) fix; **how are you ~ for cash?** wie steht's bei dir mit Geld?

fixer ['fɪk·sər] n fam (person) Schieber(in) m(f)

fixture ['fɪks·tʃər] n eingebautes Teil; **~s** pl Ausstattung f

fizz [fɪz] **I.** vi sprudeln **II.** n Sprudeln nt; **the tonic water has lost its ~** in dem Tonicwater ist keine Kohlensäure mehr

fizzle [fɪzl] vi zischen

fjord [fjɔrd] n Fjord m

FL, Fla. abbr of **Florida**

flabby ['flæb·i] adj schwabbelig

flag [flæg] **I.** n **1.** (pennant) Fahne f; (national) Flagge f **2.** (marker) Markierung f **II.** vt <-gg-> markieren **III.** vi <-gg-> (enthusiasm) abflauen; (interest) nachlassen; (strength) erlahmen

Flag Day n am 14. Juni zum Gedenken daran, dass an diesem Tag 1777 die jetzige Flagge der Vereinigten Staaten von Amerika zur Nationalfahne ernannt wurde

'flagpole, 'flagstaff n Fahnenmast m, Flaggenmast m

'flagstaff n see **flagpole**

flair [fler] n **1.** (talent) Talent nt **2.** (style) Stil m

flak [flæk] n **1.** Flakfeuer nt **2.** fig scharfe Kritik

flake [fleɪk] **I.** n **1.** (of chocolate) Raspel f; (of pastry) Krümel m; (of snow) Schneeflocke f **2.** sl (odd person) Spinner(in) m(f) **II.** vi (skin) sich schuppen

flaky ['fleɪ·ki] adj **1.** (with layers) flockig; (pastry) blättrig; (skin) schuppig **2.** sl (unreliable) schusselig

flamboyant [flæm·'bɔɪ·ənt] adj extravagant

flame [fleɪm] **I.** n Flamme f a. fig **II.** vi brennen; fig glühen

flaming ['fleɪ·mɪŋ] adj (color) flammend

flamingo <pl -s> [flə·'mɪŋ·goʊ] n Flamingo m

flammable ['flæm·ə·bəl] adj leicht entflammbar

flan [flæn] n Kuchen mit einer Füllung aus Vanillepudding

flannel [ˈflæn·l] *n* Flanell *m*

flap [flæp] **I.** *vt* <-pp-> **to ~ one's wings** mit den Flügeln schlagen **II.** *vi* <-pp-> (*flutter*) flattern; (*wings*) schlagen **III.** *n* **1.** (*flutter*) Flattern *nt* **2.** (*of cloth*) Futter *nt* **3.** *fam* (*commotion*) helle Aufregung *f*

flapjack [ˈflæp·dʒæk] *n* Pfannkuchen *m*

flare [fler] **I.** *n* Leuchtkugel *f* **II.** *vi* **1.** (*burn up*) aufflammen **2.** FASHION aufweiten

◆**flare up** *vi* **1.** auflodern *a. fig* **2.** MED sich bemerkbar machen

flash [flæʃ] **I.** *n* <*pl* -es> **1.** (*light*) [Licht]blitz *m*; (*of jewelry, metal*) [Auf]blitzen *nt kein pl*; **~ of lightning** Blitz *m* **2.** *fig* **~ of inspiration** Geistesblitz *m* **3.** PHOT Blitz *m*; **to use** [a] **~** mit Blitzlicht fotografieren ▶ **like a ~** blitzartig; **in a ~** im Nu **II.** *vt* **1.** (*light*) aufleuchten lassen **2.** *pej fam* (*flaunt*) **to ~ sth around** mit etw protzen **III.** *vi* **1.** (*shine*) blitzen **2.** *fig* (*appear*) kurz auftauchen **3.** (*move*) **to ~ by** [*or* **past**] vorbeirasen

◆**flash back** *vi* **to ~ back to sth** sich plötzlich [wieder] an etw *akk* erinnern

flashback *n* FILM Rückblende *f*

flashbulb *n* PHOT Blitz[licht]lampe *f*

flash card *n* SCH Zeigekarte *f*

flasher [ˈflæʃ·ər] *n* AUTO **~s** *pl* (*hazard lights*) Lichthupe *f*

flash flood *n* flutartige Überschwemmung

flashlight *n* Taschenlampe *f*

flashpoint *n* **1.** CHEM Flammpunkt *m* **2.** *fig* (*trouble spot*) Unruheherd *m*

flashy [ˈflæʃ·i] *adj* protzig

flask [flæsk] *n* (*bauchige*) Flasche *f*; (*for spirits*) Flachmann *m*

flat [flæt] **I.** *adj* <-tt-> **1.** (*horizontal*) flach; (*surface*) eben; (*nose*) platt **2.** (*drinks*) schal **3.** (*tire*) platt; (*person*) niedergeschlagen **4.** COMM, ECON (*slack: market*) flau **II.** *adv* <-tt-> **1.** (*horizontally*) flach; **to fall ~ on one's face** der Länge nach hinfallen **2.** (*level*) platt; **to knock sth ~** (*wall, building*) etw platt walzen **3.** *fam* (*absolutely*) rundheraus, glattweg **4. to fall ~** (*attempt*) scheitern; (*joke*) nicht ankommen **III.** *n*

1. (*level surface*) flache Seite **2.** (*tire*) Platte(r) *m*

flat 'feet *npl* Plattfüße *pl*

flat-'footed *adj* plattfüßig

flatly [ˈflæt·li] *adv* (*absolutely*) glatt[weg]

flatness [ˈflæt·nɪs] *n* Flachheit *f*; (*of ground, track*) Ebenheit *f*

flatten [ˈflæt·n] *vt* **1.** (*level*) flach machen; (*ground, path*) eben machen; (*dent*) ausbeulen **2.** (*tree*) umlegen; (*person*) niederstrecken

flatter[1] [ˈflæt·ər] *vt* **to ~ sb** jdm schmeicheln; **don't ~ yourself!** bilde dir ja nichts ein!

flatter[2] [ˈflæt·ər] *adj comp of* **flat**

flatterer [ˈflæt·ə·rər] *n* Schmeichler(in) *m(f)*

flattering [ˈflæt·ə·rɪŋ] *adj approv* schmeichelhaft; *pej* schmeichlerisch

flattery [ˈflæt·ə·ri] *n* Schmeicheleien *pl*

flaunt [flɔnt] *vt esp pej* zur Schau stellen

flautist [ˈflɔ·tɪst] *n* Flötist(in) *m(f)*

flavor [ˈfleɪ·vər] **I.** *n* (*taste*) [Wohl]geschmack *m*; (*particular taste*) Geschmacksrichtung *f* **II.** *vt* würzen

flavoring [ˈfleɪ·vər·ɪŋ] *n* Geschmacksstoff *m*

flaw [flɔ] *n* Fehler *m*; TECH Defekt *m*

flawed [flɔd] *adj* fehlerhaft; (*diamond*) unrein

flawless [ˈflɔ·lɪs] *adj* fehlerlos; (*diamond*) lupenrein; (*performance*) vollendet

flax [flæks] *n* Flachs *m*

flea [fli] *n* Floh *m*

flea market *n* Flohmarkt *m*

fled [fled] *vt, vi pt, pp of* **flee**

fledg(e)ling [ˈfledʒ·lɪŋ] **I.** *n* Jungvogel *m* **II.** *adj* neu, Jung-

flee <**fled**, **fled**> [fli] **I.** *vi* (*run away*) fliehen (**from** vor +*dat*) **II.** *vt* **to ~ the country** aus dem Land fliehen

fleece [flis] **I.** *n* **1.** (*of sheep*) Schaffell *nt* **2.** (*fabric*) Flausch *m* **3.** (*clothing*) Vliesjacke *f* **II.** *vt fig fam* (*cheat*) schröpfen

fleet [flit] *n* **1.** NAUT Flotte *f* **2.** (*group of vehicles*) Fuhrpark *m*

fleeting [ˈfli·tɪŋ] *adj* flüchtig; (*beauty*) vergänglich

flesh [fleʃ] *n* Fleisch *nt*; (*of fruit*) [Frucht]fleisch *nt* ▶ **to be** [only] **~ and blood**

auch [nur] ein Mensch sein; **in the ~** in Person

'**flesh wound** n Fleischwunde f

flew [flu] vt, vi pt, pp of **fly**

flex [fleks] I. vt, vi [sich] beugen; (muscles) [sich] [an]spannen II. n [Anschluss]kabel nt

flexibility [ˌflek·sə·ˈbɪl·ɪ·t̬i] n 1. Biegsamkeit f 2. fig Flexibilität f

flexible [ˈflek·sə·bəl] adj 1. biegsam 2. fig flexibel; **~ working hours** gleitende Arbeitszeit

flextime [ˈfleks·taɪm] n Gleitzeit f

flick [flɪk] I. n 1. (movement) kurze Bewegung; (of switch) Klicken nt; (of wrist) kurze Drehung 2. fam (movie) Film m II. vt 1. (move) **to ~ sth** etw mit einer schnellen Bewegung ausführen; (whip) schnalzen mit 2. (remove) wegwedeln

flicker [ˈflɪk·ər] I. vi flackern; (TV) flimmern; (tongue) züngeln II. n Flackern nt kein pl; (of TV pictures) Flimmern nt kein pl

flier [ˈflaɪ·ər] n 1. Flieger(in) m(f); **frequent ~** Vielflieger(in) m(f) 2. (leaflet) Flugblatt nt

flight[1] [flaɪt] n 1. (flying) Flug m; **to take ~** auffliegen 2. (of stairs) Treppe f

flight[2] [flaɪt] n (fleeing) Flucht f

'**flight deck** n 1. (on plane) Cockpit nt 2. (on ship) Flugdeck nt

'**flight number** n Flugnummer f

'**flight recorder** n Flugschreiber m

flighty [ˈflaɪ·t̬i] adj usu pej flatterhaft

flimsy [ˈflɪm·zi] adj 1. (construction) instabil, unsolide 2. (clothing) dünn, leicht 3. fig (excuse) schwach

flinch [flɪntʃ] vi (wince) [zusammen]zucken

fling [flɪŋ] I. n fig (relationship) **to have a ~ with sb** mit jdm etwas haben II. vt <flung, flung> werfen; **to ~ open** aufreißen; **to ~ oneself into sth** fig sich in etw akk stürzen

◆**fling off** vt (clothing) abwerfen a. fig; (blanket) wegstoßen

flip [flɪp] I. vt <-pp-> 1. (switch) drücken 2. (turn over) umdrehen; (coin) werfen II. vi <-pp-> 1. **to ~ [over]** sich [schnell] [um]drehen; (vehicle) sich

überschlagen 2. fig sl ausflippen III. n 1. (throw) Werfen nt 2. (movement) Ruck m; **to have a [quick] ~ through sth** etw im Schnellverfahren tun

'**flip chart** n Flipchart m o nt

flip-flop n Badelatsche f

flippant [ˈflɪp·ənt] adj leichtfertig

flipper [ˈflɪp·ər] n [Schwimm]flosse f

'**flip side** n B-Seite f

flirt [flɜrt] I. vi flirten II. n [gern] flirtende(r) Mann/Frau

flirtatious [flɜr·ˈteɪ·ʃəs] adj kokett

flit <-tt-> [flɪt] vi huschen a. fig; (fly) flattern

float [floʊt] I. n 1. (for fishing) [Kork]schwimmer m 2. (for swimming) Schwimmkork m 3. (in parade) Festzugswagen m II. vi 1. (be buoyant) schwimmen 2. (move in liquid or gas: objects) treiben; (people) sich treiben lassen III. vt 1. ECON (business) gründen; (currency) freigeben 2. (on water) treiben lassen 3. fig (idea) zur Diskussion stellen

◆**float around** vi fig (rumor) in Umlauf sein; (person) sich herumtreiben

floatation [floʊ·ˈteɪ·ʃən] n see **flotation**

floating [ˈfloʊ·t̬ɪŋ] adj (in water) schwimmend, treibend; (crane) Schwimm-

flock [flak] I. n (of animals) Herde f; (of people, birds) Schar f II. vi sich scharen

floe [floʊ] n Eisscholle f

flood [flʌd] I. n 1. (excess water) Überschwemmung f; **the F~** REL die Sintflut 2. (tide) ~ [tide] Flut f II. vt 1. (overflow) überschwemmen a. fig; (room) unter Wasser setzen 2. AUTO (engine) absaufen lassen III. vi 1. (place) überschwemmt werden; (river) über die Ufer treten 2. fig strömen

'**floodlight** n Flutlicht nt

floor [flɔr] I. n 1. (surface) [Fuß]boden m 2. (story) Stock m, Stockwerk nt II. vt 1. zu Boden schlagen 2. fig umhauen

'**floorboard** n Diele f

flooring [ˈflɔr·ɪŋ] n Boden[belag] m

'**floor lamp** n Stehlampe f

'**floor plan** n Grundriss m (eines Stockwerks)

flop [flap] I. vi <-pp-> 1. (move) sich

fallen [or plumpsen] lassen 2. (fail) ein Flop sein II. n 1. (movement) Plumps m 2. (failure: thing) Flop m

floppy ['flɑp·i] I. adj schlaff; (hair) [immer wieder] herabfallend II. n COMPUT fam Floppy [Disk] f

floral ['flɔr·əl] adj Blumen-

Florida ['flɔr·ɪ·də] n Florida nt

florist ['flɔr·ɪst] n Florist(in) m(f); ~ [shop] Blumengeschäft nt

floss [flas] I. n Zahnseide f II. vt (teeth) mit Zahnseide reinigen

flotation [floʊ·'teɪ·ʃən] n ECON Gründung f; **stock-market** ~ Börsengang m

flounder ['flaʊn·dər] vi 1. stolpern; (in snow) waten; (in water) [herum]rudern 2. fig (be in difficulty) sich abmühen

flour ['flaʊ·ər] n Mehl nt

flourish ['flɜr·ɪʃ] I. vi blühen II. vt herumfuchteln mit dat schwingen III. n (movement) schwungvolle Bewegung; (gesture) überschwängliche Geste

flourishing ['flɜr·ɪʃ·ɪŋ] adj a. fig (plants) prächtig; (business) blühend

flow [floʊ] I. vi fließen a. fig; (air, warmth) strömen; **many rivers ~ into the North Sea** viele Flüsse münden in die Nordsee II. n usu sing Fluss m a. fig ▸ **to go against/with the** ~ gegen den/mit dem Strom schwimmen

'flow chart, 'flow diagram n Flussdiagramm nt

flower ['flaʊ·ər] I. n (plant) Blume f; (blossom) Blüte f; **to be in** ~ blühen II. vi blühen a. fig

'flower bed n Blumenbeet nt

'flowerpot n Blumentopf m

flowery ['flaʊ·ə·ri] adj 1. (material) geblümt 2. fig (language) blumig

flowing ['floʊ·ɪŋ] adj flüssig; (hair) wallend

flown [floʊn] vt, vi pp of **fly**

fl. oz. n abbr of **fluid ounce** 29,57 ml

flu [flu] n short for **influenza** Grippe f

flub [flʌb] vt fam **to ~ one's lines** seinen Text verpatzen

fluctuate ['flʌk·tʃʊ·eɪt] vi schwanken; ECON fluktuieren

flue [flu] n Abzugsrohr nt; (in chimney) Rauchabzug m

fluent ['flu·ənt] adj (in a foreign language)

fließend; (style, movements) flüssig

fluff [flʌf] I. n 1. (particle) Fusseln pl 2. ORN, ZOOL Flaum m II. vt vermasseln; (exam) verhauen

fluffy ['flʌf·i] adj 1. (soft: feathers) flaumig; (animal) kuschelig [weich] 2. (light: clouds) aufgelockert; (egg whites) schaumig

fluid ['flu·ɪd] I. n Flüssigkeit f II. adj 1. flüssig 2. fig (changeable) veränderlich

fluid 'ounce n 29,57 ml

flung [flʌŋ] pt, pp of **fling**

flunk [flʌŋk] vt fam durchfallen in +dat

fluorescent [flɔ·'res·ənt] adj fluoreszierend; ~ **light** Neonlicht nt

fluoride ['flɔr·aɪd] n Fluorid nt

flurry ['flɜr·i] n 1. METEO **snow** ~ [Schnee]schauer m 2. (excitement) Unruhe f

flush¹ [flʌʃ] adj (flat) eben; ~ **with sth** mit etw dat auf gleicher Ebene

flush² [flʌʃ] I. vi 1. (blush) erröten (with vor +dat) 2. (empty) spülen; **the toilet won't** ~ die Spülung geht nicht II. vt spülen III. n usu sing Röte f kein pl

◆**flush out** vt 1. (cleanse) ausspülen 2. (drive out) hinaustreiben

flushed [flʌʃt] adj rot im Gesicht

fluster ['flʌs·tər] vt nervös machen

flute [flut] n Flöte f

flutter ['flʌt·ər] vi flattern

flux [flʌks] n **in a state of** ~ im Fluss

fly [flaɪ] I. vi <flew, flown> 1. (through the air) fliegen 2. (flag) wehen 3. (speed) sausen; **the door flew open** die Tür flog auf II. vt <flew, flown> 1. (pilot, transport) fliegen 2. (flag) wehen lassen; (kite) steigen lassen III. n 1. (insect) Fliege f 2. (zipper) Hosenschlitz m ▸ **the** ~ **in the ointment** das Haar in der Suppe IV. adj <-er, -est> sl cool

◆**fly in** vt, vi einfliegen (from aus +dat)

flyer ['flaɪ·ər] n see **flier**

flying ['flaɪ·ɪŋ] I. n Fliegen nt II. adj fliegend

FM [ˌef·'em] n abbr of **frequency modulation** FM

foal [foʊl] n Fohlen nt

foam [foʊm] n 1. (bubbles) Schaum m 2. (plastic) Schaumstoff m

foam 'rubber n Schaumgummi m

fob [fab] **I.** n Schlüsselanhänger m **II.** vt <-bb-> **to ~ sth off on sb** jdm etw andrehen

focal ['fou·kəl] adj **~ point** Brennpunkt m

focus <pl -es or form foci> ['fou·kəs] **I.** n **1.** (center) Mittelpunkt m **2. in/out of ~** scharf/nicht scharf eingestellt **II.** vi <-s- or -ss-> sich konzentrieren (**[up]on** auf +akk) **III.** vt <-s- or -ss-> **1.** (attention) konzentrieren (**on** auf +akk) **2.** (camera) scharf einstellen (**on** auf +akk); (eyes) richten (**on** auf +akk)

fodder ['fad·ər] n Futter nt

fog [fag] n Nebel m

'fogbound adj (airport) wegen Nebels geschlossen

foggy ['fa·gi] adj neblig

'foghorn n Nebelhorn nt

'fog lamp, 'fog light n Nebelscheinwerfer m

foil[1] [fɔɪl] n Folie f

foil[2] [fɔɪl] vt (thing) verhindern; (plan) durchkreuzen

fold [fould] **I.** n Falte f **II.** vt **1.** (bend) falten (**into** zu +dat); (letter) zusammenfalten; (arms) verschränken **2.** FOOD (mix) heben (**into** unter +akk) **III.** vi **1.** (bend) zusammenklappen **2.** (fail) eingehen

◆**fold up** vt, vi zusammenfalten

folder ['foul·dər] n **1.** Mappe f **2.** COMPUT Ordner m

folding ['foul·dɪŋ] adj **~ bed** Klappbett nt; **~ top** Verdeck nt

foliage ['fou·lɪ·ɪdʒ] n Laub nt

folk [fouk] **I.** n **1.** pl fam (people) Leute pl **2.** (music) Folk m **II.** adj **1.** (traditional) Volks- **2.** (connected with folk music) Folk-

'folk dance n Volkstanz m

'folk music n Folk m

folksy ['fouk·si] adj fam volkstümlich

follow ['fal·ou] **I.** vt **1.** (take same route as) folgen +dat **2.** (pursue) verfolgen **3.** (happen next) folgen auf +akk **4.** (obey) befolgen; (guidelines) sich halten an +akk **II.** vi **1.** (take the same route, happen next) folgen; **in the hours that ~ed ...** in den darauffolgenden Stunden ... **2.** (result) sich ergeben

(**from** aus +dat); (be the consequence) die Folge sein

◆**follow through** vt zu Ende verfolgen

◆**follow up I.** vt (investigate) weiterverfolgen; MED nachuntersuchen **II.** vi **to ~ up with sth** etw folgen lassen

follower ['fal·ou·ər] n Anhänger(in) m(f)

following ['fal·ou·ɪŋ] **I.** adj folgende(r, s) **II.** n **1.** + pl vb (listed) the **~** (persons) folgende Personen; (objects) Folgendes **2.** usu sing (fans) Anhänger pl **III.** prep nach +dat

'follow-up I. n Fortsetzung f **II.** adj (visit, interviews) Folge-; **~ treatment** Nachbehandlung f

fond [fand] adj (memories) teuer; (smile) liebevoll; **to be ~ of sb/sth** jdn/etw gerne mögen

fondle ['fan·dl] vt streicheln

font [fant] n TYPO Schriftart f

food [fud] n **1.** (eatables) Essen nt; **cat ~** Katzenfutter nt **2.** (foodstuff) Nahrungsmittel pl

'food chain n Nahrungskette f

'food poisoning n Lebensmittelvergiftung f

'food processor n Küchenmaschine f

'foodstuff n Nahrungsmittel pl

fool [ful] **I.** n (idiot) Dummkopf m; **to make a ~ of oneself** sich zum Narren machen **II.** adj fam blöd **III.** vt täuschen

◆**fool around** vi **1.** (carelessly) herumspielen **2.** (amusingly) herumblödeln

foolish ['fu·lɪʃ] adj töricht; **to look ~** sich blamieren

'foolproof adj idiotensicher

foot [fut] n <pl feet> **1.** (limb) Fuß m; **what size are your feet?** welche Schuhgröße haben Sie?; **to put one's feet up** die Füße hochlegen; **to set ~ in sth** einen Fuß in etw akk setzen; **at sb's feet** zu jds Füßen; **on ~** zu Fuß **2.** <pl foot or feet> (length) Fuß m (= 0,3048 Meter) **3.** <pl feet> (base) Fuß m; (of page) Ende nt ▶ **to land on one's feet** Glück haben; **to put one's ~ down** (insist) ein Machtwort sprechen; **to put one's ~ in one's mouth** ins Fettnäpfchen treten

footage ['fut·ɪdʒ] n Filmmaterial nt

foot-and-'mouth disease n Maul- und Klauenseuche f

football ['fʊt·bɔl] n 1. (game) [American] Football m 2. (ball) Football m

'footbridge n Fußgängerbrücke f

foothold n Halt m [für die Füße]

footing ['fʊt·ɪŋ] n on [an] equal ~ auf gleicher Basis

footlights npl Rampenlicht nt kein pl

'footnote n Fußnote f

'footpath n Fußweg m

'footprint n Fußabdruck m

'footrest n Fußstütze f

'footstep n Schritt m ► to follow in sb's ~ in jds Fußstapfen treten

'footstool n Fußbank f, Schemel m südd, österr

'footwear n Schuhe pl

'footwork n Beinarbeit f

for [fɔr] I. conj denn II. prep 1. für; to be all ~ sth ganz für etw akk sein; to make it easy ~ sb es jdm einfach machen; luckily ~ me zu meinem Glück; what did you do that ~? wozu hast du das getan?; to apply ~ a job sich um eine Stelle bewerben; I feel sorry ~ her sie tut mir leid; to head ~ home sich auf den Heimweg machen, auf dem Heimweg sein; to prepare ~ sth sich auf etw akk vorbereiten; say hi ~ me grüß ihn/sie von mir; to trade sth ~ sth etw gegen etw akk [ein]tauschen; to work ~ sb/sth bei jdm/etw arbeiten; a check ~ 100 dollars eine Scheck über 100 Dollar; if it hadn't been ~ him, ... ohne ihn ...; ~ your information zu Ihrer Information; to be arrested ~ murder wegen Mordes verhaftet werden; ~ various reasons aus verschiedenen Gründen; ~ rent/sale zu vermieten/verkaufen; what's the Spanish word ~ "vegetarian"? was heißt „Vegetarier" auf Spanisch? 2. (with time, distance) to practice ~ half an hour eine halbe Stunde üben; ~ the next two days in den beiden nächsten Tagen; ~ a while eine Weile; ~ a long time seit langem; ~ some time seit längerem; ~ the time being für den Augenblick; ~ the first time zum ersten Mal

forbade [fər·'bæd] pt of forbid

forbid <-dd-, forbad(e), forbidden> [fər·'bɪd] vt to ~ sb sth jdm etw verbieten; to ~ sb from doing [or to do] sth jdm verbieten, etw zu tun

forbidden [fər·'bɪd·ən] I. adj verboten II. pp of forbid

forbidding [fər·'bɪd·ɪŋ] adj abschreckend

force [fɔrs] I. n 1. (power) Kraft f; (intensity) Stärke f; to be come into [or take] ~ in Kraft treten 2. (violence) Gewalt f; by ~ mit Gewalt 3. (group) Truppe f; armed ~s Streitkräfte pl ► to join ~s sich zusammenschließen, um etw zu tun II. vt (compel) zwingen; (door) aufbrechen; to ~ sth on sb jdm etw aufzwingen

force back vt 1. (repel) zurückdrängen; fig (tears) unterdrücken 2. (push back) zurückdrücken

force down vt 1. (plane) zur Landung zwingen 2. (food) hinunterwürgen

force-feed vt zwangsernähren

force open vt mit Gewalt öffnen

forced [fɔrst] adj 1. erzwungen; ~ landing Notlandung f 2. (smile) gezwungen

forceful ['fɔrs·fəl] adj (personality) stark

forcible ['fɔr·sə·bəl] adj gewaltsam

ford [fɔrd] I. n Furt f II. vt durchqueren; (on foot) durchwaten

forearm ['fɔr·arm] n Unterarm m

forecast ['fɔr·kæst] n 1. (prediction) Prognose f 2. weather ~ [Wetter]vorhersage f

forecaster ['fɔr·kæst·ər] n METEO Meteorologe m / Meteorologin f

'forefinger n see index finger

'forefront n at the ~ an der Spitze

forego <-went, -gone> [fɔr·'goʊ] vt see forgo

foregone con'clusion n ausgemachte Sache

'foreground n Vordergrund m

'forehand n Vorhand f

forehead ['fɔr·hed] n Stirn f

foreign ['fɔr·ɪn] adj 1. (from another country) ausländisch 2. (involving other countries) ~ policy Außenpolitik f 3. (not belonging) fremd

foreign affairs npl Außenpolitik f kein pl

foreign corre'spondent n Auslandskorrespondent(in) m(f)

foreigner ['fɔr·ɪ·nər] n Ausländer(in) m(f)

foreign ex'change n Devisen pl

'foreman n 1. (workman) Vorarbeiter m 2. LAW Sprecher m (der Geschworenen)

foremost ['fɔr·moʊst] adj führend

forensic [fə·'ren·sɪk] adj forensisch

'foreplay n Vorspiel nt

foresee <-saw, -seen> [fɔr·'si] vt vorhersehen

foreseeable [fɔr·'si·ə·bəl] adj absehbar; **in the ~ future** in absehbarer Zeit

'foresight n Weitblick m; **to have the ~ to do sth** so vorausschauend sein, etw zu tun

forest ['fɔr·ɪst] n Wald m a. fig; **the Black F~** der Schwarzwald

forester ['fɔr·ɪ·stər] n Förster(in) m(f)

'forest fire n Waldbrand m

'forest ranger n Förster(in) m(f)

forestry ['fɔr·ɪ·stri] n Forstwirtschaft f

forever [fɔr·'ev·ər] adv 1. (for all time) ewig a. fig 2. (continually) ständig

forewarn [fɔr·'wɔrn] vt vorwarnen
▶ **~ed is forearmed** prov bist du gewarnt, bist du gewappnet

'foreword n Vorwort nt

forfeit ['fɔr·fɪt] vt (surrender) einbüßen; (right) verwirken

forgave [fər·'geɪv] n pt of **forgive**

forge [fɔrdʒ] I. n 1. (furnace) Glühofen m 2. (workshop) Schmiede f II. vt 1. (heat and shape) schmieden 2. (copy) fälschen

forger ['fɔr·dʒər] n Fälscher(in) m(f)

forgery ['fɔr·dʒə·ri] n Fälschung f

forget <-got, -gotten or-got> [fər·'get] vt, vi vergessen; **to ~ the past** die Vergangenheit ruhen lassen

forgetful [fər·'get·fəl] adj vergesslich

for'get-me-not n BOT Vergissmeinnicht nt

forgive <-gave, -given> [fər·'gɪv] vt **to ~ sb [for] sth** jdm etw verzeihen; (sin) vergeben; **to ~ and forget** vergeben und vergessen

forgiven [fər·'gɪv·ən] pp of **forgive**

forgiveness [fər·'gɪv·nɪs] n Vergebung f

forgiving [fər·'gɪv·ɪŋ] adj versöhnlich

forgo <-went, -gone> [fɔr·'goʊ] vt verzichten auf akk

forgot [fər·'gat] pt of **forget**

forgotten [fər·'gat·n] I. pp of **forget** II. adj vergessen

fork [fɔrk] I. n 1. (tool) Gabel f 2. (in road) Abzweigung f II. vt mit einer Gabel bearbeiten III. vi sich gabeln

● **fork out** vt **to ~ out $40** $40 springen lassen fam

forked [fɔrkt] adj gegabelt; **~ lightning** Linienblitz m

'forklift n Gabelstapler m

forlorn [fɔr·'lɔrn] adj (place) verlassen; (hope) schwach

form [fɔrm] I. n 1. (type) Form f, Art f; (of energy) Typ m; **art ~** Kunstform f; **~ of exercise** Sportart f; **life ~** Lebensform f 2. (particular way) Form f, Gestalt f; **in some ~ or other** auf die eine oder andere Art 3. (document) Formular nt; **application ~** Bewerbungsbogen m 4. (shape) Form f; (of a person) Gestalt f 5. (physical/mental condition) Form f, Kondition f II. vt 1. (shape) formen a. fig (into zu +dat); GEOG **to be ~ed from** entstehen aus 2. (arrange) bilden; **they ~ed themselves into three lines** sie stellten sich in drei Reihen auf 3. (set up) gründen; (government) bilden; **to ~ an alliance with sb** sich mit jdm verbünden III. vi sich bilden; (idea) Gestalt annehmen

formal ['fɔr·məl] adj 1. (ceremonious) formell; **~ wear** Gesellschaftskleidung f 2. (serious) förmlich

formality [fɔr·'mæl·ɪ·ṭi] n 1. (ceremoniousness) Förmlichkeit f 2. (matter of form) Formsache f

formalize ['fɔr·mə·laɪz] vt (agreement) formell bekräftigen

formally ['fɔr·mə·li] adv offiziell

format ['fɔr·mæt] I. n Format nt II. vt <-tt-> formatieren

formation [fɔr·'meɪ·ʃən] n Bildung f

former ['fɔr·mər] adj 1. (previous) ehemalig 2. (first of two) erstere(r, s)

formerly ['fɔr·mər·li] adv früher

formidable ['fɔr·mɪ·də·bəl] adj 1. (difficult) schwierig; (tremendous) kolossal; (opponent) Furcht erregend 2. (powerful) eindrucksvoll

'form letter n Briefvorlage f

formula <pl -s> ['fɔr·mjʊ·lə] n 1. For-

mel *f* **2.** FOOD Babymilchpulver *nt*

formulate [ˈfɔr·mjʊ·leɪt] *vt* ausarbeiten; (*law*) formulieren; (*theory*) entwickeln

formulation [ˌfɔr·mjʊ·ˈleɪ·ʃən] *n* (*drawing up*) Entwicklung *f*; (*of law*) Fassung *f*

fort [fɔrt] *n* Fort *nt* ▶ **to hold the ~** die Stellung halten

forth [fɔrθ] *adv* **back and ~** vor und zurück ▶ **[and so on] and so ~** und so weiter [und so fort]

forthcoming [ˌfɔrθ·ˈkʌm·ɪŋ] *adj* **1.** (*planned*) bevorstehend **2.** (*coming out soon*) in Kürze erscheinend; (*film*) in Kürze anlaufend

fortieth [ˈfɔr·ti·əθ] **I.** *adj* vierzigste(r, s) **II.** *n* **1.** (*order*) **the ~** der/die/das Vierzigste **2.** (*fraction*) Vierzigstel *nt*; *see also* **eighth**

fortification [ˌfɔr·tə·fɪ·ˈkeɪ·ʃən] *n* (*structures*) **~s** *pl* Befestigungsanlagen *pl*

fortify <-ie-> [ˈfɔr·tə·faɪ] *vt* MIL befestigen

fortress <*pl* -es> [ˈfɔr·trɪs] *n* Festung *f*

fortunate [ˈfɔr·tʃə·nɪt] *adj* glücklich; **to be ~** Glück haben

fortunately [ˈfɔr·tʃə·nɪt·li] *adv* zum Glück

fortune [ˈfɔr·tʃən] *n* **1.** (*money*) Vermögen *nt* **2.** (*luck*) **to tell sb's ~** jds Schicksal vorhersagen

fortune teller *n* Wahrsager(in) *m(f)*

forty [ˈfɔr·ti] **I.** *adj* vierzig **II.** *n* Vierzig *f*; *see also* **eight**

forum [ˈfɔr·əm] *n* Forum *nt*

forward [ˈfɔr·wərd] **I.** *adv* (*toward front*) nach vorn[e]; (*onwards*) vorwärts; **to lean ~** sich vorlehnen; **from that day ~** von jenem Tag an **II.** *adj* **1.** (*toward front*) Vorwärts- **2.** (*near front*) vordere(r, s) **3.** (*of future*) Voraus- *f*; **~ buying** Terminkauf *m* **III.** *n* SPORT Stürmer(in) *m(f)* **IV.** *vt* weiterleiten (**to** an *+akk*)

forwarding ad'dress *n* Nachsendeadresse *f*

forward-looking *adj* vorausschauend

forwards [ˈfɔr·wərdz] *adv see* **forward**

forwent [fɔr·ˈwent] *pt of* **forgo**

fossil [ˈfɑs·əl] *n* Fossil *nt*; **~ fuel** fossiler Brennstoff

foster [ˈfɑ·stər] *vt* **1.** (*child*) in Pflege nehmen **2.** (*encourage*) fördern

foster child *n* Pflegekind *nt*

fought [fɔt] *pt, pp of* **fight**

foul [faʊl] **I.** *adj* **1.** (*disgusting*) abscheulich; (*smell*) faul **2.** (*polluted*) verpestet **3.** (*mood*) fürchterlich; (*language*) anstößig **II.** *n* SPORT Foul *nt* **III.** *vt* SPORT foulen

foul-'mouthed *adj* unflätig

foul 'play *n* SPORT Foulspiel *nt*

found [faʊnd] *pt, pp of* **find**

foundation [faʊn·ˈdeɪ·ʃən] *n* **1.** (*basis*) Fundament *nt a. fig*; **to be without ~** *fig* der Grundlage entbehren **2.** (*make-up*) Grundierung *f*

foun'dation stone *n* Grundstein *m*

founder [ˈfaʊn·dər] *n* Gründer(in) *m(f)*

Founding 'Fathers *npl* Gründerväter *pl*

foundry [ˈfaʊn·dri] *n* Gießerei *f*

fountain [ˈfaʊn·tən] *n* Brunnen *m*

four [fɔr] **I.** *adj* vier **II.** *n* (*number, symbol*) Vier *f*; *see also* **eight**

four-by-four *n* AUTO allrad-/vierradangetriebenes Auto

fourfold *adj, adv* vierfach

four-'footed *adj* vierfüßig

four-leaf 'clover *n* vierblättriges Kleeblatt

four-letter 'word *n* Schimpfwort *nt*

foursome *n* Vierergruppe *f*; (*golf*) Vierer *m*

fourteen [ˌfɔr·ˈtin] **I.** *adj* vierzehn; **~ hundred hours** *spoken* vierzehn Uhr; **1400 hours** *written* 14:00 **II.** *n* Vierzehn *f*; *see also* **eight**

fourteenth [ˌfɔr·ˈtinθ] **I.** *adj* vierzehnte(r, s) **II.** *n* **1.** (*fraction*) Vierzehntel *nt* **2.** (*date*) **the ~** der Vierzehnte

fourth [fɔrθ] **I.** *adj* vierte(r, s) **II.** *n* **1.** (*order*) **the ~** der/die/das Vierte **2.** (*date*) **the ~** der Vierte **3.** (*fraction*) Viertel *nt*; *see also* **eighth**

Fourth of July *amerikanischer Unabhängigkeitstag am 4. Juli*

four-wheel 'drive *n* Allrad-/Vierradantrieb *m*

fowl <*pl* -> [faʊl] *n* Geflügel *nt kein pl*

fox [faks] **I.** *n* **1.** (*animal*) Fuchs *m a. fig*; (*fur*) Fuchspelz *m* **2.** *sl* (*attractive woman*) scharfe Braut *pej sl*; (*attractive man*) heißer Typ *pej sl* **II.** *vt* verblüffen

foxy [ˈfak·si] *adj* **1.** (*crafty*) gerissen

2. *fam* (*sexy*) sexy

foyer ['fɔɪ·ər] *n* Foyer *nt*

fracas <*pl* -es> ['freɪ·kəs] *n* lautstarke Auseinandersetzung

fraction ['fræk·ʃən] *n* **1.** (*number*) Bruchzahl *f* **2.** (*proportion*) Bruchteil *m; fig* **by a ~** um Haaresbreite

fractional ['fræk·ʃə·nəl] *adj* minimal

fracture ['fræk·tʃər] **I.** *vt, vi* brechen **II.** *n* Bruch *m*

fragile ['fræʤ·əl] *adj* **1.** (*breakable*) zerbrechlich **2.** (*unstable*) brüchig; (*peace*) unsicher

fragment ['fræg·ment] *n* **1.** (*broken piece*) Splitter *m* **2.** (*incomplete piece*) Brocken *m*

fragrance ['freɪ·grəns] *n* Duft *m*

fragrant ['freɪ·grənt] *adj* duftend

frail [freɪl] *adj* gebrechlich

frame [freɪm] **I.** *n* **1.** (*of picture*) Bilderrahmen *m* **2.** (*of door, window*) Rahmen *m* **3.** (*of eyeglasses*) **~s** *pl* Brillengestell *nt* **4.** (*body*) Körper *m* **II.** *vt* **1.** (*put in framework*) einrahmen **2.** *fam* (*falsely incriminate*) verleumden

'frame-up *n fam* abgekartetes Spiel

'framework *n* **1.** Gerüst *nt* **2.** *fig* Rahmen *m*

France [fræns] *n* Frankreich *nt*

franchise ['fræn·tʃaɪz] *n* Franchise *f*

frank¹ [fræŋk] **I.** *adj* aufrichtig; **to be ~ [with sb] [about sth]** ehrlich [zu jdm] [über etw *akk*] sein **II.** *vt* (*envelope*) frankieren

frank² [fræŋk] *n fam* (*frankfurter*) Frankfurter *f*

frankly ['fræŋk·li] *adv* offen

frantic ['fræn·tɪk] *adj* **1.** (*distracted*) verrückt (**with** vor +*dat*) **2.** (*hurried*) hektisch

fraternity [frə·'tɜr·nɪ·ti] *n* **1.** (*group*) Vereinigung *f* **2.** *UNIV* Burschenschaft *f*

fraternize ['fræt·ər·naɪz] *vi* sich verbrüdern

fraud [frɔd] *n* **1.** (*deceit*) Betrug *m* **2.** (*deceiver*) Betrüger(in) *m(f)*

fraudulent ['frɔ·dʒə·lənt] *adj* betrügerisch

fraught [frɔt] *adj* **to be ~ with difficulties** voller Schwierigkeiten stecken

fray [freɪ] *vi* (*fabric*) ausfransen

freak [frik] *n* **1.** (*abnormal thing*) etwas Außergewöhnliches; **a ~ of nature** eine Laune der Natur **2.** (*abnormal person*) Missgeburt *f*

freak out *vi fam* ausflippen

freckle ['frek·əl] *n usu pl* Sommersprosse *f*

freckled ['frek·əld] *adj* sommersprossig

free [fri] **I.** *adj* **1.** free; **~ speech** Redefreiheit *f;* **to be ~ [to do sth]** Zeit haben[, etw zu tun]; **you are ~ to come and go as you please** Sie können kommen und gehen, wann Sie wollen; **to break ~ [of** *or* **from] sth** sich [aus] etw] befreien *a. fig;* **to walk ~** straffrei ausgehen **2.** (*costing nothing*) frei
▶ **there's no such thing as a ~ lunch** nichts ist umsonst **II.** *adv* frei, gratis; **~ of charge** kostenlos **III.** *vt* freilassen; (*hands*) frei machen

free up *vt* freimachen

freebie ['fri·bi] *n fam* Werbegeschenk *nt*

freedom ['fri·dəm] *n* Freiheit *f;* **~ of information** freier Informationszugang; **~ of speech** Redefreiheit *f*

'free-for-all *n* allgemeines Gerangel

'freehand *adj* Freihand-

free 'kick *n SPORT* Freistoß *m*

freelance ['fri·læns] *n* Freiberufler(in) *m(f)*

'freeload *vi pej* schnorren (**off** bei +*dat*)

'freeloader *vi pej* Schnorrer(in) *m(f)*

freely ['fri·li] *adv* **1.** (*unrestrictedly*) frei **2.** (*without obstruction*) ungehindert **3.** (*generously*) großzügig

free 'port *n* Freihafen *m*

'free-range *adj* Freiland-

free 'speech *n* Redefreiheit *f*

free'standing *adj* frei stehend

'freestyle *n* Freistil *m*

free 'trade *n* Freihandel *m*

'freeware *n COMPUT* Freeware *f*

'freeway *n* Fern|verkehrs|straße *f*

free 'will *n* freier Wille; **to do sth of one's own ~** etw aus freien Stücken tun

freeze [friz] **I.** *n* **1.** *METEO* Frost *m* **2.** *ECON* Einfrieren *nt* **II.** *vi* <froze, frozen> **1.** (*water*) gefrieren; (*pipes*) einfrieren; **to ~ solid** festfrieren **2.** *a. fig* (*get very cold*) [sehr] frieren; **to ~ to death** erfrieren **3.** (*be still*) erstarren **III.** *vt* <froze, frozen> **1.** (*turn to ice*)

gefrieren lassen **2.** (*preserve*) einfrieren **3.** (*image*) festhalten

freeze up *vi* einfrieren

freezer ['fri·zər] *n* Gefrierschrank *m*

freezer bag *n* Kühltasche *f*

freezing ['fri·zɪŋ] **I.** *adj* frostig; **it's ~** es ist eiskalt; **I'm ~** mir ist eiskalt **II.** *n* (*preserving*) Einfrieren *nt*

freezing point *n* Gefrierpunkt *m*

freight [freɪt] *n* **1.** (*goods*) Frachtgut *nt* **2.** (*charge*) Frachtgebühr *f*

freight car *n* Güterwagen *m*

freighter ['freɪ·tər] *n* Frachter *m*

freight train *n* Güterzug *m*

French [frentʃ] **I.** *adj* französisch **II.** *n* **1.** (*language*) Französisch *nt* **2.** (*people*) **the ~** *pl* die Franzosen

French 'doors *npl* Verandatür *f*

French fries *npl* Pommes frites *pl*

French 'toast *n* FOOD armer Ritter

frenetic [frə·'net·ɪk] *adj* hektisch

frenzied ['fren·zɪd] *adj* fieberhaft; (*attack*) wild

frenzy ['fren·zi] *n* Raserei *f*

frequency ['fri·kwən·si] *n* **1.** Häufigkeit *f* **2.** RADIO Frequenz *f*

frequent ['fri·kwənt] *adj* (*often*) häufig; (*regular*) regelmäßig

frequently ['fri·kwənt·li] *adv* häufig

fresh [freʃ] *adj* **1.** frisch *a. fig*; **~ start** Neuanfang *m*; **to get a breath of ~ air** frische Luft schnappen **2.** *fam* (*cheeky*) frech

freshen ['freʃ·ən] **I.** *vt* (*drink*) auffüllen; (*room*) durchlüften **II.** *vi* (*wind*) auffrischen

freshman ['freʃ·mən] *n* **1.** (*college student*) Studienanfänger *m* **2.** (*ninthgrade high school student*) Gymnasiast *m* im ersten Jahr

freshness ['freʃ·nɪs] *n* Frische *f*

freshwater *adj* Süßwasser-

fret [fret] *vi* <-tt-> sich *dat* Sorgen machen

friction ['frɪk·ʃən] *n* Reibung *f*

Friday ['fraɪ·di] *n* Freitag *m*; *see also* **Tuesday**

fridge [frɪdʒ] *n fam* Kühlschrank *m*

fried [fraɪd] *adj* (*of food*) gebraten; **~ potatoes** Bratkartoffeln *pl*

fried 'egg *n* Spiegelei *nt*

friend [frend] *n* Freund(in) *m(f)*

friendly ['frend·li] *adj* **1.** (*showing friendship*) freundlich **2.** (*atmosphere*) angenehm

friendship ['frend·ʃɪp] *n* Freundschaft *f*

fries [fraɪz] *npl* Pommes frites *pl*

fright [fraɪt] *n* **1.** (*feeling*) Angst *f* **2.** *usu sing* (*experience*) Schrecken *m*; **to get a ~** erschrecken

frighten ['fraɪt·ən] *vt* **to ~ sb** jdm Angst machen

frighten away *vt* abschrecken

frightened ['fraɪt·ənd] *adj* verängstigt; **to be ~ of sth/sb** sich vor etw/jdm fürchten

frightening ['fraɪt·ən·ɪŋ] *adj* Furcht erregend

frigid ['frɪdʒ·ɪd] *adj* **1.** (*of manner*) frostig **2.** (*sexually*) frigid[e]

frigidity [frɪ·'dʒɪd·ɪ·ti] *n* (*of manner*) Kälte *f*

frill [frɪl] *n* Rüsche *f*

frilly ['frɪl·i] *adj* mit Rüschen

fringe [frɪndʒ] **I.** *n* **1.** (*edging*) Franse *f* **2.** (*of area*) Rand *m a. fig* **II.** *adj* **~ benefits** zusätzliche Leistungen *pl*

frisk [frɪsk] *vt* abtasten (**for** nach +*dat*)

frisky ['frɪs·ki] *adj* (*horse*) lebhaft

fritter ['frɪt·ər] *n* Fettgebackenes *nt* (*mit Obst-/Gemüsefüllung*)

frivolous ['frɪv·ə·ləs] *adj* **1.** *pej* (*person*) leichtfertig **2.** *pej* (*unimportant*) belanglos

frizzy ['frɪz·i] *adj* gekräuselt

fro [froʊ] *adv* **to and ~** hin und her

frog [frag] *n* Frosch *m*

from [fram] *prep* **1.** (*off*) von; (*out of, made of, originating in*) aus **2.** (*as seen from*) **~ here** von hier [aus]; **~ my point of view** aus meiner Sicht **3.** (*as starting location*) von; **~ the north** von Norden **4.** (*as starting time*) von, ab; **~ tomorrow on[ward]** ab morgen; **~ time to time** ab und zu **5.** (*as starting condition*) bei; **~ 25 to 200** von 25 auf 200 **6.** (*considering*) aufgrund, wegen; **~ the evidence** aufgrund des Beweismaterials **7.** (*caused by*) an +*dat*; **he died ~ his injuries** er starb an seinen Verletzungen; **the risk ~ radiation [exposure]** das Risiko einer Verstrahlung **8.** (*indicating*

protection) vor; **to protect sb ~ sth** jdn vor etw *dat* schützen

front [frʌnt] **I.** *n* **1.** *usu sing* (*forward-facing part*) Vorderseite *f;* (*of building*) Front *f;* **to lie on one's ~** auf dem Bauch liegen **2.** (*front area*) **the ~** der vordere Bereich; **at the ~** vorn[e] **3.** (*ahead of*) **in ~** vorn[e]; **in ~ of sth/sb** vor etw/jdm **4.** (*in advance*) **up ~** im Voraus **5.** MIL, METEO, POL Front *f* **II.** *adj* (*at the front*) vorder[st]e(r, s); **~ wheel** Vorderrad *nt* **III.** *vt* (*be head of*) vorstehen +*dat*

frontage ['frʌn·tɪdʒ] *n* [Vorder]front *f*

frontal ['frʌn·təl] *adj* Frontal-; **~ view** Vorderansicht *f*

front 'door *n* Haustür *f*

frontier [frʌn·'tɪr] *n* (*outlying areas*) **the ~** der ehemalige Wilde Westen der USA

front 'line *n* **1.** MIL Frontlinie *f* **2.** *fig* vorderste Front

front 'page *n* Titelseite *f*

'front-runner *n* Spitzenreiter(in) *m(f)* a. *fig*

front-wheel 'drive *n* Vorderradantrieb *m*

front 'yard *n* Vorgarten *m*

frost [frɑst] *n* Frost *m*

'frostbite *n* Erfrierung *f*

frosted ['frɑ·stɪd] *adj* (*opaque*) **~ glass** Milchglas *nt*

frosting ['frɑ·stɪŋ] *n* FOOD Glasur *f*

frosty ['frɑ·sti] *adj* frostig

froth [frɑθ] **I.** *n* Schaum *m* **II.** *vi* schäumen

frothy ['frɑ·θi] *adj* schaumig

frown [fraʊn] **I.** *vi* die Stirn runzeln; **to ~ on** [*or* **upon**] **sth** etw missbilligen **II.** *n* Stirnrunzeln *nt kein pl*

froze [froʊz] *pt of* **freeze**

frozen ['froʊ·zn] **I.** *pp of* **freeze II.** *adj* **1.** (*of water*) gefroren **2.** FOOD [tief]gefroren; **~ food** Tiefkühlkost *f*

frugal ['fru·gəl] *adj* **1.** (*economical*) sparsam **2.** (*meal*) karg

fruit [frut] **I.** *n* **1.** Frucht *f* a. *fig;* (*collectively*) Obst *nt* **II.** *vi* [Früchte] tragen

'fruitcake *n* **1.** Früchtebrot *n* **2.** *sl* (*eccentric*) Spinner(in) *m(f)*

fruition [fru·'ɪʃ·ən] *n* **to come to** [*or* **into reach**] **~** verwirklicht werden

fruitless ['frut·lɪs] *adj* fruchtlos

fruit 'salad *n* Obstsalat *m*

fruity ['fru·ti] *adj* fruchtig

frustrate ['frʌs·treɪt] *vt* **1.** (*annoy*) frustrieren **2.** (*prevent*) hindern

frustrating ['frʌs·treɪ·tɪŋ] *adj* frustrierend

frustration [frʌ·'streɪ·ʃən] *n* Frustration *f*

fry [fraɪ] *vt, vi* <-ie-> braten

frying pan ['fraɪ·ɪŋ-] *n* Bratpfanne *f*

ft. *n abbr of* **feet** ft

fuck [fʌk] *vulg* **I.** *n* **1.** (*act*) Fick *m* **2.** (*used as expletive*) **who gives a ~?** wen interessiert es schon? **II.** *inter*, Scheiße! **III.** *vt* **1.** (*have sex with*) vögeln **2.** (*damn*) [oh] **~ it!** verdammte Scheiße! **IV.** *vi* ficken

◆fuck off *vi vulg* sich verpissen

fucker ['fʌk·ər] *n vulg* **1.** (*person*) Arsch *m* **2.** (*thing*) Scheiß *m*

fucking ['fʌk·ɪŋ] *adj, adv vulg* verdammt, Scheiß-; **to be ~ useless** zu gar nichts taugen; *sl* echt, verflixt

'fuckup *n vulg, sl* (*mess*) Scheiß *m pej derb;* (*confusion*) Durcheinander *nt*

fudge [fʌdʒ] **I.** *n* Fondant *m o nt* **II.** *vt*, *vi* (*figures*) frisieren *fam*

fuel ['fju·əl] **I.** *n* Brennstoff *m* **II.** *vt* <-l-> *fig* nähren; (*resentment*) schüren

'fuel consumption *n* Treibstoffverbrauch *m*

'fuel gauge *n* Tankanzeige *f*

fuel-injection 'engine *n* Einspritzmotor *m*

'fuel pump *n* Kraftstoffpumpe *f*

fugitive ['fju·dʒɪ·tɪv] *n* Flüchtige(r) *f(m)*

fulfill [fʊl·'fɪl] *vt* **1.** (*satisfy*) erfüllen; (*potential*) ausschöpfen **2.** (*contract, promise*) erfüllen

fulfillment [fʊl·'fɪl·mənt] *n* Erfüllung *f*

full [fʊl] **I.** *adj* voll; (*after eating*) satt; (*explanation*) vollständig; (*theater*) ausverkauft; **to be ~ of sth** (*enthusiastic*) von etw *dat* ganz begeistert sein; **with one's mouth ~** mit vollem Mund; [at] **~ speed** mit voller Geschwindigkeit; **in ~ swing** voll im Gang **II.** *adv* voll **III.** *n* **in ~** zur Gänze

'fullback *n* (*in football*) Fullback *m;* (*in soccer*) Außenverteidiger(in) *m(f)*

full-'blooded *adj* **1.** (*of descent*) reinrassig **2.** (*vigorous*) kraftvoll

full-'blown *adj* (*disease*) voll ausgebrochen

full-'bodied adj (wine) vollmundig

full-'frontal adj völlig nackt

full-'grown adj ausgewachsen

full-'length I. adj (film) abendfüllend; (mirror) groß II. adv **to lie ~ on the floor** sich der Länge nach auf den Boden legen [or der Länge nach auf dem Boden liegen]

full 'moon n Vollmond m

fullness ['fʊl·nɪs] n Völle f

full-page adj ganzseitig

full-scale adj 1. (original size) in Originalgröße nach n 2. (all-out) umfassend

full 'time n (in soccer) Spielende nt

full-time I. adj Ganztags- II. adv ganztags

fully ['fʊl·i] adv völlig; **~ booked** ausgebucht

fumble ['fʌm·bəl] I. vi 1. **to ~ [around** [or **about]] for sth** nach etw dat tasten 2. SPORT den Ball fallen lassen, fumbeln II. vt (ball) fallen lassen, fumbeln III. n SPORT Fumble m

fume [fjum] vi vor Wut schäumen

fumes [fjumz] n pl Dämpfe pl; (of car) Abgase pl

fun [fʌn] I. n Spaß m; **it was lots of ~** es hat viel Spaß gemacht; **in ~** im Spaß; **have ~!** viel Spaß!; **to make ~ of sb** sich über jdn lustig machen II. adj fam lustig

function ['fʌŋk·ʃən] I. n 1. (task: of a person) Aufgabe f 2. MATH Funktion f 3. (social event) Veranstaltung f II. vi funktionieren

functional ['fʌŋk·ʃə·nəl] adj funktionstüchtig

function key n COMPUT Funktionstaste f

fund [fʌnd] I. n 1. (stock) Fonds m; **disaster ~** Notfonds m 2. (money) **~s** pl [finanzielle] Mittel II. vt finanzieren

fundamental [ˌfʌn·də·'men·təl] adj grundlegend (**to** für +akk); (difference) wesentlich

fundamentalism [ˌfʌn·də·'men·təl·ɪz·əm] n Fundamentalismus m

fundamentalist [ˌfʌn·də·'men·təl·ɪst] n Fundamentalist(in) m(f)

fundamentally [ˌfʌn·də·'ment·əl·i] adv 1. (basically) im Grunde 2. (in all important aspects) grundsätzlich

funding ['fʌnd·ɪŋ] n Finanzierung f

'fundraiser n (event) Wohltätigkeitsveranstaltung f

'fundraising I. adj **~ campaign** Spendenaktion f II. n Geldbeschaffung f

funeral ['fju·nər·əl] n Beerdigung f

'funeral director n Leichenbestatter(in) m(f)

fungus <pl -es> ['fʌŋ·gəs] n Pilz m

funicular [fju·'nɪk·ju·lər], **funicular 'railway** n Seilbahn f

funk [fʌŋk] n MUS Funk m

funky ['fʌŋ·ki] adj sl 1. (hip) flippig 2. MUS funkig

'fun-loving adj lebenslustig

funnel ['fʌn·əl] I. n 1. (tool) Trichter m 2. (on ship) Schornstein m II. vt <-l-> [mit einem Trichter] einfüllen

funnies ['fʌn·iz] npl **the ~** der Witzteil (einer Zeitung)

funny ['fʌn·i] I. adj 1. (amusing) lustig, witzig 2. (strange) komisch, merkwürdig; **to have a ~ feeling that ...** so eine Ahnung haben, dass ... 3. (dishonest) verdächtig ▶ **~ ha-ha** or **~ peculiar** [or **weird**]? lustig oder merkwürdig? II. adv fam komisch, merkwürdig

fur [fɜr] n 1. (on animal) Fell nt 2. FASHION Pelz m

furious ['fjʊr·i·əs] adj 1. (angry) [sehr] wütend; (argument) heftig; **to be ~ with sb/about** [or **at**] **sth** wütend auf jdn/über etw akk sein 2. (intense: storm) heftig; **at a ~ pace** in rasender Geschwindigkeit; **fast and ~** rasant

furnace ['fɜr·nɪs] n 1. (industrial) Hochofen m 2. (domestic) [Haupt]heizung f

furnished ['fɜr·nɪʃt] adj möbliert

furnishings ['fɜr·nɪ·ʃɪŋz] npl Einrichtung f

furniture ['fɜr·nɪ·tʃər] n Möbel pl

furor ['fjʊr·ɔr] n Aufruhr m

furrow ['fɜr·oʊ] n Furche f

furry ['fɜr·i] adj (short fur) pelzig; (long fur) wollig

further ['fɜr·ðər] I. adj comp of **far** 1. (additional) weiter; **until ~ notice** bis auf weiteres 2. (more distant) weiter [entfernt] II. adv comp of **far** 1. (to a greater degree) weiter; **to take sth ~** mit etw dat weitermachen; (pursue:

matter) etw weiterverfolgen **2.** (*more*) [noch] weiter; **I have nothing ~ to say** ich habe nichts mehr zu sagen. **3.** (*more distant*) weiter; **~ back** (*in place*) weiter zurück; (*in time*) früher

furthermore [ˈfɜr·ðər·mɔr] *adv* außerdem

furthest [ˈfɜr·ðɪst] **I.** *adj superl of* **far 1.** *fig* extremste(r, s) **2.** am weitesten entfernte(r, s) **II.** *adv superl of* **far** am weitesten

furtive [ˈfɜr·tɪv] *adj* (*glance*) verstohlen; (*action*) heimlich

fury [ˈfjʊr·i] *n* Wut *f*

fuse[1] [fjuz] *n* (*of a bomb*) Zündvorrichtung *f*

fuse[2] [fjuz] **I.** *n* Sicherung *f* **II.** *vt* verbinden

fuse box *n* Sicherungskasten *m*

fuselage [ˈfju·sə·lɑʒ] *n* [Flugzeug]rumpf *m*

fuss [fʌs] **I.** *n* **1.** (*excitement*) [übertriebene] Aufregung **2.** (*attention*) [übertriebener] Aufwand, Getue *nt pej;* **to make** [*or* **kick up**] **a ~** einen Aufstand machen **II.** *vi* (*be nervously active*) [sehr] aufgeregt sein

fussbudget *n fam* **to be a ~** penibel sein

fussy [ˈfʌs·i] *adj* **1.** *pej* (*about things*) pingelig; (*about food*) mäkelig **2.** *pej* (*overly decorated*) [zu] verspielt

futile [ˈfju·t̬əl] *adj* sinnlos

futon [ˈfu·tɑn] *n* Futon *nt*

future [ˈfju·tʃər] **I.** *n usu sing* **1.** (*in time*) Zukunft *f;* **to have no ~** keine Zukunft[saussichten] haben **2.** LING **~ tense** Futur *nt* **II.** *adj* zukünftig

futures market *n* ECON Terminbörse *f*

fuze [fjuz] *n vt see* **fuse**[1]

fuzz[1] [fʌz] *n* **1.** (*fluff*) Fussel[n] *pl* **2.** (*fluffy hair*) Flaum *m*

fuzz[2] [fʌz] *n sl* (*police*) **the ~** die Bullen *pl*

fuzzy [ˈfʌz·i] *adj* **1.** (*fluffy*) flaumig **2.** (*distorted*) verschwommen

FYI *adv fam abbr of* **for your information** z. K.

G

G <*pl* -ˈs>, **g** <*pl* -ˈs> [dʒi] *n* (*letter*) G *nt* g *nt;* **~ as in Golf** G wie Gustav

G *adj* FILM *abbr of* **General Audiences rated** ~ jugendfrei

GA, Ga. *abbr of* **Georgia**

gab [gæb] *vi* <-bb-> *pej fam* quatschen

gabble [ˈgæb·əl] *vi* quasseln

gable [ˈgeɪ·bəl] *n* Giebel *m*

gadget [ˈgædʒ·ɪt] *n* [praktisches] Gerät

gaffer [ˈgæf·ər] *n* FILM, TV ≈ Filmtechniker *m*

gag [gæg] *n* **1.** (*for mouth*) Knebel *m* **2.** (*joke*) Gag *m*

gaga [ˈgɑ·gɑ] *adj fam* vertrottelt

gage [geɪdʒ] *n vt see* **gauge**

gag order *n fam* Nachrichtensperre *f*

gaily [ˈgeɪ·li] *adv* fröhlich

gain [geɪn] **I.** *n* Zunahme *f kein pl* **II.** *v* **1.** (*obtain*) gewinnen; (*experience*) sammeln; (*independence*) erlangen; **to ~ control of sth** etw unter [seine] Kontrolle bekommen **2.** (*increase*) **to ~ sth** an etw *dat* gewinnen; (*self-confidence*) entwickeln; **to ~ speed** schneller werden; **to ~ weight** zunehmen **III.** *v* **1.** (*increase*) zunehmen **2.** (*profit*) profitieren

gait [geɪt] *n* Gang *m* *kein pl;* (*of a horse*) Gangart *f*

gala [ˈgeɪ·lə] *n* (*social event*) Gala *f*

galaxy [ˈgæl·ək·si] *n* Galaxie *f*

gale [geɪl] *n* Sturm *m*

gall [gɔl] *n* ANAT **~ bladder** Gallenblase *f*

gallery [ˈgæl·ə·ri] *n* Galerie *f*

galley [ˈgæl·i] *n* (*of a ship*) Kombüse *f;* (*of an airplane*) Bordküche *f*

gallon [ˈgæl·ən] *n* Gallone *f*

gallop [ˈgæl·əp] *vi* galoppieren

gallows [ˈgæl·oʊz] *n* + *sing vb* Galgen *m*

gallstone *n* Gallenstein *m*

galvanize [ˈgæl·və·naɪz] *vt* TECH galvanisieren

gambit [ˈgæm·bɪt] *n* **1.** (*in chess*) Gambit *nt* **2.** (*tactic, remark*) Schachzug *m*

gamble [ˈgæm·bəl] **I.** *n usu sing* Risiko *nt* **II.** *vi* [um Geld] spielen; **to ~**

on the stock market an der Börse spekulieren

gambler ['gæm·blər] n Spieler(in) m(f)

gambling ['gæm·bəlɪŋ] n Glücksspiel nt

game¹ [geɪm] n Spiel nt; **a ~ of tennis** eine Partie Tennis; **what's your ~?** fig fam was soll das?; **to play ~s with sb** fig mit jdm spielen ▶ **to beat sb at their own ~** jdn mit seinen eigenen Waffen schlagen; **two can play at that ~** was du kannst, kann ich schon lange; **the ~'s up** das Spiel ist aus

game² [geɪm] n (animal) Wild nt

'game show n Spielshow f

gaming ['geɪ·mɪŋ] n Spielen nt

gander ['gæn·dər] n Gänserich m

gang [gæŋ] n (of criminals) Bande f; (of youths) Gang f

'gangplank n Landungssteg m

gangster ['gæŋ·stər] n Gangster(in) m(f)

gang 'warfare n Bandenkrieg m

'gangway I. n NAUT, AERO Gangway f II. interj fam ~! Platz da!

gap [gæp] n Lücke f a. fig

gape [geɪp] vi glotzen

gaping ['geɪ·pɪŋ] adj weit geöffnet

garage [gə·'rɑʒ] n 1. Garage f 2. (repair shop) [Kfz-]Werkstatt f

ga'rage sale n privater Flohmarkt in der Garage

garbage ['gɑr·bɪdʒ] n Müll m a. fig

'garbage can n Mülleimer m

'garbage truck n Müllauto m

garble ['gɑr·bəl] vt durcheinanderbringen

garden ['gɑr·dən] n Garten m; ~s pl Gartenanlage f

gardener ['gɑrd·nər] n Gärtner(in) m(f)

gardening ['gɑr·dnɪŋ] n Gartenarbeit f; ~ tools Gartengeräte pl

gargle ['gɑr·gəl] vi gurgeln

garish ['ger·ɪʃ] adj pej knallbunt

garland ['gɑr·lənd] n Kranz m

garlic ['gɑr·lɪk] n Knoblauch m

garment ['gɑr·mənt] n Kleidungsstück nt

garnish ['gɑr·nɪʃ] n <pl -es> Garnierung f

garrison ['ger·ə·sən] n Garnison f

gas [gæs] I. n <pl -es> 1. (not solid or liquid) Gas nt; **natural ~** Erdgas nt 2. fam (gasoline) Benzin nt; **to step**

on the ~ fig Gas geben II. vt <-ss-> vergasen

'gasbag n pej sl Quasselstrippe f

'gas chamber n Gaskammer f

gaseous ['gæs·i·əs] adj gasförmig

'gas gauge n Benzinuhr f

'gas guzzler n fam Benzinfresser m fam

gash [gæʃ] n <pl -es> [tiefe] Schnittwunde

'gas heating n [zentrale] Gasheizung f

'gas mask n Gasmaske f

'gas meter n Gaszähler m

gasoline ['gæs·ə·lin] n Benzin nt

'gas oven n Gasherd m

gasp [gæsp] I. vi (pant) keuchen; (catch one's breath) tief einatmen; **to ~ for air** nach Luft schnappen II. vt hervorstoßen

'gas pedal n Gaspedal nt

'gas pipe n Gasleitung f

'gas pump n Zapfsäule f

'gas station n Tankstelle f

'gas stove n Gasherd m

gastric ['gæs·trɪk] adj MED Magen-

gastronomy [gæ·'strɑn·ə·mi] n Gastronomie f

gate [geɪt] n 1. (at an entrance) Tor nt; (at an airport) Flugsteig m, Gate nt 2. SPORT **starting ~** Startmaschine f

'gatecrasher n fam un[ein]geladener Gast

'gateway n 1. Eingangstor nt 2. fig Tor nt

gather ['gæð·ər] I. vt 1. (collect) sammeln; **to ~ intelligence** sich dat [geheime] Informationen beschaffen 2. FASHION kräuseln 3. (understand) verstehen; **to ~ from sb that ...** von jdm erfahren haben, dass ... II. vi (people) sich versammeln

gathering ['gæð·ər·ɪŋ] n Versammlung f

gauche [goʊʃ] adj unbeholfen

gaudy ['gɔ·di] adj knallig

gauge [geɪdʒ] I. n 1. (device) Messgerät nt; (for water level) Pegel m 2. (thickness: of metal) Stärke f; (diameter: of a gun) Durchmesser m II. vt 1. (measure) messen 2. (estimate) [ab]schätzen

gaunt [gɔnt] adj hager

gauntlet ['gɔnt·lɪt] n [Stulpen]handschuh m ▶ **to throw down the ~** den

G

Fehdehandschuh hinwerfen *geh*

gauze [gɔz] *n* Gaze *f*

gave [geɪv] *pt of* **give**

gavel ['gæv·əl] *n* Hammer *m*

gay [geɪ] *adj* (*homosexual*) schwul, gay; **~ bar** Schwulenlokal *nt*

gaze [geɪz] **I.** *vi* starren; **to ~ out of the window** aus dem Fenster starren **II.** *n* Blick *m*

gazette [gə·'zet] *n* Blatt *nt*, Anzeiger *m*

GB [ˌdʒi·'bi] *n* <*pl*-> **1.** *abbr of* **gigabyte** GByte *nt* **2.** *abbr of* **Great Britain** GB

GDP [ˌdʒi·di·'pi] *n abbr of* **gross domestic product** BIP *nt*

gear [gɪr] **I.** *n* **1.** TECH Gang *m;* **to shift ~s** schalten **2.** (*equipment*) Ausrüstung *f* **II.** *vt* ausrichten (**to** auf +*akk*)

'gearbox *n* Getriebe *nt*

'gearshift *n* Schalthebel *m*

GED [ˌdʒi·i·'di] *n abbr of* **general equivalency diploma** ≈ SfE *f* (*Kurs zur Erlangung der US-Hochschulreife auf dem zweiten Bildungsweg*)

gee [dʒi] *interj fam* Mannomann *m*

gel [dʒel] *n* Gel *nt*

gelatin, gelatine ['dʒel·ət·in] *n* Gelatine *f*

gem [dʒem] *n* Edelstein *m*

Gemini ['dʒem·ɪ·naɪ] *n* ASTROL Zwillinge *pl;* **to be a ~** [ein] Zwilling sein

gen. [dʒen] *n* **1.** *short for* **general** allgem. **2.** *short for* **generation** Gen.

gender [dʒen·dər] *n* Geschlecht *nt*

gene [dʒin] *n* Gen *nt*

genealogy [ˌdʒi·nɪ·'æl·ə·dʒi] *n* Genealogie *f*

'gene bank *n* Genbank *f*

general ['dʒen·ər·əl] **I.** *adj* allgemein; **~ idea** ungefähre Vorstellung; **~ impression** Gesamteindruck *m;* **~ meeting** Vollversammlung *f;* **it is ~ practice** es ist allgemein üblich; **in ~** [*or* **as a ~ rule**] im Allgemeinen **II.** *n* MIL General(in) *m(f)*

General A'merican *n* die amerikanische Standardsprache

general anes'thetic *n* Vollnarkose *f*

General As'sembly *n* [UNO-]Vollversammlung *f*

general de'livery *n* postlagernd

generality [ˌdʒen·ə·'ræl·ə·ti] *n* (*general statement*) **to talk in generalities** (*generalize*) verallgemeinern; **to talk about/of generalities** sich über Allgemeines unterhalten

generalization [ˌdʒen·ər·ə·lɪ·'zeɪ·ʃən] *n* Verallgemeinerung *f*

generalize ['dʒen·ər·ə·laɪz] *vt, vi* **to ~** [**about sth**] [etw] verallgemeinern

generally ['dʒen·ər·ə·li] *adv* **1.** (*usually*) normalerweise **2.** (*mostly*) im Großen und Ganzen **3.** (*widely*) **~ speaking** im Allgemeinen

general prac'titioner *n* praktischer Arzt/ praktische Ärztin

general 'public *n* **the ~** die Öffentlichkeit

general-'purpose *adj attr* Allgemein-, Universal-

general 'store *n* Gemischtwarenladen *m*

general 'strike *n* Generalstreik *m*

generate ['dʒen·ə·reɪt] *vt* (*controversy*) hervorrufen; (*electricity*) erzeugen

generation [ˌdʒen·ə·'reɪ·ʃən] *n* **1.** (*set*) Generation *f* **2.** (*production*) Erzeugung *f*

generator ['dʒen·ə·reɪ·tər] *n* Generator *m*

generic [dʒɪ·'ner·ɪk] *adj* **1.** (*general*) generisch; **~ term** Oberbegriff *m;* BIOL Gattungsbegriff *m* **2.** (*not name-brand: product*) markenlos

generosity [ˌdʒen·ə·'ras·ə·ti] *n* Großzügigkeit *f*

generous ['dʒen·ər·əs] *adj* (*person, tip*) großzügig; (*portion*) groß

genesis <*pl* -ses> ['dʒen·ə·sɪs] *n usu sing* REL **G~** das erste Buch Mose

gene 'therapy *n usu sing* Gentherapie *f*

genetic [dʒɪ·'net·ɪk] *adj* genetisch; **~ disease** Erbkrankheit *f*

genetically 'modified *adj* genmanipuliert

genetics [dʒɪ·'net·ɪks] *n* Genetik *f*

genial ['dʒi·ni·əl] *adj* freundlich

genie <*pl* -nii> ['dʒi·ni] *n* Geist *m*

genitalia [dʒen·ɪ·'teɪ·li·ə] *npl form*, **genitals** ['dʒen·ə·təlz] *npl* Geschlechtsorgane *pl*

genitive ['dʒen·ɪ·tɪv] *n* Genitiv *m*

genius <*pl* -es> ['dʒin·jəs] *n* **1.** (*person*) Genie *nt* **2.** (*intelligence, talent*)

Genialität f

genocide ['dʒen·ə·saɪd] n Völkermord m

gent [dʒent] n hum fam short for **gentleman** Gentleman m

gentian ['dʒen·tiən] n Enzian m

gentile ['dʒen·taɪl] n Nichtjude m, Nichtjüdin f

gentle ['dʒen·təl] adj sanft; (slope) leicht; ~ **exercise** leichte sportliche Betätigung

gentleman ['dʒen·təl·mən] n Gentleman m; **a perfect** ~ ein wahrer Gentleman

gentleness ['dʒen·təl·nɪs] n Sanftheit f

genuine ['dʒen·ju·ɪn] adj 1. (not fake) echt 2. (sincere) ehrlich

genus <pl -nera> ['dʒi·nəs] n BIOL Gattung f

geography [dʒi·'ɑg·rə·fi] n Erdkunde f

geologist [dʒi·'al·ə·dʒɪst] n Geologe, -in m, f

geology [dʒi·'al·ə·dʒi] n Geologie f

geometric(al) [,dʒi·ə·'met·rɪk(əl)] adj geometrisch

geometry [dʒi·'am·ə·tri] n Geometrie f

geophysics [,dʒi·oʊ·'fɪz·ɪks] n Geophysik f

Georgia ['dʒɔr·dʒə] n Georgia nt

geranium [dʒi·'reɪ·ni·əm] n Geranie f

geriatric [,dʒer·i·'æt·rɪk] adj geriatrisch

geriatrics [,dʒer·i·'æt·rɪks] n + sing vb Altersheilkunde f

germ [dʒɜrm] n MED, BIOL Keim m

German ['dʒɜr·mən] I. n 1. (person) Deutsche(r) f(m) 2. (language) Deutsch nt II. adj deutsch

German 'measles n + sing vb Röteln pl

German 'shepherd n (dog) Schäferhund m

Germany ['dʒɜr·mə·ni] n Deutschland nt

'germ-free adj keimfrei

germicide ['dʒɜr·mə·saɪd] n keimtötendes Mittel

germinate ['dʒɜr·mə·neɪt] vi keimen

germination [,dʒɜr·mə·'neɪ·ʃən] n Keimen nt

germ 'warfare n Bakterienkrieg m

gerrymander ['dʒer·ə·mæn·dər] vi POL die Wahlbezirksgrenzen manipulieren

gesticulate [dʒe·'stɪk·jə·leɪt] vi form gestikulieren

gesture ['dʒes·tʃər] I. n Geste f II. vt, vi deuten

get <got, got or gotten> [get] I. vt 1. (obtain) erhalten; **to ~ time off** frei bekommen; **where did you ~ your cell phone?** woher hast du dein Handy? 2. (receive) bekommen 3. (experience) erleben; **to ~ a surprise** überrascht sein 4. (deliver) **to ~ sth to sb** jdm etw bringen 5. (go and obtain) **to ~ [sb] sth** [or sth for sb] jdm etw besorgen 6. TRANSP (travel with: plane, taxi) nehmen; (catch) erwischen 7. + pp (cause to be) **to ~ sth confused** etw verwechseln 8. (induce) **to ~ sb/sth to do sth** jdn/etw dazu bringen, etw zu tun 9. (hear, understand) verstehen; **to ~ the message** [es] kapieren 10. (prepare: meal) zubereiten II. vi 1. (become) werden; **I got cold** mir wurde kalt; ~ **well soon!** gute Besserung!; **to ~ used to sth** sich an etw akk gewöhnen; **to ~ married** heiraten 2. (reach) kommen 3. (must) **to have got to do sth** etw machen müssen

get across vt verständlich machen

get along vi 1. (be friends) sich verstehen 2. (continue) **to ~ along with sth** (job, project) weitermachen

get around I. vi 1. **to ~ around to [doing] sth** es schaffen, etw zu tun 2. (news) sich verbreiten II. vt 1. (evade) umgehen 2. (deal with) angehen

get at vi 1. (reach) rankommen 2. fam (suggest) **to ~ at sth** auf etw akk hinauswollen 3. (discover) **to ~ at sth** etw aufdecken

get away vi 1. (leave) wegkommen 2. (escape) **to ~ away [from sb/sth]** jdm/etw entkommen 3. (avoid punishment) **to ~ away with sth** mit etw dat ungestraft davonkommen

get back I. vt (actively) zurückholen; (strength) zurückgewinnen; (passively) zurückbekommen II. vi 1. (return) zurückkommen 2. **to ~ back to [doing] sth** zu etw dat wieder zurückgehen; **to ~ back to sleep** wieder einschlafen

get behind vi 1. (support) unterstützen 2. (be slow) in Rückstand geraten

G

◆**get by** *vi* **to ~ by** [on/with sth] mit etw *dat* auskommen

◆**get down** I. *vt* (*remove*) runternehmen (**from/off** von +*dat*) II. *vi* 1. (*descend*) herunterkommen (**from/off** von +*dat*) 2. (*bend down*) sich runterbeugen 3. (*start*) **to ~ down to** [doing] **sth** sich an etw *akk* machen

◆**get in** I. *vt* 1. (*say: word*) einwerfen 2. (*bring inside*) hereinholen II. *vi* 1. (*arrive*) ankommen 2. (*return*) zurückkehren 3. (*become elected*) an die Macht kommen

◆**get into** I. *vi* 1. (*enter*) [ein]steigen in +*akk* 2. (*have interest for*) sich interessieren für II. *vt* (*argument*) verwickelt werden in +*akk*

◆**get off** I. *vi* 1. (*exit: bus, train*) aussteigen 2. (*dismount*) absteigen 3. (*evade punishment*) davonkommen II. *vt* 1. (*remove*) nehmen von; **to ~ sb off sth** (*bus, train, plane*) herausbringen aus; (*boat, roof*) herunterholen von 2. LAW freibekommen 3. (*send to sleep*) [los]schicken; **to ~ sb off to sleep** jdn in den Schlaf wiegen

◆**get on** I. *vt* (*put on*) anziehen; (*lid*) drauftun II. *vi* 1. (*be friends*) sich verstehen 2. (*continue*) weitermachen 3. (*age*) alt werden; **to be ~ting on** [in years] an Jahren zunehmen

◆**get out** I. *vi* (*secret*) herauskommen; (*news*) durchsickern II. *vt* 1. (*bring out*) rausbringen (**of** aus +*dat*) 2. (*remove*) herausbekommen

◆**get over** I. *vi* 1. **to ~ over sb/sth** über jdn/etw hinwegkommen; (*illness*) sich erholen von 2. **to ~ sth over** [with] etw hinter sich *akk* bringen II. *vt* (*idea*) rüberbringen

◆**get through** I. *vi* 1. (*make oneself understood*) **to ~ through to sb that/how ...** jdm klarmachen, dass/wie ... 2. (*contact*) **to ~ through to sb** (*on the phone*) zu jdm durchkommen II. *vt* 1. (*use up*) aufbrauchen 2. (*finish: work*) herausbekommen

◆**get together** *vi* sich treffen

◆**get up** I. *vt* 1. (*climb*) hinaufsteigen 2. *fam* (*wake*) wecken II. *vi* 1. (*get out of bed*) aufstehen 2. (*stand up*) sich erheben

'**getaway** *n fam* Flucht *f*

'**get-together** *n fam* Treffen *nt*

'**getup** *n fam* (*outfit*) Kluft *f*

geyser ['gaɪ·zər] *n* Geysir *m*

gherkin ['gɜr·kɪn] *n* Essiggurke *f*

ghetto <*pl* -s> ['get·oʊ] *n* G[h]etto *nt*

ghost [goʊst] *n* Geist *m*

ghostly ['goʊst·li] *adj* geisterhaft

'**ghost town** *n* Geisterstadt *f*

'**ghostwriter** *n* Ghostwriter *m*

GI *n fam* (*soldier*) GI *m*

giant ['dʒaɪ·ənt] I. *n* Riese *m a. fig* II. *adj* riesig

gibber ['dʒɪb·ər] *vi* stammeln

gibe [dʒaɪb] I. *n* Stichelei *f* II. *vi* **to ~ at sb/sth** über jdn/etw spötteln

giddy ['gɪd·i] *adj* schwind(e)lig

gift [gɪft] *n* 1. (*present*) Geschenk *nt a. fig* 2. (*talent*) Talent *nt;* **to have a ~ for languages** sprachbegabt sein

'**gift certificate** *n* Geschenkgutschein *m*

gifted ['gɪf·tɪd] *adj* begabt

'**gift shop** *n* Geschenkartikelladen *m*

gig [gɪg] *n* Gig *m*

gigabyte ['gɪg·ə·baɪt] *n* COMPUT Gigabyte *nt*

gigantic [dʒaɪ·'gæn·tɪk] *adj* gigantisch

giggle ['gɪg·əl] *vi* kichern (**at** über +*akk*)

gilt [gɪlt] *adj* vergoldet

gimmick ['gɪm·ɪk] *n esp pej* Trick *m;* **advertising ~** Werbetrick *m*

gin [dʒɪn] *n* (*drink*) Gin *m*

ginger ['dʒɪn·dʒər] I. *n* Ingwer *m* II. *adj* gelblich braun

'**gingerbread** *n* Lebkuchen *m*

gingerly ['dʒɪn·dʒər·li] *adv* behutsam

Gipsy *n see* **Gypsy**

giraffe <*pl* -s> [dʒə·'ræf] *n* Giraffe *f*

girder ['gɜr·dər] *n* Träger *m*

girdle ['gɜr·dəl] *n* (*corset*) Korsett *nt*

girl [gɜrl] *n* Mädchen *nt*

'**girlfriend** *n* Freundin *f*

'**Girl Scout** *n* Pfadfinderin *f*

girth [gɜrθ] *n* Umfang *m*

gist [dʒɪst] *n* **to get the ~ of sth** den Sinn von etw *dat* verstehen

give [gɪv] I. *vt* <gave, given> 1. **to ~ sb sth** jdm etw geben; (*as present*) jdm etw schenken; (*donate*) jdm etw spenden; **to ~ sb a cold** jdn mit seiner Erkältung an-

stecken; **to ~ sb his/her due** jdm Ehre erweisen; **to ~ a speech** eine Rede halten; **to ~ sb/sth a bad name** jdn/etw in Verruf bringen; **to ~ sb the news of** [*or* **about**] **sth** jdm etw mitteilen; **don't ~ me that!** *fig* komm mir doch nicht damit!; **~ her my best wishes** grüß' sie schön von mir! **2.** (*emit*) **to ~ a cry** aufschreien **3.** (*produce: result, number*) ergeben; (*warmth*) spenden **II.** *vi* <gave, given> **1.** (*donate*) spenden (**to** für +*akk*); **to ~ and take** [gegenseitige] Kompromisse machen **2.** (*bend, yield*) nachgeben; (*rope*) reißen ▶ **to ~ as good as one gets** Gleiches mit Gleichem vergelten **III.** *n* Nachgiebigkeit *f*; (*elasticity*) Elastizität *f*

give away *vt* **1.** (*offer for free*) verschenken **2.** (*betray: secret*) verraten; **to ~ oneself away** sich verraten

give back *vt* zurückgeben (**to** +*dat*)

give in *vi* **1.** (*to pressure*) nachgeben (**to** +*dat*); **to ~ in to temptation** der Versuchung erliegen **2.** (*surrender*) aufgeben

give off *vt* abgeben; (*smell, smoke*) ausströmen

give out I. *vi* **1.** (*run out*) ausgehen; (*energy*) zu Ende gehen **2.** (*stop working*) versagen **II.** *vt* **1.** (*distribute*) verteilen (**to** an +*akk*); (*books*) austeilen **2.** (*emit*) von sich *dat* geben

give over *vt* übergeben

give up I. *vi* aufgeben **II.** *vt* **1.** (*quit*) aufgeben; (*habit*) ablegen; **to ~ up doing sth** mit etw *dat* aufhören **2.** (*surrender*) überlassen; (*territory*) abtreten; **to ~ oneself up** [**to the police**] sich *akk* [der Polizei] stellen

give-and-take *n* Geben und Nehmen *nt*

giveaway I. *n* Werbegeschenk *nt* **II.** *adj* **~ price** Schleuderpreis *m*

given ['gɪv·ən] **I.** *n* gegebene Tatsache *f*; **to take sth as a ~** etw als gegeben annehmen **II.** *adj* **1.** (*certain*) gegeben **2.** (*specified*) festgelegt **III.** *prep* **~ sth** angesichts einer S. *gen* **IV.** *pp* of **give**

given name *n* Vorname *m*

giver ['gɪv·ər] *n* Spender(in) *m(f)*

glacier ['gleɪ·ʃər] *n* Gletscher *m*

glad <-dd-> [glæd] *adj* froh; **to be ~**

about sth sich über etw *akk* freuen

gladiator ['glæd·i·eɪ·t̬ər] *n* Gladiator *m*

gladly ['glæd·li] *adv* gerne

gladness ['glæd·nɪs] *n* Freude *f*

glad rags *npl hum* Festkleidung *f*

glamor ['glæm·ər] *n see* **glamour**

glamorize ['glæm·ə·raɪz] *vt* verherrlichen

glamorous ['glæm·ə·rəs] *adj* glamourös

glamour ['glæm·ər] *n* Glanz *m*

glance [glæns] **I.** *n* Blick *m*; **at first ~** auf den ersten Blick **II.** *vi* **to ~ at sth** auf etw *akk* schauen

glance off *vi* abprallen

gland [glænd] *n* Drüse *f*

glare [gler] **I.** *n* **1.** (*stare*) wütender Blick **2.** (*light*) grelles Licht **II.** *vi* (*stare*) **to ~** [**at sb**] [jdn an]starren

glaring ['gler·ɪŋ] *adj* **1.** (*staring*) stechend **2.** (*blinding*) blendend; (*light*) grell **3.** (*obvious: mistake*) eklatant

glass [glæs] *n* **1.** Glas *nt* **2.** *pl* (*spectacles*) [**a pair of**] **~es** [eine] Brille *f*

glassful *n* Glas *nt* voll

glassware *n* Glaswaren *pl*

glassy ['glæs·i] *adj* (*eyes*) glasig

glaze [gleɪz] **I.** *n* (*on food, pottery*) Glasur *f* **II.** *vt* **1.** (*food, pottery*) glasieren **2.** (*fit with glass*) verglasen

gleam [glim] **I.** *n* Schimmer *m* **II.** *vi* schimmern

gleaming ['glim·ɪŋ] *adj* glänzend

glee [gli] *n* Entzücken *nt*; (*gloating joy*) Schadenfreude *f*

glen [glen] *n* Schlucht *f*

glib <-bb-> [glɪb] *adj* (*person*) zungenfertig; (*answer*) unbedacht

glide [glaɪd] *vi* **1.** (*move smoothly*) hingleiten **2.** (*fly*) gleiten

glider ['glaɪ·dər] *n* Segelflugzeug *nt*

gliding ['glaɪ·dɪŋ] *n* Segelfliegen *nt*

glimmer ['glɪm·ər] *vi* schimmern

glimpse [glɪmps] **I.** *vt* flüchtig sehen **II.** *n* [kurzer/flüchtiger] Blick

glint [glɪnt] *vi* glitzern

glisten ['glɪs·ən] *vi* glitzern

glitch [glɪtʃ] *n fam* (*fault*) Fehler *m*; **computer ~** Computerstörung *f*

glitter ['glɪt̬·ər] *vi* glitzern; (*eyes*) funkeln ▶ **all that ~s is not gold** *prov* es ist nicht alles Gold, was glänzt

glittering ['glɪt·ər·ɪŋ] adj 1. (sparkling) glitzernd 2. (impressive: career) glanzvoll

glitz [glɪts] n Glanz m

glitzy ['glɪt·si] adj glanzvoll

gloat [gloʊt] vi sich hämisch freuen

global ['gloʊ·bəl] adj 1. (worldwide) global 2. (complete) umfassend

globalization [ˌgloʊ·bə·lɪ·ˈzeɪ·ʃən] n Globalisierung f

global 'warming n Erwärmung f der Erdatmosphäre

globe [gloʊb] n Globus m

'**globetrotter** n Globetrotter(in) m(f)

gloom [glum] n 1. (depression) Hoffnungslosigkeit f 2. (darkness) Düsterheit f; **to emerge from the ~** aus dem Dunkel auftauchen

gloomy ['glu·mi] adj 1. (dismal) trostlos 2. (dark) düster

glorify <-ie-> ['glɔr·ə·faɪ] vt verherrlichen

glorious ['glɔr·i·əs] adj 1. (victory) glorreich 2. (weather) herrlich

glory ['glɔr·i] n 1. (honor) Ruhm m 2. (splendor) Herrlichkeit f, Pracht f

gloss [glas] n 1. (shine) Glanz m; **in ~ or matte** glänzend oder matt 2. see **gloss paint**

◆**gloss over** vt schönfärben

glossary ['glas·ə·ri] n Glossar nt

'**gloss paint** n Glanzlack m

glossy ['glas·i] I. adj glänzend; **~ magazine** Hochglanzmagazin nt II. n (photo) [Hoch]glanzabzug m

glove [glʌv] n usu pl Handschuh m; **to fit like a ~** wie angegossen passen

'**glove box**, '**glove compartment** n AUTO Handschuhfach nt

glow [gloʊ] n Leuchten nt; (of a lamp) Scheinen nt; (of a cigarette) Glühen nt; **a healthy ~** eine gesunde Farbe II. vi 1. (shed light) leuchten; (fire, light) scheinen 2. (be red and hot) glühen 3. fig (look radiant) strahlen; **to ~ with health** vor Gesundheit strotzen

glower ['glaʊ·ər] vi verärgert aussehen; **to ~ at sb** jdn zornig anstarren

glowing ['gloʊ·ɪŋ] adj 1. (candle) leuchtend; (cigarette) glühend 2. (review) überschwänglich

'**glowworm** n Glühwürmchen nt

glucose ['glu·koʊs] n Traubenzucker m

glue [glu] I. n Klebstoff m II. vt 1. kleben; **to ~ sth together** etw zusammenkleben 2. fig **to be ~d to sth** an etw dat kleben; **to be ~d to the spot** wie angewurzelt dastehen

'**glue sniffing** n Schnüffeln nt

'**glue stick** n Klebestift m

glum <-mm-> [glʌm] adj niedergeschlagen

glut [glʌt] n Überangebot nt

gluten ['glu·tən] n Gluten nt

glutton ['glʌt·ən] n pej Vielfraß m

gnarled [narld] adj (branch) knorrig; (finger) knotig

gnash [næʃ] vt **to ~ one's teeth** mit den Zähnen knirschen

gnat [næt] n [Stech]mücke f

gnaw [nɔ] vi nagen a. fig (on/at/away at) an +dat)

gnawing ['nɔ·ɪŋ] adj nagend

gnome [noʊm] n Gnom m; [garden] ~ Gartenzwerg m

GNP [ˌdʒi·ɛn·ˈpi] n abbr of **Gross National Product** BSP nt

go [goʊ] I. vi <goes, went, gone> 1. (proceed) gehen; (vehicle, train) fahren; (plane) fliegen; **we have a long way to ~** wir haben noch einen weiten Weg vor uns; **to ~ toward[s] sb/sth** auf jdn/etw zugehen; **to ~ home** nach Hause gehen; **to ~ to the hospital/a party/prison/the bathroom** ins Krankenhaus/auf eine Party/ins Gefängnis/auf die Toilette gehen 2. (travel) reisen; **to ~ on vacation** in Urlaub gehen; **to ~ to Italy** nach Italien fahren; **to ~ on a trip** verreisen, eine Reise machen; **to ~ abroad** ins Ausland gehen 3. (disappear) verschwinden; **where did my keys go?** wo sind meine Schlüssel hin?; **my toothache's gone!** meine Zahnschmerzen sind weg!; **half of my salary ~es on rent** die Hälfte meines Gehaltes geht für die Miete drauf; **there ~es another one!** und wieder eine/einer weniger! 4. (leave) gehen; **let's ~!** los jetzt! 5. (do) **to ~ swimming etc.** schwimmen etc. gehen; **to ~ looking for sb/sth** jdn/etw suchen gehen 6. (attend)

to ~ **to church** in die Kirche gehen; **to ~ to school** in die Schule gehen **7.** + *adj* (*become*) werden; **to ~ bankrupt** bankrottgehen; **to ~ haywire** (*out of control*) außer Kontrolle geraten; (*malfunction*) verrücktspielen; **to ~ public** an die Öffentlichkeit treten; STOCKEX an die Börse gehen; **to ~ to sleep** einschlafen **8.** + *adj* (*be*) sein; **to ~ hungry** hungern; **to ~ unnoticed** unbemerkt bleiben **9.** (*turn out*) gehen, und, wie läuft's?; **to ~ according to plan** nach Plan laufen; **to ~ wrong** schieflaufen **10.** (*pass*) vergehen; **only two days to ~ ...** nur noch zwei Tage ... **11.** (*fail*) kaputtgehen; (*hearing, memory*) nachlassen; (*rope*) reißen **12.** (*die*) sterben **13.** (*belong*) hingehören; **the silverware ~es in this drawer** das Besteck gehört in diese Schublade **14.** (*lead: path, road*) führen **15.** (*extend*) gehen; **the meadow ~es all the way down to the stream** die Weide erstreckt sich bis hinunter zum Bach **16.** (*function: business*) laufen; **to get/keep sth ~ing** etw in Gang bringen/halten; **to keep a conversation ~ing** eine Unterhaltung am Laufen halten **17.** (*have recourse*) gehen; **to ~ to war** in den Krieg ziehen **18.** (*match, be compatible*) **to ~ together** [*or* with sth] zu etw passen; **these two colors don't ~ together** [at all] diese beiden Farben beißen sich ▶ **there** you ~ bitte schön!; **that ~es without saying** das versteht sich von selbst **II.** *aux vb future tense* to be ~ing to do sth etw tun werden; **we are ~ing to have a party tomorrow** wir geben morgen eine Party **III.** *vt* <goes, went, gone> **1.** (*travel: route*) nehmen **2.** *fam* (*say*) **she ~es to me:** I **never want to see you again!** sie sagt zu mir: ich will dich nie wiedersehen! **IV.** *n* <*pl* -es> **1.** (*turn*) **can I have a ~?** darf ich mal? **2.** (*attempt*) Versuch *m*; **in one ~** auf einen Schlag **3.** (*energy*) Antrieb *m* ▶ **from the word** ~ von Anfang an; **to make a ~ of sth** mit etw *dat* Erfolg haben

go about *vt* to ~ **about one's business** seinen Geschäften nachgehen

go after *vi* **1.** (*in succession*) to ~ **after sb/sth** nach jdm/etw gehen **2.** (*chase*) to ~ **after sb** jdn verfolgen

go against *vi* **1.** (*be negative for*) to ~ **against sb** zu jds Ungunsten *pl* ausgehen **2.** (*contradict*) **that ~es against everything I believe in** das geht gegen all das, woran ich glaube

go ahead *vi* **1.** (*go before*) vorgehen; (*in vehicle*) vorausfahren **2.** (*proceed*) vorangehen; (*event*) stattfinden; **to ~ ahead with sth** etw durchführen

go along *vi* **1.** (*on foot*) entlanggehen; (*in vehicle*) entlangfahren **2.** (*accompany*) mitgehen [*or* mitkommen] **3.** (*agree*) **to ~ along with sth/sb** etw/jdm zustimmen; (*join in*) sich etw/jdm anschließen

go around *vi* **1.** (*travel around*) **they went around Europe for two months** sie reisten zwei Monate lang durch Europa **2.** (*visit*) **to ~ around and see sb** [*or* to sb's house] bei jdm vorbeischauen **3.** (*be in circulation: rumor*) [he]rumgehen **4.** (*move in a curve*) herumgehen um +*akk;* **to ~ around the world** eine Weltreise machen ▶ **what ~es around, comes around** *saying* alles rächt sich früher oder später

go at *vi* **1.** (*attack*) **to ~ at sb** [with sth] auf jdn [mit etw *dat*] losgehen **2.** (*work hard*) **to ~ at sth** sich an etw *akk* machen; **to ~ at it** loslegen

go away *vi* **1.** (*travel*) weggehen; (*for vacation*) wegfahren **2.** (*leave*) [weg]gehen **3.** (*disappear*) verschwinden

go back *vi* **1.** (*return*) zurückgehen; (*school*) wieder anfangen; **to ~ back to sb** zu jdm zurückkehren; **to ~ back to the beginning** noch mal von vorne anfangen; **to ~ back to normal** sich wieder normalisieren **2.** (*not fulfill*) **to ~ back on one's promise** sein Versprechen nicht halten

go beyond *vi* **to ~ beyond sth 1.** (*proceed past*) an etw *dat* vorübergehen **2.** (*exceed*) über etw *akk* hinausgehen

go by *vi* **1.** (*move past*) vorbeigehen; (*vehicle*) vorbeifahren **2.** (*of time*) vergehen **3.** (*be guided by*) **to ~ by sth** nach etw *dat* gehen; **to ~ by the book**

sich an die Vorschriften halten

go down vi 1. (*move downward*) hinuntergehen; (*sun*) untergehen; (*ship a.*) sinken; (*plane*) abstürzen; **to ~ down on all fours** sich auf alle viere begeben 2. (*decrease: attendance, wind*) nachlassen; (*water level*) zurückgehen; (*prices*) sinken 3. (*break down: computer*) ausfallen 4. (*be defeated*) verlieren (**to** gegen +*akk*); (*sport etc.*) unterliegen 5. (*on foot*) entlanggehen; (*in vehicle*) entlangfahren; **she was ~ing down the road on her bike** sie fuhr auf ihrem Fahrrad die Straße entlang; **to ~ down a list** eine Liste [von oben nach unten] durchgehen 6. (*extend*) hinunterreichen

go for vi 1. (*fetch*) holen; **to ~ for a newspaper** eine Zeitung holen gehen 2. (*try to achieve*) **~ for it!** nichts wie ran! 3. (*attack*) **to ~ for the jugular** *fig* an die Gurgel springen *fam* 4. *fam* (*like*) **to ~ for sth/sb** auf etw/jdn stehen

go in vi 1. (*enter*) hineingehen 2. (*fit*) hineinpassen

go into vi 1. gehen in +*akk*; **to ~ into action** in Aktion treten; **to ~ into reverse** in den Rückwärtsgang schalten 2. (*examine*) **to ~ into sth** etw erörtern; **to ~ into detail** ins Detail gehen 3. (*join*) **to ~ into the Army** zur Armee gehen; **to ~ into the hospital** ins Krankenhaus gehen

go off vi 1. (*stop working: lights*) ausgehen; (*electricity*) ausfallen 2. (*ring: alarm clock*) klingeln 3. (*detonate: bomb*) hochgehen; (*gun*) losgehen 4. (*diverge*) abgehen; **to ~ off the subject** vom Thema abschweifen

go on vi 1. (*go further*) weitergehen; (*vehicle*) weiterfahren; **to ~ on ahead** vorausgehen; (*vehicle*) vorausfahren 2. (*extend*) sich erstrecken; (*time*) voranschreiten 3. (*continue*) weitermachen; (*fighting*) anhalten; **to ~ on with sth** mit etw *dat* fortfahren; **I can't ~ on** ich kann nicht mehr 4. (*continue speaking*) weiterreden; **sorry, please ~ on** Entschuldigung, bitte fahren Sie fort; **he went on to say that ...** dann sagte er, dass ... 5. (*happen*) passieren;

what's ~ing on here? was geht denn hier vor? 6. (*move on, proceed*) **he went on to become a teacher** später wurde er Lehrer 7. (*lights*) angehen 8. (*as encouragement*) **~ on!** los, mach schon!; **~ on, tell me!** jetzt sag' schon! 9. (*start, embark on*) anfangen; **to ~ on a diet** auf Diät gehen; **to ~ on welfare** stempeln gehen 10. (*belong on*) gehören auf +*akk*

go out vi 1. (*leave home*) [hinaus]gehen; **to ~ out to work** arbeiten gehen; **to ~ out jogging** joggen gehen 2. (*enjoy social life*) ausgehen; **to ~ out to eat** essen gehen 3. (*date*) **to ~ out with sb** mit jdm gehen 4. (*fire*) ausgehen; (*light a.*) ausfallen 5. (*tide*) zurückgehen 6. (*become unfashionable*) aus der Mode kommen ▶ **to ~ all out** sich ins Zeug legen

go over vi 1. (*cross*) hinübergehen; (*in vehicle*) hinüberfahren; (*river, street*) überqueren 2. *fig* (*change*) **to ~ over to sth** zu etw *dat* übergehen; POL zu etw *dat* überwechseln 3. (*examine*) durchgehen; (*apartment*) durchsehen 4. (*exceed*) überschreiten; **to ~ over a time limit** überziehen 5. (*be received*) **to** [**not**] **~ over well** [**with sb**] [nicht] gut ankommen [bei jdm]

go through vi 1. (*pass in and out of*) durchgehen; (*vehicle*) durchfahren 2. (*experience*) durchmachen 3. (*use up*) aufbrauchen; (*plan*) durchgehen; (*divorce*) durchkommen; (*business deal*) [erfolgreich] abgeschlossen werden 5. (*carry out*) **to ~ through with sth** durchziehen; **he has to ~ through with it now** jetzt gibt es kein Zurück mehr für ihn

go together vi zusammenpassen

go under vi 1. (*sink*) untergehen 2. (*person*) scheitern; (*business*) eingehen 3. (*move below*) **to ~ under sth** unter etw *akk* druntergehen

go up vi 1. (*move higher*) hinaufgehen; (*curtain*) hochgehen; (*balloon*) aufsteigen 2. (*increase*) steigen; **everything is ~ing up!** alles wird teurer! 3. (*approach*) **to ~ up to sb/sth** auf jdn/etw zugehen 4. (*move as far as*) **to ~ up to**

sth [bis] zu etw *dat* hingehen 5. (*ascend: mountain, street*) ansteigen

go with *vt* 1. (*accompany*) **to ~ with sb** mit jdm mitgehen 2. (*date*) **to ~ with sb** mit jdm gehen 3. (*harmonize*) passen zu

go without *vi* **to ~ without sth** ohne etw auskommen

goad [goʊd] *vt* (*provoke*) **to ~ sb into [doing] sth** jdn dazu anstacheln, etw zu tun

go-ahead ['goʊ·ə·hed] *n* Erlaubnis *f*; **to give the ~** grünes Licht geben

goal [goʊl] *n* 1. (*aim*) Ziel *nt* 2. SPORT Tor *nt*

goalie ['goʊ·li] *n fam*, **goalkeeper** ['goʊl·ki·pər] *n* Tormann, -frau *m, f*

goal line *n* Torlinie *f*

goalpost *n* Torpfosten *m*

goat [goʊt] *n* Ziege *f*

goatee [goʊ·'ti] *n* Spitzbart *m*

gobble ['gab·əl] *vt fam* [hinunter]schlingen

gobbledegook ['gab·əl·di·guk], **gobbledygook** *n pej fam* Kauderwelsch *nt*

go-between ['goʊ·bə·twin] *n* Vermittler(in) *m(f)*

go-cart *n* Gokart *m*

god [gad] *n* Gott *m*

God [gad] *n* Gott *m*; **to believe in ~** an Gott glauben; **my ~!** mein Gott!; **thank ~!** Gott sei Dank!

god-'awful *adj fam* beschissen

goddamn *vulg* I. *adj* (*emphasizing annoyance*) gottverdammt II. *interj* verdammt

goddaughter *n* Patentochter *f*

goddess <*pl* -es> ['gad·ɪs] *n* Göttin *f*; **screen ~** [Film]diva *f*

godfather *n* (*male godparent*) Patenonkel *m*; (*a. Mafia leader*) Pate *m*

godlike ['gad·laɪk] *adj* göttlich

godmother *n* Patentante *f*, Patin *f*

godsend *n* Gottesgeschenk *nt*

godson *n* Patensohn *m*

goer ['goʊ·ər] *n fam* (*person or thing that goes*) Geher *m*

goes [goʊz] *3rd pers. sing of* **go**

go-getter [goʊ·'get·ər] *n* Tatmensch *m*

goggle ['gag·əl] I. *vi fam* glotzen; **to ~ at sb/sth** jdn/etw anglotzen II. *n* [a pair

of] ~**s** [eine] [Schutz]brille *f*; **ski ~s** Skibrille *f*; **swimming ~s** Schwimmbrille *f*

going ['goʊ·ɪŋ] I. *n* 1. (*act of leaving*) Gehen *nt* 2. (*departure*) Weggang *m* 3. (*conditions*) **rough ~** ungünstige Bedingungen; **while the ~ is good** solange es gut läuft II. *adj* 1. (*current*) aktuell; **what's the ~ rate for babysitters nowadays?** wie viel zahlt man heutzutage üblicherweise für einen Babysitter? 2. (*in action*) am Laufen; **~ concern** gutgehendes Unternehmen

going-'over <*pl* goings-over> *n* **to give sth a [good] ~** (*search thoroughly*) etw gründlich durchsuchen; (*clean thoroughly*) etw gründlich reinigen

gold [goʊld] *n* Gold *nt* ▶ **[as] good as ~** mustergültig

gold dust *n* Goldstaub *m*

golden ['goʊl·dən] *adj* golden *a. fig*; **~ brown** goldbraun

goldfish *n* Goldfisch *m*

gold leaf *n* Blattgold *nt*

gold medal *n* Goldmedaille *f*

gold mine *n* Goldmine *f*; *fig* Goldgrube *f*

gold plating *n* Vergoldung *f*

goldsmith *n* Goldschmied(in) *m(f)*

golf [galf] *n* Golf *nt*

golf ball *n* Golfball *m*

golf club *n* 1. (*implement*) Golfschläger *m* 2. (*association*) Golfclub *m*

golf course *n* Golfplatz *m*

golfer ['gal·fər] *n* Golfer(in) *m(f)*

gondola ['gan·də·lə] *n* Gondel *f*

gone [gɔn] I. *pp of* **go** II. *adj* (*no longer there*) weg; (*used up*) verbraucht

goner ['gɔ·nər] *n fam* **to be a ~** (*be bound to die*) es nicht mehr lange machen; (*be irreparable*) hoffnungslos kaputt sein

gong [gaŋ] *n* Gong *m*

gonna ['gan·ə] *sl see* **going to**; **what you ~ do about it?** was willst du dagegen machen?

gonorrhea [ˌgan·ə·'ri·ə] *n* Tripper *m*

goo [gu] *n fam* Schmiere *f*

good [gʊd] I. *adj* <*better, best*> 1. gut; (*weather*) schön; (*healthy: appetite*) gesund; **have a ~ day!** schönen Tag noch!; **to have a ~ time** [viel] Spaß haben; **it's**

~ **to see you again** schön, dich wiederzusehen; ~ **dog!** braver Hund!; **to do a ~ job** gute Arbeit leisten; ~ **luck!** viel Glück!; ~ **sense** Geistesgegenwart *f*; **in ~ time** rechtzeitig; **to be ~ at sth** gut in etw *dat* sein; **he's a ~ runner** er ist ein guter Läufer; **he's not very ~ at math** er ist nicht besonders gut in Mathe; **to be ~ for nothing** zu nichts taugen; **sb looks ~ in sth** etw steht jdm; **too ~ to be true** zu schön, um wahr zu sein **2.** (*kind, understanding*) **it was very ~ of you to help us** es war sehr lieb von dir, uns zu helfen **3.** (*thorough*) gut; **to have a ~ laugh** ordentlich lachen; **to have a ~ look at sth** sich *dat* etw genau ansehen **4.** (*substantial*) beträchtlich; **to make ~ money** gutes Geld verdienen; **a ~ deal of ...** jede Menge ... **5.** (*able to provide*) **he is always ~ for a laugh** er ist immer gut für einen Witz ▶ **it's as ~ as it gets** besser wird's nicht mehr **II.** *n* **1.** (*moral force*) Gute *nt* **2.** (*benefit*) Wohl *nt;* **this will do you a world of ~** das wird Ihnen unglaublich guttun; **to do more harm than ~** mehr schaden als nützen; **for one's own ~** zu seinem eigenen Besten **3.** (*ability*) **to be no ~ at sth** wie nicht gut können

goodbye [gʊd]·'baɪ], **good-by** *interj* auf Wiedersehen; **to say ~ to sb/sth** sich von jdm/etw verabschieden; **to kiss sb ~** jdm einen Abschiedskuss geben; **to kiss sth ~** *fig* etw abschreiben

'**good-for-nothing I.** *n pej* Taugenichts *m* **II.** *adj* nichtsnutzig

Good 'Friday *n no art* Karfreitag *m*

good-'humored [ˌgʊd·'hju·mərd] *adj* fröhlich

good-'looking *adj* <more ~, most ~ *or* better-looking, best-looking> gut aussehend

good 'looks *npl* gutes Aussehen

good-'natured *adj* gutmütig

goodness ['gʊd·nɪs] *n* **1.** Güte *f* **2.** (*for emphasis*) **for ~' sake** du liebe Güte

goods [gʊdz] *npl* Waren *pl*, Güter *pl;* **sporting ~** Sportartikel *pl;* **manufactured ~** Fertigprodukte *pl*

'**good-sized** *adj* [recht] groß

'**goodwill** *n* **1.** guter Wille (**towards**

gegenüber +*dat*); **feeling of ~** Atmosphäre *f* des guten Willens **2.** ECON Goodwill *m*

goody ['gʊd·i] *n* **1.** (*desirable object*) tolle Sache *f* **2.** FOOD Leckerbissen *m*

gooey ['gu·i] *adj fam* **1.** (*sticky*) klebrig **2.** *fig, pej* schmalzig

goof [guf] *fam* **I.** *n* (*mistake*) Patzer *m* **II.** *vi* **to ~** [**up**] Mist bauen

◆**goof around** *vt* herumblödeln *fam*

goofy ['gu·fi] *adj fam* doof

goose [gus] *n* <*pl* geese> Gans *f* ▶ **to cook sb's ~** jdm die Suppe versalzen

'**goose bumps** *npl*, **goose flesh** *n*, '**goose pimples** *npl* Gänsehaut *f kein pl*

gopher ['goʊ·fər] *n* Ziesel *m*

gore[gɔr] *n* Blut *nt*

gorge[1] [gɔrdʒ] *n* Schlucht *f*

gorge[2] [gɔrdʒ] *vi* sich vollessen

gorgeous ['gɔr·dʒəs] *adj* **1.** (*very beautiful*) herrlich, großartig **2.** (*very pleasurable*) ausgezeichnet

gorilla [gə·'rɪl·ə] *n* Gorilla *m* a. fig

gory ['gɔr·i] *adj* blutig; (*film*) blutrünstig

gospel ['gas·pəl] *n* **1.** **the G~ according to Saint Mark** [*or* St Mark's Gospel] das Evangelium nach Markus **2.** (*music*) Gospel *nt*

gossamer ['gas·ə·mər] **I.** *n* Spinnfäden *pl* **II.** *adj* hauchdünn

gossip ['gas·əp] **I.** *n usu pej* **1.** (*rumors*) Klatsch *m;* **idle ~** leeres Geschwätz **2.** *pej* (*person*) Tratschbase *f* **II.** *vi* schwatzen

'**gossip column** *n* Klatschspalte *f*

gossipy ['gas·ə·pi] *adj* schwatzhaft

got [gat] *pt, pp of* **get**

gotta ['gat·ə] *fam* = [**have**] **got to** müssen

gotten ['gat·ən] *pp of* **got**

gouge [gaʊdʒ] **I.** *n* (*indentation*) Rille *f* **II.** *vt* **to ~ out** aushöhlen; (*eye*) ausstechen

goulash ['gu·laʃ] *n* Gulasch *nt*

gourd [gɔrd] *n* Kürbisflasche *f*

gourmet [gʊr·'meɪ] *n* Feinschmecker(in) *m(f)*

gout [gaʊt] *n* Gicht *f*

Gov. *n* **1.** *abbr of* **government** **2.** *abbr of* **governor**

govern ['gʌv·ərn] *vt, vi* regieren

governing ['gʌv·ərn·ɪŋ] *adj* regierend; ~ **body** Vorstand *m*

government ['gʌv·ərn·mənt] *n* Regierung *f*, Staat *m*; **local** ~ Kommunalverwaltung *f*; ~ **agency** Behörde *f*; ~ **policy** Regierungspolitik *f*; ~ **spending** Staatsausgaben *pl*; ~ **subsidy** Subvention *f*

governmental [ˌgʌv·ərn·'men·təl] *adj* Regierungs-

governor ['gʌv·ər·nər] *n* POL Gouverneur *m*

gown [gaʊn] *n* MED Kittel *m*

GP [ˌdʒi·'pi] *n* MED *abbr of* **general practitioner**

grab [græb] **I.** *n* (*snatch*) Griff *m* ► **to be up for ~s** zu haben sein **II.** *vt* <-bb-> **1.** (*sich dat*) schnappen; **to ~ hold of sb/sth** jdn/etw festhalten **2.** *fig* (*attention*) erregen; **to ~ a bite** [**to eat**] schnell einen Happen essen **III.** *vi* <-bb-> (*snatch*) grapschen

grace [greɪs] *n* **1.** (*of movement*) Grazie *f* **2.** (*of behavior*) Anstand *m kein pl*; **social ~s** gesellschaftliche Umgangsformen

graceful ['greɪs·fəl] *adj* **1.** (*in movement*) graziös **2.** (*in appearance*) elegant

graceless ['greɪs·lɪs] *adj* taktlos

gracious ['greɪ·ʃəs] **I.** *adj* **1.** (*kind*) liebenswürdig; (*merciful*) gnädig **II.** *interj* [**good** [*or* **goodness**]] ~ [**me**] [du] meine Güte

grade [greɪd] **I.** *n* **1.** (*rank*) Rang *m* **2.** (*of salary*) Gehaltsstufe *f* **3.** SCH (*score*) Note *f*; (*class*) Klasse *f* **4.** (*gradient*) Neigung *f*; [**steep**] ~ (*upwards*) [starke] Steigung; (*downwards*) [starkes] Gefälle **II.** *vt* SCH, UNIV benoten

grader ['greɪ·dər] *n* SCH **the second ~s** die Schüler, innen *m, f* der zweiten Klasse

'grade school *n* Grundschule *f*

gradient ['greɪ·di·ənt] *n* Neigung *f*

grading system Notensystem der USA mit den Buchstaben A, B, C, D, E und F, wobei A für die beste Note steht und F durchgefallen bedeutet

gradual ['grædʒ·u·əl] *adj* allmählich

graduate **I.** *n* ['grædʒ·u·ət] **1.** UNIV Absolvent(in) *m(f)*; ~ **student** Student(in) *m(f)* mit Universitätsabschluss (*Studenten mit einem „Bachelor's Degree", die*

eine weitere Stufe zur Erlangung des „Master's Degrees" absolvieren) **2.** SCH Schulabgänger(in) *m(f)* **II.** *vi* ['grædʒ·u·eɪt] **1.** UNIV einen akademischen Grad erwerben **2.** SCH die Abschlussprüfung bestehen **3.** (*complete training*) die Ausbildung abschließen; UNIV das Studium abschließen

graduated ['grædʒ·u·eɪ·tɪd] *adj* gestaffelt

graduation [ˌgrædʒ·u·'eɪ·ʃən] *n* **1.** SCH, UNIV (*completion of studies*) [Studien]abschluss *m* **2.** (*ceremony*) Abschlussfeier *f*

graffiti [grə·'fi·ti] *n* Graffiti *nt*

graft [græft] *n* **1.** MED Transplantat *nt* **2.** (*corruption*) Schiebung *f* **II.** *vt* übertragen (**on**[**to**] auf +*akk*)

grain [greɪn] *n* **1.** (*particle*) Korn *nt*, Körnchen *nt* **2.** (*crop*) Getreide *nt*

gram [græm] *n* Gramm *nt*

grammar ['græm·ər] *n* Grammatik *f*

grammatical [grə·'mæt·ɪ·kəl] *adj* grammati[kali]sch

grand [grænd] **I.** *adj* **1.** (*splendid*) prächtig, großartig; **to make a ~ entrance** einen großen Auftritt haben **2.** (*excellent*) großartig **3.** (*large, far-reaching*) ~ **ambitions** große Pläne; **on a ~ scale** in großem Rahmen **II.** *n* <*pl*-> *fam* (*one thousand dollars*) Mille *f*

grandad ['græn·dæd] *n fam see* **granddad**

'grandchild *n* Enkelkind *nt*

'granddad *n fam* **1.** (*grandfather*) Opa *m*, Opi *m* **2.** *pej* (*old man*) Opa *m*, Alter *m*

'granddaughter *n* Enkeltochter *f*

grandeur ['græn·dʒər] *n* Größe *f*; **delusions of ~** Größenwahn *m*

'grandfather *n* Großvater *m*

grand 'jury *n* Anklagejury *f*

'grandma *n fam* Oma *f*, Omi *f*

'grandmother *n* Großmutter *f*

'grandpa *n fam* Opa *m*, Opi *f*

grand pi'ano *n* [Konzert]flügel *m*

'grandson *n* Enkel[sohn] *m*

'grandstand *n* [Haupt]tribüne *f* **II.** *vi* Effekthascherei betreiben

grand 'sum, **grand 'total** *n* Gesamtsumme *f*

granite ['græn·ɪt] n Granit m

grannie ['græn·i], **granny** ['græn·i] n fam Oma f, Omi f

grant [grænt] I. n 1. UNIV Stipendium nt 2. (subsidy) Subvention f II. vt 1. (allow) to ~ sb sth jdm etw gewähren; (money) jdm etw bewilligen; (visa) jdm etw erteilen 2. (admit) zugeben; ~ed, ... zugegeben, ...

granulated ['græn·jə·leɪ·tɪd] adj ~ sugar Kristallzucker m

granule ['græn·jul] n ~s pl Granulat nt

grape [greɪp] n [Wein]traube f

grapefruit <pl -> ['greɪp·frut] n Grapefruit f

grapevine n Weinstock m ▶ I **heard** [it] on the ~ that ... es ist mir zu Ohren gekommen, dass ...

graph [græf] n Diagramm nt; ~ paper Millimeterpapier nt

graphic ['græf·ɪk] adj 1. (diagrammatic) grafisch 2. (vividly descriptive) anschaulich; in ~ detail haarklein

graphics ['græf·ɪks] npl Grafik f; ~ card Grafikkarte f

graphite ['græf·aɪt] n Graphit m

grasp [græsp] I. n 1. (grip) Griff m 2. fig Reichweite f; to be within sb's ~ zum Greifen nahe sein II. vt 1. (take firm hold) [fest] [er]greifen; to ~ sb by the arm jdn am Arm fassen 2. fig (understand) begreifen

grasping ['græs·pɪŋ] adj fig, pej habgierig

grass <pl -es> [græs] n 1. Gras nt; (lawn) Rasen m 2. sl (marijuana) Gras nt sl

grasshopper n Heuschrecke f

grassland n Grasland nt

grass'roots npl (of a party, organization) Basis f kein pl; ~ opinion Volksmeinung f

grass snake n Grasnatter f

grassy ['græs·i] adj grasbewachsen

grate [greɪt] I. n Kamin m II. vi to ~ on sb['s nerves] jdm auf die Nerven gehen III. vt FOOD reiben; (vegetables) raspeln

grateful ['greɪt·fəl] adj dankbar

grater ['greɪ·t̬ər] n Reibe f

gratifying ['græt̬·ə·faɪ·ɪŋ] adj erfreulich

grating ['greɪ·t̬ɪŋ] n Gitter nt

gratitude ['græt̬·ə·tud] n Dankbarkeit f

gratuitous [grə·'tu·ɪ·t̬əs] adj 1. (free) kostenlos 2. pej (unnecessary) überflüssig

gratuity [grə·'tu·ɪ·t̬i] n (tip) Trinkgeld n

grave [greɪv] I. n Grab nt II. adj ernst; (news) schlimm

gravel ['græv·əl] n Kies m

gravel pit n Kiesgrube f

gravely ['greɪv·li] adv ernst; ~ ill schwer krank

gravestone n Grabstein m

graveyard n Friedhof m

gravitate ['græv·ɪ·teɪt] vi to ~ to[ward] sth/sb von etw/jdm angezogen werden

gravity ['græv·ɪ·t̬i] n 1. PHYS Schwerkraft f 2. (seriousness) Ernst m

gravy ['greɪ·vi] n 1. [Braten]soße f 2. fig sl (easy money) leicht verdientes Geld

gravy boat n Sauciere f

gravy train n fig to get on the ~ sich dat ein Stück vom Kuchen abschneiden

gray [greɪ] adj grau a. fig

gray matter n fam graue Zellen pl

graze¹ [greɪz] vi grasen, weiden

graze² [greɪz] I. n Schürfwunde f II. vt streifen; to ~ one's elbow sich dat den Ellbogen aufschürfen

grease [gris] n Fett nt

greasepaint n THEAT Fettschminke f

greasy ['gri·si] adj (hair, skin) fettig; (fingers, objects a.) schmierig; (food) fett; (slippery) glitschig

great [greɪt] I. adj 1. (very big) groß; to a ~ extent im Großen und Ganzen 2. (famous) groß; (important) bedeutend 3. fam (wonderful) großartig II. adv (extremely) sehr; ~ big riesengroß III. n (person) Größe f; (in titles) Catherine the G~ Katharina die Große

Great Britain n Großbritannien nt

Greater ['greɪt̬·ər] (in cities) ~ Los Angeles Großraum m Los Angeles

great-'grandchild n Urenkel(in) m(f)

Great Lakes npl GEOG the ~ die Großen Seen

greatly ['greɪt̬·li] adv sehr; ~ impressed tief beeindruckt

greatness ['greɪt̬·nɪs] n Bedeutsamkeit f

Great Plains npl Große Ebenen pl (eine

der wichtigsten Getreideregionen der Welt)

Greece [gris] *n* Griechenland *nt*

greed [grid], **greediness** ['gri·dɪ·nɪs] *n* Gier *f*

greedy ['gri·di] *adj* gierig; *(for money, things)* habgierig

Greek [grik] **I.** *n* **1.** *(person)* Grieche, -in *m, f* **2.** *(language)* Griechisch *nt* **II.** *adj* griechisch ▸ it's **all** ~ to me das sind alles böhmische Dörfer für mich

green [grin] **I.** *n* **1.** *(color)* Grün *nt* **2.** FOOD ~s *pl* Blattgemüse *nt kein pl* **II.** *adj* **1.** grün; ~ with envy grün vor Neid **2.** *(environmental)* grün, umweltfreundlich; ~ issues *pl* Umweltschutzfragen

greenback *n fam* Dollar[schein] *m*

green card *n* Aufenthaltserlaubnis *f* mit Arbeitsgenehmigung

greenery ['gri·nə·ri] *n* Grün *nt*

greenhouse *n* Gewächshaus *nt;* ~ effect Treibhauseffekt *m*

greenish ['gri·nɪʃ] *adj* grünlich

green pepper *n* grüne Paprikaschote

greet [grit] *vt (welcome)* [be]grüßen; *(receive)* empfangen; to ~ each other [by shaking hands] sich [mit Handschlag] begrüßen

greeting ['gri·tɪŋ] *n* Begrüßung *f;* ~s *pl* Grüße *pl*

gregarious [grɪ·'ger·i·əs] *adj* gesellig

grenade [grə·'neɪd] *n* Granate *f*

grew [gru] *pt of* **grow**

grey [greɪ] *adj see* **gray**

greyhound *n* Windhund *m*

grid [grɪd] *n* **1.** Gitter *nt* **2.** ELEC Netz *nt*

griddle ['grɪd·əl] *n* Heizplatte *f*

gridiron ['grɪd·aɪ·ərn] *n* SPORT Footballfeld *nt*

gridlock ['grɪd·lɑk] *n* Verkehrskollaps *m*

grief [grif] *n* tiefe Trauer, Kummer *m*

grievance ['gri·vəns] *n* Beschwerde *f*

grieve [griv] *vi* bekümmert sein; to ~ for sb um jdn trauern; to ~ over sth über etw *akk* betrübt sein

grill [grɪl] **I.** *n (over charcoal)* [Grill]rost *m;* *(restaurant)* Grillrestaurant *nt* **II.** *vt* **1.** grillen **2.** *fig fam (interrogate)* ausquetschen

grille [grɪl] *n* Gitter *nt*

grilling ['grɪl·ɪŋ] *n fig fam* strenges Verhör

grim [grɪm] *adj* **1.** *(forbidding)* grimmig **2.** *(very unpleasant: picture)* trostlos; *(landscape)* unwirtlich; *(situation)* schlimm; things were looking ~ die Lage sah langsam düster aus

grimace ['grɪm·əs] *n* Grimasse *f*

grime [graɪm] *n* Schmutz *m*

grimy ['graɪ·mi] *adj* schmutzig

grin [grɪn] **I.** *n* Grinsen *nt kein pl* **II.** *vi* grinsen

grind [graɪnd] **I.** *n fam* the daily ~ der tägliche Trott **II.** *vt* <ground, ground> **1.** *(crush)* mahlen; *(meat)* fein hacken; to ~ sth [in]to a powder etw fein zermahlen **2.** *(sharpen)* schleifen **III.** *vi* <ground, ground> to ~ to a halt *(production)* stocken; *(negotiations)* sich festfahren

grind down *vt* **1.** *(mill)* zerkleinern **2.** *(mentally wear out)* zermürben

grind out *vt (produce continuously)* ununterbrochen produzieren

grinder ['graɪn·dər] *n* **1.** *(mill)* Mühle *f* **2.** *(mincer)* Fleischwolf *m*

grindstone ['graɪnd·stoʊn] *n* Schleifstein *m*

grip [grɪp] **I.** *n* Griff *m kein pl a. fig;* to be in the ~ of sth von etw *dat* betroffen sein; to get to ~s with sth etw in den Griff bekommen; to lose one's ~ on reality den Bezug zur Realität verlieren **II.** *vt* <-pp-> packen **III.** *vi* <-pp-> greifen

gripe [graɪp] *vi fam* nörgeln

gripping ['grɪp·ɪŋ] *adj* packend

grisly ['grɪz·li] *adj* grausig

gristle ['grɪs·əl] *n* Knorpel *m*

grit [grɪt] *n (small stones)* Splitt *m;* *(for icy roads)* Streusand *m*

gritty ['grɪt·i] *adj* **1.** *(like grit)* grob[körnig] **2.** *(full of grit)* sandig

grizzled ['grɪz·əld] *adj* ergraut

grizzly ['grɪz·li] **I.** *adj* gräulich **II.** *n* Grizzlybär *m*

groan [groʊn] **I.** *n* Stöhnen *nt kein pl* **II.** *vi* [auf]stöhnen

groceries ['groʊ·sə·riz] *npl* Lebensmittel *pl*

groggy ['grag·i] *adj* angeschlagen

G

groin [grɔɪn] n ANAT Leiste f

groom [grʊm] I. n 1. (bridegroom) Bräutigam m 2. (for horses) Pferdepfleger(in) m(f) II. vt (horse) striegeln

groove [gruv] n Rille f

groovy ['gru·vi] adj sl klasse fam, cool fam

grope [groʊp] I. vi to ~ for sth nach etw dat tasten II. vt fam to ~ sb jdn befummeln

gross [groʊs] I. adj 1. (disgusting) ekelhaft; (big and ugly) abstoßend 2. FIN Brutto- nt II. vt FIN brutto einnehmen

grossly ['groʊs·li] adv extrem

grotesque [groʊ·'tesk] adj grotesk

grouchy ['graʊ·tʃi] adj griesgrämig

ground¹ [graʊnd] I. n 1. [Erd]boden m, Erde f; below ~ unter der Erde; MIN unter Tage; to get off the ~ fig fam (plan) verwirklicht werden; to get sth off the ~ fig fam etw realisieren 2. (area of land) [ein Stück] Land nt; waste ~ brachliegendes Land; to gain ~ MIL Boden gewinnen; fig an Boden gewinnen 3. ELEC (earth) Erdung f 4. fig (area of discussion) to find common ~ Gemeinsamkeiten entdecken; to be on safe ~ sich auf sicherem Boden bewegen 5. pl ~s (reasons) Grund m; ~s for divorce Scheidungsgrund m ▶ to break new ~ Neuland betreten; to work oneself into the ~ sich kaputtmachen II. vt 1. to be ~ed fig fam Hausarrest haben 2. ELEC erden

ground² [graʊnd] I. vt pt of **grind** II. adj gemahlen

'groundbreaking adj bahnbrechend

'ground control n AVIAT Bodenkontrolle f

'ground crew n AVIAT Bodenpersonal nt kein pl

ground 'floor n Erdgeschoss nt ▶ to get in on the ~ [of sth] von Anfang an [bei etw dat] dabei sein

'ground frost n Bodenfrost m

groundhog ['graʊnd·hag] n Waldmurmeltier nt

'Groundhog Day n Murmeltiertag m

groundless ['graʊnd·lɪs] adj grundlos

'ground rules npl Grundregeln pl

'ground staff n AVIAT Bodenpersonal nt

'groundwater n Grundwasser nt

'groundwork n Vorarbeit f

group [grup] n 1. Gruppe f 2. ECON Konzern m

groupie ['gru·pi] n fam Groupie nt

group 'practice n Gemeinschaftspraxis f

group 'therapy n Gruppentherapie f

grouse [graʊs] vi fam meckern

grove [groʊv] n Wäldchen nt; olive ~ Olivenhain m

grovel <-l-> ['grav·əl] vi (behave obsequiously) to ~ [before sb] [vor jdm] zu Kreuze kriechen

grow <grew, grown> [groʊ] I. vi wachsen; to ~ taller größer werden; (sales) zunehmen; to ~ to like sth langsam beginnen, etw zu mögen II. vt 1. anbauen; (flowers) züchten; to ~ sth from seed etw aus Samen ziehen 2. (hair) wachsen lassen

◆**grow apart** vi to ~ apart from sb sich jdm [allmählich] entfremden

◆**grow into** vi hineinwachsen in +akk

◆**grow out of** vi to ~ out of a habit eine Angewohnheit ablegen

◆**grow up** vi erwachsen werden

grower ['groʊ·ər] n AGR coffee ~ Kaffeepflanzer(in) m(f)

growing ['groʊ·ɪŋ] adj 1. (boy, girl) im Wachstumsalter; ~ pains fig Anfangsschwierigkeiten pl 2. (increasing) zunehmend

growl [graʊl] vi knurren; to ~ at sb jdn anknurren

grown [groʊn] I. adj erwachsen; fully ~ ausgewachsen II. pp of **grow**

grown-up ['groʊn·ʌp] adj fam erwachsen

growth [groʊθ] n Wachstum nt

grub [grʌb] n Larve f

grubby ['grʌb·i] adj fam schmudd[e]lig; (hands) schmutzig

grudge [grʌdʒ] n Groll m kein pl

grudging ['grʌdʒ·ɪŋ] adj widerwillig

grueling ['gru·lɪŋ] adj (time) aufreibend; (journey) strapaziös

gruesome ['gru·səm] adj grausig

gruff [grʌf] adj barsch

grumble ['grʌm·bəl] vi murren

grumpy ['grʌm·pi] adj fam mürrisch brummig

grunt [grʌnt] I. n 1. (sound) Grunzen n

kein pl **2.** MIL *gemeiner Soldat/gemeine Soldatin* **II.** *vi* grunzen

G-string ['dʒiː·strɪŋ] *n* String-Tanga *m*

guarantee [ˌɡer·ən·'tiː] **I.** *n* Garantie *f;* **money-back ~** Rückerstattungsgarantie *f* **II.** *vt* garantieren; **to ~ that ...** gewährleisten, dass ...

guarantor [ˌɡer·ən·'tɔr] *n* Garant(in) *m(f);* LAW Bürge, -in *m, f*

guard [ɡɑrd] **I.** *n* **1.** (*person*) Wache *f;* (*sentry*) Wach[t]posten *m;* **security ~** Sicherheitsbeamte(r) *f(m),* -beamtin *f* **2.** (*group of guards*) Garde *f* **3.** (*protective device*) Schutz *m* **II.** *vt* (*keep watch*) bewachen; **heavily ~ed** scharf bewacht; (*protect*) [be]schützen (**against** vor *+dat*)

'guard dog *n* Wachhund *m*

guarded ['ɡɑr·dɪd] *adj* (*reserved*) zurückhaltend; (*cautious*) vorsichtig

'guardhouse *n* Wache *f*

guardian ['ɡɑr·di·ən] *n* LAW Vormund *m*

guardian 'angel *n* Schutzengel *m a. fig*

'guard rail *n* [Schutz]geländer *nt*

'guardroom *n* Wachstube *f*

'guardsman *n* (*member of National Guard*) Gardesoldat *m*

gubernatorial [ˌɡu·bər·nə·'tɔr·i·əl] *adj* Gouverneurs-

gue(r)rilla [ɡə·'rɪl·ə] *n* Guerillakämpfer(in) *m(f);* **~ warfare** Guerillakrieg *m*

guess [ɡes] **I.** *n <pl -es>* Vermutung *f;* (*estimate*) Schätzung *f;* **I'll give you three ~es** dreimal darfst du raten; **lucky ~** Glückstreffer *m;* **to take a ~ raten** ▶ **it's anyone's ~** weiß der Himmel **II.** *vi* **1.** (*conjecture*) [er]raten; **to keep sb ~ing** jdn auf die Folter spannen **2.** (*suppose*) denken; (*suspect*) annehmen; ▶ **you're right** da wirst wohl recht haben **III.** *vt* raten; **~ what?** stell dir vor!

'guessing game ['ɡes·ɪŋ·ˌɡeɪm] *n* Ratespiel *nt a. fig*

guesstimate ['ɡes·tɪ·mət] *n fam* grobe Schätzung *f*

guesswork ['ɡes·wɜrk] *n* Spekulation *f meist pl*

guest [ɡest] **I.** *n* Gast *m* **II.** *vi* als Gaststar auftreten

guesthouse *n* Gästehaus *nt,* Pension *f*

'guestroom *n* Gästezimmer *nt*

guidance ['ɡaɪ·dəns] *n* **1.** (*advice*) Beratung *f;* (*direction*) [An]leitung *f* **2.** (*steering system*) Steuerung *f*

guide [ɡaɪd] **I.** *n* Führer(in) *m(f);* TOURIST Fremdenführer(in) *m(f);* **tour ~** Reiseführer(in) *m(f)* **II.** *vt* **1.** (*show*) **to ~ sb** jdn führen *a. fig;* (*show the way*) jdm den Weg zeigen **2.** (*steer*) führen

'guidebook *n* Reiseführer *m*

guided ['ɡaɪ·dɪd] *adj* geführt; **~ tour** Führung *f*

guide dog *n* Blindenhund *m*

'guideline *n usu pl* Richtlinie *f*

guiding 'principle *n* Richtschnur *f*

guilt [ɡɪlt] *n* Schuld *f;* **feelings of ~** Schuldgefühle *pl*

guiltless ['ɡɪlt·lɪs] *adj* schuldlos

'guilt-ridden *adj* von Schuldgefühlen geplagt

guilty ['ɡɪl·ti] *adj* schuldig; **~ conscience** schlechtes Gewissen; **to feel ~ about sth** ein schlechtes Gewissen wegen einer S. *gen* haben; **to prove sb ~** jds Schuld *f* beweisen

guinea pig *n* Meerschweinchen *nt; fig* Versuchskaninchen *nt*

guise [ɡaɪz] *n* **1.** (*appearance*) Gestalt *f;* **in the ~ of a monk** als Mönch verkleidet **2.** (*pretense*) Vorwand *m*

guitar [ɡɪ·'tɑr] *n* Gitarre *f*

guitarist [ɡɪ·'tɑr·ɪst] *n* Gitarrist(in) *m(f)*

gulch [ɡʌltʃ] *n* Schlucht *f*

gulf [ɡʌlf] *n* GEOG Golf *m;* **the G~ of Mexico** der Golf von Mexiko; **the G~ states** die Golfstaaten *pl*

gull [ɡʌl] *n* Möwe *f*

gullible ['ɡʌl·ə·bəl] *adj* leichtgläubig

gulp [ɡʌlp] **I.** *n* [großer] Schluck; **to get a ~ of air** Luft holen **II.** *vt* [hinunter] schlucken **III.** *vi* **to ~ for air** nach Luft schnappen

gum¹ [ɡʌm] **I.** *n* **1.** (*sticky substance*) Gummi *nt;* (*glue*) Klebstoff *m* **2.** (*candy*) Kaugummi *m o nt* **II.** *vt <-mm->* kleben

gum² [ɡʌm] *n* ANAT **~[s]** Zahnfleisch *nt kein pl*

gumbo ['ɡʌm·boʊ] *n* Okraschote *f*

gummy ['ɡʌm·i] *adj* (*sticky*) klebrig

gumption ['ɡʌmp·ʃən] *n fam* Grips *m*

gun [gʌn] *n* (Schuss]waffe *f*; (*pistol*) Pistole *f*; (*revolver*) Revolver *m*; (*rifle*) Gewehr *nt*

◆**gun down** *vt* niederschießen

'**gunfight** *n* Schießerei *f*

'**gunfire** *n* Schießerei *f*

'**gun license** *n* Waffenschein *m*

'**gunman** *n* Bewaffnete(r) *m*

'**gunner** [gʌn·ər] *n* Artillerist *m*

'**gunpoint** *n* **at ~** mit vorgehaltener Waffe

'**gunrunner** *n* Waffenschmuggler(in) *m(f)*

'**gunshot** *n* (*shot*) Schuss *m*; **~ wound** Schusswunde *f*

gurgle ['gɜr·gəl] *vi* (*baby*) glucksen; (*water*) gluckern

gush [gʌʃ] *vi* **1.** (*flow out*) [hervor]strömen; (*at high speed*) [hervor]schießen **2.** (*praise*) [übertrieben] schwärmen

gusher ['gʌʃ·ər] *n* [natürlich sprudelnde] Ölquelle

gushing ['gʌʃ·ɪŋ] *adj* schwärmerisch

gust [gʌst] *n* [Wind]stoß *m*

gusto ['gʌs·toʊ] *n* **with ~** mit Begeisterung

gusty ['gʌs·ti] *adj* böig

gut [gʌt] **I.** *n* **1.** *fam* (*abdomen*) Bauch *m* **2.** *fam* (*courage*) **~s** *pl* Mumm *m kein pl* ▶ **to bust a ~** sich abrackern **II.** *adj fam* (*feeling*) instinktiv; (*reaction*) spontan

gutsy ['gʌt·si] *adj* mutig

gutter ['gʌt·ər] *n* (*of road*) Rinnstein *m*; (*of roof*) Dachrinne *f*

guy [gaɪ] *n* **1.** *fam* (*man*) Kerl *m*, Typ *m* **2.** *pl fam* (*people*) **are you ~s coming to lunch?** kommt ihr [mit] zum Essen?

guzzle ['gʌz·əl] *vt fam* (*drink*) in sich *akk* hineinkippen

gym [dʒɪm] *n* **1.** *short for* **gymnasium** Turnhalle *f* **2.** *short for* **PE**

gymnasium <*pl* -s> [dʒɪm·'neɪ·zi·əm] *n* Turnhalle *f*

gymnast ['dʒɪm·næst] *n* Turner(in) *m(f)*

gymnastic [dʒɪm·'næs·tɪk] *adj* turnerisch, Turn-

gymnastics [dʒɪm·'næs·tɪks] *npl* Turnen *nt kein pl*

gynecologist [ˌgaɪ·nə·'kal·ə·dʒɪst] *n* Gynäkologe, -in *m, f*

gynecology [ˌgaɪ·nə·'kal·ə·dʒi] *n* Gynäkologie *f*

Gypsy ['dʒɪp·si] *n* Zigeuner(in) *m(f)*

gyrate ['dʒaɪ·reɪt] *vi* sich drehen

gyroscope ['dʒaɪ·rə·skoʊp] *n* NAUT, AVIAT Gyroskop *nt*

H

H <*pl* -'s>, **h** <*pl* -'s> [eɪtʃ] *n* H *nt*, h *nt*; **~ as in Hotel** H wie Heinrich

habit ['hæb·ɪt] *n* **1.** (*repeated action*) Gewohnheit *f*; **a bad ~** eine schlechte [An]gewohnheit **2.** *fam* (*drug addiction*) **to have a heroin ~** heroinsüchtig sein

habitable ['hæb·ɪ·tə·bəl] *adj* bewohnbar

habitat ['hæb·ɪ·tæt] *n* Lebensraum *m*

habitual [hə·'bɪtʃ·u·əl] *adj* gewohnt

hack [hæk] **I.** *vt* **1.** (*chop*) hacken **2.** *sl* (*cope with*) aushalten; **he can't ~ it** er bringt's einfach nicht **II.** *vi* COMPUT **to ~ into sth** in etw *akk* eindringen

hacker ['hæk·ər] *n* COMPUT Hacker(in) *m(f)*

'**hacksaw** *n* Bügelsäge *f*

had [hæd, *unstressed:* həd] *vt* **1.** *pt, pp of* **have 2.** *fam* **to have ~ it** (*want to stop*) genug haben; (*to be broken*) kaputt sein

haddock <*pl* -> ['hæd·ək] *n* Schellfisch *m*

hadn't ['hæd·ənt] = **had not** *see* **have**

haggle ['hæg·əl] *vi* **to ~** [over sth] [um etw *akk*] feilschen

Hague [heɪg] *n* GEOG **The ~** Den Haag *kein art*

hail[1] [heɪl] **I.** *n* Hagel *m* **II.** *vi* hageln

hail[2] [heɪl] *vt* (*taxi*) rufen

'**hailstone** *n* Hagelkorn *nt*

hair [her] *n* (*single strand*) Haar *nt*; (*on head*) Haar *nt*, Haare *pl*

'**hairbrush** *n* Haarbürste *f*

'**hair care** *n* Haarpflege *f*

'**hair conditioner** *n* Pflegespülung *f*

'**haircut** *n* Frisur *f*

'**hairdresser** *n* Friseur *m*, Friseuse *f*

'**hair drier**, '**hair dryer** *n* Föhn *m*

hairless ['her·lɪs] *adj* unbehaart; (*person*) glatzköpfig

'**hairline** *n* Haaransatz *m*

'**hairpiece** *n* Haarteil *nt*

'**hairpin** *n* Haarnadel *f*

'**hair-raising** *adj fam* haarsträubend

'hair remover n Enthaarungsmittel nt

'hairspray n Haarspray nt

'hairstyle n Frisur f

'hairstylist n Friseur m, Friseuse f

hairy ['her·i] adj haarig

half [hæf] I. n <pl halves> 1. (fifty percent) Hälfte f; ~ an apple ein halber Apfel; three and a ~ pounds eineinhalb Kilo 2. SPORT (period) Spielhälfte f, Halbzeit f ▶ given a ~ chance wenn man die Möglichkeit hätte II. adj halbe(r, s); ~ a percent ein halbes Prozent III. adv 1. (almost) fast 2. (time) [at] ~ past nine [um] halb zehn

'halfback n SPORT Läufer(in) m(f)

'half brother n Halbbruder m

'half dozen, half a 'dozen n ein halbes Dutzend

half-'empty adj halb leer

half-'full adj halb voll

half-'hearted adj halbherzig

half 'moon n Halbmond m

half-'price adj, adv zum halben Preis

'half sister n Halbschwester f

'halftime n SPORT Halbzeit f; (break) Halbzeitpause f

'halfway I. adj halb II. adv in der Mitte; it's ~ between the two es liegt genau auf halber Strecke zwischen den beiden; ~ through dinner mitten beim Abendessen

'half-wit n pej Dummkopf m

half-'yearly adj, adv halbjährlich

hall [hɔl] n 1. (corridor) Flur m 2. (large building) Halle f; (public room) Saal m; city ~ Rathaus nt

hallmark ['hɔl·mɑrk] n Kennzeichen nt

Halloween [ˌhæl·ə·'win] n Halloween nt

hallucinate [hə·'lu·sɪ·neɪt] vi halluzinieren

hallucination [hə·ˌlu·sɪ·'neɪ·ʃən] n Halluzination f

'hallway n Flur m

halo <pl -s> ['heɪ·loʊ] n Heiligenschein m

halogen 'bulb n Halogenglühbirne f

halt [hɔlt] I. n 1. Stillstand m 2. (break) Pause f II. vt zum Stillstand bringen; (fight) beenden III. vi zum Stillstand kommen

halter ['hɔl·tər] n 1. (for animals) Halfter nt 2. FASHION see halter-top

'halter-top n FASHION rückenfreies Oberteil (mit Nackenverschluss)

halting ['hɔl·tɪŋ] adj (speech) stockend

halve [hæv] vt 1. (cut in two) halbieren 2. (lessen by 50 percent) um die Hälfte reduzieren

ham [hæm] n 1. FOOD Schinken m 2. THEAT pej Schmierenkomödiant(in) m(f)

hamburger ['hæm·bɜr·gər] n FOOD 1. (cooked) Hamburger m 2. (raw) Hackfleisch nt

ham-'fisted, ham-'handed adj pej ungeschickt

hamlet ['hæm·lət] n Weiler m

hammer ['hæm·ər] I. n 1. (tool) Hammer m 2. SPORT [Wurf]hammer m II. vt 1. (nail) einschlagen; (ball) [kräftig] schlagen; to ~ sth into sb fig jdm etw einhämmern 2. fam (defeat) New England ~ed Pittsburgh 35-3 New England war Pittsburgh mit 35:3 haushoch überlegen ▶ to ~ sth home etw dat Nachdruck verleihen III. vi hämmern a. fig

◆hammer in vt 1. (nail) einschlagen 2. fig to ~ sth into sb (fact) jdm etw einbläuen

◆hammer out vt 1. (dent) ausbeulen 2. (settlement) aushandeln

hammock ['hæm·ək] n Hängematte f

hamper¹ ['hæm·pər] n [Deckel]korb m

hamper² ['hæm·pər] vt behindern

hamster ['hæm·stər] n Hamster m

hamstring ['hæm·strɪŋ] n Kniesehne f

hand [hænd] I. n 1. ANAT Hand f; ~s up! Hände hoch!; to be good with one's ~s geschickte Hände haben; by ~ von Hand; on [one's] ~s and knees auf allen vieren 2. (control) to be in good/safe ~s in guten/sicheren Händen sein; to turn one's ~ to sth sich an etw akk machen 3. (assistance) to give [or lend] sb a ~ jdm helfen 4. (on clock) Zeiger m 5. to give sb a big ~ jdm einen großen Applaus spenden ▶ to keep a firm ~ on sth etw fest im Griff behalten; on the one ~ ... on the other [~] ... einerseits ... andererseits II. vt to ~ sb sth jdm etw [über]geben ▶ you've got to ~ it to sb man muss es jdm lassen

◆**hand back** vt zurückgeben

◆**hand down** vt weitergeben; (*tradition*) überliefern

◆**hand in** vt einreichen; (*homework*) abgeben

◆**hand out** vt (*papers, test*) austeilen (**to** an +*akk*); (*homework, advice*) geben

◆**hand over** vt **1.** (*pass*) herüberreichen; (*away from one*) hinüberreichen; (*present*) übergeben **2.** TV, RADIO weitergeben (**to** an +*akk*)

'**handbag** n Handtasche f

'**handball** n Handball m

'**handbook** n Handbuch nt

'**hand brake** n Notbremse f

'**handcuff** n ~**s** pl Handschellen pl

'**handful** n Handvoll f; **a ~ of hair** ein Büschel nt Haare; **a ~ of people** wenige Leute

'**hand grenade** n Handgranate f

'**handgun** n Handfeuerwaffe f

hand-'held adj attr tragbar

handicap ['hæn·dɪ·kæp] **I.** n Handicap nt **II.** vt <-pp-> benachteiligen

handicapped ['hæn·dɪ·kæpt] adj behindert

handicraft ['hæn·dɪ·kræft] n [Kunst]handwerk nt kein pl

handkerchief ['hæn·kər·tʃɪf] n Taschentuch nt

handle ['hæn·dəl] **I.** n Griff m; (*of a door*) Klinke f; (*of a handbag*) Bügel m ▶ **to fly off the ~** hochgehen **II.** vt **1.** (*grasp*) anfassen **2.** (*work on*) bearbeiten; (*luggage*) abfertigen; **to ~ sb's affairs** sich um jds Angelegenheiten kümmern **3.** (*deal with*) umgehen mit +*dat*, behandeln

'**handlebars** npl Lenkstange f sing

handler ['hænd·lər] n **1. baggage ~** Gepäckmann m **2.** (*dog trainer*) Hundeführer(in) m(f)

handling ['hænd·lɪŋ] n **1.** (*act of touching*) Berühren nt **2.** (*treatment*) Handhabung f

'**hand luggage** n Handgepäck nt

hand'made adj handgearbeitet

'**hand-me-down** n abgelegtes Kleidungsstück

'**handout** n Almosen nt

'**handover** n Übergabe f

hand-'picked adj handverlesen a. fig

'**handrail** n Geländer nt

'**handset** n TELEC Hörer m

'**handshake** n Händedruck m

handsome ['hæn·səm] adj gut aussehend

'**handstand** n Handstand m

'**handwriting** n Handschrift f

'**handwritten** adj handgeschrieben

handy ['hæn·di] adj **1.** (*user-friendly*) praktisch, nützlich; (*easy to handle*) handlich **2.** (*convenient*) nützlich **3.** (*conveniently close: thing*) griffbereit, greifbar

'**handyman** n Heimwerker(in) m(f)

hang [hæŋ] **I.** n **1.** (*of clothes*) Sitz m **2.** fig fam **to get the ~ of sth** bei etw dat den [richtigen] Dreh herausbekommen **II.** vt <hung, hung> **1.** (*mount*) aufhängen (**on** an +*dat*) **2.** (*decorate*) behängen **3.** <-ed, -ed> (*execute*) [auf]hängen **4.** (*head*) hängen lassen **III.** vi **1.** <hung, hung> (*be suspended*) hängen (**from** an +*dat*) **2.** <hanged, hanged> (*by execution*) hängen **3.** <hung, hung> (*mist, smell*) hängen ▶ **to ~ in there** am Ball bleiben

◆**hang around** vi **1.** (*loiter*) rumhängen fam **2.** (*waste time*) herumtrödeln fam

◆**hang back** vi (*be slow*) sich zurückhalten; (*hesitate*) zögern

◆**hang on** vi **1.** fam (*persevere*) durchhalten **2.** (*grasp*) **to ~ on to sth** sich an etw dat festhalten; (*stronger*) sich an etw akk klammern **3.** (*wait briefly*) warten; (*on the telephone*) dranbleiben; **~ on, ...** Moment mal, ...

◆**hang out I.** vt heraushängen; (*laundry*) aufhängen **vi 1.** (*project*) heraushängen **2.** sl (*loiter*) [he]rumhängen; (*waste time*) herumtrödeln ▶ **to let it all ~ out** die Sau rauslassen fam

◆**hang together** vi (*argument*) schlüssig sein

◆**hang up I.** vi auflegen **II.** vt **1.** (*suspend*) aufhängen **2.** (*phone*) auflegen

hangar ['hæŋ·ər] n AVIAT Hangar m

hanger ['hæŋ·ər] n [Kleider]bügel m

'**hang glider** n (*person*) Drachenflieger(in) m(f); (*device*) Drachen m

'**hang-gliding** n Drachenfliegen nt

hanging ['hæŋ·ɪŋ] **I.** n **1.** (execution) Hinrichtung f durch den Strang **2.** (decorative fabric) Behang m **II.** adj hängend

'**hangman** n Henker m

'**hangover** n Kater m

'**hang-up** n fam Komplex m

hankie, hanky ['hæŋ·ki] n fam short for **handkerchief** Taschentuch nt

haphazard [hæp·'hæz·ərd] adj willkürlich

happen ['hæp·ən] vi **1.** (occur) geschehen, passieren; (event) stattfinden; **these things ~** das kann vorkommen **2.** (by chance) **to ~ to do sth** zufällig etw tun

happening ['hæp·ə·nɪŋ] n usu pl Ereignis nt; (unplanned) Vorfall m

happily ['hæp·ɪ·li] adv **1.** (contentedly) glücklich; (cheerfully) fröhlich **2.** (willingly) gern

happiness ['hæp·ɪ·nɪs] n Glück nt; (contentment) Zufriedenheit f

happy ['hæp·i] adj **1.** (pleased) glücklich; (contented) zufrieden; (cheerful) fröhlich; **to be ~ about** [or **with**] **sb/sth** mit jdm/etw zufrieden sein **2.** (willing) **to be ~ to do sth** etw gerne tun **3.** (in greetings) **~ birthday** alles Gute zum Geburtstag

happy-go-'lucky adj sorglos, unbekümmert

happy 'medium n goldene Mitte

harass [hə·'ræs] vt (intimidate) schikanieren; (pester) ständig belästigen

harassment [hə·'ræs·mənt] n Schikane f; **sexual ~** sexuelle Belästigung

harbor ['har·bər] n Hafen m

hard [hard] **I.** adj **1.** (solid) hart **2.** (person) zäh, hart **3.** (difficult) schwierig; **to find sth ~ to believe** etw kaum glauben können **4.** (laborious) anstrengend; **to be ~ work** harte Arbeit sein **5.** (harmful) **to be ~ on sth** etw stark strapazieren; **to be ~ on sb** hart für jdn sein **6.** (water, drug) hart; (frost, winter) streng ▶ **~ and fast** fest; (rule) verbindlich **II.** adv **1.** (solid) hart **2.** (vigorously) fest[e], kräftig; (fight, work) hart; (rain) stark; **to try ~** sich akk sehr bemühen **3.** (severely) schwer

'**hardboard** n Hartfaserplatte f

hard-'boiled adj (egg) hart gekocht

hard 'copy n COMPUT Ausdruck m

'**hard-core, hardcore** adj **1.** (loyal: supporter) eingefleischt **2.** (explicit) hart

'**hardcover** adj gebunden

hard 'currency n harte Währung

'**hard disk, 'hard drive** n COMPUT Festplatte f

harden ['har·dən] **I.** vt **1.** (make harder) härten; (arteries) verhärten **2.** (make tougher: attitude) verhärten **II.** vi **1.** (become hard) hart werden **2.** (become tough) sich verhärten; (face) sich versteinern

hard-'fought adj (battle, match) hart

'**hard hat** n [Schutz]helm m

hard-'hearted adj hartherzig

hard 'labor n Zwangsarbeit f

'**hard'liner** n POL Hardliner m

hardly ['hard·li] adv kaum; **~ ever** so gut wie nie

hardness ['hard·nɪs] n Härte f

hard-'nosed adj nüchtern; (person) abgebrüht

hard-'pressed adj bedrängt

hard 'sell n aggressive Verkaufsmethoden pl

hardship ['hard·ʃɪp] n Not f

'**hardware** n **1.** Haushaltswaren pl **2.** COMPUT Hardware f

'**hardwood** n Hartholz nt

hard-'working adj fleißig

hardy ['har·di] adj **1.** (tough) zäh **2.** BOT winterhart

hare <pl -s> [her] n [Feld]hase m

'**harebrained** adj verrückt

harem ['her·əm] n Harem m

harm [harm] **I.** n Schaden m; **to mean no ~** es nicht böse meinen **II.** vt **to ~ sth** etw dat Schaden zufügen; **to ~ sb** jdm schaden; (hurt) jdn verletzen

harmful ['harm·fəl] adj schädlich

harmless ['harm·lɪs] adj harmlos

harmonious [har·'moʊ·ni·əs] adj harmonisch a. fig

harmonization [ˌhar·mə·nɪ·'zeɪ·ʃən] n Harmonisierung f a. fig

harmony ['har·mə·ni] n Harmonie f

harness ['har·nɪs] **I.** n <pl -es> (for animal) Geschirr nt; (for person) Gurt-

zeug nt II. vt (animal) anschirren; (person) anschnallen

harp [hɑrp] n Harfe f

harpoon [hɑr·'pun] n Harpune f

harrowing ['her·oʊ·ɪŋ] adj grauenvoll

harsh [hɑrʃ] adj 1. (winter) rau; (winter) streng; (light) grell 2. (severe) hart; (critical) scharf

harvest ['hɑr·vɪst] I. n Ernte f; (of grapes) Lese f II. vt ernten

has [hæz, həz] 3rd pers. sing of have

hash [hæʃ] n 1. FOOD Haschee nt 2. fam (shambles) **to make a ~ of sth** etw vermasseln

hash 'browns npl Kartoffelpuffer pl, ≈ Rösti pl süddt, schweiz

hasn't ['hæz·ənt] = **has not** see **have**

hassle ['hæs·əl] I. n fam Mühe f kein pl II. vt fam (pester) schikanieren; (harass) bedrängen

haste [heɪst] n Eile f; (rush) Hast f

hasten ['heɪ·sən] vi sich akk beeilen

hasty ['heɪ·sti] adj 1. eilig 2. (rash) übereilt

hat [hæt] n Hut m

hatch¹ <pl -es> [hætʃ] n 1. (opening) Durchreiche f 2. NAUT Luke f

hatch² [hætʃ] I. vi schlüpfen a. fig II. vt ausbrüten a. fig

hatchback ['hætʃ·bæk] n 1. (door) Heckklappe f 2. (vehicle) Wagen m mit Heckklappe

hatchet ['hætʃ·ɪt] n Beil nt ▸ **to bury the ~** das Kriegsbeil begraben

hate [heɪt] I. n Hass m II. vt hassen; I ~ **going to the dentist** ich hasse es, zum Zahnarzt zu gehen.

'**hate crime** n LAW Verbrechen, das aus [Rassen]hass oder Vorurteilen begangen wird

hatred ['heɪ·trɪd] n Hass m

'**hat trick** n Hattrick m

haul [hɔl] I. n Ausbeute f II. vt 1. (pull) ziehen; (sth heavy) schleppen 2. (transport) befördern

◆**haul off** vt wegziehen; **to ~ sb off to jail** fig jdn ins Gefängnis werfen

hauler ['hɔ·lər] n freight ~ Transportunternehmen nt, Spedition[sfirma] f

haunt [hɔnt] vt 1. (ghost) spuken in +dat 2. (memories) heimsuchen

haunted ['hɔn·tɪd] adj ~ **house** Gespensterhaus nt

haunting ['hɔn·tɪŋ] adj 1. (disturbing) quälend 2. (stirring) sehnsuchtsvoll

have [hæv, həv] I. aux vb <has, had, had> 1. (forming past tenses) **he** er war noch nie zuvor in New York; **we had been swimming** wir waren schwimmen gewesen 2. (render) **to ~ sth done** etw tun lassen 3. (must) **to ~ to do sth** etw tun müssen II. vt <has, had, had> 1. (possess) **to ~ sth** etw haben; ~ **a nice day!** viel Spaß!; (to customers) einen schönen Tag noch! 2. (bath) nehmen; (nap, party) machen; **to ~ a talk with sb** mit jdm sprechen 3. (food) essen; (cigarette) rauchen; **to ~ lunch** zu Mittag essen 4. (be obliged) **to ~ sth to do** etw tun müssen 5. (pregnant) **to ~ a baby** ein Baby bekommen 6. (induce) **to ~ sb do sth** jdn [dazu] veranlassen, etw zu tun ▸ **to ~ had it** (be broken) hinüber sein; (be exhausted) fix und fertig sein; **to ~ had it with sb/sth** von jdm/etw die Nase voll haben

◆**have around** vt zur Hand haben

◆**have back** vt (object) zurückhaben; (person) wieder nehmen

◆**have in** vt **to ~ sb in** [**to do sth**] jdn kommen lassen[, um etw zu tun] ▸ **to ~ it in for sb** jdn auf dem Kieker haben

◆**have on** vt 1. (clothes) tragen 2. (know about) **to ~ sth on sb/sth** (evidence, facts) etw über jdn/etw [in der Hand] haben

◆**have out** vt 1. (remove) sich dat herausnehmen lassen 2. fam (argue) **to ~ it out** [**with sb**] es [mit jdm] ausdiskutieren

◆**have over** vt **to ~ sb over** jdn zu sich dat einladen

haven't ['hæv·ənt] = **have not** see **have**

havoc ['hæv·ək] n Verwüstungen pl; **to play ~ with sth** fig etw völlig durcheinanderbringen

Hawaii [hə·'waɪ·i] n Hawaii nt

hawk [hɔk] I. n 1. (bird) Habicht m

2. POL Falke *m* **II.** *vt* **to ~ sth** mit etw *dat* hausieren gehen

hawker ['hɔ·kər] *n* Hausierer(in) *m(f)*

hawk-eyed *adj* **to be ~** Adleraugen haben

hawthorn ['hɔ·θɔrn] *n* Weißdorn *m*

hay [heɪ] *n* Heu *nt*

hay fever *n* Heuschnupfen *m*

haystack *n* Heuhaufen *m*

hazard ['hæz·ərd] *n* Gefahr *f*

hazard lights *npl* AUTO Warnblinkanlage *f*

hazardous ['hæz·ər·dəs] *adj* (*dangerous*) gefährlich; (*risky*) riskant

haze [heɪz] **I.** *n* Dunst[schleier] *m* **II.** *vt* schikanieren

hazelnut *n* Haselnuss *f*

hazy ['heɪ·zi] *adj* **1.** (*with haze*) dunstig, diesig **2.** (*confused*) unklar; (*indistinct*) verschwommen

he [hi] **I.** *pron pers* (*male person*) er; (*unspecified person*) er/sie/es **II.** *n* Er *m*

head [hed] **I.** *n* **1.** Kopf *m*; **she's got a good ~ for figures** sie kann gut mit Zahlen umgehen; **to use one's ~** seinen Verstand benutzen **2. a** [*or* **per**] **~** pro Kopf **3.** (*of bed, table*) Kopfende *nt*; (*of nail, coin*) Kopf *m*; (*of line*) Anfang *m* **4.** (*leader*) Chef(in) *m(f)*; (*of a project, department*) Leiter(in) *m(f)*; (*of church, state*) Oberhaupt *nt* ▶ **to be ~ over heels in love** bis über beide Ohren verliebt sein; **to not be able to make ~s or tails of sth** aus etw *dat* nicht schlau werden; **to go to sb's ~** jdm zu Kopf steigen **II.** *adj* leitend **III.** *vt* **1.** (*be at the front of*) anführen **2.** (*be in charge of: organization*) leiten **IV.** *vi* **to ~** [**for**] **home** sich *akk* auf den Heimweg machen

◆ **head back** *vi* zurückgehen; (*with transport*) zurückfahren

◆ **head off I.** *vt* abfangen **II.** *vi* **to ~ off to**[**ward**] **sth** sich zu etw *dat* begeben

◆ **head out** *vi* losziehen

◆ **head up** *vt* leiten

'headache *n* Kopfschmerzen *pl*

'headband *n* Stirnband *nt*

'headdress <*pl* -es> *n* Kopfschmuck *m*

header ['hed·ər] *n* **1.** (*at top of page*) Kopfzeile *f* **2.** (*in email*) Header *m*

'head'first *adv* kopfüber

'headhunter *n* Headhunter(in) *m(f)*

heading ['hed·ɪŋ] *n* Überschrift *f*

'headlamp *n* Scheinwerfer *m*

'headlight *n* Scheinwerfer *m*

'headline *n* Schlagzeile *f*

'headliner *n* Hauptattraktion *f*

'headmaster *n* Schulleiter *m*, Rektor *m*

'headmistress *n* Schulleiterin *f*, Rektorin *f*

head 'office *n* Zentrale *f*

head-'on I. *adj* Frontal- **II.** *adv* frontal; *fig* direkt

'headphones *npl* Kopfhörer *m*

'headquarters *npl* + *sing/pl vb* MIL Hauptquartier *nt*; (*of company*) Hauptsitz *m*

'headrest *n* Kopfstütze *f*

'headroom *n* lichte Höhe

'headscarf *n* Kopftuch *nt*

'headset *n* Kopfhörer *m*

head 'start *n* Vorsprung *m*

'headstrong *adj* eigensinnig

head-to-'head *adj* (*contest*) Kopf-an-Kopf-

'headwaters *n pl* Quellgewässer *pl*

'headway *n* **to make ~** [gut] vorankommen (**in** bei +*dat*, **with** mit +*dat*)

'headwind *n* Gegenwind *m*

'headword *n* LING Stichwort *nt*

heal [hil] *vt, vi* heilen

healing ['hi·lɪŋ] **I.** *adj attr* (*process*) heilsam **II.** *n* Heilung *f*

health [helθ] *n* Gesundheit *f*

'health care *n* Gesundheitsfürsorge *f*

'health center *n* Ärztehaus *nt*

'health club *n* Fitnessclub *m*

'health food *n* Reformkost *f*

'health food store *n* Naturkostladen *m*

'health hazard *n* Gesundheitsrisiko *nt*

'health insurance *n* Krankenversicherung *f*; **~ company** Krankenkasse *f*

healthy ['hel·θi] *adj* gesund *a. fig*

heap [hip] **I.** *n* a. *fig* Haufen *m* **II.** *vt* aufhäufen; *fig* **to ~ praise on sb** jdn überschwänglich loben

hear <heard, heard> [hɪr] **I.** *vt* **1.** (*perceive*) hören; **Jane ~d him go out** Jane hörte, wie er hinausging **2.** LAW (*case*) verhandeln **II.** *vi* hören (**about/of** von +*dat*)

heard [hɜrd] *pt, pp* of **hear**

hearing ['hɪr·ɪŋ] *n* 1. (*ability to hear*) Gehör *nt;* **to be hard of ~** schwerhörig sein 2. (*official examination*) Anhörung *f*

'hearing aid *n* Hörgerät *nt*

'hearing-impaired *adj* schwerhörig

hearsay ['hɪr·seɪ] *n* Gerüchte *pl*

hearse [hɜrs] *n* Leichenwagen *m*

heart [hart] *n* 1. Herz *nt;* **from the bottom of one's ~** aus tiefstem Herzen; **the ~ of the matter** der Kern der Sache; **to have one's ~ set on sth** sein [*ganzes*] Herz an etw *akk* hängen 2. (*courage*) Mut *m* 3. CARDS **~s** *pl* Herz *nt kein pl;* **queen of ~s** Herzdame *f* ► **by ~** auswendig; **to have a change of ~** sich *akk* anders besinnen

'heartache *n* Kummer *m*

'heart attack *n* Herzinfarkt *m*

'heartbeat *n* Herzschlag *m*

'heartbreaking *adj* herzzerreißend

'heartbroken *adj* todunglücklich

'heartburn *n* Sodbrennen *nt*

'heart disease *n* Herzkrankheit *f*

'heart failure *n* Herzversagen *nt*

heartily ['har·tɪ·li] *adv* herzlich; (*applaud*) begeistert

'heartland *n* (*of region*) Herz *nt*

heartless ['hart·lɪs] *adj* herzlos

'heart-rending *adj* herzzerreißend

'heartthrob *n fam* Schwarm *m*

'heart transplant *n* Herztransplantation *f*

'heartwarming *adj* herzerfreuend

hearty ['har·ti] *adj* 1. (*warm*) herzlich 2. (*breakfast*) herzhaft; (*appetite*) gesund

heat [hit] I. *n* 1. (*warmth*) Wärme *f;* (*high temperature*) Hitze *f* 2. SPORT Vorlauf *m* ► **if you can't stand the ~, get out of the kitchen** *prov* wenn es dir zu viel wird, dann lass es lieber sein II. *vt* erhitzen, heiß machen; (*food*) aufwärmen; (*house*) heizen; (*pool*) beheizen

heat up I. *vt* heiß machen; (*food*) aufwärmen; (*house*) [auf]heizen II. *vi* (*room*) warm werden; (*engine*) warm laufen; *fig* (*discussion*) sich erhitzen

heated ['hi·tɪd] *adj* 1. (*discussion*) heftig 2. (*warm*) erhitzt; (*room*) geheizt; (*pool*) beheizt

heater ['hi·tər] *n* [Heiz]ofen *m,* Heizgerät *nt;* (*in car*) Heizung *f*

heathen ['hi·ðən] *n* Heide *m,* Heidin *f*

heather ['heð·ər] *n* Heidekraut *nt*

heating ['hi·tɪŋ] *n* 1. (*action*) Heizen *nt* (*of room*) [Be]heizen *nt;* (*of substances*) Erwärmen *nt* 2. (*appliance*) Heizung *f*

'heat-resistant *adj* hitzebeständig; (*ovenware*) feuerfest

'heat shield *n* Hitzeschild *m*

'heat stroke *n* Hitzschlag *m*

'heat treatment *n* Wärmebehandlung *f*

'heat wave *n* Hitzewelle *f*

heave [hiv] I. *n* Ruck *m* II. *vt* [hoch]hieven III. *vi* 1. (*pull*) hieven 2. (*move*) sich heben und senken; (*chest, sea*) wogen

heaven ['hev·ən] *n* Himmel *m a. fig* ► **good ~s!** du lieber Himmel!

heavenly ['hev·ən·li] *adj* himmlisch

heavily ['hev·ɪ·li] *adv* 1. (*to great degree*) stark; (*gamble*) leidenschaftlich 2. (*with weight*) schwer; (*move*) schwerfällig; **~ built** kräftig gebaut 3. (*severely*) schwer; **to snow ~** stark schneien

heavy ['hev·i] I. *adj* 1. (*weighty*) schwer *a. fig;* (*fine*) hoch 2. (*rain, drinker*) stark 3. *fig* (*oppressive*) drückend; (*weather*) schwül 4. (*difficult*) schwierig; (*breathing*) schwer 5. (*beard*) dicht; (*coat*) dick; (*traffic*) stark II. *n sl* (*thug*) Schläger[typ] *m*

heavy-'duty *adj* robust; (*clothes*) strapazierfähig

heavy-'handed *adj* ungeschickt

heavy 'industry *n* Schwerindustrie *f*

heavy 'metal *n* 1. (*metal*) Schwermetall *nt* 2. (*music*) Heavymetal *m*

'heavyweight *n* Schwergewicht *nt a. fig*

Hebrew ['hi·bru] *n* 1. (*person*) Hebräer(in) *m(f);* (*language*) Hebräisch *m*

heck [hek] *interj euph sl* **where the ~ have you been?** wo, zum Teufel, bist du gewesen?

hectic ['hek·tɪk] *adj* hektisch

he'd [hid] = **he had/he would** *see* **have I, II, would**

hedge [hedʒ] *n* BOT Hecke *f*

'hedgehog *n* Igel *m*

heebie-jeebies ['hi·bɪ·'dʒi·bɪz] *npl sl* **to get the ~** Zustände kriegen

heed [hid] *form* I. *vt* beachten II. *n* Beachtung *f*; **to pay ~ to** [*or* **take ~ of**] **sth** auf etw *akk* achten

heedless ['hid·lɪs] *adj form* achtlos

heel [hil] I. *n* 1. ANAT Ferse *f* 2. (*of shoe*) Absatz *m* ▶ **to dig one's ~s in** sich auf die Hinterbeine stellen II. *interj* **~!** bei Fuß!

hefty ['hef·ti] *adj* 1. (*strong*) kräftig; (*heavy*) schwer 2. (*price, fine*) hoch, saftig *fam*

height [haɪt] *n* 1. (*top to bottom*) Höhe *f*; (*of a person*) [Körper]größe *f*; **to be 20 feet in ~** 20 Fuß hoch sein 2. (*high places*) **~s** *pl* Höhen *pl* 3. *fig* Höhepunkt *m*

heighten ['haɪ·tən] *vt* verstärken; (*tension*) steigern

heir [er] *n* Erbe *m*, Erbin *f*

heiress <*pl* -es> ['er·ɪs] *n* Erbin *f*

heirloom ['er·lum] *n* Erbstück *nt*

heist [haɪst] *n* Raub[überfall] *m*

held [held] *vt, vi pt, pp of* **hold**

helicopter ['hel·ɪ·kap·tər] *n* Hubschrauber *m*

helipad ['hel·ɪ·pæd] *n* Hubschrauberlandeplatz *m*

heliport *n* Heliport *m*, Hubschrauberlandeplatz *m*

helium ['hi·li·əm] *n* Helium *nt*

hell [hel] *n* 1. Hölle *f* 2. *fig fam* **to ~ with it!** ich hab's satt!; **to scare the ~ out of sb** jdn zu Tode erschrecken 3. *fam* (*for emphasis*) **he's one ~ of a guy!** er ist echt total in Ordnung!; **a ~ of a lot** verdammt viel ▶ **come ~ or high water** komme, was wolle; **go to ~!** scher dich zum Teufel!

he'll [hil] = **he will/he shall** *see* **will, shall**

hellish ['hel·ɪʃ] *adj* höllisch *a. fig*

hello [hə·'loʊ] I. *n* Hallo *nt* II. *interj* hallo!

helm [helm] *n* Ruder *nt a. fig*

helmet ['hel·mɪt] *n* Helm *m*

help [help] I. *n* Hilfe *f*; (*financial*) Unterstützung *f*; **to cry for ~** um Hilfe rufen II. *interj* **~!** Hilfe! III. *vi* helfen (**with** bei +*dat*) IV. *vt* 1. (*assist*) **to ~ sb** jdm helfen (**with** bei +*dat*); **can I ~ you?** (*in shop*) kann ich Ihnen behilflich sein?

2. (*improve*) verbessern; (*alleviate*) lindern 3. (*prevent*) **I can't ~ it!** ich kann nichts dagegen machen!; **sth can't be ~ed** etw ist nicht zu ändern 4. (*take*) **to ~ oneself** sich *akk* bedienen

◆**help along** *vt* **to ~ sb along** jdm [auf die Sprünge] helfen; **to ~ sth along** etw vorantreiben

◆**help out** I. *vt* **to ~ out ⇆ sb** jdm [aus] helfen II. *vi* aushelfen

◆**help up** *vt* **to ~ sb up** jdm aufhelfen

helper ['hel·pər] *n* Helfer(in) *m(f)*; (*assistant*) Gehilfe *m*, Gehilfin *f*

helpful ['help·fəl] *adj* (*person*) hilfsbereit; (*suggestion*) hilfreich

helping ['hel·pɪŋ] I. *n* (*of food*) Portion *f* II. *adj* hilfreich; **to give** [*or* **lend**] **sb a ~ hand** jdm helfen

helpless ['help·lɪs] *adj* hilflos; (*powerless*) machtlos

'**helpline** *n* Notruf *m*

helter-skelter [ˌhel·tər·'skel·tər] I. *adj* hektisch II. *adv* Hals über Kopf

hem [hem] *n* Saum *m*

◆**hem in** *vt* 1. (*surround*) umgeben 2. *fig* einengen

hemisphere ['hem·ɪ·sfɪr] *n* GEOG, ASTRON [Erd]halbkugel *f*

hemophiliac [ˌhi·moʊ·'fɪl·i·æk] *n* MED Bluter(in) *m(f)*

hemorrhage ['hem·ər·ɪdʒ] *n* MED [starke] Blutung

hemorrhoids ['hem·ər·ɔɪdz] *npl* MED Hämorrhoiden *pl*

hemp [hemp] *n* Hanf *m*

hen [hen] *n* ZOOL Henne *f*, Huhn *nt*

hence [hens] *adv* 1. *after n* (*from now*) von jetzt an; **four weeks ~** in vier Wochen 2. (*therefore*) daher

henceforth [ˌhens·'fɔrθ], **henceforward** [ˌhens·'fɔr·wərd] *adv form* von nun an

'**henpecked** *adj* **~ husband** Pantoffelheld *m*

hepatitis [ˌhep·ə·'taɪ·tɪs] *n* Leberentzündung *f*

heptathlon [hep·'tæθ·lən] *n* Siebenkampf *m*

her [hɜr] I. *pron pers* sie *in akk,* ihr *in dat;* **it was ~** sie war's II. *adj poss* ihr(e, n); (*ship, country*) sein(e, n); **what's ~ name?** wie heißt sie?

H

herald ['her·əld] n Bote m, Botin f

herb [ɜrb] n [Gewürz]kraut nt meist pl; (for medicine) [Heil]kraut nt meist pl

herbal ['ɜr·bəl] adj Kräuter-

herbicide ['hɜr·bɪ·saɪd] n Unkrautvertilgungsmittel nt

herd [hɜrd] I. n Herde f II. vt treiben
◆ **herd together** I. vt zusammentreiben II. vi sich zusammendrängen

'herd instinct n Herdentrieb m

'herdsman n Hirt[e] m

here [hɪr] I. adv hier; (with movement) hierher, hierhin; **come ~!** komm [hier] her!; **give it ~!** fam gib mal her!; **~ I am!** hier bin ich!; **~ comes the train** da kommt der Zug; **~ and now** [jetzt] sofort; **from ~ on in** [or out] von jetzt an II. interj ~! hier!

hereabout [ˌhɪr·ə·'baʊt], **hereabouts** [ˌhɪr·ə·'baʊts] adv hier [in dieser Gegend]

hereditary [hə·'red·ɪ·ter·i] adj erblich; (disease) angeboren

heredity [hə·'red·ɪ·ţi] n (transmission of characteristics) Vererbung f; (genetic makeup) Erbgut nt

heresy ['her·ə·si] n Ketzerei f

heretic ['her·ə·tɪk] n Ketzer(in) m(f)

heritage ['her·ɪ·ţɪdʒ] n Erbe nt

hermit ['hɜr·mɪt] n Eremit(in) m(f) a. fig, Einsiedler(in) m(f) a. fig

hernia <pl -s> ['hɜr·ni·ə] n MED Bruch m

hero <pl -es> ['hɪr·oʊ] n Held(in) m(f)

heroic [hɪ·'roʊ·ɪk] adj heldenhaft; **~ deed** Heldentat f

heroin ['her·oʊ·ɪn] n Heroin nt

heroine ['her·oʊ·ɪn] n Heldin f

heroism ['her·oʊ·ɪz·əm] n Heldentum nt

heron <pl -s> ['her·ən] n Reiher m

herpes ['hɜr·piz] n MED Herpes m

herring <pl -s> ['her·ɪŋ] n Hering m

hers [hɜrz] pron pers (of person/animal) ihre(r, s)

herself [hɜr·'self] pron refl 1. after vb, prep sich in akk o dat 2. emph (personally) selbst; **she told me ~** sie hat es mir selbst erzählt 3. (alone) [all] by **~** ganz alleine

he's [hiz] = **he is**/**he has** see **be**, **have** I, II

hesitant ['hez·ɪ·tənt] adj (person) un-

schlüssig; (answer) zögernd; (speech) stockend

hesitantly ['hez·ɪ·tənt·li] adv (act) unentschlossen

hesitate ['hez·ɪ·teɪt] vi zögern

hesitation [ˌhez·ɪ·'teɪ·ʃən] n (indecision) Zögern nt; (reluctance) Bedenken pl

heterogeneous [ˌhet·ər·ə·'dʒi·ni·əs] ad/ uneinheitlich

heterosexual [ˌhet·ə·roʊ·'sek·ʃu·əl] I. adj heterosexuell II. n Heterosexuelle(r) f(m)

hexagon ['hek·sə·gan] n Sechseck nt

hexagonal [hek·'sæg·ə·nəl] adv sechseckig

hey [heɪ] interj fam he!

HI abbr of **Hawaii**

hi [haɪ] interj hallo!

hibernate ['haɪ·bər·neɪt] vi Winterschlaf halten

hibernation [ˌhaɪ·bər·'neɪ·ʃən] n Winterschlaf m

hiccup, hiccough ['hɪk·ʌp] I. n 1. Schluckauf m; **to have the ~s** einen Schluckauf haben 2. fig (setback) Schwierigkeit f meist pl II. vi hicksen dial

hick [hɪk] n pej fam Provinzler(in) m(f) pej fam

hickory ['hɪk·ə·ri] n Hickory[baum] m

hid [hɪd] vt pt of **hide**

hidden ['hɪd·ən] I. vt pp of **hide** II. adj versteckt; (agenda) heimlich

hide[1] [haɪd] I. vt <hid, hidden> 1. (out of sight) verstecken (**from** vor +dat) 2. (emotions) verbergen; (facts) verheimlichen II. vi <hid, hidden> sich akk verstecken (**from** vor +dat)
◆ **hide away** I. vt verstecken II. vi sich akk verstecken
◆ **hide out, hide up** vi sich akk versteckt halten

hide[2] [haɪd] n (skin) Haut f a. fig; (with fur) Fell nt; (leather) Leder nt

'hide-and-go-seek, 'hide-and-seek n Versteckspiel nt

'hideaway n fam Versteck nt a. fig

hideous ['hɪd·i·əs] adj grässlich, scheußlich

'hideout n Versteck nt

hiding ['haɪ·dɪŋ] n **to be in ~** sich ver-

steckt halten

hierarchy ['haɪ·rar·ki] n Hierarchie f

hi-fi ['haɪ·faɪ] n short for **high fidelity** Hi-Fi-Anlage f

high [haɪ] I. adj 1. (building, speed) hoch präd, hohe(r, s) attr; (winds) stark; (marks) gut; ~ **in calories** kalorienreich; ~ **and mighty** pej herablassend 2. (on drugs) high II. adv hoch; fig **emotions were running** ~ die Gemüter erhitzten sich III. n 1. (high[est] point) Höchststand m 2. METEO Hoch nt

high 'beams npl AUTO Fernlicht nt

highbrow adj hochgeistig

highchair n Hochstuhl m

high-class adj erstklassig; (product) hochwertig

high court n see **Supreme Court**

higher edu'cation n Hochschulbildung f

high 'flier n fig Überflieger(in) m(f)

high 'frequency n Hochfrequenz f

high-'handed adj selbstherrlich

high 'heels npl 1. (shoes) hochhackige Schuhe 2. (parts of a shoe) hohe Absätze

high jump n Hochsprung m

highlands ['haɪ·ləndz] npl Hochland nt kein pl

high-level adj auf höchster Ebene nach n

high life n exklusives Leben

highlight I. n 1. (best part) Höhepunkt m 2. (in hair) ~**s** pl Strähnchen pl II. vt hervorheben; (text) markieren

highly ['haɪ·li] adv hoch; **to think** ~ **of someone** eine hohe Meinung von jdm haben

High 'Mass n Hochamt nt

Highness ['haɪ·nɪs] n **Your** ~ Eure Hoheit

high-'pitched adj (voice) hoch; (roof) steil

high point n Höhepunkt m

high-'powered adj 1. (machine) Hochleistungs-; (car) stark 2. (influential) einflussreich; (delegation) hochrangig

high-'pressure adj METEO, TECH Hochdruck-

high 'priest n REL Hohe(r) Priester m

high-'profile adj profiliert

high-'protein adj eiweißreich

high-'ranking adj hochrangig

high-reso'lution adj mit hoher Auflösung

'high-rise, high-rise 'building n Hochhaus nt

high-'risk adj hochriskant

'high school n Highschool f, ≈ Gymnasium nt

high 'seas npl hohe See; **on the** ~ auf hoher See

high 'season n Hochsaison f

high-speed 'train n Hochgeschwindigkeitszug m

high-'spirited adj ausgelassen

high 'spirits npl Hochstimmung f kein pl

'high spot n Höhepunkt m

'hightail vt, vi fam **to** ~ [it] abhauen

high-'tech adj Hightech-

high tech'nology n Hochtechnologie f

high 'tide n Flut f

high 'treason n Hochverrat m

high-'water mark n Hochwassermarke f

'highway n Highway m

hijack ['haɪ·dʒæk] I. vt entführen II. n Entführung f

hijacker ['haɪ·dʒæk·ər] n Entführer(in) m(f)

hijacking ['haɪ·dʒæk·ɪŋ] n Entführung f

hike [haɪk] I. n 1. (long walk) Wanderung f 2. fam (increase) Erhöhung f II. vi wandern III. vt fam erhöhen

hiker ['haɪ·kər] n Wanderer m, Wanderin f

hiking ['haɪ·kɪŋ] n Wandern nt

hilarious [hɪ·'ler·i·əs] adj urkomisch; (mood) ausgelassen

hill [hɪl] n Hügel m; (higher) Berg m; (slope) Steigung f

hillbilly ['hɪl·bɪl·i] n Hinterwäldler(in) m(f)

'hillside n Hang m

'hilltop n Hügelkuppe f

hilly ['hɪl·i] adj hügelig

hilt [hɪlt] n (handle) Griff m; (of sword) Heft nt

him [hɪm] pron object ihn in akk, ihm in dat; **who?** ~? wer? der?

Himalayas [ˌhɪm·ə·'leɪ·əz] npl GEOG Himalaja m

himself [hɪm·'self] pron refl 1. after vb, prep sich in akk o dat 2. emph (per-

sonally) selbst; **he told me ~** er hat es mir selbst erzählt **3.** (*alone*) **|all| by ~** ganz alleine

hind [haɪnd] *adj* hintere(r, s)

hinder ['hɪn·dər] *vt* behindern

Hindi ['hɪn·di] *n* Hindi *nt*

'hindquarters *npl* Hinterteil *nt;* (*of a horse*) Hinterhand *f*

hindrance ['hɪn·drəns] *n* Hindernis *nt*

'hindsight *n* in |*or* with |**the benefit of**|| ~ im Nachhinein

Hindu ['hɪn·du] *n* Hindu *m o f*

hinge [hɪndʒ] *n* Angel *f;* (*of gate*) Scharnier *nt*

hint [hɪnt] **I.** *n* **1.** *usu sing* (*trace*) Spur *f;* **at the slightest ~ of trouble** beim leisesten Anzeichen von Ärger **2.** (*allusion*) Andeutung *f;* **OK, I can take a ~** OK, ich verstehe schon **3.** (*advice*) Tipp *m* **II.** *vt, vi* andeuten

hip [hɪp] **I.** *n* ANAT Hüfte *f;* (*of pants*) Hüftweite *f* **II.** *adj fam* hip

'hip flask *n* Flachmann *m*

hippie ['hɪp·i] *n* Hippie *m*

hippo ['hɪp·oʊ] *n fam short for* **hippopotamus**

hippopotamus <*pl* -es> [ˌhɪp·ə·'pɑt̬·ə·məs] *n* Nilpferd *nt*

hippy ['hɪp·i] *n see* **hippie**

his [hɪz] **I.** *pron pers* seine(r, s); **some friends of ~** einige seiner Freunde **II.** *adj poss* (*of person*) sein(e)

Hispanic [hɪs·'pæn·ɪk] **I.** *adj* hispanisch **II.** *n* Hispanoamerikaner(in) *m(f)*

hiss [hɪs] **I.** *vt, vi* zischen; (*cat*) fauchen **II.** *n* <*pl* -es> Zischen *nt kein pl;* (*of cat*) Fauchen *nt kein pl*

historian [hɪ·'stɔr·i·ən] *n* Historiker(in) *m(f)*

historic [hɪ·'stɔr·ɪk] *adj* historisch

historical [hɪ·'stɔr·ɪk·əl] *adj* geschichtlich, historisch

history ['hɪs·tə·ri] *n* **1.** (*past events*) Geschichte *f* **2.** *fig* **to be ~** (*person*) vergessen sein, passé sein *fam* **3.** *usu sing* (*background*) Vorgeschichte *f;* **her family has a ~ of heart problems** Herzprobleme liegen bei ihr in der Familie

hit [hɪt] **I.** *n* **1.** (*blow*) Schlag *m* **2.** (*shot*) Treffer *m;* **to suffer a direct ~** direkt getroffen werden **3.** (*success, in baseball*) Hit *m* **4.** *fam* (*murder*) Mord *m* **5.** INET Besuch *m* einer Webseite, Hit *m* **II.** *vt* <-tt-, hit, hit> **1.** (*strike*) schlagen **2.** (*come in contact*) treffen *a. fig* **3.** (*button*) drücken; (*key*) drücken auf +*akk* **4.** (*crash into*) **to ~ sth gegen** etw akk stoßen **5.** SPORT treffen; (*basket*) erzielen **6.** *fam* (*arrive at*) **to ~ the headlines** in die Schlagzeilen kommen; **to ~ rock bottom** einen historischen Tiefstand erreichen **III.** *vi* **1.** (*strike*) **to ~ |at sb/sth|** |nach jdm/etw| schlagen; **to ~ hard** kräftig zuschlagen **2.** (*attack*) **to ~ at sb** jdn attackieren *a. fig*

hit back *vi* zurückschlagen; **to ~ back at sb** jdm Kontra geben

hit off *vt* **to ~ it off** |**with sb**| *fam* sich prächtig |mit jdm| verstehen

hit on *vt* **1.** (*think of*) kommen auf +*akk* **2.** *sl* (*make sexual advances*) **to ~ on sb** jdn anmachen

hit upon *vt* (*idea*) kommen auf +*akk*

hit-and-'miss *adj* zufällig; **a ~ affair** |rein| Glückssache

hit-and-'run *n* AUTO Fahrerflucht *f*

hitch [hɪtʃ] **I.** *n* <*pl* -es> (*difficulty*) Haken *m;* **to go off without a ~** reibungslos ablaufen **II.** *vt* **1.** (*fasten*) festmachen (**to** an +*dat*); (*trailer*) anhängen (**to** an +*akk*) **2.** *fam* (*hitchhike*) **to ~ a ride** |*or* **lift**| trampen, per Anhalter fahren **III.** *vi fam* trampen

hitch up *vt* **1.** festmachen (**to** an +*dat*); (*trailer*) anhängen (**to** an +*akk*); **to ~ a horse up to a cart** ein Pferd vor einen Wagen spannen **2.** (*pants*) hochziehen

hitcher ['hɪtʃ·ər] *n see* **hitchhiker**

'hitchhike *vi* per Anhalter fahren, trampen

'hitchhiker *n* Anhalter(in) *m(f)*, Tramper(in) *m(f)*

hi-'tech *adj see* **high-tech**

'hit man *n* Killer *m*

HIV [ˌeɪtʃ·aɪ·'vi] *n abbr of* **human immunodeficiency virus** HIV *nt*

hive [haɪv] *n* Bienenstock *m*

HMO [ˌeɪtʃ·em·'oʊ] *n abbr of* **health maintenance organization** *eine t*

der Regel vom Arbeitgeber getragene, preisgünstige Krankenversicherung mit begrenzter Ärzteauswahl

oagie ['houˑgi] *n* Riesensandwich *nt*

oard [hɔrd] **I.** *n* (*of money, food*) Vorrat *m* (**of** an +*dat*); (*treasure*) Schatz *m* **II.** *vt* horten; (*food a.*) hamstern

oarse [hɔrs] *adj* heiser

oax [houks] **I.** *n* (*deception*) Täuschung *f;* (*joke*) Streich *m;* (*false alarm*) blinder Alarm **II.** *adj* vorgetäuscht **III.** *vt* [he]reinlegen; **to ~ sb into believing** [*or* **thinking**] **sth** jdm etw weismachen

oaxer ['houks·ər] *n* jd, der falschen Alarm auslöst

obble ['hab·əl] *vi* hinken, humpeln

obby ['hab·i] *n* Hobby *nt*

obo <*pl* -s> ['hou·bou] *n* Penner(in) *m(f)*

ock [hak] *n fam* **1.** (*in debt*) **to be in ~** Schulden haben **2.** (*pawned*) **in ~** verpfändet

ockey ['hak·i] *n* [Eis]hockey *nt*

odgepodge ['hadʒ·padʒ] *n* Mischmasch *m* (**of** aus +*dat*)

oe [hou] **I.** *n* Hacke *f* **II.** *vt, vi* hacken

og [hɔg] *n* Schwein *nt*

oist [hɔɪst] **I.** *vt* hochheben; (*flag, sail*) hissen **II.** *n* Winde *f*

old [hould] **I.** *n* (*grasp*) Halt *m kein pl;* **to keep ~ of sth** etw festhalten; **to take ~** *fig* (*fire, epidemic*) übergreifen **2.** SPORT Griff *m* **3. to be on ~** auf Eis liegen *fig;* TELEC in der Warteschleife sein; **to put on ~** (*project, plans*) auf Eis legen **4.** NAUT, AVIAT Frachtraum *m* **II.** <held, held> *vt* **1.** (*grasp*) **to ~ sb/sth** [**tight** [*or* **tightly**]] jdn/etw [fest]halten; **to ~ sth in place** etw halten **2.** (*keep*) halten; **to ~ sb's attention** [*or* **interest**] jdn fesseln; **to ~ its value** seinen Wert behalten **3.** (*delay, stop*) zurückhalten; PHOT **OK, ~ it!** gut, bleib so!; TELEC **to ~ the line** am Apparat bleiben **4.** (*contain*) fassen; COMPUT speichern

hold against *vt* **to ~ sth against sb** jdm etw vorwerfen

hold back I. *vt* (*stop*) aufhalten; (*impede development*) hindern; (*information*) geheim halten **II.** *vi* (*refrain*) **to ~ back from doing sth** etw unterlassen

hold down *vt* niederhalten; (*prices*) niedrig halten

hold forth *vi* **to ~ forth** [**about sth**] sich [über etw *akk*] auslassen

hold in *vt* (*emotions*) zurückhalten; (*stomach*) einziehen

hold off I. *vt* **1.** MIL (*enemy*) abwehren **2.** (*postpone*) verschieben **II.** *vi* warten

hold on *vi* **1.** (*affix, attach*) **to be held on by** [*or* **with**] **sth** mit etw *dat* befestigt sein **2.** (*manage to keep going*) durchhalten **3.** (*wait*) **~ on!** Moment bitte!

hold onto *vt* **1.** (*grasp*) festhalten **2.** (*keep*) behalten

hold out I. *vt* ausstrecken **II.** *vi* (*manage to resist*) durchhalten

hold over *vt* **1.** (*defer*) aufschieben **2.** (*extend*) verlängern

hold to *vt* **can I ~ you to that?** bleibst du bei deinem Wort?

hold together *vt, vi* zusammenhalten

hold up I. *vt* **1.** (*raise*) hochhalten; (*hand*) heben **2.** (*support*) stützen **3.** (*delay*) aufhalten **II.** *vi* **1.** (*endure*) durchhalten, aushalten **2.** (*remain convincing*) standhalten

holder ['houl·dər] *n* **1.** (*device*) Halter *m* **2.** (*person*) Besitzer(in) *m(f)*

holding ['houl·dɪŋ] *n* **1.** (*land*) Pachtbesitz *m* **2.** FIN Beteiligung *f*

holdup ['houl·dʌp] *n* **1.** (*crime*) Raubüberfall *m* **2.** (*delay*) Verzögerung *f*

hole [houl] **I.** *n* **1.** (*gap*) Loch *nt a. fig;* (*of fox, rabbit*) Bau *m* **2.** *fig* (*fault*) **to pick ~s** [**in sth**] [etw] kritisieren **3.** *fig fam* (*difficulty*) **to get sb out of a ~** jdm aus der Patsche helfen **II.** *vt* (*in golf*) einlochen

hole up *vi fam* sich verkriechen

holiday ['hal·ɪ·deɪ] *n* Feiertag *m* ▶ **Happy ~s!** Frohe Weihnachten!

Holland ['hal·ənd] *n* Holland *nt*

holler ['hal·ər] *vt, vi fam* brüllen

hollow ['hal·ou] **I.** *adj* **1.** (*empty, sunken*) hohl **2.** *fig* wertlos; (*victory*) schal **II.** *n* **1.** (*hole*) Senke *f* **2.** (*valley*) Tal *nt* **III.** *vt* **to ~** [**out**] aushöhlen

holly ['hal·i] *n* Stechpalme *f*

holocaust ['hal·ə·kɔst] *n* **1.** (*destruction*) Inferno *nt* **2.** (*genocide*) Massenver-

nichtung f; **the H~** der Holocaust

hologram ['hal·ə·græm] n Hologramm nt

holster ['hoʊl·stər] n [Pistolen]halfter nt o f

holy ['hoʊ·li] adj heilig

Holy Com'munion n (service) heilige Kommunion

Holy 'Spirit n **the ~** der Heilige Geist

'holy water n Weihwasser nt

homage ['ham·ɪdʒ] n Huldigung f

home [hoʊm] **I.** n **1.** (abode) Zuhause nt; **a ~ away from ~** ein zweites Zuhause; **to make oneself at ~** es sich dat gemütlich machen; **at ~** zu Hause, zuhause österr, schweiz **2.** (house) Haus nt; (apartment) Wohnung f **3.** (institution) Heim nt **4.** (place of origin) Heimat f ▶ **to feel at ~ with sb** sich bei jdm wohl fühlen **II.** adv **1.** (at one's abode) zu Hause, zuhause österr, schweiz, daheim bes südd, österr, schweiz; (to one's abode) nach Hause, nachhause österr, schweiz **2.** (to sb's understanding) **to bring sth ~** [to sb] [jdm] etw klarmachen **III.** vi **to ~ in on sth** genau auf etw akk zusteuern; fig [sich dat] etw herausgreifen

'home address n Heimatadresse f

'home advantage n Heimvorteil m

home-'baked adj selbst gebacken

home 'banking n Homebanking nt

'homecoming n **1.** (return) Heimkehr f kein pl **2.** (reunion) Ehemaligentreffen nt; **~ queen** Schönheitskönigin beim Ehemaligentreffen

home 'cooking n Hausmannskost f

home eco'nomics n + sing vb Hauswirtschaft[slehre] f

'home game n Heimspiel nt

home-'grown adj aus eigenem Anbau

home 'help n Haushaltshilfe f

'homeland n (origin) Heimat f, Heimatland nt; **~ security** innere Sicherheit, Heimatschutz m

homeless ['hoʊm·lɪs] **I.** adj heimatlos; **to be ~** obdachlos sein **II.** n **the ~** pl die Obdachlosen pl

'home loan n Hypothek f

homely ['hoʊm·li] adj **1.** pej (ugly) unansehnlich **2.** (plain) schlicht aber gemütlich

home'made adj hausgemacht; (cake)

selbst gebacken

'homemaker n Hausmann, -frau m, f

homeopath ['hoʊ·mi·oʊ·pæθ] n Homöopath(in) m(f)

homeopathy [ˌhoʊ·mi·'ap·ə·θi] n Homöopathie f

'homeowner n Hausbesitzer(in) m(f)

'home page n COMPUT Homepage f

home 'plate n (in baseball) Homeplate Schlagmal nt

home 'run n (in baseball) Punkt bri gender Lauf um alle vier Male bei Baseball

home'schooling n Unterricht m z Hause

'homesick adj **to be** [or **feel**] **~** Heim weh haben

'homesickness n Heimweh nt

homestead ['hoʊm·sted] n Eigen heim nt

home'stretch n Zielgerade f a. fig

'home team n Heimmannschaft f

'home'town n Heimatstadt f

homeward ['hoʊm·wərd] adv heimwärts nach Hause

homewards ['hoʊm·wərdz] adv heim wärts

'homework n Hausaufgaben pl a. fig

homey ['hoʊ·mi] adj (cozy) heimelig

homicidal [ˌham·ɪ·'saɪ·dəl] adj gemein gefährlich

homicide ['ham·ɪ·saɪd] n LAW **1.** (mu dering) Mord m **2.** (death) Mordfall n ~ **squad** Mordkommission f

homogenize [hə·'madʒ·ə·naɪz] vt h mogenisieren

homosexual [ˌhoʊ·mə·'sek·ʃu·əl] for **I.** adj homosexuell **II.** n Homosexuelle(r) f(m)

homosexuality [ˌhoʊ·mə·sek·ʃu·'æl·ə·t n Homosexualität f

Honduras [han·'dʊr·əs] n Honduras nt

honest ['an·ɪst] adj **1.** (truthful) ehrlic **2.** (trusty) redlich

honestly ['an·ɪst·li] **I.** adv ehrlic **II.** interj **1.** (promising) [ganz] ehrlic **2.** (disapproving) also ehrlich!

honesty ['an·ɪ·sti] n Ehrlichkeit f

honey ['hʌn·i] n **1.** (from bees) Honig **2.** fam (sweet person) Schatz m

'honeybee n [Honig]biene f

honeycomb n (*wax*) Bienenwabe f; (*food*) Honigwabe f

honeydew 'melon n Honigmelone f

honeymoon n 1. (*after marriage*) Flitterwochen pl 2. *usu sing fig* Schonfrist f

honk [haŋk] I. n 1. (*of goose*) Schrei m 2. (*of horn*) Hupen nt II. vi 1. (*goose*) schreien 2. (*horn*) hupen III. vt to ~ one's horn auf die Hupe drücken

honor ['an·ər] I. n 1. (*of goose*) Ehre f 2. (*award*) Auszeichnung f II. vt ehren

honorable ['an·ər·əb·əl] adj ehrenhaft; (*person*) ehrenwert

honorary ['an·ə·rer·i] adj ehrenamtlich

honor roll n SCH, UNIV Ehrenrolle f

honors degree n UNIV akademischer Grad mit Prüfung im Spezialfach

hood[1] [hʊd] n 1. (*head covering*) Kapuze f 2. AUTO [Motor]haube f

hood[2] [hʊd] n (*gangster*) Kriminelle(r) f(m)

hood[3] [hʊd] n sl Nachbarschaft f

hoodlum ['hʊd·ləm] n (*gangster*) Kriminelle(r) f(m)

hoodwink ['hʊd·wɪŋk] vt hereinlegen

hoof [hʊf] n <pl hooves> Huf m

hook [hʊk] I. n Haken m; to leave the phone off the ~ den Telefonhörer nicht auflegen ▶ to **be** off the ~ aus dem Schneider sein; to **let** sb off the ~ jdn herauspauken II. vt 1. (*fasten*) festhaken (**to** an +dat) 2. (*grab with hook*) she ~ed the shoe out of the water sie angelte den Schuh aus dem Wasser 3. (*fish*) an die Angel bekommen

hook up I. vt 1. (*connect*) anschließen (**to** an +akk) 2. (*fasten*) zumachen 3. (*hang*) aufhängen II. vi 1. (*connect*) to ~ **up** [to sth] sich [an etw akk] anschließen 2. sl (*get together*) to ~ **up** [with sb] sich [mit jdm] treffen

hooked [hʊkt] adj 1. (*curved*) hakenförmig; ~ **nose** Hakennase f 2. (*addicted*) abhängig 3. (*interested*) to **be** ~ total begeistert sein

hooker ['hʊk·ər] n fam Nutte f sl

hooky ['hʊk·i] n fam to **play** ~ die Schule schwänzen

hooligan ['hu·lɪ·gən] n Hooligan m

hoop [hup] n Reifen m

hooray [hə·'reɪ] interj see **hurray**

hoot [hut] I. n (*owl call*) Schrei m II. vi (*owl*) schreien

hop[1] [hap] I. vi <-pp-> 1. hüpfen 2. SPORT springen II. vt <-pp-> 1. (*jump*) springen über +akk 2. fam (*board*) steigen in +akk III. n 1. (*jump*) Hüpfer m 2. fam (*flight stage*) Flugabschnitt m

◆ hop in, hop on vt, vi fam einsteigen

◆ hop off, hop out vt, vi fam aussteigen

hop[2] [hap] n BOT Hopfen m

hope [hoʊp] I. n Hoffnung f; to **give up** ~ die Hoffnung aufgeben; **in the** ~ **of doing sth** in der Hoffnung, etw zu tun II. vi hoffen (**for** auf +akk)

hopeful ['hoʊp·fəl] adj zuversichtlich; to **be** ~ **of sth** auf etw akk hoffen

hopefully ['hoʊp·fəl·i] adv 1. (*in hope*) hoffnungsvoll 2. (*it is hoped*) hoffentlich

hopeless ['hoʊp·lɪs] adj hoffnungslos; (*situation*) aussichtslos; to **be** ~ fam (*incompetent*) ein hoffnungsloser Fall sein

hopping ['hap·ɪŋ] adj fam nur hundertachtzig; to **be** ~ **mad at sb** stinksauer auf jdn sein

hopscotch ['hap·skatʃ] n Himmel und Hölle nt

horde [hɔrd] n Horde f

horizon [hə·'raɪ·zən] n Horizont m

horizontal [ˌhɔr·ɪ·'zan·təl] adj horizontal, waag[e]recht

hormone ['hɔr·moʊn] n Hormon nt

horn [hɔrn] n 1. ZOOL Horn nt 2. MUS Horn nt 3. AUTO Hupe f

hornet ['hɔr·nɪt] n Hornisse f

horny ['hɔr·ni] adj 1. (*hard*) hornartig 2. fam (*sexually excited*) geil

horoscope ['hɔr·ə·skoʊp] n Horoskop nt

horrendous [hɔ·'ren·dəs] adj schrecklich; (*conditions*) entsetzlich; (*prices*) horrend

horrible ['hɔr·ə·bəl] adj schrecklich; (*weather*) scheußlich; (*unkind*) gemein

horrific [hɔ·'rɪf·ɪk] adj 1. (*shocking*) entsetzlich, grausig 2. (*extreme: prices*) horrend

horrify <-ie-> ['hɔr·ə·faɪ] vt entsetzen

horror ['hɔr·ər] n Entsetzen nt

H

horse [hɔrs] n Pferd nt; ~ **and buggy** Pferdewagen m ► **to hear sth [straight] from the ~'s** <u>mouth</u> etw aus erster Hand haben

'horseback n **on** ~ zu Pferd

'horse chestnut n Rosskastanie f

'horseman n Reiter m

'horsepower <pl -> n Pferdestärke f

'horse race n Pferderennen nt

'horse racing n Pferderennsport m

'horseradish n Meerrettich m

'horseshoe n Hufeisen nt

'horse trailer, 'horse van n Pferdetransporter m

'horsewoman n Reiterin f

hors(e)y ['hɔr·si] adj fam pferdenärrisch

horticulture ['hɔr·tɪ·ˌkʌl·tʃər] n Gartenbau m

hose [houz] n Schlauch m

◆ **hose down, hose off** vt **to** ~ **sth** ⇄ **down** [or **off**] etw [mit einem Schlauch] abspritzen

hospice ['has·pɪs] n Hospiz nt

hospitable ['has·pɪ·tə·bəl] adj gastfreundlich

hospital ['has·pɪ·təl] n Krankenhaus nt, Spital nt schweiz

hospitality [ˌhas·pɪ·'tæl·ɪ·ti] n **1.** (welcome) Gastfreundschaft f **2.** (food) Bewirtung f

hospitalize ['has·pɪ·tə·laɪz] vt **to be** ~**d** ins Krankenhaus eingewiesen werden

host [houst] **I.** n **1.** (party giver) Gastgeber(in) m(f) **2.** TV Showmaster(in) m(f) **II.** adj ~ **country** Gastland nt **III.** vt **1.** (stage) ausrichten **2.** TV präsentieren

hostage ['has·tɪdʒ] n Geisel f

hostel ['has·təl] n Wohnheim nt; [youth] ~ Jugendherberge f

hostess <pl -es> ['hou·stɪs] n **1.** (at home, on TV) Gastgeberin f **2.** (at restaurant) Wirtin f **3.** (at exhibition) Hostess f

hostile ['has·təl] adj **1.** (unfriendly) feindselig **2.** (difficult) hart, widrig; (climate) rau **3.** ECON, MIL feindlich

hostility [ha·'stɪl·ɪ·ti] n **1.** Feindseligkeit f **2.** MIL **hostilities** pl Feindseligkeiten pl

hot [hat] adj <-tt-> **1.** (temperature) heiß; **she was** ~ ihr war heiß **2.** (food)

scharf **3.** fam (dangerous: situation) brenzlig; (stolen items) heiß **4.** sl (sexy) echt geil ► **to be all** ~ **and** <u>bothered</u> ganz aufgeregt sein

hot·'air balloon n Heißluftballon m

hot·'blooded adj (easy to anger) hitzköpfig; (passionate) heißblütig

'hot dog n (sausage) Wiener Würstchen nt; (in a bun) Hotdog m

hotel [hou·'tel] n Hotel nt

hotel 'industry n Hotelgewerbe nt

'hotfoot vt fam **to** ~ **it home** schnell nach Hause rennen

'hothead n Hitzkopf m

'hothouse n Treibhaus nt

'hotline n Hotline f; POL heißer Draht

hotly ['hat·li] adv heftig; ~ **contested** heiß umkämpft

'hotplate n (for cooking) Kochplatte f, (food warmer) Warmhalteplatte f

hot po'tato n POL heißes Eisen

'hotshot n fam Kanone f

'hot spot n **1.** (popular place) heißer Schuppen **2.** (area of conflict) Krisenherd m

hot 'stuff n **1.** fam (skillful) **to be** ~ eine Ass sein **2.** sl (sexy woman) heiße Braut, Schnecke f sl; (sexy man) heißer Typ, Schmacko m sl

hot·'tempered adj heißblütig

'hot tub n Jacuzzi® m

hot·'water bottle n Wärmflasche f

'hot·wire vt fam (car) kurzschließen

hound [haund] **I.** n [Jagd]hund m **II.** vt jagen

hour [aur] n Stunde f; **50 miles an** [or **per**] ~ 50 Meilen pro Stunde; ~**s of business** Öffnungszeiten pl; **to be paid by the** ~ pro Stunde bezahlt werden; **to work long** ~**s** lange arbeiten; **for** ~**s** stundenlang

'hour hand n Stundenzeiger m

hourly ['aur·li] adj, adv stündlich; ~ **rate** Stundensatz m

house I. n [haus] Haus nt; **the White** **H**~ das Weiße Haus; **in** ~ im Hause; **on the** ~ auf Kosten des Hauses **II.** vt [hauz] (person) unterbringen; (criminal) Unterschlupf gewähren +dat; (thing) beherbergen

'house arrest n Hausarrest m

ousebreaker *n* Einbrecher(in) *m(f)*

ousebroken *adj* stubenrein

ouse call *n* Hausbesuch *m*

ousefly *n* Stubenfliege *f*

ousehold *n* Haushalt *m*

ouseholder *n* Hauseigentümer(in) *m(f)*

ouse-hunt *vi* nach einem Haus suchen

ousehusband *n* Hausmann *m*

ousekeeper *n* Haushälter(in) *m(f)*

ousekeeping *n* Haushalten *nt*

ouse of Repre'sentatives *n* **the** ~ das Repräsentantenhaus

ouseplant *n* Zimmerpflanze *f*

ouse-to-'house *adj, adv* von Haus zu Haus

ousewarming, 'housewarming party *n* Einweihungsparty *f*

ousewife *n* Hausfrau *f*

ousework *n* Hausarbeit *f*

ousing ['haʊ·zɪŋ] *n* **1.** (*living quarters*) Wohnungen *pl* **2.** (*casing*) Gehäuse *nt*

ousing development *n* Wohnsiedlung *f*

ousing market *n* Wohnungsmarkt *m*

ousing project *n* Sozialwohnungen *pl*

OV [ˌeɪtʃ·oʊ·'vi] *n* AUTO *abbr of* **high occupancy vehicle** Fahrzeug *nt* mit mindestens zwei Insassen; **~ lane** Fahrspur *f* für Fahrzeuge mit mindestens zwei Insassen

over ['hʌv·ər] *vi* schweben; (*hawk a.*) stehen; *fig* herumlungern

overcraft <*pl* > *n* Luftkissenboot *nt*

ow [haʊ] *adv* wie; **~ are you?** wie geht es Ihnen?; **~ do you do?** (*meeting sb*) Guten Tag/Abend!; **~ come?** wie das?; **~ do you know that?** woher weißt du das?; **and ~!** und ob [*or* wie]!; **~ far/many** wie weit/viele; **~ much** wie viel

owdy ['haʊ·di] *interj fam* Tag *fam*

owever [haʊ·'ev·ər] **I.** *adv* **1.** (*showing contradiction*) jedoch; **I love ice cream — ~, I am trying to lose weight, so ...** ich liebe Eis – aber ich versuche gerade abzunehmen, daher ... **2.** + *adj* (*to whatever degree*) egal wie **3.** (*by what means*) wie um alles ... **II.** *conj* **1.** (*in any way*) wie auch immer; **~ you do it, ...** wie auch immer du es machst, ... **2.** (*nevertheless*) jedoch

howl [haʊl] **I.** *n* (*of animal, wind*) Heulen *nt kein pl* **II.** *vi* **1.** (*animal, wind*) heulen; (*person*) schreien **2.** *fam* (*laugh*) brüllen

howler ['haʊ·lər] *n* (*mistake*) Schnitzer *m*

hp [ˌeɪtʃ·'pi] *n abbr of* **horsepower** PS

HQ [ˌeɪtʃ·'kju] *n abbr of* **headquarters**

HR *n abbr of* **human resources** Personalabteilung *f*

hr. *n abbr of* **hour** Std.

ht. *n abbr of* **height**

hub [hʌb] *n* **1.** TECH Nabe *f* **2.** *fig* (*center*) Zentrum *nt*

hubbub ['hʌb·ʌb] *n* (*noise*) Lärm *m*; (*commotion*) Tumult *m*

hubby ['hʌb·i] *n hum fam* (*Ehe*)mann *m*

hubcap ['hʌb·kæp] *n* Radkappe *f*

huckleberry ['hʌk·əl·ber·i] *n* amerikanische Heidelbeere

huddle ['hʌd·əl] *n* **1.** (*close group*) [wirrer] Haufen; (*of people*) Gruppe *f* **2.** (*in football*) **to make** [*or* **form**] **a ~** die Köpfe zusammenstecken

hue [hju] *n* **1.** Farbe *f*; (*shade*) Schattierung *f* ▶ **and cry** Gezeter *nt*

huff [hʌf] **I.** *vi* **to ~ and puff** schnaufen und keuchen **II.** *n fam* **to be in a ~** eingeschnappt sein

huffy ['hʌf·i] *adj* **1.** (*easily offended*) empfindlich **2.** (*in a huff*) beleidigt

hug [hʌg] **I.** *vt* <-gg-> **1.** umarmen **2.** *fig* **the dress ~ged her body** das Kleid lag eng an ihrem Körper an **II.** *vi* <-gg-> sich umarmen **III.** *n* Umarmung *f*

huge [hjudʒ] *adj* riesig

hugely ['hjudʒ·li] *adv* ungeheuer

hulking ['hʌl·kɪŋ] *adj* massig

hull [hʌl] *n* [Schiffs]rumpf *m*

hum [hʌm] **I.** *vi* <-mm-> **1.** brausen; (*engine*) brummen; (*small machine*) surren; (*bee*) summen **2.** (*sing*) summen **II.** *vt* <-mm-> summen **III.** *n* Brausen *nt*; (*of machinery*) Brummen *nt*; (*of insects*) Summen *nt*

human ['hju·mən] **I.** *n* Mensch *m* **II.** *adj* menschlich

humane [hju·'meɪn] *adj* human

humanitarian [hju·ˌmæn·ɪ·'ter·i·ən] *adj* humanitär

humanities [hju·'mæn·ɪ·tiz] *npl* **the ~** die

Geisteswissenschaften pl

humanity [hju·'mæn·ɪ·t̬i] n **1.** (people) die Menschheit **2.** (quality) Menschlichkeit f

humanly ['hju·mən·li] adv menschlich; **to do everything ~ possible** alles Menschenmögliche tun

human 'nature n die menschliche Natur

human 'race n **the ~** die menschliche Rasse

human 'resources npl + sing vb (department) Personalabteilung f

human 'rights npl Menschenrechte pl

humble ['hʌm·bəl] adj <-r, -st> **1.** (modest) bescheiden **2.** (respectful) demütig

humdrum ['hʌm·drʌm] adj langweilig, fad[e]

humid ['hju·mɪd] adj feucht

humidifier [hju·'mɪd·ɪ·faɪ·ər] n Luftbefeuchter m

humidity [hju·'mɪd·ɪ·t̬i] n [Luft]feuchtigkeit f

humiliate [hju·'mɪl·i·eɪt] vt **1.** (humble) demütigen **2.** (embarrass) blamieren

humiliation [hju·,mɪl·i·'eɪ·ʃən] n Demütigung f

humor ['hju·mər] I. n Humor m II. vt **to ~ sb** (indulge) jdm seinen Willen lassen; (keep happy) jdn bei Laune halten fam

humorless ['hju·mər·lɪs] adj humorlos

humorous ['hju·mər·əs] adj (person) humorvoll; (book, situation) lustig; (idea) witzig

hump [hʌmp] I. n **1.** (hill) kleiner Hügel **2.** (on camel) Höcker m; (on a person) Buckel m II. vt vulg, sl (have sex with) bumsen

'humpback n **1.** (person) Buck[e]lige(r) f(m) **2.** (back) Buckel m **3.** (whale) Buckelwal m

'humpbacked adj (person) bucklig; (bridge) gewölbt

hunch [hʌntʃ] I. n <pl -es> (feeling) Gefühl nt; **to have a ~ that ...** das [leise] Gefühl haben, dass ... II. vi sich krümmen III. vt (shoulders) hochziehen; **to ~ one's back** einen Buckel machen

'hunchback n Bucklige(r) f(m)

hundred ['hʌn·drəd] I. n **1.** (number) Hundert f; **~s of cars** Hunderte von

Autos; **eight ~** achthundert **2.** th **eighteen ~s** das neunzehnte Jahrhundert II. adj hundert; **a ~ percen** hundertprozentig; **a ~ and five** [ein hundert[und]fünf

hundredth ['hʌn·drədθ] I. n **1.** (in line Hundertste(r) f(m) **2.** (fraction) Hun dertstel nt II. adj **1.** (in series) hur dertste(r, s) **2.** (in fraction) hundertste

hung [hʌŋ] pt, pp of **hang** II, III

Hungarian [hʌŋ·'ger·i·ən] I. n **1.** (pe son) Ungar(in) m(f) **2.** (language) Ur garisch nt II. adj ungarisch

Hungary ['hʌŋ·gə·ri] n Ungarn nt

hunger ['hʌŋ·gər] I. n Hunger m a. f̲ II. vi **to ~ after** [or for] sth nach etv dat hungern

hung 'over adj (from drinking) verka tert

hungry ['hʌŋ·gri] adj hungrig a. fig; **to b ~** Hunger haben

hunk [hʌŋk] n **1.** (piece) Stück nt **2.** fa (man) **a ~ of a man** ein Bild nt vo einem Mann

hunt [hʌnt] I. n **1.** (chase) Jagd **2.** (search) Suche f II. vt **1.** (chase kill) jagen **2.** (search for) Jagd mache auf +akk; **the police are ~ing the te rorists** die Polizei fahndet nach den Te roristen III. vi **1.** (chase to kill) jage **2.** (search) suchen; **to ~ through st** etw durchsuchen

hunter ['hʌn·tər] n Jäger(in) m(f)

hunting ['hʌn·tɪŋ] n Jagen nt, Jagd f

'hunting ground n Jagdrevier nt

'hunting license n Jagdschein m

'hunting season n Jagdzeit f

'huntsman n Jäger m

hurdle ['hɜr·dəl] I. n Hürde f a. fig; spo ~s pl (for people) Hürdenlauf m II. überspringen

hurdler ['hɜrd·lər] n Hürdenläufer(in) m(

hurl [hɜrl] vt schleudern; **to ~ abuse sb** jdm Beschimpfungen an den Ko̲ werfen

hurly-burly ['hɜr·li·bɜr·li] n Rummel m

hurrah [hə·'ra], **hurray** [hə·'reɪ] inte hurra

hurricane ['hɜr·ɪ·keɪn] n Orkan m; (trop cal) Hurrikan m

hurried ['hɜr·id] adj hastig; (departur̲

überstürzt

hurry ['hʌr·ɪ] I. n Eile f; **to leave in a ~** hastig aufbrechen; **to need sth in a ~** etw sofort brauchen II. vi <-ie-> sich beeilen III. vt <-ie-> **to ~ sb** jdn hetzen

hurry along I. vi sich beeilen II. vt (person) [zur Eile] antreiben; (process) beschleunigen

hurry away, hurry off I. vi schnell weggehen II. vt schnell wegbringen

hurry out I. vi hinauseilen II. vt schnell hinausbringen

hurry up I. vi sich beeilen; **~ up!** beeil dich! II. vt (person) zur Eile antreiben; (process) beschleunigen

hurt [hɜrt] I. vi <hurt, hurt> 1. (be painful) wehtun 2. (do harm) schaden a. fig II. vt <hurt, hurt> 1. a. fig (cause pain) **to ~ sb** jdm wehtun; (injure) jdn verletzen; **to ~ oneself** sich verletzen; **to ~ one's leg** sich dat am Bein wehtun 2. (harm) **to ~ sb/sth** jdm/etw schaden III. adj 1. (in pain) verletzt 2. fig (feelings) verletzt; (look, voice) gekränkt IV. n (pain) Schmerz m; (injury) Verletzung f

hurtful ['hɜrt·fəl] adj verletzend

husband ['hʌz·bənd] n Ehemann m

hush [hʌʃ] I. n Stille f II. interj **~!** pst! III. vt zum Schweigen bringen; (soothe) beruhigen

hush up vt vertuschen

'hush money n fam Schweigegeld nt

husk [hʌsk] I. n Schale f II. vt (corn) schälen

husky[1] ['hʌs·ki] adj 1. (voice) rau 2. (person) kräftig [gebaut]

husky[2] ['hʌs·ki] n (dog) Husky m, Schlittenhund m

hustle ['hʌs·əl] I. vt 1. (hurry) **to ~ sb somewhere** jdn irgendwohin treiben 2. (coerce) **to ~ sb into doing sth** jdn [be]drängen, etw zu tun II. vi 1. (work quickly) schnell erledigen 2. SPORT (play aggressively) stoßen fam III. n Gedränge nt; **~ and bustle** geschäftiges Treiben

hustler ['hʌs·lər] n 1. (swindler) Betrüger(in) m(f) 2. (prostitute) Strichjunge m, Strichmädchen nt

hut [hʌt] n Hütte f

hutch [hʌtʃ] n Käfig m; (for rabbits) Stall m

hybrid ['haɪ·brɪd] n BOT, ZOOL Kreuzung f

hydrant ['haɪ·drənt] n Hydrant m

hydraulic [haɪ·'drɑ·lɪk] adj hydraulisch

hydraulics [haɪ·'drɑ·lɪks] n + sing vb Hydraulik f

hydrocarbon [,haɪ·drə·'kar·bən] n Kohlenwasserstoff m

hydroelectric [,haɪ·droʊ·ɪ·'lek·trɪk] adj hydroelektrisch

hydrogen ['haɪ·drə·dʒən] n Wasserstoff m; **~ bomb** Wasserstoffbombe f

hyena [haɪ·'i·nə] n Hyäne f

hygiene ['haɪ·dʒin] n Hygiene f; **personal ~** Körperpflege f

hygienic [,haɪ·dʒi·'en·ɪk] adj hygienisch

hymn [hɪm] n REL Kirchenlied nt

hymnal ['hɪm·nəl], **hymnbook** ['hɪm·bʌk] n Gesangbuch nt

hype [haɪp] I. n Reklameaufwand m; **media ~** Medienrummel m II. vt (film) [in den Medien] hochjubeln

hyper ['haɪ·pər] adj fam aufgedreht, hyper sl

hyperactive [,haɪ·pər·'æk·tɪv] adj hyperaktiv

hyper'sensitive adj überempfindlich; **to be ~ to sth** auf etw akk überempfindlich reagieren

hyphen ['haɪ·fən] n (between words) Bindestrich m; (at end of line) Trennstrich m

hyphenate ['haɪ·fə·neɪt] vt mit Bindestrich schreiben

hypnosis [hɪp·'noʊ·sɪs] n Hypnose f

hypnotic [hɪp·'nɑt·ɪk] adj hypnotisierend

hypnotist ['hɪp·nə·tɪst] n Hypnotiseur(in) m(f)

hypnotize ['hɪp·nə·taɪz] vt hypnotisieren a. fig

hypochondriac [,haɪ·pə·'kan·drɪ·æk] n Hypochonder(in) m(f)

hypocrisy [hɪ·'pak·rə·si] n Heuchelei f

hypocrite ['hɪp·ə·krɪt] n Heuchler(in) m(f)

hypocritical [,hɪp·ə·'krɪt·ɪ·kəl] adj heuchlerisch

hypodermic [,haɪ·pə·'dɜr·mɪk] adj subku-

H

tan; ~ **syringe** Injektionsspritze f

hypothermia [ˌhaɪ·poʊ·ˈθɜr·mi·ə] n Unterkühlung f

hypothesis <pl -ses> [haɪ·ˈpaθ·ɪ·sɪs] n Hypothese f

hypothetical [ˌhaɪ·pə·ˈθeṭ·ɪ·kəl] adj hypothetisch

hysteria [hɪ·ˈster·i·ə] n Hysterie f

hysterical [hɪ·ˈster·ɪk·əl] adj **1.** (emotional) hysterisch **2.** fam (hilarious) ausgelassen heiter

I

I¹ <pl -'s>, **i** <pl -'s> [aɪ] n (letter) I nt, i nt; ~ **as in India** I wie Ida

I² [aɪ] pron personal ich; ~ **for one ...** ich meinerseits ...

IA, Ia. abbr of **Iowa**

ibex <pl -es> [ˈaɪ·beks] n Steinbock m

ice [aɪs] **I.** n Eis nt ▶ to **break the ~** das Eis zum Schmelzen bringen; to **put sth on ~** etw auf Eis legen **II.** vt glasieren

◆**ice over** vi (road) vereisen; (lake) zufrieren

'**Ice Age** n Eiszeit f

'**iceberg** n Eisberg m

'**icebox** n Kühlschrank m

'**icebreaker** n Eisbrecher m

'**ice cap** n Eiskappe f (an den Polen)

ice-'cold n eiskalt

'**ice cream** n Eiscreme f

'**ice-cream maker** n Eismaschine f

'**ice cube** n Eiswürfel m

iced [aɪst] adj **1.** (frozen) eisgekühlt **2.** (cake) glasiert

'**ice floe** n Eisscholle f

'**ice hockey** n Eishockey nt

Iceland [ˈaɪs·lənd] n Island nt

Icelander [ˈaɪs·lən·dər] n Isländer(in) m(f)

Icelandic [aɪs·ˈlæn·dɪk] **I.** n Isländisch nt **II.** adj isländisch

'**ice pack** n **1.** (for swelling) Eisbeutel m **2.** (sea ice) Packeis nt

'**ice pick** n Eispickel m

'**ice rink** n Schlittschuhbahn f

'**ice skate** n Schlittschuh m

'**ice-skate** vi Schlittschuh laufen, eislaufen

'**ice skating** n Schlittschuhlaufen nt

icicle [ˈaɪ·sɪ·kəl] n Eiszapfen m

icing [ˈaɪ·sɪŋ] n Zuckerguss m ▶ to **be the ~ on the cake** pej (unnecessary) [bloß] schmückendes Beiwerk sein; approv (extra) das Sahnehäubchen sein fam

icon [ˈaɪ·kan] n **1.** (painting) Ikone f **2.** COMPUT Symbol nt, Icon nt

icy [ˈaɪ·si] adj eisig [kalt]; (road) vereist

ID¹ [ˌaɪ·ˈdi] n abbr of **identification** Ausweis m

ID², Id. n abbr of **Idaho**

I'd [aɪd] = I would, I had see would, have I, II

Idaho [ˈaɪ·də·hoʊ] n Idaho nt

I'D card n [Personal]ausweis m

idea [aɪ·ˈdi·ə] n **1.** (notion) Vorstellung f, Idee f; **what gave you that ~?** wie kommst du denn auf die Idee?; **don't get any ~s!** fam komm nicht auf dumme Gedanken!; **don't give him any ~s!** fam bring ihn nicht auf dumme Gedanken! **2.** (knowledge) Begriff m; to **have an ~ of sth** eine Vorstellung von etw dat haben; to **have no ~** keine Ahnung haben

ideal [aɪ·ˈdi·əl] **I.** adj ideal **II.** n Ideal nt

idealism [aɪ·ˈdi·ə·lɪz·əm] n Idealismus m

idealist [aɪ·ˈdi·ə·lɪst] n Idealist(in) m(f)

idealistic [ˌaɪ·di·ə·ˈlɪs·tɪk] adj idealistisch

idealize [aɪ·ˈdi·ə·laɪz] vt idealisieren

ideally [aɪ·ˈdi·li] adv ideal

identical [aɪ·ˈden·tɪ·kəl] adj identisch (to mit +dat)

identifiable [aɪ·ˌden·tə·ˈfaɪ·ə·bəl] adj erkennbar; (substance) nachweisbar

identification [aɪ·ˌden·tə·fɪ·ˈkeɪ·ʃən] n **1.** (of person, criminal) Identifizierung f **2.** (sympathy) Identifikation f (with mit +dat)

identifi'cation papers npl Ausweispapiere pl

identify <-ie-> [aɪ·ˈden·tə·faɪ] **I.** vt **1.** (recognize) identifizieren **2.** (name) to **~ sb** jds Identität f feststellen **II.** vi to **~ with sb** sich mit jdm identifizieren

identity [aɪ·ˈden·tə·ti] n Identität f

i'dentity card n [Personal]ausweis m

ideological [ˌaɪ·di·ə·ˈladʒ·ɪ·kəl] *adj* ideologisch

ideology [ˌaɪ·di·ˈal·ə·dʒi] *n* Ideologie *f*

idiom [ˈɪd·i·əm] *n* LING **1.** (*phrase*) [idiomatische] Redewendung **2.** (*language*) Idiom *nt*

idiomatic [ˌɪd·i·ə·ˈmæt̬·ɪk] *adj* idiomatisch

idiot [ˈɪd·i·ət] *n* Idiot(in) *m(f)*

idiotic [ˌɪd·i·ˈat̬·ɪk] *adj* idiotisch

idle [ˈaɪ·dəl] *adj* **1.** (*lazy*) faul **2.** (*inactive*) untätig; (*machine*) außer Betrieb *präd* **3.** (*chatter*) hohl; (*threats*) leer

idol [ˈaɪ·dəl] *n* **1.** (*model*) Idol *n*. REL Götzenbild *nt*

idolize [ˈaɪ·də·laɪz] *vt* vergöttern

idyllic [aɪ·ˈdɪl·ɪk] *adj* idyllisch

i.e. [ˌaɪ·ˈi] *n abbr of* **id est** d.h.

if [ɪf] **I.** *conj* **1.** (*in case*) wenn, falls; **even ~ ...** selbst [dann,] wenn ...; **~ ..., then ...** wenn ..., dann ... **2.** (*whether*) ob **3.** (*although*) wenn auch ► **barely/hardly/ rarely ... ~ at all** kaum ..., wenn überhaupt; **~ ever** wenn [überhaupt] je[mals] **II.** *n* Wenn *nt* ► **no ~s, ands, or buts** kein Wenn und Aber *fam*

igloo [ˈɪg·lu] *n* Iglu *m* o *nt*

ignite [ɪg·ˈnaɪt] **I.** *vi* Feuer fangen; ELEC zünden **II.** *vt form* anzünden; (*arouse*) entfachen

ignition [ɪg·ˈnɪʃ·ən] *n* Zündung *f*

ignition key *n* Zündschlüssel *m*

ignition switch <-es> *n* Zündschalter *m*

ignorance [ˈɪg·nər·əns] *n* Unwissenheit *f* (**about** über +*akk*)

ignorant [ˈɪg·nər·ənt] *adj* unwissend; **to be ~ about** [*or* **of**] **sth** von etw *dat* keine Ahnung haben

ignore [ɪg·ˈnɔr] *vt* ignorieren

iguana [ɪ·ˈgwa·nə] *n* Leguan *m*

IL *abbr of* **Illinois**

ill [ɪl] **I.** *adj* **1.** (*sick*) krank; **to be critically ~** in Lebensgefahr schweben **2.** (*bad*) schädlich; (*harmful*) schädlich; (*effects*) negativ; **~ health** angegriffene Gesundheit **II.** *adv* (*badly*) schlecht; **to speak ~ of sb** schlecht über jdn sprechen

Ill. *abbr of* **Illinois**

I'll [aɪl] = **I will** *see* **will**

ill-ad·vised *adj* unklug

illegal [ɪ·ˈli·gəl] **I.** *adj* illegal **II.** *n* Illegale(r) *f(m)*

illegible [ɪ·ˈledʒ·ə·bəl] *adj* unleserlich

illegitimate [ˌɪl·ɪ·ˈdʒɪt̬·ɪ·mət] *adj* **1.** (*child*) unehelich **2.** (*unauthorized*) unzulässig

ill-e·quipped *adj* schlecht ausgestattet

ill-fitting *adj* schlecht sitzend *attr*

illicit [ɪ·ˈlɪs·ɪt] *adj* [gesetzlich] verboten

ill-in·formed *adj* schlecht informiert

Illinois [ˌɪl·ə·ˈnɔɪ] *n* Illinois *nt*

illiterate [ɪ·ˈlɪt̬·ər·ɪt] *n* Analphabet(in) *m(f)*

illness [ˈɪl·nɪs] *n* Krankheit *f*

illogical [ɪ·ˈladʒ·ɪ·kəl] *adj* unlogisch

ill-tempered *adj* schlecht gelaunt; (*by nature*) mürrisch

ill-timed *adj* ungelegen

ill-treat *vt* misshandeln

ill-treatment *n* Misshandlung *f*

illuminate [ɪ·ˈlu·mə·neɪt] *vt* erhellen; (*spotlight*) beleuchten; *fig* erläutern

illuminating [ɪ·ˈlu·mə·neɪ·t̬ɪŋ] *adj* aufschlussreich

illumination [ɪˌlu·mə·ˈneɪ·ʃən] *n* Beleuchtung *f*

illusion [ɪ·ˈlu·ʒən] *n* Illusion *f*

illusive [ɪ·ˈlu·sɪv], **illusory** [ɪ·ˈlu·sə·ri] *adj* **1.** (*deceptive*) illusorisch **2.** (*imaginary*) imaginär

illustrate [ˈɪl·ə·streɪt] *vt* **1.** illustrieren **2.** *fig* (*explain*) aufzeigen

illustration [ˌɪl·ə·ˈstreɪ·ʃən] *n* **1.** Illustration *f* **2.** *fig* (*example*) Beispiel *nt*

I'm [aɪm] = **I am** *see* **be**

image [ˈɪm·ɪdʒ] *n* **1.** (*picture*) Bild *nt* **2.** (*reputation*) Image *nt*

imaginable [ɪ·ˈmædʒ·ə·nə·bəl] *adj* erdenklich

imaginary [ɪ·ˈmædʒ·ə·ner·i] *adj* imaginär

imagination [ɪˌmædʒ·ə·ˈneɪ·ʃən] *n* Fantasie *f*

imaginative [ɪ·ˈmædʒ·ə·nə·t̬ɪv] *adj* fantasievoll

imagine [ɪ·ˈmædʒ·ɪn] *vt* **1. to ~ sb/sth** sich *dat* jdn/etw vorstellen **2.** (*suppose*) sich *dat* denken; **I can't ~ what you mean** ich weiß wirklich nicht, was du meinst ► **~ that!** stell dir das mal vor!

imbalance [ˌɪm·ˈbæl·əns] *n* Ungleichgewicht *nt*

IMF [ˌaɪ·em·'ef] n abbr of **International Monetary Fund; the ~** der IWF

imitate ['ɪm·ɪ·teɪt] vt imitieren

imitation [ˌɪm·ɪ·'teɪ·ʃən] **I.** n Imitation f **II.** adj (leather, silk) Kunst-; (pearl, gold, silver) unecht

immaculate [ɪ·'mæk·jʊ·lət] adj makellos

immature [ˌɪm·ə·'tʃʊr] adj unreif

immeasurable [ɪ·'meʒ·ər·ə·bəl] adj unermesslich

immediate [ɪ·'mi·di·ɪt] adj direkt

immediately [ɪ·'mi·di·ɪt·li] adv 1. (at once) sofort 2. (closely) direkt

immense [ɪ·'mens] adj riesig, immens

immigrant ['ɪm·ɪ·grənt] **I.** n Einwanderer m /Einwanderin f, Immigrant(in) m(f) **II.** adj attr Immigranten-, Einwanderer-

immigrate ['ɪm·ɪ·greɪt] vi einwandern, immigrieren

immigration [ˌɪm·ɪ·'greɪ·ʃən] n 1. (action) Einwanderung f, Immigration f 2. (authority) Grenzkontrolle f, ≈ Grenzschutz m (an Flughäfen)

immobile [ɪ·'moʊ·bəl] adj unbeweglich

immobility [ˌɪ·moʊ·'bɪl·ɪ·ti] n Unbeweglichkeit f

immodest [ɪ·'mad·ɪst] adj unbescheiden, eingebildet; (behavior, clothing) unanständig

immoral [ɪ·'mɔr·əl] adj unmoralisch

immortal [ɪ·'mɔr·təl] **I.** adj unsterblich **II.** n Unsterbliche(r) f(m)

immortality [ˌɪ·mɔr·'tæl·ɪ·ti] n Unsterblichkeit f

immune [ɪ·'mjun] adj pred 1. immun a. fig (to gegen/für +akk) 2. (safe) sicher (from vor +dat)

im'mune system n Immunsystem nt

immunity [ɪ·'mju·nɪ·ti] n 1. Immunität f 2. fig Unempfindlichkeit f

immunize ['ɪm·jə·naɪz] vt immunisieren

immunodeficiency [ˌɪm·jə·noʊ·dɪ·'fɪʃ·ən·si] n MED Immunschwäche f

impair [ɪm·'per] vt beeinträchtigen

impartial [ɪm·'par·ʃəl] adj unparteiisch

impasse ['ɪm·pæs] n Sackgasse f a. fig; to **reach an ~** sich festfahren

impatience [ɪm·'peɪ·ʃəns] n Ungeduld f

impatient [ɪm·'peɪ·ʃənt] adj ungeduldig (with gegenüber +dat)

impeach [ɪm·'pitʃ] vt anklagen (for wegen +gen)

impeachment [ɪm·'pitʃ·mənt] n Amtsenthebungsverfahren nt

impede [ɪm·'pid] vt behindern

impel <-ll-> [ɪm·'pel] vt [an]treiben; (force) nötigen

impending [ɪm·'pend·ɪŋ] adj attr bevorstehend

imperative [ɪm·'per·ə·tɪv] **I.** adj unbedingt erforderlich **II.** n LING **the ~** der Imperativ

imperfect [ɪm·'pɜr·fɪkt] **I.** adj fehlerhaft, unvollkommen **II.** n LING **the ~** der Imperfekt

imperial [ɪm·'pɪr·i·əl] adj 1. (of empire) Reichs-; (of emperor) kaiserlich; (imperialistic) imperialistisch 2. (measures, weights) britisch

imperialism [ɪm·'pɪr·i·ə·lɪz·əm] n Imperialismus m

imperialist [ɪm·'pɪr·i·ə·lɪst] **I.** n Imperialist(in) m(f) **II.** adj imperialistisch

impermeable [ɪm·'pɜr·mi·ə·bəl] adj undurchlässig

impersonal [ˌɪm·'pɜr·sə·nəl] adj (a. ling) unpersönlich

impersonate [ɪm·'pɜr·sə·neɪt] vt imitieren

impertinent [ɪm·'pɜr·tə·nənt] adj unverschämt

impetuous [ɪm·'petʃ·u·əs] adj impulsiv; (nature) hitzig

implant I. n ['ɪm·plænt] Implantat nt **II.** vt [ɪm·'plænt] einpflanzen

implausible [ɪm·'plɔ·zə·bəl] adj unglaubwürdig

implement I. n ['ɪm·plɪ·mənt] Gerät nt; (tool) Werkzeug nt **II.** vt ['ɪm·plɪ·ment] einführen; (plan) in die Tat umsetzen

implicate ['ɪm·plɪ·keɪt] vt 1. (involve) to **~ sb in sth** jdn mit etw dat in Verbindung bringen 2. (imply) andeuten

implied [ɪm·'plaɪd] adj indirekt

implore [ɪm·'plɔr] vt anflehen

imploring [ɪm·'plɔr·ɪŋ] adj flehend

imply <-ie-> [ɪm·'plaɪ] vt andeuten

impolite [ˌɪm·pə·'laɪt] adj unhöflich

impoliteness [ˌɪm·pə·'laɪt·nɪs] n Unhöflichkeit f

import I. vt, vi [ɪm·'pɔrt] importieren (from aus +dat) **II.** n ['ɪm·pɔrt] Import m

mportance [ɪm·ˈpɔr·təns] n Bedeutung f

mportant [ɪm·ˈpɔr·tənt] adj wichtig

mportation [ˌɪm·pɔr·ˈteɪ·ʃən] n Import m

import duty n [Import]zoll m

mpose [ɪm·ˈpoʊz] I. vt auferlegen; (order) verhängen; (law) verfügen; (taxes) erheben (**on** auf +akk) II. vi to ~ **on sb** sich jdm aufdrängen

mposing [ɪm·ˈpoʊ·zɪŋ] adj beeindruckend; (person) stattlich

mpossible [ɪm·ˈpɑs·ə·bəl] I. adj unmöglich II. n the ~ das Unmögliche

mpossibly [ɪm·ˈpɑs·ə·bli] adv unvorstellbar

mpostor, imposter [ɪm·ˈpɑs·tər] n Hochstapler(in) m(f)

mpotent [ˈɪm·pə·tənt] adj 1. machtlos 2. (sexually) impotent

mpoverished [ɪm·ˈpɑv·ər·ɪʃt] adj verarmt

mpractical [ɪm·ˈpræk·tɪ·kəl] adj unpraktisch

mprecise [ˌɪm·prɪ·ˈsaɪs] adj ungenau

mpregnate [ɪm·ˈpreɡ·neɪt] vt usu passive 1. (animal, egg) befruchten 2. (saturate) imprägnieren

mpress [ɪm·ˈpres] I. vt 1. beeindrucken 2. (convince) to ~ **sth** [up]on **sb** jdn von etw dat überzeugen II. vi Eindruck machen, imponieren; **to fail to** ~ keinen [guten] Eindruck machen

mpression [ɪm·ˈpreʃ·ən] n Eindruck m

mpressionism [ɪm·ˈpreʃ·ə·nɪz·əm] n Impressionismus m

mpressive [ɪm·ˈpres·ɪv] adj beeindruckend

mprison [ɪm·ˈprɪz·ən] vt usu passive inhaftieren

mprisonment [ɪm·ˈprɪz·ən·mənt] n Haft f

mprobability [ˌɪm·prɑb·ə·ˈbɪl·ɪ·t̬i] n Unwahrscheinlichkeit f

mprobable [ɪm·ˈprɑb·ə·bəl] adj unwahrscheinlich

mproper [ɪm·ˈprɑp·ər] adj 1. (not correct) falsch 2. (inappropriate) unpassend

mprove [ɪm·ˈpruv] I. vt verbessern II. vi sich verbessern; **to** ~ **on sth** etw [noch] verbessern; **you can't** ~ **on that!** da ist keine Steigerung mehr möglich!

improvement [ɪm·ˈpruv·mənt] n Verbesserung f; (of illness) Besserung; [home] ~[s] Renovierungsarbeiten pl (Ausbau- und Modernisierungsarbeiten am eigenen Heim)

improvisation [ɪm·ˌprɑv·ɪ·ˈzeɪ·ʃən] n Improvisation f

improvise [ˈɪm·prə·vaɪz] vt, vi improvisieren

imprudent [ɪm·ˈpru·dənt] adj leichtsinnig

impudence [ˈɪm·pjʊ·dəns] n Unverschämtheit f

impudent [ˈɪm·pjʊ·dənt] adj unverschämt

impulse [ˈɪm·pʌls] n (a. elec) Impuls m

impulsive [ɪm·ˈpʌl·sɪv] adj impulsiv

impure [ɪm·ˈpjʊr] adj unrein

in [ɪn] I. prep 1. (describing location) in +dat; **he is deaf** ~ **his left ear** er hört auf dem linken Ohr nichts; ~ **the street** auf der Straße 2. (into) in +akk; **to get** ~ **the car** ins Auto steigen 3. (describing state) ~ **pain** vor Schmerzen; ~ **secret** heimlich; **to** [**not**] **be** ~ **doubt** [nicht] zweifeln 4. ~ **French** auf Französisch 5. (during) **she assisted the doctor** ~ **the operation** sie assistierte dem Arzt bei der Operation; ~ **the end** am Ende; ~ **March** im März; ~ **the morning** morgens 6. (describing job) **she works** ~ **publishing** sie arbeitet bei einem Verlag 7. (wearing) **the woman** ~ **the hat** die Frau mit dem Hut 8. + -ing (while) ~ **attempting to save the child, ...** bei dem Versuch, das Kind zu retten, ...; ~ **doing so** dabei, damit 9. (state, condition) **to be equal** ~ **height/weight** gleich groß sein/gleich viel wiegen 10. (of every) pro; **one** ~ **ten people** jeder zehnte 11. after n **he had no say** ~ **the decision** er hatte keinen Einfluss auf die Entscheidung; **to have confidence** ~ **sb** jdm vertrauen ▶ ~ **all** [or **total**] insgesamt; ~ **between** dazwischen II. adv 1. (to speaker) herein; **come** ~**!** herein! 2. (submitted) **to hand sth** ~ etw abgeben ▶ **to let sb** ~ **on sth** jdn in etw akk einweihen III. adj 1. pred (there) da; (at home) zu

Hause **2.** (*in fashion*) in ▶ **to be ~ on sth** über etw *akk* Bescheid wissen **IV.** *n* ▶ **to know the ~s and outs of sth** sich in einer S. *gen* genau auskennen

IN *abbr of* **Indiana**

inability [ˌɪn·ə·'bɪl·ɪ·ţi] *n* Unfähigkeit *f*

inaccessible [ˌɪn·æk·'ses·ə·bəl] *adj* unzugänglich

inaccuracy [ɪn·'æk·jər·ə·si] *n* Ungenauigkeit *f*

inaccurate [ɪn·'æk·jər·ɪt] *adj* ungenau

inactive [ɪn·'æk·tɪv] *adj* untätig, inaktiv

inadequate [ɪn·'æd·ɪ·kwɪt] *adj* unangemessen

inadvisable [ˌɪn·əd·'vaɪ·zə·bəl] *adj* nicht empfehlenswert

inanimate [ɪn·'æn·ɪ·mət] *adj* leblos

inapplicable [ɪn·'æp·lɪ·kə·bəl] *adj* unanwendbar

inappropriate [ˌɪn·ə·'proʊ·pri·ɪt] *adj* unpassend

inattentive [ˌɪn·ə·'ten·tɪv] *adj* unaufmerksam

inaudible [ɪn·'ɔ·də·bəl] *adj* unhörbar

inaugural [ɪn·'ɔ·gju·rəl] *adj attr* **1.** Einweihungs- **2.** POL Antritts-

inauguration [ɪn·ˌɔ·gju·'reɪ·ʃən] *n* **1.** (*induction*) Amtseinführung *f* **2.** (*of monument, stadium*) Einweihung

in-be·tween *adj attr* Zwischen-, Übergangs-

'in box *n* COMPUT Posteingangsordner *m*

inbred ['ɪn·bred] *adj* **1.** durch Inzucht erzeugt **2.** (*inherent*) angeboren

Inc. *adj after n* ECON *abbr of* **incorporated** [als Kapitalgesellschaft] eingetragen

incapability [ɪn·ˌkeɪ·pə·'bɪl·ɪ·ţi] *n* Unfähigkeit *f*

incapable [ɪn·'keɪ·pə·bəl] *adj* unfähig (**of** *zu +dat*)

incapacity [ˌɪn·kə·'pæs·ə·ţi] *n* Unfähigkeit *f*

incense¹ ['ɪn·sens] *n* (*in church*) Weihrauch *m*

incense² [ɪn·'sens] *vt* empören

incentive [ɪn·'sen·tɪv] *n* Anreiz *m*

in'centive plan *n* Prämiensystem *nt*

incessant [ɪn·'ses·ənt] *adj* ununterbrochen

incest ['ɪn·sest] *n* Inzest *m*

incestuous [ɪn·'ses·tʃu·əs] *adj* inzestuös

inch [ɪntʃ] **I.** *n* <*pl* -es> Zoll *m* (*2,54 cm*) **II.** *vi* sich [ganz] langsam bewegen

incidence ['ɪn·sɪ·dəns] *n* Auftreten *nt*

incident ['ɪn·sɪ·dənt] *n* [Vor]fall *m*, Ereignis *nt*

incidentally [ˌɪn·sɪ·'den·təl·i] *adv* **1.** (*by the way*) übrigens **2.** (*in passing*) nebenbei; (*accidentally*) zufällig

incinerate [ɪn·'sɪn·ə·reɪt] *vt* verbrennen

incinerator [ɪn·'sɪn·ə·reɪ·ţər] *n* Verbrennungsanlage *f*

incision [ɪn·'sɪȝ·ən] *n* MED [Ein]schnitt *m*

incisor [ɪn·'saɪ·zər] *n* Schneidezahn *m*

incite [ɪn·'saɪt] *vt* aufstacheln; (*revolt, riot*) anzetteln

inclination [ˌɪn·klɪ·'neɪ·ʃən] *n* Neigung *f*

incline I. *vi* [ɪn·'klaɪn] **1.** (*tend*) tendieren (**toward[s]** zu *+dat*) **2.** (*lean*) sich neigen **II.** *vt* [ɪn·'klaɪn] **1.** *usu passive* (*dispose*) **to be ~d to do sth** dazu neigen, etw zu tun **2.** (*head*) neigen

inclined [ɪn·'klaɪnd] *adj pred* bereit; **to be ~ to agree** eher zustimmen

include [ɪn·'klud] *vt* **1.** (*contain*) enthalten; **to be ~d in sth** in etw *akk* eingeschlossen sein; **everything is ~d** alles ist inklusive; **to ~ sb/sth in sth** jdn/ etw in etw *akk* einbeziehen **2.** (*add*) beifügen

including [ɪn·'klu·dɪŋ] *prep* einschließlich

inclusion [ɪn·'klu·ʒən] *n* Einbeziehung *f*

inclusive [ɪn·'klu·sɪv] *adj* einschließlich

incognito [ˌɪn·kag·'ni·toʊ] *adv* inkognito

incoherent [ˌɪn·koʊ·'hɪr·ənt] *adj* zusammenhanglos

income ['ɪn·kʌm] *n* Einkommen *nt*

'income tax *n* Einkommensteuer *f*

incoming ['ɪn·kʌm·ɪŋ] *adj attr* **1.** ankommend; **~ call** [eingehender] Anruf; **~ freshman** *Studienanfänger an einer amerikanischen Hochschule oder Highschool* **2.** (*recently elected*) neu [gewählt]

incomparable [ɪn·'kam·pər·ə·bəl] *adj* unvergleichbar

incompatibility [ˌɪn·kəm·ˌpæţ·ə·'bɪl·ɪ·ţi] *n* Unvereinbarkeit *f*

incompatible [ˌɪn·kəm·'pæţ·ə·bəl] *adj* unvereinbar, inkompatibel; **to be ~** (*persons*) nicht zusammenpassen

ncompetence [ɪn·'kam·pə·təns], **in-competency** [ɪn·'kam·pə·tən·si] n Inkompetenz f

ncompetent [ɪn·'kam·pə·tənt] adj 1. inkompetent, unfähig 2. LAW unzuständing

ncomplete [ˌɪn·kəm·'plit] adj unvollständig

ncomprehensible [ˌɪn·kam·prɪ·'hen·sə·bəl] adj unverständlich

nconceivable [ˌɪn·kən·'si·və·bəl] adj unvorstellbar

nconsequential [ɪn·'kan·sɪ·'kwen·ʃəl] adj 1. (illogical) unlogisch 2. (unimportant) belanglos

nconsiderable [ˌɪn·kən·'sɪd·ər·ə·bəl] adj unbeträchtlich

nconsiderate [ˌɪn·kən·'sɪd·ər·ɪt] adj 1. (disregarding) rücksichtslos (toward[s] gegenüber +dat) 2. (insensitive) gedankenlos; (remark) taktlos

nconsistent [ˌɪn·kən·'sɪs·tənt] adj 1. (contradicting) widersprüchlich 2. (erratic) unbeständig

nconsolable [ˌɪn·kən·'sou·lə·bəl] adj untröstlich

nconspicuous [ˌɪn·kən·'spɪk·ju·əs] adj unauffällig

ncontestable [ˌɪn·kən·'tes·tə·bəl] adj unbestreitbar; (evidence) unwiderlegbar

ncontinent [ɪn·'kan·tə·nənt] adj MED inkontinent

nconvenience [ˌɪn·kən·'vin·jəns] I. n Unannehmlichkeit f II. vt to ~ sb jdm Unannehmlichkeiten bereiten

nconvenient [ˌɪn·kən·'vin·jənt] adj (time) ungelegen; (place) ungünstig (gelegen)

ncorrect [ˌɪn·kə·'rekt] adj 1. (untrue) falsch 2. (improper) unkorrekt

ncorruptible [ˌɪn·kə·'rʌp·tə·bəl] adj unbestechlich

ncrease I. vi [ɪn·'kriːs] (prices, rates) [an]steigen; (pain, troubles) zunehmen; (population, wealth) wachsen II. vt [ɪn·'kriːs] erhöhen; (strengthen) verstärken; (enlarge) vergrößern III. n ['ɪn·kriːs] Anstieg m, Zunahme f; (in production) Steigerung f; **to be on the ~** ansteigen

ncreasing [ɪn·'kris·ɪŋ] adj steigend, zunehmend

ncreasingly [ɪn·'kris·ɪŋ·li] adv zunehmend

incredible [ɪn·'kred·ə·bəl] adj unglaublich

incredibly [ɪn·'kred·ɪbli] adv + adj (very) unglaublich

incredulous [ɪn·'kredʒ·ə·ləs] adj ungläubig

incubator ['ɪn·kju·bei·tər] n Brutapparat m; (for babies) Brutkasten m

incur <-rr-> [ɪn·'kɜr] vt 1. sich zuziehen; (debts) machen; (losses) erleiden 2. (bring on) hervorrufen; **to ~ the anger of sb** jdn verärgern

incurable [ɪn·'kjʊr·ə·bəl] adj unheilbar

Ind. abbr of **Indiana**

indebted [ɪn·'det·ɪd] adj pred 1. FIN verschuldet 2. **to be ~ to sb for sth** jdm für etw akk dankbar sein

indecency [ɪn·'di·sən·si] n 1. (impropriety) Ungehörigkeit f 2. (assault) sexueller Übergriff m (against auf +akk)

indecent [ɪn·'di·sənt] adj 1. (improper) ungehörig 2. (lewd) unanständig; (proposal) unsittlich

indecision [ˌɪn·dɪ·'sɪʒ·ən] n Unentschlossenheit f

indecisive [ˌɪn·dɪ·'sai·sɪv] adj unentschlossen

indeed [ɪn·'did] I. adv 1. (for emphasis) wirklich; (actually) tatsächlich 2. (affirmation) allerdings 3. (for strengthening) ja II. interj (ja,) wirklich, ach, wirklich

indefinable [ˌɪn·dɪ·'fai·nə·bəl] adj undefinierbar

indefinite [ɪn·'def·ə·nɪt] adj unbestimmt

indefinite 'article n unbestimmter Artikel

indefinitely [ɪn·'def·ən·ət·li] adv auf unbestimmte Zeit

indemnify <-ie-> [ɪn·'dem·nɪ·fai] vt 1. (insure) versichern 2. (compensate) entschädigen

indemnity [ɪn·'dem·nɪ·ti] n 1. (insurance) Versicherung f 2. (compensation with liability) Schaden[s]ersatz m; (without liability) Entschädigung f

independence [ˌɪn·dɪ·'pen·dəns] n Unabhängigkeit f

Inde'pendence Day n amerikanischer Unabhängigkeitstag

independent [ˌɪn·dɪ·'pen·dənt] I. adj

unabhängig (**from** von +*dat*) II. *n* POL Parteilose(r) *f(m)*

in-depth ['ɪn·depθ] *adj attr* gründlich; (*report*) detailliert

indescribable [ˌɪn·dɪ·'skraɪ·bə·bəl] *adj* unbeschreiblich

indestructible [ˌɪn·dɪ·'strʌk·tə·bəl] *adj* unzerstörbar; (*toy*) unverwüstlich

index <*pl* -es> ['ɪn·deks] *n* 1. <*pl* -es> (*in book*) Index *m*; (*of sources*) Quellenverzeichnis *nt* 2. <*pl* -dices> (*indicator*) Index *m*, Anzeichen *nt* (**of** für +*akk*)

'index card *n* Karteikarte *f*

'index finger *n* Zeigefinger *m*

India ['ɪn·di·ə] *n* Indien *nt*

India 'ink *n* Tusche *f*

Indian ['ɪn·di·ən] I. *adj* 1. (*Asian*) indisch 2. (*native American*) indianisch, Indianer- II. *n* 1. (*Asian*) Inder(in) *m(f)* 2. (*native American*) Indianer(in) *m(f)*

Indiana [ˌɪn·di·'æn·ə] *n* Indiana *nt*

Indian 'corn *n* FOOD Mais *m*

Indian 'file *n see* **single file**

Indian 'Ocean *n* **the ~** der Indische Ozean

Indian 'summer *n* Altweibersommer *m*

indicate ['ɪn·dɪ·keɪt] *vt* 1. (*show*) [an]zeigen 2. (*imply*) auf etw *akk* hindeuten 3. (*point to*) **to ~ sb/sth** auf jdn/etw hindeuten

indication [ˌɪn·dɪ·'keɪ·ʃən] *n* 1. (*sign*) [An]zeichen *nt* (**of** für +*akk*), Hinweis *m* (**of** auf +*akk*) 2. (*on gauge, meter*) Anzeige *f*

indicator ['ɪn·dɪ·keɪ·tər] *n* 1. (*evidence*) Indikator *m* 2. TECH (*gauge, meter*) [An]zeiger *m*

indices ['ɪn·dɪ·siz] *n pl of* **index** 2

indict [ɪn·'daɪt] *vt* anklagen

indie ['ɪn·di] *adj short for* **independent** (*film, music*) Indie-

indifference [ɪn·'dɪf·ər·əns] *n* Gleichgültigkeit *f* (**to[ward]** gegenüber +*dat*)

indifferent [ɪn·'dɪf·ər·ənt] *adj* 1. (*uninterested*) gleichgültig (**to** gegenüber +*dat*) 2. (*mediocre*) [mittel]mäßig

indigenous [ɪn·'dɪdʒ·ə·nəs] *adj* [ein]heimisch

indigestible [ˌɪn·dɪ·'dʒes·tə·bəl] *adj a. fig* unverdaulich

indigestion [ˌɪn·dɪ·'dʒes·tʃən] *n* Magen-

verstimmung *f*; (*chronic*) Verdauungsstörung[en] *f[pl]*

indignant [ɪn·'dɪg·nənt] *adj* empört (**at/about** über +*akk*)

indignation [ˌɪn·dɪg·'neɪ·ʃən] *n* Empörung *f* (**at/about** über +*akk*)

indignity [ɪn·'dɪg·nɪ·ti] *n* Demütigung *f*

indigo ['ɪn·dɪ·goʊ] I. *n* Indigo *m o n* II. *adj* indigoblau

indirect [ˌɪn·dɪ·'rekt] *adj* indirekt; **~ remark** Anspielung *f*

indirect 'object *n* LING indirektes Objekt Dativobjekt *nt*

indirect 'tax *n* FIN indirekte Steuer

indiscernible [ˌɪn·dɪ·'sɜr·nə·bəl] *adj* nicht wahrnehmbar; (*invisible*) nicht erkennbar

indiscreet [ˌɪn·dɪ·'skrit] *adj* indiskret

indiscretion [ˌɪn·dɪ·'skreʃ·ən] *n* Indiskretion *f*

indiscriminate [ˌɪn·dɪ·'skrɪm·ə·nɪt] *adj* 1. (*unthinking*) unüberlegt 2. (*uncritical*) unkritisch 3. (*random*) wahllos

indispensable [ˌɪn·dɪ·'spen·sə·bəl] *adj* unentbehrlich (**for/to** für +*akk*)

indisputable [ˌɪn·dɪ·'spju·tə·bəl] *adj* unbestreitbar; (*evidence*) unanfechtbar (*skill, talent*) unbestritten

indistinct [ˌɪn·dɪ·'stɪŋkt] *adj* undeutlich (*memory*) verschwommen

indistinguishable [ˌɪn·dɪ·'stɪŋ·gwɪ·ʃə·bəl] *adj* nicht unterscheidbar; (*imperceptible*) nicht wahrnehmbar

individual [ˌɪn·dɪ·'vɪdʒ·u·əl] I. *n* 1. Einzelne(r) *f(m)*, Individuum *nt geh* 2. (*original person*) [selbstständige] Persönlichkeit II. *adj* 1. *attr* (*separate*) einzeln 2. (*particular*) individuell

individualist [ˌɪn·dɪ·'vɪdʒ·u·ə·lɪst] *n* Individualist(in) *m(f)*

individually [ˌɪn·dɪ·'vɪdʒ·u·ə·li] *adv* 1. einzeln 2. (*distinctively*) individuell

indivisible [ˌɪn·dɪ·'vɪz·ə·bəl] *adj* unteilbar

indolence ['ɪn·də·ləns] *n* Trägheit *f*

indolent ['ɪn·də·lənt] *adj* träge

Indonesia [ˌɪn·də·'ni·ʒə] *n* Indonesien *n*

Indonesian [ˌɪn·də·'ni·ʒən] I. *adj* indonesisch II. *n* 1. Indonesier(in) *m(f)* 2. (*language*) Indonesisch *nt*

indoor [ˌɪnˈdɔr] adj attr **1.** (inside) Innen-; ~ **plant** Zimmerpflanze f; SPORT Hallen- **2.** (for use inside) Haus-; SPORT Hallen-

indoors [ˌɪnˈdɔrz] adv (to inside) herein/hinein; (in building) drinnen

induce [ɪnˈdus] vt **1.** (persuade) **to ~ sb to do sth** jdn dazu bringen, etw zu tun **2.** (cause) hervorrufen **3.** MED (birth, labor) einleiten

inducement [ɪnˈdus·mənt] n Anreiz m

induct [ɪnˈdʌkt] vt usu passive **1. to be ~ed into office** in ein Amt eingesetzt werden **2.** MIL **to be ~ed [into the Army]** eingezogen werden

induction [ɪnˈdʌk·ʃən] n **1.** (into office) [Amts]einführung f; (into organization) Aufnahme f (**into** in +akk); ~ **into the military** Einberufung f [zum Wehrdienst] **2.** MED (of birth) Einleitung f **3.** ELEC, PHYS, TECH Induktion f fachspr; (of engine) Ansaugung f

indulge [ɪnˈdʌldʒ] I. vt **1.** (allow) nachgeben +dat; **to ~ sb's every wish** jdm jeden Wunsch erfüllen **2.** (spoil) verwöhnen II. vi **to ~ in sth** in etw dat schwelgen

indulgence [ɪnˈdʌl·dʒəns] n (in food, drink, pleasure) Genuss nt

indulgent [ɪnˈdʌl·dʒənt] adj nachgiebig

industrial [ɪnˈdʌs·tri·əl] adj industriell; (product, city) Industrie-; (training, development) betrieblich; ~ **area** Industriegebiet nt; ~ **output** Industrieproduktion f

industrialism [ɪnˈdʌs·tri·ə·lɪz·əm] n Industrialismus m

industrialist [ɪnˈdʌs·tri·ə·lɪst] n Industrielle(r) f(m)

industrialization [ɪnˌdʌs·tri·ə·lɪ·ˈzeɪ·ʃən] n Industrialisierung f

industrialize [ɪnˈdʌs·tri·ə·laɪz] vt industrialisieren

industrial 'park n Industriepark m

Industrial Revo'lution n HIST **the ~** die Industrielle Revolution

industrious [ɪnˈdʌs·tri·əs] adj fleißig

industry [ˈɪn·dəs·tri] n Industrie f; (trade) Branche f

inedible [ɪnˈed·ə·bəl] adj nicht essbar; (disgusting) ungenießbar

ineducable [ɪnˈedʒ·ə·kə·bəl] adj schwer erziehbar; (handicapped) lernbehindert

ineffective [ˌɪn·ɪ·ˈfek·tɪv] adj (measure) unwirksam; (person) untauglich

ineffectual [ˌɪn·ɪ·ˈfek·tʃu·əl] adj ineffektiv

inefficiency [ˌɪn·ɪ·ˈfɪʃ·ən·si] n Ineffizienz f geh; (of person) Inkompetenz f

inefficient [ˌɪn·ɪ·ˈfɪʃ·ənt] adj ineffizient

inelegant [ɪnˈel·ɪ·gənt] adj unelegant

ineligible [ɪnˈel·ɪdʒ·ə·bəl] adj (for benefits) nicht berechtigt (**for** zu +dat); (for office) nicht wählbar (**for** in +dat)

inequality [ˌɪn·ɪ·ˈkwal·ɪ·ti] n Ungleichheit f

inescapable [ˌɪn·ɪ·ˈskeɪ·pə·bəl] adj unvermeidlich; (fate) unentrinnbar; (truth) unbestreitbar

inestimable [ɪnˈes·tɪ·mə·bəl] adj unschätzbar

inevitable [ɪnˈev·ɪ·tə·bəl] I. adj unvermeidlich; (result) zwangsläufig II. n **the ~** das Unvermeidbare

inexact [ˌɪn·ɪg·ˈzækt] adj ungenau

inexcusable [ˌɪn·ɪk·ˈskju·zə·bəl] adj unverzeihlich

inexhaustible [ˌɪn·ɪg·ˈzɔs·tə·bəl] adj unerschöpflich

inexpensive [ˌɪn·ɪk·ˈspen·sɪv] adj preisgünstig

inexperience [ˌɪn·ɪk·ˈspɪr·i·əns] n Unerfahrenheit f

inexperienced [ˌɪn·ɪk·ˈspɪr·i·ənst] adj unerfahren; **to be ~ in sth** mit etw dat nicht vertraut sein; **to be ~ with sth** sich mit etw dat nicht auskennen

inexplicable [ˌɪn·ək·ˈsplɪk·ə·bəl] adj unerklärlich

infallible [ɪnˈfæl·ə·bəl] adj unfehlbar

infamous [ˈɪn·fə·məs] adj berüchtigt

infancy [ˈɪn·fən·si] n früh[este] Kindheit; fig Anfangsphase f

infant [ˈɪn·fənt] I. n Säugling m II. adj ~ **daughter** kleines Töchterchen

infanticide [ɪnˈfæn·tə·saɪd] n Kindestötung f

infantile [ˈɪn·fən·taɪl] adj pej kindisch meist pej

infant mor'tality n Säuglingssterblichkeit f

infantry [ˈɪn·fən·tri] I. n **the ~** + sing/pl

vb die Infanterie. **II.** *adj* Infanterie-
'infantryman *n* Infanterist *m*

infatuated [ɪnˈfætʃ·u·eɪ·ṭɪd] *adj* vernarrt
(**with** in +*akk*); (*in love*) verknallt *fam*
(**with** in +*akk*)

infect [ɪnˈfekt] *vt a. fig* anstecken, infizieren

infection [ɪnˈfek·ʃən] *n* Infektion *f*; **throat**
~ Halsentzündung *f*

infectious [ɪnˈfek·ʃəs] *adj a. fig* ansteckend

infer <-rr-> [ɪnˈfɜr] *vt* schließen (**from**
aus +*dat*)

inferior [ɪnˈfɪr·i·ər] **I.** *adj* **1.** minderwertig; (*mind*) unterlegen **2.** (*lower: in
rank*) rang]niedriger; (*in status*) untergeordnet **II.** *n* ~**s** *pl* Untergebene *pl*

inferi'ority complex *n* Minderwertigkeitskomplex *m*

infernal [ɪnˈfɜr·nəl] *adj a. fig* höllisch,
Höllen-

infertile [ɪnˈfɜr·ṭəl] *adj* unfruchtbar

infertility [ˌɪn·fərˈtɪl·ə·ṭi] *n* Unfruchtbar-
keit *f*

infest [ɪnˈfest] *vt* befallen (**with** mit
+*dat*)

infidelity [ˌɪn·fɪˈdel·ɪ·ṭi] *n* **1.** (*disloy-
alty*) Verrat *m* (**to** gegenüber/an +*dat*)
2. (*sexual*) Untreue *f*; **infidelities** *pl*
Seitensprünge *pl*

infiltrate [ɪnˈfɪl·treɪt] *vt* **1.** unterwan-
dern; (*building, enemy lines*) eindringen in +*akk*; (*agent, spy*) einschleusen
(**into** in +*akk*) **2.** (*idea, theory*) durchdringen

infinite [ˈɪn·fə·nɪt] *adj* **1.** unendlich
2. (*great*) grenzenlos

infinitely [ˈɪn·fən·ɪt·li] *adv* **1.** unendlich;
~ **small** winzig klein **2.** (*much*) unendlich viel

infinitive [ɪnˈfɪn·ɪ·ṭɪv] *n* Infinitiv *m*

infinity [ɪnˈfɪn·ɪ·ṭi] *n* Unendlichkeit *f*

infirm [ɪnˈfɜrm] **I.** *adj* gebrechlich **II.** *n*
the ~ *pl* die Kranken und Pflegebe-
dürftigen

infirmary [ɪnˈfɜr·mə·ri] *n* **1.** Krankenhaus *nt* **2.** (*smaller*) Krankenzimmer *nt*;
(*in prison*) Krankenstation *f*

infirmity [ɪnˈfɜr·mɪ·ṭi] *n* **1.** (*state*)
Gebrechlichkeit *f* **2.** (*illness*) Gebre-
chen *nt*

inflame [ɪnˈfleɪm] *vt* **1.** (*arouse*) entfachen **2.** (*anger*) aufbringen; (*with anger*) in Wut versetzen; (*with desire*) mit
Verlangen erfüllen

inflammable [ɪnˈflæm·ə·bəl] *adj* [leicht]
entzündbar; (*situation*) explosiv

inflammation [ˌɪn·fləˈmeɪ·ʃən] *n* Entzündung *f*

inflammatory [ɪnˈflæm·ə·tɔr·i] *adj*
1. entzündlich, Entzündungs- **2.** (*pro-
voking*) aufrührerisch

inflatable [ɪnˈfleɪ·ṭə·bəl] *adj* aufblasbar

inflate [ɪnˈfleɪt] **I.** *vt* **1.** aufblasen; (*with
pump*) aufpumpen **2.** (*exaggerate*) aufblähen *pej* **3.** (*raise*) in die Höhe treiben
II. *vi* sich mit Luft füllen

inflated [ɪnˈfleɪ·ṭɪd] *adj* aufgeblasen

inflation [ɪnˈfleɪ·ʃən] *n* **1.** ECON Inflation *f* **2.** Aufblasen *nt*; (*with pump*)
Aufpumpen *nt*

inflationary [ɪnˈfleɪ·ʃə·ne·ri] *adj* FIN infla-
tionär, Inflations-

inflect [ɪnˈflekt] *vt* LING beugen

inflexible [ɪnˈflek·sə·bəl] *adj* **1.** (*fixed*)
starr; (*person*) unflexibel **2.** (*stiff*) steif

influence [ˈɪn·flu·əns] **I.** *n* Einfluss *m* (**on**
auf +*akk*) **II.** *vt* beeinflussen

influential [ˌɪn·fluˈen·fəl] *adj* einflussreich

influenza [ˌɪn·fluˈen·zə] *n* Grippe *f*

influx [ˈɪn·flʌks] *n* Zustrom *m* (**of** an +*dat*);
(*of capital*) Zufuhr *f* (**of** an +*dat*)

infomercial [ˌɪn·fouˈmɜr·fəl] *n* TV, MEDIA
Infomercial *nt fachspr* (*als Informations-
sendung getarntes Werbevideo*)

inform [ɪnˈfɔrm] *vt* informieren

informal [ɪnˈfɔr·məl] *adj* **1.** informell;
(*atmosphere, party*) zwanglos; (*casual*)
leger **2.** (*unofficial*) inoffiziell

informant [ɪnˈfɔr·mənt] *n* Infor-
mant(in) *m(f)*

information [ˌɪn·fərˈmeɪ·ʃən] *n* **1.** Information *f*; **a piece of** ~ eine Information; **a lot of** ~ viele Informationen *pl*
2. (*phone service*) Auskunft *f*

infor'mation science *n usu pl* Informatik *f kein pl*

informative [ɪnˈfɔr·mə·ṭɪv] *adj* informativ

informed [ɪnˈfɔrmd] *adj* [gut] informiert

informer [ɪnˈfɔr·mər] *n* Infor-

mant(in) *m(f)*, Spitzel(in) *m(f)*

infotainment ['ɪn·foʊ·teɪn·mənt] *n* Infotainment *nt*

infrared ['ɪn·frə·'red] *adj* infrarot

infrastructure ['ɪn·frə·strʌk·tʃər] *n* Infrastruktur *f*

infrequent [ɪn·'fri·kwənt] *adj* selten

infringe [ɪn·'frɪndʒ] *vt* verletzen; (*law*) verstoßen (**against** gegen +*akk*)

infuriate [ɪn·'fjʊr·i·eɪt] *vt* wütend machen

ingratitude [ɪn·'græt·ə·tud] *n* Undankbarkeit *f*

ingredient [ɪn·'gri·di·ənt] *n* Zutat *f*

ingrown ['ɪn·groʊn] *adj usu attr* eingewachsen

inhabit [ɪn·'hæb·ɪt] *vt* bewohnen

inhabitant [ɪn·'hæb·ɪ·tənt] *n* Einwohner(in) *m(f)*

inhale [ɪn·'heɪl] *vt, vi* einatmen; (*smoker*) inhalieren

inherent [ɪn·'hɪr·ənt] *adj* **to be ~ in sth** etw *dat* eigen sein

inherit [ɪn·'her·ɪt] *vt, vi* erben (**from** von +*dat*)

inheritance [ɪn·'her·ɪ·təns] *n* Erbe *nt kein pl*

inhibit [ɪn·'hɪb·ɪt] *vt* **1.** (*restrict*) hindern **2.** (*deter*) hemmen

inhibition [ˌɪn·hə·'bɪʃ·ən] *n* Hemmung *f*

inhospitable [ɪn·'has·pɪ·tə·bəl] *adj* ungastlich

in-house **I.** *adj attr* hauseigen **II.** *adv* intern, im Hause

inhuman [ɪn·'hju·mən] *adj* unmenschlich

inhumane [ɪn·hju·'meɪn] *adj* barbarisch

initial [ɪ·'nɪʃ·əl] **I.** *adj attr* anfänglich, erste(r, s) **II.** *n* Initiale *f*

initialize [ɪ·'nɪʃ·ə·laɪz] *vt* COMPUT initialisieren

initially [ɪ·'nɪʃ·ə·li] *adv* anfangs

initiate [ɪ·'nɪʃ·i·eɪt] *vt* **1.** (*start*) in die Wege leiten **2.** (*admit*) einführen (**into** in +*akk*); (*officially*) [feierlich] aufnehmen (**into** in +*akk*)

initiative [ɪ·'nɪʃ·ə·tɪv] *n* Initiative *f*

inject [ɪn·'dʒekt] *vt* spritzen (**into** in +*akk*)

injection [ɪn·'dʒek·ʃən] *n* Spritze *f*; TECH Einspritzung *f*

in-joke *n* Insiderwitz *m fam*

injunction [ɪn·'dʒʌŋk·ʃən] *n* LAW [gerichtliche] Verfügung

injure ['ɪn·dʒər] *vt* verletzen

injured ['ɪn·dʒərd] **I.** *adj* verletzt **II.** **the ~** *pl* die Verletzten *pl*

injury ['ɪn·dʒə·ri] *n* Verletzung *f*

injustice [ɪn·'dʒʌs·tɪs] *n* Ungerechtigkeit *f*

ink [ɪŋk] *n* Tinte *f*; ART Tusche *f*; (*for stamp*) Farbe

ink-jet 'printer *n* Tintenstrahldrucker *m*

'ink pad *n* Stempelkissen *nt*

inland *adj* ['ɪn·lənd] *usu attr* Binnen-

in-laws ['ɪn·lɔz] *npl* Schwiegereltern *pl*

inlay *n* ['ɪn·leɪ] **1.** Einlegearbeit[en] *f[pl]* **2.** (*for tooth*) Inlay *nt*

inlet ['ɪn·let] *n* **1.** GEOG [schmale] Bucht; (*of sea*) Meeresarm *m* **2.** TECH Einlass[kanal] *m*; (*pipe*) Zuleitung *f*

inmate ['ɪn·meɪt] *n* Insasse, -in *m, f*

inn [ɪn] *n* Gasthaus *m*

innards ['ɪn·ərdz] *npl fam* Eingeweide *pl*; FOOD Innereien *pl*

innate [ɪ·'neɪt] *adj* natürlich, angeboren

inner ['ɪn·ər] *adj usu attr* innere(r, s) *attr*

inner 'city *n* Innenstadt *f*, [Stadt]zentrum *nt*

innermost ['ɪn·ər·moʊst] *adj attr* **1.** innerste(r, s) **2.** (*secret*) geheimste(r, s), intimste(r, s)

'inner tube *n* Schlauch *m*

inning ['ɪn·ɪŋ] *n* SPORT (*in baseball*) Inning *nt*

innocence ['ɪn·ə·səns] *n* Unschuld *f*

innocent ['ɪn·ə·sənt] **I.** *adj* unschuldig; (*mistake*) unbeabsichtigt **II.** *n* **to be an ~** naiv sein

innovation [ˌɪn·ə·'veɪ·ʃən] *n* **1.** Neuerung *f*; (*new product*) Innovation *f* **2.** (*creating*) [Ver]änderung *f*

innovative ['ɪn·ə·veɪ·tɪv] *adj* innovativ

innumerable [ɪ·'nu·mər·ə·bəl] *adj* unzählig

inoculate [ɪ·'nak·jə·leɪt] *vt* impfen (**against** gegen +*akk*)

inoculation [ɪ·ˌnak·jə·'leɪ·ʃən] *n* Impfung *f*

inoffensive [ˌɪn·ə·'fen·sɪv] *adj* harmlos

inoperable [ˌɪn·'ap·ər·ə·bəl] *adj* **1.** MED inoperabel **2.** (*not working*) nicht funktionsfähig

inopportune [ˌɪnˌap·ər·ˈtun] *adj* 1. (*inconvenient*) ungünstig 2. (*unsuitable*) unpassend

inorganic [ˌɪn·ɔr·ˈgæn·ɪk] *adj* CHEM anorganisch

'inpatient *n* stationärer Patient/stationäre Patientin

input ['ɪn·pʊt] *n* 1. Beitrag *m;* (*of work*) [Arbeits]aufwand *m* 2. ELEC Anschluss *m* 3. COMPUT (*data*) Input *m;* (*entering*) Eingabe *f*

inquest ['ɪn·kwest] *n* LAW gerichtliche Untersuchung [der Todesursache]

inquire [ɪn·ˈkwaɪr] *vt, vi* sich erkundigen (**about/as to** nach +*dat*); **to ~ into sth** etw untersuchen

inquiry [ɪn·ˈkwaɪ·ri] *n* 1. (*question*) Anfrage *f,* Erkundigung *f* 2. (*investigation*) Untersuchung *f;* **to make inquiries** Nachforschungen anstellen

inquisition [ˌɪn·kwɪ·ˈzɪʃ·ən] *n* 1. Verhör *nt* 2. HIST **the I~** die Inquisition

inquisitive [ɪn·ˈkwɪz·ɪ·tɪv] *adj* wissbegierig; (*curious*) neugierig; (*look, face*) fragend *attr;* (*child*) fragelustig

insane [ɪn·ˈseɪn] *adj* 1. (*mentally ill*) geistesgestört 2. *fam* (*crazy*) verrückt

insanitary [ɪn·ˈsæn·ɪ·ter·i] *adj* unhygienisch

insanity [ɪn·ˈsæn·ɪ·ti] *n* Wahnsinn *a. fig*

inscription [ɪn·ˈskrɪp·ʃən] *n* Inschrift *f;* (*in book*) Widmung *f*

insect ['ɪn·sekt] *n* Insekt *nt*

insecticide [ɪn·ˈsek·tɪ·saɪd] *n* Insektenvernichtungsmittel *nt*

insecure [ˌɪn·sɪ·ˈkjʊr] *adj* unsicher

insecurity [ˌɪn·sɪ·ˈkjʊr·ə·ti] *n* Unsicherheit *f*

inseminate [ɪn·ˈsem·ɪ·neɪt] *vt* (*woman*) [künstlich] befruchten

insemination [ɪn·ˌsem·ɪ·ˈneɪ·ʃən] *n* Befruchtung *f*

insensible [ɪn·ˈsen·sə·bəl] *adj* 1. (*unconscious*) bewusstlos 2. (*numb*) gefühllos; (*to pain*) [schmerz]unempfindlich

insensitive [ɪn·ˈsen·sɪ·tɪv] *adj* 1. (*uncaring*) gefühllos; (*remark*) taktlos 2. *usu pred* (*numb*) unempfindlich (**to** gegenüber +*dat*)

inseparable [ɪn·ˈsep·rə·bəl] *adj* 1. (*friends*) unzertrennlich 2. (*con-*

nected) untrennbar [miteinander verbunden]

insert *vt* [ɪn·ˈsɜrt] 1. [hinein]stecken; (*coins*) einwerfen 2. (*write*) einfügen; (*on form*) eintragen

'in-service *adj attr* **~ training** [innerbetriebliche] Fortbildung

inside [ɪn·ˈsaɪd] I. *n* 1. Innere *nt;* **from the ~** von innen 2. (*of hand, door*) Innenseite *f;* SPORT Innenbahn *f* II. *adv* 1. innen 2. (*indoors*) drinnen; (*direction*) hinein/herein 3. *fam* (*jailed*) hinter Gittern *fam* III. *adj attr* 1. Innen-, innere(r, s) 2. (*indoor*) Innen- IV. *prep* 1. (*direction*) **~ sth** in etw *akk* [hinein] 2. (*location*) **~ sth** in etw *dat* 3. (*within*) **~ of two hours** in[nerhalb von] zwei Stunden

insider ['ɪn·ˌsaɪ·dər] *n* Insider(in) *m(f)*

insight ['ɪn·saɪt] *n* Einblick *m* (**into** in +*akk*)

insignificant [ˌɪn·sɪg·ˈnɪf·ɪ·kənt] *adj* unbedeutend; (*remark*) belanglos; (*sum, difference*) geringfügig

insincere [ˌɪn·sɪn·ˈsɪr] *adj* unaufrichtig; (*person*) falsch; (*smile, praise*) unecht; (*flattery*) heuchlerisch

insinuate [ɪn·ˈsɪn·ju·eɪt] *vt* (*imply*) andeuten

insinuation [ɪn·ˌsɪn·ju·ˈeɪ·ʃən] *n* Anspielung *f*

insist [ɪn·ˈsɪst] I. *vi* bestehen ([up]on auf +*dat*); **to ~ [up]on doing sth** sich nicht von etw *dat* abbringen lassen II. *vt* **to ~ that ...** 1. (*claim*) fest behaupten, dass ... 2. (*demand*) darauf bestehen, dass ...

insistence [ɪn·ˈsɪs·təns] *n* Bestehen *nt* (**on** auf +*dat*)

insistent [ɪn·ˈsɪs·tənt] *adj* beharrlich; (*demand*) nachdrücklich

insofar as [ˌɪn·sou·ˈfar·əz] *adv* soweit

insole ['ɪn·soul] *n* Einlegesohle *f*

insolence ['ɪn·sə·ləns] *n* Unverschämtheit *f*

insolent ['ɪn·sə·lənt] *adj* unverschämt

insoluble [ɪn·ˈsal·jə·bəl] *adj* 1. unlösbar 2. (*minerals*) nicht löslich

insolvency [ɪn·ˈsal·vən·si] *n* Zahlungsunfähigkeit *f*

insolvent [ɪn·ˈsal·vənt] *adj* zahlungsun-

fähig

insomnia [ɪnˈsɑm·ni·ə] n Schlaflosigkeit f

inspect [ɪnˈspɛkt] vt [über]prüfen, kontrollieren

inspection [ɪnˈspɛk·ʃən] n [Über]prüfung f, Kontrolle f

inspector [ɪnˈspɛk·tər] n Inspektor(in) m(f); **tax** ~ Steuerprüfer(in) m(f)

inspiration [ɪn·spəˈreɪ·ʃən] n Inspiration f

inspire [ɪnˈspaɪr] vt **1.** inspirieren **2.** (feeling) hervorrufen (**in** bei +dat)

inspired [ɪnˈspaɪrd] adj **1.** (poet, athlete) inspiriert **2.** (excellent) großartig **3.** (motivated) motiviert

instability [ɪn·stəˈbɪl·ə·t̬i] n **1.** Instabilität f **2.** PSYCH Labilität f

install [ɪnˈstɔl] vt (machinery) aufstellen; (computer, heating) installieren; (bathroom, kitchen) einbauen; (wiring, pipes) verlegen; (phone, washing machine) anschließen

installation [ɪn·stəˈleɪ·ʃən] n **1.** (of machinery) Aufstellen nt; (of appliance, heating) Installation f; (of kitchen, bathroom) Einbau m; (of wiring, pipes) Verlegung f; (of phone, washing machine) Anschluss m **2.** (facility) Anlage f **3.** ART Installation f

installment [ɪnˈstɔl·mənt] n **1.** (part) Folge f **2.** (payment) Rate f

in'stallment purchase n Ratenkauf m

instance [ˈɪn·stəns] n **1.** (case) Fall m **2.** **for** ~ zum Beispiel

instant [ˈɪn·stənt] **I.** n **1.** Moment m, Augenblick m; **this** ~ sofort **2.** (as soon as) **the** ~ ... sobald ... **II.** adj **1.** sofortige(r, s) attr; **to take** ~ **effect** sofort wirken **2.** (in bags) Tüten-; (in cans) Dosen-; ~ **coffee** Pulverkaffee m

instantly [ˈɪn·stənt·li] adv sofort

instant 'replay n TV Wiederholung f

instead [ɪnˈstɛd] **I.** adv stattdessen **II.** prep ~ **of sb/sth** [an]statt einer Person/einer S. gen ~ **of doing sth** [an]statt etw zu tun

instinct [ˈɪn·stɪŋkt] n Instinkt m

instinctive [ɪnˈstɪŋk·tɪv] adj instinktiv

institute [ˈɪn·stɪ·tut] n Institut nt

institution [ɪn·stɪˈtu·ʃən] n **1.** (of reforms) Einführung f **2.** (building) Heim nt, Anstalt f **3.** (organization) Einrichtung f, Institution f

instruct [ɪnˈstrʌkt] vt **1.** (teach) unterrichten **2.** (order) anweisen

instruction [ɪnˈstrʌk·ʃən] n **1.** usu pl (order) Anweisung f **2.** (teaching) Unterweisung f **3.** (directions) ~**s for use** Gebrauchsanweisung f

in'struction book, in'struction manual n Handbuch nt; (for device) Gebrauchsanweisung f

instructive [ɪnˈstrʌk·tɪv] adj lehrreich, aufschlussreich

instructor [ɪnˈstrʌk·tər] n **1.** (teacher) Lehrer(in) m(f) **2.** (at university) Dozent(in) m(f)

instrument [ˈɪn·strə·mənt] n Instrument nt

instrumental [ˌɪn·strəˈmen·təl] adj **1.** MUS instrumental **2.** (influential) förderlich

'instrument panel n AUTO Armaturenbrett nt; AVIAT, NAUT Instrumententafel f

insufficient [ˌɪn·səˈfɪʃ·ənt] adj zu wenig präd, unzureichend

insular [ˈɪn·sə·lər] adj provinziell

insulate [ˈɪn·sə·leɪt] vt **1.** ELEC isolieren **2.** fig (shield) [be]schützen (**from** vor +dat)

insulating [ˈɪn·sə·leɪ·t̬ɪŋ] adj Isolier-

'insulating tape n Isolierband nt

insulation [ˌɪn·səˈleɪ·ʃən] n **1.** Isolierung f **2.** fig (protection) Schutz m

insulin [ˈɪn·sə·lɪn] n Insulin nt

insult I. vt [ɪnˈsʌlt] beleidigen **II.** n [ˈɪn·sʌlt] Beleidigung f ▸ **to add** ~ **to injury** um dem Ganzen die Krone aufzusetzen

insurance [ɪnˈʃʊr·əns] n **1.** Versicherung f; **to take out** ~ [**against sth**] sich [gegen etw akk] versichern **2.** (payout) Versicherungssumme f **3.** (premium) [Versicherungs]prämie f

in'surance agent n Versicherungsmakler(in) m(f)

in'surance company n Versicherung[s]gesellschaft] f

in'surance policy n Versicherungspolice f

in'surance premium n [Versicherungs]prämie f

insure [ɪnˈʃʊr] **I.** vt versichern **II.** vi

sich versichern (**with** bei +*dat*, **against** gegen +*akk*)

insured [ɪn·ˈʃʊrd] I. *adj* versichert II. *n* <*pl* -> **the** ~ der/die Versicherte

insurer [ɪn·ˈʃʊr·ər] *n* Versicherung(sgesellschaft) *f*

insurgent [ɪn·ˈsɜr·dʒənt] *n* POL Parteimitglied, *das sich der Parteidisziplin nicht beugt*

intact [ɪn·ˈtækt] *adj usu pred* intakt, unversehrt

intake [ɪn·ˈteɪk] I. *n* 1. (*act*) Aufnahme *f*; ~ **of breath** Luftholen *nt* 2. (*amount*) aufgenommene Menge; ~ **of calories** Kalorienzufuhr *f* II. *adj* TECH Ansaug-, Saug-

intangible [ɪn·ˈtæn·dʒə·bəl] *adj* nicht greifbar

integrate [ˈɪn·tɪ·greɪt] I. *vt* integrieren (**into** in +*akk*) II. *vi* sich integrieren

integrated [ˈɪn·tɪ·greɪ·tɪd] *adj* einheitlich; (*person*) integriert (**in** in +*akk*); ~ **school** *hist* Schule *f* ohne Rassentrennung

integrated 'circuit, I 'C *n* ELEC integrierter Schaltkreis

intellect [ˈɪn·təl·ekt] *n* Verstand *m*, Intellekt *m*

intellectual [ˌɪn·tə·ˈlek·tʃʊ·əl] I. *n* Intellektuelle(r) *f(m)* II. *adj* intellektuell, geistig

intelligence [ɪn·ˈtel·ə·dʒəns] I. *n* 1. Intelligenz *f* 2. (*department*) Geheimdienst *m* 3. (*information*) [nachrichtendienstliche] Informationen; **according to our latest** ~ unseren letzten Meldungen zufolge II. *adj* Nachrichten-; ~ **report** Geheimdienstbericht *m*

in'telligence agency *n* Geheimdienst *m*

in'telligence test *n* Intelligenztest *m*

intelligent [ɪn·ˈtel·ə·dʒənt] *adj* klug, intelligent

intend [ɪn·ˈtend] *vt* beabsichtigen; **I don't think she ~ed me to hear the remark** ich glaube nicht, dass ich die Bemerkung hören sollte; **no disrespect ~ed** [das] war nicht böse gemeint

intended [ɪn·ˈten·dɪd] *adj* beabsichtigt; **to be ~ for sth** für etw *akk* gedacht sein

intense [ɪn·ˈtens] *adj* 1. (*forceful*) intensiv; (*odor*) stechend; (*cold*) bitter;

(*desire, heat*) glühend; (*excitement*) groß; (*feeling, friendship*) tief; (*hatred*) rasend; (*love*) leidenschaftlich; (*pain*) heftig 2. (*serious*) ernst

intensify <-ie-> [ɪn·ˈten·sɪ·faɪ] I. *vt* intensivieren; (*conflict*) verschärfen; (*fears*) verstärken; (*pressure*) erhöhen II. *vi* (*heat*) stärker werden; (*feeling, competition a.*) zunehmen

intensity [ɪn·ˈten·sə·ti] *n* Stärke *f*; (*of feelings*) Intensität *f*; (*of explosion, anger*) Heftigkeit *f*

intensive [ɪn·ˈten·sɪv] *adj* intensiv; (*analysis*) gründlich; (*bombardment*) heftig

intensive 'care *n* Intensivpflege *f*; **to be in** ~ auf der Intensivstation sein

intent [ɪn·ˈtent] *n* Absicht *f*; **with ~ to do sth** mit dem Vorsatz, etw zu tun

intention [ɪn·ˈten·ʃən] *n* Absicht *f*; **full of good ~s** voller guter Vorsätze

intentional [ɪn·ˈten·ʃə·nəl] *adj* absichtlich

interact [ɪn·tər·ˈækt] *vi* aufeinander einwirken

interaction [ˌɪn·tər·ˈæk·ʃən] *n* Wechselwirkung *f*; (*of groups, people*) Interaktion *f*

interactive [ˌɪn·tər·ˈæk·tɪv] *adj* interaktiv

interbreed <-bred, -bred> [ˌɪn·tər·ˈbrid] I. *vt* kreuzen II. *vi* sich kreuzen

intercept [ˌɪn·tər·ˈsept] *vt* abfangen; ~ **a call** eine Fangschaltung legen; **to ~ a pass** SPORT einen Pass abfangen

interception [ˌɪn·tər·ˈsep·ʃən] *n* Abfangen *nt*; (*of calls*) Abhören *nt*

interceptor [ˌɪn·tər·ˈsep·tər] *n* MIL Abfangjäger *m*

interchange *n* [ˈɪn·tər·tʃeɪndʒ] 1. Austausch *m* 2. (*road*) Autobahnkreuz *nt*

interchangeable [ˌɪn·tər·ˈtʃeɪn·dʒə·bəl] *adj* austauschbar; (*word*) synonym

intercity [ˌɪn·tər·ˈsɪt·i] *adj attr* (*transportation*) Intercity-

intercom [ˈɪn·tər·kam] *n* [Gegen]sprechanlage *f*; (*for doors*) [Tür]sprechanlage *f*

intercontinental [ˌɪn·tər·ˌkan·tə·ˈnen·təl] *adj* interkontinental

intercourse [ˈɪn·tər·kɔrs] *n* 1. (*sex*) [Geschlechts]verkehr *m* 2. (*dealings*) Umgang *m*

interdict [ˌɪn·tər·ˈdɪkt] LAW I. *n* Verbot *nt*

II. *vt* verbieten

interest ['ɪn·trɪst] I. *n* 1. Interesse *nt* (**in** an +*dat*); **in the ~ of safety** aus Sicherheitsgründen 2. FIN Zinsen *pl*; **rate of ~** Zinssatz *m* II. *vt* interessieren (**in** für +*akk*)

interested ['ɪn·trɪ·stɪd] *adj* 1. (*concerned*) interessiert; **to be ~ in sb/sth** sich für jdn/etw interessieren 2. (*involved*) beteiligt; (*witness*) befangen

interest-free *adj* FIN zinslos; (*credit*) unverzinslich

interesting ['ɪn·trɪ·stɪŋ] *adj* interessant

interface *n* ['ɪn·tər·feɪs] Schnittstelle *f*; COMPUT, TECH Interface *nt*

interfere [ˌɪn·tər·ˈfɪr] *vi* 1. (*meddle*) **to ~ (in sth)** sich [in etw *akk*] einmischen 2. (*hit*) **to ~ with one another** aneinanderstoßen

interference [ˌɪn·tər·ˈfɪr·əns] *n* 1. Einmischung *f* 2. RADIO, TECH Störung *f*

interim ['ɪn·tər·ɪm] I. *n* Zwischenzeit *f* II. *adj attr* vorläufig; **~ government** Übergangsregierung *f*

interior [ɪn·ˈtɪr·i·ər] I. *adj attr* 1. (*inside*) Innen- 2. (*country*) Inlands-, Binnen- II. *n* 1. (*inside*) Innere *nt* 2. POL **the I~** das Innere; **the Department of the I~** das Innenministerium; **Secretary of the I~** Innenminister(in) *m(f)*

interior de'signer *n* Innenarchitekt(in) *m(f)*

interject [ˌɪn·tər·ˈdʒekt] I. *vt* einwerfen II. *vi* dazwischenreden

interjection [ˌɪn·tər·ˈdʒek·ʃən] *n* 1. (*interruption*) Zwischenbemerkung *f* 2. LING Interjektion *f*

intermediate [ˌɪn·tər·ˈmi·di·ɪt] *adj* 1. (*level*) mittel; (*between two things*) Zwischen-; 2. (*level of skill*) Mittel-; **~ course** Kurs *m* für fortgeschrittene Anfänger/Anfängerinnen

intermezzo <*pl* -s> [ˌɪn·tər·ˈmet·soʊ] *n* Intermezzo *nt*

interminable [ɪn·ˈtɜr·mɪ·nə·bəl] *adj* endlos

intermission [ˌɪn·tər·ˈmɪʃ·ən] *n* Pause *f*

intermittent [ˌɪn·tər·ˈmɪt·ənt] *adj* periodisch

intern I. *vt* [ɪn·ˈtɜrn] internieren II. *vi* [ɪn·ˈtɜrn] ein Praktikum absolvieren III. *n* ['ɪn·tɜrn] Praktikant(in) *m(f)*; [**hospital**] **~** Assistenzarzt, Assistenzärztin *m, f*

internal [ɪn·ˈtɜr·nəl] *adj* innere(r, s); (*within company*) innerbetrieblich; (*within country*) Binnen-; (*investigation, memo*) intern; **~ affairs** innere Angelegenheiten *pl*

internalize [ɪn·ˈtɜr·nə·laɪz] *vt* verinnerlichen

Internal 'Revenue Service *n* **the ~** ≈ das Finanzamt

international [ˌɪn·tər·ˈnæʃ·ə·nəl] *adj* international

International Court of 'Justice *n* Internationaler Gerichtshof

International 'Monetary Fund *n* Internationaler Währungsfonds

International O'lympic Committee *n* Internationales Olympisches Komitee

Internet ['ɪn·tər·net] I. *n* Internet *nt*; **to surf the ~** im Internet surfen; **on the ~** im Internet II. *adj* Internet-

Internet 'banking *n* Internetbanking *nt*

internist [ɪn·ˈtɜr·nɪst] *n* Internist(in) *m(f)*

internment [ɪn·ˈtɜrn·mənt] *n* Internierung *f*

in'ternment camp *n* Internierungslager *nt*

interpersonal [ˌɪn·tər·ˈpɜr·sə·nəl] *adj* zwischenmenschlich; **~ skills** soziale Kompetenz

interplanetary [ˌɪn·tər·ˈplæn·ə·ter·i] *adj* interplanetarisch

interplay ['ɪn·tər·pleɪ] *n* Zusammenspiel *nt* (**of** von +*dat*), Wechselwirkung *f* (**between** zwischen +*dat*)

Interpol ['ɪn·tər·pal] *n no art* Interpol *f*

interpolate [ɪn·ˈtɜr·pə·leɪt] *vt* einfügen; (*opinion*) einfließen lassen

interpret [ɪn·ˈtɜr·prɪt] I. *vt* 1. (*explain*) interpretieren; (*understand*) auslegen 2. (*perform*) wiedergeben; (*role*) auslegen II. *vi* dolmetschen

interpretation [ɪn·ˌtɜr·prɪ·ˈteɪ·ʃən] *n* Interpretation *f*; (*of rules*) Auslegung *f*; (*of dream*) Deutung *f*

interpreter [ɪn·ˈtɜr·prɪ·tər] *n* Dolmetscher(in) *m(f)*

interpreting [ɪn·ˈtɜr·prɪ·tɪŋ] *n* Dolmetschen *nt*

interrogate [ɪn·ˈter·ə·geɪt] *vt* verhören

interrogation [ɪn·ˌter·ə·ˈgeɪ·ʃən] n Verhör nt

interrogatory [ˌɪn·tə·ˈrag·ə·tɔr·i] adj fragend attr

interrupt [ˌɪn·tə·ˈrʌpt] vt, vi unterbrechen

interruption [ˌɪn·tə·ˈrʌp·ʃən] n Unterbrechung f

intersection [ˌɪn·tər·ˈsek·ʃən] n 1. Schnittpunkt m 2. (junction) [Straßen]kreuzung f

interstate [ˈɪn·tər·ˈsteɪt] I. adj attr zwischenstaatlich II. n [Bundes]autobahn f

interstate ˈhighway n [Bundes]autobahn f

interval [ˈɪn·tər·vəl] n 1. (gap) Abstand m 2. (break) Pause f, Intervall nt

intervene [ˌɪn·tər·ˈvin] vi 1. (step in) einschreiten 2. (interrupt) sich einmischen

intervening [ˌɪn·tər·ˈvin·ɪŋ] adj attr dazwischenliegend attr

intervention [ˌɪn·tər·ˈven·ʃən] n Eingreifen nt

interview [ˈɪn·tər·vju] I. n 1. (with media) Interview nt 2. (for job) Vorstellungsgespräch nt 3. (with police) Verhör nt II. vt to ~ sb (by reporter) jdn interviewen; (for job) mit jdm ein Vorstellungsgespräch führen; (by police) jdn befragen

interviewee [ˌɪn·tər·vju·ˈi] n Interviewte(r) f(m); (by police) Befragte(r) f(m); **job** ~ Kandidat(in) m(f)

interviewer [ˈɪn·tər·vju·ər] n (reporter) Interviewer(in) m(f); (in job interview) Leiter(in) m(f) des Vorstellungsgesprächs

intestine [ɪn·ˈtes·tɪn] n usu pl Darm m, Eingeweide pl

intimacy [ˈɪn·tə·mə·si] n Intimität f; (sexual) Intimitäten pl

intimate [ˈɪn·tə·mɪt] adj 1. (close) eng, vertraut; (atmosphere) gemütlich; (friend) eng; (relationship) intim 2. (detailed) gründlich; (knowledge) umfassend 3. (private) ~ details intime Einzelheiten

intimidate [ɪn·ˈtɪm·ɪ·deɪt] vt einschüchtern

intimidating [ɪn·ˈtɪm·ɪ·deɪṭ·ɪŋ] adj beängstigend; (manner) einschüchternd

intimidation [ɪn·ˌtɪm·ɪ·ˈdeɪ·ʃən] n Einschüchterung f

into [ˈɪn·tə, -tu] prep 1. (to inside) in +akk; to go ~ town in die Stadt gehen 2. (toward) in +akk; she looked ~ the mirror sie sah in den Spiegel 3. (through time) sometimes we work late ~ the evening manchmal arbeiten wir bis spät in den Abend 4. fam (interested) to be ~ sb/sth an jdm/etw interessiert sein; what kind of music are you ~? auf welche Art von Musik stehst du? 5. (transition) to translate ~ French ins Französische übersetzen

intolerable [ɪn·ˈtal·ər·ə·bəl] adj unerträglich

intolerance [ɪn·ˈtal·ər·əns] n a. MED Intoleranz f (of gegenüber +dat)

intolerant [ɪn·ˈtal·ər·ənt] adj 1. intolerant 2. MED überempfindlich (of gegenüber +dat)

intoxicating [ɪn·ˈtak·sɪ·keɪ·ṭɪŋ] adj berauschend a. fig

Intranet [ˈɪn·trə·ˈnet] n Intranet nt

intransitive [ɪn·ˈtræn·sɪ·ṭɪv] adj intransitiv

intravenous [ˌɪn·trə·ˈvi·nəs] adj intravenös

intricate [ˈɪn·trɪ·kɪt] adj kompliziert

intrigue I. vi [ɪn·ˈtrig] intrigieren II. n [ˈɪn·trig] Intrige f

intriguing [ɪn·ˈtri·gɪŋ] adj faszinierend

introduce [ˌɪn·trə·ˈdus] vt einführen; to ~ sb [to sb] jdn [jdm] vorstellen

introduction [ˌɪn·trə·ˈdʌk·ʃən] n Einführung f

intro'ductory course n Einführungskurs m

introspection [ˌɪn·trə·ˈspek·ʃən] n Selbstbeobachtung f

introvert [ˈɪn·trə·ˌvɜrt] n introvertierter Mensch

introverted [ˈɪn·trə·ˌvɜr·ṭɪd] adj introvertiert

intrude [ɪn·ˈtrud] vi stören, sich einmischen (into in +akk); am I intruding? störe ich gerade?; to ~ on sb's privacy in jds Privatsphäre eindringen

intruder [ɪn·ˈtru·dər] n Eindringling m; (thief) Einbrecher(in) m(f)

ntrusion [ɪn'tru·ʒən] *n* Störung *f*, Einmischung *f*

ntrusive [ɪn'tru·sɪv] *adj* aufdringlich

ntuition [ˌɪn·tu·'ɪʃ·ən] *n* Intuition *f*

ntuitive [ɪn·'tu·ɪ·tɪv] *adj* intuitiv

nvade [ɪn·'veɪd] **I.** *vt* **1.** to ~ a country in ein Land einmarschieren **2.** *fig* (*breach*) **to ~ sb's privacy** jds Privatsphäre verletzen **II.** *vi* einfallen

nvader [ɪn·'veɪ·dər] *n* Angreifer(in) *m(f)*; (*encroacher*) Eindringling *m*

nvalid[1] [ɪn·və·lɪd] **I.** *n* Invalide(r) *m(f)* **II.** *adj* invalide, körperbehindert

nvalid[2] [ɪn·'væl·ɪd] *adj* (*void*) ungültig; (*unsound*) nicht stichhaltig; (*theory*) nicht begründet

nvalidate [ɪn·'væl·ɪ·deɪt] *vt* (*argument*) widerlegen; (*judgment*) aufheben; (*results*) annullieren; (*theory*) entkräften

nvalidity [ˌɪn·və·'lɪd·ə·t̬i] *n* **1.** MED Invalidität *f* **2.** LAW ~ **of a contract** Nichtigkeit *f* eines Vertrags

nvaluable [ɪn·'væl·ju·ə·bəl] *adj* unbezahlbar; (*source*) unverzichtbar

nvariable [ɪn·'ver·i·ə·bəl] *adj* unveränderlich

nvariably [ɪn·'ver·i·ə·bli] *adv* ausnahmslos

nvasion [ɪn·'veɪ·ʒən] *n* **1.** MIL Invasion *f* **2.** (*interference*) Eindringen *nt kein pl* (**of** in +*akk*)

nvent [ɪn·'vent] *vt* erfinden

nvention [ɪn·'ven·ʃən] *n* Erfindung *f*; (*creativity*) Einfallsreichtum *m*

nventive [ɪn·'ven·tɪv] *adj* einfallsreich, fantasievoll

nventiveness [ɪn·'ven·tɪv·nɪs] *n* Einfallsreichtum *m*

nventor [ɪn·'ven·tər] *n* Erfinder(in) *m(f)*

nventory [ˈɪn·vən·tɔr·i] **I.** *n* Inventar *nt*, [Lager]bestand *m;* **to take ~** Inventur machen **II.** *adj* Bestands-

nvert [ɪn·'vɜrt] *vt* umkehren

nvertebrate [ɪn·'vɜr·t̬ə·brɪt] **I.** *n* wirbelloses Tier **II.** *adj* wirbellos

nvest [ɪn·'vest] **I.** *vt* investieren **II.** *vi* **to ~ in sth** [sein Geld] in etw *akk* investieren

nvestigate [ɪn·'ves·tɪ·geɪt] *vt* untersuchen

nvestigation [ɪn·ˌves·tɪ·'geɪ·ʃən] *n* Un-

tersuchung *f;* (*of affair*) [Über]prüfung *f;* (*by police*) Ermittlung *f;* (*inquiry*) Nachforschung *f*

investigator [ɪn·'ves·tɪ·geɪ·t̬ər] *n form* Ermittler(in) *m(f)*

investment [ɪn·'vest·mənt] **I.** *n* **1.** (*act*) Investierung *f* **2.** (*instance*) Investition *f* **3.** (*share*) Einlage *f* **II.** *adj* Anlage-, Investitions-, Investment-

in'vestment bank *n* FIN Investmentbank *f*

in'vestment fund *n* Investmentfonds *m*

investor [ɪn·'ves·t̬ər] *n* [Kapital]anleger(in) *m(f)*, Investor(in) *m(f)*

invigorate [ɪn·'vɪg·ə·reɪt] *vt* **1.** stärken **2.** *fig* (*stimulate*) beleben

invigorating [ɪn·'vɪg·ə·reɪ·t̬ɪŋ] *adj* **1.** stärkend **2.** *fig* (*stimulating*) belebend

invincible [ɪn·'vɪn·sə·bəl] *adj* **1.** (*unbeatable*) unschlagbar **2.** (*insuperable*) unüberwindlich

invisible [ɪn·'vɪz·ə·bəl] *adj* unsichtbar

invitation [ˌɪn·vɪ·'teɪ·ʃən] *n* **1.** (*request*) Einladung *f* (**to** zu +*dat*) **2.** (*incitement*) Aufforderung *f* (**to** zu +*dat*) **3.** (*chance*) Gelegenheit *f*

invite I. *n* [ˈɪn·vaɪt] *fam* Einladung *f* (**to** zu +*dat*) **II.** *vt* [ɪn·'vaɪt] **1.** (*to party*) einladen **2.** (*request*) **to ~ sb to do sth** jdn auffordern, etw zu tun **3.** *fig* (*cause*) herausfordern; **to ~ trouble** Unannehmlichkeiten hervorrufen

inviting [ɪn·'vaɪ·t̬ɪŋ] *adj* **1.** (*sight, weather*) einladend; (*appearance, fashion*) ansprechend **2.** (*tempting*) verlockend; (*gesture, smile*) einladend

in vitro [ɪn·'vi·troʊ] **I.** *adj* künstlich, Invitro- **II.** *adv* künstlich, in vitro *fachspr*

in vitro fertili'zation *n* künstliche Befruchtung

invoice [ˈɪn·vɔɪs] **I.** *vt* **to ~ sb** jdm eine Rechnung ausstellen **II.** *n* [Waren]rechnung *f*

involuntary [ɪn·'val·ən·ter·i] *adj* **1.** unfreiwillig **2.** (*unintentional*) unbeabsichtigt

involve [ɪn·'valv] *vt* **1.** (*include*) beinhalten; (*encompass*) umfassen; (*entail*) mit sich bringen; (*mean*) bedeuten **2.** (*affect*) betreffen; **that doesn't ~ her** sie

hat damit nichts zu tun; **this incident ~s us all** dieser Zwischenfall geht uns alle an **3.** (*bring in*) **to ~ sb in sth** jdn an etw *dat* beteiligen; (*unwillingly*) jdn in etw *akk* verwickeln; **I don't want to get ~d** ich will damit nichts zu tun haben **4.** *usu passive* **to be ~d in sth** (*be busy*) mit etw *dat* zu tun haben; (*be engrossed*) von etw *dat* gefesselt sein; **to be ~d with sb** (*have to do with*) mit jdm zu tun haben; (*relationship*) mit jdm eine Beziehung haben; (*affair*) mit jdm ein Verhältnis haben

involved [ɪnˈvalvd] *adj* kompliziert; (*affair*) verwickelt; (*issue*) komplex

involvement [ɪnˈvalv·mənt] *n* **1.** (*participation*) Beteiligung *f*, Verwicklung *f* (**in** +*dat*) **2.** (*complexity*) Komplexität *f* **3.** (*relationship*) Verhältnis *nt*

invulnerable [ɪnˈvʌl·nər·ə·bəl] *adj* **1.** unverwundbar **2.** *fig* unantastbar

inward [ˈɪn·wərd] **I.** *adj* **1.** (*ingoing*) nach innen gehend **2.** (*incoming*) Eingangs-, eindringend **3.** *usu fig* (*internal*) innere(r, s), innerlich **II.** *adv* einwärts, nach innen

inwardly [ˈɪn·wərd·li] *adv* innerlich

inwards [ˈɪn·wərdz] *adv* nach innen

IOC [ˌaɪ·oʊˈsi] *n* + *sing/pl vb abbr of* **International Olympic Committee; the ~** das IOC

iodine [ˈaɪ·ə·daɪn] *n* Jod *nt*

ion [ˈaɪ·ən] *n* Ion *nt*

IOU [ˌaɪ·oʊˈju] *n fam abbr of* **I owe you** Schuldschein *m*

Iowa [ˈaɪ·ə·wə] *n* Iowa *nt*

IQ [ˌaɪˈkju] *n abbr of* **intelligence quotient** IQ *m*

IRA [ˌaɪ·ɑrˈeɪ] *n* **1.** FIN *abbr of* **Individual Retirement Account** [steuerbegünstigte] Altersvorsorge **2.** *abbr of* **Irish Republican Army; the ~** die IRA

Iran [ɪˈræn] *n* [der] Iran

Iranian [ɪˈreɪ·ni·ən] **I.** *n* Iraner(in) *m(f)* **II.** *adj* iranisch

Iraq [ɪˈrɑk] *n* [der] Irak

Iraqi [ɪˈrɑk·i] **I.** *n* Iraker(in) *m(f)* **II.** *adj* irakisch

Ireland [ˈaɪr·lənd] *n* Irland *nt*

iris <*pl* -es> [ˈaɪ·rɪs] *n* ANAT, BOT Iris *f*

Irish [ˈaɪ·rɪʃ] **I.** *adj* irisch **II.** *n pl* **the ~** die Iren *pl*

Irishman *n* Ire *m*

Irishwoman *n* Irin *f*

iron [ˈaɪ·ərn] *n* **1.** Eisen *nt* **2.** (*appliance*) [Bügel]eisen *nt* **3.** (*club*) Golfschläger *m* ▸ **to have many/other ~s in the fire** viele/andere Eisen im Feuer haben **II.** *adj* Eisen-; *fig* (*strict*) eisern **III.** *vt, vi* bügeln

Iron Age I. *n* Eisenzeit *f* **II.** *adj* eisenzeitlich

iron curtain *n hist* **the I~ C~** der Eiserne Vorhang

ironic [aɪˈran·ɪk] *adj* ironisch

ironing [ˈaɪ·ər·nɪŋ] *n* Bügeln *nt;* (*laundry*) Bügelwäsche *f*

ironing board *n* Bügelbrett *nt*

iron lung *n* eiserne Lunge

iron ore *n* Eisenerz *nt*

ironworks *n* + *sing/pl vb* Eisenhütte *f*

irony [ˈaɪ·rə·ni] *n* Ironie *f*

irrational [ɪˈræʃ·ə·nəl] *adj* irrational

irreconcilable [ɪ·ˌrek·ən·ˈsaɪ·lə·bəl] *adj* (*ideas, views*) unvereinbar; (*enemies*) unversöhnlich

irregular [ɪˈreg·jə·lər] *adj* **1.** (*asymmetrical*) unregelmäßig; (*surface*) uneben **2.** (*unorthodox: conduct*) regelwidrig (*action*) ungesetzlich; (*dealings*) zwielichtig

irrelevant [ɪˈrel·ə·vənt] *adj* belanglos

irreparable [ɪˈrep·ər·ə·bəl] *adj* irreparabel; (*damage, loss*) unersetzlich

irreplaceable [ˌɪr·ɪ·ˈpleɪ·sə·bəl] *adj* unersetzlich; (*resources*) nicht erneuerbar

irresistible [ˌɪr·ɪ·ˈzɪs·tə·bəl] *adj* unwiderstehlich; (*argument*) schlagend

irrespective [ˌɪr·ɪ·ˈspek·tɪv] *adv* ~ **of sth** ohne Rücksicht auf etw *akk* ungeachtet einer S. *gen* ~ **of what ...** unabhängig davon, was ...

irresponsible [ˌɪr·ɪ·ˈspan·sə·bəl] *adj* **1.** (*inconsiderate*) unverantwortlich; (*person*) verantwortungslos **2.** LAW unzurechnungsfähig

irretrievable [ˌɪr·ɪ·ˈtri·və·bəl] *adj* (*losses*) unersetzlich

irreversible [ˌɪr·ɪ·ˈvɜr·sə·bəl] *adj* nicht umkehrbar, irreversibel

irrevocable [ɪˈrev·ə·kə·bəl] *adj* unwider-

ruflich, endgültig

rrigate ['ɪr·ɪ·geɪt] *vt* bewässern

rrigation [ˌɪr·ɪ'geɪ·ʃən] **I.** *n* 1. Bewässerung *f;* (*of crops*) Berieselung *f* **II.** *adj* Bewässerungs-

rritable ['ɪr·ɪ·tə·bəl] *adj* reizbar, gereizt; (*organ, tissue*) [über]empfindlich

rritant ['ɪr·ɪ·tənt] *n* 1. (*substance*) Reizstoff *m* 2. (*annoyance*) Ärgernis *nt*

rritate ['ɪr·ɪ·teɪt] *vt* 1. (*anger*) [ver]ärgern 2. (*inflame*) to ~ skin Hautreizungen hervorrufen

rritating ['ɪr·ɪ·teɪt·ɪŋ] *adj* ärgerlich, lästig; (*conduct*) irritierend

rritation [ˌɪr·ɪ'teɪ·ʃən] *n* 1. (*annoyance*) Verärgerung *f* 2. (*nuisance*) Ärgernis *nt* 3. (*inflammation*) Reizung *f;* to cause ~ eine Reizung hervorrufen

RS [ˌaɪ·ɑr·'es] *n* FIN *abbr of* **Internal Revenue Service** Finanzamt *nt*

s [ɪz] *aux vb 3rd pers. sing of* be

SBN [ˌaɪ·es·bi·'en] *n abbr of* **International Standard Book Number** ISBN-Nummer *f*

SDN [ˌaɪ·es·di·'en] *n* TELEC *abbr of* **integrated services digital network** ISDN

slam [ɪz·'lɑm] *n* [der] Islam

Islamic [ɪz·'lɑm·ɪk] *adj* islamisch

island ['aɪ·lənd] *n* Insel *f a. fig*

islander ['aɪ·lən·dər] *n* Insulaner(in) *m(f)*

isle [aɪl] *n liter* Eiland *nt*

sn't ['ɪz·ənt] = **is not** *see* **is**

isolate ['aɪ·sə·leɪt] *vt* isolieren (**from** von +*dat*); to ~ oneself sich abkapseln; to ~ a problem ein Problem gesondert betrachten

isolated ['aɪ·sə·leɪ·tɪd] *adj* 1. (*outlying*) abgelegen; (*detached: building, house*) frei stehend 2. (*solitary*) einsam [gelegen]; (*village*) abgeschieden 3. (*excluded: country*) isoliert

isolation [ˌaɪ·sə·'leɪ·ʃən] **I.** *n* Isolation *f;* (*of building, house*) Abgelegenheit *f;* ~ **from noise** Isolierung *f* gegen Schall **II.** *adj* (*block, cell*) Isolations-; (*resistor, switch*) Trenn-

iso'lation ward *n* Isolierstation *f*

ISP [ˌaɪ·es·'pi] *n* INET, TELEC *abbr of* **Internet service provider** ISP *m*

Israel ['ɪz·ri·əl] *n* Israel *nt*

Israeli [ɪz·'reɪ·li] **I.** *n* Israeli *m o f* **II.** *adj* israelisch

Israelite ['ɪz·ri·ə·laɪt] *n* Israelit(in) *m(f)*

issue ['ɪʃ·u] **I.** *n* 1. (*topic*) Thema *nt;* to make an ~ of sth etw aufbauschen 2. (*question*) Frage *f,* Problem *nt;* that's not the ~! darum geht es doch gar nicht!; to raise an ~ eine Frage aufwerfen; **the point at** ~ der strittige Punkt *f* 3. (*affair*) Sache *f* 4. (*edition*) Ausgabe *f;* date of ~ Erscheinungsdatum *nt* 5. FIN (*of shares*) Emission *f;* (*of check, document*) Ausstellung *f* **II.** *vt* 1. (*produce*) ausstellen; (*currency*) in Umlauf bringen; (*bonds*) ausgeben; (*newsletter*) veröffentlichen; (*command*) erteilen; (*ultimatum*) stellen; (*statement*) abgeben; to ~ **an arrest warrant** einen Haftbefehl erlassen 2. (*supply with*) to ~ sb with sth jdn mit etw *dat* ausstatten

it [ɪt] *pron* 1. (*unknown thing*) es; (*known thing*) er/es/sie; a room with two beds in ~ ein Raum mit zwei Betten darin 2. (*in time phrases*) what time is ~? wie spät ist es?; what day is ~? welchen Tag haben wir heute? 3. *subject* (*referring to following*) it's important/a shame that ... es ist wichtig/schade, dass ...; ~'s true I don't like **Stephanie** es stimmt, ich mag Stephanie nicht 4. (*in passive with verbs of opinion*) ~ is said that ... es heißt, dass ... 5. *emph* ~ was Paul who came here in September, not Bob Paul kam im September, nicht Bob 6. (*situation*) ~ appears that we have lost mir scheint, wir haben verloren; ~ takes me an hour to ... ich brauche eine Stunde, um ...; if ~'s convenient wenn es Ihnen/dir passt 7. (*right thing*) that's exactly ~ — what a great find! das ist genau das – ein toller Fund!; that's ~! das ist es! 8. (*the end*) that's ~ das war's ▶ go for ~! mach es!; go for ~, girl! du schaffst es, Mädchen!; this **is** ~ jetzt geht's los; <u>that's</u> ~ das ist der Punkt

IT [ˌaɪ·'ti] *n* COMPUT *abbr of* **information technology** IT *f*

Italian [ɪ·'tæl·jən] **I.** *n* 1. (*person*) Italiener(in) *m(f)* 2. (*language*) Italienisch *nt* **II.** *adj* italienisch

italic [ɪ·ˈtæl·ɪk] *adj* TYPO kursiv

italics [ɪ·ˈtæl·ɪks] *npl* TYPO Kursivschrift *f*

Italy [ˈɪt·ə·li] *n* Italien *nt*

itch [ɪtʃ] I. *n* <*pl* -es> Juckreiz *m;* I've got an ~ on my back es juckt mich am Rücken II. *vi* 1. (*prickle*) jucken 2. *fig fam* (*desire*) to be ~ing to do sth ganz wild darauf sein, etw zu tun

itchy [ˈɪtʃ·i] *adj* juckend; (*clothes*) kratzig

item [ˈaɪ·təm] *n* 1. (*thing*) Gegenstand *m;* (*in catalog*) Artikel *m;* ~ of furniture Möbelstück *nt;* luxury ~ Luxusartikel *m* 2. (*on agenda*) Punkt *m;* (*on list*) Posten *m;* ~ by ~ Punkt für Punkt

itinerary [aɪ·ˈtɪn·ə·rer·i] *n* Reiseroute *f*

it'll [ˈɪt·əl] = **it will/it shall** *see* **will**[1], **shall**

its [ɪts] *pron poss* sein(e)/ihr(e)

it's [ɪts] = **it is, it has** *see* **be, have** I, II

itself [ɪt·ˈself] *pron refl* 1. *after vb, prep* sich [selbst] 2. (*specifically*) the store ~ opened 15 years ago das Geschäft selbst öffnete vor 15 Jahren 3. (*alone*) [all] by ~ [ganz] allein

IUD [ˌaɪ·ju·ˈdi] *n abbr of* **intrauterine device** Intrauterinpessar *nt*

IV [ˌaɪ·ˈvi] *adj abbr of* **intravenous** intravenös

I've [aɪv] = **I have** *see* **have** I, II

IVF [ˌaɪ·vi·ˈef] *n abbr of* **in vitro fertilization** IVF *f*

ivory [ˈaɪ·və·ri] I. *n* Elfenbein *nt* II. *adj* Elfenbein-; ~~colored elfenbeinfarben

Ivory Coast *n* the ~ die Elfenbeinküste

ivy [ˈaɪ·vi] *n* Efeu *m*

Ivy League I. *n* the ~ *Eliteuniversitäten im Nordosten der USA* II. *n modifier* der Ivy League angehörende Eliteuniversitäten

J

J <*pl* -'s>, **j** <*pl* -'s> [dʒeɪ] *n* J *nt*, j *nt;* ~ as in Juliet J wie Julius

jab [dʒæb] I. *n* Stoß *m;* (*with knife*) Stich *m;* (*in boxing*) Gerade *f* II. *vt* <-bb-> schlagen; (*with knife*) stechen III. *vi* <-bb-> (*in boxing*) eine [kurze]

Gerade schlagen

jack [dʒæk] *n* 1. AUTO Wagenheber *r* 2. CARDS Bube *m*

jack off *vi vulg* wichsen *vulg*

jack up I. *vt* 1. (*car*) aufbocken 2. *fi* erhöhen; (*prices, rent*) in die Höhe trei ben II. *vi sl* fixen *fam*

jackal [ˈdʒæk·əl] *n* Schakal *m*

jackdaw [ˈdʒæk·dɔ] *n* Dohle *f*

jacket [ˈdʒæk·ɪt] *n* 1. FASHION Jacke 2. (*of a book*) Schutzumschlag *m*

jackhammer [ˈdʒæk·ˌhæm·ər] *n* Press lufthammer *m*

jackknife *n* Klappmesser *nt;* SPORT Hecht sprung *m*

jack-of-all-trades *n* Alleskönner(in) *m(f*

jack-o'-lantern *n* Kürbislaterne *f*

jackpot *n* Hauptgewinn *m*

Jacuzzi® [dʒə·ˈku·zi] *n* Whirlpool *m*

jade [dʒeɪd] I. *n* Jade *m o f* II. *adj* ja degrün

jagged [ˈdʒæg·ɪd] *adj* 1. gezackt; (*coast line, rocks*) zerklüftet; (*cut, tear*) ausge franst 2. *fig* (*nerves*) angeschlagen

jaguar [ˈdʒæg·war] *n* Jaguar *m*

jail [dʒeɪl] I. *n* Gefängnis *nt* II. *vt* ein sperren

jailbird *n fam* Knastbruder *m*

jailbreak *n* Gefängnisausbruch *m*

jailer [ˈdʒeɪ·lər] *n* Gefängnisaufse her(in) *m(f)*

jam[1] [dʒæm] *n* Marmelade *f*

jam[2] [dʒæm] I. *n* 1. *fam* (*awkward situ ation*) Klemme *f* 2. (*of people*) Gedrän ge *nt;* (*of traffic*) Stau *m* II. *vt* <-mm-> 1. (*block*) verklemmen; to ~ sth oper etw aufstemmen 2. (*cram inside*) [hi nein]zwängen (**into** in +*akk*) III. *v* <-mm-> sich verklemmen; (*brakes* blockieren

Jamaica [dʒə·ˈmeɪ·kə] *n* Jamaika *nt*

Jamaican [dʒə·ˈmeɪ·kən] I. *n* Jamaika ner(in) *m(f)* II. *adj* jamaikanisch

jam-packed *adj fam* (*bus, store*) geram melt voll; (*bag, box*) randvoll; (*suitcase* vollgestopft

Jan. *n abbr of* **January** Jan.

janitor [ˈdʒæn·ɪ·tər] *n* Hausmeis ter(in) *m(f)*

January [ˈdʒæn·ju·er·i] *n* Januar *m* *see also* **February**

Japan [dʒə·'pæn] n Japan nt

Japanese [ˌdʒæp·ə·'niz] I. n <pl -> 1. (person) Japaner(in) m(f) 2. (language) Japanisch nt II. adj japanisch

jar [dʒɑr] n 1. (of glass) Glas[gefäß] nt; (of metal or clay) Topf m

jargon ['dʒɑr·gən] n [Fach]jargon m

jasmine ['dʒæs·mɪn] n Jasmin m

jaundice ['dʒɔn·dɪs] n Gelbsucht f

javelin ['dʒæv·lɪn] n Speer m; (event) Speerwerfen nt

jaw [dʒɔ] n Kiefer m; lower/upper ~ Unter-/Oberkiefer m

'jawbone n Kieferknochen m

'jawbreaker n 1. FOOD großes, rundes, steinhartes Bonbon 2. fam (tongue twister) Zungenbrecher m

jay [dʒeɪ] n Eichelhäher m

'jaywalker n unachtsamer Fußgänger/ unachtsame Fußgängerin

'jaywalking n unachtsames Überqueren einer Straße

jazz [dʒæz] n 1. (music) Jazz m 2. pej fam (nonsense) Quatsch m fam ▶ and all that ~ fam und all so was

'jazz up vt fam 1. MUS verjazzen 2. fig aufpeppen

jazzy ['dʒæz·i] adj 1. MUS Jazz-, jazzartig 2. fig (colors) knallig; (piece of clothing) poppig

jealous ['dʒel·əs] adj 1. (resentful) eifersüchtig (of auf +akk) 2. (envious) neidisch (of auf +akk)

jealousy ['dʒel·ə·si] n 1. (resentment) Eifersucht f 2. (envy) Neid m

jeans [dʒinz] npl Jeans[hose] f; a pair of ~ eine Jeans[hose]

jeep [dʒip] n Jeep m, Geländewagen m

jeer [dʒɪr] I. vt ausbuhen II. vi spotten (at über +akk) III. n höhnische Bemerkung

Jehovah [dʒɪ·'hoʊ·və] n Jehova m

jell [dʒel] vi see **gel**

jellied ['dʒel·id] adj in Aspik eingelegt

Jell-O® ['dʒel·oʊ] n Wackelpudding m

jelly ['dʒel·i] n 1. FOOD Gelee m o nt 2. (substance) Gelee nt

'jellybean n bohnenförmiges Geleebonbon

'jellyfish n 1. (sea animal) Qualle f 2. pej fam (cowardly person) Wasch-

lappen m

jeopardize ['dʒep·ər·daɪz] vt gefährden; (career, future) aufs Spiel setzen

jeopardy ['dʒep·ər·di] n Gefahr f

jerk [dʒɜrk] I. n 1. (movement) Ruck m 2. pej sl (annoying person) Trottel m fam II. vi zucken; to ~ upwards hochschnellen; to ~ to a halt abrupt zum Stillstand kommen III. vt to ~ sb/sth jdn/etw mit einem Ruck ziehen; to ~ sb out of sth fig jdn aus etw dat reißen

◆jerk off vi vulg wichsen

jerkin ['dʒɜr·kɪn] n ärmellose Jacke

jerky ['dʒɜr·ki] I. adj (movement) ruckartig; (speech) abgehackt II. n luftgetrocknetes Fleisch

jersey ['dʒɜr·zi] n 1. (garment) Pullover m; SPORT Trikot nt 2. (cloth) Jersey m

jest [dʒest] n form Scherz m, Spaß m

Jesuit ['dʒez·u·ɪt] I. n Jesuit m II. adj jesuitisch, Jesuiten-

Jesus ['dʒi·zəs], **Jesus Christ** [ˌdʒi·zəs 'kraɪst] I. n Jesus m, Jesus Christus m II. interj pej sl Mensch! fam

jet [dʒet] I. n 1. AVIAT [Düsen]jet m 2. (thin stream) Strahl m 3. (nozzle) Düse f II. vi <-tt-> jetten fam

'jet-black adj pechschwarz

jet 'engine n Düsentriebwerk nt

jet 'fighter n Düsenjäger m

'jetfoil n Tragflügelboot nt

'jet lag n Jetlag m

'jet plane n Düsenflugzeug nt

jet-pro'pelled adj mit Düsenantrieb nach n

'jet set n fam Jetset m

Jew [dʒu] n Jude, Jüdin m, f

jewel ['dʒu·əl] n Edelstein m, Juwel m o nt

jeweler, jeweller ['dʒu·ə·lər] n Juwelier(in) m(f)

jewelry ['dʒu·əl·ri] n Schmuck m

Jewish ['dʒu·ɪʃ] adj jüdisch

'jigsaw n 1. (hand-operated) Laubsäge f; (electric) Stichsäge f 2. (puzzle) Puzzle[spiel] nt

jihad [dʒɪ·'had] n Dschihad m

jimmy ['dʒɪm·i] I. n Brecheisen nt II. vt <-ie-> to ~ open ⇆ sth etw aufbrechen

jingle ['dʒɪŋ·gəl] I. vt (bells) klingeln lassen; to ~ coins mit Münzen klimpern

II. *vi* (*bells*) bimmeln; (*coins*) klimpern

jive [dʒaɪv] I. *n* 1. (*dance*) Jive *m* 2. *sl* (*dishonest talk*) Gewäsch *nt fam* II. *vi* Jive tanzen

job [dʒab] *n* 1. (*employment*) Stelle *f;* **full-time/part-time** ~ Vollzeit-/Teilzeitstelle *f;* **to be out of a** ~ arbeitslos sein; **to give up one's** ~ kündigen 2. (*piece of work*) Arbeit *f;* (*task*) Aufgabe *f;* **she's only doing her** ~ sie tut nur ihre Pflicht; **to do a good** ~ **on sth** bei etw *dat* gute Arbeit leisten; **nose** ~ *fam* Nasenkorrektur *f* 3. *sl* (*crime*) Ding *nt fam*

'**job application** *n* Bewerbung *f*
jobber ['dʒab·ər] *n* Großhändler(in) *m(f)*
'**job creation** *n* Arbeitsbeschaffung *f*
'**job cuts** *npl* Stellenabbau *m kein pl*
'**job description** *n* Stellenbeschreibung *f*
'**job hunt** *n fam* Stellensuche *f*
'**job interview** *n* Bewerbungsgespräch *nt*
jobless ['dʒab·lɪs] I. *adj* arbeitslos II. *n* **the** ~ *pl* die Arbeitslosen *pl*
'**job market** *n* Arbeitsmarkt *m*
'**job-sharing** *n* Arbeitsplatzteilung *f*
'**job title** *n* Berufsbezeichnung *f*
jockey ['dʒak·i] I. *n* Jockey *m* II. *vi* **to** ~ **for sth** um etw *akk* konkurrieren
jog [dʒag] I. *n* (*run*) Dauerlauf *m;* **to go for a** ~ joggen gehen II. *vi* <-gg-> joggen
jogger ['dʒag·ər] *n* Jogger(in) *m(f)*
jogging ['dʒag·ɪŋ] *n* Joggen *nt*
john [dʒan] *n* 1. *fam* (*bathroom*) Klo *nt* 2. *sl* (*prostitute's client*) Freier *m fam*
join [dʒɔɪn] I. *vt* 1. (*connect*) **to** ~ **sth** [**to sth**] etw [mit etw *dat*] verbinden; (*add*) etw [an etw *akk*] anfügen 2. (*offer company*) **to** ~ **sb** sich zu jdm gesellen; **would you like to** ~ **us for dinner?** möchtest du mit uns zu Abend essen? 3. (*enroll*) beitreten; (*club, party*) Mitglied werden; **to** ~ **the army** Soldat werden 4. (*participate*) **to** ~ **sth** bei etw *dat* mitmachen; **let's** ~ **the dancing** lass uns mittanzen 5. (*support*) **to** ~ **sb in** [**doing**] **sth** jdm bei etw *dat* zur Seite stehen II. *vi* 1. (*connect*) **to** ~ [**with sth**] sich [mit etw *dat*] verbinden 2. (*cooperate*) **to** ~ **with sb in doing sth** sich mit jdm *dat* zusammenschlie-

ßen, um etw zu tun 3. (*enroll*) beitreten, Mitglied werden III. *n* (*seam*) Verbindung[sstelle] *f*
◆**join up** I. *vi* 1. MIL zum Militär gehen 2. (*meet*) **to** ~ **up with sb** sich mit jdm zusammentun II. *vt* **to** ~ **up** ⇆ **sth** etw [miteinander] verbinden; (*parts*) etw zusammenfügen
joint [dʒɔɪnt] I. *adj* gemeinsam II. *n* 1. (*connection*) Verbindungsstelle *f* 2. ANAT Gelenk *nt;* **to put sth out of** ~ etw ausrenken 3. *fam* (*cheap bar*) Laden *m* 4. (*cannabis cigarette*) Joint *m sl* ▶ **to be out of** ~ aus den Fugen sein
joint ac'count *n* Gemeinschaftskonto *nt*
jointly ['dʒɔɪnt·li] *adv* gemeinsam
joint 'owner *n* Miteigentümer(in) *m(f);* (*of a company*) Mitinhaber(in) *m(f)*
joint-stock 'company *n* Aktiengesellschaft *f*
joint 'venture *n* Joint Venture *nt*
joist [dʒɔɪst] *n* [Quer]balken *m*
joke [dʒoʊk] I. *n* Spaß *m;* (*trick*) Streich *m;* (*amusing thing, person*) Witz *m;* **to crack/tell** ~**s** Witze reißen/erzählen; **to make a** ~ **of sth** etw ins Lächerliche ziehen II. *vi* scherzen; **you must be joking!** das meinst du doch nicht im Ernst!; **to** ~ **about sth** sich über etw *akk* lustig machen
joker ['dʒoʊ·kər] *n* 1. (*person*) Spaßvogel *m* 2. CARDS Joker *m*
joking ['dʒoʊk·ɪŋ] I. *adj* scherzhaft II. *n* ~ **aside** Spaß beiseite
jokingly ['dʒoʊk·ɪŋ·li] *adv* im Scherz
jolly ['dʒal·i] *adj* lustig
Jolly 'Roger *n* Totenkopfflagge *f*
jolt [dʒoʊlt] *n* Stoß *m*, Ruck *m*
joss stick ['dʒas-] *n* Räucherstäbchen *nt*
jostle ['dʒas·əl] I. *vt* [an]rempeln II. *vi* [sich *akk*] drängeln
journal ['dʒɜr·nəl] *n* 1. (*periodical*) Zeitschrift *f;* (*newspaper*) Zeitung *f* 2. (*diary*) Tagebuch *nt*
journalism ['dʒɜr·nə·lɪz·əm] *n* Journalismus *m*
journalist ['dʒɜr·nə·lɪst] *n* Journalist(in) *m(f)*
journalistic [ˌdʒɜr·nə·'lɪs·tɪk] *adj* journalistisch
journey ['dʒɜr·ni] *n* Reise *f*

joy [dʒɔɪ] *n* Freude *f*, Vergnügen *nt;* **to jump for ~** einen Freudensprung machen

joyful ['dʒɔɪ·fəl] *adj* (*face, person*) fröhlich; (*event, news*) freudig

joyless ['dʒɔɪ·lɪs] *adj* freudlos

'joy ride *n* (*waghalsige*) Spritztour *(in einem gestohlenen Auto)*

'joystick *n* **1.** AVIAT Steuerknüppel *m* **2.** COMPUT Joystick *m*

JP *n abbr of* **Justice of the Peace**

Jr. *adj after n short for* **junior** jun.

jubilant ['dʒu·bɪ·lənt] *adj* glücklich; (*crowd*) jubelnd *attr*

jubilation [ˌdʒu·bɪ·'leɪ·ʃən] *n* Jubel *m*

jubilee ['dʒu·bə·li] *n* Jubiläum *nt*

Judaism ['dʒu·di·ɪz·əm] *n* Judaismus *m,* Judentum *nt*

judge [dʒʌdʒ] **I.** *n* **1.** LAW Richter(in) *m(f)* **2.** (*at a competition*) Preisrichter(in) *m(f);* (*in boxing, gymnastics, wrestling*) Punktrichter(in) *m(f);* (*in track and field, swimming*) Kampfrichter(in) *m(f)* **3.** (*expert: of literature, wine*) Kenner(in) *m(f)* **II.** *vi* **1.** (*decide*) urteilen; **~ing by his comments, ...** seinen Äußerungen nach zu urteilen, ... **2.** (*estimate*) schätzen **III.** *vt* **1.** (*decide*) beurteilen **2.** (*estimate*) schätzen **3.** SPORT **to ~ sth** bei etw *dat* Kampfrichter sein

judg(e)ment ['dʒʌdʒ·mənt] *n* **1.** LAW Urteil *nt;* **to pass ~** [**on sb/sth**] *a. fig* ein Urteil [über jdn/etw] fällen **2.** (*opinion*) Urteil *nt;* **error of ~** Fehleinschätzung *f;* **against one's better ~** wider besseres Wissen

judicial [dʒu·'dɪʃ·əl] *adj* gerichtlich; **~ authorities** Justizbehörden *pl;* **~ review** gerichtliche Überprüfung *(der Vorinstanzentscheidung)* Normenkontrolle *f (Prüfung der Gesetze auf ihre Verfassungsmäßigkeit)*

judo ['dʒu·dou] *n* Judo *nt*

jug [dʒʌg] *n* Krug *m*

juggle ['dʒʌg·əl] **I.** *vt* **to ~ sth 1.** mit etw *dat* jonglieren **2.** *fig, pej* (*manipulate*) etw manipulieren **II.** *vi* **1.** jonglieren **2.** *fig, pej* (*manipulate*) **to ~ with sth** (*facts, information*) etw manipulieren

juggler ['dʒʌg·lər] *n* Jongleur(in) *m(f)*

juice [dʒus] *n* **1.** (*of fruit, vegetables*) Saft *m;* **lemon ~** Zitronensaft *m* **2.** *pl* (*liquid in meat*) [Braten]saft *m kein pl* **3.** *fam* (*electricity*) Saft *m sl*

juicy ['dʒu·si] *adj* **1.** (*succulent*) saftig **2.** *fam* (*plentiful*) saftig; (*profit*) fett **3.** *fam* (*suggestive: joke, story*) schlüpfrig; (*details, scandal*) pikant

jukebox ['dʒuk·baks] *n* Jukebox *f*

Jul. *n abbr of* **July**

julep ['dʒu·ləp] *n* Julep *m o nt (alkoholisches Eisgetränk, oft mit Pfefferminze)*

July [dʒu·'laɪ] *n* Juli *m;* see also **February**

jumbo ['dʒʌm·bou] **I.** *adj attr* Riesen- **II.** *n* AVIAT Jumbo *m*

jumbo 'jet *n* Jumbojet *m*

jump [dʒʌmp] **I.** *n a. fig* Sprung *m;* **high/ long jump** SPORT Hoch-/Weitsprung *m;* (*in prices, temperatures*) [sprunghafter] Anstieg; (*in profits*) [sprunghafte] Steigerung; **to wake up with a ~** aus dem Schlaf hochfahren **II.** *vi* **1.** (*leap*) springen; **to ~ to one's feet** aufspringen; **to ~ up and down** herumspringen; **to ~ in[to] sth** (*car, water*) in etw *akk* [hinein]springen **2.** (*rise*) sprunghaft ansteigen, in die Höhe schnellen **3.** (*be startled*) einen Satz machen; **to make sb ~** jdn erschrecken ▶ **to ~ to conclusions** voreilige Schlüsse ziehen **III.** *vt* überspringen ▶ **to ~ the gun** *fam* überstürzt handeln

♦ **jump at** *vi* **to ~ at sth** (*idea, suggestion*) sofort auf etw *akk* anspringen *fam;* (*offer*) sich auf etw *akk* stürzen

♦ **jump in** *vi* hineinspringen

♦ **jump out** *vi* **1.** (*leave*) **to ~ out of bed** aus dem Bett springen **2.** *fig* (*stand out*) **to ~ out at sb** jdm sofort auffallen

♦ **jump up** *vi* aufspringen

jumper¹ ['dʒʌm·pər] *n* (*person*) Springer(in) *m(f);* (*horse*) Springpferd *nt*

jumper² ['dʒʌm·pər] *n* (*pinafore*) Trägerkleid *nt*

'jumper cables *npl* Starthilfekabel *nt*

'jump rope *n* Springseil *nt*

'jump-start *vt* **to ~ sb's car** jdm Starthilfe geben

'jump suit *n* Overall *m*

jumpy ['dʒʌm·pi] *adj fam* **1.** (*nervous*) nervös **2.** (*easily frightened*) schreckhaft **3.** (*unsteady: market*) unsicher

Jun. *n abbr of* **June**

junction ['dʒʌŋk·ʃən] *n* (*road*) Kreuzung *f*; (*freeway*) Autobahnkreuz *nt*

June [dʒun] *n* Juni *m; see also* **February**

jungle ['dʒʌŋ·gəl] *n a. fig* Dschungel *m*

junior ['dʒu·njər] **I.** *adj* **1.** (*younger*) junior *nach n* **2.** *attr* SPORT Junioren-, Jugend- **3.** *attr* SCH **~ college** Juniorencollege *nt* (*die beiden ersten Studienjahre umfassende Einrichtung*); **~ high school** Aufbauschule *f* (*umfasst in der Regel die Klassenstufen 6–9*) **4.** (*low rank*) untergeordnet; **~ partner** Juniorpartner(in) *m(f)* **II.** *n* **1.** (*son*) Sohn *m* **2.** (*younger*) Jüngere(r) *f(m)*; **he's two years my ~** er ist zwei Jahre jünger als ich **3.** SCH, UNIV (*third-year student*) Student(in) *m(f)* im vorletzten Studienjahr **4.** (*low-ranking person*) unterer Angestellter/untere Angestellte

juniper ['dʒu·nɪ·pər] *n* Wacholder *m*

junk¹ [dʒʌŋk] *n* **1.** (*worthless stuff*) Ramsch *m fam* **2.** *sl* (*heroin*) Stoff *m*

junk² [dʒʌŋk] *n* NAUT Dschunke *f*

'junk food *n* Schnellgerichte *pl; pej* ungesundes Essen

junkie ['dʒʌŋ·ki] *n sl* Fixer(in) *m(f) fam*; **fitness ~** *hum* Fitnessfreak *m*

'junk mail *n* Wurfsendungen *pl*, Reklame *f*

'junk shop *n* Trödelladen *m*

'junkyard *n* Schrottplatz *m*

junta ['hʊn·tə] *n* Junta *f*

Jupiter ['dʒu·pɪ·tər] *n no art* Jupiter *m*

juror ['dʒʊr·ər] *n* LAW Geschworene(r) *f(m)*

jury ['dʒʊr·i] *n* **1.** LAW **the ~** die Geschworenen *pl* **2.** (*competition*) Jury *f*

just **I.** *adv* [dʒʌst] **1.** (*in a moment*) gleich; **we're ~ about to leave** wir wollen gleich los; **I was ~ going to call you** ich wollte dich eben anrufen **2.** (*directly*) direkt, gleich **3.** (*recently*) gerade [eben], [so]eben **4.** (*now*) gerade; **to be ~ doing sth** gerade dabei sein, etw zu tun **5.** (*exactly*) genau; **that's ~ what I was going to say** genau das wollte ich

gerade sagen; **that's ~ it!** das ist es ja gerade!; **~ now** gerade; **~ then** gerade in diesem Augenblick; **~ as well** ebenso gut; **~ as/when ...** gerade in dem Augenblick, als ... **6.** (*only*) nur, bloß *fam*, (*simply*) einfach; **she's ~ a baby** sie ist noch ein Baby; **~ for fun** nur [so] zum Spaß; **[not] ~ anybody** [nicht] einfach irgendjemand **7.** (*barely*) gerade noch/mal; **~ in time** gerade noch rechtzeitig **8.** *with imperatives* **~ imagine!** stell dir das mal vor!; **~ look at this!** schau dir das mal an! ▶ **~ a minute!** (*please wait*) einen Augenblick [bitte]!; (*as interruption*) Moment [mal]!; **it's ~ one of those things** *saying* so etwas passiert eben **II.** *adj* [dʒʌst] **1.** (*fair*) gerecht (**to** gegenüber +*dat*) **2.** (*justified: punishment*) gerecht; **to have ~ cause to do sth** einen triftigen Grund haben, etw zu tun ▶ **to get one's ~ deserts** bekommen, was man verdient hat

justice ['dʒʌs·tɪs] *n* **1.** (*fairness*) Gerechtigkeit *f* **2.** (*administration of the law*) Justiz *f* **3.** (*judge*) Richter(in) *m(f)*

Justice of the 'Peace *n* Friedensrichter(in) *m(f)*

justification [‚dʒʌs·tə·fɪ·'keɪ·ʃən] *n* Rechtfertigung *f*

justified ['dʒʌs·tə·faɪd] *adj* gerechtfertigt, berechtigt

justify <-ie-> ['dʒʌs·tə·faɪ] *vt* rechtfertigen; **to ~ oneself to sb** sich jdm gegenüber rechtfertigen

justly ['dʒʌst·li] *adv* zu Recht; **to act ~** gerecht handeln

jute [dʒut] *n* Jute *f*

juvenile ['dʒu·və·naɪl] **I.** *adj* Jugend-, jugendlich **II.** *n* Jugendliche(r) *f(m)*

juvenile de'linquent *n* jugendlicher Straftäter/jugendliche Straftäterin

K

K <*pl* -'s>, **k** <*pl* -'s> [keɪ] *n* K *nt*, k *nt*; **~ as in Kilo** K wie Kaufmann

K¹ <*pl* -> *n fam* 1.000 Dollar

K² <*pl* -> *n abbr of* **kilobyte** KB

K³ <*pl* -> *n abbr of* **karat** kt.

kale [keɪl] n [Grün]kohl m

kangaroo <pl -s> [ˌkæŋ·gə·ˈru] n Känguru nt

Kans. abbr of **Kansas**

Kansas [ˈkæn·zəs] n Kansas nt

karat [ˈker·ət] n Karat nt

karate [kə·ˈrɑ·t̬i] n Karate nt

karma [ˈkɑr·mə] n Karma nt

kayak [ˈkaɪ·æk] n Kajak m o selten a. nt

kayaking n Kajakfahren nt

KB n abbr of **kilobyte** KB

kebab [kə·ˈbɑb] n Kebab m

keel [kil] n NAUT Kiel m

◆**keel over** vi **1.** NAUT kentern **2.** fam (swoon) umkippen

keen [kin] adj **1.** (enthusiastic) leidenschaftlich; **to not be ~ on [doing] sth** etw nicht [tun] wollen, etw gerne tun **2.** (perceptive: mind, eyesight) scharf **3.** (extreme: competition) scharf; (desire) heftig; (interest) lebhaft **4.** (piercing: wind) schneidend **5.** (sharp: blade) scharf

keep [kip] n [Lebens]unterhalt m II. vt <kept, kept> **1.** (hold onto) behalten; (bills, receipts) aufheben **2.** (store: medicine, money) aufbewahren **3.** (detain) **to ~ sb waiting** jdn warten lassen **4.** (prevent) **to ~ sb from doing sth** jdn davon abhalten, etw zu tun **5.** (maintain) **to ~ one's balance** das Gleichgewicht halten; **to ~ sb/sth under control** jdn/etw unter Kontrolle halten; **to ~ count of sth** etw mitzählen; **to ~ sb/sth in mind** jdn/etw im Gedächtnis behalten; **to ~ one's mouth shut** den Mund halten; **to ~ time** (watch) richtig gehen; MUS Takt halten; **to ~ track of sb/sth** jdn/etw im Auge behalten; **to ~ sb awake** jdn wach halten; **to ~ sb/sth warm** jdn/etw warm halten **6.** (not reveal) **to ~ sth from sb** jdm etw akk vorenthalten; (secret) hüten **7.** (stick to: appointment, treaty) einhalten; (oath, promise) halten **8.** (make records) **to ~ a record of sth** über etw akk Buch führen III. vi <kept, kept> **1.** (stay fresh: food) sich halten **2.** (wait) Zeit haben; **your questions can ~ until later** deine Fragen können noch warten **3.** (stay) bleiben; **to ~ quiet** still sein; **to**

~ to the left/right sich links/rechts halten **4.** (continue) **don't ~ asking silly questions** stell nicht immer so dumme Fragen; **to ~ at sth** mit etw dat weitermachen **5.** (stop oneself) **to ~ from doing sth** etw unterlassen **6.** (adhere to) **to ~ to sth** an etw dat festhalten; (not digress) bei etw dat bleiben; **to ~ to an agreement** sich an eine Vereinbarung halten; **to ~ to a schedule** einen Zeitplan einhalten

◆**keep away** I. vi sich fernhalten (from von +dat) II. vt fernhalten (from von +dat)

◆**keep back** I. vi zurückbleiben; (stay at distance) Abstand halten II. vt **1.** (restrain) zurückhalten **2.** (prevent advance) **to ~ back** ⇆ **sb** jdn aufhalten; **to ~ sb back from doing sth** jdn daran hindern, etw zu tun **3.** (withhold: information) verschweigen; (payment) einbehalten

◆**keep down** I. vi unten bleiben, sich ducken II. vt **1.** (suppress) unterdrücken **2.** (food) bei sich dat behalten ▶ **~ it down!** sei still!

◆**keep in** vt (one's anger, feelings) zurückhalten

◆**keep off** vt **1.** (not touch) **to ~ one's hands off sb/sth** die Hände von jdm/etw lassen; **"Keep Off The Grass"** „Betreten des Rasens verboten" **2.** fam (not consume) **to ~ off the booze** das Trinken lassen **3.** (not talk about) **to ~ off a subject** ein Thema vermeiden; **to ~ one's mind off sth** sich von etw dat ablenken

◆**keep on** I. vi (continue) **to ~ on doing sth** etw weiter[hin] tun II. vt ~ **your jacket on — it's cold** behalte den Mantel an, es ist kalt

◆**keep out** vi draußen bleiben; **"Keep Out"** „Zutritt verboten"; **to ~ out of sth** nicht betreten; fig sich aus etw dat heraushalten

◆**keep together** vt zusammenhalten ▶ **~ it together!** bleib bei der Sache!

◆**keep up** I. vt **1.** (maintain) fortführen; (conversation) in Gang halten; **~ it up!** [nur] weiter so! **2.** (hold up) hoch halten; **these poles ~ the tent up** diese

Stangen halten das Zelt aufrecht **3.** (*not let sleep*) wach halten **II.** *vi* **1.** (*not fall behind*) **to ~ up with sb/sth** mit jdm/ etw mithalten **2.** (*continue: noise, rain*) andauern, anhalten; (*courage, strength*) bestehen bleiben

keeper ['ki·pər] *n* (*in a zoo*) Wärter(in) *m(f)*

keeping ['ki·pɪŋ] *n* **1.** (*guarding*) Verwahrung *f;* (*care*) Obhut *f* **2.** (*obeying*) Einhalten *nt*, Befolgen *nt;* **in ~ with an agreement** entsprechend einer Vereinbarung

keepsake ['kip·seɪk] *n* Andenken *nt*

keg [keg] *n* kleines Fass

kelp [kelp] *n* Seetang *m*

kennel ['ken·əl] *n* **1.** (*dog boarding*) Hundepension *f* **2.** (*doghouse*) Hundehütte *f*

Kentucky [kən·'tʌk·i] *n* Kentucky *nt*

Kenya ['ken·jə] *n* Kenia *nt*

Kenyan ['ken·jən] **I.** *n* Kenianer(in) *m(f)* **II.** *adj* kenianisch

kept [kept] *vt, vi pt, pp of* **keep**

kernel ['kɜr·nəl] *n* **1.** (*fruit center*) Kern *m;* (*grain center*) Getreidekorn *nt* **2.** *fig* **a ~ of truth** ein Körnchen *nt* Wahrheit

kerosene, kerosine ['ker·ə·sin] *n* Kerosin *nt*

ketchup ['ketʃ·əp] *n* Ketschup *m o nt*

kettle ['ket·əl] *n* [Wasser]kessel *m* ▸ **to be a [whole] different ~ of fish** etwas ganz anderes sein

key¹ [ki] **I.** *n* **1. a.** *fig* (*for a lock*) Schlüssel *m* **2.** (*button: of a computer, piano*) Taste *f* **3.** (*to symbols*) Zeichenerklärung *f* **4.** MUS Tonart *f* **II.** *adj* (*factor, figure, role*) Schlüssel-; **~ contribution** Hauptbeitrag *m*

key² [ki] *n* [Korallen]riff *nt;* **the Florida ~s** die Florida Keys

◆ **key in** *vt* **to ~ in text** Text eingeben

keyboard **I.** *n* **1.** (*of a computer*) Tastatur *f;* (*of a piano*) Klaviatur *f* **2.** (*musical instrument*) Keyboard *nt* **II.** *vt, vi* tippen

'**keyhole** *n* Schlüsselloch *nt*

'**keynote** *n* **1.** Hauptthema *nt;* (*of a speech*) Grundgedanke *m* **2.** POL Parteilinie *f*

'**keynote address**, '**keynote speech** *n* programmatische Rede

'**keypad** *n* Tastenfeld *nt*

'**key ring** *n* Schlüsselring *m*

'**keyword** *n* **1.** (*important word*) Schlüsselwort *nt* **2.** (*for identifying*) Kennwort *nt*

kg *n abbr of* **kilogram** kg

khaki ['kæk·i] *adj* Khaki-; (*color*) khakifarben

kHz *n abbr of* **kilohertz** kHz

KIA [ˌkeɪ·aɪ·'eɪ] *adj abbr of* **killed in action** gef.

kibbutz [kɪ·'bʊts] *n* Kibbuz *m*

kick [kɪk] **I.** *n* **1.** (*with foot*) [Fuß]tritt *m*, Stoß *m;* (*in sports*) Schuss *m;* (*of a horse*) Tritt *m* **2.** *fam* (*exciting feeling*) Nervenkitzel *m* **3.** (*gun jerk*) Rückstoß *m* **II.** *vt* **1.** (*hit with foot*) [mit dem Fuß] treten; **to ~ a ball** einen Ball schießen **2.** (*get rid of: habit*) aufgeben *fam* ▸ **to ~ the bucket** ins Gras beißen **III.** *vi* (*with foot*) treten (**at** nach +*dat*); (*horse*) ausschlagen ▸ **to be alive and ~ing** gesund und munter sein

◆ **kick around** **I.** *vi fam* [he]rumliegen **II.** *vt* (*with foot*) **to ~ sth around** etw [in der Gegend] herumkicken *fam*

◆ **kick back** **I.** *vt* zurücktreten; (*ball*) zurückschießen **II.** *vi fam* (*relax*) relaxen *fam*

◆ **kick in** **I.** *vt* **1.** (*with foot: door, window*) eintreten **2.** (*contribute*) dazugeben, beisteuern **II.** *vi* **1.** (*start: drug, measure*) wirken; (*device, system*) anspringen **2.** (*to contribute*) **to ~ in for sth** einen Beitrag zu etw *dat* leisten

◆ **kick off** **I.** *vi* beginnen, anfangen; (*in soccer, football*) anstoßen **II.** *vt* (*start, launch*) beginnen

◆ **kick out** *vt* hinauswerfen

◆ **kick over** **I.** *vi* (*car*) anfahren **II.** *vt* **to ~ over ⇄ sth** etw umrempeln

◆ **kick up** *vi* **to ~ up dust** *a. fig* Staub aufwirbeln; **to ~ up a fuss** *fig* einen Wirbel machen *fam*

kicker ['kɪk·ər] *n* (*in football*) Fußballspieler(in) *m(f);* (*in soccer*) Freistoßnehmer(in) *m(f)*

'**kickoff** *n* (*in football, in soccer*) Anstoß *m*

kid [kɪd] **I.** n **1.** (*child*) Kind nt; (*young person*) Jugendliche(r) f(m); (*male*) Bursche m; (*female*) Mädchen nt; ~ **brother/sister** kleiner Bruder/kleine Schwester **2.** (*young goat*) Zicklein nt **II.** vi <-dd-> fam Spaß machen; **just ~ding!** war nur Spaß!; **no ~ding?** ohne Scherz? **III.** vt fam to ~ **sb** jdn verulken

kidnap ['kɪd·næp] **I.** vt <-pp-> entführen **II.** n Entführung f

kidnapper ['kɪd·næp·ər] n Entführer(in) m(f)

kidnapping ['kɪd·næp·ɪŋ] n Entführung f

kidney ['kɪd·ni] n ANAT, FOOD Niere f

'kidney bean n Kidneybohne f

'kidney donor n Nierenspender(in) m(f)

'kidney failure n Nierenversagen nt

'kidney-shaped adj nierenförmig

'kidney stone n Nierenstein m

kill [kɪl] **I.** n HUNT [Jagd]beute f **II.** vi (*end life: criminal*) töten; (*disease*) tödlich sein **III.** vt **1.** (*end life*) umbringen a. fig; **to ~ sb by drowning/strangling** jdn ertränken/erwürgen; **to be ~ed in an accident** bei einem Unfall ums Leben kommen **2.** (*destroy*) zerstören; **to ~ the taste of sth** etw dat den Geschmack [völlig] nehmen **3.** (*spoil: fun, joke*) [gründlich] verderben **4.** (*stop: engine, lights*) ausmachen; (*pain*) stillen; (*plan, project*) fallen lassen **5.** fam (*amuse*) **to ~ oneself with laughter** sich totlachen ▸ **to ~ time** (*spend time*) sich dat die Zeit vertreiben; (*waste time*) die Zeit totschlagen; **to ~ two birds with one stone** prov zwei Fliegen mit einer Klappe schlagen

killer ['kɪl·ər] **I.** n **1.** (*person*) Mörder(in) m(f); (*thing*) Todesursache f **2.** (*agent*) Vertilgungsmittel nt; **weed ~** Unkrautvertilgungsmittel nt **II.** adj attr (*deadly: flu, virus*) tödlich; (*hurricane, wave*) mörderisch

'killer whale n Schwertwal m

killing ['kɪl·ɪŋ] **I.** n **1.** (*act*) Tötung f **2.** (*case*) Mord[fall] m **II.** adj attr **1.** (*causing death*) tödlich **2.** fig (*difficult*) mörderisch fam

kilo ['ki·loʊ] n Kilo nt

kilobyte ['kɪl·ə·baɪt] n Kilobyte nt

kilogram ['kɪl·ə·græm] n Kilogramm nt

kilometer [kɪ·'lam·ɪ·tər] n Kilometer m

kilowatt ['kɪl·ə·wat] n Kilowatt nt

kilt [kɪlt] n Kilt m

kimono [kə·'moʊ·nə] n Kimono m

kind¹ [kaɪnd] adj **1.** (*generous, helpful*) nett; **with ~ regards** (*in a letter*) mit freundlichen Grüßen **2.** (*gentle*) **to be ~ to sb/sth** jdn/etw schonen

kind² [kaɪnd] **I.** n **1.** (*group*) Art f; **he's not that ~ of person** so einer ist der nicht fam; **all ~s of animals** alle möglichen Tiere; **to be one of a ~** einzigartig sein; **his/her ~** pej so jemand [wie er/ sie] **2.** (*limited*) **you could call this success of a ~** man könnte das als so etwas wie einen Erfolg bezeichnen **3.** (*similar*) **nothing of the ~** nichts dergleichen **II.** adv ~ **of** irgendwie; **to be ~ of interesting** irgendwie interessant sein

kindergarten ['kɪn·dər·gar·dən] n SCH Vorschule f

kind-'hearted adj gütig

kindle ['kɪn·dəl] vt **1.** (*fire*) anzünden **2.** fig (*imagination*) wecken

kindly ['kaɪnd·li] **I.** adj (*person*) freundlich; (*smile, voice*) sanft **II.** adv (*please*) freundlich, freundlicherweise; **you are ~ requested to leave the building** Sie werden freundlich[st] gebeten, das Gebäude zu verlassen

kindness <pl -es> ['kaɪnd·nɪs] n **1.** (*attitude*) Freundlichkeit f **2.** (*act*) Gefälligkeit f

kinfolk ['kɪn·foʊk] n + pl vb Verwandtschaft f

king [kɪŋ] n König m

kingdom ['kɪŋ·dəm] n **1.** (*country*) Königreich nt **2.** (*domain*) Reich nt; **animal ~** Tierreich nt

'kingfisher n Eisvogel m

'king-size(d) adj extragroß

kiosk ['ki·ask] n Kiosk m

kiss [kɪs] **I.** n <pl -es> Kuss m; **to blow sb a ~** jdm eine Kusshand zuwerfen **II.** vi [sich] küssen; **to ~ and tell** mit intimen Enthüllungen an die Öffentlichkeit gehen **III.** vt küssen; **to ~ sb goodbye** jdm einen Abschiedskuss geben ▸ **to ~ sb's ass** vulg jdm in den Arsch kriechen derb

kit [kɪt] *n* **1.** (*set*) Ausrüstung *f;* (*for a model*) Bausatz *m;* **first-aid ~** Verbandskasten *m* **2.** (*outfit*) Ausrüstung *f*

'kit bag *n* Kleidersack *m*

kitchen ['kɪtʃ·ɪn] *n* Küche *f*

kitchenette [ˌkɪtʃ·ɪ·'net] *n* Kochnische *f*

kitchen 'knife *n* Küchenmesser *nt*

kitchen 'sink *n* Spüle *f*

kitchen 'table *n* Küchentisch *m*

kite [kaɪt] *n* Drachen *m* ▶ **go fly a ~!** *fam* mach die Fliege! *sl;* **to be as high as a ~** (*drunk*) sternhagelvoll sein *fam;* (*high*) völlig zugedröhnt sein *sl*

kitsch [kɪtʃ] **I.** *n pej* Kitsch *m* **II.** *adj* kitschig

kitten ['kɪt·ən] *n* (*young cat*) Kätzchen *nt*

kitty ['kɪt·i] *n* **1.** *childspeak* (*kitten*) Miezekatze *f;* **here, ~ ~!** komm, miez, miez! **2.** (*money*) gemeinsame Kasse; (*in games*) Spiel|kasse *f*

'Kitty Litter® *n* Katzenstreu *f*

kiwi ['ki·wi] *n* (*bird, fruit*) Kiwi *m*

Kleenex® ['kli·neks] *n* Tempo|taschentuch]® *nt*

kleptomaniac [ˌklep·toʊ·'meɪ·ni·æk] *n* Kleptomane *m,* Kleptomanin *f*

km *n abbr of* **kilometer** km

knack [næk] *n* **1.** (*trick*) Kniff *m;* **to get the ~ of sth** herausfinden, wie etw geht *fam* **2.** (*talent*) Geschick *nt*

knapsack ['næp·sæk] *n* Rucksack *m*

knead [nid] *vt* (*dough*) kneten

knee [ni] **I.** *n* Knie *nt;* **to put sb on one's ~** jdn auf den Schoß nehmen ▶ **to bring sb to their ~s** jdn in die Knie zwingen *geh* **II.** *vt* **to ~ sb** jdn mit dem Knie stoßen

'kneecap I. *n* Kniescheibe *f* **II.** *vt* <-pp-> **to ~ sb** jdm die Kniescheibe zerschießen

'knee-high *n* FASHION Kniestrumpf *m*

kneel <knelt *or* kneeled, knelt *or* kneeled> [nil] *vi* knien

knelt [nelt] *pt of* **kneel**

knew [nu] *pt of* **know**

knife [naɪf] **I.** *n* <pl knives> Messer *nt* **2. to go under the ~** — MED unters Messer kommen *fam* **II.** *vt* **to ~ sb** auf jdn einstechen

knight [naɪt] **I.** *n* **1.** *hist* (*soldier*) Rit-

ter *m* **2.** CHESS Springer *m* **II.** *vt* **to ~ sb** jdn zum Ritter schlagen

knit [nɪt] **I.** *n* (*stitch*) Strickart *f* **II.** *v.* <knitted *or* knit, knitted *or* knit> **1.** (*with yarn*) stricken; (*do basic stitch*) eine rechte Masche stricken **2.** (*heal: broken bone*) zusammenwachsen **III.** *vt* <knitted *or* knit, knitted *or* knit> (*with yarn*) stricken ▶ **to ~ one's brows** die Augenbrauen zusammenziehen, die Stirn runzeln

◆knit together I. *vi* **1.** (*combine*) sich zusammenfügen **2.** (*heal: broken bone*) zusammenwachsen **II.** *vt* zusammenstricken

knitting ['nɪt·ɪŋ] *n* **1.** (*action*) Stricken *nt* **2.** (*product*) Gestrickte(s) *nt;* (*unfinished*) Strickzeug *nt*

'knitting needle *n* Stricknadel *f*

'knitwear *n* Stricksachen *pl*

knob [nab] *n* (*of a door*) Griff *m;* (*of a radio*) [Dreh]knopf *m*

knobby ['nab·i] *adj* knubbelig; (*tree, wood*) astreich

knock [nak] **I.** *n* **1.** (*sound*) Klopfen *nt;* **there was a ~ on the door** es hat [an der Tür] geklopft **2.** (*blow*) Schlag *m* **3.** *fam* (*criticism*) **he's taken a few ~s** er musste sich einiges anhören **II.** *vi* **1.** (*strike noisily*) klopfen; **to ~ at the door** an die Tür klopfen **2.** (*collide with*) stoßen (**into/against** gegen +akk) **3.** TECH (*engine, pipes*) klopfen ▶ **to ~ on wood** dreimal auf Holz klopfen **III.** *vt* **1.** (*hit*) **to ~ sth** gegen etw *akk* stoßen **2.** (*blow*) **to ~ sb** jdm einen Schlag versetzen; (*less hard*) jdm einen Stoß versetzen; **to ~ sb unconscious** jdn bewusstlos schlagen **3.** (*drive*) **to ~ sth out of sb** jdm etw austreiben; **to ~ some sense into sb** jdn zur Vernunft bringen **4.** *fam* (*criticize*) **to ~ sb/sth** jdn/etw schlechtmachen

◆knock around I. *vi fam* (*travel aimlessly*) [he]rumziehen **II.** *vt* **1.** (*beat*) **to ~ sb around** jdn verprügeln **2.** (*travel through*) **to ~ around Europe** in Europa herumreisen

◆knock back *vt fam* (*drink quickly*) hinunterkippen

◆knock down *vt* **1.** (*cause to fall*) um-

stoßen; (with a car, motorcycle) umfahren **2.** (demolish) niederreißen **3.** (reduce: price) herunterhandeln

knock off I. vt **1.** (cause to fall off) hinunterstoßen **2.** (produce quickly) schnell erledigen; (easily) etw mit links machen fam **3.** fam (stop) ~ **it off!** hör auf damit!; **to** ~ **off work early** früh Feierabend machen **4.** fam (rob) **to** ~ **off a bank** eine Bank ausräumen **5.** sl (copy) klauen fam II. vi fam Schluss machen

knock out vt **1.** (render unconscious) **to** ~ **out** ⇆ **sb** jdn bewusstlos werden lassen; (in a fight) jdn k. o. schlagen **2.** (forcibly remove) **to** ~ **out two teeth** sich dat zwei Zähne ausschlagen **3.** (eliminate) ausschalten; **to be** ~**ed out of a competition** aus einem Wettkampf ausscheiden **4.** (render useless) außer Funktion setzen **5.** fam (produce quickly) hastig entwerfen **6.** fam (astonish and impress) umhauen

knock over vt (cause to fall) umstoßen; (with a bike, car) umfahren

knock up vt sl schwängern

knockdown adj attr **1.** (very cheap) supergünstig sl; ~ **price** Schleuderpreis m fam **2.** (physically violent) **a** ~ **fight** eine handfeste Auseinandersetzung

knocker ['nɑk·ər] n **1.** (on door) Türklopfer m **2.** pl sl (breast) **big** ~**s** dicke Titten derb

knockout I. n K. o. m II. adj ~ **blow** K.-o.-Schlag m

knot [nɑt] I. n **1.** (in rope, material) Knoten m **2.** (in hair) [Haar]knoten m **3.** (in wood) Ast m **4.** (of people) Knäuel m o nt ▸ **to tie the** ~ heiraten II. vt <-tt-> knoten; (a tie) binden III. vi <-tt-> (muscles) sich verspannen; (stomach) sich zusammenkrampfen

know [noʊ] I. vt <knew, known> **1.** (have information, knowledge) wissen; (facts, results) kennen; **do you** ~ **where the post office is?** können Sie mir sagen, wo die Post ist?; I ~ **what I am talking about** ich weiß, wovon ich rede; **to** ~ **how to do sth** wissen, wie man etw macht; **to** ~ **sth by heart** etw auswendig können; **to**

let sb ~ **sth** jdn etw wissen lassen **2.** (be certain) **to not** ~ **whether ...** sich dat nicht sicher sein, ob ...; **to** ~ **for a fact that ...** ganz sicher wissen, dass ... **3.** (be acquainted with) **to** ~ **sb** jdn kennen; **she** ~**s Philadelphia well** sie kennt sich in Philadelphia gut aus; **surely you** ~ **me better than that!** du solltest mich eigentlich besser kennen!; **to** ~ **sb by name** jdn dem Namen nach kennen; **to get to** ~ **sb/each other** jdn/sich kennen lernen **4.** (have understanding) verstehen; **do you** ~ **what I mean?** verstehst du, was ich meine? **5.** (experience) I'**ve never** ~**n anything like this** so etwas habe ich noch nie erlebt **6.** (be able to differentiate) **to** ~ **right from wrong** Gut und Böse unterscheiden können ▸ **to** ~ **no bounds** keine Grenzen kennen; **to** ~ **the score** wissen, was gespielt wird; **to** ~ **a thing or two about sth** sich mit etw dat auskennen II. vi <knew, known> **1.** (have knowledge) [Bescheid] wissen; **ask Kate — she's sure to** ~ frag Kate, sie weiß es bestimmt; **as far as I** ~ so viel ich weiß; **how should I** ~? wie soll ich das wissen? **2.** fam (understand) begreifen; **I don't** ~ **why you can't ever be on time** ich begreife einfach nicht warum du nie pünktlich sein kannst ▸ **you ought to** ~ **better** du solltest es eigentlich besser wissen

know-how n Know-how nt

knowing ['noʊ·ɪŋ] adj wissend attr; (look, smile) viel sagend

knowingly ['noʊ·ɪŋ·li] adv **1.** (meaningfully) viel sagend **2.** (with full awareness) bewusst

know-it-all ['noʊ·ɪt̮·ɔl] n pej fam Besserwisser(in) m(f) pej

knowledge ['nɑl·ɪdʒ] n **1.** (body of learning) Kenntnisse pl (of in +dat); ~ **of French** Französischkenntnisse pl **2.** (acquired information, awareness) Wissen nt; **to be common** ~ allgemein bekannt sein

known [noʊn] I. vt, vi pp of **know** II. adj **1.** (publicly recognized) bekannt; **it is a little-/well-**~ **fact that ...** es ist kaum/allgemein bekannt, dass ...

2. (*understood*) bekannt; **no ~ reason** kein erkennbarer Grund **3.** (*tell publicly*) **to make sth ~** etw bekannt machen

knuckle ['nʌk·əl] *n* **1.** ANAT [Finger]knöchel *m* **2.** (*cut of meat*) Hachse *f*, Haxe *f südd*; **~ of pork** Schweinshaxe *f südd*
♦ **knuckle down** *vi* sich dahinterklemmen

KO [ˌkeɪ·'oʊ] **I.** *n abbr of* **knockout** K. o. *m* **II.** *vt <KO'd, KO'd> abbr of* **knock out; to ~ sb** jdn k. o. schlagen

koala *n*, **koala bear** [koʊ·'al·ə·] *n* Koala[bär] *m*

kooky ['ku·ki] *adj sl* ausgeflippt

Koran [kə·'ræn] *n* **the ~** der Koran

Korea [kə·'ri·ə] *n* Korea *nt;* **North/South ~** Nord-/Südkorea *nt*

Korean [kə·'ri·ən] **I.** *adj* koreanisch **II.** *n* **1.** (*inhabitant*) Koreaner(in) *m(f)* **2.** LING Koreanisch *nt*

kosher ['koʊ·ʃər] *adj a. fig* koscher

Kremlin ['krem·lɪn] *n* **the ~** der Kreml

KS *abbr of* **Kansas**

Ku Klux Klan ['ku·ˌklʌks·ˈklæn] *n + sing/ pl vb* **the ~** der Ku-Klux-Klan

kung fu [ˌkʌŋ·'fu] *n* Kung-Fu *nt*

Kurd [kɜrd] *n* Kurde *m*, Kurdin *f*

Kurdish ['kɜr·dɪʃ] **I.** *adj* kurdisch **II.** *n* LING Kurdisch *nt*

Kurdistan [ˌkɜr·dɪ·'stæn] *n* Kurdistan *nt*

Kuwait [kʊ·'weɪt] *n* Kuwait *nt*

Kuwaiti [kʊ·'weɪ·ti] **I.** *adj* kuwaitisch **II.** *n* **1.** (*inhabitant*) Kuwaiter(in) *m(f)* **2.** LING Kuwaitisch *nt*

kW <*pl* -> *n abbr of* **kilowatt** kW

Kwanzaa, Kwanza ['kwan·zə] *n* von Amerikanern afrikanischer Herkunft vom 26. Dezember bis 1. Januar gefeiertes, nicht-religiöses Fest

KY, Ky. *abbr of* **Kentucky**

L

L <*pl* -'s>, **l** <*pl* -'s> [el] *n* L *nt,* l *nt;* **~ as in Lima** L wie Ludwig

l [el] **I.** *n* **1.** *abbr of* **left** l. **2.** <*pl* ->abbr of* **liter** l **3.** <*pl* ll> TYPO *abbr of*

line Z. **II.** *adj abbr of* **left** l., L **III.** *adj abbr of* **left** l.

L. *n abbr of* **lake**

LA, La. *abbr of* **Louisiana**

lab [læb] *n short for* **laboratory** Labor *nt*

label ['leɪ·bəl] **I.** *n* **1.** (*on bottles*) Etikett *nt;* (*in clothes*) Schild[chen] *nt* **2.** (*brand name*) Marke *f* **II.** *vt <-l->* (*affix labels*) etikettieren; (*write on*) beschriften

labeling, labelling ['leɪ·bəl·ɪŋ] *n* Etikettierung *f;* (*with a price*) Auszeichnung *f*

labor ['leɪ·bər] **I.** *n* **1.** (*work*) Arbeit *f;* **manual ~** körperliche Arbeit **2.** (*workers*) Arbeitskräfte *pl* **3.** (*childbirth*) Wehen *pl;* **to go into ~** Wehen bekommen **II.** *vi* hart arbeiten, sich abmühen

laboratory ['læb·rə·ˌtɔr·i] *n* Labor[atorium] *nt*

laboratory assistant *n* Laborant(in) *m(f)*

Labor Day *n* amerikanischer Tag der Arbeit, der am ersten Montag im September gefeiert wird

labor dispute *n* Arbeitskampf *m*

laborer ['leɪb·ər·ər] *n* Hilfsarbeiter(in) *m(f)*

labor force *n + sing/pl vb* (*population*) Arbeiterschaft *f;* (*staff*) Belegschaft *f*

labor-intensive *adj* arbeitsintensiv

laborious [lə·'bɔr·i·əs] *adj* mühsam

labor market *n* Arbeitsmarkt *m*

labor-saving *adj* arbeitssparend

labor shortage *n* Arbeitskräftemangel *m*

Labrador ['læb·rə·dɔr], **Labrador retriever** *n* Labrador[hund] *m*

labyrinth ['læb·ə·rɪnθ] *n* Labyrinth *nt*

lace [leɪs] **I.** *n* **1.** (*cloth*) Spitze *f;* (*edging*) Spitzenborte *f* **2.** (*cord*) Band *nt* **shoe ~s** Schnürsenkel *pl bes nordd mitteld* **II.** *vt* **1.** (*fasten: shoes*) zubinden **2.** (*add drug*) einen Schuss [Rauschmittel] dazugeben
♦ **lace up** *vt* zuschnüren

lacerate ['læs·ə·reɪt] *vt* aufreißen

lace-ups *npl* Schnürschuhe *pl*

lack [læk] **I.** *n* Mangel *m;* **~ of funds** fehlende Geldmittel **II.** *vt* **to ~ sth** etw nicht haben

lackadaisical [ˌlæk·ə·'deɪ·zɪ·kəl] *adj* lustlos

lacking ['læk·ɪŋ] *adj pred* **to be ~ in sth**

an etw *dat* mangeln

acquer ['læk·ər] **I.** *n* Lack *m* **II.** *vt* lackieren

acrosse [lə·'kras] *n* SPORT Lacrosse *nt*

dder ['læd·ər] *n* Leiter *f*

aden ['leɪ·dən] *adj* beladen

adies' room *n* Damentoilette *f*

dle ['leɪ·dəl] **I.** *n* [Schöpf]kelle *f* **II.** *vt* austeilen

ady ['leɪ·di] *n* **1.** (*woman*) Frau *f* **2.** *form* (*polite address*) **ladies and gentlemen!** meine [sehr verehrten] Damen und Herren!

adybug *n* Marienkäfer *m*

adylike *adj* damenhaft

ag [læg] **I.** *n* (*lapse*) Rückstand *m*; (*falling behind*) Zurückbleiben *nt kein pl*; **time** ~ Zeitabstand *m* **II.** *vi* <-gg-> zurückbleiben (**behind** hinter +*dat*)

agoon [lə·'gun] *n* Lagune *f*

aid [leɪd] *pt, pp of* **lay**

aid-'back *adj fam* (*relaxed*) locker; (*calm*) gelassen

ain [leɪn] *pp of* **lie**

ake [leɪk] *n* See *m*

am [læm] *n fam* **to be on the** ~ auf der Flucht sein

amb [læm] *n* **1.** (*sheep*) Lamm *nt fam* **2.** (*meat*) Lamm[fleisch] *nt*

ambskin *n* Lammfell *nt*

ambswool *n* Lammwolle *f*

ame [leɪm] *adj* lahm

ameness ['leɪm·nɪs] *n* Lähmung *f*

ament [lə·'ment] **I.** *n* Klagelied *nt* **II.** *vt* **to** ~ **sb** um jdn trauern

aminate I. *n* ['læm·ɪ·nɪt] Laminat *nt* **II.** *vt* ['læm·ɪ·neɪt] beschichten

aminated ['læm·ɪ·neɪ·t̬ɪd] *adj* geschichtet; (*with plastic*) beschichtet

amp [læmp] *n* Lampe *f;* **street** ~ Straßenlaterne *f*

ampoon [læm·'pun] *vt* verspotten

amppost *n* Laternenpfahl *m*

ampshade *n* Lampenschirm *m*

_AN [læn] *n* COMPUT *abbr of* **local area network** LAN *nt*

ance [læns] *vt* MED aufschneiden

and [lænd] **I.** *n* Land *nt* **II.** *adj attr* **1.** MIL, AGR Boden- **2.** (*real estate*) Grundstücks **III.** *vi* **1.** AVIAT, AEROSP landen (**on** auf +*dat*) **2.** NAUT (*vessel*) an-

legen; (*people*) an Land gehen **3.** (*come down*) landen (**in/on/outside** in/auf/außerhalb +*dat*); **to** ~ **on one's feet** auf den Füßen landen; *fig* [wieder] auf die Füße fallen **IV.** *vt* **1.** (*plane*) landen; (*boat, fish*) an Land ziehen **2.** (*unload*) an Land bringen; (*cargo*) löschen

landfill *n* Deponiegelände *nt*

land forces *npl* MIL Landstreitkräfte *pl*

landing ['læn·dɪŋ] *n* **1.** (*of stairs*) Treppenabsatz *m* **2.** (*of ship, plane*) Landung *f;* **emergency** ~ Notlandung *f*

landing gear *n* Fahrgestell *nt*

landing strip *n* Landebahn *f*

landlady *n* (*owner*) Hausbesitzerin *f;* (*leaser: of apartments*) Hauswirtin *f*

landlocked *adj* von Land umgeben; ~ **country** Binnenstaat *m*

landlord *n* (*owner*) Hausbesitzer *m;* (*leaser: of apartments*) Hauswirt *m*

landmark *n* **1.** (*point of recognition*) Erkennungszeichen *nt* **2.** (*event*) Meilenstein *m*

landmine *n* MIL Landmine *f*

landowner *n* Grundbesitzer(in) *m(f)*

landscape I. *n* Landschaft *f* **II.** *adj attr* TYPO (*format*) **in** ~ **format** im Querformat

landscape architect *n* Landschaftsarchitekt(in) *m(f)*

landslide *n* **1.** (*of earth*) Erdrutsch *m* **2.** (*majority*) Erdrutsch[wahl]sieg *m;* **to win by a** ~ mit einer überwältigenden Mehrheit siegen

lane [leɪn] *n* **1.** (*road*) Gasse *f* **2.** (*of freeway*) [Fahr]spur *f;* SPORT Bahn *f*

language ['læŋ·gwɪdʒ] *n* **1.** Sprache *f;* **native** ~ Muttersprache *f* **2.** (*words*) Sprache *f;* (*style a.*) Ausdrucksweise *f;* **bad** ~ Schimpfwörter *pl*

language laboratory *n* Sprachlabor *nt*

languid ['læŋ·gwɪd] *adj* **1.** (*weak*) schwach **2.** (*listless*) gelangweilt

lank [læŋk] *adj* (*hair*) strähnig

lanky ['læŋ·ki] *adj* hoch aufgeschossen

lanolin(e) ['læn·ə·lɪn] *n* Lanolin *nt*

lantern ['læn·tərn] *n* Laterne *f*

lap¹ [læp] *n* Schoß *m*

lap² [læp] **I.** *n* SPORT Runde *f;* ~ **of honor** Ehrenrunde *f* **II.** *vt* <-pp-> (*overtake*) überrunden

L

lap³ [læp] **I.** vt lecken **II.** vi (waves) [sanft] schlagen (**against** gegen +akk)

◆**lap up** vt **1.** (drink) [auf]lecken **2.** fig (accept) [gierig] aufsaugen fig

'lapdog n **1.** (dog) Schoßhündchen nt **2.** fig (person) Spielball m

lapel [lə·'pel] n Revers nt

lapis lazuli [ˌlæp·ɪs·'læz·ə·li] n Lapislazuli m

lapse [læps] **I.** n **1.** (error) Versehen nt; (moral) Fehltritt m; **~ of memory** Gedächtnislücke f **2.** (time) Zeitspanne f; **after a ~ of a few days** nach Verstreichen einiger Tage **II.** vi **1.** (concentration) abschweifen; (quality) nachlassen **2.** (end) ablaufen; (subscription) auslaufen

lapsed [læpst] adj attr (former: Catholic) vom Glauben abgefallen; (member) ehemalig

'laptop, laptop com'puter n Laptop m

larceny ['lar·sə·ni] n JUR Diebstahl m

larch <pl -es> [lartʃ] n Lärche f

lard [lard] n Schweineschmalz m

large [lardʒ] **I.** adj **1.** (size) groß **2.** (quantity, extent) groß, beträchtlich; **a ~ amount of work** viel Arbeit ▶ **by and ~** im Großen und Ganzen **II.** n **at ~** auf freiem Fuß

largely ['lardʒ·li] adv größtenteils

largeness ['lardʒ·nɪs] n (size) Größe f; (extensiveness) Umfang m

'large-scale adj usu attr **1.** (extensive) umfangreich m **2.** (made large) in großem Maßstab nach n; **a ~ map** eine Karte mit großem Maßstab

lariat ['ler·i·ət] n Lasso nt

lark [lark] n (bird) Lerche f

larva <pl -vae> ['lar·və] n Larve f

laryngitis [ˌler·ɪn·'dʒaɪ·tɪs] n Kehlkopfentzündung f

lasagna, lasagne [lə·'zan·jə] n Lasagne f

lascivious [lə·'sɪv·i·əs] adj lüstern geh

laser ['leɪ·zər] n Laser m

'laser beam n Laserstrahl m

'laser printer n Laserdrucker m

lash¹ [læʃ] **I.** n <pl -es> **1.** (whip) Peitsche f **2.** (eyelash) [Augen]wimper f **II.** vt **1.** (whip) auspeitschen **2.** (strike) **to ~ sth** (rain) gegen etw prasseln **III.** vi (strike) schlagen (**at** gegen +akk); f (rain, wave) peitschen (**at** gegen +akk

◆**lash out** vi **1.** (attack physically) to **out at sb** [with sth] [mit etw dat] an jdn einschlagen **2.** (attack verbally, writing) **to ~ out at sb/sth** jdn/etʌ scharf kritisieren

lash² vt (tie) [fest]binden (**to** an +dat)

lasso ['læs·oʊ] **I.** n <pl -s> Lasso nt **II.** mit einem Lasso einfangen

last¹ [læst] **I.** adj **1.** attr (after all th others) **the ~ ...** der/die/das letzte ..; **to come ~** als Letzte(r) f/m/ kommer **next to ~** vorletzte(r, s); **the ~ one** der die/das Letzte; **she was the ~ one t arrive** sie kam als Letzte an **2.** (lowe in order, rank) letzte(r, s); **to be ~** Letz te(r) f/m/ sein **3.** attr (final, remainin letzte(r, s); **at the ~ moment** im letzte Moment **4.** attr (most recent, previous letzte(r, s); **~ night** gestern Abend; **th week before ~** vorletzte Woche ▶ t **have the ~ laugh** zuletzt lachen fi (show everybody) es allen zeigen; **to b the ~ straw** das Fass [endgültig] zur Überlaufen bringen fig **II.** adv **1.** (afte the others) als Letzte(r, s) **2.** (most re cently) das letzte Mal **3.** (lastly) zuletzt zum Schluss; **~ but not least** nicht zu letzt **III.** n <pl -> **1.** (one after all th others) **the ~** der/die/das Letzte; **sh was the ~ to arrive** sie kam als Letzt **2.** (final one, previous one) **the ~** der die/das Letzte **3.** fam (end) **to see th ~ of sth** fam etw nie wieder sehen müs sen; **at ~** endlich

last² [læst] **I.** vi **1.** (battle, game) [an]dau ern **2.** (car, machine) halten; (supplie etc.) ausreichen; **to make sth ~** etw sparsam verwenden **II.** vt (serve: car halten; (supplies etc.) [aus]reichen; **to ~ [sb] a lifetime** ein Leben lang halten

lasting ['læs·tɪŋ] adj dauerhaft; (impres sion) nachhaltig

lastly ['læst·li] adv schließlich

last-'minute adj in letzter Minute nach ◆

'last name n Nachname m

latch [lætʃ] n Riegel m

◆**latch on to, latch onto** vi (attac oneself to) **to ~ on to sb** sich an jdʌ hängen

'latchkey child *n* Schlüsselkind *nt*

late [leɪt] **I.** *adj* <-r, -st> **1.** (*behind time*) verspätet *attr;* **to be ~** (*bus, flight, train*) Verspätung haben; (*person*) zu spät kommen; **to be ~ for sth** zu spät zu etw *dat* kommen **2.** (*in the day*) spät; **let's go home - it's getting ~** lass uns nach Hause gehen, es ist schon spät **3.** *attr* (*towards the end*) spät; **in the ~ afternoon** spät am Nachmittag; **to be in one's ~ thirties** Ende dreißig sein **4.** *attr* (*dead*) verstorben **II.** *adv* <-r, -s> **1.** (*after the expected time*) spät; **the train arrived ~** der Zug hatte Verspätung; **to stay up ~** bis spät aufbleiben; **to work ~** Überstunden machen **2.** (*at an advanced time*) **we talked ~ into the night** wir haben bis spät in die Nacht geredet; **~ in the afternoon** am späten Nachmittag; **~ in the day** spät [am Tag]; **at the very last moment** im [aller]letzten Augenblick

'latecomer *n* Nachzügler(in) *m(f)*

lately ['leɪt·li] *adv* kürzlich, in letzter Zeit

lateness ['leɪt·nɪs] *n* Verspätung *f*

'late-night *adj* Spät-

latent ['leɪ·tənt] *adj* sci latent

later ['leɪ·tər] **I.** *adj comp of* **late 1.** *attr* (*at future time: date, time*) später **2.** *pred* (*less punctual*) später **II.** *adv comp of* **late 1.** (*at later time*) später, anschließend; **see you** [*or fam* **ya**] **~!** bis später! **2.** (*afterwards*) später, danach

lateral ['læt·ər·əl] *adj esp attr* seitlich; (*thinking*) unorthodox

latest ['leɪ·tɪst] **I.** *adj superl of* **late; the ~ …** der/die/das jüngste [*or* letzte] …; **her ~ movie** ihr neuester Film **II.** *n* **have you heard the ~?** hast du schon das Neueste gehört?

latex ['leɪ·teks] *n* Latex *m*

lathe [leɪθ] *n* Drehbank *f*

lather ['læð·ər] **I.** *n* [Seifen]schaum *m* **II.** *vt* einseifen

Latin ['læt·ən] **I.** *n* Latein *nt* **II.** *adj* (*of Latin origin*) Latein-

Latina [lə·'ti·nə] *n* Latina *f*

Latino [lə·'ti·noʊ] *n* Latino *m*

latitude ['læt·ɪ·tud] *n* Breite *f*, Breitengrad *m*

latrine [lə·'trin] *n* Latrine *f*

latter ['læt·ər] *pron* **the ~** der/die/das Letztere

lattice ['læt·ɪs] *n* Gitter[werk] *nt*

laudable ['lɔ·də·bəl] *adj* lobenswert

laugh [læf] **I.** *n* Lachen *nt kein pl* **II.** *vi* **1.** (*express amusement*) lachen (**at** über +*akk*); **to make sb ~** jdn zum Lachen bringen **2.** *fig* **to ~ at sb** (*find funny*) über jdn lachen; (*find ridiculous*) jdn auslachen ▸ **to ~ in sb's face** jdn auslachen; **no ~ing matter** nicht zum Lachen

◀laugh off *vt* mit einem Lachen abtun

laughable ['læf·ə·bəl] *adj* lächerlich *pej,* lachhaft *pej*

'laughing stock *n* **to be a ~** die Zielscheibe des Spotts sein

laughter ['læf·tər] *n* Gelächter *nt,* Lachen *nt*

launch[1] [lɔntʃ] **I.** *n* **1.** (*of boat*) Stapellauf *m;* (*of rocket, spacecraft*) Start *m* **2.** (*presentation*) Präsentation *f* **II.** *vt* **1.** (*send out: boat*) zu Wasser lassen; (*ship*) vom Stapel lassen; (*spacecraft*) starten; (*satellite*) in den Weltraum schießen **2.** (*begin*) beginnen; (*campaign, show*) starten; (*inquiry*) anstellen; **to ~ an attack** zum Angriff übergehen **3.** (*hurl*) **to ~ oneself at sb** sich auf jdn stürzen

◀launch into *vi* **to ~ into sth** sich [begeistert] in etw *akk* stürzen

launch[2] [lɔntʃ] *n* (*boat*) Barkasse *f*

'launching pad, 'launch pad *n* Abschussrampe *f*

launder ['lɔn·dər] *vt* **1.** (*wash*) waschen [und bügeln] **2.** *fig* (*money*) waschen *sl*

Laundromat® ['lɔn·drə·mæt] *n* Waschsalon *m*

laundry ['lɔn·dri] *n* **1.** (*dirty clothes*) Schmutzwäsche *f;* **to do the ~** Wäsche waschen **2.** (*washed clothes*) frische Wäsche

'laundry service *n* **1.** (*facility*) Wäscheservice *m* **2.** (*business*) Wäscherei *f*

lava ['la·və] *n* Lava *f;* (*stone*) Lavagestein *nt*

lavatory ['læv·ə·tɔr·i] *n* Toilette *f*

lavender ['læv·ən·dər] **I.** *n* Lavendel *m* **II.** *adj* lavendelfarben

lavish ['læv·ɪʃ] **I.** *adj* **1.** (*meal*) üp-

pig **2.** (*generous*) großzügig; (*praise*) überschwänglich **II.** *vt* to ~ **sth on sb** jdn mit etw *dat* überhäufen; **to ~ great effort on sth** viel Mühe in etw *akk* stecken

law [lɔ] *n* **1.** (*rule*) Gesetz *nt* **2.** (*system*) **the** ~ das Gesetz; **against the** ~ illegal **3.** (*subject*) Jura *kein art*

'lawbreaker *n* Gesetzesbrecher(in) *m(f)*

'law court *n* Gericht *nt*

'law enforcement *n* Gesetzesvollzug *m*; **in most countries, ~ is in the hands of the police** in den meisten Ländern ist es Aufgabe der Polizei, für die Einhaltung der Gesetze zu sorgen

law firm, law office *n* Anwaltsbüro *nt*, Kanzlei *f*

lawful ['lɔ·fəl] *adj* gesetzlich; (*heir*) gesetzmäßig

lawless ['lɔ·lɪs] *adj* **1.** (*without laws*) gesetzlos **2.** (*illegal*) gesetzwidrig

'lawmaker *n* Gesetzgeber(in) *m(f)*

lawn [lɔn] *n* Rasen *m*

'lawn bowling *n* Bowls *pl*

'lawnmower *n* Rasenmäher *m*

'law school *n* juristische Fakultät

'law student *n* Jurastudent(in) *m(f)*

'lawsuit *n* Klage *f*, Prozess *m*

lawyer ['lɔ·jər] *n* Rechtsanwalt, -anwältin *m, f*

lax [læks] *adj* (*careless*) lax *oft pej*; (*security*) mangelnd

laxative ['læk·sə·t̬ɪv] *n* Abführmittel *nt*

laxity ['læk·sɪ·t̬i] *n* Laxheit *f*

lay¹ [leɪ] **I.** *vt* <laid, laid> **1.** (*spread*) legen (**on** auf +*akk*), breiten (**over** über +*akk*) **2.** (*egg*) legen **3.** (*put down*) verlegen; **to ~ the blame on sb** *fig* jdn für etw *akk* verantwortlich machen **4.** (*render*) **to ~ sb/sth open to criticism** jdn/etw der Kritik aussetzen **5.** (*present*) **to ~ sth before sb** jdm etw vorlegen **6.** *vulg, sl* (*have sex*) **to get laid** flachgelegt werden *sl* ▶ **to ~ eyes on** [erstmals] zu sehen bekommen; **to ~ sth to rest** etw beschwichtigen **II.** *n* **1.** (*shape*) **the ~ of the land** *fig* die Lage **2.** *vulg, sl* (*sex partner*) **to be a good ~** gut im Bett sein *fam*

◆**lay aside** *vt* **1.** (*put away, save*) beiseitelegen **2.** *fig* (*forget: one's differ-* ences) beilegen

◆**lay down** *vt* **1.** (*deposit*) hinlegen (**on** auf +*akk*) **2.** (*weapons*) niederlegen **3.** (*rules*) festlegen ▶ **to ~ down the law** [**about sth**] [über etw *akk*] Vorschriften machen

◆**lay into** *vi fam* **to ~ into sb** (*physically*) jdn angreifen; (*verbally*) jdn zur Schnecke machen *fam*

◆**lay off** **I.** *vt* kündigen; **to ~ off ⇆ sb** jdn entlassen **II.** *vi* aufhören

◆**lay on** *vt* auftragen

◆**lay out** *vt* **1.** (*arrange*) planen; (*schedule*) organisieren **2.** *usu passive* (*design*) **to be laid out** angeordnet sein; (*garden*) angelegt sein

lay² [leɪ] *adj attr* laienhaft

lay³ [leɪ] *pt of* **lie**

layer ['leɪ·ər] **I.** *n* **1.** Schicht *f*; **~s** *pl* (*in hair*) Stufen *pl* **2.** *fig* (*level*) Stufe *f* **II.** *vt* **to ~ sth** [**with sth**] etw [abwechselnd mit etw *dat*] in Schichten anordnen

layette [leɪ·'et] *n* Babyausstattung *f*

layman *n* Laie *m*

'layoff *n* Entlassung *f*

'layout *n* **1.** (*plan: of building*) Raumaufteilung *f*; (*of town*) Plan *m* **2.** (*of text*) Layout *nt*

'layover *n* Aufenthalt *m*; (*of plane*) Zwischenlandung *f*

laze [leɪz] *vi* faulenzen

laziness ['leɪ·zɪ·nɪs] *n* Faulheit *f*

lazy ['leɪ·zi] *adj* faul

'lazybones *n* + *sing vb pej* Faulenzer(in) *m(f)*

lb. <*pl* ~> *n abbr of* **pound** Pfd.

LCD [ˌel·si·'di] *n abbr of* **liquid crystal display** LCD *nt*

lead¹ [lid] **I.** *vt* <led, led> **1.** (*command*) führen; (*delegation*) führen **2.** (*guide*) führen (**into/over/through** in/über/durch +*akk*, **to** zu +*dat*) **3.** (*go in advance*) **to ~ the way** vorangehen; (*in car*) voranfahren ▶ **to ~ sb down the garden path** *fam* jdn an der Nase herumführen **II.** *vi* <led, led> **1.** (*command*) die Leitung innehaben **2.** (*be guide*) vorangehen **3.** (*cause to happen*) **to ~ to sth** zu etw *dat* führen **4.** (*be in the lead*) führen; SPORT in Führung liegen **III.** *n* **1.** THEAT, FILM

Hauptrolle f 2. (*front position*) Führung f; **to be in the ~** führend sein; **to take over the ~** sich an die Spitze setzen 3. (*advance position*) Vorsprung m 4. (*leash*) Leine f

lead off I. vt (*initiate*) **to ~ off ⇆ sth [with sth]** etw [mit etw *dat*] eröffnen **II. vi 1.** (*begin*) beginnen **2.** (*road*) wegführen; **to ~ off to the left** nach links abgehen

lead on vt *pej* **to ~ on ⇆ sb** (*deceive*) jdm etw vormachen

lead up to *vi* **to ~ up to sth 1.** (*precede*) etw *dat* vorangehen **2.** (*approach: subject*) zu etw *akk* hinführen

lead² [led] n 1. (*metal*) Blei nt **2.** (*of pencil*) Mine f

leaded ['led·əd] *adj* (*gasoline*) verbleit

leader ['li·dər] **n 1.** (*head*) Leiter(in) m(f), Führer(in) m(f) **2.** (*competitor*) Erste(r) f(m) **3.** MUS (*conductor*) Dirigent(in) m(f)

leadership ['li·dər·ʃɪp] **n 1.** (*action*) Führung f **2.** (*position*) Leitung f, Führung f

lead-free ['led·fri] *adj* bleifrei

leading ['li·dɪŋ] *adj attr* führend

leading edge n 1. (*of wing*) Flügelvorderkante f **2.** (*of development*) **to be at the ~ [of sth]** auf dem neuesten Stand [einer S. *gen*] sein

leading question n Suggestivfrage f

lead pencil [led'-] **n** Bleistift m

lead poisoning ['led-] **n** Bleivergiftung f

lead singer [lid'-] **n** Leadsänger(in) m(f)

lead story [lid'-] **n** Leitartikel m

lead time [lid'-] **n** Vorlaufzeit f

leaf [lif] **I. n** *<pl* leaves*>* **1.** Blatt nt ► **to shake like a ~** wie Espenlaub zittern **II. vi** *<*-s, -ed*>* **to ~ through sth** etw durchblättern

leaflet ['lif·lɪt] **n** (*for advertising*) Prospekt m *österr a.* nt; (*for instructions*) Merkblatt nt; (*brochure*) Broschüre f

leafy ['li·fi] *adj* **1.** (*of place*) belaubt **2.** HORT Blatt-, blattartig

league [lig] **n 1.** (*group*) Bund m **2.** SPORT Liga f

leak [lik] **I. n** Leck nt; **gas ~** undichte Stelle in der Gasleitung **II. vi** (*container*) undicht sein; (*ship*) lecken; (*fau-*

cet) tropfen; (*tire*) Luft verlieren **III. vt 1.** (*gas, liquid*) austreten lassen **2.** *fig* (*information*) durchsickern lassen

leaky ['li·ki] *adj* leck

lean¹ [lin] **I. vi** *<*leaned, leaned*>* (*incline*) sich beugen; (*prop*) sich lehnen; **to ~ forward** sich nach vorne lehnen **II. vt** *<*leaned, leaned*>* lehnen (**against/on** an/auf +*akk*)

lean on *vi* **1.** (*rely on*) sich verlassen auf +*akk* **2.** *fam* (*put under pressure*) unter Druck setzen

lean² [lin] *adj* **1.** (*not fat*) mager; (*person a.*) schlank **2.** (*budget*) schmal *fig*

leap [lip] **I. n** *a. fig* Sprung m **II. vi** *<*leaped *or* leapt, leaped *or* leapt*>* **1.** (*jump*) springen (**across/over** über +*akk*, **from** von +*dat*); **to ~ on sth** sich auf etw stürzen **2.** (*rush*) **to ~ to sb's defense** *fig* zu jds Verteidigung eilen **3.** *fig* (*increase: prices*) in die Höhe schießen **III. vt** *<*leaped *or* leapt, leaped *or* leapt*>* springen über +*akk*, überspringen

leap out *vi* **1.** (*jump out*) herausspringen (**of** aus +*dat*) **2.** *fig* (*grab attention*) **to ~ out at sb** jdm ins Auge springen

leapfrog n Bockspringen nt

leapt [lept] *vt, vi pt, pp of* **leap**

leap year n Schaltjahr nt

learn [lɜrn] **I. vt** *<*learned *or* learnt, learned *or* learnt*>* lernen; **to ~ how to do sth** lernen, wie man etw tut ► **to ~ sth by** under**heart** etw auswendig lernen **II. vi** *<*learned *or* learnt, learned *or* learnt*>* **1.** (*master*) lernen (**about** über +*akk*) **2.** (*become aware*) **to ~ about sth** von etw *dat* erfahren

learner ['lɜr·nər] **n** Lernende(r) f(m); **to be a quick ~** schnell lernen

learnt [lɜrnt] *vt, vi pt, pp of* **learn**

lease [lis] **I. vt 1.** (*grant use*) vermieten (**to** an +*akk*) **2.** (*rent*) mieten; (*property*) pachten; (*equipment*) leasen **II. n** (*of apartment, house*) Mietvertrag m; (*of equipment*) Leasingvertrag m

leash [liʃ] **I. n** Leine f; (*for children*) Laufgurt m **II. vt** (*dog*) anleinen

leasing ['li·sɪŋ] **n 1.** (*granting of use: of land*) Verpachten nt; (*of equipment*) Leasing nt **2.** (*renting: of land*) Pach-

ten *nt;* (*of equipment*) Leasen *nt*

least [list] **I.** *adv* am wenigsten; **the ~ little thing** die kleinste Kleinigkeit; **~ of all** am allerwenigsten **II.** *adj det* (*tiniest amount*) geringste(r, s); **at ~** (*minimum*) mindestens; (*if nothing else*) zumindest

leather ['leð·ər] *n* Leder *nt*

leathery ['leð·ə·ri] *adj* led[e]rig; (*hands, skin*) ledern

leave [liv] **I.** *n* **1.** (*farewell*) Abschied *m* **2.** (*permission*) Erlaubnis *f* **3.** (*off work*) Urlaub *m* **II.** *vt* <left, left> **1.** (*depart*) verlassen; (*train*) abfahren **2.** (*permanently: husband, wife*) verlassen; (*job*) aufgeben; **to ~ school** die Schule beenden **3.** (*not take*) [zurück]lassen (**with** bei +*dat*); (*message, note*) hinterlassen **4.** (*forget*) vergessen **5.** (*cause to remain*) **to ~ sth open** etw offen lassen **6.** (*not change*) lassen **7.** (*not eat*) übrig lassen **8.** (*bequeath*) hinterlassen ▶ **to ~ sth to chance** nichts dem Zufall überlassen; **to ~ sb alone** jdn in Ruhe lassen **III.** *vi* <left, left> [weg]gehen; (*vehicle*) abfahren; (*plane*) abfliegen

♦ **leave behind** *vt* **1.** (*not take*) zurücklassen **2.** (*traces*) hinterlassen **3.** *fig* (*forget on purpose*) **to ~ behind ⇆ sth** etw hinter sich *dat* lassen

♦ **leave off** *vt* **1.** (*omit*) auslassen; **to ~ sb's name off a list** jds Namen nicht in eine Liste aufnehmen **2.** (*not put on*) **to ~ a lid off sth** keinen Deckel auf etw *akk* geben

♦ **leave out** *vt* **1.** (*omit*) auslassen; (*facts*) weglassen; (*accidentally*) vergessen **2.** (*exclude*) ausschließen

♦ **leave over** *vt usu passive* **to be left over** [**from sth**] [von etw *dat*] übrig geblieben sein

leaves [livz] *n pl of* **leaf**

leaving ['li·vɪŋ] *n* Abreise *f*

lecherous ['letʃ·ər·əs] *adj* geil *oft pej*

lectern ['lek·tərn] *n* [Redner]pult *nt*

lecture ['lek·tʃər] **I.** *n* **1.** (*speech*) Vortrag *m;* UNIV Vorlesung *f* **2.** (*criticism*) Standpauke *f fam* **II.** *vi* UNIV eine Vorlesung halten **III.** *vt* **to ~ sb on** [*or* **about**] **sth 1.** (*give speech*) jdm über etw *akk* einen Vortrag halten; UNIV vor

jdm über etw *akk* eine Vorlesung halte[n] **2.** (*criticize*) jdm wegen einer S. eine Standpauke halten *fam*

lecture hall *n* Hörsaal *m*

lecturer ['lek·tʃər·ər] *n* **1.** (*speaker*) Redner(in) *m(f)* **2.** (*university*) Do[zent(in)] *m(f)*

lecture tour *n* Vortragsreise *f*

led [led] *pt, pp of* **lead**

ledge [ledʒ] *n* Sims *m o nt;* (*of rock*) Fels[vorsprung *m*]

lee [li] *n* Windschatten *m;* GEOG, NAUT Lee *o nt fachspr*

leek [lik] *n* Lauch *m*

leer [lɪr] **I.** *vi* **to ~ at sb** jdm anzügli[che] Blicke zuwerfen **II.** *n* anzügliche[s] Grinsen

leeway ['li·wei] *n* Spielraum *m*

left¹ [left] **I.** *n* **1.** (*direction*) **from ~ to right** von links nach rechts **2.** (*turn*) **to make a ~** [nach] links abbiege[n] **3.** (*side*) **the ~** die linke Seite; POL **die Linke**; **on** [*or* **to**] **sb's ~** zu jds Linken, links von jdm **II.** *adj* linke(r, s) **III.** *adv* (*direction*) nach links; (*side*) links; **to keep ~** sich links halten ▶ **~ right and center** überall

left² [left] *pt, pp of* **leave**

left-hand *adj attr* (*on left side*) linke(r, s)

left-'handed I. *adj* (*person*) linkshändig **II.** *adv* SPORT **to throw ~** mit link[s] werfen

left-'hander *n* (*person*) Linkshänder(in) *m(f)*

leftovers *npl* (*food*) Reste *pl*

left 'wing *n* **the ~ 1.** POL die Linke **2.** MIL, SPORT der linke Flügel

left-'wing *adj* linksgerichtet, links *präd*

leg [leg] *n* **1.** (*limb, support*) Bein *n* **2.** (*meat*) Keule *f* **3.** (*stage*) Etappe *f* ▶ **to be on one's last ~s** auf dem letzten Loch pfeifen *sl;* **to pull sb's ~** *fam* jdn auf den Arm nehmen

legacy ['leg·ə·si] *n* LAW Vermächtnis *nt a. fig*

legal ['li·gəl] *adj* **1.** (*permitted by law*) legal **2.** (*statutory*) gesetzlich [vorgeschrieben] **3.** (*under law*) rechtmäßig **4.** (*of paper*) nordamerikanische Standardgröße für Papierformat: 21,6 cm x 35,6 cm

legalese [ˌli·gəl·ˈiz] *n pej fam* Juristenjargon *m oft pej*
legalize [ˈli·gə·laɪz] *vt* legalisieren *geh*
legally [ˈli·gə·li] *adv* **1.** (*permissible*) legal **2.** (*required*) **~ obliged** gesetzlich verpflichtet **3.** (*according to the law*) rechtmäßig
legal pad *n* Schreibblock *m*
legend [ˈledʒ·ənd] *n* **1.** (*saga*) Sage *f* **2.** (*person*) Legende *f*
legendary [ˈledʒ·ən·der·i] *adj* **1.** (*mythical*) sagenhaft **2.** (*famous*) legendär
leggings [ˈleg·ɪŋz] *npl* Leggings *pl*
legible [ˈledʒ·ə·bəl] *adj* lesbar
legion [ˈli·dʒən] *n* HIST Legion *f;* **the [Foreign] L~** die Fremdenlegion
Legionˈnaires' disease *n* die Legionärskrankheit
legislate [ˈledʒ·ɪ·sleɪt] *vi* ein Gesetz erlassen (**against** gegen *+akk*)
legislation [ˌledʒ·ɪ·ˈsleɪ·ʃən] *n* **1.** (*laws*) Gesetze *pl* **2.** (*lawmaking*) Gesetzgebung *f*
legislative [ˈledʒ·ɪ·sleɪ·t̬ɪv] *adj esp attr* gesetzgebend
legislator [ˈledʒ·ɪ·sleɪ·t̬ər] *n* Gesetzgeber(in) *m(f)*
legislature [ˈledʒ·ɪ·sleɪ·tʃər] *n* Legislative *f;* **member of the ~** Parlamentsmitglied *nt*
legitimate *adj* [lə·ˈdʒɪt̬·ə·mɪt] **1.** (*legal*) rechtmäßig **2.** (*reasonable*) gerechtfertigt; (*complaint*) begründet **3.** (*child*) ehelich
legitim(at)ize [lə·ˈdʒɪt̬·ə·m(ə·t)aɪz] *vt* (*make legal*) für rechtsgültig erklären
ˈlegroom *n* Beinfreiheit *f*
legume [lə·ˈgjum] *n* BOT Hülsenfrucht *f*
leisure [ˈli·ʒər] *n* Freizeit *f* ▶ **at [one's] ~** in aller Ruhe
leisurely [ˈli·ʒər·li] **I.** *adj* ruhig, geruhsam; (*picnic, breakfast*) gemütlich **II.** *adv* gemächlich
ˈleisurewear *n* Freizeit[be]kleidung *f*
lemon [ˈlem·ən] *n* **1.** (*fruit*) Zitrone *f* **2.** (*color*) Zitronengelb *nt*
lemonade [ˌlem·ə·ˈneɪd] *n* Zitronenlimonade *f*
ˈlemon peel, ˈlemon rind *n* Zitronenschale *f*
lend <lent, lent> [lend] *vt* **1.** (*loan*) leihen **2.** (*be suitable*) **to ~ itself to sth** sich für etw *akk* eignen
lender [ˈlen·dər] *n* Verleiher(in) *m(f);* (*of money*) Kreditgeber(in) *m(f)*
lending [ˈlen·dɪŋ] *n* Leihen *nt*
ˈlending library *n* Leihbibliothek *f*
length [leŋkθ] *n* **1.** (*measurement*) Länge *f;* **6 feet in ~** 6 Fuß lang **2.** (*piece*) Stück *nt;* (*of cloth*) Bahn *f* **3.** (*duration*) Dauer *f;* **at ~** (*in detail*) ausführlich ▶ **to go to great ~s** sich *dat* alle Mühe geben
lengthen [ˈleŋk·θən] **I.** *vt* verlängern; (*clothes*) länger machen **II.** *vi* [immer] länger werden
lengthwise [ˈleŋkθ·waɪz], **lengthways** [ˈleŋkθ·weɪz] *adv* der Länge nach
lengthy [ˈleŋk·θi] *adj* **1.** (*long time*) [ziemlich] lange; (*delay*) beträchtlich **2.** (*tedious*) langwierig
lenience [ˈli·ni·əns], **leniency** [ˈli·ni·ən·si] *n* Nachsicht *f,* Milde *f*
lenient [ˈli·ni·ənt] *adj* nachsichtig, milde
lens <*pl* -es> [lenz] *n* Linse *f;* (*of camera*) Objektiv *nt;* (*of glasses*) Glas *nt;* **[contact] ~** Kontaktlinse *f*
lent [lent] *vt, vi pt, pp of* **lend**
lentil [ˈlen·təl] *n* Linse *f*
Leo [ˈli·oʊ] *n* ASTRON, ASTROL **1.** *no art* der Löwe **2.** (*person*) Löwe *m;* **she is a ~** sie ist Löwe
leopard [ˈlep·ərd] *n* Leopard(in) *m(f)*
leotard [ˈli·ə·tard] *n* Trikot *nt;* (*for gymnastics a.*) Turnanzug *m*
leprosy [ˈlep·rə·si] *n* Lepra *f*
lesbian [ˈlez·bi·ən] **I.** *n* Lesbierin *f,* Lesbe *f* **II.** *adj* lesbisch
less [les] **I.** *adv comp of* **little** weniger; **the ~ ... the better** je weniger ..., umso besser; **~ and ~** immer weniger **II.** *adj comp of* **little** weniger **III.** *pron indef* weniger; **a lot ~** viel weniger; **I've been seeing ~ of her lately** ich sehe sie in letzter Zeit weniger; **~ of a problem** ein geringeres Problem
lessen [ˈles·ən] *vi* schwächer werden; (*pain*) nachlassen
lesser [ˈles·ər] *adj attr* **1.** (*smaller*) geringer; **the ~ of two evils** das kleinere Übel **2.** (*minor*) unbedeutend
lesson [ˈles·ən] *n* **1.** (*at school*) Stunde *f;*

L

~s *pl* Unterricht *m kein pl* (in in +*dat*)
2. (*experience*) Lehre *f*; to teach sb a ~
jdm eine Lektion erteilen

let¹ |let| *vt* <-tt-, let, let> 1. (*allow*) to
~ sth/sb do sth etw/jdn tun lassen;
to ~ sb go (*allow to depart*) jdn gehen
lassen; (*release from grip*) jdn loslassen;
I'll ~ you go (*on the phone*) ich will
Sie nicht länger aufhalten; to ~ sth go
(*neglect*) etw vernachlässigen; (*let pass*)
etw durchgehen lassen 2. (*give permission*) to ~ sb do sth jdn etw tun lassen
3. (*in suggestions*) ~'s go out to dinner! lass uns Essen gehen! ▶ ~ alone
... geschweige denn ...; ~ it rip *fam* es
[mal so richtig] krachen lassen *fam*

◆let down *vt* 1. to ~ down ⇆ sb (*disappoint*) jdn enttäuschen; (*fail to support*) jdn im Stich lassen 2. (*lower*) to ~
down ⇆ sth etw herunterlassen

◆let in *vt* hereinlassen; to ~ oneself in
aufschließen

◆let into *vt* to ~ sb into sth jdn in etw
akk lassen

◆let off *vt* 1. (*not punish*) to ~ sb off
with a warning jdn mit einer Verwarnung davonkommen lassen 2. (*emit*)
ausstoßen; (*bad smell*) verbreiten; to ~
off steam *a. fig* Dampf ablassen

◆let on *vi fam* to ~ on about sth [to sb]
[jdm] etwas von etw *dat* verraten

◆let out *vt* 1. (*release*) herauslassen;
I'll ~ myself out ich finde selbst hinaus 2. (*emit*) ausstoßen; to ~ out ⇆ a
shriek aufschreien 3. (*seam*) auslassen
II. *vi* enden; when does school ~ out
for the summer? wann beginnen die
Sommerferien?

◆let through *vt* durchlassen

◆let up *vi fam* (*decrease*) aufhören; (*rain
a.*) nachlassen; (*fog, weather*) aufklaren

let² |let| *n* SPORT Netzball *m*

lethal ['li·θəl] *adj* tödlich

lethargic [lɪ·ˈθɑːr·dʒɪk] *adj* 1. (*not energetic*) lethargisch 2. (*apathetic*) lustlos

letter ['let·ər] I. *n* 1. (*message*) Brief *m*;
to inform sb by ~ jdn schriftlich verständigen 2. (*of alphabet*) Buchstabe *m*
II. *adj* (*of paper*) nordamerikanische
Standardgröße für Papierformat: 21,6
cm x 27,9 cm

'letter bomb *n* Briefbombe *f*

lettuce ['let·ɪs] *n* (*plant*) Blattsalat *m*
(*with firm head*) Kopfsalat *m*

leukemia [lu·ˈki·mi·ə] *n* Leukämie *f*

level ['lev·əl] I. *adj* 1. (*plane*) horizontal, waag[e]recht 2. (*flat*) eben 3. *pre*
(*at equal height*) auf gleicher Höhe
(with mit +*dat*) 4. (*calm: voice*) ruhig
II. *n* 1. (*quantity, standard*) Niveau *nt*
(*height*) Höhe *f*; above sea ~ über dem
Meeresspiegel 2. (*extent*) Ausmaß *n*
3. (*story*) Stockwerk *nt* ~ on four im
vierten Stock 4. (*rank*) Ebene *f* III. *v.*
<-l-> 1. (*flatten: ground*) [ein]ebnen;
(*raze: building*) dem Erdboden gleich-
machen 2. (*direct: pistol*) richten (at
auf +*akk*)

◆level off, level out I. *vi* 1. (*after dropping: plane*) sich fangen; (*pilot*) das
Flugzeug abfangen; (*after rising*) horizontal fliegen 2. (*road*) flach werden
II. *vt* [ein]ebnen

◆level with *vi fam* to ~ with sb ehrlich
zu jdm sein

level-'headed *adj* vernünftig

lever ['lev·ər] I. *n* 1. Hebel *m* 2. *fig*
(*threat*) Druckmittel *nt* II. *vt* to ~ sth
up etw aufstemmen

leverage ['lev·ər·ɪdʒ] *n* 1. TECH Hebel-
kraft *f* 2. *fig* (*pressure*) Einfluss *m*

levitate ['lev·ɪ·teɪt] I. *vi* schweben II. *vt*
schweben lassen

levy ['lev·i] I. *n* Steuer *f*, Abgaben *pl*
II. *vt* <-ie-> erheben; (*tax*) auferlegen
(on +*dat*)

lewd [lud] *adj* (*indecent*) unanständig;
(*gesture*) obszön

lexical ['lek·sɪ·kəl] *adj* lexikalisch

lexicography [ˌlek·sɪ·ˈkɑg·rə·fi] *n* Lexi-
kographie *f*

lexicon ['lek·sɪ·kən] *n* Wörterbuch *nt*

liability [ˌlaɪ·ə·ˈbɪl·ɪ·ti] *n* 1. (*responsibility*) Haftung *f* 2. FIN liabilities *pl*
Verbindlichkeiten *pl* 3. (*handicap*) Belastung *f*

liable ['laɪ·ə·bəl] *adj* 1. JUR haftbar
2. (*likely*) to be ~ to do sth Gefahr
laufen, etw zu tun

liaise [lɪ·ˈeɪz] *vi* to ~ with sb/sth (*establish contact*) eine Verbindung zu jdm/
etw herstellen; (*be go-between*) als Ver-

bindungsstelle zu jdm/etw fungieren

aison ['liˑeɪˈzan] n (contact) Verbindung f; **to work in close ~ with sb** mit jdm eng zusammenarbeiten

ar ['laɪ·ər] n Lügner(in) m(f)

bel ['laɪ·bəl] JUR I. n Verleumdung f II. vt <-l-> verleumden

belous, libellous ['laɪ·bə·ləs] adj verleumderisch

beral ['lɪb·ər·əl] I. adj liberal; (attitude) tolerant II. n Liberale(r) f(m)

beral 'arts I. n pl **the ~** die Geisteswissenschaften pl II. adj geisteswissenschaftlich

beralism ['lɪb·ər·ə·lɪz·əm] n Liberalismus m

beralization [ˌlɪb·ər·ə·lɪˈzeɪ·ʃən] n Liberalisierung f

beralize ['lɪb·ər·ə·laɪz] vt liberalisieren

berate ['lɪb·ə·reɪt] vt befreien (from von +dat)

beration [ˌlɪb·əˈreɪ·ʃən] n Befreiung f (from von +dat)

iberty ['lɪb·ər·ti] n 1. (freedom) Freiheit f; **to be at ~** frei sein 2. (incorrect behavior) **to take liberties with sb** sich dat bei jdm Freiheiten herausnehmen

ibido [lɪˈbiˑdoʊ] n Libido f

Libra ['liˑbrə] n ASTRON, ASTROL 1. die Waage 2. (person) Waage f; **she is a ~** sie ist Waage

ibrarian [laɪˈbrerˑi·ən] n Bibliothekar(in) m(f)

ibrary ['laɪˈbrerˑi] n Bibliothek f; (public a.) Bücherei f; **public ~** Leihbücherei f

ice [laɪs] n pl of **louse**

license ['laɪ·səns] I. n (permit) Genehmigung f, Erlaubnis f; **driver's ~** Führerschein m II. vt **to ~ sb to do sth** jdm die Lizenz erteilen, etw zu tun

icensed ['laɪ·sənst] adj zugelassen

license plate n Nummernschild nt

license plate number n Kfz-Kennzeichen nt

icensing ['laɪ·sən·sɪŋ] n Lizenzvergabe f

ichen ['laɪ·kən] n Flechte f

ick [lɪk] I. n Lecken nt kein pl, Schlecken nt kein pl II. vt 1. lecken; (lollipop) schlecken an +dat 2. fam (beat) **to ~ sb** jdn [doch glatt] in die Tasche stecken

licking ['lɪk·ɪŋ] n fam **to give sb a [good] ~** (beating) jdm eine Tracht Prügel verpassen fam; (defeat) jdn haushoch schlagen

licorice ['lɪk·ər·ɪʃ] n Lakritze f

lid [lɪd] n 1. (cover) Deckel m 2. (eyelid) Lid nt

lie¹ [laɪ] I. n Lage f II. vi <-y-, lay, lain> 1. (repose) liegen; **to ~ awake** wach [da]liegen 2. (become horizontal) sich hinlegen 3. (be in particular state) **to ~ in wait** auf der Lauer liegen 4. (be situated) liegen; **to ~ to the east of sth** im Osten einer S. gen liegen ▶ **to ~ low** (escape search) untergetaucht sein; (avoid notice) sich unauffällig verhalten

lie around vi [he]rumliegen fam

lie ahead vi 1. (in space, position) **to ~ ahead [of sb]** vor jdm liegen 2. (in time) bevorstehen

lie back vi sich zurücklegen

lie behind vi (be cause of) **to ~ behind sth** etw dat zugrunde liegen **L**

lie down vi sich hinlegen

lie² [laɪ] I. vi <-y-> lügen; **to ~ about sb** über jdn die Unwahrheit erzählen; **to ~ to sb** jdn belügen II. n Lüge f

'lie detector n Lügendetektor m

lieu [lu] n **in ~ of sth** an Stelle einer S. gen

Lieut. n attr abbr of **Lieutenant** Lt.

lieutenant [luˈten·ənt] n 1. MIL Leutnant m 2. LAW ≈ Polizeihauptwachtmeister(in) m(f)

lieutenant 'governor n POL Vizegouverneur m

life <pl **lives**> [laɪf] n 1. [das] Leben; **to save sb's ~** jdm das Leben retten 2. (living things collectively) das Leben; **plant ~** die Pflanzenwelt 3. (energy) Lebendigkeit f; **to bring sth to ~** etw lebendiger machen 4. (time until death) das/sein Leben; **for ~** (friendship) lebenslang 5. (duration: of battery) Lebensdauer f; (of a contract) Laufzeit f ▶ **to frighten the ~ out of sb** jdn zu Tode erschrecken; **that's ~!** so ist das Leben [eben]!

'lifeboat n Rettungsboot nt

'life cycle n Lebenszyklus m

'life ex'pectancy n Lebenserwartung f
'life form n Lebewesen f
'lifeguard n (at swimming pool) Bademeister(in) m(f); (on beach) Rettungsschwimmer(in) m(f)
life im'prisonment n lebenslängliche Freiheitsstrafe
'life insurance n Lebensversicherung f
'life jacket n Schwimmweste f
'lifeless ['laɪf·lɪs] adj 1. (inanimate) leblos 2. (dull: game) langweilig; (hair) stumpf
'lifelike adj lebensecht; (imitation a.) naturgetreu
'lifeline n 1. (rope) Rettungsleine f 2. fig (vital link) [lebenswichtige] Verbindung
'life preserver n Schwimmweste f
lifer ['laɪ·fər] n fam (prisoner) Lebenslängliche(r) f(m) fam
'life raft n Rettungsfloß nt; (dinghy) Schlauchboot nt
'lifesaver n fam (thing) die Rettung fig; (person) [Lebens]retter(in) m(f) fig
life 'sentence n lebenslängliche Freiheitsstrafe
'life-size(d) adj in Lebensgröße nach n, lebensgroß
'lifestyle n Lebensstil m
'life support system n MED lebenserhaltender Apparat
'life-threatening adj (illness) lebensbedrohend; (situation) lebensgefährlich
'lifetime n usu sing 1. (time one is alive) Lebenszeit f; **to last a ~** (memories) das ganze Leben [lang] andauern 2. (time sth exists) Lebensdauer f kein pl ▸ the **chance** of a **~** eine einmalige Chance
'life vest n see **life jacket**
lift [lɪft] I. n 1. (for skiers) Skilift m 2. (act of lifting) [Hoch]heben nt kein pl 3. (ride) Mitfahrgelegenheit f; **to give sb a ~** jdn [im Auto] mitnehmen II. vt 1. (raise) [hoch]heben 2. (direct upward: eyes) aufschlagen; (head) heben 3. (airlift) fliegen; (supplies) auf dem Luftweg transportieren 4. usu passive (in surgery: face) straffen lassen, liften 5. (end: restrictions) aufheben III. vi 1. (be raised) sich heben 2. (fog) sich auflösen
◆**lift off** vi 1. (leave earth) abheben

2. (come off) sich hochheben lassen
◆**lift up** vt hochheben; (lid) hochklappen
'liftoff n AEROSP Start m
ligament ['lɪg·ə·mənt] n ANAT Band n; **to tear a ~** sich dat einen Bänderriss zuziehen
light¹ [laɪt] I. n 1. Licht nt 2. (source of brightness) Licht nt; (lamp) Lampe f; **to turn the ~ off** das Licht ausschalten 3. (fire) Feuer nt 4. usu pl (traffic light) Ampel f 5. fig (perspective) **to show sth in a good ~** etw in einem guten Licht erscheinen lassen ▸ **to come t~ ~** ans Licht kommen II. adj hell III. vt <lit or lighted, lit or lighted> 1. (erhellen); (room) beleuchten 2. (match, fire) anzünden
◆**light up** I. vt 1. (illuminate) erhelle 2. (cigar) anzünden II. vi 1. (smoke) sich dat eine [Zigarette] anstecken fam 2. (become animated: eyes) aufleuchten fig
light² [laɪt] I. adj 1. leicht 2. (for small loads) Klein-; **~ airplane** Kleinflugzeug nt 3. (low-fat) fettarm 4. (low intensity) **~ rain** Nieselregen m 5. (kiss) zart; (touch) sanft ▸ **to make ~ of sth** etw bagatellisieren II. adv **to travel ~** mit leichtem Gepäck reisen
'light bulb n Glühbirne f
lighten ['laɪ·tən] vt 1. (make less heavy) leichter machen 2. fig (make less seri ous) aufheitern; (mood) heben
◆**lighten up** vi **~ up, would you?** mach bitte nicht so ein Gesicht
lighter ['laɪ·tər] n Feuerzeug nt
light'headed adj (faint) benommen; (dizzy) schwind[e]lig
light'hearted adj unbeschwert
'lighthouse n Leuchtturm m
lighting ['laɪ·tɪŋ] n Beleuchtung f; (equipment) Beleuchtungsanlage f
lightly ['laɪt·li] adv 1. (not seriously) leichtfertig; **to not take sth ~** etw nicht leichtnehmen 2. (gently) leich (not much) wenig; **I tapped ~ o the door** ich klopfte leise an [die Tür 3. (slightly) leicht
lightness¹ ['laɪt·nɪs] n (brightness) Hel ligkeit f

ghtness² [ˈlaɪt·nɪs] n (not heaviness)
Leichtheit f

ightning [ˈlaɪt·nɪŋ] n Blitz m; **thunder
and ~** Blitz und Donner; **to be struck
by ~** vom Blitz getroffen werden

ightning rod n Blitzableiter m a. fig

light pen n COMPUT Lichtstift m

ightweight I. n (boxer) Leichtgewicht-
ler(in) m/f/ **II.** adj **1.** SPORT Leichtge-
wichts- **2.** (weighing little) leicht

light year n ASTRON Lichtjahr nt

ikable [ˈlaɪ·kə·bəl] adj liebenswert

ike¹ [laɪk] **I.** vt **1.** (enjoy) mögen; **to ~
doing sth** etw gern[e fam] tun **2.** (want)
wollen; **whether you ~ it or not** ob
es dir passt oder nicht; **would you ~
a drink?** möchten Sie etwas trinken?
3. (prefer) **I ~ to get up early** ich stehe gern[e fam] früh auf **II.** vi **as you ~**
wie Sie wollen

ike² [laɪk] **I.** prep **1.** (similar to) wie;
~ most people wie die meisten Leu-
te; **~ father, ~ son** wie der Vater, so
der Sohn; **what does it taste ~?** wie
schmeckt es?; **he looks ~ his brother**
er sieht seinem Bruder ähnlich; **there's
nothing ~ a good cup of coffee** es
geht doch nichts über eine gute Tasse
Kaffee **2.** after in (such as) wie ▸ **it
looks ~ rain** es sieht nach Regen aus
II. conj fam **1.** (the same as) wie; **let's
go swimming in the lake ~ we used
to** lass uns im See schwimmen gehen
wie früher **2.** (as if) als ob; **she acts
~ she's the boss** sie tut so, als sei sie
die Chefin

likeable [ˈlaɪ·kə·bəl] adj see **likable**

likelihood [ˈlaɪk·li·hʊd] n Wahrscheinlichkeit f

likely [ˈlaɪk·li] **I.** adj <-ier, -iest or more
~, most ~> wahrscheinlich; **please re-
mind me, because I'm ~ to forget**
erinnere mich bitte unbedingt daran,
sonst vergesse ich es wahrscheinlich
II. adv <more ~, most ~> **very ~** sehr
wahrscheinlich

like-ˈminded adj gleich gesinnt

likewise [ˈlaɪk·waɪz] adv ebenfalls, gleichfalls; **to do ~** es genauso machen

liking [ˈlaɪ·kɪŋ] n Vorliebe f; **to develop
a ~ for sth** eine Vorliebe für etw akk

entwickeln

lilac [ˈlaɪ·læk] **I.** n **1.** (bush) Flieder m
2. (color) Lila nt **II.** adj lila

lilt [lɪlt] n (of voice) singender Tonfall

lily [ˈlɪl·i] n Lilie f

limb [lɪm] n ANAT Glied nt ▸ **to risk life
and ~** [to do sth] Kopf und Kragen riskieren[, um etw zu tun] fam

limber [ˈlɪm·bər] **I.** adj <-er, -est or more
~, most ~> **1.** (supple) geschmeidig
2. (flexible) gelenkig **II.** vi **to ~ up** sich
warm machen

limbo¹ [ˈlɪm·boʊ] n **to be in ~** (plan) in
der Schwebe sein; (person) in der Luft
hängen fam

limbo² [ˈlɪm·boʊ] n (dance) Limbo m

lime¹ [laɪm] n (fruit) Limette f

lime² [laɪm] n Kalk m

ˈlimelight n Rampenlicht; **to be in the ~**
im Rampenlicht stehen

ˈlimestone n Kalkstein m

limit [ˈlɪm·ɪt] **I.** n **1.** (utmost) [Höchst]
grenze f; (boundary) Grenze f **2.** (of person) Grenze[n] f[pl]; **to reach one's ~**
an seine Grenze[n] kommen **3.** (restriction) Beschränkung f; (of blood alcohol)
Promillegrenze f; **speed ~** [zulässige]
Höchstgeschwindigkeit f ▸ **to be off
~s [to sb]** [für jdn] gesperrt sein **II.** vt
einschränken

limitation [ˌlɪm·ɪ·ˈteɪ·ʃən] n Begrenzung f

limited [ˈlɪm·ɪ·tɪd] adj begrenzt (to auf
+akk)

limited liaˈbility company n ≈ Gesellschaft f mit beschränkter Haftung

limitless [ˈlɪm·ɪt·lɪs] adj grenzenlos

limousine [ˈlɪm·ə·zin] n [Luxus]limou-
sine f

limp [lɪmp] **I.** vi hinken; fig mit Müh
und Not vorankommen **II.** n Hinken nt
III. adj **1.** (not stiff) schlaff; (cloth)
weich **2.** (weak) schlapp; (handshake)
lasch

limpid [ˈlɪm·pɪd] adj (eyes, water) klar

linchpin [ˈlɪntʃ·pɪn] n (essential element)
Stütze f

linden [ˈlɪn·dən] n Linde f

line¹ [laɪn] **I.** n **1.** (mark, contour) Linie f;
dividing ~ Trennungslinie f **2.** (wrinkle) Falte f **3.** (boundary) Grenze f

4. TELEC [Telefon]leitung *f;* (*connection*) Anschluss *m;* **please hold the ~!** bitte bleiben Sie am Apparat! **5.** (*of words, poem*) Zeile *f* **6.** (*row*) Reihe *f* **7.** (*people waiting*) Schlange *f;* **to be first in ~** an erster Stelle stehen; *fig* ganz vorne dabei sein ▶ **right down the ~** voll und ganz; **to be out of ~** (*behavior*) aus dem Rahmen fallen; (*person*) sich danebenbenehmen **II.** *vt* (*make rows*) **to ~ the streets** die Straßen säumen *geh*

◆**line up I.** *vt* **1.** (*put in row*) **to ~ up ⇆ sth** etw in einer Reihe aufstellen **2.** (*organize*) **do you have anyone ~d up to do the catering?** haben Sie jemanden für das Catering engagiert? **II.** *vi* sich [in einer Reihe] aufstellen; MIL, SPORT antreten

line² [laɪn] *vt* (*clothing*) füttern; (*drawers*) von innen auslegen

linear ['lɪn·i·ər] *adj* **1.** (*of line*) Linien- **2.** (*of length*) Längen-

linen ['lɪn·ɪn] *n* Leinen *nt;* **bed ~** Bettwäsche *f*

liner¹ ['laɪ·nər] *n* NAUT Liniendampfer *m*

liner² ['laɪ·nər] *n* (*lining*) Einsatz *m*

'linesman *n* SPORT Linienrichter *m*

'lineup *n* SPORT [Mannschafts]aufstellung *f;* (*in baseball*) Lineup *f fachspr*

linger ['lɪŋ·gər] *vi* anhalten; **the smell ~ed in the kitchen for days** der Geruch hing tagelang in der Küche

lingerie [ˌlɑn·ʒə·'reɪ] *n* [Damen]unterwäsche *f*

lingering ['lɪŋ·gər·ɪŋ] *adj attr* **1.** (*lasting*) verbleibend; (*fears*) [fort]bestehend; (*regrets*) nachhaltig **2.** ausgedehnt; (*death*) schleichend; (*illness*) langwierig

lingo <*pl* -s> ['lɪŋ·goʊ] *n esp hum fam* **1.** (*language*) Sprache *f* **2.** (*jargon*) Jargon *m*

linguist ['lɪŋ·gwɪst] *n* Linguist(in) *m(f)*

linguistics [lɪŋ·'gwɪs·tɪks] *n + sing vb* die Sprachwissenschaft

lining ['laɪ·nɪŋ] *n* **1.** (*fabric*) Futter *nt* **2.** (*of stomach*) Magenschleimhaut *f;* (*of brake*) Bremsbelag *m*

link [lɪŋk] **I.** *n* **1.** (*connection*) Verbindung *f* **2.** INET, COMPUT Link *m fachspr* **3.** (*of chain*) [Ketten]glied *nt* **II.** *vt* verbinden

'linkup *n* Verbindung *f*

linoleum [lɪ·'noʊ·li·əm] *n* Linoleum *nt*

'linseed ['lɪn·sid] *n* Leinsamen *m*

'linseed oil *n* Leinöl *nt*

lint [lɪnt] *n* MED Mull *m*

lion ['laɪ·ən] *n* **1.** Löwe *m* **2.** ASTRO Löwe *m*

lioness <*pl* -es> ['laɪ·ə·nes] *n* Löwin *f*

lip [lɪp] *n* **1.** Lippe *f* **2.** (*of pitcher*) Schnabel *m*

'lip balm *n* Lippenpflege *f*

'lip-gloss *n* Lipgloss *m*

liposuction ['lɪp·oʊ·ˌsʌk·ʃən] *n* Fettabsaugen *nt*

'lip-read <-read, -read> *vi* von den Lippen ablesen

'lip service *n pej* Lippenbekenntnis *nt;* **to pay ~ to sth** ein Lippenbekenntnis zu etw ablegen

'lipstick *n* Lippenstift *m*

liquefy <-ie-> ['lɪk·wə·faɪ] *vt, vi* [sich] verflüssigen

liqueur [lɪ·'kɜr] *n* Likör *m*

liquid ['lɪk·wɪd] **I.** *adj* **1.** (*watery*) flüssig; **~ soap** Seifenlotion *f* **2.** FIN (*free*) verfügbar **II.** *n* Flüssigkeit *f*

liquidate ['lɪk·wɪ·deɪt] *vt* **1.** ECON, FIN (*company*) auflösen; (*assets*) verfügbar machen **2.** (*kill*) liquidieren *geh*

liquidation [ˌlɪk·wɪ·'deɪ·ʃən] *n* **1.** FIN (*of company*) Auflösung *f;* **to go into ~** in Liquidation gehen **2.** (*killing*) Liquidierung *f geh*

liquidize ['lɪk·wɪ·daɪz] *vt* (*food*) pürieren

liquify ['lɪk·wə·faɪ] *vt, vi see* **liquefy**

liquor ['lɪk·ər] *n* Alkohol *m;* **hard ~** Schnaps *m*

'liquor store *n* Wein- und Spirituosengeschäft *nt*

lisp [lɪsp] *vt, vi* lispeln

list [lɪst] **I.** *n* **1.** (*list*) Liste *f;* **~ of names** Namensliste *f;* (*in books*) Namensverzeichnis *nt;* **shopping ~** Einkaufszettel *m* **II.** *vt* auflisten

listen ['lɪs·ən] *vi* **1.** (*hear*) zuhören; **to ~ to sb** jdm zuhören; **~ to this!** hör dir das an! *fam;* **to ~ to the radio** Radio hören **2.** (*heed*) zuhören; **don't ~ to them** hör nicht auf sie

◆**listen in** *vi* (*secretly*) mithören; (*without participating*) mitanhören

listener ['lɪs·nər] n Zuhörer(in) m(f)

isting ['lɪs·tɪŋ] n 1. (list) Auflistung f 2. (entry in list) Eintrag m 3. (program) **television** ~s Fernsehprogramm nt

istless ['lɪst·lɪs] adj 1. (unenergetic: person) teilnahmslos 2. (unenthusiastic) lustlos

it [lɪt] vt, vi pt, pp of **light**

iter ['li·tər] n Liter m o nt; **two ~s [of milk]** zwei Liter [Milch]

literacy ['lɪt·ə·rə·si] n Lese- und Schreibfähigkeit f

iteral ['lɪt·ər·əl] adj 1. (word-for-word) wörtlich; ~ **meaning** eigentliche Bedeutung 2. (unexaggerated) buchstäblich

iterally ['lɪt·ər·ə·li] adv 1. (word-for-word) [wort]wörtlich 2. (actually) buchstäblich

iterary ['lɪt·ə·rer·i] adj attr (criticism) Literatur-; (language) literarisch; ~ **career** Schriftstellerkarriere f

iterate ['lɪt·ər·ɪt] adj 1. (able to read and write) **to be** ~ lesen und schreiben können 2. **to be computer-~** sich mit Computern auskennen

literature ['lɪt·ər·ə·tʃər] n 1. (works) Literatur f 2. (printed matter) Informationsmaterial nt

lithe [laɪð] adj geschmeidig

lithium ['lɪθ·i·əm] n Lithium nt

lithography [lɪ·'θag·rə·fi] n Lithographie f

litigant ['lɪt·ɪ·gənt] n LAW prozessführende Partei

litigation [ˌlɪt·ɪ·'geɪ·ʃən] n LAW Prozess m

litigious [lɪ·'tɪdʒ·əs] adj LAW prozessfreudig iron

litmus ['lɪt·məs] n Lackmus m o nt

'litmus paper n Lackmuspapier nt

'litmus test n fig (indication) entscheidendes [An]zeichen

litter ['lɪt·ər] I. n 1. (trash) Müll m 2. ZOOL Wurf m II. vt 1. (make untidy) **dirty clothes ~ed the floor** dreckige Wäsche lag über den Boden verstreut 2. usu passive fig (fill) **to be ~ed with sth** mit etw dat übersät sein

'litter box n Katzenklo nt

'litterbug n fam Umweltverschmutzer(in) m(f)

little ['lɪt·əl] I. adj 1. (small, young) klein; (for emphasis) richtige(r, s), kleine(r, s)

2. attr (distance) kurz II. adv 1. (somewhat) **a** ~ ein wenig 2. (hardly) wenig; |a| ~ **more than an hour ago** vor kaum einer Stunde III. pron sing 1. (small quantity) **a** ~ ein wenig (of von +dat) 2. (not much) wenig; **as** ~ **as possible** möglichst wenig 3. (short time) **it's a** ~ **after six** es ist kurz nach sechs ▶ **precious** ~ herzlich wenig

live¹ [laɪv] I. vi 1. (be alive, spend life) leben; **will she ~?** wird sie überleben? 2. (reside) wohnen; **where do you ~?** wo wohnst du? ▶ **you'll** ~ **to regret that!** das wirst du noch bereuen! II. vt **to** ~ **one's own life** sein eigenes Leben leben ▶ **to** ~ **a lie** mit einer Lebenslüge leben

live down vt **to** ~ **down** ⇆ **sth** über etw akk hinwegkommen

live for vi **to** ~ **for sth** für etw akk leben ▶ **to** ~ **for the moment** ein sorgloses Leben führen

live off, live off of vi (depend on) **to** ~ **off sb** auf jds Kosten leben

live on vi 1. (continue) weiterleben; (tradition) fortbestehen; **to** ~ **on in memory** in Erinnerung bleiben 2. (support oneself) **to** ~ **on sth** von etw dat leben

live out vt **to** ~ **out** ⇆ **one's dreams** seine [Wunsch]träume verwirklichen

live through vi überstehen

live together vi zusammenleben

live up vt **to** ~ **it up** fam die Puppen tanzen lassen fam

live up to vi **to** ~ **up to sb's expectations** jds Erwartungen gerecht werden

live with vi 1. (cohabit) zusammenleben 2. (tolerate) sich abfinden mit +dat

live² [laɪv] I. adj 1. attr (living) lebend 2. MUS, RADIO, TV live 3. ELEC geladen; ~ **wire** Hochspannungskabel nt II. adv MUS, RADIO, TV live

livelihood ['laɪv·li·hʊd] n Lebensunterhalt m; **to lose one's** ~ seine Existenzgrundlage verlieren

liveliness ['laɪv·li·nɪs] n (of story) Lebendigkeit f; (of person) Lebhaftigkeit f

lively ['laɪv·li] adj 1. (energetic) lebhaft; (child, eyes) munter; (nature) aufge-

L

weckt **2.** (*bright: colors*) hell **3.** (*brisk*) rege; (*pace*) flott

liven ['laɪ·vən] **I.** *vt* **to ~ up ⇆ sth** Leben in etw *akk* bringen; **to ~ up ⇆ sb** jdn aufmuntern **II.** *vi* **to ~ up** (*person*) aufleben; (*party*) in Schwung kommen

liver ['lɪv·ər] *n* Leber *f*

'**liver damage** *n* Leberschaden *m*

'**liverwurst** *n* Leberwurst *f*

'**livestock** *n* Vieh *nt*, Viehbestand *m*

live wire *n* **1.** ELEC unter Strom stehende Leitung **2.** *fig fam* Feger *m*

livid ['lɪv·ɪd] *adj fam* wütend

living ['lɪv·ɪŋ] **I.** *n* **1.** *usu sing* (*livelihood*) Lebensunterhalt *m* **2.** (*lifestyle*) Lebensstil *m*; **standard of ~** Lebensstandard *m* **3.** *pl* **the ~** die Lebenden *pl* **II.** *adj* **1.** (*alive*) lebend *attr*; **~ creatures** Lebewesen *pl* **2.** (*in use*) lebendig; (*language*) lebend ▸ **to scare the ~** **daylights** **out of sb** jdn zu Tode erschrecken

'**living conditions** *n* Lebensbedingungen *pl*

'**living room** *n* Wohnzimmer *nt*

living 'will *n* LAW *Willenserklärung eines Patienten, die seine medizinische Behandlung festlegt*

lizard ['lɪz·ərd] *n* Eidechse *f*

load [loʊd] **I.** *n* **1.** (*amount carried*) Ladung *f* **2.** (*burden*) Last *f* **3.** *fam* (*lots*) **a ~ of work** ein Riesenberg *m* an Arbeit ▸ **get a ~ of this!** *fam* hör dir das an! **II.** *adv* **~s** *pl fam* tausendmal *fam* **III.** *vt* **1.** (*fill*) laden; (*container*) beladen; (*washing machine*) füllen **2.** *fig* (*burden*) **to ~ sb with responsibility** jdm sehr viel Verantwortung aufladen **3.** (*insert: DVD*) einlegen

◆**load down** *vt* (*thing*) schwer beladen

◆**load up I.** *vt* aufladen; **to ~ up ⇆ a container** einen Container beladen **II.** *vi* beladen

loaded ['loʊ·dɪd] *adj* **1.** (*carrying load*) beladen **2.** (*gun*) geladen **3.** (*excessive*) überladen (**with** mit +*dat*) **4.** *pred fam* (*rich*) steinreich **5.** *pred fam* (*drunk*) besoffen *fam*

'**loading dock** *n* Laderampe *f*

loaf¹ <*pl* **loaves**> [loʊf] *n* (*bread*) Brot *nt*; (*unsliced a.*) Brotlaib *m*

loaf² [loʊf] *vi* faulenzen; **to ~ around** herumgammeln *fam*

loafer ['loʊ·fər] *n* Faulenzer(in) *m(f) pej*

Loafer® ['loʊ·fər] *n* FASHION [leichter] Halbschuh

loan [loʊn] **I.** *n* **1.** (*money*) Kredit *m* **2. to be on ~** verliehen sein **II.** *vt* leihen

'**loanword** *n* Lehnwort *nt*

loath [loʊθ] *adj pred* **to be ~ to do sth** etw ungern tun

loathe [loʊð] *vt* (*thing*) nicht ausstehen können; (*person*) verabscheuen

loathing ['loʊ·ðɪŋ] *n* (*hate*) Abscheu *m*

loathsome ['loʊð·səm] *adj* abscheulich

loaves [loʊvz] *n pl of* **loaf**

lob [lab] **I.** *vt* <-bb-> lobben **II.** *n* **1.** (*stroke*) Lobspiel *nt kein pl* **2.** (*ball*) Lob *m*

lobby ['lab·i] **I.** *n* **1.** ARCHIT Eingangshalle *f*; **hotel ~** Hotelfoyer *nt* **2.** POL Lobby *f* **II.** *vi* <-ie-> **to ~ for sth** seinen Einfluss [mittels eines Interessensverbandes] für etw geltend machen

lobe [loʊb] *n* Lappen *m*; (*of ear*) Ohrläppchen *nt*

lobster ['lab·stər] *n* Hummer *m*

local ['loʊ·kəl] **I.** *adj* **1.** (*neighborhood*) hiesig, örtlich; **~ radio station** Lokalsender *m*; **~ bar** Stammkneipe *f fam* MED lokal **II.** *n* **1.** *usu pl* (*inhabitant*) Ortsansässige(r) *f(m)* **2.** (*trade union*) örtliches Gewerkschaftsbüro

local anes'thetic *n* örtliche Betäubung

'**local call** *n* Ortsgespräch *nt*

local 'government *n* (*of city*) Stadtverwaltung *f*; (*of community*) Kommunalverwaltung *f*

locality [loʊ·kæl·ɪ·ti] *n* Gegend *f*

localize ['loʊ·kə·laɪz] *vt* **1.** (*government*) dezentralisieren **2.** (*pinpoint*) lokalisieren *geh*

local 'newspaper *n* Lokalblatt *nt*

'**local time** *n* Ortszeit *f*

locate ['loʊ·keɪt] **I.** *vt* **1.** (*find*) ausfindig machen; (*sunken ship*) orten **2.** (*situate*) bauen; **to be centrally ~d** zentral liegen **II.** *vi* sich niederlassen

location [loʊ·'keɪ·fən] *n* **1.** (*place*) Lage *f* **2.** FILM Drehort *m* **3.** (*act*) Positionsbestimmung *f*

ock [lak] I. n 1. (*fastener*) Schloss nt 2. NAUT Schleuse f ▶ **to be under ~ and key** hinter Schloss und Riegel sitzen fam II. vt abschließen; (*suitcase*) verschließen III. vi 1. (*become secured*) schließen 2. (*become fixed*) binden

lock away vt 1. (*secure*) wegschließen 2. (*imprison*) einsperren fam

lock on vi MIL **to ~ on to a target** ein genaues Ziel ausmachen

lock out vt aussperren

lock up I. vt 1. (*shut, secure*) abschließen; (*money*) wegschließen 2. (*put in custody*) **to ~ up ⇆ sb** LAW jdn einsperren fam, jdn einlochen sl II. vi abschließen

locker ['lak·ər] n Schließfach nt; MIL, SCH, SPORT Spind m

locker room n Umkleideraum [mit Schließfächern] m

locket ['lak·ɪt] n Medaillon nt

lockout n Aussperrung f

locksmith n Schlosser(in) m(f)

lockup n Gefängnis nt; (*for drunks*) Ausnüchterungszelle f

locomotive [ˌlou·kə·'mou·ţɪv] n Lokomotive f

lode [loud] n MIN Ader f a. fig

lodge [ladʒ] I. n 1. (*house*) Hütte f 2. (*in resort*) Lodge f II. vt 1. (*submit: complaint*) einlegen; (*protest*) erheben 2. (*fix*) hineinstoßen III. vi stecken bleiben

lodger ['ladʒ·ər] n Untermieter(in) m(f)

lodging ['ladʒ·ɪŋ] n Unterkunft f

loft [laft] n (*attic*) Speicher m; (*for living*) Dachwohnung f, Loft m

lofty ['laf·ti] adj 1. (*high*) hoch [aufragend] 2. (*noble*) erhaben; (*ambitions*) hochfliegend; (*ideals*) hohe(r, s)

log [lɔg] I. n 1. (*branch*) [gefällter] Baumstamm; (*firewood*) [Holz]scheit nt 2. (*systematic record*) Aufzeichnungen pl II. vt <-gg-> 1. (*enter into record*) aufzeichnen; (*phone calls*) registrieren 2. (*trees*) fällen III. vi <-gg-> Bäume fällen

log in vi sich einloggen

log off vi sich ausloggen

log on vi sich einloggen (to in +akk)

log out vi sich ausloggen (of aus +dat)

loganberry ['lou·gən·ber·i] n Loganbeere f

logbook n NAUT Logbuch nt; AVIAT Bordbuch nt

log cabin n Blockhaus nt

logger ['lɔ·gər] n Holzfäller(in) m(f)

logic ['ladʒ·ɪk] n Logik f

logical ['ladʒ·ɪ·kəl] adj 1. logisch 2. (*sensible*) vernünftig

logistics [lou·'dʒɪs·tɪks] n + sing/pl vb Logistik f

logjam n 1. (*logs*) Anstauung f von Floßholz 2. (*deadlock*) toter Punkt; **to break a ~** wieder aus einer Sackgasse herauskommen

logo ['lou·gou] n Logo m o nt

logrolling n POL fam Kuhhandel m

loiter ['lɔɪ·ţər] vi 1. (*idle*) **to ~** [**around**] herumhängen fam 2. (*dawdle*) [herum]trödeln

loll [lal] vi (*idle*) lümmeln; (*sit*) faul dasitzen

lollipop ['lal·i·pap] n Lutscher m

lone [loun] adj attr einsam

loneliness ['loun·lɪ·nɪs] n Einsamkeit f

lonely <-ier, -iest or more ~, most ~> ['loun·li] adj 1. (*alone*) einsam 2. (*unfrequented*) abgeschieden; (*street*) still

loner ['lou·nər] n Einzelgänger(in) m(f)

lonesome ['loun·səm] adj 1. (*alone*) einsam 2. (*unfrequented*) abgelegen

long¹ [lɔŋ] I. adj 1. (*in space*) lang; (*distance*) weit; fig **to have come a ~ way** von weit her gekommen sein 2. (*in time*) lang; (*tedious*) lang[wierig]; **a ~ day** ein langer [und anstrengender] Tag; (*friendship*) langjährig; (*memory*) gut; **to work ~ hours** einen langen Arbeitstag haben ▶ **in the ~ run** auf lange Sicht [gesehen] II. adv 1. (*for a long time*) lang[e]; **I won't be ~** (*before finishing*) ich bin gleich fertig; (*before appearing*) ich bin gleich da 2. (*at a distant time*) lange; **~ ago** vor langer Zeit 3. (*after implied time*) lange; **how much ~er will it take?** wie lange wird es noch dauern? ▶ **as ~ as ...** (*during*) solange ...; (*provided that*) vorausgesetzt, dass ... III. n ▶ **before** [**very**] **~** schon [sehr] bald

long² [lɔŋ] vi sich sehnen (**for** nach +dat); **to ~ to do sth** sich danach sehnen, etw zu tun

L

long³ n GEOG abbr of **longitude** Länge f

long-'distance I. adj attr (between places) Fern-, Weit-; ~ **flight** Langstreckenflug m II. adv **to call** ~ ein Ferngespräch führen

'long-haired <longer-, longest-> adj langhaarig; (animals) Langhaar-

'longhand n Langschrift f; **to write sth in** ~ etw mit der Hand schreiben

long 'haul n 1. (long distance) Langstreckentransport m 2. (long time) **over the** ~ auf lange Sicht

long-'haul adj ~ **flight** Langstreckenflug m

'longhorn n (breed of cattle) Longhorn nt

longing ['lɒŋ·ɪŋ] n Sehnsucht f

longish ['lɒŋ·ɪʃ] adj fam ziemlich lang

longitude ['lan·dʒɪ·tud] n GEOG Länge f

'long johns npl fam lange Unterhose

'long jump n SPORT Weitsprung m

long-'lasting adj strapazierfähig

'long-life adj (batteries) langlebig

'long-lost adj attr lang verloren geglaubt; (person) lang vermisst geglaubt

'long-range adj attr Langstrecken-

'long shot n usu sing **to be a** ~ ziemlich aussichtslos sein

long-'standing adj seit langem bestehend; (friendship, relationship) langjährig

long-'suffering adj langmütig

'long-term adj attr langfristig; ~ **strategy** Langzeitstrategie f

long-'winded adj langatmig

loofa, loofah ['lu·fə] n Luffaschwamm m

look [lʊk] I. n 1. (glance) Blick m; **to get a good** ~ **at sth/sb** jdn/etw genau sehen können; **to have** [or **take**] **a** ~ **around** [for sth] sich [nach etw dat] umsehen 2. (on face) [Gesichts]ausdruck m 3. (examination) Betrachtung f; (search) **to have** [or **take**] **a** ~ **around for sb/sth** nach jdm/etw suchen 4. (appearance) Aussehen nt ▶ **if** ~s **could kill** wenn Blicke töten könnten II. interj (explanatory) pass mal auf fam; (protesting) hör mal fam III. vi 1. (glance) schauen; **to** ~ **away** wegsehen 2. (search) suchen; (in an encyclopedia) nachschlagen 3. (appear) **she**

doesn't ~ **her age** man sieht ihr ihr Alter nicht an; **to** ~ **tired** müde aussehen

to ~ **like sb** jdm ähnlich sehen 4. (face) blicken (**onto** auf +akk); (window) [hinaus]gehen (**onto** auf +akk)

◆**look after** vi (care for) **to** ~ **after sb** sich um jdn kümmern; (keep eye on) **to** ~ **after sb/sth** auf jdn/etw aufpassen

◆**look ahead** vi fig (plan) vorausschauen

◆**look around** vi 1. (glance) sich umsehen 2. (search) **to** ~ **around for sth** sich nach etw umsehen

◆**look at** vi 1. (glance) ansehen 2. (examine) **to** ~ **at sth/sb** sich dat etw/jdn ansehen 3. (regard) **to** ~ **at sth** etw betrachten

◆**look back** vi 1. (glance) zurückschauen 2. (remember) zurückblicken (**on/over/at** auf +akk) ▶ **sb never** ~**ed back** für jdn ging es bergauf

◆**look down** vi 1. (glance) nach unten sehen; **to** ~ **down at/on sb/sth** zu jdm/etw hinuntersehen 2. (examine) **to** ~ **down a list** eine Liste von oben bis unten durchgehen

◆**look for** vi (seek) **to** ~ **for sb** nach jdm suchen; **to** ~ **for a job** Arbeit suchen

◆**look forward** vi 1. (glance) nach vorne sehen 2. (anticipate) sich freuen (**to** auf +akk)

◆**look in** vi 1. (glance) hineinsehen 2. (visit) **to** ~ **in** [**on sb**] [bei jdm] vorbeischauen fam

◆**look into** vi **to** ~ **into sth** 1. (glance) in etw akk [hinein]sehen 2. (examine) etw untersuchen; **to** ~ **into a complaint** eine Beschwerde prüfen

◆**look on** vi zusehen

◆**look out** vi 1. (take care) aufpassen 2. (watch) Ausschau halten (**for** nach +dat) 3. (face) blicken (**onto/over** auf +akk); (window) hinausgehen (**onto/over** auf +akk)

◆**look over** I. vi 1. (glance) blicken über +akk; **to** ~ **over to sb** zu jdm hinübersehen 2. (offer view) blicken über +akk; (room) [hinaus]gehen auf +akk II. vt 1. (view) besichtigen 2. (examine) durchsehen; (letter) überfliegen

◆**look through** vi 1. (glance) **to** ~

through sth durch etw *akk* [hindurch] sehen **2.** (*peruse*) durchsehen; (*magazine*) durchblättern

look to *vi* (*anticipate*) **to ~ to the future** in die Zukunft blicken

look toward(s) *vi* **1.** (*glance*) **to ~ toward sth/sb** zu etw/jdm sehen **2.** (*face*) **to ~ toward sth** auf etw *akk* blicken; (*window*) auf etw *akk* [hinaus]gehen

look up I. *vi* **1.** (*glance*) **to ~ up at sb/sth** zu jdm/etw hinaufsehen **2.** (*improve*) besser werden **II.** *vt* **1.** *fam* (*visit*) **to ~ up ⊆ sb** bei jdm vorbeischauen **2.** (*search for*) nachschlagen

look upon *vi see* **look on**

look up to *vi* **to ~ up to sb** zu jdm aufsehen

'lookalike *n* Doppelgänger(in) *m(f)*

'lookout *n* **1.** (*person*) Wache *f* **2.** (*watch*) **to keep a ~** [**for sb**] [nach jdm] Ausschau halten

loom¹ [lum] *vi* **1.** (*come into view*) [drohend] auftauchen **2.** (*be ominously near*) sich drohend abzeichnen; (*storm*) sich zusammenbrauen *a. fig*

loom² [lum] *n* Webstuhl *m*

loony [ˈluːni] *n fam* Irre(r) *f(m)*

loop [luːp] **I.** *n* **1.** (*shape*) Schleife *f*; (*of string*) Schlinge *f*; (*of belt*) Schlaufen *pl* **2.** COMPUT [Programm]schleife *f* **3.** (*contraceptive*) Spirale *f* **II.** *vi* eine Schleife machen; (*road*) sich schlängeln

'loophole *n* LAW Gesetzeslücke *f*

loose [luːs] *adj* **1.** (*relaxed, not tight*) locker; (*papers*) los; (*skin*) schlaff; **~ cash/coins** Kleingeld *nt;* **to come ~** sich lösen **2.** (*hair*) offen **3.** (*not confined*) frei **4.** (*not exact*) ungefähr *attr;* (*not strict*) lose; (*translation*) frei **5.** (*clothing*) weit, locker ▶ **to hang ~** *fam* cool bleiben

'loose-leaf *adj attr* **~ binder** Ringbuch *nt*

loosely [ˈluːsli] *adv* **1.** (*not tightly*) lose; **to hang ~** schlaff herunterhängen **2.** (*not exactly*) ungefähr; **~ speaking** grob gesagt

loosen [ˈluːsən] **I.** *vt* **1.** (*collar*) aufmachen; (*tie*) lockern **2.** (*relax: muscles*) lockern ▶ **to ~ sb's tongue** jdm die

Zunge lösen **II.** *vi* sich lockern

loot [luːt] **I.** *n* **1.** (*plunder*) [Diebes]beute *f* **2.** *fam* (*money*) Zaster *m* **II.** *vt* **1.** (*plunder*) [aus]plündern **2.** (*steal*) stehlen **III.** *vi* plündern

looting [ˈluːtɪŋ] *n* Plünderei *f*

lop [lɒp] *vt* <-pp-> streichen; (*budget*) kürzen

lop off *vt* **1.** (*branches*) abhacken **2.** (*reduce: expenses*) [ver]kürzen

lope [loʊp] *vi* in großen Sätzen springen; (*hare*) hoppeln

lopsided *adj* schief

lord [lɔrd] *n* **1.** (*nobleman*) Lord *m* **2.** *fam* (*powerful man*) Herr *m*

Lord [lɔrd] *n* REL **the ~** der Herr

lose <lost, lost> [luːz] **I.** *vt* **1.** (*forfeit*) verlieren; **to ~ sth to sb** etw an jdn verlieren; **to ~ one's breath** außer Atem kommen **2.** (*through death*) **she lost her son in the fire** ihr Sohn ist beim Brand umgekommen **3.** *usu passive* **to be lost** (*things*) verschwunden sein; (*victims*) umgekommen sein; (*plane, ship*) verloren sein **4.** (*waste: opportunity*) versäumen; (*time*) verlieren **5.** (*watch*) **to ~ time** nachgehen **6.** (*not find*) verlieren; (*mislay*) verlegen; **to ~ one's way** sich verirren **7.** (*not win*) verlieren ▶ **to ~ heart** den Mut verlieren; **to ~ it** *fam* durchdrehen; **to ~ touch** [**with sb**] den Kontakt [zu jdm] verlieren **II.** *vi* (*be beaten*) verlieren (**to** gegen +*akk*) ▶ **you can't ~** du kannst nur gewinnen

lose out *vi* **1.** (*be deprived*) schlecht wegkommen *fam* **2.** (*be beaten*) **to ~ out to sb/sth** jdm/etw unterliegen

loser [ˈluːzər] *n* **1.** (*defeated person*) Verlierer(in) *m(f)* **2.** *fam* (*habitually*) Verlierer[typ] *m*

loss <*pl* -es> [lɒs] *n* Verlust *m* ▶ **to be at a ~** nicht mehr weiterwissen

lost [lɒst] **I.** *pt, pp of* **lose** **II.** *adj* **1.** (*unable to find way*) **to get ~** sich verirren; (*on foot*) sich verlaufen haben; (*using vehicle*) sich verfahren haben **2.** (*misplaced*) **to get ~** [**in the mail**] [in der Post] verschwinden **3.** *pred* (*helpless*) **to feel ~** sich verloren fühlen; **to be ~** (*not understand*) nichts verstehen

4. (*soldiers*) gefallen; (*planes, ships*) zerstört **5.** (*not won: battle, contest*) verloren ▸ **get ~!** *fam* hau ab!, zieh Leine! *sl*

lost and 'found *n* Fundbüro *nt*

loth [loʊθ] *adj see* **loath**

lotion ['loʊ·ʃən] *n* Lotion *f*

lottery ['laţ·ə·ri] *n* Lotterie *f*

lotus position *n* Lotossitz *m*

loud [laʊd] **I.** *adj* **1.** (*audible*) laut **2.** (*garish*) auffällig; (*colors*) grell, schreiend **II.** *adv* laut; **to laugh out ~** laut hals loslachen

'loudmouth *n fam* Großmaul *nt*

loudness ['laʊd·nɪs] *n* Lautstärke *f*

'loudspeaker *n* Lautsprecher *m*

Louisiana [lu·i·zi·'æn·ə] *n* Louisiana *nt*

lounge [laʊndʒ] **I.** *n* Lounge *f*; **departure ~** Abflughalle *f* **II.** *vi* (*lie*) [faul] herumliegen; (*sit*) [faul] herumsitzen

◆**lounge around** *vi* (*lie*) [faul] herumliegen; (*sit*) [faul] herumsitzen

'lounge chair *n* Klubsessel *m*

louse [laʊs] **I.** *n* [laʊs] **1.** <*pl* lice> (*parasite*) Laus *f* **2.** <*pl* -s> (*person*) miese Type *pej* **II.** *vt* [laʊz] *fam* **to ~ up ⇆ sth** etw vermasseln

lousy ['laʊ·zi] *adj* **1.** *fam* (*bad*) lausig; **I'm ~ at math** in Mathe bin ich eine absolute Null **2.** *pred* (*ill*) **to feel ~** sich hundeelend [*or* mies] fühlen **3.** (*inadequate*) armselig; **a ~ 20 dollars** lumpige 20 Dollar

louver ['lu·vər] *n* Jalousie *f*; (*slat*) Lamelle *f* [einer Jalousie]

lovable ['lʌv·ə·bəl] *adj* liebenswert

love [lʌv] **I.** *n* **1.** (*affection*) Liebe *f*; **to be in ~** verliebt sein; **to fall in ~ with sb** sich in jdn verlieben **2.** (*interest*) Leidenschaft *f*; (*with activities*) Liebe *f*; she has a great ~ of music sie liebt die Musik sehr **3.** TENNIS null **II.** *vt* (*be in love with*) lieben; (*greatly like*) sehr mögen **III.** *vi* lieben; **I would ~ for you to come to dinner tonight** ich würde mich freuen, wenn du heute zum Abendessen kämst

'love affair *n* [Liebes]affäre *f*

love-'hate relationship *n* Hassliebe *f*

loveless ['lʌv·lɪs] *adj* (*childhood, marriage*) ohne Liebe *nach n*

'love letter *n* Liebesbrief *m*

'love life *n* Liebesleben *nt kein pl*

loveliness ['lʌv·li·nɪs] *n* Schönheit *f*

lovely ['lʌv·li] *adj* **1.** (*beautiful*) schön; (*house*) wunderschön; **to look ~** reizend aussehen **2.** *fam* (*pleasant*) wunderbar, herrlich

lover ['lʌv·ər] *n* **1.** (*partner*) Liebhaber(in) *m(f)* **2.** (*fan*) Liebhaber(in) *m(f)* (of von +*dat*); **sports ~** Sportfan *m*

'love song *n* Liebeslied *nt*

'love story *n* Liebesgeschichte *f*

loving ['lʌv·ɪŋ] *adj* liebevoll

low [loʊ] **I.** *adj* **1.** (*not high*) niedrig; (*neckline, voice*) tief **2.** (*in number*) gering, wenig; (*blood pressure*) niedrig; **~ in calories** kalorienarm **3.** (*depleted*) knapp; (*stocks*) gering **4.** (*morale*) schlecht; (*quality*) minderwertig; (*self-esteem*) gering; **to have a ~ opinion of sb** von jdm nicht viel halten **II.** *adv* **1.** (*in height*) niedrig; **to be cut ~** (*dress*) tief ausgeschnitten sein **2.** (*to low level, not high-pitched*) tief; **turn the oven on ~** stell den Ofen auf kleine Hitze **III.** *n* **1.** (*low level*) Tiefpunkt *m* **2.** METEO Tief *nt*

low-'alcohol *adj* alkoholarm

'lowbrow *adj pej* (*book, film*) geistig anspruchslos, seicht

low-cal ['loʊ·kæl] *adj fam*, **low-'calorie** *adj* kalorienarm

'low-cost *adj* billig

'low-cut *adj* (*dress*) tief ausgeschnitten

'lowdown *n fam* **the ~** ausführliche Informationen

lower ['loʊ·ər] **I.** *adj* **1.** (*less high*) niedriger; (*below*) untere(r, s), Unter- **2.** (*status*) niedere(r, s), untere(r, s) **II.** *vt* **1.** (*move down*) herunterlassen; (*hem*)

herauslassen; (*lifeboat*) zu Wasser lassen; **to ~ one's eyes** die Augen niederschlagen **2.** (*decrease*) verringern; (*voice*) senken; (*quality*) mindern; **to ~ one's sights** seine Ansprüche zurückschrauben **III.** *vi* sinken

lower 'house *n* Unterhaus *nt*

low-'fat *adj* fettarm

low-key *adj* unauffällig; (*color*) gedämpft

lowland ['loʊ·lənd] *n* Flachland *nt*

low-level *adj* **1.** (*not high*) tief **2.** (*of low status*) niedrig; (*official*) klein *meist pej* **3.** COMPUT niedere(r, s)

lowly ['loʊ·li] *adj* einfach; (*status*) niedrig

lowness ['loʊ·nɪs] *n* **1.** (*in height*) Niedrigkeit *f*; (*of neckline*) Tiefe *f* **2.** (*of note*) Tiefe *f*; (*of voice*) Gedämpftheit *f*

low-'pitched *adj* tief

low 'pressure *n* PHYS Niederdruck *m*; METEO Tiefdruck *m*

low 'profile *n* Zurückhaltung *f*; **to keep a ~** sich zurückhalten; *fig* im Hintergrund bleiben

low-'spirited *adj* niedergeschlagen

low-'tech *adj* [technisch] einfach, Low-tech-

low 'tide *n* Niedrigwasser *nt*; (*of sea*) Ebbe *f*

loyal ['lɔɪ·əl] *adj* treu (**to** +dat)

loyalty ['lɔɪ·əl·ti] *n* (*faithfulness*) Treue *f*

LSD [ˌel·es·'di] *n abbr of* **lysergic acid diethylamide** LSD *nt*

lube [lub] *fam* **I.** *n see* **lubricant** **II.** *vt see* **lubricate**

lubricant ['lu·brɪ·kənt] *n* MED Gleitmittel *nt*; TECH Schmiermittel *nt*

lubricate ['lu·brɪ·keɪt] *vt* schmieren

lubrication [ˌlu·brɪ·'keɪ·fən] *n* Schmieren *nf*

lucid ['lu·sɪd] *adj* klar

luck [lʌk] **I.** *n* **1.** (*fortune*) Glück *nt*; **as ~ would have it** wie es der Zufall wollte; **just my ~!** Pech gehabt!; **to be out of ~** kein Glück haben **2.** (*success*) Erfolg *m* **II.** *vi fam* **to ~ into sth** etw durch Zufall ergattern

luckily ['lʌ·kɪ·li] *adv* glücklicherweise

lucky ['lʌk·i] *adj* **1.** (*fortunate*) glücklich **2.** (*bringing fortune*) glückbringend

lucrative ['lu·krə·t̬ɪv] *adj* einträglich

ludicrous ['lu·dɪ·krəs] *adj* (*ridiculous*)

lächerlich; (*absurd*) absurd

lug [lʌg] *vt* <-gg-> (*carry*) schleppen; (*pull*) zerren; **to ~ sth along** etw herumschleppen

luggage ['lʌg·ɪdʒ] *n* [Reise]gepäck *nt*; **piece of ~** Gepäckstück *nt*

'luggage rack *n* Gepäckablage *f*

lukewarm [ˌluk·'wɔrm] *adj* lau[warm]

lull [lʌl] *vt* **1.** (*soothe: fears*) zerstreuen; **to ~ sb to sleep** jdn in den Schlaf lullen **2.** (*trick*) einlullen; **to ~ sb into a false sense of security** jdn in trügerischer Sicherheit wiegen

lullaby ['lʌl·ə·baɪ] *n* Schlaflied *nt*

lumber¹ ['lʌm·bər] *n* (*timber*) Bauholz *nt*

lumber² ['lʌm·bər] *vi* (*person*) schwerfällig gehen; (*animal*) trotten; (*bear*) [behäbig] tapsen

lumberjack ['lʌm·bər·dʒæk] *n* Holzfäller(in) *m(f)*

'lumberyard *n* Holzlager *nt*

luminous ['lu·mə·nəs] *adj* **1.** (*bright*) leuchtend *a. fig* **2.** (*phosphorescent*) phosphoreszierend

lump [lʌmp] **I.** *n* **1.** (*chunk*) Klumpen *m* **2.** (*swelling*) Schwellung *f*; (*in breast*) Knoten *m* **II.** *vt* (*combine*) **to ~ sth with sth** etw mit etw zusammentun *fam*

lump 'sum *n* Einmalzahlung *f*

lumpy ['lʌm·pi] *adj* (*liquid*) klumpig; (*figure*) plump

lunacy ['lu·nə·si] *n* Wahnsinn *m fam*

lunar ['lu·nər] *adj attr* Mond-

lunatic ['lu·nə·t̬ɪk] **I.** *n* **1.** Geistesgestörte(r) *f(m)* **2.** (*fool*) Verrückte(r) *f(m)* **II.** *adj* verrückt *fam*

lunch [lʌntʃ] *n* <*pl* -es> **1.** (*noon meal*) Mittagessen *nt*; **to have ~** zu Mittag essen **2.** (*noon break*) Mittagspause *f* ► **to be out to ~** *hum fam* nicht ganz richtig im Kopf sein *fam*

'lunch break *n* Mittagspause *f*

'lunch hour *n* Mittagspause *f*

'lunchtime *n* (*noon*) Mittagszeit *f*; (*break*) Mittagspause *f*; **at ~** mittags

lung [lʌŋ] *n* Lungenflügel *m*; **the ~s** *pl* die Lunge[n *pl*]

'lung cancer *n* Lungenkrebs *m*

lunge [lʌndʒ] **I.** *n* Satz *m* nach vorn; (*in fencing*) Ausfall *m* **II.** *vi* **to ~ forward**

einen Satz nach vorne machen

lupin(e) ['lu·pɪn] n Lupine f

lurch [lɜrtʃ] **I.** n <pl -es> Ruck m a. fig **II.** vi (person) torkeln; (ship) schlingern

lure [lʊr] **I.** vt [an]locken; **to ~ sb away from sth** jdn von etw dat weglocken **II.** n (attraction) Reiz m

lurid ['lʊr·ɪd] adj **1.** (glaring) grell [leuchtend]; (colors) schreiend **2.** (sensational) reißerisch pej; (article) reißerisch aufgemacht pej

lurk [lɜrk] vi lauern a. fig; fig stecken (**behind** hinter +dat)

luscious ['lʌʃ·əs] adj **1.** (sweet: taste, smell) [herrlich] süß; (fruit) saftig [süß] **2.** (voluptuous: curves) üppig; (lips) voll

lush¹ [lʌʃ] adj **1.** (grass) saftig [grün]; (vegetation) üppig **2.** (décor) luxuriös

lush² [lʌʃ] n <pl -es> fam Säufer(in) m(f) pej sl

lust [lʌst] **I.** n **1.** (sexual drive) Lust f **2.** (desire) Begierde f; (greed) Gier f **II.** vi **to ~ after sth** gierig nach etw dat sein

luster ['lʌs·tər] n Glanz m

lusty ['lʌs·ti] adj (strong and healthy: person) gesund [und munter]; (cry) laut

lute [lut] n Laute f

Lutheran ['lu·θər·ən] n REL Lutheraner(in) m(f)

luxuriant [lʌg·'ʒʊr·i·ənt] adj (abundant) üppig; (hair) voll

luxuriate [lʌg·'ʒʊr·i·eɪt] vi sich aalen

luxurious [lʌg·'ʒʊr·i·əs] adj luxuriös, Luxus-

luxury ['lʌk·ʃər·i] n **1.** (self-indulgence) Luxus m **2.** (luxurious item) Luxus[artikel] m

Lycra® ['laɪ·krə] n Lycra® nt

lye [laɪ] n Lauge f

lying¹ ['laɪ·ɪŋ] vi present participle of **lie**

lying² ['laɪ·ɪŋ] **I.** adj attr verlogen, lügnerisch **II.** n Lügen nt

'lymph gland, 'lymph node n Lymphknoten m

lynch [lɪntʃ] vt lynchen

lynchpin ['lɪntʃ·pɪn] n see **linchpin**

lynx <pl -es> [lɪŋks] n Luchs m

lyric ['lɪr·ɪk] n ~**s** pl [Lied]text m

lyrical ['lɪr·ɪ·kəl] adj gefühlvoll, schwärmerisch

lyricist ['lɪr·ɪ·sɪst] n Texter(in) m(f)

M

M <pl -'s>, **m** <pl -'s> [em] n (letter) M nt, m nt; ~ **as in Mike** M wie Martha

M [em] n <pl -> abbr of **million** Mill., Mio.

m **I.** n <pl -> **1.** abbr of **mile 2.** abbr of **meter** m **3.** abbr of **minute** Min. **II.** adj **1.** abbr of **male** männl. **2.** abbr of **masculine** m **3.** abbr of **married** verh.

MA [ˌem·'eɪ] n **1.** abbr of **Master of Arts 2.** abbr of **Massachusetts**

ma [ma] n fam (mother) Mama f

Mac [mæk] n fam short for **Macintosh®** Mac m

macabre [mə·'kab·rə] adj makaber

macaroni [ˌmæk·ə·'rou·ni] n Makkaroni pl

mace [meɪs] n BOT, FOOD Mazis m

Mace® [meɪs] **I.** n ≈ Tränengas nt **II.** vt mit Tränengas besprühen

Mach [mak] n AEROSP, PHYS Mach nt

machete [mə·'ʃet·i] n Machete f

machine [mə·'ʃin] **I.** n Maschine f **II.** vt (produce) maschinell herstellen

ma'chine gun n Maschinengewehr nt

machine-'readable adj COMPUT (by device) maschinenlesbar; (by computer) computerlesbar

machinery [mə·'ʃi·nə·ri] n **1.** (machines) Maschinen pl **2.** (mechanism) Mechanismus m

ma'chine tool n Werkzeugmaschine f

machinist [mə·'ʃi·nɪst] n Maschinist(in) m(f)

macho ['matʃ·oʊ] adj pej fam machohaft, Macho-

mackerel <pl -s> ['mæk·rəl] n Makrele f

macro ['mæk·roʊ] n COMPUT Makro nt

macrobiotic [ˌmæk·roʊ·baɪ·'aṭ·ɪk] adj makrobiotisch

mad <-dd-> [mæd] adj **1.** fam (angry)

sauer; **to make sb** ~ jdn rasend machen **2.** *fam* (*insane*) wahnsinnig, verrückt; **to go** ~ den Verstand verlieren **3.** (*frantic*) **like** ~ wie verrückt **4.** *fam* (*enthusiastic*) verrückt (**about** nach +*dat*)

madam ['mæd-əm] *n* (*form of address*) gnädige Frau; (*in titles*) **M~ President** Frau Präsidentin

mad 'cow disease *n* Rinderwahnsinn *m*

maddening ['mæd-n̩-ɪŋ] *adj* äußerst ärgerlich; (*habit*) nervend

made [meɪd] **I.** *pt, pp of* **make II.** *adj* **to have** [got] **it** ~ es geschafft haben *fam*

made-to-'measure *adj* maßgeschneidert

made-'up *adj* **1.** (*imaginary*) ausgedacht **2.** (*wearing makeup*) geschminkt

madly ['mæd-li] *adv* **1.** (*insanely*) wie verrückt **2.** *fam* (*very much*) wahnsinnig

'madman *n fig fam* Verrückter *m*

madness ['mæd-nɪs] *n* Wahnsinn *m*

'madwoman *n fig fam* Verrückte *f fam*

mafia ['ma-fiə] *n* + *sing/pl vb* Mafia *f*

mag [mæg] *n fam short for* **magazine** Blatt *nt*

magazine ['mæg-ə-zin] *n* **1.** (*publication*) Zeitschrift *f* **2.** (*gun part*) Magazin *nt*

maggot ['mæg-ət] *n* Made *f*

magic ['mædʒ-ɪk] **I.** *n* **1.** (*sorcery*) Magie *f*, Zauber *m* **2.** (*tricks*) Zauberkunst[s] *m[pl]/*; **to do** ~ zaubern **II.** *adj* **1.** (*supernatural*) magisch, Zauber-; **they had no** ~ **solution** sie konnten keine Lösung aus dem Ärmel zaubern **2.** (*extraordinary: moment*) zauberhaft, wundervoll; (*powers*) magisch

magical ['mædʒ-ɪk-əl] *adj* **1.** (*magic*) magisch **2.** (*extraordinary: moment*) zauberhaft; (*powers*) magisch

magically ['mæ-dʒɪk-li] *adv* **1.** (*by magic*) wie von Zauberhand **2.** (*extraordinarily*) zauberhaft

magic 'carpet *n* fliegender Teppich

magician [mə-'dʒɪʃ-ən] *n* Zauberer *m /* Zauberin *f*; (*on stage*) Zauberkünstler(in) *m(f)*

magnate ['mæg-neɪt] *n* Magnat *m*

magnet ['mæg-nɪt] *n* Magnet *m*

magnetic [mæg-'net-ɪk] *adj* **1.** (*steel*) magnetisch; ~ **strip** Magnetstreifen *m*

2. *fig* (*attraction*) unwiderstehlich; (*charm*) anziehend

mag'netic field *n* Magnetfeld *nt*

magnetism ['mæg-nə-tɪz-əm] *n* **1.** Magnetismus *m* **2.** (*of person*) Ausstrahlung *f*

magnetize ['mæg-nə-taɪz] *vt* PHYS magnetisieren

magnification [ˌmæg-nɪ-fɪ-'keɪ-ʃən] *n* Vergrößerung *f*

magnificent [mæg-'nɪf-ɪ-sənt] *adj* (*house, concert*) wunderbar, großartig

magnify <-ie-> ['mæg-nɪ-faɪ] *vt* (*make bigger*) vergrößern; (*make worse*) verschlimmern

'magnifying glass *n* Lupe *f*

magnitude ['mæg-nɪ-tud] *n* (*size*) Größe *f*; (*of project*) Ausmaß *nt*; (*of earthquake*) Stärke *f*

magnolia [mæg-'noʊl-jə] *n* Magnolie *f*

mahogany [mə-'hag-ə-ni] *n* Mahagoni[holz] *nt*

maid [meɪd] *n* (*servant*) Dienstmädchen *nt*; (*in hotel*) Zimmermädchen *nt*

maiden ['meɪ-dən] **I.** *n old* Jungfer *f* **II.** *adj attr* (*first*) Jungfern-

'maiden name *n* Mädchenname *m*

mail¹ [meɪl] **I.** *n* Post *f*; **to send sth through** [*or* **in**] **the** ~ etw mit der Post [ver]schicken **II.** *vt* (*at post office: letter, package*) aufgeben; (*in mailbox*) einwerfen

mail² [meɪl] *n chain* ~ Kettenpanzer *m*

'mailbag *n* Postsack *m*

'mailbox *n* Briefkasten *m*

'mailing list *n* Adressenliste *f*, Mailingliste *f*

'mailman *n* Briefträger *m*, Postbote *m*

'mail order *n* [Direkt]versand *m*; (*by catalog*) Katalogbestellung *f*

maim [meɪm] *vt* verstümmeln

main [meɪn] **I.** *adj attr* Haupt- **II.** *n* TECH **water** ~ Wasserhauptleitung *f*

main 'drag *n fam* Haupt[einkaufs]straße *f*

Maine [meɪn] *n* Maine *nt*

'mainframe *n* Hauptrechner *m*

mainly ['meɪn-li] *adv* hauptsächlich, in erster Linie

'mainstream I. *n* **the** ~ *fig* der Mainstream; **to enter the** ~ **of politics** am alltäglichen politischen Alltag[sgeschäft]

teilnehmen **II.** *adj* (*book, music*) kommerziell

'main street *n* Haupt|einkaufs|straße *f*

maintain [meɪnˈteɪn] *vt* **1.** (*keep*) [bei]behalten; (*status quo*) aufrechterhalten; (*dignity*) bewahren; **to ~ the lead** in Führung bleiben **2.** (*in good condition*) instand halten **3.** (*provide for: family*) unterhalten

maintenance [ˈmeɪn·tə·nəns] *n* **1.** (*of relations*) Beibehaltung *f* **2.** (*of car*) Pflege *f*; (*of building*) Instandhaltung *f*; (*of machine*) Wartung *f* **3.** (*maintenance costs*) Unterhaltung *f*

majestic [məˈdʒes·tɪk] *adj* majestätisch; (*proportions*) stattlich

majesty [ˈmædʒ·ɪ·sti] *n* **1.** (*royal title*) |**Her/His/Your**| **M~** [Ihre/Seine/Eure] Majestät **2.** (*beauty: of sunset*) Herrlichkeit *f*; (*of person*) Würde *f*

major [ˈmeɪ·dʒər] **I.** *adj* **1.** *attr* (*important*) bedeutend, wichtig; (*main*) Haupt-; (*large*) groß **2.** *attr* (*crime*) schwer; (*illness*) schwerwiegend **II.** *n* **1.** MIL (*officer rank*) Major(in) *m(f)* **2.** UNIV (*primary subject*) Hauptfach *nt*; (*person studying*) **she was a philosophy ~** sie hat Philosophie im Hauptfach studiert **III.** *vi* UNIV **to ~ in physics** Physik als Hauptfach studieren

major ʹgeneral *n* Generalmajor(in) *m(f)*

majority [məˈdʒɔr·ɪ·ti] *n* **1.** + *sing/pl vb* (*most of cases*) in der Mehrzahl der Fälle **2.** POL (*winning margin*) |Stimmen|mehrheit *f*

make [meɪk] **I.** *n* **1.** ECON (*brand*) Marke *f* **2.** *pej* **to be on the ~** geldgierig sein **II.** *vt* <made, made> **1.** (*produce*) machen; (*manufacture*) herstellen; (*movie*) drehen; **this sweater is made of wool** dieser Pullover ist aus Wolle **2.** (*dinner*) machen; **to ~ coffee** Kaffee kochen **3.** (*become*) **I don't think he will ever ~ a good lawyer** ich glaube, aus ihm wird nie ein guter Rechtsanwalt [werden]; **to ~ |for| fascinating reading** faszinierend zu lesen sein **4.** (*cause*) machen; **to ~ sb laugh** jdn zum Lachen bringen **5.** (*force*) **to ~ sb do sth** jdn zwingen, etw zu tun **6.** + *adj* (*cause to be*) machen; **to ~ sth pub-**

lic etw veröffentlichen **7.** (*mistake, suggestion*) machen; (*appointment*) vereinbaren; (*deal*) schließen; **to ~ a call** anrufen; **to ~ an effort** sich anstrengen; **to ~ way** den Weg frei machen **8.** (*earn, get*) **he ~s 50,000 dollars a year** er verdient 50.000 Dollar im Jahr; **to ~ friends** Freundschaften schließen; **to ~ a killing** einen Riesengewinn machen **9.** *fam* (*reach*) **could you ~ a meeting at 8 a.m.?** schaffst du ein Treffen um 8 Uhr morgens?; **to ~ the finals** sich für das Finale qualifizieren; **to ~ it** es schaffen **III.** *vi* <made, made> (*pretend*) **he made as if to leave the room** er machte Anstalten, das Zimmer zu verlassen; **to ~ like ...** so tun, als ob ... ▶ **to ~ do without sth** ohne etw auskommen

♦**make for** *vi* **1.** (*head for*) zugehen auf +*akk*; (*by car or bus*) zufahren auf +*akk* **2.** (*promote*) **constant arguing doesn't ~ for a good relationship** ständiges Streiten ist einer guten Beziehung nicht gerade förderlich

♦**make of** *vt* **1.** (*understand*) **I don't know what to ~ of it** ich weiß nicht, wie ich das deuten soll **2.** (*think*) **what do you ~ of his speech?** was hältst du von seiner Rede?

♦**make off** *vi fam* **1.** (*leave*) abhauen **2.** (*steal*) **to ~ off with sth** etw mitgehen lassen *fam*

♦**make out I.** *vi fam* **1.** (*manage: person*) zurechtkommen **2.** *sl* (*kiss passionately*) [he]rummachen, [he]rumfummeln (**with** mit +*dat*) **II.** *vt* **1.** ausschreiben; (*check*) ausstellen **2.** (*see: writing*) entziffern; (*distant object*) ausmachen

♦**make over** *vt* (*change appearance: house*) umändern; (*person*) verändern

♦**make up I.** *vt* **1.** (*invent*) **to ~ up ⇆ sth: she made the whole thing up** sie hat das alles nur erfunden **2.** (*prepare*) fertig machen **3.** (*put on makeup*) **to ~ oneself up** sich schminken **4.** (*compensate: deficit*) ausgleichen; **to ~ up time** Zeit wieder gutmachen; (*train*) Zeit wieder herausarbeiten; (*repay favor*) **to ~ it up to sb** jdm gegenüber etw wiedergutmachen **II.** *vi* sich versöhnen (**with**

mit +*dat*); **kiss and ~ up** küsst euch und vertragt euch wieder

make up for *vt* entschädigen für +*akk*; (*mistake*) wiedergutmachen; **to ~ up for lost time** verlorene Zeit wieder aufholen

'**make-believe I.** *n* Fantasie *f* **II.** *vi* <made-, made-> **to ~ [that] ...** sich *dat* vorstellen, dass ...

maker ['meɪ·kər] *n* (*manufacturer*) **the ~** Hersteller(in) *m(f)*

'**makeshift** *adj* Not-, behelfsmäßig

'**makeup** *n* **1.** (*cosmetics*) Make-up; **to put on ~** sich schminken **2.** (*of group*) Zusammensetzung *f*

'**makeup artist** *n* Visagist(in) *m(f)*

making ['meɪ·kɪŋ] *n* **1.** (*production*) Herstellung *f*; **her problems with that child are of her own ~** ihre Probleme mit diesem Kind hat sie selbst verschuldet **2.** (*qualities, ingredients*) **~s** *pl* Anlagen *pl*; **she has the ~s of a great violinist** sie hat das Zeug zu einer großartigen Geigerin

maladjusted [ˌmæl·ə·ˈdʒʌs·tɪd] *adj* verhaltensgestört

malaise [mæ·ˈleɪz] *n* Unbehagen *nt*

malaria [mə·ˈler·i·ə] *n* Malaria *f*

male [meɪl] **I.** *adj* männlich; **~-dominated** von Männern dominiert **II.** *n* (*person*) Mann *m*; (*animal*) Männchen *nt*

malformation [ˌmæl·fɔr·ˈmeɪ·ʃən] *n* Missbildung *f*

malfunction [ˌmæl·ˈfʌŋk·ʃən] **I.** *vi* (*not work properly*) nicht funktionieren; (*stop working*) ausfallen **II.** *n* Ausfall *m*; (*of liver, kidney*) Funktionsstörung *f*

malice [ˈmæl·ɪs] *n* Boshaftigkeit *f*

malicious [mə·ˈlɪʃ·əs] *adj* boshaft

malignant [mə·ˈlɪg·nənt] *adj* MED bösartig

mall [mɔl] *n* [überdachtes] Einkaufszentrum

mallard <*pl* -s> [ˈmæl·ərd] *n* Stockente *f*

malleable [ˈmæl·i·ə·bəl] *adj* (*metal*) formbar; *fig* (*person*) gefügig

mallet [ˈmæl·ɪt] *n* (*hammer*) [Holz]hammer *m*; (*in croquet*) Krockethammer *m*

malnutrition [ˌmæl·nu·ˈtrɪʃ·ən] *n* Unterernährung *f*

malpractice [ˌmæl·ˈpræk·tɪs] *n* (*faulty work*) Berufsvergehen *nt*; (*criminal misconduct*) [berufliches] Vergehen; **medical ~** ärztlicher Kunstfehler

malt [mɔlt] *n* **1.** (*grain*) Malz *nt* **2.** (*malted milk*) Malzmilch *f*; **chocolate ~** Schokoladenshake mit Zusatz von Malzextrakt

mammal [ˈmæm·əl] *n* Säugetier *nt*, Säuger *m*

mammography [mə·ˈmɑg·rə·fi] *n* Mammographie *f*

mammoth [ˈmæm·əθ] **I.** *n* Mammut *nt* **II.** *adj fig* Mammut-, riesig

man [mæn] **I.** *n* <*pl* men> **1.** (*male adult*) Mann *m*; **the men's [room]** die Herrentoilette **2.** (*person*) Mensch *m*; **to be sb's right-hand ~** jds rechte Hand sein **3.** (*mankind*) der Mensch **4.** (*particular type*) **to be a family ~** ein Familienmensch *m* sein **5.** *pl* (*soldiers, workers*) Männer *pl*, Leute *pl* **II.** *interj fam* Mensch, Mann **III.** *vt* <-nn-> (*fortress*) besetzen; (*ship*) bemannen

manage [ˈmæn·ɪdʒ] **I.** *vt* **1.** (*run*) leiten **2.** (*control*) steuern; (*administer*) verwalten; (*organize*) organisieren **3.** (*accomplish*) schaffen; (*task*) bewältigen; **to ~ a smile** ein Lächeln zustande bringen **II.** *vi* **1.** (*succeed*) es schaffen; (*cope, survive*) zurechtkommen; **we'll ~!** wir schaffen das schon! **2.** (*get by*) **to ~ without sth** ohne etw auskommen

manageable [ˈmæn·ɪ·dʒə·bəl] *adj* **1.** (*doable: job*) leicht zu bewältigen; (*task*) überschaubar **2.** (*feasible*) erreichbar; (*deadline*) realistisch

management [ˈmæn·ɪdʒ·mənt] *n* **1.** (*of business*) Management *nt*, [Geschäfts]führung *f* **2.** (*managers*) Management *nt*; (*of hospital, theater*) Direktion *f* **3.** (*handling*) Umgang *m*

management 'buyout *n* Management-Buy-out *nt* (*Übernahme einer Firma durch die leitenden Direktoren*)

management con'sultant *n* Unternehmensberater(in) *m(f)*

management 'skills *npl* Führungsqualitäten *pl*

'**management studies** *n* + *sing/pl vb* Betriebswirtschaft[slehre] *f*

manager [ˈmæn·ɪ·dʒər] *n* **1.** Geschäftsführer(in) *m(f)*; (*of performer*) Ma-

M

nager(in) *m(f)*; (*of department*) Abteilungsleiter(in) *m(f)* **2.** (*chief adviser*) **campaign ~** Wahlkampfleiter *m* **3.** SPORT (*coach*) [Chef]trainer(in) *m(f)*

managerial [ˌmæn·ə·ˈdʒɪr·i·əl] *adj* Manager–; **at ~ level** auf Führungsebene

managing di'rector *n* [Haupt]geschäftsführer(in) *m(f)*

mandarin [ˈmæn·də·rɪn] *n* Mandarine *f*

Mandarin [ˈmæn·də·rɪn] *n* LING Mandarin *nt*

mandate [ˈmæn·deɪt] **I.** *n usu sing* (*authority*) Mandat *nt*; (*command*) Verfügung *f* **II.** *vt* (*order*) anordnen; (*authorize*) ein Mandat erteilen für +*akk*

mandatory [ˈmæn·də·tɔr·i] *adj* gesetzlich vorgeschrieben

mandolin [ˈmæn·də·lɪn] *n* MUS Mandoline *f*

mane [meɪn] *n* Mähne *f*

'man-eater *n* **1.** (*animal*) Tier, *das Menschen tötet* **2.** *hum fam* (*woman*) männermordender Vamp

maneuver [mə·ˈnu·vər] **I.** *n* **1.** *usu pl* (*military exercise*) Manöver *nt* **2.** (*planned move*) Manöver *nt*; *fig* Schachzug *m* **3. to have room for ~** Spielraum haben **II.** *vt* (*move*) manövrieren; (*vehicle*) lenken **III.** *vi* manövrieren

maneuverability [mə·ˌnu·vər·ə·ˈbɪl·ɪ·ti] *n* Beweglichkeit *f*, Manövrierfähigkeit *f*

maneuverable [mə·ˈnu·vər·ə·bəl] *adj* beweglich; (*ship*) manövrierfähig

mangle [ˈmæŋ·gəl] *vt usu passive* (*crush*) zerstören; (*limbs*) verstümmeln; (*car*) zerdrücken

mango <*pl* -s> [ˈmæŋ·goʊ] *n* Mango *f*

mangrove [ˈmæn·groʊv] *n* Mangrovenbaum *m*

manhandle [ˈmæn·hæn·dəl] *vt* (*handle roughly*) grob behandeln

'manhole cover *n* Einstiegsverschluss *m*

manhood [ˈmæn·hʊd] *n* (*adulthood*) Erwachsenenalter *nt* (*eines Mannes*); **to reach ~** zum Manne werden

'man-hour *n* Arbeitsstunde *f*

'manhunt *n* Verbrecherjagd *f*

mania [ˈmeɪ·ni·ə] *n* Manie *f*

maniac [ˈmeɪ·ni·æk] *n fam* Verrückte(r) *f(m)*

maniacal [mə·ˈnaɪ·ə·kəl] *adj* (*crazy*) verrückt, irrsinnig

manic [ˈmæn·ɪk] *adj* manisch; (*highly energetic*) wild

manic de'pression *n* manische Depression

manic de'pressive *n* Manisch-Depressive(r) *f(m)*

manicure [ˈmæn·ɪ·kjʊr] *n* Maniküre *f*

manicurist [ˈmæn·ɪ·kjʊr·ɪst] *n* Handpflegerin *f*

manifest [ˈmæn·ɪ·fest] **I.** *adj* offenkundig **II.** *n* TRANSP (*list of passengers*) Passagierliste *f*; (*cargo list*) [Ladungs]manifest *nt*

manifesto <*pl* -s> [ˌmæn·ɪ·ˈfes·toʊ] *n* Manifest *nt*

manifold [ˈmæn·ɪ·foʊld] *n* TECH Verteilerrohr *nt*

Manil(l)a 'envelope [mə·ˈnɪl·ə-] *n* Briefumschlag *m* aus Manilapapier

manipulate [mə·ˈnɪp·jə·leɪt] *vt* **1.** *esp pej* (*manage cleverly*) **to ~ sb** geschickt mit jdm umgehen **2.** (*with hands*) handhaben; (*machine*) bedienen; COMPUT (*text*) bearbeiten

manipulation [mə·ˌnɪp·jə·ˈleɪ·ʃən] *n* **1.** *esp pej* (*clever management*) Manipulation *f* **2.** (*handling*) Handgriff *m*

manipulative [mə·ˈnɪp·jə·lə·t̮ɪv] *adj esp pej* manipulativ

mankind [ˌmæn·ˈkaɪnd] *n* Menschheit *f*

manly [ˈmæn·li] *adj* männlich

man-'made *adj* künstlich

manna [ˈmæn·ə] *n* Manna *nt*; **~ from heaven** ein wahrer Segen

manned [mænd] *adj* AEROSP bemannt

manner [ˈmæn·ər] *n* **1.** (*way*) Weise *f*, Art *f*; **in a ~ of speaking** sozusagen **2.** (*behavior to others*) Betragen *nt* **3.** (*polite behavior*) **~s** *pl* Manieren *pl*

mannerism [ˈmæn·ə·rɪz·əm] *n* Eigenart *f*

mannish [ˈmæn·ɪʃ] *adj esp pej* (*of woman*) männlich

'manpower *n* Arbeitskräfte *pl*

mansion [ˈmæn·ʃən] *n* Villa *f*

manslaughter [ˈmæn·slɔ·t̮ər] *n* Totschlag *m*

mantel [ˈmæn·təl] *n* Kaminsims *m o nt*

'man-to-man *adj* von Mann zu Mann

manual [ˈmæn·ju·əl] **I.** *adj* manuell,

Hand-; **~ transmission** AUTO Schaltgetriebe nt II. n Handbuch nt

manually [ˈmæn·jʊ·ə·li] adv manuell

manufacture [ˌmæn·jʊˈfæk·tʃər] vt herstellen

manufacturer [ˌmæn·jʊˈfæk·tʃər·ər] n Hersteller m

manufacturing [ˌmæn·jəˈfæk·tʃər·ɪŋ] n Fertigung f

manure [məˈnʊr] n Dung m

manuscript [ˈmæn·jʊ·skrɪpt] n Manuskript nt

many [ˈmen·i] pron (a great number) viele; **too ~** zu viele; **as ~ as ...** so viele wie ...

many-ˈsided adj vielseitig; (complex) vielschichtig

map [mæp] n GEOG [Land]karte f; (of town) Stadtplan m; **road ~** Straßenkarte f

◆map out vt genau festlegen; (route) planen

maple [ˈmeɪ·pəl] n Ahorn m

ˈmaple leaf n Ahornblatt nt

maple ˈsyrup n Ahornsirup m

march [mɑrtʃ] I. n <pl -es> Marsch m II. vi marschieren III. vt **to ~ sb off** jdn wegführen; (police) jdn abführen

March <pl -es> [mɑrtʃ] n März m; see also **February**

Mardi Gras [ˈmɑr·di·ˌgrɑ] n (carnival on Shrove Tuesday) ≈ Fastnachtsdienstag m, Karneval m

mare [mer] n Stute f

margarine [ˈmɑr·dʒər·ɪn] n Margarine f

margin [ˈmɑr·dʒɪn] n 1. (outer edge) Rand m; TYPO [Seiten]rand m 2. (amount) Abstand m 3. (provision) Spielraum m; **a ~ of error** eine Fehlerspanne

marginal [ˈmɑr·dʒə·nəl] adj 1. (slight) geringfügig 2. (insignificant) nebensächlich

marginalize [ˈmɑr·dʒɪ·nə·laɪz] vt an den Rand drängen

marigold [ˈmær·ɪ·goʊld] n Studentenblume f

marijuana, marihuana [ˌmær·ɪˈwɑ·nə] n Marihuana nt

marina [məˈri·nə] n Jachthafen m

marinade [ˌmær·ɪˈneɪd] n Marinade f

marinate [ˈmær·ɪ·neɪt] vt marinieren

marine [məˈrin] I. adj attr 1. (of sea) Meeres-, See- 2. (of shipping) Schiffs- II. n Marineinfanterist m

marine biˈologist n Meeresbiologe m /-biologin f

Maˈrine Corps n Marineinfanteriekorps nt

marital [ˈmær·ɪ·təl] adj ehelich, Ehe-; **~ status** Familienstand m

maritime ˈlaw n Seerecht nt

marjoram [ˈmɑr·dʒər·əm] n Majoran m

mark [mɑrk] I. n 1. (spot, stain) Fleck m; (trace) Spur f; (fingerprint) Abdruck m 2. (identifying feature) [Kenn]zeichen nt, Merkmal nt 3. (indication) Zeichen nt **▶ to leave its/one's ~ on sb** seine Spuren bei jdm hinterlassen II. vt 1. (stain) schmutzig machen 2. (indicate) markieren 3. (commemorate) **to ~ sth** an etw akk erinnern III. vi (get dirty) schmutzig werden; (scratch) Kratzer bekommen

◆mark down vt 1. (reduce the price of) heruntersetzen 2. (give a lower grade) **to ~ down ⇆ sb** jdm eine schlechtere Note geben

◆mark off vt (separate off) abgrenzen

◆mark out vt abstecken, markieren

◆mark up vt (increase the price of) heraufsetzen

marked [mɑrkt] adj 1. (clear) deutlich; (striking) auffallend, markant; **in ~ contrast to sth** im krassen Gegensatz zu etw dat 2. (with distinguishing marks) markiert

markedly [ˈmɑr·kəd·li] adv deutlich

marker [ˈmɑr·kər] n 1. (sign, symbol) [Kenn]zeichen nt 2. (felt tip pen) Filzstift m

market [ˈmɑr·kɪt] I. n Markt m; **to put sth on the ~** etw auf den Markt bringen II. vt (sell) vermarkten

M

market 'forces npl Marktkräfte pl

marketing ['mar·kɪ·tɪŋ] n Marketing nt

market 'leader n Marktführer m

'marketplace n **1.** (place) Marktplatz m **2.** (commercial environment) Markt m

market 'research n Marktforschung f

marking ['mar·kɪŋ] n ~**s** pl Markierungen pl; (on animals) Zeichnung f kein pl

marksman ['marks·mən] n Schütze m

marksmanship ['marks·mən·ʃɪp] n Treffsicherheit f

markswoman ['marks·wʊm·ən] n Schützin f

markup ['mark·ʌp] n [Kalkulations]aufschlag m

marmalade ['mar·mə·leɪd] n Orangenmarmelade f

maroon¹ [mə·'run] vt (abandon) aussetzen

maroon² [mə·'run] adj kastanienbraun, rötlichbraun

marquee [mar·'ki] n beleuchtete Werbetafel über Kino-/Theatereingängen

marriage ['mær·ɪdʒ] n **1.** (wedding) Heirat f **2.** (relationship) Ehe f

'marriage certificate n Heiratsurkunde f

'marriage counselor n Eheberater(in) m(f)

'marriage license n Heiratserlaubnis f

'marriage vow n usu pl Ehegelübde nt geh

married ['mer·ɪd] adj verheiratet; **to get ~ [to sb]** [jdn] heiraten

marrow ['mær·oʊ] n (of bone) [Knochen]mark nt

marry ['mær·i] I. vt **1.** (wed) heiraten **2.** (officiate at ceremony) trauen, verheiraten **3.** (combine) verbinden (**to/with** mit +dat) II. vi heiraten

Mars [marz] n Mars m

marsh <pl -es> [marʃ] n Sumpf m

marshal ['mar·ʃəl] n **1.** (federal agent) Gerichtsdiener(in) m(f); **fire ~** Branddirektor(in) m(f) **2.** MIL (army officer) Marschall m

'marshland n Sumpfland nt

marshmallow ['marʃ·mel·oʊ] n Marshmallow nt

marshy ['mar·ʃi] adj sumpfig

martial 'arts npl SPORT Kampfsport m kein pl, Kampfsportarten pl

martial 'law n Kriegsrecht nt

martyr ['mar·tər] n Märtyrer(in) m(f)

martyrdom ['mar·tər·dəm] n (being a martyr) Märtyrertum nt; (death) Märtyrertod m

marvel ['mar·vəl] I. n (wonderful thing) Wunder nt II. vi <-l-> (wonder) sich wundern (**at** über +akk)

marvelous ['mar·və·ləs] adj wunderbar, großartig

Marxist ['mark·sɪst] I. n Marxist(in) m(f) II. adj marxistisch

Maryland ['mer·ə·lənd] n Maryland nt

marzipan ['mar·zɪ·pæn] n Marzipan nt o m

masc. adj abbr of **masculine**

mascara [mæ·'skær·ə] n Wimperntusche f

mascot ['mæs·kat] n Maskottchen nt

masculine ['mæs·kjə·lɪn] adj männlich, maskulin

mash [mæʃ] I. n Brei m II. vt zerdrücken, [zer]stampfen

◆ mash up vt (food) zerdrücken

mashed po'tatoes n pl Kartoffelbrei m, [Kartoffel]püree nt

mask [mæsk] I. n Maske f II. vt verbergen

masked [mæskt] adj maskiert

masking tape ['mæs·kɪŋ-] n Tesakrepp® nt

masochist ['mæs·ə·kɪst] n Masochist(in) m(f)

mason ['meɪ·sən] n Steinmetz(in) m(f)

masonry ['meɪ·sən·ri] n Mauerwerk nt

masquerade [ˌmæs·kə·'reɪd] I. n Maskerade f II. vi **to ~ as sb** sich als jdn ausgeben

mass [mæs] I. n **1.** usu sing Masse f **2.** usu sing (large quantity) Menge f; **a ~ of contradictions** eine Reihe von Widersprüchen **3.** (common people) **the ~es** pl music for the ~ Musik für die breite Masse II. vi (crowd) sich ansammeln

Mass [mæs] n REL, MUS Messe f

Mass. abbr of **Massachusetts**

Massachusetts [ˌmæs·ə·'tʃu·sɪts] n Massachusetts nt

massacre ['mæs·ə·kər] I. n Massaker nt II. vt **1.** (kill) massakrieren **2.** (defeat) vernichtend schlagen

massage [mə·'sadʒ] I. n Massage f; **to**

give sb a ~ jdn massieren II. vt (rub) massieren; to ~ **cream into the skin** Creme einmassieren

mas'sage parlor n (for sex) Massagesalon m euph

masseur [mæˈsɜr] n Masseur m

masseuse [mæˈsɜz] n Masseurin f

massive [ˈmæsɪv] adj riesig, enorm; (heart attack) schwer

mass 'market n Massenmarkt m

mass 'media n + sing/pl vb **the ~** die Massenmedien pl

mass 'murderer n Massenmörder(in) m(f)

mass-pro'duce vt serienmäßig herstellen

mass pro'duction n Massenproduktion f

mass 'transit n öffentliche Verkehrsmittel

mast [mæst] n 1. NAUT [Schiffs]mast m 2. RADIO, TV Sendeturm m

master [ˈmæstər] I. n 1. (of slave) Herr m; (of dog) Herrchen nt 2. (expert) Meister(in) m(f) II. vt 1. (cope with) meistern 2. (become proficient) beherrschen

master 'bedroom n großes Schlafzimmer

'master class n Meisterklasse f

master 'craftsman n Handwerksmeister(in) m(f)

masterful [ˈmæstərfəl] adj 1. (authoritative) bestimmend 2. (skillful) meisterhaft

'master key n Generalschlüssel m

'mastermind I. n führender Kopf II. vt federführend leiten

Master of 'Arts n ≈ Magister Artium m

Master of 'Ceremonies n Zeremonienmeister m

Master of 'Science to have a ~ ≈ ein Diplom nt in einer Naturwissenschaft haben

'masterpiece n Meisterwerk nt

'master plan n Grundplan m

Master's, Master's degree [ˈmæstərz-] n ≈ Magister m; **to study for one's ~** ≈ seinen Magister machen

'master switch n Hauptschalter m

'masterwork n see **masterpiece**

mastiff [ˈmæstɪf] n englische Dogge

masturbate [ˈmæstərbeɪt] vi masturbieren

masturbation [ˌmæstərˈbeɪʃən] n Masturbation f

mat [mæt] n 1. (for floor) Matte f; (decorative mat) Deckchen nt 2. (thick layer) **a ~ of hair** dichtes Haar; (on the head) eine Mähne fam

match[1] [mætʃ] I. n <pl -es> 1. usu sing (complement) **to be a good ~** gut zusammenpassen 2. (one of pair) Gegenstück nt 3. usu sing (equal) ebenbürtiger Gegner/ebenbürtige Gegnerin; **to have met one's ~** seine bessere Hälfte gefunden haben hum fam 4. SPORT Spiel nt; **tennis ~** Tennisspiel; CHESS Partie f 5. COMPUT (hit) Treffer m II. vi (harmonize) zusammenpassen III. vt 1. (complement) passen zu +dat 2. (find complement) **to ~ sth** [**with sth**] etw [auf etw akk] abstimmen 3. (correspond to) **to ~ sth** etw dat entsprechen, zu etw dat passen

match up I. vi (be aligned) aufeinander abgestimmt sein II. vt (find complement) **to ~ up ⇆ socks** die zusammengehörigen Socken finden

match[2] <pl -es> [mætʃ] n (for lighting) Streichholz nt

'matchbox n Streichholzschachtel f

matching [ˈmætʃ·ɪŋ] adj attr [zusammen] passend

match 'point n TENNIS Matchball m

'matchstick n Streichholz nt

mate[1] [meɪt] I. n 1. (sexual partner) Partner(in) m(f) 2. (ship's officer) Schiffsoffizier m II. vi BIOL (animals) sich paaren (with mit +dat)

mate[2] [meɪt] CHESS I. n [Schach]matt nt II. vt [schach]matt setzen

material [məˈtɪr·i·əl] I. n 1. (substance) Material nt a. fig; **raw ~** Rohmaterial nt 2. (type of cloth) Stoff m 3. (information) [Informations]material nt II. adj 1. (physical) materiell; **~ damage** Sachschaden m 2. (important) wesentlich; **to be ~ to sth** für etw akk relevant sein

materialism [məˈtɪr·i·ə·lɪz·əm] n Materialismus m

materialistic [məˌtɪr·i·ə·ˈlɪs·tɪk] adj materialistisch

materialize [məˈtɪr·i·ə·laɪz] vi (dream) sich verwirklichen, in Erfüllung gehen; (plan) in die Tat umgesetzt werden

M

maternal [məˈtɜr·nəl] *adj* mütterlich

maternity [məˈtɜr·nɪ·t̮i] *n* Mutterschaft *f*

maˈternity dress *n* Umstandskleid *nt*

maˈternity leave *n* Mutterschaftsurlaub *m*

math [mæθ] *n fam short for* **mathematics** Mathe *f*

mathematical [ˌmæθ·ə·ˈmæt̮·ɪ·kəl] *adj* mathematisch

mathematics [ˌmæθ·ə·ˈmæt̮·ɪks] *n + sing vb* Mathematik *f*

matinee [mæt·ə·ˈneɪ] *n* Matinee *f; (afternoon performance)* Frühvorstellung *f*

mating [ˈmeɪ·t̮ɪŋ] *n* Paarung *f*

matrices [ˈmeɪ·trɪ·siz] *n pl of* **matrix**

matriculate [məˈtrɪk·jə·leɪt] *vi* UNIV sich immatrikulieren

matrimonial [ˌmæt·rə·ˈmoʊ·ni·əl] *adj* form Ehe-, ehelich

matrimony [ˈmæt·rə·moʊ·ni] *n* Ehe *f;* **to be joined in holy ~** in den heiligen Stand der Ehe treten

matrix <*pl* -es> [ˈmeɪ·trɪks] *n (rectangular arrangement)* Matrix *f*

matronly [ˈmeɪ·trən·li] *adj esp hum* matronenhaft *meist pej*

matte [mæt] *adj* matt

matted [ˈmæt̮·ɪd] *adj* verflochten; *(hair)* verfilzt

matter [ˈmæt̮·ər] **I.** *n* **1.** *(material)* Materie *f;* **reading ~** Lesestoff *m* **2.** *(affair)* Angelegenheit *f*, Sache *f;* **this is a ~ for the police** das sollte man der Polizei übergeben; **a ~ of urgency** etwas Dringendes **3.** *(question)* Frage *f;* **as a ~ of fact** *(by the way)* übrigens; *(expressing agreement or disagreement)* in der Tat; **a ~ of taste** eine Geschmacksfrage **4.** *(topic)* Thema *nt;* **it's no laughing ~** das ist nicht zum Lachen **5.** *(problem)* **is anything the ~?** stimmt etwas nicht?; **what's the ~ with you?** was ist los mit dir? **II.** *vi (be of importance)* von Bedeutung sein; **that's the only thing that ~s** das ist das Einzige, was zählt; **it doesn't ~** das ist egal, das macht nichts

matter-of-ˈfact *adj* **1.** *(emotionless)* sachlich **2.** *(straightforward)* geradeheraus *präd*, direkt

mattress <*pl* -es> [ˈmæt·rɪs] *n* Matratze *f*

mature [məˈtʃʊr] **I.** *adj* **1.** *(adult)* erwachsen **2.** *(ripe)* reif; *(wine)* ausgereift **II.** *vi (physically)* erwachsen werden, heranreifen; *(mentally and emotionally)* reifer werden **III.** *vt* FOOD reifen lassen

maturity [məˈtʃʊr·ɪ·t̮i] *n* **1.** *(adulthood)* Erwachsensein *nt;* **to reach ~** *(of person)* erwachsen werden; *(of animal)* ausgewachsen sein **2.** *(developed form)* Reife *f*

maudlin [ˈmɔd·lɪn] *adj* [weinerlich] sentimental

maul [mɔl] *vt* **1.** *(wound)* verletzen; *(attack)* anfallen **2.** *(criticize)* heruntermachen

mausoleum [ˌmɔ·sə·ˈli·əm] *n* Mausoleum *nt*

mauve [moʊv] *adj* mauve

maverick [ˈmæv·ər·ɪk] *n* Einzelgänger(in) *m(f)*

max [mæks] *fam* **I.** *n short for* **maximum** max. **II.** *adv* **it'll cost you 40 dollars ~** das wird dich maximal 40 Dollar kosten

max out *vt fam* **to ~ out ⇆ sth** *(credit card)* etw ausschöpfen

maxim [ˈmæk·sɪm] *n* Maxime *f*

maximize [ˈmæk·sɪ·maɪz] *vt* maximieren

maximum [ˈmæk·sɪ·məm] **I.** *adj attr* maximal, Höchst- **II.** *n* <*pl* -ima> Maximum *nt*

maximum-security ˈprison *n* Hochsicherheitsgefängnis *nt*

may <*3rd pers. sing* may, might, might> [meɪ] *aux vb* **1.** *(indicating possibility)* können; **there ~ be side effects from the drug** diese Arznei kann Nebenwirkungen haben **2.** *(be allowed)* dürfen, können; **~ I ask you a question?** darf ich Ihnen [mal] eine Frage stellen? **3.** *(expressing wish)* mögen; **~ she rest in peace** möge sie in Frieden ruhen *form*

May [meɪ] *n* Mai *m; see also* **February**

maybe [ˈmeɪ·bi] *adv* **1.** *(perhaps)* vielleicht **2.** *(approximately)* circa, ungefähr

ˈmayday *n* Mayday *kein art (internationaler Notruf)*

mayhem [ˈmeɪ·hem] *n* Chaos *nt*

mayo ['meɪ·oʊ] *n fam short for* **mayonnaise** Mayo *f*

mayonnaise [ˌmeɪ·ə·'neɪz] *n* Mayonnaise *f*

mayor ['meɪ·ər] *n* Bürgermeister(in) *m(f)*

maze [meɪz] *n* Labyrinth *nt*

MBA [ˌem·bi·'eɪ] *n abbr of* **Master of Business Administration** MBA *m*

MC [ˌem·'si] *n abbr of* **Master of Ceremonies**

MD [ˌem·'di] *n* 1. *abbr of* **Maryland** 2. *abbr of* **Doctor of Medicine** Dr. med.

me [mi] *pron object (1st person singular)* mir *in dat,* mich *in akk;* **why are you looking at ~?** warum siehst du mich an?; **hi, it's ~** hallo, ich bin's; **between you and ~** unter uns [gesagt] ▶ **dear ~!** du liebe Güte!

ME, Me. *abbr of* **Maine**

meadow ['med·oʊ] *n* Wiese *f*

meager ['mi·gər] *adj* mager

meal[1] [mil] *n* Mahlzeit *f,* Essen *nt;* **to go out for a ~** essen gehen

meal[2] [mil] *n* AGR *(grobes)* Mehl

mealtime *n* Essenszeit *f*

mealy-mouthed *adj pej* ausweichend; *(expressions)* schönfärberisch

mean[1] [min] *adj* 1. *(unkind)* gemein, fies *fam* 2. *(vicious)* aggressiv

mean[2] <meant, meant> [min] *vt* 1. *(signify: word, symbol)* bedeuten; **no ~s no** nein heißt nein 2. *(intend to convey)* meinen; **what do you ~ by that?** was willst du damit sagen? 3. *(intend)* wollen; **it was ~t to be a surprise** das sollte eine Überraschung sein; **to ~ business** es ernst meinen; **to be ~t for each other** füreinander bestimmt sein

mean[3] [min] *adj* durchschnittlich

meander [mɪ·'æn·dər] I. *n* Windung *f* II. *vi* sich schlängeln [*or* winden]

meaning ['mi·nɪŋ] *n* Bedeutung *f*

meaningful ['mi·nɪŋ·fəl] *adj* 1. *(important)* bedeutsam, wichtig 2. *(implying something)* bedeutungsvoll

meaningless ['mi·nɪŋ·lɪs] *n (nonsensical)* sinnlos; *(empty)* nichts sagend

meanness ['min·nɪs] *n* Gemeinheit *f,* Gehässigkeit *f*

means <*pl ->* [minz] *n* 1. *(method)* Weg *m;* *(possibility)* Möglichkeit *f;* *(device)* Mittel *nt;* **~ of transport** Transportmittel *nt* 2. *(income)* **~** *pl* Geldmittel *pl;* **to live beyond one's ~** über seine Verhältnisse leben ▶ **by all ~** *form* unbedingt; *(of course)* selbstverständlich; **by no ~** auf keinen Fall

meant [ment] *pt, pp of* **mean**

meantime *n* **in the ~** inzwischen, in der Zwischenzeit

meanwhile ['min·hwaɪl] *adv* inzwischen

measles ['mi·zəlz] *n + sing vb* Masern *pl*

measly ['mi·zli] *adj pej fam* mickrig, schäbig

measurable ['meʒ·ər·ə·bəl] *adj* messbar; *(perceptible)* nachweisbar

measure ['meʒ·ər] I. *n* 1. *(unit)* Maß *nt,* Maßeinheit *f;* **a ~ of length** ein Längenmaß *nt* 2. *(measuring instrument)* Messgerät *nt;* *(ruler, indicator)* Messstab *m* 3. *usu pl (action)* Maßnahme *f* II. *vt* [ab]messen III. *vi* messen

◆measure out *vt* abmessen

◆measure up I. *vt* **to ~ up ⇆ sb** jdn einschätzen II. *vi* den Ansprüchen genügen

measured ['meʒ·ərd] *adj* gemäßigt; *(voice)* bedächtig

measurement ['meʒ·ər·mənt] *n* 1. *(size)* **sb's ~s** *pl* jds Maße *pl,* jds Größe *f* 2. *(measuring)* Messung *f*

measuring cup ['meʒ·ər·ɪŋ-] *n* Messbecher *m*

meat [mit] *n* Fleisch *nt*

meatball *n* Fleischklößchen *nt*

meat grinder *n* Fleischwolf *m*

meat loaf *n* Hackbraten *m*

Mecca ['mek·ə] *n* Mekka *nt a. fig*

mechanic [mɪ·'kæn·ɪk] *n* Mechaniker(in) *m(f)*

mechanical [mɪ·'kæn·ɪk·əl] *adj* 1. *(machines)* mechanisch; *(by machine)* maschinell 2. *(machine-like)* mechanisch

mechanical engi'neering *n* Maschinenbau *m*

mechanical 'pencil *n* Drehbleistift *m*

mechanics [mɪ·'kæn·ɪks] *n* 1. *+ sing vb* AUTO, TECH Mechanik *f* 2. *+ pl vb fam (practicalities)* Mechanismus *m*

mechanism ['mek·ə·nɪz·əm] *n* Mechanismus *m*

mechanize ['mek·ə·naɪz] vt mechanisieren

med I. adj fam see **medical** II. n fam ~**s** pl Medizin f

med. I. n abbr of **medicine** II. adj 1. abbr of **medieval** ma. 2. abbr of **medium**

medal ['med·əl] n Orden m; SPORT Medaille f

medalist ['med·əl·ɪst] n Medaillengewinner(in) m(f)

medallion [mə·'dæl·jən] n Medaillon nt

meddle ['med·əl] vi sich einmischen (**in** in +akk)

media ['mi·di·ə] n 1. pl of **medium** 2. + sing/pl vb (the press) **the** ~ die Medien pl

mediaeval [ˌmi·di·'i·vəl] adj see **medieval**

'**median** (**strip**) n Mittelstreifen m

'**media studies** npl ≈ Kommunikationswissenschaft f

mediate ['mi·di·eɪt] vi vermitteln

mediator ['mi·di·eɪ·tər] n Vermittler(in) m(f)

medic ['med·ɪk] n fam 1. MIL, NAUT Sanitäter(in) m(f) 2. (doctor) Doktor m fam

Medicaid ['med·ɪ·keɪd] n Gesundheitsfürsorgeprogramm in den USA für einkommensschwache Gruppen

medical ['med·ɪ·kəl] I. adj (facilities, research) medizinisch; (advice, treatment) ärztlich II. n fam ärztliche Untersuchung; **to have a** ~ sich ärztlich untersuchen lassen

'**medical certificate** n ärztliches Attest

medical exami'nation n ärztliche Untersuchung

Medicare ['med·ɪ·ker] n staatliche Gesundheitsfürsorge [für Senioren]

medicate ['med·ɪ·keɪt] vt usu passive (treat with drug) **to be** ~**d** medikamentös behandelt werden

medication [ˌmed·ɪ·'keɪ·ʃən] n MED Medikamente pl

medicinal [mə·'dɪs·ə·nəl] adj medizinisch

medicine ['med·ɪ·sɪn] n 1. (for illness) Medizin f 2. (substance) Medikament nt 3. (medical science) Medizin f; **to prac-**

tice ~ den Arztberuf ausüben

'**medicine cabinet**, '**medicine chest** n Hausapotheke f

medieval [ˌmi·di·'i·vəl] adj mittelalterlich

mediocre [ˌmi·di·'oʊ·kər] adj mittelmäßig

meditate ['med·ɪ·teɪt] vi 1. (think deeply) nachdenken (**on/about** über +akk) 2. (as spiritual exercise) meditieren

meditation [ˌmed·ɪ·'teɪ·ʃən] n 1. (spiritual exercise) Meditation f 2. (serious thought) Nachdenken nt

Mediterranean [ˌmed·ɪ·tə·'reɪ·ni·ən] n Mittelmeer nt

medium ['mi·di·əm] I. adj 1. (average) durchschnittlich; **of** ~ **height** von mittlerer Größe 2. FOOD (steak) halb durch II. n <pl -s> 1. (means) Medium nt; **advertising** ~ Werbeträger m 2. (art material) Medium nt

medium-'rare adj FOOD englisch

'**medium-size(d)** adj mittelgroß

medley ['med·li] n 1. (mixture) Gemisch nt 2. (of tunes) Medley nt

meek [mik] adj 1. (gentle) sanftmütig 2. pej (submissive) unterwürfig

meet [mit] I. n (sporting event) Sportveranstaltung f II. vt <met, met> 1. (by chance) treffen 2. (by arrangement) **to** ~ **sb** sich mit jdm treffen 3. (make acquaintance of) kennen lernen 4. (fulfill) erfüllen; (deadline) einhalten ▸ **to make ends** ~ über die Runden kommen III. vi <met, met> 1. (by chance) sich begegnen 2. (by arrangement) sich treffen; **to** ~ **for a drink** sich auf einen Drink treffen 3. (get acquainted) sich kennen lernen; **no, we haven't met** nein, wir kennen uns noch nicht 4. (join) zusammentreffen; (roads) zusammenlaufen

meet with vi 1. (have meeting) treffen 2. (experience: problems) stoßen auf +akk; **to** ~ **with success** Erfolg haben

meeting ['mi·tɪŋ] n (organized gathering) Versammlung f, Sitzung f, Besprechung f; **to hold a** ~ eine Besprechung abhalten

'**meeting point** n 1. (place to gather) Treffpunkt m 2. (point of contact) Schnittpunkt m

mega ['megə] adj fam Riesen-, Mega-

mega- ['megə] comp + adj fam mega-

fam; ~~**cool** megacool *sl,* geil *sl*

'**megabucks** *npl fam* Schweinegeld *nt kein pl sl*

'**megabyte** *n* Megabyte *nt*

'**megahertz** *n* Megahertz *nt*

megalomania [ˌmeg·ə·loʊ·'meɪ·ni·ə] *n* (*lust for power*) Größenwahn *m pej*

'**megaphone** *n* Megaphon *nt*

'**megawatt** *n* Megawatt *nt*

melancholy ['mel·ən·kal·i] **I.** *n* Melancholie *f* **II.** *adj* melancholisch, schwermütig

melee ['meɪ·leɪ] *n usu sing* Handgemenge *nt*

mellow ['mel·oʊ] **I.** *adj* <-er, -est *or* more ~, most ~> **1.** (*relaxed: person*) abgeklärt, locker *fam* **2.** (*not harsh*) sanft; (*flavor*) mild; (*wine*) lieblich **II.** *vi* (*colors*) weicher werden; (*flavor*) milder werden

melodic [mə·'lad·ɪk] *adj* melodisch

melodramatic [ˌmel·oʊ·drə·'mæt·ɪk] *adj* melodramatisch

melody ['mel·ə·di] *n* Melodie *f*

melon ['mel·ən] *n* Melone *f*

melt [melt] **I.** *n* **1.** (*thaw*) Schneeschmelze *f* **2.** FOOD *patty* ~ Sandwich mit geschmolzenem Käse **II.** *vt, vi* schmelzen

'**meltdown** *n* **1.** TECH [Ein]schmelzen *nt* **2.** *fam* (*collapse*) Zusammenbruch *m*

'**melting point** *n* Schmelzpunkt *m*

'**melting pot** *n fig* Schmelztiegel *m*

member ['mem·bər] *n* (*of group*) Angehörige(r) *f(m);* (*of club, party*) Mitglied *nt*

'**membership** ['mem·bər·ʃɪp] *n* **1.** (*people*) **the** ~ die Mitglieder *pl;* (*number of people*) Mitgliederzahl *f* **2.** (*being member*) Mitgliedschaft *f*

'**membership card** *n* Mitgliedsausweis *m*

membrane ['mem·breɪn] *n* Membran *f,* Häutchen *nt*

memento <*pl* -s> [mə·'men·toʊ] *n* Andenken *nt*

memoir ['mem·war] *n* **1.** (*personal account*) Erinnerung *f* **2.** (*autobiography*) ~**s** *pl* Memoiren *pl*

memo pad *n* Notizblock *m*

memorabilia [ˌmem·ər·ə·'bɪl·i·ə] *npl* Souvenirs *pl*

memorable ['mem·ər·ə·bəl] *adj* unvergesslich

memorial [mə·'mɔr·i·əl] *n* Denkmal *nt*

Me'morial Day *n* Volkstrauertag *m (wird in den Vereinigten Staaten am letzten Montag im Mai gefeiert)*

memorize ['mem·ə·raɪz] *vt* (*facts*) sich *dat* einprägen; (*poem, song*) auswendig lernen

memory ['mem·ə·ri] *n* **1.** (*ability to remember*) Gedächtnis *nt* (**for** für +*akk*) **2.** (*remembered event*) Erinnerung *f* **3.** COMPUT Speicher *m*

'**memory bank** *n* COMPUT Speicherbank *f*

men [men] *n pl of* **man**

menace ['men·əs] **I.** *n* Drohung *f* **II.** *vt* bedrohen

menacing ['men·ɪs·ɪŋ] *adj attr* drohend

mend [mend] **I.** *vt* reparieren ▶ **to** ~ **one's ways** sich bessern **II.** *vi* gesund werden *a. fig;* (*bone*) heilen

menial ['mi·ni·əl] *adj* niedrig; ~ **labor** Hilfsarbeit *f*

meningitis [ˌmen·ɪn·'dʒaɪ·t̬ɪs] *n* Gehirnhautentzündung *f*

menopause ['men·ə·pɔz] *n* Wechseljahre *pl*

'**men's room** *n* Herrentoilette *f*

menstruation [ˌmen·stru·'eɪ·ʃən] *n* Menstruation *f geh,* Periode *f*

mental ['men·t̬əl] *adj* **1.** (*of the mind*) geistig, mental; ~ **process** Denkprozess *m* **2.** (*psychological*) psychisch, seelisch; ~ **illness** Geisteskrankheit *f; fam* (*crazy*) verrückt

'**mental hospital** *n* psychiatrische Klinik

mentally ['men·t̬əl·i] *adv* **1.** (*psychologically*) psychisch **2.** (*intellectually*) geistig

menthol ['men·θɔl] *n* Menthol *nt*

mention ['men·ʃən] **I.** *n* (*reference*) Erwähnung *f* **II.** *vt* erwähnen

menu ['men·ju] *n* **1.** (*in restaurant*) Speisekarte *f* **2.** COMPUT Menü *nt*

'**menu bar** *n* COMPUT Menüleiste *f*

meow [mi·'aʊ] *vi* miauen

mercenary ['mɜr·sə·ner·i] *n* Söldner *m*

merchandise ['mɜr·tʃən·daɪz] *n* ECON Handelsware *f*

merchant ma'rine *n* Handelsmarine *f*

'**merchant ship** *n* Handelsschiff *nt*

M

merciful ['mɜr·sɪ·fəl] *adj* gnädig

merciless ['mɜr·sɪ·lɪs] *adj* **1.** (*showing no mercy*) gnadenlos **2.** (*relentless*) unnachgiebig

mercury ['mɜr·kjə·ri] *n* Quecksilber *nt*

mercy ['mɜr·si] *n* (*compassion*) Mitleid *nt*, Erbarmen *nt*; (*forgiveness*) Gnade *f* ▶ **to be at the ~ of sb** jdm auf Gnade oder Ungnade ausgeliefert sein

'mere hall *n* Kasino *nt*

mere [mɪr] *adj* nur, nichts als

merely ['mɪr·li] *adv* nur, bloß *fam*

merge [mɜrdʒ] **I.** *vi* **1.** (*join*) zusammenkommen; (*roads*) zusammenlaufen **2.** ECON (*companies*) fusionieren **3.** (*fuse*) verschmelzen (**with/into** mit +*dat*) **4.** AUTO **to ~ left** sich rechts einordnen **II.** *vt* (*companies*) zusammenschließen

merger ['mɜr·dʒər] *n* ECON Fusion *f*

meridian [mə·'rɪd·i·ən] *n* GEOG Meridian *m*

meringue [mə·'ræŋ] *n* Baiser *nt*, Meringe *f*

merit ['mer·ɪt] **I.** *n* **1.** (*worthiness*) Verdienst *nt* **2.** (*good quality*) gute Eigenschaft, Vorzug *m* **II.** *vt* verdienen

mermaid ['mɜr·meɪd] *n* Seejungfrau *f*

merry ['mer·i] *adj* fröhlich; **M~ Christmas** Frohe [*or* Fröhliche] Weihnachten

'merry-go-round *n* (*fairground ride*) Karussell *nt*

mesh [meʃ] **I.** *n* Geflecht *nt* **II.** *vi* (*gears*) ineinandergreifen

mesmerize ['mez·mə·raɪz] *vt* faszinieren

mess <*pl* -es> [mes] *n* **1.** (*messy state*) Unordnung *f*, Durcheinander *nt* **2.** *usu sing* (*disorganized state*) Chaos *nt*; **to be in a ~** sich in einem schlimmen Zustand befinden

◆ **mess around** *vi* **1.** (*behave foolishly*) herumblödeln *fam*, Unfug treiben **2.** (*waste time*) herumspielen **3.** (*tinker*) herumspielen, herumfummeln (**with** an +*dat*)

◆ **mess up** *vt fam* **1.** (*botch up*) verpfuschen; (*plan*) vermasseln **2.** (*make messy*) in Unordnung bringen

◆ **mess with** *vi* **1.** (*get involved with*) **to ~ with sb** sich mit jdm einlassen; (*cause trouble to*) jdn schlecht behandeln; **don't ~ with me!** verarsch mich

bloß nicht! *derb* **2. to ~ with sth** (*tamper*) an etw *dat* herumspielen

message ['mes·ɪdʒ] *n* (*communication*) Nachricht *f*; **to leave a ~** eine Nachricht hinterlassen ▶ **to get the ~** *fam* kapieren

messenger ['mes·ɪn·dʒər] *n* Bote *m*, Botin *f*

messy ['mes·i] *adj* **1.** (*untidy*) unordentlich; (*person*) schlampig **2.** (*dirty*) schmutzig

met [met] *vt, vi pt of* **meet**

metabolism [mɪ·'tæb·ə·lɪz·əm] *n* Stoffwechsel *m*

metal ['met·əl] **I.** *n* Metall *nt*; **precious ~** Edelmetall *nt* **II.** *adj* aus Metall *nach n*

metallic [mə·'tæl·ɪk] *adj* metallisch; **~ paint** Metalleffektlack *m*

metallurgy ['met·əl·ɜr·dʒi] *n* Metallurgie *f*

'metalwork *n* Metallarbeit *f*

metaphor ['met·ə·fɔr] *n* Metapher *f*

metaphoric(al) [met·ə·'fɔr·ɪk(əl)] *adj* metaphorisch

mete [mit] *vt* **to ~ out ⇆ sth** [**to sb**] [jdm] etw auferlegen

meteor ['mi·ti·ər] *n* Meteor *m*

meteoric [mi·ti·'ɔr·ɪk] *adj* **1.** ASTRON meteorisch **2.** (*rapid*) kometenhaft

meteorological [mi·ti·ə·rə·'lɑdʒ·ɪ·kəl] *adj* meteorologisch

meteorologist [mi·ti·ə·'rɑl·ə·dʒɪst] *n* Meteorologe *m*, Meteorologin *f*

meter[1] ['mi·tər] *n* Messuhr *f*, Zähler *m*; [**parking**] **~** Parkuhr *f*

meter[2] ['mi·tər] *n* (*unit of measurement*) Meter *m*

methane ['meθ·eɪn] *n* Methan *nt*

methanol ['meθ·ə·nɔl] *n* Methanol *nt*

method ['meθ·əd] *n* (*way of doing sth*) Methode *f*; TECH Verfahren *nt*

methodical [mə·'θɑd·ɪ·kəl] *adj* methodisch, systematisch

Methodist ['meθ·ə·dɪst] *n* Methodist(in) *m(f)*

methyl alcohol [meθ·əl·'æl·kə·hɔl] *n see* **methanol**

meticulous [mɪ·'tɪk·ju·ləs] *adj* peinlich genau; **~ detail** kleinstes Detail

metric ['met·rɪk] *adj* metrisch

metro ['met·roʊ] *adj attr short for* **met**

rropolitan Stadt-
netropolitan [ˌmet·rə-ˈpal·ə·tən] *adj* (*of large city*) weltstädtisch; **~ area** Metropolregion *f*
new [mju] *vi* miauen
Mexican [ˈmek·sɪ·kən] **I.** *n* Mexikaner(in) *m(f)* **II.** *adj* mexikanisch
Mexico [ˈmek·sɪ·kou] *n* Mexiko *nt*
ng *n* <*pl* -> *abbr of* **milligram** mg
MHz *n* <*pl* -> *abbr of* **megahertz** MHz
MI *abbr of* **Michigan**
nica [ˈmaɪ·kə] *n* Glimmererde *f*
nice [maɪs] *n pl of* **mouse**
Michigan [ˈmɪʃ·ɪ·gən] *n* Michigan *nt*
Mickey Mouse *adj attr pej fam* Scherzfam; **~ computer** Spielzeugcomputer *m*
nicrobe [ˈmaɪ·kroub] *n* Mikrobe *f*
nicrobiology [ˌmaɪ·krou-] *n* Mikrobiologie *f*
nicrochip *n* Mikrochip *m*
nicroclimate *n* Mikroklima *nt*
nicroelectronics *n* + *sing vb* Mikroelektronik *f*
nicrofilm *n* Mikrofilm *m*
nicroorganism *n* Mikroorganismus *m*
nicrophone *n* Mikrofon *nt*
nicroprocessor *n* Mikroprozessor *m*
nicroscope [ˈmaɪ·krə·skoup] *n* Mikroskop *nt*
nicroscopic [ˌmaɪ·krə·ˈskap·ɪk] *adj*
1. *fam* (*tiny*) winzig; **to look at sth in ~ detail** etw haargenau prüfen **2.** (*analysis, examination*) mikroskopisch
nicrowave I. *n* Mikrowellenherd *m*, Mikrowelle *f* **II.** *vt* in der Mikrowelle kochen/erwärmen
nidday *n* Mittag *m;* **at ~** mittags
niddle [ˈmɪd·əl] **I.** *n* **1.** (*center; between things*) Mitte *f;* (*of fruit, nuts*) Innere[s] *nt;* (*center part: of book, movie*) Mittelteil *nt* **2.** (*in time, space*) mitten; **in the ~ of the road** mitten auf der Straße; **in the ~ of the night** mitten in der Nacht; **in the ~ of nowhere** *fig* am Ende der Welt; **to be in the ~ of eating** (*busy with*) mitten dabei sein zu essen **3.** *fam* (*waist*) Taille *f* **II.** *adj attr* mittlere(r, s)
iddle 'age *n* mittleres Alter
niddle-'aged *adj* mittleren Alters *nach n*

middle 'class *n* **the ~** der Mittelstand
'middle-class *adj* Mittelstands-, mittelständisch
Middle 'East *n* **the ~** der Nahe Osten
'middleman *n* **1.** ECON (*person*) Zwischenhändler(in) *m(f)* **2.** (*go-between*) Mittelsmann *m*
middle 'name *n* zweiter Vorname
middle-of-the-'road *adj* (*film, music*) mittelmäßig
'middleweight *n* SPORT Mittelgewichtler(in) *m(f)*
Mid'east *n* **the ~** der Nahe [*or* Mittlere] Osten
midge [mɪdʒ] *n* [kleine] Mücke
midget [ˈmɪdʒ·ɪt] **I.** *n* (*dwarf*) Liliputaner(in) *m(f)* **II.** *adj* (*small*) winzig
'midnight *n* Mitternacht *f*
'midpoint *n usu sing* Mittelpunkt *m*
midriff [ˈmɪd·rɪf] *n*, **midsection** [ˈmɪd·sek·ʃən] *n* Taille *f*
mid'summer *n* Hochsommer *m*
mid'term *n* (*midpoint: of political office*) Halbzeit *f* der Amtsperiode; (*of school year*) Schulhalbjahr *nt*
midway [ˈmɪd·ˌweɪ] **I.** *adv* auf halbem Weg; **the projector broke ~ through the film** mitten im Film ging der Projektor kaputt **II.** *n* Mittelweg *einer Ausstellung oder eines Jahrmarktes, an dem sich die Hauptattraktionen befinden*
midweek *n* Wochenmitte *f*
midwife [ˈmɪd·waɪf] *n* Hebamme *f*
mid'winter *n* Mitte *f* des Winters
might¹ [maɪt] *n* **1.** (*authority*) Macht *f* **2.** (*strength*) Kraft *f;* MIL Stärke *f*
might² [maɪt] **I.** *pt of* **may II.** *aux vb* **1.** (*expressing possibility*) **I ~ go to the movies tonight** vielleicht gehe ich heute Abend ins Kino; (*could*) **someone called at six; it ~ have been him** um sechs rief jemand an, das könnte er gewesen sein; (*expressing probability*) könnte(n) **2.** *form* (*polite form of may*) **~ I ...?** dürfte ich [vielleicht] ...?; **~ I make a suggestion?** dürfte ich vielleicht einen Vorschlag machen?
mighty [ˈmaɪ·ti] **I.** *adj* (*river*) gewaltig; (*country*) mächtig; (*warrior*) stark **II.** *adv fam* sehr; **that was ~ nice of you** das war wirklich nett von dir

M

migraine ['maɪ·greɪn] n Migräne f

migrant ['maɪ·grənt] n 1. (person) Zuwanderer m, Zuwanderin f 2. (bird) Zugvogel m

migrate ['maɪ·greɪt] vi (change habitat) wandern, umherziehen; **to ~ south** (birds) nach Süden ziehen

migration [maɪ·'greɪ·ʃən] n Wanderung f; (of birds) Zug m

migratory ['maɪ·grə·tɔr·i] adj (animals) Wander-; **~ bird** Zugvogel m

mike [maɪk] n fam short for **microphone** Mikro nt

mild [maɪld] adj 1. (gentle: person) sanft; (soap) schonend; (not severe: shock) leicht; (climate) mild 2. MED (infection) leicht 3. (not strong in flavor: cheese) mild; (cigarette) leicht

mildew ['mɪl·du] n Schimmel m; (on plants) Mehltau m

mildly ['maɪld·li] adv 1. (gently) leicht; (clean) schonend; (not severely) milde 2. (as an understatement) **to put it ~** um es [mal] milde auszudrücken

mildness ['maɪld·nɪs] n 1. (of person) Sanftmut f 2. (of weather) Milde f

mile [maɪl] n 1. (distance) Meile f; **we could see for ~s and ~s** wir konnten meilenweit sehen 2. fam (far from) **to be ~s from the truth** weit von der Wahrheit entfernt sein

mileage, milage ['maɪ·lɪdʒ] n 1. (gasoline efficiency) Kraftstoffverbrauch m 2. (distance traveled) Meilenstand m

'milestone n a. fig Meilenstein m

militant ['mɪl·ɪ·tənt] adj militant

militaristic [ˌmɪl·ɪ·tə·'rɪs·tɪk] adj militaristisch

military ['mɪl·ɪ·ter·i] n pl **the ~** das Militär

military po'lice npl **the ~** die Militärpolizei

military 'service n Wehrdienst m

militia [mɪ·'lɪʃ·ə] n Miliz f

milk [mɪlk] I. n Milch f; (breast milk) Muttermilch f; (in coconuts) Kokosmilch f; **whole ~** Vollmilch f II. vt (cow) melken

milk 'chocolate n Milchschokolade f

'milkman n Milchmann m

'milk shake n Milchshake m

milky ['mɪl·ki] adj 1. (with milk) m? Milch nach n 2. (not clear: glass, wa ter) milchig; (skin) sanft

Milky 'Way n **the ~** die Milchstraße

mill [mɪl] I. n 1. (building, machine Mühle f 2. (factory) Fabrik f; **steel ~** Stahlwerk nt II. vt (grain) mahler (metal) walzen

millennium <pl -s> [mɪ·'len·i·əm] n Jahr tausend nt

miller ['mɪl·ər] n Müller(in) m(f)

millet ['mɪl·ət] n Hirse f

milligram ['mɪl·ɪ·ɡræm] n Milligramm r

milliliter ['mɪl·ɪ·ˌli·tər] n Milliliter m

millimeter ['mɪl·ɪ·ˌmi·tər] n Millimeter r

million ['mɪl·jən] n 1. (1,000,000) Mil lion f; **a ~ dollars** eine Million Dol lar 2. fam (countless number) **I've already heard that story a ~ time** diese Geschichte habe ich schon tau sendmal gehört

millionaire [ˌmɪl·jə·'ner] n Millionär m

'millstone n Mühlstein m

mime [maɪm] I. n THEAT Pantomime n Pantomimin f II. vt (conceal) pantomimisc darstellen; (mimic) mimen

mimic ['mɪm·ɪk] vt <-ck-> nachahmer (when teasing) nachäffen pej

min. I. n 1. abbr of **minimum** Mir 2. abbr of **minute** Min. II. adj abbr ‹ **minimum** min.

minaret [ˌmɪn·ə·'ret] n Minarett nt

mince [mɪns] vt FOOD hacken; (in grinde durch den Fleischwolf drehen; (onion: klein schneiden ▶ **to not ~ [one's words** kein Blatt vor den Mund neh men

'mincemeat n süße Gebäckfüllung au Dörrobst und Gewürze

mincer ['mɪn·sər] n Fleischwolf m

mind [maɪnd] n 1. (brain, intellec Geist m; (sanity a.) Verstand m; **to hav a logical ~** logisch denken können; t **use one's ~** seinen Verstand gebrauche 2. (thoughts) Gedanken pl; **what's o your ~?** woran denkst du?; **to bear st in ~** etw nicht vergessen; **to have sb sth in ~** an jdn/etw denken 3. (inte tion) **to make up one's ~** sich entsche den; **to set one's ~ to sth** sich dat et in den Kopf setzen 4. usu sing (opinio

Meinung *f;* **to change one's ~** es sich *dat* anders überlegen ▶ **to be out of one's ~** (*crazy*) übergeschnappt sein II. *vt* 1. (*be careful of, look after*) aufpassen auf +*akk* 2. (*care about*) **don't ~ me** kümmere dich nicht um mich; **I don't ~ the heat** die Hitze macht mir nichts aus 3. *fam* (*object*) **do you ~ if I smoke?** stört es Sie, wenn ich rauche?; **I wouldn't ~ a cup of coffee** gegen eine Tasse Kaffee hätte ich nichts einzuwenden ▶ **you** allerdings III. *vi* 1. (*care*) sich *dat* etwas daraus machen; **I don't ~** das ist mir egal; **never ~!** [ist doch] egal! 2. (*object*) etwas dagegen haben

'**mind-bending** *adj fam* (*puzzle*) knifflig

'**mind-blowing** *adj sl* irre *fam*

'**mind-boggling** *adj fam* irrsinnig *fam,* verrückt

minded ['maɪn·dɪd] *adj pred* **to be mathematically ~** eine mathematische Neigung haben

mindful ['maɪnd·fəl] *adj pred* **to be ~ of sb's feelings** jds Gefühle berücksichtigen

mindless ['maɪnd·lɪs] *adj* 1. (*pointless*) sinnlos; (*violence, jealousy*) blind 2. (*not intellectual: work*) geistlos; (*entertainment*) anspruchslos

'**mind reader** *n* Gedankenleser(in) *m(f)*

'**mindset** *n* Denkart *f*

mine[1] [maɪn] I. *n* 1. Bergwerk *nt; fig* (*valuable source*) Fundgrube *f* 2. MIL (*explosive*) Mine *f* II. *vt* (*coal, iron*) abbauen, fördern; (*gold*) schürfen III. *vi* **to ~ for gold** nach Gold graben

mine[2] [maɪn] *pron poss* (*belonging to me*) meine(r, s); **she's an old friend of ~** sie ist eine alte Freundin von mir

'**minefield** *n* Minenfeld *nt; fig* gefährliches Terrain

miner ['maɪ·nər] *n* Bergarbeiter(in) *m(f)*

mineral ['mɪn·ər·əl] *n* Mineral *nt*

'**mineral deposits** *npl* Erzlagerstätten *pl*

mineralogist [ˌmɪn·ə·'ral·ə·dʒɪst] *n* Mineraloge *m,* Mineralogin *f*

'**mineral water** *n* Mineralwasser *nt;* (*carbonated*) Sprudel *m*

'**minesweeper** *n* NAUT Minenräumer *m*

mingle ['mɪŋ·gəl] I. *vt usu passive* mi-

schen II. *vi* 1. (*socialize*) sich untereinander vermischen 2. (*mix*) sich vermischen

mini- ['mɪni] *comp* Mini-

miniature ['mɪn·i·ə·tʃər] I. *adj attr* Miniatur- *f* II. *n* Miniatur *f*

'**minibus** *n* Kleinbus *m*

minimal ['mɪn·ɪ·məl] *adj* minimal, Mindest-

minimize ['mɪn·ɪ·maɪz] *vt* (*reduce*) auf ein Minimum beschränken, minimieren

minimum ['mɪn·ɪ·məm] I. *n* <*pl* -**s**> Minimum *nt* II. *adj* 1. (*lowest possible*) Mindest-; **~ requirements** Mindestanforderungen *pl* 2. (*very low*) Minimal-

minimum-security 'prison *n* offenes Gefängnis

minimum 'wage *n* Mindestlohn *m*

mining ['maɪ·nɪŋ] *n* Bergbau *m*

'**mining engineer** *n* Bergbauingenieur(in) *m(f)*

'**miniskirt** *n* Minirock *m*

minister ['mɪn·ɪ·stər] *n* 1. (*protestant priest*) Pfarrer(in) *m(f)* 2. (*in government*) Minister(in) *m(f)*

ministerial [ˌmɪn·ɪ·'stɪr·i·əl] *adj* Minister-, ministeriell

ministry ['mɪn·ɪ·stri] *n* Ministerium *nt*

mink [mɪŋk] *n* <*pl* -> Nerz *m*

Minn. *abbr of* **Minnesota**

Minnesota [ˌmɪn·ɪ·'sou·tə] *n* Minnesota *nt*

minor ['maɪ·nər] I. *adj* 1. (*small, not serious: detail*) nebensächlich; (*crime*) geringfügig; (*repair*) unwichtig; (*illness*) leicht 2. (*low-ranking*) untergeordnet II. *n* (*underage person*) Minderjährige(r) *f(m)*

minority [maɪ·'nɔr·ɪ·ti] *n* Minderheit *f;* **in a ~ of cases** in wenigen Fällen

mint[1] [mɪnt] I. *n* 1. (*coin factory*) Münzanstalt *f,* Prägeanstalt *f* 2. *fam* (*lots of money*) **to make a ~** einen Haufen Geld machen *fam* II. *vt* (*money*) prägen; (*gold, silver*) münzen

mint[2] [mɪnt] *n* 1. (*herb*) Minze *f* 2. (*candy*) Pfefferminz[bonbon] *nt*

minus ['maɪ·nəs] I. *prep* MATH minus; **what is 57 ~ 39?** was ist 57 minus 39? II. *n* <*pl* -**es**> Minus[zeichen] *nt*

M

III. *adj attr* (*number*) minus; **~ ten** [degrees] **Fahrenheit** minus zehn Grad Fahrenheit

minuscule ['mɪn·ə·skjul] *adj* winzig

minute¹ ['mɪn·ɪt] **I.** *n* **1.** Minute *f* **2.** (*short time*) Moment *m;* [**wait**] **just a ~!** (*for delay*) einen Moment noch!; (*in disbelief*) Moment mal! **II.** *adj attr* **~ hand** Minutenzeiger *m*

minute² [maɪ·'nut] *adj* winzig; **in ~ detail** bis ins kleinste Detail

minutely [maɪ·'nut·li] *adv* bis ins kleinste Detail

miracle ['mɪr·ə·kəl] *n* Wunder *nt a. fig*

miraculous [mɪ·'ræk·jə·ləs] *adj* wunderbar; **to make a ~ recovery** wie durch ein Wunder genesen

mirage [mə·'raʒ] *n fig* Trugbild *nt*, Illusion *f*

mirror ['mɪr·ər] **I.** *n* Spiegel *m* **II.** *vt* widerspiegeln

mirror image *n* Spiegelbild *nt*

misapprehension [ˌmɪs·æprɪ·'hen·ʃən] *n* Missverständnis *nt*

misappropriate [ˌmɪs·ə·'prou·pri·eɪt] *vt* (*funds*) veruntreuen

misbehave [ˌmɪs·bɪ·'heɪv] *vi* (*behave badly: adult*) sich schlecht benehmen; (*child*) ungezogen sein

misbehavior [ˌmɪs·bɪ·'heɪv·jər] *n* (*by adult*) schlechtes Benehmen; (*by child*) Ungezogenheit *f*

misc. *adj short for* **miscellaneous** verschiedene(r, s)

miscalculate [ˌmɪs·'kæl·kjə·leɪt] *vt* **1.** MATH falsch berechnen **2.** (*misjudge*) falsch einschätzen

miscarriage ['mɪs·kær·ɪdʒ] *n* **1.** MED Fehlgeburt *f* **2.** LAW **~ of justice** Justizirrtum *m*

miscellaneous [ˌmɪs·ə·'leɪ·ni·əs] *adj* verschiedene(r, s), diverse(r, s)

mischief ['mɪs·tʃɪf] *n* Unfug *m;* **to keep sb out of ~** jdn davon abhalten, Dummheiten zu machen; **to mean ~** Unfrieden stiften wollen

mischievous ['mɪs·tʃə·vəs] *adj* immer zu Streichen aufgelegt; **~ child** Schlingel *m*

misconception [ˌmɪs·kən·'sep·ʃən] *n* falsche Vorstellung

misconduct [ˌmɪs·'kan·dʌkt] *n* (*bad behavior*) schlechtes Benehmen; MIL schlechte Führung; **professional ~** standeswidriges Verhalten

misconstrue [ˌmɪs·kən·'stru] *vt* missdeuten, missverstehen, falsch auslegen

misdemeanor [ˌmɪs·dɪ·'mi·nər] *n* **1.** (*minor bad action*) [leichtes] Vergehen [leichter] Verstoß **2.** LAW geringfügiges Vergehen

misdirect [ˌmɪs·dɪ·'rekt] *vt* **1.** (*send in wrong direction*) in die falsche Richtung schicken; (*letter*) falsch adressieren **2.** (*aim wrongly: hockey puck*) in die falsche Richtung lenken

miser ['maɪ·zər] *n* Geizhals *m*

miserable ['mɪz·rə·bəl] *adj* **1.** (*unhappy*) unglücklich, elend; **to make life ~** [for sb] [jdm] das Leben unerträglich machen **2.** *attr* (*bad-tempered*) griesgrämig; *fam* (*as insult*) mies, Mist-

miserably ['mɪz·ər·ə·bli] *adv* **1.** (*unhappily*) traurig **2.** (*extremely*) schrecklich furchtbar **3.** (*utterly*) jämmerlich

miserliness ['maɪ·zər·li·nɪs] *n* Geiz *m*

miserly ['maɪ·zər·li] *adj* geizig

misery ['mɪz·ə·ri] *n* **1.** (*suffering*) Elend *nt*, Not *f* **2.** (*unhappiness*) Jammer *m* ▶ **to make sb's life a ~** jdm das Leben zur Qual [*or* Hölle] machen

misfire *vi* [mɪs·'faɪr] (*engine*) eine Fehlzündung haben; (*gun*) versagen

misfit ['mɪs·fɪt] *n* Außenseiter(in) *m(f)*

misfortune [mɪs·'fɔr·tʃən] *n* (*bad luck*) Pech *nt*, Unglück *nt*

misguided [mɪs·'gaɪ·dɪd] *adj* (*attempt measures*) unsinnig; (*effort, policy*) verfehlt; (*enthusiasm*) falsch, unangebracht **to be ~ in sth** mit etw *dat* falschliegen

mishandle [mɪs·'hæn·dəl] *vt* (*misman age*) falsch behandeln; (*business*) schlecht führen; (*investigation*) [grobe] Fehler machen bei +*dat*

mishap ['mɪs·hæp] *n* Unfall *m*, Panne *f*

mishear [ˌmɪs·'hɪr] **I.** *vt* <-heard -heard> falsch hören **II.** *vi* <-heard -heard> sich verhören

mishmash ['mɪʃ·mæʃ] *n* Mischmasch *m fam*

misinform [ˌmɪs·ɪn·'fɔrm] *vt* falsch informieren

misinterpret [ˌmɪs·ɪn·ˈtɜr·prɪt] vt missverstehen; (text) falsch interpretieren

misinterpretation [ˌmɪs·ɪn·tɜr·prɪ·ˈteɪ·ʃən] n Missverständnis nt, Fehlinterpretation f

misjudge [ˌmɪs·ˈdʒʌdʒ] vt (situation) falsch einschätzen [or beurteilen]; (amount, distance) falsch schätzen

mislay <-laid, -laid> [ˌmɪs·ˈleɪ] vt verlegen

mislead <-led, -led> [ˌmɪs·ˈlid] vt (deceive) täuschen

misleading [mɪs·ˈli·dɪŋ] adj irreführend

mismanage [ˌmɪs·ˈmæn·ɪdʒ] vt falsch umgehen mit +dat; (business) schlecht führen

mismanagement [ˌmɪs·ˈmæn·ɪdʒ·mənt] n schlechte Verwaltung [or Führung]

misnomer [ˌmɪs·ˈnoʊ·mər] n (inappropriate name) unzutreffende Bezeichnung

misogynist [mɪ·ˈsɑdʒ·ə·nɪst] n Frauenfeind m

misplace [ˌmɪs·ˈpleɪs] vt verlegen

misprint [ˈmɪs·ˌprɪnt] n Druckfehler m

mispronounce [ˌmɪs·prə·ˈnaʊns] vt falsch aussprechen

misread <-read, -read> [ˌmɪs·ˈrid] vt 1. (read incorrectly) falsch lesen 2. (misinterpret) falsch verstehen

misrepresent [ˌmɪs·rep·rɪ·ˈzent] vt falsch darstellen

misrepresentation [ˌmɪs·rep·rɪ·zen·ˈteɪ·ʃən] n falsche Darstellung; LAW falsche Angabe

miss¹ [mɪs] I. n <pl -es> (failure) Fehlschlag m; SPORT (in basketball) Fehlwurf m II. vi nicht treffen; (projectile a.) danebengehen; (person, weapon a.) danebenschießen III. vt 1. (not hit) nicht treffen 2. (train) verpassen; (deadline) nicht [ein]halten 3. (be absent) versäumen; to ~ school in der Schule fehlen 4. (opportunity) verpassen 5. (not notice) nicht bemerken; (deliberately) übersehen 6. (notice loss, long for) vermissen

miss out vi zu kurz kommen; to ~ out on sth (chance, opportunity) sich dat etw entgehen lassen

miss² [mɪs] n M~ Fräulein nt

Miss. abbr of **Mississippi**

misshapen [mɪs·ˈʃeɪ·pən] adj (out of shape) unförmig

missile [ˈmɪs·əl] n MIL Flugkörper m, Rakete f

'missile base n Raketenstützpunkt m

'missile launcher n [Raketen]abschussrampe f

missing [ˈmɪs·ɪŋ] adj 1. (disappeared: thing) verschwunden; (person) vermisst; (not there) fehlend; to report sb ~ jdn als vermisst melden 2. MIL ~ in action [nach Kampfeinsatz] vermisst

missing 'link n 1. (in evolution) unbekannte Zwischenstufe 2. (connector) Bindeglied nt

missing 'person n Vermisste(r) f(m)

mission [ˈmɪʃ·ən] n 1. (task) Einsatz m, Mission f 2. (goal) Ziel nt

mission con'trol n Bodenkontrolle f

Mississippi [mɪs·ɪ·ˈsɪ·pi] n Mississippi nt

Missouri [mɪ·ˈzʊr·i] n Missouri nt

misspell <-spelled or -spelt, -spelled> [ˌmɪs·ˈspel] vt (spell wrongly) falsch buchstabieren

mist [mɪst] n 1. (light fog) [leichter] Nebel, Dunst m 2. (condensation) Beschlag m

mistake [mɪ·ˈsteɪk] I. n Fehler m, Irrtum m; spelling ~ Rechtschreibfehler m; by ~ aus Versehen, versehentlich II. vt <-took, -taken> falsch verstehen; there's no mistaking a painting by Picasso ein Gemälde von Picasso ist unverwechselbar

mistaken [mɪ·ˈsteɪ·kən] I. pp of **mistake** II. adj (announcement) irrtümlich; (idea) falsch; ~ identity Personenverwechslung f; to be ~ sich irren (about in +dat)

Mister [ˈmɪs·tər] n 1. (Mr.) Herr m 2. a. iron fam (form of address) Chef m; hey, ~! he, Sie da! fam

mistletoe [ˈmɪs·əl·toʊ] n Mistel f

mistook [mɪ·ˈstʊk] pt of **mistake**

mistreat [ˌmɪs·ˈtrit] vt misshandeln

mistress <pl -es> [ˈmɪs·trɪs] n (sexual partner) Geliebte f

mistrial [ˌmɪs·ˌtraɪ·əl] n (misconducted trial) fehlerhaftes Gerichtsverfahren

mistrust [ˌmɪs·ˈtrʌst] I. n Misstrauen nt II. vt misstrauen

M

mistrustful ['mɪs·'trʌst·fəl] *adj* misstrauisch (**of** gegenüber +*dat*)

misty ['mɪs·ti] *adj* 1. (*slightly foggy*) [leicht] neblig 2. (*blurred*) undeutlich

misunderstand <-stood, -stood> [ˌmɪs·ˌʌn·dər·'stænd] I. *vt* missverstehen II. *vi* sich irren

misunderstanding [ˌmɪs·ʌn·dər·'stæn·dɪŋ] *n* 1. (*misinterpretation*) Missverständnis *nt* 2. (*quarrel*) Meinungsverschiedenheit *f*

misuse I. *n* [ˌmɪs·'jus] (*wrong use: of funds, position*) falscher Gebrauch [*or* Umgang] II. *vt* [ˌmɪs·'juz] (*funds, position*) missbrauchen, falsch gebrauchen

mitten ['mɪt·ən] *n* Fäustling *m*

mix [mɪks] I. *n* 1. (*combination*) Mischung *f* 2. (*premixed ingredients*) Fertigmischung *f*; **sauce** ~ Fertigsauce *f* II. *vi* 1. (*combine*) sich mischen [lassen]; (*go together*) zusammenpassen 2. (*make contact with people*) unter Leute gehen; (*host*) sich unter die Gäste mischen III. *vt* 1. (*blend*) [miteinander] [ver]mischen; (*drinks*) mixen; (*paint*) mischen 2. (*sound tracks*) mischen

♦**mix in** I. *vi* sich einfügen II. *vt* untermischen

♦**mix up** *vt* 1. (*mistake for another*) verwechseln 2. (*combine ingredients*) vermischen 3. *usu passive* (*be involved with*) **to be/get ~ed up in sth** in etw *akk* verwickelt sein/werden

mixed [mɪkst] *adj* (*positive and negative*) gemischt; ~ **blessing** kein reiner Segen

mixed 'doubles *npl* SPORT gemischtes Doppel

mixed e'conomy *n* gemischte Wirtschaftsform

mixer ['mɪk·sər] *n* 1. (*machine*) Mixgerät *nt* 2. (*drink*) ~ [**drink**] Mixgetränk *nt*

mixture ['mɪks·tʃər] *n* 1. (*combination*) Mischung *f*; (*of ingredients*) Gemisch *nt* 2. (*mixed fluid substance*) Mischung *f*; AUTO Gemisch *nt*

'mix-up *n* (*confused state*) Durcheinander *nt*, Verwirrung *f*

ml <*pl* -> *n abbr of* **milliliter** ml

MLB [ˌem·el·'bi] *n* SPORT *abbr of* Major

League Baseball MLB *f*

mm *n abbr of* **millimeter** mm

MN *abbr of* **Minnesota**

MO [ˌem·'ou] *n* 1. *abbr of* **Missouri** 2. *abbr of* **modus operandi** Arbeitsweise *f* 3. *abbr of* **Medical Officer** Stabsarzt *m*, Stabsärztin *f*

mo. [mou] *n abbr of* **month**

moan [moun] I. *n* (*groan*) Stöhnen *nt*, (*of the wind*) Heulen II. *vi* 1. (*groan*) stöhnen; (*wind*) heulen 2. (*complain*) klagen, sich beschweren (**at** bei +*dat*)

mob [mab] I. *n* 1. *usu pej* (*crowd*) Mob *m*; **angry** ~ aufgebrachte Menge 2. (*criminal gang*) Verbrecherbande *f*, Gang *f*; **the M~** die Mafia II. *vt* <-bb-> (*surround*) umringen

mobile ['mou·bəl] I. *adj* 1. (*able to move, flexible*) beweglich 2. (*in a vehicle*) mobil, fahrbar; **to be** ~ motorisiert sein II. *n* (*ceiling decoration*) Mobile *nt*

mobile 'home *n* [großer] Wohnwagen *m*, Trailer *m*

mobility [mou·'bɪl·ɪ·ți] *n* Mobilität *f*

mobilize ['mou·bə·laɪz] *vt* 1. (*prepare for war: army*) mobilisieren 2. (*organize supporters*) aktivieren, mobilisieren 3. (*put to use*) einsetzen; (*snowplows*) zum Einsatz bringen

mobster ['mab·stər] *n fam* Gangster *m*

moccasin ['mak·ə·sɪn] *n* Mokassin *m*

mock [mak] I. *adj* nachgemacht, Schein-(*sympathy*) gespielt II. *vt* (*ridicule*) lächerlich machen, verspotten

mockery ['mak·ə·ri] *n* (*ridicule*) Spott *m*, Hohn *m*

'mockingbird *n* ORN Spottdrossel *f*

mode [moud] *n* 1. (*way*) Weise *f*, Methode *f*; ~ **of operation** Betriebsart 2. COMPUT, TECH (*operation*) Betriebsart *f*, Modus *m*

model ['mad·əl] I. *n* 1. Modell *nt*; COMPUT [schematische Darstellung, Simulation 2. (*example*) Vorbild *nt* 3. (*perfect example*) Muster *nt* 4. (*fashion*) Model *n* II. *vt* <-ll-> 1. (*make figure*) modellieren 2. (*on computer*) [schematisch darstellen, simulieren 3. (*show clothes*) vorführen

modem ['mou·dəm] *n* Modem *nt*

ⲙoderate I. adj ['mɑd·ər·ət] **1.** (neither large nor small: amount, quantity, size) mittlere(r, s); (prices) angemessen **2.** (not excessive) mäßig, gemäßigt; LAW (sentence) mild **II.** n ['mɑd·ər·ət] POL Gemäßigte(r) f/m **III.** vt ['mɑd·ər·eɪt] (make less extreme) mäßigen

ⲙoderation [ˌmɑd·ə·'reɪ·ʃən] n Mäßigung f; **in ~** in Maßen

ⲙoderator ['mɑd·ə·reɪ·tər] n **1.** (mediator) Vermittler(in) m/f **2.** (of discussion) Moderator(in) m/f

ⲙodern ['mɑd·ərn] adj modern

ⲙodernize ['mɑd·ər·naɪz] **I.** vt modernisieren **II.** vi modern werden

ⲙodest ['mɑd·ɪst] adj **1.** (not boastful) bescheiden **2.** (fairly small: income) bescheiden, mäßig

ⲙodesty ['mɑd·ɪ·sti] n **1.** (without boastfulness) Bescheidenheit f **2.** (chasteness) Anstand m

ⲙodification [ˌmɑd·ɪ·fɪ·'keɪ·ʃən] n Modifikation f

ⲙodifier ['mɑd·ɪ·faɪ·ər] n LING näher bestimmendes Wort; (as an adjective) Beiwort nt; (as an adverb) Umstandswort nt

ⲙodify <-ie-> ['mɑd·ɪ·faɪ] vt **1.** (change) [ver]ändern **2.** (alter: engine) modifizieren

ⲙodular ['mɑdʒ·ə·lər] adj modular, Baukasten-

ⲙodule ['mɑdʒ·ul] n Modul nt

ⲙohair ['moʊ·her] n Mohair m

ⲙoist [mɔɪst] adj feucht; (cake) saftig

ⲙoisten ['mɔɪ·sən] vt anfeuchten

ⲙoisture ['mɔɪs·tʃər] n Feuchtigkeit f

ⲙoisturize ['mɔɪs·tʃə·raɪz] vt befeuchten

ⲙoisturizer ['mɔɪs·tʃə·raɪ·zər] n Feuchtigkeitscreme f

ⲙolasses [moʊ·'læs·ɪz] n Melasse f

ⲙold¹ [moʊld] **I.** n **1.** (shape) Form f **2.** fig Typ m; **to break the ~ [of sth]** neue Wege in etw dat gehen **II.** vt formen

ⲙold² [moʊld] n BOT Schimmel m

ⲙolding ['moʊl·dɪŋ] n ARCHIT Fries m; ART [Zier]leiste f

ⲙoldy ['moʊl·di] adj (food) schimmelig

ⲙole¹ [moʊl] n ANAT [kleines] Muttermal nt

ⲙole² [moʊl] n ZOOL Maulwurf m

molecular [mə·'lek·jə·lər] adj molekular, Molekular-

molecule ['mɑl·ɪ·kjul] n Molekül nt

molehill ['moʊl·hɪl] n Maulwurfshügel m

molest [mə·'lest] vt **1.** (annoy) belästigen **2.** (attack sexually) [sexuell] belästigen

mollusk, mollusc ['mɑl·əsk] n Molluske f, Weichtier nt

molt [moʊlt] vi (birds) [sich] mausern; (cats, dogs) haaren; (snakes, insects) sich häuten

molten ['moʊl·tən] adj geschmolzen

mom [mɑm] n Mama f, Mutti f bes nordd

mom-and-pop store n Tante-Emma-Laden m fam

moment ['moʊ·mənt] n **1.** (very short time) Moment m, Augenblick m; **at any ~** jeden Augenblick; **in a ~** gleich, sofort **2.** (specific time) Zeitpunkt m; **at the ~** im Augenblick, momentan

momentarily [ˌmoʊ·mən·'ter·ɪ·li] adv **1.** (briefly) kurz, eine Weile **2.** (very soon) gleich

momentary ['moʊ·mən·ter·i] adj kurz

momentous [moʊ·'men·təs] adj bedeutsam, folgenschwer; (day) bedeutend

momentum [moʊ·'men·təm] n (force) Schwung m, Wucht f; **to gain ~** in Schwung kommen

momma ['mɑ·mə] n childspeak Mama f

mommy ['mɑm·i] n childspeak Mama f, Mami f

monarchy ['mɑn·ər·ki] n Monarchie f

monastery ['mɑn·ə·ster·i] n [Mönchs]kloster nt

monastic [mə·'næs·tɪk] adj REL mönchisch

Monday ['mʌn·di] n Montag m; see also **Tuesday**

monetary ['mɑn·ə·ter·i] adj ECON Geld-, Währungs-

money ['mʌn·i] n **1.** (cash) Geld nt; **to be short on ~** knapp bei Kasse sein fam; **to put ~ into sth** Geld in etw akk stecken fam **2.** fam (pay) Bezahlung f, Verdienst m ▶ **easy ~** leicht verdientes Geld

moneyed ['mʌn·id] adj form vermögend

'moneymaker n **1.** (person) erfolgreicher Geschäftsmann/erfolgreiche Geschäftsfrau **2.** (profitable business) gewinnbringendes Geschäft fam **3.** (profit-

M

able product) Verkaufsschlager *m fam*

'**money market** *n* Geldmarkt *m*

mongrel ['maŋ·grəl] *n* **1.** BOT, ZOOL (*result of crossing*) Kreuzung *f* **2.** *esp pej* (*dog breed*) Promenadenmischung *f hum o pej*

monitor ['man·ɪ·tər] **I.** *n* **1.** Bildschirm *m*, Monitor *m* **2.** POL (*observer*) Beobachter(in) *m(f)* **II.** *vt* **1.** (*check*) beobachten, kontrollieren **2.** RADIO, TELEC, TV (*view, listen in on*) abhören **3.** (*maintain quality, keep under surveillance*) überwachen

monk [mʌŋk] *n* Mönch *m*

monkey ['mʌŋ·ki] *n* Affe *m*

◆**monkey around** *vi fam* **1.** (*waste time*) seine Zeit verschwenden **2.** *pej* (*play*) **to ~ around with sth** mit etw *dat* herumspielen

'**monkey business** *n* **1.** (*silliness*) Blödsinn *m* **2.** (*trickery*) faule Tricks *pl*

'**monkey wrench** *n* Universal[schrauben]schlüssel *m*

monochrome ['man·ou·kroum] *adj* PHOT Schwarzweiß-

monogamy [mə·'nag·ə·mi] *n* Monogamie *f*

monogram ['man·ə·græm] *n* Monogramm *nt*

monolingual [,man·ou·'lɪŋ·gwəl] *adj* einsprachig

monologue, monolog ['man·ə·lag] *n* Monolog *m*

monopolize [mə·'nap·ə·laɪz] *vt* **1.** ECON (*control*) monopolisieren **2.** (*keep for oneself*) ganz für sich *akk* beanspruchen; (*conversation*) an sich *akk* reißen

monopoly [mə·'nap·ə·li] *n* Monopol *nt*

monorail ['man·ou·reɪl] *n* Einschienenbahn *f*

monosodium glutamate [,man·ou·sou·di·əm·'glu·tə·meɪt] *n* CHEM [Mono]natriumglutamat *nt*, Glutamat *nt*

monosyllabic [,man·ə·sɪ·'læb·ɪk] *adj pej* (*taciturn*) wortkarg

monotonous [mə·'nat·ən·əs] *adj* eintönig, monoton

monsoon [man·'sun] *n* the **~**[s] der Monsun *kein pl*

monster ['man·stər] **I.** *n* **1.** (*imaginary creature*) Monster *nt*, Ungeheuer *nt*

2. (*unpleasant person*) Scheusal *nt*; (*inhuman person*) Unmensch *m* **3.** *far* (*huge thing*) Ungetüm *nt*, Monstrum *r* **II.** *adj attr fam* (*huge*) ungeheuer

monstrous ['man·strəs] *adj* **1.** (*huge* ungeheuer, monströs **2.** (*awful*) scheuß lich; (*cruelty*) abscheulich

Mont. *abbr of* **Montana**

montage [man·'taʒ] *n* Montage *f*

Montana [man·'tæn·ə] *n* Montana *nt*

month [mʌnθ] *n* Monat *m*; **to take two-~ vacation** zwei Monate Urlau nehmen

monthly ['mʌnθ·li] **I.** *adj, adv* monatlic **II.** *n* Monatsschrift *f*

monument ['man·jə·mənt] *n* **1.** *fig* (*me morial*) Mahnmal *nt* **2.** (*historical struc ture*) Denkmal *nt*

monumental [,man·jə·'men·təl] *ac* **1.** (*tremendous*) gewaltig, kolossε **2.** ART (*large-scale*) monumental

moo [mu] *vi* muhen

mood [mud] *n* Laune *f*, Stimmung *f*; **in good ~** gut gelaunt; **to not be in the ~ to do sth** zu etw *dat* keine Lust haben

moodiness ['mu·dɪ·nɪs] *n* (*sullenness* Missmut *m*, Verdrossenheit *f*; (*grump ness*) Übellaunigkeit *f*

moody ['mu·di] *adj* **1.** (*temperamenta* launisch **2.** (*sullen*) missmutig

moon [mun] *n* ASTRON Mond *m*; **full ~** Vollmond *m* ► **to be over the ~ abou sth** über etw *akk* überglücklich sein

'**moonbeam** *n* Mondstrahl *m*

'**moonlight** **I.** *n* (*moonshine*) Mond licht *nt* **II.** *vi* <-lighted> *fam* (*work at second job*) schwarzarbeiten

'**moonshine** *n fam* (*liquor*) schwarzge brannter Alkohol

moor[1] [mʊr] *vt, vi* NAUT festmachen

moor[2] [mʊr] *n* Heideland *nt*, [Hoch moor *nt*

mooring ['mʊr·ɪŋ] *n* NAUT (*berth*) Lie geplatz *m*

moose <*pl* -> [mus] *n* Elch *m*

mop [map] **I.** *n* **1.** (*for cleaning*) Mopp *r* **2.** (*wiping*) **to give sth a ~** etw moppei **II.** *vt* <-pp-> feucht wischen

mope [moup] *vi* Trübsal blasen

◆**mope around** *vi fam* trübsinnig her umschleichen

oral ['mɔr·əl] I. adj 1. (ethical) moralisch, ethisch 2. (virtuous: person) moralisch, anständig II. n 1. (of story) Moral f 2. (standards of behavior) ~s pl Moralvorstellungen pl

norale [mə·'ræl] n Moral f

norality [mə·'ræl·ɪ·t̬i] n 1. (moral principles) moralische Grundsätze 2. (moral system) Ethik f

noralize ['mɔr·ə·laɪz] vi moralisieren

noratorium <pl -s> [ˌmɔr·ə·'tɔr·i·əm] n 1. (period of waiting) Wartefrist f 2. COMM Moratorium nt

norbid ['mɔr·bɪd] adj (unhealthy) morbid, krankhaft

nore [mɔr] I. adj comp of many, much noch mehr; **two ~ days until Christmas** noch zwei Tage bis Weihnachten; **we can't take any ~ calls** wir können keine weiteren Anrufe entgegennehmen; **some ~ coffee?** noch etwas Kaffee? II. pron 1. (greater amount) mehr; ~ **and ~ came** es kamen immer mehr; **is there any ~?** ist noch etwas da?; **no ~** nichts weiter; (countable) keine mehr 2. **all the ~** ... umso mehr ...; **the ~ the better** je mehr, desto besser III. adv 1. (forming comparatives) **let's find a ~ sensible way of doing it** wir sollten eine vernünftigere Lösung finden; ~ **importantly** wichtiger noch 2. (to a greater extent) mehr; **you should listen ~ and talk less** du solltest besser zuhören und weniger reden ▶ ~ **or less** (all in all) mehr oder weniger; (approximately) ungefähr

norgue [mɔrg] n Leichen|schau|haus nt

Mormon ['mɔr·mən] n Mormone m, Mormonin f

norning ['mɔr·nɪŋ] I. n Morgen m, Vormittag m; **tomorrow** ~ morgen Vormittag; **yesterday** ~ gestern Morgen II. interj fam Morgen!; **good** ~! guten Morgen!

morning sickness n morgendliche Übelkeit

noron ['mɔr·ɑn] n pej fam Trottel m

noronic [mɔ·'rɑn·ɪk] adj pej fam blöde

norose [mə·'roʊs] adj mürrisch

norphine ['mɔr·fin] n Morphium nt

Morse [mɔrs], **Morse 'code** n Morsealphabet nt

morsel ['mɔr·səl] n (of food) Bissen m, Happen m

mortal ['mɔr·t̬əl] adj 1. sterblich 2. (fatal) tödlich

mortality [mɔr·'tæl·ɪ·t̬i] n Sterblichkeit f

mortar ['mɔr·t̬ər] n 1. ARCHIT, TECH (mixture) Mörtel m 2. CHEM Mörser m; ~ **and pestle** Mörser m und Stößel m

'mortar shell n Mörsergranate f

mortgage ['mɔr·gɪdʒ] n Hypothek f

mortician [mɔr·'tɪʃ·ən] n Leichenbestatter(in) m(f)

mortify <-ie-> ['mɔr·t̬ə·faɪ] vt usu passive **to be mortified** (be humiliated) gedemütigt sein; (be embarrassed) sich ärgern

mortuary ['mɔr·tʃu·er·i] n Leichen|schau|haus nt

mosaic [moʊ·'zeɪ·ɪk] n Mosaik nt

Moscow ['mɑs·kaʊ] n Moskau nt

Moslem ['mɑz·ləm] adj, n see **Muslim**

mosque [mɑsk] n Moschee f

mosquito <pl -es> [mə·'ski·t̬oʊ] n Moskito m; ~ **net** Moskitonetz nt

moss <pl -es> [mɑs] n (plant) Moos nt

mossy ['mɑs·i] adj 1. (overgrown with moss) moosbedeckt 2. (resembling moss) moosartig

most [moʊst] I. pron 1. (largest quantity) **the** ~ am meisten; **at the** [very] ~ [aller]höchstens 2. pl (the majority) die Mehrheit 3. (best) **the** ~ höchstens; **to make the** ~ **of sth** das Beste aus etw dat machen II. adj 1. (greatest in amount, degree) am meisten 2. (majority of, nearly all) die meisten ▶ **for the** ~ **part** im Allgemeinen III. adv 1. (forming superlative) im Deutschen durch Superlativ ausgedrückt; ~ **easily** am leichtesten 2. form (extremely) höchst, äußerst; ~ **certainly** ganz bestimmt 3. (to the greatest extent) am meisten; **at** ~ höchstens

mostly ['moʊst·li] adv 1. (usually) meistens 2. (mainly) größtenteils 3. (chiefly) hauptsächlich

motel [moʊ·'tel] n Motel nt

moth [mɔθ] n Motte f; Nachtfalter m

'mothball I. n Mottenkugel f II. vt usu passive (put away for a while) einmotten

M

mother ['mʌð·ər] n Mutter f
'**mother-in-law** <pl mothers-> n Schwiegermutter f
motherly ['mʌð·ər·li] adj mütterlich; ~ **love** Mutterliebe f
mother-of-'pearl n Perlmutt nt
'**Mother's Day** n Muttertag m
mother 'tongue n Muttersprache f
motif [moʊ·'tif] n Motiv nt
motion ['moʊ·ʃən] I. n 1. (movement) Bewegung f; **in slow ~** in Zeitlupe 2. POL (proposal) Antrag m II. vi **to ~ to sb to do sth** jdn durch einen Wink auffordern, etw zu tun
motionless ['moʊ·ʃən·lɪs] adj bewegungslos
motion picture n [Spiel]film m
motivate ['moʊ·tə·veɪt] vt 1. (provide with motive) **they are ~d by a desire to help people** ihre Handlungsweise wird von dem Wunsch bestimmt, anderen zu helfen 2. (arouse interest) motivieren
motivation [ˌmoʊ·tə·'veɪ·ʃən] n 1. (reason) Begründung f, Veranlassung f 2. (drive) Motivation f
motive ['moʊ·tɪv] n Beweggrund m; **ulterior ~** tieferer Beweggrund
motor ['moʊ·tər] n Antriebsmaschine f, [Verbrennungs]motor m
'**motorbike** n fam Motorrad nt
'**motorboat** n Motorboot nt
'**motorcycle** n Motorrad nt
motoring ['moʊ·tər·ɪŋ] n Fahren nt
motorist ['moʊ·tər·ɪst] n Kraftfahrer(in) m(f)
motorized ['moʊ·tə·raɪzd] adj motorisiert; ~ **wheelchair** elektrisch betriebener Rollstuhl
'**motor racing** n Autorennsport m
'**motor scooter** n Motorroller m
'**motor vehicle** n Kraftfahrzeug nt
motto <pl -s> ['mɑt·oʊ] n Motto nt
mound [maʊnd] n 1. (heap) Haufen m; (small hill) Hügel m; (in baseball) **pitcher's ~** Mound m
mount [maʊnt] I. n 1. (horse) Pferd nt 2. (setting: of picture) Halterung f; (of jewel) Fassung f 3. (mountain) Berg m; **M~ Everest** Mount Everest m; **M~ Etna** der Ätna II. vt 1. (get on to ride)

[auf]steigen auf +akk 2. (fix securel] aufhängen; **to ~ a camera on a trip** eine Kamera auf ein Stativ montiere 3. (stairs) hochgehen 4. (organiz organisieren; (campaign) starten III. 1. (increase) wachsen, [an]steigen, gr ßer werden 2. (get on a horse) au steigen
mountain ['maʊn·tən] n Berg m; pl Gebirge nt
mountaineer [ˌmaʊn·tə·'nɪr] n Bergste ger(in) m(f)
mountainous ['maʊn·tə·nəs] adj geb: gig
'**mountain range** n Gebirgszug m
mounted ['maʊn·tɪd] adj beritten geh
mounting ['maʊn·tɪŋ] I. n 1. (on horse) Besteigen nt 2. (display surfac picture) Halterung f; (of machine) S ckel m II. adj attr (increasing) steigen
Mount Rushmore n Mount Rushmore (Granitfelsen, in dem die Büsten v George Washington, Thomas Jefferso Theodore Roosevelt und Abraham Li coln eingehauen sind)
mourn [mɔrn] vt, vi trauern (**for** um +ak
mourner ['mɔr·nər] n Trauernde(r) f/m
mournful ['mɔrn·fəl] adj (sad) trauri (gloomy) trübsinnig
mouse <pl mice> [maʊs] n ZOOL, COMP Maus f
'**mouse pad** n COMPUT Mauspad nt
'**mousetrap** n Mausefalle f
mousse [mus] n 1. FOOD Mousse 2. (cosmetics) Schaum m
moustache ['mʌs·tæʃ] n see **mustach**
mousy ['maʊ·si] adj farblos; (hair) mau grau
mouth [maʊθ] n 1. (of human) Mund r (of animal) Maul nt; **to have a big** fig ein großes Mundwerk haben fa 2. (opening) Öffnung f; (of river) Mü dung f
mouthful ['maʊθ·fʊl] n (of food) Bi sen m; (of drink) Schluck m
'**mouthpiece** n (of musical instrumen Mundstück nt; (of telephone) Sprec muschel f
mouth-to-'mouth, **mouth-to-mout resuscitation** n Mund-zu-Mund-Be atmung f

outhwash n Mundwasser nt

mouth-watering adj [sehr] appetitlich, köstlich

movable ['mu·və·bəl] adj beweglich

move [muv] **I.** n **1.** (movement) Bewegung f; **to be on the ~** unterwegs sein; **to make a ~** fam (leave) sich auf den Weg machen; (start) loslegen fam **2.** (step) Schritt m; (measure) Maßnahme f **3.** (in games) Zug m; **it's your ~** du bist dran **4.** (change of residence) Umzug m; (change of job) Stellenwechsel m ▶ **to get a ~ on** fam sich beeilen **II.** vi **1.** (change position) sich bewegen; **no one ~d** keiner rührte sich; **to ~ [out of the way]** aus dem Weg gehen **2.** (change) **that's my final decision, and I am not going to ~ [on it]** das ist mein letztes Wort und dabei bleibt es **3.** (progress) vorankommen; **to ~ forward** Fortschritte machen **4.** (change address) umziehen **III.** vt **1.** (change position of) bewegen; (place somewhere else) woanders hinstellen; (clear) wegräumen; (transport) befördern **2.** (transfer) verlegen; (to another job, class) versetzen **3.** (cause emotions) bewegen; **to ~ sb to tears** jdn zu Tränen rühren

move around I. vi **1.** (go around) herumgehen **2.** (travel) umherreisen **3.** (change jobs) oft wechseln; (change house) oft umziehen **II.** vt (change position of) [hin und her] bewegen; (furniture) umstellen

move along I. vt **to ~ sb** ⇄ **along** jdn zum Weitergehen bewegen **II.** vi **1.** (walk farther on) weitergehen; (drive farther on) weiterfahren **2.** (make room) aufrücken

move away I. vi **1.** (leave) weggehen; (vehicle) wegfahren **2.** (move to new house) wegziehen **II.** vt wegräumen; (push away) wegrücken

move down I. vi **1.** (change position) sich nach unten bewegen; (slip down) runterrutschen fam **2.** (change value: prices) fallen **II.** vt (change position of) nach unten bewegen; (place lower down) nach unten stellen

move in I. vi **1.** (enter a new home) einziehen; **to ~ in with sb** zu jdm ziehen **2.** (advance to attack) anrücken; **to ~ in for the kill** zum tödlichen Schlag ausholen **II.** vt **1.** (change position of) nach innen bewegen **2.** (send) einsetzen; (troops, police) einrücken lassen

move off I. vi sich in Bewegung setzen **II.** vt wegräumen

move on I. vi **1.** (continue a trip) sich wieder auf den Weg machen **2.** (progress in career) beruflich weiterkommen **3.** (change subject) **to ~ on to sth** zu etw dat übergehen **II.** vt (force to leave) vertreiben

move out I. vi **1.** (stop inhabiting) ausziehen **2.** (leave: troops) abziehen **II.** vt **1.** (clear) wegräumen; (take outside) hinausbringen **2.** (make leave: tenant) kündigen

move over I. vi **1.** (make room) Platz machen **2.** (switch) **to ~ over to sth** zu etw dat übergehen **II.** vt herüberschieben; (put aside) zur Seite räumen

move up I. vi **1.** (advance) aufrücken; (professionally, socially) aufsteigen **2.** (make room) aufrücken **3.** (increase: prices) steigen **II.** vt (change position of) nach oben bewegen

movement ['muv·mənt] n **1.** Bewegung f **2.** FIN, STOCKEX Schwankung[en] f/pl] **3.** MUS Satz m **4.** (tendency) Trend m **5.** (mechanism: of clock) Uhrwerk nt

movie ['mu·vi] n (Kino)film m; **the ~s** pl das Kino

'movie camera n Filmkamera f

'moviegoer n Kinogänger(in) m(f)

'movie star n Filmstar m

'movie theater n Kino nt

moving ['mu·vɪŋ] adj **1.** attr MECH beweglich **2.** (causing emotion) bewegend, ergreifend

mow <mowed, mowed or mown> [moʊ] vt (lawn) mähen; (field) abmähen

mower ['moʊ·ər] n Rasenmäher m

mown [moʊn] pp of **mow**

mpg [ˌem·piˈdʒiː] abbr of **miles per gallon** Meilen pro Gallone

mph [ˌem·piˈetʃ] abbr of **miles per hour** Meilen pro Stunde

Mr. ['mɪs·tər] n (title for man) Herr m

M

Mrs. ['mɪs·ɪz] n (title for married woman) Frau, Fr.

MS [‚em·'es] n 1. abbr of **Master of Science** 2. abbr of **Mississippi** Mississippi m 3. abbr of **multiple sclerosis** MS f

Ms. [mɪz] n (title for woman, married or unmarried) Fr., Frau (Alternativbezeichnung zu Mrs. und Miss, die sowohl für verheiratete als auch für unverheiratete Frauen zutrifft)

ms [‚em·'es] n 1. abbr of **manuscript** Mskr. 2. abbr of **millisecond** ms

MSG [‚em·es·'dʒi] n CHEM abbr of **monosodium glutamate**

MST [‚em·es·'ti] n abbr of **Mountain Standard Time** Mountain Standardzeit f

MT abbr of **Montana**

Mt. n abbr of **mount I** 3

much [mʌtʃ] I. adj <more, most> + sing viel; **how ~ ...?** wie viel ...?; **twice as ~** doppelt so viel II. pron 1. (relative amount) viel; **however ~ you dislike her ...** wie unsympathisch sie dir auch sein mag, ... 2. (great deal) viel; **~ of what you say is right** vieles von dem, was Sie sagen, ist richtig 3. with neg pej (poor example) **he's not ~ to look at** er sieht nicht gerade umwerfend aus III. adv <more, most> 1. (greatly) sehr; **~ to our surprise** zu unserer großen Überraschung; **to not be ~ good at sth** in etw dat nicht sehr gut sein 2. (nearly) fast; **~ the same** fast so 3. (specifying degree) **I like him as ~ as you do** ich mag ihn genauso sehr wie du; **thank you very ~** herzlichen Dank IV. conj (although) auch wenn; **~ as I like you, ...** so gern ich dich auch mag, ...

muck [mʌk] n 1. (dirt) Dreck m fam 2. euph (excrement) Haufen m fam

mucus ['mju·kəs] n Schleim m

mud [mʌd] n Schlamm m

muddle ['mʌd·əl] n Durcheinander nt

muddy ['mʌd·i] I. vt verschmutzen II. adj schlammig; (ground) matschig

'mud flap n (of car) Kotflügel m; (of bicycle) Schutzblech nt

'mudpack n Gesichtsmaske f

'mudslide n Schlammlawine f

muff [mʌf] vt fam vermasseln

muffin ['mʌf·ɪn] n Muffin nt (kleine hoher, runder, meist süßer Kuchen au Rührteig)

muffle ['mʌf·əl] vt dämpfen; fig [ab]schwä chen

muffler ['mʌf·lər] n (of car) Auspuf topf m

mug¹ [mʌg] n (cup) Becher m (mit Hen kel)

mug² [mʌg] I. n pej (face) Visage f II. <-gg-> (rob) überfallen und ausrauber

mugger ['mʌg·ər] n [Straßen]räu ber(in) m(f)

mugging ['mʌg·ɪŋ] n [Straßen]raub n Überfall m (auf offener Straße)

muggy ['mʌg·i] adv (weather) schwül

mulberry ['mʌl·ber·i] n Maulbeere f

mule¹ [mjul] n (animal) Maultier nt

mule² [mjul] n (shoe) halboffener Schuh

mull [mʌl] vt 1. (spice) **~ed wine** Glüh wein m 2. (ponder) **to ~ sth [over]** sic dat etw durch den Kopf gehen lassen

mullet ['mʌl·ɪt] n Meeräsche f

multi'colored adj mehrfarbig

multi'cultural adj multikulturell

multi'lateral adj POL multilateral geh

multi'lingual adj mehrsprachig

multi'media I. n Multimedia f II. ad multimedial

multimillion'aire n Multimillionär(in m(f)

multi'national I. n multinationaler Kon zern, Multi m fam II. adj multinationa

multiplayer ['mʌl·ti·pleɪ·ər] adj attr (com puter game) Multiplayer-

multiple ['mʌl·tə·pəl] I. adj attr vielfach vielfältig II. n Vielfache[s]

multiplex ['mʌl·tə·pleks] n Multiplex Kino nt

multiplier ['mʌl·tə·plaɪ·ər] n Multipli kator m

multiply <-ie-> ['mʌl·tə·plaɪ] vt multipli zieren (**by** mit +dat)

multi'purpose adj multifunktional Mehrzweck-

multi'racial adj gemischtrassig; **~ society** Gesellschaft, die aus den Angehörige verschiedener Rassengruppen besteht

multi'tasking n COMPUT Ausführen v mehrerer Programme, Multitasking nt

num [mʌm] *adj fam* (*silent*) still; **to keep ~** den Mund halten

numble ['mʌm·bəl] *vi* (*speak unclearly*) nuscheln

numbo jumbo [ˌmʌm·boʊ·'dʒʌm·boʊ] *n fam* Quatsch *m*

nummy ['mʌm·i] *n* Mumie *f*

numps [mʌmps] *n + sing vb* Mumps *m*

nunch [mʌntʃ] *vt, vi* mampfen

nundane [mʌn·'deɪn] *adj* (*unexciting: question*) banal; (*routine: activity, task*) alltäglich

nunicipal [mju·'nɪs·ə·pəl] *adj* Stadt-, kommunal

nunitions [mju·'nɪʃ·ənz] *npl* (*weapons*) Waffen *pl*; (*weapons and ammunition*) Kriegsmaterial *nt kein pl*; (*ammunition*) Munition *f kein pl*

nural ['mjʊr·əl] *n* Wandgemälde *nt*

nurder ['mɜr·dər] I. *n* Mord *m*, Ermordung *f* II. *vt* ermorden, umbringen *a. fig*

nurderer ['mɜr·dər·ər] *n* Mörder(in) *m(f)*

nurky ['mɜr·ki] *adj* düster; (*night*) finster; (*water*) trübe

nurmur ['mɜr·mər] *vt, vi* murmeln

nuscle ['mʌs·əl] *n* 1. (*contracting tissue*) Muskel *m* 2. *fig* (*influence*) Stärke *f* ▶ **muscle in** *vi* sich [rücksichtslos] einmischen; **to ~ in on sth** sich irgendwo [mit aller Gewalt] hineindrängeln

nuscleman *n* Muskelprotz *m*

nuscular ['mʌs·kjə·lər] *adj* 1. (*relating to muscles*) muskulär 2. (*with well-developed muscles*) muskulös

nuseum [mju·'zi·əm] *n* Museum *nt*

nush [mʌʃ] *n fam* Brei *m*, Mus *nt*

nushroom ['mʌʃ·rum] *n* Pilz *m*

nushy ['mʌʃ·i] *adj* 1. (*pulpy*) breiig 2. (*soppily romantic*) schnulzig

nusic ['mju·zɪk] *n* Musik *f*

nusical ['mju·zɪ·kəl] I. *adj* musikalisch II. *n* Musical *nt*

'music box *n* Spieluhr *f*

nusician [mju·'zɪʃ·ən] *n* Musiker(in) *m(f)*

nusk [mʌsk] *n* Moschus *m*

nuskrat ['mʌs·kræt] *n* Moschusratte *f*

Nuslim ['mʌz·ləm] I. *n* Moslem(in) *m(f)*, Muslim(in) *m(f)* II. *adj* moslemisch, muslimisch

nuss [mʌs] *vt* durcheinanderbringen

mussel ['mʌs·əl] *n* [Mies]muschel *f*

must [mʌst] I. *aux vb* 1. (*be obliged, be required*) müssen; **for security reasons, all bags ~ be left at the cloakroom** lassen Sie bitte aus Sicherheitsgründen alle Handtaschen in der Garderobe; **~ not** [*or* **~n't**] nicht dürfen; **you ~n't say anything to anyone about this matter** darüber darfst du mit niemandem sprechen 2. (*should*) **you really ~ read this book** dieses Buch sollten Sie wirklich einmal lesen 3. (*be certain to*) müssen; **she ~ be wondering where I am** sie wird sich bestimmt fragen, wo ich abgeblieben bin II. *n* Muss *nt kein pl*

mustache ['mʌs·tæʃ] *n* Schnurrbart *m*

mustang ['mʌs·tæŋ] *n* Mustang *m*

mustard ['mʌs·tərd] *n* Senf *m*

muster ['mʌs·tər] *vt* (*soldiers*) [zum Appell] antreten lassen

'must-have *adj attr fam* unentbehrlich

mustn't ['mʌs·ənt] *short for* **must not**

'must-see *n* **this film is a ~** diesen Film muss man gesehen haben

musty ['mʌs·ti] *adj* (*book*) mod[e]rig; (*room, smell*) muffig

mutation [mju·'teɪ·ʃən] *n* Mutation *f fachspr*

mute [mjut] I. *n* 1. (*person*) Stumme(r) *f(m)* 2. MUS (*quieting device*) Dämpfer *m* II. *vt* (*sound*) dämpfen III. *adj* stumm

muted ['mju·tɪd] *adj* (*not loud*) gedämpft; *fig* schweigend; (*colors*) gedeckt

mutilate ['mju·tə·leɪt] *vt* verstümmeln; *fig* verschandeln

mutilation [ˌmju·tə·'leɪ·ʃən] *n* Verstümmelung *f*; *fig* Verschandelung *f*

mutinous ['mju·tə·nəs] *adj* meuterisch; (*shareholders*) rebellisch

mutiny ['mju·tɪ·ni] I. *n* Meuterei *f* II. *vi* <-ie-> meutern

mutter ['mʌt·ər] *vi* (*mumble*) **to ~** [**to oneself**] irgendetwas [vor sich *akk* hin] murmeln

mutton ['mʌt·ən] *n* Hammelfleisch *nt*

mutual ['mju·tʃu·əl] *adj* gegenseitig; (*friends*) gemeinsam; (*agreement*) wechselseitig

M

'**mutual fund** n FIN offener Investment-fond

mutually ['mju·tʃu·ə·li] adv gegenseitig

Muzak® ['mju·zæk] n Musikberieselung f

muzzle ['mʌz·əl] I. n 1. (animal mouth) Maul nt 2. (mouth covering) Maul-korb m 3. (gun end) Mündung f II. vt (animal) einen Maulkorb anlegen; fig (person, press) mundtot machen

MW n PHYS abbr of **megawatt** MW m

my [maɪ] adj poss mein(e); ~ **brother and sister** mein Bruder und meine Schwester; **I hurt ~ foot** ich habe mir den Fuß verletzt; **I need a car of ~ own** ich brauche ein eigenes Auto

myopic [maɪ·'ap·ɪk] adj form or fig kurz-sichtig

myself [maɪ·'self] pron refl 1. (direct object of verb) mir +dat, mich +akk; **I caught sight of ~ in the mirror** ich sah mich im Spiegel 2. emph form (I, me) ich; **people like ~** Menschen wie ich 3. emph (me personally) ich persönlich; **I wrote it ~** ich schrieb es selbst 4. (me alone) **I never get an hour to ~** ich habe nie eine Stunde für mich; [all] **by ~** [ganz] alleine

mysterious [mɪ·'stɪr·i·əs] adj geheimnis-voll, mysteriös

mystery ['mɪs·tə·ri] n (secret) Geheim-nis nt; (puzzle) Rätsel nt

mystical ['mɪs·tɪ·kəl] adj mystisch

mystification [ˌmɪs·tɪ·fɪ·'keɪ·ʃən] n Ver-wunderung f

mystify <-ie-> ['mɪs·tə·faɪ] vt **to ~ sb** jdn vor ein Rätsel stellen

myth [mɪθ] n 1. (ancient story) My-thos m 2. pej (false idea) Ammen-märchen nt

mythical ['mɪθ·ɪ·kəl] adj 1. (fictional) sagenhaft 2. (supposed) imaginär

mythological [ˌmɪθ·ə·'ladʒ·ɪ·kəl] adj my-thologisch

N

N <pl -'s>, **n** <pl -'s> [en] n N nt, n nt; ~ **as in November** N wie Nordpol

N I. n abbr of **North** N m II. adj abbr of **North, Northern** nördl.

n n 1. abbr of **noun** Subst. 2. abbr (**neuter** nt

nab <-bb-> [næb] vt fam stibitzen

nag [næg] I. vi <-gg-> [herum]nörgel (**at** an +dat) II. vt <-gg-> **to ~ sb** (an noy) jdn nicht in Ruhe lassen

nagging ['næg·ɪŋ] I. n Nörgelei f II. a (persistent) quälend

nail [neɪl] I. n 1. Nagel m; **to cut one ~s** sich dat die Nägel schneiden II. 1. (fasten) nageln (**to** an +akk) 2. (catch: police) schnappen fam

'**nail-biting** adj nervenzerreißend; (filr spannend

'**nail clippers** npl Nagelknipser m

'**nail file** n Nagelfeile f

'**nail polish** n Nagellack m

'**nail scissors** npl Nagelschere f

naïve, naive [na·'iv] adj esp pej naiv pe

naked ['neɪ·kɪd] adj a. fig nackt; (flame offen; **to the ~ eye** für das bloße Auge

nakedness ['neɪ·kɪd·nɪs] n Nacktheit f

namby-pamby [ˌnæm·bi·'pæm·bi] a attr pej fam (weak: person) verweich licht

name [neɪm] I. n 1. (title) Name m **my ~'s Peter** ich heiße Peter; **first last ~** Vor-/Nachname m 2. (reputa tion) Name m, Ruf m; **to make a ~ fo oneself** sich dat einen Namen mache II. vt nennen

nameless ['neɪm·lɪs] adj namenlos

namely ['neɪm·li] adv nämlich

'**nameplate** n (on door) Türschild nt; ((company) Firmenschild nt

'**namesake** n Namensvetter m

nana ['naen·ə] n fam Omi f

nanny ['næn·i] n Kindermädchen nt

nanosecond ['nan·ə ˌsek·ənd] n Nano sekunde f

nap [næp] I. n Nickerchen nt II. <-pp-> fam ein Nickerchen machen

napkin ['næp·kɪn] n Serviette f

narc, nark [nark] n sl (narcotics agen Rauschgiftfahnder(in) m(f)

narcissus <pl -es> [nar·'sɪs·əs] n Nar zisse f

narcotic [nar·'kat·ɪk] I. n Rauschgift n II. adj MED narkotisch; (sleep-inducing einschläfernd

narrate ['nær·eɪt] vt 1. (*provide commentary*) erzählen 2. (*give account of*) schildern

narrator ['nær·eɪ·tər] n Erzähler(in) m(f)

narrow ['nær·oʊ] I. adj 1. (*thin*) eng, schmal 2. (*margin, victory*) knapp II. vi enger werden; (*gap*) sich schließen

narrowly ['nær·oʊ·li] adv (*barely*) knapp

narrow-'minded adj engstirnig

NASA ['næs·ə] n abbr of **National Aeronautics and Space Administration** NASA f

nasal ['neɪ·zəl] adj Nasen-

nastiness ['næs·ti·nɪs] n Gemeinheit f

nasturtium [nə-'stɜr·ʃəm] n [Kapuziner]kresse f

nasty ['næs·ti] adj 1. (*mean: person*) gemein; (*surprise*) böse 2. (*bad: smell*) scheußlich; (*shock*) furchtbar 3. (*serious*) schlimm, böse; **to turn ~** (*situation, animal*) unangenehm werden

nation ['neɪ·ʃən] n 1. (*country, state*) Nation f, Land nt 2. (*people*) Volk nt; **the Apache ~** der Stamm der Apachen

national ['næʃ·ə·nəl] I. adj 1. (*of a nation, nationwide: matter, organization*) national; (*flag, team*) National- 2. (*particular to a nation*) Landes-, Volks- II. n Staatsangehörige(r) f(m)

national 'anthem n Nationalhymne f

national 'debt n Staatsverschuldung f

National 'Guard n Nationalgarde f

nationalist ['næʃ·ə·nə·lɪst] I. adj nationalistisch II. n Nationalist(in) m(f)

nationality [,næʃ·ə·'næl·ə·ti] n 1. (*esp cultural*) Nationalität f 2. (*legal*) Staatsangehörigkeit f

nationalize ['næʃ·ə·nə·laɪz] vt (*company, steel industry*) verstaatlichen

national 'park, National 'Park n Nationalpark m

nation-'state n Nationalstaat m

'nationwide I. adv landesweit, im ganzen Land II. adj (*campaign*) landesweit

native ['neɪ·t̬ɪv] I. adj 1. (*of one's birth*) beheimatet; **~ country** Heimatland nt 2. (*traditions*) einheimisch; (*population*) eingeboren 3. BOT, ZOOL (*animal, plant*) beheimatet, einheimisch II. n (*local inhabitant*) Einheimische(r) f(m); (*indigenous*) Eingeborene(r) f(m)

Native A'merican n amerikanischer Ureinwohner/amerikanische Ureinwohnerin

native-'born adj gebürtig

native 'speaker n Muttersprachler(in) m(f)

na'tivity play n Krippenspiel nt

NATO ['neɪ·toʊ] n acr for **North Atlantic Treaty Organization** NATO f

natural ['nætʃ·ər·əl] I. adj 1. (*not artificial: flavor, ingredients*) natürlich; (*color*) Natur- 2. (*as in nature: harbor, reservoir*) natürlich; (*fabric, wood*) naturbelassen; **~ state** Naturzustand m 3. (*caused by nature*) natürlich; **~ disaster** Naturkatastrophe 4. (*normal*) natürlich, normal II. n approv fam Naturtalent nt

natural 'gas n Erdgas nt

natural 'history n Naturgeschichte f; (*as topic of study*) Naturkunde f

naturalistic [,nætʃ·ər·ə·'lɪs·tɪk] adj ART, LIT, PHILOS naturalistisch

naturalization [,nætʃ·ər·ə·lɪ·'zeɪ·ʃən] n Einbürgerung f

naturalize ['nætʃ·ər·ə·laɪz] vt einbürgern

naturally ['nætʃ·ər·ə·li] adv 1. natürlich; (*as expected*) verständlicherweise 2. (*without special training*) natürlich; **dancing comes ~ to him** Tanzen fällt ihm leicht

natural re'sources npl Bodenschätze pl

natural se'lection n natürliche Auslese

nature ['neɪ·tʃər] n 1. no art (*natural environment*) Natur f 2. (*innate qualities*) Art f; **by ~** von Natur aus

nature conser'vation n Naturschutz m

'nature preserve n Naturschutzgebiet nt

'nature study n Naturkunde f

'nature trail n Naturlehrpfad m

naughty ['nɔ·t̬i] adj 1. (*children*) ungezogen; iron (*adults*) ungehörig 2. hum fam (*sinful*) unanständig

nausea ['nɔ·zi·ə] n Übelkeit f; fig Ekel m

nauseate ['nɔ·zi·eɪt] vt usu passive form **to be ~d by sth** fig, pej von etw dat angeekelt sein

nauseating ['nɔ·zi·eɪ·t̬ɪŋ] adj Übelkeit erregend attr

nauseous ['nɔ·fəs] *adj* 1. (*having nausea*) **she is ~** ihr ist übel 2. *fig* (*causing nausea*) widerlich

nautical ['nɔ·tɪ·kəl] *adj* nautisch; **~ mile** Seemeile *f*

naval ['neɪ·vəl] *adj* (*of a navy*) Marine-; (*of ships*) See-; **~ base** Flottenstützpunkt *m*

navel ['neɪ·vəl] *n* ANAT Nabel *m*

navigable ['næv·ɪ·gə·bəl] *adj* (*passable*) schiffbar

navigate ['næv·ɪ·geɪt] *vt* 1. (*steer*) navigieren 2. (*pilot*) steuern; AUTO lenken

navigation [,næv·ɪ·ˈgeɪ·ʃən] *n* 1. Navigation *f* 2. (*assisting operator*) Lotsen *nt*

navigator ['næv·ɪ·geɪ·tər] *n* Navigator(in) *m(f)*; AUTO Beifahrer(in) *m(f)*

navy ['neɪ·vi] **I.** *n* **the N~** die Marine **II.** *adj* marineblau

Nazi ['nat·si] *n* Nazi *m*

Nazism ['nat·sɪz·əm], **Naziism** ['nat·si·ɪz·əm] *n hist* Nazismus *m*

NB [,en·ˈbi] *adv abbr of* **nota bene** NB

NC, N.C. *abbr of* **North Carolina**

NCO [,en·si·ˈoʊ] *n abbr of* **noncommissioned officer** Uffz. *m*

ND, N.D. *abbr of* **North Dakota**

NE *abbr of* **Nebraska**

near [nɪr] **I.** *adj* 1. (*close in space*) nahe, in der Nähe; **where's the ~est phone booth?** wo ist die nächste Telefonzelle? 2. (*close in time*) nahe **to be a ~ miss** knapp danebengehen **II.** *adv* 1. (*close in space*) nahe; **do you live somewhere ~?** wohnst du hier irgendwo in der Nähe? 2. (*close in time*) nahe; **the time is drawing ~** die Zeit rückt näher 3. (*almost*) beinahe, fast **III.** *prep* 1. (*in proximity to*) nahe [bei] +*dat;* **do you live ~ here?** wohnst du hier in der Nähe? 2. (*close to a state*) **we came ~ to being killed** wir wären beinahe getötet worden

nearby [,nɪr·ˈbaɪ] **I.** *adj* nahe gelegen **II.** *adv* in der Nähe

Near 'East *n* Naher Osten

nearly ['nɪr·li] *adv* fast, beinahe

near'sighted *adj* kurzsichtig

near'sightedness *n* Kurzsichtigkeit *f*

neat [nit] *adj* 1. (*well-maintained*) ordentlich; (*appearance*) gepflegt

2. *approv fam* (*very good*) toll 3. (*undiluted*) pur

neaten ['ni·tən] *vt* in Ordnung bringen

neatly ['nit·li] *adv* 1. (*tidily*) sauber 2. (*skillfully*) geschickt

neatness ['nit·nɪs] *n* Ordentlichkeit *f*

Nebr. *abbr of* **Nebraska**

Nebraska [nə·ˈbræs·kə] *n* Nebraska *nt*

nebulous ['neb·jə·ləs] *adj* nebelhaft; (*fear, promise*) vage

necessarily [,nes·ɪ·ˈser·ə·li] *adv* (*consequently*) notwendigerweise; (*inevitably*) unbedingt; (*of necessity*) zwangsläufig

necessary ['nes·ɪ·ser·i] *adj* notwendig

necessitate [nə·ˈses·ɪ·teɪt] *vt* erfordern

necessity [nə·ˈses·ə·ti] *n* 1. (*being necessary*) Notwendigkeit *f* 2. (*necessary thing*) **the necessities of life** das Lebensnotwendige

neck [nek] *n* 1. ANAT Hals; (*nape*) Nacken *m* 2. (*narrow part*) Hals *m* ▶ **to be breathing down sb's ~** jdm im Nacken sitzen

necklace ['nek·lɪs] *n* [Hals]kette *f*

'neckline *n* Ausschnitt *m*

'necktie *n* Krawatte *f*

nectar ['nek·tər] *n* Nektar *m*

nectarine [,nek·tə·ˈrin] *n* Nektarine *f*

née [neɪ] *adj pred* geborene

need [nid] **I.** *n* 1. (*requirement*) Bedarf *m* 2. (*yearning*) Bedürfnis *nt;* **I'm in ~ of some fresh air** ich brauche etwas frische Luft 3. (*poverty*) Not *f* **II.** *vt* 1. (*require*) brauchen 2. (*must*) **to ~ to do sth** etw tun müssen **III.** *aux vb* **~ I say more?** *iron* muss ich noch mehr sagen?

needed ['nid·ɪd] *adj* notwendig; **much-~** dringend nötig

needle ['ni·dəl] **I.** *n* Nadel *f* **II.** *vt* ärgern

needless ['nid·lɪs] *adj* unnötig; **~ to say ...** selbstverständlich ...

needn't ['ni·dənt] = **need not** *see* **need III**

needy ['ni·di] *adj* (*poor*) bedürftig, Not leidend *attr*

negate [nɪ·ˈgeɪt] *vt* (*nullify*) zunichtemachen

negative ['neg·ə·tɪv] **I.** *adj* negativ; **~ answer** ablehnende Antwort; **to be ~**

about sth etw gegenüber negativ eingestellt sein **II.** *n* **1.** (*negation*) Verneinung *f* **2.** PHOT Negativ *nt*

negatively ['neg·ə·tɪv·li] *adv* negativ; (*saying no*) ablehnend

neglect [nɪ·'glekt] **I.** *vt* vernachlässigen; **to ~ to do sth** [es] versäumen, etw zu tun **II.** *n* (*lack of care*) Vernachlässigung *f*; (*disrepair*) Verwahrlosung *f*

neglected [nɪ·'glekt·ɪd] *adj* (*uncared for*) verwahrlost; (*overlooked*) vernachlässigt

neglectful [nɪ·'glekt·fəl] *adj* nachlässig (*of* gegenüber +*dat*)

negligence ['neg·lɪ·dʒəns] *n* (*lack of care*) Nachlässigkeit *f*; (*neglect*) Vernachlässigung *f*

negligible ['neg·lɪ·dʒə·bəl] *adj* unbedeutend

negotiable [nɪ·'goʊ·ʃi·ə·bəl] *adj* **1.** (*discussable*) verhandelbar **2.** (*traversable*) passierbar; (*road*) befahrbar

negotiate [nɪ·'goʊ·ʃi·eɪt] **I.** *vt* (*discuss*) aushandeln; (*treaty*) abschließen **II.** *vi* verhandeln (**for/on** über +*akk*)

negotiation [nɪ·ˌgoʊ·ʃi·'eɪ·ʃən] *n* Verhandlung *f*

negotiator [nɪ·'goʊ·ʃi·eɪ·tər] *n* Unterhändler(in) *m(f)*

neigh [neɪ] *vi* wiehern

neighbor ['neɪ·bər] **I.** *n* (*person*) Nachbar(in) *m(f)*; *fig* (*country*) Nachbarland *nt* **II.** *vi* [an]grenzen (**on** an +*akk*)

neighborhood ['neɪ·bər·hʊd] *n* **1.** (*district*) Viertel *nt*; (*people*) Nachbarschaft *f* **2.** (*vicinity*) Nähe *f kein pl*

neighborhood watch *n* Nachbarschaftswachdienst *m*

neighboring ['neɪ·bər·ɪŋ] *adj attr* (*nearby*) benachbart; (*bordering*) angrenzend

neighborly ['neɪ·bər·li] *adj* (*community-friendly*) gutnachbarlich; (*kindly*) freundlich

neither ['ni·ðər] **I.** *adv* **1.** (*not either*) weder; **~ ... nor ...** [**nor ...**] weder ... noch ... [oder ...] **2.** (*a. not*) auch nicht ▶ **to be ~ here nor there** völlig nebensächlich sein **II.** *adj attr* keine(r, s) von beiden **III.** *pron* (*not either of two*) keine(r, s) von beiden **IV.** *conj* **1.** (*not either*) **~ ... nor ...** weder ... noch

2. *after neg* (*also not*) weder; **I can't be at the meeting, and ~ can Andrew** ich kann nicht zum Treffen kommen und Andrew auch nicht

neon ['ni·an] *n* Neon *nt*; **~ sign** Leuchtreklame *f*

neo-Nazi [ˌni·oʊ·'nat·si] *n* Neonazi *m*

nephew ['nef·ju] *n* Neffe *m*

nerd [nɜrd] *n sl* (*geek*) Streber(in) *m(f) pej*; **computer ~** Computerfreak *m sl*

nerdy ['nɜr·di] *adj fam* doof

nerve [nɜrv] *n* **1.** ANAT Nerv *m* **2.** (*courage*) Mut *m*; **to lose one's ~** die Nerven verlieren **3.** (*impudence*) Frechheit *f* ▶ **to get on sb's ~s** *fam* jdm auf die Nerven [*or* den Wecker] gehen

nerve center *n* Nervenzentrum *nt a. fig*

nerve gas *n* Nervengas *nt*

nerve-racking, nerve-wracking *adj* nervenaufreibend

nervous ['nɜr·vəs] *adj* (*high-strung*) nervös; (*tense*) aufgeregt

nervous breakdown *n* Nervenzusammenbruch *m*

nervously ['nɜr·vəs·li] *adv* nervös; (*overexcitedly*) aufgeregt; (*timidly*) ängstlich

nervousness ['nɜr·vəs·nɪs] *n* (*nervous state*) Nervosität *f*

nervous system *n* Nervensystem *nt*

nervy ['nɜr·vi] *adj pej* unverschämt

nest [nest] **I.** *n* Nest *nt* **II.** *vi* ORN nisten

nest egg *n fig* Notgroschen *m*

nesting ['nest·ɪŋ] *adj attr* **1.** (*of sets*) ineinanderstapelbar **2.** (*of nests*) Nist-

nestle ['nes·əl] **I.** *vt* **she ~d the baby lovingly in her arms** sie hielt das Baby liebevoll in ihren Armen **II.** *vi* (*object*) **to ~ in sth** in etw *akk* eingebettet sein

nestling ['nest·lɪŋ] *n* ORN Nestling *m*

Net [net] *n* INET, COMPUT **the ~** das Netz

net¹ [net] **I.** *n* Netz *nt a. fig* **II.** *vt* <-tt-> (*fish*) mit einem Netz fangen; *fig* (*criminals*) fangen

net² [net] **I.** *adj* **1.** netto, rein, Netto-, Rein-; **~ profit** Reingewinn *m* **2.** *attr fig* (*final*) End-; **~ result** Endergebnis *nt* **II.** *vt* (*after tax*) netto verdienen

Netherlands ['neð·ər·ləndz] *n* **the ~** die Niederlande *pl*

netiquette ['net·ɪ·ˌket] *n* COMPUT Netiquette *f*

netting ['net·ɪŋ] *n* Netzgewebe *nt*

nettle ['net·əl] *n* Nessel *f*; **stinging ~s** Brennnesseln *pl*

network ['net·wɜrk] **I.** *n* **1.** (*structure*) Netz[werk] *nt* **2.** *fig* (*people*) Netz *nt* **3.** TV **~ television** Sendernetz *nt* **II.** *vt* vernetzen (**to** mit +*dat*) **III.** *vi* Kontakte knüpfen

'networker *n* Networker(in) *m(f)*

networking ['net·wɜrk·ɪŋ] *n* **1.** (*making contacts*) Kontaktknüpfen *nt* **2.** COMPUT Vernetzen *nt*

neural ['nʊr·əl] *adj attr* COMPUT **~ network** Neuronennetz *nt*

neurologist [nʊ·ral·ə·dʒɪst] *n* Neurologe *m*, Neurologin *f*

neurology [nʊ·ral·ə·dʒi] *n* Neurologie *f*

neuroscience [ˌnʊr·oʊ·ˈsai·əns] *n* Neurobiologie *f*

neurosis <*pl* -ses> [nʊ·ˈroʊ·sɪs] *n* Neurose *f*

neurosurgery [ˌnʊr·oʊ·ˈsɜr·dʒə·ri] *n* Neurochirurgie *f*

neurotic [nʊ·ˈrat·ɪk] *adj* neurotisch

neuter ['nu·tər] **I.** *adj* sächlich; **~ noun** Neutrum *nt* **II.** *vt* (*male animal*) kastrieren

neutral ['nu·trəl] **I.** *adj* neutral **II.** *n* AUTO Leerlauf *m*; **in ~** im Leerlauf

neutrality [nu·ˈtræl·ə·t̮i] *n* Neutralität *f*

neutralize ['nu·trə·laɪz] *vt* (*nullify*) neutralisieren; (*bomb*) entschärfen

neutron ['nu·tran] *n* Neutron *nt*

Nev. *abbr of* **Nevada**

Nevada [nə·ˈvad·ə] *n* Nevada *nt*

never ['nev·ər] *adv* nie, niemals; **~ again!** nie wieder!; **~ before** noch nie [zuvor]

never-'ending *adj* endlos

never-'never land *n fam* Fantasiewelt *f*

nevertheless [ˌnev·ər·ðə·ˈles] *adv* dennoch

new [nu] *adj* neu; **~ boy/girl/kid** *a. fig* (*in school*) Neue(r) *f(m)*; **I'm ~ around here** ich bin neu hier

newbie ['nu·bi] *n* Anfänger(in) *m(f)*

'newborn *adj attr* neugeboren

'newcomer *n* (*new arrival*) Neuankömmling *m*; (*stranger*) Fremde(r) *f(m)*

new'fangled *adj fam* neumodisch

'newfound *adj* neu[entdeckt]

New Hampshire [ˌnu·ˈhæmp·ʃər] *n* New Hampshire *nt*

newish ['nu·ɪʃ] *adj fam* relativ neu

New Jersey [ˌnu·ˈdʒɜr·zi] *n* New Jersey *nt*

newly ['nu·li] *adv* kürzlich, neulich; **~ painted** frisch gestrichen

'newlywed *n* Jungverheiratete(r) *f(m)*

New Mexico [ˌnu·ˈmek·sɪ·koʊ] *n* New Mexico *nt*

new 'moon *n* Neumond *m*

new po'tatoes *npl* neue Kartoffeln *pl*

news [nuz] *n* **1.** (*new information*) Neuigkeit *f*; **to break the ~ to sb** jdm die schlechte Nachricht überbringen **2.** (*media*) Nachrichten *pl*; **to be in the ~** in den Schlagzeilen sein

'newscast *n* Nachrichtensendung *f*

'news conference *n* Pressekonferenz *f*

'newsflash *n* Kurzmeldung *f*

'newsgroup *n* INET Newsgroup *f*

'news item *n* Nachricht *f*

'newsletter *n* Rundschreiben *nt*

'newspaper *n* Zeitung *f*

'newsprint *n* Zeitungspapier *nt*

'news report *n* Meldung *f*

'newsroom *n* Nachrichtenredaktion *f*

'newsstand *n* Zeitungsstand *m*

'newsworthy *adj* berichtenswert

New 'Testament *n* **the ~** das Neue Testament

New 'Year *n* Neujahr *nt kein pl*; **Happy ~** gutes neues Jahr

New Year's *n fam* (*January 1*) Neujahrstag *m*; (*December 31*) Silvester *nt*

New Year's 'Day *n* Neujahr *nt*, Neujahrstag *m*

New Year's 'Eve *n* Silvester *nt*

New York [ˌnu·ˈjɔrk] *n* New York *nt*

New Zealand [ˌnu·ˈzi·lənd] *n* Neuseeland *nt*

next [nekst] **I.** *adj* **1.** (*coming immediately after*) nächste(r, s); **~ month** nächsten Monat **2.** (*next in order, space*) nächste(r, s), folgende(r, s); **who's ~?** wer ist der/die Nächste? **II.** *adv* **1.** (*subsequently*) dann, gleich darauf; **so what happened ~?** was geschah als Nächstes? **2.** (*second*) zweit-; **the ~ best thing** die zweitbeste Sache **3.** (*to one side*) **~ to sth/sb** neben etw/jdm **4.** (*almost*) **~ to nothing** fast gar nichts ▶ **what ~?** und was kommt dann? **III.** *n* (*following*

one) der/die/das Nächste

next 'door *adj pred (buildings)* nebenan *nach n; (people)* benachbart

next-'gen *adj fam* short for **next-generation** futuristisch

next of 'kin *n + sing/pl vb* nächste(r) Angehörige(r)

NH, N.H. *abbr of* New Hampshire

nibble ['nɪb·əl] *vt, vi* knabbern

Nicaragua [ˌnɪk·ə·'rag·wə] *n* Nicaragua *nt*

Nicaraguan [ˌnɪk·ə·'rag·wən] *n* Nicaraguaner(in) *m(f)*

nice [naɪs] *adj approv* 1. nett; *(pleasant)* schön, angenehm; *(neighborhood)* freundlich; **~ to meet you!** es freut mich, Sie/dich kennen zu lernen! 2. *(amiable)* nett, freundlich

nice-'looking *adj* gut aussehend, hübsch

nicely ['naɪs·li] *adv* 1. *(pleasantly)* nett, hübsch 2. *(well)* gut, nett; **that'll do ~** das reicht völlig

niche [nɪtʃ] *n* Nische *f*

nick [nɪk] *n (chip)* Kerbe *f*

nickel ['nɪk·əl] *n* 1. *(metal)* Nickel *nt* 2. *(coin)* Fünfcentstück *nt*

nickel-'plated *adj* vernickelt

nickname ['nɪk·neɪm] *n* Spitzname *m; (affectionate)* Kosename *m*

nicotine ['nɪk·ə·tin] *n* Nikotin *nt*

niece [nis] *n* Nichte *f*

nifty ['nɪf·ti] *adj approv fam (stylish)* elegant; *(skillful)* geschickt

niggle ['nɪg·əl] *vi* 1. *(criticize)* nörgeln 2. *(worry)* beunruhigen

niggling ['nɪg·lɪŋ] *adj attr (troubling)* nagend *fig*

night [naɪt] *n* 1. *(darkness)* Nacht *f;* **at ~** nachts 2. *(evening)* Abend *m;* **to have a ~ out** [abends] ausgehen

'nightcap *n (drink)* Schlaftrunk *m*

'nightclothes *npl* Nachtwäsche *f* kein *pl; (pajamas)* Schlafanzug *m*

'nightclub *n* Nachtklub *m*

'night cream *n* Nachtcreme *f*

'nightdress, 'nightgown, *fam* **nightie** ['naɪ·ti] *n* Nachthemd *nt*

nightingale ['naɪ·tɪŋ·geɪl] *n* Nachtigall *f*

'nightlife *n* Nachtleben *nt*

'nightlight *n* Nachtlicht *nt*

nightmare ['naɪt·mer] *n* Alptraum *m*

nightmarish ['naɪt·mer·ɪʃ] *adj* alptraumhaft

'night owl *n fam* Nachteule *f hum*

nights [naɪts] *adv* nachts; **to work ~** nachts arbeiten

'night school *n* Abendschule *f*

'night shift *n* Nachtschicht *f*

'nightspot *n fam* Nachtklub *m*

'nightstand *n* Nachttisch *m*

'nighttime *n* Nacht[zeit] *f*

night 'watchman *n* Nachtwächter *m*

'nightwear *n* Nachtwäsche *f*

nihilistic [ˌnaɪ·ə·'lɪs·tɪk] *adj* nihilistisch

Nikkei Index [nɪ·'keɪ-] *n* Nikkei Index *m*

nil [nɪl] *n* Nichts *nt,* Null *f*

nimble ['nɪm·bəl] *adj usu approv (agile)* gelenkig; *(quick)* flink

NIMBY <pl -s> ['nɪm·bi] *n pej acr for* **not in my back yard** *Person, die sich gegen umstrittene Bauvorhaben in der eigenen Nachbarschaft stellt, aber nichts dagegen hat, wenn diese woanders realisiert werden*

nine [naɪn] *adj* neun ▶ **the whole ~ yards** *fam* ganz und gar

9-11, 9/11 [naɪn·ɪ·'lev·ən] *n* der 11. September *(Terrorangriffe am 11.9.2001 auf das World Trade Center in New York und das Pentagon in Washington)*

nineteen [ˌnaɪn·'tin] **I.** *n* Neunzehn *f* **II.** *adj* neunzehn

nineteenth [ˌnaɪn·'tinθ] *adj* neunzehnte(r, s)

nineties ['naɪn·tiz] *npl (decade)* **the ~** die Neunziger *pl*

ninetieth ['naɪn·ti·əθ] *adj* neunzigste(r, s)

'nine-to-five *adv* **to work ~** von neun bis fünf [Uhr] arbeiten

ninety ['naɪn·ti] **I.** *n* Neunzig *f* **II.** *adj* neunzig

ninth [naɪnθ] *adj* neunte(r, s)

nip¹ [nɪp] **I.** *vt* <-pp-> *(bite)* beißen; *(pinch)* zwicken **II.** *vi* <-pp-> beißen *dat* **III.** *n* 1. *(pinch)* Kniff *m; (bite)* Biss *m* 2. *(chill)* Kälte *f;* **there's a ~ in the air** es ist frisch

nip² [nɪp] *n fam (sip)* Schluck *m*

nipple ['nɪp·əl] *n* 1. ANAT Brustwarze *f* 2. *(of baby bottle)* Sauger *m*

nippy ['nɪp·i] *adj fam* kühl

nit [nɪt] *n* Nisse *f*

nitpicking ['nɪt·pɪk·ɪŋ] I. *adj pej fam* pingelig II. *n pej fam* Krittelei *f*

nitric ['naɪ·trɪk] *adj* Stickstoff-; ~ **acid** Salpetersäure *f*

nitrogen ['naɪ·trə·dʒən] *n* Stickstoff *m*

nitroglycerin(e) [,naɪ·troʊ·'glɪs·ər·ɪn] *n* Nitroglyzerin *nt*

nitty-gritty [,nɪt·i·'grɪt·i] *n fam* **to get down to the** ~ zur Sache kommen

nitwit ['nɪt·wɪt] *n pej fam* (*stupid person*) Schwachkopf *m*

nix [nɪks] *vt fam* ablehnen

NJ, N.J. *abbr of* **New Jersey**

NM, N.M. *abbr of* **New Mexico**

no [noʊ] I. *adj* 1. (*not any*) kein(e); ~ **one** keiner 2. (*on signs*) **"~ parking"** „Parken verboten" II. *adv* 1. (*not at all*) nicht; ~ **less than sth** nicht weniger als etw 2. (*negation*) nein III. *interj* 1. (*refusal*) nein 2. (*distress*) **oh, ~!** oh nein!

Noah's ark [,noʊ·əz·'ark] *n* die Arche Noah

Nobel Prize [,noʊ·bel·'-] *n* Nobelpreis *m*

nobility [noʊ·'bɪl·ə· t̬i] *n* (*aristocracy*) **the** ~ der Adel

noble ['noʊ·bəl] I. *adj* 1. (*aristocratic*) ad[e]lig 2. *approv* (*estimable: person*) edel *geh* II. *n* Ad[e]lige(r) *f(m)*

nobody ['noʊ·bad·i] *pron indef sing* (*no people*) niemand, keiner; ~ **else** niemand anders

no-brainer ['noʊ·breɪ·nər] *n fam* **to be a** ~ ein Kinderspiel sein

nocturnal [nak·'tɜr·nəl] *adj* (*of the night*) nächtlich *attr*, Nacht-; zool (*active at night*) nachtaktiv

nod [nad] I. *n usu sing* Nicken *nt kein pl;* **to get the** ~ *fig* grünes Licht bekommen II. *vt* <-dd-> **to** ~ **one's head** mit dem Kopf nicken III. *vi* <-dd-> (*as signal*) nicken

◆**nod off** *vi* (*involuntarily*) einnicken; (*voluntarily*) ein Nickerchen machen

node [noʊd] *n* (*intersection*) Schnittpunkt *m;* comput Schnittstelle *f*

no-'fault *adj attr* Vollkasko-

no-'fly zone *n* Flugverbotszone *f*

no-'frills *adj attr* (*shop*) [schlicht und] einfach; ~ **service** Service *m* ohne Extras

no-go 'area, no-go 'zone *n* 1. (*pro-* *hibited*) verbotene Zone 2. mil Sperrgebiet *nt*

nohow ['noʊ·haʊ] *adv fam* auf gar keinen Fall

no-'iron *adj* (*clothes*) bügelfrei

noise [nɔɪz] *n* 1. (*loudness*) Lärm *m* 2. (*sound*) Geräusch *nt*

noiseless ['nɔɪz·lɪs] *adj* geräuschlos

'noise pollution *n* Lärmbelästigung *f*

noise prevention *n* Lärmvermeidung *f*

noisy ['nɔɪ·zi] *adj* laut

nomadic [noʊ·'mæd·ɪk] *adj* nomadisch, Nomaden-

nominal ['nam·ə·nəl] *adj* 1. (*titular*) nominell 2. (*small: sum of money*) gering

nominate ['nam·ə·neɪt] *vt* 1. (*propose*) nominieren 2. (*appoint*) ernennen

nomination [,nam·ə·'neɪ·ʃən] *n* 1. (*proposal*) Nominierung *f* 2. (*appointment*) Ernennung *f*

nominative ['nam·ə·nə·t̬ɪv] *n* **the** ~ der Nominativ

nominee [,nam·ə·'ni] *n* Kandidat(in) *m(f)*

nonag'gression *n* Gewaltverzicht *m;* ~ **treaty** Nichtangriffspakt *m*

nonalco'holic *adj* (*drink*) alkoholfrei

nonat'tendance *n* (*at school, a hearing*) Abwesenheit *f*

nonchalant [,nan·ʃə·'lant] *adj* gleichgültig

noncommissioned 'officer *n* mil Unteroffizier(in) *m(f)*

noncommittal [,nan·kə·'mɪt̬·əl] *adj* (*tone*) unverbindlich

noncom'pliance *n* (*with an order*) Nichtbeachtung *f*

noncon'formist *adj* nonkonformistisch

noncon'tributory *adj* beitragsfrei

noncoope'ration *n* Kooperationsverweigerung *f*

nondeposit 'bottle *n* Einwegflasche *f*

nondescript [,nan·dɪ·'skrɪpt] *adj* (*person, building*) unscheinbar; (*color, taste*) undefinierbar

none [nʌn] I. *pron* 1. (*not any*) keine(r, s); ~ **of it matters anymore** das spielt jetzt keine Rolle mehr; ~ **at all** gar keine(r, s) 2. (*no person, no one*) ~ **other than ...** kein Geringerer/keine Geringere als ... ▶ **to be** ~ **of sb's** business jdn angehen II. *adv* kein bisschen; ~ **too pleased** *form* nicht

sonderlich erfreut

nonentity [nan·'en·tə·ţi] *n pej* (*nobody*)
a ~ ein Niemand *m*

nones'sential *adj* überflüssig

nonex'istent *adj* nicht vorhanden

non'fat *adj* (*food*) fettfrei

non'fiction I. *n* Sachliteratur *f* II. *adj* ~
books Sachbücher *pl*

non'flammable *adj* (*material*) nicht entflammbar

nonne'gotiable *adj* 1. LAW (*terms*) nicht
verhandelbar 2. FIN (*document*) nicht
übertragbar

'no-no <*pl* -es> *n fam* Unding *nt;* **that's
a ~!** das macht man nicht!

nonpol'luting *adj* (*byproduct*) ungiftig

nonpro'ductive *adj* (*in-*
vestment) nicht Gewinn bringend *attr*

non'profit I. *adj* nicht gewinnorientiert
II. *n* gemeinnützige Organisation

nonre'fundable *adj* (*payment*) nicht zurückzahlbar

nonrenewable 'resources *npl* nicht
erneuerbare Energien *pl*

non'resident *adj* 1. (*not local*) auswärtig
2. COMPUT nicht resident

nonre'turnable *adj* nicht zurücknehmbar

nonsense ['nan·sens] I. *n* Unsinn *m*
II. *adj attr* unsinnig, sinnlos III. *interj*
~! Quatsch!, Unsinn!

nonsensical [ˌnan·'sen·sɪ·kəl] *adj* (*plan*)
unsinnig

non'shrink *adj* (*clothing*) einlaufsicher

non'slip *adj* (*surface*) rutschfest

non'smoking *adj* (*section*) Nichtraucher-

non'starter *n* (*idea*) Reinfall *m*

non'stick *adj* antihaftbeschichtet

non'stop *adj* 1. Nonstop- II. *adv* (*rain*)
ununterbrochen

non'toxic *adj* (*substance*) ungiftig

non'verbal *adj* (*communication*) nonverbal

non'violent *adj* (*protest*) gewaltfrei

noodle ['nu·dəl] *n* Nudel *f*

nook [nʊk] *n* Nische *f,* Ecke *f* ▶ **[in]
every ~ and cranny** in allen Ecken
und Winkeln

noon [nun] *n* Mittag *m*

no one ['noʊ·wʌn] *pron see* **nobody**

noose [nus] *n* Schlinge *f a. fig*

nope [noʊp] *adv sl* nö *fam*

nor [nɔr] *conj* noch; **neither ... ~ ...** weder ... noch ...

norm [nɔrm] *n* Norm *f*

normal ['nɔr·məl] I. *adj* 1. (*ordinary:
person, day*) normal 2. (*usual: behav-
ior*) normal (**for** für +*akk*); **as [is]** ~ wie
üblich II. *n* Normalzustand *m;* **to return to** ~ sich normalisieren

normalize ['nɔr·mə·laɪz] *vt, vi* [sich] normalisieren

normally ['nɔr·mə·li] *adv* normalerweise

north [nɔrθ] I. *n* 1. (*direction*) Norden *m;* **to the** ~ nach Norden [hin]
2. (*region*) **the N~** der Norden II. *adj*
nördlich, Nord- III. *adv* nordwärts

North A'merica *n* Nordamerika *nt*

North A'merican *adj* nordamerikanisch

North Carolina [ˌnɔrθ·ˌkær·ə·'laɪ·nə] *n*
North Carolina

North Dakota [ˌnɔrθ·də·'koʊ·də] *n* Norddakota *nt*

north'east I. *n* (*direction*) Nordosten *m*
II. *adj* nordöstlich; ~ **wind** Wind *m*
von Nordost III. *adv* nordostwärts (**of**
von +*dat*)

north'eastern *adj attr* nordöstlich, Nordost-

northerly ['nɔr·ðər·li] *adj* nördlich, Nord-

northern ['nɔr·ðərn] *adj attr* nördlich

northerner ['nɔr·ðər·nər] *n* Nordstaatler(in) *m(f)*

Northern 'Ireland *n* Nordirland *nt*

North 'Pole *n* **the** ~ der Nordpol

northward ['nɔrθ·wərd] I. *adj* (*migration*) nach Norden *nach n pl,* Nord- II. *adv*
nach Norden

north'west I. *n* Nordwesten *m;* **to the
** ~ [**of sth**] nordwestlich [von etw *dat*]
II. *adj* nordwestlich, Nordwest-

nose [noʊz] I. *n* 1. (*organ*) Nase *f;* **to
blow one's** ~ sich *dat* die Nase putzen
2. (*front*) Schnauze *f fam;* (*of aircraft*)
Flugzeugnase *f* II. *vi to* ~ **forward** sich
vorsichtig vorwärtsbewegen

◆**nose around** *vi fam* herumstöbern
fam

◆**nose out** *vt* (*secrets*) herausfinden

'nosebleed *n* Nasenbluten *nt*

'nosedive I. *n* 1. AVIAT Sturzflug *m*

2. *fig* Einbruch *m* **II.** *vi* FIN (*economy*) einbrechen

'**nose job** *n fam* Nasenkorrektur *f*

nosey ['nou·zi] *adj pej see* **nosy**

no-'smoking *adj* (*area*) Nichtraucher-

nostalgic [na·'stæl·dʒɪk] *adj* nostalgisch

no-'strike agreement *n* Streikverbotsabkommen *nt*

nostril ['nas·trəl] *n* (*of a person*) Nasenloch *nt*

nosy ['nou·zi] *adj pej* neugierig

not [nat] *adv* **1.** *after aux vb* nicht; **it's ~ unusual** das ist nicht ungewöhnlich **2.** *in tag question* **it's cold, isn't it?** es ist kalt, nicht [wahr]? **3.** *before n* kein, nicht; **it's a girl, ~ a boy** es ist ein Mädchen, kein Junge **4.** *before adj, adv* (*meaning opposite*) nicht; **~ much** nicht viel ▶ **~ at all!** (*polite answer*) überhaupt nicht!; (*denying vehemently*) überhaupt nicht!

notable ['nou·tə·bəl] *adj* **1.** (*eminent*) bedeutend **2.** (*remarkable*) beachtlich

notably ['nou·tə·bli] *adv* **1.** (*particularly*) insbesondere **2.** (*perceptibly*) merklich

notary 'public <*pl* -ies public> [ˌnou·tə·ri-] *n* Notar(in) *m(f)*

notch <*pl* -es> [natʃ] *n* Einkerbung *f*

note [nout] **I.** *n* **1.** Notiz *f*; **to leave a ~** eine Nachricht hinterlassen **2.** MUS Note *f* **II.** *vt* (*notice*) wahrnehmen; **to ~ that ...** zur Kenntnis nehmen, dass ...

'**notebook** *n* **1.** (*book*) Notizbuch *nt* **2.** COMPUT Notebook *nt*

noted ['nou·tɪd] *adj attr* bekannt

'**notepad** *n* Notizblock *m*

noteworthy ['nout·ˌwɜr·ði] *adj* (*results*) beachtenswert; **nothing ~** nichts Besonderes

not-for-'profit *adj* (*organization*) nicht auf Gewinn ausgerichtet *attr*

nothing ['nʌθ·ɪŋ] **I.** *pron indef* **1.** (*not anything*) nichts, nix *fam*; **all or ~** alles oder nichts; **~ else** nichts weiter, sonst nichts **2.** (*of no importance*) nichts; **to mean ~ to sb** jdm nichts bedeuten **3.** (*zero*) Null *f* ▶ [all] **for ~** (*vollkommen*) umsonst; **there's ~ to it** (*easy*) dazu gehört nicht viel; (*not true*) da ist nichts dran *fam* **II.** *adv* überhaupt nicht; **to look ~ like sb** jdm nicht ähnlich sehen

notice ['nou·tɪs] **I.** *vt* **1.** (*see*) bemerken; (*perceive*) wahrnehmen **2.** (*pay attention to*) beachten; **to ~ sb** (*become aware of*) auf jdn aufmerksam werden **II.** *n* **1.** (*attention*) Beachtung *f*; **to take no ~ of the fact that ...** die Tatsache ignorieren, dass ... **2.** (*information in advance*) **until further ~** bis auf weiteres **3.** (*to end an arrangement*) **to give [one's] ~** kündigen

noticeable ['nou·tɪs·ə·bəl] *adj* merklich

notification [ˌnou·tə·fɪ·'keɪ·ʃən] *n* Mitteilung *f*

notify <-ie-> ['nou·tə·faɪ] *vt* **to ~ sb** [of sth] jdn [über etw *akk*] unterrichten

notorious [nou·'tɔr·i·əs] *adj* (*temper*) notorisch; (*criminal*) berüchtigt

noun [naʊn] *n* Hauptwort *nt*, Substantiv *nt*

nourishing ['nɜr·ɪʃ·ɪŋ] *adj* (*healthy*) nahrhaft

nourishment ['nɜr·ɪʃ·mənt] *n* **1.** (*food*) Nahrung *f* **2.** (*vital substances*) Nährstoffe *pl*

Nov. *n abbr of* **November** Nov.

novel[1] ['nav·əl] *n* (*book*) Roman *m*; **detective ~** Kriminalroman *m*

novel[2] ['nav·əl] *adj* (*new*) neuartig

novelist ['nav·ə·lɪst] *n* Romanautor(in) *m(f)*

novelty ['nav·əl·ti] *n* **1.** (*new thing*) Neuheit *f* **2.** (*newness*) Neuartigkeit *f*

November [nou·'vem·bər] *n* November *m*; *see also* **February**

novice ['nav·ɪs] *n* Anfänger(in) *m(f)*

now [naʊ] **I.** *adv* **1.** (*at present*) jetzt; **until ~** bis jetzt **2.** (*at once*) [right] **~** jetzt, sofort, gleich **3.** (*up to present*) jetzt, nun; **for two years ~** seit zwei Jahren **4.** (*short time ago*) **just ~** gerade eben ▶ [it's/it was] **~ or never** saying jetzt oder nie **II.** *conj* **~ that ...** jetzt, wo ...

nowadays ['naʊ·ə·deɪz] *adv* heutzutage

nowhere ['nou·hwer] *adv* nirgends, nirgendwo; **~ to be seen** nirgends zu sehen

nozzle ['naz·əl] *n* Düse *f*; (*of gasoline pump*) [Zapf]hahn *m*

nuclear ['nu·kli·ər] *adj* Kern-, Atom-

nuclear 'family n Kernfamilie f

nuclear 'medicine n Nuklearmedizin f

nuclear 'power plant n Kernkraftwerk nt

nucleus <pl -clei> ['nu·kli·əs] n Kern m

nude [nud] I. adj nackt II. n ART Akt m

nudge [nʌdʒ] I. vt stoßen II. n 1. (push) Schubs m 2. (encouragement) Anstoß m

nudist ['nu·dɪst] n Nudist(in) m(f)

nudity ['nu·də·t̬i] n Nacktheit f

nugget ['nʌg·ɪt] n (lump) Klumpen m; **gold ~** Goldnugget nt

nuisance ['nu·səns] n 1. (pesterer) Belästigung f 2. (annoyance) Ärger m; **what a ~!** wie ärgerlich!

nuke [nuk] vt MIL sl atomar angreifen

null, null and 'void [nʌl-] adj pred LAW null und nichtig

numb [nʌm] I. adj 1. (limbs) taub; **to go ~** (limbs) einschlafen 2. (torpid) benommen II. vt 1. (deprive of feeling) taub machen 2. (lessen) **to ~ the pain** den Schmerz betäuben

number[1] ['nʌm·bər] I. n 1. (figure) Zahl f; (identifying number) Nummer f 2. + sing/pl vb (amount) [An]zahl f II. vt nummerieren

number[2] ['nʌm·ər] adj comp of **numb**

numbering ['nʌm·bər·ɪŋ] n Nummerierung f

numbness ['nʌm·nɪs] n 1. (of limbs) Taubheit f 2. (torpor) Benommenheit f

numbskull n see **numskull**

numeral ['nu·mər·əl] n Ziffer f

numerical [nu·ˈmer·ɪ·kəl] adj **in ~ order** in numerischer Reihenfolge

numeric 'keypad n COMPUT Ziffernblock m

numerous ['nu·mər·əs] adj zahlreich

numskull ['nʌm·skʌl] n Hohlkopf m pej fam

nun [nʌn] n Nonne f

nurse [nɜrs] I. n 1. (in a hospital) [Kranken]schwester f; (male) Krankenpfleger m 2. (nanny) Kindermädchen nt II. vt 1. (care for) pflegen 2. (breastfeed) stillen

nursery ['nɜr·sə·ri] n 1. (daycare) Kindergarten m; (preschool) Vorschule f 2. HORT Gärtnerei f

nursery rhyme n Kinderreim m

'nursery school n Vorschule f

nursing ['nɜr·sɪŋ] n 1. (taking care) [Kranken]pflege f 2. (feeding) Stillen nt

nut [nʌt] n 1. (fruit) Nuss f 2. TECH Mutter f 3. fam (crazy person) Bekloppte(r) f(m) sl ▶ **to go ~s** durchdrehen

'nutcracker n Nussknacker m

nutmeg ['nʌt·meg] n Muskat m

nutrient ['nu·tri·ənt] n Nährstoff m

nutrition [nu·ˈtrɪʃ·ən] n Ernährungswissenschaft f

nutritional [nu·ˈtrɪʃ·ən·əl] adj Ernährungs-; ~ **supplement** Nahrungsergänzung f

nutritionist [nu·ˈtrɪʃ·ə·nɪst] n Ernährungswissenschaftler(in) m(f)

nutritious [nu·ˈtrɪʃ·əs] adj nahrhaft

nuts [nʌts] adj pred 1. (crazy) **to be ~** verrückt sein 2. (angry) **to go ~** ausrasten 3. (enthusiastic) **to be ~ about sb** verrückt nach jdm sein

'nutshell n Nussschale f

nutty ['nʌt̬·i] adj 1. (full of nuts) mit vielen Nüssen nach n 2. (tasting like nuts: taste, aroma) nussig

nuzzle ['nʌz·əl] vt [sanft] berühren

NV abbr of **Nevada**

NY, N.Y. abbr of **New York**

nylon ['naɪ·lan] n Nylon nt

nymphomaniac [ˌnɪm·fə·ˈmeɪ·ni·æk] n pej Nymphomanin f

NZ n abbr of **New Zealand**

O

O <pl -'s>, **o** <pl -'s> [oʊ] n 1. (letter) O nt, o nt; ~ **as in Oscar** O wie Otto 2. (zero) Null f

O. abbr of **Ohio**

oaf [oʊf] n pej fam Tölpel m fam

oafish ['oʊ·fɪʃ] adj pej fam 1. (rude) rüpelhaft 2. (clumsy) tölpelig fam

oak [oʊk] n Eiche f

oar [ɔr] n Ruder nt

oasis <pl -ses> [oʊ·ˈeɪ·sɪs] n a. fig Oase f

oat [oʊt] n Hafer m

oath [oʊθ] n (promise) Eid m; **to be under ~** unter Eid stehen

'oatmeal n Haferbrei m

obedient [oʊˈbiːdiənt] *adj* gehorsam

obese [oʊˈbiːs] *adj* fett *pej*; *esp* MED fettleibig

obesity [oʊˈbiːsəti] *n* Fettheit *f pej*; *esp* MED Fettleibigkeit *f*

obey [oʊˈbeɪ] *vt*, *vi* gehorchen

obituary [oʊˈbɪtʃ·u·er·i] *n* Nachruf *m*

object[1] [ˈabˈdʒɪkt] *n* 1. (*thing, ling*) Objekt *nt* 2. (*subject*) Gegenstand *m*

object[2] [əbˈdʒɛkt] *vi* (*oppose*) dagegen sein; (*dislike*) etwas dagegen haben; **to ~ to sth** (*oppose*) gegen etw *akk* sein; (*dislike*) etwas gegen etw *akk* haben

objection [əbˈdʒɛk·ʃən] *n* Einwand *m*

objectionable [əbˈdʒɛk·ʃə·nə·bəl] *adj* (*offensive*) anstößig; (*smell*) übel

objective [əbˈdʒɛk·tɪv] I. *n* (*aim*) Ziel *nt* II. *adj* objektiv

objectively [əbˈdʒɛk·tɪv·li] *adv* (*without bias*) objektiv

ˈobject lesson *n approv* Paradebeispiel *nt*

objector [əbˈdʒɛk·tər] *n* Gegner(in) *m(f)*

obligation [ˌab·lə·ˈgeɪ·ʃən] *n* Verpflichtung *f*

obligatory [əˈblɪg·ə·tɔr·i] *adj* obligatorisch *a. hum*

oblige [əˈblaɪdʒ] I. *vt* 1. (*force*) **to be ~d to do sth** verpflichtet sein, etw zu tun 2. (*please*) **to ~ sb** [**by doing sth**] jdm [durch etw *akk*] einen Gefallen erweisen II. *vi* helfen; **I'll be happy to ~** ich werde bereitwillig helfen

obliging [əˈblaɪ·dʒɪŋ] *adj approv* (*behavior*) entgegenkommend; (*person*) zuvorkommend

oblique [oʊˈbliːk] *adj* 1. (*indirect*) indirekt 2. (*slanting*) schief

obliterate [əˈblɪt·ə·reɪt] *vt* 1. (*destroy*) vernichten 2. (*efface*) verwischen

oblivion [əˈblɪv·i·ən] *n* 1. (*obscurity*) Vergessenheit *f* 2. (*unconsciousness*) Besinnungslosigkeit *f*

oblivious [əˈblɪv·i·əs] *adj* **to be ~ of** [*or* **to**] **sth** sich *dat* einer S. *gen* nicht bewusst sein; (*not notice*) etw gar nicht bemerken

oblong [ˈab·laŋ] I. *n* Rechteck *nt* II. *adj* rechteckig

oboe [ˈoʊ·boʊ] *n* Oboe *f*

obscene [əbˈsiːn] *adj* (*offensive*) obszön;

(*joke*) zotig

obscenity [əbˈsen·ə·t̬i] *n* Obszönität *f*

obscure [əbˈskjʊr] *adj* 1. (*author, place*) unbekannt 2. (*unclear*) unbestimmt; (*text*) schwer verständlich; **for some ~ reason** aus irgendeinem unerfindlichen Grund

obscurity [əbˈskjʊr·ə·t̬i] *n* (*anonymity*) Unbekanntheit *f*; (*of no importance*) Unbedeutendheit *f*; **to sink into ~** in Vergessenheit geraten

observable [əbˈzɜr·və·bəl] *adj* wahrnehmbar

observant [əbˈzɜr·vənt] *adj approv* (*sharp-eyed*) aufmerksam

observation [ˌab·zər·ˈveɪ·ʃən] *n* Beobachtung *f*; LAW (*surveillance*) Überwachung *f*

obserˈvation tower *n* Aussichtsturm *m*

observatory [əbˈzɜr·və·tɔr·i] *n* Observatorium *nt*

observe [əbˈzɜrv] *vt* 1. (*watch closely*) beobachten; (*by police*) überwachen 2. (*study by watching: stars*) beobachten 3. *form* (*obey: ceasefire*) einhalten; (*law*) befolgen; **to ~ the speed limit** sich an die Geschwindigkeitsbegrenzung halten

observer [əbˈzɜr·vər] *n* (*watcher*) Beobachter(in) *m(f)*; (*spectator*) Zuschauer(in) *m(f)*

obsess [əbˈses] *vt* verfolgen; **to be ~ed by sb** von jdm besessen sein

obsession [əbˈsef·ən] *n* (*preoccupation*) Manie *f*; **to have an ~ with sth** von etw *dat* besessen sein

obsessive [əbˈses·ɪv] *adj* zwanghaft

obsolete [ˌab·sə·ˈliːt] *adj* veraltet; (*design*) altmodisch; (*method*) überholt

obstacle [ˈab·stə·kəl] *n* Hindernis *nt*

ˈobstacle course *n* Hindernisstrecke *f*

obstetrician [ˌab·stə·ˈtrɪʃ·ən] *n* Geburtshelfer(in) *m(f)*

obstinate [ˈab·stə·nɪt] *adj* hartnäckig; (*person*) eigensinnig

obstruct [əbˈstrʌkt] *vt* 1. (*block*) blockieren; (*path*) versperren; (*pipe*) verstopfen; (*progress*) behindern 2. SPORT sperren

obstruction [əbˈstrʌk·ʃən] *n* 1. (*blockage*) Blockierung *f*; (*med, of pipes*) Verstopfung *f*; **to cause an ~** (*for traffic*)

den Verkehr behindern 2. (*Baseball, law*) Behinderung *f*; sport Sperre *f*

obstructive [əb·ˈstrʌk·tɪv] *adj pej* hinderlich

obtain [əb·ˈteɪn] *vt* **to ~ sth [from sb]** (*to be given*) etw [von jdm] bekommen; (*to go and get*) sich *dat* etw [von jdm] verschaffen; (*permission*) erhalten

obtainable [əb·ˈteɪ·nə·bəl] *adj* erhältlich

obtuse [ab·ˈtus] *adj* MATH (*angle*) stumpf

obvious [ˈab·vi·əs] *adj* offensichtlich; (*comparison, solution*) naheliegend; (*displeasure*) deutlich; **to be ~ [that] ...** offenkundig sein, dass ...

obviously [ˈab·viəs·li] *adv* offensichtlich; **he was ~ very upset** er war sichtlich sehr aufgebracht

occasion [ə·ˈkeɪ·ʒən] *n* (*particular time*) Gelegenheit *f*; (*event*) Ereignis *nt*; **on another ~** ein anderes Mal; **on several ~s** mehrmals

occasional [ə·ˈkeɪ·ʒə·nəl] *adj* gelegentlich

occasionally [ə·ˈkeɪ·ʒə·nə·li] *adv* gelegentlich; **to see sb ~** jdn ab und zu treffen

occult [ə·ˈkʌlt] *n* **the ~** das Okkulte

occupation [ˌak·jə·ˈpeɪ·ʃən] *n* **1.** *form* (*profession*) Beruf *m* **2.** MIL Besetzung *f*

occupational [ˌak·jə·ˈpeɪ·ʃə·nəl] *adj* Berufs-, beruflich

occupational ˈtherapy *n* Beschäftigungstherapie *f*

occupier [ˈak·jə·paɪ·ər] *n* **1.** (*tenant*) Bewohner(in) *m(f)* **2.** (*conqueror*) Besatzer(in) *m(f)*

occupy <-ie-> [ˈak·ju·paɪ] *vt* **1.** (*fill*) ausfüllen; (*live in*) bewohnen **2.** (*take control of*) besetzen; **~ing forces** Besatzungstruppen *pl*

occur <-rr-> [ə·ˈkɜr] *vi* **1.** (*take place*) geschehen; (*accident*) sich ereignen; (*change*) stattfinden **2.** (*come to mind*) **to ~ to sb** jdm einfallen

occurrence [ə·ˈkɜr·əns] *n* **1.** (*event*) Vorfall *m* **2.** (*incidence*) Vorkommen *nt*

ocean [ˈoʊ·ʃən] *n* Ozean *m*

oceanography [ˌoʊ·ʃə·ˈnag·rə·fi] *n* Ozeanographie *f*

ocelot [ˈas·ə·lat] *n* Ozelot *m*

ocher, ochre [ˈoʊ·kər] *n* Ocker *m o nt*

o'clock [ə·ˈklak] *adv* **two ~** zwei Uhr

Oct. *n abbr of* **October** Okt.

octagonal [ak·ˈtæg·ə·nəl] *adj* achteckig

octane [ˈak·teɪn] *n* Oktanzahl *f*

octave [ˈak·tɪv] *n* Oktave *f*

October [ak·ˈtoʊ·bər] *n* Oktober *m*; *see also* **February**

octopus <*pl* -es> [ˈak·tə·pəs] *n* Tintenfisch *m*

OD [ˌoʊ·ˈdi] *sl abbr of* **overdose** I. *vi* **to ~ on sth** eine Überdosis einer S. *gen* nehmen *fig* II. *n* Überdosis *f*

odd [ad] I. *adj* **1.** (*strange*) merkwürdig; (*person*) eigenartig **2.** MATH ungerade **3.** *attr* (*shoe, sock*) einzeln II. *n* **~s** *pl* (*probability*) **the ~s are 3 to 1** die Chancen stehen 3 zu 1; **the ~s are ...** es ist sehr wahrscheinlich, dass ...; **the ~s on/against sb doing sth** die Chancen, dass jd etw tut/nicht tut ▶ **against all the ~s** entgegen allen Erwartungen; **~s and ends** Krimskrams *m kein pl*

oddball [ˈad·bɔl] *fam* I. *n* Verrückte(r) *f(m)* II. *adj attr* verrückt

oddity [ˈad·ə·ti] *n* Kuriosität *f*

oddly [ˈad·li] *adv* seltsam; **~ enough** merkwürdigerweise

odometer [oʊ·ˈdam·ə·tər] *n* Kilometerzähler *m*

odor [ˈoʊ·dər] *n* Geruch *m*

odorless [ˈoʊ·dər·ləs] *adj form* geruchlos

odyssey [ˈad·ɪ·si] *n usu sing liter or a. fig* Odyssee *f*

of [ʌv, əv] *prep* **1.** *after n* (*expressing relationship*) von; **the employees ~ the company** die Angestellten des Unternehmens; **the destruction ~ the rain forest** die Zerstörung des Regenwalds; **the works ~ Shakespeare** die Werke Shakespeares; **a friend ~ mine** ein Freund von mir **2.** *after n* (*relating a part to the whole*) von; **both ~ us** wir beide; **all ~ us** wir alle; **most ~ them** die meisten von ihnen; **a third ~ the people** ein Drittel der Leute; **one ~ the smartest** eine(r) der Schlauesten **3.** *after n* (*expressing quantities*) **a cup ~ coffee** eine Tasse Kaffee; **two pounds ~ apples** ein Kilo Äpfel *nt*; **a piece ~ cake** ein Stück Kuchen **4.** *after vb, n* (*consisting of*) aus; **a sweater made ~**

O

the finest lambswool ein Pullover aus feinster Schafswolle **5.** *after vb* (*concerning*) **he was accused ~ fraud** er wurde wegen Betrugs angeklagt; *after adj* **to be unsure ~ oneself** sich seiner selbst nicht sicher sein; **to be afraid ~ sb** vor jdm Angst haben; **to be fond ~ swimming** gerne schwimmen; **to be sick ~ sth** etw satthaben; *after n* **memories ~ sb/sth** Erinnerungen an jdn/etw **6.** *after n* (*expressing position*) von; **north ~** nördlich von; **on the corner ~ the street** an der Straßenecke **7.** *after n* (*in time phrases*) **the eleventh ~ March** der elfte März; (*to*) vor; **it's a quarter ~ five** es ist viertel vor fünf

off [ɔf] **I.** *prep* **1.** (*indicating removal*) von; **he wiped the dust ~ the table** er wischte den Staub von dem Tisch; **he cut a piece ~ the cheese** er schnitt ein Stück Käse ab; **to be ~ the air** RADIO, TV nicht mehr senden; **~ the record** nicht für die Öffentlichkeit bestimmt **2.** *after vb* (*moving down*) hinunter [von]; (*towards sb*) herunter [von]; **they jumped ~ the cliff** sie sprangen von der Klippe; **the boy fell ~ his bike** der Junge fiel von seinem Fahrrad herunter **3.** (*away from*) [weg] von; (*at sea*) von +*dat*; **six miles ~ the coast of Florida** sechs Meilen vor der Küste Floridas; **to lead ~ sth** von etw *dat* wegführen; **far/a long way ~ sth** weit entfernt von etw *dat* **4.** (*absent from*) **to be ~ work** am Arbeitsplatz fehlen **II.** *adv* **1.** (*not on*) aus; **to switch/turn sth ~** etw ausschalten **2.** (*away*) weg-; **to go/drive ~** weggehen/-fahren; **I'm ~ now — see you tomorrow** ich gehe jetzt – wir sehen uns morgen; **to see sb ~** jdn verabschieden **3.** (*removed*) ab-; **I'll take my jacket ~** ich ziehe meine Jacke aus; **to come ~** (*button*) abgehen **4.** (*discounted*) reduziert; **to get money ~** Rabatt bekommen **III.** *adj* **1.** (*not working*) außer Betrieb; (*switched ~*) aus[geschaltet]; (*faucet*) zugedreht **2.** (*not at work*) **to be ~** freihaben; **to take some time ~** einige Zeit freinehmen

'offbeat *adj* unkonventionell; (*sense of humor*) ausgefallen

off-'center *adj* nicht in der Mitte *präd*

'off day *n* schlechter Tag

off-'duty *adj* **to be ~** dienstfrei haben

offend [ə-'fend] **I.** *vi* (*commit a criminal act*) eine Straftat begehen **II.** *vt* (*insult*) beleidigen; (*hurt*) kränken

offender [ə-'fen-dər] *n* [Straf]täter(in) *m(f)*

offense [ə-'fens] *n* **1.** LAW Straftat *f* **2.** (*upset feelings*) Beleidigung *f*; **to cause ~** Anstoß erregen; **to take ~** [at *sth*] [wegen einer S. *gen*] gekränkt/beleidigt sein **3.** SPORT (*attack*) Angriff *m*

offensive [ə-'fen-sɪv] **I.** *adj* **1.** (*causing offense*) anstößig; (*joke*) anzüglich **II.** *n* MIL Angriff *m*; **to go on the ~** in die Offensive gehen

offer ['ɔ-fər] **I.** *n* Angebot *nt* **II.** *vt* **1.** (*present for acceptance*) anbieten **2.** (*put forward*) vorbringen; (*explanation*) abgeben; (*information*) geben

offering ['ɔ-fər-ɪŋ] *n usu pl* Spende *f*

offhand *adj* **1.** (*uninterested*) gleichgültig **2.** (*informal*) lässig; **~ remark** nebenbei fallen gelassene Bemerkung

office ['ɔ-fɪs] *n* **1.** (*room*) Büro *nt*; (*of company*) Geschäftsstelle *f* **2.** POL (*authoritative position*) Amt *nt*; **to come into ~** sein Amt antreten

'office building *n* Bürohaus *nt*

'office hours *npl* Geschäftszeit[en] *f[pl]*

officer ['ɔ-fɪ-sər] *n* **1.** MIL Offizier(in) *m(f)* **2.** (*office holder*) Beamte(r) *m*, Beamte [*or* -in] *f*; (*police*) ~ Polizeibeamte(r) *f(m)*, Polizist(in) *m(f)*

'office supplies *npl* Bürobedarf *m kein pl*

'office worker *n* Büroangestellte(r) *f(m)*

official [ə-'fɪʃ-əl] **I.** *n* **1.** (*holding public office*) Amtsperson *f*, Beamte(r) *m*, Beamte [*or* -in] *f* **2.** SPORT Schiedsrichter, -in *m, f* **II.** *adj* **1.** (*relating to an office*) offiziell, amtlich; **~ residence** Amtssitz *m* **2.** (*authorized*) offiziell; (*inquiry*) amtlich

officially [ə-'fɪʃ-ə-li] *adv* offiziell

officious [ə-'fɪʃ-əs] *adj pej* **1.** (*bossy*) schikanierend **2.** (*interfering*) aufdringlich

off-'key *adj* verstimmt

off-'limits *adj pred* **to be ~ to sb** für jdn tabu sein

off'line *adj* offline

'offload *vt* **1.** (*unload*) ausladen **2.** (*get rid of*) loswerden *fam;* **to ~ the responsibility** [**onto** sb] die Verantwortung [auf jdn] abladen

off-'peak *adj* (*telephone call*) außerhalb der Hauptsprechzeiten *nach n*

off-'piste *adv* abseits der Skipiste

'off-season *n* **the ~** die Nebensaison

offset ['ɒf·set] *vt* <-set, -set> *usu passive* (*compensate for*) **to be ~ by** [**doing**] **sth** durch etw *akk* ausgeglichen werden

off-'site *adj* Außen-

offspring <*pl*> ['ɒf·sprɪŋ] *n a. hum* (*person's child*) Nachkomme *m*

off'stage *adv* **1.** (*away from the stage*) hinter der Bühne **2.** (*privately*) privat

off-street 'parking *n* Parken auf Parkplätzen außerhalb des Stadtzentrums

off-the-'rack *adj* Konfektions-

often ['ɒ·fən] *adv* oft; **every so ~** gelegentlich

oftentimes *adv fam* häufig

ogle ['oʊ·gəl] *vt* angaffen *pej*

ogre ['oʊ·gər] *n* Menschenfresser *m; fig fam* Scheusal *nt*

OH *abbr of* **Ohio**

oh¹ [oʊ] *interj* **1.** (*to show surprise, disappointment, pleasure*) oh; **~ well** na ja **2.** (*by the way*) ach, übrigens

oh² [oʊ] *n* (*in phone numbers*) Null *f*

Ohio [oʊ·'haɪ·oʊ] *n* Ohio *nt*

oil [ɔɪl] **I.** *n* **1.** (*lubricant*) Öl *nt* **2.** (*petroleum*) [Erd]öl *nt* FOOD [Speise]öl *nt* **II.** *vt* (*lubricate*) ölen

'oilcan *n* Ölkännchen *nt*

oil change *n* Ölwechsel *m*

oil company *n* Ölfirma *f*

oil field *n* Ölfeld *nt*

oil painting *n* Ölbild *nt*

oil pipeline *n* Ölpipeline *f*

oil rig *n* Bohrinsel *f*

'oilskin *n* **~s** *pl* Ölzeug *nt kein pl*

oil tanker *n* Öltanker *m*

oil well *n* Ölquelle *f*

oily ['ɔɪ·li] *adj* **1.** (*food*) ölig **2.** (*hair*) fettig

ointment ['ɔɪnt·mənt] *n* Salbe *f*

OK, okay [oʊ·'keɪ] *fam* **I.** *adj* **1.** *pred* (*acceptable*) okay **2.** *pred* (*healthy: person*) in Ordnung **3.** *pred* (*not outstanding*) nicht schlecht **4.** *pred* (*have*

no problems) **to be ~ for money** genug Geld haben **II.** *interj* okay; **~ then** also gut **III.** *vt* **to ~ sth** zu etw *dat* sein Okay geben **IV.** *adv* gut; **did you get there ~?** bist du dort gut angekommen?

OK *abbr of* **Oklahoma**

Okla. *abbr of* **Oklahoma**

Oklahoma [oʊ·klə·'hoʊ·mə] *n* Oklahoma *nt*

okra ['oʊk·rə] *n* Okra *f*

old [oʊld] **I.** *adj* **1.** alt **2.** *after n* (*denoting an age*) alt; **three years ~** drei Jahre alt **3.** *attr* (*former*) ehemalig; (*job*) alt ▶ **you can't teach an ~ dog new tricks** *prov* der Mensch ist ein Gewohnheitstier **II.** *n* **young and ~** Jung und Alt

old 'age *n* Alter *nt*

old-'fashioned *adj esp pej* altmodisch

old 'lady *n* **1.** (*elderly female*) alte Dame **2.** *fam* (*wife, mother*) **the ~** die Alte

old 'man *n* **1.** (*elderly male*) alter Mann **2.** *fam* (*husband, father*) **the ~** der Alte *fam*

old 'master *n* alter Meister

Old 'Testament *n* **the ~** das Alte Testament

old-'timer *n fam* **1.** (*old man*) Oldie *m hum fam* **2.** (*long-time worker*) alter Hase *fam*

old 'wives' tale *n* Ammenmärchen *nt*

oleander [oʊ·li·'æn·dər] *n* Oleander *m*

olive ['al·ɪv] *n* Olive *f*

olive branch *n fig* Ölzweig *m*

'olive grove *n* Olivenhain *m*

'olive oil *n* Olivenöl *nt*

Olympic 'Games, Olympics [oʊ·'lɪm·pɪks] *n pl* **the ~** die Olympischen Spiele

omelet, omelette ['am·lət] *n* Omelett *nt*

omen ['oʊ·mən] *n* Omen *nt*

ominous ['am·ə·nəs] *adj* unheilvoll

omission [oʊ·'mɪʃ·ən] *n* Auslassung *f*

omit <-tt-> [oʊ·'mɪt] *vt* auslassen

omnivorous [am·'nɪv·ər·əs] *adj* alles fressend *attr*

on [an] **I.** *prep* **1.** (*on top of*) auf *+dat;* **the book's ~ the table** das Buch liegt auf dem Tisch **2.** *with verbs of motion* (*onto*) auf *+akk;* **to go out ~ the balcony** auf die Terrasse hinausgehen **3.** (*indicating position*) an *+dat,* auf *+dat;* **to**

lie ~ **the beach** am Strand liegen; **he had a scratch ~ his arm** er hatte einen Kratzer am Arm; ~ **the right** auf der rechten Seite 4. (*indicating contact*) an +*dat*; **I hit my head ~ the shelf** ich stieß mir den Kopf am Regal an; **to stumble ~ sth** über etw *akk* stolpern 5. (*about*) über +*akk*; **a debate ~ the crisis** eine Debatte über die Krise; **he needs some advice ~ how to dress** er braucht ein paar Tipps, wie er sich anziehen soll 6. (*based on*) auf ... hin; ~ **account of** wegen; **to rely ~ sb/sth** sich auf jdn/etw verlassen 7. (*against*) auf +*akk*; **to place a limit ~ sth** etw begrenzen 8. (*indicating a medium*) auf +*dat*; **what's ~ TV tonight?** was kommt heute Abend im Fernsehen?; **to come out ~ video** als Video herauskommen 9. (*traveling by*) in +*dat*, mit +*dat*; ~ **foot** zu Fuß 10. (*indicating date*) an +*dat*; ~ **Friday** am Freitag II. *adv* 1. (*in contact with*) auf; **to screw sth ~ etw** anschrauben 2. (*on body*) an; **to try sth ~ etw** anprobieren 3. (*indicating continuance*) weiter; **if the line's busy, keep ~ trying!** wenn besetzt ist, probier es weiter! 4. (*in forward direction*) vorwärts; **from that day ~** von diesem Tag an 5. (*functioning*) an; **to leave the light ~** das Licht anlassen; **to switch/turn sth ~ etw** einschalten 6. (*aboard*) **to get ~** (*bus, train*) einsteigen; (*horse*) aufsitzen ▶ ~ **and off** ab und zu *fam*; **you're ~!** abgemacht! *fam*

once [wʌns] I. *adv* 1. (*one time*) einmal; **just this ~** nur dieses eine Mal 2. (*in the past*) früher; ~ **upon a time ... liter** es war einmal ... ▶ **at ~** (*simultaneously*) auf einmal; (*immediately*) sofort; ~ **more** (*one more time*) noch einmal; (*again, as before*) wieder; ~ **or twice** ein paar Mal II. *conj* (*as soon as*) sobald

'**once-over** *n fam* (*cursory examination*) **to give sth the ~** etw flüchtig ansehen

oncoming ['ɒn·kʌm·ɪŋ] *adj attr* (*vehicle*) entgegenkommend; ~ **traffic** Gegenverkehr *m*

one [wʌn] I. *n* 1. (*unit*) eins; **a hundred and ~** einhundert[und]eins 2. (*numer-*

al) Eins *f* II. *adj* 1. *attr* (*not two*) ein(e); ~ **hundred** einhundert; ~ **million** eine Million 2. *attr* (*one of a number*) ein(e); **he can't tell ~ wine from another** er schmeckt bei Weinen keinen Unterschied 3. *attr* (*single, only*) einzige(r, s); **we should paint the bedroom ~ color** wir sollten das Schlafzimmer nur in einer Farbe streichen 4. *attr* (*some future*) irgendein(e); ~ **day** irgendwann 5. *attr* (*some in the past*) ein(e); ~ **evening** eines Abends ▶ ~ **way or another** (*somehow*) irgendwie III. *pron* 1. (*single item*) eine(r, s); **not a single ~** kein Einziger/keine Einzige/kein Einziges; ~ **after another** eine(r, s) nach dem/der anderen; **this/that ~** diese(r, s)/jene(r, s) 2. (*single person*) eine(r); **she thought of her loved ~s** sie dachte an ihre Lieben; ~ **by ~** nacheinander; **she's ~ of my favorite writers** sie ist eine meiner Lieblingsautoren 3. (*expressing alternatives*) ~ **or the other** der/die/das eine oder der/die/das andere 4. *form* (*any person, most people*) man; (*I*) ich; ~ **gets the impression that ...** man hat den Eindruck, dass ... ▶ **to be ~ of the family** zur Familie gehören *fig*; **in ~s and twos** (*in small numbers*) immer nur ein paar; (*alone or in a pair*) allein oder paarweise

'**one-armed** *adj* einarmig

'**one-eyed** *adj attr* einäugig

one-'handed I. *adv* mit einer Hand II. *adj attr* einhändig

one-'liner *n* Einzeiler *m*

one-night 'stand *n* 1. (*sexual relationship*) Abenteuer *nt* für eine Nacht 2. (*performance*) einmaliges Gastspiel

one-piece, one-piece 'swimsuit *n* Einteiler *m*

oneself [wʌn·'self] *pron refl* 1. *after vb, prep* (*direct object*) sich 2. (*personally*) selbst; **to see sth for ~** etw selbst sehen 3. (*alone*) [**all**] **by ~** [ganz] alleine

'**one-sided** *adj* einseitig

'**one-time** *adj attr* 1. (*former*) ehemalig 2. (*happening only once*) einmalig

one-track 'mind *n* **to have a ~** immer nur eins im Kopf haben

one-way 'street n Einbahnstraße f

one-way 'ticket n einfache Fahrkarte, Einzelfahrschein m

ongoing ['ɑn·goʊ·ɪŋ] adj laufend attr

onion ['ʌn·jən] n Zwiebel f

online [ˌɑn·'laɪn] COMPUT I. adj Online-II. adv online

onlooker ['ɑn·lʊk·ər] n a. fig Zuschauer(in) m(f)

only ['oʊn·li] I. adj attr einzige(r, s); the ~ one der/die/das Einzige; the ~ way die einzige Möglichkeit II. adv 1. (exclusively) nur; **for members** ~ nur für Mitglieder 2. (just) erst 3. (merely) nur, bloß; **not** ~ ..., **but also** ... nicht nur ..., sondern auch ... 4. (unavoidably) nur, unweigerlich; **the situation can** ~ **get better** die Situation kann sich nur verbessern III. conj (however) aber, jedoch; **he's a good athlete,** ~ **he smokes too much** er ist ein guter Sportler, bloß raucht er zu viel

onset ['ɑn·set] n Beginn m

onshore ['ɑn·ʃɔr] adv an Land

on-'site I. adj Vor-Ort- II. adv vor Ort

onstage [ˌɑn·'steɪʤ, ˌɑn-] adv auf die Bühne

on-the-job 'training n Ausbildung f am Arbeitsplatz

onward ['ɑn·wərd] I. adj attr (of trip) Weiter- II. adv 1. (into the future) **from that day** ~ von diesem Tag an 2. (of direction) weiter

onyx ['ɑn·ɪks] n Onyx m

oops [ʊps] interj fam hoppla

ooze [uz] I. vi (seep out) tropfen (**from** aus +dat); (water) sickern; **to** ~ **with oil** vor Öl triefen II. vt fig (overflow with: charm) ausstrahlen; (sex appeal) versprühen

opal ['oʊ·pəl] n Opal m

opalescent [ˌoʊ·pə·'les·ənt] adj schillernd

opaque [oʊ·'peɪk] adj (not transparent) undurchsichtig; (window) trüb

OPEC ['oʊ·pek] n acr for **Organization of Petroleum Exporting Countries** OPEC f

open ['oʊ·pən] I. adj 1. (not closed) offen, geöffnet, auf präd; (book) aufgeschlagen; (flower) aufgeblüht; **wide** ~ [sperrangel]weit geöffnet; **to burst** ~ (case) aufgehen 2. pred (for customers: shop) geöffnet, offen 3. (not yet decided: question) offen; **to keep an** ~ **mind** unvoreingenommen bleiben 4. (not enclosed) offen; **to be in the** ~ **air** an der frischen Luft sein 5. pred (frank: person) offen 6. pred (exposed) offen, ungeschützt; **to be** ~ **to criticism** kritisierbar sein II. vi 1. (from closed) sich öffnen, aufgehen 2. (for business: shop) öffnen; (for the first time) eröffnen 3. (story) beginnen, anfangen 4. (play) Premiere haben III. vt 1. (book) aufschlagen; (window, bottle) aufmachen; (eyes, letter) öffnen; a. fig (mouth) aufmachen 2. (bank account) eröffnen ▶ **to** ~ **sb's <u>eyes</u> to sb** jdm die Augen über jdn öffnen IV. n 1. (out of doors) [out] **in the** ~ draußen; (in the open air) im Freien 2. (not secret) **to come out into the** ~ ans Licht kommen

◆open out I. vi 1. (move apart) sich ausbreiten 2. (map) sich auffalten lassen; (flower) aufblühen 3. (grow wider) sich erweitern; (river) breiter werden II. vt (unfold) **to** ~ **⇆ a map** eine [Land]karte auseinanderfalten

◆open up I. vi 1. (store, etc.) eröffnen 2. (start shooting) das Feuer eröffnen, losfeuern II. vt 1. (pipe) passierbar machen; (house) aufschließen; (door) aufmachen 2. (make available) **to** ~ **up ⇆ sth** [**to sb/sth**] [jdm/etw] etw zugänglich machen

'open-air adj im Freien nach n

opener ['oʊ·pə·nər] n (opening device) Öffner m

open-'faced adj (sandwich) belegt

open-heart 'surgery n Operation f am offenen Herzen

opening ['oʊ·pə·nɪŋ] n 1. (action) Öffnen nt 2. (hole) Öffnung f; (in traffic) Lücke f 3. (job) freie Stelle 4. (introduction: of a film) Anfang m

'opening hours npl Öffnungszeiten pl

'**opening time** n Öffnungszeit f

openly ['ou·pən·li] adv **1.** (frankly) offen **2.** (publicly) öffentlich

open 'market n offener Markt

open-'minded adj (to new ideas) aufgeschlossen; (not prejudiced) unvoreingenommen

openness ['ou·pən·nəs] n Offenheit f

opera ['ap·rə] n Oper f

'**opera house** n Opernhaus nt

operate ['ap·ə·reɪt] I. vi **1.** (work) funktionieren **2.** (perform surgery) **to ~ on sb** jdn operieren **3.** (do business) operieren geh II. vt (work) bedienen

'**operating room** n MED Operationssaal m

'**operating system, OS** [ou·'es] n COMPUT Betriebssystem nt

operation [ap·ə·'reɪ·ʃən] n **1.** (way of functioning) Funktionsweise f; **day-to-day ~** gewöhnlicher Betriebsablauf **2.** (functioning state) Betrieb m; **to come into ~** (law) in Kraft treten **3.** (process) Vorgang m **4.** (activity) Unternehmung f; MIL Operation f; **rescue ~** Rettungsaktion f **5.** (surgery) Operation f

operational [ap·ə·'reɪ·ʃə·nəl] adj (functioning) betriebsbereit

operative ['ap·ər·ə·tɪv] I. n (in a factory) [Fach]arbeiter(in) m(f) II. adj (functioning) in Betrieb präd

operator ['ap·ə·reɪ·tər] n **1.** (worker) Bediener(in) m(f) **2.** (switchboard worker) Telefonist(in) m(f)

operetta [ap·ə·'ret·ə] n Operette f

ophthalmologist [af·θəl·'mal·ə·dʒɪst] n Augenarzt, -ärztin m, f

opiate ['ou·pi·ɪt] n Opiat nt

opinion [ə·'pɪn·jən] n **1.** (belief) Meinung f **2.** (view on topic) Einstellung f, Standpunkt m; **difference of ~** Meinungsverschiedenheit f; **to have a high ~ of sb** von jdm eine hohe Meinung haben

opinionated [ə·'pɪn·jə·neɪ·tɪd] adj pej rechthaberisch

o'**pinion poll** n Meinungsumfrage f

opium ['ou·pi·əm] n Opium nt

opossum <pl -s> [ə·'pas·əm] n Opossum nt

opponent [ə·'pou·nənt] n POL Widersa-

cher(in) m(f); SPORT Gegner(in) m(f)

opportune [ap·ər·'tun] adj angebracht

opportunism [ap·ər·'tu·nɪz·əm] n Opportunismus m

opportunist [ap·ər·'tu·nɪst] n Opportunist(in) m(f)

opportunity [ap·ər·'tu·nə·ti] n **1.** (occasion) Gelegenheit f; **a window of ~** eine Chance **2.** (for advancement) Möglichkeit f

oppose [ə·'pouz] vt **1.** (disapprove) ablehnen **2.** (resist) **to ~ sb/sth** gegen jdn/etw vorgehen **3.** SPORT **to ~ sb** gegen jdn antreten

opposed [ə·'pouzd] adj pred **to be ~ to sth** gegen etw akk sein

opposing [ə·'pou·zɪŋ] adj attr entgegengesetzt; (opinion) gegensätzlich; (team) gegnerisch

opposite ['ap·ə·zɪt] I. n Gegenteil nt II. adj **1.** (contrary) gegensätzlich **2.** (facing) gegenüberliegend; (directions) entgegengesetzt III. adv gegenüber IV. prep (across from) gegenüber

opposition [ap·ə·'zɪʃ·ən] n **1.** (resistance) Widerstand m **2.** (party not in power) Opposition[spartei] f; (opposing team) gegnerische Mannschaft

oppression [ə·'preʃ·ən] n Unterdrückung f

oppressive [ə·'pres·ɪv] adj **1.** (regime) unterdrückerisch **2.** (heat, weather) drückend

opt [apt] vi **to ~ for sth** sich für etw akk entscheiden

◆**opt in** vi sich beteiligen

◆**opt out** vi nicht mitmachen; (withdraw) aussteigen fam

optical ['ap·tɪ·kəl] adj optisch

optician [ap·'tɪʃ·ən] n Optiker(in) m(f)

optimism ['ap·tə·mɪz·əm] n Optimismus m

optimist ['ap·tə·mɪst] n Optimist(in) m(f)

optimize ['ap·tə·maɪz] vt optimieren

optimum ['ap·tə·məm] adj optimal

option ['ap·ʃən] n Wahl f; (possibility) Möglichkeit f; **to not be an ~** nicht in Frage kommen

optional ['ap·ʃə·nəl] adj wahlfrei

opulence ['ap·jə·ləns] n (luxury) Luxus m

opulent ['ap·jə·lənt] adj **1.** (affluent)

wohlhabend **2.** (*luxurious*) luxuriös

OR *n abbr of* **Oregon**

or [ɔr] *conj* **1.** (*as a choice*) oder **2.** (*otherwise*) sonst; **either ... ~ ...** entweder...[,] oder **3.** (*and a. not*) **not ... ~ ...** weder ... noch ...

oral ['ɔr·əl] **I.** *adj* mündlich **II.** *n* ~s *pl* mündliches Examen

orange ['ɔr·ɪndʒ] **I.** *n* (*fruit*) Orange *f* **II.** *adj* orange[farben]

orange juice *n* Orangensaft *m*

orange peel *n* Orangenschale *f*

orangutan [ɔ·'ræŋ·ə·tæn], **orangoutang** [ɔ·'ræŋ·ə·tæŋ] *n* Orang-Utan *m*

orator ['ɔr·ə·tər] *n* Redner(in) *m(f)*

orbit ['ɔr·bɪt] **I.** *n* **1.** (*constant course*) Umlaufbahn *f*; **in ~ around the earth** in einer Erdumlaufbahn **2.** *fig* (*influence*) [Einfluss]bereich *m* **II.** *vt* (*circle around*) umkreisen

orchard ['ɔr·tʃərd] *n* Obstgarten *m*

orchestra ['ɔr·kɪ·strə] *n* Orchester *nt*

orchestral [ɔr·'kes·trəl] *adj* orchestral

orchestra pit *n* Orchestergraben *m*

orchestra seats *npl* Parkett *nt*

orchestrate ['ɔr·kɪ·streɪt] *vt* **1.** (*arrange for orchestra*) orchestrieren **2.** *fig* (*event*) organisieren

orchid ['ɔr·kɪd] *n* Orchidee *f*

ordeal [ɔr·'dil] *n fig* (*painful experience*) Zerreißprobe *f*

order ['ɔr·dər] **I.** *n* **1.** (*neatness*) Ordnung *f* **2.** (*sequence*) Reihenfolge *f*; **word ~** Wortstellung *f*; **in alphabetical ~** in alphabetischer Reihenfolge **3.** (*command*) Befehl *m*; **doctor's ~s** ärztliche Anweisung **4.** Bestellung *f*; (*request to make sth a.*) Auftrag *m* **5.** (*correct behavior*) Ordnung *f*; **to restore ~** die Ordnung wiederherstellen **6.** (*condition*) Zustand *f*; **to be in working ~** (*ready for use*) funktionsbereit sein; (*functioning*) funktionieren; **"out of ~"** „außer Betrieb" **7.** (*intention*) **in ~ to do sth** um etw zu tun **II.** *vi* bestellen **III.** *vt* **1.** (*command*) befehlen **2.** COMM (*request from company or in restaurant*) bestellen

order around *vt* herumkommandieren *fam*

order form *n* Bestellformular *nt*

orderly ['ɔr·dər·li] **I.** *n* (*hospital attendant*) ≈ [Kranken]pfleger(in) *m(f)* **II.** *adj* **1.** (*methodical*) geordnet; (*neat*) ordentlich **2.** (*demonstration*) friedlich

ordinal, ordinal number ['ɔr·də·nəl-] *n* Ordinalzahl *f*

ordinary ['ɔr·də·ner·i] **I.** *adj* gewöhnlich, normal **II.** *n* (*normal state*) **nothing out of the ~** nichts Ungewöhnliches

ore [ɔr] *n* Erz *nt*

Ore. *n abbr of* **Oregon**

oregano [ə·'reg·ə·noʊ] *n* Oregano *m*

Oregon ['ɔr·ɪ·gən] *n* Oregon *nt*

organ ['ɔr·gən] *n* **1.** MUS Orgel *f* **2.** ANAT Organ *nt*

organ donor *n* Organspender(in) *m(f)*

organic [ɔr·'gæn·ɪk] *adj* **1.** AGR **~ fruit** Obst *nt* aus biologischem Anbau **2.** organisch

organism ['ɔr·gə·nɪz·əm] *n* Organismus *m*

organist ['ɔr·gə·nɪst] *n* Organist(in) *m(f)*

organization [ˌɔr·gə·nɪ·'zeɪ·ʃən] *n* Organisation *f*

Organization of Petroleum Exporting Countries *n* die Organisation Erdöl exportierender Länder

organize ['ɔr·gə·naɪz] *vt* **1.** (*activities*) organisieren; (*books, files*) ordnen; (*space*) aufteilen **2.** vorbereiten; (*committee, team*) zusammenstellen

organized ['ɔr·gə·naɪzd] *adj* organisiert

organized crime *n* organisiertes Verbrechen

organizer ['ɔr·gə·naɪ·zər] *n* **1.** (*book*) Terminplaner *m* **2.** (*person*) Organisator(in) *m(f)*

orgasm ['ɔr·gæz·əm] *n* Orgasmus *m*

orgy ['ɔr·dʒi] *n* Orgie *f*

orient ['ɔr·i·ənt] **I.** *n* GEOG **the O~** der Orient **II.** *vt* (*determine position*) **to ~ oneself [by sth]** sich [nach etw *dat*] orientieren

oriental [ˌɔr·i·'en·təl] *adj* orientalisch

orientation [ˌɔr·i·en·'teɪ·ʃən] *n* Orientierung *f*; **sexual ~** sexuelle Neigung

orienteering [ˌɔr·i·en·'tɪr·ɪŋ] *n* Orientierungslauf *m*

origin ['ɔr·ə·dʒɪn] *n* **1.** (*beginning, source*) Ursprung *m* **2.** (*place sth/sb comes from*) Herkunft *f kein pl*

original [ə·'rɪdʒ·ɪ·nəl] **I.** *n* Original *nt*

II. adj **1.** (first) ursprünglich; **the ~ version** die Originalversion; (of a book) die Originalausgabe **2.** (unique) originell; (innovative) bahnbrechend **3.** (from creator) original; **~ painting** Original nt

originality [ə·ˌrɪdʒ·ɪ·ˈnæl·ə·t̬i] n Originalität f

originally [ə·ˈrɪdʒ·ɪ·nə·li] adv ursprünglich

originate [ə·ˈrɪdʒ·ɪ·neɪt] **I.** vi entstehen; **to ~ from sth** aus etw dat stammen **II.** vt erfinden

ornament [ˈɔr·nə·mənt] n **1.** Ziergegenstand m; (figurine) Figürchen nt **2.** (adornment) Schmuck m

ornamental [ˌɔr·nə·ˈmen·t̬əl] adj Zierde

ornate [ɔr·ˈneɪt] adj (object) prunkvoll; (music) ornamentreich; (language, style) kunstvoll

ornithology [ˌɔr·nə·ˈθal·ə·dʒi] n Ornithologie f fachspr

orphan [ˈɔr·fən] n Waise f

orphanage [ˈɔr·fə·nɪdʒ] n Waisenhaus nt

orthodontist [ˌɔr·θə·ˈdan·tɪst] n Kieferorthopäde, -in m, f

orthodox [ˈɔr·θə·daks] adj **1.** (generally accepted) herkömmlich **2.** (strictly religious) strenggläubig **3.** REL **Greek ~** griechisch orthodox; **the O~ Church** die christlich orthodoxe Kirche

orthopedic [ˌɔr·θə·ˈpi·dɪk] adj orthopädisch

orthopedist [ˌɔr·θə·ˈpi·dɪst] n Orthopäde, -in m, f

OS [ˌoʊ·ˈes] n COMPUT abbr of **operating system**

oscillate [ˈas·ə·leɪt] vi (swing) schwingen

oscillation [ˌas·ə·ˈleɪ·ʃən] n (movement) Schwingung f

osmosis [az·ˈmoʊ·sɪs] n BIOL, CHEM Osmose f fachspr

ostensible [a·ˈsten·sə·bəl] adj angeblich

ostensibly [a·ˈsten·sab·li] adv angeblich

ostentatious [ˌas·tən·ˈteɪ·ʃəs] adj prahlerisch; (lifestyle) protzig

osteoporosis [ˌas·ti·oʊ·pə·ˈroʊ·sɪs] n MED Osteoporose f fachspr

ostracize [ˈas·trə·saɪz] vt ächten

ostrich [ˈas·trɪtʃ] n ORN Strauß m

other [ˈʌð·ər] **I.** adj det **1.** (different) andere(r, s); **in ~ words** mit anderen Worten; **~ people** andere [Leute] **2.** (additional) andere(r, s), weitere(r, s) **3.** (alternative) andere(r, s); **on the ~ hand** andererseits; **every ~** jede(r, s) zweite **II.** pron (the remaining one) **the ~** der/die/das andere; **one or the ~** eines davon; **the ~s** die anderen

otherwise [ˈʌð·ər·waɪz] **I.** adv **1.** (differently) anders; **unless you let me know ~, …** sofern ich nichts Gegenteiliges von dir höre, … **2.** (except for this) sonst **II.** conj andernfalls

otter [ˈat̬·ər] n Otter m

ouch [aʊtʃ] interj aua, autsch

ought [ɔt] aux vb **1.** (indicating duty) **~ to do sth** jd sollte etw tun; **we ~ to have agreed** wir hätten nicht zustimmen sollen **2.** (indicating probability) **we ~ to be home by 7 o'clock** um sieben müssten wir eigentlich zu Hause sein; **ten minutes ~ to be enough time** zehn Minuten müssten eigentlich genügen

ounce [aʊns] n Unze f

our [aʊr] adj poss unser(e)

ours [aʊrz] pron poss (belonging to us) unsere(r, s); **he's a cousin of ~** er ist ein Cousin von uns

ourselves [aʊr·ˈselvz] pron refl **1.** after vb, prep (direct object) uns; **we enjoyed ~ at the party very much** wir hatten großen Spaß bei der Party **2.** emph (personally) wir persönlich; **to see sth for ~** etw selbst sehen

oust [aʊst] vt (expel) vertreiben; (by taking their position) verdrängen

out [aʊt] **I.** adj pred **1.** (not at a place) **to be ~** nicht da sein; (not at home) nicht zu Hause sein; **to be ~ and about** unterwegs sein; (after an illness) wieder auf den Beinen sein **2.** (outside) **to be ~** draußen sein; (prisoner) [wieder] draußen sein fam **3.** (visible) **to be ~** (sun, moon, stars) am Himmel stehen; (in blossom) blühen; (available) erhältlich sein; (on the market) auf dem Markt sein **4.** (known) **to be ~** heraus sein; (secret) gelüftet sein; (news) bekannt sein **5.** (finished) aus; **before**

the month is ~ vor Ende des Monats **6.** SPORT **to be ~** (*not playing*) nicht [mehr] im Spiel sein; (*in cricket, baseball*) aus sein; (*outside a boundary*) im Aus sein **7.** (*light, TV*) erloschen **II.** *adv* **1.** (*not in sth*) außen; (*not in a room, apartment*) draußen; (*outdoors*) draußen, im Freien; **to keep sb ~** jdn nicht hereinlassen **2.** (*outwards*) heraus; (*seen from inside*) hinaus; (*facing the outside*) nach außen; (*out of a room, building a.*) nach draußen; **get ~!** raus hier! *fam* **3.** (*away from home, for a social activity*) **to eat ~** im Restaurant essen; **to go ~** ausgehen **4.** (*removed*) [he]raus; (*extinguished*) aus; **to put a fire ~** ein Feuer löschen; **to cross sth ~** etw ausstreichen **5.** (*fully*) burned ~ *a. fig* ausgebrannt; (*fuse*) durchgebrannt **6.** (*aloud*) **to call to sb** jdm zurufen; **to cry ~ in pain** vor Schmerzen aufschreien **7.** (*unconscious*) **to knock sb ~** jdn bewusstlos schlagen **8.** (*open*) **to open sth ~** (*unfold*) etw auseinanderfalten; (*spread out*) etw ausbreiten **III.** *vt* **to ~ sb** (*homosexual*) jdn outen *fam* **IV.** *prep fam* aus +*dat*; **to run ~ the door** zur Tür hinausrennen

out-and-out *adj attr* ausgemacht

'**outback** *n* Hinterland *nt* [Australiens]

out'bid <-bid, -bid> *vt* überbieten

'**outboard**, **outboard** '**motor** *n* Außenbordmotor *m*

'**outbreak** *n* (*of a disease, a war*) Ausbruch *m*

'**outburst** *n* Ausbruch *m*

'**outcast** *n* Ausgestoßene(r) *f(m)*; **social ~** gesellschaftlicher Außenseiter/gesellschaftliche Außenseiterin

'**outclass** *vt* in den Schatten stellen

'**outcome** *n* Ergebnis *nt*

'**outcry** *n* lautstarker Protest

out'dated *adj* veraltet; (*ideas, views*) überholt

out'do <-did, -done> *vt* übertreffen

'**outdoor** *adj* (*clothes*) für draußen *nach n*; **~ swimming pool** Freibad *nt*

'**outdoors** [ˌaʊtˈdɔːrz] *adv* im Freien

outdoorsy [ˌaʊtˈdɔːr·zi] *adj fam* **to be ~** gern in der freien Natur [*or* an der frischen Luft] sein

'**outer** [ˈaʊ·tər] *adj* **1.** (*external*) äußerlich **2.** (*far from center*) äußere(r, s)

'**outermost** [ˈaʊ·tər·moʊst] *n attr* äußerste(r, s)

'**outfield** *n* Outfield *nt*

'**outfit** *n* **1.** (*clothes*) Kleidung *f*; **cowboy ~** Cowboykostüm *nt* **2.** *fam* (*group*) Verein *m*; (*musicians*) Truppe *f*

'**outflow** *n* Ausfluss *m*

'**out'going** *adj approv* (*extrovert*) kontaktfreudig

out'grow <-grew, -grown> *vt* (*become too big for*) **to ~ sth** aus etw *dat* herauswachsen

'**outgrowth** *n* Auswuchs *m a. fig*; (*development*) Weiterentwicklung *f*

'**outing** [ˈaʊ·tɪŋ] *n* **1.** (*trip*) Ausflug *m*; **to go on an ~** einen Ausflug machen **2.** (*revealing homosexuality*) Outing *nt*

out'last *vt* überdauern; **to ~ sb** jdn überleben

'**outlaw** [ˈaʊt·lɔ] *n* (*criminal*) Bandit(in) *m(f)*; (*fugitive from law*) Geächtete(r) *f/m*

'**outlay** *n* Aufwendungen *pl*

'**outlet** *n* **1.** ELEC Steckdose *f* **2.** (*exit*) Ausgang *m*; (*for water*) Abfluss *m* **3.** (*means of expression*) Ventil *nt fig* **4.** (*store*) Verkaufsstelle *f*; **factory ~** Fabrikverkauf *m*

'**outline I.** *n* **1.** (*brief description*) Übersicht *f* **2.** (*contour*) Umriss *m* **II.** *vt* **to ~ sth 1.** (*draw*) die Umrisse von etw *dat* zeichnen **2.** (*summarize*) etw [kurz] umreißen

out'live *vt* (*live longer than*) **to ~ sb** jdn überleben; **to ~ sth** etw überdauern

'**outlook** *n* **1.** (*view*) Aussicht *f* **2.** (*future prospect*) Aussicht[en] *f[pl]* **3.** (*attitude*) Einstellung *f*

'**outlying** *adj attr* (*region, town*) abgelegen

outma'neuver *vt* ausmanövrieren

outmoded [ˌaʊtˈmoʊ·dɪd] *adj pej* altmodisch; (*ideas*) überholt

out'number *vt* zahlenmäßig überlegen sein

'**out of** *prep* **1.** *after vb* (*towards outside*) aus **2.** *after vb* (*situated away from*) außerhalb; **she's ~ the office at the moment** sie ist zurzeit nicht an ihrem

O

[Arbeits]platz; *after n* außerhalb **3.** *after vb* (*from*) von; **she had to pay for it ~ her own pocket** sie musste es aus der eigenen Tasche bezahlen **4.** (*excluded from*) aus; **I'm glad to be ~ it** ich bin froh, dass ich das hinter mir habe; **to be ~ the question** nicht in Frage kommen **5.** *after n* (*ratio of*) von; **nine times ~ ten** neun von zehn Malen **6.** (*without*) **they were ~ luck** sie hatten kein Glück [mehr]; **to run ~ cash** kein Bargeld mehr haben **7.** (*beyond*) außer; **~ reach** außer Reichweite; **~ focus** (*photo*) unscharf; **get ~ the way!** aus dem Weg!
▶ **~ sight, ~ <u>mind</u>** aus den Augen, aus dem Sinn; **~ place** fehl am Platz

out-of-court 'settlement *n* LAW außergerichtliche Einigung

out of 'date *adj pred*, **'out-of-date** *adj attr* veraltet; (*clothing*) altmodisch; (*ideas*) überholt

out of the 'way *adj pred*, **'out-of-the-way** *adj attr* (*place*) abgelegen

'outpatient *n* ambulanter Patient/ambulante Patientin

out'play *vt* **to ~ sb** besser spielen als jd

'outpost *n* **1.** MIL (*base*) Stützpunkt *m* **2.** (*remote branch*) Außenposten *m*

'outpouring *n* (*of emotion*) Ausbruch *m*

'output I. *n* ECON Ausstoß *m;* COMPUT Ausgabe *f* **II.** *vt* (*data*) ausgeben

'outrage I. *n* Empörung *f;* (*deed*) Schandtat *f;* (*disgrace*) Schande *f kein pl* **II.** *vt* (*arouse indignation*) [**to be**] **~d by sth** entrüstet über etw *akk* [sein]

outrageous [aʊtˈreɪˌdʒəs] *adj* **1.** (*terrible*) empörend; (*unacceptable*) unerhört **2.** (*unusual and shocking*) außergewöhnlich; (*outfit a.*) gewagt **3.** (*exaggerated*) ungeheuerlich; (*story*) unwahrscheinlich; (*lie*) schamlos

'outreach *adj* **~ work** soziales Engagement; **~ program** Programm *nt* zur sozialen Unterstützung

'outright I. *adj attr* **1.** (*total*) total; (*disaster*) absolut **2.** (*undisputed*) offensichtlich; (*winner*) eindeutig **II.** *adv* **1.** (*totally*) total **2.** (*clearly*) eindeutig **3.** (*immediately*) sofort; **to be killed ~** auf der Stelle tot sein

out'run <-ran, -run, -nn-> *vt* **to ~ sb** jdm

davonlaufen

'outset *n* Anfang *m; from the ~ vo[m]* Anfang an

out'side I. *n* **1.** (*exterior*) Außenseite (*of a fruit*) Schale *f; from the ~ fig* vo[n] außen **2.** (*external appearance*) o[n] **the ~** äußerlich **II.** *adj attr* **1.** (*oute[r] door*) äußere(r, s); **~ wall** Außenmauer[n] **2.** (*external*) außenstehend; **the wor[ld] ~** die Welt draußen **III.** *adv* **1.** (*not [in a] building*) außen **2.** (*in open air*) im Fre[i]en **IV.** *prep* außerhalb (**of** von +*dat*)

outsider [ˌaʊtˈsaɪˌdər] *n* Außensei[t]er(in) *m(f)*

'outsize *adj attr* (*very large*) übergroß

'outskirts [ˈaʊtˌskɜrts] *npl* Stadtrand *m*

'outsourcing [ˈaʊtˌsɔrˌsɪŋ] *n* Outsou[r]cing *nt fachspr;* (*of production*) Produk[tionsauslagerung *f*

outspoken [ˌaʊtˈspoʊˌkən] *adj* offe[n] (*criticism*) unverblümt; (*opponent*) en[t]schieden

out'standing *adj* **1.** (*excellent*) auße[r]gewöhnlich; (*effort, contribution*) be[merkenswert; (*performance*) brillan[t] (*achievement*) überragend **2.** (*not dea[lt] with*) unerledigt; (*problems*) ungelöst

out'stay *vt* (*stay too long*) **to ~ one[s'] welcome** länger bleiben, als man e[r]wünscht ist

outstretched [ˌaʊtˈstretʃt] *adj* ausge[streckt

out'strip <-pp-> *vt* **1.** (*surpass*) übertre[f]fen **2.** (*be greater*) übersteigen

out'vote *vt* überstimmen

'outward I. *adj attr* **1.** (*exte[rior*) äußere(r, s), Außen-; (*superficia[l*) äußerlich **2.** (*going out*) ausgehend; **flight** Hinflug *m* **II.** *adv* nach außen

outwardly [ˈaʊtˌwərdˌli] *adv* äußerlich[;] nach außen hin

outwards [ˈaʊtˌwərdz] *adv* nach außen

out'weigh *vt* (*in importance*) **to ~ s[th]** etw wettmachen; **the advantages ~ th[e] disadvantages** die Vorteile überwiege[n] die Nachteile

out'wit <-tt-> *vt* austricksen

oval [ˈoʊˌvəl] *adj* oval

Oval 'Office *n* POL **the ~** das Oval Offic[e] (*Büro des US-Präsidenten*)

ovary [ˈoʊˌvəˌri] *n* Eierstock *m*

ovation [oʊˈveɪ·ʃən] n Applaus m

oven [ˈʌv·ən] n [Back]ofen m

ovenproof adj hitzebeständig

oven-ready adj bratfertig, backfertig

over [ˈoʊ·vər] I. adv pred 1. (across) hinüber; ~ here hier herüber; (on the other side) drüben; ~ there dort drüben 2. (another way up) to turn ~ umdrehen 3. (downwards) to fall ~ hinfallen; to knock sth ~ etw umstoßen 4. (finished) to be ~ vorbei sein 5. (remaining) übrig 6. (again) noch einmal; ~ and ~ immer wieder 8. prep 1. (across) über 2. (on the other side of) über 3. (above) über; (moving above) über; a flock of geese passed ~ eine Schar von Gänsen flog über uns hinweg 4. (everywhere) [überall] in; all ~ the world in der ganzen Welt 5. (during) in, während; ~ the years, he became more and more depressed mit den Jahren wurde er immer deprimierter 6. (through) he told me ~ the phone er sagte es mir am Telefon 7. (more than) über; this shirt cost me ~ $50! dieses Hemd hat mich über 50 Dollar gekostet! 8. (past) to get ~ sb/sth über jdn/etw hinweg kommen

overa'bundant adj übermäßig

over'act vi THEAT übertreiben

overall I. n [ˈoʊ·vər·ɔl] ~s pl Latzhose f II. adj [ˈoʊ·vər·ɔl] attr Gesamt- III. adv [ˌoʊ·vər·ˈɔl] insgesamt

over'bearing adj pej (arrogant) anmaßend

overboard adv NAUT über Bord ▶ to go ~ zu weit gehen, es übertreiben

over'book I. vt usu passive to be ~ed überbucht sein II. vi zu viele Buchungen vornehmen

over'cast adj (sky) bedeckt

over'charge vi zu viel berechnen

overcoat n Mantel m

over'come <-came, -come> I. vt 1. (fear) überwinden; (temptation) widerstehen; (enemy forces) besiegen 2. usu passive (render powerless) to be ~ by sth (sleep) von etw dat überwältigt werden; (fumes) von etw dat ohnmächtig werden II. vi siegen

over'compensate vi to ~ for sth etw akk überkompensieren

over'confident adj (extremely self-assured) übertrieben selbstbewusst; (too optimistic) übertrieben zuversichtlich

over'crowded adj überfüllt; (town) übervölkert

over'do <-did, -done> vt to ~ it sich überanstrengen; (go too far) zu weit gehen

over'done adj (overcooked: in water) verkocht; (in oven) verbraten

overdose I. n [ˈoʊ·vər·doʊs] Überdosis f II. vi [ˌoʊ·vər·ˈdoʊs] eine Überdosis nehmen

'overdraft n Kontoüberziehung f

over'draw <-drew, -drawn> vt (account) überziehen

over'dress vi sich zu fein anziehen

'overdrive n 1. AUTO Schongang m 2. fig (effort) to be in ~ auf Hochtouren laufen

over'due adj usu pred überfällig

over 'easy adj, adv usu pred ~ egg auf beiden Seiten gebratenes Spiegelei

over'eat <-ate, -eaten> vi zu viel essen

over'emphasize vt überbetonen

overestimate [ˌoʊ·vər·ˈes·tə·meɪt] vt überschätzen

overex'cited adj usu pred to be ~ ganz aufgeregt sein

overex'pose vt to be ~d 1. PHOT überbelichtet sein 2. usu passive to be ~d to risks zu starken Risiken ausgesetzt sein

overex'tend vt to ~ oneself [on sth] sich [bei etw dat] [finanziell] übernehmen

overflow I. n [ˈoʊ·vər·floʊ] 1. (act of spilling) Überlaufen nt 2. (overflowing liquid) überlaufende Flüssigkeit 3. (outlet) Überlauf m II. vi [ˌoʊ·vər·ˈfloʊ] (river, tank) überlaufen

overhang [ˌoʊ·vər·ˈhæŋ] vt <-hung, -hung> (project over) to ~ sth über etw akk hinausragen

overhaul vt [ˌoʊ·vər·ˈhɔl] (repair) überholen

overhead I. n [ˈoʊ·vər·hed] (running costs of business) laufende Geschäftskosten II. adj [ˈoʊ·vər·hed] attr (above head level) Hoch-; ELEC oberirdisch III. adv [ˌoʊ·vər·ˈhed] in der Luft; a plane circled ~ ein Flugzeug kreiste

O

über uns

over'hear <-heard, -heard> *vt* to ~ sth etw zufällig mithören; **to ~ sb** jdn unabsichtlich belauschen

over'heat *vi* sich erhitzen *a. fig*

overin'dulge *vi* (*eat too much*) sich *dat* den Bauch vollschlagen *fam*; (*drink too much*) sich volllaufen lassen *fam*

overjoyed [ˌoʊ·vər·ˈdʒɔɪd] *adj pred* überglücklich

'overkill *n pej* (*excessiveness*) Übermaß *nt*

overland I. *adj* [ˈoʊ·vər·lænd] *attr* Überland- **II.** *adv* [ˌoʊ·vər·ˈlænd] auf dem Landweg

overlap I. *n* [ˈoʊ·vər·læp] **1.** (*overlapping part*) Überlappung *f* **2.** (*similarity*) Überschneidung *f* **II.** *vi* <-pp-> [ˌoʊ·vər·ˈlæp] **1.** (*lie edge over edge*) sich überlappen **2.** (*be partly similar*) sich überschneiden

overload I. *n* [ˈoʊ·vər·loʊd] **1.** ELEC Überlast[ung] *f;* TRANSP Übergewicht *nt* **2.** (*excess*) Überbelastung *f* **II.** *vt* [ˌoʊ·vər·ˈloʊd] (*overburden: vehicle*) überladen; (*system, person*) überlasten

overlook *vt* [ˌoʊ·vər·ˈlʊk] **1.** (*look out onto*) überblicken **2.** (*not notice*) übersehen

overly [ˈoʊ·vər·li] *adv* allzu

over'night I. *adj* **1.** *attr* (*for a night*) Nacht-; ~ **stay** Übernachtung *f* **2.** (*for next day: delivery*) über Nacht **3.** (*sudden*) ganz plötzlich; ~ **success** Blitzerfolg *m* **II.** *adv* **1.** (*until next day*) in der Nacht, über Nacht **2.** *fig* (*suddenly*) in kurzer Zeit

'overpass *n* Überführung *f*

over'pay <-paid, -paid> *vt* für etw *akk* zu viel bezahlen

over'populated *adj* überbevölkert

over'powering *adj* überwältigend; (*smell*) durchdringend

overpro'duce *vt* to ~ sth von etw *dat* zu viel produzieren

over'rated *adj pej* überbewertet

over'reach *vt* to ~ oneself sich übernehmen

overre'act *vi* überreagieren

over'ride I. *n* Übersteuerung *f;* **manual** ~ Automatikabschaltung *f* **II.** *vt* <-rid, -ridden> **1.** (*outweigh*) überwiegen **2.** (*control*) abschalten

over'riding *adj attr* vorrangig

over'rule *vt* überstimmen; (*objection*) zurückweisen

over'run I. *vt* <-ran, -run> **1.** MIL (*occupy*) überrollen **2.** (*spread over*) sich in etw *dat* ausbreiten **3.** (*budget*) überschreiten **II.** *vi* <-ran, -run> (*exceed time*) überziehen

overseas I. *adj* [ˈoʊ·vər·siz] *attr* (*abroad*) Übersee-, in Übersee *nach n* **II.** *adv* [ˌoʊ·vər·ˈsiz] (*in foreign country*) im Ausland; (*to foreign country*) ins Ausland

over'see <-saw, -seen> *vt* beaufsichtigen

overseer [ˈoʊ·vər·ˌsi·ər] *n* Aufseher, -in *m, f*

over'shadow *vt* **1.** (*make insignificant*) in den Schatten stellen **2.** (*cast gloom over*) überschatten

'overshoe *n* Überschuh *m*

over'shoot <-shot, -shot> *vt* to ~ sth über etw *akk* hinausschießen; **the plane overshot the runway** das Flugzeug schoss über die Rennbahn hinaus

'oversight *n* (*mistake*) Versehen *nt;* **by an** ~ aus Versehen

over'simplify <-ie-> *vt* grob vereinfachen

'oversize, 'oversized *adj* überdimensional

over'sleep <-slept, -slept> *vi* verschlafen

over'spend <-spent, -spent> **I.** *vi* zu viel [Geld] ausgeben **II.** *vt* (*budget*) überschreiten

over'staffed *adj* überbesetzt

over'state *vt* übertreiben; **to ~ a case** einen Fall übertrieben darstellen

over'stay *vt* to ~ a visa ein Visum überschreiten

over'supply *n* (*supply*) Überangebot *nt*

overt [ˈoʊ·vɜrt] *adj* offenkundig; (*racism*) unverhohlen

over'take <-took, -taken> *vt* überholen *a. fig*

over-the-'counter *adj attr* (*drugs, remedies*) rezeptfrei

over-the-'top *adj fam* übertrieben

overthrow I. *n* [ˈoʊ·vər·θroʊ] (*removal from power*) Sturz *m* **II.** *vt* <-threw,

-thrown> [ˈoʊ·vər·ˈθroʊ] (*topple*) stürzen; (*regime*) zu Fall bringen

over·time I. n 1. (*extra work*) Überstunden pl 2. SPORT (*extra time*) Verlängerung f II. adv to work ~ Überstunden machen

over·tired adj übermüdet

over·ture [ˈoʊ·vər·tʃər] n Ouvertüre f

over·turn I. vi umstürzen; (*boat*) kentern II. vt 1. (*turn upside down*) umstoßen 2. (*reverse*) revidieren; (*government*) stürzen

over·value vt (*give excessively high value to*) überbewerten

'over·view n Überblick m

over·weight [ˌoʊ·vər·ˈweɪt] adj zu schwer; (*person a.*) übergewichtig

over·whelm [ˌoʊ·vər·ˈwelm] vt 1. (*affect powerfully*) überwältigen 2. (*enemy*) besiegen

over·whelming [ˌoʊ·vər·ˈwel·mɪŋ] adj (*very powerful*) überwältigend; (*need*) unwiderstehlich; (*grief*) unermesslich

over·work I. vi [ˌoʊ·vər·ˈwɜrk] sich überarbeiten II. vt [ˌoʊ·vər·ˈwɜrk] to ~ sb jdn [mit Arbeit] überlasten

ovu·la·tion [ˌav·ju·ˈleɪ·ʃən] n Eisprung m

ow [aʊ] interj au

owe [oʊ] vt 1. (*be in debt*) schulden; to ~ sb an explanation jdm eine Erklärung schuldig sein; to ~ sb thanks jdm zu Dank verpflichtet sein 2. (*be indebted*) to ~ sth to sb jdm etw verdanken

owing [ˈoʊ·ɪŋ] adj pred ausstehend

'owing to prep form ~ sth wegen einer S. gen

owl [aʊl] n Eule f; barn ~ Schleiereule f

own [oʊn] I. pron (*belonging, relating to*) his time is his ~ er kann über seine Zeit frei verfügen; to make sth [all] one's ~ sich dat etw [ganz] zu eigen machen; to have ideas of one's ~ eigene Ideen haben ▶ [all] on one's ~ [ganz] allein[e] II. adj attr 1. (*belonging to, individual*) eigene(r, s) 2. (*for oneself*) to make up one's ~ mind sich akk entscheiden ▶ in one's ~ right (*not due to others*) aus eigenem Recht; (*through one's talents*) aufgrund der eigenen Begabung III. vt (*possess*) besitzen

◆**own up** vi es zugeben

owner [ˈoʊ·nər] n Besitzer(in) m(f)

owner-'occupied adj vom Eigentümer/ von der Eigentümerin selbst bewohnt

ox <pl -en> [aks] n Ochse m

oxi·dize [ˈak·sɪ·daɪz] vt, vi oxidieren

oxtail 'soup n Ochsenschwanzsuppe f

oxy·acety·lene [ˌak·si·ə·ˈset·ə·lin] n Azetylensauerstoff m

oxy·gen [ˈak·sɪ·dʒən] n Sauerstoff m

'oxygen mask n Sauerstoffmaske f

oys·ter [ˈɔɪ·stər] n Auster[nmuschel] f

oz, oz. <pl -> n abbr of **ounce**

ozone [ˈoʊ·zoʊn] n Ozon nt

'ozone layer n Ozonschicht f

P

P <pl -'s>, **p** <pl -'s> [pi] n p nt, P nt; ~ as in Papa P wie Paula

p. [pi] n <pl pp> abbr of **page** S.

p [pi] adv MUS abbr of **piano** p

PA, Pa. n abbr of **Pennsylvania**

pace [peɪs] I. n 1. (*speed*) Tempo nt 2. (*step*) Schritt m; to keep ~ with sb mit jdm Schritt halten II. vi gehen

'pace·maker n 1. (*for heart*) [Herz]schrittmacher m 2. SPORT (*speed setter*) Schrittmacher(in) m(f)

Pa·cif·ic [pə·ˈsɪf·ɪk] n the ~ der Pazifik

paci·fier [ˈpæs·ə·faɪ·ər] n (*for baby*) Schnuller m

paci·fist [ˈpæs·ə·fɪst] n Pazifist(in) m(f)

paci·fy [ˈpæs·ə·faɪ] vt beruhigen

pack [pæk] I. n 1. (*packet*) Packung f 2. (*backpack*) Rucksack m 3. (*of cards*) [Karten]spiel nt 4. (*group*) Gruppe f II. vi packen III. vt 1. (*put into a container: articles, goods*) [ein]packen 2. a. fig (*cram*) vollpacken (**with** mit +dat); to be ~ed [**with people**] gerammelt voll [mit Leuten] sein fam

◆**pack away** vt wegpacken

◆**pack in** vt 1. (*cram in*) hineinstopfen; (*people, animals*) hineinpferchen 2. einpacken

◆**pack into** vt 1. (*put*) [ein]packen 2. (*cram*) [hinein]stopfen 3. fig (*fit*) [hinein]packen

◆**pack off** vt fam wegschicken

◆**pack up** I. vt zusammenpacken II. vi fam **to ~ up and leave** seine Sachen packen und gehen

package ['pæk·ɪdʒ] I. n 1. (parcel) Paket nt 2. (pack: of cookies etc.) Packung f II. vt 1. (pack) verpacken 2. fig präsentieren

packaged [pæk·ɪdʒd] adj (food) verpackt

'**package deal** n Pauschalangebot nt

packaging ['pæk·ɪ·dʒɪŋ] n Verpackung f

packer ['pæk·ər] n [Ver]packer(in) m(f)

packet ['pæk·ɪt] n Packung f, Schachtel f

pact [pækt] n Pakt m

pad[1] [pæd] I. n 1. (wad) Pad m o nt 2. (protector) Polster nt 3. (of paper) Block m 4. AEROSP, AVIAT **launch ~** Abschussrampe f II. vt <-dd-> [aus]polstern

pad[2] [pæd] vi trotten; (walk softly) tappen

padded ['pæd·ɪd] adj [aus]gepolstert

padding ['pæd·ɪŋ] n Polsterung f

paddle[1] ['pæd·əl] I. n Paddel nt II. vi paddeln

paddle[2] ['pæd·əl] vi planschen

paddy ['pæd·i] n Reisfeld nt

padlock ['pæd·lak] n Vorhängeschloss nt

page[1] [peɪdʒ] I. n (single sheet) Blatt nt; COMPUT (single side) Seite f II. vi COMPUT **to ~ up/down** auf der Seite nach oben/unten gehen

page[2] [peɪdʒ] vt (over loudspeaker) ausrufen; (by pager) anpiepsen

pageant ['pædʒ·ənt] n 1. (show) **beauty ~** Schönheitswettbewerb m 2. (play) Historienspiel nt

pager ['peɪ·dʒər] n Pager m, Piepser m

pagination [ˌpædʒ·ə·'neɪ·ʃən] n Seitennummerierung f

paid [peɪd] I. pt, pp of **pay** II. adj attr bezahlt

pail [peɪl] n Eimer m

pain [peɪn] n 1. (feeling) Schmerz m; **a ~ in one's leg** Schmerzen pl im Bein 2. (physical suffering) Schmerz[en] m[pl] 3. (effort) **~s** pl Mühe f; **to go to great ~s to do sth** keine Mühe scheuen, etw zu tun

painful ['peɪn·fəl] adj schmerzhaft; (death) qualvoll

painfully ['peɪn·fəl·i] adv unter Schmerzen

'**painkiller** n Schmerzmittel nt

painless ['peɪn·lɪs] adj 1. (without pain) schmerzlos 2. fig (without trouble) schmerzlos

painstaking ['peɪnz·ˌteɪ·kɪŋ] adj [sehr] sorgfältig

paint [peɪnt] I. n 1. (substance) Farbe f; (on car) Lack m 2. (art color) **~s** pl Farben pl II. vi 1. ART malen 2. (decorate rooms) streichen III. vt 1. (make picture) malen 2. (house) anstreichen; (wall) streichen

'**paintbrush** n [Farb]pinsel m

painter ['peɪn·tər] n 1. (artist) [Kunst]maler(in) m(f) 2. (sb who paints buildings) Maler(in) m(f)

painting ['peɪn·tɪŋ] n 1. (picture) Bild nt 2. (house decorating) Streichen nt

'**paintwork** n (of a house) Anstrich m

pair [per] n Paar nt; **a ~ of gloves** ein Paar nt Handschuhe; **a ~ of pants** eine Hose

◆**pair off** I. vi einen Partner/eine Partnerin finden II. vt **to ~ sb off [with sb]** jdn [mit jdm] verkuppeln fam

pajamas [pə·'dʒɑ·məz] npl Pyjama m

pal [pæl] n fam Kumpel m

palace ['pæl·əs] n Palast m

palatial [pə·'leɪ·ʃəl] adj prachtvoll

pale [peɪl] I. adj blass II. vi (go white) bleich werden

Palestinian [ˌpæl·ə·'stɪn·i·ən] I. n Palästinenser(in) m(f) II. adj palästinensisch

palette ['pæl·ɪt] n ART Palette f

pall [pɔl] vi an Reiz verlieren

pallet ['pæl·ɪt] n Palette f

palliative ['pæl·i·ə·tɪv] adj schmerzstillend attr

pallid ['pæl·ɪd] adj (very pale) fahl

pallor ['pæl·ər] n Blässe f

palm[1] [pɑm] n Handfläche f

palm[2] [pɑm] n (tree) Palme f

Palm 'Sunday n Palmsonntag m

palpable ['pæl·pə·bəl] adj 1. (obvious) offenkundig 2. (tangible) spürbar

palpitations [ˌpæl·pə·'teɪ·ʃənz] npl Herzklopfen nt kein pl

paltry ['pɔl·tri] adj (small) armselig; (sum)

lächerlich

Pampas ['pæm·pəz] *n* + *sing/pl vb* Pampa *f*

pamper ['pæm·pər] *vt* verwöhnen

pamphlet ['pæm·flɪt] *n* [kleine] Broschüre *f*

pan[1] [pæn] **I.** *n* Pfanne *f* **II.** *vt* <-nn-> *fam* (*criticize*) verreißen

pan[2] [pæn] *vi* **to ~ to the left** nach links schwenken

▶ **pan out** *vi* sich entwickeln

panacea [,pæn·ə·'si·ə] *n* Allheilmittel *nt*

panache [pə·'næʃ] *n* Elan *m*

Panama Ca'nal *n* **the ~** der Panamakanal

pancake *n* Pfannkuchen *m*

pancreas <*pl* -es> ['pæŋ·kri·əs] *n* Bauchspeicheldrüse *f*

panda ['pæn·də] *n* Panda *m*

pandemonium [,pæn·də·'mou·ni·əm] *n* **1.** Chaos *nt* **2.** *fig* (*uproar*) Tumult *m*

pane [peɪn] *n* [Fenster]scheibe *f*

panel ['pæn·əl] **I.** *n* **1.** (*wooden*) [Holz]paneel *nt*; (*metal*) Blech *nt* **2.** **instrument ~** AVIAT Instrumentenbrett *nt*; AUTO Armaturenbrett *nt* **II.** *vt* <-l-> täfeln (**with** mit +*dat*)

paneling ['pæn·ə·lɪŋ] *n* [Holz]täfelung *f*

panelist ['pæn·ə·lɪst] *n* (*on expert team*) Mitglied *nt* [einer Expertengruppe]

panhandle *vi* schnorren

panhandler *n fam* Schnorrer(in) *m(f)*

panic ['pæn·ɪk] **I.** *n* Panik *f* **II.** *vi* <-ck-> in Panik geraten

panicky ['pæn·ɪ·ki] *adj* panisch

panic-stricken *adj* von Panik ergriffen

panorama [,pæn·ə·'ræm·ə] *n* Panorama *nt*

panoramic [,pæn·ə·'ræm·ɪk] *adj* Panorama-

pansy ['pæn·zi] *n* (*flower*) Stiefmütterchen *nt*

pant[1] [pænt] *vi* (*breathe rapidly*) keuchen

pant[2] [pænt] *n* FASHION **~s** *pl* **a pair of ~s** eine [lange] Hose ▶ **to be caught with one's ~s down** *fam* auf frischer Tat ertappt werden

panther <*pl* -> ['pæn·θər] *n* Puma *m*

panties ['pæn·tiz] *npl fam* [Damen]slip *m*

pantomime ['pæn·tə·maɪm] *n* Pantomime *f*

pantsuit, 'pants suit *n* Hosenanzug *m*

pantyhose *npl* Strumpfhose *f*

papa ['pa·pə] *n childspeak fam* Papa *m*

papacy ['peɪ·pə·si] *n* Pontifikat *nt*

papal ['peɪ·pəl] *adj* päpstlich

paparazzi [,pa·pə·'ra·tsi] *npl* Paparazzi *pl*

papaya [pə·'paɪ·ə] *n* Papaya *f*

paper ['peɪ·pər] *n* **1.** Papier *nt*; **recycled ~** Altpapier *nt* **2.** (*newspaper*) Zeitung *f* **3.** *usu pl* (*document*) Dokument *nt*; (*credentials*) [Ausweis]papiere *pl*

'paperback *n* Taschenbuch *nt*

paper 'bag *n* Papiertüte *f*

paper chase *n* Schnitzeljagd *f*

'paper clip *n* Büroklammer *f*

'paper cup *n* Pappbecher *m*

'paper mill *n* Papierfabrik *f*

paper money *n* Papiergeld *nt*

paper-'thin *adj, adv* hauchdünn

paper 'towel *n* Papierhandtuch *nt*

'paperweight *n* Briefbeschwerer *m*

papery ['peɪ·pə·ri] *adj* (*skin*) pergamenten

papier-mâché [,peɪ·pər·mə·'ʃeɪ] *n* Pappmaschee *nt*

papyrus <*pl* -es> [pə·'paɪ·rəs] *n* Papyrus *m*

par [par] *n* **1.** (*standard*) **below ~** unter dem Durchschnitt **2.** (*equality*) **to be on [a] ~ with each other** einander ebenbürtig sein

par. ['perə] *n short for* **paragraph** Absatz *m*

parable ['pær·ə·bəl] *n* Parabel *f*

parachute ['pær·ə·ʃut] **I.** *n* Fallschirm *m* **II.** *vi* mit dem Fallschirm abspringen

'parachute jump *n* Fallschirmabsprung *m*

parachutist ['pær·ə·ʃu·tɪst] *n* Fallschirmspringer(in) *m(f)*

parade [pə·'reɪd] **I.** *n* (*procession*) Parade *f* **II.** *vi* **1.** (*walk in procession*) einen Umzug machen **2.** (*show off*) **to ~ around** auf und ab stolzieren **III.** *vt* **1.** MIL (*troops*) aufmarschieren lassen **2.** *fig* (*knowledge, wealth*) zur Schau tragen

paradise ['pær·ə·daɪs] *n* Paradies *nt*

paradoxical [,pær·ə·'dak·sɪ·kəl] *adj* paradox

paraffin ['pær·ə·fɪn] *n*, **paraffin wax** *n* Paraffin *nt*

P

paragraph ['pær·ə·græf] n 1. (*text*) Absatz m 2. (*newspaper article*) [kurze] Zeitungsnotiz

parakeet ['pær·ə·kit] n Sittich m

paralegal [ˌpe·rə·'li·gəl] n juristische Hilfskraft

parallel ['pær·ə·lel] I. adj 1. (*lines*) parallel 2. (*corresponding*) ~ **example** Parallelbeispiel nt II. n (*similarity*) Parallele f III. adv parallel; **to run ~ to sth** zu etw dat parallel verlaufen

parallel bars npl Barren m

parallel 'line n Parallele f

paralysis <pl -ses> [pə·'ræl·ə·sɪs] n Lähmung f a. fig

paralyze ['pær·ə·laɪz] vt 1. MED a. fig lähmen 2. (*bring to halt*) lahmlegen

paramedic [ˌpær·ə·'med·ɪk] n Sanitäter(in) m(f)

parameter [pə·'ræm·ə·tər] n usu pl (*set of limits*) ~**s** pl Leitlinien pl

paranoia [ˌpær·ə·'nɔɪ·ə] n PSYCH Paranoia f geh

paranoid ['pær·ə·nɔɪd] adj paranoid

paranormal [pær·ə·'nɔr·məl] n **the ~** übernatürliche Erscheinungen

paraplegic [ˌpær·ə·'pli·dʒɪk] n doppelseitig Gelähmte(r) f(m)

parasite ['pær·ə·saɪt] n Parasit m a. fig

parasol ['pær·ə·sɔl] n Sonnenschirm m

paratrooper ['pær·ə·ˌtru·pər] n Fallschirmjäger(in) m(f)

paratroops ['pær·ə·trups] npl Fallschirmtruppen pl

parboil ['par·bɔɪl] vt **to ~ food** Lebensmittel kurz vorkochen (*um sie dann weiterzuverarbeiten*)

parcel ['par·səl] I. n Paket nt II. vt <-l-> einpacken

parcel 'post n Paketpost f

parched [partʃt] adj (*dried out*) vertrocknet; (*throat*) ausgedörrt

Parcheesi® [par·'tʃi·zi] n Mensch-ärgere-dich-nicht[-Spiel] nt

parchment ['partʃ·mənt] n Pergament nt

pardon ['par·dən] I. n LAW Begnadigung f II. vt 1. (*forgive*) verzeihen, entschuldigen 2. LAW begnadigen III. interj (*apology*) **I beg your ~!** [or ~ **me!**] Entschuldigung!, tut mir Leid!; (*request for repetition*) wie bitte?; (*reply to of-*

fensiveness) na, hören Sie mal!

parent ['per·ənt] n (*of a child*) Elternteil m; ~**s** Eltern pl

parental [pə·'ren·təl] adj elterlich

parent 'company n Muttergesellschaft f

parenthesis <pl -ses> [pə·'ren·θə·sɪs] n usu pl (*runde*) Klammern pl

parenthood ['per·ənt·hʊd] n Elternschaft f

parent 'teacher association n Eltern-Lehrer-Organisation f

parishioner [pə·'rɪʃ·ə·nər] n Gemeindemitglied nt

parity ['pær·ɪ·ti] n Gleichheit f

park [park] I. n Park m II. vt AUTO (*ein*) parken III. vi parken

parka ['par·kə] n Parka m

parking ['par·kɪŋ] n Parkplatz m

parking garage n Parkhaus nt

parking lot n Parkplatz m

parking meter n Parkuhr f

parking place, parking space n Parkplatz m

parking ticket n Strafzettel m für unerlaubtes Parken

park ranger n Parkaufseher(in) m(f)

parkway n Schnellstraße f

parliament ['par·lə·mənt] n (*institution*) P~ Parlament nt

parliamentary [ˌpar·lə·'men·tə·ri] adj parlamentarisch

parlor ['par·lər] n Salon m; **funeral ~** Bestattungsinstitut nt

parlor game n Gesellschaftsspiel nt

Parmesan, Parmesan cheese ['par·mə·zan-] n Parmesan[käse] m

parochial [pə·'roʊ·ki·əl] adj 1. REL Gemeinde- 2. pej (*provincial*) provinziell

parochial 'school n Konfessionsschule f

parody ['pær·ə·di] I. n a. pej (*imitation*) Parodie f II. vt <-ie-> parodieren

parole [pə·'roʊl] n bedingte Haftentlassung

parrot ['pær·ət] n Papagei m

parse [pars] vt COMPUT **to ~ a text** einer Text parsen fachspr

parsley ['pars·li] n Petersilie f

parsnip ['pars·nɪp] n Pastinak m

parson ['par·sən] n Pastor(in) m(f)

part [part] I. n 1. Teil m; **for the most ~** zum größten Teil; **body ~** Körperteil m,

[spare] ~s Ersatzteile *pl* 2. (*unit*) [An]teil *m* 3. FILM, TV Folge *f* 4. *usu pl* GEOG Gegend *f*; **around these ~s** *fam* in dieser Gegend 5. THEAT *a. fig* Rolle *f* II. *adv* teils, teilweise III. *vi* 1. (*separate*) sich trennen 2. (*become separated: curtains*) aufgehen; (*lips*) sich öffnen IV. *vt* 1. trennen 2. (*hair*) scheiteln ▶ **to ~ company** sich trennen

part with *vi* **to ~ with sth** sich von etw *dat* trennen

parted ['pɑr·tɪd] *adj* 1. (*separated*) getrennt (**from** von +*dat*) 2. (*hair*) **her hair is ~ on the side** sie trägt einen Seitenscheitel

partial ['pɑr·ʃəl] *adj* 1. (*incomplete*) Teil-; (*paralysis*) partiell 2. (*biased*) parteiisch

partiality [ˌpɑr·ʃiˈæl·ɪ·t̬i] *n* (*bias*) Parteilichkeit *f*

partially ['pɑr·ʃə·li] *adv* teilweise

participant [pɑr·ˈtɪs·ə·pənt] *n* Teilnehmer(in) *m(f)*

participate [pɑr·ˈtɪs·ə·peɪt] *vi* teilnehmen

participation [pɑr·ˌtɪs·ə·ˈpeɪ·ʃən] *n* Teilnahme *f*

participle ['pɑr·tɪ·sɪ·pəl] *n* Partizip *nt*

particle ['pɑr·tɪ·kəl] *n* Teilchen *nt*

particular [pər·ˈtɪk·jə·lər] I. *adj* 1. *attr* (*individual*) bestimmt 2. *attr* (*special*) besondere(r, s) 3. *pred* (*demanding*) anspruchsvoll (**about** hinsichtlich +*gen*) II. *n* (*information*) ~s *pl* Einzelheiten *pl* ▶ **in** ~ insbesondere

particularly [pər·ˈtɪk·jə·lər·li] *adv* besonders, vor allem

parting '**shot** *n* letztes [sarkastisches] Wort

partisan ['pɑr·t̬ɪ·zən] *n* MIL Partisan(in) *m(f)*

partition [pɑr·ˈtɪʃ·ən] I. *n* 1. POL Teilung *f* 2. (*structure*) Trennwand *f* II. *vt* (*divide*) [unter]teilen

partly ['pɑrt·li] *adv* zum Teil, teilweise

partner ['pɑrt·nər] *n* 1. (*owner*) Teilhaber(in) *m(f)* 2. (*in sports*) Partner(in) *m(f)* 3. (*spouse*) Ehepartner(in) *m(f)*; (*unmarried*) [Lebens]partner(in) *m(f)*

partnership ['pɑrt·nər·ʃɪp] *n* Partnerschaft *f*

'**partnership agreement** *n* Gesellschaftsvertrag *m*

part of '**speech** <*pl* parts-> *n* LING Wortart *f*

part-'time I. *adj* Teilzeit- II. *adv* **to work ~** halbtags arbeiten

part-time '**job** *n* Teilzeitarbeit *f*

part-'timer *n* Halbtagskraft *f*

party ['pɑr·t̬i] I. *n* 1. (*celebration*) Party *f* 2. POL Partei *f* 3. (*group*) [Reise]gruppe *f* II. *vi* <-ie-> *fam* feiern

party '**line** *n* POL Parteilinie *f*

party '**politics** *n* + *sing/pl vb* Parteipolitik *f*

pass [pæs] I. *n* <*pl* -es> 1. (*road, sports*) Pass *m* 2. SCH, UNIV (*grade*) „Bestanden" 3. (*permit*) Passierschein *m* II. *vt* 1. (*go past*) **to ~ sb/sth** an jdm/etw vorbeigehen; (*in car*) an jdm/etw vorbeifahren 2. (*overtake*) überholen 3. (*hand to*) **to ~ sb sth** [*or* **to ~ sth to sb**] jdm etw geben 4. SPORT **to ~ the ball to sb** jdm den Ball zuspielen 5. (*succeed: exam, test*) bestehen, ablegen ▶ **to ~ the buck to sb** *fam* die Verantwortung auf jdn abwälzen III. *vi* 1. (*move by*) vorbeigehen; (*car*) vorbeifahren; **to ~ unnoticed** unbemerkt bleiben 2. (*overtake*) überholen 3. (*go away*) vorübergehen 4. SPORT (*of a ball*) zuspielen 5. SCH (*succeed*) bestehen 6. (*time*) vergehen 7. (*be accepted as*) **I don't think you'll ~ for 18** keiner wird dir abnehmen, dass du 18 bist

◆**pass along** *vt* **to ~ along ⇄ sth** etw weitergeben

◆**pass around** *vt* herumreichen

◆**pass away** *vi euph* (*die*) entschlafen *geh*

◆**pass by** I. *vi* 1. (*time*) vergehen 2. (*go past*) [an jdm/etw] vorbeigehen II. *vt* (*miss sb*) **sth ~es sb by** etw geht an jdm vorbei

◆**pass down** *vt* 1. *usu passive* (*bequeath*) **to be ~ed down** (*tradition*) weitergegeben werden 2. (*hand down*) hinunterreichen

◆**pass off** *vt* **to ~ sth off as sth** etw *akk* als etw ausgeben

◆**pass on** *vt* 1. (*information*) weitergeben 2. (*disease*) übertragen 3. *usu*

passive **to be ~ed on** (*clothes*) weitergegeben werden; (*fortune*) [weiter] vererbt werden

◆ **pass out** *vi* in Ohnmacht fallen

◆ **pass over** *vt* **1.** *usu passive* (*not promote*) **to be ~ed over** [**for promotion**] [bei der Beförderung] übergangen werden **2.** (*disregard*) übergehen

◆ **pass through** *vi* durchreisen

◆ **pass up** *vt* **to ~ up ⇆ sth** sich *dat* etw entgehen lassen

passable ['pæs·ə·bəl] *adj* **1.** (*traversable*) passierbar **2.** (*satisfactory*) [ganz] passabel

passage ['pæs·ɪdʒ] *n* **1.** (*narrow corridor*) Gang *m* **2.** LIT (*excerpt*) [Text]passage *f;* Stück *nt* **3.** (*progression: of time*) Voranschreiten *nt*

'**passageway** *n* Korridor *m*, [Durch]gang *m*

passenger ['pæs·ən·dʒər] *n* (*on a bus*) Fahrgast *m;* (*on an airline*) Passagier(in) *m(f);* (*in a car*) Mitfahrer(in) *m(f)*

'**passenger seat** *n* (*in car*) Beifahrersitz *m*

passer-by <*pl* passers-> [,pæs·ər·'baɪ] *n* Passant(in) *m(f)*

passing ['pæs·ɪŋ] **I.** *adj attr* **1.** (*vehicle*) vorbeifahrend; (*pedestrian*) vorbeigehend; **with each ~ day** mit jedem weiteren Tag[, der vergeht] **2.** (*remark*) beiläufig **3.** (*resemblance*) gering **II.** *n* SPORT Passen *nt*

passion ['pæʃ·ən] *n* **1.** (*große*) Leidenschaft **2.** (*fancy*) Vorliebe *f;* **to have a ~ for doing sth** etw leidenschaftlich gerne tun

passionate ['pæʃ·ə·nɪt] *adj* leidenschaftlich

'**passion fruit** *n* Passionsfrucht *f*

passive ['pæs·ɪv] *adj* **1.** (*role*) passiv **2.** (*submissive*) unterwürfig; **to be too ~** sich *dat* zu viel gefallen lassen

'**passkey** *n* **1.** see **master key 2.** see **skeleton key**

Passover ['pæs·,oʊ·vər] *n* Passah[fest] *nt*

passport ['pæs·pɔrt] *n* [Reise]pass *m*

'**passport control** *n* Passkontrolle *f*

'**password** *n* Parole *f;* COMPUT Passwort *nt*

past [pæst] **I.** *n* Vergangenheit *f;* (*past*

life) Vorleben *nt* **II.** *adj* **1.** *attr* (*preceding*) vergangen; (*former*) frühere(r, s) **2.** (*over*) vorüber, vorbei **III.** *adv* **to go ~ sb** an jdm vorbeigehen; (*vehicle*) an jdm vorbeifahren **IV.** *prep* **1.** (*to other side*) an ... vorbei; **to drive ~** vorbeifahren; (*at other side*) hinter, nach **2.** (*after the hour of*) nach; **it's a quarter ~ five** es ist Viertel nach Fünf

pasta ['pas·tə] *n* Nudeln *pl*

paste [peɪst] **I.** *n* **1.** (*soft substance*) Paste *f* **2.** (*sticky substance*) Kleister *m* **II.** *vt* **1.** (*affix*) kleben (**on[to]** auf +*akk*) **2.** COMPUT einfügen

pastel [pæ·'stel] *adj* pastellfarben

pasteurize ['pæs·tʃə·raɪz] *vt usu passive* pasteurisieren

pastor ['pæs·tər] *n* Pfarrer *m*, Pastor *m*

past 'participle *n* Partizip Perfekt *nt*

past 'perfect, past 'perfect tense *n* Plusquamperfekt *nt*

pastry ['peɪ·stri] *n* **1.** (*dough*) [Kuchen]teig *m* **2.** (*cake*) Gebäckstück *nt*

'**pastry chef, 'pastry cook** *n* Konditor(in) *m(f)*

past 'tense *n* Vergangenheit *f*

pasture ['pæs·tʃər] *n* Weide *f*

pasty ['pæs·ti] *adj pej* (*complexion*) bleich, käsig *fam*

pat [pæt] **I.** *vt* <-tt-> tätscheln **II.** *n* **1.** (*tap*) [freundlicher] Klaps **2. a ~ of butter** ein Stückchen *nt* Butter

patch [pætʃ] **I.** *n* <*pl* -es> **1.** (*piece of fabric*) Flicken *m;* (*for an eye*) Augenklappe *f* **2.** (*spot*) Fleck[en] *m;* **in ~es** stellenweise **II.** *vt* (*cover*) flicken

◆ **patch up** *vt* **1.** (*repair*) zusammenflicken *fam* **2.** *fig* (*conciliate*) **to ~ up an argument** einen Streit beilegen

'**patchwork** *n* Patchwork *n*

patchy ['pætʃ·i] *adj* **1.** METEO ~ **fog** stellenweise Nebel **2.** *fig* (*inconsistent*) von sehr unterschiedlicher Qualität *nach n, präd;* (*knowledge*) lückenhaft

pâté [pa·'teɪ] *n* Pastete *f*

patent ['pæt·ənt] *n* LAW Patent *nt;* **to take out a ~ on sth** [sich *dat*] etw patentieren lassen

patented ['pæt·ən·tɪd] *adj* (*copyrighted*) patentiert

patent 'leather *n* Lackleder *nt*

'patent office n Patentamt nt

paternal [pə-'tɜr·nəl] adj väterlich

pa'ternity leave n Vaterschaftsurlaub m

pa'ternity suit n Vaterschaftsprozess m

path [pæθ] n 1. (way) Weg m, Pfad m; **to cross sb's ~** jdm über den Weg laufen 2. (direction) Weg m; (of a bullet) Bahn f

pathetic [pə-'θet·ɪk] adj 1. (heart-rending) Mitleid erregend 2. pej (pitiful) jämmerlich; (excuse) schwach

pathologist [pə-'θɑl·ə·dʒɪst] n Pathologe, -in f

pathos ['peɪ·θɑs] n Pathos nt geh

'pathway n Weg m a. fig

patience ['peɪ·ʃəns] n Geduld f

patient ['peɪ·ʃənt] I. adj geduldig; **to be ~ with sb** mit jdm Geduld haben II. n MED Patient(in) m(f)

patina ['pæt·ən·ə] n CHEM, SCI, TECH Film m; (on copper, brass) Patina f

patio ['pæt·i·oʊ] n Terrasse f

patriarchal [ˌpeɪ·tri·'ɑr·kəl] adj patriarchalisch

patricide ['pæt·rə·saɪd] n Vatermord m

patriotic [ˌpeɪ·tri·'ɑt·ɪk] adj patriotisch

patrol [pə-'troʊl] I. vi <-ll-> patrouillieren II. n Patrouille f; **highway ~** Polizei, die die Highways überwacht

pa'trol car n Streifenwagen m

pa'trolman n Streifenpolizist(in) m(f), Polizeiwachtmeister(in) m(f)

patron ['peɪ·trən] n (benefactor) Schirmherr m; **~ of the arts** Mäzen(in) m(f) der [schönen] Künste

patronize ['peɪ·trə·naɪz] vt pej **to ~ sb** jdn herablassend behandeln

patronizing ['peɪ·trə·naɪ·zɪŋ] adj pej (attitude) herablassend; (look) gönnerhaft

patron 'saint n Schutzpatron(in) m(f)

patter ['pæt·ər] vi (feet) trippeln; (rain) prasseln

pattern ['pæt·ərn] n Muster nt

patterned ['pæt·ərnd] adj gemustert

patty ['pæt·i] n Pastetchen nt; **burger ~** Fleischbratling m

paunch <pl -es> [pɔntʃ] n Bauch m

paunchy ['pɔn·tʃi] adj dickbäuchig

pauper ['pɔ·pər] n Arme(r) f(m)

pause [pɔz] I. n Pause f II. vi eine [kur-ze] Pause machen; (speaker) innehalten III. vt anhalten

pavement ['peɪv·mənt] n Asphalt m

paving ['peɪ·vɪŋ] n das Pflastern

'paving stone n Pflasterstein m

paw [pɔ] I. n Pfote f; (of a big cat, bear) Pranke f sl II. vt fam (touch) begrabschen

pawn¹ [pɔn] vt verpfänden

pawn² [pɔn] n CHESS Bauer m

'pawnbroker n Pfandleiher(in) m(f)

pay [peɪ] I. n (wages) Lohn m; (salary) Gehalt nt II. vt <paid, paid> (give) [be]zahlen; **~ out** etw [aus]zahlen; **to ~ in cash** [in] bar [be]zahlen 2. (settle) bezahlen; **to ~ one's dues** (debts) seine Schulden bezahlen; fig (obligations) seine Schuldigkeit tun III. vi <paid, paid> 1. (give money) [be]zahlen 2. (be profitable) rentabel sein; **it ~s to do sth** es lohnt sich, etw zu tun fig (suffer) **to ~ [for sth]** [für etw akk] bezahlen

pay back vt 1. (give back) zurückzahlen; (debts) bezahlen 2. fig (for revenge) **to ~ sb back for sth** jdm etw heimzahlen

pay off I. vt 1. (repay) abbezahlen; (settle: debt) [vollständig] begleichen 2. **to ~ off ⇆ sb** jdn kaufen II. vi fig fam sich auszahlen

pay out I. vt ausgeben II. vi FIN **to ~ out [on a policy]** [be]zahlen

pay up vi [be]zahlen

'paycheck n Lohnscheck m

'payday n Zahltag m

payer ['peɪ·ər] n Zahler(in) m(f)

paying ['peɪ·ɪŋ] adj attr zahlend

'payload n TRANSP, AEROSP Nutzlast f

payment ['peɪ·mənt] n (sum) Zahlung f

'payoff n 1. fam (reward) Lohn m 2. fam (bribe) Bestechung f

'payout n FIN Ausschüttung f

pay-per-'view n Pay-Per-View nt (System, bei dem der Zuschauer nur für die Sendungen zahlt, die er auch tatsächlich gesehen hat)

'pay phone n Münzfernsprecher m

'pay raise n (for white-collar worker) Gehaltserhöhung f; (for blue-collar worker) Lohnerhöhung f

pay TV n fam Pay-TV nt

P

PBS [ˌpiːbiːˈes] *n abbr of* **Public Broadcasting Service** *amerikanischer Fernsehsender*

PC [ˌpiːˈsiː] I. *n* 1. *abbr of* **personal computer** PC *m* 2. *abbr of* **political correctness** II. *adj abbr of* **politically correct** pc

p.c. [ˌpiːˈsiː] *n abbr of* **percent** p.c.

PDA [ˌpiːdiːˈeɪ] *n abbr of* **personal digital assistant** PDA *m*

PE [ˌpiːˈiː] *n abbr of* **physical education**

pea [piː] *n* Erbse *f*

peace [piːs] *n* 1. Frieden *m* 2. (*social order*) Ruhe *f*

ꞌ**peace conference** *n* Friedenskonferenz *f*

peaceful [ˈpiːsfəl] *adj* friedlich; (*calm*) ruhig

ꞌ**peaceꞌkeeping** I. *n* Friedenssicherung *f* II. *adj* ~ **force** Friedenstruppe *f*

ꞌ**peace-loving** *adj* friedliebend

ꞌ**peacemaking** *n* Befriedung *f geh*

ꞌ**peace movement** *n* Friedensbewegung *f*

ꞌ**peace settlement** *n* Friedensabkommen *nt*

ꞌ**peacetime** *n* Friedenszeiten *pl*

ꞌ**peace treaty** *n* Friedensvertrag *m*

peach [piːtʃ] *n* <*pl* -es> Pfirsich *m*

peachy [ˈpiːtʃi] *adj fam* wunderbar, toll

peacock [ˈpiːkak] *n* Pfau *m*

peak [piːk] I. *n* Gipfel *m* II. *vi* (*athletes*) [seine] Höchstleistung erbringen; (*production*) den Höchststand erreichen

peal [piːl] I. *n* (*sound*) Dröhnen *nt kein pl* II. *vi* (*bells*) läuten

peanut [ˈpiːnʌt] *n* 1. (*nut*) Erdnuss *f* 2. *fam* (*very little*) ~s *pl* Klacks *m*

ꞌ**peanut butter** *n* Erdnussbutter *f*

pear [per] *n* Birne *f*

pearl [pɜrl] *n* Perle *f*

peasant [ˈpezənt] *n* [Klein]bauer, [Klein]bäuerin *m*, *f*

peat [piːt] *n* Torf *m*

ꞌ**peat bog** *n* Torfmoor *nt*

pebble [ˈpebəl] *n* Kieselstein *m*

pecan [prˈkan] *n* Pekannuss *f*

peck [pek] I. *n* 1. (*bite*) Picken *nt kein pl* 2. *fam* (*quick kiss*) Küsschen *nt* II. *vt* 1. (*bite*) hacken nach +*dat* 2. *fam* (*kiss quickly*) **to ~ sb on the cheek** jdn flüchtig auf die Wange küssen III. *vi* (*with the beak*) picken

ꞌ**pecking order** *n* Hackordnung *f*

pectoral [ˈpektərəl] *adj* Brust-, pektoral *fachspr*

peculiar [prˈkjuːljər] *adj* 1. (*strange*) seltsam, merkwürdig 2. (*belonging to, special: to sb*) typisch

peculiarity [prˌkjuːliˈærɪti] *n* 1. (*strangeness*) Eigenartigkeit *f* 2. (*idiosyncrasy*) Eigenart *f*

peculiarly [prˈkjuːljərli] *adv* eigenartig

pedal [ˈpedəl] I. *n* Pedal *nt* II. *vi* <-l-> Rad fahren

pedantic [pəˈdæntɪk] *adj* pedantisch

peddle [ˈpedəl] *vt* **to ~ sth** *esp pej* (*sell*) etw verscherbeln *pej*

peddler [ˈpedlər] *n* Drogenhändler(in) *m(f)*

pedestal [ˈpedɪstəl] *n* Sockel *m*

pedestrian [pəˈdestriːən] *n* Fußgänger(in) *m(f)*

pedestrian crossing *n* Zebrastreifen *m*

pedestrianize [pəˈdestriːənaɪz] *vt* in eine Fußgängerzone umwandeln

pedestrianized [prˈdestriːənaɪzd] *adj* ~ **area** Fußgängerzone *f*

pedestrian ꞌmall *n* Fußgängerzone *f*

pediatrician [ˌpiːdiːəˈtrɪʃən] *n* Kinderarzt, -ärztin *m*, *f*

pedicure [ˈpedɪkjʊr] *n* Pediküre *f*

pedigree [ˈpedɪɡriː] *n* Stammbaum *m*

pedometer [prˈdamətər] *n* Pedometer *nt*

pedophile [ˈpedəfaɪl] *n* Pädophile(r) *m*

pee [piː] *fam* I. *n* 1. (*urine*) Pipi *nt Kindersprache* 2. (*act*) Pinkeln *nt*; **to go ~** *esp childspeak* Pipi machen II. *vi* pinkeln *fam*; **to ~ in one's pants** in die Hose[n] machen

peek [piːk] I. *n* flüchtiger Blick II. *vi* blinzeln; **to ~ over sth** über etw *akk* gucken

◆**peek out** *vi* hervorgucken

peel [piːl] I. *n* Schale *f* II. *vt* (*fruit*) schälen; **to ~ the paper off sth** etw auswickeln III. *vi* (*paint, wallpaper*) sich lösen; (*skin*) sich schälen

◆**peel off** I. *vt* schälen; (*adhesive strip*) abziehen II. *vi* (*come off*) sich lösen

peeler [ˈpiːlər] *n* (*utensil*) Schäler *m*

peelings [ˈpiːlɪŋz] *npl* Schalen *pl*

peep[1] [piːp] I. *n usu sing* 1. (*bird sound*) Piep[ser] *m* 2. (*answer, statement*)

Laut *m*; **to not hear [so much as] a ~ out of** [*or* **from**] **sb** keinen Mucks von jdm hören **II.** *vi* piepsen

peep² [piːp] **I.** *n* (*look*) [verstohlener] Blick **II.** *vi* **1.** verstohlen blicken, spähen **2.** (*appear*) hervorkommen (**through** durch +*akk*)

◆**peep out** *vi* (*toe, finger*) herausgucken

'peephole *n* Guckloch *nt*, Spion *m*

peeping 'Tom *n* Spanner *m fam*

peer [pɪr] *vi* (*look closely*) spähen; **to ~ over sb's shoulder** jdm über die Schulter gucken

peeved [piːvd] *adj fam* sauer

peevish ['piː·vɪʃ] *adj* mürrisch

peg [peg] **I.** *n* (*hook*) Haken *m*; (*stake*) Pflock *m* **II.** *vt* <-gg-> **to ~ prices** Preise stützen

pejorative [pɪ·'dʒɔr·ə·tɪv] *adj form* abwertend

Pekinese <*pl* -> [ˌpiː·kə·'niːz] *n* (*dog*) Pekinese *m*

pelican ['pel·ɪ·kən] *n* Pelikan *m*

pellet ['pel·ɪt] *n* **1.** (*ball*) Kugel *f* **2.** (*gunshot*) Schrot *nt o m kein pl*

pelt [pelt] *vt* **to ~ sb with sth** jdn mit etw *dat* bewerfen

pelvis <*pl* -es> ['pel·vɪs] *n* Becken *nt*

pen¹ [pen] *n* (*writing utensil*) Feder *f*; **ballpoint ~** Kugelschreiber *m*

pen² [pen] *n* (*enclosed area*) Pferch *m*

◆**pen in** *vt* (*animal*) einsperren; **to be ~ned in** (*people*) eingeschlossen sein

pen³ [pen] *n fam short for* **penitentiary** Knast *m fam*

penal ['piː·nəl] *adj attr* **~ code** Strafgesetz *nt*

penalize ['piː·nə·laɪz] *vt* **to ~ sb** [**for sth**] jdn [für etw *akk*] bestrafen

penalty ['pen·əl·ti] *n* LAW *a. fig* Strafe *f*

'penalty area *n* Strafraum *m*

'penalty box *n* **1.** (*in soccer*) Strafraum *m* **2.** (*in hockey*) Strafbank *f*

'penalty clause *n* [restriktive] Vertragsklausel

'penalty shot *n* **to award a ~** (*in hockey*) einen Strafschuss verhängen; (*in soccer*) einen Elfmeter geben

penance ['pen·əns] *n* Buße *f*

pencil ['pen·səl] **I.** *n* (*writing utensil*) Bleistift *m*; FASHION **eyeliner ~** Eye-

linerstift *m* **II.** *vt* <-l-> mit Bleistift schreiben

◆**pencil in** *vt* vormerken

'pencil case *n* Federmäppchen *nt*

'pencil sharpener *n* [Bleistift]spitzer *m*

pendant ['pen·dənt] *n* Anhänger *m*

pending ['pen·dɪŋ] *adj* LAW anhängig; (*deal*) bevorstehend

pendulum ['pen·dʒə·ləm] *n* Pendel *nt*

penetrate ['pen·ɪ·treɪt] *vt* **to ~ sth 1.** (*move into*) in etw *akk* eindringen **2.** (*spread through: smell*) etw durchdringen

penetrating ['pen·ɪ·treɪ·tɪŋ] *adj* durchdringend *attr*; (*analysis*) eingehend

penguin ['peŋ·gwɪn] *n* Pinguin *m*

penicillin [ˌpen·ɪ·'sɪl·ɪn] *n* Penicillin *nt*

peninsula [pə·'nɪn·sə·lə] *n* Halbinsel *f*

penis <*pl* -es> ['piː·nɪs] *n* Penis *m*

penitent ['pen·ɪ·tənt] *n* REL reuiger Sünder/reuige Sünderin

penitentiary [ˌpen·ɪ·'ten·tʃə·ri] *n* Gefängnis *nt*

'penknife *n* Taschenmesser *nt*

'pen name *n* Pseudonym *nt*

pennant ['pen·ənt] *n* (*flag*) Wimpel *m*; SPORT Siegeswimpel *m*

penniless ['pen·i·lɪs] *adj* mittellos

Pennsylvania [ˌpen·sɪl·'veɪ·ni·ə] *n* Pennsylvania *nt*

penny <*pl* -nies> ['pen·i] *n* Penny *m*
▶ **to be worth** every **~** sein Geld wert sein

'penny-pinching *adj* geizig

'pen pal *n* Brieffreund(in) *m(f)*

pension ['pen·ʃən] *n* Rente *f*

'pension fund *n* Pensionskasse *f*

'pension plan *n* Altersversorgungsplan *m*

pensive ['pen·sɪv] *adj* nachdenklich

pentagon ['pen·tə·gən] *n* Fünfeck *nt*

Pentagon ['pen·tə·gən] *n* **the ~** das Pentagon

pentathlon [pen·'tæθ·lən] *n* Fünfkampf *m*

penthouse ['pent·haʊs] *n* Penthaus *nt*

'pent-up *adj* (*emotions*) aufgestaut

peony ['piː·ə·ni] *n* Pfingstrose *f*

people ['piː·pəl] **I.** *n* **1.** *pl* (*persons*) Leute *pl*, Menschen *pl*; **rich ~** die Reichen *pl* **2.** *pl* (*nation*) Volk *nt* **II.** *adj* **~ skills** Menschenkenntnis *f kein pl*

pep [pep] **I.** *n fam* Elan *m*, Schwung *m*

P

II. *vt* <-pp-> **to ~ sb ⇆ up** jdn in Schwung bringen; **to ~ sth ⇆ up** aufpeppen (**with** mit +*dat*)

pepper ['pep·ər] **I.** *n* **1.** (*spice*) Pfeffer *m;* **black ~** schwarzer Pfeffer **2.** (*vegetable*) Paprika *f* **II.** *vt* (*add pepper*) pfeffern

'**peppercorn** *n* Pfefferkorn *nt*

'**pepper mill** *n* Pfeffermühle *f*

'**peppermint** *n* Pfefferminz(bonbon) *nt*

pepperoni [pep·ə·'rou·ni] *n* Salami *f*

'**pepper shaker** *n* Pfefferstreuer *m*

peppery ['pep·ə·ri] *adj* pfeffrig; (*dish*) scharf

'**pep pill** *n* Aufputschmittel *nt*

'**pep talk** *n* Motivationsgespräch *nt*

per [pɜr] *prep* **1.** (*for every, in every*) pro **2.** (*according to*) **as ~ usual** wie gewöhnlich

per annum [pər·'æn·əm] *adv form* per annum

per capita [pər·'kæp·ɪ·tə] *adj attr form* Pro-Kopf-

perceive [pər·'siv] *vt* wahrnehmen

percent [pər·'sent] **I.** *n* Prozent *nt;* **what ~ ...?** wie viel Prozent ...? **II.** *adv* -prozentig

percentage [pər·'sen·tɪdʒ] *n* Prozentsatz *m;* **what ~ ...?** wie viel Prozent ...?

per'centage point *n* Prozentpunkt *m*

perceptible [pər·'sep·tə·bəl] *adj* wahrnehmbar

perception [pər·'sep·ʃən] *n usu sing* Wahrnehmung *f kein pl*

perceptive [pər·'sep·tɪv] *adj* einfühlsam; (*observer*) aufmerksam; (*remark*) scharfsinnig

perch [pɜrtʃ] **I.** *n* <*pl* -es> (*for birds*) Sitzstange *f* **II.** *vi* (*bird*) sitzen (**on** auf +*dat*); (*person*) thronen (**on** auf +*dat*)

percolate ['pɜr·kə·leɪt] *vt* filtrieren; **to ~ coffee** Filterkaffee zubereiten **II.** *vi* (*water*) durchsickern

percolator ['pɜr·kə·leɪ·tər] *n* Kaffeemaschine *f*

percussion [pər·'kʌʃ·ən] *n* Percussion *f,* Schlagzeug *nt*

peregrine 'falcon *n* Wanderfalke *m*

peremptory [pə·'remp·tə·ri] *adj* gebieterisch

perennial [pə·'ren·i·əl] **I.** *n* mehrjährige Pflanze **II.** *adj attr* (*lasting through many years*) mehrjährig

perfect I. *adj* ['pɜr·fɪkt] vollkommen, perfekt **II.** *vt* [pər·'fekt] perfektionieren

perfection [pər·'fek·ʃən] *n* Perfektion *f*

perfectionist [pər·'fek·ʃə·nɪst] *n* Perfektionist(in) *m(f)*

perfectly ['pɜr·fɪkt·li] *adv* vollkommen, perfekt; **~ clear** absolut klar *fam*

perforate ['pɜr·fə·reɪt] *vt* perforieren (*once*) durchstechen

perforation [pɜr·fə·'reɪ·ʃən] *n* Loch *nt*

perform [pər·'fɔrm] **I.** *vt* **1.** (*entertain*) vorführen; (*play, symphony*) aufführen; (*on an instrument*) spielen **2.** (*function*) erfüllen **3.** (*surgical procedure*) durchführen **II.** *vi* **1.** (*on stage*) auftreten; (*play*) spielen **2.** (*function*) funktionieren; (*car*) laufen **3.** (*do, act*) **to ~ well** gut sein

performance [pər·'fɔr·məns] *n* **1.** (*entertaining, showing*) Vorführung *f;* (*of a play, ballet*) Aufführung *f;* (*of a part*) Darstellung *f;* **to give a ~** eine Vorstellung geben **2.** (*effectiveness, level of achievement*) Leistung *f*

performer [pər·'fɔr·mər] *n* Künstler(in) *m(f)*

perfume I. *n* ['pɜr·fjum] **1.** (*scented liquid*) Parfüm *nt* **2.** (*of a flower*) Duft *m* **II.** *vt* [pər·'fjum] parfümieren

perfunctory [pər·'fʌŋk·tə·ri] *adj* flüchtig

perhaps [pər·'hæps] *adv* **1.** (*maybe*) vielleicht **2.** (*approximately*) ungefähr

peril ['per·əl] *n form* (*danger*) Gefahr *f;* (*risk*) Risiko *nt*

perimeter [pə·'rɪm·ə·tər] *n* Grenze *f*

period ['pɪr·i·əd] **I.** *n* **1.** (*length of time*) Zeitspanne *f,* Periode *f;* **for a ~ of three months** für die Dauer von drei Monaten **2.** (*time in history, development*) Zeit *f;* (*distinct time*) Zeitabschnitt *m;* (*phase*) Phase *f;* **~ of office** Amtszeit *f* **3.** *fam* (*menstruation*) Periode *f* **4.** LING *a. fig* Punkt *m* **II.** *adj* (*clothing, novel*) historisch

periodical [pɪr·i·'ad·ɪ·kəl] *n* Zeitschrift *f;* (*specialist journal a.*) Periodikum *nt fachspr*

peripheral [pə·'rɪf·ər·əl] **I.** *adj* **1.** (*minor*) unbedeutend **2.** (*at the edge*) Rand- **II.** *n* COMPUT Peripherie *f fachspr*

periscope ['per·ɪ·skoup] *n* Periskop *nt*

perishable ['per·ɪʃ·ə·bəl] *adj* (*food*) [leicht] verderblich

perjury ['pɜr·dʒə·ri] *n* Meineid *nt;* **to commit ~** einen Meineid schwören

perk [pɜrk] *n* Vergünstigung *f*

perk up I. *vi* 1. (*cheer up*) aufleben; (*become more awake*) munter werden 2. (*recover*) sich erholen II. *vt* 1. (*cheer up*) aufheitern 2. (*energize*) aufmuntern

perky ['pɜr·ki] *adj* (*lively*) munter

perm¹ [pɜrm] *n* short for **permanent** Dauerwelle *f*

perm² [pɜrm] *vt* **to ~ hair** Dauerwellen machen

permafrost ['pɜr·mə·frɔst] *n* Dauerfrost[boden] *m*

permanence ['pɜr·mə·nəns], **permanency** ['pɜr·mə·nən·si] *n* Beständigkeit *f*

permanent ['pɜr·mə·nənt] *adj* permanent, ständig; (*relationship*) dauerhaft; (*ink*) wasserfest; **~ address** fester Wohnsitz; **~ damage** bleibender Schaden

permeable ['pɜr·mi·ə·bəl] *adj a. fig form* durchlässig *a. fig*

permissible [pər·'mɪs·ə·bəl] *adj* gestattet

permission [pər·'mɪʃ·ən] *n* Erlaubnis *f;* (*from an official body*) Genehmigung *f*

permissive [pər·'mɪs·ɪv] *adj pej* nachgiebig; (*sexually*) freizügig

permit I. *n* ['pɜr·mɪt] Genehmigung *f* II. *vt* <-tt-> [pər·'mɪt] 1. (*give permission*) gestatten, erlauben 2. (*make possible*) **to ~ sb to do sth** jdm ermöglichen, etw zu tun III. *vi* [pər·'mɪt] **weather ~ting** vorausgesetzt, das Wetter spielt mit

permitted [pər·'mɪt·ɪd] *adj* zulässig

peroxide [pə·'rak·saɪd] *n* Peroxyd *nt*

perpendicular [,pɜr·pən·'dɪk·ju·lər] I. *adj* senkrecht II. *n* Senkrechte *f;* MATH, ARCHIT the ~ das Lot

perpetrate ['pɜr·pə·treɪt] *vt form* begehen

perpetrator ['pɜr·pə·treɪ·tər] *n form* Täter(in) *m(f)*

perpetual [pər·'petʃ·u·əl] *adj attr* ständig

perpetuate [pər·'petʃ·u·eɪt] *vt* aufrechterhalten

perplex [pər·'pleks] *vt* (*puzzle*) verblüffen

perplexed [pər·'plekst] *adj* perplex; (*puzzled a.*) verblüfft

perplexity [pər·'plek·sɪ·ti] *n* Verblüffung *f*

persecute ['pɜr·sɪ·kjut] *vt usu passive* verfolgen

persecution [,pɜr·sɪ·'kju·ʃən] *n usu sing* Verfolgung *f*

perseverance [,pɜr·sə·'vɪr·əns] *n* Beharrlichkeit *f,* Ausdauer *f*

persevere [,pɜr·sə·'vɪr] *vi* nicht aufgeben; **to ~ with sth** an etw *dat* festhalten; (*continue*) mit etw *dat* weitermachen

persevering [,pɜr·sə·'vɪr·ɪŋ] *adj* beharrlich

Persian ['pɜr·ʒən] *n* (*cat*) Perserkatze *f*

persist [pər·'sɪst] *vi* 1. (*continue to exist*) andauern; (*cold, rain*) anhalten 2. (*to not give up*) beharrlich bleiben 3. (*continue*) **to ~ in doing sth** nicht aufhören, etw zu tun

persistence [pər·'sɪs·təns] *n* 1. (*continuation*) Anhalten *nt* 2. (*perseverance*) Hartnäckigkeit *f*

persistent [pər·'sɪs·tənt] *adj* 1. (*difficulties*) anhaltend; (*cough*) hartnäckig 2. (*demand*) ständig

person <*pl* **people** *or form* **-s**> ['pɜr·sən] *n* (*human*) Person *f,* Mensch *m;* **not a single ~ came** kein Mensch kam; **cat ~** Katzenliebhaber(in) *m(f);* **night ~** Nachtmensch *m*

persona <*pl* **-nae**> [pər·'sou·nə] *n* Fassade *f meist pej*

personal ['pɜr·sə·nəl] *adj* persönlich; (*private a.*) privat; **~ data** Personalien *pl;* **~ quality** Charaktereigenschaft *f*

personal ad *n* Kontaktanzeige *f*

personal com'puter *n* Personal Computer *m*

personal digital as'sistant *n* PDA *m,* [handflächengroßer] Taschencomputer

personality [,pɜr·sə·'næl·ɪ·ti] *n* (*character, a celebrity*) Persönlichkeit *f*

personally ['pɜr·sə·nə·li] *adv* persönlich

personal 'pronoun *n* Personalpronomen *nt*

personnel [,pɜr·sə·'nel] *n* 1. *pl* (*employees*) Personal *nt kein pl* 2. (*department*) Personalabteilung *f*

person'nel department *n* Personalabteilung *f*

personnel 'manager *n* Personalchef(in) *m(f)*

P

perspective [pər·'spek·tɪv] n (viewpoint) Perspektive f; **from a historical ~** aus geschichtlicher Sicht; **in ~** perspektivisch; **to get sth in ~** etw nüchtern betrachten

perspiration [ˌpɜr·spə·'reɪ·ʃən] n Schweiß m

perspire [pər·'spaɪr] vi schwitzen

persuade [pər·'sweɪd] vt überreden; (convince) überzeugen

persuasion [pər·'sweɪ·ʒən] n usu sing (talking into) Überredung f; (convincing) Überzeugung f

persuasive [pər·'sweɪ·sɪv] adj überzeugend

pert [pɜrt] adj 1. (attractively small) wohl geformt 2. (impudent) frech

pertinent ['pɜr·tən·ənt] adj form relevant; (question) sachdienlich; (remark) treffend

perturb [pər·'tɜrb] vt form beunruhigen

pervasive [pər·'veɪ·sɪv] adj (widespread) weit verbreitet

perversion [pər·'vɜr·ʒən] n pej 1. (unnatural behavior) Perversion f 2. **~ of justice** Rechtsbeugung f

pervert I. n ['pɜr·vɜrt] pej (sexual deviant) Perverse(r) f(m) II. vt [pər·'vɜrt] pej (truth) verdrehen

perverted [pər·'vɜr·tɪd] adj (sexually deviant) pervers

pesky ['pes·ki] adj fam verdammt fam

pessimist ['pes·ə·mɪst] n Pessimist(in) m(f)

pessimistic [ˌpes·ə·'mɪs·tɪk] adj pessimistisch

pest [pest] n 1. (destructive animal) Schädling m 2. fig fam (annoying person) Nervensäge f fam

'**pest control** n Schädlingsbekämpfung f

pester ['pes·tər] vt belästigen; **to ~ sb to do sth** jdn drängen, etw zu tun

pesticide ['pes·tə·saɪd] n Schädlingsbekämpfungsmittel nt

pestle ['pes·əl] n Stößel m

pet [pet] I. n Haustier nt II. adj 1. (concerning animals) **~ cat** Hauskatze f 2. (project, theory, charity) Lieblings- III. vt <-tt-> streicheln

petal ['pet·əl] n Blütenblatt nt

petite [pə·'tit] adj approv (person) zierlich

petition [pə·'tɪʃ·ən] I. n 1. (signed document) Petition f 2. LAW (written request) Gesuch nt II. vi LAW (request formally) einen Antrag stellen

petitioner [pə·'tɪʃ·ən·ər] n LAW Kläger(in) m(f)

pet 'name n Kosename m

petrified ['pet·rə·faɪd] adj 1. (fossilized) versteinert 2. (terrified) gelähmt fig; **to be ~ of sth** vor etw dat panische Angst haben

petrochemical [ˌpet·roʊ·'kem·ɪ·kəl] adj attr petrochemisch

petroleum [pə·'troʊ·li·əm] n Erdöl nt

petting ['pet·ɪŋ] n Petting nt

petty ['pet·i] adj pej 1. (insignificant) unbedeutend 2. (small-minded) kleinkariert

petty 'cash n Portokasse f

'**petty officer** n NAUT ≈ Marineunteroffizier m

pew [pju] n Kirchenbank f

pewter ['pju·tər] n Zinn nt

PG [ˌpi·'dʒi] adj abbr of **parental guidance**; **to be rated ~** bedingt jugendfrei sein

pH [ˌpi·'eɪtʃ] n usu sing pH-Wert m

phallic ['fæl·ɪk] adj phallisch

phantom ['fæn·təm] I. n (ghost) Geist m II. adj attr (caused by mental illusion) Phantom-

pharaoh ['fer·oʊ] n Pharao m

pharmaceutical [ˌfar·mə·'su·tɪ·kəl] adj attr pharmazeutisch

pharma'ceutical industry n Pharmaindustrie f

pharmacist ['far·mə·sɪst] n Apotheker(in) m(f)

pharmacy ['far·mə·si] n 1. (drugstore) Apotheke f 2. (profession) Pharmazie f

phase [feɪz] n Phase f

◆**phase in** vt stufenweise einführen

◆**phase out** vt auslaufen lassen

phat [fæt] adj sl toll, krass sl

PhD [ˌpi·eɪtʃ·'di] n abbr of **Doctor of Philosophy** Dr., Doktor m

pheasant <pl -s> ['fez·ənt] n Fasan m

phenomena [fə·'nam·ə·nə] n pl of **phenomenon**

phenomenal [fə·'nam·ə·nəl] adj (great) phänomenal

phenomenon <pl -mena> [fə·'nam·ə·

nan] n Phänomen nt geh

phew [fju] interj fam puh

philately [fɪ·ˈlæt·ə·li] n Philatelie f

Philippines [ˈfɪl·ə·pinz] npl **the ~** die Philippinen pl

philistine [ˈfɪl·ɪ·stin] n pej Banause m

philosopher [fɪ·ˈlɑs·ə·fər] n Philosoph(in) m(f)

philosophic(al) [ˌfɪl·ə·ˈsɑf·ɪk(əl)] adj (calm) gelassen

philosophy [fɪ·ˈlɑs·ə·fi] n Philosophie f

phlegm [flɛm] n Schleim m

phobia [ˈfoʊ·bi·ə] n Phobie f

phone [foʊn] **I.** n Telefon nt; **to answer the ~** ans Telefon gehen; **on the ~** am Telefon **II.** vt anrufen **III.** vi telefonieren

◆**phone back** vt, vi zurückrufen

◆**phone in** vi anrufen, sich telefonisch melden

◆**phone up** vt anrufen

'phone book n Telefonbuch nt

'phone booth n Telefonzelle f

'phone card n Telefon[kredit]karte f

phonetic [fə·ˈnɛt·ɪk] adj LING phonetisch fachspr

phony, phoney [ˈfoʊ·ni] pej **I.** adj fam (accent, smile) aufgesetzt, künstlich; (documents) gefälscht **II.** n (impostor) Hochstapler(in) m(f); (fake) Fälschung f

phooey [ˈfu·i] interj hum fam pfui

phosphate [ˈfɑs·feɪt] n Phosphat nt

phosphorescent [ˌfɑs·fə·ˈrɛs·ənt] adj phosphoreszierend

photo [ˈfoʊ·toʊ] n short for **photograph** Foto nt

'photo album n Fotoalbum nt

'photocopier n [Foto]kopierer m

'photocopy I. n [Foto]kopie f **II.** vt [foto]kopieren

photo 'finish n SPORT Fotofinish nt fachspr

photogenic [ˌfoʊ·toʊ·ˈdʒɛn·ɪk] adj fotogen

photograph [ˈfoʊ·tə·græf] **I.** n Fotografie f, Foto nt; **aerial ~** Luftaufnahme f **II.** vt fotografieren

photographer [fə·ˈtɑg·rə·fər] n Fotograf(in) m(f)

photography [fə·ˈtɑg·rə·fi] n Fotografie f

photo'journalism n Fotojournalismus m

photo oppor'tunity n Fototermin m

photo'sensitive adj lichtempfindlich

photo'synthesis n BIOL, CHEM Photosynthese f

phrasal 'verb n LING Phrasal Verb nt (Grundverb mit präpositionaler oder adverbialer Ergänzung)

phrase [freɪz] n (words) Satz m; (idiomatic expression) Ausdruck m

'phrase book n Sprachführer m

pH value [ˈpi·eɪtʃ·ˌ-] n pH-Wert m

physical [ˈfɪz·ɪ·kəl] **I.** adj (condition, love) körperlich; **to have a ~ disability** körperbehindert sein; **~ contact** Körperkontakt m **II.** n MED Untersuchung f

physical edu'cation n Sport[unterricht] m

physically [ˈfɪz·ɪ·kəl·i] adv körperlich

physical 'therapist n Physiotherapeut(in) m(f) fachspr

physical 'therapy n Physiotherapie f fachspr

physician [fɪ·ˈzɪʃ·ən] n Arzt, Ärztin m, f

physicist [ˈfɪz·ɪ·sɪst] n Physiker(in) m(f)

physics [ˈfɪz·ɪks] n + sing vb Physik f

physiologist [ˌfɪz·i·ˈɑl·ə·dʒɪst] n Physiologe, -in m, f

physique [fɪ·ˈzik] n Körperbau m

pianist [ˈpi·æn·ɪst] n Klavierspieler(in) m(f); (professional) Pianist(in) m(f)

piano [pi·ˈæn·oʊ] n Klavier nt, Piano nt

piazza [pɪ·ˈat·sə] n Marktplatz m

pick¹ [pɪk] **I.** n (choice) Auswahl f **II.** vt **1.** (select) aussuchen; **to ~ sth at random** etw [völlig] willkürlich aussuchen **2.** (harvest) pflücken **3.** (scratch) **to ~ sth** an etw dat kratzen; **to ~ one's nose** in der Nase bohren **4.** (take) **to ~ sth from/off [of] sth** etw aus/von etw dat nehmen **5.** (lock) knacken **III.** vi **1.** (be choosy) aussuchen **2.** (toy with) **to ~ at one's food** in seinem Essen herumstochern

◆**pick off** vt (shoot) **to ~ off ⇆ sb** jdn einzeln abschießen

◆**pick on** vi herumhacken auf +dat

◆**pick out** vt **1.** (select) aussuchen **2.** (recognize) erkennen

◆**pick over, pick through** vt **to ~ sth ⇆ over** etw gut durchsehen

◆**pick up I.** vt **1.** (lift) aufheben; **to ~**

up the phone [den Hörer] abnehmen
2. (*acquire*) erwerben; **to ~ up an illness** sich mit einer Krankheit anstecken
3. (*collect*) abholen **4.** sl (*for sexual purposes*) **to ~ up ⇄ sb** jdn abschleppen **5.** (*signal*) empfangen **6.** *fam* (*pay for*) **to ~ up the tab** die Rechnung bezahlen II. *vi* **1.** (*improve*) sich bessern; (*numbers*) steigen **2.** (*resume*) **to ~ up where one left off** da weitermachen, wo man aufgehört hat

pick² [pɪk] *n* (*pickax*) Spitzhacke *f*
'**pickax**, **pickaxe** *n* Spitzhacke *f*
picker ['pɪk·ər] *n* (*of crops*) Erntehelfer(in) *m(f)*
picket ['pɪk·ɪt] *n* **1.** (*stake*) Palisade *f* **2.** (*striker*) Streikposten *m*
picket 'fence *n* Palisadenzaun *m*
'**picket line** *n* Streikpostenkette *f*
pickings ['pɪk·ɪŋz] *npl* **slim ~** magere Ausbeute
pickle ['pɪk·əl] **I.** *n* FOOD saure Gurke **II.** *vt* FOOD einlegen
pickled ['pɪk·əld] *adj* eingelegt
'**pick-me-up** *n fam* Muntermacher *m*
'**pickpocket** *n* Taschendieb(in) *m(f)*
'**pickup** *n* **1.** (*pickup truck*) (offener) Kleintransporter **2.** *fam* (*casual sexual acquaintance*) Eroberung *f hum*
'**pickup truck** *n* (offener) Kleintransporter
picky ['pɪk·i] *adj pej fam* pingelig; (*eater*) wählerisch
picnic ['pɪk·nɪk] *n* Picknick *nt*
picture ['pɪk·tʃər] **I.** *n* **1.** (*painting, drawing*) Bild *nt*; (*photograph a.*) Foto *nt* **2.** (*on TV screen*) [Fernseh]bild *nt* **3.** FILM **motion ~** Film *m* **II.** *vt* (*imagine*) sich *dat* vorstellen
'**picture book** *n* (*for children*) Bilderbuch *nt*
'**picture frame** *n* Bilderrahmen *m*
'**picture library** *n* Bildarchiv *nt*
picturesque [ˌpɪk·tʃə·ˈresk] *adj* (*scenery*) malerisch; (*language*) bildhaft
'**picture window** *n* Panoramafenster *nt*
piddle ['pɪd·əl] *vi vulg* pinkeln
pidgin ['pɪdʒ·ɪn] *n* LING Pidgin *nt fachspr*
pie [paɪ] *n* [Obst]torte *f*; **spinach ~** Spinatpastete *f*
piece [pis] **I.** *n* **1.** (*bit*) Stück *nt*; (*part*)

Teil *nt o m*; (*of bread*) Scheibe *f*; (*of cake*) Stück *nt*; [**all**] **in one ~** heil; **to break sth in**[**to**] [*or to*] **~s** etw in Stücke brechen; **~ by ~** Stück für Stück **2.** (*item, coin*) Stück *nt*; **~ of baggage** Gepäckstück *nt*; **a ~ of evidence** ein Beweis *m* **3.** (*in chess*) Figur *f* **4.** MUS, THEAT Stück *nt* ▶ **a ~ of the action** ein Stück *nt* des Kuchens; **to be a ~ of cake** *fam* kinderleicht sein **II.** *vt* **to ~ together ⇄ sth** etw zusammensetzen; (*reconstruct*) etw rekonstruieren
piecemeal **I.** *adv* (*bit by bit*) Stück für Stück **II.** *adj* (*bit by bit*) stück[chen]weise
'**piece rate** *n* Akkordlohn *m*
'**piecework** *n* Akkordarbeit *f*
pier [pɪr] *n* NAUT Pier *m o fachspr f*; (*dock*) Landungsbrücke *f*
pierce [pɪrs] *vt* (*make hole in*) durchstechen; (*break through*) durchbrechen; **to have ~d ears** Ohrlöcher haben
piercing ['pɪr·sɪŋ] **I.** *adj* **1.** durchdringend; (*voice*) schrill **2.** (*cold*) eisig **3.** (*question, reply, wit*) scharf **II.** *n* (*hole in body*) Piercing *nt*
pig [pɪg] *n* **1.** Schwein *nt a. fig* **2.** *fam* (*greedy person*) Vielfraß *m*
● **pig out** *vi fam* **to ~ out** [**on sth**] sich [mit etw *dat*] vollstopfen
pigeon ['pɪdʒ·ən] *n* Taube *f*
'**pigeonhole I.** *n* [Post]fach *nt*, Ablage *f* **II.** *vt* (*categorize*) in eine Schublade stecken
'**pigeon-toed** *adj* mit einwärtsgerichteten Füßen nach *n*
piggish ['pɪg·ɪʃ] *adj pej* (*behavior*) schweinisch
piggy ['pɪg·i] *n childspeak fam* Schweinchen *nt*
'**piggyback** *n* **to give sb a ~** [**ride**] jdn huckepack nehmen
'**piggy bank** *n* Sparschwein *nt*
pig'headed *adj pej* stur
pigment ['pɪg·mənt] *n* Pigment *nt*
Pigmy ['pɪg·mi] *n adj see* **Pygmy**
'**pigskin** *n* **1.** (*leather*) Schweinsleder *nt* **2.** SPORT *fam* Leder *nt* (*Ball beim American Football*)
'**pigsty** *n pej, a. fig* Schweinestall *m*
'**pigtail** *n* Zopf *m*

pike¹ [paɪk] n ZOOL Hecht m

pike² [paɪk] n short for **turnpike** Mautstraße f ▶ sth **comes** down the ~ etw kommt auf uns zu

pile¹ [paɪl] I. n 1. (stack) Stapel m; fam (heap) Haufen m 2. sl (fortune) Vermögen nt II. vt stapeln (**on**[to] auf +dat)
♦**pile in** vi in etw akk [hinein]strömen
♦**pile on** vt anhäufen; **you're really piling on the compliments tonight** du bist ja heute Abend so großzügig mit Komplimenten
♦**pile up** vt, vi [sich] anhäufen

pile² [paɪl] n (fabric surface) Flor m

piles [paɪlz] npl fam see **hemorrhoids**

'pile-up n fam Massenkarambolage f

pilfer ['pɪl·fər] vt, vi klauen

pilgrim ['pɪl·grɪm] n Pilger(in) m(f)

pill [pɪl] n 1. (tablet) Tablette f 2. (contraceptive) **the** ~ die Pille

pillar ['pɪl·ər] n Pfeiler m

pillow ['pɪl·ou] n 1. (for bed) [Kopf]-kissen nt 2. (decorative cushion) Kissen nt

'pillowcase n [Kopf]kissenbezug m

pilot ['paɪ·lət] I. n 1. AVIAT Pilot(in) m(f); NAUT Lotse, -in m, f 2. TV Pilotfilm f II. vt AVIAT, NAUT (aircraft) fliegen; (ship) lotsen

'pilot light n Zündflamme f

'pilot's license n Pilotenschein m

pimento [pɪ·'men·tou], **pimiento** [pɪ·'mjen·tou] n 1. (sweet red pepper) [rote] Paprika 2. (spice) Piment m o nt

pimp [pɪmp] n Zuhälter m

pimple ['pɪm·pəl] n Pickel m

pimply ['pɪm·pli] adj pickelig

pin [pɪn] I. n 1. (sharp object) Nadel f 2. (brooch) Brosche f II. vt <-nn-> 1. (attach with pin) befestigen ([up] on/[on]to an +dat) 2. (hold firmly) to ~ sb to the floor jdn auf den Boden drücken
♦**pin down** vt 1. (define exactly) genau definieren 2. (make decide) to ~ down ⇆ sb [to sth] jdn auf etw akk festnageln
♦**pin up** vt anstecken; (hair) hochstecken

PIN [pɪn] n abbr of **personal identification number** PIN

pinafore ['pɪn·ə·fɔr] n [große] Schürze

'pinball n Flipper m

pincer ['pɪn·sər] n ~**s** pl [Kneif]zange f

pinch [pɪntʃ] I. vt 1. (nip) kneifen 2. sl (steal) klauen II. vi kneifen; (boots, shoes) drücken III. n <pl -es> 1. (nip) Kneifen nt 2. (small quantity) Prise f ▶ to take sth with a ~ **of** salt etw mit Vorsicht genießen

pinch·'hit vi SPORT einspringen

pinch 'hitter n SPORT Ersatzspieler(in) m(f)

'pincushion n Nadelkissen nt

pine¹ [paɪn] n Kiefer f

pine² [paɪn] vi sich sehnen (**for** nach +dat)

pineapple ['paɪn·æp·əl] n Ananas f

'pinecone n Kiefernzapfen m

ping [pɪŋ] I. n (sound) [kurzes] Klingeln II. vi [kurz] klingeln

Ping-Pong ['pɪŋ·ˌpaŋ] n fam Tischtennis nt, Pingpong nt

'pinhead n Stecknadelkopf m

pinion ['pɪn·jən] n TECH Ritzel nt

pink [pɪŋk] adj (pale red) rosa, pink; (cheeks) rosig

pinkie ['pɪŋ·ki] n fam kleiner Finger

pink slip n fam 1. (notice) Kündigung f 2. AUTO (ownership document) Kraftfahrzeugbrief m

'pinpoint I. vt [genau] feststellen II. adj attr sehr genau; ~ **accuracy** hohe Genauigkeit

'pinprick n Nadelstich m

pint [paɪnt] n Pint nt (0,473 l)

'pintsize(d) adj fam winzig; fig unbedeutend

'pinup n [Star]poster nt o m

pioneer [ˌpaɪ·ə·'nɪr] n Pionier(in) m(f)

pioneering [ˌpaɪ·ə·'nɪr·ɪŋ] adj bahnbrechend; (innovative) innovativ

pious ['paɪ·əs] adj fromm

pip [pɪp] n 1. (on playing card) Farbe f 2. HORT Kern m

pipe [paɪp] n 1. TECH (tube) Rohr nt; (small tube) Röhre f; (for gas, water) Leitung f 2. (for smoking) Pfeife f II. vt (gas, water) leiten
♦**pipe down** vi fam (be quiet) den Mund halten; (be quieter) leiser sein
♦**pipe up** vi den Mund aufmachen

'pipe cleaner n Pfeifenreiniger m

P

'pipeline *n* Pipeline *f;* **in the ~** *fig* in Planung

piping ['paɪ·pɪŋ] *adv* **~ hot** kochend heiß

piquant ['pi·kənt] *adj* pikant; *fig (stimulating)* interessant

pique [pik] *n* Ärger *m*

piracy ['paɪ·rə·si] *n* **1.** (*at sea*) Piraterie *f,* Seeräuberei *f* **2.** (*of copyrights*) Raubkopieren *nt*

pirate ['paɪ·rət] **I.** *n* **1.** (*buccaneer*) Pirat(in) *m(f)* **2.** (*plagiarizer*) Raubkopierer(in) *m(f)* **II.** *adj attr* (*video, CD*) raubkopiert

Pisces <*pl ->* ['paɪ·siz] *n* ASTROL Fische *pl,* kein art

piss [pɪs] *vulg* **I.** *n* **1.** (*urine*) Pisse *f derb* **2.** *usu sing* (*action*) **to take a ~** schiffen *derb* **II.** *vi* pinkeln *fam*

pissed [pɪst] *adj vulg* [stink]sauer

pissed off [pɪst·ɔf] *adj* **to be ~ at sb** auf jdn sauer sein

pistachio [pɪ·ˈstæʃ·i·oʊ] *n* Pistazie *f*

pistol ['pɪs·təl] *n* Pistole *f*

piston ['pɪs·tən] *n* Kolben *m*

pit[1] [pɪt] **I.** *n* **1.** (*hole in ground*) Grube *f* **2.** (*mine*) Bergwerk *nt* **3.** (*scar*) Narbe *f* **4.** *sl* (*the worst*) **the ~s** *pl* das Allerletzte **II.** *vt* <-tt-> (*place in competition*) **to ~ oneself against sb/sth** sich mit jdm/ etw messen

pit[2] [pɪt] FOOD **I.** *n* Kern *m* **II.** *vt* <-tt-> entkernen

pita, pita bread ['pi·tə·] *n* Pitabrot *nt*

pitch[1] [pɪtʃ] **I.** *n* <*pl -es*> **1.** (*delivery from pitcher*) Pitch *m,* Wurf *m* **2.** (*tone*) Tonhöhe *f;* (*of a voice*) Stimmlage *f* **3.** (*persuasion*) [sales] **~** [Verkaufs]sprüche *pl a. pej fam* **II.** *vt* **1.** (*throw*) pitchen, werfen **2.** (*set up*) aufstellen; (*tent*) aufschlagen **3.** MUS (*instrument*) stimmen **4.** (*target*) **to be ~ed at sb** (*book, film*) sich an jdn richten **III.** *vi* SPORT (*in baseball*) pitchen, werfen

♦ pitch in *vi fam* (*contribute*) mit anpacken

pitch[2] [pɪtʃ] *n* Pech *nt*

'pitch-black *adj* pechschwarz

pitcher[1] ['pɪtʃ·ər] *n* SPORT (*in baseball*) Pitcher(in) *m(f) fachspr*

pitcher[2] ['pɪtʃ·ər] *n* (*jug*) [Henkel]krug *m*

pith [pɪθ] *n* **1.** (*of orange etc.*) weiße Innenhaut **2.** (*in plants*) Mark *nt*

pithy ['pɪθ·i] *adj* **1.** (*succinct*) prägnant **2.** (*of citrus fruits*) dickschalig

pitiful ['pɪt·ɪ·fəl] *adj* **1.** (*arousing pity*) bemitleidenswert; (*sight*) traurig **2.** (*unsatisfactory*) jämmerlich

pitiless ['pɪt·ɪ·lɪs] *adj* erbarmungslos

'pit stop *n* **1.** AUTO Boxenstopp *m* **2.** *usu sing hum* (*journey break*) Reiseunterbrechung *f*

pittance ['pɪt·əns] *n usu sing pej* Hungerslohn *m*

pity ['pɪt·i] **I.** *n* **1.** (*compassion*) Mitleid *nt;* **to feel ~ for sb** mit jdm Mitleid haben **2.** (*shame*) **to be a ~** schade sein **II.** *vt* <-ie-> Mitleid haben mit +*dat*

pivot ['pɪv·ət] **I.** *n* MECH, TECH (*shaft*) [Dreh]zapfen *m* **II.** *vi* **to ~ around sth** *a. fig* um etw *akk* kreisen

pixel ['pɪk·səl] *n* Pixel *nt fachspr*

pizza ['pit·sə] *n* Pizza *nt*

placate ['pleɪ·keɪt] *vt* beschwichtigen

place [pleɪs] **I.** *n* **1.** (*location*) Ort *m,* **~ of birth** Geburtsort *m;* **~ of work** Arbeitsplatz *m;* **in ~s** stellenweise **2.** (*home*) **I'm looking for a ~ to live** ich bin auf Wohnungssuche **3.** *fig* (*position, rank*) Stellung *f;* **if I were in your ~ ...** ich an deiner Stelle ..., wenn ich du wäre ... **4.** (*proper position*) **to be in ~** an seinem Platz sein; *fig* (*completed*) fertig sein; (*arrangements*) abgeschlossen; **to be out of ~** nicht an der richtigen Stelle sein; (*person*) fehl am Platz[e] sein **5.** (*job, position*) Stelle *f;* (*seat, on team*) Platz *m* **6.** (*ranking*) Platz *m* **▶ in the first/second ~** (*firstly, secondly*) erstens/zweitens; **to go ~s** *fam* weit kommen, es zu etw *dat* bringen; **to take ~** stattfinden **II.** *vt* **1.** (*position*) **to ~ an ad in the paper** eine Anzeige in die Zeitung setzen; **to ~ a bet on sth** auf etw *akk* wetten **2.** (*impose: embargo*) verhängen (**on** über +*akk*); **to ~ a limit on sth** etw begrenzen **3.** (*ascribe*) **to ~ the blame on sb** jdm die Schuld geben; **to ~ importance on sth** etw *akk* Wert legen **4.** (*put in certain condition*) **to ~ sb under surveillance** jdn unter Beobachtung stellen **5.** (*appoint*

to a position) **to ~ sb in charge** [of sth] jdm die Leitung [von etw *dat*] übertragen **III.** *vi* SPORT sich platzieren; (*finish first or second*) **to bet** [a horse] **to ~** eine Platzwette abschließen

placebo [plə·'si·bou] *n* MED Placebo *nt*

place kick *n* SPORT Place-Kick *m*, Platzkick *m*

place mat *n* Set *nt o m,* Platzdeckchen *nt*

placement ['pleɪs·mənt] *n* **1.** (*being placed*) Platzierung *f* **2.** (*by job service*) Vermittlung *f;* (*job itself*) Stelle *f*

place name *n* Ortsname *m*

placid ['plæs·ɪd] *adj* ruhig, friedlich; (*person a.*) gelassen

plague [pleɪg] **I.** *n* **1.** (*disease*) Seuche *f*; **the ~** die Pest **2.** (*of insects*) Plage *f* **II.** *vt* bedrängen; (*irritate*) ärgern

plaice <*pl* -> [pleɪs] *n* Scholle *f*

plaid [plæd] *n* FASHION Schottenmuster *nt*

plain [pleɪn] **I.** *adj* **1.** (*simple, uncomplicated*) einfach; **~ and simple** ganz einfach **2.** (*clear*) klar, offensichtlich; **to make sth ~** etw klarstellen **3.** (*unattractive*) unscheinbar **II.** *adv fam* (*downright*) einfach **III.** *n* GEOG Ebene *f*

plainclothes *adj attr* Zivil-

plainly ['pleɪn·li] *adv* **1.** (*simply*) einfach **2.** (*clearly*) deutlich; (*obviously*) offensichtlich

plainness ['pleɪn·nɪs] *n* **1.** (*simplicity*) Einfachheit *f* **2.** (*unattractiveness*) Unscheinbarkeit *f*

plainspoken *adj* direkt

plaintiff ['pleɪn·tɪf] *n* Kläger(in) *m(f)*

plan [plæn] **I.** *n* **1.** **to go according to ~** wie geplant verlaufen **2.** (*intention*) Plan *m,* Absicht *f;* **what are your ~s for this weekend?** was hast du dieses Wochenende vor? **II.** *vt* <-nn-> planen **III.** *vi* **1.** (*prepare*) planen **2.** **to ~ on sth** (*expect*) mit etw *dat* rechnen; (*intend*) etw vorhaben

plane[1] [pleɪn] *n* **1.** (*aircraft*) Flugzeug *nt;* **by ~** mit dem Flugzeug **2.** (*level*) Ebene *f*

plane[2] [pleɪn] *n* Hobel *m*

plane[3] [pleɪn] *n* (*tree*) Platane *f*

plane crash *n* Flugzeugunglück *nt*

planet ['plæn·ɪt] *n* Planet *m;* **to be from**

a different ~ *fig* aus einer anderen Welt sein

plank [plæŋk] *n* (*timber*) Brett *nt;* (*in house*) Diele *f*

planner ['plæ·nər] *n* Planer(in) *m(f)*

planning ['plæ·nɪŋ] *n* Planung *f*

plant [plænt] **I.** *n* **1.** (*organism*) Pflanze *f* **2.** (*factory*) Werk *nt,* Betrieb *m* **3.** (*machinery*) Maschinen *pl* **II.** *vt* **1.** pflanzen **2.** *fam* (*frame*) [heimlich] platzieren; **to ~ sth on sb** jdm etw unterschieben

plantain ['plæn·tɪn] *n* FOOD, BOT Kochbanane *f*

plantation [plæn·'teɪ·ʃən] *n* Plantage *f*

planter ['plæn·tər] *n* **1.** (*plantation owner*) Pflanzer(in) *m(f)* **2.** (*container*) Blumentopf *m*

plaque [plæk] *n* **1.** (*plate*) Tafel *f*; **brass ~** Messingschild *nt* **2.** MED [Zahn]belag *m*

plasma ['plæz·mə] *n* Plasma *nt*

plaster ['plæs·tər] **I.** *n* ARCHIT [Ver]putz *m* **II.** *vt* (*mortar*) verputzen

plastered ['plæs·tərd] *adj pred fam* stockbesoffen

plastic ['plæs·tɪk] **I.** *n* Plastik *nt kein pl* **II.** *adj* **1.** (*of plastic*) Plastik- **2.** *pej* (*artificial*) künstlich

plastic bag *n* Plastiktüte *f*

plastic bullet *n* Gummigeschoss *nt*

plastic explosive *n* Plastiksprengstoff *m*

plastic surgery *n* Schönheitschirurgie *f*

plastic wrap *n* Frischhaltefolie *f*

plate [pleɪt] *n* **1.** (*dish*) Teller *m* **2.** (*metal layer*) **gold ~** Vergoldung *f* **3.** AUTO **license ~** Nummernschild *nt*

plateau <*pl* -s> [plæ·'tou] *n* **1.** GEOG (*upland*) [Hoch]plateau *nt* **2.** ECON (*flat period*) **to reach a ~** stagnieren

plated ['pleɪ·tɪd] *adj* überzogen

plateful ['pleɪt·fʊl] *n* Teller *m;* **a ~ of lasagna** ein Teller *m* [voll] Lasagne

plate glass *n* Flachglas *nt fachspr*

platform ['plæt·fɔrm] *n* **1.** (*elevated area*) Plattform *f* **2.** RAIL Bahnsteig *m* **3.** (*stage*) Podium *nt*

platform shoes *npl* Plateauschuhe *pl*

plating ['pleɪ·tɪŋ] *n* Überzug *m*

platinum ['plæt·nəm] *n* Platin *nt*

platonic [plə·'tan·ɪk] *adj* platonisch

platoon [plə·'tun] *n* MIL Zug *m*

platter ['plæt̬·ər] *n* Platte *f*

P

plausibility [ˌplɔ·zə·ˈbɪl·ɪ·ti] *n* Plausibilität *f*

plausible [ˈplɔ·zə·bəl] *adj* plausibel

play [pleɪ] I. *n* 1. (*recreation*) Spiel *nt* 2. THEAT [Theater]stück *nt* 3. (*space for movement*) Spielraum *m* II. *vi* 1. spielen; **to ~ for money** um Geld spielen ▶ **to ~ for time** versuchen, Zeit zu gewinnen III. *vt* 1. (*take part in*) spielen; **to ~ cards** Karten spielen 2. (*compete against*) **to ~ sb** gegen jdn spielen 3. MUS, THEAT **to ~ the lead** die Hauptrolle spielen 5. (*gamble*) **to ~ the stock market** an der Börse spekulieren 6. (*perpetrate*) **to ~ a trick on sb** jdn hochnehmen *fig fam*; (*practical joke*) [jdm] einen Streich spielen 7. (*execute*) **to ~ a shot** schießen; (*in pool*) stoßen ▶ **to ~ ball** *sl* mitspielen *fam*; **to ~ one's cards right** geschickt taktieren; **to ~ it safe** auf Nummer sicher gehen

◆ **play along** *vi* **to ~ along with sth** etw [zum Schein] mitmachen

◆ **play around** *vi* 1. (*mess around: children*) spielen; **stop ~ing around!** hör mir dem Blödsinn auf! *fam* 2. (*experiment*) **to ~ around with sth** etw *dat* [herum]spielen; (*try out*) etw ausprobieren

◆ **play back** *vt* noch einmal abspielen

◆ **play down** *vt* herunterspielen

◆ **play off** *vt* **to ~ off ⇆ sb against sb** jdn gegen jdn ausspielen

◆ **play on** *vi* 1. (*exploit*) **to ~ on sth** etw ausnutzen 2. (*keep playing*) weiterspielen

◆ **play out** I. *vt* 1. *usu passive* (*take place*) **to be ~ed out** (*scene*) sich abspielen 2. (*play to end*) **to ~ out the last few seconds** SPORT die letzten Sekunden spielen II. *vi* zu Ende gehen

◆ **play through** *vt* MUS [von Anfang bis Ende] [durch]spielen

◆ **play up** I. *vt* hochspielen II. *vi fam* **to ~ up to sb** sich bei jdm einschmeicheln

◆ **play with** *vi* 1. (*entertain oneself with*) **to ~ with sth** mit etw *dat* spielen 2. (*play together*) **to ~ with sb** mit jdm spielen 3. (*manipulate nervously*) **to ~**

with sth mit etw *dat* herumspielen *fam* II. *vt vulg, fam* **to ~ with oneself** an sich *dat* herumspielen

'**playback** *n* Playback *nt*

'**playboy** *n usu pej* Playboy *m*

player [ˈpleɪ·ər] *n* 1. Spieler(in) *m(f)*; **baseball ~** Baseballspieler(in) *m(f)* 2. (*playback machine*) **CD ~** CD-Player *m* 3. POL (*participant*) **a key ~** Schlüsselfigur *f*

playful [ˈpleɪ·fəl] *adj* spielerisch

'**playground** *n* Spielplatz *m*

'**playhouse** *n* Spielhaus *nt (für Kinder)*

playing card [ˈpleɪ·ɪŋ-] *n* Spielkarte *f*

playing field [ˈpleɪ·ɪŋ-] *n* Sportplatz *m*

'**playoff** I. *n* Play-off *nt* II. *adj* ~ **game** Entscheidungsspiel *nt*

'**playpen** *n* Laufstall *m*

'**playroom** *n* Spielzimmer *nt*

'**plaything** *n* Spielzeug *nt*

'**playtime** *n* (*in school*) Pause *f*

'**playwright** *n* Dramatiker(in) *m(f)*

plaza [ˈpla·zə] *n* [**shopping**] ~ Einkaufszentrum *nt*

plea [pli] *n* 1. (*appeal*) Appell *m* 2. LAW **to enter a ~** eine Einrede erheben

'**plea bargaining** *n* LAW *Vereinbarung zwischen Staatsanwalt und Angeklagtem, der sich zu einem geringeren Straftatbestand bekennen soll*

plead <pleaded *or* pled, pleaded *or* pled> [plid] I. *vi* 1. (*implore*) [flehentlich] bitten, flehen; **to ~ with sb** [**to do sth**] jdn anflehen[, etw zu tun] 2. LAW (*as advocate*) plädieren; (*speak for*) **to ~ for sb** jdn verteidigen 3. + *adj* LAW (*answer charge*) **to ~ guilty** sich schuldig bekennen II. *vt* 1. (*claim*) behaupten 2. (*argue for*) **to ~ a case** LAW eine Sache vor Gericht vertreten

pleading [ˈpli·dɪŋ] *adj* flehend

pleasant [ˈplez·ənt] *adj* 1. (*experience*) angenehm 2. (*friendly*) freundlich

please [pliz] I. *interj* 1. (*in requests*) bitte 2. (*when accepting sth*) ja, bitte; **more potatoes? — ~** noch Kartoffeln? — gern II. *vt* (*make happy*) gefallen; **to be hard to ~** schwer zufrieden zu stellen sein III. *vi* **eager to ~** [unbedingt] gefallen wollen

pleased [plizd] *adj* (*happy*) froh, erfreut;

(*content*) zufrieden; **to be ~ that ...** froh sein, dass ...

pleasing ['pli·zɪŋ] *adj* angenehm; **to be ~ to the ear** hübsch klingen

pleasurable ['pleʒ·ər·ə·bəl] *adj* angenehm

pleasure ['pleʒ·ər] *n* Freude *f;* **to give sb ~** jdm Freude bereiten; **to take ~ in doing sth** Vergnügen daran finden, etw *akk* zu tun

pleat [plit] *n* Falte *f*

pled [pled] *vt, vi pt, pp of* **plead**

pledge [pledʒ] I. *n* 1. (*promise*) Versprechen *nt;* **to make a ~ that ...** geloben, dass ... II. *vt* versprechen

plentiful ['plen·tɪ·fəl] *adj* reichlich *präd*

plenty ['plen·ti] I. *n form* (*abundance*) Reichtum *m* II. *adv fam* **~ more** noch viel mehr III. *pron* 1. (*more than enough*) mehr als genug; **~ of money/ time** viel Geld/Zeit 2. (*a lot*) genug; **~ to see** viel zu sehen

pliable ['plaɪ·ə·bəl] *adj* biegsam

pliers ['plaɪ·ərz] *npl* Zange *f*

plight [plaɪt] *n* Not[lage] *f*

plod [plɑd] *vi* <-dd-> 1. (*walk slowly*) stapfen 2. (*work slowly*) **to ~ through sth** sich durch etw *akk* hindurcharbeiten

◆**plod away** *vi* vor sich *akk* hin arbeiten

plop [plɑp] *vi* <-pp-> 1. (*fall into liquid*) platschen *fam* 2. (*drop heavily*) plumpsen *fam*

plot [plɑt] I. *n* 1. (*conspiracy*) Verschwörung *f* 2. LIT (*story line*) Handlung *f* 3. (*of land*) Parzelle *f;* **vegetable ~** Gemüsebeet *nt* II. *vt* <-tt-> (*conspire*) [im Geheimen] planen *a. hum* III. *vi* <-tt-> **to ~ against sb** sich gegen jdn verschwören

◆**plot out** *vt* 1. (*route*) [grob] planen 2. (*scene, story*) umreißen

plotter ['plɑt·ər] *n* 1. (*conspirator*) Verschwörer(in) *m(f)* 2. COMPUT Plotter *m*

plow [plaʊ] I. *n* Pflug *m* II. *vt, vi* AGR pflügen

◆**plow into** I. *vi* **to ~ into sth** in etw *akk* hineinrasen II. *vt* **to ~ sth into sth** in etw *akk* investieren

◆**plow up** *vt* (*land*) umpflügen; (*lawn*) umgraben

ploy [plɔɪ] *n* Plan *m*

pluck [plʌk] I. *n* Mut *m* II. *vt* 1. (*pick*) **to ~ sth** [**from sth**] (*flower*) etw [von etw *dat*] abpflücken 2. (*feathers*) ausrupfen; (*hair*) entfernen

◆**pluck up** *vt* **to ~ up the courage** [**to do sth**] allen Mut zusammennehmen[, um etw zu tun]

plug [plʌg] I. *n* 1. (*connector*) Stecker *m;* **to pull the ~** [**on sth**] den Stecker [aus etw *dat*] herausziehen 2. (*socket*) Steckdose *f* 3. (*for sink*) Stöpsel *m* II. *vt* <-gg-> 1. (*leak*) stopfen, [zu]stopfen (**with** mit +*dat*) 2. (*publicize*) anpreisen

◆**plug away** *vi* verbissen arbeiten (**at** an +*dat*)

◆**plug in** I. *vt* einstöpseln II. *vi* (*electrical device*) sich anschließen lassen

◆**plug up** *vt* zustopfen

'plug-in *n* Zusatz *m*

plum [plʌm] I. *n* Pflaume *f* II. *adj* 1. (*color*) pflaumenfarben 2. *attr* (*desirable*) **~ job** Traumberuf *m*

plumb¹ [plʌm] I. *vt* (*determine depth*) [aus]loten II. *adj pred* gerade III. *adv* 1. *fam* (*squarely*) genau 2. *fam* (*completely*) **~ crazy** total verrückt

plumb² [plʌm] *vt* **to ~ sth into sth** etw an etw *akk* anschließen

'plumb bob *n* Lot *nt*

plumber ['plʌm·ər] *n* Klempner(in) *m(f)*

plumbing ['plʌm·ɪŋ] *n* Wasserleitungen *pl*

plume [plum] *n* 1. (*large feather*) Feder *f* 2. (*cloud*) **~ of smoke** Rauchwolke *f*

plummet ['plʌm·ɪt] I. *vi* 1. (*plunge*) fallen 2. (*prices*) in den Keller purzeln *fam* II. *n see* **plumb bob**

plump [plʌmp] *adj* (*rounded*) rund; *euph* (*person*) füllig

◆**plump down** *fam* I. *vt* **to ~ down ⇆ sth** etw hinplumpsen lassen *fam* II. *vi* **to ~ down in a chair** sich auf einen Stuhl fallen lassen

◆**plump up** *vt* (*cushion*) aufschütteln

plumpness ['plʌmp·nɪs] *n* Fülligkeit *f*

plunder ['plʌn·dər] I. *vt, vi* plündern II. *vi* plündern III. *n* (*booty*) Beute *f*

plunge [plʌndʒ] I. *n* (*drop*) Sprung *m;* (*fall*) Sturz *m;* (*dive*) **to make a ~** tauchen II. *vi* 1. (*fall*) stürzen (**into** in

P

+*akk*) **2.** (*decrease dramatically*) dramatisch sinken **III.** *vt* (*immerse*) **to ~ sth into sth** etw in etw *akk* eintauchen; (*in cooking*) etw in etw *akk* geben
♦ **plunge in** *vi* **1.** (*dive in*) eintauchen **2.** *fig* (*get involved*) sich einmischen

plunger ['plʌn·dʒər] *n* Saugpumpe *f*

plunk [plʌŋk] **I.** *n fam* (*sound*) Ploppen *nt* **II.** *vt fam* **1.** (*set down heavily*) **to ~ sth somewhere** etw irgendwo hinknallen **2.** (*sit heavily*) **to ~ oneself down on a chair** sich auf einen Stuhl plumpsen lassen
♦ **plunk down** *vt fam* **to ~ oneself down** sich hinplumpsen lassen

pluperfect ['plu·ˌpɜr·fɪkt] *n* LING **the ~** das Plusquamperfekt

plural ['plʊr·əl] *n* **the ~** der Plural

plus [plʌs] **I.** *prep* plus **II.** *n* <*pl* -es> Plus *nt kein pl fam* **III.** *adj* **1.** *attr* (*above zero*) **~ two degrees** zwei Grad plus **2.** *pred* (*or more*) mindestens; **20 ~** mindestens 20

plush [plʌʃ] **I.** *adj* (*luxurious*) exklusiv **II.** *n* Plüsch *m*

'plus sign *n* Pluszeichen *nt*

plutonium [plu·'toʊ·ni·əm] *n* Plutonium *nt*

ply[1] [plaɪ] *n* **1.** (*thickness*) Stärke *f* **2.** (*layer*) Schicht *f*

ply[2] <-ie-> [plaɪ] *vt* **1.** (*sell: drugs*) handeln **2.** (*supply continuously*) **to ~ sb with wine** jdn mit Wein abfüllen *fam*

'plywood *n* Sperrholz *nt*

pm, p.m. [ˌpiː·'em] *adv abbr of* **post meridian; eight ~** acht Uhr abends, zwanzig Uhr

PMS [ˌpiː·em·'es] *n* MED *abbr of* **premenstrual syndrome** PMS *nt*

pneumonia [nu·'moʊn·jə] *n* Lungenentzündung *f*

PO [ˌpiː·'oʊ] *n abbr of* **Post Office**

poach[1] [poʊtʃ] *vt* pochieren

poach[2] [poʊtʃ] *vt* **1.** (*catch illegally*) wildern **2.** (*ideas*) stehlen **3.** (*employee*) abwerben (**from** +*dat*)

poacher ['poʊ·tʃər] *n* Wilderer *m*

P'O box *n abbr of* **Post Office Box** Postfach

pocket ['pak·ɪt] **I.** *n* **1.** (*in clothing*) Tasche *f* **2.** (*on bag*) Fach *nt* **3.** *fig* (*financial resources*) **out of one's own ~** aus eigener Tasche **II.** *vt* **1.** (*put in one's pocket*) in die Tasche stecken **2.** (*keep sth for oneself*) behalten

'pocketbook *n* Handtasche *f*

'pocketknife *n* Taschenmesser *nt*

pocket money *n* Taschengeld *nt*

'pocket-size(d) *adj* im Taschenformat, nach *n*

pod [pad] *n* (*seed container*) Hülse *f*, (*pea*) Schote *f*

podiatrist [pə·'daɪ·ə·trɪst] *n* Fußpfleger(in) *m(f)*

podium <*pl* -dia> ['poʊ·di·əm] *n* Podium *nt*

poem ['poʊ·əm] *n a. fig* Gedicht *nt*

poet ['poʊ·ət] *n* Dichter(in) *m(f)*

poetic(al) [poʊ·'et̬·ɪk(əl)] *adj* (*relating to poetry*) dichterisch; **~ language** Dichtersprache *f*

poetry ['poʊ·ɪ·tri] *n* Dichtung *f*

poignant ['pɔɪn·jənt] *adj* bewegend

poinsettia [pɔɪn·'set̬·i·ə] *n* Weihnachtsstern *m*

point [pɔɪnt] **I.** *n* **1.** (*sharp end*) Spitze *f* **2.** (*decimal point*) Komma **3.** (*position*) Punkt *m*; **~ of contact** Berührungspunkt *m* **4.** (*particular time*) Zeitpunkt *m*; **at that ~** zu diesem Zeitpunkt; (*then*) in diesem Augenblick **5.** (*argument, issue*) Punkt *m*; **she made the ~ that ...** sie wies darauf hin, dass ...; (*stress*) sie betonte, dass ...; **ok, ~ taken** o. k., ich hab schon begriffen *fam* **6.** (*most important idea*) **to come to the ~** auf den Punkt kommen **7.** (*purpose*) Sinn *m*, Zweck *m* **8.** (*stage in process*) Punkt *m*; **from that ~ on ...** von diesem Moment an ...; **up to a ~** bis zu einem gewissen Grad **9.** SPORT Punkt *m* **10.** (*important characteristic*) Merkmal *nt*; **good ~s** gute Seiten **II.** *vi* **1.** (*with finger*) zeigen (**at/to** auf +*akk*) **2.** (*be directed*) weisen; **to ~ west** nach Westen zeigen **3.** (*indicate*) hinweisen (**to** auf +*akk*) **III.** *vt* **1.** (*aim*) **to ~ sth at sb** (*weapon*) etw [auf jdn] richten **2.** (*direct*) **to ~ sb in the direction of sth** jdm den Weg zu etw *dat* beschreiben
♦ **point out** *vt* **1.** (*show*) **to ~ out ⇆ sth** [**to sb**] [jdn] auf etw hinweisen; (*with*

finger) [jdn] etw zeigen **2.** (*inform*) to ~ **out that ...** darauf aufmerksam machen, dass ...

point-'blank *adv* **1.** (*at very close range*) aus nächster Nähe **2.** (*bluntly*) geradewegs

pointed ['pɔɪn·tɪd] *adj* **1.** (*with sharp point*) spitz **2.** (*emphatic*) pointiert *geh*; (*criticism*) scharf

pointer ['pɔɪn·tər] *n* **1.** (*on dial*) Zeiger *m* **2.** *usu pl fam* (*tip*) Tipp *m*

pointless ['pɔɪnt·lɪs] *adj* sinnlos, zwecklos

point of 'view <*pl* **points of view**> *n* Ansicht *f*

poise [pɔɪz] **I.** *n* Haltung *f* **II.** *vt usu passive* **1.** (*balance*) balancieren; (*hover*) **to be ~d** schweben **2.** *fig* **to be ~d to do sth** (*about to*) nahe daran sein, etw zu tun

poised [pɔɪzd] *adj* beherrscht

poison ['pɔɪ·zən] **I.** *n* Gift *nt* **II.** *vt* vergiften

poison 'gas *n* Giftgas *nt*

poisoning ['pɔɪ·zə·nɪŋ] *n* **1.** (*act*) Vergiften *nt* **2.** (*condition*) Vergiftung *f*; **blood ~** Blutvergiftung *f*

poison 'ivy *n* Giftsumach *m*

poisonous ['pɔɪ·zə·nəs] *adj* giftig

poke¹ [poʊk] **I.** *n* (*jab*) Stoß *m* **II.** *vt* **1.** (*prod*) anstoßen; (*with umbrella, stick*) stechen; **to ~ a hole in sth** in etw *akk* ein Loch in etw *akk* bohren **2. to ~ sth into/through sth** (*prod with*) etw in/durch etw *akk* stecken **3.** (*fire*) schüren
  ► **to ~ one's nose into sb's business** *fam* seine Nase in jds Angelegenheiten stecken **III.** *vi* **1.** (*jab repeatedly*) herumfummeln *fam* (**at** an +*dat*) **2.** (*break through*) durchscheinen
  ◆ **poke around** *vi fam* herumstöbern
  ◆ **poke out I.** *vi* **to ~ out** [**of sth**] [aus etw *dat*] hervorgucken **II.** *vt* (*tongue*) herausstrecken
  ◆ **poke up** *vi* hervorragen

poke² [poʊk] *n* ► **to buy a pig in a ~** *pej* die Katze im Sack kaufen *fig*

poker¹ ['poʊ·kər] *n* (*card game*) Poker *m o nt*

poker² ['poʊ·kər] *n* (*fireplace tool*) Schürhaken *m*

pokey, poky ['poʊ·ki] *adj pej* (*slow*) lahm

Poland ['poʊ·lənd] *n* Polen *nt*

'polar bear *n* Eisbär *m*

polarize ['poʊ·lə·raɪz] *vt, vi* [sich] polarisieren

pole¹ [poʊl] *n* **1.** GEOG, ELEC Pol *m* **2.** (*extreme*) **to be ~s apart** Welten voneinander entfernt sein

pole² [poʊl] *n* Stange *f*; **flag~** Fahnenmast *m*

'pole vault *n* Stabhochsprung *m kein pl*

'pole-vaulter *n* Stabhochspringer(in) *m(f)*

police [pə·'lis] **I.** *n* + *pl vb* **1.** (*force*) **the ~** die Polizei *kein pl*; **to call the ~** die Polizei rufen **2.** (*police officers*) Polizisten, -innen *pl* **II.** *vt* **1.** (*maintain law and order*) überwachen **2.** (*regulate*) **to ~ sth** etw kontrollieren

po'lice car *n* Polizeiauto *nt*

po'lice department *n* Polizeidienststelle *f*

po'lice dog *n* Polizeihund *m*

po'lice force *n* **1.** (*the police*) **the ~** die Polizei **2.** (*unit of police*) Polizeieinheit *f*

po'liceman *n* Polizist *m*

po'lice officer *n* Polizeibeamte(r) *m*, Polizeibeamte [*or* -in] *f*

po'lice station *n* Polizeiwache *f*

po'licewoman *n* Polizistin *f*

policy¹ ['pal·ə·si] *n* **1.** (*plan*) Programm *nt* **2.** Politik *f*

policy² ['pal·ə·si] *n* (*for insurance*) Police *f*

'policyholder *n* Versicherungsnehmer(in) *m(f)*

'policymaker *n* Parteiideologe, -ideologin *m, f*

polio [,poʊ·li·oʊ], **poliomyelitis** [,poʊ·li·oʊ·ˌmaɪ·ə·'laɪ·təs] *n spec* Kinderlähmung *f*

polish ['pal·ɪʃ] **I.** *n* **1.** (*substance*) Politur *f*; **shoe ~** Schuhcreme *f* **2.** *fig* (*refinement*) [gesellschaftlicher] Schliff **II.** *vt* polieren; (*shoes*) putzen
  ◆ **polish off** *vt* **1.** (*food*) verdrücken *fam* **2.** *fam* (*beat*) abfertigen, abservieren

Polish ['poʊ·lɪʃ] **I.** *n* Polnisch *nt* **II.** *adj* polnisch

polished ['pal·ɪʃt] *adj* **1.** (*gleaming*) glän-

zend *attr* **2.** (*performance*) großartig

polite [pə-ˈlaɪt] *adj* höflich

politeness [pə-ˈlaɪt-nɪs] *n* Höflichkeit *f*

political [pə-ˈlɪt-ɪ-kəl] *adj* politisch; ~ **leaders** politische Größen *pl*

political cor'rectness *n* politische Korrektheit

politically cor'rect *adj* politisch korrekt

politician [ˌpal-ə-ˈtɪʃ-ən] *n* Politiker(in) *m(f)*

politics [ˈpal-ə-tɪks] *npl* **1.** + *sing vb* Politik *f kein pl;* **to go into** ~ in die Politik gehen **2.** + *sing/pl vb* (*within group*) **office** ~ Büroklüngelei *f pej*

polka [ˈpoʊl-kə] *n* Polka *f*

'polka dot *n usu sg* Tupfen *m*

poll [poʊl] **I.** *n* **1.** (*public survey*) Erhebung *f;* **an opinion** ~ eine Meinungsumfrage **2.** (*number of votes cast*) Wahlbeteiligung *f* **II.** *vt* **1.** (*canvass in poll*) befragen **2.** (*receive*) **the party ~ed 67% of the vote** die Partei hat 67 % der Stimmen erhalten

pollen [ˈpal-ən] *n* Blütenstaub *m*

'pollen count *n* Pollenflug *m kein pl*

polling [ˈpoʊl-ɪŋ] *n* Wahl *f*

'polling booth *n* Wahlkabine *f*

pollutant [pə-ˈlu-tənt] *n* Schadstoff *m*

pollute [pə-ˈlut] *vt* verschmutzen

polluter [pə-ˈlu-tər] *n* Umweltverschmutzer(in) *m(f)*

pollution [pə-ˈlu-ʃən] *n* Verschmutzung *f;* **environmental** ~ Umweltverschmutzung *f*

polo [ˈpoʊ-loʊ] *n* Polo *nt*

'polo shirt *n* Polohemd *nt*

polyester [ˌpal-i-ˈes-tər] *n* Polyester *m*

polyethylene [ˌpal-i-ˈeθ-ə-lin] *n* Polyäthylen *nt*

polygamous [pə-ˈlɪg-ə-məs] *adj* polygam *geh*

polygon [ˈpal-i-gan] *n* Vieleck *nt,* Polygon *nt fachspr*

polygraph [ˈpal-i-græf] *n* Lügendetektor *m*

polyp [ˈpal-ɪp] *n* MED, ZOOL Polyp *m*

polystyrene [ˌpal-i-ˈstaɪ-rin] *n* Styropor® *nt*

polytechnic [ˌpal-i-ˈtek-nɪk] **I.** *adj* (*institute*) Technische Hochschule *f* **II.** *n* Fachhochschule *f*

polyunsaturated fats [ˌpal-i-ʌn-ˈsætʃ-ə-

reɪ-tɪd-], **polyunsaturates** [ˌpal-i-ʌn-ˈsætʃ-ə-reɪts] *npl* (*fatty acids*) mehrfach ungesättigte Fettsäuren; (*fats*) Fette mit einem hohen Anteil an mehrfach ungesättigten Fettsäuren

polyurethane [ˌpal-i-ˈjʊr-ə-θeɪn] *n* Polyurethan *nt*

pomegranate [ˈpam-græn-ɪt] *n* Granatapfel *m*

pompon [ˈpam-pan], **pompom** [ˈpam-pam] *n* **1.** (*of cheerleader*) Pompon *m* **2.** (*yarn ball*) Quaste *f*

pompous [ˈpam-pəs] *adj* **1.** (*person*) selbstgefällig **2.** (*language*) geschraubt *pej*

poncho [ˈpan-tʃoʊ] *n* Poncho *m*

pond [pand] *n* **1.** (*body of water*) Teich *m* **2.** *hum* (*Atlantic Ocean*) **the** ~ der große Teich

ponder [ˈpan-dər] **I.** *vt* durchdenken **II.** *vi* nachdenken

pone [poʊn] *n* [**corn**] ~ Maisbrot *nt*

pontificate [pan-ˈtɪf-ɪ-kɪt] *vi pej* **to** ~ **about sth** sich über etw *akk* auslassen

pontoon [pan-ˈtun] *n* Ponton *m*

pontoon 'bridge *n* Pontonbrücke *f*

pony [ˈpoʊ-ni] *n* (*small horse*) Pony *nt*

'ponytail *n* Pferdeschwanz *m*

poo [pu] *n childspeak sl* Aa *nt kein pl*

poodle [ˈpu-dəl] *n* Pudel *m*

poof [puf] *interj fam* hui!

pooh [pu] *interj fam* (*in disgust*) pfui!, igitt!

pooh-pooh [ˌpu-ˈpu] *vt fam* abtun

pool[1] [pul] **I.** *n* Becken *nt;* [**swimming**] ~ Schwimmbecken *nt;* (*private*) Swimmingpool *m;* (*public*) Schwimmbad *nt* **II.** *vi* (*liquid*) sich stauen

pool[2] [pul] **I.** *n* SPORT Poolbillard *nt* **II.** *vt* zusammenlegen

'pool hall *n* Billardzimmer *nt*

'pool table *n* Poolbillardtisch *m*

poop[1] [pup] *n* (*of ship*) Heck *nt*

poop[2] [pup] **I.** *n euph* (*excrement*) Aa *nt;* **dog** ~ Hundedreck *m fam* **II.** *vi fam* (*defecate*) Aa machen *Kindersprache*

poop 'out *vi* **1.** (*become tired*) schlappmachen **2.** (*not persevere*) sich geschlagen geben

pooped [pupt] *adj fam* erschöpft, [fix und] fertig

pooper scooper ['pu·pər·ˌsku·pər] n fam Kotschaufel f (Schaufel zum Entfernen von Hundekot)

poor [pʊr] adj 1. (lacking money) arm 2. (inadequate) unzureichend, schlecht; **to be in ~ health** in schlechtem gesundheitlichen Zustand sein 3. attr (deserving of pity) arm

poorly ['pʊr·li] adv ~ **dressed** ärmlich gekleidet

poor re'lation n arme(r) Verwandte(r) f/m

pop[1] [pap] I. n 1. (noise) Knall m 2. usu sing sl **a ~** pro Stück II. adv **to go ~** (make noise) einen Knall machen III. vi <-pp-> 1. (make noise) knallen 2. (burst) platzen IV. vt <-pp-> 1. (burst) platzen lassen 2. (put quickly) **~ the pizza in the oven** schieb' die Pizza in den Ofen ▶ **to ~ pills** Pillen schlucken

pop in vi vorbeischauen

pop out vi herausspringen

pop up vi 1. (appear unexpectedly) auftauchen 2. (in baseball: hit a short, high fly ball) einen Popup schlagen

pop[2] [pap] n fam Papa m

pop[3] [pap] n (music) Pop m

pop art n Pop-Art f

popcorn n Popcorn nt

pope [poʊp] n Papst m

poplar ['pap·lər] n Pappel f

poplin ['pap·lɪn] n Popelin m

pop music n Popmusik f

poppy ['pap·i] n Mohnblume f

Popsicle® ['pap·sɪ·kəl] n Eis nt am Stiel

pop singer n Popsänger(in) m(f)

popular ['pap·jə·lər] adj 1. (widely liked) beliebt 2. attr (not highbrow) populär 3. attr (widespread) weit verbreitet; **it is a ~ belief that ...** viele glauben, dass ...

popularity [ˌpap·jə·'lær·ɪ·t̬i] n Beliebtheit f

popularize ['pap·jə·lə·raɪz] vt (make accessible) breiteren Kreisen zugänglich machen

popularly ['pap·jə·lər·li] adv (commonly) allgemein; **as is ~ believed** wie man allgemein annimmt

populate ['pap·jə·leɪt] vt usu passive (inhabit) **to be ~d** bevölkert sein; (island) bewohnt sein

population [ˌpap·jə·'leɪ·ʃən] n 1. usu sing (inhabitants) Bevölkerung f kein pl 2. (number of people) Einwohnerzahl f

population 'density n Bevölkerungsdichte f

population ex'plosion n Bevölkerungsexplosion f

porcelain ['pɔr·sə·lɪn] n Porzellan nt

porch [pɔrtʃ] n <pl -es> 1. (veranda) Veranda f

porcupine ['pɔr·kjʊ·paɪn] n Stachelschwein nt

pore[1] [pɔr] vi (examine) brüten (**over** über +dat)

pore[2] [pɔr] n Pore f

pork [pɔrk] n Schweinefleisch nt

'pork chop n Schweinekotelett nt

porky ['pɔr·ki] adj pej fam fett

porn [pɔrn] n short for **pornography** fam Porno m

pornographic [ˌpɔr·nə·'græf·ɪk] adj (containing pornography) pornografisch, Porno-

pornography [pɔr·'nag·rə·fi] n Pornografie f

porous ['pɔr·əs] adj porös

porpoise ['pɔr·pəs] n Tümmler m

porridge ['pɔr·ɪdʒ] n Porridge m o nt

port[1] [pɔrt] n 1. (harbor) Hafen m 2. (town) Hafenstadt f

port[2] [pɔrt] n AVIAT, NAUT Backbord nt

port[3] [pɔrt] n COMPUT Anschluss m, Port m fachspr

port[4] [pɔrt] n (wine) Portwein m

portable ['pɔr·t̬ə·bəl] adj tragbar

portal ['pɔr·t̬əl] n form Portal nt

porter ['pɔr·t̬ər] n Gepäckträger m

portfolio [pɔrt·'foʊ·li·oʊ] n 1. (of drawings) Mappe f 2. FIN Portefeuille nt fachspr

'porthole n NAUT Bullauge nt; AVIAT Kabinenfenster nt

portion ['pɔr·ʃən] I. n 1. (part) Teil m 2. (serving) Portion f; (piece) Stück m II. vt **to ~ out** ⇆ sth etw aufteilen

portrait ['pɔr·trɪt] I. n Porträt nt II. adj TYPO **in ~ format** im Hochformat

portray [pɔr·'treɪ] vt 1. (paint) porträtieren 2. (describe) darstellen

Portugal ['pɔr·tʃə·gəl] n Portugal nt

P

pose [pouz] **I.** *n* **1.** (*bodily position*) Haltung *f* **2.** *usu sing* (*pretence*) Getue *nt* **II.** *vi* **1.** (*adopt position*) posieren **2.** (*pretend*) **to ~ as** sich ausgeben als **III.** *vt* **1.** (*cause*) aufwerfen; **to ~ a threat to sb** eine Bedrohung für jdn darstellen **2.** (*question*) stellen

poser ['pou·zər] *n pej fam* (*person*) Angeber(in) *m(f)*

posh [pɑʃ] *adj fam* vornehm

position [pə·'zɪʃ·ən] **I.** *n* **1.** (*place*) Platz *m*; (*building*) Lage *f* **2.** (*in navigation*) Position *f* **3.** (*posture*) Stellung *f*; **to change one's ~** eine andere Stellung einnehmen **4.** SPORT (*in team*) [Spieler] position *f* **5.** (*rank*) Position *f*; (*in race, competition*) Platz *m* **II.** *vt* platzieren

positive ['pɑz·ɪ·t̮ɪv] *adj* **1.** (*certain*) bestimmt; **to be ~ about sth** sich *dat* einer S. *gen* sicher sein **2.** (*optimistic, med, math, elec*) positiv

positively ['pɑz·ɪ·t̮ɪv·li] *adv* **1.** (*definitely*) bestimmt; (*promise*) fest **2.** (*think*) positiv

posse ['pɑs·i] *n hist* (*summoned by sheriff*) [Hilfs]trupp *m*

possess [pə·'zes] *vt* **1.** besitzen **2.** *usu passive* (*control*) **to be ~ed by the Devil** vom Teufel besessen sein

possession [pə·'zef·ən] *n* **1.** (*having*) Besitz *m*; **to be in sb's ~** sich in jds Besitz befinden **2.** *usu pl* (*something owned*) Besitz *m kein pl*

possessive [pə·'zes·ɪv] *adj* **1.** (*not sharing*) eigen **2.** (*jealous*) besitzergreifend

possibility [ˌpɑs·ə·'bɪl·ɪ·t̮i] *n* **1.** Möglichkeit *f*; **there's a ~ that ...** es kann sein, dass ... **2.** (*potential*) **possibilities** *pl* Möglichkeiten *pl*

possible ['pɑs·ə·bəl] *adj* möglich; **it's just not ~** das ist einfach nicht machbar; **as much as ~** so viel wie möglich

possibly ['pɑs·ə·bli] *adv* **1.** (*feasibly*) **he couldn't ~ have known that** das kann er doch unmöglich gewusst haben! **2.** (*perhaps*) möglicherweise; **very ~** durchaus möglich

possum <*pl* -> ['pɑs·əm] *n* Opossum *nt*

post¹ [poust] **I.** *n* **1.** (*pole*) Pfosten *m* **2.** *fam* **goal ~** [Tor]pfosten *m* **II.** *vt* COMPUT **to ~ sth on the [Inter]net** etw

über das Internet bekannt geben

post² [poust] *n* MIL Stützpunkt *m*

postage ['pou·stɪdʒ] *n* Porto *nt*

'postage meter *n* Frankiermaschine *f*

postal ['pou·stəl] *adj attr* Post- ▶ **to g◄ ~ sl** Amok laufen

'postcard *n* Postkarte *f*

post'date *vt* (*give later date*) vordatie ren

poster ['pou·stər] *n* [Werbe]plakat *nt*

post'graduate *n* Postgraduierte(r) *f/m fachspr*

posthumous ['pɑs·tʃə·məs] *adj* form post[h]um

posting ['pou·stɪŋ] *n* COMPUT (*message* Posting *nt*

'postmark I. *n* Poststempel *m* **II.** *vt us. passive* **to be ~ed** abgestempelt sein

'postmaster *n* Leiter *m* einer Post dienststelle

post'modern *adj* post-modern

postmortem [ˌpoust·'mɔr·t̮əm] **I.** *◄* **1.** MED *see* autopsy **2.** *fam* (*discussion* Manöverkritik *f hum* **II.** *adj attr* (*don◄ after death*) nach dem Tod *nach n*

'post office *n* **the ~** die Post *kein pl*

postpone [poust·'poun] *vt* verschieben

'postscript *n* Postskript[um] *nt*

posture ['pɑs·tʃər] *n* [Körper]haltung *f*

posy ['pou·zi] *n* Sträußchen *nt*

pot¹ [pɑt] **I.** *n* **1.** Topf *m*; **coffee ~** Kaf feekanne *f* **2.** (*for plants*) Blumentopf *n* **II.** *vt* <-tt-> (*plants*) eintopfen

pot² [pɑt] *n sl* Pot *m*

potassium [pə·'tæs·i·əm] *n* Kalium *nt*

potato <*pl* -es> [pə·'teɪ·t̮ou] *n* Kartoffel *.* **baked ~** Ofenkartoffel *f*

po'tato chip *n usu pl* Kartoffelchip *m*

po'tato peeler *n* Kartoffelschäler *m*

potbellied ['pɑt·ˌbelid] *adj* dickbäuchig

potency ['pou·tən·si] *n* **1.** (*strength* Stärke *f*; (*of temptation, a spell*) Macht *(of a drug*) Wirksamkeit *f* **2.** (*sexua* Potenz *f*

potent ['pou·tənt] *adj* **1.** (*strong*) mäch tig; (*drink*) stark; (*argument*) schlagkräf tig **2.** (*sexual*) potent

potential [pə·'ten·ʃəl] **I.** *adj* potenzie geh, möglich **II.** *n* Potenzial *nt geh*

potentially [pə·'ten·ʃə·li] *adv* potenzi ell *geh;* **~ disastrous** möglicherweise

verheerend; **sth is ~ fatal** etw kann tödlich sein

potholder n Topflappen m

pothole n (in road) Schlagloch nt

pot'luck n attr FOOD (communal meal) **~ dinner** Abendessen, zu dem jeder eine Speise mitbringt

potpourri [ˌpou·pu·'ri] n Potpourri nt

pot roast n Schmorbraten m

potshot n 1. (with gun) blinder Schuss 2. fig (verbal attack) Seitenhieb m

potter ['pɑt·ər] n Töpfer(in) m(f)

pottery ['pɑt·ə·ri] n 1. Keramik f kein pl 2. (factory) Töpferei f

potty ['pɑt·i] n Töpfchen nt

pouch <pl -es> [paʊtʃ] n 1. (small bag) Beutel m 2. ZOOL (of kangaroo) Beutel m

poultry ['poʊl·tri] n pl Geflügel nt kein pl

pounce [paʊns] vi 1. (jump) losspringen; (animal) einen Satz machen 2. fig (seize opportunity) zuschlagen

pound[1] [paʊnd] n (unit of weight) ≈ Pfund nt (454 g)

pound[2] [paʊnd] I. vt 1. (hit repeatedly) **to ~ sth** auf etw akk hämmern 2. MIL (bombard) **to ~ enemy positions** die feindlichen Stellungen bombardieren II. vi (beat: pulse) schlagen; (heart a.) pochen

pounding ['paʊn·dɪŋ] I. n 1. (noise: of guns) Knattern nt; (in head) Pochen nt; (of waves) Brechen nt 2. (attack) Beschuss m kein pl; **to take a ~** unter schweren Beschuss geraten 3. (defeat) Niederlage f; (in election, match) Schlappe f II. adj (drum) dröhnend; (head) pochend

pour [pɔr] I. vt 1. (cause to flow) gießen (**into/onto** in/auf +akk); **to ~ sb sth** jdm etw einschenken 2. fig (give in large amounts: resources) fließen lassen (**into** +akk); (energy) stecken (**into** in +akk) II. vi 1. (flow) fließen (**into/out of** in/aus +akk) 2. impers (rain) **it's ~ing** [rain] es schüttet wie aus Kübeln fam

◆**pour in** vi hereinströmen, hineinströmen; (letters, donations) massenweise eintreffen

◆**pour out** I. vt 1. (liquids) ausgießen, herauskippen; (solids) ausschütten 2. (produce quickly) ausstoßen II. vi (come out) ausströmen; (smoke) herausquellen

pout [paʊt] I. vi einen Schmollmund machen II. n Schmollmund m

poverty ['pɑv·ər·ti] n Armut f

'**poverty line** n **the ~** die Armutsgrenze

'**poverty-stricken** adj bitterarm

POW [ˌpi·oʊ·'dʌb·əl·ju] n abbr of **prisoner of war** KG

powder ['paʊ·dər] I. n Pulver nt II. vt pudern

powdered ['paʊ·dərd] adj 1. (in powder form) Pulver-; **~ sugar** Puderzucker m 2. (covered with powder) gepudert

powdery ['paʊ·də·ri] adj pulv[e]rig; (finer) pud[e]rig

power ['paʊ·ər] I. n 1. POL (control) Macht f; (influence) Einfluss m; **to seize ~** die Macht ergreifen 2. (nation) [Führungs]macht f 3. (person, group) Macht f 4. (ability) Vermögen nt; **to do everything in one's ~** alles in seiner Macht Stehende tun 5. (strength) Kraft f; (output a.) Leistung f; (of sea, wind, explosion) Gewalt f; (of nation) Stärke f 6. (electricity) Strom m; **nuclear ~** Atomenergie f II. vt antreiben

◆**power down** I. vt ELEC, TECH abschalten; (computer) herunterfahren II. vi COMPUT herunterfahren; TECH zum Stillstand kommen

◆**power up** I. vt ELEC, TECH einschalten; (computer) hochfahren II. vi TECH, COMPUT hochfahren

power-as'sisted adj attr Servo-

'**powerboat** n see **motorboat**

power 'brakes npl Servobremsen pl

'**power cable** n Stromkabel nt

powerful ['paʊ·ər·fəl] adj 1. (mighty) mächtig; (influential) einflussreich 2. (physically strong) stark, kräftig 3. (effect, influence) stark; (argument) schlagkräftig

powerfully ['paʊ·ər·fə·li] adv 1. (strongly) stark; (very much) sehr 2. (using great force) kraftvoll

powerless ['paʊ·ər·lɪs] adj machtlos

'**power line** n Stromkabel nt

'**power outage** n Stromausfall m

P

'power plant n Kraftwerk nt

power 'steering n Servolenkung f

'power tool n Motorwerkzeug nt; (electric) Elektrowerkzeug nt

PR [piː'ɑːr] n abbr of public relations PR

practical ['præk·tɪ·kəl] adj 1. (not theoretical) praktisch 2. approv (good at doing things) praktisch [veranlagt] 3. (possible) realisierbar

practicality [ˌpræk·tɪ·'kæl·ɪ·ṭi] n 1. (feasibility) Durchführbarkeit f 2. (practical aspect) the practicalities pl die praktische Seite

practically ['præk·tɪk·li] adv (almost) praktisch

practice ['præk·tɪs] I. n 1. (preparation) Übung f; to be out of ~ aus der Übung sein 2. (training session) [Übungs]stunde f; SPORT Training nt 3. (actual performance, usual procedure) Praxis f; in ~ in der Praxis 4. (custom) Sitte f II. vt (rehearse) to ~ [doing] sth etw üben; (improve particular skill) an etw dat arbeiten III. vi 1. (improve skill) üben 2. (work in a profession) praktizieren

practiced ['præk·tɪst] adj (experienced) erfahren; ~ eye geübtes Auge

practicing ['præk·tɪs·ɪŋ] adj attr praktizierend

practitioner [præk·'tɪʃ·ə·nər] n form medical ~ praktischer Arzt/praktische Ärztin

pragmatic [præg·'mæṭ·ɪk] adj (attitude) pragmatisch; (idea) vernünftig

prairie ['prer·i] n [Gras]steppe f; (in North America) Prärie f

'prairie dog n ZOOL Präriehund m

praise [preɪz] I. vt loben II. n (approval) Lob nt; to win ~ for sth für etw akk [großes] Lob ernten

praiseworthy ['preɪz·ˌwɜr·ði] adj lobenswert

prank [præŋk] n Streich m

pray [preɪ] vi beten

prayer [prer] n 1. Gebet nt; to say a ~ for sb für jdn beten 2. fig (hope) Hoffnung f; to not have a ~ fam kaum Chancen haben

'prayer book n Gebetbuch nt

'prayer meeting n Gebetsstunde f

'prayer rug n Gebetsteppich m

preach [priːtʃ] I. vi 1. (give a sermon) predigen (to vor +dat) 2. pej (lecture) to ~ to sb [about sth] jdm eine Predigt [über etw akk] halten fig II. vt to ~ a sermon eine Predigt halten

preacher ['priː·tʃər] n 1. (priest) Geistliche(r) f(m) 2. Prediger(in) m(f)

prearrange [ˌpriː·ə·'reɪndʒ] vt usu passive vorplanen

precarious [prɪ·'ker·i·əs] adj (balance) unsicher

precaution [prɪ·'kɔ·ʃən] n Vorkehrung f

precede [prɪ·'siːd] vt 1. (in rank) rangieren vor dat (in importance) wichtiger sein als 2. (in time) vorausgehen dat

precedence ['pres·ə·dəns] n Vorrang m

precedent ['pres·ə·dənt] n vergleichbarer Fall, Präzedenzfall m geh

preceding [prɪ·'si·dɪŋ] adj attr vorhergehend; the ~ page die vorige Seite

precinct ['priː·sɪŋkt] n 1. (electoral district) Wahlbezirk m 2. (police station) Revier nt

precious ['preʃ·əs] I. adj (of great value) wertvoll; to be ~ to sb jdm viel bedeuten II. adv fam ~ little herzlich wenig

precipice ['pres·ə·pɪs] n (steep drop) Abgrund m; (cliff face) Steilhang m

precipitate [prɪ·'sɪp·ɪ·teɪt] I. vi 1. METEO einen Niederschlag bilden 2. CHEM to ~ [out] ausfallen fachspr II. n Satz m

precipitation [prɪ·ˌsɪp·ɪ·'teɪ·ʃən] n 1. METEO Niederschlag m 2. (forming into a solid) Setzen nt

precise [prɪ·'saɪs] adj genau

precisely [prɪ·'saɪs·li] adv 1. (exactly) genau, präzise 2. approv (carefully) sorgfältig

precision [prɪ·'sɪʒ·ən] n Genauigkeit f

precocious [prɪ·'koʊ·ʃəs] adj 1. (developing early) frühreif; ~ talent frühe Begabung 2. pej (maturing too early) altklug

preconceived [ˌpriː·kən·'siːvd] adj esp pej vorgefasst

preconception [ˌpriː·kən·'sep·ʃən] n esp pej vorgefasste Meinung

precondition [ˌpriː·kən·'dɪʃ·ən] n Voraussetzung f

precooked [ˌpriː·'kʊkt] adj vorgekocht

predator ['pred·ə·tər] n 1. (animal)

Raubtier *nt;* (*bird*) Raubvogel *m* **2.** *pej* (*person*) Profiteur(in) *m(f)*

redatory ['pred·ə·tɔr·i] *adj* **1.** (*preying*) Raub-, räuberisch **2.** *esp pej* (*exploitative*) raubtierhaft

redecessor ['pred·ə·ses·ər] *n* Vorgänger(in) *m(f)*

redetermine [,pri·dɪ·'tɜr·mən] *vt usu passive* vor|her|bestimmen; **at a ~d signal** auf ein verabredetes Zeichen hin

redicament [prɪ·'dɪk·ə·mənt] *n* Notlage *f*

redict [prɪ·'dɪkt] *vt* vorhersagen; (*sb's future etc.*) prophezeien

redictable [prɪ·'dɪk·tə·bəl] *adj* **1.** (*foreseeable*) vorhersehbar **2.** *pej* (*not very original*) berechenbar

rediction [prɪ·'dɪk·ʃən] *n* (*forecast*) Vorhersage *f;* ECON, POL Prognose *f*

redominance [prɪ·'dam·ə·nəns] *n* **1.** (*greater number*) zahlenmäßige Überlegenheit **2.** (*predominant position*) Vorherrschaft

redominant [prɪ·'dam·ə·nənt] *adj* vorherrschend; **to be ~** führend sein

reempt [,pri·'empt] *vt form* (*act in advance*) **to ~ sth** etw zuvorkommen

reemptive [pri·'emp·tɪv] *adj* **1.** (*preventive*) vorbeugend **2.** MIL (*forestalling the enemy*) präventiv

reen [prin] *vi* **1.** (*bird*) sich putzen **2.** *pej* (*person*) sich auftakeln

re-exist [,pri·ɪg·'zɪst] *vi form* vorher existieren

refabricated [,pri·'fæb·rɪ·keɪ·tɪd] *adj* vorgefertigt

reface ['pref·ɪs] *n* (*introduction*) Einleitung *f;* (*to a novel etc.*) Vorwort *nt*

refect ['pri·fekt] *n* (*official*) Präfekt(in) *m(f)*

refer <-rr-> [prɪ·'fɜr] *vt* **to ~ doing sth** [**to doing sth**] etw lieber [als etw] tun

referable ['pref·rə·bəl] *adj* besser

referably ['pref·rə·bli] *adv* vorzugsweise

reference ['pref·rəns] *n* **1.** (*priority*) Priorität *f;* **to be given ~** Vorrang haben **2.** (*greater liking*) Vorliebe *f*

referential [,pref·ə·'ren·ʃəl] *adj attr* Vorzugs-; **to get ~ treatment** bevorzugt behandelt werden

referred [prɪ·'fɜrd] *adj attr* bevorzugt,

Lieblings-

prefix ['pri·fɪks] *n* <*pl* -es> LING Präfix *nt fachspr*

pregnancy ['preg·nən·si] *n* Schwangerschaft *f*

pregnant ['preg·nənt] *adj* (*woman*) schwanger; (*animal*) trächtig

prehistoric [,pri·hɪ·'stɔr·ɪk] *adj* **1.** prähistorisch **2.** *pej fam* (*outdated*) steinzeitlich *fig*

prejudge [,pri·'dʒʌdʒ] *vt* vorschnell ein Urteil fällen über +*akk*

prejudice ['predʒ·ə·dɪs] **I.** *n* (*preconceived opinion, bias*) Vorurteil *nt;* **racial ~** Rassenvorurteil *nt* **II.** *vt* **1.** (*harm*) **to ~ sb's chances** jds Chancen beeinträchtigen **2.** (*bias*) **to ~ sb [against/in favor of sb/sth]** jdn [gegen/für jdn/etw] einnehmen

prejudiced ['predʒ·ə·dɪst] *adj* voreingenommen; **to be ~ against sb** Vorurteile gegen jdn haben

prelim ['pri·lɪm] *n* SPORT *fam short for* **preliminary** Vorrunde *f*

preliminary [prɪ·'lɪm·ə·ner·i] **I.** *adj attr* einleitend; **~ arrangements** Vorbereitungen *pl* **II.** *n* **1.** (*introduction*) Einleitung *f* **2.** SPORT Vorrunde *f*

prelude ['prel·jud] *n usu sing* (*preliminary*) Vorspiel *nt*

premarital [,pri·'mær·ɪ·təl] *adj* vorehelich *attr*

premature [,pri·mə·'tʃʊr] *adj* **1.** voreilig **2.** MED **~ baby** Frühgeburt *f*

premeditated [,pri·'med·ɪ·teɪ·tɪd] *adj* geplant

premeditation [,pri·med·ɪ·'teɪ·ʃən] *n form* **with ~** (*of a crime*) mit Vorsatz

premenstrual [,pri·'men·stru·əl] *adj attr* prämenstruell

premier [prɪ·'mɪr] **I.** *n* Premierminister(in) *m(f)* **II.** *adj attr* **the ~ sporting event** der bedeutendste Wettkampf

premiere, première [prɪ·'mɪr] **I.** *n* Premiere *f* **II.** *vt* uraufführen

premise ['prem·ɪs] *n* Prämisse *f geh;* **to start from the ~ that ...** von der Voraussetzung ausgehen, dass ...

premium ['pri·mi·əm] **I.** *n* **1.** (*insurance payment*) [Versicherungs]prämie *f* **2.** (*extra charge*) Zuschlag *m* **3.** (*gaso-*

P

line) Super[benzin] *nt* II. *adj attr* (*top-quality*) Spitzen-; **the ~ brand** die führende Marke

premonition [ˌpriːməˈnɪʃ·ən] *n* [böse] Vorahnung *f*

prenatal [ˌpriːˈneɪ·təl] *adj attr* vorgeburtlich

preoccupation [ˌpriːakjəˈpeɪ·ʃən] *n* **1.** (*dominant concern*) Sorge *f* **2.** (*state of mind*) [a] **~ with sth** ständige [gedankliche] Beschäftigung mit etw *dat*

preoccupied [priˈak·ju·paɪd] *adj* **1.** (*distracted*) gedankenverloren; (*absorbed*) nachdenklich **2.** (*worried*) besorgt

preordain [ˌpriːɔrˈdeɪn] *vt usu passive form* **to be ~ed** vorherbestimmt sein; (*path*) vorgezeichnet; **sb is ~ed to succeed** der Erfolg ist jdm sicher

prep [prep] *n fam* Vorbereitung *f*

preparation [ˌprep·əˈreɪ·ʃən] *n* **1.** (*getting ready*) Vorbereitung *f;* (*of food*) Zubereitung *f;* **to do a lot of ~ [for sth]** sich sehr gut [auf etw *akk*] vorbereiten **2.** (*measures*) **~s** *pl* Vorbereitungen *pl*

preparatory [prɪˈpær·ə·tɔr·i] *adj* vorbereitend *attr;* Vorbereitungs-

prepare [prɪˈper] I. *vt* **1.** (*get ready*) vorbereiten (**for** +*akk*); **to ~ the way [for sb/sth]** den Weg [für jdn/etw] bereiten **2.** (*make*) zubereiten; (*meal*) machen II. *vi* **to ~ for sth** sich auf etw *akk* vorbereiten

prepared [prɪˈperd] *adj* **1.** *pred* (*ready*) bereit, fertig *fam;* **to be ~ for sth** auf etw vorbereitet sein **2.** *pred* (*willing*) **to be ~ to do sth** bereit sein, etw zu tun

prepay <-paid, -paid> [ˌpriːˈpeɪ] *vt* im Voraus bezahlen

prepayment [ˌpriːˈpeɪ·mənt] *n* Vorauszahlung *f*

preposition [ˌprep·əˈzɪʃ·ən] *n* Verhältniswort *nt,* Präposition *f*

preposterous [prɪˈpas·tər·əs] *adj* absurd, unsinnig

preppy, preppie [ˈprep·i] I. *n Schüler(in) einer privaten „prep school", der/die großen Wert auf gute Kleidung und das äußere Erscheinungsbild legt* II. *adj* (*appearance*) adrett; (*clothes, look*) popperhaft *meist pej fam*

prerogative [prɪˈrag·ə·ṭɪv] *n usu sing*

form (*right*) Recht *nt;* (*privilege*) Vorrecht *nt*

preschool [ˈpriː·skul] *n* Kindergarten *m*

prescribe [prɪˈskraɪb] *vt* (*medical*) **to sth [for sb]** [jdm] etw verschreiben

prescription [prɪˈskrɪp·ʃən] *n* (*medica* Rezept *nt;* **to be available by ~ onl** verschreibungspflichtig sein

presence [ˈprez·əns] *n* **1.** (*attendance* Anwesenheit *f;* **in my ~** in meiner Gegenwart **2.** *approv* (*dignified bearing* Haltung *f*

present¹ [ˈprez·ənt] I. *n* (*now*) **the** die Gegenwart; **at ~** zurzeit, gegenwärtig II. *adj* **1.** *attr* (*current*) derzeitig gegenwärtig; (*month*) laufend; **at the ~ moment** im Moment **2.** *attr* (*case* vorliegend **3.** *usu pred* (*in attendance* anwesend

present² I. *n* [ˈprez·ənt] Geschenk *nt;* **t get sth as a ~** etw geschenkt bekommen II. *vt* [prɪˈzent] **1.** (*give formally* **to ~ sth [to sb/sth]** (*gift*) [jdm] etw schenken; (*award*) [jdm] etw überreichen **2.** (*hand over, show*) **to ~ sth [t sb/sth]** [jdm/etw] etw vorlegen **3.** (*pi forward*) **to ~ sth [to sb/sth]** [jdm/etw] etw präsentieren; (*proposal*) unterbreiten **4.** (*confront*) **to ~ sb with the facts** jdm die Fakten vor Augen führe **5.** (*arise*) **to ~ itself** (*opportunity, solu tion*) sich bieten

presentable [prɪˈzen·tə·bəl] *adj* (*person* vorzeigbar; (*thing*) ansehnlich

presentation [ˌpre·zənˈter·ʃən] *n* **1.** (*giv ing*) Präsentation *f;* (*of a thesis*) Vorlage *f;* (*of awards*) [Preis]verleihung *f* **2.** (*lecture*) Präsentation *f* **3.** (*of photo graphs, works*) Ausstellung *f*

present-day *adj usu attr* heutig *attr*

presenter [prɪˈzen·tər] *n* Moderator(in) *m(f)*

presently [ˈprez·ənt·li] *adv* **1.** (*now*) ge genwärtig **2.** (*soon*) bald, gleich

present tense *n* LING Präsens *nt*

preservation [ˌprez·ərˈveɪ·ʃən] *n* **1.** (*up keep*) Erhaltung *f* **2.** (*conservation* Bewahrung *f;* (*of order*) Aufrechterha tung *f;* (*of food*) Konservierung *f*

preservative [prɪˈzɜr·və·ṭɪv] *n* Konservierungsstoff *m*

reserve [prɪˈzɜrv] I. *vt* 1. (*maintain*) erhalten; (*customs*) bewahren 2. (*conserve*) konservieren; (*wood*) [mit Holzschutzmittel] behandeln; (*fruit*) einmachen II. *n* 1. *usu pl* (*jam or jelly*) Marmelade *f*; (*cooked whole*) Eingemachte(s) *nt kein pl* 2. (*reserve*) **nature ~** Naturschutzgebiet *nt*

reserved [prɪˈzɜrvd] *adj* 1. (*maintained*) konserviert; (*building*) erhalten 2. **~ food** konservierte Lebensmittel

reside [prɪˈzaɪd] *vi* **to ~ over sth** etw leiten

residency [ˈprez·ɪ·dən·si] *n* Präsidentschaft *f*

resident [ˈprez·ɪ·dənt] *n* (*of country*) Präsident(in) *m(f)*; (*of company, corporation*) [Vorstands-]vorsitzende(r)

residential [ˌprez·ɪ·ˈden·tʃəl] *adj usu attr* POL (*of president*) Präsidenten-; (*of office*) Präsidentschafts-

Presidents' Day *n* Präsidententag *m* (*nationaler Feiertag am dritten Montag im Februar*)

press [pres] I. *n* <*pl* -es> 1. (*push*) Druck *m;* **at the ~ of a button** auf Knopfdruck 2. (*news media*) **the ~** die Presse; (*publicity*) **to get good ~** eine gute Presse bekommen II. *vt* 1. (*push*) **to ~ sth** [auf] etw *akk* drücken; **to ~ sth into sth** etw in etw *akk* hineindrücken 2. (*flatten*) zusammendrücken; (*flowers*) pressen 3. (*iron*) bügeln III. *vi* 1. (*push*) drücken 2. (*be urgent*) drängen

press ahead *vi* **to ~ ahead** [**with sth**] etw vorantreiben

press on I. *vi* **to ~ on** [**with sth**] [mit etw *dat*] [zügig] weitermachen II. *vt* **to ~ sth on sb** jdm etw aufdrängen

press agency *n* Nachrichtenagentur *f*

press clipping *n* Zeitungsausschnitt *m*

press conference *n* Pressekonferenz *f*

pressing [ˈpres·ɪŋ] *adj* (*issue*) dringend; (*requests*) nachdrücklich

press office *n* Pressestelle *f*

press release *n* Pressemitteilung *f*

pressure [ˈpreʃ·ər] I. *n* 1. Druck *m;* **to apply ~** Druck ausüben 2. (*stress*) Druck *m;* (*stronger*) Überlastung *f;* **to be under ~ to do sth** unter Druck ste-

hen, etw zu tun 3. (*insistence*) **to put ~ on sb** [**to do sth**] jdn unter Druck setzen[, damit er/sie etw tut] II. *vt* **to ~ sb to do sth** jdn [massiv] dazu drängen, etw zu tun

pressure cooker *n* Schnellkochtopf *m*

pressure gauge *n* Druckmesser *m*

pressurize [ˈpreʃ·ə·raɪz] *vt* druckfest halten

prestige [preˈstiʒ] *n* Prestige *nt,* Ansehen *nt*

presumably [prɪˈzu·mə·bli] *adv* vermutlich

presume [prɪˈzum] *vt* (*suppose, believe*) annehmen; **to be ~d innocent** als unschuldig gelten

presumption [prɪˈzʌmp·ʃən] *n* (*assumption*) Annahme *f*

presumptuous [prɪˈzʌmp·tʃu·əs] *adj* (*attitude*) überheblich; (*forward*) unverschämt

pretax [ˌpriˈtæks] *adj* vor Abzug der Steuern *nach n,* Brutto-

pretend [prɪˈtend] I. *vt* 1. (*behave falsely*) vorgeben, vortäuschen; **to ~ that one is asleep** sich schlafend stellen 2. (*imagine*) **to ~ to be sth** so tun, als sei man etw; **I'll just ~ that I didn't hear that** ich tue einfach so, als hätte ich das nicht gehört II. *vi* (*feign*) **to ~ to sb that ...** jdm vormachen, dass ...

pretender [prɪˈten·dər] *n* (*title*) Anwärter, Anwärterin *m, f*

pretense [ˈpri·tens] *n* (*false behavior*) Vortäuschung *f;* **under false ~s** unter Vorspiegelung falscher Tatsachen

pretension [prɪˈten·ʃən] *n* 1. *usu pl* (*claim*) Anspruch *m* 2. *pej see* **pretentiousness**

pretentious [prɪˈten·ʃəs] *adj pej* (*person*) großspurig; (*manner, speech, style*) hochgestochen

pretentiousness [prɪˈten·ʃəs·nɪs] *n* (*arrogance*) Überheblichkeit *f,* Anmaßung *f*

pretext [ˈpri·tekst] *n* Vorwand *m*

pretty [ˈprɪt·i] I. *adj* (*person*) hübsch; (*thing*) hübsch II. *adv fam* 1. (*fairly*) ~ **good** *fam* ganz gut; ~ **damn quick** *fam* verdammt schnell 2. (*almost*) ~ **much everything** beinah alles

P

pretzel ['pret·səl] n Brezel f

prevail [prɪ·'veɪl] vi 1. (triumph) siegen; (person) sich durchsetzen 2. (induce) **to ~ [up]on sb to do sth** jdn dazu bewegen, etw zu tun

prevailing [prɪ·'ver·lɪŋ] adj attr (wind) vorherrschend; (law) geltend

prevalent ['prev·ə·lənt] adj (common) vorherrschend attr; (disease) weit verbreitet

prevent [prɪ·'vent] vt verhindern; (crime) verhüten; **to ~ sb from doing sth** jdn daran hindern, etw zu tun

preventative [prɪ·'ven·tə·t̮ɪv] adj see **preventive**

prevention [prɪ·'ven·ʃən] n (of disaster) Verhinderung f; (of accident) Vermeidung f

preventive [prɪ·'ven·t̮ɪv] adj vorbeugend

preview ['pri·vju] n (of a film) sneak ~ Vorpremiere f; (trailer) Vorschau f

previous ['pri·vi·əs] adj attr 1. (former) vorig; (prior) vorherig; ~ **conviction** Vorstrafe f 2. (preceding) vorig, vorhergehend; **on the ~ day** am Tag davor

previously ['pri·vi·əs·li] adv (beforehand) zuvor; (formerly) früher; ~ **unreleased** bisher unveröffentlicht

prey [preɪ] I. n (victim) Beute f II. vi (exploit) **to ~ on sb** jdn ausnutzen; (abuse) jdn ausnehmen

price [praɪs] I. n Preis m; **to pay full ~ for sth** den vollen Preis bezahlen; **not at any ~** um keinen Preis II. vt **to be reasonably ~d** einen angemessenen Preis haben

'**price cut** n Preissenkung f

'**price fixing** n Preisabsprache f

priceless ['praɪs·lɪs] adj unbezahlbar

'**price range** n Preislage f

'**price tag**, '**price ticket** n Preisschild nt

'**price war** n Preiskrieg m

pricey ['praɪ·si] adj fam teuer

pricing ['praɪ·sɪŋ] n Preisgestaltung f

prick [prɪk] I. n 1. (act of piercing) Stechen nt; fig (sharp pain) Stich m 2. vulg (penis) Schwanz m II. vt stechen; **to ~ one's finger** sich dat o akk in den Finger stechen

◆ **prick up** vt **to ~ up one's ears** die Ohren spitzen

prickle ['prɪk·əl] n 1. (thorn) Dorn m 2. (sensation) Kratzen nt

prickly ['prɪk·li] adj 1. (thorny) stachelig 2. fam (easily offended) [leicht] reizbar

prickly 'pear n Kaktusfeige f

pride [praɪd] I. n 1. (satisfaction) Stolz m; **to take ~ in sth** stolz auf etw sein 2. (arrogance) Hochmut m 3. (animal group) **a ~ of lions** ein Rudel n Löwen II. vt **to ~ oneself on sth** au etw akk [besonders] stolz sein

priest [prist] n Priester m

prim <-mm-> [prɪm] adj pej steif

primarily [praɪ·'mer·ə·li] adv vorwiegend, in erster Linie

primary ['praɪ·mer·i] I. adj (principal) primär geh, Haupt-; ~ **concern** Hauptanliegen nt II. n POL (election) Vorwahl f

primary 'color n Grundfarbe f

'**primary school** n Grundschule f

primate ['praɪ·meɪt] n ZOOL (mammal) Primat m

prime [praɪm] I. adj attr 1. (main) wesentlich, Haupt-; ~ **suspect** Hauptverdächtige(r) f(m) 2. (best) erstklassig II. n Blütezeit f fig; **to be in one's ~** im besten Alter sein III. vt 1. (prepare) vorbereiten 2. (canvas, wood) grundieren

prime 'number n Primzahl f

primer ['praɪ·mər] n Grundierfarbe f

'**prime time** n Hauptsendezeit f

primitive ['prɪm·ɪ·t̮ɪv] adj primitiv

prince [prɪns] n (royal) Prinz m

princess <pl -es> ['prɪn·sɪs] n Prinzessin f

principal ['prɪn·sə·pəl] I. adj attr Haupt-, hauptsächlich II. n 1. (in a school) Direktor(in) m(f), Schulleiter(in) m(f); (in a play) Hauptdarsteller(in) m(f) 2. usu sing (of investment) Kapitalsumme f

principally ['prɪn·səp·li] adv hauptsächlich, in erster Linie

principle ['prɪn·sə·pəl] n 1. Prinzip nt; **basic ~** Grundprinzip nt 2. (basis) Grundlage f ▶ **on** ~ aus Prinzip

print [prɪnt] n 1. (lettering) Gedruckte(s) nt; **to read the fine ~** das Kleingedruckte lesen 2. (printed form) Druck m; **out of ~** vergriffen 3. (photo)

Abzug m; (copy of artwork) Druck m II. vt 1. TYPO drucken 2. PUBL veröffentlichen; (in magazine, newspaper) abdrucken 3. COMPUT ausdrucken III. vi (write in unjoined letters) in Druckschrift schreiben

printable ['prɪn·tə·bəl] adj druckfähig; (manuscript) druckfertig

printed 'circuit board n Leiterplatte f

printer ['prɪn·tər] n 1. (machine) Drucker m 2. (person) Drucker(in) m(f)

printing ['prɪn·tɪŋ] n 1. (act) Drucken nt 2. (handwriting) Druckschrift f

printout n Ausdruck m

print run n Auflage f

print shop n Grafikhandlung f

prior ['praɪ·ər] adj attr (earlier) frühere(r, s)

prioritize [praɪ'ɔr·ɪ·taɪz] vt 1. (order) der Priorität nach ordnen 2. (give preference to) vorrangig behandeln

priority [praɪ'ɔr·ɪ·ti] n 1. (deserving greatest attention) vorrangige Angelegenheit; **top ~** Angelegenheit f von höchster Priorität; **to get one's priorities straight** seine Prioritäten richtig setzen 2. (precedence) Vorrang m 3. (right of way) Vorfahrt f

prior to prep **to ~ sth** vor etw dat

prism ['prɪz·əm] n Prisma nt

prison ['prɪz·ən] n a. fig (jail) Gefängnis nt a. fig; **to be in ~** im Gefängnis sitzen

prison camp n (for POWs) [Kriegs]gefangenenlager nt; (for political prisoners) Straflager nt

prisoner ['prɪz·ə·nər] n a. fig Gefangene(r) f/m a. fig, Häftling m

prisoner of 'war <pl prisoners-> n Kriegsgefangene(r) f/m

prison sentence n Freiheitsstrafe f

privacy ['praɪ·və·si] n 1. (personal realm) Privatsphäre f; **in the ~ of one's [own] home** in den eigenen vier Wänden pl 2. (time alone) Zurückgezogenheit f

private ['praɪ·vət] I. adj 1. (personal, not open to public) privat 2. (confidential) vertraulich; **to keep sth ~** etw für sich akk behalten 3. (secluded) abgelegen II. n 1. (not in public) **to speak to sb in ~** jdn [or mit jdm] unter vier Augen

sprechen 2. (soldier) Gefreiter m

private 'eye n fam Privatdetektiv(in) m(f)

privately ['praɪ·vət·li] adv 1. (not in public) privat 2. (secretly) heimlich

privatization [ˌpraɪ·və·tɪ'zeɪ·ʃən] n Privatisierung f

privatize ['praɪ·və·taɪz] vt privatisieren

privilege ['prɪv·ə·lɪdʒ] I. n 1. (special right) Privileg nt 2. (honor) Ehre f II. vt usu passive (give privileges to) privilegieren

privileged ['prɪv·ə·lɪdʒd] adj 1. (with privileges) privilegiert 2. LAW (information) vertraulich

prize[1] [praɪz] I. n (sth won) Preis m; (in lottery) Gewinn m II. adj attr (prize-winning) preisgekrönt III. vt usu passive **to ~ sth highly** etw hoch schätzen

prize[2] [praɪz] vt **to ~ sth open** etw [mit einem Hebel] aufbrechen

'prize-winning adj attr preisgekrönt

pro[1] [proʊ] I. n Pro nt; **the ~s and cons of sth** das Pro und Kontra einer S. gen II. prep (in favor of) für

pro[2] [proʊ] n fam Profi m

proactive [proʊ'æk·tɪv] adj initiativ geh

probability [ˌprɑb·ə·'bɪl·ɪ·ti] n Wahrscheinlichkeit f

probable ['prɑb·ə·bəl] adj wahrscheinlich

probably ['prɑb·ə·bli] adv wahrscheinlich

probation [proʊ'beɪ·ʃən] n 1. (trial period) Probezeit f; **to be on ~** Probezeit haben; (employee) auf Probe eingestellt sein 2. LAW Bewährung f

pro'bation officer n Bewährungshelfer(in) m(f)

probe [proʊb] I. vi 1. (investigate) forschen (for nach +dat); **to ~ into sb's private life** in jds Privatleben herumschnüffeln pej fam 2. (physically search) Untersuchungen durchführen II. vt untersuchen III. n 1. (investigation) Untersuchung f 2. MED, ELEC, ASTRON Sonde f

problem ['prɑb·ləm] n 1. (difficulty) Schwierigkeit f; **no ~** (sure) kein Problem; (don't mention it) keine Ursache; **what's the ~?** fam was ist denn los? 2. (task) Aufgabe f; **that's her ~!** das ist ihre Sache!

procedure [prə'siːdʒər] n 1. (*particular course of action*) Verfahren *nt*; **standard ~** übliche Vorgehensweise 2. (*operation*) Vorgang *m* 3. LAW **court ~** Gerichtsverfahren *nt*

proceed [prou'siːd] *vi form* 1. (*make progress*) fortschreiten, vorangehen 2. (*continue*) fortfahren 3. (*go on*) **to ~ to do sth** sich anschicken, etw zu tun

proceeding [prou'siːdɪŋ] n 1. (*action*) Vorgehen *nt kein pl* 2. *usu pl* (*legal action*) Verfahren *nt*

proceeds ['prouːsiːdz] *npl* Einnahmen *pl*

process ['prasˑes] I. n <*pl* -es> 1. (*series of actions*) Prozess *m* 2. (*method*) Verfahren *nt* 3. (*passage*) Verlauf *m*; **in the ~** dabei II. *vt* 1. (*deal with*) bearbeiten 2. COMPUT verarbeiten 3. (*treat*) bearbeiten, behandeln

processing ['prasˑesˑɪŋ] n 1. (*of application*) Bearbeitung *f* 2. TECH Weiterverarbeitung *f*; FOOD Konservierung *f* 3. COMPUT Verarbeitung *f*

procession [prə'sefˑən] n Umzug *m*

processor [pra'sesˑər] n 1. **food ~** Küchenmaschine *f* 2. COMPUT Prozessor *m*

pro-'choice *adj* für das Recht auf Abtreibung

procreate ['prouːkriˑeɪt] *vi* sich fortpflanzen

proctor ['praktər] SCH, UNIV I. n (*for exam*) [Prüfungs]aufsicht *f* II. *vi* Aufsicht führen

procure [prou'kjʊr] *vt form* beschaffen

procurement [prou'kjʊrˑmənt] n *form* Beschaffung *f*

prod [prad] I. n 1. (*tool*) Ahle *f* 2. (*poke*) Schubs *m fam*, [leichter] Stoß 3. *fig* (*incitation*) Anstoß *m fig*; (*reminder*) Gedächtnisanstoß *m* II. *vt* <-dd-> stoßen

prodigal ['pradˑɪˑgəl] *adj* verschwenderisch

prodigy ['pradˑəˑdʒi] n **child ~** Wunderkind *nt*

produce I. *vt* [prə'duːs] 1. (*make*) herstellen; (*coal, oil*) fördern; (*electricity*) erzeugen 2. (*bring about*) bewirken; (*effect, profits*) erzielen 3. FILM produzieren; THEAT (*play*) inszenieren II. *vi* [prə'duːs] 1. (*bring results*) Ergebnisse erzielen 2. (*give output*) produzieren; (*mine*) fördern III. n ['praˑduːs] (*fruits and veg-*

etables) Obst *nt* und Gemüse *nt*

producer [prə'duːsər] n 1. (*manufacturer*) Hersteller *m*; AGR Erzeuger *m* 2. FILM, TV Produzent(in) *m(f)*; THEAT Regisseur(in) *m(f)*

product ['pradˑəkt] n 1. (*sth produced*) Erzeugnis *nt*, Produkt *nt* 2. (*result*) Ergebnis *nt*

production [prə'dʌkˑʃən] n 1. Produktion *f*, Herstellung *f*; (*of energy*) Erzeugung *f* 2. FILM, TV, RADIO, MUS Produktion *f*; THEAT Inszenierung *f*

pro'duction line n Fließband *nt*

production 'manager n Produktionsleiter(in) *m(f)*

productive [prə'dʌkˑtɪv] *adj* 1. (*with large output*) produktiv; (*land, soil*) fruchtbar, ertragreich; *fig* (*conversation*) fruchtbar 2. (*profitable*) rentabel

productivity [ˌprouˑdəkˈtɪvˑɪˑti] n Produktivität *f*

prof [praf] n *fam short for* **professor** Prof *m*

profanity [prou'fænˑɪˑti] n 1. (*blasphemy*) Gotteslästerung *f* 2. (*swearing*) Fluchen *nt*

professed [prə'fest] *adj attr* (*openly declared: communist*) erklärt

profession [prə'fefˑən] n 1. (*field of work*) Beruf *m* 2. (*body of workers*) **the legal ~** der Anwaltsberuf

professional [prə'fefˑəˑnəl] I. *adj* 1. (*of a profession*) beruflich, Berufs- 2. (*not tradesman*) freiberuflich, akademisch 3. (*expert*) fachmännisch 4. *approv* (*businesslike*) professionell; **to do a ~ job** etw fachmännisch erledigen 5. (*not amateur*) Berufs-; SPORT Profi- II. n 1. (*not an amateur*) Fachmann, Fachfrau *m, f*; SPORT Profi *m* 2. (*not a tradesman*) Angehörige(r) *f(m)* der freien [*or* akademischen] Berufe

professionalism [prə'fefˑəˑnəˑlɪzˑəm] n (*skill and experience*) Professionalität *f*; (*attitude*) professionelle Einstellung

professionally [prə'fefˑəˑnəˑli] *adv* 1. (*by a professional*) von einem Fachmann/einer Fachfrau 2. (*not as an amateur*) berufsmäßig

professor [prə'fesˑər] n Professor(in) *m(f)*

proficient [prə·ˈfɪʃ·ənt] *adj* to be ~ **in a language** eine Sprache beherrschen

profile [ˈproʊ·faɪl] *n* 1. (*side view*) Profil *nt* 2. (*description*) Porträt *nt fig* 3. (*public image*) ▶ **to raise sb's ~** jdn hervorheben ▶ **to keep a <u>low</u> ~** sich zurückhalten

profit [ˈpraf·ɪt] I. *n* Gewinn *m*; net ~ Reingewinn *m* II. *vi* profitieren

profitability [ˌpraf·ɪ·t̬ə·ˈbɪl·ɪ·t̬i] *n* Rentabilität *f*

profitable [ˈpraf·ɪ·t̬ə·bəl] *adj* 1. (*in earnings*) Gewinn bringend, rentabel 2. (*advantageous*) nützlich

profiteer [ˌpraf·ɪ·ˈtɪr] I. *n pej* Profitjäger(in) *m(f)* II. *vi* (*make excessive profit*) riesige Gewinne erzielen

profiteering [ˌpraf·ɪ·ˈtɪr·ɪŋ] *n* Wucher *m pej*

'profit margin *n* Gewinnspanne *f*

'profit sharing *n* Gewinnbeteiligung *f*

profound [prə·ˈfaʊnd] *adj* 1. (*extreme*) tief gehend; (*change*) tief greifend; (*impression*) tief 2. (*strongly felt*) tief, heftig; (*compassion*) tief empfunden 3. (*intellectual*) tiefsinnig *a. iron,* tiefgründig

profuse [prə·ˈfjus] *adj* überreichlich; (*bleeding*) stark

prognosis <*pl* -ses> [prag·ˈnoʊ·sɪs] *n* Prognose *f*; **to make a ~** eine Prognose stellen

program [ˈproʊ·græm] I. *n* 1. RADIO, TV, COMPUT Programm *nt*; (*single broadcast*) Sendung *f* 2. (*list of events*) Programm *nt*; THEAT Programmheft *nt* II. *vt* <-mm-> TECH, COMPUT (*instruct*) programmieren

programmer [ˈproʊ·græm·ər] *n* COMPUT Programmierer(in) *m(f)*

'programming language *n* COMPUT Programmiersprache *f*

progress I. *n* [ˈprag·res] 1. (*onward movement*) Vorwärtskommen *nt*; **to make good ~** gut vorwärtskommen 2. Fortschritt *m* II. *vi* [prə·ˈgres] (*develop*) Fortschritte machen; **how's the work ~ing?** wie geht's mit der Arbeit voran?

progression [prə·ˈgreʃ·ən] *n* 1. (*development*) Entwicklung *f* 2. MATH (*series*) Reihe *f*

progressive [prə·ˈgres·ɪv] *adj* 1. (*gradual*) fortschreitend; (*gradually increasing*) zunehmend 2. (*forward-looking*) progressiv

prohibit [proʊ·ˈhɪb·ɪt] *vt* verbieten

prohibition [ˌproʊ·ə·ˈbɪʃ·ən] *n* 1. (*ban*) Verbot *nt* 2. *hist* (*US alcohol ban*) **P~** *no art* die Prohibition

prohibitive [proʊ·ˈhɪb·ɪ·t̬ɪv] *adj* 1. (*price*) unerschwinglich 2. (*prohibiting*) ~ **measures** Verbotsmaßnahmen *pl*

project I. *n* [ˈpra·dʒekt] 1. (*undertaking*) Projekt *nt* 2. (*plan*) Plan *m* II. *vt* [prə·ˈdʒekt] 1. (*forecast*) vorhersagen; (*profit, number*) veranschlagen 2. (*film*) projizieren III. *vi* [prə·ˈdʒekt] (*protrude*) hervorragen, [hinaus]ragen (**over** über +*akk*)

projectile [prə·ˈdʒek·t̬əl] *n* (*thrown object*) Wurfgeschoss *nt*

projection [prə·ˈdʒek·ʃən] *n* 1. (*forecast*) Prognose *f*; (*of expenses*) Voranschlag *m* 2. (*protrusion*) Vorsprung *m*

projectionist [prə·ˈdʒek·ʃə·nɪst] *n* Filmvorführer(in) *m(f)*

project 'manager *n* Projektmanager(in) *m(f)*

projector [prə·ˈdʒek·tər] *n* Projektor *m*

proletarian [ˌproʊ·lə·ˈter·i·ən] I. *n* Proletarier(in) *m(f)* II. *adj* proletarisch

pro-'life *adj* gegen das Recht auf Abtreibung

proliferate [proʊ·ˈlɪf·ə·reɪt] *vi* stark zunehmen; (*animals*) sich stark vermehren

prolific [proʊ·ˈlɪf·ɪk] *adj* 1. (*productive*) produktiv 2. *pred* (*abundant*) **to be ~** in großer Zahl vorhanden sein

prologue, prolog [ˈproʊ·lag] *n* Vorwort *nt*

prolong [proʊ·ˈlaŋ] *vt* verlängern

prom *n* Ball am Ende des Schuljahres der High School

promenade [ˌpram·ə·ˈneɪd] *n* (*walkway*) [Strand]promenade *f*

prominence [ˈpram·ə·nəns] *n* 1. (*conspicuousness*) Unübersehbarkeit *f*; **to give sth ~** etw in den Vordergrund stellen 2. (*importance*) Bedeutung *f*

prominent [ˈpram·ə·nənt] *adj* 1. (*pro-*

P

jecting) vorstehend *attr* **2.** (*distinguished*) prominent

promiscuity [ˌprɑm·ɪ·ˈskjuː·ɪ·ti] *n* Promiskuität *f geh*

promiscuous [prə·ˈmɪs·kju·əs] *adj pej* promisk

promise [ˈprɑm·ɪs] **I.** *vt, vi* versprechen; **I ~!** ich verspreche es! **II.** *n* **1.** (*pledge*) Versprechen *nt* **2.** (*potential*) **to show ~** (*person*) viel versprechend sein

promising [ˈprɑm·ɪ·sɪŋ] *adj* viel versprechend

promontory [ˈprɑm·ən·tɔr·i] *n* GEOG Vorgebirge *nt*

promote [prə·ˈmoʊt] *vt* **1.** (*raise in rank*) befördern (**to** zu +*dat*) **2.** (*encourage*) fördern; **to ~ awareness of sth** etw ins Bewusstsein rufen **3.** (*advertise*) für etw *akk* werben

promoter [prə·ˈmoʊ·tər] *n* (*organizer*) Veranstalter(in) *m(f)*

promotion [prə·ˈmoʊ·ʃən] *n* **1.** (*in rank*) Beförderung *f* **2.** (*advertising campaign*) Werbekampagne *f*

prompt [prɑmpt] **I.** *vt* **1.** THEAT (*remind of lines*) soufflieren **2.** COMPUT auffordern **II.** *adj* **1.** (*swift*) prompt; (*action*) sofortig **2.** (*punctual*) pünktlich **III.** *n* **1.** COMPUT Prompt *m fachspr* **2.** THEAT Stichwort *nt*

promptly [ˈprɑmpt·li] *adv* **1.** (*quickly*) prompt *m* **2.** *fam* (*immediately afterward*) gleich danach, unverzüglich

prong [prɑŋ] *n* Zacke *f*

pronoun [ˈproʊ·naʊn] *n* Pronomen *nt*

pronounce [prə·ˈnaʊns] *vt* **1.** (*speak*) aussprechen **2.** (*verdict*) verkünden **3.** (*declare*) **to ~ sb dead** jdn für tot erklären

pronounced [prə·ˈnaʊnst] *adj* deutlich; (*accent*) ausgeprägt

pronouncement [prə·ˈnaʊns·mənt] *n* Erklärung *f*

pronto [ˈprɑn·toʊ] *adv fam* fix

pronunciation [prə·ˌnʌn·sɪ·ˈeɪ·ʃən] *n* Aussprache *f*

proof [pruf] **I.** *n* **1.** (*confirmation*) Beweis *m* **2.** TYPO (*trial impression*) Korrekturfahne *f* **3.** (*of alcohol*) Alkoholgehalt *m* **II.** *vt* (*make waterproof*) wasserdicht machen

proofread <-read, -read> *vt, vi* Korrektur lesen

proofreader *n* Korrektor(in) *m(f)*

prop[1] [prɑp] **I.** *n* Stütze *f* **II.** *vt* stützen

prop[2] [prɑp] *n usu pl* THEAT Requisite *f*

propaganda [ˌprɑp·ə·ˈɡæn·də] *n usu pej* Propaganda *f*

propagate [ˈprɑp·ə·ɡeɪt] **I.** *vt* **1.** (*plants*) vermehren **2.** *form* (*disseminate*) verbreiten **II.** *vi* (*plants*) sich vermehren

propane [ˈproʊ·peɪn] *n* Propan *nt*

propel <-ll-> [prə·ˈpel] *vt* antreiben

propellant [prə·ˈpel·ənt] *n* **1.** (*fuel*) Treibstoff *m* **2.** (*gas*) Treibgas *nt*

propeller [prə·ˈpel·ər] *n* Propeller *m*

proper [ˈprɑp·ər] *adj* **1.** (*real, correct*) echt **2.** (*socially respectable*) anständig

properly [ˈprɑp·ər·li] *adv* **1.** (*correctly*) richtig **2.** (*socially respectably*) anständig

proper ˈnoun, proper ˈname *n* Eigenname *m*

property [ˈprɑp·ər·ti] *n* **1.** (*things owned*) Eigentum *nt*; (*owned buildings*) Immobilienbesitz *m*; **private ~** Privatbesitz *m* **2.** (*attribute*) Eigenschaft *f*

prophecy [ˈprɑf·ə·si] *n* Prophezeiung *f*

prophesy <-ie-> [ˈprɑf·ə·saɪ] *vt* prophezeien

prophet [ˈprɑf·ɪt] *n a. fig* Prophet *m*

prophetic [prə·ˈfet·ɪk] *adj* prophetisch

proponent [prə·ˈpoʊ·nənt] *n* Befürworter(in) *m(f)*

proportion [prə·ˈpɔr·ʃən] *n* **1.** (*part*) Anteil *m* **2.** (*relation*) Verhältnis *nt*; **to be out of ~** [**to sth**] in keinem Verhältnis zu etw *dat* stehen

proportional [prə·ˈpɔr·ʃə·nəl] *adj* proportional (**to** zu +*dat*); **inversely ~** umgekehrt proportional

proportioned [prə·ˈpɔr·ʃənd] *adj* **beautifully ~** ebenmäßig proportioniert

proposal [prə·ˈpoʊ·zəl] *n* **1.** (*suggestion*) Vorschlag *m* **2.** (*offer of marriage*) Antrag *m*

propose [prə·ˈpoʊz] **I.** *vt* **1.** (*suggest*) vorschlagen **2.** (*intend*) **to ~ doing sth** beabsichtigen, etw zu tun **II.** *vi* **to ~** [**to sb**] [jdm] einen [Heirats]antrag machen

proposition [ˌprɑp·ə·ˈzɪʃ·ən] *n* **1.** (*as-*

sertion) Aussage f 2. (proposal) Vorschlag m; business ~ geschäftliches Angebot

proprietary [prə·ˈpraɪ·ə·ter·i] adj ECON, LAW urheberrechtlich geschützt

proprietor [prə·ˈpraɪ·ə·tər] n Inhaber(in) m(f)

propulsion [prə·ˈpʌl·ʃən] n Antrieb m

prorate [ˌproʊ·ˈreɪt] vt anteilmäßig aufteilen

prose [proʊz] n Prosa f

prosecute [ˈpras·ɪ·kjut] I. vt LAW **to ~ sb** [**for sth**] jdn [wegen einer S. gen] strafrechtlich verfolgen II. vi (in court) für die Anklage zuständig sein

prosecuting [ˈpras·ɪ·kju·tɪŋ] adj attr ~ **attorney** Staatsanwalt, Staatsanwältin m, f

prosecution [ˌpras·ɪ·ˈkju·ʃən] n 1. (legal action) strafrechtliche Verfolgung 2. (legal team) **the ~** die Anklagevertretung 3. (case) Anklage[erhebung] f

prosecutor [ˈpras·ɪ·kju·tər] n Ankläger(in) m(f)

prospect [ˈpras·pekt] I. n 1. Aussicht f 2. (opportunities) ~s pl Aussichten pl, Chancen pl II. vi nach Bodenschätzen suchen

prospective [prə·ˈspek·tɪv] adj voraussichtlich; (customer) potenziell

prospector [ˈpras·pek·tər] n MIN Prospektor(in) m(f) fachspr

prospectus [prə·ˈspek·təs] n Prospekt m

prosperity [pra·ˈsper·ɪ·ti] n Wohlstand m

prosperous [ˈpras·pər·əs] adj (well-off) wohlhabend

prostitute [ˈpras·tə·tut] n Prostituierte f; **male ~** Stricher m pej

prostitution [ˌpras·tɪ·ˈtu·ʃən] n Prostitution f

prostrate [ˈpras·treɪt] adj 1. (face downward) ausgestreckt 2. (overcome) überwältigt

protect [prə·ˈtekt] vt schützen (**against** gegen +akk, **from** vor +dat)

protection [prə·ˈtek·ʃən] n 1. (defense) Schutz m; (of interests) Wahrung f 2. (paid to criminals) Schutzgeld nt

protective [prə·ˈtek·tɪv] adj 1. (affording protection) Schutz- 2. (wishing to protect) fürsorglich (**of/toward** gegen-

über +dat)

protector [prə·ˈtek·tər] n Beschützer(in) m(f)

protégé, protégée [ˈproʊ·tə·ʒeɪ] n Protegé m geh

protein [ˈproʊ·tin] n Eiweiß nt

protest I. n [ˈproʊ·test] 1. (strong complaint) Protest m 2. (demonstration) Protestkundgebung f II. vi [proʊ·ˈtest] protestieren

Protestant [ˈpraˌɪ·stənt] n Protestant(in) m(f)

protester [prə·ˈtes·tər] n (objector) Protestierende(r) f(m); (demonstrator) Demonstrant(in) m(f)

'protest march n Protestmarsch m

protocol [ˈproʊ·tə·kɔl] n Protokoll nt

proton [ˈproʊ·tan] n PHYS Proton nt

prototype [ˈproʊ·tə·taɪp] n Prototyp m

protractor [proʊ·ˈtræk·tər] n MATH Winkelmesser m

protrude [proʊ·ˈtrud] vi hervorragen (**from** aus +dat)

protruding [proʊ·ˈtru·dɪŋ] adj attr (ears) abstehend; (eyes) vortretend

protrusion [proʊ·ˈtru·ʒən] n Vorsprung m

proud [praʊd] adj 1. stolz (**of** auf +akk) 2. pej (arrogant) eingebildet

proudly [ˈpraʊd·li] adv 1. (with pride) stolz 2. pej (haughtily) hochnäsig fam

prove <-d, -d or proven> [pruv] I. vt (establish) beweisen II. vi + n/adj sich erweisen; **to ~ successful** sich als erfolgreich erweisen

proven [ˈpru·vən] I. vt, vi pp of **prove** II. adj nachgewiesen; (remedy) erprobt

proverb [ˈprav·ɜrb] n Sprichwort nt

proverbial [prə·ˈvɜr·bi·əl] adj fig (well-known) sprichwörtlich

provide [prə·ˈvaɪd] I. vt zur Verfügung stellen; (explanation) liefern; **to ~ sb with sth** jdn mit etw dat versorgen II. vi **to ~ for oneself** für sich selbst sorgen

provided [prə·ˈvaɪ·dɪd] I. adj beigefügt II. conj see **providing [that]**

provider [prə·ˈvaɪ·dər] n 1. (supplier) Lieferant(in) m(f) 2. (breadwinner) Ernährer(in) m(f)

providing (that) [prə·ˈvaɪ·dɪŋ-] conj (as long as) sofern

province ['prɑv·ɪns] n 1. (*territory*) Provinz f 2. (*area of knowledge*) [Fach]gebiet nt

provincial [prə·'vɪn·ʃəl] adj 1. (*of a province*) Provinz- 2. pej (*unsophisticated*) provinziell

provision [prə·'vɪʒ·ən] n 1. (*providing*) Versorgung f; (*financial precaution*) Vorkehrung f 2. (*something supplied*) Vorrat m 3. (*stipulation*) **with the ~ that ...** unter der Bedingung, dass ...

provisional [prə·'vɪʒ·ə·nəl] adj vorläufig

proviso [prə·'vaɪ·zoʊ] n Vorbehalt m

provocation [ˌprɑv·ə·'keɪ·ʃən] n Provokation f

provoke [prə·'voʊk] vt 1. (*vex*) **to ~ sb [into doing sth]** jdn [zu etw dat] provozieren 2. (*outrage*) hervorrufen

prow [praʊ] n Bug m

prowl [praʊl] I. n (*search*) Streifzug m, Suche f II. vt durchstreifen III. vi **to ~ [around]** umherstreifen

prowler ['praʊ·lər] n Herumtreiber(in) m(f) fam

proximity [prɑk·'sɪm·ɪ·ti] n Nähe f

proxy ['prɑk·si] n Bevollmächtigte(r) f(m)

prudent ['pru·dənt] adj vorsichtig; (*action*) klug

prudish ['pru·dɪʃ] adj prüde

prune[1] [prun] n (*plum*) Dörrpflaume f

prune[2] [prun] vt HORT [be]schneiden; fig reduzieren; (*costs*) kürzen

pry[1] <-ie-> [praɪ] vi **to ~ into sth** seine Nase in etw akk stecken fam

pry[2] <-ie-> [praɪ] vt **to ~ sth open** etw [mit einem Hebel] aufbrechen

prying ['praɪ·ɪŋ] adj pej neugierig

PS [ˌpi·'es] n abbr of **postscript** PS nt

psalm [sɑm] n REL Psalm m

pseudo ['su·doʊ] adj Pseudo-

pseudonym ['su·də·nɪm] n Pseudonym nt

PST [ˌpi·es·'ti] n abbr of **Pacific Standard Time** pazifische Zeit

psych [saɪk] vt fam (*prepare*) **to ~ oneself up** sich akk [psychisch] aufbauen

psyched [saɪkt] adj pred sl (*excited*) aufgedreht fam, aufgeputscht

psychedelic [ˌsaɪ·kə·'del·ɪk] adj psychedelisch

psychiatric [ˌsaɪ·ki·'æt·rɪk] adj psychiatrisch

psychiatrist [saɪ·'kaɪ·ə·trɪst] n Psychiater(in) m(f)

psychiatry [saɪ·'kaɪ·ə·tri] n Psychiatrie f

psychic ['saɪ·kɪk] I. n Medium nt II. adj übernatürlich

psychoanalysis [ˌsaɪ·koʊ·ə·'næl·ə·sɪs] n Psychoanalyse f

psychological [ˌsaɪ·kə·'lɑdʒ·ɪ·kəl] adj (*of the mind, not physical*) psychisch

psychologist [saɪ·'kɑl·ə·dʒɪst] n Psychologe, -in m, f

psychology [saɪ·'kɑl·ə·dʒi] n Psychologie f

psychopath ['saɪ·kə·pæθ] n Psychopath(in) m(f)

psychotherapist [ˌsaɪ·koʊ·'θer·ə·pɪst] n Psychotherapeut(in) m(f)

psychotic [saɪ·'kɑt̬·ɪk] adj psychotisch

pt.[1] abbr of **part** I 2, 3

pt.[2] abbr of **point** I

pt.[3] abbr of **pint** Pint nt (0,568 l)

PTA [ˌpi·ti·'eɪ] abbr of **Parent-Teacher Association** Eltern-Lehrer-Organisation f

PTO [ˌpi·ti·'oʊ] abbr of **Parent-Teacher Organization** ≈ Elternbeirat m

pub [pʌb] n Kneipe f

puberty ['pju·bər·ti] n Pubertät f

public ['pʌb·lɪk] I. adj öffentlich II. n + sing/pl vb 1. (*the people*) **the ~** die Öffentlichkeit 2. (*patrons*) Anhängerschaft f; **the viewing ~** Zuschauer pl

public-ad'dress system n Lautsprecheranlage f

publication [ˌpʌb·lɪ·'keɪ·ʃən] n 1. (*publishing*) Veröffentlichung f 2. (*published work*) Publikation f

public 'holiday n gesetzlicher Feiertag

public 'interest n öffentliches Interesse

publicist ['pʌb·lɪ·sɪst] n Publizist(in) m(f)

publicity [pʌb·'lɪs·ɪ·ti] n 1. (*promotion*) Publicity f 2. (*attention*) Aufsehen nt

publicize ['pʌb·lɪ·saɪz] vt bekannt machen

public 'library n öffentliche Bibliothek

publicly ['pʌb·lɪk·li] adv öffentlich

public o'pinion n öffentliche Meinung

public re'lations npl MEDIA, POL Public Relations pl

public 'school n öffentliche [or staatliche] Schule

public 'sector *n* öffentlicher Sektor

public 'television *n* öffentlich-rechtliches Fernsehen

public transpor'tation *n* öffentliche Verkehrsmittel

public u'tility *n* (*company*) öffentlicher Versorgungsbetrieb

publish ['pʌb·lɪʃ] *vt* (*article, result*) veröffentlichen; (*book, newspaper*) herausgeben

publisher ['pʌb·lɪ·ʃər] *n* MEDIA 1. (*company*) Verlag *m* 2. (*newspaper owner*) Herausgeber(in) *m(f)*

publishing ['pʌb·lɪ·ʃɪŋ] *n* Verlagswesen *nt*

'publishing house *n* Verlag *m*

puck [pʌk] *n* SPORT Puck *m*

pucker ['pʌk·ər] I. *vt* in Falten legen; (*lips*) spitzen II. *vi* to ~ [up] (*cloth*) sich kräuseln; (*lips*) sich spitzen

pudding ['pʊd·ɪŋ] *n* Pudding *m*

puddle ['pʌd·əl] *n* Pfütze *f*

pudgy ['pʌdʒ·i] *adj* rundlich; (*face*) schwammig; (*person*) pummelig

Puerto Rican [ˌpwer·tə·'ri·kən] I. *n* Puerto-Ricaner(in) *m(f)* II. *adj* puertoricanisch

Puerto Rico [ˌpwer·tə·'ri·koʊ] *n* Puerto Rico *nt*

puff [pʌf] I. *n* 1. *fam* (*short blast: of breath*) Atemstoß *m;* (*of wind*) Windstoß *m* 2. (*pastry*) Blätterteig *m* II. *vi* 1. (*breathe heavily*) schnaufen 2. (*smoke*) to ~ on a cigar eine Zigarre qualmen III. *vt fam* (*praise*) aufbauschen

pull apart *vt* auseinanderziehen

puff out *vt* aufblähen; (*feathers*) aufplustern

puff up I. *vt fig* to ~ oneself up (*person*) sich aufblasen II. *vi* [an]schwellen

puffy ['pʌf·i] *adj* geschwollen, verquollen

'pug nose *n* Stupsnase *f*

puke [pjuk] I. *vt vulg* to ~ sth ⇆ [up] etw [aus]kotzen *sl* II. *vi sl* kotzen *sl*

pull [pʊl] I. *n* 1. (*tug*) Zug *m* 2. (*force*) Zugkraft *f;* (*of the earth*) Anziehungskraft *f* 3. (*on a cigarette*) Zug *m;* (*on a bottle*) Schluck *m* 4. (*attraction*) Anziehung *f* II. *vt* 1. (*draw*) ziehen; (*trigger*) abdrücken 2. MED (*muscle*) zerren 3. *fam* (*gun*) ziehen ▶ to ~

sb's **leg** *fam* jdn auf den Arm nehmen; to ~ **strings** Beziehungen spielen lassen III. *vi* (*draw*) to ~ [at sth] [an etw *dat*] ziehen

pull ahead *vi* 1. (*overtake*) to ~ ahead of sb jdn überholen 2. SPORT in Führung gehen

pull apart *vt* auseinanderziehen

pull aside *vt* to ~ sb aside jdn zur Seite nehmen

pull away I. *vi* to ~ away from sb/ sth 1. (*leave*) sich von jdm/etw wegbewegen 2. SPORT (*runner*) sich vom Feld absetzen 3. (*recoil*) vor jdm zurückweichen II. *vt* wegreißen

pull back *vi* 1. (*recoil*) zurückschrecken 2. MIL (*withdraw*) sich zurückziehen

pull down *vt* 1. (*move down*) herunterziehen 2. (*building*) abreißen 3. *sl* (*earn*) kassieren

pull in I. *vi* TRANSP (*train*) einfahren; (*bus*) anhalten II. *vt* 1. (*attract*) anziehen 2. *fam* (*earn*) [ab]kassieren

pull off *vt* 1. (*take off*) [schnell] ausziehen 2. *fam* (*succeed*) durchziehen; (*deal*) zustande bringen

pull on *vt* [schnell] überziehen

pull out I. *vi* 1. (*move out: vehicle*) ausscheren 2. (*depart: train*) ausfahren; (*car*) herausfahren 3. (*withdraw*) aussteigen *fam* II. *vt* 1. MIL to ~ out troops Truppen abziehen 2. (*take out*) herausziehen

pull over I. *vt* (*vehicle*) anhalten II. *vi* (*vehicle*) zur Seite fahren

pull through *vi* (*survive*) durchkommen

pull together *vt* (*regain composure*) to ~ oneself together sich zusammennehmen

pull up I. *vt* 1. (*pull toward one*) heranziehen 2. (*raise*) hochziehen 3. (*floorboards*) herausreißen II. *vi* [heranfahren und] anhalten

pull-down 'menu *n* Pulldown-Menü *nt*

pulley ['pʊl·i] *n* Flaschenzug *m*

'pullout *n* 1. MIL Rückzug *m* 2. PUBL [Sonder]beilage *f*

pulp [pʌlp] I. *n* 1. (*mush*) Brei *m* 2. FOOD Fruchtfleisch *nt kein pl* II. *vt* zu Brei verarbeiten

pulpit ['pʊl·pɪt] n Kanzel f

pulsate ['pʌl·seɪt] vi pulsieren; (with noise) vibrieren

pulse [pʌls] n 1. (heartbeat) Puls m; **to take sb's ~** jds Puls fühlen 2. fig (mood) **to have one's finger on the ~** am Ball sein

pulverize ['pʌl·və·raɪz] vt pulverisieren

puma ['pu·mə] n Puma m

pumice ['pʌm·ɪs], **pumice stone** ['pʌm·ɪs-] n Bimsstein m

pump¹ [pʌmp] I. n (device) Pumpe f II. vt pumpen

pump² [pʌmp] n (shoe) Pumps m

pumpernickel ['pʌm·pər·nɪk·əl] n Pumpernickel nt

pumpkin ['pʌmp·kɪn] n [Garten]kürbis m

pumpkin pie n eine Art Kürbiskuchen, der vor allem an Thanksgiving und Weihnachten serviert wird

pun [pʌn] n Wortspiel nt

punch¹ [pʌntʃ] I. n (piercing tool) Stanzwerkzeug nt; [hole] ~ (for paper) Locher m II. vt (metal) [aus]stanzen; (paper) lochen

punch² [pʌntʃ] I. n <pl -es> 1. (hit) [Faust]schlag m; (in boxing) Punch m kein pl fachspr 2. (strong effect) Durchschlagskraft f kein pl; (of arguments) Überzeugungskraft f kein pl II. vt (hit) **to ~ sb** jdn [mit der Faust] schlagen

punch³ [pʌntʃ] n (hot or cold) Punsch m; (cold) Bowle f

'**punch bowl** n Punschschüssel f, Bowlengefäß nt

'**punch line** n Pointe f

punctual ['pʌŋk·tʃu·əl] adj pünktlich

punctuation [ˌpʌŋk·tʃu·'eɪ·ʃən] n Zeichensetzung f

punctu'ation mark n Satzzeichen nt

puncture ['pʌŋk·tʃər] I. vt 1. (pierce) durchstechen 2. fig (hope) zerstören; (mood) verderben II. vi (burst: tire) ein Loch bekommen

pungent ['pʌn·dʒənt] adj 1. a. pej (strong: taste, smell) scharf 2. fig (wit, words) scharf a. pej; (comment) bissig pej

punish ['pʌn·ɪʃ] vt 1. (penalize) bestrafen 2. (treat roughly) strapazieren; (treat badly) malträtieren

punishable ['pʌn·ɪʃ·ə·bəl] adj LAW (offense) strafbar; **a ~ infraction of the rules** ein Regelverstoß, der zu ahnden ist

punishing ['pʌn·ɪ·ʃɪŋ] I. adj attr fig 1. (heavy) mörderisch fig fam 2. (tough) hart, schwer, anstrengend II. n (severe handling) Strapazierung f; (rough treatment) Malträtierung f; **to take a ~** (equipment) stark beansprucht werden; (boxer) Prügel beziehen

punishment ['pʌn·ɪʃ·mənt] n 1. (penalty) Bestrafung f, Strafe f; **capital ~** Todesstrafe f 2. (severe handling) Strapazierung f; (rough handling) grobe Behandlung; (strain) Strapaze f

punk [pʌŋk] n 1. pej fam (worthless person) Dreckskerl m 2. (music) Punk[rock] m; (fan) Punker(in) m(f)

punt [pʌnt] SPORT I. vt, vi punten II. n Punt m

puny ['pju·ni] adj pej 1. (person) schwächlich 2. fig (lacking in power) schwach; (attempt) schüchtern

pupil¹ ['pju·pəl] n Schüler(in) m(f)

pupil² ['pju·pəl] n ANAT Pupille f

puppet ['pʌp·ɪt] n (theater doll) [Hand]puppe f; (on strings) Marionette f a. pej, fig

'**puppet show** n Puppenspiel nt, Marionettentheater nt

puppy ['pʌp·i] n (baby dog) junger Hund, Welpe m

purchase ['pɜr·tʃəs] I. vt form (buy) kaufen II. n (something bought, act of buying) Kauf m

purchaser ['pɜr·tʃə·sər] n Käufer(in) m(f)

'**purchasing power** n Kaufkraft f kein pl

pure [pjʊr] adj 1. (unmixed) rein, pur 2. (air, water) sauber 3. fig (utter) rein, pur

'**purebred** adj reinrassig

purée [pju·'reɪ] I. vt <puréed, puréeing> pürieren II. n Püree nt

purely ['pjʊr·li] adv 1. (completely) rein, ausschließlich 2. (merely) bloß

purge [pɜrdʒ] I. vt a. fig (cleanse) reinigen (of von +dat); **to ~ oneself of sth** (guilt) sich von etw dat reinwaschen II. n POL Säuberung[saktion] f

purification [ˌpjʊr·ə·fɪˈkeɪ·ʃən] n Reinigung f

purify [ˈpjʊr·ə·faɪ] vt reinigen (**of/from** von +dat)

purist [ˈpjʊr·ɪst] n Purist(in) m(f)

puritanical [ˌpjʊr·ɪ·ˈtæn·ɪ·kəl] adj usu pej puritanisch

purity [ˈpjʊr·ɪ·t̬i] n 1. (cleanness) Sauberkeit f 2. (freedom from admixture) Reinheit f

purl [pɜrl] n linke Masche

purple [ˈpɜr·pəl] adj (red/blue mix) violett; (more red) lila[farben]; (crimson) purpurrot

Purple 'Heart n Verwundetenabzeichen nt

purpose [ˈpɜr·pəs] n 1. (reason) Grund m 2. (goal) Absicht f, Ziel nt 3. (resoluteness) **lack of ~** Unentschlossenheit f

purposeful [ˈpɜr·pəs·fəl] adj 1. (singleminded) zielstrebig 2. (resolute) entschlossen

purposely [ˈpɜr·pəs·li] adv absichtlich, bewusst

purr [pɜr] vi (cat) schnurren

purse [pɜrs] n 1. (handbag) Handtasche f 2. SPORT (prize money) Preisgeld nt

purser [ˈpɜr·sər] n AVIAT Purser m; NAUT Zahlmeister(in) m(f) fachspr

pursue [pər·ˈsu] vt 1. a. fig verfolgen 2. (investigate) weiterverfolgen 3. (engage in) betreiben; (studies) nachgehen

pursuer [pər·ˈsu·ər] n Verfolger(in) m(f)

pursuit [pər·ˈsut] n 1. (chase) Verfolgung[sjagd] f; (of knowledge, fulfillment) Streben nt 2. (activity) Beschäftigung f

pus [pʌs] n Eiter m

push [pʊʃ] I. n <pl -es> 1. (shove) Stoß m; (slight push) Schubs m fam; to **give sb/sth a ~** jdm/etw einen Stoß versetzen 2. (press) Druck m; **at the ~ of a button** auf Knopfdruck a. fig 3. (concerted effort) Anstrengung[en] f[pl], Kampagne f II. vt 1. (shove) schieben; (in a crowd) drängeln; (violently) stoßen, schubsen; **to ~ sth to the back of one's mind** fig etw verdrängen 2. (move forcefully) schieben; (give a push) stoßen 3. (pressure) **to ~ sb into doing sth** jdn [dazu] drängen, etw zu tun; (force) jdn

zwingen, etw zu tun 4. (press) **to ~ sth** auf etw akk drücken 5. (demand a lot) **to ~ oneself** sich dat alles abverlangen 6. sl (promote) propagieren; (sell illegal drugs) pushen sl III. vi 1. (exert force) dräng[el]n; (move) schieben; **to ~ and pull** hin- und herschieben 2. **to ~ past sb** sich an jdm vorbeidrängen

♦**push around** vt 1. (violently) herumstoßen 2. fig, pej (bully) herumkommandieren

♦**push back** vt 1. (move backwards) zurückschieben, zurückdrängen 2. fig (delay: date) verschieben

♦**push down** vt 1. (lever) hinunterdrücken 2. (prices) [nach unten] drücken

♦**push forward** I. vt 1. approv, a. fig (development) [ein großes Stück] voranbringen 2. (present forcefully) in den Vordergrund stellen II. vi (continue) weitermachen

♦**push in** vt (press against) eindrücken

♦**push off** I. vi fig, a. pej fam (leave) sich verziehen II. vt NAUT abstoßen

♦**push out** vt 1. (force out) hinausjagen 2. (dismiss) hinauswerfen

♦**push over** vt umwerfen, umstoßen

♦**push through** I. vi (maneuver through) **to ~ through sth** sich durch etw akk drängen II. vt POL (motion) durchdrücken fam

♦**push up** vt 1. (move higher) **to ~ sb ⇆ up** jdn hochheben 2. ECON (demands) steigern; (prices) hochtreiben

'**pushbutton** I. adj (automated) Druckknopf-, [voll]automatisch II. n Druckknopf m

pusher [ˈpʊʃ·ər] n pej Dealer(in) m(f)

'**pushover** n 1. fig, pej fam (easily defeated opponent) leichter Gegner/leichte Gegnerin 2. approv, fig fam (easy success) Kinderspiel nt kein pl

'**pushpin** n Reißzwecke f

'**pushup** n Liegestütz m

pushy [ˈpʊʃ·i] adj fig fam 1. pej aufdringlich 2. (ambitious) tatkräftig

pussy [ˈpʊs·i] n 1. (cat) Mieze[katze] f fam 2. fig, pej vulg (woman's genitals) Muschi f

'**pussyfoot** vi pej fam (move cautiously) **to ~ around** herumreden fam

'**pussy willow** *n* Salweide *f*

put <-tt-, put, put> [pʊt] *vt* **1.** (*place*) to ~ **sth somewhere** etw irgendwohin stellen; (*lay down*) etw irgendwohin legen; **she ~ some milk in her coffee** sie gab etwas Milch in ihren Kaffee; **to ~ oneself in sb's place** sich in jds Situation versetzen; **I ~ clean sheets on the bed** ich habe das Bett frisch bezogen; **she ~ her arm round him** sie legte ihren Arm um ihn; **to ~ sb to bed** jdn ins Bett bringen **2.** (*invest*) **to ~ effort into sth** Mühe in etw *akk* stecken **3.** (*impose*) **to ~ the blame on sb** jdm die Schuld geben; **to ~ pressure on sb** jdn unter Druck setzen; **to ~ sb to the test** jdn auf die Probe stellen **4.** (*include*) **to ~ sth on the agenda** etw auf die Tagesordnung setzen **5.** (*indicating change of condition*) **to ~ sb at risk** jdn in Gefahr bringen; **to ~ one's affairs in order** seine Angelegenheiten in Ordnung bringen; **to ~ a stop to sth** etw beenden **6.** (*express*) **how should I ~ it?** wie soll ich mich ausdrücken?

◆**put across** *vt* (*make understood*) **to ~ one's point across** etw verständlich machen

◆**put aside** *vt* **1.** (*save*) zurücklegen; (*money a.*) sparen; **to ~ sth aside for sb** etw *akk* für jdn auf die Seite legen **2.** (*postpone*) **to ~ aside ⇆ sth** (*book etc.*) etw beiseitelegen

◆**put away** *vt* **1.** (*tidy up*) wegräumen; (*in storage place*) einräumen **2.** (*save*) auf die hohe Kante legen **3.** *fam* (*eat a lot*) **to ~ away ⇆ sth** etw in sich *akk* hineinstopfen

◆**put back** *vt* **1.** (*replace*) zurückstellen **2.** (*reassemble*) **to ~ sth back together** etw wieder zusammensetzen

◆**put down** *vt* **1.** (*set down*) ablegen **2.** (*lower: arm, feet*) herunternehmen; **to ~ sb ⇆ down** jdn runterlassen **3.** (*spread*) **to ~ down roots** *a. fig* Wurzeln schlagen **4.** (*write*) aufschreiben; **to ~ sth down** jdn für etw *akk* eintragen **5.** ECON (*leave as deposit*) anzahlen **6.** (*deride*) **to ~ down ⇆ sb/oneself** jdn/sich schlechtmachen

◆**put forward** *vt* (*idea*) vorbringen; (*can-*

didate) vorschlagen

◆**put in** **I.** *vt* **1.** (*place in*) hineinsetzen/-legen/-stellen **2.** (*food, ingredients*) hinzufügen **3.** (*install*) installieren **4.** (*enter, submit*) **to ~ in an order for sth** etw bestellen **II.** *vi* **to ~ in for sth** (*job*) sich um etw *akk* bewerben; (*pay raise, transfer*) etw beantragen

◆**put off** *vt* **1.** (*delay*) verschieben **2.** (*persuade to not act*) vertrösten **3.** (*discourage*) **to ~ sb off from doing sth** jdm etw *akk* verleiden [*or* madigmachen]

◆**put on** *vt* **1.** (*clothes, shoes*) anziehen; (*makeup*) auflegen; *fig* (*smile*) aufsetzen **2.** (*turn on*) einschalten **3.** (*provide*) bereitstellen; (*exhibition*) veranstalten **4.** (*increase*) **to ~ on weight** zunehmen

◆**put out** *vt* **1.** (*place outside*) **to ~ the laundry out** [**to dry**] die Wäsche draußen aufhängen **2.** (*hand, foot*) ausstrecken **3.** MEDIA (*publish*) veröffentlichen **4.** (*place ready*) **to ~ sth out** [**for sb**] (*chairs, clothes*) [jdm] etw hinstellen **5.** (*fire*) löschen; (*cigarette*) ausmachen; (*lights*) ausschalten

◆**put over** *vt fam* (*fool*) **to ~ one over on sb** sich mit jdm einen Scherz erlauben

◆**put through** *vt* **1.** (*insert through*) **to ~ sth through sth** etw durch etw *akk* schieben; (*pierce*) etw durch etw *akk* stechen **2.** TELEC (*connect*) **to ~ sb through to sb** jdn mit jdm verbinden **3.** (*carry through: plan, proposal*) durchbringen

◆**put together** *vt* **1.** (*assemble*) zusammensetzen; (*machine, model, radio*) zusammenbauen **2.** (*make*) zusammenstellen; (*list*) aufstellen **3.** MATH (*add*) **to ~ 10 and 15 together** 10 und 15 zusammenzählen; **she earns more than all the rest of us ~ together** *fig* sie verdient mehr als wir alle zusammengenommen

◆**put up** *vt* **1.** (*hang up*) aufhängen; (*flag, sail*) hissen **2.** (*raise*) hochheben; (*feet*) hochlegen; (*hair*) aufstecken **3.** (*build*) bauen **4.** (*offer*) **to ~ sth up for sale** etw zum Verkauf anbieten **5.** (*give shel-*

ter) unterbringen

 ▸ **put up with** *vi* **I'm not ~ing up with this any longer** ich werde das nicht länger dulden

'putdown *n* verächtliche Bemerkung

putrid ['pju·trɪd] *adj form* 1. (*smell*) faulig 2. BIOL (*organic matter*) verfault

putt [pʌt] SPORT I. *vt, vi* putten II. *n* Putt *m*

putter¹ ['pʌt·ər] *n* SPORT (*golf club*) Putter *m*

putter² ['pʌt·ər] *vi* (*do nothing in particular*) vor sich akk hin werkeln *fam*

putty ['pʌt·i] I. *n* (*Dichtungs*)kitt *m* II. *vt* <-ie-> [ver]kitten, [ver]spachteln

puzzle ['pʌz·əl] *n* 1. (*question, test of ingenuity*) Rätsel *nt*; **jigsaw ~** Puzzle *nt* 2. (*test of patience*) Geduldsspiel *nt*

puzzled ['pʌz·əld] *adj* ratlos

puzzling ['pʌz·əl·ɪŋ] *adj* rätselhaft

PVC [ˌpi·vi·'si] *n abbr of* **polyvinyl chloride** PVC *nt*

Pygmy ['pig·mi] *n pej, a. fig* Zwerg(in) *m(f)*

pylon ['paɪ·lɑn] *n* AUTO (*traffic cone*) Pylon *m*

pyramid ['pɪr·ə·mɪd] *n* Pyramide *f*

Pyrex® ['paɪ·reks] *n* Pyrex-Glas®

python <*pl* -s> ['paɪ·θən] *n* Python *m*

Q

Q <*pl* -'s>, **q** <*pl* -'s> [kju] *n* Q *nt*, q *nt*; **~ as in Quebec** Q wie Quelle

Q. [kju] *n* ECON *abbr of* **quarter** Quartal *nt*

q. [kju] *n* 1. FOOD *abbr of* **quart** Quart *nt (0,95 l)* 2. *abbr of* **question** Frage *f*

qt., **qt** *n* FOOD *abbr of* **quart** Quart *nt (0,95 l)*

Q-tip® ['kju·tɪp] *n* Wattestäbchen *nt*

quack¹ [kwæk] I. *n* Quaken *nt* II. *vi* quaken

quack² [kwæk] *n pej* (*fake doctor*) Quacksalber(in) *m(f) pej*

quad¹ [kwad] *n short for* **quadrangle** Geviert *nt*; (*on campus*) Hof

quad² [kwad] *n fam short for* **quadruplet** Vierling *m*

quadrangle ['kwad·ræŋ·gəl] *n* (*square*)

Geviert *nt*

quadrant ['kwad·rənt] *n* MATH Viertelkreis *m*

quadraphonic [ˌkwad·rə·'fan·ɪk] *adj* quadrophon[isch]

quadrilateral [ˌkwad·rɪ·'læt̬·ər·əl] *n* Viereck *nt*

quadruped ['kwad·rə·ped] *n* Vierfüßer *m*

quadruple [kwa·'dru·pəl] I. *vt* vervierfachen II. *adj* vierfach *attr*

quadruplet [kwa·'dru·plɪt] *n* Vierling *m*

quagmire ['kwæg·maɪr] *n* Morast[boden] *m*

quail <*pl* -s> [kweɪl] *n* ZOOL Wachtel *f*

quaint [kweɪnt] *adj* 1. (*charming*) reizend; (*village*) malerisch; (*cottage*) urig 2. (*old-fashioned*) altertümlich

quake [kweɪk] I. *n fam* [Erd]beben *nt* II. *vi* (*earth*) beben

Quaker ['kweɪ·kər] *n* Quäker(in) *m(f)*

qualification [ˌkwal·ə·fɪ·'keɪ·ʃən] *n* 1. (*skill*) Qualifikation *f* 2. (*condition*) [notwendige] Voraussetzung *f* 3. (*restriction*) Einschränkung *f*

qualified ['kwal·ɪ·faɪd] *adj* 1. (*competent*) qualifiziert 2. (*restricted*) bedingt; **to make a ~ statement** eine Erklärung unter Einschränkungen abgeben

qualifier ['kwal·ɪ·faɪ·ər] *n* Qualifikant(in) *m(f)*

qualify <-ie-> ['kwal·ɪ·faɪ] I. *vt* 1. (*make competent*) qualifizieren 2. (*make eligible*) **to ~ sb to do sth** jdn berechtigen, etw zu tun 3. (*restrict*) einschränken; **to ~ a remark** eine Bemerkung unter Vorbehalt äußern II. *vi* 1. (*prove competence*) sich qualifizieren (**for** für +akk) 2. (*meet requirements*) die [nötigen] Voraussetzungen erfüllen

qualifying ['kwal·ɪ·faɪ·ɪŋ] *adj attr* 1. (*restrictive*) einschränkend 2. SPORT (*round*) Qualifikations-

qualitative ['kwal·ɪ·ter·tɪv] *adj* qualitativ

quality ['kwal·ɪ·ti] I. *n* 1. (*standard*) Qualität *f*; **~ of life** Lebensqualität *f* 2. (*feature*) Merkmal *nt*; **managerial qualities** Führungsqualitäten *pl* II. *adj* [qualitativ] hochwertig

'quality control *n usu sing* Qualitätskontrolle *f*

Q

quality time *n* die Zeit, die man dafür aufbringt, familiäre Beziehungen zu entwickeln und zu pflegen

qualm [kwam] *n* **1.** (*doubt*) ~s *pl* Bedenken *pl* **2.** (*uneasiness*) ungutes Gefühl

quandary ['kwan·də·ri] *n usu sing* Unentschiedenheit *f;* **to be in a ~** sich nicht entscheiden können

quantify <-ie-> ['kwan·tə·faɪ] *vt* mengenmäßig messen

quantitative ['kwan·tə·teɪ·ţɪv] *adj* quantitativ *geh*

quantity ['kwan·tɪ·ţi] *n* **1.** (*amount*) Menge *f;* (*of individual items*) Stückzahl *f* **2.** (*large amount*) große Menge *f*

quarantine ['kwɔr·ən·ˌtin] *n* Quarantäne *f*

quarrel ['kwɔr·əl] **I.** *n* (*argument*) Streit *m;* **to have a ~** sich streiten **II.** *vi* <-l-> **1.** (*argue*) sich streiten (**about** über +*akk*) **2.** (*disagree with*) **to ~ with sth** etwas an etw *dat* aussetzen

quarrelsome ['kwɔr·əl·səm] *adj* streitsüchtig

quarry[1] ['kwɔr·i] **I.** *n* Steinbruch *m* **II.** *vt* <-ie-> brechen

quarry[2] ['kwɔr·i] *n* (*animal*) Jagdbeute *f*

quart [kwɔrt] *n* Quart *nt (0,95 l);* **a ~ of milk** ein Quart *nt* Milch

quarter ['kwɔr·ţər] **I.** *n* **1.** (*fourth*) Viertel *m;* **the bottle was a ~ full** es war noch ein Viertel in der Flasche; **to divide sth into ~s** etw in vier Teile teilen **2.** (*coin*) Vierteldollar *m* **3.** (*time*) Viertel *nt;* (*of year*) Quartal *nt;* **a ~ to/after three** Viertel vor/nach drei **4.** SPORT (*period*) Viertel *nt* **5.** (*area*) Gegend *f;* **the French Q~** das französische Viertel **6.** (*lodgings*) ~s *pl* Wohnung *f;* MIL Quartier *nt* ▶ **at close ~s with sb** in jds Nähe **II.** *vt* vierteln

quarterback *n* **1.** SPORT Quarterback *m fachspr* **2.** (*leader*) Gruppenleiter(in) *m(f)*

quarterfinal *n* Viertelfinale *nt*

quarterly ['kwɔr·ţər·li] *adv, adj* vierteljährlich

quartermaster ['kwɔr·ţər·ˌmæs·tər] *n* MIL Quartiermeister *m*

quarter note *n* MUS Viertelnote *f*

quartet, quartette [kwɔr·'tet] *n* Quartett *nt*

quartz [kwɔrts] *n* Quarz *m;* **rose ~** Rosenquarz *m*

quash [kwɑʃ] *vt* **1.** (*destroy*) zermalmen; *fig* (*hopes*) zunichtemachen **2.** (*suppress: rebellion*) niederschlagen; (*rumors*) zum Verstummen bringen

quasi- ['kwɑ·zi] *comp* (*resembling*) Quasi-, quasi-

quaver ['kweɪ·vər] *vi* **1.** (*tremble: person*) zittern; (*voice a.*) beben **2.** (*speak*) mit zitternder Stimme sprechen

quay [ki] *n* Kai *m*

queasy ['kwi·zi] *adj* **1.** (*stomach*) [über]empfindlich **2.** (*upset*) übel *nach n*

queen [kwin] *n* **1.** (*chess*) Dame *f* **3.** *fam* (*gay*) Tunte *f pej fam;* **drag ~** Transvestit *m*

queer [kwɪr] **I.** *adj* **1.** (*strange*) seltsam; **to have ~ ideas** schräge Ideen haben **2.** *offensive fam* (*homosexual*) schwul *fam* **II.** *n offensive fam* Schwule(r) *m fam;* (*female*) Lesbe *f fam*

quell [kwel] *vt* **1.** (*suppress: revolt*) niederschlagen **2.** *fig* (*doubts, fears*) zerstreuen

quench [kwentʃ] *vt* löschen; *fig* dämpfen

query ['kwɪr·i] **I.** *n* Rückfrage *f* **II.** *vt* <-ie-> *form* **1.** (*doubt*) in Frage stellen **2.** (*ask*) befragen

quest [kwest] *n* Suche *f*

question ['kwes·tʃən] **I.** *n* **1.** (*query*) Frage *f;* **to pop the ~** jdm einen [Heirats]antrag machen **2.** (*doubt*) Zweifel *m;* **there's no ~ about it** keine Frage; **without ~** zweifellos **3.** (*matter*) Frage *f;* **to be out of the ~** nicht in Frage kommen **II.** *vt* **1.** (*ask*) befragen (**about** über +*akk*) **2.** (*interrogate*) verhören (**about** zu +*dat*)

questionable ['kwes·tʃə·nə·bəl] *adj* **1.** (*uncertain*) zweifelhaft; (*future*) ungewiss **2.** (*shady*) fragwürdig

questioning ['kwes·tʃə·nɪŋ] **I.** *n* (*by police*) Verhör *nt* **II.** *adj* (*look*) fragend

question mark *n* Fragezeichen *nt a. fig*

questionnaire [ˌkwes·tʃə·'ner] *n* Fragebogen *m*

queue [kju] COMPUT **I.** *n* Schlange *f* **II.** *vi* anstehen, Schlange stehen

quibble ['kwɪb·əl] I. n (*criticism*) Krittelei f II. vi sich streiten (**about** über +akk); **no one would ~ with that** das würde niemand bestreiten

quiche <pl -> [kiʃ] n Quiche f

quick [kwɪk] I. adj 1. (*fast*) schnell; **in ~ succession** in schneller [Ab]folge; **to have a ~ temper** ein rasch aufbrausendes Temperament haben 2. (*short*) kurz; **to have a ~ look at sth** sich dat etw kurz ansehen 3. (*alert*) [geistig] gewandt; **~ wit** Aufgewecktheit f; (*in replying*) Schlagfertigkeit f II. adv schnell, rasch III. interj schnell

'quick-acting adj schnell wirksam

quickie ['kwɪk·i] I. n 1. (*fast thing*) kurze Sache f 2. (*sex*) Quickie m II. adj **~ divorce** schnelle und unkomplizierte Scheidung

quickly ['kwɪk·li] adv schnell, rasch

quickness ['kwɪk·nɪs] n 1. (*speed*) Schnelligkeit f 2. (*alertness*) **~ of mind** scharfer Verstand

'quicksand n Treibsand m

'quickstep n the **~** der Quickstepp

quick-'tempered adj hitzköpfig

quick-'witted adj (*alert*) aufgeweckt; (*reply*) schlagfertig

quid pro quo ['kwɪd·proʊ·'kwoʊ] n Gegenleistung f

quiet ['kwaɪ·ət] I. adj <-er, -est or more ~, most ~> 1. (*not loud*) leise 2. (*silent*) ruhig; **please be ~** Ruhe bitte! 3. (*not talking*) still; (*child*) ruhig; (*taciturn*) schweigsam 4. (*secret*) heimlich; **to keep sth ~** etw für sich akk behalten 5. (*street*) ruhig ▶ **as ~ as a mouse** mucksmäuschenstill fam II. n 1. (*silence*) Stille f 2. (*lack of excitement*) Ruhe f; **peace and ~** Ruhe und Frieden

◆quiet down I. vi 1. (*become quiet*) leiser werden 2. (*become calm*) sich beruhigen II. vt 1. (*make less noisy*) zur Ruhe bringen 2. (*calm*) beruhigen

quietly ['kwaɪət·li] adv 1. (*not loudly*) leise 2. (*silently*) still; **to wait ~** ruhig warten 3. (*unobtrusively*) unauffällig; **to be ~ confident** insgeheim überzeugt sein

quietness ['kwaɪ·ət·nɪs] n Ruhe f; (*silence*) Stille f

quill [kwɪl] n 1. (*feather*) Feder f 2. (*of porcupine*) Stachel m

quilt [kwɪlt] I. n Steppdecke f; **patchwork ~** Flickendecke f II. vt [ab]steppen

quinine ['kwaɪ·naɪn] n Chinin nt

quintessential [ˌkwɪn·tə·'sen·ʃəl] adj essentiell

quintet, quintette [kwɪn·'tet] n Quintett nt

quintuplet [kwɪn·'tʌp·lɪt] n Fünfling m

quip [kwɪp] n witzige Bemerkung

quirk [kwɜrk] n 1. (*habit*) Marotte f 2. (*oddity*) Merkwürdigkeit f kein pl

quirky ['kwɜr·ki] adj schrullig fam

quit <quit or quitted, quit or quitted> [kwɪt] I. vi 1. (*worker*) kündigen; (*official*) zurücktreten 2. COMPUT aussteigen 3. (*give up*) aufgeben II. vt 1. (*stop*) **~ wasting my time** hör auf, meine Zeit zu verschwenden; **to ~ smoking** das Rauchen aufgeben 2. (*give up*) aufgeben; (*job*) kündigen 3. COMPUT (*end*) aussteigen aus +dat

quite [kwaɪt] adv 1. (*fairly*) ziemlich; **I had to wait ~ a long time** ich musste ganz schön lange warten fam 2. (*completely*) ganz, völlig; **~ honestly, ...** ehrlich gesagt ...

quits [kwɪts] adj pred quitt (**with** mit +dat); **to call it ~** fam es gut sein lassen

quiver ['kwɪv·ər] vi zittern

quixotic [kwɪk·'sat·ɪk] adj (*idea, vision*) unrealistisch; (*attempt*) naiv

Q

quiz [kwɪz] I. n <pl -zes> SCH, UNIV (*kurze*) Prüfung f. vt (*question*) abfragen (**about** zu +dat)

'quiz show n Quizsendung f

quorum ['kwɔr·əm] n Quorum nt geh

quota ['kwoʊ·tə] n Quote f

quotation [kwoʊ·'teɪ·ʃən] n 1. (*citation*) Zitat nt 2. STOCKEX [Kurs]notierung f

quo'tation marks npl Anführungszeichen pl

quote [kwoʊt] I. n 1. (*citation*) Zitat nt 2. (*quotation mark*) **~s** pl Gänsefüßchen pl fam 3. (*estimate*) Kostenvoranschlag m II. vt 1. (*cite*) zitieren; **to ~ sb on sth** jdn zu etw dat zitieren 2. (*give: price*) nennen 3. STOCKEX notieren III. vi zitieren; **to ~ from sb**

jdn zitieren

quotient ['kwoʊ·ʃənt] n Quotient m

QWERTY keyboard [ˌkwɜr·ti·'ki·bɔrd] n englische Standardtastatur

R

R <pl -'s>, **r** <pl -'s> [ar] n R nt, r nt; ~ **as in Romeo** R wie Richard

r adv abbr of **right** r.

R[1] [ar] adj abbr of **right** r.

R[2] [ar] adv FILM abbr of **Restricted; rated** ~ nicht für Jugendliche unter 17 Jahren

rabbi ['ræb·aɪ] n Rabbiner m

rabbit ['ræb·ɪt] n Kaninchen nt

'**rabble-rousing** adj [auf]hetzerisch

rabid ['ræb·ɪd] adj (dog) tollwütig; fig fanatisch

rabies ['reɪ·biz] n + sing vb Tollwut f

raccoon [ræ·'kun] n Waschbär(in) m(f)

race[1] [reɪs] n Rasse f; (species) Spezies f

race[2] [reɪs] I. n (run) Rennen nt; (competition) Wettkampf m II. vi Rennen laufen; (vehicles) Rennen fahren; (rush) rennen; **to** ~ **by** (time) schnell vergehen III. vt **to** ~ **sb** gegen jdn antreten

'**racecar** n Rennwagen m

'**racecourse** n Rennbahn f

'**racehorse** n Rennpferd nt

racer ['reɪ·sər] n [Renn]läufer(in) m(f); (horse) Rennpferd nt; (bicycle) Rennrad nt; (car) Rennwagen m

'**racetrack** n Rennbahn f

racial ['reɪ·ʃəl] adj Rassen-; (racist) rassistisch

racism ['reɪ·sɪz·əm] n Rassismus m

racist ['reɪ·sɪst] I. n Rassist(in) m(f) II. adj rassistisch

rack [ræk] I. n Regal nt; **clothes** ~ Kleiderständer m; **magazine** ~ Zeitschriftenständer m II. vt **to** ~ **one's brains** sich dat den Kopf zerbrechen

racket[1] ['ræk·ɪt] n SPORT Schläger m

racket[2] ['ræk·ɪt] n fam 1. Krach m 2. **extortion** ~ Schutzgelderpressung f

racketeering [ˌræk·ə·'tɪr] n dunkle Machenschaften pl

racoon [ræ·'kun] n see **raccoon**

racy ['reɪ·si] adj 1. anzüglich; (clothing)

gewagt 2. (person) draufgängerisch

radar ['reɪ·dar] n Radar m o nt

radiant ['reɪ·di·ənt] adj (smile) strahlend

radiate ['reɪ·di·eɪt] I. vi ausstrahlen II. vt ausstrahlen; (heat) abgeben

radiation [ˌreɪ·di·'eɪ·ʃən] n Strahlung f; (process) Abstrahlen nt

radiator ['reɪ·di·eɪ·tər] n Heizkörper m; (on car) Kühler m

radio ['reɪ·di·oʊ] I. n 1. Radio nt südd, österr, schweiz a. m; (communicator) Funkgerät nt; **on/over the** ~ über Funk 2. (broadcasting) Radio nt; **to listen to the** ~ Radio hören II. vi **to** ~ **for help** über Funk Hilfe anfordern

radioactive [ˌreɪ·di·oʊ·'æk·tɪv] adj radioaktiv

radioactivity [ˌreɪ·di·oʊ·æk·'tɪv·ɪ·ti] n Radioaktivität f

radiologist [ˌreɪ·di·'al·ə·dʒɪst] n Radiologe(in) m(f)

radiology [ˌreɪ·di·'al·ə·dʒi] n Radiologie f

'**radio station** n Radiosender m

radish <pl -es> ['ræd·ɪʃ] n Rettich m

radium ['reɪ·di·əm] n Radium nt

radius <pl -dii> ['reɪ·di·əs] n Radius m

raffle ['ræf·əl] I. n Tombola f II. vt verlosen

raft [ræft] n Floß nt

rafting ['ræf·tɪŋ] n Rafting nt

rag [ræg] n Lumpen m; (for cleaning) Lappen m; (for dust) Staubtuch nt

♦ **rag on** <-gg-> fam **to** ~ **on sb** jdn nerven sl; (scold) auf jdm herumhacken fam

rage [reɪdʒ] I. n 1. Wut f; **to get in a** ~ sich aufregen 2. **to be** [all] **the** ~ der letzte Schrei sein fam II. vi toben; (at sb) anschreien; (fire) wüten

ragged ['ræg·ɪd] adj zerlumpt; (group) unorganisiert

raging ['reɪ·dʒɪŋ] adj (river) reißend; (fire) lodernd; (inferno) flammend; (thirst) schrecklich

'**ragtime** n Ragtime m

raid [reɪd] I. n Angriff m; (by police) Razzia f; (by bandits) Überfall m II. vt 1. überfallen; (bomb) bombardieren;

(*town*) plündern **2.** (*rob*) ausplündern; (*bank*) überfallen

rail [reɪl] *n* **1.** Bahn *f;* **by ~** mit der Bahn **2.** (*track*) Schiene *f* **3.** (*on stairs*) Geländer *nt;* (*pole*) Stange *f*

railing ['reɪ·lɪŋ] *n* Geländer *nt*

'railroad *n* **1.** [Eisen]bahn *f* kein pl **2.** (*track*) Schienen *pl;* (*stretch*) Strecke *f*

'railroad crossing *n* Bahnübergang *m*

'railroad station *n* Bahnhof *m*

rain [reɪn] **I.** *n* Regen *m;* **in the ~** im Regen **II.** *vi impers* **it's ~ing** es regnet

rainbow ['reɪn·boʊ] *n* Regenbogen *m*

'rain cloud *n* Regenwolke *f*

'raincoat *n* Regenmantel *m*

'raindrop *n* Regentropfen *m*

'rainfall *n* Niederschlag *m;* (*quantity*) Niederschlagsmenge *f*

'rain forest *n* Regenwald *m*

'rainproof *adj* wasserdicht

'rainstorm *n* starke Regenfälle *pl*

rainy ['reɪ·ni] *adj* regnerisch

raise [reɪz] **I.** *n* Gehaltserhöhung *f* **II.** *vt* **1.** heben; (*anchor*) lichten; (*eyebrow, blinds*) hochziehen; (*flag, sail*) hissen **2.** (*increase*) erhöhen; (*quality*) verbessern **3.** (*mention*) vorbringen; (*issue*) aufwerfen **4.** (*capital*) aufbringen **5.** (*children*) aufziehen **6.** (*breed*) züchten

raisin ['reɪ·zən] *n* Rosine *f*

rake [reɪk] **I.** *n* Harke *f* **II.** *vt* [zusammen]rechen; (*soil*) harken **III.** *vi* **to ~ through sth** etw durchsuchen
  ♦ rake in *vt* rechen, *fam* (*money*) kassieren

rally ['ræl·i] **I.** *n* **1.** [Massen]versammlung *f;* (*of troops*) Versammlung *f* **2.** sport Ballwechsel *m* **3.** (*race*) Rallye *f* **II.** *vt* <-ie-> (*troops*) sammeln; (*support*) gewinnen; (*supporters*) mobilisieren **III.** *vi* <-ie-> (*prices*) sich erholen
  ♦ rally 'around *vi* unterstützen

ram [ræm] **I.** *n* **1.** Widder *m* **2.** (*weapon*) Rammbock *m* **II.** *vt* <-mm-> rammen

Ramadan [ˌræm·ə·'dan] *n* Ramadan *m*

ramble ['ræm·bəl] **I.** *n* Wanderung *f* **II.** *vi* **1.** wandern **2.** *pej fam* faseln *fam*

rambling ['ræm·blɪŋ] **I.** *n* **~s** *pl* Gefasel *nt* kein pl *pej* **II.** *adj* **1.** (*incoherent*) unzusammenhängend **2.** **~ rose** Kletterrose *f*

ramification [ˌræm·ɪ·fɪ·'keɪ·ʃən] *n usu pl* Auswirkung *f*

ramp [ræmp] *n* Rampe *f*

rampage ['ræm·peɪdʒ] **I.** *n* Randale *f;* **on the ~** angriffslustig **II.** *vi* randalieren

rampant ['ræm·pənt] *adj* ungezügelt, wuchernd; (*inflation*) galoppierend

ramshackle ['ræm·ʃæk·əl] *adj* klapp[e]rig; (*building*) baufällig

ran [ræn] *pt of* **run**

ranch [ræntʃ] *n <pl -es>* Ranch *f*

rancher ['ræn·tʃər] *n* Viehzüchter(in) *m(f);* (*worker*) Farmarbeiter(in) *m(f)*

rancid ['ræn·sɪd] *adj* ranzig

rancor ['ræŋ·kər] *n* Verbitterung *f,* Groll *m*

R & B [ˌar·ənd·'bi] *n abbr of* **rhythm and blues** R & B *m*

random ['ræn·dəm] **I.** *n* **at ~** willkürlich; (*by chance*) zufällig **II.** *adj* zufällig; **~ sample** Stichprobe *f*

rang [ræŋ] *pt of* **ring**

range [reɪndʒ] **I.** *n* **1.** Auswahl *f;* (*selection*) Angebot *nt* **2.** (*limits*) Bereich *m* **3.** (*distance*) Entfernung *f;* **in/out of ~** in/außer Reichweite **4.** (*mountains*) Bergkette *f* **5.** (*stove*) [Koch]herd *m* **II.** *vi* schwanken; **to ~ from sth to sth** von etw *dat* bis [zu etw *dat*] reichen

ranger ['reɪn·dʒər] *n* Aufseher(in) *m(f);* (*soldier*) Ranger(in) *m(f);* **park ~** Parkranger *m*

rank¹ [ræŋk] **I.** *n* **1.** Position *f;* MIL Dienstgrad *m* **2.** (*row*) Reihe *f;* **to close ~s** die Reihen schließen; *fig* sich zusammenschließen **II.** *vi* **to ~ second in the world** auf Platz zwei der Weltrangliste stehen; **to ~ above sb** einen höheren Rang als jd einnehmen **III.** *vt* einstufen

rank² [ræŋk] *adj* **1.** (*smelly*) stinkend **2.** *attr* absolut; (*outsider*) total

ransack ['ræn·sæk] *vt* durchwühlen; *hum* plündern; (*rob*) ausrauben

ransom ['ræn·səm] **I.** *n* Lösegeld *nt* **II.** *vt* auslösen

rant [rænt] **I.** *n* Geschimpfe *nt* **II.** *vi* [vor sich *akk* hin] schimpfen

rap¹ [ræp] **I.** *n* **1.** Klopfen *nt* kein pl; *fam* (*rebuke*) Anpfiff *m fam* **2.** *sl* **to take**

the ~ **[for sth]** die Schuld [für etw *akk*] zugeschoben kriegen **II.** *vt* <-pp-> klopfen; *fig* (*criticize*) scharf kritisieren

rap² [ræp] **I.** *n* MUS Rap *m* **II.** *vi* MUS rappen

rape [reɪp] **I.** *n* Vergewaltigung *f*; *fig* Zerstörung *f* **II.** *vt* vergewaltigen

rapid ['ræp·ɪd] *adj* schnell; (*change, growth*) rasch; (*rise*) steil; (*sudden*) plötzlich

rapids ['ræp·ɪdz] *npl* Stromschnellen *pl*

rapist ['reɪ·pɪst] *n* Vergewaltiger(in) *m(f)*

rapport [ræ·'pɔːr] *n* Harmonie *f*

rapture ['ræp·tʃər] *n* Verzückung *f*

rare [rer] *adj* **1.** selten **2.** (*meat*) blutig

rarely ['rer·li] *adv* selten

rarity ['rer·ɪ·t̬i] *n* Seltenheit *f*

rascal ['ræs·kəl] *n* Schlingel *m*; (*child*) Frechdachs *m*

rash [ræʃ] **I.** *n* <*pl* -es> Ausschlag *m* **II.** *adj* übereilt

raspberry ['ræz·ˌber·i] *n* Himbeere *f*

Rastafarian [ˌræs·tə·'far·i·ən] *n* Rastafari *m*

rat [ræt] *n* Ratte *f*

rate [reɪt] **I.** *n* **1.** Geschwindigkeit *f*; (*measure*) Maß *nt*; (*payment, tax*) Satz *m*; **unemployment ~** Arbeitslosenrate *f* **2. at any ~** (*whatever happens*) auf jeden Fall; (*at least*) zumindest **II.** *vt* [ein]schätzen, halten (**as für** +*akk*)

rather ['ræð·ər] *adv* **1.** lieber, vielmehr; **I'd ~ rather stay** ich würde lieber bleiben **2.** (*very*) ziemlich **3. or ~ ...** oder besser gesagt ... **4.** (*on the contrary*) eher

ratification [ˌræt̬·ə·fɪ·'keɪ·ʃən] *n* Ratifizierung *f*

ratify <-ie-> ['ræt̬·ə·faɪ] *vt* ratifizieren

rating ['reɪ·t̬ɪŋ] *n* Einschätzung *f*, Einstufung *f*; TV **~s** *pl* [Einschalt]quoten *pl*

ratio ['reɪ·ʃi·oʊ] *n* Verhältnis *nt*

ration ['ræʃ·ən] **I.** *n* Ration *f* **II.** *vt* rationieren

rational ['ræʃ·ə·nəl] *adj* rational

rationalize ['ræʃ·ə·nə·laɪz] *vt, vi* rationalisieren

rationing ['ræʃ·ə·nɪŋ] *n* Rationierung *f*

rat race *n* ewiger Konkurrenzkampf

rattle ['ræt̬·əl] **I.** *n* **1.** Klappern *nt*; (*of chains*) Rasseln *nt* **2.** (*toy*) Rassel *f* **II.** *vi* **1.** klappern; (*keys*) rasseln **2.** (*move*) rattern **3. to ~ on** [drauflos]quasseln *fam*

III. *vt* (*keys*) rasseln; (*person*) durcheinanderbringen

rattlesnake *n* Klapperschlange *f*

raucous ['rɔ·kəs] *adj* rau, heiser

raunchy ['rɔn·tʃi] *adj* schlüpfrig *fam*; (*video, film*) heiß *fam*

ravage ['ræv·ɪdʒ] *vt* verwüsten

rave [reɪv] **I.** *n* Rave *m o nt* **II.** *adj attr* (*reviews*) glänzend **III.** *vi* **1. to [rant and] ~** toben **2.** *fam* (*praise*) schwärmen

raven ['reɪ·vən] *n* Rabe *m*

ravenous ['ræv·ə·nəs] *adj* ausgehungert; (*appetite*) unbändig

ravine [rə·'vin] *n* Schlucht *f*

raving ['reɪ·vɪŋ] **I.** *n* **~s** *pl* Hirngespinste *pl* **II.** *adj attr* total **III.** *adv* **to be [stark] ~ mad** *fam* völlig verrückt sein

ravioli [ræv·i·'oʊ·li] *n* Ravioli *pl*

ravishing ['ræv·ɪ·ʃɪŋ] *adj* hinreißend

raw [rɔ] *adj* **1.** roh **2.** (*inexperienced*) unerfahren **3.** (*sore*) wund; *fig* (*nerves*) empfindlich

raw ma'terial *n* Rohstoff *m*

ray¹ [reɪ] *n* Strahl *m*

ray² [reɪ] *n* (*fish*) Rochen *m*

rayon ['reɪ·ɑn] *n* Viskose *f*

razor ['reɪ·zər] **I.** *n* Rasierapparat *m* **II.** *vt* [ab]rasieren

'razor blade *n* Rasierklinge *f*

'razor-sharp *adj pred*, **razor-sharp** *adj attr* **to be ~** scharf wie ein Rasiermesser sein; *fig* [äußerst] scharfsinnig

Rd. *n abbr of* **road** Str.

reach [ritʃ] **I.** *n* <*pl* -es> **1.** (*arm length, power*) Reichweite *f*; TV, RADIO [Sende]bereich *m* **2.** (*distance to travel*) **to be within [easy] ~** [ganz] in der Nähe sein **II.** *vi* **1.** (*stretch*) greifen **2.** (*touch*) herankommen **3.** (*extend*) reichen **III.** *vt* **1.** (*arrive at*) erreichen; (*destination*) ankommen **2.** (*audience*) erreichen; (*agreement*) erzielen **3.** (*road*) **to ~ sth** bis zu etw *dat* führen; (*hair, clothing*) bis zu etw *dat* reichen **4.** (*touch*) **to be able to ~ sth** an etw *akk* herankommen **5.** (*contact*) erreichen; (*on the phone*) [telefonisch] erreichen **6.** *fam* (*give*) hinüberreichen

♦**reach down** *vi* hinabreichen, herunterreichen

◆**reach out I.** *vt* to ~ out ⇆ one's hand die Hand ausstrecken **II.** *vi* greifen nach +*dat*

◆**reach out to** *vi* to ~ out to sb (*stretch*) die Hand nach jdm ausstrecken; (*help*) für jdn da sein

◆**reach over** *vi* hinübergreifen

◆**reach up** *vi* nach oben greifen

react [rɪˈækt] *vi* reagieren

reaction [rɪˈækʃən] *n* Reaktion *f*

reactionary [rɪˈækʃəˌnɛri] **I.** *adj pej* reaktionär **II.** *n pej* Reaktionär(in) *m(f)*

reactor [rɪˈæktər] *n* Reaktor *m;* **nuclear** ~ Kernreaktor *m*

read¹ [rid] **I.** *n usu sing* **1.** *fam* **to be a good** ~ sich gut lesen [lassen] **2.** (*act*) Lesen *nt* **II.** *vt* <read, read> lesen; (*aloud*) vorlesen; (*emotion*) erraten; **to ~ sb** jdn verstehen; **to ~ sth in sb's face** jdm etw vom Gesicht ablesen **III.** *vi* <read, read> lesen; **to ~ aloud** laut vorlesen; **to ~ well** (*book*) sich gut lesen

◆**read off** *vt* herunterlesen; (*dial*) ablesen

◆**read out** *vt* laut vorlesen; COMPUT auslesen

◆**read over, read through** *vt* [schnell] durchlesen

◆**read up** *vi* nachlesen; **to ~ up on sth** sich *akk* über etw *akk* informieren

read² [red] **I.** *vt, vi pt, pp of* **read II.** *adj* **well** ~ belesen

reader [ˈriːdər] *n* Leser(in) *m(f)*; (*aloud*) Vorleser(in) *m(f)*; (*proofreader*) Lektor(in) *m(f)*

readily [ˈrɛdˌə·li] *adv* bereitwillig; (*easily*) ohne weiteres

readiness [ˈrɛdˌɪnɪs] *n* **1.** Bereitwilligkeit *f;* (*preparedness a.*) Bereitschaft *f* **2.** (*quickness*) Schnelligkeit *f*

reading [ˈriːdɪŋ] *n* **1.** Lesen *nt* **2.** (*material*) Lesestoff *m* **3.** (*recital*) Lesung *f*

reading glasses *npl* Lesebrille *f*

readjust [ˌriːəˈdʒʌst] **I.** *vt* [wieder] neu anpassen; (*tie*) zurechtrücken; (*machine*) neu einstellen **II.** *vi* **1.** (*machine*) sich neu einstellen; (*clock*) sich neu stellen **2.** (*readapt*) sich wieder gewöhnen

ready [ˈrɛdi] *adj* **1.** *pred* fertig; **to get ~**

sich *akk* fertig machen; **to be ~ to go** bereit zum Gehen sein **2.** (*available*) verfügbar **3.** *attr esp approv* (*quick*) prompt ▶ **~, set, go!** auf die Plätze, fertig, los!

ready-'made *adj* **1.** (*ready for use*) gebrauchsfertig; FOOD fertig **2.** FASHION Konfektions- **3.** (*available*) vorgefertigt

'ready-to-wear *adj* Konfektions-

reaffirm [ˌri·əˈfɜrm] *vt* bestätigen

real [riːl] **I.** *adj* **1.** wirklich; (*genuine*) echt; (*beauty*) wahr; **a ~ bargain** ein echt günstiges Angebot **2.** *fam* (*disaster*) echt ▶ **the ~ thing** (*not fake*) das Wahre; (*true love*) die wahre Liebe; **get ~!** *fam* mach dir doch nichts vor! **II.** *adv fam* wirklich *fam*

'real estate *n* Immobilien *pl*

'real estate agent *n* Immobilienmakler(in) *m(f)*

realism [ˈriː·lɪz·əm] *n* Realismus *m*

realist [ˈriː·lɪst] *n* Realist(in) *m(f)*

realistic [ˌriː·əˈlɪs·tɪk] *adj* realistisch

reality [riːˈæl·ɪ·ti] *n* **1.** Realität *f;* **in ~** in Wirklichkeit **2.** (*fact*) Tatsache *f;* **to become a ~** wahr werden

realization [ˌriː·ə·lɪˈzeɪ·ʃən] *n* **1.** (*awareness*) Erkenntnis *f* **2.** (*fulfillment*) Realisierung *f*

realize [ˈriː·əˌlaɪz] *vt* **1.** **to ~ sth** sich *dat* einer S. *gen* bewusst sein; (*become aware of*) etw erkennen **2.** (*dream*) verwirklichen

really [ˈriː·ə·li] **I.** *adv* wirklich; (*seriously*) ernsthaft **II.** *interj* (*in surprise*) wirklich; (*in annoyance*) also wirklich

realm [rɛlm] *n* **1.** Reich *nt* **2. within the ~s of possibility** im Bereich des Möglichen

reap [rip] *vt* ernten *a. fig;* (*field*) abernten; (*profits*) realisieren

reappear [ˌri·əˈpɪr] *vi* wieder auftauchen [*or* erscheinen]

reapply <-ie-> [ˌri·əˈplaɪ] *vi* **to ~ for sth** sich nochmals um etw *akk* bewerben

reappraisal [ˌri·əˈpreɪ·zəl] *n* Neubewertung *f*

rear¹ [rɪr] **I.** *n* **1.** (*back*) **the ~** der hintere Teil **2.** *fam* (*buttocks*) Hintern *m* **II.** *adj attr* Hinter-; AUTO Heck-; **~ wheel** Hinterrad *nt*

rear² [rɪr] I. *vt usu passive* großziehen; (*animal*) aufziehen; (*breed*) züchten II. *vi* 1. (*horse*) sich aufbäumen 2. to ~ **above sth** etw überragen

rearm [ˌriˈɑrm] *vi* sich *akk* wieder bewaffnen

rearview 'mirror *n* Rückspiegel *m*

rear-wheel 'drive *n* Hinterradantrieb *m*

reason [ˈriːzən] I. *n* 1. Grund *m;* **there is every ~ to ...** es spricht alles dafür, ...; **for some ~** aus irgendeinem Grund 2. (*sense*) Vernunft *f;* (*sanity*) Verstand *m* II. *vi* 1. (*judge*) ausgehen 2. to ~ **with sb** vernünftig mit jdm reden III. *vt* to ~ **that ...** schlussfolgern, dass ...

reasonable [ˈriːzənəbəl] *adj* 1. (*sensible*) vernünftig 2. (*understanding*) einsichtig; **be ~!** sei [doch] vernünftig! 3. (*justified*) angebracht 4. (*price*) akzeptabel

reasonably [ˈriːzənəbli] *adv* 1. (*sensibly*) vernünftig 2. (*fairly*) ziemlich 3. ~ **priced** preiswert

reasoning [ˈriːzənɪŋ] *n* logisches Denken

reassure [ˌriːəˈʃʊr] *vt* [wieder] beruhigen

reassuring [ˌriːəˈʃʊrɪŋ] *adj* beruhigend

rebate [ˈriːbeɪt] *n* Rückzahlung *f;* (*discount*) [Preis]nachlass *m*

rebel I. *n* [ˈrebəl] Rebell(in) *m(f)* II. *adj* [ˈrebəl] aufständisch III. *vi* <-ll-> [rɪˈbel] *a. fig* rebellieren

rebellion [rɪˈbeljən] *n* Rebellion *f*

rebellious [rɪˈbeljəs] *adj* rebellisch; (*child*) aufsässig

rebirth [ˌriˈbɜrθ] *n* Wiedergeburt *f*

rebound [rɪˈbaʊnd] I. *vi* abprallen; (*in basketball*) rebounden II. *vt* (*in basketball*) rebounden *n* [ˈriːbaʊnd] Abprallen *nt;* (*in basketball*) Rebound *m*

rebuff [rɪˈbʌf] I. *vt* [schroff] zurückweisen II. *n* Zurückweisung *f*

rebuild <rebuilt, rebuilt> [ˌriˈbɪld] *vt* wieder aufbauen

recall I. *vt* [rɪˈkɔl] 1. sich *akk* erinnern 2. (*product*) zurückrufen II. *n* [ˈriːkɔl] Rückruf *m*

recede [rɪˈsid] *vi* 1. (*sea, tide*) zurückgehen 2. *fig* (*diminish*) weniger werden 3. (*hair*) zurückgehen

receipt [rɪˈsit] *n* 1. Erhalt *m* 2. (*payment slip*) Quittung *f*

receive [rɪˈsiv] I. *vt* 1. erhalten; (*salary*) beziehen; (*degree*) erhalten; (*prize*) [verliehen] bekommen *m* TV empfangen II. *vi* SPORT den Ball bekommen

receiver [rɪˈsivər] *n* (*of telephone*) Hörer *m;* (*of radio*) Empfänger *m*

recent [ˈriːsənt] *adj* kürzlich; **in ~ times** in der letzten Zeit

recently [ˈriːsəntli] *adv* kürzlich; **until ~** bis vor kurzem

reception [rɪˈsepʃən] *n* Empfang *m;* (*guest area*) Rezeption *f;* ~ **desk** Rezeption *f*

receptionist [rɪˈsepʃənɪst] *n* Empfangschef *m;* (*female*) Empfangsdame *f;* (*in office*) Empfangssekretärin *f*

recess [ˈriːses] I. *n* <*pl* -es> 1. (*niche*) Nische *f* 2. [Sitzungs]pause *f;* SCH Pause *f* II. *vt* 1. (*cut out*) aussparen 2. (*suspend*) vertagen

recession [rɪˈseʃən] *n* Rezession *f*

recharge [ˌriˈtʃɑrdʒ] *vt* [neu] aufladen; **to ~ one's batteries** *fig* neue Kräfte tanken

rechargeable [ˌriˈtʃɑrdʒəbəl] *adj* [wieder]aufladbar

recipe [ˈresəpi] *n* Rezept *nt*

recipient [rɪˈsɪpiənt] *n* Empfänger(in) *m(f)*

reciprocal [rɪˈsɪprəkəl] *adj* (*mutual*) beidseitig; (*favor*) gegenseitig; (*reverse*) umgekehrt

recital [rɪˈsaɪtəl] *n* Aufzählung *f;* (*of poetry*) Vortrag *m;* (*of dance*) Aufführung *f*

recite [rɪˈsaɪt] *vt* aufzählen; (*poem*) vortragen; (*at school*) [auswendig] aufsagen

reckless [ˈreklɪs] *adj* rücksichtslos; (*not cautious*) leichtsinnig

recklessness [ˈreklɪsnɪs] *n* Leichtsinn *m;* (*of driving*) Rücksichtslosigkeit *f*

reckon [ˈrekən] *vt* 1. (*calculate*) berechnen 2. **I ~ you won't be seeing her again** ich denke nicht, dass du sie je wiedersehen wirst

reckon with *vt* to ~ **with sth/sb** etw/jdm rechnen

reckoning ['rek·nɪŋ] *n* Berechnung *f*

reclaim [rɪ·'kleɪm] *vt* zurückverlangen; (*luggage*) abholen; **to ~ land from the sea** dem Meer Land abgewinnen

recline [rɪ·'klaɪn] I. *vi* sich *akk* zurücklehnen. II. *vt* **to ~ one's seat** die Rückenlehne seines Sitzes nach hinten stellen

recluse ['rek·lus] *n* Einsiedler(in) *m(f)*

recognition [ˌrek·əg·'nɪʃ·ən] *n* 1. [Wieder]erkennen *nt* 2. (*appreciation*) Anerkennung *f*

recognizable ['rek·əg·naɪ·zə·bəl] *adj* erkennbar

recognize ['rek·əg·naɪz] *vt* (*identify*) erkennen; (*know again*) wiedererkennen; (*acknowledge*) anerkennen

recoil [rɪ·'kɔɪl] I. *vi* zurückspringen; (*draw back*) zurückweichen; (*rubber band, spring*) zurückschnellen II. *n* Rückstoß *m*

recollect [ˌrek·ə·'lekt] *vt* sich *akk* erinnern an +*akk*

recollection [ˌrek·ə·'lek·ʃən] *n* Erinnerung *f*

recommend [ˌrek·ə·'mend] *vt* empfehlen; (*doctor a.*) raten

recommendation [ˌrek·ə·mən·'deɪ·ʃən] *n* Empfehlung *f*; (*advice a.*) Rat *m*

recompense ['rek·əm·ˌpens] *n* Belohnung *f*; (*retribution*) Entschädigung *f*

reconcile ['rek·ən·saɪl] *vt* versöhnen; (*conflict*) schlichten; (*differences*) beilegen

reconciliation [ˌrek·ən·ˌsɪl·i·'eɪ·ʃən] *n* Versöhnung *f*; (*of differences*) Beilegung *f*

recondition [ˌri·kən·'dɪʃ·ən] *vt* (*engine*) [general]überholen

reconnaissance [rɪ·'kɑn·ə·səns] *n* MIL Aufklärung *f*

reconnoiter [ˌri·kə·'nɔɪ·tər] *vt* MIL auskundschaften

reconsider [ˌri·kən·'sɪd·ər] *vt* [noch einmal] überdenken

reconstruct [ˌri·kən·'strʌkt] *vt* wieder aufbauen; (*restore*) wiederherstellen; (*crime*) rekonstruieren

reconstruction [ˌri·kən·'strʌk·ʃən] *n* Rekonstruktion *f*; (*restoration*) Wiederaufbau *m*

record I. *n* ['rek·ərd] 1. Aufzeichnungen *pl*; (*document*) Akte *f*; (*of attendance*) Liste *f*; (*minutes*) Protokoll *nt* 2. **criminal ~** Vorstrafenregister *nt*; **medical ~** Krankenblatt *nt* 3. (*music*) [Schall]platte *f* 4. SPORT Rekord *m* ▶ **to say sth on/off the ~** etw offiziell/inoffiziell sagen II. *adj* ['rek·ərd] Rekord- III. *vt* [rɪ·'kɔrd] 1. (*store*) aufzeichnen, registrieren; (*feelings, ideas*) niederschreiben 2. (*measure*) messen 3. FILM, MUS aufnehmen

'**record-breaking** *adj attr* Rekord-

recorder [rɪ·'kɔr·dər] *n* 1. **video ~** Videorekorder *m*; **tape ~** Kassettenrekorder 2. MUS Blockflöte *f*

'**record holder** *n* Rekordhalter(in) *m(f)*

recording [rɪ·'kɔr·dɪŋ] *n* Aufnahme *f*; (*of program*) Aufzeichnung *f*

'**record player** *n* [Schall]plattenspieler *m*

recount[1] [rɪ·'kaʊnt] *vt* [ausführlich] erzählen

recount[2] I. *vt* [ˌri·'kaʊnt] nachzählen II. *n* ['ri·kaʊnt] erneute Stimmenauszählung

recourse ['ri·kɔrs] *n* Zuflucht *f*

recover [rɪ·'kʌv·ər] I. *vt* wiederbekommen; (*stolen goods*) sicherstellen; (*composure*) wiederfinden; (*data*) wiederherstellen; **to be fully ~ed** völlig genesen sein II. *vi* sich *akk* erholen

recovery [rɪ·'kʌv·ə·ri] *n* Erholung *f*; (*getting back*) Wiedererlangen *nt*; (*of survivor*) Bergung *f*

recreation [ˌrek·ri·'eɪ·ʃən] *n* Freizeitbeschäftigung *f*; (*fun*) Erholung *f*

recreational [ˌrek·ri·'eɪ·ʃə·nəl] *adj* Freizeit-

recreational 'vehicle *n* Wohnwagen *m*

rec room ['rek·rum] *n* Aufenthaltsraum *m*

recruit [rɪ·'krut] I. *vt* einstellen; (*members*) werben; (*soldiers*) rekrutieren; (*volunteers*) finden II. *vi* (*army*) Rekruten anwerben; (*company*) Neueinstellungen vornehmen; (*club*) neue Mitglieder werben III. *n* MIL Rekrut(in) *m(f)*; (*to party, club*) neues Mitglied; (*staff*) neu eingestellte Arbeitskraft

rectangle ['rek·tæŋ·gəl] *n* Rechteck *nt*

rectangular [rek·'tæŋ·gjə·lər] *adj* rechteckig

rectify <-ie-> ['rek·tə·faɪ] *vt* (*set right*) korrigieren; (*omission*) nachholen

rector [ˈrek·tər] n Pfarrer m; UNIV Rektor(in) m(f)

rectory [ˈrek·tə·ri] n Pfarrhaus nt

rectum <pl -ta> [ˈrek·təm] n MED Mastdarm m

recuperate [rɪˈkuː·pə·reɪt] vi sich akk erholen

recur <-rr-> [rɪˈkɜr] vi sich wiederholen, wiederkehren

recycle [ˌriˈsaɪ·kəl] vt recyceln; fig wiederverwenden

recycling [ˌriˈsaɪ·kəl·ɪŋ] n Recycling nt

red [red] I. adj <-dd-> rot; (eyes) gerötet II. n Rot nt; **to be in the ~** in den roten Zahlen sein

Red ˈCross n **the ~** das Rote Kreuz

redden [ˈred·ən] I. vi sich röten; (person) rot werden; (sky) sich rot färben II. vt rot färben

reddish [ˈred·ɪʃ] adj rötlich

redecorate [ˌriˈdek·ə·reɪt] I. vt neu streichen; (wallpaper) neu tapezieren II. vi renovieren

redeem [rɪˈdiːm] vt wiederherstellen; (mistake) wettmachen; (pay off) ab[be]zahlen; (mortgage) tilgen; (pledge) einlösen

redevelop [ˌriˌdɪˈvel·əp] vt sanieren

ˈred-eye n fam Nachtflug m

red-ˈhanded adj **to catch sb ~** jdn auf frischer Tat ertappen

ˈredhead [ˈred·hed] n Rothaarige(r) f(m)

red-ˈheaded adj rothaarig

red ˈherring n Ablenkungsmanöver nt

red-ˈhot adj 1. **to be ~** [rot] glühen; fig glühend heiß sein 2. (news) brandaktuell

red-ˈlight district n Rotlichtviertel nt

red ˈmeat n dunkles Fleisch (wie Rind, Lamm und Kalb)

ˈredneck n pej fam weißer Arbeiter aus den Südstaaten, oft mit reaktionären Ansichten

redness [ˈred·nɪs] n Röte f

redouble [rɪˈdʌb·əl] vt verdoppeln

red ˈpepper n rote(r) Paprika

redress [rɪˈdres] vt wiedergutmachen

Red ˈSea n **the ~** das Rote Meer

ˈredskin n pej fam Rothaut f pej

red ˈtape n Bürokratie f

reduce [rɪˈduːs] vt verringern; (prices)

heruntersetzen; (taxes) senken; (photo) verkleinern; (fraction) kürzen; **he was ~d to begging for help** er war gezwungen, seine Eltern um Hilfe zu bitten

reduced [rɪˈduːst] adj attr (price) heruntergesetzt; **to be in ~ circumstances** in verarmten Verhältnissen leben

reduction [rɪˈdʌk·ʃən] n Reduzierung f (of photo) Verkleinerung f; (in taxes) Senkung f; (in salary) Kürzung f

redundant [rɪˈdʌn·dənt] adj überflüssig

red ˈwine n Rotwein m

reed [riːd] n Schilf[gras] nt; (in instrument) Rohrblatt nt

reef [riːf] n Riff nt

reek [riːk] vi übel riechen, stinken

reel [riːl] n Rolle f; (for film, tape) Spule f (for fishing line) Angelrolle f

re-elect [ˌriˌɪˈlekt] vt wiederwählen

re-enter [ˌriˈen·tər] vt (bus, car) wieder einsteigen in +akk; (country) wieder einreisen in +akk; (house, store) wieder hineingehen in +akk; (room) wieder betreten; (earth's atmosphere) wieder eintreten in +akk

ref [ref] n abbr of **referee** fam Schiri m fam

ref. [ref] n abbr of **reference** AZ

refectory [rɪˈfek·tə·ri] n UNIV Mensa f

refer <-rr-> [rɪˈfɜr] I. vt verweisen; **he was ~red to a specialist** er wurde an einen Facharzt überwiesen II. vi 1. **to ~ to sb/sth** sich akk auf jdn/etw beziehen; **~ring to your letter, ...** Bezug nehmend auf Ihren Brief ... 2. (consult) **to ~ to sth** (dictionary) in etw dat nachschlagen

referee [ˌref·əˈri] n Schiedsrichter(in) m(f), (arbitrator) Schlichter(in) m(f)

reference [ˈref·ər·əns] n 1. Verweis m 2. (allusion: indirect) Anspielung f; (direct) Bemerkung f; (direct mention) Bezugnahme f; **in ~ to sb/sth** mit Bezug auf jdn/etw 3. (in correspondence) Aktenzeichen nt 4. (recommendation) Empfehlungsschreiben nt

ˈreference book n Nachschlagewerk nt

ˈreference number n Aktenzeichen nt, (on goods) Artikelnummer f

referendum <pl -s> [ˌref·əˈren·dəm] n POL Referendum nt

refill I. n ['riː·fɪl] **1. to give sb a ~** fam jdm nachschenken **2.** (replacement) Nachfüll-, Ersatz- II. vt [ˌriː·ˈfɪl] **to ~ a cup** eine Tasse wieder füllen

refine [rɪ·ˈfaɪn] vt raffinieren; (improve) verfeinern

refined [rɪ·ˈfaɪnd] adj raffiniert; (food) aufbereitet; (metal) veredelt; fig kultiviert

refinement [rɪ·ˈfaɪn·mənt] n Raffinieren nt; (of metal) Veredelung f; fig Verfeinerung f

refinery [rɪ·ˈfaɪ·nə·ri] n Raffinerie f

reflect [rɪ·ˈflekt] I. vt **1.** widerspiegeln; (light, sound) reflektieren **2.** (show) zeigen II. vi **1.** reflektieren **2.** (ponder) nachdenken **3. to ~ badly on sth** ein schlechtes Licht auf etw akk werfen

reflection [rɪ·ˈflek·ʃən] n **1.** (reflecting) Reflexion f **2.** (image) Spiegelbild nt; fig (sign) Ausdruck m, Zeichen nt **3.** (consideration) Betrachtung f

reflective [rɪ·ˈflek·tɪv] adj reflektierend; (person) nachdenklich

reflex <pl -es> ['riː·fleks] n Reflex m

reform [rɪ·ˈfɔːm] I. vt reformieren; (criminal) bessern II. vi sich akk bessern III. n Reform f; (of criminal) Besserung f

reformation [ˌref·ər·ˈmeɪ·ʃən] n hist **the R~** die Reformation

reformer [rɪ·ˈfɔːr·mər] n Reformer(in) m(f)

re'form school n Erziehungsheim nt

refrain [rɪ·ˈfreɪn] vi sich akk zurückhalten; **to ~ from smoking** das Rauchen unterlassen

refresh [rɪ·ˈfreʃ] vt erfrischen; fig (skills) auffrischen; **to ~ one's memory** seinem Gedächtnis auf die Sprünge helfen; **to ~ sb's drink** jds Glas nachfüllen

re'fresher course [rɪ·ˈfreʃ·ər·] n Auffrischungskurs m

refreshing [rɪ·ˈfreʃ·ɪŋ] adj erfrischend; (pleasing) [herz]erfrischend

refreshment [rɪ·ˈfreʃ·mənt] n Erfrischung f; **~s** (drinks) Erfrischungen pl; (food) Snacks pl

refrigerator [rɪ·ˈfrɪdʒ·ə·reɪ·tər] n Kühlschrank m

refuel <-l-> [ˌriː·ˈfjuː·əl] vt, vi auftanken

refuge ['ref·juːdʒ] n Zufluchtsort m; **women's ~** Frauenhaus nt

refugee [ˌref·jʊ·ˈdʒiː] n Flüchtling m

'refugee camp n Aufnahmelager nt

refund I. vt [ˌriː·ˈfʌnd] zurückerstatten II. n ['riː·fʌnd] Rückzahlung f

refurbish [ˌriː·ˈfɜːr·bɪʃ] vt aufpolieren; (house) renovieren

refusal [rɪ·ˈfjuː·zəl] n Ablehnung f; (of offer) Zurückweisung f; (of invitation) Absage f; (of food, visa) Verweigerung f

refuse¹ [rɪ·ˈfjuːz] I. vt ablehnen; (horse) verweigern II. vt ablehnen; (offer) ausschlagen

refuse² ['ref·juːs] n form Abfall m

reg. adj abbr of **regular**

regain [rɪ·ˈɡeɪn] vt wiederbekommen; (lost ground) zurückgewinnen; (consciousness) wiedererlangen

regal ['riː·ɡəl] adj majestätisch

regard [rɪ·ˈɡɑːrd] I. vt **1.** betrachten; **to ~ sb/sth as sth** jdn/etw als etw betrachten, jdn/etw für etw akk halten **2.** (concerning) **as ~s** was ... angeht, II. n **1.** Rücksicht f; **without ~ for sb/sth** ohne Rücksicht auf jdn/etw **2.** (respect) Achtung f **3.** (aspect) **in this ~** in dieser Hinsicht **4.** (concerning) **with ~ to ...** in Bezug auf ... +akk

regarding [rɪ·ˈɡɑr·dɪŋ] prep bezüglich +gen

regardless [rɪ·ˈɡɑrd·lɪs] adv trotzdem; **~ of the expense** ungeachtet der Kosten; **to press on ~** trotzdem weitermachen

regards [rɪ·ˈɡɑrdz] n pl **[best] ~** [viele] Grüße; **Jim sends his ~** Jim lässt grüßen

regenerate [rɪ·ˈdʒen·ə·reɪt] I. vt erneuern; (tissue) neu bilden II. vi sich regenerieren; (tissue) sich neu bilden

regent ['riː·dʒənt] n Regent(in) m(f)

reggae ['reg·eɪ] n Reggae m

regime [rə·ˈʒiːm] n Regime nt

regiment ['redʒ·ə·mənt] I. n Regiment nt II. vt in Gruppen einordnen

region ['riː·dʒən] n Region f; (administrative) [Verwaltungs]bezirk m

regional ['riː·dʒə·nəl] adj regional

register ['redʒ·ɪ·stər] I. n **1.** Register nt **2.** (till) **cash ~** Kasse f II. vt **1.** registrieren; (birth, death) anmelden; (copyright) eintragen **2.** (measure) anzeigen **3.** (letter, package) per Einschreiben schicken

R

4. to ~ surprise sich überrascht zeigen **III.** *vi* **1.** sich melden; (*to vote*) sich eintragen; (*to take classes*) sich einschreiben; **to ~ with the authorities** sich behördlich anmelden **2.** (*dial*) anzeigen **3.** (*show*) sich zeigen

registrar ['redʒ·ɪ·strar] *n* Standesbeamte(r) *m*, Standesbeamte [*or* -in] *f*; UNIV höchster Verwaltungsbeamter/höchste Verwaltungsbeamte [*or*-in]

registration [ˌredʒ·ɪ·'streɪ·ʃən] *n* **1.** Anmeldung *f*, Registrierung *f*; (*at school*) Einschreibung *f*; UNIV Immatrikulation *f* **2.** (*document*) (**motor vehicle**) ~ Kraftfahrzeugschein *m*

regret [rɪ·'gret] **I.** *vt, vi* <-tt-> bedauern; **I ~** (**to have**) **to inform you that** ... leider muss ich Ihnen mitteilen, dass ... **II.** *n* Bedauern *nt kein pl;* **to have no ~s about sth** etw nicht bereuen; **to send one's ~s** sich entschuldigen [lassen]

regretful [rɪ·'gret·fəl] *adj* bedauernd; (*smile*) wehmütig

regrettable [rɪ·'gret·ə·bəl] *adj* bedauerlich

regular ['reg·jə·lər] **I.** *adj* **1.** regelmäßig; (*price*) regulär; (*procedure*) üblich; (*surface*) gleichmäßig; **to keep ~ hours** sich an feste Zeiten halten; **~ gasoline** Normalbenzin *nt* **2.** *attr* **~ fries** normale Portion Pommes Frites **II.** *n* Stammgast *m*

regularity [ˌreg·jə·'ler·ɪ·ti] *n* (*in time*) Regelmäßigkeit *f*; (*of shape*) Ebenmäßigkeit *f*

regularly ['reg·jə·lər·li] *adv* regelmäßig; (*equally*) gleichmäßig

regulate ['reg·jʊ·leɪt] *vt* regeln; (*adjust*) regulieren

regulation [ˌreg·jʊ·'leɪ·ʃən] *n* Vorschrift *f*; **in accordance with the ~s** vorschriftsmäßig; **fire ~s** Brandschutzbestimmungen *pl*

rehearsal [rɪ·'hɜr·səl] *n* Probe *f*

rehearse [rɪ·'hɜrs] *vt, vi* proben

reign [reɪn] **I.** *vi* **1.** regieren; **to ~ over a country** ein Land regieren **2.** (*be dominant*) dominieren; **confusion ~s** es herrscht Verwirrung **II.** *n* Herrschaft *f*

rein [reɪn] *n usu pl* Zügel ▸ **to give**

free ~ to sb jdm freie Hand lassen

reincarnation [ˌri·ɪn·kar·'neɪ·ʃən] *n* Wiedergeburt *f*

reindeer <*pl* -> ['reɪn·dɪr] *n* Rentier *nt*

reinforce [ˌri·ɪn·'fɔrs] *vt* (*strengthen, troops*) verstärken; (*concrete*) armieren; (*findings*) bestätigen

reinforcement [ˌri·ɪn·'fɔrs·mənt] *n* **1.** Verstärkung *f*; **steel ~** Stahlträger *m, meist pl* **2.** **~s** *pl* Verstärkungstruppen *pl*; (*equipment*) Verstärkung *f*

reinstate [ˌri·ɪn·'steɪt] *vt* wieder einstellen; (*tax*) wieder einführen; (*law and order*) wiederherstellen

reject I. *vt* [rɪ·'dʒekt] ablehnen; (*excuse*) nicht annehmen; (*snub*) abweisen; (*drug*) nicht vertragen; (*transplant*) abstoßen; **to feel ~ed** sich als Außenseiter(in) fühlen **II.** *n* ['ri·dʒekt] Ausschussware *f*; (*person*) Außenseiter(in) *m(f)*

rejection [rɪ·'dʒek·ʃən] *n* Ablehnung *f*, MED Abstoßung *f*

rejoice [rɪ·'dʒɔɪs] *vi* sich freuen

rejoicing [rɪ·'dʒɔɪ·sɪŋ] *n* Freude *f*

rejoin [ˌri·'dʒɔɪn] *vt* sich wieder vereinigen

relapse I. *n* ['ri·læps] MED Rückfall *m*; (*in economy*) Rückschlag *m* **II.** *vi* [rɪ·'læps] MED einen Rückfall haben; (*economy*) einen Rückschlag erleiden

relate [rɪ·'leɪt] **I.** *vt* **1.** in Verbindung bringen **2.** (*narrate*) erzählen; **to ~ sth to sb** jdm etw berichten **II.** *vi* **1.** *fam* (*get along*) **to ~ to sb/sth** eine Beziehung zu jdm/etw finden **2.** (*be about*) **to ~ to sb/sth** von jdm/etw handeln; **chapter nine ~s to inflation** in Kapitel neun geht es um die Inflation

related [rɪ·'leɪ·tɪd] *adj* **1.** verbunden; **to be directly ~ to sth** in direktem Zusammenhang mit etw *dat* stehen **2.** (*species*) verwandt; **to be ~ by blood** blutsverwandt sein; **distantly ~** entfernt verwandt

relating to [rɪ·'leɪ·tɪŋ-] *prep* in Zusammenhang mit +*dat*

relation [rɪ·'leɪ·ʃən] *n* **1.** Bezug *m*; **in ~ to** in Bezug auf +*akk* **2.** (*relative*) Verwandte(r) *f(m)*; **is Julia any ~ to you?** ist Julia irgendwie mit dir verwandt?

3. (*between countries*) **~s** pl Beziehungen pl

relationship [rɪ·ˈleɪ·ʃən·ʃɪp] n 1. (*connection*) Beziehung f 2. (*in family*) Verwandtschaftsverhältnis nt 3. (*association*) Verhältnis nt; **to be in a ~ with sb** mit jdm eine feste Beziehung haben

relative [ˈrel·ə·tɪv] I. adj relevant; (*corresponding*) jeweilig(r, s); (*comparative*) relativ; **to be ~ to sth** von etw dat abhängen II. n Verwandte(r) f(m)

relaunch [ˌriː·ˈlɔːntʃ] I. vt (*rocket*) erneut starten; (*product*) erneut auf den Markt bringen II. n (*of rocket*) Zweitstart m; (*of ship*) zweiter Stapellauf; (*of brand*) Wiedereinführung f

relax [rɪ·ˈlæks] I. vi sich entspannen; **~!** entspann dich!; (*don't worry*) beruhige dich! II. vt lockern; (*muscles a.*) entspannen; (*security*) einschränken

relaxation [rɪ·læk·ˈseɪ·ʃən] n Entspannung f; (*of discipline*) Nachlassen nt; (*of laws*) Liberalisierung f; (*of rules*) Lockerung f

relaxed [rɪ·ˈlækst] adj entspannt; (*easygoing*) locker; (*manner*) lässig

relay [ˈriː·leɪ] I. vt mitteilen; (*message*) weiterleiten; (*TV*) übertragen II. n Staffellauf m

release [rɪ·ˈliːs] I. vt 1. freilassen; (*prisoner*) [aus der Haft] entlassen; (*brake*) lösen; (*shutter*) betätigen; (*steam*) freisetzen; (*grip*) lockern 2. (*circulate*) verbreiten; (*issue*) veröffentlichen; (*CD*) herausbringen II. n 1. Entlassung f; (*of hostage*) Freilassung f; (*of funds*) Freigabe f; (*of gases*) Entweichen nt 2. (*mechanism*) Auslöser m 3. (*publication*) Veröffentlichung f; **press ~** Pressemitteilung f 4. (*new CD*) Neuerscheinung f

relegate [ˈrel·ə·geɪt] vt usu passive **the story was ~d to the middle pages of the newspaper** die Story wurde in den Mittelteil der Zeitung verschoben

relent [rɪ·ˈlent] vi nachgeben; (*wind, rain*) nachlassen

relentless [rɪ·ˈlent·lɪs] adj unnachgiebig; (*rain*) unablässig; (*persecution*) gnadenlos; (*pressure*) unaufhörlich

relevance [ˈrel·ə·vəns], **relevancy** [ˈrel·ə·vən·si] n Bedeutsamkeit f; (*significance*) Bedeutung f

relevant [ˈrel·ə·vənt] adj relevant; (*important*) bedeutend

reliability [rɪ·ˌlaɪ·ə·ˈbɪl·ɪ·ti] n Zuverlässigkeit f; (*trustworthiness*) Vertrauenswürdigkeit f

reliable [rɪ·ˈlaɪ·ə·bəl] adj zuverlässig; (*credible*) glaubwürdig; (*criterion*) sicher; (*trustworthy*) vertrauenswürdig

reliance [rɪ·ˈlaɪ·əns] n Verlass m; (*trust*) Vertrauen nt

reliant [rɪ·ˈlaɪ·ənt] adj abhängig

relic [ˈrel·ɪk] n a. fig, hum Relikt nt

relief [rɪ·ˈliːf] n 1. Entlastung f; (*of suffering*) Linderung f; (*of tension*) Erleichterung f; **tax ~** Steuerermäßigung f; **to breathe a sigh of ~** erleichtert aufatmen 2. (*welfare*) Hilfsgüter pl 3. (*next shift*) Ablösung f 4. (*sharpness*) Kontrast m; **to stand out in sharp ~** sich deutlich von etw dat abheben

re·lief worker n Mitarbeiter(in) m(f) einer Hilfsorganisation; (*in third-world countries*) Entwicklungshelfer(in) m(f)

relieve [rɪ·ˈliːv] vt 1. erträglicher machen; (*pressure*) verringern; (*tension*) abbauen; (*pain*) lindern 2. (*unburden*) **to ~ sb of sth** jdm etw abnehmen; hum (*steal*) jdm um etw akk erleichtern; **to ~ oneself** hum sich akk erleichtern euph 3. (*take over*) ablösen

relieved [rɪ·ˈliːvd] adj erleichtert; **to be ~ to hear sth** etw mit Erleichterung hören

religion [rɪ·ˈlɪdʒ·ən] n Religion f; (*beliefs*) Glaube m; (*system*) Kult m

religious [rɪ·ˈlɪdʒ·əs] adj religiös; (*pious a.*) fromm; **~ organization** Glaubensgemeinschaft f

relish [ˈrel·ɪʃ] I. n 1. Genuss m; **with ~** genüsslich 2. (*sauce*) Relish nt II. vt genießen; **to ~ the thought that ...** sich darauf freuen, dass ...

reload [ˌriː·ˈloʊd] I. vt nachladen; (*camera*) neu laden; (*ship*) wieder beladen II. vi nachladen

reluctance [rɪ·ˈlʌk·təns] n Widerwillen m

reluctant [rɪ·ˈlʌk·tənt] adj widerwillig; **to be ~ to do sth** sich dagegen sträuben, etw zu tun

rely [rɪ·ˈlaɪ] vi 1. **to ~ on sb/sth** sich auf

R

jdn/etw verlassen; **to ~ on sb/sth to do sth** sich darauf verlassen, dass jd/etw etw tut **2.** (*depend on*) **to ~ on sb/sth** von jdm/etw abhängen; **to ~ on sb/sth for** [*or to do*] **sth** darauf angewiesen sein, dass jd/etw etw tut

remain [rɪ'meɪn] *vi* **1.** bleiben; **to ~ behind** zurückbleiben **2.** + *n or adj* bleiben; **to ~ untreated** nicht behandelt werden **3.** (*survive*) übrig bleiben; (*person*) überleben; **much ~s to be done** es muss noch vieles getan werden; **the fact ~s that ...** das ändert nichts an der Tatsache, dass ...

remainder [rɪ'meɪn·dər] *n* Rest *m*

remaining [rɪ'meɪ·nɪŋ] *adj attr* übrig

remains [rɪ'meɪnz] *npl* Überbleibsel *pl; form* (*corpse*) sterbliche Überreste

remake I. *vt* <-made, -made> [ˌriː'meɪk] (*film*) neu drehen **II.** *n* ['riː·meɪk] Neuverfilmung *f*

remark [rɪ'mɑrk] **I.** *vt* bemerken **II.** *vi* eine Bemerkung machen; **to ~ on sth** sich über etw äußern **III.** *n* Bemerkung *f*

remarkable [rɪ'mɑr·kə·bəl] *adj* bemerkenswert; (*ability*) beachtlich; (*surprising*) merkwürdig

remarkably [rɪ'mɑr·kə·bli] *adv* bemerkenswert; (*surprisingly*) überraschenderweise

remarry <-ie-> [ˌriː'mær·i] *vi* wieder heiraten

rematch ['riː·mætʃ] *n* Rückspiel *nt*

remedy ['rem·ə·di] *n* Heilmittel *nt;* (*solution*) Mittel *nt*

remember [rɪ'mem·bər] **I.** *vt* sich erinnern; (*memorize*) sich *dat* merken; (*commemorate*) gedenken +*gen;* **I never ~ her birthday** ich denke nie an ihren Geburtstag; **to ~ doing sth** sich daran erinnern, etw getan zu haben **II.** *vi* sich erinnern; **to ~ [that] ...** sich daran erinnern, [dass] ...

remind [rɪ'maɪnd] *vt* erinnern; **that ~s me!** das erinnert mich an etwas!; **to ~ sb about sth** jdn an etw *akk* erinnern

reminder [rɪ'maɪn·dər] *n* Erinnerung *f;* (*for bill*) Mahnung *f;* **as a ~ to oneself that ...** um sich *akk* daran zu erinnern, dass ...

remnant ['rem·nənt] *n* Rest *m;* **~ sale** Resteverkauf *m*

remorse [rɪ'mɔrs] *n* Reue *f;* **without ~** erbarmungslos

remorseless [rɪ'mɔrs·lɪs] *adj* gnadenlos (*attack*) brutal; (*relentless*) unerbittlich

remote <-r, -st> [rɪ'moʊt] *adj* **1.** fern (*isolated*) abgelegen; (*in time*) lang vergangen; (*past, future*) fern **2.** (*standoffish*) distanziert

remote con'trol *n* (*device*) Fernbedienung *f;* (*action*) Fernsteuerung *f*

remote-con'trolled *adj* ferngesteuert

removal [rɪ'muː·vəl] *n* Beseitigung *f;* (*taking off*) Abnahme *f;* (*of stain a.*) Entfernung *f*

remove [rɪ'muv] *vt* **1.** entfernen; (*obstacle*) beseitigen; (*car*) abschleppen; (*mine*) räumen; (*makeup*) entfernen **2.** *form* **to ~ sb** [**from office**] jdn [aus dem Amt] entlassen

remover [rɪ'mu·vər] *n* Reinigungsmittel *nt;* **nail polish ~** Nagellackentferner *m*

Renaissance [ˌren·ə·'sɑns] *n* **the ~** die Renaissance

render ['ren·dər] *vt form* **1.** **she was ~ed unconscious** sie wurde ohnmächtig; **to ~ sb speechless** jdn sprachlos machen **2.** (*interpret*) wiedergeben; (*song*) vortragen **3.** (*offer*) leisten

rendering ['ren·dər·ɪŋ] *n* **1.** (*performance*) Interpretation *f;* (*of song*) Vortrag *m;* (*of role*) Darstellung *f* **2.** (*account*) Schilderung *f*

rendezvous ['ran·deɪ·vu] **I.** *n* <*pl* -> **1.** Rendezvous *nt* **2.** (*place*) Treffpunkt *m* **II.** *vi* sich heimlich treffen

renegade ['ren·ə·geɪd] **I.** *n* Abtrünnige(r) *f(m) pej* **II.** *adj attr* abtrünnig

renew [rɪ'nu] *vt* erneuern; (*passport*) verlängern; (*repair*) reparieren; (*patch*) ausbessern; **to ~ a relationship** eine Beziehung wieder aufnehmen

renewal [rɪ'nu·əl] *n* Erneuerung *f;* (*regeneration*) Entwicklung *f;* (*of passport*) Verlängerung *f*

renewed [rɪ'nud] *adj* erneuert *attr;* (*interest*) wieder erwacht

renovate ['ren·ə·veɪt] *vt* renovieren

renovation [ˌren·ə·'veɪ·ʃən] *n* Renovie-

renowned [rɪˈnaʊnd] *adj form, liter* berühmt

rent [rent] **I.** *n* Miete *f;* (*for land*) Pacht *f;* **"for ~"** „zu vermieten" **II.** *vt* mieten; (*land*) pachten; (*dress*) ausleihen; (*rent out*) vermieten **III.** *vi* vermietet werden; **to ~ for sth** gegen etw *akk* zu mieten sein

rental [ˈren·təl] *n* Miete *f;* **~ agency** Verleih *m;* **car ~ agency** Autoverleih *m*

rent-free *adj* mietfrei

reopen [ri·ˈoʊ·pən] **I.** *vt* wieder aufmachen; (*shop*) wieder eröffnen; (*negotiations*) wieder aufnehmen **II.** *vi* wieder eröffnen

reorganize [ri·ˈɔr·gə·naɪz] *vt, vi* reorganisieren

rep [rep] *n fam* (*salesperson*) *short for* **representative** Vertreter(in) *m(f)*

repaint [ri·ˈpeɪnt] *vt* neu streichen

repair [ri·ˈper] **I.** *vt* reparieren; (*defect*) beheben; (*road*) ausbessern; (*put right*) [wieder] in Ordnung bringen; (*damage*) wiedergutmachen **II.** *n* Reparatur *f;* (*repaired place*) ausgebesserte Stelle; **beyond ~** irreparabel; **to be in good ~** in gutem Zustand sein; **~s** *pl* Reparaturarbeiten *pl;* **to do ~s** Reparaturen durchführen

reparable [ˈrep·ər·ə·bəl] *adj* reparabel

repatriate [ri·ˈpeɪ·tri·eɪt] *vt* [in das Heimatland] zurückschicken

repatriation [ri·ˌpeɪ·tri·ˈeɪ·ʃən] *n* Repatriierung *f*

repay <-paid, -paid> [ri·ˈpeɪ] *vt* **1.** zurückzahlen; (*loan*) tilgen; **to ~ sb** jdm Geld zurückzahlen **2. to ~ a favor** sich für eine Gefälligkeit erkenntlich zeigen; **to ~ sth by doing sth** etw mit etw *dat* vergelten

repeal [ri·ˈpil] **I.** *vt* aufheben **II.** *n* Aufhebung *f*

repeat [ri·ˈpit] **I.** *vt* wiederholen; **~ after me** bitte mir nachsprechen; **don't ~ this but ...** sag es nicht weiter, [aber] ... **II.** *vi* sich wiederholen **III.** *n* Wiederholung *f*

repeatedly [ri·ˈpi·tɪd·li] *adv* wiederholt; (*several times*) mehrfach

repel <-ll-> [ri·ˈpel] *vt* **1.** zurückweisen; *form* (*repulse*) abwehren **2. she was ~led by the sight** sie war abgestoßen von dem Anblick

repellent [ri·ˈpel·ənt] **I.** *n* Insektenspray *nt* **II.** *adj* abstoßend

repetition [ˌrep·ə·ˈtɪʃ·ən] *n* Wiederholung *f*

repetitious [ˌrep·ə·ˈtɪʃ·əs], **repetitive** [ri·ˈpeṭ·ə·tɪv] *adj* sich wiederholend *attr*

replace [ri·ˈpleɪs] *vt* ersetzen; (*return*) [an seinen Platz] zurücklegen; (*receiver*) wieder auflegen; (*bandage*) wechseln

replacement [ri·ˈpleɪs·mənt] **I.** *n* Ersatz *m;* (*person*) Vertretung *f;* (*substituting*) Ersetzung *f* **II.** *adj attr* Ersatz-; **~ hip joint** künstliches Hüftgelenk

replay **I.** *vt* [ˌri·ˈpleɪ] (*game*) wiederholen; (*video*) nochmals abspielen **II.** *n* [ˈri·pleɪ] (*recording*) Wiederholung *f;* (*game*) Wiederholungsspiel *nt*

replica [ˈrep·lɪ·kə] *n* Kopie *f*

reply [ri·ˈplaɪ] **I.** *vi* <-ie-> antworten; **to ~ to letters/a question** Briefe/eine Frage beantworten **II.** *n* Antwort *f*

report [ri·ˈpɔrt] **I.** *n* Meldung *f;* (*statement*) Bericht *m* **II.** *vt* **1. to ~ sth** etw berichten; **he was ~ed missing in action** er wurde als vermisst gemeldet; **to ~ a crime** ein Verbrechen anzeigen **2.** (*denounce*) melden; (*to the police*) anzeigen **3. the new management is ~ed to be more popular among the staff** es heißt, dass die neue Geschäftsleitung bei der Belegschaft beliebter sei **III.** *vi* **1.** Bericht erstatten; **to ~ on sth to sb** (*once*) jdm über etw *akk* Bericht erstatten; (*ongoing*) jdn über etw *akk* auf dem Laufenden halten; **to ~ [that] ...** mitteilen, [dass] ... **2.** (*be accountable to*) **to ~ to sb** jdm unterstehen **3.** (*arrive*) sich zur Arbeit melden; (*to the police*) sich bei der Polizei melden

◆**report back I.** *vt* **to ~ back sth [to sb]** [jdm] über etw *akk* berichten **II.** *vi* Bericht erstatten; **to ~ back on sth [to sb]** [jdm] über etw *akk* Bericht erstatten

reporter [ri·ˈpɔr·ţər] *n* Reporter(in) *m(f)*

repossess [ˌri·pə·ˈzes] *vt* wieder in Besitz nehmen

represent [ˌrep·ri·ˈzent] *vt* repräsentieren;

R

(*depict*) darstellen; (*symbolize*) symbolisieren; (*be typical of*) widerspiegeln

representation [ˌrep·rɪ·zen·ˈteɪ·ʃən] n [Stell]vertretung f; (*that depicts*) Darstellung f

representative [ˌrep·rɪ·ˈzen·tə·tɪv] I. adj repräsentativ; (*typical*) typisch II. n [Stell]vertreter(in) m(f); POL Abgeordnete(r) f(m)

repressive [rɪ·ˈpres·ɪv] adj repressiv geh; (*regime*) unterdrückerisch

reprimand [ˈrep·rə·mænd] I. vt tadeln II. n Rüge f

reprint I. vt [ˌriˈprɪnt] nachdrucken II. n [ˈriˈprɪnt] Nachdruck m

reprisal [rɪ·ˈpraɪ·zəl] n Vergeltungsmaßnahme f

reproach [rɪ·ˈproʊtʃ] I. vt to ~ sb [for doing sth] jdm [wegen einer S. gen] Vorwürfe machen II. n <pl -es> Vorwurf m

reproachful [rɪ·ˈproʊtʃ·fəl] adj vorwurfsvoll

reproduce [ˌri·prə·ˈdus] I. vi sich fortpflanzen; (*multiply*) sich vermehren II. vt reproduzieren; (*in large numbers*) vervielfältigen

reproduction [ˌri·prə·ˈdʌk·ʃən] n Fortpflanzung f; (*multiplying*) Vermehrung f; (*copy*) Reproduktion f; **sound ~** Wiedergabe f II. adj ~ **furniture** Stilmöbel pl

reproductive [ˌri·prə·ˈdʌk·tɪv] adj Fortpflanzungs-

reptile [ˈrep·taɪl] n Reptil nt

republic [rɪ·ˈpʌb·lɪk] n Republik f

Republican [rɪ·ˈpʌb·lɪ·kən] POL I. n Republikaner(in) m(f) II. adj republikanisch

repulsion [rɪ·ˈpʌl·ʃən] n Abscheu m

repulsive [rɪ·ˈpʌl·sɪv] adj abstoßend

reputable [ˈrep·jə·tə·bəl] adj angesehen

reputation [ˌrep·jʊ·ˈteɪ·ʃən] n Ruf m; (*high regard*) Ansehen nt; **to have a ~ for sth** für etw akk bekannt sein; **to have a ~ as sth** einen Ruf als etw haben

repute [rɪ·ˈpjut] n Ansehen nt; **of good ~** von gutem Ruf

reputed [rɪ·ˈpju·tɪd] adj vermutet; (*supposed*) mutmaßlich

request [rɪ·ˈkwest] I. n 1. Bitte f; **on ~** auf Anfrage 2. (*formal*) Antrag m; **to**

submit a ~ that ... beantragen, dass ... 3. (*in radio*) [Musik]wunsch m II. v 1. to ~ sth form um etw akk bitten; **as ~ed** wie gewünscht 2. (*in radio*) to ~ sth [sich dat] etw wünschen

require [rɪ·ˈkwaɪr] vt 1. brauchen; to **be ~d for sth** für etw akk erforderlich sein; **~d reading** Pflichtlektüre f 2. (*demand*) to ~ **sth** [of sb] etw [von jdm verlangen 3. (*order*) **the rules ~ that ...** die Vorschriften besagen, dass ...

requirement [rɪ·ˈkwaɪr·mənt] n Voraussetzung f; **it is a legal ~ that ...** es ist gesetzlich vorgeschrieben, dass ...; **to meet the ~s** die Voraussetzungen erfüllen

requisite [ˈrek·wɪ·zɪt] I. adj attr form erforderlich II. n usu pl Notwendigkeit f

rescue [ˈres·kju] I. vt retten; (*free*) befreien; **to ~ sb from danger** jdn aus einer Gefahr retten II. n Rettung f; **to come to sb's ~** jdm zu Hilfe kommen III. adj Rettungs-

research I. n [ˈri·sɜrtʃ] 1. Forschung f (*specific*) Erforschung f; **to conduct ~** [into sth] [etw er]forschen 2. (*studies*) Untersuchungen pl II. vi [rɪ·ˈsɜrtʃ forschen; **to ~ in[to] sth** etw erforschen III. vt [rɪ·ˈsɜrtʃ] erforschen; (*reporter* recherchieren

researcher [rɪ·ˈsɜrtʃ·ər] n Forscher(in) m(f

resemblance [rɪ·ˈzem·bləns] n Ähnlichkeit f; **to bear a ~ to sb/sth** jdm/etw ähnlich sehen

resemble [rɪ·ˈzem·bəl] vt ähneln

resent [rɪ·ˈzent] vt sich [sehr] ärgern; **to ~ doing sth** etw [äußerst] ungern tun

resentment [rɪ·ˈzent·mənt] n Verbitterung f

reservation [ˌrez·ər·ˈveɪ·ʃən] n 1. Reservierung f; **to make a ~** reservieren 2. usu pl (*doubt*) Bedenken pl 3. (*land*) Reservat nt

reserve [rɪ·ˈzɜrv] I. n 1. Reserve f; **to put sth on ~** [for sb] etw [für jdn] reservieren 2. (*area*) Reservat nt; **wildlife ~** Naturschutzgebiet nt 3. SPORT Ersatzspieler(in) m(f) 4. (*restraint*) Reserviertheit f II. vt aufheben; (*save*) reservieren; (*room, tickets a.*) vorbestellen; **to ~ the right to do sth** sich dat das Recht vorbehalten, etw zu tun

reserved [rɪˈzɜrvd] *adj* reserviert; (*restrained*) reserviert; (*smile*) verhalten

reservoir [ˈrez·ər·vwar] *n* Wasserreservoir *nt; fig* Reservoir *nt*

reset <-tt-, -set, -set> [ˌriˈset] *vt* (*clock*) neu stellen; (*bone*) [ein]richten; COMPUT neu starten

residence [ˈrez·ɪ·dəns] *n* 1. *form* (*domicile*) Wohnsitz *m*; **to take up ~ in a country** sich in einem Land niederlassen 2. (*building*) Wohngebäude *nt*; (*of monarch*) Residenz *f* 3. (*for research*) Forschungsaufenthalt *m*; (*for teaching*) Lehraufenthalt *m*

resident [ˈrez·ɪ·dənt] I. *n* Bewohner(in) *m(f)*; **local** ~ Anwohner(in) *m(f)*; **"~s only"** „Anlieger frei" II. *adj* 1. ansässig; (*in-house*) hauseigen 2. (*fears*) tief sitzend

residential [ˌrez·ɪˈden·ʃəl] *adj* Wohn-; ~ **district** Wohngebiet *nt*

residue [ˈrez·ə·du] *n usu sing* Rückstand *m*

resign [rɪˈzaɪn] I. *vi* kündigen; **to ~ from office** von einem Amt zurücktreten II. *vt* 1. aufgeben; (*post*) niederlegen 2. (*accept*) **to ~ oneself to sth** sich mit etw abfinden

resignation [ˌrez·ɪɡˈneɪ·ʃən] *n* (*letter, act*) Kündigung *f*; (*from post*) Rücktritt *m*; (*acceptance*) Resignation *f*

resigned [rɪˈzaɪnd] *adj* resigniert; **to be ~ to sth** sich mit etw *dat* abgefunden haben

resilience [rɪˈzɪl·jəns], **resiliency** [rɪˈzɪl·jən·si] *n* Widerstandskraft *f*

resilient [rɪˈzɪl·jənt] *adj* zäh; (*health*) unverwüstlich

resin [ˈrez·ɪn] *n* Harz *nt*

resist [rɪˈzɪst] I. *vt* 1. (*oppose*) **to ~ sth** etw *dat* Widerstand leisten; **to ~ arrest** LAW sich der Verhaftung widersetzen 2. (*refuse*) **to ~ sth** sich gegen etw *akk* wehren 3. (*temptation*) widerstehen +*dat* II. *vi* sich wehren; (*refuse*) widerstehen

resistance [rɪˈzɪs·təns] *n* Widerstand *m*; (*to illness*) Widerstandskraft *f*; ~ **to a disease** Resistenz *f* gegen eine Krankheit

resistant [rɪˈzɪs·tənt] *adj* resistent

resolute [ˈrez·ə·lut] *adj form* entschlos-

sen; (*belief*) fest

resolution [ˌrez·əˈlu·ʃən] *n* 1. Entschlossenheit *f*; (*decision*) Entscheidung *f*; (*intention*) Vorsatz *m*; **New Year's** ~ gute Vorsätze fürs Neue Jahr 2. (*of image*) Auflösung *f*

resolve [rɪˈzalv] I. *vt* 1. (*differences*) beilegen; **the crisis ~d itself** die Krise legte sich von selbst 2. *form* (*decide*) **to ~ that ...** beschließen, dass ... II. *vi* beschließen; **to ~ to do sth** beschließen, etw zu tun III. *n* Entschlossenheit *f*

resolved [rɪˈzalvd] *adj pred* entschlossen

resonance [ˈrez·ə·nəns] *n* [Nach]hall *m*

resonant [ˈrez·ə·nənt] *adj* [wider]hallend; **to be ~ with sth** von etw *dat* widerhallen

resort [rɪˈzɔrt] I. *n* Urlaubsort *m*; (*recourse*) Einsatz *m*; **as a last** ~ als letzten Ausweg; **you're my last** ~! du bist meine letzte Hoffnung! II. *vi* **to ~ to sth** auf etw *akk* zurückgreifen

resound [rɪˈzaʊnd] *vi* Furore machen; **the rumor ~ed throughout the world** das Gerücht ging um die ganze Welt

resounding [rɪˈzaʊn·dɪŋ] *adj attr* schallend; (*emphatic*) unglaublich; (*success*) durchschlagend

resource [ˈri·sɔrs] *n pl* Ressourcen *pl*; (*wealth*) [finanzielle] Mittel; **natural ~s** Bodenschätze *pl*

resourceful [rɪˈsɔrs·fəl] *adj* einfallsreich

respect [rɪˈspekt] I. *n* Respekt *m*; (*consideration*) Rücksicht *f*; **to have** ~ **for sb** Rücksicht auf jdn nehmen; **to have no** ~ **for sth** etw nicht respektieren; **to pay one's ~s** [**to sb**] jdm einen Besuch abstatten; **to pay one's last ~s to sb** jdm die letzte Ehre erweisen ▶ **in many ~s** in vielen Punkten; **in every** ~ in jeglicher Hinsicht II. *vt* respektieren

respectable [rɪˈspek·tə·bəl] *adj* (*decent*) anständig; (*salary*) ansehnlich; (*deserving respect*) respektabel; (*person*) angesehen

respected [rɪˈspek·təd] *adj* angesehen

respectful [rɪˈspekt·fəl] *adj* respektvoll; **to be ~ of sth** etw respektieren

respective [rɪˈspek·tɪv] *adj attr* jeweilig

respectively [rɪˈspek·tɪv·li] *adv* bezie-

hungsweise

respirator [ˈres·pə·reɪ·tər] n Beatmungsgerät nt; (mask) Atem[schutz]gerät nt

respond [rɪˈspɑnd] I. vt to ~ that ... erwidern, dass ... II. vi antworten; (react) reagieren

response [rɪˈspɑns] n Antwort f; (reaction) Reaktion f; **to meet with a good ~** eine gute Resonanz finden; **in ~ to sth** in Erwiderung auf etw akk

responsibility [rɪˌspɑn·sə·ˈbɪl·ɪ·ti] n Verantwortung f; (duty) Verantwortlichkeit f; **to claim ~ for sth** sich für etw akk verantwortlich erklären; **to carry a lot of ~** eine große Verantwortung tragen

responsible [rɪˈspɑn·sə·bəl] adj verantwortlich; (in charge a.) zuständig; (sensible) verantwortungsbewusst; (job) verantwortungsvoll; **to hold sb ~** jdn verantwortlich machen

responsive [rɪˈspɑn·sɪv] adj gut reagierend; **to be ~ to treatment** auf eine Behandlungsmethode ansprechen

rest[1] [rest] I. n 1. Erholung f; (period) [Ruhe]pause f; **to have a [little] ~** eine [kurze] Pause machen; **for a ~** zur Erholung 2. (support) Stütze f II. vt 1. to ~ one's eyes seine Augen ausruhen 2. (support) lehnen III. vi 1. [aus]ruhen; **to not ~ until ...** [so lange] nicht ruhen, bis ... 2. (be supported) ruhen 3. (depend) ruhen; (be based) beruhen ▶ **[you can] ~ assured [that ...]** seien Sie versichert, dass ...

rest[2] [rest] n + sing/pl vb **the ~** der Rest

restaurant [ˈres·tər·ant] n Restaurant nt

restful [ˈrest·fəl] adj beruhigend; (atmosphere) entspannt; (place) friedlich

'rest home n Altersheim nt

restless [ˈrest·lɪs] adj unruhig; (uneasy) rastlos; (wakeful) ruhelos; (night) schlaflos; **to get ~** anfangen, sich unwohl zu fühlen

restoration [ˌres·tə·ˈreɪ·ʃən] n (act) Restaurieren nt; (instance) Restaurierung f

restore [rɪˈstɔr] vt restaurieren; (re-establish) wiederherstellen; **to ~ sb's faith in sth** jdm sein Vertrauen in etw akk zurückgeben; **to ~ sb to life** jdn ins Leben zurückbringen; **to ~ sb to power** jdn

wieder an die Macht bringen

restrain [rɪˈstreɪn] vt zurückhalten; (forcefully) bändigen; **to ~ sb from [doing] sth** jdn davon abhalten, etw zu tun; **to ~ oneself** sich beherrschen

restrained [rɪˈstreɪnd] adj beherrscht; (criticism) verhalten; (manners) gepflegt

restraint [rɪˈstreɪnt] n Beherrschung f; (restriction) Einschränkung f; **to exercise ~** Zurückhaltung üben

restrict [rɪˈstrɪkt] vt beschränken; (number) begrenzen; **to ~ sb from [doing] sth** jdm etw untersagen

restricted [rɪˈstrɪk·tɪd] adj begrenzt; (space) eng; (subject to limitation) eingeschränkt

restriction [rɪˈstrɪk·ʃən] n Begrenzung f; (act) Einschränken nt; **to lift ~s** Restriktionen aufheben

restrictive [rɪˈstrɪk·tɪv] adj einschränkend; (measures) restriktiv

'restroom n Toilette f

restructure [ˌri·ˈstrʌk·tʃər] vt umstrukturieren

result [rɪˈzʌlt] I. n Folge f; (outcome) Ergebnis nt; (math a.) Resultat nt; (satisfactory) Erfolg m; **to have good ~s with sth** gute Ergebnisse mit etw dat erzielen II. vi resultieren; **to ~ in sth** etw zur Folge haben

resume [rɪˈzum] I. vt wieder aufnehmen; (journey) fortsetzen; **to ~ doing sth** fortfahren, etw zu tun II. vi wieder beginnen; (after short interruption) weitergehen

résumé [ˈrez·u·meɪ] n Lebenslauf m

resumption [rɪˈzʌmp·ʃən] n (act) Wiederaufnahme f; (instance) Wiederbeginn m kein pl

retail [ˈri·teɪl] I. n Einzelhandel m II. vi **this model of computer ~s for 650 dollars** im Einzelhandel kostet dieses Computermodell 650 Dollar

retailer [ˈri·teɪ·lər] n Einzelhändler(in) m(f)

retain [rɪˈteɪn] vt behalten; (attention) halten; (dignity) bewahren; (hold in place) zurückhalten; (not lose) speichern; (thought) behalten; **to ~ control of sth** etw weiterhin in der Gewalt haben; **to ~ the right to do sth** LAW sich

das Recht vorbehalten, etw zu tun

etainer [rɪ'teɪ·nər] n Vorschuss m

etake I. vt <-took, -taken> [ˌriˈteɪk] (regain) wiedergewinnen; (exam) wiederholen; (scene) nochmals drehen **II.** n ['riˈteɪk] Neuaufnahme

etaliate [rɪˈtæl·i·eɪt] vi Vergeltung üben; (for insults) sich revanchieren

etaliation [rɪˌtæl·iˈeɪ·ʃən] n Vergeltung f; (act) Vergeltungsschlag m

etaliatory [rɪˈtæl·i·ə·tɔr·i] adj attr Vergeltungs-

etard ['riˈtɑrd] n pej sl Idiot m pej

etarded [rɪˈtɑr·dɪd] adj pej fam zurückgeblieben

etch [retʃ] vi würgen; **to make sb ~** jdn zum Würgen bringen

ethink I. vt <-thought, -thought> [ˌriˈθɪŋk] überdenken **II.** n ['riˈθɪŋk] Überdenken nt; **to have a ~** etw noch einmal überdenken

etina <pl -s> ['ret·ən·ə] n Netzhaut f

etinue ['ret·ən·u] n Gefolge nt kein pl

etire [rɪˈtaɪr] vi **1.** in den Ruhestand treten; (worker) in Rente gehen; (civil servant) in Pension gehen; (self-employed) sich zur Ruhe setzen; (soldier) aus der Armee ausscheiden; (athlete) seine Karriere beenden **2.** form (withdraw) sich zurückziehen

etired [rɪˈtaɪ·ərd] adj im Ruhestand präd; (worker) in Rente präd; (civil servant) pensioniert

etirement [rɪˈtaɪr·mənt] n Ruhestand m; (act) Ausscheiden nt aus dem Arbeitsleben; (of civil servant) Pensionierung f; (of soldier) Verabschiedung f; (of athlete) Zurücktreten nt

re'tirement plan n Vorsorgeplan m

etiring [rɪˈtaɪ·ər·ɪŋ] adj zurückhaltend

etort [rɪˈtɔrt] **I.** vt **to ~ that ...** scharf erwidern, dass ... **II.** vi scharf antworten **III.** n scharfe Antwort

etouch [ˌriˈtʌtʃ] vt retuschieren

etrace [riˈtreɪs] vt zurückverfolgen; (in mind) [geistig] nachvollziehen; **to ~ one's steps** denselben Weg zurückgehen

etract [rɪˈtrækt] **I.** vt **1.** zurückziehen; (offer) zurücknehmen **2.** (draw back) zurückziehen; (into body) einziehen

II. vi eingezogen werden

retrain [riˈtreɪn] **I.** vt umschulen **II.** vi umgeschult werden

retreat [rɪˈtrit] **I.** vi zurückweichen; (floodwaters) zurückgehen; (withdraw) sich zurückziehen; (hide) sich verstecken; **to ~ into oneself** sich in sich selbst zurückziehen **II.** n Abwendung f; MIL Rückzug m; (place) Zufluchtsort m

retrial ['riˈtraɪl] n LAW Wiederaufnahmeverfahren nt

retribution [ˌret·rəˈbju·ʃən] n form Vergeltung f

retrieval [rɪˈtri·vəl] n Wiedererlangen nt; (rescuing) Rettung f; (of wreckage) Bergung f; **data ~** Datenabruf m; (when lost) Datenrückgewinnung f

retrieve [rɪˈtriv] vt wiederfinden; (fetch) zurückholen; (rescue) retten; (from wreckage) bergen; (data) abrufen

retriever [rɪˈtri·vər] n Retriever m

retro ['ret·roʊ] adj fam (fashion) Retro-

retroactive [ˌret·roʊˈæk·tɪv] adj rückwirkend

retrospect ['ret·rə·spekt] n **in ~** im Rückblick

retrospective [ˌret·rəˈspek·tɪv] **I.** adj rückblickend; (mood) nachdenklich **II.** n Retrospektive f

return [rɪˈtɜrn] **I.** n **1.** Rückkehr f; (of illness) Wiederauftreten nt; **~ home** Heimkehr f **2.** (giving back) Rückgabe f; (stroke) Rückschlag m; (proceeds) Gewinn m; **~ on capital** Rendite f **3.** (key) Returntaste f **II.** adj attr (trip) Rück- **III.** vi **1.** zurückkommen; (illness) wiederkommen; **to ~ home** nach Hause gehen/kommen; (after long absence) heimkehren; **~ to sender** zurück an Absender **2.** (revert) **to ~ to sth** etw wieder aufnehmen; **to ~ to normal** (things) sich wieder normalisieren; (person) wieder zu seinem alten Ich zurückfinden **IV.** vt **1.** zurückgeben; **to ~ sth to its place** etw an seinen Platz zurückstellen **2.** (reciprocate) erwidern; **to ~ a wave** zurückwinken; **to ~ sb's call** jdn zurückrufen **3.** (volley) annehmen

re'turn key n Eingabetaste f

reunification [riˌju·nə·frˈkeɪ·ʃən] n Wiedervereinigung f

R

reunion [ˌriː·ˈjuːn·jən] *n* **1.** Treffen *nt* **2.** *form* (*bringing together*) Wiedervereinigung *f;* (*coming together*) Wiedersehen *nt*

reunite [ˌriː·juː·ˈnaɪt] **I.** *vt* wieder zusammenführen; **to ~ sb with sb** jdn mit jdm [wieder] zusammenbringen **II.** *vi* sich wiedervereinigen; (*people*) wieder zusammenkommen

reusable [ˌriː·ˈjuː·zə·bəl] *adj* wiederverwendbar

reuse [ˌriː·ˈjuːz] *vt* wiederverwenden

rev¹ [rev] *n fam short for* **revolution** Drehzahl *f;* **~s** *pl* Umdrehungen *pl* [pro Minute]

rev² <-vv-> [rev] *vt* auf Touren bringen; (*noisily*) aufheulen lassen

● **rev up I.** *vi* auf Touren kommen; (*noisily*) aufheulen **II.** *vt* auf Touren bringen

Rev. *n abbr of* **Reverend**

revamp [ˌriː·ˈvæmp] *vt fam* aufpeppen; (*room*) aufmöbeln; (*image*) aufpolieren

reveal [rɪ·ˈviːl] *vt* zeigen; (*disclose*) enthüllen; (*secret*) verraten; (*identity*) zu erkennen geben; **to ~ that ...** enthüllen, dass ...; (*admit*) zugeben, dass ...

revealing [rɪ·ˈviː·lɪŋ] *adj* freizügig; (*dress*) gewagt; (*interview*) aufschlussreich

revel <-l-> [ˈrev·əl] *vi* feiern

● **revel in** *vi* **to ~ in sth** seine wahre Freude an etw *dat* haben

revelation [ˌrev·ə·ˈleɪ·ʃən] *n* Enthüllung *f* ▶ **to be [quite] a ~ to sb** jdm die Augen öffnen

revelry [ˈrev·əl·ri] *n* [ausgelassenes] Feiern; *usu pl* (*festivity*) [ausgelassenes] Feier

revenge [rɪ·ˈvendʒ] **I.** *n* Rache *f;* (*desire*) Rachedurst *m;* **to get one's ~** sich rächen; **~ killing** Vergeltungsmord *m* **II.** *vt* rächen

revenue [ˈrev·ə·nu] *n* Einkünfte *pl;* (*of state*) Staatseinkünfte *pl;* **sales ~s** Verkaufseinnahmen *pl;* **tax ~s** Steueraufkommen *nt*

revere [rɪ·ˈvɪr] *vt form* verehren; (*work*) hoch schätzen

reverence [ˈrev·ər·əns] *n* Verehrung *f;* **to treat sth/sb with ~** etw/jdn ehrfürchtig behandeln

reverend [ˈrev·ər·ənd] *n* ≈ Pfarrer *m*

reverent [ˈrev·ər·ənt] *adj* ehrfürchtig; (*be-*

havior) ehrerbietig

reverential [ˌrev·ə·ˈren·ʃəl] *adj form* ehr fürchtig

reversal [rɪ·ˈvɜr·səl] *n* (*effect*) Wende (*situation*) Umkehrung *f;* (*misfortune* Rückschlag *m;* **~ of a trend** Trendwen de *f;* **role ~** Rollentausch *m*

reverse [rɪ·ˈvɜrs] **I.** *vt* umkehren; (*tur over*) umdrehen; (*coat*) wenden; (*car* zurücksetzen **II.** (*car*) rückwärtsfah ren; (*briefly*) zurücksetzen **III.** *n* **1. th ~ das** Gegenteil; **to do sth in ~** etw umgekehrt tun **2.** (*gear*) Rückwärts gang *m;* **to go into ~** in den Rückwärts gang schalten **3.** (*back*) Rückseite *f;* (*coin a.*) Kehrseite *f* **IV.** *adj* umgekehr (*direction*) entgegengesetzt

reversible [rɪ·ˈvɜr·sə·bəl] *adj* zum Wen den *nach n;* (*alterable*) umkehrbar; coat Wendejacke *f*

revert [rɪ·ˈvɜrt] *vi* **to ~ to sth** zu etw *da* zurückkehren; (*bad state*) in etw *ak* zurückfallen; **to ~ to a method** auf ein Methode zurückgreifen

review [rɪ·ˈvju] **I.** *vt* **1.** (*erneut*) [über]prü fen; (*reconsider*) überdenken; (*salaries* revidieren **2.** (*look back over*) zurück blicken auf +*akk;* (*lesson*) wiederholen **let's ~ what has happened so far** füh ren wir uns vor Augen, was bis jetzt pas siert ist **3.** (*criticize*) besprechen; (*book play*) rezensieren **4. to ~ the troop** eine Parade abnehmen **II.** *vi* lerne **III.** *n* **1.** Überprüfung *f;* **to come un der ~** überprüft werden; (*case*) wiede aufgenommen werden **2.** (*summary* Überblick *m;* (*of lesson*) Wiederholung. **month under ~** ECON Berichtsmonat *m* **wage** [*or* **salary**] **~** Gehaltsrevision *f;* **for an exam** Prüfungsvorbereitung **3.** (*of book, play*) Rezension *f;* **movie ~** Filmbesprechung *f*

reviewer [rɪ·ˈvjuː·ər] *n* Kritiker(in) *m(f* (*of plays a.*) Rezensent(in) *m(f)*

revise [rɪ·ˈvaɪz] *vt* umändern; (*manu script*) überarbeiten; (*book*) redigieren (*reconsider*) überdenken; **to ~ sth up wards/downwards** etw nach oben unten korrigieren

revision [rɪ·ˈvɪʒ·ən] *n* (*act*) Überarbei tung *f;* (*version*) Neufassung *f;* (*of book*

überarbeitete Ausgabe; (*alteration*) Änderung *f*

evitalize [riːˈvaɪ.tə.laɪz] *vt* wieder beleben

revival [rɪˈvaɪ.vəl] *n* **1.** Wiederbelebung *f*; (*of idea*) Wiederaufleben *f*; (*of custom a.*) Renaissance *f*; **economic ~** wirtschaftlicher Aufschwung **2.** (*new production*) Neuauflage *f*; (*of film*) Neuverfilmung *f*; (*of play*) Neuaufführung *f*

revive [rɪˈvaɪv] **I.** *vt* wiederbeleben; (*give new energy*) beleben; (*resurrect*) wieder aufleben lassen; (*economy*) ankurbeln; (*idea*) wieder aufgreifen; (*interest*) wiedererwecken; (*spirits*) wieder heben; **to ~ sb's hopes** jdm neue Hoffnungen machen **II.** *vi* (*to consciousness*) wieder zu sich *dat* kommen; (*to health*) sich erholen; (*be resurrected*) sich erholen; (*economy a.*) wieder aufblühen; (*custom*) wieder aufleben; (*confidence*) zurückkehren; (*suspicions*) wieder aufkeimen

revolt [rɪˈvoʊlt] **I.** *vi* rebellieren **II.** *vt* **to ~ sb** jdn abstoßen; **to be ~ed by sth** von etw *dat* angeekelt sein **III.** *n* Revolte *f*; **~ against the government** Regierungsputsch *m*

revolting [rɪˈvoʊl.tɪŋ] *adj* abstoßend; (*person*) widerlich; (*smell*) ekelhaft

revolution [ˌrev.əˈluː.ʃən] *n* Revolution *f*; TECH Umdrehung *f*; **~s per minute** Drehzahl *f*

revolutionary [ˌrev.əˈluː.ʃə.ner.i] **I.** *n* Revolutionär(in) *m(f)* **II.** *adj* revolutionär; *fig* bahnbrechend

revolutionize [ˌrev.əˈluː.ʃə.naɪz] *vt* revolutionieren

revolve [rɪˈvɑlv] *vi* sich drehen; **to ~ on an axis** sich um eine Achse drehen

revolve around *vi* **to ~ around sth** sich um etw *akk* drehen

revolver [rɪˈvɑl.vər] *n* Revolver *m*

revolving [rɪˈvɑl.vɪŋ] *adj attr* rotierend; **~ door** Drehtür *f*

revue [rɪˈvjuː] *n* Revue *f*

reward [rɪˈwɔrd] **I.** *n* Belohnung *f*; (*for service*) Anerkennung *f*; (*finder's fee*) Finderlohn *m* **II.** *vt* belohnen

rewarding [rɪˈwɔr.dɪŋ] *adj* befriedigend; (*experience*) lohnend; (*task*) dankbar

rewind **I.** *vt* <-wound, -wound> [ˌriːˈwaɪnd] aufwickeln; (*cassette*) zurückspulen; (*watch*) aufziehen **II.** *vi* <-wound, -wound> [ˌriːˈwaɪnd] zurückspulen **III.** *adj* [ˈriːwaɪnd] Rückspul-

rewrite <-wrote, -written> **I.** *vt* [ˌriːˈraɪt] neu schreiben; (*revise*) überarbeiten; (*recast*) umschreiben; **to ~ history** *fig* die Geschichte neu schreiben **II.** *n* [ˈriːraɪt] Überarbeitung *f*

rhapsody [ˈræp.sə.di] *n* Rhapsodie *f*

rhetoric [ˈret.ər.ɪk] *n* (*persuasive*) Redegewandtheit *f*; (*bombastic*) Phrasendrescherei *f pej*; **empty ~** leere Worte

rhetorical [rɪˈtɔr.ɪ.kəl] *adj* rhetorisch; (*overdramatic*) übertrieben dramatisch

rheumatic [ruˈmæt.ɪk] *adj* rheumatisch; (*joint a.*) rheumakrank

rheumatism [ˈruː.mə.tɪz.əm] *n* Rheuma *nt*

Rhine [raɪn] *n* GEOG **the ~** der Rhein

rhino [ˈraɪ.noʊ] *n fam short for* **rhinoceros** Nashorn *nt*

rhinoceros <*pl* -es> [raɪˈnɑs.ər.əs] *n* Nashorn *nt*

Rhode Island [ˌroʊdˈaɪ.lənd] *n* Rhode Island *nt*

Rhodes [roʊdz] *n* Rhodos *nt*

rhubarb [ˈruː.bɑrb] *n* Rhabarber *m*

rhyme [raɪm] **I.** *n* Reim *m*; (*poem*) Reim[vers] *m*; (*word*) Reimwort *nt*; **in ~** gereimt **II.** *vi* **to ~** [**with sth**] sich [auf etw *akk*] reimen **III.** *vt* reimen

rhythm [ˈrɪð.əm] *n* Rhythmus *m*

rhythmic(al) [ˈrɪð.mɪk(əl)] *adj* rhythmisch

RI, R.I. *abbr of* **Rhode Island**

rib [rɪb] **I.** *n* Rippe *f*; **~s** (*food*) Rippchen *pl*; **to break a ~** sich *dat* eine Rippe brechen **II.** *vt* <-bb-> *fam* **to ~ sb** jdn aufziehen

ribbon [ˈrɪb.ən] *n* Band *nt*; *fig* Streifen *m*; **in ~s** in Fetzen; **to cut sb/sth to ~s** jdn/etw zerfetzen; *fig* jdn/etw in der Luft zerreißen

rib cage *n* Brustkorb *m*

rice [raɪs] *n* Reis *m*; **brown ~** Naturreis *m*

rich [rɪtʃ] **I.** *adj* reich; (*land*) fruchtbar; (*soil a.*) fett; (*vegetation*) üppig; (*reward*) großzügig; (*food*) gehaltvoll; (*hard to digest*) schwer; (*intense*) satt; (*flavor*)

R

reich; (*smell*) schwer; (*taste*) voll; (*interesting*) reich; (*life a.*) erfüllt; (*history*) bedeutend; **to get ~ quick** schnell zu Reichtum kommen; **~ in detail** sehr detailliert **II. n the ~** *pl* die Reichen

richness ['rɪtʃ·nɪs] *n* Reichtum *m*; (*fattiness*) Reichhaltigkeit *f*; (*intensity*) Stärke *f*; (*of color*) Sattheit *f*; **~ of detail** Detailgenauigkeit *f*

ricksha(w) ['rɪk·ʃa, -ʃɔ] *n* Rikscha *f*

ricochet ['rɪk·ə·ʃeɪ] **I.** *n* (*act*) Abprallen *nt*; (*ball*) Abpraller *m*; (*bullet*) Querschläger *m* **II.** *vi* abprallen

rid <-dd-, rid, rid> [rɪd] *vt* **to ~ sth/sb of sth** etw/jdn von etw *dat* befreien; **to be ~ of sb/sth** jdn/etw los sein; **to get ~ of sb/sth** jdn/etw loswerden

riddance ['rɪd·əns] *n* ▶ **good ~ [to him]**! Gott sei Dank[, dass wir den los sind]!

ridden ['rɪd·ən] *pp of* **ride**

riddle ['rɪd·əl] *n* Rätsel *nt*

ride [raɪd] **I.** *n* **1.** Fahrt *f*; (*on horse*) Ritt *m*; (*carousel*) Karussellfahrt *f*; **to go for a ~** eine Fahrt machen; (*with horse*) ausreiten **2.** (*lift*) Mitfahrgelegenheit *f*; **to give sb a ~** jdn [im Auto] mitnehmen ▶ **to take sb for a ~** *fam* jdn übers Ohr hauen **II.** *vt* <rode, ridden> fahren; (*horse*) reiten; **I ~ my bicycle to work** ich fahre mit dem Fahrrad zur Arbeit; **to ~ the bus/train** Bus/Zug fahren **III.** *vi* <rode, ridden> reiten

rider ['raɪ·dər] *n* Reiter(in) *m(f)*; (*of vehicle*) Fahrer(in) *m(f)*

ridge [rɪdʒ] *n* Grat *m*; (*of roof*) Dachfirst *m*; **~ of high/low pressure** Hoch-/Tiefdruckkeil *m*

ridicule ['rɪd·ɪ·kjul] **I.** *n* Spott *m*; **to hold sth up to ~** sich über etw lustig machen **II.** *vt* verspotten

ridiculous [rɪ·'dɪk·jʊ·ləs] *adj* lächerlich; (*inane*) absurd

rife [raɪf] *adj pred* weit verbreitet; **~ with** voller +*gen*

riffraff ['rɪf·ræf] *n* + *sing/pl vb pej* Gesindel *nt kein pl*

rifle[1] ['raɪ·fəl] *n* Gewehr *nt*

rifle[2] ['raɪ·fəl] **I.** *vi* durchwühlen **II.** *vt* plündern

'rifle range *n* Schießstand *m*

rift [rɪft] *n* Spalt *m*; GEOL [Erd]spalt *m*; *f*, (*disagreement*) Spaltung *f*; (*in friend ship*) Bruch *m*

rig [rɪg] **I.** *n* Vorrichtung *f*; **drilling ~** Bohrinsel *f*; **gas/oil ~** Gas-/Ölbohrin sel *f*; **big ~** [mehrachsiger] Sattelschlep per **II.** *vt* <-gg-> (*boat*) takeln; (*sails* anschlagen *fachspr*; (*shelter*) [behelfs mäßig] zusammenbauen; (*manipulate* manipulieren

rigging ['rɪg·ɪŋ] *n* (*on ship*) Takelung *f* (*manipulation*) Manipulation *f*; **ballot-~** Wahlmanipulation *f*

right [raɪt] **I.** *adj* **1.** (*good*) richtig; (*fair* gerecht; **to do the ~ thing** das Richtige tun; **you're ~ to be annoyed** du bist zu Recht verärgert **2.** (*exact*) genau; **to get sth ~** etw richtig machen; **you were ~ about him** was ihn angeht, haben Sie Recht gehabt; **to be just ~** *fam* genau das Richtige sein **3. ~?** oder? **4.** (*best* richtig; **he's the ~ person for the job** er ist der Richtige für den Job; **to be in the ~ place at the ~ time** zur rechter Zeit am rechten Ort sein **5.** *pred* (*functioning*) in Ordnung; **is your watch ~?** geht deine Uhr richtig? **6.** (*not left* rechte(r, s); **to make a ~ turn** rechts abbiegen **II.** *adv* **1.** (*completely*) völlig; **she walked ~ past me** sie lief direkt an mir vorbei; **to be ~ behind sb** voll [und ganz] hinter jdm stehen **2.** (*all the way*) ganz; (*directly*) direkt **3.** (*well* gut; **things have been going ~ for me** es läuft gut für mich **4.** (*not left*) rechts; **to turn ~** [nach] rechts abbiegen **III.** *n* **1.** (*goodness*) Recht *nt* **2.** (*morally correct*) das Richtige; **the ~s and wrongs of sth** das Für und Wider einer S. *gen* **3.** (*claim*) Recht *nt*; **~ of** [*or* **to**] **free speech** Recht *nt* auf freie Meinungsäußerung; **women's ~s** die Rechte *p* der Frau[en] **4.** (*right side*) rechte Seite; **on the ~** rechts; **on my/her ~** rechts [von mir/ihr] **5.** POL **the R~** die Rechte; **the far ~** die Rechtsextremen *pl* **IV.** *vt* **1.** (*correct position*) aufrichten; (*correct condition*) in Ordnung bringen **2.** (*rectify*) wiedergutmachen **V.** *interj fam* **1.** (*okay*) in Ordnung; **~ you are!** in Ordnung! **2.** (*as introduction*) **~, let's**

go also, nichts wie los *fam*

'right away *adv* sofort; **we have to leave ~ away** wir müssen unverzüglich aufbrechen

rightful ['raɪt-fəl] *adj attr* rechtmäßig

'right-hand *adj attr* rechte(r, s); (*with right hand*) mit der Rechten *nach n;* ~ **punch** rechter Haken

right-hand 'man *n* **sb's** ~ jds rechte Hand

rightly ['raɪt-li] *adv* richtig; (*justifiably*) zu Recht

right-'minded *adj* vernünftig

'right of 'way <*pl* rights of way> *n* Durchgangsrecht *nt;* (*on road*) Vorfahrt *f*

right-'wing *adj* rechts *präd,* rechte(r, s)

rigid ['rɪdʒ-ɪd] *adj* steif; (*unalterable*) starr; (*stringent*) streng

rigidity [rɪ-'dʒɪd-ɪ-ti] *n* Steifheit *f; pej* (*intransigence*) Starrheit *f*

rigmarole ['rɪg-mə-roʊl] *n usu sing pej* Gelabere *nt pej;* (*procedures*) Prozedur *f*

rigor ['rɪg-ər] *n* Genauigkeit *f;* (*strictness*) Strenge *f*

rigor mortis [ˌrɪg-ər-'mɔr-tɪs] *n* Leichenstarre *f*

rigorous ['rɪg-ər-əs] *adj* peinlich genau; (*disciplined*) strikt; (*demanding*) hart

rile [raɪl] *vt fam* ärgern; **to get sb ~d** jdn verärgern

rim [rɪm] *n* Rand *m;* (*of wheel*) Felge *f;* **on the Pacific R~** am Rande des Pazifiks **2.** *usu pl* (*of spectacles*) Fassung *f* II. *vt* <-mm-> umgeben; (*frame*) umrahmen

rind [raɪnd] *n* Schale *f;* [grated] **lemon ~** [geriebene] Zitronenschale

ring¹ [rɪŋ] I. *n* Ring *m;* (*of people, things*) Kreis *m;* (*clique*) Kartell *nt;* **spy ~** Spionagering *m* II. *vt usu passive* umringen

ring² [rɪŋ] I. *n* **1.** Klingeln *nt;* (*sound*) Klirren *nt;* **your name has a familiar ~** Ihr Name kommt mir bekannt vor **2.** *usu sing* (*phone call*) **to give sb a ~** jdn anrufen II. *vi* <rang, rung> (*phone*) klingeln; (*ears*) klingen; **the room rang with laughter** der Raum war von Lachen erfüllt III. *vt* <rang, rung> läuten

♦**ring out** *vi* ertönen

'ring binder *n* Ringbuch *nt*

ringer ['rɪŋ-ər] *n* ► **to be a** dead ~ **for sb** jdm aufs Haar gleichen

'ring finger *n* Ringfinger *m*

ringing ['rɪŋ-ɪŋ] I. *adj attr* schallend; ~ **cheer** lauter Jubel II. *n* Klingeln *nt*

'ringleader *n* Anführer(in) *m(f)*

ringlet ['rɪŋ-lɪt] *n usu pl* Locke *f*

rink [rɪŋk] *n* Bahn *f;* **ice** ~ Eisbahn *f*

rinse [rɪns] I. *n* Spülung *f;* (*for mouth*) Mundspülung *f;* (*conditioner*) [Haar]spülung *f;* (*for tinting hair*) Tönung *f* II. *vt* spülen; (*hands*) abspülen; (*mouth*) ausspülen III. *vi* spülen

riot ['raɪ-ət] I. *n* **1.** Krawall *m;* (*uproar*) Aufstand *m;* **a** ~ **of color**(s) eine Farbenpracht **2. to run** ~ (*people*) Amok laufen; (*emotions*) verrückt spielen; **my imagination ran** ~ die Fantasie ist mit mir durchgegangen II. *vi* randalieren; *fig* wild feiern

rioter ['raɪ-ə-tər] *n* Aufständische(r) *f(m)*

rioting ['raɪ-ə-tɪŋ] *n* Randalieren *nt*

rip [rɪp] I. *n* **1.** (*tear*) Riss *m* **2.** *usu sing* (*act*) Zerreißen *nt;* (*with knife*) Zerschlitzen *nt* II. *vt* <-pp-> zerreißen; **to ~ sth to shreds** etw zerfetzen; **to ~ sth open** etw aufreißen; (*with knife*) etw aufschlitzen III. *vi* <-pp-> reißen; (*seams*) platzen

♦**rip off** *vt fam* (*steal*) mitgehen lassen; (*ideas*) klauen; **to ~ off ⇆ sb** (*overcharge*) jdn übers Ohr hauen

♦**rip out** *vt* herausreißen

♦**rip up** *vt* zerreißen; (*carpet*) herausreißen

RIP [ˌar-aɪ-'pi] *abbr of* rest in peace R.I.P.

ripe [raɪp] *adj* reif; (*matured*) ausgereift; (*intense*) beißend; **to be** ~ **for sth** reif für etw *akk* sein; **to live to a** ~ **old age** ein hohes Alter erreichen

ripen ['raɪ-pən] *vi* [heran]reifen

ripeness ['raɪp-nɪs] *n* Reife *f*

'rip-off *n fam* Wucher *m;* (*fraud*) Schwindel *m;* **that's just a** ~ **of my idea!** da hat doch bloß einer meine Idee geklaut! *fam*

ripple ['rɪp-əl] I. *n* leichte Welle *f;* (*feeling*) Schauer *m;* (*sound*) Raunen *nt;* (*reac-*

R

tion) Wirkung *f;* **a ~ of laughter** ein leises Lachen **II.** *vi* (*water*) sich kräuseln; (*stream*) plätschern; (*grain*) wogen; **his muscles ~d under his skin** man sah das Spiel seiner Muskeln [unter der Haut] **III.** *vt* (*water*) kräuseln; (*muscles*) spielen lassen

rip-'roaring *adj attr fam* sagenhaft

rise [raɪz] **I.** *n* **1.** Hochgehen *nt;* (*of sun*) Aufgehen *nt;* (*in society*) Aufstieg *m;* **~ to power** Aufstieg *m* an die Macht **2.** (*height*) Höhe *f;* (*hill*) Anhöhe *f* **3.** (*increase*) Anstieg *m* **II.** *vi* <rose, risen> **1.** steigen; (*curtain*) aufgehen; (*sun*) aufgehen; (*from chair*) sich erheben; (*voice*) höher werden; (*become louder*) lauter werden; (*wind*) aufkommen; (*ground*) ansteigen; (*improve status*) aufsteigen; **to ~ to fame** berühmt werden; **to ~ against sb/sth** sich gegen jdn/etw auflehnen **2.** (*increase*) [an] steigen; (*river, prices*) steigen; (*dough*) aufgehen; (*temper*) sich erhitzen ▸ **to ~ to the bait** anbeißen; **~ and shine!** los, raus aus den Federn!

♦ **rise above** *vi* **to ~ above sth** (*tower*) sich über etw *dat* erheben; (*person*) über etw *akk* stehen; **to ~ above difficulties** Schwierigkeiten überwinden

♦ **rise up** *vi* (*mutiny*) sich auflehnen; (*be visible*) aufragen

risen ['rɪz·ən] *pp of* **rise**

rising ['raɪ·zɪŋ] *adj attr* (*politician*) aufstrebend; (*floodwaters*) steigend; (*sun*) aufgehend; (*costs*) steigend; (*wind*) aufkommend; (*fury*) wachsend; (*ground*) [auf]steigend

risk [rɪsk] **I.** *n* Risiko *nt;* **health ~** Gesundheitsrisiko *nt;* **to take a ~** ein Risiko eingehen **II.** *vt* riskieren; **to ~ life and limb** Leib und Leben riskieren

risky ['rɪs·ki] *adj* riskant

rite [raɪt] *n usu pl* Ritus *m;* **last ~s** Sterbesakramente *pl*

ritual ['rɪtʃ·u·əl] **I.** *n* Ritual *nt* **II.** *adj attr* rituell

rival ['raɪ·vəl] **I.** *n* Rivale(in) *m(f);* ECON Konkurrent *m;* **arch ~** Erzrivale(in) *m(f);* **bitter ~s** scharfe Rivalen; **~ team** gegnerische Mannschaft **II.** *vt* <-l-> konkurrieren

rivalry ['raɪ·vəl·ri] *n* Rivalität *f;* ECON Konkurrenz *f;* **friendly ~** freundschaftlicher Wettstreit

river ['rɪv·ər] *n* Fluss *m;* **down/up ~** stromab-/aufwärts

'river bed *n* Flussbett *nt*

'riverside *n* [Fluss]ufer *nt*

rivet ['rɪv·ɪt] **I.** *n* Niete *f* **II.** *vt* **to ~ sth** [**together**] etw [zusammen]nieten; (*fig*) **to be ~ed to the spot** *fig* wie angewurzelt stehen bleiben

riveting ['rɪv·ɪ·tɪŋ] *adj fam* fesselnd

RN [ˌɑr·'en] *n abbr of* **registered nurse** examinierte Krankenschwester; (*male*) examinierter Krankenpfleger

roach <*pl* -es> [routʃ] *n fam* Küchenschabe *f;* sl (*butt*) eingedrehter Pappfilter

road [roʊd] *n* Straße *f; fig* Weg *m;* **busy ~** stark befahrene Straße; **side ~** Nebenstraße *f;* **on the ~ to recovery** auf dem Wege der Besserung

'roadblock *n* Straßensperre *f*

'road hog *n pej fam* Verkehrsrowdy *m*

'roadhouse *n* Raststätte *f*

roadie ['roʊ·di] *n fam* Roadie *m*

'roadkill *n* totgefahrenes Tier; (*action*) Überfahren *nt* eines Tiers

'road map *n* Straßenkarte *f*

'road rage *n* aggressives Verhalten im Straßenverkehr

'roadside **I.** *n* Straßenrand *m* **II.** *adj* Straßen-; (*café*) am Straßenrand gelegen

'road sign *n* Verkehrsschild *nt*

'road-test *vt* Probe fahren

'roadway *n* Fahrbahn *f*

'roadwork *n* Straßenbauarbeiten *pl*

roam [roʊm] **I.** *vi* **1. to ~ around/over/ through** umherstreifen **2.** (*thoughts*) abschweifen **II.** *vt* **to ~ the streets** durch die Straßen ziehen *fam;* (*dog*) herumstreunen

'roaming *n* Roaming *nt* (*per Handy Auslandsgespräche führen*)

roar [rɔr] **I.** *n* Brüllen *nt;* (*of cannon*) Donnern *nt;* (*of engine*) [Auf]heulen *nt,* (*of fire*) Prasseln *nt;* (*of thunder*) Grollen *nt;* (*of waves*) Tosen *nt;* (*laughter*) schallendes Gelächter **II.** *vi* brüllen; (*cannon*) donnern; (*engine*) [auf]heulen; (*fire*) prasseln; (*thunder*) grollen

(waves) tosen; (wind) heulen; **to ~ with laughter** in schallendes Gelächter ausbrechen; **to ~ at sb** jdn anbrüllen

oast [rəʊst] **I.** vt rösten; (meat) braten; **to ~ sb** mit jdm hart ins Gericht gehen **II.** vi braten; fig [vor Hitze] umkommen fam **III.** adj attr Brat-; **~ beef** Rinderbraten m; **~ chicken** Brathähnchen nt **IV.** n (process) Rösten nt; (of coffee) Röstung f

oasting ['rəʊstɪŋ] adj fam knallheiß

ob <-bb-> [rɑb] vt **1.** (person) bestehlen; (violently) rauben +dat; (bank) ausrauben **2.** usu passive fam (overcharge) ausnehmen **3.** (deprive) **to ~ sb of sth** jdn um etw akk bringen

obber ['rɑb·ər] n Räuber(in) m(f)

obbery ['rɑb·ə·ri] n Raubüberfall m; (theft a.) Raub m; **bank ~** Bankraub m

obe [rəʊb] n usu pl (formal) Talar m; (bathrobe) Morgenmantel m

obot ['rəʊ·bɑt] n Roboter m

obotics [rəʊ·'bɑt·ɪks] n + sing vb Robotik f kein pl

obust [rəʊ·'bʌst] adj kräftig; (appetite) gesund; (sturdy) widerstandsfähig; (view) bodenständig; (food) deftig; (wine) kernig

obustness [rəʊ·'bʌst·nɪs] n Widerstandsfähigkeit f; (determination) Entschlossenheit f

ock¹ [rɑk] n Stein m; GEOL Gestein nt; fam (diamond) Klunker m; (boulder) Felsbrocken m; (embedded) Fels[en] m; (in sea) Riff nt; fig Fels m in der Brandung ► **on the ~s** zum einen Ende; (marriage) kaputt fam; (drink) mit Eis

ock² [rɑk] **I.** n Rockmusik f; (sway) Schaukeln nt **II.** vt schaukeln; (gently) wiegen; (quake) erschüttern **III.** vi schaukeln; (dance) rocken fam; (play music) Rock[musik] spielen; **he really ~s!** fam ist er ein Supertyp!

ock-and-'roll n see **rock 'n' roll**

ock 'bottom n Tiefpunkt m; **to be at ~** am Tiefpunkt [angelangt] sein; (person a.) am Boden zerstört sein

ocker ['rɑk·ər] n (chair) Schaukelstuhl m; (of cradle) [Wiegen]kufe; (musician) Rockmusiker(in) m(f); (fan) Rockfan m ► **to be off one's ~** übergeschnappt sein

rocket ['rɑk·ɪt] **I.** n (Marsch]flugkörper m; (for space travel) Rakete f; (firework) [Feuerwerks]rakete f **II.** vi **to ~ [up]** hochschnellen; **to ~ to fame** über Nacht berühmt werden

Rockies ['rɑk·iz] n **the ~** die Rocky Mountains pl

'rocking chair n Schaukelstuhl m

'rocking horse n Schaukelpferd nt

'rock music n Rockmusik f

rock 'n' 'roll n Rock and Roll m

'rock salt n Steinsalz nt

'rock star n Rockstar m

rocky ['rɑk·i] adj felsig; (soil) steinig; (difficult) schwierig; (future) unsicher

Rocky 'Mountains n **the ~** die Rocky Mountains pl

rod [rɑd] n Stange f; (for punishing) Rute f; (cane) Rohrstock m; (for fishing) [Angel]rute f ► **to rule sb/sth with a ~ of iron** jdn/etw mit eiserner Hand regieren

rode [rəʊd] pt of **ride**

rodent ['rəʊ·dənt] n Nagetier nt

rodeo ['rəʊ·di·oʊ] n Rodeo nt

roger ['rɑdʒ·ər] interj ~! verstanden!

rogue [rəʊg] **I.** n Gauner(in) m(f); (rascal) Spitzbube m **II.** adj skrupellos; **~ state** Schurkenstaat m

role [rəʊl] n Rolle f; (function a.) Funktion f; **supporting ~** Nebenrolle f

'role model n Rollenbild nt

'role play, 'role playing n Rollenspiel nt

roll [rəʊl] **I.** n **1.** Rolle f; (of cloth) Ballen m **2.** (list) [Namens]liste f; (register) Verzeichnis nt **3.** (bread) Brötchen nt **4.** (movement) Rollen nt; (overturn) Herumrollen nt; (wallowing) Herumwälzen nt; (of ship) Schlingern nt **5.** usu sing (of thunder) [G]rollen nt kein pl; **drum ~** Trommelwirbel m ► **to be on a ~** fam eine Glückssträhne haben **II.** vt **1.** rollen; (eyes) verdrehen; (turn over) drehen; **to ~ one's car** sich mit dem Auto überschlagen **2. to ~ sth into sth** etw zu etw dat rollen; **he ~ed the clay into a ball** er formte den Ton zu einer Kugel **3.** (wind) aufrollen; (cigarette) drehen; (wrap) **to ~ sth in sth** etw in etw akk einwickeln **4.** (flatten) walzen; (pastry) ausrollen **III.** vi rol-

len; (*overturn*) sich herumrollen; (*wallow*) sich [herum]wälzen; (*flow*) rollen; (*tears*) kullern; (*ship*) schlingern; (*person*) schwanken; (*undulate*) wallen; (*thunder*) [g]rollen; (*operate*) laufen; **to keep sth ~ing** etw in Gang halten; **to ~ by** (*elapse*) vorbeiziehen

◆roll back *vt* zurückrollen; (*push back*) zurückschieben; (*fold back*) zurückschlagen; (*lower*) senken; *fig* (*advances*) umkehren; **to ~ back the years** die Uhr zurückdrehen *fig*

◆roll down I. *vt* hinunterrollen; (*bring down*) herunterrollen; (*window*) herunterkurbeln II. *vi* hinunterrollen; (*come down*) herunterrollen; (*tears a.*) herunterlaufen

◆roll in I. *vi* hineinrollen; (*come in*) hereinrollen; *fam* (*offers*) [massenhaft] eingehen; (*money*) reinkommen *fam;* *fam* (*arrive*) hereinplatzen *fam* ▸ **to be ~ing in money** *fam* im Geld schwimmen II. *vt* herein-/hineinrollen

◆roll on *vi* weitergehen; (*time*) verfliegen

◆roll out I. *vt* hinaus-/herausrollen; (*dough*) ausrollen; (*metal*) auswalzen; (*product*) herausbringen II. *vi* (*product*) herauskommen

◆roll over I. *vi* herumrollen; (*dog, bather*) sich umdrehen; (*car*) umkippen; (*boat*) kentern; **to ~ onto one's side** sich auf die Seite rollen II. *vt* umdrehen

◆roll up I. *vt* hochrollen; (*sleeves*) hochkrempeln; (*window*) hochkurbeln; (*coil*) aufrollen; (*string*) aufwickeln II. *vi* hochrollen; *fam* (*arrive*) aufkreuzen

'roll call *n* Namensaufruf *m kein pl*

roller ['rou·lər] *n* Rolle *f;* (*for hair*) Lockenwickler *m;* TECH Walze *f*

'Rollerblade® I. *n* Rollerblade® *m* II. *vi* inlineskaten

'roller coaster *n* Achterbahn *f*

'roller skate *n* Rollschuh *m*

'roller-skate *vi* Rollschuh laufen

'roller skater *n* Rollschuhläufer(in) *m(f)*

rolling ['rou·lɪŋ] *adj attr* (*hills*) sanft ansteigend; (*gait*) [sch]wankend

'rolling pin *n* Nudelholz *nt*

'roll-on *n* Deoroller *m*

roly-poly [ˌrou·li·'pou·li] *adj hum fam* rundlich; (*baby*) moppelig *fam;* (*child*) pummelig

ROM [rɑm] *n abbr of* **Read Only Memory** ROM *m o nt*

Roman ['rou·mən] I. *adj* römisch II. *n* Römer(in) *m(f)*

Roman 'Catholic I. *adj* römisch-katholisch II. *n* Katholik(in) *m(f)*

romance [rou·'mæns] *n* Romantik *f;* (*love*) romantische Liebe; (*affair*) Romanze *f;* (*movie*) Liebesfilm *m;* (*book*) Liebesroman *m*

Romania [rou·'meɪ·ni·ə] *n* Rumänien *n*

Romanian [rou·'meɪ·ni·ən] I. *adj* rumänisch II. *n* Rumäne(in) *m(f);* (*language*) Rumänisch *nt*

romantic [rou·'mæn·tɪk] I. *adj* romantisch II. *n* Romantiker(in) *m(f)*

Rome [roum] *n* Rom *nt*

romp [rɑmp] I. *vi* tollen II. *n* Tollerei *f;* (*book*) Klamauk *m*

roof [ruf] *n* Dach *nt;* (*attic*) Dachboden *m;* (*ceiling*) Decke *f;* (*of mouth*) Gaumen *m*

'roof rack *n* Dachgepäckträger *m*

'rooftop *n* Dach *nt*

rook [rʊk] *n* CHESS Turm *m*

rookie ['rʊk·i] *n fam* Neuling *m;* MIL Rekrut(in) *m(f)*

room [rum] I. *n* Zimmer *nt;* (*space*) Platz *m;* (*scope a.*) Raum *m;* **the whole ~ laughed** alle, die im Zimmer waren, lachten; **double ~** Doppelzimmer *nt;* **~ for maneuver** Bewegungsspielraum *m* II. *vi* wohnen; **to ~ with sb** mit jdm zusammen wohnen

'rooming house *n* Pension *f*

'roommate *n* (*in room*) Zimmergenosse(in) *m(f);* (*in apartment*) Mitbewohner(in) *m(f)*

'room service *n* Zimmerservice *m*

room 'temperature *n* Zimmertemperatur *f*

roomy ['ru·mi] *adj* geräumig

roost [rust] I. *n* Rastplatz *m;* (*for sleep*) Schlafplatz *m* II. *vi* rasten

rooster ['ru·stər] *n* Hahn *m*

root¹ [rut] *n* Wurzel *f;* (*of potato*) Knolle *f;* (*of tulip*) Zwiebel *f;* *fig* (*origin*) Wurzel *f;* (*essential*) Kern *m;* MATH Wurzel *f;* **t**

take ~ Wurzeln schlagen; **square** ~ Quadratwurzel *f*

root² [rʊt] *vi fam* **to** ~ **for a team** eine Mannschaft anfeuern

root around *vi fam* herumwühlen

root out *vt* (*weeds*) ausgraben; (*evil*) ausrotten; (*find*) aufstöbern

root beer *n* eine Art Limonade aus verschiedenen Pflanzenextrakten

root vegetable *n* Wurzelgemüse *nt*; (*potato*) Knolle *f*

rope [roʊp] **I.** *n* Seil *nt*; NAUT Tau *nt*; (*lasso*) Lasso *nt* **II.** *vt* anseilen; **to** ~ **calves** Kälber mit dem Lasso [ein]fangen

rope in *vt fam* einspannen

rope off *vt* **to** ~ **off** ⇆ **an area** ein Gebiet [mit Seilen/einem Seil] absperren

rope ladder *n* Strickleiter *f*

rosary ['roʊ·zə·ri] *n* Rosenkranz *m*

rose¹ [roʊz] **I.** *n* Rose *f*; (*bush*) Rosenbusch *m*; (*tree*) Rosenbäumchen *nt*; (*color*) Rosa *nt* **II.** *adj* rosa

rose² [roʊz] *pt of* **rise**

rosebud *n* Rosenknospe *f*

rosebush *n* Rosenstrauch *m*

rose hip *n* Hagebutte *f*

rosemary ['roʊz·mer·i] *n* Rosmarin *m*

roster ['ras·tər] *n* Liste *f*; (*plan*) Plan *m*; **duty** ~ Dienstplan *m*

rostrum <*pl* -s> ['ras·trəm] *n* Tribüne *f*

rosy ['roʊ·zi] *adj* rosig

rot [rat] **I.** *n* (*process*) Fäulnis *f*; (*matter*) Verfaultes *nt*; BOT Fäule *f* **II.** *vi* <-tt-> verrotten; (*teeth, meat*) verfaulen; (*woodwork*) vermodern; (*deteriorate*) verkommen

rot away *vi* verfaulen

rotary ['roʊ·tə·ri] *n see* **traffic circle**

rotate ['roʊ·teɪt] **I.** *vi* rotieren; (*alternate*) wechseln **II.** *vt* drehen; (*troops*) auswechseln; (*crops*) im Fruchtwechsel anbauen; **to** ~ **duties** Aufgaben turnusmäßig [abwechselnd] verteilen

rotation [roʊ·'teɪ·ʃən] *n* Umdrehung *f*; **crop** ~ Fruchtwechsel *m*; **in** ~ im Wechsel

rote [roʊt] *n* **by** ~ auswendig

rotor ['roʊ·tər] *n* Rotor *m*

rotten ['rat·ən] *I. adj* verfault; (*fruit*) verdorben; (*tooth*) faul; (*wood*) modrig; (*corrupt*) korrupt; *fam* (*bad*) mies; (*joke*) gemein; (*cook*) hundsmiserabel

II. *adv fam* total *fam*; **spoiled** ~ (*child*) völlig verzogen

rouble ['ru·bəl] *n see* **ruble**

rouge [ruʒ] *n* Rouge *nt*

rough [rʌf] **I.** *adj* rau; (*ground*) uneben; (*landscape*) unwirtlich; (*fur*) struppig; (*hard*) hart; (*wine*) sauer; *fam* (*difficult*) schwer; (*makeshift*) primitiv; (*unrefined*) ungehobelt; (*imprecise*) grob; **to give sb a** ~ **time** jdm das Leben ganz schön schwer machen; **a** ~ **idea** eine ungefähre Vorstellung **II.** *n* (*in golf*) **the** ~ das Rough *fachspr* **III.** *vt fam* **to** ~ **it** [ganz] primitiv leben

roughage ['rʌf·ɪdʒ] *n* Ballaststoffe *pl*; (*fodder*) Raufutter *nt*

'rough-and-tumble *adj attr* ~ **atmosphere** raue Atmosphäre

rough 'draft *n* Rohfassung *f*; (*sketch*) Entwurf *m*

roughen ['rʌf·ən] **I.** *vt* aufrauen **II.** *vi* rau werden; (*society*) verrohen; (*weather*) stürmisch werden

'roughhouse *vi* Radau machen *fam*; (*fight*) sich prügeln; (*playfully*) sich raufen

roughly ['rʌf·li] *adv* grob; ~ **sketched** skizzenhaft; ~ **speaking** ganz allgemein gesagt; ~ **the same** ungefähr gleich

'roughneck *n fam* Rohling *m*; (*rig worker*) Bohrarbeiter(in) *m(f)*

roughness ['rʌf·nɪs] *n* Rauheit *f*; (*of ground*) Unebenheit *f*; (*of game*) Härte *f*

'roughshod *adv* **to ride** ~ **over sb** *fig* jdn unterdrücken

roulette [ru·'let] *n* Roulette *nt*

round [raʊnd] **I.** *adj* <-er, -est> rund; (*face*) rundlich; (*vowel*) gerundet **II.** *n* (*of drinks*) Runde *f*; (*series*) Folge *f*; SPORT Runde *f*; (*routine*) Trott *m*; ~ **of talks** Gesprächsrunde *f*; ~ **of applause** Beifall *m*; ~ **of ammunition** Ladung *f* **III.** *vt* **to** ~ **the corner** um die Ecke biegen

round down *vt* abrunden

round off *vt* abrunden

round up *vt* (*sum*) aufrunden; (*people*) zusammentrommeln *fam*; (*things*) zusammentragen; (*cattle*) zusammentreiben; (*support*) holen

roundabout ['raʊnd·ə·baʊt] *adj* umständlich; **to take a** ~ **route** einen Um-

R

weg machen; **to ask sb in a ~ way** jdn durch die Blumen fragen

rounded ['raʊn·dɪd] *adj* rund; (*edges*) abgerundet

roundly ['raʊnd·li] *adv form* gründlich; (*criticize*) heftig; (*defeat*) haushoch

round 'robin *n* Wettkampf, in dem jeder gegen jeden antritt

round'table *adj attr* **~ discussion** Gespräch *nt* am runden Tisch

'round-the-clock *adj* rund um die Uhr nach *n*

round 'trip I. *n* Rundreise *f* **II.** *adv* **to fly ~** ein Rückflugticket haben

round-trip 'ticket *n* Hin- und Rückfahrkarte *f*; AVIAT Hin- und Rückflugticket *nt*

'roundup *n* Versammlung *f*; (*of suspects*) Festnahme *f*; (*of cattle*) Zusammentreiben *nt*; (*summary*) Zusammenfassung *f*

rouse [raʊz] *vt* wecken; **to ~ sb to action** jdn zum Handeln bewegen

rousing ['raʊ·zɪŋ] *adj* mitreißend; (*cheer*) stürmisch

route [raʊt] *n* Strecke *f*; (*of parade*) Verlauf *m*; (*delivery path*) Runde *f*; (*bus number*) Linie *f*; **the ~ to success** der Weg zum Erfolg; **to have a paper ~** Zeitungen austragen

Route 66 *n* berühmte Straße von Chicago nach Los Angeles

routine [ru·'tin] **I.** *n* Routine *f*; (*dancing*) Figur *f*; (*gymnastics*) Übung *f*; COMPUT Programm *nt* **II.** *adj* routinemäßig; (*performance a.*) durchschnittlich; **~ inspection** Routineuntersuchung *f*; **to become ~** zur Gewohnheit werden

row¹ [roʊ] *n* Reihe *f*; **in ~s** reihenweise; **in a ~** (*in succession*) hintereinander

row² [roʊ] *vt, vi* rudern

row³ [raʊ] **I.** *n* Streit *m* **II.** *vi fam* streiten

rowboat ['roʊ·boʊt] *n* Ruderboot *nt*

rowdy ['raʊ·di] *adj* rüpelhaft; (*party*) wild

'row house *n* Reihenhaus *nt*

rowing ['roʊ·ɪŋ] *n* Rudern *nt*

royal ['rɔɪ·əl] **I.** *adj* <-er, -est> königlich; *fig* fürstlich **II.** *n fm* Angehörige(r) *f(m)* der königlichen Familie

royalty ['rɔɪ·əl·ti] *n* **1.** + *sing/pl vb*

Königshaus *nt*; **to treat sb like ~** jdn fürstlich behandeln **2.** PUBL **royalties** *pl* Tantiemen *pl*

rpm <*pl* -> [,ar·pi·'em] *n abbr of* **revolutions per minute** U/min

RR [,ar·'ar] *n abbr of* **railroad**

RSVP [,ar·es·vi·'pi] *abbr of* **répondez s'il vous plaît** u. A. w. g.

rub [rʌb] **I.** *n* Reiben *nt*; **to give sth a ~** (*hair*) etw trocken rubbeln; (*material*) etw polieren **II.** *vt* <-bb-> einreiben; (*polish*) polieren; **to ~ one's hands together** sich *dat* die Hände reiben **III.** *vi* <-bb-> reiben; (*shoes*) scheuern

♦ **rub down** *vt* abreiben; (*child*) abfrottieren

♦ **rub in** *vt* einreiben; **to ~ it in** *fam* etw *dat* herumreiten ▸ **don't keep on ~bing my nose in it!** hör auf, es mir unter die Nase zu reiben!

♦ **rub off I.** *vi* wegreiben; (*stains*) rausgehen; **sth ~s off on sb** *fam* etw färbt auf jdn ab **II.** *vt* wegwischen

♦ **rub out I.** *vt* ausradieren; **to ~ out ⇆ sb** *sl* jdn abmurksen *sl* **II.** *vi* herausgehen; (*erase*) sich ausradieren lassen

rubber ['rʌb·ər] *n* Gummi *m o nt*; *sl* (*condom*) Gummi *m*; **~s** *pl* (*shoes*) Überschuhe *pl* (*aus Gummi*)

rubber 'band *n* Gummiband *nt*

rubber 'boot *n* Gummistiefel *m*

rubber 'check *n sl* ungedeckter Scheck

rubberneck ['rʌb·ər·nek] *sl* **I.** *n see* **rubbernecker II.** *vi* gaffen *fam*

rubbernecker ['rʌb·ər·nek·ər] *n sl* Gaffer(in) *m(f) pej fam*

'rubber plant *n* Gummibaum *m*

'rubber stamp *n* Stempel *m*; *fig* Genehmigung *f*

rubber-'stamp *vt* genehmigen; (*decision*) bestätigen

'rubber tree *n* Kautschukbaum *m*

rubbery ['rʌb·ə·ri] *adj* gummiartig; (*meat*) zäh; (*legs*) wackelig

rubbish ['rʌb·ɪʃ] *n* Müll *m*; *fam* (*nonsense*) Quatsch *m*; *fam* (*junk*) Gerümpel *nt*

rubble ['rʌb·əl] *n* Trümmer *pl*; (*for building*) Bauschutt *m*; **to reduce sth to ~** etw in Schutt und Asche legen

rubella [ru·'bel·ə] *n* Röteln *pl*

uble, rouble ['ru·bəl] n Rubel m

uby ['ru·bi] I. n Rubin m II. adj Rubin-; (color) rubinrot

ucksack ['rʌk·sæk] n Rucksack m

uckus ['rʌk·əs] n fam Krawall m

udder ['rʌd·ər] n [Steuer]ruder nt

ude [rud] adj unhöflich; (behavior) unverschämt; (gesture) ordinär; (joke) unanständig; (surprise) böse

udimentary [ˌru·də·'men·tə·ri] adj elementar; (primitive) primitiv; (method) einfach

udiments ['ru·də·mənts] npl **the ~** die Grundlagen pl

uffian ['rʌf·i·ən] n Schlingel m

uffle ['rʌf·əl] vt durcheinanderbringen; (hair) zerzausen; (upset) aus der Ruhe bringen ▸ **to ~ sb's feathers** jdn auf die Palme bringen fam

ug [rʌg] n Teppich m; sl (wig) Haarteil nt

ugby ['rʌg·bi] n Rugby nt

ugged ['rʌg·ɪd] adj uneben; (cliff) zerklüftet; (coast) wild; (robust) kräftig; (looks) markant; (vehicle) robust; (solid) fest; (honesty) unerschütterlich

uin ['ru·ɪn] I. vt zerstören; (dress, name) ruinieren; (hopes) zunichtemachen; **to ~ sb's day** jdm den Tag vermiesen; **to ~ sb's chances** jdm die Suppe versalzen II. n Ruine f; (bankruptcy) Ruin m; **~s** pl (of building) Ruinen pl; (of reputation) Reste pl; (of hopes) Trümmer pl; **to be in ~s** eine Ruine sein; (after fire) in Schutt und Asche liegen; fig zerstört sein

uinous ['ru·ə·nəs] adj ruinös

ule [rul] I. n 1. (instruction) Regel f; **~s and regulations** Regeln und Bestimmungen; **to be against the ~s** gegen die Regeln verstoßen 2. (control) Herrschaft f; **the ~ of law** die Rechtsstaatlichkeit ▸ **as a** [general] **~** in der Regel II. vt 1. (govern) regieren 2. (control) beherrschen 3. (draw) ziehen III. vi herrschen; (sovereign a.) regieren

rule out vt ausschließen

rule book n Vorschriftenbuch nt

ruler ['ru·lər] n Herrscher(in) m(f); (device) Lineal nt

ruling ['ru·lɪŋ] I. adj attr (governing)

herrschend; (primary) hauptsächlich; (passion) größte(r, s) II. n Entscheidung f

rum [rʌm] n Rum m

Rumania [roʊ·'meɪ·ni·ə] see **Romania**

rumble ['rʌm·bəl] I. n Grollen nt; (of stomach) Knurren nt; fam Schlägerei f II. vi rumpeln; (stomach) knurren; (thunder) grollen

rumbling ['rʌm·bəl·ɪŋ] I. n Grollen nt; (of distant guns) Donnern nt; **~s** pl (indications) [erste] Anzeichen pl II. adj grollend attr

rummage ['rʌm·ɪdʒ] vi **to ~ through sth** etw durchstöbern

rummage sale n Flohmarkt m

rummy ['rʌm·i] n CARDS Rommé nt

rumor ['ru·mər] I. n Gerücht nt II. vt passive **the president is ~ed to be seriously ill** der Präsident soll angeblich ernsthaft krank sein; **it is ~ed that ...** es wird gemunkelt, dass ...

rump [rʌmp] n 1. (of animal) Hinterbacken pl 2. (beef) Rumpsteak nt 3. hum (buttocks) Hinterteil nt fam

rumpus ['rʌm·pəs] n fam Krawall m

run [rʌn] I. n 1. Lauf m; **to go for a ~** laufen gehen 2. (course) Strecke f 3. (period) Dauer f; **~ of good luck** Glückssträhne f 4. (enclosure) Gehege nt 5. SPORT (in baseball) Run m 6. (in stocking) Laufmasche f 7. fam **the ~s** pl (diarrhea) Dünnpfiff m fam ▸ **in the long ~** auf lange Sicht gesehen; **in the short ~** kurzfristig II. vi <ran, run> 1. laufen; **to ~ for** schnell in Deckung gehen; **to ~ for one's life** um sein Leben rennen 2. (operate) fahren; (engine) laufen; (machine) in Betrieb sein; **work is ~ning smoothly at the moment** die Arbeit geht im Moment glatt von der Hand 3. (travel) laufen; (lead) verlaufen; (ski) gleiten; **the route ~s through the mountains** die Strecke führt durch die Berge 4. (last) [an]dauern; **the film ~s for two hours** der Film dauert zwei Stunden 5. (flow) fließen; **my nose is ~ning** meine Nase läuft; **the river ~s** [down] **to the sea** der Fluss mündet in das Meer 6. (candidate) kandidieren; **to ~ for President** für das

Präsidentenamt kandidieren **7.** (*fray*) eine Laufmasche bekommen ▸ **to ~ in the family** in der Familie liegen; **to ~ low** [langsam] ausgehen **III.** *vt* <ran, run> **1.** (*pass*) **he ran a vacuum cleaner over the carpet** er saugte den Teppich ab; **to ~ one's fingers through one's hair** sich *dat* mit den Fingern durchs Haar fahren **2.** (*machine*) bedienen; (*program, engine*) laufen lassen **3.** (*manage*) leiten; (*farm*) betreiben; (*government, household*) führen; **don't tell me how to ~ my life!** erklär mir nicht, wie ich mein Leben leben soll! **4.** (*conduct*) anbieten; (*test*) durchführen **5.** (*water*) laufen lassen; (*bath*) einlaufen lassen **6. to ~ a red light** *fam* eine rote Ampel überfahren ▸ **to ~ the show** verantwortlich sein

◆ **run across** *vi* zufällig treffen; **to ~ across a problem** auf ein Problem stoßen

◆ **run after** *vi* hinterherlaufen

◆ **run along** *vi fam* ~**!** troll dich!

◆ **run around** *vi* herumlaufen; (*bustle*) herumrennen *fam*; **to ~ around with sb** sich mit jdm herumtreiben *fam*

◆ **run away** *vi* weglaufen; (*liquid*) abfließen; **to ~ away from sb** (*wife*) jdn verlassen

◆ **run down I.** *vt* überfahren; (*boat*) rammen; (*reduce*) reduzieren; (*production*) drosseln; (*supplies*) einschränken; *fam* (*belittle*) runtermachen **II.** *vi* (*battery*) leer werden; (*become reduced*) reduziert werden

◆ **run into** *vi* hineinrennen; **he ran into a tree on his motorcycle** er fuhr mit seinem Motorrad gegen einen Baum; **to ~ into sb** (*bump into*) jdm über den Weg laufen; **to ~ into difficulties** auf Schwierigkeiten stoßen

◆ **run off I.** *vi* abhauen; (*drain*) ablaufen **II.** *vt* **he quickly ran off some copies** er machte schnell ein paar Kopien

◆ **run on** *vi* **1. the game ran on for too long** das Spiel zog sich zu lange hin **2. to ~ on sth** mit etw *dat* betrieben werden

◆ **run out** *vi* ausgehen; (*expire*) auslaufen; **the milk has ~ out** die Milch ist alle

◆ **run over I.** *vt* überfahren **II.** *vi* (*bath*) überlaufen; (*review*) durchgehen

◆ **run through** *vi* (*examine*) durchgehe **(**(*practice*) durchspielen

◆ **run up I.** *vt* (*debt*) machen; (*costume* nähen **II.** *vi* **to ~ up against problem** auf Probleme stoßen

'**runaround** *n fig* **to give sb the ~** jd **(** keine klare Auskunft geben

'**runaway I.** *adj attr* (*out of control*) auße **(** Kontrolle geraten; (*prices*) galoppierend **(** (*prisoner*) entlaufen; (*horse*) durchge **(** gangen **II.** *n* Ausreißer(in) *m(f) fam*

'**rundown I.** *n* zusammenfassender Be **(** richt **II.** *adj* verwahrlost; (*building* **(** baufällig; (*worn out*) abgespannt

rung[1] [rʌŋ] *n* Sprosse *f; fig* Stufe *f*

rung[2] [rʌŋ] *pp of* **ring**

'**run-in** *n fam* Krach *m*

runner ['rʌn·ər] *n* Läufer(in) *m(f);* (*horse* **(** Rennpferd *nt;* (*messenger*) Bote(in) *m(* **(**

runner-'up *n* Zweite(r); **to be the ~** de **(** zweiten Platz belegen

running ['rʌn·ɪŋ] **I.** *n* **1.** Laufen *N* **(** **2.** (*management*) Leitung *f;* (*of ma* **(** *chine*) Bedienung *f* ▸ **to be out of th** **(** ~ nicht mehr im Rennen sein **II.** *a* **(** **1.** *after n* (*in a row*) nacheinander *nac* **(** *n* **2.** (*ongoing*) [fort]laufend **3.** (*opera* **(** *ing*) betriebsbereit

runny ['rʌn·i] *adj* (*nose*) laufend *att* **(** (*jam*) dünnflüssig

run-of-the-'mill *adj* durchschnittlich

runt [rʌnt] *n* zurückgebliebenes Jungtie **(** *pej sl* (*person*) Wicht *m; little ~* Würn **(** chen *nt*, kleines Ding

'**run-through** *n* THEAT Durchlaufprobe **(** (*examination*) Durchgehen *nt*

'**run-up** *n* Anlauf *m* [zum Absprung]; *fi* **(** (*prelude*) Vorlauf *m*

'**runway** *n* Start- und Landebahn *f;* (*ca* **(** *walk*) Laufsteg *m*

rupture ['rʌp·tʃər] **I.** *vi* zerreißen; (*ap* **(** *pendix*) durchbrechen; (*artery*) platze **(** **II.** *vt* zerreißen; **to ~ a blood ves** **(** **sel** ein Blutgefäß zum Platzen bringe **(** **III.** *n* Zerreißen *nt;* (*of artery*) Platzen *n* **(** (*hernia*) Bruch *m;* (*torn muscle*) [Mus **(** kel]riss *m*

rural ['rʊr·əl] *adj* ländlich

ruse [ruz] *n* List *f*

rush¹ [rʌʃ] **I.** n **1.** Eile f; **to be in a ~** in Eile sein **2.** (rapid movement) Ansturm m; (press) Gedränge nt **3.** (surge) Schwall m; (of emotions) Anfall m **II.** vi **1.** eilen; **stop ~ing!** hör auf zu hetzen!; **to ~ in** hineinstürmen; (water) hineinschießen; **to ~ out** hinausstürzen; (water) herausschießen; **to ~ toward sb** auf jdn zueilen **2. to ~ into sth** (decision) etw überstürzen **III.** vt **1. she was ~ed to the hospital** sie wurde auf schnellstem Weg ins Krankenhaus gebracht **2.** (pressure) **to ~ sb [into sth]** jdn [zu etw dat] treiben; **don't ~ me!** dräng mich nicht! **3. let's not ~ things** lass uns nichts überstürzen

rush² [rʌʃ] n BOT Binse f

rush hour n Hauptverkehrszeit f

rush order n Eilauftrag m

Russia ['rʌʃ·ə] n Russland nt

Russian ['rʌʃ·ən] **I.** adj russisch **II.** n Russe(in) m(f); (language) Russisch nt

rust [rʌst] **I.** n Rost m; (color) Rostbraun nt **II.** vi rosten; **to ~ away/ through** ver-/durchrosten

rustic ['rʌs·tɪk] adj rustikal; (simple) grob [zusammen]gezimmert; fig schlicht

rustle ['rʌs·əl] **I.** vi rascheln; (silk) rauschen **II.** vt **1. to ~ paper** mit Papier rascheln **2.** (cattle) stehlen **III.** n Rascheln nt; (of silk) Knistern nt

rustler ['rʌs·lər] n Viehdieb(in) m(f)

rustproof adj rostbeständig; **~ paint** Rostschutzfarbe f

rusty ['rʌs·ti] adj rostig; fig eingerostet; **my Russian is a little ~** ich bin mit meinem Russisch etwas aus der Übung

rut [rʌt] n Furche f; fig Trott m

ruthless ['ruθ·lɪs] adj skrupellos; (measure) hart; (dictatorship) erbarmungslos

ruthlessness ['ruθ·lɪs·nɪs] n Unbarmherzigkeit f; (of behavior) Rücksichtslosigkeit f; (of action) Skrupellosigkeit f

RV [ar·'vi] n abbr of **recreational vehicle**

rye [raɪ] n Roggen m; **~ [whiskey]** Roggenwhiskey m

S

S <pl -'s>, **s** <pl -'s> [es] n S nt, s nt; **~ as in Sierra** S wie Siegfried

S [es] n adj **1.** abbr of **south, southern** S **2.** abbr of **small** S

s <pl -> abbr of **second** Sek.

Sabbath ['sæb·əθ] n Sabbat m

saber ['seɪ·bər] n Säbel m

sable ['seɪ·bəl] n Zobel m; (fur) Zobelpelz m

sabotage ['sæb·ə·taʒ] **I.** vt sabotieren; (plans) zunichtemachen **II.** n Sabotage f

saccharin ['sæk·ər·ɪn] n Süßstoff m

sachet [sæ·'ʃeɪ] n Päckchen nt

sack¹ [sæk] **I.** n Sack m; **~ of potatoes** Sack m Kartoffeln **II.** vt rausschmeißen fam

sack² [sæk] vt plündern

sackful n Sack m kein pl

sacrament ['sæk·rə·mənt] n Sakrament nt

sacred ['seɪ·krɪd] adj heilig; (tradition) geheiligt

sacrifice ['sæk·rə·faɪs] **I.** vt opfern; (give up a.) aufgeben **II.** vi **to ~ to the gods** den Göttern Opfer bringen **III.** n Opfer nt; **at great personal ~** unter großem persönlichen Verzicht; **to make ~s** Opfer bringen

sacrilege ['sæk·rə·lɪdʒ] n Sakrileg nt geh; fig Verbrechen nt

sad <-dd-> [sæd] adj traurig; (regrettable a.) bedauerlich; (incident) betrüblich; (pathetic) bedauernswert; **to look ~** betrübt aussehen; **to make sb ~** jdn traurig machen; **~ to say** bedauerlicherweise

sadden ['sæd·ən] vt traurig machen; (distress) schwer treffen

saddle ['sæd·əl] **I.** n Sattel m; **to be in the ~** im Sattel sein; fig (in charge) im Amt sein **II.** vt satteln; **to be ~d with sth** fam etw akk am Hals haben; **to ~ sb with sth** fam jdm etw akk anhalsen

sadism ['seɪ·dɪz·əm] n Sadismus m

sadist ['seɪ·dɪst] n Sadist(in) m(f)

sadistic [sə·'dɪs·tɪk] adj sadistisch

sadly ['sæd·li] adv traurig; (regrettably) leider; (fully) völlig

sadness ['sæd·nɪs] n Traurigkeit f

safari [sə·'far·i] *n* Safari *f*

safe [seɪf] **I.** *adj* sicher; (*certain*) [relativ] sicher; (*driver*) vorsichtig; [**have a**] ~ **trip!** gute Reise!; **to keep sth in a** ~ **place** etw sicher aufbewahren ▸ **to be in** ~ **hands** in guten Händen sein; **to play it** ~ auf Nummer Sicher gehen *fam* **II.** *n* Tresor *m*

safe-de'posit box *n* Tresorfach *nt*

safe'keeping *n* **to be in sb's** ~ in jds Gewahrsam sein; **to give sth to sb for** ~ jdm etw in Verwahrung geben

safely ['seɪf·li] *adv* sicher; (*avoiding risk*) vorsichtig; (*without harm: person*) wohlbehalten; (*object*) heil

safe 'sex *n* Safer Sex *m*

safety ['seɪf·ti] *n* Sicherheit *f*; (*of medicine*) Unbedenklichkeit *f*

'safety belt *n* Sicherheitsgurt *m*

'safety catch *n* Sicherung *f*

'safety measures *npl* Sicherheitsmaßnahmen *pl*

'safety pin *n* Sicherheitsnadel *f*

'safety regulations *npl* Sicherheitsvorschriften *pl*

saffron ['sæf·rən] **I.** *n* Safran *m* **II.** *adj* safrangelb

sag [sæg] **I.** *vi* <-gg-> [herab]hängen; (*bed, rope*) durchhängen; (*courage*) sinken **II.** *n* Durchhängen *nt*

saga ['sa·gə] *n* Saga *f*; (*novel*) Familienroman *m*; *pej* [lange] Geschichte

sage [seɪdʒ] *n* Salbei *m*

Sagittarius [,sædʒ·ə·'ter·i·əs] *n* ASTROL Schütze *m*

said [sed] *pt, pp of* **say**

sail [seɪl] **I.** *n* Segel *nt*; (*of windmill*) Flügel *m*; (*journey*) [Segel]törn *m* ▸ **to set** ~ in See stechen **II.** *vi* (*by ship*) reisen; (*by yacht*) segeln; **the ball ~ed over the fence** der Ball segelte über den Zaun; **she ~ed into the room** sie kam ins Zimmer gerauscht ▸ **to** ~ **close to the wind** sich hart an der Grenze des Erlaubten bewegen **III.** *vt* (*ship*) steuern; (*yacht*) segeln; **to** ~ **the Pacific** den Pazifik befahren

'sailboard *n* Surfbrett *nt*

'sailboat *n* Segelboot *nt*

sailing ['seɪ·lɪŋ] *n* Segeln *nt*; (*sport*) Segelsport *m*

sailor ['seɪ·lər] *n* Matrose *m*; (*on sailing boat*) Segler(in) *m(f)*

saint [seɪnt, sənt] *n* Heilige(r) *f(m)*; **to make sb a** ~ jdn heiligsprechen; **S- Peter** der heilige Petrus; **to be no** ~ *hum* nicht gerade ein Heiliger/eine Heilige sein

saintly ['seɪnt·li] *adj* heilig

Saint Patrick's Day *n* der 17. März, an dem die irische Gemeinschaft in den USA ihren heiligen Schutzpatron feiert

'saint's day *n* Heiligenfest *nt*

sake [seɪk] *n* **for the** ~ **of sth** um einer S. *gen* willen; **for sb's** ~ jdm zuliebe ▸ **for goodness'** [*or* **heaven's**] ~ um Gottes [*or* Himmels] willen

salad ['sæl·əd] *n* Salat *m*

salami [sə·'la·mi] *n* Salami *f*

salary ['sæl·ə·ri] *n* Gehalt *nt*; (*wage packet*) Lohntüte *f*

sale [seɪl] *n* **1.** Verkauf *m*; (*amount sold*) Absatz *m*; **for** ~ zu verkaufen; **to be on** ~ erhältlich sein **2.** (*at cut prices*) Ausverkauf *m*; (*auction*) Auktion *f*; **to be on** ~ im Angebot sein

'sales clerk *n* Verkäufer(in) *m(f)*

'salesman *n* Verkäufer *m*; **door-to-door** ~ Hausierer *m*

'salesperson *n* Verkäufer(in) *m(f)*

'sales tax *n* Umsatzsteuer *f*

'saleswoman *n* Verkäuferin *f*

saliva [sə·'laɪ·və] *n* Speichel *m*

salmon ['sæm·ən] *n* <*pl* -> Lachs *m*

salmonella [,sæl·mə·'nel·ə] *n* Salmonelle[n] *f[pl]*

saloon [sə·'lun] *n dated* Saloon *m*

salt [sɔlt] **I.** *n* Salz *nt*; **a pinch of** ~ eine Prise Salz ▸ **to take sth with a pinch of** ~ etw mit Vorsicht genießen *fam* **II.** *vt* salzen

'salt flats *npl* Salzwüste *f*

salt 'lake *n* Salzsee *m*

'salt shaker *n* Salzstreuer *m*

'salt water *n* Salzwasser *nt*

salty ['sɔl·ti] *adj* salzig

salutation [,sæl·jə·'ter·ʃən] *n* Anrede *f*, *liter* (*greeting*) Gruß *m*

salute [sə·'lut] **I.** *vt* **1.** *form* grüßen; (*welcome*) begrüßen **2.** MIL **to** ~ **sb** vor jdm salutieren **II.** *vi* MIL salutieren **III.** *n* Gruß *m*; MIL Salut *m*; (*of guns*)

Salut[schuss] *m*; **to give a ~** salutieren

salvage ['sæl·vɪdʒ] *vt* (*cargo*) bergen; (*reputation*) wahren

salvation [sæl·'ver·ʃən] *n* Rettung *f*; REL Erlösung *f*

Salvation 'Army *n* Heilsarmee *f*

Samaritan [sə·'mer·ɪ·tən] *n* REL **the good ~** der barmherzige Samariter

same [seɪm] **I.** *adj attr* **1.** (*similar*) **the ~ ...** der/die/das gleiche ...; (*identical*) der-/die-/dasselbe; **she's the ~ age as me** sie ist genauso alt wie ich **2.** (*not another*) **the ~ ...** der/die/das gleiche ...; **at the ~ time** gleichzeitig; (*nevertheless*) trotzdem ▶ **to be in the ~ boat** [**as sb**] im gleichen Boot wie jd sitzen **II.** *pron* **the ~** der-/die-/dasselbe; **things will never be the ~ again** nichts wird mehr so sein wie früher; **to be one and the ~** ein und der-/die-/dasselbe sein ▶ **all the ~** trotzdem **III.** *adv* **I feel just the ~** [**as you do**] mir geht es genauso [wie dir]

sample ['sæm·pəl] **I.** *n* Probe *f*; (*of fabric*) Muster *nt*; (*for test*) Stichprobe *f*; **blood ~** Blutprobe *f* **II.** *vt* [aus]probieren; (*food*) kosten

sampler ['sæm·plər] *n* Probeset *nt*

sanction ['sæŋk·ʃən] **I.** *n* Strafmaßnahme *f*; POL Sanktion *f* **II.** *vt* unter Strafe stellen

sanctuary ['sæŋk·tʃu·er·i] *n* Heiligtum *nt*; (*refuge*) Zuflucht *f*; (*for animals*) Schutzgebiet *nt*

sand [sænd] **I.** *n* Sand *m*; **~s** *pl* (*beach*) Sandstrand *m*; (*of desert*) Sand *m* kein *pl* **II.** *vt* [ab]schmirgeln

sandal ['sæn·dəl] *n* Sandale *f*

'sandalwood *n* Sandelholz *nt*

'sandbag I. *n* Sandsack *m* **II.** *vt* <-gg-> mit Sandsäcken schützen; *fig* niederschlagen

'sandbox *n* Sandkasten *m*

'sandcastle *n* Sandburg *f*

'sand dune *n* Sanddüne *f*

'sandpaper I. *n* Schmirgelpapier *nt* **II.** *vt* abschmirgeln

'sandstone *n* Sandstein *m*

'sandstorm *n* Sandsturm *m*

sandwich ['sænd·wɪtʃ] **I.** *n* <*pl* -es> Sandwich *m o nt* ▶ **to be one ~ short of a**

picnic *hum fam* völlig übergeschnappt sein **II.** *vt* einklemmen; **to ~ sth** [**in**] **between sth** *fig* etw zwischen etw *dat* dazwischenschieben

'sandwich board *n* Reklametafel *f* (*mittels verbindendem Schulterriemen von einer Person auf Brust und Rücken als doppelseitiges Werbeplakat getragen*)

sandy ['sæn·di] *adj* sandig; (*color*) sandfarben

sane [seɪn] *adj* geistig gesund; LAW zurechnungsfähig; (*action*) vernünftig

sang [sæŋ] *pt of* **sing**

sanitary ['sæn·ɪ·ter·i] *adj* hygienisch; (*installations*) sanitär

'sanitary napkin *n* Damenbinde *f*

sanitation [sæn·ɪ·'ter·ʃən] *n* Hygiene *f*; (*toilets*) sanitäre Anlagen; (*water disposal*) Abwasserkanalisation *f*

sanity ['sæn·ɪ·ţi] *n* gesunder Verstand; LAW Zurechnungsfähigkeit *f*; (*sensibleness*) Vernünftigkeit *f*; *hum* Verstand *m fam*

sank [sæŋk] *pt of* **sink**

Santa, Santa Claus [sæn·tə·'klɔz] *n* der Weihnachtsmann

sap¹ [sæp] *n* **1.** (*of tree*) Saft *m* **2.** *sl* (*dope*) Trottel *m fam*

sap² [sæp] *vt* <-pp-> **to ~ sb's energy** an jds Energie *gen* zehren

sapling ['sæp·lɪŋ] *n* junger Baum

sapphire ['sæf·aɪr] *n* Saphir *m*

Saran® Wrap, Saran® wrap [sə·'ræn-] *n* Frischhaltefolie *f*

sarcasm ['sar·kæz·əm] *n* Sarkasmus *m*

sarcastic [sar·'kæs·tɪk] *adj* sarkastisch; (*tongue*) scharf

sardine [sar·'din] *n* Sardine *f*; **packed like ~s** wie die Ölsardinen zusammengepfercht

Sardinia [sar·'dɪn·i·ə] *n* Sardinien *nt*

sari ['sa·ri] *n* Sari *m*

SARS, Sars [sarz] *n* MED *acr for* **severe acute respiratory syndrome** SARS *kein art*

SASE [es·eɪ·es·'i] *n abbr of* **self-addressed stamped envelope** adressierter und frankierter Rückumschlag

sash¹ <*pl* -es> [sæʃ] *n* Schärpe *f*

sash² <*pl* -es> [sæʃ] *n* (*in windows*) Fensterrahmen *m*; (*in doors*) Türrahmen *m*

sat [sæt] *pt, pp of* **sit**

Satan ['seɪ·tən] *n* Satan *m*

satchel ['sætʃ·əl] *n* [Schul]ranzen *m*

satellite ['sæt·ə·laɪt] *n* Satellit *m;* (ASTRON *a.*) Trabant *m*

'**satellite dish** *n* Satellitenschüssel *f fam*

satin ['sæt·ən] *n* Satin *m*

satire ['sæt·aɪr] *n* Satire *f*

satirical [sə·'tɪr·ɪ·kəl] *adj* satirisch; (*mocking*) ironisch

satirist ['sæt·ər·ɪst] *n* Satiriker(in) *m(f)*

satirize ['sæt·ə·raɪz] *vt* satirisch darstellen

satisfaction [ˌsæt·ɪs·'fæk·ʃən] *n* Zufriedenheit *f;* (*sth producing satisfaction*) Genugtuung *f geh;* **to sb's ~** zu jds Zufriedenheit; **to my great ~** zu meiner großen Genugtuung

satisfactory [ˌsæt·ɪs·'fæk·tə·ri] I. *adj* befriedigend II. *n* Ausreichend *nt kein pl* (*Mindestnote für das Bestehen einer Prüfung*)

satisfy <-ie-> ['sæt·ɪs·faɪ] *vt* zufrieden stellen; (*need*) befriedigen; (*condition*) erfüllen; **to ~ sb that ...** jdn überzeugen, dass ...

satisfying ['sæt·ɪs·faɪ·ɪŋ] *adj* zufrieden stellend

saturate ['sætʃ·ə·reɪt] *vt* durchnässen; (*fill*) [völlig] auslasten; CHEM sättigen

saturated ['sætʃ·ə·reɪ·t̬ɪd] *adj* durchnässt; (*soil*) aufgeweicht; CHEM gesättigt

saturation [ˌsætʃ·ə·'reɪ·ʃən] *n* CHEM Sättigung *f;* **~ point** Sättigungspunkt *m*

Saturday ['sæt·ər·deɪ] *n* Samstag *m; see also* **Tuesday**

Saturn ['sæt·ərn] *n* Saturn *m*

sauce [sɔs] I. *n* 1. Soße *f;* **tomato ~** Tomatensoße *f;* **apple ~** Apfelmus *nt* 2. *pej sl* (*alcohol*) Alkohol *m* II. *vt fam* **to ~ sth up** etw würzen

'**saucepan** *n* Kochtopf *m*

saucer ['sɔ·sər] *n* Untertasse *f*

Saudi ['sau·di] I. *n* (*male*) Saudi[-Araber] *m;* (*female*) Saudi-Araberin *f* II. *adj* saudisch

Saudi A'rabia *n* Saudi-Arabien *nt*

Saudi A'rabian I. *n* Saudi-Araber(in) *m(f)* II. *adj* saudi-arabisch

sauerkraut ['sau·ər·kraut] *n* Sauerkraut *nt*

sauna ['sɔ·nə] *n* Sauna *f*

saunter ['sɔn·tər] *vi* bummeln *fam;* (*amble*) schlendern; **to ~ along** herumschlendern

sausage ['sɔ·sɪdʒ] *n* Wurst *f;* (*small*) Würstchen *nt;* (*type*) Wurstsorte *f*

sauté [sɔ·'teɪ] *vt* <sautéed *or* sautéd> [kurz] [an]braten

savage ['sæv·ɪdʒ] I. *adj* wild; (*fierce*) brutal II. *n usu pej* Wilde(r) *f(m) pej,* (*barbarian*) Barbar(in) *m(f)* III. *vt* anfallen; *fig* attackieren

savagery ['sæv·ɪdʒ·ri] *n* Brutalität *f*

savanna(h) [sə·'væn·ə] *n* Savanne *f*

save [seɪv] I. *vt* 1. retten; **to ~ sb's life** jds Leben retten 2. (*retain*) aufheben; (*money*) sparen 3. (*collect*) sammeln 4. (*time, energy*) sparen 5. COMPUT speichern 6. (*goal*) verhindern; (*penalty*) abwehren ▶ **a stitch in time ~s nine** *prov* was du heute kannst besorgen, das verschiebe nicht auf morgen *prov* II. *vi* 1. (*money*) sparen; **to ~ with a bank** ein Sparkonto bei einer Bank haben 2. **to ~ on sth** bei etw *dat* sparen III. *n* Abwehr *f*

saving ['seɪ·vɪŋ] *n* 1. **~s** *pl* Ersparnisse *pl* 2. (*act*) Einsparung *f;* (*result*) Ersparnis *f*

savings account ['seɪ·vɪŋz·ə·ˌkaunt] *n* Sparkonto *nt*

'**savings bank** *n* Sparkasse, *die nicht auf* Profitbasis arbeitet und auch für kleine Einlagen Zinsen bietet

savior ['seɪv·jər] *n* Retter(in) *m(f);* **the S~** REL der Erlöser

savor ['seɪ·vər] I. *n* Geschmack *m* II. *vt* auskosten

savory ['seɪ·və·ri] *adj* pikant; (*salty*) salzig, (*appetizing*) appetitanregend

savvy ['sæv·i] *fam* I. *adj* ausgebufft *sl* II. *n* Köpfchen *nt;* (*practical*) Können *nt*

saw[1] [sɔ] I. *n* Säge *f* II. *vt* <-ed, -ed *or* sawn> [zer]sägen; **to ~ a tree down** einen Baum fällen III. *vi* sägen

saw[2] [sɔ] *pt of* **see**

'**sawdust** *n* Sägemehl *nt*

'**sawmill** *n* Sägemühle *f*

sawn [sɔn] *pp of* **saw**

Saxony ['sæk·sə·ni] *n* Sachsen *nt*

saxophone ['sæk·sə·foun] *n* Saxophon *n...*

saxophonist ['sæk·sə·fou·nɪst] n Saxophonist(in) m(f)

say [seɪ] I. vt <said, said> 1. sagen; **to ~ sth to sb** jdm etw sagen (**about** über +akk); **to ~ goodbye to sb** sich von jdm verabschieden; **to have nothing to ~** nichts zu sagen haben; **to ~ nothing of the cost** ganz zu schweigen von den Kosten; **it goes without ~ing that ...** es versteht sich von selbst, dass ... 2. (recite) aufsagen; (prayer) sprechen 3. (show) sagen; **the sign ~s ...** auf dem Schild steht ...; **it ~s on the bottle ...** auf der Flasche heißt es ...; **my watch ~s 3 o'clock** auf meiner Uhr ist es 3 [Uhr]; **the way he drives ~s a lot about his character** sein Fahrstil sagt eine Menge über seinen Charakter aus 4. (instruct) **she said to call her back** sie sagte, du sollst sie zurückrufen; **to ~ whether/where etc.** sagen, ob/wo usw.; **~ when!** sag stopp! ▶ **~ no more!** fam alles klar!; **you don't ~!** was du nicht sagst!; **you said it!** fam du sagst es! II. vi <said, said> sagen; **where was he going? — he didn't ~** wo wollte er hin? – das hat er nicht gesagt; **hard to ~** schwer zu sagen; **that's not for me to ~** es steht mir nicht zu, das zu entscheiden III. n Meinung f; **to have a/no ~ in sth** bei etw dat ein/kein Mitspracherecht haben IV. interj 1. fam (doubting) **~s who?** wer sagt das? 2. (approving) **~, that's a great idea!** Mensch, das ist ja eine tolle Idee! fam

saying ['seɪ·ɪŋ] n Sprichwort nt

'say-so n fam Erlaubnis f

SC, S.C. abbr of **South Carolina**

scab [skæb] n 1. Kruste f 2. pej fam (strikebreaker) Streikbrecher(in) m(f)

scabby ['skæb·i] adj schorfig; pej fam schäbig

scabies ['skeɪ·biz] n Krätze f

scaffold ['skæf·əld] n [Bau]gerüst nt; hist (for executions) Schafott nt

scaffolding ['skæf·əl·dɪŋ] n [Bau]gerüst nt

scald [skɔld] I. vt verbrühen; (cook) erhitzen; (fruit) dünsten; (milk) abkochen II. n Verbrühung f

scalding ['skɔl·dɪŋ] adj kochend; **~ hot**

kochend heiß

scale¹ [skeɪl] I. n Schuppe f II. vt (fish) [ab]schuppen

scale² [skeɪl] I. n 1. Skala f; (of map) Maßstab m; **to ~** maßstab[s]getreu 2. (extent) Umfang m; **on a national ~** auf nationaler Ebene; **on a large/small ~** im großen/kleinen Rahmen 3. MUS Tonleiter f II. vt (besteigen); **to ~ a wall** auf eine Mauer klettern

◆ **scale down** I. vt reduzieren; (production) einschränken II. vi verkleinern

◆ **scale up** vt erweitern; (production) erhöhen

scale³ [skeɪl] n usu pl Waage f; **to tip the ~s** fig den [entscheidenden] Ausschlag geben

scallop ['skal·əp] n Kammmuschel f; (served) Jakobsmuschel f; **veal ~** Schnitzel nt

scalp [skælp] I. n Kopfhaut f II. vt skalpieren; pej (tickets) unter der Hand verkaufen

scalpel ['skæl·pəl] n Skalpell nt

scalper ['skæl·pər] n pej Schwarzhändler(in) m(f) (für Eintrittskarten)

scaly ['skeɪ·li] adj schuppig; (kettle) verkalkt

scam [skæm] n fam Betrug m

scamper ['skæm·pər] vi flitzen fam

scan [skæn] I. vt <-nn-> absuchen; (glance) überfliegen; COMPUT einscannen II. n Abtastung f; (med a.) Scan m; (glance) [flüchtige] Durchsicht

scandal ['skæn·dəl] n Skandal m; (disgrace a.) Schande f; (gossip) Skandalgeschichten pl

scandalize ['skæn·də·laɪz] vt schockieren; (offend) empören

scandalous ['skæn·də·ləs] adv skandalös; (shocking) schockierend

Scandinavia [ˌskæn·dɪˈneɪ·vi·ə] n Skandinavien nt

Scandinavian [ˌskæn·dɪˈneɪ·vi·ən] I. adj skandinavisch II. n Skandinavier(in) m(f)

scanner ['skæn·ər] n Scanner m

scant [skænt] adj attr gering, dürftig

scanty ['skæn·ti] adj knapp; (inadequate) unzureichend; (evidence) unzulänglich

scapegoat ['skeɪp·goʊt] n Sündenbock m

S

scar [skar] **I.** n Narbe f **II.** vt <-rr-> **to be ~red** [**by sth**] [von etw dat] gezeichnet sein; **to be ~red for life** fürs [ganze] Leben gezeichnet sein

scarce [skers] adj knapp; (rare) rar; **to make oneself ~** sich akk aus dem Staub machen fam

scarcely ['skers·li] adv kaum

scarcity ['sker·sɪ·ti] n Knappheit f

scare [sker] **I.** n Schreck[en] m; (public panic) Hysterie f; **bomb ~** Bombendrohung f; **to give sb a ~** jdm einen Schrecken einjagen **II.** vt **to ~ sb** jdm Angst machen ▸ **to ~ the living daylights out of sb** jdn zu Tode erschrecken
♦**scare away, scare off** vt verscheuchen; (discourage) abschrecken

scarecrow ['sker·kroʊ] n Vogelscheuche f

scaremonger ['sker·ˌmaŋ·gər] n Panikmacher(in) m(f)

scarf <pl -s or scarves> [skarf] n Schal m

scarlet ['skar·lət] **I.** n Scharlachrot nt **II.** adj scharlachrot

scarlet **fever** n Scharlach m

scary ['sker·i] adj Furcht erregend; (uncanny) unheimlich

scat [skæt] interj fam ~! hau ab!

scathing ['sker·ðɪŋ] adj versengend; (criticism) scharf; (remark) bissig

scatter ['skæt̬·ər] **I.** vt verstreuen **II.** vi sich zerstreuen **III.** n liter [vereinzeltes] Häufchen

'scatterbrain n zerstreute Person

'scatterbrained adj zerstreut

scattered ['skæt̬·ərd] adj verstreut; (far apart) weit verstreut; (sporadic) vereinzelt

scavenge ['skæv·ɪndʒ] **I.** vi stöbern; (feed) nach Essen suchen **II.** vt (find) aufstöbern; (get) ergattern fam

scavenger ['skæv·ɪn·dʒər] n Aasfresser m; pej (person) Aasgeier m pej fam

scenario [sə·'ner·i·oʊ] n Szenario nt; **worst-case ~** schlimmster Fall

scene [sin] n **1.** Szene f; (setting) Schauplatz m; (scenery) Kulisse f; **behind the ~s a.** fig hinter den Kulissen; **crime ~** Tatort m **2.** (real-life event) Szene f; (milieu) **drug ~** Drogenszene f

scenery ['si·nə·ri] n Landschaft f; THEAT Bühnenbild nt

scenic ['si·nɪk] adj landschaftlich schön

scent [sent] **I.** n Duft m; (perfume) Parfüm nt; (of animal) Fährte f; **to be on sb's/sth's ~ a.** fig jdm/etw auf der Fährte sein a. fig **II.** vt wittern; (detect) ahnen

scepter ['sep·tər] n Zepter nt

schedule ['skedʒ·ul] **I.** n Zeitplan m, (of events) Programm nt; TRANSP Fahrplan m; SPORT Spielplan m; SCH, UNIV Stundenplan m; **ahead of ~** früher als geplant; **behind ~** im Verzug; **on ~** termingerecht; **work ~** Dienstplan m **II.** vt usu passive planen; (meeting) ansetzen; **they've ~d him to speak at three o'clock** sie haben seine Rede für drei Uhr geplant

scheduled ['skedʒ·uld] adj attr geplant; TRANSP planmäßig

schematic [ski·'mæt̬·ɪk] adj schematisch

scheme [skim] **I.** n **1.** (sinisterer) Plan; POL Verschwörung f **2.** (pattern) Gesamtbild nt; **it fits into his ~ of things** das passt in sein Bild; **color ~** Farb[en]zusammenstellung f **II.** vi planen

scheming ['ski·mɪŋ] **I.** adj attr pej intrigant geh; (cleverly) raffiniert **II.** n Intrigieren nt

schizophrenia [ˌskɪt·sə·'fri·ni·ə] n Schizophrenie f; fam (behavior) schizophrenes Verhalten nt

schizophrenic [ˌskɪt·sə·'fren·ɪk] **I.** adj schizophren **II.** n Schizophrene(r) f(m)

scholar ['skal·ər] n Gelehrte(r) f(m); (good learner) fleißiger Student/fleißige Studentin

scholarly ['skal·ər·li] adj wissenschaftlich; (erudite) gelehrt

scholarship ['skal·ər·ʃɪp] n **1. her book is a work of great ~** ihr Buch ist eine großartige wissenschaftliche Arbeit **2.** (award) Stipendium nt

school[1] [skul] **I.** n Schule f; (faculty) Fakultät f; (smaller) Institut nt; **elementary ~** Grundschule f; **public ~** staatliche Schule f; **to attend ~** zur Schule gehen; **driving ~** Fahrschule f; **graduate ~** hohe Stufe innerhalb des Hochschulsystems, die das Studium bis zum Master's degree oder dem PhD

umfasst II. vt erziehen; (train) schulen; (dog) dressieren

school² [skuːl] n ZOOL Schule f; (shoal) Schwarm m

'school age n schulpflichtiges Alter

'school bag n Schultasche f

'school board n Schulbehörde f

'schoolbook n Schulbuch nt

'schoolboy n Schuljunge m, Schüler m

'schoolchild n Schulkind nt

'schoolgirl n Schulmädchen nt, Schülerin f

schooling ['skuːlɪŋ] n Schulbildung f; (training) Ausbildung f

'schoolroom n Klassenzimmer nt

'schoolteacher n Lehrer(in) m(f)

'schoolwork n Schularbeiten pl

'schoolyard n Schulhof m

schooner ['skuːnər] n Schoner m

science ['saɪəns] n [Natur]wissenschaft f; (discipline) Wissenschaft f; **applied** ~ angewandte Wissenschaft

science 'fiction n Sciencefiction f

scientific [ˌsaɪən'tɪf·ɪk] adj naturwissenschaftlich; (method) wissenschaftlich

scientist ['saɪ·ən·tɪst] n Wissenschaftler(in) m(f)

sci-fi ['saɪ.faɪ] n short for **science fiction** Sciencefiction f

scissors ['sɪz·ərz] npl Schere f; **a pair of** ~ eine Schere

sclerosis [sklɪ·'rou·sɪs] n Sklerose f

scoff [skaf] vi spotten; (laugh) lachen; **to** ~ **at sb/sth** sich über jdn/etw lustig machen

scold [skould] vt ausschimpfen

scolding ['skoul·dɪŋ] n Schimpfen nt; **to get a [good]** ~ [furchtbar] ausgeschimpft werden

scone [skoun] n weiches, krustenloses Gebäck, das entweder nur mit Butter oder mit Butter und Marmelade gegessen wird

scoop [skuːp] I. n 1. Schaufel f; (ladle) Schöpflöffel m; **measuring** ~ Messlöffel m 2. (amount) Löffel m; (of ice cream) Kugel f 3. JOURN fam Knüller m fam 4. fam (Insider)informationen pl II. vt 1. schaufeln; (ice cream) löffeln 2. JOURN **we were ~ed by a rival paper** eine konkurrierende Zeitung kam

uns zuvor

▸ **scoop up** vt hochheben

scoot [skuːt] vi fam rennen

scooter ['skuː·tər] n [Tret]roller m; **motor** ~ Motorroller m

scope [skoup] n Rahmen m; (possibility) Möglichkeit f; (freedom) Spielraum m

scorch [skɔrtʃ] I. vt versengen III. vi versengt werden III. n <pl -es> versengte Stelle; ~ **mark** Brandfleck m

scorcher ['skɔr·tʃər] n fam sehr heißer Tag

scorching ['skɔr·tʃɪŋ] adj sengend; (heat) glühend

score [skɔr] I. n 1. Punktestand m; (of game) Spielstand m; **final** ~ Endstand m 2. (dispute) Streit[punkt] m; **to settle a** ~ eine Rechnung begleichen 3. MUS Partitur f 4. (notch) Kerbe f 5. (twenty) zwanzig; (three ~ years and ten) siebzig Jahre; ~**s of** Dutzende von ▸ **to know the** ~ wissen, wie der Hase läuft fam; **what's the** ~? fam wie sieht's aus? II. vt 1. SPORT treffen; (goal) schießen; (run) scoren 2. (achieve) erreichen; **to** ~ **points** fig sich dat einen Vorteil verschaffen 3. (cut) einkerben 4. fam (drugs) beschaffen III. vi 1. scoren; (in basketball) einen Punkt machen; (in soccer) ein Tor schießen 2. (achieve) abschneiden 3. sl [sich dat] Stoff beschaffen 4. sl (have sex) jdn ins Bett kriegen

'scoreboard n Anzeigetafel f

scorer ['skɔr·ər] n Torschütze, -schützin m, f; (scorekeeper) Scorer m; **the leading** ~ Torschützenkönig m; (in basketball, football) Spieler, der die meisten Punkte erzielt hat

scorn [skɔrn] I. n Verachtung f II. vt verachten; (refuse) ablehnen ▸ **hell hath no fury like a woman** ~**ed** saying die Hölle kennt keinen schlimmeren Zorn als den einer verlachten Frau

scornful ['skɔrn·fəl] adj verächtlich

Scorpio ['skɔr·pi·ou] n ASTROL Skorpion m

scorpion ['skɔr·pi·ən] n Skorpion m

Scot [skat] n Schotte, Schottin m, f

Scotch <pl -es> [skatʃ] n Scotch m

Scotch 'tape® n Tesa[film]® m

scot-'free adv straffrei; (unchallenged)

S

unbehelligt; (*unharmed*) ungeschoren

Scotland ['skɒt·lənd] *n* Schottland *nt*

Scots [skɒts] **I.** *adj* schottisch **II.** *n* Schottisch *nt*

'Scotsman *n* Schotte *m*

'Scotswoman *n* Schottin *f*

Scottish ['skɒt·ɪʃ] **I.** *adj* schottisch **II.** *n* **the ~** *pl* die Schotten *pl*

scoundrel ['skaʊn·drəl] *n* Schuft *m*

scour[1] ['skaʊ·ər] **I.** *n* Scheuern *nt* **II.** *vt* scheuern; (*torrent*) auswaschen; (*wind*) abtragen

scour[2] ['skaʊ·ər] *vt* **to ~ sth [for sb/sth]** etw [nach jdm/etw] absuchen; (*newspaper*) etw [nach jdm/etw] durchforsten

scourer ['skaʊ·ər·ər] *n* Topfreiniger *m*

scourge [skɜrdʒ] *n* Geißel *f geh;* (*critic*) Kritiker(in) *m(f)*

scout [skaʊt] **I.** *n* Pfadfinder(in) *m(f);* (*talent seeker*) Talentsucher(in) *m(f)* **II.** *vi* kundschaften; **to ~ for new talent** nach neuen Talenten suchen **III.** *vt* auskundschaften

'scoutmaster *n* Pfadfinderführer(in) *m(f)*

scowl [skaʊl] **I.** *n* mürrischer [Gesichts] ausdruck **II.** *vi* mürrisch [drein]blicken

scrabble ['skræb·əl] *vi* [herum]wühlen; **to ~ for sth** nach etw *dat* greifen

scram <-mm-> [skræm] *vi fam* abhauen

scramble ['skræm·bəl] **I.** *n* Kletterpartie *f;* (*rush*) Gedrängel *nt fam* **II.** *vi* klettern; (*rush*) hasten; **to ~ to one's feet** sich hochrappeln *fam* **III.** *vt* (*eggs*) verrühren; (*encode*) verschlüsseln

scrambled 'eggs *npl* Rührei *nt*

scrap [skræp] **I.** *n* Stück[chen] *nt;* (*of paper*) Fetzen *m;* (*metal*) Schrott *m;* **~s** *pl* (*leftovers*) Speisereste *pl* **II.** *vt* <-pp-> (*throw away*) wegwerfen; (*metal*) verschrotten; (*abolish*) abschaffen; *fam* (*abandon*) aufgeben

'scrapbook *n* [Sammel]album *nt*

scrape [skreɪp] **I.** *n* [Ab]kratzen *nt;* (*on skin*) Abschürfung *f;* (*scratch*) Kratzer *m; fam* (*situation*) Klemme *f* **II.** *vt* **1.** [ab]schaben; (*dirt*) [ab]kratzen **2. to ~ sth** (*graze*) sich *dat* etw aufschürfen; (*car*) etw verkratzen **III.** *vi* (*rub*) reiben; (*brush*) bürsten; (*scratch*) kratzen; (*economize*) sparen

◆**scrape by** *vi* mit Ach und Krach durch-

kommen *fam*

◆**scrape through** *vi* gerade [mal] so durchkommen *fam*

◆**scrape together, scrape up** *vt* zusammenbekommen; (*money*) zusammenkratzen *fam*

scraper ['skreɪ·pər] *n* Spachtel *m o f;* (*for windshields*) Kratzer *m;* (*for shoes*) Abkratzer *m*

'scrap heap *n* Schrotthaufen *m;* **to be on the ~** *fig* zum alten Eisen gehören *fam;* (*plan*) verworfen worden sein

'scrap iron *n* Alteisen *nt*

scrappy ['skræp·i] *adj* rauflustig

scratch [skrætʃ] **I.** *n <pl -es>* **1.** (*cut*) Kratzer *m* **2.** (*itch*) **to give oneself a ~** sich *akk* kratzen **3. to start [sth] from ~** [mit etw *dat*] bei null anfangen **II.** *vt* zerkratzen; (*person*) kratzen; (*mark*) verkratzen; (*itch*) kratzen; **to ~ one's head** sich am Kopf kratzen **III.** *vi* kratzen; (*itch*) sich kratzen

◆**scratch out** *vt* auskratzen; (*word*) durchstreichen

'scratch card *n* Rubbellos *nt*

'scratch paper *n* Schmierpapier *nt;* (*for draft*) Konzeptpapier *nt*

scratchy ['skrætʃ·i] *adj* kratzig

scrawl [skrɔl] **I.** *vt* [hin]kritzeln *fam* **II.** *n* Gekritzel *nt;* (*note*) hingekritzelte Notiz *fam*

scrawny ['skrɔ·ni] *adj* dürr; (*vegetation*) mager

scream [skrim] **I.** *n* Schrei *m;* (*of animal*) Gekreisch[e] *nt kein pl;* (*of engine*) Heulen *nt;* (*of plane*) Dröhnen *nt;* **~ for help** Hilfeschrei *m* **II.** *vi* schreien; (*with joy*) kreischen; (*engine*) heulen; (*plane*) dröhnen; **to ~ at sb** jdn anschreien **III.** *vt* schreien; (*shout*) lauthals schreien

screech [skritʃ] **I.** *n <pl -es>* Schrei *m;* (*of animal*) Kreischen *nt kein pl;* (*of tires*) Quietschen *nt kein pl* **II.** *vi* schreien; (*animal*) kreischen; (*tires*) quietschen

screen [skrin] **I.** *n* **1.** Leinwand *f;* (*of television*) Bildschirm *m;* (*for radar*) Schirm *m* **2.** (*panel*) Trennwand *f;* (*for protection*) Schutzschirm *m;* (*against insects*) Fliegengitter *nt* **3.** (*that conceals*)

Tarnung f II. vt (conceal) abschirmen; (shield) schützen; (examine) überprüfen; (show) vorführen; TV senden; **to ~ sb for sth** MED jdn auf etw akk hin untersuchen

screening ['skri·nɪŋ] n Vorführen nt; (of TV program) Ausstrahlung f; (testing) Überprüfung f; MED Untersuchung f; **health ~** Vorsorgeuntersuchung f; (X-ray) Röntgenuntersuchung f

'**screen saver** n Bildschirmschoner m

screw [skru] I. n Schraube f; (turn) Drehung f ▶ **to have a ~ loose** hum jdm nicht ganz dicht sein pej II. vt 1. **to ~ sth to sth** etw an etw akk schrauben 2. (twist) **to ~ sth tight** etw fest zudrehen; **to ~ sth into/on sth** etw in/auf etw akk schrauben 3. vulg, sl (have sex with) vögeln derb

screw around fam I. vi herumblödeln; (waste time) herumtrödeln II. vt **to ~ sb around** (mess about) jdm auf die Nerven gehen; (waste time) jds Zeit f verschwenden

screw on vi (cap) sich zuschrauben lassen; (nut) sich anziehen lassen

screw up I. vt 1. sl (spoil) vermasseln fam; (exam) versieben; **to ~ it up** Mist bauen fam 2. (twist) verziehen; **to ~ up one's eyes** blinzeln II. vi sl **to ~ up [on sth]** [bei etw dat] Mist bauen fam

'**screwball** n 1. (in baseball) Screwball m 2. fam Spinner(in) m(f) pej

'**screwdriver** n Schraubenzieher m

screwed [skrud] adj pred sl festgefahren; (in hopeless situation) geliefert

'**screw top** n Schraubverschluss m

'**screwup**, '**screw-up** n sl Schnitzer m fam

screwy ['skru·i] adj fam verrückt

scribble ['skrɪb·əl] I. vt [hin]kritzeln II. vi kritzeln; hum (write) schriftstellern fam III. n Gekritzel nt kein pl pej; (handwriting) Klaue f pej sl

scrimp [skrɪmp] vi **to ~ and save** knausern pej fam

script [skrɪpt] n 1. Drehbuch nt; (of play) Regiebuch nt; (of broadcast) Skript nt 2. (writing style) Schrift f, Schriftart f

'**scriptwriter** n Drehbuchautor(in) m(f); RADIO Rundfunkautor(in) m(f)

scroll [skroʊl] I. n [Schrift]rolle f II. vi COMPUT scrollen

Scrooge [skrudʒ] n pej Geizhals m

scrounge [skraʊndʒ] fam I. vt pej **to ~ sth [off sb]** etw [von jdm] schnorren II. vi 1. **to ~ [around] for sth** nach etw dat herumsuchen 2. pej schnorren

scrounger ['skroʊn·dʒər] n pej fam Schnorrer(in) m(f)

scrub¹ [skrʌb] I. n to give sth a [good] ~ etw [gründlich] [ab]schrubben fam II. vt <-bb-> [ab]schrubben fam; fam (cancel) fallen lassen; (project) abblasen II. vi <-bb-> schrubben fam

scrub² [skrʌb] n (bushes) Gestrüpp nt; (area) Busch m

scrubber ['skrʌb·ər], '**scrub brush** n Schrubber m; (smaller) Scheuerbürste f

scruffy ['skrʌf·i] adj schmuddelig pej fam; (person) vergammelt pej fam; (place) heruntergekommen fam

scruple ['skru·pəl] n **~s** pl Skrupel pl

scrupulous ['skrup·ju·ləs] adj gewissenhaft; (careful) [peinlich] genau

scrutinize ['skru·tə·naɪz] vt [genau] untersuchen; (text) studieren

scrutiny ['skru·tə·ni] n [genaue] [Über]prüfung f

'**scuba diving** n Sporttauchen nt

scuff [skʌf] vt verschrammen; (wear away) abwetzen; **to ~ one's feet** schlurfen

scuffle ['skʌf·əl] I. n Handgemenge nt II. vi sich balgen

sculpt [skʌlpt] I. vt [heraus]meißeln; (in clay) modellieren; (shape) formen II. vi bildhauern fam

sculptor ['skʌlp·tər] n Bildhauer(in) m(f)

sculpture ['skʌlp·tʃər] I. n (art) Bildhauerei f; (object) Skulptur f II. vt [heraus]meißeln; (in clay) modellieren; (shape) formen; (model) modellieren III. vi bildhauern fam

scum [skʌm] n Schaum m; (residue) Rand m; (layer) Schmutzschicht f; pej (evil people) Abschaum m

'**scumbag** n pej sl (man) Mistkerl m fam; (woman) Miststück nt fam

scurry ['skɜr·i] vi <-ie-> eilen; (mouse) huschen

scuttle ['skʌt·əl] vi hasten; (mouse) huschen

scythe [saɪð] I. n Sense f II. vt [mit der Sense] [ab]mähen; **to ~ sb/sth** [**down**] fig jdn/etw niedermähen fam III. vi preschen

SD, S.D. abbr of **South Dakota**

sea [si] n **1.** the ~ das Meer; **at the bottom of the ~** auf dem Meeresboden; **by the ~** am Meer; **the high ~s** die hohe See; **the Dead ~** das Tote Meer **2.** (sea state) Seegang m kein pl ▶ **to be** [all] **at ~** [ganz] ratlos sein

'seabed n Meeresgrund m
'seaboard n Küste f
'sea dog n Seebär m fam
'seafood n Meeresfrüchte pl
'seafront n Strandpromenade f; (beach) Strand m
'seagull n Möwe f
'sea horse n Seepferdchen nt

seal¹ [sil] I. n **1.** (stamp) Siegel nt **2.** (join) Verschluss m II. vt **1.** (stamp) siegeln **2.** (close) [fest] verschließen; (airtight) luftdicht verschließen; (watertight) wasserdicht verschließen; (gaps) abdichten; (with seal) versiegeln; (for customs) plombieren; (with adhesive) zukleben; (border) schließen

◆ **seal up** vt [fest] verschließen; (with seal) versiegeln; (with adhesive) zukleben; (gaps) abdichten

seal² [sil] n ZOOL Seehund m

'sea level n Meeresspiegel m; **above ~** über dem Meeresspiegel

'sealing wax n Siegelwachs nt

'sea lion n Seelöwe m

seam [sim] n Naht f; (of coal) Schicht f; **to be bursting at the ~s** fig aus allen Nähten platzen fam

'seaman ['si·mən] n Seemann m; (rank) Matrose m

seamless ['sim·lɪs] adj nahtlos; a. fig (robe) ohne Nähte nach n

seamlessly ['sim·lɪs·li] adv nahtlos

seamy ['si·mi] adj heruntergekommen, (dubious) zwielichtig; **the ~ side of life** die Schattenseite des Lebens

'seaplane n Wasserflugzeug nt

'seaport n Seehafen m

search [sɜrtʃ] I. n Suche f; (for drugs) Durchsuchung f; (of person) Leibesvisitation f; COMPUT Suchlauf m; **to go off**

in ~ of sth sich auf die Suche nach etw dat machen II. vi suchen; **to ~ for sb/sth** nach jdm/etw suchen; **to ~ through sth** etw durchsuchen III. vt durchsuchen; (place) absuchen; (conscience) prüfen; (memory) durchforschen

◆ **search out** vt ausfindig machen

'search engine n COMPUT Suchmaschine f

searching ['sɜr·tʃɪŋ] adj (look) forschend; (inquiry) eingehend; (question) tief gehend

'searchlight n Suchscheinwerfer m

'search party n Suchtrupp m

'search warrant n Durchsuchungsbefehl m

'seashell n Muschel f

'seashore n Strand m; (coast) [Meeres]-küste f

'seasick adj seekrank

'seasickness n Seekrankheit f

'seaside I. n the ~ die [Meeres]küste; **at the ~** am Meer II. adj attr See-

season ['si·zən] I. n **1.** Jahreszeit f; **the Christmas ~** die Weihnachtszeit; **the rainy ~** die Regenzeit **2.** (period) Saison f; (business a.) Hauptzeit f; **oysters are out of ~ at the moment** zurzeit gibt es keine Austern; **at the height of the ~** in der Hochsaison; **high ~** Hochsaison f II. vt würzen; (wood) ablagern lassen

seasonal ['si·zə·nəl] adj ~ **adjustment** Saisonbereinigung f; ~ **work** Saisonarbeit f

seasoned ['si·zənd] adj (timber) abgelagert; (spiced) gewürzt

seasoning ['si·zə·nɪŋ] n Gewürz nt; (salt and pepper) Würze f

'season ticket n Dauerkarte f; SPORT Saisonkarte f

seat [sit] I. n **1.** [Sitz]platz m; (in car) Sitz m; (in bus, train) Sitzplatz m; (in theater) Platz m; **to take a ~** sich [hin] setzen **2.** usu sing (of chair) Sitz m; (of pants) Hosenboden m **3.** (base) Sitz m II. vt **to ~ 2500** 2500 Menschen fassen; **his car ~s five** in seinem Auto haben fünf Leute Platz

'seat belt n Sicherheitsgurt m; **to fasten one's ~** sich anschnallen

seating ['si:tɪŋ] *n* Sitzgelegenheiten *pl*; (*arrangement*) Sitzordnung *f*; **~ for 6** Sitzplätze *pl* für 6 Personen

'seating arrangements *npl*, **'seating plan** *n* Sitzordnung *f*

'seawater *n* Meerwasser *nt*

'seaweed *n* (See)tang *m*

sec. [sek] *n short for* **second; wait a ~!** Moment mal!; **hold on** [*just*] **a ~!** warte einen Moment!

secluded [sɪˈkluːdɪd] *adj* abgelegen; (*area*) abgeschieden; (*life*) zurückgezogen

seclusion [sɪˈkluːʒən] *n* Zurückgezogenheit *f*; (*of place*) Abgelegenheit *f*

second¹ ['sekənd] *n* Sekunde *f*; (*short time a.*) Augenblick *m*; **I'll only be a ~** ich bin gleich da

second² ['sekənd] **I.** *adj* **1.** *usu attr* zweite(r, s); **the ~ time** das zweite Mal; **to finish ~** Zweite(r) werden; **to be in ~ place** auf Platz zwei sein **2.** **~-largest** zweitgrößte(r, s); **Germany's ~ city** Deutschlands zweitwichtigste Stadt; **to be ~ to none** unübertroffen sein **3.** *attr* (*another*) zweite(r, s); **to give sb a ~ chance** jdm eine zweite Chance geben; **to have ~ thoughts** es sich *dat* noch einmal überlegen ▶ **to play ~ fiddle to sb** in jds Schatten stehen **II.** *n* AUTO zweiter Gang **III.** *adv* **to finish ~** den zweiten Platz belegen **IV.** *vt* (*motion*) unterstützen

secondary ['sekəndəri] *adj* **1.** zweitrangig; **to play a ~ role** eine untergeordnete Rolle spielen **2.** **~ education** höhere Schulbildung

'secondary school *n* SCH Highschool *f*

second 'best *n* **to settle for ~** sich mit weniger zufriedengeben

second-'best *adj* zweitbeste(r, s)

second 'class I. *n* zweite Klasse **II.** *adv* **to travel ~** zweiter Klasse reisen

second-'guess I. *vt* **to ~ sb** jdn/etw im Nachhinein kritisieren **II.** *vi* vorhersagen, was jd tun wird

'secondhand I. *adj* **1.** **~ car** Gebrauchtwagen *m*; **~ clothes** Secondhandkleidung *f* **2.** (*information*) aus zweiter Hand *nach n* **II.** *adv* gebraucht; (*from intermediary*) aus zweiter Hand

second 'hand *n* Sekundenzeiger *m*

secondly ['sekəndli] *adv* zweitens

second-'rate *adj pej* zweitklassig

secrecy ['si:krəsi] *n* Geheimhaltung *f*; (*ability*) Verschwiegenheit *f*; (*secretiveness*) Heimlichtuerei *f pej*; **in ~** im Geheimen

secret ['si:krɪt] **I.** *n* Geheimnis *nt*; **to keep a ~** ein Geheimnis für sich *akk* behalten; **in ~** insgeheim; **to do sth in ~** etw heimlich tun **II.** *adj* geheim; (*hidden*) verborgen; (*done in secret*) heimlich

secret 'agent *n* Geheimagent(in) *m(f)*

secretary ['sekrətəri] *n* Sekretär(in) *m(f)*

Secretary ['sekrətəri] *n* Minister, -in *m, f*; **~ of Defense** Verteidigungsminister(in) *m(f)*

Secretary 'General <*pl* Secretaries General> *n* Generalsekretär(in) *m(f)*

Secretary of 'State *n* Außenminister(in) *m(f)*

secretive ['si:krɪtɪv] *adj* geheimnisvoll; (*character*) verschlossen

'Secret Service *n* **the ~** der Geheimdienst

sect [sekt] *n* Sekte *f*

section ['sekʃən] *n* **1.** Teil *nt*; (*of road*) Teilstrecke *f*; TECH [Bau]teil *nt*; (*of statute*) Paragraph *m*; (*of book*) Abschnitt *m*; (*of document*) Absatz *m* **2.** (*area*) Bereich *m*; **nonsmoking ~** (*in restaurant*) Nichtraucherbereich *m*; (*on train*) Nichtraucherabteil *nt*; **woodwind ~** Holzbläser *pl* **3.** (*division*) Abteilung *f* **4.** (*cut*) Schnitt *m*; **cesarean ~** Kaiserschnitt *m*

◆**section off** *vt* abteilen

sector ['sektər] *n* Sektor *m*; (*of land a.*) Zone *f*

secure [sɪˈkjʊr] **I.** *adj* <-r, -st> sicher; (*guarded*) bewacht; (*phone*) abhörsicher; (*rope*) fest; (*door*) fest verschlossen; **financially ~** finanziell abgesichert **II.** *vt* **1.** (*rights*) sich *dat* sichern **2.** (*make safe*) [ab]sichern; **to ~ sb/ sth against sth** jdn/etw vor etw *dat* schützen **3.** (*fasten*) befestigen; (*door*) fest schließen

security [sɪˈkjʊrɪti] *n* **1.** Sicherheit *f*;

(*guards*) Sicherheitsdienst *m;* **tight ~** strenge Sicherheitsvorkehrungen; **to tighten ~ die** die Sicherheitsmaßnahmen verschärfen **2.** *usu sing* (*safeguard*) Sicherheit *f* **3.** FIN **securities** *pl* (*investments*) Wertpapiere *pl;* (*government securities*) Staatspapiere *pl*

Se'curity Council *n* Sicherheitsrat *m*

se'curity forces *npl* Sicherheitskräfte *pl*

se'curity guard *n* Sicherheitsbeamte(r), -beamtin *m, f*

sedan [sɪ'dæn] *n* Limousine *f*

sedate [sɪ'deɪt] *vt* MED ruhigstellen

sedation [sɪ'deɪ·ʃən] *n* MED Ruhigstellung *f*

sedative ['sed·ə·tɪv] *n* Beruhigungsmittel *nt*

sediment ['sed·ə·mənt] *n* Sediment *nt;* (*in wine*) [Boden]satz *m*

seduce [sɪ'dus] *vt* verführen; **to ~ sb into doing sth** jdn dazu verleiten, etw zu tun

seduction [sɪ'dʌk·ʃən] *n* Verführung *f;* (*quality*) Verlockung *f*

seductive [sɪ'dʌk·tɪv] *adj* verführerisch; (*offer*) verlockend

see <saw, seen> [si] **I.** *vt* **1.** sehen; (*movie*) [sich *dat*] [an]sehen **2.** (*understand*) verstehen; (*discern*) erkennen; **I ~ what you mean** ich weiß, was du meinst; **~ what I mean?** siehst du? **3.** (*consider*) **this is how I ~ it** so sehe ich die Sache; **to ~ sth in a new light** etw mit anderen Augen sehen **4.** (*learn*) **I'll ~ who it is** ich schaue mal nach, wer es ist; **that remains to be ~n** das wird sich zeigen; **to ~ into the future** in die Zukunft schauen **5.** (*meet*) sehen; (*by chance*) [zufällig] treffen; **we're ~ing friends this weekend** wir treffen uns am Wochenende mit Freunden; **~ you later!** *fam* (*until later*) bis später!; (*goodbye*) tschüs! *fam;* **to be ~ing sb** (*dating*) mit jdm zusammen sein *fam;* **I'm not ~ing anyone at the moment** ich habe im Moment keine Freundin/keinen Freund **6.** (*talk to*) sprechen; (*receive*) empfangen; **Ms. Miller can't ~ you now** Frau Miller ist im Moment nicht zu sprechen; **to ~ a doctor** zum Arzt gehen **7.** (*accompany*) **to ~ sb**

home/to the door jdn nach Hause/zur Tür bringen ▶ **to the last of sb** [endlich] jdn los sein *fam;* **to ~ the for-est for the trees** den Wald vor [lauter] Bäumen nicht sehen *hum* **II.** *vi* **1.** sehen; **let me ~!** lass mich mal sehen!; **can you ~?** (*in theater etc.*) können Sie noch sehen? **2.** (*understand*) oh, I ~! aha!; **I ~** ich verstehe; **I ~ from your re-port ...** Ihrem Bericht entnehme ich, ...; **we'll ~ about that** das wird sich zeigen ▶ **to not ~ eye to eye [with sb]** nicht derselben Ansicht sein [wie jd]

◆**see in** *vt* hineinbringen; **to ~ the New Year in** das neue Jahr begrüßen

◆**see off** *vt* verabschieden; **to ~ sb off at the airport** jdn zum Flughafen bringen

◆**see out** *vt* **1.** (*escort*) hinausbegleiten **2.** (*continue to end of*) durchstehen; (*last until end of*) überstehen; (*project*) bis zum Ende mitmachen

◆**see through** *vt* **1.** **to ~ through sth** durch etw *akk* hindurchsehen **2.** (*plan*) durchschauen **3.** (*sustain*) **to ~ sb through** jdm über die Runden helfen *fam;* (*comfort*) jdm beistehen; **will 30 dollars be enough to ~ you through?** reichen dir 30 Dollar? **4.** (*project*) zu Ende bringen

◆**see to** *vt* **to ~ to sb/sth** sich um jdn/ etw kümmern; **to ~ to it that ...** dafür sorgen, dass ...

seed [sid] **I.** *n* **1.** Samen *m;* (*of grain*) Korn *nt;* **~s** *pl* AGR Saat *f kein pl* **2.** (*seeds*) Samen *pl;* **to go to ~** Samen bilden; (*plants*) schießen; *fig* (*person*) herunterkommen *fam* **II.** *vt* **1.** (*sow*) besäen; **to ~ itself** sich aussäen **2.** (*fruit*) entkernen **3.** *usu passive* SPORT **to be ~ed** platziert sein

'seedbed *n* Samenbeet *nt; fig* Grundlage *f*

seedless ['sid·lɪs] *adj* kernlos

seedy ['si·di] *adj* zwielichtig; (*character*) zweifelhaft; (*clothes*) schäbig

seeing ['si·ɪŋ] *conj* **~ that ...** da ...

seek <sought, sought> [sik] *vt* **1.** *form* suchen; (*try to obtain a.*) erstreben; (*jus-tice*) streben **2.** (*ask for*) erbitten geh; (*approval*) einholen; **to ~ advice from sb** jdn um Rat bitten

◆**seek out** vt ausfindig machen; (*informa-tion*) herausfinden

seem [siːm] vi **1.** **he's sixteen, but he ~s younger** er ist sechzehn, wirkt aber jünger; **he ~s like a very nice man** er scheint ein sehr netter Mann zu sein; (*it ~s all right to me*) das scheint mir ganz in Ordnung zu sein; **it ~ed like a good idea at the time** damals hielt ich das für eine gute Idee **2.** **there ~s to have been some mistake** da liegt anscheinend ein Irrtum vor; **it ~s [that]** **...** anscheinend ...; **it ~s as if ...** es scheint, als ob ...; **it ~s to me that he isn't the right person** ich finde, er ist nicht der Richtige

seemingly ['siːmɪŋlɪ] adv scheinbar

seen [siːn] pp of **see**

seep [siːp] vi sickern; fig (*truth*) durch-sickern

◆**seep away** vi versickern

seesaw ['siːsɔː] **I.** n Wippe f; fig Auf und Ab nt **II.** vi wippen; fig sich auf und ab bewegen; (*prices*) steigen und fallen; (*mood*) schwanken

seethe [siːð] vi **1.** (*be very angry*) kochen fam **2.** (*be crowded*) wimmeln

'**see-through** adj durchsichtig

segment ['seɡmənt] n Teil m; (*of popu-lation*) Gruppe f; (*of worm*) Segment nt

segregation [ˌseɡrəˈɡeɪʃən] n Tren-nung f; **racial ~** Rassentrennung f

seize [siːz] vt **1.** (*grab*) ergreifen **2.** usu passive fig **to be ~d with sth** von etw dat ergriffen werden **3.** (*capture*) ein-nehmen; (*criminal*) festnehmen; (*hos-tage*) nehmen; (*power*) ergreifen; (*more aggressively*) an sich akk reißen **4.** (*con-fiscate*) beschlagnahmen

◆**seize on** vt (*idea*) aufgreifen; (*excuse*) greifen

◆**seize up** vi (*engine*) stehen bleiben; (*brain*) aussetzen

seizure ['siːʒər] n MED Anfall m

seldom ['seldəm] adv selten; **~ if ever** fast nie

select [səˈlekt] **I.** adj (*high-class*) exklu-siv; (*chosen*) ausgewählt; (*team*) aus-erwählt; (*fruit*) ausgesucht **II.** vt aus-suchen; (*person*) auswählen; (*team*) aufstellen **III.** vi **to ~ from sth** aus etw

dat [aus]wählen

selection [səˈlekʃən] n Auswahl f; BIOL Selektion f geh; **to make one's ~** seine Wahl treffen

selective [səˈlektɪv] adj wählerisch; (*buyer*) kritisch; (*choosing the best*) ausgewählt; (*process*) gezielt

self <pl **selves**> [self] n **one's ~** das Selbst; **to be [like** or **back to]] one's former ~** wieder ganz der/die Alte sein

self-addressed stamped 'envelope n adressierter frankierter Rückumschlag

self-ad'hesive adj selbstklebend

self-ap'pointed adj selbst ernannt

self-as'surance n Selbstvertrauen nt

self-as'sured adj selbstbewusst

self-'centered adj egozentrisch

self-com'posed adj beherrscht; **to re-main ~** gelassen bleiben

self-con'fessed adj attr **she's a ~ thief** sie bezeichnet sich selbst als Diebin

self-'confidence n Selbstvertrauen nt

self-'conscious adj gehemmt; (*smile*) verlegen

self-con'tained adj selbstgenügsam; (*community*) autark; (*apartment*) se-parat

self-con'trol n Selbstbeherrschung f

self-de'ceit, self-de'ception n Selbst-betrug m

self-de'fense n Selbstverteidigung f; **to kill sb in ~** jdn in Notwehr töten

self-de'struct vi sich selbst zerstören; (*materials*) zerfallen

self-'discipline n Selbstdisziplin f

self-ef'facing adj bescheiden

self-em'ployed **I.** adj selbständig **II.** n **the ~** pl die Selbständigen pl

self-es'teem n Selbstwertgefühl nt

self-'evident adj offensichtlich; **it is ~ that ...** es liegt auf der Hand, dass ...

self-ex'planatory adj **to be ~** keiner weiteren Erklärung bedürfen

self-ex'pression n Selbstdarstellung f

self-'help n Selbsthilfe f

self-im'portance n Selbstgefälligkeit f

self-im'portant adj selbstgefällig

self-im'posed adj selbst verordnet

self-in'dulgence n Luxus m; (*act*) Hem-mungslosigkeit f

self-in'dulgent *adj* genießerisch

self-in'flicted *adj* selbst zugefügt

self-'interest *n* Eigeninteresse *f*

selfish ['sel·fɪʃ] *adj* selbstsüchtig; (*motive*) eigennützig

selfishness ['sel·fɪʃ·nɪs] *n* Selbstsucht *f*

selfless ['self·lɪs] *adj* selbstlos

self-'made *adj* selbst gemacht; **~ man** Selfmademan *m*

self-'portrait *n* Selbstbildnis *nt;* **to draw a ~** sich selbst porträtieren

self-pos'sessed *adj* selbstbeherrscht

self-preser'vation *n* Selbsterhaltung *f*

self-re'spect *n* Selbstachtung *f*

self-re'specting *adj* **no ~ person** niemand, der was auf sich hält

self-'righteous *adj* selbstgerecht

self-rising 'flour *n* Mehl, dem Backpulver beigemischt ist

self-'sacrifice *n* Selbstaufopferung *f*

self-'service *n* Selbstbedienung *f*

self-suf'ficiency *n* Selbstversorgung *f*

self-suf'ficient *adj* selbständig

self-'taught *adj* selbst erlernt; (*acquired*) autodidaktisch

sell [sel] **I.** *vt* <sold, sold> **1.** verkaufen; **to ~ sb sth** [*or* sth **to sb**] jdm etw [zu]schicken; **to ~ sth in the mail** etw mit der Post verkaufen (**for** für +*akk*) **2.** (*persuade*) **to ~ sth** [**to sb**] jdn für etw *akk* gewinnen; **to ~ an idea to sb** jdm eine Idee schmackhaft machen **II.** *vi* <sold, sold> verkaufen; (*attract customers*) sich verkaufen ▶ **to ~ like hotcakes** wie warme Semmeln weggehen **III.** *n* Ware *f*; **to be a hard/soft ~** schwer/leicht verkäuflich sein

◆ **sell off** *vt* verkaufen

◆ **sell out I.** *vi* **to be/have sold out** (*product, shop, play*) ausverkauft sein; **to ~ to sb** (*business*) [seine Firma] an jdn verkaufen; (*give in to*) sich *akk* an jdn verkaufen **II.** *vt* **1. to be sold out** ausverkauft sein **2.** *fam* (*betray*) verraten

seller ['sel·ər] *n* Verkäufer(in) *m(f)*; (*product*) Verkaufsschlager *m*

'selling price *n* Kaufpreis *m*

'sellout *n* Ausverkauf *m*; (*betrayal*) Auslieferung *f*; **the concert was a ~** das Konzert war ausverkauft

selves [selvz] *n pl of* **self**

semen ['si·mən] *n* Sperma *nt*

semester [sə·'mes·tər] *n* Semester *nt*

semi <*pl* -s> ['sem·i] *n fam* **1.** (*truck*) Sattelschlepper *m* **2.** SPORT ~**s** *pl* Halbfinale *nt*

semiauto'matic *adj* MIL halbautomatisch

'semicircle *n* Halbkreis *m*

semi'circular *adj* halbkreisförmig

'semicolon *n* Semikolon *nt*

semicon'ductor *n* Halbleiter *m*

semi'conscious *adj* halb bewusstlos

semi'final *n* Halbfinale *nt*

semi'finalist *n* Halbfinalist(in) *m(f)*

seminar ['sem·ə·nar] *n* Seminar *nt*

semi'precious *adj* **~ stone** Halbedelstein *m*

semi'skilled *adj* angelernt

semo'lina [ˌsem·ə·'li·nə] *n* Gries *m*

Sen. *n* POL *abbr of* **senator**

senate ['sen·ɪt] *n* Senat *m*

senator ['sen·ə·tər] *n* Senator(in) *m(f)*

send <sent, sent> [send] *vt* **1. to ~** [**sb**] **sth** [*or* sth **to sb**] jdm etw [zu]schicken; **to ~ sth in the mail** etw mit der Post schicken; **to ~ a signal to sb** jdm etw signalisieren **2.** (*dispatch*) schicken; **to ~ sb for sth** jdn nach etw *dat* [los] schicken; **to ~ sb to prison** jdn ins Gefängnis stecken **3.** (*transmit*) senden; (*signal*) schicken; (*pass on*) **to ~ sb sth** jdm etw übermitteln [lassen]; **Maggie ~s** [**you**] **her love** Maggie lässt [dich] grüßen **4.** (*cause*) **the news sent him running back to the house** die Nachricht ließ ihn wieder ins Haus laufen; **to ~ sb into a panic** jdn in Panik versetzen ▶ **to ~ sb flying** jdn zu Boden schicken

◆ **send away I.** *vi* **to ~ away for sth** sich *dat* etw zuschicken lassen **II.** *vt* wegschicken

◆ **send back** *vt* zurückschicken

◆ **send for** *vi* (*summon*) rufen; (*brochure*) anfordern; (*help*) holen

◆ **send in I.** *vt* (*bill*) einreichen; (*report*) einschicken; (*order*) aufgeben; (*troops*) einsetzen **II.** *vi* **to ~ in for sth** sich *dat* etw zuschicken lassen; (*for information*)

etw anfordern

send off I. vt abschicken; (package) aufgeben; (dispatch) fortschicken; **to be sent off for fighting** (player) einen Platzverweis wegen Rauferei bekommen **II.** vi **to ~ off for sth** etw anfordern

send out I. vi **to ~ out for sth** etw telefonisch bestellen **II.** vt aussenden; (letter) verschicken; (email) versenden

send up vt (prices) ansteigen lassen; (pass on) zuschicken; fam (imprison) hinter Gitter bringen

sender ['sen·dər] n Absender(in) m(f)

'sendoff n Verabschiedung f; **to give sb a ~** jdn verabschieden

Senegal [,sen·ɪ·ˈɡɔl] n Senegal m

senile ['si·naɪl] adj senil

senility [sə·ˈnɪl·ɪ· t̬i] n Senilität f

senior ['sin·jər] **I.** adj **1.** form älter **2.** (employee) vorgesetzt **3.** attr SCH, UNIV Senior- **II.** n **1.** Senior(in) m(f); (employee) Vorgesetzte(r) f/m; **she's my ~ by three years** sie ist drei Jahre älter als ich **2.** SCH, UNIV Bezeichnung für Schüler einer Highschool- oder einer Collegeabgangsklasse

senior 'citizen n **~s** (pl) ältere Menschen

senior 'high school n (Schulform nach der Junior High School, welche die Stufen 9, 10, 11 und 12 enthält)

seniority [sin·ˈjɔr·ɪ· t̬i] n Alter nt; (rank) Dienstalter nt

senior 'partner n Seniorpartner(in) m(f)

sensation [sen·ˈseɪ·ʃən] n **1.** Gefühl nt; **~ of cold** Kälteempfindung f; **burning ~** Brennen nt **2.** (stir) Sensation f; **to cause a ~** Aufsehen erregen

sensational [sen·ˈseɪ·ʃə·nəl] adj sensationell; (very good a.) fantastisch; (shocking a.) spektakulär

sensationalism [sen·ˈseɪ·ʃən·əl·ɪ·zəm] n Sensationsmache m pej

sense [sens] **I.** n **1.** Verstand m; **sb's ~s** pl jds gesunder Menschenverstand; **it's time you came to your ~s** es wird Zeit, dass du zur Vernunft kommst **2. to make** (good) **~** sinnvoll sein; **to see the ~ in sth** den Sinn in etw dat sehen; **there's no ~ in doing sth** es hat keinen Sinn, etw zu tun **3.** (faculty) Sinn m; **~**

of hearing Gehör nt; **~ of sight** Sehvermögen nt; **~ of smell** Geruchssinn m; **sixth ~** sechster Sinn **4.** (feeling) Gefühl nt; **~ of duty** Pflichtgefühl nt; **~ of justice** Gerechtigkeitssinn m **5.** (meaning) Bedeutung f; **to make ~** einen Sinn ergeben; **in every ~** in jeder Hinsicht **II.** vt wahrnehmen; (danger) wittern; **to ~ that ...** spüren, dass ....

senseless ['sens·lɪs] adj (waste) sinnlos; (foolish) töricht; (unconscious) bewusstlos

sensible ['sen·sə·bəl] adj vernünftig; (decision) weis; (person) klug; (suitable) angemessen

sensibly ['sen·sə·bli] adv vernünftig; (suitably) angemessen; (dressed) passend

sensitive ['sen·sɪ· t̬ɪv] adj **1.** verständnisvoll; **to be ~ to sth** für etw akk Verständnis haben **2.** (secret) vertraulich **3.** (responsive) empfindlich; **to be ~ to cold** kälteempfindlich sein; **~ feelings** verletzliche Gefühle

sensitivity [,sen·sə·ˈtɪv·ɪ· t̬i] n Verständnis nt; (confidentiality) Vertraulichkeit f; (reaction) Überempfindlichkeit f; **~ to light** Licht[über]empfindlichkeit f

sensor ['sen·sər] n Sensor m

sensual ['sen·ʃu·əl] adj sinnlich

sensuality [,sen·ʃu·ˈæl·ɪ· t̬i] n Sinnlichkeit f

sent [sent] pt, pp of **send**

sentence ['sen·təns] **I.** n **1.** Urteil nt; (punishment) Strafe f; **life ~** lebenslängliche Haftstrafe; **to serve a ~** eine Strafe verbüßen **2.** (words) Satz m **II.** vt verurteilen

sentiment ['sen·tə·mənt] n **1.** usu pl Ansicht f; **my ~s exactly!** ganz meine Meinung!; **popular ~** allgemeine Meinung **2.** (emotion) Rührseligkeit f

sentimental [,sen·tə·ˈmen·təl] adj **1.** gefühlvoll; **~ value** ideeller Wert **2.** (emotional) sentimental; (music) kitschig; (story) rührselig

sentimentality [,sen·tə·men·ˈtæl·ɪ· t̬i] n Sentimentalität f

sentry ['sen·tri] n Wache f

separate I. adj ['sep·ər·ɪt] getrennt; (independent) einzeln attr; **a ~ piece of paper** ein extra Blatt nt Papier; **to keep**

S

sth ~ etw getrennt halten **II.** vt ['sep-ə·reɪt] trennen **III.** vi ['sep-ə·reɪt] sich trennen; CHEM sich scheiden; (*couple*) sich trennen; (*divorce*) sich scheiden lassen; **she is ~d from her husband** sie lebt von ihrem Mann getrennt

separation [ˌsep·ə·'reɪ·ʃən] n Trennung f; (*living apart*) [eheliche] Trennung

separatist ['sep·ə·rə·tɪst] n Separatist(in) m(f)

Sept. n abbr of **September** Sept.

September [sep·'tem·bər] n September m; see also **February**

sequel ['si·kwəl] n Fortsetzung f; (*follow-up*) Nachspiel nt

sequence ['si·kwəns] n **1.** Reihenfolge f; (*of programs*) Sendefolge f; (*connected series*) Abfolge f **2.** (*part of film*) Sequenz f; **closing ~** Schlussszene f

sequin ['si·kwɪn] n Paillette f

Serb [sɜrb] n Serbe, Serbin m, f

Serbia ['sɜr·bi·ə] n Serbien nt

Serbian ['sɜr·bi·ən] **I.** adj serbisch **II.** n Serbe, Serbin m, f; (*language*) Serbisch nt

Serbo-Croatian [ˌsɜr·bou·krou·'eɪ·ʃən] n Serbokroatisch nt

serenade [ˌser·ə·'neɪd] **I.** n Serenade f; (*by lover*) Ständchen nt **II.** vt ein Ständchen bringen

sergeant ['sar·dʒənt] n Unteroffizier m; (*police*) ≈ Polizeimeister(in) m(f)

sergeant major n Oberfeldwebel m

serial ['sɪr·i·əl] **I.** n Fortsetzungsgeschichte f **II.** adj Serien-

'serial killer n Serienmörder(in) m(f)

'serial number n Seriennummer f

series <pl -> ['sɪr·iz] n Reihe f; (*succession*) Folge f; (*products*) Serie f

serious ['sɪr·i·əs] adj **1.** ernst; (*threat, argument*) ernsthaft; (*accident*) schwer; (*dangerous*) gefährlich; (*allegation*) schwerwiegend **2.** attr (*careful*) ernsthaft **3.** (*significant*) bedeutend; (*thought-provoking*) tiefgründig; (*writer*) anspruchsvoll

seriously ['sɪr·i·əs·li] adv **1.** ernst; (*badly*) schwer; (*dangerously*) ernstlich **2.** fam (*very*) äußerst; **~ funny** urkomisch

seriousness ['sɪr·i·əs·nɪs] n Ernst m; (*sincerity*) Ernsthaftigkeit f; **in all ~** ganz im Ernst

sermon ['sɜr·mən] n Predigt f; pej (*lecture*) [Moral]predigt f

serrated [sə·'reɪ·t̬ɪd] adj gezackt

serum <pl -s> ['sɪr·əm] n Serum nt

servant ['sɜr·vənt] n Bedienstete(r) f(m); (*for public*) Angestellte(r) f(m) (im öffentlichen Dienst)

serve [sɜrv] **I.** n Aufschlag m; (*in volleyball*) Angabe f **II.** vt **1.** (*customer*) bedienen; (*food*) servieren; **this ~s 4 to 5** das ergibt 4 bis 5 Portionen **2.** (*complete*) ableisten; (*prison sentence*) absitzen fam **3.** **to ~ a purpose** einen Zweck erfüllen; **if my memory ~s me right** wenn ich mich recht erinnere **4.** **to ~ the ball** Aufschlag haben; (*in volleyball*) Angabe haben ▸ **~ him right!** fam das geschieht ihm recht! **III.** vi servieren; (*work for*) dienen; (*function a.*) fungieren; (*in tennis*) aufschlagen; (*in volleyball*) angeben

✦**serve up** vt servieren

server ['sɜr·vər] n Server m

service ['sɜr·vɪs] n **1.** Service m; (*paid*) Dienstleistung f; (*at shop*) Bedienung f; **customer ~** Kundendienst m **2.** form **to be of ~** [to sb] [jdm] von Nutzen sein; **to need the ~s of an expert** einen Gutachter/eine Gutachterin brauchen **3.** **ambulance ~** Rettungsdienst m; **civil ~** öffentlicher Dienst **4.** **to be out of/in ~** außer/in Betrieb sein; **postal ~** Postwesen nt **5.** Aufschlag m; (*in volleyball*) Angabe f **6.** **the ~s** das Militär nt kein pl **7.** Gottesdienst m; **morning/evening ~** Frühmesse/Abendandacht f **8.** (*maintenance*) Wartung f; AUTO Inspektion f

'service area n Raststätte f

'service center n Reparaturwerkstatt f; (*garage*) Werkstatt f

'service charge n Bedienungsgeld nt

'serviceman n Militärangehöriger m

'service station n Tankstelle f

'servicewoman n MIL Militärangehörige f

servile ['sɜr·vəl] adj pej unterwürfig; (*obedience*) sklavisch

serving ['sɜr·vɪŋ] **I.** n (*a ~ of rice*) eine Portion Reis **II.** adj attr **the longest-~ mayor** der dienstälteste Bürgermeister/

die dienstälteste Bürgermeisterin

sesame ['ses·ə·mi] *n* Sesam *m*

session ['sef·ən] *n* Sitzung *f*; (*period*) Sitzungsperiode *f*; (*for specific activity*) Stunde *f*; ~ **recording** ~ Aufnahme *f*

set[1] [set] **I.** *adj* **1.** *pred* (*ready*) bereit, fertig; **ready,** [get] ~**, go!** auf die Plätze, fertig, los!; **to be** [all] ~ [for sth] [für etw *akk*] bereit sein **2.** (*pattern, time*) fest[gesetzt]; ~ **phrase** feststehender Ausdruck **3.** (*look*) starr **4.** *attr* (*assigned*) vorgegebene(r, s); (*subject a.*) bestimmte(r, s) **II.** *vt* <set, set> **1.** (*place*) stellen; (*on its side*) legen; **to** ~ **foot in/on sth** etw betreten **2.** *usu passive* "**West Side Story**" **is** ~ **in New York** "West Side Story" spielt in New York **3. his remarks** ~ **me thinking** seine Bemerkungen gaben mir zu denken; **to** ~ **one's/sb's mind at ease** sich/jdn beruhigen; **to** ~ **sth in motion** etw in Bewegung setzen [*or fig a.* ins Rollen bringen] **4.** (*prepare*) vorbereiten; (*table*) decken; **to** ~ **the scene for sth** (*create conditions*) die Bedingungen für etw *akk* schaffen; (*facilitate*) den Weg für etw *akk* frei machen **5.** (*adjust*) einstellen; (*clock*) stellen **6.** (*fix*) festsetzen; (*budget*) festlegen; (*date, time*) ausmachen; (*deadline*) setzen **7.** (*record*) aufstellen; (*pace*) vorgeben; **to** ~ **a good example for sb** jdm ein Vorbild sein **8.** (*dislocation*) einrenken; (*bone*) einrichten **9.** (*hair*) legen **10.** TYPO setzen **11. to** ~ **sail for ...** nach ... losfahren **III.** *vi* <set, set> (*bones*) zusammenwachsen; (*concrete*) fest werden; (*sun*) untergehen

set[2] [set] *n* **1.** (*Satz*) Satz *m*; (*pair*) Paar *nt*; **coffee** ~ Kaffeeservice *nt* **2.** THEAT Bühnenbild *nt*; FILM Szenenaufbau *m*; **on the** ~ bei den Dreharbeiten; (*on location*) am Set **3.** (*appliance*) Gerät *nt*; (*television*) Fernseher *m*; (*radio*) Radio[gerät] *nt* **4.** (*in tennis*) Satz *m*

◆ **set about** *vi* **to** ~ **about doing sth** sich daran machen, etw zu tun

◆ **set apart** *vt* **to** ~ **sth** ~ **sb/sth** ⇆ **apart from sb/sth** etw unterscheidet jdn/etw von jdm/etw; **to be** ~ **apart for sth** für etw *akk* reserviert sein

◆ **set aside** *vt* beiseitelegen; (*clothes*) sich *dat* zurücklegen lassen; (*money*) sparen; (*time*) einplanen; (*differences*) begraben

◆ **set back** *vt* **1.** (*delay*) zurückwerfen; (*deadline*) verschieben **2.** (*position*) zurücksetzen; **their garden is** ~ **back from the road** ihr Garten liegt nicht direkt an der Straße

◆ **set down** *vt* absetzen; (*plane*) landen; **to** ~ **sth down in writing** aufschreiben

◆ **set in** *vi* (*weather*) einsetzen; (*complications*) sich einstellen

◆ **set off I.** *vi* sich auf den Weg machen; (*in car*) losfahren **II.** *vt* (*trigger*) auslösen; (*bomb*) zünden; **to** ~ **sb off** jdn verärgern

◆ **set on** *vt fam* **to** ~ **an animal on sb** ein Tier auf jdn hetzen

◆ **set out I.** *vt* (*arrange*) auslegen; (*chairs*) aufstellen; (*idea*) darlegen **II.** *vi* aufbrechen; **to** ~ **out to do sth** beabsichtigen, etw zu tun

◆ **set up** *vt* (*camp*) aufschlagen; (*business*) einrichten; (*program*) installieren; (*system*) konfigurieren; *fam* (*deceive*) übers Ohr hauen *fam*

'setback *n* Rückschlag *m*

setting ['set·ɪŋ] *n usu sing* Lage *f*; (*surroundings*) Umgebung *f*; (*in film*) Schauplatz *m*; (*for jewel*) Fassung *f*

settle ['set·əl] **I.** *vi* sich niederlassen; (*in chair*) es sich *dat* bequem machen; (*build up*) sich anhäufen; (*end dispute*) sich einigen; (*weather*) beständig werden **II.** *vt* **1.** (*decide*) entscheiden; (*deal with*) regeln; (*end*) erledigen; (*argument*) beilegen; **that** ~**s that** damit hat sich das erledigt **2.** (*colonize*) besiedeln ▶ **to** ~ **a score** [**with sb**] [mit jdm] abrechnen

◆ **settle down I.** *vi* sich [häuslich] niederlassen; (*in chair*) es sich *dat* bequem machen; (*calm down*) sich beruhigen **II.** *vt* **1. to** ~ **oneself down** es sich *dat* bequem machen **2.** (*calm down*) beruhigen

◆ **settle for** *vi* **to** ~ **for sth** mit etw *dat* zufrieden sein

◆ **settle in** *vi* sich einleben

S

◆ **settle on** vi to ~ on sth sich für etw akk entscheiden; (agree on) sich auf etw akk einigen; (on name) sich für etw akk entscheiden

settled ['set·əld] adj 1. pred to be ~ sich eingelebt haben; to feel ~ sich heimisch fühlen 2. (calm) ruhig; (life-style) geregelt

settlement ['set·əl·mənt] n 1. (resolution) Übereinkunft f; (agreement) Vereinbarung f; LAW Vergleich m; (of conflict) Lösung f; (of matter) Regelung f; (of strike) Schlichtung f; **they reached an out-of-court ~** sie einigten sich außergerichtlich 2. (colony) Siedlung f; (colonization) Besiedlung f; (people) Ansiedlung f

settler ['set·lər] n Siedler(in) m(f)

'**setup** n Aufbau m; (arrangement) Einrichtung f; fam (deception) abgekartetes Spiel

seven ['sev·ən] I. adj sieben; see also **eight** II. n Sieben f; see also **eight**

'**sevenfold** adj siebenfach

seventeen [,sev·ən·'tin] I. adj siebzehn; see also **eight** II. n Siebzehn f; see also **eight**

seventeenth [,sev·ən·'tinθ] I. adj siebzehnte(r, s) II. n 1. (date, ordinal) **the ~** der Siebzehnte 2. (fraction) Siebzehntel nt

seventh ['sev·ənθ] I. adj siebte(r, s) II. n 1. (date, ordinal) **the ~** der Siebte 2. (fraction) Siebtel nt

seventieth ['sev·ən·ti·əθ] I. adj siebzigste(r, s) II. n 1. Siebzigste(r, s); (fraction) Siebzigstel nt

seventy ['sev·ən·ti] I. adj siebzig II. n Siebzig f

several ['sev·ər·əl] I. adj einige; (various) verschiedene II. pron einige

'**severance pay** n Abfindung f

severe [sə·'vɪr] adj schwer; (pain) heftig; (cutbacks) drastisch; (criticism) hart; (strict) streng; (storm) heftig; (cold) eisig; (frost) streng; (violent) gewaltig; (reprimand) scharf

severity [sə·'ver·ɪ·ti] n Schwere f; (of situation) Ernst m; (harshness) Härte f; (strictness) Strenge f; (of criticism) Schärfe f; (extreme nature) Rauheit f

Seville [sə·'vɪl] n Sevilla nt

sew <sewed, sewn or sewed> [soʊ] I. vt [an]nähen II. vi nähen

◆ **sew up** vt 1. zunähen; (wound) nähen 2. fam (end) zum Abschluss bringen; to be ~n up unter Dach und Fach sein

sewage ['su·ɪdʒ] n Abwasser nt

sewer ['su·ər] n Abwasserkanal m

sewerage ['su·ər·ɪdʒ] n Kanalisation f

sewing ['soʊ·ɪŋ] n Nähen nt; (things) Näharbeit f

'**sewing basket** n Nähkorb m

'**sewing machine** n Nähmaschine f

sewn [soʊn] pp of **sew**

sex <pl -es> [seks] n 1. Geschlecht nt; **the opposite ~** das andere Geschlecht 2. (intercourse) Sex m; to have ~ Sex haben; to have ~ with sb mit jdm schlafen

'**sex appeal** n Sexappeal m

'**sex education** n Sexualerziehung f

sexism ['sek·sɪz·əm] n Sexismus m

sexist ['sek·sɪst] I. adj sexistisch II. n Sexist(in) m(f)

'**sex life** n Sexualleben nt

'**sex symbol** n Sexsymbol nt

sextet [sek·'stet] n Sextett nt

sexual ['sek·ʃu·əl] adj geschlechtlich; (erotic) sexuell; ~ **equality** Gleichheit f der Geschlechter

sexual discrimi'nation n Diskriminierung f aufgrund des Geschlechts

sexual 'harassment n sexuelle Belästigung

sexual 'intercourse n Geschlechtsverkehr m

sexuality [,sek·ʃu·'æl·ɪ·ti] n Sexualität f

sexy ['sek·si] adj fam sexy; (arousing) erregend; (exciting) heiß

Seychelles [seɪ·'ʃelz] n **the ~** die Seychellen pl

Sgt. n abbr of **sergeant** Uffz.

shabby ['ʃæb·i] adj schäbig; (clothing) gammelig; (poorly dressed) ärmlich gekleidet; (unfair) schäbig; (mediocre) mittelmäßig; (excuse) fadenscheinig

shack [ʃæk] n Hütte f

◆ **shack up** vi fam to ~ up with sb mit jdm zusammenziehen; to be ~ed up with sb mit jdm zusammenleben

shackle ['ʃæk·əl] I. n ~s pl Fesseln f pl;

fig Zwänge *m pl* **II.** *vt* [mit Ketten] fesseln; *fig* behindern

shade [ʃeɪd] **I.** *n* **1.** Schatten *m;* **patch of ~** schattiges Plätzchen; **in the ~** im Schatten **2.** (*lampshade*) [Lampen]schirm *m* **3.** (*color*) [Farb]ton *m* **4.** *fam* (*sunglasses*) **~s** *pl* Sonnenbrille *f* **II.** *vt* **1.** [vor der Sonne] schützen; (*eyes*) beschirmen **2.** (*draw*) schattieren

shading [ʃeɪ·dɪŋ] *n* Schattierung *f*

shadow [ʃæd·oʊ] **I.** *n* Schatten *m;* (*under eye*) Augenring *m;* (*trace*) Hauch *m;* **not a ~ of doubt** nicht der leiseste Zweifel **II.** *vt* verdunkeln; (*follow*) beschatten; (*player*) decken

shadowboxing *n* Schattenboxen *nt*

shadowy [ʃæ·doʊ·i] *adj* schattig; (*dark*) düster; (*dubious*) zweifelhaft; **~ figure** schemenhafte Figur; *fig* rätselhaftes Wesen

shady [ʃeɪ·di] *adj* schattig; *fam* fragwürdig; (*dishonest*) unehrlich

shaft [ʃæft] **I.** *n* (*hole*) Schacht *m;* (*handle*) Schaft *m;* (*in engine*) Welle *f;* **~ of sunlight** Sonnenstrahl *m* **II.** *vt fam* betrügen

shaggy [ʃæg·i] *adj* struppig; (*unkempt*) zottelig

Shah [ʃɑ] *n hist* Schah *m*

shake [ʃeɪk] **I.** *n* **1.** Schütteln *nt;* **she gave the box a ~** sie schüttelte die Schachtel **2.** *fam* (*milkshake*) Shake *m* ▸ **to be no great ~s at sth** bei etw *dat* nicht besonders gut sein **II.** *vt* <shook, shaken> schütteln; *fig* erschüttern; **~ well before using** vor Gebrauch gut schütteln; **the news has ~n the whole country** die Nachricht hat das ganze Land schwer getroffen; **to ~ oneself** sich schütteln; **to ~ sth over sth** etw über etw *akk* streuen **III.** *vi* <shook, shaken> beben; (*with fear a.*) zittern (**with** vor +*dat*) ▸ **to ~ like a leaf** wie Espenlaub zittern

◆**shake off** *vt* abschütteln; (*get rid of*) überwinden; (*habit*) ablegen; (*illness*) besiegen; (*person*) loswerden; (*pursuer*) abschütteln

◆**shake out** *vt* ausschütteln

◆**shake up** *vt* (*mix*) mischen; (*shock*) aufwühlen; (*alter*) umkrempeln; (*reor-*ganize) umstellen

shaken [ʃeɪ·kən] **I.** *vt, vi pp of* **shake** **II.** *adj* erschüttert

shaker [ʃeɪ·kər] *n* Mixbecher *m;* **salt/pepper ~** Salz-/Pfefferstreuer *m*

shakily [ʃeɪ·kɪ·li] *adv* wack[e]lig; (*speak*) zitt[e]rig; (*uncertainly*) unsicher

shaky [ʃeɪ·ki] *adj* zittrig; (*ladder*) wack[e]lig; (*basis*) unsicher; (*economy*) instabil; **to feel a bit ~** (*physically*) noch etwas wack[e]lig auf den Beinen sein; (*emotionally*) beunruhigt sein; **to get off to a ~ start** mühsam in Gang kommen

shall [ʃæl] *aux vb liter* **1.** (*future*) **I ~ ...** ich werde ... **2.** (*ought to*) **I/he ~ ...** ich/er soll ...

shallow [ʃæl·oʊ] *adj* seicht; *fig a.* oberflächlich

sham [ʃæm] **I.** *n* **1.** *usu sing* Betrug *m kein pl* **2.** (*pretense*) Verstellung *f* **II.** *adj* gefälscht; **~ marriage** Scheinehe *f* **III.** *vt* <-mm-> vortäuschen **IV.** *vi* <-mm-> sich verstellen

shambles [ʃæm·bəlz] *n + sing vb fam* **to be [in] a ~** sich in einem chaotischen Zustand befinden

shame [ʃeɪm] **I.** *n* **1.** Scham *f;* (*disgrace*) Schande *f;* (*a pity*) Jammer *m;* **what a ~!** wie schade!; **~ on you!** *a. hum* schäm dich!; **to bring ~ on sb** Schande über jdn bringen; **it's a [great] ~ that ...** es ist [jammer]schade, dass ... **II.** *vt* **1.** beschämen **2.** (*bring shame on*) **to ~ sb/sth** jdm/etw Schande machen

shamefaced [ʃeɪm·feɪst] *adj* verschämt

shameful [ʃeɪm·fəl] *adj* schimpflich; (*defeat*) schmachvoll; (*disgraceful*) empörend; **it's ~ that ...** es ist eine Schande, dass ...

shameless [ʃeɪm·lɪs] *adj* schamlos

shampoo [ʃæm·ˈpu] **I.** *n* Shampoo *nt* **II.** *vt* shampoonieren

shamrock [ʃæm·rɑk] *n* weißer Feldklee

shape [ʃeɪp] **I.** *n* **1.** Form *f;* BIOL Gestalt *f;* MATH Figur *f;* **in any ~ or form** *fig* in jeder Form; **all ~s and sizes** alle Formen und Größen; **to take ~** Form annehmen **2. to be in bad ~** (*things*) in schlechtem Zustand sein; (*people*) in schlechter Verfassung sein; SPORT nicht in Form sein; **to be in great ~** in Hochform sein ▸ **to**

S

<u>whip</u> sb/sth into ~ jdn/etw auf Vordermann bringen *fam* II. *vt* |aus|formen; (*influence*) prägen; (*character*) formen; (*destiny*) gestalten

shapeless [ˈʃeɪp·lɪs] *adj* formlos; (*ideas*) vage; (*not shapely*) unförmig

shapely [ˈʃeɪp·li] *adj* wohlgeformt; (*figure*) schön; (*woman*) gut gebaut

shard [ʃard] *n* Scherbe *f;* (*of metal*) Splitter *m*

share [ʃer] I. *n* Anteil *m;* (*in company a.*) Aktie *f;* **one's ~ of the blame** seine Mitschuld; **the lion's ~ of sth** der Löwenanteil von etw *dat* **to have had one's fair ~ of sth** *iron* etw reichlich abbekommen haben; **to have a ~ in sth** an etw *dat* teilhaben II. *vi* teilen; **to ~ in sth** an etw *dat* teilhaben; (*participate*) in etw *dat* beteiligt sein III. *vt* 1. teilen; **to ~ responsibility** Verantwortung gemeinsam tragen 2. (*have in common*) gemeinsam haben; (*opinion*) teilen; **to ~ an interest** ein gemeinsames Interesse haben 3. (*communicate*) **to ~ sth with sb** etw an jdn weitergeben; **to ~ one's thoughts with sb** jdm seine Gedanken anvertrauen

'shareholder *n* Aktionär(in) *m(f)*

shark <*pl* -s> [ʃark] *n* Hai|fisch| *m; pej fam* Hai *m;* **loan ~** Kredithai *m*

sharp [ʃarp] I. *adj* scharf; (*pointed*) spitz; (*features*) kantig; (*stabbing*) stechend; (*sudden*) plötzlich; (*marked*) drastisch; (*rise*) stark; (*clear-cut*) scharf, deutlich, klar; (*perceptive*) scharfsinnig; (*eyes*) scharf; (*penetrating*) schrill; **to bring sth into ~ focus** etw klar und deutlich herausstellen II. *adv* **at 7:30 ~** um Punkt 7.30 Uhr; **to turn ~ left/right** scharf links/rechts abbiegen

sharpen [ˈʃar·pən] *vt a. fig* schärfen; (*pencil*) spitzen; (*knife*) schleifen; (*intensify*) verschärfen

sharpener [ˈʃar·pən·ər] *n* **pencil ~** Bleistiftspitzer *m*

sharp-'eyed *adj* scharfsichtig

'sharpshooter *n* Scharfschütze *m*

sharp-'tempered *adj* leicht erregbar

sharp-'tongued *adj* scharfzüngig

sharp-'witted *adj* scharfsinnig

shat [ʃæt] *vi pt, pp of* shit

shatter [ˈʃæt·ər] I. *vi* zerspringen II. *vt* zertrümmern; (*health*) zerrütten; *fig* vernichten; (*calm*) zerstören; (*dreams*) zunichtemachen

shattered [ˈʃæt·ərd] *adj fam* am Boden zerstört

shattering [ˈʃæt·ər·ɪŋ] *adj fam* (*upsetting*) erschütternd; (*destructive*) vernichtend

shatterproof [ˈʃæt·ər·ˌpruf] *adj* bruchsicher; (*windshield*) splitterfrei

shave [ʃeɪv] I. *n* Rasur *f;* **I need a ~** ich muss mich rasieren; **close ~** Glattrasur *f; fig* knappes Entkommen; **to have a close ~** gerade noch davonkommen II. *vi* <-d, -d *or* shaven> sich rasieren III. *vt* <-d, -d *or* shaven> rasieren

shaven [ˈʃeɪ·vən] *adj* rasiert; (*head*) kahl geschoren

shaver [ˈʃeɪ·vər] *n* Rasierapparat *m*

'shaving brush *n* Rasierpinsel *m*

'shaving cream *n* Rasiercreme *f*

'shaving foam *n* Rasierschaum *m*

shawl [ʃɔl] *n* Schultertuch *nt*

she [ʃi] I. *pron* sie; (*country*) es; (*ship*) sie II. *n usu sing* **a ~** eine Sie; (*animal*) ein Weibchen *nt*

shear <-ed, -ed *or* shorn> [ʃɪr] *vt* scheren

shears [ʃɪrz] *npl* |große| Schere *f*

shed¹ <-dd-, shed, shed> [ʃed] I. *vt* ablegen; (*leaves*) abwerfen; (*hair*) verlieren; (*blood, tears*) vergießen; (*light*) verbreiten; **to ~ a few pounds** ein paar Kilo abnehmen; **to ~ one's skin** sich häuten II. *vi* sich häuten; (*cats*) haaren

shed² [ʃed] *n* Schuppen *m;* **garden ~** Gartenhäuschen *nt*

sheep <*pl* -> [ʃip] *n* Schaf *nt;* **flock of ~** Schafherde *f*

'sheepdog *n* Schäferhund *m*

sheepish [ˈʃi·pɪʃ] *adj* unbeholfen; (*smile*) verlegen

'sheepskin *n* Schaffell *nt*

sheer [ʃɪr] *adj* 1. ~ **bliss** eine wahre Wonne; ~ **nonsense** blanker Unsinn 2. (*cliff*) steil

sheet [ʃit] *n* Laken *nt;* (*of paper*) Blatt *nt;* (*of metal*) Platte *f*

'sheet metal *n* Blech *nt*

'sheet music *n* Noten *pl*

sheik(h) [ʃik] *n* Scheich *m*

shelf <pl **shelves**> [ʃelf] n [Regal]brett nt; (set of shelves) Regal nt

shelf life n Haltbarkeit f

shell [ʃel] **I.** n **1.** Schale f; (of tortoise) Panzer m; (of pea) Hülse f; (on beach) Muschel f **2.** (artillery) Granate f; (cartridge) Patrone f ▸ **to come out of one's ~** aus sich dat herausgehen **II.** vt schälen; (nut) knacken; (pea) enthülsen; (bombard) [mit Granaten] bombardieren

◆ **shell out** fam **I.** vt blechen **II.** vi **to ~ out for sb/sth** für jdn/etw bezahlen

'**shellfish** <pl -> n Schalentier nt

shelling ['ʃəl·ɪŋ] n Bombardierung f

'**shell-shocked** adj fam völlig geschockt

shelter ['ʃel·tər] **I.** n Schutz m; (structure) Unterstand m; (to sit in) Häuschen nt; (for the needy) Heim nt **II.** vi Schutz suchen **III.** vt schützen

sheltered ['ʃəl·tərd] adj geschützt; (childhood) [über]behütet

shepherd ['ʃep·ərd] **I.** n Schäfer(in) m(f) **II.** vt hüten; **to ~ sb toward the door** jdn zur Tür führen

sherbet ['ʃɜr·bət], **sherbert** ['ʃɜr·bərt] n Fruchteis nt

sheriff ['ʃer·ɪf] n Sheriff m

sherry ['ʃer·i] n Sherry m

shield [ʃild] **I.** n [Schutz]schild m; (with coat of arms) [Wappen]schild m o nt; (eyes) schützen

shift [ʃɪft] **I.** vt [weg]bewegen; (furniture) verschieben; (blame) abwälzen; (emphasis) verlagern; **to ~ gears** schalten **II.** vi sich bewegen; (change position) die [or seine] Position verändern; **it won't ~** es lässt sich nicht bewegen; **to ~ into reverse** den Rückwärtsgang einlegen **III.** n **1.** Wechsel m; **a ~ in the balance of power** eine Verlagerung im Gleichgewicht der Kräfte **2.** (work, people) Schicht f

◆ **shift down** vi herunterschalten

◆ **shift up** vi hochschalten

'**shift key** n COMPUT Shifttaste f

'**shift work** n Schichtarbeit f

'**shift worker** n Schichtarbeiter(in) m(f)

shifty ['ʃɪf·ti] adj hinterhältig; **to look ~** verdächtig aussehen

Shiite ['ʃi·aɪt] **I.** n Schiit(in) m(f) **II.** adj schiitisch

shimmer ['ʃɪm·ər] **I.** vi schimmern **II.** n usu sing Schimmer m

shin [ʃɪn] n Schienbein nt

shindig ['ʃɪn·dɪg] n fam [wilde] Fete

shine [ʃaɪn] **I.** n Glanz m ▸ **[come] rain or ~** komme, was da wolle **II.** vi <shone or shined, shone or shined> scheinen; (stars) leuchten; (metal) glänzen; (eyes) strahlen; (excel) glänzen **III.** vt <shone or shined, shone or shined> **1.** **to ~ a light at sb/sth** jdn/etw anstrahlen **2.** (polish) polieren

◆ **shine out** vi [auf]leuchten; (excel) herausragen

shiner ['ʃaɪ·nər] n fam Veilchen nt

shining ['ʃaɪ·nɪŋ] adj glänzend; (eyes) strahlend; (outstanding) hervorragend; (example) leuchtend

shiny ['ʃaɪ·ni] adj glänzend; (metal) [spiegel]blank

ship [ʃɪp] **I.** n Schiff nt; **by ~** mit dem Schiff; (goods) per Schiff **II.** vt <-pp-> verschiffen; (transport) transportieren

◆ **ship off** vt verschiffen; (goods) per Schiff verschicken; fam (send away) wegschiffen

◆ **ship out I.** vt per Schiff senden **II.** vi fam sich verziehen

'**shipbuilder** n Werft f

'**shipbuilding** n Schiffbau m

'**shipload** n Schiffsladung f

shipment ['ʃɪp·mənt] n Sendung f; (dispatching) Transport m

'**shipowner** n (inland) Schiffseigner(in) m(f); (ocean) Reeder(in) m(f)

shipper ['ʃɪp·ər] n Spediteur(in) m(f); (business a.) Spedition f

shipping ['ʃɪp·ɪŋ] n **1.** Transport m; (by mail) Versand m; (by ship) Verschiffung f **2.** (costs) Transportkosten pl; (by mail) Postversand m; (by sea) Versand m auf dem Seeweg **3.** (ships) Schiffe pl [eines Landes]

'**shipping lane** n Schifffahrtsweg m

'**shipshape** adj pred fam aufgeräumt; **to make sth ~** etw aufräumen

'**shipwreck I.** n Schiffbruch m; (remains) [Schiffs]wrack nt **II.** vt usu passive **to be ~ed** Schiffbruch erleiden; (fail) scheitern

'shipyard n [Schiffs]werft f

shirk [ʃɜrk] vt meiden; **to ~ one's responsibilities** sich seiner Verantwortung entziehen

shirt [ʃɜrt] n Hemd nt ▶ **keep your~ on!** fam reg dich ab!

'shirtsleeve n usu pl Hemdsärmel m; **in ~s** in Hemdsärmeln

shit [ʃɪt] vulg I. n Scheiße f derb; **Jackie doesn't take any ~ from anyone** Jackie lässt sich von niemandem was gefallen fam ▶ **to beat the ~ out of sb** aus jdm Hackfleisch machen fam; **the ~ hits the fan** es gibt Ärger; **to not know ~ about** sb/sth keinen blassen Schimmer von jdm/etw haben fam II. interj ~! Scheiße! derb III. vi <-tt-, shit or shitted or shat, shit or shitted or shat> scheißen derb IV. vt <-tt-, shit or shitted or shat, shit or shitted or shat> **to ~ one's pants** sich dat [vor Angst] in die Hosen machen fam

shitty [ˈʃɪt·i] adj vulg beschissen derb

shiver [ˈʃɪv·ər] I. n Schauder m; **to give sb the ~s** fam jdn das Fürchten lehren II. vi zittern; **to ~ with cold** frösteln

shoal [ʃoʊl] n Schwarm m

shock [ʃɑk] I. n Schock m; (electric) [elektrischer] Schlag; (health condition) Schock[zustand] m; **prepare yourself for a ~** mach dich auf etwas Schlimmes gefasst; **a ~ to the system** eine schwierige Umstellung; **to be in [a state of] ~** unter Schock stehen II. vt schockieren; (deeply) erschüttern

'shock absorber n Stoßdämpfer m

shocker [ˈʃɑk·ər] n fam Schocker m; **the headline was a deliberate ~** die Schlagzeile sollte schockieren

shocking [ˈʃɑk·ɪŋ] adj schockierend; (crime) abscheulich; (surprising) völlig überraschend

'shockproof adj bruchsicher

'shock therapy, 'shock treatment n Schocktherapie f

'shock wave n Druckwelle f; **the news sent ~s through the financial world** die Nachricht erschütterte die Finanzwelt

shoddy [ˈʃɑd·i] adj schlampig [gearbeitet] fam; (run down) schäbig; (goods) minderwertig; (reprehensible) schäbig

shoe [ʃu] I. n Schuh m; (horseshoe) Hufeisen nt; **a pair of ~s** ein Paar nt Schuhe ▶ **to put oneself in sb's ~s** sich in jds Lage versetzen; **if I were in your ~s** fam an deiner Stelle II. vt <shod or shoed, shod or shodden or shoed> (horse) beschlagen

'shoehorn n Schuhlöffel m

'shoelace n usu pl Schnürsenkel m

'shoemaker n Schuster(in) m(f)

'shoe polish n Schuhcreme f

'shoe size n Schuhgröße f

'shoestring n usu pl Schnürsenkel m ▶ **to do sth on a ~** fam etw mit wenig Geld tun

shone [ʃoʊn] pt, pp of **shine**

shoo [ʃu] fam I. interj ~! husch [husch]! II. vt wegscheuchen

shook [ʃʊk] pt of **shake**

shoot [ʃut] I. n (on plant) Trieb m; (hunt) Jagd f; PHOT Aufnahmen pl II. vi <shot, shot> 1. schießen; **to ~ to kill** mit Tötungsabsicht schießen 2. + adv/prep **to ~ past** vorbeischießen 3. (film) filmen; (take photos) fotografieren 4. (target) **to ~ for sth** etw anstreben III. vt <shot, shot> 1. **to ~ sth** (gun) mit etw dat schießen; (arrow) etw abschießen; (bullet) etw abfeuern 2. (hit) anschießen; (dead) erschießen; **to be shot in the leg** ins Bein getroffen werden 3. (movie) drehen; (photo) machen 4. **to ~ questions at sb** jdn mit Fragen bombardieren 5. (goal) schießen

◆**shoot down** vt abschießen; (kill) erschießen; fam (accusation) niedermachen

◆**shoot off** I. vi schnell losfahren; (people) eilig aufbrechen II. vt abschießen ▶ **to ~ one's mouth off** sl sich dat das Maul zerreißen

◆**shoot out** I. vi plötzlich hervorschießen; (water) herausschießen; (flames) hervorbrechen II. vt 1. **he shot out a hand** er streckte blitzschnell die Hand aus 2. **to ~ it out** etw [mit Schusswaffen] austragen

◆**shoot up** I. vi 1. (price) schnell ansteigen; (skyscraper) in die Höhe schießen 2. fam (child) schnell wachsen 3. sl sich

dat einen Schuss verpassen *sl* **II.** *vt* sich *dat* spritzen

hooting ['ʃu·tɪŋ] *n* **1.** Schießerei *f;* (*killing*) Erschießung *f;* (*sport*) Jagen *nt* **2.** FILM Drehen *nt*

shooting range *n* Schießstand *m*

hooting 'star *n* Sternschnuppe *f;* (*person*) Shootingstar *m*

shootout *n* Schießerei *f*

hop [ʃap] **I.** *n* Laden *m;* (*garage*) Werkstatt *f;* **to set up ~** ein Geschäft eröffnen; (*start out in business*) ein Unternehmen eröffnen **II.** *vi* <-pp-> einkaufen

shopkeeper *n* Ladeninhaber(in) *m(f)*

shoplifter *n* Ladendieb(in) *m(f)*

shoplifting *n* Ladendiebstahl *m*

hopper ['ʃap·ər] *n* Käufer(in) *m(f)*

shopping ['ʃap·ɪŋ] *n* Einkaufen *nt;* **to go ~** einkaufen [gehen]

shopping bag *n* Einkaufstasche *f*

shopping basket *n* Einkaufskorb *m*

shopping cart *n* Einkaufswagen *m*

shopping center *n* Einkaufszentrum *nt*

shopping list *n* Einkaufsliste *f*

shopping mall *n* überdachtes Einkaufszentrum

hore [ʃor] *n* Küste *f;* (*bank*) Ufer *nt;* (*beach*) Strand *m;* **on ~** an Land

shoreline *n* Küstenlinie *f*

horn [ʃɔrn] *pp of* **shear**

short [ʃɔrt] **I.** *adj* **1.** kurz; (*person*) klein; **at ~ range** aus kurzer Entfernung; **in the ~ term** kurzfristig; **Bob's ~ for Robert** Bob ist die Kurzform von Robert **2.** **we're still one person ~** uns fehlt noch eine Person; **to be in ~ supply** schwer zu beschaffen sein; **sb is ~ of sth** jdm mangelt es an etw *dat* **we're a bit ~ of coffee** wir haben nur noch wenig Kaffee; **to be ~ [of cash]** knapp bei Kasse sein; **to be ~ of breath** außer Atem sein ► **to have a ~ fuse** schnell wütend werden; **to draw the ~ straw** den Kürzeren ziehen **II.** *adv* **to cut sth ~** etw abkürzen; **to fall ~ of expectations** den Erwartungen nicht entsprechen ► **in ~** kurz gesagt

shortage ['ʃɔr·tɪdʒ] *n* Mangel *m kein pl*

shortbread *n* Shortbread *nt* (*Buttergebäck*)

short'change *vt* **to ~ sb** jdm zu wenig

Wechselgeld herausgeben

short 'circuit *n* Kurzschluss *m*

short-'circuit **I.** *vt* kurzschließen; (*avoid*) abkürzen **II.** *vi* einen Kurzschluss haben

'shortcoming *n usu pl* Mangel *m;* (*of person*) Fehler *m;* (*of system*) Unzulänglichkeit *f*

'shortcut *n* Abkürzung *f*

shorten ['ʃɔr·tən] **I.** *vt* kürzen; (*name*) abkürzen **II.** *vi* kürzer werden

'shortfall *n* Mangel *m kein pl;* (*deficit*) Defizit *nt*

'shorthand *n* Kurzschrift *f*

short-'handed *adj* unterbesetzt; **to be ~** zu wenig Personal haben

'short list *n* **to be on the ~** in der engeren Wahl sein

'short-list *vt* in die engere Wahl ziehen

short-lived [-'lɪvd] *adj* kurzlebig

shortly ['ʃɔrt·li] *adv* in Kürze; **~ afterwards** kurz danach

'short-range *adj* Kurzstrecken-; (*forecast*) kurzfristig

shorts [ʃɔrts] *n pl* kurze Hose; (*underpants*) Unterhose *f*

short'sighted *adj* kurzsichtig *a. fig*

'short-term *adj* kurzfristig

shot[1] [ʃat] *n* **1.** Schuss *m* **2.** (*in basketball*) Wurf *m;* (*in tennis, golf*) Schlag *m;* (*in soccer, hockey*) Schuss *m* **3.** (*photograph*) Aufnahme *f;* FILM Einstellung *f* **4.** *fam* (*injection*) Spritze *f; fig* Schuss *m* **5.** *fam* (*attempt*) Gelegenheit *f;* **to give it a ~** es mal versuchen *fam* **6.** (*of alcohol*) Schuss *m* **7.** (*remark*) **to take a ~ at sb** jdn runtermachen; (*attack verbally*) über jdn herfallen ► **like a ~** *fam* wie der Blitz

shot[2] [ʃat] **I.** *vt, vi pt, pp of* **shoot** **II.** *adj fam* ausgeleiert *fam;* **my nerves are ~** ich bin mit meinen Nerven am Ende

'shotgun *n* Schrotflinte *f* ► **to ride ~** *fam* auf dem Beifahrersitz mitfahren *(im Auto/auf dem Motorrad)*

'shot put *n* SPORT **the ~** Kugelstoßen *nt kein pl*

'shot putter *n* SPORT Kugelstoßer(in) *m(f)*

should [ʃʊd] *aux vb* **you ~ be ashamed of yourselves** ihr solltet euch [was] schämen; **~ I apologize to him?** soll[te]

S

ich mich bei ihm entschuldigen?; **there ~n't be any problems** es dürfte eigentlich keine Probleme geben; **I ~ have known that ...** ich hätte es eigentlich wissen müssen, dass ...; **why ~ I?** warum sollte ich?; **where's Stuart? — how ~ I know?** wo ist Stuart? – woher soll[te] ich das wissen?

shoulder ['ʃoʊl·dər] **I.** n Schulter f; (of road) Bankett nt; **to shrug one's ~s** mit den Achseln zucken **II.** vt **1.** (accept) auf sich akk nehmen; (blame) übernehmen **2.** (push) **to ~ one's way somewhere** sich irgendwohin drängen

'**shoulder bag** n Umhängetasche f

'**shoulder blade** n Schulterblatt nt

'**shoulder pad** n Schulterpolster nt

shout [ʃaʊt] **I.** n Ruf m; **a ~ of laughter** lautes Gelächter **II.** vi schreien; **to ~ at sb** jdn anschreien; **to ~ to sb** jdm zurufen **III.** vt rufen; **to ~ sth at sb** jdm etw zurufen; **to ~ abuse at sb** jdn lautstark beschimpfen

◆**shout down** vt niederschreien fam

◆**shout out** vt [aus]rufen

shouting ['ʃaʊ·tɪŋ] **I.** n Schreien nt **II.** adj ▶ **within ~ distance** in Rufweite; fig nahe [an] +dat

shove [ʃʌv] **I.** n Ruck m; **to give sth a ~** etw [weg]rücken **II.** vt schieben; **to ~ sb around** jdn herumstoßen fam; **to ~ sth into a bag** etw in eine Tasche stecken **III.** vi drängen

◆**shove off** vi fam abhauen sl

shovel ['ʃʌv·əl] **I.** n Schaufel f; (of bulldozer) Baggerschaufel f; **a ~ of snow** eine Schaufel [voll] Schnee **II.** vt, vi <-l-> schaufeln a. fig

show [ʃoʊ] **I.** n **1.** Demonstration f; **~ of solidarity** Solidaritätsbekundung f geh **2.** (display) Schau f; **just for ~** nur der Schau wegen **3.** (event) Ausstellung f; **slide ~** Diavortrag m; **to be on ~** ausgestellt sein **4.** (entertainment) Show f; (on TV a.) Unterhaltungssendung f; (at theater) Vorstellung f ▶ **let's get this ~ on the road** fam lasst uns die Sache [endlich] in Angriff nehmen; **the ~ must go on** saying die Show muss weitergehen **II.** vt <showed, shown or showed> **1.** (film) zeigen; (exhibit)

ausstellen; (perform) vorführen; (passport) vorzeigen; **to ~ sb respect** jdm Respekt erweisen **2.** (reveal) zeigen; **he started to ~ his age** man konn te ihm langsam sein Alter ansehen; **to ~ common sense** gesunden Menschen verstand beweisen **3.** (explain) zeigen; **to ~ sb the way** jdm den Weg zeigen **4.** (record) anzeigen; (statistics) [aus] zeigen; (profit) aufweisen **5.** (prove) beweisen; **to ~ [sb] how ...** [jdm] zeigen wie ...; **to ~ oneself [to be]** sich als etw erweisen ▶ **to ~ one's true col ors** Farbe bekennen; **that will ~ you** fam das wird dir eine Lehre sein **III.** v <showed, shown or showed> **1.** (be visible) zu sehen sein; **to let sth ~** sich dat etw anmerken lassen **2.** (film) lau fen fam; **now ~ing at a theater nea you!** jetzt in Ihrem Kino!

◆**show around** vt herumführen; **to ~ sb around the house** jdm das Hau zeigen

◆**show in** vt her-/hineinführen

◆**show off I.** vt **to ~ off** ⇄ sb/sth mi jdm/etw angeben **II.** vi angeben

◆**show through** vi durchschimmern

◆**show up I.** vi **1.** (appear) sich zeigen **the drug does not ~ up in blood tests** das Medikament ist in Blutproben nich nachweisbar **2.** fam (arrive) auftaucher **II.** vt **1.** (expose) zeigen **2.** (embarrass) bloßstellen

show biz ['ʃoʊ·bɪz] n fam short for **show business** Showbiz nt

'**show business** n Showbusiness nt

'**showcase** n Schaukasten m; (opportu nity) Schaufenster nt

shower ['ʃaʊ·ər] **I.** n Schauer m; (fo bathing) Dusche f; **to take a ~** duscher **II.** vt bespritzen; **to ~ sb with compli ments** jdn mit Komplimenten überhäu fen **III.** vi duschen

'**shower cap** n Duschhaube f

showing ['ʃoʊ·ɪŋ] n usu sing Ausstel lung f; (broadcasting) Übertragung f (performance) Vorstellung f

'**show jumping** n Springreiten nt

'**showman** n Showman m

shown [ʃoʊn] vt, vi pp of **show**

'**showoff** n Angeber(in) m(f)

howroom n Ausstellungsraum m

howtime n Aufführung[szeit] f ▶ **it's ~!** es geht los!

howy [ˈʃoʊ·i] adj auffällig

hrank [ʃræŋk] vt, vi pt of **shrink**

hrapnel [ˈʃræp·nəl] n Granatsplitter pl

hred [ʃred] I. n Streifen m; (of hope) Funke m; **there isn't a ~ of evidence** es gibt nicht den geringsten Beweis; **to be in ~s** zerfetzt sein; **to rip sth to ~s** etw in Fetzen reißen II. vt <-dd-> zerkleinern; (vegetables) hacken

hredder [ˈʃred·ər] n Reißwolf m; (paper) Shredder m

hrew [ʃru] n Spitzmaus f

hrewd [ʃrud] adj schlau; (eye) scharf; (move) geschickt

hriek [ʃrik] I. n [schriller, kurzer] Schrei II. vi kreischen; (with laughter) brüllen; (with pain) [auf]schreien III. vt [auf]schreien

hrill [ʃrɪl] adj schrill

hrimp <pl -s> [ʃrɪmp] n Garnele f; pej fam (person) Zwerg m hum

hrine [ʃraɪn] n Heiligtum nt; (for relics) Schrein m a. fig; (tomb) Grabmal nt; (for worship) Pilgerstätte f

hrink [ʃrɪŋk] I. vi <shrank or shrunk, shrunk or shrunken> **1.** schrumpfen; (sweater) eingehen **2. to ~ away** zurückweichen **3. to ~ from [doing] sth** sich vor etw dat drücken fam II. vt <shrank or shrunk, shrunk or shrunken> schrumpfen lassen III. n fam Psychiater(in) m(f)

hrink-wrap n Plastikfolie f II. vt in Frischhaltefolie einpacken; (book) einschweißen

hrivel <-l-> [ˈʃrɪv·əl] vi [zusammen] schrumpfen; (fruit) schrumpeln; (plants) welken; (skin) faltig werden; (profits) schwinden

hrivel up vi zusammenschrumpfen; (fruit) schrumpeln

hrove Tuesday [ʃroʊv·ˈtuz·deɪ] n no art Fastnachtsdienstag m

hrub [ʃrʌb] n Strauch m

hrubbery [ˈʃrʌb·ə·ri] n Sträucher pl; (area) Gebüsch nt

hrug [ʃrʌg] I. n Achselzucken nt II. vi <-gg-> die Achseln zucken III. vt

to ~ one's shoulders die Achseln zucken

shrunk [ʃrʌŋk] vt, vi pt, pp of **shrink**

shrunken [ˈʃrʌŋ·kən] I. adj geschrumpft II. vt, vi pp of **shrink**

shudder [ˈʃʌd·ər] I. vi zittern; (ground) beben; I ~ **to think what ...** mir graut vor dem Gedanken, was ...; **to ~ to a halt** mit einem Rucken zum Stehen kommen II. n Schaudern nt; **to send a ~ through sb** jdn erschaudern lassen pej

shuffle [ˈʃʌf·əl] I. n Mischen nt (von Karten); (rearrangement) Neuordnung f; (of feet) Schlurfen nt; **to give the cards a ~** die Karten mischen II. vt mischen; (feet) schlurfen; **to ~ sth around** etw hin- und herschieben III. vi Karten mischen; (with feet) schlurfen

shun <-nn-> [ʃʌn] vt meiden; **to ~ sb** jdm aus dem Weg gehen

shush [ʃʊʃ] I. interj pst! II. vt fam **to ~ sb** jdm sagen, dass er/sie still sein soll

shut [ʃʌt] I. adj geschlossen; (curtains) zugezogen; **to slam a door ~** eine Tür zuschlagen II. vt <-tt-, shut, shut> (close) schließen; (book) zuklappen; (shop) schließen ▶ **~ your mouth!** Klappe! sl III. vi <-tt-, shut, shut> schließen

shut away vt einsperren

shut down I. vt abstellen; (factory) stilllegen; (computer) herunterfahren II. vi zumachen

shut in vt einsperren

shut off I. vt abstellen; (computer) herunterfahren; **to ~ oneself off** sich zurückziehen II. vi sich [automatisch] ausschalten

shut out vt ausschließen; (thoughts) verdrängen; (light) abschirmen

shut up I. vt **1.** schließen; **to ~ up shop** das Geschäft schließen; (stop business) seine Tätigkeit einstellen **2.** fam (silence) zum Schweigen bringen II. vi fam den Mund halten

shutdown n Schließung f

shuteye n fam Nickerchen nt

shutter [ˈʃʌt·ər] n Fensterladen m; PHOT [Kamera]verschluss m

shuttle [ˈʃʌt·əl] n (train) Pendelzug m;

S

(*plane*) Pendelmaschine *f;* **space ~** Raumfähre *f*

shuttle bus *n* [kostenloser] Zubringer[bus]

shuttlecock ['ʃʌt·əl·kak] *n* Federball *m*

shy [ʃaɪ] *adj* schüchtern; (*smile*) scheu

shy away from *vt* **to ~ away from** [doing] sth vor etw *dat* zurückschrecken

shyness ['ʃaɪ·nɪs] *n* Schüchternheit *f*

Siamese [ˌsaɪ·ə·'miːz] **I.** *n <pl>* Siamese, Siamesin *m, f;* (*cat*) Siamkatze *f;* (*language*) Siamesisch *nt* **II.** *adj* siamesisch

Siamese 'twins *npl* siamesische Zwillinge

Sicilian [sɪ·'sɪl·jən] **I.** *n* Sizilianer(in) *m(f)* **II.** *adj* sizilianisch

Sicily ['sɪs·ɪ·li] *n* Sizilien *nt*

sick [sɪk] **I.** *adj* **1.** krank; (*mentally*) geisteskrank; (*machine, engine*) angeschlagen; **to call in ~** sich krankmelden **2.** *pred* **to be ~** (*vomit*) sich erbrechen; **to feel ~** sich schlecht fühlen **3.** *pred fam* **to be ~ and tired of sth** etw [gründlich] satthaben; **to be ~ of sb/sth** von jdm/etw die Nase voll haben **4.** *fam* (*cruel*) geschmacklos; (*person*) pervers; (*mind*) abartig ▶ **to be worried ~** *fam* krank vor Sorge sein **II.** *n* **the ~** *pl* die Kranken *pl*

sicken ['sɪk·ən] **I.** *vi* erkranken **II.** *vt* (*upset*) krank machen *fam;* (*disgust*) anekeln

sickening ['sɪk·ən·ɪŋ] *adj* entsetzlich; (*smell*) widerlich; (*annoying*) [äußerst] ärgerlich

sickle ['sɪk·əl] *n* Sichel *f*

'sick leave *n* MED **to be on ~** krankgeschrieben sein

sickly ['sɪk·li] *adj* kränklich; (*complexion*) blass

sickness <*pl* -es> ['sɪk·nɪs] *n* Krankheit *f;* (*nausea*) Übelkeit *f*

'sick pay *n* Krankengeld *nt*

side [saɪd] **I.** *n* **1.** Seite *f;* (*of hill*) Hang *m;* (*of house*) [Seiten]wand *f;* (*of plate, field*) Rand *m;* (*of river*) [Fluss]ufer *nt;* (*of road*) [Straßen]rand *m;* **this ~ up!** oben!; **on all ~s** auf allen Seiten; **to stay at sb's ~** jdm zur Seite stehen; **at the ~ of sth** neben etw *dat* **2.** (*half*

of bed) Hälfte *f;* (*of town, road*) Seite **3. to take sb to one ~** jdn auf die Sei nehmen **4.** (*party*) Partei *f;* (*team a* Mannschaft *f;* **to change ~s** sich auf d andere Seite schlagen; **to take ~s** Part ergreifen **5. I've listened to your ~ o the story** ich habe jetzt deine Versio der Geschichte gehört ▶ **the other ~ of the coin** die Kehrseite der Medaill **to be on the large/small ~** zu groß klein sein **II.** *adj* **~ job** Nebenbeschäfti gung *f* **III.** *vi* **to ~ against sb** sich gege jdn stellen; **to ~ with sb** zu jdm halte

'sideburns *npl* Koteletten *pl*

'sidecar *n* AUTO Seitenwagen *m*

'side dish *n* FOOD Beilage *f*

'side effect *n* Nebenwirkung *f*

'sideshow *n* Nebenaufführung *f;* (*exhib tion*) Sonderausstellung *f*

'sidestep I. *vt* <-pp-> **to ~ sb/sth** jdm etw ausweichen **II.** *vi* <-pp-> auswe chen **III.** *n* Schritt *m* zur Seite; *fig* Au weichmanöver *nt*

'side street *n* Seitenstraße *f*

'sidetrack *vt* ablenken

'sidewalk *n* Bürgersteig *m*

sideways ['saɪd·weɪz] **I.** *adv* seitwär (*awry*) schief **II.** *adj* seitlich; (*loo* von der Seite

siding ['saɪ·dɪŋ] *n* Rangiergleis *nt*

siege [siːdʒ] *n* MIL Belagerung *f;* **to lay to sth** etw belagern

sieve [sɪv] **I.** *n* Sieb *nt* ▶ **to have mind like a ~** *fam* ein Gedächtnis w ein Sieb haben **II.** *vt* sieben

sift [sɪft] *vt* **1.** sieben; **~ some sugar ov the cake** bestäuben Sie den Kuchen m Zucker **2.** (*examine*) durchsieben; (*e dence*) [gründlich] durchgehen

sigh [saɪ] **I.** *n* Seufzer *m;* **to heave a** einen Seufzer ausstoßen **II.** *vi* seufze (*wind*) säuseln; **to ~ with relief** vor F leichterung [auf]seufzen

sight [saɪt] *n* **1.** [**sense of**] **~** Sehverm gen *nt* **2.** (*access*) Sicht *f;* (*range* Sichtweite *f;* **get out of my ~!** *fam* g mir aus den Augen!; **to be in/out of** in/außer Sichtweite sein; **to keep c of ~** sich nicht sehen lassen **3.** (*a* Anblick *m;* **love at first ~** Liebe auf d ersten Blick; **to know sb by ~** jdn vo

Sehen [her] kennen **4.** (*attractions*) ~s *pl* Sehenswürdigkeiten *pl* **5.** (*on gun*) Visier *nt* ▶ **out of ~, out of mind** *prov* aus den Augen, aus dem Sinn *prov;* **to set one's ~s on sth** sich *dat* etw zum Ziel machen

sightseeing *n* Besichtigungen *pl;* **to go ~** Sehenswürdigkeiten besichtigen

sightseer ['saɪt·siː·ər] *n* Tourist(in) *m(f)*

sign [saɪn] **I.** *n* **1.** Zeichen *nt;* **to make the ~ of the cross** sich bekreuzigen **2.** (*notice*) [Straßen]schild *nt;* (*signboard*) Schild *nt;* (*traffic* ~) Verkehrsschild *nt* **3.** (*symbol*) Zeichen *nt;* (*of zodiac*) Sternzeichen *nt* **4.** (*indication*) [An]zeichen *nt;* (*trace*) Spur *f;* **~ of life** Lebenszeichen *nt* **II.** *vt* (*letter*) unterschreiben; (*contract*) unterzeichnen; (*book*) signieren **III.** *vi* unterschreiben; **to ~ for a delivery** eine Lieferung gegenzeichnen

sign in I. *vi* sich eintragen **II.** *vt* eintragen

sign off *vi* (*end letter*) zum Schluss kommen; (*end work*) Schluss machen

sign on I. *vi* sich verpflichten; (*for class*) sich einschreiben **II.** *vt* verpflichten

sign out *vt* (*books*) ausleihen

sign over *vt* übertragen

sign up *vi* sich verpflichten; (*for class*) sich einschreiben

signal ['sɪg·nəl] **I.** *n* Signal *nt;* (*reception*) Empfang *m;* (*gesture*) Zeichen *nt;* (*traffic light*) Ampel *f;* (*for trains*) Signal *nt;* (*on car*) Blinker *m* **II.** *vi* <-l-> signalisieren; **she ~ed to them to be quiet** sie gab ihnen ein Zeichen, ruhig zu sein

signature ['sɪg·nə·tʃər] *n* **1.** Unterschrift *f;* (*of artist*) Signatur *f* **2.** (*characteristic*) Erkennungszeichen *nt*

significance [sɪg·'nɪf·ɪ·kəns] *n* Wichtigkeit *f;* (*meaning*) Bedeutung *f;* **to be of no ~** bedeutungslos sein

significant [sɪg·'nɪf·ɪ·kənt] *adj* bedeutend; (*important*) bedeutsam; (*date, event*) wichtig; (*difference*) deutlich; (*increase*) beträchtlich; (*look*) viel sagend; **do you think it's ~ that ...** glaubst du, es hat etwas zu bedeuten, dass ...

signify <-ie-> ['sɪg·nə·faɪ] **I.** *vt* andeuten **II.** *vi* **it doesn't ~** es macht nichts

signpost I. *n* Wegweiser *m* **II.** *vt* ausschildern

Sikh [siːk] *n* Sikh *m*

silence ['saɪ·ləns] **I.** *n* Stille *f;* (*of person*) Schweigen *nt;* (*discretion*) Stillschweigen *nt;* (*calmness*) Ruhe *f;* **to work in ~** still arbeiten ▶ **~ is golden** *prov* Schweigen ist Gold **II.** *vt* zum Schweigen bringen; (*doubts*) verstummen lassen

silencer ['saɪ·lən·sər] *n* Schalldämpfer *m*

silent ['saɪ·lənt] *adj* still; (*not talking a.*) schweigsam; **to be ~** schweigen; **to keep ~** still sein; **to go ~** verstummen

silhouette [ˌsɪl·uˈet] **I.** *n* Silhouette *f* **II.** *vt* **to be ~d against sth** sich von etw *dat* abheben

silicon ['sɪl·ɪ·kən] *n* Silizium *nt*

silicon 'chip *n* COMPUT, ELEC Siliziumchip *m*

silicone ['sɪl·ɪ·koʊn] *n* Silikon *nt*

Silicon 'Valley *n* Silicon Valley *nt*

silk [sɪlk] *n* Seide *f*

'silkworm *n* Seidenraupe *f*

silky ['sɪl·ki] *adj* seidig; (*voice*) samtig

sill [sɪl] *n* Fensterbank *f*

silly ['sɪl·i] *adj* albern; **don't be ~!** (*make silly suggestions*) red keinen Unsinn!; (*do silly things*) mach keinen Quatsch! *fam;* **to be bored ~** zu Tode gelangweilt sein

silo ['saɪ·loʊ] *n* Silo *m o nt*

silver ['sɪl·vər] **I.** *n* Silber *nt;* (*coins*) Münzgeld *nt;* (*cutlery*) [Tafel]silber *nt* **II.** *adj* Silber- ▶ **every cloud has a ~ lining** *saying* jedes Unglück hat auch sein Gutes

'silverfish <*pl* -> *n* Silberfischchen *nt*

similar ['sɪm·ə·lər] *adj* ähnlich (**to** +*dat*)

similarity [ˌsɪm·əˈler·ɪ·ti] *n* Ähnlichkeit *f*

simple <-r, -st> ['sɪm·pəl] *adj* einfach; (*straightforward*) schlicht; (*ignorant*) naiv; **the ~ things in life** die einfachen Dinge des Lebens; **for the ~ reason that ...** aus dem schlichten Grund, dass ...

simple-'minded *adj* einfach; (*naive*) einfältig

simplicity [sɪmˈplɪs·ɪ·ti] *n* Einfachheit *f;*

S

~ **itself** die Einfachheit selbst

simplification [ˌsɪm·plə·fɪ·ˈkeɪ·ʃən] n Vereinfachung f

simplify <-ie-> [ˈsɪm·plə·faɪ] vt vereinfachen

simply [ˈsɪm·pli] adv einfach; (just) nur; (humbly) bescheiden

simulate [ˈsɪm·jʊ·leɪt] vt simulieren; (resemble) nachahmen; (feign) vortäuschen

simulation [ˌsɪm·jʊ·ˈleɪ·ʃən] n Simulation f; (feigning) Vortäuschung f

simulator [ˈsɪm·jʊ·leɪ·tər] n Simulator m

simultaneous [ˌsaɪ·məl·ˈteɪ·ni·əs] adj gleichzeitig

sin [sɪn] I. n Sünde f; [as] **ugly as** ~ unglaublich hässlich II. vi <-nn-> sündigen

since [sɪns] I. adv seitdem; **we haven't seen her** ~ seitdem haben wir sie nicht mehr gesehen; **long** ~ seit langem; **not long** ~ vor kurzem [erst] II. prep seit III. conj da; [**ever**] ~ seit

sincere [sɪn·ˈsɪr] adj ehrlich; (gratitude) aufrichtig

sincerely [sɪn·ˈsɪr·li] adv ehrlich; (in letter) mit freundlichen Grüßen

sinew [ˈsɪn·ju] n Sehne f

sing <sang or sung, sung> [sɪŋ] vt, vi singen; (kettle) pfeifen; (locusts) zirpen; (wind) pfeifen; (ring) dröhnen

◆**sing out** I. vi laut singen; fam (call out) schreien II. vt fam ausrufen

sing. I. n abbr of **singular** Sg. II. adj abbr of **singular** im Sing. nach n

Singapore [ˈsɪŋ·ə·pɔr] n Singapur nt

Singaporean [ˈsɪŋ·ə·pɔr·i·ən] I. adj aus Singapur nach n II. n Singapurer(in) m(f)

singe [sɪndʒ] I. vt ansengen; (slightly) versengen II. vi angesengt werden; (slightly) versengt werden

singer [ˈsɪŋ·ər] n Sänger(in) m(f)

singing [ˈsɪŋ·ɪŋ] n Singen nt

single [ˈsɪŋ·gəl] I. adj einzige(r, s); (having one part) einzelne(r, s); (unmarried) ledig; ~ **mother** allein erziehende Mutter; **not a** ~ **soul** keine Menschenseele; **every** ~ **time** jedes Mal II. n (record) Single f; (room) Einzelzimmer nt; (in baseball) Single m

◆**single out** vt auswählen; (rejects) he[rausgreifen]

single ʼfile n **in** ~ im Gänsemarsch

single-ʼhanded I. adv [ganz] allei[n] II. adj allein

single-ʼminded adj zielstrebig

ʼ**singles bar** n Singlekneipe f

single-ʼsex adj nach Geschlechtern ge[trennt]

singly [ˈsɪŋ·gli] adv einzeln

singular [ˈsɪŋ·gjə·lər] I. adj Singular-; **t[o] be** ~ im Singular stehen; ~ **form** Singu[larform f] II. n Singular m

Sinhalese [ˌsɪn·hə·ˈliz] I. adj singhale[sisch] II. n Singhalese, Singhalesin m, [f]; (language) Singhalesisch nt

sinister [ˈsɪn·ɪ·stər] adj unheimlich; fa[r] (ominous) unheilvoll; (forces) dunkel

sink [sɪŋk] I. n Spülbecken nt; (wash[basin]) Waschbecken nt II. vi <san[k] or sunk, sunk> vi sinken; (in mud) einsinken; (sun) untergehen; (subside[)] sich senken; (head) herabsinken; (sales) zurückgehen; (standards) nachlassen[;] **to** ~ **to the ground** (person) zu Boden sinken; **to** ~ **to the bottom** auf den Bo[den] den sinken ► **sb's heart** ~s (sad) jd[m] wird das Herz schwer; (discouraged) je[m] verliert den Mut III. vt <sank or sunk[,] sunk> versenken; (well) bohren; (ruin[)] zunichtemachen

◆**sink in** vi einsinken; (liquid) einzie[hen; (be understood) ins Bewusstsein[] dringen

◆**sink into** vi **to** ~ **into sth** in etw dat[] einsinken; (lotion) in etw akk einziehen[;] (lie back) in etw akk [hinein]sinken; **to** ~ **into bed** sich ins Bett fallen lassen; **to** ~ **into a coma** ins Koma fallen

sinking [ˈsɪŋ·kɪŋ] adj attr sinkend; **a** ~ **feeling** ein flaues Gefühl [in der Ma[gengegend]; **with a** ~ **heart** resignier[t] ► **to leave the** ~ **ship** das sinkend[e] Schiff verlassen

sinner [ˈsɪn·ər] n Sünder(in) m(f)

Sioux [su] I. adj Sioux- II. n <pl -[>] Sioux m o f; (language) Sioux nt

sip [sɪp] I. vt <-pp-> nippen; (carefully[)] etw in kleinen Schlucken trinken II. [n] Schlückchen nt

siphon [ˈsaɪ·fən] I. n Saugheber m II. [vt]

[mit einem Saugheber] absaugen

sir [sɜr] *n* Herr *m;* **excuse me, ~** entschuldigen Sie bitte; **no, ~!** *fam* auf keinen Fall!; **Dear S~** [*or* **Madam**] Sehr geehrte Damen und Herren

siren ['saɪ·rən] *n* Sirene *f*

sister ['sɪs·tər] *n* Schwester *f;* (*nun*) [Ordens]schwester *f*

sister city *n* Partnerstadt *f*

'sister-in-law *<pl* sisters-> *n* Schwägerin *f*

sisterly ['sɪs·tər·li] *adj* schwesterlich

sit <-tt, sat, sat> [sɪt] **I.** *vi* sitzen; (*perch a.*) hocken; (*sit down*) sich hinsetzen; (*be located*) liegen; (*in session*) tagen; (*court*) zusammenkommen; (*fit*) passen; (*clothes*) sitzen; *fam* (*baby-sit*) babysitten; **~!** (*to dog*) Platz! ▶ **to be ~ting pretty** fein heraus sein; **to ~ tight** sich nicht rühren **II.** *vt* **to ~ oneself** sich *akk* setzen

sit around *vi* herumsitzen

sit back *vi* sich zurücklehnen; (*do nothing*) die Hände in den Schoß legen

sit down I. *vi* sich [hin]setzen; (*be sitting*) sitzen; **to ~ down to dinner** sich zum Essen an den Tisch begeben **II.** *vt* setzen; **to ~ oneself down** sich hinsetzen

sit in *vi* **1.** dabeisitzen; **to ~ in on a meeting** einem Treffen beisitzen **2.** (*hold sit-in*) ein Sit-in halten

sit on *vi* **1. to ~ on a committee** Mitglied eines Komitees sein **2.** *fam* (*not act*) **to ~ on sth** auf etw *dat* sitzen

sit out *vt* auslassen; (*until end*) bis zum Ende ausharren

sit through *vt* über sich *akk* ergehen lassen

sit up *vi* aufrecht sitzen; **to ~ up straight** sich gerade hinsetzen; **to ~ up and take notice** *fam* aufhorchen

sitcom ['sɪt·kɑm] *n fam short for* **situation comedy** Sitcom *f*

site [saɪt] **I.** *n* Stelle *f;* (*plot*) Grundstück *nt;* (*of crime*) Tatort *m;* **building ~** Baustelle *f;* **camping ~** Campingplatz *m;* **on ~** vor Ort; **Web ~** Website *f* **II.** *vt* einen Standort bestimmen; **to be ~d out of town** außerhalb der Stadt liegen

'sit-in *n* Sit-in *nt*

sitter ['sɪt·ər] *n* Babysitter(in) *m(f)*

situated ['sɪtʃ·u·eɪ·tɪd] *adj pred* **1.** gelegen; **~ near the church** in der Nähe der Kirche **2. to be well ~** [finanziell] gutgestellt sein

situation [ˌsɪtʃ·u·eɪ·ʃən] *n* Lage *f;* (*location a.*) Standort *m*

six [sɪks] **I.** *adj* sechs; *see also* **eight** **II.** *pron* sechs; *see also* **eight** ▶ **~ of one and half a dozen of the other** gehupft wie gesprungen *fam* **III.** *n* Sechs *f; see also* **eight**

'six-pack *n* Sechserpack *m;* (*of beer*) Sixpack *m*

sixteen [sɪk·ˈstin] **I.** *adj* sechzehn; *see also* **eight** **II.** *n* Sechzehn *f; see also* **eight**

sixteenth [ˌsɪk·ˈstinθ] **I.** *adj* sechzehnte(r, s) **II.** *pron* **the ~** der/die/das sechzehnte **III.** *adv* als sechzehnte(r, s) **IV.** *n* Sechzehntel *nt*

sixth [sɪksθ] **I.** *adj* sechste(r, s) **II.** *pron* **the ~** der/die/das sechste **III.** *adv* als sechste(r, s) **IV.** *n* Sechstel *nt*

sixtieth ['sɪk·sti·əθ] **I.** *adj* sechzigste(r, s) **II.** *pron* **the ~** der/die/das sechzigste **III.** *adv* als sechzigste(r, s) **IV.** *n* Sechzigstel *nt*

sixty ['sɪk·sti] **I.** *adj* sechzig **II.** *pron* sechzig **III.** *n* Sechzig *f*

size [saɪz] *n* Größe *f;* (*of debt*) Höhe *f;* **to double in ~** seine Größe verdoppeln; **to increase in ~** größer werden; **shirt/ shoe ~** Hemd-/Schuhgröße *f*

sizzle ['sɪz·əl] *vi* brutzeln; *fam* aufregend sein

skate [skeɪt] **I.** *n* (*for ice*) Schlittschuh *m;* (*roller skate*) Rollschuh *m* **II.** *vi* (*on ice*) Schlittschuh laufen; (*on roller skates*) Rollschuh fahren ▶ **to be skating on thin ice** sich auf dünnem Eis bewegen

skateboard ['skeɪt·bɔrd] **I.** *n* Skateboard *nt* **II.** *vi* skaten

skater ['skeɪ·tər] *n* (*on ice*) Schlittschuhläufer(in) *m(f);* (*on roller skates*) Rollschuhfahrer(in) *m(f);* **figure ~** Eiskunstläufer(in) *m(f);* **speed ~** Eisschnellläufer(in) *m(f)*

skating ['skeɪ·tɪŋ] *n* (*on ice*) Eislaufen *nt;* (*roller skating*) Rollschuhlaufen *nt;* **figure ~** Eiskunstlauf *m;* **speed ~** Eis-

S

schnelllauf *m*

'skating rink *n* (*of ice*) Eisbahn *f*; (*for roller skating*) Rollschuhbahn *f*

skeleton ['skel·ɪ·tən] *n* Skelett *nt*; (*of boat*) Gerippe *nt*; (*of building*) Skelett *nt*; (*of report*) Entwurf *m* ▶ **to have ~s in the <u>closet</u>** eine Leiche im Keller haben *fam*

skeptic ['skep·tɪk] *n* Skeptiker(in) *m(f)*

skeptical *adj* skeptisch

sketch [sketʃ] I. *n* <*pl* -es> Skizze *f*; (*outline*) Überblick *m*; (*comedy*) Sketch *m* II. *vt* skizzieren; (*outline*) umreißen III. *vi* Skizzen machen

'sketchbook *n* Skizzenbuch *nt*

sketchy ['sketʃ·i] *adj* flüchtig; (*incomplete*) lückenhaft

skewer ['skju·ər] I. *n* Spieß *m* II. *vt* anstechen; (*criticize*) sticheln

ski [ski] I. *n* Ski *m* II. *vi* Ski fahren; **to ~ down the slope** die Piste hinunterfahren

skid [skɪd] *vi* <-dd-> rutschen; (*in vehicle*) schleudern; **to ~ to a halt** schlitternd zum Stehen kommen

'skid mark *n* Reifenspur *f*; (*from braking*) Bremsspur *f*

skier ['ski·ər] *n* Skifahrer(in) *m(f)*

skiing ['ski·ɪŋ] *n* Skifahren *nt*

'ski jump *n* Sprungschanze *f*; (*jump*) Skisprung *m*; (*event*) Skispringen *nt*

skill [skɪl] *n* Geschick *nt*; (*ability*) Fähigkeit *f*; (*technique*) Fertigkeit *f*; **language ~s** Sprachkompetenz *f*

skilled [skɪld] *adj* ausgebildet; (*skillful*) geschickt; **highly ~ job** hoch qualifizierte Tätigkeit

skillful ['skɪl·fəl] *adj* geschickt; (*showing skill*) gekonnt

skim <-mm-> [skɪm] *vt* streifen; (*read*) überfliegen; (*froth*) abschöpfen

'ski mask *n* Skimaske *f*

skin [skɪn] I. *n* Haut *f*; (*hide*) Fell *nt*; (*of fruit*) Schale *f*; **to be soaked to the ~** nass bis auf die Haut sein ▶ **it's no ~ off my <u>nose</u>** das ist nicht mein Problem; **by the ~ of one's <u>teeth</u>** nur mit knapper Not II. *vt* <-nn-> häuten; (*fruit*) schälen; **to ~ one's knees** sich *dat* die Knie aufschürfen; **to ~ sb alive** *hum* Hackfleisch aus jdm machen *fam*

'skinhead *n* Skinhead *m*

skinny ['skɪn·i] *adj* mager

'skin-tight *adj* hauteng

skip [skɪp] I. *vi* <-pp-> 1. hüpfen; (*with rope*) seilspringen; **to ~ with joy** einen Freudensprung machen 2. (*omit*) **to ~ over sth** etw überspringen; **let's ~ to the next one** lasst uns direkt zum Nächsten übergehen II. *vt* <-pp-> 1. **to ~ rope** seilspringen 2. (*omit*) überspringen 3. (*not participate*) nicht teilnehmen; (*dance*) auslassen; (*class*) schwänzen *fam*; (*work*) blau machen *fam*; (*meeting*) etw sausen lassen III. *n* Hüpfer *m*

skirmish <*pl* -es> ['skɜr·mɪʃ] *n* Gefecht *nt*; (*argument*) Wortgefecht *nt*

skirt [skɜrt] *n* Rock *m* II. *vt* umgeben; (*move around*) umfahren; (*avoid*) [bewusst] umgehen

'ski slope *n* Skipiste *f*

skulk [skʌlk] *vi* herumlungern *fam*; (*move*) schleichen

skull [skʌl] *n* Schädel *m*

skunk [skʌŋk] *n* Stinktier *nt*

sky [skaɪ] *n* Himmel *m*; **in the ~** am Himmel ▶ **the ~'s the <u>limit</u>** alles ist möglich

'sky-blue *adj attr* himmelblau

'skydiving *n* Fallschirmspringen *nt*

'skylight *n* Oberlicht *nt*; (*in roof*) Dachfenster *nt*

'skyline *n* (*of city*) Skyline *f*; (*horizon*) Horizont *m*

'skyscraper *n* Wolkenkratzer *m*

slab [slæb] *n* Platte *f*; (*of wood*) Tafel *f*; (*of food*) [dicke] Scheibe

slack [slæk] I. *adj* schlaff; (*not busy*) ruhig; (*market*) flau; (*lazy*) träge; **discipline has become very ~ lately** die Disziplin hat in letzter Zeit sehr nachgelassen II. *n* **the men pulled on the rope to take up the ~** die Männer zogen am Seil, um es zu spannen; **to cut sb some ~** *fam* jdm Spielraum einräumen *m*

◆ **slack off** *vi* es langsamer angehen lassen

slacken ['slæk·ən] I. *vt* locker lassen; (*grip*) lockern; (*pace*) verlangsamen II. *vi* sich lockern; (*diminish*) langsamer

werden; (*demand*) nachlassen

slacks [slæks] *npl* Hose *f;* **a pair of ~** eine Hose

slain [sleɪn] *vt, vi pp of* **slay**

slalom ['slɑːləm] *n* Slalom *m*

slam [slæm] **I.** *n* Knall *m;* (*of door*) Zuschlagen *nt;* (*punch*) Schlag *m;* (*push*) harter Stoß **II.** *vt* <-mm-> (*door*) zuschlagen; (*hit*) schlagen; *fam* (*criticize*) heruntermachen **III.** *vi* <-mm-> zuschlagen; **to ~ on the brakes** voll auf die Bremse treten

slander ['slæn·dər] **I.** *n* üble Nachrede; (*statement*) Verleumdung *f* **II.** *vt* verleumden

slang [slæŋ] *n* Slang *m;* **army ~** Militärjargon *m*

slant [slænt] **I.** *vi* sich neigen **II.** *n* Neigung *f;* (*perspective*) Tendenz *f;* **to have a right-wing ~** rechtsgerichtet sein

slanting ['slæn·tɪŋ] *adj* schräg

slap [slæp] **I.** *n* Klaps *m fam;* (*noise*) Klatschen *nt;* **~ in the face** Ohrfeige *f; fig* Schlag *m* ins Gesicht **II.** *vt* <-pp-> **1.** schlagen; **to ~ sb on the back** jdn auf den Rücken schlagen; (*in congratulations*) jdm [anerkennend] auf die Schulter klopfen **2.** *fam* **to ~ a fine on sth** eine Geldstrafe auf etw *akk* draufschlagen

'slapstick *n* Slapstick *m*

slash [slæʃ] **I.** *vt* **1.** **to ~ sb's tires** jds Reifen aufschlitzen *fam;* **to ~ one's wrists** sich *dat* die Pulsadern aufschneiden **2.** (*budget*) kürzen; (*prices*) senken; (*staff*) abbauen; (*workforce*) verringern **II.** *n* <*pl* -es> Schnittwunde *f;* (*in object*) Schnitt *m;* (*punctuation*) Schrägstrich *m*

slate [sleɪt] **I.** *n* Schiefer *m;* (*on roof*) [Dach]schindel *f* ▸ **to wipe the ~ clean** reinen Tisch machen **II.** *adj* Schiefer- **III.** *vt* **to be ~d for sth** für etw *akk* vorgesehen sein

slaughter ['slɔ·tər] **I.** *vt* abschlachten; (*animal*) schlachten; *fam* (*defeat*) vom Platz fegen **II.** *n* Abschlachten *nt;* (*of animals*) Schlachten *nt; fam* (*defeat*) Schlappe *f*

Slav [slɑv] **I.** *n* Slawe, Slawin *m, f* **II.** *adj* slawisch

slave [sleɪv] **I.** *n* Sklave, Sklavin *m, f* **II.** *vi* schuften; **to ~** [**away**] **at sth** sich mit etw *dat* herumschlagen

slavery ['sleɪ·və·ri] *n* Sklaverei *f*

Slavic ['slɑ·vɪk] *adj* slawisch

slavish ['sleɪ·vɪʃ] *adj* sklavisch

Slavonic [slə·'vɑn·ɪk] *adj* slawisch

slay <slew, slain> [sleɪ] *vt* **to be slain** ermordet werden

sled [sled] **I.** *n* Schlitten *m* **II.** *vi* <-dd-> **to go ~ding** Schlittenfahren gehen

sledge [sledʒ] *n* Schlitten *m*

'sledgehammer *n* Vorschlaghammer *m*

sleek [slik] *adj* geschmeidig; (*streamlined*) elegant; (*car*) schnittig; *fig* (*in manner*) [aal]glatt *pej;* (*well-groomed*) gepflegt

sleep [slip] **I.** *n* Schlaf *m;* **to go to ~** einschlafen; **to put sb to ~** jdn einschlafen lassen ▸ **he can do it in his ~** er beherrscht es im Schlaf **II.** *vi* <slept, slept> schlafen; **~ tight!** schlaf schön!; **to ~ late** lange schlafen; **to ~ soundly** [tief und] fest schlafen; **to ~ with sb** mit jdm schlafen ▸ **to ~ on it** eine Nacht darüber schlafen

♦**sleep in** *vi* ausschlafen

♦**sleep off** *vt* (*hangover*) ausschlafen; (*headache*) sich gesund schlafen

sleeper ['sli·pər] *n* **1. to be a light ~** einen leichten Schlaf haben **2.** (*train*) Zug *m* mit Schlafwagenabteil; (*sleeping car*) Schlafwagen *m* **3.** (*pajamas*) **~s** *pl* Schlafanzug *m* **4.** (*spy*) Schläfer *m*

sleepiness ['sli·pɪ·nɪs] *n* Schläfrigkeit *f*

sleeping ['sli·pɪŋ] *adj attr* **let ~ dogs lie** *prov* schlafende Hunde soll man nicht wecken *prov*

'sleeping bag *n* Schlafsack *m*

'sleeping pill *n* Schlaftablette *f*

sleepless ['slip·lɪs] *adj* schlaflos

'sleepwalk *vi* schlafwandeln

'sleepwalker *n* Schlafwandler(in) *m(f)*

sleepy ['sli·pi] *adj* schläfrig; (*town*) verschlafen *fam*

sleet [slit] **I.** *n* Eisregen *m* **II.** *vi impers* **it's ~ing** es fällt Eisregen

sleeve [sliv] *n* Ärmel *m;* (*for record*) [Schallplatten]hülle *f;* **to roll up one's ~s** die Ärmel hochkrempeln ▸ **to have sth up one's ~** etw im Ärmel haben

sleigh [sleɪ] *n* Pferdeschlitten *m*

S

slender ['slen·dər] *adj* schlank; (*object*) schmal; (*means*) knapp

slept [slept] *pt, pp of* **sleep**

slew [slu] *pt of* **slay**

slice [slaɪs] **I.** *n* Scheibe *f;* (*of cake*) Stück *nt;* (*portion*) Anteil *m* **II.** *vt* in Scheiben schneiden; (*cake*) in Stücke schneiden **III.** *vi* to **~ through sth** etw durchschneiden
slice off *vt* abschneiden
slice up *vt* in Scheiben schneiden; (*bread*) aufschneiden; (*cake*) in Stücke schneiden; (*profits*) aufteilen

slick [slɪk] **I.** *adj* gekonnt; (*great*) geil *sl;* (*performance*) tadellos; (*answer*) glatt; (*clever*) gewieft; (*hair*) geschniegelt *fam;* (*road*) glatt **II.** *n* Ölteppich *m* **III.** *vt* to **~ back one's hair** *sich dat* die Haare nach hinten klatschen *fam*

slide [slaɪd] **I.** *vi* <slid, slid *or* slidden> rutschen; (*smoothly*) gleiten; (*currency*) sinken **II.** *vt* <slid, slid *or* slidden> **she slid the hatch open** sie schob die Luke auf **III.** *n* (*at playground*) Rutsche *f;* (*in photography*) Dia *nt;* **rock ~** Felslawine *f*

slight [slaɪt] **I.** *adj* gering; (*mistake*) klein; (*injury*) leicht; (*slim*) zierlich; **there's been a ~ improvement** es hat sich geringfügig gebessert; **he has a ~ tendency to exaggerate** er neigt etwas zu Übertreibungen; **not in the ~est** nicht im Geringsten

slightly ['slaɪt·li] *adv* ein wenig; **to know sb ~** jdn flüchtig kennen

slim [slɪm] *adj* <-mm-> schlank; (*waist*) schmal; (*object*) dünn; (*chance*) gering; **~ pickings** magere Ausbeute
slim down **I.** *vi* abnehmen **II.** *vt* reduzieren

slime [slaɪm] *n* Schleim *m*

slimy ['slaɪ·mi] *adj* schleimig *a. fig*

sling [slɪŋ] **I.** *n* Schlinge *f;* (*for baby*) Tragetuch *nt;* (*weapon*) Schleuder *f* **II.** *vt* <slung, slung> **1.** schleudern **2.** (*hang*) **to be slung from sth** von etw *dat* herunterhängen

slip [slɪp] **I.** *n* **1.** Fall *m* **2.** (*form*) Formular *nt;* (*sales slip*) Kassenzettel *m;* **a ~ of paper** ein Stück *nt* Papier **3.** (*mistake*) Flüchtigkeitsfehler *m;* **~ of**

the tongue Versprecher *m* ▶ **to give sb the ~** jdn abhängen **II.** *vi* <-pp-> **1.** ausrutschen; (*hand*) abrutschen; (*tires*) wegrutschen; (*clutch*) schleifen **2.** to **~ into the house** ins Haus schleichen; **to ~ through a gap** durch ein Loch schlüpfen **3.** to **~ into sth more comfortable** [sich] etwas Bequemeres anziehen **4.** (*price*) sinken **5.** (*make mistake*) sich versprechen; **to let sth ~ etw** ausplaudern **6.** to **~ into bad habits** sich *dat* schlechte Gewohnheiten aneignen ▶ **to ~ through sb's fingers** jdm entkommen **III.** *vt* <-pp-> **1.** she **~ped the key under the mat** sie schob den Schlüssel unter die Matte; **he ~ped the letter into his pocket** er steckte den Brief in seine Tasche **2.** to **~ sb's attention** jds Aufmerksamkeit entgehen; **sth ~s sb's mind** jd vergisst etw
slip away *vi* sich wegstehlen; (*time*) verstreichen *geh;* (*control*) entgleiten
slip by *vi* vorbeihuschen; (*years*) verfliegen; (*mistake*) durchgehen
slip down *vi* herunterrutschen
slip in **I.** *vt* einbringen **II.** *vi* sich hereinschleichen
slip off **I.** *vi* sich davonstehlen; (*fall off*) herunterrutschen **II.** *vt* abstreifen
slip on *vt* anziehen; (*ring*) sich *dat* anstecken
slip out *vi* **1.** to **~ out for a second** kurz weggehen **2.** (*secret*) herausrutschen
slip up *vi* einen Fehler begehen

'slip-on **I.** *adj attr* **~ shoes** Slipper *pl* **II.** *n* **~s** *pl* Slipper *pl*

slipper ['slɪp·ər] *n* Hausschuh *m*

slippery ['slɪp·ə·ri] *adj* rutschig; (*situation*) unsicher; (*road*) glatt; (*untrustworthy*) windig *fam* ▶ **to be as ~ as an eel** aalglatt sein

slit [slɪt] **I.** *vt* <-tt-, slit, slit> aufschlitzen; **to ~ one's wrists** sich *dat* die Pulsadern aufschneiden **II.** *n* Schlitz *m;* (*of door*) Spalt *m*

slob [slab] *n pej fam* Gammler(in) *m(f)*

slog [slag] *fam* **I.** *n* Schufterei *f;* (*hike*) [Gewalt]marsch *m* **II.** *vi* <-gg-> **1.** to **~ up the hill** sich auf den Hügel schleppen **2.** (*work*) sich durcharbeiten

slogan ['slou·gən] *n* Slogan *m;* **campaign ~** Wahlspruch *m*

slop [slap] *fam* I. *n* 1. *pej* (*food*) Schlabber *m* 2. (*waste*) **~s** *pl* Abfälle *pl;* (*food waste*) Essensreste *pl* II. *vt* <-pp-> verschütten III. *vi* <-pp-> überschwappen

slope [sloup] I. *n* Hang *m;* (*angle*) Neigung *f;* (*of roof*) Schräge *f* II. *vi* (*ground*) abfallen; (*roof*) geneigt sein; **to ~ down/up** abfallen/ansteigen

sloping ['slou·pɪŋ] *adj attr* schräg; (*upwards*) ansteigend; (*downwards*) abfallend

sloppy ['slap·i] *adj* schlampig; (*romantic*) kitschig

slot [slat] *n* Schlitz *m;* (*for money*) Geldeinwurf *m;* (*for mail*) Briefschlitz *m;* (*on TV*) Sendezeit *f*

sloth [slaθ] *n* Faultier *nt*

'slot machine *n* Spielautomat *m*

slouch [slautʃ] I. *n* <*pl* -es> krumme Haltung ▸ **to be no** ‹**at** [doing] sth› *fam* etw gut können II. *vi* gebeugt stehen; **to ~ along the street** die Straße entlangschlendern

Slovak ['slou·vak] I. *n* Slowake, Slowakin *m, f;* (*language*) Slowakisch *nt* II. *adj* slowakisch

Slovakia [slou·'va·ki·ə] *n* die Slowakei

Slovakian [slou·'va·ki·ən] I. *n* Slowake, Slowakin *m, f;* (*language*) Slowakisch *nt* II. *adj* slowakisch

Slovene ['slou·vin] I. *n* Slowene, Slowenin *m, f;* (*language*) Slowenisch *nt* II. *adj* slowenisch

Slovenia [slou·'vi·ni·ə] *n* Slowenien *nt*

Slovenian [slou·'vi·ni·ən] I. *n* Slowene, Slowenin *m, f;* (*language*) Slowenisch *nt* II. *adj* slowenisch

slow [slou] *adj* 1. langsam; (*business*) flau 2. (*dumb*) begriffsstutzig; **to be** [a little] **~ on the uptake** [ein wenig] schwer von Begriff sein 3. (*clock*) nachgehen; **to be** [10 minutes] **~** [10 Minuten] nachgehen II. *vi* langsamer werden; **to ~ to a crawl** fast zum Stillstand kommen

◆**slow down** I. *vt* verlangsamen; (*speed*) drosseln II. *vi* langsamer werden; (*car*) langsamer fahren; (*speak*) langsamer sprechen; (*walk*) langsamer laufen; (*relax*) kürzertreten *fam*

'slowdown *n* **economic ~** Konjunkturabschwächung *f*

slowly ['slou·li] *adv* langsam; **~ but surely** langsam, aber sicher

slowness ['slou·nɪs] *n* Langsamkeit *f*

sludge [slʌdʒ] *n* Schlamm *m*

slug[1] [slʌg] *n* Nacktschnecke *f*

slug[2] [slʌg] *fam* I. *vt* <-gg-> **to ~ sb** jdm eine verpassen *sl;* **to ~ it out** es untereinander ausfechten II. *n* gehöriger Schlag

sluggish ['slʌg·ɪʃ] *adj* träge; (*market*) flau; (*engine*) lahm

slum [slʌm] *n* Slum *m*

slump [slʌmp] I. *n* [plötzliche] Abnahme; (*recession*) Rezession *f;* **~ in prices** Preissturz *m;* **economic ~** Wirtschaftskrise *f* II. *vi* 1. (*prices*) stürzen; (*sales*) zurückgehen 2. (*fall heavily*) fallen

slung [slʌŋ] *pt, pp of* **sling**

slur [slɜr] I. *vt* <-rr-> undeutlich artikulieren; (*drunkard*) lallen; (*damage*) verleumden II. *n* Verleumdung *f;* **to cast a ~ on sb/sth** jdn/etw in einem schlechten Licht erscheinen lassen

slurp [slɜrp] *fam* I. *vi* schlürfen II. *vt* schlürfen III. *n* Schlürfen *nt*

slush [slʌʃ] *n* [Schnee]matsch *m; pej* (*kitsch*) Gefühlsduselei *f*

slut [slʌt] *n pej* Schlampe *f derb*

sly [slaɪ] *adj* verstohlen; (*smile*) verschmitzt; (*cunning*) gerissen; **on the ~** heimlich

smack [smæk] I. *n* [klatschender] Schlag; (*noise*) Knall *m;* (*kiss*) Schmatz *m* II. *adv* **~ in the middle** genau in der Mitte; **I walked ~ into it** ich lief voll dagegen III. *vt* **to ~ sb** jdm eine knallen *fam;* **to ~ sb's butt** jdm den Hintern versohlen

small [smɔl] *adj* klein; (*amount a.*) gering; (*insignificant*) unbedeutend; **in ~ quantities** in kleinen Mengen; **~ child** Kleinkind *nt;* **~ consolation** ein schwacher Trost; **to make sb feel ~** jdn niedermachen *fam* ▸ **it's a ~ world!** *prov* die Welt ist klein!

small 'change *n* Kleingeld *nt*

'small fry *n* + *sing/pl vb fam* kleine Fische; (*child*) junges Gemüse *hum*

small-'minded *adj* engstirnig

small 'print *n* the ~ das Kleingedruckte

'small talk *n* Smalltalk *m o nt*

'small-time *adj* unbedeutend; ~ crook kleiner Gauner

'small-town *adj attr* Kleinstadt-

smart [smart] I. *adj* schlau; (*stylish*) schick; (*quick*) [blitz]schnell; to make a ~ move klug handeln II. *n* 1. *sl* the ~s *pl* die [nötige] Intelligenz 2. (*pain*) Schmerz *m* III. *vi* brennen

smart aleck [ˌsmart·'æl·ek] *n pej fam* Schlauberger(in) *m(f) fam*

'smart-ass *n pej vulg* Klugschei-ßer(in) *m(f) sl*

smarten ['smar·tən] I. *vt* to ~ sth ⇆ up etw herrichten; (*house*) etw verschö-nern; to ~ oneself ⇆ up sich in Schale werfen *fam* II. *vi* to ~ up mehr Wert auf sein Äußeres legen

smash [smæʃ] I. *n* <*pl* -es> 1. Kra-chen *nt*; *sport* Schlag *m*; forehand/backhand ~ Vorhand-/Rückhand-schmetterball *m* 2. *fam* (*song*) Super-hit *m*; box-office ~ Kassenschlager *m* II. *vt* zerschlagen; (*window*) einschla-gen; (*strike*) schmettern; (*record*) bre-chen; (*ball*) schmettern III. *vi* zerbre-chen; (*strike*) prallen

✦ smash in *vt* einschlagen

✦ smash up *vt* zertrümmern; (*crush*) zer-drücken; (*car*) zu Schrott fahren

smashing ['smæʃ·ɪŋ] *adj* vernichtend; to be a ~ success *fam* ein durchschlagen-der Erfolg sein

'smashup *n* schwerer Unfall; (*pile-up*) Karambolage *f*

smear [smɪr] I. *vt* 1. to ~ sth on sth etw mit etw *dat* beschmieren 2. (*slur*) verunglimpfen II. *n* Fleck *m*; (*slur*) Ver-leumdung *f*

smell [smel] I. *n* Geruch *m*; (*of perfume*) Duft *m*; (*bad*) Gestank *m*; sense of ~ Geruchssinn *m* II. *vi* <smelled *or* smelt, smelled *or* smelt> 1. riechen 2. ~ + *adj* (*give off odor*) riechen; (*pleasantly*) duften; (*stink*) stinken III. *vt* <smelled *or* smelt, smelled *or* smelt> riechen ▶ to ~ a rat den Braten riechen *fam*

✦ smell out *vt* aufspüren

smelly ['smel·i] *adj* stinkend *attr*

smelt [smelt] *vt, vi pt, pp of* smell

smile [smaɪl] I. *n* Lächeln *nt*; to give sb a ~ jdm zulächeln II. *vi* lächeln; to ~ at sb jdn anlächeln

smiley ['smaɪ·li], 'smiley face *n* INET Smiley *m*

smirk [smɜrk] I. *vi* grinsen; to ~ at sb jdn süffisant anlächeln II. *n* Grinsen *nt*

smith [smɪθ] *n* Schmied *m*

smock [smɑk] *n* [Arbeits]kittel *m*

smog [smɑg] *n* Smog *m*

smoke [smoʊk] I. *n* 1. Rauch *m* 2. to have a ~ eine rauchen *fam* 3. *fam* (*cigarettes*) ~s *pl* Glimmstängel *pl* ▶ to go up in ~ in Rauch [und Flammen] aufgehen II. *vt* rauchen; FOOD räuchern ▶ put that in your pipe and ~ it! schreib dir das hinter die Ohren! III. *vi* rauchen

✦ smoke out *vt* ausräuchern; *fig* entlarven

smoked [smoʊkt] *adj* geräuchert; ~ fish Räucherfisch *m*

smoker ['smoʊ·kər] *n* Raucher(in) *m(f)*; (*compartment*) Raucherabteil *nt*; ~'s cough Raucherhusten *m*

'smokescreen *n* Vorwand *m*

smoking ['smoʊ·kɪŋ] *n* Rauchen *nt*; ~ ban Rauchverbot *nt*

smoky ['smoʊ·ki] *adj* verraucht; (*emit-ting*) rauchend *attr*; (*tasting*) rauchig

smolder ['smoʊl·dər] *vi* schwelen; (*ciga-rette*) glimmen; (*dispute*) schwelen; to ~ with rage vor Zorn glühen

smooth [smuð] I. *adj* glatt; (*sea*) ruhig; (*without difficulty*) problemlos; (*flight*) ruhig; (*landing*) sanft; (*mild*) mild; (*suave*) [aal]glatt; ~ operator gewiefte Person II. *vt* 1. to ~ the path [to sth] den Weg [zu etw *dat*] ebnen 2. (*rub in*) einmassieren

✦ smooth down *vt* glatt streichen

✦ smooth over *vt* in Ordnung bringen

smoothly ['smuθ·li] *adv* reibungslos; (*suavely*) aalglatt *pej*; to go ~ glatt-laufen *fam*

smother ['smʌð·ər] *vt* ersticken; (*sup-press*) unterdrücken; to be ~ed in sth von etw *dat* völlig bedeckt sein

smudge [smʌdʒ] I. *vt* verwischen; (*dirty*) beschmutzen II. *vi* verlaufen; (*ink*) klecksen; (*mascara*) verschmiert III. *n* Fleck *m*

smug <-gg-> [smʌg] *adj* selbstgefällig

smuggle ['smʌg·əl] *vt* schmuggeln

smuggler ['smʌg·lər] *n* Schmuggler(in) *m(f)*

smuggling ['smʌg·lɪŋ] *n* Schmuggel *m*

snack [snæk] *n* Snack *m*

'snack bar *n* Imbissstube *f*

snag [snæg] I. *n fam;* (*rip*) gezogener Faden; to hit a ~ auf Schwierigkeiten stoßen II. *vt* <-gg-> don't ~ your coat on the barbed wire pass auf, dass du mit deiner Jacke nicht am Stacheldraht hängen bleibst

snail [sneɪl] *n* Schnecke *f*

'snail mail *n hum fam* Schneckenpost *f*

snake [sneɪk] *n* Schlange *f*

'snake bite *n* Schlangenbiss *m*

'snakeskin *n* Schlangenhaut *f*; FASHION Schlangenleder *nt*

snap [snæp] I. *n* Knacken *nt;* (*sound*) Knacks *m;* (*fastener*) Druckknopf *m;* it was a ~! *fam* es war ein Kinderspiel! II. *vi* <-pp-> auseinanderbrechen; (*whip*) peitschen; (*bite*) schnappen; her patience finally ~ped *fig* ihr riss schließlich der Geduldsfaden; to ~ at sb (*speak sharply*) jdn anfahren III. *vt* <-pp-> entzweibrechen; to ~ off etw abbrechen; to ~ sth shut etw zuknallen; (*book*) etw zuklappen; to ~ one's fingers mit den Fingern schnippen; to ~ sb's head off jdm den Kopf abreißen *fam*

snap out *vi* ~ out of it! krieg dich wieder ein!

snappy ['ʃnæp·i] *adj* 1. *fam* (*smart*) schick; (*quick*) zackig; make it ~! mach fix! *fam*

'snapshot *n* Schnappschuss *m*

snare [sner] I. *n* Falle *f;* (*noose*) Schlinge *f* II. *vt* [mit einer Falle] fangen

snarl [snɑrl] I. *vi* knurren; to ~ at sb jdn anknurren II. *n* Knurren *nt*

snatch [snætʃ] I. *n* <pl -es> 1. to make a ~ at sth nach etw *dat* greifen 2. (*fragment*) Fetzen *m* 3. to do sth in ~es etw mit Unterbrechungen tun *vt* II. *vt* schnappen; (*steal*) sich *dat* greifen III. *vi* greifen

sneak [snik] I. *vi* <-ed *or* snuck, -ed *or* snuck> schleichen; to ~ up on sb/

sth sich an jdn/etw heranschleichen II. *vt* <-ed *or* snuck, -ed *or* snuck> to ~ a look at sb/sth einen verstohlenen Blick auf jdn/etw werfen; to ~ sb/sth in jdn/etw hineinschmuggeln III. *n pej* Schleicher, -in *m, f*

sneaker ['sni·kər] *n usu pl* Turnschuh *m*

sneaky ['sni·ki] *adj* raffiniert

sneer [snɪr] I. *vi* spöttisch grinsen; (*utter*) spotten II. *n* spöttisches Lächeln

sneeze [sniz] I. *vi* niesen ▶ not to be ~d at nicht zu verachten II. *n* Niesen *nt*

sniff [snɪf] I. *vi* 1. die Luft einziehen; (*animal*) wittern; to ~ at sth an etw *dat* schnuppern; (*animal*) die Witterung von etw *dat* aufnehmen 2. (*show disdain*) to ~ at sth über etw *akk* die Nase rümpfen II. *vt* to ~ sth an etw *dat* riechen

sniff out *vt* aufspüren; *fig* entdecken

snip [snɪp] I. *n* Schnitt *m* II. *vt* schneiden

snipe [snaɪp] *vi* aus dem Hinterhalt schießen; (*criticize*) attackieren

sniper ['snaɪ·pər] *n* Heckenschütze *m*

snitch [snɪtʃ] I. *vt fam* klauen II. *vi pej sl* to ~ on sb jdn verpetzen III. *n* <pl -es> *pej sl* Petze(r) *f/m*

snivel ['snɪv·əl] I. *vi* <-l-> schniefen *fam;* (*cry*) flennen *pej fam* II. *n* Geplärre *nt pej fam;* (*sad*) Schniefen *nt*

sniveling ['snɪv·əl·ɪŋ] I. *n* Geheul *nt pej fam* II. *adj attr* weinerlich

snob [snab] *n* Snob *m*

snobbery ['snab·ə·ri] *n* Snobismus *m*

snoop [snup] *vi fam* [herum]schnüffeln; (*pry*) [herum]spionieren; to ~ on sb jdn ausspionieren

snooze [snuz] *fam* I. *vi* ein Nickerchen machen II. *n* Nickerchen *nt*

snore [snɔr] I. *vi* schnarchen II. *n* Schnarchen *nt kein pl*

snorkel ['snɔr·kəl] I. *n* Schnorchel *m* II. *vi* <-l-> schnorcheln

snort [snɔrt] I. *vi* schnauben II. *vt* [verächtlich] schnauben; to ~ cocaine *sl* Kokain schnupfen III. *n* Schnauben *nt kein pl*

snot [snat] *n fam* Rotz *m*

snotty ['snat·i] *adj fam* Rotz-; (*handkerchief*) vollgerotzt; *pej* (*rude*) rotzfrech *sl;*

(*answer*) pampig; (*look*) unverschämt

snout [snaʊt] *n* Schnauze *f*; (*of pig*) Rüssel *m*; (*nose*) Rüssel *m sl*

snow [snoʊ] **I.** *n* Schnee *m*; (*snowfall*) Schneefall *m* **II.** *vi impers* it's ~ing es schneit

◆**snow in** *vt* to be ~ed in eingeschneit sein

'**snowball** *n* Schneeball *m*

'**snowboard I.** *n* Snowboard *nt* **II.** *vi* Snowboard fahren

'**snowbound** *adj* eingeschneit; (*road*) wegen Schnees gesperrt

'**snow chains** *npl* Schneeketten *pl*

'**snowdrift** *n* Schneewehe *f*

'**snowfall** *n* Schneefall *m*; (*amount*) Schneemenge *f*

'**snowflake** *n* Schneeflocke *f*

'**snowman** *n* Schneemann *m*

'**snowplow** *n* Schneepflug *m*

'**snowshoe** *n usu pl* Schneeschuh *m*

'**snowstorm** *n* Schneesturm *m*

snow-'**white** *adj* schneeweiß; (*sheets a.*) blütenweiß; (*face*) kalkweiß

Snow '**White** *n* Schneewittchen *nt*

snowy ['snoʊ·i] *adj* schneereich; (*snow-covered*) verschneit; (*mountain*) schneebedeckt; (*color*) schneeweiß

'**snub-nosed** *adj attr* stupsnasig; (*gun*) mit kurzem Lauf *nach n*

snuff [snʌf] **I.** *n* Schnupftabak *m* **II.** *vt* to ~ it *fam* abkratzen *sl*

◆**snuff out** *vt* auslöschen; (*cigarette*) ausdrücken; (*with one's foot*) austreten; (*hopes*) zunichtemachen

snug [snʌg] *adj* kuschelig, gemütlich, mollig warm; (*tight*) eng

so [soʊ] **I.** *adv* he's pretty nice; more ~ than I was led to believe er ist ganz nett, viel netter als ich angenommen hatte; what are you looking ~ unhappy about? warum bist du denn so traurig?; what's ~ wrong about that? was ist denn daran so falsch?; I have an enormous amount of work to do — ~ do I ich habe jede Menge Arbeit – ich auch; can I watch television? — I suppose ~ darf ich fernsehen? – na gut, meinetwegen; I'm afraid ~ ich fürchte ja; ~ they say so sagt man; I told you ~ ich habe es dir ja gesagt; is that ~?

stimmt das?; if ~ ... wenn das so ist ...; and ~ it was und so kam es dann auch; and ~ forth und so weiter; ~ to speak sozusagen ▸ ~ long bis dann; ~ what? na und? *fam* **II.** *conj* I couldn't find you ~ I left ich konnte dich nicht finden, also bin ich gegangen; ~ what's the problem? wo liegt denn das Problem?; be quiet ~ she can concentrate sei still, damit sie sich konzentrieren kann ▸ ~ long as ... (*if*) sofern; (*for the time*) solange **III.** *adj sl* that's ~ 70's das ist typisch 70er

soak [soʊk] **I.** *n* Einweichen *nt kein pl* **II.** *vt* einweichen; (*in alcohol*) einlegen; (*wet*) durchnässen **III.** *vi* eingeweicht werden

◆**soak in I.** *vi* einziehen; (*be understood*) in den Schädel gehen *fam*; will it ever ~ in? ob er/sie das wohl jemals kapiert? *fam* **II.** *vt* einsaugen; *fig* in sich *akk* aufnehmen

◆**soak up** *vt* aufsaugen; *fig* [gierig] in sich *akk* aufnehmen; (*atmosphere*) in sich *akk* aufnehmen; (*sun/shine*) sich aalen

soaked [soʊkt] *adj* (*wet*) to be ~ pitschnass sein *fam*; ~ in sweat schweißgebadet; (*shirt*) völlig durchgeschwitzt

soaking ['soʊ·kɪŋ] **I.** *n* Einweichen *nt kein pl*; (*becoming wet*) Nasswerden *nt kein pl*; to get a ~ patschnass werden *fam* **II.** *adj* ~ [wet] klatschnass *fam*

so-and-so ['soʊ·ən·soʊ] *n fam* Herr/ Frau Soundso; (*thing*) das und das; what a mean old ~! das ist ein alter Fiesling! *sl*

soap [soʊp] **I.** *n* Seife *f*; (*soap opera*) Seifenoper *f* **II.** *vt* einseifen

'**soap opera** *n* Seifenoper *f*

soapy ['soʊ·pi] *adj* seifig; ~ water Seifenwasser *nt*

soar [sɔr] *vi* aufsteigen; (*peaks*) sich erheben; (*prices*) in die Höhe schnellen; (*bird*) [in großer Höhe] segeln; (*glider*) gleiten

sob [sab] **I.** *n* Schluchzen *nt kein pl* **II.** *vi* <-bb-> schluchzen **III.** *vt* <-bb-> schluchzen

sober ['soʊ·bər] **I.** *adj* nüchtern; (*thought a.*) sachlich; (*color*) gedeckt; (*truth*) einfach **II.** *vt* ernüchtern

◆**sober up I.** vi nüchtern werden **II.** vt nüchtern machen

sobering ['sou·bər·ɪŋ] adj ernüchternd

so-called [ˌsou·'kɔld] adj attr so genannt

soccer ['sak·ər] n Fußball m

'soccer mom n pej fam Bezeichnung für Mütter aus den Vorortsiedlungen, die viel Zeit damit verbringen, ihre Kinder von einer Sportveranstaltung zur nächsten zu fahren

sociable ['sou·ʃə·bəl] adj gesellig; (friendly) umgänglich

social ['sou·ʃəl] **I.** adj gesellschaftlich; (of human behavior) sozial; **I'm a ~ drinker** ich trinke nur, wenn ich in Gesellschaft bin **II.** n Treffen nt; **church ~** Gemeindefest nt

socialism ['sou·ʃə·lɪz·əm] n Sozialismus m

socialist ['sou·ʃə·lɪst] **I.** n Sozialist(in) m(f) **II.** adj sozialistisch

socialize ['sou·ʃə·laɪz] **I.** vi **to ~ with sb** mit jdm gesellschaftlich verkehren **II.** vt sozialisieren; (offender) [re]sozialisieren

socially ['sou·ʃə·li] adv gesellschaftlich; **to meet sb ~** jdn privat treffen

social se'curity n Sozialhilfe f; (pension) Sozial|versicherungs|rente f

social 'service n Sozialarbeit f; **~s** pl (welfare) staatliche Sozialleistungen

'social work n Sozialarbeit f

'social worker n Sozialarbeiter(in) m(f)

society [sə·'saɪ·ɪ·ti] n Gesellschaft f; (elite) die [feine] Gesellschaft; (organization) Verein m

sociologist [ˌsou·si·'al·ə·dʒɪst] n Soziologe, Soziologin m, f

sociology [ˌsou·si·'al·ə·dʒi] n Soziologie f

sock¹ [sak] n Socke f

sock² [sak] vt schlagen; (in soccer) schießen

socket ['sak·ɪt] n Steckdose f; (for lamps) Fassung f; **eye ~** Augenhöhle f

soda ['sou·də] n **1.** see **soft drink** **2.** see **soda water**

'soda water n Sodawasser nt

sodden ['sad·ən] adj durchnässt; (grass) durchweicht

sodium ['sou·di·əm] n Natrium nt

sodium bi'carbonate n see **baking**

soda

sodium 'chloride n Natriumchlorid nt

sofa ['sou·fə] n Sofa nt

'sofa bed n Schlafcouch f

soft [sɔft] adj weich; (skin) zart; (leather) geschmeidig; (hair) seidig; (weak) schlaff; (colors) zart; (music) gedämpft; (voice) leise

'softball n Softball m

soft-'boiled adj weich [gekocht]

'soft drink n Limo[nade] f

soften ['sɔ·fən] **I.** vi weich werden; (ice cream) schmelzen; (moderate) nachgiebiger werden **II.** vt weich werden lassen; (moderate) mildern; (color) dämpfen

◆**soften up I.** vt weicher machen; (win over) erweichen; (persuade) rumkriegen fam **II.** vi weich werden

softener ['sɔ·fə·nər] n Weichmacher m; (for kettle) Enthärter m; **fabric ~** Weichspüler m

soft'hearted adj weichherzig; (gullible) leichtgläubig

softie ['sɔf·ti] n fam see **softy**

softly ['sɔft·li] adv sanft; (quietly) leise; (dimly) schwach

softness ['sɔft·nɪs] n Weichheit f; (smoothness) Weichheit f; (of skin) Glätte f; (of hair) Seidigkeit f; (of lighting) Gedämpftheit f; (of colors) Zartheit f

soft-'spoken adj **to be ~** leise sprechen; **~ manner** freundliche und sanfte Art

software ['sɔft·wer] n COMPUT Software f

softy ['sɔf·ti] n fam Softie m sl

soggy ['sag·i] adj durchnässt; (boggy) glitschig fam; (soil) aufgeweicht; FOOD matschig

soil [sɔɪl] n Erde f; (territory) Boden m

solace ['sal·ɪs] n Trost m

solar ['sou·lər] adj Solar-

solar 'cell n Solarzelle f

solar e'clipse n Sonnenfinsternis f

solar 'energy n Solarenergie f

solarium <pl -aria> [sou·'ler·i·əm] n Solarium nt; (porch) Glasveranda f

'solar system n Sonnensystem nt

sold [sould] pt, pp of **sell**

solder ['sad·ər] **I.** vt löten **II.** n Lötmetall nt

soldier ['soul·dʒər] n Soldat(in) m(f)

S

sold 'out *adj* ausverkauft

sole¹ [soʊl] *n* [Fuß]sohle *f*; (*of shoe*) [Schuh]sohle *f*

sole² [soʊl] *adj attr* einzig; (*exclusive*) Allein-

solely ['soʊl·li] *adv* einzig und allein

solemn ['sal·əm] *adj* feierlich; (*oath*) heilig; (*grave*) ernst; (*voice*) getragen

solicitor [sə·'lɪs·ɪ·tər] *n* POL Rechtsreferent(in) *m(f)* (*einer Stadt*)

solid ['sal·ɪd] **I.** *adj* fest; (*wall*) solide; (*foundation*) stabil; (*punch*) kräftig; (*rock*) massiv; (*not hollow*) massiv; (*substantial*) verlässlich; (*evidence*) handfest; (*uninterrupted*) durchgehend; (*dependable*) zuverlässig; (*marriage*) stabil; (*investment*) sicher; **~ silver** massives Silber **II.** *n* **~s** *pl* feste Nahrung *kein pl* **III.** **frozen ~** hart gefroren; (*plants*) steif gefroren

solidarity [ˌsal·ə·'der·ɪ·t̬i] *n* Solidarität *f*; **S~** (*movement*) Solidarität *f*

solidify <-ie-> [sə·'lɪd·ə·faɪ] *vi* fest werden; (*lava*) erstarren; (*cement*) hart werden; (*water*) gefrieren; *fig* (*plans*) sich konkretisieren; (*idea*) konkret[er] werden

solidity [sə·'lɪd·ɪ·t̬i] *n* fester Zustand; (*of wood*) Härte *f*; (*of foundation*) Stabilität *f*; (*of facts*) Zuverlässigkeit *f*; (*of argument*) Stichhaltigkeit *f*; (*of judgment*) Fundiertheit *f*; (*of commitment*) Verlässlichkeit *f*; (*of investment*) Solidität *f*; (*of company*) finanzielle Stärke; (*strength*) Stabilität *f*

solitaire ['sal·ə·ter] *n* Patience *f*

solitary ['sal·ə·ter·i] *adj* einzelne(r, s) *attr*; (*lonely*) einsam; (*remote*) abgeschieden

solitude ['sal·ə·tud] *n* Alleinsein *nt*; (*loneliness*) Einsamkeit *f*; **in ~** alleine

solo ['soʊ·loʊ] **I.** *adj attr* Solo- **II.** *adv* allein; MUS solo **III.** *n* MUS Solo *nt*

soloist ['soʊ·loʊ·ɪst] *n* Solist(in) *m(f)*

solution [sə·'lu·ʃən] *n* Lösung *f*; (*to puzzle*) [Auf]lösung *f*; (*act*) Lösen *nt*; **software ~s** Softwareanwendungen *pl*

solve [salv] *vt* lösen; (*crime*) aufklären; (*mystery*) aufdecken

Somali [soʊ·'ma·li] **I.** *n* <*pl* -> Somalier(in) *m(f)*; (*language*) Somali *nt* **II.** *adj* somalisch

Somalia [soʊ·'mal·i·ə] *n* Somalia *nt*

somber ['sam·bər] *adj* düster; (*setting*) ernst; (*dark*) dunkel; (*day*) trüb

some [sʌm] **I.** *adj attr* **1.** (*unknown amount:* + *sing*) etwas; **there's ~ cake in the kitchen** es ist noch Kuchen in der Küche; **~ more** noch etwas **2.** (*certain:* + *pl*) gewisse **3.** (*unknown*) irgendein(e); **he's in ~ kind of trouble** er steckt in irgendwelchen Schwierigkeiten; **~ day or another** irgendwann **4.** (*noticeable:* to **~ extent** bis zu einem gewissen Grad **5.** (*slight*) **there is ~ hope that ...** es besteht noch etwas Hoffnung, dass ... **II.** *pron* **1.** (*unspecified number of persons or things*) welche **2.** (*unspecified amount of sth*) **if you need money, I can lend you ~** wenn du Geld brauchst, kann ich dir gerne welches leihen **3.** (*at least a small number*) einige **4.** + *pl vb* (*among larger number*) **~ of you have already met Betsey** einige von euch kennen Betsey bereits **III.** *adv* **~ sixty or sixty-five feet deep** ungefähr zwanzig Meter tief

somebody ['sʌm·bad·i] *pron indef* **1.** jemand; **~ or other** irgendwer; **~ else** jemand anders; **there's ~ at the door** jemand ist an der Tür **2.** (*one person*) irgendwer **3.** **to be ~** jemand [*or* etwas] sein

somehow ['sʌm·haʊ] *adv* irgendwie

someone ['sʌm·wʌn] *pron see* **somebody**

someplace ['sʌm·pleɪs] *adv* irgendwo; **~ else** woanders/woandershin

somersault ['sʌm·ər·sɔlt] **I.** *n* (*on ground*) Purzelbaum *m*; (*in air*) Salto *m* **II.** *vi* einen Purzelbaum schlagen; (*in air*) einen Salto machen; (*car*) sich überschlagen

something ['sʌm·θɪŋ] *pron indef* etwas; **~ else** etwas anderes; **~ special/sharp/stronger** etwas Besonderes/Scharfes/Stärkeres; **to do ~** [about sb/sth] etwas [gegen jdn/etw] unternehmen; **I need ~ to write with** ich brauche etwas zum Schreiben; **is there ~ you'd like to say?** möchtest du mir etwas sagen?; **it was ~ of a surprise** es war eine kleine

Überraschung; **she works for a bank or ~** sie arbeitet für eine Bank oder so was; **~ like ...** ungefähr wie ...; (*approximately*) um die ... ▶ **that's** (**really**) **~** das ist schon was; **there's ~ in it** es ist etwas dran

sometime ['sʌm·taɪm] *adv* irgendwann; **come up and see me ~** komm mich mal besuchen; **~ soon** demnächst irgendwann

sometimes ['sʌm·taɪmz] *adv* manchmal

somewhere ['sʌm·hwer] *adv* irgendwo/irgendwohin; **~ else** woanders/woandershin; **~ between 30 and 40** so zwischen 30 und 40

son [sʌn] *n* Sohn *m*

sonar ['soʊ·nɑr] *n* Sonar[gerät] *nt*

sonata [sə·'nɑ·tə] *n* Sonate *f*

song [sɔŋ] *n* Lied *nt*; (*singing*) Gesang *m*; (*of cricket*) Zirpen *nt*

son-in-law <*pl* sons-> *n* Schwiegersohn *m*

sonnet ['sɑn·ɪt] *n* Sonett *nt*

soon [sun] *adv* bald; (*early*) früh; **~ after sth** kurz nach etw *dat* **how ~** wie bald; **~er rather than later** lieber früher als später; **as ~ as possible** so bald wie möglich; **the ~er the better** je eher, desto besser; **not a moment too ~** gerade noch rechtzeitig; **I'd ~er not speak to him** ich würde lieber nicht mit ihm sprechen

soot [sʊt] *n* Ruß *m*

soothe [suð] *vt* beruhigen; (*relieve*) lindern

sooty ['sʊt·i] *adj* verrußt

sop [sɑp] *vt* **to ~ up ⇆ sth** etw aufsaugen

sophisticated [sə·'fɪs·tə·keɪ·t̬ɪd] *adj* [geistig] verfeinert; (*cultured*) kultiviert; (*audience*) anspruchsvoll; (*restaurant*) gepflegt; (*highly developed*) hoch entwickelt; (*method*) raffiniert; (*approach*) differenziert

sophomore ['sɑf·ə·mɔr] *n* (*in college*) Student(in) *m(f)* im zweiten Studienjahr; (*in high school*) Schüler(in) *m(f)* einer Highschool im zweiten Jahr

sopping ['sɑp·ɪŋ] *fam* **I.** *adj* klatschnass **II.** *adv* **~ wet** klatschnass

soppy ['sɑp·i] *adj fam* gefühlsdus[e]lig

(*film*) schmalzig

soprano [sə·'præn·oʊ] *n* Sopranistin *f*; (*range*) Sopran *m*

sorcerer ['sɔr·sər·ər] *n* Zauberer *m*

sorcery ['sɔr·sə·ri] *n* Zauberei *f*

sordid ['sɔr·dɪd] *adj* schmutzig; (*squalid*) schäbig; (*apartment*) verkommen

sore [sɔr] *adj* schlimm; (*overused*) wund [gescheuert]; **~ muscles** Muskelkater *m*; **~ point** *fig* wunder Punkt **II.** *n* wunde Stelle; **to open an old ~** *fig* alte Wunden aufreißen

sorely ['sɔr·li] *adv* arg; **to be ~ tempted to do sth** stark versucht sein, etw zu tun

sorrow ['sar·oʊ] *n* Kummer *m*; (*experience*) Leid *nt*

sorry ['sar·i] **I.** *adj* **1.** *pred* **I'm/she's ~** es tut mir/ihr leid; **to be ~ about sth** etw bedauern; **to say ~ [to sb]** sich [bei jdm] entschuldigen; **we were ~ to hear [that] ...** es tat uns leid zu hören, dass ...; **sb feels ~ for sb/sth** jd/etw tut jdm leid **2.** *attr* (*wretched*) armselig **II.** *interj* **~!** Verzeihung!

sort [sɔrt] **I.** *n* **1.** (*type*) Sorte *f* **2.** *fam* **I had a ~ of feeling that ...** ich hatte so ein Gefühl, dass ... **3.** **I know your ~!** Typen wie euch kenne ich [zur Genüge]! *fam* **II.** *adv fam* **~ of 1. that's ~ of difficult to explain** das ist nicht so einfach zu erklären **2.** (*not exactly*) mehr oder weniger **III.** *vt* sortieren **IV.** *vi* **to ~ through sth** etw sortieren

sort out *vt* ordnen; (*mess*) in Ordnung bringen; (*resolve*) klären; (*problem*) lösen; (*choose*) aussuchen; (*for throwing out or giving away*) aussortieren

SOS [ˌes·oʊ·'es] *n* SOS *nt*; *fig* Hilferuf *m*

so-so ['soʊ·soʊ] *fam* **I.** *adj* so lala *präd* **II.** *adv* so lala

sought [sɔt] *pt, pp of* seek

sought-after *adj* begehrt

soul [soʊl] *n* **1.** Seele *f*; (*feeling a.*) Gefühl *nt*; **not a ~** keine Menschenseele **2.** *mus* Soul *m*

soul-destroying *adj* nervtötend; (*discouraging*) zermürbend

soul mate *n* Seelenverwandte(r) *f(m)*

soul-searching *n* Prüfung *f* des Gewissens

S

sound¹ [saʊnd] **I.** n Geräusch nt; (of bell) Klang m; (TV) Ton m; LING Laut m; PHYS Schall m; **don't make a ~!** sei still! **II.** vi **1.** erklingen; (alarm) ertönen; (alarm clock) klingeln; (bell) läuten **2.** fam (complain) **to ~ off** herumtönen **3.** + adj (seem) klingen **III.** vt (alarm) auslösen; (car horn) hupen

sound² [saʊnd] **I.** adj (healthy) gesund; (in good condition) in gutem Zustand; (trustworthy) solide; (reasonable) vernünftig; (advice) gut; (argument) schlagend; (sleep) tief; **to be of ~ mind** bei klarem Verstand sein **II.** adv **to be ~ asleep** tief [und fest] schlafen

'sound bite n prägnanter Ausspruch (eines Politikers)

soundly ['saʊnd·li] adv gründlich; (clearly) eindeutig; (severely) schwer fam; (reliably) fundiert geh; (sleep) tief

'soundproof I. adj schalldicht **II.** vt schalldicht machen

soup [sup] n Suppe f

'soup kitchen n Armenküche f

sour ['saʊ·ər] **I.** adj sauer; (ill-tempered) griesgrämig; (embittered) verbittert **II.** vt sauer machen; (make unpleasant) trüben **III.** vi sauer werden; fig getrübt werden

source [sɔrs] n Quelle f; (reason) Grund m; **~s** pl (references) Quellen[angaben] pl; **according to government ~s** wie in Regierungskreisen verlautete

south [saʊθ] **I.** n Süden m; **to the ~ of sth** südlich von etw; **the S~** die Südstaaten pl **II.** adj südlich **III.** adv **my room faces ~** mein Zimmer ist nach Süden ausgerichtet; **to drive ~** Richtung Süden fahren

South 'Africa n Südafrika nt

South 'African I. adj südafrikanisch **II.** n Südafrikaner(in) m(f)

South A'merica n Südamerika nt

South A'merican I. adj südamerikanisch **II.** n Südamerikaner(in) m(f)

South Carolina [ˌsaʊθ·ˌkær·ə·ˈlaɪ·nə] n Südkarolina nt

South Dakota [ˌsaʊθ·də·ˈkoʊ·t̬ə] n Süddakota nt

south'east I. n Südosten m **II.** adj südöstlich **III.** adv südostwärts

southerly ['sʌð·ər·li] **I.** adj südlich **II.** adv südlich; (going south) südwärts; (coming from south) von Süden **III.** n Südwind m

southern ['sʌð·ərn] adj südlich

southerner ['sʌð·ər·nər] n Südstaatler(in) m(f)

southernmost ['sʌð·ərn·moʊst] adj **the ~ ...** der/die/das südlichste ...

South Ko'rea n Südkorea nt

South Ko'rean I. adj südkoreanisch **II.** n Südkoreaner(in) m(f)

South 'Pole n Südpol m

southward ['saʊθ·wərd] **I.** adj südlich **II.** adv südwärts

southwards ['saʊθ·wərdz] adv see **southward II**

south'west I. n Südwesten m **II.** adj südwestlich **III.** adv südwestwärts

south'western adj südwestlich

souvenir [ˌsu·və·ˈnɪr] n Andenken nt

sovereign ['sav·rɪn] **I.** n Herrscher(in) m(f) **II.** adj attr oberste(r, s); (state) souverän; **~ power** Hoheitsgewalt f

sow¹ <sowed, sown or sowed> [soʊ] **I.** vt säen; a. fig (mines) legen; (doubts) wecken **II.** vi säen

sow² [saʊ] n (pig) Sau f

sown [soʊn] vt, vi pp of **sow¹**

'soybean n Sojabohne f

'soy sauce n Sojasoße f

spa [spa] n [Bade]kurort m; (spring) Heilquelle f; **health ~** Heilbad nt

space [speɪs] n Raum m; (gap, vacancy) Platz m; (between two things) Zwischenraum m; (for photo) freie Stelle; (between words) Zwischenraum m; (premises) Fläche f; (for living) Wohnraum m; (seat) [Sitz]platz m; (cosmos) Weltraum m; **blank ~** Lücke f; **parking ~** Parklücke f

'space bar n COMPUT Leertaste f

'spacecraft <pl -> n Raumfahrzeug nt

spaced-'out adj sl **to be ~** geistig weggetreten sein fam; (scatterbrained) schusselig sein fam

'spaceman n [Welt]raumfahrer m

'space-saving adj Platz sparend

'spaceship n Raumschiff nt

'space station n [Welt]raumstation f

'spacewoman n Raumfahrerin f

spacious ['speɪ·ʃəs] *adj* geräumig; (*area*) weitläufig

spade [speɪd] *n* Spaten *m*; CARDS Pik *nt*

spaghetti [spə·'ɡeṭ·i] *n* Spaghetti *pl*

spaghetti 'western *n fam* Italowestern *m*

Spain [speɪn] *n* Spanien *nt*

spam [spæm] *n* COMPUT Spam *m*

span [spæn] **I.** *n usu sing* Spanne *f*; (*distance*) Breite *f*; (*scope*) Umfang *m*; **life ~** Lebensspanne *f* **II.** *vt* <-nn-> überspannen; (*cross*) führen

spangle ['spæŋ·ɡəl] *n* Paillette *f*

spangled ['spæŋ·ɡəld] *adj* mit Pailletten besetzt; (*shiny*) glitzernd

Spaniard ['spæn·jərd] *n* Spanier(in) *m(f)*

spaniel ['spæn·jəl] *n* Spaniel *m*

Spanish ['spæn·ɪʃ] **I.** *n* **1.** (*language*) Spanisch *nt* **2.** + *pl vb* **the ~** die Spanier *pl* **II.** *adj* spanisch

spank [spæŋk] *vt* **to ~ sb** jdm den Hintern versohlen; (*sexually*) jdm einen Klaps auf den Hintern geben

spanking ['spæŋ·kɪŋ] **I.** *n* Tracht *f* Prügel **II.** *adv* **~ new** funkelnagelneu

spare [sper] *vt* verschonen; (*go easy on*) schonen; (*avoid*) ersparen; (*not use*) sparen; **could you ~ [me] 10 dollars?** kannst du mir 10 Dollar leihen?; **to ~ no cost** keine Kosten scheuen **II.** *adj* Ersatz-; **~ [bed]room** Gästezimmer *nt* **III.** *n* AUTO Ersatzreifen *m*

spare 'parts *n pl* Ersatzteile *pl*

'spareribs *npl* [Schäl]rippchen *pl*

spare 'time *n* Freizeit *f*

spare 'tire *n* Ersatzreifen *m; fam* (*fat*) Rettungsring *m*

sparing ['sper·ɪŋ] *adj* sparsam

spark [spark] **I.** *n* Funke[n] *m*; **~ of hope** Fünkchen *nt* Hoffnung; **a bright ~** ein Intelligenzbolzen *m fam* **II.** *vt* entfachen *a. fig*; (*interest*) wecken; (*problems*) verursachen **III.** *vi* Funken sprühen

sparkle ['spar·kəl] **I.** *vi* funkeln; *fig* (*be witty*) sprühen (**with** vor +*dat*) **II.** *n* Funkeln *nt*; **sth lacks ~** einer *S. dat* fehlt es an Schwung

sparkling ['spark·lɪŋ] *adj* glänzend; (*eyes*) funkelnd; (*lively*) vor Leben sprühend; (*drink*) mit Kohlensäure *nach n*; (*wine*) schäumend

'spark plug *n* Zündkerze *f*

sparrow ['sper·oʊ] *n* Spatz *m*

sparse [spars] *adj* spärlich; (*meager*) dürftig

Spartan ['spar·tən] **I.** *adj* spartanisch **II.** *n* Spartaner(in) *m(f)*

spasm ['spæz·əm] *n* Krampf *m*; (*surge*) Anfall *m*

spastic ['spæs·tɪk] *adj* spastisch; *fig, offensive sl* schwach

spat [spæt] *vt, vi pt, pp of* **spit**

spate [speɪt] *n* **a ~ of sth** eine Flut von etw *dat*

spatter ['spæṭ·ər] **I.** *vt* bespritzen; **to ~ sb with water** jdn nass spritzen **II.** *vi* prasseln

spatula ['spætʃ·ə·lə] *n* Spachtel *m o f*

spawn [spɔn] **I.** *vt* (*frog*) ablegen; *fig* hervorbringen. **II.** *vi* (*frog*) laichen **III.** *n* (*eggs*) Laich *m*

speak <spoke, spoken> [spik] **I.** *vi* sprechen; (*make speech a.*) reden; (*converse*) sich unterhalten; **scientifically ~ing** wissenschaftlich gesehen; **strictly ~ing** genau genommen; **to ~ to [or with] sb [about sth]** mit jdm [über etw *akk*] reden **II.** *vt* sagen; **to not ~ a word** kein Wort herausbringen; **to ~ one's mind** sagen, was man denkt; **to ~ English fluently** fließend Englisch sprechen

⬩**speak against** *vi* **to ~ against sth** sich gegen etw *akk* aussprechen

⬩**speak for** *vi* **to ~ for sb** in jds Namen sprechen; **to ~ for oneself** für sich selbst sprechen ▶ **~ for yourself!** *fam* du vielleicht!

⬩**speak out** *vi* seine Meinung deutlich vertreten; **to ~ out against sth** sich gegen etw *akk* aussprechen

⬩**speak up** *vi* lauter sprechen; (*support*) seine Meinung sagen; **to ~ up for sb/ sth** für jdn/etw eintreten

speaker ['spi·kər] *n* Redner(in) *m(f)*; (*loudspeaker*) Lautsprecher *m*; **native ~** Muttersprachler(in) *m(f)*; **the S~ of the House** der/die Vorsitzende des Repräsentantenhauses

speaking ['spi·kɪŋ] **I.** *n* Sprechen *nt*; (*holding speech*) Reden *nt* **II.** *adj* ▶ **to be on ~ terms** miteinander bekannt sein; **they are no longer on ~ terms**

S

with each other sie reden nicht mehr miteinander

spear [spɪr] I. n Speer m II. vt durchbohren

'**spearhead** I. n Speerspitze f; fig Spitze f II. vt a. fig anführen

'**spearmint** n grüne Minze

special ['speʃ·əl] I. adj besondere(r, s); (circumstances) außergewöhnlich; (for particular purpose) speziell; (for particular use) Spezial-; **on ~ occasions** zu besonderen Gelegenheiten; **to be ~ to sb** jdm sehr viel bedeuten II. n 1. (meal) Tagesgericht nt 2. pl (bargains) **~s** Sonderangebote pl

special e'dition n Sonderausgabe f

special effect n usu pl Spezialeffekt m

specialist ['speʃ·ə·lɪst] n Spezialist(in) m(f)

specialization [ˌspeʃ·ə·lɪˈzei·ʃən] n Spezialisierung f; (skill) Spezialgebiet nt

specialize ['speʃ·ə·laɪz] vi sich spezialisieren

specialized ['speʃ·ə·laɪzd] adj spezialisiert; (particular) spezial; **~ knowledge** Fachwissen f; **~ magazine** Fachzeitschrift f

specially ['speʃ·əl·i] adv speziell; (particularly) insbesondere; (very) besonders

special 'offer n Sonderangebot nt

specialty ['speʃ·əl·ti] n Spezialität f; (skill) Fachgebiet nt

species <pl -> ['spi·fiz] n Art f

specific [spə·'sɪf·ɪk] adj genau; (particular) speziell; **could you be a little more ~?** könntest du dich etwas klarer ausdrücken?; **~ details** besondere Einzelheiten

specifically [spə·'sɪf·ɪk·li] adv speziell; (clearly) ausdrücklich

specification [ˌspes·ə·fɪˈkei·ʃən] n 1. (specifying) Angabe f 2. (plan) **~s** pl detaillierter Entwurf; (for building) Bauplan m 3. (description) genaue Angabe; (for patent) Patentschrift f; (for machines) Konstruktionsplan m

specify <-ie-> ['spes·ə·faɪ] vt angeben; (list) spezifizieren; (expressly) ausdrücklich angeben

specimen ['spes·ə·mən] n Exemplar nt; MED Probe f

speck [spek] n Fleck m; (of blood) Spritzer m; (particle) Körnchen m

speckle ['spek·əl] n Tupfen m

speckled ['spek·əld] adj gesprenkelt

specs [speks] npl fam short for **spectacles** Brille f

spectacle ['spek·tə·kəl] n Spektakel nt; (event) Schauspiel nt; (sight) Anblick m

spectacles ['spek·tə·kəlz] npl old Brille f

spectacular [spek·'tæk·ju·lər] adj atemberaubend; (striking) spektakulär

spectator [spek·'tei·tər] n Zuschauer(in) m(f)

spectrum <pl -tra> ['spek·trəm] n Spektrum nt; (range) Palette f

speculate ['spek·ju·leɪt] vi spekulieren

speculation [ˌspek·ju·'lei·ʃən] n Spekulation f

speculative ['spek·jə·lə·tɪv] adj spekulativ

speculator ['spek·ju·leɪ·tər] n Spekulant(in) m(f)

sped [sped] pt, pp of **speed**

speech <pl -es> [spitʃ] n Sprache f; (style a.) Redestil m; (oration) Rede f; (shorter) Ansprache f; (act) Sprechen nt; **in everyday ~** in der Alltagssprache; **freedom of ~** Redefreiheit f

speechless ['spitʃ·lɪs] adj sprachlos

speed [spid] I. n Geschwindigkeit f; (quickness) Schnelligkeit f; (of engine) Drehzahl f; sl (drug) Speed nt; **full ~ ahead!** volle Kraft voraus! II. vi <sped, sped> sausen; (car) rasen

speed up I. vt beschleunigen; **to ~ up ⇆ sb/sth** jdn/etw antreiben II. vi beschleunigen; (person) sich beeilen

'**speedboat** n Rennboot nt

'**speed bump** n Bodenschwelle f

'**speed dating** n organisierte Partnersuche, wobei man mit jedem Kandidaten nur wenige Minuten spricht

speeding ['spi·dɪŋ] n Geschwindigkeitsüberschreitung f

'**speed limit** n Geschwindigkeitsbegrenzung f

speedometer [spɪ·'dam·ɪ·tər] n Tachometer m o nt

'**speed skating** n Eisschnelllauf m

'**speed trap** n Radarfalle f

speedy ['spi·di] adj schnell; (decision, recovery a.) rasch; (delivery) prompt

spell[1] <spelled *or* spelt, spelled *or* spelt> [spel] **I.** *vt* buchstabieren; (*signify*) bedeuten **II.** *vi* [richtig] schreiben; (*aloud*) buchstabieren
◆ **spell out** *vt* buchstabieren; (*explain*) klarmachen

spell[2] [spel] *n* Zauber *m;* (*words*) Zauberspruch *m;* **to cast a ~ on sb** jdn verzaubern; **to be under sb's ~** von jdm verzaubert sein

spell[3] [spel] *n* **to go through a bad ~** eine schwierige Zeit durchmachen; **~ of sunny weather** Schönwetterperiode *f;* **to suffer from dizzy ~s** unter Schwindelanfällen leiden

spellbinding ['spel·baɪn·dɪŋ] *adj* fesselnd

spellbound ['spel·baʊnd] *adj* gebannt; **to hold sb ~** jdn fesseln

'**spellchecker** *n* COMPUT Rechtschreibhilfe *f*

spelling ['spel·ɪŋ] *n* Rechtschreibung *f;* (*activity*) Buchstabieren *nt kein pl*

'**spelling bee** *n* Buchstabierwettbewerb *m*

spelt[1] [spelt] *pt, pp of* **spell**

spelt[2] [spelt] *n* Dinkel *m*

spend [spend] **I.** *vt* <spent, spent> ausgeben; (*time*) verbringen **II.** *vi* <spent, spent> Geld ausgeben

spending ['spen·dɪŋ] *n* Ausgaben *pl*

spent [spent] **I.** *pt, pp of* **spend** **II.** *adj* verbraucht; (*tired*) erschöpft

sperm <*pl* ~> [spɜrm] *n* Samenzelle *f;* *fam* (*semen*) Sperma *nt*

'**sperm whale** *n* Pottwal *m*

spew [spju] **I.** *vt* ausspeien; (*lava*) auswerfen; (*exhaust*) ausstoßen; (*vomit*) erbrechen; (*blood*) spucken **II.** *vi* austreten; (*ash*) herausgeschleudert werden; (*flames*) hervorschlagen; (*water*) hervorsprudeln; (*vomit*) erbrechen

sphere [sfɪr] *n* Kugel *f;* (*earth*) Erdkugel *f;* (*area*) Bereich *m*

spherical ['sfɪr·ɪ·kəl] *adj* kugelförmig

spice [spaɪs] **I.** *n* Gewürz *nt;* *fig* Pep *m* **II.** *vt* würzen; *fig* aufpeppen *fam*

spicy ['spaɪ·si] *adj* würzig; (*hot*) scharf; (*story*) pikant

spider ['spaɪ·dər] *n* Spinne *f*

spike [spaɪk] **I.** *n* Nagel *m;* (*of fence*) Spitze *f;* (*of animal*) Stachel *m;* (on shoes) Spike *m pl* **II.** *vt* **1.** *fam* **to ~ sb's drink** einen Schuss Alkohol in jds Getränk geben **2.** (*injure*) verletzen **3.** *fam* (*story*) ablehnen; (*plan*) einstellen

spill [spɪl] **I.** *n* Verschüttete(s) *nt;* (*pool*) Lache *f;* (*stain*) Fleck *m;* oil ~ Ölteppich *m* **II.** *vt* <spilled *or* spilt, spilled *or* spilt> verschütten; *fam* (*reveal*) ausplaudern ▶ **to ~ the beans** das Geheimnis lüften **III.** *vi* überlaufen; (*flour*) verschüttet werden; (*crowd*) strömen; (*conflict*) sich ausbreiten **IV.** *adj* ▶ **don't cry over ~ed milk** *saying* was passiert ist, ist passiert

spilt [spɪlt] *pt, pp of* **spill**

spin [spɪn] **I.** *n* **1.** Drehung *f;* (*in washing machine*) Schleudern *nt* **2.** (*drive*) Spritztour *f fam;* **to send a car into a ~** ein Auto zum Schleudern bringen **II.** *vi* <-nn-, spun, spun> rotieren; (*washing machine*) schleudern; (*make thread*) spinnen; **to ~ out of control** außer Kontrolle geraten; **my head is ~ning** mir dreht sich alles *fam* **III.** *vt* <-nn-, spun, spun> drehen; (*clothes*) schleudern; (*yarn*) spinnen
◆ **spin out I.** *vi* **to ~ out of control** (*car*) außer Kontrolle geraten **II.** *vt* **to ~ out** ⇆ **sth** etw ausdehnen

spinach ['spɪn·ɪtʃ] *n* Spinat *m*

'**spinal column** *n* Wirbelsäule *f*

spindle ['spɪn·dəl] *n* Spindel *f*

spindly ['spɪnd·li] *adj* spindeldürr

'**spin doctor** *n* ≈ Pressesprecher(in) *m(f);* POL Spindoktor *m*

'**spin-dry** *vt* schleudern

'**spin-dryer** *n* Wäscheschleuder *f*

spine [spaɪn] *n* Wirbelsäule *f;* (*of book*) [Buch]rücken *m;* (*spike*) Stachel *m*

spine-chilling ['spaɪn·ˌtʃɪl·ɪŋ] *adj* gruselig

spineless ['spaɪn·lɪs] *adj pej* rückgratlos

spinning ['spɪn·ɪŋ] *n* Spinnen *nt*

'**spinning wheel** *n* Spinnrad *nt*

'**spinoff**, '**spin-off I.** *n* Nebenprodukt *nt* **II.** *adj attr* **~ effect** Folgewirkung *f*

spiny ['spaɪ·ni] *adj* stach[e]lig; (*plant a.*) dornig

spiral ['spaɪ·rəl] **I.** *n* Spirale *f* **II.** *adj attr* spiralförmig **III.** *vi* <-l-> sich hoch-/hi-

S

nunterwinden; (*smoke, hawk*) spiralförmig auf-/absteigen; (*prices*) ansteigen

spirit ['spɪr·ɪt] n 1. Geist m; (*ghost a.*) Gespenst nt; (*mood*) Stimmung f; (*vitality*) Temperament nt; **the Holy S~** der Heilige Geist; **team ~** Teamgeist m 2. (*alcohol*) ~s pl Spirituosen pl

spirited ['spɪr·ɪ·tɪd] adj temperamentvoll; (*discussion*) lebhaft; (*person*) beherzt; (*reply*) mutig

spiritual ['spɪr·ɪ·tʃu·əl] I. adj geistig; (*leader*) religiös II. n Spiritual nt

spit [spɪt] I. n Spucke f II. vi <-tt-, spat or spit, spat or spit> spucken; **to ~ at sb** jdn anspucken III. vt <-tt-, spat or spit, spat or spit> ausspucken; (*flames*) ausstoßen

◆**spit out** vt ausspucken; fam (*say angrily*) fauchen; **~ it out!** spuck's schon aus!

spite [spaɪt] I. n Bosheit f; **in ~ of sth** trotz einer S. gen II. vt ärgern

spiteful ['spaɪt·fəl] adj gehässig

spitting 'image n Ebenbild nt

splash [splæʃ] I. n <pl -es> Platschen nt; (*of sauce*) Klecks m fam; (*in drink*) Spritzer m II. vt verspritzen; (*spray*) bespritzen; **her picture was ~ed all over the newspapers** ihr Bild erschien groß in allen Zeitungen III. vi klatschen; (*spill out*) spritzen

splatter ['splæt·ər] I. vt bespritzen II. vi spritzen

spleen [splin] n Milz f

splendid ['splen·dɪd] adj großartig

splendor ['splen·dər] n Pracht f; ~s pl Herrlichkeiten pl

splint [splɪnt] n Schiene f

splinter ['splɪn·tər] n Splitter m

'**splinter group** n POL Splittergruppe f

split [splɪt] I. n Riss m; (*in wood*) Spalt m; (*in opinion*) Kluft f; (*in party*) Spaltung f; (*of couple*) Trennung f; (*sharing*) Aufteilung f II. vt <-tt-, split, split> teilen; (*in half*) halbieren; (*party*) spalten; (*seam*) aufplatzen lassen; **to ~ the difference** fig sich akk auf halbem Weg einigen; **to ~ one's head open** sich dat den Kopf aufschlagen III. vi <-tt-, split, split> [entzwei]brechen; (*seam*) aufplatzen; (*hair*) splissen; (*couple*) sich trennen; **to ~ into groups** sich aufteilen; **to ~ from**

sth (*group*) sich von etw dat abspalten

◆**split off** I. vt abbrechen; (*with axe*) abschlagen; (*separate*) abtrennen II. vi sich lösen; **to ~ off from sth** (*group*) sich von etw dat abspalten

◆**split up** I. vt aufteilen; (*group*) teilen II. vi 1. **to ~ up into groups** sich in Gruppen aufteilen 2. (*couple*) sich trennen

'**split-up** n Trennung f

splutter ['splʌt·ər] I. vi stottern; (*fire*) zischen II. vt **to ~ an excuse** eine Entschuldigung hervorstoßen III. n Prusten nt; (*of car*) Stottern nt; (*of fire*) Zischen nt

spoil [spɔɪl] I. n ~s pl Beute f II. vt <spoiled or spoilt, spoiled or spoilt> verderben; (*pamper*) verwöhnen; (*child*) verziehen; **to ~ sb's chances** jds Chancen ruinieren; **to be spoiled for choice** eine große Auswahl haben III. vi <spoiled or spoilt, spoiled or spoilt> schlecht werden

spoiled [spɔɪld] adj verdorben; (*child*) verzogen

spoilsport ['spɔɪl·spɔrt] n fam Spielverderber(in) m(f)

spoilt [spɔɪlt] vt, vi pt, pp of **spoil**

spoke¹ [spoʊk] n Speiche f

spoke² [spoʊk] pt of **speak**

spoken [spoʊ·kən] I. pp of **speak** II. adj attr gesprochen

spokesman ['spoʊks·mən] n Sprecher m

'**spokesperson** <pl -people> n Sprecher(in) m(f)

'**spokeswoman** n Sprecherin f

sponge [spʌndʒ] n Schwamm m

◆**sponge off** I. vt **to ~ off ⇆ sb/sth** jdn/etw schnell [mit einem Schwamm] [ab]waschen II. vi pej fam ausnutzen

'**sponge cake** n Rührkuchen m; (*without fat*) Biskuit[kuchen] m

sponger ['spʌn·dʒər] n pej Schmarotzer(in) m(f)

sponsor ['span·sər] I. vt sponsern; (*candidate*) unterstützen II. n Sponsor(in) m(f); (*of charity*) Förderer, Förderin m, f

spontaneous [span·'teɪ·ni·əs] adj spontan; (*laughter*) impulsiv

spook [spuk] n fam Gespenst nt

spooky ['spu·ki] *adj fam* schaurig; (*uncanny*) unheimlich; (*film*) gespenstisch

spool [spul] *n* Rolle *f*

spoon [spun] *n* Löffel *m*

spoon-feed <-fed, -fed> ['spun·fid] *vt to ~ sb* jdn mit einem Löffel füttern; (*supply*) jdm alles vorgeben

spoonful <*pl* -s *or* spoonsful> ['spun·ful] *n* Löffel *m*

sporadic [spə·'ræd·ɪk] *adj* sporadisch

sport [spɔrt] *n* Sport *m;* (*type*) Sportart *f;* **to be a [good]/bad ~** *fam* ein/kein Spielverderber/eine/keine Spielverderberin sein; **~s** *pl* Sport *m;* **to be good at ~s** sportlich sein

sports car *n* Sportwagen *m*

sportsman *n* Sportler *m*

sportsmanship *n* Fairness *f*

sportswoman *n* Sportlerin *f*

sporty ['spɔr·ʈi] *adj* (*athletic*) sportlich; (*car*) schnell

spot [spat] **I.** *n* Fleck *m;* (*dot*) Punkt *m;* (*pattern*) Tupfen *m;* (*place*) Stelle *f;* (*on TV*) Beitrag *m;* **on the ~** an Ort und Stelle **II.** *vt* <-tt-> entdecken; (*notice*) bemerken

spot 'check *n* Stichprobe *f*

spotless ['spat·lɪs] *adj* makellos; (*unblemished* a.) tadellos

spotlight I. *n* Scheinwerfer *m;* **to be in the ~** *fig* im Rampenlicht stehen **II.** *vt* <-lighted *or* -lit, -lighted *or* -lit> **to ~ sth** etw beleuchten; *fig* auf etw *akk* aufmerksam machen

spotted ['spat·ɪd] *adj* getupft; (*covered*) gesprenkelt

spout [spaʊt] **I.** *n* Ausguss *m* **II.** *vt* speien; *pej* (*rant*) faseln *fam* **III.** *vi* hervorschießen; *pej* (*rant*) Reden schwingen *fam*

sprain [spreɪn] **I.** *vt to ~ one's ankle* sich *dat* den Knöchel verstauchen **II.** *n* Verstauchung *f*

sprang [spræŋ] *pt of* **spring**

sprawl [sprɔl] **I.** *n* Ausdehnung *f* **II.** *vi* sich ausbreiten; (*slouch*) herumlümmeln *pej fam*

sprawling ['sprɔ·lɪŋ] *adj pej* ausgedehnt; (*irregular*) unregelmäßig

spray [spreɪ] **I.** *n* Spray *m o nt;* (*cloud*) Sprühnebel *m;* (*of perfume*) Wolke *f;* (*of water*) Gischt *m o f* **II.** *vt* besprühen; (*plants*) spritzen; (*paint*) sprühen **III.** *vi* spritzen

spread [spred] **I.** *n* Verbreitung *f;* (*range*) Vielfalt *f;* (*am* (*meal*) Festessen *nt;* (*on bread*) Aufstrich *m;* (*news*) Doppelseite *f* **II.** *vi* <spread, spread> sich ausbreiten; (*panic*) sich verbreiten; (*stretch*) sich erstrecken **III.** *vt* <spread, spread> ausbreiten; (*net*) auslegen; (*bread*) bestreichen; (*sand*) verteilen; (*fertilizer*) streuen; (*disease*) übertragen; (*panic*) verbreiten; (*rumors*) verbreiten

spread-eagled ['spred·'i·gəld] *adj* ausgestreckt

'spreadsheet *n* Tabellenkalkulation *f*

spree [spri] *n* **shopping ~** Einkaufstour *f*

sprightly ['spraɪt·li] *adj* munter; (*old person*) rüstig

spring [sprɪŋ] **I.** *n* (*season*) Frühling *m;* TECH Feder *f;* (*water*) Quelle *f* **II.** *vi* <sprang *or* sprung, sprung> springen; (*appear*) auftauchen; **to ~ to mind** in den Kopf schießen

'springboard *n* Sprungbrett *nt*

spring-'clean I. *vi* Frühjahrsputz machen **II.** *vt* **to ~ a house** in einem Haus Frühjahrsputz machen

'spring roll *n* Frühlingsrolle *f*

'springtime *n* Frühling *m*

sprinkle ['sprɪŋ·kəl] **I.** *vt* streuen; (*cover*) bestreuen; (*with liquid*) besprengen **II.** *n* **a ~ of snow** leichter Schneefall; **chocolate ~s** Schokosplitter *pl*

sprinkler ['sprɪŋ·klər] *n* Bewässerungsanlage *f;* (*for lawn*) Sprinkler *m;* (*for fires*) Sprinkler *m*

sprinkling ['sprɪŋ·klɪŋ] *n* **a ~ of ...** ein paar ...; **a ~ of salt** eine Prise Salz

sprint [sprɪnt] **I.** *vi* sprinten **II.** *n* Sprint *m*

sprinter ['sprɪn·tər] *n* Sprinter(in) *m(f)*

sprout [spraʊt] **I.** *n* Spross *m;* **Brussels ~s** *pl* Rosenkohl *m* **II.** *vi* sprießen; (*buds*) austreiben *geh;* (*germinate*) keimen **III.** *vt* treiben

sprout up *vi* aus dem Boden schießen

spruce [sprus] *n* Fichte *f*

sprung [sprʌŋ] *pt, pp of* **spring**

spud [spʌd] *n sl* Kartoffel *f*

spun [spʌn] *pt, pp of* **spin**

spur [spɜr] I. n Sporn m; fig Ansporn m ▶ **on the ~ of the moment** spontan II. vt <-rr-> ansornen; (persuade) bewegen; (incite) anstacheln

spurt [spɜrt] I. n Strahl m; (surge) Schub m; **to do sth in ~s** etw schubweise machen; **to put on a ~** einen Spurt hinlegen II. vt [ver]spritzen III. vi spritzen

sputter ['spʌt·ər] I. n Knattern nt II. vi zischen; (car) stottern III. vt heraussprudeln; (stutter) stottern

spy [spaɪ] I. n Spion(in) m(f) II. vi spionieren; **to ~ on sb** jdm nachspionieren III. vt sehen; (spot) entdecken

squabble ['skwab·əl] I. n Zankerei f II. vi sich zanken

squad [skwad] n Mannschaft f; MIL Trupp m

'squad car n Streifenwagen m

squadron ['skwad·rən] n Schwadron f; (air force) Staffel f; (navy) Geschwader nt

squalid ['skwal·ɪd] adj schmutzig; (neglected) verwahrlost; (immoral) verkommen

squalor ['skwal·ər] n Schmutz m; (immorality) Verkommenheit f

squander ['skwan·dər] vt verschwenden; (opportunity) vertun

square [skwer] I. n Quadrat nt; (in town) Platz m; (tool) Winkelmaß nt; MATH Quadratzahl f II. adj quadratisch; (face) kantig; (on each side) im Quadrat; (when squared) zum Quadrat; (foot, mile) Quadrat-; **to be** [all] ~ fam auf gleich sein III. vt 1. **to ~ sth with sth** etw mit etw dat in Übereinstimmung bringen 2. (settle) in Ordnung bringen ◆ **square up** vi fam abrechnen

squarely ['skwer·li] adv aufrecht; (directly) direkt

square 'root n MATH Quadratwurzel f

squash¹ [skwaʃ] n (pumpkin) Kürbis m

squash² [skwaʃ] I. n Squash nt II. vt zerdrücken; (rumors) aus der Welt schaffen; **to ~ sth flat** etw platt drücken

squat [skwat] I. vi <-tt-> 1. hocken; **to ~** [down] sich hinhocken 2. (on land) sich illegal ansiedeln; **to ~** [in a house] ein Haus besetzen II. n Hocke f; (exercise) Kniebeuge f; (building) besetztes Haus III. adj <-tt-> gedrungen

squatter ['skwat·ər] n Hausbesetzer(in) m(f)

squaw [skwɔ] n offensive Squaw f

squawk [skwɔk] I. vi kreischen II. n Kreischen nt

squeak [skwik] I. n Quietschen nt; (of animal) Quieken nt; (of mouse) Piep[s]er m fam; (of person) Quiekser m fam II. vi quietschen; (animal, person) quieken; (mouse) piepsen

'squeaky-clean adj blitzsauber fam

squeal [skwil] I. n [schriller] Schrei; (of tires) Quietschen nt; (of brakes) Kreischen nt; (of pig) Quieken nt II. vi kreischen; (pig) quieken; (tires) quietschen; (brakes) kreischen

squeamish ['skwi·mɪʃ] I. adj zimperlich; **he is ~ about seeing blood** er ekelt sich vor Blut II. npl **to be not for the ~** nichts für schwache Nerven sein

squeeze [skwiz] I. n 1. Drücken nt; **to give sth a ~** etw drücken 2. (limit) Beschränkung f 3. (fit) Gedränge nt; **it'll be a tight ~** es wird eng werden II. vt drücken; (orange) auspressen; (sponge) ausdrücken; (push in) [hinein]zwängen; (push through) [durch]zwängen; (constrict) einschränken III. vi **to ~ in/past/through** sich hinein-/vorbei-/durchzwängen

squid <pl -> [skwɪd] n Tintenfisch m

squiggle ['skwɪg·əl] n Schnörkel m

squint [skwɪnt] vi blinzeln; **to ~ at sb/sth** einen Blick auf jdn/etw werfen

squirm [skwɜrm] I. vi sich winden; **to ~ in pain** sich vor Schmerzen krümmen II. n **to give a ~ of embarrassment** sich vor Verlegenheit winden

squirrel ['skwɜr·əl] n Eichhörnchen nt

squirt [skwɜrt] I. vt spritzen; **to ~ sb with sth** jdn mit etw dat bespritzen II. vi **to ~ out** herausspritzen III. n Spritzer m

Sri Lanka [ˌsri·'lɑn·kə] n Sri Lanka nt

Sri Lankan [ˌsri·'lɑn·kən] I. adj sri-lankisch; **to be ~** aus Sri Lanka sein II. n Sri-Lanker(in) m(f)

southwest SSW

st. n **1.** abbr of **street** Str. **2.** abbr of **saint** St.

tab [stæb] I. vt <-bb-> **to ~ sb/sth** auf jdn/etw einstechen; **to ~ sth with a fork** mit einer Gabel in etw dat herumstochern; **to ~ the air [with sth]** [mit etw dat] in der Luft herumfuchteln II. vi <-bb-> **to ~ at sb/sth** auf jdn/etw einstechen III. n Stich m; (wound) Stichwunde f; (pain) Stich m ► **to take a ~ at [doing] sth** etw [einmal] probieren

stabbing ['stæ·bɪŋ] I. n Messerstecherei f II. adj stechend; (fear) durchdringend

stability [stə·'bɪl·ɪ·ţi] n Stabilität f

stabilization [ˌsteɪ·bə·lɪ·'zeɪ·ʃən] n Stabilisierung f

stabilize ['steɪ·bə·laɪz] I. vt stabilisieren; (prices a.) festigen II. vi sich stabilisieren; **his condition has now ~d** sein Zustand ist jetzt stabil

stable¹ <-r, -st or more ~, most ~> ['steɪ·bəl] adj stabil; (relationship) fest; PSYCH ausgeglichen

stable² ['steɪ·bəl] n Stall m

stack [stæk] I. n Stapel m; (of papers) Stoß m; fam (amount) Haufen m; (hi-fi) Stereoturm m II. vt [auf]stapeln; (dishwasher) einräumen; (shelves) auffüllen

stadium <pl -s> ['steɪ·di·əm] n Stadion nt

staff [stæf] I. n **1.** + sing/pl vb Belegschaft f; **nursing ~** Pflegepersonal nt **2.** (stick) [Spazier]stock m II. vt usu passive **many charities are ~ed by volunteers** viele Wohltätigkeitsvereine beschäftigen ehrenamtliche Mitarbeiter

stag [stæg] n Hirsch m

stage [steɪdʒ] I. n **1.** Etappe f; (of race a.) Abschnitt m; (level) Stufe f; **crucial ~** entscheidende Phase **2.** THEAT Bühne f; **to take center ~** im Mittelpunkt [des Interesses] stehen II. vt aufführen; (concert) geben; (meeting) veranstalten; (strike) organisieren; (game) austragen

stage fright n Lampenfieber nt

stage-manage vt inszenieren

stage manager n Bühnenmeister(in) m(f)

stage name n Künstlername m

stagger ['stæg·ər] I. vi wanken; (waver a.) schwanken; **to ~ to one's feet** sich aufrappeln II. vt erstaunen III. n Wanken nt

staggering ['stæg·ər·ɪŋ] adj erstaunlich; (news) unglaublich; (shocking) erschütternd

stagnant ['stæg·nənt] adj stagnierend; (pool) still; (water) stehend

stagnate ['stæg·neɪt] vi stagnieren; (stream) ins Stocken geraten

stagnation [stæg·'neɪ·ʃən] n Stagnation f

stain [steɪn] I. vt verfärben; (wood) [ein]färben; (spot) Flecken machen auf +dat; (reputation) schaden II. vi abfärben; (discolor) sich verfärben; (take dye) sich färben III. n Verfärbung f; (blemish) Makel m

stained [steɪnd] adj verfärbt; (with spots) fleckig; (dyed) gefärbt

'stained-glass window n Buntglasfenster nt

stainless 'steel n rostfreier Stahl

'stain remover n Fleckenentferner m

stair [ster] n Treppenstufe f; **~s** pl Treppe f; **flight of ~s** Treppe f

'staircase n Treppenhaus nt; **spiral ~** Wendeltreppe f

'stairway n Treppe f

stake [steɪk] I. n **1.** Pfahl m **2.** usu pl (bet) Einsatz m **3.** (interest) Anteil m ► **to be at ~** (in question) zur Debatte stehen; (at risk) auf dem Spiel stehen II. vt **1.** (animal) anbinden; (plant) hochbinden **2.** (bet) setzen; **to ~ one's future on sth** seine Zukunft auf etw akk aufbauen

stake out vt **1.** (watch) überwachen **2.** (mark) markieren; (border) abstecken

stakeholder n Teilhaber(in) m(f)

stalactite [stə·'læk·taɪt] n Tropfstein m

stalagmite [stə·'læg·maɪt] n Tropfstein m

stale [steɪl] adj schal; (beer) abgestanden; (air) muffig; (bread) alt; (unoriginal) fantasielos; (joke) abgedroschen; (without zest) abgestumpft

stalemate ['steɪl·meɪt] I. n Patt nt; (deadlock) Stillstand m II. vt patt setzen; (deadlock) zum Stillstand bringen

stalk¹ [stɔk] n Stiel m

stalk² [stɔk] **I.** vt jagen; **to ~ sb** jdm nachstellen **II.** vi stolzieren; (angrily) marschieren

stalker [stɔ·kər] n Stalker(in) m(f); (hunter) Jäger(in) m(f)

stall¹ [stɔl] **I.** n Stall m; (booth) [Verkaufs]stand m; (for parking) [markierter] Parkplatz; (toilet) Toilette f **II.** vi stehen bleiben; (aircraft) abrutschen; (negotiations) zum Stillstand kommen **III.** vt abwürgen

stall² [stɔl] **I.** vi zögern; **to ~ for time** Zeit gewinnen **II.** vt verzögern; **to ~ sb** fam jdn hinhalten

stallion [ˈstæl·jən] n Hengst m

stamina [ˈstæm·ə·nə] n Durchhaltevermögen nt

stammer [ˈstæm·ər] **I.** n Stottern nt **II.** vi stottern

stamp [stæmp] **I.** n **1.** Stempel m; **~ of approval** Genehmigungsstempel m; **postage ~** Briefmarke f **2.** (step) Stampfer m fam; (sound) Stampfen nt **II.** vt **1.** [ab]stempeln; **to ~ a letter** einen Brief frankieren **2.** zertreten; **to ~ one's foot** mit dem Fuß aufstampfen **III.** vi stampfen; (walk a.) stapfen; **to ~ on sth** auf etw akk treten

◆ **stamp out** vt ausmerzen; (crime) bekämpfen; (disease) ausrotten; (fire) austreten

'**stamp collector** n Briefmarkensammler(in) m(f)

stampede [stæm·ˈpid] **I.** n wilde Flucht; (of people) [Menschen]auflauf m **II.** vi durchgehen; (people) stürzen

stance [stæns] n Haltung f; (attitude) Standpunkt m

stand [stænd] **I.** n **1.** Stellung f; (view) Einstellung f; **to take a ~ on sth** sich für etw akk einsetzen **2.** (seating) ~s pl [Zuschauer]tribüne f **3.** (support) Ständer m **4.** LAW **the ~** der Zeugenstand; **to take the ~** vor Gericht aussagen **5.** **to make a ~** klar Stellung beziehen **6.** **taxi ~** Taxistand m **II.** vi <stood, stood> **1.** stehen; **~ against the wall** stell dich an die Wand; **to ~ clear** aus dem Weg gehen; **to ~ still** stillstehen **2.** (be located) stehen/liegen; **to ~ in sb's way** jdm im Weg stehen **3.** + adj **to ~ open/**

empty/in second place offen/leer/an zweiter Stelle stehen; **with the situation as it ~s right now ...** so wie die Sache im Moment aussieht, ... **4.** (remain valid) gelten; **does that offer still ~?** ist das Angebot noch gültig? ▸ **to ~ on one's own two <u>feet</u>** auf eigenen Füßen stehen **III.** vt <stood, stood> **1.** **to ~ sth somewhere** etw irgendwohin stellen; **to ~ sth on its head** etw auf den Kopf stellen **2.** (bear) ertragen; **she can't ~ anyone touching her** sie kann es nicht leiden, wenn man sie anfasst; **to ~ the test of time** die Zeit überdauern **3.** **to ~ trial** sich vor Gericht verantworten müssen ▸ **to ~ sb in <u>good</u> stead** jdm von Nutzen sein

◆ **stand around** vi herumstehen

◆ **stand back** vi (take detached view) etw aus der Distanz betrachten; (not get involved) tatenlos zusehen; (be set back from) abseitsliegen

◆ **stand by** vi bereitstehen; (observe) dabeistehen; (promise) halten; **to ~ by sb/one's word** zu jdm/zu seinem Wort stehen

◆ **stand for** vi **1.** (tolerate) **to not ~ for sth** sich dat etw nicht gefallen lassen **2.** (represent) **to ~ for sth** für etw akk stehen

◆ **stand in** vi **to ~ in for sb** für jdn einspringen

◆ **stand out** vi hervorragen; (be distinguishable) zu unterscheiden sein; (be identifiable) gekennzeichnet sein; **to ~ out in a crowd** sich von der Menge abheben

◆ **stand up** vi aufstehen; (stand) stehen

standard [ˈstæn·dərd] **I.** n **1.** Standard m; (criterion) Gradmesser m; **to raise ~s** das Niveau heben **2.** (principles) ~s pl Wertvorstellungen pl **II.** adj Standard-; (average) durchschnittlich

standardization [ˌstæn·dər·dɪ·ˈzeɪ·ʃən] n Standardisierung f

standardize [ˈstæn·dər·daɪz] vt standardisieren; (compare) vereinheitlichen

standby <pl -s> [ˈstænd·baɪ] **I.** n Reserve f; **on ~** in Bereitschaft **II.** adj Ersatz-

stand-in n Vertretung f; (actor) Ersatz m

tanding ['stæn·dɪŋ] I. n 1. (status) Ansehen nt 2. to be of long ~ von langer Dauer sein II. adj attr (upright) [aufrecht] stehend; (permanent) ständig; (stationary) stehend

tanding o'vation n stehende Ovationen pl

standpoint n Standpunkt m

standstill n Stillstand m; to be at a ~ zum Erliegen kommen

standup adj attr • comedy Stand-up-Comedy f; ~ comedian Stand-up-Comedian m

tank [stæŋk] pt of stink

staple ['ster·pəl] I. n Heftklammer f II. vt heften; to ~ sth together etw zusammenheften

staple gun n Heftmaschine f

tapler ['ster·plər] n Hefter m

star [stɑr] I. n 1. Stern m; (asterisk) Sternchen nt; (performer) Star m II. vt <-rr-> "King Lear" ~ring John Smith as Lear „King Lear" mit John Smith als Lear III. vi <-rr-> to ~ in a film in einem Film die Hauptrolle spielen IV. adj attr Star-; ~ witness Hauptzeuge, -zeugin m, f

tarboard ['stɑr·bərd] n Steuerbord nt kein pl

tarch [stɑrtʃ] n Stärke f

tare [ster] I. n Starren nt; (directed) fester Blick II. vi starren; (gawk) große Augen machen; to ~ at sb/sth jdn/etw anstarren III. vt to ~ sb in the eye jdn anstarren; to ~ sb up and down jdn anstieren fam ► to be staring sb in the face auf der Hand liegen

tarfish n Seestern m

taring ['stɑr·ɪŋ] adj starrend

tark [stɑrk] I. adj krass; to be a ~ reminder drastisch an etw akk erinnern II. adv ~ naked splitterfasernackt fam; ~ raving mad hum, iron völlig übergeschnappt fam

tarling ['stɑr·lɪŋ] n Star m

tarry-eyed adj blauäugig

Stars and Stripes [ˌstɑrz·ənd·'straɪps] npl + sing vb the ~ die Stars and Stripes pl (Nationalflagge der USA)

tar sign n Sternzeichen nt

Star-Spangled 'Banner n the ~ das Sternenbanner (die Nationalflagge der USA); (anthem) der Star Spangled Banner (die Nationalhymne der USA)

start [stɑrt] I. n 1. Anfang m; SPORT Start m; it was an exciting ~ es fing spannend an; to make a fresh ~ einen neuen Anfang machen; to have a good ~ in life einen guten Start ins Leben haben 2. to give a ~ zusammenzucken II. vi 1. anfangen; (on trip) losfahren; (car) anspringen; (happen) beginnen; ~ing tomorrow ab morgen; to ~ with (at first) anfangs; (firstly) zunächst einmal 2. (jump) zusammenfahren III. vt anfangen; (switch on) einschalten; (machine) anstellen; (motor) anlassen; (car) starten; (family) gründen; (initiate) ins Leben rufen; when do you ~ your new job? wann fängst du mit deiner neuen Stelle an?; to ~ a fire Feuer machen; to ~ doing sth anfangen, etw zu tun

start back vi sich auf den Rückweg machen

start off I. vi they ~ed off by reading through the script zuerst lasen sie das Skript durch; to ~ off as sth seine Laufbahn als etw beginnen; to ~ off with sb/sth bei jdn/etw anfangen II. vt to ~ sth ⇆ off etw beginnen; to ~ sb off doing sth jdn zu etw dat veranlassen; to ~ sb off with sth jdm den Start bei etw dat erleichtern

start out vi aufbrechen; (begin) anfangen

start up I. vt gründen; (motor) anlassen II. vi beginnen; (engine) anspringen

'starting point n Ausgangspunkt m

startle ['stɑr·t̬əl] vt erschrecken

startling ['stɑr·t̬əl·ɪŋ] adj überraschend; (alarming) erschreckend

'start-up n [Neu]gründung f; (of machine) Inbetriebnahme f; COMPUT Hochfahren nt; ~ disk Startdiskette f

starvation [stɑr·'veɪ·ʃən] n Unterernährung f; (fatal) Hungertod m; to die of ~ verhungern

starve [stɑrv] I. vi hungern; (die) verhungern; (be malnourished) unterernährt sein; fam am Verhungern sein fam; (crave) hungern (for nach +dat) II. vt

S

aushungern; **to ~ oneself to death** sich zu Tode hungern; **to be ~d of sth** um etw *akk* gebracht werden

starving ['star·vɪŋ] *adj* ausgehungert; **I'm ~!** ich bin am Verhungern!

stash [stæʃ] I. *n <pl -es>* [geheimes] Lager, Vorrat *m* II. *vt fam* verstecken; (*money*) bunkern

state [steɪt] I. *n* **1.** Zustand *m;* (*bodily*) körperliche Verfassung; **~ of war** Kriegszustand *m;* **a good ~ of health** ein guter Gesundheitszustand; **~ of mind** Gemütszustand *m* **2.** (*nation*) Staat *m;* (*government a.*) Regierung *f;* (*in USA*) [Bundes]staat *m;* (*in Germany*) Land *nt;* **the S~s** *pl fam* (*the USA*) die Staaten *pl* II. *vt* aussprechen; (*objections*) vorbringen; (*source*) angeben; (*fix*) nennen; (*demands*) stellen; **to ~ why ...** darlegen, warum ...

'**State Department** *n* **the ~** das US-Außenministerium

stately ['steɪt·li] *adj* würdevoll; (*splendid*) prächtig

statement ['steɪt·mənt] *n* Erklärung *f;* (*formal*) Stellungnahme *f;* **to make a ~ to the press** eine Presseerklärung abgeben; **bank ~** [Konto]auszug *m*

state of the 'art, state-of-the-'art *adj attr* auf dem neuesten Stand der Technik *nach n*

'**stateside** I. *adj* in den Staaten *präd* II. *adv* in die Staaten

'**statesman** *n* Staatsmann *m*

'**stateswoman** *n* Staatsfrau *f*

state 'visit *n* Staatsbesuch *m*

static ['stæt·ɪk] I. *adj* statisch; (*not changing*) konstant II. *n* statische Elektrizität

static elec'tricity *n* statische Elektrizität

station ['steɪ·ʃən] *n* **1. train ~** Bahnhof *m;* **subway ~** U-Bahn-Haltestelle *f;* **police ~** Polizeiwache *f;* **power ~** Kraftwerk *nt* **2.** TV Sender *m*

stationary ['steɪ·ʃə·ner·i] *adj* ruhend; (*not changing*) unverändert

stationery ['steɪ·ʃə·ner·i] *n* Schreibwaren *pl;* (*writing paper*) Schreibpapier *nt*

'**station house** *n* Polizeiwache *f*

'**station wagon** *n* Kombi[wagen] *m*

statistics [stə·'tɪs·tɪks] *npl* Statistik *f*

statue ['stætʃ·u] *n* Statue *f*

Statue of 'Liberty *n* **the ~** die Frei heitsstatue

stature ['stætʃ·ər] *n* Statur *f;* (*reputation*) Prestige *nt;* **short ~** kleiner Wuchs

status ['stæ·təs] *n* Status *m;* (*prestige a.*) Prestige *nt;* **legal ~** Rechtsposition *f*

'**status symbol** *n* Statussymbol *nt*

statute ['stætʃ·ut] *n* Satzung *f;* (*law*) Ge setz *nt;* **by ~** satzungsgemäß

'**statute book** *n* Gesetzbuch *nt*

statute of limi'tations *n* Verjährungs gesetz *nt*

staunch [stɔntʃ] *adj* standhaft; (*Catholic* überzeugt; (*opponent*) erbittert

stave off *vt* hinauszögern; (*prevent*) ab wenden; (*hunger*) stillen; **to ~ off ⇆ s** jdn hinhalten *fam*

stay [steɪ] I. *n* Aufenthalt *m;* **overnigh ~** Übernachtung *f* II. *vi* **1.** bleiber **to ~ put** *fam* (*keep standing*) stehe bleiben; (*not stand up*) sitzen bleiber (*not move*) sich nicht vom Fleck rühre **2.** (*reside temporarily*) untergebrach sein; **to ~ overnight** übernachten **3.** *n or adj* bleiben; **the stores ~ ope until 8 p.m.** die Läden haben bis 2 Uhr geöffnet; **to ~ in touch** in Verbin dung bleiben III. *vt* ▶ **to ~ the cours** durchhalten

◆ **stay away** *vi* fernbleiben; (*avoid*) me den

◆ **stay behind** *vi* [noch] [da]bleiben; **to ~ behind after school** nachsitzen

◆ **stay in** *vi* zu Hause bleiben

◆ **stay on** *vi* [noch] bleiben; (*lid*) draufble ben; (*sticker*) haften; (*light*) an bleiben (*device*) eingeschaltet bleiben

◆ **stay out** *vi* wegbleiben; **~ out of th kitchen!** bleib aus der Küche!; **to ~ out of trouble** sich *dat* Ärger vom Ha halten *fam*

◆ **stay together** *vi* immer zusamme sein; (*always*) unzertrennlich sein (*group*) zusammenbleiben; (*loyally*) z sammenhalten

◆ **stay up** *vi* aufbleiben

steady ['sted·i] I. *adj* fest; (*regular*) kont nuierlich; (*pulse*) regelmäßig; (*increase* stetig; (*rain*) anhaltend; (*speed*) kor stant; (*voice*) fest; (*pain*) permanen

steak [hand] ruhig; (calm) verlässlich; (nerves) stark **II.** vt <-ie-> stabilisieren; (ladder) festhalten; (nerves) beruhigen; **to ~ oneself** ins Gleichgewicht kommen, Halt finden **III.** adv **to hold ~** (prices) stabil bleiben; **to hold sth ~** etw festhalten

steak [steɪk] n Rindfleisch nt; (slice) [Beef]steak nt

steal [stiːl] **I.** vt <stole, stolen> stehlen; (heart) erobern; **she stole a glance at her watch** sie lugte heimlich auf ihre Armbanduhr; **to ~** [sb's] **ideas** [jds] Ideen klauen fam **II.** vi <stole, stolen> stehlen; **he stole out of the room** er stahl sich aus dem Zimmer

stealth [stelθ] n Heimlichkeit f; **by ~** heimlich

stealthy ['stel·θi] adj heimlich

steam [stiːm] **I.** n Dampf m; **to let off ~** Dampf ablassen **II.** vi dampfen
◆ **steam up I.** vi [sich] beschlagen **II.** vt **the windows are ~ed up** die Fenster sind beschlagen; **to get all ~ed up** [about sth] fam sich [über etw akk] unheimlich aufregen

'**steamboat** n Dampfschiff nt, Dampfer m

steamer ['stiː·mɚ] n Dampfer m; (pot) Dampfkochtopf m

'**steamroller I.** n Dampfwalze f **II.** vt niederwalzen; **to ~ sb into doing sth** jdn unter Druck setzen, etw zu tun

'**steamship** n Dampfschiff nt

steamy ['stiː·mi] adj feuchtheiß; fam (sexy) heiß; (novel a.) prickelnd

steel [stiːl] **I.** n Stahl m; **nerves of ~** Nerven pl wie Drahtseile **II.** vt **to ~ oneself against/for sth** sich gegen/für etw akk wappnen; **to ~ oneself** [to do sth] all seinen Mut zusammennehmen[, um etw zu tun]

'**steelworker** n Stahlarbeiter(in) m(f)

'**steelworks** npl + sing vb Stahlwerk nt

steep [stiːp] adj steil; (slope) abschüssig; (steps) hoch; (dramatic) drastisch; (decline) deutlich; (expensive) überteuert

steepen ['stiː·pən] vi steiler werden; (slope) ansteigen

steeple ['stiː·pəl] n Turmspitze f; (of church) Kirchturm m

'**steeplechase** n Hindernislauf m; (for horses) Hindernisrennen nt

steer[1] [stɪr] vt, vi steuern

steer[2] [stɪr] n junger Ochse

steering ['stɪr·ɪŋ] n Lenkung f; NAUT Steuerung f

'**steering wheel** n Steuer[rad] nt; (of car a.) Lenkrad nt

stem [stem] **I.** n Stamm m; (of leaf) Stiel m; (of grain) Halm m; (of glass) [Glas]stiel m **II.** vi <-mm-> **to ~ back to sth** auf etw akk zurückgehen; **to ~ from sb/sth** auf jdn/etw zurückzuführen sein

stench [stentʃ] n Gestank m

stencil ['sten·səl] n Schablone f; (picture) Schablonenzeichnung f

step [step] **I.** n Schritt m; (measure a.) Vorgehen nt; (of dance) [Tanz]schritt m; (stair) Stufe f; (of ladder) Sprosse f; **"watch your ~"** „Vorsicht, Stufe!"; **to be one ~ ahead** [of sb] [jdm] einen Schritt voraus sein; **~ by ~** Schritt für Schritt; **to take drastic ~s** zu drastischen Mitteln greifen; **in ~** im Takt; fig im Einklang; **to walk in ~** im Gleichschritt laufen **II.** vi <-pp-> **1. to ~ on sb's foot** jdm auf den Fuß treten; **to ~ over sth** über etw akk steigen **2.** (walk) **to ~ somewhere** irgendwohin gehen; **would you care to ~ this way please, sir?** würden Sie bitte hier entlanggehen, Sir?; **to ~ aside** zur Seite gehen; **to ~ out of line** fig sich danebenbenehmen **III.** vi treten (**on** auf +akk); **~ on it!** gib Gas! fam
◆ **step back** vi zurücktreten; (reconsider) Abstand nehmen
◆ **step down** vi zurücktreten; (witness) den Zeugenstand verlassen
◆ **step in** vi eintreten; (car) einsteigen; (intervene) eingreifen
◆ **step up** vt verstärken; (pace) beschleunigen; (volunteer) vortreten

'**stepbrother** n Stiefbruder m

'**stepdaughter** n Stieftochter f

'**stepfather** n Stiefvater m

'**stepladder** n Stehleiter f

'**stepmother** n Stiefmutter f

'**stepping stone** n [Tritt]stein m; fig Sprungbrett nt

'**stepsister** n Stiefschwester f

S

'stepson n Stiefsohn m

stereo ['ster·i·ou] I. n <pl -os> Stereo nt; fam (unit) Stereoanlage f II. adj Stereo-

stereotype ['ster·i·ə·taɪp] I. n Stereotyp nt; (character) stereotype Figur f II. vt to ~ sb/sth jdn/etw in ein Klischee zwängen

sterile ['ster·əl] adj steril

sterilization [ˌster·ə·lɪ·ˈzeɪ·ʃən] n Sterilisierung f

sterilize ['ster·ə·laɪz] vt sterilisieren; (disinfect) desinfizieren; (water) abkochen

stern¹ [stɜrn] adj ernst; (strict) streng; (difficult) hart

stern² [stɜrn] n NAUT Heck nt

steroid ['ster·ɔɪd] n Steroide pl

stethoscope ['steθ·ə·skoup] n Stethoskop nt

stew [stu] I. n Eintopf m II. vt schmoren III. vi (vor sich hin) schmoren

steward ['stu·ərd] n Flugbegleiter m; (on cruise) Schiffsbegleiter m; (at event) Ordner(in) m(f)

stewardess <pl -es> ['stu·ər·dɪs] n Flugbegleiterin f; (on cruise) Schiffsbegleiterin f

stick [stɪk] I. n 1. (implement) Zweig m; (implement) Stock m; walking ~ Spazierstock m; hockey ~ Hockeyschläger m; celery ~s Selleriestangen pl; a ~ of chewing gum ein Stück nt Kaugummi 2. a ~ in the ribs ein Stoß m in die Rippen II. vi <stuck, stuck> 1. kleben; this glue won't ~ dieser Klebstoff hält nicht 2. (not move) feststecken; (car) stecken bleiben; (be unmovable) festsitzen; (door) klemmen; to ~ in sb's mind jdm in Erinnerung bleiben 3. (persevere) to ~ with sth an etw dat dranbleiben 4. to ~ to one's budget sich an sein Budget halten; to ~ to a diet eine Diät einhalten 5. to ~ by sb/sth zu jdm/etw halten ▶ to ~ to one's guns nicht lockerlassen III. vt <stuck, stuck> 1. kleben (to an +akk); ~ your things wherever you like fam stellen Sie Ihre Sachen irgendwo ab; to ~ one's head around the door seinen Kopf durch die Tür stecken 2. fam (burden) to be stuck with sb jdn am Hals haben ▶ to ~ one's nose

into sb's business seine Nase in jds Angelegenheiten stecken

◆**stick around** vi fam da bleiben

◆**stick in** I. vi stecken bleiben II. vt fam to ~ sth in sth etw in etw akk einkleben; to ~ sth in|to| sth etw in etw akk hineinstecken

◆**stick out** I. vt ausstrecken; (tongue) herausstrecken; to ~ it out (endure) es |bis zum Ende| durchhalten II. vi (her-) vorstehen; (ears) abstehen; (be obvious) offensichtlich sein; to ~ out like a sore thumb wie ein bunter Pudel auffallen fam

◆**stick together** I. vt zusammenkleben II. vi zusammenkleben; fig immer zusammen sein; (always) unzertrennlich sein; (group) zusammenbleiben; (loyally) zusammenhalten

◆**stick up** I. vt fam überfallen II. vi emporragen; (on end) abstehen; to ~ up for sb/sth sich für jdn/etw einsetzen

sticker ['stɪk·ər] n Aufkleber m, (for collecting) Sticker m; price ~ Preisschild|chen| nt

'stick insect n Gespenstheuschrecke f

'stick-in-the-mud I. n fam Muffel m II. adj attr rückständig

stickler ['stɪk·lər] n Pedant(in) m(f) pej; to be a ~ for accuracy pingelig auf Genauigkeit achten

'stick-on adj attr Klebe-

'stick-up n sl Überfall m

sticky ['stɪk·i] adj klebrig; (weather) schwül; (air) stickig; to be ~ with sth mit etw dat verklebt sein

stiff [stɪf] I. adj (paper, dough) fest; (paste) dick; (opposition) stark; (breeze) steif; (criticism) herb II. adv to be ~ scared = zu Tode erschrocken sein

stiffen ['stɪf·ən] I. vi sich versteifen; (muscles) sich verspannen; (with nervousness) sich verkrampfen; (with fear) erstarren II. vt versteifen; (collar) stärken

stiff-necked ['stɪf·nekt] adj halsstarrig; (arrogant) arrogant

stifle ['staɪ·fəl] I. vi ersticken II. vt ersticken; (suppress) unterdrücken; to ~ the urge to laugh sich dat das Lachen verbeißen

stifling ['staɪ·flɪŋ] *adj* erstickend; (*air*) zum Ersticken *nach n, präd*; (*heat*) drückend; (*room*) stickig; (*repressive*) erdrückend

stiletto <*pl* -os> [stɪ·'let·oʊ] *n* Pfennigabsatz *m*; **~s** *pl* Schuhe *pl* mit Pfennigabsätzen

stiletto 'heel *n* Pfennigabsatz *m*

still [stɪl] **I.** *n* Stille *f*; (*photo*) Standfoto *nt* **II.** *adj* ruhig; (*motionless*) reglos; (*water*) ohne Kohlensäure *nach n*; **to keep ~ still halten, sich nicht bewegen **III.** *adv* **1.** (*immer*) noch, noch immer; (*in future as in past*) nach wie vor; **there's ~ time for us to ...** wir können es noch schaffen, ... zu ... **2.** (*nevertheless*) trotzdem; **..., but he's ~ your brother ...,** [aber] er ist immer noch dein Bruder **3. to want ~ more** immer noch mehr wollen

'stillbirth *n* Totgeburt *f*

'stillborn *adj* tot geboren

still 'life <*pl* -s> *n* Stillleben *nt*; (*style*) Stilllebenmalerei *f*

stilt [stɪlt] *n usu sing* Stelze *f*

stimulant ['stɪm·jə·lənt] *n* Anreiz *m*; (*drug*) Stimulans *nt*; SPORT Aufputschmittel *nt*

stimulate ['stɪm·jə·leɪt] **I.** *vt* ankurbeln; (*excite*) stimulieren **II.** *vi* mitreißen

stimulating ['stɪm·jə·leɪ·tɪŋ] *adj* stimulierend; (*sexually a.*) erregend; (*conversation*) anregend; (*atmosphere*) animierend; (*exercise*) belebend

stimulation [ˌstɪm·jə·'leɪ·ʃən] *n* Anregung *f*; (*physical*) belebende Wirkung; (*sexual*) Stimulieren *nt*; (*motivation*) Ankurbelung *m*; (*of interest*) Erregung *f*

stimulus <*pl* -li> ['stɪm·jə·ləs] *n* Anreiz *m*; (*motivation*) Ansporn *m*; BIOL Reiz *m*

sting [stɪŋ] **I.** *n* Stich *m*; (*from ointment, jellyfish*) Brennen *nt*; (*from needle*) Stechen *nt* **2.** *sl* (*raid*) Coup *m* **II.** *vi* <stung, stung> stechen; (*sunburn*) brennen; (*cut*) schmerzen; (*words*) schmerzen **III.** *vt* <stung, stung> stechen; **to ~ sb's eyes** jdm in den Augen brennen; **he was stung by her criticism** ihre Kritik hat ihn tief getroffen

stinger ['stɪŋ·ər] *n* Stachel *m*

stingray ['stɪŋ·reɪ] *n* Stechrochen *m*

stingy ['stɪn·dʒi] *adj fam* geizig

stink [stɪŋk] **I.** *n usu sing* Gestank *m*; *fam* (*trouble*) Stunk *m* **II.** *vi* <stank *or* stunk, stunk> stinken (**of** nach +*dat*); *fam* (*suck*) stinken; *fam* (*be wrong*) zum Himmel stinken *sl*; **his acting ~s** *fam* er ist ein miserabler Schauspieler

'stink bomb *n* Stinkbombe *f*

stipulate ['stɪp·jə·leɪt] *vt* verlangen; (*contract*) festlegen; (*law*) vorschreiben

stipulation [ˌstɪp·jə·'leɪ·ʃən] *n* Bedingung *f*; (*clause*) Klausel *f*

stir [stɜr] **I.** *n usu sing* **1.** (*with spoon*) [Um]rühren *nt* **2.** (*movement*) Bewegung *f*; (*of emotion*) Erregung *f*; (*excitement*) Aufruhr *f*; **to cause a ~** Aufsehen erregen **II.** *vt* <-rr-> **1.** rühren; **to ~ sth into sth** etw in etw *akk* [hin]einrühren **2.** (*move*) rühren **3.** (*arouse*) bewegen; (*anger*) erregen; (*emotions*) aufwühlen **4. to ~ sb into action** jdn zum Handeln bewegen **III.** *vi* <-rr-> rühren; (*move*) sich regen; (*water*) sich bewegen; (*awaken*) wach werden; **to ~ within sb** sich in jdm regen

'stir-fry **I.** *n* Wok *m* **II.** *vt* <-ie-> kurz anbraten

stirring ['stɜr·ɪŋ] **I.** *n* Regung *f* **II.** *adj* aufwühlend

stirrup ['stɜr·əp] *n* Steigbügel *m*

stitch [stɪtʃ] **I.** *n* <*pl* -es> Stich *m*; (*in knitting*) Masche *f*; (*method*) Stichart *f*; (*pain*) Seitenstechen *nt*; **to not have a ~ on** splitterfasernackt sein ► **to be in ~es** *fam* sich schieflachen **II.** *vi* sticken; (*sew*) nähen **III.** *vt* nähen

stock [stɑk] **I.** *n* **1.** (*supply*) Vorrat *m*; Bestand *m*; (*livestock*) Viehbestand *m*; **to be in ~** vorrätig sein **2. ~s** *pl* (*in company*) Aktien *pl* **3.** FOOD Brühe *f*; **fish ~** Fischfond *m* **II.** *adj attr* Vorrats-; (*standard*) Standard- **III.** *vt* vorrätig haben; (*fill*) füllen; (*shelves*) auffüllen; (*supply*) beliefern

'stockbroker *n* Börsenmakler(in) *m(f)*

'stock exchange *n* Börse *f*

'stockholder *n* Aktionär(in) *m(f)*

stocking ['stɑk·ɪŋ] *n* **~s** *pl* Strümpfe *pl*

'stock market *n* [Wertpapier]börse *f*

'stockpile **I.** *n* Vorrat *m* **II.** *vt* **to ~ sth** Vorräte an etw *dat* anlegen; **to ~ weapons** ein Waffenarsenal anlegen

stock-'still *adj pred* stocksteif

stocky ['stak·i] *adj* stämmig

stoic ['stoʊ·ɪk] **I.** *n* stoischer Mensch **II.** *adj* stoisch

stoicism ['stoʊ·ɪ·sɪz·əm] *n* stoische Ruhe; *(about sth specific)* Gleichmut *m*

stoke [stoʊk] *vt* schüren; *(furnace)* beschicken

stole [stoʊl] *pt of* steal

stomach ['stʌm·ək] **I.** *n* Magen *m*; *(abdomen)* Bauch *m*; **upset ~** Magenverstimmung *f*; **to have no ~ for sth** keinen Appetit auf etw *akk* haben; *(desire)* keine Lust haben, etw zu tun **II.** *vt fam* **to not be able to ~ sth** etw *akk* nicht ertragen können

'stomachache *n usu sing* Magenschmerzen *pl*

stomp [stamp] **I.** *n* Stampfen *nt* **II.** *vi* stapfen; *(intentionally)* trampeln; **to ~ on sb/sth** auf jdn/etw treten; *(suppress)* jdn/etw niedertrampeln **III.** *vt* *(rebellion)* niederschlagen; **to ~ one's feet** mit den Füßen [auf]stampfen

stone [stoʊn] **I.** *n* Stein *m*; *(in fruit a.)* Kern *m*; *(jewel)* [Edel]stein *m*; **to be [just] a ~'s throw away** [nur] einen Katzensprung [weit] entfernt sein **II.** *adj attr* Stein–; **~ statue** Statue *f* aus Stein **III.** *vt* steinigen

'Stone Age *n* **the ~** die Steinzeit

stone-'cold **I.** *adj* eiskalt **II.** *adv* **~ sober** stocknüchtern *fam*

stoned [stoʊnd] *adj* entsteint; *sl (drugged)* high; *(drunk)* betrunken; **to be ~ out of one's mind** total zu[gedröhnt] sein

stone-'deaf *adj* stocktaub *fam*

'stonemason *n* Steinmetz(in) *m(f)*

stony ['stoʊ·ni] *adj* steinig; *(unfeeling)* steinern; *(silence)* eisig

stood [stʊd] *pt, pp of* stand

stool [stul] *n* Hocker *m*; *(feces)* Stuhl *m*

stoop[1] [stup] **I.** *n usu sing* Buckel *m* **II.** *vi* sich beugen; **we had to ~ to go through the doorway** wir mussten den Kopf einziehen, um durch die Tür zu gehen; **to ~ down** sich bücken; **to ~ so low as to do sth** so weit sinken, dass man etw tut

stoop[2] [stup] *n* offene Veranda

stop [stap] **I.** *vt* <-pp-> anhalten; *(traf-* *fic)* aufhalten; *(make cease)* beenden; *(temporarily)* unterbrechen; *(bleeding)* stillen; *(clock)* anhalten; *(machine)* abstellen; *(cease)* aufhören mit +*dat*; **~ that man!** haltet den Mann!; **this will ~ the pain** davon gehen die Schmerzen weg *fam*; **~ it!** hör auf [damit]!; **to ~ sb [from] doing sth** jdn davon abhalten, etw zu tun **II.** *vi* <-pp-> stehen bleiben; *(car)* [an]halten; *(bus)* halten; *(machine)* nicht mehr laufen; *(rain)* aufhören; *(pain)* abklingen; *(payments)* eingestellt werden; **~! halt!; to ~ dead** abrupt innehalten; **to ~ [doing sth]** aufhören[, etw zu tun], [mit etw *dat*] aufhören; **she ~ped drinking** sie trinkt nicht mehr ▸ **to ~ at nothing** vor nichts zurückschrecken **III.** *n* Halt *m*; *(break)* Pause *f*; *(for bus)* Haltestelle *f*; **to come to a ~** stehen bleiben; *(car a.)* anhalten; *(rain)* aufhören; *(project)* eingestellt werden; **to put a ~ to sth** etw *dat* ein Ende setzen

stop by *vi* vorbeischauen; **to ~ by sb's house** bei jdm vorbeischauen

stop off *vi* kurz bleiben; *(while traveling)* eine Zwischenstation machen

stop over *vi* eine Zwischenstation machen

stop up *vt* verstopfen; *(hole)* [zu]stopfen

'stopgap *n* Notlösung *f*

'stoplight *n* [Verkehrs]ampel *f*; *(brake light)* Bremslicht *nt*

'stopover *n* Zwischenlandung *f*; *(duration)* Zwischenaufenthalt *m*

stoppage ['stap·ɪdʒ] *n* Arbeitseinstellung *f*; *(unintentional)* Unterbrechung *f*

stopper ['stap·ər] *n* Stöpsel *m*

'stop sign *n* Stoppschild *nt*

'stopwatch *n* Stoppuhr *f*

storage ['stɔr·ɪdʒ] *n* Lagerung *f*; *(of books)* Aufbewahrung *f*; *(of data, power)* Speicherung *f*; **to put sth into ~** etw [ein]lagern

store [stɔr] **I.** *n* **1.** Vorrat *m*; *fig* Schatz *m*; **~s** *pl* Vorräte *pl*; **to be in ~ [for sb]** *fig* [jdm] bevorstehen; **we have a surprise in ~ for your father** wir haben für deinen Vater eine Überraschung auf Lager **2.** *(business)* Laden *m*; *(larger)*

Geschäft nt; (department store) Kaufhaus nt; (warehouse) Lager nt II. vt [auf]speichern; (supplies) lagern; (data) [ab]speichern

'**storeroom** n Lagerraum m; (for food) Vorratskammer f

stork [stɔːk] n Storch m

storm [stɔːm] I. n Sturm m; (with thunder) Gewitter nt; (with rain) Unwetter nt; ~ **of applause** Beifallssturm m; **to raise a ~ of protest** einen [Protest]sturm hervorrufen ▶ **to take sth/sb by ~** etw/ jdn im Sturm erobern II. vi 1. impers it's ~**ing** es stürmt 2. (race) stürmen; **to ~ out** hinausstürmen III. vt stürmen

'**storm cloud** n Gewitterwolke f

stormy ['stɔːmi] adj stürmisch; (fierce) stürmisch; (life) bewegt; (debate) hitzig

story[1] ['stɔːri] n Geschichte f; (lie a.) [Lügen]märchen nt fam; (narrative) Erzählung f; (plot) Handlung f; (rumor) Gerücht nt; (report) Beitrag m; (in newspaper) Artikel m; **the ~ goes that ...** man erzählt sich, dass ... ▶ **to make a long ~ short** um es kurz zu machen

story[2] ['stɔːri] n Stockwerk nt; **a three-~ house** ein dreistöckiges Haus

'**storyteller** n Geschichtenerzähler(in) m(f); fam (liar) Lügner(in) m(f)

stout [staʊt] adj beleibt; (woman) füllig euph; (strong) kräftig; (shoes) fest

stoutly ['staʊtli] adv stämmig; (strongly) stabil; (firmly) entschieden; **to ~ believe in sth** fest an etw akk glauben

stove [stəʊv] n Herd m; (heater) Ofen m

'**stovepipe** n Ofenrohr nt

stow [stəʊ] vt verstauen; (hide) verstecken; (fill) vollmachen; (goods) verladen

◆ **stow away** I. vt verstauen; (hide) verstecken II. vi als blinder Passagier reisen

stowaway ['stəʊ·ə·weɪ] n blinder Passagier/blinde Passagierin

straddle ['stræd·əl] I. vt 1. **to ~ sth** (standing) mit gespreizten Beinen über etw akk stehen; (sitting) rittlings auf etw dat sitzen; (jumping) [mit gestreckten Beinen] über etw akk springen 2. (legs) spreizen 3. **to ~ an issue** bei einer Frage nicht klar Stellung beziehen II. vi breitbeinig [da]stehen; (sit) mit gespreizten Beinen [da]sitzen

straggler ['stræg·lər] n Nachzügler(in) m(f)

straight [streɪt] I. adj 1. gerade; (hair) glatt; (skirt) gerade geschnitten; (road, row) [schnur]gerade; **the picture isn't ~** das Bild hängt schief 2. (frank) offen; (honest) ehrlich; (answer) klar 3. (heterosexual) heterosexuell 4. (factual) tatsachengetreu 5. (plain) einfach; (undiluted) pur 6. pred (in order) in Ordnung; (clarified) geklärt; **to set things ~** (tidy) Ordnung schaffen; (organize) etwas auf die Reihe kriegen fam; **to set sb ~ about sth** jdm Klarheit über etw akk verschaffen II. adv 1. (in a line) gerade[aus]; **go ~ down this road** folgen Sie immer dieser Straße; **to look ~ ahead** geradeaus schauen 2. **to get ~ to the point** sofort zur Sache kommen 3. **I can't think ~ anymore** ich kann nicht mehr klar denken

straighten ['streɪ·tən] I. vt gerade machen; (hair) glätten; (river) begradigen; (tie) zurechtrücken II. vi sich aufrichten; (river) gerade werden; (hair) sich glätten

◆ **straighten out** I. vt gerade machen; (clothes) glatt streichen; (tidy up) in Ordnung bringen; (clarify) klarstellen; (misunderstanding) aus der Welt schaffen II. vi gerade werden

◆ **straighten up** I. vi sich aufrichten; (ship) [wieder] geradeaus fahren; (aircraft) [wieder] geradeaus fliegen II. vt gerade machen; (tidy) aufräumen; (put in order) regeln

straightforward [ˌstreɪt·ˈfɔr·wərd] adj direkt; (explanation) unumwunden; (look) gerade; (honest) aufrichtig; (easy) einfach

strain[1] [streɪn] I. n usu sing Druck m; (overexertion) [Über]beanspruchung f; (muscle) Zerrung f; **to be under a lot of ~** unter hohem Druck stehen II. vi **to ~ at the leash** an der Leine zerren III. vt ziehen an +dat; (muscle) zerren; (overexert) [stark] beanspruchen; (eyes) überanstrengen; (coffee) filtern; (vegetables) abgießen

S

strain² [streɪn] n Rasse f; (of plants) Sorte f; (of virus) Art f

strained [streɪnd] adj bemüht; (artificial) gekünstelt; (relations) angespannt; (stressed) abgespannt

strainer ['streɪ·nər] n Sieb nt

'straitjacket n Zwangsjacke f

strait-laced ['streɪt·leɪst] adj puritanisch

strand [strænd] n Faden m; (of rope) Strang m; (of tissue) Faser f; (of hair) Strähne f; ~ **of the plot** Handlungsstrang m

stranded ['stræn·dɪd] adj gestrandet; **to be ~** fig festsitzen; **to leave sb ~** jdn sich dat selbst überlassen

strange [streɪndʒ] adj sonderbar; (unusual) ungewöhnlich; (weird) seltsam; (exceptional) erstaunlich; (uneasy) komisch; (unwell) unwohl; (not known) fremd; (unfamiliar) nicht vertraut

strangely ['streɪndʒ·li] adv merkwürdig; **she was ~ calm** sie war auffällig still; **~ enough** seltsamerweise

stranger ['streɪn·dʒər] n Fremde(r) f/m; (new to a place) Neuling m; **are you a ~ here, too?** sind Sie auch fremd hier?

strangle ['stræŋ·gəl] vt erdrosseln; **to ~ sth** fig etw unterdrücken

'stranglehold n Würgegriff m; fig Vormacht[stellung] f

strangulation [ˌstræŋ·gjʊ·'leɪ·ʃən] n Erdrosselung f

strap [stræp] I. n Riemen m; (for safety) Gurt m; (for clothes) Träger m; (hold in vehicle) Halteschlaufe f; **watch ~** Uhrarmband nt II. vt <-pp-> **to ~ sth [to sth]** etw [an etw dat] befestigen

strategic [strə·'ti·dʒɪk] adj strategisch

strategist ['stræt·ə·dʒɪst] n Stratege, -in m, f

strategy ['stræt·ə·dʒi] n 1. Strategie f; fig a. Taktik f 2. (art of planning) Taktieren nt; (of war) Kriegsstrategie f

stratum <pl -ta> ['streɪ·təm] n Schicht f

straw [strɔ] n Stroh nt; (stem, tube) Strohhalm m; **to draw ~s** losen ▶ **to be the final ~** das Fass zum Überlaufen bringen

strawberry ['strɔ·ˌber·i] n Erdbeere f

stray [streɪ] I. vi streunen; (go astray) sich verirren; (move casually) umherstreifen; (digress) abweichen; (thoughts) abschweifen; **her eyes kept ~ing to the clock** ihre Blicke wanderten immer wieder zur Uhr II. adj attr streunend; (lost) umherirrend; (isolated) vereinzelt; (occasional) gelegentlich; **to be hit by a ~ bullet** von einem Blindgänger getroffen werden

streak [strik] I. n Streifen m; (on window) Schliere f; (run) Strähne f; **lucky ~** Glückssträhne f; **~s** pl (in hair) Strähnen pl II. vt usu passive **to be ~ed** gestreift sein; **~ed with gray** (hair) von grauen Strähnen durchzogen III. vi flitzen fam

streaker ['stri·kər] n fam Flitzer(in) m(f)

stream [strim] I. n Bach m; (flow) Strahl m; (of people) Strom m; (series) Schwall m; (current) Strömung f II. vi strömen; (water) fließen; (nose) laufen; (eyes) tränen

streamer ['stri·mər] n Wimpel m; (decoration) Luftschlange f

streamlined ['strim·laɪnd] adj stromlinienförmig; (car a.) windschnittig; (efficient) rationalisiert; (simplified) vereinfacht

street [strit] n Straße f; **in the ~** auf der Straße; **I live on Main St~** ich wohne in der Main Street; **side ~** Seitenstraße f ▶ **the average man/woman/person on the ~** der Mann/die Frau von der Straße

'streetcar n Straßenbahn f

'street lamp n Straßenlaterne f

'streetlight n Straßenlicht nt

strength [streŋkθ] n Kraft f; (of structure) Belastbarkeit f; (potency) Stärke f; (of alcoholic drink a.) Alkoholgehalt m; (of drug) Konzentration f; (of medicine) Wirksamkeit f; (effectiveness) Wirkungsgrad m; (of argument) Überzeugungskraft f; (intensity) Intensität f; (of color) Leuchtkraft f; (of belief) Stärke f; **physical ~** körperliche Kraft; **to gain ~** wieder zu Kräften kommen; **to gather ~** an Stabilität gewinnen; **to show great ~ of character** große Charakterstärke zeigen; **to draw ~ from sth** aus etw dat Kraft ziehen; **sb's ~s and weaknesses** jds Stärken und Schwächen; **to turn out in ~** in Massen anrücken ▶ **on the ~ of**

sth aufgrund einer S. *gen*

strengthen ['streŋk·θən] I. *vt* kräftigen; (*fortify*) befestigen; (*increase*) [ver]stärken; (*intensify*) intensivieren; (*improve*) verbessern; (*currency*) stabilisieren II. *vi* stärker werden; (*muscles*) kräftiger werden; (*wind*) auffrischen; (*market*) an Wert gewinnen; (*currency*) zulegen

strenuous ['stren·ju·əs] *adj* anstrengend; (*energetic*) energisch; **despite ~ efforts** trotz angestrengter Bemühungen

stress [stres] I. *n* <*pl* -es> Stress *m*; (*emphasis*) Betonung *f*; (*force*) Belastung *f*; (*tension*) Spannung *f*; (*pressure*) Druck *m*; **to be under ~** starken Belastungen ausgesetzt sein; (*at work*) unter Stress stehen II. *vt* 1. betonen; **I'd just like to ~ that ...** ich möchte lediglich darauf hinweisen, dass ... 2. (*strain*) belasten; **to ~ sb [out]** jdn stressen

stressed [strest] *adj* gestresst; (*pronounced*) betont

stressful ['stres·fʊl] *adj* aufreibend; **~ situation** Stresssituation *f*

stretch [stretʃ] I. *n* <*pl* -es> 1. (*exercise*) Dehnungsübungen *pl* 2. (*section*) Stück *nt*; (*of road*) Streckenabschnitt *m*; (*of time*) Zeitspanne *f*; **~ of train tracks** Bahnstrecke *f*; **~ of water** Wasserfläche *f* II. *vi* sich dehnen; (*clothes*) weiter werden; (*body*) sich [recken und] strecken; (*exercise*) Dehnungsübungen machen III. *vt* [aus]dehnen; (*tighten*) straff ziehen; (*sauce*) verlängern; **we're already fully ~ed** wir sind schon voll ausgelastet; **to ~ one's legs** sich *dat* die Beine vertreten; **to ~ the limit** über das Limit hinausgehen; **to ~ sb's patience** jds Geduld auf eine harte Probe stellen

stretcher ['stretʃ·ər] *n* Tragbahre *f*

strew <strewed, strewn *or* strewed> [stru] *vt* [ver]streuen; (*cover*) bestreuen

strict [strɪkt] *adj* streng; (*boss*) strikt; (*penalty*) hart; (*vegetarian*) überzeugt; (*limit*) festgesetzt; (*neutrality*) strikt; (*absolute*) streng; **in the ~est confidence** streng vertraulich

strictly ['strɪkt·li] *adv* streng; **~ defined** genau definiert; **~ speaking** genau genommen

stride [straɪd] I. *vi* <strode, stridden>

schreiten; **to ~ forward** *fig* vorankommen II. *n* Schritt *m*; **to hit one's ~** in Schwung kommen; **to take sth in one's ~** mit etw *dat* gut fertigwerden; **to make ~s forward** Fortschritte machen

strike [straɪk] I. *n* 1. Angriff *m*; **preemptive ~** Präventivschlag *m*; *fig* vorbeugende Maßnahme 2. (*of labor*) Streik *m*; **to be [out] on ~** streiken; **to call for a ~** einen Streik ausrufen 3. (*discovery*) Fund *m* 4. (*in baseball*) Strike *m* II. *vt* <struck, struck *or* stricken> 1. schlagen; (*soccer ball*) schießen; **to ~ sth** (*bang against*) gegen etw *akk* schlagen; (*bump into*) gegen etw *akk* stoßen; (*drive against*) gegen etw *akk* fahren; (*collide with*) mit etw *dat* zusammenstoßen; **to ~ one's fist on the table** mit der Faust auf den Tisch schlagen 2. *usu passive* **to be struck by lightning** vom Blitz getroffen werden 3. **to ~ a blow** zuschlagen; **to ~ a blow against sb/sth** *fig* jdm/etw einen Schlag versetzen 4. (*devastate*) heimsuchen; **the flood struck New Orleans** die Flut brach über New Orleans herein 5. **she doesn't ~ me as [being] very motivated** sie scheint mir nicht besonders motiviert [zu sein] 6. (*impress*) **to be struck by sth** von etw *dat* beeindruckt sein 7. (*achieve*) erreichen; **to ~ a deal with sb** mit jdm eine Vereinbarung treffen 8. **to ~ the hour** die [volle] Stunde schlagen 9. **has it ever struck you that ...?** ist dir je der Gedanke gekommen dass ...? 10. (*match*) anzünden 11. **to ~ oil** auf Öl stoßen; **to ~ it rich** das große Geld machen III. *vi* <struck, struck> 1. treffen; (*lightning*) einschlagen; **to ~ at the heart of sth** etw vernichtend treffen; **to ~ home** ins Schwarze treffen 2. (*act*) zuschlagen; (*attack*) angreifen; (*illness*) ausbrechen; (*fate*) zuschlagen 3. (*clock*) schlagen 4. (*not work*) streiken

◆**strike back** *vi* zurückschlagen

◆**strike down** *vt* **to ~ down ⇆ sb** jdn niederschlagen; (*kill*) jdn töten; (*epidemic*) jdn dahinraffen

◆**strike out** I. *vt* 1. (*delete*) **to ~ out ⇆ sth** etw [aus]streichen 2. (*in baseball*) **to**

~ **out** ⇆ **sb** jdn ausstreiken II. *vi* 1. zuschlagen; **to ~ out at sb** nach jdm schlagen; (*fig*) jdn scharf angreifen 2. **to ~ out on one's own** eigene Wege gehen

◆**strike up** *vt* anfangen; **to ~ up a friendship with sb** sich mit jdm anfreunden

'**strikebreaker** *n* Streikbrecher(in) *m(f)*

striker ['straɪkər] *n* Streikende(r) *f/m;* (*in soccer*) Stürmer(in) *m(f)*

striking ['straɪkɪŋ] *adj* 1. bemerkenswert; (*differences*) erheblich; (*feature*) herausragend; (*parallel*) erstaunlich; (*personality*) beeindruckend; (*goodlooking*) umwerfend; **the most ~ aspect of sth** das Bemerkenswerteste an etw *dat* 2. **within ~ distance [of sth]** in unmittelbarer Nähe [einer S. *gen*]; (*short distance*) einen Katzensprung [von etw *dat*] entfernt

string [strɪŋ] I. *n* Schnur *f;* MUS, SPORT Saite *f;* (*chain*) Kette *f;* (*series a.*) Reihe *f;* **ball of ~** Knäuel *m o nt;* **to pull [some] ~s** seine Beziehungen spielen lassen; **[with] no ~s attached** ohne Bedingungen; **~ of pearls** Perlenkette *f;* **the ~s** *pl* (*instruments*) die Streichinstrumente *pl;* (*players*) die Streicher *pl* II. *vt* <strung, strung> (*fit*) besaiten; (*racket*) bespannen; (*attach*) auffädeln

◆**string up** *vt fam* jdn [auf]hängen

string 'bean *n* grüne Bohne

string(ed) instrument [ˌstrɪŋd'-] *n* Saiteninstrument *nt*

'**string quartet** *n* Streichquartett *nt*

stringy ['strɪŋ·i] *adj* faserig; (*hair*) strähnig

strip [strɪp] I. *n* Streifen *m* II. *vt* <-pp-> 1. (*house*) leer räumen; **to ~ sth bare** etw kahl fressen 2. (*undress*) **to ~ sb** jdn ausziehen 3. *usu passive* **to ~ sb of sth** jdn einer S. *gen* berauben; **to ~ sb of his/her title** jdm seinen Titel aberkennen III. *vi* <-pp-> sich ausziehen; **~ped to the waist** mit nacktem Oberkörper

stripe [straɪp] *n* Streifen *m;* MIL [Ärmel]streifen *m*

'**strip light** *n* Neonröhre *f*

stripper ['strɪp·ər] *n* Stripper(in) *m(f);* (*solvent*) Farbentferner *m*

'**strip search** *n* Leibesvisitation, bei der

sich der/die Durchsuchte ausziehen muss

'**striptease** *n* Striptease *m*

strive <strove *or* -d, striven> [straɪv] *vi* sich bemühen; **to ~ after sth** nach etw *dat* streben; **to ~ for sth** um etw *akk* ringen

strode [stroʊd] *pt of* **stride**

stroke [stroʊk] I. *vt* streicheln; **to ~ sth** über etw *akk* streichen; **to ~ sb's hair** jdm übers Haar streichen II. *n* Streicheln *nt;* (*mark*) Strich *m;* (*hit*) Schlag *m;* **at the ~ of midnight** um Punkt Mitternacht; **to suffer a ~** einen Schlaganfall bekommen; **breast ~** Brustschwimmen *nt;* **by a ~ of fate** durch eine Fügung des Schicksals; **~ of luck** Glücksfall *m;* **~ of genius** genialer Einfall

stroll [stroʊl] I. *n* Spaziergang *m;* (*around town*) Stadtbummel *m;* **to go for a ~** einen Spaziergang machen II. *vi* schlendern

stroller ['stroʊ·lər] *n* [Kinder]sportwagen *m*

strong [strɔŋ] I. *adj* stark; (*desire*) brennend; (*economy*) gesund; (*currency*) hart; (*incentive*) groß; (*reaction*) heftig; (*resistance*) erbittert; (*rivalry*) ausgeprägt; (*effective*) gut; (*robust*) stabil; (*tough*) stark; (*deep-seated*) überzeugt; (*conviction*) fest; (*objections*) stark; (*tendency*) deutlich; (*bright*) hell; (*light*) grell; (*pungent*) streng; (*flavor*) kräftig; (*smell*) beißend; **tact is not her ~ point** Takt ist nicht gerade ihre Stärke; **~ language** derbe Ausdrucksweise; **to be as ~ as an ox** bärenstark sein II. *adv fam* **to come on ~** (*sexually*) rangehen *fam;* (*aggressively*) in Fahrt kommen *fam;* **still going ~** noch gut in Form

'**strong-arm** I. *adj attr pej* brutal II. *vt* **to ~ sb** jdn einschüchtern

'**strongbox** *n* [Geld]kassette *f*

'**stronghold** *n* Stützpunkt *m;* *fig* Hochburg *f;* (*sanctuary*) Zufluchtsort *m*

strongly ['strɔŋ·li] *adv* stark; (*advise*) nachdrücklich; (*criticize*) heftig; (*deny*) energisch; (*recommend*) dringend; (*smell*) stark; **~ built** kräftig gebaut

strong-'minded *adj* willensstark

strong-'willed adj willensstark

strove [strouv] pt of **strive**

struck [strʌk] pt, pp of **strike**

structural ['strʌk·tʃər·əl] adj strukturell; (of building) baulich

structure ['strʌk·tʃər] I. n Aufbau m; (system) Struktur f; (construction) Bau[werk] nt; (makeup) Konstruktion f II. vt strukturieren; (construct) konstruieren; (life) regeln

struggle ['strʌg·əl] I. n Kampf m; **uphill ~** harter Kampf II. vi kämpfen; (toil) sich abmühen; **to ~ with sth** sich mit etw dat herumschlagen; **to ~ to one's feet** sich mühsam aufrappeln; **to ~ for survival** ums Überleben kämpfen

strum [strʌm] I. vt <-mm-> herumzupfen auf +dat; (guitar) herumklimpern auf +dat II. vi <-mm-> [herum]klimpern III. n usu sing (sound of strumming) Klimpern nt

strung [strʌŋ] pt, pp of **string**

strut [strʌt] I. vi <-tt-> **to ~ around/past** herum/vorbeistolzieren II. vt <-tt-> **to ~ one's stuff** esp hum fam (dance) zeigen, was man hat; (showcase) zeigen, was man kann III. n Strebe f

strychnine ['strɪk·naɪn] n Strychnin nt

stub [stʌb] I. n (of check) Abriss m; (of pencil) Stummel m II. vt <-bb-> **to ~ one's toes** sich die Zehen anstoßen

stubble ['stʌb·əl] n Stoppeln pl

stubbly ['stʌb·li] adj Stoppel-

stubborn ['stʌb·ərn] adj starrköpfig; (persistent) hartnäckig; (problem) vertrackt

stuck [stʌk] I. pt, pp of **stick** II. adj 1. fest; **the door is ~** die Tür klemmt 2. pred **I hate being ~ behind a desk** ich hasse Schreibtischarbeit; **to be ~ in** sth in etw dat feststecken; **to be ~ with sb** jdn am Hals haben 3. pred (at a loss) **to be ~** nicht klarkommen fam; **I'm really ~** ich komme einfach nicht weiter

stuck-'up adj pej fam hochnäsig, fam

stud[1] [stʌd] n Stecker m; (for collar) Kragenknopf m; (for shirt) Hemdknopf m; (for cuff) Manschettenknopf m; (in snow tire) Spike m

stud[2] [stʌd] n Deckhengst m; (farm) Gestüt nt; sl (man) geiler Typ

student ['stu·dənt] n Student(in) m(f);

(pupil) Schüler(in) m(f)

student 'teacher n Referendar(in) m(f)

studied ['stʌd·id] adj wohl überlegt

studio ['stu·di·ou] n Atelier nt; (for photography) Studio nt; (company) Filmgesellschaft f; (apartment) Appartement nt

study ['stʌd·i] I. vt <-ie-> studieren; (at school) lernen; (look at) eingehend betrachten; **to ~ for an exam** auf eine Prüfung lernen; **to ~ how/whether ...** erforschen, wie/ob ... II. vi <-ie-> studieren; (at school) lernen III. n 1. Untersuchung f; (academic) Studie f 2. (studying) Lernen nt; (at university) Studieren nt 3. (room) Arbeitszimmer nt 4. (drawing) Studie f

stuff [stʌf] I. n 1. fam (indeterminate) Zeug nt oft pej fam; **to know one's ~** sich auskennen 2. (possessions) Sachen pl 3. (material) Stoff m II. vt stopfen; (fill) ausstopfen; (turkey) füllen; **to ~ oneself** fam sich vollstopfen

stuffed animal n Kuscheltier nt

stuffing ['stʌf·ɪŋ] n Füllung f

stumble ['stʌm·bəl] vi stolpern; (while speaking) stocken; **to ~ on sth** über etw akk stolpern; **to ~ around** herumtappen; **to ~ across sb/sth** [zufällig] auf jdn/etw stoßen

'stumbling block n Stolperstein m

stump [stʌmp] I. n Stumpf m; (of arm) Armstumpf m; (of leg) Beinstumpf m; (of tooth) Zahnstummel m; **out on the ~** POL im Wahlkampf II. vt verwirren; **we're all completely ~ed** wir sind mit unserem Latein am Ende

stun <-nn-> [stʌn] vt betäuben; (amaze) verblüffen; **~ned silence** fassungsloses Schweigen

stung [stʌŋ] pt, pp of **sting**

stunk [stʌŋk] pt, pp of **stink**

stunning ['stʌn·ɪŋ] adj fantastisch; (amazing) unfassbar; (blow) betäubend

stunt[1] [stʌnt] vt (growth) hemmen

stunt[2] [stʌnt] n Stunt m; (for publicity) Gag m; **to pull a ~** fig fam etwas Verrücktes tun

stunted ['stʌn·t̬ɪd] adj verkümmert; (underdeveloped) unterentwickelt

'stuntman n Stuntman m

S

stupid ['stu·pɪd] I. *adj* <-er, -est> dumm; (*silly*) blöd *fam* II. *n fam* Blödmann *m*

stupidity [stu·'pɪd·ɪ·ti] *n* Dummheit *f*

stupor ['stu·pər] *n* Benommenheit *f*; **in a drunken ~** im Vollrausch

sturdy ['stɜr·di] *adj* (*robust: chair, wall*) stabil; (*material*) robust; (*shoes*) fest; (*arms*) kräftig; (*body*) stämmig

stutter ['stʌt·ər] I. *vt, vi* stottern II. *n* Stottern *nt kein pl*

sty [staɪ] *n* Schweinestall *m*

style [staɪl] I. *n* Stil *m*; (*stylishness a.*) Schick *m*; **in the ~ of sth** im Stil einer Person/einer S. *gen* **that's not my ~** *fam* das ist nicht mein Stil; **to have real ~** Klasse haben; **to do things in ~** alles im großen Stil tun; **the latest ~** die neueste Mode II. *vt* gestalten; (*hair*) frisieren

styling ['staɪ·lɪŋ] *n* Styling *nt*; (*of hair*) Frisur *f*

stylish ['staɪ·lɪʃ] *adj* elegant; (*smart*) flott *fam*; (*fashionable*) modisch; (*polished*) stilvoll

stylistic [staɪ·'lɪs·tɪk] *adj* stilistisch

sub [sʌb] I. *n* **1.** *fam short for* **substitute** Vertretung *f* **2.** *fam short for* **submarine** U-Boot *nt* II. *vi* <-bb-> *short for* **substitute; to ~ for sb** für jdn einspringen

subconscious [ˌsʌb·'kan·ʃəs] I. *n* Unterbewusstsein *nt* II. *adj attr* unterbewusst

subcontractor [ˌsʌb·kən·træk·tər] *n* Subunternehmer(in) *m(f)*

subculture ['sʌb·kʌl·tʃər] *n* Subkultur *f*

subdue [səb·'du] *vt* unter Kontrolle bringen; (*into subjection*) unterwerfen; (*suppress*) unterdrücken; (*emotion*) bändigen

subdued [sʌb·'dud] *adj* beherrscht; (*reticent*) zurückhaltend; (*voice, lighting*) gedämpft; (*quiet*) leise; (*mood*) gedrückt

subject I. *n* ['sʌb·dʒɪkt] Thema *nt*; (*person*) Versuchsperson *f*; (*field*) Fach *nt*; (*specific*) Spezialgebiet *nt*; (*at school*) [Schul]fach *nt* II. *adj* ['sʌb·dʒɪkt] **to be ~ to sth** etw *dat* ausgesetzt sein; (*contingent on*) von etw *dat* abhängig sein; **to be ~ to a high rate of tax** einer ho-

hen Steuer unterliegen; **~ to payment** vorbehaltlich einer Zahlung III. *vt* [səb·'dʒekt] **to ~ sb/sth to sth** jdn/etw etw *dat* aussetzen; **to ~ sb to torture** jdn foltern

subjective [səb·'dʒek·tɪv] *adj* subjektiv

submachine gun [ˌsʌb·mə·'ʃin·ˌgʌn] *n* Maschinenpistole *f*

submarine ['sʌb·mə·rin] I. *n* U-Boot *nt* II. *adj* Unterwasser-

submerge [səb·'mɜrdʒ] I. *vt* tauchen; (*inundate*) überschwemmen II. *vi* untertauchen

submission [səb·'mɪʃ·ən] *n* Unterwerfung *f*; (*to orders*) Gehorsam *m*

submit <-tt-> [səb·'mɪt] I. *vt* **1.** **to ~ oneself to sb/sth** sich jdm/etw unterwerfen; **to ~ oneself to treatment** sich einer Behandlung unterziehen **2.** (*hand in*) einreichen; **to ~ sth to sb** jdm etw vorlegen II. *vi* aufgeben; (*yield*) nachgeben; (*unconditionally*) sich unterwerfen

subordinate I. *n* [sə·'bɔr·dən·ɪt] Untergebene(r) *f(m)* II. *adj* [sə·'bɔr·dən·ɪt] zweitrangig; (*lower in rank*) rangniedriger

subpoena [sə·'pi·nə] LAW I. *vt* <-ed, -ed or -'d, -'d> vorladen II. *n* Ladung *f*; **to serve a ~ on sb** jdn vorladen

subscribe [səb·'skraɪb] I. *vi* **1.** **to ~ to sth** (*magazine*) etw abonnieren **2.** (*donate*) spenden II. *vt* spenden

subscriber [səb·'skraɪ·bər] *n* Abonnent(in) *m(f)*; (*service*) Kunde, Kundin *m, f*

subscription [səb·'skrɪp·ʃən] *n* Abonnement *nt*, Abonnementgebühr *f*

subsequent ['sʌb·sɪ·kwənt] *adj* [nach]folgend; (*later*) später

subsequently ['sʌb·sɪ·kwənt·li] *adv* anschließend

subservient [səb·'sɜr·vi·ənt] *adj* unterwürfig

subside [səb·'saɪd] *vi* nachlassen; (*anger*) sich legen

subsidence [səb·'saɪ·dəns] *n* Absenken *nt*

subsidiary [səb·'sɪd·i·er·i] *adj* **~ [company]** Tochtergesellschaft *f*

subsidize ['sʌb·sə·daɪz] *vt* subventionieren

subsidy ['sʌb·sə·di] n Subvention f

substance ['sʌb·stəns] n 1. Substanz f; (material) Materie f; chemical ~ Chemikalie f 2. (significance) Substanz f; (decisive) Gewicht nt; the book lacks ~ das Buch hat inhaltlich wenig zu bieten 3. (main point) Wesentliche(s) nt

substandard [ˌsʌb·'stæn·dərd] adj unterdurchschnittlich

substantial [səb·'stæn·ʃəl] adj attr solide; (facts) bedeutend; (contribution) wesentlich; (difference) erheblich; (improvement) deutlich; (weighty) überzeugend; ~ evidence hinreichender Beweis

substantially [səb·'stæn·ʃə·li] adv erheblich; (mainly) im Wesentlichen

substantiate [səb·'stæn·ʃi·eɪt] vt bekräftigen; (report) bestätigen; (claim) begründen

substitute ['sʌb·stə·tut] I. vt austauschen; (players) auswechseln II. vi einspringen; (deputize) als Stellvertreter fungieren III. n Ersatz m; (player) Ersatzspieler(in) m(f); there's no ~ for him! es geht doch nichts über ihn!

substitution [ˌsʌb·stə·'tu·ʃən] n Ersetzung f; (act) Austausch m; (of player) [Spieler]wechsel m

subterfuge ['sʌb·tər·fjudʒ] n List f

subterranean [ˌsʌb·tə·'reɪ·ni·ən] adj unterirdisch; fig Untergrund-

subtitle ['sʌb·taɪ·təl] I. vt untertiteln II. n Untertitel m

subtle <-r, -st> ['sʌt·əl] adj subtil; (flavor) fein; (charm) unaufdringlich; (astute) scharfsinnig; (strategy) geschickt; ~ tact ausgeprägtes Taktgefühl

subtlety ['sʌt·əl·ti] n Subtilität f; (astuteness) Scharfsinnigkeit f

subtotal ['sʌb·ˌtoʊ·təl] n Zwischensumme f

subtract [səb·'trækt] vt abziehen (from von +dat)

subtraction [səb·'træk·ʃən] n Subtraktion f

subtropical [ˌsʌb·'trap·ɪ·kəl] adj subtropisch

suburb ['sʌb·ɜrb] n Vorort m; the ~s pl der Stadtrand

suburban [sə·'bɜr·bən] adj Vorstadt-; pej

(provincial) spießig fam

suburbia [sə·'bɜr·bi·ə] n Vororte pl; (people) Vorstadtbewohner pl

subversive [səb·'vɜr·sɪv] I. adj umstürzlerisch II. n Umstürzler(in) m(f)

subway ['sʌb·weɪ] n U-Bahn f; by ~ mit der U-Bahn; ~ station U-Bahn-Station f

subzero [sʌb·'zɪ·roʊ] adj unter null [Grad] nach n; ~ temperatures Minusgrade pl

succeed [sək·'sid] I. vi 1. Erfolg haben; (plan) gelingen; she ~ed in doing it es gelang ihr, es zu tun 2. (follow) die Nachfolge antreten; to ~ to the throne die Thronfolge antreten II. vt to ~ sb in office jds Amt übernehmen

succeeding [sək·'si·dɪŋ] adj attr aufeinanderfolgend; in the ~ weeks in den darauf folgenden Wochen

success [sək·'ses] n Erfolg m; to be a big ~ with sb bei jdm einschlagen fam; to achieve ~ erfolgreich sein; box-office ~ (film) Kassenschlager m fam

successful [sək·'ses·fəl] adj erfolgreich; (lucrative a.) lukrativ; (effective) gelungen

succession [sək·'seʃ·ən] n 1. Folge f; (of events a.) Serie f; in [close] ~ [dicht] hintereinander 2. (line of inheritance) Nachfolge f; ~ to the throne Thronfolge f

successive [sək·'ses·ɪv] adj attr aufeinanderfolgend; six ~ weeks sechs Wochen hintereinander

successor [sək·'ses·ər] n Nachfolger(in) m(f)

succinct [sək·'sɪŋkt] adj kurz [und bündig]

such [sʌtʃ] I. adj 1. attr solcher(r, s); I had never met ~ a person before so ein Mensch war mir noch nie begegnet; ~ a thing so etwas; there's no ~ thing as ghosts so etwas wie Geister gibt es nicht 2. he's ~ an idiot! er ist so ein Idiot!; why are you in ~ a hurry? warum bist du derart in Eile? II. pron solche(r, s); (suchlike) dergleichen; ~ is life so ist das Leben; ~ as wie; as ~ an [und für] sich III. adv so; she's ~ an arrogant person sie ist dermaßen arrogant;

S

I've never had ~ good coffee ich habe noch nie [einen] so guten Kaffee getrunken; ~ ... that ... so ..., dass ...

suchlike ['sʌtʃ.laɪk] *pron* dergleichen

suck [sʌk] **I.** *n* Saugen *nt*; (*on popsicle*) Lutschen *nt* **II.** *vt* **to ~ sth** an etw *dat* saugen; (*sweets*) etw lutschen; **to be ~ed into sth** *fig* in etw *akk* hineingezogen werden **III.** *vi* saugen; (*on candy*) lutschen; sl ätzend sein

◆**suck up** **I.** *vt* aufsaugen **II.** *vi pej fam* **to ~ up to sb** sich bei jdm einschmeicheln

sucker ['sʌk.ər] **I.** *n fam* Einfaltspinsel *m*; **to be a ~ for sth** nach etw *dat* verrückt sein **II.** *vt* **to ~ sb into sth** jdn zu etw *dat* verleiten

suction ['sʌk.ʃən] *n* [Ab]saugen *nt*; (*force*) Saugwirkung *f*

suction cup *n* Saugfuß *m*

Sudan [suˈdæn] *n* Sudan *m*

Sudanese [ˌsu.dəˈniz] **I.** *n* Sudanese, Sudanesin *m, f* **II.** *adj* sudan[es]isch

sudden ['sʌd.ən] *adj* plötzlich; (*departure*) überhastet; (*movement*) abrupt; **all of a ~** *fam* [ganz] plötzlich

sudden infant death syndrome *n* plötzlicher Kindstod

suddenly ['sʌd.ən.li] *adv* plötzlich

suds [sʌdz] *npl* Seifenwasser *nt*; (*foam*) Schaum *m*; *sl* (*beer*) Bier *nt*

sue [su] **I.** *vt* verklagen; **to ~ sb for damages/libel** jdn auf Schadenersatz/ wegen Beleidigung verklagen; **to ~ sb for divorce** gegen jdn die Scheidung einreichen **II.** *vi* prozessieren; **to ~ for sth** etw einklagen

suede [sweɪd] *n* Wildleder *nt*

suffer ['sʌf.ər] **I.** *vi* leiden; (*deteriorate a.*) Schaden erleiden; **to ~ from sth** unter etw *dat* zu leiden haben **II.** *vt* erleiden; (*put up with*) ertragen; **to ~ neglect** vernachlässigt werden; **to not ~ fools gladly** mit dummen Leuten keine Geduld haben

sufferer ['sʌf.ər.ər] *n* (*chronic*) Leidende(r) *f(m)*; (*acute*) Erkrankte(r) *f(m)*; **AIDS ~** AIDS-Kranke(r) *f(m)*; **asthma ~** Asthmatiker(in) *m(f)*

suffering ['sʌf.ər.ɪŋ] *n* Leiden *nt*; (*distress*) Leid *nt*

sufficiency [səˈfɪʃ.ən.si] *n* Hinlänglichkeit *f*; (*quantity*) ausreichende Menge

sufficient [səˈfɪʃ.ənt] *adj* ausreichend, genügend; **to be ~ for sth/sb** für etw/ jdn ausreichen

suffocate ['sʌf.ə.keɪt] *vt, vi* ersticken

suffocating ['sʌf.ə.keɪ.tɪŋ] *adj* erstickend; *fig* erdrückend; (*air*) stickig

suffrage ['sʌf.rɪdʒ] *n* Wahlrecht *nt*

sugar ['ʃʊg.ər] *n* Zucker *m*; (*endearment*) Schätzchen *nt fam*

'**sugar beet** *n* Zuckerrübe *f*

'**sugar cane** *n* Zuckerrohr *nt*

'**sugar cube** *n* Stück *nt* Zucker

'**sugar daddy** *n* wohlhabender älterer Mann, der ein junges Mädchen aushält

sugary ['ʃʊg.ə.ri] *adj* zuckerhaltig; (*sugarlike*) zuckerig; *fig* zuckersüß; (*smile*) süßlich

suggest [səgˈdʒest] *vt* **1.** **to ~ sth [to sb]** [jdm] etw vorschlagen **2.** (*indicate*) hinweisen; **the footprints ~ that ...** die Fußspuren lassen darauf schließen, dass ... **3.** (*insinuate*) **to ~ sth** etw andeuten; **to ~ that ...** darauf hindeuten, dass ...; **are you ~ing that ...?** willst du damit sagen, dass ...?

suggestion [səgˈdʒes.tʃən] *n* Vorschlag *m*; (*hint*) Andeutung *f*; (*indication*) Hinweis *m*; (*trace*) Spur *f*; **to be always open to ~s** immer ein offenes Ohr haben

suggestive [səgˈdʒes.tɪv] *adj* andeutend; (*risqué*) anzüglich

suicidal [ˌsu.ɪˈsaɪ.dəl] *adj* selbstmörderisch; (*person*) selbstmordgefährdet; (*disastrous*) [selbst]zerstörerisch; **that would be ~** das wäre glatter Selbstmord

suicide ['su.ɪ.saɪd] *n* Selbstmord *m*; **to commit ~** Selbstmord begehen

suit [sut] **I.** *n* Anzug *m*; (*jacket and skirt*) Kostüm *nt*; CARDS Farbe *f*; **ski ~** Skianzug *m* ▸ **to follow ~** dem dasselbe tun **II.** *vt* **to ~ sb** jdm passen; (*clothes*) jdm stehen; **to ~ oneself** tun, was man will; **~ yourself!** [ganz,] wie du willst!

suitable ['su.tə.bəl] *adj* geeignet; (*clothing*) angemessen

'**suitcase** *n* Koffer *m*

suite [swit] *n* Suite *f*; (*furniture*) Garni-

tur f; **~ of offices** Reihe f von Büroräumen; **bedroom ~** Schlafzimmereinrichtung f

sulfur ['sʌl·fər] n Schwefel m

sulfuric 'acid n Schwefelsäure f

sulk [sʌlk] I. vi schmollen II. n **to be in a ~** schmollen

sulky ['sʌl·ki] adj beleidigt; (face) mürrisch

sultan ['sʌl·tən] n Sultan m

sultry ['sʌl·tri] adj schwül; (sexy) sinnlich

sum [sʌm] n Summe f

➤ **sum up** I. vi zusammenfassen; (judge) resümieren II. vt zusammenfassen; (evaluate) einschätzen; **to ~ up a situation at a glance** eine Situation auf einen Blick erfassen

summarize ['sʌm·ə·raɪz] vt, vi [kurz] zusammenfassen; **to ~, ...** kurz gesagt, ...

summary ['sʌm·ə·ri] I. n Zusammenfassung f; (of contents) [kurze] Inhaltsangabe II. adj knapp; (dismissal) fristlos

summer ['sʌm·ər] I. n Sommer m; **a ~'s day** ein Sommertag m; **in [the] ~** im Sommer II. vi den Sommer verbringen

summer house n Ferienhaus nt

summertime n Sommerzeit f; **in the ~** im Sommer

summer 'vacation n Sommerurlaub m; SCH Sommerferien pl

summit ['sʌm·ɪt] n Gipfel m; fig a. Höhepunkt m

summon ['sʌm·ən] vt zu sich dat bestellen; LAW vorladen; (help) holen; **to ~ a meeting** eine Versammlung einberufen; **to ~ up the courage to do sth** den Mut aufbringen, etw zu tun

summons ['sʌm·ənz] I. n <pl -es> LAW [Vor]ladung f; (call) Aufforderung f; **to issue a ~** [vor]laden II. vt LAW **to ~ sb** jdn vorladen lassen

sumptuous ['sʌmp·tʃu·əs] adj luxuriös; (dinner) üppig

sun [sʌn] I. n Sonne f; **to sit in the ~** in der Sonne sitzen; **everything under the ~** alles Mögliche II. vt <-nn-> **to ~ oneself** sich sonnen

sunbathe vi sonnenbaden

sunbeam n Sonnenstrahl m

sunblock n Sunblocker m

sunburn I. n Sonnenbrand m II. vi

<-ed or-burnt, -ed or-burnt> sich verbrennen

sunburned, 'sunburnt adj sonnengebräunt; (red) sonnenverbrannt

sundae ['sʌn·di] n Eisbecher m

Sunday ['sʌn·deɪ] n Sonntag m; see also **Tuesday**

Sunday school n Sonntagsschule f

sundial n Sonnenuhr f

sundown n Sonnenuntergang m

sundries ['sʌn·driz] n pl Verschiedenes nt kein pl

sundry ['sʌn·dri] adj attr verschiedene(r, s) ▶ **all and ~** fam Hinz und Kunz pej

sunflower n Sonnenblume f

sung [sʌŋ] pp of **sing**

sunglasses npl Sonnenbrille f

sunk [sʌŋk] pp of **sink**

sunken ['sʌŋ·kən] adj attr tief[er] liegend attr; (bathtub) eingelassen; (cheeks) eingefallen

sunlight n Sonnenlicht nt

sunlit adj sonnenbeschienen; (room) sonnig

sunny ['sʌn·i] adj sonnig; (cheery) heiter; **~ intervals** Aufheiterungen pl

sunrise n Sonnenaufgang m

sunroof n Schiebedach nt

sunscreen n Sonnenschutzmittel nt

sunset n Sonnenuntergang m

sunshade n Sonnenblende f; (umbrella) Sonnenschirm m

sunshine n sonniges Wetter; (sunlight) Sonnenschein m

sunstroke n Sonnenstich m

suntan n Sonnenbräune f; **to get a ~** braun werden

suntan lotion n Sonnencreme f

suntanned adj sonnengebräunt

sunup n Sonnenaufgang m

super ['su·pər] fam I. adj klasse II. interj super!, spitze! III. adv besonders

superb [sə·'pɜrb] adj ausgezeichnet; (impressive) erstklassig; (view) großartig

Super Bowl n Finale des professionellen amerikanischen Fußballs

superficial [ˌsu·pər·'fɪʃ·əl] adj oberflächlich; (damage) geringfügig; (apparent) äußerlich; (treatment) flüchtig

superfluous [su·'pɜr·flu·əs] adj überflüssig

S

super'human *adj* übermenschlich

superimpose [ˌsu·pər·ɪm·'pouz] *vt* überlagern

superintendent [ˌsu·pər·ɪn·'ten·dənt] *n* Aufsicht *f*; (*of schools*) Oberschulrat, -rätin *m, f*; (*police officer*) Polizeichef(in) *m(f)*

superior [sə·'pɪr·i·ər] I. *adj* vorgesetzt; (*excellent*) überragend; (*taste*) erlesen; (*better*) überlegen; *pej* (*arrogant*) überheblich; **to be ~ in numbers** in der Überzahl sein II. *n* Vorgesetzte(r) *f(m)*

superiority [sə·ˌpɪr·i·'ɔr·ɪ·ti] *n* Überlegenheit *f*; *pej* (*arrogance*) Überheblichkeit *f*

'superman *n* Superman *m*

supermarket ['su·pər·ˌmar·kɪt] *n* Supermarkt *m*

supernatural [ˌsu·pər·'næt͡ʃ·ər·əl] I. *adj* übernatürlich; (*extraordinary*) außergewöhnlich II. *n* **the ~** das Übernatürliche

supersonic [ˌsu·pər·'san·ɪk] *adj* Überschall-

superstar ['su·pər·star] *n* Superstar *m*

superstition [ˌsu·pər·'stɪʃ·ən] *n* Aberglaube[n] *m*

superstitious [ˌsu·pər·'stɪʃ·əs] *adj* abergläubisch

superstore ['su·pər·stɔr] *n* Großmarkt *m*

supervise ['su·pər·vaɪz] *vt* beaufsichtigen

supervision [ˌsu·pər·'vɪʒ·ən] *n* Beaufsichtigung *f*; (*of prisoners*) Überwachung *f*

supervisor ['su·pər·vaɪ·zər] *n* Aufsichtsbeamte(r), -beamtin *m, f*; (*in shop*) Abteilungsleiter(in) *m(f)*; (*in factory*) Vorarbeiter(in) *m(f)*; scн Betreuungslehrer(in) *m(f)*; univ Betreuer(in) *m(f)*

supervisory [ˌsu·pər·'vaɪ·zə·ri] *adj* Aufsichts-

supper ['sʌp·ər] *n* Abendessen *nt*

supple ['sʌp·əl] *adj* geschmeidig; (*mind*) flexibel; (*skin*) weich

supplement ['sʌp·lə·mənt] I. *n* Ergänzung *f*; (*book*) Supplement *nt*; (*section*) Beilage *f*; (*information*) Nachtrag *m* II. *vt* ergänzen; **to ~ one's income** sein Einkommen aufbessern

supplementary [ˌsʌp·lə·'men·tə·ri], **supplemental** [sʌp·lə·'men·təl] *adj* zusätzlich

supplier [sə·'plaɪ·ər] *n* Lieferant(in) *m(f)*; (*company a.*) Lieferfirma *f*; (*of services*) Dienstleister(in) *m(f)*

supply [sə·'plaɪ] I. *vt* <-ie-> bereitstellen; (*provide sb with sth*) versorgen; (*drugs*) beschaffen; (*act as source*) liefern II. *n* 1. Vorrat *m*; (*action*) Versorgung *f*; **oil ~** Ölzufuhr *f* 2. ECON Angebot *nt*; **to be in short ~** Mangelware sein 3. **supplies** *pl* Versorgung *f*; (*amount needed*) Bedarf *m*; **to cut off supplies** die Lieferungen einstellen

support [sə·'pɔrt] I. *vt* 1. **to ~ oneself on sth** sich auf etw *akk* stützen; **the ice is thick enough to ~ our weight** das Eis ist so dick, dass es uns trägt 2. (*fund*) (*finanziell*) unterstützen; (*lifestyle*) finanzieren; (*family*) unterhalten; **to ~ sb** für jds Lebensunterhalt aufkommen 3. (*back*) unterstützen; (*plan*) befürworten; **to ~ a team** für ein Team sein II. *n* 1. Stütze *f*; **to give sth ~** etw *dat* Halt geben 2. (*funds*) Unterstützung *f*; LAW Unterhalt *m* 3. (*backing*) Stütze *f*; (*services*) Support *m*; **to give sb moral ~** jdn moralisch unterstützen

supporter [sə·'pɔr·tər] *n* Anhänger(in) *m(f)*; (*of campaign*) Befürworter(in) *m(f)*; (*of theory*) Verfechter(in) *m(f)*

supportive [sə·'pɔr·tɪv] *adj* **to be ~ of sb** jdm eine Stütze sein; **to be ~ of sth** etw unterstützen

suppose [sə·'pouz] *vt* 1. **to ~ [that]** ... annehmen, dass ...; **I ~ you think that's funny** du hältst das wohl auch noch für komisch; **I don't ~ you could ...** Sie könnten mir nicht zufällig ...; **you're ~d to be asleep** du solltest eigentlich schon schlafen 2. (*believe*) glauben; **her new book is ~d to be very good** ihr neues Buch soll sehr gut sein ► **I ~ so** wenn du meinst

supposed [sə·'pouzd] *adj attr* angenommen; (*killer*) mutmaßlich

supposedly [sə·'pou·zɪd·li] *adv* angeblich; (*apparently*) anscheinend

supposing [sə·'pou·zɪŋ] *conj* **~ he doesn't show up?** was, wenn er nicht erscheint?

supposition [ˌsʌp·ə·'zɪʃ·ən] *n* Spekula-

tion f; (belief) Vermutung f; **on the ~ that ...** vorausgesetzt, dass ...

suppository [sə'paz·ə·tɔr·i] n Zäpfchen nt

suppress [sə·'pres] vt unterdrücken; (revolution) niederschlagen; (terrorism) bekämpfen; (information) zurückhalten; (inhibit) hemmen; (weaken) schwächen; (reaction) abschwächen; (memories) verdrängen

suppression [sə·'pref·ən] n Unterdrückung f; (of revolt) Niederschlagung f; (of terrorism) Bekämpfung f; (of information) Zurückhaltung f; (weakening) Hemmung f

supremacy [sə·'prem·ə·si] n Vormachtstellung f; SPORT Überlegenheit f

supreme [sə·'prim] adj höchste(r, s); (extreme) äußerste(r, s); (wonderful) überragend; (moment) einzigartig

Supreme 'Court n oberstes Gericht

surcharge ['sɜr·tʃardʒ] n Zuschlag m; (penalty) Strafgebühr f

sure [ʃʊr] I. adj pred sicher; **I'm not really ~** ich weiß nicht so genau; **to feel ~ [that] ...** überzeugt [davon] sein, dass ...; **to be ~ [that] ...** [sich dat] sicher sein, dass ...; **to be ~ to ...** daran denken, dass ...; **be ~ to close the door** vergiss nicht, die Tür zuzumachen ► **~ thing** fam sicher!; (of course) [na] klar! fam; **to be ~ of oneself** sehr von sich dat überzeugt sein; **to make ~ [that] ...** darauf achten, dass ... II. adv fam echt; **I ~ am hungry!** hab ich vielleicht einen Hunger! III. interj fam – **I will!** aber klar doch!

surely ['ʃʊr·li] adv sicher[lich]; **~ you don't expect me to believe that!** du erwartest doch wohl nicht, dass ich dir das abnehme! fam; **slowly but ~** langsam, aber sicher

surf [sɜrf] I. n Brandung f II. vi surfen; (windsurf) windsurfen III. vt **to ~ the Internet** im Internet surfen

surface ['sɜr·fɪs] I. n Oberfläche f; (of lake) Spiegel m; road ~ Straßenbelag m ► **to scratch the ~ [of sth]** [etw] streifen II. vi auftauchen

'surface mail n Postsendung, die auf dem Land- bzw. Seeweg befördert wird

surfboard ['sɜrf·bɔrd] n Surfbrett nt

surfer ['sɜr·fər] n Surfer(in) m(f); (windsurfer) Windsurfer(in) m(f)

surfing ['sɜr·fɪŋ] n Surfen nt; (windsurfing) Windsurfen nt

surge [sɜrdʒ] I. vi wogen; (sea) branden; (profits) [stark] ansteigen; **to ~ [up]** (emotion) aufwallen; (cheer) aufbrausen II. n [plötzlicher] Anstieg; (wave) Woge f; fig Ansturm m; (of emotion) Woge f

surgeon ['sɜr·dʒən] n Chirurg(in) m(f)

surgery ['sɜr·dʒə·ri] n chirurgischer Eingriff

surgical ['sɜr·dʒɪ·kəl] adj chirurgisch; (orthopedic) medizinisch

surmount [sər·'maʊnt] vt meistern; (obstacle) überwinden

surname ['sɜr·neɪm] n Familienname m

surpass [sər·'pæs] vt **to ~ oneself** sich selbst übertreffen

surplus ['sɜr·pləs] I. n <pl -es> Überschuss m II. adj zusätzlich; (dispensable) überschüssig

surprise [sər·'praɪz] I. n Überraschung f; **~!** fam Überraschung!; **to take sb by ~** jdn überraschen; **to one's [great] ~** zu seinem [großen] Erstaunen II. vt überraschen; **to ~ sb doing sth** jdn bei etw dat überraschen III. adj attr überraschend

surprised [sər·'praɪzd] adj überrascht; (amazed) erstaunt; pred (disappointed) enttäuscht; **I wouldn't be ~ if ...** es würde mich nicht wundern, wenn ...; **pleasantly ~** angenehm überrascht

surprising [sər·'praɪ·zɪŋ] adj überraschend

surprisingly [sər·'praɪ·zɪŋ·li] adv erstaunlich; (unexpectedly) überraschenderweise

surrender [sə·'ren·dər] I. vi aufgeben; MIL kapitulieren; (give in a.) nachgeben; **to ~ to sb** sich jdm ergeben; **to ~ to temptation** der Versuchung erliegen II. n Kapitulation f

surrogate 'mother n Leihmutter f

surround [sə·'raʊnd] vt umgeben; (encircle) einkreisen; MIL umstellen

surrounding [sə·'raʊn·dɪŋ] adj attr **~ area** Umgebung f

surroundings npl Umgebung f; (living conditions a.) [Lebens]verhältnisse pl

surveillance [sər·'veɪ·ləns] n Überwachung f

survey I. vt [sər'veɪ] (*passers-by*) befragen; (*look at*) betrachten; (*carefully*) begutachten; (*overview*) umreißen II. n ['sɜr-veɪ] Untersuchung f; (*research*) Studie f; (*overview*) Übersicht f; (*of topic*) Überblick m; (*of land*) Vermessung f; **nationwide ~** landesweite Umfrage

surveyor [sər'veɪ-ər] n [Land]vermesser(in) m(f)

survival [sər'vaɪ-vəl] n Überleben nt

survive [sər'vaɪv] I. vi überleben; *fig a.* erhalten bleiben; (*monument*) überdauern; (*tradition*) fortbestehen; **to ~ on sth** sich mit etw *dat* am Leben halten II. vt überleben; *fig* hinwegkommen; (*fire*) überstehen

surviving [sər'vaɪ-vɪŋ] adj noch lebend; (*relative*) hinterblieben; *fig* [noch] vorhanden

survivor [sər'vaɪ-vər] n Überlebende(r) f(m); (*tough person*) Überlebenskünstler(in) m(f); **she's a cancer ~** sie hat den Krebs besiegt

susceptible [sə'sep-tə-bəl] adj **to be ~ to sth** für etw *akk* empfänglich sein

suspect I. vt [sə'spekt] vermuten; (*consider guilty*) verdächtigen; (*doubt*) anzweifeln; (*motives*) misstrauen; **to be ~ed of sth** einer S. *gen* verdächtigt werden II. n ['sʌs·pekt] Verdächtige(r) f(m) III. adj ['sʌs·pekt] verdächtig; (*possibly defective*) zweifelhaft

suspend [sə'spend] vt 1. [vorübergehend] aussetzen; (*worker*) suspendieren; (*student*) [zeitweilig] [vom Unterricht] ausschließen; (*player*) sperren; **to ~ judgment** mit seiner Meinung zurückhalten 2. (*hang*) herabhängen

suspender [sə'spen·dər] n **~s** pl Hosenträger pl

suspense [sə'spens] n Spannung f; **to keep sb in ~** jdn im Ungewissen lassen

suspension [sə'spen·ʃən] n 1. [zeitweilige] Einstellung f; (*of worker, student*) Suspendierung f; (*of player*) Sperrung f 2. AUTO Radaufhängung f

sus'pension bridge n Hängebrücke f

suspicion [sə'spɪʃ·ən] n Verdacht m; (*mistrust*) Misstrauen nt; **to be above ~** über jeglichen Verdacht erhaben sein

suspicious [sə'spɪʃ·əs] adj verdächtig; (*distrustful*) misstrauisch; **to be ~ of sth** einer S. *dat* gegenüber skeptisch sein

sustain [sə'steɪn] vt aufrechterhalten; (*keep alive*) [am Leben] erhalten; (*family*) unterhalten; (*emotionally*) unterstützen

sustainable [sə'steɪ·nə·bəl] adj haltbar; (*argument*) stichhaltig; (*resources*) erneuerbar; (*development*) nachhaltig

sustained [sə'steɪnd] adj anhaltend; (*determined*) nachdrücklich

swab [swab] I. n Tupfer m; (*sample*) Abstrich m II. vt <-bb-> abtupfen

swagger ['swæg·ər] I. vi stolzieren; (*behave*) prahlen II. n Prahlerei f

swallow¹ ['swal·oʊ] I. n Schlucken nt; (*quantity*) Schluck m II. vt [hinunter]schlucken; (*greedily*) verschlingen; *fam* (*believe*) schlucken; **to be ~ed [up] by sth** von etw *dat* geschluckt werden *fam*; **to ~ sth whole** etw *akk* unzerkaut [hinunter]schlucken III. vi schlucken

swallow² ['swal·oʊ] n (*bird*) Schwalbe f

swam [swæm] vt, vi *pt of* **swim**

swamp [swamp] I. vt überschwemmen; **I'm ~ed with work at the moment** im Moment ersticke ich in Arbeit II. n Sumpf m

'swampland, 'swamplands npl Sumpfland nt

swan [swan] n Schwan m

swap [swap] I. n Tausch m; (*interchange*) Austausch m; (*deal*) Tauschhandel m II. vt <-pp-> tauschen; (*stories*) austauschen III. vi <-pp-> tauschen; **to ~ with sb** mit jdm tauschen

swarm [swɔrm] I. n Schwarm m; (*people*) Schar f II. vi schwärmen; **to be ~ing with sth** von etw *dat* [nur so] wimmeln

swat [swat] I. vt <-tt-> totschlagen; (*ball*) schmettern II. n [heftiger] Schlag; (*swatter*) Fliegenklatsche f

sway [sweɪ] I. vi schwanken; (*trees*) sich wiegen; II. vt schwenken; (*wind*) wiegen; (*alter*) ändern; **to be ~ed by sb/sth** sich von jdm/etw beeinflussen lassen; (*change mind*) von jdm/etw umgestimmt werden

swear <swore, sworn> [swer] I. vi fluchen; (*take oath*) schwören II. vt

schwören; (*oath*) leisten

swear in *vt* vereidigen

'**swearing** *n* Fluchen *nt*

'**swear word** *n* Fluch *m*

sweat [swet] I. *n* Schweiß *m; to work oneself into a ~* [*about sth*] sich [wegen einer S. *dat*] verrückt machen *fam* II. *vi* <sweat *or* sweated, sweat *or* sweated> schwitzen III. *vt* <sweat *or* sweated, sweat *or* sweated> ▶ *to ~* **blood** Blut [und Wasser] schwitzen *fam*

sweat out *vt to ~ it out* zittern *fam*

sweater ['swet·ər] *n* Pullover *m*

'**sweatpants** *n pl* Jogginghose *f*

'**sweatshirt** *n* Sweatshirt *nt*

'**sweatshop** *n* Ausbeuterbetrieb *m pej*

'**sweaty** ['swet·i] *adj* verschwitzt; (*work*) schweißtreibend

Swede [swid] *n* Schwede *m*, Schwedin *f*

Sweden ['swi·dən] *n* Schweden *nt*

Swedish ['swi·dɪʃ] I. *n* Schwedisch *nt* II. *adj* schwedisch

sweep [swip] I. *n* Kehren *nt;* (*with saber*) ausholender Hieb; (*range*) Reichweite *f* II. *vt* <swept, swept> 1. kehren; **she swept the pile of papers into her bag** sie schaufelte den Stapel Papiere in ihre Tasche **2.** *to ~* **sth** (*epidemic*) über etw *akk* kommen III. *vi* <swept, swept> kehren; (*move*) gleiten

sweep aside *vt* [hin]wegfegen; (*dismiss*) beiseiteschieben

sweep away *vt* [hin]wegfegen; *fig* beiseiteschieben; (*carry away*) mitreißen

sweep out I. *vt* auskehren II. *vi* hinausstürmen

sweep up I. *vt* zusammenkehren II. *vi* aufkehren

sweeper ['swi·pər] *n* Kehrmaschine *f;* (*person*) [Straßen]kehrer(in) *m(f);* (*in soccer*) Libero *m*

sweeping ['swi·pɪŋ] *adj* weitreichend; (*changes*) einschneidend; (*cuts*) drastisch; (*general*) pauschal; (*generalization*) grob; (*curves*) weit

sweepstakes ['swip·steɪks] *npl* + *sing/pl vb* Art Lotterie, wobei mit kleinen Einsätzen u. A. auf Pferde gesetzt wird und diese Einsätze an den Gewinner gehen

sweet [swit] I. *adj* süß; (*pleasant a.*) angenehm; (*endearing*) niedlich; (*wine,*

voice) lieblich; (*temper*) sanft; (*kind*) lieb II. *n* ~**s** *pl* Süßigkeiten *pl*

'**sweet-and-sour** *adj* süßsauer

'**sweet corn** *n* [Zucker]mais *m*

sweeten ['swi·tən] *vt* süßen; *to ~* [*up* ⇆] *sb* jdn günstig stimmen

sweetener ['swi·tən·ər] *n* Süßstoff *m;* (*pill*) Süßstofftablette *f;* (*inducement*) Versuchung *f*

'**sweetheart** *n* Liebling *m*

sweetness ['swit·nɪs] *n* Süße *f;* (*pleasantness*) Freundlichkeit *f;* (*of victory*) süßes [*or* wohliges] Gefühl

swell <swelled, swelled *or* swollen> [swel] I. *vt* [an]steigen lassen; (*sales*) steigern II. *vi* 1. *to ~* [*up*] anschwellen 2. (*increase*) zunehmen; (*population*) ansteigen; (*get louder*) lauter werden III. *n* (*of sound*) zunehmende Lautstärke; (*of music*) Anschwellen *nt;* (*of sea*) Seegang *m*

swelling ['swel·ɪŋ] *n* Schwellung *f;* (*sudden*) Beule *f;* (*activity*) Anschwellen *nt*

sweltering ['swel·tər·ɪŋ] *adj* drückend heiß; (*heat*) schwül

swept [swept] *vt, vi pt of* **sweep**

swerve [swɜrv] I. *vi* [plötzlich] ausweichen; (*car*) ausscheren; (*line*) eine Schwenkung vollziehen *geh; to ~ from one's principles* von seinen seinen Grundsätzen abweichen II. *n* Schlenker *m;* (*evasion*) Ausweichbewegung *f; fig* Abweichung *f; a ~* **to the left/right** ein Ausscheren *nt* nach links/rechts

swift [swɪft] I. *adj* schnell II. *n* Mauersegler *m*

swiftly ['swɪft·li] *adv* schnell

swiftness ['swɪft·nɪs] *n* Schnelligkeit *f*

swill [swɪl] I. *n* Schweinefutter *nt; fig, pej* (*drink*) Gesöff *nt fam;* (*food*) Fraß *m fam* II. *vt usu pej fam* hinunterstürzen; (*beer*) hinunterkippen

swim [swɪm] I. *vi* <swam, swum, -mm-> schwimmen; (*whirl*) verschwimmen II. *vt* <swam, swum, -mm-> durchschwimmen; *to ~* **a few strokes** ein paar Züge schwimmen III. *n to go for a ~* schwimmen gehen

swimming ['swɪm·ɪŋ] *n* Schwimmen *nt*

'**swimming cap** *n* Badekappe *f*

'**swimming pool** *n* Schwimmbecken *nt;*

(*private*) Swimmingpool *m;* (*public*) Schwimmbad *nt;* **indoor/outdoor ~** Hallen-/Freibad *nt*

'**swimsuit** *n* Badeanzug *m;* (*trunks*) Badehose *f*

'**swim trunks**, '**swimming trunks** *npl* Badehose *f*

swindle ['swɪn·dəl] I. *vt* betrügen; **to ~ sb out of sth** jdn um etw *akk* betrügen II. *n* Betrug *m*

swindler ['swɪnd·lər] *n* Betrüger(in) *m(f)*

swine <*pl* -> [swaɪn] *n* Schwein *nt;* *pej fam* (*person*) Schwein *nt*

swing [swɪŋ] I. *n* Schwingen *nt;* (*punch*) Schlag *m;* (*in baseball*) Schwung *m;* (*seat*) Schaukel *f;* (*change*) Schwankung *f;* POL Umschwung *m* ▸ **to be in full** ~ voll im Gang sein II. *vi* <swung, swung> 1. [hin und her] schwingen; (*in circles*) sich drehen; (*baseball bat*) schwingen; (*mood*) schwanken; **the door swung open in the wind** die Tür ging durch den Schlag auf 2. (*try to hit*) zum Schlag ausholen; **to ~ at sb** nach jdm schlagen 3. (*party*) swingen ▸ **to ~ into action** loslegen *fam* III. *vt* <swung, swung> [hin- und her] schwingen; **do you think you could** ~ **the job for me?** *fam* glaubst du, du könntest die Sache für mich schaukeln?; **to ~ it** es deichseln

swing around I. *vi* sich schnell umdrehen; (*in fear*) herumfahren; **she swung around the corner at full speed** sie kam mit vollem Tempo um die Ecke geschossen II. *vt to* ~ **sth around** etw [her]umdrehen; (*in circles*) etw herumschwingen; **to ~ a conversation around to sth** ein Gespräch auf etw *akk* bringen

swipe [swaɪp] I. *vi* schlagen II. *vt fam* (*steal*) klauen III. *n* Schlag *m;* **to take a** ~ **at sb/sth** auf jdn/etw losschlagen

swirl [swɜrl] I. *vi* wirbeln II. *n* (*of water*) Strudel *m;* (*of snow, wind*) Wirbel *m;* (*of dust*) Wolke *f*

Swiss [swɪs] I. *adj* Schweizer- II. *n* <*pl* -> Schweizer(in) *m(f)*

switch [swɪtʃ] I. *n* <*pl* -es> 1. Schalter *m;* **to flick a** ~ (*on*) einen Schalter anknipsen; (*off*) einen Schalter ausknip-

sen 2. (*substitution*) Wechsel *m;* (*alteration*) Änderung *f;* (*change*) Wechsel *m* II. *vi* wechseln III. *vt* 1. (*adjust settings*) umschalten 2. (*direction*) wechseln; (*substitute*) auswechseln

◆ **switch off** I. *vt* ausschalten II. *vi* ausschalten; (*lose attention*) abschalten *fam*

◆ **switch on** I. *vt* einschalten; (*TV a.*) anmachen II. *vi* einschalten

◆ **switch over** *vi* wechseln

'**switchblade** *n* Klappmesser *nt*

'**switchboard** *n* Vermittlung *f*

Switzerland ['swɪt·sər·lənd] *n* Schweiz *f*

swivel ['swɪv·əl] I. *vt* <-l-> drehen II. *vi* <-l-> sich drehen

swollen ['swoʊ·lən] I. *pp of* **swell** II. *adj* geschwollen; (*face*) aufgequollen; (*larger*) angeschwollen

swoop [swup] I. *n* Sturzflug *m;* *fam* (*attack*) Überraschungsangriff *m* II. *vi* herabstoßen; **to ~ in on sb/sth** *fam* jdn/etw angreifen; (*police*) bei jdm/etw eine Razzia machen

sword [sɔrd] *n* Schwert *nt*

'**swordfish** *n* Schwertfisch *m*

swore [swɔr] *pt of* **swear**

sworn [swɔrn] I. *pp of* **swear** II. *adj attr* ~ **statement** eidliche Aussage; ~ **enemy** Todesfeind(in) *m(f)*

swum [swʌm] *pp of* **swim**

swung [swʌŋ] *pt, pp of* **swing**

sycamore ['sɪk·ə·mɔr] *n* Platane *f*

syllable ['sɪl·ə·bəl] *n* Silbe *f*

syllabus <*pl* -es> ['sɪl·ə·bəs] *n* Lehrplan *m;* (*list*) Leseliste *f*

symbiosis [ˌsɪm·bɪ·'oʊ·sɪs] *n* Symbiose *f*

symbiotic [ˌsɪm·bɪ·'ɑt·ɪk] *adj* symbiotisch

symbol ['sɪm·bəl] *n* Symbol *nt*

symbolic [sɪm·'bɑl·ɪk] *adj* symbolisch

symbolize ['sɪm·bə·laɪz] *vt* symbolisieren

symmetrical [sɪ·'met·rɪ·kəl] *adj* symmetrisch; (*face*) ebenmäßig

symmetry ['sɪm·ə·tri] *n* Symmetrie *f;* (*evenness*) Ebenmäßigkeit *f;* (*correspondence*) Übereinstimmung *f*

sympathetic [ˌsɪm·pə·'θet·ɪk] *adj* verständnisvoll; (*sympathizing*) mitfühlend; (*likeable*) sympathisch; **to be ~ about sth** für etw *akk* Verständnis haben; **to**

be ~ to|ward] sb/sth mit jdm/etw sympathisieren

sympathize [ˈsɪm·pə·θaɪz] *vi* Verständnis haben; (*show compassion*) Mitleid haben; (*agree with*) sympathisieren

sympathizer [ˈsɪm·pə·θaɪ·zər] *n* Sympathisant(in) *m(f)*

sympathy [ˈsɪm·pə·θi] *n* Mitleid *nt;* (*commiseration*) Mitgefühl *nt;* (*understanding*) Verständnis *nt;* (*agreement*) Übereinstimmung *f;* (*affection*) Sympathie *f;* **sympathies** *pl* (*condolences*) Beileid *nt*

symphony [ˈsɪm·fə·ni] *n* Symphonie *f*

symptom [ˈsɪmp·təm] *n* Symptom *nt; fig a.* [An]zeichen *nt*

symptomatic [ˌsɪmp·təˈmæt̬·ɪk] *adj* symptomatisch

synagogue [ˈsɪn·ə·gag] *n* Synagoge *f*

synchronize [ˈsɪŋ·krə·naɪz] **I.** *vt* aufeinander abstimmen; **to ~ watches** Uhren gleichstellen **II.** *vi* zeitlich zusammenfallen

synchronous [ˈsɪŋ·krə·nəs] *adj* synchron

syndicate [ˈsɪn·də·kɪt] *n* Syndikat *nt;* JOURN Pressesyndikat *nt*

syndrome [ˈsɪn·droʊm] *n* Syndrom *nt*

synergy [ˈsɪn·ər·dʒi] *n* Synergismus *m;* (*energy*) Synergie *f*

synonym [ˈsɪn·ə·nɪm] *n* Synonym *nt*

synonymous [sɪˈnɑn·ɪ·məs] *adj* synonym

synopsis <*pl* -ses> [sɪˈnæp·sɪs] *n* Zusammenfassung *f*

synthesis <*pl* -theses> [ˈsɪn·θə·sɪs] *n* Synthese *f*

synthesize [ˈsɪn·θə·saɪz] *vt* künstlich herstellen

synthesizer [ˈsɪn·θə·saɪ·zər] *n* Synthesizer *m*

synthetic [sɪn·ˈθet̬·ɪk] **I.** *adj* synthetisch; *fig, pej* (*fake*) künstlich; **~ fiber** Kunstfaser *f* **II.** *n* synthetischer Stoff

syphilis [ˈsɪf·ə·lɪs] *n* Syphilis *f*

Syria [ˈsɪr·i·ə] *n* Syrien *nt*

Syrian [ˈsɪr·i·ən] **I.** *adj* syrisch **II.** *n* Syr[i]er(in) *m(f)*

syringe [sə·ˈrɪndʒ] *n* Spritze *f*

syrup [ˈsɪr·əp] *n* Sirup *m;* **maple ~** Ahornsirup

system [ˈsɪs·təm] *n* System *nt*

systematic [ˌsɪs·təˈmæt̬·ɪk] *adj* systematisch

T

T <*pl* -'s>, **t** <*pl* -'s> [ti] *n* T *nt,* t *nt;* **~ as in Tango** T wie Theodor

t. *n abbr of* **ton** t

tab [tæb] *n* Lasche *f;* (*on file*) [Kartei]reiter *m; fam* (*bill*) Rechnung *f;* **to pick up the ~** die Rechnung übernehmen ▶ **to keep ~s on sth/sb** *fam* etw/jdn [genau] im Auge behalten

tabby [ˈtæb·i] *adj,* **n ~** [**cat**] Tigerkatze *f*

'tab key *n* COMPUT Tabulatortaste *f*

table [ˈteɪ·bəl] *n* Tisch *m;* (*list*) Tabelle *f;* **to set the ~** den Tisch decken ▶ **to turn the ~s on sb** jdm gegenüber den Spieß umdrehen

'tablecloth *n* Tischtuch *nt*

'table manners *npl* Tischmanieren *pl*

'tablespoon *n* Esslöffel *m*

tablet [ˈtæb·lɪt] *n* Tablette *f;* (*commemorative*) [Gedenk]tafel *f*

'table tennis *n* Tischtennis *nt*

tabloid [ˈtæb·lɔɪd] *n* Boulevardzeitung *f*

taboo [tə·ˈbu] **I.** *n* Tabu *nt* **II.** *adj* tabu, Tabu-

tack [tæk] **I.** *n* kurzer Nagel; (*pin*) Reißzwecke *f;* (*stitch*) Heftstich *m;* **to try a different ~** *fig* eine andere Richtung einschlagen **II.** *vt* festnageln; (*sew*) anheften; (*hem*) heften

tackle [ˈtæk·əl] **I.** *n* Ausrüstung *f;* (*hoist*) Winde *f;* (*in football*) Tackle *m;* (*in soccer*) Angriff *m;* **block and ~** Flaschenzug *m* **II.** *vt* in Angriff nehmen; (*problem*) angehen; (*manage*) fertigwerden; (*in football*) tackeln; (*in soccer*) angreifen

tacky [ˈtæk·i] *adj* klebrig; *pej fam* (*in bad taste*) billig; *pej fam* (*shoddy*) schäbig

tact [tækt] *n* Taktgefühl *nt;* (*sensitiveness*) Feingefühl *nt*

tactful [ˈtækt·fəl] *adj* taktvoll

tactic [ˈtæk·tɪk] *n* Taktik *f*

tactical [ˈtæk·tɪ·kəl] *adj* taktisch; (*skillful*) geschickt

tactless [ˈtækt·lɪs] *adj* taktlos

tadpole [ˈtæd·poʊl] n Kaulquappe f

taffeta [ˈtæf·ɪ·tə] n Taft m

tag [tæg] I. n Schild[chen] nt; (on clothes) Etikett nt; (on car) Steuerplakette f; (on suitcase) [Koffer]anhänger m; (security tag) Sicherungsetikett nt; (for person) elektronische Fessel II. vt <-gg-> mit einem Schild versehen; (suitcase) mit einem Anhänger versehen; (electronically) ein Sicherungsetikett anbringen; (person) eine elektronische Fessel anlegen

◆**tag along** vi fam hinterherlaufen; (join) mitkommen

tail [teɪl] I. n Schwanz m; (of car) Heck nt; fam (follower) Beschatter(in) m(f); **heads or ~s?** Kopf oder Zahl?; **to have sb on one's ~** jdn auf den Fersen haben; **to put a ~ on sb** jdn beschatten lassen ▶ **I can't make <u>heads</u> or ~s of it** ich werde daraus einfach nicht schlau II. vt fam beschatten

◆**tail off** vi nachlassen; (voice) schwächer werden

'tailgate I. n Heckklappe f; (of truck) Ladeklappe f; (of van) Laderampe f II. vt, vi fam [zu] dicht auffahren

'taillight n Rücklicht nt

tailor [ˈteɪ·lər] I. n Schneider(in) m(f) II. vt [nach Maß] schneidern

tailor-'made adj maßgeschneidert; **to be ~ for sb/sth** für jdn/etw maßgeschneidert sein

'tailpipe n Auspuffrohr nt

taint [teɪnt] vt verderben; (reputation) beflecken

Taiwan [ˌtaɪ·ˈwɑn] n Taiwan nt

Taiwanese [ˌtaɪ·wə·ˈniz] I. adj taiwanisch II. n Taiwaner(in) m(f)

Tajikistan [tɑ·ˈdʒɪ·kɪ·ˌstɑn] n Tadschikistan nt

take [teɪk] I. n Einnahmen pl; (scene) Take m o nt fachspr ▶ **to <u>be</u> on the ~** fam Bestechungsgelder nehmen II. vt <took, taken> 1. (accept) annehmen; (criticism) akzeptieren; **to ~ sth badly** etw schlecht aufnehmen 2. (transport) bringen; **to ~ sb to the train station** jdn zum Bahnhof fahren 3. (seize) nehmen; (power) ergreifen; (city) einnehmen; (win) gewinnen; **to ~ sb by the hand/throat** jdn bei der Hand nehmen/

am Kragen packen 4. (tolerate) ertragen; (abuse) hinnehmen 5. (hold) aufnehmen; **my car ~s five people** mein Auto hat Platz für fünf Leute 6. (require) erfordern; **I ~ [a] size five [or a size five shoe]** ich habe Schuhgröße fünf; **it ~s ...** man braucht ...; **hold on, it won't ~ long** warten Sie, es dauert nicht lange 7. (receive) erhalten 8. (remove) [weg]nehmen; (steal a.) stehlen; (chess piece) schlagen 9. (travel by) nehmen; **to ~ the bus** mit dem Bus fahren 10. (consume) zu sich dat nehmen; (medicine) einnehmen 11. (engage in) machen; (bath) nehmen; (exam) schreiben; (notes) sich dat machen; (pictures) machen 12. (feel) **to ~ notice of sb/sth** jdn/etw beachten; **to ~ offense** beleidigt sein 13. **I ~ it [that] ...** ich nehme an, [dass] ... 14. (order) nehmen ▶ **to ~ sb by surprise** jdn überraschen; **what do you ~ me for?** wofür hältst du mich?

◆**take aback** vt verblüffen; (shock) schockieren

◆**take along** vt mitnehmen

◆**take apart** vt auseinandernehmen

◆**take away** vt [weg]nehmen; **to ~ away sb's fear** jdm die Angst nehmen; **to ~ away ⇄ sb** jdn mitnehmen; (police) jdn abführen ▶ **to ~ sb's <u>breath</u> away** jdm den Atem verschlagen

◆**take back** vt zurücknehmen; (return) [wieder] zurückbringen; (repossess) [sich dat] zurückholen; (territory) zurückerobern; **to ~ sb back [home]** jdn nach Hause bringen

◆**take down** vt [sich dat] notieren; (particulars) aufnehmen; (remove) abnehmen; (from higher position) herunternehmen; (picture) abhängen; (tent) abschlagen; (scaffolding) abbauen

◆**take in** vt 1. hineinbringen; (person a.) hineinführen; (to police station) festnehmen; (accommodate) aufnehmen; (child) zu sich dat nehmen; (admit) aufnehmen; (university) zulassen; (deceive) hereinlegen; (understand) aufnehmen; **to be ~n in [by sb/sth]** sich [von jdm/ etw] täuschen lassen; **to ~ in a situation** eine Situation erfassen 2. (tuck)

enger machen

◆**take off I.** vt abnehmen; (clothes) ausziehen; (coat a.) ablegen; (hat) absetzen; **to ~ sth off sb** fam jdm etw wegnehmen; **he was ~n off to the hospital** er wurde ins Krankenhaus gebracht **II.** vi abheben; fam (leave) verschwinden; (flee) abhauen; (idea) ankommen; (product a.) einschlagen

◆**take on** vt auf sich akk nehmen; (job) annehmen; (employ) einstellen; (load) laden; (passengers) aufnehmen

◆**take out** vt herausbringen; (trash) hinausbringen; (invite) ausführen; (insurance) abschließen; (loan) aufnehmen; (money) abheben; sl (kill) beseitigen; (destroy) vernichten; **to ~ sb out to dinner** jdn zum Abendessen einladen

◆**take over I.** vt übernehmen; fig in Beschlag nehmen; (power) ergreifen **II.** vi **to ~ over [from sb]** jdn ablösen; **the night shift ~s over at 10 p.m.** die Nachtschicht übernimmt um 22.00 Uhr

◆**take to** vi **1.** (like) **to ~ to sb/sth** an jdm/etw Gefallen finden **2. to ~ to drink** anfangen, zu trinken; **to ~ to doing sth** anfangen, etw zu tun ▶ **to ~ to sth like a duck to water** bei etw dat gleich in seinem Element sein

◆**take up I.** vt hinaufbringen; (carpet) herausreißen; (skirt) kürzen; (start doing) anfangen; (job) antreten; (accept) annehmen; (opportunity) wahrnehmen; **my job ~s up all my time** mein Beruf frisst meine ganze Zeit auf; **to ~ sth up with sb** etw mit jdm erörtern; **to ~ up a point** einen Punkt aufgreifen; **to ~ up space** Raum einnehmen **II.** vi **to ~ up with sb** sich mit jdm einlassen

taken ['teɪ·kən] **I.** vt, vi pp of **take** **II.** adj **to be ~ with sb/sth** von jdm/ etw angetan sein

'**takeoff** n Start m; sport Absprungstelle f; **to be ready for ~** startklar sein

'**take-out** n Imbissbude f; (food) Essen nt zum Mitnehmen

'**takeover** n Übernahme f

taker ['teɪ·kər] n Wettende(r) f(m); (at sale) Interessent(in) m(f); (buyer) Käufer(in) m(f); **any ~s?** wer nimmt die

Wette an?

taking ['teɪ·kɪŋ] n **-s** pl Einnahmen pl ▶ **to be there for the ~** zum Mitnehmen sein; (not settled) [noch] offen sein

talc [tælk], **talcum** (**powder**) ['tæl·kəm-(pau·dər)] n Talkpuder m; (perfumed) Körperpuder m

tale [teɪl] n Geschichte f; lit Erzählung f; (true story) Bericht m; **fairy ~** Märchen nt; **tall ~** [Lügen]märchen nt ▶ **to live to tell the ~** fam überleben

talent ['tæl·ənt] n Talent nt

talented ['tæl·ən·tɪd] adj begabt

Taliban ['tæ·li·bæn] n Taliban f

talisman <pl -s> ['tæl·ɪs·mən] n Talisman m

talk [tɔk] **I.** n Gespräch nt; (conversation) Unterhaltung f; (private) Unterredung f; (lecture) Vortrag m; (things said) Worte pl; **to have a ~ with sb** mit jdm reden; (conversation) sich mit jdm unterhalten; **idle ~** leeres Gerede **II.** vi reden; (converse) sich unterhalten; **to ~ to sb on the phone** mit jdm telefonieren ▶ **look who's ~ing** fam du hast es gerade nötig, etwas zu sagen **III.** vt fam **to ~ politics** über Politik sprechen ▶ **to ~ about ...** so was von ... fam

◆**talk around I.** vt **to ~ sb around** jdn überreden **II.** vi **to ~ around sth** um etw akk herumreden

◆**talk back** vi eine freche Antwort geben; **don't ~ back!** keine Widerrede!

◆**talk down** vi **to ~ down to sb** mit jdm herablassend reden

◆**talk out** vt **to ~ one's way out of sth** sich aus etw dat herausreden; **to ~ sb out of [doing] sth** jdm ausreden, etw zu tun

◆**talk over** vt durchsprechen

◆**talk through** vt durchsprechen; **to ~ sb through sth** jdm bei etw dat gut zureden

talkative ['tɔ·kə·tɪv] adj gesprächig

talking ['tɔk·ɪŋ] **I.** adj sprechend **II.** n Sprechen nt; **"no ~, please!"** „Ruhe bitte!"

'**talk show** n Talkshow f

tall [tɔl] adj hoch; (person) groß; (price) ziemlich hoch; **to grow ~** groß werden

tally <-ie-> ['tæl·i] **I.** *vi* übereinstimmen **II.** *vt* **1.** to ~ sth ⇄ [up] etw zusammenzählen **2.** (*check off*) nachzählen; (*score*) notieren **III.** *n usu sing* Strichliste *f*; **to keep a ~** eine [Strich]liste führen

talon ['tæl·ən] *n* Klaue *f*

tambourine [ˌtæm·bə·'rin] *n* Tamburin *nt*

tame [teɪm] **I.** *adj* zahm; (*harmless*) friedlich; (*book, joke*) lahm **II.** *vt* zähmen; (*anger*) bezähmen; (*impatience*) zügeln

tamper ['tæm·pər] *vi* to ~ **with sth** etw [in betrügerischer Absicht] verändern

tampon ['tæm·pɑn] *n* Tampon *m*

tan [tæn] **I.** *vi* <-nn-> braun werden **II.** *vt* <-nn-> bräunen; (*leather*) gerben; **to be ~ned** braun gebrannt sein **III.** *n* [Sonnen]bräune *f*; (*color*) Gelbbraun *nt* **IV.** *adj* gelbbraun

tandem ['tæn·dəm] *n* Tandem *nt*

tang [tæŋ] *n* [scharfer] Geruch; (*taste*) [scharfer] Geschmack

tangent ['tæn·dʒənt] *n* ▶ to **fly off on a ~** [plötzlich] das Thema wechseln

tangerine [ˌtæn·dʒə·'rin] *n* Mandarine *f*

tangible ['tæn·dʒə·bəl] *adj* fassbar; (*real*) real; (*advantage*) echt; (*evidence*) handfest

tangle ['tæŋ·gəl] **I.** *n* [wirres] Knäuel; (*of wires*) Gewirr *nt*; (*confusion*) Durcheinander *nt*; **to get into a ~** sich verfangen **II.** *vt* durcheinanderbringen; (*threads*) verwickeln **III.** *vi* verfilzen; (*wires*) sich verwickeln

tangle up I. *vt* durcheinanderbringen **II.** *vi* verfilzen; (*wires*) sich *akk* verwickeln

tango ['tæŋ·goʊ] **I.** *n* Tango *m* **II.** *vi* Tango tanzen

tangy ['tæŋ·i] *adj* scharf; (*smell*) durchdringend

tank [tæŋk] *n* Tank *m*; MIL Panzer *m*; *fish* ~ Aquarium *nt*

tanker ['tæŋ·kər] *n* Tanker *m*; (*truck*) Tankwagen *m*

tanned [tænd] *adj* braun [gebrannt]; (*leather*) gegerbt

'tanning bed *n* Sonnenbank *f*

tantalize ['tæn·tə·laɪz] **I.** *vt* reizen; (*fascinate*) in den Bann ziehen; (*keep in*

suspense) auf die Folter spannen **II.** *vi* reizen

tantalizing ['tæn·tə·laɪ·zɪŋ] *adj* verlockend; (*smile*) verführerisch

tantamount ['tæn·tə·maʊnt] *adj* to be ~ **to sth** mit etw *dat* gleichbedeutend sein

tantrum ['tæn·trəm] *n* Wutanfall *m*; to **throw a ~** einen Wutanfall bekommen

Tanzania [ˌtæn·zə·'ni·ə] *n* Tansania *nt*

tap¹ [tæp] **I.** *n* **1.** (*leichter*) Schlag **2.** (*dancing*) Stepp[tanz] *m* **II.** *vt* <-pp-> [leicht] klopfen; **to ~ sb on the shoulder** jdm auf die Schulter tippen **III.** *vi* <-pp-> [leicht] klopfen

tap² [tæp] **I.** *n* **1.** Hahn *m*; **to be on ~** *fig* [sofort] verfügbar sein **2.** TELEC Abhörgerät *nt* **II.** *vt* <-pp-> **1.** (*intercept*) abhören **2.** (*energy*) erschließen **3.** (*drain*) [ab]zapfen; (*barrel*) anstechen; (*beer*) zapfen **III.** *vi fam* to ~ **into new markets** neue Märkte erschließen

'tap dance I. *n* Stepptanz *m* **II.** *vi* steppen

tape [teɪp] **I.** *n* Band *nt*; SPORT (*at finish*) Zielband *nt*; (*for measuring*) Maßband *nt*; (*adhesive*) Klebeband *nt*; (*for recording*) [Ton-/Magnet]band *nt*; **audio** ~ Audiokassette *f*; **Scotch** ~® Tesafilm® *m* **II.** *vt* **1.** **she ~d a note to the door** sie heftete eine Nachricht an die Tür **2.** (*record*) aufnehmen

'tape deck *n* Tapedeck *nt*

'tape measure *n* Maßband *nt*

taper ['teɪ·pər] *vi* sich verjüngen

taper off *vi* sich verjüngen; (*decrease*) [allmählich] abnehmen; (*interest*) nachlassen

'tape recorder *n* Tonbandgerät *nt*

tapestry ['tæp·əs·tri] *n* Gobelin *m*

'tapeworm *n* Bandwurm *m*

'tap water *n* Leitungswasser *nt*

tar [tɑr] **I.** *n* Teer *m* **II.** *vt* <-rr-> teeren ▶ **to be ~red with the same brush** um kein Haar besser sein

tarantula [tə·'ræn·tʃə·lə] *n* Tarantel *f*

tardy ['tɑr·di] *adj* unpünktlich; (*overdue*) verspätet; (*sluggish*) langsam; (*progress*) schleppend

target ['tɑr·gɪt] **I.** *n* **1.** Ziel *nt*; **to hit the ~** ins Schwarze treffen; **to be on ~** auf [Ziel]kurs liegen; (*analysis*) zutreffen

2. (goal) Zielsetzung f; **to be on ~** im Zeitplan liegen **II.** vt <-t-> [ab]zielen **III.** adj Ziel-; (profit) angestrebt

target practice n Übungsschießen nt

tarnish ['tɑr·nɪʃ] **I.** vi stumpf werden; (discolor) anlaufen; fig (lose shine) an Glanz verlieren; (honor) beschmutzt werden **II.** vt trüben; (discolor) anlaufen lassen; fig den Glanz nehmen; (reputation) beflecken **III.** n Belag m; fig Makel m

tarpaulin [tɑr·ˈpɔ·lɪn] n [Abdeck]plane f

tarragon ['tær·ə·gən] n Estragon m

tart¹ [tɑrt] adj scharf; (sour) sauer; (irony) beißend; (remark) bissig

tart² [tɑrt] n (Obst)törtchen nt; usu pej (whore) Schlampe f; **jam ~** Marmeladentörtchen nt

Tartar ['tɑr·tər] n Tatar(in) m(f); (language) Tatarisch nt

task [tæsk] n Aufgabe f **▶ to take sb to ~** jdn zur Rede stellen

task force n Arbeitsgruppe f; MIL Eingreiftruppe f; (police) Spezialeinheit f

Tasmania [tæz·ˈmeɪ·ni·ə] n Tasmanien nt

Tasmanian [tæz·ˈmeɪ·ni·ən] **I.** n Tasmanier(in) m(f) **II.** adj tasmanisch

tassel ['tæs·əl] n Quaste f

taste [teɪst] **I.** n Geschmack m; (liking) Vorliebe f; (encounter) Kostprobe f; **sense of ~** Geschmackssinn m; **to acquire a ~ for sth** etw dat Geschmack finden; **to have a ~ of sth** einen Vorgeschmack von etw dat bekommen **II.** vt schmecken; (test) probieren; (success) [einmal] erleben **III.** vi schmecken; **to ~ sweet** süß schmecken

tasteful ['teɪst·fəl] adj geschmackvoll

tasteless ['teɪst·lɪs] adj geschmacksneutral; (unappetizing) fad[e]; (beer) schal; (offensive) geschmacklos

tasty ['teɪ·sti] adj schmackhaft

tatter ['tæ·tər] n usu pl Fetzen m; **to be in ~s** zerfetzt sein; fig (reputation) ruiniert sein

tattered ['tæt·ərd] adj zerlumpt; (flag) zerrissen; (reputation) ramponiert

tattoo [tæ·ˈtu] **I.** n Tattoo m o nt **II.** vt tätowieren

taught [tɔt] pt, pp of **teach**

taunt [tɔnt] **I.** vt verspotten; (provoke) sticheln **II.** n spöttische Bemerkung; (tease) Hänselei f; (provocation) Stichelei f

Taurus ['tɔr·əs] n ASTROL Stier m

taut [tɔt] adj straff [gespannt]; (muscle) gespannt; (rubber band) stramm; (face) angespannt

tax [tæks] **I.** n <pl -es> Steuer f; (burden) Belastung f; (on resources) Beanspruchung f; **income ~** Einkommensteuer f; **to impose a ~ on sth** etw besteuern **II.** vt besteuern; (burden) belasten; (make demands) beanspruchen; (confront) beschuldigen; **to be ~ed [heavily]** [hoch] besteuert werden

taxable ['tæk·sə·bəl] adj steuerpflichtig

taxation [tæk·ˈseɪ·ʃən] n Besteuerung f; (money) Steuereinnahmen pl

'tax collector n Steuerbeamte(r), -beamtin m, f

tax-ded'uctible adj steuerlich absetzbar

'tax dodger n fam, **'tax evader** n Steuerhinterzieher(in) m(f)

'tax evasion n Steuerhinterziehung f

'tax-exempt adj von der Mehrwertsteuer befreit

tax-'free adj steuerfrei

taxi ['tæk·si] n Taxi nt

taxidermist ['tæk·sɪ·ˌdɜr·mɪst] n [Tier]präparator(in) m(f)

taxidermy ['tæk·sɪ·ˌdɜr·mi] n Taxidermie f

'taxi driver n Taxifahrer(in) m(f)

taxing ['tæk·sɪŋ] adj anstrengend; (hard) schwierig

'taxi stand n Taxistand m

'taxman n Finanzbeamte(r), -beamtin m, f; **the ~** das Finanzamt

'taxpayer n Steuerzahler(in) m(f)

'tax return n Steuererklärung f

TB [ˌti·ˈbi] n abbr of **tuberculosis** TB

tbsp. <pl -> n abbr of **tablespoon** EL

tea [ti] n Tee m

'tea bag n Teebeutel m

teach <taught, taught> [titʃ] **I.** vt **1.** unterrichten; **to ~ sb sth** [or sth to sb] jdm etw beibringen; **to ~ school** Lehrer(in) m(f) sein **2. this has taught him a lot** daraus hat er viel gelernt; **to ~ sb a lesson** jdm eine Lehre erteilen **II.** vi unterrichten

teacher ['ti·tʃər] n Lehrer(in) m(f)

teaching ['ti·tʃɪŋ] I. n Unterrichten nt; (profession) Lehrberuf m II. adj Lehr-

'teacup n Teetasse f

teak [tik] n Teak[holz] nt; (tree) Teakbaum m

team [tim] I. n Mannschaft f; **research ~** Forschungsgruppe f II. vi 1. fam (gather) ein Team bilden 2. (join) sich [in eine Gruppe] einfügen
◆**team up** vi 1. ein Team bilden 2. (join) sich [in eine Gruppe] einfügen

team 'spirit n Teamgeist m

'teamwork n Teamarbeit f

'teapot n Teekanne f

tear¹ [ter] I. n Riss m II. vt <tore, torn> zerreißen; **to ~ a muscle** sich dat einen Muskelriss zuziehen III. vi <tore, torn> 1. [zer]reißen; (lining) ausreißen 2. fam (rush) **to ~ away** losrasen
◆**tear apart** vt zerreißen; (play) verreißen
◆**tear away** vt to **~ sb ⇆ away** jdn wegreißen; **to ~ oneself away** sich losreißen; **to ~ sth ⇆ away** etw abreißen
◆**tear down** vt abreißen
◆**tear off** vt abreißen; **to ~ off one's clothes** sich dat die Kleider vom Leib reißen
◆**tear out** vt ausreißen; (page) herausreißen
◆**tear up** vt zerreißen; (destroy) kaputtmachen fam; (road) aufreißen

tear² [tɪr] n Träne f

teardrop ['tɪr·drap] n Träne f

'tear gas n Tränengas nt

'tearjerker n fam Schnulze f

tease [tiz] I. n Quälgeist m fam; (playfully) neckische Person; (erotic) Aufreißer(in) m(f) II. vt aufziehen; (playfully) necken; (provoke) provozieren

teaser ['ti·zər] n neckische Person; (riddle) harte Nuss fam

'teaspoon n Teelöffel m

teat [tit] n Zitze f

technical ['tek·nɪ·kəl] adj technisch; (detailed) Fach-; **~ term** Fachausdruck m

technicality [ˌtek·nə·ˈkæl·ɪ·ti] n Formsache f; (triviality) unnötiges Detail

technician [tek·ˈnɪʃ·ən] n Techniker(in) m(f)

technique [tek·ˈnik] n Technik f; (method) Methode f

technology [tek·ˈnal·ə·dʒi] n Technologie f

teddy ['ted·i] n Teddybär m; (undergarment) Body m

'teddy bear n Teddybär m

tedious ['ti·di·əs] adj langweilig; (job a.) öde; (conversation) zäh

tedium ['ti·di·əm] n Langeweile f

tee [ti] n Tee nt
◆**tee off** I. vi abschlagen II. vt fam **to get ~d off** sauer werden fam

teeming ['tim·ɪŋ] adj überfüllt

teen [tin] n Teenager m

teenage(d) ['tin·eɪdʒ(d)] adj attr jugendlich; (person) im Teenageralter nach n

teenager ['tin·eɪ·dʒər] n Teenager m

teens [tinz] npl Jugendjahre pl

tee shirt ['ti·ʃɜrt] n T-Shirt m

teeter ['ti·tər] vi + adv/prep taumeln; **to ~ on the brink of a disaster** fig sich am Rande einer Katastrophe bewegen

teeth [tiθ] npl pl of **tooth** ▶ **in the ~ of sth** (against) angesichts einer S. gen; (despite) trotz einer S. gen

teethe [tið] vi zahnen

teetotaler [ˌti·ˈtou·təl·ər] n Abstinenzler(in) m(f)

tel. n abbr of **telephone number** Tel.

telecommunications ['tel·ɪ·kə·ˌmju·nɪ·ˈkeɪ·ʃənz] npl + sing vb Fernmeldewesen nt

telecommuting ['tel·ɪ·kə·ˌmju·tɪŋ] n Telearbeit f

telegenic [ˌtel·ə·ˈdʒen·ɪk] adj telegen

telegram ['tel·ɪ·græm] n Telegramm nt

telegraph ['tel·ɪ·græf] I. n Telegraf m II. vt telegrafieren; (inform) telegrafisch benachrichtigen

telepathic [ˌtel·ə·ˈpæθ·ɪk] adj telepathisch

telepathy [tə·ˈlep·ə·θi] n Telepathie f

telephone ['tel·ə·foun] I. n Telefon nt; **cell[ular] ~** Handy nt; **by ~** telefonisch II. vt anrufen III. vi telefonieren

'telephone book n Telefonbuch nt

'telephone booth n Telefonzelle f

'telephone call n Telefonanruf m

'telephone directory n Telefonverzeichnis nt

'telephone number n Telefonnummer f

'telephone operator n Vermittlung f

telescope ['tel·ə·skoʊp] I. n Teleskop nt II. vt ineinanderschieben III. vi sich ineinanderschieben

telescopic [ˌtel·ə·'skap·ɪk] adj Teleskop-; (powered) ausfahrbar; (ladder) ausziehbar; **~ lens** Teleobjektiv nt

televise ['tel·ə·vaɪz] vt [im Fernsehen] übertragen

television ['tel·ə·vɪʒ·ən] n Fernsehgerät nt; (broadcasting) Fernsehen nt; **on ~** im Fernsehen

'television set n Fernsehapparat m

telex ['tel·eks] n <pl -es> Telex nt

tell [tel] I. vt <told, told> sagen; (joke, story) erzählen; (discern) erkennen; (notice) [be]merken; (know) wissen; (determine) feststellen; **can you ~ me the way to the train station?** können Sie mir sagen, wie ich zum Bahnhof komme?; **to ~ a lie** lügen; **to ~ [the] time** die Uhr lesen II. vi <told, told> to ~ [on sb] jdn verraten

'tell apart vt auseinanderhalten

'tell off vt ausschimpfen

teller ['tel·ər] n Kassierer(in) m(f)

telling ['tel·ɪŋ] adj aufschlussreich

telltale ['tel·teɪl] adj verräterisch

temp [temp] fam I. n Gelegenheitsarbeiter(in) m(f) II. vi jobben fam

temp. [temp] n abbr of **temperature** Temp.

temper ['tem·pər] n usu sing Laune f; **she has a very sweet ~** sie hat ein sehr sanftes Wesen; **to be in a bad temper** wütend sein; **to lose one's ~** die Geduld verlieren

temperament ['tem·prə·mənt] n Temperament nt; **fit of ~** Temperamentsausbruch m; (angrier) Wutanfall m

temperamental [ˌtem·prə·'men·təl] adj launisch

temperate ['tem·pər·ɪt] adj gemäßigt

temperature ['tem·pər·ə·tʃər] n Temperatur f; **to have a ~** Fieber haben

tempest ['tem·pɪst] n Sturm m

temple ['tem·pəl] n Tempel m; (on head) Schläfe f

tempo <pl -s> ['tem·poʊ] n Tempo nt

temporary ['tem·pə·rer·i] adj vorüberge-

hend; (with specific limit) befristet; **~ staff** Aushilfspersonal nt

tempt [tempt] vt in Versuchung führen; (attract) reizen; **to be ~ed** schwach werden; **to ~ sb into doing sth** jdn dazu verleiten, etw zu tun ▶ **to ~ fate** das Schicksal herausfordern

temptation [temp·'teɪ·ʃən] n Versuchung f; (thing) Verlockung f

tempting ['temp·tɪŋ] adj verführerisch

ten [ten] I. adj zehn; see also **eight** II. n Zehn f; **~s of thousands** zehntausende; see also **eight**

tenant ['ten·ənt] n Mieter(in) m(f); (of leasehold) Pächter(in) m(f)

tend¹ [tend] vi **1. to ~ to[ward]** sth zu etw dat neigen; **he ~s to come early** er kommt meistens früh **2.** (be directed toward) tendieren; **to ~ upwards** eine Tendenz nach oben aufweisen

tend² [tend] vt sich kümmern

'tend to vi sich kümmern um +akk

tendency ['ten·dən·si] n Tendenz f; (inclination) Neigung f; (trend) Trend m

tender¹ ['ten·dər] adj zart; (affectionate) zärtlich; (heart) weich

tender² ['ten·dər] I. n Angebot nt II. vt **to ~ one's resignation** die Kündigung einreichen; (from office) seinen Rücktritt anbieten

tender'hearted adj weichherzig

tenderloin ['ten·dər·lɔɪn] n Lendenstück nt

tenderly ['ten·dər·li] adv zärtlich; (lovingly) liebevoll

tenderness ['ten·dər·nɪs] n Zärtlichkeit f

tendon ['ten·dən] n Sehne f

tendril ['ten·drəl] n Ranke f

tenement ['ten·ə·mənt] n heruntergekommene Mietwohnung f

Tenn. abbr of **Tennessee**

Tennessee [ˌten·ɪ·'si] n Tennessee nt

tennis ['ten·ɪs] n Tennis nt

'tennis court n Tennisplatz m

'tennis racket n Tennisschläger m

'tennis shoe n Turnschuh m

tenor ['ten·ər] n Tenor m; (voice a.) Tenorstimme f

tense [tens] I. adj angespannt; (moment) spannungsgeladen II. vt anspannen

tense up vi sich [an]spannen

tension ['ten·ʃən] n Spannung f; (of muscle) Verspannung f; (uneasiness) [An]spannung f; (strain) Spannung[en] f[pl]; **to ease the ~** die Spannungen reduzieren

tent [tent] n Zelt nt; **to pitch a ~** ein Zelt aufschlagen

tentacle ['ten·tə·kəl] n Tentakel m; (sensor) Fühler m

tenterhooks ['ten·tər·hʊks] npl ► **to be [kept] on ~** wie auf glühenden Kohlen sitzen

tenth [tenθ] I. n the ~ der Zehnte; **a ~** ein Zehntel nt II. adj attr zehnte(r, s); **to be ~** Zehnte(r, s) sein III. adv als Zehnte(r, s)

tepee ['ti·pi] n Indianerzelt nt

tepid ['tep·ɪd] adj lau[warm]; (applause) schwach

term [tɜrm] I. n 1. Semester nt; (trimester) Trimester nt; (of office) Amtszeit f; (range) Dauer f; **prison ~** Gefängnisstrafe f; **in the short ~** kurzfristig 2. (phrase) Ausdruck m; **to be on friendly ~s with sb** mit jdm auf freundschaftlichem Fuß stehen; **in no uncertain ~s** unmissverständlich II. vt bezeichnen

terminal ['tɜr·mɪ·nəl] I. adj (fatal) End-; **~ disease** tödlich verlaufende Krankheit II. n 1. Terminal m o nt; **airport ~** Flughafengebäude nt; **bus ~** Busbahnhof m 2. (in circuit) Anschluss m

terminate ['tɜr·mɪ·neɪt] I. vt beenden; (contract) aufheben; (pregnancy) abbrechen II. vi enden

termination [ˌtɜr·mɪ·'neɪ·ʃən] n Beendigung f; (of contract) Aufhebung f

terminology [ˌtɜr·mɪ·'nɑl·ə·dʒi] n Terminologie f

termite ['tɜr·maɪt] n Termite f

'term paper n UNIV Seminararbeit f

terrace ['ter·əs] I. n Terrasse f II. vt terrassenförmig anlegen

terrain [te·'reɪn] n Gelände nt

terrestrial [tə·'res·tri·əl] adj form terrestrisch geh, Erd-; (animal, plant) Land-

terrible ['ter·ə·bəl] adj schrecklich; **to look ~** schlimm aussehen; **to be a ~ nuisance** schrecklich lästig sein

terribly ['ter·ə·bli] adv schrecklich; fam (extremely) außerordentlich

terrier ['ter·i·ər] n Terrier m

terrific [tə·'rɪf·ɪk] adj fam toll fam; (great) gewaltig

terrified ['ter·ə·faɪd] adj erschrocken; (scared) verängstigt; **to be ~ of sth** [große] Angst vor etw dat haben

terrify <-ie-> ['ter·ə·faɪ] vt fürchterlich erschrecken

terrifying ['ter·ə·faɪ·ɪŋ] adj entsetzlich; (speed) Angst erregend; (experience) schrecklich

territorial [ˌter·ə·'tɔr·i·əl] adj territorial; (plant) regional begrenzt

territory ['ter·ə·tɔr·i] n Gebiet nt; POL Hoheitsgebiet nt; BIOL Revier nt; **forbidden ~** fig verbotenes Terrain; **familiar ~** fig vertrautes Gebiet ► **it comes with the ~** es gehört dazu

terror ['ter·ər] n schreckliche Angst; (political violence) Terror m; **reign of ~** Schreckensherrschaft f; **war on ~** Bekämpfung f des Terrorismus

'terror cell n Terrorzelle f

terrorism ['ter·ə·rɪz·əm] n Terrorismus m; **act of ~** Terroranschlag m

terrorist ['ter·ə·rɪst] I. n Terrorist(in) m(f) II. adj attr terroristisch; **~ attack** Terroranschlag m

terrorize ['ter·ə·raɪz] vt in Angst und Schrecken versetzen; (bully) terrorisieren

'terror-stricken, 'terror-struck adj starr vor Schreck nach n

terse [tɜrs] adj kurz und bündig; (reply) kurz

test [test] I. n Test m; SCH Klassenarbeit f; UNIV Klausur f; (challenge) Herausforderung f; **blood ~** Blutuntersuchung f; **driving ~** Fahrprüfung f; **to pass/fail a ~** eine Prüfung bestehen/nicht bestehen; **to put sb/sth to the ~** etw/jdn auf die Probe stellen ► **to stand the ~ of time** die Zeit überdauern II. vt testen; (by touching) prüfen; (by tasting) probieren; (examine) untersuchen; (performance) überprüfen III. vi einen Test machen

testament ['tes·tə·mənt] n Testament nt; **the New/Old T~** das Neue/Alte Testament

'test drive n Probefahrt f

tester ['tes·tər] n Prüfer(in) m(f); (machine) Prüfgerät nt

testicle ['tes·tɪ·kəl] n Hoden m

testify <-ie-> ['tes·tɪ·faɪ] vi (als Zeuge/Zeugin) aussagen; **to ~ to sth** etw bezeugen; fig von etw dat zeugen geh

testimonial [ˌtes·tɪ·'moʊ·ni·əl] n Bestätigung f; (tribute) Ehrengabe f

testimony ['tes·tɪ·moʊ·ni] n [Zeugen]aussage f; (proof) Beweis m

testing ['tes·tɪŋ] n Testen m

'test tube n Reagenzglas nt

testy ['tes·ti] adj leicht reizbar; (answer) gereizt

tetanus ['tet·ə·nəs] n Tetanus m

tether ['teθ·ər] I. n (Halte)seil nt ▸ **to be at the <u>end</u> of one's ~** am Ende seiner Kräfte sein II. vt anbinden

Tex. abbr of **Texas**

Texan ['tek·sən] I. n Texaner(in) m(f) II. adj texanisch

Texas ['tek·səs] n Texas nt

text [tekst] I. n Text m; (of document) Inhalt m; (writings) Schrift f; (textbook) Lehrbuch nt; ~ **message** SMS f II. vt **to ~ [sb] sth** [jdm] eine SMS[-Nachricht] senden

textbook I. n Lehrbuch nt II. adj attr Parade-; ~ **landing** Bilderbuchlandung f

textile ['teks·taɪl] n Stoff m; ~**s** pl Textilien pl

'text message n SMS f

texture ['teks·tʃər] n Struktur f; (of surface) [Oberflächen]beschaffenheit f; (consistency) Konsistenz f

Thai [taɪ] I. n Thai m o f, Thailänder(in) m(f); (language) Thai nt II. adj thailändisch

Thailand ['taɪ·lənd] n Thailand nt

Thames [temz] n Themse f

than [ðən] I. prep bigger ~ größer als; rather ~ anstatt +gen; other ~ außer +dat; other ~ that, ... abgesehen davon, ... II. conj als

thank [θæŋk] vt **to ~ sb** jdm danken; ~ **you [very much]!** danke [sehr]!; no/yes, ~ **you** nein, danke/ja, bitte ▸ **thank <u>goodness</u>!** Gott sei Dank!

thankful ['θæŋk·fəl] adj dankbar; (pleased) froh

thankfully ['θæŋk·fəl·i] adv glücklicherweise; (gratefully) dankbar

thankless ['θæŋk·lɪs] adj undankbar

thanks [θæŋks] npl Dank m; (thank you) danke; **many ~!** vielen Dank!; **to express one's ~** seinen Dank zum Ausdruck bringen geh

thanksgiving [ˌθæŋks·'gɪv·ɪŋ] n Dankbarkeit f; **prayer of ~** Dankgebet nt; **T~** Thanksgiving nt (amerikanisches Erntedankfest)

'thank you n Danke[schön] nt

that [ðæt] I. adj dem der/die/das; **who is ~ girl?** wer ist das Mädchen? II. pron **1.** dem ~**'s a good idea** das ist eine gute Idee; ~**'s why** deshalb **2.** dem, after prep **after/before** ~ danach/davor; **like ~** (in such a way) so; (of such a kind) derartig; fam (effortlessly) einfach so **3.** dem ~**'s it!** jetzt reicht's!; **I won't agree to it and** ~**'s** ~ ich stimme dem nicht zu, und damit Schluss **4.** rel der/die/das; (when) als; **the year** ~ **Anna was born** das Jahr, in dem Anna geboren wurde III. conj dass; **so** ~ damit IV. adv so; **it wasn't [all]** ~ **good** so gut war es [nun] auch wieder nicht

thatched [θætʃt] adj reetgedeckt

thaw [θɔ] I. n Tauwetter nt a.fig II. vi auftauen; (ice) schmelzen III. vt **to ~ sth** ⇆ **out** etw auftauen

the [ðə, ði] I. art definite **1.** der/die/das; **it's on** ~ **table** es ist auf dem Tisch; ~ **Smiths** die Schmidts; ~ **inevitable** das Unvermeidliche; ~ **highest/longest** ... der/die/das höchste/längste ... **2.** ~ ... der/die/das ...; **Harry's Bar is** ~ **place to go** Harry's Bar ist in der Szene total in fam **3.** (with measurements) pro; **sold by** ~ **liter** literweise verkauft **II.** adv + comp **all** ~ **better/worse** umso besser/schlechter; ~ **colder it got,** ~ **more she shivered** je kälter es wurde, desto mehr zitterte sie

theater ['θi·ə·tər] n Theater nt; **movie** ~ Kino nt; MIL Schauplatz m; **to go to the** ~ ins Kino/Theater gehen

theatergoer n Theaterbesucher(in) m(f)

theatrical [θɪ·'æt·rɪ·kəl] adj Theater-; (exaggerated) theatralisch; ~ **agent** Theateragent(in) m(f)

theft [θeft] n Diebstahl m

their [ðer] adj poss ihr(e); **the children brushed ~ teeth** die Kinder putzten sich die Zähne; **has everybody got ~ passport?** hat jeder seinen Pass dabei?

theirs [ðerz] pron ihr(e, es); **they think everything is ~** sie glauben, dass ihnen alles gehört; **a favorite game of ~** eins ihrer Lieblingsspiele

them [ðem] pron pers sie in akk, ihnen in dat; (him/her) ihm/ihr in dat, ihn/sie in akk; **we want to show every customer that we appreciate ~** wir wollen jedem Kunden zeigen, wie sehr wir ihn schätzen

theme [θim] n Thema nt; (music) Melodie f

'theme music n Titelmusik f

themselves [ðəm·'selvz] pron refl **the children behaved ~ [very well]** die Kinder benahmen sich [sehr gut]; **they tried it for ~** sie versuchten es selbst; **everyone who considers ~ a race car driver** jeder, der sich selbst für einen Rennfahrer hält

then [ðen] adv damals; (after that) dann; **before ~** davor; **by/until ~** bis dahin; **but ~** aber schließlich

theological [ˌθi·ə·'lɑdʒ·ɪ·kəl] adj Theologie-

theology [θɪ·'al·ə·dʒi] n Glaubenslehre f; (study) Theologie f

theorem ['θi·ər·əm] n Lehrsatz m

theoretical [ˌθi·ə·'reṭ·ɪ·kəl] adj theoretisch

theorize ['θi·ə·raɪz] vi Theorien aufstellen

theory ['θi·ə·ri] n Theorie f; **in ~** theoretisch

therapeutic [ˌθer·ə·'pju·ṭɪk] adj therapeutisch; (beneficial) gesundheitsfördernd

therapist ['θer·ə·pɪst] n Therapeut(in) m(f)

therapy ['θer·ə·pi] n Therapie f

there [ðer] I. adv 1. dort; (to place) dorthin; **~'s that book you were looking for** hier ist das Buch, das du gesucht hast; **the museum is closed today — we'll go ~ tomorrow** das Museum ist heute zu — wir gehen morgen hin; **here and ~** hier und da; **in/up ~** drin[nen]/oben; **to get ~** hinkommen; fig (succeed) es schaffen; (understand)

es verstehen **2. ~ are lives at stake** es stehen Leben auf dem Spiel; **~ goes my raise** das war's dann wohl mit meiner Gehaltserhöhung; **~'s a good dog** braver Hund; **~ comes a point where ...** es kommt der Punkt, an dem .. ▶ **been ~, done that** fam kalter Kaffee; **~ you have it** na siehst du II. inter schau!; (expressing satisfaction) na bitte!; **~, ~!** schon gut!

'thereby adv dadurch

therefore ['ðer·fɔr] adv deshalb

thermal ['θɜr·məl] I. n **~s** pl Thermounterwäsche f II. adj attr Thermal-

thermal 'underwear n Thermounterwäsche f

thermometer [θər·'mam·ə·ṭər] n Thermometer nt

Thermos®, Thermos® bottle ['θɜr·məs-] n Thermosflasche f

thermostat ['θɜr·mə·stæt] n Thermostat m

thesaurus <pl -es> [θɪ·'sɔr·əs] n Synonymwörterbuch nt

these [ðiz] I. adj pl of **this** II. pron dem pl of **this** diese; **are ~ your bags?** sind das hier deine Taschen?; **~ are my kids** das sind meine Kinder; **~ here** die da

thesis <pl -ses> ['θi·sɪs] n wissenschaftliche Arbeit; (for diploma) Diplomarbeit f, (for master's degree) Magisterarbeit f

they [ðeɪ] pron pers sie; (he/she) er/sie; **where are my glasses? ~'re gone!** wo ist meine Brille? sie ist weg!; **ask a friend if ~ can help** frag einen Freund, ob er helfen kann; **~ say ...** es heißt, ...

they'll [ðeɪl] = **they will** see **will**[1]

they're [ðer] = **they are** see **be**

they've [ðeɪv] = **they have** see **have** I, II

thick [θɪk] I. adj dick; (viscous a.) zähflüssig; (dense) dicht; (hair a.) voll ▶ **to have ~ skin** ein dickes Fell haben II. n fam **in the ~ of sth** mitten[drin] in etw dat III. adv **the snow lay ~ on the path** auf dem Weg lag eine dicke Schneedecke ▶ **the complaints were coming ~ and fast** es hagelte Beschwerden; **to lay it on ~** dick auftragen

thicken ['θɪk·ən] I. vt eindicken II. vi dick[er] werden; (denser) dicht[er] werden

thicket ['θɪk·ɪt] n Dickicht nt

thickness [ˈθɪk·nɪs] *n* Dicke *f;* (*denseness*) Dichte *f*

thick-skinned *adj* dickhäutig

thief <*pl* **thieves**> [θiːf] *n* Dieb(in) *m(f)*

thigh [θaɪ] *n* (Ober)schenkel *m*

thimble [ˈθɪm·bəl] *n* Fingerhut *m*

thin <-nn-> [θɪn] **I.** *adj* dünn; (*line*) fein; (*too slim*) hager; (*fog*) leicht; (*crowd*) klein; (*fluid*) dünn[flüssig]; (*feeble*) schwach; (*disguise*) dürftig; (*excuse*) fadenscheinig ▶ **to disappear into ~ air** sich in Luft auflösen; **to be on ~ ice** sich auf dünnem Eis bewegen **II.** *vt* verdünnen; (*less dense*) ausdünnen

thing [θɪŋ] *n* Ding *nt;* (*unspecified*) Sache *f;* (*matter a.*) Thema *nt;* **one ~ leads to another** das eine führt zum anderen; **sure ~!** na klar!; **you lucky ~!** du Glückliche(r)!; [**the**] **poor ~** der/die Ärmste; (*child*) das arme Ding; **to know a ~ or two** eine ganze Menge wissen; **to be not sb's ~** nicht jds Ding *nt* sein *fam;* **the whole ~** das Ganze; **to do one's own ~** *fam* seinen [eigenen] Weg gehen; **just the ~** *fam* genau das Richtige; **~s** *pl* (*possessions*) Besitz *m;* (*specific*) Sachen *pl;* **swimming ~s** Schwimmzeug *nt* ▶ **to be just one of those ~s** (*unavoidable*) einfach unvermeidlich sein; (*typical*) typisch sein; **to be onto a good ~** *fam* etwas Gutes auftun

think [θɪŋk] **I.** *vi* <thought, thought> **1.** denken; (*reflect*) überlegen; **to ~ better of sth** sich *dat* etw anders überlegen; **yes, I ~ so** ich glaube schon; **not everybody ~s like you** nicht jeder denkt wie du; **I thought as much!** das habe ich mir schon gedacht!; **to ~ highly of sb/sth** viel von jdm/etw halten; **to ~ of doing sth** erwägen, etw zu tun **2.** (*come up with*) **to ~ of sth** sich *dat* etw ausdenken; **to ~ of a solution** auf eine Lösung kommen ▶ **I can't hear myself ~!** ich kann mein eigenes Wort nicht mehr verstehen! **II.** *vt* <thought, thought> **to ~ the world of sb/sth** große Stücke auf jdn/etw halten; **who do you ~ you are?** für wen hältst du dich eigentlich?; **to ~ to do sth** daran denken, etw zu tun **III.** *n fam* **to give**

sth a ~ sich *dat* etw überlegen

◆**think about** *vi* **to ~ about sth** über etw *akk* denken; (*reflect*) über etw *akk* nachdenken; (*consider*) sich *dat* etw überlegen

◆**think ahead** *vi* vorausdenken; (*be foresighted*) sehr vorausschauend sein

◆**think back** *vi* zurückdenken

◆**think over** *vt* überdenken; **I'll ~ it over** ich überleg's mir noch mal

◆**think through** *vt* [gründlich] durchdenken

◆**think up** *vt fam* sich *dat* ausdenken

thinker [ˈθɪŋ·kər] *n* Denker(in) *m(f)*

thinking [ˈθɪŋ·kɪŋ] **I.** *n* Denken *nt;* (*reasoning*) Überlegung *f;* **good ~!** gut gedacht!; **to do some ~ about sth** sich *dat* über etw *akk* Gedanken machen **II.** *adj attr* denkend

'think tank *n* Expertenkommission *f*

thinner [ˈθɪn·ər] **I.** *n* Verdünnungsmittel *nt;* **paint ~** Farbverdünner *m* **II.** *adj comp of* **thin**

thin-'skinned *adj* sensibel

third [θɜrd] **I.** *n* Dritte(r, s); (*fraction*) Drittel *nt;* (*gear*) dritter Gang; **the ~ of September** der dritte September **II.** *adj* dritte(r, s); **~ best** drittbeste(r, s)

third de'gree *n* Polizeimaßnahme *f (zur Erzwingung eines Geständnisses);* **to give sb the ~** *fam* jdn in die Mangel nehmen

third 'party *n* Dritte(r) *f(m)*

Third 'World *n* **the ~** die Dritte Welt; **~ country** Drittweltland *nt*

thirst [θɜrst] *n* Durst *m;* (*desire*) Verlangen *nt;* **to die of ~** verdursten; **~ for knowledge** Wissensdurst *m*

thirsty [ˈθɜr·sti] *adj* durstig; **to be ~** Durst haben; **to be ~ for sth** nach etw *dat* hungern

thirteen [θɜrˈtin] **I.** *n* Dreizehn *f; see also* **eight** **II.** *adj* dreizehn; *see also* **eight**

thirteenth [θɜrˈtinθ] **I.** *n* **1. the ~** der/die/das Dreizehnte; (*date*) der Dreizehnte; *see also* **eighth 2.** (*fraction*) Dreizehntel *nt; see also* **eighth II.** *adj* dreizehnte(r, s); *see also* **eighth III.** *adv* als Dreizehnte(r, s); *see also* **eighth**

thirtieth [ˈθɜr·ti·əθ] **I.** *n* Dreißigste(r, s); (*fraction*) Dreißigstel *nt;* **the ~** (*date*)

T

der Dreißigste; *see also* **eighth** **II.** *adj* dreißigste(r, s); *see also* **eighth** **III.** *adv* als Dreißigste(r, s); *see also* **eighth**

thirty ['θɜr·ti] **I.** *n* Dreißig *f;* **the thirties** *pl* die dreißiger Jahre; **to be in one's thirties** in den Dreißigern sein; *see also* **eight** **II.** *adj* dreißig; *see also* **eight**

this [ðɪs] **I.** *adj attr* diese(r, s); ~ **minute** sofort; **by ~ time** dann **II.** *pron is ~ your bag?** ist das deine Tasche?; ~ **is my husband Steve** das ist mein Ehemann Steve; **what's ~?** was soll das?; ~ **is what I was talking about** davon spreche ich ja; **every time I do ~, it hurts** jedes Mal, wenn ich das mache, tut es weh; **like ~** so ▸ so; **and that** *fam* dies und das **III.** *adv so* so; ~ **far and no further** bis hierher und nicht weiter

thistle ['θɪs·əl] *n* Distel *f*

thong [θaŋ] *n* Lederband *nt;* (*G-string*) Tanga *m;* ~**s** *pl* (*flip-flop*) Flip-Flops *pl*

thorn [θɔrn] *n* Dorn *m*

thorny ['θɔr·ni] *adj* dornig; (*difficult*) schwierig; (*issue*) heikel

thorough ['θɜr·oʊ] *adj* genau; (*careful*) sorgfältig; (*reform*) durchgreifend

thoroughbred **I.** *n* Vollblut[pferd] *nt* **II.** *adj* reinrassig

thoroughly ['θɜr·oʊ·li] *adv* genau; (*completely*) völlig; (*enjoy*) ausgiebig

thoroughness ['θɜr·oʊ·nɪs] *n* Sorgfältigkeit *f*

those [ðoʊz] **I.** *adj det pl of* **that**; **how much are ~ brushes?** wie viel kosten die Bürsten da?; **I like ~ cookies with the almonds** ich mag die Kekse mit den Mandeln **II.** *pron pl of* **that**; **these peaches aren't ripe — try ~ on the table** diese Pfirsiche sind noch nicht reif, versuch die auf dem Tisch; ~ **are my kids over there** das sind meine Kinder da drüben; ~ **who ...** diejenigen, die ...; **one of ~** eine(r) davon

though [ðoʊ] **I.** *conj* obwohl; (*however*) [je]doch; **as ~** als ob **II.** *adv* trotzdem

thought [θɔt] **I.** *n* Nachdenken *nt;* (*idea*) Gedanke *m;* **to be deep in ~** tief in Gedanken versunken sein; **to give sb some ~** sich *dat* Gedanken über etw *akk* machen ▸ **it's the ~ that** <u>counts</u>

fam der gute Wille zählt **II.** *vt, vi pt, pp of* **think**

thoughtful ['θɔt·fəl] *adj* aufmerksam; (*contemplative*) nachdenklich; (*careful*) sorgfältig

thoughtless ['θɔt·lɪs] *adj* rücksichtslos; (*without thinking*) unüberlegt

'**thought-provoking** *adj* nachdenklich stimmend

thousand ['θaʊ·zənd] **I.** *n* Tausend *f,* **two ~** zweitausend; (*year*) [das Jahr] zweitausend; **a ~ dollars** [ein]tausend Dollar; ~**s** *Tausende pl* **II.** *adj det, attr* tausend; **I've said it a ~ times** ich habe es jetzt unzählige Male gesagt

thousandth ['θaʊ·zəntθ] **I.** *n* Tausendste(r, s); (*fraction*) Tausendstel *nt* **II.** *adj so;* tausendste(r, s); **the ~ ...** der/die/das tausendste ...; **a ~ part** ein Tausendstel *nt*

thrash [θræʃ] *vt* verprügeln; *fam* (*defeat*) haushoch schlagen

thrashing ['θræʃ·ɪŋ] *n* Prügel *pl;* **to give sb a** [**good**] ~ jdm eine [anständige] Tracht Prügel verpassen

thread [θred] **I.** *n* Garn *nt;* (*fiber*) Faden *m;* (*groove*) Gewinde *nt;* INET Thread *m* **II.** *vt* **1.** (*put through*) einfädeln; **she ~ed her way through the crowd** sie schlängelte sich durch die Menge **2.** (*put onto a string*) auffädeln

threat [θret] *n* Drohung *f;* (*risk*) Gefahr *f;* **to pose a ~ to sb/sth** eine Gefahr für jdn/etw darstellen; **to be under ~ of sth** von etw *dat* bedroht sein

threaten ['θret·ən] **I.** *vt* bedrohen; (*be danger*) gefährden; **to ~ sb with sth** jdm mit etw *dat* drohen; (*with weapon*) jdn mit etw *dat* bedrohen **II.** *vi* drohen; **to ~ to do sth** damit drohen, etw zu tun

threatening ['θret·ə·nɪŋ] *adj* drohend; (*menacing*) bedrohlich; (*clouds*) dunkel; ~ **letter** Drohbrief *m*

three [θri] **I.** *n* Drei *f;* (*quantity*) drei; (*time*) drei [Uhr]; **in ~s** in Dreiergruppen; **the ~ of diamonds** die Karodrei; **at ~ p.m.** um drei Uhr [nachmittags]; *see also* **eight** ▸ **two's company,** ~**'s a crowd** drei sind einer zu viel **II.** *adj* drei; **I'll give you ~ guesses** dreimal darfst du raten; *see also* **eight**

▶ ~ **cheers** [**for** *sb*/*sth*]! ein dreifaches Hoch [auf jdn/etw]!

three-'D *adj fam,* **three-di'mensional** *adj* dreidimensional

three-'quarter *adj attr* dreiviertel

three-'wheeler *n* dreirädriges Auto; (*tricycle*) Dreirad *nt*

thresh [θreʃ] *vt* dreschen

'threshing machine *n* Dreschmaschine *f*

threshold ['θreʃ·həʊld] *n* [Tür]schwelle *f*; *fig* Anfang *m*; (*limit*) Grenze *f*; **pain** ~ Schmerzgrenze *f*

threw [θruː] *pt of* **throw**

thrift [θrɪft] *n* Sparsamkeit *f*

'thrift shop, **'thrift store** *n* Laden, in dem gespendete, meist gebrauchte Waren verkauft werden, um Geld für wohltätige Zwecke zu sammeln

thrifty ['θrɪf·ti] *adj* sparsam

thrill [θrɪl] **I.** *n* Erregung *f*; (*titillation*) Nervenkitzel *m* **II.** *vt* erregen; (*fascinate*) faszinieren; (*frighten*) Angst machen; (*delight*) entzücken

thriller ['θrɪl·ər] *n* Thriller *m*

thrilling ['θrɪl·ɪŋ] *adj* aufregend; (*story*) spannend

thriving ['θraɪ·vɪŋ] *adj* (*community*) gut funktionierend

throat [θroʊt] *n* Kehle *f*; (*inside neck*) Rachen *m*; **a sore** ~ Halsschmerzen *pl*; **to cut** *sb's* ~ jdm die Kehle durchschneiden ▶ **to have a lump in one's** ~ einen Kloß im Hals haben; **to jump down** *sb's* ~ jdn anschnauzen

throb [θrab] **I.** *n* Klopfen *nt*; (*of heart*) Pochen *nt*; (*of bass*) Dröhnen *nt* **II.** *vi* <-bb-> klopfen; (*heart*) pochen; (*bass*) dröhnen; **his head was** ~**bing** er hatte rasende Kopfschmerzen

throne [θroʊn] *n* Thron *m*; REL Stuhl *m*

throng [θraŋ] **I.** *n* [Menschen]menge *f* **II.** *vt* visitors ~ed **the narrow streets** die engen Straßen wimmelten nur so von Besuchern

throttle ['θrat·əl] **I.** *n* Drosselklappe *f*; **at full** ~ mit voller Geschwindigkeit; *fig* mit Volldampf **II.** *vt* würgen; (*strangle*) erdrosseln; *fig* (*hinder*) drosseln

through [θruː] **I.** *prep* durch *+akk*; (*because of a.*) wegen *+gen*; (*during*) während *+gen*; (*by means of*) über *+akk*;

she looked ~ her mail sie sah ihre Post durch; **we're open Monday** ~ **Friday** wir haben Montag bis Freitag geöffnet; **I can't hear you** ~ **all this noise** ich kann dich bei diesem Lärm nicht verstehen; **we were cut off halfway** ~ **the conversation** unser Gespräch wurde mittendrin unterbrochen; ~ **chance** durch Zufall; **to get** ~ *sth* (*endure*) etw durchstehen **II.** *adj* **1.** *pred* (*finished*) fertig; **we're** ~ (*relationship*) mit uns ist es aus; (*job*) es ist alles erledigt **2.** *pred* (*successful*) durch; **Henry is** ~ **to the final** Henry hat sich für das Finale qualifiziert **3.** *attr* (*bus*) durchgehend **III.** *adv* **1. the train goes** ~ **to Hamburg** der Zug fährt bis nach Hamburg durch **2.** (*from beginning to end*) [ganz] durch; **to be halfway** ~ *sth* etw halb durch haben **3.** ~ **and** ~ durch und durch; **cooked** ~ durchgegart

through'out [θruː·'aʊt] **I.** *prep* **1. people** ~ **the country** Menschen im ganzen Land **2.** (*at times during*) während *+gen*; ~ **the performance** die ganze Vorstellung über **II.** *adv* vollständig; (*the whole time*) die ganze Zeit [über]

throw [θroʊ] **I.** *n* Wurf *m*; **a stone's** ~ [**away**] *fig* nur einen Steinwurf von hier **II.** *vi* <threw, thrown> werfen **III.** *vt* <threw, thrown> **1.** werfen; (*hurl*) schleudern; (*wrestler*) zu Fall bringen; (*rider*) abwerfen; (*direct*) zuwerfen; **to** ~ **a fit/tantrum** *fam* einen Anfall/Wutanfall bekommen; **to** ~ **a party** eine Party geben; **to** ~ **a punch at** *sb* jdm einen Schlag versetzen; **to** ~ *sb sth* [*or sth to sb*] jdm etw zuwerfen; **to** ~ **oneself onto** *sb*/*sth* sich auf jdn stürzen/auf etw *akk* werfen; **to** ~ **oneself at** *sb* (*embrace*) sich jdm an den Hals werfen; (*attack*) sich auf jdn stürzen; **to** ~ *sth* **against** *sth* etw gegen etw *akk* schleudern **2.** *fam* (*confuse*) **to** ~ *sb* [**off**] jdn durcheinanderbringen ▶ **to** ~ **caution to the wind** eine Warnung in den Wind schlagen

◆**throw away** *vt* wegwerfen; **to** ~ **money away on** *sth* Geld für etw *akk* zum Fenster hinauswerfen

◆**throw back** *vt* nach hinten werfen;

T

(*curtains*) aufreißen ▶ **to ~ sth back in sb's face** jdm etw wieder auftischen
◆**throw off** *vt* herunterreißen; (*clothes*) schnell ausziehen; **to ~ oneself off sth** sich von etw *dat* hinunterstürzen; **to ~ sb ⇌ off** (*escape*) jdn abschütteln; (*fluster*) jdn aus dem Konzept bringen
◆**throw on** *vt* **1. ~ a log on the fire, will you?** legst du bitte noch einen Scheit aufs Feuer?; **to ~ oneself on sb** sich auf jdn stürzen **2.** (*clothes*) eilig anziehen **3. to ~ suspicion on sb** den Verdacht auf jdn lenken
◆**throw out** *vt* hinauswerfen; (*discard*) wegwerfen; (*dismiss*) entlassen; (*player*) vom Platz stellen; (*lawsuit*) abweisen
◆**throw up I.** *vt* hochwerfen; (*hands*) hochreißen; *fam* (*vomit*) erbrechen **II.** *vi fam* sich übergeben

throwaway ['θrou·ə·wei] *adj attr* wegwerfbar; (*unimportant*) achtlos dahingeworfen *attr*; ~ **razor** Einwegrasierer *m*
thrown [θroun] *pp of* **throw**
thru [θru] *prep, adv fam see* **through**
thrush <*pl* -es> [θrʌʃ] *n* Drossel *f*
thrust [θrʌst] **I.** *n* Stoß *m*; (*impetus*) Stoßrichtung *f*; **the main ~ of an argument** die Hauptaussage eines Arguments **II.** *vi* <thrust, thrust> **to ~ at sb with a knife** nach jdm mit einem Messer stoßen **III.** *vt* <thrust, thrust> **to ~ money into sb's hand** jdm Geld in die Hand stecken; **to ~ sth on sb** jdm etw auferlegen; **to ~ oneself on sb** sich jdm aufdrängen
thud [θʌd] **I.** *vi* <-dd-> dumpf aufschlagen **II.** *n* dumpfer Schlag
thug [θʌg] *n* Schlägertyp *m*
thumb [θʌm] **I.** *n* Daumen *m* ▶ **to stand out like a sore ~** unangenehm auffallen **II.** *vt* **1.** *fam* **to ~ a ride** per Anhalter fahren **2.** (*book*) durchblättern **III.** *vi* **to ~ through a newspaper** durch die Zeitung blättern
thumb 'index *n* Daumenregister *nt*
'**thumbnail** *n* Daumennagel *m*
'**thumbtack** *n* Reißzwecke *f*
thump [θʌmp] **I.** *n* dumpfer Knall **II.** *vt* schlagen **III.** *vi* schlagen; (*heart*) klopfen
thunder ['θʌn·dər] **I.** *n* Donner *m*; (*loud*

sound) Getöse *nt*; **rumble of ~** Donnergrollen *nt* ▶ **to steal sb's ~** jdm die Schau stehlen **II.** *vi* donnern; (*declaim*) schreien; **to ~ by** vorbeidonnern; **to ~ about sth** sich lautstark über etw *akk* äußern **III.** *vt* brüllen
'**thunderbolt** *n* Blitzschlag *m*
'**thundercloud** *n usu pl* Gewitterwolke *f*
thundering ['θʌn·dər·ɪŋ] **I.** *n* Donnern *nt* **II.** *adj* tosend; (*voice*) dröhnend; (*enormous*) enorm; (*success a.*) riesig
thunderous ['θʌn·dər·əs] *adj attr* donnernd; ~ **applause** Beifallsstürme *pl*
'**thunderstorm** *n* Gewitter *nt*
'**thunderstruck** *adj pred* wie vom Donner gerührt
Thursday ['θɜrz·dei] *n* Donnerstag *m*; *see also* **Tuesday**
thus [ðʌs] *adv* folglich; (*in this way*) so
thwart [θwɔrt] *vt* vereiteln; (*escape*) verhindern; (*plan*) durchkreuzen
thyme [taim] *n* Thymian *m*
thyroid ['θai·rɔid] *n* Schilddrüse *f*
tiara [tɪ·ˈær·ə] *n* Tiara *f*
tibia <*pl* -biae> ['tɪb·i·ə] *n* Schienbein *nt*
tic [tɪk] *n* [nervöses] Zucken
tick¹ [tɪk] **I.** *n* Ticken *nt* **II.** *vi* ticken ▶ **what makes sb ~** was jdn bewegt
◆**tick off** *vt fam* auf die Palme bringen
tick² [tɪk] *n* ZOOL Zecke *f*
ticker-tape pa'rade *n* Konfettiparade *f*
ticket ['tɪk·ɪt] *n* Karte *f*; (*tag*) Etikett *nt*; **concert ~** Konzertkarte *f*; **lottery ~** Lottoschein *m*; **plane ~** Flugticket *nt*; **price ~** Preisschild *nt*; (*for fine*) Strafzettel *m*
'**ticket collector** *n* Schaffner(in) *m(f)*
'**ticking** ['tɪk·ɪŋ] *n* Ticken *nt*
tickle ['tɪk·əl] **I.** *vi* kitzeln **II.** *vt* kitzeln; **to ~ sb's fancy** jdn reizen *f*; **~** Jucken *nt*; **~ in one's throat** Kratzen *nt* im Hals
ticklish ['tɪk·lɪʃ] *adj* kitzlig; (*delicate*) heikel
tick-tack-toe, tic-tac-toe [ˌtɪk·ˌtæk·ˈtou] *n* Tic Tac Toe *nt*
'**tidal wave** *n* Flutwelle *f*; *fig* Flut *f*
tidbit ['tɪd·bɪt] *n* Leckerbissen *m*; **juicy ~s** *fig* pikante Einzelheiten
tiddlywinks ['tɪd·li·wɪŋks] *n pl* Flohhüpfen *nt*

tide [taɪd] *n* Gezeiten *pl;* (*opinion*) öffentliche Meinung; (*trend*) Welle *f;* the ~ has turned die Meinung ist umgeschlagen; **high** ~ Flut *f;* **low** ~ Ebbe *f;* **to swim against the** ~ gegen den Strom schwimmen

tide over *vt* **to** ~ **sb over** jdm über die Runden helfen *fam*

tidiness ['taɪ·dɪ·nɪs] *n* Ordnung *f*

tidy ['taɪ·di] **I.** *adj* ordentlich; *fam* (*sum*) beträchtlich **II.** *vt* aufräumen

tie [taɪ] **I.** *n* **1.** (*necktie*) Krawatte *f;* **bow** ~ Fliege *f* **2.** *pl* diplomatic ~s diplomatische Beziehungen; **family** ~s Familienbande *pl* **3.** **to end in a** ~ mit einem Unentschieden enden **II.** *vi* <-y-> **1.** schließen; **to** ~ **in the front/back** vorne/hinten zugebunden werden **2.** **to** ~ **with sb/sth** denselben Platz wie jd/etw belegen **III.** *vt* <-y-> **1.** fesseln; (*knot*) machen; (*necktie*) binden **2.** (*restrict*) **to be** ~d **to sth/somewhere** an etw *akk*/einen Ort gebunden sein ▸ **sb's hands are** ~d jds Hände sind gebunden

tie back *vt* zurückbinden

tie down *vt* festbinden; **to be** ~d **down** (*restricted*) gebunden sein; **to** ~ **sb down to sth** *fam* jdn auf etw *akk* festlegen

tie in *vi* **to** ~ **in with sth** mit etw *dat* übereinstimmen

tie up *vt* festbinden; (*hair*) hochbinden; (*delay*) aufhalten; (*capital*) binden; (*game*) den Ausgleich erzielen; **to be** ~d **up** (*busy*) beschäftigt sein ▸ **to** ~ **up some loose ends** etwas erledigen

tiebreaker, '**tiebreak** *n* Tie-Break *m o nt*

tier [tɪr] *n* Reihe *f;* (*level*) Lage *f;* ~ **of management** Managementebene *f*

tie-up *n* Stillstand *m*

tiff [tɪf] *n fam* Plänkelei *f;* **to have a** ~ eine Meinungsverschiedenheit haben

tiger ['taɪ·gər] *n* Tiger *m*

tight [taɪt] **I.** *adj* **1.** fest; (*clothes*) eng; (*close*) dicht; (*taut*) gespannt; (*muscles*) verspannt; (*face*) angespannt; (*severe*) streng; (*bend*) eng; (*budget*) knapp; ~ **spot** *fig* Zwickmühle *f* **2.** *pej fam* (*miserly*) knauserig ▸ **to run a** ~ **ship** ein

strenges Regime führen **II.** *adv pred* straff; (*seal*) fest; **to hang on** ~ **to sb/sth** sich an jdm/etw festklammern

tighten ['taɪ·tən] **I.** *vt* festziehen; (*rope*) festbinden; (*screw*) anziehen; (*boost*) verstärken ▸ **to** ~ **one's belt** den Gürtel enger schnallen **II.** *vi* straff werden

tight'fisted *adj pej fam* geizig

tight-'fitting *adj* eng anliegend

'**tightrope** *n* Drahtseil *nt;* ~ **walker** Seiltänzer(in) *m(f)*

tights [taɪts] *npl* (**pair of**) ~ Strumpfhose *f;* (*for dancing*) Leggings *pl*

tile [taɪl] **I.** *n* Fliese *f* **II.** *vt* fliesen

till[1] [tɪl] *prep, conj see* **until**

till[2] [tɪl] *n* Kasse *f* ▸ **to be caught with one's hand in the** ~ auf frischer Tat ertappt werden

tilt [tɪlt] **I.** *n* Neigung *f* ▸ [**at**] **full** ~ mit voller Kraft **II.** *vt* neigen; **to** ~ **the balance** einen Meinungsumschwung herbeiführen **III.** *vi* sich neigen; (*opinion*) sich ab-/zuwenden

timber ['tɪm·bər] *n* Bauholz *nt;* (*beam*) Holzplanke *f*

time [taɪm] **I.** *n* **1.** Zeit *f;* (*occasion*) Mal *nt;* MUS Takt *m;* ~ **stood still** die Zeit stand still; ~**'s up** *fam* die Zeit ist um; **it will take some** ~ es wird eine Weile dauern; ~**s are changing** die Zeiten ändern sich; **to keep** ~ den Takt halten; **as** ~ **goes by** im Lauf[e] der Zeit; **for all** ~ für immer; **to go through a difficult** ~ eine schwere Zeit durchmachen; **free** ~ Freizeit *f;* **period of** ~ Zeitraum *m;* **a long** ~ **ago** vor langer Zeit; **to be pressed for** ~ in Zeitnot sein; **to take one's** ~ sich *dat* Zeit lassen; **for the** ~ **being** vorläufig; **to tell the** ~ die Uhr lesen; **on** ~ pünktlich; **for the first** ~ zum ersten Mal; **from** ~ **to** ~ ab und zu; **three** ~**s a week** drei Mal in der Woche; **for the hundredth** ~ zum hundertsten Mal; **to be behind the** ~**s** seiner Zeit hinterherhinken; **to not have much** ~ **for sb** jdn nicht mögen; **to do** ~ *fam* [im Knast] sitzen **2.** **two** ~**s five is ten** zwei mal fünf ist zehn ▸ ~ **is of the essence** die Zeit drängt; [**only**] ~ **will tell** *saying* erst die Zukunft wird es zeigen **II.** *vt* **to** ~ **sb in the 100**

T

meters jds Zeit beim 100-Meter-Lauf nehmen; **to ~ sth** [**right**] den richtigen Zeitpunkt wählen

'**time bomb** n Zeitbombe f

'**time-consuming** adj zeitintensiv

timeless ['taɪm·lɪs] adj zeitlos; (beauty) immer während attr

time limit n Frist f

timely ['taɪm·li] adj rechtzeitig; (remark) passend; (manner) rasch

'**timeout** I. n <pl times-> SPORT Auszeit f; **to call a ~** ein Time-out nehmen II. interj Auszeit!

timer ['taɪ·mər] n Timer m; (for eggs) Eieruhr f

'**time-saving** adj Zeit sparend

'**timetable** n Fahrplan m; (for events) Programm nt; (for appointments) Zeitplan m

'**time zone** n Zeitzone f

timid <-er, -est> ['tɪm·ɪd] adj ängstlich; (shy) schüchtern; (lacking courage) zaghaft

timing ['taɪ·mɪŋ] n Timing nt; (measuring) Zeitabnahme f; (of race) Stoppen nt

tin [tɪn] n Zinn nt; (for baking) Backform f; **cake ~** Kuchenform f

tin 'can n Blechdose f

'**tinfoil** ['tɪn·fɔɪl] n Alufolie f

tinge [tɪndʒ] I. n Hauch m; (of emotion) Anflug m; **~ of red** [leichter] Rotstich II. vt usu passive **to be ~d with orange** mit Orange [leicht] getönt sein; **~d with regret** mit einer Spur von Bedauern

tingle ['tɪŋ·gəl] I. vi kribbeln; **to ~ with excitement** vor Aufregung zittern II. n Kribbeln nt

tinker ['tɪŋ·kər] vi **to ~** [**around**] [**with sth**] [an etw dat] herumbasteln

tinkle ['tɪŋ·kəl] I. vi klimpern; (bell) klingen; (fountain) plätschern; (urinate) Pipi machen II. vt **to ~ a bell** mit einer Glocke klingeln III. n Klingen nt; (of water) Plätschern nt; fam (urine) Pipi nt

tinny ['tɪn·i] adj blechern

tinsel ['tɪn·səl] n Lametta nt

tint [tɪnt] I. n Farbton m; (dye) Tönung f II. vt tönen

tiny ['taɪ·ni] adj winzig

tip¹ [tɪp] n Spitze f ▶ **it's on the ~ of my**

tongue es liegt mir auf der Zunge

tip² [tɪp] I. vt <-pp-> umkippen; (tilt) neigen; **to ~ the balance** den Ausschlag geben II. vi <-pp-> kippen

tip³ [tɪp] I. n Trinkgeld nt; (suggestion) Tipp m; **to leave a 15% ~** 15 % Trinkgeld geben II. vt <-pp-> Trinkgeld geben; (inform) einen Tipp geben III. v <-pp-> Trinkgeld geben

◆**tip off** vt einen Tipp geben

◆**tip over** vt, vi umkippen

'**tip-off** n fam Tipp m

tiptoe ['tɪp·toʊ] I. **n on ~**[**s**] auf Zehenspitzen II. vi auf Zehenspitzen gehen

tire¹ [taɪr] I. vt ermüden; **to ~ oneself doing sth** von etw dat müde werden II. vi müde werden; **to ~ of sth/sb** etw/jdn satthaben; **to never ~ of doing sth** nie müde werden, etw zu tun

tire² [taɪr] n Reifen m; **spare ~** Ersatzreifen m; fig fam Rettungsring m

tired <-er, -est> ['taɪrd] adj müde; (excuse) lahm; (phrase) abgedroschen; **to be sick and ~ of sth/sb** von etw/jdm die Nase gestrichen voll haben fam

tireless ['taɪr·lɪs] adj unermüdlich

tiresome ['taɪr·səm] adj mühsam; (habit) unangenehm

tiring ['taɪr·rɪŋ] adj ermüdend

tissue ['tɪʃ·u] n Seidenpapier nt; (for nose) Tempo® nt; BIOL Gewebe nt

tit¹ [tɪt] n (bird) Meise f ▶ **~ for tat** wie du mir, so ich dir

tit² [tɪt] n vulg, sl (breast) Titte f

title ['taɪt·əl] I. n Titel m; **job ~** Berufsbezeichnung f II. vt betiteln

'**title deed** n LAW Eigentumsurkunde f

'**title page** n Titelblatt nt

titter ['tɪt·ər] I. vi kichern II. n Gekicher nt

TN abbr of **Tennessee**

to [tu] I. prep **they go ~ work on the bus** sie fahren mit dem Bus zur Arbeit; **we moved ~ Germany last year** wir sind letztes Jahr nach Deutschland gezogen; **she goes ~ college** sie geht auf die Universität; **I've asked them ~ dinner** ich habe sie zum Essen eingeladen; **tie the leash ~ the fence** mach die Leine am Zaun fest; **I prefer beef ~ seafood** ich ziehe Rindfleisch Meeresfrüchten

vor; **and ~ this day ...** und bis auf den heutigen Tag ...; **he converted ~ Islam** er ist zum Islam übergetreten; **it's twenty ~ six** es ist zwanzig vor sechs; **here's ~ you!** auf Ihr Wohl!; **the record is dedicated ~ her mother** die Schallplatte ist ihrer Mutter gewidmet; **give that gun ~ me** gib mir das Gewehr; **to be married ~ sb** mit jdm verheiratet sein; **to tell sth ~ sb** jdm etw erzählen; **ten ~ the third power** zehn hoch drei; **the north** nördlich; **from place ~ place** von Ort zu Ort; **to point ~ sth** akk zeigen; **cheek ~ cheek** Wange an Wange **II.** *to form infin* **I'll have ~ tell him** ich werde es ihm sagen müssen; **he told me ~ wait** er sagte mir, ich solle warten; **I asked her ~ give me a call** ich bat sie, mich anzurufen; **would you like to go? — yes, I'd love ~** möchtest du hingehen? – ja, sehr gern; **I'm sorry ~ hear that** es tut mir leid, das zu hören; **I don't know what ~ do** ich weiß nicht, was ich tun soll; **to be about ~ do sth** gerade etw tun wollen; **easy ~ use** leicht zu bedienen; **~ be honest** um ehrlich zu sein **III.** *adv* zu; **to come ~** zu sich *dat* kommen

'oad [toʊd] *n* Kröte *f*

'oadstool *n* Giftpilz *m*

:oady ['toʊ·di] *pej* **I.** *n* Speichellecker *m* **II.** *vi* <-ie-> kriechen

:o and 'fro I. *adv* hin und her; *(back and forth)* vor und zurück **II.** *vi fam* **to be toing and froing** vor- und zurückgehen; *(be indecisive)* hin und her schwanken

:oast¹ [toʊst] **I.** *n* Toast *m;* **slice of ~** Scheibe *f* Toast ▶ **to be ~** *hum fam* erledigt sein *fam* **II.** *vt* toasten; *(nuts)* rösten

:oast² [toʊst] **I.** *n* Toast *m;* **to drink a ~ to sb** auf jdn trinken **II.** *vt* trinken

:oaster ['toʊ·stər] *n* Toaster *m*

:obacco [tə·'bæk·oʊ] *n* Tabak *m*

:o-be [tə·'bi] *comp* zukünftige(r, s) *attr;* **mother-~** werdende Mutter

:oboggan [tə·'bɑg·ən] **I.** *n* Schlitten *m* **II.** *vi* Schlitten fahren

:oday [tə·'deɪ] **I.** *adv* heute; *(nowadays)* heutzutage **II.** *n* heutiger Tag; **what's the date ~?** welches Datum haben wir

heute?; **cars of ~** Autos *pl* von heute

toddler ['tɑd·lər] *n* Kleinkind *nt*

to-do [tə·'du] *n usu sing fam* Getue *nt pej;* *(confrontation)* Wirbel *m;* **to make a big ~ about sth** ein großes Theater um etw *akk* machen

to-'do list *n* Besorgungsliste *f*

toe [toʊ] **I.** *n* Zehe *f;* *(of sock)* Spitze *f* ▶ **to keep sb on their ~s** jdn auf Zack halten **II.** *vt* **to ~ the party line** der Parteilinie folgen

'toehold *n* Vorteil *m*

'toenail *n* Zehennagel *m*

toffee ['tɔ·fi] *n* Toffee *nt*

together [tə·'geð·ər] **I.** *adv* zusammen; *(collectively a.)* gemeinsam; *(simultaneously)* gleichzeitig; *(close ~)* nah beisammen; **all ~ now** jetzt alle miteinander **II.** *adj fam* ausgeglichen

togetherness [tə·'geð·ər·nɪs] *n* Zusammengehörigkeit *f*

Togo ['toʊ·goʊ] *n* Togo *nt*

Togolese [ˌtoʊ·goʊ·'liz] **I.** *adj* togoisch **II.** *n* Togoer(in) *m(f)*

toilet ['tɔɪ·lɪt] *n* Toilette *f*

'toilet bowl *n* Toilettenschüssel *f*

'toilet paper *n* Toilettenpapier *nt*

toiletries ['tɔɪ·lɪ·triz] *npl* Toilettenartikel *pl*

'toilet seat *n* Toilettensitz *m*

toing and froing [ˌtu·ɪŋ·ənd·'froʊ·ɪŋ] *n* Hin und Her *nt;* *(back and forth)* Vor und Zurück *nt*

token ['toʊ·kən] **I.** *n* Zeichen *nt;* *(chip)* Chip *m* ▶ **by the same ~** aus demselben Grund **II.** *adj attr* nominell; *(fine)* symbolisch; **the ~ woman** die Alibifrau

told [toʊld] *pt, pp of* **tell**

tolerance ['tɑl·ər·əns] *n* Toleranz *f;* *(capacity a.)* Widerstandsfähigkeit *f;* **~ to alcohol** Alkoholverträglichkeit *f*

tolerant ['tɑl·ər·ənt] *adj* tolerant; *(resistant)* widerstandsfähig; *(plant)* resistent

tolerate ['tɑl·ə·reɪt] *vt* tolerieren; *(person)* ertragen; *(heat, pain)* aushalten; *(drug)* vertragen

toleration [ˌtɑl·ə·'reɪ·ʃən] *n* Toleranz *f*

toll [toʊl] *n* Maut *f;* *(for phone call)* [Fernsprech]gebühr *f;* **death ~** Opferzahl *f*

'toll bridge *n* Mautbrücke *f*

'toll-free *adj* gebührenfrei; ~ **number** gebührenfreie Telefonnummer

tomahawk ['tɑ·mə·hak] *n* Tomahawk *m*

tomato <*pl* -es> [tə·'meɪ·toʊ] *n* Tomate *f*

tomb [tum] *n* Grab *nt*; (*mausoleum*) Gruft *f*; (*below ground*) Grabkammer *f*

tombstone ['tum·stoʊn] *n* Grabstein *m*

tomcat ['tɑm·kæt] *n* Kater *m*

tomorrow [tə·'mɑr·oʊ] I. *adv* morgen II. *n* der morgige Tag; ~'s **problems** Probleme *pl* von morgen; **a better ~** eine bessere Zukunft ► ~ **is another day** *saying* morgen ist auch noch ein Tag

ton <*pl* -> [tʌn] *n* Tonne *f*; **how much money does he have?** — ~s *fam* wie viel Geld besitzt er? – jede Menge; **a ~ of money** *fam* ein Haufen *m* Geld; **to weigh a ~** *fam* Unmengen wiegen ► **to come down on sb like a ~ of bricks** jdn völlig fertigmachen

tone [toʊn] *n* Klang *m*; (*of speaking*) Ton *m*; (*of color*) Farbton *m*; **dial ~** Wählton *m*; **disrespectful ~** respektloser Ton

◆tone down *vt* abmildern; (*color*) abschwächen

'tone-deaf *adj* **to be ~** unmusikalisch sein

toner ['toʊ·nər] *n* Toner *m*; ~ **cartridge** Tonerpatrone *f*

Tonga ['tɑŋ·gə] *n* Tonga *nt*

Tongan ['tɑŋ·gən] I. *adj* tongaisch II. *n* Tongaer(in) *m(f)*; (*language*) Tongasprache *f*

tongs [tɑŋz] *npl* Zange *f*

tongue [tʌŋ] *n* Zunge *f*; **cat got your ~?** hat es dir die Sprache verschlagen?; **to bite one's ~** sich *dat* in die Zunge beißen; ~ **of land** Landzunge *f* ► **to say sth ~ -in cheek** etw als Scherz meinen

'tongue-tied *adj* sprachlos

'tongue twister *n* Zungenbrecher *m*

tonic¹ ['tɑn·ɪk] *n* Tonikum *nt*; (*sth that rejuvenates*) Erfrischung *f*

tonic² ['tɑn·ɪk], **tonic water** ['tɑnɪk-] *n* Tonic[water] *nt*

tonight [tə·'naɪt] I. *adv* heute Abend; (*until after midnight*) heute Nacht II. *n* der heutige Abend

tonsillitis [ˌtɑn·sə·'laɪ·tɪs] *n* Mandelent-

zündung *f*

tonsils ['tɑn·səlz] *npl* Mandeln *pl*

too [tu] *adv* **1.** zu; **to be ~ bad** wirklich schade sein; **far ~ difficult** vie zu schwierig; **to be not ~ sure i ...** sich *dat* nicht ganz sicher sein, ob ... **2.** (*also*) auch; **me ~!** ich auch! **3.** (*moreover*) überdies

took [tʊk] *vt, vi pt of* **take**

tool [tul] *n* Werkzeug *nt*; (*aid*) Mittel *nt,* **to be a ~ of the trade** zum Handwerkszeug gehören

'toolbox *n* Werkzeugkiste *f*

'tool chest, 'toolkit *n* Werkzeugkasten *m*

toot [tut] I. *n* Hupen *nt* II. *vt* anhupen; **to ~ a horn** auf die Hupe drücken

tooth <*pl* teeth> [tuθ] *n* Zahn *m*; (*o, comb*) Zinke *f*; (*of saw*) [Säge]zahn *m,* (*of cog*) Zahn *m*; **to brush one's teeth** die Zähne putzen; **to grit one's teeth** die Zähne zusammenbeißen ► **to sink one's teeth into sth** sich in etw *akk* hineinstürzen

'toothache *n* Zahnschmerzen *pl*

'toothbrush *n* Zahnbürste *f*

'toothpaste *n* Zahnpasta *f*

'toothpick *n* Zahnstocher *m*

top¹ [tɑp] I. *n* **1.** oberes Ende; (*of mountain*) [Berg]gipfel *m*; (*of tree*) [Baum]krone *f*; (*highest rank*) Spitze *f*; **there was a pile of books on ~ of the table** auf dem Tisch lag ein Stoß Bücher; **from ~ to bottom** von oben bis unten; **to be at the ~ of one's class** Klassenbeste(r) *f(m)* sein; **to get on ~ of sth** *fig* etw in den Griff bekommen **2.** FASHION Top *nt* **3.** (*lid*) Deckel *m* ► **off the ~ of one's head** *fam* aus dem Stegreif; **to go over the ~** überreagieren II. *adj attr* oberste(r, s); (*best*) beste(r, s); (*maximum*) höchste(r, s); ~ **floor** oberstes Stockwerk; **sb's ~ choice** jds erste Wahl; ~ **athlete** Spitzensportler(in) *m(f)*; ~ **speed** Höchstgeschwindigkeit *f* III. *vt* <-pp-> anführen; (*surpass*) übertreffen; **to ~ a list** oben auf einer Liste stehen

◆top off *vt* garnieren; (*tank*) auffüllen; (*conclude*) abrunden; (*crown*) krönen

top² [tɑp] *n* (*toy*) Kreisel *m*

topaz ['toʊ·pæz] *n* Topas *m*

'top hat *n* Zylinder *m*

p-'heavy adj kopflastig

pic ['tap·ɪk] n Thema nt

pical ['tap·ɪ·kəl] adj aktuell; (by topics) hematisch

picality [,tap·ɪ·'kæl·ɪ·ţi] n Aktualität f

pless ['tap·lɪs] adj oben ohne präd

pmost adj attr oberste(r, s)

pography [tə·'pag·rə·fi] n Topographie f

pping ['tap·ɪŋ] n Garnierung f

pple ['tap·əl] I. vt umwerfen; (overthrow) stürzen II. vi stürzen; (prices) fallen

topple over I. vt umwerfen II. vi umfallen

p 'quality n Spitzenqualität f

p 'secret adj streng geheim

p 'speed n Höchstgeschwindigkeit f

psy-turvy [,tap·sɪ·'tɜr·vi] fam I. adj chaotisch II. adv to turn sth ~ etw auf den Kopf stellen

rch [tɔrtʃ] I. n <pl -es> Fackel f; (blowtorch) Lötlampe f; Olympic ~ olympisches Feuer II. vt fam in Brand setzen

rchlight n Fackelschein m

re [tɔr] vt, vi pt of tear

rment I. n ['tɔr·ment] Qual f; (physical) starke Schmerzen pl; (torture) Tortur f II. vt [tɔr·'ment] quälen; to be ~ed by grief großen Kummer haben

rn [tɔrn] I. vt, vi pp of tear II. adj pred innerlich] zerrissen

rnado <pl -s> [tɔr·'neɪ·doʊ] n Tornado m

rpedo [tɔr·'pi·doʊ] I. n <pl -es> Torpedo m II. vt torpedieren

rrent ['tɔr·ənt] n Sturzbach m; (large amount) Strom m

rrential [tɔ·'ren·ʃəl] adj sintflutartig

rso ['tɔr·soʊ] n Rumpf m; (statue) Torso m

rtoise ['tɔr·ţəs] n [Land]schildkröte f

rtoiseshell n Schildpatt nt

rtuous ['tɔr·tʃu·əs] adj gewunden; (complicated) umständlich; (process) langwierig

rture ['tɔr·tʃər] I. n Folter f; (suffering) Qual f II. vt foltern; (disturb) quälen

ss <pl -es> [tɔs] I. n Wurf m II. vt werfen; (fling) schleudern; (horse) abwerfen; (one's head) zurückwerfen;

(salad) schwenken III. vi ▶ to ~ and turn sich hin und her wälzen

toss out vt hinauswerfen

tot [tat] n fam Knirps m

total ['toʊ·ţəl] I. n Gesamtsumme f; in ~ insgesamt II. adj gesamt; (absolute) völlig; (disaster) rein; to be a ~ stranger vollkommen fremd sein III. vt <-l-> zusammenrechnen; fam (car) zu Schrott fahren; their debts ~ 8,000 dollars ihre Schulden belaufen sich auf 8.000 Dollar

total up vt zusammenrechnen

totalitarian [toʊ·,tæl·ə·'ter·i·ən] adj totalitär

totalitarianism [toʊ·,tæl·ə·'ter·i·ə·nɪz·əm] n Totalitarismus m

totally ['toʊ·ţə·li] adv völlig

'tote bag n Einkaufstasche f

totem ['toʊ·ţəm] n Totem nt

totter ['tat·ər] vi wanken

tottery ['tat·ə·ri] adj wackelig; (person) zittrig

toucan ['tu·kæn] n Tukan m

touch [tʌtʃ] I. n <pl -es> 1. Tasten nt; (instance) Berührung f; the material was soft to the ~ das Material fühlte sich weich an; at the ~ of a button auf Knopfdruck; to be/keep in ~ with sb/sth mit jdm/etw in Kontakt stehen/ bleiben 2. (of salt) Spur f; a ~ of the flu fam eine leichte Grippe ▶ to be a soft ~ fam leichtgläubig sein II. vt berühren; (contact) in Berührung kommen; (border) grenzen; (emotions) bewegen ▶ to ~ a [raw] nerve einen wunden Punkt berühren III. vi sich berühren

touch down vi landen

touch on, touch upon vi ansprechen

touch up vt auffrischen; (photograph) retuschieren

touch-and-'go adj unentschieden; to be ~ whether ... auf Messers Schneide stehen, ob ...

'touchdown n Landung f; sport Touchdown m

touched [tʌtʃt] adj pred gerührt

touchiness ['tʌtʃ·ɪ·nɪs] n fam Überempfindlichkeit f; (delicacy) Empfindlichkeit f

touching ['tʌtʃ·ɪŋ] adj rührend

T

touchy ['tʌtʃ·i] *adj fam* empfindlich; *(delicate)* heikel

tough [tʌf] *adj* robust; *(hardy, fibrous)* zäh; *(difficult, harsh)* schwierig; *(climate)* rau; *(competition)* hart; *(winter, laws)* streng; *(violent)* rau; **to be as ~ as nails** nicht unterzukriegen sein

◆**tough out** *vt fam* aussitzen; **to ~ it out** es durchhalten

toughen ['tʌf·ən] I. *vt* verstärken; *(glass)* härten II. *vi* stärker werden

toupee [tu·'peɪ] *n* Toupet *nt*

tour [tʊr] I. *n* Reise *f*; *(period of duty)* Tournee *f*; *(guided ~)* Führung *f* II. *vt* bereisen; *(professionally)* besuchen; **to ~ Germany** eine Deutschlandtournee machen III. *vi* **to ~ [with sb]** [mit jdm] auf Tournee gehen

'**tour guide** *n* Reiseführer *m*; *(person a.)* Fremdenführer(in) *m(f)*

touring ['tʊr·ɪŋ] *n* Reisen *nt*; **to do some ~** herumreisen

tourism ['tʊr·ɪz·əm] *n* Tourismus *m*

tourist ['tʊr·ɪst] *n* Tourist(in) *m(f)*

'**tourist office** *n* Fremdenverkehrsamt *nt*

'**tourist season** *n* Hauptsaison *f*

tournament ['tɜr·nə·mənt] *n* Turnier *nt*

tousled ['taʊ·zəlt] *adj* zerzaust

tow [toʊ] I. *n* Schleppen *nt*; **to have sb in ~** jdn im Schlepptau haben II. *vt* ziehen; *(car)* abschleppen

toward(s) [tɔrd(z)] *prep* in Richtung; **she walked ~ him** sie ging auf ihn zu; **we're up ~ the front of the line** wir sind nahe dem Anfang der Schlange; **~ midnight** gegen Mitternacht; **to count ~ sth** auf etw *akk* angerechnet werden

towel ['taʊ·əl] I. *n* Handtuch *nt*; **paper ~** Papiertuch *nt* ▶ **to throw in the ~** das Handtuch werfen II. *vt* <-ll-> **to ~ sth dry** etw trockenreiben

'**towel rack** *n* Handtuchhalter *m*

tower ['taʊ·ər] *n* Turm *m* ▶ **a ~ of strength** ein Fels in der Brandung

◆**tower above, tower over** *vi* aufragen; **to ~ above sb/sth** jdn/etw überragen

towering ['taʊ·ər·ɪŋ] *adj* hoch aufragend; *(great)* überragend

town [taʊn] *n* Stadt *f*; **home ~** Heimatstadt *f*; **the whole ~** die ganze Stadt; **to be in ~** in der Stadt sein ▶ **to go**

to ~ [on sth] sich [bei etw *dat*] i[ns] Zeug legen

town 'clerk *n* Magistratsbeamte(r), -be[amtin *m, f*

town 'hall *n* Rathaus *nt*

'**tow truck** *n* Abschleppwagen *m*

toxic ['tak·sɪk] *adj* giftig; **~ waste** Gi[ft]müll *m*

toxicology [ˌtak·sɪ·'kal·ə·dʒi] *n* Toxik[o]logie *f*

toxin ['tak·sɪn] *n* Toxin *nt*

toy [tɔɪ] *n* Spielzeug *nt*; **stuffed ~** K[uschel]scheltier *nt*

◆'**toy with** *vi* spielen mit +*dat*

'**toy store** *n* Spielwarengeschäft *nt*

trace [treɪs] I. *n* Spur *f*; **without a** spurlos; **to put a ~ on a phone call** e[i]nen Anruf zurückverfolgen II. *vt* 1. au[s]finden; *(phone call)* zurückverfolge[n]; **to ~ sb** jds Spur verfolgen 2. *(throu[gh] paper)* durchpausen; *(with finger)* nach[zeichnen] malen

'**trace element** *n* Spurenelement *nt*

'**tracing paper** *n* Pauspapier *nt*

track [træk] I. *n* 1. Weg *m*; RAIL Bah[n]steig *m*; **~s** *pl* Gleise *pl*; **to get one's li[fe] back on ~** sein Leben wieder in die Re[ihe] bringen 2. *usu pl (prints)* Spur *f*; *(of deer)* Fährte *f* 3. SPORT Laufbahn *f*; *(f[ür] racecars)* Rennstrecke *f*; *(for bikes)* Ra[d]rennbahn *f* 4. *(athletics)* Leichtathletik 5. *(in film)* Soundtrack *m* ▶ **to be o[ff] the beaten ~** abgelegen sein; **to keep ~ of sb/sth** jdn/etw im Auge behalten; **[to] stop in one's ~s** vor Schreck erstar[ren] II. *vt* verfolgen; *(find)* aufspüren; **to ~ s[b]** jds Spur verfolgen

◆'**track down** *vt* aufspüren; *(informatio[n])* ausfindig machen

track and 'field *n* Leichtathletik *f*

'**trackball** *n* Rollkugel *f*

'**track record** *n* Streckenrekord *m*; *([of] company)* Erfolgsbilanz *f*

'**track shoe** *n* Laufschuh *m*

'**tracksuit** *n* Trainingsanzug *m*

tract [trækt] *n* Gebiet *nt*; *(propert[y])* Grundstück *nt*; **respiratory ~** Atem[wege *pl*

traction ['træk·ʃən] *n* **to be in ~** [im] Streckverband liegen

tractor ['træk·tər] *n* Traktor *m*

'tractor-trailer *n* Sattelschlepper *m*

trade [treɪd] **I.** *n* Handel *m*; (*business type*) Branche *f*; (*handicraft*) Handwerk *nt*; **building** ~ Baugewerbe *nt*; **to learn a** ~ ein Handwerk erlernen **II.** *vi* tauschen; (*do business*) Geschäfte machen **III.** *vt* austauschen; **to** ~ **places [with sb]** [mit jdm] den Platz tauschen

◆**trade in** *vt* in Zahlung geben

'trade agreement *n* Handelsabkommen *nt*

'trade fair *n* Messe *f*

'trade-in *n* Tauschware *f*; ~ **value** Gebrauchtwert *m*

'trademark *n* Warenzeichen *nt*; (*of person*) charakteristisches Merkmal

'trade name *n* Markenname *m*

'trader ['treɪdər] *n* Händler(in) *m(f)*; (*broker*) Wertpapierhändler(in) *m(f)*

'trade route *n* Handelsweg *m*

trade 'secret *n* Betriebsgeheimnis *nt*

tradesman ['treɪdz·mən] *n* Handwerker *m*

'trade union *n* Gewerkschaft *f*

'trade wind *n* Passat *m*

trading ['treɪ·dɪŋ] *n* Handel *m*

tradition [trə·'dɪʃ·ən] *n* Tradition *f*; (*custom a.*) Brauch *m*; (*style a.*) Stil *m*

traditional [trə·'dɪʃ·ə·nəl] *adj* traditionell; (*person*) konservativ

traditionalist [trə·'dɪʃ·ə·nə·lɪst] *n* Traditionalist(in) *m(f)*

traffic ['træf·ɪk] **I.** *n* Verkehr *m*; (*trade*) illegaler Handel; **to get stuck in** ~ im Verkehr stecken bleiben; **data** ~ Datenverkehr *m* **II.** *vi* <-ck-> handeln; **to** ~ **in arms** Waffenhandel betreiben

'traffic accident *n* Verkehrsunfall *m*

'traffic circle *n* Kreisverkehr *m*

'traffic cop *n fam* Verkehrspolizist(in) *m(f)*

'traffic island *n* Verkehrsinsel *f*; (*median*) Mittelstreifen *m*

'traffic jam *n* [Rück]stau *m*

'trafficker ['træf·ɪk·ər] *n* Händler(in) *m(f)*

'traffic light *n* Ampel *f*

tragedy ['trædʒ·ə·di] *n* Tragödie *f*; **it's a** ~ **that** ... es ist tragisch, dass ...

tragic ['trædʒ·ɪk] *adj* tragisch

trail [treɪl] **I.** *n* Weg *m*; (*track*) Spur *f*; **to be on the** ~ **of sth/sb** etw/jdm auf der Spur sein **II.** *vt* **to** ~ **sb** jdm auf der Spur sein; (*competitor*) hinter jdm liegen

III. *vi* schleifen; (*vines*) sich ranken; (*be losing*) zurückliegen; **to** ~ **after sb** hinter jdm her trotten

◆**trail away** *vi* verstummen

◆**trail behind I.** *vi* zurückbleiben **II.** *vt* hinterherlaufen

◆**trail off** *vi* verstummen

trailblazer ['treɪl·bleɪ·zər] *n* Wegbereiter(in) *m(f)*

trail-blazing ['treɪl·bleɪ·zɪŋ] *adj attr* bahnbrechend

trailer ['treɪ·lər] *n* Anhänger *m*; (*home*) Wohnwagen *m*; (*advertisement*) Trailer *m*

'trailer park *n* Wohnwagenabstellplatz *m*

'trailer trash *n pej sl* weißer Abschaum *pej*

train [treɪn] **I.** *n* Zug *m*; (*retinue*) Gefolge *nt*; (*procession*) Zug *m*; (*part of dress*) Schleppe *f*; **to lose one's** ~ **of thought** den roten Faden verlieren **II.** *vi* trainieren **III.** *vt* ausbilden; (*dog*) abrichten; (*vines*) ziehen; (*gun*) richten

trained [treɪnd] *adj* ausgebildet; (*dog*) abgerichtet; (*eye*) geschult

trainee [treɪ·'ni] *n* Auszubildende(r) *f(m)*

trainer ['treɪ·nər] *n* Trainer(in) *m(f)*; (*of animals*) Dresseur(in) *m(f)*; (*in circus*) Dompteur *m*, Dompteuse *f*

training ['treɪ·nɪŋ] *n* Ausbildung *f*; (*of new employee*) Schulung *f*; (*of dog*) Abrichten *nt*; (*practice*) Training *nt*

'training camp *n* Trainingscamp *nt*

'train station *n* Bahnhof *m*

trait [treɪt] *n* Eigenschaft *f*; **genetic** ~ genetisches Merkmal

traitor ['treɪ·tər] *n* Verräter(in) *m(f)*

trajectory [trə·'dʒek·tə·ri] *n* Flugbahn *f*

tramp [træmp] **I.** *vi* marschieren; (*heavily*) trampeln **II.** *n* Vagabund(in) *m(f)*; *pej* (*woman*) Flittchen *nt*

trample ['træm·pəl] **I.** *vt* niedertrampeln; (*crops*) zertrampeln; **to be ~d to death** zu Tode getrampelt werden **II.** *vi* herumtrampeln

trampoline ['træm·pə·lin] *n* Trampolin *nt*

trance [træns] *n* Trance *f*; (*music*) Trance-Musik *f*

tranquil ['træn·kwɪl] *adj* ruhig; (*expression*) gelassen

tranquility [træn·'kwɪl·ɪ·ţi] *n* Ruhe *f*

tranquilize ['træŋ·kwɪ·laɪz] *vt* ruhigstellen

tranquilizer ['træŋ·kwɪ·laɪ·zər] *n* Beruhigungsmittel *nt*

tranquillity [træŋ·'kwɪl·ɪ·ti] *n see* **tranquility**

tranquillize ['træŋ·kwɪ·laɪz] *vt see* **tranquilize**

tranquillizer ['træŋ·kwɪ·laɪ·zər] *n see* **tranquilizer**

transact [træn·'zækt] *vt* abschließen; (*negotiations*) durchführen

transaction [træn·'zæk·ʃən] *n* Transaktion *f;* **business ~** Geschäft *nt*

transatlantic [ˌtræns·ət·'læn·tɪk] *adj* transatlantisch; (*voyage*) über den Atlantik

transcendental [ˌtræn·sen·'den·təl] *adj* transzendent[al]

transcript ['træn·skrɪpt] *n* Abschrift *f;* **~s** *pl* SCH, UNIV Zeugnisse *pl*

transfer [træns·'fɜr] I. *vt* <-rr-> [træns·'fɜr] (*money*) überweisen; (*reassign*) versetzen; (*power*) abgeben; (*responsibility*) übertragen; (*call*) weiterleiten II. *vi* <-rr-> [træns·'fɜr] (*employee*) überwechseln; (*passenger*) umsteigen III. *n* ['træns·fɜr] **1.** Verlegung *f;* (*of money*) Überweisung *f;* (*of ownership*) Übertragung *f;* (*at work*) Versetzung *f;* (*player*) Transferspieler(in) *m(f)* **2.** (*pattern*) Abziehbild *nt;* **heat ~** Wärmeübertragung *f*

transfigure [træns·'fɪg·jər] *vt* verwandeln

transfix [træns·'fɪks] *vt usu passive* **to be ~ed by sth/sb** von etw/jdm fasziniert sein; **to be ~ed with horror** starr vor Entsetzen sein

transform [træns·'fɔrm] *vt* verwandeln

transformation [ˌtræns·fər·'meɪ·ʃən] *n* Verwandlung *f*

transformer [træns·'fɔr·mər] *n* Transformator *m*

transfusion [træns·'fju·ʒən] *n* Transfusion *f*

transient ['træn·zi·ənt] *n* Durchreisende(r) *f(m)*

transistor [træn·'zɪs·tər] *n* Transistor *m*

transit ['træn·zɪt] *n* **1.** Transit *m;* **passengers in ~** Transitreisende *pl* **2.** (*public transport*) öffentliches Verkehrswesen;

mass ~ öffentlicher Nahverkehr

'transit desk *n* Transitschalter *m*

transition [træn·'zɪʃ·ən] *n* Übergang *m;* **to be in ~** in einer Übergangsphase sein

transitional [træn·'zɪʃ·ə·nəl] *adj* Übergangs-

'transit visa *n* Transitvisum *nt*

translate ['træns·leɪt] I. *vt* übersetzen; (*simplify*) einfacher ausdrücken; (*ideas*) umsetzen; **to ~ sth from Greek to Spanish** etw aus dem Griechischen ins Spanische übersetzen II. *vi* übersetzen; (*transfer*) sich umsetzen lassen; **to ~ from Hungarian to Russian** aus dem Ungarischen ins Russische übersetzen

translation [træns·'leɪ·ʃən] *n* Übersetzung *f;* (*act*) Übersetzen *nt;* (*conversion*) Umsetzung *f*

translator ['træns·leɪ·tər] *n* Übersetzer(in) *m(f)*

transmission [træns·'mɪʃ·ən] *n* Übertragen *nt;* (*broadcast*) Sendung *f;* (*gears*) Getriebe *nt*

transmit <-tt-> [træns·'mɪt] I. *vt* übertragen; (*impart*) übermitteln; (*knowledge*) vermitteln II. *vi* senden

transmitter [træns·'mɪt·ər] *n* Sender *m*

transparency [træns·'per·ən·si] *n* Lichtdurchlässigkeit *f;* (*slide*) Dia *nt*

transparent [træns·'per·ənt] *adj* durchsichtig; *fig* transparent

transpire [træn·'spaɪ·ər] *vi* sich ereignen; (*become known*) sich herausstellen

transplant I. *vt* [træns·'plænt] transplantieren; (*relocate*) umsiedeln II. *n* ['træns·plænt] Transplantation *f;* (*organ*) Transplantat *nt*

transplantation [ˌtræns·plæn·'teɪ·ʃən] *n* Transplantation *f*

transport I. *vt* [træns·'pɔrt] befördern; **to ~ sb to a time** jdn in eine Zeit versetzen II. *n* ['træns·pɔrt] Beförderung *f;* (*traffic*) Verkehrsmittel *nt;* (*vehicle*) [Transport]fahrzeug *nt;* **means of ~** Transportmittel *nt*

transportation [ˌtræns·pər·'teɪ·ʃən] *n* Beförderung *f;* (*means*) Transportmittel *nt;* **through ~** Transitverkehr *nt;* **to provide ~** ein Beförderungsmittel zur Verfügung stellen

transporter [træns·'pɔr·tər] *n* Transporter *m*

transvestite ['træns·'ves·taɪt] *n* Transvestit *m*

trap [træp] **I.** *n* Falle *f*; (*ambush*) Hinterhalt *m*; **to set a ~** eine Falle aufstellen; **to fall into a ~** in die Falle gehen; **shut your ~!** *sl* Klappe! **II.** *vt* <-pp-> **1.** [in einer Falle] fangen **2.** *usu passive* (*confine*) **to be ~ped** eingeschlossen sein; **to feel ~ped** sich gefangen fühlen **3.** (*trick*) in die Falle locken; **to ~ sb into sth/doing sth** jdn dazu bringen, etw zu tun **4.** (*finger*) sich *dat* einklemmen

'trapdoor *n* Falltür *f*; THEAT Versenkung *f*

trapeze [træ·'piz] *n* Trapez *nt*

trappings ['træp·ɪŋz] *npl* Drumherum *nt fam*; **the ~ of power** die Insignien *pl* der Macht

trash [træʃ] **I.** *n* Abfall *m*; *pej fam* Plunder *m*; (*literature*) Schund *m*; (*people*) Gesindel *nt*; (*nonsense*) Mist *m* **II.** *vt fam* kaputt machen; (*place*) verwüsten; (*criticize*) auseinandernehmen; **to ~ sb** über jdn herziehen

'trash can *n* Mülltonne *f*

trashy ['træʃ·i] *adj pej fam* wertlos; **~ novels** Kitschromane *pl*

trauma <*pl -s*> ['trɔ·mə] *n* Trauma *nt*

traumatic [trɔ·'mæt·ɪk] *adj* traumatisch; (*upsetting*) furchtbar

traumatize ['trɔ·mə·taɪz] *vt usu passive* **to be ~d by sth** durch etw *akk* traumatisiert sein

travel ['træv·əl] **I.** *vi* <-l-> reisen; (*by air*) fliegen; (*by train*) fahren; (*move*) sich [fort]bewegen; **to ~ badly** lange Reisen nicht vertragen; (*freight*) lange Transporte nicht vertragen **II.** *vt* <-l-> **to ~ the world** die Welt bereisen **III.** *n* Reisen *nt*; **~s** *pl* (*journeys*) Reisen *pl*

travel agency *n* Reisebüro *nt*

travel agent *n* Reisebürokaufmann *m*, Reisebürokauffrau *f*

traveler ['træv·ə·lər] *n* Reisende(r) *f(m)*

traveler's check *n* Reisescheck *m*

travel expenses *npl* Reisekosten *pl*

travel guide *n* Reiseführer *m*

traveling ['træv·ə·lɪŋ] *n* Reisen *nt*

traveller *n see* **traveler**

travelling *see* **traveling**

travelog ['træv·ə·lɔg] *n* Reisebericht *m*; (*film*) Reisebeschreibung *f*

travesty ['træv·ɪ·sti] *n* Karikatur *f*; (*burlesque*) Travestie *f*; **~ of justice** Hohn *m* auf die Gerechtigkeit

trawl [trɔl] **I.** *vt* mit dem Schleppnetz fangen; (*search*) durchkämmen **II.** *vi* **1.** **to ~ [for sth]** mit dem Schleppnetz [nach etw *dat*] fischen **2.** (*search*) **to ~ through sth** etw durchsuchen

trawler ['trɔ·lər] *n* Trawler *m*

tray [treɪ] *n* Tablett *nt*; (*for papers*) Ablage *f*

treacherous ['tretʃ·ər·əs] *adj* verräterisch; (*disloyal*) treulos; (*dangerous*) tückisch; (*sea*) trügerisch

treachery ['tretʃ·ə·ri] *n esp hist* Verrat *m*

tread [tred] **I.** *vi* <trod *or* treaded, trodden *or* trod> **1.** (*step*) treten; **to ~ in/on sth** in/auf etw *akk* treten **2.** (*maltreat*) **to ~ on sb** jdn treten ▸ **to ~ carefully** vorsichtig vorgehen **II.** *vt* <trod *or* treaded, trodden *or* trod> **to ~ sth down** etw niedertreten; **to ~ water** Wasser treten **III.** *n* Tritt *m*; (*step*) Stufe *f*; (*of tire*) [Reifen]profil *nt*; (*of shoe*) [Schuh]profil *nt*

treadmill ['tred·mɪl] *n* Heimtrainer *m*; (*routine*) Tretmühle *f fam*

treason ['tri·zən] *n* [Landes]verrat *m*; **high ~** Hochverrat *m*

treasure ['treʒ·ər] **I.** *n* Schatz *m*; **~s** *pl* Schätze *pl* **II.** *vt* [hoch]schätzen; (*memories*) bewahren

'treasure hunt *n* Schatzsuche *f*

treasurer ['treʒ·ər·ər] *n* Schatzmeister(in) *m(f)*; (*of club*) Kassenwart(in) *m(f)*

'treasure trove *n* Fundgrube *f*

treasury ['treʒ·ə·ri] *n* Schatzkammer; **the T~** das Finanzministerium

'Treasury Secretary *n* Finanzminister(in) *m(f)*

treat [trit] **I.** *vt* behandeln; (*regard*) betrachten; (*sewage*) klären; **to ~ sb/sth badly** jdn/etw schlecht behandeln; **to ~ sth with contempt** etw mit Verachtung begegnen; **to ~ sb [to sth]** jdn [zu etw *dat*] einladen; **to ~ oneself [to sth]** sich *dat* etw gönnen **II.** *vi fam* Jack's ~ing! Jack gibt einen aus! **III.** *n* [it's] my ~ das geht auf meine Rechnung; **it is a special ~ to do that** es ist ein besonderes

T

Vergnügen, das zu tun; **to give oneself a ~** sich *dat* etw gönnen

treatise ['triː·tɪs] *n* Abhandlung *f*

treatment ['triːt·mənt] *n* Behandlung *f*; (*of waste*) Verarbeitung *f*; **to respond to ~** auf eine Behandlung ansprechen

treaty ['triː·ti] *n* Vertrag *m*

treble ['treb·əl] **I.** *adj attr* Diskant-; **~ voice** Sopranstimme *f* **II.** *n* Sopran *m*

tree [triː] *n* Baum *m*

'tree house *n* Baumhaus *nt*

'tree-lined *adj* von Bäumen gesäumt

'tree surgeon *n* Baumchirurg(in) *m(f)*

'treetops *npl* **the ~** die [Baum]wipfel *pl*

trek [trek] **I.** *vi* <-kk-> wandern **II.** *n* Wanderung *f*; (*hike*) Marsch *m*

tremble ['trem·bəl] **I.** *vi* zittern; (*voice*) beben; **to ~ like a leaf** zittern wie Espenlaub **II.** *n* Zittern *nt*

tremendous [trɪ·'men·dəs] *adj* enorm; (*scope*) riesig; (*help*) riesengroß *fam*; (*good*) klasse *fam*

tremor ['trem·ər] *n* Zittern *nt*; MED Tremor *m*; (*earthquake*) Beben *nt*; (*fluctuation*) Schwanken *nt*

tremulous ['trem·jʊ·ləs] *adj* zitternd; (*voice*) zittrig

trench <*pl* -es> [trentʃ] *n* Graben *m*; MIL Schützengraben *m*

'trench coat *n* Trenchcoat *m*

trend [trend] *n* Trend *m*; (*style a.*) Mode *f*; **the latest ~** der letzte Schrei *fam*

trendsetter ['trend·ˌset·ər] *n* Trendsetter(in) *m(f)*

trendy ['tren·di] *adj* modisch

trespass ['tres·pəs] *vi* unbefugt eindringen; **to ~ on sb's land** jds Land unerlaubt betreten

trespasser ['tres·pæs·ər] *n* Eindringling *m;* **"~s will be prosecuted!"** „unbefugtes Betreten wird strafrechtlich verfolgt!"

trial ['traɪ·əl] *n* Prozess *m*; (*test*) Probe *f*; **clinical ~s** klinische Tests *pl;* **~ by jury** Schwurgerichtsverhandlung *f;* **to stand ~** vor Gericht stehen

triangle ['traɪ·æŋ·gəl] *n* Dreieck *nt*; (*object*) dreieckiges Objekt; (*percussion*) Triangel *f*; (*drawing aid*) Zeichendreieck *nt*

triangular [traɪ·'æŋ·gjʊ·lər] *adj* dreieckig

tribal ['traɪ·bəl] *adj* (*ethnic*) Stammes-; *fam* (*group*) Gruppen-

tribe [traɪb] *n* Stamm *m*; *fam* (*group*) Sippe *f*

tribunal [traɪ·'bjuː·nəl] *n* Gericht *nt*; (*investigative body*) Untersuchungsausschuss *m*

tribune ['trɪb·juːn] *n* Tribüne *f*

tributary ['trɪb·jə·ter·i] *n* Nebenfluss *m*

tribute ['trɪb·juːt] *n* Tribut *m;* **to pay ~ to sb/sth** jdm/etw Tribut zollen *geh;* **to be a ~ to sb/sth** (*beneficial*) jdm/etw Ehre machen

trick [trɪk] **I.** *n* Trick *m;* (*knack*) Kunstgriff *m;* **he knows all the ~s of the trade** er ist ein alter Hase; **to play a ~ on sb** jdm einen Streich spielen; **dirty ~** gemeiner Trick; **~ of the light** optische Täuschung ▶ **to not miss a ~** keine Gelegenheit auslassen; **to do the ~** klappen *fam* **II.** *adj attr* (*question*) Fang-; (*acrobatic*) Kunst- **III.** *vt* hintergehen; (*fool*) reinlegen *fam;* **to ~ sb into doing sth** jdn dazu bringen, etw zu tun

trickery ['trɪk·ə·ri] *n* Betrug *m*; (*repeated*) Betrügerei *f*

trickle ['trɪk·əl] **I.** *vi* sickern; (*in drops*) tröpfeln; (*sand*) rieseln; (*tear*) kullern; (*details*) durchsickern; **people ~d back into the theatre** die Leute kamen in kleinen Gruppen in den Theatersaal zurück **II.** *vt* tröpfeln **III.** *n* Rinnsal *nt geh*, (*in drops*) Tropfen *pl;* **a ~ of people** wenige Leute

'trick question *n* Fangfrage *f*

tricky ['trɪk·i] *adj* betrügerisch; (*sly*) raffiniert; (*awkward*) schwierig; (*difficult*) kniff[e]lig

tricycle ['traɪ·sɪ·kəl] *n* Dreirad *nt*

trident ['traɪ·dənt] *n* Dreizack *m*

tried [traɪd] *vt, vi pt, pp of* **try**

trifle ['traɪ·fəl] *n* Kleinigkeit *f;* **a ~ surprised** etwas erstaunt

trifling ['traɪ·flɪŋ] *adj* unbedeutend; (*sum*) geringfügig

trigger ['trɪg·ər] **I.** *n* Abzug *m;* (*cause*) Auslöser *m;* **to pull the ~** abdrücken **II.** *vt* auslösen

trill [trɪl] **I.** *n* Trillern *nt*; MUS Triller *m* **II.** *vt, vi* trillern

trillion ['trɪl·jən] n **1.** <pl -> Billion f **2.** pl fam ~s pl Tausende pl

trilogy ['trɪl·ə·dʒi] n Trilogie f

trim [trɪm] **I.** n Nachschneiden nt; (edging) Applikation f **II.** adj <-mer, -mest> ordentlich; (lawn) gepflegt; (slim) schlank **III.** vt <-mm-> [nach]schneiden; (beard) stutzen; (reduce) kürzen; (costs a.) verringern; (decorate) schmücken

trimming ['trɪm·ɪŋ] n **the ~s** pl das Zubehör; **turkey with all the ~s** Truthahn m mit allem Drum und Dran

Trinidad ['trɪn·ɪ·dæd] n Trinidad nt

Trinidadian ['trɪn·ɪ·dæd·i·ən] **I.** adj trinidadisch **II.** n Trinidader(in) m(f)

trinity ['trɪn·ɪ·t̬i] n **the** [**Holy**] **T~** die [Heilige] Dreifaltigkeit

trinket ['trɪŋ·kɪt] n wertloser Schmuckgegenstand; ~**s** pl Plunder m

trio <pl -s> ['triː·oʊ] n Trio nt

trip [trɪp] **I.** n **1.** Reise f; (outing) Ausflug m; **round ~** Rundreise f; **ego ~** Egotrip m **2.** (stumble) Stolpern nt **II.** vi <-pp-> stolpern; fam (be on drugs) auf einem Trip sein sl; **to ~ off one's tongue** leicht von der Zunge gehen **III.** vt <-pp-> **to ~ sb** jdm ein Bein stellen

◆**trip over** vi stolpern; **to ~ over one's words** über seine Worte stolpern

◆**trip up** vi. vt **1.** (unbalance) **to ~ up ⇄ sb** jdm ein Bein stellen ⇄ (problem) zu Fall bringen **2.** (slip) einen Fehler machen

tripe [traɪp] n Kutteln pl; fam (nonsense) Quatsch m

triple ['trɪp·əl] **I.** adj attr dreifach; (of three parts) Dreier- **II.** adv dreimal so viel **III.** vt verdreifachen **IV.** vi sich verdreifachen; (in baseball) einen Triple schlagen **V.** n Triple m

triplet ['trɪp·lɪt] n usu pl Drilling m

tripod ['traɪ·pad] n Stativ nt

trite [traɪt] adj abgedroschen

triumph ['traɪ·ʌmf] **I.** n Triumph m; (joy) Siegesfreude f **II.** vi triumphieren

triumphant [traɪ·ʌm·fənt] adj siegreich; (successful) erfolgreich; (exulting) triumphierend

trivia ['trɪv·i·ə] npl Lappalien pl

trivial ['trɪv·i·əl] adj trivial; (issue) be-

langlos; (details) bedeutungslos; (petty) kleinlich

triviality [ˌtrɪv·i·ˈæl·ɪ·t̬i] n Belanglosigkeit f; (unimportant thing) Trivialität f

trivialize ['trɪv·i·ə·laɪz] vt trivialisieren

trod [trad] pt, pp of **tread I, II**

trodden ['trad·ən] pp of **tread I, II**

Trojan ['troʊ·dʒən] **I.** n Trojaner(in) m(f) **II.** adj trojanisch

trolley ['tral·i] n Straßenbahn f

'trolley bus n Oberleitungsbus m

trombone [tram·ˈboʊn] n Posaune f

troop [truːp] **I.** n Truppe f; (of animals) Schar f; (of soldiers) Trupp m **II.** vi **to ~ off** abziehen fam

trooper ['truː·pər] n [einfacher] Soldat; **state ~** Polizist(in) m(f)

trophy ['troʊ·fi] n Preis m; (memento) Trophäe f; **war ~** Kriegsbeute f

tropic ['trap·ɪk] n **the T~ of Cancer/Capricorn** der Wendekreis des Krebses/Steinbocks; **the ~s** pl die Tropen pl

tropical ['trap·ɪ·kəl] adj Tropen-; (weather) tropisch

trot [trat] **I.** n Trab m; (of horse) Trott **II.** vi <-tt-> trotten; (horse) traben; (ride) im Trab reiten; (run) laufen

◆**trot along** vi traben

◆**trot off** vi fam losziehen

trotter ['trat̬·ər] n [pig] ~**s** pl Schweinshaxen pl

trouble ['trʌb·əl] **I.** n Schwierigkeiten pl; (annoyance) Ärger m; (problem) Problem[e] nt/pl/; (cause of worry) Sorge f; (inconvenience) Umstände pl; (malfunction) Störung f; (strife) Unruhe f; **the only ~ is that ...** der einzige Haken [dabei] ist, dass ...; **it's no ~ at all** das macht gar keine Umstände; **to spell ~** fam nichts Gutes bedeuten; **to stay out of ~** sauber bleiben hum fam; **to get oneself into a bit of ~** sich in Schwierigkeiten bringen; **engine ~** Motorschaden m **II.** vt beunruhigen; (grieve) bekümmern; (cause pain) plagen; **to ~ sb for sth** form jdn um etw akk bemühen geh

troubled ['trʌb·əld] adj bedrängt; (times) unruhig; (worried) besorgt

'trouble-free adj problemlos

'troublemaker n Unruhestifter(in) m(f)

'troubleshooting n Fehler-/Störungsbeseitigung f; (searching) Fehlersuche f; (mediation) Vermittlung f

troublesome ['trʌb·əl·səm] adj schwierig

'trouble spot n Unruheherd m

trough [trɔf] n Trog m; (low) Tiefpunkt m

troupe [trup] n Truppe f

trouser ['trau·zər] n [pair of] ~s Hose f

trout <pl -s> [traut] n Forelle f

trowel ['trau·əl] n Maurerkelle f; (for gardening) kleiner Spaten

Troy [trɔɪ] n hist Troja nt

truancy ['tru·ən·si] n [Schule]schwänzen nt fam

truant ['tru·ənt] n Schulschwänzer(in) m(f) fam

truce [trus] n Waffenstillstand m

truck [trʌk] n Last[kraft]wagen m; pickup ~ Lieferwagen m ▶ to have no ~ with sb/sth fam mit jdm/etw nichts zu tun haben

'truck driver, trucker ['trʌk·ər] n Lastwagenfahrer(in) m(f); (over long distances) Fernfahrer(in) m(f)

trucking ['trʌk·ɪŋ] n Lkw-Transport m; ~ company Spedition[sfirma] f

'truck stop n Fernfahrerraststätte f

trudge [trʌdʒ] I. vi wandern, trotten II. n [anstrengender] Fußmarsch

true [tru] I. adj <-r, -st> wahr; (accurate) richtig; (aim) genau; (actual) echt; (loyal) treu; it is ~ [to say] that ... es stimmt, dass ...; ~ love wahre Liebe; to be ~ to one's word zu seinem Wort stehen ▶ sb's ~ colors jds wahres Gesicht; ~ to form wie zu erwarten II. adv 1. to ring ~ glaubhaft klingen 2. (accurately) genau

'true-blue adj attr treu; (genuine) waschecht fam

true 'love n sb's ~ jds Geliebte(r) f(m)

truffle ['trʌf·əl] n Trüffel f o m

truly ['tru·li] adv wahrhaftig; (very) wirklich; (genuinely a.) echt ▶ yours ~ meine Wenigkeit hum; Yours ~ (at end of letter) mit freundlichen Grüßen

trump [trʌmp] I. n Trumpf m; ~s pl Trumpffarbe f II. vt übertrumpfen; (better) ausstechen

◆trump up vt erfinden

trumpet ['trʌm·pət] I. n Trompete f II. vi trompeten III. vt ausposaunen fam

trumpeter ['trʌm·pə·tər] n Trompeter(in) m(f)

truncheon ['trʌn·tʃən] n Schlagstock m

trundle ['trʌn·dəl] I. along zuckeln

trunk [trʌŋk] n Stamm m; (body) Rumpf m; (of elephant) Rüssel m; (of car) Kofferraum m; [swim[ming]] ~s pl Badehose f

trust [trʌst] I. n Vertrauen nt; position of ~ Vertrauensposten m; in sb's ~ in jds Obhut f II. vt vertrauen; to ~ sb to do sth jdm zutrauen, dass er/sie etw tut III. vi to ~ in sb/sth auf jdn/etw vertrauen; to ~ [that] ... hoffen, [dass] ...

trusted ['trʌs·tɪd] adj attr getreu geh; (proved) bewährt

trustful ['trʌst·fəl] adj vertrauensvoll; (gullible) leichtgläubig

trusting ['trʌs·tɪŋ] adj see trustful

trusty ['trʌs·ti] adj attr zuverlässig; (loyal) treu

truth <pl -s> [truθ] n Wahrheit f; (principle) Grundprinzip nt; in what she says es ist nichts Wahres an dem, was sie sagt

truthful ['truθ·fəl] adj wahr; (sincere) ehrlich; (accurate) wahrheitsgetreu

try [traɪ] I. n Versuch m; to give sth a ~ etw ausprobieren II. vi <-ie-> versuchen; (make an effort) sich bemühen III. vt <-ie-> versuchen; (experiment a.) probieren; (sample) [aus]probieren; (put on trial) vor Gericht stellen; to ~ sb for sth jdn wegen einer S. gen anklagen

◆try for vi sich bemühen

◆try on vt anprobieren

◆try out vt ausprobieren; to ~ out ⇆ sb/ sth jdn/etw testen

trying ['traɪ·ɪŋ] adj anstrengend; (difficult) hart; (time) schwierig

T-shirt ['ti·ʃɜrt] n T-Shirt nt

tsp. <pl -> n abbr of teaspoon[ful] TL

T-square ['ti·skwɛr] n Reißschiene f

tsunami [tsu·'na·mi] n Tsunami m

tub [tʌb] n Kübel m; fam (bath) [Bade]-wanne f; (carton) Becher m

tuba ['tu·bə] n Tuba f

tubby ['tʌb·i] adj pummelig

tube [tub] n Röhre f; (bigger) Rohr nt;

(*container*) Tube *f*; **inner ~** Schlauch *m*; **test ~** Reagenzglas *nt*; **the ~** *fam* (*TV*) die Glotze *pej sl* ▶ **to go** <u>down</u> **the ~[s]** den Bach runter gehen *fam*

tuberculosis [tu‧ˌbɜr‧kjə‧ˈlou‧sɪs] *n* Tuberkulose *f*

tuck [tʌk] I. *n* Abnäher *m*; **tummy ~ Operation, bei der am Bauch Fett abgesaugt wird** II. *vt* **to ~ sb into bed** jdn ins Bett [ein]packen *fam*; **to ~ one's legs under oneself** seine Beine unterschlagen

✦tuck away *vt* verstauen; (*hide*) verstecken

✦tuck in *vt* (*shirt*) in die Hose stecken; (*put to bed*) zudecken

Tuesday [ˈtuz‧dər] *n* Dienstag *m*; **[on] ~ afternoon/evening** [am] Dienstagnachmittag/-abend; **on ~ afternoons/evenings** dienstagnachmittags/-abends; **a week/two weeks from ~** Dienstag in einer Woche/zwei Wochen; **a week/two weeks ago ~** Dienstag vor einer Woche/zwei Wochen; **every ~** jeden Dienstag; **last/next/this ~** [am] letzten/[am] nächsten/diesen Dienstag; **~ before last/after next** vorletzten/übernächsten Dienstag; **[on] ~** [am] Dienstag; **on ~ March 4th** am Dienstag, den 4. März; **[on] ~s** dienstags

tuft [tʌft] *n* Büschel *nt*

tug [tʌg] I. *n* Ruck *m*; (*boat*) Schlepper *m*; **to give sth a ~** an etw *dat* zerren II. *vt* <-gg-> ziehen III. *vi* <-gg-> zerren

tug of war *n* Tauziehen *nt*; (*struggle a.*) Hin und Her *nt*

tuition [tu‧ˈɪʃ‧ən] *n* Studiengebühr *f*; (*at school*) Schulgeld *nt*; (*teaching*) Unterricht *m*; **private ~** Einzelunterricht *m*

tulip [ˈtu‧lɪp] *n* Tulpe *f*

tumble [ˈtʌm‧bəl] I. *vi* fallen; (*faster*) stürzen; (*prices*) [stark] fallen II. *n* Sturz *m*; **to take a ~** stürzen

✦tumble over *vi* hinfallen; (*collapse*) umfallen

'tumbledown *adj attr* baufällig

'tumble dryer *n* Wäschetrockner *m*

tumbler [ˈtʌm‧blər] *n* [Trink]glas *nt*; (*acrobat*) Bodenakrobat(in) *m(f)*

tumbleweed [ˈtʌm‧bəl‧wid] *n* Steppenhexe *f*

tummy [ˈtʌm‧i] *n fam* Bauch *m*

tumor [ˈtu‧mər] *n* Geschwulst *f*

tumult [ˈtu‧mʌlt] *n* Krach *m*; (*disorder*) Tumult *m*; (*agitation*) Verwirrung *f*

tumultuous [tu‧ˈmʌl‧tʃu‧əs] *adj* lärmend; (*applause*) stürmisch; (*confused*) turbulent; (*excited*) aufgeregt

tuna [ˈtu‧nə] *n <pl -s>* Thunfisch *m*

tune [tun] I. *n* Melodie *f*; **to the ~ of 2 million dollars** in Höhe von 2 Millionen Dollar; **to be out of ~** falsch spielen ▶ **to** <u>change</u> **one's ~** einen anderen Ton anschlagen II. *vt* (*piano*) stimmen; (*radio*) einstellen; (*car*) tunen

✦tune in *vi* 1. einschalten; **to ~ in to a station** einen Sender einstellen 2. *fam* (*be sensitive*) **to be ~d in to sth** eine Antenne für etw *akk* haben

tuner [ˈtu‧nər] *n* Empfänger *m*; (*person*) Stimmer(in) *m(f)*

'tune-up *n* **to give a car a ~** einen Wagen [neu] einstellen

tunic [ˈtu‧nɪk] *n* Kittel *m*

'tuning fork *n* Stimmgabel *f*

Tunisia [tu‧ˈni‧ʒə] *n* Tunesien *nt*

Tunisian [tu‧ˈni‧ʒən] I. *n* Tunesier(in) *m(f)* II. *adj* tunesisch

tunnel [ˈtʌn‧əl] I. *n* Tunnel *m* ▶ **to** <u>see</u> [**the**] <u>light</u> **at the end of the ~** das Licht am Ende des Tunnels sehen II. *vi* <-l-> einen Tunnel graben; **to ~ under a river** einen Fluss untertunneln III. *vt* <-l-> **to ~ one's way out** sich herausgraben

'tunnel vision *n* Tunnelblick *m*; *fig* Scheuklappendenken *nt*

turban [ˈtɜr‧bən] *n* Turban *m*

turbine [ˈtɜr‧bɪn] *n* Turbine *f*

'turbocharged *adj* mit Turboaufladung nach *n*; *sl* (*energetic*) Turbo-

'turbocharger *n* Turbolader *m*

turbulence [ˈtɜr‧bjʊ‧ləns] *n* Turbulenz *f*; **air ~** Turbulenzen *pl*

turbulent [ˈtɜr‧bjʊ‧lənt] *adj* turbulent; (*sea a.*) unruhig

turd [tɜrd] *n vulg* Scheißhaufen *m derb*

turf *<pl -s or turves>* [tɜrf] *n* Rasen *m*; *fam* (*territory*) Revier *nt*; *fam* (*expertise*) Spezialgebiet *f*; **artificial ~** Kunstrasen *m*

Turk [tɜrk] *n* Türke *m*, Türkin *f*

turkey ['tɜr·ki] *n* Pute(r) *f(m);* (*meat*) Putenfleisch *nt*

Turkey ['tɜr·ki] *n* Türkei *f*

Turkish ['tɜr·kɪʃ] I. *adj* türkisch II. *n* Türkisch *nt*

turmoil ['tɜr·mɔɪl] *n* Tumult *m;* **her mind was in ~** sie war völlig durcheinander

turn [tɜrn] I. *n* Drehung *f;* (*change in direction*) Kurve *f;* **"no left ~"** „Links abbiegen verboten"; **things took an ugly ~** *fig* die Sache nahm eine üble Wendung; **it's my ~ now!** jetzt bin ich dran!; **the ~ of the century** die Jahrhundertwende; **to take ~s doing sth** etw abwechselnd tun; **to do sb a good ~** jdm einen guten Dienst erweisen ▶ **one good ~ deserves another** *saying* eine Hand wäscht die andere II. *vt* drehen; (*switch direction a.*) wenden; (*aim*) richten; **the shock ~ed her hair gray overnight** durch den Schock wurde sie über Nacht grau; **to ~ the corner** um die Ecke biegen; **to ~ one's attention to sth** seine Aufmerksamkeit etw *dat* zuwenden; **to ~ sth/sb into sth** etw/ jdn in etw *akk* umwandeln; **to ~ sth [over]** umdrehen; (*page*) umblättern ▶ **to ~ sb's back on sb/sth** sich von jdm/etw abwenden; **to ~ a blind eye to sth** die Augen vor etw *dat* verschließen III. *vi* 1. sich drehen; **to ~ around [and around]** sich umdrehen 2. (*wind*) drehen; *fig* sich wenden; **to ~ around** (*person*) sich umdrehen; (*car*) wenden; **to ~ left/right** [nach] links/rechts abbiegen; **to ~ on one's heels** auf dem Absatz kehrtmachen 3. **to ~ to sb for help** jdn um Hilfe bitten 4. (*change*) werden; (*milk*) sauer werden; (*leaves*) sich verfärben; (*luck*) sich wenden; **his face ~ed green** er wurde ganz grün im Gesicht; **to ~ into sth** zu etw *dat* werden 5. **to ~ to sth** (*subject*) sich etw *dat* zuwenden 6. **to ~ 20** 20 werden ▶ **to ~ [over] in one's grave** sich im Grabe umdrehen

◆**turn against** I. *vi* sich auflehnen II. *vt* **to ~ sb against sb/sth** jdn gegen jdn/ etw aufwiegeln

◆**turn away** I. *vi* sich abwenden II. *vt* wegrücken; (*repulse*) abweisen

◆**turn back** I. *vi* [wieder] zurückgehen; **there's no ~ing back now!** *fig* jetzt gibt es kein Zurück [mehr]! II. *vt* zurückschicken; (*at border*) zurückweisen; (*sheet*) zurückschlagen

◆**turn down** *vt* abweisen; (*offer*) ablehnen; (*heat*) niedriger stellen; (*music*) leiser stellen; (*sheet*) zurückschlagen; (*collar*) herunterschlagen

◆**turn in** I. *vt* 1. (*to police: thing*) abgeben; (*person*) verpfeifen; **to ~ oneself in to the police** sich der Polizei stellen 2. (*submit*) einreichen 3. (*inwards*) nach innen drehen II. *vi* 1. *fam* (*go to bed*) sich in die Falle hauen 2. (*drive in*) einbiegen

◆**turn off** I. *vt* abschalten; (*engine*) abstellen; (*gas*) abdrehen; (*lights*) ausmachen; (*TV*) ausschalten; **to ~ sb off** jdm die Lust nehmen; (*be sexually unappealing*) jdn abtörnen *sl* II. *vi* abbiegen

◆**turn on** I. *vt* einschalten; (*heat*) aufdrehen; (*lights*) anmachen; *fam* (*excite*) anmachen; (*sexually a.*) antörnen *sl* II. *vi* einschalten; **to ~ on sb** auf jdn losgehen

◆**turn out** I. *vi* sich entwickeln; (*be revealed to be*) sich herausstellen; (*arrive*) erscheinen; **how did it ~ out?** wie ist es gelaufen? *fam* II. *vt* ausmachen; (*kick out*) [hinaus]werfen *fam;* (*empty*) [aus] leeren; (*pockets*) umdrehen; (*products*) produzieren

◆**turn over** I. *vi* sich umdrehen; (*boat*) kentern; (*car*) sich überschlagen; (*pages*) umblättern; (*sell*) laufen; (*engine*) laufen; (*start*) anspringen II. *vt* umdrehen; (*mattress*) wenden; (*page*) umblättern; (*soil*) umgraben; (*ponder*) sorgfältig überdenken; **to ~ over ⇆ sth to sb** (*delegate responsibility*) jdm etw übertragen; (*give*) jdm etw [über]geben; **to ~ sth over in one's head** sich *dat* etw durch den Kopf gehen lassen ▶ **to ~ over a new leaf** einen [ganz] neuen Anfang machen

◆**turn up** I. *vi* erscheinen; (*become available*) sich ergeben; (*solution*) sich finden; (*happen*) passieren II. *vt* aufdrehen; (*music*) lauter machen; (*heat*) höher stellen; (*collar*) hochschlagen;

(*find*) finden

'**turnabout** n Umschwung m

'**turnaround** n Wende f; (*of health*) Besserung f; (*of company*) Aufschwung m; (*sudden reversal*) Kehrtwendung f

'**turning point** n Wendepunkt m

turnip ['tɜr·nɪp] n [Steck]rübe f

'**turnoff** ['tɜrn·ɔf] n Abzweigung f; (*sth unappealing*) Gräuel nt; **to be a real ~** (*sexually*) abtörnen sl

'**turnout** ['tɜrn·aʊt] n Teilnahme f; POL Wahlbeteiligung f

'**turnover** ['tɜrn·ɔʊ·vər] n **1.** apple ~ Apfeltasche f **2.** (*of staff*) Fluktuation f geh; (*of business*) Umsatz m

'**turnstile** n Drehkreuz nt

'**turntable** n Drehscheibe f; (*for records*) Plattenteller m

turpentine ['tɜr·pən·taɪn] n Terpentin nt

turquoise ['tɜr·kwɔɪz] **I.** n Türkis m **II.** adj türkis[farben]

turtle <pl -> ['tɜr·təl] n Schildkröte f

'**turtledove** n Turteltaube f

'**turtleneck** n Rollkragen m; (*sweater*) Rollkragenpullover m

tush [tʊʃ] n sl Hintern m fam

tusk [tʌsk] n Stoßzahn m

tussle ['tʌs·əl] **I.** vi sich balgen; **to ~ [with sb] over sth** [mit jdm] über etw akk streiten **II.** n Rauferei f; (*argument*) Streiterei f

tut [tʌt] interj ~ ~ na, na!

tutor ['tu·tər] **I.** n Nachhilfelehrer(in) m(f); (*private teacher*) Privatlehrer(in) m(f) **II.** vt (*in addition to school lessons*) Nachhilfestunden geben; (*private tuition*) Privatunterricht erteilen

tuxedo [tʌk·'si·doʊ] n Smoking m

TV [ˌti·'vi] n abbr of **television** Fernseher m; (*programming*) Fernsehen nt; **on ~** im Fernsehen

twang [twæŋ] **I.** n Doing nt **II.** vt zupfen **III.** vi einen sirrenden Ton von sich geben

tweak [twik] **I.** vt zupfen; (*adjust*) gerade ziehen; **this proposal still needs some ~ing** an diesem Vorschlag muss noch etwas gefeilt werden **II.** n Zupfen nt

tweed [twid] n Tweed m

tweet [twit] **I.** vi piepsen **II.** n Piepsen nt

tweeter ['twi·tər] n Hochtonlautsprecher m

tweezers ['twi·zərz] npl [**pair of**] ~ Pinzette f

twelfth [twelfθ] **I.** adj zwölfte(r, s) **II.** adv als zwölfte(r, s) **III.** n ~ der/die/das Zwölfte; (*date*) der Zwölfte

twelve [twelv] **I.** adj zwölf; see also **eight II.** n Zwölf f; see also **eight**

twentieth ['twen·ti·əθ] **I.** adj zwanzigste(r, s) **II.** adv an zwanzigster Stelle **III.** n the ~ der/die/das Zwanzigste; (*date*) der Zwanzigste

twenty ['twen·ti] **I.** adj zwanzig; see also **eight II.** n Zwanzig f; see also **eight**

twice [twaɪs] adv zweimal; (*doubly*) doppelt; **~ a day** zweimal täglich; **she is ~ his age** sie ist doppelt so alt wie er

twiddle ['twɪd·əl] vt [herum]drehen; **to ~ one's thumbs** Däumchen drehen

twig [twɪg] n [kleiner] Zweig

twilight ['twaɪ·laɪt] n Zwielicht nt

twin [twɪn] **I.** n Zwilling m; (*thing*) Pendant nt geh; **identical/fraternal ~s** eineiige/zweieiige Zwillinge **II.** adj Zwillings-; (*rooms*) miteinander verbunden; (*cities*) Partner- **III.** vt <-nn-> **to ~ sth [with sth]** etw [mit etw dat] [partnerschaftlich] verbinden

twine [twaɪn] **I.** n Schnur f **II.** vi sich schlingen **III.** vt **to ~ sth together** etw ineinanderschlingen

twinge [twɪndʒ] n Stechen nt; **~ of pain** stechender Schmerz; **~ of guilt** Anflug m eines schlechten Gewissens

twinkle ['twɪŋ·kəl] **I.** vi funkeln **II.** n Funkeln nt; **to do sth with a ~ in one's eye** etw mit einem [verschmitzten] Augenzwinkern tun

twinkling ['twɪŋ·klɪŋ] **I.** adj funkelnd **II.** n kurzer Augenblick; **in the ~ of an eye** im Handumdrehen

twin 'room n Zweibettzimmer nt

'**twinset, 'twin set** n Twinset nt

twirl [twɜrl] **I.** vt wirbeln **II.** vt rotieren lassen; (*in dancing*) [herum]wirbeln **III.** n Wirbel m; (*in dancing*) Drehung f

twist [twɪst] **I.** vt [ver]drehen; (*coil*) herumwickeln; (*sprain*) sich verrenken; **to ~ sth off** etw abdrehen; **to ~ sb's arm** fig auf jdn Druck ausüben **II.** vi

sich winden; **to ~ and turn** (*road*) sich schlängeln **III.** *n* Drehung *f;* (*bend*) Kurve *f;* (*change*) Wendung *f;* **to give sth a ~** etw [herum]drehen; **cruel ~ of fate** grausame Wendung des Schicksals

twisted ['twɪs·tɪd] *adj* verdreht; (*ankle*) gezerrt; (*winding*) verschlungen; (*path*) gewunden

twister ['twɪs·tər] *n fam* Tornado *m*

twitch [twɪtʃ] **I.** *vi* zucken **II.** *vt* zucken mit +*dat;* (*tug*) zupfen; **to ~ one's nose** (*rabbit*) schnuppern **III.** *n* <*pl* -es> **1. to have a [nervous] ~** nervöse Zuckungen *pl* haben **2.** (*tug*) Ruck *m*

twitter ['twɪt·ər] *vi* zwitschern; **to ~ away** (*chatter*) vor sich hinplappern

two [tu] **I.** *adj* zwei; **~ [o'clock]** zwei [Uhr]; **to break sth in ~** etw entzwei brechen; **the ~ of you** ihr beide; *see also* **eight** ▶ **to throw in one's ~ cents [worth]** seinen Senf dazugeben; **to be ~ of a [kind]** aus dem gleichen Holz geschnitzt sein; **to be of ~ [minds]** hin- und hergerissen sein; **there are no ~ [ways] about it** es gibt keine andere Möglichkeit **II.** *n* Zwei *f; see also* **eight**

'**two-bit** *adj attr pej fam* billig *pej*

'**two-di·men·sion·al** *adj* zweidimensional; *pej* (*plot*) flach

'**two-faced** *adj pej* falsch

twofold ['tu·foʊld] **I.** *adj* zweifach; (*with two parts*) zweiteilig **II.** *adv* zweifach; **to increase sth ~** etw verdoppeln

'**two-piece** *n* Bikini *m;* (*suit*) Zweiteiler *m*

twosome ['tu·səm] *n* Duo *nt;* (*couple*) Paar *nt;* **as a ~** zu zweit

'**two-time** *vt fam* **to ~ sb [with sb]** jdn [mit jdm] betrügen

TX *abbr of* **Texas**

TXT *vt short for* **text; to ~ sth** etw texten

tycoon [taɪ·'kun] *n* [Industrie]magnat(in) *m(f)*

tyke [taɪk] *n fam* Gör *nt*

type [taɪp] **I.** *n* **1.** Art *f;* (*of skin*) Typ *m;* (*of food*) Sorte *f* **2.** (*character*) Typ *m;* **to be one's ~** jds Typ sein *fam* **3.** (*lettering*) Schriftart *f;* **italic ~** Kursivschrift *f* **II.** *vt* tippen; (*classify*) typisieren *geh*

III. *vi* Maschine schreiben

◆**type out** *vt* tippen

◆**type up** *vt* erfassen

'**typecast** *vt irreg, usu passive* **to be ~** auf eine Rolle festgelegt sein/werden

'**typeface** *n* Schrift[art] *f*

'**typescript** *n* maschinengeschriebenes Manuskript

'**typesetter** *n* Setzmaschine *f;* (*printer*) [Schrift]setzer(in) *m(f)*

'**typesetting** *n* Setzen *nt*

'**typewrite** *vt irreg* tippen

'**typewriter** *n* Schreibmaschine *f*

'**typewritten** *adj* maschinengeschrieben

typhoid ['taɪ·fɔɪd], **typhoid 'fever** *n* Typhus *m*

typhoon [taɪ·'fun] *n* Taifun *m*

typhus ['taɪ·fəs] *n* Typhus *m*

typical ['tɪp·ɪ·kəl] *adj* typisch; (*symptom a.*) charakteristisch

typically ['tɪp·ɪ·kəl·i] *adv* typisch; **~, ...** normalerweise ...

typing ['taɪ·pɪŋ] *n* Tippen *nt*

typist ['taɪ·pɪst] *n* Schreibkraft *f*

typo ['taɪ·poʊ] *n fam* Druckfehler *m*

tyrannical [tɪ·'ræn·ɪ·kəl] *adj* tyrannisch

tyrannize ['tɪr·ə·naɪz] *vt* tyrannisieren

tyranny ['tɪr·ə·ni] *n* Tyrannei *f*

tyrant ['taɪ·rənt] *n* Tyrann(in) *m(f);* (*bossy man*) [Haus]tyrann *m pej;* (*bossy woman*) [Haus]drachen *m pej fam*

Tyrol [tɪ·'roʊl] *n* **the ~** Tirol *nt*

tzar [zar] *n see* **czar**

U

U <*pl* -'s>, **u** <*pl* -'s> [ju] *n* (*letter*) U *nt, u nt;* **~ as in Uniform** U wie Ulrich

U¹ [ju] *n* CHEM *see* **uranium** U *nt*

U² [ju] *fam abbr of* **university** Uni *f*

UAE [ju·eɪ·'i] *n pl abbr of* **United Arab Emirates; the ~** die VAE

U-boat ['ju·boʊt] *n* U-Boot *nt*

UFO <*pl* -s> [ju·ef·'oʊ] *n abbr of* **unidentified flying object** UFO *nt*

ugh [ʌɡ] *interj fam* igitt!

ugliness ['ʌɡ·li·nɪs] *n* Hässlichkeit *f; fig a.* Scheußlichkeit *f*

ugly ['ʌɡ·li] *adj* **1.** (*not beautiful*) hässlich

2. (*unpleasant: rumors*) übel; (*mood*) unerfreulich; **to turn ~** eine üble Wendung nehmen

UHF [ˌjuːeɪtʃˈef] n abbr of **ultrahigh frequency** UHF

UK [juːˈkeɪ] n abbr of **United Kingdom; the ~** das Vereinigte Königreich

Ukraine [juːˈkreɪn] n die Ukraine

ulcer [ˈʌlsər] n Geschwür nt

ulterior [ʌlˈtɪriər] adj **~ motive** Hintergedanke m

ultimate [ˈʌltəmɪt] adj attr **1.** (*unbeatable*) bester(r, s) **2.** (*highest*) höchste(r, s); (*deterrent*) wirksamste(r, s) **3.** (*final*) endgültig; **~ destination** Endziel nt

ultimately [ˈʌltəmɪtli] adv (*in the end*) letzten Endes; (*eventually*) letztlich

ultimatum <pl -ta> [ʌltəˈmeɪtəm] n Ultimatum nt

ultrahigh ˈfrequency n Ultrahochfrequenz f

ultramaˈrine adj ultramarin[blau]

ultraˈsonic adj Ultraschall-

ultraˈviolet adj ultraviolett

um [əm] interj fam hm, äh

umˈbilical cord n Nabelschnur f

umbrella [ʌmˈbrelə] n Regenschirm m; **folding ~** Knirps® m

umpire [ˈʌmpaɪr] n SPORT (*esp baseball*) Schiedsrichter(in) m(f)

umpteen [ˈʌmptiːn] adj fam zig; **~ times** zigmal

UN [juːˈen] n pl abbr of **United Nations; the ~** die UN [or UNO]

unable [ʌnˈeɪbəl] adj **to be ~ to do sth** etw nicht tun können

unabridged [ʌnəˈbrɪdʒd] adj ungekürzt

unacceptable [ʌnəkˈseptəbəl] adj inakzeptabel; (*offer*) unannehmbar

unaccompanied [ʌnəˈkʌmpənid] adj ohne Begleitung nach n, präd; (*baggage*) herrenlos

unaccounted-for [ʌnəˈkaʊntɪdˌfɔr] adj pred **1.** (*unexplained*) ungeklärt **2.** (*not included in count*) nicht erfasst; (*person*) vermisst

unaccustomed [ʌnəˈkʌstəmd] adj **to be ~ to doing sth** es nicht gewohnt sein, etw zu tun

unaddressed [ʌnəˈdrest] adj (*enve-*

lope) nicht adressiert

unadorned [ʌnəˈdɔrnd] adj schlicht

unadulterated [ʌnəˈdʌltəˌreɪtɪd] adj unverfälscht; (*alcohol*) rein

unadventurous [ʌnədˈventʃərəs] adj (*person*) wenig unternehmungslustig

unaffected [ʌnəˈfektɪd] adj **1.** (*unchanged*) unberührt; (*unmoved*) unbeeindruckt **2.** (*natural*) natürlich; (*manner*) ungekünstelt

unaided [ʌnˈeɪdɪd] adj ohne fremde Hilfe nach n

unaltered [ʌnˈɔltərd] adj unverändert

unambiguous [ʌnæmˈbɪgjuːəs] adj unzweideutig; (*statement*) eindeutig

un-American [ʌnəˈmɛrɪkən] adj unamerikanisch; **~ activities** ≈Landesverrat m (*gegen den amerikanischen Staat gerichtete Umtriebe*)

unanimous [juːˈnænəməs] adj einstimmig

unanswerable [ʌnˈænsərəbəl] adj **1. to be ~** nicht zu beantworten sein **2.** (*irrefutable*) unwiderlegbar

unanswered [ʌnˈænsərd] adj unbeantwortet

unapproachable [ʌnəˈproʊtʃəbəl] adj unzugänglich; (*person a.*) unnahbar

unarmed [ʌnˈɑrmd] adj unbewaffnet

unasked [ʌnˈæskt] adj **1.** ungefragt; **an ~ question** eine Frage, die keiner zu stellen wagt **2.** (*not requested*) **~-for** ungebeten

unassuming [ʌnəˈsuːmɪŋ] adj bescheiden

unattached [ʌnəˈtætʃt] adj **1.** (*not connected*) einzeln **2.** (*bachelor*) ungebunden

unattended [ʌnəˈtendɪd] adj **1.** (*alone*) unbegleitet; (*baggage*) unbeaufsichtigt **2.** (*unmanned*) nicht besetzt

unattractive [ʌnəˈtræktɪv] adj unattraktiv; (*personality*) wenig anziehend

unauthorized [ʌnˈɔθəˌraɪzd] adj nicht autorisiert; (*person, access*) unbefugt attr

unavailable [ʌnəˈveɪləbəl] adj (*not in*) nicht verfügbar; (*person*) nicht erreichbar

unavoidable [ʌnəˈvɔɪdəbəl] adj unvermeidlich

U

unaware [ˌʌn·ə·ˈwer] adj to be ~ of sth sich dat einer S. gen nicht bewusst sein

unawares [ˌʌn·ə·ˈwerz] adv to catch sb ~ jdn überraschen

unbalanced [ʌn·ˈbæl·ənst] adj 1. (uneven) schief; (account) nicht ausgeglichen; (diet) unausgewogen 2. (unstable) labil

unbearable [ʌn·ˈber·ə·bəl] adj unerträglich

unbeatable [ʌn·ˈbi·tə·bəl] adj 1. unschlagbar; (army) unbesiegbar 2. (perfect) unübertrefflich

unbeaten [ʌn·ˈbi·tən] adj ungeschlagen

unbeknown [ˌʌn·bɪ·ˈnoʊn], **unbeknownst** [ˌʌn·bɪ·ˈnoʊnst] adv ~ to sb ohne jds Wissen

unbelievable [ˌʌn·bɪ·ˈli·və·bəl] adj 1. (surprising) unglaublich 2. fam (extraordinary) sagenhaft

unbelieving [ˌʌn·bɪ·ˈli·vɪŋ] adj ungläubig

unbend [ʌn·ˈbend] I. vt <bent, bent> strecken II. vi <bent, bent> (straighten out) [wieder] gerade werden; (person) sich aufrichten

unbiased [ʌn·ˈbaɪ·əst] adj unparteiisch; (report) objektiv

unbleached [ʌn·ˈblitʃt] adj ungebleicht

unborn [ʌn·ˈbɔrn] adj ungeboren

unbreakable [ʌn·ˈbreɪ·kə·bəl] adj unzerbrechlich; (habit) fest verankert; (promise) bindend; (rule) unumstößlich

unbroken [ʌn·ˈbroʊ·kən] adj 1. unbeschädigt; (record) ungebrochen 2. (sleep) ungestört

unbuckle [ʌn·ˈbʌk·əl] vt aufschnallen; (seatbelt) öffnen

unburden [ʌn·ˈbɜr·dən] vt to ~ oneself [to sb] [jdm] sein Herz ausschütten

unbutton [ʌn·ˈbʌt·ən] vt, vi aufknöpfen

uncalled for adj pred, **uncalled-for** [ʌn·ˈkɔld·fɔr] adj attr unnötig; (remark) unpassend

uncanny [ʌn·ˈkæn·i] adj unheimlich

uncared for adj pred, **uncared-for** [ʌn·ˈkerd·fɔr] adj attr ungepflegt

unceasing [ʌn·ˈsi·sɪŋ] adj unaufhörlich; (efforts) unablässig

uncertain [ʌn·ˈsɜr·tən] adj 1. (unsure) unsicher; **in no ~ terms** klar und deutlich 2. (unpredictable) ungewiss; (tem-

per) launenhaft

uncertainty [ʌn·ˈsɜr·tən·ti] n 1. (doubtfulness) Ungewissheit f 2. (hesitancy) Unsicherheit f

unchallenged [ʌn·ˈtʃæl·ɪndʒd] adj unwidersprochen; **to go ~** unangefochten bleiben

unchanged [ʌn·ˈtʃeɪndʒd] adj unverändert

uncharted [ʌn·ˈtʃar·tɪd] adj fig ~ **territory** Neuland nt

unchecked [ʌn·ˈtʃekt] adj 1. (unrestrained) unkontrolliert; **to continue ~** ungehindert weitergehen 2. (not examined) ungeprüft

unclaimed [ʌn·ˈkleɪmd] adj nicht beansprucht; (baggage) nicht abgeholt

unclassified [ʌn·ˈklæs·ɪ·faɪd] adj nicht geheim

uncle [ˈʌŋ·kəl] n Onkel m ▸ **to cry** [or **say**] ~ fam klein beigeben

unclean [ʌn·ˈklin] adj 1. (unhygienic) verunreinigt 2. (impure) schmutzig

unclear [ʌn·ˈklɪr] adj 1. (not certain) unklar 2. (vague) vage

Uncle 'Sam n Uncle Sam m (Bezeichnung für die USA)

uncluttered [ʌn·ˈklʌt·ərd] adj 1. (tidy) aufgeräumt 2. fig (mind) frei

uncomfortable [ʌn·ˈkʌm·fər·tə·bəl] adj 1. (causing discomfort) unbequem 2. (uneasy) unbehaglich; (silence) gespannt

uncommitted [ˌʌn·kə·ˈmɪt·ɪd] adj unentschieden

uncommon [ʌn·ˈkam·ən] adj selten

uncommunicative [ˌʌn·kə·ˈmju·nɪ·kə·tɪv] adj to be ~ about sth wenig über etw sprechen

uncompromising [ʌn·ˈkam·prə·maɪ·zɪŋ] adj kompromisslos

unconcerned [ˌʌn·kən·ˈsɜrnd] adj 1. (not worried) unbekümmert 2. (indifferent) desinteressiert

unconditional [ˌʌn·kən·ˈdɪʃ·ə·nəl] adj bedingungslos; (love a.) rückhaltlos

unconfirmed [ˌʌn·kən·ˈfɜrmd] adj unbestätigt

unconscious [ʌn·ˈkan·ʃəs] adj bewusstlos; **to be ~ of sth** sich dat einer S. gen nicht bewusst sein

unconsciously [ʌn·ˈkan·ʃəs·li] *adv* unbewusst

unconsciousness [ʌn·ˈkan·ʃəs·nɪs] *n* Bewusstlosigkeit *f*

unconstitutional [ʌn·kan·stɪ·ˈtu·ʃə·nəl] *adj* verfassungswidrig

uncontested [ʌn·kən·ˈtes·tɪd] *adj* 1. (*unchallenged*) unbestritten; (*claim*) unstreitig 2. LAW ~ **divorce** einvernehmliche Scheidung

uncontrollable [ʌn·kən·ˈtrou·lə·bəl] *adj* unkontrollierbar; (*bleeding*) unstillbar

uncontrolled [ʌn·kən·ˈtrould] *adj* unkontrolliert; (*aggression*) unbeherrscht

unconventional [ʌn·kən·ˈven·ʃə·nəl] *adj* unkonventionell

unconvincing [ʌn·kən·ˈvɪn·sɪŋ] *adj* 1. (*not persuasive*) nicht überzeugend 2. (*not credible*) unglaubwürdig

uncooked [ʌn·ˈkʊkt] *adj* roh

uncooperative [ʌn·kou·ˈap·ər·ə·tɪv] *adj* unkooperativ

uncountable [ʌn·ˈkaʊn·tə·bəl] *adj* unzählbar; (*countless*) zahllos

uncouple [ʌn·ˈkʌp·əl] *vt* MECH abkuppeln

uncover [ʌn·ˈkʌv·ər] *vt* 1. (*bare*) freilegen 2. (*disclose*) entdecken; (*secret*) aufdecken

uncritical [ʌn·ˈkrɪt·ɪ·kəl] *adj* unkritisch

uncrowned [ʌn·ˈkraʊnd] *adj* ungekrönt *a. fig*

uncut [ʌn·ˈkʌt] *adj* 1. ungeschnitten 2. (*not shortened: version*) ungekürzt

undated [ʌn·ˈdeɪ·tɪd] *adj* undatiert

undecided [ʌn·dɪ·ˈsaɪ·dɪd] *adj* 1. (*hesitant*) unentschlossen; **to be ~ about sth** sich *dat* über etw *akk* [noch] unklar sein 2. (*vote*) unentschieden

undeclared [ʌn·dɪ·ˈklerd] *adj* 1. FIN nicht deklariert 2. (*unofficial*) ~ **war** Krieg *m* ohne Kriegserklärung

undefined [ʌn·dɪ·ˈfaɪnd] *adj* 1. unbestimmt 2. (*lacking clarity*) vage

undelivered [ʌn·dɪ·ˈlɪv·ərd] *adj* nicht zugestellt

undemocratic [ʌn·dem·ə·ˈkræt·ɪk] *adj* undemokratisch

undemonstrative [ʌn·dɪ·ˈman·strə·tɪv] *adj* zurückhaltend

undeniable [ʌn·dɪ·ˈnaɪ·ə·bəl] *adj* ~ **evi-**

dence eindeutiger Beweis

undeniably [ʌn·dɪ·ˈnaɪ·ə·bli] *adv* unbestreitbar

under [ˈʌn·dər] I. *prep* 1. (*below*) unter +*dat; with verbs of motion* unter +*akk* 2. (*less than*) unter +*dat;* **to cost ~ 5 dollars** weniger als fünf Dollar kosten 3. (*governed by*) unter +*dat;* ~ **the supervision of sb** unter jds Aufsicht 4. (*in state of*) unter +*dat;* ~ **arrest** unter Arrest; ~ [**no**] **circumstances** unter [keinen] Umständen II. *adv* 1. (*down*) **to go** ~ untergehen; (*company*) Pleite machen 2. (*less*) **suitable for kids aged five and** ~ geeignet für Kinder von fünf Jahren und darunter

under·a·chieve *vi* weniger leisten als erwartet

under·age *adj* minderjährig

underarm *n* Achselhöhle *f*

under·charge *vt, vi* zu wenig berechnen

underclothes *npl see* **underwear**

undercoat I. *n* 1. (*paint*) Grundierung *f* 2. (*fur*) Wollhaarkleid *nt* II. *vt* grundieren

undercover I. *adj attr* geheim; ~ **police officer** Geheimpolizist(in) *m(f)* II. *adv* geheim

undercurrent *n* 1. (*of sea*) Unterströmung *f* 2. *fig* Unterton *m*

underde·veloped *adj* unterentwickelt

underdog *n* Außenseiter(in) *m(f)*

underdone *adj* (*undercooked*) nicht gar; (*meat*) blutig

under·dressed *adj* (*too casual*) zu einfach gekleidet

undere·quipped *adj* unzureichend ausgerüstet

under·estimate *vt* unterschätzen

underex·pose *vt* (*photo*) unterbelichten

under·fed *adj* unterernährt

under·funding *n* Unterfinanzierung *f*

under·go <-went, -gone> *vt* **to ~ surgery** sich einer Operation unterziehen

under·graduate *n* Student(in) *m(f)*

underground I. *adj* 1. unterirdisch; ~ **cable** Erdkabel *nt* 2. POL Untergrund-II. *adv* 1. GEOG unter der Erde 2. POL **to go** ~ in den Untergrund gehen

undergrowth *n* Dickicht *nt*

underhand I. *adj* (*devious*) hinterhäl-

U

tig; ~ **dealings** betrügerische Machenschaften **II.** *adv* SPORT mit der Hand von unten

underin'sured *adj* unterversichert

under'lay *vt pt of* **underlie**

under'lie <-y-, -lay, -lain> *vt* zugrunde liegen

'**underline** *vt* **1.** (*draw line*) unterstreichen **2.** (*emphasize*) betonen

under'lying *adj attr* zugrunde liegend

under'manned *adj* unterbesetzt

under'mine *vt* (*weaken*) untergraben; (*confidence*) schwächen

underneath [ʌn·dər·'niθ] **I.** *prep* unter +*dat*; *with vbs of motion* unter +*akk* **II.** *adv* darunter

under'nourished *adj* unterernährt

under'paid *adj* unterbezahlt

'**underpants** *npl* Unterhose *f*

under'pay <-paid, -paid> *vt usu passive* unterbezahlen

under'play *vt* herunterspielen

under'populated *adj* unterbevölkert

under'privileged *adj* unterprivilegiert

under'rated *adj* unterschätzt

under'sell <-sold, -sold> *vt* **1.** (*offer cheaper: competitor*) unterbieten **2.** (*undervalue*) unterbewerten

'**undershirt** *n* Unterhemd *nt*

'**underside** *n usu sing* Unterseite *f*

under'signed <*pl* -> *n form* **the** ~ der/ die Unterzeichnete

'**underskirt** *n* Unterrock *m*

under'staffed *adj* unterbesetzt

understand <-stood, -stood> [ʌn·dər·'stænd] **I.** *vt* **1.** (*perceive meaning*) verstehen; **to not** ~ **a single word** kein einziges Wort verstehen; **to** ~ **one another** sich verstehen **2.** (*comprehend significance*) begreifen **3.** (*sympathize with*) **to** ~ **sb** für jdn Verständnis haben **4.** (*be informed*) **to** ~ [**that**] ... hören, dass ... **II.** *vi* **1.** (*comprehend*) verstehen, kapieren *fam* **2.** (*infer*) **to** ~ **from sth that** ... aus etw *dat* schließen, dass ...

understandable [ʌn·dər·'stæn·də·bəl] *adj* verständlich

understanding [ʌn·dər·'stæn·dɪŋ] **I.** *n* **1.** (*comprehension*) Verständnis *nt* **2.** (*agreement*) Übereinkunft *f*; **tacit** ~

stillschweigendes Abkommen **3.** (*condition*) Bedingung *f*; **to do sth on the** ~ **that** ... etw unter der Bedingung machen, dass ... **II.** *adj* verständnisvoll

understatement [ʌn·dər·'steɪt·mənt] *n* Untertreibung *f*, Understatement *nt*

understood [ʌn·dər·'stʊd] *pt, pp of* **understand**

understudy ['ʌn·dər·ˌstʌd·i] *n* THEAT Zweitbesetzung *f*

undertake <-took, -taken> [ʌn·dər·'teɪk] *vt* **1.** (*take on*) durchführen **2.** (*guarantee*) **to** ~ **to do sth** sich verpflichten, etw zu tun

undertaker ['ʌn·dər·ˌteɪ·kər] *n see* **funeral director**

undertaking [ʌn·dər·'teɪ·kɪŋ] *n* **1.** (*project*) Unternehmung *f* **2.** (*pledge*) Verpflichtung *f*

'**undertone** *n* gedämpfte Stimme

under'used, under'utilized *adj* nicht [voll] ausgelastet

under'value *vt* unterbewerten; (*person*) unterschätzen

'**underwater I.** *adj* Unterwasser- **II.** *adv* unter Wasser

'**underwear** *n* Unterwäsche *f*

'**underweight** *adj* untergewichtig

'**underworld** *n* Unterwelt *f*

under'write <-wrote, -written> *vt* **to** ~ **a loan** für einen Kredit bürgen

'**underwriter** *n* Versicherer, Versicherin *m, f*

undesirable [ʌn·dɪ·'zaɪ·rə·bəl] *adj* unerwünscht

undeveloped [ˌʌn·dɪ·'vel·əpt] *adj* **1.** (*land*) unerschlossen **2.** ECON unterentwickelt

undid [ʌn·'dɪd] *pt of* **undo**

undies ['ʌn·diz] *npl fam* Unterwäsche *f kein pl*

undiscovered [ˌʌn·dɪ·'skʌv·ərd] *adj* unentdeckt

undisputed [ʌn·dɪ·'spju·t̬ɪd] *adj* unumstritten

undisturbed [ʌn·dɪ·'stɜrbd] *adj* **1.** (*untouched*) unberührt **2.** (*uninterrupted*) ungestört

undivided [ʌn·dɪ·'vaɪ·dɪd] *adj* ungeteilt

undo <-did, -done> [ʌn·'du] **I.** *vt* **1.** (*unfasten*) öffnen; (*button, zipper*) aufmachen **2.** (*cancel: damage*) beheben; **to** ~

the good work die gute Arbeit zunichtemachen **II.** *vi* (*button*) aufgehen

undone [ʌnˈdʌn] **I.** *vt pp of* **undo** **II.** *adj* offen; **to come ~** aufgehen

undoubted [ʌnˈdaʊ·tɪd] *adj* unbestritten

undoubtedly [ʌnˈdaʊ·tɪd·li] *adv* zweifellos

undreamed of *adj pred*, **undreamed-of** [ʌnˈdrimd·ˌʌv] *adj attr*, **undreamt of** *adj pred*, **undreamt-of** [ʌnˈdremt·ˌʌv] *attr* unvorstellbar; (*success*) ungeahnt

undress [ʌnˈdres] *vt, vi* [sich] ausziehen

undressed [ʌnˈdrest] *adj pred* unbekleidet

undue [ʌnˈdu] *adj* ungebührlich; **~ pressure** übermäßiger Druck

unduly [ʌnˈdu·li] *adv* unangemessen; (*concerned*) übermäßig

undying [ʌnˈdaɪ·ɪŋ] *adj attr* unvergänglich; (*love*) ewig

unearned [ʌnˈɜrnd] *adj* **1.** (*undeserved*) unverdient **2.** (*not worked for*) nicht erarbeitet

unearth [ʌnˈɜrθ] *vt* (*discover*) entdecken; (*truth*) ans Licht bringen

unearthly [ʌnˈɜrθ·li] *adj* **1.** (*eerie*) gespenstisch; (*noise*) grässlich **2.** *fam* (*inconvenient*) **at some ~ hour** zu einer unchristlichen Zeit

unease [ʌnˈiz], **uneasiness** [ʌnˈiz·ɪ·nɪs] *n* Unbehagen *nt*

uneasy [ʌnˈi·zi] *adj* **1.** (*anxious*) besorgt; (*smile*) gequält **2.** (*causing anxiety*) unangenehm; (*relationship*) gespannt

uneconomic [ʌn·ek·ə·ˈnɑm·ɪk] *adj* unwirtschaftlich

uneducated [ʌnˈedʒ·ə·keɪ·tɪd] *adj* ungebildet

unemotional [ʌn·ɪ·ˈmoʊ·ʃə·nəl] *adj* **1.** (*not feeling emotions*) kühl **2.** (*not revealing emotions*) emotionslos

unemployable [ʌn·ɪm·ˈplɔɪ·ə·bəl] *adj* unvermittelbar

unemployed [ʌn·ɪm·ˈplɔɪd] **I.** *n* **the ~** *pl* die Arbeitslosen **II.** *adj* arbeitslos

unemployment [ʌn·ɪm·ˈplɔɪ·mənt] *n* Arbeitslosigkeit *f*

unemployment compen'sation, unemployment in'surance *n* Arbeitslosenunterstützung *f*, Arbeitslosengeld *nt*

unemployment office *n* Arbeitsamt *nt*

unenviable [ʌn·ˈen·vi·ə·bəl] *adj* wenig beneidenswert

unequal [ʌnˈi·kwəl] *adj* **1.** (*different*) unterschiedlich; **~ triangle** ungleichseitiges Dreieck **2.** (*unjust*) ungerecht; (*contest*) ungleich

unequaled, unequalled *adj* [ʌn·ˈi·kwəld] unübertroffen

UNESCO [ju·ˈnes·koʊ] *n acr for* **United Nations Educational, Scientific and Cultural Organization**; [the] **~** die UNESCO

unethical [ʌnˈeθ·ɪ·kəl] *adj* unmoralisch

uneven [ʌnˈi·vən] *adj* **1.** (*not level*) uneben **2.** (*not parallel*) ungleich; **~ bars** (*gymnastics*) Stufenbarren *m* **3.** (*unfair*) unterschiedlich; (*contest*) ungleich **4.** (*odd*) ungerade

uneventful [ʌn·ɪ·ˈvent·fəl] *adj* ereignislos

unexceptional [ʌn·ɪk·ˈsep·ʃə·nəl] *adj* nicht außergewöhnlich

unexciting [ʌn·ɪk·ˈsaɪ·tɪŋ] *adj* (*uneventful*) ereignislos

unexpected [ʌn·ɪk·ˈspek·tɪd] **I.** *adj* unerwartet; (*opportunity*) unvorhergesehen **II.** *n* **the ~** das Unerwartete

unexplained [ʌn·ɪk·ˈspleɪnd] *adj* unerklärt

unexpressed [ʌn·ɪk·ˈsprest] *adj* unausgesprochen

unfailing [ʌnˈfeɪ·lɪŋ] *adj* beständig; (*loyalty*) unerschütterlich

unfair [ʌnˈfer] *adj* ungerecht

unfaithful [ʌnˈfeɪθ·ful] *adj* untreu

unfamiliar [ʌn·fə·ˈmɪl·jər] *adj* unvertraut; (*experience*) ungewohnt; (*place*) unbekannt

unfashionable [ʌnˈfæʃ·ə·nə·bəl] *adj* unmodisch

unfasten [ʌnˈfæs·ən] **I.** *vt* (*button, belt*) öffnen **II.** *vi* aufgehen

unfavorable [ʌnˈfeɪ·vər·ə·bəl] *adj* **1.** (*adverse*) ungünstig; (*decision*) negativ **2.** (*disadvantageous*) nachteilig

unfeeling [ʌnˈfi·lɪŋ] *adj* gefühllos

unfilled [ʌnˈfɪld] *adj* leer; (*job*) offen

unfinished [ʌnˈfɪn·ɪʃt] *adj* **1.** (*incomplete*) unvollendet; **~ business** offene Fragen *pl* **2.** (*rough*) halbfertig

unfit [ʌnˈfɪt] *adj* **1.** (*unhealthy*) nicht fit;

U

to be ~ for work arbeitsuntauglich sein 2. (*incompetent*) ungeeignet

unflappable [ʌnˈflæp·ə·bəl] *adj fam* unerschütterlich

unflinching [ʌnˈflɪn·tʃɪŋ] *adj* unerschrocken; (*determination*) unbeirrbar

unfold [ʌnˈfoʊld] I. *vt* (*open*) entfalten; (*furniture*) aufklappen II. *vi* 1. (*develop*) sich entwickeln 2. (*open*) aufgehen

unforeseeable [ʌn·fɔrˈsi·ə·bəl] *adj* unvorhersehbar

unforeseen [ʌn·fɔrˈsin] *adj* unvorhergesehen

unforgettable [ʌn·fərˈgeṭ·ə·bəl] *adj* unvergesslich

unforgivable [ʌn·fərˈgɪv·ə·bəl] *adj* unverzeihlich

unfortunate [ʌnˈfɔr·tʃə·nɪt] *adj* 1. (*unlucky*) unglücklich 2. (*regrettable*) bedauerlich; (*manner*) ungeschickt

unfortunately [ʌnˈfɔr·tʃə·nɪt·li] *adv* unglücklicherweise

unfriendly [ʌnˈfrend·li] *adj* unfreundlich; (*hostile*) feindlich; **environmentally ~** umweltschädlich

unfulfilled [ʌn·fʊlˈfild] *adj* (*promise, life*) unerfüllt

unfurnished [ʌnˈfɜr·nɪʃt] *adj* unmöbliert

ungainly [ʌnˈgeɪn·li] *adj* unbeholfen

UN General 'Assembly *n* UN-Vollversammlung *f*

ungentlemanly [ʌnˈdʒen·təl·mən·li] *adj* ungalant *geh*

ungrateful [ʌnˈgreɪt·fəl] *adj* undankbar

unhappy [ʌnˈhæp·i] *adj* unglücklich

unharmed [ʌnˈhɑrmd] *adj* unversehrt

unhealthy [ʌnˈhel·θi] *adj* 1. (*unwell*) kränklich 2. (*harmful*) ungesund

unheard [ʌnˈhɜrd] *adj* ungehört

un'heard-of *adj* 1. (*unknown*) unbekannt 2. (*unthinkable*) undenkbar

unhelpful [ʌnˈhelp·fʊl] *adj* (*person*) nicht hilfsbereit

unhoped-for [ʌnˈhoʊpt·fɔr] *adj* unverhofft

unhurt [ʌnˈhɜrt] *adj* unverletzt

UNICEF [ˈju·nɪ·sef] *n acr for* **United Nations (International) Children's (Emergency) Fund** UNICEF *f*

unidentified [ʌn·aɪˈden·tə·faɪd] *adj* (*unknown*) nicht identifiziert

unification [ju·nɪ·fɪˈkeɪ·ʃən] *n* Vereinigung *f*

uniform [ˈju·nə·fɔrm] I. *n* 1. (*outfit*) Uniform *f* 2. *fam* (*police officer*) Polizist(in) *m(f)* II. *adj* 1. (*same*) einheitlich 2. (*consistent*) gleich bleibend; (*color*) einförmig

uniformity [ju·nəˈfɔr·mə·ṭi] *n* 1. (*sameness*) Einheitlichkeit *f* 2. (*consistency*) Gleichmäßigkeit *f*

unilateral [ju·nəˈlæt·ər·əl] *adj* einseitig

unimaginable [ʌn·ɪˈmædʒ·ə·nə·bəl] *adj* unvorstellbar

unimportant [ʌn·ɪmˈpɔr·tənt] *adj* unwichtig

uninhabited [ʌn·ɪnˈhæb·ɪ·ṭɪd] *adj* (*building*) unbewohnt; (*land a.*) unbesiedelt

uninhibited [ʌn·ɪnˈhɪb·ɪ·ṭɪd] *adj* ungehemmt

uninjured [ʌnˈɪn·dʒərd] *adj* unverletzt

unintelligent [ʌn·ɪnˈtel·ɪ·dʒənt] *adj* unintelligent

unintelligible [ʌn·ɪnˈtel·ɪ·dʒə·bəl] *adj* unverständlich

unintentional [ʌn·ɪnˈten·ʃə·nəl] *adj* unabsichtlich

uninterested [ʌnˈɪn·trɪ·stɪd] *adj* uninteressiert; **to be ~ in sth/sb** kein Interesse an etw/jdm haben

uninteresting [ʌnˈɪn·trɪ·stɪŋ] *adj* uninteressant

uninterrupted [ʌn·ɪn·tərˈʌp·tɪd] *adj* ununterbrochen; (*rest*) ungestört

union [ˈjun·jən] *n* 1. (*state*) Union *f* 2. (*organization*) Verband *m*; (*labor union*) Gewerkschaft *f*

unique [juˈnik] *adj* 1. (*only*) einzigartig 2. (*exceptional*) einzigartig; (*opportunity*) einmalig

unisex [ˈju·nɪ·seks] *adj* unisex

unison [ˈju·nɪ·sən] *n* **to sing in ~** einstimmig singen; **to act in ~** in Übereinstimmung handeln

unit [ˈju·nɪt] *n* 1. (*standard*) Einheit *f* 2. (*group*) Abteilung *f* 3. (*furniture*) Element *nt* 4. MATH Einer *m*

'unit cost *n* COMM Kosten *pl* pro Einheit

unite [juˈnaɪt] *vt, vi* [sich] vereinigen

united [juˈnaɪ·ṭɪd] *adj* 1. (*joined*) verei-

nigt ▶ **we stand, divided we fall**
saying nur gemeinsam sind wir stark

United 'Kingdom *n* the ~ das Vereinigte
Königreich

United 'Nations *n* the ~ die Vereinten
Nationen *pl*

United 'States *n* + *sing vb* the ~ [of
America] die Vereinigten Staaten *pl*
[von Amerika]

universal [ju·nə·'vɜr·səl] *adj* universell;
(*agreement*) allgemein; ~ **truth** allgemein gültige Wahrheit

universe ['ju·nə·vɜrs] *n* the ~ das Universum

university [ju·nə·'vɜr·sɪ·ţi] *n* Universität *f*

unjust [ʌn·'dʒʌst] *adj* ungerecht

unjustifiable [ʌn·ˌdʒʌs·tɪ·'faɪ·ə·bəl] *adj*
nicht zu rechtfertigen *präd*

unjustified [ʌn·'dʒʌs·tɪ·faɪd] *adj* unge-
rechtfertigt; (*complaint*) unberechtigt

unkind [ʌn·'kaɪnd] *adj* (*mean*) unfreundlich, gemein

unknowing [ʌn·'noʊ·ɪŋ] *adj* ahnungslos

unknown [ˌʌn·'noʊn] **I.** *adj* unbekannt
II. *n* the ~ das Unbekannte

unlawful [ʌn·'lɔ·fəl] *adj* rechtswidrig

unleaded [ʌn·'led·ɪd] *adj* (*gasoline*) bleifrei

unleavened [ʌn·'lev·ənd] *adj* ~ **bread**
ungesäuertes Brot

unless [ən·'les] *conj* he won't come ~
he has time er wird nicht kommen,
außer wenn er Zeit hat

unlicensed [ʌn·'laɪ·sənst] *adj* ohne Lizenz *nach n*

unlike [ʌn·'laɪk] *prep* **1.** (*different*) **to be**
~ **sb/sth** jdm/etw nicht ähnlich sein
2. (*not normal for*) **to be** ~ **sb** für jdn
nicht typisch sein

unlikely [ʌn·'laɪk·li] *adj* **1.** (*improbable*)
unwahrscheinlich **2.** (*unconvincing*)
nicht überzeugend

unlimited [ʌn·'lɪm·ɪ·ţɪd] *adj* unbegrenzt

unlisted [ʌn·'lɪs·tɪd] *adj* **1.** STOCKEX nicht
notiert **2.** TELEC (*securities*) unnotiert
nicht verzeichnet

unload [ʌn·'loʊd] **I.** *vt* **1.** (*vehicle*) entladen; (*container*) ausladen; (*dishwasher*)
ausräumen **2.** (*get rid*) abstoßen; (*garbage*) abladen **II.** *vi* **1.** (*empty*) abladen
2. ECON entladen; (*ship*) löschen

unlock [ʌn·'lak] *vt* aufschließen

unlocked [ʌn·'lakt] *adj* unverschlossen

unlucky [ʌn·'lʌk·i] *adj* **1.** (*unfortunate*)
glücklos **2.** (*causing bad luck*) **to be** ~
Unglück bringen

unmanageable [ʌn·'mæn·ɪ·dʒə·bəl] *adj*
unkontrollierbar; (*child*) außer Rand und
Band *pred*

unmanned [ʌn·'mænd] *adj* unbemannt

unmarked [ʌn·'markt] *adj* **1.** (*without
mark*) unbeschädigt **2.** (*grave*) namenlos; ~ [**police**] **car** Zivilfahrzeug *nt* der
Polizei

unmarried [ʌn·'mær·ɪd] *adj* unverhei-
ratet

unmatched [ʌn·'mætʃt] *adj* unübertroffen

unmentionable [ʌn·'men·ʃə·nə·bəl] *adj*
unaussprechlich; **to be** ~ tabu sein

unmistakable [ʌn·mɪ·'steɪ·kə·bəl] *adj*
unverkennbar; (*symptom*) eindeutig

unmitigated [ʌn·'mɪţ·ɪ·geɪ·ţɪd] *adj* absolut; (*disaster*) total

unmoved [ʌn·'muvd] *adj usu pred* unbewegt; (*emotionless*) ungerührt

unnamed [ʌn·'neɪmd] *adj* ungenannt

unnatural [ʌn·'næʧ·ər·əl] *adj* unnatürlich;
PSYCH abnorm

unnecessarily [ʌn·ˌnes·ə·'ser·ə·li] *adv*
unnötigerweise

unnecessary [ʌn·'nes·ə·ser·i] *adj* unnötig

unnerve [ʌn·'nɜrv] *vt* nervös machen

unnoticed [ʌn·'noʊ·ţɪst] *adj pred* unbemerkt

UN ob'server *n* UNO-Beobachter(in) *m(f)*

unobtainable [ʌn·əb·'teɪ·nə·bəl] *adj* unerreichbar

unobtrusive [ʌn·əb·'tru·sɪv] *adj* unaufdringlich

unoccupied [ʌn·'ak·jə·paɪd] *adj* (*seat*)
frei

unofficial [ʌn·ə·'fɪʃ·əl] *adj* inoffiziell

unorganized [ʌn·'ɔr·gə·naɪzd] *adj* unorganisiert

unorthodox [ʌn·'ɔr·θə·daks] *adj* unkonventionell; (*method*) ungewöhnlich

unpack [ʌn·'pæk] *vt, vi* auspacken; (*car*)
ausladen

unpaid [ʌn·'peɪd] *adj* unbezahlt; (*invoice
a.*) ausstehend

unpalatable [ʌn·'pæl·ə·tə·bəl] *adj* (*dis-*

tasteful) unangenehm

unperturbed [ˌʌn·pər·'tɜrbd] *adj* nicht beunruhigt

unpick [ʌn·'pɪk] *vt* (*a seam*) auftrennen

unplaced [ʌn·'pleɪst] *adj* SPORT unplatziert

unpleasant [ʌn·'plez·ənt] *adj* 1. (*not pleasing*) unangenehm 2. (*unfriendly*) unfreundlich

unplug <-gg-> [ʌn·'plʌg] *vt* ausstecken

unpolluted [ˌʌn·pə·'lu·t̬ɪd] *adj* unverschmutzt

unpopular [ʌn·'pap·jə·lər] *adj* 1. (*not liked*) unbeliebt 2. (*not accepted*) unpopulär

unpopularity [ʌn·ˌpap·jə·'ler·ə·t̬i] *n* (*of person*) Unbeliebtheit *f*

unprecedented [ʌn·'pres·ə·den·t̬ɪd] *adj* noch nie da gewesen; (*action*) beispiellos

unpredictable [ˌʌn·prɪ·'dɪk·tə·bəl] *adj* unvorhersehbar; (*weather*) unberechenbar

unprejudiced [ʌn·'predʒ·ə·dɪst] *adj* unvoreingenommen; (*opinion*) objektiv

unpretentious [ˌʌn·prɪ·'ten·ʃəs] *adj* bescheiden; (*tastes*) einfach

unproductive [ˌʌn·prə·'dʌk·tɪv] *adj* unproduktiv; (*land*) unfruchtbar

unprofessional [ˌʌn·prə·'feʃ·ə·nəl] *adj* 1. (*amateurish*) unprofessionell 2. (*unethical*) gegen die Berufsehre *präd;* ~ **conduct** berufswidriges Verhalten

unprofitable [ʌn·'praf·ɪ·t̬ə·bəl] *adj* unrentabel

unprompted [ʌn·'pramp·tɪd] *adj* unaufgefordert

unprovoked [ˌʌn·prə·'voʊkt] *adj* grundlos

unpublished [ʌn·'pʌb·lɪʃt] *adj* unveröffentlicht

unqualified [ʌn·'kwal·ə·faɪd] *adj* 1. unqualifiziert 2. (*unreserved*) bedingungslos; (*success*) voll

unquestionable [ʌn·'kwes·tʃə·nə·bəl] *adj* fraglos; (*honesty*) unzweifelhaft

unquestioning [ʌn·'kwes·tʃə·nɪŋ] *adj* bedingungslos; (*obedience*) absolut

unquote ['ʌn·kwoʊt] *vi* **quote ...** ~ Zitatanfang ... Zitatende

unravel <-l-> [ʌn·'ræv·əl] I. *vt* 1. (*undo*)

auftrennen 2. (*knot*) aufmachen 3. (*mystery*) lösen II. *vi* sich auftrennen

unreadable [ʌn·'ri·də·bəl] *adj* 1. (*illegible*) unleserlich 2. (*dull*) schwer zu lesen *präd*

unreal [ʌn·'ril] *adj* unwirklich

unrealistic [ʌn·ˌri·ə·'lɪs·tɪk] *adj* unrealistisch

unreasonable [ʌn·'ri·zə·nə·bəl] *adj* 1. unvernünftig 2. (*demand*) überzogen

unrefined [ʌn·rɪ·'faɪnd] *adj* 1. CHEM nicht raffiniert 2. (*coarse*) unkultiviert

unregistered [ʌn·'redʒ·ɪ·stərd] *adj* nicht registriert; (*birth*) nicht eingetragen

unrelated [ˌʌn·rɪ·'leɪ·t̬ɪd] *adj* 1. (*not of family*) nicht [miteinander] verwandt 2. (*unconnected*) **to be** ~ nicht zusammenhängen (**to** mit +*dat*)

unreliable [ˌʌn·rɪ·'laɪ·ə·bəl] *adj* unzuverlässig

unrelieved [ˌʌn·rɪ·'livd] *adj* ununterbrochen; (*boredom*) dauernd

unremarkable [ˌʌn·rɪ·'mar·kə·bəl] *adj* nicht bemerkenswert

unrepeatable [ˌʌn·rɪ·'pi·t̬ə·bəl] *adj* nicht wiederholbar

unrepentant [ˌʌn·rɪ·'pen·tənt] *adj* reue[e]los

unreserved [ˌʌn·rɪ·'zɜrvd] *adj* 1. (*without reservations*) uneingeschränkt; (*support*) voll 2. (*not booked*) nicht reserviert

unreservedly [ˌʌn·rɪ·'zɜrv·ɪd·li] *adv* vorbehaltlos

unrest [ʌn·'rest] *n* Unruhen *pl;* **social** ~ soziale Spannungen

unrestrained [ˌʌn·rɪ·'streɪnd] *adj* uneingeschränkt; (*laughter*) ungehemmt

unrestricted [ˌʌn·rɪ·'strɪk·tɪd] *adj* uneingeschränkt; (*access*) ungehindert

unripe [ʌn·'raɪp] *adj* unreif

unroll [ʌn·'roʊl] I. *vt* aufrollen II. *vi* sich abrollen [lassen]

unruly <-ier, -iest *or* more ~, most ~> [ʌn·'ru·li] *adj* 1. (*disorderly*) ungebärdig; (*crowd*) aufrührerisch 2. (*hair*) nicht zu bändigen *präd*

unsafe [ʌn·'seɪf] *adj* (*dangerous*) unsicher; (*sex*) ungeschützt

unsaid [ʌn·'sed] *adj* ungesagt ► **what's said cannot be** ~ *prov* gesagt ist gesagt

UN 'sanction n UN-Sanktion f

unsatisfactory [ʌn·sæt·ɪs·ˈfæk·tə·ri] adj **1.** unzureichend; (answer) unbefriedigend **2.** SCH (grade) ungenügend

unsatisfied [ʌn·ˈsæt·ɪs·faɪd] adj unzufrieden

unsaturated [ʌn·ˈsætʃ·ə·reɪ·tɪd] adj CHEM, FOOD ungesättigt attr

unsavory [ʌn·ˈseɪ·və·ri] adj **1.** (unpalatable) unappetitlich **2.** (asocial) fragwürdig; (character) zwielichtig

unscathed [ʌn·ˈskeɪðd] adj **to emerge ~ from sth** fig etw unbeschadet überstehen

unscheduled [ʌn·ˈskedʒ·ʊld] adj außerplanmäßig; (stop, landing) außerfahrplanmäßig

unscrew [ʌn·ˈskru] **I.** vt **1.** (detach) abschrauben **2.** (open) aufschrauben **II.** vi (detach) sich abschrauben lassen

unscripted [ʌn·ˈskrɪp·tɪd] adj improvisiert

unscrupulous [ʌn·ˈskru·pjə·ləs] adj skrupellos

unseal [ʌn·ˈsil] vt entsiegeln

unsecured [ʌn·sɪ·ˈkjʊrd] adj **1.** FIN **an ~ loan** Blankokredit m **2.** (unfastened) unbefestigt

UN Se'curity Council n UN-Sicherheitsrat m

unseen [ʌn·ˈsin] adj ungesehen

unselfish [ʌn·ˈsel·fɪʃ] adj selbstlos

unsettle [ʌn·ˈset·əl] vt verunsichern

unsettled [ʌn·ˈset·əld] adj **1.** (political climate) unruhig; (weather) unbeständig **2.** (unresolved) noch anstehend

unsettling [ʌn·ˈset·əl·ɪŋ] adj beunruhigend

unshakable, unshakeable [ʌn·ˈʃeɪ·kə·bəl] adj (belief) unerschütterlich; (alibi) felsenfest

unsightly <-ier, -iest or more ~, most ~> [ʌn·ˈsaɪt·li] adj unansehnlich

unsigned [ʌn·ˈsaɪnd] adj nicht unterschrieben; (painting) unsigniert

unskilled [ʌn·ˈskɪld] adj **1.** (inept) ungeschickt **2.** (laborer) ungelernt

unsociable [ʌn·ˈsoʊ·ʃə·bəl] adj (person) ungesellig

unsocial [ʌn·ˈsoʊ·ʃəl] adj unsozial

unsold [ʌn·ˈsoʊld] adj unverkauft

unsolved [ʌn·ˈsalvd] adj (mystery, problem) ungelöst

unsophisticated [ʌn·sə·ˈfɪs·tə·keɪ·tɪd] adj (naive) naiv; (taste) einfach

unsound [ʌn·ˈsaʊnd] adj **1.** (unstable) instabil **2.** (argument) nicht stichhaltig; (judgment) anfechtbar

unspecified [ʌn·ˈspes·ɪ·faɪd] adj unspezifiziert

unspoiled [ʌn·ˈspɔɪld] adj (person) natürlich; (landscape) unberührt

unspoken [ʌn·ˈspoʊ·kən] adj (agreement) stillschweigend

unsportsmanlike [ʌn·ˈspɔrts·mən·laɪk] adj unsportlich; (behavior) unfair

unstable [ʌn·ˈsteɪ·bəl] adj **1.** (not firm) nicht stabil; (furniture) wackelig **2.** fig instabil

unsteady [ʌn·ˈsted·i] adj **1.** (unstable) nicht stabil **2.** (wavering) zittrig

unstuck [ʌn·ˈstʌk] adj **to come ~** sich [ab] lösen; fam (fail) scheitern

unsubstantial [ʌn·səb·ˈstæn·ʃəl] adj unwesentlich

unsuccessful [ʌn·sək·ˈses·fəl] adj erfolglos; (candidate) unterlegen; **to be ~ in sth** bei etw dat keinen Erfolg haben

unsuitable [ʌn·ˈsu·tə·bəl] adj nicht geeignet

unsung [ʌn·ˈsʌŋ] adj unbesungen; (hero) unbeachtet

unsure [ʌn·ˈʃʊr] adj unsicher; **to be ~ why ...** nicht genau wissen, warum ...

unsuspecting [ʌn·sə·ˈspek·tɪŋ] adj ahnungslos

unsympathetic [ʌn·sɪm·pə·ˈθet·ɪk] adj **1.** ohne Mitgefühl nach n **2.** (disapproving) verständnislos; **to be ~ toward sb** für jdn kein Verständnis haben

untangle [ʌn·ˈtæŋ·gəl] vt entwirren a. fig; (mystery) lösen

untapped [ʌn·ˈtæpt] adj (resources) ungenutzt

untaxed [ʌn·ˈtækst] adj (tax-free) steuerfrei

unthinkable [ʌn·ˈθɪŋ·kə·bəl] adj undenkbar

unthinking [ʌn·ˈθɪŋ·kɪŋ] adj unbedacht;

(*unintentional*) unabsichtlich

untidy [ʌnˈtaɪ·di] *adj* (*disordered*) unordentlich; (*appearance*) ungepflegt

untie <-y-> [ʌnˈtaɪ] *vt* **1.** (*undo*) lösen **2.** (*boat*) losbinden

until [ənˈtɪl] **I.** *prep* **1.** (*up to*) bis +*akk;* **two more days ~ Easter** noch zwei Tage bis Ostern **2.** (*beginning at*) bis +*akk;* **we didn't eat ~ midnight** wir aßen erst um Mitternacht **II.** *conj* **1.** (*up to time when*) bis; **I laughed ~ tears rolled down my face** ich lachte, bis mir die Tränen kamen **2.** (*not before*) **to not do sth ~ ...** etw erst [dann] tun, wenn ...

untimely [ʌnˈtaɪm·li] *adj* (*inopportune*) ungelegen

untold [ʌnˈtoʊld] *adj attr* unsagbar; (*damage*) immens; (*wealth*) unermesslich

untouched [ˌʌnˈtʌtʃt] *adj* **1.** (*not touched*) unberührt **2.** (*unaffected*) **to be ~ by sth** von etw *dat* nicht betroffen sein

untoward [ʌnˈtɔrd] *adj* **1.** (*unfortunate*) ungünstig **2.** (*remark*) unpassend

untrained [ʌnˈtreɪnd] *adj* ungeübt; (*eye*) ungeschult

untranslatable [ˌʌn·trænsˈleɪ·tə·bəl] *adj* unübersetzbar

untreated [ʌnˈtri·t̬ɪd] *adj* unbehandelt; **~ sewage** ungeklärte Abwässer *pl*

untried [ʌnˈtraɪd] *adj* (*inexperienced*) unerfahren

untrue [ʌnˈtru] *adj* unwahr

untrustworthy [ʌnˈtrʌst·ˌwɜr·ði] *adj* unzuverlässig

untruthful [ʌnˈtruθ·fəl] *adj* unwahr; (*person*) unaufrichtig

unused¹ [ʌnˈjuzd] *adj* unbenutzt; **to go ~** nicht genutzt werden

unused² [ʌnˈjuzd] *adj pred* **to be ~ to sth** an etw *akk* nicht gewöhnt sein

unusual [ʌnˈju·ʒu·əl] *adj* ungewöhnlich

unusually [ʌnˈju·ʒu·ə·li] *adv* ungewöhnlich

unveil [ʌnˈveɪl] *vt* enthüllen

unwanted [ʌnˈwan·t̬ɪd] *adj* unerwünscht; (*clothes*) abgelegt

unwelcome [ʌnˈwel·kəm] *adj* unwillkommen; **to make sb feel ~** jdm das

Gefühl geben, nicht willkommen zu sein

unwell [ʌnˈwel] *adj pred* **sb is ~** jdm geht es nicht gut; **to feel ~** sich unwohl fühlen

unwilling [ʌnˈwɪl·ɪŋ] *adj* **to be ~ to do sth** nicht gewillt sein, etw zu tun

unwillingly [ʌnˈwɪl·ɪŋ·li] *adv* ungern

unwind <unwound, unwound> [ʌnˈwaɪnd] **I.** *vi* **1.** (*unroll*) sich abwickeln **2.** (*relax*) sich entspannen **II.** *vt* abwickeln

unwise [ʌnˈwaɪz] *adj* unklug

unwittingly [ʌnˈwɪt̬·ɪŋ·li] *adv* **1.** (*without realizing*) unwissentlich **2.** (*unintentionally*) unbeabsichtigterweise

unworkable [ʌnˈwɜr·kə·bəl] *adj* undurchführbar

unworldly [ʌnˈwɜrld·li] *adj* (*naive*) weltfremd

unworthy [ʌnˈwɜr·ði] *adj* unwürdig; **~ of interest** nicht von Interesse

unwrap <-pp-> [ʌnˈræp] *vt* (*contents*) auspacken

unwritten [ʌnˈrɪt·ən] *adj* nicht schriftlich fixiert; (*agreement*) stillschweigend

unzip <-pp-> [ʌnˈzɪp] *vt* **1.** (*open*) **to ~ sth** den Reißverschluss einer S. *gen* aufmachen **2.** COMPUT auspacken

up [ʌp] **I.** *adv* **1.** (*to higher*) nach oben; **halfway ~** auf halber Höhe **2.** (*erect*) aufrecht; **lean it ~ against the wall** lehnen Sie es gegen die Wand **3.** (*out of bed*) auf; **~ and about** auf den Beinen **4.** (*at higher*) oben; **~ there** da oben **5.** (*toward*) **to sb/sth** auf jdn/ etw zu; **to walk ~ to sb** auf jdn zugehen **6.** (*to point of*) **~ until** [*or* to] bis +*akk;* **~ to 300 dollars** bis zu 300 Dollar **II.** *prep* **1.** (*to higher*) hinauf/ herauf; **~ the ladder** die Leiter hinauf/ herauf **2.** (*along*) [*just*] **~ the road** ein Stück die Straße hinauf/herauf; **~ and down** auf und ab **3.** (*against*) **up the river** flussauf[wärts] **4.** (*at top of*) **he's ~ that ladder** er steht dort oben auf der Leiter ▸ **~ yours!** *vulg, sl* du könnt/ du kannst mich mal! **III.** *adj* **1.** *attr* (*rising*) nach oben **2.** *pred* (*finished*) vorbei, um; **your time is ~!** Ihre Zeit ist um! **3.** *pred fam* (*happening*) **what's**

~? was ist los? **IV.** n fam Hoch nt; **~s and downs** Höhen und Tiefen pl **V.** vt <-pp-> erhöhen; (price, tax) anheben; **to ~ the stakes** den Einsatz erhöhen

up-and-'coming adj attr aufstrebend

upbeat ['ʌp·biːt] adj fam **1.** optimistisch; (mood) fröhlich

upbringing ['ʌp·brɪŋ·ɪŋ] n usu sing Erziehung f

upcoming ['ʌp·ˌkʌm·ɪŋ] adj bevorstehend

update I. vt [ʌp·'deɪt] **1.** (modernize) aktualisieren; (hardware) nachrüsten **2.** (inform) auf den neuesten Stand bringen **II.** n ['ʌp·deɪt] Update nt fachspr

upend [ʌp·'end] vt hochkant stellen

upfront [ʌp·'frʌnt] adj **1.** pred (frank) offen; **to be ~ about sth** etw offen sagen **2.** attr (advance) Voraus-; **~ payment** Anzahlung f

upgrade ['ʌp·greɪd] **I.** vt **1.** COMPUT erweitern; (hardware) nachrüsten **2.** (promote) befördern **II.** n **1.** COMPUT Aufrüsten nt **2.** (version) verbesserte Version

upheaval [ʌp·'hiː·vəl] n Aufruhr m; **political ~** politische Umwälzung[en] f/pl/

uphill [ʌp·'hɪl] adv, adj bergauf

uphold <-held, -held> [ʌp·'hoʊld] vt aufrechterhalten; (verdict) bestätigen

upholstery [ʌp·'hoʊl·stə·ri] n (padding) Polsterung f; (covering) Bezug m

upkeep ['ʌp·kiːp] n **1.** (maintenance) Instandhaltung f **2.** (of person) Unterhalt m; (of animals) Haltungskosten f

uplift [ʌp·'lɪft] vt **1.** (raise) anheben **2.** (inspire) [moralisch] aufrichten

uplifting [ʌp·'lɪf·tɪŋ] adj erbaulich

upon [ə·'pɑn] prep form **1.** (on top of) auf +dat; with verbs of motion auf +akk **2.** (hanging on) an +dat **3.** (at time of) **once ~ a time** [es war einmal] vor langer Zeit

upper ['ʌp·ər] adj attr **1.** (higher) obere(r, s); (arm, lip) Ober- **2.** (rank) höhere(r, s) **3.** (location) höher gelegen

'upper case n TYPO **in ~** in Großbuchstaben

upper 'class n Oberschicht f

upper 'deck n Oberdeck nt

uppermost ['ʌp·ər·moʊst] adj oberste(r, s)

uppity ['ʌp·ɪ·ţi] adj pej fam hochnäsig

upright ['ʌp·raɪt] **I.** adj **1.** (vertical) senkrecht; (erect) aufrecht **2.** (honest) anständig **II.** adv (vertical) senkrecht; (erect) aufrecht; **bolt ~** kerzengerade **III.** n SPORT Pfosten m

uprising ['ʌp·raɪ·zɪŋ] n Aufstand m

uproar ['ʌp·rɔr] n **1.** (noise) Lärm m **2.** (protest) Aufruhr m

uproot [ʌp·'ruːt] vt **1.** (extract) herausreißen; (tree) entwurzeln **2.** **to ~ oneself** seine Heimat verlassen

upscale [ʌp·'skeɪl] adj (goods) hochwertig

upset I. vt [ʌp·'set] **1.** (push over) umwerfen; (a glass) umstoßen **2.** (unsettle) aus der Fassung bringen; (distress) mitnehmen **II.** adj [ʌp·'set] **1.** pred (nervous) aufgeregt; (angry) aufgebracht; (distressed) bestürzt **2.** **to have an ~ stomach** sich den Magen verdorben haben **III.** n ['ʌp·set] Ärger m; (argument) Verstimmung f

upsetting [ʌp·'set·ɪŋ] adj erschütternd; (saddening) traurig

upshot ['ʌp·ʃɑt] n [End]ergebnis nt

upside 'down I. adj (inverted) auf dem Kopf stehend attr; **that picture is ~** das Bild hängt verkehrt herum **II.** adv verkehrt herum; **to turn sth ~** etw auf den Kopf stellen a. fig

upstage ['ʌp·steɪdʒ] vt **to ~ sb** jdm die Schau stehlen

upstairs [ʌp·'sterz] **I.** adj oben präd, obere(r, s) attr **II.** adv (to higher) nach oben; (at higher) oben

upstart ['ʌp·stɑrt] n pej Emporkömmling m

upstate ['ʌp·steɪt] adj im ländlichen Norden [des Bundesstaates] nach n; **in ~ New York** im ländlichen Teil New Yorks

upstream [ʌp·'striːm] adv flussaufwärts

upswing ['ʌp·swɪŋ] n ECON Aufschwung m

uptake [ʌp·'teɪk] n ▶ **to be slow on the ~** fam schwer von Begriff sein

uptight [ʌp·'taɪt] adj fam **1.** (nervous) nervös; (anxious) ängstlich **2.** (inhibited) verklemmt

'up-to-date adj attr (information) aktuell

up-to-the-'minute adj hochaktuell

U

uptown ['ʌp·taʊn] *adj* **to live in ~ Manhattan** im nördlichen Teil Manhattans leben

upturn ['ʌp·tɜrn] *n* Aufschwung *m*

upturned [ʌp·'tɜrnd] *adj* nach oben gewendet; (*boat*) gekentert

upward ['ʌp·wərd] I. *adj* Aufwärts- II. *adv* nach oben; **from childhood ~** von Kindheit an

upwardly ['ʌp·wərd·li] *adv* nach oben, aufwärts; **~ mobile** aufstrebend und erfolgreich

upwards ['ʌp·wərdz] *adv* nach oben, aufwärts

uranium [ju·'reɪ·ni·əm] *n* Uran *nt*

urban ['ɜr·bən] *adj attr* städtisch; **~ area** Stadtgebiet *nt*

urbane [ɜr·'beɪn] *adj* weltmännisch; (*manner*) kultiviert

urbanization [ˌɜr·bə·nɪ·'zeɪ·ʃən] *n* Verstädterung *f*

urchin ['ɜr·tʃɪn] *n* 1. ZOOL Seeigel *m* 2. (*child*) [street] **~** Straßenkind *nt*

urge [ɜrdʒ] I. *n* Verlangen *nt;* (*compulsion*) Drang *m* II. *vt* 1. (*persuade*) **to ~ sb** [**to do sth**] jdn drängen[, etw zu tun] 2. (*advocate*) **to ~ sth** auf etw *akk* dringen, zu etw *dat* drängen; **to ~ caution** zur Vorsicht mahnen

urgency ['ɜr·dʒən·si] *n* Dringlichkeit *f;* **to be a matter of ~** äußerst dringend sein

urgent ['ɜr·dʒənt] *adj* (*imperative*) dringend; (*on letter*) „eilt"

urgently ['ɜr·dʒənt·li] *adv* dringend

urinate ['jʊr·ə·neɪt] *vi* urinieren

urine ['jʊr·ɪn] *n* Urin *m*

URL [ˌju·ar·'el] *n abbr of* **uniform resource locator** URL *m*

urn [ɜrn] *n* (*vase*) Krug *m;* (*for remains*) [Grab]urne *f*

us [əs, *stressed:* ʌs] *pron* (*object of we*) uns *dat o akk;* **let ~ know** lassen Sie es uns wissen; **both of ~** wir beide; **it's ~** wir sind's

U.S., US [ju·'es] *n abbr of* **United States; the ~** die USA *pl*

USA, U.S.A. [ˌju·es·'eɪ] *n abbr of* **United States of America; the ~** die USA *pl*

USAF [ˌju·es·eɪ·'ef] *n abbr of* **United States Air Force; the ~** die US-Luft-

waffe

usage ['ju·sɪdʒ] *n* 1. (*practice*) Usus *m geh* 2. (*of word*) Verwendung *f*

use I. *vt* [juz] 1. (*utilize*) benutzen; (*skills, talent*) nutzen; (*method*) anwenden; (*dictionary, idea*) verwenden; **I could ~ some help** ich könnte etwas Hilfe gebrauchen; **to ~ drugs** Drogen nehmen 2. (*employ*) einsetzen; **to ~ common sense** seinen gesunden Menschenverstand benutzen 3. (*consume*) verbrauchen; **this radio ~s four AAA batteries** für dieses Radio braucht man vier AAA Batterien 4. (*exploit*) ausnutzen II. *n* [jus] 1. (*utilization*) Verwendung *f;* (*of dictionary a.*) Benutzung *f;* (*of talent, experience*) Nutzung *m;* (*of method*) Anwendung *f;* **directions for ~** Gebrauchsanweisung *f;* **for external ~ only** nur zur äußerlichen Anwendung; **to find a ~ for sth** für etw *akk* Verwendung finden; **to make ~ of sth** etw benutzen; (*experience, talent*) etw nutzen 2. (*consumption*) Verwendung *f* 3. (*usefulness*) Nutzen *m;* **can I be of any ~?** kann ich vielleicht irgendwie behilflich sein?; **it's no ~** [doing sth] hat keinen Zweck[, etw zu tun]

use up *vt* verbrauchen; (*completely*) [völlig] aufbrauchen

used¹ [juzd] *vt only in past* **my father ~ to say ...** mein Vater sagte [früher] immer, ...

used² [juzd] *adj* (*old*) gebraucht

used³ [juzd] *adj* (*accustomed*) **to be ~ to sth** etw gewohnt sein

useful ['jus·fəl] *adj* 1. (*practical*) nützlich (**for** für +*akk*) 2. (*advantageous*) wertvoll; **to come in ~** gut zu gebrauchen sein

usefulness ['jus·fəl·nɪs] *n* Nützlichkeit *f;* (*applicability*) Verwendbarkeit *f*

useless ['jus·lɪs] *adj* 1. (*pointless*) sinnlos 2. *fam* (*inept*) zu nichts zu gebrauchen *präd;* **he's a ~ goalkeeper** er taugt nichts als Torwart 3. (*unusable*) unbrauchbar

user ['ju·zər] *n* Benutzer(in) *m(f);* (*of software, system a.*) Anwender(in) *m(f);* (*of electricity, gas*) Verbraucher(in) *m(f)*

'user-friendly *adj* COMPUT benutzer-

freundlich

user 'interface *n* COMPUT Benutzeroberfläche *f*

USP [ˌjuˈesˈpi] *n* ECON *abbr of* **unique selling proposition** USP *m*

USPS [ˌjuˈesˈpiˈes] *n abbr of* **United States Postal Service** *US-amerikanische staatliche Postgesellschaft*

USS [ˌjuˈesˈes] *n abbr of* **United States Ship** *Schiff aus den Vereinigten Staaten*

usual [ˈjuˈʒuˈəl] *adj* üblich, normal; **to find sth in its ~ place** etw an seinem gewohnten Platz vorfinden

usually [ˈjuˈʒuˈəˈli] *adv* normalerweise; **more ... than ~** mehr ... als sonst

usurp [juˈsɜrp] *vt* 1. (*power*) an sich *akk* reißen 2. (*oust*) verdrängen

UT, Ut. *abbr of* **Utah**

Utah [ˈjuˈtɔ] *n* Utah *nt*

utensil [juˈtenˈsəl] *n* Utensil *nt;* **kitchen ~s** Küchengeräte *pl*

utility [juˈtɪlˈɪˈti] I. *n* 1. (*usefulness*) Nützlichkeit *f* 2. (*provider*) **public ~** öffentlicher Versorgungsbetrieb II. *adj* **~ vehicle** Mehrzweckfahrzeug *nt*

u'tility room *n* Raum, in dem Haushaltsgeräte, wie z. B. Waschmaschine und Trockner stehen, und der ebenfalls als Vorratskeller dient

utilization [ˌjuˈtɪˈlɪˈzeɪˈʃən] *n* Verwendung *f*

utilize [ˈjuˈtɪˈlaɪz] *vt* nutzen

utmost [ˈʌtˈmoʊst] *adj attr* größte(r, s); **of the ~ importance** von äußerster Wichtigkeit

utter[1] [ˈʌtˈər] *adj attr* vollkommen; **~ nonsense** absoluter Blödsinn

utter[2] [ˈʌtˈər] *vt* 1. (*give voice to*) von sich *dat* geben; **without ~ing a word** ohne ein Wort zu sagen 2. (*speak out*) sagen; (*curse*) ausstoßen

utterly [ˈʌtˈərˈli] *adv* vollkommen; **to be ~ convinced that ...** vollkommen [davon] überzeugt sein, dass ...

U-turn [ˈjuˈtɜrn] *n* 1. (*of car*) Wende *f* 2. (*change*) Kehrtwendung *f*

V

V <*pl* -'s> *n,* **v** <*pl* -'s> [vi] *n* (*letter*) V *nt,* v *nt;* **~ as in Victor** V wie Viktor

v [vi] I. *n* LING *abbr of* **verb** v II. *prep abbr of* **verse, verso, versus** vs. III. *adv abbr of* **very**

VA, Va. *abbr of* **Virginia**

vac [væk] I. *n fam short for* **vacuum cleaner** Staubsauger *m* II. *vt, vi* <-cc-> *fam short for* **vacuum clean** [staub]saugen

vacancy [ˈveɪˈkənˈsi] *n* 1. (*room*) freies Zimmer; **"no vacancies"** „belegt" 2. (*job*) freie Stelle; **to fill a ~** eine [freie] Stelle besetzen

vacant [ˈveɪˈkənt] *adj* 1. (*empty: bed, seat*) frei; (*land*) unbebaut 2. (*job*) unbesetzt

vacate [ˈveɪˈkeɪt] *vt* räumen; (*place, seat*) frei machen

vacation [veɪˈkeɪˈʃən] I. *n* 1. (*holiday*) Ferien *pl,* Urlaub *m;* **to take a ~** Urlaub machen; **on ~** im Urlaub 2. UNIV Semesterferien *pl;* LAW Gerichtsferien *pl* II. *vi* Urlaub machen

vacationer [veɪˈkeɪˈʃəˈnər] *n* Urlauber(in) *m(f)*

vaccinate [ˈvækˈsəˈneɪt] *vt* impfen

vaccination [ˌvækˈsəˈneɪˈʃən] *n* [Schutz]impfung *f*

vaccine [ˈvækˈsin] *n* Impfstoff *m*

vacuum <*pl* -s> [ˈvækˈjum] I. *n* 1. Vakuum *nt* 2. *fig* (*gap*) Vakuum *nt,* Lücke *f* 3. (*vacuum cleaner*) Staubsauger *m* II. *vt* [staub]saugen

'vacuum cleaner *n* Staubsauger *m*

'vacuum-packed *adj* vakuumverpackt

vagina <*pl* -s> [vəˈdʒaɪˈnə] *n* ANAT Vagina *f,* Scheide *f*

vagrant [ˈveɪˈgrənt] *n* Obdachlose(r) *f/m)*

vague [veɪg] *adj* 1. ungenau, vage; (*blurred*) verschwommen 2. (*person*) zerstreut

vagueness [ˈveɪgˈnəs] *n* Unbestimmtheit *f*

vain [veɪn] *adj* 1. (*conceited*) eingebildet; (*about one's looks*) eitel 2. (*futile*) sinnlos; (*hope*) töricht 3. (*unsuccessful*) **in ~** vergeblich

valance ['væl·əns] *n* **1.** (*on bed*) Volant *m* **2.** (*on curtain rail*) Querbehang *m*

valedictorian [,væl·ə·dɪk·'tɔːr·i·ən] *n* Abschiedsredner(in) *m(f)* (*Jahrgangsbeste(r), die/der bei Schul- oder Universitätsentlassungsfeiern eine Abschiedsrede hält*)

valedictory [,væl·ə·'dɪk·tə·ri] *adj* (*school-leaving*) ~ **address** Abschiedsrede *f*

valentine ['væl·ən·taɪn] *n* Valentinskarte *f*

'Valentine's Day *n* Valentinstag *m*

'valet parking *n* Parkservice *m*

valid ['væl·ɪd] *adj* **1.** (*well-founded*) begründet; (*argument*) stichhaltig; (*criticism*) gerechtfertigt **2.** (*in force*) gültig

validate ['væl·ə·deɪt] *vt* bestätigen

validity [və·'lɪd·ə·ṭi] *n* Gültigkeit *f;* (*value*) Wert *m*

valley ['væl·i] *n* Tal *nt*

valuable ['væl·ju·ə·bəl] **I.** *adj* wertvoll **II.** *n usu pl* Wertsachen *pl*

valuation [,væl·ju·'eɪ·ʃən] *n* **1.** (*appraisal*) **to make a ~ of sth** etw schätzen **2.** (*price*) Schätzwert *m*

value ['væl·ju] **I.** *n* **1.** Wert *m;* **to be of little ~** wenig Wert haben **2.** (*ethics*) ~**s** *pl* Werte *pl* **II.** *vt* schätzen

valued ['væl·jud] *adj* geschätzt

valueless ['væl·ju·lɪs] *adj* wertlos

valve [vælv] *n* Ventil *nt*

vampire ['væm·paɪr] *n* Vampir(in) *m(f)*

van [væn] *n* (*truck*) Transporter *m;* **delivery ~** Lieferwagen *m*

vandal ['væn·dəl] *n* Vandale(in) *m(f) pej*

vandalism ['væn·də·lɪz·əm] *n* Vandalismus *m*

vanguard ['væn·gɑrd] *n fig* (*leader*) **to be in the ~ of sth** zu den Vorreitern einer S. *gen* gehören

vanilla [və·'nɪl·ə] **I.** *n* Vanille *f* **II.** *adj fig* (*ordinary*) **plain ~** nullachtfuffzehn *fam*

vanish ['væn·ɪʃ] *vi* verschwinden; **to ~ into thin air** sich in Luft auflösen

'vanishing point *n* Fluchtpunkt *m*

vanity ['væn·ə·ṭi] *n* Eitelkeit *f*

vantage ['væn·tɪdʒ] *n* Aussichtspunkt *m*

'vantage point *n* **1.** (*outlook*) Aussichtspunkt *m* **2.** *fig* (*perspective*) Blickpunkt *m*

vapor ['veɪ·pər] *n* Dampf *m*

vaporization [,veɪ·pər·ɪ·'zeɪ·ʃən] *n* Verdampfung *f*

vaporize ['veɪ·pə·raɪz] *vt, vi* verdampfen

vaporizer ['veɪ·pə·raɪ·zər] *n* Inhalator *m*

'vapor trail *n* Kondensstreifen *m*

variable ['vær·i·ə·bəl] **I.** *n* Variable *f* **II.** *adj* variabel, veränderlich; (*weather*) unbeständig

variance ['vær·i·əns] *n* **1.** **to be at ~ with sth** mit etw *dat* nicht übereinstimmen **2.** (*variation*) Abweichung *f*

variant ['vær·i·ənt] *n* Variante *f*

variation [,vær·i·'eɪ·ʃən] *n* **1.** (*variability*) Abweichung *f* **2.** (*difference*) Schwankung[en] *f[pl]*

varied ['vær·id] *adj* unterschiedlich; (*career*) bewegt; (*group*) bunt gemischt

variegated ['vær·i·ə·geɪ·ṭɪd] *adj* (*multicolored*) mischfarbig; (*leaves*) bunt

variety [və·'raɪ·ə·ṭi] *n* **1.** (*diversity*) Verschiedenartigkeit *f;* (*in job a.*) Abwechslungsreichtum *m* **2.** (*assortment*) Vielfalt *f* **3.** (*category*) Art *f;* BIOL Spezies *f*

va'riety show *n* Varieteeshow *f*

various ['vær·i·əs] *adj* verschieden

varnish ['vɑr·nɪʃ] **I.** *n* <*pl* -es> Lack *m* **II.** *vt* lackieren

vary <-ie-> ['vær·i] **I.** *vi* **1.** (*differ*) variieren, verschieden sein; **to ~ greatly** stark voneinander abweichen **2.** (*change*) sich verändern **II.** *vt* variieren

varying ['veri·ɪŋ] *adj* unterschiedlich

vase [veɪs] *n* Vase *f*

vast [væst] *adj* gewaltig; (*country*) weit; (*majority*) überwältigend

vat [væt] *n* Fass *nt*

Vatican ['væt̬·ɪ·kən] *n* **the ~** der Vatikan

vault [vɔlt] **I.** *n* **1.** (*arch*) Gewölbebogen *m* **2.** (*strong room*) Tresorraum *m;* (*safe*) Magazin *nt* **3.** (*jump*) Sprung *m* **II.** *vt* **to ~ sth** über etw *akk* springen

vaulted ['vɔl·tɪd] *adj* gewölbt

VCR [,vi·si·'ɑr] *n abbr of* **videocassette recorder** Videorekorder *m*

veal [vil] *n* Kalbfleisch *nt*

veg <-gg-> [vedʒ] *vi fam* **to ~ out** herumhängen

vegan ['vi·gən] *n* Veganer(in) *m(f)*

vegetable ['vedʒ·tə·bəl] *n* **1.** (*edible plant*) Gemüse *nt* **2.** (*not animal or mineral*) Pflanze *f*

'**vegetable fat** n pflanzliches Fett

'**vegetable garden** n Gemüsegarten m

'**vegetable oil** n pflanzliches Öl

vegetarian [ˌvedʒ·ə·ˈter·i·ən] n Vegetarier(in) m(f)

vegetate [ˈvedʒ·ə·teɪt] vi vegetieren

vegetation [ˌvedʒ·ə·ˈteɪ·ʃən] n Pflanzen pl

veggie [ˈvedʒ·i] n fam short for **vegetable**

vehement [ˈvi·ə·mənt] adj vehement, heftig; (critic) scharf

vehicle [ˈvi·ə·kəl] n Fahrzeug nt

veil [veɪl] n Schleier m a. fig

veiled [veɪld] adj fig (hidden) verschleiert; (threat) versteckt

vein [veɪn] n 1. (vessel) Vene f 2. BOT, ZOOL, MIN Ader f

veined [veɪnd] adj geädert

Velcro® [ˈvel·kroʊ] n Klettverschluss m

velocity [və·ˈlas·ə·ti] n Geschwindigkeit f

velvet [ˈvel·vɪt] n Samt m

velvety [ˈvel·və·ti] adj samtig

vend [vend] vt verkaufen

vendetta [ven·ˈdet·ə] n Vendetta f

'**vending machine** n Automat m

vendor [ˈven·dər] n Straßenverkäufer(in) m(f)

veneer [və·ˈnɪr] n 1. (layer) Furnier nt 2. fig (front) Fassade f

venerable [ˈven·ər·ə·bəl] adj ehrwürdig; (tradition) alt

venereal [və·ˈnɪr·i·əl] adj ~ **disease** Geschlechtskrankheit f

venetian 'blind n Jalousie f

Venezuela [ˌven·ə·ˈzweɪ·lə] n Venezuela nt

vengeance [ˈven·dʒəns] n Rache f

venison [ˈven·ɪ·sən] n Rehfleisch nt

venom [ˈven·əm] n Gift nt

venomous [ˈven·ə·məs] adj giftig a. fig

vent [vent] I. n 1. (outlet) Abzug m; **air ~** Luftschacht m 2. fig (release) Ventil nt; **to give ~ to one's anger** seinem Ärger Luft machen II. vt **~ one's anger on sb** seine Wut an jdm auslassen

ventilate [ˈven·tə·leɪt] vt lüften

ventilation [ˌven·tə·ˈleɪ·ʃən] n Belüftung f

ventilator [ˈven·tə·leɪ·tər] n Ventilator m

ventriloquist [ven·ˈtrɪl·ə·kwɪst] n Bauchredner(in) m(f)

venture [ˈven·tʃər] I. n Projekt nt II. vt (opinion) vorsichtig äußern

'**venture capital** n Risikokapital nt

venue [ˈven·ju] n (site) Veranstaltungsort m; (for competition) Austragungsort m

veranda(h) [və·ˈræn·də] n Veranda f

verb [vɜrb] n Verb nt

verbal [ˈvɜr·bəl] adj mündlich

verbalize [ˈvɜr·bə·laɪz] vt ausdrücken

verbally [ˈvɜr·bə·li] adv mündlich

verbatim [vɜr·ˈbeɪ·tɪm] adv wortwörtlich

verbose [vɜr·ˈboʊs] adj wortreich; (speech) weitschweifig

verdict [ˈvɜr·dɪkt] n Urteil nt; **~ of not guilty** Freispruch m; **unanimous ~** einstimmiges Urteil; **to return a ~** ein Urteil verkünden

verdigris [ˈvɜr·dɪ·grɪs] n Grünspan m

verge [vɜrdʒ] n 1. (edge) Rand m 2. fig (brink) **to be on the ~ of collapse** kurz vor dem Zusammenbruch stehen

verifiable [ˌver·ə·ˈfaɪ·ə·bəl] adj (fact) überprüfbar; (theory) nachweisbar

verification [ˌver·ə·fɪ·ˈkeɪ·ʃən] n Verifizierung f geh; (checking) Überprüfung f

verify <-ie-> [ˈver·ə·faɪ] vt (check) überprüfen; (confirm) belegen

vermicelli [ˌvɜr·mə·ˈtʃel·i] npl Fadennudeln pl

vermin [ˈvɜr·mɪn] npl (animals) Schädlinge pl; **to control ~** Ungeziefer bekämpfen

Vermont [vɜr·ˈmant] n Vermont nt

vermouth [vɜr·ˈmuθ] n Wermut m

vernacular [vɜr·ˈnæk·jə·lər] n (umgangssprache f; (dialect) Dialekt m

versatile [ˈvɜr·sə·təl] adj vielseitig

versatility [ˌvɜr·sə·ˈtɪl·ə·ti] n Vielseitigkeit f

verse [vɜrs] n 1. (poetry) Dichtung f; **in ~** in Versen m 2. (poem, song) Strophe f

versed [vɜrst] adj **to be [well] ~ in sth** (knowledgeable about) in etw dat [sehr] versiert sein geh

version [ˈvɜr·ʒən] n (variant) Version f; (of book, text) Fassung f; **abridged ~** Kurzfassung f

versus [ˈvɜr·səs] prep gegen

vertebra <pl -brae> [ˈvɜr·tə·brə] n Wirbel m

V

vertebrate ['vɜr·tə·brɪt] n Wirbeltier nt

vertical ['vɜr·tə·kəl] adj senkrecht

vertigo ['vɜr·tə·gou] n Schwindel m

verve [vɜrv] n Begeisterung f

very ['ver·i] I. adv 1. (extremely) sehr, außerordentlich 2. (to great degree) sehr; ~ much sehr 3. + superl (to add force) aller-; to do the ~ best one can sein Allerbestes geben; at the ~ most allerhöchstens; the ~ next day schon am nächsten Tag II. adj attr at the ~ bottom zuunterst; the ~ fact that ... allein schon die Tatsache, dass ...; they're the ~ opposite of one another sie sind völlig unterschiedlich

vessel ['ves·əl] n 1. (ship) Schiff nt 2. (container) Gefäß nt

vest [vest] n [Anzug]weste f

vestibule ['ves·tə·bjul] n (foyer) Vorraum m; (in theater) Foyer nt

vestige ['ves·tɪdʒ] n (trace) Spur f

vestry ['ves·tri] n Sakristei f

vet¹ [vet] n Tierarzt, Tierärztin m, f

vet² [vet] n fam short for **veteran** Veteran(in) m(f)

veteran ['vet·ər·ən] n (expert, ex-military) Veteran(in) m(f) hum, alter Hase hum

Veteran's Day n Veteranentag m (der 11. November als Andenken an den Waffenstillstand zwischen Deutschland und den Alliierten 1918)

veterinarian [ˌvet·ər·ə·'ner·i·ən] n Tierarzt, Tierärztin m, f

veterinary ['vet·ər·ə·ner·i] adj attr tierärztlich; ~ **medicine** Tiermedizin f

veto ['vi·tou] I. n <pl -es> 1. (nullification) Veto nt 2. (right of refusal) Vetorecht nt II. vt 1. (refuse) ein Veto einlegen gegen +akk 2. (forbid) untersagen

vex [veks] vt verärgern

VHF [ˌvi·eɪtʃ·'ef] n abbr of **very high frequency** UKW f

via ['vaɪ·ə] prep 1. (through) über 2. (using) per, via

viable ['vaɪ·ə·bəl] adj 1. (successful) existenzfähig 2. (feasible) machbar

viaduct ['vaɪ·ə·dʌkt] n Viadukt m o nt

vibe [vaɪb] n usu pl sl (atmosphere) Schwingungen pl; (general feeling) Klima nt

vibrant ['vaɪ·brənt] adj 1. (person) leb-

haft 2. (atmosphere, place) lebendig 3. (color) leuchtend

vibrate ['vaɪ·breɪt] vi vibrieren

vibration [vaɪ·'breɪ·ʃən] n Vibration f; (of earthquake) Erschütterung f

vicarious [vɪ·'ker·i·əs] adj nachempfunden; (pleasure) indirekt; ~ **satisfaction** Ersatzbefriedigung f

vice¹ [vaɪs] n Laster nt

vice² [vaɪs] n see **vise**

vice 'chairman n stellvertretende(r) Vorsitzende(r)

Vice 'President, vice 'president n Vizepräsident(in) m(f)

'vice squad n Sittendezernat nt

vice versa [ˌvaɪ·sə·'vɜr·sə] adv umgekehrt

vicinity [və·'sɪn·ə·ti] n Nähe f; **in the ~ [of sth]** in der Nähe [einer S. gen]

vicious ['vɪʃ·əs] adj (malicious) boshaft, gemein; (crime) grauenhaft; (dog) bissig

vicious 'circle, vicious 'cycle n Teufelskreis m

victim ['vɪk·tɪm] n 1. (harmed) Opfer nt 2. (sufferer) **cancer ~** Krebskranke(r) f/m

victimize ['vɪk·tə·maɪz] vt ungerecht behandeln

victor ['vɪk·tər] n Sieger(in) m(f)

Victorian [vɪk·'tɔr·i·ən] adj (era) viktorianisch

victory ['vɪk·tə·ri] n Sieg m

video ['vɪd·i·ou] n Video nt

'video camera n Videokamera f

videocas'sette recorder, VCR n Videorekorder m

'videoconference n Videokonferenz f

'video game n Videospiel nt

'videophone n Bildtelefon nt

'videotape n 1. (cassette) Videokassette f 2. (tape) Videoband nt

Vienna [vi·'en·ə] n Wien nt

Viennese [ˌvi·ə·'niz] I. n <pl -> Wiener(in) m(f) II. adj Wiener-, wienerisch

Vietnam [ˌvi·et·'nam] n Vietnam nt

Vietnamese [vi·et·nə·'miz] I. adj vietnamesisch II. n Vietnamese, -mesin m, f

view [vju] I. n 1. (sight) Sicht f; **in full ~ of all the spectators** vor den Augen aller Zuschauer; **to come into ~** sichtbar

werden 2. (*panorama*) [Aus]blick *m;* he paints rural ~s er malt ländliche Motive 3. (*opinion*) Ansicht *f,* Meinung *f;* it's my ~ that the price is much too high meiner Meinung nach ist der Preis viel zu hoch; point of ~ Standpunkt *m;* from my point of ~ ... meiner Meinung nach ... 4. (*perspective*) Ansicht *f;* in ~ of sth angesichts einer S. *gen* II. *vt* 1. (*watch*) to ~ sb/sth [from sth] etw [von jdm/etw aus] betrachten; (*spectator*) etw *dat* [von etw *dat* aus] zusehen 2. (*consider*) to ~ sb/sth [as sb/sth] jdn/etw [als jdn/etw] betrachten; we ~ the situation with concern wir betrachten die Lage mit Besorgnis

viewer ['vju·ər] *n* 1. (*person*) [Fernseh]zuschauer(in) *m(f)* 2. (*for film*) Filmbetrachter *m*

'viewfinder *n* PHOT [Bild]sucher *m*

viewing ['vju·ɪŋ] *n* FILM Anschauen *nt;* TV Fernsehen *nt*

'viewpoint *n* 1. (*opinion*) Standpunkt *m* 2. (*place*) Aussichtspunkt *m*

vigilant ['vɪdʒ·ɪ·lənt] *adj* wachsam

vigor ['vɪg·ər] *n* 1. (*liveliness*) Energie *f;* with ~ mit vollem Eifer 2. (*forcefulness*) Ausdruckskraft *f*

vigorous ['vɪg·ər·əs] *adj* 1. (*strong*) kräftig, kraftvoll 2. (*walk*) stramm 3. (*passionate*) leidenschaftlich; (*criticism*) heftig; (*denial*) energisch

vile [vaɪl] *adj* abscheulich

village ['vɪl·ɪdʒ] *n* Dorf *nt*

villager ['vɪl·ə·dʒər] *n* Dorfbewohner(in) *m(f)*

villain ['vɪl·ən] *n* (*in novel, film*) Bösewicht *m*

VIN ['vi·'aɪ·'en] *n* AUTO *acr for* **vehicle identification number** Kfz-Kennzeichen *nt*

vinaigrette [ˌvɪn·ə·'gret] *n* Vinaigrette *f*

vindicate ['vɪn·də·keɪt] *vt* (*justify: thing*) rechtfertigen; (*person*) verteidigen

vindictive [vɪn·'dɪk·tɪv] *adj* nachtragend; (*vengeful*) rachsüchtig

vine [vaɪn] *n* 1. (*of grape*) Weinrebe *f* 2. (*creeper*) Rankengewächs *nt*

vinegar ['vɪn·ə·gər] *n* Essig *m*

vineyard ['vɪn·jərd] *n* Weinberg *m*

vintage ['vɪn·tɪdʒ] I. *n* 1. (*wine*) Jahr-

gangswein *m* 2. (*year*) Jahrgang *m* II. *adj* 1. (*classic*) erlesen; this film is ~ Disney dieser Film ist ein Disneyklassiker 2. AUTO ~ car Oldtimer *m*

vinyl *n* ['vaɪ·nəl] Vinyl *nt*

viola [vi·'ou·lə] *n* MUS Viola *f,* Bratsche *f*

violate ['vaɪ·ə·leɪt] *vt* (*breach*) brechen; (*regulation*) verletzen; to ~ a law gegen ein Gesetz verstoßen

violation [ˌvaɪ·ə·'leɪ·ʃən] *n* Verletzung *f,* Verstoß *m*

violence ['vaɪ·ə·ləns] *n* 1. (*behavior*) Gewalt *f* 2. (*force*) Heftigkeit *f*

violent ['vaɪ·ə·lənt] *adj* 1. (*brutal*) gewalttätig; (*person a.*) brutal; (*death*) gewaltsam 2. (*strong*) heftig; (*argument*) heftig

violet ['vaɪ·ə·lɪt] I. *n* Veilchen *nt* II. *adj* violett

violin [ˌvaɪ·ə·'lɪn] *n* Violine *f,* Geige *f*

violinist [ˌvaɪ·ə·'lɪn·ɪst] *n* Violinist(in) *m(f),* Geiger(in) *m(f)*

V.I.P., VIP [vi·aɪ·'pi] *n abbr of* **very important person** Promi *m fam*

virgin ['vɜr·dʒɪn] I. *n* 1. (*chaste*) Jungfrau *f* 2. (*novice*) unbeschriebenes Blatt *fam* II. *adj attr* jungfräulich

Virginia [vər·'dʒɪn·jə] *n* Virginia *nt*

Virgin Islands *npl* the ~ die Jungferninseln *pl*

virginity [vər·'dʒɪn·ə·ti] *n* Jungfräulichkeit *f*

Virgo ['vɜr·gou] *n no art* ASTROL Jungfrau *f*

virile ['vɪr·əl] *adj* potent; (*masculine*) männlich

virtual ['vɜr·tʃu·əl] *adj* 1. (*almost*) so gut wie, quasi; to be a ~ unknown praktisch unbekannt sein 2. COMPUT, PHYS virtuell

virtually ['vɜr·tʃu·ə·li] *adv* praktisch, eigentlich

virtual re'ality *n* virtuelle Realität

virtue ['vɜr·tʃu] *n* 1. (*quality*) Tugend *f* 2. (*advantage*) Vorteil *m* 3. (*benefit*) Nutzen *m*

virtuoso [ˌvɜr·tʃu·'ou·sou] *n < pl -s>* Virtuose, -in *m, f*

virus ['vaɪ·rəs] *n < pl -es>* 1. MED Virus *nt o fam m* 2. COMPUT Virus *m*

visa ['vi·zə] *n* Visum *nt*

V

vis-à-vis [ˌvi·zə·'vi] *prep* (*concerning*) bezüglich +*gen*

viscose ['vɪs·koʊs] *n* Viskose *f*

viscous ['vɪs·kəs] *adj* zähflüssig

vise [vaɪs] *n* Schraubstock *m*

visibility [ˌvɪz·ə·'bɪl·ə·t̬i] *n* **1.** (*view*) Sichtweite *f* **2.** (*being seen*) Sichtbarkeit *f*

visible ['vɪz·ə·bəl] *adj* sichtbar; **to be barely ~** kaum zu sehen sein

vision ['vɪʒ·ən] *n* **1.** (*sight*) Sehvermögen *nt;* **to have blurred ~** verschwommen sehen **2.** (*mental image*) Vorstellung *f* **3.** (*forethought*) Weitblick *m*

visionary ['vɪʒ·ə·ner·i] *n* Visionär(in) *m(f)* geh

visit ['vɪz·ɪt] **I.** *n* **1.** Besuch *m;* **to have a ~ from sb** von jdm besucht werden **2.** *fam* (*chat*) Plauderei *f* **II.** *vt* besuchen **III.** *vi* einen Besuch machen; **to ~ with sb** sich mit jdm treffen

'visiting hours *npl* Besuchszeiten *pl*

visitor ['vɪz·ɪ·t̬ər] *n* Besucher(in) *m(f);* (*at hotel*) Gast *m*

visor ['vaɪ·zər] *n* **1.** (*of cap*) Schild *nt* **2.** AUTO Sonnenblende *f*

vista ['vɪs·tə] *n* Aussicht *f*

visual ['vɪʒ·u·əl] **I.** *adj* visuell; **~ imagery** Bildersymbolik *f* **II.** **~s** *pl* Bildmaterial *nt*

visual 'aid *n* Anschauungsmaterial *nt*

visualize ['vɪʒ·u·ə·laɪz] *vt* **to ~ sth** (*imagine*) sich *dat* etw vorstellen

vital ['vaɪ·t̬əl] *adj* (*essential*) unerlässlich; (*stronger*) lebensnotwendig; **to be of ~ importance** von entscheidender Bedeutung sein

vitality [vaɪ·'tæl·ə·t̬i] *n* Vitalität *f*

vital 'signs *n pl* MED Lebenszeichen *pl*

vitamin ['vaɪ·t̬ə·mɪn] *n* Vitamin *nt*

'vitamin deficiency *n* Vitaminmangel *m*

vittles ['vɪt̬·əls] *n pl hum* Lebensmittel *pl*

vivacious [vɪ·'veɪ·ʃəs] *adj* (*lively*) lebhaft; (*cheerful*) munter

vivid ['vɪv·ɪd] *adj* **1.** (*graphic*) anschaulich; (*memories*) lebhaft **2.** (*colors*) kräftig

vixen ['vɪk·sən] *n* Füchsin *f*

vocabulary [voʊ·'kæb·jə·ler·i] *n* Wortschatz *m*

vocal ['voʊ·kəl] **I.** *adj* **1.** stimmlich **2.** (*outspoken*) laut; (*minority*) lautstark **II.** *n* MUS Vokalpartie *f* fachspr

'vocal cords *n pl* Stimmbänder *pl*

vocalist ['voʊ·kə·lɪst] *n* Sänger(in) *m(f)*

vocalize ['voʊ·kə·laɪz] *vt* LING (*express*) aussprechen; (*thoughts*) in Worte fassen

vocation [voʊ·'keɪ·ʃən] *n* Berufung *f*

vocational [voʊ·'keɪ·ʃə·nəl] *adj* beruflich; **~ training** Berufsausbildung *f*

vodka ['vad·kə] *n* Wodka *m*

vogue [voʊg] *n* Mode *f*

voice [vɔɪs] **I.** *n* **1.** Stimme *f;* **at the top of one's ~** in voller Lautstärke; **inner ~** innere Stimme; **to keep one's ~ down** leise sprechen **2.** (*expression*) **to give ~ to sth** etw zum Ausdruck bringen **II.** *vt* zum Ausdruck bringen; (*complaint*) vorbringen

voiceless ['vɔɪs·lɪs] *adj* stumm *a. fig*

'voice mail *n* Voicemail *f*

'voice-over *n* TV, FILM Offkommentar *m* fachspr

void [vɔɪd] **I.** *n* (*empty space*) Leere *f*, kein *pl a. fig;* (*in building*) Hohlraum *m* ► **to fill a** [*or* **the**] **~** die innere Leere ausfüllen **II.** *adj* (*invalid*) nichtig **III.** *vt* (*annul*) aufheben

vol. *n abbr of* **volume** (*book*) Bd.; (*measure*) vol.

volatile ['val·ə·t̬əl] *adj* **1.** (*changeable*) unbeständig; (*unstable*) instabil **2.** (*explosive*) explosiv

volcanic [val·'kæn·ɪk] *adj* vulkanisch

volcano <*pl* -es> [val·'keɪ·noʊ] *n* Vulkan *m a. fig*

volition [voʊ·'lɪʃ·ən] *n* **of one's own ~** aus freien Stücken

volley ['val·i] **I.** *n* **1.** (*salvo*) Salve *f* **2.** SPORT (*in tennis*) Volley *m* fachspr **II.** *vi* SPORT (*in tennis*) einen Volley schlagen fachspr

volleyball ['val·i·bɔl] *n* Volleyball *m*

volt [voʊlt] *n* Volt *nt*

voltage ['voʊl·tɪdʒ] *n* Spannung *f*

voluble ['val·jə·bəl] *adj* redselig

volume ['val·jum] *n* **1.** (*space*) Volumen *nt* **2.** (*sound*) Lautstärke *f* **3.** (*book*) Band *m*

'volume control *n* Lautstärkeregler *m*

voluntary ['val·ən·ter·i] *adj* freiwillig; ~ **work** ehrenamtliche Tätigkeit

voluntary organi'zation *n* Freiwilligenorganisation *f*

volunteer [,val·ən·'tɪr] **I.** *n* **1.** (*worker*) ehrenamtlicher Mitarbeiter/ehrenamtliche Mitarbeiterin **2.** (*helper*) Freiwillige(r) *f(m)* **II.** *vt* (*information*) bereitwillig geben; (*one's services*) anbieten **III.** *vi* **to ~ to do sth** sich [freiwillig] anbieten, etw zu tun

voluptuous [və·'lʌp·tʃu·əs] *adj* üppig; (*woman a.*) kurvenreich; (*sumptuous*) verschwenderisch

vomit ['vam·ɪt] *vi* [sich] erbrechen

voodoo ['vu·du] *n* Voodoo *m*

vortex <*pl* -es> ['vɔr·teks] *n* Wirbel *m*

vote [voʊt] **I.** *n* **1.** (*choice*) Stimme *f* **2.** (*election*) Abstimmung *f* **3.** (*right*) **the ~** das Wahlrecht **II.** *vi* **1.** (*elect*) wählen; **to ~ against sb** für jdn stimmen **2.** (*decide*) abstimmen (**on** über +*akk*) **III.** *vt* **1.** (*elect*) **to ~ sb into office** jdn ins Amt wählen **2.** (*declare*) **she was ~d the winner** sie wurde zur Siegerin erklärt

◆vote down *vt* niederstimmen

voter ['voʊ·tər] *n* Wähler(in) *m(f)*

voter regis'tration *n* Eintragung *f* ins Wählerverzeichnis

'voter turnout *n* Wahlbeteiligung *f*

voting ['voʊ·tɪŋ] *n* Wählen *nt*

'voting booth *n* Wahlkabine *f*

'voting machine *n* Wahlmaschine *f*

vouch [vaʊtʃ] *vi* **to ~ for sb** sich für jdn verbürgen

voucher ['vaʊ·tʃər] *n* Gutschein *m*; **school ~** *öffentliche Mittel, die in Amerika bereitgestellt werden, damit Eltern ihre Kinder in Privatschulen schicken können*

vow [vaʊ] **I.** *vt* geloben *geh* **II.** *n* Versprechen *nt*; **~s** *pl* (*of marriage*) Eheversprechen *nt*

vowel ['vaʊ·əl] *n* Vokal *m*

voyage ['vɔɪ·ɪdʒ] *n* Reise *f*; (*by sea*) Seereise *f*

voyeur [vɔɪ·'jɜr] *n* Voyeur(in) *m(f)*

VP [,vi·'pi] *n abbr of* **vice president** Vizepräsident(in) *m(f)*

vs. *prep abbr of* **versus** vs.

VT, Vt. *abbr of* **Vermont**

vulcanize ['vʌl·kə·naɪz] *vt* vulkanisieren

vulgar ['vʌl·gər] *adj* ordinär, vulgär; (*bad taste*) abgeschmackt

vulnerable ['vʌl·nər·ə·bəl] *adj* verletzlich; **to be ~ to sth** anfällig für etw *akk* sein; **to be ~ to criticism** Kritik ausgesetzt sein; **to feel ~** sich verwundbar fühlen

vulture ['vʌl·tʃər] *n* Geier *m a. fig*

W

W <*pl* -'s>, **w** <*pl* -'s> ['dʌb·əl·ju] *n* W *nt*, w *nt*; **~ as in Whiskey** W wie Wilhelm

W¹ **I.** *adj* **1.** *abbr of* **West** W- **2.** *abbr of* **western** I **II.** *n abbr of* **West** W

W² <*pl* -> *n abbr of* **Watt** W

WA *abbr of* **Washington**

wacko ['wæk·oʊ] *n pej sl* (*person*) Querkopf *m*

wacky ['wæk·i] *adj fam* (*person, idea*) verrückt

wad [wad] *n* **1.** (*mass*) Knäuel *nt*; (*of cotton*) Wattebausch *m* **2.** *fam* (*bundle*) **~s** *pl* **of money** schöne Stange Geld *fam*

waddle ['wad·əl] *vi* watscheln

wade [weɪd] *vi* waten

wader ['weɪ·dər] *n* Watvogel *m*

wafer ['weɪ·fər] *n* (*cookie, cracker*) Waffel *f*

wafer-'thin *adj, adv* hauchdünn

waffle¹ ['waf·əl] *n* (*food*) Waffel *f*

waffle² ['waf·əl] *vi pej fam* herumdrucksen *fam*

'waffle iron *n* Waffeleisen *nt*

wag [wæg] **I.** *vt* <-gg-> **to ~ one's finger** mit dem Finger drohen **II.** *vi* <-gg-> wedeln

wage [weɪdʒ] **I.** *n* Lohn *m*; **minimum ~** Mindestlohn *m* **II.** *vt* **to ~ war on sth** *fig* gegen etw *akk* vorgehen

'wage earner *n* Lohnempfänger(in) *m(f)*

'wage freeze *n* Lohnstopp *m*

wagon ['wæg·ən] *n* Wagen *m*

waif [weɪf] *n* (*child*) verwahrlostes Kind

wail [weɪl] *vi* jammern; (*siren*) heulen

wailing ['weɪ·lɪŋ] *adj* jammernd; (*sirens*) heulend

W

waist [weɪst] n Taille f

'waistband n Bund m

waist-'deep adv bis zur Taille

'waistline n Taille f

wait [weɪt] I. n Warten nt ▸ to lie in ~ [for sb] [jdm] auflauern II. vi warten (for auf +akk); ~ a minute! Moment mal! III. vt (serve) to ~ tables als Kellner/Kellnerin arbeiten

wait around vi warten

wait behind vi zurückbleiben

wait on vt (serve) to ~ on sb jdn bedienen

wait up vi ~ up! warte mal!

waiter ['weɪ·tər] n Bedienung f, Kellner m; ~! Herr Ober!

'waiting list n Warteliste f

'waiting room n Wartezimmer nt

waitress <pl -es> ['weɪ·trɪs] n Kellnerin f, Bedienung f

waive [weɪv] vt verzichten auf +akk

waiver ['weɪ·vər] n Verzichterklärung f

wake¹ [weɪk] n NAUT Kielwasser nt; in the ~ of sth fig infolge einer S. gen

wake² <woke or waked, woken or waked> [weɪk] I. vi aufwachen II. vt aufwecken

wake up I. vi aufwachen a. fig II. vt aufwecken

wakeful ['weɪk·fəl] adj ~ night schlaflose Nacht

waken ['weɪ·kən] I. vi aufwachen II. vt [auf]wecken

walk [wɔk] I. n 1. (going) Gehen nt; (as recreation) Spaziergang m; to go for a ~ einen Spaziergang machen 2. (path) Wanderweg m II. vt 1. to ~ the streets (wander) durch die Straßen gehen; (prostitute) auf den Strich gehen sl 2. (dog) ausführen III. vi 1. (go) zu Fuß gehen 2. (for recreation) spazieren gehen

walk away vi 1. (withdraw) sich zurückziehen (from von +dat) 2. fam (steal) to ~ away with sth etw mitgehen lassen fam

walk in vi hereinkommen

walk in on vt to ~ in on sb bei jdm hereinplatzen fam

walk off vi 1. (leave) weggehen 2. fam (steal) to ~ off with sth etw mitgehen

lassen fam

walk out vi 1. (leave) to ~ out on sb jdn im Stich lassen 2. (strike) streiken

walk over vt fam to ~ [all] over sb jdn ausnutzen

walk through vt to ~ sb through sth etw mit jdm durchgehen

walker ['wɔ·kər] n Fußgänger(in) m(f); (for recreation) Spaziergänger(in) m(f)

walkie-talkie [ˌwɔ·ki·'tɔ·ki] n Walkie-Talkie nt

'walk-in adj (closet) begehbar; (clinic) Klinik, für die keine Voranmeldung nötig ist

walking ['wɔ·kɪŋ] I. n 1. (going) Gehen nt; (as recreation) Spazierengehen nt II. adj attr within ~ distance zu Fuß erreichbar

'walking shoes npl Wanderschuhe pl

'walking stick n Spazierstock m

Walkman® <pl -men> ['wɔk·mən] n Walkman® m

'walk-on adj attr THEAT, FILM ~ part [or role] Statistenrolle f

'walkout n Arbeitsniederlegung f

'walkover n leichter Sieg

'walkway n [Fuß]weg m

wall [wɔl] n Mauer f; (in room) Wand f; the Great W~ of China die Chinesische Mauer

wall in vt usu passive ummauern

wall off vt usu passive durch eine Mauer abtrennen

'wall chart n Schautafel f

'wall clock n Wanduhr f

wallet ['wɔ·lɪt] n (for money) Brieftasche f; (for documents) Dokumentenmappe f

'wall hanging n Wandteppich m

'wall map n Wandkarte f

wallop ['wɔ·ləp] fam I. vt schlagen II. n Schlag m

wallow ['wɔ·loʊ] vi to ~ in self-pity in Selbstmitleid zerfließen

'wallpaper I. n Tapete f II. vt tapezieren

'Wall Street n Wall Street f

wall-to-'wall adj 1. ~ carpeting Teppichboden m 2. fig (constant) ständig; ~ coverage Berichterstattung f rund um die Uhr

walnut ['wɔl·nʌt] n Walnuss f

walrus <pl -> ['wɔl·rəs] n Walross nt

waltz [wɔlts] **I.** n <pl -es> Walzer m **II.** vi Walzer tanzen

◆**waltz in** vi hereintanzen fam

wand [wɔnd] n Zauberstab m

wander ['wɒn·dər] **I.** vt **to ~ the streets** (stroll) durch die Straßen schlendern; (be lost) durch die Straßen irren **II.** vi (lose concentration) **my attention is ~ing** ich bin nicht bei der Sache

wandering ['wɒn·dər·ɪŋ] adj attr wandernd; (tribe) nomadisierend

wane [weɪn] vi abnehmen; **to wax and ~** zu- und abnehmen

wangle ['wæŋ·gəl] vt fam deichseln; **to ~ one's way out of sth** sich aus etw dat herauswinden

wanna ['wɒ·nə] fam = **want to** see **want II**

wannabe ['wɒ·nə·bi] adj pej fam Möchtegern- ∘ iron fam

want [wɒnt] **I.** n **1.** (need) Bedürfnis nt; **to be in ~ of sth** etw benötigen **2.** (lack) Mangel m **II.** vt **1.** (desire) wünschen, wollen; (politely) mögen; **to be ~ed by the police** polizeilich gesucht werden **2.** (need) brauchen ▶ **waste** not, ~ not prov spare in der Zeit, dann hast du in der Not prov

◆**want in** vi fam **to ~ in** [on sth] [bei etw dat] dabei sein wollen

◆**want out** vi fam **to ~ out** [of sth] [aus etw dat] aussteigen wollen

wanting ['wɒn·tɪŋ] adj pred unzulänglich

wanton ['wɒn·tən] adj leichtfertig; **~ destruction** mutwillige Zerstörung

WAP [wæp] n INET acr for **Wireless Application Protocol** WAP nt

war [wɔr] n Krieg m; **at ~** im Kriegszustand a. fig; **to go to ~** in den Krieg ziehen

'**war baby** n Kriegskind nt

warbler ['wɔr·blər] n Grasmücke f

'**war correspondent** n Kriegsberichterstatter(in) m(f)

'**war crime** n Kriegsverbrechen nt

'**war criminal** n Kriegsverbrecher(in) m(f)

ward [wɔrd] n Station f

◆**ward off** vt abwehren

warden ['wɔr·dən] n **1.** (in prison) Gefängnisdirektor(in) m(f) **2.** (official) **game ~** Jagdaufseher(in) m(f)

wardrobe ['wɔrd·roʊb] n **1.** (armoire) [Kleider]schrank m **2.** (clothing) Garderobe f

warehouse ['wer·haʊs] n Lagerhaus nt

warfare ['wɔr·fer] n Krieg[s]führung f

warhead ['wɔr·hed] n Sprengkopf m

warily ['wer·ɪ·li] adv vorsichtig; (suspiciously) misstrauisch

warlike ['wɔr·laɪk] adj **1.** (military) kriegerisch **2.** (hostile) militant

warlord n Kriegsherr m

warm [wɔrm] **I.** adj **1.** (not cool) warm **2.** (hearty) warm; (person) warmherzig; (welcome) herzlich **II.** vt wärmen; (food) aufwärmen

◆**warm up I.** vi **1.** (engine) warm laufen **2.** (limber up) aufwärmen **II.** vt (engine) warm laufen lassen; (food) aufwärmen

warm-'blooded adj warmblütig

'**warm front** n METEO Warmfront f

warm-'hearted adj warmherzig

warmly ['wɔrm·li] adv **1. to dress ~** sich warm anziehen **2.** (heartily) herzlich

warmth [wɔrmθ] n **1.** (heat) Wärme f **2.** (affection) Herzlichkeit f

'**warm-up** n [Sich]aufwärmen nt kein pl

warn [wɔrn] **I.** vi warnen (of vor +dat) **II.** vt warnen (about vor +dat); **to ~ sb not to do sth** jdn davor warnen, etw zu tun

warning ['wɔr·nɪŋ] n **1.** (notice) Warnung f **2.** (threat) Drohung f

'**warning sign** n **1.** (signboard) Warnschild nt **2.** usu pl (symptom) Anzeichen nt

warp [wɔrp] **I.** vt, vi verziehen **II.** n **~ and weft** Kette und Schuss

'**warpath** n **to be on the ~** auf dem Kriegspfad sein hum

warped [wɔrpt] adj **1.** (bent) verzogen **2.** (perverted) verschroben pej

warrant ['wɔr·ənt] **search ~** Durchsuchungsbefehl m

'**warrant officer** n ranghöchster Unteroffizier

warranty ['wɔr·ən·ti] n Garantie f

warren ['wɔr·ən] n **1.** (burrows) Kaninchenbau m **2.** (maze) Labyrinth nt

warship ['wɔr·ʃɪp] n Kriegsschiff nt

wart [wɔrt] *n* Warze *f* ▶ **~s and all** *fam* mit all seinen/ihren Fehlern und Schwächen

'wartime *n* Kriegszeit[en] *f[pl]*

wary ['wer·i] *adj* vorsichtig

'war zone *n* Kriegsgebiet *nt*

was [waz] *pt of* **be**

wash [waʃ] I. *n* <*pl* -**es**> *usu sing* (*cleaning*) Waschen *nt kein pl;* **to give sth a** [**good**] **~** etw [gründlich] waschen II. *vt* 1. (*clean*) waschen; (*dishes*) spülen ▶ **to ~ one's hands of sth** von etw nichts zu tun haben wollen III. *vi* sich waschen

◆**wash away** *vt* 1. (*sea*) wegspülen 2. (*clean*) auswaschen

◆**wash down** *vt* 1. (*swallow*) hinunterspülen 2. (*clean*) waschen

◆**wash off** I. *vi* sich abwaschen lassen II. *vt* abwaschen

◆**wash out** I. *vi* sich herauswaschen lassen II. *vt* 1. (*clean*) auswaschen 2. (*remove*) herauswaschen

◆**wash over** *vi* (*flow over*) **to ~ over sb** über jdn [hinweg]spülen

◆**wash up** *vi* 1. (*wash oneself*) sich waschen 2. *usu passive* (*burn out*) **to be ~ed up** [völlig] ausgebrannt sein

Wash. *abbr of* **Washington**

washable ['waʃ·ə·bəl] *adj* (*garment*) waschbar; (*surface*) abwaschbar; **machine~~** waschmaschinenfest

wash-and-'wear *adj* bügelfrei

'washbasin *n* Waschbecken *nt*

'washcloth *n* Waschlappen *m*

washed-out [ˌwaʃtˈaʊt] *adj* 1. (*clothes*) verwaschen 2. (*tired*) fertig *fam*

washer ['waʃ·ər] *n* 1. (*machine*) Waschmaschine *f* 2. (*ring*) Unterlegscheibe *f;* (*seal*) Dichtung *f*

'washing machine *n* Waschmaschine *f*

Washington ['waʃ·ɪŋ·tən] *n* Washington *nt*

'washout *n usu sing fam* Reinfall *m fam*

'washroom *n* Toilette *f*

wasn't ['wʌz·ənt] = **was not** *see* **be**

wasp [wasp] *n* Wespe *f*

'wasps' nest *n* Wespennest *nt*

waste [weɪst] I. *n* 1. (*misuse*) Verschwendung *f;* **~ of time** Zeitverschwendung *f* 2. (*matter*) Abfall *m;*

industrial ~ Industriemüll *m* 3. (*excrement*) Exkremente *pl* II. *vt* 1. (*misuse*) verschwenden; **don't ~ my time!** stieh mir nicht meine wertvolle Zeit! 2. *fam* **to ~ sb** jdn umlegen

◆**waste away** *vi* immer dünner werden

'wastebasket *n* Papierkorb *m*

wasted ['weɪs·tɪd] *adj sl* 1. (*high on drugs*) mit Drogen vollgepump 2. (*drunk*) betrunken

'waste disposal *n* Abfallbeseitigung *f*

wasteful ['weɪst·fəl] *adj* verschwenderisch (**of** mit +*dat*)

waste 'management *n* Abfallwirtschaft *f*

'waste pipe *n* Abflussrohr *nt*

'waste product *n* Abfallprodukt *nt*

waster ['weɪ·stər] *n* Verschwender(in) *m(f)*

watch [watʃ] I. *n* 1. (*timepiece*) Armbanduhr *f* 2. (*duty*) Wache *f;* **on ~** auf Wache II. *vt* 1. (*look at*) beobachten; **to ~ TV** fernsehen 2. (*keep vigil*) aufpassen auf +*akk* 3. (*be careful*) **~ it!** pass auf!; **to ~ one's weight** auf sein Gewicht achten ▶ **to ~ one's step** aufpassen III. *vi* 1. (*look*) zusehen 2. (*be attentive*) aufpassen

◆**watch out** *vi* **~ out!** Achtung!

'watchband *n* Uhr[arm]band *nt*

'watchdog *n* 1. (*dog*) Wachhund *m* 2. (*organization*) Überwachungsgremium *nt*

watcher ['watʃ·ər] *n* Zuschauer(in) *m(f)*

watchful ['watʃ·fəl] *adj* wachsam

watchmaker ['watʃ·ˌmeɪ·kər] *n* Uhrmacher(in) *m(f)*

'watchman *n* **night ~** Nachtwächter *m*

'watchtower *n* Wachturm *m*

water ['wɔ·tər] I. *n* 1. (*liquid*) Wasser *nt* 2. (*urine*) **to pass ~** Wasser lassen ▶ **to be ~ under the bridge** Schnee von gestern sein *fam;* **like a fish out of ~** wie ein Fisch auf dem Trocknen II. *vt* bewässern; (*plants*) gießen III. *vi* 1. (*eyes*) tränen 2. (*salivate*) **my mouth is ~ing** mir läuft das Wasser im Munde zusammen

◆**water down** *vt* (*dilute*) verdünnen

'waterborne *adj* **~ disease** durch das Wasser übertragene Krankheit

'water bottle *n* Wasserflasche *f*

'water buffalo *n* ZOOL Wasserbüffel *m*

'water cannon n Wasserwerfer m

'water color n **1.** (paint) Aquarellfarbe f **2.** (picture) Aquarell nt

'water-cooled adj wassergekühlt

'water cooler n [Trink]wasserspender m

'watercress n Brunnenkresse f

'waterfall n Wasserfall m

'waterfowl n pl Wasservögel pl

'waterfront n (shore) Ufer nt; (area) Hafengebiet nt

watering ['wɔːtər·ɪŋ] n (of land) Bewässerung f; (of plants) Gießen nt

'watering can n Gießkanne f

'watering hole n **1.** (pond) Wasserloch nt **2.** hum fam (bar) Kneipe f fam

'water level n (of surface water) Wasserstand m; (of river) Pegel[stand] m

'water lily n Seerose f

'waterline n Wasserlinie f

'waterlogged adj (ground) feucht

'water main n Haupt[wasser]leitung f

'watermark n (on paper) Wasserzeichen nt

'watermelon n Wassermelone f

'water meter n Wasserzähler m

'water pipe n Wasserleitung f

'water pistol n Wasserpistole f

'water pollution n Wasserverschmutzung f

'water polo n Wasserball m kein pl

'water power n Wasserkraft f

'water pressure I. n Wasserdruck m

'waterproof I. adj wasserdicht **II.** vt wasserundurchlässig machen

water-re'pellent adj Wasser abweisend

'watershed n fig (change) Wendepunkt m

'water shortage n Wassermangel m kein pl

'water-ski vi Wasserski fahren

water-'soluble adj wasserlöslich

'water supply n (for area) Wasservorrat m; (for households) Wasserversorgung f

'water table n Grundwasserspiegel m

'water tank n Wassertank m

'watertight ['wɔːtər·taɪt] adj wasserdicht

'water vapor n Wasserdampf m

'waterway n Wasserstraße f

'waterworks npl (facility) Wasserwerk nt
► **to turn on the ~** fam losheulen fam

watery <more, most or -ier, -iest> ['wɔː·tə·ri] adj **1.** (drink) dünn; (soup) wässrig **2.** (light, sunshine) fahl

watt [wɑt] n Watt nt

wattage ['wɑt·ɪdʒ] n Wattzahl f

wave [weɪv] **I.** n **1.** (of water, hair) Welle f **2.** fig (feeling) ~ **of panic** Welle der Panik **3.** (of hand) Wink m; **to give sb a** ~ jdm [zu]winken **II.** vi **1.** (greet) winken; **I ~d at him across the room** ich winkte ihm durch den Raum zu **2.** (flag) wehen **III.** vt (with hand) to ~ **goodbye to sb** jdm zum Abschied [nach]winken

♦ wave aside vt **to ~ aside ⇆ an objection** einen Einwand abtun

♦ wave down vt anhalten

♦ wave through vt durchwinken

'waveband n Wellenbereich m

'wavelength n Wellenlänge f

waver ['weɪ·vər] vi **1.** wanken; (concentration) nachlassen **2.** (be indecisive) schwanken

wavy ['weɪ·vi] adj wellig; (hair) gewellt

wax [wæks] **I.** n Wachs nt **II.** vt **1.** (polish) wachsen; (floor) bohnern **2.** (remove hair) enthaaren

wax 'paper n Butterbrotpapier nt

waxy ['wæk·si] adj Wachs-, aus Wachs nach n

way [weɪ] **I.** n **1.** (road) Weg m; **one-~ street** Einbahnstraße f **2.** (route) **we have to go by ~ of Chicago** wir müssen über Chicago fahren; **to ask the ~** nach dem Weg fragen; **to be on the ~** (letter, baby) unterwegs sein; **to get under ~** in Gang kommen; **to go the wrong ~** sich verlaufen; (in car) sich verfahren; **to lead the ~** vorausgehen; **to lose one's ~** sich verirren **3.** (distance) Weg m; **to be a long ~ off** (in space) weit entfernt sein; (in time) fern sein **4.** (direction) **this ~ around** so herum; **which ~ are you going?** in welche Richtung gehst du? **5.** (manner) Art f, Weise f; **that is definitely not the ~ to do it** so macht man das auf gar keinen Fall!; **~s and means** Mittel und Wege; **one ~ or another** so oder so; **no ~** auf gar keinen Fall; **no ~!** sl ausgeschlossen!, kommt nicht in die Tüte! fam **II.** adv fam weit; **to be ~ past sb's bedtime** für jdn allerhöchste Zeit zum Schlafengehen sein

wayward ['weɪ·wərd] adj eigenwillig

we [wi] pron pers wir; **in this section ~ discuss ...** in diesem Abschnitt besprechen wir ..

weak [wik] adj **1.** schwach; (coffee, tea) dünn **2.** (ineffective: leader) unfähig; (argument, attempt) schwach

weaken ['wi·kən] I. vi schwächer werden II. vt schwächen

weakling ['wik·lɪŋ] n Schwächling m

weakness <pl -es> ['wik·nɪs] n Schwäche f

wealth [welθ] n Reichtum m; (fortune) Vermögen nt

'wealth tax n Vermögenssteuer f

wealthy ['wel·θi] adj reich

wean [win] vt (baby) abstillen

weapon ['wep·ən] n Waffe f a. fig; **~s of mass destruction** Massenvernichtungswaffen pl

weaponry ['wep·ən·ri] n Waffen pl

wear [wer] I. n **1.** (clothing) Kleidung f **2.** (damage) ~ **and tear** Verschleiß m II. vt <wore, worn> tragen ▶ **to ~ one's heart on one's sleeve** das Herz auf der Zunge tragen III. vi <wore, worn> (clothes) abtragen

◆ **wear away** vi sich abnutzen

◆ **wear down** vt (tire) fertigmachen fam; (weaken) zermürben

◆ **wear off** vi nachlassen

◆ **wear out** I. vi abnutzen II. vt erschöpfen

wearable ['wer·ə·bəl] adj tragbar

weary ['wɪr·i] adj müde

weasel ['wi·zəl] n Wiesel nt

weather ['weð·ər] I. n Wetter nt; (climate) Witterung f ▶ **to be under the ~** fam angeschlagen sein fam II. vi verwittern

'weather-beaten adj verwittert

'weather chart n Wetterkarte f

'weather conditions npl Witterungsverhältnisse pl

'weather forecast n Wettervorhersage f

'weatherman n Wettermann m fam

'weatherproof adj wetterfest

weave [wiv] vt, vi <wove or weaved, woven or weaved> weben

weaver ['wi·vər] n Weber(in) m(f)

web [web] n **1.** (of spider) Netz nt

2. fig **a ~ of intrigue** ein Netz nt von Intrigen

'web browser n INET [Web-]Browser m fachspr

web-footed ['web·ˌfʊt·ɪd] adj mit Schwimmfüßen nach n

webmaster ['web·mæs·tər] n INET Web-Administrator(in) m(f)

'web page n INET Webseite f

'website n INET Website f

webzine ['web·zin] n INET Webzine nt (Onlinemagazin)

we'd [wid] **1.** = **we had** see **have** I, II **2.** = **we would** see **would**

wedding ['wed·ɪŋ] n Hochzeit f

'wedding anniversary n Hochzeitstag m

'wedding cake n Hochzeitstorte f

'wedding day n Hochzeitstag m

'wedding dress n Brautkleid nt

'wedding night n Hochzeitsnacht f

'wedding present n Hochzeitsgeschenk nt

'wedding ring n Ehering m, Trauring m

wedge [wedʒ] I. n Keil m II. vt einkeilen

Wednesday ['wenz·deɪ] n Mittwoch m; see also **Tuesday**

wee [wi] adj winzig; **in the ~ hours** zwischen 1 und 2 Uhr

weed [wid] I. n Unkraut nt kein pl II. vt (garden) jäten

weedy ['wi·di] adj fam [spindel]dürr

week [wik] n **1.** (seven days) Woche f; **twice a ~** zweimal die Woche **2.** (work period) **five-day ~** 5-Tage-Woche

'weekday n Wochentag m

weekend n Wochenende nt; **on the ~|s|/on ~s** am Wochenende/an Wochenenden

weekly ['wik·li] I. adj, adv wöchentlich II. n (magazine) Wochenzeitschrift f; (newspaper) Wochenzeitung f

weep [wip] vi <wept, wept> weinen

weeping willow n Trauerweide f

weigh [weɪ] I. vi **1.** (in measurement) wiegen **2.** fig **to ~ heavily** eine große Bedeutung haben II. vt [ab]wiegen

◆ **weigh down** vt niederdrücken; **to be ~ed down with sth** schwer mit etw dat beladen sein

◆ **weigh in** vi **1.** **to ~ in at 132 pounds**

132 Pfund auf die Waage bringen **2.** *fam* (*intervene*) **to ~ in with sth** (*opinion*) etw einbringen

'weigh-in *n* SPORT Wiegen *nt*

weight [weɪt] **I.** *n* **1.** Gewicht; **to put on** [*or* **gain**] **~** zunehmen ▶ **to** <u>**throw**</u> **one's ~ around** *fam* seinen Einfluss geltend machen **II.** *vt* **to ~ sth down** etw beschweren

weightless ['weɪt·lɪs] *adj* schwerelos

'weightlifter *n* Gewichtheber(in) *m(f)*

weighty ['weɪ·ti] *adj* **1.** (*heavy*) schwer **2.** *fig* (*important*) [ge]wichtig

weird [wɪrd] *adj fam* seltsam, komisch

weirdo <*pl* -os> ['wɪr·doʊ] *n pej fam* seltsame Person, Freak *m*

welcome ['wel·kəm] **I.** *vt* **1.** (*greet*) willkommen heißen **2.** (*be glad of*) begrüßen **II.** *n* **1.** (*reception*) **to give sb a warm ~** jdm einen herzlichen Empfang bereiten **2.** (*approval*) Zustimmung *f* ▶ **to** <u>**overstay**</u> **one's ~** länger bleiben, als man erwünscht ist **III.** *adj* **1.** willkommen **2. thank you very much — you're ~** vielen Dank – nichts zu danken

welcoming ['wel·kə·mɪŋ] *adj* **~ smile** freundliches Lächeln

weld [weld] **I.** *vt* schweißen **II.** *n* Schweißnaht *f*

welder ['wel·dər] *n* Schweißer(in) *m(f)*

welfare ['wel·fer] *n* Sozialhilfe *f*; **to be on ~** von [der] Sozialhilfe leben

'welfare payments *npl* Sozialabgaben *pl*

'welfare services *npl* + *sing vb* (*office*) Sozialamt *nt*

we'll [wɪl] = **we will** *see* **will**[1]

well[1] [wel] **I.** *adj* <better, best> *usu pred* **1.** (*healthy*) gesund; **to feel ~** sich gut fühlen; **to get ~** gesund werden **2.** (*okay*) **all's ~ here** hier ist alles in Ordnung; **all ~ and good** gut und schön **II.** *adv* <better, best> **1.** (*in a good way*) gut; **~ done!** gut gemacht!, super! *fam*; **to be money ~ spent** gut angelegtes Geld sein; **to mean ~** es gut meinen **2.** (*thoroughly*) gut; **to know sb ~** jdn gut kennen **3.** (*used for emphasis*) [sehr] wohl; **to be ~ aware of sth** sich *dat* einer S. *gen* durchaus bewusst sein;

~ and truly ganz einfach **4.** (*also*) **as ~** auch; (*and*) **as ... as ... ...** sowie ... **III.** *interj* (*introducing, continuing*) nun [ja], also; (*hesitating, resignedly*) tja *fam*; (*surprised*) **~ I, ~!** sieh mal einer an!

well[2] [wel] *n* **1.** (*for water*) Brunnen *m* **2. oil ~** Ölquelle *f*

well-ad'vised *adj pred* **to be ~ to do sth** gut beraten sein, etw zu tun

well ap'pointed *adj pred*, **well-ap'pointed** *adj attr* gut ausgestattet

well 'balanced *adj pred*, **well-'balanced** *adj attr* **1.** (*report*) objektiv; (*team*) harmonisch **2.** (*diet*) ausgewogen

well be'haved *adj pred*, **well-be'haved** *adj attr* (*child*) artig; (*dog*) brav

well-'being *n* feeling of **~** wohliges Gefühl

well 'bred *adj pred*, **well-'bred** *adj attr* (*with good manners*) wohlerzogen *geh*; (*refined*) gebildet

well 'chosen *adj pred*, **well-'chosen** *adj attr* gut gewählt; **to say a few ~ words** ein paar passende Worte [sagen]

well con'nected *adj pred*, **well-con'nected** *adj attr* **to be ~** gute Beziehungen haben

well de'served *adj pred*, **well-de'served** *adj attr* wohlverdient

well de'veloped *adj pred*, **well-de'veloped** *adj attr* gut entwickelt

well 'done *adj pred*, **well-'done** *adj attr* **1.** (*of meat*) gut durch[gebraten] **2.** (*of work*) gut gemacht

well 'dressed *adj pred*, **well-'dressed** *adj attr* gut gekleidet

well 'educated *adj pred*, **well-'educated** *adj attr* gebildet

well 'founded *adj pred*, **well-'founded** *adj attr* [wohl]begründet

well 'groomed *adj pred*, **well-'groomed** *adj attr* gepflegt

well 'heeled *adj pred*, **well-'heeled** *adj attr fam* [gut] betucht

well in'formed *adj pred*, **well-in'formed** *adj attr* **to be ~ on a subject** über ein Thema gut Bescheid wissen

well in'tentioned *adj pred*, **well-in'tentioned** *adj attr* gut gemeint

well 'kept *adj pred*, **well-'kept** *adj attr* **1.** (*tended*) gepflegt **2.** (*hidden*) **a ~ se-**

W

cret ein gut gehütetes Geheimnis

well 'known *adj pred*, well-'known *adj attr* [allgemein] bekannt; (*famous*) berühmt

well 'meaning *adj pred*, well-'meaning *adj attr* ~ **advice** gut gemeinte Ratschläge

'wellness *n* Wohlbefinden *nt*

well 'off <better-, best-> *adj pred*, well-'off *adj attr* wohlhabend

well pro'portioned *adj pred*, well-pro'portioned *adj attr* wohlproportioniert

well 'read *adj pred*, well-'read *adj attr* [sehr] belesen

well 'spoken *adj pred*, well-'spoken *adj attr* (*polite*) höflich; (*refined*) beredt

well 'timed *adj pred*, well-'timed *adj attr* **his remark was** ~ seine Bemerkung kam zur rechten Zeit

well-to-'do *adj fam* [gut] betucht

'well-wisher *n* wohlwollender Freund/ wohlwollende Freundin; (*supporter*) Sympathisant(in) *m(f)*

well 'worn *adj pred*, well-'worn *adj attr* (*clothes*) abgetragen; (*object*) abgenützt

went [went] *pt of* go

wept *pt*, *pp of* weep

were [wɜr] *pt of* be

we're [wɪr] = we are *see* be

weren't [wɜrnt] = were not *see* be

west [west] I. *n* 1. (*direction*) Westen *m*; to be to the ~ of sth westlich von etw *dat* liegen 2. POL the W~ die westliche Welt 3. *adj attr* westlich, West-; the ~ coast of Florida die Westküste Floridas III. *adv* westwärts; to travel ~ nach Westen reisen

'westbound *adj* in Richtung Westen

westerly ['wes·tər·li] *adj* westlich

western ['wes·tərn] I. *adj attr* West-, westlich; ~ Europe Westeuropa *nt* II. *n* (*film*) Western *m*

westerner ['wes·tər·nər] *n* Abendländer(in) *m(f)*

West Vir'ginia *n* West Virginia *nt*

westward(s) ['west·wərd(z)] *adj* westlich; (*road*) nach Westen *nach n*

wet [wet] I. *adj* <-tt-> 1. (*soaked*) nass; soaking ~ [völlig] durchnässt 2. (*cov-*

ered with moisture) feucht 3. (*not dried*) "~ paint!" „frisch gestrichen!" II. *vt* <-tt-, wet *or* wetted, wet *or* wetted> 1. (*moisten*) anfeuchten; (*soak*) nass machen 2. (*urinate*) **to** ~ **the bed** das Bett nass machen

'wetback *n pej sl* illegaler Einwanderer/ illegale Einwanderin aus Mexiko

wet 'dream *n fam* feuchter Traum

'wetness *n* Nässe *f*

'wetsuit *n* Tauceranzug *m*

we've [wiv] = we have *see* have I, II

whack [hwæk] I. *vt sl* (*murder*) **to** ~ **sb** jdn umlegen *fam* II. *n* (*blow*) Schlag *m*

whacko ['wæ·koʊ] *adj sl see* wacko

whale [hweɪl] *n* Wal *m*

whaling ['hweɪ·lɪŋ] *n* der Walfang

wharf <*pl* wharves> [hwɔrf] *n* Kai *m*

what [hwʌt] I. *pron* 1. *interrog* was; ~ **is your name?** wie heißt du?; ~ **about sb/sth?** *fam* was ist mit jdm/ etw?; ~ **for?** (*for what purpose?*) wofür?; *fam* (*why?*) warum?; ~ **if ...?** was ist, wenn ...?; **so** ~? *fam* na und? 2. *rel* was; **I can't decide** ~ **to do next** ich kann mich nicht entschließen, was ich als nächstes tun soll 3. *rel* (*whatever*) was; **do** ~ **you can** tu, was du kannst II. *adj* 1. (*which*) welche(r, s); ~ **time is it?** wie spät ist es? 2. (*emphasizing*) was für; ~ **a shame!** wie schade! III. *interj* 1. (*pardon?*) ~? **I can't hear you** was? ich höre dich nicht 2. (*showing surprise, disbelief*) ~!? **you left him there alone!?** was?! du hast ihn da allein gelassen?

whatchamacallit ['hwʌtʃ·ə·mə·ˌkɔl·ɪt] *n fam* Dingsda *m o f o nt fam*; (*object a.*) Dings *nt fam*

whatever [hwʌt·'ev·ər] I. *pron* 1. was [auch immer]; **I eat** ~ **I want** ich esse, was ich will 2. *fam* **or** ~ wie du willst II. *adj* 1. (*any*) was auch immer; **take** ~ **action is needed** mach, was auch immer nötig ist 2. (*regardless*) gleichgültig welche(r, s) III. *adv with neg* überhaupt

whatnot ['hwʌt·nat] *n fam* **and** ~ und was weiß ich noch alles

whatsoever [ˌhwʌt·soʊ·'ev·ər] *adv* überhaupt

wheat [hwit] *n* Weizen *m*

'**wheat germ** *n* Weizenkeim *m*

wheel [hwil] *n* **1.** Rad *nt;* **rear** ~ Hinterrad *nt* **2.** *(for steering)* Steuer *nt;* AUTO Lenkrad *nt;* **to be at the** ~ am Steuer sitzen **3.** *fam (vehicle)* ~**s** *pl* fahrbarer Untersatz *hum*

◆ **wheel around** *vi* sich schnell umdrehen; *(esp shocked)* herumfahren

'**wheelbarrow** *n* Schubkarre *f*

'**wheelchair** *n* Rollstuhl *m*

'**wheeler-dealer** [ˌhwi·lər·'di·lər] *n* Schlitzohr *nt*

wheeling ['hwi·lɪŋ] *n* ~ **and dealing** Abzockerei *f sl;* *(shady)* Gemauschel *nt*

wheeze [hwiz] **I.** *vi* keuchen **II.** *n* Keuchen *nt kein pl*

when [hwen] **I.** *adv* **1.** *interrog* wann; ~ **do you want to go?** wann möchtest du gehen? **2.** *rel (during)* wenn, wo; **there are times** ~ ... es gibt Momente, wo ... **II.** *conj* **1.** *(once in past)* als; *(several times in past)* wenn; **I loved that film** ~ **I was a child** als Kind liebte ich diesen Film **2.** *(after, whenever)* wenn

whenever [hwen·'ev·ər] *conj* **1.** wann auch immer **2.** *(every time)* jedes Mal, wenn ...

where [hwer] *adv* **1.** *interrog* wo; *(to where)* wohin; *(from where)* woher; ~ **are you going?** wohin gehst du? **2.** *rel* wo; *(to where)* wohin; *(from where)* woher; **Boston,** ~ **Phil comes from ...** Boston, wo Phil herkommt ... ▸ **to see** ~ **sb's coming from** verstehen, was jd meint

whereabouts I. *n* ['hwer·ə·baʊts] + *sing/pl vb* Aufenthaltsort *m* **II.** *adv* [ˌhwer·ə·'baʊts] wo *(genau);* ~ **in Manhattan do you live?** wo genau in Manhattan wohnst du?

whereas [hwer·'æz] *conj (in contrast to)* während

wherever [ˌhwer·'ev·ər] **I.** *conj* **1.** *(to whatever place)* wohin auch immer **2.** *(in all places)* wo auch immer **II.** *adv (in every case)* wann immer; ~ **possible** wenn möglich

whether ['hweð·ər] *conj* **1.** *(if)* ob; **to ask** ~ **...** fragen, ob ...; **she can't decide** ~ **to tell him** sie kann sich nicht entschei-

den, ob sie es ihm sagen soll **2.** *(no matter)* ~ **you like it or not** ob es dir [nun] gefällt oder nicht

whew [hwu] *interj* puh

which [hwɪtʃ] **I.** *pron* **1.** *interrog (one)* welche(r, s); ~ **[one] is mine?** welches gehört mir? **2.** *rel (with defining clause)* der/die/das; **the conference,** ~ **ended on Friday** die Konferenz, die am Freitag geendet hat **3.** *rel (with non-defining clause)* was; **she says it's Anna's fault,** ~ **is ridiculous** sie sagt, das ist Annas Schuld, was aber Blödsinn ist **II.** *adj interrog (one)* welche(r, s); ~ **doctor did you see?** bei welchem Arzt warst du?

whichever [hwɪtʃ·'ev·ər] **I.** *pron* wer/ was auch immer **II.** *adj attr* **1.** *(any one)* ~ ... der-/die-/dasjenige, der/ die/das ...; **choose** ~ **brand you prefer** wähle die Marke, die du lieber hast **2.** *(regardless)* egal welche(r, s), welche(r, s) ... auch immer

whiff [hwɪf] *n usu sing* Hauch *m kein pl*

while [hwaɪl] **I.** *n* Weile *f;* **in a** ~ in Kürze **II.** *conj* **1.** *(during)* während **2.** *(although)* obwohl; ~ **I completely understand your point of view, ...** wenn ich Ihren Standpunkt auch vollkommen verstehe, ...

whim [hwɪm] *n* Laune *f*

whimper ['hwɪm·pər] *vi (person)* wimmern; *(dog)* winseln

whimsical ['hwɪm·zɪ·kəl] *adj* **1.** *(playful)* skurril *geh* **2.** *(capricious)* launenhaft

whimsy, whimsey ['hwɪm·zi] *n* **1.** *(whim)* Laune *f* **2.** *(playfulness)* Spleenigkeit *f*

whine [hwaɪn] *vi* **1.** *(utter sound)* jammern; *(animal)* jaulen **2.** *(complain)* meckern

whip [hwɪp] **I.** *n* Peitsche *f* **II.** *vt* <-pp-> **1.** *(hit)* [mit der Peitsche] schlagen; *(horse)* die Peitsche geben **2.** *fam (defeat)* [vernichtend] schlagen

◆ **whip out** *vt* zücken

◆ **whip up** *vt* **1.** *(excite)* **to** ~ **up support** Unterstützung finden **2.** *(cook)* zaubern *fig, hum*

'**whiplash** *n* ~ **[injury]** Schleudertrauma *nt*

W

whipped [wɪpt] *adj* ~ **cream** Schlagsahne *f*

whippet ['hwɪp·ɪt] *n* Whippet *m*

whipping ['hwɪp·ɪŋ] *n* 1. (*punishment*) **to get a** ~ Prügel beziehen 2. *fam* (*defeat*) Schlappe *f fam*

'**whipping cream** *n* Schlagsahne *f*

whir [hwɜr] *vi* <-rr-> surren

whirl [hwɜrl] I. *vt, vi* wirbeln II. *n* 1. (*action*) Wirbeln *nt* 2. (*activity*) Trubel *m*

whirligig ['hwɜr·lɪ·gɪg] *n* (*top*) Kreisel *m*

whirlpool ['hwɜrl·pul] *n* Whirlpool *m*

whirlwind ['hwɜrl·wɪnd] *n* Wirbelwind *m*

whisk [hwɪsk] I. *n* Schneebesen *m* II. *vt* (*cream*) schlagen

whisker ['hwɪs·kər] *n* 1. (*of animal*) Schnurrhaar[e] *nt/pl* 2. (*beard*) ~**s** *pl* Bartstoppeln *pl* ▶ **by a** ~ um Haaresbreite

whiskey, whisky ['hwɪs·ki] *n* Whisk[e]y *m*

whisper ['hwɪs·pər] I. *vi* flüstern II. *n* Flüstern *nt kein pl*; **to speak in a** ~ etw im Flüsterton sagen

whispering ['hwɪs·pər·ɪŋ] I. *n* Flüstern *nt* II. *adj attr* flüsternd

whist [hwɪst] *n* Whist *nt*; **game of** ~ Partie *f* Whist

whistle ['hwɪs·əl] I. *vi* 1. pfeifen 2. (*bird*) zwitschern II. *vt* pfeifen III. *n* 1. (*sound*) Pfeifen *nt* 2. (*device*) Pfeife *f*; **as clean as a** ~ blitzsauber

white [hwaɪt] I. *n* 1. Weiß *nt* 2. (*of eye*) Weiße *nt* 3. (*person*) Weiße(r) *f/m* II. *adj* 1. weiß; **black and** ~ schwarzweiß 2. (*coffee*) mit Milch *nach* O 3. ~ **bread** Weißbrot *nt* 4. (*Caucasian*) weiß ▶ **as** ~ **as a sheet** weiß wie die Wand, kreidebleich

'**white-collar** *adj* ~ **worker** Angestellte(r) *f/m*

white flag *n* weiße Fahne

'**White House** *n* **the** ~ das Weiße Haus

white lie *n* Notlüge *f*

'**white meat** *n* helles Fleisch

whiten ['hwaɪ·tən] I. *vt* weiß machen; (*teeth*) bleichen II. *vi* weiß werden

whitener ['hwaɪ·nər] *n* (*for coffee*) Kaffeeweißer *m*

'**whiteout** *n* 1. METEO [starker] Schneesturm 2. TYPO Korrekturflüssigkeit *f*

'**white sale** *n* Weißwäscheausverkauf *m*

'**whitewash** I. *n* 1. (*solution*) Tünche *f* 2. (*cover-up*) Schönfärberei *f* II. *vt* 1. (*paint*) weiß anstreichen 2. (*conceal*) schönfärben

white wine *n* Weißwein *m*

whiting <*pl* -> ['hwaɪ·tɪŋ] *n* (*fish*) Weißfisch *m*

Whitsun ['hwɪt·sən] *n* Pfingsten *nt*

whittle ['hwɪt·əl] *vt* schnitzen

◆ **whittle down** *vt* reduzieren

whiz, whizz [hwɪz] I. *vi* 1. **to** ~ **by** vorbeijagen 2. (*time*) rasen II. *vt* [mit dem Mixer] verrühren III. *n fam* **computer** ~ Computerass *nt fam*

whiz kid *n* Wunderkind *nt, fam* Genie *nt oft hum*

who [hu] *pron* 1. *interrog* (*which person*) wer; ~ **did this?** wer war das? 2. *interrog* (*whom*) wem *dat*, wen *akk*; ~ **do you want to talk to?** mit wem möchten Sie sprechen? 3. *rel* der/die/das; **I think it was your dad** ~ **called** ich glaube, das war dein Vater, der angerufen hat

whoa [hwoʊ] *interj* 1. *fam* (*slow down!*) langsam! 2. *fam* (*wow!*) wow *sl*, toll! *fam*

whodunit, whodunnit [,hu·'dʌn·ɪt] *n fam* Krimi *m fam*

whoever [hu·'ev·ər] *pron rel* **come out,** ~ **you are** kommen Sie heraus, wer auch immer Sie sind

whole [hoʊl] I. *adj* 1. (*entire*) ganz; **the** ~ [**wide**] **world** die ganze [weite] Welt 2. (*in one piece*) ganz; (*intact*) intakt II. *n* 1. (*entire thing*) **a** ~ ein Ganzes *nt* 2. (*entirety*) **the** ~ das Ganze 3. (*in total*) **on the** ~ im Großen und Ganzen III. *adv* ganz; **a** ~ **new approach** ein ganz neuer Ansatz

'**whole food** *n* Vollwertkost *f*

wholehearted [,hoʊl·'har·tɪd] *adj* 1. (*sincere*) aufrichtig 2. (*committed*) engagiert

whole milk *n* Vollmilch *f*

'**whole note** *n* MUS ganze Note

'**whole rest** *n* MUS ganze Pause

wholesale ['hoʊl·seɪl] I. *adj* 1. *attr* ~ **business** Großhandel *m* 2. (*extensive*) ~ **reform** umfassende Reform II. *adv* (*in*

bulk) in Großmengen

wholesaler ['hoʊl·seɪ·lər] n Großhändler(in) m(f)

wholesome ['hoʊl·səm] adj wohltuend; (healthy) gesund

'**whole-wheat** adj attr ~ **bread** Vollkornbrot nt

who'll [hul] = **who will** see **who**

wholly ['hoʊ·li] adv ganz, völlig

whom [hum] pron form 1. (interrog) wem dat, wen akk; ~ **did she marry?** wen hat er geheiratet? 2. (rel) das/der/die; **none of** ~ ... keiner, der ...

'**whooping cough** n Keuchhusten m

whoops [hwʊps] interj fam hoppla; ~-a-**daisy** hopsala

whop [hwap] vt <-pp-> fam schlagen

whopper ['hwap·ər] n fam 1. (huge thing) Apparat m sl; **that's a ~ of a fish** das ist ja ein Riesenfisch 2. (lie) faustdicke Lüge fam

whore [hɔr] n pej Nutte f sl

who's [huz] = **who is**, **who has** see **who**

whose [huz] I. adj 1. (in questions) wessen; ~ **round is it?** wer ist dran? 2. (indicating possession) dessen; **she's the woman** ~ **car I rode in** sie ist die Frau, in deren Auto ich gefahren bin II. pron poss, interrog wessen

why [hwaɪ] adv 1. (for what reason) warum; ~ **did she say that?** warum hat er das gesagt? 2. (for that reason) **the reason** ~ **I** ... der Grund, warum ich ...

WI abbr of **Wisconsin**

wick [wɪk] n Docht m

wicked ['wɪk·ɪd] I. adj 1. (evil) böse 2. (cunning) raffiniert 3. fam (good) saugut sl II. interj fam super fam

wicker ['wɪk·ər] n Korbgeflecht nt

wicker 'furniture n Korbmöbel pl

wicket ['wɪk·ɪt] n (croquet hoop) Tor nt

wide [waɪd] I. adj 1. (broad) breit 2. (considerable) enorm, beträchtlich 3. (open) geweitet; (eyes) groß 4. (varied) breit gefächert; ~ **range of goods** großes Sortiment an Waren II. adv weit; ~ **apart** weit auseinander

wide-angle 'lens n PHOT Weitwinkelobjektiv nt fachspr

'**wide-a'wake** adj pred, **wide-a'wake** adj attr hellwach

widely ['waɪd·li] adv 1. (broadly) breit 2. (extensively) weit; ~ **admired** weithin bewundert 3. (considerably) beträchtlich

'**widespread** adj weit verbreitet

widow ['wɪd·oʊ] n Witwe f

widower ['wɪd·oʊ·ər] n Witwer m

width [wɪdθ] n Breite f

wiener ['wi·nər] n 1. (hot dog) Wiener Würstchen nt 2. childspeak fam (penis) Pimmel m fam

wife <pl **wives**> [waɪf] n [Ehe]frau f

wig [wɪg] n Perücke f

wiggle ['wɪg·əl] vt, vi wackeln

wigwam ['wɪg·wam] n Wigwam m

wild [waɪld] I. adj 1. (undomesticated) wild 2. (uncultivated: landscape) rau, wild; ~ **flowers** wild wachsende Blumen 3. (uncontrolled) unbändig; (behavior) undiszipliniert 4. (stormy) rau, stürmisch 5. fam (angry) wütend 6. fam (enthusiastic) **to be ~ about sb** auf jdn ganz wild sein II. adv wild; **to run ~** (child) sich dat selbst überlassen sein; (animals) frei herumlaufen III. n 1. (natural environment) **the ~** die Wildnis f; fig (remote places) **the ~s** pl die Pampa f kein pl oft hum fam

wild 'boar n Wildschwein nt

'**wildcard** n 1. CARDS Joker m 2. COMPUT Wildcard f

'**wildcat** n Wildkatze f

wilderness <pl -es> ['wɪl·dər·nɪs] n Wildnis f; (desert) Wüste f

'**wildfire** n **to spread like ~** fig sich wie ein Lauffeuer verbreiten

'**wildfowl** n Federwild nt kein pl; FOOD Wildgeflügel nt kein pl

wild-'goose chase n (venture) fruchtloses Unterfangen

'**wildlife** I. n [natürliche] Tier- und Pflanzenwelt f II. adj ~ **sanctuary** Wildschutzgebiet nt

wildly ['waɪld·li] adv 1. (in uncontrolled way) wild; **to talk ~** wirres Zeug reden fam 2. (haphazardly) ungezielt; **to guess ~** [wild] drauflosraten fam

wild 'rice n Wildreis m

Wild West n **the ~** der Wilde Westen

wiles [waɪlz] npl Trick m; **to use all one's ~** mit allen Tricks arbeiten

W

wilful ['wɪl·fəl] *adj see* **willful**

will¹ <would, would> [wɪl] *aux vb* **1.** (*in future tense*) **do you think he ~ come?** glaubst du, dass er kommt [*or* kommen wird]? **2.** (*repeating question*) **you won't forget to tell him, ~ you?** du vergisst aber nicht, es ihm zu sagen, oder? **3.** (*expressing intention*) werden; **I ~ always love you** ich werde dich immer lieben **4.** (*expressing facts*) **fruit ~ keep longer in the fridge** Obst hält sich im Kühlschrank länger

will² [wɪl] **I.** *n* **1.** Wille *m* **2.** LAW Testament *nt* **II.** *vt* **to ~ sb to do sth** jdn [durch Willenskraft] dazu bringen, etw zu tun

wilful, willful ['wɪl·fəl] *adj* **1.** (*deliberate*) bewusst; (*damage*) mutwillig **2.** (*self-willed*) eigensinnig; (*obstinate*) starrsinnig

willies ['wɪl·iz] *npl fam* **sb has the ~** jd kriegt Zustände

willing ['wɪl·ɪŋ] *adj* **1.** (*unopposed*) bereit **2.** (*enthusiastic*) willig

willingness ['wɪl·ɪŋ·nɪs] *n* (*readiness*) Bereitschaft *f*; (*enthusiasm*) Bereitwilligkeit *f*

willow ['wɪl·oʊ] *n* Weide *f*

willpower *n* Willenskraft *f*

wily ['waɪ·li] *adj* listig

wimp [wɪmp] *n fam* Waschlappen *m*

win [wɪn] **I.** *vt* <won, won> **1.** (*be victorious*) gewinnen **2.** (*get*) gewinnen, bekommen; (*recognition*) finden ▶ **you can't ~ them [*or* 'em] all** *saying* man kann nicht immer Glück haben **II.** *vi* <won, won> gewinnen; **to ~ hands down** spielend gewinnen ▶ **may the best man ~** dem Besten der Sieg **III.** *n* Sieg *m*

◆ **win back** *vt* **1.** SPORT **to ~ back ⇆ the trophy** den Pokal zurückholen **2.** (*customers*) zurückgewinnen

◆ **win over** *vt* (*persuade*) überzeugen

◆ **win around** *vt* überzeugen

winch [wɪntʃ] *n* <*pl* -es> Winde *f*

wind¹ [wɪnd] *n* **1.** (*air*) Wind *m*; **to see which way the ~ is blowing** sehen, woher der Wind weht *a. fig* **2.** (*breath*) Atem *m* **3.** (*flatulence*) Blähungen *pl*

wind² [waɪnd] **I.** *vt* <wound, wound>

1. (*wrap*) wickeln; (*yarn*) aufwickeln; (*film*) spulen **2.** (*watch*) aufziehen **3.** (*turn*) winden **II.** *vi* <wound, wound> **1.** (*meander*) sich schlängeln **2.** (*coil*) sich wickeln

◆ **wind down I.** *vt* (*business*) auflösen; (*production*) drosseln **II.** *vi* (*relax*) [sich] entspannen

◆ **wind up I.** *vt* **1.** (*end*) abschließen; (*meeting, speech*) beenden **2.** (*annoy*) **to ~ up ⇆ sb** jdn auf die Palme bringen **3.** (*clock*) aufziehen **II.** *vi fam* **1.** (*end*) schließen *fam;* (*speech*) abschließend bemerken **2.** (*land*) enden; **to ~ up in prison** im Gefängnis landen *fam*

windbreak *n* Windschutz *m*

wind energy *n* Windenergie *f*

winder ['waɪn·dər] *n* Aufziehschraube *f*; (*on watch*) Krone *f*

windfall *n* **1.** (*money*) warmer [Geld]regen *fam* **2.** (*fruit*) ~s *pl* Fallobst *nt kein pl*

wind farm *n* Windpark *m*

wind generator *n* Windgenerator *m*

winding ['waɪn·dɪŋ] **I.** *adj* gewunden; (*road*) kurvenreich **II.** *n* ELEC Wicklung *f*

wind instrument *n* Blasinstrument *nt*

windmill *n* **1.** (*for grinding*) Windmühle *f* **2.** (*turbine*) Windrad *nt*

window ['wɪn·doʊ] *n* **1.** (*a. comput*) Fenster *nt*; (*of shop*) Schaufenster *nt*; **rear ~** Heckscheibe *f* **2.** (*opportunity*) Gelegenheit *f*

window box *n* Blumenkasten *m*

window cleaner *n* **1.** (*person*) Fensterputzer(in) *m(f)* **2.** (*detergent*) Glasreiniger *m*

window display *n* Schaufensterauslage *f*

window frame *n* Fensterrahmen *m*

window-shopping *n* Schaufensterbummel *m*

windowsill *n* (*inside*) Fensterbank *f*; (*outside*) Fenstersims *m o nt*

windpipe *n* Luftröhre *f*

wind power *n* (*energy*) Windenergie *f*

windshield *n* Windschutzscheibe *f*

windshield wiper *n* Scheibenwischer *m*

windsurfer ['wɪnd·ˌsɜr·fər] *n* Windsurfer(in) *m(f)*

windswept *adj* **1.** (*beach*) windge-

peitscht **2.** (*appearance*) [vom Wind] zerzaust

'wind tunnel n Windkanal m

'wind turbine n Windturbine f

windward ['wɪnd·wərd] *adj, adv* windwärts

windy¹ ['wɪn·di] *adj* METEO windig

windy² ['waɪn·di] *adj* (*road*) kurvenreich

wine [waɪn] **I.** n Wein m **II.** vi **to ~ and dine** fürstlich essen

'wine bottle n Weinflasche f

'wine cellar n Weinkeller m

'wineglass n Weinglas nt

winegrower ['waɪn·ˌgroʊ·ər] n Winzer(in) m(f)

winegrowing ['waɪn·ˌgroʊ·ɪŋ] n Wein[an]bau m

'wine list n Weinkarte f

winery ['waɪ·nə·ri] n Weinkellerei f

'winetasting n Weinprobe f

wing [wɪŋ] n **1.** Flügel m **2.** THEAT **to be waiting in the ~s** in den Kulissen warten

'wing chair n Ohrensessel m

winger ['wɪŋ·ər] n SPORT (*left*) Linksaußen m; (*right*) Rechtsaußen m

'wing nut n Flügelmutter f

'wingspan n Flügelspannweite f

wink [wɪŋk] **I.** vi (*one eye*) zwinkern; **to ~ at sb** jdm zuzwinkern **II.** n [Augen]zwinkern nt ▶ **to not sleep a ~** kein Auge zutun

winner ['wɪn·ər] n (*victor*) Gewinner(in) m(f); (*in competition*) Sieger(in) m(f)

winning ['wɪn·ɪŋ] **I.** *adj attr* (*in competition*) Sieger-; (*victorious*) siegreich; **to be on a ~ streak** eine Glückssträhne haben **II.** n **~s** pl Gewinn m

winter ['wɪn·tər] n Winter m

winter 'sports npl Wintersport m kein pl

'wintertime n Winterzeit f

wintry ['wɪn·tri], **wintery** ['wɪn·tə·ri] *adj* winterlich

wipe [waɪp] **I.** vt **1.** (*clean*) abwischen; (*feet*) abtreten; (*nose*) putzen **2.** (*dishes*) abtrocknen **II.** n Reinigungstuch nt

◆**wipe down** vt abwischen; (*with water*) abwaschen

◆**wipe off** vt (*clean*) wegwischen; (*from surface*) abwischen

◆**wipe out** vt **1.** (*destroy*) auslöschen; (*disease*) ausrotten **2.** (*kill*) beseitigen

◆**wipe up** vt aufwischen

wire ['waɪr] **I.** n **1.** (*thread*) Draht m **2.** ELEC (*cable*) Leitung f **II.** vt **1.** (*fasten*) mit Draht binden **2.** ELEC (*connect*) mit elektrischen Leitungen versehen

'wire cutters npl [pair of] ~ Drahtschere f

'wireless *adj* drahtlos; ~ **network** Funknetz nt

wiretapping ['waɪr·ˌtæp·ɪŋ] n Abhören nt von Telefonleitungen

wiring ['waɪ·rɪŋ] n **1.** (*wires*) elektrische Leitungen pl **2.** (*installation*) Stromverlegen nt

'wiring diagram n Schaltplan m

wiry ['waɪ·ri] *adj* **1.** (*hair*) borstig **2.** *fig* (*lean*) drahtig

Wis. *abbr of* **Wisconsin**

Wisconsin [wɪs·'kɑn·sɪn] n Wisconsin nt

wisdom ['wɪz·dəm] n Weisheit f

'wisdom tooth n Weisheitszahn m

wise [waɪz] *adj* **1.** (*sage*) klug; **to be older and ~r** durch Schaden klug geworden sein **2.** (*sensible*) vernünftig; **a ~ choice** eine gute Wahl **3.** *pred fam* (*aware*) **to get ~ to sb** jdn durchschauen

◆**wise up** vi fam aufwachen

wisecrack ['waɪz·kræk] **I.** n Witzelei[en] f[pl] **II.** vi witzeln

'wise guy n fam Klugschwätzer m pej fam

wish [wɪʃ] **I.** n <pl -es> **1.** (*desire*) Wunsch m, Verlangen nt **2.** (*thing desired*) Wunsch m; **to grant sb a ~** jdm einen Wunsch erfüllen **3.** (*regards*) **~es** pl Grüße pl **II.** vt **1.** (*be desirous*) wünschen; **whatever you ~** was immer du möchtest **2.** (*make a magic wish*) **to ~** [that] ... sich dat wünschen, dass ... **3.** (*express wishes*) **to ~ sb happy birthday** jdm zum Geburtstag gratulieren **III.** vi **1.** (*want*) wollen **2.** (*make a wish*) wünschen

wishbone ['wɪʃ·boʊn] n Gabelbein nt

wishful 'thinking n Wunschdenken nt

wishy-washy ['wɪʃ·i·ˌwɑʃ·i] *adj* (*colors*) wässrig

wisp [wɪsp] n Büschel nt; ~**s of smoke** [kleine] Rauchfahnen

W

wispy ['wɪs·pi] *adj* dünn; (*hair*) strähnig

wisteria [wɪ·'stɪr·i·ə] *n* BOT Glyzin[i]e *f*

wistful ['wɪst·fəl] *adj* (*smile*) wehmütig; (*look*) sehnsüchtig

wit [wɪt] *n* 1. (*humor*) Witz *m*; **dry ~** trockener Humor 2. (*intelligence*) **~s** *pl* geistige Fähigkeiten; **to keep one's ~s** seine fünf Sinne zusammenhalten *fam*

witch <*pl* -es> [wɪtʃ] *n* Hexe *f*

'**witchcraft** *n* Hexerei *f*

'**witch doctor** *n* Medizinmann *m*

'**witch-hunt** *n* Hexenjagd *f*

with [wɪð, wɪθ] *prep* 1. (*having*) mit +*dat*; **~ a little luck** mit ein wenig Glück 2. (*accompanied*) **~ friends** mit Freunden 3. (*concerning*) **to have something to do ~ sb/sth** etwas mit jdm/etw zu tun haben 4. (*using*) **she paints ~ watercolors** sie malt mit Wasserfarben 5. (*while*) **~ things the way they are** so wie die Dinge sind 6. (*in state of*) vor +*dat*; **she was shaking ~ rage** sie zitterte vor Wut 7. (*in company of*) bei +*dat*; **to stay ~ relatives** bei Verwandten übernehmen

withdraw <-drew, -drawn> [wɪð·'drɔ] I. *vt* 1. (*remove*) herausziehen; **to ~ one's hand** seine Hand zurückziehen 2. (*money*) abheben 3. (*take back: coins*) aus dem Verkehr ziehen II. *vi* sich zurückziehen

withdrawal [wɪð·'drɔ·əl] *n* 1. FIN [Geld]abhebung *f* 2. MIL Rückzug *m* 3. (*taking back*) Zurücknehmen *nt*; (*cancel*) Zurückziehen *nt*; (*of funds*) Entzug *m*; (*of allegation*) Widerruf *m*; (*from contract*) Rücktritt *m*

with'drawal symptoms *npl* Entzugserscheinungen *pl*

wither ['wɪð·ər] *vi* verdorren

withhold <-held, -held> [wɪð·'hould] *vt* 1. (*not give*) zurückhalten; **to ~ information** Informationen verschweigen 2. (*not pay*) etw nicht zahlen; **to ~ benefit payments** Leistungen nicht auszahlen

within [wɪð·'ɪn] I. *prep* 1. (*inside*) innerhalb +*gen* 2. (*in limit of*) **~ reach** in Reichweite II. *adv* innen; **from ~** von innen [heraus]

'**with-it** *adj fam* 1. (*trendy*) modisch;

to be ~ auf dem neuesten Stand sein 2. (*alert*) aufmerksam

without [wɪð·'aut] *prep* ohne +*akk*

withstand <-stood, -stood> [wɪð·'stænd] *vt* **to ~ sth** etw standhalten; **to ~ rough treatment** eine unsanfte Behandlung aushalten

witness ['wɪt·nɪs] I. *n* <*pl* -es> Zeuge, -in *m, f*; **expert ~** Gutachter(in) *m(f)* II. *vt* beobachten; **to ~ sb doing sth** sehen, wie jd etw tut

'**witness stand** *n* Zeugenstand *m kein p*

witty ['wɪt·i] *adj* (*clever*) geistreich; (*funny*) witzig

wizard ['wɪz·ərd] *n* Zauberer *m*

wobble ['wab·əl] I. *vi* 1. (*move*) wackeln; (*wheel*) eiern *fam*; (*knees*) zittern 2. (*tremble: voice*) zittern II. *vt* rütteln III. *n* Wackeln *nt kein pl*

wobbly ['wab·li] *adj* wack[e]lig

wok [wak] *n* Wok *m*

woke [wouk] *vt, vi pt of* **wake**

woken ['wou·kən] *vt, vi pp of* **wake**

wolf [wʊlf] I. *n* <*pl* wolves> Wolf *m* ▶ **to cry ~** blinden Alarm schlagen II. *vt* **to ~ down** etw verschlingen

'**wolf cub** *n* Wolfsjunge(s) *nt*

'**wolfhound** *n* Wolfshund *m*

'**wolf whistle** *n* bewundernder Pfiff

woman ['wʊm·ən] *n* <*pl* women> Frau *f*

womanizer ['wʊm·ə·nai·zər] *n* Weiberheld *m oft pej*

womanly ['wʊm·ən·li] *adj* weiblich

womb [wum] *n* Gebärmutter *f*

womenfolk ['wɪm·ɪn·fouk] *npl* Frauen *p*

women's lib [ˌwɪm·ɪnz·'lɪb] *n fam short for* **women's liberation** die Frauen[rechts]bewegung

won [wʌn] *vt, vi pt, pp of* **win**

wonder ['wʌn·dər] I. *vi* 1. (*ask*) sich fragen; **why do you ask? — I was just ~ing** warum fragst du? – ach, nur so; **to ~ about sth** sich Gedanken über etw machen 2. (*surprised*) **to ~ at sth** sich über etw wundern II. *n* 1. (*surprise*) Staunen *nt*, Verwunderung *f* 2. (*marvel*) Wunder *nt*; **no ~ ...** kein Wunder dass ...; **to work ~s** [wahre] Wunder wirken

'**wonder boy** *n iron, hum fam* Wunderknabe *m*

'**wonder drug** n Wundermittel nt

'**wonderful** ['wʌn·dər·fəl] adj wunderbar

'**wonderland** n Wunderland nt; **winter ~** winterliche Märchenlandschaft

won't [woʊnt] = **will not** see **will**[1]

woo [wu] vt to ~ voters Wähler umwerben

'**wood** [wʊd] n 1. Holz nt; **plank of ~** [Holz]brett nt 2. (forest) ~**s** pl Wald m ▸ **to not be out of the ~[s]** (still critical) noch nicht über den Berg sein fam; (still difficult) noch nicht aus dem Schneider sein fam; **knock on ~!** unberufen!

'**woodcarving** n ART 1. (art genre) Holzschnitzerei f 2. (object) [Holz]schnitzerei f

'**woodchuck** n ZOOL Waldmurmeltier nt

'**woodcut** n ART Holzschnitt m

'**wooded** ['wʊd·ɪd] adj ~ **area** Waldgebiet nt

'**wooden** ['wʊd·ən] adj 1. Holz-, aus Holz nach n 2. (stiff: movements) hölzern

'**woodland** n ~[s pl] Wald m

'**woodpecker** n Specht m

'**woodpile** n Holzstoß m

'**wood pulp** n Zellstoff m

'**woodwind** n pl the ~**s** die Holzbläser pl

'**woodwork** n (of building) Holzwerk nt ▸ **to come out of the ~** ans Licht kommen

'**woodworking** n (carpentry) Tischlern nt; (business) Tischlerei f

'**woodworm** <pl -> n Holzwurm m

woof [wʊf] vi (dog) bellen; ~, ~! wau, wau

'**woofer** ['wʊf·ər] n Tieftonlautsprecher m

wool [wʊl] n Wolle f

'**woolen, woollen** ['wʊl·ən] adj wollen, aus Wolle nach n

'**wooly, woolly** ['wʊl·i] adj 1. Woll-, wollen 2. (vague) verschwommen; (thoughts) wirren

'**woozy** ['wu·zi] adj fam (dizzy) benommen; (drunk) beschwipst fam

'**word** [wɜrd] I. n 1. Wort nt; **in other ~s** mit anderen Worten; **in a ~** um es kurz zu sagen 2. (talk) [kurzes] Gespräch; **to have a ~ with sb [about sth]** mit jdm [über etw akk] sprechen 3. (promise) Wort nt; **to go back on one's ~** sein

Wort brechen 4. (lyrics) ~**s** pl Text m ▸ **by ~ of mouth** mündlich II. vt formulieren

'**wording** ['wɜr·dɪŋ] n Formulierung f

'**wordless** ['wɜrd·lɪs] adj wortlos, ohne Worte

'**word order** n Wortstellung f

word-'perfect adj textsicher

'**wordplay** n Wortspiel nt

'**word processor** n COMPUT 1. (computer) Textverarbeitungssystem nt 2. (program) Textverarbeitungsprogramm nt

'**word wrap** n COMPUT [automatischer] Zeilenumbruch

wore [wɔr] vt, vi pt of **wear**

'**work** [wɜrk] I. n 1. (activity) Arbeit f; **to be hard ~** (strenuous) anstrengend sein; (difficult) schwierig sein 2. (employment) Arbeit f; **to look for ~** auf Arbeitssuche sein; **to be at ~** bei der Arbeit sein 3. (opus) Werk nt; ~**s of art** Kunstwerke pl 4. (factory) ~**s** + sing vb Werk nt, Fabrik f 5. fam (all) **the ~s** pl das ganze Drum und Dran kein pl II. vi 1. (do job) arbeiten; **to ~ hard** hart arbeiten; **to ~ together** zusammenarbeiten 2. (be busy) arbeiten; **to ~ at/on sth** an etw dat arbeiten 3. (function) funktionieren; **my cell phone doesn't ~** mein Handy geht nicht 4. (succeed) funktionieren, klappen fam; (medicine) wirken III. vt 1. (operate: machine) bedienen; (equipment) etw betätigen 2. (move) **to ~ sth free** etw losbekommen 3. (pay by working) **to ~ one's way through college** sich dat sein Studium finanzieren ▸ **to ~ one's fingers to the bone [for sb/sth]** fam sich dat [für jdn/etw] den Rücken krummarbeiten

◆**work away** vi vor sich hinarbeiten

◆**work for** vt 1. (be employed by) arbeiten für +akk 2. (appeal to) **to [not] ~ for sb** jdm [nicht] zusagen

◆**work in** vt (mix in) einarbeiten; (on skin) einreiben

◆**work off** vt (counteract) abarbeiten; (energy) loswerden

◆**work out** I. vt 1. (calculate) errechnen 2. (develop) ausarbeiten 3. (figure out) **to ~ out ⇆ sth** hinter etw akk kom-

men **4.** (*solve itself*) things usually ~ **themselves out** die Dinge erledigen sich meist von selbst **II.** *vi* **1.** (*amount to*) to ~ **out cheaper** billiger kommen **2.** (*develop*) sich entwickeln; to ~ **out well** gut laufen *fam* **3.** (*do exercise*) trainieren

◆**work through** *vt* durcharbeiten; (*problems*) aufarbeiten

◆**work toward** *vt* to ~ **toward a deadline** auf einen Termin hinarbeiten

◆**work up I.** *vt* **1.** (*generate*) to ~ **up an appetite** Appetit bekommen **2.** (*upset*) to ~ **oneself up** sich aufregen **3.** (*develop*) to ~ **up a sweat** ins Schwitzen kommen **II.** *vi* (*progress to*) to ~ **up to sth** sich zu etw *dat* hocharbeiten

workable ['wɜrk·ə·bəl] *adj* **1.** (*feasible*) durchführbar **2.** (*able to be manipulated*) bearbeitbar; ~ **land** bebaubares Land

workaholic ['wɜrk·ə·ho·lɪk] *n fam* Arbeitssüchtige(r) *f(m)*

workbench *n* Werkbank *f*

workbook *n* Arbeitsbuch *nt*

work camp *n* Lager, in dem Freiwillige gemeinnützige Arbeiten verrichten

workday *n* **1.** (*work time*) Arbeitstag *m* **2.** (*not holiday*) Werktag *m*

worker ['wɜr·kər] *n* (*employee*) Arbeiter(in) *m(f)*; **blue-collar** ~ [Fabrik]arbeiter(in) *m(f)*

work ethic *n* Arbeitsethos *nt*

workforce *n* Belegschaft *f*

working ['wɜr·kɪŋ] *adj attr* **1.** (*employed*) berufstätig **2.** (*for work*) ~ **conditions** Arbeitsbedingungen *pl* **3.** (*functioning*) funktionierend *attr*; **in** ~ **order** betriebsfähig

working 'class *n* **the** ~ die Arbeiterklasse *kein pl*

workload *n* Arbeitspensum *nt kein pl*; TECH Leistungsumfang *m*

workman *n* **1.** (*worker*) Arbeiter *m* **2.** (*craftsman*) Handwerker *m*

workmanlike *adj* fachmännisch

workmanship ['wɜrk·mən·ʃɪp] *n* Verarbeitung[sgüte] *f*

work of 'art *n* Kunstwerk *nt*

workout *n* Fitnesstraining *nt*

work permit *n* Arbeitserlaubnis *f*

workplace *n* Arbeitsplatz *m*

workshop *n* **1.** (*room*) Werkstatt *f* **2.** (*meeting*) Workshop *m*

workstation *n* **1.** COMPUT Workstation *f fachspr* **2.** (*work area*) Arbeitsplatz *m*

work surface *n* Arbeitsfläche *f*

world [wɜrld] *n* **1.** (*earth*) **the** ~ die Welt [*or* Erde] **2.** (*planet*) Welt *f*; **beings from other ~s** Außerirdische *pl* **3.** (*society*) **the ancient** ~ die antike Welt ▶ **to be out of this** ~ *fam* himmlisch sein; **not for [all] the** ~ nie im Leben

World 'Bank *n* **the** ~ die Weltbank

world-class *adj* von Weltklasse *nach n*

world-'famous *adj* weltberühmt

world popu'lation *n* Weltbevölkerung *f*

world 'power *n* Weltmacht *f*

world 'record *n* Weltrekord *m*

World Series *npl* Finale der US-amerikanischen Baseball-Profiliga

World's 'Fair *n* Weltausstellung *f*

world view *n* Weltanschauung *f*

world 'war *n* Weltkrieg *m*; **W~ W~ II** der 2. Weltkrieg

worldwide ['wɜrld·ˌwaɪd] *adj, adv* weltweit

World Wide 'Web *n* INET **the** ~ das World Wide Web, das Internet

worm [wɜrm] **I.** *n* (*comput*) Wurm *m* **II.** *vt* (*treat for worms: an animal*) entwurmen

worm-eaten *adj* wurmzerfressen

worn [wɔrn] **I.** *vt, vi pp of* **wear** **II.** *adj* (*damaged*) abgenutzt; (*carpet*) abgetreten

worn 'out *adj pred*, **'worn-out** *adj attr* **1.** (*tired*) erschöpft **2.** (*shoes*) durchgelaufen

worried ['wɜr·id] *adj* beunruhigt, besorgt; **to be** ~ **about sb/sth** sich *dat* um jdn/etw Sorgen machen

worry ['wɜr·i] **I.** *vi* <-ie-> sich *dat* Sorgen machen (**about** um +*akk*); **I'm sorry — don't** ~ **about it** tut mir leid — das macht doch nichts **II.** *vt* <-ie-> beunruhigen **III.** *n* Sorge *f*

worrying ['wɜ·ri·ɪŋ] *adj* Besorgnis erregend

worse [wɜrs] **I.** *adj comp of* **bad** schlechter; (*harder, uglier*) schlimmer **II.** *adv comp of* **badly** (*less well*) schlechter;

(*more seriously*) schlimmer **III.** *n* **to change for the** ~ schlechter werden

worsen ['wɜr·sən] *vt, vi* [sich] verschlechtern

worship ['wɜr·ʃɪp] **I.** *n* **1.** (*service*) Verehrung *f* **2.** (*service*) Gottesdienst *m* **II.** *vt* <-p-> **1.** (*revere*) **to ~ a deity** einer Gottheit huldigen *geh* **2.** (*adore*) vergöttern ▸ **to ~ the ground sb walks on** jdn abgöttisch verehren *fam* **III.** *vi* <-p-> beten

worshiper, worshipper ['wɜr·ʃɪp·ər] *n* Kirchgänger(in) *m(f)*; **devil ~** Teufelsanbeter(in) *m(f)*

worst [wɜrst] **I.** *adj superl of* **bad 1.** (*poorest, least*) **the ~ ...** der/die/das schlechteste ... **2.** (*most dangerous*) schlimmste(r, s) **3.** (*least advantageous*) ungünstigste(r, s) **II.** *adv superl of* **badly 1.** (*most severely*) am schlimmsten **2.** (*least well*) am schlechtesten **III.** *n* **at** ~ schlimmstenfalls ▸ **to be at one's** ~ sich von seiner schlechtesten Seite zeigen

worsted ['wʊs·tɪd] *n* Kammgarn *m*

worth [wɜrθ] **I.** *adj pred* **1.** (*valued, meriting*) wert; **to be ~ one's weight in gold** Gold wert sein ▸ **if a thing is ~ doing, it's ~ doing well** *saying* wenn schon, denn schon *fam;* **for what it's ~** *fam* übrigens *fam* **II.** *n* Wert *m;* **of little ~** von geringem Wert

worthless ['wɜrθ·lɪs] *adj* wertlos *a. fig*

worthwhile [ˌwɜrθ·'hwaɪl] *adj* **to be ~** sich lohnen

worthy ['wɜr·ði] *adj* **1.** (*estimable*) würdig **2.** (*meriting*) ~ **of praise** lobenswert

would [wʊd] *aux vb* **1.** (*in indirect speech*) **they promised that they ~ help** sie versprachen zu helfen **2.** (*expressing condition*) **what ~ you do if ...?** was würdest du tun, wenn ...? **3.** (*expressing inclination*) **sb ~ rather do sth** jd würde lieber etw tun

'would-be *adj attr* Möchtegern- *pej fam*

wouldn't ['wʊd·ənt] = **would not** *see* **would**

wound[1] [wund] **I.** *n* Wunde *f;* **gunshot ~** Schussverletzung *f* **II.** *vt* verwunden

wound[2] [waʊnd] *vt, vi pt, pp of* **wind**

wounded ['wun·dɪd] **I.** *adj* verletzt **II.** *n* **the ~** *pl* MIL die Verwundeten *pl*

wove [woʊv] *vt, vi pt of* **weave**

woven ['woʊ·vən] **I.** *vt, vi pp of* **weave II.** *adj* (*on loom*) gewebt; **~ fabric** Gewebe *nt*

wow [waʊ] *interj fam* wow *sl,* toll! *fam*

wrangle ['ræŋ·gəl] **I.** *vi* streiten **II.** *n* Gerangel *nt*

wrap [ræp] **I.** *n* **1.** (*robe*) Umhang *m* **2.** (*packaging*) Verpackung *f;* **plastic ~** Frischhaltefolie *f* **3.** FOOD Tortillawrap *m* **II.** *vt* <-pp-> **1.** (*cover*) einpacken; (*in paper*) einwickeln **2.** (*draw around*) **to ~ sth around sb** etw um jdn wickeln ▸ **to ~ sb around one's little finger** jdn um den kleinen Finger wickeln

wraparound ['ræp·ə·ˌraʊnd] **I.** *adj* herumgezogen **II.** *n* **1.** FASHION Wickelrock *m* **2.** COMPUT Zeilenumbruch *m*

wrap up I. *vt* **1.** (*cover*) einwickeln **2.** (*deal*) unter Dach und Fach bringen **II.** *vi usu passive* **to be ~ped up in sb** mit jdm ganz beschäftigt sein

wrapper ['ræp·ər] *n* (*packaging*) Verpackung *f;* **candy ~** Bonbonpapier *nt*

'wrapping paper *n* (*for package*) Packpapier *nt;* (*for present*) Geschenkpapier *nt*

wreak [rik] *vt* **to ~ damage [on sth]** Schaden [an etw *dat*] anrichten

wreath [riθ] *n* Kranz *m*

wreck [rek] **I.** *n* **1.** (*of ship*) Schiffbruch *m* **2.** (*remains*) Trümmerhaufen *m* **3.** (*accident*) Unfall *m* **II.** *vt* **1.** (*sink*) **to be ~ed** (*ship*) Schiffbruch erleiden **2.** (*destroy*) zerstören **3.** (*spoil*) ruinieren; (*hopes*) zunichtemachen

wreckage ['rek·ɪdʒ] *n* Wrackteile *pl*

wrecker ['rek·ər] *n* **1.** (*destroyer*) Zerstörer(in) *m(f)* **2.** (*truck*) Abschleppwagen *m*

wren [ren] *n* Zaunkönig *m*

wrench [rentʃ] **I.** *n* <*pl* -es> **1.** (*tool*) Schraubenschlüssel *m;* **screw ~** Franzose *m* **2.** *usu sing* (*twisting*) Ruck *m* **II.** *vt* (*muscle*) zerren; (*joint*) verrenken

wrestle ['res·əl] *vi* SPORT ringen

wrestler ['res·lər] *n* Ringer(in) *m(f);* **Sumo ~** Sumoringer(in) *m(f)*

W

wrestling ['res·lɪŋ] n Ringen nt

'**wrestling bout**, '**wrestling match** n Ringkampf m

wretched ['retʃ·ɪd] adj 1. (unhappy) unglücklich 2. (state) jämmerlich

wriggle ['rɪg·əl] vi 1. (twist) sich winden; **to ~ free [of sth]** sich [aus etw dat] herauswinden 2. (move) schlängeln

wring <wrung, wrung> [rɪŋ] vt 1. (twist) auswringen 2. (break) **to ~ sb's neck** jdm den Hals umdrehen a. fig

wrinkle ['rɪŋ·kəl] I. n (crease) Knitterfalte f; (in face) Falte f II. vt, vi zerknittern

wrinkled ['rɪŋ·kli] adj zerknittert; (face, skin) faltig

wrist [rɪst] n Handgelenk nt

'**wristband** n 1. (strap) Armband nt 2. (absorbent) Schweißband nt

'**wristwatch** n Armbanduhr f

writ [rɪt] n [gerichtliche] Verfügung; **to issue a ~ against sb** jdn vorladen

write <wrote, written or old writ> [raɪt] I. vt 1. (pen) schreiben; **to ~ a letter to sb** jdm einen Brief schreiben 2. (fill out) ausstellen II. vi (pen letters) schreiben; **to know how to read and ~** Lesen und Schreiben können

♦ **write away** vi **to ~ away for sth** etw [schriftlich] anfordern

♦ **write back** vt, vi zurückschreiben

♦ **write down** vt aufschreiben

♦ **write in** I. vt **to ~ sth** (in text) etw einfügen; (in form) etw eintragen II. vi schreiben; **he wrote in expressing his dissatisfaction** er schickte einen Brief, um seine Unzufriedenheit auszudrücken

♦ **write off** I. vi **to ~ off for sth** etw [schriftlich] anfordern II. vt abschreiben

♦ **write out** vt 1. (put in writing) aufschreiben 2. (in full) ausschreiben

♦ **write up** vt (notes) ausarbeiten; (report) aufschreiben fam

'**write-in** adj POL **a ~ candidate** ein nachträglich auf der Liste hinzugefügter Kandidat

'**write-off** n FIN Abschreibung f

'**write-protected** adj COMPUT schreibgeschützt

writer ['raɪ·tər] n 1. (person) Verfasser(in) m(f) 2. (author) Autor(in) m(f)

'**write-up** n (of film) Kritik f; (of book a.) Rezension f

writing ['raɪ·tɪŋ] n 1. (skill) Schreiben nt, **in ~** schriftlich 2. (literature) Literatur f 3. (handwriting) [Hand]schrift f

'**writing desk** n Schreibtisch m

'**writing pad** n Schreibblock m

'**writing paper** n Schreibpapier nt

written ['rɪt·ən] I. vt, vi pp of **write** II. adj **the ~ word** das geschriebene Wort ► **to have sth ~ all over one's face** jdm steht etw ins Gesicht geschrieben

wrong [rɒŋ] I. adj 1. (incorrect) falsch; **it's all ~** das ist völlig verkehrt; **to be proven ~** widerlegt werden; **to be ~ about sth** sich bei etw dat irren 2. (amiss) **what's ~ with you today?** was ist denn heute mit dir los? ► **to get hold of the ~ end of the stick** etw in den falschen Hals bekommen fam II. adv 1. (incorrectly) falsch 2. **to go ~** (things) schiefgehen fam III. n **to know right from ~** Richtig und Falsch unterscheiden können ► **to be in the ~** (mistaken) sich irren

wrongdoer ['rɒŋ·ˌdu·ər] n Übeltäter(in) m(f)

wrongful ['rɒŋ·fəl] adj unrechtmäßig

wrong-headed adj querköpfig pej; (idea) hirnverbrannt fam

wrongly ['rɒŋ·li] adv 1. (mistakenly) fälschlicherweise 2. (incorrectly) falsch

wrote [roʊt] vt, vi pt of **write**

wrought [rɔt] adj attr (silver, gold) gehämmert

wrought 'iron n Schmiedeeisen nt

wrung [rʌŋ] vt pt, pp of **wring**

wry <-ier, -iest or -er, -est> [raɪ] adj usu attr (humor) trocken; (smile) bitter

wt. n abbr of **weight** Gew.

wuss [wʊs] n pej fam Schlappschwanz m pej sl

WV, W.V. abbr of **West Virginia**

WY abbr of **Wyoming**

Wyo. abbr of **Wyoming**

Wyoming [waɪ·'oʊ·mɪŋ] n Wyoming nt

X

X <pl -'s>, **x** <pl -'s> [eks] n X nt, x nt; ~ **as in X-ray** X wie Xanthippe

x [eks] **I.** vt to ~ [out ⇄] sth [aus]streichen **II.** n MATH x nt; **~-axis** x-Achse f

X 'chromosome n X-Chromosom nt

xenophobia [ˌzen·ə·'fou·bi·ə] n Fremdenhass m

xerox ['zɪr·aks] vt kopieren

Xerox® ['zɪr·aks] n Kopie f

Xmas <pl -es> ['krɪs·məs] n fam short for **Christmas** Weihnachten f

X-ray ['eks·reɪ] **I.** n **1.** (picture) Röntgenbild nt **2.** (examination) Röntgenuntersuchung f; **to have an ~** sich röntgen lassen **II.** vt röntgen

xylophone ['zaɪ·lə·foun] n Xylophon nt

Y

Y <pl -'s>, **y** <pl -'s> [waɪ] n Y nt, y nt; ~ **as in Yankee** Y wie Ypsilon

y [waɪ] n MATH y nt; **~-axis** y-Achse f

yacht [jat] n Jacht f

'yachtsman n **around-the-world ~** Weltumsegler m

yak [jæk] vi <-kk-> fam quasseln

yam [jæm] n Jamswurzel f

yank [jæŋk] fam **I.** n usu pej fam Ruck m **II.** vt [ruckartig] ziehen an +dat

◆ **yank out** vt herausreißen

Yank [jæŋk] n usu pej fam Ami m

Yankee ['jæŋ·ki] n usu pej fam **1.** (person from northern US) Nordstaatler(in) m(f) **2.** (American) Ami m

yap [jæp] vi <-pp-> **1.** (dog) kläffen **2.** fam (talk) quasseln

yard¹ [jard] n usu pl fam Yard nt; **to sell sth by the ~** etw in Yards verkaufen

yard² [jard] n **1.** (lawn) Garten m **2.** (worksite) Werksgelände nt; (for storage) Lagerplatz m

'yardstick n Maßstab m

yarn [jarn] n Garn nt

yawn [jɔn] **I.** vi gähnen a. fig **II.** n Gähnen nt kein pl

yawning ['jɔ·nɪŋ] adj gähnend a. fig

yd. n abbr of **yard¹**

yeah [jeə] adv fam (yes) ja[wohl]; **oh ~!** [or ~, ~!] iron ja klar!

year [jɪr] n **1.** Jahr nt; **five times a ~** fünfmal im [or pro] Jahr; **two ~s' work** zwei Jahre Arbeit; **last ~** letztes Jahr **2.** (age) [Lebens]jahr nt; **a two-~-old child** ein zweijähriges Kind **3.** SCH Schuljahr nt; UNIV Studienjahr nt; (group) Klasse f

'yearbook n SCH, UNIV Jahrbuch nt

yearly ['jɪr·li] adj, adv jährlich; **twice-~** zweimal pro Jahr

yearn [jɜrn] vi sich sehnen (**for** nach +dat)

yeast [jist] n Hefe f

yell [jel] **I.** n **1.** (shout) [Auf]schrei m **2.** (cheer) Schlachtruf m **II.** vi **to ~ for help** um Hilfe rufen; **to ~ at sb** jdn anschreien

yellow ['jel·ou] **I.** adj **1.** (color) gelb; (yellowed) vergilbt **2.** fam (cowardly) feige **II.** vi vergilben

yellow 'fever n Gelbfieber nt

yellowish ['jel·ou·ɪʃ] adj gelblich

'Yellow Pages® npl **the ~** die Gelben Seiten

yelp [jelp] vi (dog) kläffen; (person) aufschreien

yen¹ <pl -> [jen] n Yen m

yen² [jen] n fam Faible nt; **to have a ~ to do sth** den Drang haben, etw zu tun

yep [jep] adv fam ja

yes [jes] **I.** adv **1.** ja; **~, please** ja bitte; **to say ~** [to sth] ja [zu etw dat] sagen, etw bejahen **2.** (contradicting) aber ja [doch] **II.** n <pl -[s]es> Ja nt

'yes-man n fam Jasager m

yesterday ['jes·tər·deɪ] **I.** adv gestern **II.** n Gestern nt

yet [jet] **I.** adv **1.** (until now) bis jetzt; + superl **the best ~** der/die/das Beste bisher **2.** (already) schon; **is it time to go ~? — no, not ~** ist es schon Zeit zu gehen? – nein, noch nicht **3.** (despite that) trotzdem; (but) aber [auch]; (in spite of everything) schon **II.** conj doch

yew [ju] n Eibe f

Yiddish ['jɪd·ɪʃ] n Jiddisch nt

yield [jild] **I.** n **1.** Ertrag m **2.** MIN Aus-

beute *f* II. *vt* 1. (*produce*) hervorbringen; (*grain*) erzeugen; (*results*) liefern 2. FIN abwerfen; **the bonds are currently ~ing 6-7%** die Pfandbriefe bringen derzeit 6-7 % III. *vi* (*give right of way*) **to ~ to sb** jdm den Vortritt lassen

YMCA [ˌwaɪ-ɛm-siː-ˈeɪ] *n + sing/pl vb abbr of* **Young Men's Christian Association** CVJM *m*

yoga [ˈjoʊ-gə] *n* Yoga *nt*

yogurt, yoghurt [ˈjoʊ-gərt] *n* Joghurt *m o nt*

yoke [joʊk] I. *n* (*for pulling*) Joch *nt a. fig* II. *vt fig* **to ~ sth together** etw [miteinander ver]koppeln

yolk [joʊk] *n* Eigelb *nt*

you [ju] *pron* 1. (*singular*) du *in nomin,* dich *in akk,* dir *in dat;* (*polite form*) Sie *in nomin, akk,* Ihnen *in dat;* **if I were ~** wenn ich du/Sie wäre, an deiner/Ihrer Stelle 2. (*plural*) ihr *in nomin,* euch *in akk, dat;* (*polite form*) Sie *in nomin, akk,* Ihnen *in dat;* **how many of ~ are there?** wie viele seid ihr? 3. (*one*) man; **~ learn from experience** aus Erfahrung wird man klug; **it's not good for ~** das ist nicht gesund

you'll [jul] = **you will** *see* **will**[1]

young [jʌŋ] *adj* jung; **she's ~ for sixteen** für sechzehn ist sie noch recht kindlich; **to be ~ at heart** im Herzen jung [geblieben] sein

youngster [ˈjʌŋ-stər] *n* Jugendliche(r) *f/m*

your [jʊr] *adj poss* 1. (*singular*) dein(e); (*plural*) euer/eure; (*polite form*) Ihr(e) 2. (*one's*) sein(e); **it's enough to break ~ heart** es bricht einem förmlich das Herz

you're [jʊr] = **you are** *see* **be**

yours [jʊrz] *pron poss* 1. deine/deiner/dein[e]s, Ihre/Ihrer/Ihr[e]s; **is this pen ~?** ist das dein Stift?; **the choice is ~** Sie haben die Wahl 2. (*in letter*) **Y~ truly** mit freundlichen Grüßen

yourself <*pl* **yourselves**> [jʊr-ˈsɛlf] *pron* 1. (*singular*) dich *akk,* dir *dat;* (*plural*) euch; (*polite form, sing/pl*) sich; **how would you describe ~?** wie würden Sie sich beschreiben?; **help yourselves, boys** bedient euch, Jungs 2. (*oneself*) sich; **to have sth [all] to ~** etw für dich

[*or* sich] allein haben 3. (*personally*) selbst; **you can do that ~** du kannst das selbst machen; **to be ~** du selbst sein; **to try sth for ~** etw selbst versuchen

youth [juθ] *n* 1. (*period*) Jugend *f* 2. (*young man*) Jugendliche(r) *m* 3. *pl* (*young people*) **the ~ of today** die Jugend von heute

'**youth center,** '**youth club** *n* Jugendzentrum *nt*

youthful [ˈjuːθ-fəl] *adj* jugendlich

'**youth hostel** *n* Jugendherberge *f*

you've [juv] = **you have** *see* **have** I, II

yo-yo <*pl* -s> [ˈjoʊ-joʊ] I. *n* Jo-Jo *nt* II. *vi fam* (*vacillate*) schwanken

yucky [ˈjʌk-i] *adj fam* ek[e]llig

Yukon Territory [ˈjuː-kən-] *n* Yukon Territory *nt*

'**yule log** *n* großes Holzscheit, das zur Weihnachtszeit im offenen Feuer brennt

yum [jʌm] *interj fam* lecker!

yuppie [ˈjʌp-i] *n* Yuppie *m*

Z

Z <*pl* -'s>, **z** <*pl* -'s> [ziː] *n* Z *nt,* z *nt;* **~ as in Zulu** Z wie Zacharias

z [ziː] *n* MATH z *nt;* **~-axis** z-Achse *f*

zany [ˈzeɪ-ni] *adj* ulkig

zap [zæp] *fam* I. *vt* <-pp-> 1. (*person*) erledigen; (*thing*) kaputtmachen 2. COMPUT (*delete*) löschen II. *vi* <-pp-> TV zappen III. *interj* schwups!

zeal [ziːl] *n* Eifer *m*

zealous [ˈzɛl-əs] *adj* [über]eifrig

zebra <*pl* -s> [ˈziː-brə] *n* Zebra *nt*

zero [ˈzɪr-oʊ] I. *n* <*pl* -s> 1. MATH Null *f* 2. (*point on scale*) Nullpunkt *m;* **10 degrees below ~** zehn Grad unter null II. *adj* **~ hour** die Stunde null III. *vt* auf null einstellen

♦ **zero in** *vi* (*aim*) **to ~ in on a target** ein Ziel anvisieren

zero 'tolerance *n* LAW Nulltoleranz *f*

zest [zɛst] *n* 1. (*enthusiasm*) Eifer *m* 2. **lemon ~** Zitronenschale *f*

zigzag [ˈzɪg-zæg] I. *n* Zickzack *m* II. *vi* <-gg-> sich im Zickzack bewege

zinc [zɪŋk] *n* Zink *nt*

zip [zɪp] **I.** *n* **1.** *fam* (*vigor*) Schwung *m* **2.** (*Zip Code*) ≈ Postleitzahl *f* **II.** *pron fam* null; **I know ~ about computers** ich habe null Ahnung von Computern **III.** *vt* <-pp-> (*close*) **could you help me ~** [up] **my dress?** könntest du mir vielleicht helfen, den Reißverschluss an meinem Kleid zuzumachen?; **to ~ sth together** etw mit einem Reißverschluss zusammenziehen **IV.** *vi* <-pp-> **1.** (*fasten*) **it ~s** [up] **at the back** es hat hinten einen Reißverschluss **2.** (*speed*) rasen; **to ~ through** (*job*) im Eiltempo erledigen

'Zip Code *n* ≈ Postleitzahl *f*

zipper ['zɪp·ər] *n* Reißverschluss *m*

zodiac ['zoʊ·di·æk] *n* **sign of the ~** Tierkreiszeichen *nt*

zombie ['zam·bi] *n* Zombie *m*

zone [zoʊn] *n* Zone *f*; **danger ~** Gefahrenzone *f*; **no-fly ~** Flugverbotszone *f*

zoning ['zoʊn·ɪŋ] **I.** *n* Bodenordnung *f* **II.** *adj* **~ restriction** Planungsbeschränkung *f*

zoo [zu] *n* Zoo *m*

zoologist [zoʊ·'al·ə·dʒɪst] *n* Zoologe, Zoologin *m, f*

zoology [zoʊ·'al·ə·dʒi] *n* Zoologie *f*

zoom [zum] **I.** *n* **~** [lens] Zoom[objektiv] *nt* **II.** *vi* **1.** (*speed*) rasen; **to ~ ahead** [*or* **off**] davonsausen; (*in race*) vorpreschen **2.** PHOT zoomen

◆zoom in *vi* [nahe] heranfahren, heranzoomen

◆zoom out *vi* wegzoomen

zucchini <*pl* -s> [zu·'ki·ni] *n* Zucchini *f*

Liste der unregelmäßigen deutschen Verben
List of the irregular German verbs

Die einfachen Zeiten unregelmäßiger Verben sind in den Spitzklammern (< >) nach dem Stichwort angegeben. Zusammengesetzte oder präfigierte Verben, deren Formen denen des Grundverbs entsprechen, sind auf der Deutsch-Englischen Seite mit *irreg* markiert. Außerdem gibt das Wörterbuch die unregelmäßigen Formen zusammengesetzter Verben an, die sich anders verhalten als ihre Grundverben. Die Verben, die mit *sein* oder alternativ mit *sein* oder *haben* konjugiert werden, sind entsprechend im Wörterbucheintrag gekennzeichnet. Wenn das Hilfsverb nicht eigens angegeben ist, wird die Perfektform mit *haben* gebildet.

Inflections of irregular verbs are given in angle brackets (< >) after the headword in the main part of the dictionary. Compound verbs and prefixed verbs whose conjugated forms correspond to those of the base verb are marked *irreg* on the German-English side of the dictionary. Conjugated forms of compound verbs are provided, however, when they differ from the conjugated forms of the base verb. Verbs that take *sein* and those that take *sein* or *haben* in the compound past tenses are marked accordingly in the dictionary entry. Whenever the auxiliary verb is not specifically given, one may assume that the compound past tenses are formed with *haben*.

Infinitiv infinitive	Präteritum Simple past	Partizip Perfekt past participle
backen	backte *o alt* buk	gebacken
befehlen	befahl	befohlen
beginnen	begann	begonnen
beißen	biss	gebissen
bergen	barg	geborgen
bersten	barst	geborsten
bewegen	bewog	bewogen
biegen	bog	gebogen
bieten	bot	geboten
binden	band	gebunden
bitten	bat	gebeten
blasen	blies	geblasen
bleiben	blieb	geblieben
bleichen	bleichte *o alt* blich	gebleicht *o alt* geblichen
braten	briet	gebraten
brechen	brach	gebrochen
brennen	brannte	gebrannt
bringen	brachte	gebracht
denken	dachte	gedacht
dreschen	drosch	gedroschen
dringen	drang	gedrungen

Infinitiv infinitive	Präteritum Simple past	Partizip Perfekt past participle
dürfen	durfte	dürfen, gedurft
empfangen	empfing	empfangen
empfehlen	empfahl	empfohlen
empfinden	empfand	empfunden
essen	aß	gegessen
fahren	fuhr	gefahren
fallen	fiel	gefallen
fangen	fing	gefangen
fechten	focht	gefochten
finden	fand	gefunden
flechten	flocht	geflochten
fliegen	flog	geflogen
fliehen	floh	geflohen
fließen	floss	geflossen
fressen	fraß	gefressen
frieren	fror	gefroren
gären	gärte *o* gor	gegärt *o* gegoren
gebären	gebar	geboren
geben	gab	gegeben
gedeihen	gedieh	gediehen
gefallen	gefiel	gefallen
gehen	ging	gegangen
gelingen	gelang	gelungen
gelten	galt	gegolten
genesen	genas	genesen
genießen	genoss	genossen
geraten	geriet	geraten
geschehen	geschah	geschehen
gestehen	gestand	gestanden
gewinnen	gewann	gewonnen
gießen	goss	gegossen
gleichen	glich	geglichen
gleiten	glitt	geglitten
glimmen	glimmte *o selten* glomm	geglimmt *o selten* geglommen
graben	grub	gegraben
greifen	griff	gegriffen

Infinitiv infinitive	Präteritum Simple past	Partizip Perfekt past participle
haben	hatte	gehabt
halten	hielt	gehalten
hängen	hing (hängte)	gehangen, (gehängt)
heben	hob	gehoben
heißen	hieß	geheißen
helfen	half	geholfen
kennen	kannte	gekannt
klimmen	klimmte *o* klomm	geklommen *o* geklimmt
klingen	klang	geklungen
kneifen	kniff	gekniffen
kommen	kam	gekommen
können	konnte	können, gekonnt
kriechen	kroch	gekrochen
laden	lud	geladen
lassen	ließ	gelassen *nach Infinitiv* lassen
laufen	lief	gelaufen
leiden	litt	gelitten
leihen	lieh	geliehen
lesen	las	gelesen
liegen	lag	gelegen
lügen	log	gelogen
mahlen	mahlte	gemahlen
meiden	mied	gemieden
melken	melkte *o veraltend* molk	gemolken
messen	maß	gemessen
misslingen	misslang	misslungen
mögen	mochte	mögen, gemocht
nehmen	nahm	genommen
nennen	nannte	genannt
pfeifen	pfiff	gepfiffen
preisen	pries	gepriesen
quellen	quoll	gequollen
raten	riet	geraten
reiben	rieb	gerieben
reißen	riss	gerissen
reiten	ritt	geritten

Infinitiv infinitive	Präteritum Simple past	Partizip Perfekt past participle
rennen	rannte	gerannt
reichen	roch	gerochen
ringen	rang	gerungen
rinnen	rann	geronnen
rufen	rief	gerufen
salzen	salzte	gesalzen *o selten* gesalzt
saufen	soff	gesoffen
saugen	sog *o* saugte	gesogen *o* gesaugt
schaffen	schuf	geschaffen
schallen	schallte *o* scholl	geschallt
scheiden	schied	geschieden
scheinen	schien	geschienen
scheißen	schiss	geschissen
schelten	schalt	gescholten
scheren	schor	geschoren
schieben	schob	geschoben
schießen	schoss	geschossen
schinden	schindete	geschunden
schlafen	schlief	geschlafen
schlagen	schlug	geschlagen
schleichen	schlich	geschlichen
schleifen	schliff	geschliffen
schließen	schloss	geschlossen
schlingen	schlang	geschlungen
schmeißen	schmiss	geschmissen
schmelzen	schmolz	geschmolzen
schnauben	schnaubte *o veraltet* schnob	geschnaubt *o veraltet* geschnoben
schneiden	schnitt	geschnitten
schrecken *vt* *vi*	schreckte schrak	geschreckt geschrocken
schreiben	schrieb	geschrieben
schreien	schrie	geschrie[e]n
schreiten	schritt	geschritten
schweigen	schwieg	geschwiegen
schwellen	schwoll	geschwollen
schwimmen	schwamm	geschwommen
schwinden	schwand	geschwunden

Infinitiv infinitive	Präteritum Simple past	Partizip Perfekt past participle
schwingen	schwang	geschwungen
schwören	schwor	geschworen
sehen	sah	gesehen
senden	sandte *o* sendete	gesandt *o* gesendet
sieden	siedete *o* sott	gesiedet *o* gesotten
singen	sang	gesungen
sinken	sank	gesunken
sinnen	sann	gesonnen
sitzen	saß	gesessen
sollen	sollte	sollen, gesollt
spalten	spaltete	gespalten *o* gespaltet
speien	spie	gespie[e]n
spinnen	spann	gesponnen
sprechen	sprach	gesprochen
sprießen	spross *o* spießte	gesprossen
springen	sprang	gesprungen
stechen	stach	gestochen
stecken	steckte *o geh* stak	gesteckt
stehen	stand	gestanden
stehlen	stahl	gestohlen
steigen	stieg	gestiegen
sterben	starb	gestorben
stieben	stob *o* stiebte	gestoben *o* gestiebt
stinken	stank	gestunken
stoßen	stieß	gestoßen
streichen	strich	gestrichen
streiten	stritt	gestritten
tragen	trug	getragen
treffen	traf	getroffen
treiben	trieb	getrieben
treten	trat	getreten
triefen	triefte *o geh* troff	getrieft *o geh* getroffen
trinken	trank	getrunken
trügen	trog	getrogen
tun	tat	getan
verbieten	verbot	verboten
verbrechen	verbrach	verbrochen

Infinitiv infinitive	Präteritum Simple past	Partizip Perfekt past participle
verderben	verdarb	verdorben
vergessen	vergaß	vergessen
verlieren	verlor	verloren
verraten	verriet	verraten
verstehen	verstand	verstanden
verwenden	verwendete *o* verwandte	verwendet *o* verwandt
verzeihen	verzieh	verziehen
wachsen	wuchs	gewachsen
waschen	wusch	gewaschen
weben	webte *o geh* wob	gewebt *o geh* gewoben
weichen	wich	gewichen
weisen	wies	gewiesen
wenden	wendete *o geh* gewandt	gewendet *o geh* gewandt
werben	warb	geworben
werden	wurde	worden, geworden
werfen	warf	geworfen
wiegen	wog	gewogen
winden	wand	gewunden
winken	winkte	gewinkt *o dial* gewunken
wissen	wusste	gewusst
wollen	wollte	wollen, gewollt
wringen	wrang	gewrungen
ziehen	zog	gezogen
zwingen	zwang	gezwungen

Die Hilfsverben *sein, haben* und *werden*
The auxiliary verbs *sein, haben,* and *werden*

sein

Präsens Present	Präteritum Simple Past	Perfekt Present Perfect	Plusquamperfekt Past Perfect
bin	war	bin gewesen	war gewesen
bist	warst	bist gewesen	warst gewesen
ist	war	ist gewesen	war gewesen
sind	waren	sind gewesen	waren gewesen
seid	wart	seid gewesen	wart gewesen
sind	waren	sind gewesen	waren gewesen

Futur Future	Konjunktiv I Subjunctive I	Konjunktiv II Subjunctive II	Imperativ Imperative
werde sein	sei	wäre	
wirst sein	seist	wär[e]st	sei
wird sein	sei	wäre	
werden sein	seien	wären	seien wir
werdet sein	seiet	wär[e]t	seid
werden sein	seien	wären	seien Sie

haben

Präsens Present	Präteritum Simple Past	Perfekt Present Perfect	Plusquamperfekt Past Perfect
habe	hatte	habe gehabt	hatte gehabt
hast	hattest	hast gehabt	hattest gehabt
hat	hatte	hat gehabt	hatte gehabt
haben	hatten	haben gehabt	hatten gehabt
habt	hattet	habt gehabt	hattet gehabt
haben	hatten	haben gehabt	hatten gehabt

Futur Future	Konjunktiv I Subjunctive I	Konjunktiv II Subjunctive II	Imperativ Imperative
werde haben	habe	hätte	
wirst haben	habest	hättest	hab[e]
wird haben	habe	hätte	
werden haben	haben	hätten	haben wir
werdet haben	habet	hättet	habt
werden haben	haben	hätten	haben Sie

werden

Präsens Present	Präteritum Simple Past	Perfekt Present Perfect	Plusquamperfekt Past Perfect
werde	wurde	bin geworden	war geworden
wirst	wurdest	bist geworden	warst geworden
wird	wurde	ist geworden	war geworden
werden	wurden	sind geworden	waren geworden
werdet	wurdet	seid geworden	wart geworden
werden	wurden	sind geworden	waren geworden

Futur Future	Konjunktiv I Subjunctive I	Konjunktiv II Subjunctive II	Imperativ Imperative
werde werden	werde	würde	
wirst werden	werdest	würdest	werd[e]
wird werden	werde	würde	
werden werden	werden	würden	werden wir
werdet werden	werdet	würdet	werdet
werden werden	werden	würden	werden Sie

Die Modalverben
The modal verbs

können

Präsens Present	Präteritum Simple Past	Perfekt Present Perfect	Plusquamperfekt Past Perfect
kann	konnte	habe gekonnt	hatte gekonnt
kannst	konntest	hast gekonnt	hattest gekonnt
kann	konnte	hat gekonnt	hatte gekonnt
können	konnten	haben gekonnt	hatten gekonnt
könnt	konntet	habt gekonnt	hattet gekonnt
können	konnten	haben gekonnt	hatten gekonnt

Futur Future	Konjunktiv I Subjunctive I	Konjunktiv II Subjunctive II
werde können	könne	könnte
wirst können	könntest	könntest
wird können	könne	könnte
werden können	können	könnten
werdet können	könn[e]t	könntet
werden können	können	könnten

dürfen

Präsens Present	Präteritum Simple Past	Perfekt Present Perfect	Plusquamperfekt Past Perfect
darf	durfte	habe gedurft	hatte gedurft
darfst	durftest	hast gedurft	hattest gedurft
darf	durfte	hat gedurft	hatte gedurft
dürfen	durften	haben gedurft	hatten gedurft
dürft	durftet	habt gedurft	hattet gedurft
dürfen	durften	haben gedurft	hatten gedurft

Futur Future	Konjunktiv I Subjunctive I	Konjunktiv II Subjunctive II
werde dürfen	dürfe	dürfte
wirst dürfen	dürftest	dürftest
wird dürfen	dürfe	dürfte
werden dürfen	dürfen	dürften
werdet dürfen	dürf[e]t	dürftet
werden dürfen	dürfen	dürften

mögen

Präsens Present	Präteritum Simple Past	Perfekt Present Perfect	Plusquamperfekt Past Perfect
mag	mochte	habe gemocht	hatte gemocht
magst	mochtest	hast gemocht	hattest gemocht
mag	mochte	hat gemocht	hatte gemocht
mögen	mochten	haben gemocht	hatten gemocht
mögt	mochtet	habt gemocht	hattet gemocht
mögen	mochten	haben gemocht	hatten gemocht

Futur Future	Konjunktiv I Subjunctive I	Konjunktiv II Subjunctive II
werde mögen	möge	möchte
wirst mögen	mögest	möchtest
wird mögen	möge	möchte
werden mögen	mögen	möchten
werdet mögen	mög[e]t	möchtet
werden mögen	mögen	möchten

müssen

Präsens Present	Präteritum Simple Past	Perfekt Present Perfect	Plusquamperfekt Past Perfect
muss	musste	habe gemusst	hatte gemusst
musst	musstest	hast gemusst	hattest gemusst
muss	musste	hat gemusst	hatte gemusst
müssen	mussten	haben gemusst	hatten gemusst
müsst	musstet	habt gemusst	hattet gemusst
müssen	mussten	haben gemusst	hatten gemusst

Futur Future	Konjunktiv I Subjunctive I	Konjunktiv II Subjunctive II
werde müssen	müsse	müsste
wirst müssen	müssest	müsstest
wird müssen	müsse	müsste
werden müssen	müssen	müssten
werdet müssen	müss[e]t	müsstest
werden müssen	müssen	müssten

sollen

Präsens Present	Präteritum Simple Past	Perfekt Present Perfect	Plusquamperfekt Past Perfect
soll	sollte	habe gesollt	hatte gesollt
sollst	solltest	hast gesollt	hattest gesollt
soll	sollte	hat gesollt	hatte gesollt
sollen	sollten	haben gesollt	hatten gesollt
sollt	solltet	habt gesollt	hattet gesollt
sollen	sollten	haben gesollt	hatten gesollt

Futur Future	Konjunktiv I Subjunctive I	Konjunktiv II Subjunctive II
werde sollen	solle	sollte
wirst sollen	solltest	solltest
wird sollen	solle	sollte
werden sollen	sollen	sollten
werdet sollen	soll[e]t	solltet
werden sollen	sollen	sollten

wollen

Präsens Present	Präteritum Simple Past	Perfekt Present Perfect	Plusquamperfekt Past Perfect
will	wollte	habe gewollt	hatten gewollt
willst	wolltest	hast gewollt	hattest gewollt
will	wollte	hat gewollt	hatte gewollt
wollen	wollten	haben gewollt	hatten gewollt
wollt	wolltet	habt gewollt	hattet gewollt
wollen	wollten	haben gewollt	hatten gewollt

Futur / Future	Konjunktiv I / Subjunctive I	Konjunktiv II / Subjunctive II
werde wollen	wolle	wollte
wirst wollen	wollest	wolltest
wird wollen	wolle	wollte
werden wollen	wollen	wollten
werdet wollen	woll[e]t	wolltet
werden wollen	wollen	wollten

Übersicht über die wichtigsten unregelmäßigen englischen Verben
List of the most important irregular English verbs

Infinitiv Infinitive	Präteritum Simple past	Partizip Perfekt Past participle
abide	abode, abided	abode, abided
arise	arose	arisen
awake	awoke, awaked	awoken, awaked
be	was *sing*, were *pl*	been
bear	bore	born(e)
beat	beat	beaten, beat
become	became	become
begin	began	begun
behold	beheld	beheld
bend	bent	bent
beset	beset	beset
bet	bet, betted	bet, betted
bid	bid, bade	bid, bidden
bind	bound	bound
bite	bit	bitten
bleed	bled	bled
bless	blessed, blest	blessed, blest
blow	blew	blown
break	broke	broken
breed	bred	bred
bring	brought	brought
broadcast	broadcast, broadcasted	broadcast, broadcasted
build	built	built
burn	burned, burnt	burned, burnt
burst	burst	burst
bust	bust, busted	bust, busted
buy	bought	bought
can	could	–
cast	cast	cast

Infinitiv Infinitive	Präteritum Simple past	Partizip Perfekt Past participle
catch	caught	caught
choose	chose	chosen
cling	clung	clung
clothe	clothed, clad	clothed, clad
come	came	come
cost	cost	cost
creep	crept	crept
cut	cut	cut
deal	dealt	dealt
dig	dug	dug
dive	dived, dove	dived, dove
do	did	done
draw	drew	drawn
dream	dreamed, dreamt	dreamed, dreamt
drink	drank	drunk
drive	drove	driven
dwell	dwelt, dwelled	dwelt, dwelled
eat	ate	eaten
fall	fell	fallen
feed	fed	fed
feel	felt	felt
fight	fought	fought
find	found	found
fit	fitted, fit	fitted, fit
flee	fled	fled
fling	flung	flung
fly	flew	flown
forbid	forbad(e)	forbidden
forecast	forecast, forecasted	forecast, forecasted
forget	forgot	forgotten
forgive	forgave	forgiven
freeze	froze	frozen
get	got	gotten, got
give	gave	given

Infinitiv Infinitive	Präteritum Simple past	Partizip Perfekt Past participle
go	went	gone
grind	ground	ground
grow	grew	grown
hang	hung, LAW hanged	hung, LAW hanged
have	had	had
hear	heard	heard
hide	hid	hidden, hid
hit	hit	hit
hold	held	held
hurt	hurt	hurt
keep	kept	kept
kneel	knelt, kneeled	knelt, kneeled
knit	knitted, knit	knitted, knit
know	knew	known
lay	laid	laid
lead	led	led
lean	leaned	leaned
leap	leaped, leapt	leaped, leapt
learn	learned, learnt	learned, learnt
leave	left	left
lend	lent	lent
let	let	let
lie	lay	lain
light	lit, lighted	lit, lighted
lose	lost	lost
make	made	made
may	might	–
mean	meant	meant
meet	met	met
mistake	mistook	mistaken
mow	mowed	mowed, mown
pay	paid	paid
prove	proved	proved, proven
put	put	put

Infinitiv Infinitive	Präteritum Simple past	Partizip Perfekt Past participle
quit	quit, quitted	quit, quitted
read	read	read
rid	rid, ridded	rid, ridded
ride	rode	ridden
ring	rang	rung
rise	rose	risen
run	ran	run
saw	sawed	sawed, sawn
say	said	said
see	saw	seen
seek	sought	sought
sell	sold	sold
send	sent	sent
set	set	set
sew	sewed	sewn, sewed
shake	shook	shaken
shave	shaved	shaved, shaven
shear	sheared	sheared, shorn
shed	shed	shed
shine	shone	shone
shit	shit, shitted, shat	shit, shitted, shat
shoe	shod, shoed	shod, shodden, shoed
shoot	shot	shot
show	showed	shown, showed
shrink	shrank, shrunk	shrunk, shrunken
shut	shut	shut
sing	sang	sung
sink	sank	sunk
sit	sat	sat
slay	slew	slain
sleep	slept	slept
slide	slid	slid, slidden
sling	slung	slung
slink	slunk	slunk

Infinitiv Infinitive	Präteritum Simple past	Partizip Perfekt Past participle
slit	slit	slit
smell	smelled, smelt	smelled, smelt
sow	sowed	sown, sowed
speak	spoke	spoken
speed	speeded, sped	speeded, sped
spell	spelled, spelt	spelled, spelt
spend	spent	spent
spill	spilled, spilt	spilled, spilt
spin	spun	spun
spit	spat, spit	spat, spit
split	split	split
spoil	spoiled, spoilt	spoiled, spoilt
spread	spread	spread
spring	sprang, sprung	sprung
stand	stood	stood
stave	staved, stove	staved, stove
steal	stole	stolen
stick	stuck	stuck
sting	stung	stung
stink	stank, stunk	stunk
strew	strewed	strewn, strewed
stride	strode	stridden
strike	struck	struck
string	strung	strung
strive	strove, strived	striven
swear	swore	sworn
sweat	sweat, sweated	sweat, sweated
sweep	swept	swept
swell	swelled	swelled, swollen
swim	swam	swum
swing	swung	swung
take	took	taken
teach	taught	taught
tear	tore	torn

Infinitiv Infinitive	Präteritum Simple past	Partizip Perfekt Past participle
tell	told	told
think	thought	thought
thrive	thrived, throve	thrived, thriven
throw	threw	thrown
thrust	thrust	thrust
tread	trod	trodden
understand	understood	understood
wake	woke, waked	woken, waked
wear	wore	worn
weave	wove	woven
wed	wed, wedded	wed, wedded
weep	wept	wept
wet	wet, wetted	wet, wetted
win	won	won
wind	wound	wound
withhold	withheld	withheld
wring	wrung	wrung
write	wrote	written

Die Zahlwörter

Numerals

Die Kardinalzahlen

Cardinal numbers

null	0	nought, zero
eins	1	one
zwei	2	two
drei	3	three
vier	4	four
fünf	5	five
sechs	6	six
sieben	7	seven
acht	8	eight
neun	9	nine
zehn	10	ten
elf	11	eleven
zwölf	12	twelve
dreizehn	13	thirteen
vierzehn	14	fourteen
fünfzehn	15	fifteen
sechzehn	16	sixteen
siebzehn	17	seventeen
achtzehn	18	eighteen
neunzehn	19	nineteen
zwanzig	20	twenty
einundzwanzig	21	twenty-one
zweiundzwanzig	22	twenty-two
dreiundzwanzig	23	twenty-three
dreißig	30	thirty
einunddreißig	31	thirty-one
zweiunddreißig	32	thirty-two
vierzig	40	forty
einundvierzig	41	forty-one
fünfzig	50	fifty
einundfünfzig	51	fifty-one
sechzig	60	sixty
einundsechzig	61	sixty-one
siebzig	70	seventy
einundsiebzig	71	seventy-one

achtzig	80	eighty
einundachtzig	81	eighty-one
neunzig	90	ninety
einundneunzig	91	ninety-one
hundert	100	a [o one] hundred
hundert(und)eins	101	hundred and one
hundert(und)zwei	102	hundred and two
hundert(und)zehn	110	hundred and ten
zweihundert	200	two hundred
dreihundert	300	three hundred
vierhundert(und)einundfünfzig	451	four hundred and fifty-one
tausend	1000	a [o one] thousand
zweitausend	2000	two thousand
zehntausend	10 000	ten thousand
eine Million	1 000 000	a [o one] million
zwei Millionen	2 000 000	two million
eine Milliarde	1 000 000 000	a [o one] billion
eine Billion	1 000 000 000 000	a [o one] trillion

Die Ordnungszahlen   Ordinal numbers

erste	1.	1st	first
zweite	2.	2nd	second
dritte	3.	3rd	third
vierte	4.	4th	fourth
fünfte	5.	5th	fifth
sechste	6.	6th	sixth
siebente	7.	7th	seventh
achte	8.	8th	eighth
neunte	9.	9th	ninth
zehnte	10.	10th	tenth
elfte	11.	11th	eleventh
zwölfte	12.	12th	twelfth
dreizehnte	13.	13th	thirteenth
vierzehnte	14.	14th	fourteenth
fünfzehnte	15.	15th	fifteenth
sechzehnte	16.	16th	sixteenth
siebzehnte	17.	17th	seventeenth

achtzehnte	18.	18th	eighteenth
neunzehnte	19.	19th	nineteenth
zwanzigste	20.	20th	twentieth
einundzwanzigste	21.	21st	twenty-first
zweiundzwanzigste	22.	22nd	twenty-second
dreiundzwanzigste	23.	23rd	twenty-third
dreißigste	30.	30th	thirtieth
einunddreißigste	31.	31st	thirty-first
vierzigste	40.	40th	fortieth
einundvierzigste	41.	41st	forty-first
fünfzigste	50.	50th	fiftieth
einundfünfzigste	51.	51st	fifty-first
sechzigste	60.	60th	sixtieth
einundsechzigste	61.	61st	sixty-first
siebzigste	70.	70th	seventieth
einundsiebzigste	71.	71st	seventy-first
achtzigste	80.	80th	eightieth
einundachtzigste	81.	81st	eighty-first
neunzigste	90.	90th	ninetieth
hundertste	100.	100th	(one) hundredth
hundertunderste	101.	101st	hundred and first
zweihundertste	200.	200th	two hundredth
dreihundertste	300.	300th	three hundredth
vierhundert(und)einund-fünfzigste	451.	451st	four hundred and fifty-first
tausendste	1000.	1000th	(one) thousandth
tausend(und)einhundertste	1100.	1100th	thousand and (one) hundredth
zweitausendste	2000.	200th	two thousandth
einhunderttausendste	100 000.	100 000th	(one) hundred thousandth
millionste	1 000 000.	1 000 000th	millionth
zehnmillionste	10 000 000.	10 000 000th	ten millionth

Die Bruchzahlen   Fractions

ein halb	$^1/_2$	one [*o a*] half
ein Drittel	$^1/_3$	one [*o a*] third
ein Viertel	$^1/_4$	one [*o a*] quarter
ein Fünftel	$^1/_5$	one [*o a*] fifth
ein Zehntel	$^1/_{10}$	one [*o a*] tenth
ein Hundertstel	$^1/_{100}$	one hundredth
ein Tausendstel	$^1/_{1000}$	one thousandth
ein Millionstel	$^1/_{1000000}$	one millionth
zwei Drittel	$^2/_3$	two thirds
drei Viertel	$^3/_4$	three quarters
zwei Fünftel	$^2/_5$	two fifths
drei Zehntel	$^3/_{10}$	three tenths
anderthalb	$1^1/_2$	one and a half
zwei(und)einhalb	$2^1/_2$	two and a half
fünf drei achtel	$5^3/_8$	five and three eighths
eins Komma eins	1,1 1.1	one point one
zwei Komma drei	2,3 2.3	two point three

Vervielfältigungszahlen   Multiples

einfach	single	vierfach	fourfold, quadruple
zweifach	double	fünffach	fivefold
dreifach	threefold, treble, triple	hundertfach	(one) hundredfold

Gewichte und Maße

Das Dezimalsystem

Giga	1 000 000 000	G	giga
Mega	1 000 000	M	mega
Hektokilo	100 000	hk	hectokilo
Myria	10 000	ma	myria
Kilo	1 000	k	kilo
Hekto	100	h	hecto
Deka	10	da	deca
Dezi	0,1	d	deci
Centi	0,01	c	centi
Milli	0,001	m	milli
Dezimilli	0,000 1	dm	decimilli
Centimilli	0,000 01	cm	centimilli
Mikro	0,000 001	µ	micro

Weights and measures

Decimal system

Umrechnungstabellen

In den USA ist immer noch das anglo-amerikanische Maßsystem in Gebrauch. In Großbritannien ist man offiziell auf das Dezimalsystem umgestiegen, jedoch bevorzugen viele immer noch das alte System. Für Temperaturen wird die Fahrenheit-Skala verwendet. Nur diejenigen anglo-amerikanischen Maße, die immer noch in Umlauf sind, werden in den Tabellen aufgeführt. Man erhält ein angloamerikanisches Maß, indem man das entsprechende metrische mit dem **fett** gedruckten Umrechnungsfaktor multipliziert. Umgekehrt gilt: Ein imperiales Maß, das durch den gleichen Faktor dividiert wird, ergibt das metrische.

Conversion tables

Only U.S. Customary units still in common use are given here. To convert a metric measurement to U.S. Customary measures, multiply by the conversion factor in **bold**. Likewise dividing a U.S. Customary measurement by the same factor will give the metric equivalent. Note that the decimal comma is used throughout rather than the decimal point.

| **Das metrische System** **Metric measurement** | | | **Anglo-amerikanisches Maßsystem** **U.S. Customary System** | | | |

Längenmaße / Length measures

Seemeile	1 852 m	–	nautical mile			
Kilometer	1 000 m	km	kilometer	**0,62**	mile (= 1760 yards)	m, mi
Hektometer	100 m	hm	hectometer			
Dekameter	10 m	dam	decameter			
Meter	1 m	m	meter	**1,09** **3,28**	yard (= 3 feet) foot (= 12 inches)	yd ft
Dezimeter	0,1 m	dm	decimeter			
Zentimeter	0,01 m	cm	centimeter	**0,39**	inch	in
Millimeter	0,001 m	mm	millimeter			
Mikron	0,000 001 m	µ	micron			
Millimikron	0,000 000 001 m	mµ	millimicron			
Angström	0,000 000 000 1 m	Å	angstrom			

Flächenmaße / Surface measures

Quadratkilometer	1 000 000 m²	km²	square kilometer	**0,386**	square mile (= 640 acres)	sq. m., sq. mi.
Quadrathektometer Hektar	10 000 m²	hm² ha	square hectometer hectare	**2,47**	acre (= 4840 square yards)	a.
Quadratdekameter Ar (SCHWEIZ: Are)	100 m²	dam² a	square decameter are			
Quadratmeter	1 m²	m²	square meter	**1.196** **10,76**	square yard (9 square feet) square feet (= 144 square inches)	sq. yd sq. ft
Quadratdezimeter	0,01 m²	dm²	square decimeter			
Quadratzentimeter	0,000 1 m²	cm²	square centimeter	**0,155**	square inch	sq. in.
Quadratmillimeter	0,000 001 m²	mm²	square millimeter			

Kubik- und Hohlmaße   Volume and capacity

Kubikkilo-meter	1 000 000 000 m³	km³	cubic kilo-meter			
Kubikmeter	1 m³	m³	cubic meter	**1,308**	cubic yard (= 27 cubic feet)	cu. yd
Ster		st	stere	**35,32**	cubic foot (= 1728 cubic inches)	cu. ft
Hektoliter	0,1 m³	hl	hectoliter			
Dekaliter	0,01 m³	dal	decaliter			
Kubik-dezimeter	0,001 m³	dm³	cubic deci-meter	**0,26**	gallon	gal.
Liter		l	liter	**2,1**	pint	Pt
Deziliter	0,000 1 m³	dl	deciliter			
Zentiliter	0,000 01 m³	cl	centiliter	**0,352** **0,338**	fluid ounce	fl. oz
Kubik-zentimeter	0,000 001 m³	cm³	cubic cen-timeter	**0,061**	cubic inch	cu. in.
Milliliter	0,000 001 m³	ml	milliliter			
Kubik-millimeter	0,000 000 001 m³	mm³	cubic milli-meter			

Gewichte   Weight

Tonne	1 000 kg	t	ton	**1,1**	[short] ton (= 2000 pounds)	t.
Quintal	100 kg	q	quintal			
Kilogramm	1 000 g	kg	kilogram	**2,2**	pound (= 16 ounces)	lb
Hekto-gramm	100 g	hg	hectogram			
Dekagramm	10 g	dag	decagram			
Gramm	1 g	g	gram	**0,035**	ounce	oz
Karat	0,2 g	–	carat			
Dezigramm	0,1 g	dg	decigram			
Zentigramm	0,01 g	cg	centigram			
Milligramm	0,001 g	mg	milligram			
Mikro-gramm	0,000 001 g	µg, g	microgram			

Temperaturumrechnung   Temperature conversion

Fahrenheit – Celsius		Celsius – Fahrenheit	
°F	°C	°C	°F
0	–17,8	–10	14
32	0	0	32
50	10	10	50
70	21,1	20	68
90	32,2	30	86
98,4	37	37	98,4
212	100	100	212
zur Umrechnung 32 abziehen und mit $5/9$ multiplizieren		zur Umrechnung mit $9/5$ multiplizieren und 32 addieren	
To convert subtract 32 and multiply by $5/9$		To convert multiply by $9/5$ and add 32	

Notes

Notes

Notes

Zeichen und Abkürzungen

phraseologischer Block	▶	phrase block
trennbares Verb	|	separable verb
Kontraktion	=	contraction
Partizip ohne *ge-*	*	German past participle formed without *ge-*
entspricht etwa	≈	comparable to
alte Schreibung	ALT	unreformed German spelling
reformierte Schreibung	RR	reformed German spelling
zeigt variable Stellung des Objektes und der Ergänzung bei Phrasal Verbs auf	⇌	indicates the variable position of the object in phrasal verb sentences
Warenzeichen	®	trade mark
auch	a.	also
Abkürzung	*Abk* *abbr*	abbreviation
Akronym	*acr*	acronym
Adjektiv	*adj*	adjective
Verwaltung	ADMIN	administration
Adverb	*adv*	adverb
Raum- und Luftfahrt	AEROSP	aerospace
Landwirtschaft	AGR	agriculture
Akkusativ	*akk*	accusative
Akronym	*Akr*	acronym
Anatomie	ANAT	anatomy
aufwertend	*approv*	approving
Archäologie	ARCHÄOL ARCHEOL	archaeology
Architektur	ARCHIT	architecture
Artikel	*art*	article
Kunst	ART	art
Astrologie	ASTROL	astrology
Astronomie	ASTRON	astronomy
attributiv	*attr*	attributive
Hilfsverb	*aux*	auxiliary verb
Luftfahrt	AVIAT	aviation
Bauwesen	BAU	construction
Bergbau	BERGB	mining
Biologie	BIOL	biology
Botanik	BOT	botany
Binnendeutsch	BRD	German of Germany
Chemie	CHEM	chemistry
Handel	COMM	commerce
komparativ in Komposita	*comp*	comparative in compounds
Informatik	COMPUT	computing

Symbols and abbreviations

Konjunktion	*conj*	conjunction
Dativ	*dat*	dative
bestimmt	*def*	definite
dekliniert	*dekl*	declined
demonstrativ	*dem*	demonstrative
derb	*derb*	vulgar language
Bestimmungswort	*det*	determiner
dialektal	DIAL	dialect
Diminutiv	*dim*	diminutive
Ökologie	ECOL	ecology
Wirtschaft	ECON	economy
Elektrizität	ELEK ELEC	electricity
emphatisch	*emph*	emphatic
Europäische Union	EU	European Union
euphemistisch	*euph*	euphemistic
Femininum	*f*	feminine
fachsprachlich	*fachspr*	specialist term
umgangssprachlich	*fam*	informal
Fußball	FBALL	football
feminine Form	*fem*	feminine form
bildlich	*fig*	figurative
Finanzen	FIN	finance
Kochkunst	FOOD	food and cooking
förmlicher Sprachgebrauch	*form*	formal
gehobener Sprachgebrauch	*geh*	formal
Genitiv	*gen*	genitive
Geographie	GEOG	geography
Geologie	GEOL	geology
historisch	*hist*	historical
Geschichte	HIST	history
Gartenbau	HORT	gardening
scherzhaft	*hum*	humorous
Jagd	HUNT	hunting
Imperfekt	*imp*	imperfect
Imperativ	*imper*	imperative
unpersönliches Verb	*impers*	impersonal use
unbestimmt	*indef*	indefinite
Internet	INET	internet
Infinitiv	*infin*	infinitive
Interjektion	*interj*	interjection
fragend	*interrog*	interrogative
unveränderlich	*inv*	invariable
ironisch	*iron*	ironic
unregelmäßig	*irreg*	irregular
Journalismus	JOURN	journalism
Jura	JUR	law

Zeichen und Abkürzungen

Symbols and abbreviations

Karten	KARTEN	cards
Kochkunst	KOCHK	food and cooking
Konjunktion	konj	conjunction
Kunst	KUNST	art
Jura	LAW	law
Linguistik	LING	linguistics
Literatur	LIT	literature
literarisch	liter	literary
Luftfahrt	LUFT	aviation
Maskulinum	m	masculine
maskuline Form	masc	masculine form
Mathematik	MATH	mathematics
Mechanik	MECH	mechanics
Medizin	MED	medicine
Medien	MEDIA	media
Meteorologie	METEO	meteorology
Militär	MIL	military
Bergbau	MIN	mining
Mode	MODE	fashion
Musik	MUS	music
Substantiv	n	noun
Seefahrt	NAUT	navigation
verneinend, Verneinung	neg	negative, negation
Nominativ	nomin	nominative
Norddeutsch	NORDD	language of Northern Germany
Neutrum	nt	neuter
Ökologie	ÖKOL	ecology
Wirtschaft	ÖKON	economics
veraltet	old	old
Vogelkunde	ORN	ornithology
österreichisches Deutsch	ÖSTERR	Austrian German
Partizip	part	participle
abwertend	pej	pejorative
Personal(pronomen)	pers	personal pronoun
Person	pers.	person
Pharmazie	PHARM	pharmacy
Philosophie	PHILOS	philosophy
Fotografie	PHOT	photography
Physik	PHYS	physics
plural	pl	plural
poetisch	poet	poetic
Politik	POL	politics
possessiv	poss	possessive
Partizip Perfekt	pp	past participle
Präposition	präp	preposition
Prädikativ	pred	predicative
Präposition	prep	preposition

Präsens	pres	present
Pronomen	pron	pronoun
Sprichwort	prov	proverb
erste Vergangenheit	pt	past tense
Verlagswesen	PUBL	publishing
Rundfunk	RADIO	radio broadcasting
Eisenbahnwesen	RAIL	railway
selten	rare	rare
Raumfahrt	RAUM	aerospace
reflexiv	refl	reflexive
Religion	rel	religion
Sache	S.	thing
Schule	SCH	school
schweizerisches Deutsch	SCHWEIZ	Swiss German
Naturwissenschaften	SCI	science
trennbar	sep	separable
Einzahl	sing	singular
salopp	sl	slang
Soziologie	SOZIOL SOCIOL	sociology
fachsprachlich	spec	specialist term
Sport	SPORT	sports
Börse	STOCKEX	stock exchange
Süddeutsch	SÜDD	language of Southern Germany
Superlativ	superl	superlative
Technik	TECH	technology
Nachrichtentechnik	TELEK TELEC	telecommunications
Tennis	TENNIS	tennis
Theater	THEAT	theatre
Tourismus	TOURIST	tourism
Transport und Verkehr	TRANSP	transportation
Fernsehen	TV	television
Buchdruck	TYPO	typography
Universität	UNIV	university
gewöhnlich	usu	usually
veraltend	veraltend	dated
veraltet	veraltet	old
Verlagswesen	VERLAG	publishing
intransitives Verb	vi	intransitive verb
reflexives Verb	vr	reflexive verb
transitives Verb	vt	transitive verb
vulgär	vulg	vulgar language
Zoologie	ZOOL	zoology